2002

ALMANAC *Plus*

107TH CONGRESS
2ND SESSION

VOLUME LVIII

Congressional Quarterly Inc.

1255 22nd Street N.W.
Washington, D.C. 20037

President & Publisher Robert W. Merry
Executive Editor, Sr. V.P. David Rapp

Executive Editors
Susan Benkelman, Mike Mills

Managing Editors
Scott Montgomery, Chuck Hawkins

Senior Editors
Jan Austin, David Hawkings

Art and Production Director
Chris Fruitrich

Department Editors
Randy Wynn, Mike Christensen, Caitlin Hendel,
Jonathan Broder, John Cranford

Deputy Editors
Virginia Barazia, Daniel J. Parks, Art Brodsky,
Adriel Bettelheim, Colin Clark

Associate Editors
Martha Angle, Brian Nutting, H. Amy Stern,
Katherine Rizzo

Senior Writers
Mary Agnes Carey, John Cochran, David Nather,
Alan K. Ota, Andrew Taylor, Pat Towell

Reporters
Rebecca Adams, Jonathan Allen, Joseph C. Anselmo,
Jill Barshay, Peter Cohn, Jennifer A. Dlouhy,
Susan Ferrechio, Helen Fessenden, Gregory L. Giroux,
Samuel Goldreich, Adam Graham-Silverman,
Siobhan Hughes, Mary Clare Jalonick, Martin Kady II,
Gebe Martinez, Stephen J. Norton, Keith Perine,
Jonathan Riehl, Joseph J. Schatz, Kate Schuler,
Carolyn Skorneck, Niels C. Sorrells,
Allison Stevens, Bill Swindell

CQ
2002
ALMANAC *Plus*

Editor
Jan Austin

Production Editor
Melinda W. Nahmias

Deputy Editors, Publications
Pat Joy, Tina Johnson-Marcel, John Bicknell,
Jack Deutsch

Copy Editors
Arwen Bicknell, Yolie Dawson, Chris Joaquim,
Melinda W. Nahmias, Kathleen Silvassy,
Charles Southwell, Lisa Weintraub

Staff Photographer Scott J. Ferrell

Graphic Artist Marilyn Gates-Davis

News Research
Nell Benton (supervisor)
Alecia Marzullo Burke (senior researcher)
Andrew Freedman, Peter E. Harrell,
Jay Millikan, Sarah Molenkamp

Indexer Susan Nedrow

Systems Editor Ron Brodmann

Editorial Assistant Adam Satariano

HOUSE ACTION REPORTS
Managing Editor Kerry Jones

CQ.COM ON CONGRESS
Associate Managing Editor Peter Roybal

CQ HOMELAND SECURITY
Editor Jeff Stein

POLITICS
Politics Editor Bob Benenson

BUSINESS OFFICES
General Manager, Sr. V.P. Keith A. White

Circulation Marketing Director Bob Shew

Circulation Sales Director Jim Gale

Ad Sales, V.P. Joan Daly

Chief Financial Officer Diane Atwell

Product Development, V.P. Michael K. Connelly

Customer Support Services Manager LaWanda Council

**CQ Press
General Manager, Sr. V.P.** John A. Jenkins

**Published by
CONGRESSIONAL QUARTERLY INC.**

Chairman Andrew Barnes
Vice Chairman Andrew P. Corty
Founder Nelson Poynter
(1903-1978)

Congressional Quarterly Inc.

Congressional Quarterly Inc. is a publishing and information services company and the recognized national leader in political journalism. For more than half a century, CQ has served clients in the fields of business, government, news and education with complete, timely and nonpartisan information on Congress, politics and national issues.

The flagship publication is the CQ Weekly, a news magazine on Congress and its legislative activities. The publication tracks legislation as it is created in subcommittee, committee, floor, House-Senate conferences and leadership offices, providing detail and analysis unavailable anywhere else.

CQ Today, formerly the CQ Daily Monitor, is a legislative newsdaily providing a morning news report on Congress and the scheduled hearings and markups of congressional committees. It provides a comprehensive breaking news report of everything that just happened or is about to happen on Capitol Hill.

CQ also offers the most comprehensive, detailed and up-to-the-minute legislative tracking information on the World Wide Web. CQ.com provides immediate access to exclusive CQ coverage of bill action, votes, schedules and member profiles, with direct links to relevant texts of bills, committee reports, testimony and verbatim transcripts.

CQ Press, a division of Congressional Quarterly Inc., serves the academic and education markets with a variety of reference works and political science text books, both in print and online, plus reference books on the federal government, national elections and politics.

The CQ Press catalogue includes the signature CQ reference work, "Politics in America," with original profiles of every member of the 108th Congress, written and edited by the CQ staff.

CQ Press also publishes a unique weekly publication — The CQ Researcher — with each week's issue focused exclusively on a single topic of current interest. And CQ Press offers a line of print and Web-based directories, such as the Congressional Staff Directory.

The "Congressional Quarterly Almanac®," published annually, provides a legislative history for each session of Congress. "Congress and the Nation," published every four years, provides a record of government for a presidential term.

Library of Congress Catalog Number 47-41081
ISBN: 1-56802-638-2   ISSN: 0095-6007

CONGRESSIONAL QUARTERLY OFFERS A COMPLETE LINE OF PUBLICATIONS AND RESEARCH SERVICES.

The CQ Almanac 'Plus'

The 2002 edition of the CQ Almanac rounds out the story of the 107th Congress, providing narrative accounts of every major piece of legislation that lawmakers considered in the second session.

The volume contains 19 legislative chapters, each written especially for the book to summarize and review the year's events in Congress. We added "Plus" to our title in 2001 to highlight this original material. Edited by Jan Austin, a 16-year veteran of the CQ newsroom, the Almanac contains complete retellings of more than 75 bills, based on reporting and analysis done throughout the year by Congressional Quarterly's news staff.

The second session was one of contrasts. Congress left a firm imprint on history with major bills creating a new Department of Homeland Security, approving a pre-emptive war in Iraq and clearing the biggest increase in defense spending since the Vietnam war. Congress also produced a sweeping overhaul of campaign finance rules, a new six-year farm act, so-called trade promotion authority guaranteeing up-or-down votes on new trade agreements, a landmark bill to regulate the accounting industry and crack down on corporate fraud, and a new federal terrorism insurance program.

At the same time, Congress failed in its most fundamental task — appropriating money to pay for the operations of the federal government. Only two of the fiscal 2003 spending bills — for defense and military construction — were enacted. The 11 non-defense bills were kicked over to the next Congress, leaving federal departments and programs operating month to month at fiscal 2002 levels.

The Almanac provides a detailed look at each major bill considered in 2002 — whether or not it became law. It examines how the bills were shaped as they moved from committee markup to floor votes and conference negotiations. The stories also identify and explain the main provisions of the bills and look at the roles played by individual members of Congress.

In addition, the Almanac contains a number of data-filled appendixes, including:

- **Congress and its members:** An 11-page glossary of terms that arise in discussing Congress and legislation, a list of members of the House and Senate in the second session of the 107th Congress, and a box listing membership changes.
- **Vote studies.** CQ's popular study of the roll call votes cast in Congress during the year. Separate studies analyze the level of presidential support, party unity and member participation during the year, providing aggregate scores for each chamber along with individual ratings for every member.
- **Key votes.** An account of the votes chosen by the CQ editors as most critical in determining the outcome of congressional action on major issues during the year.
- **Texts.** Presidential statements, Democratic responses and other key documents from the year.
- **Public laws.** A detailed list of all the bills enacted into law during the year.
- **Political report.** Official, state-by-state results of the 2002 midyear election, plus results of special elections.
- **Roll call votes.** A complete set of roll call vote charts for both chambers, describing every vote and every member's position on each vote.

CQ produces the Almanac for public policy specialists, scholars, journalists and all interested citizens and students of the U.S. legislative system.

This volume is the 58th in a series that began in 1946. We believe it remains true to the mandate laid out more than 50 years ago by CQ founders Nelson and Henrietta Poynter: "Congressional Quarterly presents the facts in as complete, concise and unbiased form as we know how. The editorial comment on the acts and votes of Congress, we leave to our subscribers."

David Rapp
Editor & Senior Vice President

CQ

"By providing a link between the local newspaper and Capitol Hill we hope Congressional Quarterly can help to make public opinion the only effective pressure group in the country. Since many citizens other than editors are also interested in Congress, we hope that they too will find Congressional Quarterly an aid to a better understanding of their government."

Foreword, Congressional Quarterly, Vol. I, 1945
Henrietta Poynter, 1901-1968
Nelson Poynter, 1903-1978

SUMMARY TABLE OF CONTENTS

Table of Contents

Chapter 1 – Inside Congress

Chapter 2 – Appropriations

Chapter 3 – Abortion

Chapter 4 – Agriculture

Chapter 5 – Banking & Financial Services

Chapter 6 – Budget

Chapter 7 – Defense

Chapter 8 – Energy & Environment

Chapter 9 – Foreign Policy

Chapter 10 – Health

Chapter 11 – Industry & Regulation

Chapter 12 – Labor & Employment

Chapter 13 – Law & Judiciary

Chapter 14 – Politics & Elections

Chapter 15 — Social Policy

Chapter 16 — Taxes

Chapter 17 — Technology & Science

Chapter 18 — Trade

Chapter 19 — Transportation

Appendixes

Chapter 1

INSIDE CONGRESS

ς

Politics, Security Shape Agenda

It did not have the dramatic twists and turns that made the first session so exceptional, but the second session of the 107th Congress left its mark on history. It approved the biggest reorganization of government since World War II, and it opened the door to a fundamental shift in U.S. foreign policy by authorizing President Bush to launch pre-emptive strikes to disarm Iraq.

Most of the year was shaped by the ongoing impact of the terrorist attacks of Sept. 11, 2001, which continued to redraw the political landscape at home and abroad. In an effort to help the government do a better job of preventing future attacks, Congress passed legislation creating the Cabinet-level Department of Homeland Security that combined all or part of 22 federal agencies under one roof to coordinate their counterterrorism efforts.

And to eliminate the possibility that Iraq could launch attacks against the United States or its neighbors with weapons of mass destruction, or give such weapons to terrorist organizations such as al Qaeda, Congress authorized Bush to take military action against Saddam Hussein. The resolution encouraged Bush to seek the support of the United Nations first, but it authorized the United States to go to war with or without U.N. approval.

All the while, the session was dominated by the political struggle for control of the Senate, where the change of just one seat in the November elections threatened to shift the majority from the Democrats to the Republicans. With 50 Democrats, 49 Republicans and one independent, the margin of control was so close that the two parties could not avoid fighting over it.

That struggle slowed the Senate even more than usual. Republicans sought to paint Majority Leader Tom Daschle, D-S.D., as an obstructionist and incompetent leader, and Daschle resorted to stronger legislative tactics to keep the chamber's focus on Democratic priorities and minimize the political differences within his caucus. House Republicans pushed through a number of measures designed more to inoculate themselves from political attacks — and turn up the heat on Daschle — than to be signed into law.

Bush, bolstered by strong public approval of his handling of the war on terrorism, accused Democrats of delaying the passage of the homeland security bill — originally a Democratic initiative. The popular president campaigned for GOP candidates in the crucial last two weeks before the November election, a gamble that helped Republicans win back the Senate and guaranteed a unified Republican government for the 108th Congress.

The homeland security bill eventually was approved in a

lame-duck session. However, the 107th Congress adjourned Nov. 22 without completing a more fundamental task: It left all 11 of the fiscal 2003 non-defense appropriations bills unfinished, punting the job to the next Congress.

The power struggle exposed the dual political reality of the 107th Congress after the Sept. 11 attacks, in which lawmakers generally were unified on the war against terrorism but as divided on domestic issues as before the attacks. Moreover, the fight for control of the Senate guaranteed gridlock on virtually all legislation that did not have an immediate urgency with the public. "When it got done, it got done under the lash of events," said Ross K. Baker, a political scientist at Rutgers University. "They did it because the public demanded action . . . and it would have been embarrassing if they had not acted."

What Did, and Did Not, Get Done

From the moment Bush entered the House chamber Jan. 29 to deliver his first official State of the Union address, it was clear that domestic issues would have a hard time competing with the war on terrorism and everything that could be linked to it. Bush spent the first half of his speech promising to continue the fight against al Qaeda and other terrorist groups, make Americans more secure at home and keep "regimes that sponsor terror" from threatening the United States or its allies. In a phrase that marked a new focus on countries his administration saw as growing threats, Bush singled out Iraq, Iran and North Korea as an "axis of evil" that was "arming to threaten the peace of the world."

With the nation in an economic slump, however, Bush also promised "economic security" for Americans. "My budget supports three great goals for America," he said. "We will win this war, we will protect our homeland, and we will revive our economy." (*Text, p. D-3*)

Protecting the homeland became the underlying theme of the second session. In addition to passing the homeland security bill and authorizing U.S. war in Iraq, Congress created an independent commission to investigate the Sept. 11 attacks. It passed legislation to strengthen the security of the nation's seaports and oil and natural gas pipelines, gave airline pilots permission to carry guns in cockpits, and created a federal terrorism insurance program to protect commercial property and insurance companies in case of terrorist attacks.

On other fronts, lawmakers sought to address the anger many Americans felt at corporate scandals such as the collapse of Enron Corp. and WorldCom Inc., both fueled by accounting fraud, that forced massive layoffs, devastated workers' retirement savings and added to the stock market tur-

Highlights: 107th Congress, Second Session

✔ CONGRESS DID

- Create a new Department of Homeland Security, consolidating all or parts of 22 federal agencies in the largest government reorganization since World War II.
- Write a new farm bill, reversing a six-year policy of limiting federal crop subsidies.
- Agree to consider trade deals proposed by the president on a fast track, by accepting or rejecting them without amendment.
- Create an independent commission to investigate intelligence and other government mistakes that preceded the terrorist attacks of Sept. 11.
- Set federal corporate accounting and governance standards, the biggest increase in the regulation of publicly traded companies since the Depression.
- Authorize the president to use military force against Iraq.
- Increase the limit on government borrowing by $450 billion, to $6.4 trillion.
- Increase the defense budget by 11 percent, the biggest one-year increase in two decades.
- Make the federal government the insurer of last resort for losses due to major terrorist attacks.
- Rewrite campaign finance rules to ban "soft money" and restrict issue advocacy advertising.
- Set the first federal standards for the states' conduct of elections in response to the disputed 2000 presidential contest.
- Expel a House member for the first time since 1980.
- Confirm 72 federal judges, meaning President Bush won approval for 77 percent of his nominees in his first two years.

- Extend unemployment benefits for 13 weeks as part of a $94 billion, five-year economic stimulus plan.
- Bolster efforts to stockpile vaccines and otherwise prepare for biological and chemical attacks.

✗ CONGRESS DID NOT

- Adopt an annual budget resolution, only the second such failure since the current budget law was enacted in 1974.
- Clear any of the 11 non-defense appropriations bills for fiscal 2003, which began Oct. 1.
- Rewrite federal bankruptcy law, primarily to make it more difficult for people to erase their debts.
- Create a prescription drug benefit as part of Medicare.
- Expand patients' rights in managed-care medical insurance plans.
- Protect employee pension investments from corporate malfeasance.
- Extend unemployment insurance benefits beyond the year's end.
- Pass a long-term rewrite of welfare programs.
- Widen faith-based groups' role in providing federally funded social services.
- Overhaul export control law.
- Extend the 2001 tax cuts beyond their 2010 expiration date.
- Deregulate the market for broadband Internet service over telephone lines.
- Overhaul federal energy policy to encourage conservation as well as production, including opening portions of the Arctic National Wildlife Refuge to drilling.
- Ban human cloning.

---

moil that played havoc with the finances of millions of Americans. That public anger led to the passage of a corporate accountability bill tougher than many members of Congress thought possible, including new rules for accounting firms, new disclosure and conflict-of-interest rules for publicly traded companies, and stronger criminal penalties for securities fraud.

After seven years of Senate filibusters and other setbacks, Congress passed a bill overhauling the nation's campaign finance laws. Lawmakers granted fast-track trade negotiating authority to Bush, agreeing to take straight up-or-down votes on his trade agreements without the possibility of amendments. They passed a six-year farm bill that reversed a 1996 policy of limiting federal price supports. And they responded to the turmoil of the 2000 presidential election by creating new standards for federal elections and authorizing $3.9 billion in grants to the states over three years to meet them.

But the 107th Congress also left a long list of unfinished business, allowing some of the biggest domestic initiatives to fall victim to politics. Unable to agree on a bottom line for fiscal 2003 domestic spending, Congress failed to produce a budget resolution. That, in turn, opened the way for a meltdown on the 11 non-defense spending bills, which left much of the government running on a short-term continuing resolution until mid-January 2003.

Divided over how to modify the 1996 welfare overhaul, Congress left it to run on autopilot through annual appropriations. Lawmakers were unable to reauthorize the 1975 Individuals with Disabilities Education Act, also because of disagreement over how much the law should be rewritten. Differences over how much to spend on prescription drug coverage and whether it should be provided through Medicare or the private sector left that agenda item unfinished as well. Efforts to create a national energy policy stalled over such issues as electricity market restructuring and whether to allow oil and gas exploration in Alaska's Arctic National Wildlife Refuge (ANWR).

Bush failed to win congressional approval for his initiative to increase aid to faith-based social programs, a top priority left over from his presidential campaign, as Democrats worried that the initiative would lead to subsidized religious discrimination. Like the previous two Congresses, the 107th was unable to agree on a patients' rights bill after a longstanding dispute over the right to sue managed-care plans proved fatal to the entire effort. And, for the third time in as many Congresses, members tried but failed to bring a bankruptcy overhaul bill to enactment.

Efforts to pass a stimulus bill to address the nation's economic slump bogged down in deep partisan and ideological divisions. The only thing to come of the effort was a 13-

week extension of unemployment benefits and a few tax breaks to help businesses recover from the Sept. 11 attacks. Failure to pass a further unemployment extension just before adjournment minimized even that achievement.

"Members of Congress do want to pass legislation, but they also want other things. They want to win re-election, and they want their party to prevail," observed Jack Pitney, a professor of government at Claremont McKenna College in Southern California. "Sometimes a failed bill is more powerful than a bill that's passed."

The Shrinking Stimulus

Republicans began the year hoping to jump-start the lackluster economy with broad tax relief for individuals and businesses, including acceleration of Bush's 10-year $1.35 trillion tax cut package (PL 107-16) enacted in 2001. Democrats, however, wanted to extend unemployment benefits and spend more on infrastructure and homeland security. The debate had been raging since the end of the first session. *(2001 Almanac, p. 18-15)*

In the Senate, both parties gave up trying to settle their ideological differences and passed a simple 13-week extension of unemployment benefits Feb. 6. House Republicans resisted, sending a new stimulus bill to the Senate, partly to keep the heat on Daschle. The Senate lobbed another straight unemployment extension to the House, exposing a rare split between House and Senate Republicans. "It's the difference between a House Republican who wants to fight for America, and a Senate Republican who doesn't," said House Majority Leader Dick Armey, R-Texas.

Finally in March, rank-and-file House Republicans talked their leaders into striking a compromise that resulted in a measure that included the 13-week extension of unemployment benefits and a few tax breaks to help businesses recover from the Sept. 11 attacks. The House passed the bill March 7 and the Senate cleared it the next day (PL 107-147) — just after Federal Reserve Board Chairman Alan Greenspan declared that the recession was over.

Budget Paralysis

In the meantime, Bush sent Congress a $2.16 trillion fiscal 2003 budget Feb. 4, calling for a 9 percent increase in discretionary spending, virtually all of it for defense, and annual deficits until fiscal 2005.

The House, under a Republican majority that was Bush's most valuable ally in Congress during much of the session, adopted a budget resolution (H Con Res 353) on March 20 that largely tracked the president's proposals.

In the Senate, Budget Committee Chairman Kent Conrad, D-N.D., won approval from his committee for a cautious budget (S Con Res 100) that exposed the divisions among Democratics without attracting any GOP support. Fiscally conservative Democrats said there was too little emphasis on reducing the federal debt, while liberals complained it did not promise enough for social programs. The measure allowed $9 billion more in discretionary spending than was available under the House version.

Education funding was a particularly sensitive issue. Democrats and moderate Republicans had backed the 2001 education overhaul law (PL 107-110), dubbed "No Child Left Behind" by Bush, largely on the condition that the an-

nual reading and math tests required in grades 3-8 would be accompanied by a substantial increase in funding to help poor schools meet the new standards. But a Democratic analysis concluded that Bush's budget would cut the programs covered by the new law by $90 million. "He actually cuts funding for programs in the bill he just signed and that he's been going around the country touting," said Tom Harkin, D-Iowa, chairman of the Senate Labor, Health and Human Services (HHS), and Education Appropriations Subcommittee. "Of course I'm going to insist on increases."

Unable to bridge the differences, Daschle quietly shelved plans to bring the budget resolution to the floor. That deprived Democrats of one of their best vehicles for highlighting differences with the Republicans, which often involved spending priorities. Republicans blasted Daschle as unable to conduct the basic business of the Senate.

With the Senate paralyzed on the budget, the GOP-controlled House required its appropriators to abide by the discretionary spending limits in the House resolution. Bush threatened to veto spending bills that exceeded those limits, but appropriators in both chambers continued to work under the assumption that they eventually would get more money. Senate appropriators marked up all 13 spending bills before the August recess. House appropriators delayed action on some of the biggest spending bills, including the Labor-HHS measure, hoping that GOP leaders would loosen the purse strings toward the end of the year.

Conservative House Republicans were afraid that was exactly what was going to happen. In July, they won a promise from Speaker J. Dennis Hastert, R-Ill., that he would bring the Labor-HHS bill to a vote after the August recess, before any more spending bills had reached the floor. That decision had the enthusiastic support of the Bush administration. But moderate Republicans rebelled, complaining that the education funding in the bill was inadequate. Lacking the votes to pass the bill, Republican leaders kept it off the House floor — creating a backlog of unfinished domestic spending bills behind it.

Corporate Scandals and Campaign Finance

Meanwhile, the fallout from the collapse of Enron Corp. in December 2001 was bringing new life to old initiatives and putting new ones on the congressional agenda.

The most immediate impact was a boost for the stalled campaign finance overhaul bill, which had passed the Senate in 2001 but was pulled from the House floor that year after moderate Republicans joined with Democrats to defeat a complicated leadership-backed rule setting the terms of the House debate. *(2001 Almanac, p. 6-3)*

At its heart, the Enron scandal was about fraudulent accounting and the toll it took on workers' lives after their 401(k) savings were decimated. But because the energy giant had escaped questioning for so long, the scandal also drew attention to the political clout it had wielded through its campaign contributions to both parties. That revelation, politically embarrassing for Republicans and Democrats alike, made it an urgent priority for them to rewrite the rules that made such special-interest influence possible.

Since Hastert was in no hurry to bring the bill — sponsored by Christopher Shays, R-Conn., and Martin T. Meehan, D-Mass. — to the floor, the only way to force a vote

107th Congress, 2nd Session: By the Numbers

The second session of the 107th Congress began, as the Constitution requires, at noon on Jan. 23, 2002. Under the terms of the annual adjournment resolution (S Con Res 160), the Senate adjourned sine die at 6:12 p.m. on Nov. 20; the House adjourned sine die at 2:23 p.m. on Nov. 22. The following are some statistical comparisons of the two chambers over the past decade:

		2002	2001	2000	1999	1998	1997	1996	1995	1994	1993
Days in Session	Senate	149	173	141	162	143	153	132	211	138	153
	House	123	142	135	137	119	132	122	168	123	142
Time in Session (hours)	Senate	1,043	1,236	1,018	1,184	1,095	1,093	1,037	1,839	1,244	1,270
	House	772	922	1,054	1,125	999	1,004	919	1,525	905	982
Avg. Length Daily Session (hours)	Senate	7	7.1	7.2	7.3	7.7	7.1	7.9	8.7	9.0	8.3
	House	6.3	6.5	7.8	8.2	8.4	7.6	7.5	9.1	7.4	6.9
Public Laws Enacted		241	136	410	170	241	153	245	88	255	210
Bills/Resolutions Introduced	Senate	1,563	2,203	1,546	2,352	1,321	1,839	860	1,801	999	2,178
	House	2,711	4,318	2,701	4,241	2,253	3,662	1,899	3,430	2,104	4,543
	TOTAL	4,274	6,521	4,247	6,593	3,574	5,501	2,759	5,231	3,103	6,721
Recorded Votes	Senate	253	380	298	374	314	298	306	613	329	395
	House[1]	484	512	603	611	547	640	455	885	507	615
	TOTAL	739	892	901	985	861	938	761	1,498	836	1,010
Vetoes		0	0	7[2]	5	5	3[3]	6	11	0	0

SOURCE: Congressional Record

[1] includes quorum calls
[2] includes pocket vetoes
[3] does not include line-item vetoes

was to get 218 signatures on a discharge petition. That strategy rarely works, and Shays and Meehan had been trying for months with little success. But the Enron scandal put them over the top. The campaign finance bill was forced to the floor Feb. 14 and passed by a solid margin, over the opposition of House Republican leaders. In the Senate, sponsors John McCain, R-Ariz., and Russell D. Feingold, D-Wis., negotiated to win passage of virtually the same version of the bill, avoiding a conference that opponents could have used to kill the measure. The Senate cleared the bill March 20, and Bush quietly signed it into law (PL 107-155).

Lawmakers also grasped for ways to address the root causes of the Enron scandal. They quickly focused on two issues: new regulations for the accounting industry, which was complicit in the shady dealings that led to Enron's collapse; and legislation to overhaul 401(k) plans to prevent other employees from suffering such disastrous losses.

The accounting legislation was the only part of the plan that actually became law. The House passed a bill in April that would have set up a new accounting oversight board, but many of the details would have been left to the Securities and Exchange Commission. Democrats pressed for a stronger bill, but their amendments were turned back.

Then in June, WorldCom Inc. admitted it had overstated its income by $3.9 billion. The news made the Senate's version of the accounting bill unstoppable and allowed the approval of Democratic amendments that broadened it further, such as mandating prison terms of up to 10 years for se-

curities fraud. Bush insisted that Congress send him a bill before the August recess, and the final version (PL 107-204) largely reflected the Senate bill.

The pension proposals, however, never quite took off. In April, the House passed a bill that would have given workers participating in 401(k) plans more flexibility to sell employer stock from those accounts; it also would have allowed financial services firms that manage retirement accounts to give investment advice to workers. But two Senate committees came up with conflicting proposals, and Daschle abandoned plans to put a compromise bill on the floor in September when it became clear that it would become a magnet for amendments intended as last-minute efforts to revive other stalled legislation.

Security on the Home Front

In May, Democrats headed by Sen. Joseph I. Lieberman of Connecticut, already seen as a potential challenger to Bush in 2004, proposed consolidating dozens of federal agencies into a Cabinet-level Department of Homeland Security. At the time, the effort was motivated partly by a desire to elevate the job of Homeland Security Director Tom Ridge to Cabinet-level status so he could no longer refuse to testify before Congress, as he had since his appointment by Bush in September 2001.

On May 22, the Senate Governmental Affairs Committee, which Lieberman chaired, approved the homeland security bill. An identical bill sponsored by William M. "Mac"

Thornberry, R-Texas, awaited action in the House. Publicly, the Bush administration was cool to the plan, prompting most congressional Republicans to oppose it. "I don't think you're going to be able to reorganize the executive branch without the cooperation of the executive branch. It's just not going to happen," said Sen. Fred Thompson of Tennessee, the ranking Republican on the Governmental Affairs panel.

Two weeks later, the Bush administration did an about-face and put its own stamp on the idea.

On June 6, Bush released his own proposal — which turned out to have been in the works since April — with a barrage of briefings and color charts, topped off with a presidential address. His plan was broader than anyone in Congress had contemplated, and he challenged lawmakers to approve it by the end of the year. "As we have learned more about the plans and capabilities of the terrorist network, we have concluded that our government must be reorganized to deal more effectively with the new threats of the 21st century," Bush said during a prime-time television address.

Coming so late in the year, that challenge created a major disruption in an agenda that was already significantly backed up. Still, Congress had no choice but to make room for it. Failing to get it done by the end of the year would have given Bush the ultimate reason to rail against a "do-nothing Congress," a label no one, particularly Democrats, wanted on an issue that seemed so important to Americans' safety.

In the House, Hastert and Minority Leader Richard A. Gephardt, D-Mo., created a nine-member Select Committee on Homeland Security to merge proposals from a number of committees on the homeland security bill. The Senate did not create any new committees to deal with the legislation. Instead, Lieberman took charge of the effort, assembling the new legislation to be brought to the Senate floor as an amendment to his original homeland security bill.

The House passed its version of the bill by a substantial margin July 26, despite a new controversy that arose over Bush's insistence on broad flexibility to hire, fire, promote and set salaries for the estimated 170,000 workers in the new department. But the issue gave rise to considerable turmoil in the Senate, causing the debate to drag on through September and into October as the White House, Senate Democrats and a handful of moderates from both parties tried to work out a compromise. Senators from both parties remained so divided over the personnel issue that Congress left town Oct. 17 without a homeland security bill to send to Bush's desk.

Bush and his GOP supporters said he needed broad flexibility in personnel rules to hire the most qualified people to deal with a wide range of terrorist threats. Democrats and their labor allies said the provision was simply an excuse to deny union representation to government workers. Bush regarded the flexibility as so crucial to the success of the future department that he threatened to veto any bill that did not contain it. In a Sept. 23 speech, he attacked Democrats for putting up such a fight over labor issues, charging that the Senate was "more interested in special interests in Washington and not interested in the security of the American people." When he read news reports about the speech, Daschle stormed to the Senate floor. With Daniel K. Inouye, D-Hawaii, who lost an arm in World War II, sitting behind him, the normally soft-spoken Daschle yelled himself hoarse. "You tell Sen. Inouye he is not interested in the security of the American people," Daschle said. "You tell those who fought in Vietnam and in World War II they are not interested in the security of the American people."

That conflict erupted in the middle of tense negotiations over the resolution approving the use of force in Iraq, but Democrats also had been stewing over what they saw as Bush's attempt to steal their idea for a homeland security department. By digging in over the work rules, however, Democrats effectively handed Bush an opening to attack them as opponents of their own idea. The White House was just as unwilling to compromise, if not more so, analysts said — but the standoff hurt Democrats more than it hurt Bush.

Other Troubles for Daschle

That was not the only failure of high-profile legislation in the Senate. In July, four competing proposals to establish prescription drug coverage for seniors failed after the House had passed a Republican plan that relied on the private sector to offer the coverage.

Daschle and Gephardt blamed Republicans for the Senate defeat and criticized the House bill as inadequate, but Republicans said the deadlock over homeland security and prescription drugs proved Daschle was unable to get the nation's most important priorities through the Senate. "There's no question that the Senate is not doing its job," said Minority Leader Trent Lott, R-Miss. Mitch McConnell, R-Ky., complained that "this has been the most unproductive session of the Senate in the 18 years I've been here."

If so, it was not because Daschle was a hands-off majority leader. Indeed, he began to use increasingly strong tactics not just to get bills moving in the closely divided Senate, but to steer them toward the results he wanted.

Daschle brought his favorite prescription drug proposal, sponsored by Bob Graham, D-Fla., straight to the Senate floor as an amendment to a drug pricing bill after the Finance Committee failed to meet a deadline to produce an alternative. He brought an energy bill directly to the floor to avoid the Energy and Natural Resources Committee, where Democrats did not have the votes to defeat a proposal to open ANWR to oil and gas exploration. And he filed a cloture motion to limit debate on a bill to strengthen penalties for "hate crimes" immediately after bringing it to the floor — exactly the kind of tactic he complained about when Lott used it as majority leader. The cloture vote failed, and the hate crimes measure never came back to the floor.

The House, meanwhile, spent much of the year passing bills it knew had no chance in the closely divided Senate but that promised political benefit to House Republicans. From a prescription drug bill to limits on liability for medical malpractice, three failed economic stimulus bills and half a dozen measures to make all or parts of the 2001 tax cuts permanent, Republicans could blame the Senate — and particularly Daschle — if the bills failed in that chamber.

Debate Over War in Iraq

The other part of Bush's doctrine for preventing new attacks in the United States — pre-emptive strikes against nations that could use weapons of mass destruction or pass them on to terrorists — led to a far more divisive debate

over whether to go to war to disarm Iraq.

Through the summer, Bush had been signaling the possibility of military strikes, arguing that Saddam had failed to dismantle his nuclear, chemical and biological weapons programs as he had committed to do in April 1991 under the agreement that ended the Gulf War. *(1991 Almanac, p. 437)*

The Bush administration argued that previous congressional and U.N. resolutions gave it all the authority it needed to go to war. But, facing the prospect of a pre-emptive war that some feared could last for years, many lawmakers were unwilling to buy that argument. "This is not merely a legal issue," said Daschle. "The issue is whether the president should seek to obtain the full support of the American people and their elected representatives before sending U.S. troops into combat in Iraq." Sen. Arlen Specter, R-Pa., said Congress has "a responsibility institutionally under the Constitution to declare war, and we have a responsibility to acquaint the American people as to what is involved."

On Sept. 4, Bush conceded, announcing he would seek congressional approval before launching any military strikes against Iraq. But he made it clear he wanted a vote before Nov. 5 — a decision that changed the dynamics of both the congressional debate and the midterm elections. The timing made it harder for congressional Democrats to hold out for more limits on Bush's authority to go to war. It exposed the split between many rank-and-file members, who wanted stronger language requiring Bush to seek the support of other countries and work through the United Nations, and some in the leadership who did not want Democrats to be portrayed as weak on international threats so close to the elections.

The ensuing debate turned on questions such as whether Bush should be required to form an international coalition to share in the military action, whether he should be authorized to launch a pre-emptive strike, how broad the goals of any war should be, and how much oversight Congress would have. Many Republicans thought it would set a dangerous precedent to tie Bush's hands if the United States was threatened, but some thought the language originally proposed by Bush — giving him authority to "restore international peace and security in the region" — was too broad and amounted to a blank check.

After negotiating with Republican and Democratic leaders, the Bush administration agreed to limit any military strikes to Iraq and to invoke the 1973 War Powers Act, which would limit Bush's ability to wage war without congressional oversight. But the White House held firm against any language that would require Bush to get permission from other countries before launching military actions that he believed were necessary to protect U.S. security. When Daschle held out for more concessions, the White House cut him out of the talks and reached a separate deal with Gephardt on language that would give Bush broad authority to decide whether and when to go to war against Iraq. For a variety of reasons, including his likely campaign for the presidency in 2004, Gephardt was wary of having Democrats appear complacent about Iraq's weapons of mass destruction.

The House adopted the resolution Oct. 10, with most Democrats voting "no" in defiance of Gephardt. The following day in the Senate, most Democrats — including a reluctant Daschle — voted for the resolution, giving Bush a 3-to-

1 margin in that chamber. Republican support was almost unanimous in both houses.

GOP Midterm Election Victory

The timing of the Iraq debate was a boost to Republicans and a source of annoyance to Democrats. It enabled GOP candidates to focus on the foreign policy issues that tended to favor them, while drowning out Democrats' efforts to talk about the economy and domestic issues, which they saw as Bush's greatest vulnerabilities. Speaking to a reporter, Rep. David R. Obey, D-Wis., said, "[Bush political adviser] Karl Rove gets up every morning, and his No. 1 job is to get people like you to ask people like me about Iraq, rather than the economy and corporate malfeasance."

However, Democrats themselves had asked for the Iraq debate, and it rapidly became clear they did not have a unified plan for the economy anyway. The party was painfully divided between the majority that wanted to criticize Bush's 2001 tax cut and a significant minority that had voted for it. Senate Democrats tried to blur the differences by giving their candidates a choice of three economic messages to use in their campaigns: Cancel that portion of the 2001 tax cut that had not yet taken effect, raise the minimum wage, or pass new tax cuts aimed at low-income people rather than the wealthy.

In the last two weeks before the election, Bush went on a campaign tour for GOP candidates, a move that was considered a risk by many political analysts because it made him personally invested in an election in which Republicans could have done poorly. There were about a half-dozen close races for Senate seats held by Democrats and about the same number for Republican-held seats, so a small shift in voter turnout could have made the difference in which party would control the Senate.

Bush's gamble paid off. His pleas for a GOP-controlled Senate that would enable him to enact his agenda helped motivate Republican voters to show up at the polls, while many Democratic voters, angry at their party for not fighting harder against a war with Iraq and for domestic priorities, stayed home. Republicans held the House, and with a net shift of two seats, they recaptured the Senate.

Lame-Duck Session

Before breaking for the elections, lawmakers had left most of the government running on a short-term appropriation (PL 107-244) that was due to expire Nov. 22. That alone guaranteed there would be a post-election, lame-duck session. With the Senate so closely divided, and a Republican majority certain in January, any lingering hopes vanished that lawmakers might break the appropriations logjam when they returned. A seventh stopgap spending bill (PL 107-294), cleared Nov. 19, kept the government operating until Jan. 11, 2003. Other items still on the agenda included the homeland security bill, terrorism insurance, defense authorization, port security, bankruptcy overhaul and another extension of unemployment insurance.

Lott, who was set to become Senate majority leader, had pushed for a quick lame-duck session that would fund the government into the following year and leave the homeland security effort for the next Congress. But a newly resurgent Bush said it was "imperative" that lawmakers send him the

Pelosi to Lead House Democrats

The rise of Nancy Pelosi to become the first woman to lead a political party in Congress took less than a year.

Before January 2002, the 62-year-old California Democrat was not even in the leadership. She vaulted directly into the No. 2 leadership slot Jan. 15, becoming House minority whip. She had been elected in October 2001 to replace David E. Bonior of Michigan, who gave up the post to concentrate on his race for governor.

Less than 10 months later, the top slot opened up. After Democrats once again failed to regain the House majority in the November 2002 election, Minority Leader Richard A. Gephardt of Missouri resigned from the leadership. He said he bore special responsibility for Democrats' failure to retake the majority four times in a row under his leadership, but it had been well known for months that he was likely to step down to focus on a bid for the 2004 Democratic presidential nomination.

Pelosi and Martin Frost of Texas, the Democratic Caucus chairman, had been gearing up for a battle for the top slot if Gephardt stepped down. Frost cast himself as a moderate alternative to the liberal Pelosi. "I think her politics are to the left, and for the party to be successful, we must speak to the broad center of the country," he said.

Just three days after the midterm election, however, Frost concluded that Pelosi had the majority of the votes locked up and dropped out of the race. Harold E. Ford Jr. of Tennessee jumped in, presenting himself as the new moderate candidate. The 32-year-old Ford said the elections proved the Democratic caucus needed a change, adding, "I don't think Ms. Pelosi represents that change."

But Pelosi was right in declaring she already had the election sewn up. In the Nov. 14 leadership election, Pelosi won 177 votes, compared with just 29 votes for Ford.

Some Republicans salivated at the prospect of a "San Francisco liberal" running the Democratic caucus. But leading Democrats — including newly elected Minority Whip Steny H. Hoyer of Maryland, who had lost to Pelosi in his previous bid for the minority whip job — said her political and legislative skills should not be underestimated. As a Californian, she had the support of the largest delegation in the House, and she had built up strong loyalty among House Democrats for years as a leading fundraiser and organizer.

"I don't think they chose me as an outspoken San Francisco liberal," she said. "I think they chose me as a person who can lead the caucus to victory, as a person who can build coalitions among the various segments of our caucus and as a person who represents various points of view within the caucus. The next leader had to come from some segment of the party, and I'm the one who got the votes."

homeland security bill before the end of the 107th Congress. Bush also called for "immediate" passage of a terrorism insurance bill.

Moderate senators who had been trying to broker a compromise on personnel rules for the new Homeland Security Department gave up. They settled for language that gave unions two months to review new personnel rules and seek mediation, though the Homeland Security Department could still impose the rules after two months even if the disputes had not been settled. "It's not a compromise. It's only an agreement to get this bill passed," said John B. Breaux, D-La. "It's the best we could get. It's not what I would have written." The House quickly assembled a new version of the bill and passed it Nov. 13. The Senate passed it Nov. 19, and the House gave final approval Nov. 22.

On terrorism insurance, Bush pushed relentlessly to get House Republicans to accept a deal he had struck with Senate Democrats before the election. Bush had dropped a ban on punitive damages, strongly backed by House leaders. The bill consolidated terrorism-related civil lawsuits in federal court and provided that punitive damages not count as insured losses subject to government aid. House GOP leaders, angry that Bush had cut a deal with Daschle, refused for several weeks to support the compromise. Bush repeatedly pushed GOP leaders to drop their opposition. They relented after Bush agreed to champion legislation in 2003 to curb punitive damage awards.

The conference report on the bankruptcy overhaul, still considered live legislation at the start of the lame-duck session, died in the House on Nov. 14 when abortion foes and others managed to defeat the rule for floor debate. The chief objection was a provision that was aimed at abortion protesters.

The Senate cleared the fiscal 2003 defense authorization bill Nov. 13, after compromising with Bush on a provision aimed at allowing military retirees to receive both veterans' pensions and disability payments.

But in a sign of how completely economic issues had been pushed off the agenda, Congress failed in a last-minute effort to pass another extension of unemployment benefits, which were due to expire Dec. 28 for more than 800,000 laid-off workers.

The Senate passed a 13-week extension, a compromise worked out by Senate Minority Whip Don Nickles, R-Okla., and Hillary Rodham Clinton, D-N.Y. But the House refused to reconsider its version, drafted by Ways and Means Committee Chairman Bill Thomas, R-Calif., which called for a five-week extension and would have canceled a scheduled cut in Medicare payments to physicians, a move opposed by the top Republican and Democrat on the Senate Finance Committee. Bush declined to intervene, and the 107th Congress adjourned without resolving the dispute.

Congressional Turnover

Even as they completed the lame-duck session, members were organizing for the 108th Congress. Senate Republicans

Public Gaffe Costs Lott Leadership Job

Trent Lott said he was simply trying to make Strom Thurmond feel good on his 100th birthday. Instead, the Mississippi Republican reopened old wounds of racism and segregation — and became the first Senate majority leader in history to be forced out of his job.

In his final months in the Senate, Thurmond had become known mainly for his longevity, and senator after senator had paid tribute to him. They carefully talked around the fact that the South Carolina Republican, who had served in the Senate for 47 years, was once a staunch opponent of civil rights legislation who ran for president against Harry S Truman in 1948 as the segregationist "Dixiecrat" candidate. (*Thurmond retirement, p. 1-12*)

Then, at a 100th birthday party for Thurmond on Dec. 5, Lott brought all of those memories back. "I want to say this about my state: When Strom Thurmond ran for president, we voted for him. We're proud of it," the Senate Republican leader said from the podium. "And if the rest of the country had followed our lead, we wouldn't have had all these problems over all these years, either."

At first, the statement got little attention. Then, Web columnists started to write about it. Then the national media. Conservative columnists, particularly African-American conservatives, pounced on Lott for seeming to confirm the worst stereotypes about Republicans being behind the curve on race relations.

Senate Majority Leader Tom Daschle, who had to work with Lott on a daily basis, initially gave him a pass. The South Dakota Democrat said Lott's comments were just another case in which "he and I go to the microphone . . . [and] say things we meant to say differently." But outraged members of the Congressional Black Caucus said Lott deserved no such mercy, and Daschle and other prominent Democrats quickly moved to condemn Lott's comments.

Senate Republicans stayed quiet, hoping the episode would fade after a few days. It did not. Instead, it erupted into a full-blown firestorm, one that only got worse every time Lott tried to apologize — particularly after it was revealed that Lott had made similar statements about Thurmond in the past.

At first, both Lott and his spokesman dismissed the comments. Then, Lott issued a written statement Dec. 9 apologizing "to anyone who was offended." Two days later, he made telephone calls to two talk shows — Sean Hannity's radio show and CNN's Larry King Live — to give more elaborate apologies and explain that he never meant to endorse segregation. "It basically is saying [to Thurmond], 'You know, you would have made a great president.' He lights up, he smiles at that," Lott told Hannity. "That's the vein that it was in. It was never intended to say, 'Because of the policies you were advocating in 1948.'"

None of Lott's comments put the issue to rest, and any chance that he could have survived the scandal was

and House Democrats saw an almost complete turnover in their leaderships, while the House GOP leadership endured its own shifts with the retirement of Armey. Only the Senate Democratic leadership remained stable; as much as Republicans tried to criticize his effectiveness, the affable and low-key Daschle was too popular with his Democratic colleagues to face a challenge.

In the Senate Republican Conference, McConnell was elected whip for the 108th Congress, replacing Nickles, who was leaving the No. 2 leadership job because of self-imposed GOP term limits to become chairman of the Budget Committee. Rick Santorum of Pennsylvania remained as chairman of the Senate Republican Conference, the third-ranking leadership post, but Jon Kyl of Arizona was set to take over as chairman of the Republican Policy Committee, replacing the term-limited Larry E. Craig of Idaho.

There was little suspense about who would be the Senate majority leader. Lott had served as Senate Republican leader since 1996 and was set to be re-elected without opposition.

Then, a careless birthday speech for 100-year-old Republican Sen. Strom Thurmond of South Carolina ended Lott's leadership career. After remarks suggesting that the nation would have been better off if Thurmond had succeeded in his segregationist presidential campaign of 1948, Lott was pummeled by embarrassed conservatives and outraged Democrats, and forced to step down as Senate Republican leader.

Bill Frist of Tennessee, a smart and telegenic heart surgeon who was considered unlikely to make the same kinds of stumbles on racial issues, took his place. (*Lott, above*)

In the House, Gephardt gave up his post as minority leader after Democrats failed to regain the majority for the fourth time since he became House Democratic leader. Nancy Pelosi, the Democratic whip, moved into Gephardt's slot, giving House Democrats the uncompromising liberal voice many thought Gephardt had abandoned when he endorsed the Iraq resolution. (*Pelosi, p. 1-9*)

Steny H. Hoyer of Maryland was elected without opposition to take Pelosi's place as Democratic whip. And Robert Menendez of New Jersey became the highest-ranking Hispanic lawmaker in congressional history when he was elected chairman of the Democratic Caucus, defeating Rosa DeLauro of Connecticut by one vote, 104-103. Menendez replaced Martin Frost of Texas, who was barred by party rules from seeking another term. James E. Clyburn of South Carolina replaced Menendez as vice chairman of the caucus.

On the Republican side, Hastert was elected to a third term as House GOP leader, no surprise for the popular Speaker. Tom DeLay of Texas moved up from the No. 3 position of majority whip to the No. 2 position of majority leader — putting the outspoken conservative, known for his strategic skill in holding Republican votes together, in charge of shaping the GOP congressional agenda in 2003.

dashed Dec. 12, when President Bush publicly criticized him. "Recent comments by Sen. Lott do not reflect the spirit of our country," Bush told a mostly black audience in Philadelphia, to thunderous applause. "He has apologized, and rightly so."

For Bush and his allies, there were bigger issues at stake than the survival of one Republican leader. Bush had campaigned as a "different kind of Republican," one who would pursue "compassionate conservative" policies and improve his party's record on civil rights. As a presidential candidate in 2000, he had told the National Association for the Advancement of Colored People that "the party of Lincoln has not always carried the mantle of Lincoln." Lott's comments had put all of those efforts at risk.

As the pressure mounted, Lott quickly set up a televised press conference in his hometown of Pascagoula, Miss., on Dec. 13. "Segregation is a stain on our nation's soul," Lott said. "I have asked and am asking for people's forbearance and forgiveness as I continue to learn from my own mistakes and as I continue to grow as both a person and a leader."

Three days later, he told an astonished interviewer for Black Entertainment Television (BET) that he supported affirmative action.

To Republicans, Lott's numerous apologies were looking increasingly desperate — particularly his endorsement of affirmative action, which most conservatives saw as a sellout. On Dec. 15, Don Nickles of Oklahoma, the outgoing Senate Republican whip and a longtime rival of Lott, issued a statement suggesting Lott "had been weak-ened to the point that it may jeopardize his ability to enact our agenda."

That was the cue for which other Republicans were waiting. Although Lott already had been re-elected as Senate Republican leader before the controversy, Senate Republican Conference Chairman Rick Santorum of Pennsylvania scheduled a new meeting for Jan. 6 to decide Lott's fate. Virginia Sen. George Allen suggested to Bill Frist of Tennessee, a heart surgeon who had strengthened his party's credentials on health care issues, that he consider challenging Lott for the Senate majority leader job.

There had been speculation about Frist as a possible successor ever since the scandal erupted, and the White House had sent not-so-subtle signals that Bush would be happy if Frist took Lott's place. But Frist always had presented himself as someone who would have to be drafted for the job.

In reality, his reluctance faded quickly. On Dec. 19, Frist released a statement that "if it is clear that a majority of the Republican Caucus believes a change in leadership would benefit the institution of the United States Senate, I will likely step forward for that role." Within hours, Republicans rallied behind him so solidly that Lott's re-election became impossible.

On Dec. 20, Lott announced he would no longer be a candidate for the majority leader job. Eager to put the nightmarish publicity behind them, Senate Republicans canceled their January meeting and, in a Dec. 23 telephone conference call, elected Frist by acclamation to be the Senate majority leader for the 108th Congress.

DeLay's protégé, Roy Blunt of Missouri, was elected to succeed him as majority whip, while Deborah Pryce of Ohio was elected to the No. 4 position of House Republican Conference chairman.

The leadership situation became especially murky in the Senate during the lame-duck session, when the close margin made it possible that the shift of a single seat could have returned Republicans to the majority before the end of the session.

That almost happened with the Missouri seat held by Democrat Jean Carnahan. She was defeated by Republican Jim Talent in the Nov. 5 election, and once his election was certified, Republicans were guaranteed to regain control of the Senate, since Talent's victory would give them the one-seat shift they needed. Talent, however, was not sworn in until Nov. 25, three days after the 107th Congress adjourned.

Untimely Departures

Congress also mourned the death of two liberal icons. Democratic Rep. Patsy T. Mink of Hawaii, first elected to the House in 1964 and nearing the end of her 12th term, died Sept. 28 of viral pneumonia after contracting chicken pox. Ed Case, a moderate who declared himself independent of Hawaii's long-dominant Democratic Party machine, won a special election to fill out the remainder of Mink's term — after the 107th had already adjourned — and defeated 43 other candidates in another special election Jan. 4 to win a full term in the 108th.

In the Senate, Democrat Paul Wellstone of Minnesota, an outspoken liberal firebrand who was just finishing his second term, was fighting an uphill battle for re-election against Republican Norm Coleman, the popular former mayor of St. Paul. On Oct. 25, just 10 days before the election, Wellstone's twin-engine plane crashed in freezing rain and light snow in northern Minnesota. The senator, his wife Sheila, his daughter Marcia, three campaign aides and two pilots all were killed.

A stunned Coleman put his campaign on hold, and grieving Democrats scrambled to find a last-minute candidate to replace Wellstone. Walter F. Mondale, the former senator (1964-76), vice president and Democratic presidential nominee, stepped in, calling his weeklong campaign a tribute to Wellstone. Coleman, faced with the sensitive task of restarting his campaign so soon after his opponent's death, simply asked voters to "look with me into the future."

The day before the election, Minnesota Gov. Jesse Ventura appointed Dean Barkley, a fellow Independence Party member and longtime ally, to serve the remainder of Wellstone's term. On Nov. 5, Coleman defeated Mondale by 2 percentage points — a GOP coup that helped Republicans regain control of the Senate. ◆

Strom Thurmond Retires at Age 99

When he gaveled the 107th Congress to a close on Nov. 20, Strom Thurmond left the Senate chamber on his own terms, just two weeks shy of his 100th birthday. On a personal level, he had a singular determination to finish out his service. On a broader political level, he performed to the end with constant accommodation to his South Carolina constituents.

Though he served for more than 47 years at the Capitol, Thurmond was not simply a creature of Congress. He was really a product of the South, in particular the politics of South Carolina and its century-long re-emergence from the debilitating and (to Southerners) emasculating era of Reconstruction.

The segregationist politics in the first half of Thurmond's career personified the spiteful resistance to giving African-Americans an equal place in U.S. society. The second half embodied the recognition, however grudging, that they were entitled to full citizenship. In short, the civil rights laws of the 1960s and 1970s forced politicians of Thurmond's era and region to adapt or fall by the wayside. Strom Thurmond not only survived but thrived as a political force to be reckoned with.

Thurmond always prided himself on "standing with the people." In the first three decades of his 74-year political career, "the people" — those who voted — were exclusively white. The landmark 1965 Voting Rights Act (PL 89-110) forced him to redefine "the people" to include blacks as well as whites. (*1965 Almanac, p. 553*)

Thurmond incorporated both races into his own brand of hands-on politics with such success that he could count on 15 percent of the black vote every six years — and perhaps more important, he encountered almost no organized opposition from black political groups. He was a formidable retail politician who loved the person-to-person contact and had a gift for connecting names and faces, and the stories that went with them. He touched lives literally and figuratively in every county of the state. Simply put, his constituents left it up to him when to quit.

By the time Thurmond had cast his "aye" vote for the 1982 Voting Rights Act — and boasted about it to the NAACP's chief lobbyist on his way into the Senate chamber — his political realignment and that of the Senate's Old Southern Guard were complete.

Civil rights activist Victoria DeLee captured the essence of his success when she told reporters in 1972, "I'm for whoever is getting the job done, and Strom is getting the job done. What a man was yesterday doesn't matter. It's what he is today that counts."

In the Blood

For all of his years in Washington, Thurmond left a modest legislative record. There are few major laws named after him, although he is well honored on South Carolina real estate. He is remembered for how long he served, the unprecedented span of his career in public life.

Remarkably, Thurmond had a rich political career in South Carolina before he came to Washington. That long and varied service — superintendent of schools, state senator, judge, governor and (less successfully) third-party presidential candidate — was instrumental in his political survival when the 1965 Voting Rights Act transformed the South Carolina electorate. He loved public life and treated constituents as his lifeblood. He knew every inch of South Carolina and had deep ties and connections in every county. Those ties counted for something when change came.

The basic benefit of incumbency also was a critical factor in Thurmond's long tenure. His Senate service at the height of the civil rights struggle insulated him somewhat from the turmoil. Though he hurled invective from the Senate floor in opposition to every civil rights bill, he was one step removed from the battleground — being neither a mayor ordering police to arrest protesters nor a governor standing in the schoolhouse door.

When the time came to examine his record at the end of a term, his incendiary rhetoric could be offset by the concrete actions of an attentive politician with an extraordinary common touch.

The Write-In Senator

Like much of his life, Thurmond's arrival in the Senate was unusual. He was the only senator ever elected as a write-in candidate, defeating state Sen. Edgar Brown in 1954. Brown had been chosen by Democratic Party leaders to take the place of incumbent Burnet Maybank (1941-54), who died unexpectedly two months before the election. Thurmond promised that if he won, he would step down and run again for a full term in 1956. He did so and won without opposition.

From the start of his political career with his election as Edgefield superintendent of education in 1928, Thurmond was a Democrat. There really was no other party in the South, the result of smoldering anger over the Civil War — which had ended only 63 years before — and the Republican-led Reconstruction.

When he won election as governor in 1946, he campaigned as a progressive and began his term in that vein, advocating more money for education, encouraging women to serve in government and dispatching a special prosecutor to try the brutal lynching of a black man. But by the end of 1947, Thurmond was drawn inexorably into the conflict over civil rights policy between the Southern wing of the party and northern Democrats.

Right after President Harry S Truman was nominated by the Democrats in July 1948 for election in his own right, Thurmond headed to Birmingham and a meeting there of "states' rights" Democrats. Yielding to urgent entreaties, he agreed to be the insurgents' presidential candidate. More prominent governors and Southern senators, chief among them Richard Russell of Georgia (1933-71) and James O. Eastland of Mississippi (1941, 1943-78), declined to bolt the party to make a run for the White House, recognizing that if they lost, they risked their seniority in the Senate.

If Thurmond was an unlikely choice — a recently elected governor with no national following — he had none of that political power to lose and, at a minimum, something to gain by the name recognition afforded him during the fall campaign. His acceptance speech in Birmingham — an incendiary blast about there not being "enough troops in the Army" to force integration — would become attached to him like a tattoo.

Thurmond and his running mate, Gov. Fielding L. Wright of Mississippi (1946-52), were dubbed the "Dixiecrats." They carried only Alabama, Louisiana, Mississippi and South Carolina — 39 electoral votes in all, although less than 1.2 million votes. But if winning only 2 percent nationwide was a poor showing, it nonetheless planted the seeds of a political realignment to come.

Thurmond's initial reputation as a progressive governor gave way to a more reactionary profile. The Senate became his new platform, and although he took a back seat to his Southern elders, Russell and Eastland, on most matters, Thurmond was the moving force behind the 1956 "Southern Manifesto," a broadside that called for resistance to the Supreme Court's school desegregation mandates in *Brown v. Board of Education*.

The next year he conducted what is still the longest live filibuster in history — 24 hours, 18 minutes — in opposition to President Dwight D. Eisenhower's modest civil rights bill (PL 85-315). Thurmond's performance bore no resemblance to today's decorous stalling tactics, which allow the mere threat of extended debate to bring Senate action to a halt. In 1957, Thurmond was on the floor for the entire time, reading state voting procedures and hoping that word of his marathon effort would prompt Southern supporters to call or wire their senators to join him. *(1957 Almanac, p. 553)*

The filibuster was unsuccessful, but Thurmond took his opposition to the stump, using the federal government's actions to integrate Little Rock's high school as an occasion to vent his criticism. "We in the South are not about to surrender, not now or in the future," he said. He reserved a special blast for the Supreme Court, whom he called "nine puppets of the NAACP" for refusing to give Arkansas authorities more time to work out a compromise. He promised that Southerners would "maintain an adequate system of mass education for all people — either public or private — and that we will maintain it segregated."

It may have been Russell who devised the Southern strategy in opposition to the major civil rights legislation of the 1960s, which sought to open public accommodations (1964) and ensure voting rights (1965). But Thurmond was more than a reliable vote; he was a cheerleader for the cause. He opposed the legislation in speech after speech and took on the nomination of Thurgood Marshall to the federal judiciary, belittling Marshall's many legal victories and wondering aloud whether he was versed properly in the Constitution.

Where others might venerate the Fifth and 14th Amendments — equal protection and due process guarantees — Thurmond was a 10th Amendment man. He revered the clause that reserved powers not specified elsewhere to the states. He could give a 10th Amendment speech on a moment's notice, reminding listeners that the Constitution does not say a word about education or the running of hotels, restaurants or barber shops, which to him meant the federal government had no business interfering in those affairs.

Jumping to the GOP

By 1964, Thurmond had grown increasingly disaffected with the Democrats. Fond of Arizona Republican Sen. Barry Goldwater (1953-65, 1969-87), he decided to switch parties in September 1964, right after Goldwater won the GOP nomination to challenge President Lyndon B. Johnson.

His announcement of the party switch was a 22-count indictment against the Democrats, who had "forsaken the people to become the party of minority groups, power-hungry union leaders, political bosses and businessmen looking for government contracts and favors," and had "invaded the private lives of people by using the powers of government for coercion and intimidation of individuals . . . encouraged lawlessness, civil unrest and mob actions." Continued Democratic rule, he claimed, would mean that "freedom as we have known it in this country is doomed, and individuals will be destined to lives of regulation, control, coercion, intimidation and subservience to a power elite who shall rule from Washington."

Thurmond would not be the most important Southern Republican in the coming decades, but he was the first, a marker for the evolving political realignment throughout the region. The old Dixiecrats were turning into the new Southern Republicans — distrustful of an imposing federal government, resentful of the new race consciousness.

Thurmond was up for re-election in 1966 and should have been a prime target for defeat. He was running as a Republican in a state that still was traditionally Democratic. On top of that, the 1965 Voting Rights Act had taken effect, and black registered voters — many of them with memories dating to 1948 or earlier — would be going to the polls in significant numbers. But Thurmond prevailed, winning a third full term with 62 percent.

Two years later, he threw his considerable energy behind the presidential candidacy of Richard M. Nixon, serving as a linchpin of the vaunted Southern strategy.

Thurmond faced his most formidable opponent in 1978. In a race that drew national attention, he beat the attractive and much younger Charles "Pug" Ravenel. Widowed since 1960, Thurmond had remarried in 1966, to Nancy Moore, a former Miss South Carolina who was 44 years his junior. By now he was the father of four young children.

The image of this youthful, vigorous family campaigning for husband and father proved to be a help.

Two other factors were important: what was by now a half-century relationship with the South Carolina electorate, and Thurmond's own recognition of a new political reality. He had been the first South Carolina lawmaker to hire a black on his staff. He began courting the growing number of black elected officials, and he tended to his black constituents' needs with the same care he always had given white Carolinians.

In the Senate, Thurmond could play rough politics, literally and figuratively. A fitness buff, he was proud of the fact that he was stronger and in better shape than many other, younger colleagues, even if he was a bit vain. Well-versed in Senate procedure, he knew the importance of committee

quorums. Without them, a panel cannot act. In 1964, he famously wrestled Texas Democrat Ralph Yarborough (1957-71) to the ground outside a committee room in the Dirksen Senate Office Building to prevent Yarborough from making a quorum to consider legislation that Thurmond opposed.

In 1978, when Republicans were shifting committee assignments among themselves, Thurmond exercised his seniority to take the ranking seat on Judiciary, jumping over his much more moderate GOP colleague, Charles McC. Mathias Jr. of Maryland (1969-87). Thurmond had been the ranking member on Armed Services, but he was sure he could better protect GOP interests on a Judiciary Committee now chaired by Massachusetts Democrat Edward M. Kennedy instead of Mississippi's Eastland, who had retired.

When Republicans took over the Senate in 1981, Thurmond's decision proved critical. The election results meant that the old Dixiecrat would become Judiciary chairman, presiding over civil rights legislation and judicial nominations.

The ensuing debate over renewing the all-important Voting Rights Act (PL 97-205) turned into a lesson in the importance of that law and Thurmond's own accommodations to the new order: Thurmond now had a black constituency. While Jesse Helms, R-N.C., and other conservatives mounted a filibuster against it, Thurmond declined to play obstructionist politics and ultimately supported the measure when the final votes were cast. (*1982 Almanac, p. 373*)

Waning Powers

When Republicans again won control of the Senate in 1994, after six years in the minority, Thurmond switched committees to chair Armed Services. But at 92, he was little more than a figurehead. Republican John W. Warner of Virginia was the functional chairman. Under pressure from his GOP colleagues, Thurmond relinquished control of the panel at the end of 1998 and focused on the ceremonial role of Senate president pro tempore. Early in 2001, he had to give up those duties, too frail to make the walk from his office to open the Senate every day that the chamber was in session.

As a sign of goodwill toward him, colleagues created the honorary position of "president pro tempore emeritus." In previous years there had been other acknowledgments of respect. When Joseph R. Biden Jr., D-Del., took over Judiciary in 1987, he delayed announcing his reorganization plans until he could tell Thurmond first. He tracked him down in South Carolina, on the reviewing stand for a local parade that Thurmond had promised to attend.

Thurmond was loyal to those who were loyal to him. Increasingly frail in the waning weeks of his last session, he mustered up the energy in October for one final blast on the Senate floor, excoriating the Judiciary Committee for not moving on the nomination of one of his most trusted aides, Dennis Shedd, to a new federal appellate court position. Shedd ultimately was confirmed. (*Nominations, p. 13-12*)

It was vintage Strom Thurmond, calling to mind another such moment, one of the periodic dinners with former aides back home in Columbia. A few got up to tell stories after the dishes were cleared, and then Thurmond spoke, delivering a Borscht Belt routine but with a Southern accent. When the program was over and most guests had filtered out, the remaining few realized the senator was not with them. They scoured the room and finally found him in the back, shaking hands one by one with the kitchen help. He was thanking them for their work.

Where once he had seen only servants, now it was Strom who bowed to his constituents. ◆

Two Veteran Members Leave in Disgrace

Ethics transgressions led to the departure of two members of Congress in 2002. One gave up a faltering re-election bid; the other was forced out after being sentenced to eight years in prison.

Sen. Torricelli Admonished, Resigns

Democratic Sen. Robert G. Torricelli of New Jersey was "severely admonished" by the Senate Ethics Committee on July 30 for improperly accepting expensive gifts from a former campaign supporter. It was the harshest ethical rebuke of a senator in seven years. Two months later, amid plummeting poll ratings, Torricelli abandoned his campaign for a second term in the Senate.

In January, the Justice Department ended a four-year investigation into Torricelli's campaign fundraising activities and allegations that he had improperly accepted and failed to report expensive gifts from David Chang, a former supporter who was then serving an 18-month sentence for making illegal campaign contributions to Torricelli's 1996 Senate campaign. Prosecutors said they lacked sufficient credible evidence for an indictment, but they forwarded their files to the Ethics Committee. (*2001 Almanac, p. 6-9*)

Ethics Chairman Harry Reid, D-Nev., recused himself from the probe, after news reports revealed that he had contributed $500 to Torricelli's legal defense fund in 2001. Daniel K. Inouye, D-Hawaii, took over at Reid's behest.

After six months of closed-door staff work, the panel invited Torricelli to meet with committee lawyers to answer questions under oath, which he did. Chang offered to testify from prison, but he was rebuffed. On July 30, after hearing from no other witnesses, the six Ethics members (three from each party) issued a surprisingly sharp letter that "severely admonished" Torricelli for violating Senate rules prohibiting members from accepting gifts of more than $50 in value. The panel concluded that Torricelli's relationship with Chang "created at least the appearance of impropriety," and it ordered Torricelli to pay Chang the fair-market cost of the items he accepted. The full Senate was not required to act. Torricelli took the floor and apologized to the Senate and to his constituents.

While he continued his re-election campaign, his relatively unknown GOP opponent, businessman Douglas Forrester, took a double-digit lead in most polls. Torricelli withdrew from the race Sept. 30. Democrats successfully petitioned the New Jersey Supreme Court to order the distribution of ballots using the name of their replacement candidate — Frank R. Lautenberg, who had been senator from 1982 until 2001 — notwithstanding a state law that set a deadline of 51 days before an election for replacing candidates. The U.S. Supreme Court declined to reconsider that decision, and Lautenberg won the Senate seat in November.

Rep. Traficant Expelled

On July 24, six days before he was sentenced and led away in handcuffs to begin an eight-year prison term, James A. Traficant Jr., D-Ohio, was expelled from the House of Representatives on a vote of 420-1. Traficant was only the fifth House member ever expelled, and only the second since the Civil War. *(House vote 346, p. H-108)*

The expulsion vote in some ways was the final defiant act of the bombastic Traficant, whose nearly nine terms in office were spent railing against federal conspiracies, unproven cover-ups, China's influence on the U.S. government and the long arm of the IRS. Most lawmakers convicted of crimes resigned rather than force their colleagues to go through an uncomfortable expulsion debate and vote. Traficant refused to depart willingly, getting his last say — and the maximum number of paydays — before his colleagues threw him out.

He also ran for re-election from his prison cell as an independent. He received 15 percent of the vote.

Traficant was accused of demanding kickbacks from some of his congressional aides and using his position for personal gain. On April 11, a federal court jury in Cleveland found him guilty of conspiracy to commit bribery, seeking and accepting illegal gratuities, racketeering, obstruction of justice and filing false federal income tax returns — all of the 10 counts that had been brought the year before by a federal grand jury. *(2001 Almanac, p. 6-8)*

A subcommittee of the House ethics committee examined 10 ethics counts that were based on the criminal proceeding, heard three days of testimony and deliberated for five hours. On July 18, the panel decided that Traficant had violated House rules, finding him guilty on nine of 10 ethics counts. Later that day, the full Committee on Standards of Official Conduct recommended his expulsion.

On the House floor six days later, Traficant offered a rambling, 45-minute defense, in which he maintained that he was the victim of a government vendetta. Then, in an uncharacteristically quiet and weary voice, he told his colleagues, "Vote your conscience. Nothing personal." Only Gary A. Condit, D-Calif., opposed the expulsion resolution (H Res 495). The last member expelled before Traficant was Michael J. "Ozzie" Myers, D-Pa. (1976-80), who had accepted bribes from undercover FBI agents in the sting operation known as Abscam. ◆

GAO Loses Attempt to Sue Vice President Cheney

There was plenty of disagreement over whether the General Accounting Office (GAO) was staying true to its mission when it sued Vice President Dick Cheney to force him to release records from an energy task force he headed in 2001. But there was little dispute that in losing the battle, the investigative and auditing arm of Congress suffered a setback that could hinder its ability to enforce even routine requests for information from the White House.

The legal battle arose after Democrats accused the White House of relying heavily on advice from big business in 2001 to draft a national energy policy. They asked the administration to release documents related to private meetings of Cheney's National Energy Policy Development Group. When the administration refused, House Democrats John D. Dingell of Michigan and Henry A. Waxman of California asked the GAO to look into the task force. They did not try to use committee subpoenas to get the information, because the House GOP majority almost certainly would have blocked them.

But Comptroller General David M. Walker, who headed the GAO, took up their cause and repeatedly demanded information from the White House about the task force. When Cheney refused, the GAO filed a federal lawsuit Feb. 22 seeking to compel Cheney to provide the names of everyone who participated in task force meetings. It was the first time the GAO had sued the executive branch to disclose documents.

The White House insisted its deliberations and consultations with federal employees and outsiders were private matters, protected by the Constitution. The case was assigned to U.S. District Judge John D. Bates, a former member of Independent Counsel Kenneth W. Starr's legal team, who recently had been named to the federal bench by President Bush.

In arguments before the court in September, Cheney's lawyer, Paul D. Clement, asked Bates to dismiss the case, saying the GAO lacked the standing to sue the vice president and that Congress had other ways of obtaining the information, such as issuing subpoenas. The GAO, however, argued that a dismissal of the case would cripple its ability to investigate federal programs. Such a move would "essentially put the GAO out of business" because it would encourage other federal agencies to deny requests for information, said attorney Carter G. Phillips.

On Dec. 9, Bates dismissed the lawsuit, echoing Cheney's argument that the GAO lacked the standing to compel the disclosure of the task force records. In addition, he said the court should not get involved in the separation-of-powers struggle that would result if the congressional office was allowed to force Cheney to release the records. "Such an excursion by the judiciary would be unprecedented and would fly in the face of the restricted role of the federal courts under the Constitution," Bates wrote.

Bates wrote that the GAO was only "an agent of Congress" and noted that there had been no subpoena for the information from the House, the Senate or any congressional committee.

Waxman called the court ruling "convoluted and bizarre" and urged the GAO to appeal the decision. He said Bates appeared to have ignored a 1983 Supreme Court ruling, in *Bowsher v. Merck*, that a pharmaceutical company had to give the GAO records of its business with federal agencies even though the accounting office was only responding to the request of individual lawmakers.

After consulting with congressional leaders from both parties, however, Walker concluded an appeal would be too risky and expensive. On Feb. 7, 2003, he announced the GAO would not appeal the decision because such an appeal would require an "investment of significant time and resources over several years." In addition, because Bates did not actually rule on the merits of GAO's argument, "it has no effect on GAO's statutory audit rights or on the obligation of agencies to provide GAO with information," the

congressional office said.

That view contradicted the arguments of Democratic leaders, including House Minority Leader Nancy Pelosi of California, who had urged the GAO to appeal the ruling. "Everyone should be held accountable, including the president and the vice president," a Pelosi spokesman said. Waxman called the decision not to appeal Bates' ruling "a tremendous setback for open government."

Ironically, private organizations had better luck forcing the Bush administration to turn over some of the task force documents. In February 2001, U.S. District Judge Gladys Kessler ordered the Energy Department to turn over thousands of pages of records related to the task force that had been requested by the Natural Resources Defense Council, an environmental group. The lawsuit forced the department to release 11,000 pages of documents, though critics said the administration deleted important information from them. ◆

Chapter 2

APPROPRIATIONS

Eleven Spending Bills Postponed

The appropriations process all but collapsed in 2002, leaving 11 of the 13 annual spending bills unfinished and forwarding the problem to the 108th Congress. The only fiscal 2003 spending bills to become law were for the Department of Defense (PL 107-248) and military construction (PL 107-249). All non-defense programs were funded at fiscal 2002 levels under a series of five continuing resolutions, the last of which was good through Jan. 11, 2003. (*Bush budget, p. 6-3*)

The stalemate was the result of divisions between Democrats and Republicans, and among Republicans themselves, over how closely to stick to the limit set by President Bush for total discretionary spending. Bush's fiscal 2003 budget called for a total of $759 billion in discretionary funds. However, that included a request for a $10 billion defense reserve fund, a blank check that appropriators refused to write. As a result, all parties eventually accepted $749 billion as the Bush discretionary request.

Within that total, Bush sought a 13 percent increase for defense while essentially freezing non-defense appropriations at $366 billion. Appropriators in both parties on both sides of the Capitol made it clear they did not think that was enough to enable them to write 13 bills that could garner the support needed to get through both chambers.

The prescription for trouble was written early in the year, when the House and Senate failed to agree on a fiscal 2003 budget resolution. Without a budget resolution to establish a common spending limit for both chambers, lawmakers went their separate ways. It was only the second time that had happened since the start of the modern budget process in 1974. (*Budget resolution, p, 6-8*)

The House adopted a budget resolution (H Con Res 353) with a $749 billion discretionary total, plus $10 billion set aside for Bush's defense reserve; members subsequently voted to make that limit binding on the House appropriators. The Senate Budget Committee approved a discretionary limit of $768 billion with no defense reserve, but Democratic leaders concluded they did not have the votes in the full Senate and never brought the measure (S Con Res 100) to the floor. Appropriators in both chambers said the Senate total was the minimum they needed. Bush said he would veto spending bills that exceeded the House total.

House, Senate on Separate Paths

Using a strategy that had proved successful in the recent past, House appropriators moved several politically popular domestic spending bills to the end of the queue, underfunding them at the outset on the assumption that GOP leaders eventually would loosen the purse strings — even if it meant breaking Bush's discretionary spending limit. In July, the House passed three domestic spending bills — for the Interior Department, legislative branch, and the Treasury Department and Postal Service.

Recognizing a familiar pattern, a small band of fiscal conservatives intervened in mid-July. They won a promise from Speaker J. Dennis Hastert, R-Ill., to move the biggest of the domestic bills — for the departments of Labor, Health and Human Services (HHS) and Education — to the front of the line after the August recess. When it became apparent in September that GOP leaders could not get the votes to pass the Labor-HHS measure without spending more than the $130.9 billion in discretionary funds proposed by Bush, the appropriations process came to a halt in the House.

In the Senate, Appropriations Committee Chairman Robert C. Byrd, D-W.Va., moved all 13 bills through his panel by the end of July, with solid GOP support. The bills exceeded Bush's domestic spending request by about $13 billion, including some advance appropriations. The only domestic spending bill that made it through the full Senate, however, was for the legislative branch. Senate floor action on appropriations largely stopped after the August recess.

The exception to the stalemate was defense. Bush had insisted all year that Congress act on defense first, and, given the war against terrorism and the threat of action against Iraq, lawmakers readily complied. Once the defense bill and the smaller military construction bill cleared in October, Bush had little incentive to compromise on the remaining measures.

Bush Holds Line in Lame-Duck Session

House appropriators still hoped for a freer spending environment after the midterm elections. But Republican gains on Nov. 5 strengthened Bush's determination to hold firm.

When House Appropriations Committee Chairman C.W. Bill Young, R-Fla., and the ranking Republican on Senate Appropriations, Ted Stevens of Alaska, went to the White House on Nov. 15 hoping to get an additional $10 billion, Bush cautioned them not to go much beyond about $750 billion. Hastert had promised Young before the election that action on spending bills would occur during the lame-duck session, but that plan was quickly scotched. Hastert and other GOP leaders decided instead to return to the appropriations bills in January, when the party would control both chambers of Congress.

To allow that to happen, the House voted 270-143 on Nov. 13 to pass a short-term spending bill (H J Res 124) that would keep domestic programs operating at 2002 levels until Jan. 11, 2003. The Senate cleared the continuing resolution, 92-2, on Nov. 19, and Bush signed it Nov. 23 (PL 107-294). (*House vote 474, p. H-148; Senate vote 253, p. S-52*)

The continuing resolution included language to extend expiring provisions of the landmark 1996 welfare overhaul law (PL 104-193). It also contained a provision giving the secretary of the new Department of Homeland Security limited flexibility to transfer funds between agencies of the new Cabinet department. That flexibility, strongly resisted by appropriators who feared their wishes could be rewritten by executive fiat, was limited to a total of $500 million and could not exceed 2 percent of any given account. The measure also provided $140 million in unspent appropriations as seed money for the new agency. (*Welfare, p. 15-3; Homeland Security Department, p. 7-3*) ◆

Appropriations Mileposts
107th Congress — Second Session

Bill	House Action	Senate Action	House Final*	Senate Final*	President Signed	Story
Agriculture (HR 5263, S 2801)	Committee approved 7/11/02	Committee approved 7/25/92				2-5
Commerce-Justice-State (S 2778)		Committee approved 7/18/02				2-7
Defense (HR 5010 — PL 107-248)	Passed 6/27/02	Passed 8/1/02	10/10/02	10/16/02	10/23/02	2-9
District of Columbia (HR 5521, S 2809)	Committee approved 9/26/02	Committee approved 7/25/02				2-14
Energy-Water Development (HR 5431, S 2784)	Committee approved 9/5/02	Committee approved 7/24/02				2-16
Foreign Operations (HR 5410, S 2779)	Committee approved 9/12/02	Committee approved 7/18/02				2-18
Interior (HR 5093, S 2708)	Passed 7/17/02	Floor debate ended 9/25/02				2-21
Labor-HHS-Education (HR 5320, S 2766)		Committee approved 7/18/02				2-24
Legislative Branch (HR 5121, S 2720)	Passed 7/18/02	Passed 7/25/02				2-27
Military Construction (HR 5011 — PL 107-249)	Passed 6/27/02	Passed 7/18/02	10/10/02	10/11/02	10/23/02	2-30
Transportation (HR 5559, S 2808)	Committee approved 10/1/02	Committee approved 7/25/02				2-32
Treasury-Postal Service (HR 5120, S 2740)	Passed 7/24/02	Committee approved 7/16/02				2-35
VA-HUD (HR 5605, S 2797)	Committee approved 10/9/02	Committee approved 7/25/02				2-38
FY 2003 Continuing Resolutions (H J Res 111 — PL 107-229) (H J Res 112 — PL 107-235) (H J Res 122 — PL 107-240) (H J Res 123 — PL 107-244) (H J Res 124 — PL 107-294)	Passed 9/26/02 10/3/02 10/10/02 10/16/02 11/13/02	Passed 9/26/02 10/3/02 10/11/02 10/16/02 11/19/02			9/30/02 10/4/02 10/11/02 10/18/02 11/23/02	2-3
FY 2002 Supplemental (HR 4775 — PL 107-206)	Passed 5/24/02	Passed 6/7/02	7/23/02	7/24/02	8/2/02	2-40

* Adoption of conference report

Farm Subsidy Fight Put Off

House and Senate appropriators completed work on separate versions of a fiscal 2003 agricultural appropriations bill, but the measure stalled as part of the yearlong dispute over non-defense spending. Programs funded by the annual bill were left to operate at fiscal 2002 levels until Jan. 11, 2003, under a stopgap spending law (PL 107-294).

Both versions of the bill would have provided about $74.3 billion — compared with $73.5 billion requested by President Bush and $73.4 billion appropriated for fiscal 2002.

About one-fourth of the total — $17.6 billion in the House bill, $18 billion in the Senate version — was discretionary spending for programs such as rural development; supplemental nutrition for women, infants and children; and the Food and Drug Administration. The other three-fourths was mandatory spending required under separate law for programs such as commodity price and income supports, food stamps and child nutrition.

Both committees put off decisions on controversial issues left over from debate on the new six-year farm bill (PL 107-171), including demands for tighter limits on federal subsidies to individual farmers and a proposal to diversify the livestock industry by requiring that one-fourth of all livestock be purchased on the open market before slaughter. The two issues pitted lawmakers from the Midwest, where farms tend to be smaller and production costs lower, against those from the South and West. *(Farm bill, p. 4-3)*

Midwesterners hoped to limit annual payments to individual farmers to $275,000, arguing that it would allow Congress to direct more money to conservation and other programs that help small farmers. The farm law had reduced the limit from $460,000 to $360,000 but allowed the continuation of generic certificates that have cash value and do not count against the caps. Many lawmakers from the South and West argued that smaller payments would be unfair to farmers in their regions who had higher production costs.

Among other disputes waiting to erupt if either bill reached the floor was a move by House appropriators to provide only minimal funding for a nationwide conservation program that Senate Agriculture Committee Chairman Tom Harkin, D-Iowa, had worked into the new farm law. The appropriators wanted to limit the program to a pilot project in Harkin's home state. Also, Sen. Byron L. Dorgan, D-N.D., promised to offer a floor amendment — strongly opposed by the administration and House Republicans — to allow U.S. banks to finance food sales to Cuba.

Much of the increase in discretionary spending in both bills would have gone to the Women, Infants and Children (WIC) program, which provides nutrition assistance for low-income pregnant women and young children; the Food

BoxScore **2003** Fiscal Year
Agriculture

Bills:
HR 5263, S 2801
Legislative Action:
House Appropriations Committee approved HR 5263 (H Rept 107-623) by voice vote July 11.
Senate Appropriations Committee approved S 2801 (S Rept 107-223), 29-0, July 25.

for Peace program, which supplies foreign governments with commodities to combat malnutrition and famine; and a 2.6 percent pay raise for Agriculture Department employees.

WIC was slated to get $4.776 billion under the House bill, a $428 million increase over fiscal 2002 and $25 million more than Bush requested. The Senate bill met Bush's request for $4.751 billion. Food for Peace would have gotten $1.357 billion under the House bill, and $1.328 billion under the Senate version, compared with $999 million in fiscal 2002.

Overall, spending for domestic food programs was expected to increase by $4.1 billion under both bills, due mainly to a 14 percent increase for food stamps that reflected higher demand because of the sagging economy as well as increased benefits under the 2002 farm law.

Both bills generally kept farm programs at existing levels. Funding for the Commodity Credit Corporation was down by $3 billion, but that was because the CCC had reduced its net realized losses and was expected to need less new money.

Legislative Action

House Subcommittee, Committee Action

The House Agriculture Appropriations Subcommittee approved its bill by voice vote June 26. Because of a printing delay, subcommittee members had only about two hours to look over the draft before the markup, and they approved it in minutes. Subcommittee Chairman Henry Bonilla, R-Texas, held off amendments on policy issues such as the limit on farm subsidies. "This is an agriculture appropriations bill and not a vehicle or means by which major legislation can be rewritten," he told the panel.

The full Appropriations Committee gave voice vote approval to the bill (HR 5263 — H Rept 107-623) on July 11.

Again, members generally avoided controversial amendments. Marcy Kaptur of Ohio, ranking Democrat on the subcommittee, planned to offer an amendment to tighten the limits on farm subsidies, but she backed off when Bonilla threatened to counter with an amendment to strip funding for 23 projects from the bill, including 18 in Ohio. GOP leaders denied they had bullied Kaptur into backing down.

An attempt by Maurice D. Hinchey, D-N.Y., to provide $250 million in crop disaster assistance for specialty crops was rejected, 29-31.

Kaptur succeeded in getting voice vote approval of two amendments. One was to transfer $1 million of the increase in funding for the Commodity Futures Trading Commission to the inspector general to investigate suspicious activities

Where the Money Goes

Agriculture Spending

(figures are in thousands of dollars of new budget authority)

	Fiscal 2002 Appropriation	Fiscal 2003 Bush Request	House Panel Approved	Senate Panel Approved
GRAND TOTAL	**$73,355,443**	**$73,530,527**	**$74,263,068**	**$74,330,233**
Total adjusted for scorekeeping*	**$73,463,827**	**$74,062,330**	**$74,305,871**	——
MAIN COMPONENTS				
Domestic food programs	$37,894,627	$41,871,651	$41,971,942	$41,927,865
Agricultural programs	29,227,688	25,197,007	25,373,392	25,593,038
Rural development programs	2,581,924	2,587,065	2,823,288	2,745,988
Foreign food and export assistance	1,124,518	1,449,591	1,491,081	1,464,385
Conservation programs	962,139	1,000,944	1,020,579	1,044,212
Food and Drug Administration, other agencies	1,456,651	1,424,269	1,464,586	1,498,249

* Based on Congressional Budget Office criteria for determining discretionary spending; adjusted total is used to assess compliance with 302(b) allocations.

TABLE: House and Senate Appropriations committees

of Enron Corp. The other was to bar "expatriate" corporations — companies that are incorporated in offshore tax havens, such as Bermuda, but whose securities are traded mostly in the United States — from being awarded new federal agriculture contracts.

Tom Latham, R-Iowa, indicated that he would offer an amendment on the floor aimed at improving market access for small, independent meatpacking houses by requiring that a quarter of slaughtered livestock be purchased on the open market. The proposal also would have barred meatpackers from owning or controlling livestock within two weeks of slaughter.

Senate Subcommittee, Committee Action

The Senate Agriculture Appropriations Subcommittee approved its own version of the bill by voice vote July 23.

The full committee approved the measure (S 2801 — S Rept 107-223), 29-0, on July 25.

Harkin held back an amendment to prohibit meatpackers from owning livestock but vowed to offer it on the floor. "It's got to be done," he said. "I'll do everything I can to get this done."

Dorgan likewise promised a floor amendment to allow farmers to borrow money from U.S. banks to finance food sales to Cuba, something the Bush administration strongly opposed. The first farm products in 23 years had been shipped from North Dakota to Cuba in 2001, Dorgan said, but they had to be paid for in cash. The money was borrowed from French banks.

Harkin did succeed in restoring funds for his national conservation program, which had been sharply cut in the House bill. ◆

Senate Panel Approves CJS Bill

The Senate Appropriations Committee approved a fiscal 2003 spending bill for the departments of Commerce, Justice and State and related agencies, but no other action was taken in either chamber. Like most of the other appropriations bills, the measure was sidetracked by a yearlong dispute over non-defense spending, and the departments were funded at fiscal 2002 levels until Jan. 11, 2003, under a continuing resolution (PL 107-294).

The Senate bill would have appropriated nearly $47.1 billion, $3.2 billion more than President Bush requested and $2.8 billion more than was provided for fiscal 2002. The main focus for Senate appropriators was homeland security, which accounted for $12.8 billion out of the $43.5 billion in discretionary budget authority in the bill. Programs marked for increases included FBI intelligence and anti-terrorism activities, border security programs and plans to upgrade security at U.S. embassies. To free up the money, appropriators proposed freezing spending on most other programs.

The most notable exception was the Securities and Exchange Commission (SEC). The agency was pushed to the head of the line and slated for a $292 million increase over fiscal 2002 spending in the wake of corporate accounting scandals at Enron Corp., WorldCom Inc. and elsewhere. (*Corporate accounting, p. 11-3*)

While the spending bill had an easy start in committee, it was expected to face numerous problems down the road. The measure funded a broad range of agencies and institutions, including the federal courts, the Equal Employment Opportunity Commission, the Census Bureau and the Small Business Administration. All had defenders on Capitol Hill who hoped to spare their favorite programs from cuts.

House appropriators said they were awaiting the outcome of the debate on creating a Department of Homeland Security. But they also faced the same clash of priorities as their Senate colleagues. Aides said lawmakers in both chambers were hoping the Appropriations committees would allocate more money for the bill before they had to cut a final deal. The inability to get an agreement on more discretionary spending ultimately halted work on all of the non-defense spending bills for fiscal 2003.

Legislative Action

Senate Committee Action

The Senate CJS Appropriations Subcommittee approved the measure by voice vote in less than 10 minutes July 16. The full committee approved the bill (S 2778 — S Rept 107-218) by a vote of 28-0 on July 18.

The bill included nearly $25.8 billion for the Justice De-

BoxScore **2003** Fiscal Year

Commerce-Justice-State

Bill:

S 2778

Legislative Action:

Senate Appropriations Committee approved S 2778 (S Rept 107-218), 28-0, on July 18.

partment, almost $3 billion more than Bush requested; $6 billion for the Commerce Department, about $325 million more than requested; $5 billion for the federal judiciary, about $275 million less than requested, and $7.4 billion for the State Department, about $215 million less than requested.

The $43.5 billion in discretionary spending was $1.9 billion more than Congress appropriated in fiscal 2002. Winners included:

● **U.S. embassies.** Appropriators approved $1.3 billion for security at the nation's embassies and for construction of a new facility in Beijing. About $30 million of the total was to enhance security at "soft targets," overseas properties such as American schools affiliated with the United States but not owned by the government.

● **INS.** The bill included $6.3 billion for the Immigration and Naturalization Service (INS) — about the same amount as requested but $150 million above the fiscal 2002 level. Homeland security initiatives accounted for $948 million of the INS appropriation, including $141 million authorized by the new border security law (PL 107-173) enacted in May. (*Border security, p. 13-7*)

● **FBI.** The FBI was slated to get $4.2 billion, including an increase of $493 million solely for homeland security initiatives such as intelligence analysis, the agency's Joint Terrorism Task Forces and information technology.

● **SEC.** Senate appropriators included $751 million for the SEC, a 65 percent increase over fiscal 2002. Bush initially asked for $467 million but requested an additional $100 million July 9.

Most other programs not connected to homeland security would have remained essentially at fiscal 2002 levels, though the measure included an across-the-board 4.1 percent pay raise for employees at the departments, and $4.6 billion for the federal prison system, $2.5 million more than the administration sought.

The Census Bureau would have received $497 million, considerably less than the $705 million the White House requested to help the agency re-engineer the census in time for 2010 and expand its annual nationwide population survey. In a sampling of controversies to come, Pete V. Domenici, R-N.M., argued that more funding was critical for the bureau's annual population survey, which ultimately could replace the decennial census. Democrat Dianne Feinstein of California and Republican Kay Bailey Hutchison of Texas said the bill should include money, not requested by Bush, to reimburse states and local governments for the costs of jailing illegal aliens.

The committee did increase funds for two programs that were popular with lawmakers but not the administration. Members included $185 million for Advanced Technology

Commerce-Justice-State Spending

(figures are in thousands of dollars of new budget authority)

	Fiscal 2002 Appropriation	Fiscal 2003 Bush Request	Senate Panel Approved
GRAND TOTAL	**$44,272,536**	**$43,907,072**	**$47,067,043**
BILL COMPONENTS			
Department of Justice	$23,704,045	$22,800,337	$25,780,035
FBI	4,269,864	4,203,837	4,203,837
Drug Enforcement Administration	1,481,783	1,545,919	1,530,470
Immigration and Naturalization Service	6,192,220	6,343,458	6,341,763
Department of State	7,361,559	7,631,875	7,417,823
Department of Commerce	5,820,500	5,638,500	5,962,105
Bureau of the Census	490,800	705,316	496,846
National Oceanic and Atmospheric Administration	3,258,848	3,130,614	3,345,941
The Judiciary	4,707,155	5,241,610	4,965,151
Securities and Exchange Commission	458,605	466,900	750,504
Small Business Administration	888,514	783,048	788,537
Equal Employment Opportunity Commission	310,406	308,822	317,206

TABLE: Senate Appropriations Committee

Program grants, created during the Clinton administration to help companies develop technologies with commercial potential. Bush wanted the program cut to $108 million. Appropriators also restored funding for local law enforcement grants, including Clinton's Community Oriented Policing Services (COPS) grants, a perennial favorite with lawmakers and their constituents back home. Bush requested no new money for hiring police officers under the COPS program. The Senate bill included $330 million — equal to the fiscal 2002 level. ◆

No Expense Spared on Defense Bill

Congress cleared a fiscal 2003 Defense Department spending bill that reflected wide agreement among lawmakers after the Sept. 11, 2001, attacks that no dollars should be spared in the war on terrorism and on a looming showdown with Iraq. The $355.1 billion bill provided $37.5 billion more than Congress appropriated for fiscal 2002, $20.7 billion more if supplemental spending was included.

The bill was one of only two fiscal 2003 appropriations measures to clear before the session's end. The 11 others — all non-defense bills — stalled in a dispute over discretionary spending. The defense bill cleared Oct. 16, and President Bush signed it into law Oct. 23 (HR 5010 — PL 107-248).

The final bill was $1.6 billion less than what Bush sought — excluding a $10 billion contingency request that appropriators did not fund — but it largely tracked administration plans to transform the military into a lighter, more agile force. As was customary, it closely followed the outlines of the annual defense authorization bill (PL 107-314). *(Defense authorization, p. 7-12)*

Lawmakers worked furiously to complete the spending bill — along with the companion fiscal 2003 military construction bill (PL 107-249) — before Congress recessed for the Nov. 5 midterm elections. With the war on terrorism, the growing possibility of an attack on Iraq and political delays to legislation creating a new Department of Homeland Security, members were eager to show their commitment on defense. The significant increase in spending also reduced conflicts over priorities. Even Bush's request to spend $7.8 billion on a missile defense system, a highly contentious issue in previous years, drew little criticism.

Lawmakers also accepted Defense Secretary Donald H. Rumsfeld's decision to cancel the Army's Crusader mobile cannon, despite fierce opposition earlier in the year and strong support for the $11 billion program from members of the GOP leadership in both chambers. The fate of the Crusader dominated much of the debate on the bill.

Appropriators did balk at the White House request for a $10 billion contingency fund for future expenses associated with the war on terrorism, saying it would amount to a blank check. They deferred action on the issue until the administration submitted a detailed request.

Highlights

The final defense bill included $71.5 billion for weapons procurement, $57.8 billion for research and development,

BoxScore 2003 *Fiscal Year*

Defense

Bill:
HR 5010 — PL 107-248
Legislative Action:
House passed HR 5010 (H Rept 107-532), 413-18, on June 27.
Senate passed HR 5010, amended (S Rept 107-213), 95-3, on Aug. 1.
House adopted the conference report (H Rept 107-732), 409-14, on Oct. 10.
Senate cleared the bill, 93-1, on Oct. 16.
President signed Oct. 23.

$114.8 billion for operations and maintenance and $93.6 billion for personnel.

It provided $37.5 billion more than the fiscal 2002 appropriation, marking the largest increase in defense spending since the Vietnam War. Two supplemental spending bills (PL 107-117 and PL 107-206), which added about $16.8 billion to fiscal 2002 spending, reduced the difference to $20.7 billion.

The following are major components of the measure:

● **Crusader.** No funds. Lawmakers ultimately agreed to cancel the Army's mobile cannon and reallocated the money to speed development of a new, lighter cannon, which they hoped would incorporate technology and salvage jobs linked to the Crusader. Rumsfeld had announced May 8 that he would cancel the 40-ton cannon as part of an effort to build a lighter, more mobile force.

● **Missile defense.** $7.4 billion for the program to develop and build an anti-missile system, about $43 million less than requested and $318 million below the fiscal 2002 level.

● **Joint Strike Fighter.** $3.5 billion, as requested, to develop the multi-role fighter aircraft.

● **F/A-18 E and F.** $3.2 billion to buy 46 of the planes, the Navy's upgrade of the F/A-18 C and D aircraft.

● **F-22 Raptor.** $4.1 billion, as requested, for 23 of the Air Force's controversial next-generation fighter, plus $809 million for research and development on the aircraft.

● **Destroyers.** $2.3 billion for two DDG-51 *Arleigh Burke*-class guided missile destroyers, as requested.

● **Submarine conversion.** $825 million to replace ballistic nuclear missiles with long-range conventional Tomahawk cruise missiles on four submarines.

● **New attack submarine.** $1.5 billion, as requested, to buy the fourth in the *Virginia*-class of new attack submarines to replace the retiring *Los Angeles*-class submarines.

● **Military pay.** A 4.1 percent pay raise for military personnel, equal to the president's request, with targeted pay increases of up to 6.5 percent for senior personnel.

● **Russian nuclear security.** $417 million to assist in the dismantling of nuclear weapons in the former Soviet Union.

Legislative Action

House Subcommittee, Committee Action

The full House Appropriations Committee approved its version of the bill (H Rept 107-532) by voice vote June 24. The Defense Subcommittee had approved a draft of the bill

Where the Money Goes

Defense Spending

(figures are in thousands of dollars of new budget authority)

	Fiscal 2002 Appropriation	Fiscal 2003 Bush Request	House Bill	Senate Bill	Conference Report
GRAND TOTAL	$317,623,747	$366,671,630***	$354,712,914	$355,405,941	$355,107,380
Total adjusted for scorekeeping*	$320,869,347	$366,671,630	$354,712,914	$355,405,941	$355,107,380
MAIN COMPONENTS					
Operation and maintenance	$105,047,644	$131,553,902	$114,780,366	$114,821,468	$114,780,258
Military personnel	82,056,651	94,247,858	93,424,834	93,825,528	93,577,552
Procurement	60,864,948	67,220,034	70,285,272	71,526,725	71,548,217
Research and development	48,921,641	53,702,299	57,754,286	56,137,243	58,608,506
Revolving and management funds	1,745,394	2,433,785	2,777,085	2,719,085	2,727,585
Other Defense Department programs	20,491,353	17,076,268	17,108,019	17,524,968	17,372,813
Related agencies	447,929	392,754	407,254	422,754	468,979
General provisions	-2,832,813	44,730	-1,824,202	-1,571,830	-3,976,530
Counterterrorism	881,000	**	**	**	**

*Adjustments based on Congressional Budget Office criteria for determining discretionary spending; adjusted total is used to assess compliance with 302(b) allocations.

**Counterterrorism funds included in other accounts in fiscal 2003 bill.

***President Bush's request initially was calculated as $366,794,095.

TABLE: House Appropriations Committee

by voice vote June 19. As was customary, the subcommittee met behind closed doors and disclosed few details, but members made clear their determination to save jobs related to the Crusader.

• **Crusader.** The full committee complied with Rumsfeld's request to eliminate funding for the cannon and redistribute the $476 million initially requested for the project to other accounts. The administration had submitted a formal request to that effect May 29. But the committee stressed in its report accompanying the bill that it was acting "with some degree of trepidation" and directed the Army to build a replacement cannon that incorporated many of the technologies developed for the Crusader. The conference report on the supplemental spending bill (PL 107-206), cleared July 24, already had directed the Army to enter a contract to use Crusader technology in developing a lightweight tank.

The committee shifted $280 million, as requested, to develop lightweight rocket launchers, highly accurate rockets and cannon shells, and other artillery upgrades. But it devoted the remaining $196 million specifically to accelerating development of a new long-range mobile artillery piece using Crusader-based technologies. The report cited such features as a liquid-cooled barrel that would allow the Crusader to fire a 100-pound shell every six seconds. The appropriators added $173 million to the effort to ensure the development of a vehicle and munitions suitable for the new technology and mission.

Subcommittee members Martin Olav Sabo, D-Minn., and Rodney Frelinghuysen, R-N.J., in particular, pressed hard to secure this endorsement of a cannon based on Crusader technology. Crusader contractor United Defense LP and its subcontractors employed about 800 people from Sabo's Minneapolis district and the surrounding area. Frelinghuysen's district was home to the Army's Picatinny Arsenal, where about 250 jobs were linked to the Crusader.

• **Comanche.** The bill included $915 million, as requested, to continue development of the Army's Comanche scout helicopter. But the report excoriated the service for repeated delays and cost increases that had plagued the program. The committee's support for Comanche "is now in jeopardy unless the Army can show marked progress over the next fiscal year," the panel said, adding that the Army should start considering cheaper alternatives.

• **"Smart" weapons.** The committee took more drastic steps on two Army plans to develop "smart" weapons. Appropriators said the projects were taking too long and costing too much, on top of which the weapons were not performing as promised. They denied the $12 million requested to buy small, robot tank-killers called wide area munitions, and they provided only 20 percent of the $190 million requested to continue developing the "brilliant anti-tank" warhead, a yard-long glider intended to pick out specific enemy vehicles and dive down to attack.

• **F-22.** The bill included the $4.6 billion requested to buy 23 F-22s, as Lockheed Martin continued to increase production. However, the panel expressed concern over the rapid production schedule, given the aircraft's history of cost overruns and technical problems. The report specified that before ordering more than 16 of the planes, Pentagon officials would have to certify to Congress that the advantages of faster production outweighed the risk of the planes having to be modified extensively if problems were discovered later.

• **Aircraft carrier.** The bill included $250 million in unrequested funds for improvements to the CVN-77, the Navy's next nuclear aircraft carrier that would serve as a transition ship from the *Nimitz* class of nuclear carriers to the next generation, designated the CVNX. Earlier in the year, the Navy had dropped plans to incorporate a new type of radar in the CVN-77 that would give a commander a more comprehensive view of the ship's surroundings. Criticizing that

decision as shortsighted, the appropriators added the funds to install the modern radar.

House Floor Action

With the issue of the Crusader largely resolved, the House passed a $354.7 billion version of the bill June 27 by an overwhelming vote of 413-18. The bill was virtually unchanged from the version approved by the committee. It was $2.1 billion below Bush's request, not counting the $10 billion contingency request. The difference was made available for the military construction bill, which was $540 million above its allocation, and defense programs in the Energy and Water spending bill. (*Military construction, p. 2-30; Energy and water, p. 2-16; House vote 270, p. H-88*)

During the debate, GOP leaders easily turned back an effort to hamstring Bush's missile defense program. By a vote of 112-314, members rejected an amendment that would have eliminated $122 million earmarked for construction of five anti-missile interceptor launch silos at Fort Greely in Alaska. (*House vote 269, p. H-88*)

Critics of the missile defense system, including the amendment's sponsor, John F. Tierney, D-Mass., argued that the administration was rushing work on the silos so it could claim by the 2004 election that a missile defense had been deployed, and further contended that interceptor missiles had not been adequately tested. The silos were part of an expanded network of test facilities scattered around the eastern Pacific for more realistic testing of missile defense. The administration said the test interceptors in the five Fort Greely silos could provide a rudimentary defense against a missile fired from North Korea.

By voice vote, the House adopted an amendment by John M. Spratt Jr., D-S.C., to transfer $30 million from development of a satellite-launched anti-missile interceptor to a project in which modified Boeing 747s would carry lasers capable of destroying missiles as they rise from their launch sites. The amendment restored half of the $60 million that the Appropriations Committee had cut from the $598 million requested for the Airborne Laser.

Senate Committee Action

The Senate Appropriations Committee approved a $355.4 billion version of the defense appropriations bill (S Rept 107-213) by a vote of 28-0 on July 18. The measure, which exceeded the House bill by $693 million, honored most of the administration's major Pentagon initiatives, including the decision to cancel the Crusader. The Defense Subcommittee had approved it by voice vote July 16.

The bill totaled $1.4 billion less than Bush requested, not counting the contingency fund. Appropriators trimmed the $1.4 billion from the defense bill in order to add funds to the military construction and Energy and Water appropriations bills.

● **Crusader**. Like the House, the Senate committee accepted Rumsfeld's proposal to reallocate the $476 million initially requested for the Crusader. Rather than dividing the money among specific programs as Rumsfeld proposed, however, the Senate panel added the $476 million to the budget for Future Combat Systems, the Army's program to deploy a new class of light combat vehicles and artillery beginning in 2008.

Also like the House, the Senate committee added $173

million to accelerate work on a lightweight replacement cannon that capitalized on the labor and technologies that had been dedicated to the heavy cannon. "To the extent possible, the men and women who are working on [the Crusader] will not be put on the streets," said Daniel K. Inouye of Hawaii, ranking Democrat on the subcommittee. Besides the artillery-related funds, the committee added $105 million to the Future Combat Systems request, bringing the total to $813 million.

● **C-17.** The committee added $586 million to the $2.7 billion requested for C-17 wide-body cargo jets, which would allow the Air Force to continue to buy the planes at a rate of 15 per year. To defer some costs to future budgets, the Air Force had requested funds to buy only 12 planes.

● **Missile defense.** The bill included the $7.8 billion Bush requested for missile defense programs, but following the lead in the Senate version of the defense authorization bill, the committee appropriated only $6.9 billion of it outright, giving Bush discretion to use the remaining $814 million either for missile defense or counterterrorism costs. By voice vote, the committee adopted an amendment by Chairman Robert C. Byrd, D-W.Va., requiring the president to tell Congress how he intended to spend the $814 million.

● **F/A-18 E and F.** The committee added $136 million to the $3.1 billion the Navy requested to buy 44 F/A-18 E and F model combat jets. The additional money would enable the Navy to buy a total of 48 planes.

● **Aircraft carrier.** Appropriators added $229 million to the $244 million requested for components for use in the new aircraft carrier designated CVNX. They included a new nuclear power plant and huge electrically powered catapults to assist takeoff. Bush had proposed delaying the start of construction of the new carrier from 2006 to 2007. The added funds would eliminate half of that delay.

In approving the bill, appropriators made a handful of larger cuts in the president's request, effectively creating a kitty of upward of $2 billion that allowed them to add member-backed projects without increasing the bill's total cost. The cuts included $850 million in anticipation of improvements in Pentagon business practices, $400 million to force reductions in the cost of information technology and $373 million in anticipation of health care costs for military retirees coming in under budget.

Many of the committee's additions to the president's request involved projects in states of panel members, including Inouye, ranking committee Republican Ted Stevens of Alaska, and Democrat Byron L. Dorgan of North Dakota.

Senate Floor Action

The Senate passed its $355.4 billion defense bill, 95-3, on Aug. 1, though the usually quick floor action took longer than expected because John McCain, R-Ariz., balked at a plan to lease Boeing jets to replace the Air Force's 40-year-old refueling tankers. (*Senate vote 204, p. S-41*)

Enacted as part of the fiscal 2002 defense spending bill (PL 107-117), the $20 billion deal allowed the Air Force to lease 100 new, modified 767 jets from Boeing to replace the service's fleet of tankers. McCain assailed the deal as a bailout for the troubled company, saying it ultimately would cost $6 billion more than proponents claimed. (*2001 Almanac, p. 2-13*)

When the Senate took up the fiscal 2003 defense bill July 31, McCain challenged what amounted to an offshoot of the leasing deal — a provision to appropriate $31 million toward the $400 million cost of a six-year lease on four of the Boeing aircraft for use in shuttling senior Pentagon officials around the world. By voice vote, the Senate adopted a McCain amendment to require "full and open" competition for the leasing of the four planes.

McCain, a member of the Armed Services Committee, then offered an amendment to require approval by the defense authorizers of all leasing deals. "It's basically a matter of whether the Senate Armed Services Committee maintains its relevance," he said.

Stevens insisted that the deal was necessary in light of the Air Force's aging aircraft. "To fly a plane built in Harry Truman's administration is laughable," Stevens said. McCain eventually abandoned his challenge, but he was one of three senators to vote against the bill.

The Senate adopted several other amendments by voice vote, including:

• A proposal by Paul Wellstone, D-Minn., to bar the Pentagon from awarding contracts to companies that set up paper headquarters in offshore tax havens after Dec. 31, 2001. Democrats were trying to make corporate expatriates a campaign issue and vowed to amend as many bills as possible with contract prohibitions.

• An amendment by Byrd to limit Pentagon use of government credit cards. The General Accounting Office had reported cases in which such cards were improperly used for personal expenses, including escort services.

• An amendment by Richard G. Lugar, R-Ind., to allow the president to waive certain congressionally mandated restrictions on providing money to help Russia dispose of its huge stockpiles of lethal chemical weapons left over from the Cold War. Bush sought the waiver to free his hands in allocating funds under the so-called Nunn-Lugar program, created in the 1990s to help former Soviet republics dispose of nuclear, chemical and biological weapons and their delivery systems. The bill included $417 million, as requested, to continue the Nunn-Lugar program.

• A Wellstone amendment to require the Defense Department to investigate cases of domestic violence in the military. The issue had moved to the forefront after four murders at Fort Bragg, N.C., in which service members were charged with killing their wives. Some of the service members recently had returned from fighting in Afghanistan.

Conference/Final Action

When Congress returned from its August recess, the military was preparing for a potential war with Iraq and Republicans and the Bush administration were stepping up pressure to finish the defense bill. "The American people are not going to like it if they see the Congress playing politics with the defense bill when we're at war," Bush warned Sept. 5.

House and Senate conferees announced agreement Oct. 9 on a $355.1 billion bill. The House adopted the conference report (H Rept 107-732), 409-14, on Oct. 10, shortly after voting to approve the use of military force against Iraq. The Senate cleared the bill, 93-1, on Oct. 16, with Russell D. Feingold, D-Wis., casting the sole "nay" vote. (*House vote 457, p. H-144; Senate vote 239, p. S-49*)

The following are among the issues settled in conference:

• **Missile defense.** The final bill appropriated $7.4 billion for missile defense programs, roughly equal to the House and Senate bills.

• **Shipbuilding.** The conferees approved $9 billion for Navy shipbuilding, an increase of $842 million over Bush's request. The extra funds largely were to cover cost overruns on ships funded in earlier budgets. The administration requested $645 million for these prior-year costs; the conference report added $635 million. The House bill would have provided $645 million, the Senate bill $1.5 billion.

Of the amount added, $311 million was to pay for shifting several shipbuilding contracts among shipyards in Maine, Louisiana and Mississippi. The complicated swap, which the Navy said would save time and money over the long run, would give the Louisiana yard, owned by Northrop Grumman, construction of 12 large amphibious landing transports, four of which had been slated for construction at the General Dynamics shipyard in Bath, Maine. In return, Northrop Grumman would transfer to Bath the contracts to build four Aegis destroyers that had been slated for construction in Northrop's yard in Pascagoula, Miss.

• **New aircraft carriers.** The conferees added $160 million to the $244 million requested to begin work on the first ship in the new CVNX class of aircraft carriers. The administration would have delayed the start of construction on the ship by one year, to 2007. The ship was to be built by General Dynamics' Newport News Shipbuilding and Drydock division, the only shipyard in the country that built nuclear-powered carriers. The Senate bill would have added $229 million.

The conferees also added $90 million, rather than the $250 million approved by the House, to upgrade the electronic warfare system for the CVN-77.

• **Other ships.** The negotiators approved, with minor changes, requests for $2.3 billion for two Aegis destroyers, $1.5 billion for the fourth boat in the *Virginia* class of new nuclear-powered submarines, and $825 million for conversion of four big missile-launching subs to carry cruise missiles rather than Trident nuclear-armed ballistic missiles. They also approved a requested $243 million to continue building a $1.5 billion helicopter carrier, designated an LHD, designed to carry 1,700 Marines plus the helicopters and landing craft to haul them ashore.

• **Fighter aircraft.** As requested, the conferees approved $4.1 billion for 23 additional Lockheed Martin F-22 fighters intended to replace the F-15 and F-16 and designed to have both air-to-air and air-to-ground fighter capabilities. But they also agreed to the House language limiting the purchase to 16 planes unless top Pentagon officials justified the need for faster production to Congress.

The bill provided $3.2 billion for 46 Navy F/A-18 E/F fighters built in St. Louis by Boeing — an addition of two planes and $120 million to Bush's budget request and to the House level. As requested, the bill included $3.5 billion to continue development of the new F-35 Joint Strike Fighter, slated to replace several 1970s-vintage warplanes.

• **Cargo, tanker aircraft.** The bill provided $4.2 billion to purchase 15 additional C-17 wide-body cargo jets. Bush had sought partial funding of $3.7 billion, but conferees rejected that approach and added $586 million to fully fund purchase

of the 15 planes.

● **"Smart" bombs.** As requested, the bill provided $765 million for JDAM satellite-guided "smart" bombs — more than triple the amount requested. To accelerate production of the Predator drone aircraft, used to spot targets in Afghanistan, the conferees approved $131 million, $26 million more than requested.

● **Crusader.** Accepting the administration's decision to cancel development of the Army's Crusader mobile cannon, the conferees earmarked $369 million to develop a replacement cannon. Combined with changes in other artillery-related programs either proposed by the administration or initiated by Congress, that brought the total for new artillery programs to $591 million — an increase of $115 million over the administration's original budget request.

● **Helicopters.** As requested, conferees included $915 million to continue developing the Army's missile-armed Comanche helicopter, a joint production of Boeing and the Sikorsky division of United Technologies.

The conference report also included $270 million to buy 19 Sikorsky Blackhawk helicopters — an increase of seven aircraft and $117 million over the Bush request. The House had called for four extra Blackhawks; the Senate called for nine. Some of the choppers would go to Army Reserve units.

● **Armored cars.** The conferees strongly endorsed the Army's plan to field six brigades equipped with lightweight armored cars, called Strykers. The provision came in response to reports that top Pentagon officials might reduce the number of such units to save money. The bill provided the $812 million requested to continue buying the armored cars and developing a version equipped with a large cannon. The conferees also added $60 million to accelerate the purchase of other equipment that would be used by the Stryker brigades. The brigades were an interim step in the transformation of the Army to a lighter, more mobile force.

● **Other.** As they had done for years, the conferees added funds to the defense bill for cancer research: $150 million for breast cancer and $85 million for prostate cancer.

To make room for their own initiatives funded in the bill, conferees agreed to cut more than $2 billion from Bush's request, targeting spending that they insisted would not affect defense readiness. The cuts included $820 million to reflect the reduction in air patrols over U.S. territory, $850 million to force a reduction in the amount spent by the Pentagon on consultants, $409 million to reflect lower-than-anticipated spending for a new health care benefit for military retirees and $97 million to enforce greater discipline in the use of government credit cards. ◆

Appropriators Generous to D.C.

The fiscal 2003 District of Columbia bill, the smallest of the 13 annual appropriations measures, was blocked by the logjam that held up all of the domestic spending bills. It won committee approval in both chambers but did not reach the floor in either. The versions approved by House and Senate appropriators would have provided $517 million to the District — 37 percent more than President Bush requested — and ratified the city's own, $7.4 billion annual budget.

Del. Eleanor Holmes Norton, D-D.C., said those looking for proof that the District of Columbia's credibility with Congress had grown need look no further. It had been just a year since the financial control board imposed on the city in 1995 was disbanded.

Although appropriators were skeptical about the long-term budget outlook — a decline in tourism following the Sept. 11, 2001, terrorist attacks, coupled with the economic downturn, had hurt the District — they were pleased with the city's financial turnaround. "There is a significant growth in confidence in the District of Columbia," said Senate D.C. Appropriations Subcommittee Chairwoman Mary L. Landrieu, D-La. "There are good things happening to the District in terms of fiscal management."

Despite the general good will, however, a number of social policy riders seemed likely to cause trouble if the fiscal 2003 bill had gone further. The topics were familiar from past fights on the annual measure. The Senate bill would have allowed the city to begin using local — but not federal — funds for a needle-exchange program to reduce HIV transmission among drug addicts, as well as for an initiative seeking voting rights in Congress. House Republicans opposed both proposals. Both the House and Senate bills would have banned the use of federal or local money for abortions, except in cases of rape, incest or danger to the life of the woman, and for carrying out a ballot initiative on medical marijuana. Both bills included language to allow the use of local funds to pay health benefits to unmarried domestic partners of city employees.

Both versions of the bill met most of Bush's $379 million request for federal funds, while adding $138 million for items not in the president's budget.

The following are highlights of the two bills:

● **D.C. courts.** The bulk of the federal funds under both bills was for the courts and judicial services — $347 million in the House bill, $365 million in the Senate version. Bush requested $346 million. This covered the D.C. courts, defender services, and the Court Services and Offender Supervision Agency for the District.

● **Sewage management.** The biggest single addition to

Bills:
HR 5521, S 2809

Legislative Action:
Senate Appropriations Committee approved S 2809 (S Rept 107-225), 29-0, July 25.
House Appropriations Committee approved HR 5521 (H Rept 107-716) by voice vote Sept. 26.

Bush's request in both bills was $50 million to begin implementing a plan to fix the city's outdated combined sewer system. Built in the late 1800s, the system dumped raw sewage into the Potomac and Anacostia Rivers as often as 75 times a year during heavy rains.

● **Emergency communications center.** Appropriators also added money — $19 million in the House bill, $10 million in the Senate version — for a unified communication center to coordinate first responders such as police, firefighters and emergency personnel. The funds were part of an add-on for capital infrastructure development of $24 million in the House and $15 million in the Senate.

● **Charter schools.** House appropriators added $16 million, Senate appropriators $20 million, to construct and renovate public charter school facilities.

● **D.C. budget.** By law, the city had to win congressional approval before it could spend its own funds. Both bills approved $7.4 billion in District spending, including $5.8 billion in operating expenses, as requested by D.C. officials.

In the absence of a completed appropriations bill, the District received federal funds at the fiscal 2002 level under a series of stopgap spending bills, the last of which (PL 107-294) was good until Jan. 11, 2003.

The fiscal 2002 D.C. appropriations bill (PL 107-96) provided $408 million in federal funds for the district. A new continuing resolution (PL 108-2) enacted Jan. 10, 2003, permitted the District of Columbia to spend local funds while Congress was completing the fiscal 2003 bill. (*2001 Almanac, p. 2-18*)

Legislative Action

Senate Committee Action

The Senate Appropriations Committee approved its version of the bill (S 2809 — S Rept 107-225) on July 25 by a vote of 29-0. The District of Columbia Subcommittee had approved it, 4-1, on July 23.

Kay Bailey Hutchison, R-Texas, lost an attempt in subcommittee to impose a $195-per-hour limit on attorneys' fees in special education cases, with a per-case maximum of $3,000. The vote was 1-4. She withheld the amendment at the full committee markup at the request of Chairman Robert C. Byrd, D-W.Va., but she said she would offer it again on the floor.

Under federal law, parents could take legal action to ensure that the city provided special education to qualifying children. Hutchison argued that attorneys were drumming up cases in

Where the Money Goes

District of Columbia Spending

(figures are in thousands of dollars of new budget authority)

	Fiscal 2002 Appropriation	Fiscal 2003 Bush Request	House Panel Approved	Senate Panel Approved
TOTAL FEDERAL FUNDS	**$607,879**	**$378,752**	**$517,000**	**$517,000**
TOTAL DISTRICT OF COLUMBIA FUNDS	**$7,306,616**	**$7,307,787**	**$7,443,535**	**$7,419,887**
FEDERAL FUND COMPONENTS				
D.C. Court Operations	$112,280	$159,045	$160,545	$173,193
Defender Services	34,285	32,000	32,000	37,000
Court Services and Offender Supervision	147,205	154,707	154,707	154,707
Resident Tuition Aid	17,000	17,000	17,000	17,000
Emergency Planning	16,058	15,000	15,000	15,000
Capital Development	—	—	24,298	15,100
Chief Financial Officer	8,300	—	23,450	15,000

TABLE: House and Senate Appropriations committees

order to make money for themselves without regard to whether the children they represented really needed the services. She said such cases had generated $13 million to $18 million a year for local attorneys since an earlier cap on attorneys' fees was lifted in the fiscal 2002 D.C. appropriations bill.

House Committee Action

The full House Appropriations Committee approved HR 5521 (H Rept 107-716) by voice vote Sept. 26.

Norton issued a written statement declaring the markup "the smoothest of my 12 years in Congress." ◆

Bill Boosts Funds for Energy, Water

The House and Senate Appropriations committees each approved versions of a fiscal 2003 energy and water bill, but neither measure reached the floor. The bill — which funds the Department of Energy, the Army Corps of Engineers and Interior Department water projects — stalled because of a yearlong dispute over all non-defense appropriations. Energy and water programs were left to operate at fiscal 2002 levels until Jan. 11, 2003, under a stopgap spending law (PL 107-294).

Both the House and Senate versions exceeded the $26.2 billion limit that President Bush wanted to set for the bill. Senate appropriators approved a $26.8 billion bill; the House version was $26.5 billion. The totals reflected senators' desire to boost funding for nuclear security, and the desire of appropriators in both chambers to protect water projects run by the Corps. The fiscal 2002 appropriation was $25.1 billion (PL 107-66), an amount that rose to $25.8 billion with additional funding in the supplemental spending bill (PL 107-38) enacted after the Sept. 11, 2001, terrorist attacks. *(2001 Almanac, p. 2-21)*

The following are the main components of the two bills:

● **Energy Department.** Senate appropriators allocated $21 billion for Energy, $433 million more than the president requested, including $6.1 billion for nuclear weapons-related activities, a $242 million increase over Bush's budget. House appropriators agreed to $20.7 billion for Energy, with $115 million less than Bush sought for the nuclear programs. Both bills included $1.1 billion for environmental cleanup at nuclear weapons facilities, as Bush requested. But only the House endorsed an administration proposal for an annual cleanup account.

● **Corps of Engineers.** The White House wanted to cut spending for the Corps of Engineers to $4.2 billion, nearly 10 percent below fiscal 2002, with no new construction projects. Although the Corps had been criticized for overstating the economic rationale for some of its water projects, documented most recently in a June report by the General Accounting Office, Congress showed little interest in changing the agency's organizational structure or cutting its budget. Lawmakers counted on the hundreds of flood control, navigation, storm damage reduction and environmental restoration projects to bring dollars to their districts.

The Senate bill included $4.6 billion for the Corps, roughly what it had received in fiscal 2002; House appropriators increased that to $4.8 billion. In fiscal 2002, Congress had agreed to a 4 percent cut.

● **Interior Department.** Both bills rejected an administration proposal to cut funding for Interior Department water

---

BoxScore **2003** Fiscal Year

Energy-Water

Bills:
HR 5431, S 2784

Legislative Action:

Senate Appropriations Committee approved S 2784 (S Rept 107-220), 29-0, on July 24.

House Appropriations Committee approved HR 5431 (H Rept 107-681) by voice vote Sept. 5.

---

projects in Western states. Bush requested $881 million, a 7 percent reduction from fiscal 2002. The Senate bill included $956 million, the House version $948 million.

● **Nuclear waste.** The two committees were divided over funding for Yucca Mountain, Nev., which had been designated as the permanent repository for the nation's high-level nuclear waste. The House bill included $525 million, as requested by Bush, but Senate Democratic Whip Harry Reid of Nevada, chairman of the Senate Energy and Water Appropriations Subcommittee and a bitter opponent of the plan to store nuclear waste in his home state, agreed to provide only $336 million.

Legislative Action

House Subcommittee, Committee Action

The House Energy and Water Appropriations Subcommittee approved a draft bill by voice vote after only a few minutes of debate July 10. The full Appropriations Committee approved the $26.5 billion bill (HR 5431 — H Rept 107-681) by voice vote Sept. 5. The panel had held off for a month after returning from the August recess out of fear that fiscal conservatives, eager to hold down spending, might ambush the measure on the House floor.

David R. Obey of Wisconsin, ranking Democrat on the committee, said appropriators had done what they could, given the spending limits demanded by the administration, but he said he would try on the floor or in conference to add $235 million for nuclear plant security that Bush had declined to spend under the fiscal 2002 emergency spending law (PL 107-206). *(Supplemental, p. 2-40)*

The committee bill included no money for the California Federal Bay Delta (CALFED) project, a sprawling system of water collection and management projects in the San Francisco Bay and Sacramento River areas. The project's authorization had expired in 2000.

Senate Subcommittee, Committee Action

The Senate Appropriations Committee approved its version of the bill (S 2784 — S Rept 107-220), 29-0, on July 24, two days after the Energy and Water Development Subcommittee approved the draft by voice vote.

Traditionally, the House and Senate emphasize different sections of the annual bill, with the House seeking large spending increases for Corps projects in members' districts, and senators instead adding extra money for the Energy Department's nuclear weapons programs. This time, however, Senate appropriators joined in the call for more money for the Corps. They included $4.6 billion, $475 million more

Where the Money Goes

Energy and Water Spending

(figures are in thousands of dollars of new budget authority)

	Fiscal 2002 Appropriation	Fiscal 2003 Bush Request	House Panel Approved	Senate Panel Approved
GRAND TOTAL	**$25,795,359**	**$26,163,457**	**$26,541,000**	**$26,785,991**
Total adjusted for scorekeeping*	$25,305,359	$25,876,981	$26,027,000	——
MAIN COMPONENTS				
Corps of Engineers (Defense Department)	$4,657,096	$4,172,954	$4,765,712	$4,647,953
Interior Department	951,520	881,149	947,520	956,149
Energy Department	19,966,226	20,894,976	20,675,871	20,961,784
Atomic Energy Defense Activities	(15,003,600)	(15,700,859)	(15,601,867)	(15,775,217)
Independent Agencies	220,517	214,378	151,897	220,105
Nuclear Regulatory Commission	(79,627)	(86,047)	(58,505)	(58,505)
Emergency Supplemental	600,359	——	——	——
Rescissions	−55,000	——	——	——

* Based on Congressional Budget Office criteria for determining discretionary spending; adjusted total is used to assess compliance with 302(b) allocations.

TABLE: House and Senate Appropriations committees

than the administration requested. "In order to get a bill out of the House, [appropriators] had to add a lot of water money, so we added water money, too," said Pete V. Domenici of New Mexico, ranking Republican on the subcommittee. Other senators said they did not want to cut funding for the Corps at a time when it was trying to improve its management of water projects.

But there also were areas of significant disagreement.

● **Yucca Mountain.** While Senate appropriators agreed to increase overall spending for the Energy Department, at Reid's insistence they sought to sharply reduce funding for work on Yucca Mountain, providing $188 million less than Bush's request. Reid's efforts to cut funding had touched off a dispute between the House and Senate in 2001, and was expected to do so again. *(Nuclear waste site, p. 8-8)*

● **CALFED.** The Senate bill would have provided $30 mil-lion indirectly for the CALFED project, which was zeroed out in the House version.

● **Nuclear Waste.** Both bills would have funded the administration's initial request for $800 million for nuclear waste cleanup at Energy Department sites, plus an additional $300 million that the White House told appropriators it needed. But the House bill did not specify where the money should be used, while the Senate version allocated the money to specific cleanup projects. "Reid is not going to give [the department] $1.1 billion without any strings," said a Senate Democratic aide. Hinting at the possibility of further legislative changes to the program, Domenici criticized the department's slow progress in cleaning up sites in several states without meeting required regulatory milestones. "We cannot keep doing this forever," he told the Appropriations Committee. ◆

Annual Abortion Fight Delayed

The House and Senate Appropriations committees each approved versions of the fiscal 2003 foreign operations spending bill, but the legislation did not reach the floor of either chamber. It was delayed by conflicts over abortion and stopped by a broader dispute between Congress and the White House over non-defense spending. Programs covered by the bill — most foreign aid, contributions to international financial institutions and military assistance — were funded at fiscal 2002 levels until Jan. 11, 2003, under a continuing resolution (PL 107-294).

The foreign operations bill approved by the Senate Appropriations Committee in July would have provided $16.4 billion, about $229 million more than President Bush's original request. House appropriators approved a $16.6 billion version in September that included an additional $350 million requested by Bush on Sept. 3 for international HIV/AIDS programs and for aid to Israel and the Palestinians. The new total was roughly the same as the fiscal 2002 level if supplemental spending was included.

Had the bill gone further, it would have met with several problems, most of them familiar from past foreign aid battles.

● **Family planning.** The fiercest fight was expected to be over aid for international family planning programs. At the urging of anti-abortion groups, Bush decided July 22 not to release $34 million that had been appropriated in fiscal 2002 for the U.N. Fund for Population Activities (UNFPA). A carefully written compromise in the fiscal 2002 foreign operations law (PL 107-115) permitted but did not require the United States to contribute to the agency. The White House said contributions to the U.N. family planning agency could end up aiding forced abortions as part of China's one-child family planning program. U.N. officials insisted that they worked only in regions of China where such policies had been lifted. *(2001 Almanac, p. 2-25)*

The Senate bill included $50 million for UNFPA in fiscal 2003 — Bush had requested only $25 million to be held in reserve for the group — as well as other international family planning provisions that were certain to draw opposition from Bush and the GOP-controlled House.

● **Andean Counterdrug Initiative.** Both bills included funds for U.S. anti-drug efforts in Colombia and neighboring countries, but Senate appropriators decided to trim Bush's request and earmark much of the money. The Andean Counterdrug Initiative was launched in 2001 in an attempt to block narcotics shipments to the United States. As part of the fiscal 2002 supplemental spending law (PL 107-206), Congress agreed to support a broader campaign aimed at left-wing guerrillas and other paramilitary groups, as well as at drug traffickers.

BoxScore **2003** Fiscal Year

Foreign Operations

Bills:
HR 5410, S 2779.

Legislative Action:
Senate Appropriations Committee approved S 2779 (S Rept 107-219), 28-0, July 18.

House Appropriations Committee approved HR 5410 (H Rept 107-663) by voice vote Sept. 12.

Senate Committee Action

The Senate Appropriations Committee approved its $16.4 billion foreign aid bill (S 2779 — S Rept 107-219) by a vote of 28-0 on July 18. Two days earlier, the Foreign Operations Subcommittee approved the measure by voice vote.

● **Family planning.** In a clear signal of its frustration with Bush, who had delayed a decision on releasing the fiscal 2002 UNFPA funds, the committee included $50 million for the U.N. agency in fiscal 2003. The bill also sought to revise the law that was later cited by the administration in withholding the $34 million. Known as the Kemp-Kasten amendment, the law prohibited aid to any group that "supports or participates in the management" of a program of coercive abortion or involuntary sterilization. The provision had been included in every foreign operations spending bill since it was first enacted in 1985. *(1985 Almanac, p. 367)*

The bill would have changed the language to bar funds only to organizations or programs that "directly participate" in coercive abortion or involuntary sterilization. It also sought to roll back one of Bush's first acts in office: his reinstatement of President Ronald Reagan's "Mexico City" prohibition against funding private family planning organizations that perform or promote abortions, even if they use their own funds to do so.

There were other, less controversial departures from the administration's proposals.

● **HIV/AIDS.** The bill called for a $200 million contribution to a multilateral fund to fight HIV/AIDS overseas — $100 million more than requested. Richard J. Durbin, D-Ill., vowed to fight for additional money on the Senate floor.

● **Andean initiative.** The bill also called for $637 million for the Andean initiative, including $88 million of the $98 million requested to protect a key Colombian oil pipeline. The total was $94 million less than Bush requested. Appropriators specified that $215 million of the money be used by USAID for social and economic programs, and earmarked other money for specific purposes.

● **Indonesia.** In the biggest fight during subcommittee markup, Daniel K. Inouye, D-Hawaii, and Ted Stevens of Alaska, ranking Republican on the full committee, said it was time to relax restrictions on military training aid to Indonesia. The restrictions (PL 106-113) were put in place in 1999 after repeated accusations of human rights violations by the Indonesian military, particularly during East Timor's successful struggle for independence.

Stevens argued that the United States needed the aid of Indonesia, a predominantly Muslim nation, in the ongoing war on terror, and said aid restrictions hurt the relationship.

Where the Money Goes

Foreign Operations Spending

(figures are in thousands of dollars of new budget authority)

	Fiscal 2002 Appropriation	Fiscal 2003 Bush Request	Senate Panel Approved	House Panel Approved
GRAND TOTAL	**$15,440,780***	**$16,492,896**	**$16,395,200**	**$16,594,574**
MAIN COMPONENTS				
Bilateral Economic Assistance	$9,624,529	$10,050,780	$10,136,111	$10,369,280
Military Assistance	3,855,000	4,295,450	4,272,250	4,285,200
Multilateral Assistance	1,383,296	1,747,497	1,587,558	1,535,997
Export and Investment Assistance	577,955	399,281	399,281	404,097

* Only includes funds in fiscal 2002 spending bill (PL 107-115). Does not include supplemental spending.

TABLE: House and Senate Appropriations committees

He also noted that Indonesia had installed a new government since the 1999 East Timor massacres. That did not sway Foreign Operations Subcommittee Chairman Patrick J. Leahy, D-Vt., who had been pressing sanctions since 1999. "It's the same military," he said.

House Subcommittee Action

The House Foreign Operations Appropriations Subcommittee approved a $16.6 billion version of the bill Sept. 5, after some quick juggling to accommodate Bush's last-minute request for an extra $350 million to combat mother-to-child transmission of HIV/AIDS overseas and provide extra aid to Israel and the Palestinians.

The money originally was included in the fiscal 2002 supplemental spending law, but Bush objected to its designation as "emergency spending" and refused to use it. Instead, he asked lawmakers to add $350 million to the foreign aid spending bill — but without exceeding the overall budget limits.

"We're going to have to make some creative adjustments," said Appropriations Chairman C.W. Bill Young, R-Fla., who addressed part of the problem by agreeing to increase the subcommittee's allocation by $200 million. Committee aides said the remaining $150 million would be offset with cuts from aid the panel had planned to provide Afghanistan and other programs focusing on HIV/AIDS.

As requested, the subcommittee added $200 million to the $2.7 billion in military and economic assistance already in the bill for Israel. It increased humanitarian aid to the West Bank and Gaza by $50 million, bringing the total to about $125 million for fiscal 2003.

The extra $100 million to fight HIV/AIDS brought total bilateral HIV/AIDS funding to $536 million. The bill also called for contributing $250 million to a global fund for fighting AIDS, tuberculosis and malaria. Nancy Pelosi, D-Calif., sought to earmark an additional $400 million for HIV/AIDS efforts, but subcommittee Chairman Jim Kolbe, R-Ariz., objected that the increase would come at the expense of other health programs. The amendment was rejected, 6-7.

During the four-hour markup, members sidestepped a number of contentious issues, saying they would tackle them when the bill got to full committee.

● **Family planning.** Kolbe attempted a compromise by designating $25 million for UNFPA but setting several conditions, including a requirement that the U.S. contribution be reduced dollar-for-dollar by the amount UNFPA spent in China. Other family planning issues were put off.

● **Andean initiative.** The panel agreed to fully fund Bush's request of $731 million for the Andean Counterdrug Initiative and did not try to allocate funds for specific purposes. Ranking Democrat, Nita M. Lowey of New York, failed on a 4-6 vote to retain an existing requirement that the administration certify twice a year that Bogota was meeting human rights conditions spelled out in the spending bill. Kolbe successfully argued for only one certification per year, saying the second could slow the U.S. anti-drug effort.

● **Palestine.** In one of the most passionate debates, David R. Obey of Wisconsin, ranking Democrat on the full committee, sought to delete provisions tying aid to a future Palestinian state to the presence of a democratically elected leadership. "This would be the only country in the world that would have to be a democracy to get aid," Obey said angrily. "I care more about whether they're trying to kill us than whether they're a Jeffersonian democracy." But Lowey and others defeated the amendment on a 3-6 vote, arguing that different standards should apply to a new Palestinian government than to existing states.

● **Indonesia.** The panel rejected, 6-7, an amendment by Lowey to limit training of Indonesian military officers to non-military subjects, such as civilian-military relations. Democrats said the Indonesian military had yet to account for its alleged abuses in East Timor. But Kolbe said the aid was needed to prevent terrorism from taking root in the world's largest Muslim nation.

House Committee Action

The full House Appropriations Committee approved the bill (HR 5410 — H Rept 107-663) by voice vote Sept. 12, after again putting off the debate on overseas family planning aid. Democrats could barely hide their disdain during the markup. "What happened this year is, in my opinion, unacceptable," said Lowey.

Despite objections from Obey, the committee agreed by

voice vote to transfer the allocation for the extra $200 million from the fiscal 2003 defense appropriations bill (HR 5010), which already had passed the House, to the foreign operations bill. Young said no money actually would be taken from the defense bill; the allocation was being used simply to protect the foreign operations bill from a point of order when it got to the floor. When that would occur was not clear, however; lawmakers had begun to talk of putting off the spending bills for a lame-duck session, or even for the 108th Congress.

During the markup, most members refrained from offering contentious amendments, choosing instead to air their grievances without forcing uncomfortable votes.

● **Serbia.** The only recorded vote came when Steny H. Hoyer, D-Md., tried to block aid to Serbia until the administration could certify that Belgrade was cooperating with an international criminal tribunal. The amendment was rejected, 15-30. Hoyer argued that Serbia had not yet shown its commitment to democracy and human rights and that providing aid without controls would be like writing a blank check. But Kolbe countered that setting conditions on the aid would punish the many Serbs who were acting to reintegrate the nation into the West after years of isolation and multiple wars with its neighbors.

● **Afghanistan.** Members of both parties united to increase aid for Afghanistan beyond the $148 million requested by Bush. "There are not sufficient funds in here to do what we know needs to be done in Afghanistan," Kolbe said. "We can't abandon humanitarian and all other necessary work." He and Lowey scraped together money from other funds to bring total aid to Afghanistan to $296 million. Kolbe called the proposal "the minimum amount needed to prevent Afghanistan from sliding back into chaos."

Their amendment was adopted by voice vote. The money was earmarked from funding in already established accounts for disaster assistance, refugee programs and anti-terrorism.

● **Cuba.** As originally drafted, the bill would have dropped a longstanding law that allowed the United States to cooperate with Cuba on counternarcotics programs. George Nethercutt, R-Wash., and others opposed the change, arguing that it would cut off a potential ally in fighting the drug trade. "I will deal with the devil if I have to, to stay the flow of drugs into my district," said José E. Serrano, D-N.Y.

Kolbe argued that the Cuban government did not cooperate with the United States anyway, but he agreed to amend the bill to clarify that assistance should be blocked to "the government of Cuba" as opposed to just "Cuba." The amendment was adopted by voice vote.

● **Palestinians.** Kolbe and Lowey won voice vote approval for an amendment to limit assistance to any potential Palestinian state until the administration could certify that the new government was dedicated to peace with Israel and to democracy. ◆

Logging Dispute Halts Senate Bill

The House passed a $19.8 billion bill to fund the Interior Department and related agencies in fiscal 2003, but a protracted fight over logging in national forests halted floor action on a $19.3 billion Senate version. That left programs covered by the bill to be funded at fiscal 2002 levels under a series of continuing resolutions, the last of which was good until Jan. 11, 2003 (PL 107-294).

The Interior bill initially was expected to be among the least controversial and easiest to pass of the fiscal 2003 measures. The annual bill pays for the management of public lands by the Interior Department's Bureau of Land Management and National Park Service, and by the Agriculture Department's Forest Service. It also funds health, education and other programs for American Indians, as well as an array of cultural programs such as the national endowments for the humanities and arts.

House appropriators kept their version of the bill relatively free of the controversial policy riders that often trip it up, but they added $700 million in emergency spending to fight wildfires and borrowed some money from other spending bills to pay for conservation programs. That caught the eye of fiscal conservatives, who worried that appropriators would exceed the president's budget in the early bills, then give Congress the choice of underfunding the later bills or breaking the budget. The White House also objected to the emergency spending, saying the proper place to debate it would be on a fiscal 2002 supplemental spending bill that was pending.

After initially holding up the Interior bill, the budget hawks allowed it to proceed, along with the spending bills for the Treasury Department and legislative branch, in return for early consideration of the biggest domestic spending measure, the bill for the departments of Labor, Health and Human Services (HHS), and Education. That deal allowed House passage of the Interior bill, although it ultimately led to the breakdown of the appropriations process.

In the Senate, the bill was caught up in lengthy policy disputes, mainly over forest management and how to reduce the threat of future wildfires like the ones that were consuming forests in Colorado, Arizona and other Western states. The two parties were at odds over how much logging to allow as a way to thin forests and whether to waive environmental laws. Neither side could get the 60 votes needed to avoid a filibuster, and Senate action stalled.

Concern over the wildfires was a constant theme in debate on the bill. By the time of the committee markups in late June, 2.5 million acres, or three times the 10-year average, were ablaze. The wildfires were expected to require hundreds of millions of dollars in additional fiscal 2002

BoxScore 2003 *Fiscal Year*

Interior

Bill:
HR 5093
Legislative Action:
House passed HR 5093
(H Rept 107-564), 377-46, on July 17.
Senate began debate on HR 5093, amended (S Rept 107-201), on Sept. 4.

funds. The National Forest Service and the Bureau of Land Management could borrow temporarily from other accounts to make up for the shortfall, but the money had to be repaid. The shortfall was expected to be about $650 million.

Highlights

The following are highlights of the two bills:
- **Wildfires.** The House bill included $2.2 billion in fiscal 2003 to fight wildfires; Senate appropriators approved $2 billion. In addition, the House bill included $700 million in emergency fiscal 2002 money.
- **National parks.** Both measures included $2.4 billion for the National Park Service, about $1.6 billion of it for national park operations.
- **Indian Health Service.** The Senate bill included $2.8 billion, as requested, for the Indian Health Service. The House bill allocated $2.9 billion.
- **Arts.** The National Endowment for the Arts (NEA) was slated to get $126 million under the House bill, $118 million under the Senate version. The National Endowment for the Humanities (NEH) would have received $131 million under the House bill and $128 million under the Senate version.

House Committee Action

The House Appropriations Committee quickly approved its $19.8 billion Interior bill (HR 5093 — H Rept 107-564) by voice vote July 9. The bill was $519 million above the fiscal 2002 level and $269 million more than President Bush requested. Working from a draft approved by the Interior Subcommittee on June 25, the full committee added $60 million for conservation programs and $700 million in emergency fiscal 2002 funds for fighting wildfires. Counting the emergency funds, the bill totalled $20.4 billion.

The supplemental firefighting money was added by Norm Dicks, D-Wash., and approved by voice vote. Of the total, $500 million was for the Forest Service and $200 million for the Bureau of Land Management. The $60 million in conservation funding was for the Land Conservation Protection Infrastructure Improvement fund, created in 2000 (PL 106-291) and dedicated to acquiring, conserving and protecting public lands. To cover the extra money, the committee agreed by voice vote to reallocate $30 million each from the unfinished spending bills for the departments of Commerce, Justice and State, and for the departments of Veterans Affairs, and Housing and Urban Development. (*2000 Almanac, pp. 2-83, 10-6*)

The committee also gave voice vote approval to an amendment by its ranking Democrat, David R. Obey of

Where the Money Goes

Interior Spending

(figures are in thousands of dollars of new budget authority)

	Fiscal 2002 Appropriation	Fiscal 2003 Bush Request	House Passed	Senate Panel Approved
GRAND TOTAL	**$19,167,770**	**$18,938,916**	**$20,414,125**	**$19,346,920**
Total adjusted for scorekeeping*	**$19,272,770**	**$19,522,916**	**$19,792,125**	**$19,346,920**
MAIN COMPONENTS				
Interior Department	$9,496,419	$9,450,753	$9,969,175	$9,626,866
Bureau of Land Management	1,872,597	1,825,422	2,110,542	1,880,042
U.S. Fish and Wildlife Service	1,276,424	1,283,364	1,396,091	1,282,531
National Park Service	2,380,074	2,355,561	2,395,139	2,373,444
U.S. Geological Survey	914,002	867,338	928,405	926,667
Bureau of Indian Affairs	2,222,876	2,245,804	2,270,758	2,270,829
Forest Service	4,130,416	3,948,711	4,645,250	4,027,880
Department of Energy	1,766,470	1,717,241	1,892,643	1,830,991
Smithsonian Institution	518,860	527,960	527,960	537,960

* Based on Congressional Budget Office criteria for determining discretionary spending; adjusted total is used to assess compliance with 302(b) allocations.

TABLE: House and Senate Appropriations committees

Wisconsin, to prohibit use of funds in the bill for any activity related to energy development in the Arctic National Wildlife Refuge.

House Floor Action

The House passed the $19.8 billion bill, 377-46, on July 17, after GOP leaders quelled an uprising by budget conservatives angry about the $700 million in emergency spending — money that did not count against spending limits — and the decision to shift money from unfinished spending bills. *(House vote 318, p. H-102)*

Ignoring pleas from GOP appropriators, the dissidents held up the bill with floor amendments, though attempts to trim money from the measure were defeated soundly. They backed off only after securing a pledge from the leadership that the Labor-HHS-Education bill (HR 5320) would be the first spending measure considered after the August recess. "The issue is very simply [that] some of us think that our budget process has gone awry," said Patrick J. Toomey of Pennsylvania, a member of the Republican Study Committee, which led the uprising. *(Labor-HHS, p. 2-24)*

The running argument over money was punctuated by a series of policy debates and amendments. Members agreed to:

• Bar use of funds in the bill to allow new oil and gas drilling off the California coast. The amendment, by Lois Capps, D-Calif., was adopted, 252-172, after California lawmakers argued that Bush had given the same protection to Florida by executive order in May. *(House vote 315, p. H-100)*

• Increase funding for the NEA by $10 million and the NEH by $5 million, offset by reductions in the administrative accounts for the Interior Department and the Forest Service. The amendment, by Louise M. Slaughter, D-N.Y., who chaired the Congressional Arts Caucus, was adopted, 234-192. *(House vote 310, p. H-98)*

• Prohibit use of funds in the bill to plan or construct improvements to Pennsylvania Avenue in front of the White House without approval of the appropriators. The amendment, by Del. Eleanor Holmes Norton, D-D.C. , was intended to prevent the administration from permanently closing the street to vehicular traffic without congressional input. It was approved by voice vote.

• Block efforts to abbreviate an audit of Indian trust funds, which the Interior Department allegedly had mishandled for generations. Lawmakers from Arizona tried to limit the investigation to the years since 1985, but the House voted, 281-144, to extend the accounting back to 1887. *(House vote 311, p. H-100)*

• Reject, 201-223, an amendment by Earl Blumenauer, D-Ore., to protect wildlife on the Lower Klamath and Tule Lake National Wildlife refuges in Oregon and California by preventing farmers from renewing their leases to grow row crops or alfalfa in the refuges. *(House vote 316, p. H-100)*

• Block funds for an expansion of the Grand Staircase-Escalante National Monument, which President Bill Clinton designated in 1996 to protect the area from development. Clinton's action angered many Utah officials. The amendment, by Resources Committee Chairman James V. Hansen, R-Utah, shifted the funds intended to buy land near the monument and specified that they be used instead to pay for completing a visitors' center at Bear River refuge. It was adopted by voice vote.

• Accept by voice vote a compromise policy on grazing that would increase the amount of funding for environmental assessments of grazing land.

House leaders avoided a potentially bitter environmental debate over whether to restore a Clinton administration ban on roadbuilding on 58.5 million acres of National Forest Service land in 39 states. Jay Inslee, D-Wash., dropped his planned amendment to restore the Clinton policy because of restrictions in the rule for floor debate.

The rule also allowed Hansen and Transportation and Infrastructure Chairman Don Young, R-Alaska, to strike two provisions relating to a 36-year, $7.8 billion restoration pro-

ject for the Florida Everglades. One provision would have strengthened the Interior Department's role in the project at the expense of the Army Corps of Engineers. Environmental lobbyists and their congressional allies thought Interior would look out for environmental concerns as the project proceeded. The second provision would have required owners of a few dozen homes to move from an area that might be flooded by the project. Democrats offered an amendment to restore both provisions, but Young challenged it on a point of order and was sustained.

Senate Committee Action

Moving quickly to clear its agenda before the July Fourth recess, the Senate Appropriations Committee approved a $19.3 billion version of the bill (S 2708 — S Rept 107-201) by a vote of 29-0 on June 27. In an attempt to bring the bill closer to the president's budget request, Chairman Robert C. Byrd, D-W.Va., and ranking Republican Ted Stevens of Alaska agreed before the markup to cut almost $344 million in funds for firefighting, the Indian Health Service, abandoned mine reclamation and historical preservation from the original draft. Byrd also urged restraint on earmarks, saying homeland security projects had to take priority in spending decisions.

Senate Floor Action

Senators took up the bill Sept. 4, but quickly reached an impasse over forest policy. After three weeks of fruitless debate, they gave up Sept. 25.

Before setting the bill aside, the Senate agreed by voice vote to add $6 billion in emergency disaster aid for drought-stricken farmers. The amendment, by Majority Leader Tom Daschle, D-S.D., was adopted Sept. 10, after Daschle prevailed, 79-16, on a motion to waive budget restrictions that would have blocked the add-on. The aid was popular with senators of both parties, though it was seen as particularly helpful to Tim Johnson, Daschle's Democratic colleague from South Dakota, who was in a tight re-election race. (*Senate vote 212, p. S-43*)

Most of the debate, however, was over rival forest policy amendments. Forest experts said increased undergrowth and dead wood in forests, resulting from decades of fire suppression, was feeding the wildfires and making them burn hotter. The GOP solution, reflecting a "healthy forests" initiative outlined by Bush in August, was to allow timber companies to do more logging as an inducement to removing forest debris.

The GOP amendment, offered by Senate Republican Policy Chairman Larry E. Craig of Idaho and Pete V. Domenici, R-N.M., would have allowed cutting on up to 10

million acres of public land. It would have waived environmental laws such as the 1969 National Environmental Policy Act (PL 91-190), which requires agencies to conduct environmental impact studies before launching projects. And it proposed to limit lawsuits against government forest thinning practices. Suits would have to be filed within seven days of a project being proposed; courts would have 360 days to review them and could not issue restraining orders in the meantime. A project could be blocked only if it was done in an "arbitrary and capricious" manner. The 1969 law allowed citizens to appeal a project before filing a lawsuit, but the amendment would block appeals for fire-prone areas.

Environmental groups and most congressional Democrats charged that the plan was aimed primarily at increasing logging on public lands.

Democrats, led by Energy and Natural Resources Committee Chairman Jeff Bingaman of New Mexico, planned to offer a competing amendment to allow thinning on 2.5 million acres in addition to 2.5 million acres already available. The only limit on lawsuits would have been a ban on filing challenges under the 1969 law against projects within half a mile of buildings, aides said. Seventy percent of funds would have gone to thinning projects near buildings. Environmental analyses would not have been required for small projects.

The battle was fought out over the arcane question of whether to invoke cloture — thus limiting debate — on a proposal by Byrd to spend $825 million to repay agencies for their firefighting efforts. Democrats were eager to close the debate because that also would have eliminated the GOP amendment. But three attempts to garner the necessary 60 votes failed. The votes were 50-49 on Sept. 17, 49-46 on Sept. 23, and 51-47 on Sept. 25. (*Senate votes 217, 221 and 224; pp. S-44, S-45 and S-46*)

Ron Wyden, D-Ore., and Dianne Feinstein, D-Calif., tried to broker a compromise with Craig and his allies, but it was nixed by other Western Republicans. The Wyden-Feinstein compromise would have created a one-year program to allow thinning on 7 million acres in national forests most vulnerable to wildfires. Lawsuits challenging tree-cutting practices would have been allowed but limited. Unlike the original Craig proposal, the Wyden-Feinstein plan would have allowed a court to issue a temporary restraining order, though plaintiffs would have to reapply every 60 days.

With the November elections approaching, the Interior bill, like most of the other spending bills, was pushed to the lame-duck session. After the election, appropriators tried to get more money for the spending bills; when they failed, they threw in the towel and agreed to leave the problem to the next Congress. ◆

Labor Bill Brings Process to a Halt

Although Congress got an unusually early start on the fiscal 2003 Labor, Health and Human Services (HHS) and Education appropriations bill, the measure never made it to a floor vote in either chamber because of a larger disagreement over spending levels. The programs covered by the bill were funded at fiscal 2002 levels until Jan. 11, 2003, under a continuing resolution (PL 107-294).

The only action on the bill was in the Senate, but the drama came in the House, where the bill turned into a roadblock that brought the appropriations process to a halt.

The annual Labor-HHS spending bill — historically the largest and most controversial of the appropriations measures — frequently languishes until the end of the session. At that point, lawmakers often are willing to set aside budget constraints and provide whatever extra money is needed to finish the bill and get out of town. This time, however, fiscal conservatives decided to use the bill to make a stand for tighter fiscal discipline. They got an agreement from Speaker J. Dennis Hastert, R-Ill., to make it the first of the appropriations bills brought to the floor after the August recess, putting it before most of the other domestic spending measures.

House Appropriations Chairman C.W. Bill Young, R-Fla., privately acknowledged that the amount allocated for the bill was not sufficient to win over a majority of members, but he agreed to honor Hastert's pledge. On Sept. 4, the day Congress returned from its recess, he introduced a Labor-HHS bill (HR 5320) that mirrored President Bush's request for $130.9 billion in discretionary budget authority. The bill quickly ran into an intra-party stalemate, with GOP moderates saying it would short-change education and other programs, while conservatives insisted on sticking with Bush's budget.

In the Senate, by contrast, a more generous Labor-HHS bill (S 2766) glided through the Appropriations Committee with relatively little trouble in mid-July. Iowa Democrat Tom Harkin, chairman of the Labor-HHS-Education Appropriations Subcommittee, worked with ranking Republican Arlen Specter of Pennsylvania to write a bill that boosted funding for education and health services while restoring cuts Bush sought in the Labor Department budget.

The bill had a discretionary spending total of $136.4 billion, including advance funding for future years. That was a 7 percent increase over fiscal 2002 and $5.2 billion more than Bush requested. The discretionary funding that was under dispute actually accounted for less than a third of the Labor-HHS bill. The remainder was for entitlement programs, such as Medicaid, the federal-state health program for the poor; Medicare, the health program for the elderly and disabled; Supplemental Security Income for poor el-

BoxScore 2003 *Fiscal Year*

Labor-HHS-Education

Bills:

HR 5320, S 2766

Legislative Action:

Senate Appropriations Committee approved S 2766 (S Rept 107-216), 29-0, on July 18.

derly and disabled people; and unemployment insurance. For those programs, spending levels are determined by eligibility formulas and other criteria already set in law. Counting the mandatory funds, the bill totaled $432.5 billion, compared with $426.2 billion requested by Bush.

Highlights

The following are highlights of the Senate committee-approved bill and the president's proposal. Appropriators said the House bill was identical to Bush's request.

● **Labor.** Senate appropriators rejected Bush's request to cut the department's discretionary funding by 7 percent, to $11.5 billion. Instead, the bill called for $12.4 billion, about the same as the fiscal 2002 level, including a $657 million increase over fiscal 2002 in assistance for dislocated workers. Bush sought a $505 million cut. Other increases in the bill included $1 billion more than Bush requested for the Employment and Training Administration, for a total of $10.8 billion; $79 million for the Migrant and Seasonal Farmworker program, which Bush proposed to eliminate; and $225 million for Youth Opportunity Grants, rather than a reduction to $44.5 million as Bush proposed.

● **HHS.** The Senate bill included $61.5 billion in discretionary funds for HHS, an increase of about $4.4 billion over fiscal 2002 and $2 billion more than Bush wanted. Senate appropriators agreed with Bush's request for $27.2 billion for the National Institutes of Health (NIH), a $3.7 billion increase over fiscal 2002 that would complete a five-year effort to double NIH's budget. They agreed to provide $332 million more than Bush sought for Head Start, $620 million more for the Centers for Disease Control and Prevention (CDC), and $300 million more for LIHEAP, which provides home heating assistance to low-income people.

● **Education.** The Senate committee proposed $53.2 billion in discretionary funding for education, a $4.2 billion increase over fiscal 2002 and $2.8 billion more than Bush requested. The bill included $11.8 billion for Title I grants for poor and disadvantaged students, a $1.5 billion increase over fiscal 2002, and $500 million more than requested. It included $3.1 billion for programs to improve the quality of teaching in the nation's classrooms, $250 million more than in fiscal 2002 or in Bush's budget.

The bill called for a $1 billion increase, as requested, for special education, but Democrats said they would fight to make the money mandatory, rather than leaving it to the annual discretion of Congress. Bush and many Republicans said they first wanted changes to the 1975 Individuals with Disabilities Education Act (PL 94-142).

Where the Money Goes

Labor-HHS-Education Spending

(figures are in thousands of dollars of new budget authority)

	Fiscal 2002 Appropriation	Fiscal 2003 Bush Request	Senate Panel Approved
GRAND TOTAL	**$411,276,875**	**$426,171,807**	**$432,502,509**
MAIN COMPONENTS			
Department of Health and Human Services	$305,720,364	$317,776,875	$319,983,563
National Institutes of Health	23,455,843	27,167,926	27,192,926
Children and Family Services	8,428,574	8,593,364	8,864,054
Centers for Disease Control	4,303,256	3,874,444	4,493,572
Department of Education	51,421,993	52,841,371	55,698,270
Education for the disadvantaged	12,346,900	13,385,400	14,087,400
Student financial assistance	12,285,500	12,767,500	13,162,000
Special education	8,672,804	9,687,804	9,696,424
School improvement programs	7,837,473	6,784,484	8,303,834
Labor Department	14,576,697	13,304,891	14,536,706
Employment and Training Administration	10,925,361	9,750,567	10,771,559
Occupational Safety and Health Administration	443,498	437,019	469,604

TABLE: Senate Appropriations Committee

Legislative Action

Senate Committee Action

The Senate Appropriations Committee approved its version of the bill (S 2766 — S Rept 107-216) on July 18 with unanimous approval and rare comity. The vote was 29-0. The Labor-HHS-Education Subcommittee had approved the measure by voice vote two days earlier. The bill's path was smoothed by a discretionary spending allocation of $134.1 billion, $5 billion more than was available to the House Labor-HHS-Education Subcommittee. Taking into account advance funding for future years, the Senate bill contained a total of $136.4 billion in discretionary funds.

Harkin and other Democrats focused particularly on education, saying Bush was not seeking the funding necessary to carry out the landmark 2001 education law (PL 107-110) that he had signed proudly in January. "If our schools are going to be held accountable for their performance . . . then they need the resources to meet these new, higher standards," Harkin said. *(2001 Almanac, p. 8-3)*

The 2001 law, which reauthorized the 1994 Elementary and Secondary Education Act (ESEA), required states to start administering statewide reading and math tests for grades 3 through 8 by the 2005-06 school year, and it included other measures to help disadvantaged children catch up with their peers in more affluent districts. It authorized a record $21.9 billion for elementary and secondary education programs in fiscal 2002, according to the Congressional Research Service (CRS). But it included few specific authorization levels in subsequent years, leaving lawmakers to wrangle over how much money was needed to achieve success. Bush proposed $22 billion for ESEA programs in fiscal 2003, about $50 million more than the previous fiscal year, according to CRS. Senate appropriators approved $24.3 billion.

The committee gave voice vote approval to one amendment, a proposal by Harkin to increase the discretionary allocation for the bill by $144 million, mainly to add money for the CDC.

House Bill

Working with a total for discretionary spending that many on the committee said was too low, House appropriators allotted the Labor-HHS-Education Subcommittee $129.9 billion and an overall total of $418.7 billion for the bill. Panel Republicans warned that trying to pass such a lean bill would force their GOP colleagues in tough re-election races to cast politically difficult votes. They were particularly worried about trying to provide education funding below the levels authorized in the landmark 2001 education law.

"Obviously, at $129 billion, we can't do everything people want to get done," said Subcommittee Chairman Ralph Regula, R-Ohio.

When Young acceded to the Speaker's wishes and introduced the bill in September, he made it clear that it was not produced by his committee. An Appropriations press release stated: "House Appropriations Committee Chairman C.W. Bill Young today introduced the president's budget request for the Labor, Health and Human Services and Education appropriations bill. This action was taken to fulfill a House Republican leadership commitment to conservative members of the conference to take up the Labor-HHS bill on the floor before any other appropriations bill. For details on the bill please refer to the Appendix of the [president's] FY03 Budget Request."

Regula and Young sent White House budget director Mitchell E. Daniels Jr. a letter in October asking him for a list of education programs the administration believed were not working and could be cut in order to provide more money for better uses. "I don't question there are many of them,

but it's hard to ferret them out," Regula said.

At a GOP business forum Oct. 9, Regula asked Daniels "to suggest to me how you'd get a conference, and a conference report, with a Democratic Senate when you're $6 billion apart, and most of those are programs that people like."

Daniels responded, "You will never outbid the Senate, and this is part of the House's lot in life."

The bill never reached the floor. ◆

Debate Over Capitol Police Postponed

The fiscal 2003 spending bill for congressional operations was one of only three annual appropriations bills to make it through both chambers, but action on the measure stopped there because of a broader dispute over non-defense spending. That left the legislative branch, like much of the federal government, operating at fiscal 2002 levels under a series of stopgap laws, the last of which (PL 107-294) was good until Jan. 11, 2003.

Although lawmakers never got a chance to reconcile the $2.7 billion House bill with the Senate's $2.4 billion version, the final bill was expected to total about $3.3 billion. By custom, the chambers set funding levels for their own operations and do not alter each other's figures.

The annual bill covers staff salaries, office expenses, mail, police and maintenance of the Capitol complex. It also funds agencies and offices that primarily serve Congress, including the Library of Congress, the General Accounting Office (GAO) and the Government Printing Office (GPO).

The main sticking point, had the bill reached conference, was a Senate plan to merge the Capitol Police and the Library of Congress police into a single force. House members had opposed such a move in the past as costly and ineffective. Supporters said it would provide more seamless security for the Capitol.

Highlights

The following are highlights of the two bills:
● **Capitol Police.** The House included $219 million for salary and expenses of the Capitol Police, compared with $210 million in the Senate bill. Both chambers endorsed a 5 percent pay raise for the police on top of the 4.1 percent increase that the bills assumed for all Capitol Hill employees. Members hoped the raise, plus increased benefits including a tuition reimbursement plan, would help stem the flight of officers to other federal law enforcement agencies, which had been recruiting heavily since the Sept. 11, 2001, terrorist attacks.
● **Library of Congress.** The House called for $422 million, a 5 percent increase over fiscal 2002 level. The Senate proposed $410 million.
● **GPO.** The printing office was slated to get $120 million under the House bill, $5 million more than in fiscal 2002, and $122 million under the Senate version. A potential red flag for the White House, which was seeking to privatize much of the government's printing work, was language the Senate included that directed the administration to send printing requests to the GPO.

BoxScore **2003** *Fiscal Year*

Legislative Branch

Bill:

HR 5121

Legislative Action:

House passed HR 5121 (H Rept 107-576), 365-49, on July 18.

Senate passed HR 5121, 85-14, on July 25, after inserting the text of its own bill (S 2720 — S Rept 107-209).

● **GAO.** The GAO was to receive $454 million under both bills, $24 million more than in 2002.
● **Architect of the Capitol.** The House bill included $303 million, the Senate bill $388 million. Each by custom excluded spending on the other chamber's buildings. Unlike the House bill, the Senate measure proposed to create a position of Deputy Architect to act as the chief operating officer for the Architect of the Capitol.
● **Congressional staff.** The House bill included funding to increase the monthly public transportation subsidy for staff to $100 from $65. It also included funding and authorizing language to provide student loan payments to House workers. Senate workers already received such a benefit.

Legislative Action

House Subcommittee Action

The House Legislative Branch Appropriations Subcommittee approved a $2.7 billion draft of the bill by voice vote June 27. The measure included $960 million for House operations.

Members of both parties used the subcommittee markup to complain bitterly about construction plans for the new Capitol Visitor Center, due to begin in the summer. The construction was expected to severely limit parking on the East Front Plaza of the Capitol. Hundreds of members regularly drove their cars onto the plaza to reach the floor quickly for votes. "Particularly for older members and members with handicaps, this is going to cause a very big problem," said Ray LaHood, R-Ill.

Democrats also used the markup to attack House GOP leaders for barring them from offering a Democratic substitute for the Medicare prescription drug bill (HR 4954). As a protest, David R. Obey of Wisconsin, ranking Democrat on the full committee, offered a motion to strike all funding for the House of Representatives from the bill. "The gutless, spineless leadership [will not] allow members to work their will on prescription drugs," Obey said. His motion was defeated by voice vote.

The night before the markup, the House passed by voice vote a separate bill (HR 5018) aimed at improving the pay and working conditions of the Capitol Police. The measure cosponsored by Bob Ney, R-Ohio, and Steny H. Hoyer, D-Md. — the chairman and ranking member of the House Administration Committee — also called for a 5 percent pay raise for officers, as well as an increase in their annual leave.

Where the Money Goes

Legislative Branch Spending

(figures are in thousands of dollars of new budget authority)

	Fiscal 2002 Appropriation	Fiscal 2003 Bush Request	House Passed	Senate Passed
GRAND TOTAL*	**$2,543,712**	**$2,652,401**	**$2,671,900**	**$2,417,108**
MAIN COMPONENTS				
House of Representatives	$919,907	$949,642	$960,406	—
Senate	641,385	683,300	—	672,593
Capitol Police	157,190	212,626	256,175	209,803
Architect of the Capitol	378,470	335,184	303,066	387,970
Library of Congress	481,663	511,734	508,484	496,920
General Accounting Office	429,444	454,802	453,534	454,534

*Totals do not include the other chamber's amount

TABLE: House and Senate Appropriations committees

House Committee Action

The full Appropriations Committee approved the bill (HR 5121 — H Rept 107-576) by voice vote July 11. The committee gave voice vote approval to amendments by:

• James P. Moran, D-Va., to withhold $590,000 from the Joint Committee on Taxation until it released a report on tax evasion by expatriates. Democrats were trying to dislodge a report requested three years before by then-Ways and Means Committee Chairman Bill Archer, R-Texas (1971-2001), that had yet to be released. Moran said he believed the report was complete, but that Republicans were withholding it because of the study's results.

• Subcommittee Chairman Charles H. Taylor, R-N.C., to provide additional benefits to Capitol Police officers, including a new tuition reimbursement benefit of up to $10,000 a year, for a maximum of $40,000, in exchange for serving at least three years on the force. Other provisions included extra pay for officers with special duties, such as the bomb squad or providing protection for members and visiting dignitaries, and reimbursement of most back pay to officers who worked large amounts of overtime following the Sept. 11, 2001, terrorist attacks. "Mr. Taylor's amendment will go a long way toward stabilizing our police force," said Hoyer.

House Floor Action

The House passed the bill, 365-49, on July 18. (*House vote 321, p. H-102*)

Appropriators had hoped to use the debate to spotlight the boost in spending on the Capitol Police. Instead, much of the focus was on Moran's proposal to withhold funds from the Joint Tax Committee. The provision was struck from the bill on a point of order on the grounds that it was legislating on an appropriations bill. Moran was allowed to introduce it as an amendment, but it was rejected along largely partisan lines, 206-213. (*House vote 320, p. H-102*)

Lawmakers also struck a provision that would have given the Capitol Police chief the authority to determine recruitment bonuses, tuition reimbursements, salaries for new employees, relocation bonuses and other personnel and pay issues. That, too, was considered legislating on a spending bill.

Senate Committee Action

The Senate Appropriations Committee approved a $2.4 billion version of the bill (S 2720 — S Rept 107-209) that included $675 million for Senate operations, but not the $960 million for the House. The panel approved the bill by voice vote July 11, hours after the Legislative Branch Subcommittee gave its approval, also by voice vote.

The bill contained several provisions not in the House version, including:

• The proposed merger over three years of the 1,208-member Capitol Police and the 122 police for the Library of Congress into a single force. Richard J. Durbin, D-Ill., and Robert F. Bennett, R-Utah, the chairman and ranking member of the subcommittee, said the move would make the two forces more efficient by placing them under a unified command structure. "We don't need to have two large police forces for an area that's this small," said Bennett, and putting them under a single command structure "makes a lot of sense."

• A restructuring of the office of the Architect of the Capitol, which bore the burden of cleaning up the Capitol complex after the 2001 anthrax attacks, by creating a new position for a deputy architect who would also act as the office's chief operating officer.

• A directive to the Bush administration to comply with a 107-year-old law requiring that all government documents be printed by the GPO. The language was written in response to a May 3 memorandum from the Office of Management and Budget (OMB) that ordered federal agencies to use private printers if they could do a job faster and cheaper. In doing so, the appropriators said, the administration would "completely disregard a law which has been in place since 1895."

The OMB memorandum said GPO premiums and fees were costing federal agencies an extra $50 million to $70 million a year. The arrangement "unfairly penalizes both taxpayers and efficient would-be competitors," OMB charged.

The Senate appropriators, however, said in the report accompanying the bill that the memorandum showed the pro-

posed change could increase the government's costs by as much as $335 million in the first year.

• $50 million for a backup computing facility for the House, Senate and other congressional offices. A lack of computer access was a serious problem when offices were evacuated after anthrax-tainted letters were sent to Capitol Hill in the fall of 2001. The bill also included increased funding for screening mail addressed to Capitol Hill.

Senate Floor Action

The Senate quickly passed HR 5121 by a vote of 85-14 on July 25, after substituting the text of its own bill. (*Senate vote 191, p. S-39*)

Durbin and Bennett said they would press House members to accept the proposed police force merger. "The House has resisted the merger in the past," Bennett said. "But I think they'll be more open to it this time around." ◆

Congress Fights for Family Housing

The military construction spending bill was one of only two fiscal 2003 appropriations measures cleared before the 107th Congress adjourned. President Bush signed it into law Oct. 23 (HR 5011 — PL 107-249), along with the huge defense appropriations bill.

The general dispute over fiscal 2003 spending levels that left the domestic spending bills stranded had little impact on the $10.5 billion military construction measure. Typically the least controversial of the 13 regular appropriations bills, it paid for building and repairing barracks, family housing and other facilities as well as for the costs associated with base closings.

The fiscal 2003 bill provided $835 million more than Bush requested, though that was still $105 million below the fiscal 2002 level (PL 107-64).

Of the total, $5.6 billion was for military construction, $4.2 billion for family housing, and $561 million for environmental cleanup and other projects related to base closings. Ninety-seven of 495 major bases had been closed since 1988.

The bill included $1.2 billion for new construction and modernization of the nation's 12,819 barracks spaces, nearly half of which were at least 30 years old. Recognizing that the all-volunteer force meant more service members with families, Congress provided $2.9 billion for existing family housing and $1.3 billion for new housing. The latter was $135 million more than the fiscal 2002 level. (*2001 Almanac, p. 2-41*)

Congress also more than doubled the president's request for National Guard and reserve programs to $688 million.

Although the bill was signed in mid-October, many of the new programs remained on hold for several weeks until Congress cleared the fiscal 2003 defense authorization bill (PL 107-314), which provided authority for the government to spend the money. (*Defense authorization, p. 7-12*)

Legislative Action

House Subcommittee, Committee Action

The House Appropriations Committee approved a $10.1 billion version of the spending bill (H Rept 107-533) by voice vote June 27. The panel's Military Construction Subcommittee had approved a draft by voice vote June 12, after adding more than $1 billion, or 13 percent, to Bush's original request.

Bush initially had requested $9 billion for military construction, $1.7 billion less than was appropriated for fiscal

---

BoxScore **2003** Fiscal Year

Military Construction

Bill:
HR 5011 — PL 107-249

Legislative Action:

House passed HR 5011 (H Rept 107-533), 426-1, on June 27.

Senate passed HR 5011, amended (S Rept 107-202), 96-3, on July 18.

House adopted the conference report (H Rept 107-731), 419-0, on Oct. 10.

Senate cleared the bill by voice vote Oct. 11.

President signed Oct. 23.

2002. At the same time, he sought a significant increase in defense spending — $48 billion more than enacted for fiscal 2002. In the report accompanying the bill, the GOP-led Appropriations Committee criticized the president's priorities. "It strains credulity that additional military construction spending could not be found with an increase of this magnitude," the report said. "The unavoidable conclusion is that the administration's rhetoric regarding the importance of quality of life for troops and their families does not coincide with the facts."

To permit a spending increase, House appropriators shifted $594 million from the Defense budget to the military construction bill. The Pentagon had ruled that the money, part of Bush's defense request, was military construction funding to be spent improving security at U.S. facilities. The appropriators also added $541 million from other accounts. The House Armed Services Committee had made similar changes in its version of the fiscal 2003 authorization bill (HR 4546).

The resulting bill proposed: $5.3 billion for military construction programs, $4.2 billion for family housing and $545 million for base-closure costs. Of the total, $673 million would go to improve security at military facilities, $168 million for chemical demilitarization programs, $1.3 billion for new family housing, $2.9 billion to maintain existing housing and $485 million for environmental cleanup.

Subcommittee members also used the bill to fund construction at bases in their home states — both to improve the local installations and to build up the facilities in hopes of making them off limits for the next round of base closings in 2005.

House Floor Action

The House passed the bill, 426-1, in less than an hour June 27. (*House vote 277, p. H-90*)

Several Democrats bemoaned the fact that the $10.1 billion measure still was about $520 million below the fiscal 2002 level. "In the wake of Sept. 11, there is so much more that we should be doing," said John W. Olver of Massachusetts, ranking Democrat on the Military Construction Subcommittee. But full committee Chairman C.W. Bill Young, R-Fla., praised the measure because of its programs to upgrade military housing.

Senate Committee Action

The Senate Appropriations Committee approved a $10.6 billion version of the bill (S 2709 — S Rept 107-202) by

Where the Money Goes

Military Construction Spending

(figures are in thousands of dollars of new budget authority)

	Fiscal 2002 Appropriation	Fiscal 2003 Bush Request	House Passed	Senate Passed	Conference Report
GRAND TOTAL	**$10,604,400**	**$9,664,041**	**$10,083,000**	**$10,622,000**	**$10,499,000**
MAIN COMPONENTS					
Military Construction	$5,886,150	$4,704,243	$5,121,858	$5,580,278	$5,564,648
NATO infrastructure	162,600	168,200	168,200	168,200	167,200
Family housing	4,095,739	4,246,460	4,247,804	4,228,384	4,206,014
Base closure and realignment	632,713	545,138	545,138	645,138	561,138
General provisions	−172,802	—	—	—	—

TABLE: House and Senate Appropriations committees

voice vote June 27. By that point, the president's request included not only the original $9 billion, plus the $594 million for increased security protection, but also an additional $122 million. The revised request had not come to the Hill in time to be incorporated into the House version. The Senate bill still was $900 million more costly than Bush's request, a fact that drew sharp criticism from the White House.

Funding differences between the House and Senate bills included:

● **Members' projects.** The Senate bill included $957 million for projects added by individual members, compared with $541 million in the House version. Each chamber had an almost entirely different list of add-ons.

● **Base closings.** Senate appropriators approved $645 million for base closing costs, $100 million more than in the House version or the administration request. The extra money was earmarked for cleanup costs. "Until the environmental cleanup is completed, these closed bases are the equivalent of giant white elephants," said Sen. Dianne Feinstein, D-Calif., chairman of the Military Construction Subcommittee.

● **National Guard and Reserve.** Senate appropriators added $290 million to the $319 million requested by the president. The House had added $210 million to the request.

● **Modernization.** Another $200 million was added to the Senate bill, evenly split for Army and Air Force infrastructure modernization programs.

● **NATO.** Like the House, the Senate recommended against funding two NATO programs in Greece and Spain, concerned that growing NATO commitments would drain funds from priority U.S. projects.

Senate Floor Action

The Senate passed HR 5011 by a vote of 96-3 on July 18, after substituting the text of its own bill. Senate action had been delayed by Jon Kyl, R-Ariz., who placed a hold on the bill until he got a guarantee from appropriators that they would fund $1.1 billion in another spending bill to help fight fires that had scorched the West during the summer. (*Senate vote 181, p. S-37*)

Conference/Final Action

House and Senate conferees finished work on the bill Oct. 9. The House adopted the conference report (H Rept 107-731) by a vote of 419-0 on Oct. 10. The Senate cleared the bill by voice vote early Oct. 11. (*House vote 458, p. H-144*)

Although the bill's $10.5 billion bottom line represented a victory over initial White House proposals, appropriators still felt shortchanged. The total was closer to the Senate's $10.6 billion, but the House had agreed by voice vote Sept. 10 to instruct its conferees to insist on the higher of the House or Senate funding levels for most items. Appropriators said they had to fight for every dollar. ◆

Highway Funds at Center of Debate

Disputes over highway spending dominated debate on Transportation appropriations for fiscal 2003. Declining gasoline tax revenue forced the Bush administration to cut its highway budget request, and though lawmakers wanted to restore spending, they could not agree on how much to provide. The issue never was settled because the bill was halted by a broader dispute over the budget. Transportation spending was extended at fiscal 2002 levels under a series of continuing resolutions, the last of which (PL 107-294) was good until Jan. 11, 2003.

The Senate Appropriations Committee acted first on the bill, approving a $64.7 billion version in July that exceeded President Bush's request by $8.6 billion. The difference was due mainly to added Senate spending for highways and for Amtrak, the national passenger railroad.

The House Appropriations Committee approved a $60 billion version of the bill in October that was $4 billion above Bush's request. Extra highway funding was the major factor in the House increase.

In addition to highways and Amtrak, the annual bill funded other transportation agencies including the Federal Aviation Administration, the Coast Guard, the Federal Transit and Railroad administrations, and the National Highway Traffic Safety Administration. Two-thirds of the spending was mandatory, required under highway and aviation funding laws enacted in 1998 and 2000. That left $21.7 billion in discretionary spending in the House bill and $22.2 billion in the Senate version.

When the Transportation bill stalled in October as part of the larger meltdown over limits on non-defense spending, the dispute over highway spending spilled into late-session efforts to keep the government running at previous-year levels under a series of stopgap spending bills.

Highlights

The following are the main issues that arose in debate on the two versions of the bill:

● **Highways.** Bush requested $23.3 billion in Highway Trust Fund spending, $8.5 billion less than the $31.8 billion appropriated for fiscal 2002. The cut was required under a mechanism known as revenue aligned budget authority, enacted as part of the 1998 surface transportation law, or TEA-21 (PL 105-178). *(1998 Almanac, p. 24-3)*

The 1998 law guaranteed minimum levels of highway spending through 2003, including $27.7 billion in fiscal 2003. But it also tied each year's spending to the amount of gas tax revenues flowing into the Highway Trust Fund. Rising revenue for the first four years of TEA-21 gave Congress

---

BoxScore 2003
Fiscal Year

Transportation

Bills:
HR 5559, S 2808

Legislative Action:
Senate Appropriations Committee approved S 2808 (S Rept 107-224) by voice vote July 25.
House Appropriations Committee approved HR 5559 (H Rept 107-722) by voice vote Oct. 1.

---

plenty of money to spend on roads. But for fiscal 2003, the White House Office of Management and Budget (OMB) forecast an $8.5 billion drop in gasoline tax revenue, leading the administration to cut a corresponding amount from its budget request.

Spurred by state officials and road builders, the transportation authorizing committees tried to ensure that fiscal 2003 spending would at least equal the $27.7 billion minimum that was guaranteed by TEA-21. The House passed a separate bill (HR 3694) on May 14 authorizing the extra $4.4 billion, and appropriators later won administration approval to include the authorization in a fiscal 2002 supplemental spending bill (PL 107-206) signed in August. *(Supplemental p. 2-40)*

In writing the appropriations bill, the House committee called for $27.7 billion in Highway Trust Fund spending, while Senate appropriators provided for $31.8 billion.

When the appropriations process broke down, Congress set fiscal 2003 spending for highways at $27.7 billion as part of the short-term bills that kept the government running. The last of those bills let highway money actually flow to the states at an annual rate of $31.8 billion, though total spending for the year still was limited to $27.7 billion.

● **Amtrak.** Funding for the financially strapped national passenger railroad also was in dispute. Bush asked for $521 million and insisted that any spending beyond that be tied to management changes. In June, the administration released a set of principles for overhauling Amtrak that included increased state funding, an end to Amtrak's reliance on federal operating subsidies and the opening of intercity routes to competition. Amtrak proponents on Capitol Hill, many of them Democrats, disagreed, saying the federal money had to come first to keep the service solvent.

The House bill included $762 million for Amtrak, along with a requirement for improved financial reporting. The Senate bill included $1.2 billion and criticized some of the changes sought by the administration.

Amtrak was about $4 billion in debt and avoided a shutdown in early July only after Congress and the White House provided $305 million in bailout money. That was expected to keep trains running into fiscal 2003, although Amtrak officials said the line could face another shutdown if it did not receive the $1.2 billion it requested.

● **TSA.** The Transportation Security Administration (TSA), the agency in charge of securing the nation's transportation system under the 2001 aviation security bill (PL 107-71), also presented problems for appropriators. Costs had increased as the agency took over responsibility for security at the nation's airports. The TSA estimated it would need 67,000 employees, more than twice the 30,000 Con-

Where the Money Goes

Transportation Spending

(figures are in thousands of dollars of new budget authority)

	Fiscal 2002 Appropriation	Fiscal 2003 Bush Request	House Panel Approved	Senate Panel Approved
GRAND TOTAL	**$24,376,970**	**$21,345,680**	**$21,740,930**	**$22,173,468**
Total adjusted for scorekeeping*	**$24,317,670**	**$22,126,680**	**$21,689,930**	**—**
Limits on obligations and exempt obligations	**($42,073,108)**	**($33,883,018)**	**($38,306,767)**	**($42,475,231)**
MAIN COMPONENTS				
Federal Aviation Administration	$10,528,500	$10,182,225	$10,199,225	$10,186,225
Federal Highway Administration**	542,000	—	100,00	200,000
Federal Railroad Administration	1,044,633	711,265	957,614	1,422,589
Federal Transit Administration	3,272,700	1,445,000	1,445,000	1,545,000
Transportation Security Administration	3,464,800***	2,572,000	2,317,309	2,176,000
Coast Guard	5,494,659	6,057,978	6,060,978	5,771,978
National Highway Traffic Safety Administration	129,780	128,445	133,433	143,000
Secretary of Transportation	155,171	140,760	181,031	171,669
General Provisions	148,525	—	—	360,000

* Adjustments based on Congressional Budget Office criteria for determining discretionary spending; adjusted total is used to assess compliance with 302(b) allocations.

** Does not include money from trust funds, which are budgeted as limits on obligations.

*** Includes emergency supplemental appropriations.

TABLE: House and Senate Appropriations committees

gress originally anticipated. Meanwhile, the agency was behind schedule in meeting several deadlines, including a Dec. 31 deadline for screening all airline baggage for explosives.

A total of $5.8 billion was appropriated for the TSA in fiscal 2002. Bush initially requested $4.8 billion for fiscal 2003, but increased that to $5.3 billion midyear. The passenger and cargo fees that originally were supposed to pay for the agency were expected to raise only about $2.7 billion. The Senate bill included $4.95 billion for the TSA in fiscal 2003. The House, acting after Bush asked for an extra $546 million, provided for $5.1 billion.

● **Coast Guard.** Bush requested $6.1 billion for the Coast Guard, which had taken a lead role in port and maritime security after Sept. 11. The House bill essentially matched the request, which was a half billion dollars over the fiscal 2002 level. The Senate bill proposed $5.8 billion for the Coast Guard, also requiring that the Coast Guard dedicate more time to traditional missions, such as search and rescue, that had taken a lower priority since Sept. 11.

Legislative Action

Senate Committee Action

The Senate Transportation Appropriations Subcommittee approved its $64.7 billion version of the bill by voice vote July 24, and the full committee followed suit July 25 (S 2808 — S Rept 107-224). Chairman Robert C. Byrd, D-W.Va., was pushing to get all 13 of the regular spending bills through his committee before the August recess.

● **Highways.** The bill written by the subcommittee restored $8.5 billion in highway funds that Bush proposed cutting for fiscal 2003, bringing the total to the fiscal 2002 level of $31.8 billion. Subcommittee Chairwoman Patty Mur-

ray, D-Wash., said the increased highway spending was needed to preserve more than 350,000 road construction jobs nationwide.

● **Amtrak.** The committee proposed $1.2 billion for Amtrak and required none of the managerial or budgetary changes sought by the administration. "States are $40 billion short in their own state budgets," said Murray. "We need to work with the states to keep Amtrak funded as we work to try and figure out how the allocations in the individual states can participate in Amtrak funding in the future."

"One thing I've learned as [a former] chairman of this [sub]committee is that throwing money at Amtrak will not solve its problems," responded Richard C. Shelby of Alabama, the ranking Republican on the panel.

● **TSA.** The Senate also exceeded Bush's request for the TSA, providing for $4.9 billion in fiscal 2003, a $150 million increase. (This was before Bush increased his request to $5.3 billion.) Democrats signaled that pressure from the White House to add more money could lead to an extended budget dispute. "I don't know where they are suggesting we take [additional money] from," Murray said.

House Committee Action

The House Appropriations Committee approved a $60 billion version of the bill (HR 5559 — H Rept 107-722) by voice vote Oct. 1.

● **Highways.** House appropriators took a compromise stance on highway spending, providing the $27.7 billion authorized under the supplemental spending bill. An amendment by Chet Edwards, D-Texas, to increase highway spending to $31.8 billion was defeated on a 26-29 party-line vote. Edwards stressed the economic necessity of more highway spending, but Transportation Appropriations Subcommittee Chairman Harold Rogers, R-Ky., said it would be fiscally irresponsible.

● **Amtrak.** The committee bill included $762 million for the struggling passenger rail service, $241 million above the president's request. When the markup began Sept. 26, committee Republicans defeated a proposal by Martin Olav Sabo, D-Minn., to increase the amount to $1.2 billion, as in the Senate version. It was rejected on a 25-35 party line vote.

Sabo argued that the total was "simply not enough to sustain Amtrak for the next fiscal year." But Rogers maintained that an additional $438 million for the rail line would rupture the spending cap imposed on the bill and subject it to points of order. "If we go to the floor with this we'll be shut down in a matter of seconds. This is a poison pill," he said.

Rogers included language in a manager's amendment to limit spending on long-distance trains to $150 million, 75 percent of what Amtrak said it needed to keep all the trains running. Amtrak would have to seek contributions from the states or other non-federal sources to make up the difference, or cut some long-distance routes. The amendment was approved by voice vote.

● **TSA.** The bill included $5.1 billion in fiscal 2003 for the TSA, $200 million below the president's revised request.

An attempt by James P. Moran, D-Va., to increase spending on airport modifications to support the installation of explosive detection machines was defeated by voice vote. It would have increased funding by $425 million to a total of $700 million, offsetting the money by eliminating 1,701 TSA positions as "shoe and bin runners," responsible for handling passenger possessions at screening checkpoints at airports. Rogers argued that there was more than enough money already for airport modifications. ◆

Treasury Bill Draws Veto Threats

The bill for the Treasury Department, Postal Service and related agencies was the last of five fiscal 2003 spending bills to win House passage in 2002. The Senate Appropriations Committee approved its own version of the bill, but the measure never made it to the floor. Instead, the accounts covered by the bill were kept alive at fiscal 2002 levels under a series of stopgap bills, the last of which (PL 107-294) was good until Jan. 11, 2003.

Both the House and Senate versions of the Treasury-Postal bill contained about $18.5 billion in discretionary spending. Although the White House had requested $18 billion, it said the congressional figure was acceptable. The bills also included $16.6 billion in mandatory spending, mostly for federal employee retirement plans, bringing the total to $34.8 billion ($35.1 billion in the House version, after scorekeeping adjustments).

The annual measure funded the Treasury Department — including the IRS and Customs Service — the White House, general government overhead and other nuts-and-bolts agencies such as the Office of Personnel Management (OPM). While the bill itself was relatively noncontroversial, it routinely attracted controversial policy riders.

The White House threatened to veto the fiscal 2003 bill over language aimed at barring enforcement of a ban on travel by U.S. citizens to Cuba. A veto threat in 2001 prompted conferees to drop a similar provision from the fiscal 2002 measure (PL 107-67). (*2001 Almanac, p. 2-47*)

The White House also warned of a veto over language in both versions that would have prevented the administration from setting numerical goals, targets or quotas for "outsourcing" federal jobs. The provisions were intended to rein in the White House's management agenda, which included a program to determine whether jobs that were "commercial in nature," such as food service, could be provided through contracts with private businesses.

One issue that often dogged the Treasury-Postal bill — whether members of Congress would get annual pay raises — did not arise in 2002. The pay raises were automatic unless Congress blocked them, which it did four times in the 1990s. This time, however, the House rejected an attempt to block the pay increase. As a result, members' pay was set to increase to $154,700 on Jan. 1, 2003, up from $150,000.

Treasury Department agencies such as the FBI, Customs Service and Secret Service played key roles in the fight against terrorism. As a result, the pending creation of a Homeland Security Department, and government efforts to enhance domestic safety in the meantime, dominated much of the debate on the bill.

BoxScore 2003 Fiscal Year
Treasury-Postal Service

Bills:
HR 5120, S 2740
Legislative Action:
Senate Appropriations Committee approved S 2740 (S Rept 107-212), 29-0, on July 16.
House passed HR 5120 (H Rept 107-575), 308-121, on July 24.

Highlights

The following are major components of the two bills:

● **IRS.** More than half the discretionary spending in the measure — $9.9 billion in the House version, almost $10 billion in the Senate — was for the IRS, whose role in processing tax returns and enforcing tax laws provided a huge source of revenue for the federal government.

● **Customs.** The Customs Service, a central component of the proposed Homeland Security Department, was to receive $3.1 billion under both versions. That was a slight increase over fiscal 2002 and about $300 million more than requested. However, both bills rejected an administration proposal to raise $250 million in revenue by increasing Customs fees on airplane and cruise ship passengers entering the country.

● **Secret Service.** The Secret Service, which like Customs was expected to move from the Treasury to the new department, was scheduled to get $1 billion under both bills, which was in line with what it got in fiscal 2002.

● **BATF.** The House-passed bill included $891 million for the Bureau of Alcohol, Tobacco and Firearms. Senate appropriators proposed $890 million.

● **White House.** The House bill included $1 billion for the Executive Office of the President, $249 million more than requested. The main difference was $200 million added by the House to modernize voting equipment, pending completion of a separate measure (PL 107-252) to overhaul the regulation of federal elections. Senate appropriators included $731 million for the office of the president, $55 million less than requested. They did not include money for the election overhaul. (*Election overhaul, p. 14-3*)

Both bills added money for the Office of Homeland Security — $24 million in the House bill, $25 million in the Senate version. The office was expected to remain even after the creation of the new department. As they had the previous year, appropriators in both chambers rejected a request from President Bush to consolidate all the accounts for the Executive Office of the President into one, saying they were unwilling to cede that much latitude to the White House.

● **Office of Personnel Management.** Virtually all of the mandatory spending, $16.6 billion in both bills, was for OPM. All but about $300 million of it was for employee health, disability and retirement benefits.

● **Post Office.** Although the Postal Service was largely self-financing, it received a small amount of appropriated money each year, much of it to pay for reduced mailing rates for the blind. Both bills called for $108 million in fiscal 2003, though the House wanted part of the money paid in fiscal 2004.

Where the Money Goes

Treasury-Postal Service Spending

(figures are in thousands of dollars of new budget authority)

	Fiscal 2002 Appropriation*	Fiscal 2003 Bush Request	House Passed	Senate Panel Approved
GRAND TOTAL	**$33,713,862**	**$34,276,280**	**$34,821,460**	**$34,766,450**
Total adjusted for scorekeeping **	$34,027,862	$35,294,266	$35,086,446	—
MAIN COMPONENTS				
Office of Personnel Management	$15,619,078	$16,558,859	$16,559,041	$16,560,856
Treasury Department	15,646,178	15,865,446	16,168,789	16,303,655
IRS	9,470,604	9,915,853	9,898,593	9,995,221
Customs Service	3,087,352	2,834,113	3,129,197	3,141,614
Secret Service	1,028,841	1,013,954	1,021,411	1,020,466
Executive Office of the President	797,571	786,002	1,034,536	730,581
General Services Administration	598,593	516,614	510,566	620,727
Postal Service	596,093	76,619	76,619	107,633

* Includes supplemental appropriations enacted in 2001.

** Based on Congressional Budget Office criteria for determining discretionary spending; adjusted total is used to assess compliance with 302(b) allocations.

TABLE: House and Senate Appropriations committees

● **Federal pay raise.** Both versions of the bill called for a 4.1 percent pay raise for federal civilian employees, which would bring civilian pay increases in line with those provided for the military under the fiscal 2003 defense appropriations law (PL 107-248).

Legislative Action

House Subcommittee Action

The House Treasury, Postal Service and General Government Appropriations Subcommittee approved a draft of the bill by voice vote June 26, putting off most contentious issues for full committee.

The panel agreed by voice vote to increase federal workers' pay by 4.1 percent, instead of the 2.6 percent increase proposed by Bush. The amendment, by ranking Democrat Steny H. Hoyer of Maryland and Frank R. Wolf, R-Va., was estimated to cost $1.3 billion, which would have to be borne by the individual departments and agencies. Such pay parity had existed for 14 of the previous 16 years; it was included in the fiscal 2002 Treasury-Postal spending law against Bush's wishes.

The subcommittee rejected, 25-34, an attempt by Carrie P. Meek, D-Fla., to increase appropriations for the "First Accounts" program, which subsidized accounts for low- and moderate-income people in areas underserved by banks. Meek sought to match the 2002 level of $10 million, instead of the $4 million contained in the bill, and wanted to remove restrictions on the program added by subcommittee Chairman Ernest Istook, R-Okla. Istook said grants made with fiscal 2002 funds resulted in costs of up to $1,468 for each new account opened.

House Committee Action

The full Appropriations Committee approved the bill (HR 5120 — H Rept 107-575) by voice vote July 9, after adopting two controversial amendments.

The first, by Rosa DeLauro, D-Conn., sought to bar agencies funded under the bill from contracting with companies that were incorporated in offshore tax havens but whose stock was traded on U.S. exchanges. The amendment was part of an ongoing campaign by Democrats to curb the ability of companies to avoid U.S. taxes by reincorporating in offshore tax havens. DeLauro, a staunch liberal, won on a 41-17 vote with help from conservative Republicans such as Zach Wamp of Tennessee and Anne M. Northup of Kentucky. "I'm outraged by corporations who leave this country purely to avoid paying taxes," Northup said.

The second amendment, offered by Northup and backed by the National Association of Realtors, aimed to block national banks from acting as real estate brokers. Under the amendment, the Treasury Department would have to wait a year before it could finalize a rule proposed by the Clinton administration to declare real estate brokering as "financial in nature." Under the 1999 Gramm-Leach-Bliley financial service overhaul law (PL 106-102), such a declaration would allow banks into the real estate business.

House Floor Action

The House passed the bill, 308-121, on July 24, after adopting several amendments that made the measure a prime candidate for a presidential veto. *(House vote 341, p. H-108)*

● **Cuba.** The House voted 262-167 to lift the 42-year ban on travel by U.S. citizens to Cuba. The amendment, by conservative Republican Jeff Flake of Arizona, proposed to block the use of federal money to enforce the ban. Seventy-three Republicans broke with the White House to support it. "This is all about freedom," Flake said. "Our government should not tell us where we can and cannot travel." *(House vote 331, p. H-104)*

The White House had warned of a veto if the final bill included such a provision. GOP leaders mounted a vigor-

ous campaign to derail the amendment. Select Intelligence Committee Chairman Porter J. Goss, R-Fla., offered an alternative that would have tied any lifting of the travel ban to a presidential certification that Cuba did not have and was not developing biological weapons, providing such technology to terrorists or providing aid to terrorists. Those who favored lifting the ban said Goss' alternative was little more than an attempt to use the terrorism issue to undercut Flake. It was rejected, 182-247. *(House vote 330, p. H-104)*

The House adopted a second amendment by Flake to allow Cuban Americans to send more money to their families back home by blocking enforcement of the $1,200 annual limit on such remittances. The vote was 251-177. *(House vote 332, p. H-106)*

Also, Jerry Moran, R-Kan., won voice vote adoption of a proposal to block enforcement of sanctions against private sales of food or medicine to Cuba.

The only Cuba amendment to meet defeat was a bid by Charles B. Rangel, D-N.Y., to lift the Cuba embargo altogether. It was rejected, 204-226. *(House vote 333, p. H-106)*

"There's a bipartisan group here that has come together and who realize that the status quo doesn't work and it's time for a change," said Jim McGovern, D-Mass. "They threw the most difficult amendment they could throw at us with the Goss amendment, and it was overwhelmingly defeated."

"Those votes reflected a nation that's got a different attitude on [Cuba] than it had three, four, five years ago," acknowledged Majority Leader Dick Armey, R-Texas.

● **Private contracting.** The bill attracted another piece of veto bait July 24, with the adoption of an amendment by James P. Moran, D-Va., to bar the administration from using numerical goals, targets or quotas in "outsourcing" federal jobs to private sector contractors. The vote was 261-166. *(House vote 336, p. H-106)*

The White House said that "prohibiting the funding for public-private competitions is akin to mandating a monopoly regardless of the impact on services to citizens and the added costs to taxpayers," and warned of a veto if the language was included in the final version of the bill. Thomas M. Davis III, R-Va., chairman of the House GOP campaign committee, supported the amendment, shrugging off the veto language. "It's an idle threat. He's not going to veto it over that," he said.

In other action on the bill:

● Davis succeeded in striking the DeLauro provision aimed at barring contracts with companies incorporated offshore to avoid taxes.

● Bernard Sanders, I-Vt., won adoption, 308-121, of language to block companies from switching from defined benefit pension plans, in which workers are guaranteed a certain level of benefits when they retire, to cash balance plans, a hybrid between traditional defined benefit plans and defined contribution plans such as 401(k)s. *(House vote 339, p. H-108)*

● A bipartisan group of lawmakers teamed up to block freshman Jim Matheson, D-Utah, from offering an amendment to kill members' automatic cost of living adjustment for fiscal 2003. The vote to block the amendment was 258-156; it came on a procedural vote on the rule (H Res 488) governing floor debate on the bill. *(House vote 322, p. H-102)*

Fiscal conservatives had threatened to hold up floor action on the Treasury-Postal bill because it exceeded Bush's request by $537 million. They said the additional funding, though relatively small, came at the expense of larger and more difficult-to-pass domestic spending bills. They wanted the Treasury bill to advance only after the House had considered the bill for the departments of Labor, Health and Human Services (HHS), and Education, traditionally the most difficult to pass. They backed off after being promised that Labor-HHS would be the first spending bill considered in September.

Senate Committee Action

The Senate Appropriations Committee approved its version of the bill (S 2740 — S Rept 107-212) on July 16 by a vote of 29-0. The bill's $18.5 billion discretionary funding level was virtually identical to that of the House measure. The Treasury and General Government Subcommittee had approved a draft by voice vote July 11.

Like the House-passed bill, the measure drafted by Subcommittee Chairman Byron L. Dorgan, D-N.D., included language to end effectively the ban on travel to Cuba. During the subcommittee markup, Dorgan won a 4-3 party-line vote to add a provision barring executive branch agencies from using quotas when contracting federal jobs to private sector companies.

Mary L. Landrieu, D-La., said that when the bill reached the floor she would offer an amendment, identical to language in the House bill, to block the proposed Treasury Department rule that would permit banks to act as real estate brokers. Landrieu chose not to offer the amendment in committee, in deference to Chairman Robert C. Byrd, D-W.Va., who did not like to spend time debating controversial matters in committee that would be revisited on the floor. ◆

Lean Times for VA-HUD Bill

The fiscal 2003 spending bill for the departments of Veterans Affairs (VA) and Housing and Urban Development (HUD) and 20 independent agencies went through the House and Senate Appropriations committees with relative ease, but the legislation stalled behind the controversial Labor-HHS spending bill and never made it to the floor of either chamber. Programs covered by the VA-HUD bill were funded under a series of short-term laws, the last of which was good until Jan. 11, 2003 (PL 107-294).

Senate appropriators approved a version of the bill in July that included $91.4 billion in discretionary spending. That was $2 billion less than President Bush requested and $4 billion below the fiscal 2002 level. The House version, which won committee approval in October, would have provided $91 billion in discretionary funds. Both versions also included $31.6 billion in mandatory funding that was required under other laws, primarily for veterans' benefits. That brought the total to $124.5 billion in the Senate and $122.6 billion in the House.

In addition to the veterans and housing programs, the measure funded such diverse agencies as NASA, the EPA, the Federal Emergency Management Agency (FEMA), the National Science Foundation (NSF) and a variety of other programs. With homeland security the top priority and more high-profile spending bills claiming a larger share of the funding, VA-HUD appropriators found it even more difficult than usual to stretch spending to meet the wide-ranging needs of their bill.

One cost-cutting proposal by the Bush administration — that veterans with annual incomes of $24,000 or more be required to pay a $1,500 deductible for medical care — was quickly rejected. With midterm elections approaching and veterans complaining of continuing backlogs at VA medical centers, appropriators in both chambers saw the deductible as a political non-starter. The decision was a victory for veterans groups, but it put an even greater squeeze on funding for other agencies and programs.

House appropriators, who were working with a tighter limit on discretionary spending than their Senate counterparts, responded in part by simply leaving out some items such as the AmeriCorps volunteer program and assuming they would be funded when the bill reached conference.

Highlights

The following are highlights of the two bills:
- **Veterans.** Both committee bills exceeded Bush's request of $56.9 billion for the Department of Veterans Affairs by about $3.5 billion. Both called for $58.1 billion for the de-

---

BoxScore | **2003** Fiscal Year

VA-HUD

Bills:
HR 5605, S 2797
Legislative Action:
Senate Appropriations Committee approved S 2797 (S Rept 107-222), 29-0, on July 25.
House Appropriations Committee approved HR 5605 (H Rept 107-740) by voice vote Oct. 9.

---

partment, including $23.9 billion for veterans' medical care — $1.1 billion more than Bush requested and a $2.4 billion increase over fiscal 2002.
- **Housing.** Senate appropriators proposed $32.1 billion for HUD, a $734 million increase over Bush's request. The House committee complied with Bush's request for $31.4 billion.
- **FEMA.** Neither committee met Bush's overall request for $6.7 billion for FEMA. The Senate bill called for $4.4 billion; the House bill included $3.6 billion.

The Senate bill included $1.8 billion for disaster relief programs as requested, but made $1.5 billion of it emergency money not subject to the discretionary spending limits. The House cut Bush's request by $22 million less.

Bush also sought $3.5 billion for a FEMA "first responder" initiative to help states and local governments purchase equipment and prepare for possible terror attacks. The administration expected the funds to be administered by the proposed Homeland Security Department, which had not yet been approved. House appropriators instead provided $817 million for emergency planning and assistance, $450 million of it for grants to local firefighters. The Senate bill included $1.7 billion, $900 million of it for grants to local fire agencies.
- **EPA.** Both committees rejected Bush's request that they cut environmental programs by 6 percent, to $7.6 billion. The Senate provided for $8.3 billion, the House for $8.2 billion.
- **NASA.** Both bills were close to the $15 billion that Bush requested for NASA. The House proposed $15.3 billion, the Senate $15.2 billion.
- **NSF.** The National Science Foundation would have received $5.4 billion under the House bill, a 13 percent increase over fiscal 2002. The Senate bill included $5.35 billion for the foundation. Bush had requested $5 billion.

Legislative Action

Senate Committee Action

The Senate Appropriations Committee approved its version of the bill (S 2797 — S Rept 107-222) by a vote of 29-0 on July 25. The VA, HUD and Independent Agencies Subcommittee had approved it two days earlier by voice vote. "This is indeed a year of austerity," noted Subcommittee Chairman Barbara A. Mikulski, D-Md.

Mikulski said she allocated $23.9 billion for veterans' health benefits, as opposed to the $22.8 billion requested by Bush, because the system was being overwhelmed by veterans seeking prescription drug coverage that was not available under the Medicare program. "VA medical care is in

Where the Money Goes

Veterans, Housing, EPA, NASA Spending

(figures are in thousands of dollars of new budget authority)

	Fiscal 2002 Appropriation	Fiscal 2003 Bush Request	Senate Panel Approved	House Panel Approved
GRAND TOTAL	**$119,907,308**	**$121,358,580**	**$124,507,956**	**$122,572,881**
Total adjusted for scorekeeping*	**$123,820,208**	**$124,979,700**	**$124,509,956**	**$122,596,881**
MAIN COMPONENTS				
Department of Veterans Affairs	$51,137,398	$54,513,675	$58,089,545	$58,131,067
Veterans Health Administration	21,768,895	23,207,850	24,359,020	24,369,020
Department of Housing and Urban Development	32,148,695	31,348,851	32,082,924	31,346,314
Public and Indian Housing	21,997,535	23,619,088	23,854,434	22,959,722
Environmental Protection Agency	8,078,813	7,620,513	8,299,141	8,204,465
Hazardous Substance Superfund	1,221,242	1,148,978	1,173,978	1,323,978
NASA	14,901,700	15,000,000	15,200,000	15,300,000
FEMA	7,924,725	6,703,912	4,435,117	3,611,895
National Science Foundation	4,789,240	5,028,220	5,353,360	5,422,942
Corporation for National and Community Service	406,980	636,342	521,342	5,000

*Adjustments based on Congressional Budget Office criteria for determining discretionary spending; adjusted total is used to assess compliance with 302(b) allocations.

TABLE: House and Senate Appropriations committees

crisis," agreed Christopher S. Bond of Missouri, the subcommittee's ranking Republican. "It troubles me that veterans with severe disabilities are being forced to wait several months to see a doctor."

The appropriators decisively rejected the proposed $1,500 deductible for veterans' medical care, although they agreed to extend the VA's existing authority to charge veterans co-payments for prescription drugs. Without the co-payments, the appropriators would have had to come up with an additional $600 million.

Mikulski allocated $15.2 billion for NASA, a $200 million increase over the president's request that would help fund the International Space Station and a proposed mission to Pluto. Mikulski had suggested a $1 billion annual increase for the next three years, but she said that figure was unrealistic.

The Senate committee rejected a Bush plan to transfer other science programs, such as the National Oceanic and Atmospheric Administration's Sea Grant program and the EPA environmental education program, to the NSF. Mikulski said she thought her committee would not get an increase in funding if all those programs were included under the NSF.

House Committee Action

The House Appropriations Committee approved its version of the bill (HR 5605 — H Rept 107-740) by voice vote Oct. 9, two days after its Subcommittee on Veterans Affairs, Housing and Urban Development and Independent Agencies gave its approval, also by voice vote. The $90.9 billion in discretionary spending — $500 million less than in the Senate bill — reflected House GOP leaders' determination not to exceed the president's budget.

"Our problem is not the Senate; it's our allocation," said a frustrated James T. Walsh, R-N.Y., chairman of the subcommittee. "I feel like Sisyphus."

By the time of the markup, House Republicans were pressing for even tighter limits on the VA-HUD bill in order to free up more money for the departments of Labor, Health and Human Services, and Education while staying within the president's budget limits.

The bill closely followed the Senate version, though there were some notable exceptions that allowed the House to stay within its budget limits. House appropriators included only half as much money for FEMA's first-responder programs. Also, Walsh was under instructions from House GOP leaders not to follow the Senate in reducing the bottom line by designating part of the disaster relief money as "emergency funding" that would not count against the bill's discretionary spending limits.

David R. Obey of Wisconsin, ranking Democrat on the full committee, said the House appropriations process had become a charade, and the bill's price tag eventually would balloon in a House-Senate conference committee.

Walsh also omitted any money for AmeriCorps and other federally administered volunteer programs, which were touted as a Bush administration priority. Bush requested $631 million; Senate appropriators included $515 million. Walsh said he withheld the funding to prevent House conservatives from cutting AmeriCorps, a program from the Clinton administration that they long had opposed, to fund veterans programs. But he assured lawmakers that AmeriCorps would be funded in conference committee.

Walsh said the decision to provide $23.9 billion for veterans' health care came in response to veterans' complaints over the backlog at VA medical centers. Veterans' outcries also led the appropriators to reject the proposal to charge some veterans a new $1,500 deductible.

Maurice D. Hinchey, D-N.Y., tried to add $16 million to the $18.2 billion in the bill for the EPA. He said the extra money would fund an additional 122 full-time positions for enforcers that environmentalists argued were needed to crack down on polluters. The amendment was defeated by voice vote. ◆

Extra Funds for Defense, Security

Congress cleared a $28.9 billion fiscal 2002 supplemental spending bill in July devoted mainly to defense and homeland security. In a test of strength over spending limits, President Bush used the threat of a veto to force House and Senate appropriators to give up what would have been an additional $2 billion in net spending. Bush signed the bill into law Aug. 2 (HR 4775 — PL 107-206).

The bill contained $31.9 billion in new appropriations and $3 billion in rescissions and other offsets, producing the bottom line of $28.9 billion in discretionary spending. About half the total, $14.4 billion, went to the Pentagon, with most of the remainder devoted to homeland security, recovery assistance for New York in the aftermath of the Sept. 11, 2001, attacks, and foreign assistance and embassy security. In addition, the bill provided $1.1 billion in mandatory spending for veterans' compensation and pensions.

Final agreement was delayed for weeks as House and Senate conferees struggled to stay within the spending limit set by the administration.

Bush had submitted a request in March for $27.1 billion in emergency spending to combat terrorism — including $14 billion for the Pentagon, $5.5 billion for New York City and $4.4 billion for the new agency created to improve transportation security. Analysis by both parties in the Senate Budget Committee — and not rebutted by the White House — subsequently put Bush's request at $28.4 billion by including a separate $1.3 billion administration request for additional funds for Pell Grant college loans.

House appropriators initially planned to advance a $30 billion package, saying that was close enough to the request. But the White House's Office of Management and Budget (OMB) objected, and appropriators made changes — primarily a scoring adjustment that Democrats derided as a gimmick — that brought the bill down to $28.8 billion. The House passed the measure May 24, giving the White House a marker on Capitol Hill. Despite threats that a larger bill would be vetoed, the Senate passed a version in June with a price tag of $31.5 billion, much of it additional homeland security spending.

Bipartisan negotiations initially produced a $30.4 billion compromise, but the White House intervened, declared the bill unacceptable and forced appropriators back to the drawing board. The final result was the $28.9 billion bill. Of the total, $5.1 billion was designated as contingency emergency spending; the president was given 30 days to decide whether to use all or none of the money. On Aug. 13, Bush turned

---

BoxScore 2002
Fiscal Year

Defense Supplemental

Bill:
HR 4775 — PL 107-206
Legislative Action:
House passed HR 4775 (H Rept 107-480), 280-138, May 24.
Senate passed HR 4775, 71-22, on June 7, after substituting the text of S 2551 (S Rept 107-156).
House adopted the conference report (H Rept 107-593), 397-32, on July 23.
Senate cleared the bill, 92-7, on July 24.
President signed Aug. 2.

---

down the $5.1 billion, effectively cutting the bill's total to $23.8 billion. The biggest cuts were in homeland security, which was reduced to $4.4 billion. Bush subsequently asked Congress to provide $996 million from the bill in fiscal 2003 but said it should not add to total spending for the year.

Highlights

The following are the main components of the bill as enacted:

● **Defense.** $14.4 billion, including $11.9 billion for the Defense Emergency Response Fund to pay the incremental costs of the global war on terrorism, such as military operations, increased personnel and additional intelligence gathering.

● **Homeland security.** $6.7 billion, including $3.9 billion for the Transportation Security Administration (TSA), created after the Sept. 11 attacks (PL 107-71) to improve airport, airline and baggage security. The total also included funds for first responder grants, fire department grants, FBI activities, added security at nuclear facilities, Coast Guard expenses and other needs.

● **New York City.** $5.5 billion, including $2.7 billion in emergency disaster relief, $1.8 billion to repair damage to the transit system and $783 million in block grants to restore the area hit by the attacks.

● **Foreign assistance and embassy security.** $2.1 billion, including $200 million for HIV/AIDS programs, $200 million for Israel, $50 million for the Palestinians and $211 million for embassy construction and renovation in Afghanistan and Tajikistan.

● **Pell grants.** $1 billion to avert an expected shortfall in the student loan program.

● **Veterans.** $1.1 billion in funding for veterans' disability payments. The spending was mandatory, which meant it was not included in the bill's discretionary total.

Legislative Action

House Committee Action

The House Appropriations Committee approved a $29.4 billion version of the bill (H Rept 107-480) by voice vote May 15. What most members hoped would be a quick debate turned into a markup that lasted 20 hours over three days, punctuated by fights over spending and a host of unrelated riders.

Conservatives succeeded in trimming the $30 billion

draft brought to the committee by Chairman C.W. Bill Young, R-Fla., and ranking Democrat David R. Obey of Wisconsin, to $29.4 billion, according to the Congressional Budget Office (CBO). Most of the additions to Bush's request could be used only if the president specifically asked for the money and declared it emergency spending. The bill's main components were:

• **Defense.** $15.8 billion for the military — $14 billion requested by Bush, plus $1.8 billion in unrequested money for a contingency fund to help pay for the war in Afghanistan.

• **Homeland security.** $5.8 billion, including $3.9 billion for the TSA.

• **New York City.** $5.5 billion, as requested.

• **Foreign assistance.** $1.6 billion, about $350 million more than proposed, mainly for security aid to the "frontline" states in the war on terrorism, but also including $200 million for a global AIDS fund, $250 million for Israel and the Palestinians, and $370 million for recovery efforts in Afghanistan.

• **Offsets.** $1.7 billion in offsetting spending cuts and rescissions, including $643 million from the airline assistance fund created after the Sept. 11 attacks (PL 107-42).

Both parties used the markup to advance their agendas on everything from the national debt to illegal immigrants and the Crusader missile.

In at least one case, the panel overrode itself. On May 10, members agreed, 32-31, to add controversial language proposed by Nita M. Lowey, D-N.Y., requiring the president to release $34 million in previously appropriated U.N. family planning funds by July 10 if a White House commission concluded that Chinese family planning clinics did not perform forced abortions. But after warnings from GOP leaders that the provision could sink the entire bill, the committee subsequently voted, 32-30, to replace the amendment with language giving the president more discretion over how much to spend.

In other action, the committee agreed:

• By voice vote to ask the administration to continue work on the Crusader mobile artillery system until Congress weighed in on the program. The amendment was adopted after a proposal to prevent the administration from canceling the Crusader was dropped.

• By voice vote to allow Bush to give Israel as much as $200 million to fight terrorism, while giving the Palestinians as much as $50 million in disaster assistance.

• By 38-18, to prohibit U.S. participation in or cooperation with the International Criminal Court, restrict military aid to any nation that ratified the treaty creating the court, and grant the president sweeping authority to use military force to retrieve U.S. or allied personnel detained by the court. The amendment, by Majority Whip Tom DeLay, R-Texas, also proposed to restrict U.S. participation in certain peacekeeping operations unless there were guarantees that they would not be under the court's jurisdiction. Obey and four other Democrats voted "present" to signal their view that the matter should be the purview of the International Relations Committee.

• By voice vote to delete language in the draft that would have doubled, to $10, the airline ticket surcharge created in 2001 to help finance the operations of the new Transportation Security Administration. The provision — intended to generate $150 million in revenue to offset other spending — drew immediate opposition from the airline industry and its allies in Congress, who said the extra expense for consumers would harm the travel industry just as it was recovering from Sept. 11. To keep the bill's cost from growing, the committee voted instead to trim some midyear spending on the new agency, including some money for airlines to strengthen cockpit doors.

The committee rejected:

• By 27-34, an amendment urging Homeland Security Director Tom Ridge to give formal congressional testimony, which he had refused to do on the grounds that he was a presidential adviser and not the head of a department or agency with budget authority.

• By 27-32, an amendment by José E. Serrano, D-N.Y., to include new amnesty provisions for illegal immigrants.

• By 23-33, a Serrano amendment to prohibit the Immigration and Naturalization Service from using local and state police for civil enforcement.

House Floor Action

The House passed the bill, 280-138, in the pre-dawn hours of May 24, after a bitter debate that stretched over 16 hours. CBO put the bill's discretionary total at $30.1 billion, but OMB "rescored" a key provision, enabling the leadership to call it a $28.8 billion bill. (*House vote 206, p. H-68*)

The climax came May 22, when GOP leaders quelled a brewing rebellion among their own appropriators and succeeded in adding a package of controversial provisions that had not been considered by the committee. The changes were made as part of the rule for floor debate, which was adopted 216-209. (*House vote 194, p. H-66*)

The following amendments were added by the rule:

• **Debt limit.** To provide an increase in the statutory debt ceiling without requiring members to take a politically difficult up-or-down vote, GOP leaders inserted language pledging that Congress would protect "the full faith and credit of the government." That laid the groundwork to add the actual debt limit increase to the supplemental when it went to conference. The existing $5.95 trillion debt limit was expected to run out by the end of June. (*Debt limit, p. 6-10*)

Democrats wanted a chance to debate and vote on the increase. They blamed the growing debt on Bush's $1.35 trillion, 10-year tax cut (PL 107-16) enacted in 2001 and argued that any increase in borrowing would eventually be paid out of Social Security surpluses. Amid complaints that Republicans were ducking the issue, Democrats engineered what they said was a clean up-or-down vote. The rule allowed one motion to send the bill back to committee for changes, and they used it to request that the debt limit language be stripped. The motion failed, 201-215, on May 24. (*House vote 205, p. H-68*)

• **Spending limit.** The rule also inserted language that set a discretionary spending limit for the House's fiscal 2003 appropriations bills. The provision "deemed" or declared that the House version of the fiscal 2003 budget resolution (H Con Res 353), adopted March 20, would "have force and effect in the House" as if it had been agreed to by both chambers. Reflecting Bush's position, the House budget limited discretionary spending to $759 billion. Senate appropriators were using a figure of $768 billion, based on a budget

Appropriations

(S Con Res 100) approved by the Senate Budget Committee but never adopted on the floor.

- **Medicare hospital payments.** Medicare reimbursement rates were increased for hospitals in several counties in New York and Pennsylvania.
- **Textiles.** Fulfilling a promise to textile-state Republicans, including Jim DeMint of South Carolina and Robin Hayes of North Carolina, the leadership added a requirement that knit and woven fabrics be dyed and finished in the United States in order to qualify for duty-free treatment under the 2000 African and Caribbean trade law (PL 106-200). The promise had been made in exchange for their votes in December 2001 to pass a bill (PL 107-210) reviving the president's fast-track trade authority. (*Fast track, p. 18-3*)

After losing the opening vote on the rule, Obey orchestrated an all-out, two-day war of rhetoric and parliamentary maneuvers against the bill. With the enthusiastic participation of rank-and-file Democrats, Obey prepared hundreds of amendments. He and Young virtually dared one another to see who was more willing to keep the House in session into the Memorial Day holiday weekend. After concluding the Democrats were serious, exasperated Republicans pulled the bill from the floor the night of May 23 and wrote a new rule that allowed only one hour of debate and no amendments. Just after 2 a.m. the next morning, the rule was adopted, 213-201, along party lines, and the Democratic blockade was broken. "They have taken abusive power to a new level," Obey charged. (*House vote 204, p. H-68*)

Several provisions of the committee-reported bill were dropped under the second rule, including part of the proposal to rescind money appropriated for the airline assistance fund and the provision giving the president additional discretion to determine how much of the $34 million appropriated for family planning funds to withhold.

Senate Committee Action

The Senate Appropriations Committee approved a $31 billion version of the bill (S 2551 — S Rept 107-156) by a vote of 29-0 on May 22.

Drawn up by Chairman Robert C. Byrd, D-W.Va., the bill included:

- **Defense.** $14 billion, as requested by Bush, but not the additional $1.8 billion in contingency funds endorsed by House appropriators.
- **New York City.** $5.5 billion, as requested.
- **Homeland security.** $8.3 billion, $2.5 billion more than the House, including $4.7 billion for the TSA. Byrd said testimony by state and local officials, including police, fire and medical personnel, confirmed the need for the added funding.
- **Veterans' benefits.** $1.1 billion in mandatory benefit payments to veterans added to the bill at the administration's request. The benefits were required by law.
- **Offsets.** About $1.2 billion.

The most controversial part of the bill was an "all or none" provision inserted by Byrd that would require Bush to release all the non-defense money in the measure or none of it. The language was a response to signals from the White House that Bush might not spend all the money.

The Senate bill also contained language requiring Bush to release the $34 million in family planning aid by July 10 if

the White House commission found that U.N. workers did not aid or abet forced abortion or sterilization in China. And it proposed requiring confirmation of Ridge as Homeland Security director. Byrd had unsuccessfully tried to obtain testimony from Ridge. Unrequested funds added by senators for favorite projects also drew administration ire.

Senate Floor Action

Despite a veto threat from the White House, the Senate passed the bill June 7 by a vote of 71-22, enough to override the president. The vote came after four days of debate in which Republicans tried but failed to trim the package. Twenty-six of 49 Republicans backed the bill, and only two Democrats voted against it. Including amendments added on the floor, the bill appropriated $31.5 billion. (*Senate vote 145, p. S-30*)

In a statement issued June 4, the White House said the measure exceeded the president's request for non-defense programs by more than $4 billion and warned that the president's advisers would recommend a veto if it were not changed.

But Minority Leader Trent Lott, R-Miss., noted that the administration's veto threat was not from Bush himself, and Ted Stevens of Alaska, the top Republican on the Appropriations Committee, called it a negotiating "tactic." Stevens urged fiscal conservatives such as Phil Gramm, R-Texas, to give up a threat to bog down the bill unless its price tag was cut. "I will guarantee you: The bill that comes out of conference will be a bill the president will accept," Stevens said.

When admonishments were not enough, the Senate agreed, 87-10, on June 6 to invoke cloture, ending the threat of a conservative filibuster. However, the motion came at a cost: It also barred non-germane amendments, thereby scuttling bipartisan hopes of using the bill to carry an agreement on spending limits for fiscal 2003, as well as a plan to increase the limit on the national debt. (*Senate vote 135, p. S-29*)

During debate on the bill, the Senate rejected:

- An attempt by Don Nickles, R-Okla., to strike the "all or none" provision. Nickles' amendment was tabled (killed) by a vote of 58-26. Byrd also won a 69-25 vote to retain the emergency designation for the bill's non-defense spending. (*Senate votes 143, 144, p. S-30*)
- Three attempts by John McCain, R-Ariz., to cut funding for specific programs — the National Defense Center of Excellence for Research in Oceanic Sciences, a Smithsonian Institution storage facility and Agriculture Research Service facilities. All three amendments were tabled by overwhelming majorities. (*Senate votes 136, 137, 138, p. S-29*)
- An effort by Health, Education, Labor and Pensions Committee Chairman Edward M. Kennedy, D-Mass., to add $150 million to help schools offer summer programs. The amendment fell, 38-60, on a procedural motion. "I support the amendment but not on this bill, not on this bill. I have a job to do," said Byrd, as he fought to keep the bill on track. (*Senate vote 132, p. S-29*)
- A five-year extension of budget enforcement rules that were set to expire Sept. 30. The amendment fell after sponsors Judd Gregg, R-N.H., and Russell D. Feingold, D-Wis., failed, 49-49, to protect it from a procedural challenge. (*Senate vote 133, p. S-29*)

The Senate adopted amendments to:

• Eliminate all proposed rescissions of money appropriated for the airline assistance fund — the House bill still included some — adding $393 million to the bill's cost. The amendment, adopted 91-4, was pushed mainly by senators from states served by US Airways. Rick Santorum, R-Pa., said the rescission would mean "certain death" for that airline. *(Senate vote 131, p. S-29)*

• Double funding in the bill for international HIV/AIDS programs to $200 million. The amendment, adopted 79-14, was sponsored by Jesse Helms, R-N.C., and Bill Frist, R-Tenn. *(Senate vote 141, p. S-30)*

• Bar aid to, or cooperation with, the International Criminal Court and restrict U.S. participation in certain peacekeeping missions unless they were outside the court's jurisdiction. The amendment, by John W. Warner, R-Va., was adopted 75-19. *(Senate vote 140, p. S-30)*

Conference/Final Action

House and Senate conferees agreed July 18 to a $28.9 billion bill — $31.9 billion in new discretionary spending and $3 billion in offsets. The total was $100 million more than the House bill, as estimated by OMB, $2.5 billion less than the Senate bill, and approximately $500 million more than Bush requested, with most of the difference going to homeland defense. The House adopted the conference report (H Rept 107-593), 397-32, on July 23, and the Senate cleared the bill the next day, 92-7. *(House vote 328, p. H-104; Senate vote 188, p. S-38)*

House and Senate appropriators initially agreed on a $30.4 billion bill, hoping that the administration would relent. But before they could hold a formal conference session to approve it, the White House stepped in. Budget director Mitchell E. Daniels Jr. came to the Capitol the night of July 11 to serve notice that the additional spending for the appropriators' own priorities was not a price Bush was willing to pay. GOP leaders backed the White House, and Speaker J. Dennis Hastert, R-Ill., said he would not put a conference agreement before the full House unless Bush had indicated he would sign it.

The appropriators were furious, but they set about to shave the cost of the bill. They requested a list of suggested cuts or offsets from the White House but dismissed the paperwork delivered the next morning as too sketchy and too late to be of any use. They reached a final agreement July 18 and filed the conference report the next day.

The following are the main elements of the compromise:

• **Defense.** The $14.4 billion for defense was about $330 million more than in the Senate bill or Bush's request, but $1.4 billion less than the House had wanted. Conferees adopted the Senate level of $100 million for nuclear non-proliferation activities, compared with $5 million in the House bill. It made $390 billion in defense funds available to reimburse key frontline states for support provided for U.S. military operations but required prior approval of the Appropriations committees before the funds could be released.

• **New York City.** The $5.5 billion for expenses related to the Sept. 11 attack reflected Bush's request and the actions of both chambers.

• **Homeland security.** The biggest difference from the president's request was the addition of $2.4 billion for homeland security, bringing the total to $6.7 billion. Agreeing with the House, conferees trimmed Bush's request for the Transportation Security Administration by $550 million, leaving $3.9 billion. They specified that $738 million be used for baggage security, $630 million to buy explosive detection systems for checked baggage screening, $125 million for port security and $15 million for intercity bus security. The conference report directed the agency to begin publishing monthly performance information in a number of areas.

• **Foreign assistance.** The bill provided $2.1 billion — $500 million more than requested but roughly equal to the House and Senate bills.

• **"All or none" provision.** Conferees scaled back the Senate-passed plan to require Bush to use all or none of the non-defense spending in the bill. Instead, they applied the restriction to $5.1 billion, primarily for items added by lawmakers, and gave the president 30 days to decide. If he chose to use the $5.1 billion, he would have to request that it be classified as emergency spending.

• **International family planning.** The final bill dropped the Senate language requiring release of the $34 million in family planning funds. On July 23, Bush decided to withhold the money.

• **Amtrak.** Conferees agreed to provide $205 million in cash to assist the struggling passenger train service. The House bill contained no funding; the Senate provided $55 million. White House officials indicated no opposition, although they proposed a loan instead.

• **Firefighting and flood recovery.** Conferees provided $100 million but pledged to seek additional emergency funds in the fiscal 2003 Interior spending bill.

• **Pell grants.** Like the House and Senate, the conferees agreed to $1 billion for Pell grants, $255 million less than requested.

• **Airline loans.** Conferees rejected the administration's proposal to offset part of the bill's cost by suspending the post-Sept. 11 airline loan guarantee program.

• **Election overhaul.** The bill included $400 million for new voting technology and equipment, subject to enactment of an authorization bill. The total was $50 million less than the House level; the Senate bill contained no funds. *(Election overhaul, p. 14-3)*

• **Offsets.** Appropriators brought down the cost of the bill nearly to the president's level, primarily by finding offsets and rescissions, rather than reducing or eliminating their preferred programs and earmarks. The $3 billion in rescissions and other offsets included cuts of $455 million from an export enhancement program in the Agriculture Department, $739 million from several housing and economic development programs in the Department of Housing and Urban Development, $60 million in international development assistance funds and $45 million in overhead at the departments of Labor, Health and Human Services and Education.

• **International Criminal Court.** As under the House and Senate bills, the agreement restricted U.S. involvement with the new court.

• **Highway funding.** Conferees adopted language from the House bill restoring a projected $4.4 billion cut in highway funding. The aim was to ensure $27.7 billion in fiscal 2003 highway spending, the base level required by

the 1998 surface transportation law, known as TEA-21 (PL 105-178). (*Transportation appropriations, p. 2-32; 1998 Almanac, p. 24-3*)

● **Medicare.** Conferees rejected the House proposal to boost Medicare reimbursement rates for certain hospitals in New York and Pennsylvania.

● **Textile trade.** The final bill retained House language limiting knit and woven fabrics eligible for duty-free treatment in the United States.

● **Debt.** The final bill did not include language added in the House on the debt limit. The debt ceiling was increased in a separate bill (PL 107-199) enacted June 28.

The bill's funding included $417 million to enhance veterans' medical care, $158 million for nuclear emergency response programs, $31 million for the Securities and Exchange Commission to enhance enforcement, $23 million to reimburse the Washington, D.C., government for security expenses and for facilities at the regional Bioterrorism Hospital Preparedness Program, and $16 million for the Capitol Police. ◆

Chapter 3

ABORTION

House Acts to Limit Abortions

Abortion opponents in the House succeeded in passing several bills aimed at scaling back the availability of abortion, but only one measure survived the Senate. The one bill that became law (HR 2175 — PL 107-207) protected infants who are born alive at any point, even if the birth occurs during an attempted abortion.

The House also passed:

• A bill (HR 4965) to ban a procedure opponents called "partial birth" abortion.

• A bill (HR 4691) to allow hospitals and other health care providers to refuse to perform abortions without losing federal funds.

• A bill (HR 476) to make it a crime to knowingly take a minor across state lines for an abortion to circumvent parental consent laws.

Infant Protection Bill Cleared

Legislation guaranteeing legal protection to babies born alive at any stage of development was signed into law Aug. 5 (PL 107-207). The House passed the bill by voice vote March 12 under expedited procedures; the Senate cleared it by voice vote July 18. The measure had the White House's support and was relatively non-controversial, especially because many states already had such laws.

The bill established in statute that fetuses "born alive" are human beings legally alive and entitled to the same constitutional protections as other individuals. A fetus "born alive" was defined as one that has been expelled from the woman and is breathing, has a beating heart, a pulsating umbilical cord or muscle movement. Backers said the bill was needed to protect infants who survive late-term abortions.

The House Judiciary Committee, which had approved the bill (H Rept 107-186), 25-2, on July 24, 2001, stated that it did not intend to mandate medical treatment for infants in cases where doctors did not advise it. The bill also stated that it was not intended to grant any more rights than were already recognized for a fetus. That provision convinced Democrats that the measure would do nothing more than duplicate state laws. "This legislation is, I believe, unnecessary but harmless," said Jerrold Nadler, D-N.Y. There are "no such things as born-alive abortions."

A similar bill passed the House in 2000 but was never acted on by the Senate. The Senate had voted, 98-0, to add a similar bill to patients' rights legislation (S 1050) in 2001.

'Partial Birth' Ban

One of the most closely watched anti-abortion bills was a measure (HR 4965) passed by the House in July to outlaw a late-term procedure that opponents called "partial birth" abortion. The procedure was defined as one in which a doctor "intentionally vaginally delivers a living fetus . . . for the purpose of performing an overt act that the [doctor] knows will kill the partially delivered living fetus."

The bill would have allowed the procedure only when it was necessary to save a woman's life. Those who performed the procedure for other reasons — including risks to a woman's health that were short of life-threatening — would have faced fines and up to two years in prison. The woman would not have been criminally liable.

The House Judiciary Committee approved the bill (H Rept 107-604) on a 20-8 party-line vote July 17. The Constitution Subcommittee had approved it, 8-3, on July 11. Democrats said the language should be broadened to allow exceptions to avoid health problems for the woman. Bill supporters argued that such a procedure was never needed to protect a woman's health. Some also questioned whether protecting a woman's health should be given higher priority than protecting the life of a fetus. "That little thing is not a diseased appendix," said longtime abortion foe Henry J. Hyde, R-Ill. "It is not a pair of infected tonsils. It is a tiny little member of the human family."

Republicans on the full committee turned back six Democratic amendments to limit the scope of the bill — including two that would have provided some kind of exception for cases where the procedure was necessary for the woman's health.

The House passed the bill July 24 by a vote of 274-151, with one member abstaining by voting "present." The leadership brought the bill up under a closed rule that barred amendments. Democrats had hoped to offer a number of amendments to make exceptions for cases where a woman's health was threatened but her life was not in danger. Instead, they tried to recommit the bill to the Judiciary Committee with instructions to include such an exception. The motion failed, 187-241. House GOP leaders immediately called for the Senate to take up the measure, but with Democrats in control, the Senate was never expected to do so. (*House votes 343, 342, p. H-108*)

The anti-abortion movement had tried for years to enact legislation to outlaw partial-birth abortions. Congress cleared bills banning the practice in the 104th and 105th Congresses, but both were vetoed by President Bill Clinton. Backers did not have the necessary votes to override the vetoes. (*1997 Almanac, p. 6-12; 1996 Almanac, p. 6-43*)

Both chambers passed similar bills again in the 106th Congress, but action was halted in 2000 after the Supreme Court struck down a similar state law. The court ruled in *Stenberg v. Carhart* that a Nebraska law prohibiting partial-birth abortion violated a woman's constitutional rights. The court found that the law was unconstitutionally vague and failed to include an exception to protect the health of the woman. (*2000 Almanac, p. 3-3*)

Right to Refuse Abortions

On Sept. 25, the House passed a bill (HR 4691) to let hospitals and other health care providers refuse to perform abortions or to refer women elsewhere for such services without losing Medicaid funds or other federal money. Insurance companies would be allowed to refuse to pay for abortions without losing federal funds. The vote was 229-189, with 37 Democrats voting in favor and 24 Republicans

voting against the bill. (*House vote 412, p. H-130*)

The legislation had been bottled up in the Energy and Commerce Committee, so Majority Leader Dick Armey, R-Texas, moved it directly to the House floor for a vote. The bill was certain to go nowhere in the Democratic-controlled Senate, but with midterm elections weeks away, it sparked an emotional debate that gave each party a chance to restate positions important to its base.

The bill's sponsor, Energy and Commerce Health Subcommittee Chairman Michael Bilirakis, R-Fla., said the measure was "not intended to be an expansion of what is already in current law." He said it would clarify a "conscience clause" in the 1944 Public Health Services Act (PL 78-410) that explicitly protected doctors who refused to perform abortions from being penalized by the federal government or any state or local government that received federal money. The bill would have rewritten the law to say that "health care entities" covered by the clause should include "other health professionals, a hospital, a provider-sponsored organization, a health maintenance organization, a health insurance plan and any other kind of health care facility, organization or plan."

Supporters, including Joe Pitts, R-Pa., said the change was needed to counter recent state court interpretations that excluded hospitals from the conscience clause. They cited a 1997 Alaska Supreme Court ruling that a hospital in that state had to allow doctors to perform abortions there because it was the only area hospital, making it a quasi-public facility.

Opponents said the bill would greatly expand existing law and weaken a woman's legal right to an abortion by limiting its availability. They said it would not allow exemptions in cases of rape or incest or to save the life of the woman, and would allow hospitals and insurers to stop physicians and others from providing abortions or even referring women to others for abortion services.

Catholic hospital groups and secular medical chains lobbied for the bill to guarantee not only that they could continue to receive federal funding while refusing to perform abortions, but also that they would not face sanctions under state laws or regulations.

The rule for floor debate allowed no amendments. An attempt by Sherrod Brown of Ohio, ranking Democrat on the Health Subcommittee, to send the bill back to committee failed on a vote of 191-230. (*House vote 411, p. H-130*)

Parental Consent

The House voted 260-161 on April 17 to pass a bill (HR 476) that would make it a crime to circumvent state parental consent laws by knowingly taking a minor across state lines for an abortion. Violators would face fines of up to $100,000 and a year in prison. The measure included an exception from prosecution if the abortion was necessary to save the life of the minor; the minor could not be prosecuted under the bill. (*House vote 97, p. H-36*)

The House had passed similar bills in the 105th and 106th Congresses, but the Senate did not act on them. (*1999 Almanac, p. 3-3; 1998 Almanac, p. 3-3*)

The bill was designed to buttress laws in states that required pregnant girls to get their parents' permission before obtaining abortions. Twenty-seven states required notification of or consent by a parent before a minor could have an abortion. Most of the state laws also allowed a minor to get permission from a judge for an exemption from parental notification or consent requirements. "Parents are in the best position to make decisions about their minor children," insisted Steve Chabot, R-Ohio.

But Lynn Woolsey, D-Calif., argued that the measure could have the opposite effect. "This bill is not going to encourage teens to talk to their parents," Woolsey said. Instead, she said, the measure would prompt teenagers to "seek unsafe, illegal abortions." Democrats also argued that it was impractical and unfair to expect minors to seek permission from a judge in order to receive an abortion.

The rule governing the April 17 debate did not allow for floor amendments, but Democrats tried to send the bill back to the Judiciary Committee for additional language that would exempt siblings, grandparents or clergy who transported a minor across state lines for an abortion. The motion, by Sheila Jackson-Lee of Texas, was rejected 173-246. (*House vote 96, p. H-36*)

The Judiciary Committee had approved the bill (H Rept 107-397) on a 19-6 party-line vote March 20. Republicans easily fended off Democratic amendments, including a proposal to exempt grandparents and adult siblings. Democrats also tried but failed to add an exemption for girls who become pregnant as a result of sex with a parent or other guardian. Chabot and Spencer Bachus, R-Ala., argued that the amendment would allow a pregnant victim of incest to secretly obtain an abortion and then return to a harmful home environment without the abuse being discovered. ◆

Chapter 4

AGRICULTURE

'02 Farm Bill Revives Subsidies

Congress cleared a sprawling, six-year farm bill May 8 that overturned a central tenet of the 1996 "Freedom to Farm" act. The new law re-established farm subsidies that had been abolished under the 1996 act, while renewing fixed annual payments that had been instituted as a way to wean farmers off of the subsidies. President Bush signed the bill into law May 13 (HR 2646 — PL 107-171).

At the time of enactment, the total cost of all programs under the bill was estimated at $440.8 billion over six years, $45.1 billion more than the cost of continuing existing law. Over 10 years, the cost was estimated at $746.9 billion, a $73.5 billion increase over existing law. The numbers were based on estimated cost of the programs in April 2001. Unlike funds provided in most authorization bills, the amounts in the farm bill were mandatory spending, not subject to annual appropriations.

In addition to providing large subsidy increases for the major row crops — wheat, corn, oats, rice, cotton and soybeans — the 2002 law added support for dry peas, lentils and chickpeas; created a new national dairy program; and revamped the peanut subsidy program. Spending rose for conservation, rural development and research, with a new focus on energy development. The law also set tighter limits on annual federal payments to farmers, reinstated food stamps for legal immigrants, and began a country-of-origin labeling program for meat, fish, fruit, vegetables and peanuts.

A large part of the cost — $535.1 billion over 10 years — was for nutrition programs, mainly food stamps, although most of that would have been spent under existing law. The increases under the new law were mainly for farm programs.

The 1996 farm law (PL 104-127), which expired Oct. 1, 2002, had been written by Republicans after they took control of Congress in 1995. The aim was to deregulate agriculture programs and move farmers away from federal subsidies. The law replaced a decades-old policy of providing subsidies when market prices dropped and requiring farmers to plant the same crop every year. Instead, it guaranteed farmers fixed but declining annual payments regardless of market prices. By removing planting restrictions, it allowed farmers to rotate their crops to take advantage of weather conditions and market prices.

Backers of the law hoped it would encourage farmers to base their production decisions on the market rather than on government supports. But a wave of financial crises around the world, particularly in Asia, caused commodity prices to collapse. Instead of being weaned off government support, farmers returned to Congress for a series of emergency farm aid packages totaling $30.5 billion between 1998 and 2001.

When work on a replacement farm bill began in 2001,

BoxScore

Bill:
HR 2646 — PL 107-171
Legislative Action:
Senate passed HR 2646, amended (S Rept 107-117), 58-40, on Feb. 13.
House adopted the conference report (H Rept 107-424), 280-141, on May 2.
Senate cleared the bill, 64-35, on May 8.
President signed May 13.

there was significant interest from the White House and key congressional Democrats in reducing the emphasis on support for growers of traditional crops — programs that provided disproportionate benefits to huge "factory farms." Instead, they proposed to spend more on conservation programs that helped small farmers who agreed to set aside or otherwise preserve land.

But the push for more conservation spending could not withstand a drive by many farm-state lawmakers to expand traditional commodity-based support programs for row crops. Election-year pressures played a major role, especially in the Senate, where party control was up for grabs in 2002 and the most vulnerable incumbents were from farm states.

Although the final bill increased conservation spending by nearly 80 percent, the total — $38.5 billion over 10 years — still paled by comparison to the $124.8 billion provided for commodity support programs. Supporters hoped the increased subsidies would end the need for emergency appropriations to supplement farm income.

Highlights

The following are highlights of the new farm act:
● **Fixed payments.** The law expanded the main subsidy program of the 1996 law, which provided fixed but declining annual cash payments to producers of the major program crops. The payments were not linked to the amount or type of crops produced or the prevailing market price for the crop. Soybeans and other oilseeds were added to the list of eligible crops.
● **Marketing loans.** The law reauthorized marketing assistance loans and loan deficiency payments to producers of major program crops and soybeans. Marketing assistance loans allowed producers to borrow money from the government using their crops as collateral, with loan rates set by statute. If a crop sold for less than the price established in the loan program, farmers could forfeit the crop to the government as full payment. Loan deficiency payments were direct payments to producers for the difference between the going rate for their crop and the marketing assistance loan rate.
● **Countercyclical payments.** The law also created a new program to aid producers of major program crops and soybeans when market prices dropped below a target price defined in the law. The government would make up the difference between the average market price, plus the fixed payment, and the target price. The aim was to provide a safety net similar to what was in place before the 1996 farm law.
● **Payment limits.** The combined cap on annual payments to individual farmers was reduced from $460,000 under pri-

or law to $360,000. Beginning in the 2003 crop year, fixed payments were limited to $40,000 per person, marketing loan gains and loan deficiency payments to $75,000 per person, and countercyclical payments to $65,000 per person. Allowances for additional farms effectively doubled those amounts. The law left in place an exemption for Agriculture Department commodity certificates that had cash value.

● **Dairy support.** The law reauthorized the existing milk price support program, under which Agriculture Department purchases of surplus milk products enabled dairy processors to pay farmers a set price for milk. It also created a new program of direct countercyclical payments to dairy farmers when prices fell below a set level.

● **Peanuts.** A new peanut program was created, similar to the one for major crops, with fixed payments, countercyclical payments and marketing loans. The existing peanut quota program was terminated and quota holders were eligible for compensation for five years to ease the transition.

● **Other commodities.** The bill established marketing assistance loans and loan deficiency programs — similar to those for major program crops — for wool, mohair, unshorn pelts, honey, small chickpeas, lentils and dry peas.

● **Conservation programs.** The law provided an increase of $17.1 billion over 10 years for a number of conservation programs, including the Conservation Reserve Program, the Wetlands Reserve Program, the Farmland Protection Program, the Wildlife Habitat Incentives Program, the Environmental Quality Incentives Program, the Water Conservation Program and the Small Watershed Rehabilitation Program.

The total included $2 billion for a new Conservation Security Program to provide incentive payments for maintaining and increasing farm and ranch stewardship practices, and $254 million for a new Grassland Reserve Program, designed to enroll up to 2 million acres of virgin and improved pastureland into a preservation program.

● **Trade restrictions.** As part of the Uruguay Round of world trade talks, the United States was limited to no more than $19.1 billion in annual farm subsidies defined as likely to distort trade. The bill authorized the Agriculture secretary to adjust commodity subsidies to keep them within that limit; Congress assumed that the annual fixed payments would not count against the cap.

● **Food stamps.** The food stamp program was reauthorized through fiscal 2007, with some modifications, such as allowing states to provide transitional benefits for five months to families leaving welfare for work. Like the Senate bill, it restored food stamp benefits to legal permanent residents who had lived in the country for five years, recently arrived children, the disabled and refugees.

Background

Farm-state lawmakers originally had hoped to clear a new, multi-year farm bill in 2001. Although the 1996 law was not due to expire until Oct. 1, 2002, they were anxious to lay claim to $73.5 billion in new spending for farm programs that had been set aside under the fiscal 2002 budget resolution. With the federal surplus vanishing, they feared the money might not be available if they waited. But regional and party differences foiled plans for quick action. By

year's end, the House had passed a 10-year farm bill, while the Senate was deadlocked over a bigger, five-year bill. (*2001 Almanac, p. 3-3*)

The House passed its version of the bill Oct. 5, agreeing to $73.5 billion in new spending for agriculture programs over 10 years, most of it to maintain and expand subsidies for growers of row crops. Members narrowly defeated an amendment that embraced the idea of de-emphasizing traditional crop subsidies in favor of conservation initiatives available to every farmer. The debate pitted a powerful and close-knit coalition of farm-state lawmakers who wanted to maintain the status quo against a group of urban and suburban members who hoped to bring about broad changes.

In the Senate, Agriculture Committee Chairman Tom Harkin, D-Iowa, set out to write a bill that would restructure farm policy to emphasize conservation payments that would benefit small farmers. He succeeded in increasing funding for conservation, but to win support for the bill, he agreed to add even more money to revive and expand the commodity-based support policies of the past. The Congressional Budget Office (CBO) estimated that the evolving Senate bill would provide $73.4 billion in new spending calculated over 10 years, more than half of which would be spent in the first five years.

The bills that emerged from the House and Senate were based on the same general principles: fixed federal payments to farmers; new countercyclical aid tied to a guaranteed per-bushel target price; marketing loans for grains, cotton and oilseeds, and planting flexibility with no supply controls. The Senate bill, however, put more benefits into loan deficiency payments linked to prices, while the House bill put more money into the fixed payments. The Senate bill was front-loaded so that more of the money would be spent in the first five years.

The White House objected to the House bill, but it disliked the costlier Senate bill even more. The Office of Management and Budget said the price supports in both measures would encourage overproduction, increase government support in a time of declining revenue, and risk violating the restrictions on agriculture subsidies in global trade agreements.

The administration favored putting more money into conservation programs and de-emphasizing commodity price supports, but it remained aloof from the bill-writing process. After Sept. 11, the White House's main goal for the farm bill was to postpone a vote in the Senate, thereby delaying the conference until 2002 when it could focus on the issue. Barring that, officials favored a late entry, a proposal by Republicans Pat Roberts of Kansas and Thad Cochran of Mississippi that focused on farm savings accounts — rather than target-price payments — that would be matched by government funds when prices were down. Although that proposal failed, Senate Republicans held firm to block three attempts in December to bring the underlying bill to a vote.

Legislative Action

Senate Floor Action

After six days of floor debate and amendments, the Senate passed its version of the farm bill, 58-40, on Feb. 13. The biggest change was a controversial amendment to reduce

the total federal payments that individual farmers could receive each year. *(Senate vote 30, p. S-10)*

The White House lobbied the Senate to reject the bill, and all but nine Republicans voted against it. Richard G. Lugar of Indiana, ranking Republican on the Agriculture Committee, complained that the measure would go "in the wrong direction" by continuing a system that awarded two-thirds of the subsidies to 4 percent of all farmers.

At the time of the Senate vote, CBO said the bill would increase spending by $73.5 billion over 10 years, the amount allowed in the fiscal 2002 budget resolution, which continued to govern the bill. Total spending over 10 years, including nutrition and rural development programs, was estimated at $578.5 billion in the Senate and House versions. Over five years, however, the Senate bill was expected to cost $45 billion in new spending, $9 billion more than the House bill. Harkin said the bill was front-loaded because farmers needed the help immediately, but the higher five-year cost was also the result of election-year pressures in the Senate for more spending, particularly for row crops.

In all major areas of the bill — conservation, rural development, trade, research and energy — the Senate plan was more expensive. Another $2.4 billion in emergency agriculture assistance was added after Max Baucus, D-Mont., succeeded, 69-30, in exempting the package from budget restrictions. The assistance included $1.8 billion for crop losses and $500 million for livestock producers. *(Senate vote 25, p. S-9; drought aid, p. 4-11)*

● **Payment limit.** Senators stunned the agriculture community Feb. 7 by agreeing to sharply reduce the total federal subsidies that any one farmer or farm operation could receive. In place of the existing $460,000 annual cap, the Senate endorsed a limit of $225,000 for individuals and $275,000 for couples. The change, contained in an amendment by Byron L. Dorgan, D-N.D., and Charles E. Grassley, R-Iowa, was adopted by voice vote after an attempt by Blanche Lincoln, D-Ark., to table (kill) it failed, 31-66. *(Senate vote 18, p. S-8)*

The Agriculture Committee had voted to increase the cap to $500,000. Harkin had tried to reduce it but compromised on the limit to get the bill out of his committee. The House bill proposed raising the limit to $550,000 per farm.

To make the limits even stricter, the amendment required that commodity certificates — which were issued by the Agriculture Department and were the equivalent of cash — be counted. Exclusion of the certificates under existing law allowed some farmers to greatly exceed the cap. The amendment also proposed to eliminate the "three entity rule," which allowed a farmer to receive full benefits for the first farm and up to half the amount for two additional farms, effectively doubling the overall cap.

The stricter payment limits were backed by Midwestern senators who represented regions with small farms and by many members from urban areas who opposed government payments to large agribusinesses. An environmental group had drawn public attention to the issue in 2001 by posting a list on its Web site of every federal farm subsidy recipient between 1996 and 2000. Drawn from Agriculture Department data, the list showed that the top 10 percent of 2.4 million recipients of federal crop subsidies received two-thirds of all payments.

But senators from the South and West who represented regions with large farms adamantly opposed the lower cap, saying it did not take into account the high operating costs for their regional commodities. Tim Hutchinson, R-Ark., called it "nothing less than war on Southern farmers."

● **Meatpacking industry.** Another controversial Senate provision sought to prohibit meatpackers from owning or controlling livestock for more than 14 days before slaughter, with exceptions for farmer cooperatives and small packers. The provision — inserted by a group of Midwestern senators led by Grassley and Tim Johnson, D-S.D. — was aimed at halting consolidation in the meatpacking industry. Critics said a handful of corporations, such as ConAgra Foods and Smithfield Foods Inc., had gained a stranglehold on beef and pork processing and prices.

The proposal was pushed mainly by lawmakers from the Great Plains who represented small livestock operations that had been getting squeezed out of the market. It was strongly opposed by lawmakers from the South and West, including House Agriculture Committee Chairman Larry Combest, R-Texas, who represented large cattle and hog operations.

Harkin and Grassley amended the bill on the floor to clarify that the ban would not affect marketing arrangements where the packer did not exercise operational, managerial or supervisory control over the livestock or the farming operation that produced the livestock. A motion by Larry E. Craig, R-Idaho, to table (kill) the amendment failed, 46-53. *(Senate vote 23, p. S-9)*

● **Dairy program.** In addition to continuing the existing milk price support program, the Senate bill proposed a new, three-year, $2 billion program to provide countercyclical payments to dairy farmers. For the Northeastern states, the payments would kick in when prices fell below a target price; for other states, payments would occur when milk prices fell below the five-year average for that quarter. The program was a priority for the six Northeastern states that had been part of the Northeast Dairy Compact, a regional system that had allowed members to set prices for their dairy farmers above federally guaranteed levels. The compact had expired Sept. 30, 2001, and efforts to reauthorize it had been blocked by members from Western and Midwestern states with large dairy operations.

An attempt by Pete V. Domenici, R-N.M., to substitute flat, direct fixed payments to dairy producers was tabled by a vote of 56-42. *(Senate vote 29, p. S-10)*

In other floor action, the Senate:

● **Food stamps.** Adopted, 96-1, an amendment by Richard J. Durbin, D-Ill., to restore food stamp benefits to legal immigrants that were eliminated in the 1996 welfare law (PL 104-193). The amendment followed Bush administration policy, but it included a provision by Phil Gramm, R-Texas, to end benefits if an immigrant lost legal status for at least 12 months. *(Senate vote 17, p. S-8)*

● **Bankruptcy.** Adopted, 93-0, an amendment by Jean Carnahan, D-Mo., to make permanent Chapter 12 of the bankruptcy code, which covered farmers. The provision had expired Sept. 30. *(Senate vote 20, p. S-8)*

● **Farm savings accounts.** A small, $18 million test program was all that remained in the bill of the national farm savings accounts plan proposed by Roberts and backed by

the White House. An amendment by Harkin that would have created a $510 million, four-year program in 10 states was rejected, 17-80. Harkin proposed the idea during a larger partisan fight over nutrition spending, a move that Roberts called "disingenuous." The Senate chairman argued that he had given Republicans a chance to support the plan. "I was willing to give it a shot to see if it works," he said. "I sure didn't find much support for it." (*Senate vote 26, p. S-9*)

● **Water rights.** Westerners opposed an attempt to require farmers and ranchers to lease or sell water rights to the federal government if they took part in a new conservation program. Harry Reid, D-Nev., modified the plan to make it a test program in seven states, with the states having discretion on how to resolve water conservation problems. That did not satisfy critics such as Michael D. Crapo, R-Idaho, who offered an amendment to remove the language. His motion was tabled, 55-45. (*Senate vote 24, p. S-9*)

On other amendments, the Senate:

● Rejected, 11-85, a proposal by Lugar that would have replaced the commodity subsidy programs with annual payments of $7,000 per eligible farmer. (*Senate vote 19, p. S-8*)

● Rejected, 44-52, an amendment by Paul Wellstone, D-Minn., that would have maintained a cap on the amount of cost-share aid that new or expanding large-scale animal feeding operations could receive under the Environmental Quality Incentives Program. (*Senate vote 15, p. S-7*)

● Adopted, 82-14, a Harkin amendment to give farmers with beef and pork production contracts the same rights as poultry producers to discuss contracts with bankers, lawyers or federal and state officials. (*Senate vote 16, p. S-8*)

Conference/Final Action

It took House and Senate conferees nearly two months to agree on a final bill. The House adopted the conference report (H Rept 107-424) by a vote of 280-141 on May 2. The Senate cleared the bill, 64-35, on May 8. (*House vote 123, p. H-46; Senate vote 103, p. S-23*)

"I've never voted for a farm bill conference report. I will vote for this one. That's how good I feel about this farm legislation," said Senate Majority Leader Tom Daschle, D-S.D., who helped iron out the final details.

His enthusiasm was not shared by many in the House, who argued during the final debate that the new bill was a throwback to New Deal-era government support policies. Two House conferees, Cal Dooley, D-Calif., and John A. Boehner, R-Ohio, refused to sign the final report. "It represents the most sweeping non-military expansion of the federal government since the Great Society and will create more problems than it will solve," they said in a joint statement.

Combest argued that the conference report was "the best compromise that we are likely to see. In addition to desperately needed help for farmers, it contains the largest single increase in conservation funding in history, significant gains for food stamp and nutrition funding, more resources for agricultural research, increased incentives for renewable fuels production, and a strengthened commitment to our rural communities. And it is all accomplished within limits of the budget."

Revising the Senate Bill

Senate negotiators had come into the conference in an awkward position. House and Senate aides had already begun poring over the competing versions of the bill when CBO found it had underestimated the 10-year cost of the Senate version by $6.1 billion. Instead of matching the 10-year funding increase of $73.5 billion in the House-passed bill — the figure that the administration and congressional leaders had agreed to — the Senate version was calculated to boost spending by $79.6 billion.

"I am not trying to blame the Senate," said Combest, "but if one has an extra $6.1 billion, one can make a lot more of the competing interests satisfied." Combest had publicly questioned how the Senate had managed to propose higher spending for every major section of the bill and still stay within the $73.5 billion limit.

Harkin said the mistake occurred because CBO had missed a major change made in the original Senate bill (S 1628) and contained in subsequent rewrites. Traditionally, direct commodity payments to farmers were calculated on 85 percent of their eligible acreage, but the Senate bill provided that they be based on 100 percent of a farmer's acreage. "It is a disappointment that CBO has made an error of this magnitude," Harkin said.

The revised estimate meant that Harkin had to negotiate cuts with senators who had voted for the bill because of its largess. A suggestion by Combest that the Senate simply drop all its extra provisions, including the dairy program, was a non-starter. In the end, senators dug deeply into proposed conservation and nutrition programs, and also into smaller items, such as a farmers' credit plan, to preserve the funding increases for the commodity subsidies that were key to winning Senate support.

The House agreed March 19 to let the Senate use the modified numbers as a starting point for negotiations.

Splitting Their Differences

The main differences during negotiations were between populist Senate Democrats, whose bill was designed to help small farmers and livestock producers, and House members from both parties who wanted a more traditional farm bill. In many areas, they split the difference. Even the six-year term of the final bill was a compromise between the Senate's five-year bill and the 10-year House measure.

● **Payment limits.** The final bill drew loud criticism in the House from members who wanted sharp limits on federal payments to farmers. Although the original House-passed bill would have increased the annual limit to $550,000, the House subsequently voted, 265-158, to instruct its conferees to agree to the Senate position in favor of a $275,000 limit. The final compromise was a $360,000 limit; conferees dropped Senate proposals to count commodity certificates under the cap and to eliminate the three-entity rule. (*House vote 100, p. H-38*)

"They carved out exceptions that would basically blow the lid off of any limitation," complained Rep. Ron Kind, D-Wis. Kind, with Nick Smith, R-Mich., tried to send the conference report back to the drawing board with instructions to adopt the $275,000 payment cap and divert more money to conservation, nutrition, rural development and energy programs, but the motion failed, 172-251. (*House vote 122, p. H-46*)

• **Commodity supports.** Commodity support programs were increased by $47.8 billion over 10 years. The Senate had proposed raising loan price supports used to help farmers get bank financing. House conferees argued that a farmer would have to produce to get the higher loan rates, leading to overproduction. Instead, they pushed for fixed cash payments. The agreement contained higher loan rates during the first two years of the bill, and then a decline.

• **Meatpacking plants.** Conferees dropped the Senate ban on meatpackers owning cattle, hogs or sheep within 14 days of their slaughter. Midwestern lawmakers did win inclusion of another provision they sought: a requirement that meat, fish, fruit and vegetables be labeled with their country of origin — a provision largely directed at meat from Canada. Conferees agreed to a voluntary labeling provision that would become mandatory after two years.

• **Dairy.** The final bill reauthorized the milk price support program, as both chambers had recommended, and it created a new, three-and-a-half-year national dairy program to give farmers additional help when dairy prices dropped below a fixed level. The cost was estimated at $1.3 billion through Sept. 30, 2005. The Senate's separate program for the Northwest was not included.

Dooley, whose state of California was the nation's largest dairy state, argued that the provisions would effectively increase consumer prices for the types of milk products made in California, such as powdered milk and butter, by at least 20 cents. "That's a huge impact in the market prices because of an effort to hand out money to dairy farmers across the country," Dooley said. But the dairy program was needed to secure the votes of Northeastern lawmakers.

• **Conservation.** The final bill provided $17.1 billion in new spending for conservation programs, compared with $21.5 billion in the Senate bill and $15.8 billion passed by the House. Harkin expressed particular satisfaction that the bill provided $2 billion for his proposed Conservation Security Program, which would pay farmers and ranchers for land, water and wildlife conservation efforts. Harkin had originally sought $3.2 billion. Environmental groups were critical of Senate negotiators for backing away from the Senate's higher total for conservation.

Part of the increase in conservation funding went to the Environmental Quality Incentives Program to help large hog producers comply with new EPA rules. Rep. Tom Latham, R-Iowa, contended that this funding to large operators was "a reward for not taking care of the environment." He voted against the bill.

• **Bankruptcy.** The conference agreement extended Chapter 12 of the bankruptcy code to Dec. 31, 2002. A provision to make Chapter 12 permanent had been included in a separate bankruptcy overhaul bill, but that measure was stalled in conference. Chapter 12 had expired Oct. 1, 2001. *(Bankruptcy, p. 5-3)*

The Senate farm bill would have re-enacted Chapter 12 with no expiration date. Although the House version had no comparable provision, the House voted 424-3 on April 10 to instruct conferees to accept the Senate provision. *(House vote 86, p. H-32)*

In separate action, the House on April 16 passed a bill to restore Chapter 12 for eight months, retroactive to Oct. 1, 2001. The vote was 407-3. The Senate cleared the bill by voice vote April 23, and Bush signed it May 7 (PL 107-170). *(House vote 95, p. H-36)*

• **Disaster funds.** The final bill did not include the $2.4 billion in disaster assistance proposed by the Senate. It did include a Senate plan to give $94 million in assistance to apple producers.

• **Cuba.** Conferees dropped a Senate provision that would have repealed statutory restrictions against private financing of agricultural sales to Cuba, thereby allowing U.S. banks to finance such exports. The House-passed bill did not address the issue, but the House voted 273-143 on April 23 to instruct conferees to agree to the Senate provision. *(House vote 105, p. H-40)* ◆

Provisions of the Farm Bill

Following are the major provisions of the 2002 farm bill (HR 2646 — PL 107-171) signed into law May 13:

Commodity Programs

The bill reauthorized through 2008 many provisions of existing law related to core commodity programs, including fixed payments and marketing loans, while making some modifications to those programs. It created a new countercyclical program to assist farmers affected by low market prices, thereby establishing a system of payments similar to the "safety net" structure that was abolished by the 1996 farm law (PL 104-127). The bill also reauthorized and made changes to the programs for sugar, peanuts, and fruits and vegetables, and created a new national dairy program.

• **Fixed payments.** The bill extended through 2008 fixed payments created under the 1996 law. The payments, which were not tied to specific crops or market prices, were originally intended to wean farmers away from crop subsidies. The bill added soybeans and other oilseeds to the program.

• **Market loans.** The measure reauthorized marketing assistance loans and loan deficiency payments to producers of major program crops and soybeans. Marketing assistance loans allow producers to borrow money from the government using their crops as collateral. If the crop sells for less than the loan rate, producers are allowed to repay their loans at the lower rate. Loan deficiency payments are direct federal payments to producers for the difference between the going rate for their crop and the marketing assistance loan rate.

• **Countercyclical payments.** A new subsidy was created for producers of major program crops and soybeans, with payments based on fluctuations in market prices to counter downturns in the farm economy. The payments would be triggered whenever a crop's effective price fell below a target price defined in the bill.

• **Peanuts.** The Depression-era peanut quota system, which limited the amount farmers produced in order to maintain high market prices, was scrapped. Instead, peanuts were treated similarly to major program crops, with fixed and countercyclical payments and market-

ing loans. Quota holders were to be compensated at 11 cents per pound per year for five years to transition out of the old program.

- **Sugar.** The bill repealed a 1-cent-per-pound penalty in the 1996 bill that was imposed on sugar producers when they forfeited sugar that was used as collateral against government loans.
- **Dairy.** The new law created a 3½-year national dairy program, retroactive to Dec. 1, 2001, to give farmers additional financial aid when prices dropped below a target price. Monthly payments were to equal 45 percent of the difference between $16.94 per hundredweight and the Boston Class I price. Producers were eligible for payments on up to 2.4 million pounds of production annually. The U.S. Department of Agriculture (USDA) was to report to Congress on the program's effectiveness one year after the bill's enactment.
- **Other commodities.** The bill reinstated wool and mohair subsidies that were deleted in 1996 and also added honey and crops such as small chickpeas, lentils and dry peas. Also, $94 million was included in direct aid for apple growers, and the federal government was to spend $200 million annually to purchase other fruits and vegetables and other specialty crops.
- **Payment limits.** The annual cap on total federal payments to farmers was lowered from $460,000 to $360,000. The limit for fixed payments was $40,000 per person, the cap for marketing loan gains and loan deficiency payments was $75,000 per person, and the limit for new countercyclical payments was $65,000 per person. The bill continued the use of generic certificates and the three-entity rule, under which some producers could receive higher total federal benefits than the cap would otherwise allow. Congress also mandated a system to track benefits going to farmers or corporations.
- **Trade compliance.** The Uruguay Round Agreement on agriculture set a ceiling of $19.1 billion per year on domestic farm support programs that were considered most likely to distort production and trade. The farm bill stated that the secretary of Agriculture would adjust expenditures if necessary to avoid exceeding the limit and report to Congress.

Conservation Programs

The bill reauthorized existing conservation programs and created two new ones: the Conservation Security Program and the Grassland Reserve Program.

- **Conservation Security Program.** Under the new program, farmers would receive payments for employing soil, water or wildlife habitat conservation methods on working lands. Land enrolled in the Conservation Reserve Program, the Wetlands Reserve Program or the Grassland Reserve Program, as well as land that had been idle for four of the last six years, would not be eligible for enrollment in this program, which was expected to cost $2 billion over 10 years.
- **Conservation Reserve Program.** Under this voluntary program, farmers received annual rental payments in return for removing highly erodible land from production for 10 years and devoting it to conservation uses. The program was reauthorized at an estimated cost of $1.5 billion over 10 years. The law increased the enrollment cap from 36.4 million acres to 39.2 million acres and expanded a wetlands pilot project to 1 million acres in all states.
- **Wetlands Reserve Program.** Under the wetlands reserve program, farmers agreed to preserve wetlands in exchange for annual or lump-sum payments from the Agriculture Department, as well as cost-sharing payments, to restore an area to the original wetland condition. The $1.5 billion, 10-year cost allowed for the amount of eligible acres to increase to 2.3 million.
- **Environmental Quality Incentives Program.** The program, created under the 1996 law, provided technical assistance and cost-sharing and incentive payments to encourage livestock producers

and farmers to manage the use of nutrients and manure so as to improve water quality. The bill increased annual payments to $1.3 billion in a series of steps, totaling $9 billion over 10 years. Sixty percent of the funds would go to livestock producers and 40 percent to crop producers. The increase was a major factor in the $17.1 billion overall increase for conservation in the bill.

- **Grassland Reserve Program.** The aim of the new program was to enroll up to 2 million acres of virgin and improved pastureland under 10-, 15- or 20-year contracts. The 10-year cost was $254 million.
- **Other conservation programs.** The bill authorized the Farmland Protection Program (at a cost of $985 million over 10 years); the Wildlife Habitat Incentives Program ($700 million over 10 years); the Water Conservation Program ($600 million over 10 years); the Small Watershed Rehabilitation Program ($275 million over 10 years); and a $200 million, 10-year plan to help conserve desert terminal lakes. The Farmland Protection Program, which paid farmers near urban areas to keep their land in production, included a plan by the Dracut Land Trust in Massachusetts to protect from development the farm operated by American Airlines Captain John Ogonowski, the pilot of Flight 11 that was hijacked Sept. 11 and crashed into the World Trade Center. The Water Conservation Program sets aside $50 million for producers in the Klamath Basin region in the Northwest.

Trade

- **Market Access Program.** Funding for the program — which provided financial assistance to U.S. producers and exporters for promotional activities abroad — was increased to $200 million annually by 2006.
- **Food for Progress.** The program provided commodities on credit or on a grant basis to developing countries and emerging democracies. It also was intended to help U.S. producers by removing surpluses from the domestic market. The law reauthorized the program at a cost of $308 million over 10 years and increased the cap on the amount of funds spent to transport the commodities.
- **Other trade provisions.** Other programs that were reauthorized included the Food for Peace program, adding conflict prevention as a program objective; Technical Assistance for Specialty Crops, which provided exporter assistance to address barriers against U.S. specialty crops; and the Foreign Market Development Cooperator Program, which promoted value-added products such as wheat flour and soybean oil. The George McGovern-Robert Dole International Food for Education and Child Nutrition Program, a maternal, infant and child nutrition program, also was extended. The bill also authorized the establishment of a program to provide live lamb on an emergency food relief basis to Afghanistan. The Farmers From Africa and Caribbean Basin Program was added to the Farmer-to-Farmer program with a $10 million authorization to establish and administer bilateral exchange programs to provide technical assistance to farmers in Africa and the Caribbean Basin.

Nutrition

- **Food stamps.** The $6.4 billion nutrition program modified previous law by allowing states to provide transitional food stamp benefits for five months to families leaving welfare for work under Temporary Assistance for Needy Families.

The bill also restored food stamp benefits to legal permanent residents who had lived in the country for five years, effective April 2003, recently arrived children, the disabled and refugees. The 1996 welfare overhaul law (PL 104-193) revoked the eligibility of most legal immigrants to receive food stamps. In 1998, the benefits were restored to children and the elderly who arrived in the country before 1996.

The law included new procedures to simplify and streamline the food stamp program to align it with other public assistance programs and to improve the quality control system. States with a high or significantly improved performance in the food stamp program would be eligible for bonuses from a $48-million-per-year fund beginning in fiscal 2003. The bill also consolidated nutrition assistance funding for Puerto Rico and American Samoa, set aside $5 million a year beginning in fiscal 2002 for community food project grants, and authorized $140 million a year in commodities purchases for The Emergency Food Assistance Program, which provided commodities to food banks and soup kitchens.

- **Commodity distribution.** The new law reauthorized the distribution of surplus commodities to special nutrition projects and the Commodity Supplemental Food Program, and set aside $60 million for emergency food aid.
- **Child nutrition and related programs.** The law encouraged institutions participating in the school lunch program and the school breakfast program to include in their food purchases locally produced foods. A pilot program would make available to students in 25 elementary or secondary schools in each of four states and on one American Indian reservation free fresh and dried fruits and fresh vegetables throughout the school day.

Funding was increased for the Women, Infants and Children Farmers' Market Nutrition Program and for the Seniors Farmers' Market Nutrition Program.

The Congressional Hunger Fellows Program was created to encourage the pursuit of careers in humanitarian service.

Credit

- **Farm ownership loans.** Beginning farmers and ranchers were given greater access to USDA farm credit programs through loan guarantees. The loan repayment program for beginning farmers and ranchers was increased to 15 years. Under a pilot program, beginning farmers or ranchers in at least five states were to get loan guarantees to help purchase farms on a land contract basis.
- **Emergency loans.** The measure authorized loans in response to emergency quarantines imposed by the USDA under plant protection or animal quarantine laws as well as natural disasters.
- **Farm credit.** The secretary of Agriculture was authorized to provide unused funds allocated for socially disadvantaged farmers and ranchers within a state to other states that had pending loan applications for socially disadvantaged farmers and ranchers.

The secretary was authorized to make an operating loan to a borrower who had received debt forgiveness on not more than one occasion that directly and primarily resulted from a natural disaster as designated by the president.

Rural Development

- **Miscellaneous grants.** The law authorized $30 million per year for water or wastewater disposal grants; $15 million for rural business opportunity grants; $30 million a year for the Community Water Assistance program to maintain water quality in rural communities, particularly in emergencies; $10 million per year for grants to nonprofit organizations to finance the construction, refurbishing and servicing of individually owned household well water systems in rural areas for low- to moderate-income individuals; $60 million in grants and loans for water and waste facilities for American Indian tribes; grants for water systems for rural and native villages in Alaska; rural cooperative development grants; and $10 million per year in grants for rural tribal college and university facilities and the development of day care facilities in rural areas.
- **Value-added agricultural products market development.** The law expanded the eligibility for grants under this program, with

$40 million authorized each year. Five percent of the funds were to be used for the Agriculture Marketing Resource Center.

- **Renewable energy systems.** The law allowed low-interest (4 percent) loans, loan guarantees and grants to be used by producers for energy systems and improvements, including wind systems and anaerobic digesters.
- **Rural electronic commerce.** The law created a new rural electronic commerce extension program to help small businesses and microenterprises in rural areas. It authorized $360 million over six years for grants to eligible regional development centers and land grant colleges to develop business strategies and provide training.
- **Rural telework.** Nonprofit or educational institutions or American Indian tribes were eligible to apply for grants of up to $2 million to use telecommunications to perform work functions at rural work centers located outside an employer's place of business.
- **Historic barn preservation.** The law called for preservation of barns that were at least 50 years old and were eligible for listing on national, state or local registers or inventories of historic structures.
- **Delta regional authority.** The bill included $7 million per year for grants to develop state-of-the-art technology in animal nutrition and value-added manufacturing to promote economic development.
- **Northern Great Plains Regional Authority.** The bill provided $30 million per year for grants to the authority — which included Iowa, Minnesota, Nebraska, North Dakota and South Dakota — for transportation improvements, telecommunications networking, job training, business development, aid to distressed areas and other economic development programs.
- **Rural Business Investment Program.** The program provided $280 million in guarantees for rural business investment companies to provide equity investment for businesses. The six-year cost of the program was $100 million.
- **Rural Strategic Investment Program.** Under the law, regional investment boards could receive up to $3 million for economic development. The six-year cost was $100 million.
- **Rural broadband access.** The Rural Electrification Act of 1936 was amended to provide funds to allow rural consumers to receive high-speed broadband service at a six-year cost of $100 million, as well as to allow for expansion of 911 telephone service.
- **SEARCH grants.** The law authorized $51 million per year for grants to small communities for environmental projects.
- **Rural television loan guarantees.** The law authorized $80 million over six years for loan guarantees to ensure that local television broadcast signals reached rural residents in unserved or underserved areas. Unused funds could be used to expand broadband access.
- **Rural development backlogs.** The law authorized $360 million over six years to speed processing of applications for water and wastewater programs.
- **Farm worker training.** A program to train farm workers in new technologies required for higher-value crops was authorized for $10 million per year.
- **Rural firefighters and emergency personnel grant program.** The law authorized $50 million over six years to train rural firefighters and emergency personnel.

Research

- **Agriculture extensions.** The law continued numerous programs totaling $1.3 billion over six years, including policy research centers; the Human Nutrition Intervention and Health Promotion Program; the pilot research program to combine medical and agricultural research; the Nutrition Education Program; continuing animal health and disease research program; an increase from $15 million to $25 million a year for grants to upgrade

agricultural and food sciences facilities at land-grant colleges; national research and training virtual centers; Hispanic-serving institutions; competitive grants for international agricultural science and education programs; university research; supplemental and alternative crops; aquaculture research facilities; rangeland research; a national genetics resources program; a nutrient management research and extension initiative; an agricultural telecommunications program; an assistive technology program for farmers with disabilities; partnerships for high-value agricultural product quality research; bio-based products; integrated research; an education and extension competitive grants program; the equity in educational land-grant status act of 1994; 1994 institution research grants; an endowment for 1994 institutions; precision agriculture; the Thomas Jefferson initiative for crop diversification; research regarding diseases of wheat, triticale, and barley caused by fusarium graminearum or by tilletia indica; the Office of Pest Management Policy; National Agricultural Research, the Extension, Education, and Economics Advisory Board; grants for research on production and marketing of alcohols and industrial hydrocarbons from agricultural commodities and forest products; agricultural experiment stations research facilities; and competitive, special and facilities research grants for the National Research Initiative.

- **Initiative for future agriculture and food systems.** The program, which studied future food production, environmental quality and natural resources management, farm income and rural economic, business and community development, received a funding increase from $120 million a year to $200 million.
- **Bovine Johne's disease control program.** The USDA was authorized to conduct research, testing and evaluation of programs for management of Johne's disease in livestock.
- **Biosecurity.** In addition to the usual agricultural research, extension and education funding, the bill gave special authorization for such sums as necessary for biosecurity planning and response.

Forestry

- **Forest land enhancement program.** New funding totaling $100 million was committed for a new cost-share program to assist private non-industrial forest landowners in adopting sustainable forest management practices.
- **Enhanced community fire protection.** The bill authorized $35 million per year to coordinate efforts to prevent and fight wildland fires.

Energy

- **Federal procurement of biobased products.** The bill authorized $6 million for a new program under which federal agencies would purchase biobased products — industrial products, other than food and feeds, made from renewable plant and animal material.
- **Biodiesel fuel education.** The bill created a grant program to educate government and private fuel consumers about the benefits of biodiesel fuel use, at a cost of $5 million.
- **Renewable energy system and energy efficiency improvements.** The bill established a loan guarantee and grant program to assist farmers in purchasing renewable energy systems and making energy efficiency improvements, at a cost of $115 million.
- **Biomass Research and Development Act of 2000.** The act was reauthorized and funded through 2007, at a cost of $75 million.
- **Bio-energy program.** The bill authorized $204 million over six years to allow the secretary of Agriculture to continue making payments to bio-energy producers who purchased agricultural commodities for the purpose of expanding production of biodiesel and fuel grade ethanol.

Miscellaneous

- **Country of origin labeling.** The bill required the USDA to provide guidelines for voluntary labeling of meat, fruits, vegetables, fish and peanuts by Sept. 30, 2002. The program was to become mandatory in two years. For a commodity to be labeled a U.S.A. product, it had to be born, raised and processed in the United States. Commodities that were ingredients in processed products would not fall under the labeling requirement.
- **Crop insurance.** The Adjusted Gross Revenue pilot crop insurance program offered coverage for crops for which traditional crop insurance was not available. It was initially offered in five states and then expanded to 17 states. The new law required that at least eight counties in California and at least eight counties in Pennsylvania be added to the pilot program in 2003.
- **Disaster assistance.** Eligibility and aid were expanded in several areas under the bill, including $94 million for apple producers for the loss of markets during the 2000 crop year; livestock producers affected by shortages of feed or sudden increases in production costs; and $10 million for onion farmers in New York's Orange County who suffered losses during one or more of the 1996 through 2000 crop years.
- **Orchard assistance.** Farmers with commercial orchards who suffered more than a 15 percent loss due to a natural disaster were to be reimbursed 75 percent of the cost of replanting trees.
- **Animal welfare.** The law prohibited interstate movement of animals for animal fighting.
- **Animal health protection.** Under the bill, the secretary of Agriculture could prohibit or restrict entry of any animal or related material if necessary to prevent spread of any livestock pest or disease. The secretary also could prohibit or restrict exports to prevent the spread of disease from or within the United States. The secretary's authority extended to holding, seizing, treating or destroying any animal or limiting the interstate movement of animals and acting to detect, control or eradicate any pest or disease of livestock. Owners would be paid based on fair market value of destroyed animals and related material.
- **Livestock.** Growers with swine production contracts would be provided the same statutory protections as livestock sellers and poultry growers under the law. Also, livestock and poultry producers could discuss contracts with state and federal agencies and other individuals having a fiduciary or familial relationship, notwithstanding a confidentiality provision in any contract between a producer and a processor for the sale of livestock or poultry.
- **Specialty crops.** The secretary of Agriculture was authorized to use not less than $50 million each fiscal year to purchase fresh fruits and vegetables for distribution to schools and service institutions. The bill included $10 million for a cranberry acreage reserve program, which involved purchasing permanent easements on wetlands or on buffer strips adjacent to wetlands that were environmentally sensitive and had been or were currently used for cranberry cultivation. Another $10 million per year cost-share pilot program was established to create demonstration projects intended to increase fruit and vegetable consumption and to promote healthful eating. The bill also provided $94 million of Commodity Credit Corporation (CCC) funds for 2002 to pay apple producers who suffered market losses during the 2000 crop year, with eligible crops not to exceed 5 million pounds. CCC funds totaling $10 million also were to be used to assist onion producers in Orange County, N.Y., who suffered losses between 1996 and 2000. A program to promote the expansion of farmers markets was included.
- Organic products. A National Organic Certification Cost Share Program was created to help producers and handlers get certification under the National Organic Program. Also, farmers who produced and marketed solely 100 percent organic products and

did not produce any non-organic products were exempt from assessments under commodity promotion laws.

• **Assistant secretary of Agriculture for Civil Rights.** The bill created an office to ensure USDA's compliance with civil rights laws.

• **Socially disadvantaged farmers and ranchers.** The bill provided assistance for socially disadvantaged farmers and ranchers, including an Indian tribal community college, an Alaska native cooperative college, West Virginia State College, and a Hispanic-serving institution. The law also required the secretary of Agriculture to report on participation rates of socially disadvantaged farmers and ranchers by race, ethnicity and gender.

• **Catfish and ginseng.** The law stated that only fish classified within the family Ictaluridae could be labeled or advertised as "catfish." Also, "ginseng" could be considered a common name only for any herb or herbal ingredient derived from a plant classified within the genus Panax.

• **Food safety.** The bill provided for the establishment of a 15-member Food Safety Commission to recommend how to improve food safety.

• **Irradiation.** The term "pasteurization" was redefined to include other processes besides heat treatment for eliminating microbial pathogens, potentially allowing foods treated with irradiation, high pressure, or ultraviolet light to be labeled as pasteurized. The secretary of Health and Human Services was to issue a final rule to regulate labeling of irradiated foods.

• **Biotechnology education.** A public education program about the safety of foods produced using biotechnology was established.

• **Downed livestock.** The secretary of Agriculture was to investigate and report to Congress on non-ambulatory animals — livestock too sick or injured to stand — and enforce new regulations.

• **Commercial fisheries failure.** Emergency disaster relief was made available to the commercial fishery industry in the Northeast.

• **Plant protection.** Criminal penalties were increased for anyone who knowingly destroyed records, moved pests in commerce or committed multiple violations of the Plant Protection Act.

• **Family farmer bankruptcy.** Chapter 12 Bankruptcy provisions were extended to Dec. 31, 2002. ◆

Senate Seeks Additional Farm Aid

Farm-state senators tried repeatedly but without success to pass emergency legislation to aid farmers and ranchers stricken by drought in 2001 and 2002. Their attempts stretched from an early effort to get emergency money into the 2002 farm bill to an end-of-session bid to pass a separate farm aid measure. The Bush administration and many Republicans argued that any aid should come out of the 2002 farm bill (PL 107-171) enacted in May, or that it should be offset by spending cuts.

In February, the Senate added $2.4 billion to its version of the six-year farm bill to aid farmers and ranchers who suffered weather-related disasters in 2001. The assistance included $1.8 billion for crop losses and $500 million for livestock producers. It was approved by voice vote Feb. 12, after Max Baucus, D-Mont., succeeded, 69-30, in exempting the amendment from budget restrictions. (*Farm bill, p. 4-3; Senate vote 25, p. S-9*)

But the provision drew a veto threat from the White House, and it was dropped in conference. A major rationale for the large agriculture subsidies in the underlying farm bill was that they would eliminate the need for annual emergency aid for farmers.

Just before the August recess, Senate Agriculture Committee Chairman Tom Harkin, D-Iowa, scheduled a markup for a disaster aid bill (S 2801) introduced by Baucus, but postponed it because members could not agree on how to pay for the assistance. Harkin, Majority Leader Tom Daschle of South Dakota and other Senate Democrats wanted the aid treated as emergency spending that would not count against allocations for the fiscal 2003 agriculture appropriations bill; committee Republicans called for offsets.

Ignoring the administration's opposition, the Senate voted overwhelmingly Sept. 10 to attach nearly $6 billion in drought assistance to the fiscal 2003 Interior spending bill

(HR 5093). The amendment, by Daschle, was adopted by voice vote after he won a procedural motion, 79-16. Eager to help drought-stricken farmers and to protect themselves politically, 31 Republicans joined Democrats to support the amendment. (*Senate vote 212, p. S-43*)

The measure, based on the Baucus bill, would have provided emergency support to farmers and ranchers who had lost income because of weather-related disasters in 2001 and 2002. While the Congressional Budget Office estimated the cost at $5.9 billion, others said that because of the severity of the drought, it could cost much more.

House Majority Leader Dick Armey, R-Texas, said the drought aid clearly was aimed at improving the re-election prospects of Democrats such as Sen. Tim Johnson, Daschle's colleague from South Dakota, who was in a close race with Republican Rep. John Thune. "Anybody who does not recognize that is walking through life with blinders on," Armey told reporters.

"Well, if I just did it to help Democrats," Daschle responded, "I guess I am puzzled why so many Republicans would help us."

GOP lawmakers said they expected money in the Daschle amendment to be reduced in conference. Senate Republican Policy Committee Chairman Larry E. Craig of Idaho voted for the amendment to show concern for his state's farmers, but he predicted that farm aid in the final bill would be reduced to around $3 billion. "This amendment is a budget buster," he said. "That's why this amount will never become law." The issue became moot, however, because the Senate never completed the Interior bill.

Baucus made a last-ditch effort Nov. 19, seeking to bring up a Daschle bill (S 3099) that was similar to the Interior amendment, but Minority Leader Trent Lott, R-Miss., objected, saying the cost was unclear.

Although Bush consistently had said the farm bill he signed in May included more than enough entitlement spending to deal with weather conditions and bad crops, the administration abruptly changed course a few weeks before the election. On Sept. 19, Agriculture Secretary Ann M. Veneman appeared at a press conference with Thune and other farm-state Republicans to announce plans to spend $752 million to aid Midwestern livestock producers whose herds had been ravaged by heat and drought. The money was drawn from excess customs fees, money that usually went to child nutrition programs and commodity purchases. ◆

Chapter 5

BANKING & FINANCIAL SERVICES

Bankruptcy Rewrite Stalls Again

For the third time in as many Congresses, legislation to overhaul the nation's bankruptcy laws faltered just short of the finish line. House and Senate conferees reached agreement on a bill (HR 333), but the conference report was scuttled in the closing days of the session by Republican anti-abortion activists in the House, who opposed a provision aimed at protesters fined for anti-abortion activities.

The measure, which would have made it harder for consumers to walk away from their debts, was a top priority for banks and credit card companies but a target for consumer groups and bankruptcy attorneys. It would have forced more individuals filing for bankruptcy to use Chapter 13 of the code, which requires repayment of most debts, rather than Chapter 7, which allows individuals to escape remaining debts after liquidating their assets. The bill would have capped at $125,000 the amount of home equity a debtor could shield from creditors in bankruptcy proceedings for a home purchased within 40 months of the bankruptcy filing.

The year began with the legislation stalled in a conference that was trying to reconcile separate versions passed by the House and Senate in 2001. By mid-May, negotiators had narrowed the differences to a single issue: a Senate provision aimed at preventing demonstrators — particularly protesters at abortion clinics — from filing for bankruptcy to avoid paying court-ordered fines and judgments. The dispute pitted Senate sponsor Charles E. Schumer, D-N.Y., against abortion foe Rep. Henry J. Hyde, R-Ill.

For months the longtime adversaries refused to budge. But the pressure to advance the bill, fueled by large campaign contributions from the financial services industry, finally forced them to reach a compromise in late July.

Hyde agreed to bar debtors from filing for bankruptcy to escape fines for "intentional, knowing or reckless actions" that interfered with or caused violence against people who provided "lawful goods or services." Schumer agreed that the bill would make clear that the restriction was not intended to cover activities protected by the First Amendment, including peaceful picketing, prayer or other similar types of demonstrations.

GOP leaders were set to bring the conference report to the House floor before the August recess, but protests by a group of anti-abortion Republicans led them to abandon their plans. The leadership tried again during the lame-duck session, but the opponents managed to defeat the rule for debate on the measure.

On Nov. 15, the House passed the bill again after dropping the protest provision as well as language authorizing 28 new bankruptcy judgeships. That maneuver killed any chances of clearing the rewrite in the Senate.

BoxScore

Bill:
HR 333
Legislative Action:
House rejected the rule for debate on the conference report to HR 333 (H Rept 107-617), 172-243, on Nov. 14.
House passed HR 333, amended, 244-116, Nov. 15.

Highlights

Key provisions of the conference report on the bankruptcy bill would have:

● **Means test.** Made it more difficult for debtors to file for Chapter 7 bankruptcy, which allows them to escape debts still unpaid after they liquidate their assets. Individuals would have been ineligible for Chapter 7 if they had sufficient income to repay $10,000 or 25 percent of their debts over five years. Such cases would be handled under Chapter 13, which requires repayment of most debts. Debtors earning less than the median family income for their state would be exempt from the means test.

● **Homestead exemption.** Allowed debtors to shield from creditors no more than $125,000 in home equity. The limit applied to homes bought within 40 months of filing for bankruptcy.

● **Secured credit.** Required debtors to pay in full for cars and other goods bought on credit within 2½ years of filing for bankruptcy.

● **Tax returns.** Required people filing for bankruptcy to submit their most recent federal tax returns to bankruptcy courts, though they would not have to include attachments.

● **Small business.** Expedited handling of cases for small businesses with $2 million or less in debt filing under Chapter 11 of the bankruptcy code.

● **Farmers.** Made Chapter 12 bankruptcy protection for family farmers permanent. It would have doubled the eligibility limit to include farmers with up to $3 million in sales, and extended coverage to family fishing businesses.

● **Extra expenses.** Allowed debtors to claim an additional allowance for housing and utilities if the expenses were shown to be necessary and reasonable.

● **Enforcing fines.** Prohibited debtors from filing bankruptcy to escape fines and penalties incurred for crimes that involved intentional acts or threats that obstructed, intimidated or interfered with a person involved in obtaining and providing lawful goods or services. Fines would be imposed for intentional or repeated violations of court orders protecting access to a facility, such as a health or abortion clinic, that provided lawful goods or services. The language specified that fine enforcement provisions should not be construed to affect any "expressive conduct," such as peaceful picketing or prayer vigils, that are protected by the First Amendment.

Background

The drive to rewrite the bankruptcy code began in response to a spike in consumer bankruptcy filings in the mid-to late 1990s. The soaring numbers — which peaked at 1,398,182 in 1998 — prompted complaints that many

Farm Protection Renewed

Although the broad bankruptcy overhaul bill (HR 333) collapsed, Congress did clear a temporary measure that extended bankruptcy protection for family farmers. The House passed the measure (HR 5472) by voice vote Oct. 1, and the Senate cleared it Nov. 20, also by voice vote. The bill renewed Chapter 12 bankruptcy protection for six months, beginning Jan. 1, 2003, when it was set to expire. President Bush signed it into law Dec. 19 (PL 107-377).

Chapter 12 of the bankruptcy code allowed bankrupt family farmers to restructure debts without losing their land.

House Judiciary Committee Chairman F. James Sensenbrenner Jr., R-Wis., introduced the short-term extension as a way of keeping pressure on lawmakers to clear the broader bill, which would have made Chapter 12 permanent. But the broad bill collapsed Nov. 14, blocked by conservative House Republicans who opposed a provision aimed at anti-abortion protesters. The Senate then cleared the Chapter 12 extension. (*Bankruptcy, p. 5-3*)

More than 21,000 farmers had filed for bankruptcy protection under Chapter 12 since it was enacted in 1986. It originally was viewed as a temporary fix for a flood of farmers filing for protection under other sections of the nation's bankruptcy code, which require some assets to be liquidated to repay debts.

wealthier people were able to exploit the system to erase debts they could afford to pay. Opponents countered that the proposals to toughen bankruptcy requirements were an unwarranted attack on protections for the middle class, adding they had little sympathy for credit card companies that flooded consumers with offers of easy credit.

Consumer filings actually dropped in 1999 and 2000, only to hit a new high of 1,452,030 in 2001. Experts said the increase stemmed from a combination of a souring economy and a marketing blitz by bankruptcy lawyers who warned debtors to file for protection before the law was changed.

Bankruptcy overhaul legislation had come close to enactment twice; conference reports were completed in 1998 and 2000. The first one died in the Senate, where Democrats were angry over the watering down of consumer protections. The second was pocket-vetoed by President Bill Clinton, who cited deletion of an earlier version of Schumer's provision aimed at anti-abortion protesters. He also criticized as too lenient a proposed $100,000 cap on the homestead exemption, applied only to homes held for two years or less before a filing. (*2000 Almanac, p. 5-3; 1998 Almanac, p. 5-15*)

Still, the bill seemed to be in for an easy ride in 2001. The combination of a GOP-controlled Congress and Bush in the White House had supporters optimistic for early enactment. The House and Senate each passed bills by wide margins in March. But action stalled after James M. Jeffords, I-Vt., left the GOP, giving control of the Senate to the Democrats. The shift in power gave greater leverage to senators such as Schumer, who dug in his heels over the abortion provision.

An initial conference session scheduled for Sept. 12 was canceled after the Sept. 11 terrorist attacks. Conferees finally exchanged opening statements in a meeting Nov. 14, but got no further. (*2001 Almanac, p. 4-3*)

The two main sticking points were a revised version of Schumer's Senate provision, strongly opposed by House Republicans, and differences over the homestead exemption. The Senate proposed capping the exemption for all homes at $125,000. The House, backed by the White House, set the cap at $100,000 for homes purchased within two years of a filing.

Legislative Action

Conference

House and Senate conferees held a handful of formal meetings in 2002, with a great deal of the negotiating going on behind the scenes. The chairmen of the House and Senate Judiciary committees, Rep. F. James Sensenbrenner Jr., R-Wis., and Sen. Patrick J. Leahy, D-Vt., came tantalizingly close to a final agreement April 23. Conferees resolved all of the issues but one: what to do with Schumer's amendment. House Republicans hated it; Senate Democrats said they would reject the bill without it. Another session in May failed to break the logjam. Finally on July 25, with little warning, Schumer and Hyde reached a deal and conferees signed off on a final agreement (H Rept 107-617).

● **Abortion.** Backers of bankruptcy overhaul had been astonished at the intransigence of Hyde and Schumer, who seemed willing to kill the landmark legislation over the abortion protest language. For Schumer, the provision was an effort to put teeth into a 1994 law (PL 103-259) he championed that made it a crime to bar access to abortion clinics. He and other Senate Democrats said the provision was essential to prevent protesters from dodging fines levied under that law.

Hyde, who opposed the 1994 clinic access law, said the provision would penalize peaceful protesters who mistakenly violated a police order. "This could hurt some little nun that's saying the Rosary and stepping across some line that some policeman draws," he said. "There will be more give and take. . . . But I can be as stubborn as [Schumer] can be." (*1994 Almanac, p. 355*)

Schumer's provision came in response to several cases in which abortion opponents, such as Randall Terry of Operation Rescue, had filed bankruptcy in an attempt to write off debts they incurred after being fined for illegally trying to shut down abortion clinics. Schumer also cited violent fringe anti-abortion groups that had detailed plans to take advantage of the existing system.

Senate Democrats maintained that the real obstacle was Hyde, a passionate opponent of abortion and a revered figure in the House. They said House negotiators would have accepted Schumer's language except for the fear of offending Hyde. In fact, the anti-abortion lobby did not work hard to support Hyde, while women's groups were adamant in their support of Schumer.

But late on July 25, after a meeting that lasted nearly five hours, Hyde and Schumer managed to reach an agreement. The compromise — nearly identical to an offer Schumer had made just two weeks before — proposed barring individ-

uals from using bankruptcy protection to escape fines and civil judgments if they had interfered with, intimidated, obstructed or injured those who provide "lawful goods or services," including abortions. Schumer's original provision applied solely to anti-abortion protesters. The agreement also specified that the language was not intended to cover activities protected by the First Amendment, such as picketing, public prayer and other peaceful demonstrations.

● **Homestead exemption.** The other chief sticking point — differences on the homestead exemption — had been resolved in April. The conferees adopted the Senate's $125,000 limit, but applied it only to homes purchased within 40 months of a bankruptcy filing. Previously, the amount of home equity shielded under bankruptcy had been set by the states, five of which had no limits. Two of those states, Texas and Florida, were known as havens for debtors who moved across state lines to buy expensive homes, knowing that creditors would not be able to seize them after they filed for bankruptcy.

House Action

On July 26, just hours before the House was to take up the conference report, a coalition of anti-abortion Republicans, led by Christopher H. Smith of New Jersey and Joe Pitts of Pennsylvania, objected to the Schumer-Hyde compromise, saying they were concerned that it went too far and could overly penalize some peaceful protesters.

Pitts said he worried about "sidewalk counselors" at abortion clinics "who go in front of the abortion clinics day after day, just to pray or offer someone a pamphlet." If they were shown to have willfully obstructed access to an abortion clinic, "they could be fined and could spend the rest of their life sending checks to Planned Parenthood," Pitts said.

Calling Hyde "the icon of the pro-life movement," Pitts said he "felt terrible having to go against the leadership, the administration and Sensenbrenner." Hyde later said his heart was with Pitts and Smith. "I'm on their side," he said. "But I made a deal with Schumer, and I'm going to live up to it."

Uncertain that they had the votes, House GOP leaders decided to postpone action on the conference report until September rather than risk an embarrassing defeat on the floor. Further delays in September allowed abortion foes more time to press their colleagues. By then, the midterm elections were just weeks away, and the leadership was unwilling to push a bill that might alienate the party's political base. That pushed the measure into the lame-duck session.

Finally, on Nov. 14, GOP leaders were ready to bring the conference report to the floor. But in a rare procedural defeat, they lost a vote on the rule for floor debate. The vote was 172-243, with 87 Republicans voting against the rule. (*House vote 478, p. H-150*)

The vote was held open for about an hour while Pitts and other anti-abortion Republicans stood at the well, lobbying against the measure. After GOP leaders acknowledged that the rule was doomed, Republicans rushed to change their votes. So many switched from "aye" to "nay" that the clerk's office had to double- and triple-check the numbers.

Republican leaders then regrouped and decided to try another strategy designed to get bankruptcy legislation through the House. They offered a new version of the bill that dropped the abortion protest provision and struck language that would have established 28 new bankruptcy judgeships. That provision was removed as part of the procedural move to reopen debate.

Members passed the new version of the bill, 244-116, early the morning of Nov. 15. Senate Majority Leader Tom Daschle, D-S.D., said the Senate would not pass it without the abortion provisions. (*House vote 484, p. H-150*)

Lobbyists who had worked on the legislation for years, only to see it collapse at the last minute, said they were weary of the fight. "A lot of the groups that have been working so hard on this bill have lost their stomach for it," said Tracy Mullin, chief executive officer of the National Retail Federation, which had lobbied furiously for the bill. Still, lobbyists said they would try again. ◆

House Votes to Boost FDIC Coverage

A string of bank failures and a steady erosion of deposit insurance reserves spurred efforts in both chambers to increase insurance coverage for depositors and make other changes to the nation's deposit insurance system. The House passed a bill by an overwhelming majority in May, but a companion Senate measure never got out of the Banking Committee.

The bills (HR 3717, S 1945) proposed to merge the two existing federal deposit insurance funds; increase deposit insurance coverage for individuals from $100,000 per account to $130,000, with future increases linked to inflation, and more than double coverage for individual retire-

BoxScore

Bills:
HR 3717, S 1945
Legislative Action:
House passed HR 3717 (H Rept 107-467), 408-18, on May 22.

ment accounts. To add stability to the deposit insurance funds, the Federal Deposit Insurance Corporation (FDIC) would be given authority to impose premiums on well-capitalized and well-managed banks that were not paying anything under the existing system.

Smaller banks wanted the increase in deposit insurance, hoping it would enable them to attract more depositors. But large banks, which were not as dependent on deposits as a source of lending capital, worried that increased coverage levels for depositors would lead to higher FDIC premiums for the banks.

Sponsors of the House bill — Michael G. Oxley, R-Ohio,

chairman of the Financial Services Committee, and Spencer Bachus, R-Ala., chairman of the Subcommittee on Financial Institutions and Credit — were able to win swift passage. But the Senate version, sponsored by Financial Institutions Subcommittee Chairman Tim Johnson, D-S.D., died in the full Banking, Housing and Urban Affairs Committee. The measure was not a priority for Banking Chairman Paul S. Sarbanes, D-Md., and was staunchly opposed by the panel's top Republican, Phil Gramm of Texas. "The $100,000 is a very high number," Gramm said of the existing coverage. "I think, with our agenda, this is a pretty low-priority item."

Background

The FDIC and the federal deposit insurance system were established in 1934 to stabilize the nation's banking system in the wake of a national run on banks and thrifts. Under the deposit insurance system, the federal government guarantees the funds of bank depositors in the event of a bank failure. Initially, the FDIC insured deposits up to $2,500. Congress periodically increased the limit, most recently in 1980 when the previous $40,000 limit was increased to $100,000 per account (PL 96-221). (*1980 Almanac, p. 275*)

In the late 1980s and early 1990s, Congress modified the deposit insurance system in response to the savings and loan crisis and bank failures. Among other things, Congress eliminated the separate agency that had insured savings and loans (the Federal Savings and Loan Insurance Corporation) and established two distinct insurance funds under the FDIC — the Bank Insurance Fund (BIF), which insured commercial banks, and the Savings Association Insurance Fund (SAIF), which did the same for thrifts.

The two funds were required by law to maintain reserves equal to $1.25 for every $100 in insured deposits. If the BIF fell below that level, premiums of up to 23 cents for every $100 of insured deposits would be assessed automatically on all banks — including well-capitalized, low-risk institutions — until the funds climbed above the reserve ratio. (*1989 Almanac, p. 117*)

In reality, both funds exceeded the legally required ratio; neither fund had dipped below it since 1996. The FDIC estimated that 92 percent of banks paid no premiums and that more than 900 institutions chartered since 1996 had never paid them. But the BIF ratio had been declining, both because of bank failures and because the uncertain stock market had led investors to shift funds into insured deposits.

Investment firms such as Merrill Lynch & Co. Inc. and Salomon Smith Barney Inc. were pouring money into insured bank deposit accounts. By spreading deposits among several of their affiliated banks, they were able to tout aggregate FDIC protection as high as $1 million. According to the FDIC, the two firms had swept a total of $73 billion into BIF-insured accounts between March 2000 and September 2001, automatically sending the FDIC's reserve ratio to about 1.32 percent, uncomfortably close to the 1.25 percent trigger level. The investment firms were among the institutions that paid no premiums.

Commercial banks did not like the idea that they would be required to bear part of the burden if the reserve ratio fell much further. The FDIC argued that the system was too

cyclical, with most banks paying too little in a healthy economy, then facing drastic premium assessments in a sour one when they could least afford to pay them. Even opponents of premium increases wanted some adjustments to avoid a sudden 23 basis point assessment when reserves dipped too low.

Highlights

The following are the major elements of both bills:
- **Deposit insurance coverage.** Both bills proposed to increase deposit insurance coverage from $100,000 per account to $130,000 and require future increases indexed to inflation every five years. This was the key provision for the smaller banks. Opponents said it would expose the insurance fund to greater losses and invite a flood of deposits that would reduce the ratio of fund reserves to insured deposits. The administration, the FDIC and the Federal Reserve all opposed raising the coverage limit.
- **Retirement account coverage.** The bills included increased coverage for certain types of retirement accounts, such as IRAs, 401(k)s and Keogh plans. The coverage would rise from $100,000 per account under existing law to $260,000 under the House bill and $250,000 under the Senate version.
- **Premium assessments.** The most contentious provision was a plan to eliminate the statutory 1.25 reserve ratio and allow the FDIC to establish an annual reserve ratio. The House bill specified that it be within a range of $1.15 to $1.40 for every $100 of insured deposits. The Senate bill included a range of $1.00 to $1.50 per $100 in deposits. The FDIC would be authorized to impose risk-based premium assessments on all banks and thrifts whenever deposit insurance fund balances declined below the threshold.
- **Merger of BIF and SAIF.** Perhaps the least controversial provision in both bills was a proposal to combine the two FDIC insurance funds. There was widespread agreement among federal regulators and the private sector that the separation was anachronistic after years of cross-pollination that had led to commingled ownership of banks and thrifts.
- **Municipal deposits.** Eighty percent of deposits held by in-state banks for local governments in excess of $130,000 would be insured, up to $2 million under the House-passed bill and up to $5 million under the Senate version.

Legislative Action

House Subcommittee Action

The bill won easy voice vote approval from the Financial Institutions and Credit Subcommittee on March 7. But opposition to increased coverage levels also was evident. Carolyn B. Maloney, D-N.Y., pointedly referred to March 6 letters from Treasury Secretary Paul H. O'Neill and Federal Reserve Chairman Alan Greenspan to John J. LaFalce of New York, ranking Democrat on the full committee, reiterating their opposition to raising the coverage level. "There is no evidence that an increase in the coverage level would promote competition or materially improve the ability of community banks to obtain funds," O'Neill wrote.

Bachus won voice vote approval for a manager's amendment that included provisions to allow the FDIC to set re-

serves at between 1.15 percent and 1.4 percent of insured deposits, rather than 1 percent and 1.5 percent under the original bill. Periodic indexing of insurance coverage was changed to every five years, rather than every 10. A new provision would allow the FDIC to impose a special assessment on financial institutions whose insured deposits grew "well in excess of industry averages." The provision was aimed at banks affiliated with the investment firms that were shifting billions of dollars of previously uninsured deposits into the system. "I, for one, feel there should not be any free riders," Bachus said.

The only other amendment was a proposal by Maxine Waters of California, the senior subcommittee Democrat, to allow a 50 percent premium discount to banks that offered "lifeline accounts" to low-income customers, based on the deposits held in those accounts. The amendment was adopted by voice vote.

House Committee Action

The full Financial Services Committee approved the bill (H Rept 107-467) by a vote of 52-2 on April 17. LaFalce scolded junior members for supporting the bill, saying they would face tough questions from constituents. "Why did you oppose the unanimous recommendation of the financial sector's regulators?" he asked. "What did you know that they didn't?"

In action on amendments, the committee:

• Adopted by voice vote an amendment by Richard H. Baker, R-La., to allow Congress to vote on periodic, inflation-based increases in deposit insurance coverage, rather than simply making them automatic. If Congress failed to act within a certain time, the increases would take effect. The amendment also would change the standard used to determine inflation-based increases from the Consumer Price Index to the Personal Consumption Expenditures Chain-Type Index.

• Adopted by voice vote an amendment by Bob Ney, R-Ohio, to change the criteria used by the FDIC to impose new fees on institutions with increased deposits.

• Rejected by voice vote a LaFalce amendment that would have required any coverage increase to be accom-panied by an increase in the reserve ratio if the FDIC determined that the coverage change would increase systemic risk.

• Rejected, 16-32, a LaFalce attempt to delete the bill's new treatment of municipal deposit insurance and instead call for a study of the possible effects of increasing municipal deposit insurance coverage.

• Rejected by voice vote a LaFalce proposal to restore the 1.25 percent standard used in determining when deposit insurance reserves were too low.

• Defeated by voice vote an amendment by Maloney that would have maintained the standard deposit insurance coverage level for individuals at $100,000, adjusted for inflation.

• Rejected, 23-34, an attempt by Eric Cantor, R-Va., to eliminate the provision added by Waters allowing a discount on premiums for institutions that offered "lifeline" accounts.

• Rejected by voice vote a Waters amendment to allow the FDIC to deny dividends and credits to institutions with low ratings or poor records in combating money laundering, or institutions under investigation by federal banking agencies for violations such as deceptive practices.

House Floor Action

The bill breezed through the House, 408-18, on May 22 under expedited procedures that barred amendments and required a two-thirds majority. *(House vote 190, p. H-64)*

Before bringing the bill to the floor, GOP leaders lowered, to $2 million from the original $5 million, a cap on partial insurance coverage for local government deposits greater than $130,000. They also dropped the provision that would have allowed the FDIC to charge extra premiums to banks that disproportionately add deposits to the system.

The Waters amendment giving premium discounts to banks that provided "lifeline" accounts boosted Democratic support for the bill. But some Republicans opposed it, agreeing to vote for the legislation only after receiving assurances that GOP leaders would press to drop the language in conference negotiations with the Senate.

With the Senate bill stuck in committee, the House leadership never had to make good on the promise. ◆

Chapter 6

BUDGET

Bush Budget Focuses on Security

President Bush submitted a $2.16 trillion fiscal 2003 budget to Congress on Feb. 4, with domestic security and the war on terrorism as his top priorities. To make room for substantial increases in those areas, the White House recommended freezing or cutting most domestic programs. Bush also called for $656 billion in tax cuts over 10 years, including making permanent the tax cuts enacted in 2001. He called for Congress to hold total discretionary spending — the money the appropriators would have available to allocate for fiscal 2003 — to $747 billion.

The Congressional Budget Office (CBO), Congress' official scorekeeper, did its own calculations in March, putting Bush's discretionary budget request at $759.1 billion. Both the White House and Congress agreed to use that number.

CBO projected that if all Bush's proposals were enacted, the government would run a deficit of $121 billion in fiscal 2003, returning to surplus in fiscal 2005. The agency projected a cumulative surplus of $681 billion over 10 years; without counting the Social Security surplus, however, the deficit would continue through that period. The White House's Office of Management and Budget (OMB), which prepares the president's budget, put the fiscal 2003 deficit at $80 billion, returning to surplus in 2005, with a cumulative surplus for fiscal 2003-12 of $1 trillion. A year earlier, both OMB and CBO were forecasting a $5.6 trillion surplus for fiscal 2002-11. *(Deficit, p. 6-13)*

With broad agreement on the need for military action abroad and stepped up security at home, lawmakers in both parties were left debating where to cut other accounts and whether to take the political risk of exceeding the president's overall total.

Opposition Democrats focused on the huge change in the long-term surplus forecasts, and on the return — possibly for years to come — of the practice of borrowing from the surpluses in the Social Security trust funds to pay for other government spending. "It just seems so eerily familiar," said Rep. James P. Moran, D-Va., recalling the Reagan administration. "We have a popular president again who's promising deep tax cuts, dramatic increases in defense spending, and yet he says that it's going to be OK, we're going to balance our budgets."

Although Democrats and many Republicans were unhappy with the austerity of Bush's domestic budget, they were hemmed in by their support for the president's war efforts, their reluctance to push the country deeper into deficit and the constraints imposed by a weak economy. At the ideological extremes, fiscal conservatives wanted to clamp down even harder on domestic spending, while a handful of liberal Democrats favored delaying or repealing the 2001 tax cuts (PL 107-16). Other Democrats and even some Republicans

wanted to trade some of the defense spending sought by Bush for more spending on domestic programs such as highway construction, education and job training. But the White House warned lawmakers not to try tapping the Pentagon or homeland security budgets to fund domestic priorities. "We'll resist that, and I think pretty strongly," warned OMB Director Mitchell E. Daniels Jr.

Spending Priorities

The following are major elements of Bush's Feb. 4 budget:
- **Defense.** According to CBO calculations, the budget called for $392.8 billion in discretionary spending for defense, including a $10 billion "war reserve" for combating terrorism in Afghanistan and elsewhere. That was a jump of $45 billion, or 13 percent, over the fiscal 2002 level. Most of the funds were under the Defense appropriations bill, but the request also covered military construction, as well as nuclear weapons programs under the energy and water spending bill. It included a 4.1 percent increase in military pay, funding for upgraded weapons systems and $7.8 billion for development of a ballistic missile defense system.
- **Non-defense programs.** Bush requested a 1 percent increase in non-defense discretionary spending, to $366.3 billion, but that became a 1 percent decrease when the homeland security component was removed. Increases proposed for a few accounts — such as foreign operations, veterans' medical care, the Coast Guard and airport security — meant even sharper reductions for other programs. Bush recommended cuts in programs related to agriculture, commerce, community and regional development, the administration of justice, natural resources and the environment, along with less-than-inflation increases in other areas such as energy.

John M. Spratt Jr. of South Carolina, top Democrat on the House Budget Committee, said the administration's budget was $15.8 billion short of the amount needed to maintain the existing level of government services, exclud-

Bush's Budget Totals

The president's fiscal 2003 budget proposed $2.16 trillion in new spending, or budget authority. Actual outlays from the Treasury, including spending approved in previous years, would total $2.13 trillion. In fiscal 2002 through 2004, the administration forecast outlays to exceed revenues, with resulting budget deficits.

(fiscal years, in billions of dollars)

	Estimated	Proposed				
	2002	2003	2004	2005	2006	2007
Budget authority	$2,085.0	$2,162.9	$2,210.2	$2,309.7	$2,414.7	$2,529.0
Outlays	2,052.3	2,128.2	2,189.1	2,276.9	2,369.1	2,467.7
Revenues	1,946.1	2,048.1	2,175.4	2,338.0	2,455.3	2,571.7
BALANCE	−106.2	−80.1	−13.7	61.1	86.2	104.0

SOURCE: Office of Management and Budget

Proposals by Appropriations Panel

Bush's fiscal 2003 requests for discretionary budget authority, in billions of dollars, for programs under the jurisdiction of the 13 House and Senate Appropriations subcommittees.

	2001 Enacted	2002 Estimate	2003 Proposed	Change 2002-03
Agriculture	$ 16.7	$ 16.9	$ 17.2	$ 0.3
Commerce, Justice, State	39.7	40.5	41.2	0.7
Defense	296.6	320.5	360.4	40.0
District of Columbia	0.5	0.4	0.4	< 0.05
Energy and water development	24.4	24.8	25.3	0.5
Foreign operations	14.6	15.5	16.1	0.7
Interior	19.5	19.6	19.5	– 0.1
Labor, HHS, Education	110.5	124.6	131.2	6.6
Legislative branch	2.8	3.1	3.5	0.4
Military construction	9.1	10.5	9.0	–1.6
Transportation	17.8	16.4	19.7	3.3
Treasury, Postal Service	16.7	17.9	18.7	0.9
VA, HUD, NASA and EPA	81.7	85.8	93.5	7.7
Allowances	—	—	– 0.4	– 0.4
Emergency Response Fund *	20.0	20.0	10.0	– 10.0
Less effects of altering allocation of federal retiree benefit costs	– 8.1	– 8.5	– 9.0	– 0.4
TOTALS	**$662.6**	**$707.9**	**$756.5**	**$48.5**

* The fiscal 2001 and 2002 amounts reflect the supplemental appropriations (PL 107-38) enacted Sept. 18.
NOTE: Figures may not add due to rounding   SOURCE: President's fiscal 2003 budget

ing defense and homeland security.

• **Homeland security.** Bush requested $36 billion in discretionary budget authority for homeland security programs, including border security, protecting against biological attacks, and grants to state and local police and firefighters. Of the total, $10 billion was for defense, about $8 billion for the Department of Transportation, more than $7 billion for the Department of Justice, more than $4 billion for the Department of Health and Human Services, and $3.5 billion for the Federal Emergency Management Agency.

The White House calculated that $27 billion in discretionary spending had been appropriated for homeland security in fiscal 2002 — $18 billion in the regular spending bills and $8 billion in the emergency supplemental (PL 107-117) enacted Jan. 10. (*2001 Almanac, p. 2-59*)

Appropriators from both parties were dismayed at some of Bush's domestic proposals. Beyond the cuts in favorite programs, they were stung by a new feature in the fiscal 2003 budget: special sections in many chapters complaining about congressional earmarks. They were particularly incensed over a proposal to rescind $1.3 billion in earmarks added to the fiscal 2002 Labor-HHS-Education spending bill (PL 107-116) and use that money to cover a shortfall in the popular Pell Grant program. "Unless the Constitution is amended," House Appropriations Committee Chairman C.W. Bill Young, R-Fla., wrote in a Feb. 6 letter to OMB, "Congress will continue to exercise its discretion over feder-

al funds and will earmark those funds for purposes we deem appropriate."

Another administration proposal — to shift the costs of some retirement benefits from the mandatory to the discretionary side of the ledger — was a non-starter on Capitol Hill. It would have meant that benefits previously paid directly by the Treasury would instead soak up part of the discretionary spending available for each appropriations bill — a total of about $9 billion in 2003, according to CBO.

CBO dropped the $9 billion when it recalculated the president's budget at $759.1 billion. The House followed suit, adopting a fiscal 2003 budget resolution (H Con Res 353) that gave appropriators $759 billion in discretionary spending to allocate among the 13 bills. The Senate Budget Committee also ignored the accounting proposal, but instead of dropping the $9 billion, it added it to the pot of discretionary money available to the appropriators, bringing the Senate total to $768 billion. The difference was never settled. (*Budget resolution, p. 6-8*)

Proposed Tax Cuts

As calculated by the Joint Committee on Taxation, which provides the tax numbers used by Congress and CBO, Bush's budget called for $602 billion in tax cuts in 2003 through 2012. An additional $80 billion in proposed tax credits brought the total to $682 billion. The biggest item in the package was $353 billion over 10 years to extend the 2001 tax cuts. Other elements included:

• $68 billion over 10 years for a package of health care incentives, including a refundable tax credit to enable certain uninsured people to purchase health insurance, a deduction for long-term care insurance premiums, and allowing families to claim a personal exemption for ill or disabled persons living with them.

• $62 billion in 2002 and $65 billion in 2003 for tax cuts as part of an economic stimulus plan. The 10-year cost was estimated at $44 billion.

• $9.1 billion over 10 years in tax incentives for energy production and conservation, including tax credits for alternative electricity production, the purchase of fuel-efficient vehicles and energy production from landfills.

• $4.2 billion over 10 years for an education tax credit, including credits of up to $2,500 to families that transferred their children from failing public schools to better-performing private schools.

Economic Assumptions

The president's budget was based on economic assumptions that included a powerful economic rebound in 2003.
(*Continued on p. 6-8*)

Bush's Fiscal 2003 Proposal by Agency

A breakdown, in millions of dollars per fiscal year, as it would apply to the individual departments of the federal government.

	BUDGET AUTHORITY			OUTLAYS		
	2001 Actual	2002 Estimate	2003 Proposed	2001 Actual	2002 Estimate	2003 Proposed
Legislative Branch	$3,326	$3,706	$3,874	$3,135	$3,625	$3,970
The Judiciary	4,597	5,052	5,592	4,519	4,977	5,497
Agriculture	73,664	76,509	75,796	68,599	76,565	74,443
Commerce	5,301	5,468	5,449	5,137	5,495	5,670
Defense-Military	312,979	332,994	378,622	293,995	330,553	360,989
Education	39,955	55,330	56,498	35,748	47,587	53,800
Energy	17,849	19,215	19,892	16,490	19,093	19,784
Health and Human Services	435,337	468,454	491,854	426,767	459,366	488,794
Housing and Urban Development	32,425	34,326	35,043	33,994	30,948	34,600
Interior	9,965	10,721	10,589	8,249	10,290	10,822
Justice	22,459	26,294	27,060	21,296	23,073	29,385
Labor	44,090	59,375	56,498	39,367	58,579	56,554
State	8,409	9,481	9,828	7,524	11,132	9,883
Transportation	67,136	64,373	63,079	54,838	60,788	58,843
Treasury	392,848	383,062	399,418	390,569	382,616	398,188
Veterans Affairs	48,237	51,663	56,568	45,839	51,451	56,513
Corps of Engineers	4,813	4,753	4,151	4,834	4,975	4,347
Other Defense-Civil Programs	34,375	35,660	41,045	34,167	35,537	40,933
Environmental Protection Agency	7,724	7,995	7,538	7,490	7,790	8,061
Executive Office of the President	13,314	336	337	254	464	334
FEMA	4,894	7,312	6,174	4,426	5,789	7,550
General Services Administration	479	641	241	−1	586	−52
International Assistance Programs	11,387	12,175	12,891	11,792	13,287	12,969
NASA	14,361	15,013	15,118	14,199	14,484	14,885
National Science Foundation	4,553	4,930	5,177	3,696	4,564	4,886
Office of Personnel Management	53,169	56,321	68,730	50,919	54,277	67,940
Small Business Administration	−48	1,197	800	−550	1,073	587
Social Security Administration						
(On-budget)	43,870	44,737	47,341	40,614	46,922	48,034
(Off-budget)	428,825	447,410	462,634	421,412	445,749	461,621
Other Independent Agencies						
(On-budget)	14,721	18,272	17,545	11,650	17,952	18,706
(Off-budget)	4,064	2,813	5,154	2,302	2,015	−1,448
Allowances		25,724	7,600		27,000	6,356
Undistributed offsetting receipts	−199,344	−206,282	−235,214	−199,344	−206,282	−235,214
(On-budget)	(−122,623)	(−120,217)	(−141,801)	(−122,623)	(−120,217)	(−141,801)
(Off-budget)	(−76,721)	(−86,065)	(−93,413)	(−76,721)	(−86,065)	(−93,413)
TOTALS	**$1,959,734**	**$2,085,030**	**$2,162,922**	**$1,863,926**	**$2,052,320**	**$2,128,230**

Figures may not add due to rounding.
SOURCE: President's fiscal 2003 budget

Bush's Fiscal 2003 Proposal by Function

A breakdown, in millions of dollars per fiscal year, of governmental spending categories that cross agency lines.

	BUDGET AUTHORITY			OUTLAYS		
	2001 Actual	2002 Estimate	2003 Proposed	2001 Actual	2002 Estimate	2003 Proposed
NATIONAL DEFENSE						
Department of Defense — military	$312,979	$332,994	$378,622	$293,995	$330,553	$360,989
Atomic energy defense activities	14,416	16,009	16,458	13,037	15,863	16,294
Defense-related activities	1,630	1,719	1,721	1,501	1,570	1,729
Total, National defense	**$329,025**	**$350,722**	**$396,801**	**$308,533**	**$347,986**	**$379,012**
INTERNATIONAL AFFAIRS						
International development and humanitarian assistance	7,715	7,993	8,685	7,208	7,713	8,596
International security assistance	5,668	6,110	6,581	6,560	7,548	6,660
Conduct of foreign affairs	6,327	7,064	7,285	5,127	8,674	7,240
Foreign information and exchange activities	881	820	840	816	904	914
International financial programs	−1,928	286	485	−3,110	−1,319	−943
Total, International affairs	**$18,663**	**$22,273**	**$23,876**	**$16,601**	**$23,520**	**$22,467**
GENERAL SCIENCE, SPACE AND TECHNOLOGY						
General science and basic research	7,708	8,102	8,394	6,566	7,765	8,093
Space flight, research and supporting activities	13,424	14,077	14,280	13,330	13,994	14,075
Total, General science, space and technology	**$21,132**	**$22,179**	**$22,674**	**$19,896**	**$21,759**	**$22,168**
ENERGY						
Energy supply	−1,084	−768	−944	−1,100	−707	−867
Energy conservation	810	916	905	763	831	897
Emergency energy preparedness	150	180	189	160	173	190
Energy information, policy and regulation	292	284	368	266	264	346
Total, Energy	**$168**	**$612**	**$518**	**$89**	**$561**	**$566**
NATURAL RESOURCES AND ENVIRONMENT						
Water resources	5,502	5,582	4,926	5,377	5,962	5,277
Conservation and land management	9,164	9,512	9,922	7,489	9,151	9,662
Recreational resources	3,024	3,098	3,074	2,331	2,956	3,174
Pollution control and abatement	7,899	8,155	7,698	7,661	7,958	8,227
Other natural resources	4,171	4,516	4,347	3,477	4,211	4,261
Total, Natural resources and environment	**$29,760**	**$30,863**	**$29,967**	**$26,335**	**$30,238**	**$30,601**
AGRICULTURE						
Farm income stabilization	25,054	24,746	19,633	22,761	24,578	19,887
Agricultural research and services	4,187	4,243	4,180	3,792	4,252	4,339
Total, Agriculture	**$29,241**	**$28,989**	**$23,813**	**$26,553**	**$28,830**	**$24,226**
COMMERCE AND HOUSING CREDIT						
Mortgage credit	1,963	−514	296	−1,138	−6,654	−4,799
Postal Service	4,157	3,409	5,231	2,395	2,786	−1,371
(On-budget)	(93)	(596)	(77)	(93)	(771)	(77)
(Off-budget)	(4,064)	(2,813)	(5,154)	(2,302)	(2,015)	(−1,448)
Deposit insurance	1	1	1	−1,413	218	1,349
Other advancement of commerce	6,311	7,761	8,557	6,186	7,414	8,521
Total, Commerce and housing credit	**$12,432**	**$10,657**	**$14,085**	**$6,030**	**$3,764**	**$3,700**
(On-budget)	(8,368)	(7,844)	(8,931)	(3,728)	(1,749)	(5,148)
(Off-budget)	(4,064)	(2,813)	(5,154)	(2,302)	(2,015)	(−1,448)
TRANSPORTATION						
Ground transportation	44,040	43,989	39,786	35,843	37,630	36,757
Air transportation	18,395	16,461	18,806	14,367	18,932	17,973
Water transportation	4,890	5,446	5,113	4,731	5,331	4,701
Other transportation	252	229	23	279	237	18
Total, Transportation	**$67,577**	**$66,125**	**$63,728**	**$55,220**	**$62,130**	**$59,449**
COMMUNITY AND REGIONAL DEVELOPMENT						
Community development	5,859	7,587	5,544	5,319	5,923	6,815
Area and regional development	3,360	3,039	2,827	2,807	3,068	2,909
Disaster relief and insurance	4,684	7,906	6,370	3,851	6,374	7,665
Total, Community and regional development	**$13,903**	**$18,532**	**$14,741**	**$11,977**	**$15,365**	**$17,389**
EDUCATION, TRAINING, EMPLOYMENT, AND SOCIAL SERVICES						
Elementary, secondary and vocational education	26,047	32,929	34,505	22,867	27,044	32,194
Higher education	10,477	19,110	18,845	9,578	16,767	18,394
Research and general education aids	3,201	2,899	2,893	2,827	3,334	2,989
Training and employment	7,801	7,620	6,908	7,200	8,147	8,009
Other labor services	1,513	1,604	1,583	1,336	1,563	1,769
Social services	14,670	15,420	16,148	13,494	14,842	15,668
Total, Educ., training, employment and social services	**$63,709**	**$79,582**	**$80,882**	**$57,302**	**$71,697**	**$79,023**

	BUDGET AUTHORITY			OUTLAYS		
	2001 Actual	2002 Estimate	2003 Proposed	2001 Actual	2002 Estimate	2003 Proposed
HEALTH						
Health care services	157,832	173,540	203,201	152,053	170,600	204,386
Health research and training	21,583	24,493	28,070	18,021	21,724	24,518
Consumer and occupational health and safety	2,658	3,006	3,027	2,560	2,913	3,031
Total, Health	**$182,073**	**$201,039**	**$234,298**	**$172,634**	**$195,237**	**$231,935**
MEDICARE						
Medicare	217,176	230,338	234,467	217,464	226,395	234,361
INCOME SECURITY						
General retirement and disability insurance	6,882	6,538	6,374	5,777	5,223	5,278
Federal employee retirement and disability	82,537	86,513	91,176	80,978	84,993	89,783
Unemployment compensation	32,694	47,291	43,429	30,242	47,368	43,429
Housing assistance	25,144	27,546	29,423	30,110	32,085	32,875
Food and nutrition assistance	35,039	38,937	42,461	34,062	38,838	40,932
Other income security	91,128	99,347	106,466	88,601	102,226	107,383
Total, Income security	**$273,424**	**$306,172**	**$319,329**	**$269,770**	**$310,733**	**$319,680**
SOCIAL SECURITY						
Social Security	440,543	461,322	476,938	433,129	459,662	475,925
(On-budget)	(11,718)	(13,912)	(14,304)	(11,717)	(13,913)	(14,304)
(Off-budget)	(428,825)	(447,410)	(462,634)	(421,412)	(445,749)	(461,621)
VETERANS' BENEFITS AND SERVICES						
Income security for veterans	24,435	26,079	27,687	22,464	26,004	27,561
Veterans' education, training and rehabilitation	1,662	1,940	2,195	1,247	2,029	2,511
Hospital and medical care for veterans	21,655	23,026	24,528	21,683	22,849	24,336
Veterans' housing	−914	−871	516	−917	−919	519
Other veterans' benefits and services	1,529	1,576	1,678	1,351	1,564	1,655
Total, Veterans' benefits and services	**$48,367**	**$51,750**	**$56,604**	**$45,828**	**$51,527**	**$56,582**
ADMINISTRATION OF JUSTICE						
Federal law enforcement activities	26,570	16,175	16,048	12,470	15,288	15,566
Federal litigative and judicial activities	8,684	10,479	12,264	8,497	10,547	12,409
Federal correctional activities	4,416	4,745	5,994	4,318	4,320	6,211
Criminal justice assistance	5,354	5,863	3,932	5,158	4,287	6,433
Total, Administration of justice	**$45,024**	**$37,262**	**$38,238**	**$30,443**	**$34,442**	**$40,619**
GENERAL GOVERNMENT						
Legislative functions	2,509	2,993	3,121	3,394	3,067	3,290
Executive direction and management	510	579	591	465	614	580
Central fiscal operations	9,862	10,416	10,884	9,657	10,519	10,772
General property and records management	783	966	798	210	993	537
Central personnel management	180	192	223	194	195	222
General purpose fiscal assistance	2,473	2,498	2,041	2,308	2,542	2,075
Other general government	2,123	1,470	1,597	1,814	1,770	1,587
Deductions for offsetting receipts	−1,889	−1,438	−1,431	−1,889	−1,438	−1,431
Total, General government	**$16,551**	**$17,676**	**$17,824**	**$15,153**	**$18,262**	**$17,632**
NET INTEREST						
Interest on Treasury debt securities (gross)	359,507	338,833	353,078	359,507	338,833	353,078
Interest received by on-budget trust funds	−75,302	−74,287	−77,245	−75,302	−74,287	−77,245
Interest received by off-budget trust funds	−68,811	−76,822	−83,849	−68,811	−76,822	−83,849
Other interest	−9,198	−8,964	−10,541	−9,195	−8,965	−10,541
Other investment income	0	−802	−802	0	−374	−784
Total, Net interest	**$206,196**	**$178,386**	**$180,659**	**$206,199**	**$178,385**	**$180,659**
(On-budget)	(275,007)	(255,208)	(264,508)	(275,010)	(255,207)	(264,508)
(Off-budget)	(−68,811)	(−76,822)	(−83,849)	(−68,811)	(−76,822)	(−83,849)
Total, Allowances	**$0**	**$1,092**	**$−417**	**$0**	**$27,000**	**$6,356**
Total, Undistributed offsetting receipts	**$−55,230**	**$−55,173**	**$−74,120**	**$−55,230**	**$−55,173**	**$−74,120**
(On-budget)	(−47,320)	(−45,930)	(−64,556)	(−47,320)	(−45,930)	(−64,556)
(Off-budget)	(−7,910)	(−9,243)	(−9,564)	(−7,910)	(−9,243)	(−9,564)
TOTALS	**$1,959,734**	**$2,085,030**	**$2,162,922**	**$1,863,926**	**$2,052,320**	**$2,128,230**
(On-budget)	(1,603,566)	(1,720,872)	(1,788,547)	(1,516,933)	(1,690,621)	(1,761,470)
(Off-budget)	(356,168)	(364,158)	(374,375)	(346,993)	(361,699)	(366,760)

Figures may not add due to rounding.
SOURCE: President's fiscal 2003 budget

Economic Forecasts Compared

	2002	2003	2004	2005	2006	2007
Real GDP growth (*chain-weighted*)						
OMB	0.7%	3.8%	3.7%	3.6%	3.2%	3.1%
CBO	0.8	4.1	3.7	3.2	3.2	3.2
Blue Chip	1.0	3.4	3.4	3.3	3.2	3.1
Inflation (*CPI*)						
OMB	1.8	2.2	2.3	2.4	2.4	2.4
CBO	1.8	2.5	2.5	2.5	2.5	2.5
Blue Chip	1.7	2.4	2.6	2.7	2.7	2.7
Unemployment						
OMB	5.9	5.5	5.2	5.0	4.9	4.9
CBO	6.1	5.9	5.4	5.2	5.2	5.2
Blue Chip	6.1	5.7	4.9	4.9	4.8	4.9
91-Day Treasury bills						
OMB	2.2	3.5	4.0	4.3	4.3	4.3
CBO	2.2	4.5	4.9	4.9	4.9	4.9
Blue Chip	2.1	3.4	4.5	4.7	4.8	4.8
10-Year Treasury notes						
OMB	5.1	5.1	5.1	5.1	5.2	5.2
CBO	5.0	5.5	5.8	5.8	5.8	5.8
Blue Chip	5.1	5.6	5.7	5.7	5.7	5.8

This comparison of the forecasts of the White House's Office of Management and Budget (OMB), the Congressional Budget Office (CBO) and the "Blue Chip" consensus of private economists uses year-over-year percentage change in inflation-adjusted gross domestic product (GDP) and the Consumer Price Index (CPI). The unemployment rate and the T-bill and T-note interest rates are annual averages. The OMB forecast assumes enactment of the president's budget and therefore is not strictly comparable with those of CBO and the Blue Chip.

SOURCE: President's fiscal 2003 budget

While CBO had predicted an even more optimistic 4.1 percent growth rate in January, it reduced that to 3.4 percent in March. Higher growth boosts tax collections.

OMB had somewhat more optimistic views of inflation, unemployment, interest rates and corporate profits in 2003 than either CBO or the "Blue Chip" group of private forecasters. OMB also assumed enactment of an economic stimulus bill that added 0.5 percent to its predictions of economic growth. (*Chart, this page*)

Subsequent Requests

In the months that followed release of the budget, Bush added a number of specific requests for fiscal 2003 spending, including $200 million to help Israel fight terrorism, $200 million for AIDS prevention overseas, $546 million for the Transportation Security Administration, and $50 million in humanitarian aid for the West Bank and Gaza Strip. Congress had provided comparable funding in the fiscal 2002 supplemental spending law (PL 107-206), but it was part of $5.1 billion in "contingent emergency" funds that Bush decided not to spend. (*Supplemental, p. 2-40*)

Other subsequent requests included $800 million for firefighting and $366 million for the Energy Department. The administration said all the funding should come out of the $759 billion in fiscal 2003 discretionary spending envisioned by the House-adopted budget resolution, but the White House did not suggest what should be cut. ◆

(*Continued from p. 6-4*)
OMB's assumptions fell within the boundaries of Wall Street's forecasts, particularly the more optimistic ones. OMB predicted economic growth of 3.8 percent in 2003.

A Year With No Budget Resolution

With both parties focused on sharpening their differences in advance of the November elections — and no compromise in sight on overall spending — Congress failed to produce a fiscal 2003 budget resolution. It was only the second time since the modern budget process was created in 1974 that the House and Senate had been unable to agree on a common set of numbers to guide their spending and tax decisions. It signaled a breakdown in the budget process that would stop Congress from clearing any of the fiscal 2003 non-defense spending bills, forcing a lame-duck session and, ultimately, a continuing resolution to keep the government going into 2003. (*Appropriations, p. 2-3*)

The chief sticking point was discretionary spending — the amount available to appropriators for the 13 regular fiscal 2003 spending bills. GOP leaders steered a budget resolution (H Con Res 353) through the House in March that reflected President Bush's demand for a $759 billion discretionary limit. In the Senate, Democrats pushed a budget plan (S Con Res 100) with a $768 billion limit through the Budget Committee, but they lacked the votes to prevail in the full Senate and never brought the measure to the floor. Though the two chambers were only $9 billion apart, it was enough to produce gridlock.

Appropriators in both chambers agreed that the $768 billion Senate figure was the minimum necessary to ensure that they could muster majorities for the 13 fiscal 2003 bills, especially given the extra expenses for the war on ter-

rorism and homeland security. But Bush held firm, warning April 16 that he would veto domestic spending bills that exceeded his limit, and House Republican leaders refused to budge.

Adding to the disarray, budget enforcement laws that had helped restrain spending increases and tax cuts since 1990 were set to expire Sept. 30, and lawmakers were unwilling to extend them without a budget agreement. "We don't have budget numbers, we don't have enforcement mechanisms," lamented Senate Minority Leader Trent Lott, R-Miss., before the August recess.

While lawmakers knew a budget deal would help them adjourn the 107th Congress early enough for a few weeks of uninterrupted campaigning, they also knew that recent elections had not been good to politicians who took bold action to combat the deficit. President George Bush lost his 1992 re-election bid after breaking his "read my lips" promise and backing a tax increase in the name of curbing a record deficit. Democrats lost control of Congress in 1994 after enacting President Bill Clinton's tax-heavy deficit reduction package. *(1992 Almanac, p. 3-A; 1994 Almanac, p. 561)*

BoxScore

Bills:

H Con Res 353, S Con Res 100

Legislative Action:

House passed H Con Res 353 (H Rept 107-376), 221-209, on March 20.

Senate Budget Committee approved S Con Res 100 (S Rept 107-141), 12-10, on March 21.

keep its overall total about $5 billion below the president's, to $2.158 trillion, by making small trims to a number of mandatory programs. The move carried no enforcement weight, and the authorizing committees were expected to ignore it. But it allowed Republicans to argue that the budget would be in balance, at least by their accounting, were it not for a package of unemployment and tax benefits (PL 107-147) enacted in March. In other words, Democrats shared responsibility for a $45.6 billion deficit projection for fiscal 2003.

While praising Bush's conduct of the war on terrorism and pledging full support for his defense budget, Democrats attacked the proposed cuts in domestic spending and charged that Republicans were setting the country up for massive deficits. They presented no plan of their own, however, instead offering amendments to increase funding for various domestic programs in the GOP budget. Republicans cited that as further evidence that Democrats were not serious about reining in deficits.

Legislative Action

House Committee Action

After rejecting numerous Democratic amendments, Republicans on the House Budget Committee united March 13 to approve a budget resolution (H Con Res 353 — H Rept 107-376) that closely tracked Bush's request. The vote was 23-17.

The resolution included a discretionary spending limit of $759 billion, a 7 percent increase over fiscal 2002. That was the amount the Congressional Budget Office (CBO) calculated would be required to pay for the president's budget proposals. Most of the increase — $45.1 billion — was for the military, which was slated to get $392.7 billion under the House plan, including a $10 billion contingency fund requested by Bush for anti-terrorism efforts. That left $366.3 billion for non-defense spending, most of it for domestic programs. The committee ignored an administration request for an additional $9 billion in discretionary funds to pay for a proposal to shift certain federal retiree benefit costs from the mandatory to the discretionary part of the ledger.

The House resolution called for $28 billion in additional tax cuts over five years but did not instruct committees to prepare a "reconciliation" bill to make such changes.

Republicans made a few other changes to Bush's request, for example, boosting funds for a 10-year Medicare drug benefit and Medicare modernization plan to $350 billion, $190 billion more than Bush sought. Democrats said the total was still inadequate. The resolution also exceeded Bush's requests for transportation by $1.2 billion and for veterans programs by $1.1 billion.

Even with those additions, the committee was able to

House Floor Action

The House adopted the budget March 20 by a mostly party-line vote of 221-209, after GOP leaders headed off a potential revolt by Armed Services Committee members. *(House vote 79, p. H-30)*

The defense hawks wanted guarantees that their committee would have influence over the $10 billion reserve requested by Bush to conduct the war on terrorism; they said the Pentagon needed the money immediately for infrastructure improvements. But lawmakers such as Duncan Hunter, R-Calif., backed off after being shuttled to the White House to meet with Bush, who promised to add more military modernization funds to his fiscal 2002 supplemental appropriations request. *(Supplemental, p. 2-40)*

Democrats were angry because the GOP-controlled Rules Committee allowed no floor amendments. But Republicans said the Democrats had offered no comprehensive budget of their own and should not be able to simply fire off amendments attacking the GOP plan. "The Democrats took a walk," said John E. Sununu, R-N.H.

John M. Spratt Jr. of South Carolina, top Democrat on the Budget Committee, said fiscal conditions made it impossible to produce a budget plan that Democrats could feel comfortable with. "Frankly, we tried to produce a budget resolution, and we found . . . we would have to use the gimmicks and the devices the other side used," he said.

Senate Committee Action

The Democratic-controlled Senate Budget Committee approved its budget resolution (S Con Res 100 — S Rept 107-141) on a party-line vote of 12-10 on March 21. Signaling trouble ahead, however, some Democrats, including Russell D. Feingold of Wisconsin and Ernest F. Hollings of South Carolina, said they would not support the budget on the floor. With only a one-vote margin in the Senate, Dem-

ocrats could not afford to lose a single Democratic vote.

On the key issue of fiscal 2003 discretionary spending, Chairman Kent Conrad, D-N.D., proposed a $768.1 billion limit — $392.8 billion for defense and $375.3 billion for non-defense accounts. The chief difference came on the domestic side, where Conrad's plan exceeded the House resolution by $9 billion. Conrad ignored Bush's proposal to convert federal employee benefits into discretionary spending, instead leaving the retirement accounts to be funded by mandatory spending as before. But while the House had left out the $9 billion Bush requested to pay for the shift, Conrad took the money and used it to restore cuts proposed by Bush in domestic programs.

Republicans criticized the move, but a senior aide acknowledged that a draft GOP plan — which was not offered at the markup — would have recommended about as much appropriated spending as Conrad's.

Although the Democrats' resolution assumed no change in Bush's 2001 tax cuts, it included a trigger that would have required the committee to produce a five-year balanced-budget plan for fiscal 2004 without using Social Security funds if CBO determined that the government was borrowing from Social Security surpluses to fund other programs. Zell Miller, D-Ga., an early and enthusiastic supporter of the 2001 tax cut, cried foul. "It looks to me like you're in effect doing away with the tax cut," he said.

The most substantive debate concerned the question of extending budget enforcement caps on appropriations. Caps had been in place since 1990, and the most recent version, set in the 1997 budget law (PL 105-33), was to expire Oct. 1. While the caps routinely were breached in times of surplus, they had proven useful in the past in enforcing deficit reduction.

The committee rejected, on an 11-11 tie, an amendment by Judd Gregg, R-N.H., and Feingold to set new discretionary caps for the following five years. Proposals that exceeded the caps would have been subject to a point of order that took 60 votes to overcome. The amendment was opposed by Conrad and by Appropriations Chairman Robert C. Byrd, D-W.Va., who also sat on the Budget panel. Byrd objected to what he saw as an assault on the ap-propriators' authority.

The committee also rejected, by a party-line 10-12 vote, a GOP amendment that would have fully funded the president's defense spending request for fiscal 2005 through 2012. The resolution as approved put $244.6 billion requested for defense during those years into a special fund that could be used either for that purpose or for debt reduction.

Treating the defense money as a reserve, as well as proposing to freeze existing tax law, allowed Conrad to claim his budget would provide more than the president's for education, transportation and health care while paying down more debt. He said it would reduce the national debt held by the public by $1.16 trillion — to a new total of $2.36 trillion — in fiscal 2012, compared with $2.89 trillion that would remain under Bush's budget.

Fallout for Appropriations

With general agreement on the total for defense, Congress was able to clear two fiscal 2003 appropriations bills — for the Defense Department (PL 107-248) and for military construction (PL 107-249).

The remaining 11 bills — covering the departments of Agriculture, Commerce, Education, Energy, Interior, Health and Human Services, Housing and Urban Development, Justice, Labor, State, Treasury, Transportation and Veterans Affairs, as well as foreign operations, the legislative branch, the District of Columbia and myriad agencies — never cleared. Instead, those agencies were funded at fiscal 2002 levels under a series of continuing resolutions, the last of which (PL 107-294) was good until Jan. 11, 2003.

Appropriators said they simply did not have enough money. The House, where GOP leaders insisted appropriators live within limits set by the president's budget, passed only three of the non-defense bills. Although Senate appropriators had an additional $9 billion to work with, they still had trouble writing bills that could satisfy enough members to prevail in the closely divided chamber. The legislative branch bill (HR 5121) was the only one of the non-defense spending measures to pass the Senate. ◆

Congress Raises Borrowing Ceiling

To the immense relief of the Bush administration, the House cleared a bill June 27 raising the legal limit on the federal debt by $450 billion, to $6.4 trillion. President Bush signed the bill the following day (S 2578 — PL 107-199), and the Treasury Department immediately announced plans to resume debt auctions.

The return of federal deficits had put Bush and congressional Republicans, who regularly castigated Democrats as big spenders, in the uncomfortable position of leading the drive for a debt increase. Treasury had said the ceiling on the accumulated debt had to be increased by June 28 to allow new government borrowing. Otherwise, the government risked defaulting on U.S. securities, halting the payment of Social Security and Medicare benefits and interrupting government operations, including the battle against terrorism. "If it hadn't been increased," Treasury Secretary Paul H. O'Neill said afterward, "it would have put us in the position of defaulting on the full faith and credit of the U.S., or in the alternative, using potentially fraudulent accounting devices to paper over a lack of action by the Congress."

O'Neill had begun asking Congress in December 2001 to increase the debt ceiling to $6.7 trillion. The administration repeated its request for a $750 billion increase throughout the spring of 2002.

But House Republicans wanted to avoid an up-or-down vote on a debt increase. GOP leaders repeatedly postponed

floor action, hoping instead to attach the measure to the fiscal 2002 anti-terrorism supplemental spending bill (HR 4775 — PL 107-206), which would have allowed them to portray the debt increase as an unforeseen consequence of the Sept. 11 terrorist attacks.

For their part, Democrats saw the must-pass debt increase as a chance to paint Republicans as fiscally irresponsible — with particular emphasis on Bush's $1.35 trillion, 10-year tax cut (PL 107-16) enacted in 2001. Senate Majority Leader Tom Daschle, D-S.D., would not acquiesce in attaching the debt increase to the supplemental. In the House, Minority Leader Richard A. Gephardt, D-Mo., offered little comfort. He said Republicans who voted for the Bush tax cut should bear the political burden now. "If you order the meal, you pay the bill," he said June 12.

The delays forced O'Neill to engage in the same kind of short-term accounting methods that Republicans had lambasted Clinton administration Treasury Secretary Robert E. Rubin for using when he sought to avoid default in 1995-96.

In late March, Treasury reduced the number of bonds it normally auctioned in an attempt to stay under the debt ceiling until the influx of income tax receipts after April 15. In April, O'Neill temporarily suspended investment in the Government Securities Investment Fund, or G-Fund, a kind of 401(k) program for federal employees. Treasury also redeemed some government assets in the Civil Service Retirement and Disability Trust Fund, which funds the pensions of federal workers. In both cases, the Treasury supplied IOUs to be replaced, with interest, when the debt crunch eased. That created enough extra borrowing authority to allow the government to meet the April federal payroll and pay Social Security, Medicare, Medicaid and other mandatory government obligations.

The April 15 cash flow temporarily eased the situation, but officials insisted they were running out of room to maneuver. On May 1, Treasury said that without congressional action the debt limit would be breached by late June, when payments to several trust funds, including Social Security, were due.

With the House still hesitating, Senate leaders from both parties took the unusual step of advancing their own debt ceiling bill, a measure that by custom originates in the House.

Background

The statutory ceiling on the national debt covers federal debt held by the public — in the form of Treasury securities, savings bonds and other government notes — as well as the government's obligations to the federal trust funds, primarily for Social Security and Medicare.

Though the public debt had been reduced during the surplus era — fiscal 1998-2001 — the total national debt had continued to grow as bonds piled up in the Social Se-

BoxScore

Bill:

S 2578 — PL 107-199

Legislative Action:

Senate passed S 2578, 68-29, on June 11.

House cleared S 2578, 215-214, on June 27.

President signed June 28.

curity trust funds. The return to deficits in fiscal 2002 meant the Treasury also was engaging in significant new public borrowing. The combination brought borrowing dangerously close to the legal limit.

Because a default was unthinkable, Congress had never failed to raise the cap when it was necessary. But lawmakers often took the opportunity to score political points about deficit spending or to use must-pass debt limit bills to advance other legislation.

A debt ceiling increase was the vehicle used to advance the 1985 Gramm-Rudman-Hollings law (PL 99-177), which required across-the-board budget cuts if Congress failed to meet deficit-reduction targets. As part of the package, Congress agreed to breach the $2 trillion mark, setting a new $2.079 trillion debt limit. (*1985 Almanac, p. 457*)

In 1990, Congress passed a series of short-term increases in the debt ceiling while wrangling with President George Bush over the major deficit-reduction deal (PL 101-508) of his presidency. (*1990 Almanac, p. 165*)

In 1995, with the debt approaching a limit of $4.9 trillion, Republicans tried to use the issue to force President Bill Clinton to back a GOP deficit-reduction bill. The move flopped, and Republicans took a beating in public opinion polls after the federal government was forced into a partial shutdown. (*1995 Almanac, p. 2-63*)

The following year, with Treasury Secretary Rubin's options dwindling and Wall Street growing nervous, the debt ceiling was increased to $5.5 trillion, but not without a popular change in Social Security benefits and a provision to help small businesses challenge government regulation. Budget hawks also were rewarded with a controversial line-item veto measure (PL 104-130) that was linked to the debt-ceiling bill. (*1996 Almanac, p. 2-25*)

The last increase in the debt ceiling came during a rare time of peace in the budget wars, when the GOP-controlled Congress and Clinton came together to enact the landmark 1997 balanced-budget law (PL 105-33), including the $5.95 trillion ceiling. (*1997 Almanac, p. 2-47*)

Legislative Action

Senate Action

The Senate passed its debt limit bill (S 2578) on June 11 by a solid bipartisan margin of 68-29. The measure, which Daschle had introduced a week earlier, proposed to increase the debt ceiling by $450 billion, to $6.4 trillion. (*Senate vote 148, p. S-31*)

Daschle was eager to move the bill along, and Minority Leader Trent Lott, R-Miss., snapped up what he said was a good offer. "He came up with a responsible number, a reasonable number," Lott said. "We both told our conferences this is not the kind of thing you play games with."

The Treasury estimated that the increase would keep the government solvent at least until the middle of December,

and possibly into 2003, depending mainly on how well the economy performed.

House Action

The Senate's action, and the lack of more politically palatable alternatives, finally pushed the House to act. On June 27, House GOP leaders managed to clear the bill, 215-214, with three Democrats voting in favor and six Republicans opposed. Democrats said they would support a short-term increase to provide time for a budget summit aimed at erasing the deficit, but that it was up to those who voted for the 2001 tax cut to provide the votes for a longer-term increase. Republicans argued that the recession and the Sept. 11 attacks were the principal reasons for having to raise the debt limit. (*House vote 279, p. H-90*)

The bill came to the floor in a highly unusual manner. With almost no warning, Republicans amended the rule on the fiscal 2003 military construction spending bill (HR 5011) to permit the House to consider the Senate-passed debt bill. The move provided minimal notice — and minimal debate, just one hour.

Speaker J. Dennis Hastert, R-Ill., had insisted for weeks that the debt limit would end up on the fiscal 2002 supplemental spending bill, saying GOP leaders simply could not corral enough Republican votes to pass a stand-alone debt bill. The leadership had amended the House version of the supplemental to state that the government would take all steps necessary to avoid a default. The goal was to punt the issue to conference, where precise language on the debt limit could be added to the conference agreement. The amendment was inserted into the House supplemental as part of the rule that governed the floor debate. The rule was adopted, 216-209, on May 22, with all but one Democrat opposed. (*House vote 194, p. H-66*)

Even after the Senate passed the separate bill, Hastert and Majority Leader Dick Armey, R-Texas, stuck to their plan. But the supplemental was stalled in a slow-moving conference, and the White House wanted quick action on the debt. "As we fight for freedom," Bush wrote to House leaders on June 25, "we must not imperil the full faith and credit of the United States government and the soundness and strength of the American economy." Daschle, meanwhile, seemed to be looking for a way to force Republicans to back more money for fiscal 2003 spending as the price for a debt-limit increase.

"If the choice is between passing a stand-alone bill to increase the debt limit or agreeing to Senate demands for more spending, the House should pass a stand-alone bill," said John Shadegg of Arizona, the leader of the conservative Republican Study Committee.

With lawmakers preparing to leave for the July Fourth recess, Hastert decided the night of June 26 to move to a quick vote the next day, clearing the Senate-passed bill. ◆

Budget Enforcement Rules Expire

Budget enforcement laws aimed at controlling federal deficits were allowed to expire Sept. 30, after lawmakers were unable to agree on a means for extending them. The Senate adopted a limited set of rules that applied only in that chamber and were good through April 15, 2003.

Statutory spending "caps" on discretionary appropriations and pay-as-you-go (PAYGO) rules for new tax cuts and entitlement programs had been in place since 1990 (PL 101-508). They were extended as part of deficit reduction laws in 1993 (PL 103-66) and 1997 (PL 105-33). (*1990 Almanac, p. 161; 1993 Almanac, p. 124; 1997 Almanac, p. 2-48*)

The PAYGO law theoretically triggered across-the-board spending reductions if tax cuts or new entitlement spending was not offset by revenue increases or entitlement cuts. The spending caps allowed budget points of order to be lodged against appropriations bills that exceeded the dollar targets. In the House, a simple majority can overcome a budget point of order, but in the Senate, 60 votes are required, making the caps a more potent tool in that chamber.

However, Congress averted PAYGO cuts each year by simply adopting language wiping the PAYGO scorecard clean. In November, lawmakers cleared a bill (PL 107-312) erasing a $127 billion PAYGO deficit amassed in previously enacted legislation. The law also erased any PAYGO deficits for fiscal 2004-06. Congress also routinely evaded spending caps by ignoring them in session-ending budget deals.

Still, budget hawks said the rules had had a restraining effect on Congress. They warned that it would be easier for members to move a raft of deficit-worsening measures if the rules were not extended, a particularly worrisome prospect since the budget already had returned to deficit after four years of surplus.

The obvious vehicle for extending the rules would have been the annual congressional budget resolution, but lawmakers could not agree on one for fiscal 2003. When it became clear that a broad, multi-year deal would not advance, budget writers tried several times to move more skeletal, short-term plans to impose an appropriations cap and extend PAYGO. Their only success was the Senate's short-term extension of PAYGO rules.

Legislative Action

Budget Resolution

The House agreed May 22 — as part of the rule for debate on a fiscal 2002 supplemental spending bill (PL 107-206) — to treat the fiscal 2003 House budget resolution as if it had been agreed to by both chambers. The resolution (H Con Res 353), adopted March 20, limited discretionary spending for fiscal 2003 to $759 billion. President Bush reinforced the House limit, threatening April 16 to veto spending bills that exceeded it.

The Senate's fiscal 2003 budget resolution (S Con Res

100), approved in committee March 21, set a one-year $768 billion discretionary limit. The committee rejected, on an 11-11 tie, an amendment by Judd Gregg, R-N.H., and Russell D. Feingold, D-Wis., that would have provided discretionary spending caps for five years. Feingold warned that he — and perhaps a few other Senate Democrats — probably would not support the budget resolution on the floor without tougher budget enforcement provisions. With a one-vote margin, and other defections threatened, Democratic leaders concluded they did not have the votes to get the budget resolution adopted and never brought it to the floor.

Trying to Hitch a Ride

With the budget resolution stalled, the chairmen and ranking Republicans on the Senate Budget and Appropriations committees looked for another vehicle to carry both the $768.1 billion limit on fiscal 2003 appropriations and language extending the expiring budget enforcement mechanisms. Top candidates included must-pass legislation to increase the federal debt limit (PL 107-199) and a midyear supplemental spending bill (PL 107-206). But the strategy drew opposition from Senate Minority Leader Trent Lott of Mississippi and other GOP leaders because the fiscal 2003 cap exceeded the $759 billion limit demanded by Bush. Appropriators from both parties in both chambers said $768 billion in discretionary spending was a minimum if they were to get support for the annual spending bills.

On June 20, the Senate came within one vote of going on record in favor of the plan. Feingold offered an amendment to the fiscal 2003 defense authorization bill that would have extended for five years statutory limits on discretionary spending — including a $768 billion cap in fiscal 2003 — and PAYGO rules. Pete V. Domenici of New Mexico, ranking Republican on the Budget Committee, implored his colleagues to support the plan even though it was at odds with Bush's budget. He said Bush could use his veto to hold spending below $768 billion, but that the enforcement tools were critical. "I wouldn't join this if I didn't see down the road something a lot more onerous," Domenici said.

But the White House lobbied strenuously against the amendment, and it fell on a 59-40 vote to waive a budget point of order; 60 votes were required. The point of order was raised by Phil Gramm, R-Texas, who remained a staunch foe of the plan through much of the session. Eight Republicans broke ranks to join all the Democrats and the Senate's independent in the majority. (*Senate vote 159, p. S-33*)

Senate Extension

After months of maneuvering, the Senate agreed by voice vote Oct. 16 to a widely backed resolution (S Res 304) to restore the PAYGO rules until April 15, 2003. The resolution also revived recently expired Senate points of order against tax cuts or mandatory spending not provided for in a budget resolution. The 15 points of order, which required 60 votes to overcome, were a potentially powerful tool to block those who, under the Senate's freewheeling rules, offered popular but costly floor amendments to spend money or cut taxes. "Of all the issues to be voted on, the most significant opportunity to save taxpayers money over the next year is this little resolution," Domenici said.

Although popular, the action had been delayed for

months by objections from Gramm, who said the enforcement rules had done little to deter appropriators from spending more money, but had been effective in blocking tax cuts. Gramm threatened a filibuster of the resolution, which would have pushed off a vote until the week of Oct. 21. Instead, he reached agreement with proponents such as Domenici and Budget Chairman Kent Conrad, D-N.D., to extend the rules for only six months instead of through Sept. 30, as originally proposed. The rules applied only to Senate procedures and could be changed by subsequent votes in the Senate. By contrast, violations of the statutory PAYGO law and appropriations caps would have sparked automatic across-the-board spending cuts.

A Clean Slate

In an ironic coda, Congress cleared a separate bill shortly before adjourning that erased the $127 billion PAYGO deficit and any deficits for fiscal 2004-06. The House passed the bill, 366-19, on Nov. 14, and the Senate cleared it the next day by voice vote. Bush signed the bill Dec. 2. (*House vote 482, p. H-150*)

Congress regularly passed such language before the end of a session, but the provision usually was buried in a must-pass bill. This time, however, GOP appropriators refused to include the language in the final stopgap spending bill (PL 107-294). Tired of being singled out by party leaders for failing to exercise fiscal discipline, they decided to make the point that recently enacted tax cuts and new mandatory spending in the 2002 farm bill and elsewhere dwarfed any discretionary spending they were seeking to add to the budget. The result was the separate roll call vote on a relatively routine measure intended to block automatic spending cuts. ◆

Surplus Streak Broken

The federal government ended fiscal 2002 in the red, concluding a four-year streak of budget surpluses. The final deficit was $157.8 billion — $317.5 billion not counting the surplus in the Social Security trust funds.

The return to deficit spending did not evoke the kind of outcry that was common in the 1980s and 1990s. Securing the United States against a future terrorist attack and the war on terrorism abroad were now the priorities, making a balanced budget seem almost a luxury. The war in Afghanistan and a possible war with Iraq meant that defense spending, in particular, was on the rise. Federal revenue in fiscal 2002 fell by $138 billion from the previous year, with virtually all of the decrease coming from a decline in individual income tax receipts. The Congressional Budget Office attributed that decline to the weak economy and to President Bush's 2001 tax package (PL 107-16).

Republicans generally regarded the tax cuts as a stimulus to the economy, which reduced longstanding GOP worries about deficit spending. "If there's things we can do to grow the economy, to help the economy, that's how you get back to balanced budgets," said House Speaker J. Dennis Hastert, R-Ill. "If you can stimulate the economy, then you are reducing deficits."

Indeed, a new group of "growth hawks" was emerging

within the Republican Party, led by Bush and drawing on a younger generation of lawmakers — such as Roy Blunt of Missouri, the incoming House majority whip for the 108th Congress — who were more pragmatic in their approach to deficits.

Democrats, meanwhile, continued to push for spending increases in a broad array of domestic programs, saying the assault on red ink should come on the revenue side of the ledger, not through spending cuts.

Another factor reducing concern about the deficit was its relatively modest size in relation to the economy as a whole. The fiscal 2002 deficit amounted to 1.5 percent of the gross domestic product (GDP), the annual value of all goods and services produced. That was well below the deficits of the mid-1980s and early 1990s, which frequently topped 4 percent of GDP. ◆

Chapter 7

DEFENSE

Homeland Department Created

After nearly a year of often bitter debate, Congress authorized the creation of a Cabinet-level Department of Homeland Security, combining all or part of 22 federal agencies responsible for counterterrorism. The consolidation was the largest reorganization of the federal bureaucracy since defense and intelligence agencies were restructured at the start of the Cold War. President Bush signed the bill into law Nov. 25 (HR 5005 — PL 107-296).

The idea of combining federal agencies responsible for counterterrorism and clarifying lines of authority originated in the House and Senate in 2001, following the Sept. 11 terrorist attacks on the World Trade Center and the Pentagon. The Bush administration initially resisted, arguing the job could be handled out of the White House Office of Homeland Security. But the office's director, Tom Ridge, who was not subject to Senate confirmation, frustrated lawmakers by repeatedly declining to testify on the administration's plans. *(2001 Almanac, p. 10-4)*

In May 2002, the Senate Governmental Affairs Committee approved a bill (S 2452), sponsored by Chairman Joseph I. Lieberman, D-Conn., to create a Cabinet-level homeland security department and a separate White House Office for Combating Terrorism, and to elevate Ridge's job to Cabinet-level status.

In June, amid increased congressional scrutiny of pre-Sept. 11 intelligence failures and declining public approval ratings, the Bush administration abruptly reversed course. In a June 6 announcement that caught official Washington and even some Cabinet secretaries by surprise, Bush issued a proposal for the creation of a new homeland security department — a sprawling bureaucracy with at least 170,000 employees and a budget of $37.5 billion that would include the Federal Emergency Management Agency (FEMA), the Coast Guard, the Immigration and Naturalization Service (INS), Secret Service, Border Patrol, U.S. Customs Service and the newly created Transportation Security Administration (TSA). The proposal included an information analysis office to synthesize intelligence provided by the CIA, FBI and other agencies.

The plan also called for "significant flexibility" in hiring, pay and personnel management. The White House Office of Homeland Security would continue as a separate entity advising the president.

A nine-member House Select Committee on Homeland Security, chaired by Majority Leader Dick Armey, R-Texas, assembled recommendations from 11 committees to produce a bill (HR 5005) that closely resembled the White House blueprint. The panel approved the bill July 19. The

BoxScore

Bill:
HR 5005 — PL 107-296
Legislative Action:
House passed HR 5005
(H Rept 107-609), 295-132, on
July 26.
House passed HR 5710, 299-121, on Nov. 13.
Senate passed HR 5005, 90-9, on Nov. 19, after substituting the text of HR 5710.
House cleared HR 5005, by voice vote, Nov. 22.
President signed Nov. 25.

House passed the measure July 26, after a stormy floor debate in which Democrats and moderate Republicans tried but failed to add protections for unionized government workers.

In the Democratic-controlled Senate, the Governmental Affairs panel approved a reworked version of Lieberman's bill July 25. While the measure followed some of the administration's proposals for the department's structure, it affirmed employees' rights to union representation unless their jobs were materially changed after their transfer to the new department. The White House issued a veto threat, arguing the language would diminish the president's existing power.

The Senate floor debate, which dragged on until Congress broke for the November midterm elections, focused on the work rules. Republicans charged that Democrats were tying the president's hands and jeopardizing national security in order to cater to organized labor. Democrats countered that the administration and its allies were using homeland security as a smokescreen to gut civil service protections.

Following GOP victories on Election Day, Bush declared the bill the "single most important item of unfinished business" for Congress and advised lawmakers not to adjourn before finishing it. A small group of Senate moderates, who had been working for months to find a middle ground on work rules, gave up and reluctantly accepted GOP language allowing the new department to write its own personnel rules.

The House passed a new version of the bill (HR 5710) in a bid to quicken the pace of the lame-duck session. Senate Majority Leader Tom Daschle, D-S.D., made a last-minute bid to strip several favors to corporations added at the last minute by Republicans — a move that would have sent the bill back to the House, which had all but left for the year. Daschle's amendment was defeated, with key Democratic moderates siding with Republicans. The Senate inserted the compromise into HR 5005 and passed it Nov. 19. The House cleared the bill in a pro forma session Nov. 22.

Confident the bill would pass, Bush had had members of his homeland security office working on a transition plan for months. Before signing the bill Nov. 25, he announced that Ridge was his choice to head the new department.

Highlights

Following are the main components of the new law:
• **Transferred agencies.** The department absorbed 22 existing federal agencies involved in border security, bioterrorism defenses and disaster management. Major agencies shifted to the new department included the Coast Guard, TSA,

FEMA, U.S. Customs Service, Secret Service and the agricultural import and entry inspection functions of the Animal and Plant Health Inspection Service.

● **INS.** The law abolished the INS and split the agency into two separate components — an immigration enforcement bureau and a citizenship bureau — both of which were placed within the new department.

● **Departmental structure.** The law organized the department into four primary divisions:

— Border and Transportation Security, made up of various border control and transportation agencies, was responsible for setting U.S. visa policy and securing U.S. borders and transportation systems.

— Emergency Preparedness and Response, which combined FEMA and the functions of other agencies charged with preparing for and responding to terror attacks.

— Science and Technology, combining various science and technology programs. It was charged with developing countermeasures against terror threats involving weapons of mass destruction, including chemical, biological, radiological and nuclear attacks.

— Information Analysis and Infrastructure Protection, charged with analyzing all intelligence information on possible terror attacks on the United States and evaluating critical U.S. infrastructure for vulnerabilities to terrorism.

● **Employee policies.** The secretary of the new department was given broad authority to reorganize the transferred agencies and functions within the new bureaucracy, and was allowed to create new personnel and pay grades outside of the Civil Service system. The measure set up a procedure for employee and union feedback on personnel and pay proposals, with a 30-day review period and subsequent 30-day negotiation period, after which the department could impose its new rules despite any employee objections. The authority was to expire after five years.

The president could strip employees of their union representation if the mission of their agency or division changed "materially" or if a majority of the employees within that union worked primarily with intelligence, counterintelligence or investigations related to terrorism. The president was required to give advance notice of his intent to take such actions and submit a written explanation to Congress.

● **Liability limits.** The law limited legal liability for certain anti-terrorism products, including voiding pending lawsuits against drugmakers that made mercury-based vaccine additives. Some doctors suspected the additives caused autism in children. Republican leaders said the provision was needed to ensure that health professionals were not subject to lawsuits for administering vaccines to help prevent or treat bioterrorism threats.

The bill also extended through 2003 the federal Aviation War Risk Insurance program and the liability limits of commercial airlines whose aircraft were used in terror attacks.

● **Airport baggage screening.** The law extended for one year, until Dec. 31, 2003, the deadline for airports to install explosive detection equipment to check airline passenger baggage for bombs. It also limited the legal liability of certain airport screening companies and allowed non-citizen U.S. nationals to work as airport passenger and baggage screeners.

● **Arming pilots.** The TSA was required to establish a program under which trained commercial airline pilots would be allowed to carry guns aboard aircraft.

● **BATF.** The Bureau of Alcohol, Tobacco and Firearms (BATF) was transferred from the Treasury Department to the Justice Department. The law required the bureau to establish a new explosives training center, and it set new federal restrictions on the possession and use of explosives.

● **Smallpox vaccinations.** The Department of Health and Human Services (HHS) was authorized to administer the smallpox vaccine to segments of the population if it determined there was a public health threat posed by smallpox. The law protected drug companies and health professionals from legal liability for any adverse health reactions to the smallpox vaccine, provided for claims against the government for people who suffered such reactions and gave liability protections to drug companies that made certain additives or components of other vaccines.

● **Charitable deduction.** The law provided for the creation of tax-deductible charitable funds that could be used to compensate families of military personnel, FBI agents, intelligence agents and other U.S. government representatives who died in the line of duty as a result of a terror attack.

● **Exemptions.** Certain activities of the new department were exempted from several "good government" rules that generally applied to federal agencies, including the Freedom of Information Act and the Federal Advisory Committee Act.

● **Corporate tax avoidance.** The law prohibited the department from issuing contracts to companies that moved their headquarters overseas to avoid U.S. taxes, but waived the restriction if the contracts were necessary for national security, to prevent the loss of U.S. jobs or to prevent additional government costs.

Background

Though virtually every member of Congress supported the idea of coordinating the federal fight against terrorism, heated deliberations were almost inevitable given the stakes involved, the sweep of the plan and the way it would allow the new department to rearrange functions, eliminate agencies and transfer significant amounts of money between agencies without seeking prior congressional approval.

The 52-page draft plan submitted by the Bush administration in June also lacked important details on how to handle so-called dual-purpose agencies such as the Coast Guard and the U.S. Customs Service, which had both significant homeland security functions and core missions that had little to do with protecting the nation.

House leaders decided to allow 11 committees with jurisdiction over the issue to mark up the Bush plan, which made it more permissible for members of both parties to air their criticisms. Though most party leaders endorsed creating the department as quickly as possible, some House Democrats voiced concern that Bush's plan was inadequate and potentially counterproductive because it might enlarge the bureaucracy without making the parts work together more smoothly. Democrats also contended that the proposal was not "budget neutral," as the White House claimed, but would require substantial additional revenues beyond what the existing agencies already were spending.

Administration officials argued the department would not cost more if Congress gave the proposed secretary of homeland security significant leeway in management rules, including hiring and procurement. The White House also sought to ease concerns that the flexibility it was seeking to manage the new department could erode federal employees' civil service protections and change their pay scales. Bush denied that any such plans were contemplated but asked for the right to cross-train workers and transfer some within the new department.

As the debate wore on and Senate Democrats continued to resist calls for flexibility, Bush characterized congressional dissent over his plan as the result of turf wars between lawmakers unable to put aside parochial concerns in the name of national security. But the crux of the dispute turned equally on how much power lawmakers were willing to cede to the executive branch. Administration insistence that the proposed department's unique missions and the threat of global terrorism justified broad exemptions from some laws and, by extension, congressional oversight, rankled many powerful lawmakers. So did White House demands that the new department have the ability to transfer appropriated money within its constituent agencies, diluting the power of appropriators accustomed to controlling most aspects of federal spending. In the end, Republican gains in the midterm elections gave the administration the leverage it needed to prevail in the power struggle between the branches.

Legislative Action

House Committee Action: Eleven Panels Weigh In

The 11 House committees with jurisdiction over the president's plan held a frenzied series of markups the week of July 8 that produced some radically different versions of what a Cabinet-level homeland security department should look like.

The panels were racing to meet a July 12 deadline imposed by House leaders, who had hopes of passing the bill before the anniversary of the Sept. 11 attacks. But the boldness with which the committees disagreed with the president, and the many ways in which they sliced and diced his plan, left tough choices for the newly created Select Committee on Homeland Security, which was charged with blending the recommendations into a single bill.

During the House markups:

• The administration backed down on a proposal to move all of the Agriculture Department's Animal and Plant Health Inspection Service to the new department after farm groups complained. Under a compromise worked out with the House Agriculture Committee, only functions involving import and border inspection would be transferred, while other functions would remain where they were.

• The Appropriations Committee rejected an administration request for broad control over the financing of the proposed department, especially authority to transfer within the department up to 5 percent of the money appropriated for individual programs, as well as 5 percent of unobligated balances available to agencies being relocated to the new department.

• The Energy and Commerce Committee rebuffed an administration plan to transfer health research from HHS. Instead, the panel voted to give the new department HHS' responsibility for overseeing the transfer of dangerous pathogens and toxins used in research laboratories.

• The Government Reform Committee agreed to administration requests to move the Coast Guard, FEMA, INS and Secret Service to the new department, while backing down from a plan to defy the administration and shift all visa services from the State Department. Over the objections of most Republicans, the panel agreed to allow employees who moved to the new department to retain their collective bargaining agreements if their jobs were unchanged.

• The Select Intelligence Committee voted to create a separate intelligence agency within the new department that would be responsible for gathering information from other intelligence agencies, analyzing it and disseminating it to state and local governments.

• The International Relations Committee backed the White House plan to have the State Department continue issuing visas, but stipulated that the proposed new department would set policy.

• The Judiciary Committee defied the administration by opting to move only the law enforcement functions of the INS into the new department, instead of the entire agency. The committee's recommendation was nearly identical to an INS restructuring bill (HR 3231) written by Chairman F. James Sensenbrenner Jr., R-Wis., and passed by the House in April. The committee also bucked the White House by voting to transfer the Secret Service from the Treasury Department to Justice, instead of to the new department. It also agreed to shift only a small portion of FEMA, leaving most of the agency independent.

• The Science Committee opted to block the proposed transfer of the National Institute of Standards and Technology's computer security division to the proposed department. In another departure from the administration plan, it called for creation of a corps of volunteers called NET Guard, to help communities recover from terrorist attacks on computer and communications systems.

• The Transportation and Infrastructure Committee rejected the administration's proposal to move the Coast Guard and FEMA into the new department. It also proposed that the TSA remain within the Transportation Department until it met deadlines to put security screeners and explosive detection systems in place at all airports.

House Committee Action: Select Panel Writes Bill

Signaling that the administration would get most of what it wanted from the House, the nine-member Select Committee on Homeland Security ignored many of the departures proposed by the various committees and approved a bill (HR 5005 — H Rept 107-609, Part 1) on July 19 that stuck close to the White House plan. After a daylong markup, the committee approved the measure, 5-4, along party lines.

The select panel did agree with the Judiciary Committee recommendation to split the INS and include only its enforcement and border protection services within the new department, instead of merging the entire agency intact.

And, anticipating major disagreements over the administration's personnel proposals, Armey opted not to include

them in the 216-page draft bill. Compromise language offered by panel member Rob Portman, R-Ohio, and accepted by voice vote at the markup, affirmed workers' bargaining rights but proposed to allow the secretary of the new department to exclude individuals who were involved in national security matters.

The panel tried to produce a compromise on appropriations by allowing for the new department to reprogram 2 percent of appropriated funds for up to two years, subject to 15 days' advance notice. The select panel also asserted itself in the area of privacy, including language in the bill that would prohibit national identification cards. While there was no pending legislation to create such cards, the administration, in a homeland security strategy released July 16, called for uniform standards for state driver's licenses.

The functions of the TSA were the object of considerable attention. Armey included language in the draft to delay indefinitely the Dec. 31, 2002, deadline set by the 2001 aviation security law (PL 107-71) for all airports to check screened baggage for explosives. Committee Democrats argued the language would relieve the agency and airports of having to implement key safety measures by a date certain. Eventually, the panel adopted, 6-3, a compromise by J.C. Watts Jr., R-Okla., to allow airports that could not meet existing deadlines to obtain a one-year waiver from the TSA.

The panel rejected, on a 5-4 party-line vote, language by Nancy Pelosi, D-Calif., that would have established the White House Office of Homeland Security in law and made its director subject to Senate confirmation. Republicans said the language amounted to congressional micromanagement of the Executive Office of the President.

House Floor Action

The House passed the bill, 295-132, on July 26, after Democrats unexpectedly won adoption of a proposal to bar the new department from contracting with any U.S. company, or its subsidiaries, that had its headquarters in an overseas tax haven. *(House vote, 367, p. H-116)*

The language was added on a "motion to recommit" — a procedural gambit to alter a bill on the verge of passage — offered by Rosa DeLauro, D-Conn. It gained support from some Republicans who were eager to make a political statement in the midst of a series of corporate scandals that began with the December 2001 collapse of Enron Corp. After 101 Republicans who initially opposed the motion switched their votes, the final tally for DeLauro's language was 318-110. *(House vote 366, p. H-114)*

● **Work rules.** Much of the floor debate focused on federal personnel rules, and whether worker protection language would diminish the president's powers. The House adopted, 229-201, an amendment by Christopher Shays, R-Conn., that affirmed union members' rights but allowed the president to set aside collective bargaining agreements that could have an "adverse impact" on the new department's ability to keep the nation secure. *(House vote 356, p. H-112)*

The Shays amendment was designed as an alternative to a proposal by Constance A. Morella, R-Md., that would have affirmed employees' rights to union representation unless their jobs were changed materially after they were transferred to the new department. Morella's amendment, which drew a veto threat from the White House, was reject-

ed, 208-222. *(House vote 357, p. H-112)*

Some observers said the personnel rules were detracting from more substantive debates on homeland security. They questioned the wisdom of trying to use a national defense bill to reshape a government personnel system that was widely derided as cumbersome and ineffective.

"There are things to criticize in both camps," said Steven J. Kelman, a professor of public management at Harvard University's John F. Kennedy School of Government. "The administration's efforts to remove collective bargaining protections is provocative and ties into a Republican anti-labor agenda. And public employee unions have strenuously opposed even moderate efforts to create flexible personnel systems."

● **Visas.** The House rejected, 118-309, another amendment strongly opposed by the White House that would have transferred the office that issues visas from the State Department to the new Homeland Security Department. The proposal was offered by Curt Weldon, R-Pa. *(House vote 365, p. H-114)*

● **Airport security.** An amendment by James L. Oberstar, D-Minn., to drop the one-year extension for airports to install bomb-detecting equipment was rejected, 211-217. *(House vote 362, p. H-114)*

Senate Committee Action

The Senate Governmental Affairs Committee approved a revised version of Lieberman's bill (S 2452) by a vote of 12-5 at the end of a two-day markup July 25. Lawmakers were divided, mostly along party lines, over how much power to cede to the executive branch in the sweeping reorganization. "We have some very fundamental disagreements with regard to the president's authority," said Fred Thompson of Tennessee, ranking Republican on the panel.

The legislation came in the form of a comprehensive amendment by Lieberman.

The Bush administration turned up pressure on senators even before they finished work on the bill, threatening to veto the measure and contending it would not give the executive branch enough flexibility to manage the department in order to respond to terror threats. Lieberman said the bill gave the president 85 percent to 90 percent of what he had requested, and vowed to continue to negotiate with the administration.

● **Work rules.** The biggest disagreement again focused on work rules for the new department. The Senate bill affirmed employees' rights to union representation unless their jobs were changed materially after the transfer to the new department. Democrats said they wanted to assure that some 50,000 employees in the proposed department who were represented by federal worker unions would continue to enjoy collective bargaining protections. They pointed to a Bush administration decision in January to end union representation for about 500 workers at several Justice Department agencies as justification for the language.

Republicans tried to carve out exemptions for the proposed department, citing the need to shift employees within constituent agencies to respond to various threats.

In considering amendments, the committee:

● Rejected, 7-10, an attempt by Thompson to strike language affirming union rights.

● Rejected, 7-10, a Thompson amendment to give the

new department's secretary broad discretion in hiring, firing, recruiting and transferring employees.

• Adopted by voice vote a set of proposals by George V. Voinovich, R-Ohio, that, among other things, would give the proposed department and other federal agencies power to raise the salaries of experienced managers from $166,700 to $192,600 and give agencies expanded powers to offer early retirement buyouts to restructure the work force.

• Rejected, on an 8-8 tie, a Voinovich amendment to lift a 5,000-worker limit on the number of federal employees that could be involved in experimental personnel demonstration projects.

• Rejected, on an 8-9 party-line vote, an attempt by Thompson to give the proposed department so-called fast-track reorganization authority, which had existed government-wide from 1973 to 1984. The authority allowed a Cabinet secretary to submit a plan to Congress and reorganize agencies within 75 days. Democrats said the new secretary would have sufficient flexibility under existing law to get the department established.

• **Appropriated funds.** The administration lobbied for the ability to redirect up to 5 percent of the funding appropriated for any agencies transferred to the new department. But an agreement between Lieberman; Senate Appropriations Committee Chairman Robert C. Byrd, D-W.Va.; and ranking Republican Ted Stevens of Alaska left Congress with authority over appropriated funds. The committee adopted by voice vote an amendment, offered by Stevens and modified by Lieberman, requiring that most funding and assets transferred to the department be used only for the purposes originally intended. The money could not be used to fund new positions created under the bill.

• **Coast Guard.** The panel adopted additional barriers to reprogramming money, especially for the Coast Guard, which had a strong constituency and perennially was strapped for funds to meet its many responsibilities. The committee adopted, 9-7, an amendment by Stevens and Susan Collins, R-Maine, to create a special status for the Coast Guard in the new department and prevent its assets from being diverted permanently from core missions, such as search and rescue, fisheries enforcement and maritime navigation. The secretary of the new department would be permitted to assign the Coast Guard specific homeland security duties.

• **Intelligence.** Moving closer to the administration's position on intelligence sharing, the committee:

• Adopted, by voice vote, an amendment by Carl Levin, D-Mich., to maintain the CIA's counterterrorism center as the government's focal point for receiving and analyzing information about terror threats. The new department would review the threats and connect them to known vulnerabilities, and could direct other agencies to address those threats. Lieberman had proposed establishing a terrorism directorate within the proposed department to serve as the focal point, but he acknowledged Levin's plan would avoid duplication.

• Rejected, 8-8, an attempt by Thompson to put responsibility for information analysis and infrastructure protection under a single directorate in the new department.

• Adopted, by voice vote, an amendment by Robert F. Bennett, R-Utah, and Levin to exempt from Freedom of In-

formation Act disclosure requirements some proprietary information that companies voluntarily provide to the department about infrastructure vulnerabilities. The amendment also narrowed the bill's definition of what constituted voluntary submission of information to ensure that applications for grants, permits, licenses or other government benefits would remain subject to disclosure.

Senate Floor Action

The Senate took up the bill Sept. 3, opening what would turn out to be weeks of futile floor debate and behind-the-scenes negotiations that focused primarily on the issue of employee rights in the new department. By the time the regular session ended to allow for the midterm elections, the chamber was so deadlocked that Daschle pulled the bill from the floor.

Most of the debate and amendments in September were on a Lieberman substitute that reflected the revised bill approved by the Governmental Affairs Committee in July.

• **Workers' rights.** Democrats and Republicans vied over rival compromises on workers' rights, with neither side able to muster the 60 votes needed to head off a filibuster.

Most Republicans backed a substitute by Phil Gramm, R-Texas, and Zell Miller, D-Ga., that followed the president's original plans for the new department and included House language that would allow the government to remove employees from unions for national security reasons after giving notice in writing.

Democrats rallied around a proposal by centrists John B. Breaux, D-La.; Ben Nelson, D-Neb.; and Lincoln Chafee, R-R.I., to allow the president to remove employees from unions for national security reasons but allow the employees to appeal. The president would have to provide a detailed explanation for removing workers, and appeals would be lodged with the Federal Labor Relations Authority — an independent agency that administers labor-management relations programs for federal workers. The appeal would have to include "clear and convincing evidence" that the president's decision was not justified.

Republicans wanted a "clean" vote on the Gramm-Miller substitute; Democrats were intent on amending that proposal with the Breaux-Nelson-Chafee plan.

In back-to-back votes Sept. 26, the Senate rejected, 50-49, an attempt to invoke cloture on the Democratic version of the bill offered by Lieberman — 10 votes short of the necessary 60-vote majority. An attempt to limit debate on the Gramm-Miller substitute failed, 44-53. (*Senate votes 226, 227, p. S-46*)

The Senate already had rejected two earlier attempts to cut off debate on the Lieberman plan, a step that would have sharply limited Republicans' ability to offer changes. On Sept. 19, the day Gramm and Miller unveiled their substitute amendment, senators rejected a Democratic cloture motion, 50-49. A second attempt at cloture was rejected, 49-49 on Sept. 25. (*Senate votes 218, 225, pp. S-44 and S-46*)

• **Byrd's crusade.** Through much of the Senate debate, Byrd conducted a lonely crusade against what he saw as administration pressure on Congress to rubber-stamp a sweeping government reorganization. His initial efforts to slow the process forced Daschle to delay bringing the bill up until after the August recess.

Byrd slowed the debate with lengthy floor speeches critical of what he said was the administration's disregard for congressional oversight. "With the level of endorsement the Congress has given to this idea, you would think that the proposal for a new Homeland Security Department had been engraved in the stone tablets that were handed down to Moses at Mount Sinai," Byrd said in one animated floor speech. "But in reality, the idea was developed by four presidential staffers in the basement of the White House. For all we know, it could have been drafted on the back of a cocktail napkin."

On Sept. 24, the Senate rejected, 28-70, an amendment by Byrd that would have required the administration to consult with Congress about the reorganization in three stages over 13 months. (*Senate vote 222, p. S-45*)

On at least two other occasions, the Senate rejected attempts to extend Congress' reach into White House decision-making.

Senators agreed, by voice vote, Sept. 17 to an amendment by Thompson to eliminate provisions that would have established the White House Office of Homeland Security by statute and required that its director be confirmed by the Senate. The Senate had rejected, 41-55, an attempt by Lieberman to kill Thompson's amendment. The Senate also rejected, 48-49 on Sept. 12, an amendment by Ernest F. Hollings, D-S.C., to require that the secretary of the new department and the attorney general be made statutory members of the National Security Council.(*Senate votes 214, 215, p. S-43*)

● **Intelligence commission.** For a time, it seemed that the homeland security bill would become the vehicle for creating an independent commission to investigate intelligence failures leading up to the Sept. 11 attacks. On Sept. 26, the Senate adopted, 90-8, a Lieberman amendment to establish such a commission. But when it became clear that the homeland bill was bogged down in the fight over workers' rights, Lieberman and others switched their attention to the intelligence authorization bill (PL 107-306), which ultimately carried the proposal to enactment. (*Senate vote 223, p. S-45; intelligence bill, p. 7-18*)

On other issues, the Senate:

● Adopted, by voice vote, a proposal by Barbara Boxer, D-Calif., and Robert C. Smith, R-N.H., to require the Transportation Department to deputize qualified pilots of commercial passenger and cargo planes to use lethal force in defense of their aircraft. Under the amendment, selected pilots would be allowed to carry guns in the cockpit, after receiving training similar to that offered to federal law enforcement officers.

● Agreed, by voice vote, to an amendment by Paul Wellstone, D-Minn., to withhold homeland security department contracts from companies that reincorporated abroad to avoid U.S. taxes.

Final Action

The Republican victory in the midterm elections gave Bush the clout he needed to break the deadlock on the bill. "The single most important item of unfinished business on Capitol Hill is to create a unified Department of Homeland Security," Bush declared in his post-election press conference Nov. 7. "It's imperative that the Congress send me a bill that I can sign before the 107th Congress ends."

Bush directed Republican leaders to reconcile the House and Senate bills, and aides worked through the weekend to write the final legislation. The president also told GOP senators to keep amendments off the bill in order to push it quickly through the lame-duck session without the time-consuming process of a House-Senate conference.

Breaux, Chafee and Nelson reluctantly agreed to allow the administration to create a new personnel system for the department outside of civil service rules. The compromise gave the president the power to remove workers from union representation on national security grounds. "It's the best we could get," said Breaux. "It's not what I would have written."

The House passed the new language, introduced as HR 5710, by a vote of 299-121 on Nov. 13. (*House vote 477, p. H-148*)

Senate leaders moved to expedite deliberations by cutting off floor debate and limiting amendments. Democrats made one final attempt to shape the legislation, when Daschle tried to remove several special-interest provisions added by House GOP leaders at the last minute, including one to limit liability for pharmaceutical companies.

Republicans prevailed in the final showdown Nov. 19; moderates sided with the administration and defeated Daschle's amendment, 47-52. GOP leaders argued that the amendment would gut important provisions and kill the legislation for the year. Moderate Republicans Collins, Chafee and Olympia J. Snowe of Maine won assurances from House and Senate GOP leaders during the roll call vote that the provisions in dispute would be stripped early in the 108th Congress. The Senate then inserted the House-passed language into HR 5005 and passed the final measure, 90-9. (*Senate votes 245, 249, p. S-51*)

The final House vote clearing the bill was a formality, done by unanimous consent in pro forma session Nov. 22. ◆

Homeland Security Provisions

Following are the main provisions of the law (HR 5005 — PL 107-296)— cleared Nov. 22 and signed Nov. 25 — that created the Cabinet-level Department of Homeland Security:

Homeland Security Department: Mission and Structure

• **Mission.** The mission of the new department is to prevent terrorist attacks within the United States, reduce the nation's vulnerability to such acts and make sure the country is prepared to deal with any disaster that results from an attack.

The department is not allowed to investigate or prosecute acts of terrorism. That function remains in the hands of federal agencies such as the FBI, and local and state authorities. Otherwise, the law gives the secretary of Homeland Security wide-ranging powers, including making grants, agreeing to contracts and making agreements with other federal agencies. The secretary also is directed to make sure all the disparate databases and computer systems throughout the department are integrated so that they can share information.

• **Structure.** The new agency incorporates all or part of 22 federal agencies. It is divided into four substantive divisions: Information Analysis and Infrastructure Protection; Science and Technology; Border and Transportation Security; and Emergency Preparedness and Response. A fifth division handles management. Each is headed by an undersecretary and has several assistant secretaries.

Information Analysis and Infrastructure Protection

• **Mission.** The division is responsible for receiving, analyzing and assessing terrorism information from the CIA, FBI and other intelligence agencies, and issuing reports on the seriousness of the threat. It is directed to make a nationwide assessment of the nation's "critical infrastructure," much of which is privately owned, including power plants, water systems, railroads, highways, bridges, the Internet, telecommunications networks, financial networks and the electrical grids. And it is responsible for sharing information on threats to the nation or its critical infrastructure with states, local governments and private-sector entities as needed.

• **Personnel.** Employees from the State Department, CIA, FBI, National Imagery and Mapping Agency, National Security Agency and Defense Intelligence Agency can be assigned to this division to help with information analysis.

• **Agencies transferred.** The following is a list of agencies moved to this division (and their previous agencies or departments):

- National Infrastructure Protection Center (FBI).
- National Communications System (Defense).
- Critical Infrastructure Assurance (Commerce).
- National Infrastructure Simulation and Analysis Center (Energy).
- Federal Computer Incident Response Center (GSA).

• **FOIA protections.** Private businesses that own or manage anything deemed "critical infrastructure" voluntarily may submit information that reveals vulnerabilities, and that information can be kept secret and exempt from disclosure under the Freedom of Information Act. This FOIA exemption also limits the liabilities of such companies from lawsuits that can arise if weaknesses in their security are revealed. Anyone who leaks this critical infrastructure information to the public or news media can be fined and sen-

tenced to up to one year in prison.

• **Privacy officer.** The secretary of Homeland Security is required to appoint a privacy officer to act as an in-house watchdog to make sure department policies and use of technology do not erode individual privacy. The privacy officer is required to make an annual report to Congress and enforce the provisions of the 1974 Privacy Act (PL 93-579), which bars the government from using personal, private information collected for one purpose for a totally different purpose. (*1974 Almanac, p. 292*)

• **Net Guard.** The undersecretary for information analysis and infrastructure protection has authority to create a volunteer organization called Net Guard made up of technology experts or professionals who can help localities prepare for and defend against cyberattacks on critical information systems.

• **Information sharing.** The law includes provisions of the Homeland Security Information Sharing Act, which encourages the federal government to coordinate its terrorist intelligence gathering and to share information as needed with state and local governments. This information may need to be unclassified or edited in order to share it with some local or state law enforcement agents. The department is directed to develop information systems that allow people with higher security clearance to access classified information, while allowing other law enforcement officials access to unclassified information. These information systems should pull from the National Law Enforcement Telecommunications System, the Regional Information Sharing System and the Terrorist Threat Warning System of the FBI.

• **Cybersecurity.** The law increases penalties for hackers or computer criminals who intentionally try to injure or kill while carrying out cyberattacks. Sentences of up to life in prison are provided for cybercriminals who attempt to cause death through computer crimes.

Science and Technology

• **Mission.** This is the research and development division, charged with improving law enforcement technologies and biological terrorism preparedness, while establishing training centers for homeland security. It is to help develop, test, study and approve products, equipment or technologies that the department could use in the war against terrorism.

• **Advisory groups.** Special committees are to be created to advise and consult with the department about anti-terrorism technologies that could be used by federal, state or local governments. They include a 20-member Homeland Security Science and Technology Advisory Committee. The advisory committees are exempt from some federal open meeting rules.

• **Agencies transferred.** The following is a list of agencies moved to this division (and their previous agencies or departments):

- Chemical, radiological and biological preparedness division (Energy).
- National Bio-Weapons Defense Analysis Center, part of the Lawrence Livermore National Laboratory (Defense).
- Plum Island Animal Disease Center (Agriculture).

• **Smallpox.** The Homeland Security Department is directed to coordinate a smallpox vaccination plan with the Department of

Health and Human Services (HHS). The law limits federal liability for health problems that arise from the smallpox vaccine.

- **Research centers.** A Homeland Security Advanced Research Projects Agency was established and authorized at $500 million for fiscal 2003. The agency is intended to be similar to the Defense Advanced Research Project Agency (DARPA). The law also establishes a system of university-based homeland security research centers.

Border and Transportation Security

- **Mission.** Border and Transportation Security, by far the largest division, is charged with protecting air, land and sea transportation; protecting the nation's borders and territorial waters; and enforcing immigration and visa laws.
- **Agencies transferred.** Agencies moved to this division (and their previous departments) are:
  - U.S. Customs Service (Treasury).
  - U.S. Border Patrol (Justice).
  - Transportation Security Administration (Transportation).
  - Federal Protective Service, which provides security for federal buildings (GSA).
  - Office of Domestic Preparedness (Justice).
  - Federal Law Enforcement Training Center (Treasury).
  - Immigration and Naturalization Service (Justice).
- **INS.** The functions of the Immigration and Naturalization Service (INS) are transferred to the Homeland Security Department, and the INS is abolished. The law requires that the INS' immigration services and border security functions be organized into two separate bureaus in the department. The bureaus must submit separate budget requests, accompanied by reorganization plans sent to the Judiciary and Appropriations committees of both chambers.

The law also allows government buyouts for employees who choose to leave or retire under the INS restructuring. An employee who takes a buyout and decides to return to the department within five years must repay the government the bonus for leaving.

- **Bureau of Border Security.** The new bureau is to enforce the nation's immigration laws, absorbing INS enforcement operations including the Border Patrol, inspections, investigations, intelligence, and detention and removal.
- **Customs Service.** The Customs Service function of stopping contraband from entering the country is placed under the Border and Transportation Security Department. Certain revenue collection and trade enforcement functions, however, remain under the Treasury Department.
- **Agricultural inspectors.** The inspection functions of the Animal Plant and Health Inspection Service (APHIS) are transferred to the department, while quarantine duties remain in the Agriculture Department. APHIS inspectors are charged with identifying and preventing "agroterrorism" — intentional efforts to poison the food supply or introduce malicious viruses into produce or food products.
- **Transportation Security Administration.** The law shifts the TSA to the new department but specifies that it remain a distinct entity within the Border and Transportation Security department for at least two years.

The law also extends the deadline for certain airports to install explosives detection systems for baggage until Dec. 31, 2003. The original law (PL 107-296) that created TSA set the deadline for Dec. 31, 2002. (*2001 Almanac, p. 20-4*)

- **Visas.** The department is responsible for setting guidelines for visas for foreigners who want to visit the United States. State De-

partment consular offices will still issue visas, but they must follow rules set by Homeland Security. The secretary of Homeland Security is authorized to assign personnel to overseas consulates if he believes it is in the interests of homeland security. A special provision bans all "third party" screening for visas in Saudi Arabia and requires that Homeland Security employees approve or reject Saudi visas. Every visa application rejected must be put into an electronic database to better track the names of people denied visas.

- **Border fence.** The law expresses the sense of Congress that finishing a 14-mile fence along the U.S.-Mexico border at San Diego should be a high priority.
- **Immigrant children.** Authority to deal with children of illegal aliens is transferred to the director of the office of refugee resettlement at HHS, who is encouraged to keep the children's best interests in mind and attempt to reunite immigrant children with parents overseas. These children must be protected from smugglers, traffickers and other criminal elements. The law prohibits children from being released on their own recognizance if they are under 18.
- **Employee discipline.** The secretary of Homeland Security and the attorney general are authorized to create within this division pilot projects to try out different ways of disciplining employees. Certain unions and managers are exempt from such pilot programs.
- **Immigration reports.** The secretary of Homeland Security is required to submit reports to the president and Congress with detailed statistics about immigration applications and demographics of new immigrants.
- **Immigration office.** The law gives the attorney general authority over the Executive Office for Immigration Review.

Emergency Preparedness and Response

- **Mission.** The division is instructed to focus on preparing for and responding to terrorist attacks. Responsibilities include disaster aid, as well as the stockpiling of treatments and vaccines for biological or chemical weapons attacks.
- **Agencies transferred.** Agencies moved to this division (and their previous departments) are:
  - Federal Emergency Management Agency.
  - Integrated Hazard Information System of the National Oceanic and Atmospheric Administration (Commerce). This system will be renamed "Firesat" under the new department.
  - National Domestic Preparedness Office (FBI).
  - Office of Emergency Preparedness (HHS).
  - National Stockpile of Vaccines (HHS).
  - Nuclear Incident Response Team (Energy).
- **Public health.** HHS is directed to work with Homeland Security on a national strategy for preparing public health workers to respond to a terrorist attack.
- **FEMA.** FEMA is designated as the emergency response agency for terrorist attacks but is still required to carry out its role of responding to other disasters such as hurricanes and floods.
- **Commercial technologies.** To the maximum extent practicable, the department is directed to use off-the-shelf technologies — those readily available in the commercial market — in building information systems that share intelligence. The department also is directed to buy many of its products or services from the private sector.

Other Agencies

In addition to the five divisions, several other agencies are transferred to or created in the new department.

- **Coast Guard.** The Commandant of the Coast Guard reports di-

rectly to the secretary of Homeland Security. The Coast Guard is to work closely with the Under Secretary of Border and Transportation Security as well as maintain its existing independent identity as a military service. If there is a declaration of war or when the president so directs, the Coast Guard would operate as an element of the Department of Defense, consistent with existing law. The Coast Guard remains a separate unit and must continue its non-homeland security duties, including search and rescue, marine safety and environmental protection measures. The secretary of Homeland Security is not allowed to decrease the Coast Guard's work force in these non-homeland areas, except in emergencies.

The secretary, along with the commandant of the Coast Guard, is required within 90 days of enactment to submit a report on the deepwater program, a program to replace the Coast Guard's offshore ships and planes. The report is supposed to include ways to accelerate the deepwater overhaul from a 20-year program to a 10-year program.

● **Bureau of Citizenship and Immigration Services.** The immigration services of the INS are taken over by a new Bureau of Citizenship and Immigration Services under the deputy secretary of Homeland Security. The bureau is directed to develop pilot programs to eliminate the backlog of immigrant-related paperwork such as green cards.

● **Secret Service.** The Secret Service and all its functions are transferred to the Homeland Security Department, but the Secret Service remains independent of the four directorates under homeland security.

● **Office for State and and Local Government Coordination.** The law creates a special office responsible for overseeing and coordinating department programs for and liaison with state and local governments.

Department Management

● **Undersecretary.** An undersecretary of Homeland Security for management is to oversee budget, human resources, procurement, information technology, department grants, internal audits, building management, and security for employees and department facilities. The undersecretary is responsible for collecting immigration statistics from the Border and Transportation Security division. The undersecretary also is to oversee the chief information officer, chief financial officer and chief human capital officer.

● **Human resources.** The Homeland Security secretary is authorized to create and modify a unified human resources management system for all the agencies being merged. The system must be "flexible" and "contemporary," but it must maintain protections for whistleblowers and union members. The law requires collaboration with employees and unions for any changes to existing personnel rules. The authority to set new personnel rules expires five years after the law took effect Nov. 25, 2002.

● **Union rights.** The president or the Homeland Security secretary is allowed to remove employees from unions or collective bargaining units if their jobs have "materially changed" or if the majority of employees within a collective bargaining unit have jobs that involve intelligence or investigative work.

● **Civil rights.** The management division includes a director of civil rights and civil liberties whose job is to assess all allegations of discrimination, while enforcing civil rights rules in the department.

● **Employee rights.** The department is not exempt from existing laws protecting whistleblowers and must provide equal employment protections required in other federal agencies.

● **Salary and benefits.** The secretary of Homeland Security is required to submit a plan within 90 days of enactment that ensures there is no disparity in pay or benefits between the agencies that have been transferred into the department.

● **Inspector general.** An inspector general's office within the department will serve as the in-house investigator, but the secretary of Homeland Security has unusual authority to prohibit any inspector general's investigation if he thinks it would not be in the interest of national security. This provision also allows assistant inspectors general to carry guns and make arrests if necessary, if they have been given permission by the attorney general.

Contractors and Liability

The Homeland Security secretary has procurement power to fund research projects and approve pilot programs for new homeland security products or technologies. The secretary also may employ outside consultants or experts without having to follow certain government pay limitations.

● **Acquisition authority.** The department has authority to make some purchases without going through a contracting process. "Micropurchases" for supplies and products of up to $7,500 are allowed for certain Homeland Security employees. The secretary has authority to sign contracts of up to $200,000 for purchases made inside the United States and up to $300,000 for purchases made outside the country without having to go through a competitive bidding process.

The secretary also can authorize purchases of commercial products up to $7.5 million under expedited procurement procedures. The normal limit is $5 million. The law also gives emergency acquisition authority to agency heads to make immediate purchases to help in recovery from a terrorist attack.

● **Unsolicited proposals.** The Homeland Security Department is authorized to review unsolicited ideas for homeland security products or technologies in order to encourage innovation.

● **Anti-terrorism technologies.** The law allows the secretary of Homeland Security to create a list of anti-terrorism technologies or products that the department will buy.

● **Liability limits.** Lawsuits are limited for the use of products that make the list. The law prohibits punitive damages — monetary awards for pain and suffering — against contractors whose homeland security products make the list. Lawsuits for economic damages — recovery of lost wages, salary or property — are allowed, but plaintiffs must prove that the contractor acted fraudulently or negligently.

The law allows pain-and-suffering judgments against individuals or governments that sponsor terrorist acts.

● **Liability insurance.** The law requires Homeland Security contractors to carry the maximum amount of liability insurance available for their industry.

Miscellaneous Provisions

● **Homeland Security Council.** The law establishes a Homeland Security Council within the Executive Office of the President to advise the president on homeland security matters. Members include the president, vice president, secretary of Homeland Security, attorney general, secretary of Defense and anyone else designated by the president. The council has a staff headed by an executive secretary appointed by the president.

● **BATF.** The Bureau of Alcohol, Tobacco and Firearms (BATF) is transferred from the Treasury Department to the Justice Depart-

ment. The law requires the bureau to establish a new explosives training center. It also establishes new federal restrictions on the possession and use of explosives.

● **Airline liability.** The law extends until the end of 2003 the federal Aviation War Risk Insurance program and the liability limits of commercial airlines whose aircraft were used in terror attacks.

● **Arming pilots.** The TSA is required to develop a program under which trained commercial airline pilots would be allowed to carry guns aboard aircraft. Volunteer pilots may be deputized as federal flight deck officers and allowed to carry firearms after receiving training and achieving proficiency comparable to that for air marshals, and meeting other TSA requirements.

● **Department transition.** The department has one year from enactment to complete the merger of the 22 agencies. Sixty days after enactment, the president is required to submit a plan for transferring agencies into the department, identifying the funds and functions that will be transferred into Homeland Security.

● **Congressional committees.** The law calls on Congress to review its committee structure and possibly reorganize to handle the creation of the Homeland Security Department.

● **National ID program.** The law specifies that the Homeland Security Act should not be used as a justification to create a national identification program.

● **Advisory committees.** The Homeland Security secretary is authorized to create advisory committees to consult with the department on various security matters. These committees terminate after two years.

● **Reorganization.** The secretary is allowed to discontinue or reorganize divisions within the Homeland Security Department but is barred from eliminating agencies or units that are required to remain under the law.

● **Sale of property.** The secretary is allowed to sell excess property that belongs to the department.

● **Budget request.** The president is required to submit an annual homeland security budget proposal, starting with the 2004 budget. The law requires the budget request, starting in fiscal 2005, to include future year projections for homeland security.

● **Limits on secretary's power.** The secretary is prohibited from having any power over the military, and is not given any war powers. ◆

Congress Backs Defense Buildup

Embracing President Bush's call for an increase in defense spending that was the largest since the Vietnam War, Congress cleared a $392.9 billion defense authorization bill for fiscal 2003. The total was roughly equal to Bush's $392.8 billion request and $43 billion more than was authorized for fiscal 2002.

With U.S. troops seeking to root out al Qaeda terrorists in Afghanistan and shipping off to the Persian Gulf region for an anticipated war in Iraq, lawmakers were not disposed to make many major changes to Bush's proposal. The political pressures of the coming midterm elections also contributed to an atmosphere that left many members unwilling to take on a wartime president. Congress cleared the measure Nov. 13, and Bush signed it into law Dec. 2 (HR 4546 — PL 107-314).

More than a third of the authorization — $139.8 billion — was dedicated to operations and maintenance. The bill also authorized $73.8 billion for weapons procurement; $56.7 billion for research and development, $2.9 billion more than requested; $93.8 billion for

BoxScore

Bill:
HR 4546 — PL 107-314

Legislative Action:

House passed HR 4546 (H Rept 107-436), 359-58, on May 10.

Senate passed S 2514 (S Rept 107-151) 97-2, on June 27, then incorporated the text into HR 4546 and passed it by voice vote.

House adopted the conference report (H Rept 107-772) by voice vote, Nov. 12.

Senate cleared the bill by voice vote Nov. 13.

President signed Dec. 2.

fate of the Crusader cannon, whether to accept Bush's request for a $10 billion contingency fund to spend as needed for the war on terrorism and a politically explosive dispute over proposed changes in the payment of benefits to disabled veterans. The latter issue pitted the Bush administration against a bipartisan, bicameral group of lawmakers and delayed final action on the bill until the post-election lameduck session.

The decision to cancel the Crusader was a follow-on to Bush's promises during the 2000 campaign that, as president, he would create the "military of the next century," scrapping the congressionally popular conventional weapons designed for the Cold War to make room for the high-technology weapons suited to an agile, lightweight force. Time constraints for the new administration and the Sept. 11, 2001, attacks made it difficult for Bush to follow through on that promise in his first year.

In 2002, however, Defense Secretary Donald H. Rumsfeld took the initial step May 8, announcing that he would cancel the Crusader cannon, the heir to the Paladin howitzer and an $11 billion program derided by critics as an example of weaponry designed to counter a long-gone Soviet threat. Rumsfeld said

personnel; $10.4 billion for military construction and family housing; and $16.5 billion for defense-related activities carried out by the Energy Department.

Major issues that did arise during the debate included the

the 40-ton cannon was too heavy for rapid deployment to distant conflicts. The decision drew immediate opposition from several lawmakers, including two Oklahoma Republicans — Senate Minority Whip Don Nickles and House Republican Conference Chairman J.C. Watts Jr., in whose district the big gun was to be built. United Defense LP, the Crusader's politically well-connected contractor, launched a lobbying campaign.

But Bush and senior Pentagon officials were determined to eliminate the program, and the White House threatened to veto the entire defense authorization bill if Congress spared the Crusader. In the end, Congress went along with Bush.

The biggest fight, however, was over a proposal by both chambers to change a 111-year-old law that barred veterans from receiving full disability compensation while still receiving full pension benefits. Veterans organizations had lobbied for years to eliminate this ban on "concurrent receipts," which they said affected at least 450,000 veterans. The White House strongly opposed such a change, saying it could add as much as $58 billion to defense spending over 10 years. Pentagon officials also argued that military veterans were well compensated, drawing full pensions that were indexed for inflation and included lifetime health care and other benefits.

Highlights

The following are the major components of the bill:
- **Missile defense.** $7.8 billion for development of a missile defense system, roughly the same amount as requested by the administration.
- **Crusader.** No funds. Despite resistance from members worried about losing jobs, the bill endorsed Rumsfeld's decision to cancel the program. The administration originally had requested $476 million for the weapon.
- **F-22 Raptor.** $4.1 billion, as requested, for 23 of the Air Force's next-generation fighter plane, with an additional $627 million for research and development.
- **Joint Strike Fighter.** $3.5 billion, roughly the same amount as requested, for the multipurpose aircraft to be used by the Air Force, Navy and Marine Corps.
- **F/A-18 E and F.** $3.4 billion for 48 aircraft, the Navy's upgrade of the existing F/A-18 C/D.
- **Assault ship.** $969 million for Navy's next generation surface combat ship, the DD(X).
- **Drones.** Nearly $1 billion for unmanned aerial vehicles similar to those used in Afghanistan.
- **Destroyer.** $2.4 billion, as requested, for two *Arleigh Burke*-class guided missile destroyers, the DDG-51.
- **New attack submarine.** $1.6 billion, as the administration sought, to purchase the fifth boat in the *Virginia* class of attack submarines to replace the *Los Angeles*-class subs, which were being retired.
- **Anti-terrorism.** $7.3 billion, as requested, for Defense Department programs to combat terrorism.
- **Military pay raise.** A minimum 4.1 percent pay increase, as requested, for military personnel, with higher raises for mid-grade and senior noncommissioned officers, and mid-grade officers.
- **Veterans' benefits.** A change in law that allowed veterans to receive both their full military pension and their full disability payment — if the disability resulted from a combat wound for which they earned a Purple Heart or their disability rating was at least 60 percent a result of "combat-related" disability.
- **Contingency fund.** $10 billion as a contingency fund for future war costs, as requested. However, the money was never appropriated.

Legislative Action

House Subcommittee Action

Five subcommittees of the House Armed Services Committee approved portions of the bill during the last two weeks of April. The markups included:
- **Military readiness.** Environmental laws generated the most controversy when the Military Readiness Subcommittee approved its portion of the bill by voice vote April 25. The panel recommended $147.7 billion for operations and maintenance programs, a $22.7 billion increase over fiscal 2002.

Just days before the panel met, the Pentagon asked lawmakers for eight exemptions from environmental laws to facilitate training exercises. The subcommittee endorsed two changes. It agreed to a waiver for training exercises in which some treaty-protected birds could be killed. On March 13, a federal judge had ruled that the Navy was violating the 1918 Migratory Bird Treaty Act by using a small island near Guam as a bombing range.

The other provision was an amendment to the Endangered Species Act of 1973 (PL 93-205) to bar the Interior Department from designating as a "critical habitat" any area on a base that was governed by a natural resources management plan agreed to by federal and state environmental officials and the Pentagon. By law, activities in critical habitats were restricted tightly. (*1973 Almanac, p. 670*)

Pentagon officials, with the backing of several Armed Services Committee members, argued that it was increasingly difficult for military units to conduct realistic training because of the combination of environmental laws and restrictions imposed by urban development.
- **Military installations and facilities.** The panel gave voice vote approval April 25 to $10 billion for military construction projects in fiscal 2003, after rejecting, 3-13, a proposal by Gene Taylor, D-Miss., to cancel a round of military base closings slated for 2005. The bill was about $1 billion above the administration's original request.

"How do you grow your forces and shrink your bases at the same time?" argued Taylor. "The House was forced into voting for [base closures] by a bad situation." The House version of the fiscal 2002 defense authorization bill (PL 107-107) did not address base closures. But Senate support for the proposal and pressure from the White House forced House members to sign on to the deal in conference. Most members who voted against the Taylor amendment said they opposed more base closures, but thought it was too late to rework the fiscal 2002 law. Others worried that reopening the issue could have unintended consequences, such as moving the next round of closures up to 2003. (*2001 Almanac, p. 7-3*)

● **Procurement.** The subcommittee gave voice vote approval April 30 to $75 billion in military procurement spending, $3.2 billion more than the president requested. The extra money was targeted to boost accounts for ship-building programs, upgrade F-15 and F-16 aircraft, and buy Navy training aircraft. The authorizers proposed tapping into the president's requested $10 billion war reserve for most of the extra money.

House Committee Action

The full House Armed Services Committee approved a $383.4 billion version of the bill (H Rept 107-436) in a nine-hour marathon session May 1. The vote was 57-1, with Cynthia A. McKinney, D-Ga., casting the only "nay" vote.

The total was $32.6 billion above the fiscal 2002 level. The committee described it as the largest inflation-adjusted increase since 1966. Most of the increase went to cover inflation, higher costs for routine operations than previously estimated and other basic expenses, prompting several defense hawks to complain that Bush should ask for more in fiscal 2004. "Even this sizeable defense budget does not fully address all of the military's pressing needs," said Armed Services Chairman Bob Stump, R-Ariz.

● **Contingency fund.** The panel went along with much of Bush's budget proposal, but it balked at the request for a $10 billion, no-strings-attached contingency fund for the war on terrorism. Many lawmakers said they would not write a blank check, and the committee asked Bush to submit more details. In the meantime, the committee agreed to use $3.7 billion of the $10 billion to pay for ongoing military operations in Afghanistan and homeland security activities.

To keep within the discretionary spending cap set in the House budget resolution, the committee shifted the $3.7 billion (later revised to $3.1 billion) worth of programs to a separate bill (HR 4547). That created room in the main bill for members' priorities. The committee subsequently approved HR 4547 (H Rept 107-603) by a vote of 50-1 on July 18, after adding language to allocate much of the rest of the $10 billion to specific projects. The House passed the bill by a near-unanimous vote of 413-3, on July 24. Members expected the bill to be folded into the larger authorization bill in conference. (*House vote 335, p. H-106*)

● **Missile defense.** The bill added $21 million to the $7.8 billion requested by Bush to develop and deploy a missile defense system. The committee rejected, 26-32, an amendment by John M. Spratt Jr., D-S.C., to shift funds within the total for missile defense. An attempt by Spratt to prohibit the development of nuclear-tipped interceptor missiles to destroy attacking missiles was defeated, 24-31. No missile defense programs in development used nuclear warheads, but some Pentagon officials had raised the possibility.

● **Crusader.** The bill included the $476 million originally requested for the Crusader cannon. In its report on the bill, the committee directed the Pentagon not to halt the program until it had completed a study of the alternatives.

● **Veterans' benefits.** The committee proposed that the most severely disabled military retirees, those whose disabilities were 60 percent or more combat-related, be allowed to receive both their full retirement pay and their full VA disability payments by 2007.

● **Nuclear weapons.** Several conservative Democrats joined Republicans in rejecting Democratic-sponsored amendments aimed at restricting nuclear weapons programs. In a "nuclear posture review," made public in January, the administration had said it was considering putting some decommissioned warheads in reserve, and it indicated that it wanted to reduce the time it would take to resume nuclear tests. Republicans argued that the Democratic proposals would limit a president's future options, "taking chips that the president has, and may want to use, off the table," in the words of Duncan Hunter, R-Calif. The committee:

● Rejected, 25-32, an amendment by Ellen O. Tauscher, D-Calif., expressing the sense of Congress that the United States should reduce the number of deployed nuclear warheads to 1,700 and dismantle those removed from service. The amendment also would have stricken from the bill an endorsement of the development of earth-penetrating nuclear warheads intended to obliterate command posts and chemical weapons factories buried underground.

● Rejected, 25-31, an amendment by Spratt that would have required the executive branch to give Congress at least 12 months notice of any intention to resume underground nuclear test explosions. The United States had conducted no such tests since 1992, and Bush had said he did not intend to resume testing. However, a Pentagon advisory panel had recommended that the Energy Department shorten the time it would need to resume testing to a year or less, rather than the estimated two to three years.

● Adopted, 25-16, an amendment by Hunter directing the Energy Department to draw up a plan on how to reduce to one year the time that would be needed to resume testing.

● **Environment.** The committee bill included limited waivers from the Endangered Species Act and the Migratory Bird Treaty Act. The committee:

● Rejected, by voice vote, an amendment by Jim Maloney, D-Conn., that would have dropped the prohibition on designating a "critical habitat" on certain bases. Maloney and other Democrats said the Pentagon already could get a waiver from the Endangered Species Act to allow training. But Hunter insisted the pendulum had swung too far toward environmental protection at the expense of combat readiness.

● Rejected, 22-34, an amendment that would have eliminated a provision to designate as wilderness 500,000 acres owned by the Interior Department. The land, south of the Great Salt Lake in Utah, was under the airspace of a sprawling complex of bombing ranges and testing areas.

● **Base closings.** The committee rejected, 19-38, an amendment by Taylor to cancel the next round of shutdowns.

● **Other amendments.** The committee accepted, by voice vote, a proposal by Taylor to limit U.S. troops in Colombia to no more than 500. The vote came only after the panel adopted, 31-28, a second-degree amendment by Saxby Chambliss, R-Ga., to allow the secretary of Defense to waive the limitation on grounds of national security.

Reprising similar votes from recent years, the committee rejected, 24-34, an amendment by Loretta Sanchez, D-Calif., that would have allowed female service members or military dependents stationed abroad to obtain abortions in local U.S. military hospitals, provided they paid for the procedure.

• **Other changes.** The committee made a number of other changes to the president's request to address specific concerns among the members. The committee:

• Added $550 million to boost the number of active-duty personnel by 12,652, an increase of nearly 1 percent. In testimony before the committee, the service chiefs had expressed concern about overextending the troops on various missions, including the war in Afghanistan and the Balkans. Ike Skelton of Missouri, the ranking Democrat on the committee, pushed for an increase in the active-duty numbers.

• Added $229 million to the $244 million requested to buy components for a nuclear-powered aircraft carrier, which would allow construction of the ship to begin a year earlier than previously planned.

• Added $810 million — the largest single block of money added to the bill — to increase the Navy's shipbuilding budget, which members of both parties had decried as woefully inadequate to sustain the fleet at its existing level of about 300 ships.

House Floor Action

The House passed the $383.4 billion bill by a vote of 359-58 on May 10, after GOP leaders easily turned back a number of Democratic challenges. (*House vote 158, p. H-54*)

• **Nuclear weapons.** Democrats continued to express concern that the administration was reversing a decades-old bipartisan goal of reducing both the number of nuclear weapons and U.S. reliance on them. Heather A. Wilson, R-N.M., who chaired the House Republican Policy Committee's panel on defense, argued that a new international dynamic required a new approach toward nuclear weapons. "The relationship with Russia has profoundly changed: We're not each other's worst enemy anymore," she said. "But there are other people we both have to worry about."

The House:

• Rejected, 172-243, an amendment by Edward J. Markey, D-Mass., that would have prohibited research on a nuclear "bunker-buster" that would destroy command posts and chemical weapons plants buried deep underground. The program was the centerpiece of the administration's new vision for nuclear weapons. (*House vote 141, p. H-50*)

• Adopted, 362-53, an amendment by Curt Weldon, R-Pa., to allow research and development but bar the construction of a prototype nuclear bunker-buster. The fiscal 1994 defense authorization law (PL 103-160) prohibited the Pentagon from researching or developing new low-yield nuclear weapons, which it defined as those that produce an explosion equivalent to 5,000 tons (5 kilotons) or less of TNT — about one-third the explosive power of the bombs that the United States dropped on Hiroshima and Nagasaki in World War II. The intent was to ban the use of such weapons. (*House vote 142, p. H-50; 1993 Almanac, p. 433*)

• **Missile defense.** The House:

• Rejected, 159-253, an amendment by John F. Tierney, D-Mass., to prohibit development of "space-based" missile defense programs. Tierney said his amendment was intended to block deployment of anti-missile weapons in space. But Republicans complained that it was so broadly worded that missile detection and communications satellites used by ground-based anti-missile systems would be undermined. (*House vote 145, p. H-52*)

• Adopted, by voice vote, a Spratt proposal to add $135 million to the Israeli Arrow and U.S. PAC-3 anti-missile systems by cutting funds from other missile defense programs.

• Rejected, 192-223 a Spratt motion to recommit the bill to the Armed Services Committee with instructions to add language banning use of funds to develop or deploy nuclear-tipped anti-missile interceptors. (*House vote 157, p. H-54*)

• **Other amendments.** The House also:

• Rejected, 202-215, an amendment by Sanchez to allow female service members and dependents stationed overseas to obtain abortions at local U.S. military hospitals, provided they paid for the procedure. (*House vote 153, p. H-54*)

• Adopted 264-152, an amendment by Ron Paul, R-Texas, expressing the sense of the House that no funds authorized by the bill should be used to cooperate with the International Criminal Court. (*House vote 155, p. H-54*)

• Adopted, 232-183, an amendment by Virginia independent Virgil H. Goode to authorize military personnel to assist the Immigration and Naturalization Service and the Customs Service, if requested. (*House vote 154, p. H-54*)

Senate Committee Action

The Senate Armed Services Committee on May 9 approved a $393.4 billion version of the bill (S 2514 — S Rept 107-151) that cut Bush's plan for missile defense and shifted the money to shipbuilding. The vote was 17-8.

• **Missile defense.** The committee, on a party-line vote, reduced Bush's request for missile defense by $814 million and shifted $690 million to the Navy's shipbuilding account. Committee Chairman Carl Levin, D-Mich., said national security was being "shortchanged by the focus on missile defense." John W. Warner of Virginia, the committee's ranking Republican, responded that the vote "fails to send a clear message to America's allies and adversaries that the Congress will provide the necessary resources to defend our homeland and our troops."

• **Nuclear weapons.** The bill prohibited spending $15 million that Bush requested to develop the nuclear bunker-buster.

• **Contingency fund.** In a break with the House, the Senate panel included the $10 billion war reserve fund without dipping into it. "We did not touch it. It ought to be held for the war on terrorism," said Levin.

• **Crusader.** The bill included the $476 million originally requested for the Crusader. Rumsfeld's announcement about canceling the program came as the Senate Armed Services Committee was in the middle of the defense authorization process. But Levin left open the possibility that the funding might be dropped after the committee received details from the Pentagon.

• **Shipbuilding.** The bill added $1.1 billion to Bush's $8.2 billion shipbuilding request. The increase included $690 million cut from the missile defense request and divvied up to buy components for ships that would be funded in future budgets — $415 million for a nuclear-powered submarine, $150 million for amphibious landing transports, designated LPDs, and $125 million for Aegis destroyers.

The committee's shipbuilding increase also included $229 million, in addition to the $244 million requested, for components for a nuclear powered aircraft carrier. The ship,

which would be built at Newport News Shipbuilding and Drydock Co. in Virginia, had been slated for the fiscal 2006 budget, but limited budgets forced the Navy to slow that schedule. The Senate committee's increase, which matched what the House provided, would put the carrier back on schedule for funding in fiscal 2006.

The Senate panel included two non-controversial provisions requested by the Pentagon that would allow the Defense Department to work out agreements with state and local governments and private organizations to forestall private development on land adjacent to military bases.

Senate Floor Action

The Senate passed a $393.3 billion version of the bill June 27 by a vote of 97-2, after Bush persuaded the Democratic-controlled body to endorse his $7.8 billion request for a missile defense development program. *(Senate vote 165, p. S-34)*

● **Missile defense.** Faced with a presidential veto threat issued June 19, Democrats agreed June 26 to authorize the full $7.8 billion requested for missile defense, but to specify that Bush could use $814 million of it for missile defense or to fight terrorism at home and abroad. Warner offered the amendment giving Bush discretion over the $814 million. Levin insisted on additional language to stipulate that counterterrorism was the higher priority. For nearly two days, Republicans resisted. In the end, they took the money and let the Democrats have the rhetoric, but only after administration lawyers assured them that the compromise language would give Bush a free hand on missile defense. Both the Levin and Warner amendments were adopted by voice vote.

In further action on missile defense, the Senate:

● Adopted by voice vote June 26 an amendment by Dianne Feinstein, D-Calif., and Ted Stevens, R-Alaska, to bar development or deployment of nuclear-armed missile defense interceptors.

● Adopted by voice vote June 27 an amendment by Armed Services Strategic Forces Subcommittee Chairman Jack Reed, D-R.I., that would require the Pentagon to send Congress a report in both a classified and unclassified form within 120 days of a missile defense test. In early June, the Pentagon had stated that it would reduce greatly the amount of information released about future tests of the ground-based interceptor missile slated for deployment in Alaska. Critics charged that Rumsfeld was trying to shield the program from tough technical scrutiny by exempting it from some of the detailed oversight applied to other major weapons programs.

● **Crusader.** The Senate approved an amendment June 19 that gave Rumsfeld a nearly free hand to kill the cannon. The amendment shifted the $476 million designated for the cannon to the Army's Future Combat Systems, a new generation of lightweight tanks, troop carriers, long-range artillery and other equipment. The amendment also required that the Army complete a comparative analysis of the Crusader and three alternatives and report to Rumsfeld and Congress within 30 days of the bill's enactment. Thereafter, Rumsfeld would be free to seek from the House and Senate Armed Services and Appropriations committees permission to reprogram the $476 million to accelerate other artillery programs and pay a cancellation fee to United Defense LP.

The Armed Services Committee had approved the amendment, 13-6, on June 13 after receiving additional in-

formation from the Pentagon about the program.

Warner, the administration's point man on the issue, agreed that the Army should complete its study, but he argued that the White House would not accept a bill that blocked cancellation of the Crusader. As a compromise, Warner offered a second-degree amendment to Levin's, dropping the requirement that the four committees approve Rumsfeld's proposal on how to spend the Crusader funds.

After the Senate approved Warner's proposal by voice vote, lawmakers adopted the revised Levin amendment, 96-3. New York Democrats Charles E. Schumer and Hillary Rodham Clinton joined George V. Voinovich, R-Ohio, in voting against the amendment. The Army's Watervliet Arsenal near Albany, N.Y., was counting on manufacturing the Crusader's gun as a major source of work for its roughly 500 employees, beginning in 2006. *(Senate vote 158, p. S-33)*

● **Veterans' benefits.** Brushing aside a fresh veto threat, the Senate adopted, by voice vote, an amendment that would repeal over five years the law under which veterans' pensions were reduced dollar-for-dollar to offset their disability payments.

Majority Whip Harry Reid, D-Nev., a longtime leader of the effort to repeal the ban, dismissed the veto threat. "President George W. Bush would not veto this bill because of what veterans get," Reid said as he dropped the statement from the administration into a wastebasket on the Senate floor. Thomas R. Carper, D-Del., warned that Reid might be underestimating Bush's determination to control expenditures. "How do we pay for this?" Carper demanded. "Whatever sense of fiscal responsibility held sway here in the past is ebbing away."

● **Other amendments.** In other action, the Senate:

● Agreed, 50-49, on June 25 to table (kill) an amendment by Edward M. Kennedy, D-Mass., that would have required the Pentagon to conduct public-private competitions for many contracts that it routinely awarded to private companies. Democrats Max Baucus of Montana and John B. Breaux of Louisiana joined a solid Republican bloc to block the amendment. *(Senate vote 162, p. S-34)*

● Adopted, 93-0, on June 24 a proposal by Robert C. Smith, R-N.H., to prohibit any military superior from requiring or pressuring female service members stationed in Saudi Arabia to wear an abaya, the traditional religious garment that enshrouds a woman from head to toe. The Pentagon had required female personnel in Saudi Arabia to wear the garment when leaving their base on grounds that it would respect local customs and protect the Americans against being singled out by terrorists. *(Senate vote 161, p. S-34)*

● Adopted by voice vote June 26 an amendment to beef up the Energy Department's programs to help other countries prevent terrorists from acquiring nuclear material. Of the $1.2 billion that the bill would authorize for anti-proliferation activities, the amendment would allow the department to reallocate $100 million for new initiatives, including $15 million to develop ways to detect and deal with a so-called dirty bomb, a conventional explosive device used to scatter radioactive debris.

● Adopted by voice vote an amendment by Armed Services Personnel Subcommittee Chairman Max Cleland, D-Ga., that would give the services discretion to increase their active-duty manpower by 12,000 — just under 1 percent

over the level of 1.39 million requested by Bush. The amendment did not address the $500 million cost of such an increase.

• Adopted, 52-40, on June 21 an amendment by Patty Murray, D-Wash., that would allow female service members or dependents stationed abroad to obtain abortions in local U.S. military hospitals, provided they paid for the procedure. (*Senate vote 160, p. S-34*)

Conference/Final Action

House and Senate negotiators were not able to reach final agreement on the bill until mid-November. The House adopted the conference report (H Rept 107-772) by voice vote Nov. 12, and the Senate cleared the bill for the president by voice vote Nov. 13.

Conferees had hoped to finish before Congress adjourned in mid-October, but their dispute with the White House over veterans' benefits delayed final action until after the November elections.

By then, the fiscal 2003 defense appropriations bill — the bill that actually provided most of the money — had become law (PL 107-248). Still, without the authorization, many programs would have died. Among the items in jeopardy were $10.4 billion in military building programs, a pay raise aimed at encouraging mid-level officers to stay in the armed forces and authorization to end work on the Crusader cannon. Authorizers also worried that if they failed to complete work on the bill, future decisions on defense programs might be shifted from the authorizers to the Appropriations committees, ceding even more power to the spending panels.

• **Veterans' benefits.** For months, the administration fought demands by veterans and lawmakers to repeal the 19th century ban on concurrent receipts. Under the law, a retiree's disability pay was deducted from his pension. The Senate bill would have eliminated the ban outright over five years, affecting about 700,000 retirees. The House bill would have phased it out over five years for about 90,000 of the most severely disabled retirees. Administration officials threatened to veto any bill that repealed existing law. Many lawmakers and lobbyists bet that Bush would not veto the bill over the provision, given veterans' political clout and the fact that 90 percent of the House and 83 percent of the Senate had cosponsored legislation to liberalize the restriction. But the subject was too hot to handle before the election.

Following the election, the administration and Congress were able to compromise. The deal, largely engineered by Warner, was expected to cost $2 billion over 10 years. It extended full retirement and disability benefits to any retiree disabled as a result of enemy fire and to retirees classified as at least 60 percent disabled because of injuries suffered in combat, training or other hazardous duty. Warner termed the deal "Purple Heart Plus Others." Veterans groups vowed to push in the 108th Congress for complete repeal.

• **Crusader.** The final bill redirected the $476 million requested for the crusader to the Army's Future Combat System and directed that by fiscal 2008, the Army should be provided with an alternative non-line-of-sight cannon. The bill added $293 million to aid the Army in developing a cannon that made use of Crusader technology.

• **Environmental laws.** Conferees accepted a deal worked out by Levin that gave the Pentagon a temporary reprieve from the Migratory Bird Treaty Act while the Interior Department worked out a long-term solution. The House bill would have amended the act to exempt training activities. House Republicans were forced to abandon efforts to loosen the Endangered Species Act.

• **Missile defense.** The final bill provided $7.8 billion for missile defense, with some additional oversight. The money included funds for an initial deployment of the system in Alaska. The bill gave the president the option of redirecting up to $814 million of the amount to the war on terrorism. The agreement prohibited the use of any fiscal 2003 funds for research, development, testing, evaluation, procurement or deployment of nuclear armed interceptors for a missile defense system. The Senate bill contained an outright ban; the House bill had no similar provision.

• **Base closings.** Conferees dropped a House provision that would have made it harder to close military installations when a new round of closures began in 2005. It would have required a unanimous vote by the nine-member commission before additional facilities could be added to the list of bases set for closure. Existing law required seven members to vote for an addition. Instead, the final bill simply included a House requirement that two commission members visit a base before it could be slated for closure.

• **Reporting requirements.** The bill eliminated or modified requirements for 22 periodic reports to Congress mandated by earlier legislation, most of which covered narrow subjects or had been overtaken by events. At the same time, it required new reports on some major weapons programs such as the Army's Comanche helicopter. It also included provisions designed to improve scrutiny of some programs by top-level Pentagon agencies, particularly those that viewed programs from a "joint," or multiservice, perspective. The Pentagon grudgingly accepted the reporting provisions in the bill.

• **Contingency fund.** The final bill authorized the $10 billion that Bush requested as an unallocated contingency fund to cover future operations in the war against terrorism. But the authorizers' action was irrelevant because the companion defense appropriations bill did not include the $10 billion. Neither the House nor the Senate Appropriations committee would give the administration that much money without congressional oversight or control. (*Defense appropriations, p. 2-9*)

• **Comanche helicopter.** The bill authorized $915 million, as requested, to continue developing the Comanche, a missile-armed reconnaissance helicopter with a "stealthy" design intended to shield it from radar and infrared detectors. But in their report the conferees made clear their unhappiness with the Army's management of the program. The helicopter's budget and schedule had been changed for the sixth time since 1988. The bill required detailed quarterly reports to Congress on Comanche's status.

• **Shipbuilding.** The bill authorized a total of $9.1 billion for shipbuilding — $920 million more than Bush requested. Defense hawks had decried the Pentagon budget as too small to sustain the fleet for the long term at its existing size of about 300 ships. However, the increase did not add any new ships to the five in the administration's request. Most of

the increase went to pay for cost increases in ships funded in earlier years ($488 million), refueling a nuclear-powered submarine that otherwise would have been mothballed despite being fit for years of additional service ($200 million), and buying components for the next aircraft carrier so construction could be started sooner than the administration planned ($229 million).

The bill authorized $4 million to begin designing a so-called littoral combat ship. Although the funds had not been requested, the Navy planned to buy these for missions close to enemy coasts. While providing funds to accelerate their purchase, the bill also required close review of the Navy's rationale for the new ship.

● **Refueling tankers.** One of the most contentious weapons issues in the bill was a controversial effort by the Air Force and Boeing Co. to set up an $18 billion program to lease 767 jetliners for use as midair refueling tankers. The bill prohibited any agreement unless it was funded by law or Rumsfeld made a formal "reprogramming" request to the Senate and House Armed Services and Appropriations committees asking that he be allowed to begin leasing the planes with funds Congress has appropriated for other Pentagon programs.

In its statement on the bill, the White House said it would construe that provision as requiring that Rumsfeld make the request before signing the lease — but not that he needed to wait for congressional approval.

● **Abortion.** The final bill dropped the Senate amendment that would have allowed privately funded abortions for U.S. military personnel at overseas military facilities.

● **Colombia.** The final bill did not include the House amendment setting a cap of 500 U.S. troops in Colombia. There was an existing cap of 400 on the number of U.S. military personnel who could operate in Colombia. ◆

Intelligence Bill Creates 9/11 Panel

Congress cleared a fiscal 2003 intelligence authorization bill Nov. 15 after reaching a last-minute agreement with the White House on an independent commission to investigate the Sept. 11, 2001, terrorist attacks. The annual intelligence bill authorized the activities of 11 agencies, including the CIA and National Security Agency, and intelligence agencies in the State, Energy and Defense departments. President Bush signed it into law Nov. 27 (HR 4628 — PL 107-306).

Although the White House had consistently opposed an independent probe, it ultimately agreed to a power-sharing arrangement designed to ensure that neither party could turn the investigation into a political vehicle. The House included the establishment of a commission in its version of the intelligence bill, passed in July. Although the Senate bill had no comparable language, the Senate voted overwhelmingly in September for a full independent investigation, adding it to a separate homeland security bill (HR 5005). Support for an independent panel grew over the summer as members of the House and Senate Intelligence committees investigating Sept. 11-related failures became increasingly frustrated over their inability to get information from the intelligence agencies.

The final agreement, reached after the midterm elections, allowed Bush to name the commission chairman. Democrats failed in a bid to name a co-chairman with equal powers. But advocates of a strong probe won one concession. Senate Minority Leader Trent Lott, R-Miss., promised

BoxScore

Bill:
HR 4628 — PL 107-306
Legislative Action:
House passed HR 4628 (H Rept 107-592) by voice vote July 25.
Senate passed HR 4628, amended (S Rept 107-149), by voice vote Sept. 25.
House adopted the conference report (H Rept 107-789), 366-3, on Nov. 15.
Senate cleared the bill by voice vote Nov. 15.
President signed Nov. 27.

that one of his choices for the panel would be vetted by Senate Republicans who supported a strong investigation.

Lawmakers said compromises on the rest of the legislation had been worked out weeks before the bill was finally cleared. The provisions were largely non-controversial and mostly classified. The total was classified but was reported to be between $35 billion and $40 billion, about a 25 percent increase over fiscal 2002 authorization levels.

Background

The failure of U.S. intelligence agencies to anticipate or prevent the Sept. 11 attacks on the World Trade Center in New York and on the Pentagon led to a debate in the fall of 2001 over the best way to examine what went wrong. Lawmakers working on the fiscal 2002 intelligence authorization bill (PL 107-108) ultimately rejected proposals to create an outside commission, deciding that Congress itself should conduct any inquiry. Senate Select Intelligence Committee Chairman Bob Graham, D-Fla., said conferees agreed that "if there is going to be a commission, it should be done at the level of the president and leadership of Congress." (*2001 Almanac, p. 11-3*)

On Feb. 14, 2002, the House and Senate Intelligence committees launched a joint investigation into intelligence failures and activities before and after the Sept. 11 attacks. The panels moved at their own pace for months, hiring staff, poring through gathered documents and planning hearings. Members periodically voiced concerns that

the panels were too close to the CIA to do a thorough job, or that the investigation was too narrowly focused on the intelligence agencies, or that the committees were slow-walking the probe. But most members seemed satisfied to let them proceed.

During the summer, however, lawmakers began to get impatient with the slow pace of the joint investigation, and support for an outside commission slowly grew. Public hearings originally expected in May or June slipped to summer and eventually to September. Richard C. Shelby of Alabama, ranking Republican on Senate Select Intelligence, and others began to accuse the CIA and other intelligence agencies of delaying the release of documents and information in hopes of running out the clock until the joint investigation expired in the spring of 2003.

Meanwhile, families of Sept. 11 victims persistently lobbied Congress and the White House to create an independent commission. Momentum intensified after joint hearings in September revealed several pieces of information that could have helped predict the attacks. At that point, most members of the Intelligence committees agreed that setting up an independent probe was the only way to get the necessary answers.

On Sept. 20, the White House switched course, sending a letter to House Speaker J. Dennis Hastert, R-Ill., advocating an independent inquiry as a follow-on to the congressional investigation. The Intelligence committees held their last hearing Oct. 17 and began writing a report to be issued in early 2003.

Legislative Action

House Committee, Floor Action

The House version of the intelligence authorization bill was approved by voice vote in a closed session of the Select Intelligence Committee on May 15 (H Rept 107-592).

The bill came to the House floor July 24 and passed by voice vote after an acrimonious debate that stretched into the early-morning hours of July 25. The debate was not on the bill itself but on a proposal to create a 10-member independent commission to examine intelligence failures leading up to Sept. 11. The amendment, by Tim Roemer, D-Ind., was adopted, 219-188, and reflected lawmakers' growing impatience with the ongoing congressional probe. At the time, it was assumed that the provisions would die in a House-Senate conference. (*House vote 347, p. H-110*)

In its original form, Roemer's amendment called for a commission that would look not only at intelligence failures but also at a broad array of other problem areas, including border and transportation security. But GOP leaders said such a wide-ranging probe was beyond the scope of the intelligence authorization bill and would fall under the jurisdiction of several other committees. So Roemer redrafted the measure to have the independent panel join the Intelligence committees in looking only at intelligence-related failures.

Most House Democrats supported the amendment, as did a group of moderate Northeast Republicans whose districts included families of Sept. 11 victims. They were joined by a band of conservatives unhappy with the performance of the CIA and other intelligence agencies, as well as with Con-

gress' oversight of their work. "I'm not satisfied that we in this body can do justice to an investigation of intelligence," said Curt Weldon, R-Pa., a senior member of the House Armed Services Committee who voted in favor of the amendment. "The Intelligence committees don't want to take on the CIA aggressively enough."

Republicans on the House Select Intelligence Committee dismissed the vote as a politically motivated attempt to embarrass Bush, who had spoken out against the idea of an independent commission.

The controversy over an outside commission overshadowed debate on the details of the bill, which lawmakers said would provide spy agencies with the largest single-year percentage increase in at least two decades.

Jerry Lewis, R-Calif., chairman of the Defense Appropriations Subcommittee, said the administration was seeking a 25 percent increase for intelligence in its fiscal 2003 budget for the Defense Department, which funded about 85 percent of the intelligence community. If such an increase became law, the fiscal 2003 budget for the CIA and other intelligence agencies could be in excess of $35 billion — significantly more than the $26.7 billion that CIA Director George J. Tenet revealed publicly in 1998. "This bill turns a corner on rebuilding our intelligence capabilities," said Porter J. Goss, R-Fla., chairman of the House Select Intelligence Committee. (*1998 Almanac, p. 8-25*)

The White House Office of Management and Budget (OMB) issued a statement July 24 that largely was supportive of the legislation but repeated Bush's view that an investigation of the Sept. 11 attacks should be left to the House and Senate panels. The commission idea "is duplicative and would cause a further diversion of essential personnel from their duties in fighting the war" on terrorism, the OMB statement said.

The bill did not call for the broad legislative overhaul of intelligence gathering that many independent intelligence experts said was needed. The Intelligence committees were waiting for their joint inquiry to end in February 2003 before trying such a politically daunting task. Instead, the bill included a series of smaller steps to improve intelligence, such as authorizing a $10 million grant program for college instruction to address the lack of foreign language specialists. It also proposed to curtail the ability of foreign governments to make requests under the Freedom of Information Act (FOIA) to obtain documents from spy agencies.

Senate Committee, Floor Action

The Senate passed the bill by voice vote Sept. 25 after substituting the text of its own version (S 2506 — S Rept 107-149). The Senate Intelligence committee had approved the measure by voice vote May 8.

The bill included provisions to hire more human spies, enable the super-secret National Security Agency to improve equipment for eavesdropping on fiber-optic communications and make possible better analysis of intelligence data. It also called for a commission to assess the future of intelligence research and development. Intelligence officials were concerned that the United States might be losing its cutting-edge capabilities in areas such as satellites and telecommunications.

Aides said there were few significant differences between the House and Senate versions of the bill.

There was no attempt to adopt an amendment calling for a Sept. 11 commission because the Senate had added the language the day before to the Homeland Security bill. The proposal — by Joseph I. Lieberman, D-Conn., and John McCain, R-Ariz. — was much stronger than what Roemer had been able to add to the House intelligence bill. It called for a 10-member commission with broad authority to investigate all circumstances of the Sept. 11 attacks, including intelligence failures. The panel would have subpoena powers and the power to investigate all branches of government. The Senate agreed to the amendment, 90-8, on Sept. 24. (*Senate vote 223, p. S-45; Homeland Security, p. 7-3*)

Lieberman and McCain had introduced the plan in December 2001. Although the Governmental Affairs Committee, which Lieberman chaired, approved the bill (S 1867 — S Rept 107-150) on March 21, the measure had languished for months before being revived in September.

Conference/Final Action

With few differences between the bills, the House-Senate conference was expected to be swift and painless. Instead, it dragged into the lame-duck session. Conferees did not sign off on their report until Nov. 14. The House adopted the conference report (H Rept 107-789) by a vote of 366-3 on Nov. 15; the Senate cleared the bill the same day by voice vote. (*House vote 483, p. H-150*)

The bill was held up by the prolonged dispute over an independent Sept. 11 commission. With the homeland security bill bogged down in a fight over workers' rights, Lieberman and others had switched their attention to the intelligence bill as it headed to conference. Supporters pushed for a broad-ranging investigation that might last up to two years; White House officials insisted on having some controls over the direction of the probe. Members thought they had a deal Oct. 10, but the plug was suddenly pulled because of White House objections.

Committee leaders had agreed to limit the investigation to post-Sept. 11 operations, as the White House wanted, and to employ extra safeguards to protect information about sources and methods used by intelligence agencies. They also agreed not to repeat unnecessarily any work conducted by the joint House-Senate inquiries. Investigation into the administration's "response" to the attacks would be limited to the "immediate response." The president would name one co-chairman of the 10-member commission, which would have two years to finish its job.

White House officials refused to sign off on the deal, and House GOP leaders sided with them. Stephen Push, representing the group Families of September 11, said House Intelligence Chairman Goss backed out of the deal after a phone call from Vice President Dick Cheney.

At that point, lawmakers handed off the negotiations to family members of Sept. 11 victims, who spent the better part of a week talking with White House officials. The White House insisted on a presidentially appointed chairman, rather than co-chairmen appointed by the two parties. It also insisted on limiting or dropping the notion of full subpoena powers. "The heart and soul of an independent commission is the composition and subpoena powers," said Roemer, who was working closely with the fami-

lies. "That's what we're down to."

The negotiations continued after the November elections, finally producing a deal that all sides accepted. The length of the probe was restricted to 18 months, ensuring it would end well before the 2004 elections — a key White House demand — and the funding was kept to a relatively modest $2 million. Senate Republicans agreed that one of their designees for the 10-member panel would be vetted by two strong backers of the probe, McCain and Shelby. That selection, combined with the five appointments to be made by Democrats, gave commission proponents an effective majority and the votes needed to issue subpoenas.

In return, the president was allowed to pick the commission's chairman, giving his designee substantial control over the direction and tone.

Postscript

Report of Joint House-Senate Panel

On Dec. 11, the House and Senate Intelligence committees released their recommendations and some of their findings, though their full report of some 450 pages had yet to be declassified. As hinted during the September hearings, the joint investigation found no instances where any U.S. agent had specific information related to the Sept. 11 attacks. But the report did find several missed chances in which investigators either ignored suspicions about possible attacks or failed to comprehend the importance of information at hand. It was harsh in its assessment of the intelligence agencies' preparedness to deal with terrorism, arguing that as terrorists prepared to launch the Sept. 11 attacks on the World Trade Center and the Pentagon, U.S. agents still were operating under Cold War rules as if they were competing against a nation, not a loose-knit transnational group of terrorists.

The two main recommendations were to create a Cabinet-level director of national intelligence that would coordinate efforts among all the various agencies, and to study the creation of a domestic intelligence agency, similar to Britain's MI5, to supplement the FBI. The panel also urged more investment in technology at covert agencies and more funding for agencies to hire linguists.

The report recommended that the president review federal classification procedures. Legislators complained repeatedly during the investigation about the slow pace at which documents were declassified, hinting that the agencies were using classification as a tool for covering up errors.

Aides said the final recommendations were approved by voice vote, with some dissensions, while the panel's findings were approved by a unanimous voice vote.

The Defense Department's patrons in Congress consistently had fought the idea of creating an intelligence czar because it would mean wresting control of the bulk of covert operations from the Pentagon. Tom Ridge, designated as secretary of the new Department of Homeland Security, was lukewarm to the idea. "I'm not sure that we need it, but if Congress passes it, we'll have to deal with it," he said Dec. 11. Graham acknowledged that it would be tough to overcome institutional disdain for a new intelligence czar. But he argued that the lack of communication among agencies

leading up to and following Sept. 11 highlighted the need for a single coordinator. "Someone needs to command the entire fleet," he said. "Why is there a better chance [of doing it now]? Fundamentally because 3,025 people were killed because of gaps in our intelligence."

Independent Commission

The independent commission created under the intelligence authorization law got off to a rocky start. The two men appointed as chairman and vice chairman resigned before the investigation even began. Former Secretary of State Henry A. Kissinger, Bush's choice for chairman, and former Sen. George J. Mitchell, D-Maine (1980-95), the Democrats' pick, withdrew in the face of arguments from family members of Sept. 11 victims that they could not function if there was an appearance of conflict of interest at their full-time jobs. Mitchell dropped out Dec. 11, saying his job at the law firm Piper Rudnick might keep him from devoting the necessary time to the investigation. Kissinger followed suit Dec. 13. He insisted he had no conflicts of interest, but said the perception that there could be some would keep him from performing the investigation properly.

On Dec. 16, Bush named former New Jersey Gov. Tom Kean to replace Kissinger as chairman. Democrats had chosen former Rep. Lee Hamilton, D-Ind. (1965-99) to serve as vice chairman. Other Democrats on the commission were Georgia Sen. Max Cleland, Indiana Rep. Tim Roemer, Richard Ben-Veniste and Jamie Gorelick. Republicans were former Washington Sen. Slade Gorton (1981-87, 1989-2001), Jim Thompson, John Lehman and Fred Fielding. ◆

Veterans to Benefit From Two Bills

Congress cleared two veterans bills in 2002: one to create or expand a series of veterans' benefits, the other to set up emergency preparedness centers at Department of Veterans Affairs (VA) hospitals. A third measure — a health care package — was left for the 108th Congress after lawmakers failed to reach agreement.

Veterans' Benefits

The veterans' benefits package (S 2237 — PL 107-330) reflected a compromise between the House and Senate Veterans' Affairs committees on S 2237 and a series of veterans bills that the House had passed earlier in the Congress.

Among its main provisions, the compromise bill:

• Extended VA health care eligibility to the surviving spouses of veterans when the spouse remarried after age 55.

• Expanded eligibility for special compensation for women veterans with service-related loss of breast tissue, including by mastectomy or radiation treatment.

• Shielded National Guard personnel from certain actions, such as evictions and foreclosures, if they were called up by a governor for a national emergency. Prior law protected only active-duty military.

• Expanded benefits for veterans with hearing loss.

• Permitted veterans to retain Veterans' Mortgage Life Insurance beyond age 70.

• Increased the annual benefit for Medal of Honor recipients from $600 to $1,000.

• Authorized the creation of a Battle of the Bulge memorial at Arlington National Cemetery.

Sen. Bill Nelson, D-Fla., temporarily slowed work on the bill in November to protest the deletion of a provision that would have made it illegal for companies to offer lump-sum cash payments in exchange for a veteran's monthly benefits checks. The lump-sum payments were smaller than the lifelong value of the benefits.

The Senate passed S 2237 (S Rept 107-234) by voice vote Sept. 26. The House passed the bill by voice vote Nov. 15, after inserting the compromise measure. The Senate cleared the bill by voice vote Nov. 18, and President Bush signed it Dec. 6.

Emergency Preparedness

The second bill (HR 3253 — PL 107-287) authorized $100 million over five years to set up four centers where VA doctors could plan the appropriate response to various kinds of terrorist attacks. Bill sponsors said VA doctors were uniquely qualified for this work because the health problems affecting veterans often were caused by the same kinds of toxins or the type of violence that could occur in terrorist attacks.

The four centers were to conduct research and develop detection, diagnosis, prevention and treatment methods for chemical and biological agents, as well as serve as clearinghouses for information going to other health care providers. The VA also was directed to develop education and training programs on medical response to terrorist activities.

The bill gave the VA what Rep. James P. Moran, D-Va., said was "a formal role in the national disaster medical system" and authorized VA hospitals to treat first responders, military forces responding to domestic attacks and members of the public who were victims of a terrorist attack.

Implementation had to be delayed, however, until appropriators provided funds for the program, a step both Veterans' Affairs committee members and appropriators said would occur when the 108th Congress convened.

The bill was lobbed back and forth between the House and Senate, beginning in May. The Senate passed the final compromise version by voice vote Oct. 15, and the House cleared it the next day, also by voice vote. The bill was signed Nov. 7.

Health Benefits Stall

The House passed a veterans' health care bill (HR 3645 — H Rept 107-600) by voice vote July 22. The Senate Veterans' Affairs Committee approved a separate version (S 2043 — S Rept 107-231) on June 6, but the bill went no further. One of the major stumbling blocks was a House proposal to overhaul the VA's procurement system to institute national buying guidelines, instead of allowing each facility to negotiate its own purchase deals.

Senators argued that the plan was too ambitious and said it would be best to give the VA time to come up with its own more limited overhaul. The Senate also objected to House proposals to require more oversight of research and educational companies that operate at VA facilities. ◆

Chapter 8

ENERGY & ENVIRONMENT

Stakes Too High on Energy Bill

House Republicans and Senate Democrats fought to a draw over what would have been the first comprehensive energy legislation since 1992. With the public focused on national security and the sagging economy — and lawmakers far apart on fundamental energy issues — the legislation collapsed of its own weight before the midterm elections.

The House had passed a bill in 2001 that closely tracked business-friendly recommendations of a White House energy policy task force chaired by Vice President Dick Cheney. In concert with President Bush and the task force, the House bill aimed to achieve greater energy independence by increasing domestic production — including opening parts of Alaska's Arctic National Wildlife Refuge (ANWR) to drilling. It included $33.5 billion in tax incentives tilted toward increased production.

Senate Democratic leaders took a sharply different tack, emphasizing energy conservation. The Senate bill, passed in April 2002, included provisions to encourage fuel efficiency and greater use of renewable energy sources. It rejected drilling in ANWR and called for $15.2 billion in tax incentives, split nearly evenly between proposals to boost production and promote conservation. It also called for easing electricity regulations, strengthening the ability of federal regulators to review mergers involving utilities, and requiring greater use of ethanol in gasoline — topics not addressed in the House bill.

Negotiations to reconcile the House and Senate bills began in June but quickly stalled over basic issues such as ANWR, electricity market restructuring and clean air mandates. Conferees set those questions aside and proceeded through a six-month debate that focused on regional issues such as the proposed mandate to use more ethanol and a ban on the gasoline additive methyl tertiary butyl ether (MTBE).

But the big issues remained, and in October conferees finally gave up on a comprehensive bill. They could not even agree on a bare-bones plan that included nuclear liability protections. The only fragment Congress cleared was a bill to improve pipeline safety and security. *(Pipeline safety, p. 8-7)*

The acrimonious debate ended where it began. Most Republicans said the country had to find more domestic sources of fuel to reduce its dependence on foreign oil, especially in such dangerous times. Most Democrats said the country could become more energy independent through conservation.

Background

Although the House passed its energy bill in 2001, the Senate was unable to get a bill out of committee. Frank Murkowski, R-Alaska, who chaired the Energy and Natural Resources Committee for the first half of the session, intro-

BoxScore

Bill:
HR 4
Legislative Action:
Senate passed HR 4, 88-11, on April 25, after substituting the text of S 517.

duced a comprehensive energy bill that focused on developing coal, oil and natural gas resources, and nuclear power; a companion bill called for an array of tax incentives for energy producers.

But before the committee could mark up Murkowski's proposal, the Senate shifted to Democratic control and Jeff Bingaman, D-N.M., took over as committee chairman. Bingaman introduced his own bill, which focused on electricity, but committee action was delayed first by the August recess and then by Sept. 11. In October, Bingaman was ready to try again, but Majority Leader Tom Daschle, D-S.D., had the markup canceled and a new bill drafted when it became clear that a majority on the committee would support drilling in ANWR. *(2001 Almanac, p. 9-3)*

Legislative Action

Senate Floor Action

After six weeks of debate in which both sides held their ground on major issues, the Senate passed its energy bill, 88-11, on April 25. The vote came on HR 4, after the Senate substituted the text of its own bill (S 517). A number of Republicans voted for the bill, assembled largely by the Democratic leadership, in order to get to conference, where they hoped House provisions on ANWR and other issues would prevail. *(Senate vote 94, p. S-21)*

Daschle drew intense GOP criticism for bringing the bill directly to the floor Feb. 15, bypassing the committee process. One exception was the $16 billion package of energy tax incentives, which the Finance Committee had approved Feb. 13.

Politics clearly dominated the debate, as it had in the House. "There's no sense of urgency," said Olympia J. Snowe, R-Maine, who bucked party leaders on several conservation issues. "We're all consumed with the political aspects of the debate instead of the policy."

During the extended floor debate, senators considered a long list of amendments:

● **Renewable fuels.** Bingaman fended off a variety of attempts to alter a provision he wrote requiring that utilities generate at least 10 percent of their electricity from renewable sources, such as the wind or sun, by 2020. At the time, less than 3 percent of the nation's electricity came from renewables, not including hydropower. Bingaman's proposal was intended to replace a requirement in the 1978 Public Utility Regulatory Policies Act (PURPA) (PL 95-617) that utilities buy power from renewable energy sources when it was available. Utilities complained that the law forced them to pay too much for power. *(1978 Almanac, p. 639)*

Bingaman exempted municipal power companies and rural electric cooperatives and included language that would

have allowed utilities to buy from a portfolio of renewables including solar, wind, landfill gas, geothermal and biomass. Environmentalists argued that it would do little to increase the use of renewable energy.

An attempt by James M. Jeffords, I-Vt., chairman of the Environment and Public Works Committee, to require utilities to produce 20 percent of their electricity from renewables by 2020 was defeated, 29-70, on March 14. (*Senate vote 50, p. S-13*)

An amendment by Jon Kyl, R-Ariz., to leave the issue of renewable energy to the states was defeated, 40-58, on March 21. Kyl said the federal government had no business requiring the use of renewable sources. He warned that the Northeast — which had less ability to generate energy from wind and the sun than such areas as the Southwest — would have to buy credits because it could not meet the standards. "Get ready," Kyl said to Northeastern senators. "You're going to be sending a lot of money to states like those in the Southwest." (*Senate vote 55, p. S-14*)

A second Kyl amendment, to allow states to opt out of the federal requirement for renewables, was defeated, 37-58, on March 21. (*Senate vote 59, p. S-15*)

An amendment by Murkowski, who was then the ranking Republican on the Energy and Natural Resources Committee, that would have exempted states that had their own renewables policy was defeated, 39-57, on March 21. (*Senate vote 58, p. S-15*)

Shortly before passing the bill, the Senate agreed to an amendment by Don Nickles, R-Okla., to halve the cost of penalties for utilities that violated the renewable energy requirement. A motion to table (kill) his amendment failed 38-59. (*Senate vote 83, p. S-20*)

● **Fuel efficiency standards.** Under existing Corporate Average Fuel Economy (CAFE) standards, each manufacturer's fleet had to average 27.5 miles per gallon (mpg) for cars and 20.7 mpg for light trucks, including sport utility vehicles (SUVs) and minivans. The manufacturers had lobbied aggressively for years against increasing the standards, urging Congress instead to approve tax incentives for technology that would improve fuel efficiency. The White House favored increasing automobile fuel economy, but asked Congress to leave the Transportation Department free to determine how best to do it.

The Senate voted, 62-38, on March 13 in favor of a proposal by Carl Levin, D-Mich., and Christopher S. Bond, R-Mo., to require the National Highway Traffic Safety Administration (NHTSA) to increase mileage standards for light trucks, including SUVs, within 15 months and for cars within two years. If it did not act in that time, or if it set standards lawmakers did not like, Congress could step in. "It could be a 1 mile per gallon increase," acknowledged cosponsor George V. Voinovich, R-Ohio, "but it has to be an increase." If the federal agency did not meet the timetable, Congress would be free to act. The effect would be to freeze congressional action for two years. (*Senate vote 47, p. S-13*)

The House bill required that automakers save 5 billion gallons of oil over the six years, but did not set specific standards. The House had rejected an amendment that would have raised combined standards for cars and light trucks to 27.5 mpg by 2007.

The White House and the auto industry lobbied hard for the Levin-Bond plan, which they much preferred to an alternative by John Kerry, D-Mass., and John McCain, R-Ariz., that would have increased the standard to 36 mpg by 2015 for both cars and light trucks. Under the Kerry-McCain plan, manufacturers that could not reach that level would be able to buy "emissions credits" from other automakers or industries, allowing them to reduce their fleet average to 32.4 mpg.

The auto industry, unions, business lobbyists, and rural and suburban minivan and truck drivers converged on Capitol Hill to lobby against Kerry-McCain. Some ads claimed that people would lose their SUVs if the amendment was adopted. As it turned out, the proposal was never offered.

While the outcome on fuel economy was expected, Kerry supporters had hoped that the vote would be closer.

The Senate also added language by Zell Miller, D-Ga., to exempt pickup trucks from any increase in CAFE standards. It was adopted, 56-44, with even Daschle voting for it. "Anyone smart enough to get elected to the U.S. Senate should know that you can't ignore pickup pops, just like you can't ignore soccer moms," Miller told reporters outside the Senate chamber. (*Senate vote 48, p. S-13*)

Proponents of stricter fuel standards tried again April 25 with an amendment by Thomas R. Carper, D-Del., to require regulations for automobiles manufactured after model year 2006 that would reduce the amount of oil consumed by at least 1 million barrels per day by 2015. Most Republicans and some Democrats from oil and automobile producing states joined to table the amendment, 57-42. (*Senate vote 90, p. S-21*)

● **Electricity.** The Senate bill proposed to repeal the 1935 Public Utility Holding Company Act (PUHCA), which restricted the territory and businesses in which utilities could operate, as well as PURPA, the 1978 law that required them to buy power from renewable energy sources when it was available. The bill substituted other, less stringent requirements. (*1978 Almanac, p. 639*)

Craig Thomas, R-Wyo., won voice vote approval March 14 for an amendment to give the power industry and regional authorities a stronger role in ensuring the reliability of the nation's electric power grid. Western Democrats supported Thomas' amendment and helped him muster the 60 votes needed to overcome a budget point of order raised by Democratic leaders; the vote was 60-40. (*Senate vote 49, p. S-13*)

The main difference between the Democratic and Republican approaches was the amount of federal oversight. Democrats wanted the Federal Energy Regulatory Commission (FERC) to write and oversee policies to avoid power failures. Thomas' amendment would have given electricity producers and regional reliability boards greater sway. Both approaches would replace the existing voluntary guidelines of the North American Electric Reliability Council, created more than 30 years before among utilities and rural cooperatives to ensure grid reliability.

The action came a day after the Senate adopted, by voice vote, a series of lower-profile electricity amendments addressing rules governing mergers, pricing, state authority and federal purchase requirements.

An attempt by Larry E. Craig, R-Idaho, to delete the electricity deregulation section of the bill was defeated, 32-67, on

April 10. Craig, Murkowski and others argued that the complex provisions should not be included without committee scrutiny and markup. Some public power and consumer groups opposed the Democratic language on electricity, saying it could weaken consumer protections and limit competition to provide wholesale power. (*Senate vote 62, p. S-16*)

The Senate adopted by voice vote an amendment by Carper to restore a portion of PURPA by requiring utilities to buy power from industries, such as some hospitals and universities, that converted their waste heat to electricity. A motion to table the amendment failed, 37-60, on April 24. (*Senate vote 82, p. S-19*)

● **Ethanol.** At the behest of Daschle and other Midwestern senators, the Senate bill had a provision requiring smog-prone states such as California and New York to discontinue use of MTBE — a petroleum-based additive that adds oxygen to fuel and reduces air pollution in engines. MTBE had been found to contaminate groundwater and already was banned in a number of states. Instead, the states would be required to use ethanol — alcohol distilled mainly from corn — as an additive.

Dianne Feinstein, D-Calif., led the opposition, arguing that gasoline prices in California and New York would rise sharply because ethanol would cost more to ship and because corn shortages could affect supplies. Because gasohol — motor fuel spiked with ethanol — was taxed at a lower rate than gasoline, some states also feared that they would lose highway construction money because federal fuel tax revenue would decline.

After a heated debate that pitted California and New York senators against those from Midwestern farm states, the Senate on April 11 voted, 61-36, to table a Feinstein amendment that would have allowed states to get expedited 30-day waivers from the EPA if ethanol supplies were low. "I don't intend to vote for the bill if the mandate remains in its current form," Feinstein said. (*Senate vote 67, p. S-17*)

An attempt by Feinstein to delay implementation of the ethanol requirement from 2004 to 2005 was tabled, 60-39, on April 25. (*Senate vote 88, p. S-20*)

● **ANWR.** The Senate on April 18 rejected the centerpiece of Bush's energy plan — oil and gas exploration in ANWR. Daschle forced a vote on whether to invoke cloture, thereby limiting debate, on a Murkowski proposal to allow the drilling. The cloture motion was defeated, 46-54, demonstrating that Republicans could not muster a majority, let alone the 60 votes they needed to prevail. GOP leaders were unable to persuade even one undecided senator to support their proposal on ANWR, despite continued unrest in the Middle East, political turmoil in OPEC member nation Venezuela and an offer by some lawmakers to link the opening of ANWR with aid for the beleaguered steel industry. (*Senate vote 71, p. S-18*)

The vote left many senators resigned to stalemate over energy policy, in many ways a reflection of the public's ambivalence on the subject. "We're doing very good at stopping things. We're not doing very good at doing things," said John B. Breaux of Louisiana, one of five Senate Democrats who backed Murkowski's amendment.

● **Global warming.** Senators agreed by voice vote April 25 to soften a requirement in the bill that industries report their greenhouse gas emissions. The new provision would make it voluntary, unless less than 60 percent of gases were reported within five years.

● **Nuclear liability.** On March 7, senators agreed, 78-21, to add a 10-year extension of the 1957 Price-Anderson Act (PL 100-408), which limited the nuclear industry's liability for accidents. The law, which expired in August, capped industry liability at $9.4 billion. The House had passed a separate 15-year reauthorization bill (HR 2983) on Nov. 27, 2001. (*Senate vote 42, p. S-12*)

● **Derivatives.** Feinstein tried but failed to restore the authority of the Commodity Futures Trading Commission (CFTC) to regulate private trading in energy derivatives — futures contracts for electricity and fuel. The derivatives played a role in both the 2001 spike in California power prices and the collapse of Enron Corp. Feinstein withdrew the amendment April 10, after the Senate rejected, 48-50, an attempt to limit debate on it. Publicly traded energy futures already were regulated. (*Senate vote 61, p. S-16*)

Feinstein argued that the change would help regulators investigate cases of market fraud. Opponents, led by Phil Gramm, R-Texas, said the CFTC already had the authority to sanction companies that engaged in securities fraud.

● **Other amendments.** On other issues, the Senate:

● Adopted, 69-30, on April 11 an amendment by Richard J. Durbin, D-Ill., that would create a consumer energy commission to investigate seasonal spikes in energy prices and how to prevent them. Durbin specifically focused on gasoline and natural gas prices. Previously, the Senate agreed to create a consumer advocate's office within the Department of Justice. (*Senate vote 66, p. S-17*)

● Adopted, 93-5, on March 6 a proposal by Daschle to require the use of the so-called southern route for a proposed natural gas pipeline from Prudhoe Bay via Fairbanks to the lower 48 states. (*Senate vote 41, p. S-12*)

● Agreed, 78-21, on March 7 to ask the EPA to study a process for oil and gas drilling known as hydraulic fracturing, which is used to split rock formations. (*Senate vote 43, p. S-12*)

● Adopted, 94-0, on March 8 an amendment by McCain to reauthorize and strengthen pipeline safety programs. The Senate had passed the proposal (S 235), 98-0, in 2001, but the House had not acted on it. (*Senate vote 45, p. S-13*)

Daschle finally managed to bring debate on the bill to a close with a cloture motion that was adopted, 86-13, on April 23. (*Senate vote 77, p. S-19*)

Neither side showed much enthusiasm for what remained of the Senate bill after six weeks — a modest collection of inducements for greater energy production, conservation and the use of renewable fuels and insulation.

Conference

Despite the odds, House Energy and Commerce Committee Chairman Billy Tauzin, R-La., pushed relentlessly for a bill that could be enacted in 2002. As chairman of the House-Senate conference on the bill, Tauzin set a Sept. 30 deadline for reaching a final deal and laid out an extensive plan detailing how, week by week, negotiators would progress toward a final agreement.

Conferees were able to agree on a number of smaller issues, but most big-ticket items — ANWR, electricity dereg-

ulation, ethanol — remained unresolved. By the time Congress adjourned for the midterm elections, conferees had all but given up on completing an omnibus energy bill in the 107th Congress.

Tauzin could not even get support in the lame-duck session for a bare-bones conference report that would have extended liability protection for the nuclear industry and updated pipeline safety laws. All that survived of the energy bill was the pipeline safety proposal, which cleared Nov. 11 (PL 107-355).

Hard-Fought Issues

On most of the biggest issues, the stakes for each party were too great — and the potential advantage of lambasting the other side too tempting — to allow room for compromise.

● **ANWR.** Republican conferees dangled several possible compromises: In return for allowing drilling in ANWR, they said they might be willing to set aside additional areas in the refuge as wilderness that would be off-limits to development, require utilities to generate 10 percent of their electricity from renewable sources by 2020, or discuss a plan to track climate change.

Senate Democrats said simply that they would not entertain any proposal to allow drilling in the refuge, while Republican Joe L. Barton of Texas, who chaired the House Energy and Commerce Subcommittee on Energy and Air Quality, said the bill was not worth salvaging if Democrats did not compromise on ANWR.

● **Electricity deregulation.** Revamping the way electricity was regulated and marketed was one of the original catalysts for the energy debate, but it became one of the biggest obstacles to a final agreement. The White House insisted that the bill rewrite regulations to spur investment in the energy sector, which was in a deep slump.

Because the House bill had no comparable provisions, House conferees decided, after five hours of debate and a 8-6 vote, to use a bill developed by Barton. Barton's plan called for repealing PUHCA and adding incentives for utilities in every part of the country to join regional transmission networks, independent operations that manage electricity transmission within a geographical area.

The Senate version was more modest. White House officials and Republicans, such as Thomas, had negotiated for weeks during the spring to reach a compromise with Democrats on a proposal to repeal PUHCA and, as markets developed, ease provisions in PURPA that required utilities to buy power from renewable energy sources when they were available. The Senate bill was silent on regional transmission organizations.

Negotiators focused on at least four issues: how much authority FERC should have in reviewing company mergers; whether all utilities that benefited from improvements in electricity grids, such as those in the Midwest and Northeast, should be required to pay for costs; how to address a controversial FERC proposal that aimed to create a seamless national grid for transmitting electricity; and the extent to which utilities should be required to use more renewable fuels in electricity generation.

The issues divided lawmakers along regional as well as partisan lines. Westerners and Southerners — including Senate Minority Leader Trent Lott, R-Miss., Craig and Sen.

Maria Cantwell, D-Wash. — wanted to use the energy bill to kill the proposed FERC rule, which they feared could hurt their consumers. Known as "standard market design," the rule sought to eliminate state control over power transmission lines and establish uniform regulations for trading electricity around the country. The goal was to finish the job of creating competitive markets for electricity begun in 1992. (*1992 Almanac, p. 231*)

State regulators and public power companies, which were exempt from FERC oversight, called the rule a power grab aimed at expanding the commission's control over utilities. The Bush administration supported the general goals of the FERC proposal, although some changes were expected before it became final.

Tauzin proposed adding language that would allow the rule to become final only after FERC had met a series of conditions, including showing that prices would drop, that transmission or construction of new power lines would not be affected adversely, and that the regulation would not hamper the ability of state regulators to protect consumers.

Democrats also were unhappy with a provision in Barton's draft that would revoke FERC's authority to review power industry mergers, leaving antitrust reviews to the Department of Justice and the Federal Trade Commission. If PUHCA was repealed, analysts expected a number of mergers in the industry.

Democrats said proof that FERC oversight was necessary could be seen in allegations that companies such as Enron Corp., Avista Corp. and El Paso Electric Co. schemed to inflate wholesale electricity prices during the 2001 California energy crisis.

● **Renewable resources.** Another controversy centered on the Senate provision to require utilities to generate at least 10 percent of their electricity from renewable sources by 2020. Republicans wanted to stretch the definition of which fuels could be considered "renewable" by including, for example, waste heat. Environmentalists opposed that broader definition, while conservatives argued that utilities should not have any mandate at all.

● **Ethanol.** House and Senate negotiators exchanged proposals on ethanol but reached no agreement. The Senate bill proposed to triple the use of ethanol to nearly 5 billion gallons annually by 2012, while phasing out the use of MTBE within four years. It also would have protected ethanol-based fuel producers from some lawsuits.

A counteroffer from House conferees would have started the mandated increase of ethanol in 2005, rather than 2004, and would have set a goal of tripling the use of the fuel additive by 2014, rather than 2012. Unlike the Senate bill, the House offer did not propose banning MTBE nationwide. That irritated some environmentalists and the oil industry, which faced a patchwork of different standards as various states acted on their own to ban MTBE. Also, the House added liability protection for the producers of fuel mixed with oxygenates such as MTBE.

Lawmakers in the Northeast and California continued to oppose both the Senate and House provisions, but said the House plan was worse because it had more liability protections for industry and no ban on MTBE.

"It's a stick-it-to-California bill," complained Democratic

Rep. Henry A. Waxman of California.

Meanwhile, ethanol producers opposed the House offer, fearing it would unravel the carefully balanced agreement reached in the Senate. The industry was concerned that the mandate to use more ethanol would take effect later under the House proposal.

● **Climate change.** House negotiators rejected provisions in the Senate bill on climate change. The language was based on provisions of a bill (S 1008) introduced by Robert C. Byrd, D-W.Va., and Ted Stevens, R-Alaska, that would establish a greenhouse gas registry and set up a White House Office of Climate Change Response to develop and implement a plan to reduce global warming.

In a Sept. 25 letter to Bingaman, Byrd said that if conferees dropped the Byrd-Stevens provisions, he would have "serious reservations" about supporting the conference report. But on Oct. 3, House conferees rejected the Senate proposal, 2-15. Waxman and Edward J. Markey, D-Mass., who backed the climate change proposal, said the Senate provision was modest. It would track pollution and would not impose penalties on polluters.

Issues Resolved

At least two high-profile issues were resolved in conference, but the compromises died along with the overall bill.

● **CAFE standards.** Conferees did agree to a new motor vehicle fuel economy provision. It called for the NHTSA to issue regulations for SUVs and minivans that would save 5 billion gallons of oil over six years, an increase of about one mile per gallon over the existing standard. The increase would be required for model years 2006-12. Negotiators also adopted the Senate language to exempt pickup trucks from increases and struck provisions requiring the NHTSA to consider the effects that tougher standards would have on vehicle safety and autoworker jobs.

● **Nuclear liability.** Conferees agreed in September to extend the Price-Anderson Act for 15 years, but that provision also died along with the rest of the bill. ◆

Congress Clears Pipeline Safety Bill

Completing an effort that started in early 2001, Congress cleared a bill aimed at improving the safety and security of 1.8 million miles of pipeline in the United States. President Bush signed it into law (HR 3609 — PL 107-355) on Dec. 17.

The bill required that half of all interstate oil and gas pipelines be inspected within five years, and that all get an initial inspection within a decade. Reinspection would occur every seven years. The bill increased, from $25,000 to $100,000 per incident, the civil penalties for a pipeline operator who violated safety requirements. The maximum penalty for a related series of violations was raised from $500,000 to $1 million.

The measure, introduced in response to a number of pipeline accidents, gained new momentum after the Sept. 11, 2001, attacks, which increased concern about the vulnerability of pipelines to terrorism.

The House passed the bill in July, after markups by the Transportation and Energy and Commerce committees. The Senate had passed its version (S 235) in February 2001. House and Senate negotiators ultimately worked out their differences as part of the conference on omnibus energy legislation (HR 4). When that energy measure died at the end of the session, the pipeline security provisions were broken out and cleared separately. *(Energy, p. 8-3)*

BoxScore

Bill:
HR 3609 — PL 107-355
Legislative Action:
House passed HR 3609
(H Rept 107-605, Parts 1, 2),
423-4, on July 23.
Senate passed HR 3609,
amended, by voice vote
Nov. 13.
House cleared the bill by voice
vote Nov. 15.
President signed Dec. 17.

dollars in damage to property. Accidents generally were attributed to aging pipes and the expansion of suburbs into previously rural areas, which brought residents closer to oil and gas pipelines. With the Sept. 11 attacks, concern over pipeline safety grew as part of the general review of the vulnerability of the nation's infrastructure to hostile acts.

Federal regulation of pipeline safety was the responsibility of the Office of Pipeline Safety within the Transportation Department. The office had been criticized for failing to address safety concerns or implement congressional mandates, such as regular inspections. The office's authorization expired at the end of fiscal 2001.

The Senate bill (S 235), passed 98-0 on Feb. 8, 2001, would have required a first round of inspections within five years of enactment and inspection updates every five years. Maximum civil penalties for violations would have risen from $25,000 to $500,000, with the maximum for a series of safety violations rising from $500,000 to $1 million. The bill proposed to authorize a total of $86 million in federal spending and $57 million for state grants for pipeline safety.

Background

Pipeline accidents over the previous decade had resulted in hundreds of deaths, thousands of injuries and millions of

Legislative Action

House Committee Action

Two committees — Transportation and Infrastructure, and Energy and Commerce — approved separate versions of the House bill, with some provisions in conflict.

The Transportation and Infrastructure Committee, which had primary jurisdiction, went first, approving its bill (HR 3609 — H Rept 107-605, Part 1) on May 22 by a vote of 55-13. The bill required the Transportation Department to issue rules for inspecting gas pipelines and to inspect all those pipelines within 10 years of the bill's enactment. It authorized $162.2 million for the Office of Pipeline Safety through fiscal 2005. Limits on civil penalties for pipeline operators' safety violations would increase to $50,000 per incident, with a $750,000 limit for repeat violators.

Some Democrats and environmentalists expressed concern about a provision to allow the Transportation Department to "streamline" environmental reviews of pipeline repair, saying it could allow the department to overturn decisions made by the EPA.

The Energy and Commerce Committee approved its version (H Rept 107-605, Part 2) by voice vote June 13, after making several changes that infuriated Transportation Committee Chairman Don Young, R-Alaska.

The changes — by Joe L. Barton, R-Texas, chairman of the Energy and Commerce Subcommittee on Energy and Air Quality — included higher caps on civil penalties for pipeline operators' safety violations: $100,000 per incident, with a $1 million limit for repeat violations.

Barton also dropped the provision that would allow the Transportation Department to streamline environmental reviews of pipeline repairs and substituted a requirement for an interagency committee to consider streamlining.

Young called Energy and Commerce Committee Chairman Billy Tauzin, R-La., to complain about the changes and threatened to stop the bill unless he could get the amendments removed.

House Floor Action

The House passed HR 3609 on July 23 by an overwhelming vote of 423-4, after the leadership struck a compromise on the disputed provisions. The bill authorized up to $189.7 million for the Transportation Department for pipeline safety and security. (*House vote 334, p. H-106*)

The measure retained the interagency study of streamlining environmental rules sought by Transportation Committee Democrats and the Energy and Commerce Committee, as well as whistleblower protections for pipeline employees who reported safety violations. It included the higher fines for violations supported by Energy and Commerce. But Republicans on the Transportation Committee won inclusion of a regime that called for pipelines to be inspected within 10 years of the bill's enactment, with reinspections every seven years. Democrats had wanted inspections repeated every five years.

The bill established a five-year, $100 million research program to be run by the Transportation and Energy departments, along with others, that would look for ways to improve pipeline safety. Operators would be required to provide pipeline data to the Transportation Department to create a national pipeline mapping system.

Final Action

Rather than going to conference with the Senate, House members decided to resolve the issue as part of negotiations on the omnibus energy bill (HR 4). John McCain, R-Ariz., sponsor of the Senate-passed pipeline bill, had added the language to the Senate version of the energy bill March 8. The vote on his amendment was 94-0. (*Senate vote 45, p. S-13*)

On Sept. 12, the energy conferees announced an agreement on the pipeline safety provisions that was less restrictive than the Senate's bill but required earlier inspections and stiffer penalties than the House version.

When it became clear that the energy bill was hopelessly bogged down, the Senate passed HR 3609, amended to reflect the compromise, by voice vote Nov. 13. The House cleared the bill Nov. 15, also by voice vote. ◆

Bush, Hill Back Nuclear Waste Site

Congress endorsed a decision by President Bush to make Yucca Mountain in Nevada the permanent repository for high-level radioactive waste from the nation's nuclear power plants. The joint resolution, which Bush signed July 23 (H J Res 87 — PL 107-200), overrode a veto of the project by the governor of Nevada. It was the latest chapter in a 20-year controversy that was expected to move next to the courts. Nevada state officials and environmentalists had several lawsuits pending in federal court and planned to file more. Meanwhile, the states had an estimated 77,000 tons of nuclear waste waiting to be transported and buried in tunnels hundreds of feet beneath the Nevada desert.

Safely storing the waste from nuclear reactors, which remains lethal for thousands of years, had been a major impediment for the nuclear power industry. In 1982, Congress promised the 39 states that were temporarily storing nuclear waste that it would settle on a single, permanent repository. Though several sites were considered, Congress in 1987 di-

rected the government to focus exclusively on Yucca Mountain, a desolate volcanic ridge in the desert 100 miles northwest of Las Vegas. Officials in Nevada, the nation's fastest-growing state, battled the project for years, arguing that it was a potential health threat to their region.

The climax came in 2002. On Jan. 10, Energy Secretary Spencer Abraham notified Nevada's governor, Republican Kenny Guinn, that he would recommend Yucca Mountain officially be designated as the permanent waste repository. On Feb. 15, Bush formally accepted Abraham's recommendation. Under the 1987 law designating Yucca Mountain as the only place to be considered for the waste repository, Nevada's governor and legislature then had 60 calendar days to disapprove of Bush's action. Congress had another 90 days to overturn the veto by passing a resolution by majority vote in both chambers.

On April 9, Guinn vetoed the decision, as expected. Despite determined lobbying by the Nevada delegation, the

House voted overwhelmingly in May to override the veto. Though Senate Democratic Whip Harry Reid of Nevada had the support of Majority Leader Tom Daschle, D-S.D., in opposing the resolution, the Senate followed suit July 9.

The Energy Department planned to seek a license from the Nuclear Regulatory Commission in 2004 to begin moving the 77,000 tons of waste into the repository by 2010.

Background

The 1982 Nuclear Waste Policy Act (PL 97-425) set up a timetable for the Energy Department to begin disposing of used nuclear fuel in a geological repository by Jan. 31, 1998, and prescribed a process for selecting a disposal site. It also set up the Nuclear Waste Fund to collect fees from utilities to finance construction of a permanent storage site. In 1986, the Energy Department issued environmental assessments for five potential geologic disposal sites, including Yucca Mountain. (*1982 Almanac, p. 304*)

The 1987 law (PL 100-203) required the department to focus research and evaluation exclusively on Yucca Mountain as the permanent site. It also authorized construction of a temporary storage site, an interim solution backed by the nuclear power companies. But the Energy Department was not allowed to select a short-term site until it had recommended the construction of the permanent Yucca Mountain site. (*1987 Almanac, p. 307*)

No short-term site was ever named, and the federal government defaulted on its obligation to begin removing used nuclear fuel from reactor sites by Jan. 31, 1998.

In 1998 and 1999, the Energy Department issued a series of reports concluding that Yucca Mountain could be used as the permanent site with no adverse impact on public health or safety and providing a design for the storage site. In 2001, the department issued a study concluding that the proposed repository could meet the EPA's radiation protection standard.

While the scientific studies were being conducted, high-level radioactive waste was accumulating, stored in 131 above-ground facilities composed of temporary concrete-encased pools in 39 states. Nearly 161 million people lived within 75 miles of those sites.

The Yucca Mountain site was expected to store that waste, along with future waste projected at 2,000 tons per year, in specially designed containers buried 1,000 feet underground. It was estimated that the waste could be safely stored there for 10,000 years, although opponents questioned the validity of those estimates.

Opposition came primarily from members of the Nevada delegation — both Republicans and Democrats — and environmentalists concerned with potential threats to human health and environmental integrity. They cited a number of studies that raised questions about the project, including a report by the Nuclear Waste Technical Review Board (created to provide an independent assessment of the project), that questioned the technical basis for the Energy Department's safety estimates. Opponents worried that the nuclear

BoxScore

Bill:

H J Res 87 — PL 107-200

Legislative Action:

House passed H J Res 87 (H Rept 107-425), 306-117, on May 8.

Senate cleared H J Res 87 by voice vote July 9.

President signed July 23.

waste eventually could seep into groundwater or that containers could be ruptured by earthquakes. They also raised concerns over transporting the waste through 43 states and within one mile of 50 million Americans. Opponents maintained that this presented not only a significant risk for accidents, but also a potential target for terrorists.

Supporters countered that 20 years worth of scientific studies demonstrated the unique suitability and safety of the site. They pointed to the Energy Department's flawless safety record in shipping defense-related waste to a site in New Mexico and argued that a greater terrorist threat was presented by leaving the waste scattered at stationary sites throughout the country. Officials and members of the public in the 39 states with existing temporary facilities were eager to be rid of the waste and wanted the federal government to honor its commitment to remove it.

Opening Yucca Mountain also was seen as crucial to sustaining the health of the nuclear energy industry, which provided about 20 percent of the nation's electricity. But advocates of nuclear energy acknowledged that opening the site did not mean the nuclear industry would begin building new plants. After the partial meltdown at Pennsylvania's Three Mile Island in 1979, federal safety regulators imposed regulations that made new nuclear plants uneconomical, and many utilities were forced to abandon partially built power plants. No new reactors had been ordered since 1978.

"This is just another step on a long road," said Frank H. Murkowski of Alaska, ranking Republican on the Senate Energy and Natural Resources Committee. "The terms of trying to permit and license a new reactor are still overwhelming, and we're going to have to come a long way before we see any new applications."

Legislative Action

House Action

In the House, where the vote was never in doubt, the joint resolution passed, 306-117, on May 8. The Energy and Commerce Committee had approved the measure (H Rept 107-425), 41-6, on April 25. Many lawmakers were eager to send waste piling up at commercial sites across their states to Nevada. (*House vote 133, p. H-48*)

Senate Action

After months of maneuvering and debate, the Senate on July 9 voted 60-39 to proceed to debate on the resolution, then adopted H J Res 87 by voice vote. The Energy and Natural Resources Committee had approved the measure (S J Res 34 — S Rept 107-159) by a vote of 13-10 on June 5. (*Senate vote 167, p. S-35*)

Several senators who voted for the resolution said their support had little to do with backing the desert repository. They were motivated by the more parochial desire to pre-

vent waste from remaining in their own states if the Nevada project was rejected.

Nevada hired John Podesta, White House chief of staff under President Bill Clinton, to help coordinate its message and make its case. The state's congressional delegation focused not only on the strong opposition in Nevada, but also on potential risks of transporting the waste. Sen. John Ensign, R-Nev., gave every senator he visited a list of which highways in their states would carry waste shipments.

But in the end, it was not enough to overcome an all-out campaign by the administration and the nuclear utility industry. ◆

Bill to Aid Brownfields Cleanup Passes House, Dies in Senate

The House passed a bill in June designed to make it easier for communities to use federal programs to clean up contaminated former industrial sites known as "brownfields," but the Senate did not act and the measure died at the end of the session.

The bill (HR 2941) would have formally authorized the Housing and Urban Development Department (HUD) brownfields redevelopment grant program and eased requirements that discouraged smaller communities from applying for the grants. The House Financial Services Committee approved the measure by voice vote April 11 (H Rept 107-448), and the full House passed it by voice vote June 4.

The United States was estimated to have approximately 500,000 brownfields sites — urban industrial and commercial sites that were contaminated but not polluted enough to qualify for coverage under the superfund hazardous waste cleanup program. A consensus had emerged on the need

and desirability of cleaning up these often abandoned sites as a means of promoting their redevelopment and revitalizing the communities around them.

The House bill was aimed at increasing access to capital for smaller communities that traditionally had been unable to get HUD assistance. Specifically, it proposed to eliminate a HUD requirement that local governments obtain Community Development Block Grant (CDBG) Section 108 loan guarantees before they could receive HUD brownfields grants. Small cities, in particular, had trouble getting the loan guarantees.

The House bill contained provisions to:
• Formally authorize the HUD brownfields program through fiscal 2007.
• Eliminate a requirement that communities receiving brownfields grants obtain a CDBG Section 108 loan guarantee.
• Require HUD, in choosing grant recipients, to consider what other federal money a community had received and whether it had been used to encourage private developers to clean up and redevelop brownfields.
• Expand HUD's definition of brownfields to include land damaged by mining.
• Authorize a pilot revolving loan program to serve as a pool for economic development loans that would be available to eligible local governments on a competitive basis.

The bill was seen as a complement to a law (PL 107-118) cleared in December 2001 that formally established the separate brownfields program run by the EPA and provided $200 million a year to states and local governments for brownfields cleanup programs. The law also protected owners of restored brownfields sites from having to pay any future cleanup costs. Fear of liability for future cleanup costs had been a major obstacle to developing the sites. (*2001 Almanac, p. 9-11*)

The EPA program focused on assessment and cleanup, while HUD's program focused more on cleanup. ◆

Chapter 9

FOREIGN POLICY

Hill Backs Use of Force in Iraq

President Bush won congressional passage of a resolution authorizing the use of military force against Iraq — with or without support from the United Nations. Despite the gravity of the matter, the outcome was never in doubt. Bipartisan support for the president's request was overwhelming in both chambers. Congress cleared the measure Oct. 11, and Bush signed it into law Oct. 16 (H J Res 114 — PL 107-243).

It was the first time Congress had been asked to endorse a possible pre-emptive strike against a sovereign nation. When the United States fought Iraq 11 years earlier, it was with broad international support to reverse Saddam Hussein's seizure of Kuwait. Even then, Congress set a high bar, demanding cost-sharing among allies and clear entry and exit strategies before authorizing the war.

This time, Bush asked Congress to look beyond the United States' tradition of never striking first and permit him to unleash the armed forces when he concluded that diplomacy had failed to disarm Iraq. United Nations support would be sought but not required. The White House negotiated the language with House Minority Leader Richard A. Gephardt, D-Mo., after efforts to strike a bargain with Senate Democrats and Republicans bogged down.

The resolution authorized the president to use U.S. forces "as he determines to be necessary and appropriate in order to (1) defend the national security of the United States against the continuing threat posed by Iraq and (2) enforce all United Nations Security Council resolutions regarding Iraq." (*Text, p. D-16*)

Bush hailed the outcome, describing it as a message to the world that "America speaks with one voice." But the votes belied a deep ambivalence and substantial fears among lawmakers.

During three days of debate in the House and five in the Senate, lawmakers posed and sought answers to dozens of questions. Why threaten to wage war alone if diplomacy fails? Why the urgency to act when there was no proof of an imminent chemical, biological or nuclear threat by Iraqi President Saddam Hussein? And what, precisely, was the connection between Iraq and the Sept. 11, 2001, terrorist attacks, a connection Bush said justified taking on Saddam?

Bush's allies argued that waiting would only give Saddam more time to increase his arsenal. "A gun smokes only after it has been fired, and that may be too late," said freshman Rep. Rob Simmons, R-Conn.

Also working in Bush's favor was the searing national memory of Sept. 11. Some lawmakers feared that if they failed to give Bush the power to act against Iraq, the na-

BoxScore

Bill:

H J Res 114 — PL 107-243

Legislative Action:

House passed H J Res 114 (H Rept 107-721), 296-133, on Oct. 10.

Senate cleared H J Res 114, 77-23, on Oct. 11.

President signed Oct. 16.

tion would be vulnerable to further strikes. Others, despite their reservations, worried they would be labeled unpatriotic if they voted against a popular president in the final weeks before a national election. In the end, many of those who had earlier questioned Bush's talk of war joined in an unexpectedly broad coalition behind the president.

Despite the wide margin of Bush's victory, however, analysts cautioned that Bush still had much convincing to do. "The president has run a successful campaign to win a vote," said Thomas E. Mann, a senior political scholar at the Brookings Institution. "The president has not persuaded the public or the Congress that a full, careful cost-benefit analysis has been done and that this is the wisest course to follow. He has maneuvered very effectively to get their votes. I don't think he has won their minds."

Background

Talk of war with Iraq had escalated with almost dizzying speed. After Sept. 11, the goal of U.S. policy toward Iraq shifted from containment to regime change. In his 2002 State of the Union address, Bush singled out Iraq as part of an "axis of evil" in the world. He was more explicit in a June speech at West Point, where he described a new U.S. policy of pre-emptive attacks against countries suspected of developing weapons of mass destruction. (*Text, p. D-3*)

In August, Vice President Dick Cheney and other Bush allies publicly articulated a rationale for using force unilaterally to overthrow Saddam. Other senior Republicans, including former national security adviser Brent Scowcroft and former Secretary of State James A. Baker III, took exception, raising doubts about the wisdom of going it alone. Members of Congress, returning from their August recess, insisted on the need for consultation.

After initially insisting that Bush had all the legal justification he needed for military action without further congressional or U.N. authority, the White House acceded. On Sept. 4, Bush announced that he would come to Congress for approval to "do whatever is necessary to deal with the threat posed by Saddam Hussein's regime."

On Sept. 12, Bush took his message to the United Nations, where he stated his case for war against Iraq and warned that the United States was prepared to act with or without Security Council sanction. The administration pressed for the Security Council to adopt a new, no-nonsense arms inspection regime for Baghdad and be prepared to use force if Saddam failed to disarm. If the Security Council fell short, Bush made clear, the United States would take unilateral action.

Legislative Action

Assembling the Resolution

The precise language of the resolution was negotiated between congressional leaders and the White House before the measure ever reached the committee room or floor of either chamber. The outlines began to take shape Sept. 19 when the White House, bowing to congressional demands for a voice in the decision to go to war, submitted a draft (S J Res 45). Over the next 10 days, White House negotiations focused largely on the Democratic-controlled Senate. The administration agreed to drop language authorizing force to "restore international peace and security to the region" — which critics feared could justify wider military action. They included a reference to the 1973 War Powers Act (PL 93-148), absent from the original proposal, which required congressional notification before any military action or "as soon thereafter as may be feasible." And they added language putting the burden on Bush to certify that reliance on diplomacy "will not adequately protect" U.S. interests before going to war.

At that point, Republican leaders said they had made enough concessions. But Senate Majority Leader Tom Daschle, D-S.D., said Democrats still wanted more clarity about what Bush could do under the resolution and specific requirements to "explore other options" before taking unilateral action.

Frustrated, White House aides decided Oct. 1 to switch gears and try to cut a separate deal with Gephardt. They also persuaded Henry J. Hyde, R-Ill, chairman of the House International Relations Committee, to schedule a markup for the next day, increasing the pressure on Gephardt to reach a deal. Bush announced the resulting compromise in a Rose Garden ceremony Oct. 2, with dozens of lawmakers from both parties flanking him in a display of unified U.S. determination. Conspicuously absent from the gathering was Daschle.

The compromise gave Bush the latitude he wanted in deciding whether and why to go to war against Iraq. As he demanded in the negotiations, he could cite numerous existing U.N. resolutions as grounds for an attack. But at Gephardt's insistence, the resolution required the president to report to Congress within 60 days of the start of hostilities — rather than the 90 days proposed by Bush. It also required a presidential ruling that diplomacy was no longer working and that any war would not affect the wider war against terrorism. "Iraq is a problem. It presents a problem after 9/11 that it did not before, and we should deal with it diplomatically if we can, militarily if we must. And I think this resolution does that," Gephardt said.

Senate Democrats were stunned by Gephardt's move, which left Daschle out in the cold. Some saw Gephardt as trying to improve his own chances as a presidential candidate in 2004 by ensuring that he did not look weak on national security. Gephardt said presidential politics had nothing to do with his decision. He said he regretted his vote in 1991 against the resolution (PL 102-1) that authorized the first war against Iraq. "I didn't know everything that I know now," he said. Some Democrats pointed to Gephardt's need to recover from a major embarrassment in his caucus, creat-

ed when vocal anti-war Democrats Jim McDermott of Washington and David E. Bonior of Michigan publicly called Bush's Iraq policy into question while on a trip to Baghdad. (*1991 Almanac, p. 437*)

House Committee Action

The House International Relations Committee approved the compromise bill (H J Res 114 — H Rept 107-721) by a vote of 31-11 on Oct. 3. The resolution had been introduced the previous day by Speaker J. Dennis Hastert, R-Ill., and Gephardt.

Some Democrats remained unhappy with the language, saying it would grant Bush too much latitude to wage war. Their frustrations were on display at the markup, where they mounted nine challenges to the proposed resolution. Under orders from Hyde and ranking Democrat Tom Lantos of California, every one was defeated.

House Floor Action

The House passed the resolution, 296-133, on Oct. 10. Gephardt was joined by 80 other Democrats in support of Bush, while just six Republicans opposed him. (*House vote 455, p. H-142*)

Republicans said the compromise supported Bush's policy of toppling Saddam without tying the president's hands. They also viewed it as offering little more than lip service to the United Nations.

But Gephardt and many Democrats supported it because they said it would strengthen Secretary of State Colin L. Powell's effort to win U.N. Security Council support to confront Saddam over his weapons of mass destruction. "The only way to get the United Nations to treat the issue seriously is for Congress and the international community to support the use of military force," said Howard L. Berman, D-Calif.

The House defeated all attempts to change the resolution. Lawmakers rejected:

• 155-270, an amendment by John M. Spratt Jr., D-S.C., that would have required the president to seek a new U.N. Security Council resolution authorizing use of force before taking military action. If the administration decided to proceed alone, it should first seek congressional authorization. Spratt maintained that since three in eight House members voted for the amendment, the administration should be aware that congressional support remained fragile. (*House vote 453, p. H-142*)

• 77-355, an amendment by Barbara Lee, D-Calif., that would have urged the president to work through the United Nations to ensure that Iraq was not developing weapons of mass destruction and urged the use of peaceful means to resolve the issue, including the return of weapons inspectors. (*House vote 452, p. H-142*)

• 101-325, a motion by Dennis J. Kucinich, D-Ohio, to send the bill back to committee with instructions to insert language requiring the president to report to Congress prior to using military force as to the potential effects on the U.S. economy, Iraqi citizens and international stability. (*House vote 454, p. H-142*)

Many of those who voted for the resolution raised questions in their speeches that indicated ambivalence: Was war really necessary? If so, when would it begin, and how would

it be executed and paid for? If the United States moved alone, was it willing to bear the responsibility of further destabilization in the Middle East region that could follow an invasion? Why Iraq, when there were other groups and nations that posed more serious threats to international security? And what would happen to the unfinished war against terrorism in Afghanistan?

To these and other questions, Hyde replied that while a united Congress would pressure the United Nations to pass an equally forceful resolution against Iraq, the United States should not fear acting alone. "On whom does the final responsibility for protecting ourselves rest?" Hyde asked. "Is it ours or do we share it with others? Are decisions regarding our fate to be made in common with others?" Hyde's answer: "We have no choice but to act as a sovereign country, prepared to defend ourselves, with our friends and allies if possible, but alone if necessary."

In the end, the fear of not acting superseded most concerns. "I abhor the idea of the U.S. making a pre-emptive strike," said Vernon J. Ehlers, R-Mich. "Our philosophy has always been to take the first punch before we act," he said in a statement. "But when the first punch can destroy a city and kill hundreds of thousands of people, we must consider ways to stop that punch."

Majority Leader Dick Armey, R-Texas, who until the week of Oct. 7 challenged the propriety of a possible pre-emptive strike, ended up delivering the closing speech on the president's behalf. "The snake is out of his hole," he said. "We are not striking an innocent here. We are correcting an error of complacency." His voice quavering, Armey addressed his speech to the president: "We trust to you the best we have to give. . . . Use them well."

Senate Action

Ten hours later, in the early morning hours of Oct. 11, the Senate cleared the measure on a 77-23 roll call. Daschle was among the solid majority of Democrats — 29 out of 50 — who voted with Bush. Among Republicans, only Rhode Island's Lincoln Chafee voted no. (*Senate vote 237, p. S-48*)

Daschle, the last of the four top congressional leaders to endorse the resolution, did so after unveiling a list of conditions that he said should be met before undertaking a military campaign, top among them that the president be forthright about the threat and cost. "Public support for military action can evaporate quickly if the American people come to believe that they have not been given all the facts," he warned. "If that should happen, no resolution Congress might pass will be able to unify our nation."

Robert C. Byrd, D-W.Va., mounted a quixotic, one-man campaign to persuade the Senate to flex its constitutional muscle and slow the march toward war. At the least, debate over a possible invasion of Iraq should not be conducted amid the passions of an election campaign, he argued.

"This is a fateful decision," Byrd said. "It involves the treasure of this country. It involves the blood of our fighting men and women. It is too momentous and too far-reaching a decision to be signed, sealed and delivered by 10:15 tomorrow morning," he said Oct. 9, on the eve of a vote limiting time for debate.

"The longer we wait, the more dangerous [Saddam] becomes," responded John McCain, R-Ariz., a prisoner of war

during the Vietnam conflict and a proponent of the resolution. He and others argued strongly against Byrd's complaints that the resolution would give the president unlimited authority to wage war, akin to the 1964 Gulf of Tonkin resolution (PL 88-408) authorizing military action during the Vietnam War. "That's just ludicrous," McCain said. "The one lesson of the Vietnam War that we will never forget is: Never let a resolution just sit out there as a reason to conduct a conflict Americans don't support."

After several rounds of negotiating with Daschle, Byrd cut short his threat to filibuster the resolution. In any case, the chances that such a filibuster could have succeeded were quashed Oct. 10, when the Senate voted, 75-25, to invoke cloture, and thereby limit debate, on an amendment that made the Senate language virtually identical to the House's. (*Senate vote 233, p. S-48*)

The Senate rejected, 14-86, an amendment by Byrd that would have stated that the resolution would not "alter the constitutional authorities of the Congress to declare war." (*Senate vote 234, p. S-48*)

The Senate also roundly defeated, 31-66, a Byrd amendment to put a two-year limit on any congressional authorization of military action. (*Senate vote 232, p. S-48*)

In other action, the Senate rejected, 24-75, an amendment by Carl Levin, D-Mich., that would have allowed the use of force only if it had been authorized by the United Nations and only for the purpose of eliminating weapons of mass destruction in Iraq. It also would have required the president to certify to Congress that the United States had exhausted diplomatic and other peaceful means to obtain compliance by Iraq with a new U.N. resolution. (*Senate vote 235, p. S-48*)

Finally, senators rejected, 30-70, an amendment by Richard J. Durbin, D-Ill., that would have authorized the use of force to meet "an imminent threat posed by Iraq's weapons of mass destruction," a higher threshold than the "continuing threat posed by Iraq" that was cited in the resolution. (*Senate vote 236, p. S-48*)

"International law has never, never, gotten to the point where anything less than imminent threat was used as being sufficient," Levin said in the debate. He noted that the lower standard for a pre-emptive strike could apply to North Korea, Iran or other nations possessing weapons of mass destruction.

The uncertainty could be sensed in the uneasy stillness of the Senate chamber as the roll was called for the climactic vote starting at 12:50 a.m. Oct. 11. In votes on the most momentous matters — the impeachment trial of President Bill Clinton in 1999, the most recent example — senators declare their votes aloud while sitting at their desks, then wait in silence for the outcome to be announced. In this case, however, senators simply slipped out of the chamber and into the night after casting their ballots.

Postscript

After nearly two months of arduous negotiations, the U.N. Security Council gave unanimous approval to a resolution that gave Iraq a "final opportunity" to comply with its disarmament obligations; required Iraq to declare within 30 days all of its programs for weapons of mass destruction; insisted that U.N. weapons inspectors have unconditional and

unrestricted access to any suspected weapons site; and warned Iraq that it would face "serious consequences" for failing to comply with these requirements.

Bush praised the U.N. action but added: "America will be making only one determination: Is Iraq meeting the terms of the Security Council resolution or not? The United States has agreed to discuss any material breach with the Security Council, but without jeopardizing our freedom of action to defend our country. If Iraq fails to fully comply, the United States and other nations will disarm Saddam Hussein." ◆

State Bill Highlights U.N. Funds

As tension mounted in the fall over possible U.S. intervention in Iraq, Congress cleared a bill that reauthorized the State Department for fiscal 2002-03 and took several steps to boost U.S. ties to the United Nations. The law released $322 million in U.S. back payments to the world body, temporarily increased the U.S. share of the U.N. peacekeeping budget and funded the United States' return to the U.N. Education, Scientific and Cultural Organization (UNESCO). President Bush signed the bill into law Sept. 30 (HR 1646 — PL 107-228).

The U.N. funds were the highlight of a measure that authorized $13.8 billion for fiscal 2003 — $8.6 billion for State Department and related operations, including efforts to enhance security at U.S. embassies and other diplomatic missions overseas, and $5.2 billion for military aid and counterterrorism.

The legislation had languished for months, stalled by House-Senate differences over drug certification and other issues. Compromise suddenly became imperative when Bush delivered a speech to the U.N. General Assembly on Sept. 12, calling for a tough new Security Council resolution on Iraq. Eager to support the president's efforts, House and Senate negotiators moved quickly to bury their differences.

"Our bill clearly demonstrates Congress' commitment to multilateralism and offers a vote of confidence in the United Nations," declared Tom Lantos of California, ranking Democrat on the House International Relations Committee. "It's now time for the United Nations to prove itself worthy of such confidence."

Highlights

The major funding authorized by the bill included:
- **State Department.** $4 billion in fiscal 2003 for State Department operations, including $564 million for worldwide security upgrades.
- **Embassy security.** $555 million for embassy security, construction and maintenance, on top of the $1 billion per year in fiscal 2002-04 authorized under the fiscal 2000 omnibus appropriations act (PL 106-113).
- **International broadcasting.** $486 million, including

BoxScore

Bill:
HR 1646 — PL 107-228
Legislative Action:
House passed HR 1646 (H Rept 107-57), 352-73, on May 16, 2001.
Senate passed HR 1646, amended, by voice vote May 1, 2002.
House adopted the conference report (H Rept 107-671) by voice vote Sept. 25.
Senate cleared the bill by voice vote Sept. 26.
President signed Sept. 30.

---

funding for Radio Free Asia, broadcasts to Cuba and Voice of America services to the Middle East.
- **International organizations.** $891 million for assessed contributions to international organizations in fiscal 2003, much of it for the United Nations. In addition, the law authorized $726 million for assessed U.S. contributions to the United Nations and regional organizations for international peacekeeping activities in fiscal 2003.
- **U.N. arrearages.** $322 million in back payments to the United Nations — $244 million for the fiscal 2003 payment, plus $78 million in U.S. dues that had accumulated since Congress began considering the legislation in 2001.
- **Foreign military sales and training.** $4.1 billion for foreign military sales programs, particularly military funding for Israel and Egypt. The bill also authorized $85 million for International Military Education and Training (IMET), $5 million more than requested, which conferees said reflected "the managers' strong support for the IMET program."

Background

The bill authorized funding for State Department programs, contributions to multilateral organizations and activities, and U.S. foreign broadcasting operations. It did not include most bilateral U.S. aid to foreign countries, which was authorized separately. The authorization expired every two years. Lawmakers regularly avoided passing a stand-alone renewal, instead attaching reauthorizing language to the annual appropriations bill for the Commerce, Justice and State departments. A separate authorization bill had not been enacted since 1994. (*1994 Almanac, p. 454*)

Efforts to clear a broad State Department reauthorization bill in 2001 stalled after the Sept. 11 terrorist attacks, which pushed other priorities to the fore. The House passed an $8.2 billion authorization bill (HR 1646 — H Rept 107-57) on May 16. The Senate Foreign Relations Committee approved an $18.4 billion companion bill (S 1803 — S Rept 107-60) on Sept. 4.

The House bill initially included release of $826 million in back U.N. dues — $582 million in fiscal 2002 and

$244 million in 2003. These were the second and third installments of a plan negotiated in December 2000, under which the United States agreed to pay a total of $926 million in back dues in exchange for a reduction in U.S. contributions and other organizational changes at the United Nations. The plan had been written into the fiscal 2000 omnibus appropriations law, but release of the second and third payments required separate authorizing legislation. *(1999 Almanac, p. 14-3)*

The House was poised to provide the authorization, but shortly before it took up the State Department bill, the United States lost its seat on the U.N. Human Rights Commission. Members retaliated by voting to hold up the third installment until the United States regained its seat. The second installment was not affected.

The Sept. 11 terrorist attacks sidetracked the State Department bill. But with the administration trying to build a global coalition against terrorism, Congress cleared a separate bill (PL 107-46) in October 2001 to release the $582 million installment for fiscal 2002 and adjust statutory contributions limits to allow the payment to go forward. *(2001 Almanac, p. 11-13)*

As frequently occurred, the need for a fiscal 2002 State Department authorization was waived under the Commerce-Justice-State appropriations bill (PL 107-77).

Legislative Action

Senate Floor Action

The Senate took up HR 1646 on May 1 and passed it by voice vote without debate after substituting the text of its own bill (S 1803 — S Rept 107-122).

Conference/Final Action

With Congress focused on a request by Bush for sweeping war powers against Iraq, House and Senate conferees met Sept. 18 and quickly agreed on a compromise State Department bill. The House adopted the conference report (H Rept 107-671) by voice vote Sept. 25. The Senate cleared the bill the next day, also by voice vote.

The following are among the main issues settled by the conferees:

• **U.N. back payments.** In addition to releasing the $322 million to the United Nations, the bill modified conditions set in U.S. law for paying the arrears, bringing them close to the agreement reached with the United Nations in 2000. For two years, the cap on U.S. contributions to the U.N. peacekeeping budget would be increased from 25 percent to slightly more than 27 percent. The United Nations had been calculating the U.S. share at 30 percent, which contributed to the buildup of U.S. arrears. U.S. payments to the U.N. general budget were set at 22 percent of the total.

The conference report also expressed the sense of Congress that the United States should move toward paying its U.N. dues in January, rather than October, to coincide with the U.N. budget cycle. The fact that the United States was perpetually behind was a major factor in the arrears.

• **International broadcasting.** Final negotiations bogged down briefly over an attempt by House International Relations Committee Chairman Henry J. Hyde, R-Ill., to include a bill on U.S. government broadcasting and international exchange programs in the final conference report. The bill (HR 3969), passed by the House in July, sought to shake up the nation's "public diplomacy" bureaucracy and authorize an additional $255 million for international outreach and media programs, including expanded efforts to improve the U.S. image in the Arab world. But Senate Foreign Relations Committee Chairman Joseph R. Biden Jr., D-Del., objected to Hyde's plans to alter the role of the Broadcasting Board of Governors, charged with overseeing U.S. government broadcasters. Unable to resolve the dispute, conferees left the provisions out of the bill.

• **Drug certification.** The bill suspended the State Department's annual drug certification program for two years. Secretary of State Colin L. Powell requested the moratorium, saying the grading process insulted allies such as Mexico and hurt U.S. anti-drug operations. A country that did not get a passing grade indicating it was complying with U.S. anti-drug programs faced a possible cutoff of U.S. aid. The Senate bill called for a three-year suspension; the House would have left the existing process in place.

• **Russia.** The bill included several provisions to bolster ties with Russia, a permanent member of the Security Council whose support Bush needed for a strong new anti-Iraq resolution.

Conferees adopted a Senate-passed initiative to forgive certain Russian debts in exchange for investments in nonproliferation programs. Russia had assumed the Soviet Union's debts and owed roughly $2.7 billion to the United States. Up to 10 percent of the funds saved by Russia because of any debt relief was to be used to promote independent media and the rule of law in Russia.

The measure also revived a State Department program to relocate Russian scientists to the United States in an effort to prevent them from taking jobs with U.S. enemies, such as Iraq. From 1992 through its expiration in 1996, the program (PL 102-509) allowed up to 750 highly skilled scientists and their families to be admitted to the United States without meeting the normal requirement that they first be recruited by a U.S. employer. The conference agreement extended the program for four years and increased to 950 the total number of scientists who could be admitted.

• **Taiwan.** The bill authorized the sale of four *Kidd*-class Navy destroyers to Taiwan. It also boosted Taipei's standing in the pecking order of U.S. military sales, raising it to the status of a "major non-NATO ally."

• **Lebanon.** Conferees agreed to scale back a House amendment that would have blocked $35 million in military training funds to Lebanon until that nation adequately controlled its southern border with Israel. The area was dominated by Hezbollah guerrillas, who regularly launched rocket attacks on Israel. The compromise freed $25 million but held the remaining $10 million in escrow until Lebanon asserted its authority in the south.

• **Jerusalem.** The conference agreement expressed Congress' commitment to relocating the U.S. embassy in Israel to Jerusalem and urged the president to immediately begin the process of relocation called for in a 1995 law (PL 104-45). The bill also prohibited the use of funds to operate a U.S. consulate or diplomatic facility in Jerusalem that was not under the supervision of the U.S. ambassador and pro-

hibited the publication of any government document that listed countries and their capitals and did not identify Jerusalem as the capital of Israel.

● **Palestinians.** The bill required the president to report every six months on whether the Palestine Liberation Organization (PLO) and Palestinian Authority were abiding by commitments to renounce violence and assume responsibility over all PLO personnel. Failure of the Palestinians to comply could result in U.S. sanctions. ◆

No Agreement Reached On HIV/AIDS Bill

House and Senate negotiators came close to a last-minute compromise on legislation (HR 2069) aimed at increasing U.S. support for overseas HIV/AIDS programs, but differences over money and the scope of the bill proved insurmountable.

The House had passed a bill by voice vote Dec. 11, 2001, that would have authorized $1.4 billion in fiscal 2002 to target AIDS, particularly in sub-Saharan Africa. Although the region had only 10 percent of the world's population, it accounted for 70 percent of all HIV/AIDS cases and 80 percent of all AIDS-related deaths. The proposed authorization included $750 million for a global fund or other multilateral efforts to combat AIDS, $560 million for bilateral programs operated primarily by the U.S. Agency for International Development, and $50 million for a pilot program to help African nations buy medicines to treat AIDS.

The Senate passed its version of the bill by voice vote July 12, 2002, after substituting language approved June 13 by the Foreign Relations Committee (S 2525 — S Rept 107-206). The bill would have authorized $4.7 billion in fiscal 2003-04, including $2.2 billion for the Global Fund to Fight AIDS, Tuberculosis and Malaria, established in January 2002. The total also included $1.7 billion for bilateral programs and $500 million in fiscal 2003 for international activities administered by the Department of Health and Human Services (HHS), primarily the Centers for Disease Control and Prevention. The bill also called for more debt relief for AIDS-afflicted countries and included authorization for additional funds for vaccine programs and programs to treat tuberculosis and malaria, which often plague AIDS victims.

The end-of-session compromise would have authorized $4 billion for international AIDS programs over two years, with a $2 billion cap on money for the new global fund. It dropped Senate provisions on debt relief for AIDS-afflicted countries and on HIV/AIDS programs operated by HHS. House Financial Services Committee Chairman Michael G. Oxley, R-Ohio, and Energy and Commerce Committee Chairman Billy Tauzin, R-La., had objected to the provisions, saying they intruded on their committees' jurisdictions. ◆

Lawmakers Endorse Radio Free Afghanistan

The House on Feb. 12 cleared legislation to establish Radio Free Afghanistan, a U.S.-government-sponsored broadcasting service similar to Radio Free Europe. The bill authorized $17 million in fiscal 2002 — $8 million for broadcast operations and $9 million for capital improvements. It provided for eight hours of daily broadcasts. President Bush signed the bill into law (HR 2998 — PL 107-148) on March 11.

In clearing the bill, 421-2, the House agreed to Senate amendments that reduced both the cost and broadcasting hours. (*House vote 15, p. H-12*)

The initial House version, passed Nov. 7, 2001, would have authorized a total of $27.5 million in fiscal 2002 and 2003 and provided for 12 hours of daily broadcasts. The Senate passed the amended version by voice vote Feb. 7, 2002.

During the war in Afghanistan, the United States increased broadcasts to the Central Asian nation through the existing Voice of America. ◆

Congress Supports Treaties, Child Protection

Congress sent President Bush a bill to implement two recently ratified international treaties aimed at cracking down on terrorists and their financial backers. The measure was signed into law June 25 (HR 3275 — PL 107-197).

The bill, which the House cleared by voice vote June 18, updated U.S. law to comply with the International Convention for the Suppression of Terrorism Bombings (Treaty Doc 106-6) and the International Convention for the Suppression of Financing of Terrorism (Treaty Doc 106-49). The Senate had ratified those accords Dec. 5, 2001.

The House had first passed the implementing bill Dec. 19, 2001, by a vote of 381-36. The Senate passed it, 83-1, on June 14, after making several changes that required a second House vote. (*Senate vote 154, p. S-33*)

Under the revised bill, prosecutors can seek the death penalty for terrorist bombings, but only on the more limited grounds outlined in a law that prohibits the use of weapons of mass destruction. The original bill would have extended the death penalty to any individual guilty of violating the new statute. The amended bill also required prosecutors to show that a suspect knew he or she was helping to fund terrorists, a requirement lacking in the original House bill.

In separate action, the Senate on June 18 ratified by voice vote two optional protocols (Treaty Doc 106-37) to the Convention on the Rights of the Child that prohibited using children as soldiers and sought to combat child pornography, child prostitution and child slavery. ◆

Chapter 10

HEALTH

No Deal on Prescription Benefit

Congress debated but could not agree on legislation to add a prescription drug benefit to Medicare, the federal health insurance program for elderly and disabled Americans. Republicans passed a prescription drug bill in the House, but partisan differences doomed each of four proposals considered in the narrowly divided Senate.

Although election-year politics and partisan bickering contributed to the deadlock, members of both parties said the philosophical differences were so great that agreement would have been difficult under the best of conditions.

Republicans insisted that any prescription drug coverage should conform to the demands of the marketplace, with private insurers setting the premiums, deductibles and coverage terms within guidelines. Democrats said the government should design and manage a guaranteed benefit that would be uniform across the nation, available to all seniors and embedded in the traditional Medicare fee-for-service program. Democrats favored broad coverage despite the cost, while Republicans were willing to have beneficiaries pick up the full tab for some of their drug expenses.

"That's the fundamental divide, and it's pretty hard to mask over that divide," said Senate Majority Leader Tom Daschle, D-S.D.

The GOP House-passed bill, which would have cost $350 billion over 10 years, would have allowed Medicare beneficiaries to buy new private insurance policies for prescription drugs. House Democrats offered a far more generous plan costing $800 billion over 10 years. It would have given the federal government the authority to determine premium rates and the details of coverage for all enrollees.

The Senate initially debated three prescription drug proposals: a government-run plan backed by Democrats; a "tripartisan" approach proposed by moderates that included both private and public sector coverage options; and a more modest GOP plan that would have given beneficiaries access to discount drug cards and offered coverage on a sliding income scale for people with extremely high annual drug costs.

When none of the plans were adopted — all failed to get the 60 votes needed to overcome objections that they exceeded Senate spending limits — a small group of Democrats and moderate Republicans offered a scaled-back alternative aimed at helping poor seniors and those with high annual drug bills. But that, too, failed to win 60 votes. Finally, the Senate passed the underlying bill, which would have made it harder for big drug companies to block approval of cheaper generic drugs, but the measure died in the House. (*Generic drugs, p. 10-8*)

Lawmakers from both parties vowed in their re-election campaigns to resolve the issue in the 108th Congress.

BoxScore

Bills:
HR 4954, S 812
Legislative Action:
House passed HR 4954 (H Rept 107-539, Part 1, H Rept 107-542, Part 1), 221-208, on June 28.

Major Issues

All of the comprehensive bills proposed a voluntary prescription drug benefit for Medicare beneficiaries under a new "Part D" of the program. The following are some of the major issues that differentiated the bills:

● **Government, private sector roles.** Republican plans relied completely or in part on private insurers to design and provide new drug-only insurance policies. To encourage insurers to offer such policies, they included government subsidies and other financial incentives, in effect absorbing part of the risk. The overall plan would be administered through a new Medicare office.

Under the Democrats' plans, prescription drug coverage would be designed and administered by Medicare, which would contract with private sources such as pharmacy benefit managers and health plans. The government would bear most of the risk.

● **Coverage.** Under the GOP approach, benefits could differ from one region to another, but there would be a minimum or "standard" level. Democrats favored a uniform benefit set by the government and available to all enrollees.

The potential cost to the enrollee varied considerably among plans. Republicans proposed an annual deductible, plus monthly premiums that would be set by the insurer and vary by region. After the deductible was met, a percentage of costs would be covered by insurance up to a limit of about $2,000. Beyond that, the beneficiary would bear all of the cost until his or her out-of-pocket expenses reached an upper threshold of nearly $4,000, after which the government and the insurer would pay all of the costs.

The Democrats generally favored full coverage with no gap, although enrollees might have to chose from a list of covered drugs.

● **Low-income beneficiaries.** All of the plans included subsidies for low-income beneficiaries, although coverage differed, ranging from 135 percent of the federal poverty level to 170 percent.

Background

Beginning with a proposal for a prescription drug benefit offered by President Bill Clinton in 1999, the two parties had been arguing over how such a benefit should be delivered, what the government role should be and how much it should cost. (*1999 Almanac, p. 16-31*)

Democrats made the addition of such a benefit to Medicare one of their top legislative priorities. They argued that use of prescription drugs was an increasingly important part of health care treatment, and that seniors should receive drug coverage as part of their Medicare benefits. Medicare

did not pay for outpatient prescription drugs unless a senior joined a managed-care plan that offered benefits. The addition of a drug benefit would be one of the most expensive expansions of the program since it was created in 1965.

Recognizing the public interest in a drug benefit, House Republicans presented their own plan in 2000. It relied on the private insurance market to develop coverage and proposed federal subsidies to help insurers cover the costs. The bill squeaked through the House, 217-214, far short of the votes needed to override Clinton's promised veto. But the Health Insurance Association of America (HIAA), a key industry trade group, surprised its longtime GOP allies by opposing the plan as unworkable. Industry officials said such policies would not be profitable, given the fact that the purchasers would tend to be seniors with particularly high drug bills. (*2000 Almanac, p. 12-16*)

There was little action on the issue in 2001, as lawmakers focused on other priorities, from President Bush's tax cut plan and a massive overhaul of education law to the Sept. 11 attacks. (*2001 Almanac, p. 12-7*)

In 2002, hoping to inoculate their party from Democratic criticisms on the issue during an election year, House GOP leaders worked again to introduce a prescription drug bill. The legislation that the House ultimately passed in June was based on the bill that Republicans had written two years earlier. This time, with more money in the bill for them, the insurers were on board. "There is now a much better chance that our members will offer the benefit, " HIAA President Donald A. Young, told Ways and Means Chairman Bill Thomas, R-Calif., in a letter June 18.

A separate issue that complicated the debate in 2002 involved reimbursements for Medicare providers, who argued their payments had been cut too deeply under the 1997 Balanced Budget Act (PL 105-33). The House bill included $30 billion over 10 years, which helped win over some wavering Republicans but also cut into the total funds available for the prescription drug benefit. (*Medicare reimbursements, p. 10-5*)

Legislative Action

House Committee Action

The House Republican bill, introduced June 18, was considered by two committees — Ways and Means and Energy and Commerce.

Coverage limits were dictated in part by GOP leaders' decision to stay within the parameters of the House-passed fiscal 2003 budget resolution (H Con Res 353), which allowed $350 billion for the bill over 10 years. To do that, they proposed to cover 80 percent of an enrollee's prescription costs from $251 to $1,000, then 50 percent of the next $1,000. The enrollee would pay all of the costs between $2,001 and a "catastrophic cap" of $4,500. Beyond that, the federal government and insurers would pick up the entire cost. The gap in coverage, dubbed the "doughnut hole," was an easy mark for Democratic critics.

The bill was more generous than the Republicans' 2000 plan, which would have covered 30 percent of pharmaceutical costs between $1,250 and $1,350, rising to 90 percent once a beneficiary's annual bill reached $6,000 or more.

Premiums would vary by region; sponsors estimated that they would average $34 per month. To encourage private insurers to offer policies even in areas where it might not otherwise be profitable, the bill called for federal subsidies of 65 percent or more of the cost of providing coverage.

In addition to the prescription drug provisions, GOP drafters included more than $30 billion to increase payments to Medicare health care providers. Doctors, hospitals and others were threatening to leave the program unless they got more money, and sympathetic lawmakers, particularly those from rural areas, made their support for the drug plan contingent upon getting help for their local providers.

The bill also included policy changes that proponents said would contain Medicare spending and help ensure that the program could handle the coming wave of Baby Boomers. Those provisions were key for many Republicans, including Thomas, a cosponsor of the measure.

● **Ways and Means Committee.** After a bitterly partisan, 13-hour markup, the House Ways and Means Committee approved the bill (HR 4954 — H Rept 107-539, Part 1) in the early morning hours of June 19. The vote was 22-16 along mostly party lines. The measure had the backing of the health insurance industry and key health provider groups but drew criticisms from some consumer and seniors' lobbying groups.

At the insistence of some Republicans, the cap on out-of-pocket expenses was reduced to $3,800.

Democrats had no luck in changing the bill. More than a dozen Democratic amendments were rejected, including a substitute offered by Charles B. Rangel of New York. The Democrats' $800 billion, 10-year plan called for a more generous benefit to seniors through the existing government-run, fee-for-service Medicare program, rather than requiring beneficiaries to buy separate drug-only policies from private insurers. Enrollees would pay a $25 monthly premium and a $100 annual deductible. Medicare would pick up 80 percent of drug costs until the enrollee had paid $2,000, then cover 100 percent of costs after that.

Health Subcommittee Chairwoman Nancy L. Johnson, R-Conn., who introduced the GOP bill, called the Democrats' plan "breathtakingly irresponsible." Pete Stark of California, the ranking Democrat on the subcommittee, responded that the Democratic alternative was more costly because a meaningful drug benefit "doesn't come on the cheap. It's a matter of priorities."

● **Energy and Commerce Committee.** One day after the Ways and Means markup began, the House Energy and Commerce Committee started its own marathon session. Chairman Billy Tauzin, R-La., broke the legislation into 13 narrower bills, allowing him to rule many of the proposed Democratic amendments out of order. All of the Democratic amendments that were offered were rejected. The markup continued past midnight and finally concluded at about 8:30 on the morning of June 21 when the committee voted, 30-23, to approve a bill (HR 4988 — H Rept 107-542, Part 1) that reunited the separate pieces.

The only major area of bipartisan agreement came on a $34.5 billion package of increased payments to Medicare providers. The entire bill would have cost $341 billion over 10 years, according to the Congressional Budget Office (CBO).

Medicare 'Givebacks' Languish

Despite high hopes and considerable lobbying, doctors, hospitals and other Medicare providers failed to roll back payment cuts enacted in 1997 as part of a drive to reduce the deficit. The proposal had wide support in Congress, but it was packaged with prescription drug legislation that died at the end of the session.

The House included $30 billion for Medicare providers over 10 years as part of a $350 billion bill to add prescription drug coverage to Medicare. The bill passed in June, but partisan conflicts doomed the legislation in the Senate.

For five years, providers who cared for Medicare's nearly 40 million recipients had complained that the 1997 Balanced Budget Act (PL 105-33) cut their reimbursements too deeply. Twice, in 1999 and 2000, Congress increased payments to providers in what came to be known as "giveback" legislation. (*1997 Almanac, p. 6-3*)

In 1999, Congress included a $16 billion, five-year package of givebacks in an omnibus appropriations law (PL 106-113). Medicare providers pressed for a second installment in 2000, winning about $35 billion over five years as part of yet another omnibus spending bill (PL 106-554). (*1999 Almanac, p. 16-31; 2000 Almanac, p. 12-25*)

Renewed Effort in 2002

The providers, including physicians, hospitals, nursing homes and home health agencies, began pushing early in 2002 for a third giveback bill. The $30 billion included in the House prescription drug bill (HR 4954) helped win votes for that measure, particularly among lawmakers from rural areas. It also raised providers' hopes that Congress would hear their concerns. (*Medicare prescriptions, p. 10-3*)

While there was bipartisan support in the Senate for more provider funds, no givebacks were included in the various versions of the Medicare prescription drug benefit that were offered on the Senate floor in July. All those proposals failed.

Provider groups used the August recess to make their case for more funds. The American Medical Association was especially aggressive, arguing that physicians would leave Medicare in droves unless Congress reversed a cut in physician payments scheduled to take effect early in 2003.

In October, Senate Finance Committee Chairman Max Baucus, D-Mont., and the panel's ranking Republican, Charles E. Grassley of Iowa, introduced a $43 billion giveback bill (S 3018). Baucus attempted to get a floor vote on the bill Oct. 4, but Minority Whip Don Nickles, R-Okla., objected, saying it should not be considered without giving lawmakers a chance to offer amendments.

Baucus and Grassley had been unable to get their measure out of the Finance Committee because panel members Olympia J. Snowe, R-Maine, and John B. Breaux, D-La., were determined to attach their version of a prescription drug benefit bill. They said Congress should not give health care providers more money without first providing drug coverage to seniors.

AARP, the powerful seniors lobbying group, had said the same, as had the White House, which raised fears that President Bush might veto a measure that dealt only with providers.

Just before adjourning, the House added increased Medicare doctor payments to a broader bill (HR 5063) that included welfare and unemployment provisions. But in the Senate, Majority Leader Tom Daschle, D-S.D., as well as Baucus and Grassley, objected, saying Congress should act to increase payments to all Medicare providers, not just physicians.

The key showdown occurred early on, when the committee rejected, 23-30, the $800 billion Democratic substitute for the drug benefit provisions. The amendment was offered by ranking Democrat John D. Dingell of Michigan.

Republicans rejected, 31-24, a Democratic proposal to set a $35 premium in law that would rise annually in proportion to the growth in per capita Medicare drug costs. Other defeated Democratic amendments included proposals to close the coverage gap, which in the Energy and Commerce version would have hit an upper limit of $3,700 before Medicare picked up the full cost; give the Health and Human Services (HHS) secretary the authority to negotiate price discounts with drug manufacturers; and guarantee enrollees the lowest prescription drug price available.

House Floor Action

The House passed HR 4954 on a near-party line vote of 221-208 that concluded at 2:30 a.m. on June 28. Passage followed an extraordinary day of lobbying by Speaker J. Dennis Hastert, R-Ill., the White House and health industry trade

groups. In the end, eight Republicans strayed from the fold to vote against the bill, while an equal number of Democrats voted for it. (*House vote 282, p. H-90*)

Before the bill came to the floor, the GOP-controlled Rules Committee made several changes to the version approved by the Ways and Means Committee. The bill proposed a $3,700 ceiling on out-of-pocket costs, as approved by the Energy and Commerce Committee, rather than the $3,800 in the Ways and Means version. It increased the subsidy for insurers from 65 percent of the cost of providing coverage to 67 percent. It also dropped a Ways and Means provision that would have established a co-payment for home health care.

Republican leaders faced dissension within their own ranks right up to the opening moments of the debate. Action was delayed for hours June 27 as the leadership lobbied more than three dozen members who had either expressed concerns about the measure or said they intended to vote against it. Several industry groups, including the Pharmaceutical Research and Manufacturers of America, were

called in to help get members on board. White House aides visited members' offices, and Republican leaders granted favors. At one point, Hastert threatened to hold the House in session into the weekend, delaying the start of the Fourth of July recess if necessary, to ensure action on the bill.

To maintain control and force Democrats into an up-or-down vote, the Rules Committee had approved a closed rule for debate that barred amendments. The 218-213 vote to adopt the rule gave GOP leaders confidence they had enough support to pass the bill. (*House vote 280, p. H-90*)

As the floor debate dragged into the early morning of June 28, Democrats accused Republicans of designing the bill to please their allies in the drug and insurance industry rather than to give seniors the prescription drug coverage they needed. They said the bill was the first step toward privatization of Medicare and pointed to criticism from groups such as Consumers Union, Families USA, and the seniors' group AARP. In a June 18 letter to Thomas, AARP Executive Director and Chief Executive Officer William D. Novelli had said the bill's "large coverage gap is a strong disincentive to enrollment."

The Democrats were particularly angry that Republicans refused to let them offer their plan as a substitute. They were allowed only a motion to recommit, which failed, 204-223. (*House vote 281, p. H-90*)

Republicans accused Democrats of designing a drug bill more for political gain than to help seniors and said it would bust the federal budget. "Democrats care only about outbidding Republicans in an attempt to score political points for the election," said Michael Bilirakis, R-Fla., chairman of the Energy and Commerce Health Subcommittee.

Among Republicans who voted against the bill were Jo Ann Emerson of Missouri and Gil Gutknecht of Minnesota, who led an effort to lower drug costs by allowing the wholesale importation of U.S. drugs from Canada, where they were cheaper, and tightening patent laws to make it harder for manufacturers of brand-name drugs to impede low-cost generic competition.

Senate Floor Action

Daschle called the House-passed measure "a terrible bill" and said House Republicans were "so far to the right on this issue that it is a challenge to see how we can reconcile our differences." In hopes of spurring a compromise, he gave the Senate Finance Committee a deadline of July 15 to report a bill for floor consideration.

With several factions competing for support, the committee missed the deadline. Some Finance members, including ranking Republican Charles E. Grassley of Iowa, later complained that the panel could have produced a bill if given more time, but Daschle said the committee had had its chance.

On July 15, Daschle began floor consideration of legislation (S 812) intended to lower prices by making it difficult for brand-name drugmakers to extend their patents. The measure served as the vehicle for the larger prescription drug debate. Because the Senate had not adopted a fiscal 2003 budget resolution, any proposal had to be within the $300 billion approved for a Medicare plan in the fiscal 2002 budget resolution (H Con Res 83). Anything costing more was subject to a point of order that required 60 votes to overcome, a hurdle that ultimately proved too

high for all of the proposals.

Three major prescription drug plans were offered as amendments to S 812.

● **Democratic plan.** Most Democrats, including Daschle, supported a bill (S 2625) sponsored by Bob Graham of Florida, Zell Miller of Georgia and Edward M. Kennedy of Massachusetts. The bill called for a uniform benefit available to all Medicare beneficiaries with a $25 monthly premium, plus co-payments of $10 for each generic drug and $40 for each brand-name drug on a list of approved drugs. There would be no deductible, and the beneficiary's out-of-pocket costs would be capped at $4,000 a year. The plan would be run by HHS, which would contract with private sources such as pharmacy benefit managers and health plans. CBO said the bill would cost $594 billion over 10 years.

Republicans found it too expensive and government-driven. An attempt to waive the budget limits got the support of all 50 Democrats, plus Peter G. Fitzgerald, R-Ill., and James M. Jeffords, I-Vt. But the 52-47 vote was short of the 60 needed, and the amendment fell July 23. (*Senate vote 186, p. S-38*)

● **Tripartisan plan.** A second proposal, known as the tripartisan plan, was sponsored by Republican Grassley, Democrat John B. Breaux of Louisiana and independent Jeffords. It offered three different options for coverage: the traditional fee-for-service Medicare program, a Medicare managed-care plan or a stand-alone drug policy to be offered by private insurers. It included a $24 monthly premium, a $250 deductible and a 50 percent cost share for expenses of between $251 and $3,450. Insurers could alter the premiums, benefits and co-payments if they got approval from the government. A special Medicare Competitive Agency would be established in HHS to administer the plan. The bill was estimated to cost $370 billion over 10 years.

That proposal, too, failed to get the necessary 60 votes. It had the backing of 45 Republicans, Jeffords, and Louisiana Democrats Breaux and Mary L. Landrieu. It fell, 48-51, on July 23. (*Senate vote 187, p. S-38*)

● **Discount card.** A third alternative, by Chuck Hagel, R-Neb., would have provided a discount card to help low-income seniors buy drugs at reduced prices, along with financial help to seniors who had extremely high annual drug costs. The estimated cost was $150 billion over eight years.

Democrats said the benefits were too limited. Hagel failed, 51-48, to overcome a point of order on July 24. He was backed by 47 Republicans and four Democrats. (*Senate vote 189, p. S-38*)

● **Graham-Smith compromise.** Finally, in a last-ditch effort, Graham and Republican Gordon H. Smith of Oregon offered a scaled-back proposal to provide prescription drug coverage to Medicare recipients with incomes of less than 200 percent of the federal poverty level. It also would have provided catastrophic coverage for those with drug costs above $3,300 per year for an annual payment of $25.

Some members hoped that the fear of leaving for the August recess empty-handed would push the Senate to overcome its differences, and the Graham-Smith compromise seemed to offer the best hope for a deal. But like the other plans, it needed 60 votes to overcome a budget point of order because its cost exceeded the $300 billion limit. The

vote July 31 was 49-50, well short of the required 60 votes. Four Republicans voted for the plan; five Democrats voted against it. (*Senate vote 199, p. S-40*)

"I think a lot of people are concerned about leaving out so much of the middle . . . people are legitimately concerned about backlash from a large group of seniors," said Breaux, about the Graham-Smith compromise.

After two weeks of debate over the prescription drug proposals, the Senate passed the underlying generic drug bill, 78-21, with 28 Republicans in favor, on July 31. CBO estimated that the bill would reduce total spending on prescription drugs by $60 billion, or 1.3 percent, over 10 years; the measure later died in the House. (*Senate vote 201, p. S-41*) ◆

No Accord on Patients' Rights Bill

Legislation to give patients new rights in dealing with their managed-care plans died quietly at the end of the 107th Congress. Neither chamber formally appointed conferees to resolve differences over the bill (HR 2563) that had set off heated battles between Senate Democrats and House Republicans in 2001. Informal efforts to find a compromise between a Senate-passed patients' rights bill and the House version, favored by the White House, foundered over the same issue that had sunk previous patients' rights bills: whether and how to cap the liability of health plans that denied treatment to a patient.

The House-passed bill would have capped damages at $1.5 million and sharply limited opportunities for punitive damages. The Senate version, far more friendly to plaintiffs, would have allowed up to $5 million in damages in federal court and no federal limits in state courts.

Democrats claimed the two sides could not reach a deal because the administration was catering to the insurance industry. Republicans accused Democrats of being too closely aligned with trial lawyers and said their proposal would dramatically increase the cost of health insurance.

In fact, given the narrow partisan divide in Congress, the impending midterm elections, and the fact that voters were focused on other issues such as national security and the sagging economy, there was little incentive for either side to make dramatic concessions.

Democrats recognized that the health care environment had changed since the late 1990s when they began championing patients' rights legislation in earnest. Their chief argument then was that health plans, particularly health maintenance organizations, or HMOs, were unfairly denying patients the care they needed.

In the intervening years, patients had gained some leverage. Responding to complaints from workers and their employers, managed-care plans had loosened some of the restrictions that had tamped down health care spending. State courts began entertaining novel new challenges by patients that cracked the liability shield of insurers. Patients began choosing preferred provider organizations and other looser types of networks that offered discounts without the sharp restrictions that closed-network HMOs imposed. Given these gains, many Democrats felt little need to compromise on liability, which was so important to their supporters, particularly plaintiffs' attorneys.

Republicans concluded that the political sting had dissipated from the patients' rights debate and that voters were more concerned about other issues. As a result, they too saw no need to compromise. Conservatives also were concerned that the rising costs of health care would be exacerbated by the liability provisions and coverage requirements in the patients' rights legislation.

A June 20 decision by the Supreme Court also may have factored into the lack of progress. In *Rush Prudential HMO v. Moran*, the court affirmed that states have the right to pass laws giving patients an external review when their insurers deny them coverage of a treatment. Creating such independent reviews was key to both versions of the patients' rights bill. If the court had struck down the Illinois law at the center of the case, Congress might have been more inclined to act; instead, the ruling reduced the urgency for a federal law.

Background

Democrats had made the patients' rights bill the first order of business when they took control of the Senate in June 2001. Their bill — sponsored by John McCain, R-Ariz., Edward M. Kennedy, D-Mass., and John Edwards, D-N.C. — passed 59-36 on June 29, with universal backing from Democrats and the support of eight Republicans, three of whom were up for re-election. (*2001 Almanac, p. 12-3*)

The Senate bill would have allowed millions of Americans for the first time to sue their health plans in federal court when they believed they had been injured by the plan's coverage decision. Plaintiffs could have collected civil damages of up to $5 million and unlimited economic and non-economic damages. Patients challenging their plan's influence over medical decisions could sue in state court, where damages would be determined by state laws.

The House seemed poised to pass a similar bill, but the day before the vote one of the main sponsors, Charlie Norwood, R-Ga., suddenly abandoned his Democratic allies and struck a separate deal with President Bush on a more industry-friendly bill that passed, 226-203, on Aug. 2.

The measure proposed capping punitive and compensatory damages at $1.5 million each in state or federal courts, with punitive damages available only in the rare instance when a plan ignored the recommendation of an external review panel. The House bill also would have banned patients from using the Racketeer Influenced and Corrupt Organizations (RICO) law (PL 91-452) against insurers.

In a new protection for insurers, a patient who lost an appeal to an external reviewer would have to overcome a "rebuttable presumption" that the insurer had been correct in denying care. The patient would have to provide clear and convincing evidence that this was false. Patients would not have been given the same presumption.

Additionally, patients would have had to prove that a denial was "the" proximate cause of an injury — not just "a" cause, potentially among many others.

2002: No Progress

Lawmakers struggled behind the scenes in 2002 to find a compromise that could blend the two approaches. For months, the cosponsors of the Senate-passed bill — McCain, Kennedy and Edwards — worked quietly with the Bush administration in an effort to reconcile their bill and the House proposal that Bush favored. However, they could not resolve differences over liability caps. Democrats insisted on giving patients broad rights to sue their health insurers when a denial of coverage resulted in harm. Republicans insisted on caps on damages and limits to any lawsuits.

Giving up on the informal negotiations, Senate Majority Leader Tom Daschle, D-S.D., moved to appoint conferees on Aug. 1, but Republicans objected, saying they had not been given sufficient notice. As the congressional midterm elections and the final days of the session approached, the debate collapsed in partisan bickering over liability. ◆

Senate Seeks to Lower Drug Prices

With the debate over creating a prescription drug benefit for seniors stalled in Congress, Senate Democrats looked for ways to attack the high price of prescription drugs for Americans of all ages. In July, the Senate passed a bill to tighten patent laws in order to make generic drugs more readily available, and to allow the so-called reimportation of U.S.-made drugs from Canada, where they often were less expensive. The bill had significant Republican support, and Democrats hailed its passage as a major victory for their party, although their hopes of also using it as a vehicle to carry wide-ranging Medicare prescription drug legislation fizzled. (*Medicare prescriptions, p. 10-3*)

House Republicans never took up the Senate bill. They preferred to keep the focus on the fact that they had passed a Medicare prescription drug benefit (HR 4954) in June and the Democratic-controlled Senate had not, a point they hoped would resonate with voters in the midterm elections.

On Oct. 21, two weeks before the elections, President Bush unveiled his own plan to get more generic drugs on the market, a message to voters that he and congressional Republicans cared about lowering drug prices.

Background

The focus of the debate on generic drugs was a 1984 law (PL 98-417) known as the Hatch-Waxman act for its original sponsors, Sen. Orrin G. Hatch, R-Utah, and Rep. Henry A. Waxman, D-Calif. Although the law was designed to speed generic versions of brand-name drugs to market, critics said it often had the opposite effect.

Lobbyists for the drug industry and their allies on Capitol Hill replied that Hatch-Waxman was working as Congress intended and that abuses were rare. They noted that, since the bill's enactment, the generic industry's share of the overall market had jumped from less than 20 percent to almost 50 percent. Drugmakers also pointed to the cost of developing new lifesaving drugs — $800 million on average to get a new drug to market, they said — and warned that further limits on their ability to protect their patents would reduce

BoxScore

Bill:

S 812

Legislative Action:

Senate passed S 812, 78-21, on July 31.

their incentive for research and development. (*1984 Almanac, p. 451*)

Dr. Gregory J. Glover, who testified on behalf of the Pharmaceutical Research and Manufacturers of America (PhRMA) at a Senate hearing May 8, called Hatch-Waxman "one of the most successful pieces of consumer legislation in history." He told the Health, Education, Labor and Pensions Committee, "What is a loophole in the eyes of the generics is a fundamental procedure that protects the intellectual property rights of the innovators."

But Democrats and many Republicans said that pharmaceutical companies had abused the law to unfairly extend the life of their patents, blocking competition and keeping drug prices high. A report issued by the Federal Trade Commission (FTC) on July 30 detailed abuses and recommended legislative action to modify two provisions of the law that the FTC said provided particular opportunities for drugmakers to keep generic drugs off the market.

Under Hatch-Waxman, a brand-name drugmaker facing a patent challenge could file suit to stop the generic from entering the market, automatically blocking the Food and Drug Administration (FDA) from approving the generic for 30 months while the legal issues were resolved. The pharmaceutical company could then list additional patents for variants on the drug, providing new grounds to file suit and getting multiple 30-month stays resulting in years of protection.

At the May 8 hearing, Charles E. Schumer, D-N.Y., cited the example of the pain medication Ultram, whose manufacturer, Johnson & Johnson, won a new patent by developing a new dosing schedule: taking one-fourth of a pill, and slowly building to a full dose. He said the new patent allowed the company to extend its exclusive right to the drug.

The FTC report recommended a single 30-month stay.

The second provision of Hatch-Waxman singled out by the FDA gave a generic that successfully challenged a brand-name drug 180 days of exclusive access to the market before other generics could come in. In some cases, brand-name companies had turned what was meant as an incentive into another barrier. A company, for example, could make a deal

with the generic to put off actually bringing the product to market, which could delay the start of the 180-day period and hold off other generics. The FTC recommended that drugmakers and producers of generics be required to file certain of their communications with the agency.

Highlights

The Senate bill, sponsored by Schumer and John McCain, R-Ariz., contained provisions to tighten the Hatch-Waxman law, as well as language added on the floor by Byron L. Dorgan, D-N.D., to allow reimportation of certain U.S.-made drugs. The following are the main components of the bill, as passed by the Senate:

● **30-month stay.** A pharmaceutical company would get only one 30-month stay against FDA approval of a generic drug whose entry into the market was being challenged by the pharmaceutical company.

● **"Rolling" 180-day exclusivity.** A generic company that won a patent challenge would have exclusive access to the market for 180 days, but if it did not bring out the generic, because it had reached a financial settlement with the brand company or for other reasons, the 180-day exclusivity would pass automatically to the next applicant in line.

● **Timely suit.** A brand company would have to bring a suit within 45 days of being challenged by a generic. Otherwise, it would forfeit its right to sue on that patent against that generic drug.

● **Drug reimportation.** Licensed pharmacists and wholesalers would be allowed to import FDA-approved, U.S.-manufactured drugs from Canada under strict safety procedures.

Legislative Action

Senate Committee Action

The Senate Health, Education, Labor and Pensions Committee approved the Schumer-McCain bill (S 812), by a vote of 16-5 on July 11. In an indication of the issue's political appeal, half the committee's 10 Republicans voted for the bill; all five were facing re-election in the fall.

As introduced, the bill would have eliminated the automatic 30-month delay in FDA approval of generic drugs when the brand company filed suit. A substitute, adopted by voice vote in the committee, allowed for a single 30-month stay per application from a generic producer under limited circumstances.

The amended bill also allowed generic drugmakers to seek a declaratory judgment in federal civil court to challenge brand-name patents listed in the so-called Orange Book, the FDA's registry of pharmaceutical products, formulations and applications that are protected from competition. Under existing law, the FDA simply listed the patents without evaluating them; only the listing company could remove them from the list.

The declaratory judgment language was the subject of the most intense debate, with some Republicans charging it would lead to a proliferation of lawsuits.

The committee adopted a separate amendment by voice vote to clarify that the generic cause-of-action language would not authorize award of damages and would be allowed only in challenges to patents within 30 days of approval of a brand-name application.

Senate Floor Action

The Senate passed the bill, 78-21, on July 31, after two and a half weeks of debate, much of it spent trying to add various Medicare prescription drug amendments. All attempts to amend the bill with a prescription drug plan failed. John B. Breaux, D-La., was the only Democrat to vote against the bill; 28 Republicans voted for it. (*Senate vote 201, p. S-41*)

Dorgan won voice vote approval for his amendment to allow pharmacists and wholesalers to import FDA-approved, U.S.-manufactured drugs from Canada. He said consumers could save as much as $38 billion a year.

The amendment was a narrower version of a law (PL 106-387) enacted in 2000 that allowed re-imports from all major industrialized countries. Health and Human Service secretaries in both the Clinton and Bush administrations had chosen not to implement the law, citing concerns about the safety of drugs purchased outside the United States. Dorgan and his cosponsors, including Maine Republicans Susan Collins and Olympia J. Snowe, said that narrowing the bill to Canada should ease any worries over the safety of the drugs. (*2000 Almanac, p. 2-8*)

Other amendments adopted on the floor included an additional $9 billion in Medicaid and social services funding to help states cope with rising Medicaid costs.

The Senate voted 56-43 to allow states to use their volume purchasing power to buy lower-priced drugs for uninsured people who do not qualify for Medicaid. (*Senate vote 182, p. S-37*)

On July 30 the Senate voted 57-42 to table (kill) an amendment by Mitch McConnell, R-Ky., that would have put caps on punitive damages and attorneys' fees in medical malpractice cases. (*Senate vote 197, p. S-40*)

House Bill

House Republican leaders had no interest in taking up the Senate bill or a companion House measure. "We want to keep the pressure on the Senate to do a drug benefit," explained John Feehery, a spokesman for Speaker J. Dennis Hastert, R-Ill.

Minority Leader Richard A. Gephardt, D-Mo., and McCain circulated a "discharge petition" in an attempt to force the House version (HR 1862) to the floor for a vote, but they were able to gather only 150 signatures out of the 218 they needed.

Hastert's office described the discharge effort as "another desperate attempt to change the subject away from another major House accomplishment — passage of a fair, fiscally responsible and comprehensive plan to strengthen Medicare with prescription drug coverage."

Bush's Plan

On Oct. 21, Bush surprised Capitol Hill by issuing a plan to make regulatory changes affecting the Hatch-Waxman act. The changes included allowing only one 30-month automatic stay when a brand name challenged a generic's attempt to enter the market and imposing penalties for "frivolous" patents — such as those to change a pill's bottle or its

color — that were listed in the FDA's Orange Book. Administration officials said the president's plan would save consumers $35 billion over the coming decade. The Congressional Budget Office had estimated that the Senate-passed plan would save $60 billion over the same period.

The drug industry, a longtime ally and potent fundraiser for Bush and the Republican Party, stood to lose billions with the Bush plan, but the industry perceived it as far less onerous than the Senate bill.

Jeff Trewhitt, a spokesman for PhRMA, called Bush's proposal "an important development that needs to be weighed very carefully." ◆

New Law Targets Bioterrorism

Congress cleared a bill authorizing $4.2 billion in fiscal 2003 and additional amounts in future years to help federal, state and local governments prepare for and respond to biological attacks and other public health emergencies. President Bush signed the measure into law (HR 3448 — PL 107-188) on June 12.

The bill authorized increases in the nation's stockpiles of medicines and vaccines, expansion of facilities and labs run by the Centers for Disease Control and Prevention (CDC), tighter controls on biological agents, and steps to safeguard the nation's food and water supplies. It also reauthorized drug company user fees to speed Food and Drug Administration (FDA) review and approval of new drugs.

The FDA provision was added in conference and drew an angry response from critics who said it threatened to make the FDA a captive of the industry it regulated. But supporters, including Sen. Edward M. Kennedy, D-Mass., said the bill balanced speedy approval of life-saving drugs with new money and authority to conduct ongoing safety studies of drugs once they landed on pharmacy shelves.

BoxScore

Bill:
HR 3448 — PL 107-188
Legislative Action:
House passed HR 3448, 418-2, on Dec. 12, 2001.
Senate passed HR 3448 by voice vote Dec. 20, after substituting the text of S 1765.
House adopted the conference report (H Rept 107-481), 425-1, on May 22, 2002.
Senate cleared the bill, 98-0, on May 23.
President signed June 12.

and handling of dangerous biological agents and toxins. HHS was directed to establish a comprehensive national database on every individual who possessed, used or transferred certain dangerous toxins or agents, such as anthrax and smallpox. Anyone who possessed these agents was required to register with HHS, report any transfer of the agents and submit to screening and inspections. The Agriculture Department was given similar authority to regulate agents that could threaten crops or farm animals.

● **Food safety.** Authorized $100 million in fiscal 2002, and unspecified sums in fiscal 2003 through 2006, to improve food safety efforts, particularly at ports of entry, with special emphasis on detecting the intentional adulteration of food. The FDA could hold food items for up to 30 days if there was credible evidence that they posed a serious health threat to humans or animals. All facilities that manufactured, processed, packed or held food for consumption in the United States were required to register with the FDA.

Food importers were required to provide the FDA with details about food shipments before they arrived at a port of entry. If notice was not provided, the food could not enter the United States. The FDA could ban importers who repeatedly violated U.S. food safety regulations.

● **Drug imports.** Required foreign manufacturers to register annually before being allowed to import drugs and medical devices into the United States.

● **Drinking water safety.** Authorized $160 million in fiscal 2002, and unspecified sums in succeeding years, to protect the safety of drinking water systems. Drinking water systems across the country were required to provide the EPA with assessments of their vulnerability to terrorist attacks and to develop emergency plans to prepare for and respond to such attacks. In response to concerns over security at the EPA, the law exempted the assessments from release under the Freedom of Information Act, required the agency to take steps to secure and limit access to the documents, and set criminal penalties for anyone who disclosed the contents.

● **Prescription drug user fees.** Reauthorized the FDA's user fee program for prescription drug manufacturers through fis-

Highlights

The main provisions of the new law:
● **Emergency medical stockpiles.** Authorized $1.15 billion in fiscal 2002, and unspecified sums in succeeding years, for the Department of Health and Human Services (HHS) to expand stockpiles of vaccines, medicines and other supplies. The total included $509 million to purchase additional smallpox vaccines.

● **State and local preparedness.** Authorized $1.6 billion in fiscal 2003, and unspecified amounts in fiscal 2004 through 2006, for grants to states, local governments, and public and private health care facilities to improve planning and preparedness, increase laboratory capacity, train health care personnel, and develop new drugs, therapies and vaccines. A total of $520 million was set aside for state grants to help hospitals and other health facilities prepare for biological attacks.

● **Biological agents.** Tightened controls on the possession

cal 2007 and specified the fees should generate a total of $1.2 billion over five years. The funds were to be used by the FDA to review new drugs for safety and effectiveness, and to enhance the safety review of drugs already on the market.

Background

The legislation was introduced in 2001 out of concern that the nation's public health system was unprepared to handle a major bioterror attack. Federal and local officials had trouble dealing with a handful of anthrax cases in Florida, New York, Connecticut and Washington, D.C. Five people died after exposure to anthrax, most likely sent through the mail.

Congress had appropriated $2.5 billion for bioterrorism programs in fiscal 2002 without waiting for the separate authorization bill, but authorizers pressed ahead, saying their bill was necessary to provide clear guidance and legal certainty to federal and state governments.

The House passed a $2.9 billion version of the authorization bill Dec. 12. The Senate followed Dec. 20 with a $3.2 billion bill. Both versions authorized funds to develop and produce anthrax vaccines, antibiotics and other medicines to combat bioterrorism. Both authorized grants to states, local governments and public health departments to prepare for health emergencies. Both also authorized aid to hospitals, the CDC, public health networks and food safety programs. *(2001 Almanac, p. 12-9)*

Differences included provisions in the House bill, but not the Senate version, authorizing funds to improve the safety of public water supplies. The Senate bill had more detailed food safety inspection requirements. It also included a provision — opposed by John D. Dingell of Michigan, ranking Democrat on the House Energy and Commerce Committee — to give drug companies a limited antitrust exemption so they could collaborate on drugs to prevent and fight a biological attack. Another controversial Senate provision would have given companies accelerated approval of drugs by allowing them to use expedited research procedures with animals. Critics worried that such abbreviated research could compromise safety.

Legislative Action

Conference/Final Action

After weeks of quiet staff work, House and Senate conferees agreed on a final bill and filed a conference report (H Rept 107-481) on May 21. The House adopted the conference report, 425-1, on May 22, and the Senate cleared the bill, 98-0, the next day. *(House vote 189, p. H-64; Senate vote 124, p. S-27)*

The following were among the issues resolved in conference:

● **FDA user fee.** The biggest change was the addition of the user fee provisions to allow the FDA to hire additional employees to review new pharmaceutical products. The reauthorization was a priority for Billy Tauzin, R-La., chairman of the House Energy and Commerce Committee, and Kennedy, chairman of the Senate Health, Education, Labor and Pensions Committee. They settled on the bill as the best way to renew the fees, created in 1992 (PL 102-571), before they expired Sept. 30.

● **Drug testing.** Democrats tried but failed to include language codifying an FDA rule that required drugmakers to conduct separate pediatric safety tests for drugs prescribed for both adults and children. A bill (S 2394 — S Rept 107-300) to enforce the rule was approved by Kennedy's committee Aug. 1, but went no further. Republicans argued that financial incentives for such testing enacted in 2001 (PL 107-109) made the rule unnecessary. *(2001 Almanac, p. 12-10)*

● **Medical devices.** Manufacturers of medical devices tried to add a user fee program, modeled after the drug user fee system, to speed approvals of new medical devices. But Kennedy balked at a provision sought by device manufacturers to allow private contractors to review medical device safety. Modified user fee provisions were cleared in a separate bill (PL 107-250). *(Medical devices, 10-12)*

● **Water treatment plants.** At Tauzin's insistence, conferees dropped a Senate proposal that wastewater treatment plants be required to report to the EPA on safety plans and assessments of vulnerability to terrorism. Tauzin cited objections from House Transportation and Infrastructure Committee Chairman Don Young, R-Alaska, whose panel had jurisdiction over water safety issues.

● **CDC.** The final bill authorized $300 million per year in fiscal 2002 and 2003 to upgrade and expand CDC facilities. The House bill had included $300 million; the Senate included just under $120 million.

● **Antitrust exemption.** Conferees dropped the Senate provision that would have given antitrust exemptions to drugmakers preparing to provide critical vaccines. ◆

Medical Device User Fee Enacted

Congress cleared a bill creating new user fees for manufacturers of medical devices, modeled on a similar fee paid by drug companies. The legislation was a top priority for the industry, which agreed to pay the fees in return for getting swifter reviews of their products by the Food and Drug Administration (FDA). President Bush signed the bill into law Oct. 26 (HR 5651 — PL 107-250).

The bill authorized the FDA to collect $150 million over five years to defray the cost of hiring new regulators to speed up its review process. It set time goals for the FDA and allowed device manufacturers to hire independent contractors to conduct some safety inspections of their factories. The measure codified an agreement that the Bush administration had struck with the medical device industry in May.

The bill was a victory for industry groups that had lobbied for years to get a dedicated funding source for FDA reviews in hopes of getting their products to market more quickly. They complained that the average FDA review time in 2001 for pre-market approval applications was 411 days, more than twice the 180-day statutory requirement. The industry did not get all it wanted, however. A proposal to allow private contractors to review and recommend approval for many new medical devices was scaled back. Instead, the bill allowed private contractors to assume some of the FDA's duties to inspect manufacturing facilities.

The medical device user fee program was based on the one already in place for drugmakers. Created in 1992, the drug user fee was reauthorized in 2002 as part of a law (PL 107-188) funding efforts to battle bioterrorism. Manufacturers had hoped to tack the medical device fee onto the bill as well, but Democrats resisted, saying the proposal was too broad. Critics also contended that the shift to user fees risked turning the FDA into a captive of the industries it was regulating. The user fee applied to companies making a broad variety of products including breast implants, defibrillators and respirators. *(Bioterrorism, p. 10-10)*

Highlights

The following are the main elements of the new law:
- **User fees.** The bill authorized the FDA to collect $150 million in user fees from the medical device industry — $25 million in fiscal 2003, $27 million in 2004, $30 million in 2005, $33 million in 2006 and $35 million in 2007. The initial benchmark fee for pre-market applications was $154,000 in fiscal 2003. The FDA was required to use the fees to meet performance goals and speed up its review and approval process.
- **Small-business waivers.** Fees were waived for first-time

BoxScore

Bill:
HR 5651 — PL 107-250

Legislative Action:
House passed HR 3580 (H Rept 107-728), 406-3, Oct. 9.
House passed HR 5651 by voice vote Oct. 16.
Senate cleared HR 5651 by voice vote Oct. 17.
President signed Oct. 26.

applications from companies with annual sales under $30 million.
- **Federal spending.** The law called for Congress to provide an additional $15 million per year for the program from general funds. If lawmakers did not appropriate $60 million through fiscal 2006, the user fees would expire.
- **Third-party inspections.** Device manufacturers could hire independent contractors to conduct safety inspections of their factories. The contractors had to be approved by the FDA, and the agency had to perform every third inspection of domestic facilities.
- **Post-market studies.** At Democrats' insistence, the bill authorized $3 million in fiscal 2003 and $6 million in 2004 to expand FDA studies of the safety of new products after they reached the market.
- **Reprocessed medical devices.** The bill established new regulations governing the sterilization and re-use of catheters and other products that previously were approved only for single use. Such products had to be clearly labeled so patients would know they were safe and effective according to FDA standards.

Legislative Action

House Action

The House passed a medical device user fee bill (HR 3580 — H Rept 107-728) on Oct. 9 by a vote of 406-3. The Energy and Commerce Committee had approved the bill by voice vote Oct. 2. *(House vote 450, p. H-142)*

The measure contained most of the provisions that ultimately were enacted into law. Like the final bill, it did not set an exact amount for individual fees, but provided a total to be collected each year. It set a benchmark pre-market application fee of $139,000 in fiscal 2003. In addition, the bill called for the FDA to receive an extra $15 million per year in appropriations. Companies with less than $10 million in sales would pay reduced fees or be exempted altogether. The user fees would expire after fiscal 2005 if the agency had not received $45 million in matching federal money over three years.

Although the bill got overwhelming support in the House, some Senate Democrats who supported the measure, particularly Edward M. Kennedy, D-Mass., chairman of the Senate Health, Education, Labor and Pensions Committee, still had safety concerns about third-party plant inspections and about broader sterilization and re-use of disposable items such as catheters and syringes.

Final Action

Rather than passing a separate Senate bill and reconciling the two versions in conference, a group of senior House

and Senate lawmakers negotiated a bipartisan compromise that was introduced as a clean bill (HR 5651) on Oct. 16. The House passed it by voice vote several hours later, and the Senate cleared it by voice vote the next day.

At Kennedy's urging, the original House bill was amended to specify that the FDA would conduct every third inspection of a domestic medical device factory, allowing independent contractors to do other reviews.

The bill also was revised to expand the number of companies exempted from some user fees. It waived fees for first-time applications for firms with annual sales under $30 million, instead of the $10 million in the original bill. The Advanced Medical Technology Association, which led negotiations with the White House on the user fee plan, wanted to limit the threshold to $10 million. The group feared that if more companies were exempted, total user fee revenue could fall short and trigger automatic fee increases on those that did pay. The rival Medical Device Manufacturers Association sought a waiver for up to $100 million in sales but agreed to $30 million.

The bill required Congress to appropriate an additional $60 million in general funds over four years or see the user fee program expire. ◆

House GOP Passes Malpractice Bill

House Republicans succeeded in passing a sweeping bill to limit damage awards and plaintiff attorneys' fees in medical malpractice lawsuits, but the Senate had already rejected a more limited plan, making it clear the legislation would not be enacted in the 107th Congress.

The Senate proposal would have capped punitive damages in medical malpractice cases at twice the compensatory damages, limited attorneys' fees and required lawsuits to be filed within two years of the discovery of an injury. It failed July 30 when offered as a floor amendment to an unrelated generic drug bill (S 812). Six Republicans joined all 50 Democrats and James M. Jeffords, I-Vt., to kill the proposal, 57-42. (*Senate vote 197, p. S-40*)

The House bill (HR 4600), passed Sept. 26, mirrored a proposal by President Bush. It included a $250,000 cap on non-economic damages, restrictions on attorneys' fees, strict limits on punitive damages, and protection for drug and medical device manufacturers whose products were approved by the Food and Drug Administration (FDA).

The American Medical Association (AMA), which had made overhauling liability laws its top legislative priority, endorsed the House bill. "As medical liability insurance becomes unaffordable or unavailable, physicians are forced to limit services, leave their practices or relocate — seriously impeding patient access to health care," said AMA president-elect Dr. Donald J. Palmisano.

Both Democrats and Republicans agreed on the need to address the soaring cost of malpractice insurance; premiums had increased by nearly 50 percent in a number of states over the previous two years. But the two sides had sharply conflicting views on the causes and proper remedies.

Republicans, joined by doctors and insurance companies, blamed rising jury awards for the huge premium increases. Democrats, backed by trial lawyers and consumer groups, pointed to the insurance industry as the culprit, saying insurers were using a handful of cases to justify rate increases so they could recoup stock market losses and make up for

BoxScore

Bill:
HR 4600

Legislative Action:
Senate killed, 57-42, on July 30 an amendment to S 812 to cap medical malpractice awards.

House passed HR 4600 (H Rept 107-693, Parts 1 and 2), 217-203, on Sept. 26.

bad business decisions in the 1990s. Some suggested ending the industry's partial exemption from antitrust laws.

Highlights

The House-passed bill applied to any health care lawsuit brought in federal or state court or subject to an alternative dispute resolution system. It would have:

• **Economic damages.** Allowed full economic damages — defined as "objectively verifiable monetary losses" incurred as a result of an injury, such as past and future medical expenses, loss of past and future earnings, the cost of obtaining domestic services, loss of employment, and loss of business or employment opportunities.

• **Non-economic damages.** Limited non-economic damages to $250,000, regardless of the number of defendants or the number of separate claims resulting from the same incident. The bill defined non-economic damages as damages for physical and emotional pain, suffering, inconvenience, physical impairment, mental anguish, disfigurement, loss of enjoyment of life, loss of society and companionship, loss of consortium, hedonic damages, injury to reputation, and all other non-economic losses. The jury would not be informed of the damage cap.

• **Punitive damages.** Limited punitive damages that could be awarded in a health care lawsuit to two times economic damages, or $250,000, whichever was greater.

Punitive damages were defined in the bill as those awarded "for the purpose of punishment or deterrence." Again, the jury would not be informed of the cap.

A plaintiff would be able to file for punitive damages only after the court had found a "substantial probability" that he or she would prevail in the claim. Punitive damages could be awarded only if it was proven "by clear and convincing evidence" that the defendant acted with malicious intent to injure, or that the defendant "deliberately failed to avoid unnecessary injury" that it knew the plaintiff was "substantially certain" to suffer. Punitive damages could not

be awarded if there were no compensatory damages.

● **Joint and several liability.** Prohibited the use of joint and several liability, under which plaintiffs could recover all or part of the damages from any one or all of the defendants found responsible for the injury. Instead, each defendant would be liable for his or her share of the damages, as determined by the judge or jury.

● **FDA-approved medical products.** Shielded drug manufacturers and makers of medical devices from punitive damages if their products were approved by the FDA or were generally considered safe. The exemption would not apply if the manufacturer had knowingly withheld information from the FDA.

● **Statute of limitations.** Required that a health care lawsuit be filed within three years of the date of the injury, or one year after the plaintiff discovers — or should have discovered — the injury, whichever occurred first. The deadline could be extended if there was proof of fraud or intentional concealment.

● **Attorneys' fees.** Capped attorney "contingent fees" — a predetermined percentage of any amount awarded by the court to the client. The total of all contingent fees for representing all plaintiffs in a health care lawsuit could not exceed 40 percent of the first $50,000 recovered, 33.3 percent of the next $50,000, 25 percent of the next $500,000 and 15 percent of any amount over $600,000.

● **State laws.** Pre-empted state laws that conflicted with the application of any provision in the bill. However, the bill would not pre-empt any state statutory limit on the amount of compensatory, punitive or total damages awarded in a health care lawsuit, whether the state total was higher or lower than the caps provided for in the bill. The provisions dealing with caps on awards would apply only to those states that had no set statutory limits on damage awards in health care lawsuits.

Background

The problem of malpractice costs began to grow in the 1970s, when a number of private insurers stopped offering coverage, saying the costs were prohibitive. With congressional Democrats deflecting efforts to curb malpractice insurance lawsuits, the states took the lead. Several states passed laws limiting damages, most of them modeled on California's 1975 Medical Injury Compensation Reform Act (MICRA). Doctors who hoped to stave off rising rates in the future banded together to create physician-owned insurance companies.

A decade later, when premiums once again started to rise, state legislatures passed more laws. California addressed the issue again with comprehensive insurance regulations through an initiative known as "Proposition 103," which affected a wide range of industries including health care.

All told, more than three dozen states passed damage caps, although some had been repealed or ruled unconstitutional. According to the National Council of State Legislatures, all states had some sort of limits on tort litigation, such as a requirement that defendants pay only the share of damages for which they were responsible, limits on attorneys' fees, provisions to allow periodic payments of awards, or caps on some awards.

Legislative Action

House Committee Action

The House bill was considered by two committees: Judiciary and Energy and Commerce.

● **Judiciary Committee.** The Judiciary Committee went first, approving the bill (H Rept 107-693, Part 1) by voice vote Sept. 10.

Reversing the parties' traditional roles on states' rights, Republicans defeated a series of Democratic amendments aimed at protecting state laws and otherwise limiting the scope of the bill. "We need to do something about this national problem, and we need a national law," argued F. James Sensenbrenner Jr., R-Wis., chairman of the committee. Jerrold Nadler, D-N.Y., meanwhile, charged that the bill's central provision, capping awards for non-economic damages, would "gut" state statutes that set higher limits.

The panel rejected several amendments by Robert C. Scott, D-Va. — all by voice vote — including proposals to limit the bill to cases in federal courts; drop the time limit on filing medical malpractice suits; strike the limits on non-economic damages and the requirement that liability be shared by lawsuit defendants based on their percentage share of fault; strike the limit on punitive damages; strike the limits on lawyers' contingency fees; and drop a provision that would override state court rulings that defendants could not reduce damages by showing that a plaintiff had been compensated by an insurer.

The closest Democrats came was a 14-14 vote rejecting a bid by Nadler to index damage awards to inflation. The committee rejected, 7-15, a Nadler proposal that the bill's restrictions on medical malpractice awards not supersede any caps set by states. The panel rejected other Nadler amendments, mostly on 6-16 votes, including proposals to extend the time limit for filing a medical malpractice lawsuit; exempt U.S. companies headquartered offshore for tax haven purposes from damage limits in medical malpractice lawsuits; and bar the sealing of court rulings or opinions in medical malpractice lawsuits unless a judge determined that doing so was in the greater public interest than disclosure or when sealing was no broader than necessary to protect privacy interests.

Sheila Jackson-Lee, D-Texas, tried unsuccessfully to limit the bill's scope to cases filed by plaintiffs who were at least 12 years old at the time the claim arose, or who were below the age of 65 when the claim arose.

● **Energy and Commerce Committee.** The Energy and Commerce Committee approved the bill (H Rept 107-693, Part 2) on Sept. 18 by a vote of 27-22, after Republicans defeated a series of Democratic amendments aimed at reducing the scope of the bill or allowing higher damage awards.

Democrats Jane Harman of California and Ralph M. Hall of Texas crossed party lines to vote for the bill. Republicans Lee Terry of Nebraska and Robert L. Ehrlich Jr. of Maryland voted against it.

"America's doctors work under constant threat of lawsuits from contingency-fee lawyers seeking exorbitant settlements," argued committee Chairman Billy Tauzin, R-La.

John D. Dingell of Michigan, the committee's ranking Democrat, retorted that the bill was an ill-considered effort offered at the bidding of insurance companies and medical

care providers seeking to escape responsibility for their actions. He said he had asked the General Accounting Office to examine the practices of malpractice insurers during the previous decade to determine the extent to which rising rates were caused by poor investment decisions and efforts to compete by slashing premiums.

The only amendment that survived was a symbolic sense of Congress provision written by Charlie Norwood, R-Ga., stating that a health insurer should be liable for damages when a patient is harmed by a decision as to what care is medically necessary or appropriate.

Democratic amendments were rejected as they had been in the Judiciary Committee. The committee:

• Defeated, 22-27, a proposal by Henry A. Waxman, D-Calif., to drop the ban on punitive damages for FDA-approved drugs and medical devices.

• Rejected, 21-29, an amendment by Anna G. Eshoo, D-Calif., to drop the limit on non-economic damages in cases involving product liability.

• Defeated, 20-29, an attempt by Eshoo to strike the punitive damage limits.

• Rejected, 19-33, a proposal by Diana DeGette, D-Colo., to eliminate the cap on non-economic damages.

• Rejected, 21-23, an amendment by Gene Green, D-Texas, to replace the bill with a sense of Congress resolution affirming that states and not the federal government have authority to regulate insurance.

• Rejected, 19-31, a proposal by Edward J. Markey, D-Mass., to allow juries to impose damages that exceeded limits in the bill and require defendants to pay the difference into a trust fund that would be used to reduce medical malpractice insurance rates.

• Defeated, by voice vote, an amendment by Mike Doyle, D-Pa., to raise the caps on non-economic damages to $1.5 million, with annual increases pegged to growth in the Consumer Price Index.

• Rejected, 21-28, an attempt by Bart Stupak, D-Mich., to change time limits on filing a medical malpractice suit to within two years of date of injury (instead of three years) or within two years of discovery of an injury (instead of one year), whichever was later (instead of whichever occurred first). The amendment also would have eliminated a three-year deadline to file a lawsuit in the absence of proof of fraud, intentional concealment or the presence of a foreign object unintentionally left in the injured person.

• Rejected by voice vote a proposal by Frank Pallone Jr., D-N.J., to create a federal reinsurance fund that would be available to all medical malpractice insurers in cases of lawsuit claims in excess of $250,000.

House Floor Action

The House passed the bill Sept. 26 on a largely party-line vote of 217-203, with each side accusing the other of supporting positions that would put the nation's health care system at risk. Only 14 Democrats voted for the legislation; 15 Republicans voted against it. The bill was considered under a closed rule for debate that barred all amendments. (*House vote 421, p. H-132*)

Before the vote, about 150 white-coated physicians attended a rally to warn that health professionals and hospitals around the nation were curbing or dropping services because of high malpractice premiums.

Democrats argued that the bill would not help doctors or patients, and that the only beneficiaries would be the insurance companies.

Before passing the bill, the House rejected, 193-225, a motion by John Conyers Jr., D-Mich., to send it back to committee with instructions to include language stating that none of the provisions would pre-empt state laws on the liability of health maintenance organizations. (*House vote 420, p. H-132*) ◆

Health Centers Reauthorized

Congress reauthorized funding through fiscal 2006 for community health centers, the National Health Service Corps, telehealth and rural health care programs in a bill signed into law Oct. 26 (S 1533 — PL 107-251).

The bill was part of a plan by President Bush to increase funding sufficiently to ensure a doubling by 2006 of the more than 11 million patients being served by community health centers. Approximately 40 percent of the patients seeking treatment at such centers were uninsured; one-third of those were children. It was one of the few steps taken by the 107th Congress to address the surge in the ranks of the uninsured, which jumped almost 15 percent to 41.2 million in 2001, according to the Census Bureau.

The new law included provisions to:

• Authorize $1.3 billion in fiscal 2002 and unspecified amounts through fiscal 2006 for community health centers.

• Reauthorize the National Health Service Corps, allotting $146 million in scholarship and loan repayment incentives in fiscal 2002 and "such sums as may be necessary" through 2006 as incentives to health profession students who agreed to serve as primary care clinicians in underserved areas in exchange for the educational support. The health service corps had placed more than 22,000 health care providers in rural communities, urban centers and other areas with a shortage of physicians and other health professionals during the previous 30 years.

• Authorize $40 million in fiscal 2002 and unspecified funds in future years for grants to improve the quality of rural health care services. The bill also created a new grant program to promote the use of telecommunications technology to give patients and health care providers in rural areas access to high-quality health care services and information.

• Create a new Healthy Communities Access Program to help communities and groups of health care providers develop coordinated health care services for the uninsured. Both private and public organizations would be eligible for grants under the program, of which no more than 35 could be awarded each year through fiscal 2006. The bill also authorized $50 million over five years for state grants to innovative programs that addressed the needs of areas with limited access to dental care.

As initially passed by the Senate April 16, the bill authorized $1.4 billion for community health centers in fiscal 2002 and unspecified sums through fiscal 2006. The House on Oct. 1 passed a similar bill (HR 3450) for fiscal 2003 through 2006. The final bill — which the House passed, 392-5, on Oct. 16 and the Senate cleared by voice vote Oct. 17 — was a compromise between the two. (*House vote 466, p. H-146*) ◆

Chapter 11

INDUSTRY & REGULATION

New Rules for Corporations

In a stark reversal of the deregulatory mood that had prevailed on Capitol Hill, Congress cleared a landmark bill to regulate the accounting industry and crack down on corporate fraud. The bill came together in late July, as a wave of corporate scandals battered the stock market and members scrambled to take action before the August recess. President Bush signed the measure into law July 30 (HR 3763 — PL 107-204).

The new law created an independent board, supervised by the Securities and Exchange Commission (SEC), to police the accounting industry, with powers to set standards and to investigate and discipline violators. Accounting firms were generally barred from providing many lucrative consulting services to the companies whose books they audited. The law required that a company's audit committee — rather than company executives — assume responsibility for hiring and working with outside accounting firms. It also imposed new reporting and disclosure requirements on public companies and substantially increased criminal penalties for corporate fraud.

The impetus for the bill was a string of corporate scandals that began with the collapse of the Houston-based Enron Corp. in December 2001. On Capitol Hill, at least 10 committees rushed to investigate the Enron collapse, the largest bankruptcy in U.S. history. An overhaul of the accounting industry seemed all but certain.

The House passed an accounting regulation bill (HR 3763) in April that called for, but would not have created, a new public organization to oversee the auditing of publicly traded companies. The measure, sponsored by Financial Services Committee Chairman Michael G. Oxley, R-Ohio, would have increased financial disclosure requirements and barred auditors from providing some consulting services to the companies they audited.

Many Democrats complained the bill lacked teeth, but by then the Enron scandal had receded from the headlines, subsumed by homeland security issues and a crisis in Israeli-Palestinian affairs. Conflicting congressional strategies and moves by the SEC to strengthen regulation on its own seemed to point toward stalemate.

The dynamic shifted dramatically in late June, however, when communications giant WorldCom Inc. disclosed that it had improperly accounted for $3.9 billion in expenses and the Xerox Corp. revealed it had improperly accounted for $2 billion in revenue. The news jolted the stock markets, already suffering from a lack of investor confidence, and reinvigorated prospects for a much tougher bill (S 2673) in the Senate, sponsored by Paul S. Sarbanes, D-Md., chairman of

BoxScore

Bill:
HR 3763 — PL 107-204
Legislative Action:
House passed HR 3763 (H Rept 107-414), 334-90, on April 24.
Senate passed S 2673 (S Rept 107-205), 97-0, on July 15, then inserted the text into HR 3763.
House adopted the conference report (H Rept 107-610), 423-3, on July 25.
Senate cleared the bill, 99-0, on July 25.
President signed July 30.

the Banking Committee.

When the Sarbanes bill passed the Senate July 15 without a single "nay" vote, the GOP-controlled House upped the ante, passing a separate measure (HR 5118) to increase criminal penalties for corporate fraud above even those in the broader Senate bill. With Bush and most members calling for final action before the August recess, the House and Senate quickly reached agreement, based largely on the Senate-passed bill.

The new law marked a shift away from the laissez-faire approach to business regulation of the previous several decades and toward more federal oversight of corporations, stock markets and accounting firms. "The dramatic increase in huge audit failures has had an enormous psychological impact on investors and stock market levels," said Joel Seligman, a securities law expert and dean of the Washington University School of Law in St. Louis. "What you are seeing at the moment is the clearest instance since the 1920s and 1930s that Congress is legislating precisely because they are concerned that investor confidence has been undermined."

Highlights

The following are the main components of the new accounting law:
- **Oversight board.** The law established a new, independent regulatory body — the Public Company Accounting Oversight Board — to police the auditing of publicly traded companies. The board, overseen by the SEC, would have authority to establish and enforce auditing standards and to investigate and discipline accountants or firms that violated the standards. Only two of the board's five members could be accountants. To assure its independence, the board was to be funded by fees paid by public companies.
- **Auditor independence.** The law required that auditors be hired by, and report to, a company's audit committee. Accounting firms could not audit corporations whose top officials previously worked for the auditor and participated in the company's audit the previous year. Accounting firms were barred from performing eight specific services — including financial systems design, internal auditing, management consulting and legal services — for public companies that they audited. Accounting firms had to rotate their lead audit partners at client corporations every five years.
- **Corporate responsibility.** Chief executive officers (CEOs) and chief financial officers (CFOs) were required to certify the accuracy of annual and quarterly financial re-

ports. Willful violation could be punished by up to $5 million in fines and up to 20 years in prison. If the company was subsequently forced to restate its earnings, the CEO and CFO would have to pay back any bonuses or profits on company stock sales earned in the prior 12 months.

The SEC was directed to adopt new rules to prevent conflicts of interest by stock analysts, and to place any civil penalties collected from corporate executives in a new fund that would be used to compensate victims who lost money because of the executives' violations of law.

- **Securities fraud.** The law established a new securities fraud penalty with a maximum prison sentence of up to 25 years and new criminal penalties of up to 20 years imprisonment for shareholder fraud and document shredding. It also gave corporate whistleblowers federal protection against retaliation.
- **Accounting standards.** A majority of members of the Financial Accounting Standards Board (FASB), the private standards-setting body for accountants, could not have been affiliated with accounting firms in the previous two years.
- **SEC authorization.** The bill authorized $776 million for SEC operations in fiscal 2003, including $103 million to increase the salaries of SEC professionals and $98 million to hire 200 new employees.

Background

Under federal law, all corporations that sell stocks or bonds to the public are required to disclose detailed information about their financial condition. The financial statements are prepared by the company itself, in accordance with generally accepted accounting principles. They are then certified by independent outside auditors, using random and systemic checks of company records and finances to verify the statements' accuracy.

Prior to enactment of the accounting bill, the SEC had broad authority to regulate corporate accounting and the auditing of publicly traded companies, but it was limited by a lack of resources. As a result, it tended to investigate and take enforcement action in only the most egregious cases. The state boards of accountancy, which were responsible for licensing accountants to practice within their states, lacked the ability to investigate companies at a national level.

The most comprehensive supervision of accountants and auditors came from the industry's own trade association, the American Institute of Certified Public Accountants (AICPA), a voluntary organization funded entirely by the industry. While AICPA disciplined accountants, critics claimed that it generally resolved cases by issuing confidential letters to the parties involved rather than suspending or expelling the accountant from AICPA, which could disqualify the accountant from auditing some publicly traded companies.

The industry also had a peer review process under which accounting firms examined the audit work performed by other firms to determine whether it was done properly. That process was monitored by the Public Oversight Board, another body created and funded by the accounting industry. Since the board's creation in 1977 no major firm had ever failed a peer review, despite a series of accounting scandals, including the savings and loan crisis in the late 1980s.

Shock Waves From Enron

Just months before the energy giant Enron declared bankruptcy, it had been widely regarded as one of the most innovative, fastest growing and best managed businesses in the nation. It also enjoyed close contacts with top Bush administration officials. But it turned out that the company's profitability was largely the result of creative accounting. Massive amounts of debt had been moved off Enron's books to special partnerships to prevent the losses from appearing on the company's financial statements. The shady bookkeeping was sanctioned by the company's auditor, Arthur Andersen LLP, which also earned millions of dollars in consulting fees from Enron. The accounting firm was later convicted of obstructing justice for shredding documents related to the Enron probe.

In response to the Enron scandal, SEC Chairman Harvey L. Pitt in January called for a new private-sector body under the SEC to oversee and discipline auditors, replacing the supervisory functions performed by AICPA and the Public Oversight Board. The SEC also initiated numerous new reporting and disclosure rule-makings. Although Pitt promised to cooperate with Congress on legislation, he cautioned lawmakers not to go too far in mandating remedies.

As momentum for legislation built on Capitol Hill, Bush sought to shape the debate, releasing a 10-point set of recommendations in March that relied heavily on SEC enforcement of existing laws. "Existing regulations should be clearer; penalties for wrongdoing should be tougher," he said March 7. Bush proposed blocking outside auditors from performing internal audits for the same client they audited, and giving investors greater access to corporate financial data. He called for more rapid disclosure of stock transactions by corporate executives, and said that CEOs should be required to vouch personally for corporate financial statements and surrender bonuses based on erroneous statements. One omission that drew immediate criticism from Democrats was any mention of additional funding for the beleaguered SEC.

Meanwhile, many public companies began improving their financial reporting practices on their own in an effort to reduce investor wariness and demonstrate that they could police themselves. The trend included prominent companies such as General Electric, IBM Corp. and Intel Corp. Federal Reserve Board Chairman Alan Greenspan said market mechanisms were taking care of many issues that Congress was seeking to address through legislation.

Legislative Action

House Committee Action

The House Financial Services Committee approved Oxley's bill (HR 3763 — H Rept 107-414) on April 16 by a vote of 49-12, with the support of 16 Democrats.

The bill called for the SEC to develop and oversee the operations of a new regulatory body for the accounting industry, with the organization's composition and powers left mainly to the SEC. It also called on the SEC to modify its own rules to prohibit accounting firms from performing two specific services — internal audits and designing financial information systems — for their audit clients.

Top committee Democrat John J. LaFalce of New York

tried but failed to change the bill with a series of amendments aimed at strengthening the proposed new oversight board, including giving it subpoena powers, adding to the list of services that accounting firms would be barred from performing for their audit clients, and requiring greater accountability from corporate officers.

Some Democrats, however, urged restraint. "Most of the accounting firms in this country have not been indicted for malpractice," said Paul E. Kanjorski, D-Pa. "I don't think the failures of the Enron situation justify the heavy hand of government coming down."

House Floor Action

The House passed the bill April 24 by a vote of 334-90. While ongoing criticism from Democrats spelled trouble ahead in the Senate, Oxley's immediate priority was to get a bill through the House. Democrats argued that Republicans had steered clear of a tougher measure because of their close ties to Wall Street. (House vote 110, p. H-42)

The key floor vote came on a substitute by LaFalce, similar to the proposals he had offered in committee. It was narrowly defeated on a near-party-line vote of 202-219. (House vote 108, p. H-40)

LaFalce argued that the duties and responsibilities of the new regulatory body should be spelled out, rather than be left to the SEC. The amendment would have required the SEC to create an organization with the authority to set auditing rules and standards, the ability to compel testimony from an accounting firm and its employees, and expanded powers to discipline accountants who violated auditing rules and standards. It also proposed a longer list of non-auditing services that a firm would be barred from performing for companies that it audited and a requirement that a corporation's auditing committee approve any other services provided by its outside auditor.

Other provisions included requiring a corporation's CEO and CFO to certify the accuracy and veracity of the company's financial statements, requiring the SEC to prohibit stock analysts from owning stock in any of the companies they covered, and compelling corporate executives and directors who engaged in misconduct to forfeit the proceeds of any associated stock transactions.

Republicans countered that a lighter touch was needed to avoid saddling the private sector with burdensome new regulations. "In our zeal to act, we can easily do more harm than good," said Oxley. "We can damage the capital markets and the economy in the process."

AICPA hailed Oxley's bill as "unprecedented and rigorous" and pledged to cooperate with its provisions. Privately, accounting industry lobbyists hoped that any new law would not go much beyond Oxley's approach, particularly with respect to rules regarding what types of consulting services accounting firms could perform for their audit clients. A new regulatory body that scrutinized accounting firms for conflicts of interest would obviate the need for an outright ban on consulting services, they said.

By then, the SEC was moving aggressively to police public companies under existing securities law, without waiting for a new congressional mandate. Some saw that as offering political cover if lawmakers got bogged down and did no more than boost the SEC's appropriation for fiscal 2003.

In separate action, the committee had given voice vote approval April 11 to a bill (HR 3764 — H Rept 107-415) to authorize $776 million for the SEC for fiscal 2003, 62 percent more than Bush requested.

Senate Committee Action

The Senate Banking, Housing and Urban Affairs Committee approved Sarbanes' bill (S 2673 — S Rept 107-205) on June 18 in a bipartisan vote of 17-4. The markup, which came after a last-minute deal that softened some provisions, ended a monthlong standoff between Sarbanes and the panel's ranking Republican, Phil Gramm of Texas.

The vote was a surprise to accounting industry lobbyists, who had fiercely opposed Sarbanes' approach. The chairman pulled off the stealth victory by striking a deal the night before the markup with the Senate's only accountant — Michael B. Enzi, R-Wyo. — that resulted in several changes to the draft.

The bill called for a new regulatory board under SEC oversight to monitor the accounting industry, with powers to investigate and punish wrongdoing. It specified eight non-audit services or categories of service that auditors would not be able to provide to the companies they audited. The oversight board would be able to make exceptions on a company-by-company basis. CEOs and CFOs would have to certify company financial statements, and lead audit partners could not be in charge of reviewing a single company's books for more than five consecutive years. Insider stock sales would be barred during "blackout" periods, when employees were forbidden from selling shares from their retirement accounts.

Gramm failed, 9-12, to eliminate the list of services that accounting firms could not sell to their auditing clients.

A Sarbanes-Enzi amendment, adopted by voice vote, added a requirement that two of the five members of the regulatory board be accountants. Consumer advocates said that would increase the chance that the new board would be dominated by the accounting industry. Another change under the Sarbanes-Enzi compromise required the board to keep its disciplinary proceedings confidential.

Senate Floor Action

The Senate passed the Sarbanes bill July 15 by a vote of 97-0, then inserted the text into HR 3763 and sent it back to the House. With retirement portfolios dwindling and investors anxiously watching the markets, the potential political fallout of failing to act had become obvious to all sides. Although Bush initially backed Oxley's approach, he signaled after the Senate vote that he would sign whatever bill Congress could get on his desk before the August recess. (Senate vote 176, p. S-36)

The pace had quickened in late June, as revelations of shaky bookkeeping by WorldCom and Xerox reinvigorated Democrats and sent many Republicans rushing for cover. "The growing list of corporations under question makes clear that we aren't just talking about one or two isolated cases," Senate Majority Leader Tom Daschle, D-S.D., said pointedly, but "a deregulatory, permissive atmosphere that has relied too much on corporate America to police itself."

"The appearance and the potential for conflict is obvious," acknowledged Minority Leader Trent Lott, R-Miss.

"Something's going to have to change."

Rushing to get ahead of the debate, Bush had gone to Wall Street on July 9 to chastise corporate executives and propose several legal and regulatory changes. Bush called for doubling prison sentences for mail and wire fraud, and announced the creation of a corporate fraud task force to coordinate criminal investigations. "In the long run, there's no capitalism without conscience; there is no wealth without character," Bush said.

During debate on the bill, the Senate agreed to:

• Add several of Bush's proposals, including doubling jail sentences for mail and wire fraud from five years to 10, and tightening existing law on obstruction of justice involving document shredding. The amendment, by Lott, was adopted, 97-0. (*Senate vote 171, p. S-35*)

• Mandate prison terms of up to 10 years for shareholder fraud and obstruction of justice involving document shredding. The amendment, by Patrick J. Leahy, D-Vt., was adopted, 97-0. (*Senate vote 169, p. S-35*)

• Increase penalties for federal pension law violations; make penalties for conspiracy the same as for the underlying crime; and require corporate officials to certify financial reports or face criminal penalties. The plan, by Joseph R. Biden Jr., D-Del., was adopted, 96-0. (*Senate vote 170, p. S-35*)

• Clarify that a provision requiring corporate executives to certify financial reports also would apply to executives of corporations that had moved offshore. The proposal, by Byron L. Dorgan, D-N.D., was adopted by voice vote.

• Prohibit companies from making some personal loans to executives or directors, and require that the SEC study the use of off-balance-sheet transactions. The two amendments, by Charles E. Schumer, D-N.Y., were adopted by voice vote.

• Require disclosure within two days of all stock sales by top corporate executives and directors. Such reports had been taking as long as 40 days to become public. The proposal, by Jean Carnahan, D-Mo., was adopted, 97-0. (*Senate vote 174, p. S-36*)

• Direct the SEC to establish rules requiring attorneys to report corporate wrongdoing to a company's officers or, if necessary, to its directors. The amendment, by John Edwards, D-N.C, was adopted, 97-0. (*Senate vote 175, p. S-36*)

Amendments blocked or rejected on the floor included:

• An attempt by Mitch McConnell, R-Ky., to make unions subject to financial reporting procedures comparable to those required of corporations. The amendment was killed (tabled), 55-43. (*Senate vote 168, p. S-35*)

• A proposal by John McCain, R-Ariz., to force businesses to report stock options as expenses for tax purposes. Democratic leaders prevented a vote on the amendment.

• An attempt by Carl Levin, D-Mich., to require that the FASB review the treatment of stock options and adopt a rule governing that treatment. It was blocked by Gramm.

House Response

After the Senate vote, House GOP deputy whips Mark Foley of Florida and Mike Rogers of Michigan urged House Speaker J. Dennis Hastert, R-Ill., to pass the Senate version. "Immediate action is required to get a bill to the president's desk," they wrote. But House Republican leaders decided instead to stake out a position on new and tougher criminal penalties for corporate fraud. The new bill (HR 5118),

passed 392-28 on July 16, proposed to quadruple criminal penalties for mail and wire fraud to 20 years from five, and to mandate criminal penalties for filing false statements with the SEC, among other provisions. (*House vote 299, p. H-96*)

After briefly asserting that user fees in the Sarbanes bill violated the constitutional requirement that all revenue measures originate in the House, Hastert backed down and all but promised to have a bill on Bush's desk by July 26, when the House was scheduled to begin its August recess. Earlier that day, a GOP pollster had warned Republicans that they would court disaster if they departed for a month-long vacation while the markets fell, without completing a bill. Also, Republicans were eager to put a halt to Democratic election-year attacks on the GOP as too cozy with business interests at a time when workers were losing their savings because of corporate fraud.

Conference/Final Action

The conference report (H Rept 107-610), completed July 24, largely reflected the Senate bill and represented an ideological capitulation by congressional Republicans. Bush had outflanked members of his own party by calling on Congress to send him a bill before the August recess. That left Republicans little choice but to abandon their traditional hands-off approach to securities market regulation.

The House adopted the conference report in a nearly unanimous, 423-3 vote on July 25, and the Senate cleared the bill, 99-0, the same day. (*House vote 348, p. H-110; Senate vote 192, p. S-39*)

While the Senate bill was the base text used by House and Senate negotiators, the increased penalties for corporate fraud also drew on the second House bill. House negotiators won some provisions, such as a requirement for real-time public disclosure of material changes in companies' financial conditions, as well as the requirement that civil penalties for securities law violations go into a fund for defrauded investors. Republicans also were able to rein in the independence of the new oversight board and place it more firmly under the aegis of the SEC than it would have been under the Senate-passed bill. New language in the conference report made it clear the SEC was empowered to require record-keeping by the board and to inspect the board's activities.

Still, some Republicans decried what they said was a blind rush to clear the bill. "This is an election year, and we're in the middle of a stampede by a bunch of politicians who want to pass something," said Rep. John A. Boehner of Ohio. Gramm criticized the measure as a "one-size-fits-all prescription when clearly that one size does not fit all." Both men voted to clear the bill, however.

The accounting industry, whose lobbyists had wielded considerable influence on Capitol Hill, was largely eclipsed by the quick pace of events. "This is a bit of a tsunami tide," said Bruce Josten, an executive vice president at the U.S. Chamber of Commerce.

Insurance companies won a minor change when Democrats agreed to allow accounting firms that audited insurers also to perform work related to audits required by state insurance regulators. Financial services lobbyists persuaded Sarbanes to change a provision that barred many company loans to corporate executives in order to make an exception

for margin accounts held by employees of securities firms.

Noticeably absent from the bill was any mention of the accounting treatment of stock options. Under existing law, companies were not required to list stock options as expenses on their income statements. Critics blamed the liberal use of stock options for fostering a corporate culture that focused on short-term gains at the expense of long-term stability. Opponents of mandatory expensing of stock options, including high-tech firms, said expensing would paint an unfair picture of a company's financial health, which could drive down stock prices

Postscript

Because the fiscal 2003 appropriations process broke down, the SEC had to wait to get extra funding to carry out its new responsibilities. The agency ultimately got $716 mil-

lion under the fiscal 2003 omnibus spending bill (PL 108-7) enacted in January 2003. That was less than the $776 million authorized under the accounting law, but significantly more than the $567 million requested by Bush.

Meanwhile, Pitt abruptly resigned as SEC chairman Nov. 5. He was facing an internal SEC probe as well as the wrath of Sarbanes and others over his handling of appointments to the oversight board. Pitt failed to tell the SEC commission before it confirmed William H. Webster III as chairman, that Webster had served as chairman of the audit committee for financially troubled U.S. Technologies Inc. Webster later resigned. On Dec. 10, Bush picked William H. Donaldson to replace Pitt, subject to Senate confirmation. Donaldson, who co-founded the investment firm Donaldson, Lufkin & Jenrette, was a former chairman and CEO of Aetna Inc., and a former chairman of the New York Stock Exchange. ◆

Provisions of the Corporate Fraud Bill

The following are provisions of the new law overhauling regulation of the accounting industry and increasing corporate accountability. The measure was signed into law July 30 (HR 3763 — PL 107-204).

Oversight Board

● **Board.** The law created a new, independent regulatory body, the Public Company Accounting Oversight Board, to oversee the auditing of publicly traded companies in order to protect the interests of investors. The board, which is classified as a District of Columbia-based nonprofit corporation, operates under Securities and Exchange Commission (SEC) oversight. All the board's rules, decisions and sanctions must be submitted to the SEC for approval. The SEC can censure or limit the board's activities, operations and members for cause.

● **Membership.** The board is composed of five full-time members appointed by the SEC in consultation with the Federal Reserve chairman and the Treasury secretary. No more than two of the board members may have worked previously as certified public accountants. Board members serve for five years with staggered terms. They must serve full time, and are not to be employed in any other business or professional activity during their terms. Board members are limited to two terms.

● **Registration and inspection.** Accounting firms that audit publicly traded companies are required to register with the oversight board. The board must conduct annual inspections of accounting firms that regularly audit more than 100 publicly traded companies, and inspect other accounting firms at least once every three years. Foreign public accounting firms that audit companies whose shares trade on U.S. exchanges are subject to the new law.

● **Powers.** The board has the authority to establish and enforce auditing standards, and to investigate and discipline accountants or accounting firms that violate those standards. It is empowered to require registered accounting firms to provide documents and testimony in the course of an investigation. It also can ask other companies and individuals to provide documents and testimony, as well as request the SEC issue subpoenas.

● **Penalties**. The board can suspend or bar individuals from being associated with registered accounting firms, and suspend or revoke accounting firms' registration. It can levy civil money penalties of

not more than $100,000 for an individual or $2 million for a corporation. Intentional, knowing or reckless conduct is punishable by a penalty of up to $750,000 for an individual and $15 million for a corporation.

● **Funding.** To ensure its independence, the board is funded through annual accounting fees assessed on publicly traded companies, with each company's assessment determined by its average annual market capitalization (the company's share price multiplied by the number of shares issued).

● **Auditing standards.** The board is required to establish or adopt standards for audits of public companies. The standards must require registered accounting firms to prepare and maintain audit work papers for seven years, including an evaluation of the internal financial controls of their public company clients.

Accounting Standards

● **Funding.** To ensure its independence, the Financial Accounting Standards Board (FASB), which sets national accounting standards, must be funded by fees assessed on publicly traded companies.

● **Membership.** A majority of FASB's board must be composed of individuals who have not been affiliated with accounting firms during their service or in the two years prior to their service.

● **Accounting system.** FASB is directed to conduct a study on the possible use of a "principles-based" accounting system, in which accounting guidelines are loosely drawn and based on principle, rather than the existing "rules-based" accounting system, which relies on specifically enumerated rules.

Auditor Independence

● **Audit committees.** Auditors must be hired by, and report to, a company's audit committee (or if there is no audit committee, the company's entire board of directors). The audit committee is to set compensation levels for outside accountants and be able to seek outside advice at company expense. Accounting firms must report to audit committees regarding accounting policies and procedures, alternative treatments of financial information that the auditors have discussed with company management, if any, and material written communications between the auditors and company man-

agement. Audit committees must set up a procedure for receiving complaints regarding the company's accounting and auditing, as well as confidential, anonymous information provided by company employees.

Each member of a corporation's audit committee must be "independent" — not part of the company's management and not receiving any compensation from the company for consulting or other services. The SEC can make exceptions.

Accounting firms are prohibited from auditing a corporation if the chief executive officer (CEO), chief financial officer (CFO), controller, chief accounting officer, or any person serving in an equivalent position previously worked for the accounting firm and participated in the company audit during the previous year.

● **Non-audit services.** Auditors are barred from providing specified non-audit services to the same publicly traded companies they audit. Barred services include: bookkeeping or other services related to accounting records or financial statements; financial information systems design and implementation; appraisal or valuation services; actuarial services; internal audits; management or human resources; broker/dealer, investment adviser or investment banking services; legal and expert services; or other services the board decides are not permitted. The board can grant case-by-case exceptions to the banned services.

Accounting firms can provide certain other non-audit services, including tax services, to a corporation, if approved in advance by the audit committee. Prior approval by the audit committee, or a designated subset of the audit committee, is not required if combined compensation for all such non-audit services is 5 percent or less of the total compensation paid by the corporation to the auditor during the fiscal year, or if such services were not recognized as non-audit services by the client at the time of engagement, or if such services are promptly brought to the audit committee's attention and approved by either the audit committee or one or more of its members before the completion of the audit.

● **Auditor rotation.** Accounting firms must periodically rotate their lead audit partners, and the review partners, so that no one partner either leads an audit for a specific public company or reviews it for more than five years in a row.

● **GAO study.** The Comptroller General is directed to study the possible impact of requiring mandatory rotation of entire accounting firms on audits of publicly traded companies.

Corporate Responsibility

● **Executive responsibility.** Corporate CEOs and CFOs and those persons performing similar functions at publicly traded companies — including U.S. companies that establish a shell headquarters abroad — are required to certify the accuracy of annual and quarterly company financial reports to the SEC. The executives must attest that they have reviewed the report and, based on their knowledge, vouch that it does not contain any untruths or misstatements of any significant facts and that they represent an accurate description of the company's financial condition in all material respects. They also must verify that they have established, and are maintaining and periodically evaluating, internal controls so that they can become aware of any material changes in the company's financial condition.

● **Improper influence on audits.** Company officers and directors are forbidden from, directly or indirectly, fraudulently influencing, coercing, manipulating or misleading the company's outside auditors.

● **CEO and CFO forfeitures.** If a company is later forced to restate its earnings because of material non-compliance or misconduct regarding financial reporting requirements, the CEO and CFO will be required to repay the company any bonuses or compensation based on incentives or stock, as well as any profits they

earned from sales of company stock during the 12 months following the initial financial statement. The SEC can make exceptions.

● **Officer and director bars.** The SEC can ask a federal court to bar persons from serving as officers or directors of publicly traded companies if the person's conduct demonstrates "unfitness." The previous standard was "substantial unfitness."

● **Stock trading restrictions.** The new law prohibits corporate directors or executive officers from buying, selling or transferring company stock during "blackout" periods of at least three consecutive business days when at least 50 percent of all participants and beneficiaries in the company-sponsored pension or 401(k) plan are barred from doing so. If an executive illegally conducts a stock transaction during blackout periods, the company may go to court to recover any profits made from the transaction, subject to a two-year statute of limitations. Shareholders can also go to court, after waiting 60 days for the company to take action.

Applicable blackout periods do not include regularly scheduled blackout periods that are part of the plan and disclosed to employees, or those that are imposed when participants or beneficiaries either begin or cease to be part of the plan as a result of a merger, acquisition, divestiture or similar transaction that involves either the retirement plan or the plan sponsor.

Plan administrators are generally required to notify participants and beneficiaries 30 days in advance of any blackout period — including the reasons for the blackout and when it is expected to begin and end — and issue a statement advising the participants or beneficiaries to review their individual investment decisions in light of the blackout period. The secretary of Labor may fine plan administrators up to $100 per day per participant or beneficiary for failing or refusing to provide required notices.

● **Attorney responsibility.** Within 180 days of enactment, the SEC must issue rules requiring attorneys who appear and practice before the commission on behalf of publicly traded companies to report material securities law violations, breaches of fiduciary duty or similar violations to the company's chief legal counsel or its CEO. If those officers do not appropriately respond to the report, the attorney is required to inform either the company's audit committee, another committee of independent directors or the entire board of directors.

● **Fund for defrauded investors.** Money collected through court-ordered disgorgements (refunds of money by defendants because of securities law violations), settlements involving disgorgements, or civil penalties must, at the SEC's discretion, be put into a fund to be paid to victims of the particular violation. The SEC also can accept gifts and bequests made to the United States for the fund.

The SEC is required to study its own enforcement actions during the previous five years to identify ways to effectively pay restitution to defrauded investors, and report to the House Financial Services and Senate Banking committees within 180 days.

Disclosure and Transparency Requirements

● **Off-balance-sheet disclosures.** Corporations must include in their annual and quarterly financial reports to the SEC any information on off-balance-sheet transactions or partnerships that may have an effect on the company's financial condition. A company's "pro forma" financial statements, such as preliminary reports or releases issued in advance of quarterly and annual SEC reports, may not contain any untrue material statements or omit material information that makes the statement misleading, and must depict the financial conditions and operations of the company under generally accepted accounting principles.

● **Special-purpose entities.** The SEC will study filings by publicly traded companies to determine the extent to which off-balance-sheet transactions and special-purpose entities (complex business arrangements that can be used to transfer and hide debt) are used,

and whether generally accepted accounting rules provide for transparent disclosure to investors. The SEC is required to report to the president, the Senate Banking and the House Financial Services committees as to the number of off-balance-sheet transactions employed by publicly traded companies, the extent to which special-purpose entities are used as part of such transactions, whether generally accepted accounting principles or SEC rules provide for transparent disclosure of off-balance-sheet transactions, and issue SEC recommendations for improving the reporting of off-balance-sheet transactions.

● **Conflicts of interest.** Publicly traded companies are barred from making loans to directors or officers. Exceptions include home improvement and manufactured home loans; consumer credit; charge cards; and margin accounts for employees of securities brokers and dealers, so long as they are provided in the ordinary course of the company's consumer credit business and made available to the public on terms that are at least as favorable.

The prohibition also does not apply to loans made or maintained by insured depository institutions if the loans are subject to prior restrictions on insider lending.

Directors, officers, and owners of more than 10 percent of stock in a publicly traded company must file statements with the SEC indicating the amount of stock held and any changes in ownership before the end of the second business day that follows the day the relevant transaction occurred.

● **Internal controls.** Annual company reports to the SEC must contain statements of management responsibility for establishing and maintaining internal controls and financial reporting procedures, along with an assessment of their effectiveness. The company's outside accounting firm also must evaluate those statements and assessments.

● **Codes of ethics.** Public companies are required to report to the SEC regarding whether or not they have codes of ethics for their senior financial officers. Companies also must immediately disclose any changes to or waivers of their codes of ethics.

● **Audit committee financial experts.** Public companies must report to the SEC as to whether at least one member of the audit committee is a "financial expert," defined as someone who understands generally accepted accounting principles, including for estimates, accruals and reserves; has experience in preparing or auditing financial statements at similar companies; and has experience with internal accounting controls as well as an understanding of the role of audit committees.

● **Enhanced SEC review.** The SEC is required to review public company filings at least once every three years, paying particular attention to companies that have restated their financial results, have especially volatile stock prices, have the largest market capitalizations and "significantly affect" particular economic sectors.

● **Real-time disclosures.** Publicly traded companies must plainly and publicly disclose "on a rapid and current basis" any material changes in their operations or financial conditions.

Securities Analysts

● **Conflicts of interest.** The SEC, or registered securities associations or national securities exchanges that the SEC designates, must adopt rules to prevent conflicts of interest by stock analysts.

The rules must limit the ability of investment bankers who underwrite stocks to supervise or affect the compensation of stock analysts who work for the same firm; restrict advance approval of analyst reports by investment bankers; prevent investment bankers from retaliating against affiliated stock analysts who issue unfavorable recommendations against stocks; and create structural and informational firewalls to separate the investment and research divisions of investment banks.

The rules must define periods surrounding initial public offer-

ings of stock during which involved brokers and dealers should not publish or distribute research reports on the stock of the issuing company.

They also must require a stock analyst, in preparing research reports and when making public appearances, to disclose the extent to which he owns the stock being discussed; whether the analyst or his employer has received any income from the company whose stock is being discussed; whether his employer has had any business dealings in the past year with the company; and whether the analyst's compensation was tied to investment banking revenues collected by his employer.

SEC Resources and Authority

● **Fiscal 2003 authorization.** The law authorizes $776 million for the SEC for fiscal 2003, $317.4 million more than the agency's fiscal 2002 appropriation. Of that amount, $102.7 million is designated for commission salaries and benefits, $108.4 million for information technology, security, and recovery from the Sept. 11 terrorist attacks, and $98 million for hiring not fewer than 200 additional staff members.

● **Additional SEC authority.** The SEC can censure or bar from appearing or practicing before the commission any person whom it finds to be lacking in qualifications or integrity, or to have engaged in improper or unethical conduct.

● **Penny stock bars.** Courts have the authority to bar persons found to have engaged in misconduct from any offering of penny stocks, which are high-risk stocks that typically sell for less than one dollar per share. The SEC can grant exceptions.

Studies and Reports

● **Accounting firm consolidation.** The law directs the Comptroller General to study the consolidation of public accounting firms since 1989, along with the impact on stock markets and capital formation and any problems faced by businesses because of "limited competition" among public accounting firms. The findings, as well recommendations on increasing competition, are to be submitted to the Senate Banking and House Financial Services committees.

● **SEC reports.** The SEC is required to submit studies to the Senate Banking and House Financial Services committees concerning: the role and function of credit rating agencies; securities law violations by accountants, investment bankers, brokers, attorneys and others between Jan. 1, 1998, and Dec. 31, 2001; and the SEC's own enforcement actions during the past five years involving reporting violations and financial restatements, along with an analysis of which reporting requirements are most susceptible to fraud.

● **Investment banking.** The Comptroller General is required to report to Congress on whether investment banks and financial advisers had a hand in concealing the true financial condition of publicly traded companies, especially Enron Corp. and Global Crossing Ltd., with recommended regulatory or legislative steps to address concerns.

Corporate Fraud

● **Document falsification and shredding.** Knowingly altering, falsifying or destroying records, documents or tangible objects with the intent to obstruct justice is punishable by a fine and/or up to 20 years in prison.

● **Audit records.** Accountants must keep audit and review records for five years after the end of the fiscal period during which the audit or review occurred. The SEC is required to establish rules within 180 days. Violation of the five-year retention requirement is punishable by a fine and/or up to 10 years in prison.

● **Debts in bankruptcy.** Federal bankruptcy law is amended so that debts resulting from judgments, orders or settlements incurred because of securities law violations or common law fraud are non-

dischargeable in bankruptcy proceedings.

- **Statute of limitations.** In a provision backed by plaintiff lawyers, the statute of limitations for civil lawsuits related to securities fraud is expanded to up to two years after discovery of the fraud or five years after the fraud occurred. Previously, the limit was one year after discovery of the fraud or three years after the fraud occurred.

- **Whistleblower protections.** Publicly traded companies and their agents are prohibited from retaliating against whistleblowers who provide information or otherwise assist in an investigation being conducted by the company, federal regulators or law enforcement, or members of Congress or congressional committees. Whistleblowers who claim they have been retaliated against have 90 days to file a complaint to the secretary of Labor. If there is no final decision in the dispute within 180 days, the whistleblower can seek redress in federal court.

- **Securities fraud felony.** A "scheme or artifice" to defraud shareholders or to obtain money or property in connection with securities fraud is punishable by a fine and/or up to 25 years in prison.

White-Collar Crime

- **Mail and wire fraud.** Criminal penalties for mail and wire fraud are increased to a maximum of 20 years in prison, up from five.

- **Pension law violations.** Violations of the Employee Retirement Income Security Act of 1974 (PL 93-406) are punishable by a fine of up to $100,000 and/or 10 years in prison; the old penalty was a fine of up to $5,000 and one year in prison. Corporations are subject to a fine of up to $500,000; the old penalty was a fine of up to $100,000.

- **Review by U.S. Sentencing Commission.** The U.S. Sentencing Commission has 180 days to review — and amend, as appropriate — federal sentencing guidelines related to securities fraud.

- **Certification of financial reports.** CEOs and CFOs must certify that SEC filings fully comply with legal requirements and that they fairly describe, in all material respects, the company's opera-

tions and financial condition. Knowing violations are punishable by a fine of up to $1 million and 10 years in prison. Willful violations are punishable by a fine of up to $5 million and 20 years in prison.

- **Attempt and conspiracy.** Attempting or conspiring to commit offenses under the chapter are crimes that carry punishments equal to those for committing the crime itself.

Corporate Tax Returns

- **Sense of the Senate.** The sense of the Senate is that CEOs should sign corporate federal income tax returns.

Corporate Fraud Accountability

- **Record tampering.** Destroying or tampering with records, documents or other objects, or attempting to do so, to obstruct or impede official proceedings is subject to a fine and/or up to 20 years in prison.

- **Temporary freeze authority.** The SEC can petition a federal court to order that extraordinary payments by a public company under investigation to its officers, directors, employees or other persons be held in escrow for up to 90 days.

- **Officer and director bars.** The SEC is empowered to prohibit persons, either temporarily or permanently, from serving as officers or directors of publicly traded companies upon a finding that they are unfit to do so.

- **Increased criminal penalties.** Violations of the Securities and Exchange Act of 1934 are punishable by a fine of up to $5 million and/or 20 years in prison; the old penalties were a $1 million fine and/or 10 years in prison. Corporations are subject to a fine of up to $25 million; the old penalty was a fine of up to $2.5 million.

- **Whistleblower protections.** Anyone who knowingly retaliates against a person who provides truthful information to a law enforcement officer shall be fined and/or imprisoned for up to 10 years. ◆

Terrorism Insurers Get Federal Help

With a major push from the real estate and commercial insurance industries — and personal lobbying by President Bush — Congress cleared a bill Nov. 19 establishing a three-year federal terrorism insurance program. The program placed a cap on potential losses for commercial property and casualty insurers in the event of a cataclysmic terrorist attack. The aim was to encourage the insurance industry to provide commercial terrorism coverage at affordable prices in the wake of the Sept. 11, 2001, terrorist attacks, while giving it time to develop a market-based system for absorbing the risks.

Enactment was a major victory for Bush, who had made the legislation one of his top domestic priorities. It also was a win for congressional Democrats, who successfully resisted the inclusion of a ban on punitive damages in terrorism cases. Bush signed the bill into law Nov. 26 (HR 3210 — PL 107-297).

The measure required the government to cover 90 percent of an insurance company's terrorism-related losses, once insured losses exceeded a specific trigger level. Total federal responsibility was capped at $100 billion per year.

Lobbyists for commercial property and casualty insurers came to Congress shortly after Sept. 11, saying that while claims from the attacks would be paid, the industry could not continue to offer terrorism coverage unless the federal government stepped in to share the risk. The reinsurance industry, which had played that role, was planning to stop covering terrorism insurance as soon as Jan. 1, 2003.

The House and Senate initially took very different approaches. The House bill, passed in November 2001, would have created a federal terrorism insurance loan program to cover 90 percent of insured losses once industry-wide losses reached $1 billion. The plan was to recoup the money from the insurers and their policyholders. Under the Senate bill, passed in June 2002, the threshold for federal intervention would have been much higher — $10 billion in losses industry-wide — but the money would have been a subsidy, not a loan. Both bills capped total federal assistance at $100 billion.

The chief dispute — one that almost sank the bill — was whether to bar punitive damages in civil lawsuits related to terrorism. Many Senate Republicans, including Mitch Mc-

Connell of Kentucky and Phil Gramm of Texas, insisted that such a ban be part of any terrorism insurance bill. But their plan was anathema to many Senate Democrats, especially Majority Leader Tom Daschle of South Dakota, who feared it would establish a wedge for the so-called tort reform movement.

The deadlock finally was broken in October, when Bush struck a deal with Senate Democrats to drop the punitive damages provision and provide for civil lawsuits arising from terrorist acts to be consolidated in federal court. Punitive damages awarded in a lawsuit would not count as insured losses subject to government aid.

The agreement was followed quickly by a deal on the entire bill between the White House, Senate Democrats and House Financial Services Committee Chairman Michael G. Oxley, R-Ohio, just before Congress adjourned for the November elections. Republicans, angry that Bush had cut a deal with Daschle, refused for several weeks to support the compromise. They relented after House Speaker J. Dennis Hastert, R-Ill., extracted a promise from Bush that he would champion legislation in 2003 to curb punitive damage awards.

Highlights

The following are major components of the new law:

● **Federal safety net.** The federal government would pay 90 percent of claims arising from terrorist attacks once industry-wide insured losses exceeded a trigger level of $10 billion in 2003, $12.5 billion in 2004 and $15 billion in 2005. Losses covered by the program were capped at $100 billion per year for the industry as a whole.

An individual company could qualify for aid before the industry-wide threshold was reached, if its terrorism losses exceeded a certain percentage of the company's premiums. The threshold — essentially a deductible — was 7 percent in 2003, 10 percent in 2004 and 15 percent in 2005. The company was responsible for 100 percent of losses up to those thresholds.

Government aid paid out after an insurance company met its deductible but before the larger industry-wide threshold was reached was subject to repayment by commercial policyholders.

Once the $100 billion cap was met, no further federal funds would be provided and insurers that had covered their deductible for the year would not be required to cover any additional losses.

● **Terrorism lawsuits.** The law required that all civil lawsuits arising from a terrorist attack be grouped together and considered in federal, rather than state, court. Amounts awarded as punitive damages in such cases would not count as insured losses under the federal program.

● **Terrorism coverage.** The new law voided any state actions that exempted insurance companies from providing

---

BoxScore

Bill:
HR 3210 — PL 107-297

Legislative Action:
Senate passed S 2600, 84-14, June 18, subsequently inserting the text into HR 3210.
House adopted the conference report (H Rept. 107-779) by voice vote Nov. 14.
Senate cleared the bill, 86-11, on Nov. 19.
President signed Nov. 26.

---

terrorism coverage. As a result, upon enactment, all existing commercial property and casualty policies provided terrorism coverage. Insurers were expected to immediately send out notices of increased premiums for such coverage.

Background

Before Sept. 11, commercial insurance policies routinely included terrorism coverage. Following the terrorist attacks, insurers gave assurances that they were well capitalized and could pay the estimated $40 billion in claims. But the large reinsurance companies, which insured the insurers, announced they would not continue covering terrorism insurance when policies came up for renewal, many of them on Jan. 1, 2003. That led to dire predictions of catastrophe for the insurance industry and turmoil for the economy as a whole. (*2001 Almanac, p. 4-6*)

Congress at first seemed ready to act. The House passed a bill Nov. 29, 2001, that called for a one-year federal program, with a possible two-year extension. Under the bill:

● The federal government would cover 90 percent of insured losses from future acts of terrorism once the industry-wide losses exceeded $1 billion. Each company, however, would be responsible for covering 100 percent of its first $5 million in losses. Smaller insurance companies that suffered disproportionately large terrorist-related losses could receive federal aid once industry-wide losses exceeded $100 million.

● Federal assistance would be capped at $100 billion.

● The federal money would be a loan, with the first $20 billion recouped through direct assessments on insurance companies and amounts from $20 billion to $100 billion recovered through surcharges on policyholders.

● Any lawsuit involving losses or injuries caused by acts of terrorism would have to be considered in federal court. Economic damages in such cases would be limited and punitive damages banned. Attorney fees would be capped at 20 percent of the court-ordered damages or settlement.

In the more fractious Senate, however, the legislation became ensnared in a debate over how or whether to ban punitive damages in civil suits arising from future terrorist acts. A bipartisan group of Banking Committee members negotiated a proposal with the White House that called for a straight subsidy. But Daschle blocked committee Chairman Paul S. Sarbanes, D-Md., from introducing the bill or moving it through the committee, mainly because it contained a ban on punitive damages. The fight went into the final hours of the first session, to no avail, and Congress adjourned in December without finishing a bill.

Under the bipartisan plan:

● Insurance companies would be responsible for the first $10 billion in terrorism-related losses in one year.

● The federal government would pay 90 percent of claims after that, up to $100 billion.

● Terrorism-related lawsuits would be considered in fed-

eral court, punitive damages would be barred and attorney fees capped.

Lobbying Campaign Retooled

By the time Congress resumed work in 2002, the sense of urgency had receded. There were anecdotal examples of property owners and construction companies in major cities being unable to get sufficient insurance, but the effects were gradual and not the catastrophe that backers of the bill had predicted. Meanwhile, a string of corporate scandals, highlighted by the massive bankruptcy of Enron Corp. in December 2001, made members leery of taking action that could be seen as a handout to business.

What turned the situation around, ultimately leading to the bill's enactment, was a retooled lobbying campaign led by real estate interests and the direct and sustained involvement of the president.

The insurers had gotten permission from most state regulators to eliminate terrorism coverage from their policies. That left the commercial real estate industry grappling with skyrocketing insurance rates and scarce terrorism coverage. Encouraged by Karl Rove, Bush's chief domestic policy adviser, the real estate lobbyists swung into action, redefining the bill as essential to keep commercial construction going and shore up the faltering economy. They bombarded Capitol Hill with statistics on the interruption of commercial construction and the downgrading of commercial mortgage-backed securities that they said demonstrated an overwhelming need for the bill.

The strategy was a win-win for Rove: If a bill cleared, Bush could claim credit; if it did not, Republicans could use it to bash Daschle and a "do nothing" Democratic-controlled Senate.

Bush touted the bill as critical to his efforts to jump-start the economy, saying the lack of terrorism risk insurance had caused wary firms to forgo $15 billion in construction projects costing 300,000 jobs. In speeches across the country, the president hammered on Congress to send him a bill. While the numbers were disputed by consumer groups, business lobbyists were able to convince Democrats that a bill was needed.

Legislative Action

Senate Floor Action

On June 18, the Senate voted 84-14 in favor of a terrorism insurance bill (S 2600) sponsored by Christopher J. Dodd, D-Conn. Subsequently, in order to go to conference, the Senate agreed July 25 to insert the text into HR 3210. (*Senate vote 157, p. S-33*)

The bill covered one year, with a possible extension for one more. Under the Senate bill:

- The federal government would cover 80 percent of insured losses below $10 billion and 90 percent of total losses that exceeded $10 billion. Each insurer would have to satisfy a deductible based on its market share before receiving assistance. The federal assistance would not have to be paid back.
- Federal assistance would be capped at $100 billion.
- Lawsuits involving losses or injuries caused by acts of

terrorism would have to be considered in federal court. Punitive damages would not be covered by the federal program.

Despite Bush's high-profile involvement, the bill had remained stalled through the spring. Daschle refused to bring a version to the floor that included a ban on punitive damages, and Gramm and other Republicans refused to let him bring up a bill that did not. The impasse was broken June 10 when Bush's senior economic advisers sent a letter to Minority Leader Trent Lott, R-Miss., saying they would advise the president not to sign a bill if it did not ban punitive damages.

The path to passage was cleared once the Senate voted to invoke cloture, thus limiting debate on the bill. Democratic leaders enlisted the White House to win the procedural victory at the expense of GOP leaders, who wanted their rank and file to have the option of offering additional amendments. Business lobbyists frantically canvassed GOP senators before the vote.

The vote for cloture was 65-31, five more than the required minimum; 17 Republicans voted "yea." The vote was complicated by the fact that Sam Brownback, R-Kan., was seeking to force a test vote on an unrelated amendment to ban human cloning. Majority Whip Harry Reid, D-Nev., said it was the first time since Democrats had taken control of the Senate the year before that they had prevailed on a cloture vote over the active opposition of GOP leaders. (*Senate vote 157, p. S-33*)

During debate on the bill, the Senate also:

- Agreed, 50-46, to table (kill) an amendment by McConnell that would have prohibited punitive damages unless a defendant was convicted of a criminal offense related to the plaintiff's injury. (*Senate vote 152, p. S-32*)
- Agreed, 70-24, to table an amendment by Bill Nelson, D-Fla., that would have regulated terrorism insurance premiums. (*Senate vote 153, p. S-32*)
- Adopted, 81-3, an amendment by George Allen, R-Va., to allow victims of terrorism to recover damages from the frozen assets of terrorists, terrorist organizations or state sponsors of terrorist acts. (*Senate vote 155, p. S-33*)

Gramm was one of 14 Republicans who voted against the bill. He cited provisions that would have allowed individual insurance companies to get taxpayer assistance before overall losses reached an industry-wide threshold. Gramm said those provisions made sense in 2001, when insurers were scrambling to deal with the abrupt loss of reinsurance. But with many commercial policies having been renewed since then — at substantially higher premiums — Gramm said the provisions would give insurers "windfalls" because the government would assume much more of the risk.

Consumer advocates shared that criticism, arguing that the commercial insurance market already had adjusted.

Conference/Final Action

House-Senate negotiations on a final bill did not begin in earnest until well after the August recess. The final agreement was struck Oct. 17, after many in Congress had left for the campaign trail, pushing final action into the lame-duck session. The House adopted the conference report (H Rept 107-779) by voice vote Nov. 14. The Senate cleared the bill, 86-11, on Nov. 19. (*Senate vote 252, p. S-52*)

Negotiations had sputtered until Oct. 16, when the

White House, in a startling reversal, agreed to discard the provision on punitive damages. Ultimately, the administration decided it was better to back away from the provision than to end up with language that could undercut existing legal standards in states that either banned punitive damages or had caps on such awards.

Like both the House and Senate versions of the bill, the conference agreement required that civil lawsuits related to terrorism be consolidated in federal courts, a win for the "tort reform" movement, which argued that it would prevent venue-shopping by plaintiffs' attorneys in state courts.

The compromise, backed by Oxley, enabled negotiators to iron out their other differences quickly. They agreed on a three-year bill, under which the government would pay 90 percent of claims after insured losses from terrorism surpassed $10 billion in the first year, $12.5 billion in the second year and $15 billion in the third year, up to a cap of $100 billion.

Government assistance would be available after individual insurer deductibles had been met, but before the industry-wide threshold was crossed. That aid would be re-paid through surcharges on commercial policyholders, at the discretion of the Treasury secretary. Oxley and Richard H. Baker, R-La., the architects of the House version, insisted on some form of payback.

House GOP leaders, particularly Majority Whip Tom De-Lay of Texas, were sufficiently irritated with the White House for cutting a bilateral deal with Daschle and his Senate Democratic allies that they kept Bush waiting until very near the end of the 107th Congress before agreeing to adopt the conference report. Many of them mulled whether to let the bill die in favor of trying again in the next Congress, when the GOP would control both chambers. But Bush relentlessly pushed Republican leaders to drop their opposition, promising to champion a conservative tort reform agenda in the 108th Congress to set broad new limits on civil litigation.

The bill faced one last obstacle. Gramm refused to allow a final vote until the Senate had passed a bill (PL 107-296) to create a Cabinet Department of Homeland Security. That made the vote to clear the terrorism insurance bill the second to last Senate roll call vote of the 107th Congress. ◆

Chapter 12

LABOR & EMPLOYMENT

Pension Security Bills Falter

Legislation to protect employee retirement savings from corporate misdeeds died in the Senate because of an end-of-session disagreement over whether to attach non-pension items such as business tax breaks. The issue of pension safety, which arose in response to the collapse of Enron Corp. and WorldCom Inc., brought out fundamental differences between the political parties over whether the government should impose specific restrictions to safeguard pension plans, or give employees choices that would allow them to protect their own retirement funds.

The bankruptcy of energy giant Enron and the resulting evaporation of its employees' retirement savings prompted the Bush administration in February to propose legislation to safeguard 401(k) retirement plans. President Bush's proposal, combined with intense interest on Capitol Hill, appeared to virtually guarantee that Congress would take some action to remedy flaws in the pension system illustrated by the Enron debacle.

In the House, the Education and the Workforce and Ways and Means committees took different approaches, and the GOP leadership assembled a compromise package (HR 3762), which the House passed in April. The bill would have given workers participating in 401(k) plans more flexibility in selling employer stock from those accounts and would have allowed financial services firms that manage retirement accounts to give investment advice to workers. Existing law prohibited such conduct if the adviser could benefit from the transaction.

Democrats unsuccessfully pushed an alternative that would have made more widespread changes to pension laws, then struggled to decide whether to break with their party to support the GOP bill or risk having to defend a vote against "pension reform" in an election year.

Partisan tensions were more pronounced in the Senate. The Health, Education, Labor and Pensions Committee, under Chairman Edward M. Kennedy, D-Mass., approved a sweeping measure (S 1992) in March that would have limited the amount of company stock that workers could acquire in their 401(k) plans. Virtually everyone agreed that the bill, which was championed by labor and consumer groups, would never make it through the full Senate. Finance Committee Chairman Max Baucus, D-Mont., and ranking Republican Charles E. Grassley of Iowa took a different tack, winning committee approval in July for a bill (S 1971) that more closely resembled the House measure.

Majority Leader Tom Daschle, D-S.D., promised to put pension legislation before the Senate in September and urged Baucus and Kennedy to come up with a compromise. The resulting language would have allowed employees to sell stock

BoxScore

Bills:
HR 3762, S 1992, S 1971

Legislative Action:

Senate Health, Education, Labor and Pensions Committee approved S 1992 (S Rept 107-226), 11-10, on March 21.

House passed HR 3762 (H Rept 107-383), 255-163, April 11.

Senate Finance Committee approved S 1971 (S Rept 107-242) by voice vote July 11.

in their company in as little as three years after they received it as matching shares in their 401(k) accounts — a provision that addressed former Enron employees' complaints that the company prohibited them from selling such shares until they reached age 50, leaving them helpless when the stock went through the floor. Daschle abandoned plans to put the bill before the Senate, however, when it became apparent it would be a magnet for floor amendments aimed at reviving a variety of otherwise stalled legislation. That reality, combined with organized labor's criticisms that the compromise did not include employee representation on boards that manage 401(k) plans, scuttled the bill.

Background

A generation ago, most workers who were eligible for company-provided retirement savings — particularly those represented by unions — were covered by defined-benefit plans. Under those plans, the company contributes annually to a pension trust fund, and the employee is guaranteed a set yearly benefit after retiring. A trustee or fiduciary appointed by the employer decides how to invest the funds in the pension plan. Under the 1974 Employee Retirement Income Security Act (PL 93-406), known as ERISA, the fiduciary is required to act solely in the best interests of those covered by the plan. (*1974 Almanac, p. 244*)

Along with a decline in union membership, the number of workers in such plans fell from 30 million in 1983 to 22.3 million in 2000. Many workers instead participated in defined-contribution plans, such as 401(k) retirement savings accounts, first authorized by Congress in 1978 (PL 95-600). (*1978 Almanac, p. 219*)

Under these plans, the employee makes pre-tax contributions to his or her own retirement account. Employers often match a portion of those savings by contributing either cash or company stock. The employee is responsible for deciding how to invest the funds, usually by choosing from a range of alternatives selected by the employer or the fiduciary; company stock is frequently one of the options. The value of the retirement benefit depends on the balance in the account — the sum of all contributions, plus interest, dividends, and capital gains or losses. The Pension Benefit Guaranty Corporation, established by ERISA, insures only defined-benefit plans, not defined-contribution plans. Companies originally were given broad leeway to run their 401(k) programs in the hope of encouraging more of them to participate.

Enron Collapse Spurs Action

The drive to assert more control over defined-contribution plans began in early 2002, after revelations

that thousands of employees at Enron had lost much of their retirement nest eggs because Enron's contributions to its 401(k) plans were almost entirely in the form of company stock, which became worthless. Workers at WorldCom Inc., which was driven toward insolvency in June by nearly $4 billion in accounting wrongdoing, also had invested heavily in company stock.

On Feb. 1, Bush presented a plan that would have required firms to give their employees more flexibility in selling company stock held in their 401(k) plans, while allowing businesses to provide independent investment advice to their workers. It also would have barred executives from selling company stock during so-called blackout periods when employees were blocked from doing so.

The speed with which the administration produced the 401(k) overhaul proposal, just three weeks after assembling a Cabinet-level task force, suggested the political potency of the issue. "Employees who have worked hard and saved all their lives should not have to risk losing everything if their company fails," Bush said in his Jan. 29 State of the Union address. (*Text, p. D-3*)

The next step was up to Congress, where the labor and tax-writing committees had long battled for control of the pension issue and Democrats and Republicans were at odds over solutions. The labor panels had jurisdiction over ERISA, which governs pension plans and contains civil and criminal penalties for breaches of a pension plan manager's fiduciary duties. The House Ways and Means and Senate Finance committees had jurisdiction over the Internal Revenue Code, which contains the qualification requirements pension plans must meet to receive tax benefits; the tax code also contains the penalty excise taxes often used to keep companies in line.

Legislative Action

House Ways and Means Committee

The House Ways and Means Committee went first, approving a bill (HR 3669 — H Rept 107-382, Part 1) on March 14 that would have required companies that provide their own stock as a matching contribution in employee 401(k) accounts to allow the workers to begin selling those shares after they had participated in the plan for three years. The vote was 36-2.

Chairman Bill Thomas, R-Calif., decided to go ahead with the markup despite an agreement worked out by House GOP leaders with the Ways and Means, Education and the Workforce, Energy and Commerce, and Financial Services committees to work toward a common pension bill, to be assembled by the House Rules Committee. The markup was preceded by a series of explosive closed-door meetings between Thomas and John A. Boehner, R-Ohio, chairman of the Education and the Workforce Committee, concerning whose panel would have primary control over the process.

The Ways and Means bill proposed penalty excise taxes for employers who failed to provide quarterly "education notices" to participants in 401(k) programs, including information on the merits of diversifying investments. Excise taxes would also apply if employers failed to provide 30 days' notice before implementing a blackout period in which

workers were barred from trading in their accounts.

Under the bill's diversification requirements, workers immediately would be able to begin selling the company stock that they had bought in their 401(k) plans. They could sell the employer's matching contribution after three years, and other employer contributions after five years. The percentage of company stock that employees could sell would be phased in gradually to prevent a large-scale sell-off. Workers could use a portion of their salary through tax-free payroll deductions to purchase professional investment advice.

In action on amendments, the committee:

• Rejected, 16-22, a proposal by ranking Democrat Charles B. Rangel of New York to impose a 20 percent excise tax on an executive's sale of company stock during any period when 401(k) participants could not trade their company shares.

• Adopted, by voice vote, a substitute amendment by Thomas that would, among other things, exempt employee stock options or stock purchase plans from payroll taxes. The IRS had not imposed such taxes in the past, but the Treasury Department issued proposed rules in November 2001 to begin applying them in January 2003. Therefore the Ways and Means provision, initially projected to have no cost, carried a cost of $23 billion over 10 years.

House Education and the Workforce Committee

The House Education and the Workforce Committee approved its own bill (HR 3762 — H Rept 107-383, Part 1) on March 20 by a mostly partisan vote of 28-19.

The bill placed no limits on the amount of its own stock that a company could provide in its 401(k) plan. Employees would be free to sell those shares after being in the plan for three years or after holding the stock for three years. Quarterly account statements would have to include information on the benefits of diversifying. Employees could receive investment advice from the same financial service providers that managed their 401(k) plans as long as the firm disclosed fees and any potential conflicts of interest. Employers would be responsible for workers' savings during blackout periods.

House Floor Action

The House passed HR 3762 on April 11 by a vote of 255-163. In a deal worked out by Majority Leader Dick Armey, R-Texas, the bill consisted largely of Boehner's bill, plus certain provisions from the Ways and Means version. Despite an intense effort by Democratic leaders, who condemned the bill as favoring employers over employees, 46 Democrats joined 208 Republicans to support it. (*House vote 92, p. H-34*)

The resulting bill contained provisions to:

• **Diversification.** Allow workers to sell company-issued matching stock after holding the shares for three years. Companies would have the option of allowing sale of the matching stock after the employee had been in the plan for three years. In order to prevent a market-disrupting sell-off, employees could sell the employer-contributed stock already in their plans before the bill took effect in 20 percent increments over a five-year period, beginning in 2003.

• **Blackout periods.** Give 30-day advance notice to plan participants before any blackout period of more than three days. Employers could not sell any company stock during a blackout period.

● **Investment advice.** As in the Boehner bill, employees could get advice from financial service providers who managed their 401(k) plans as long as the advisers disclosed fees and potential conflicts of interest. Employees also could use a portion of their salaries through a pre-tax payroll deduction to purchase professional investment advice, as under the Thomas bill.

The House rejected, 187-232, a Democratic substitute offered by George Miller of California, ranking member on the Education and the Workforce Committee. The proposal would have allowed workers to sell company-issued stock in their 401(k) plans after participating in the plan for three years. Employees could sell company stock already in their 401(k) plans one year after enactment. Employers that offered company stock as an investment option in their 401(k) plans would have to provide independent investment advice to employees. Like the bill, the amendment required a 30-day advance notice of a blackout period, but it applied the notice to a blackout of any length, not just to those lasting more than three days. The substitute also required equal representation of employees and employers on 401(k) boards. *(House vote 90, p. H-34)*

The House rejected, 204-212, a motion by Miller to send the bill back to committee to add language that effectively would have made deferred compensation to top executives subject to bankruptcy claims. *(House vote 91, p. H-34)*

Consumer groups and Democrats remained opposed to the idea of allowing workers to get advice from the same firms that managed their 401(k) plans.

They also opposed a provision eliminating a requirement that allowed a pension plan to receive favorable tax treatment only if it met specific standards in balancing the benefits between rank-and-file employees and top executives. They contended the provision would allow a company to set up a pension plan for top executives while neglecting the needs of all other employees.

Senate Health, Education, Labor and Pension

The Senate Health, Education, Labor and Pension Committee approved the Kennedy bill (S 1992 — S Rept 107-226) on an 11-10 party-line vote March 21.

Under the bill, those companies that did not offer traditional defined-benefit pension plans could offer their stock either as a matching 401(k) contribution or as an investment option for employees, but not both. Employees would be allowed to sell company stock in their 401(k) plans after three years of service. Employees could receive investment advice from third parties not connected with the retirement plan. Company executives would be held liable for knowingly taking or concealing actions that harmed the interests of 401(k) plan participants. Kennedy's bill would have allowed employees to serve on company boards that oversee pension plans. And workers could file suit against company executives alleging malfeasance to recover 401(k) losses.

Republicans immediately pronounced the Kennedy bill dead on arrival. They were critical particularly of the proposal to limit employee investments in company stock. Democrats argued that some degree of diversification should be required in a retirement plan that provided no guaranteed pension benefit upon retirement.

The committee rejected, 10-11, an attempt by Michael B. Enzi, R-Wyo., and Tim Hutchinson, R-Ark., to strike the provision, which Hutchinson called a "backdoor cap."

Senate Finance Committee

The Senate Finance Committee approved the Baucus bill (S 1971 — S Rept 107-242) by voice vote July 11, after the chairman agreed not to offer it as an amendment to the accounting regulation bill (S 2673) that was before the Senate. In return, Daschle promised to put pension legislation on the floor in September and urged Baucus and Kennedy to come up with a compromise in the interim.

Under the Finance Committee bill, employees would be allowed to sell company stock offered as matching contributions after three years of service. Companies would be required to notify employees 30 days before a blackout period. They also would have to notify employees promptly after an executive sold company stock. Like the Kennedy bill, the measure allowed a company to hire a financial firm to provide employee investment advice only if it did not administer the company's 401(k) plan.

Baucus incorporated eight amendments, including a proposal by John Kerry, D-Mass., to allow workers 55 years or older immediately to divest company stock out of a 401(k) plan. In an effort to rein in various corporate perks that had come under scrutiny in the recent scandals, the bill proposed that deferred compensation held by executives in offshore trusts be taxed. Company loans to executives would be treated as compensation that could be taxed unless the official put up collateral, arranged for a fixed payment schedule or signed a promissory note. Bonuses and commissions that totaled $1 million or more annually would be subject to withholding taxes at the top tax rate of 38.6 percent, rather than the supplemental wage rate of 27 percent.

Baucus also included an amendment that he sponsored requiring a chief executive officer to sign a company's federal tax return under penalty of perjury. "I think this is ridiculous," said Don Nickles, R-Okla. "There is not a CEO in the country that prepares a tax return." Baucus said CEOs would have to have a "woeful, willful and almost intentional knowledge" of wrongdoing to be convicted.

Senate Floor Action

Congress returned from its August recess with a full agenda, limited time and the political pressures of the impending midterm election. Appropriations bills, homeland security and a potential war with Iraq were the dominant priorities, leaving little time for fractious disputes that could eat up valuable floor time. With that in mind, Daschle sought to broker a compromise on a narrow pension bill, which he planned to bring to the floor the week of Sept. 23. "I'm afraid we just don't have a lot of time" Kennedy said, acknowledging that he would have to give up much of his bill. "We may try to offer some of these things as amendments on the floor." But the threat of controversial amendments from various corners quickly made the project too unwieldy, and Daschle gave up.

The most substantive provision that remained in the compromise bill was a requirement that employees be allowed to sell matching contributions of company stock in their 401(k) plans after holding them for three years.

The bill did not contain controversial provisions to limit the amount of company stock that could be held in 401(k) plans, a restriction that would be similar to an existing 10 percent cap on holdings of company stock in traditional pension fund assets.

Unions, fearful that the bill was being eviscerated, backed a Kennedy floor amendment that would have required employees to be represented on trustee boards that managed 401(k) plans. Unions said employee members would keep co-workers informed about any problems in retirement plans. But such an amendment was almost certain to trigger a GOP filibuster. "We think this is a stalking horse for something unions have always wanted: seats on corporate boards," said Grassley. "That isn't going to happen." Kennedy also was considering language to require companies to limit the ways in which employees could invest, such as stock options, donated shares and stock-purchase plans. Republicans said such investment decisions should be left in the hands of workers, not government.

Meanwhile, since the pension bill would be one of the last vehicles for floor amendments aimed at reviving stalled legislation, Baucus and Grassley were seeking to add a wide range of business tax breaks as well as tax penalties for companies that moved headquarters offshore. In short, the potential baggage was too heavy.

Postscript

Although the pension bills died at the end of the Congress, lawmakers did set new requirements for pension plan blackout periods as part of the corporate accountability law (PL 107-204) enacted July 30. The law required companies to notify workers 30 days before a blackout period of three days or more that restricted employees' ability to sell stock in their 401(k) accounts. Employers were required to tell workers why they could not access their 401(k) accounts, as well as the stop and start dates of the blackout. The law also prohibited senior executives from selling company stock during such blackout periods. ◆

Jobless Benefits End for Millions

Congress agreed in March to extend federal unemployment benefits for 13 weeks, in part because payments were about to run out for workers who had been laid off after the Sept. 11, 2001, terrorist attacks. However, an attempt at the end of the session to continue the extension into 2003 collapsed, leaving an estimated 2.1 million jobless workers without benefits in the new year and punting the problem to the 108th Congress.

Jobless workers typically could apply to states to receive up to 26 weeks of unemployment insurance. Reacting to the economic downturn and the plight of those who lost their jobs after the attacks, Congress began working in late 2001 on a broad economic stimulus bill that included an additional 13 weeks of federally provided unemployment benefits. But partisan disputes over the rest of the package doomed the bill. Lawmakers finally gave up and settled for a scaled-back measure consisting of the unemployment benefits and several business tax breaks. The bill cleared March 8 and was signed into law the following day (HR 3090 — PL 107-147). The unemployment benefits were scheduled to expire Dec. 28. (*Stimulus, p. 16-3*)

Both chambers passed bills during the November lame-duck session aimed at avoiding the cutoff, but differences over the length of the extension and unrelated provisions on Medicare physician payments scuttled the effort.

The House passed a bill (HR 5063) by voice vote Nov. 14 calling for a five-week extension of benefits at an esti-

BoxScore

Bills:
HR 3090 — PL 107-147;
HR 5063; HR 3529

Legislative Action:
President signed HR 3090 on March 9.
House passed HR 5063 by voice vote Nov. 14, after substituting unemployment provisions.
Senate passed HR 3529 by voice vote Nov. 14, amended with unemployment provisions.

mated cost of $900 million. But the bill also contained provisions added by Ways and Means Committee Chairman Bill Thomas, R-Calif., to block a 4.4 percent cut in the Medicare reimbursement rate for physicians that was scheduled to take effect Feb. 1, 2003. (*Medicare reimbursements, p. 10-5*)

Hours later, the Senate passed a bill (HR 3529) by voice vote that provided for another 13-week extension. The Senate bill did not contain the Medicare rider because the top Republican and Democrat on the Senate Finance Committee insisted that doctors receive no additional funds unless other Medicare providers did. The other providers also were scheduled for reimbursement cuts. Thomas refused to budge, and House leaders insisted that anything more than a five-week extension could deplete too much of the $29 billion in the federal unemployment trust funds. They said they would reassess the nation's unemployment situation in January.

Senators, including the unlikely duo of Hillary Rodham Clinton, D-N.Y., and GOP Whip Don Nickles of Oklahoma, sought a compromise and lobbied the Bush administration to get involved. Seven senators wrote to President Bush on Nov. 19 urging him to endorse the Senate bill. "Too many of these Americans have worked hard, played by the rules, and paid into the unemployment trust fund," the senators wrote. "Yet, as the holiday season approaches, they are facing an end to their critically needed benefits."

The letter was signed by Clinton, Majority Leader Tom

Daschle, D-S.D.; Gordon H. Smith, R-Ore.; Maria Cantwell, D-Wash.; Arlen Specter, R-Pa.; Paul S. Sarbanes, D-Md.; and Edward M. Kennedy, D-Mass.

The White House declined to enter the fray. Nickles on Nov. 19 offered a nine-week extension and made a pitch to Thomas, according to a Senate GOP aide. But the House held to its all-or-nothing stance. "The House has already acted," said an aide to Speaker J. Dennis Hastert, R-Ill.

Democrats made the most of the bill's collapse. "I have to say, this is a story right out of Charles Dickens," said Daschle, referring to the prospect of benefits ending three days after Christmas. ◆

Chapter 13

LAW & JUDICIARY

New Era of Oversight for Justice

For the first time in 20 years, Congress cleared legislation reauthorizing the Department of Justice. Lawmakers hoped the bill, signed into law Nov. 2 (HR 2215 — PL 107-273), would be a tool for reasserting congressional oversight of the department, after years of scant attention.

The bill authorized $17.6 billion for the department in fiscal 2002 and $20.5 billion in fiscal 2003.

It required Justice to submit regular reports to Congress, including reports on the operation of the Office of Justice Programs and on the FBI's use of a highly secretive e-mail surveillance program known as Carnivore. It also incorporated provisions from a number of other bills ranging from drug treatment programs to patent and trademark law.

The last full-fledged Justice Department reauthorization had been enacted in 1979 (PL 96-132), with extensions in 1980 and 1981. Since then, the department's operations had been authorized on a year-to-year basis as part of the annual appropriations bill for the Commerce, Justice and State departments, a method that did not allow for review of long-term policy goals by the House and Senate Judiciary committees.

"We cannot continue to neglect our responsibility to exercise responsible oversight of the Justice Department," said Orrin G. Hatch of Utah, ranking Republican on the Senate Judiciary Committee.

The measure came at a time when the department was taking on increased responsibilities as part of the war on terrorism. The House and Senate Judiciary committees were concerned over lapses in internal security at the department, perceived mismanagement at a number of Justice agencies, and disagreements with Justice officials over the reach of Congress' oversight powers. Senate Judiciary Committee Chairman Patrick J. Leahy, D-Vt., and his House counterpart, F. James Sensenbrenner Jr., R-Wis., complained in particular about Justice's failure to respond to their inquiries about the implementation of a sweeping anti-terrorism law enacted in 2001 (PL 107-56), known as the USA Patriot Act.

Highlights

The bill included the following authorizations:

- **Justice Department operations.** $17.6 billion in fiscal 2002 for Justice Department operations and $20.5 billion in fiscal 2003. The bill also required the president to submit a Justice Department authorization request for fiscal 2004 and fiscal 2005 when he submitted his fiscal 2004 budget.
- **Immigration and Naturalization Service.** $4.1 billion — $3.3 billion of it for the border patrol.

BoxScore

Bill:
HR 2215 — PL 107-273
Legislative Action:
House passed HR 2215 (H Rept 107-125) by voice vote July 23, 2001.
Senate passed, amended, by voice vote Dec. 20.
House adopted the conference report (H Rept 107-685), 400-4, on Sept. 26, 2002.
Senate cleared the bill by voice vote Oct. 3
President signed Nov. 2

- **Prisons.** $4.6 billion for the federal prison system.
- **FBI.** $4.3 billion for the detection, investigation and prosecution of federal crimes. The bill included a number of requirements aimed at improving security at the agency. This was in part a response to a series of blunders, including the discovery in 2001 that top special agent Robert Hanssen had been spying for Russia for more than a decade. That news followed revelations that hundreds of documents the FBI had agreed to give to attorneys for Oklahoma City bomber Timothy J. McVeigh never had been turned over. More recently, lawmakers were angered by reports of evidence and opportunities missed in the months before the Sept. 11, 2001, terrorist attacks.
- **Inspector general.** $66 million for the Office of the Inspector General, with specific authority to investigate all allegations of criminal or administrative misconduct by Justice Department employees, including FBI personnel. This codified a rule issued by Attorney General John Ashcroft in July 2001 expanding the inspector general's jurisdiction over the FBI. The bill authorized $2 million to hire 25 full-time employees to conduct an increased number of audits, inspections and investigations of alleged misconduct by FBI employees. And it required a report to Congress on whether an inspector general should be established for the FBI.
- **U.S. attorneys.** $1.6 billion for the 94 U.S. attorneys and their offices and the Executive Office of U.S. Attorneys. At least $10 million was to be used to augment the investigation and prosecution of intellectual property crimes. Also, 200 assistant U.S. attorneys from the six litigating divisions were to be transferred from the main FBI headquarters in Washington, D.C., to various field offices around the country.
- **Other bills.** Separate bills folded into the conference report included measures on juvenile justice, drug abuse, trademark law, federal judgeships and the Violence Against Women Act.

Background

The House first passed the bill (HR 2215) by voice vote July 23, 2001. The Senate amended the measure and passed it by voice vote Dec. 20.

Both versions sought to improve congressional oversight of the department by, among other things, requiring it to submit regular reports to Congress. Both included provisions to require the department's inspector general to give Congress an oversight plan for the FBI, and provided for creation of a Violence Against Women Office in the department.

The main difference was the addition by the Senate of

several other bills — including measures on juvenile justice, drug treatment programs and the establishment of additional federal judgeships — that threatened to snag the bill.

For years, controversial riders had doomed efforts to reauthorize the Justice Department. In 1998, for example, a similar reauthorization easily won House passage, but the Senate Judiciary Committee did not act on it until September, and disputes over wiretapping provisions and other language in the measure stalled action in that body. In other years, fights over gun control provisions slowed the bill's progress in the Senate.

Conference/Final Action

With minor differences on the core Justice Department provisions easily resolved, conference negotiations centered on the Senate add-ons. In the end, Senate Democrats largely prevailed. The conference report (H Rept 107-685) was filed Sept. 25, and the House adopted it by a vote of 400-4 the next day. Final Senate action was held up briefly by Republicans who were angry over Leahy's handling of President Bush's judicial nominations or upset over unrelated bills being folded into the conference report. The Senate cleared the bill by voice vote Oct. 3, but only after the leadership won a 93-5 vote to invoke cloture, thus limiting the debate. (*House vote 422, p. H-132; Senate vote 229, p. S-47; judges, p. 13-12*)

Some of the provisions that negotiators attached to the bill built on the core mission of reasserting Congress' power to oversee the department. Others, such as language on patents and trademarks, had no easy connection to the original measure. The following were among the main conference decisions:

● **Judgeships.** Like the Senate bill, the final version authorized eight new permanent district court judgeships — five in California, two in Texas and one in North Carolina. In addition, four temporary judgeships were made permanent — two in Illinois and one each in New York and Virginia. The bill also created seven new temporary judgeships — one each in Alabama, Arizona, California, Florida, New Mexico, North Carolina and Texas — and extended the temporary judgeship in Ohio for five years. The House-passed bill did not provide for any new federal judgeships. Conferees debated how many more judges were needed and where to put them. Some questioned whether the Justice Department bill was the proper place for the provisions.

● **Drug abuse.** The Senate also won inclusion of a number of provisions from a bill (S 304), approved by the Senate Judiciary Committee in 2001, authorizing grants to states for jail-based substance abuse programs. The House bill had no comparable provisions. The controversy here was over jurisdiction. House Energy and Commerce Committee Chairman Billy Tauzin, R-La., and ranking Democrat, John D. Dingell of Michigan, objected to the language and said the issue should be handled as part of their committee's work in 2004 to reauthorize the Substance Abuse and Mental Health Services Administration.

● **Juvenile justice.** The agreement incorporated, with some modifications, provisions of two bills passed by the House in 2001. The first (HR 863) authorized juvenile crime prevention grants to the states for three years. The second (HR 1900) reauthorized the Juvenile Justice and Delinquency Prevention Act, consolidating under one umbrella five juvenile justice programs including boot camps, mentoring services and child

abuse treatment services. (*2001 Almanac, p. 14-17*)

● **Trademark and patents.** The conference agreement incorporated provisions from a bill (HR 741) modifying U.S. trademark laws to allow companies to take advantage of the international trademark treaty known as the Madrid Protocol. The bill had passed in the House in 2001 but was stuck in the Senate. Conferees also attached a bill (S 1754) reauthorizing the Patent and Trademark Office from fiscal 2003 through 2008, authorizing the office to receive appropriations in amounts equal to the fees it collected each year, and directing the office to develop a user-friendly electronic system for filing and processing patent and trademark applications. Also included was language from a bill (S 487 — S Rept 107-31) amending the 1976 Copyright Act (PL 94-553) to allow teachers to send digitized books, music and movies over the Internet without first getting permission. The Senate had passed the bill in 2001; the House Judiciary Committee approved a revised version Sept. 25.

● **FBI.** Many of the provisions aimed at boosting security and oversight at the bureau and improving its computer systems were drawn from an FBI overhaul bill (S 1974 — S Rept 107-148) approved April 25 by the Senate Judiciary Committee. It included statutory authority for an FBI police force to protect buildings and personnel. The FBI also was directed to submit a plan to Congress for implementing the Webster Commission's recommendations on FBI internal security functions in the wake of the Hanssen espionage case.

Other provisions required the attorney general and FBI director to submit a report to Congress on the use of the Carnivore system; authorized "danger pay" for FBI agents in hazardous duty locations outside the United States; and required the FBI director to report to Congress on the bureau's information management and technology programs, including recommendations for any legislation needed to enhance their effectiveness. The bill authorized an additional $2 million in fiscal 2003 for the FBI to hire 14 full-time employees for the bureau's Office of Professional Responsibility.

● **Violence Against Women Act.** Like both the House and Senate versions, the final bill established a Violence Against Women Office, with a director appointed by the president and confirmed by the Senate. The director was authorized to award all grants and contracts under the office and was responsible for generally carrying out the responsibilities of the Violence Against Women Act (PL 106-386).

In other provisions, the new law:

● **Boys and Girls Clubs.** Authorized grants to the Boys and Girls Clubs of America to help establish 1,200 additional clubs with the goal of having 4,000 Boys and Girls Clubs in operation by 2007.

● **Disaster litigation.** Incorporated the text of a bill (HR 860) passed by the House in 2001 to streamline and consolidate the process by which multidistrict litigation governing disasters was adjudicated.

● **Judicial Improvements Act.** Included provisions from a bill (HR 3892), which the House passed by voice vote July 22, to reorganize and clarify existing mechanisms for filing complaints against federal judges. The changes were intended to provide more guidance to circuit chief judges when evaluating complaints, while providing individuals with more information on the status of their cases and making the process more user-friendly. ◆

House Targets Crimes Against Kids

The House passed an omnibus bill to combat crimes against children, but many of the provisions were too sweeping for members of the Senate, and that chamber did not consider it. The package (HR 5422), assembled by Judiciary Committee Chairman F. James Sensenbrenner Jr., R-Wis., was built around a popular bill aimed at speeding up the development of a federal alert system for abducted children, known as the AMBER Plan.

Many of the other pieces had already passed in the House as separate bills but were stalled in the Senate. They included proposals for lifetime supervision of sex offenders (HR 4679), new prohibitions on sex tourism (HR 4477), a two-strikes-and-you're-out policy for sex offenses against children (HR 2146), wiretapping in child sex crime investigations (HR 1877), and stiffer penalties for sex crimes against children.

The House Judiciary Committee approved the omnibus bill by voice vote Oct. 2 (H Rept 107-723, Part 1). The House passed it Oct. 8 by an overwhelming vote of 390-24. (*House vote 446, p. H-140*)

Highlights

The following are highlights of the bills and provisions that made up the House package:

AMBER Plan

The centerpiece of the package was a bill to provide national coordination and assistance to states and localities that participated in the AMBER Plan, a partnership between law enforcement agencies and broadcasters that was credited with having saved 30 abducted children. Most recently, the AMBER Plan had been credited with saving the lives of two California teenagers kidnapped from their cars in August.

The system — named after Amber Hagerman, a 9-year-old girl abducted and killed in Arlington, Texas, in 1996 — used the Emergency Alert System, similar to what was used to broadcast severe weather emergencies, to issue an alert when a child was abducted, including descriptions of the abducted child, the suspected abductor and any vehicle involved. Twenty-four states had developed statewide plans, with many states linking together through regional systems. But the system was still a patchwork, with large areas not covered; communication across state and local systems often was not possible.

The Senate had passed its own version of the bill — S 2896 sponsored by Kay Bailey Hutchison, R-Texas — by voice vote Sept. 10. President Bush supported the bill and urged House GOP leaders to finish it in time for an Oct. 1 conference on missing, exploited and runaway children.

At that conference, Bush announced that he was direct-

BoxScore

Bill:
HR 5422
Legislative Action:
House passed HR 5422 (H Rept 107-723, Part 1), 390-24, on Oct. 8.

ing the attorney general to establish an AMBER alert coordinator in the Justice Department to serve as a nationwide point of contact for state and local officials and to establish national standards for the plans.

The following are the bill's main provisions:

● **National coordinator.** A national coordinator would be established within the Justice Department to work with state and local officials to develop the AMBER alert network. The coordinator would:

● Work to eliminate gaps in the network, including gaps in areas of interstate travel; help states to develop more AMBER plans; and support efforts to ensure regional coordination.

● Notify and consult with the FBI, the Transportation Department and the Federal Communications Commission (FCC) about each alert issued for an abducted child through the AMBER network.

● Work with the Transportation Department, the FCC, and state and local broadcasters and law enforcement agencies to establish voluntary minimum standards for broadcasting alerts throughout the AMBER network.

● **Highway grant program.** The bill would establish a matching grant program within the Transportation Department and authorize $20 million in fiscal 2003. The program would help states develop electronic message boards and other forms of communication along highways to spread the word about abducted children.

● **Development grants.** A matching grant program would be created within the Justice Department, authorized at $5 million in fiscal 2003, to help states support the AMBER alert network, including education and training, law enforcement programs and equipment.

● **National Center for Missing and Exploited Children.** The bill would increase a grant to the center from $10 million to $20 million per year in fiscal 2003 and 2004.

Lifetime Consequences for Sex Offenders

The package included a bill, passed by the House in June, that would permit judges to order lifetime supervision of sex offenders who had completed their sentences. It would apply to those convicted of sexual abuse, sexual exploitation and other abuse of of children, transportation for illegal sexual activity, and sex trafficking of children by force, fraud or coercion. It would also apply to those convicted of coercion and enticement, the use of interstate facilities to transmit information about a minor, and kidnapping of a minor under the age of 18. Under existing law, federal judges could order up to five years of post-incarceration supervision of sex offenders.

The House originally passed the bill (HR 4679 — H Rept 107-527), 409-3, under suspension of the rules June 25. (*House vote 255, p. H-84*)

Stiffer Penalties for Sex Crimes Against Children

The omnibus bill also included provisions to increase penalties for sex crimes against children. The bill would make murder involving child abuse, child assault or torture a first degree murder charge. It included the following increases in maximum penalties:

- From 20 to 30 years for sexual exploitation of a child. For anyone with a prior sex offense conviction, the maximum penalty would increase from 30 to 50 years.
- From 15 to 20 years, for shipping, receiving or distributing by any means, including by computer, child pornography or any visual depictions of minors engaged in sexually explicit conduct. For those with a prior sex offense conviction, the maximum sentence would increase from 30 to 40 years. The maximum penalty for possession of such material would increase from five to 10 years, and from 10 to 20 years for those with a prior sexual offense conviction.
- From 15 to 30 years for transporting a minor for prostitution and for traveling in interstate or foreign commerce to have sex with minors.
- From 20 to 40 years for forced sex trafficking of minors.

The bill also would direct the U.S. Sentencing Commission to increase the minimum sentencing for kidnapping, originally ranging from 51 months to 63 months, to 121 months to 151 months. It would repeal a provision in the existing sentencing guidelines that decreased the minimum sentencing levels if the victim was released within 24 hours. The bill also increased the sentencing range for kidnappers who sexually exploited the victim, and provided for a mandatory minimum sentence of 20 years for the kidnapping of a person under the age of 18.

Sex Tourism Prohibition

The package included provisions of a bill passed by the House in June to make it easier to prosecute those who travel to another country to have sex with a minor, regardless of whether the person originally intended to do so.

The bill would:

- Make it a crime, punishable by up to 15 years in prison, to travel into the United States for the purpose of engaging in any illicit sexual conduct.
- Make it a crime for a U.S. citizen or permanent resident traveling abroad to engage or attempt to engage in illicit sexual conduct, even if the individual did not travel with the intent of engaging in these acts. As a result, prosecutors would no longer have to prove intent for those traveling in foreign countries. Violation would be punishable by fines and up to 15 years in prison.
- Make it an offense, punishable by up to 15 years in prison, to arrange, induce, procure or facilitate the travel of a person knowing that the individual was traveling in interstate or foreign commerce for the purpose of engaging in illicit sexual conduct.
- Define an illicit sexual act as a sexual act that would be illegal under certain statutes if it occurred in the special maritime and territorial jurisdiction of the United States, or any commercial sex act with a person under the age of 18.
- Specify that only those who knew or should have known that they were engaging in sexual activity with a minor under the age of 18 could be charged. Defendants would have to prove by a "preponderance of the evidence" that they reasonably believed the person was at least 18 years old.
- Make it an offense, punishable by up to 15 years in prison, to attempt or conspire to violate these provisions.

The House had passed the bill (HR 4477 — H Rept 107-525) by a vote of 418-8 on June 26 under suspension of the rules. (*House vote 259, p. H-84*)

Two Strikes and You're Out

The bill provided for a mandatory sentence of life in prison for anyone convicted a second time of a sexual offense against a child. Specifically, it called for a life sentence, unless the death penalty was imposed, against an individual convicted of a federal sex offense against a child under the age of 17 if the perpetrator had been convicted of a previous federal or state sexual offense against a child. If the prior offense was under state law, it would have to have been an offense under federal law had the crime taken place in a federal jurisdiction.

The measure would apply to second convictions for seven specific crimes — aggravated sexual abuse, sexual abuse, sexual abuse of a minor or ward, abusive sexual contact, sexual abuse resulting in death, the selling or buying of children, and transporting a minor in interstate or foreign commerce for the purposes of prostitution or for illegal sexual purposes under a state law.

The House had passed these provisions as a separate bill (HR 2146 — H Rept 107-373) by a vote of 382-34 on March 14. (*House vote 64, p. H-26*)

Wiretapping in Child Sex Crimes

The bill would authorize the use of wiretaps and other electronic surveillance in investigating crimes of child pornography, the buying and selling of children for sexual exploitation, inducing or coercing someone to cross state lines to engage in illegal sexual activities and transporting minors for illegal sexual activity.

The House had passed these provisions (HR 1877 — H Rept 107-468), 396-11, under suspension of the rules May 21. (*House vote 175, p. H-60*)

Other Provisions

The bill also contained provisions to:

- Abolish the statute of limitations for the prosecution of child abduction and felony sex offenses against minors, meaning a perpetrator could be prosecuted for the crime regardless of how much time had passed since it occurred. The provision would not apply to military cases.
- Deny pre-trial release for anyone charged with rape or kidnapping of a minor.
- Require federal, state and local law enforcement agencies to report each case of a missing person under the age of 21, up from age 18 under existing law, to the National Crime Information Center of the Department of Justice.
- Require the Justice Department to report to Congress on the number of times since 1993 that the department had inspected the records of producers of pornographic material to ensure that minors were not being used in such productions, including the number of prosecutions resulting from the inspection. ◆

Cracking Down on Border Security

Congress cleared legislation May 8 designed to tighten U.S. border security and prevent terrorists from entering the country, while also making it harder for aliens to overstay their visas without detection. Lawmakers took pains to stress that their goal was to catch terrorists, not to stem the flow of legal immigrants from Mexico and elsewhere. But provisions that would have made it easier for thousands of illegal immigrants to apply for legal residency were dropped from the bill and died at the end of the session. President Bush signed the bill into law May 14 (HR 3525 — PL 107-173).

The legislation, written after the Sept. 11, 2001, terrorist attacks, included an increase in numbers and salaries for U.S. border inspectors, tighter monitoring of foreign students in the United States and the use of tamper-resistant travel documents with biometric identifiers such as a fingerprint.

The House passed the bill easily in December 2001, but a companion bill stalled in the Senate. In March, the House attached the provisions to a separate bill (HR 1885) that would have extended a visa program known as 245(i). The program allowed immigrants whose visas had expired to remain in the United States while waiting to receive their green card. When it became clear that combining the two bills was only complicating efforts to clear the border security provisions, the Senate turned back to the House's stand-alone measure. With a few changes, that bill cleared. (*Visa program, 2001 Almanac, p. 14-13*)

Highlights

The new border security law contained provisions to:
● Increase the number of Immigration and Naturalization Service (INS) inspectors and Customs Service agents at U.S. ports of entry.
● Establish a government-wide data-sharing system, known as Chimera, to identify potential terrorists who apply for U.S. visas or try to enter the United States.
● Require the use of machine-readable visas and passports including biometric identifiers to allow U.S. officials to better monitor those entering and exiting the country.
● Bar most citizens of countries considered to be state sponsors of terrorism from receiving temporary U.S. visas.
● Establish an electronic system to track foreign students in the United States.
● Require all vessels entering or leaving the United States to supply manifests of their passengers and crew, with a requirement that all manifests be in an electronic format by 2003. Failure to comply could result in a $1,000 fine.

BoxScore

Bill:
HR 3525 — PL 107-173
Legislative Action:
Senate passed HR 3525, amended, 97-0, on April 18.
House cleared the bill, 411-0, on May 8.
President signed May 14.

Background

The border security bill was a response to the many weaknesses in the immigration system revealed by the Sept. 11 terrorist attacks. One of the suspected hijackers who died in the attacks, for example, had come into the United States as a student but never attended classes, a fact the school had not reported to the government.

The House passed the border security measure by voice vote Dec. 19, and it was expected to fly through the Senate before adjournment. But Robert C. Byrd, D-W.Va., put a hold on the measure, saying it was so sweeping and would authorize so much new spending that members should have time to debate it and offer amendments. (*2001 Almanac, p. 14-14*)

Legislative Action

In an effort to prod Senate action on border security, the House agreed 275-137 on March 12 to attach the provisions to the visa extension bill and send the package to the Senate. (*House vote 53, p. H-24*)

That only seemed to complicate efforts. Byrd warned that he would continue to object to leadership attempts to bring up the bill under a unanimous consent agreement that allowed no amendments or debate. "This senator from West Virginia will not be pressured into passing legislation," he said on the floor March 18. Byrd also objected to the immigration provisions as rewarding lawbreakers. "If waiving tougher penalties for illegal aliens is not a form of amnesty, then I don't know what is," he said.

However, pressure was building in the Senate to break the logjam. "The longer we wait to send this bill to the president . . . the longer it will take for our nation's border and visa procedures to be made more secure," sponsors warned in a letter to Majority Leader Tom Daschle, D-S.D.

Bowing to Byrd, Senate leaders brought the stand-alone border security bill (HR 3525) to the floor April 18. Byrd won several changes, including a delay in the deadlines for some of the security requirements and more stringent penalties on schools that failed to adequately track their foreign students. The Senate then passed the amended bill, 97-0. (*Senate vote 75, p. S-18*)

After securing Senate agreement to drop one provision, the House accepted the Senate changes May 8, clearing the bill, 411-0. The disputed provision would have permitted the attorney general to circumvent the normal bidding process in developing the Chimera terrorist database. The Senate adopted a resolution May 8 striking the language. (*House vote 131, p. H-48*) ◆

Border Security Provisions

Following are major provisions of the border security law (PL 107-173):

Border Controls

● **Additional inspectors.** The Immigration and Naturalization Service (INS) was authorized to hire an additional 200 inspectors and 200 investigative personnel each year for five years, beginning in fiscal 2002.

● **Computer upgrades.** The law authorized $150 million for technology upgrades at INS inspection facilities. The money was for upgrading old computer systems and buying electronic scanners to check travel documents, such as visas and passports.

● **Salary increases.** Higher wages were authorized for INS border patrol agents and inspection assistants.

● **Training.** INS officers were required to get ongoing training.

Visa System

● **Temporary visas.** The bill prohibited the issuance of temporary visas for business or travel to citizens of countries judged to be state sponsors of terrorism, unless it was determined that the individual was not a security risk. Seven nations — Iran, Iraq, Syria, Libya, Cuba, North Korea and Sudan — were classified as state sponsors of terrorism.

● **Student visas.** Schools that admitted foreign students were required to track the students' participation and notify the government of any who did not show up for classes. Schools that failed to comply with the reporting requirements would lose the right to accept foreign students. The bill required that universities and other institutions certified to receive foreign students be reviewed every two years by the Education secretary, the secretary of State and the INS commissioner.

● **Chimera terrorist database.** The bill mandated the establishment of a government-wide, electronic data-sharing system on persons with terrorist ties that could be used by federal officials to conduct more thorough background checks of people trying to enter the United States. The system, known as Chimera, was to include the names of suspected terrorists and other information from a wide variety of agencies, including the FBI. The president was given responsibility for forming a nine-member federal commission to monitor the database and report annually to Congress.

U.S. consular offices and embassies were directed to form committees to watch for suspected terrorists and make sure their names were entered into the Chimera system.

Travel Documents and Manifests

● **Stolen passports.** Countries that participated in the Visa Waiver Program were required to inform U.S. officials about thefts of blank passports. The waiver program allowed citizens from a select group of mostly industrialized countries to enter the United States for short visits for business or pleasure without having to get a visa. The attorney general or the secretary of State could bar a country from the program for failing to report passport thefts.

● **High-tech visas.** Beginning Oct. 26, 2003, the State Department was required to issue only machine-readable, tamper-resistant visas that included biometric identifiers, such as fingerprints. Biometric scanners to read these passports had to be installed at all U.S. ports of entry by that date.

All nations participating in the Visa Waiver Program had to issue passports with the same high-tech features by that date.

● **Passenger manifests.** All commercial airlines and vessels entering or leaving the United States were required to supply immigration officials with manifests listing all passengers and crew. By 2003, the manifests had to be in an electronic format. Airplanes or ships that failed to comply with the rule would be fined $1,000. ◆

INS Abolished, Duties Divided

The Immigration and Naturalization Service (INS), long a target of congressional criticism, was abolished under the law (PL 107-296) that created the new Department of Homeland Security. It was replaced with two, separate bureaus in the new department — one to handle immigration services, the other to protect the borders and keep out illegal immigrants. (*Homeland Security, p. 7-3*)

Congress had sought for decades to reinvent the troubled agency, which was charged with the sometimes conflicting missions of tracking down and deporting those in the United States illegally, while assisting legal immigrants to work their way through the cumbersome process to become citizens. Complaints of mismanagement, ineffective border control and a growing backlog of immigrant applications and petitions were common.

In the early 1990s, Congress established the U.S. Commission on Immigration Reform to review and evaluate the immigration system. In 1997, the commission, chaired by former Rep. Barbara Jordan, D-Texas (1973-79), recommended that the federal immigration system be fundamentally restructured, including the dismantling of the INS. The commission found that the INS suffered from conflicting priorities and mission overload, and that its service and enforcement missions were incompatible.

While the Clinton administration agreed with the commission's findings on INS management problems, it rejected the recommendation to abolish the agency. Instead, it proposed to restructure the INS by separating immigration and enforcement functions. However, the plan was never aggressively pursued.

Bills introduced in the 105th and 106th Congresses offered a variety of approaches for restructuring the INS, including dismantling the agency, but none went beyond the subcommittee level.

Congress substantially increased the INS' budget — from $1.4 billion in fiscal 1992 to $5.6 billion in fiscal 2002 — in

hopes of improving the agency's performance. However, the problems continued, particularly in processing immigration applications, along with the agency's inability to stem the flow of undocumented workers and to track workers, students and visitors once they arrived in the country.

House Judiciary Committee Chairman F. James Sensenbrenner Jr., R-Wis., made overhauling the agency a priority in the 107th Congress, and he was joined by Attorney General John Ashcroft, who in 2001 announced an administration plan to restructure the agency. The House passed a bill to split the INS (HR 3231 — H Rept 107-413) by a vote of 405-9 on April 25. (*House vote 116, p. H-42*)

The Senate did not act on the separate INS restructuring bill because the Bush administration decided to include immigration functions in the new Homeland Security Department just as that chamber was preparing to enter the INS debate.

Both the House bill and the administration proposal called for abolishing the INS and dividing it into separate bureaus to guard the borders and to handle immigration services. What they did not agree on was how the top of the new agency would be structured. The administration wanted a strong central figure to oversee immigration; Sensenbrenner wanted to give more authority to those in charge of the two bureaus.

Under the homeland security bill, it appeared there would be no strong, central immigration figure except the attorney general. The INS' immigration services were turned over to the Bureau of Citizenship and Immigration Services, which reported to the deputy secretary of Homeland Security. The bureau was directed to develop pilot programs to eliminate the backlog of immigrant-related paperwork such as green cards.

INS enforcement operations — including the Border Patrol, inspections, investigations, intelligence, and detention and removal — were absorbed by the Bureau of Border Security in the Border and Transportation Division. ◆

Bill to Limit Class Action Suits Dies

The House in March passed a bill to limit class action suits, but the measure went no further, halted by Democratic opposition in the Senate and reluctance by many members to be seen as protecting businesses in the midst of a series of corporate scandals. The bill (HR 2341) would have given jurisdiction over most class action lawsuits to federal district courts and established a "bill of rights" for plaintiffs in federal class action lawsuits. It was sponsored by Republican Robert W. Goodlatte and Democrat Rick Boucher, both of Virginia.

Even before House passage, Senate Judiciary Committee Chairman Patrick J. Leahy, D-Vt., made clear that the issue was not on his to-do list for the rest of the 107th Congress. Democrats, who controlled the Senate, generally favored leaving the civil litigation system unchanged, arguing that it offered an appropriate means for aggrieved consumers to band together to fight well-financed companies. Their view had been bolstered by the Enron Corp.'s December 2001 bankruptcy filing, which prompted class action lawsuits filed by thousands of employees who lost their life savings because they were invested in what became worthless company stock.

Republicans, who controlled the House, had long sought to protect businesses from the cost of fighting class action suits in state courts. Businesses said existing law allowed attorneys in class action suits to shop nationwide for the venue they determined would be most sympathetic to their case, and that it inappropriately allowed state courts to make decisions that could affect hundreds or thousands of people across the country.

The House passed a similar bill in the 106th Congress, but it died in the Senate in the face of a filibuster threat. (*2000 Almanac, p. 15-39*)

BoxScore

Bill:
HR 2341

Legislative Action:
House passed HR 2341
(H Rept 107-370), 233-190,
March 13.

Background

Class action suits are filed by large groups of people who allege that similar harm was caused them by a company or industry for the same reason. They allow people who are financially unable to sue on their own to pool their resources and create an "affected class." Attorneys for such plaintiffs preferred being heard in state courts because the rules there often were considered friendlier to plaintiffs, and jury awards tended to be larger.

Under existing law, the only class action cases heard in federal court were those in which every plaintiff stood to receive at least $75,000 and in which the defendant and the lead plaintiff lived in different states.

The bill was supported by the National Association of Manufacturers, National Federation of Independent Business, U.S. Chamber of Commerce, Independent Insurance Agents of America and National Association of Wholesaler Distributors. Opponents included the Association of Trial Lawyers of America, Consumers Union, Consumer Federation of America, U.S. Public Interest Research Group, Public Citizen and the National Conference of State Legislatures.

Highlights

Under the main provisions of the House-passed bill:
• Class action cases could be heard in federal court if the expected total jury award was at least $2 million, there were at least 100 members in the affected class and any of them lived in a state or country different from that of the defendant.
• This would not apply if a substantial majority of the

plaintiffs and defendants were from one state, the claims primarily involved the laws of the state where the action was originally filed, or the primary defendants were state governments or state officials.

• All plaintiffs in a class action would have to be given easy-to-understand settlement explanations. Supporters said that in some instances the complex legal jargon used to inform claimants that they had "won" a case masked the fact that they would not receive actual cash awards.

Legislative Action

House Committee Action

The Judiciary Committee approved the bill (H Rept 107-370) 16-10 on March 7 after Republicans easily fended off several Democratic amendments. The committee:

• Rejected, 9-16, a proposal by Jerrold Nadler, D-N.Y., to require that more class action settlements be made public. "It's important for the public to be aware of health and safety dangers so they can take steps to preserve their lives," Nadler argued.

• Defeated, 11-17, an amendment by Adam B. Schiff, D-Calif., to allow suits filed by private citizens and authorized by state attorneys general "on behalf of the public interest" to be heard in state courts.

• Rejected, 9-15, an amendment by Melvin Watt, D-N.C., specifically designed to scuttle the bill.

House Floor Action

With the last-minute endorsement of the Bush administration, the bill won a solid 233-190 majority in the House on March 13. The vote went largely along party lines; only 17 Democrats voted for the bill, and five Republicans voted against it. (House vote 62, p. H-26)

Again, a series of Democratic amendments were easily defeated. The House:

• Rejected, 191-234, a proposal by Barney Frank, D-Mass., to specify that suits not certified as class actions subject to a federal court's jurisdiction could then be tried in state court. The case would not later be subject to removal to federal court unless it met the existing party diversity standards. (House vote 60, p. H-26)

• Rejected, 202-223, a proposal by John Conyers Jr., D-Mich., to prevent a company from moving a case from state to federal court by incorporating a new company abroad and acquiring the original company. (House vote 58, p. H-24)

• Rejected, 174-251, an attempt by Maxine Waters, D-Calif., to require that anyone who withheld or shredded documents that were required to be handed over through a discovery motion in a class action lawsuit be found to have admitted to the facts of that motion. (House vote 56, p. H-24)

• Rejected, 194-231, an attempt by Zoe Lofgren, D-Calif., to strike a provision in the bill that would exclude civil suits brought on behalf of the general public by local prosecutors from being deemed class actions. (House vote 57, p. H-24)

• Rejected, 177-248, a proposal by Sheila Jackson-Lee, D-Texas, to block a party in a class action suit from moving the case's venue to federal court if that party destroyed, falsified or altered material evidence. (House vote 59, p. H-26)

• Rejected, 191-235, a motion to send the bill back to the House Judiciary Committee with instructions to add language blocking defendants who knowingly committed a terrorist act from moving a class action suit to federal court. (House vote 61, p. H-26) ◆

Court Ruling Holds On 'Virtual' Child Porn

Both chambers passed bills to ban "virtual" child pornography — the House on June 25, the Senate on Nov. 14 — but they were not able to agree on a final version before the 107th Congress adjourned.

The legislation was a response to a Supreme Court ruling in April that the original law addressing the issue (PL 104-208) was overly broad and thus unconstitutional. That 1996 law prohibited any image that "is, or appears to be, of a minor engaging in sexually explicit conduct." The ban included images that were simulated by computer technology, or that used adults who looked like children. The high court found in *Ashcroft v. The Free Speech Coalition* that extending the reach of child pornography laws to computer-generated and other images involving no real children would also prohibit visual depictions, such as films, art or medical manuals, that had redeeming social value. (1996 Almanac, p. 5-38)

The House bill (HR 4623 — H Rept 107-526), which passed 413-8 on June 25, proposed to bar any computer-generated image that was "nearly indistinguishable . . . from that of a minor engaging in sexually explicit conduct." The bill's sponsor, Lamar Smith, R-Texas, and other supporters said they believed the new version would pass constitutional muster because it was more narrowly drawn than the law it would replace. They also argued that it would prevent child pornographers from using a familiar legal argument — that there is no proof the images they distribute show real children. (House vote 256, p. H-84)

Critics, however, said the latest legislation was no more constitutional than the 1996 law. Robert C. Scott, D-Va., said it tried to do "exactly what the Supreme Court said you cannot do."

The Senate bill (S 2520), passed by voice vote Nov. 14, began as an effort by Judiciary Committee ranking Republican Orrin G. Hatch of Utah and panel Chairman Patrick J. Leahy, D-Vt., to write a law more likely to withstand constitutional scrutiny. But before the Judiciary Committee approved the bill by voice vote Nov. 14, it adopted two amendments by Hatch that brought the measure closer to its House counterpart. Critics said the resulting bill was constitutionally weaker and indicated that Congress was increasingly seeking to test the bounds of the Constitution in this area.

As introduced, the Hatch-Leahy bill would have made it a crime to pander, or solicit, material that "conveys the impression that the material is, or contains, an obscene visual depiction of a minor engaging in sexually explicit conduct." One of the amendments expanded the definition of a minor to include "a computer or computer-generated image that is virtually indistinguishable from an actual minor." The other amendment expanded the pandering portion of the bill to

include "purported material" that conveys the impression that a minor is engaging in obscene sexual behavior.

The high court consistently had maintained that pornography was protected speech unless it was ruled to be obscene — but it also had held that pornography involving minors could be banned, regardless of whether it was obscene, because of the compelling interest in protecting children.

Frederick Schauer, a conservative Harvard University constitutional law professor who served on the Meese Commission on pornography, said the change in the Senate pandering language "would push well over the constitutional edge a provision that is now right up against that edge, but probably barely on the constitutional side of it." ◆

Congress Alters Royalty, Trademark Rules

Congress cleared several pieces of trademark legislation, including a bill to simplify international trademark registration for U.S. business firms, as well as a bill limiting the royalties paid by small Internet music broadcasters. All but the Webcaster bill were enacted Nov. 2 as part of a law (PL 107-273) reauthorizing the Justice Department. *(Justice, p. 13-3)*

● **Madrid Protocol.** The Justice Department bill incorporated the provisions of a separate measure (HR 741), the Madrid Protocol Implementation Act, which modified U.S. trademark laws to allow companies to take advantage of the international trademark treaty known as the Madrid Protocol. The treaty, which had been in effect since 1996, provided a centralized, one-stop international system that enabled trademark owners to apply to register their trademarks in up to 70 member countries simultaneously.

The United States had not previously participated because the Senate had never ratified the treaty. On Oct. 17, the Senate ratified the Madrid Protocol by voice vote, allowing the implementing provisions to take effect.

The House had passed HR 741 (H Rept 107-19) in March 2001; the Senate Judiciary Committee had marked up its own version of the bill (S 407 — S Rept 107-46) in July 2001.

● **Internet royalties.** The Internet royalties bill codified a two-year agreement between the recording industry and small Webcasters on the royalty rates that the Webcasters would pay to performers and record companies. The deal applied only to Webcasters with gross revenues of $500,000 or less in 2003, and $1.25 million or less in 2004. The Senate passed the bill Nov. 14 and the House cleared it Nov. 15, both on voice votes. The measure was signed into law Dec. 4 (HR 5469 — PL 107-321).

Small Webcasters had argued that a new royalty schedule proposed in June by the Library of Congress — which was responsible for overseeing copyright matters such as the payment rates for the use of musical performances — would have put them out of business.

The House initially passed the bill by voice vote on Oct. 7. However, Jesse Helms, R-N.C., held up action in the Senate after receiving complaints from non-commercial and religious radio webcasters that they had not been included.

The final version delayed the imposition of any new royalties for six months. It allowed Webcasters to pay royalties based on their expenses or revenue — which they said would mean less out-of-pocket expenses for them. And it provided a potentially lower-cost option for tax-exempt, non-commercial Webcasters.

● **Patent and Trademark Office.** The Justice Department bill included language reauthorizing the Patent and Trademark Office for five years, through fiscal 2008, in amounts equal to the fees taken in by the office in each year. It also required the office to develop a user-friendly electronic system for filing and processing patent and trademark applications. It required that the system be completed within three years and authorized $50 million each in fiscal 2003, 2004 and 2005 to make that happen. Both chambers had passed similar legislation (S 487, HR 2047) earlier in the session.

● **Teachers' online copyright exemption.** The Justice Department law also made it easier for teachers to use digital content for Web instruction. The provisions amended a 1976 copyright law (PL 94-553) to allow teachers to send digitized books, music and movies over the Internet without first getting permission from the copyright holder. The Senate had passed this as a separate bill (S 487) in 2001. ◆

Republicans Block Efforts To Expand Hate Crimes Ban

Although Democrats considered it a priority, legislation to broaden the federal definition of hate crimes failed to get a floor vote in either chamber. Democratic leaders pulled a hate crimes bill from the Senate floor in June after sponsors were unable to muster the votes needed to limit debate. In the House, supporters tried but failed to get enough signatures on a discharge petition to bring a similar bill directly to the floor.

The bills would have expanded hate crime laws to cover offenses committed because of a victim's gender, sexual orientation or disability. Existing law (PL 90-284), enacted in 1968, allowed federal prosecution of crimes based on race, color, religion or national origin. It could be used only under six specified situations of federal involvement, including crimes committed against victims while they voted or were on federal property. *(1968 Almanac, p. 152)*

The Senate began June 10 to consider a hate crimes bill (S 625 — S Rept 107-147), sponsored by Edward M. Kennedy, D-Mass., that had been approved by the Judiciary Committee in 2001. Opponents drafted several amendments — many related only loosely, if at all, to the underlying bill — and threatened a protracted debate on the legislation.

To stave off the amendments, Majority Leader Tom Daschle, D-S.D., filed a motion to invoke cloture, or limit the debate. Republicans lobbied a handful of bill supporters in their own caucus, arguing it was too early to stop debate and that cloture would block legitimate amendments. The bill's proponents campaigned, too, but were unable to get the 60 votes needed to limit debate. The cloture motion failed, 54-43, on June 11. Republican opponents persuaded

two GOP cosponsors, John Ensign of Nevada and Arlen Specter of Pennsylvania, to vote with them against limiting debate. Four GOP senators — all cosponsors of the bill — voted for cloture: Gordon H. Smith of Oregon, Lincoln Chafee of Rhode Island, and Susan Collins and Olympia J. Snowe, both of Maine.

Proponents of similar legislation in the House (HR 1343) made a last-ditch effort to force the bill to the floor with a discharge petition. They had 208 cosponsors when the 107th Congress adjourned, still short of the 218 needed to prevail. The House bill was sponsored by John Conyers Jr., D-Mich. ◆

Acrimony Reigns Over Judicial Picks

The fight over President Bush's selections for federal judgeships was one of the harshest partisan disputes of the 107th Congress. Senate Republicans made a priority of trying to help Bush reshape the federal judiciary in a more conservative vein, while the Democratic majority and its allies in liberal advocacy groups were intent on setting boundaries for that effort. Both parties viewed the fight — which focused on a handful of appellate court seats and on the pace of Senate action on Bush's nominees — as a dress rehearsal for a showdown over the next Supreme Court nominee. The Senate had not been called on to confirm a high court justice since 1994.

The Senate confirmed 100 presidential nominees to the federal appellate and district courts. The Judiciary Committee rejected two of Bush's picks; 28 nominees did not get votes in the committee. Bush's 77 percent success rate on judicial nominees during his first two years in office was lower than that of the previous two presidents.

It was rare for the Judiciary Committee to vote down a judicial nomination. According to the Congressional Research Service, it had happened only nine times since 1977. Usually, if nominees ran into trouble in the Senate, they did not get a committee hearing or a vote, or they withdrew rather than face a negative vote from the committee.

When the 107th Congress adjourned, there were 34 vacancies on the federal trial courts (5 percent of the total authorized judgeships) and 25 vacancies (or 14 percent) on the appeals courts. But with Republicans regaining control of the Senate in the 108th Congress, Bush was expected to renominate all of the judicial nominees not confirmed in the first two years of his presidency.

● **Pickering.** The nomination of Charles W. Pickering Sr. for the 5th Circuit Court of Appeals in New Orleans was the first of the year to prove publicly controversial. Civil rights and other liberal interest groups mounted an aggressive campaign against Pickering, who was a federal judge for the Southern District of Mississippi. They cited his work in 1976 on a Republican Party platform plank that called for a constitutional amendment banning abortion. They also criticized his votes as a Mississippi state lawmaker in favor of spending bills that included money for the Sovereignty Commission, established in the 1950s to fight desegregation efforts.

Pickering's allies, led by Minority Leader Trent Lott, R-Miss., said his 12 years as a U.S. district judge showed he was fair and impartial, and the American Bar Association rated Pickering as "well-qualified," its highest rating. Republicans said Pickering had shown great personal courage during the civil rights struggles in his home state, where as a county attorney in 1967, he helped the FBI investigate and prosecute the Ku Klux Klan and testified against a Klan imperial wizard. They said his decisions typically were upheld on appeal and that his rate of reversal was lower than the national average for a district court judge.

The nomination effectively died for the year March 14, when the Judiciary Committee voted, 10-9 along party lines, against forwarding it to the full Senate.

Committee Chairman Patrick J. Leahy, D-Vt., was unapologetic. "When the president sends us a nominee who raises concerns over qualification or has a misunderstanding of the appropriate role of a federal judge, I intend to make my concerns known," he said. "And this is one of those times."

An emotional Lott took to the Senate floor after the vote, saying Pickering was a personal friend and that he took the rejection as a slap against himself and his state. Lott slowed Senate action for a time to protest the vote and to try to force Judiciary Committee action on Bush's other nominees.

Some committee Democrats said Pickering was paying the price for the hardball tactics the GOP used to delay and defeat Clinton nominees to the federal bench. "They are exactly right," Arlen Specter, R-Pa., said of the Democrats' complaints. "When President Clinton was in the White House, this committee did not act properly." Specter called for a truce, suggesting that any nomination that failed on a party-line vote be brought to the full Senate. Democrats rejected the idea.

"I think that this is payback," said Lott. "The problem with payback is, when does it ever end?"

● **Owen.** Six months later, on Sept. 5, the Judiciary Committee by an identical vote rejected Priscilla Owen for the same court. Again, the nominee's views on abortion rights were central to the opposition of the Democrats, who focused on Owen's opinions as a Texas Supreme Court justice regarding the state's parental consent law. Her cause was not helped by the fact that a one-time colleague on that court, Alberto R. Gonzales, who had since become the White House counsel, had labeled one of Owen's opinions "an unconscionable act of judicial activism."

Owen's supporters said she was a brilliant legal mind and noted that she received the highest score on the Texas Bar exam in her class.

● **Estrada.** The committee never voted on Bush's nomination of Miguel A. Estrada to become the first Hispanic on the D.C. Circuit Court of Appeals, widely viewed as the pre-eminent appeals court because it handles so many gov-

ernment policy disputes.

Estrada was a partner in the law firm that represented Bush before the Supreme Court during the disputed 2000 election. During a hearing Sept. 26, Judiciary panel Democrats noted that one of Estrada's supervisors when he was an assistant to the solicitor general in the Clinton administration had said that he lacked the judgment necessary to serve on the appellate bench. An Hispanic group maintained that his pro-bono work on anti-loitering statutes caused "grave concerns" about how well he represented the Hispanic com-munity. Estrada's supporters hailed him as a rising star and one of the nation's most impressive young lawyers.

● **Shedd.** The final judge confirmed in 2002 was Dennis Shedd for a seat on the 4th Circuit Court of Appeals in Richmond. The vote was 55-44 on Nov. 19, and the confirmation largely was seen as an act of senatorial courtesy to the retiring Strom Thurmond, R-S.C., who had employed Shedd as a top aide. Shedd, like Estrada, had been criticized by liberal groups as a conservative ideologue. He had been waiting for a vote since May 2001. (*Senate vote 250, p. S-32*) ◆

Chapter 14

POLITICS &
ELECTIONS

New Voting Standards Enacted

Nearly two years after the closest and most hotly disputed election in modern U.S. history, Congress cleared a bill that for the first time set nationwide standards for the conduct of elections and authorized nearly $3.9 billion in federal aid over three years to help states meet those standards. President Bush signed the measure into law on Oct. 29 (HR 3295 — PL 107-252).

The most immediate assistance was authorization for $650 million in "early grants" to help states train election workers and replace outdated voting machines. Each state was eligible for at least $5 million.

Most of the remaining money was to be distributed later by a new commission to help states meet election requirements, train poll workers, provide voter education and administer elections. To qualify for the federal grants, states had to implement a set of broad national standards.

The legislation was aimed primarily at preventing a repeat of the disputed 2000 presidential contest between Bush and Democrat Al Gore. Arguments over the narrow outcome in Florida, where electoral votes held the key to the presidency, lasted 34 days until a 5-4 Supreme Court decision effectively awarded the election to Bush.

The bipartisan election bill was the product of months of difficult talks that nearly broke down several times, with the president essentially on the sidelines throughout. The original idea simply was to make it easier to vote. Noting reports that 4 million to 6 million Americans were denied the right to vote in the 2000 election, Democrats pressed for legislation to replace outdated voting equipment and allow voters to cast "provisional ballots" if there were any question about their eligibility. Republicans, however, insisted on adding new protections against voter fraud.

The logjam began to break toward the end of 2001, when the House passed its initial version of the bill and a bipartisan framework for a deal was reached in the Senate. But it took until April 2002 for the Senate to pass its bill and another six months to produce a final compromise.

The Senate version was more generous than the House bill — $3.5 billion over five years compared with $2.65 billion over three — and its standards were more explicit. State and local officials, who wanted flexibility in deciding how to meet the standards, opposed the more specific Senate requirements. But the main dispute was over Senate provisions aimed at preventing voter fraud.

Sen. Christopher S. Bond, R-Mo., was the most outspoken advocate of stiffer voter registration requirements.

BoxScore

Bill:
HR 3295 — PL 107-252
Legislative Action:
House passed HR 3295 (H Rept 107-329), 362-63, on Dec. 12, 2001.
Senate passed HR 3295 by voice vote April 11, 2002, after substituting the text of S 565, passed, 99-1, earlier in the day.
House adopted the conference report (H Rept 107-730), 357-48, on Oct. 10.
Senate cleared the bill, 92-2, on Oct. 16.
President signed Oct. 29.

"If your vote is canceled out by a dog or a dead person, it's as if you did not have the right to vote," said Bond, who blamed voter fraud for the GOP loss in the Missouri Senate race in 2000. But many Democrats, along with a coalition of civil rights and voting rights groups, warned that new restrictions could disenfranchise low-income and minority voters. The challenge, in Bond's words, was to strike a balance that made it "easier to vote and harder to cheat."

Both sides expressed satisfaction with the final bill, though Democrats were more qualified in their praise. Acknowledging that it was the only way to get enough GOP support to clear the bill, Democrats agreed to a requirement that first-time voters show one of several forms of identification at the polls. Republicans agreed, however, that a voter could use something other than a driver's license or other photo ID. As a backup, voters in every state would be able to cast a provisional ballot if they had no identification. The ballots would be counted later if the voter could prove his or her eligibility to vote.

Democrats backed away from a demand that individuals be allowed to sue over violations of the new election standards, a proposal strongly opposed by Republicans and by state and election officials. Instead, individuals could go through alternative dispute resolution systems designed and run by the states; the Justice Department could file lawsuits if individuals did not get their problems resolved.

"It is not a perfect bill. But it is a good bill, a balanced bill, a bill that will make our democracy work better," said Christopher J. Dodd, D-Conn., chairman of the Senate Rules and Administration Committee and lead sponsor of the Senate bill. John Conyers Jr. of Michigan, ranking Democrat on the House Judiciary Committee, said the voter identification requirement was "not a provision I would have wanted," but added that "its inclusion in this agreement cannot possibly overshadow the tremendous step forward the bill represents."

One of the biggest questions left after the law was enacted was whether the government would provide the money to pay for it. Lawmakers included $400 million in the fiscal 2002 supplemental appropriations law (PL 107-206), but it was part of $5.1 billion in emergency funds that Bush chose not to spend. Hopes that money would be provided in the fiscal 2003 Treasury-Postal spending bill collapsed when Congress adjourned without completing any of the domestic appropriations bills. The problem was left to the next Congress.

Highlights

The following are the main components of the new law. The voter fraud provisions took effect Jan. 1, 2003, but most changes in state and local election systems were not expected to be felt before the runup to the 2004 congressional and presidential elections.

- **Election standards.** The law established broad federal election standards, but left the means of achieving them to the discretion of the states. The standards — to be in place by 2004, with a possible delay in most cases until 2006 — included allowing voters to check for and correct errors made in casting their votes, providing at least one voting machine per precinct for disabled voters, allowing voters whose eligibility was in doubt to cast provisional ballots subject to later verification, and establishing a computerized statewide voter registration database to ensure accurate voter lists.
- **Election commission.** A four-member, presidentially appointed Election Assistance Commission was established to make grants and oversee the creation of election standards.
- **Federal grants.** The commission was authorized to distribute a total of $3 billion in grants over three years to help states meet election standards, train poll workers and administer elections. Additional funds were authorized for grants to increase access to polling places for disabled voters, improve voting technology, and test new voting machines and other equipment.
- **Voting machine replacement.** The law authorized $325 million for one-time payments to states to replace punch card and lever voting machines with new equipment. A state could receive $4,000 for each of its polling precincts.
- **Election fraud.** First-time voters would be required to produce a valid photo identification at some point during the registration process. Those without a driver's license could use the last four digits of their Social Security number or be assigned unique identifiers.

Background

Lawmakers began calling for an overhaul of the nation's balloting procedures after the 2000 presidential elections exposed them as an unreliable hodgepodge of local standards, inconsistent procedures and old equipment. Congress rushed to devise remedies, but the work soon slowed to a crawl. There were simply too many competing interests in the debate and not enough lingering public outrage to force Congress to resolve any disputes quickly.

The delay cost Congress any opportunity it might have had to affect the 2002 elections. However, a flurry of action before the end of the first session in December 2001 renewed hopes that lawmakers could institute changes at least in time for the 2004 presidential elections.

The House on Dec. 12 passed a bipartisan bill (HR 3295) that had been introduced after months of negotiations by House Administration Committee Chairman Bob Ney, R-Ohio, and Steny H. Hoyer of Maryland, the committee's ranking Democrat. Meanwhile across the Capitol, a bipartisan group of senators broke a months-long impasse to announce a compromise on a package of election changes. The agreement was inserted into a bill by Dodd (S 565) that had won Democrats-only approval in his Rules and Administration Committee in November. (*2001 Almanac, p. 15-3*)

Legislative Action

Senate Floor Action

The Senate passed S 565, 99-1, on April 11, then inserted the language into HR 3295 and passed that bill by voice vote in order to go to conference with the House. The lone dissenter was Conrad Burns, R-Mont., who complained that the bill would impose "a one-size-fits-all solution" that would shortchange rural states. (*Senate vote 65, p. S-17*)

The floor debate had begun two months earlier, but quickly bogged down in a dispute over how to curb fraud at the polls without disenfranchising voters. Reflecting the bipartisan compromise reached in December, the bill required that a first-time voter who registered by mail prove his or her identity by providing a copy of an identifying document such as a valid driver's license, pay stub, utility bill, bank statement or government check. The provision was included at Bond's insistence.

Democrats Charles E. Schumer of New York and Ron Wyden of Oregon argued that the requirement would disenfranchise poor and disabled people. They proposed that new voters be allowed to vouch for their identities with a signature, which would be matched against records on file with state or local election officials. Republicans said that would invite additional fraud.

An attempt by Bond to table (kill) Schumer's amendment failed, 46-51, on Feb. 27. Republicans responded by saying they would stop any additional work on the bill unless the amendment was withdrawn. (*Senate vote 38, p. S-11*)

After two unsuccessful attempts to limit debate, Majority Leader Tom Daschle, D-S.D., pulled the bill and moved on to other business. The first vote, on March 1, was 49-39, 11 votes short of the 60 required to invoke cloture. The second, on March 4, was 51-44, nine votes shy. (*Senate votes 39, 40, p. S-12*)

Another three weeks of off-the-floor negotiations produced a plan, adopted by unanimous consent March 22, that allowed the Senate to finish work on the bill.

With Republicans signaling they would bury the bill otherwise, Democrats agreed — at least for the time being — to give up trying to scale back the anti-fraud provisions. That still left the question of what to do about Oregon and Washington, which already had vote-by-mail systems in place. Oregon relied exclusively on mail-in ballots, and the system accounted for about two-thirds of Washington's turnout in 2000.

The solution was to allow voters in those two states who registered by mail to submit their driver's license number or the last four digits of their Social Security number, then mark their ballots with that same number as a means of proving their identity. In other states, voters who registered by mail would have to prove their identities at the polls with a driver's license, utility bill, canceled government check or some other proof of residence and identity.

Before passing the bill April 11, the Senate also:

• Dropped a requirement that election officials notify provisional ballot voters within 30 days as to whether their vote was counted. The proposal to strike the provision, by Pat Roberts, R-Kan., was adopted 56-43. (*Senate vote 63, p. S-16*)

• Rejected, 48-52, an amendment by Hillary Rodham Clinton, D-N.Y., that would have required the government to set a "residual vote error rate" but allow a waiver for areas with historically high rates of intentional undervoting. (*Senate vote 64, p. S-17*)

In earlier action on Feb. 14, the Senate:

• Rejected, 44-50, a proposal by Richard J. Durbin, D-Ill., to require states to allow all voters, including those using punch-card voting machines, to verify their votes and correct any errors. The underlying bill required states that used other voting technologies to permit such verification, but sponsors argued that because nearly one-third of Americans used punch-card machines, Durbin's proposal would be too burdensome. (*Senate vote 32, p. S-10*)

• Rejected, 31-63, a proposal by Harry Reid, D-Nev., and Arlen Specter, R-Pa., to restore voting rights to felons who had served their full sentences. (*Senate vote 31, p. S-10*)

• Rejected, 46-49, an amendment by Joseph I. Lieberman, D-Conn., to allow federal employees to take time off to serve as nonpartisan poll workers in federal elections. (*Senate vote 33, p. S-10*)

• Rejected, 40-55, a proposal by Burns to allow states to purge the rolls of people who failed to vote in federal elections for four consecutive years. (*Senate vote 34, p. S-10*)

• Agreed, by voice vote, to add language specifying that six states would retain exemptions from the National Voter Registration Act of 1993 (PL 103-31). The 1993 "motor voter" law required states to allow citizens to register to vote when they apply for a drivers' license. Idaho, Minnesota, New Hampshire, North Dakota, Wisconsin and Wyoming were exempt because they either did not require voter registration or allowed same day registration at polling stations. (*1983 Almanac, p. 199*)

Conference/Final Action

House and Senate negotiators reached an agreement on the bill Oct. 4, nearly six months after Senate passage. Bond's insistence on the anti-fraud provisions and the backing he got from other Republicans were among the factors that delayed completion of the conference.

The House adopted the conference report (H Rept 107-730), 357-48, on Oct. 10. The Senate cleared the bill, 92-2, on Oct. 16. The two "no" votes in the Senate were cast by Clinton and Schumer, who said the anti-fraud provisions would still discriminate against millions of New Yorkers who did not have driver's licenses. (*House vote 462, p. H-144; Senate vote 238, p. S-49*)

The final deal was worked out in a marathon series of meetings among Dodd, Bond, Ney, Hoyer and Mitch McConnell of Kentucky, ranking Republican on the Senate Rules and Administration Committee.

Civil rights groups generally regarded the final bill as a good compromise. "I think it's going to help tremendously," said Hilary O. Shelton, director of the NAACP's Washington bureau. He said he was encouraged because the bill would ban states from enforcing the identification requirements in discriminatory ways, meaning they could not be applied more strictly to black voters than to white voters.

State and local officials said most of their issues had been addressed — particularly because the agreement did not grant individuals the right to sue, a provision states had fought aggressively to avoid being tied up in expensive litigation. But the solution — relying on the Justice Department to investigate and file suit over violations — rankled African-American Democrats and the NAACP, who expressed concern over Attorney General John Ashcroft's level of commitment to voting rights. ◆

Election Overhaul Provisions

The following are the main provisions of the election overhaul law (HR 3295 — PL 107-252) signed Oct. 29.

Buyout of Outdated Voting Machines

• **Machine replacement.** The law authorized $325 million for one-time payments to help states replace punch-card and lever voting machines. A state could get $4,000 for each polling precinct that used a punch-card or lever machine in the 2000 election.

• **Administering elections.** To improve the administration of elections, the law authorized $325 million in payments to states, to be distributed on the basis of the state's voting age population. The grants could be used to train election officials and poll workers.

Election Commission

The bill created a four-member Election Assistance Commission, its members nominated by the president and subject to confirmation by the Senate.

• **Authority.** The commission was to serve as a clearinghouse of information on voting equipment; set voluntary guidelines to help states comply with the new election standards; make the annual grant payments to the states; provide for testing and certification of voting system hardware and software; conduct studies on subjects such as military and overseas voting, voters who register by mail, and the impact of the use of Social Security numbers in elections; and establish the Help America Vote College Program to encourage college students to serve as poll workers or assistants.

• **Limitation on authority.** The commission did not have the authority to issue any rules or regulations, except as permitted under the National Voter Registration Act of 1993 (PL 103-31), also known as the "motor voter" law.

Grants

The measure authorized $3 billion over three years — $1.4 billion in fiscal 2003, $1 billion in fiscal 2004 and $600 million in fiscal 2005 — for a grant program administered by the commission to help states meet election requirements, train poll workers, provide voter education and administer elections.

In addition, it authorized:

• $100 million over three years to make polling places physically accessible to voters with disabilities.

• $20 million in fiscal 2003 for research on improving voting equipment and technology.

• $10 million in fiscal 2003 for a pilot program to test improvements to voting equipment and technology.

• $30 million over three years to establish the new Election Assistance Commission.

• $30 million over three years for state protection and advocacy programs.

• $5 million in fiscal 2003 to establish the Help America Vote College Program to encourage college students to serve as poll workers or assistants.

• $5 million in fiscal 2003 to establish the Help America Vote Foundation to recruit secondary school students to serve as poll workers or assistants.

• $200,000 in fiscal 2003 to conduct mock elections for students and parents.

Election Standards

To make sure eligible voters were not denied the right to vote, the bill required each state to comply with certain "uniform and nondiscriminatory" requirements, including the following:

• **Correcting voting errors.** Voters had to be able to check for and correct errors on their ballots in a private and independent way. Effective in 2006.

• **Provisional voting.** A voter whose eligibility was questioned had to be able to cast a provisional ballot, which would be counted if state or local election officials later determined that he or she was eligible to vote. Voters who cast provisional ballots had to sign an affidavit stating their belief that they were registered in that jurisdiction and eligible to vote in that election. They could check a "free access system," such as a toll-free telephone number or a Web site, to determine whether their votes were counted. Effective by 2004.

• **Voting extensions.** If a federal or state court ordered a polling place to remain open beyond the closing time set by state law, all votes cast after the normal closing time had to be provisional, and those ballots had to be separated from other provisional ballots.

• **Statewide voter registration list.** Each state had to have a uniform, centralized and computerized statewide voter registration list. A unique identification number had to be assigned to each registered voter. Each state had to design a system to make sure its list was accurate and updated regularly. Consistent with the 1993 voter registration law, voters who did not respond to a notice in the mail and then failed to vote in two consecutive general elections in federal election years could be removed from the list, but they could not be removed solely for not voting. Effective in 2004, with a possible waiver until 2006.

• **Access for voters with disabilities.** Each precinct had to have at least one voting machine that allowed voters with disabilities to vote in a private and independent manner. Effective in 2006. In addition, any new voting system purchased with federal funds starting in 2007 had to be accessible to people with disabilities.

• **Voting definition.** States had to adopt a "uniform and nondiscriminatory" definition of what constituted a legal vote and what would be counted as a vote for each type of voting machine used in the state. Effective in 2006.

• **Error rates.** Each state had to have a voting system with an error rate that did not exceed the rate established by the Federal Election Commission's Office of Election Administration. The job of setting the rate was to be transferred to the new Election Assistance Commission. Effective in 2006.

• **Multilingual accessibility.** States had to continue to provide alternative language accessibility pursuant to Section 203 of the 1965 Voting Rights Act (PL 89-110).

Anti-Fraud Protections

• **Voter registration.** Individuals had to provide a driver's license number when registering to vote. People without a driver's license could provide the last four digits of their Social Security number. Those possessing neither a driver's license nor a Social Security number would be assigned a unique identifier. Effective in 2004, with a possible waiver until 2006.

• **Voter identification.** First-time voters who registered by mail had to provide proof of identity at some point in the process — when they registered, or when they voted in person or by mail. They could provide a current, valid photo identification or a copy of a bank statement, paycheck, utility bill or other government document that showed their name and address. If they could not produce any of those documents, they could cast provisional ballots that would be counted only if officials later verified they were eligible to vote. Effective in 2003.

Enforcement

• **By the states.** States receiving funds under the bill had to establish an administrative procedure for resolving grievances. Anyone who believed the new election standards had been violated, or were about to be violated, could file a complaint and request a hearing. The state had to make a decision within 90 days, either by providing a remedy or dismissing the complaint. If the state failed to meet the deadline, an alternative dispute resolution procedure had to be available to resolve the complaint within 60 days.

• **By the United States.** The Justice Department was authorized to file a civil action in federal court to seek relief, including an injunction or restraining order, against any state or jurisdiction that did not apply the new requirements in a uniform and nondiscriminatory manner. Individuals did not have a right to sue. States that did not accept funds under the bill had to either establish a grievance procedure or submit a compliance plan with the Justice Department.

Military and Overseas Voting

• **State regulation.** Each state was required to designate a single office to provide information to members of the armed forces about registration and absentee voting in that state. States had to report to the Election Assistance Commission the number of military and overseas applications they received and the number of ballots they received. They were prohibited from disqualifying ballots that were received too early, and if they rejected registration applications from military or overseas voters, they had to give those voters a reason why the applications were rejected.

• **Federal regulation.** The Defense Department was required to guarantee, to the maximum extent possible, that military voting assistance officers had the time and resources they needed to help military personnel vote. The Pentagon also had to make certain, to the maximum extent possible, that all military ballots had postmarks or other official proof of the mailing date in order to ensure that no such ballots arrived after Election Day. ◆

Finance Battle Shifts to the Courts

Bill:

HR 2356 — PL 107-155

Legislative Action:

House passed HR 2356
(H Rept 107-131, Part 1), 240-
189, on Feb. 14.

Senate cleared HR 2356, 60-
40, on March 20.

President signed March 27.

After numerous filibusters, years of debate and hundreds of votes, Congress cleared a major rewrite of the nation's campaign finance laws, the first in three decades. But the final Senate vote in March only moved the battle over regulating campaign funding into a new phase: The two sides would fight on in the courts.

The year began with a remarkable reversal of fortune for the supporters of campaign finance legislation in the House. Their bill (HR 2356) had been stalled since the summer of 2001 in a standoff with Republican leaders over the rules for floor debate. Then came the collapse of Enron Corp. in December 2001. The massive bankruptcy exposed the energy trader's network of political giving and influence and triggered a panic among both Democrats and Republicans who had benefited from the company's largess. Many lawmakers faced uncomfortable questions about their campaign fundraising and were looking to distance themselves from the debacle.

One day after Congress reconvened in January, backers of the House campaign finance bill, led by Republican Christopher Shays of Connecticut and Democrat Martin T. Meehan of Massachusetts, collected the last of the 218 signatures they needed to force their measure back to the floor under rules to their liking.

At the heart of the House measure was a ban on "soft money" — the unregulated contributions to political parties from corporations, labor unions and wealthy individuals — plus new restrictions on the campaign advertising that soft money had gone to support. But to win votes and align their measure with the bill (S 27) that the Senate had passed in 2001, the sponsors had to make some significant changes on the floor — for example, raising the limit on "hard money" — the contributions made directly to candidates — from $1,000 to $2,000.

House Republican leaders did their best to sink the bill on the floor or change it enough to force a conference with the Senate, but the existing system had grown impossible to defend and the measure's momentum proved unstoppable. The House passed the bill early on Feb. 14, sending it back to the Senate.

Most lawmakers expected one last fight. But President Bush had indicated he would sign whatever Congress sent him, and both sides already were turning their attention to the courts, where opponents promised to try to overturn the measure once it became law. The Senate cleared the bill March 20. Although Bush signed the measure March 27 (PL 107-155), he described it as "flawed" and pointedly avoided the traditional signing ceremony that would have brought the bill's sponsors, including his rival, Republican Sen. John McCain of Arizona, to the White House.

Immediately after the bill became law, longtime opponent Sen. Mitch McConnell, R-Ky., and a diverse coalition of groups sued to overturn it, saying it trampled on the rights of Americans to speak out and participate freely in the political process. A provision calling for "expedited judicial review" put the measure on a fast track to the Supreme Court, with hearings before a special three-judge panel in U.S. District Court in Washington held in December.

Meanwhile, the four principal sponsors of the new campaign finance law challenged the Federal Election Commission (FEC) regulations implementing the statute. Shays and Meehan sued in U.S. District Court in October to overturn the FEC's new soft money rules. The rules, approved in July, narrowed the definition of solicitation, which the sponsors said would permit parties to set up "sham" entities that would be able to raise and spend soft money on the parties' behalf. Restricted by Senate ethics rules from joining a lawsuit as a plaintiff, McCain and cosponsor Russell D. Feingold, D-Wis., instead promised to lead a legislative challenge in the 108th Congress by filing a resolution under the Congressional Review Act (PL 104-121), which provides a process for Congress to overturn agency rulemaking.

Highlights

The following are key provisions of the law:

● **Soft money.** National party committees cannot accept or spend soft money. State and local party committees can spend soft money on voter registration and mobilization in federal elections only under certain conditions: The effort must not mention a federal candidate. No donor may give more than $10,000 per year. Soft money may not be raised by federal candidates or national parties, and it may not go to broadcast advertising, except for ads that mention only state or local candidates. State and local parties must spend soft money in a mix with hard money. Party committees may not collaborate with each other to raise the money, and they may not transfer it to national parties, candidate committees or any other organization.

● **Hard money.** The limit on individual contributions to House and Senate candidates is $2,000 per election, double the old limit, and it is indexed to grow with inflation. The aggregate contribution limit for individuals is $95,000 per two-year election cycle — $37,500 to candidates and $57,500 to parties and political action committees (PACs). To give the two-year maximum, at least $20,000 must go to national parties. Individuals may give $10,000 per year to state party committees.

● **Broadcast advertising.** Labor unions, for-profit corporations and nonprofits cannot fund broadcast advertising directly if the ad refers to a federal candidate, reaches at least 50,000 people within the candidate's electorate, and runs within 60 days of a general election or 30 days before a pri-

mary. Such ads can be paid for only through a PAC and with regulated hard-money contributions.

- **Independent and coordinated expenditures.** Independent expenditures of $1,000 or more made on a candidate's behalf within 20 days of an election must be reported to the FEC within 24 hours. Further out from elections, independent expenditures of $10,000 or more made on a candidate's behalf must be reported within 48 hours. When spending to help a candidate, political parties must choose in each election whether to work independently or in concert with the candidate. They may not do both in the same election. Coordinated expenditures are limited; independent expenditures are not. Any money spent by a person, other than a candidate, in concert with a political party will be treated as a contribution to the party. The FEC must issue new rules regulating coordination between candidates or parties and outside groups. The law specifies that the new regulations shall not require evidence of formal coordination or agreements between outside groups and candidates or parties to establish that election activity is "coordinated."

- **Self-financed candidates.** The law raises the limits on hard-money contributions to House and Senate candidates who face wealthy, self-financed opponents. It also increases the limits on what political parties may spend in concert with those candidates.

- **Fundraising by candidates.** Federal candidates and officeholders may not raise or spend soft money for federal election activities. The prohibition applies to political action committees associated with federal candidates, known as leadership PACs. The law makes an exception for federal officeholders who are running for state office, as long as the money is not spent on advertising or other activities that mention federal candidates.

- **Fundraising for nonprofits.** Candidates and officeholders may help nonprofits raise money for voter registration and mobilization, soliciting individual contributions of up to $20,000 per year. Candidates and officeholders are prohibited from soliciting such contributions from labor unions and corporations. They can solicit general contributions for nonprofits from any source, including corporations and labor unions, if the nonprofit's principal purpose is not voter registration or get-out-the-vote activities and the solicitation does not specify how the money will be spent.

Background

The safest bet in Washington had long been that Congress never would overhaul the campaign finance system. The status quo logic of incumbency argued against it. Powerful outside interest groups, key to the base of each major party, opposed it. And, with the courts leery of anything that might restrict political speech, the legal ground was uncertain.

The House and Senate had debated since 1980 whether to revamp the system, which had not changed significantly since a rewrite (PL 93-433) passed in 1974, in the wake of the Watergate scandal. Both parties repeatedly promised an overhaul, but made little effort to deliver it. (*1974 Almanac, p. 611*)

Nevertheless, momentum for an overhaul had been building at least since the 1994 elections, when the parties took in a record-breaking $102 million in soft money. The Enron scandal of late 2001 put the legislation over the top,

but it was only the final push.

Soft money — called "non-federal funds" by the FEC because it fell outside the reach of federal limits on direct-to-candidate contributions — was supposed to go to "party-building" activities, such as voter mobilization and registration. But it came to be used for campaign activities, particularly broadcast advertising. The U.S. Supreme Court opened the door for broader use of soft money with a June 1996 ruling that parties could spend an unlimited amount to promote their positions on issues as long as they did not coordinate the activity directly with candidates. (*1996 Almanac, p. 5-47*)

The amount of soft money flowing through the system more than quadrupled in the 2000 election: to $495 million for the two major parties combined. Tales of questionable fundraising tactics on both sides piled up.

Meanwhile, supporters of an overhaul were shaping and reshaping their legislation, making compromises, dropping some proposals as unworkable or politically unpalatable. The heart of the measure that finally cleared Congress — the ban on soft money and restrictions on political advertising by outside groups — took shape gradually.

In 1997, McCain and Feingold introduced a measure that included a ban on soft money, free or discounted television advertising and postage for candidates who adhered to voluntary spending limits, as well as new restrictions intended to draw a clearer line between spending to promote candidates and spending to promote issues. Shays and Meehan introduced a companion bill in the House. (*1997 Almanac, p. 1-26*)

Shays and Meehan managed twice, in 1998 and 1999, to use the threat of a discharge petition to force votes on their version of the bill. It passed both times. (*1999 Almanac, p. 8-3; 1998 Almanac, p. 18-3*)

The last pieces began coming together with the 2000 elections. McCain made "campaign finance reform" the foundation of his presidential bid, boosting him and the cause to national prominence. Turnover in the Senate, where McCain and Feingold had been blocked for years by McConnell's filibusters, also shifted the balance in favor of an overhaul. The measure finally passed the Senate in March 2001, after an extraordinary two weeks of debate.

However, the bill stalled in the House in July 2001, when Democrats and a few Republicans voted down a rule for floor debate that had been drafted by GOP leaders. The rule would have made it difficult for Shays and Meehan to alter their bill on the floor to bring it in line with the Senate-passed measure and avoid sending it back to the Senate for another debate. Shays-Meehan supporters quickly began gathering signatures on a discharge petition to force the bill back to the House floor under rules more to their liking. By the end of the year, they had gathered 215 of the 218 signatures they needed, putting them within striking distance of their ultimate goal. (*2001 Almanac, p. 6-3*)

Legislative Action

House Floor Action

After hours of debate, the House passed the Shays-Meehan bill, 240-189, in the early morning of Feb. 14. (*House vote 34, p. H-16*)

Shays and Meehan had finally gathered the last of the

218 signatures needed to bring the bill to the floor. But signatures were not the same as votes, and the sponsors still faced opposition and uncertainty from many members.

House Democrats had provided the bulk of the votes to pass similar bills in 1998 and 1999, but once the Senate passed the measure and it appeared close to becoming law, some Democrats grew increasingly uneasy. They worried that the ban on soft money and the higher limits on hard money, which Republicans historically were better at raising, would put their party at a competitive disadvantage.

Republican leaders, meanwhile, sought to weigh down the measure with amendments that the Senate would never accept, while also providing cover for members who wanted to say they had voted for overhaul. If they were unable to block the bill outright on the floor, they hoped to force it into a conference committee, where they would have a better chance of killing or significantly altering it.

Shays and Meehan succeeded in defending a revised version of their bill against two GOP-sponsored substitutes.

• In a surprise gambit, GOP leaders offered an old version of Shays-Meehan, the one that passed in 1999, as one of their substitutes. It was now out of sync with the Senate-passed measure — missing, for example, the provision raising contribution limits for candidates facing wealthy opponents — and would have forced a conference.

"A couple of people backing off of Shays-Meehan want this vote so they can say they voted for reform," said Bob Ney, R-Ohio, who offered the substitute. "They would like to have a chance to vote the way they did in 1999. That was the pure bill." Ney, however, said he would not vote for his own substitute. The House rejected it 53-377. (*House vote 20, p. H-12*)

• The other GOP substitute, offered by Majority Leader Dick Armey, R-Texas, would have banned all soft money at the national, state and local levels — a more sweeping prohibition than Shays and Meehan proposed. It also would have prohibited corporations, unions and tax-exempt groups from using soft money for voter registration and get-out-the-vote activities. "If in fact my colleagues have the courage of their convictions and they want to put their … soft money where their soft-spoken mouth is, vote for Armey and get rid of soft money now," Armey said. "We are either for a ban on soft money now or we are not."

The Armey substitute was defeated 179-249, with 44 Republicans joining 204 Democrats and Vermont Independent Bernard Sanders to oppose it. (*House vote 19, p. H-12*)

• The last substitute offered was the revised Shays-Meehan bill, which was adopted, 240-191. (*House vote 21, p. H-12*)

Shays and Meehan then went on to beat back all amendments that they considered "poison pills" designed to derail the legislation in the Senate.

• The closest vote came on an amendment by Charles W. "Chip" Pickering Jr., R-Miss., that would have exempted communications about gun rights from the advertising restrictions in the bill. More than a dozen Southern Republicans voted with a majority of Republicans in favor of the amendment. Several Republicans said the proposal was aimed at winning the votes of Southern Democrats and creating political havoc in the midterm elections for those who did not support the measure. The National Rifle Association had placed the vote on its congressional scorecard. Nevertheless, the amendment was rejected,

209-219. (*House vote 24, p. H-14*)

• The House rejected, 160-268, an amendment by Roger Wicker, R-Miss., that would have banned non-U.S. citizens, including permanent legal residents, from donating to campaigns. The House had accepted a similar amendment in 1999. The debate was rancorous, with amendment supporters charging that the existing system gave "enemies of the state access to our political system." That comment prompted angry responses from Hispanic and other minority lawmakers, who said it was a slur against immigrants. (*House vote 30, p. H-14*)

• The House also turned back amendments that would have lifted the bill's advertising restrictions when the content related to civil rights; to advocacy for veterans, military personnel, senior citizens and families; and to advocacy for workers, farmers and family issues. (*House votes 25, 26, 27, p. H-14*)

Shays-Meehan supporters offered three amendments aimed at winning votes and aligning their measure with the Senate-passed bill.

• The first, by Zach Wamp, R-Tenn., doubled hard money limits for candidates from $1,000 to $2,000 per election. It was adopted, 218-211. (*House vote 28, p. H-14*)

• The second, offered by Shelley Moore Capito, R-W.Va., and adopted by voice vote, raised the limits still further for candidates facing wealthy opponents who pumped large amounts of their own money into their campaigns.

• The third amendment, by Gene Green, D-Texas, stripped out a Senate provision that would have guaranteed cheap television ad rates to candidates and political parties close to Election Day. Supporters feared the provision would jeopardize the bill in the House. Senate sponsors already had approved the change, and the House adopted it, 327-101. (*House vote 23, p. H-14*)

Before the House passed the bill, Ney offered as a substitute an alternative bill he cosponsored with Albert R. Wynn, D-Md., that would have capped, not banned, soft money. The House rejected it, 181-248 (*House vote 33, p. H-16*)

Although Bush was no fan of the legislation, he had stayed out of the congressional debate from the beginning, and he rejected a plea from House Speaker J. Dennis Hastert, R-Ill., to help beat back the bill. The White House further undercut efforts to keep Republicans united against the measure by signaling, just as the battle was getting under way on the House floor, that the president would sign the bill. In the end, 41 House Republicans bucked their leadership and voted for the bill; 12 Democrats opposed it.

Final Action

The Senate cleared the bill March 20 by a vote of 60-40, with one in five Republicans breaking from their leadership to support it. (*Senate vote 54, p. S-14*)

McConnell, long the bill's leading opponent, had filibustered earlier campaign finance measures and was being coy enough this time to keep the bill's supporters guessing, even after House passage. He managed to delay action for more than a month, forcing bill supporters to prove they had the 60 votes required to overcome a filibuster, which they did in a 68-32 vote March 20. (*Senate vote 53, p. S-14*)

But McConnell conceded eventual defeat even before the bill reached the floor. He was turning his attention to the courts, where he would lead the attempt to overturn the law. ◆

Chapter 15

SOCIAL POLICY

No Accord on Welfare Rewrite

Astrong push by President Bush and passage of a bill by the House were not enough to break the logjam over rewriting the 1996 welfare overhaul law. Lawmakers agreed instead to extend major provisions of the 1996 law, which expired Sept. 30, until Jan. 11, 2003, and embark on a full reauthorization in the 108th Congress.

Bush made updating the welfare law a centerpiece of his social agenda for the year. The debate in Congress lacked the stark ideological divides of 1996, when the choice was whether to end 60 years of welfare as an open-ended entitlement. But while most members no longer questioned the idea of welfare as temporary aid, there were sharp disputes over the details.

Bush and most congressional Republicans said the 1996 law largely had been successful, with welfare case loads falling by more than half since enactment. "History tells us we were right, absolutely right in what we did in taking people out of a life of dependence," said Rep. E. Clay Shaw Jr., R-Fla., the main author of the 1996 measure. Republicans generally wanted to maintain the basic spending levels, while nudging additional recipients into the work force.

Most Democrats and some moderate Republicans argued that any increase in work requirements had to be tied to a significant increase in aid, particularly for decent child care. They also stressed the importance of training and counseling to enable recipients to stay in the work force.

The issue that polarized lawmakers, however, was whether to restore welfare benefits for legal immigrants. Pressure to revive those benefits, which were cut under the 1996 law, came from state officials, influential senators and Hispanic voters, whose support was being courted intensely for the midterm election. But House conservatives insisted that the 1996 law discouraged welfare dependency among immigrants and ensured that those who sponsored new arrivals would take responsibility for their care.

Bush opened the debate over the welfare law Feb. 26, proposing that recipients be required to work a full 40-hour week, rather than the 30 hours required under the 1996 law, and that states have 70 percent of their welfare recipients in jobs or actively seeking work by 2007, compared with 50 percent under existing law. In a nod to conservatives, he also proposed new, federally funded programs to promote marriage and encourage teenagers to abstain from sex.

The House welfare bill, passed in May, closely tracked the administration's proposal, including the work and caseload requirements and $250 million to promote marriage and teen sexual abstinence. Conservatives agreed to add $1

BoxScore

Bill:
HR 4737

Legislative Action:
House passed HR 4737, 229-197, on May 16.
Senate Finance Committee approved HR 4737, amended (S Rept 107-221), 13-8, on June 26.

billion over five years to mandatory spending for child care grants.

The Senate Finance Committee approved an alternative version of the bill that would have maintained the 30-hour workweek for recipients, made it easier for them to take college classes or get vocational training, increased mandatory child care subsidies by $5.5 billion over five years, and allowed states to use federal money to provide cash benefits to legal immigrants. Though the plan had the support of some moderate Republicans, Majority Leader Tom Daschle, D-S.D., opposed it and vowed to seek more child care funding on the Senate floor.

At one point, it seemed a deal might be possible in the lame-duck session. But Republicans set that idea aside after their victory at the polls in November promised to give them a freer hand in the 108th Congress. With no agreement in sight, cash-strapped state officials pressed Congress for a three-year extension of the 1996 law to guarantee continued funding.

Congress opted instead for short-term extensions. The first stopgap appropriations bill (PL 107-229), enacted Sept. 30, kept welfare programs alive through Dec. 31. The final continuing resolution of the year (PL 107-294) extended those programs until Jan. 11, 2003.

Highlights

The following is a comparison of the main provisions in the House and Senate welfare bills:

● **Work requirements.** Both bills would have required states to gradually increase the portion of welfare recipients who worked from 50 percent to 70 percent by 2007. The House bill would have increased from 30 to 40 the number of hours per week that welfare recipients had to work, with at least 24 hours spent at a work site. The Senate bill left the required workweek at 30 hours, with at least 24 hours at a work site.

● **Definition of 'work.'** On-the-job training would count as work under the House bill, but vocational training and time spent searching for a job would not. However, up to three months in a two-year period could be spent on any activity, including drug treatment. Recipients could spend four months in a two-year period in training that led to a job. Under the Senate bill, vocational training could be counted as work for 24 months rather than 12, as under existing law. Job searches would count as work for eight weeks rather than six, and drug treatment programs could be counted as work for limited periods.

● **Child care.** The House proposed a $1 billion increase over five years in mandatory spending on child care block grants, with offsets identified elsewhere in the budget. The

bill also would have authorized an additional $3 billion over five years in discretionary child care spending. The Senate bill proposed a $5.5 billion increase over five years in mandatory spending, without identifying offsets. A separate bill (S 2758) approved by the Senate Health, Education, Labor and Pensions Committee proposed a one-year $1 billion increase in discretionary child care assistance.

● **Legal immigrants.** Under the Senate measure, states could restore federal cash welfare benefits to legal immigrants and could extend health insurance benefits to some immigrants, including children and pregnant women. The House bill retained the 1996 ban on welfare payments to most legal immigrants.

● **State waivers.** The House bill would have allowed states to win special permission — so-called super waivers from certain federal requirements — to combine anti-poverty block grants from welfare, housing, nutrition and other programs in demonstration projects.

● **Marriage, abstinence and teen pregnancy.** The House bill would have authorized up to $300 million per year for programs aimed at promoting marriage; the Senate bill called for $200 million per year. Both measures would have authorized $50 million a year to discourage teen pregnancy. The House version focused on sexual abstinence; the Senate bill included education about contraceptives.

Background

The 1996 welfare overhaul law (PL 104-193) ended a six-decade-old guarantee of cash benefits to all eligible low-income mothers and children, replacing it with a block grant program aimed at moving those on welfare into the work force. The new Temporary Assistance for Needy Families (TANF) program took the place of Aid to Families with Dependent Children (AFDC), providing fixed block grants for programs designed and operated by the states. The law authorized $16.5 billion per year for TANF block grants through fiscal 2002. (*1996 Almanac, p. 6-3*)

States had broad discretion in deciding how to use the funds — including providing cash assistance, child care, education, job training and transportation — and in determining who would be eligible for various TANF-funded benefits and services.

However, the law did set certain criteria. To receive federal welfare funds, states were required to spend at least 75 percent of what they spent on AFDC and similar programs in fiscal 1994. States were barred from using federal welfare funds to aid most legal immigrants unless they had been in the United States for at least five years. The states could use their own funds to provide benefits to recent immigrants, but fewer than half did.

The law also required that 50 percent of the families receiving assistance under TANF engage in some kind of work-related activity for at least 30 hours each week. No family could receive federally funded assistance for more than five years. Families that received aid entirely from state funds were not subject to the federal five-year limit. About 20 states had time limits shorter than five years, but states often provided exceptions for some groups of families that met certain criteria.

Legislative Action

House Education and the Workforce Committee

The Education and the Workforce Committee approved its version of the bill (HR 4092 — H Rept 107-452, Part 1) by a party-line vote of 25-20 on May 2. The measure included the 40-hour-per-week work requirement, with at least 24 hours at a work site, and the mandate that states increase the portion of welfare recipients who worked from 50 percent to 70 percent by 2007.

In response to complaints from Democratic committee members that the GOP bill demanded more work from welfare clients without helping them pay for child care and other expenses, the panel agreed to authorize $2.3 billion for discretionary child care programs in fiscal 2003, a $200 million increase over the original proposal. The amendment, by Michael N. Castle, R-Del., was adopted, 25-21, on May 1.

The bill also included a proposal for super waivers that would allow states to combine two or more block grants in a demonstration project in areas such as employment, adult literacy and child care. Other provisions included a denial of cash assistance to those who failed to show up to work for more than two consecutive months and up to $200 million in federal funds for programs to promote marriage.

During the two-day markup May 1-2, the committee also:

● Adopted by voice vote an amendment by Chairman John A. Boehner, R-Ohio, to add funding guarantees for some programs and to clarify that child care grants in the bill were intended for all low-income families, not just those in the TANF program.

● Rejected, 22-25, an amendment by George Miller, D-Calif., to devote $8 billion annually to discretionary child care block grants.

● Rejected, 22-26, a proposal by Dale E. Kildee, D-Mich., to strike the super waiver provision.

● Rejected, 17-24, a proposal by Dennis J. Kucinich, D-Ohio, to allow families of welfare recipients to continue receiving benefits even if the recipient did not report to work for a month.

● Rejected, 18-26, an amendment by Robert C. Scott, D-Va., to prohibit religious discrimination against beneficiaries by charitable organizations that contracted with a state to provide assistance.

● Rejected, 9-36, a proposal by Patsy T. Mink, D-Hawaii, to allow therapy for physical and mental disabilities, literacy training or drug rehabilitation to count toward work requirements.

● Rejected, 20-26, a Mink amendment to add domestic and sexual violence counseling to the list of required services for recipients.

House Ways and Means Committee

The House Ways and Means Committee approved its version of the bill (HR 4090 — H Rept 107-460, Part 1) on May 2, the same day the Education and the Workforce Committee acted. The party-line vote was 23-16.

The committee proposed to hold mandatory spending on child care grants to $2.7 billion annually through fiscal 2005. (Ways and Means had jurisdiction over the mandatory grants, while Education and the Workforce had oversight

of discretionary spending. Mandatory spending did not require separate appropriations.)

An attempt by Pete Stark, D-Calif., to boost the funds by by $11.3 billion over five years failed, 13-21. Committee Chairman Bill Thomas, R-Calif., said he would support adding $2 billion over five years when the bill was prepared formally for the House floor in the Rules Committee.

Like the Education and the Workforce version, the Ways and Means bill required that 70 percent of welfare recipients be working by fiscal 2007, and that they work 40 hours per week. Other provisions increased from 30 percent to 50 percent the portion of TANF funds that states could transfer to their child care block grants and authorized $300 million annually for programs to promote stable marriages, including premarital education, counseling and research into keeping families together.

During the markup, the committee:

• Rejected by voice vote an amendment by Jim McDermott, D-Wash., to maintain the 30-hour minimum weekly requirement for work and work-related activities.

• Rejected, 15-22, an amendment by Xavier Becerra, D-Calif., that would have restored most welfare benefits for legal immigrants.

• Rejected, 16-23, a proposal by Charles B. Rangel, D-N.Y., to extend eligibility for TANF grants to Puerto Rico, the Virgin Islands and Guam.

• Rejected, 15-20, a proposal by Benjamin L. Cardin, D-Md., to include the first 20 hours of vocational training and education as part of an individual's minimum work requirement.

House Floor Action

After hours of debate, the House on May 16 passed a new bill (HR 4737) introduced by the GOP leadership that incorporated the work of the two committees with some changes. The vote was 229-197, with 14 Democrats supporting the bill. (*House vote 170, p. H-58*)

The bill would have increased annual mandatory child care grants from $2.7 billion to $2.9 billion, a total increase of $1 billion over five years. It would have authorized $2.3 billion in discretionary spending on child care in fiscal 2003, an increase of $200 million. An additional $200 million would be authorized for each succeeding year, reaching a total of $3.1 billion in fiscal 2007. States would be allowed to shift up to 50 percent of their welfare grants to child care each year, up from 30 percent.

Other provisions included authorizing up to $300 million a year in federal and matching state grants for marriage-promotion programs and $50 million a year for initiatives aimed at encouraging teenagers to abstain from sex.

Democrats said the measure demanded more of low-income parents without helping them get adequate education and training, or paying for care for their children while they worked. A Democratic substitute, offered by Cardin, would have increased mandatory spending on child care by $11 billion over five years, maintained the 30-hour-per-week work requirement, allowed legal immigrants to receive benefits, and increased TANF funding annually to keep up with inflation. It was rejected, 198-222. "Thank God, there's a Senate, and thank God they are working in a much more bipartisan way," Cardin said later. (*House vote 168, p. H-58*)

Bush praised the House for passing the legislation and urged the Senate to follow up quickly.

The bill reached the floor after a last-minute debate within the GOP caucus over the super waiver proposals. Thomas and other backers of the idea hoped it would allow states to provide creative services for welfare families, such as putting food stamp coupons and welfare payments on the same debit cards or designing a single application for housing and job-training aid. But appropriators and authorizers complained that the provision would allow states to flout restrictions that Congress had placed on grant programs. The leadership revised the bill slightly to clarify that states could not get waivers for congressional restrictions on funding, especially bans on moving funds from one account to another.

Senate Finance Committee

Senate Finance Committee Chairman Max Baucus, D-Mont., pushed a more bipartisan version of the bill — a necessity if the measure was to have a chance of passing in the narrowly divided chamber. The Finance Committee approved the bill June 26 by a vote of 13-8, with the help of three Republicans — Orrin G. Hatch of Utah, Frank H. Murkowski of Alaska and Olympia J. Snowe of Maine. However, Baucus lost the backing of Daschle, who served on the committee and cast the one Democratic "no" vote.

The bill (HR 4737 — S Rept 107-221) retained the existing requirement that adults on welfare work 30 hours per week. It called for extending health care coverage to some legal immigrants. And it included an additional $5.5 billion in mandatory child care spending over five years — significantly more than the $1 billion, five-year increase called for in the House-passed bill. The committee had jurisdiction over the mandatory funds.

Some Senate Democrats wanted to add as much as $11.3 billion over five years for child care, arguing that low-income parents needed significantly more help in paying for day care as they worked their way off welfare. Daschle and others planned a fight on the issue later in the summer when the bill was expected to reach the floor. "If we are serious about moving people from assistance to self-sufficiency, we need to give them the tools to do so," Daschle said.

Although the Republicans who backed the bill in committee wanted more child care aid than the House-passed bill would provide, Hatch cautioned against asking Bush to go too high. "The worst thing we can do is load it up with a lot of spending that guarantees its demise," he said.

During the markup, the Finance Committee:

• Approved, 12-9, an amendment by Bob Graham, D-Fla., to give states the option of allowing some legal immigrants, including children and pregnant women, to receive health insurance coverage under Medicaid and the State Children's Health Insurance Program. Graham said his amendment, expected to cost $660 million over five years, would help bring health care to 176,000 people, including many children.

Republicans winced at the price tag. Jon Kyl, R-Ariz., noted that legal immigrants entering the United States had to have a local sponsor who pledged to provide financial backing if needed, including medical expenses. "We don't need to provide an incentive for people to immigrate here who are a burden on society," Kyl said.

• Rejected, 8-12, a Kyl proposal to provide $120 million

a year to states for costs of providing emergency hospital care for undocumented aliens.

• Approved by voice vote a series of amendments that would have allowed states to count college courses as fulfilling a recipient's work requirement, transfer up to 10 percent of their cash assistance grants into the social services block grant and waive the work requirement for an adult who was the only able-bodied person caring for a disabled family member. States also would be allowed to continue applying for waivers to develop innovative local programs not specifically authorized under the 1996 welfare law.

Jeff Bingaman, D-N.M., dropped a proposal to add an additional $1.5 billion for child care grants after Hatch objected to more mandatory spending. Hatch's support was crucial because other Republicans were expected to follow his lead when the bill reached the floor.

Senate Health, Education, Labor and Pensions

On Sept. 4, the Senate Health, Education, Labor and Pensions Committee gave voice vote approval to a separate bill (S 2758) that called for a $1 billion increase in discretionary child care subsidies in fiscal 2003, bringing the total authorization for that year to $3.1 billion. The Senate was expected to merge the bill with the Finance Committee version of HR 4737.

The bill, sponsored by Christopher J. Dodd, D-Conn., required that states set aside 10 percent of the grant money to improve the quality of child care and 5 percent to increase payment for child care providers. Chairman Edward M. Kennedy, D-Mass., said only one in seven daycare centers provided a level of quality that promoted healthy development and that the annual turnover rate for child care workers was more than 30 percent. Senate Democrats and a few Republicans said many eligible families were denied subsidies because the program did not have enough money.

The committee rejected, by voice vote, a substitute offered by ranking Republican Judd Gregg of New Hampshire that would have added $1 billion in discretionary money over five years. ◆

Charitable Choice by Executive Order

President Bush came into office eager to expand the role of religious organizations in providing federally subsidized social services. He also wanted to create new federal tax breaks to encourage private giving to charities.

The House passed a bill (HR 7) in 2001 that reflected much of Bush's wish list, but by the time the measure left the Senate Finance Committee in 2002, it contained only the tax breaks. Even that proposal was too controversial to reach the floor in the Democratic-controlled chamber, and the bill died at the end of the session.

In the absence of congressional action, Bush ordered Cabinet departments to carry out many of the provisions by executive order.

Bush had begun the year hoping to revive his faith-based initiative, which had languished after the House passed its bill in July 2001. His prospects turned on a bipartisan Senate compromise developed by Joseph I. Lieberman, D-Conn., and Rick Santorum, R-Pa. Like the House-passed bill, the Lieberman-Santorum plan (S 1924) would have increased tax breaks for charitable donations and required equal treatment for faith-based organizations competing to deliver a range of federally funded social services. But unlike the House bill, the Lieberman-Santorum plan did not seek to exempt religious groups from state and local anti-discrimination laws outside the scope of federal law or allow federal agencies to offer indirect aid to religious groups, such as vouchers needy families could take to religious groups to pay for drug treatment or day care.

Many Senate Democrats still objected, fearing the bill

BoxScore

Bill:
HR 7

Legislative Action:
Senate Finance Committee approved H 7, amended (S Rept 107-211), by voice vote June 18.

would leave the door open for groups to practice hiring discrimination while using federal funds. Instead, the Senate Finance Committee reported only the tax portion. Lieberman and Santorum hoped to add their charitable choice provisions on the Senate floor, but the bill never made it that far.

Background

The basic charitable choice provisions of the House bill — allowing religious groups to deliver federal services on an equal basis with other organizations without playing down their religious mission or hiring people who do not share their faith — were not new. They were an expansion of provisions in the 1996 welfare overhaul (PL 104-193), which allowed religious groups to provide federally funded family assistance services, foster care and adoption assistance without removing religious icons or giving up their exemption under the 1964 Civil Rights Act to use religious beliefs in their hiring and firing decisions. The groups could not discriminate against beneficiaries, however. Subsequent laws added several more services that such groups could provide.

What ignited controversy over the House bill was the proposed expansion of charitable choice to virtually the entire range of social services, including crime prevention, housing grants, job training and programs for older Americans. Many Democrats and moderate Republicans worried about allowing religious groups to discriminate in hiring with federal funds. They also worried that the bill would supersede state and local anti-discrimination laws, particularly

those that protected the hiring of gays and lesbians and provided domestic partner benefits. (*2001 Almanac, p. 17-3*)

Legislative Action

Senate Committee Action

The response of the Senate Finance Committee was to approve a more limited version of the House bill (H 7 — S Rept 107-211) that left out the charitable choice provisions. The amended bill, approved by voice vote June 18, consisted of a tax package to help spur charitable giving and assist small nonprofit groups and low-income taxpayers.

The bill included provisions to:

• Create a special tax deduction for taxpayers who did not itemize their deductions and could not deduct charitable donations under existing law. Non-itemizers would be able to deduct contributions of between $250 and $500; the deduction for couples would be between $500 and $1,000. The House bill included a deduction by 2010 of up to $100 for individuals and $200 for couples.

• Restore funding for the Social Services Block Grant, which helped states pay for day care and other services for the poor. Up to 10 percent of the Temporary Assistance for Needy Families program funds could go to the grant.

• Allow tax-free deductions from individual retirement accounts for contributions to qualified charities.

• Create tax-free savings accounts, or individual development accounts, for low-income individuals and families.

• Authorize up to $10 million per year in matching funds to nonprofit groups that helped low-income taxpayers prepare tax returns.

Sponsors hoped to take up the bill in the lame-duck session, but they held off because they were unable to line up enough votes to defeat an amendment that some saw as a poison pill. The proposal, which Jack Reed, D-R.I., planned to offer, would have prohibited religious groups from using federal funds to hire based on their religious beliefs.

Executive Action

Bush announced Dec. 12 that key provisions of the stalled legislation would be implemented by executive order. He directed all federal agencies to maintain what he called "a level playing field for faith-based organizations" when awarding social service grants and specified that groups could retain their religious identity while carrying out federally funded programs. He called specifically on the Federal Emergency Management Agency and the departments of Housing and Urban Development and Health and Human Services to revise their policies to give equal consideration to religious organizations. The White House also issued a guidebook explaining what faith-based groups needed to do to qualify for government grants, including the proper uses of federal money. Bush made his remarks at a White House Conference on Faith-Based and Community Initiatives held in Philadelphia. ◆

Chapter 16

TAXES

Modest Stimulus Bill Enacted

After fighting to an impasse over legislation to stimulate the economy, Republicans and Democrats agreed on a scaled-back bill built around unemployment benefits and limited business tax breaks. The bill cleared March 8 and was signed into law the following day (HR 3090 — PL 107-147).

The measure, which was expected to cost $94 billion through 2007, gave an extra 13 weeks of unemployment benefits to workers who had exhausted them and provided $43 billion worth of temporary business tax breaks, including an immediate 30 percent deduction of the cost of new equipment purchased through 2003. It also provided tax incentives for rebuilding lower Manhattan and temporarily extended a package of narrow business tax provisions, most of which had expired at the end of 2001.

Enactment capped a long debate between and within the two parties over the best way to try to jump-start the economy. Republicans promoted a broad package of tax relief for individuals and businesses, while Democrats focused on aid for the jobless and new spending on infrastructure and homeland security.

Even as those approaches were running aground in a bitterly divided Senate, a consensus was there for the asking on a set of proposals that included extension of unemployment benefits, temporary tax relief for new investment, tax incentives for New York City and tax relief for money-losing corporations.

Still, House Republicans and Senate Democrats focused for months on expanding the package to include party-defining proposals that had no chance of enactment. As the debate wore on, signs that the economy was recovering undercut the pressure for an economic stimulus.

Finally, with six months of benefits about to expire for workers unemployed since the Sept. 11, 2001, terrorist attacks, House Republicans persuaded their leadership to drop the gamesmanship in favor of a bill that could become law.

All sides declared victory, though few found much to savor. "Bingo! Congress passes half a stimulus!" quipped Senate Minority Whip Don Nickles, R-Okla. On the other side of the Capitol, Rep. Jim McDermott, D-Wash., told his colleagues, "I urge everyone to vote for a bad compromise."

"We sort of filibustered our way through the recession, and the argument is not there for it anymore," said John B. Breaux, D-La., who worked for months with other Senate centrists to try to broker a deal on a stimulus package.

BoxScore

Bill:
HR 3090 — PL 107-147

Legislative Action:

House passed HR 3090 (H Rept 107-251), 216-214, on Oct. 24, 2001.

Senate passed HR 622, amended, by voice vote, Feb. 6, 2002.

House passed HR 622, amended, 225-199, on Feb. 14.

Senate passed HR 3090, amended, by voice vote Feb. 14.

House passed HR 3090, amended, 417-3, on March 7.

Senate cleared HR 3090, 85-9, on March 8.

President signed March 9.

Highlights

The following are the main elements of the new law:

- **Unemployment insurance.** Up to 13 additional weeks of unemployment compensation for those who had exhausted their 26 weeks of regular benefits. Workers in states that continued to experience unemployment rates of 4 percent or higher would receive an additional 13 weeks of benefits. Estimated six-year cost: $13.1 billion.

- **Accelerated depreciation.** An extra 30 percent first-year deduction for equipment purchased on or since Sept. 11, 2001. The provision was good for three years. The business lobby argued that depreciation schedules, which determine the pace at which companies can write off equipment purchases over time, needed updating to reflect the rapid pace of technological innovation. The high-tech community, in particular, lobbied heavily for the provision. Estimated six-year cost: $59.5 billion.

- **Net operating loss carryback.** A temporary extension — from two years to five — of the period over which businesses could use net operating losses to offset past tax liability. The provision, meant to aid businesses that suffered losses during the recession, applied to losses in 2001 and 2002. Estimated six-year cost: $4.3 billion.

- **Expired tax breaks.** Extension, generally through Dec. 31, 2003, of a set of narrow tax breaks, most of which had expired at the end of 2001. The provisions, orphaned for months by the political wrangling over the economic stimulus bill, included tax credits for employers who hired hard-to-place workers, credits for buying electric vehicles, and an extension through 2006 of a provision that allowed U.S. financial services firms or financing subsidiaries operating overseas to defer payment of U.S. taxes on income earned abroad. Estimated six-year cost: $12.8 billion.

- **New York City.** Tax incentives to encourage investment and rebuilding in the area of lower Manhattan affected most directly by the Sept. 11 terrorist attacks. The bill included up to $2,400 in wage credits to firms affected by the attacks, a bonus 30 percent tax deduction for property investment in the area, an increase from $24,000 to $35,000 in deduction for small businesses that owned property in the area, and authorization for up to $17 billion in new or refinanced tax-exempt bonds to rebuild or rehabilitate property in the zone. Estimated six-year cost: $4.8 billion.

Background

The Sept. 11 attacks — which destroyed the twin towers of the World Trade Center, closed the New York Stock Exchange for four days of trading and sent shock waves through the economy — set off an intense debate over what Congress should do to stimulate a recovery. Lawmakers already had approved a $1.35 trillion, 10-year tax cut (PL 107-16) in the first session. But the finding in November by the National Bureau of Economic Research that a recession had begun in March 2001, combined with the uncertainties growing out of Sept. 11, created new pressure for Congress to act.

There was wide agreement on the need to accelerate the rate at which business could write off capital purchases, extend the period during which firms could write off losses against past tax liability and renew a package of temporary tax provisions. All sides also agreed on the need to extend unemployment insurance and provide $300 rebate checks for those working poor who had not received checks earlier in the year as part of President Bush's tax cut.

But there also were deep partisan differences. Republicans wanted to speed up some individual rate cuts enacted in the Bush tax law and to repeal the corporate alternative minimum tax (AMT), which prevented companies from using tax breaks to avoid any taxes. Democrats insisted that the bill expand eligibility for unemployment insurance, subsidize 75 percent of COBRA continuation health coverage premiums for those who had lost their jobs, and expand Medicaid to cover those ineligible for employer-sponsored COBRA plans. Created in 1986 (PL 99-272), COBRA allowed the jobless to maintain coverage through former employers' plans if they paid up to 102 percent of the cost. The ultimate compromise contained none of those items.

An early version of HR 3090 squeaked through the Republican-controlled House in October 2001 by a vote of 216-214. The bill, estimated to cost $99.5 billion in 2002, consisted of individual and business tax cuts, including retroactive repeal of the corporate AMT, a 30 percent first-year deduction for new business equipment, accelerated depreciation for certain business purchases and extension of the net operating loss carryback. It also would have reduced capital gains taxes, made the 25 percent tax rate in Bush's 2001 tax law effective in 2002, rather than in 2006, and sent $300 tax rebates ($600 for couples) to the working poor. Democrats tried but failed to delete the AMT repeal, add a one-year extension of unemployment benefits and provide a 75 percent federal subsidy of COBRA premiums.

In the Senate, Democrats pushed an equally partisan, $66.4 billion version of HR 3090 through the Finance Committee, but Republicans were able to block floor action. The bill included a 13-week extension of unemployment benefits, a 75 percent COBRA subsidy, a more limited set of business tax breaks and rebate checks for the working poor, as well as $1.8 billion to rebuild New York City, help for Amtrak and $6 billion in aid to farmers.

When efforts to produce a compromise failed, the House on Dec. 20 passed a new $89.8 billion stimulus bill (HR 3529) by a vote of 224-193, with nine Democrats and all but two Republicans voting in favor. The bill was built on the consensus provisions, including the 13-week extension of unemployment benefits, rebate checks, expansion of the net operating loss carryback, tax benefits for New York City and renewal of expiring tax provisions. But it lost the support of most Democrats by including vouchers to cover 60 percent of the cost of premiums for COBRA or other health coverage, the immediate reduction of the 27 percent income tax rate to 25 percent, and AMT relief for corporations. The Senate did not take up the bill. (*2001 Almanac, p. 18-15*)

Legislative Action

House, Senate Exchange Bills

In the early weeks of 2002, Democrats and Republicans resumed what they all recognized as an exercise in futility. Signs of improvement in the economy reduced pressure for a deal. And what had been billed in advance as a strong call from Bush in his State of the Union message to get the economic stimulus bill back on track came out sounding lukewarm to some. "For the sake of American workers, let's pass a stimulus package," Bush said. (*Text, p. D-3*)

Majority Leader Tom Daschle, D-S.D., brought a revised plan to the Senate floor the week of Jan. 21 that included the 13-week extension of jobless worker benefits, the $300 rebate, a 30 percent first-year deduction for the cost of new business equipment, and a plan to send federal money to states to help them pay for Medicaid. GOP conservatives said the measure was far too limited, and many questioned whether it was worth the trouble. "At some point, you have to decide: Can we do this, and is it worth having?" said Minority Leader Trent Lott, R-Miss.

Daschle pulled the plug on the bill Feb. 6, after both sides fell short of the 60 votes needed to overcome procedural hurdles. Democrats failed, 56-39, to invoke cloture, or limit debate, on their plan. Republicans failed, 48-47, to move forward on an $89 billion plan that mirrored the bill passed by the House in December 2001. At that point, senators of both parties agreed to give up on an economic stimulus bill. Instead, the Senate passed by voice vote a stripped-down bill (HR 622) containing only the 13-week extension of unemployment benefits. (*Senate votes 13, 14, p. S-7*)

Despite private pleas from Senate GOP leaders, the House voted 225-199 on Feb. 14 to send HR 622 back to the Senate after substituting a text nearly identical to the December House-passed stimulus measure. More than half of the fiscal 2002 cost of the $80.9 billion House bill was for business tax breaks. "It's the difference between a House Republican who wants to fight for America, and a Senate Republican who doesn't," an exasperated House Majority Leader Dick Armey, R-Texas, told reporters Feb. 14. (*House vote 38, p. H-16*)

Senate Republicans were not impressed. The same day, they joined with Democrats to agree by voice vote to send HR 3090 back to the House — after substituting the text of HR 622, their unemployment extension.

Final Action

After a weeklong congressional recess, House GOP leaders decided their next move would be to advance a bill that combined a 13-week extension of unemployment benefits with a health care tax credit for the unemployed. They

planned to bring up the bill under suspension of the rules, which required a two-thirds majority and allowed no amendments. The bill would fail, but not before it put Democrats, who vehemently opposed the tax credit approach for health insurance, in a bind. "If Mr. Daschle wants to block health insurance for the unemployed, we think that's unfortunate," said John Shadegg of Arizona, chairman of the conservative Republican Study Committee.

But with workers who lost their jobs after Sept. 11 about to exhaust their six months of regular benefits, rank-and-file Republicans were losing patience. At a meeting March 6, House Republicans called on their leaders to put together a consensus bill that could pass the Senate. The tax cuts were narrowed to those with wide support. Gone were the individual cuts and corporate AMT repeal pushed by the Republicans. Gone, too, was the Democrats' plan to subsidize health care insurance for the unemployed.

The House passed the bill March 7 on a 417-3 vote. The Senate cleared it the next day, 85-9. (*House vote 52, p. H-22; Senate vote 44, p. S-13*) ◆

GOP Seeks Permanent Tax Cuts

House Republicans passed a series of bills in the first half of the year aimed at making various pieces of President Bush's signature 2001 tax law permanent. The offensive — dubbed the "flaming arrow strategy" by proponents — largely was ignored by the Democratic-controlled Senate, but it gave Republicans a chance to showcase their tax policies in an election year and to draw a clear distinction between themselves and most Democrats.

In an early test, the House voted 235-218 on Feb. 6 to support a nonbinding resolution (H Con Res 312) stating that the tax cuts should not expire in 2010 as specified in the law. The House subsequently passed bills to repeal the expiration date on the estate tax repeal, marriage tax breaks, pension incentives and other provisions. (*House vote 10, p. H-8*)

The expiration, or sunset, provision was the price Republicans and their newly elected president had paid to get Bush's $1.35 trillion, 10-year tax cut (PL 107-16) through Congress in May 2001. Many Republicans hoped that in 2002 they could make the cuts permanent, a goal that Bush reaffirmed in his Jan. 29 State of the Union speech and assumed in his fiscal 2003 budget. But changed circumstances made that an uphill battle. The peace, prosperity and budget surpluses of early 2000 had given way to the war on terrorism, a sagging economy and a return to budget deficits. (*Text, p. D-3*)

Republicans said the economic effects of the Sept. 11, 2001, terrorist attacks and the downturn in the economy that began in mid-2000 were to blame for renewed deficits, and they argued that further tax relief would encourage spending and investment. Democratic leaders pointed to Bush's tax cuts as the chief culprit. Some, including Sen. Edward M. Kennedy, D-Mass., went further, calling for a delay or even a repeal of some of Bush's cuts.

BoxScore

Bills:

HR 586 (sunset repeal);

HR 2143 (estate tax);

HR 4019 (marriage tax);

HR 4800 (adoption);

HR 4823 (Holocaust payments)

HR 4931 (pensions)

Legislative Action:

House passed HR 586, 229-198, on April 18.

House passed HR 4800, 391-1, and HR 4823, 392-1, June 4.

House passed HR 2143, 256-171, on June 6.

House passed HR 4019, 271-142, on June 13.

House passed HR 4931, 308-70, on June 21.

Background

The 2001 tax law, which fulfilled a top Bush campaign pledge, cut income tax rates across the board and created a new 10 percent bracket for a portion of income previously taxed at 15 percent.

The measure also provided tax breaks for married couples, starting in 2005; doubled the child tax credit by 2010; repealed the estate tax in 2010 after cutting the top rate from 55 percent to 45 percent; and increased annual contribution limits on individual retirement accounts (IRAs) and other retirement savings. It also temporarily increased the income limits exempting taxpayers from the alternative minimum tax (AMT) through 2004. (*2001 Almanac, p. 18-3*)

To keep costs within limits set in the fiscal 2002 budget resolution (H Con Res 83), and to satisfy Senate budget rules that disqualified provisions on a reconciliation bill that would reduce revenues for more than 10 years, all provisions were set to expire Dec. 31, 2010. After that date, the tax code would revert to previous law.

Almost as soon as the tax measure became law, legislation was introduced to make the cuts permanent.

Legislative Action

Repeal of Sunset Provision

On April 18, the House voted 229-198 to make Bush's tax cuts permanent. The vehicle was a Senate-passed bill (HR 586) aimed at expanding a tax credit for foster care payments. The House replaced those provisions with a proposal to repeal the sunset date for, among other provisions, the reductions in individual marginal rates, the repeal of the estate tax, the increase in the child tax credit, and the in-

crease in the standard deduction for married couples. The Joint Committee on Taxation, Congress' final word on the cost of tax bills, estimated the price tag at $372.8 billion for 2002 to 2012. (*House vote 103, p. H-38*)

The bill also included proposals to change penalty and interest provisions in the tax code to protect taxpayers, and alter internal IRS rules and disciplinary procedures. "This is a vote between the parties that is a philosophical difference," Thomas M. Davis III of Virginia, chairman of the National Republican Congressional Committee, said April 18. "That's why we have campaigns: to fight over this."

"Let me assure you that this vote is going to be the subject of a lot of campaigns for the House this fall," said Minority Leader Richard A. Gephardt, D-Mo. "We intend to raise this vote as the vote on whether or not you want to keep Social Security strong, or whether you don't care about Social Security." Nine Democrats backed the bill, as opposed to 28 who had voted for the 2001 overhaul. "The bottom line is, times have changed," said Jim Matheson, D-Utah, who backed the 2001 bill but voted "no" on repealing the sunset requirement.

Estate Tax Repeal

On June 6, the House endorsed a permanent repeal of the estate tax (HR 2143) on a bipartisan 256-171 vote. Joint Tax estimated the bill's cost in 2011-2012 at $80.7 billion. (*House vote 219, p. H-72*)

Republicans viewed the estate tax repeal as the portion of the 2001 law most worth fighting for. Not only did it appeal to their political base, but it also had important Democratic support. While the repeal affected only a relatively small number of taxpayers — the majority of estates, those valued at less than $675,000, were exempt from taxation even before the 2001 law — Republicans successfully cast the debate as a fight to preserve family farms and family-controlled small businesses. That made the repeal attractive in farm states, where several Democratic senators were in tight re-election races.

But the momentum behind the legislation collapsed a week later in the Senate. Phil Gramm, R-Texas, tried to waive budget rules in order to get a vote on a permanent repeal, but failed on a 54-44 vote. While the supporters had a majority, they were short of the 60 votes required to waive the point of order. Majority Leader Tom Daschle, D-S.D., said the tally fulfilled a commitment he had made to allow a vote on the estate tax repeal in June and that he planned to let it stand as the Senate's final word on the tax cut permanency question for the year. (*Senate vote 151, p. S-32*)

Two Democratic alternatives to a full repeal also fell on budget-related points of order. The first, by Byron L. Dorgan of North Dakota, would have exempted the first $4 million of an estate from taxation and provided a full deduction for family-owned businesses starting in 2003. It was rejected, 44-54. The second, by Kent Conrad, also of North Dakota,

would have set a top estate tax rate of 50 percent and exempted the first $3 million. It fell, 38-60. (*Senate votes 149, 150, pp. S-31, S-32*)

Marriage Tax Breaks

On June 13, the House voted 271-142 to pass legislation (HR 4019) to make the tax breaks for married couples permanent. Sixty Democrats voted for the bill, as did every Republican who voted. (*House vote 229, p. H-76*)

The provisions in question gradually increased the standard deduction for married couples to twice that for individuals, and changed the portion of their income subject to the 15 percent rate to double that of a single person. By 2008, a married couple would be able to earn $3,000 more than a single person and still qualify for the earned-income tax credit. Extending those provisions for two years, through 2012, would cost an additional $41.9 billion, according to the Joint Tax Committee.

Pension Incentives

On June 21, the House voted to remove the expiration date on tax incentives for pension and retirement contributions contained in the 2001 law. The vote on the bill (HR 4931) was 308-70. (*House vote 248, p. H-82*)

The incentives included increased contribution limits for IRAs and elective deferral plans such as 401(k)s; "catch-up" contributions for individuals age 50 and older; modifications to rollover rules for workers who moved their pension savings when changing jobs; faster vesting of pension plans; and modifications to pension security, enforcement and small-business regulations. The bill did not apply to a temporary non-refundable tax credit for contributions to eligible retirement plans by certain middle- and low-income taxpayers, scheduled to expire in 2006.

An amendment by Richard E. Neal, D-Mass., that would have provided additional benefits for lower-level employees and placed additional restrictions on retirement plan tax breaks for top executives was rejected 182-204. (*House vote 246, p. H-82*)

Adoption, Holocaust Survivors

On June 4, the House voted to make permanent two other popular pieces of the 2001 tax law. One of the bills (HR 4800) would have repealed the sunset on provisions that increased the adoption tax credit from $5,000 ($6,000 for children with special needs) to $10,000, and that doubled to $10,000 the amount an employer could deduct for employee-adoption assistance. The second (HR 4823) was to retain an income exclusion for Holocaust restitution payments. The bills passed on votes of 391-1 and 392-1, respectively, with Charles W. Stenholm, D-Texas, casting the only "nay" votes. He said the dwindling surplus meant it was not the time to deny the Treasury revenue. (*House votes 207, 208, p. H-70*) ◆

Add-Ons Sink Investor Tax Breaks

House Republican leaders were hoping in October to pass a pre-election package of tax breaks aimed at helping the 84 million Americans whose investments in stocks and mutual funds had suffered losses during the continuing decline in the stock market. The tax benefits would have relaxed retirement savings rules and increased the immediate write-off for stock market losses. But intraparty disputes over provisions that Ways and Means Committee Chairman Bill Thomas, R-Calif., tried to add to the package prompted GOP leaders to put off further action until 2003.

At the behest of the Republican leadership, the Ways and Means Committee approved two investor-friendly tax bills in October. One (HR 1619) would have raised to $8,250 the amount of capital losses taxpayers could deduct each year from ordinary income. The other (HR 5558) would have increased the amount people could contribute tax-free to Individual Retirement Accounts (IRAs), 401(k)s and other retirement savings accounts, while gradually increasing to 70½ the age at which retirees were required to make annual withdrawals.

The leadership planned to combine the bills into a $65 billion, 10-year package and win passage before the midterm elections. The proposals had wide backing among Republicans, and many Democrats supported some elements, particularly the retirement savings breaks.

But just before the measure was to go to the floor, Thomas inserted several controversial provisions, including a proposal to retroactively penalize U.S. companies that relocated their headquarters to Bermuda or other offshore locations in order to reduce their federal income taxes.

The provisions drew objections from rank-and-file Republicans, as well as from Majority Leader Dick Armey, R-Texas, killing the tax package for the year.

Legislative Action

House Committee Action

The House Ways and Means Committee approved both bills Oct. 8. Thomas had drafted the proposals reluctantly under instructions from Speaker J. Dennis Hastert, R-Ill., Armey, and Majority Whip Tom DeLay, R-Texas, but he insisted that they go through his committee.

Democrats on the committee opposed the tax breaks, arguing that their combined cost would worsen the deficit, and that they would benefit rich investors more than middle-income ones. Thomas said the breaks would not do much to stimulate the economy, but would "help build market confidence and restore the losses of America's investors."

● **Capital loss deduction.** The first bill (HR 1619 — H Rept 107-734) was approved on a party-line vote of 24-11.

BoxScore

Bills:

HR 1619, HR 5558

Legislative Action:

House Ways and Means Committee approved HR 1619 (H Rept 107-734), 24-11, and HR 5558 (H Rept 107-733), 24-10 — both on Oct. 8.

It proposed to increase from $3,000 to $8,250 the amount of capital losses an investor could deduct from ordinary income. The amount would be indexed for inflation after 2002.

Under existing law, there was no limit to the amount of losses a taxpayer could claim, as long as they were deducted against capital gains. The limit came into play if his or her losses exceeded gains that year. Up to $3,000 of the additional losses could be subtracted from ordinary income, but amounts above $3,000 had to be carried over to future years when they could be deducted from gains.

Democrats argued that the proposal might actually have a negative effect on the markets because it would encourage people to sell stocks and cause the market to tumble further. Republicans defeated an amendment by Earl Pomeroy, D-N.D., to make the increased deduction a one-year break for 2002 and grant it only to individuals who made less than $75,000 ($150,000 for couples).

● **Retirement savings.** The second bill (HR 5558 — H Rept 107-733), approved on another party-line vote of 24-10, was aimed at increasing retirement savings.

The bill would have allowed investors to keep their money longer in tax-deferred retirement accounts, gradually raising the age when individuals had to start making withdrawals to 75 from 70½. Republicans said the change, which was projected to cost the U.S. Treasury almost $27 billion over 10 years, would allow more time for retirees' portfolios to rebound with the stock market. Under existing law, required withdrawals did not force the sale of stock; the assets could be shifted from retirement accounts to regular accounts, with tax then paid on the withdrawals.

The other main provision would have allowed individuals to contribute more money tax-free to retirement savings accounts such as IRAs and 401(k)s. It would have made effective in 2003 increases that were not scheduled to be phased in until 2008 under the 2001 tax cut law (PL 107-16). For example, an individual would be able to contribute $5,000 tax-free to an IRA in 2003, rather than the $3,000 maximum under existing law. Republicans argued that a fresh wave of money into the market could help boost stock prices and inspire investor confidence. (*2001 Almanac p. 18-12*)

The measure was a scaled-back version of legislation proposed by Rob Portman, R-Ohio, and Benjamin L. Cardin, D-Md. Cardin voted against the bill in committee, saying it should not be rushed through.

House Floor Action

Plans to bring the bill to the floor Oct. 11 were thwarted when Thomas defied GOP leaders with several new provi-

Corporate Inversions and Taxes

In the wake of a wave of corporate scandals, many in Congress were eager to show they were cracking down on corporate misbehavior. Several bills targeted U.S. companies that reincorporated in places such as Bermuda or the Cayman Islands where there was little or no taxation on businesses in order to minimize their U.S. tax bills. Only one relatively weak provision was enacted, however: The law (PL 107-296) creating the Department of Homeland Security prohibited the awarding of some federal contracts to such companies.

The practice was known as corporate inversion, because the company first created an offshore subsidiary — often nothing more than a post office box — and then inverted its corporate structure by making the subsidiary the parent. The location of the company's actual operations remained unchanged, with most employees still working in the United States.

Conservatives and some business trade groups, including the U.S. Chamber of Commerce, fought efforts to curb the practice, arguing that the best way to avoid corporate expatriation was to cut corporate taxes in the United States.

In June, the Senate Finance Committee approved two bills (S 2119, S 2498), but neither was brought to the floor. In July, House Ways and Means Committee Chairman Bill Thomas, R-Calif., introduced a bill to overhaul the tax treatment of income earned abroad (HR 5095) that sought to strip the advantages of registering a head-

quarters overseas. The bill was widely opposed and never put before the committee.

Democratic lawmakers found some success with a less direct approach: a push to deny federal contracts to companies that moved their headquarters offshore. On July 26, the House voted, 318-110, for language by Rosa DeLauro, D-Conn., to attach such a ban to the initial House homeland security bill (HR 5005). (*House vote 366, p. H-114*)

On Sept. 5, Sen. Paul Wellstone, D-Minn., won voice vote adoption of a similar amendment to the Senate version of the homeland bill. But in final negotiations, language was added allowing the Homeland Department secretary to waive the restriction. Three moderate Senate Republicans said they had assurances the waiver would be revisited in 2003. Stronger anti-inversion legislation was written in the fall but went no further. Thomas included a retroactive moratorium on offshore relocations in a draft investor tax cut package, but opposition from Republican leaders effectively scuttled the bill. Senate Finance Committee Chairman Max Baucus, D-Mont., proposed ending the tax breaks for inversions to help offset the cost of a small-business tax cut, but a lack of consensus doomed his package. (*Investor tax cuts, p. 16-7*)

In November, the Treasury Department proposed requiring companies to disclose the full costs and tax consequences of inversion transactions to shareholders.

sions, including small-business tax cuts, a limited extension of unemployment benefits and a plan to retroactively penalize U.S. companies that relocated their headquarters to Bermuda and other offshore locations to reduce their taxes.

With the White House ambivalent on new tax cuts and the Senate poised to kill the bill, Thomas saw the effort as a waste of time and preferred laying down a marker for legislation to come in the 108th Congress, when real

solutions to corporate tax dodging and foreign tax disputes could be addressed.

The corporate expatriate provision not only upset GOP conservatives, it was a particularly insulting goodbye gift to Armey, who was retiring. Armey had argued for years that rather than punishing companies for moving offshore, Congress should reduce the incentives for such action by cutting corporate income taxes. ◆

Chapter 17

TECHNOLOGY & SCIENCE

Broadband Deregulation Blocked

The House passed a bill to deregulate the market for high-speed Internet service over telephone lines. But the measure — the largest and most controversial piece of telecommunications legislation in the 107th Congress — went no further. Senate Commerce, Science and Transportation Committee Chairman Ernest F. Hollings, D-S.C., blocked action in the Senate.

The House bill (HR 1542) — sponsored by Energy and Commerce Committee Chairman Billy Tauzin, R-La., and ranking Democrat John D. Dingell of Michigan — would have loosened certain legal restrictions imposed on the regional Bell phone companies by the 1996 Telecommunications Act (PL 104-104).

Specifically, it would have allowed the Bells to transmit high-speed Internet traffic over telephone lines outside their service regions without first having to meet requirements in the 1996 law that they open their local systems to competition. The bill also would have rolled back regulatory requirements that allowed rivals to use a Bell's advanced lines and equipment at a discount to provide high-speed Internet services. Bells said that acted as a disincentive to spending the amounts needed to upgrade the equipment. The aim was to enable the Bells to compete head-to-head with unregulated cable TV operators in the high-speed, broadband market.

After spending most of 2001 pushing the bill through the committee process, Tauzin began the year with a commitment from House GOP leaders to bring the measure to a quick vote. The Bells were among the largest employers in many districts, and they targeted an extensive advertising and lobbying campaign at House members. Still, some holdouts voiced concerns about how much access Bell competitors would have to the companies' high-speed networks. (*2001 Almanac, p. 16-4*)

In the end, a surprisingly large majority of House members accepted Tauzin and Dingell's arguments that the 1996 law needed to be overhauled to address the advent of new data services. But House passage of the bill Feb. 27 was the high-water mark for the legislation.

Hollings, who had a leading role in writing the 1996 act and was a staunch foe of the Bells, denounced the Tauzin-Dingell bill and vowed to kill it even as the House was debating the measure. In a fiery hearing March 20, Hollings belittled the bill in several sharp exchanges with Tauzin, while reserving grudging praise for both sponsors' persistence. He said the bill would tilt the competitive balance in the telecommunications market in favor of regional Bells and help them consolidate control over local phone markets. "I've said time and again, the only thing I like about [HR] 1542 is the authors," Hollings said.

Dingell's blunt response: "If you can do it better than we did, we challenge you to do it; we urge you to do it, and we hope you succeed."

BoxScore

Bill:
HR 1542

Legislative Action:

House passed HR 1542, 273-157, on Feb. 27.

Background

There was widespread agreement on the importance of promoting broadband — high-speed networks that could transmit huge volumes of voice, video and computer data over long distances. But there was significant disagreement over what role, if any, the government should have.

Cable companies, with about a 70 percent share of the residential broadband market, were largely unregulated and free to hook up their Internet customers via the same fiber-optic lines they used to deliver video signals.

The Bells — Verizon Communications, SBC Communications Inc., BellSouth Corp. and Qwest Communications International Inc. — could use their lines to provide Internet services to their customers, but they had technological and competitive problems not faced by the cable companies. First, their copper phone lines could only provide broadband Internet services to homes located within a mile or two of the phone company's central switching office. To take this digital subscriber line, or DSL service, farther required the Bells to run fiber-optic lines into residential neighborhoods, then connect to the copper lines going into individual homes in order to limit the distance DSL signals had to travel over the copper wire.

Bells also had to meet a series of pro-competitive provisions in the 1996 law before they could transmit computer data outside of local service regions. The conditions included opening their local phone networks to competitors, and allowing rivals to lease individual parts of their networks at below-retail prices. In 1999, the Federal Communications Commission (FCC) ruled that the line-sharing requirements also applied to advanced equipment and lines used for DSL broadband services, meaning that competitors could use the Bell's local lines to provide DSL services at a discount. (*1996 Almanac, p. 3-43*)

Legislative Action

House Floor Action

The House passed the Tauzin-Dingell bill Feb. 27 by a vote of 273-157. The outcome, which had been predicted for weeks, put the House on record as siding with the FCC and its deregulation-minded chairman, Michael K. Powell, who wanted to eliminate rules he said had been made obsolete by rapid technological change. (*House vote 45, p. H-20*)

Much of the daylong debate focused on competing views of how much access rivals should have to the Bells' high-speed networks. The Bells balked at building out new fiber optic lines to provide DSL service if it meant they would be required under the 1996 law to share them with competitors at below-retail cost.

Bill opponents, led by Chris Cannon, R-Utah, and John Conyers Jr., D-Mich., offered language that would have maintained the access requirements of the 1996 law. It was effectively killed, 173-256, on a procedural motion. *(House vote 44, p. H-20)*

An alternative — by Tauzin-Dingell supporters Steve Buyer, R-Ind., and Edolphus Towns, D-N.Y. — proposed separate rules for fiber optic and copper lines. Bells using fiber optic lines to provide broadband Internet services would be required to carry competitor's broadband services at "just and reasonable" rates and terms set by the FCC — a change from the existing requirement that competitors be able to lease individual elements of the network at below-retail prices. Competitors could continue leasing the DSL portion of a Bell's copper lines at discount rates if the service was provided exclusively over a copper line, but that limited the discount to homes near a phone company's central office. The language was added by voice vote after a lengthy series of parliamentary maneuvers.

The rule for floor debate on the bill automatically made another change that had been negotiated by the Energy and Commerce and Judiciary committees. The provisions required Bells that planned to transmit high-speed data services across long-distance boundaries — but had not gained FCC approval to provide long-distance voice services in those areas — to notify the Justice Department at least 30 days before starting the data transmissions. Judiciary Chairman F. James Sensenbrenner Jr., R-Wis., had originally wanted to require the Bells to get approval from the Justice Department before entering the long-distance market.

The rule also clarified that the 1996 law did not override or diminish federal antitrust laws, thereby overturning *Goldwasser v. Ameritech*, a 2000 decision by the 7th U.S. Circuit Court of Appeals that held that a Bell's refusal to allow a rival to connect to its local network was not an antitrust violation. Overturning the decision was also a Sensenbrenner priority.

The House adopted, 421-7, an amendment by Fred Upton, R-Mich., and Gene Green, D-Texas, to increase FCC penalties on phone companies that violated requirements of the 1996 act. It increased the maximum fine per violation from $120,000 to $1 million per day, with a cap for continuing violations rising from $1.2 million to $10 million. For repeat offenders, the penalty per violation was doubled to $2 million per day, with a cap of $20 million. The amendment also doubled, from one year to two, the statute of limitations for the FCC to bring enforcement actions against phone companies. *(House vote 43, p. H-20)*

Senate Action

In the Senate, Hollings held several hearings on telecommunications competition but did not allow the bill to advance. Commerce Committee ranking Republican John McCain of Arizona, once a proponent of even more sweeping deregulation, surprised observers by branding the Tauzin-Dingell bill as special-interest legislation.

John B. Breaux, D-La., the leading voice in the Senate for overhauling the telecommunications rules, joined with Don Nickles, R-Okla., to offer what was seen as a milder version of Tauzin-Dingell. The bill (S 2430) would have given the FCC four months to come up with rules that ensured "regulatory parity" between all broadband providers — DSL, cable TV and satellites. That would have given the Bells some of the same relief offered by Tauzin-Dingell, but Breaux would have explicitly maintained requirements of the 1996 law relating to voice services. The FCC would have had exclusive jurisdiction over broadband.

Hollings and allies, such as Ted Stevens, R-Alaska, and Daniel K. Inouye, D-Hawaii, said Breaux's approach was little more than the Tauzin-Dingell bill in sheep's clothing. Hollings introduced his own bill (S 2448) calling for loans and grants to encourage broadband deployment, especially in rural and underserved areas. Money collected from the 3 percent federal telephone excise tax would have financed the program, established wireless technology pilot projects and funded research.

Hollings also introduced a bill (S 1364) to split each of the Bells into separate retail and wholesale companies in order to spur more local telephone competition. ◆

FCC Spectrum Auction Delayed

Congress and the White House acted swiftly in June to delay indefinitely a Federal Communications Commission (FCC) auction of part of the airwaves used by television broadcasters. President Bush signed the bill into law June 19 (HR 4560 — PL 107-195).

The delay was enacted at the behest of a number of wireless telecommunications firms that argued the FCC should not auction the electromagnetic spectrum in the 700 MHz band without a comprehensive spectrum management plan in place. The companies also cited the struggling economy and signs that TV broadcasters were less than willing to vacate that part of the airwaves before a 2007 deadline.

The auction, scheduled for June 19, was required under budget and appropriations laws enacted in 1997 and 2000. The anticipated revenue was used at the time as a bookkeeping device to offset deficits, but even then, there was skepticism over whether it would materialize.

The House initially passed the bill by voice vote May 7, shortly after the Energy and Commerce Committee had given its approval, also by voice vote (H Rept 107-443). The initial version simply would have postponed all auctions of the 700 MHz band indefinitely.

The Senate passed the bill by voice vote June 18, with an amendment allowing the FCC to proceed with auctioning a slice of the 700 MHz band. The change was negotiated with Sen. Ted Stevens, R-Alaska, who was concerned that many smaller, rural wireless telecommunications carriers, including some in his home state, would not have enough spectrum to offer advanced services in rural areas. The House cleared the amended bill by voice vote the same day.

The final bill postponed the scheduled auction, except for two blocks of the lower 700 MHz band. The FCC was required to auction that lower portion as early as Aug. 19 and no later than Sept. 19. It was left to the FCC when to reschedule auctions of the upper 700 MHz band.

Background

To prepare for a transition from analog to digital television, the FCC in 1997 allocated every television station an additional band of electromagnetic spectrum in which to begin broadcasting a digital signal. The stations were expected to continue their analog broadcasts as well while they made the transition. Congress codified many of the FCC's deadlines for this transition in the 1997 Balanced Budget Act (PL 105-33), with a final requirement that all stations broadcast digital signals by the end of 2006. At that point, broadcasters would be required to discontinue their analog broadcasts

BoxScore

Bill:

HR 4560 — PL 107-195

Legislative Action:

House passed HR 4560 (H Rept 107-443) by voice vote May 7.

Senate passed HR 4560, amended, by voice vote June 18.

House cleared HR 4560 by voice vote June 18.

President signed June 19.

and return that spectrum to the FCC for reassignment to other users.

In order to count the revenue within the five years covered by the bill, however, the law required that the returned analog spectrum be auctioned off for other uses by Sept. 30, 2002 — more than four years before the return deadline. The law required that television spectrum in the upper 700 MHz band, corresponding to TV channels 60 to 69, be allocated between public safety services and commercial uses, with the commercial auctions to begin after Jan. 1, 2001. (*1997 Almanac, p. 3-34*)

In 1999, Congress advanced the timetable for auctioning the channel 60 to 69 spectrum, requiring that the proceeds from this auction be deposited in the U.S. Treasury no later than Sept. 30, 2000. The anticipated revenue was used to offset part of the cost of the fiscal 2000 omnibus appropriations act (PL 106-113). The FCC repeatedly postponed the auction. ◆

Attempt to Ban Cloning Stalls

Attempts in the Senate to pass a ban on human cloning collapsed in a dispute over whether to ban the cloning of all human embryos, or allow it for the purpose of creating human tissue for biomedical research.

In revisiting a debate that consumed the chamber in 1998 but was left similarly unresolved, senators faced profound questions, such as whether early-stage embryos are the moral equivalent of human beings. Biomedical research advocates cited potential therapies derived from cloning that might cure such conditions as juvenile diabetes and Parkinson's disease. But abortion foes argued that cloning to create tissue for research is the same as murder, because it involves destroying embryos to extract the cells.

The House took a clear stand in favor of a comprehensive ban in 2001, voting 265-162 for a bill (HR 2505) that would have imposed penalties of at least 10 years in prison and $1 million in fines on anyone who attempted to clone a human embryo for any purpose. Members rejected, with equal strength, an attempt by James C. Greenwood, R-Pa., to outlaw human cloning for the purpose of creating a child, while allowing it for medical research. The vote was 175-251. (*2001 Almanac, p. 16-3*)

Senate proponents of a broad ban (S 1899), led by sponsors Sam Brownback, R-Kan., and Mary L. Landrieu, D-La., vowed to bring the issue to the floor and pass a measure mirroring the House-passed bill.

Those who supported cloning for medical research backed a bill (S 2439) by Arlen Specter, R-Pa., Edward M. Kennedy, D-Mass., and Dianne Feinstein, D-Calif., that

would have made it a crime to try to create a human baby through cloning or to implant a cloned organism in a womb. But it would have permitted cloning to extract cells for biomedical research.

That bill got a boost in the spring, when GOP conservatives Orrin G. Hatch of Utah and Strom Thurmond of South Carolina announced that they would break with anti-abortion colleagues to back it. "A critical part of being pro-life is to support measures that help the living," Hatch said. Cloning opponents denounced Hatch's decision, but his announcement, and Thurmond's, were not unexpected. Hatch had sided with biomedical groups on patent issues and federal support for stem-cell research. Thurmond, whose daughter suffered from diabetes, had endorsed research using fetal tissue a decade earlier. He said in a statement May 3 that "support for regenerative medicine is the essence of the pro-life position."

A third bill (S 2076) by Byron L. Dorgan, D-N.D., proposed banning the implantation of a cloned organism into the womb for purposes of creating a human being. Dorgan depicted the measure as a middle ground, though critics said it would allow implantation of a cloned embryo for unspecified periods of time.

With 12 to 15 senators uncommitted, none of the proposals had the 60 votes needed to cut off a filibuster. The end came June 12, when Brownback and Majority Leader Tom Daschle, D-S.D., were unable to agree on how to bring the issue to the floor.

Daschle offered eight hours of debate between the Brown-

back-Landrieu bill and the Specter-Kennedy-Feinstein alternative. After the debate, there would have been up-or-down votes on each. Brownback wanted Specter's bill to come up first, allowing up to four amendments. Brownback hoped to offer a two-year moratorium on all cloning — a fallback proposal he hoped would stop senators from joining the other side in the debate. When Democratic Whip Harry Reid of Nevada objected, the discussion ended. ◆

Chapter 18

TRADE

Victory for Bush on Fast Track

After nearly 18 months of debate and delays that ended in two weeks of frenzied deal-making, Congress granted President Bush authority to negotiate international trade pacts without fear of last-minute changes from Congress. An appearance on Capitol Hill by the president and the support of a handful of Democrats helped break the logjam. The bill cleared Aug. 1, and Bush signed it into law (HR 3009 — PL 107-210) on Aug. 6, vowing to make quick use of it to jump-start trade talks with Chile, Singapore and Morocco. The administration was also looking ahead to the next round of global trade talks and to negotiations on a free-trade zone for most of the Western Hemisphere.

Even with fast track, however, negotiations with other nations were expected to be difficult. Bush had lost the free-trade high ground when, in a quest to win votes in Congress for fast track and better position himself for a 2004 re-election run in battleground states, he had agreed to tariffs of up to 30 percent for certain steel imports and backed a farm bill (PL 107-171) that included increased export subsidies.

The new law renewed fast-track trade negotiating authority, which the Bush administration renamed Trade Promotion Authority (TPA). It required Congress to vote up or down on trade agreements within 90 days of receiving them from the president and barred all amendments. Fast-track authority had lapsed in 1994. The law included a Democratic priority — a $12 billion expansion of the Trade Adjustment Assistance (TAA) program for workers dislocated as a result of trade deals. It also renewed an expired Andean trade preferences law that lowered tariffs on goods imported from Colombia, Bolivia, Ecuador and Peru.

The trade bill had moved in fits and starts in the first session of the 107th Congress, passing the House by just one vote on Dec. 6, 2001. The Senate Finance Committee approved its own version Dec. 12, but Majority Leader Tom Daschle, D-S.D., put off floor action until 2002. The main opposition to the bill came from Democrats who were unwilling to give the president a free hand to negotiate trade deals that they said could end up hurting American workers and undermining U.S. trade and environmental laws.

When the Senate took up its version of the bill (HR 3009) in May 2002, Democrats made substantial changes, linking fast track to a major expansion of the three-decade-old program of assistance to displaced workers, as well as adding language that would have allowed Congress to alter trade deals to protect U.S. anti-dumping laws.

Daschle hoped to use informal talks to reach a quick deal

BoxScore

Bill:

HR 3009 — PL 107-210

Legislative Action:

House passed HR 3005 (H Rept 107-249, Part 1), 215-214, on Dec. 6, 2001.

Senate passed HR 3009, amended, 66-30, on May 23.

House adopted H Res 450 (H Rept 107-518), 216-215, on June 26.

House adopted the conference report (H Rept 107-624), 215-212, on July 27.

Senate cleared HR 3009, 64-34, on Aug. 1.

President signed Aug. 6.

on a final bill, but House Ways and Means Committee Chairman Bill Thomas, R-Calif., resisted. Meanwhile, Bush was insisting the bill be sent to him before Congress left for its August recess, and all sides agreed that the closer they got to the fall elections, the less chance they would have for a compromise. A House-Senate conference finally convened in September with the daunting task of finding a deal that would hold the support of Senate Democrats, minimize the loss of GOP conservatives and attract enough House Democrats to offset any defections.

Just when the goal seemed to slip out of reach, Thomas and Senate Finance Committee Chairman Max Baucus, D-Mont., struck a deal and the bill cleared. The sudden turnaround was part of a spate of legislating before the August recess by lawmakers who were worried about looking passive at a time of reeling stock markets, unfolding tales of corporate fraud and an unsteady economy.

Highlights

The following were the main elements of the new law:

- **Expedited procedures.** The law authorized special trade promotion authority, formerly known as fast-track procedures, for congressional consideration of trade agreements reached before June 1, 2005, with an optional extension to June 1, 2007. Congress had 90 days after receiving a trade agreement from the president to pass or reject an implementing bill. No amendments would be allowed.

- **Consultations.** The U.S. trade representative (USTR) was required to consult with relevant congressional committees, as well as a newly created Congressional Oversight Group, before initialing any agreement. Failure to consult with Congress would make the trade agreement ineligible for fast-track procedures, if both chambers agreed.

Also, the president was required to report to Congress in advance of any proposals in trade negotiations that could require changes to U.S. trade remedy laws.

- **Unemployed worker benefits.** The TAA program for workers who lost their jobs or had their wages reduced as a result of increased imports was extended for five years, as was assistance to firms that faced layoffs because of foreign competition. The bill created a tax credit for laid-off workers equal to 65 percent of their health insurance costs. It extended benefits to secondary workers, such as employees of companies that supplied businesses affected by trade, and provided benefits to workers whose plants moved anywhere overseas. Previously, benefits were available only to workers whose plants moved to Mexico or Canada under

the North American Free Trade Agreement (NAFTA).

● **Negotiating objectives.** The law set a number of overall objectives for U.S. trade negotiators — including more open, equitable and reciprocal market access; agreement from trade partners not to weaken domestic labor or environmental laws in an effort to promote trade; and respect for worker rights and the rights of children consistent with International Labor Organization (ILO) core labor standards.

It also established a set of "principal trade negotiating objectives" that included preserving the ability of the United States to rigorously enforce its trade laws.

● **Andean trade.** The law reinstated through 2006 the duty-free treatment of over 6,000 products, including textiles, from the Andean countries of Bolivia, Colombia, Ecuador and Peru.

● **African and Caribbean trade.** The law increased the quantities of certain imported apparel eligible for duty-free treatment. It increased the cap for apparel made in the Caribbean from knit fabric made of U.S. yarn and clarified that T-shirts and other "knit-to-shape" items were included. It also increased a cap on apparel made in sub-Saharan Africa from regional fabric and temporarily loosened some restrictions on apparel from Botswana and Namibia.

● **GSP.** The agreement renewed tariff breaks for developing nations under the General System of Preferences (GSP), which extends duty-free treatment to thousands of products from more than 140 countries.

● **Customs Service.** The Customs budget was reauthorized with increased funding for border security.

Background

The Constitution gave Congress the exclusive power to set tariffs and regulate foreign commerce, but since the 1930s, lawmakers had delegated that authority in one way or another to the president, who was seen as less vulnerable to pressure from individual industries and interests. The turning point was the 1930 Smoot-Hawley Act, which set prohibitively high tariffs that were considered partially responsible for the Great Depression. In 1934, President Franklin D. Roosevelt pushed Congress to enact the first reciprocal trade agreements act, which gave the president authority to negotiate mutual tariff reductions with U.S. trading partners. Congress renewed the authority repeatedly over the years, and successive presidents used the power to help reduce global tariff barriers.

Fast-track procedures to expedite Congress' approval of trade agreements were first enacted in the 1974 Trade Act (PL 93-618). The procedures were first used during the Carter administration for the General Agreement on Tariffs and Trade (GATT) Tokyo Round Agreements, which were approved and implemented in the Trade Agreements Act of 1979 (PL 96-39). That act also renewed the procedures for another eight years; they were extended again in 1988 (PL 100-418), with a third extension in 1993 (PL 103-49) to cover the Uruguay Round agreements under GATT. *(1974 Almanac, p. 553; 1979 Almanac, p. 293; 1988 Almanac, p. 209; 1993 Almanac, p. 182)*

Fast-track procedures were used in 1993, when Congress narrowly approved NAFTA (PL 103-182), establishing a free-trade zone in Canada, the United States and Mexico, as well as in 1994 to implement the Uruguay Round agreements (PL 103-465), including U.S. participation in the World Trade Organization (WTO). *(1993 Almanac, p. 171; 1994 Almanac, p. 123)*

Fast-track negotiating authority expired for agreements reached after April 15, 1994. President Bill Clinton sought an extension, but the House, largely because of opposition from most Democrats, defeated a renewal bill in 1998. Jordan and Vietnam completed trade agreements with the United States without fast-track procedures, but many countries were unwilling to do so without a guarantee that the deal would not subsequently be amended by Congress. *(1998 Almanac, p. 23-3; 2001 Almanac, pp. 19-6, 19-11)*

Renewing fast-track authority was a top priority for the Bush administration, particularly for negotiations to extend NAFTA to other parts of Latin America, and to reach new multilateral accords involving foreign direct investment, intellectual property, agriculture, and labor and environmental policies related to trade. An agreement to begin formal negotiations in these areas had been reached in November 2001 at the WTO ministerial meetings in Doha, Qatar.

Action in 2001

The bill (HR 3005 — H Rept 107-249, Part 1) passed by the House on Dec. 6, 2001, was limited largely to renewing fast-track procedures. It included some labor and environmental protection as negotiating goals, but it did not satisfy many Democrats who wanted sanctions or other mechanisms to enforce labor and environmental provisions in trade agreements. Speaker J. Dennis Hastert, R-Ill., repeatedly put off floor action because he lacked the votes. In the end, the bill squeaked by, 215-214, with 194 Republicans and 21 Democrats voting "yes." GOP leaders held the balloting open for an extra 20 minutes while they rounded up the last critical vote. Several Republicans said they put aside qualms about broadening the president's trade negotiating authority in order to support Bush in a time of war. *(2001 Almanac, p. 19-3)*

The Senate Finance Committee approved a version of the bill (HR 3005 — S Rept 107-139) on Dec. 12, with minor changes to make it more palatable to Democrats in the areas of labor, congressional review and product dumping. Baucus and ranking Republican Charles E. Grassley of Iowa allowed no amendments, putting off Democratic demands for tougher labor and anti-dumping provisions for the floor.

Congress took action on two other trade bills in 2001 that were ultimately folded into the new trade law.

● **TAA.** Both chambers moved bills to reauthorize trade adjustment assistance. The program, enacted under the 1974 statute that created fast-track procedures, had expired Sept. 30, 2001. TAA included assistance for workers and firms, with a third program added in 1993 to cushion the effects of NAFTA.

Hoping to build momentum for the fast-track bill, the House Ways and Means Committee on Oct. 5 approved a bill (HR 3008 — H Rept 107-244) reauthorizing TAA for workers and firms with minor changes through September 2003. The House passed the bill Dec. 6 by a vote of 420-3, before voting on its separate fast-track bill.

On Dec. 4, Senate Finance approved a broader TAA bill (S 1209 — S Rept 107-134). In addition to expanding the

program and reauthorizing it through fiscal 2006, the bill would have subsidized 75 percent of the premium for COBRA health coverage for workers eligible for TAA assistance. COBRA — part of the 1986 Consolidated Omnibus Budget Reconciliation Act (PL 99-272) — allowed workers to continue coverage under their former employer's plan. But paying the employer's portion of the cost often was too expensive for people looking for new jobs. The subsidy, estimated to cost $3.3 billion through 2011, was the Republicans' chief complaint against the bill. The committee approved the bill by voice vote only after Grassley and Baucus agreed that it would be kept separate from fast track. The bill also included a reauthorization of the Customs Service. *(1986 Almanac, p. 252)*

The bill added TAA for communities hurt by imports and required country-of-origin labeling for imported food and fish. It reauthorized the Customs Service, the USTR's office and the U.S. International Trade Commission.

● **Andean trade.** The House on Nov. 16 passed a bill by voice vote (HR 3009 — H Rept 107-290) to extend and expand trade preferences for four Andean nations. The measure, strongly opposed by some Democrats, proposed extending through 2006 a 1991 law (PL 102-182) that provided duty-free treatment for about 6,000 products from Bolivia, Ecuador, Colombia and Peru. The bill also called for ending tariffs on several goods previously exempt from the law, including tuna, petroleum products, footwear and sugar. And it extended trade benefits for apparel covered under the 2000 African and Caribbean Basin trade law (PL 106-200). *(1991 Almanac, p. 127; 2000 Almanac, p. 20-24)*

Sponsors argued that the Andean law helped anti-drug efforts by strengthening the economies of Andean nations, a major source of cocaine. Critics worried that it could hurt the domestic tuna and textile industries.

The Senate Finance Committee approved a revised version of the Andean trade bill (HR 3009 — S Rept 107-126) on Nov. 29 that included fewer trade benefits for Andean textile exporters. The committee also adopted an amendment by John B. Breaux, D-La., to limit duty-free imports of canned tuna from Ecuador. According to the office of Bob Graham, D-Fla., since the Andean law was enacted, total two-way trade between the United States and the Andean region had more than doubled to $28.5 billion a year.

Authorization for the Andean trade preferences expired Dec. 4, 2001. On Feb. 14, Bush extended the duties for 90 days pending congressional renewal of the popular measure.

Legislative Action

Senate Floor Action

After 18 days of debate and the adoption of several major amendments, the Senate passed its trade legislation (HR 3009) the night of May 23. The vote was 66-30, with 41 Republicans, 24 Democrats and independent James M. Jeffords of Vermont in support. Voting against the measure were five Republicans and 25 Democrats. *(Senate vote 130, p. S-28)*

The changes that allowed the bill to advance through the Senate, particularly the expansion of aid to dislocated workers, sparked significant opposition from House Republicans. Another change — an amendment allowing Congress to alter a trade pact in order to protect U.S. trade laws —

brought a veto threat from the White House. The Senate made its revisions not to the House's fast-track bill, but to the separate, House-passed Andean trade bill.

Daschle kicked off the Senate debate with a wide-ranging amendment that paired trade promotion authority with the worker assistance provisions from S 1209.

Republicans argued that the worker provisions were too expansive and much too expensive, but they also were under strong White House pressure to win fast-track authority for the president. Daschle made it clear they would not get one without the other. While speakers marked time on the floor, senators from both parties and the White House engaged in lengthy negotiations over the worker assistance proposals. Finally, on May 9, Baucus and Grassley announced a deal that gave Democrats many, but not all, of their main goals. The following day, Baucus introduced the package as a substitute amendment that effectively became the underlying bill for the remainder of the debate. The Senate adopted the Baucus substitute by voice vote May 23, after voting, 68-29, the previous day to limit further debate. *(Senate vote 122, p. S-27)*

● **Worker assistance.** Under the bipartisan agreement, trade-displaced workers would for the first time be eligible for government-subsidized health insurance, in the form of tax credits covering 70 percent of their premiums. Democrats had proposed a subsidy to cover 75 percent of COBRA premiums. Republicans favored a 60 percent tax credit for the purchase of insurance. Under the compromise, the percentage was closer to what Democrats wanted, while the mechanism for the subsidy reflected the GOP plan. Those who already had individual health insurance could only use the tax credit for six months.

Also, TAA eligibility would be extended to so-called secondary workers, who were harmed indirectly because they worked for companies that supplied the firms affected firsthand by globalization. A wage insurance pilot program would cover as much as $5,000 annually in lost wages for trade-displaced workers older than age 50.

As part of the compromise, Democrats dropped a provision sought by Daschle that would have made retired steelworkers eligible for one year for a tax credit to cover 73 percent of their health insurance premiums. The two sides agreed to allow the chief sponsors, Democrats Barbara A. Mikulski of Maryland and John D. Rockefeller IV of West Virginia, a chance to try to restore it on the floor.

Democrats also agreed to drop a proposal to make truck drivers who lost their jobs to trade with Mexico eligible for trade adjustment assistance. Republicans accepted a provision that tied GSP benefits to updated ILO standards, including bans on child labor and workplace discrimination.

White House lobbyists eventually persuaded GOP critics to go along with the deal, but their discomfort with the compromise was palpable. On May 16, Judd Gregg, R-N.H., tried unsuccessfully to delete the pilot program for older workers. His amendment was tabled (killed), 58-38. *(Senate vote 114, p. S-25)*

In the days that followed, the Senate voted on a number of amendments, including the following:

● **Dayton-Craig.** Despite an explicit veto threat, senators on May 14 voted to carve a wide exception from the core of the fast-track concept. Under the amendment — sponsored

by Republican Policy Committee Chairman Larry E. Craig of Idaho and Mark Dayton, D-Minn. — a simple Senate majority could remove any part of a trade agreement that altered U.S. anti-dumping or other trade remedy laws. The amendment was adopted by voice vote, after a motion to table it was rejected by a filibuster-proof majority of 38-61. Sixteen Republicans, 44 Democrats and Jeffords voted to keep the proposal alive. (*Senate vote 110, p. S-24*)

The amendment went to the heart of one of the most widespread congressional concerns about fast track: that in their zeal to tear down trade barriers, U.S. negotiators would sell domestic producers short and agree to deals that would deprive them of remedies under U.S. law.

● **Labor and environmental standards.** Democrats made several unsuccessful attempts to limit fast-track procedures to trade deals that included enforceable labor and environmental standards.

By 54-44, senators May 15 tabled an amendment by Joseph I. Lieberman, D-Conn., that would have deleted a provision in the fast-track bill barring the United States or a trading partner from retaliating for failure to enforce labor or environmental standards. (*Senate vote 112, p. S-25*)

By 69-30 the same day, the Senate tabled an amendment by Richard J. Durbin, D-Ill., that would have required any trade pact considered under fast-track procedures to compel the parties to uphold their domestic labor and environmental standards, under penalty of trade remedy laws. (*Senate vote 113, p. S-25*)

By 52-46, senators May 16 tabled an amendment by Christopher J. Dodd, D-Conn., that would have required trade agreements negotiated under fast track to include a central provision of the U.S.-Jordan free trade agreement. Endorsed by Congress in 2001 (PL 107-43), the pact prohibited the signatories from weakening their labor or environmental laws in order to facilitate trade. (*Senate vote 115, p. S-25; 2001 Almanac, p. 19-6*)

● **Textiles.** Highlighting the importance of regional and industry considerations, the Senate on May 15 adopted, 66-33, a proposal by Democrats John Edwards of North Carolina and Zell Miller of Georgia to require U.S. negotiators to seek competitive deals for U.S. exports of textile products, extend TAA income support to some laid-off textile workers and provide grants for community colleges in hard-hit areas to enhance retraining programs. (*Senate vote 111, p. S-24*)

● **Steel workers.** On May 21, senators failed to block a GOP filibuster against Rockefeller and Mikulski's proposal to make retired steel workers eligible for one year for the 70 percent health insurance tax credit. The vote was 56-40, four votes short of the 60 required to limit debate, and the amendment was dropped. A handful of GOP conservatives said they would rather see fast track die than provide such an unprecedented benefit. (*Senate vote 117, p. S-26*)

● **Foreign investment.** Conservatives also threatened to sink the bill if the Senate adopted an amendment by John Kerry, D-Mass., to make it more difficult for foreign trading partners to win trade disputes claiming compensation for U.S. health, labor or other laws they consider trade barriers. Kerry said he wanted to ensure that trade agreements did not give foreign investors greater protection than was available to U.S. companies. But the White House said in a statement issued May 8 that the amendment would "funda-

mentally weaken longstanding protection for U.S. companies abroad, leaving our investors vulnerable to unfair treatment by foreign governments." The Senate tabled the amendment, 55-41, on May 21. (*Senate vote 121, p. S-27*)

Baucus provided an alternative May 14, with an amendment clarifying that foreign investors would not be accorded greater legal protection than U.S. investors under the investment provisions of trade agreements. It was adopted 98-0. (*Senate vote 109, p. S-24*)

An attempt by George Allen, R-Va., to make low-interest government loans for mortgage payments available to displaced workers was tabled, 50-49. Vice President Dick Cheney, who was in the Capitol to attend the weekly GOP caucus luncheon, cast the tie-breaking vote, the third in his 16 months in office. (*Senate vote 119, p. S-26*)

By a vote of 60-38, the Senate on May 22 tabled a proposal by Bill Nelson, D-Fla., that would have limited the president's authority to reduce tariffs on products, such as frozen orange juice concentrate, that were under anti-dumping or countervailing duty orders. (*Senate vote 123, p. S-27*)

On May 23, Mary L. Landrieu, D-La., offered an amendment to extend TAA benefits to stevedores and other maritime workers put out of work as a result of Bush's import tariffs on steel. She failed, 50-46, to overcome a budget point of order against the amendment; 60 votes were required. (*Senate vote 128, S-28*)

By voice vote May 22, the Senate adopted an amendment by Carl Levin, D-Mich., to instruct trade negotiators to make opening foreign markets for U.S. automobiles and auto parts a priority. The next day senators adopted by voice vote an amendment by Paul Wellstone, D-Minn., to make protection of human rights and democracy a goal of trade negotiations.

By the time the marathon debate ended, Republicans felt they had paid a heavy price to preserve one of the president's top legislative priorities.

Further House Floor Action

Before going to conference on HR 3009, the House agreed by the narrowest of margins to specify that the negotiations include the House-passed version of the fast-track bill (HR 3005), as well as specific House provisions on a number of other trade matters. None of these provisions were in HR 3009 as passed by the House.

The plan (H Res 450 — H Rept 107-518) was drawn up by Ways and Means Chairman Thomas and adopted by a vote of 216-215 on June 26. Thirteen members who had voted in favor of the House bill in December defected. Many of the 10 Democrats in the group favored liberalized international trade but opposed Thomas' strategy of going to conference with a package of provisions never fully voted on by the House. (*House vote 264, p. H-86*)

In addition to HR 3005, Thomas' resolution added the House-passed TAA bill (HR 3008) with new provisions related to health care benefits for displaced workers; provisions similar to those in the House version of a supplemental appropriations bill (HR 4775) to restrict certain textile imports from the Caribbean and Africa; language from a House-passed resolution (H Con Res 262) expressing congressional concern regarding WTO dispute panels and anti-dumping agreements; a House-passed Customs border security bill (HR 3129); and a measure to renew GSP (HR 3010)

not considered by the House.

The resolution also appointed House members of the conference committee.

House GOP leaders had to pull the resolution from the floor agenda June 20 because they lacked the votes, but with appeals to party loyalty and free-trade philosophy, they finally managed to eke out a one-vote victory for the controversial proposal.

Conference/Final Action

With less than a day to go before the House was scheduled to begin its August recess, conferees reached agreement on a final bill. House leaders pulled out a 215-212 victory on the conference report (H Rept 107-624) in a vote taken after 3 a.m. on Saturday, July 27. The Senate, which was not due to leave for another week, cleared the bill on a relatively drama-free 64-34 vote Aug. 1. *(House vote 370, p. H-116; Senate vote 207, p. S-41)*

The conference opened July 23 with Republicans intent on reversing some of the concessions made in the Senate. Baucus, however, made it clear that any deal would have to include health insurance benefits for displaced workers. Republicans were loath to relent, fearful of setting a precedent for future health care legislation. The November elections were approaching, labor unions were elevating their anti-fast-track rhetoric and leaders in both chambers were wary of forcing members to take such a controversial vote. The bill's prospects seemed increasingly dim, save for the possibility of a vote during a lame-duck session.

But with Bush insisting on quick action to aid the economy and lawmakers eager to convince voters that Congress was willing to act decisively, Thomas and Baucus held a lengthy meeting the evening of July 25 and reached agreement on a final bill. With victory still uncertain in the House, Bush visited the Capitol the next day to make a personal plea for passage. When the measure finally came to the floor in the pre-dawn hours, Bush's persistence paid off.

GOP leaders picked up five additional pro-business Democrats who resisted pressure from their party leadership. Free-trade Democrat Cal Dooley of California claimed credit for most of those votes. At Thomas' request, Dooley had corralled 25 Democrats with ties to business and put them through back-to-back meetings, with direct pitches from Baucus and Breaux, then U.S. Trade Representative Robert B. Zoellick, chief White House lobbyist Nick Calio and Commerce Secretary Donald L. Evans. A handful of Republicans also got on board. With victory assured, Republicans in districts with strong anti-fast-track constituencies, like Robin Hayes of textile-rich North Carolina, were let off the hook by their leaders and voted "no."

Senate opponents had their last gasp on Aug. 1, attacking the bill as an abrogation of congressional power and a nail in the coffin of the U.S. manufacturing sector. "We're going out of business, and nobody wants to talk about it," thundered South Carolina Democrat Ernest F. Hollings.

Minutes after the final vote, Baucus and Grassley gathered in the Capitol with administration officials to present a different view. The conference report "sends a message of certainty to this economy, to the financial markets, to the equities markets," said Evans. Bush placed a congratulatory phone call to the group, hailing the measure as a "jobs bill." And Grassley presented Baucus with a T-shirt — made in Mexico — reading "TPA Works for America."

Key Compromises

The following were the major compromises reached in conference on the bill:

● **TAA.** The Senate prevailed on the $12 billion expansion of benefits to workers and firms injured by foreign competition. The program was extended through fiscal 2007, as the Senate wanted. The House would have extended it for two years, at an estimated cost of $500 million a year, through fiscal 2004. The program was expanded not only to suppliers of trade-affected firms, as endorsed by the House, but to downstream workers affected by NAFTA and workers whose factories moved abroad because of trade agreements or foreign competition. The bill increased job search and relocation allowances, established an alternate assistance program for older workers and created a TAA program for farmers and ranchers.

● **Health insurance.** As part of the worker assistance package, conferees agreed to a tax credit covering 65 percent of the cost of health care insurance under COBRA or certain state-based group plans. Democrats favored a subsidy covering 70 percent of premiums; Republicans wanted a tax credit for 60 percent of coverage. Thomas attempted to mold the provision into an individual private insurance policy tax credit, but Democrats would not budge.

● **Dayton-Craig.** The final bill did not include the Dayton-Craig amendment, which would have allowed the Senate to alter portions of trade agreements that could weaken anti-dumping or other U.S. trade remedy laws. That was the trade-off Baucus made to get House agreement to the TAA package. Instead, Baucus included language elevating protection of those laws to the status of a principal negotiating objective, and requiring the president to give Congress 180 days' advance notice before signing an agreement that would affect those laws. Daschle predicted a congressional mutiny if Bush started putting U.S. trade remedy laws on the table. "I would see the trade representative at the table negotiating something and we, in a very public way, admonish him to do something else," he said. "It would be very hard for him to negotiate with his trading partners with any authority or credibility if the Congress has taken a different point of view."

● **Andean trade.** In renewing and expanding trade benefits for Andean countries, the Caribbean and Africa, the conference report closely followed the House version and provided less protection for the domestic textile industry than the Senate had wanted. It allowed trade preferences for Ecuadoran tuna but excluded canned tuna.

● **Labor and environment.** The final bill fell far short of Democratic demands that trade agreements eligible for fast track include enforceable labor and environmental provisions. Democrats had lost that fight in both chambers. Instead, it included as official U.S. negotiating objectives ensuring that trade and environmental policies were mutually supportive and promoting respect for worker rights and the rights of children. Also, the president was required to review the impact of future trade agreements on U.S. employment. ◆

Provisions of the Trade Bill

The following are the main provisions of the 2002 Trade Act (PL 107-210) signed by the president on Aug. 6:

Trade Authority

● **Negotiating authority.** The law renews the president's authority to negotiate certain reductions in tariffs and non-tariff barriers to trade, including unlimited authority to negotiate reciprocal duty-elimination on a sector basis within the World Trade Organization (WTO) forum. The authority covers trade agreements signed before June 1, 2005, with a possible extension to June 1, 2007.

● **Fast-track procedures.** The law authorizes special trade promotion authority, formerly known as fast-track procedures, for legislation to implement trade agreements entered into before July 1, 2005. Once such legislation is introduced, Congress has 90 days to complete work; the bill is subject to up or down votes in each chamber with no amendments. Trade promotion authority may be extended to cover agreements entered into before July 1, 2007, if the president requests it and neither chamber adopts a resolution of disapproval.

● **Notification and consultation.** The president must notify and consult with the House Ways and Means and Senate Finance committees, a new congressional oversight group and other relevant congressional committees at least 90 calendar days before entering into negotiations. In the case of negotiations already under way with Chile and Singapore, and negotiations to create a Free Trade Area of the Americas, the president is required to consult with Congress as soon as is feasible.

The president also must notify the House and Senate at least 90 days before signing a trade agreement governed by the bill.

● **Agriculture, textiles.** Before initiating negotiations on tariff reductions in agriculture and textiles, the president must assess whether U.S. tariffs on products bound by the Uruguay Round Agreements are lower than the tariffs set by the countries with which the president is negotiating, and whether the negotiation provides an opportunity to address any disparity.

The president must consult with the House Ways and Means and Senate Finance committees, as well as the Agriculture committees in the case of agricultural products, concerning the results of this assessment, whether it is appropriate for the United States to agree to further tariff reductions, and how all applicable negotiating objectives would be met.

The law includes a new definition of import sensitive agriculture to encompass products subject to tariff rate quotas, as well as products subject to the lowest tariff reductions in the Uruguay Round Agreement.

● **Congressional Oversight Group.** The law creates a new Congressional Oversight Group, composed of the chairmen and ranking members of the House Ways and Means and Senate Finance committees, together with three additional members of those committees, and the chairmen and ranking members of committees with jurisdiction over laws affected by specific trade agreements. The members are to be accredited as official advisers to U.S. delegations negotiating agreements. The USTR is directed to develop guidelines to facilitate useful and timely exchange of information, including regular briefings, access to pertinent documents and coordination with Congress at all critical periods during negotiations, including at negotiation sites.

● **U.S. trade remedy laws.** At least 180 days before signing a trade agreement, the president must transmit a report to the House Ways and Means and Senate Finance committees on proposals advanced in negotiations that could change U.S. trade remedy laws.

● **Proposed changes to existing laws.** Within 60 days of signing an agreement, the president must submit to Congress a preliminary list of existing laws that would need to be changed to bring the United States into compliance with the accord.

● **Trade agreement submission.** After entering into a trade agreement, the president is required to submit the draft agreement, the implementing legislation and a statement of administrative action to Congress. There is no deadline for this submission.

● **Expedited procedures.** At this point, procedures of the Trade Act of 1974 apply. Specifically, the same day the president formally submits the legislation, the bill is introduced (by request) by the majority leaders of the House and the Senate. House committees of jurisdiction have 45 legislative days to report the bill. The House must vote on the bill within 15 legislative days after it has been reported or discharged from the committees. Senate committees then have 15 days, with another 15 days for Senate floor action. The total period for congressional consideration is 90 legislative days. No amendments are allowed in committee or on the floor; the bill is subject to up or down votes.

● **Limitations on trade promotion authority.** An implementing bill will not be eligible for expedited treatment if both chambers separately agreed to a resolution of disapproval stating that the president had failed to meet requirements for notifying and consulting with Congress. The law also provides that any trade agreement or understanding with a foreign government that is not disclosed to Congress will have no effect under U.S. law.

● **Mock markups.** The absence of a time limit for the president to submit an implementing bill provides time for the committees of jurisdiction to conduct informal "mock markups" of the draft bill in consultation with the administration. The purpose is to allow Congress, the public, and the private sector to weigh in before the bill is formally submitted and changes are prohibited.

Trade Adjustment Assistance

● **Reauthorization.** The law reauthorizes the Trade Adjustment Assistance (TAA) program through fiscal 2007 for workers who lose their jobs or have their wages reduced as a result of increased imports. The total cost of the program is estimated at $12 billion over 10 years. A second TAA program, which provides technical assistance to firms that face layoffs due to foreign competition, is reauthorized through fiscal 2007 at $16 million.

● **Health insurance tax credit.** As part of the package for displaced workers, the bill establishes a refundable tax credit to cover 65 percent of the cost of monthly health insurance premiums. The credit can be used to subsidize the cost of company-based (COBRA) or pooled health insurance policies, and for individual insurance in cases when a worker purchased such a policy one month before losing a job. The tax credit, which will be granted in advance, and is good for 12 months, is available to eligible TAA recipients and to Pension Benefit Guaranty Corporation (PBGC) pension recipients. The bill also provides seed and support money for state high-risk pools, and authorizes National Emergency Grant funds to assist workers with health insurance costs on an interim basis.

● **Eligibility expansion.** The law extends TAA eligibility for the first time to secondary workers who are suppliers to trade-affected businesses, and to downstream workers affected by trade with Mexico or Canada. Benefits also are extended to workers whose plants

move anywhere overseas, if the relocation results from a U.S. trade agreement. Previously, benefits were available only to workers whose plants moved to Mexico or Canada under NAFTA.

● **Unified TAA programs.** A third TAA program under NAFTA is merged into the regular program for displaced workers.

● **Older workers.** A two-year pilot program is created for trade-affected workers age 50 or older who take a new job at lower pay. The program provides wage insurance for part of the gap between old and new earnings for up to $10,000 over two years.

● **Farmers and ranchers.** A new TAA program will serve family farmers (with exceptions for some farmers receiving assistance under other laws) and ranchers. The Commerce secretary is directed to study the feasibility of extending TAA benefits to fishermen.

● **Worker training.** The existing worker training budget is doubled to $220 million.

● **Income benefits.** The bill extends the maximum period during which a worker can receive trade adjustment allowances from 52 to 78 weeks, and provides an additional 26 weeks of income support for workers requiring remedial education, including English as a second language.

● **Cash benefits.** The maximum job search allowance is increased from $800 per worker to $1,250 per worker and the maximum relocation allowance goes from $800 per worker to $1,250 per worker.

Negotiating Objectives

The bill sets out overall U.S. trade objectives, specifies the principal objectives to be pursued in trade talks, and adds a list of priorities for the president, and by extension, U.S. trade negotiators.

● **Overall objectives.** Overall U.S. trade objectives include obtaining more open, equitable and reciprocal market access; reducing or eliminating barriers and other trade distorting policies and practices; further strengthening the system of international trading agreements and procedures, including dispute settlement; and fostering economic growth and full employment in the U.S. and the global economies. The list also includes ensuring that trade and environmental policies are mutually supportive; promoting respect for worker rights and the rights of children consistent with International Labor Organization (ILO) core labor standards; seeking provisions under which the parties strive to ensure that they do not weaken their labor and environmental protection laws to promote trade; ensuring that small businesses have equal access to global markets; reducing trade barriers that particularly affect small businesses; and promoting full compliance with ILO convention aimed at eliminating the worst forms of child labor.

● **Principal negotiating objectives.** The principal objectives to be pursued in trade negotiations include reducing barriers to trade in services; lowering barriers to foreign investment while ensuring that foreign investors are not accorded greater rights than U.S. investors in the United States; and preserving the ability of the United States to rigorously enforce its trade laws, including anti-dumping and countervailing duty laws. Negotiators must seek to eliminate government policies that unduly threaten sustainable development; gain market access for U.S. environmental technologies; and ensure that labor, environmental, health or safety policies and practices of parties to trade agreements do not arbitrarily or unjustifiably discriminate against U.S. exports or serve as disguised barriers to trade.

Additional objectives include protecting intellectual property rights; obtaining reciprocal market access for U.S. exports of agricultural commodities, textiles and apparel; and ensuring that trade protections apply to electronic commerce. Trade negotiators also must respect a declaration adopted at the WTO Ministerial in November 2001 that granted poor countries certain exemptions from intellectual property protections afforded to Western-produced

pharmaceuticals, especially those related to treating HIV/AIDS.

● **Presidential priorities.** Many of the priorities set out for U.S. trade negotiators require reports to Congress. Priorities include strengthening the ability of U.S. trading partners to promote respect for core labor standards and to set environmental and health standards. The president also is required to review the impact of future agreements on U.S. employment.

Customs Service

● **Customs authorization.** The law authorizes $1.4 million per year in fiscal 2003-04 for non-commercial operations (functions related to individuals entering and exiting the United States), and $1.6 billion per year in fiscal 2003-04 for commercial activities (import and export of goods by commercial entities).

● **Mail searches.** Customs investigators are permitted to search unsealed, outbound U.S. mail weighing 16 ounces or more for weapons of mass destruction, firearms, illegal drugs, unreported monetary instruments and other contraband. Investigators still will need a warrant to search mail weighing less than 16 ounces.

● **Immunity.** Customs officers are granted immunity from civil lawsuits arising from personal searches of people entering the country, as long as the search is conducted in good faith with reasonable means. Customs border facilities must post notices of personal search policies, including the prohibition of racial profiling.

● **U.S.-Canada border.** The law earmarks $25 million for 285 new Customs officers to serve at the U.S.-Canada border, and $90 million for anti-terrorism and narcotics detection equipment for the U.S.-Mexico border, the U.S.-Canada border and Florida and Gulf Coast seaports.

● **Security regulations.** The Customs Service is required to promulgate new regulations regarding mandatory electronic information on imports and exports of cargo and documentation for waterborne cargo. The Treasury secretary is directed to establish a joint task force to evaluate secure systems of transportation.

● **Textile trans-shipments.** The General Accounting Office (GAO) will audit the Customs Service's system for monitoring the illegal trans-shipment of textile and apparel products through third countries in order to claim preferential U.S. tariff treatment, and recommend improvements. The law authorizes $10 million to enhance the Customs Service's textile trans-shipment enforcement operations.

● **Africa trade.** The law authorizes $1.3 million for the Customs Service to provide technical assistance to sub-Saharan African countries to develop and implement effective visa and anti-transshipment systems to prevent the illegal trans-shipment of textiles and other goods as required in the African Growth and Opportunity Act (PL 106-200).

● **World Trade Center.** The law authorizes funds to re-establish Customs Service operations, including a textile monitoring and enforcement center, formerly located at the World Trade Center in New York. The Congressional Budget Office estimates it will cost $100 million to replace the facilities.

● **Personnel practices.** Customs is required to report to Congress on a number of its personnel practices, including performance standards, the effect of the collective bargaining process on its drug interdiction efforts and a comparison of duty rotation policies of the Customs Service and other federal agencies of similarly situated enforcement personnel.

The law also requires the Customs Service to conduct a study to ensure that appropriate training is being provided to personnel who are responsible for financially auditing importers; mandates the imposition of a cost-accounting system for the Customs Service to effectively explain its expenditures; and directs the GAO to determine whether current user fees are appropriately set at a level commensurate with the service provided for the fee.

• **Child cyber-smuggling.** The law authorizes $10 million to carry out a program established by the Child Cyber-Smuggling Center to prevent child pornography and child sexual exploitation.

Andean Trade

• **Reauthorization.** The law renews the 1991 Andean Trade Preferences Act (PL 102-182) through 2006, retroactive to Dec. 4, 2001, granting preferential treatment to more than 6,000 products made in Bolivia, Ecuador, Peru and Colombia.

• **Expansion.** Added to the duty-free list are Andean apparel made from U.S. fabric and a limited amount of Andean apparel made from Andean fabric, some kinds of packaged (non-canned) tuna caught from U.S. or Andean flagged vessels, as well as shoes, watches, petroleum products and some leather items.

African and Caribbean Trade

The law expands the African and Caribbean Basin trade law of 2000 (PL 106-200) by raising caps for duty-free textile imports to the United States and by expanding the list of duty-free products.

• **African apparel.** More knit products can enter duty free from Africa, as long as they are made from U.S. or African yarn. African-made merino wool sweaters are added to the duty-free list. Botswana and Namibia are added to the list of nations permitted — for a two-year transition period — duty-free importation of knitted apparel made from third-country yarn.

• **Caribbean apparel.** Caribbean nations may export to the United States more knitted apparel duty free, but all the knits must be made from U.S. yarn. The law clarifies that so-called knit-to-shape items, such as T-shirts, made in the Caribbean are duty-free.

Other Provisions

• **GSP.** The General System of Preferences (GSP) is reauthorized through 2006. This is the fifth renewal of the program, which provides duty-free entry to the United States for more than 6,000 products from about 140 developing countries. Nations qualifying for GSP must meet a set of conditions, such as abiding by U.S. intellectual property laws. The new law denies eligibility to countries that engage in the worst forms of child labor, fail to conform to certain fundamental labor rights or do not support U.S. efforts against terrorism.

• **Wool.** Reduced duties on worsted wool fabric are extended to 2005, as are payments to U.S. manufacturers to encourage them to make worsted wool garments.

• **Nuclear generators.** Nuclear steam generators can be imported duty free.

• **Sugar quotas.** The Agriculture Department and Customs Service are directed to monitor synthetic molasses and other altered sugar products that are circumventing quotas on sugars and syrups, and to devise a plan to counter this subversion.

• **USTR.** The office of the U.S. Trade Representative is reauthorized at $65 million over two years.

• **WTO dispute fund.** The law creates a $50 million fund to pay WTO fines.

• **ITC.** The U.S. International Trade Commission is reauthorized at $111 million over two years. ◆

Export-Import Bank Reauthorized

Congress agreed to reauthorize the Export-Import (Ex-Im) Bank of the United States through fiscal 2006, while calling for changes in bank programs aimed at combating "tied aid" provided by other countries. The Ex-Im Bank provides loans, credit guarantees and credit insurance to help U.S. exporters compete with foreign companies that receive public financing. President Bush signed the bill (S 1372 — PL 107-189) into law June 14.

The law increased the total amount of bank loans, guarantees and insurance that could be outstanding at any one time from $75 billion to $100 billion by 2006. It directed the bank to double the share of its financing used to boost exports of businesses with fewer than 100 employees, as well as those owned by women or by socially and economically disadvantaged individuals. Other provisions called for human rights impact assessments for any bank project over $10 million and authorized $80 million to upgrade the bank's technology.

The legislation won approval from House and Senate committees in 2001, but its journey from there to the president's desk was tortuous. Two Nebraska Republicans, Rep. Doug Bereuter and Sen. Chuck Hagel, led efforts to make the bank more independent. They were upset that the Treasury Department had blocked a bank grant aimed at helping a Nebraska-based company, Valmont Industries, sell farm equipment to China. The company lost a $5 million contract to a competitor.

Bereuter, chairman of the House Financial Services sub-committee with jurisdiction over the bank, added language stating that the Treasury could not veto such tied-aid decisions, but conferees eventually agreed to a compromise that gave the president final say over the grants. Tied aid was provided on a long-term low-interest basis for public sector capital projects in developing countries. The purpose was to counter the aid that other countries used to help their businesses beat out direct U.S. competitors.

While Congress deliberated, the bank operated under a series of three short-term authorizations. The last one (PL 107-186) expired June 14.

Legislative Action

Senate Floor Action

The Senate passed the bill — which had been approved by the Banking, Housing and Urban Finance Committee in July 2001 (S Rept 107-52) — by voice vote March 14. It proposed to authorize the bank through fiscal 2006, and called for the bank to increase from 10 percent to 18 percent the portion of its assistance used to finance exports by small businesses.

Rather than explicitly reining in the Treasury Department, the committee included language in its report endorsing an agreement that had been reached between Treasury and the Ex-Im Bank on standards and procedures for making

tied-aid grants. Banking Committee Chairman Paul S. Sarbanes, D-Md., said his view of whether legislative change was needed would depend on whether the agreement was working. The report did state that if all of the procedures were followed, the case-by-case responsibility for deciding on tied aid would belong to the Ex-Im Bank.

House Floor Action

The House passed the bill by voice vote May 1, after substituting the text of its own measure (HR 2871 — H Rept 107-292), which had been approved by the Financial Services Committee in 2001. The bill directed Treasury and the Ex-Im Bank to jointly develop standards and procedures for the tied-aid grant program, which would be renamed the "Export Competitiveness Program and Fund." Bereuter included language in the bill stating that Treasury could not veto a specific tied-aid grant decision.

Before passing the bill, the House rejected, 135-283, an amendment by Bernard Sanders, I-Vt., that would have barred companies that laid off a higher percentage of workers in the United States than overseas from getting Ex-Im Bank help. (*House vote 120, p. H-44*)

Conference/Final Action

House and Senate conferees reached a final agreement May 24, after last-minute negotiations with the White House over the tied-aid fund. The House adopted the con-

BoxScore

Bill:
S 1372 — PL 107-189
Legislative Action:
Senate passed S 1372 (S Rept 107-52) by voice vote March 14.
House passed S 1372, amended (H Rept 107-292), by voice vote May 1.
House adopted the conference report (H Rept 107-487), 344-78, on June 5.
Senate cleared S 1372 by voice vote June 6.
President signed June 14.

ference report (H Rept 107-487) by a vote of 344-78 on June 5. The Senate cleared the bill by voice vote without debate June 6. (*House vote 210, p. H-70*)

Treasury had warned that it would recommend a veto of any bill that took away its control over the tied-aid fund. After two days of talks with the White House, conferees agreed to make the president, not the Treasury, the final arbiter over the use of the fund.

Despite the amount of attention it received, the so-called tied-aid war chest was a relatively small part of the bank's work. Of the estimated $3.1 billion needed to implement the bill from fiscal 2002 through 2006, tied aid was expected to account for $128 million, or 4 percent.

Liberal Democrats and conservative Republicans opposed the conference report in the House, describing the Ex-Im bank's work as a form of "corporate welfare" that could end up hurting rather than helping American workers. But sponsors were able to win the support of other Democrats by including language requiring the bank to consider the impact of a bank loan or grant on U.S. employment.

To assuage other lawmakers, the final version of the bill required the bank to look at foreign nations' records on fighting terrorism in providing loans. It also prohibited the bank from extending loans to foreign companies found in violation of U.S. trade laws and required that the bank double, to 20 percent, its share of transactions with small businesses. ◆

No Change to Controls On High-Tech Exports

An industry-led effort to ease export controls on "dual use" technologies — those with both military and commercial applications — failed once again, after free-traders and national security conservatives were unable to reach a compromise.

The legislation would have reauthorized the 1979 Export Administration Act (PL 96-72), which expired in 1994. The law, which had been kept in place by short-term extensions and by executive order — allowed the executive branch to block the export of high-technology equipment that could be used to construct advanced weapons.

Technology industry lobbyists said the export control system was out of date and hurt U.S. businesses, often blocking the export of devices that were readily available on world markets. But efforts to rewrite the law had collapsed repeatedly in disputes over whether the Commerce or Defense department should play the main role in deter-

mining what exports to restrict.

A bill (HR 2581 — H Rept 107-297, Part 1) approved by the House International Relations Committee on Aug. 1, 2001, and a similar measure (S 149 — S Rept 107-10) passed by the Senate on Sept. 6, 2001, would have divided authority for regulating exports among the Commerce, State and Defense departments. (*2001 Almanac, p. 19-8*)

In 2002, amid heightened security concerns growing out of the Sept. 11, 2001, terrorist attacks, the House Armed Services Committee amended the bill with provisions to enhance the Pentagon's role in regulating exports. The committee approved its version of HR 2581 (H Rept 107-297, Part 2), 44-6, on March 6. Among other things, the Armed Services version would have reinstated a special list of items that were determined to be critical to U.S. military superiority. The list itself would have been controlled by the secretary of Defense, and items that were listed could not have been exported without Pentagon approval.

The dim prospects for reconciling this bill with the more business-friendly Senate version halted further action in the 107th Congress. ◆

Chapter 19

TRANSPORTATION

Airline Security Law Refined

The federal government's role in securing the nation's air transport system got a modest makeover, as Congress worked to refine the sweeping 2001 aviation security law. The changes were enacted as part of the law creating the new Department of Homeland Security (HR 5005 — PL 107-296).

The Transportation Security Administration (TSA), created under the 2001 law (PL 107-71) to handle security operations for aviation and all other modes of transportation, was moved from the Transportation Department to the Department of Homeland Security, with the proviso that it remain a separate entity for at least two years. (*Homeland security, p. 8-3*)

In addition, the homeland law included provisions to:

• Arm and train airline pilots of passenger aircraft as "federal flight deck officers."

• Give airports an additional year, where necessary, to have machines in place to screen all airline baggage for explosives.

• Allow the TSA to hire U.S. nationals — legal residents of U.S. territories — as passenger and baggage screeners at airports. The original law required that all screeners be U.S. citizens.

• Provide some liability protection for airlines, including extending the federal Aviation War Risk Insurance program through the end of 2003. (*Airline aid, p. 19-4*)

Arming Pilots

The homeland security law required the TSA to establish a program to deputize volunteer commercial airline pilots as federal "flight deck officers" and allow them to carry guns aboard the aircraft. The purpose was to provide a last line of defense against potential hijackers. Before they could bring guns aboard, the pilots had to achieve a level of training and proficiency comparable to that required of air marshals, and to meet other TSA requirements. Preference was given to former military or law enforcement personnel. The law generally exempted the pilots and airlines from any liability that might result from defending a plane against terrorist acts.

Background

The 2001 law gave the Transportation Department discretion to begin arming some airline pilots, but the Bush administration chose not to implement the plan. Undersecretary John W. Magaw, the first director of the TSA, told the Senate Commerce, Science and Transportation Committee on May 21 that pilots should not be armed. "Pilots need to concentrate on flying the plane," Magaw testified. "My feeling is you secure the cockpit, and if something does happen on that plane, they really have to be in control of the aircraft."

The airline industry lobbied against arming pilots out of concern over liability and the potential cost of weapons training. Commerce, Science and Transportation Committee Chairman Ernest F. Hollings, D-S.C., who had jurisdiction over the issue in the Senate, initially opposed arming pilots, although he later agreed to give the program a chance.

The pilots, however, lobbied heavily to be able to carry firearms on flights, and congressional sentiment favored the pilots. "The government already has told us that if terrorists take control of one of our cockpits, they will send military aircraft to shoot down the airliner and all its crew and passengers," said Duane Woerth, president of the Air Line Pilots Association, which represented some 26,000 pilots. "We do not understand why these same government officials refuse to give pilots a last chance to prevent such a tragedy."

Magaw, who was unpopular with industry groups and members of Congress for a number of reasons, was removed July 18 and replaced by James M. Loy, a former commandant of the U.S. Coast Guard who had been second in command at the TSA. Loy quickly promised to review the policy of arming pilots.

Legislative Action

The House voted, 310-113, on July 10 to create a two-year demonstration program, under which at least 250 and up to 1,400 specially trained commercial airline pilots would be allowed to carry guns aboard aircraft. (*House vote 292, p. H-94*)

The bill (HR 4635) was the result of a bipartisan compromise worked out in the Transportation and Infrastructure Subcommittee on Aviation. The panel amended the original version to greatly limit the number of pilots who could be armed and make the program a two-year demonstration. The full Transportation and Infrastructure Committee approved the bill by voice vote June 26 (H Rept 107-555, Part 1).

On Sept. 5, the Senate agreed by voice vote to add similar language to the homeland security bill (HR 5005), although without limits that would be set under the House bill. The provisions were included in the final version of the homeland bill.

Baggage Screening

The homeland security law extended for one year, until Dec. 31, 2003, the deadline for some airports to have in place explosive detection machines capable of checking all airline baggage. The TSA director was authorized to grant the extension on a case-by-case basis. Until the machines were in place, the TSA had to use alterative methods, including hand searches, to ensure that 100 percent of the checked baggage was screened and the TSA director had to report to Congress monthly on the airport's progress in meeting the extended deadline.

The law also allowed non-citizen U.S. nationals to work as airport passenger and baggage screeners.

Background

While the TSA met its Nov. 19 deadline for deploying federal screeners at 429 national airports, it was clear early

Airlines Get Only Modest Help

Congress agreed to extend through 2003 a program that allowed domestic airlines to qualify for federal war risk insurance. The war risk program was designed to provide insurance to commercial aircraft and ships that traveled to high-risk areas to serve foreign policy and national security needs and could not get commercial insurance on reasonable terms.

The extension was enacted as part of the law that created the Department of Homeland Security (HR 5005 — PL 107-296). The law also extended through 2003 a $100 million limit on an airline's liability for injuries suffered as a result of terrorist attacks.

The airline industry had asked Congress for a much more generous follow-on to a $15 billion bailout (PL 107-42) it received in 2001. That package — aimed at helping airlines weather the effects of the Sept. 11 terrorist attacks — included $5 billion in cash and $10 billion in loan guarantees and other aid, including six months of eligibility for the war risk insurance program and the $100 million liability limit.

Most airlines had not recovered financially from the drop in air travel after Sept. 11, and company executives came to Congress to plead for more help in 2002. The bailout money had been exhausted, and the war risk insur-

ance kept alive by a string of 60-day extensions in response to continued airline lobbying. The industry wanted the government to renew the terrorism insurance and pick up a portion of its security costs. For instance, it wanted to end the $2.50-per-leg passenger fee that helped defray the costs of airport security assumed by the government under the 2001 aviation security law (PL 107-71). The airlines were absorbing the fee rather than raising ticket prices because fewer people were flying. (*2001 Almanac, p. 20-4*)

But Congress had little appetite for another bailout package. "We simply can't help every troubled industry, even if we wanted to," said John D. Rockefeller IV, D-W.Va., chairman of the Senate Commerce, Science and Transportation Subcommittee on Aviation. (*2001 Almanac, p. 20-3*)

Instead, bills passed by the Senate on Nov. 18 and approved by the House Transportation Committee's Aviation Subcommittee on Oct. 2 proposed modest relief, mainly by extending the war risk insurance program. The House bill (HR 5506) would have extended the insurance for a year, while the version passed by the Senate (S 2949 — S Rept 107-293) would have extended it for nine months. In the end, the issue was handled as part of the homeland security bill.

on that it would not be able to meet the second deadline set in the 2001 law: to have machinery in place by Dec. 31 to screen all checked baggage for explosives.

Many airports had to make structural changes to accommodate the minivan-sized machines. Loy, who was winning rave reviews from lawmakers for his common-sense approach to the job, testified Sept. 10 that the agency would find it "virtually impossible" to meet the deadline at some larger airports without inconveniencing passengers. In some cases, he said, engineering and installation problems could force travelers out to the curb as they waited in line at security checkpoints. Airports, particularly the Dallas-Fort Worth International Airport and McCarran International Airport in Las Vegas, lobbied heavily for some relief from the deadline.

Legislative Action

The Senate passed a bill by voice vote Nov. 18 to provide leeway for up to 40 airports. The Commerce, Science and

Transportation Committee had approved the measure (S 2949 — S Rept 107-293) by voice vote Sept. 19.

The proposal was the result of negotiations between the TSA, Hollings and ranking committee Republican John McCain of Arizona; all had acknowledged that the Dec. 31 deadline would be impossible to meet at some of the largest airports. The bill as introduced would have given airports six more months to meet the requirement, but an amendment by Kay Bailey Hutchison, R-Texas, adopted by voice vote, extended the deadline by one year. Hutchison said six months was not long enough for large airports with engineering challenges, such as Dallas-Fort Worth.

The bill also included a provision to remove the requirement that airport screeners be U.S. citizens, instead requiring only that they be U.S. nationals, a category that includes resident aliens or residents of a territory such as American Samoa.

The House version of the homeland security bill, passed July 26, included the one-year extension for airports. ◆

Law Calls for Tighter Port Security

Congress cleared a port security bill that for the first time required a comprehensive anti-terrorism plan for the nation's 361 commercial seaports. It also expanded and formalized the preeminent role in port security assumed by the Coast Guard following the Sept. 11, 2001, terrorist attacks.

However, the new law's impact on the safety of U.S. maritime commerce seemed likely to be limited by a lack of money. Lawmakers could not agree on how to come up with an estimated $4 billion over six years to pay for the improvements and left the funding, instead, to the Bush administration and the next Congress. The bill cleared Nov. 14, and President Bush signed it into law Nov. 25 (S 1214 — PL 107-295).

The Senate bill, sponsored by Ernest F. Hollings, D-S.C., chairman of the Commerce, Science and Transportation Committee, initially passed in December 2001. The House passed its own version in June 2002. Both bills called for nationwide assessments of port vulnerability and a grant program to help with security upgrades. However, a House-Senate conference agreement on a final bill was held up for months by a dispute over whether to impose user fees to help pay for it.

Republicans objected to a proposal by Hollings for a user fee on cargo and passengers coming in and out of U.S. ports that would have raised an estimated $700 million a year. Senate Minority Leader Trent Lott, R-Miss., House Ways and Means Committee Chairman Bill Thomas, R-Calif., and others attacked it as a new tax and an unnecessary burden on trade. Shipping companies and manufacturers lobbied heavily against it.

House and Senate conferees were able to finish the bill only after Hollings relented and dropped the proposed fees. The final bill required the administration to submit a funding plan to address port security vulnerabilities within six months of enactment.

Conferees also faced a protracted, though less-publicized, dispute over background checks for dockworkers. The Senate bill listed specific crimes for which workers could be denied security credentials, but the International Longshore and Warehouse Union objected. The House version did not list specific crimes. Conferees eventually agreed to leave it to the Transportation secretary to decide who would receive credentials, which would be in the form of a transportation worker identity card.

Highlights

The following are the main provisions of the new law. Most tasks assigned to the Department of Transportation were expected to shift to the new Homeland Security

BoxScore

Bill:
S 1214 — PL 107-295
Legislative Action:
House passed S 1214, amended (H Rept 107-405), by voice vote June 4.
Senate adopted the conference report (H Rept 107-177), 95-0, on Nov. 14.
House cleared the bill by voice vote Nov. 14.
President signed Nov. 25.

Department, which was taking over responsibility for the Coast Guard. (*Homeland Security Department, p. 7-3*)

● **Anti-terrorism planning.** The law required the Coast Guard to conduct vulnerability assessments of U.S. ports, vessels and other shoreline facilities, such as nuclear power plants or chemical facilities, that were vulnerable to attack. Detailed vulnerability assessments of those sites would be used to develop and implement local and national security plans, as well as customized plans for specific facilities and vessels seen as vulnerable.

● **Local coordination.** Area security advisory committees were to be created at each port to coordinate planning among law enforcement, intelligence agencies, the Customs Service, Coast Guard, immigration, port authorities, shipping companies and port workers.

● **Response teams.** The Coast Guard was directed to establish maritime safety and security teams that could be deployed rapidly in the event of terrorist threats or criminal actions against vessels, ports, facilities or cargo in U.S. waters. The Coast Guard already had deployed port security units specially trained in port and waterway security to help patrol several major ports.

● **"Sea marshals."** The measure authorized armed Coast Guard personnel to act as "sea marshals," boarding incoming vessels to prevent or respond to acts of terrorism. The provision gave statutory authority to a program the Coast Guard already had established.

● **Anti-terrorism grants.** The law created a new grant program through fiscal 2008 to assist ports, as well as state and local governments, in upgrading port security.

It also authorized $15 million a year through fiscal 2008 for research and development of technologies to help the Customs Service target suspicious cargo and detect explosives, chemical and biological agents, and nuclear materials.

Another $5.5 million a year was authorized to train maritime security workers.

● **Security cards.** The Transportation Department was to develop and issue a new, national transportation security card that would allow eligible port workers, merchant mariners and truck drivers to work in "secure" areas of ports and other transportation facilities. Vessels and port facilities had to identify "secure" areas where access would be restricted to those with valid federal transportation security cards.

● **Foreign port assessments.** The Coast Guard was required to assess security measures at certain foreign ports and authorized to bar vessels from entering U.S. ports if they came from a foreign port that failed to meet security standards.

● **Container and cargo security.** The law required the Transportation Department to develop and maintain an anti-terrorism cargo identification, tracking and screening

system for containerized cargo shipped through U.S. ports. It also required the department to develop standards for container seals and locks, and systems to detect tampering.

The Customs Service was formally authorized to require shippers to provide advance electronic information on cargo being shipped to or from the United States. The information was to be shared with other federal agencies.

- **Intelligence.** The Transportation Department was to establish a maritime intelligence program to collect and analyze information concerning any vessel operating in U.S. waters in order to evaluate potential threats.
- **U.S. territorial limits.** The law extended the U.S. territorial sea from three miles offshore to 12 miles.
- **Tracking system.** Most commercial vessels, including passenger vessels, operating in U.S. waters had to be equipped with transponders that identified the vessel and its location; the Transportation Department was directed to establish a long-range vessel tracking system using satellite technologies.
- **Coast Guard authorization.** The law authorized $6 billion for the Coast Guard in fiscal 2003, including $4.3 billion for Coast Guard operations. It was the first time the Coast Guard had been authorized since 1998.

Background

Well before Sept. 11, 2001, U.S. officials were concerned about the vulnerability of busy commercial seaports to terrorism. About 2 percent of the 6 million cargo containers entering the country each year were inspected; a month after the terrorist attacks, a suspected member of the terrorist organization al Qaeda was caught trying to travel from Italy to Canada in a container.

"Our 361 sea and river ports handle 95 percent of U.S. international trade," Hollings often pointed out. "These ports annually transfer more than 2 billion tons of freight — often in huge containers from ships directly onto trucks and rail cars that immediately head onto our highways and rail systems," he said. Hollings called the fact that less than 2 percent of the containers were checked by customs or law enforcement officials "a gaping hole in our national security that must be fixed."

Before Sept. 11, the Coast Guard, whose mission ranged from boating safety and drug interdiction to law enforcement and military activity, was planning to spend only about 14 percent of its resources on port safety and security. The lion's share of its $5.4 billion fiscal 2002 budget was to have gone to drug interdiction, fisheries enforcement, and search and rescue.

Immediately after the terrorist attacks, the Coast Guard reoriented its priorities to put 58 percent of its resources into port security and cut back on other missions. Cutters and smaller patrol boats that protected against poaching by foreign fishing trawlers in the days before the attacks were redeployed to guard key waterways, such as New York Harbor and the Los Angeles-Long Beach port complex. Reservists were summoned to duty in several harbors.

The Coast Guard also worked with local port police on a sea marshal program under which armed personnel boarded suspicious ships, interviewed crews, reviewed cargo manifests and then escorted the ships into harbor. Special attention was paid to cruise ships or vessels carrying hazardous cargo, such as natural gas, and ships from the Middle East. The Coast Guard also established a half-dozen intelligence centers to analyze happenings on the high seas that could compromise U.S. security.

Senate Maritime Security Bill

The Senate bill, passed on Dec. 20, 2001, had been drafted in July, before the terrorist attacks that made homeland security a top government priority. The aim was to establish a coordinated national policy to protect seaports from crime and terrorism. The bill required the Coast Guard to evaluate the vulnerability of the nation's 50 most important ports and called for national and local committees to upgrade port security and coordinate federal, state and local responses to security threats. The bill would have authorized $3.3 billion in loan guarantees and grants for improving port security infrastructure. It also would have authorized $1.1 billion over six years for additional Customs Service personnel, better training and security improvements such as dockside cameras and guard dogs. It would have required vessels to provide electronic cargo manifest and crew information before arriving in a U.S. port.

The bill called for an extension of tonnage duties through 2006 on cargo entering or leaving U.S. ports, with up to $59 million annually used to help pay for stepped up security measures.

Legislative Action

The House passed S 1214 by voice vote June 4, after substituting the text of its own bill (HR 3983 — H Rept 107-405). The Transportation and Infrastructure Committee had approved the bill by voice vote March 20.

The measure, sponsored by committee Chairman Don Young, R-Alaska, authorized $83 million per year in grants for port security improvements in fiscal 2003 through 2005 and required the creation of a comprehensive maritime anti-terrorism plan. It included provisions to:

- Require the Coast Guard to conduct vulnerability assessments of U.S. ports, and use the results to plan and implement national, state and local security plans.
- Require the Coast Guard to evaluate security systems in certain foreign ports and to deny entry to vessels coming from foreign ports that did not maintain effective security.
- Authorize the Transportation secretary to issue port security cards, which could only be denied if an individual was found to be a terrorist risk.
- Require the Transportation Security Administration to develop an anti-terrorism identification and screening system for containerized cargo going into and out of the United States through a foreign port. The bill also required new standards for containers and locks.
- Authorize $4.2 billion for the Coast Guard in fiscal 2002. The House had passed this as a separate bill (HR 3507) in December 2001, but the Senate never acted on it.
- Establish anti-terrorism teams to patrol U.S. waters, authorize Coast Guard sea marshals to prevent or respond to terrorist threats in ports and aboard vessels, and continue a practice begun in late 2001 that required all captains of arriving vessels to give the Coast Guard 96 hours' notice before entering a 12-mile "security zone." Commercial vessel

operators would have to provide a manifest of passengers and crew members.

Conference/Final Action

House and Senate negotiators reached a tentative deal on the bill Oct. 17 after Hollings dropped his insistence that the bill's cost be covered by an extension of tonnage duties or a new cargo user fee. By then, however, members were already leaving to campaign, pushing final action into the post-election lame-duck session.

The Senate adopted the conference report (H Rept 107-777) by a vote of 95-0 on Nov. 14. The House cleared the bill by voice vote the same day. *(Senate vote 243, p. S-50)*

Hollings said that he proposed a new cargo fee and an extension of Customs Service tonnage duties because he doubted that Congress would be able to make room for port security programs in the fiscal 2003 budget.

Thomas and Young insisted that port security funding should come from general revenue, a point that was reinforced by an impressive array of lobbying interests including groups such as the American Association of Exporters and Importers, which represented General Electric Co., General Motors Corp. and other corporate giants.

Another barrier to Hollings' proposal was the constitutional requirement that all revenue bills originate in the House. Had the bill included the cargo tonnage duty, it would have been subject to a "blue slip" referring the entire measure to the Ways and Means Committee.

"While I preferred to include a guaranteed funding source for port security enhancements," Hollings said in a statement, "I believe it is critical that we approve the essential elements of the legislation before this session ends." ◆

Amtrak Funding Bill Loses Steam

Lawmakers were unable to agree on legislation to reauthorize Amtrak, which left the struggling passenger rail line to survive on emergency cash infusions. The last authorization expired Sept. 30. The future of federal support for Amtrak was put off for the 108th Congress, when it was expected to come up as part of a scheduled reauthorization of surface transportation programs.

The Transportation Department gave Amtrak a $100 million loan in June to avert a shutdown, and Congress provided $205 million in supplemental funding (PL 107-206) a month later. Proponents said Amtrak needed more money, at least $1.2 billion, to keep it running through fiscal 2003. Meanwhile, the railroad endured a spate of summertime accidents that injured more than 100 passengers and damaged or destroyed 13 passenger cars.

A House bill (HR 4545), sponsored by Transportation and Infrastructure Committee Chairman Don Young, R-Alaska, would have authorized the railroad for one year at $1.9 billion, while requiring Amtrak to submit business plans to the Transportation Department inspector general and the House and Senate transportation committees. The measure won approval from the panel's Railroads Subcommittee, but it stalled after Young insisted it be paired with a high-speed rail bill (HR 2950), which was bogged down by a dispute between organized labor and House Republicans.

In the Senate, Commerce, Science and Transportation Committee Chairman Ernest F. Hollings, D-S.C., sponsored a much more generous five-year bill (S 1991) that would have authorized up to $4.6 billion annually through fiscal 2007, with additional short-term spending for security and tunnel safety improvements. The Commerce Committee approved Hollings' bill April 18, but it languished on the Senate calendar.

BoxScore

Bills:
S 1991, HR 4545, HR 2950
Legislative Action:
Senate Commerce, Science and Transportation Committee approved S 1991 (S Rept 107-157), 20-3, on April 18.
House Transportation and Infrastructure subcommittee approved HR 4545 and HR 2950 by voice vote May 8.

Background

Congress had last bailed out Amtrak with an extra infusion of cash in 1997 (PL 105-134), but it was with the understanding that the railroad would be self-sufficient by 2002. *(1997 Almanac, p. 3-22)*

Not only had Amtrak not turned a profit since then, but some lawmakers said the railroad's managers misled them into thinking it was close to the goal when it was not. Amtrak lost $1.1 billion in fiscal 2001 and continued losing millions of dollars each day. Unable to profit from the public's uneasiness with flying after Sept. 11, 2001, it lacked the money needed to repair dozens of damaged and run-down rail cars and aging stations. The railroad carried less than 1 percent of all intercity traffic. Few cities on Amtrak's routes had more than one train a day.

A report by the General Accounting Office (GAO) in April said that Amtrak had failed to carry out much of a network growth strategy it had announced two years before. It had started three of 12 planned new routes, and one of those was canceled when it failed to pick up freight business Amtrak executives were counting on.

"The thing with Amtrak is that — outside the Northeast Corridor — this is something that touches no one's life in any meaningful way except for hobbyists. People who love trains are well organized," said Ron Utt, a senior research fellow at the Heritage Foundation, a conservative think tank in Washington.

But Amtrak remained popular with city officials even if the public did not ride it much. Some liked having a trans-

portation alternative and a potential remedy for traffic congestion. Others hoped to develop high-speed connections to neighboring metropolitan areas.

Meanwhile, organized labor, a major factor because of the influence it could bring to bear on Congress, was fighting to save thousands of railroad jobs, whether they remained with Amtrak or ended up being transferred to new companies operating passenger rail service.

Legislative Action

Senate Committee Action

The Senate Commerce, Science and Transportation Committee approved its five-year passenger rail measure (S 1991 — S Rept 107-157) by a vote of 20-3 on April 18. The bill would have authorized $1.4 billion in fiscal 2003 for security and tunnel safety improvements; $7.8 billion over five years for high-speed rail projects; and $13.3 billion over five years for Amtrak. The bill also would have authorized $35 billion for loans and loan guarantees under the Railroad Rehabilitation and Infrastructure Financing program, which was created, but not funded, under the 1998 surface transportation law (PL 105-178). (*1998 Almanac, p. 24-3*)

In addition, the bill would have repealed the requirement in the 1997 Amtrak Reform and Accountability Act that Amtrak be operationally self-sufficient by the end of 2002. "No national rail passenger system in the world operates without some form of subsidy, either operating or capital funding, or both," the committee report said. It also predicted that "proper funding of Amtrak's capital needs would help to reduce Amtrak's operating expenses, obviating the need for short-term borrowing to cover operating expenses."

Before approving the bill, the panel adopted by voice vote an amendment requiring that 50 percent of the rail security funds be spent outside the Northeast Corridor, which runs between Washington, D.C., and Boston. Other provisions included labor protections and requirements that Amtrak continue to operate as a national system, that it implement new financial planning and accounting methods, and that it put any net revenues from non-passenger operations into maintaining sufficient working capital to prevent major service disruptions.

On other amendments, the committee:

• Rejected, 5-18, a proposal by ranking Republican John McCain of Arizona to establish an Amtrak Control Board to monitor the rail company's finances, approve Amtrak's budgets and provide management assistance.

• Rejected, 10-13, another McCain amendment, which would have required Amtrak to have the Transportation secretary's approval before taking on new debt.

• Adopted by voice vote a McCain amendment to require that new high-speed rail projects funded under the bill be subject to a competitive bidding process.

• Adopted by voice vote a McCain proposal to allow states to put up some of the funds for high-speed rail projects. The underlying bill required a 100 percent federal share.

• Adopted by voice vote an amendment by Gordon H. Smith, R-Ore., to clarify that the bill would not preclude Amtrak from maintaining non-high-speed service in certain parts of the country. Another Smith amendment, also approved by voice vote, added Portland, Ore., to the list of high-speed rail priority locations.

• Adopted by voice vote a proposal by John D. Rockefeller IV, D-W.Va., to make non-railroad entities eligible for loans and loan guarantees under the bill.

• Adopted by voice vote two amendments by Ron Wyden, D-Ore. — to require the Transportation Department to hire an independent consultant to examine Amtrak route and service planning decisions, and to apply executive branch conflict of interest standards to Amtrak board members and Amtrak officers.

• Adopted by voice vote an amendment by Bill Nelson, D-Fla., to designate the Tampa-to-Orlando corridor as a priority for high-speed rail service.

House Subcommittee Action

On May 8, following a rally by union members and other Amtrak supporters at a Capitol Hill park, the House Transportation and Infrastructure Railroads Subcommittee gave voice vote approval to a pair of passenger rail bills — a $1.9 billion Amtrak reauthorization bill for fiscal 2003 and legislation to authorize $59 billion over 10 years to build high-speed rail lines in several areas of the country.

The authorization bill (HR 4545) included $1.2 billion requested by the railroad for operations, capital improvements and retirement payments and $775 million for security and repairs to tunnels in New York, Baltimore and Washington. In return, it required greater supervision of Amtrak by the Transportation Department, congressional committees and the GAO.

The committee planned to take up a long-term Amtrak reauthorization in 2003.

The high-speed rail bill (HR 2950) reflected the findings of the Amtrak Reform Council and others that the future of passenger rail in the United States lay in high-speed routes over limited distances — up to about 300 miles — where it could compete on service and price with airlines. Amtrak's only solidly profitable route was its high-speed Northeast Corridor.

The bill would have allowed states to issue tax-exempt and tax-credit bonds for high-speed rail lines — up to $2.4 billion worth of bonds each year through 2012. States that issued the bonds would be required to pay for some rail improvements, such as eliminating grade crossings and rehabilitating or building stations. The bill also included $35 billion for the Railroad Rehabilitation and Infrastructure Financing program.

Young argued that passenger service had a chance if it was high speed, and the legislation would have allowed the development of corridors not necessarily part of Amtrak. Also, he insisted that the Amtrak reauthorization bill be considered together with the high-speed rail measure.

On May 22, Young withdrew both measures from a full committee markup because of a dispute among House Republicans, the Association of American Railroads and unions representing construction and railroad workers. The unions were trying to ensure that they got a majority of the potential jobs from the bond program and that new employees were covered by federal railroad labor laws, including the Railway Labor Act of 1926 and a 1974 railroad retirement bill (PL 93-445). Republican lawmakers and the railroad association said the unions' proposal could not be accommodated within existing rail labor laws. ◆

Appendix A

CONGRESS
AND ITS MEMBERS

Glossary of Congressional Terms

Act — The term for legislation once it has passed both chambers of Congress and has been signed by the president or passed over his veto, thus becoming law. Also used in parliamentary terminology for a bill that has been passed by one house and engrossed. (*Also see engrossed bill.*)

Adjournment sine die — Adjournment without a fixed day for reconvening — literally, "adjournment without a day." Usually used to connote the final adjournment of a session of Congress. A session can continue until noon Jan. 3 of the following year, when, under the 20th Amendment to the Constitution, it automatically terminates. Both chambers must agree to a concurrent resolution for either chamber to adjourn for more than three days.

Adjournment to a day certain — Adjournment under a motion or resolution that fixes the next time of meeting. Under the Constitution, neither chamber can adjourn for more than three days without the concurrence of the other. A session of Congress is not ended by adjournment to a day certain.

Amendment — A proposal by a member of Congress to alter the language, provisions or stipulations in a bill or in another amendment. An amendment usually is printed, debated and voted upon in the same manner as a bill.

Amendment in the nature of a substitute — Usually an amendment that seeks to replace the entire text of a bill by striking out everything after the enacting clause and inserting a new version of the bill. An amendment in the nature of a substitute can also refer to an amendment that replaces a large portion of the text of a bill.

Appeal — A member's challenge of a ruling or decision made by the presiding officer of the chamber. A senator can appeal to members of the Senate to override the decision. If carried by a majority vote, the appeal nullifies the chair's ruling. In the House, the decision of the Speaker traditionally has been final; seldom are there appeals to the members to reverse the Speaker's stand. To appeal a ruling is considered an attack on the Speaker.

Appropriations bill — A bill that gives legal authority to spend or obligate money from the Treasury. The Constitution disallows money to be drawn from the Treasury "but in Consequence of Appropriations made by Law."

By congressional custom, an appropriations bill originates in the House. It is not supposed to be considered by the full House or Senate until a related measure authorizing the funding is enacted. An appropriations bill grants the actual budget authority approved by the authorization bill, though not necessarily the full amount permissible under the authorization.

If the 13 regular appropriations bills are not enacted by the start of the fiscal year, Congress must pass a stopgap spending bill or the departments and agencies covered by the unfinished bills must shut down.

About half of all budget authority, notably that for Social Security and interest on the federal debt, does not require annual appropriations; those programs exist under permanent appropriations. (*Also see authorization bill, budget authority, budget process, supplemental appropriations bill.*)

Authorization bill — Basic, substantive legislation that establishes or continues the legal operation of a federal program or agency either indefinitely or for a specific period of time, or which

sanctions a particular type of obligation or expenditure. Under the rules of both chambers, appropriations for a program or agency may not be considered until the program has been authorized, although this requirement is often waived.

An authorization sets the maximum amount of funds that can be given to a program or agency, although sometimes it merely authorizes "such sums as may be necessary." (*Also see backdoor spending authority.*)

Backdoor spending authority — Budget authority provided in legislation outside the normal appropriations process. The most common forms of backdoor spending are borrowing authority, contract authority, entitlements and loan guarantees that commit the government to payments of principal and interest on loans — such as guaranteed student loans — made by banks or other private lenders. Loan guarantees result in actual outlays only when there is a default by the borrower.

In some cases, such as interest on the public debt, a permanent appropriation is provided that becomes available without further action by Congress.

Bills — Most legislative proposals before Congress are in the form of bills and are designated according to the chamber in which they originate — HR in the House of Representatives or S in the Senate — and by a number assigned in the order in which they are introduced during the two-year period of a congressional term.

"Public bills" deal with general questions and become public laws if they are cleared by Congress and signed by the president. "Private bills" deal with individual matters, such as claims against the government, immigration and naturalization cases or land titles, and become private laws if approved and signed. (*Also see private bills, resolution.*)

Bills introduced — In both the House and Senate, any number of members may join in introducing a single bill or resolution. The first member listed is the sponsor of the bill, and all subsequent members listed are cosponsors.

Many bills are committee bills and are introduced under the name of the chairman of the committee or subcommittee. All appropriations bills fall into this category. A committee frequently holds hearings on a number of related bills and may agree to one of them or to an entirely new bill. (*Also see clean bill.*)

Bills referred — After a bill is introduced, it is referred to the committee or committees that have jurisdiction over the subject with which the bill is concerned. Under the standing rules of the House and Senate, bills are referred by the Speaker in the House and by the presiding officer in the Senate. In practice, the House and Senate parliamentarians act for these officials and refer the vast majority of bills. (*Also see discharge a committee.*)

Borrowing authority — Statutory authority that permits a federal agency to incur obligations and make payments for specified purposes with borrowed money.

Budget — The document sent to Congress by the president early each year estimating government revenue and expenditures for the ensuing fiscal year.

Budget Act — The common name for the Congressional Budget and Impoundment Control Act of 1974, which established the

current budget process and created the Congressional Budget Office. The act also put limits on presidential authority to spend appropriated money. It has undergone several major revisions since 1974. (*Also see budget process, impoundments.*)

Budget authority — Authority for federal agencies to enter into obligations that result in immediate or future outlays. The basic forms of budget authority are appropriations, contract authority and borrowing authority. Budget authority may be classified by (1) the period of availability (one-year, multiple-year or without a time limitation), (2) the timing of congressional action (current or permanent) or (3) the manner of determining the amount available (definite or indefinite). (*Also see appropriations, outlays.*)

Budget process — The annual budget process was created by the Congressional Budget and Impoundment Control Act of 1974, with a timetable that was modified in 1990. Under the law, the president must submit his proposed budget by the first Monday in February. Congress is supposed to complete an annual budget resolution by April 15, setting guidelines for congressional action on spending and tax measures.

Budget rules enacted in the 1990 Budget Enforcement Act and updated in 1993 and 1997 set caps on discretionary spending through fiscal 2002. The caps could be adjusted annually to account for changes in the economy and other limited factors. In addition, pay-as-you-go (PAYGO) rules required that any tax cut, new entitlement program or expansion of existing entitlement benefits that would increase a deficit be offset by an increase in taxes or a cut in entitlement spending.

The rules held Congress harmless for budget-deficit increases that lawmakers did not explicitly cause — for example, increases due to a recession or to an expansion in the number of beneficiaries qualifying for Medicare or food stamps. PAYGO did not apply when there was a budget surplus.

If Congress exceeded the discretionary spending caps in its appropriations bills, the law required an across-the-board cut — known as a sequester — in non-exempt discretionary spending accounts. If Congress violated the PAYGO rules, entitlement programs were subject to a sequester. Supplemental appropriations were subject to similar controls, with the proviso that if both Congress and the president agreed, spending designated as an emergency could exceed the caps.

Budget resolution — A concurrent resolution that is passed by both chambers of Congress but does not require the president's signature. The measure sets a strict ceiling on discretionary budget authority, along with non-binding recommendations about how the spending should be allocated. The budget resolution may also contain "reconciliation instructions" requiring authorizing and tax-writing committees to propose changes in existing law to meet deficit-reduction goals. The Budget Committee in each chamber then bundles those proposals into a reconciliation bill and sends it to the floor. (*Also see reconciliation.*)

By request — A phrase used when a senator or representative introduces a bill at the request of an executive agency or private organization but does not necessarily endorse the legislation.

Calendar — An agenda or list of business awaiting possible action by each chamber. The House uses six legislative calendars. They are the Consent, Corrections, Discharge, House, Private and Union calendars. (*Also see individual listings.*)

In the Senate, all legislative matters reported from committee go on one calendar. They are listed there in the order in which committees report them or the Senate places them on the calendar, but they may be called up out of order by the majority leader,

either by obtaining unanimous consent of the Senate or by a motion to call up a bill. The Senate also has one non-legislative calendar, which is used for treaties and nominations. (*Also see executive calendar.*)

Call of the calendar — Senate bills that are not brought up for debate by a motion, unanimous consent or a unanimous consent agreement are brought before the Senate for action when the calendar listing them is "called." Bills must be called in the order listed. Measures considered by this method usually are non-controversial, and debate on the bill and any proposed amendments is limited to five minutes for each senator.

Chamber — The meeting place for the membership of either the House or the Senate; also the membership of the House or Senate meeting as such.

Clean bill — Frequently after a committee has finished a major revision of a bill, one of the committee members, usually the chairman, will assemble the changes and what is left of the original bill into a new measure and introduce it as a "clean bill." The revised measure, which is given a new number, is referred back to the committee, which reports it to the floor for consideration. This often is a timesaver, as committee-recommended changes in a clean bill do not have to be considered and voted on by the chamber. Reporting a clean bill also protects committee amendments that could be subject to points of order concerning germaneness.

Clerk of the House — An officer of the House of Representatives who supervises its records and legislative business. Many former administrative duties were transferred in 1992 to a new position, the director of non-legislative and financial services.

Cloture — The process by which a filibuster can be ended in the Senate other than by unanimous consent. A motion for cloture can apply to any measure before the Senate, including a proposal to change the chamber's rules. A cloture motion requires the signatures of 16 senators to be introduced. To end a filibuster, the cloture motion must obtain the votes of three-fifths of the entire Senate membership (60 if there are no vacancies), except when the filibuster is against a proposal to amend the standing rules of the Senate and a two-thirds vote of senators present and voting is required.

The cloture request is put to a roll call vote one hour after the Senate meets on the second day following introduction of the motion. If approved, cloture limits each senator to one hour of debate. The bill or amendment in question comes to a final vote after 30 hours of consideration, including debate time and the time it takes to conduct roll calls, quorum calls and other procedural motions. (*Also see filibuster.*)

Committee — A division of the House or Senate that prepares legislation for action by the parent chamber or makes investigations as directed by the parent chamber.

There are several types of committees. Most standing committees are divided into subcommittees, which study legislation, hold hearings and report bills, with or without amendments, to the full committee. Only the full committee can report legislation for action by the House or Senate. (*Also see standing, oversight, select and special committees.*)

Committee of the Whole — The working title of what is formally "The Committee of the Whole House [of Representatives] on the State of the Union." The membership is composed of all House members sitting as a committee. Any 100 members who are present on the floor of the chamber to consider legislation com-

prise a quorum of the committee. Any legislation, however, must first have passed through the regular legislative or appropriations committee and have been placed on the calendar.

Technically, the Committee of the Whole considers only bills directly or indirectly appropriating money, authorizing appropriations or involving taxes or charges on the public. Because the Committee of the Whole need number only 100 representatives, a quorum is more readily attained and legislative business is expedited. Before 1971, members' positions were not individually recorded on votes taken in the Committee of the Whole.

When the full House resolves itself into the Committee of the Whole, it replaces the Speaker with a "chairman." A measure is debated and amendments may be proposed, with votes on amendments as needed. (*Also see five-minute rule.*)

When the committee completes its work on the measure, it dissolves itself by "rising." The Speaker returns, and the chairman of the Committee of the Whole reports to the House that the committee's work has been completed. At this time, members may demand a roll call vote on any amendment adopted in the Committee of the Whole. The final vote is on passage of the legislation.

In 1993 and 1994, the four delegates from the territories and the resident commissioner of Puerto Rico were allowed to vote on questions before the Committee of the Whole. If their votes were decisive in the outcome, however, the matter was automatically re-voted, with the delegates and resident commissioner ineligible. They could vote on final passage of bills or on separate votes demanded after the Committee of the Whole rises. This limited voting right was rescinded in 1995.

Committee veto — A requirement added to a few statutes directing that certain policy directives by an executive department or agency be reviewed by certain congressional committees before they are implemented. Under common practice, the government department or agency and the committees involved are expected to reach a consensus before the directives are carried out. (*Also see legislative veto.*)

Concurrent resolution — A concurrent resolution, designated H Con Res or S Con Res, must be adopted by both chambers, but it is not sent to the president for approval and, therefore, does not have the force of law. A concurrent resolution, for example, is used to fix the time for adjournment of a Congress. It is also used to express the sense of Congress on a foreign policy or domestic issue. The annual budget resolution is a concurrent resolution.

Conference — A meeting between representatives of the House and the Senate to reconcile differences between the two chambers on provisions of a bill. Members of the conference committee are appointed by the Speaker and the presiding officer of the Senate.

A majority of the conferees for each chamber must agree on a compromise, reflected in a "conference report" before the final bill can go back to both chambers for approval. When the conference report goes to the floor, it is difficult to amend. If it is not approved by both chambers, the bill may go back to conference under certain situations, or a new conference may be convened. Many rules and informal practices govern the conduct of conference committees.

Bills that are passed by both chambers with only minor differences need not be sent to conference. Either chamber may "concur" with the other's amendments, completing action on the legislation. Sometimes leaders of the committees of jurisdiction work out an informal compromise instead of having a formal conference. (*Also see custody of the papers.*)

Confirmations — (*See nominations.*)

Congressional Record — The daily, printed account of proceedings in both the House and Senate chambers, showing substantially verbatim debate, statements and a record of floor action. Highlights of legislative and committee action are given in a Daily Digest section of the Record, and members are entitled to have their extraneous remarks printed in an appendix known as "Extension of Remarks." Members may edit and revise remarks made on the floor during debate, although the House in 1995 limited members to technical or grammatical changes.

The Congressional Record provides a way to distinguish remarks spoken on the floor of the House and Senate from undelivered speeches. In the Senate, all speeches, articles and other matter that members insert in the Record without actually reading them on the floor are set off by large black dots, or bullets. However, a loophole allows a member to avoid the bulleting if he or she delivers any portion of the speech in person. In the House, undelivered speeches and other material are printed in a distinctive typeface. The record is also available in electronic form. (*Also see Journal.*)

Congressional terms of office — Terms normally begin on Jan. 3 of the year following a general election. Terms are two years for representatives and six years for senators. Representatives elected in special elections are sworn in for the remainder of a term. Under most state laws, a person may be appointed to fill a Senate vacancy and serve until a successor is elected; the successor serves until the end of the term applying to the vacant seat.

Consent Calendar — Members of the House may place on this calendar most bills on the Union or House Calendar that are considered non-controversial. Bills on the Consent Calendar normally are called on the first and third Mondays of each month. On the first occasion that a bill is called in this manner, consideration may be blocked by the objection of any member. The second time, if there are three objections, the bill is stricken from the Consent Calendar. If fewer than three members object, the bill is given immediate consideration.

A member may also postpone action on the bill by asking that the measure be passed over "without prejudice." In that case, no objection is recorded against the bill and its status on the Consent Calendar remains unchanged. A bill stricken from the Consent Calendar remains on the Union or House Calendar. The Consent Calendar has seldom been used in recent years.

Continuing resolution — A joint resolution, cleared by Congress and signed by the president, to provide new budget authority for federal agencies and programs until the regular appropriations bills have been enacted. Also known as "CRs" or continuing appropriation, continuing resolutions are used to keep agencies operating when, as often happens, Congress fails to finish the regular appropriations process by the start of the new fiscal year.

The CR usually specifies a maximum rate at which an agency may incur obligations, based on the rate of the prior year, the president's budget request or an appropriations bill passed by either or both chambers of Congress but not yet enacted.

Contract authority — Budget authority contained in an authorization bill that permits the federal government to enter into contracts or other obligations for future payments from funds not yet appropriated by Congress. The assumption is that funds will be provided in a subsequent appropriations act. (*Also see budget authority.*)

Corrections Calendar, Corrections Day — A House calendar established in 1995 to speed consideration of bills aimed at eliminating burdensome or unnecessary regulations. Bills on the Cor-

rections Calendar can be called up on the second and fourth Tuesday of each month, called Corrections Day. They are subject to one hour of debate without amendment, and require a three-fifths majority for passage. (*Also see calendar.*)

Correcting recorded votes — Rules prohibit members from changing their votes after the result has been announced. Occasionally, however, a member may announce hours, days or months after a vote has been taken that he or she was "incorrectly recorded." In the Senate, a request to change one's vote almost always receives unanimous consent, so long as it does not change the outcome. In the House, members are prohibited from changing votes if they were tallied by the electronic voting system.

Cosponsor — (*See bills introduced.*)

Current services estimates — Estimated budget authority and outlays for federal programs and operations for the forthcoming fiscal year based on continuation of existing levels of service without policy changes but with adjustments for inflation and for demographic changes that affect programs. These estimates, accompanied by the underlying economic and policy assumptions upon which they are based, are transmitted by the president to Congress when the budget is submitted.

Custody of the papers — To reconcile differences between the House and Senate versions of a bill, a conference may be arranged. The chamber with "custody of the papers" — the engrossed bill, engrossed amendments, messages of transmittal — is the only body empowered to request the conference. By custom, the chamber that asks for a conference is the last to act on the conference report.

Custody of the papers sometimes is manipulated to ensure that a particular chamber acts either first or last on the conference report. (*Also see conference.*)

Deferral — Executive branch action to defer, or delay, the spending of appropriated money. The 1974 Congressional Budget and Impoundment Control Act requires a special message from the president to Congress reporting a proposed deferral of spending. Deferrals may not extend beyond the end of the fiscal year in which the message is transmitted. A federal district court in 1986 struck down the president's authority to defer spending for policy reasons; the ruling was upheld by a federal appeals court in 1987. Congress can prohibit proposed deferrals by enacting a law doing so; most often, cancellations of proposed deferrals are included in appropriations bills. (*Also see rescission.*)

Dilatory motion — A motion made for the purpose of killing time and preventing action on a bill or amendment. House rules outlaw dilatory motions, but enforcement is largely within the discretion of the Speaker or chairman of the Committee of the Whole. The Senate does not have a rule barring dilatory motions except under cloture.

Discharge a committee — Occasionally, attempts are made to relieve a committee of jurisdiction over a bill that is before it. This is attempted more often in the House than in the Senate, and the procedure rarely is successful.

In the House, if a committee does not report a bill within 30 days after the measure is referred to it, any member may file a discharge motion. Once offered, the motion is treated as a petition needing the signatures of a majority of members (218 if there are no vacancies). After the required signatures have been obtained, there is a delay of seven days.

Thereafter, on the second and fourth Mondays of each month,

except during the last six days of a session, any member who has signed the petition must be recognized, if he or she so desires, to move that the committee be discharged. Debate on the motion to discharge is limited to 20 minutes. If the motion is carried, consideration of the bill becomes a matter of high privilege.

If a resolution to consider a bill is held up in the Rules Committee for more than seven legislative days, any member may enter a motion to discharge the committee. The motion is handled like any other discharge petition in the House. Occasionally, to expedite non-controversial legislative business, a committee is discharged by unanimous consent of the House, and a petition is not required. In 1993, the signatures on pending discharge petitions — previously kept secret — were made a matter of public record. (*For Senate procedure, see discharge resolution.*)

Discharge Calendar — The House calendar to which motions to discharge committees are referred when they have the required number of signatures (218) and are awaiting floor action. (*Also see calendar.*)

Discharge petition — (*See discharge a committee.*)

Discharge resolution — In the Senate, a special motion that any senator may introduce to relieve a committee from consideration of a bill before it. The resolution can be called up for Senate approval or disapproval in the same manner as any other Senate business. (*For House procedure, see discharge a committee.*)

Discretionary spending caps — (*See budget process.*)

Division of a question for voting — A practice that is more common in the Senate but also used in the House whereby a member may demand a division of an amendment or a motion for purposes of voting. Where an amendment or motion can be divided, the individual parts are voted on separately when a member demands a division. This procedure occurs most often during the consideration of conference reports.

Enacting clause — Key phrase in bills beginning, "Be it enacted by the Senate and House of Representatives . . ." A successful motion to strike it from legislation kills the measure.

Engrossed bill — The final copy of a bill as passed by one chamber, with the text as amended by floor action and certified by the clerk of the House or the secretary of the Senate.

Enrolled bill — The final copy of a bill that has been passed in identical form by both chambers. It is certified by an officer of the chamber of origin (clerk of the House or secretary of the Senate) and then sent on for the signatures of the House Speaker, the Senate president pro tempore and the president of the United States. An enrolled bill is printed on parchment.

Entitlement program — A federal program that guarantees a certain level of benefits to people or other entities who meet requirements set by law. Examples include Social Security and unemployment benefits. Some entitlements have permanent appropriations; others are funded under annual appropriations bills. In either case, it is mandatory for Congress to provide the money.

Executive Calendar — A non-legislative calendar in the Senate that lists presidential documents such as treaties and nominations. (*Also see calendar.*)

Executive document — A document, usually a treaty, sent to the Senate by the president for consideration or approval. Execu-

tive documents are referred to committee in the same manner as other measures. Unlike legislative documents, treaties do not die at the end of a Congress but remain "live" proposals until acted on by the Senate or withdrawn by the president.

Executive session — A meeting of a Senate or House committee (or occasionally of either chamber) that only its members may attend. Witnesses regularly appear at committee meetings in executive session — for example, Defense Department officials during presentations of classified defense information. Other members of Congress may be invited, but the public and news media are not allowed to attend.

Filibuster — A time-delaying tactic associated with the Senate and used by a minority in an effort to prevent a vote on a bill or amendment that probably would pass if voted upon directly. The most common method is to take advantage of the Senate's rules permitting unlimited debate, but other forms of parliamentary maneuvering may be used.

The stricter rules of the House make filibusters more difficult, but delaying tactics are employed occasionally through various procedural devices allowed by House rules. (*Also see cloture.*)

Fiscal year — Financial operations of the government are carried out in a 12-month fiscal year, beginning on Oct. 1 and ending on Sept. 30. The fiscal year carries the date of the calendar year in which it ends. (From fiscal 1844 to fiscal 1976, the fiscal year began July 1 and ended the following June 30.)

Five-minute rule — A debate-limiting rule of the House that is invoked when the House sits as the Committee of the Whole. Under the rule, a member offering an amendment and a member opposing it are each allowed to speak for five minutes. Debate is then closed. In practice, amendments regularly are debated for more than 10 minutes, with members gaining the floor by offering pro forma amendments or obtaining unanimous consent to speak longer than five minutes. (*Also see Committee of the Whole, hour rule, strike out the last word.*)

Floor manager — A member who has the task of steering legislation through floor debate and amendment to a final vote in the House or the Senate. Floor managers usually are chairmen or ranking members of the committee that reported the bill. Managers are responsible for apportioning the debate time granted to supporters of the bill. The ranking minority member of the committee normally apportions time for the minority party's participation in the debate.

Frank — A member's facsimile signature, which is used on envelopes in lieu of stamps for the member's official outgoing mail. The "franking privilege" is the right to send mail postage-free.

Germane — Pertaining to the subject matter of the measure at hand. All House amendments must be germane to the bill being considered. The Senate requires that amendments be germane when they are proposed to general appropriations bills or to bills being considered once cloture has been adopted or, frequently, when the Senate is proceeding under a unanimous consent agreement placing a time limit on consideration of a bill. The 1974 budget act also requires that amendments to concurrent budget resolutions be germane.

In the House, floor debate must be germane, and the first three hours of debate each day in the Senate must be germane to the pending business.

Gramm-Rudman-Hollings Deficit Reduction Act — (*See sequester.*)

Grandfather clause — A provision that exempts people or other entities already engaged in an activity from rules or legislation affecting that activity.

Hearings — Committee sessions for taking testimony from witnesses. At hearings on legislation, witnesses usually include specialists, government officials and spokesmen for individuals or entities affected by the bill or bills under study. Hearings related to special investigations bring forth a variety of witnesses. Committees sometimes use their subpoena power to summon reluctant witnesses. The public and news media may attend open hearings but are barred from closed, or "executive," hearings. The vast majority of hearings are open to the public. (*Also see executive session.*)

Hold-harmless clause — A provision added to legislation to ensure that recipients of federal funds do not receive less in a future year than they did in the current year if a new formula for allocating funds authorized in the legislation would result in a reduction to the recipients. This clause has been used most often to soften the impact of sudden reductions in federal grants.

Hopper — Box on House clerk's desk into which members deposit bills and resolutions to introduce them.

Hour rule — A provision in the rules of the House that permits one hour of debate time for each member on amendments debated in the House of Representatives sitting as the House. Therefore, the House normally amends bills while sitting as the Committee of the Whole, where the five-minute rule on amendments operates.

House as in the Committee of the Whole — A procedure that can be used to expedite consideration of certain measures such as continuing resolutions and, when there is debate, private bills. The procedure can be invoked only with the unanimous consent of the House or a rule from the Rules Committee and has procedural elements of both the House sitting as the House of Representatives, such as the Speaker presiding and the previous question motion being in order, and the House sitting as the Committee of the Whole, with the five-minute rule being in order. (*See Committee of the Whole.*)

House Calendar — A listing for action by the House of public bills that do not directly or indirectly appropriate money or raise revenue. (*Also see calendar.*)

Immunity — The constitutional privilege of members of Congress to make verbal statements on the floor and in committee for which they cannot be sued or arrested for slander or libel. Also, freedom from arrest while traveling to or from sessions of Congress or on official business. Members in this status may only be arrested for treason, felonies or a breach of the peace, as defined by congressional manuals.

Joint committee — A committee composed of a specified number of members of both the House and Senate. A joint committee may be investigative or research-oriented, an example of the latter being the Joint Economic Committee. Others have housekeeping duties; examples include the joint committees on Printing and on the Library of Congress.

Joint resolution — Like a bill, a joint resolution, designated H J Res or S J Res, requires the approval of both chambers and the

signature of the president, and has the force of law if approved. There is no practical difference between a bill and a joint resolution. A joint resolution generally is used to deal with a limited matter such as a single appropriation.

Joint resolutions are also used to propose amendments to the Constitution. In that case they require a two-thirds majority in both chambers. They do not require a presidential signature, but they must be ratified by three-fourths of the states to become a part of the Constitution. (*Also see concurrent resolution, resolution.*)

Journal — The official record of the proceedings of the House and Senate. The Journal records the actions taken in each chamber, but, unlike the Congressional Record, it does not include the substantially verbatim report of speeches, debates, statements and the like.

Law — An act of Congress that has been signed by the president or passed, over his veto, by Congress. Public bills, when signed, become public laws and are cited by the letters PL and a hyphenated number. The number before the hyphen corresponds to the Congress, and the one or more digits after the hyphen refer to the numerical sequence in which the president signed the bills during that Congress. Private bills, when signed, become private laws. (*Also see bills, private bills.*)

Legislative day — The "day" extending from the time either chamber meets after an adjournment until the time it next adjourns. Because the House normally adjourns from day to day, legislative days and calendar days usually coincide. But in the Senate, a legislative day may, and frequently does, extend over several calendar days. (*Also see recess.*)

Line-item veto — Presidential authority to strike individual items from appropriations bills, which presidents since Ulysses S. Grant have sought. Congress gave the president a form of the power in 1996 (PL 104-130), but this "enhanced rescission authority" was struck down by the Supreme Court in 1998 as unconstitutional because it allowed the president to change laws on his own.

Loan guarantees — Loans to third parties for which the federal government guarantees the repayment of principal or interest, in whole or in part, to the lender in the event of default.

Lobby — A group seeking to influence the passage or defeat of legislation. Originally the term referred to people frequenting the lobbies or corridors of legislative chambers to speak to lawmakers.

The definition of a lobby and the activity of lobbying is a matter of differing interpretation. By some definitions, lobbying is limited to direct attempts to influence lawmakers through personal interviews and persuasion. Under other definitions, lobbying includes attempts at indirect, or "grass-roots," influence, such as persuading members of a group to write or visit their district's representative and state's senators or attempting to create a climate of opinion favorable to a desired legislative goal.

The right to attempt to influence legislation is based on the First Amendment to the Constitution, which says Congress shall make no law abridging the right of the people "to petition the government for a redress of grievances."

Majority leader — Floor leader for the majority party in each chamber. In the Senate, in consultation with the minority leader, the majority leader directs the legislative schedule for the chamber. He or she is also his party's spokesperson and chief strategist. In the House, the majority leader is second to the Speaker in the majority party's leadership and serves as the party's legislative strategist. (*Also see Speaker, whip.*)

Manual — The official handbook in each chamber prescribing in detail its organization, procedures and operations.

Marking up a bill — Going through the contents of a piece of legislation in committee or subcommittee to, for example, consider the provisions, act on amendments to provisions and proposed revisions to the language, and insert new sections and phraseology. If the bill is extensively amended, the committee's version may be introduced as a separate (or "clean") bill, with a new number, before being considered by the full House or Senate. (*Also see clean bill.*)

Minority leader — Floor leader for the minority party in each chamber.

Morning hour — The time set aside at the beginning of each legislative day for the consideration of regular, routine business. The "hour" is of indefinite duration in the House, where it is rarely used. In the Senate, it is the first two hours of a session following an adjournment, as distinguished from a recess. The morning hour can be terminated earlier if the morning business has been completed.

Business includes such matters as messages from the president, communications from the heads of departments, messages from the House, the presentation of petitions, reports of standing and select committees and the introduction of bills and resolutions.

During the first hour of the morning hour in the Senate, no motion to proceed to the consideration of any bill on the calendar is in order except by unanimous consent. During the second hour, motions can be made but must be decided without debate. Senate committees may meet while the Senate conducts the morning hour.

Motion — In the House or Senate chamber, a request by a member to institute any one of a wide array of parliamentary actions. He or she "moves" for a certain procedure, such as the consideration of a measure. The precedence of motions, and whether they are debatable, is set forth in the House and Senate manuals.

Nominations — Presidential appointments to office subject to Senate confirmation. Although most nominations win quick Senate approval, some are controversial and become the topic of hearings and debate. Sometimes senators object to appointees for patronage reasons — for example, when a nomination to a local federal job is made without consulting the senators of the state concerned. In some situations a senator may object that the nominee is "personally obnoxious" to him. Usually other senators join in blocking such appointments out of courtesy to their colleagues. (*Also see senatorial courtesy.*)

One-minute speeches — Addresses by House members at the beginning of a legislative day. The speeches may cover any subject but are limited to one minute's duration.

Outlays — Actual spending that flows from the liquidation of budget authority. Outlays associated with appropriations bills and other legislation are estimates of future spending made by the Congressional Budget Office (CBO) and the White House's Office of Management and Budget (OMB). CBO's estimates govern bills for the purpose of congressional floor debate, while OMB's numbers govern when it comes to determining whether legislation exceeds spending caps.

Outlays in a given fiscal year may result from budget authority provided in the current year or in previous years. (*Also see budget authority, budget process.*)

Override a veto — If the president vetoes a bill and sends it

back to Congress with his objections, Congress may try to override his veto and enact the bill into law. Neither chamber is required to attempt to override a veto. The override of a veto requires a recorded vote with a two-thirds majority of those present and voting in each chamber. The question put to each chamber is: "Shall the bill pass, the objections of the president to the contrary notwithstanding?" (*Also see pocket veto, veto.*)

Oversight committee — A congressional committee or designated subcommittee that is charged with general oversight of one or more federal agencies' programs and activities. Usually, the oversight panel for a particular agency is also the authorizing committee for that agency's programs and operations.

Pair — A voluntary, informal arrangement that two lawmakers, usually on opposite sides of an issue, make on recorded votes. In many cases the result is to subtract a vote from each side, with no effect on the outcome.

Pairs are not authorized in the rules of either chamber, are not counted in tabulating the final result and have no official standing. However, members pairing are identified in the Congressional Record, along with their positions on such votes, if known. A member who expects to be absent for a vote can pair with a member who plans to vote, with the latter agreeing to withhold his or her vote.

There are three types of pairs:

(1) A live pair involves a member who is present for a vote and another who is absent. The member in attendance votes and then withdraws the vote, announcing that he or she has a live pair with colleague "X" and stating how the two members would have voted, one in favor, the other opposed. A live pair may affect the outcome of a closely contested vote, since it subtracts one "yea" or one "nay" from the final tally. A live pair may cover one or several specific issues.

(2) A general pair, widely used in the House, does not entail any arrangement between two members and does not affect the vote. Members who expect to be absent notify the clerk that they wish to make a general pair. Each member then is paired with another desiring a pair, and their names are listed in the Congressional Record. The member may or may not be paired with another taking the opposite position, and no indication of how the members would have voted is given.

(3) A specific pair is similar to a general pair, except that the opposing stands of the two members are identified and printed in the Congressional Record.

Pay-as-you go (PAYGO) rules — (*See budget process.*)

Petition — A request or plea sent to one or both chambers from an organization or private citizens' group seeking support for particular legislation or favorable consideration of a matter not yet receiving congressional attention. Petitions are referred to appropriate committees. In the House, a petition signed by a majority of members (218) can discharge a bill from a committee. (*Also see discharge a committee.*)

Pocket veto — The act of the president in withholding his approval of a bill after Congress has adjourned. When Congress is in session, a bill becomes law without the president's signature if he does not act upon it within 10 days, excluding Sundays, from the time he receives it. But if Congress adjourns sine die within that 10-day period, the bill will die even if the president does not formally veto it.

The Supreme Court in 1986 agreed to decide whether the president could pocket veto a bill during recesses and between sessions of the same Congress or only between Congresses. The justices in 1987 declared the case moot, however, because the bill in question was invalid once the case reached the court. (*Also see adjournment sine die, veto.*)

Point of order — An objection raised by a member that the chamber is departing from rules governing its conduct of business. The objector cites the rule violated, with the chair sustaining his or her objection if correctly made. Order is restored by the chair's suspending proceedings of the chamber until it conforms to the prescribed "order of business."

Both chambers have procedures for overcoming a point of order, either by vote or, what is most common in the House, by including language in the rule for floor consideration that waives a point of order against a given bill. (*Also see rules.*)

President of the Senate — Under the Constitution, the vice president of the United States presides over the Senate. In his absence, the president pro tempore, or a senator designated by the president pro tempore, presides over the chamber.

President pro tempore — The chief officer of the Senate in the absence of the vice president — literally, but loosely, the president for a time. The president pro tempore is elected by his fellow senators. Recent practice has been to elect the senator of the majority party with the longest period of continuous service.

Previous question — A motion for the previous question, when carried, has the effect of cutting off all debate, preventing the offering of further amendments and forcing a vote on the pending matter. In the House, a motion for the previous question is not permitted in the Committee of the Whole, unless a rule governing debate provides otherwise. The motion for the previous question is a debate-limiting device and is not in order in the Senate.

Printed amendment — A House rule guarantees five minutes of floor debate in support and five minutes in opposition, and no other debate time, on amendments printed in the Congressional Record at least one day prior to the amendment's consideration in the Committee of the Whole.

In the Senate, while amendments may be submitted for printing, they have no parliamentary standing or status. An amendment submitted for printing in the Senate, however, may be called up by any senator.

Private bill — A bill dealing with individual matters such as claims against the government, immigration or land titles. When a private bill is before the chamber, two members may block its consideration, thereby recommitting the bill to committee. The backers still have recourse, however. The measure can be put into an "omnibus claims bill" — several private bills rolled into one. As with any bill, no part of an omnibus claims bill may be deleted without a vote. When the private bill goes back to the House floor in this form, it can be deleted from the omnibus bill only by majority vote.

Private Calendar — The House calendar for private bills. The Private Calendar must be called on the first Tuesday of each month, and the Speaker may call it on the third Tuesday of each month as well. (*Also see calendar, private bill.*)

Privileged questions — The order in which bills, motions and other legislative measures are considered on the floor of the Senate and House is governed by strict priorities. A motion to table, for instance, is more privileged than a motion to recommit. Thus, if a member moves to recommit a bill to committee for further consideration, another member can supersede the first action by moving

to table it, and a vote will occur on the motion to table (or kill) before the motion to recommit. A motion to adjourn is considered "of the highest privilege" and must be considered before virtually any other motion.

Pro forma amendment — *(See strike out the last word.)*

Public Laws — *(See law.)*

Questions of privilege — These are matters affecting members of Congress individually or collectively. Matters affecting the rights, safety, dignity and integrity of proceedings of the House or Senate as a whole are questions of privilege in both chambers.

Questions involving individual members are called questions of "personal privilege." A member rising to ask a question of personal privilege is given precedence over almost all other proceedings. For instance, if a member feels that he or she has been improperly impugned in comments by another member, he or she can immediately demand to be heard on the floor on a question of personal privilege. An annotation in the House rules points out that the privilege rests primarily on the Constitution, which gives members a conditional immunity from arrest and an unconditional freedom to speak in the House.

In 1993, the House changed its rules to allow the Speaker to delay for two legislative days the floor consideration of a question of the privileges of the House unless it is offered by the majority leader or minority leader.

Quorum — The number of members whose presence is necessary for the transaction of business. In the Senate and House, it is a majority of the membership. In the Committee of the Whole House, a quorum is 100. If a point of order is made that a quorum is not present, the only business that is in order is either a motion to adjourn or a motion to direct the sergeant-at-arms to request the attendance of absentees. In practice, however, both chambers conduct much of their business without a quorum present. *(Also see Committee of the Whole House.)*

Reading of bills — Traditional parliamentary procedure required bills to be read three times before they were passed. This custom is of little modern significance. Normally a bill is considered to have its first reading when it is introduced and printed, by title, in the Congressional Record. In the House, a bill's second reading comes when floor consideration begins. (The actual reading of a bill is most likely to occur at this point, if at all.) The second reading in the Senate is supposed to occur on the legislative day after the measure is introduced, but before it is referred to committee. The third reading (again, usually by title) takes place when floor action has been completed on amendments.

Recess — A recess, as distinguished from adjournment, does not end a legislative day and therefore does not interrupt unfinished business. (The rules in each chamber set forth certain matters to be taken up and disposed of at the beginning of each legislative day.) The House usually adjourns from day to day. The Senate often recesses, thus meeting on the same legislative day for several calendar days or even weeks at a time.

Recognition — The power of recognition of a member is lodged in the Speaker of the House and the presiding officer of the Senate. The presiding officer names the member to speak first when two or more members simultaneously request recognition. The order of recognition is governed by precedents and tradition for many situations. In the Senate, for instance, the majority leader has the right to be recognized first.

Recommit to committee — A motion, made on the floor after a bill has been debated, to return it to the committee that reported it. If approved, recommittal usually is considered a death blow to the bill. In the House, the right to offer a motion to recommit is guaranteed to the minority leader or someone he or she designates.

A motion to recommit may include instructions to the committee to report the bill again with specific amendments or by a certain date. Or the instructions may direct that a particular study be made, with no definite deadline for further action.

If the recommittal motion includes instructions to "report the bill back forthwith" and the motion is adopted, floor action on the bill continues with the changes directed by the instructions automatically incorporated into the bill; the committee does not actually reconsider the legislation.

Reconciliation — The 1974 budget act created a "reconciliation" procedure for bringing existing tax and spending laws into conformity with ceilings set in the congressional budget resolution. Under the procedure, the budget resolution sets specific deficit-reduction targets and instructs tax-writing and authorizing committees to propose changes in existing law to meet those targets. Those recommendations are consolidated without change by the Budget committees into an omnibus reconciliation bill, which then must be considered and approved by both chambers of Congress.

Special rules in the Senate limit debate on a reconciliation bill to 20 hours and bar extraneous or non-germane amendments. *(Also see budget resolution, sequester.)*

Reconsider a vote — Until it is disposed of, a motion to reconsider the vote by which an action was taken has the effect of putting the action in abeyance. In the Senate, the motion can be made only by a member who voted on the prevailing side of the original question or by a member who did not vote at all. In the House, it can be made only by a member on the prevailing side.

A common practice in the Senate after close votes on an issue is a motion to reconsider, followed by a motion to table the motion to reconsider. On this motion to table, senators vote as they voted on the original question, which allows the motion to table to prevail, assuming there are no switches. That closes the matter, and further motions to reconsider are not entertained.

In the House, as a routine precaution, a motion to reconsider usually is made every time a measure is passed. Such a motion almost always is tabled immediately, thus shutting off the possibility of future reconsideration except by unanimous consent.

Motions to reconsider must be entered in the Senate within the next two days the Senate is in session after the original vote has been taken. In the House, they must be entered either on the same day or on the next succeeding day the House is in session. Sometimes on a close vote, a member will switch his or her vote to be eligible to offer a motion to reconsider.

Recorded vote — A vote upon which each member's stand is individually made known. In the Senate, this is accomplished through a roll call of the entire membership, to which each senator on the floor must answer "yea," "nay" or "present." Since January 1973, the House has used an electronic voting system for recorded votes, including yea-and-nay votes formerly taken by roll calls.

When not required by the Constitution, a recorded vote can be obtained on questions in the House on the demand of one-fifth (44 members) of a quorum or one-fourth (25) of a quorum in the Committee of the Whole. Recorded votes are required in the House for appropriations, budget and tax bills. *(Also see yeas and nays.)*

Report — Both a verb and a noun as a congressional term. A

committee that has been examining a bill referred to it by the parent chamber "reports" its findings and recommendations to the chamber when it completes consideration and returns the measure. The process is called "reporting" a bill. In some cases, a bill is reported without a written report.

A "report" is the document setting forth the committee's explanation of its action. Senate and House reports are numbered separately and are designated S Rept or H Rept. When a committee report is not unanimous, the dissenting committee members may file a statement of their views, called minority or dissenting views and referred to as a minority report. Members in disagreement with some provisions of a bill may file additional or supplementary views. Sometimes a bill is reported without a committee recommendation.

Legislative committees occasionally submit adverse reports. However, when a committee is opposed to a bill, it usually fails to report the bill at all. Some laws require that committee reports — favorable or adverse — be made.

Rescission — Cancellation of budget authority that was previously appropriated but has not yet been spent.

Resolution — A "simple" resolution, designated H Res or S Res, deals with matters entirely within the prerogatives of a single chamber. It requires neither passage by the other chamber nor approval by the president, and it does not have the force of law. Most resolutions deal with the rules or procedures of one chamber. They are also used to express the sentiments of a single chamber, such as condolences to the family of a deceased member, or to comment on foreign policy or executive business. A simple resolution is the vehicle for a "rule" from the House Rules Committee. (*Also see concurrent and joint resolutions, rules.*)

Rider — An amendment, usually not germane, that its sponsor hopes to get through more easily by including it in other legislation. A rider becomes law if the bill to which it is attached is enacted. Amendments providing legislative directives in appropriations bills are examples of riders, though technically legislation is banned from appropriations bills.

The House, unlike the Senate, has a strict germaneness rule; thus, riders usually are Senate devices to get legislation enacted quickly or to bypass lengthy House consideration and, possibly, opposition.

Rules — Each chamber has a body of rules and precedents that govern the conduct of business. These rules deal with issues such as duties of officers, the order of business, admission to the floor, parliamentary procedures on handling amendments and voting, and jurisdictions of committees. They are normally changed only at the start of each Congress.

In the House, a rule may also be a resolution reported by the Rules Committee to govern the handling of a particular bill on the floor. The committee may report a rule, also called a special order, in the form of a simple resolution. If the House adopts the resolution, the temporary rule becomes as valid as any standing rule and lapses only after action has been completed on the measure to which it pertains.

The rule sets the time limit on general debate. It may also waive points of order against provisions of the bill in question such as nongermane language or against certain amendments expected on the floor. It may even forbid all amendments or all amendments except those proposed by the legislative committee that handled the bill. In this instance, it is known as a "closed" rule as opposed to an "open" rule, which puts no limitation on floor amendments, thus leaving the bill completely open to alteration by the adoption of germane amendments. (*Also see point of order.*)

Secretary of the Senate — Chief administrative officer of the Senate, responsible for overseeing the duties of Senate employees, educating Senate pages, administering oaths, overseeing the registration of lobbyists and handling other tasks necessary for the continuing operation of the Senate. (*Also see Clerk of the House.*)

Select or special committee — A committee set up for a special purpose and, usually, for a limited time by resolution of either the House or Senate. Most special committees are investigative and lack legislative authority: Legislation is not referred to them, and they cannot report bills to their parent chambers.

Senatorial courtesy — A general practice with no written rule — sometimes referred to as "the courtesy of the Senate" — applied to consideration of executive nominations. Generally, it means that nominations from a state are not to be confirmed unless they have been approved by the senators of the president's party of that state, with other senators following their colleagues' lead in the attitude they take toward consideration of such nominations. (*Also see nominations.*)

Sequester — Automatic, across-the-board spending cuts, generally triggered after the close of a session by a report issued by the Office of Management and Budget. Under the 1985 Gramm-Rudman anti-deficit law, modified in 1987, a year-end sequester was triggered if the deficit exceeded a pre-set maximum. However, the Budget Enforcement Act of 1990, updated in 1993 and 1997, effectively replaced that procedure through fiscal 2002.

Instead, if Congress exceeded an annual cap on discretionary budget authority or outlays, a sequester was triggered for all eligible discretionary spending to make up the difference. If Congress violated pay-as-you-go rules by allowing the net effect of legislated changes in mandatory spending and taxes to increase the deficit, a sequester was triggered for all non-exempt entitlement programs. Similar procedures applied to supplemental appropriations bills. (*Also see budget process.*)

Sine die — (*See adjournment sine die.*)

Speaker — The presiding officer of the House of Representatives, selected by his party caucus and formally elected by the whole House. While both parties nominate candidates, choice by the majority party is tantamount to election. In 1995, House rules were changed to limit the Speaker to four consecutive terms.

Special session — A session of Congress after it has adjourned sine die, completing its regular session. Special sessions are convened by the president.

Spending authority — The 1974 budget act defines spending authority as borrowing authority, contract authority and entitlement authority for which budget authority is not provided in advance by appropriation acts.

Sponsor — (*See bills introduced.*)

Standing committees — Committees that are permanently established by House and Senate rules. The standing committees of the House were reorganized in 1974, with some changes in jurisdictions and titles made when Republicans took control of the House in 1995. The last major realignment of Senate committees was in 1977. The standing committees are legislative committees: Legislation may be referred to them, and they may report bills and resolutions to their parent chambers.

Standing vote — A non-recorded vote used in both the House and Senate. (A standing vote is also called a division vote.) Members in favor of a proposal stand and are counted by the presiding officer. Then members opposed stand and are counted. There is no record of how individual members voted.

Statutes at large — A chronological arrangement of the laws enacted in each session of Congress. Though indexed, the laws are not arranged by subject matter, and there is no indication of how they changed previously enacted laws. (*Also see law, U.S. Code.*)

Strike from the Record — A member of the House who is offended by remarks made on the House floor may move that the offending words be "taken down" for the Speaker's cognizance and then expunged from the debate as published in the Congressional Record.

Strike out the last word — A motion whereby a House member is entitled to speak for five minutes on an amendment then being debated by the chamber. A member gains recognition from the chair by moving to "strike out the last word" of the amendment or section of the bill under consideration. The motion is pro forma, requires no vote and does not change the amendment being debated. (*Also see five-minute rule.*)

Substitute — A motion, amendment or entire bill introduced in place of the pending legislative business. Passage of the substitute kills the original measure by supplanting it. The substitute may also be amended. (*Also see amendment in the nature of a substitute.*)

Supplemental appropriations bill — Legislation appropriating funds after the regular annual appropriations bill for a federal department or agency has been enacted. Supplemental appropriations bills often arrive about halfway through the fiscal year, when needs that Congress and the president did not anticipate (or may not have wanted to fund) become pressing. In recent years, supplementals have been driven by spending to help victims of natural disasters and to carry out peacekeeping commitments.

Suspend the rules — A time-saving procedure for passing bills in the House. The wording of the motion, which may be made by any member recognized by the Speaker, is: "I move to suspend the rules and pass the bill . . ." A favorable vote by two-thirds of those present is required for passage. Debate is limited to 40 minutes, and no amendments from the floor are permitted. If a two-thirds favorable vote is not attained, the bill may be considered later under regular procedures. The suspension procedure is in order every Monday and Tuesday and is intended to be reserved for non-controversial bills.

Table a bill — Motions to table, or to "lay on the table," are used to block or kill amendments or other parliamentary questions. When approved, a tabling motion is considered the final disposition of that issue. One of the most widely used parliamentary procedures, the motion to table is not debatable, and adoption requires a simple majority vote.

In the Senate, however, different language sometimes is used. The motion may be worded to let a bill "lie on the table," perhaps for subsequent "picking up." This motion is more flexible, keeping the bill pending for later action, if desired. Tabling motions on amendments are effective debate-ending devices in the Senate.

Treaties — Executive proposals — in the form of resolutions of ratification — which must be submitted to the Senate for approval by two-thirds of the senators present. Treaties are normally sent to the Foreign Relations Committee for scrutiny before the Senate takes action. Foreign Relations has jurisdiction over all treaties, regardless of the subject matter. Treaties are read three times and debated on the floor in much the same manner as legislative proposals. After approval by the Senate, treaties are formally ratified by the president.

Trust funds — Funds collected and used by the federal government for carrying out specific purposes and programs according to terms of a trust agreement or statute such as the Social Security and unemployment compensation trust funds. Such funds are administered by the government in a fiduciary capacity and are not available for the general purposes of the government.

Unanimous consent — A procedure used to expedite floor action. Proceedings of the House or Senate and action on legislation often take place upon the unanimous consent of the chamber, whether or not a rule of the chamber is being violated. It is frequently used in a routine fashion, such as by a senator requesting the unanimous consent of the Senate to have specified members of his or her staff present on the floor during debate on a specific amendment. A single member's objection blocks a unanimous consent request.

Unanimous consent agreement — A device used in the Senate to expedite legislation. Much of the Senate's legislative business, dealing with both minor and controversial issues, is conducted through unanimous consent or unanimous consent agreements. On major legislation, such agreements usually are printed and transmitted to all senators in advance of floor debate. Once agreed to, they are binding on all members unless the Senate, by unanimous consent, agrees to modify them. An agreement may list the order in which various bills are to be considered; specify the length of time for debate on bills and contested amendments and when they are to be voted upon; and, frequently, require that all amendments introduced be germane to the bill under consideration.

In this regard, unanimous consent agreements are similar to the "rules" issued by the House Rules Committee for bills pending in the House.

Union Calendar — Bills that directly or indirectly appropriate money or raise revenue are placed on this House calendar according to the date they are reported from committee. (*Also see calendar.*)

U.S. Code — A consolidation and codification of the general and permanent laws of the United States arranged by subject under 50 titles, the first six dealing with general or political subjects, and the other 44 alphabetically arranged from agriculture to war. The U.S. Code is updated annually, and a new set of bound volumes is published every six years. (*Also see law, statutes at large.*)

Veto — Disapproval by the president of a bill or joint resolution (other than one proposing an amendment to the Constitution). When Congress is in session, the president must veto a bill within 10 days, excluding Sundays, after he has received it; otherwise, it becomes law without his signature. When the president vetoes a bill, he returns it to the chamber of origin along with a message stating his objections. (*Also see pocket veto, override a veto.*)

Voice vote — In either the House or Senate, members answer "aye" or "no" in chorus, and the presiding officer decides the result. The term is also used loosely to indicate action by unanimous consent or without objection. (*Also see yeas and nays.*)

Whip — In effect, the assistant majority or minority leader, in either the House or Senate. His or her job is to help marshal votes in support of party strategy and legislation.

Without objection — Used in lieu of a vote on non-controversial motions, amendments or bills that may be passed in either chamber if no member voices an objection.

Yeas and nays — The Constitution requires that yea-and-nay votes be taken and recorded when requested by one-fifth of the members present. In the House, the Speaker determines whether one-fifth of the members present requested a vote. In the Senate, practice requires only 11 members. The Constitution requires the yeas and nays on a veto override attempt. (*Also see recorded vote.*)

Yielding — When a member has been recognized to speak, no other member may speak unless he or she obtains permission from the member recognized. This permission is called yielding and usually is requested in the form, "Will the gentleman (or gentlelady) yield to me?" While this activity occasionally is seen in the Senate, the Senate has no rule or practice to parcel out time.

In the House, the floor manager of a bill usually apportions debate time by yielding specific amounts of time to members who have requested it. ◆

Members of the 107th Congress, 2nd Session . . .

(As of Nov. 22, 2002, when the House adjourned sine die.)

Representatives
R 223; D 208; I 1
3 vacancies

— A —

Abercrombie, Neil, D-Hawaii (1)
Ackerman, Gary L., D-N.Y. (5)
Aderholt, Robert B., R-Ala. (4)
Akin, Todd, R-Mo. (2)
Allen, Tom, D-Maine (1)
Andrews, Robert E., D-N.J. (1)
Armey, Dick, R-Texas (26)

— B —

Baca, Joe, D-Calif. (42)
Bachus, Spencer, R-Ala. (6)
Baird, Brian, D-Wash. (3)
Baker, Richard H., R-La. (6)
Baldacci, John, D-Maine (2)
Baldwin, Tammy, D-Wis. (2)
Barcia, James A., D-Mich. (5)
Barr, Bob, R-Ga. (7)
Barrett, Thomas M., D-Wis. (5)
Bartlett, Roscoe G., R-Md. (6)
Barton, Joe L., R-Texas (6)
Bass, Charles, R-N.H. (2)
Becerra, Xavier, D-Calif. (30)
Bentsen, Ken, D-Texas (25)
Bereuter, Doug, R-Neb. (1)
Berkley, Shelley, D-Nev. (1)
Berman, Howard L., D-Calif. (26)
Berry, Marion, D-Ark. (1)
Biggert, Judy, R-Ill. (13)
Bilirakis, Michael, R-Fla. (9)
Bishop, Sanford D. Jr., D-Ga. (2)
Blagojevich, Rod R., D-Ill. (5)
Blumenauer, Earl, D-Ore. (3)
Blunt, Roy, R-Mo. (7)
Boehlert, Sherwood, R-N.Y. (23)
Boehner, John A., R-Ohio (8)
Bonilla, Henry, R-Texas (23)
Bonior, David E., D-Mich. (10)
Bono, Mary, R-Calif. (44)
Boozman, John, R-Ark. (3)
Borski, Robert A., D-Pa. (3)
Boswell, Leonard L., D-Iowa (3)
Boucher, Rick, D-Va. (9)
Boyd, Allen, D-Fla. (2)
Brady, Kevin, R-Texas (8)
Brady, Robert A., D-Pa. (1)
Brown, Corrine, D-Fla. (3)
Brown, Henry E. Jr., R-S.C. (1)
Brown, Sherrod, D-Ohio (13)
Bryant, Ed, R-Tenn. (7)
Burr, Richard M., R-N.C. (5)
Burton, Dan, R-Ind. (6)
Buyer, Steve, R-Ind. (5)

— C —

Callahan, Sonny, R-Ala. (1)
Calvert, Ken, R-Calif. (43)
Camp, Dave, R-Mich. (4)
Cannon, Christopher B., R-Utah (3)
Cantor, Eric, R-Va. (7)
Capito, Shelley Moore, R-W.Va. (2)
Capps, Lois, D-Calif. (22)
Capuano, Michael E., D-Mass. (8)
Cardin, Benjamin L., D-Md. (3)
Carson, Brad, D-Okla. (2)
Carson, Julia, D-Ind. (10)
Castle, Michael N., R-Del. (AL)
Chabot, Steve, R-Ohio (1)
Chambliss, Saxby, R-Ga. (8)
Clay, William Lacy, D-Mo. (1)
Clayton, Eva, D-N.C. (1)
Clement, Bob, D-Tenn. (5)
Clyburn, James E., D-S.C. (6)
Coble, Howard, R-N.C. (6)
Collins, Mac, R-Ga. (3)
Combest, Larry, R-Texas (19)
Condit, Gary A., D-Calif. (18)
Conyers, John Jr., D-Mich. (14)

Cooksey, John, R-La. (5)
Costello, Jerry F., D-Ill. (12)
Cox, Christopher, R-Calif. (47)
Coyne, William J., D-Pa. (14)
Cramer, Robert E. "Bud," D-Ala. (5)
Crane, Philip M., R-Ill. (8)
Crenshaw, Ander, R-Fla. (4)
Crowley, Joseph, D-N.Y. (7)
Cubin, Barbara, R-Wyo. (AL)
Culberson, John, R-Texas (7)
Cummings, Elijah E., D-Md. (7)
Cunningham, Randy "Duke," R-Calif. (51)

— D —

Davis, Danny K., D-Ill. (7)
Davis, Jim, D-Fla. (11)
Davis, Jo Ann, R-Va. (1)
Davis, Susan A., D-Calif. (49)
Davis, Thomas M. III, R-Va. (11)
Deal, Nathan, R-Ga. (9)
DeFazio, Peter A., D-Ore. (4)
DeGette, Diana, D-Colo. (1)
Delahunt, Bill, D-Mass. (10)
DeLauro, Rosa, D-Conn. (3)
DeLay, Tom, R-Texas (22)
DeMint, Jim, R-S.C. (4)
Deutsch, Peter, D-Fla. (20)
Diaz-Balart, Lincoln, R-Fla. (21)
Dicks, Norm, D-Wash. (6)
Dingell, John D., D-Mich. (16)
Doggett, Lloyd, D-Texas (10)
Dooley, Cal, D-Calif. (20)
Doolittle, John T., R-Calif. (4)
Doyle, Mike, D-Pa. (18)
Dreier, David, R-Calif. (28)
Duncan, John J. "Jimmy" Jr., R-Tenn. (2)
Dunn, Jennifer, R-Wash. (8)

— E —

Edwards, Chet, D-Texas (11)
Ehlers, Vernon J., R-Mich. (3)
Ehrlich, Robert L. Jr., R-Md. (2)
Emerson, Jo Ann, R-Mo. (8)
Engel, Eliot L., D-N.Y. (17)
English, Phil, R-Pa. (21)
Eshoo, Anna G., D-Calif. (14)
Etheridge, Bob, D-N.C. (2)
Evans, Lane, D-Ill. (17)
Everett, Terry, R-Ala. (2)

— F —

Farr, Sam, D-Calif. (17)
Fattah, Chaka, D-Pa. (2)
Ferguson, Mike, R-N.J. (7)
Filner, Bob, D-Calif. (50)
Flake, Jeff, R-Ariz. (1)
Fletcher, Ernie, R-Ky. (6)
Foley, Mark, R-Fla. (16)
Forbes, J. Randy, R-Va. (4)
Ford, Harold E. Jr., D-Tenn. (9)
Fossella, Vito J., R-N.Y. (13)
Frank, Barney, D-Mass. (4)
Frelinghuysen, Rodney, R-N.J. (11)
Frost, Martin, D-Texas (24)

— G —

Gallegly, Elton, R-Calif. (23)
Ganske, Greg, R-Iowa (4)
Gekas, George W., R-Pa. (17)
Gephardt, Richard A., D-Mo. (3)
Gibbons, Jim, R-Nev. (2)
Gilchrest, Wayne T., R-Md. (1)
Gillmor, Paul E., R-Ohio (5)
Gilman, Benjamin A., R-N.Y. (20)
Gonzalez, Charlie, D-Texas (20)
Goode, Virgil H. Jr., R-Va. (5)
Goodlatte, Robert W., R-Va. (6)
Gordon, Bart, D-Tenn. (6)
Goss, Porter J., R-Fla. (14)
Graham, Lindsey, R-S.C. (3)
Granger, Kay, R-Texas (12)
Graves, Sam, R-Mo. (6)
Green, Gene, D-Texas (29)
Green, Mark, R-Wis. (8)
Greenwood, James C., R-Pa. (8)
Grucci, Felix J. Jr., R-N.Y. (1)
Gutierrez, Luis V., D-Ill. (4)
Gutknecht, Gil, R-Minn. (1)

— H —

Hall, Ralph M., D-Texas (4)
Hansen, James V., R-Utah (1)
Harman, Jane, D-Calif. (36)
Hart, Melissa A., R-Pa. (4)
Hastert, J. Dennis, R-Ill. (14)
Hastings, Alcee L., D-Fla. (23)
Hastings, Doc, R-Wash. (4)
Hayes, Robin, R-N.C. (8)
Hayworth, J.D., R-Ariz. (6)
Hefley, Joel, R-Colo. (5)
Herger, Wally, R-Calif. (2)
Hill, Baron P., D-Ind. (9)
Hilleary, Van, R-Tenn. (4)
Hilliard, Earl F., D-Ala. (7)
Hinchey, Maurice D., D-N.Y. (26)
Hinojosa, Rubén, D-Texas (15)
Hobson, David L., R-Ohio (7)
Hoeffel, Joseph M., D-Pa. (13)
Hoekstra, Peter, R-Mich. (2)
Holden, Tim, D-Pa. (6)
Holt, Rush D., D-N.J. (12)
Honda, Michael M., D-Calif. (15)
Hooley, Darlene, D-Ore. (5)
Horn, Steve, R-Calif. (38)
Hostettler, John, R-Ind. (8)
Houghton, Amo, R-N.Y. (31)
Hoyer, Steny H., D-Md. (5)
Hulshof, Kenny, R-Mo. (9)
Hunter, Duncan, R-Calif. (52)
Hyde, Henry J., R-Ill. (6)

— I, J —

Inslee, Jay, D-Wash. (1)
Isakson, Johnny, R-Ga. (6)
Israel, Steve, D-N.Y. (2)
Issa, Darrell, R-Calif. (48)
Istook, Ernest, R-Okla. (5)
Jackson, Jesse L. Jr., D-Ill. (2)
Jackson-Lee, Sheila, D-Texas (18)
Jefferson, William J., D-La. (2)
Jenkins, Bill, R-Tenn. (1)
John, Chris, D-La. (7)
Johnson, Eddie Bernice, D-Texas (30)
Johnson, Nancy L., R-Conn. (6)
Johnson, Sam, R-Texas (3)
Johnson, Timothy V., R-Ill. (15)
Jones, Stephanie Tubbs, D-Ohio (11)
Jones, Walter B., R-N.C. (3)

— K —

Kanjorski, Paul E., D-Pa. (11)
Kaptur, Marcy, D-Ohio (9)
Keller, Ric, R-Fla. (8)
Kelly, Sue W., R-N.Y. (19)
Kennedy, Mark, R-Minn. (2)
Kennedy, Patrick J., D-R.I. (1)
Kerns, Brian, R-Ind. (7)
Kildee, Dale E., D-Mich. (9)
Kilpatrick, Carolyn Cheeks, D-Mich. (15)
Kind, Ron, D-Wis. (3)
King, Peter T., R-N.Y. (3)
Kingston, Jack, R-Ga. (1)
Kirk, Mark Steven, R-Ill. (10)
Kleczka, Gerald D., D-Wis. (4)
Knollenberg, Joe, R-Mich. (11)
Kolbe, Jim, R-Ariz. (5)
Kucinich, Dennis J., D-Ohio (10)

— L —

LaFalce, John J., D-N.Y. (29)
LaHood, Ray, R-Ill. (18)
Lampson, Nick, D-Texas (9)
Langevin, Jim, D-R.I. (2)
Lantos, Tom, D-Calif. (12)
Larsen, Rick, D-Wash. (2)
Larson, John B., D-Conn. (1)
Latham, Tom, R-Iowa (5)
LaTourette, Steven C., R-Ohio (19)
Leach, Jim, R-Iowa (1)
Lee, Barbara, D-Calif. (9)
Levin, Sander M., D-Mich. (12)
Lewis, Jerry, R-Calif. (40)
Lewis, John, D-Ga. (5)
Lewis, Ron, R-Ky. (2)
Linder, John, R-Ga. (11)
Lipinski, William O., D-Ill. (3)

LoBiondo, Frank A., R-N.J. (2)
Lofgren, Zoe, D-Calif. (16)
Lowey, Nita M., D-N.Y. (18)
Lucas, Frank D., R-Okla. (6)
Lucas, Ken, D-Ky. (4)
Luther, Bill, D-Minn. (6)
Lynch, Stephen F., D-Mass. (9)

— M —

Maloney, Carolyn B., D-N.Y. (14)
Maloney, Jim, D-Conn. (5)
Manzullo, Donald, R-Ill. (16)
Markey, Edward J., D-Mass. (7)
Mascara, Frank R., D-Pa. (20)
Matheson, Jim, D-Utah (2)
Matsui, Robert T., D-Calif. (5)
McCarthy, Carolyn, D-N.Y. (4)
McCarthy, Karen, D-Mo. (5)
McCollum, Betty, D-Minn. (4)
McCrery, Jim, R-La. (4)
McDermott, Jim, D-Wash. (7)
McGovern, Jim, D-Mass. (3)
McHugh, John M., R-N.Y. (24)
McInnis, Scott, R-Colo. (3)
McIntyre, Mike, D-N.C. (7)
McKeon, Howard P. "Buck," R-Calif. (25)
McKinney, Cynthia A., D-Ga. (4)
McNulty, Michael R., D-N.Y. (21)
Meehan, Martin T., D-Mass. (5)
Meek, Carrie P., D-Fla. (17)
Meeks, Gregory W., D-N.Y. (6)
Menendez, Robert, D-N.J. (13)
Mica, John L., R-Fla. (7)
Millender-McDonald, Juanita, D-Calif. (37)
Miller, Dan, R-Fla. (13)
Miller, Gary G., R-Calif. (41)
Miller, George, D-Calif. (7)
Miller, Jeff, R-Fla. (1)
Mollohan, Alan B., D-W.Va. (1)
Moore, Dennis, D-Kan. (3)
Moran, James P., D-Va. (8)
Moran, Jerry, R-Kan. (1)
Morella, Constance A., R-Md. (8)
Murtha, John P., D-Pa. (12)
Myrick, Sue, R-N.C. (9)

— N —

Nadler, Jerrold, D-N.Y. (8)
Napolitano, Grace F., D-Calif. (34)
Neal, Richard E., D-Mass. (2)
Nethercutt, George, R-Wash. (5)
Ney, Bob, R-Ohio (18)
Northup, Anne M., R-Ky. (3)
Norwood, Charlie, R-Ga. (10)
Nussle, Jim, R-Iowa (2)

— O —

Oberstar, James L., D-Minn. (8)
Obey, David R., D-Wis. (7)
Olver, John W., D-Mass. (1)
Ortiz, Solomon P., D-Texas (27)
Osborne, Tom, R-Neb. (3)
Ose, Doug, R-Calif. (3)
Otter, C. L. "Butch," R-Idaho (1)
Owens, Major R., D-N.Y. (11)
Oxley, Michael G., R-Ohio (4)

— P —

Pallone, Frank Jr., D-N.J. (6)
Pascrell, Bill Jr., D-N.J. (8)
Pastor, Ed, D-Ariz. (2)
Paul, Ron, R-Texas (14)
Payne, Donald M., D-N.J. (10)
Pelosi, Nancy, D-Calif. (8)
Pence, Mike, R-Ind. (2)
Peterson, Collin C., D-Minn. (7)
Peterson, John E., R-Pa. (5)
Petri, Tom, R-Wis. (6)
Phelps, David, D-Ill. (19)
Pickering, Charles W. "Chip" Jr., R-Miss. (3)
Pitts, Joe, R-Pa. (16)
Platts, Todd R., R-Pa. (19)
Pombo, Richard W., R-Calif. (11)
Pomeroy, Earl, D-N.D. (AL)
Portman, Rob, R-Ohio (2)
Price, David E., D-N.C. (4)
Pryce, Deborah, R-Ohio (15)
Putnam, Adam H., R-Fla. (12)

. . . Governors, Supreme Court, Cabinet-Rank Officers

— Q, R —

Quinn, Jack, R-N.Y. (30)
Radanovich, George P., R-Calif. (19)
Rahall, Nick J. II, D-W.Va. (3)
Ramstad, Jim, R-Minn. (3)
Rangel, Charles B., D-N.Y. (15)
Regula, Ralph, R-Ohio (16)
Rehberg, Denny, R-Mont. (AL)
Reyes, Silvestre, D-Texas (16)
Reynolds, Thomas M., R-N.Y. (27)
Riley, Bob, R-Ala. (3)
Rivers, Lynn, D-Mich. (13)
Rodriguez, Ciro D., D-Texas (28)
Roemer, Tim, D-Ind. (3)
Rogers, Harold, R-Ky. (5)
Rogers, Mike, R-Mich. (8)
Rohrabacher, Dana, R-Calif. (45)
Ros-Lehtinen, Ileana, R-Fla. (18)
Ross, Mike, D-Ark. (4)
Rothman, Steven R., D-N.J. (9)
Roukema, Marge, R-N.J. (5)
Roybal-Allard, Lucille, D-Calif. (33)
Royce, Ed, R-Calif. (39)
Rush, Bobby L., D-Ill. (1)
Ryan, Paul D., R-Wis. (1)
Ryun, Jim, R-Kan. (2)

— S —

Sabo, Martin Olav, D-Minn. (5)
Sanchez, Loretta, D-Calif. (46)
Sanders, Bernard, I-Vt. (AL)
Sandlin, Max, D-Texas (1)
Sawyer, Tom, D-Ohio (14)
Saxton, H. James, R-N.J. (3)
Schaffer, Bob, R-Colo. (4)
Schakowsky, Jan, D-Ill. (9)
Schiff, Adam B., D-Calif. (27)
Schrock, Ed, R-Va. (2)
Scott, Robert C., D-Va. (3)
Sensenbrenner, F. James Jr., R-Wis. (9)
Serrano, José E., D-N.Y. (16)
Sessions, Pete, R-Texas (5)
Shadegg, John, R-Ariz. (4)
Shaw, E. Clay Jr., R-Fla. (22)
Shays, Christopher, R-Conn. (4)
Sherman, Brad, D-Calif. (24)
Sherwood, Donald L., R-Pa. (10)
Shimkus, John, R-Ill. (20)
Shows, Ronnie, D-Miss. (4)
Shuster, Bill, R-Pa. (9)
Simmons, Rob, R-Conn. (2)
Simpson, Mike, R-Idaho (2)
Skeen, Joe, R-N.M. (2)
Skelton, Ike, D-Mo. (4)
Slaughter, Louise M., D-N.Y. (28)
Smith, Adam, D-Wash. (9)
Smith, Christopher H., R-N.J. (4)
Smith, Lamar, R-Texas (21)
Smith, Nick, R-Mich. (7)
Snyder, Vic, D-Ark. (2)
Solis, Hilda L., D-Calif. (31)
Souder, Mark, R-Ind. (4)
Spratt, John M. Jr., D-S.C. (5)
Stark, Pete, D-Calif. (13)
Stearns, Cliff, R-Fla. (6)
Stenholm, Charles W., D-Texas (17)
Strickland, Ted, D-Ohio (6)
Stump, Bob, R-Ariz. (3)
Stupak, Bart, D-Mich. (1)
Sullivan, Jim, R-Okla. (1) *
Sununu, John E., R-N.H. (1)
Sweeney, John E., R-N.Y. (22)

— T —

Tancredo, Tom, R-Colo. (6)
Tanner, John, D-Tenn. (8)
Tauscher, Ellen O., D-Calif. (10)
Tauzin, Billy, R-La. (3)
Taylor, Charles H., R-N.C. (11)
Taylor, Gene, D-Miss. (5)
Terry, Lee, R-Neb. (2)
Thomas, Bill, R-Calif. (21)
Thompson, Bennie, D-Miss. (2)
Thompson, Mike, D-Calif. (1)
Thornberry, William M. "Mac," R-Texas (13)
Thune, John, R-S.D. (AL)
Thurman, Karen L., D-Fla. (5)
Tiahrt, Todd, R-Kan. (4)

Tiberi, Pat, R-Ohio (12)
Tierney, John F., D-Mass. (6)
Toomey, Patrick J., R-Pa. (15)
Towns, Edolphus, D-N.Y. (10)
Turner, Jim, D-Texas (2)

— U, V —

Udall, Mark, D-Colo. (2)
Udall, Tom, D-N.M. (3)
Upton, Fred, R-Mich. (6)
Velázquez, Nydia M., D-N.Y. (12)
Visclosky, Peter J., D-Ind. (1)
Vitter, David, R-La. (1)

— W —

Walden, Greg, R-Ore. (2)
Walsh, James T., R-N.Y. (25)
Wamp, Zach, R-Tenn. (3)
Waters, Maxine, D-Calif. (35)
Watkins, Wes, R-Okla. (3)
Watson, Diane, D-Calif. (32)
Watt, Melvin, D-N.C. (12)
Watts, J.C. Jr., R-Okla. (4)
Waxman, Henry A., D-Calif. (29)
Weiner, Anthony, D-N.Y. (9)
Weldon, Curt, R-Pa. (7)
Weldon, Dave, R-Fla. (15)
Weller, Jerry, R-Ill. (11)
Wexler, Robert, D-Fla. (19)
Whitfield, Edward, R-Ky. (1)
Wicker, Roger, R-Miss. (1)
Wilson, Heather A., R-N.M. (1)
Wilson, Joe, R-S.C. (2)
Wolf, Frank R., R-Va. (10)
Woolsey, Lynn, D-Calif. (6)
Wu, David, D-Ore. (1)
Wynn, Albert R., D-Md. (4)

— X, Y, Z —

Young, C.W. Bill, R-Fla. (10)
Young, Don, R-Alaska (AL)

Delegates

Acevedo-Vilá, Aníbal, D-P.R.
Christensen, Donna M.C., D-Virgin Is.
Faleomavaega, Eni F.H., D-Am. Samoa
Norton, Eleanor Holmes, D-D.C.
Underwood, Robert A., D-Guam

Senators
R 49; D 49; I 2

Akaka, Daniel K., D-Hawaii
Allard, Wayne, R-Colo.
Allen, George, R-Va.
Baucus, Max, D-Mont.
Barkley, Dean, I-Minn.
Bayh, Evan, D-Ind.
Bennett, Robert F., R-Utah
Biden, Joseph R. Jr., D-Del.
Bingaman, Jeff, D-N.M.
Bond, Christopher S., R-Mo.
Boxer, Barbara, D-Calif.
Breaux, John B., D-La.
Brownback, Sam, R-Kan.
Bunning, Jim, R-Ky.
Burns, Conrad, R-Mont.
Byrd, Robert C., D-W.Va.
Campbell, Ben Nighthorse, R-Colo.
Cantwell, Maria, D-Wash.
Carnahan, Jean, D-Mo.
Carper, Thomas R., D-Del.
Chafee, Lincoln, R-R.I.
Cleland, Max, D-Ga.
Clinton, Hillary Rodham, D-N.Y.
Cochran, Thad, R-Miss.
Collins, Susan, R-Maine
Conrad, Kent, D-N.D.
Corzine, Jon, D-N.J.
Craig, Larry E., R-Idaho
Crapo, Michael D., R-Idaho
Daschle, Tom, D-S.D.
Dayton, Mark, D-Minn.
DeWine, Mike, R-Ohio

Dodd, Christopher J., D-Conn.
Domenici, Pete V., R-N.M.
Dorgan, Byron L., D-N.D.
Durbin, Richard J., D-Ill.
Edwards, John, D-N.C.
Ensign, John, R-Nev.
Enzi, Michael B., R-Wyo.
Feingold, Russell D., D-Wis.
Feinstein, Dianne, D-Calif.
Fitzgerald, Peter G., R-Ill.
Frist, Bill, R-Tenn.
Graham, Bob, D-Fla.
Gramm, Phil, R-Texas
Grassley, Charles E., R-Iowa
Gregg, Judd, R-N.H.
Hagel, Chuck, R-Neb.
Harkin, Tom, D-Iowa
Hatch, Orrin G., R-Utah
Helms, Jesse, R-N.C.
Hollings, Ernest F., D-S.C.
Hutchinson, Tim, R-Ark.
Hutchison, Kay Bailey, R-Texas
Inhofe, James M., R-Okla.
Inouye, Daniel K., D-Hawaii
Jeffords, James M., I-Vt.
Johnson, Tim, D-S.D.
Kennedy, Edward M., D-Mass.
Kerry, John, D-Mass.
Kohl, Herb, D-Wis.
Kyl, Jon, R-Ariz.
Landrieu, Mary L., D-La.
Leahy, Patrick J., D-Vt.
Levin, Carl, D-Mich.
Lieberman, Joseph I., D-Conn.
Lincoln, Blanche, D-Ark.
Lott, Trent, R-Miss.
Lugar, Richard G., R-Ind.
McCain, John, R-Ariz.
McConnell, Mitch, R-Ky.
Mikulski, Barbara A., D-Md.
Miller, Zell, D-Ga.
Murkowski, Frank H., R-Alaska
Murray, Patty, D-Wash.
Nelson, Ben, D-Neb.
Nelson, Bill, D-Fla.
Nickles, Don, R-Okla.
Reed, Jack, D-R.I.
Reid, Harry, D-Nev.
Roberts, Pat, R-Kan.
Rockefeller, John D. IV, D-W.Va.
Santorum, Rick, R-Pa.
Sarbanes, Paul S., D-Md.
Schumer, Charles E., D-N.Y.
Sessions, Jeff, R-Ala.
Shelby, Richard C., R-Ala.
Smith, Gordon H., R-Ore.
Smith, Robert C., R-N.H.
Snowe, Olympia J., R-Maine
Specter, Arlen, R-Pa.
Stabenow, Debbie, D-Mich.
Stevens, Ted, R-Alaska
Thomas, Craig, R-Wyo.
Thompson, Fred, R-Tenn.
Thurmond, Strom, R-S.C.
Torricelli, Robert G., D-N.J.
Voinovich, George V., R-Ohio
Warner, John W., R-Va.
Wyden, Ron, D-Ore.

Governors
R 27; D 21; I 2

Ala. — Donald Siegelman, D
Alaska — Tony Knowles, D
Ariz. — Jane Dee Hull, R
Ark. — Mike Huckabee, R
Calif. — Gray Davis, D
Colo. — Bill Owens, R
Conn. — John G. Rowland, R
Del. — Ruth Ann Minner, D
Fla. — Jeb Bush, R
Ga. — Roy Barnes, D
Hawaii — Benjamin J. Cayetano, D
Idaho — Dirk Kempthorne, R
Ill. — George Ryan, R
Ind. — Frank L. O'Bannon, D
Iowa — Tom Vilsack, D
Kan. — Bill Graves, R
Ky. — Paul E. Patton, D

La. — Mike Foster, R
Maine — Angus King, I
Md. — Parris N. Glendening, D
Mass. — Jane Swift, R
Mich. — John Engler, R
Minn. — Jesse Ventura, I
Miss. — Ronnie Musgrove, D
Mo. — Bob Holden, D
Mont. — Judy Martz, R
Neb. — Mike Johanns, R
Nev. — Kenny Guinn, R
N.H. — Jeanne Shaheen, D
N.J. — James E. McGreevey, D
N.M. — Gary E. Johnson, R
N.Y. — George E. Pataki, R
N.C. — Michael F. Easley, D
N.D. — John Hoeven, R
Ohio — Bob Taft, R
Okla. — Frank Keating, R
Ore. — John Kitzhaber, D
Pa. — Mark Schweiker, R
R.I. — Lincoln C. Almond, R
S.C. — Jim Hodges, D
S.D. — William J. Janklow, R
Tenn. — Don Sundquist, R
Texas — Rick Perry, R
Utah — Michael O. Leavitt, R
Vt. — Howard Dean, D
Va. — Mark Warner, D
Wash. — Gary Locke, D
W.Va. — Bob Wise, D
Wis. — Scott McCallum, R
Wyo. — Jim Geringer, R

Supreme Court

Rehnquist, William H. — Va., Chief Justice
Breyer, Stephen G. — Mass.
Ginsburg, Ruth Bader — N.Y.
Kennedy, Anthony M. — Calif.
O'Connor, Sandra Day — Ariz.
Scalia, Antonin — Va.
Souter, David H. — N.H.
Stevens, John Paul — Ill.
Thomas, Clarence — Ga.

Cabinet

Abraham, Spencer — Energy
Ashcroft, John — Attorney General
Chao, Elaine L. — Labor
Evans, Donald L. — Commerce
Martinez, Mel — HUD
Mineta, Norman Y. — Transportation
Norton, Gale A. — Interior
O'Neill, Paul H. — Treasury
Paige, Rod — Education
Powell, Colin L. — State
Principi, Anthony J. — Veterans Affairs
Rumsfeld, Donald H. — Defense
Thompson, Tommy G.— HHS
Veneman, Ann M. — Agriculture

Other Executive Branch Officers

Cheney, Dick — Vice President
Card, Andrew H. Jr. — Chief of Staff
Daniels, Mitchell E. Jr. — OMB Director
Lindsey, Lawrence — Chairman, National Economic Council
Negroponte, John D.— U.N. Representative
Rice, Condoleezza — National Security Adviser
Tenet, George J. — Director of Central Intelligence
Whitman, Christine Todd — EPA Administrator
Zoellick, Robert B. — U.S. Trade Representative

Membership Changes

Died (2)

Name, Party, State (District)	Date	Began Service	Age	Successor
Rep. Patsy T. Mink, D-Hawaii (2)	Sept. 9, 2002	1964	74	Ed Case, D, sworn in 1/4/2003
Sen. Paul Wellstone, D-Minn.	Oct. 25, 2002	1991	58	Dean Barkley, I, sworn in 11/12/02

Resigned (3)

Name, Party, State (District)	Date	Began Service	Age	Successor
Rep. Tony P. Hall, D-Ohio (3)	Sept. 9, 2002	U.N. ambassador	60	Michael R. Turner, R, sworn in 1/7/03
Rep. Steve Largent, R-Okla. (1)	Feb. 15, 2002	Run for governor	47	John Sullivan, R, sworn in 2/27/02
Sen. Frank H. Murkowski, R-Alaska	Nov. 5, 2002	Run for governor	69	Lisa Murkowski, R, sworn in 1/7/03

Expelled (1)

Name, Party, State (District)	Date	Began Service	Age	Successor
Rep. James A. Traficant Jr., D-Ohio (17)	July 24, 2002	Corruption	61	Tim Ryan, D*

*Tim Ryan defeated Ann Womer Benjamin, R, and James A. Traficant Jr., I, after defeating Rep. Tom Sawyer in the primary.

Defeated In Primary (9)

Name, Party, State (District)	Winner
Rep. Bob Barr, R-Ga. (7)	Rep. John Linder, R-Ga. (11)
Rep. Gary A. Condit, D-Calif. (18)	Dennis Cardoza
Rep. Earl F. Hilliard, D-Ala. (7)	Artur Davis
Rep. Brian Kerns, R-Ind. (7)	Rep. Steve Buyer, R-Ind. (5)
Rep. Frank R. Mascara, D-Pa. (20)	Rep. John P. Murtha, D-Pa. (12)
Rep. Cynthia A. McKinney, D-Ga. (4)	Denise Majette
Rep. Lynn Rivers, D-Mich. (13)	Rep. John D. Dingell, D-Mich. (16)
Rep. Tom Sawyer, D-Ohio (14)	Tim Ryan, D
Sen. Robert C. Smith, R-N.H.	Rep. John E. Sununu, R-N.H. (1)

Defeated In General Election (11)

Name, Party, State (District)	Winner
Sen. Jean Carnahan D-Mo.	Jim Talent, R
Sen. Max Cleland, D-Ga.	Rep. Saxby Chambliss, R
Sen. Tim Hutchinson, R-Ark.	Mark Pryor, D
Rep. George W. Gekas, R-Pa. (17)	Rep. Tim Holden, D
Rep. Felix J. Grucci Jr., R-N.Y. (1)	Timothy H. Bishop, D
Rep. Bill Luther, D-Minn. (6)	John Kline, R
Rep. Jim Maloney, D-Conn. (5)	Rep. Nancy L. Johnson, R-Conn.
Rep. Constance A. Morella, R-Md. (8)	Chris Van Hollen, D
Rep. David Phelps, D-Ill. (19)	Rep. John Shimkus, R
Rep. Ronnie Shows, D-Miss. (4)	Rep. Charles W. "Chip" Pickering Jr., R
Rep. Karen L. Thurman, D.-Fla. (5)	Ginny Brown-Waite, R

Retiring Senators (5)

Name, Party, State	Began Service
Phil Gramm, R-Texas	1985
Jesse Helms, R-N.C.	1973
Fred Thompson, R-Tenn.	1994
Strom Thurmond, R-S.C.	1954[†]
Robert G. Torricelli, D-N.J.	1997

[†]Did not serve April to November 1956

Sought Other Office (19)

Name, Party, State (District)	Goal/Outcome
Rep. John Baldacci, D-Maine (2)	Governor/won
Rep. James A. Barcia, D-Mich (5)	State Senate/won
Rep. Thomas M. Barrett, D-Wis. (5)	Governor/lost
Rep. Ken Bentsen, D-Texas (25)	Senate/lost
Rep. Rod R. Blagojevich, D-Ill. (5)	Governor/won
Rep. David E. Bonior, D-Mich. (10)	Governor/lost
Rep. Ed Bryant, R-Tenn. (7)	Senate/lost
Rep. Saxby Chambliss, R-Ga. (8)	Senate/won
Rep. Bob Clement D-Tenn. (5)	Senate/lost
Rep. John Cooksey, R-La. (5)	Senate/lost
Rep. Robert H. Ehrlich Jr., R-Md. (2)	Governor/won
Rep. Greg Ganske, R-Iowa (4)	Senate/lost
Rep. Lindsey Graham, R-S.C. (3)	Senate/won
Rep. Van Hilleary, R-Tenn. (4)	Governor/lost
Sen. Frank H. Murkowski, R-Alaska[§]	Governor/won
Rep. Bob Riley, R-Ala. (3	Governor/won
Rep. John E. Sununu, R-N.H. (1)	Senate/won
Rep. John Thune, R-S.D. (AL)	Senate/lost
Del. Robert A. Underwood, D-Guam	Governor/lost

Retiring House Members (18)

Name, Party, State (District)	Began Service
Dick Armey, R-Texas (26)	1985
Robert A. Borski, D-Pa. (3)	1983
Sonny Callahan, R-Ala. (1)	1985
Eva Clayton, D-N.C. (1)	1992
William J. Coyne, D-Pa. (14)	1981
Benjamin A. Gilman, R-N.Y. (20)	1973
James V. Hansen, R-Utah (1)	1981
Steve Horn, R-Calif. (38)	1993
John J. LaFalce, D-N.Y. (29)	1975
Carrie P. Meek, D-Fla. (17)	1993
Dan Miller, R-Fla. (13)	1993
Tim Roemer, D-Ind. (3)	1991
Marge Roukema, R-N.J. (5)	1981
Bob Schaffer, R-Colo. (4)	1997
Joe Skeen, R-N.M. (2)	1980
Bob Stump, R-Ariz. (3)	1977
Wes Watkins, R-Okla. (3)[§]	1997
J.C. Watts Jr., R-Okla. (4)	1995

[§]Served as a Democrat 1977-91

Appendix B

VOTE STUDIES

Lessons for a New Congress

This was supposed to be the Congress in which getting anything done at all would have been a major accomplishment. Yet somehow, the 107th Congress — the most evenly divided in half a century — was able to pass a significant roster of legislation. It also gave up on some of its most pressing tasks, such as passing the annual appropriations bills and resolving major health care issues that have been on the agenda for years.

For the 108th Congress, therefore, the most important guide for how to get things done — what to do and what not to do — will be the lessons it can take from the successes and failures of the 107th Congress.

The challenges that lawmakers will face for the two years beginning Jan. 7 are far different from those of the two years now ending. In 2003, lawmakers would seem to have little excuse for stalemating, given that Republicans will control the House, the Senate and the White House. In reality, of course, the margins of control will not be much wider than they were in the 107th, and with only 51 seats in the Senate, the GOP will have a hard time advancing bills by itself. And there is no reason to assume that passing bills will be the Democrats' goal, given how well the attacks on the failures of the Democratic Senate worked for Republicans in the November election.

Those who do want to pass bills, however, can take a number of cues from the experiences of the 107th. Many of the most pertinent lessons come from the second session, which adjourned Nov. 22, when Congress sought to tackle the unfinished business that was left from the crisis-filled session of 2001. Those lessons will be important, congressional scholars say, if the 108th is to take on the increasingly complicated challenges that will be laid at its doorstep.

"The things that were easiest to get done have gotten done," said David W. Rohde, a professor of political science at Michigan State University. For example, if the next Congress is asked to attempt a reorganization of the intelligence community, as a joint House-Senate panel recommended Dec. 11, "that's not going to be nearly as easy as passing a homeland security bill," Rohde said.

Perhaps the most important lesson from the 107th was the road map for how to build true bipartisan coalitions. Not the narrow kind — Republicans plus the most conservative Democrat, Zell Miller of Georgia, or Democrats plus the most liberal Senate Republican, Lincoln Chafee of Rhode Island — but the broad kind, in which there is enough strength on both sides to carry a controversial bill from beginning to end.

The Congress that just ended often appeared to be more bipartisan than it actually was. The wave of legislation that followed the Sept. 11 attacks, from the far-reaching anti-terrorism law (PL 107-56) to the creation of the Department of Homeland Security (PL 107-296), was never really in danger because neither party could afford to stand in the way of the war on terrorism. And some of the most divisive disputes between the two parties, particularly in 2002, never made it to the floor at all. (*Party unity, p. B-9*)

But there also were examples of bills that might not have reached Bush's desk had there not been enough committed

supporters from both parties to steer them through the toughest controversies. Both the education overhaul (PL 107-110), and the law that created new federal election standards (PL 107-252) were built on tradeoffs that gave large numbers of Republicans and Democrats a strong incentive to support them.

Those solid bipartisan coalitions are not always necessary; the 107th certainly had its share of bills that were forced upon one party or another. The lesson, however, is that in a closely divided Congress, forcing a bill only works when one party has substantially more credibility on the issue than the other. A big push from the president helps as well.

Bush won Democratic support for his $1.35 trillion tax cut (PL 107-16) largely because Democrats knew they were vulnerable on taxes, not because the majority of the party wanted a tax cut that large. Likewise, Democrats won GOP support for the criminal penalties in the accounting overhaul measure (PL 107-204) largely because Republicans knew they could not oppose such an idea in the heat of the corporate scandals, not because the deal had been negotiated with them. When the two parties tried to force their vastly different economic stimulus bills upon each other, however, neither could prevail — because neither one had a strong advantage in public confidence in their economic plans.

Another lesson is one that by its nature may not have much effect on strategy: A closely divided Congress can pass even the most controversial legislation if there is a crisis or scandal strong enough to make inaction politically impossible.

Issues such as Medicare prescription drug coverage and an overhaul of bankruptcy laws languished largely because the public did not seem to consider those crises severe in the near term. But the horror of Sept. 11 made it possible to pass anti-terrorism measures that would have been unthinkable otherwise, and the bitterness over the corporate scandals that devastated retirement savings made it impossible for Congress not to pass a tough accounting bill.

"They did it because the public demanded action . . . and it would have been embarrassing if they had not acted," said Ross K. Baker, a political scientist at Rutgers University. "Had the supporters of bankruptcy reform had the benefit of a massive bankruptcy scandal, they might have gotten that through."

If the 108th wants a track record of accomplishments, analysts say, members will have to build an agenda that addresses the full range of issues that are important to the public — and that truly gives both sides a stake in its success. (*Presidential support, p. B-5*)

Of the many lessons that are being offered from the paper trail of the 107th Congress, these are half a dozen that may become applicable early in the new year:

Education: Don't Be Afraid of Compromise

Teachers and education groups will be arguing for years over whether the 2001 rewrite of federal education law was good policy. But as a model for legislative strategy in a closely divided Congress, it is hard to find a more successful ex-

ample from the 107th Congress than the reauthorization of the 1965 Elementary and Secondary Education Act (ESEA), which began with bipartisan negotiations and never gave up on them. (*2001 Almanac, p. 8-3*)

Like so many domestic issues, education had been one that was impossible to take on without ideological fights over nearly everything, including federal versus state and local control, school vouchers, and guns in schools. The political environment had been so toxic that the 106th Congress failed to reauthorize ESEA, leaving its programs to run on autopilot as they received an extra year of appropriations under the old rules. (*2000 Almanac, p. 9-3*)

Bush, however, put education at the top of his agenda, and he laid out his plan to Congress shortly after taking office in January 2001. It included provisions that no one expected to survive, such as private school vouchers, and Bush did not fight very hard for them. But its centerpiece — annual testing in reading and math for students in grades 3 through 8, with rewards for the best-performing schools and penalties for the worst — was important enough to him that his White House team tried to work out bipartisan agreements early on.

Top Republicans and Democrats conducted two separate sets of negotiations, one in the Senate Health, Education, Labor and Pensions Committee and the other in the House Education and the Workforce Committee, to work out bipartisan bills that the committees' leaders would fight for. The basic deal was the same in each case: annual testing for Bush, more state and local flexibility for congressional Republicans and big increases in funding for Democrats.

Those early tradeoffs angered some in both parties, but they also gave the top committee Republicans and Democrats an incentive to fight off amendments that could have toppled their delicate balance. They also built enough support to carry the bill through by huge margins on both sides of the Capitol — no small feat in such a divided Congress.

That gave the bill the momentum it needed to survive months of negotiations, as well as the period after Sept. 11 when the issue was starved for attention.

Voting Standards: Find Something for Everyone

There were times when the effort to overhaul federal election law, in response to the debacle of the 2000 election, appeared to be on its deathbed because there had been so many compromises that no one was pushing for it anymore. In the end, however, those tradeoffs were precisely the reason the bill became law — they gave both sides a reason to keep it alive.

Unlike the education bill, the election overhaul did not start out as a bipartisan initiative. Eventually, however, the two sides discovered the winning formula. Republicans would give Democrats most of the national standards they wanted in exchange for new anti-fraud protections, which were a higher priority to Republicans than the measures to get rid of outdated voting equipment and let voters correct errors on their ballots.

At first, it was not clear the deal would hold. The anti-fraud language was so objectionable to civil rights and voting rights groups that it almost neutralized their support. The changes did not build any new support among state and local election officials, who never wanted the new federal mandates. And the balancing act was so precarious that the final House-Senate negotiations turned into loud, public partisan squabbles more than once.

But if the tradeoff gave both sides something to hate about the bill, it also gave both sides something to like. Ultimately, that was enough to keep them talking — and to win lopsided votes for the final bill. (*Election overhaul, p. 14-3*)

Accounting Regulation: Don't Underreach

The most common advice Republicans have received for the next Congress — when they will control both elected branches of government — is not to overreach. But the lesson of the accounting standards bill, which ended up tougher than anyone expected, may be exactly the opposite: Do not underestimate how much the public wants Congress to do in addressing an urgent crisis.

In this case, the crisis was the corporate scandals that led to the collapse of Enron Corp. and WorldCom Inc. After the Enron disaster, the House passed a bill that would have created an accounting oversight board, but Democrats roundly criticized it as a weak response. A tougher Senate bill faced an uncertain future as the momentum from Enron faded. But once WorldCom admitted it had overstated its income by a whopping $3.9 billion, there was no holding back. The Senate beefed up its bill by adding Democratic provisions to mandate prison terms of up to 10 years for securities fraud and to lengthen the statute of limitations

---

CQ Vote Study Guide

Congressional Quarterly has conducted studies analyzing the voting behavior of members of Congress since 1945. This is how the studies are carried out:

● **Selecting votes.** CQ bases its vote studies on all roll call votes on which members were asked to vote "yea" or "nay." In 2002 there were 253 such votes in the Senate and 483 in the House. The study excludes quorum calls (there was one in the House in 2002) because they require only that members vote "present."

The totals do include House votes to approve the Journal (36 in 2002) and Senate votes to instruct the sergeant at arms to request members' presence in the chamber (two in 2002).

The presidential support and party unity studies are based on votes selected from the total according to the criteria described on pages B-14 and B-20.

● **Individual scores.** Members' scores in the accompanying charts are based only on the votes each member actually cast. The same method is used for leading scorers on pages B-7, B-11 and B-13.

● **Overall scores.** For consistency with previous years, graphs and breakdowns by chamber, party and region are based on all yea-or-nay votes. In those cases, absences lower scores. (*Methodology, 1987 Almanac, p. 22-C*)

● **Rounding.** Scores are rounded to the nearest percentage point, although rounding is not used to bring any score up to 100 percent.

for civil lawsuits.

By the time House Financial Services Committee Chairman Michael G. Oxley, R-Ohio, urged a "cooling-off period" during the August recess, he looked irrelevant — particularly after Bush essentially promised to sign whatever Congress sent him before August. (*Corporate accounting, p. 11-3*)

Prescription Drug Benefit: Start Early, Avoid Extremes

To make a serious effort to break the deadlock over prescription drug coverage in the 108th, lawmakers will have to avoid two crucial mistakes that caused the effort to fail in the 107th: starting too late and putting too much faith in the classic bargaining strategy of staking out extreme positions to get better concessions later.

One reason the education bill succeeded, with the numerous divisive issues it had to address, was that lawmakers started at the beginning of the 107th. In the case of prescription drugs, lawmakers did not have bills ready until the middle of 2002 — not nearly enough time to reach a compromise on such a complicated effort, even if they had wanted one so close to the elections.

In addition, however, the effort suffered from the fact that each side staked out a position it knew offered the other side little or nothing to work with. The House passed a Republican bill (HR 4954) that would have relied on the private sector to design prescription drug coverage at a time when most Democrats wanted it to be part of the Medicare program. Both sides were so divided over the cost of such a plan that four successive versions failed in the Senate.

That squared with the classic bargaining strategy of asking for more than one expects to get and making tradeoffs later, but it also served as a warning to the 108th that lawmakers who rely on that strategy can end up with nothing. (*Medicare prescriptions, p. 10-3*)

Budget and Appropriations: Unite or Lose

There were many causes for the breakdown of the budget and appropriations process in 2002, but the simplest — internal divisions among Republicans and among Democrats — should remind the 108th of a classic rule on budgetary politics: When Congress is divided over what it wants, the president will always get what he wants.

As conservative House Republicans dueled with their moderate colleagues over the right spending level for the Labor, Health and Human Services, and Education appropriations bill, the entire series of spending bills stalled along with it. That failure was the reason Bush was able to force appropriators to cut the fiscal 2003 spending bills to meet his funding levels — just as President Bill Clinton was so often able to force divided congressional Republicans to fatten their spending bills to meet his requests. (*Appropriations, p. 2-3*)

Unemployment Benefits: Finger-Pointing Is Not Enough

Lawmakers from both parties decry the "blame game," but the truth is they often get political mileage out of it. The 108th may find, however, that there is no political mileage to be had in the failure of the 107th to extend unemployment benefits to the jobless workers who lost them on Dec. 28.

In November, the Senate passed a measure (HR 3529) by the unlikely team of Hillary Rodham Clinton, D-N.Y., and Republican Whip Don Nickles of Oklahoma that would have provided a three-month extension of benefits for $4.9 billion. The House already had passed its version — a five-week extension (HR 5063), coupled with a controversial provision to prevent cuts in Medicare payments to doctors.

Neither side would budge. "The House has already acted," said an aide to Speaker J. Dennis Hastert, R-Ill. Senate Majority Leader Tom Daschle, D-S.D., responded that, "The Republican message to unemployed workers can be summed up in two words: Bah humbug."

In January, both sides will find out whether the 800,000 laid-off workers who lost their benefits find that to be a useful debate. (*Unemployment, p. 12-6*) ◆

Bush's 'Politics of the Possible'

The Senate was in Democratic hands and wartime unity had given way to election-year partisanship, but President Bush's success rate on congressional votes during 2002 was still higher than that of any president since Lyndon B. Johnson.

By keeping his agenda narrow, working closely with a loyal Republican leadership in the House and employing a strategic mix of compromise and muscle, Bush got his way 88 percent of the time. Of the 98 votes on which he took a clear position, he won all but 12.

That record was slightly better than Bush's 87 percent in 2001, and the best posted by a president since 1965, when Johnson, also in the second year of his administration, prevailed on 93 percent of the votes on which he took sides.

CQ Vote Studies	
Presidential support	B-5
Top scorers	B-7
Party unity	B-9
Top scorers	B-11
Participation	B-12
Top scorers	B-13
Background	B-14

Bush ended the year in an even better position to advance his agenda in the 108th Congress, which will see Republican majorities in both chambers guided by leaders grateful to their popular president for helping to regain GOP control of the Senate.

Congressional Quarterly's calculation of presidential support measures only how often a majority of the House or Senate voted the way the president wanted. The study does not reflect whether the president's proposals became law. CQ looks at each House and Senate floor vote, determines whether the president took a clear position before the vote and notes the outcome. Since 1953, when CQ started tracking presidential support, winning percent-

PRESIDENTIAL SUCCESS ▸ History

Percentage of the time the president won on roll call votes on which he took a clear position:

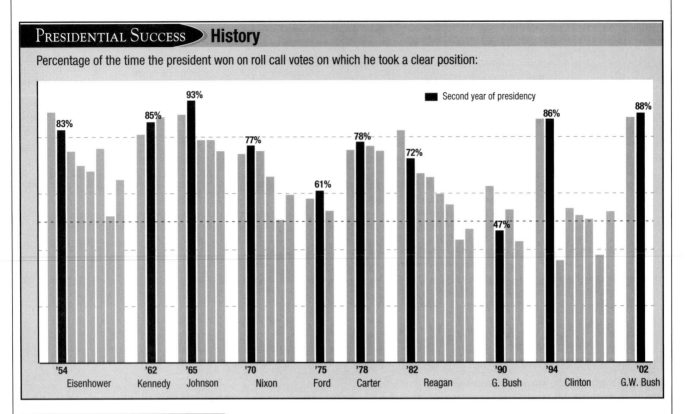

2002 Data

Senate	53 victories
	5 defeats
House	33 victories
	7 defeats
Total Bush success rate:	88%

As in 2001, the number of 2002 floor votes on which Bush took a clear position was relatively small. And more than a third of this year's presidential support votes were on confirmation of judicial and executive branch nominees. Bush won every vote in that category because the nominations opposed most strenuously by Senate Democrats were blocked in committee.

The range of legislation on which the president chose to invest significant political capital was quite limited. The bipartisanship that followed the Sept. 11, 2001, terrorist attacks had dissolved by early 2002, particularly as Democrats worked to refocus the election-year debate on the faltering economy. But homeland security and foreign policy were central to Bush's agenda, and the president's position as a wartime commander in chief continued to be a source of power, as demonstrated by the November election results.

Also high on Bush's agenda was trade — an issue that creates coalitions that blur partisan divisions. Bush won a prize that had eluded the executive branch since 1994 —

ages have ranged from Johnson's high in 1965, when Democrats had a tight grip on both the House and Senate, to a low of 36 percent in 1995, when Democrat Bill Clinton faced the first Republican-controlled Congress in 40 years.

fast-track trade promotion authority — after forcing Republicans to accede to Democratic demands for expansion of Trade Adjustment Assistance (TAA) for laid-off workers.

Budget issues also continued to be important to the administration, with Bush determined to hold a line on non-defense spending. Bush took on Republicans as well as Democrats and threatened a veto in a successful battle to keep the cost of a fiscal 2002 supplemental spending package (PL 107-206) close to his own proposal. Although Bush gave some ground, the confrontation set an important marker for the fiscal 2003 appropriations process.

On his priority issues, the president relied on the formula that guided his dealings with Congress during the first year of his administration: He focused on a few essentials, ceded ground when necessary to reach his ultimate objective and relied on Republican leaders to keep the troops in line.

"He learned the key lessons of calling his shots carefully," said Kenneth R. Weinstein of the conservative Hudson Institute. "And also knowing when it makes sense to take something that he may not love. . . . He's willing to compromise when there are larger principles at issue."

Stephen Hess, a Brookings Institution senior scholar, likened Bush's approach to that of President Dwight D. Eisenhower, whom Hess served as a speechwriter. Eisenhower surrounded himself with experienced, disciplined and tight-lipped aides and focused on a narrow set of issues, including creation of the Interstate Highway System. Eisenhower's 1953 success rate — 89 percent — remains the record high for a Republican president in CQ's vote studies. (*1953 Almanac, p. 77*)

Going With the Flow

Bush showed more clearly in 2002 that when the political momentum is against him, he is willing to change course

Leading Scorers: Presidential Support

Support indicates those who in 2002 voted most often for President Bush's position. **Opposition** shows those who voted most often against the president's position. Scores are based on actual votes cast. Members who missed half or more of the votes are not listed. Scores are rounded to one decimal; lawmakers with identical scores are listed alphabetically.

Senate Support

Republicans		Democrats	
Frist. Tenn.	100.0%	Miller, Ga.	91.8%
Lott, Miss.	100.0	Nelson, Neb.	91.1
Lugar, Ind.	100.0	Lincoln, Ark.	89.5
Thompson, Tenn.	100.0	Baucus, Mont.	87.9
Hagel, Neb.	98.3	Breaux, La.	87.9
Hatch, Utah	98.2	Landrieu, La.	83.6
Nickles, Okla.	98.2	Cantwell, Wash.	81.0
Bennett, Utah	98.2	Bayh, Ind.	79.3
DeWine, Ohio	98.2	Graham, Fla.	79.3
Bond, Mo.	98.1	Kohl, Wis.	79.3
Brownback, Kan.	98.1	Bingaman, N.M.	78.9
Hutchinson, Ark.	97.9	Carper, Del.	78.9

Senate Opposition

Republicans		Democrats	
Shelby, Ala.	13.5%	Akaka, Hawaii	36.7%
Collins, Maine	12.1	Kennedy, Mass.	36.4
Sessions, Ala.	11.8	Corzine, N.J.	35.8
Specter, Pa.	11.3	Boxer, Calif.	35.2
Snowe, Maine	10.3	Sarbanes, Md.	35.1
McCain, Ariz.	9.6	Wellstone, Minn.	34.6
Smith, Ore.	9.3	Conrad, N.D.	34.5
Warner, Va.	9.3	Levin, Mich.	34.5
		Stabenow, Mich.	34.5
		Torricelli, N.J.	34.0

House Support

Republicans		Democrats	
Skeen, N.M.	95.0%	Lucas, Ky.	78.0%
Oxley, Ohio	94.7	Hall, Texas	70.0
DeLay, Texas	92.3	Cramer, Ala.	61.5
Dunn, Wash.	92.3	Holden, Pa.	60.0
Goss, Fla.	92.3	Barcia, Mich.	59.4
Hart, Pa.	92.3	Pomeroy, N.D.	58.0
Hastings, Wash.	92.3	Skelton, Mo.	58.0
Hyde, Ill.	92.3	John, La.	57.9
Sununu, N.H.	92.3	Tanner, Tenn.	56.4
Thornberry, Texas	92.3	Murtha, Pa.	54.8
Gillmor, Ohio	92.1	Gordon, Tenn.	53.8
Knollenberg, Mich.	92.1	McIntyre, N.C.	53.8
Schrock, Va.	92.1	Peterson, Minn.	53.8
Watts, Okla.	92.1	Phelps, Ill.	53.8

House Opposition

Republicans		Democrats	
Paul, Texas	48.7%	Frank, Mass.	86.5%
Morella, Md.	47.4	McDermott, Wash.	86.5
Duncan, Tenn.	38.0	Lofgren, Calif.	85.0
Gilman, N.Y.	30.8	Payne, N.J.	84.2
Flake, Ariz.	30.0	Slaughter, N.Y.	83.8
Leach, Iowa	30.0	Watson, Calif.	83.8
Weldon, Pa.	28.9	Hilliard, Ala.	83.3
Hostettler, Ind.	28.0	Nadler, N.Y.	81.6
Jones, N.C.	28.0	Solis, Calif.	81.6
Moran, Kan.	28.0	Carson, Ind.	80.6
Goode, Va.	25.6	Coyne, Pa.	80.6
Johnson, Conn.	25.0	Hinchey, N.Y.	80.0
		Lantos, Calif.	80.0
		McKinney, Ga.	80.0
		Udall, N.M.	80.0

and take advantage of it. Most notable was his request in June for legislation creating a Department of Homeland Security — a proposal he had opposed for months. By embracing the plan and making it his own, Bush seized the initiative and positioned himself for some of his most significant legislative victories of 2002.

The homeland security bill (PL 107-296) was trapped in the Senate in the fall by a partisan dispute over collective bargaining rights. But after the Nov. 5 elections, dispirited Democrats dropped their objections and accepted Bush's demands.

With the help of House Speaker J. Dennis Hastert, R-Ill., and other Republican leaders, the president focused his legislative agenda on laying the groundwork for the midterm elections.

Many of the votes on which Bush prevailed came as the House considered domestic legislation that was clearly going nowhere in the Senate. Among them were several bills that would have extended all or parts of the 2001 tax cut package (PL 107-16), one to limit class-action lawsuits (HR 2341) and another to allow hospitals and doctors to refuse to provide abortions without losing federal funds (HR 4691).

Those measures appealed to the GOP base and helped build the platform from which Bush would campaign successfully during the weeks leading up to the midterm elections.

None of the bills had any reasonable chance of enactment, and Bush did not work hard to force votes in the Senate. "Why waste the energy when the cards are stacked against you?" asked Stephen Wayne, a professor of government at Georgetown University. "Particularly when there was a chance to reshuffle the deck."

Focused Lobbying

On the limited set of issues where Bush chose to make a determined stand, the White House showed what a focused

and relentless lobbying campaign can accomplish.

The White House understood early that a deal on TAA would be the key to Senate passage of fast track (PL 107-210), which allows the president to negotiate trade deals without congressional tinkering. Administration staff met once or twice a week with Senate aides for about six months to hammer out a deal, according to a Democratic Finance Committee aide involved in the discussions.

The most conservative Senate Republicans, including Phil Gramm of Texas, were unhappy, describing a TAA expansion as a government handout for dying industries that are no longer competitive in their markets.

"The administration focuses on the critical things to get the legislation to the floor," the Democratic aide said. "They understood that TAA would be a problem and they had to get ahead of it early. That was the issue they had to get past, and they had to put out brush fires on both sides of the aisle."

In the House, where the GOP held a majority, the administration used a different approach, coaxing just enough Republicans to vote for fast track over the objections of most Democrats. Bush traveled to the Capitol in July to tell House Republicans that the economic future of the country was at stake.

"Once they made the decision that they were going to do it on a partisan basis, they did a brilliant job," said Rep. Robert T. Matsui of California, one of the normally pro-trade Democrats who voted against the final legislation.

The president's efforts on fast track were focused and persistent, said Bill Lane, chief lobbyist for construction equipment manufacturer Caterpillar Inc. "He never lost focus on the ultimate goal."

A presidential action opposed by Caterpillar and other free-trade proponents was another factor in Bush's success on the trade issue.

The imposition of tariffs on some steel imports helped the administration win votes for fast track from 55 of the 120 members of the Congressional Steel Caucus.

"Throughout the process, you knew the president was absolutely determined to get fast track, and he was willing to make compromises to get it," Lane said. "The entire campaign had an air of inevitably. The question was not whether he would get fast track. It was what compromises he would make to get it."

Caution on Other Issues

On other issues, including some of the most contentious of the year, Bush kept his positions fluid — or sidestepped the debate entirely.

Bush took an unambiguous position on only nine of 24 "key votes" that CQ identified for 2002. The votes were chosen because they involved matters of great controversy, were a test of presidential or political power, or had potentially great impact on the nation and lives of Americans. (*Key votes*, p. C-3)

In January, when the campaign finance debate roared back to life in the House, Bush rebuffed Hastert's plea for presidential assistance in blocking the overhaul that eventually became law (PL 107-155). The White House sent mixed signals — that the president wanted reform, then that Bush was endorsing nothing. He later called the legislation, which he signed without public ceremony, "flawed."

Bush stayed on the sidelines, too, while House and Senate negotiators hammered out legislation (PL 107-252) to overhaul the nation's electoral system, an issue that sprang from his own contested election in 2000.

The president belatedly entered the debate over legislation to address a string of corporate scandals — and never pinned himself firmly to one piece of legislation.

Decline in Tests of Presidential Support

For the first time since the Eisenhower administration, the number of presidential support votes identified by Congressional Quarterly slipped below 100 in 2002 — about half the typical number of such votes in the 1980s.

The current decline began during the Clinton administration. The recent exception was in 1995, when President Bill Clinton squared off against the newly ascendant Republican Congress.

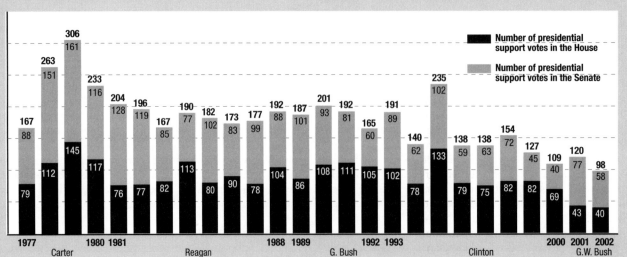

In response to growing public concern, Bush released a set of principles in March for addressing the problem. Then he reluctantly backed a bill (HR 3763) the House passed in April. But when the momentum shifted to a more stringent Senate measure, he told Congress to send him a bill before the August recess, then got out of the way. The measure Bush eventually signed (PL 107-204) closely tracked the Senate bill.

When Bush did take a stand, many of the disagreements already had played out behind the scenes. As in 2001, Bush often endorsed what Congress already had drafted and was inclined to support.

Short-Lived Losses

The president's success rate on floor votes varied by issue. Bush's lowest figure was on defense and foreign policy votes: He lost five of 15 votes, for a score of 67 percent. By contrast, his score on votes related to economic affairs and trade was 85 percent. On domestic issues, Bush won nearly 83 percent of the time.

But two of Bush's defeats on defense and foreign policy were short-lived, showing the president's ability to refocus after a loss and work with Congress behind the scenes to shift legislative language closer to his position.

In July, against the president's wishes, the House passed an intelligence authorization bill that included a provision Bush opposed: an independent commission on the Sept. 11 terrorist attacks. By the time he signed the legislation into law (PL 107-306), the commission's role had grown, but he had gained the right to appoint the chairman.

"He always said in Texas that he was able to reach out to Democrats and work with them," said Weinstein of the Hudson Institute. "And here, he has shown he can reach out and run with an idea his opponents proposed."

Bush also lost an initial House vote on a provision in the fiscal 2003 defense authorization bill that would have allowed disabled military retirees to collect both pensions and disability payments. Bush declared that too expensive, but the administration later struck a deal that permitted "concurrent receipt" of payments to retirees with combat-related disabilities (PL 107-314).

As he demonstrated during the first year of his administration, Bush often chooses to declare victory when Congress has moved only as far in his direction as it is willing to go.

House Democrats and Republicans working on a major farm policy rewrite (HR 2646) ignored administration warnings that the bill's crop subsidy increases would lead to overproduction and lower prices.

But after the Senate passed a more expensive version, the administration embraced the House bill as the more palatable alternative. The White House worked to make the cost of the final measure closer to the House figure, and endorsed the final deal (PL 107-171). Bush also got two things he wanted: resumption of food stamp benefits for legal immigrants and an agreement to delete a provision that would have relaxed restrictions on trading food and medicine with Cuba. ◆

Votes on Partisan Issues Decline

Some of the most partisan congressional battles of 2002 never made it to a floor vote — making the House and Senate appear, statistically speaking, much more bipartisan than they were.

Congressional observers said an agenda that focused on national security and international terrorism contributed to the recent decline in partisan voting. Only 45 percent of the votes in the Senate pitted a majority of one party against a majority of the other, a 10-percentage-point decline from 2001. In the House, 43 percent of the roll calls developed into these sort of "party unity votes" calculated annually by Congressional Quarterly — an increase from the 40 percent figure of the previous year but identical to the percentage in 2000.

President Bush's "domestic agenda really just dropped off the table for quite a while," said David T. Canon, a political science professor at the University of Wisconsin at Madison. "The controversial domestic agenda has been basically postponed."

Little was even attempted on such frequently polarizing topics as taxes and Social Security, Canon said. In addition, Congress did not clear any of the 11 non-defense appropriations bills in 2002, which reduced the number of partisan fights. In 2001, a single spending bill — the one that funds veterans, housing, space and environmental programs — provoked 14 partisan votes in the House and two in the Senate. In 2002, that bill was one of eight that never came to the

floor in either chamber. Congressional leaders have committed to clearing the unfinished fiscal 2003 spending bills at the start of the 108th Congress before tackling another budget cycle. That effort could bring a rash of partisan votes on controversial amendments that Congress managed to avoid.

In raw numbers, the Senate had 115 party unity votes in 2002, 95 fewer than in 2001. The House had 209 such votes, five more than the year before but 50 fewer than in 2000. Behind the low numbers, particularly in the Senate, was a lack of agreement on many issues, particularly appropriations and energy policy. When a measure seemed unlikely to pass, leaders dropped it.

House Republican leaders, to no one's surprise, blamed the Democratic-controlled Senate for the lack of action on appropriations bills, as well as some other measures. Roy Blunt of Missouri, the incoming House Republican whip, said the Democratic Senate's inability to adopt its version of a fiscal 2003 budget resolution (S Con Res 100) was a primary factor in thwarting progress on appropriations bills. "It's very difficult in an election year to ask our members to take votes that are challenging for them when they know that the Senate doesn't have" a budget plan, he said.

House GOP leaders, for their part, failed to resolve a dispute between appropriators and fiscal conservatives over spending levels, holding up consideration of the non-defense measures.

PARTY UNITY ▸ Partisan Voting by Chamber

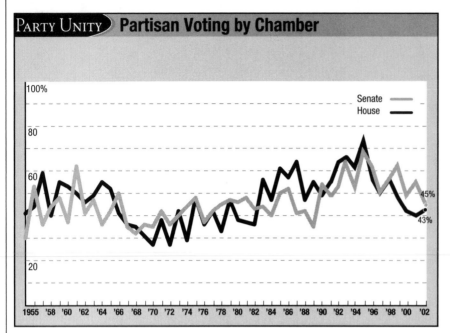

2002 Data			
	PARTISAN VOTES	TOTAL VOTES	PERCENTAGE
Senate	115	253	45%
House	209	483	43%

For More Information

No Tax Cut Fight

In 2001, the battle over Bush's tax cut (PL 107-16) produced 49 Senate party unity votes, the most of any issue that year. No such significant fiscal fight was on the agenda this time. (*2001 Almanac, p. 18-3*)

In 2002, the Senate recorded the most party unity votes, 21, on an energy package (S 517) that ultimately went unfinished and likely will be revisited by the 108th Congress.

Overall, the Senate saw its fewest number of party unity votes since 1989. And the percentage of Senate votes that were partisan was the lowest it has been since that year as well.

While the GOP-led House saw a slight increase in the percentage of partisan votes since 2001, the figure remained below 50 percent for the fourth year in a row. The votes that did divide the parties in the House included seven "question of privilege" procedure motions and five resolutions urging Senate action on House-passed bills.

Shrinking Moderates

For all the talk of the power held by Republican moderates and conservative Democrats, it rarely showed on floor votes in either chamber. Moderates in both chambers spent the year "picking and choosing their fights," said Sarah Binder, a political science professor at George Washington University who has studied voting patterns. In the House in particular, she said, "when push comes to shove, they quite often vote with their leadership."

Just one House vote turned on the conservative Blue Dog coalition of Democrats. That vote, on a rent-to-own contracts bill (HR 1701), succeeded by a 14-vote margin. Nineteen of the 33 Blue Dogs supported the measure, which most Democrats voted against, helping to offset the opposition of 43 Republicans.

In the Senate, centrists who tried to cobble together legislative compromises often found their work ignored or bypassed. Their limited impact was illustrated on the bill (PL 107-296) creating a new Department of Homeland Security.

Amid the bipartisan haste at the end of the session to clear the measure and adjourn for the year, the centrists gave up their fight against several provisions in the bill that some considered "pork." The bill passed 90-9, and the centrists settled for a promise that their complaints would be revisited in 2003.

Sen. Blanche Lincoln, D-Ark., vowed that she and other moderates would continue to "reach out to everybody, even the most unlikely people," in the quest for compromise. "Even though the majority has changed, the margins are still close," Lincoln said. "The leadership has the opportunity to either work in a bipartisan way or not."

In the Senate, just 28 votes were decided by five votes or less, limiting the ability of the small group of centrists to affect the outcome. Eight of those were cloture votes to cut off debate and proceed to a vote, and all failed. In a chamber where much of the heavy lifting occurs before floor action, none of the tight votes in the Senate came on final passage of a bill.

GOP More Unified

Both parties showed they could bring their dissidents closer to the fold than in previous years. Republicans continued their tendency to be the more ideologically homogenous party, and the departure of some high-profile moderates in the House will bolster that trend. "Our conference is a pretty conservative one," Blunt said.

Constance A. Morella of Maryland was defeated Nov. 5; Greg Ganske of Iowa lost a bid for the Senate; and Marge Roukema of New Jersey and Benjamin A. Gilman of New York retired.

Jim Kolbe of Arizona, a GOP moderate on social issues, said losing Morella and the others did not portend tougher times for GOP moderates. "I wouldn't read too much into that," Kolbe said.

But Brian L. Lawson, an assistant professor of political science at the University of Cincinnati and former House aide, said having lawmakers who are able to reach across party lines can be a benefit. "In terms of the internal organization of the House, it's not helpful if you don't have those people there," Lawson said.

Some leading Democrats disagree. "We have found that the moderates in the Republican caucus very often, when it makes

Leading Scorers: Party Unity

Support indicates those who in 2002 voted most often with their party's majority against the other party. **Opposition** shows those who voted most often against their party's majority. Scores are based on actual votes cast. Members who missed half or more of the votes are not listed. Scores are rounded to one decimal; lawmakers with identical scores are listed alphabetically.

Senate Support

Republicans		Democrats	
Nickles, Okla.	99.1%	Wellstone, Minn.	100.0%
Lott, Miss.	98.2	Sarbanes, Md.	98.3
Frist, Tenn.	97.4	Leahy, Vt.	98.2
Bunning, Ky.	97.4	Reed, R.I.	98.2
McConnell, Ky.	96.5	Durbin, Ill.	97.4
Kyl, Ariz.	96.5	Kennedy, Mass.	97.3
Inhofe, Okla.	96.3	Mikulski, Md.	96.5
Roberts, Kan.	95.6	Corzine, N.J.	95.6
Santorum, Pa.	95.6	Dayton, Minn.	95.5
Thomas, Wyo.	95.6	Levin, Mich.	94.8
Gramm, Texas	95.5	Stabenow, Mich.	94.8
		Schumer, N.Y.	94.7
		Boxer, Calif.	94.7

Senate Opposition

Republicans		Democrats	
Chafee, R.I.	45.6%	Miller, Ga.	60.0%
Collins, Maine	42.6	Nelson, Neb.	48.7
Snowe, Maine	42.6	Breaux, La.	44.7
Specter, Pa.	39.8	Lincoln, Ark.	39.5
Smith, Ore.	34.2	Landrieu, La.	35.4
Fitzgerald, Ill.	22.6	Baucus, Mont.	33.3
McCain, Ariz.	20.0	Cleland, Ga.	31.3
Shelby, Ala.	19.6	Bayh, Ind.	29.8
Gregg, N.H.	18.8	Carper, Del.	26.1
Warner, Va.	18.0	Graham, Fla.	23.5
Campbell, Colo.	17.9	Nelson, Fla.	22.8
		Bingaman, N.M.	21.8
		Daschle, S.D.	20.0

House Support

Republicans		Democrats	
Riley, Ala.	99.4%	Becerra, Calif.	100.0%
Cantor, Va.	99.0	Solis, Calif.	100.0
Keller, Fla.	99.0	McGovern, Mass.	99.0
Sessions, Texas	99.0	Markey, Mass.	99.0
Armey, Texas	99.0	Tierney, Mass.	99.0
Miller, Calif.	99.0	Olver, Mass.	99.0
Vitter, La.	99.0	Velázquez, N.Y.	99.0
Largent, Okla.	98.9	Coyne, Pa.	99.0
Stump, Ariz.	98.6	Filner, Calif.	99.0
Goodlatte, Va.	98.6	Conyers, Mich.	99.0
Culberson, Texas	98.5	Roybal-Allard, Calif.	99.0
DeLay, Texas	98.5	Schakowsky, Ill.	99.0
Everett, Ala.	98.5	Stark, Calif.	99.0
Wicker, Miss.	98.5		
Pence, Ind.	98.5		
Doolittle, Calif.	98.5		

House Opposition

Republicans		Democrats	
Morella, Md.	42.2%	Hall, Texas	59.6%
Leach, Iowa	28.6	Lucas, Ky.	58.4
Johnson, Conn.	24.6	Shows, Miss.	40.9
Paul, Texas	24.4	Stenholm, Texas	40.6
Gilman, N.Y.	23.4	Cramer, Ala.	39.3
Simmons, Conn.	22.3	Taylor, Miss.	36.5
Houghton, N.Y.	22.0	John, La.	36.0
Horn, Calif.	21.4	Peterson, Minn.	35.8
Boehlert, N.Y.	21.1	Barcia, Mich.	35.7
Castle, Del.	20.6	Holden, Pa.	32.5
		Phelps, Ill.	30.8
		Tanner, Tenn.	29.6

a difference, aren't there," said Steny H. Hoyer, D-Md.

The list of lawmakers who were willing to buck their parties frequently in 2002 contains few surprises, although the leading opposition scores were lower than in 2001.

The exceptions in the Senate were Democrats Zell Miller of Georgia, Ben Nelson of Nebraska and John B. Breaux of Louisiana, each of whom posted higher opposition scores than in 2001. Miller joined Republicans on 60 percent of party unity votes, the highest percentage in the Senate. "Miller is way over there," Binder said.

Lincoln Chafee of Rhode Island led Senate Republicans in voting against a majority of his party for the third straight year, although in 2002 his opposition score of 46 percent was lower than in 2001, when it was 50 percent, or than in 2000, when it was 63 percent.

For the second consecutive year, Morella was the only

House Republican who voted against her party more than 30 percent of the time. Her opposition score of 42 percent was higher than in 2001, yet still one of the lowest in her House career.

House Democrats, meanwhile, had 12 lawmakers who hit the 30 percent opposition mark, not counting James A. Traficant Jr. of Ohio, who voted only once before being expelled July 24. *(Ethics, p. 1-14)*

The top Democratic maverick in the House was Ralph M. Hall of Texas, who sided with Republicans 60 percent of the time. That is less than the previous year, when he joined the GOP on three of every four party unity votes.

The list of the most loyal House Democrats was dominated by lawmakers from California, New York and Massachusetts; 16 of the top 20 scorers hailed from those three states. ◆

Voting Participation Still High

When Thomas M. Barrett missed a House vote in March on legislation requiring life imprisonment for repeat child sex offenders, Wisconsin Republicans pounced. State GOP Chairman Rick Graber said the Milwaukee Democrat, who was running for governor at the time, owed the people of the state an explanation for why he "skipped the chance to crack down on child molesters."

Barrett sought to defuse the criticism, explaining he had missed the vote, and 11 others that week, because he was having hernia surgery. He eventually lost the primary to state Attorney General Jim Doyle, who went on to win the governorship. But Barrett spokesman Brigid O'Brien said the missed votes in no way contributed to the defeat.

Members of Congress now answer the call to vote "yea" or "nay" from the wells of the chambers of the House and Senate far more frequently than they once did — a collective 94.8 percent of the time in 2002. Although that was a slight decrease from the 96.5 percent recorded the previous year, the 2002 score made this the 10th consecutive year when the overall congressional voting participation score hovered around 95 percent. The score only routinely climbed above 90 percent in the 1980s; it had never risen above that benchmark until 1975, and during the 1960s it rarely met or exceeded 85 percent.

The consistency of the high voting participation rates of the past decade appears attributable to a combination of reasons, including a desire among members to avoid the political danger of being seen as not doing their jobs, and the fact that congressional leaders now schedule roll calls in a way that makes it easier for members to cast their votes.

Voting is "what it's all about," argued the Senate's historian, Richard A. Baker. "If you can't be there to vote on a fairly reasonable basis, what's more important than that?"

Maintaining a good record of voting has been made easier by the leaderships of both parties on both sides of the Capitol. In recent years, they have collectively bent over backward to schedule the lion's share of recorded votes in the middle of the week, to inconvenience the fewest number of colleagues with long commutes back to their home districts.

The Barrett incident highlights another motivator: the potential for too many missed votes to make a lawmaker vulnerable to defeat. But this article of faith among political strategists does not appear to be borne out by the election results of recent years, which reveal no noticeable correlation between voting participation scores and political survival.

Overall, in 2002, senators logged a 96.3 percent voter participation rate, down from 98.2 percent in 2001. Since 1954, CQ has found that voting participation has declined in almost every election year, then increased slightly in the year between elections. However, the Senate held only 253 recorded votes in 2002, one-third fewer than the 380 in 2001. That sharp drop was largely the result of partisan gridlock, where agreements to bring legislation to the floor were hard to come by.

In the House, voter participation dipped to 94.6 percent, or 1.6 percentage points lower than in 2001. The 483 votes on which a "yea" or "nay" was called was a slight drop from the 507 of the year before.

House and Senate freshmen, traditionally the most vulnerable in re-elections, performed better than the chambers as a whole. Their combined voter participation rate was 97.9 percent.

House freshman Jim Langevin, D-R.I., is a good example of the participation trends. He did not miss one of the 507 voting opportunities he had during his first year in Congress. In 2002, he slipped, missing two votes when, he said, he was caught at a meeting too far away from the Capitol to make it back.

Some Capitol Hill veterans advise freshmen to miss a couple of less important votes early on to avoid starting a streak that could become all-consuming. Langevin rejected that counsel.

"I see it as my primary responsibility to vote and speak on behalf of my constituents," he said. "I take every vote as critically important."

Senate historian Baker argued that members do not have much of an ex-

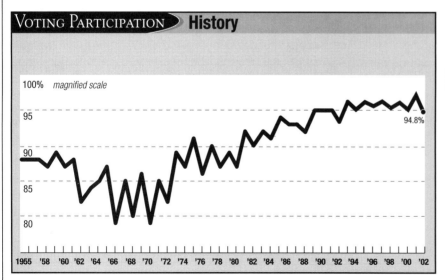

VOTING PARTICIPATION ▶ History

100% *magnified scale*
95 — 94.8%
90
85
80

1955 '58 '60 '62 '64 '66 '68 '70 '72 '74 '76 '78 '80 '82 '84 '86 '88 '90 '92 '94 '96 '98 '00 '02

2002 Data		
	RECORDED VOTES	PARTICIPATION RATE
Senate	253	96.3%
House	483	94.6%
Total	736	94.8%

For More Information	

cuse to miss votes these days, given the accommodations of their leadership and the improved transportation that makes it easier than ever for lawmakers to return to Washington.

But former Rep. Bill Frenzel, R-Minn. (1971-91), contended that a high voting participation rate is not the only measuring stick by which to judge lawmakers, who juggle many responsibilities. For instance, he said, should a member skip out on a meeting with a constituent to vote on a meaningless resolution?

"Sometimes congressmen have more important things to do than vote," said Frenzel, now a guest scholar at the Brookings Institution.

Frenzel also said that while he traditionally had a voting participation rate near the bottom of his state delegation, "Only one chap ever brought it up in an election contest. . . . I invited him to single out which one I missed that I should have voted on. The guy had no way to explain that, and it all went away."

Leading Scorers: Voting Participation

The following 27 lawmakers were the only to cast "yea" or "nay" votes on every roll call ballot conducted in 2002:

HOUSE REPUBLICANS
John Boozman of Arkansas
Michael N. Castle of Delaware
Ander Crenshaw of Florida
Tom Latham of Iowa
Frank A. LoBiondo of New Jersey
Mike Rogers of Michigan
Pat Tiberi of Ohio
Fred Upton of Michigan

HOUSE DEMOCRATS
Marion Berry of Arkansas
Susan A. Davis of California
Bob Etheridge of North Carolina
Jesse L. Jackson Jr. of Illinois
Dale E. Kildee of Michigan
Michael R. McNulty of New York

SENATE REPUBLICANS
Susan Collins of Maine
Charles E. Grassley of Iowa
Richard G. Lugar of Indiana
Olympia J. Snowe of Maine

SENATE DEMOCRATS
Maria Cantwell of Washington
John Edwards of North Carolina
Russell D. Feingold of Wisconsin
Bob Graham of Florida
Ernest F. Hollings of South Carolina
Herb Kohl of Wisconsin
Carl Levin of Michigan
Debbie Stabenow of Michigan
Ron Wyden of Oregon

NOTE: Independent Dean Barkley of Minnesota voted on all of the 14 Senate roll calls for which he was eligible after being appointed Nov. 4.

Case Studies

Results from the November election suggest that voting participation is not a key factor in the outcome of a campaign. For example, Illinois Democrat Rod R. Blagojevich took heat this year for missing House votes as he campaigned for governor. He won the race easily, despite posting the fourth worst voter participation score — 56 percent — among House members this year. And Republican Bob Riley won his race for governor of Alabama despite having a 58 percent voting participation rate in the House.

But the flip side of a low voting record often means a heavy campaign schedule back home, which would be expected to help a candidate's prospects.

In fact, staying in Washington to vote might hinder a candidate. Republican Rep. John Thune made it to 99 percent of the votes in the House and nonetheless narrowly lost his bid for the Senate in South Dakota against incumbent Democrat Tim Johnson, who himself had a 98 percent participation score.

There have been mixed results on the voting participation's effectiveness as a campaign weapon. For instance, in his 1998 campaign for a fourth Senate term, New York Republican Alfonse M. D'Amato hammered Democratic Rep. Charles E. Schumer for having a poor voting participation record. There were several other factors in the race, and Schumer won anyway.

And a strong voting record was not enough to save GOP Rep. Jay C. Kim of California, who in 1997 pleaded guilty to accepting $250,000 in illegal contributions during his first run for Congress. Kim touted his near-perfect voting streak in his 1998 bid for a fourth House term, but it did not work; he lost in the primary.

But two decades earlier, Republican Rudy Boschwitz was able to capitalize on the extended absences of incumbent Democrat Wendell Anderson (1976-78) from the Senate to beat the Democrat. The story of that Minnesota Senate contest still looms in the minds of some as the best example of someone's poor voting attendance sealing his fate.

"If you miss a few votes, it's not important. But if you miss a whole series, it is important," said Boschwitz, who served for 12 years and is now chairman of the family business in Minneapolis. Indeed, as Boschwitz still remembers, Anderson had the second worst voting record in the Senate in 1978 — making it to only 49 percent of the votes.

Democrat William H. Natcher of Kentucky remains something of a legend on Capitol Hill, casting 18,401 consecutive roll call votes between the start of his House career in 1953 and March 2, 1994, when he was wheeled into the House chamber on a gurney to cast his final ballot. He died four weeks later.

Though they may not be trying to match that streak, 14 House members — five of them freshmen — posted 100 percent voting records. Thirteen senators in office all year also posted perfect scores. (*Leading scorers, above*)

Iowa Republican Charles E. Grassley extended the longest active voting streak in the Senate to nine consecutive years and 3,364 votes. In the House, Michigan Republican Fred Upton has the longest active perfect record: He has not missed the last 2,732 votes since 1998.

On the other end of the spectrum, James A. Traficant Jr. compiled a microscopic 0.3 percent voting participation score. The Ohio Democrat voted just once in 344 votes for which he was eligible. He was convicted on federal racketeering charges in April; the House expelled him in July.

In the Senate, the retiring Jesse Helms, R-N.C., who underwent heart surgery, had the lowest voting rate of any senator, with 38 percent. ◆

Presidential Support Background

Congressional Quarterly selects roll call votes for its presidential support study based on statements made by the president or his authorized spokesmen.

Members' **support** shows the percentage of the time members voted *in agreement* with the president. **Opposition** shows the percentage of the time members voted *against* the president's position.

Presidential **success** is the percentage of the selected votes on which the president prevailed. Absences lower parties' scores. Scores for 2001 are given for comparison.

Presidential Success by Issue

"Economic affairs" includes votes on trade and on omnibus and supplemental spending bills, which may fund both domestic and defense/foreign policy programs. "Average" column only, includes Senate confirmation votes.

	Defense/Foreign Policy		Domestic		Economic Affairs		Average	
	2002	2001	2002	2001	2002	2001	2002	2001
Senate	100%	67%	0%	68%	76%	89%	91%	88%
House	62	75	91	78	94	94	83	84
Congress	67	71	83	73	85	92	88	87

Average Presidential Support by Party

	Support					Opposition			
	Republicans		Democrats				Republicans		Democrats	
	2002	2001	2002	2001			2002	2001	2002	2001
Senate	89%	94%	71%	66%		**Senate**	5%	4%	26%	32%
House	82	86	32	31		**House**	15	12	64	67

Average Presidential Support by Region *

	Support									Opposition							
	East		West		South		Midwest			East		West		South		Midwest	
	2002	2001	2002	2001	2002	2001	2002	2001		2002	2001	2002	2001	2002	2001	2002	2001
Republicans									**Republicans**								
Senate	89%	91%	89%	93%	86%	94%	93%	96%	**Senate**	7%	9%	5%	3%	4%	3%	3%	3%
House	79	80	83	86	83	88	82	84	**House**	17	18	14	11	14	9	14	14
Democrats									**Democrats**								
Senate	66	65	72	65	79	69	70	65	**Senate**	29	34	24	32	18	28	28	34
House	30	29	27	29	39	37	31	29	**House**	66	69	70	69	58	60	63	68

Presidential Success Rate History

Average score for both chambers of Congress

Eisenhower		**Johnson**		**Ford**				**Clinton**	
1953	89.0%	1964	88.0%	1974	58.2%	1983	67.1	1993	86.4%
1954	82.8	1965	93.0	1975	61.0	1984	65.8	1994	86.4
1955	75.0	1966	79.0	1976	53.8	1985	59.9	1995	36.2
1956	70.0	1967	79.0			1986	56.1	1996	55.1
1957	68.0	1968	75.0	**Carter**		1987	43.5	1997	53.6
1958	76.0			1977	75.4%	1988	47.4	1998	50.6
1959	52.0	**Nixon**		1978	78.3			1999	37.8
1960	65.0	1969	74.0%	1979	76.8	**Bush**		2000	55.0
		1970	77.0	1980	75.1	1989	62.6%	**Bush**	
Kennedy		1971	75.0			1990	46.8	2001	87.0%
1961	81.0%	1972	66.0	**Reagan**		1991	54.2	2002	87.8
1962	85.4	1973	50.6	1981	82.4%	1992	43.0		
1963	87.1	1974	59.6	1982	72.4				

* **Regions:** Congressional Quarterly defines regions of the United States as follows: **East:** Conn., Del., Maine, Md., Mass., N.H., N.J., N.Y., Pa., R.I., Vt., W.Va. **West:** Alaska, Ariz., Calif., Colo., Hawaii, Idaho, Mont., Nev., N.M., Ore., Utah, Wash., Wyo. **South:** Ala., Ark., Fla., Ga., Ky., La., Miss., N.C., Okla., S.C., Tenn., Texas, Va. **Midwest:** Ill., Ind., Iowa, Kan., Mich., Minn., Mo., Neb., N.D., Ohio, S.D., Wis.

2002 House Presidential Position Votes

The following is a list of 40 House roll-call votes in 2002 on which the president took a clear position. Votes are listed by roll-call number in broad categories and identified by topic.

Domestic Policy

10 Victories

Vote Number	Description
62	Class action suits
97	Abortion
133	Nuclear waste
170	Welfare
256	Crime
343	Abortion
357	Federal employees
359	Liability
412	Abortion
421	Medical malpractice

1 Defeat

Vote Number	Description
336	Federal employees

Economic Affairs

15 Victories

Vote Number	Description
79	Budget
92	Pensions
103	Taxes
130	Trade (steel tariffs)
206	Appropriations
207	Taxes
208	Taxes
217	Taxes
219	Taxes
229	Taxes
248	Taxes
279	Debt limit
328	Appropriations
329	Trade (Vietnam)
370	Trade (fast track)

1 Defeat

Vote Number	Description
371	Taxes

Defense and Foreign Policy

8 Victories

Vote Number	Description
53	Border security
145	Missile defense
333	Cuba
365	Visas
367	Homeland security
455	Iraq
476	Sept. 11 commission
477	Homeland security

5 Defeats

Vote Number	Description
176	Terrorism victims
292	Arming pilots
331	Cuba
347	Sept. 11 commission
463	Military retiree benefits

House Success Score

Victories	33
Defeats	7
Total	40
Success rate	**82.5%**

2002 Senate Presidential Position Votes

The following is a list of 58 Senate roll call votes in 2002 on which the president took a clear position. Votes are listed by roll call number in broad categories and identified by topic.

Domestic Policy

0 Victories

Vote Number	Description

1 Defeat

Vote Number	Description
30	Farm bill

Defense and Foreign Policy

2 Victories

Vote Number	Description
237	Iraq
249	Homeland security

0 Defeats

Vote Number	Description

Economic Affairs and Trade

13 Victories

Vote Number	Description
112	Trade (fast track)
113	Trade (fast track)
115	Trade (fast track)
121	Trade (fast track)
123	Trade (fast track)
127	Trade (fast track)
128	Trade (fast track)
130	Trade (fast track)
148	Debt limit
159	Budget
188	Appropriations
207	Trade (fast track)
252	Terrorism insurance

4 Defeats

Vote Number	Description
110	Trade (fast track)
143	Appropriations
151	Taxes
212	Appropriations

Nominations

38 Victories (0 Defeats)

Vote Number	Description	Vote Number	Description
4	Marcia S. Krieger	205	Henry E. Autrey
5	James C. Mahan	208	Terrence F. McVerry
11	Callie V. Granade	211	Kenneth A. Marra
12	Philip R. Martinez	213	Timothy J. Corrigan
21	Michael J. Melloy	216	Arthur J. Schwab
22	Jay C. Zainey	219	Reena Raggi
35	Robert E. Blackburn	250	Dennis W. Shedd
37	Cindy K. Jorgenson		
46	Ralph R. Beistline		
51	David C. Bury		
52	Randy Crane		
68	Terrence L. O'Brien		
69	Lance M. Africk		
76	Legrome D. Davis		
79	Jeffrey R. Howard		
85	Percy Anderson		
86	John F. Walter		
95	Joan E. Lancaster		
96	William C. Griesbach		
98	Michael M. Baylson		
99	Cynthia M. Rufe		
104	Leonard E. Davis		
105	Andrew S. Hanen		
106	Samuel H. Mays Jr.		
107	Thomas M. Rose		
108	Paul G. Cassell		
184	Richard R. Clifton		
194	Julia Smith Gibbons		
195	Joy Flowers Conti		
196	John E. Jones III		
202	D. Brooks Smith		

Senate Success Score

Victories	53
Defeats	5
Total	58
Success rate	**91.4%**

ALABAMA	1	2	3
Shelby	87	13	90
Sessions	88	12	88
ALASKA			
Stevens	95	5	98
Murkowski	96	4	84
ARIZONA			
McCain	90	10	90
Kyl	96	4	95
ARKANSAS			
Hutchinson	98	2	83
Lincoln	89	11	98
CALIFORNIA			
Feinstein	76	24	100
Boxer	65	35	93
COLORADO			
Campbell	91	9	97
Allard	96	4	98
CONNECTICUT			
Dodd	68	32	91
Lieberman	77	23	97
DELAWARE			
Biden	77	23	97
Carper	79	21	98
FLORIDA			
Graham	79	21	100
Nelson	78	22	95
GEORGIA			
Cleland	78	22	100
Miller	92	8	84
HAWAII			
Inouye	76	24	88
Akaka	63	37	a84
IDAHO			
Craig	95	5	95
Crapo	96	4	97
ILLINOIS			
Fitzgerald	95	5	100
Durbin	67	33	98
INDIANA			
Lugar	100	0	100
Bayh	79	21	100

IOWA	1	2	3
Grassley	95	5	100
Harkin	69	31	93
KANSAS			
Brownback	98	2	90
Roberts	96	4	91
KENTUCKY			
McConnell	96	4	91
Bunning	96	4	98
LOUISIANA			
Breaux	88	12	100
Landrieu	84	16	95
MAINE			
Snowe	90	10	100
Collins	88	12	100
MARYLAND			
Sarbanes	65	35	98
Mikulski	68	32	97
MASSACHUSETTS			
Kennedy	64	36	95
Kerry	72	28	93
MICHIGAN			
Levin	66	34	100
Stabenow	66	34	100
MINNESOTA			
Wellstone[1]	65	35	95
Dayton	68	32	97
MISSISSIPPI			
Cochran	96	4	95
Lott	100	0	97
MISSOURI			
Bond	98	2	91
Carnahan	72	28	98
MONTANA			
Burns	93	7	97
Baucus	88	12	100
NEBRASKA			
Hagel	98	2	100
Nelson	91	9	97
NEVADA			
Reid	71	29	100
Ensign	96	4	95

NEW HAMPSHIRE	1	2	3
Smith	96	4	93
Gregg	96	4	93
NEW JERSEY			
Torricelli	66	34	86
Corzine	64	36	91
NEW MEXICO			
Domenici	96	4	91
Bingaman	79	21	98
NEW YORK			
Schumer	68	32	97
Clinton	67	33	98
NORTH CAROLINA			
Helms	100	0	28
Edwards	76	24	100
NORTH DAKOTA			
Conrad	66	34	100
Dorgan	70	30	97
OHIO			
DeWine	98	2	95
Voinovich	96	4	91
OKLAHOMA			
Nickles	98	2	97
Inhofe	96	4	93
OREGON			
Wyden	74	26	100
Smith	91	9	93
PENNSYLVANIA			
Specter	89	11	91
Santorum	96	4	93
RHODE ISLAND			
Reed	66	34	97
Chafee	93	7	100
SOUTH CAROLINA			
Thurmond	93	7	97
Hollings	71	29	100
SOUTH DAKOTA			
Daschle	75	25	98
Johnson	68	32	98
TENNESSEE			
Thompson	100	0	90
Frist	100	0	97

Key

Democrats • **Republicans**
Independents

TEXAS	1	2	3
Gramm	96	4	97
Hutchison	96	4	95
UTAH			
Hatch	98	2	98
Bennett	98	2	95
VERMONT			
Leahy	67	33	98
Jeffords	71	29	95
VIRGINIA			
Warner	91	9	93
Allen	93	7	100
WASHINGTON			
Murray	75	25	98
Cantwell	81	19	100
WEST VIRGINIA			
Byrd	70	30	98
Rockefeller	71	29	100
WISCONSIN			
Kohl	79	21	100
Feingold	67	33	100
WYOMING			
Thomas	94	6	91
Enzi	93	7	95

ND Northern Democrats   SD Southern Democrats

Southern states - Ala., Ark., Fla., Ga., Ky., La., Miss., N.C., Okla., S.C., Tenn., Texas, Va.

Presidential Support
and Opposition: Senate

1. Presidential Support Score. Percentage of recorded votes cast in 2002 on which President Bush took a position and on which the senator voted "yea" or "nay" in agreement with the president's position. Failure to vote did not lower an individual's score.

2. Presidential Opposition Score. Percentage of recorded votes cast in 2002 on which President Bush took a position and on which the senator voted "yea" or "nay" in disagreement with the president's position. Failure to vote did not lower an individual's score.

3. Participation in Presidential Support Votes. Percentage of the 58 recorded Senate votes on which President Bush took a position and on which the senator was present and voted "yea" or "nay."

[1] *Sen. Dean Barkley, I-Minn., was sworn in Nov. 12, 2002, to replace Sen. Paul Wellstone, D-Minn., who died Oct. 25, 2002. The first vote for which Barkley was eligible was vote 240. Barkley was eligible for three presidential position votes. His presidential support score was 67 percent. The last vote for which Wellstone was eligible was vote 239. Wellstone was eligible for 55 presidential position votes.*

Presidential Support
and Opposition: House

1. Presidential Support Score. Percentage of recorded votes cast in 2002 on which President Bush took a position and on which the member voted "yea" or "nay" in agreement with the president's position. Failure to vote did not lower an individual's score.

2. Presidential Opposition Score. Percentage of recorded votes cast in 2002 on which President Bush took a position and on which the member voted "yea" or "nay" in disagreement with the president's position. Failure to vote did not lower an individual's score.

3. Participation in Presidential Support Votes. Percentage of the 40 recorded House votes on which President Bush took a position and on which a member was present and voted "yea" or "nay."

[1] Rep. Patsy T. Mink, D-Hawaii, died Sept. 28, 2002. The last vote for which she was eligible was vote 423. Mink was eligible for 36 presidential position votes.

[2] The Speaker votes only at his discretion, usually to break a tie or to emphasize the importance of a matter.

[3] Rep. Tony P. Hall, D-Ohio, resigned effective Sept. 9, 2002. The last vote for which he was eligible was vote 377. He was eligible for 34 presidential position votes.

[4] Rep. James A. Traficant Jr., D-Ohio, was expelled from the House of Representatives July 24, 2002. The last vote for which he was eligible was vote 346. He was eligible for 27 presidential position votes.

[5] Rep. John Sullivan, R-Okla., was sworn in Feb. 27, 2002. The first vote for which he was eligible was vote 42. Sullivan was eligible for 40 presidential position votes. Sullivan succeeds Republican Steve Largent, who resigned effective Feb. 15, 2002, to run for governor of Oklahoma. The last vote for which Largent was eligible was vote 38. He was eligible for no presidential position votes.

[6] Rep. Virgil H. Goode Jr. of Virginia switched his party affiliation from independent to Republican, effective Aug. 1, 2002.

Key

Democrats • **Republicans**
Independents

	1	2	3
ALABAMA			
1 *Callahan*	84	16	78
2 *Everett*	85	15	98
3 *Riley*	81	19	78
4 *Aderholt*	82	18	100
5 Cramer	62	38	98
6 *Bachus*	89	11	90
7 Hilliard	17	83	90
ALASKA			
AL *Young*	86	14	93
ARIZONA			
1 *Flake*	70	30	100
2 Pastor	28	72	100
3 *Stump*	90	10	75
4 *Shadegg*	87	13	98
5 *Kolbe*	82	18	100
6 *Hayworth*	85	15	98
ARKANSAS			
1 Berry	42	58	100
2 Snyder	41	59	98
3 *Boozman*	85	15	100
4 Ross	50	50	100
CALIFORNIA			
1 Thompson	26	74	95
2 *Herger*	82	18	100
3 *Ose*	84	16	93
4 *Doolittle*	84	16	93
5 Matsui	24	76	95
6 Woolsey	25	75	100
7 Miller	22	78	100
8 Pelosi	23	77	98
9 Lee	25	75	100
10 Tauscher	35	65	100
11 *Pombo*	84	16	93
12 Lantos	20	80	100
13 Stark	23	77	98
14 Eshoo	24	76	95
15 Honda	21	79	98
16 Lofgren	15	85	100
17 Farr	25	75	100
18 Condit	44	56	85
19 *Radanovich*	89	11	95
20 Dooley	51	49	98
21 *Thomas*	90	10	98
22 Capps	32	68	100
23 *Gallegly*	82	18	100
24 Sherman	28	72	100
25 *McKeon*	90	10	100
26 Berman	24	76	93
27 Schiff	32	68	95
28 *Dreier*	92	8	100
29 Waxman	25	75	90
30 Becerra	23	77	98
31 Solis	18	82	95
32 Watson	16	84	93
33 Roybal-Allard	22	78	100
34 Napolitano	21	79	98
35 Waters	21	79	98
36 Harman	42	58	100
37 Millender-McD.	27	73	93
38 *Horn*	77	23	98

	1	2	3
39 *Royce*	82	18	100
40 *Lewis*	87	13	95
41 *Miller*	90	10	98
42 Baca	28	72	98
43 *Calvert*	89	11	95
44 *Bono*	84	16	95
45 *Rohrabacher*	77	23	98
46 Sanchez	21	79	95
47 *Cox*	86	14	93
48 *Issa*	85	15	98
49 Davis	35	65	100
50 Filner	22	78	100
51 *Cunningham*	86	14	93
52 *Hunter*	78	22	100
COLORADO			
1 DeGette	25	75	100
2 Udall	33	67	98
3 *McInnis*	89	11	95
4 *Schaffer*	85	15	100
5 *Hefley*	85	15	100
6 *Tancredo*	76	24	95
CONNECTICUT			
1 Larson	30	70	100
2 *Simmons*	78	22	100
3 DeLauro	22	78	100
4 *Shays*	82	18	100
5 Maloney	45	55	100
6 *Johnson*	75	25	100
DELAWARE			
AL *Castle*	78	22	100
FLORIDA			
1 *Miller*	85	15	100
2 Boyd	50	50	100
3 Brown	29	71	95
4 *Crenshaw*	90	10	100
5 Thurman	34	66	95
6 *Stearns*	82	18	83
7 *Mica*	90	10	98
8 *Keller*	87	13	98
9 *Bilirakis*	87	13	98
10 *Young*	88	12	100
11 Davis	48	52	100
12 *Putnam*	88	12	100
13 *Miller*	87	13	98
14 *Goss*	92	8	100
15 *Weldon*	85	15	100
16 *Foley*	90	10	100
17 Meek	31	69	98
18 *Ros-Lehtinen*	85	15	100
19 Wexler	29	71	95
20 Deutsch	41	59	93
21 *Diaz-Balart*	87	13	95
22 *Shaw*	92	8	100
23 Hastings	27	73	93
GEORGIA			
1 *Kingston*	85	15	100
2 Bishop	52	48	100
3 *Collins*	82	18	98
4 McKinney	20	80	88
5 Lewis	21	79	83
6 *Isakson*	85	15	100
7 *Barr*	79	21	98
8 *Chambliss*	90	10	98
9 *Deal*	82	18	95
10 *Norwood*	82	18	95
11 *Linder*	90	10	98
HAWAII			
1 Abercrombie	32	68	95
2 Mink [1]	33	67	83
IDAHO			
1 *Otter*	87	13	98
2 *Simpson*	92	8	100
ILLINOIS			
1 Rush	28	72	90
2 Jackson	25	75	100
3 Lipinski	47	53	75
4 Gutierrez	31	69	88
5 Blagojevich	36	64	70
6 *Hyde*	92	8	98
7 Davis	24	76	95
8 *Crane*	86	14	93
9 Schakowsky	25	75	100
10 *Kirk*	85	15	100
11 *Weller*	88	12	100
12 Costello	40	60	100
13 *Biggert*	82	18	100

ND Northern Democrats SD Southern Democrats

	1	2	3
14 Hastert[2]	100	0	35
15 Johnson	80	20	100
16 Manzullo	82	18	95
17 Evans	24	76	93
18 LaHood	82	18	98
19 Phelps	54	46	98
20 Shimkus	80	20	100
INDIANA			
1 Visclosky	22	78	100
2 Pence	84	16	95
3 Roemer	40	60	100
4 Souder	89	11	95
5 Buyer	83	17	88
6 Burton	84	16	78
7 Kerns	80	20	100
8 Hostettler	72	28	100
9 Hill	45	55	100
10 Carson	19	81	90
IOWA			
1 Leach	70	30	100
2 Nussle	88	12	100
3 Boswell	40	60	100
4 Ganske	81	19	90
5 Latham	85	15	100
KANSAS			
1 Moran	72	28	100
2 Ryun	88	12	100
3 Moore	40	60	100
4 Tiahrt	88	12	100
KENTUCKY			
1 Whitfield	87	13	98
2 Lewis	85	15	100
3 Northup	90	10	98
4 Lucas	78	22	100
5 Rogers	87	13	95
6 Fletcher	87	13	98
LOUISIANA			
1 Vitter	85	15	98
2 Jefferson	40	60	100
3 Tauzin	88	12	100
4 McCrery	87	13	95
5 Cooksey	84	16	93
6 Baker	82	18	98
7 John	58	42	95
MAINE			
1 Allen	36	64	98
2 Baldacci	35	65	100
MARYLAND			
1 Gilchrest	80	20	88
2 Ehrlich	81	19	93
3 Cardin	35	65	100
4 Wynn	33	67	100
5 Hoyer	33	67	100
6 Bartlett	79	21	98
7 Cummings	25	75	100
8 Morella	53	47	95
MASSACHUSETTS			
1 Olver	27	73	93
2 Neal	28	72	98
3 McGovern	22	78	100
4 Frank	14	86	93
5 Meehan	26	74	85
6 Tierney	23	77	98
7 Markey	25	75	100
8 Capuano	21	79	98
9 Lynch	33	67	100
10 Delahunt	24	76	93
MICHIGAN			
1 Stupak	33	67	100
2 Hoekstra	88	12	100
3 Ehlers	87	13	98
4 Camp	85	15	100
5 Barcia	59	41	93
6 Upton	83	17	100
7 Smith	90	10	98
8 Rogers	85	15	100
9 Kildee	38	62	100
10 Bonior	26	74	68
11 Knollenberg	92	8	95
12 Levin	28	72	100
13 Rivers	21	79	98
14 Conyers	21	79	98
15 Kilpatrick	27	73	93
16 Dingell	26	74	95

	1	2	3
MINNESOTA			
1 Gutknecht	78	22	100
2 Kennedy	90	10	98
3 Ramstad	82	18	100
4 McCollum	25	75	100
5 Sabo	25	75	100
6 Luther	40	60	100
7 Peterson	54	46	98
8 Oberstar	28	72	98
MISSISSIPPI			
1 Wicker	85	15	100
2 Thompson	22	78	90
3 Pickering	85	15	100
4 Shows	49	51	98
5 Taylor	45	55	100
MISSOURI			
1 Clay	32	68	93
2 Akin	90	10	100
3 Gephardt	33	67	98
4 Skelton	58	42	100
5 McCarthy	29	71	95
6 Graves	79	21	95
7 Blunt	91	9	83
8 Emerson	81	19	93
9 Hulshof	88	12	100
MONTANA			
AL Rehberg	85	15	100
NEBRASKA			
1 Bereuter	85	15	100
2 Terry	84	16	95
3 Osborne	88	12	100
NEVADA			
1 Berkley	42	58	100
2 Gibbons	88	12	100
NEW HAMPSHIRE			
1 Sununu	92	8	98
2 Bass	82	18	100
NEW JERSEY			
1 Andrews	41	59	98
2 LoBiondo	80	20	100
3 Saxton	87	13	95
4 Smith	80	20	100
5 Roukema	83	17	45
6 Pallone	30	70	100
7 Ferguson	88	12	100
8 Pascrell	48	52	100
9 Rothman	32	68	95
10 Payne	16	84	95
11 Frelinghuysen	85	15	100
12 Holt	30	70	100
13 Menendez	28	72	90
NEW MEXICO			
1 Wilson	90	10	100
2 Skeen	95	5	100
3 Udall	20	80	100
NEW YORK			
1 Grucci	82	18	100
2 Israel	41	59	98
3 King	84	16	95
4 McCarthy	45	55	100
5 Ackerman	32	68	95
6 Meeks	26	74	98
7 Crowley	39	61	95
8 Nadler	18	82	95
9 Weiner	24	76	95
10 Towns	32	68	95
11 Owens	21	79	98
12 Velázquez	24	76	95
13 Fossella	87	13	98
14 Maloney	34	66	95
15 Rangel	24	76	95
16 Serrano	26	74	95
17 Engel	44	56	98
18 Lowey	26	74	95
19 Kelly	80	20	100
20 Gilman	69	31	98
21 McNulty	28	72	100
22 Sweeney	85	15	100
23 Boehlert	78	22	100
24 McHugh	85	15	100
25 Walsh	87	13	98
26 Hinchey	20	80	100
27 Reynolds	92	8	100
28 Slaughter	16	84	93
29 LaFalce	32	68	93

	1	2	3
30 Quinn	84	16	95
31 Houghton	77	23	88
NORTH CAROLINA			
1 Clayton	28	72	98
2 Etheridge	50	50	100
3 Jones	72	28	100
4 Price	38	62	100
5 Burr	92	8	100
6 Coble	82	18	100
7 McIntyre	54	46	98
8 Hayes	82	18	98
9 Myrick	88	12	100
10 Ballenger	90	10	100
11 Taylor	85	15	98
12 Watt	25	75	100
NORTH DAKOTA			
AL Pomeroy	58	42	100
OHIO			
1 Chabot	85	15	100
2 Portman	92	8	100
3 Hall[3]	46	54	70
4 Oxley	95	5	95
5 Gillmor	92	8	95
6 Strickland	32	68	100
7 Hobson	90	10	100
8 Boehner	92	8	93
9 Kaptur	24	76	95
10 Kucinich	26	74	95
11 Jones	24	76	85
12 Tiberi	88	12	100
13 Brown	22	78	100
14 Sawyer	28	72	98
15 Pryce	92	8	93
16 Regula	90	10	100
17 Traficant[4]	0	0	0
18 Ney	90	10	100
19 LaTourette	82	18	98
OKLAHOMA			
1 Sullivan[5]	88	12	100
2 Carson	52	48	100
3 Watkins	90	10	98
4 Watts	92	8	95
5 Istook	85	15	100
6 Lucas	88	12	100
OREGON			
1 Wu	42	58	100
2 Walden	90	10	100
3 Blumenauer	25	75	100
4 DeFazio	24	76	95
5 Hooley	37	63	95
PENNSYLVANIA			
1 Brady	31	69	98
2 Fattah	28	72	98
3 Borski	39	61	90
4 Hart	92	8	98
5 Peterson	84	16	95
6 Holden	60	40	100
7 Weldon	71	29	95
8 Greenwood	82	18	98
9 Shuster	88	12	100
10 Sherwood	89	11	95
11 Kanjorski	42	58	100
12 Murtha	55	45	78
13 Hoeffel	38	62	98
14 Coyne	19	81	90
15 Toomey	88	12	100
16 Pitts	88	12	100
17 Gekas	88	12	100
18 Doyle	38	62	100
19 Platts	82	18	100
20 Mascara	51	49	93
21 English	87	13	98
RHODE ISLAND			
1 Kennedy	40	60	100
2 Langevin	35	65	100
SOUTH CAROLINA			
1 Brown	82	18	100
2 Wilson	82	18	100
3 Graham	82	18	98
4 DeMint	85	15	100
5 Spratt	42	58	100
6 Clyburn	31	69	98
SOUTH DAKOTA			
AL Thune	82	18	100

	1	2	3
TENNESSEE			
1 Jenkins	86	14	93
2 Duncan	62	38	100
3 Wamp	82	18	100
4 Hilleary	84	16	93
5 Clement	53	47	95
6 Gordon	54	46	98
7 Bryant	88	12	100
8 Tanner	56	44	98
9 Ford	46	54	98
TEXAS			
1 Sandlin	50	50	100
2 Turner	44	56	98
3 Johnson, Sam	89	11	95
4 Hall	70	30	100
5 Sessions	87	13	98
6 Barton	90	10	98
7 Culberson	85	15	100
8 Brady	85	15	100
9 Lampson	36	64	98
10 Doggett	22	78	100
11 Edwards	47	53	95
12 Granger	85	15	100
13 Thornberry	92	8	98
14 Paul	51	49	98
15 Hinojosa	41	59	93
16 Reyes	41	59	93
17 Stenholm	45	55	100
18 Jackson-Lee	21	79	98
19 Combest	86	14	73
20 Gonzalez	28	72	100
21 Smith	89	11	95
22 DeLay	92	8	98
23 Bonilla	88	12	100
24 Frost	35	65	100
25 Bentsen	38	62	100
26 Armey	92	8	100
27 Ortiz	42	58	90
28 Rodriguez	25	75	100
29 Green	31	69	98
30 Johnson	22	78	100
UTAH			
1 Hansen	83	17	88
2 Matheson	48	52	100
3 Cannon	87	13	95
VERMONT			
AL Sanders	18	82	100
VIRGINIA			
1 Davis	82	18	100
2 Schrock	92	8	95
3 Scott	23	77	98
4 Forbes	85	15	98
5 Goode[6]	74	26	98
6 Goodlatte	88	12	100
7 Cantor	90	10	100
8 Moran	42	58	100
9 Boucher	49	51	98
10 Wolf	82	18	100
11 Davis	82	18	95
WASHINGTON			
1 Inslee	28	72	100
2 Larsen	38	62	100
3 Baird	32	68	100
4 Hastings	92	8	98
5 Nethercutt	87	13	98
6 Dicks	36	64	98
7 McDermott	14	86	93
8 Dunn	92	8	98
9 Smith	38	62	93
WEST VIRGINIA			
1 Mollohan	34	66	95
2 Capito	80	20	100
3 Rahall	28	72	100
WISCONSIN			
1 Ryan	82	18	98
2 Baldwin	23	77	98
3 Kind	29	71	95
4 Kleczka	30	70	100
5 Barrett	33	67	90
6 Petri	82	18	100
7 Obey	32	68	100
8 Green	82	18	100
9 Sensenbrenner	85	15	100
WYOMING			
AL Cubin	85	15	98

Southern states - Ala., Ark, Fla., Ga., Ky., La., Miss., N.C., Okla., S.C., Tenn., Texas, Va.

Party Unity Background

Roll call votes used for the party unity study are those on which a majority of voting Democrats opposed a majority of voting Republicans.

Support indicates the percentage of the time that members voted *in agreement* with a majority of their party on these party unity votes.

Opposition indicates the percentage of the time members voted *against* a majority of their party on party unity votes.

The scores below show the **average** of members' scores by party, chamber and region.

(Party switchers are accounted for; failure to vote lowers support and opposition scores for chambers and parties.)

Average Party Unity Scores by Chamber

	Republicans		Democrats			Republicans		Democrats	
	2002	2001	2002	2001		2002	2001	2002	2001
Support					**Opposition**				
Senate	84%	88%	83%	89%	Senate	12%	10%	15%	10%
House	90	91	86	83	House	7	6	10	14

Average Party Support/Opposition by Party and Region*

Senate	Support	Opposition	House	Support	Opposition
Northern Republicans	83%	15%	Northern Republicans	88%	8%
Southern Republicans	87	7	Southern Republicans	93	4
Northern Democrats	86	12	Northern Democrats	88	8
Southern Democrats	68	31	Southern Democrats	80	17

*Southern Democrats and Republicans are those from Ala., Ark., Fla., Ga., Ky., La., Miss., N.C., Okla., S.C., Tenn., Texas, Va. All others are considered Northern.

2002 Party Victories

The number of times each party won on party unity votes:

	Senate	House	Total
Republicans won	73	170	243
Democrats won	42	39	81

Unanimous Voting by Parties

The number of times each party voted unanimously on party unity votes:

	Senate		House		Total	
	2002	2001	2002	2001	2002	2001
Republicans voted unanimously	23	55	54	66	77	121
Democrats voted unanimously	12	37	37	1	49	38

Party Unity Average Scores by Year

Average score by party in both chambers of Congress:

Year	Republicans	Democrats	Year	Republicans	Democrats
1967	71%	66%	1985	75%	79%
1968	63	57	1986	71	78
1969	62	62	1987	74	81
1970	59	57	1988	73	79
1971	66	62	1989	73	81
1972	64	57	1990	74	81
1973	68	68	1991	78	81
1974	62	63	1992	79	79
1975	70	69	1993	84	85
1976	66	65	1994	83	83
1977	70	67	1995	91	80
1978	67	64	1996	87	80
1979	72	69	1997	88	82
1980	70	68	1998	86	83
1981	76	69	1999	86	84
1982	71	72	2000	87	83
1983	74	76	2001	90	85
1984	72	74	2002	89	86

2002 Party Unity Votes

Following are the votes, by roll call number, on which a majority of Democrats voted against a majority of Republicans.

House

(209 of 483 "yea/nay" votes)

8	34	61	96	141	194	216	274	312	338	361	397	430	468
10	36	62	97	145	196	217	275	313	339	362	398	433	469
19	37	63	101	151	197	218	276	314	340	363	400	434	470
21	38	75	102	152	198	219	278	315	342	364	401	435	472
22	42	76	103	153	199	224	279	316	343	367	410	436	473
24	44	77	105	154	200	225	280	317	347	368	411	438	474
25	49	78	106	155	201	228	281	319	352	369	412	440	475
26	51	79	108	157	202	229	282	320	353	370	413	441	476
27	53	83	109	164	203	238	288	323	354	371	414	453	477
28	55	85	114	165	204	241	289	330	355	387	415	454	478
29	56	87	120	166	205	243	291	331	356	391	416	455	479
30	57	88	122	168	206	246	303	332	357	392	419	459	480
31	58	90	133	169	211	247	308	333	358	393	420	460	481
32	59	91	135	170	214	264	310	336	359	394	421	461	484
33	60	92	136	192	215	269	311	337	360	395	429	467	

Senate

(115 of 253 "yea/nay" votes)

2	25	39	57	71	101	118	130	149	168	200	221	236
3	28	40	58	80	103	119	132	150	172	202	222	241
6	29	47	59	81	110	121	133	151	179	203	224	244
8	30	48	60	82	111	123	137	152	182	206	225	245
13	31	49	61	83	112	125	139	156	186	207	226	246
14	32	50	63	84	113	126	141	159	187	214	227	247
15	33	53	64	87	114	127	143	160	189	215	228	250
23	34	54	66	89	115	128	144	162	197	217	232	
24	38	55	70	90	117	129	147	167	199	218	235	

Proportion of Partisan Roll Calls

How often a majority of Democrats voted against a majority of Republicans:

Year	House	Senate	Year	House	Senate	Year	House	Senate	Year	House	Senate
1959	55%	48%	1970	27%	35%	1981	37%	48%	1992	64%	53%
1960	53	37	1971	38	42	1982	36	43	1993	65	67
1961	50	62	1972	27	36	1983	56	44	1994	62	52
1962	46	41	1973	42	40	1984	47	40	1995	73	69
1963	49	47	1974	29	44	1985	61	50	1996	56	62
1964	55	36	1975	48	48	1986	57	52	1997	50	50
1965	52	42	1976	36	37	1987	64	41	1998	56	56
1966	41	50	1977	42	42	1988	47	42	1999	47	63
1967	36	35	1978	33	45	1989	55	35	2000	43	49
1968	35	32	1979	47	47	1990	49	54	2001	40	55
1969	31	36	1980	38	46	1991	55	49	2002	43	45

Party Unity and
Party Opposition: House

1. Party Unity. Percentage of recorded party unity votes in 2002 on which a member voted "yea" or "nay" in agreement with a majority of his or her party. (Party unity votes are those on which a majority of voting Democrats opposed a majority of voting Republicans.) Percentages are based on votes cast; thus, failure to vote did not lower a member's score.

2. Party Opposition. Percentage of recorded party unity votes in 2002 on which a member voted "yea" or "nay" in disagreement with a majority of his or her party. Percentages are based on votes cast; thus, failure to vote did not lower a member's score.

3. Participation in Party Unity Votes. Percentage of the 209 recorded House party unity votes in 2002 on which a member was present and voted "yea" or "nay."

[1] Rep. Patsy T. Mink, D-Hawaii, died Sept. 28, 2002. The last vote for which she was eligible was vote 423. Mink was eligible for 179 party unity votes.

[2] The Speaker votes only at his discretion, usually to break a tie or to emphasize the importance of a matter.

[3] Rep. Tony P. Hall, D-Ohio, resigned effective Sept. 9, 2002. The last vote for which he was eligible was vote 377. He was eligible for 159 party unity votes.

[4] Rep. James A. Traficant Jr., D-Ohio, was expelled from the House of Representatives July 24, 2002. The last vote for which he was eligible was vote 346. He was eligible for 140 party unity votes.

[5] Rep. John Sullivan, R-Okla., was sworn in Feb. 27, 2002. The first vote for which he was eligible was vote 42. Sullivan was eligible for 190 party unity votes. Sullivan succeeds Republican Steve Largent, who resigned effective Feb. 15, 2002, to run for governor of Oklahoma. The last vote for which Largent was eligible was vote 38. He was eligible for 19 party unity votes. His party unity score was 95 percent.

[6] Rep. Virgil H. Goode Jr. of Virginia switched his party affiliation from independent to Republican, effective Aug. 1, 2002.

Key

Democrats   •   **Republicans**
Independents

	1	2	3
ALABAMA			
1 *Callahan*	95	5	86
2 *Everett*	99	1	98
3 *Riley*	99	1	76
4 *Aderholt*	96	4	98
5 Cramer	61	39	99
6 *Bachus*	98	2	93
7 Hilliard	92	8	95
ALASKA			
AL *Young*	94	6	94
ARIZONA			
1 *Flake*	89	11	100
2 Pastor	92	8	99
3 *Stump*	99	1	70
4 *Shadegg*	98	2	99
5 *Kolbe*	88	12	99
6 *Hayworth*	98	2	100
ARKANSAS			
1 Berry	79	21	100
2 Snyder	85	15	100
3 *Boozman*	95	5	100
4 Ross	73	27	99
CALIFORNIA			
1 Thompson	93	7	93
2 *Herger*	98	2	98
3 *Ose*	86	14	95
4 *Doolittle*	98	2	93
5 Matsui	97	3	99
6 Woolsey	99	1	99
7 Miller	97	3	91
8 Pelosi	99	1	99
9 Lee	99	1	99
10 Tauscher	86	14	100
11 *Pombo*	96	4	97
12 Lantos	94	6	96
13 Stark	99	1	94
14 Eshoo	95	5	95
15 Honda	99	1	99
16 Lofgren	94	6	99
17 Farr	99	1	99
18 Condit	82	18	84
19 *Radanovich*	96	4	92
20 Dooley	72	28	95
21 *Thomas*	91	9	99
22 Capps	93	7	100
23 *Gallegly*	94	6	99
24 Sherman	95	5	100
25 *McKeon*	95	5	99
26 Berman	96	4	95
27 Schiff	92	8	100
28 *Dreier*	93	7	100
29 Waxman	98	2	91
30 Becerra	100	0	97
31 Solis	100	0	99
32 Watson	98	2	93
33 Roybal-Allard	99	1	99
34 Napolitano	98	2	97
35 Waters	97	3	95
36 Harman	83	17	97
37 Millender-McD.	96	4	94
38 *Horn*	79	21	99

	1	2	3
39 *Royce*	97	3	98
40 *Lewis*	92	8	97
41 *Miller*	99	1	96
42 Baca	91	9	99
43 *Calvert*	96	4	99
44 *Bono*	89	11	96
45 *Rohrabacher*	94	6	99
46 Sanchez	96	4	96
47 *Cox*	95	5	95
48 *Issa*	94	6	98
49 Davis	92	8	100
50 Filner	99	1	97
51 *Cunningham*	97	3	98
52 *Hunter*	94	6	99
COLORADO			
1 DeGette	98	2	97
2 Udall	93	7	99
3 *McInnis*	96	4	94
4 *Schaffer*	94	6	98
5 *Hefley*	92	8	97
6 *Tancredo*	96	4	98
CONNECTICUT			
1 Larson	95	5	99
2 *Simmons*	78	22	97
3 DeLauro	96	4	100
4 *Shays*	80	20	99
5 Maloney	76	24	96
6 *Johnson*	75	25	99
DELAWARE			
AL *Castle*	79	21	100
FLORIDA			
1 *Miller*	98	2	100
2 Boyd	71	29	96
3 Brown	95	5	95
4 *Crenshaw*	98	2	100
5 Thurman	89	11	95
6 *Stearns*	96	4	93
7 *Mica*	96	4	98
8 *Keller*	99	1	97
9 *Bilirakis*	98	2	98
10 *Young*	94	6	97
11 Davis	85	15	99
12 *Putnam*	98	2	99
13 *Miller*	97	3	99
14 Goss	95	5	99
15 *Weldon*	98	2	99
16 *Foley*	90	10	99
17 Meek	94	6	94
18 *Ros-Lehtinen*	93	7	99
19 Wexler	89	11	96
20 Deutsch	86	14	92
21 *Diaz-Balart*	94	6	96
22 *Shaw*	93	7	99
23 Hastings	93	7	90
GEORGIA			
1 *Kingston*	98	2	97
2 Bishop	80	20	98
3 *Collins*	96	4	99
4 McKinney	91	9	86
5 Lewis	96	4	90
6 *Isakson*	94	6	99
7 *Barr*	96	4	96
8 *Chambliss*	98	2	99
9 *Deal*	96	4	94
10 *Norwood*	96	4	95
11 *Linder*	98	2	93
HAWAII			
1 Abercrombie	89	11	98
2 Mink [1]	95	5	88
IDAHO			
1 *Otter*	94	6	99
2 *Simpson*	95	5	99
ILLINOIS			
1 Rush	95	5	94
2 Jackson	96	4	100
3 Lipinski	75	25	86
4 Gutierrez	95	5	87
5 Blagojevich	81	19	69
6 *Hyde*	97	3	98
7 Davis	96	4	94
8 *Crane*	98	2	92
9 Schakowsky	99	1	100
10 *Kirk*	85	15	100
11 *Weller*	96	4	99
12 Costello	80	20	100
13 *Biggert*	89	11	100

ND Northern Democrats   SD Southern Democrats

	1	2	3
14 *Hastert* [2]	100	0	24
15 *Johnson*	85	15	99
16 *Manzullo*	95	5	97
17 Evans	97	3	98
18 *LaHood*	92	8	97
19 Phelps	69	31	99
20 *Shimkus*	94	6	99

INDIANA

	1	2	3
1 Visclosky	92	8	99
2 *Pence*	99	1	98
3 Roemer	79	21	100
4 *Souder*	94	6	98
5 *Buyer*	97	3	92
6 *Burton*	97	3	82
7 *Kerns*	95	5	100
8 *Hostettler*	88	12	100
9 Hill	76	24	99
10 Carson	96	4	96

IOWA

	1	2	3
1 *Leach*	71	29	99
2 *Nussle*	93	7	99
3 Boswell	81	19	100
4 *Ganske*	85	15	91
5 *Latham*	92	8	100

KANSAS

	1	2	3
1 *Moran*	89	11	100
2 *Ryun*	98	2	99
3 Moore	82	18	99
4 *Tiahrt*	96	4	97

KENTUCKY

	1	2	3
1 *Whitfield*	94	6	95
2 *Lewis*	98	2	100
3 *Northup*	95	5	98
4 Lucas	42	58	100
5 *Rogers*	95	5	99
6 *Fletcher*	96	4	98

LOUISIANA

	1	2	3
1 *Vitter*	99	1	96
2 Jefferson	92	8	97
3 *Tauzin*	97	3	99
4 *McCrery*	97	3	99
5 *Cooksey*	97	3	83
6 *Baker*	96	4	96
7 John	64	36	96

MAINE

	1	2	3
1 Allen	95	5	97
2 Baldacci	93	7	94

MARYLAND

	1	2	3
1 *Gilchrest*	86	14	93
2 *Ehrlich*	90	10	87
3 Cardin	90	10	99
4 Wynn	87	13	98
5 Hoyer	89	11	99
6 *Bartlett*	94	6	99
7 Cummings	95	5	99
8 *Morella*	58	42	98

MASSACHUSETTS

	1	2	3
1 Olver	99	1	98
2 Neal	96	4	95
3 McGovern	99	1	100
4 Frank	97	3	99
5 Meehan	98	2	89
6 Tierney	99	1	99
7 Markey	99	1	99
8 Capuano	98	2	99
9 Lynch	94	6	97
10 Delahunt	97	3	96

MICHIGAN

	1	2	3
1 Stupak	89	11	97
2 *Hoekstra*	91	9	99
3 *Ehlers*	85	15	99
4 *Camp*	95	5	100
5 Barcia	64	36	94
6 *Upton*	92	8	100
7 *Smith*	89	11	96
8 *Rogers*	96	4	100
9 Kildee	89	11	100
10 Bonior	95	5	74
11 *Knollenberg*	96	4	97
12 Levin	95	5	100
13 Rivers	96	4	99
14 Conyers	99	1	96
15 Kilpatrick	98	2	95
16 Dingell	96	4	97

MINNESOTA

	1	2	3
1 *Gutknecht*	94	6	99
2 *Kennedy*	97	3	95
3 *Ramstad*	84	16	100
4 McCollum	98	2	99
5 Sabo	96	4	99
6 Luther	85	15	99
7 Peterson	64	36	98
8 Oberstar	94	6	98

MISSISSIPPI

	1	2	3
1 *Wicker*	99	1	99
2 Thompson	94	6	94
3 *Pickering*	97	3	98
4 Shows	59	41	97
5 Taylor	63	37	99

MISSOURI

	1	2	3
1 Clay	94	6	90
2 *Akin*	98	2	100
3 Gephardt	93	7	97
4 Skelton	73	27	99
5 McCarthy	95	5	98
6 *Graves*	95	5	99
7 *Blunt*	98	2	91
8 *Emerson*	93	7	97
9 *Hulshof*	95	5	97

MONTANA

	1	2	3
AL *Rehberg*	95	5	100

NEBRASKA

	1	2	3
1 *Bereuter*	86	14	98
2 *Terry*	92	8	99
3 *Osborne*	89	11	100

NEVADA

	1	2	3
1 *Berkley*	87	13	99
2 *Gibbons*	96	4	99

NEW HAMPSHIRE

	1	2	3
1 *Sununu*	93	7	98
2 *Bass*	85	15	99

NEW JERSEY

	1	2	3
1 Andrews	88	12	99
2 *LoBiondo*	84	16	100
3 *Saxton*	91	9	99
4 *Smith*	89	11	99
5 *Roukema*	82	18	40
6 Pallone	95	5	100
7 *Ferguson*	87	13	99
8 Pascrell	89	11	99
9 Rothman	87	13	99
10 Payne	98	2	96
11 *Frelinghuysen*	84	16	98
12 Holt	94	6	99
13 Menendez	87	13	99

NEW MEXICO

	1	2	3
1 *Wilson*	90	10	100
2 *Skeen*	92	8	100
3 *Udall*	98	2	100

NEW YORK

	1	2	3
1 *Grucci*	88	12	97
2 Israel	83	17	99
3 *King*	92	8	98
4 McCarthy	84	16	98
5 Ackerman	93	7	98
6 Meeks	94	6	99
7 Crowley	93	7	95
8 Nadler	97	3	94
9 Weiner	95	5	98
10 Towns	94	6	94
11 Owens	98	2	98
12 Velázquez	99	1	98
13 *Fossella*	94	6	96
14 Maloney	93	7	94
15 Rangel	98	2	94
16 Serrano	96	4	97
17 Engel	89	11	97
18 Lowey	94	6	98
19 *Kelly*	90	10	100
20 Gilman	77	23	96
21 McNulty	90	10	100
22 *Sweeney*	91	9	99
23 *Boehlert*	79	21	100
24 McHugh	90	10	94
25 Walsh	88	12	99
26 Hinchey	99	1	97
27 *Reynolds*	96	4	99
28 Slaughter	98	2	92
29 LaFalce	93	7	93
30 Quinn	84	16	97
31 *Houghton*	78	22	87

NORTH CAROLINA

	1	2	3
1 Clayton	97	3	93
2 Etheridge	87	13	100
3 Jones	89	11	99
4 Price	92	8	100
5 *Burr*	95	5	98
6 *Coble*	95	5	100
7 McIntyre	72	28	96
8 *Hayes*	97	3	99
9 *Myrick*	97	3	99
10 *Ballenger*	96	4	99
11 *Taylor*	97	3	97
12 Watt	97	3	98

NORTH DAKOTA

	1	2	3
AL Pomeroy	78	22	100

OHIO

	1	2	3
1 *Chabot*	96	4	100
2 *Portman*	95	5	99
3 Hall [3]	84	16	86
4 *Oxley*	96	4	91
5 *Gillmor*	93	7	95
6 Strickland	90	10	99
7 Hobson	94	6	99
8 Boehner	97	3	97
9 Kaptur	96	4	96
10 Kucinich	96	4	99
11 Jones	98	2	95
12 *Tiberi*	95	5	100
13 Brown	98	2	99
14 Sawyer	98	2	96
15 *Pryce*	95	5	93
16 Regula	94	6	100
17 Traficant [4]	0	0	0
18 *Ney*	95	5	99
19 *LaTourette*	89	11	97

OKLAHOMA

	1	2	3
1 *Sullivan* [5]	99	1	99
2 Carson	74	26	96
3 *Watkins*	97	3	99
4 *Watts*	97	3	97
5 *Istook*	94	6	98
6 *Lucas*	98	2	100

OREGON

	1	2	3
1 Wu	88	12	99
2 *Walden*	95	5	100
3 Blumenauer	96	4	100
4 DeFazio	94	6	97
5 Hooley	87	13	94

PENNSYLVANIA

	1	2	3
1 Brady	94	6	100
2 Fattah	97	3	95
3 Borski	91	9	93
4 *Hart*	97	3	100
5 *Peterson*	94	6	95
6 Holden	67	33	100
7 *Weldon*	86	14	94
8 *Greenwood*	81	19	98
9 *Shuster*	98	2	100
10 *Sherwood*	96	4	99
11 Kanjorski	79	21	100
12 Murtha	75	25	89
13 Hoeffel	93	7	100
14 Coyne	99	1	97
15 *Toomey*	96	4	97
16 *Pitts*	97	3	97
17 *Gekas*	94	6	100
18 Doyle	90	10	99
19 *Platts*	85	15	99
20 Mascara	85	15	81
21 *English*	93	7	99

RHODE ISLAND

	1	2	3
1 Kennedy	89	11	99
2 Langevin	91	9	99

SOUTH CAROLINA

	1	2	3
1 *Brown*	95	5	99
2 *Wilson*	97	3	99
3 *Graham*	89	11	97
4 *DeMint*	97	3	100
5 Spratt	88	12	99
6 Clyburn	97	3	99

SOUTH DAKOTA

	1	2	3
AL *Thune*	83	17	99

TENNESSEE

	1	2	3
1 *Jenkins*	97	3	96
2 *Duncan*	91	9	99
3 *Wamp*	90	10	99
4 *Hilleary*	95	5	85
5 Clement	73	27	93
6 Gordon	74	26	97
7 *Bryant*	98	2	96
8 Tanner	70	30	94
9 Ford	87	13	97

TEXAS

	1	2	3
1 Sandlin	83	17	99
2 Turner	74	26	99
3 *Johnson, Sam*	98	2	98
4 Hall	40	60	99
5 *Sessions*	99	1	97
6 *Barton*	98	2	99
7 *Culberson*	99	1	98
8 *Brady*	97	3	91
9 Lampson	87	13	94
10 Doggett	95	5	100
11 Edwards	76	24	99
12 *Granger*	96	4	97
13 *Thornberry*	94	6	98
14 *Paul*	76	24	96
15 Hinojosa	89	11	89
16 Reyes	85	15	91
17 Stenholm	59	41	99
18 Jackson-Lee	97	3	98
19 *Combest*	96	4	77
20 Gonzalez	94	6	99
21 *Smith*	97	3	96
22 *DeLay*	99	1	99
23 *Bonilla*	97	3	98
24 Frost	86	14	99
25 Bentsen	90	10	99
26 *Armey*	99	1	99
27 Ortiz	82	18	94
28 Rodriguez	96	4	98
29 Green	86	14	98
30 Johnson	95	5	99

UTAH

	1	2	3
1 *Hansen*	98	2	97
2 Matheson	76	24	100
3 *Cannon*	96	4	94

VERMONT

	1	2	3
AL *Sanders*	98	2	99

VIRGINIA

	1	2	3
1 *Davis*	96	4	99
2 *Schrock*	97	3	97
3 Scott	96	4	99
4 *Forbes*	98	2	99
5 *Goode* [6]	93	7	100
6 *Goodlatte*	99	1	99
7 *Cantor*	99	1	100
8 Moran	84	16	98
9 Boucher	81	19	97
10 *Wolf*	89	11	100
11 *Davis*	90	10	97

WASHINGTON

	1	2	3
1 Inslee	96	4	99
2 Larsen	88	12	98
3 Baird	92	8	99
4 *Hastings*	98	2	99
5 *Nethercutt*	94	6	95
6 Dicks	85	15	99
7 McDermott	97	3	99
8 *Dunn*	93	7	99
9 Smith	81	19	95

WEST VIRGINIA

	1	2	3
1 Mollohan	78	22	99
2 *Capito*	89	11	100
3 Rahall	88	12	99

WISCONSIN

	1	2	3
1 *Ryan*	92	8	94
2 Baldwin	99	1	99
3 Kind	86	14	99
4 Kleczka	95	5	98
5 Barrett	95	5	91
6 *Petri*	86	14	99
7 Obey	94	6	99
8 *Green*	94	6	100
9 *Sensenbrenner*	94	6	99

WYOMING

	1	2	3
AL *Cubin*	97	3	86

Southern states - Ala., Ark, Fla., Ga., Ky., La., Miss., N.C., Okla., S.C., Tenn., Texas, Va.

	1	2	3
ALABAMA			
Shelby	80	20	93
Sessions	87	13	99
ALASKA			
Stevens	89	11	96
Murkowski	93	7	95
ARIZONA			
McCain	80	20	96
Kyl	96	4	99
ARKANSAS			
Hutchinson	87	13	95
Lincoln	61	39	99
CALIFORNIA			
Feinstein	83	17	99
Boxer	95	5	98
COLORADO			
Campbell	82	18	92
Allard	91	9	99
CONNECTICUT			
Dodd	94	6	97
Lieberman	85	15	99
DELAWARE			
Biden	89	11	99
Carper	74	26	100
FLORIDA			
Graham	77	23	100
Nelson	77	23	99
GEORGIA			
Cleland	69	31	100
Miller	40	60	96
HAWAII			
Inouye	90	10	92
Akaka	91	9	91
IDAHO			
Craig	93	7	98
Crapo	92	8	94
ILLINOIS			
Fitzgerald	77	23	100
Durbin	97	3	100
INDIANA			
Lugar	91	9	100
Bayh	70	30	99

	1	2	3
IOWA			
Grassley	88	12	100
Harkin	92	8	98
KANSAS			
Brownback	94	6	96
Roberts	96	4	99
KENTUCKY			
McConnell	97	3	100
Bunning	97	3	99
LOUISIANA			
Breaux	55	45	99
Landrieu	65	35	98
MAINE			
Snowe	57	43	100
Collins	57	43	100
MARYLAND			
Sarbanes	98	2	100
Mikulski	96	4	99
MASSACHUSETTS			
Kennedy	97	3	96
Kerry	92	8	97
MICHIGAN			
Levin	95	5	100
Stabenow	95	5	100
MINNESOTA			
Wellstone [1]	100	0	100
Dayton	95	5	96
MISSISSIPPI			
Cochran	86	14	100
Lott	98	2	99
MISSOURI			
Bond	89	11	99
Carnahan	84	16	100
MONTANA			
Burns	88	12	97
Baucus	67	33	94
NEBRASKA			
Hagel	94	6	100
Nelson	51	49	100
NEVADA			
Reid	94	6	98
Ensign	90	10	97

	1	2	3
NEW HAMPSHIRE			
Smith	88	12	98
Gregg	81	19	97
NEW JERSEY			
Torricelli	91	9	89
Corzine	96	4	99
NEW MEXICO			
Domenici	89	11	87
Bingaman	78	22	96
NEW YORK			
Schumer	95	5	99
Clinton	93	7	99
NORTH CAROLINA			
Helms	100	0	42
Edwards	84	16	100
NORTH DAKOTA			
Conrad	86	14	100
Dorgan	88	12	99
OHIO			
DeWine	89	11	100
Voinovich	88	12	97
OKLAHOMA			
Nickles	99	1	99
Inhofe	96	4	95
OREGON			
Wyden	87	13	100
Smith	66	34	99
PENNSYLVANIA			
Specter	60	40	98
Santorum	96	4	99
RHODE ISLAND			
Reed	98	2	99
Chafee	54	46	99
SOUTH CAROLINA			
Thurmond	90	10	97
Hollings	85	15	100
SOUTH DAKOTA			
Daschle	80	20	91
Johnson	85	15	96
TENNESSEE			
Thompson	94	6	96
Frist	97	3	100

Key

Democrats ● **Republicans**
Independents

	1	2	3
TEXAS			
Gramm	96	4	97
Hutchison	92	8	97
UTAH			
Hatch	93	7	96
Bennett	94	6	92
VERMONT			
Leahy	98	2	99
Jeffords	88	12	95
VIRGINIA			
Warner	82	18	97
Allen	90	10	99
WASHINGTON			
Murray	86	14	100
Cantwell	82	18	100
WEST VIRGINIA			
Byrd	82	18	99
Rockefeller	90	10	100
WISCONSIN			
Kohl	84	16	100
Feingold	84	16	100
WYOMING			
Thomas	96	4	99
Enzi	95	5	97

ND Northern Democrats   SD Southern Democrats

Southern states - Ala., Ark., Fla., Ga., Ky., La., Miss., N.C., Okla., S.C., Tenn., Texas, Va.

Party Unity and Party Opposition: Senate

1. Party Unity. Percentage of recorded party unity votes in 2002 on which a senator voted "yea" or "nay" in agreement with a majority of his or her party. (Party unity roll calls are those on which a majority of voting Democrats opposed a majority of voting Republicans.) Percentages are based on votes cast; thus, failure to vote did not lower a member's score.

2. Party Opposition. Percentage of recorded party unity votes in 2002 on which a senator voted "yea" or "nay" in disagreement with a majority of his or her party. Percentages are based on votes cast; thus, failure to vote did not lower a member's score.

3. Participation in Party Unity Votes. Percentage of the 115 recorded Senate party unity votes in 2002 on which a senator was present and voted "yea" or "nay."

[1] Sen. Dean Barkley, I-Minn., was sworn in Nov. 12, 2002, to replace Sen. Paul Wellstone, D-Minn., who died Oct. 25, 2002. The first vote for which Barkley was eligible was vote 240. Barkley was eligible for six party unity votes. The last vote for which Wellstone was eligible was vote 239. Wellstone was eligible for 109 party unity votes.

Key

Democrats • **Republicans**
Independents

	1	2
ALABAMA		
Shelby	95	96
Sessions	95	96
ALASKA		
Stevens	97	97
Murkowski	91	91
ARIZONA		
McCain	92	92
Kyl	98	98
ARKANSAS		
Hutchinson	90	90
Lincoln	99	99
CALIFORNIA		
Feinstein	99	99
Boxer	96	96
COLORADO		
Campbell	95	95
Allard	98	98
CONNECTICUT		
Dodd	94	94
Lieberman	98	98
DELAWARE		
Biden	97	97
Carper	99	99
FLORIDA		
Graham	100	100
Nelson	98	98
GEORGIA		
Cleland	99	99
Miller	92	92
HAWAII		
Inouye	89	88
Akaka	90	90
IDAHO		
Craig	96	96
Crapo	92	92
ILLINOIS		
Fitzgerald	99	99
Durbin	99	99
INDIANA		
Lugar	100	100
Bayh	99	99

	1	2
IOWA		
Grassley	100	100
Harkin	96	96
KANSAS		
Brownback	96	96
Roberts	96	96
KENTUCKY		
McConnell	98	98
Bunning	97	97
LOUISIANA		
Breaux	99	99
Landrieu	97	97
MAINE		
Snowe	100	100
Collins	100	100
MARYLAND		
Sarbanes	99	99
Mikulski	97	97
MASSACHUSETTS		
Kennedy	93	93
Kerry	96	96
MICHIGAN		
Levin	100	100
Stabenow	100	100
MINNESOTA		
Wellstone [1]	99	99
Dayton	96	96
MISSISSIPPI		
Cochran	99	99
Lott	98	98
MISSOURI		
Bond	97	97
Carnahan	98	98
MONTANA		
Burns	96	96
Baucus	96	96
NEBRASKA		
Hagel	99	99
Nelson	98	98
NEVADA		
Reid	99	99
Ensign	95	95

	1	2
NEW HAMPSHIRE		
Smith	98	98
Gregg	95	95
NEW JERSEY		
Torricelli	85	85
Corzine	96	96
NEW MEXICO		
Domenici	89	89
Bingaman	95	95
NEW YORK		
Schumer	98	98
Clinton	99	99
NORTH CAROLINA		
Helms	38	37
Edwards	100	100
NORTH DAKOTA		
Conrad	99	99
Dorgan	98	98
OHIO		
DeWine	99	99
Voinovich	94	94
OKLAHOMA		
Nickles	97	97
Inhofe	96	96
OREGON		
Wyden	100	100
Smith	98	98
PENNSYLVANIA		
Specter	97	97
Santorum	97	97
RHODE ISLAND		
Reed	99	99
Chafee	99	99
SOUTH CAROLINA		
Thurmond	97	97
Hollings	100	100
SOUTH DAKOTA		
Daschle	94	94
Johnson	98	98
TENNESSEE		
Thompson	93	93
Frist	99	99

	1	2
TEXAS		
Gramm	96	96
Hutchison	97	97
UTAH		
Hatch	96	96
Bennett	94	94
VERMONT		
Leahy	99	99
Jeffords	94	94
VIRGINIA		
Warner	96	96
Allen	99	99
WASHINGTON		
Murray	99	99
Cantwell	100	100
WEST VIRGINIA		
Byrd	99	99
Rockefeller	99	99
WISCONSIN		
Kohl	100	100
Feingold	100	100
WYOMING		
Thomas	97	97
Enzi	95	95

ND Northern Democrats   SD Southern Democrats

Southern states - Ala., Ark., Fla., Ga., Ky., La., Miss., N.C., Okla., S.C., Tenn., Texas, Va.

Voting Participation: Senate

1. Voting Participation. Percentage of 253 recorded votes in 2002 on which a senator voted "yea" or "nay."

2. Voting Participation (without motions to instruct). Percentage of 251 recorded votes in 2002 on which a senator voted "yea" or "nay." In this version of the study, two votes to instruct the sergeant at arms to request the attendance of absent senators were excluded.

Absences because of illness. Congressional Quarterly no longer designates members who missed votes because of illness. In the past, notations to that effect were based on official statements published in the Congressional Record, but these were found to be inconsistently used.

Rounding. Scores are rounded to the nearest percentage, except that no scores are rounded up to 100 percent. Senators with a 100 percent score participated in all recorded votes for which they were eligible.

[1] Sen. Dean Barkley, I-Minn., was sworn in Nov. 12, 2002, to replace Sen. Paul Wellstone, D-Minn., who died Oct. 25, 2002. The first vote for which Barkley was eligible was vote 240. His participation score was 100 percent. The last vote for which Wellstone was eligible was vote 239.

Key

Democrats • **Republicans**
Independents

Voting Participation: House

1. **Voting Participation.** Percentage of 483 recorded votes in 2002 on which a representative voted "yea" or "nay."

2. **Voting Participation (without Journal votes).** Percentage of 447 recorded votes in 2002 on which a member voted "yea" or "nay." In this version of the study, 36 votes on approval of the House Journal were excluded.

Absences because of illness. Congressional Quarterly no longer designates members who missed votes because of illness. In the past, notations to that effect were based on official statements published in the Congressional Record, but these were found to be inconsistently used.

Rounding. Scores are rounded to the nearest percentage, except that no scores are rounded up to 100 percent. Members with a 100 percent score participated in all recorded votes for which they were eligible.

[1] Rep. Patsy T. Mink, D-Hawaii, died Sept. 28, 2002. The last vote for which she was eligible was vote 423.

[2] The Speaker votes only at his discretion, usually to break a tie or to emphasize the importance of a matter.

[3] Rep. Tony P. Hall, D-Ohio, resigned effective Sept. 9, 2002. The last vote for which he was eligible was vote 377.

[4] Rep. James A. Traficant Jr., D-Ohio, was expelled from the House of Representatives July 24, 2002. The last vote for which he was eligible was vote 346.

[5] Rep. John Sullivan, R-Okla., was sworn in Feb. 27, 2002. The first vote for which he was eligible was vote 42. Sullivan succeeds Republican Steve Largent, who resigned effective Feb. 15, 2002, to run for governor of Oklahoma. The last vote for which Largent was eligible was vote 38. His participation score was 89 percent.

[6] Rep. Virgil H. Goode Jr. of Virginia switched his party affiliation from independent to Republican, effective Aug. 1, 2002.

	1	2
ALABAMA		
1 *Callahan*	80	81
2 *Everett*	93	93
3 *Riley*	58	58
4 *Aderholt*	98	98
5 Cramer	98	99
6 *Bachus*	92	92
7 Hilliard	91	91
ALASKA		
AL *Young*	85	88
ARIZONA		
1 *Flake*	99	98
2 Pastor	99	99
3 *Stump*	70	70
4 *Shadegg*	97	97
5 *Kolbe*	99	99
6 *Hayworth*	97	97
ARKANSAS		
1 Berry	100	100
2 Snyder	96	96
3 *Boozman*	100	100
4 Ross	99	99
CALIFORNIA		
1 Thompson	95	95
2 *Herger*	95	96
3 *Ose*	93	93
4 *Doolittle*	93	93
5 Matsui	96	97
6 Woolsey	97	97
7 Miller	87	87
8 Pelosi	97	97
9 Lee	99	99
10 Tauscher	99	99
11 *Pombo*	94	94
12 Lantos	93	93
13 Stark	92	93
14 Eshoo	98	98
15 Honda	97	97
16 Lofgren	98	98
17 Farr	99	99
18 Condit	84	83
19 *Radanovich*	92	92
20 Dooley	90	90
21 *Thomas*	96	96
22 Capps	99	99
23 *Gallegly*	94	95
24 Sherman	99	99
25 *McKeon*	98	98
26 Berman	90	91
27 Schiff	99	99
28 *Dreier*	99	99
29 Waxman	89	89
30 Becerra	92	92
31 Solis	95	95
32 Watson	91	91
33 Roybal-Allard	98	98
34 Napolitano	95	96
35 Waters	90	91
36 Harman	96	96
37 Millender-McD.	89	89
38 *Horn*	98	98

	1	2
39 *Royce*	98	98
40 *Lewis*	93	93
41 *Miller*	94	94
42 Baca	99	99
43 *Calvert*	95	96
44 *Bono*	93	94
45 *Rohrabacher*	99	99
46 Sanchez	94	94
47 *Cox*	91	91
48 *Issa*	97	97
49 Davis	100	100
50 Filner	95	96
51 *Cunningham*	98	98
52 *Hunter*	95	96
COLORADO		
1 DeGette	96	96
2 Udall	98	98
3 *McInnis*	94	94
4 *Schaffer*	87	88
5 *Hefley*	98	98
6 *Tancredo*	90	96
CONNECTICUT		
1 Larson	98	98
2 *Simmons*	97	97
3 DeLauro	99	99
4 *Shays*	96	97
5 Maloney	94	95
6 *Johnson*	98	98
DELAWARE		
AL *Castle*	100	100
FLORIDA		
1 *Miller*	98	98
2 Boyd	98	98
3 Brown	89	90
4 *Crenshaw*	100	100
5 Thurman	94	94
6 *Stearns*	94	93
7 *Mica*	97	98
8 *Keller*	96	97
9 *Bilirakis*	97	96
10 *Young*	91	92
11 Davis	96	97
12 *Putnam*	98	98
13 *Miller*	98	98
14 *Goss*	98	98
15 *Weldon*	97	98
16 *Foley*	98	98
17 Meek	89	92
18 *Ros-Lehtinen*	94	94
19 Wexler	92	93
20 Deutsch	90	91
21 *Diaz-Balart*	92	92
22 *Shaw*	98	98
23 Hastings	85	85
GEORGIA		
1 *Kingston*	95	96
2 Bishop	97	97
3 *Collins*	94	95
4 McKinney	85	86
5 Lewis	84	84
6 *Isakson*	99	99
7 *Barr*	92	92
8 *Chambliss*	97	97
9 *Deal*	93	94
10 *Norwood*	95	95
11 *Linder*	94	94
HAWAII		
1 Abercrombie	96	96
2 Mink [1]	86	86
IDAHO		
1 *Otter*	99	99
2 *Simpson*	96	97
ILLINOIS		
1 Rush	90	91
2 Jackson	100	100
3 Lipinski	82	82
4 Gutierrez	82	82
5 Blagojevich	56	56
6 *Hyde*	95	96
7 Davis	94	94
8 *Crane*	88	88
9 Schakowsky	98	98
10 *Kirk*	98	99
11 *Weller*	98	98
12 Costello	97	97
13 *Biggert*	99	99

ND Northern Democrats   SD Southern Democrats

	1	2
14 Hastert[2]	13	13
15 Johnson	99	99
16 Manzullo	94	94
17 Evans	98	97
18 LaHood	94	94
19 Phelps	97	97
20 Shimkus	99	99

INDIANA

	1	2
1 Visclosky	99	99
2 Pence	98	98
3 Roemer	99	99
4 Souder	93	94
5 Buyer	90	91
6 Burton	76	76
7 Kerns	99	99
8 Hostettler	99	99
9 Hill	99	98
10 Carson	92	92

IOWA

	1	2
1 Leach	98	98
2 Nussle	98	98
3 Boswell	99	99
4 Ganske	92	92
5 Latham	100	100

KANSAS

	1	2
1 Moran	99	99
2 Ryun	98	98
3 Moore	99	99
4 Tiahrt	97	97

KENTUCKY

	1	2
1 Whitfield	95	96
2 Lewis	99	99
3 Northup	95	96
4 Lucas	99	99
5 Rogers	99	99
6 Fletcher	97	97

LOUISIANA

	1	2
1 Vitter	95	96
2 Jefferson	93	93
3 Tauzin	95	96
4 McCrery	95	96
5 Cooksey	80	79
6 Baker	95	95
7 John	91	91

MAINE

	1	2
1 Allen	97	97
2 Baldacci	91	92

MARYLAND

	1	2
1 Gilchrest	92	92
2 Ehrlich	81	83
3 Cardin	98	98
4 Wynn	95	96
5 Hoyer	97	97
6 Bartlett	99	99
7 Cummings	97	98
8 Morella	96	96

MASSACHUSETTS

	1	2
1 Olver	96	96
2 Neal	93	93
3 McGovern	99	99
4 Frank	97	97
5 Meehan	92	91
6 Tierney	98	98
7 Markey	98	98
8 Capuano	96	97
9 Lynch	93	93
10 Delahunt	92	93

MICHIGAN

	1	2
1 Stupak	97	98
2 Hoekstra	97	97
3 Ehlers	99	99
4 Camp	99	99
5 Barcia	93	93
6 Upton	100	100
7 Smith	92	93
8 Rogers	100	100
9 Kildee	100	100
10 Bonior	69	68
11 Knollenberg	96	96
12 Levin	98	98
13 Rivers	98	98
14 Conyers	85	86
15 Kilpatrick	91	91
16 Dingell	95	96

MINNESOTA

	1	2
1 Gutknecht	99	98
2 Kennedy	95	95
3 Ramstad	99	99
4 McCollum	99	99
5 Sabo	98	98
6 Luther	96	96
7 Peterson	96	96
8 Oberstar	97	98

MISSISSIPPI

	1	2
1 Wicker	98	98
2 Thompson	96	96
3 Pickering	98	98
4 Shows	96	96
5 Taylor	99	99

MISSOURI

	1	2
1 Clay	84	86
2 Akin	99	99
3 Gephardt	93	95
4 Skelton	99	99
5 McCarthy	98	98
6 Graves	99	99
7 Blunt	93	93
8 Emerson	92	92
9 Hulshof	92	93

MONTANA

	1	2
AL Rehberg	99	100

NEBRASKA

	1	2
1 Bereuter	97	97
2 Terry	98	98
3 Osborne	99	99

NEVADA

	1	2
1 Berkley	99	99
2 Gibbons	98	98

NEW HAMPSHIRE

	1	2
1 Sununu	95	95
2 Bass	99	99

NEW JERSEY

	1	2
1 Andrews	97	97
2 LoBiondo	100	100
3 Saxton	97	97
4 Smith	98	98
5 Roukema	41	41
6 Pallone	99	99
7 Ferguson	98	98
8 Pascrell	97	97
9 Rothman	95	95
10 Payne	93	94
11 Frelinghuysen	97	97
12 Holt	98	98
13 Menendez	95	95

NEW MEXICO

	1	2
1 Wilson	99	99
2 Skeen	99	99
3 Udall	99	100

NEW YORK

	1	2
1 Grucci	97	97
2 Israel	97	97
3 King	95	95
4 McCarthy	98	98
5 Ackerman	95	95
6 Meeks	93	93
7 Crowley	94	94
8 Nadler	88	87
9 Weiner	94	94
10 Towns	89	90
11 Owens	93	93
12 Velázquez	93	93
13 Fossella	93	93
14 Maloney	93	93
15 Rangel	93	94
16 Serrano	95	95
17 Engel	97	97
18 Lowey	97	97
19 Kelly	99	99
20 Gilman	95	95
21 McNulty	100	100
22 Sweeney	92	92
23 Boehlert	97	97
24 McHugh	95	95
25 Walsh	96	96
26 Hinchey	94	94
27 Reynolds	98	97
28 Slaughter	90	91
29 LaFalce	92	92
30 Quinn	94	94
31 Houghton	88	88

NORTH CAROLINA

	1	2
1 Clayton	90	91
2 Etheridge	100	100
3 Jones	97	97
4 Price	99	99
5 Burr	97	97
6 Coble	99	99
7 McIntyre	97	97
8 Hayes	99	99
9 Myrick	98	98
10 Ballenger	96	97
11 Taylor	90	91
12 Watt	98	98

NORTH DAKOTA

	1	2
AL Pomeroy	98	98

OHIO

	1	2
1 Chabot	99	99
2 Portman	98	98
3 Hall[3]	81	82
4 Oxley	91	92
5 Gillmor	95	95
6 Strickland	99	99
7 Hobson	99	99
8 Boehner	94	94
9 Kaptur	93	94
10 Kucinich	99	99
11 Jones	90	91
12 Tiberi	100	100
13 Brown	98	98
14 Sawyer	95	95
15 Pryce	87	88
16 Regula	99	99
17 Traficant[4]	0	0
18 Ney	99	99
19 LaTourette	95	95

OKLAHOMA

	1	2
1 Sullivan[5]	98	98
2 Carson	95	95
3 Watkins	91	91
4 Watts	89	89
5 Istook	94	94
6 Lucas	98	99

OREGON

	1	2
1 Wu	98	99
2 Walden	99	99
3 Blumenauer	98	98
4 DeFazio	97	97
5 Hooley	95	95

PENNSYLVANIA

	1	2
1 Brady	94	95
2 Fattah	92	92
3 Borski	86	86
4 Hart	99	99
5 Peterson	93	93
6 Holden	99	99
7 Weldon	92	93
8 Greenwood	93	93
9 Shuster	99	99
10 Sherwood	99	99
11 Kanjorski	98	98
12 Murtha	82	83
13 Hoeffel	99	99
14 Coyne	92	93
15 Toomey	97	97
16 Pitts	96	97
17 Gekas	99	99
18 Doyle	94	95
19 Platts	96	98
20 Mascara	74	74
21 English	97	98

RHODE ISLAND

	1	2
1 Kennedy	95	96
2 Langevin	99	99

SOUTH CAROLINA

	1	2
1 Brown	99	99
2 Wilson	99	99
3 Graham	98	98
4 DeMint	99	99
5 Spratt	97	97
6 Clyburn	98	98

SOUTH DAKOTA

	1	2
AL Thune	99	99

TENNESSEE

	1	2
1 Jenkins	91	91
2 Duncan	99	99
3 Wamp	98	98
4 Hilleary	75	76
5 Clement	86	87
6 Gordon	94	95
7 Bryant	92	92
8 Tanner	94	94
9 Ford	95	96

TEXAS

	1	2
1 Sandlin	97	98
2 Turner	99	99
3 Johnson, Sam	95	95
4 Hall	99	99
5 Sessions	94	95
6 Barton	95	96
7 Culberson	98	98
8 Brady	95	94
9 Lampson	95	96
10 Doggett	99	99
11 Edwards	99	99
12 Granger	97	97
13 Thornberry	98	98
14 Paul	96	96
15 Hinojosa	89	90
16 Reyes	89	89
17 Stenholm	99	99
18 Jackson-Lee	96	96
19 Combest	83	83
20 Gonzalez	99	99
21 Smith	95	95
22 DeLay	96	98
23 Bonilla	96	97
24 Frost	95	95
25 Bentsen	95	95
26 Armey	96	97
27 Ortiz	93	93
28 Rodriguez	97	97
29 Green	98	98
30 Johnson	99	99

UTAH

	1	2
1 Hansen	92	92
2 Matheson	99	100
3 Cannon	87	86

VERMONT

	1	2
AL Sanders	92	93

VIRGINIA

	1	2
1 Davis	99	99
2 Schrock	96	96
3 Scott	99	99
4 Forbes	99	99
5 Goode[6]	98	99
6 Goodlatte	99	99
7 Cantor	99	99
8 Moran	95	95
9 Boucher	95	95
10 Wolf	99	99
11 Davis	95	95

WASHINGTON

	1	2
1 Inslee	99	99
2 Larsen	98	98
3 Baird	99	98
4 Hastings	96	96
5 Nethercutt	92	92
6 Dicks	98	98
7 McDermott	92	93
8 Dunn	98	98
9 Smith	92	92

WEST VIRGINIA

	1	2
1 Mollohan	96	96
2 Capito	99	99
3 Rahall	98	98

WISCONSIN

	1	2
1 Ryan	94	94
2 Baldwin	99	99
3 Kind	97	97
4 Kleczka	95	95
5 Barrett	89	89
6 Petri	99	99
7 Obey	97	97
8 Green	99	100
9 Sensenbrenner	99	99

WYOMING

	1	2
AL Cubin	87	87

Southern states - Ala., Ark., Fla., Ga., Ky., La., Miss., N.C., Okla., S.C., Tenn., Texas, Va.

Appendix C

KEY VOTES

Strategic Muscle, Political Will

In any Congress, lawmaking succeeds by a mix of legislative strategy and political will. For the closely divided 107th Congress, each of the two sessions offered distinct portraits that first emphasized one of these elements and then the other.

The first year of the 107th unfolded as a primer in legislative tactics, with Republicans and Democrats taking victories and losses based largely on their success at gamesmanship over such matters as tax cuts and education policy. Republicans and Democrats each sought to maneuver the other into untenable political positions that forced just enough of them to vote against type to provide a margin of victory.

But in the second session, it was most often the gathering of momentum behind political will that determined winners and losers. The standing danger of any closely divided Congress — that just a few party strays will upend the most carefully conceived floor maneuver — struck home for Republican House leaders on bankruptcy overhaul and Senate leaders on prescription drugs.

The result in 2002 was a legislative record marked not by the closest votes, in which one side out-whipped the other to claim a scant majority, but rather by lopsided votes in which the desire to legislate reached a tipping point and overwhelmed the impulses of partisans to argue over details.

On the issues where no such momentum had built — where the tipping point had not yet been reached — details were parsed, positions held firm, and close votes in one chamber led nowhere in the other.

The key votes of the year, as selected by the editors of Congressional Quarterly, illustrate that dichotomy of fortunes.

CQ's tradition of declaring the key congressional votes of the year usually yields a collection of votes whose outcomes had been in doubt, or which largely determined the fate of an issue. This time, however, outcomes most often were determined by shifts in political momentum. As a result, CQ editors chose some votes that lacked suspense but reflected a point in the debate when an issue's momentum became inexorable. Others show predictable outcomes but were on issues of such national importance that they almost automatically were considered key votes, such as the vote to authorize the use of force in Iraq.

On the issues where Republicans and Democrats were driven by political momentum, primarily though not exclusively on national security issues, the votes in the House and Senate were almost without drama but were conclusive to the matters at hand.

On the issues where the parties concluded that there still was a fight worth having, primarily on domestic policy ques-

How CQ Picks Key Votes

Since 1945, Congressional Quarterly has selected a series of key votes on major issues of the year.

An issue is judged to be a key vote by the extent to which it represents:

- a matter of major controversy
- a matter of presidential or political power
- a matter of potentially great impact on the nation and lives of Americans.

For each group of related votes on an issue, one key vote is usually chosen — one that, in the opinion of CQ editors, was most important in determining the outcome.

tions, the votes on the floor were hard-won, unpredictable and more valuable as indicators of where the battle will begin in the 108th Congress than where they ended in the 107th.

The weight of political momentum was nowhere more evident than in the on-and-off quest to regulate the accounting industry. At the beginning of the year, the historic bankruptcy of Enron Corp., the energy trading giant in Houston, generated an intense but ultimately brief drive on Capitol Hill to call the auditing industry to account for the way one of its leaders, Arthur Andersen LLP, failed to note Enron's financial trouble. Despite enormous investor losses and the teary-eyed appearance of bankrupted Enron employees before congressional committees, the sentiment in Congress did not coalesce behind an urgent need to respond.

Then, a string of smaller business collapses through the spring culminated with the June announcement that WorldCom Inc. had hidden nearly $4 billion in expenses and vastly overstated its earnings. The reaction on Capitol Hill was nearly instantaneous. The plodding move toward possible action on pension rules, accounting standards and tax havens swiftly became a charge known as corporate accountability.

Before members left for the August recess, a new accounting oversight system, essentially written by Sen. Paul S. Sarbanes, D-Md., had been endorsed by Congress and sent to President Bush, who promptly signed it (PL 107-204). WorldCom and an increasingly pessimistic stock market had tipped the scale of politics and Sarbanes' bill, once greeted coolly, rocketed out of the Senate on a 97-0 vote that set the stage for equally swift and decisive House passage.

The dynamics on homeland security were much the same, though it was not scandal but the midterm election that provided the momentum. After spending the summer generally in agreement that a Homeland Security Department needed to be created, Republicans and Democrats argued to a standstill over whether employees of the department should have civil service and collective bargaining rights. The strong votes for passage of the bill (HR 5005 — PL 107-296) — with the Republican provisions curtailing civil service protections — came during the lame-duck session in November.

The critical votes in the House and Senate, however, occurred during the summer, when the course was set to make labor issues the central fight, and the midterm election the driving force to determine which way the issue would tip. In that election, Republicans gained three Senate seats and retook control of the chamber, while padding their majority in the House. At least one Democratic incumbent, Sen. Max Cle-

land of Georgia, lost to a GOP challenger, Rep. Saxby Chambliss, who focused on the way Democrats had stalled passage of the homeland security legislation over employee rights.

Close Votes, No Deals

The close votes often reflected stalemate between the parties. The debate over creating a prescription drug benefit for Medicare recipients clearly showed that it is an issue on which Republicans and Democrats still see a fight worth having. Without a pivotal event to swing both parties onto one plan, the issue remained intractable.

Republicans labored over a program that would rely heavily on private insurers to offer coverage and House leaders muscled it through the chamber, over the objections of some of their own members. But the hard-won passage of the bill (HR 4954) on a 221-108 vote gave Senate Democrats little to work with. The Senate tried but could not agree on one plan, choosing instead to kill every alternative on procedural votes known as budget points of order.

In the end, the GOP bill was the only prescription plan passed at all by the 107th Congress, making it a likely starting point for discussion in the 108th.

There were, of course, exceptions to the tipping point principle that largely governed lawmaking in 2002. There were a few close votes on issues that ultimately became law.

Chief among them was passage of the Trade Promotion Authority Bush had sought. Although the Senate vote was decisive, the House voted 215-212 to pass the measure (HR 3009 — PL 107-210) giving Bush greater latitude to negotiate trade deals.

Free trade breaks along regional lines as much as by party affiliation, and some Republicans in districts where the local economy was threatened by overseas trade were not easily persuaded to vote with Bush.

Republicans also suffered as a result of failed legislative strategy. The long, labored effort to overhaul bankruptcy law to make it more difficult for consumers to dodge their debts through the courts ran into new trouble despite the efforts of House GOP leaders.

A provision in the conference report on the bill (HR 333) specified that abortion protesters could not evade fines levied against them through bankruptcy. The language was the product of months of negotiation. But even with the support of Henry J. Hyde, R-Ill., the dean of anti-abortion forces in the House, abortion foes were adamant that the report not be adopted with the protest language included.

House leaders had tried once in July to secure adoption of the conference report, but were forced to pull it when it became clear abortion foes had mustered the votes to ensure defeat.

When GOP leaders tried again in October, believing that abortion opponents would have less clout after the midterm election, their gamble cost them dearly. The rule for debate of the conference report was defeated.

The key votes for 2002 follow, listed in the order of their original vote numbers.

34 Campaign Finance

Vote: Passage of the campaign finance overhaul bill brought to the floor after advocates succeeded in using a discharge petition to force consideration.

Ever since the Senate passed its initial version of the campaign finance bill in March 2001, supporters of the companion legislation in the House (HR 2356) had been fighting uncertainty and restlessness among Democrats.

House Democrats had provided the bulk of the votes for passage of similar bills twice before, in 1998 and 1999. But now that the Senate hurdle had finally been overcome and the legislation appeared close to becoming law, some Democrats were uneasy with the provision at the heart of the bill, a ban on unregulated "soft money" contributions from businesses, unions and the wealthy to the political parties. Another issue for some Democrats was the bill's increased limits on "hard money" giving — regulated donations directly to candidates — that Republicans had proved themselves better at. (*1999 Almanac, p. 8-3;*

1998 Almanac, p. 18-3)

The measure had stalled in the House in July 2001 when Democrats and a few Republicans voted down a rule for its floor consideration that had been drafted by GOP leaders. The rule would have made it difficult for sponsors Christopher Shays, R-Conn., and Martin T. Meehan, D-Mass., to alter their bill on the floor to bring it in line with the Senate-passed measure and avoid sending it back to the Senate for another debate. (*2001 Almanac, p. 6-3)*

On Jan. 24, 2002, after months of effort, Shays and Meehan gathered the last of the 218 signatures they needed on a "discharge petition" to bring their bill to the floor under debate rules more to their liking. The sponsors also had the benefit of momentum, thanks to the collapse of Enron Corp. and revelations regarding the energy trader's network of political giving and legislative influence.

GOP leaders were preparing a series of amendments they hoped would sink the bill. Their goal was to attach amendments that the Senate would never accept, while also providing political cover for lawmakers who wanted to say they had voted for a change in the system.

In the end, the momentum for the campaign finance overhaul designed by Meehan and Shays — and their Senate counterparts, John McCain, R-Ariz., and Russell D. Feingold, D-Wis. — proved unstoppable. The Shays-Meehan coalition largely held in the House, and mixed signals from the White House undercut efforts to unify House Republicans against the legislation. Speaker J. Dennis Hastert, R-Ill., asked President Bush for help before the debate began, but Bush chose to keep his distance. Just as the battle on the House floor was beginning

Feb. 13, White House spokesman Ari Fleischer signaled that Bush would sign any bill that would improve the campaign finance system.

Not long after, the president himself said he was endorsing nothing but would look closely at whatever Congress sent him. By then, supporters of the bill were on their way to victory.

Despite the intense pressure Republican leaders put on their caucus and more than 14 hours of maneuvering on the floor aimed at bringing down the bill, the House rejected every amendment that bill supporters feared would force a conference with the Senate. The climax — and key vote — came in the early morning hours of Feb. 14, when 41 Republicans joined the solid majority in the House to pass the bill. Only 12 Democrats voted no. The vote was 240-189: R 41-176; D-198-12 (ND 150-6, SD 48-6); I: 1-1. (*House vote 34, p. C-18*)

The campaign finance bill was on its way back to the Senate, which cleared it on March 20. Bush called the measure "flawed" but signed it (PL 107-155) a week later.

44 Broadband/Internet Service

Vote: Defeat of a motion to recommit the Tauzin-Dingell bill to the Commerce Committee for revision, which signaled the presence of a bipartisan majority to pass the intensely lobbied legislation.

Telecommunications legislation tends to be among the most technically intricate and heavily lobbied measures in Congress. And when a bill comes to the floor, the parliamentary maneuvering can be just as intense.

There was just one major telecommunications bill during the year. It was sponsored by House Energy and Commerce Committee Chairman Billy Tauzin, R-La., and ranking panel Democrat John D. Dingell of Michigan. As might be expected, it attracted considerable attention and money from the telecommunications industry. And, given the complex issues involved, the key vote came on an obscure procedural question without precedent in 92 years.

The Tauzin-Dingell bill (HR 1542) would have deregulated interstate high-speed Internet services provided over telephone lines by the four regional Bell companies — Verizon, SBC Communications, BellSouth and Qwest Communications — and allowed them to offer the services without opening their local telephone markets to competitors, which is a requirement under the 1996 telecommunications policy law (PL 104-104). (*1996 Almanac, p. 3-43*)

As the bill was readied for floor action, a complex strategy evolved. Christopher B. Cannon, R-Utah, and John Conyers Jr. of Michigan, the senior Democrat on the House Judiciary Committee, wanted to offer an amendment to restore the state and federal regulatory authority that the legislation would remove.

Steve Buyer, R-Ind., and Edolphus Towns, D-N.Y., countered with an amendment to restore some of the Federal Communications Commission's regulatory authority, but still keep the Bell-friendly spirit of the bill. The pivotal decision was for Buyer and Towns to ask that their amendment be considered as a second-degree amendment to Cannon-Conyers, meaning that Buyer-Towns would be voted on first, and if it were adopted, the Cannon-

Conyers language would not be voted on at all.

As the debate proceeded in the House, everyone waited for the expected sequence to take place. But Cannon did not offer his amendment during the time allocated.

There was great puzzlement on the floor, until Cannon's ally, Edward J. Markey, D-Mass., offered a motion to recommit, or send, the bill back to committee with instructions to add the Cannon-Conyers language. His reasoning, Markey said, was that Cannon-Conyers deserved its own up-or-down vote, and this was the only way to accomplish that. Buyer was upset because his move to block Cannon-Conyers had been countered. A recommittal motion is typically a tool used by lawmakers in the minority party. But this bill was hardly typical — members of both parties were on each side of the bill.

The showdown commenced when the presiding officer, Ray LaHood, R-Ill., ordered a vote on the "previous question," essentially moving to stop debate on the Markey recommittal motion. If approved, the vote on the Markey motion could proceed. But it failed, 173-256: R 62-157; D 109-99 (ND 98-56; SD 11-43); I 2-0. (*House vote 44, p. C-18*)

Congressional Research Service (CRS) called the episode "an unusual parliamentary process," marking the first time since 1910 that a motion on the previous question on a motion to recommit was defeated.

More immediately, the vote was a harbinger that Markey — the leading opponent of the Baby Bells' crusade — did not have nearly enough votes to derail the Tauzin-Dingell bill. Soon after, another rare occurrence came into play. Buyer and Towns were allowed to add their amendment to Markey's recommittal motion and to the bill itself without need for a separate recorded vote on their measure. Some protested that the recommittal process was being abused, but in the end the underlying bill passed, 273-157, a tally that closely mirrored the outcome of the key vote on Markey's parliamentary maneuver.

158 Defense Authorization

Vote: Passage of a bill to authorize the largest percentage increase in defense spending in decades without a single attempt to amend the bill to lower spending.

Ever since the boom years of the Clinton administration, the partisan divide over defense spending had been muddled. Democrats, normally opposed to big increases in the military, went along with larger defense authorizations as long as there was enough money to fund their domestic priorities.

But that political equation changed in 2001 when the tax cuts that were President Bush's top priority slashed projected federal budget surpluses. Bush insisted that domestic spending be kept tight at the same time that he proposed a $30 billion increase over the fiscal 2001 budget for defense — the last Clinton defense plan.

That year's House vote on the fiscal 2002 defense authorization bill may not have reflected members' fundamental policy views since it came only two weeks after the Sept. 11 terrorist attacks.

It was the vote on the fiscal 2003 defense authorization bill that could have tested House Democrats' resolve for challenging the size of the defense budget. Although the

House version of the bill amounted to $13 billion less than Bush requested, that difference reflected some technical bookkeeping decisions. Essentially, the bill endorsed Bush's request for a $45 billion increase in defense spending — the largest since the Vietnam War.

More than two-thirds of the Democrats voted for it.

The House GOP leadership barred consideration of several floor amendments, including one that would have cut $1.8 billion from the F-22 fighter program and another that would have eliminated $475 million authorized for the Army's Crusader cannon, which Defense Secretary Donald H. Rumsfeld had decided to cancel, but which the House version of the defense authorization bill (HR 4546) approved.

But the Democrats made their stand on a very narrow beachhead of issues. They presented a series of amendments designed to restrict the administration's study of the use of tactical nuclear weapons in wartime. They also proposed several amendments that would have restrained Bush's missile defense program, though none that would have reduced the $7.8 billion anti-missile budget for fiscal 2003.

The House, splitting largely along party lines, rejected all of these amendments. In the end, in a vote that ensured the Bush administration an unimpeded road to an enormous military build-up, the House passed the bill May 10 by a vote of 359-58: R 212-1; D 146-56 (ND 100-51; SD 46-5); I 1-1. (*House vote 158, p. C-18*)

170 Welfare Reauthorization

Vote: Passage of a Republican plan to renew the principle of welfare-to-work that was the cornerstone of the 1996 welfare system overhaul.

The 104th Congress ended more than 60 years of unfettered public assistance by writing a landmark welfare law (PL 104-193) in 1996 that tied payments to tough new work requirements. It was the most sweeping social policy change won by the Republicans who had just taken over the Capitol. Many Democrats, who thought the terms of the overhaul were too tough, predicted that a future Congress would rue the day.

But in 2002, most members of the 107th Congress, in both parties, demonstrated that they were generally satisfied with the basics of the measure, mindful that welfare caseloads had declined by more than half since its enactment. Instead, they debated whether work or education and training would best lead welfare recipients out of poverty, and how much flexibility states should be given to run the programs.

With major provisions slated to end Sept. 30, Congress needed to reauthorize the law or let it expire. President Bush made reauthorization a 2002 priority, calling for even tougher work rules for adult recipients and significant funding for programs that promote marriage. House Republicans wrote a bill (HR 4737) that tracked Bush's priorities and — they knew — would serve as the most conservative possible counterweight to what they expected would be a much softer welfare bill coming out of the Democratic-controlled Senate.

The GOP proposed requiring recipients to work 40 hours a week. States would be required to have at least 70 percent of their recipients employed by 2007, up from 50 percent required under the 1996 law. House Democrats said that while recipients should be required to work, they

should also be given more opportunities to take vocational training or attend adult education classes. They argued that many adults still on welfare were the toughest cases — drug-addicted, mentally ill or illiterate — who could not easily find employment.

By the time the debate reached the House floor May 16, any hope that the House might find a middle ground had been abandoned. Instead, the debate broke along party lines, and featured well-used partisan brickbats over social policy.

In the end, only 14 conservative Democrats voted for the GOP bill, and only four Republicans voted against it. The vote was 229-197: (R 214-4; D 14-192; ND 7-147; SD 7-45; I 1-1). (*House vote 170, p. C-18*)

Despite the partisan character of the debate and of the vote, the bill's passage demonstrated a recognition on Capitol Hill, even among some Democrats, that there would be no retreat from the 1996 decision to require work of welfare recipients. The Senate Finance Committee later amended the House bill to retain the 30-hour work requirement and provide for $5.5 billion in child care funding, but the measure died thereafter, forcing lawmakers to pass a temporary extension into 2003 only.

Still, the refining of Washington's new welfare posture will be a major social policy effort of the 108th Congress, and the vote to pass the House bill in 2002 will provide a clear demarcation of where the conservative edge of Congress' views lies.

194 Discretionary Spending Limit

Vote: Adoption of a measure, over the fierce objections of GOP appropriators, that committed the House to live under President Bush's spending ceiling for fiscal 2003.

A single House procedural vote one spring evening heralded one of the most bruising annual fights over discretionary spending in modern times. The outcome was locked in such intractable divisions — between Republican factions in Congress, between the House and the Senate, and between Congress and President Bush — that the year ended with none of the domestic spending bills enacted for fiscal 2003.

The vote came after the House Republican majority had adopted a budget resolution (H Con Res 353) that endorsed Bush's budget proposal, with an overall limit on discretionary spending of $759 billion. That figure included Bush's request for a $10 billion defense reserve fund to be spent at the administration's discretion, an idea Congress quickly rejected.

Bush had proposed a big increase in defense spending, but not even an inflationary increase for the rest of government. Republicans on the Appropriations Committee reluctantly supported the budget resolution, expecting to be able to exceed the spending limit later in the process or to negotiate a higher level with the Senate.

Senate Budget Committee Democrats marked up a budget (S Con Res 100) calling for about $9 billion more in non-defense spending than the House. Their plan had little chance of adoption on the floor, however, lacking any Republican support and facing the threat of Democratic defections. Majority Leader Tom Daschle, D-S.D., never brought a budget up for debate, but the Senate Appropriations Committee pressed ahead, marking up bills

with the Senate Budget Committee's $768 billion grand total as their target.

With no prospect that a final budget would be written, Republican House appropriators sought to ignore their own version. They began talking openly about producing spending bills with a total roughly equivalent to the Senate's more expensive bottom line.

House leaders soon came under pressure, from the White House as well as from fiscal conservatives in their ranks, to hold the appropriators in check. To that end, Republican leaders called on the House to cast another vote committing itself to living under the spending ceiling in its budget.

Although by itself the language they proposed would have imposed no enforceable restraint on spending, appropriators from both parties were furious. It was an unusual move, and the appropriators feared that the provision's adoption would doom them to a year of frustration — unable to win passage of domestic spending bills written under the ceiling.

The key vote came May 22 on a procedural measure setting the rules for floor debate on the fiscal 2002 supplemental appropriations bill (PL 107-206). Republican leaders had drafted the rule so that, if adopted, it would automatically attach the spending limit language to the widely popular appropriations bill. The only option that GOP appropriators had was to defeat the rule for consideration of the supplemental bill. Such procedural matters are normally considered party loyalty votes, but in this case GOP leaders were stung by a handful of defections. Appropriations subcommittee chairmen Sonny Callahan of Alabama and Jim Kolbe of Arizona went against their party, as did fellow GOP appropriator Roger Wicker of Mississippi. Three other Republican appropriators registered their protest by voting "present": Zach Wamp of Tennessee, George Nethercutt of Washington and Henry Bonilla of Texas, another subcommittee chairman. Several other GOP appropriators waited until late in the roll call to vote, forcing party leaders to work hard to head off other defections. But in the end, the rule was adopted, 216-209: R 214-3; D 1-205 (ND 1-153; SD 0-52); I 1-1. (*House vote 194, p. C-18*)

While its Senate counterparts, operating under a higher spending ceiling, approved all 13 of their fiscal 2003 spending bills on unanimous votes, the House committee never tried to mark up two of the largest domestic spending bills, one covering the Commerce, Justice and State departments and the other (HR 5320) for the Labor, Health and Human Services, and Education departments. The House passed only five of the 13 bills, and the 107th Congress adjourned with only two measures enacted: defense (PL 107-248) and military construction (PL 107-249).

282 Medicare Prescription Coverage

<u>Vote:</u> Passage of a GOP proposal that drew enough Republican moderates and Democrats to provide a clear picture of where the House stood as the Senate prepared for its own debate.

Congressional Republicans, especially the more conservative ones who ran the House, had long espoused a limited role for government in health care. And to the ex-

tent that they had in the past supported a prescription drug benefit for Medicare, it had been a very modest offering. A House-passed plan in 2000 would have cost $40 billion over five years.

So it was significant when Republican leaders decided in the summer of 2002 that it was imperative for the House to pass a Medicare drug benefit with a cost pegged at $350 billion over 10 years. Taking action would send the powerful message that the GOP-led House could deliver a Medicare drug bill before the Democratic-led Senate on one of the Democrats' core campaign issues. And if the Senate did act, the House would be ready with its conference position.

But it turned out that the Republican plan (HR 4954), cosponsored by Ways and Means Chairman Bill Thomas of California and Energy and Commerce Chairman Billy Tauzin of Louisiana, was not the easy election-year sell that House leaders thought it would be.

First, they had to wrestle with demands from rural Republicans and others in the rank and file that the bill include $30 billion over 10 years for health care providers. There was pressure to spare doctors and other health care professionals from more payment cuts scheduled under the Balanced Budget Act of 1997 (PL 105-33).

Next, leaders had to squelch a group of about three dozen Republican dissidents who had joined with Democrats in seeking provisions that would lower drug costs by directly restricting how the pharmaceutical industry does business. Those provisions included one to allow the wholesale importation of drugs sold more cheaply in Canada, and another to tighten patent laws to make it more difficult for manufacturers of brand-name drugs to impede low cost generic competition.

The legislation would have allowed Medicare enrollees to purchase private insurance policies covering prescription drugs, beginning in 2005, with a monthly premium estimated at $33. Patients would pay the first $250 of their drug costs each year, 20 percent of costs from $251 to $1,000, and 50 percent of the next $1,000. The patient would have to pay all drug costs from $2,001 to $3,700, after which insurers would pay the entire cost. The bill offered subsidies for low-income seniors to reduce or eliminate their insurance premiums and limit their co-payments.

AARP, the nation's largest advocacy group for Americans age 50 and older, criticized the plan as a poor deal for Medicare enrollees. Democrats denounced it as a sellout to the insurance industry.

Negotiations among Republicans over provider payments, drug pricing and other issues of contention continued right up to the point when the rule for debate came to the House floor. Thomas, Tauzin and Speaker J. Dennis Hastert of Illinois led a two-hour GOP conference meeting to try to sell members on the bill. More than two dozen Republicans expressed concerns about the bill.

GOP leaders tried to "educate" the dissidents into supporting the bill and, when necessary, leaned a little harder. Policy aides from the White House visited members' offices. And at one point during the week, Hastert threatened to hold the House in session into the weekend, delaying the start of the Fourth of July recess if necessary, to act on the bill.

To maintain control and force Democrats into an up-or-down vote, the Rules Committee barred amendments on the floor. The 218-213 vote to adopt that closed rule for floor debate gave GOP leaders confidence they had the votes to pass the bill.

It also allowed Hastert to declare victory as the House voted 221-208 on July 28 to pass the bill: R 212-8; D 8-199 (ND 6-148, SD 2-51); I 1-1. (*House vote 282, p. C-18*)

The measure never became law, but it demonstrated that House Republicans were willing to expand the scope of benefits under the 1965 Medicare program to meet demands of seniors, provided they could do so through private insurers, not the government.

347 | Independent Sept. 11 Commission

Vote: Adoption of an amendment to the intelligence authorization bill to create an independent commission to examine government agencies' failures in advance of the Sept. 11, 2001, terrorist attacks.

Hopes seemed dim for much of the year for those — most vocally the families of people who died in the Sept. 11 terrorist attacks — who wanted an independent commission to conduct a broad inquiry into government actions that not only failed to prevent those attacks but might have precipitated and even exacerbated them. Such a panel, in their view, would have looked at everything from immigration policy to federal construction standards.

Although a joint inquiry into the attacks by the House and Senate Intelligence committees was well under way by summer, some members of the House panel, led by Democrat Tim Roemer of Indiana, felt a broader investigation was necessary. They had come to this conclusion because the congressional inquiry was limited to the actions of covert agencies and because some panel members were not convinced they were receiving candid answers from the intelligence community.

Roemer, backed by lawmakers in both parties, threatened to amend the fiscal 2003 intelligence authorization legislation (HR 4628) to include authorization for an independent panel with the power to investigate any government policy or program that might have contributed to the al Qaeda terrorists' ability to hijack four commercial jetliners on Sept. 11, 2001.

Roemer's proposal was based on legislation (S 1867) first put forward in the Senate in late 2001 by Joseph I. Lieberman, D-Conn., and John McCain, R-Ariz. As chairman of the Governmental Affairs Committee, Lieberman had managed to get the measure through his panel in March 2002, but he was unable to secure a promise from the Senate leadership to bring the bill to the floor.

Momentum for their cause did not grow after revelations in May that FBI headquarters had ignored warnings — received in the summer of 2001 from an agent in Phoenix — hinting that terrorists were taking flight lessons with the intention of piloting jets into buildings. In addition, the White House opposed an independent investigation, especially while Congress was conducting its own inquiry.

Under pressure from the White House, the GOP leadership wrote a rule for debate on the House's intelligence

bill that allowed only a very narrow amendment. Roemer responded with an amendment proposing a commission to review intelligence agency efforts to implement recommendations by the joint House-Senate inquiry and other investigative panels. It also provided for the commission to review resource allocation, recommend organizational changes and determine technological needs in the intelligence community.

Roemer and his supporters saw the amendment as the camel's nose under the tent for winning a broader independent inquiry later. And that is precisely what happened. On July 25, the House adopted the amendment with 25 Republicans — many of whom had not indicated support for a probe in the past — bucking the president and the GOP leadership and voting for the idea of an independent commission. The vote was 219-188: R 25-183; D 193-4 (ND 145-1, SD 48-3) I 1-1. (*House vote 347, p. C-20*)

The vote offered clear evidence that Congress did not want its own inquiry to be the final word on the matter. By the time lawmakers returned from their August recess, the White House was preparing to reverse its position by expressing willingness to work out a deal with them on some sort of independent commission. On Sept. 24 the Senate applied more pressure, voting 90-8 to create a panel with a broad mandate as part of its version of the homeland security bill (HR 5005).

Negotiations stretched into November as probe backers and the White House bickered about the details of the new commission's scope and makeup. A compromise was finally reached under which the president would name the chairman of the panel, but members of Congress who backed the commission would name most of its members. The president signed the provision into law as part of the intelligence authorization bill Nov. 27.

357 | Homeland Security

Vote: Defeat of an amendment that would have extended civil service union protections to many workers in a new Department of Homeland Security, thus clarifying the political strength of the White House opposition to such protections.

The debate over creating a Homeland Security Department evolved into a bitter political fight over a single issue: the rights of federal workers. The administration was insistent on having the authority to write personnel rules for the new department that eliminated standard civil service protections. Democrats, longtime allies of federal workers' unions, ardently disagreed.

In particular, the two sides were at odds over the administration's view that in designing a new personnel system, it should have the broad power to fire and transfer workers and exempt some department employees from union representation on national security grounds. Organized labor argued that the administration was using homeland security as a smoke screen to gut collective bargaining protections. The administration tried to give assurances that existing protections, such as fair labor standards and civil rights rules, would apply in the new department. But labor groups and their Democratic friends were not mollified, and it was becoming increasingly clear that the question of workers' rights would be central to

the outcome of the legislation creating the new security department.

After a nine-member Select Committee on Homeland Security in the Republican-controlled House reported out a bill (HR 5005) that accommodated most of the administration's wishes, Constance A. Morella, R-Md., offered an amendment during floor debate that would have stipulated that workers transferred to the new department would retain their collective bargaining rights, unless their job descriptions were significantly changed.

The White House branded the language a non-starter, saying it would diminish powers that presidents had enjoyed since 1962, when John F. Kennedy asserted his authority to exclude unions from agencies primarily concerned with intelligence, investigations or security. The authority was codified by the 1978 Civil Service Reform Act (PL 95-454). *(1978 Almanac, p. 818)*

Faced with the prospect of moderate Republicans siding with Morella's amendment on worker rights, House Republican leaders sought to give wavering lawmakers an alternative. They arranged for Christopher Shays, R-Conn., to offer an amendment before Morella's that similarly would affirm union members' rights but would allow the president a waiver to set aside collective bargaining agreements that could have an "adverse impact" on the department's ability to keep the nation secure. All but two Republicans voted for the language, while 11 conservative Democrats crossed over to vote for it as well, and it was adopted, 229-201.

Morella then offered her amendment. The eight-term congresswoman faced a tough re-election fight in a predominantly Democratic district that is home to thousands of federal workers. She proposed effectively nullifying the waiver that would have been created under the Shays amendment. Morella raised the possibility of an "arbitrary" application of the national security waiver of collective bargaining rights, saying federal workers needed more ironclad assurances they would retain their rights.

With the Shays amendment adopted, the vote on Morella's proposal offered a clear window into the depth of House support for taking the union point of view — and rebuffing the president — in resolving the workers' rights dispute. But on the key vote, Morella persuaded only four moderate Republicans to join her, while seven Democrats voted against her language. As a result, it was rejected, 208-222, on July 26. (R 5-214; D 202-7; ND 153-2; SD 49-5; I 1-1) *(House vote 357, p. C-20)*

Senate Democrats included language virtually identical to Morella's in the homeland security bill approved by the Governmental Affairs Committee, but it was dropped in negotiations over the final version of the legislation. And the congresswoman lost her bid for a ninth term in November.

370 | Fast-Track Trade Procedures

Vote: Adoption of the conference report giving President Bush authority to submit trade pacts to Congress for consideration without amendments.

After the Senate in May joined the House in passing legislation to revive fast-track procedures for congressional action on trade deals, the stage was set for a summer of contentious conference negotiations. The main stumbling block to an easy deal was the Senate bill (HR 3009), which included a 10-year, $12 billion expansion of Trade Adjustment Assistance (TAA) programs for those who lost their jobs as a consequence of expanded trade. Many Republicans viewed TAA as an overly generous entitlement for workers in outdated industries.

Even after House Ways and Means Committee Chairman Bill Thomas, R-Calif., and Senate Finance Committee Chairman Max Baucus, D-Mont., settled a bizarre public spat over which of them would chair the conference (Thomas prevailed), disagreements over the worker provisions continued to impede progress. Though supportive of the bill's central purpose — giving the president the power to reach trade agreements with other nations that Congress could reject or endorse, but not tinker with — GOP fiscal conservatives were reluctant to embrace the TAA expansion as a price for their support.

Democrats in both chambers threatened to oppose any bill that did not include something as generous as the Senate TAA package. In addition, as the midterm elections approached, labor and environmental groups were becoming increasingly vocal in their opposition to the fast-track bill. With Democrats newly emboldened by the backlash against corporate accounting scandals, GOP leaders were talking about delaying the final vote on the trade bill until a post-election, lame-duck session.

At that point the White House ratcheted up the pressure for a compromise, pushing hard to get a bill on President Bush's desk before the congressional August recess. A frenzied week of conference negotiations followed, culminating in a three-hour, closed-door session late the evening of July 25 between Thomas and Baucus. The House chairman agreed to accept most of the Senate TAA package. The Senate chairman agreed to a revision of Senate language that would have allowed the Senate to amend trade deals if they affected U.S. anti-dumping laws.

Still, as the ink dried on the conference report, its fate was by no means assured. Administration officials showed up to lobby pro-business Democrats. Bush himself came to the Capitol to rally the House Republican rank and file to support the top trade objective of his presidency.

Textile state lawmakers, who proved vital in the original House vote, were not convinced the conference report protected their industries adequately. House appropriators were angry that the package, which did not go through their committee, would expand federal spending in a way they could not control.

But Bush's persistence — and some last-minute deals — paid off. The president telephoned to assuage Appropriations Committee Chairman C.W. Bill Young, R-Fla. Five pro-business Democrats — Adam Smith and Rick Larsen of Washington, Ellen O. Tauscher and Jane Harman of California, and Harold E. Ford Jr. of Tennessee — resisted pressure from their party leadership and voted for the conference agreement after having opposed the initial House bill in December.

Amid all the narrow but potentially decisive crosscurrents, the GOP leadership navigated the fragile deal to a bare embrace. After an overnight debate that started the Friday that the chamber's summer recess was to begin, the

House adopted the conference report with essentially one vote to spare. The final tally shortly after 3 a.m. on Saturday, July 27, was 215-212: R 190-27; D 25-183 (ND 11-143, SD 14-40); I 0-2. (*House vote 370, p. C-20*)

455 Iraq Use of Force Resolution

Vote: Passage of the resolution granting President Bush authority to wage war against Iraq as part of the effort to disarm it, thus endorsing a doctrine of pre-emptive strikes.

One of President Bush's central themes since he took office was the threat posed to U.S. national security by Iraq's attempts to develop chemical, biological and nuclear weapons. In his 2002 State of the Union address, Bush included Iraq as part of an "axis of evil" — a trio of nations, also including Iran and North Korea, all of which were trying to acquire unconventional weapons. Bush warned that the United States had no choice but to confront this threat. (*Text, p. D-3*)

The president went much further in a speech he delivered in June at the U.S. Military Academy at West Point. There, Bush explained that his administration would confront unconventional threats with a policy of military pre-emption. This new policy — unprecedented in U.S. history — meant that Bush was prepared to wage war against countries to prevent them from developing and using weapons of mass destruction against the United States.

Congress worried that Bush was leading the country to war without its approval, and lawmakers insisted that he submit a war resolution to Congress.

At first White House officials said Bush did not need congressional approval to defend the country. But in early September, he agreed to submit a resolution.

Once Bush made it clear he would respect Congress' role in the decision to use force against Iraq, he was assured a victorious vote. Despite deep reservations about Bush's muscular policy toward Iraq, many lawmakers — Democrats and Republicans — were reluctant to vote against the popular president on a matter of national security on the eve of midterm elections.

For Bush, however, the issue was his margin of victory on Capitol Hill. He did not want a repeat of the 1991 Persian Gulf War resolution (PL 102-1), in which Congress narrowly gave his father, President George Bush, approval to end Iraq's occupation of Kuwait. (*1991 Almanac, p. 437*)

He also wanted strong bipartisan support to strengthen his hand in negotiations with the United Nations, which had yet to vote on its own resolution to deal with Iraq.

As the White House and lawmakers negotiated for mutually acceptable wording, Bush was unable to reach a compromise with Senate Majority Leader Tom Daschle, D-S.D. As a result, Bush struck a deal with House Minority Leader Richard A. Gephardt, D-Mo., that gave him broad authority for launching a war against Iraq and a free hand to act without approval from the United Nations.

With Gephardt on the president's side and Daschle politically isolated, the House easily passed a measure (H J Res 114) authorizing military action against Iraq by a vote of 296-133. (R 215-6; D 81-126 (ND 49-105, SD 32-21); I 0-1). (*House vote 455, p. C-20*)

478 Abortion Opponents' Rights

Vote: Defeat of a rule to govern debate on a bankruptcy overhaul compromise that would have limited the rights of abortion protesters in bankruptcy proceedings.

A single provision in a comprehensive overhaul of the nation's bankruptcy code provided abortion opponents with their most significant victory of the year.

On a late-session procedural move to bring a conference report to the House floor, anti-abortion forces not only proved they still held sway over Republicans in a way that even the financial services lobbyists did not, but they also ensured that another year would lapse without the enactment of a bankruptcy bill under discussion since 1997.

The provision that caught their attention was aimed at preventing abortion protesters from filing for bankruptcy in order to avoid paying court-ordered judgments. It resulted from painstaking negotiations between Sen. Charles E. Schumer, D-N.Y., who wanted a strict crackdown on such practices, and Rep. Henry J. Hyde, R-Ill., who had become something of a patron saint of abortion foes.

The language provoked enough concern among Hyde's anti-abortion colleagues that they stalled consideration of the conference agreement on the bill (HR 333) in August. But, in November, with the election recently behind them, Republican leaders thought it was a good bet they could win a majority for the measure. A "yes" vote in the House was sure to be matched by a vote to clear the bill by the Senate.

To protect the conference agreement from parliamentary attacks, House GOP leaders wrote a resolution to set the rules for floor debate Nov. 14. Votes in favor of the rule were slow in coming, and many that showed up on the electronic tally in the "aye" column soon switched to "nay."

In the well of the House, Republicans were caught in a tug of war between their leadership, which was trying to make good on a promise to their financial services industry backers, and their conservative colleagues, who were never willing to stray too far from the anti-abortion forces that made up their base of political support. In the end, the anti-abortion side won the votes of two-fifths of the Republicans that day, more than enough to counterbalance the one-quarter of the Democrats who voted with the rest of the GOP to keep the bill alive.

The rejection of the rule, 172-243, killed the bankruptcy bill for the 107th Congress: R 124-87; D 48-155 (ND 24-127, SD 24-28); I 0-1. (*House vote 478, p. C-20*)

Majority Whip Tom DeLay of Texas worked the well feverishly, trying to persuade Republicans not to hand the party an embarrassing loss. But his formidable vote-getting skills were trumped by the work of Republican anti-abortion lawmakers such as Joe Pitts of Pennsylvania and Christopher H. Smith of New Jersey, who were working in concert with the Christian Coalition, Concerned Women for America and the U.S. Conference of Catholic Bishops.

About 20 minutes after the vote began, Speaker J. Dennis Hastert, R-Ill., who by custom does not vote, cast his vote in favor of the rule, creating a tie at 204. That was the closest Republican leaders got to winning. After GOP leaders acknowledged that their bid was doomed, many Republicans who had supported the rule out of loyalty to their lead-

ers rushed to change their votes.

Once the bankruptcy overhaul had become entangled in abortion politics — and anti-abortion Republicans showed they could trump the lobbying might of the business community within the GOP — the bill's future looked bleak.

"It becomes the 108th Congress' abortion vote," said Samuel J. Gerdano, executive director of the nonpartisan American Bankruptcy Institute. "It's entirely in this other realm, which, if you're an advocate of the bill, is not very comfortable because you don't have any control over it."

30   Farm Bill

Vote: Passage of a bill repudiating the 1996 "Freedom to Farm" act.

A basic tenet of the politics of agriculture in Congress is that the fault lines are always regional and hardly ever ideological. The most notable exception came six years ago, when the newly ascendant Republicans won enactment of a law (PL 104-127) designed to wean farmers from a federal subsidy system. But in the 107th Congress, there was never much doubt that the 1996 law would be repudiated. The big questions were how much more to spend and — reviving the regional battles of old — which commodities to treat a bit better than others.

The first question was answered in 2001. In October, the House passed a farm, conservation, nutrition and rural development package promising a double-digit increase in spending for the new decade. The Senate took up the bill (HR 2646) and by year's end signaled it would seek to spend even more. The question this year was what else the Senate would need to do to advance the bill, especially in an election year in which some of the most competitive Senate races were in farming or ranching states.

Republican senators from farm states railed against the farm bill that two Midwest Democrats — Majority Leader Tom Daschle of South Dakota and Agriculture Committee Chairman Tom Harkin of Iowa — had written. The bill was pushed to relatively easy passage Feb. 13, but only after it was altered to bring an array of senators on board.

That was the key agriculture policy vote of the year — because it set the stage for negotiations during the next two months on a six-year farm bill (PL 107-171) that generally maintained the regional deals embodied in the Senate measure. The vote was 58-40: R 9-38; D 48-2 (ND40-1; SD 8-1); I 1-0. (*Senate vote 30, p. C-22*)

A $2 billion support program for small dairy farmers persuaded Maine's two Republican senators, Susan Collins and Olympia J. Snowe, as well as Pennsylvania Republican Arlen Specter to support the bill. The hefty dairy program

also won over James M. Jeffords, I-Vt. Similarly, a $4.4 billion program for peanut farmers brought the Republican Senate delegations from Alabama and Virginia, while also guaranteeing the support of Georgia's two Democratic senators, Zell Miller and Max Cleland.

Daschle and Harkin were able to keep almost all of the remaining Democratic senators in line by warning that if their bill did not pass quickly, under the congressional budget rules, the $73.5 billion in additional spending that had been earmarked by Congress in 2001 was at strong risk of evaporating. Democratic senators who were not from states with large agricultural sectors were warned that a vote against the bill could cost Democrats control of the Senate.

Only two Democrats voted against the Senate bill: Jon Corzine of New Jersey, who viewed the package as too expensive, and Blanche Lincoln of Arkansas, who did not find the benefits for the rice and cotton farmers of her state sufficiently generous.

47   Fuel Economy Standards

Vote: Adoption of an amendment to delay congressional action on gas mileage requirements, guaranteeing that tougher standards would not be part of the year's energy bill.

Senate debate on an omnibus energy bill (HR 4) mirrored a seeming contradiction in the national psyche: Americans think it is more important to protect the environment than to drill for more oil, but they are unwilling to give up their big, fuel-guzzling vehicles in order to reduce demand.

Mindful of voter ambivalence, Congress has not done much to force the issue. Corporate Average Fuel Economy (CAFE) standards adopted in 1975 had been virtually unchanged since 1985; between 1995 and 1999, House Republicans added language to annual transportation spending laws blocking even a study of new standards.

As President Bush took office, however, the climate appeared to be changing. Faced with growing political pressure to emphasize conservation, leading Republicans said they were willing to consider higher CAFE standards. In the House-passed energy bill, this translated into a modest increase: a requirement that automakers implement changes to save 5 billion gallons of oil over the next six years.

In the Senate, plans were being laid for a more ambitious CAFE goal. Democrat John Kerry of Massachusetts and Republican John McCain of Arizona drafted a proposal that would require all classes of cars and light trucks to average 36 mpg by 2015, a jump of between 5 mpg and 10 mpg across the fleets. Proponents contended that automakers had or were developing the technology to make such a figure attainable.

As the Senate debate approached, the auto industry lobbied hard for more flexibility, similar to the approach in the House bill. Opponents of the Kerry-McCain plan argued that higher fuel efficiency would mean smaller, lighter and more dangerous cars — and fewer jobs for autoworkers. Left unsaid was that expensive sport utility vehicles, with their high profit margins, had become Detroit's bread and butter.

The opponents of higher CAFE standards decided their best approach was to offer an alternative. The amendment — by Carl Levin, D-Mich., and Christopher S. Bond, R-Mo. — would have required the National Highway Traffic

Safety Administration to increase mileage standards for light trucks, including SUVs, within 15 months and for cars within two years.

Industry officials said the Levin amendment ensured that some increase would occur, but not under the "aggressive" timetable envisioned by Kerry and McCain. The choice was cast as between a mandate that would be imposed by Congress, at the cost of jobs and vehicle safety, and a more considered decision by an agency that would have to take economics into consideration. A phalanx of interests, including the auto industry, unions, rural and suburban minivan and truck drivers, and business lobbyists, converged on Capitol Hill to lobby — and on March 13 the amendment by Levin and Bond was adopted, 62-38: R 43-6; D 19-31 (ND 14-27, SD 5-4) I 0-1. (*Senate vote 47, p. C-22*)

54 Campaign Finance

Vote: Clearing of the bill that rewrote the way federal campaigns would be funded.

The battle over whether to rewrite the campaign finance law on the books since Watergate had stretched over more than a decade, through one veto and hundreds of votes. Even after the measure (HR 2356) was passed by the House on Feb. 14 and came roaring back to the Senate, most lawmakers expected one last fight on the floor.

Mitch McConnell, R-Ky., long the bill's leading opponent, had filibustered earlier campaign finance measures and was being coy enough this time to keep the bill's supporters guessing. Majority Leader Tom Daschle, D-S.D., prepared to muscle it through the chamber with a complicated series of procedural votes designed to break a filibuster.

In the end, McConnell managed to delay action on the bill for more than a month and forced its supporters to prove they had the 60 votes required to overcome a filibuster. But he had conceded defeat even before the bill reached the floor. The March 20 vote to clear the legislation was 60-40, as one in five Republicans broke from their leadership to support enactment: R 11-38; D 48-2 (ND 40-1, SD 8-1); I 1-0. President Bush signed the bill into law (PL 107-155) on March 27. (*Senate vote 54, p. C-22*)

As examples of questionable fundraising practices on both sides piled up, supporters of an overhaul shaped and reshaped their legislation, making compromises and dropping some proposals as politically unpalatable. Abandoned, for example, was a provision that would have banned contributions from political action committees — part of the first campaign finance bill introduced in 1995 by Sens. John McCain, R-Ariz., and Russell D. Feingold, D-Wis.

The heart of the final bill — the ban on soft money and restrictions on political advertising funded with those unregulated contributions — took shape gradually. The final pieces began coming together during the 2000 elections. McCain made campaign finance the foundation of his presidential race, boosting him and the cause to national prominence. His popularity and tenacity helped keep the bill moving forward.

When the 107th Congress began, turnover in the Senate, where McCain and Feingold had been blocked for years by filibusters, shifted the balance of power. Seven senators who voted to block the 1999 campaign finance bill were re-

placed by supporters of McCain and Feingold. Another five Republicans who had opposed the measure in the past switched their votes. The first to announce a change of heart was Thad Cochran of Mississippi, who said he had watched his colleagues struggle against a tide of opposition money and concluded that McCain had been right.

65 Federal Election Standards

Vote: Passage of a bill to set federal standards for elections, combining provisions to simplify voting with greater safeguards against fraud.

Before the terrorism of Sept. 11 and the anthrax attacks, perhaps the most immediate crisis the 107th Congress promised to address was the calamity of Election Day 2000, which had cast doubt on the outcome of the presidential contest and deepened voter skepticism about the reliability and fairness of the entire electoral process. But it was not until 17 months after that election — when the Senate in April passed an election overhaul bill embodying a set of carefully balanced tradeoffs — that Republicans and Democrats cemented a pact that would carry the legislation through a summer of negotiations to President Bush's desk.

To ensure that eligible voters would never again be denied the right to vote, Democrats wanted to set the first federal standards for conducting elections and provide money to help carry out those requirements. They likened the effort to a revival of the civil rights legislative campaigns of the 1960s.

After fits and starts, the House passed a bipartisan bill (HR 3295) at the end of 2001 that set broad minimum standards while giving states considerable flexibility in deciding how to meet them. And at the same time, it appeared that a similar bridging of the breach had been accomplished in the Senate. The key was a willingness by Democrats to include anti-fraud protections as a condition of winning Republican support. Sen. Christopher S. Bond, R-Mo., blamed fraud for defeats of Republican colleagues in both the Senate and gubernatorial races in Missouri the year before, so the only election bill that he and many other Republicans would support was one that would make it "easier to vote and harder to cheat."

As soon as the compromise (S 565) came to the Senate floor in February, however, the anti-fraud provisions ran into trouble. Democrats Charles E. Schumer of New York and Ron Wyden of Oregon argued that the language — to require voters who had registered by mail to produce proof of identity and residency when they voted for the first time — would have disenfranchised poor and minority voters. Civil rights and voting rights group took their side. Schumer and Wyden tried to replace the language they disliked with language allowing new voters to vouch for their identities with a signature. The Senate, by 46-51, rejected a move that would have tabled, and thereby killed, the Democrats' alternative.

That was the moment that almost caused the fragile deal to unravel. Republicans refused to continue work on the bill unless the amendment was withdrawn, and the legislation was pulled from the floor for a month.

Ultimately, however, Democrats decided they had to leave the anti-fraud provisions in the bill for it to pass. The best Schumer and Wyden could get was an exception allowing voters in Oregon and Washington — where most voting was

conducted by mail — to submit their driver's license numbers or part of their Social Security numbers to prove their identities. When the bill returned to the floor in April, the nearly unanimous support for the package's basic bargain — easier access to the polls in return for tougher rules to restrict fraud — was made clear. The vote for passage was 99-1: R 48-1; D 50-0 (ND 41-0, SD 9-0); I 1-0. (*Senate vote 65, p. C-22*)

The vote would not be the last hurdle for the bill. Conference negotiations almost fell apart several times, but the tradeoff that had been finalized by the Senate proved to be enough to keep Democrats and Republicans talking. Ultimately, it was the tradeoff at the core of the measure (PL 107-252) that Bush signed Oct. 29 — almost two years after the disputed election that started it all.

71 Arctic National Wildlife Refuge

Vote: Defeat of a motion to end debate on an amendment to permit drilling for oil in ANWR, thus killing the proposal.

The promise of oil beneath the coastal plain of Alaska's Arctic National Wildlife Refuge (ANWR) was a centerpiece of President Bush's energy strategy and the focus of nearly two years of debate in Congress. In 2001, the oil industry, the administration, its congressional allies and the Teamsters Union framed the debate in economic terms — energy independence and jobs — and were able to win House passage of an energy bill (HR 4) that would allow oil and gas exploration on ANWR's coast, with actual development limited to 2,000 acres.

Shaken by the House vote, environmental groups poured resources into stopping the proposal in the Senate. They recruited officials from other unions to fight the plan and aired pleas from celebrities not to allow drilling in ANWR, which many consider the crown jewel of public lands because it is so unspoiled. Environmental groups — citing polls showing that a majority of Americans feared that drilling would pose ecological harm — made it clear that senators who voted for drilling would be held accountable in November.

Those who favored drilling also had lost some momentum by the time of the debate in the spring. Bush did not publicly insist that he would veto an energy bill without an ANWR drilling provision. Concerns about an electricity shortage on the West Coast had subsided and gasoline prices were down, easing the pressure for more energy resources.

Through weeks of Senate debate, the parties maneuvered for advantage. Republicans repeatedly demanded Senate action while avoiding a vote by failing to submit an ANWR amendment because they lacked the 60 votes required to shut off a promised Democratic filibuster. After threatening to file for cloture on the entire energy bill, which would have precluded an ANWR amendment, Majority Leader Tom Daschle, D-S.D., finally brought the issue to a head April 18, arranging a vote on whether to bring the debate on the ANWR question to a close. Sixty votes were required, and proponents of the drilling came up 14 short. The vote on invoking cloture was 46-54: R 41-8; D 5-45 (ND 2-39, SD 3-6); I 0-1. (*Senate vote 71, p. C-22*)

The defection of eight Republicans denied the amendment sponsors even the simple majority they might have cited in conference as evidence of Senate support for drilling.

130 Fast-Track Trade Procedures

Vote: Passage of a bill giving President Bush greater trade negotiating authority, but only if coupled with an expansion of aid to trade-displaced workers.

Since fast-track trade authority lapsed in 1994, deep congressional divisions over the impact of free trade on U.S. industry and the environment prevented the White House from regaining broad latitude to negotiate trade deals. Fast-track authority requires Congress to vote for or against a trade agreement within 90 days of its receipt from the president, but prohibits amendments.

Soon after entering office in 2001, President Bush made renewing fast track one of his top international policy objectives. Dubbing it "trade promotion authority," Bush said he needed to assure trading partners that Congress would not tinker with deals after they had been negotiated.

Most Democrats and some Republicans feared that the U.S. would lose manufacturing jobs to overseas competitors paying lower wages and operating under weaker environmental standards. But House Republican leaders managed to pass their fast-track bill (HR 3005) by a single vote in December 2001. (*2001 Almanac p. 19-3*)

While the Senate is generally more inclined to support trade liberalization, Democratic leaders had to consider the fears of their political base in the labor and environmental communities. Majority Leader Tom Daschle of South Dakota and Finance Committee Chairman Max Baucus of Montana decided that the best way to appease those groups was to compel Bush and the GOP to accept — as a condition of reviving fast track — a substantial expansion of Trade Adjustment Assistance (TAA) programs, which provide financial assistance and job training to workers who are laid off as a consequence of foreign competition.

The White House expressed support for a generous TAA package, but the most conservative Republicans in the Senate balked, describing an expansion as essentially a government handout for industries that were dying because they could no longer stay competitive in their markets. Particularly troublesome for those senators was a proposed subsidy for trade-displaced workers to help them cover the cost of medical insurance. Negotiations among Baucus, Finance ranking Republican Charles E. Grassley of Iowa and Phil Gramm, R-Texas, dragged on until the White House persuaded Gramm to accept a compromise. It called for a $12 billion TAA expansion over 10 years that included a tax credit — but not a direct subsidy — for health care.

But the legislation before the Senate (HR 3009) faced other hurdles. Mark Dayton, D-Minn., and Larry E. Craig, R-Idaho, won solid backing for an amendment that would allow the Senate to strip trade pacts, by a simple majority vote, of any language that would undercut U.S. antidumping laws. The vote came even though business groups turned out en masse to oppose the amendment, pledging campaign retribution against supporters. Bush said he would veto the entire trade package if the Dayton-Craig language landed on his desk.

The year's most important trade vote in the Senate, therefore, came May 23 on passage of trade legislation

written with the policy objectives of both parties in mind. With the Democrats split almost evenly and the Republicans breaking eight-to-one in favor, the vote was 66-30: R 41-5; D 24-25 (ND 16-24, SD 8-1); I 1-0. *(Senate vote 130, p. C-22)*

The tally gave Bush's trade agenda substantial momentum, but it also demonstrated the resolve of Senate Democrats to be important players in U.S. trade policy — and the willingness of the Republicans to go along. In the end, the Senate-passed bill became the framework for the measure ultimately enacted (PL 107-210). Much of the TAA expansion was retained at Democratic insistence, and the Dayton-Craig provision was dealt away in the bargaining. As a result, the Senate vote to clear the bill was nearly the same as its vote for initial passage, 64-34.

151 Extending the 2001 Tax Cut

Vote: Defeat of a motion to waive budget rules in order to permit an indefinite extension of the estate tax repeal; the vote killed the proposal.

Since the day in June 2001 that President Bush put his signature on the deepest tax reduction in a generation, its sunset provision had been labeled by the statute's Republican proponents as its most noteworthy blemish. While efforts to extend all or parts of the law (PL 107-16) came up short in 2002, the Senate did cast one ballot that buoyed advocates' hope of someday making the year's cut "permanent."

Neither the president, nor his allies at the Capitol, ever intended to confine the duration of his signature tax cut. But budget rules and the limits of Republican power in the 107th Congress forced the GOP to agree that the package would expire altogether on Dec. 31, 2010. The $1.35 trillion total was set by a congressional budget resolution, meaning that all of the revenue had to be forgone within the 10-year time frame of that budget — unless, as a practical matter, three-fifths of the entire Senate was willing to create an exception.

No such Senate supermajority existed in 2001, which is why the sunset provision was part of the law. And — given the return of deficits and the polarizing effect of the tax debate in an election year — the votes to extend the cuts were still lacking in 2002. So, while House Republicans pushed through such a bill (HR 586) along party lines in April, any similar measure was always a non-starter in the Senate.

Political pragmatists in the GOP were willing to settle for something less: a Senate test vote on indefinitely extending one broadly popular provision. Although the chance of winning even that was a long shot, the GOP viewed such a vote as an opportunity to draw a clear distinction in the minds of voters between themselves and most Democrats.

For their campaign, the GOP chose the repeal of the estate tax, which had a broad and bipartisan base of support but also the shortest life span under the law. After a gradual reduction in the top rate to 46 percent from 55 percent by 2007, the tax would be wiped off the books altogether — but only for heirs of people who died in 2010. Only a few thousand people annually would be affected by the tax's resurrection the following year, because the great majority of estates (those valued at less than $675,000) were exempt from tax-

ation before the 2001 law and because a majority of the tax was paid on inherited stocks, bonds, real estate or other non-business assets. Still, Republicans successfully painted the debate as a fight to preserve family farms and family-controlled small businesses, which drew support from Democrats who represented farm country or large numbers of small businesses.

The test vote, in the GOP view, allowed the party to win no matter the outcome: Either enough politically vulnerable Democrats would be pressed to vote "yes" to create an upset victory, or the Republicans would have an issue to use against those senators in the midterm elections.

Majority Leader Tom Daschle, D-S.D., promised to allow the year's key Senate vote on tax policy in return for a loosening of Senate Republican objections to the year's energy legislation (HR 4). On June 12, senators voted 54-44 to waive the budgetary restrictions preventing an extension of the estate tax repeal: R 45-2; D 9-41 (ND 4-37, SD 5-4); I 0-1. *(Senate vote 151, p. C-22)*

Although insufficient to advance the tax cutters' quest — 60 votes were required to prevail — the vote allowed Republicans to boast that a solid Senate majority favored the idea.

At the same time, Democrats claimed some success at resisting the GOP maneuver. Only three of the 14 Democratic senators then seeking re-election — Finance Committee Chairman Max Baucus of Montana, Max Cleland of Georgia and Mary L. Landrieu of Louisiana — voted with the Republicans. And six of the 12 Democrats who had voted to enact the tax law in 2001 voted against allowing an extension of the estate tax repeal.

157 Terrorism Insurance

Vote: Passage of a bill to create a government-backed re-insurance pool, including a provision on civil liability that provided the foundation for a final compromise on the issue.

In the wake of the terrorist attacks of Sept. 11, 2001, which resulted in an estimated $40 billion in insurance claims, commercial property and casualty insurers said that — absent a federal backstop — they would no longer routinely insure businesses, sports stadiums and skyscrapers against the risk of such catastrophic terrorism.

The House passed a bill (HR 3210) in November 2001 to make the federal government the insurer of last resort, but the Senate remained hamstrung over the question of whether to ban punitive damages in civil lawsuits arising from terrorist acts. Such a ban, which was included in the House bill, was unthinkable to Senate Majority Leader Tom Daschle, D-S.D. He derailed a Senate Banking Committee compromise that would have barred such awards. But Senate Republicans, such as Phil Gramm of Texas and Mitch McConnell of Kentucky, said a ban was necessary to prevent trial lawyers from profiting from terrorism.

For months, Republicans thwarted Daschle's attempts to bring a bill without a punitive damages ban to the floor. They finally relented in June after senior Bush administration officials sent a letter to Minority Leader Trent Lott, R-Miss., saying they would recommend that Bush not sign a bill that "leaves the American economy and victims of terrorist acts subject to predatory lawsuits and punitive damages."

Republicans took the letter as a sign that Bush would not abandon them during House-Senate conference negotiations. They allowed Daschle to bring a bill (S 2600) to the floor that did not ban punitive damages, but stipulated that such awards would not be insured losses subject to government aid.

But the key vote — because it displayed the united resolve of Senate Democrats to stick to their guns in subsequent conference negotiations — came on June 18 when the Senate voted to pass the bill. The vote was 84-14: R 34-14; D 49-0 (ND 40-0, SD 9-0); I 1-0. (*Senate vote 157, p. C-23*)

That overwhelming show of support for the bill demonstrated that most Senate Republicans cared more about establishing a federal terrorism insurance program than about setting new ground rules for tort law. The vote also reflected that Senate Democrats were prepared to steadfastly oppose the addition of a punitive damages ban during negotiations with the White House, which was eager to complete the bill as a means of helping stimulate the economy.

The White House relented on the issue of punitive damages when it became clear that Senate Democrats would not agree to language specifying that federal legislation would not necessarily infringe on state legal standards. That was important because a handful of states already banned punitive damages awards.

Bush then successfully lobbied congressional Republicans, especially the House GOP leaders who strongly supported a punitive damages ban, to swallow their misgivings and adopt the conference report. The president signed the bill (PL 107-297) on Nov. 26.

176 Corporate Regulation

Vote: Passage of a bill to strengthen federal accounting and corporate governance regulation, which had been stalled until new business scandals changed the political dynamic and made broad legislation inevitable.

The year began with indignant lawmakers lining up to castigate current and former executives of the bankrupt Enron Corp. Numerous congressional investigations and legislative proposals were not far behind as Congress responded to a series of corporate scandals.

But by early summer, momentum for legislative action had dissipated. In April, the House had passed a Bush administration-backed bill (HR 3763) that was dismissed by critics as a tepid response to a debilitating crisis in investor confidence. The administration's push for creation of a Department of Homeland Security, along with a burgeoning Middle East crisis, diverted attention from the corporate accounting issue, and from an effort by Senate Banking Committee Chairman Paul S. Sarbanes, D-Md., to move a more stringent bill. Some Democrats fretted that Sarbanes had squandered the corporate accountability mandate by waiting until May to unveil his bill and until June to begin a markup.

Then came the June 25 revelation that telecommunications giant WorldCom Inc. improperly counted $3.9 billion in expenses as capital costs. Literally overnight, corporate fraud legislation went from a sidetracked casualty of gridlock to must-pass legislation that practically no one on Capitol Hill or in the administration dared to oppose.

By the time Sarbanes' bill reached the Senate floor after the July Fourth recess, a crackdown on corporate cheating had become unstoppable. Several amendments were adopted during a week of debate, including one offered by Judiciary Committee Chairman Patrick J. Leahy, D-Vt., that mandated prison terms for shareholder fraud and obstruction of justice involving document shredding. Across the Capitol, House Financial Services Committee Chairman Michael G. Oxley, R-Ohio, dryly observed that at that moment "summary execution would get about 85 votes."

In the end, not a single senator voted against the most sweeping corporate regulatory measure since the Depression — a clear signal that the Senate's approach would be very nearly the package that became law. That signal was sent July 15 with the 97-0 vote to pass the bill: R 46-0; D 50-0 (ND 41-0, SD 9-0); I 1-0. (*Senate vote 176, p. C-23*)

Senate Democrats rode that wave of support through a quick conference with the House. The absence of dissent in the Senate, combined with President Bush's insistence that Congress send him a bill before it left town for its August recess, allowed Senate Democrats to largely dictate to Republicans the terms of the conference report. Just two weeks after the vote, Bush signed a law (PL 107-204) closely tracking the Senate's bill, with creation of an oversight board to set standards for audits and oversee the accounting industry, and a prohibition on auditors providing other services to the publicly traded companies they audit.

199 Medicare Prescription Coverage

Vote: Defeat of a motion that would have exempted a prescription drug proposal from budgetary requirements, thus killing a bipartisan compromise proposal.

After the House passed a bill June 28 to create a Medicare prescription drug benefit, the pressure was on the Democrats who led the Senate to respond in kind. In the middle of July, Majority Leader Tom Daschle, D-S.D., called up a bill (S 812) designed to speed government approval of less expensive generic drugs, using it as a vehicle for a floor fight over a Medicare prescription drug benefit.

All year, Daschle had blocked the Finance Committee from considering a Medicare drug bill, because he knew centrists John B. Breaux, D-La., and James M. Jeffords, I-Vt., would side with panel Republicans to report a version similar to the House bill (HR 4954) — an approach anathema to a majority of Senate Democrats. But he also knew, well before the floor debate began, that his own side lacked the 60 votes needed to overcome procedural hurdles.

As the floor debate unfolded, it was clear there was still a "fundamental divide," as Daschle called it, over whether private insurance companies or the government-run Medicare program should deliver a drug benefit to senior citizens. Off the floor, sponsors of competing plans worked to develop a compromise — just as they had earlier in the year. But one by one, alternative proposals, including fallback plans seeking to bridge the partisan divide, were rejected. Neither side could muster the 60 votes necessary to waive budget points of order that were raised, because most plans exceeded the $300 billion, 10-year cost that had been sanctioned in the fiscal 2002 budget resolution.

A proposal by Democrats Bob Graham of Florida, Zell Miller of Georgia and Edward M. Kennedy of Massachusetts failed to surmount the point of order, 52-47. A competing amendment — known as the "tripartisan plan" because it was sponsored by Republican Charles E. Grassley of Iowa along with Breaux and Jeffords — fell, 48-51. A far more limited plan by Chuck Hagel, R-Neb., and John Ensign, R-Nev., failed on a different procedural challenge, 51-48. It would have offered a discount card to help low-income Medicare beneficiaries buy drugs and would have capped out-of-pocket costs based on a sliding income scale.

By the end of the week, both sides voiced frustration at the stalemate, and the atmosphere appeared ripe for a compromise. Graham, working with Republican Gordon H. Smith of Oregon, attempted to build on the Hagel proposal with a $400 billion, 10-year plan that would cover all Medicare recipients who earned up to double the poverty level and those with annual drug bills in excess of $3,300.

The proposal was endorsed by AARP, the biggest lobbying group for senior citizens and those nearing retirement. While AARP preferred a more comprehensive program, with four days left before the August recess, the Graham-Smith amendment was seen as the last best chance for a Medicare prescription drug benefit to pass the Senate in the 107th Congress. The vote on this plan — technically another vote on whether to waive a budget point of order — would be key.

Sponsors believed that members' fear of going home empty-handed would outweigh their objections to this particular proposal. But it, too, failed, 49-50. R 4-44, D 45-5 (ND 38-3, SD 7-2); 0-1. (*Senate vote 199, p. C-23*)

The closeness of the vote again showed the philosophical divide on Medicare, though a handful of senators on both sides voted against the majority of their party. The vote was a setback for Daschle and the Democrats, who felt they had moved as far as they could to win GOP support. But opponents, most of them Republicans, continued to insist that the issue should be returned to the Finance Committee, where they knew they could prevail on their preferred version.

223 | Independent Sept. 11 Commission

Vote: Adoption of an amendment to launch an independent inquiry into intelligence shortcomings that may have helped to precipitate the 2001 terrorist attacks.

By the time they were called on to decide whether to launch an independent investigation of government lapses before the Sept. 11, 2001, terrorist attacks, senators were more than ready to take up another tool to force additional answers out of the Bush administration.

At the time of the vote, Sept. 24, 2002, the House and Senate Intelligence committees had been at work for almost four months on their own joint inquiry into government intelligence failures before the attacks, and they were receiving few answers they viewed as credible. Lawmakers such as Richard C. Shelby of Alabama, the ranking Republican on Senate Intelligence, had begun to accuse the CIA and other covert agencies of stonewalling and blocking the release of information in hopes of waiting out the inquiry, scheduled to close early in 2003.

Slowly senators began re-examining legislation (S 1867)

originally put forward by Joseph I. Lieberman, D-Conn., and John McCain, R-Ariz., in December 2001. The bill proposed an independent commission with subpoena powers and the power to investigate all branches of the government to see what, if anything, could have been done to prevent the four hijackings that resulted in the worst terrorist attack ever on the United States.

Lieberman, chairman of the Governmental Affairs Committee, had won his panel's backing for the proposal in March. But the measure languished as Lieberman failed to secure any promises from the Senate leadership to bring it to the floor.

Momentum started to build in July, and in the House. Tim Roemer, D-Ind., a member of the House Intelligence Committee, also had grown dissatisfied with the pace of the congressional probe. Blocked by the Republican leadership from winning a vote on broad language similar to Lieberman's, Roemer nonetheless was able to secure adoption in the House of a proposal to create an independent commission with the narrow mandate of reviewing the intelligence agencies' implementation of recommendations from the joint House-Senate inquiry and from other investigations.

Within weeks, it became clear the sentiment existed in Congress to go beyond that. By the time Congress left for its August recess, several Republican senators, including Fred Thompson of Tennessee and Pat Roberts of Kansas, indicated that they would support an independent investigation similar to Lieberman's original proposal. Four days before the vote took place, the White House publicly reversed course to signal it would support the idea.

As a result, the Senate majority was overwhelming. With only eight of the president's most loyal allies in dissent, the Senate voted 90-8 to make the creation of an independent commission with a broad mandate part of a larger bill (HR 5005) to establish a Homeland Security Department: R 41-8; D 48-0 (ND 39-0, SD 9-0); I 1-0. (*Senate vote 223, p. C-23*)

But the homeland security bill quickly became tied up in a partisan dispute about workers' rights and did not move further until after the election. In the interim, proponents of a broadly constituted commission — prodded by families of the victims of Sept. 11 — learned that White House support for an independent panel did not necessarily mean the president supported the kind of commission envisioned by Congress.

The level of support in the Senate vote Sept. 24 served as crucial leverage in getting the administration to compromise on some of its demands about the scope and powers of the probe. The pressure ultimately yielded an agreement in the lame-duck session under the fiscal 2003 intelligence authorization law (PL 107-306), which President Bush signed Nov. 27, to create an 18-month probe with a chairman appointed by the president and a majority of its members appointed by supporters of an aggressive investigation.

226 | Homeland Security

Vote: Defeat of a motion to limit debate on a proposal for a new Homeland Security Department that included civil service protections for employees, heralding the loss of momentum for the Democrats on the issue.

The most divisive issue blocking the creation of a new

Homeland Security Department pitted federal employees' unions against the White House over "management flexibility" giving the department authority to write its own personnel rules. As the midterm election neared, the debate escalated from a philosophical difference into an increasingly acerbic and entrenched political fight. The venue was the Senate floor, where the bill (HR 5005) had languished since the House passed its version in July.

In the weeks before Election Day, moderates tried to broker a compromise over the president's powers to remove employees from their collective bargaining agreements on national security grounds. Bush wanted to preserve authority the president has had since 1962 to prevent the unionization of intelligence and national security workers.

Unions, fearful the president would use the powers to eliminate them from the new department, wanted to narrow the exemption to employees who were given substantially new jobs as part of the reorganization.

The pleas by moderates to step up negotiations were drowned out by the rhetoric of Republicans and Democrats, each blaming the other for stalling the bill. GOP leaders said Democrats were more interested in protecting the power of their top union contributors than in protecting national security. Democratic leaders charged that Republicans only wanted an election issue, not a compromise.

Majority Leader Tom Daschle, D-S.D., resorted to a tactic he rarely used — and had vilified Republicans for employing extensively in the past. He "filled the amendment tree," a parliamentary maneuver in the Senate that allows one side to shut down a debate by preventing any additional motions or amendments from being offered.

Reflecting the partisan tenor of the moment, the Senate voted along nearly precise party lines Sept. 26 to reject a bid to push the debate toward a climax. The key vote came on a bid to invoke cloture, and thereby restrict debate, on the Democratic version of the homeland measure, by Governmental Affairs Committee Chairman Joseph I. Lieberman of Connecticut. The vote was 50-49: R 1-48; D 48-1 (ND 41-0, SD 7-1); I 1-0. The majority was 10 short of the 60 votes required for cloture. (*Senate vote 226, p. C-23*)

The vote was pivotal because it heralded the high-water mark for whatever momentum the Democrats had built for fundamentally reshaping the homeland bill — and especially its labor provisions — to their liking. Because the Democrats were unable to draw any more GOP votes to their cause, the outcome made it clear that the decisive issue in the debate would not be resolved before the election. Republicans refused to allow further action unless promised that their version of the employment language, the one Bush insisted upon, would not be altered.

Democratic leaders hoped that on Election Day the voters might revive the momentum in their direction. In fact, the opposite happened. The Democrats lost control of the Senate for the 108th Congress, in part because swing voters in some close races signaled that they did not like the party's pro-union emphasis. Soon after, Republicans were able to leverage substantial victories on the measure (PL 107-296) that Bush signed Nov. 25.

237 Iraq Use of Force Resolution

Vote: Clearing of the measure giving President Bush authority to wage war against Iraq as part of the effort to disarm it, thus endorsing a doctrine of pre-emptive strikes.

Little daylight existed between President Bush and his civilian leaders in the Pentagon over the commander in chief's desire to confront Iraq. But throughout August and September, there were loud hints that Secretary of State Colin L. Powell, the Vietnam War veteran who rose to the rank of chairman of the Joint Chiefs of Staff, had misgivings about another Persian Gulf conflict.

In the Senate, senior members of the Foreign Relations Committee reflected Powell's cautionary view, in part because of the good relations the top diplomat had cultivated in Congress since taking over at State. Powell's Democratic and Republican allies were looking out for his interests even if he was unwilling to express his doubts publicly.

Faced with Bush's request for far-reaching authority to challenge Iraq, embodied by the initial resolution (H J Res 45) the White House sent to Congress on Sept. 19, Foreign Relations Committee Chairman Joseph R. Biden Jr., D-Del., and Richard G. Lugar, R-Ind., joined forces in writing a narrower measure. It would have limited the war authorization to efforts to uncover and disarm Iraq's nuclear, chemical and biological weapons. It also would have required the president, before using force, to either win backing of the U.N. Security Council or state that the threat was "so grave" that immediate action was warranted — an approach that emphasized the need for diplomacy.

Separately, Senate Armed Services Committee Chairman Carl Levin, D-Mich., wrote a proposal that would condition U.S. action against Iraq on U.N. support.

Bush sought to reach a compromise with Senate Democratic leaders in order to quash any public opposition and to strengthen his hand in negotiations about Iraq at the U.N. Security Council, with Powell and National Security Adviser Condoleezza Rice negotiating with the senators.

When that failed, Bush turned to House Minority Leader Richard A. Gephardt, D-Mo., a possible presidential rival in 2004 who had taken a hard line toward Iraq earlier in the year. Gephardt and Bush compromised on a resolution that would give the president the broadest latitude on deciding if and when to go to war against Iraq.

Once the two reached agreement Oct. 1, all momentum for the Biden-Lugar and Levin alternatives was gone, and passage of the Bush-Gephardt resolution was assured.

Sen. Robert C. Byrd, D-W.Va., was one of the few to muster a voice in opposition, saying expediency had won in a "fateful decision. It involves the treasure of this country. It involves the blood of our fighting men and women."

But hours after the Senate overwhelmingly rejected Byrd amendments to limit the authorization Oct. 10, the chamber voted resoundingly to clear the measure (PL 107-243) that would permit the first pre-emptive strike ever by the United States against a foreign nation. The vote was 77-23: R 48-1; D 29-21 (ND 21-20, SD 8-1); I 0-1. (*Senate vote 237, p. C-23*) ◆

34. HR 2356. Campaign Finance Overhaul/Passage. Passage of the bill that would ban "soft money" donations to national political parties but allow up to $10,000 in soft-money donations to state and local parties for voter registration and get-out-the-vote activities. The bill would prevent issue ads from targeting specific candidates within 60 days of a general election or 30 days of a primary. The bill also would increase the individual contribution limit from $1,000 to $2,000 per election for House and Senate candidates, both of which would be indexed for inflation. Passed 240-189: R 41-176; D 198-12 (ND 150-6, SD 48-6); I 1-1. Feb. 14, 2002 (in the session that began and the Congressional Record dated Feb. 13, 2002). (*Story, p. C-4*)

44. HR 1542. High-Speed Internet Access/Previous Question. Motion to order the previous question (thus ending debate and possibility of amendment) on the Markey, D-Mass., motion to recommit the bill to the House Energy and Commerce Committee with instructions to add language that would maintain the ability of the states and the Federal Communications Commission to enforce current telecommunications law regulations over the Bells' entry into the high-speed Internet access market. Motion rejected 173-256: R 62-157; D 109-99 (ND 98-56, SD 11-43); I 2-0. Feb. 27, 2002. (*Story, p. C-5*)

158. HR 4546. Fiscal 2003 Defense Authorization/Passage. Passage of the bill that would authorize $383.4 billion for defense programs for fiscal 2003. It would include the president's request of $7.8 billion for missile defense systems and $7.3 billion for counterterrorism programs. It would provide $475 million for the Crusader artillery system. The bill also would exempt military activities from certain environmental regulations and include an average 4.7 percent pay increase for military personnel. Passed 359-58: R 212-1; D 146-56 (ND 100-51, SD 46-5); I 1-1. May 10, 2002 (in the session that began and the Congressional Record dated May 9, 2002). (*Story, p. C-5*)

170. HR 4737. Welfare Renewal/Passage. Passage of the bill that would authorize $16.5 billion to renew the Temporary Assistance for Needy Families block grant program through fiscal 2007 and require new welfare aid conditions. The bill would require individuals to work 40 hours per week to be eligible for assistance and require states to have 70 percent or more of their families working by 2007. It would authorize additional funding for child care and marriage promotion activities. The bill also would allow states to combine different types of block grants but bar them from using a waiver to transfer funds from one welfare account to another. Motion agreed to 229-197: R 214-4; D 14-192 (ND 7-147, SD 7-45); I 1-1. A two-thirds majority of those present and voting (282 in this case) is required for passage under suspension of the rules. A "yea" was a vote in support of the president's position. May 16, 2002. (*Story, p. C-6*)

194. HR 4775. Fiscal 2002 Supplemental Appropriations/Rule. Adoption of the rule (H Res 428) that would provide for House floor consideration of the bill that would provide $28.8 billion in supplemental appropriations for fiscal 2002, more than half of which would go toward military operations. Adopted 216-209: R 214-3; D 1-205 (ND 1-153, SD 0-52); I 1-1. May 22, 2002. (*Story, p. C-6*)

282. HR 4954. Prescription Drug Coverage/Passage. Passage of the bill that would allow Medicare recipients to cover prescription drug costs through private insurance policies beginning in 2005. The bill would cost $350 billion over 10 years. Patients would pay a $33 monthly premium, with a $250 annual deductible. Patients would pay 20 percent of drug costs from $251 to $1,000 and 50 percent of the next $1,000. They would pay all costs from $2,001 to $3,700, after which insurers would pay the entire cost. Subsidies would reduce premiums and co-payments for low-income patients. Passed 221-208: R 212-8; D 8-199 (ND 6-148, SD 2-51); I 1-1. June 28, 2002 (in the session that began and the Congressional Record that is dated June 27, 2002). (*Story, p. C-7*)

[1] *The Speaker votes only at his discretion, usually to break a tie or to emphasize the importance of a matter.*

[2] *Rep. John Sullivan, R-Okla., was sworn in Feb. 27, 2002. The first vote for which he was eligible was Vote 42. Sullivan succeeded Republican Steve Largent, who resigned effective Feb. 15, 2002, to run for governor of Oklahoma. The last vote for which Largent was eligible was Vote 38.*

Key

Y	Voted for (yea).
#	Paired for.
+	Announced for.
N	Voted against (nay).
X	Paired against.
–	Announced against.
P	Voted "present."
C	Voted "present" to avoid possible conflict of interest.
?	Did not vote or otherwise make a position known.

Democrats   **Republicans**
Independents

	34	44	158	170	194	282
ALABAMA						
1 *Callahan*	N	N	Y	N	Y	Y
2 *Everett*	N	N	Y	Y	Y	Y
3 *Riley*	–	N	+	Y	Y	Y
4 *Aderholt*	N	N	Y	Y	Y	Y
5 Cramer	Y	N	Y	Y	N	N
6 *Bachus*	N	N	Y	Y	Y	Y
7 Hilliard	N	N	Y	N	N	N
ALASKA						
AL *Young*	N	N	Y	Y	Y	Y
ARIZONA						
1 *Flake*	N	Y	Y	Y	Y	N
2 Pastor	Y	N	Y	N	N	N
3 *Stump*	N	N	Y	Y	Y	Y
4 *Shadegg*	N	Y	Y	Y	Y	Y
5 *Kolbe*	N	Y	Y	Y	N	Y
6 *Hayworth*	N	Y	Y	Y	Y	Y
ARKANSAS						
1 Berry	Y	N	Y	N	N	N
2 Snyder	Y	N	Y	N	N	N
3 *Boozman*	N	N	Y	Y	Y	Y
4 Ross	Y	N	Y	N	N	N
CALIFORNIA						
1 Thompson	Y	Y	Y	N	N	N
2 *Herger*	N	N	Y	Y	Y	Y
3 Ose	Y	N	+	Y	Y	Y
4 *Doolittle*	N	N	Y	Y	Y	Y
5 Matsui	Y	Y	Y	N	N	N
6 Woolsey	Y	Y	N	N	N	N
7 Miller, George	Y	Y	N	N	N	N
8 Pelosi	Y	Y	Y	N	N	N
9 Lee	Y	Y	N	N	N	N
10 Tauscher	Y	N	Y	N	N	N
11 *Pombo*	N	Y	?	Y	Y	Y
12 Lantos	Y	Y	Y	N	N	N
13 Stark	Y	Y	N	N	N	N
14 Eshoo	Y	Y	N	N	N	N
15 Honda	Y	Y	N	N	N	N
16 Lofgren	Y	Y	N	N	N	N
17 Farr	Y	Y	N	N	N	N
18 Condit	Y	Y	Y	N	N	Y
19 *Radanovich*	N	N	Y	Y	Y	Y
20 Dooley	Y	Y	N	N	N	N
21 *Thomas*	N	N	Y	Y	Y	Y
22 Capps	Y	Y	N	N	N	N
23 *Gallegly*	N	N	Y	Y	Y	Y
24 Sherman	Y	Y	N	N	N	N
25 *McKeon*	N	N	Y	Y	Y	Y
26 Berman	Y	Y	N	N	N	N
27 Schiff	Y	N	Y	N	N	N
28 *Dreier*	N	N	Y	Y	Y	Y
29 Waxman	Y	Y	?	N	N	N
30 Becerra	Y	Y	N	N	N	N
31 Solis	Y	Y	N	N	N	N
32 Watson	Y	Y	?	N	N	N
33 Roybal-Allard	Y	Y	N	N	N	N
34 Napolitano	Y	Y	N	N	N	N
35 Waters	Y	Y	N	N	N	N
36 Harman	Y	Y	N	N	N	N
37 Millender-McD.	Y	Y	N	N	N	N
38 Horn	Y	N	Y	Y	Y	Y

	34	44	158	170	194	282
39 *Royce*	N	Y	Y	Y	Y	Y
40 *Lewis*	N	Y	Y	Y	Y	Y
41 *Miller, Gary*	N	N	Y	Y	Y	Y
42 Baca	Y	N	Y	N	N	N
43 *Calvert*	N	N	Y	Y	Y	Y
44 *Bono*	Y	N	Y	Y	Y	Y
45 *Rohrabacher*	N	Y	Y	Y	Y	Y
46 Sanchez	Y	N	Y	N	N	N
47 *Cox*	N	Y	Y	Y	Y	Y
48 *Issa*	N	N	Y	Y	Y	Y
49 Davis	Y	Y	N	N	N	N
50 Filner	Y	N	N	N	N	N
51 *Cunningham*	N	N	Y	Y	Y	Y
52 *Hunter*	N	N	Y	Y	Y	Y
COLORADO						
1 DeGette	Y	Y	N	N	N	N
2 Udall	Y	Y	N	N	N	N
3 *McInnis*	N	Y	Y	Y	Y	Y
4 *Schaffer*	N	Y	Y	Y	Y	Y
5 *Hefley*	?	Y	Y	Y	Y	Y
6 *Tancredo*	N	N	Y	Y	Y	Y
CONNECTICUT						
1 Larson	Y	N	N	N	N	N
2 *Simmons*	Y	N	Y	Y	Y	Y
3 DeLauro	Y	Y	N	N	N	N
4 *Shays*	Y	Y	Y	N	N	N
5 Maloney	Y	N	Y	N	N	Y
6 *Johnson*	Y	Y	Y	Y	Y	Y
DELAWARE						
AL *Castle*	Y	Y	Y	Y	Y	Y
FLORIDA						
1 *Miller, J.*	N	N	Y	Y	Y	Y
2 Boyd	Y	N	Y	Y	N	N
3 Brown	Y	N	Y	N	N	N
4 *Crenshaw*	N	N	Y	Y	Y	Y
5 Thurman	Y	Y	Y	N	N	N
6 *Stearns*	N	N	Y	Y	Y	Y
7 *Mica*	N	N	Y	Y	Y	Y
8 *Keller*	N	Y	Y	Y	Y	Y
9 *Bilirakis*	N	N	Y	Y	Y	Y
10 *Young*	N	Y	Y	Y	Y	Y
11 Davis	Y	Y	Y	N	N	N
12 *Putnam*	N	N	Y	Y	Y	Y
13 *Miller, D.*	N	N	Y	Y	Y	Y
14 *Goss*	N	N	Y	Y	Y	Y
15 *Weldon*	N	N	Y	Y	Y	Y
16 *Foley*	Y	N	Y	Y	Y	Y
17 Meek	Y	N	Y	N	N	N
18 *Ros-Lehtinen*	Y	N	Y	Y	Y	Y
19 Wexler	Y	N	Y	N	?	N
20 Deutsch	Y	N	Y	?	?	N
21 *Diaz-Balart*	N	N	Y	Y	Y	Y
22 *Shaw*	N	N	Y	Y	Y	Y
23 Hastings	Y	N	Y	N	N	N
GEORGIA						
1 *Kingston*	N	Y	Y	Y	Y	Y
2 Bishop	Y	N	Y	N	N	N
3 *Collins*	N	N	Y	Y	Y	Y
4 McKinney	Y	Y	N	N	N	N
5 Lewis	Y	N	?	N	N	N
6 *Isakson*	N	N	Y	Y	Y	Y
7 *Barr*	N	N	Y	Y	Y	Y
8 *Chambliss*	N	Y	Y	Y	Y	Y
9 *Deal*	N	N	Y	Y	Y	Y
10 *Norwood*	N	Y	Y	Y	Y	Y
11 *Linder*	N	Y	Y	Y	Y	Y
HAWAII						
1 Abercrombie	Y	Y	Y	N	N	N
2 Mink	Y	Y	Y	N	N	N
IDAHO						
1 *Otter*	N	N	Y	Y	Y	Y
2 *Simpson*	N	N	Y	Y	Y	Y
ILLINOIS						
1 Rush	Y	N	Y	N	N	N
2 Jackson	Y	N	N	N	N	N
3 Lipinski	N	Y	N	Y	N	?
4 Gutierrez	Y	N	Y	N	N	N
5 Blagojevich	Y	N	N	N	N	N
6 *Hyde*	N	N	Y	Y	Y	Y
7 Davis	Y	N	Y	N	N	N
8 *Crane*	N	N	?	Y	Y	Y
9 Schakowsky	Y	Y	N	N	N	N
10 *Kirk*	Y	N	Y	Y	Y	Y
11 *Weller*	N	N	Y	Y	Y	Y
12 Costello	Y	Y	N	N	N	N
13 *Biggert*	N	Y	Y	Y	Y	Y

ND Northern Democrats   SD Southern Democrats

Member	34	44	158	170	194	282
14 **Hastert**[1]	N		Y	Y	Y	Y
15 **Johnson**	Y	N	Y	Y	Y	Y
16 **Manzullo**	N	N	Y	Y	Y	N
17 Evans	Y	?	Y	N	N	N
18 **LaHood**	N	N	Y	Y	Y	Y
19 Phelps	Y	Y	Y	Y	N	N
20 **Shimkus**	N	N	Y	Y	Y	Y
INDIANA						
1 Visclosky	Y	N	Y	N	N	N
2 **Pence**	N	N	Y	Y	Y	Y
3 Roemer	Y	Y	Y	N	N	N
4 **Souder**	N	N	Y	Y	Y	Y
5 **Buyer**	N	N	Y	?	Y	Y
6 **Burton**	N	N	+	Y	+	Y
7 **Kerns**	N	N	Y	N	Y	Y
8 **Hostettler**	N	N	Y	N	Y	N
9 Hill	Y	N	Y	N	N	N
10 Carson	Y	Y	Y	N	N	N
IOWA						
1 **Leach**	Y	Y	Y	Y	Y	Y
2 **Nussle**	N	N	Y	Y	Y	Y
3 Boswell	Y	Y	Y	N	N	Y
4 **Ganske**	Y	N	Y	Y	Y	Y
5 **Latham**	N	Y	Y	Y	Y	Y
KANSAS						
1 **Moran**	N	Y	Y	Y	Y	Y
2 **Ryun**	N	Y	Y	Y	Y	Y
3 Moore	Y	Y	Y	N	N	N
4 **Tiahrt**	N	N	Y	Y	Y	Y
KENTUCKY						
1 **Whitfield**	N	N	Y	Y	Y	Y
2 **Lewis**	N	N	Y	Y	Y	Y
3 **Northup**	N	N	Y	Y	Y	Y
4 Lucas	Y	N	Y	Y	N	Y
5 **Rogers**	N	N	Y	Y	Y	Y
6 **Fletcher**	N	N	Y	Y	Y	Y
LOUISIANA						
1 **Vitter**	N	N	Y	Y	Y	Y
2 Jefferson	Y	N	Y	N	N	?
3 **Tauzin**	N	N	Y	Y	Y	Y
4 **McCrery**	N	N	Y	Y	Y	Y
5 **Cooksey**	N	N	Y	Y	Y	Y
6 **Baker**	N	N	Y	Y	Y	Y
7 John	Y	N	?	N	N	N
MAINE						
1 Allen	Y	N	Y	N	N	N
2 Baldacci	Y	?	Y	N	N	N
MARYLAND						
1 **Gilchrest**	Y	Y	Y	Y	Y	Y
2 **Ehrlich**	N	Y	Y	Y	Y	Y
3 Cardin	Y	N	Y	N	N	N
4 Wynn	Y	N	Y	N	N	N
5 Hoyer	Y	N	Y	N	N	N
6 **Bartlett**	N	Y	Y	Y	Y	Y
7 Cummings	Y	N	Y	N	N	N
8 **Morella**	Y	N	Y	N	Y	Y
MASSACHUSETTS						
1 Olver	Y	Y	N	N	N	N
2 Neal	Y	N	Y	N	N	N
3 McGovern	Y	N	N	N	N	N
4 Frank	Y	Y	N	N	N	N
5 Meehan	Y	Y	Y	N	N	N
6 Tierney	Y	Y	N	N	N	N
7 Markey	Y	Y	N	N	N	N
8 Capuano	Y	N	N	N	N	N
9 Lynch	Y	N	Y	N	N	N
10 Delahunt	Y	Y	N	N	N	N
MICHIGAN						
1 Stupak	Y	Y	Y	N	N	N
2 **Hoekstra**	N	Y	Y	Y	Y	Y
3 **Ehlers**	N	N	Y	Y	Y	Y
4 **Camp**	N	N	Y	Y	Y	Y
5 Barcia	N	N	Y	Y	N	N
6 **Upton**	Y	N	Y	Y	Y	Y
7 **Smith**	Y	N	Y	Y	Y	N
8 **Rogers**	N	Y	Y	Y	Y	Y
9 Kildee	Y	N	Y	N	N	N
10 Bonior	Y	N	N	N	N	N
11 **Knollenberg**	N	N	Y	Y	Y	Y
12 Levin	Y	N	Y	N	N	N
13 Rivers	Y	Y	N	N	N	N
14 Conyers	Y	Y	N	N	N	N
15 Kilpatrick	Y	Y	N	N	N	N
16 Dingell	Y	N	Y	N	N	N
MINNESOTA						
1 **Gutknecht**	N	N	Y	Y	Y	N
2 **Kennedy**	N	N	+	Y	Y	Y
3 **Ramstad**	Y	Y	Y	Y	Y	Y
4 McCollum	Y	Y	Y	N	N	N
5 Sabo	Y	Y	Y	N	N	N
6 Luther	Y	Y	Y	Y	N	N
7 Peterson	N	Y	Y	Y	N	Y
8 Oberstar	Y	Y	N	N	N	N
MISSISSIPPI						
1 **Wicker**	N	Y	Y	Y	N	Y
2 Thompson	N	N	Y	N	N	N
3 **Pickering**	N	Y	Y	Y	Y	Y
4 Shows	N	N	Y	Y	N	N
5 Taylor	Y	N	Y	Y	N	N
MISSOURI						
1 Clay	Y	N	?	N	N	?
2 **Akin**	N	N	Y	Y	Y	Y
3 Gephardt	Y	Y	Y	N	N	N
4 Skelton	Y	Y	Y	N	N	N
5 McCarthy	Y	Y	Y	N	N	N
6 **Graves**	N	N	Y	Y	Y	Y
7 **Blunt**	N	N	Y	Y	Y	Y
8 **Emerson**	N	N	Y	Y	+	N
9 **Hulshof**	N	N	Y	Y	Y	Y
MONTANA						
AL **Rehberg**	N	N	Y	Y	Y	Y
NEBRASKA						
1 **Bereuter**	Y	Y	Y	Y	Y	Y
2 **Terry**	N	N	Y	Y	Y	Y
3 **Osborne**	Y	N	Y	Y	Y	Y
NEVADA						
1 Berkley	Y	Y	Y	N	N	N
2 **Gibbons**	N	N	Y	Y	Y	Y
NEW HAMPSHIRE						
1 **Sununu**	N	Y	Y	Y	Y	Y
2 **Bass**	Y	N	Y	Y	Y	Y
NEW JERSEY						
1 Andrews	Y	Y	Y	N	N	N
2 **LoBiondo**	Y	N	Y	Y	Y	Y
3 **Saxton**	N	N	Y	Y	Y	Y
4 **Smith**	N	N	Y	Y	Y	Y
5 **Roukema**	?	Y	?	Y	Y	?
6 Pallone	Y	Y	Y	N	N	N
7 **Ferguson**	Y	N	Y	Y	Y	Y
8 Pascrell	Y	N	Y	N	N	N
9 Rothman	Y	Y	Y	N	N	N
10 Payne	Y	Y	N	N	N	N
11 **Frelinghuysen**	Y	Y	Y	Y	Y	Y
12 Holt	Y	Y	Y	N	N	N
13 Menendez	Y	N	Y	N	N	N
NEW MEXICO						
1 **Wilson**	N	Y	Y	Y	Y	Y
2 **Skeen**	N	Y	Y	Y	Y	Y
3 Udall	Y	Y	Y	N	N	N
NEW YORK						
1 **Grucci**	Y	N	Y	Y	Y	Y
2 Israel	Y	Y	Y	N	N	Y
3 **King**	N	N	Y	?	Y	Y
4 McCarthy	Y	N	Y	N	N	N
5 Ackerman	Y	N	Y	N	N	N
6 Meeks	Y	N	N	N	N	N
7 Crowley	Y	Y	Y	N	N	N
8 Nadler	Y	Y	N	N	N	N
9 Weiner	Y	Y	N	N	N	N
10 Towns	Y	N	N	N	N	?
11 Owens	Y	Y	N	N	N	N
12 Velázquez	Y	Y	N	N	N	N
13 **Fossella**	N	N	Y	Y	Y	Y
14 Maloney	Y	Y	Y	N	N	N
15 Rangel	Y	Y	N	N	N	N
16 Serrano	Y	N	N	N	N	N
17 Engel	Y	N	Y	N	N	N
18 Lowey	Y	Y	Y	N	N	N
19 **Kelly**	N	N	Y	Y	Y	Y
20 **Gilman**	Y	–	Y	Y	Y	Y
21 McNulty	Y	N	Y	N	N	N
22 **Sweeney**	N	N	Y	Y	Y	Y
23 **Boehlert**	Y	N	Y	Y	Y	Y
24 **McHugh**	Y	N	Y	Y	Y	Y
25 **Walsh**	Y	N	Y	Y	Y	Y
26 Hinchey	Y	Y	N	N	N	N
27 **Reynolds**	N	N	Y	Y	Y	Y
28 Slaughter	Y	Y	Y	N	N	N
29 LaFalce	Y	Y	Y	N	N	N
30 **Quinn**	Y	N	Y	Y	Y	Y
31 **Houghton**	Y	N	Y	Y	Y	Y
NORTH CAROLINA						
1 Clayton	Y	N	N	N	N	N
2 Etheridge	Y	Y	Y	N	N	N
3 **Jones**	N	Y	Y	Y	Y	Y
4 Price	Y	N	Y	N	N	N
5 **Burr**	N	N	Y	Y	Y	Y
6 **Coble**	N	N	Y	Y	Y	Y
7 McIntyre	Y	N	Y	N	N	N
8 **Hayes**	N	N	Y	Y	Y	Y
9 **Myrick**	N	N	Y	Y	Y	Y
10 **Ballenger**	N	N	Y	Y	Y	Y
11 **Taylor**	N	N	Y	Y	Y	Y
12 Watt	Y	Y	N	N	N	N
NORTH DAKOTA						
AL Pomeroy	Y	Y	Y	Y	N	N
OHIO						
1 **Chabot**	N	Y	Y	Y	Y	Y
2 **Portman**	N	N	Y	Y	Y	Y
3 Hall	Y	N	?	N	N	N
4 **Oxley**	N	N	Y	Y	Y	Y
5 **Gillmor**	N	N	Y	Y	Y	Y
6 Strickland	Y	N	Y	N	N	N
7 **Hobson**	N	Y	Y	Y	Y	Y
8 **Boehner**	N	N	Y	Y	Y	Y
9 Kaptur	Y	Y	Y	N	N	N
10 Kucinich	Y	Y	N	N	N	N
11 Jones	Y	Y	N	N	N	N
12 **Tiberi**	N	N	Y	Y	Y	Y
13 Brown	Y	Y	N	N	N	N
14 Sawyer	Y	N	Y	N	N	N
15 **Pryce**	N	N	Y	Y	Y	Y
16 **Regula**	N	N	Y	Y	Y	Y
17 Traficant	?	?	?	?	?	?
18 **Ney**	N	N	Y	Y	Y	Y
19 **LaTourette**	Y	N	Y	Y	Y	Y
OKLAHOMA						
1 **Largent**[2]	N					
1 **Sullivan**[2]		N	Y	Y	Y	Y
2 Carson	Y	Y	Y	N	N	N
3 **Watkins**	N	N	Y	Y	Y	Y
4 **Watts**	N	Y	Y	Y	Y	Y
5 **Istook**	N	N	Y	Y	Y	N
6 **Lucas**	N	N	Y	Y	Y	Y
OREGON						
1 Wu	Y	Y	N	Y	N	N
2 **Walden**	N	N	Y	Y	Y	Y
3 Blumenauer	Y	Y	N	N	N	N
4 DeFazio	Y	Y	N	N	N	N
5 Hooley	Y	Y	Y	N	N	N
PENNSYLVANIA						
1 Brady	Y	N	Y	N	N	N
2 Fattah	Y	Y	N	N	N	N
3 Borski	Y	Y	Y	N	N	N
4 **Hart**	N	N	Y	Y	Y	Y
5 **Peterson**	N	Y	Y	Y	Y	Y
6 Holden	Y	N	Y	Y	N	N
7 **Weldon**	Y	N	Y	Y	Y	Y
8 **Greenwood**	Y	N	Y	Y	Y	Y
9 **Shuster, Bill**	N	N	Y	Y	Y	Y
10 **Sherwood**	N	N	Y	Y	Y	Y
11 Kanjorski	Y	Y	Y	N	Y	N
12 Murtha	N	N	Y	?	N	N
13 Hoeffel	Y	Y	Y	N	N	N
14 Coyne	Y	Y	N	N	N	N
15 **Toomey**	N	N	Y	Y	Y	Y
16 **Pitts**	N	Y	Y	Y	Y	Y
17 **Gekas**	N	N	Y	Y	Y	Y
18 Doyle	Y	Y	Y	N	N	N
19 **Platts**	Y	Y	Y	Y	Y	Y
20 Mascara	Y	Y	Y	–	?	N
21 **English**	N	N	Y	Y	Y	Y
RHODE ISLAND						
1 Kennedy	Y	N	Y	N	N	N
2 Langevin	Y	N	Y	N	N	N
SOUTH CAROLINA						
1 **Brown**	N	N	Y	Y	Y	Y
2 **Wilson**	N	N	Y	Y	Y	Y
3 **Graham**	Y	N	Y	Y	Y	Y
4 **DeMint**	N	Y	Y	Y	Y	Y
5 Spratt	Y	N	Y	N	N	N
6 Clyburn	Y	N	Y	N	N	N
SOUTH DAKOTA						
AL **Thune**	Y	Y	Y	Y	Y	Y
TENNESSEE						
1 **Jenkins**	N	Y	Y	Y	Y	Y
2 **Duncan**	N	Y	Y	Y	Y	Y
3 **Wamp**	Y	Y	Y	Y	P	Y
4 **Hilleary**	N	N	Y	Y	Y	Y
5 Clement	Y	N	Y	N	N	N
6 Gordon	Y	N	Y	N	N	N
7 **Bryant**	N	N	Y	Y	Y	Y
8 Tanner	Y	N	Y	?	N	N
9 Ford	Y	N	Y	N	N	N
TEXAS						
1 Sandlin	Y	N	Y	N	N	N
2 Turner	Y	N	Y	N	N	N
3 **Johnson, Sam**	N	Y	Y	Y	Y	Y
4 Hall	N	N	Y	Y	N	Y
5 **Sessions**	N	N	Y	Y	Y	Y
6 **Barton**	N	N	Y	Y	Y	Y
7 **Culberson**	N	N	Y	Y	Y	Y
8 **Brady**	?	N	Y	Y	Y	Y
9 Lampson	Y	N	Y	?	N	N
10 Doggett	Y	Y	N	N	N	N
11 Edwards	Y	N	Y	Y	N	N
12 **Granger**	N	N	Y	Y	Y	Y
13 **Thornberry**	N	N	Y	Y	Y	Y
14 **Paul**	N	Y	N	N	Y	?
15 Hinojosa	Y	N	Y	N	N	N
16 Reyes	Y	N	?	N	N	N
17 Stenholm	Y	N	Y	N	N	N
18 Jackson-Lee	Y	N	N	N	N	N
19 **Combest**	N	Y	?	?	Y	Y
20 Gonzalez	Y	N	Y	N	N	N
21 **Smith**	N	N	Y	Y	Y	Y
22 **DeLay**	N	N	Y	Y	Y	Y
23 **Bonilla**	N	N	Y	Y	P	Y
24 Frost	Y	N	Y	N	N	N
25 Bentsen	Y	N	Y	N	N	N
26 **Armey**	N	N	Y	Y	Y	Y
27 Ortiz	Y	N	Y	N	N	N
28 Rodriguez	Y	N	Y	N	N	N
29 Green	Y	N	Y	N	N	N
30 Johnson, E.B.	Y	Y	Y	N	N	N
UTAH						
1 **Hansen**	N	Y	Y	Y	Y	Y
2 Matheson	Y	N	Y	N	N	Y
3 **Cannon**	N	Y	?	Y	Y	Y
VERMONT						
AL Sanders	Y	Y	N	N	N	N
VIRGINIA						
1 **Davis, Jo Ann**	N	N	Y	Y	Y	Y
2 **Schrock**	N	N	Y	Y	Y	Y
3 Scott	N	Y	Y	N	N	N
4 **Forbes**	N	Y	Y	Y	Y	Y
5 Goode	N	Y	Y	Y	Y	Y
6 **Goodlatte**	N	N	Y	Y	Y	Y
7 **Cantor**	N	Y	Y	Y	Y	Y
8 Moran	Y	Y	Y	N	N	N
9 Boucher	N	N	Y	N	N	N
10 **Wolf**	Y	Y	Y	Y	Y	Y
11 **Davis, T.**	N	Y	Y	Y	Y	Y
WASHINGTON						
1 Inslee	Y	Y	Y	N	N	N
2 Larsen	Y	N	Y	N	N	N
3 Baird	Y	Y	Y	N	N	N
4 **Hastings**	N	Y	Y	Y	Y	Y
5 **Nethercutt**	N	N	+	Y	P	Y
6 Dicks	Y	N	Y	N	N	N
7 McDermott	Y	Y	N	N	N	N
8 **Dunn**	N	Y	Y	Y	Y	Y
9 Smith	Y	N	Y	N	N	N
WEST VIRGINIA						
1 Mollohan	N	N	Y	N	N	N
2 **Capito**	Y	N	Y	Y	Y	Y
3 Rahall	N	N	Y	N	N	N
WISCONSIN						
1 **Ryan**	N	N	Y	Y	Y	Y
2 Baldwin	Y	N	N	N	N	N
3 Kind	Y	N	N	N	N	N
4 Kleczka	Y	Y	N	N	N	N
5 Barrett	Y	Y	N	N	N	N
6 **Petri**	Y	N	Y	Y	Y	Y
7 Obey	Y	Y	N	N	N	N
8 **Green**	N	N	Y	Y	Y	Y
9 **Sensenbrenner**	N	Y	Y	Y	Y	Y
WYOMING						
AL **Cubin**	?	?	Y	Y	Y	Y

Southern states - Ala., Ark., Fla., Ga., Ky., La., Miss., N.C., Okla., S.C., Tenn., Texas, Va.

347. HR 4628. Fiscal 2003 Intelligence Authorization/Sept. 11 Task Force. Roemer, D-Ind., amendment that would establish a National Commission on Terrorist Attacks Upon the United States. The commission would review the implementation by the intelligence agencies of recommendations of a joint House-Senate investigation and other inquiries into the Sept. 11, 2001, terrorist attacks. Adopted 219-188: R 25-183; D 193-4 (ND 145-1, SD 48-3); I 1-1. A "nay" was a vote in support of the president's position. (Subsequently, the House passed the bill by voice vote.) July 25, 2002 (in the session that began and the Congressional Record that is dated July 24, 2002). *(Story, p. C-8)*

357. HR 5005. Homeland Security/Union Membership. Morella, R-Md., amendment that would give federal employees who transfer into the Homeland Security Department the right to join a union if they were under union protection before the transfer. The president could exempt employees from union membership when duties are directly related to the war on terrorism. Rejected 208-222: R 5-214; D 202-7 (ND 153-2, SD 49-5); I 1-1. A "nay" was a vote in support of the president's position. July 26, 2002. *(Story, p. C-8)*

370. HR 3009. Trade Promotion Authority/Conference Report. Adoption of the conference report on the bill that would allow special trade promotion authority for congressional consideration of trade agreements reached before June 1, 2005, and extend duty-free status to certain products from Bolivia, Colombia, Ecuador and Peru. It also would reauthorize and expand a program to provide retraining assistance to U.S. workers hurt by trade agreements, create a 65 percent tax credit for health insurance costs for displaced workers, and authorize a five-year extension of the Generalized System of Preferences. Adopted (thus sent to the Senate) 215-212: R 190-27; D 25-183 (ND 11-143, SD 14-40); I 0-2. A "yea" was a vote in support of the president's position. July 27, 2002 (in the session that began and the Congressional Record dated July 26, 2002). *(Story, p. C-9)*

455. H J Res 114. Use of Force/Passage. Passage of the joint resolution that would authorize the use of force against Iraq and require the administration to report to Congress that diplomatic options have been exhausted no later than 48 hours after military action has begun. The president also would be required to submit a progress report to Congress at least every 60 days. Passed 296-133: R 215-6; D 81-126 (ND 49-105, SD 32-21); I 0-1. A "yea" was a vote in support of the president's position. Oct. 10, 2002. *(Story, p. C-10)*

478. HR 333. Bankruptcy Overhaul/Rule. Adoption of the rule (H Res 606) to provide for House floor consideration of the conference report on the bill that would require debtors able to repay $10,000 or 25 percent of their debts over five years, to file under Chapter 13, which requires a reorganization of debts under a repayment plan, instead of seeking to discharge their debts under Chapter 7. It also would block those protesting abortion and other issues from declaring bankruptcy to avoid paying court-ordered fines and judgments. Rejected 172-243: R 124-87; D 48-155 (ND 24-127, SD 24-28); I 0-1. Nov. 14, 2002. *(Story, p. C-10)*

[1] *Rep. Patsy T. Mink, D-Hawaii, died Sept. 28, 2002. The last vote for which she was eligible was vote 423.*

[2] *The Speaker votes only at his discretion, usually to break a tie or to emphasize the importance of a matter.*

[3] *Rep. Tony P. Hall, D-Ohio, resigned effective Sept. 9, 2002. The last vote for which he was eligible was vote 377.*

[4] *Rep. James A. Traficant Jr., D-Ohio, was expelled from the House of Representatives on July 24, 2002. The last vote for which he was eligible was vote 346.*

[5] *Rep. Virgil H. Goode Jr. of Virginia switched his party affiliation from independent to Republican, effective Aug. 1, 2002.*

Key

Y	Voted for (yea).
#	Paired for.
+	Announced for.
N	Voted against (nay).
X	Paired against.
–	Announced against.
P	Voted "present."
C	Voted "present" to avoid possible conflict of interest.
?	Did not vote or otherwise make a position known.

Democrats **Republicans**
Independents

	347	357	370	455	478
ALABAMA					
1 *Callahan*	?	N	Y	Y	?
2 *Everett*	N	N	Y	Y	N
3 *Riley*	N	N	Y	Y	Y
4 *Aderholt*	N	N	Y	Y	N
5 Cramer	Y	Y	N	Y	Y
6 *Bachus*	N	N	Y	Y	Y
7 Hilliard	Y	Y	N	N	N
ALASKA					
AL *Young*	?	N	N	Y	Y
ARIZONA					
1 *Flake*	N	N	Y	Y	N
2 Pastor	Y	Y	N	N	N
3 *Stump*	?	N	?	?	?
4 *Shadegg*	N	N	Y	Y	N
5 *Kolbe*	N	N	Y	Y	Y
6 *Hayworth*	N	N	Y	Y	N
ARKANSAS					
1 Berry	Y	Y	N	Y	Y
2 Snyder	Y	Y	N	Y	Y
3 *Boozman*	N	N	Y	Y	N
4 Ross	Y	Y	N	Y	N
CALIFORNIA					
1 Thompson	Y	Y	N	N	Y
2 *Herger*	N	N	Y	Y	Y
3 *Ose*	N	N	Y	Y	Y
4 *Doolittle*	N	N	Y	Y	?
5 Matsui	Y	Y	N	N	N
6 Woolsey	Y	Y	N	N	N
7 Miller, George	Y	Y	N	N	N
8 Pelosi	Y	Y	N	N	N
9 Lee	Y	Y	N	N	N
10 Tauscher	Y	Y	Y	Y	Y
11 *Pombo*	N	N	Y	Y	N
12 Lantos	Y	Y	N	Y	N
13 Stark	Y	Y	N	N	N
14 Eshoo	Y	Y	N	N	N
15 Honda	Y	Y	N	N	N
16 Lofgren	Y	Y	N	N	N
17 Farr	Y	Y	N	N	N
18 Condit	?	Y	N	Y	Y
19 *Radanovich*	N	N	Y	Y	Y
20 Dooley	Y	N	Y	Y	Y
21 *Thomas*	N	N	Y	Y	Y
22 Capps	Y	Y	N	N	N
23 *Gallegly*	N	N	Y	Y	N
24 Sherman	Y	Y	N	Y	N
25 *McKeon*	N	N	Y	Y	N
26 Berman	Y	Y	N	Y	N
27 Schiff	Y	Y	N	Y	N
28 *Dreier*	N	N	Y	Y	Y
29 Waxman	Y	Y	N	Y	N
30 Becerra	Y	Y	N	N	N
31 Solis	Y	Y	N	N	N
32 Watson	Y	Y	N	N	N
33 Roybal-Allard	Y	Y	N	N	N
34 Napolitano	Y	Y	N	N	N
35 Waters	Y	Y	N	N	N
36 Harman	Y	Y	N	N	N
37 Millender-McD.	Y	Y	N	N	N
38 *Horn*	N	N	Y	N	Y

	347	357	370	455	478
39 *Royce*	N	N	Y	Y	Y
40 *Lewis*	N	N	Y	Y	N
41 *Miller, Gary*	N	N	Y	Y	N
42 Baca	Y	Y	N	N	N
43 *Calvert*	N	N	Y	N	N
44 *Bono*	N	N	Y	Y	N
45 *Rohrabacher*	N	N	Y	Y	N
46 Sanchez	Y	Y	N	N	N
47 *Cox*	?	N	Y	Y	Y
48 *Issa*	?	N	Y	Y	N
49 Davis	Y	Y	N	N	N
50 Filner	Y	Y	N	N	N
51 *Cunningham*	N	N	Y	Y	N
52 *Hunter*	N	N	Y	Y	N
COLORADO					
1 DeGette	Y	Y	N	N	N
2 Udall	Y	Y	N	N	N
3 *McInnis*	N	N	Y	Y	N
4 *Schaffer*	N	N	Y	Y	N
5 *Hefley*	N	N	Y	Y	N
6 *Tancredo*	Y	N	Y	Y	N
CONNECTICUT					
1 Larson	Y	Y	N	N	N
2 *Simmons*	N	Y	N	Y	Y
3 DeLauro	Y	Y	N	N	N
4 *Shays*	N	N	Y	Y	Y
5 Maloney	Y	Y	N	N	Y
6 *Johnson*	Y	N	Y	Y	Y
DELAWARE					
AL *Castle*	N	N	Y	Y	Y
FLORIDA					
1 *Miller, J.*	N	N	Y	Y	N
2 Boyd	N	N	N	Y	?
3 Brown	Y	Y	N	N	N
4 *Crenshaw*	N	N	Y	Y	Y
5 Thurman	Y	Y	N	Y	N
6 *Stearns*	–	N	N	Y	N
7 *Mica*	N	N	Y	Y	N
8 *Keller*	N	N	Y	Y	N
9 *Bilirakis*	N	N	Y	Y	N
10 *Young*	N	N	Y	Y	N
11 Davis	Y	Y	N	Y	Y
12 *Putnam*	N	N	Y	Y	N
13 *Miller, D.*	N	N	Y	Y	N
14 *Goss*	N	N	Y	Y	Y
15 *Weldon*	N	N	Y	Y	N
16 *Foley*	N	N	Y	Y	Y
17 Meek	Y	Y	N	N	N
18 *Ros-Lehtinen*	N	N	Y	Y	N
19 Wexler	Y	Y	N	N	N
20 Deutsch	Y	Y	N	Y	N
21 *Diaz-Balart*	N	N	Y	Y	?
22 *Shaw*	N	N	Y	Y	Y
23 Hastings	Y	Y	N	N	N
GEORGIA					
1 *Kingston*	N	N	Y	Y	Y
2 Bishop	Y	Y	N	Y	N
3 *Collins*	N	?	Y	Y	Y
4 McKinney	Y	Y	N	N	?
5 Lewis	Y	Y	N	N	N
6 *Isakson*	N	N	Y	Y	Y
7 *Barr*	Y	N	Y	N	N
8 *Chambliss*	N	N	Y	Y	Y
9 *Deal*	N	N	Y	Y	Y
10 *Norwood*	N	N	N	Y	N
11 *Linder*	N	N	Y	Y	Y
HAWAII					
1 Abercrombie	Y	Y	N	N	N
2 Mink [1]	Y	Y	N		
IDAHO					
1 *Otter*	?	N	Y	Y	N
2 *Simpson*	N	N	Y	Y	Y
ILLINOIS					
1 Rush	Y	Y	N	N	N
2 Jackson	Y	Y	N	N	N
3 Lipinski	Y	Y	?	N	N
4 Gutierrez	+	Y	N	N	N
5 Blagojevich	Y	Y	N	Y	?
6 *Hyde*	N	N	Y	Y	Y
7 Davis	Y	Y	N	N	N
8 *Crane*	N	N	Y	Y	Y
9 Schakowsky	Y	Y	N	N	N
10 *Kirk*	N	N	Y	Y	Y
11 *Weller*	Y	N	Y	Y	Y
12 Costello	Y	Y	N	Y	Y
13 *Biggert*	N	N	Y	Y	Y

ND Northern Democrats   SD Southern Democrats

	347	357	370	455	478
14 ***Hastert*** [2]	N		Y	Y	Y
15 ***Johnson***	N	N	Y	Y	N
16 ***Manzullo***	N	N	Y	Y	N
17 Evans	Y	Y	N	N	N
18 ***LaHood***	N	N	Y	Y	N
19 Phelps	Y	Y	N	Y	N
20 ***Shimkus***	N	N	Y	Y	N
INDIANA					
1 Visclosky	Y	Y	N	N	N
2 ***Pence***	N	N	Y	Y	N
3 Roemer	Y	Y	N	Y	N
4 ***Souder***	N	N	Y	Y	N
5 ***Buyer***	N	N	Y	Y	Y
6 ***Burton***	Y	N	Y	Y	N
7 ***Kerns***	N	N	Y	Y	N
8 ***Hostettler***	N	N	N	N	N
9 Hill	Y	N	Y	Y	Y
10 Carson	Y	Y	N	N	N
IOWA					
1 ***Leach***	Y	N	Y	N	Y
2 ***Nussle***	N	N	Y	Y	Y
3 Boswell	Y	Y	N	Y	Y
4 ***Ganske***	Y	N	Y	Y	Y
5 ***Latham***	N	N	Y	Y	Y
KANSAS					
1 ***Moran***	N	N	Y	Y	N
2 ***Ryun***	N	N	Y	Y	N
3 Moore	Y	Y	Y	Y	Y
4 ***Tiahrt***	N	N	Y	Y	N
KENTUCKY					
1 ***Whitfield***	N	N	Y	Y	N
2 ***Lewis***	N	N	Y	Y	N
3 ***Northup***	N	N	Y	Y	Y
4 Lucas	Y	N	Y	Y	Y
5 ***Rogers***	N	N	Y	Y	Y
6 ***Fletcher***	N	N	Y	Y	Y
LOUISIANA					
1 ***Vitter***	N	N	Y	Y	N
2 Jefferson	Y	Y	Y	Y	N
3 ***Tauzin***	N	N	Y	Y	N
4 ***McCrery***	N	N	Y	Y	Y
5 ***Cooksey***	N	N	Y	Y	?
7 John	Y	Y	Y	Y	N
MAINE					
1 Allen	Y	Y	N	N	N
2 Baldacci	Y	Y	N	N	N
MARYLAND					
1 ***Gilchrest***	Y	N	Y	Y	Y
2 ***Ehrlich***	Y	N	Y	Y	?
3 Cardin	Y	Y	N	N	N
4 Wynn	Y	Y	N	Y	Y
5 Hoyer	Y	Y	N	Y	N
6 ***Bartlett***	Y	N	N	Y	N
7 Cummings	Y	Y	N	N	N
8 ***Morella***	Y	Y	Y	N	Y
MASSACHUSETTS					
1 Olver	Y	Y	N	N	N
2 Neal	Y	Y	N	N	N
3 McGovern	Y	Y	N	N	N
4 Frank	Y	Y	N	N	N
5 Meehan	Y	?	?	Y	N
6 Tierney	Y	Y	N	N	N
7 Markey	Y	Y	N	Y	N
8 Capuano	Y	Y	N	N	N
9 Lynch	Y	Y	N	Y	N
10 Delahunt	Y	Y	N	N	N
MICHIGAN					
1 Stupak	Y	Y	N	N	N
2 ***Hoekstra***	N	N	N	Y	N
3 ***Ehlers***	N	N	Y	Y	N
4 ***Camp***	N	N	Y	Y	Y
5 Barcia	Y	Y	N	Y	N
6 ***Upton***	N	N	Y	Y	Y
7 ***Smith***	N	N	Y	Y	Y
8 ***Rogers***	N	N	Y	Y	N
9 Kildee	Y	Y	N	N	N
10 Bonior	?	Y	N	N	N
11 ***Knollenberg***	–	N	Y	Y	Y
12 Levin	Y	Y	N	N	N
13 Rivers	Y	Y	N	N	Y
14 Conyers	Y	Y	N	N	N
15 Kilpatrick	Y	Y	N	N	N
16 Dingell	Y	Y	N	N	N
MINNESOTA					
1 ***Gutknecht***	Y	N	Y	Y	N
2 ***Kennedy***	N	N	Y	Y	N
3 ***Ramstad***	N	N	Y	Y	Y
4 McCollum	Y	Y	N	N	N
5 Sabo	Y	Y	N	N	N
6 Luther	Y	Y	N	Y	N
7 Peterson	Y	Y	N	Y	N
8 Oberstar	Y	Y	N	N	N
MISSISSIPPI					
1 ***Wicker***	N	N	Y	Y	N
2 Thompson	Y	Y	N	N	N
3 ***Pickering***	N	N	Y	Y	N
4 Shows	Y	Y	N	Y	N
5 Taylor	Y	N	N	Y	N
MISSOURI					
1 Clay	?	Y	N	N	N
2 ***Akin***	N	N	Y	Y	N
3 Gephardt	Y	Y	N	Y	N
4 Skelton	Y	Y	Y	Y	Y
5 McCarthy	+	Y	N	N	N
6 ***Graves***	N	N	Y	Y	Y
7 ***Blunt***	?	?	?	Y	Y
8 ***Emerson***	N	N	Y	Y	Y
9 ***Hulshof***	N	N	Y	Y	Y
MONTANA					
AL ***Rehberg***	N	N	Y	Y	N
NEBRASKA					
1 ***Bereuter***	N	N	Y	Y	Y
2 ***Terry***	N	N	Y	Y	N
3 ***Osborne***	N	N	Y	Y	N
NEVADA					
1 Berkley	Y	Y	N	Y	N
2 ***Gibbons***	N	N	Y	Y	Y
NEW HAMPSHIRE					
1 ***Sununu***	N	N	Y	Y	N
2 ***Bass***	N	N	Y	Y	Y
NEW JERSEY					
1 Andrews	Y	Y	N	Y	N
2 ***LoBiondo***	Y	N	N	Y	N
3 ***Saxton***	N	N	Y	Y	N
5 ***Roukema***	?	N	?	?	?
6 Pallone	Y	Y	N	N	N
7 ***Ferguson***	Y	N	Y	Y	N
8 Pascrell	Y	Y	N	Y	N
9 Rothman	Y	Y	N	Y	Y
10 Payne	Y	Y	N	N	N
11 ***Frelinghuysen***	Y	N	Y	Y	Y
12 Holt	Y	Y	N	N	N
13 Menendez	Y	Y	N	N	N
NEW MEXICO					
1 ***Wilson***	N	N	Y	Y	Y
2 ***Skeen***	N	N	Y	Y	Y
3 Udall	Y	Y	N	N	N
NEW YORK					
1 ***Grucci***	N	N	Y	Y	+
2 Israel	Y	Y	N	Y	Y
3 ***King***	N	N	Y	Y	Y
4 McCarthy	Y	Y	N	Y	Y
5 Ackerman	Y	Y	N	Y	N
6 Meeks	Y	Y	N	N	Y
7 Crowley	Y	Y	N	Y	Y
8 Nadler	Y	Y	N	N	N
9 Weiner	Y	Y	N	Y	N
10 Towns	Y	Y	N	N	N
11 Owens	Y	Y	N	N	N
12 Velázquez	Y	Y	N	N	N
13 ***Fossella***	N	N	Y	Y	Y
14 Maloney	Y	Y	N	Y	Y
15 Rangel	Y	Y	N	N	N
16 Serrano	Y	Y	N	N	N
17 Engel	Y	Y	N	Y	N
18 Lowey	Y	Y	N	Y	N
19 ***Kelly***	N	N	Y	Y	Y
20 ***Gilman***	Y	N	Y	Y	Y
21 McNulty	Y	Y	N	Y	N
22 ***Sweeney***	N	N	Y	Y	Y
23 ***Boehlert***	N	N	Y	Y	Y
24 ***McHugh***	N	N	N	Y	Y
25 ***Walsh***	N	N	N	Y	Y
26 Hinchey	Y	Y	N	N	N
27 ***Reynolds***	N	N	Y	Y	Y
28 Slaughter	?	Y	N	N	N
29 LaFalce	?	Y	N	N	N
30 ***Quinn***	N	N	N	Y	Y
31 ***Houghton***	N	N	Y	N	?
NORTH CAROLINA					
1 Clayton	Y	Y	N	N	N
2 Etheridge	Y	Y	Y	Y	Y
3 ***Jones***	Y	N	N	Y	N
4 Price	Y	Y	N	N	Y
5 ***Burr***	N	N	Y	Y	Y
6 ***Coble***	N	N	N	Y	Y
7 McIntyre	Y	Y	N	Y	N
8 ***Hayes***	N	N	N	Y	N
9 ***Myrick***	N	N	Y	Y	Y
10 ***Ballenger***	N	N	Y	Y	N
11 ***Taylor***	N	N	N	Y	Y
12 Watt	Y	Y	N	N	N
NORTH DAKOTA					
AL Pomeroy	N	Y	N	Y	N
OHIO					
1 ***Chabot***	N	N	Y	Y	Y
2 ***Portman***	N	N	Y	Y	N
3 Hall [3]	?	Y	N		
4 ***Oxley***	N	N	Y	Y	Y
5 ***Gillmor***	N	N	Y	Y	Y
6 Strickland	Y	Y	N	N	Y
7 ***Hobson***	N	N	Y	Y	Y
8 ***Boehner***	?	N	Y	Y	Y
9 Kaptur	Y	Y	N	N	N
10 Kucinich	Y	Y	N	N	N
11 Jones	Y	Y	N	N	N
12 ***Tiberi***	N	N	Y	Y	Y
13 Brown	Y	Y	N	N	N
14 Sawyer	Y	Y	N	N	N
15 ***Pryce***	N	N	Y	Y	Y
16 ***Regula***	N	N	N	Y	Y
17 Vacant [4]					
18 ***Ney***	N	N	Y	Y	Y
19 ***LaTourette***	Y	N	N	Y	Y
OKLAHOMA					
1 ***Sullivan***	N	N	Y	Y	N
2 Carson	Y	Y	Y	Y	Y
3 ***Watkins***	N	N	Y	Y	Y
4 ***Watts***	N	N	Y	Y	N
5 ***Istook***	N	N	Y	Y	N
6 ***Lucas***	N	N	Y	Y	Y
OREGON					
1 Wu	Y	Y	N	N	Y
2 ***Walden***	N	N	Y	Y	Y
3 Blumenauer	Y	Y	N	N	N
4 DeFazio	Y	Y	N	N	N
5 Hooley	Y	Y	N	N	?
PENNSYLVANIA					
1 Brady	Y	Y	N	N	N
2 Fattah	Y	Y	N	N	N
3 Borski	Y	Y	N	Y	N
4 ***Hart***	N	N	Y	Y	Y
5 ***Peterson***	N	N	Y	Y	Y
6 Holden	Y	Y	N	Y	N
7 ***Weldon***	Y	N	N	Y	N
8 ***Greenwood***	N	N	Y	Y	Y
9 ***Shuster, Bill***	N	N	Y	Y	N
10 ***Sherwood***	N	N	Y	Y	Y
11 Kanjorski	Y	Y	N	Y	N
12 Murtha	?	Y	N	Y	N
13 Hoeffel	Y	Y	N	Y	N
14 Coyne	Y	Y	N	N	N
15 ***Toomey***	N	N	Y	Y	?
16 ***Pitts***	N	N	Y	Y	N
17 ***Gekas***	N	N	Y	Y	Y
18 Doyle	Y	Y	N	N	N
19 ***Platts***	N	N	Y	Y	Y
20 Mascara	Y	Y	N	Y	N
21 ***English***	N	N	Y	Y	Y
RHODE ISLAND					
1 Kennedy	Y	Y	N	Y	N
2 Langevin	Y	Y	N	N	N
SOUTH CAROLINA					
1 ***Brown***	N	N	Y	Y	Y
2 ***Wilson***	N	N	N	Y	N
3 ***Graham***	N	N	N	Y	N
4 ***DeMint***	N	N	Y	Y	N
5 Spratt	Y	Y	N	Y	Y
6 Clyburn	Y	Y	N	N	N
SOUTH DAKOTA					
AL ***Thune***	N	N	Y	Y	N
TENNESSEE					
1 ***Jenkins***	N	N	Y	Y	Y
2 ***Duncan***	Y	N	N	N	Y
3 ***Wamp***	N	N	Y	Y	N
4 ***Hilleary***	Y	N	Y	Y	N
5 Clement	Y	Y	N	Y	Y
6 Gordon	?	Y	N	Y	Y
7 ***Bryant***	N	N	Y	Y	N
8 Tanner	N	Y	Y	Y	Y
9 Ford	Y	Y	Y	Y	Y
TEXAS					
1 Sandlin	Y	Y	N	Y	N
2 Turner	?	Y	N	Y	Y
3 ***Johnson, Sam***	N	N	Y	Y	N
4 Hall	N	N	Y	Y	N
5 ***Sessions***	N	N	Y	Y	Y
6 ***Barton***	N	N	Y	Y	Y
7 ***Culberson***	N	N	Y	Y	Y
8 ***Brady***	N	N	Y	Y	Y
9 Lampson	Y	Y	N	Y	Y
10 Doggett	Y	Y	N	N	N
11 Edwards	Y	Y	N	Y	Y
12 ***Granger***	N	N	Y	Y	Y
13 ***Thornberry***	N	N	Y	Y	N
14 ***Paul***	N	N	N	N	N
15 Hinojosa	Y	Y	Y	N	Y
16 Reyes	Y	Y	N	N	N
17 Stenholm	Y	N	Y	Y	Y
18 Jackson-Lee	Y	Y	N	N	N
19 ***Combest***	?	N	?	Y	?
20 Gonzalez	Y	Y	N	N	Y
21 ***Smith***	N	N	Y	Y	Y
22 ***DeLay***	N	N	Y	Y	Y
23 ***Bonilla***	N	N	Y	Y	Y
24 Frost	Y	Y	N	Y	Y
25 Bentsen	Y	Y	Y	Y	Y
26 ***Armey***	N	N	Y	Y	Y
27 Ortiz	Y	Y	N	+	N
28 Rodriguez	Y	Y	N	N	N
29 Green	Y	Y	N	Y	N
30 Johnson, E.B.	Y	Y	N	N	Y
UTAH					
1 ***Hansen***	?	N	?	Y	Y
2 Matheson	Y	Y	Y	Y	Y
3 ***Cannon***	N	N	Y	Y	Y
VERMONT					
AL *Sanders*	Y	Y	N	N	N
VIRGINIA					
1 ***Davis, Jo Ann***	N	N	N	Y	N
2 ***Schrock***	N	N	Y	Y	Y
3 Scott	Y	Y	N	N	N
4 ***Forbes***	N	N	Y	Y	N
5 ***Goode*** [5]	N	N	N	Y	N
6 ***Goodlatte***	N	N	Y	Y	N
7 ***Cantor***	N	N	Y	Y	Y
8 Moran	Y	Y	Y	N	Y
9 Boucher	?	Y	N	Y	Y
10 ***Wolf***	Y	N	Y	Y	N
11 ***Davis, T.***	?	N	Y	Y	?
WASHINGTON					
1 Inslee	Y	Y	N	N	N
2 Larsen	Y	Y	Y	N	Y
3 Baird	Y	Y	N	N	Y
4 ***Hastings***	N	N	Y	Y	Y
5 ***Nethercutt***	Y	N	Y	Y	Y
6 Dicks	Y	Y	Y	Y	Y
7 McDermott	Y	Y	N	N	N
8 ***Dunn***	N	N	Y	Y	Y
9 Smith	?	Y	Y	Y	Y
WEST VIRGINIA					
1 Mollohan	Y	Y	N	N	N
2 ***Capito***	Y	Y	N	Y	Y
3 Rahall	Y	Y	N	N	N
WISCONSIN					
1 ***Ryan***	N	N	Y	Y	Y
2 Baldwin	Y	Y	N	N	N
3 Kind	Y	Y	N	Y	Y
4 Kleczka	Y	Y	N	N	N
5 Barrett	Y	Y	N	N	N
6 ***Petri***	N	Y	Y	Y	Y
7 Obey	Y	Y	N	N	N
8 ***Green***	N	N	Y	Y	Y
9 ***Sensenbrenner***	N	N	Y	Y	Y
WYOMING					
AL ***Cubin***	N	N	Y	Y	N

Southern states - Ala., Ark., Fla., Ga., Ky., La., Miss., N.C., Okla., S.C., Tenn., Texas, Va.

	30	47	54	65	71	130	151
ALABAMA							
Shelby	Y	Y	N	Y	Y	?	Y
Sessions	Y	Y	N	Y	Y	N	Y
ALASKA							
Stevens	N	Y	N	Y	Y	Y	Y
Murkowski	N	Y	N	Y	Y	Y	Y
ARIZONA							
McCain	N	N	Y	Y	Y	Y	Y
Kyl	N	Y	N	Y	Y	Y	Y
ARKANSAS							
Hutchinson	N	Y	N	Y	Y	Y	Y
Lincoln	N	Y	Y	Y	N	Y	Y
CALIFORNIA							
Feinstein	Y	N	Y	N	Y	N	Y
Boxer	Y	N	Y	Y	N	N	N
COLORADO							
Campbell	N	Y	N	Y	Y	N	Y
Allard	N	Y	N	Y	Y	Y	Y
CONNECTICUT							
Dodd	Y	N	Y	Y	N	N	N
Lieberman	Y	N	Y	Y	N	Y	N
DELAWARE							
Carper	Y	Y	Y	Y	Y	N	Y
Biden	Y	N	Y	Y	N	Y	N
FLORIDA							
Graham	Y	N	Y	Y	N	Y	Y
Nelson	Y	N	Y	Y	N	Y	Y
GEORGIA							
Miller	Y	Y	Y	Y	Y	Y	Y
Cleland	Y	Y	Y	Y	N	Y	Y
HAWAII							
Inouye	Y	N	Y	Y	Y	?	N
Akaka	Y	N	Y	Y	Y	N	N
IDAHO							
Craig	N	Y	N	Y	Y	Y	Y
Crapo	N	Y	N	Y	Y	Y	?
ILLINOIS							
Durbin	Y	N	Y	Y	N	N	N
Fitzgerald	Y	Y	Y	N	Y	Y	Y
INDIANA							
Lugar	N	Y	Y	Y	Y	Y	Y
Bayh	Y	Y	Y	Y	N	Y	Y

	30	47	54	65	71	130	151
IOWA							
Grassley	Y	Y	N	Y	Y	Y	Y
Harkin	Y	N	Y	Y	N	Y	N
KANSAS							
Brownback	N	Y	N	Y	Y	?	Y
Roberts	N	Y	N	Y	Y	Y	Y
KENTUCKY							
McConnell	N	Y	N	Y	Y	Y	Y
Bunning	N	Y	N	Y	Y	Y	Y
LOUISIANA							
Breaux	Y	Y	N	Y	Y	Y	N
Landrieu	Y	Y	Y	Y	Y	Y	N
MAINE							
Snowe	Y	N	Y	Y	N	Y	Y
Collins	Y	N	Y	Y	N	Y	Y
MARYLAND							
Sarbanes	Y	Y	Y	Y	N	N	N
Mikulski	Y	Y	Y	Y	N	N	N
MASSACHUSETTS							
Kennedy	Y	N	Y	Y	N	N	N
Kerry	Y	N	Y	Y	N	Y	N
MICHIGAN							
Levin	Y	Y	Y	Y	N	N	N
Stabenow	Y	Y	Y	Y	N	N	N
MINNESOTA							
Wellstone	Y	N	Y	Y	N	N	N
Dayton	Y	N	Y	Y	N	N	N
MISSISSIPPI							
Cochran	N	Y	Y	Y	Y	Y	Y
Lott	N	Y	N	Y	Y	Y	Y
MISSOURI							
Bond	N	Y	N	Y	Y	Y	Y
Carnahan	Y	Y	Y	Y	N	N	N
MONTANA							
Baucus	Y	Y	Y	Y	N	Y	Y
Burns	N	Y	N	N	Y	Y	Y
NEBRASKA							
Nelson	Y	Y	N	Y	Y	Y	Y
Hagel	N	Y	N	Y	Y	Y	Y
NEVADA							
Reid	Y	N	Y	Y	N	N	N
Ensign	N	Y	N	Y	Y	N	Y

	30	47	54	65	71	130	151
NEW HAMPSHIRE							
Smith	N	Y	N	Y	N	Y	Y
Gregg	N	N	N	Y	Y	N	Y
NEW JERSEY							
Corzine	N	N	Y	N	N	N	N
Torricelli	Y	N	Y	Y	N	N	N
NEW MEXICO							
Domenici	?	Y	Y	Y	Y	Y	Y
Bingaman	Y	N	Y	Y	N	Y	N
NEW YORK							
Clinton	Y	N	Y	Y	N	N	N
Schumer	Y	N	Y	Y	N	N	N
NORTH CAROLINA							
Helms	N	Y	N	Y	Y	?	+
Edwards	Y	N	Y	Y	N	Y	N
NORTH DAKOTA							
Conrad	Y	Y	Y	Y	N	N	N
Dorgan	Y	Y	Y	Y	N	N	N
OHIO							
DeWine	N	Y	N	Y	N	Y	Y
Voinovich	N	Y	N	Y	Y	Y	Y
OKLAHOMA							
Nickles	N	Y	N	Y	Y	Y	Y
Inhofe	N	Y	N	Y	Y	Y	Y
OREGON							
Wyden	Y	N	Y	Y	N	Y	Y
Smith	N	N	N	Y	Y	Y	Y
PENNSYLVANIA							
Specter	Y	Y	Y	Y	Y	Y	Y
Santorum	N	Y	N	Y	Y	Y	Y
RHODE ISLAND							
Reed	Y	N	Y	Y	N	N	N
Chafee	N	N	Y	N	Y	N	N
SOUTH CAROLINA							
Thurmond	N	Y	N	Y	Y	Y	Y
Hollings	Y	N	Y	Y	N	N	N
SOUTH DAKOTA							
Daschle	Y	N	Y	Y	N	Y	N
Johnson	Y	Y	Y	Y	N	N	N
TENNESSEE							
Thompson	N	Y	Y	Y	Y	Y	Y
Frist	N	Y	N	Y	Y	Y	Y

Key

Y	Voted for (yea).
#	Paired for.
+	Announced for.
N	Voted against (nay).
X	Paired against.
–	Announced against.
P	Voted "present."
C	Voted "present" to avoid possible conflict of interest.
?	Did not vote or otherwise make a position known.

Democrats **Republicans**
Independents

	30	47	54	65	71	130	151
TEXAS							
Gramm	N	Y	N	Y	Y	Y	Y
Hutchison	N	Y	N	Y	Y	Y	Y
UTAH							
Hatch	N	Y	N	Y	Y	Y	Y
Bennett	?	Y	N	Y	Y	Y	Y
VERMONT							
Leahy	Y	N	Y	Y	N	N	N
Jeffords	Y	N	Y	Y	N	N	N
VIRGINIA							
Warner	Y	Y	Y	Y	Y	Y	Y
Allen	Y	Y	N	Y	Y	Y	Y
WASHINGTON							
Cantwell	Y	N	Y	Y	N	Y	N
Murray	Y	N	Y	Y	N	Y	N
WEST VIRGINIA							
Byrd	Y	Y	Y	Y	N	N	N
Rockefeller	Y	N	Y	Y	N	N	N
WISCONSIN							
Kohl	Y	Y	Y	Y	Y	N	N
Feingold	Y	Y	Y	Y	N	N	N
WYOMING							
Thomas	N	Y	N	Y	Y	Y	Y
Enzi	N	Y	N	Y	Y	Y	Y

ND Northern Democrats   SD Southern Democrats

Southern states - Ala., Ark., Fla., Ga., Ky., La., Miss., N.C., Okla., S.C., Tenn., Texas, Va.

30. HR 2646. Farm Bill/Passage. Passage of the bill that would reauthorize federal agriculture programs for five years, including a dairy provision that would authorize $2 billion in direct federal subsidies to milk producers. It also would re-establish programs that supply payments to farmers when commodity prices fall below a specified level. Passed 58-40: R 9-38; D 48-2 (ND 40-1, SD 8-1); I 1-0. A "nay" was a vote in support of the president's position. (Before passage, the Senate struck all after the enacting clause, and inserted the text of S 1731, as amended, into the bill.) Feb. 13, 2002. (*Story, p. C-11*)

47. S 517. Energy Plan/CAFE Standards. Levin, D-Mich., amendment to the Daschle, D-S.D., substitute amendment. The Levin amendment would strike the CAFE standard in the substitute and replace it with language directing the National Highway Traffic Safety Administration (NHTSA) to set a new standard in 15 months. Congress would be permitted to raise the standard if NHTSA did not act within the 15-month time period. Adopted 62-38: R 43-6; D 19-31 (ND 14-27, SD 5-4); I 0-1. March 13, 2002. (*Story, p. C-11*)

54. HR 2356. Campaign Finance Overhaul/Passage. Passage of the bill that would ban "soft money" donations to national political parties but allow up to $10,000 in soft-money donations to state and local parties for voter registration and get-out-the-vote activity. The bill also would increase the individual contribution limit from $1,000 to $2,000 per election for House and Senate candidates, both of which would be indexed for inflation. Passed (thus cleared for the president) 60-40: R 11-38; D 48-2 (ND 40-1, SD 8-1); I 1-0. March 20, 2002. (*Story, p. C-12*)

65. S 565. Election Overhaul/Passage. Passage of the bill that would impose detailed voting-procedure requirements on states. It would require states to let voters verify their votes before casting ballots, allow voters to change their ballots before submitting their votes and notify voters if they vote for more than one candidate for an office. Passed 99-1: R 48-1; D 50-0 (ND 41-0, SD 9-0); I 1-0. April 11, 2002. (*Story, p. C-12*)

71. S 517. Energy Plan/Cloture. Motion to invoke cloture (thus limiting debate) on the Murkowski, R-Alaska, amendment to the Daschle, D-S.D., substitute amendment. The Murkowski amendment would allow for oil and gas development in a portion of the Arctic National Wildlife Refuge if the president certifies to Congress that production in the area is in the nation's economic and security interests. It would limit the amount of surface disturbances to 2,000 acres, impose an export ban on oil produced from the refuge, and designate an additional 1.5 million acres as wilderness in exchange for opening to drilling approximately 1.5 million acres of non-wilderness in the coastal plain region of the refuge. The substitute amendment would overhaul the nation's energy policies, restructure the electricity system and provide for $16.04 billion in energy-related tax incentives. It also would give the National Highway Traffic Safety Administration 15 months to two years to set new CAFE standards. Motion rejected 46-54: R 41-8; D 5-45 (ND 2-39,SD 3-6); I 0-1. Three-fifths of the total Senate (60) is required to invoke cloture. April 18, 2002. (*Story, p. C-13*)

130. HR 3009. Trade Promotion Authority/Passage. Passage of the bill that would extend duty-free status to certain products from Bolivia, Colombia, Ecuador and Peru, renew the president's fast-track authority and reauthorize and expand a program to provide retraining and relocation assistance to U.S. workers hurt by trade agreements. Passed 66-30: R 41-5; D 24-25 (ND 16-24, SD 8-1); I 1-0. A "yea" was a vote in support of the president's position. (Before passage, the Senate adopted the Baucus substitute amendment, as amended, by voice vote.) May 23, 2002. (*Story, p. C-13*)

151. HR 8. Estate Tax/Permanent Repeal. Gramm, R-Texas, motion to waive the Budget Act with respect to the Conrad, D-N.D., point of order against the Gramm amendment that would permanently extend the repeal of the estate tax contained in last year's $1.35 trillion tax cut law. Motion rejected 54-44: R 45-2; D 9-41 (ND 4-37, SD 5-4); I 0-1. A three-fifths majority vote (60) of the total Senate is required to waive the Budget Act. A "yea" was a vote in support of the president's position. (Subsequently the point of order was sustained and the Gramm amendment fell.) June 12, 2002. (*Story, p. C-14*)

Key Senate Votes 157, 176, 199, 223, 226, 237

	157	176	199	223	226	237
ALABAMA						
Shelby	Y	Y	N	Y	N	Y
Sessions	N	Y	N	Y	N	Y
ALASKA						
Stevens	Y	Y	N	Y	N	Y
Murkowski	Y	Y	N	Y	N	Y
ARIZONA						
McCain	Y	Y	N	Y	N	Y
Kyl	N	Y	N	Y	N	Y
ARKANSAS						
Hutchinson	Y	Y	Y	Y	N	Y
Lincoln	Y	Y	Y	Y	Y	Y
CALIFORNIA						
Feinstein	Y	Y	Y	Y	Y	Y
Boxer	Y	Y	Y	Y	Y	N
COLORADO						
Campbell	N	Y	N	Y	N	Y
Allard	Y	Y	N	Y	N	Y
CONNECTICUT						
Dodd	Y	Y	Y	Y	Y	Y
Lieberman	Y	Y	Y	Y	Y	Y
DELAWARE						
Carper	Y	Y	Y	Y	Y	Y
Biden	Y	Y	Y	Y	Y	Y
FLORIDA						
Graham	Y	Y	Y	Y	Y	N
Nelson	Y	Y	Y	Y	Y	Y
GEORGIA						
Miller	Y	Y	Y	Y	N	Y
Cleland	Y	Y	Y	Y	Y	Y
HAWAII						
Inouye	Y	Y	Y	?	Y	N
Akaka	Y	Y	Y	Y	Y	N
IDAHO						
Craig	N	+	N	Y	N	Y
Crapo	Y	+	N	Y	N	Y
ILLINOIS						
Durbin	Y	Y	Y	Y	Y	N
Fitzgerald	Y	Y	N	Y	N	Y
INDIANA						
Lugar	Y	Y	N	N	N	Y
Bayh	Y	Y	Y	Y	Y	Y

	157	176	199	223	226	237
IOWA						
Grassley	N	Y	N	Y	N	Y
Harkin	Y	Y	N	Y	Y	Y
KANSAS						
Brownback	Y	Y	N	Y	N	Y
Roberts	Y	Y	N	Y	N	Y
KENTUCKY						
McConnell	N	Y	N	Y	N	Y
Bunning	Y	Y	N	Y	N	Y
LOUISIANA						
Breaux	Y	Y	N	Y	Y	Y
Landrieu	Y	Y	Y	Y	?	Y
MAINE						
Snowe	Y	Y	N	Y	N	Y
Collins	Y	Y	Y	Y	N	Y
MARYLAND						
Sarbanes	Y	Y	Y	Y	Y	N
Mikulski	Y	Y	Y	Y	Y	N
MASSACHUSETTS						
Kennedy	Y	Y	Y	Y	Y	N
Kerry	+	Y	Y	Y	Y	Y
MICHIGAN						
Levin	Y	Y	Y	Y	Y	N
Stabenow	Y	Y	Y	Y	Y	N
MINNESOTA						
Wellstone	Y	Y	Y	Y	Y	N
Dayton	Y	Y	Y	Y	Y	N
MISSISSIPPI						
Cochran	Y	Y	N	N	N	Y
Lott	Y	Y	N	N	N	Y
MISSOURI						
Bond	Y	Y	N	N	N	Y
Carnahan	Y	Y	Y	Y	Y	Y
MONTANA						
Baucus	Y	Y	Y	?	Y	Y
Burns	N	Y	N	Y	N	Y
NEBRASKA						
Nelson	Y	Y	N	Y	Y	Y
Hagel	Y	Y	N	Y	N	Y
NEVADA						
Reid	Y	Y	Y	Y	Y	Y
Ensign	Y	Y	N	Y	N	Y

	157	176	199	223	226	237
NEW HAMPSHIRE						
Smith	N	Y	N	Y	N	Y
Gregg	Y	Y	N	N	N	Y
NEW JERSEY						
Corzine	Y	Y	Y	Y	Y	N
Torricelli	Y	Y	Y	Y	Y	Y
NEW MEXICO						
Domenici	Y	Y	N	Y	N	Y
Bingaman	Y	Y	Y	Y	Y	N
NEW YORK						
Clinton	Y	Y	Y	Y	Y	Y
Schumer	Y	Y	Y	Y	Y	Y
NORTH CAROLINA						
Helms	?	+	–	Y	N	Y
Edwards	Y	Y	Y	Y	Y	Y
NORTH DAKOTA						
Conrad	Y	Y	Y	Y	Y	N
Dorgan	Y	Y	Y	Y	Y	Y
OHIO						
DeWine	Y	Y	N	Y	N	Y
Voinovich	Y	Y	N	N	N	Y
OKLAHOMA						
Nickles	N	Y	N	Y	N	Y
Inhofe	Y	Y	N	Y	N	Y
OREGON						
Wyden	Y	Y	Y	Y	Y	N
Smith	Y	Y	Y	Y	N	Y
PENNSYLVANIA						
Specter	Y	Y	Y	Y	Y	N
Santorum	N	Y	N	Y	N	Y
RHODE ISLAND						
Reed	Y	Y	Y	Y	Y	N
Chafee	Y	Y	N	Y	Y	N
SOUTH CAROLINA						
Thurmond	Y	Y	N	Y	N	Y
Hollings	Y	Y	N	Y	Y	Y
SOUTH DAKOTA						
Daschle	Y	Y	Y	Y	Y	Y
Johnson	Y	Y	Y	Y	Y	Y
TENNESSEE						
Thompson	Y	Y	N	Y	N	Y
Frist	Y	Y	N	Y	N	Y

	157	176	199	223	226	237
TEXAS						
Gramm	N	Y	N	N	N	Y
Hutchison	N	Y	N	Y	N	Y
UTAH						
Hatch	Y	Y	N	Y	N	Y
Bennett	Y	Y	N	Y	N	Y
VERMONT						
Leahy	Y	Y	Y	Y	Y	N
Jeffords	Y	Y	N	Y	Y	N
VIRGINIA						
Warner	Y	Y	N	Y	N	Y
Allen	Y	Y	N	Y	N	Y
WASHINGTON						
Cantwell	Y	Y	Y	Y	Y	N
Murray	Y	Y	Y	Y	Y	N
WEST VIRGINIA						
Byrd	Y	Y	Y	Y	Y	Y
Rockefeller	Y	Y	Y	Y	Y	Y
WISCONSIN						
Kohl	Y	Y	Y	Y	Y	Y
Feingold	Y	Y	N	Y	Y	N
WYOMING						
Thomas	N	Y	N	N	N	Y
Enzi	N	Y	N	Y	N	Y

Key

Y   Voted for (yea).
Paired for.
+   Announced for.
N   Voted against (nay).
X   Paired against.
–   Announced against.
P   Voted "present."
C   Voted "present" to avoid possible conflict of interest.
?   Did not vote or otherwise make a position known.

Democrats   ***Republicans***
Independents

ND Northern Democrats   SD Southern Democrats

Southern states - Ala., Ark., Fla., Ga., Ky., La., Miss., N.C., Okla., S.C., Tenn., Texas, Va.

157. S 2600. Terrorism Insurance/Passage. Passage of the bill that would require the federal government to reimburse insurance companies for 90 percent of catastrophic losses related to terrorism between $10 billion and $100 billion in 2002, with an option to renew the program the following year to cover 90 percent of claims between $15 billion and $100 billion. Passed 84-14: R 34-14; D 49-0 (ND 40-0, SD 9-0); I 1-0. June 18, 2002. *(Story, p. C-14)*

176. S 2673. Accounting Industry Overhaul/Passage. Passage of the bill that would require more complete disclosure of corporate finances and overhaul regulation of the accounting industry. The bill would establish a new oversight board to police accounting firms, and forbid firms from providing investment banking, management consulting and other services for publicly traded companies. It would create new criminal penalties for shareholder fraud and obstruction of justice involving document shredding and require chief executive officers and chief financial officers to attest to the accuracy of financial statements included in SEC filings. Passed 97-0: R 46-0; D 50-0 (ND 41-0, SD 9-0); I 1-0. July 15, 2002. *(Story, p. C-15)*

199. S 812. Drug Patents/Prescription Drugs. Graham, D-Fla., motion to waive the Budget Act with respect to the Frist, R-Tenn., point of order against the Graham amendment to the Dorgan, D-N.D., amendment. The Graham amendment would provide prescription drug coverage for Medicare recipients with incomes of up to 200 percent of the poverty level. It also would provide catastrophic coverage for drug costs over $3,300 per year for an annual payment of $25 per year. All recipients would be eligible for a discount of 5 percent or more on prescription drugs. The Dorgan amendment would authorize the Secretary of Health and Human Services (HHS) to promulgate regulations permitting pharmacists and wholesalers to import prescription drugs from Canada into the United States. It also would require Canadian pharmacies and wholesalers that provide drugs for importation to register with HHS and allow individuals to import prescription drugs from Canada if the medication is for personal use and is less than a 90-day supply. Motion rejected 49-50: R 4-44; D 45-5 (ND 38-3, SD 7-2); I 0-1. A three-fifths majority vote (60) of the total Senate is required to waive the Budget Act. (Subsequently, the chair upheld the point of order, and the amendment fell.) July 31, 2002. *(Story, p. C-15)*

223. HR 5005. Homeland Security/Independent Commission. Lieberman, D-Conn., amendment to the Lieberman substitute amendment. The amendment would establish the National Commission on Terrorist Attacks Upon the United States to investigate the facts and circumstances relating to the Sept. 11 terrorist attacks. The commission would be required to report its initial findings and recommendations to the president and to Congress within six months of its first meeting, followed by a second report within one year. Adopted 90-8: R 41-8; D 48-0 (ND 39-0, SD 9-0); I 1-0. Sept. 24, 2002. *(Story, p. C-16)*

226. HR 5005. Homeland Security/Cloture. Motion to invoke cloture (thus limiting debate) on the Lieberman, D-Conn., substitute amendment that would create a Cabinet-level Homeland Security Department charged with protecting domestic security. Motion rejected 50-49: R 1-48; D 48-1 (ND 41-0, SD 7-1); I 1-0. Three-fifths of the total Senate (60) is required to invoke cloture. Sept. 26, 2002. *(Story, p. C-16)*

237. H J Res 114. Use of Force/Passage. Passage of the joint resolution that would authorize the use of force against Iraq and require the administration to report to Congress that diplomatic options have been exhausted no later than 48 hours after military action has begun. The president also would be required to submit a progress report to Congress at least every 60 days. Passed (thus cleared for the president) 77-23: R 48-1; D 29-21 (ND 21-20, SD 8-1); I 0-1. A "yea" was a vote in support of the president's position. Oct. 11, 2002 (in the session that began and the Congressional Record dated Oct. 10, 2002). *(Story, p. C-17)*

Appendix D

TEXTS

Bush Says National Security And Economic Revival Will Require Deficit Spending

Following is a transcript of President Bush's first State of the Union address, delivered to a joint session of Congress the night of Jan. 29, as recorded by eMediaMillWorks Inc.

Mr. Speaker, Vice President Cheney, members of Congress, distinguished guests, fellow citizens: As we gather tonight, our nation is at war, our economy is in recession and the civilized world faces unprecedented dangers. Yet the state of our union has never been stronger.

We last met in an hour of shock and suffering. In four short months, our nation has comforted the victims, begun to rebuild New York and the Pentagon, rallied a great coalition, captured, arrested and rid the world of thousands of terrorists, destroyed Afghanistan's terrorist training camps, saved a people from starvation and freed a country from brutal oppression.

The American flag flies again over our embassy in Kabul. Terrorists who once occupied Afghanistan now occupy cells at Guantanamo Bay. And terrorist leaders who urged followers to sacrifice their lives are running for their own.

America and Afghanistan are now allies against terror. We will be partners in rebuilding that country. And this evening we welcome the distinguished interim leader of a liberated Afghanistan: Chairman Hamid Karzai.

The last time we met in this chamber, the mothers and daughters of Afghanistan were captives in their own homes, forbidden from working or going to school. Today, women are free, and are part of Afghanistan's new government. And we welcome the new minister of women's affairs, Dr. Sima Samar.

Our progress is a tribute to the spirit of the Afghan people, to the resolve of our coalition and to the might of the United States military.

When I called our troops into ac-tion, I did so with complete confidence in their courage and skill. And tonight, thanks to them, we are winning the war on terror. The men and women of our armed forces have delivered a message now clear to every enemy of the United States: Even 7,000 miles away, across oceans and continents, on mountaintops and in caves you will not escape the justice of this nation.

For many Americans, these four months have brought sorrow and pain that will never completely go away. Every day, a retired firefighter returns to ground zero to feel closer to his two sons who died there. At a memorial in New York, a little boy left his football with a note for his lost father: "Dear Daddy, please take this to Heaven. I don't want to play football until I can play with you again someday." Last month, at the grave of her husband, Michael, a CIA officer and Marine who died in Mazar-e-Sharif, Shannon Spann said these words of farewell: "Semper fi, my love."

'Our Cause Is Just'

Shannon is with us tonight. Shannon, I assure you and all who have lost a loved one that our cause is just, and our country will never forget the debt we owe Michael and all who gave their lives for freedom.

Our cause is just, and it continues. Our discoveries in Afghanistan confirmed our worst fears and showed us the true scope of the task ahead. We have seen the depth of our enemies' hatred in videos where they laugh about the loss of innocent life. And the depth of their hatred is equaled by the madness of the destruction they design. We have found diagrams of American nuclear power plants and public water facilities, detailed instructions for making chemical weapons, surveillance maps of American cities, and thorough descriptions of landmarks in America and throughout the world.

What we have found in Afghanistan confirms that, far from ending there, our war against terror is only beginning. Most of the 19 men who hijacked planes on September the 11th were trained in Afghanistan's camps. And so were tens of thousands of others. Thousands of dangerous killers, schooled in the methods of murder, often supported by outlaw regimes, are now spread throughout the world like ticking time bombs, set to go off without warning.

Thanks to the work of our law enforcement officials and coalition partners, hundreds of terrorists have been arrested, yet tens of thousands of trained terrorists are still at large. These enemies view the entire world as a battlefield, and we must pursue them wherever they are. So long as training camps operate, so long as nations harbor terrorists, freedom is at risk, and America and our allies must not, and will not, allow it.

Our nation will continue to be steadfast, and patient and persistent in the pursuit of two great objectives. First, we will shut down terrorist camps, disrupt terrorist plans and bring terrorists to justice. And second, we must prevent the terrorists and regimes who seek chemical, biological or nuclear weapons from threatening the United States and the world.

Our military has put the terror training camps of Afghanistan out of business, yet camps still exist in at least a dozen countries. A terrorist underworld — including groups like Hamas, Hezbollah, Islamic Jihad and Jaish-i-Mohammed — operates in remote jungles and deserts, and hides in the centers of large cities.

While the most visible military action is in Afghanistan, America is acting elsewhere. We now have troops in the Philippines helping to train that country's armed forces to go after terrorist cells that have executed an American and still hold hostages. Our

soldiers, working with the Bosnian government, seized terrorists who were plotting to bomb our embassy. Our Navy is patrolling the coast of Africa to block the shipment of weapons and the establishment of terrorist camps in Somalia.

My hope is that all nations will heed our call and eliminate the terrorist parasites who threaten their countries and our own. Many nations are acting forcefully. Pakistan is now cracking down on terror, and I admire the strong leadership of President Musharraf. But some governments will be timid in the face of terror. And make no mistake about it: If they do not act, America will.

'Axis of Evil'

Our second goal is to prevent regimes that sponsor terror from threatening America or our friends and allies with weapons of mass destruction. Some of these regimes have been pretty quiet since Sept. 11, but we know their true nature.

North Korea is a regime arming with missiles and weapons of mass destruction, while starving its citizens.

Iran aggressively pursues these weapons and exports terror, while an unelected few repress the Iranian people's hope for freedom.

Iraq continues to flaunt its hostility toward America and to support terror. The Iraqi regime has plotted to develop anthrax and nerve gas and nuclear weapons for over a decade. This is a regime that has already used poison gas to murder thousands of its own citizens, leaving the bodies of mothers huddled over their dead children. This is a regime that agreed to international inspections then kicked out the inspectors. This is a regime that has something to hide from the civilized world.

States like these, and their terrorist allies, constitute an axis of evil, arming to threaten the peace of the world. By seeking weapons of mass destruction, these regimes pose a grave and growing danger. They could provide these arms to terrorists, giving them the means to match their hatred. They could attack our allies or attempt to blackmail the United States. In any of these cases, the price of indifference would be catastrophic.

We will work closely with our coali-

tion to deny terrorists and their state sponsors the materials, technology and expertise to make and deliver weapons of mass destruction. We will develop and deploy effective missile defenses to protect America and our allies from sudden attack. And all nations should know: America will do what is necessary to ensure our nation's security.

We'll be deliberate, yet time is not on our side. I will not wait on events while dangers gather. I will not stand by as peril draws closer and closer. The United States of America will not permit the world's most dangerous regimes to threaten us with the world's most destructive weapons.

Our war on terror is well begun, but it is only begun. This campaign may not be finished on our watch, yet it must be and it will be waged on our watch.

We can't stop short. If we stopped now, leaving terror camps intact and terror states unchecked, our sense of security would be false and temporary. History has called America and our allies to action, and it is both our responsibility and our privilege to fight freedom's fight.

Budget Priorities

Our first priority must always be the security of our nation, and that will be reflected in the budget I send to Congress. My budget supports three great goals for America: We will win this war, we will protect our homeland, and we will revive our economy.

Sept. 11 brought out the best in America and the best in this Congress, and I join the American people in applauding your unity and resolve.

Now Americans deserve to have this same spirit directed toward addressing problems here at home. I am a proud member of my Party. Yet as we act to win the war, protect our people and create jobs in America, we must act first and foremost not as Republicans, not as Democrats, but as Americans.

It costs a lot to fight this war. We have spent more than a billion dollars a month — over $30 million a day— and we must be prepared for future operations. Afghanistan proved that expensive precision weapons defeat the enemy and spare innocent lives, and we need more of them. We need to replace aging aircraft and make our mili-

tary more agile to put our troops anywhere in the world quickly and safely.

Our men and women in uniform deserve the best weapons, the best equipment and the best training, and they also deserve another pay raise.

My budget includes the largest increase in defense spending in two decades, because while the price of freedom and security is high, it is never too high. Whatever it costs to defend our country, we will pay.

The next priority of my budget is to do everything possible to protect our citizens and strengthen our nation against the ongoing threat of another attack.

Time and distance from the events of September the 11th will not make us safer unless we act on its lessons. America is no longer protected by vast oceans. We are protected from attack only by vigorous action abroad and increased vigilance at home.

My budget nearly doubles funding for a sustained strategy of homeland security, focused on four key areas: bioterrorism, emergency response, airport and border security, and improved intelligence.

We will develop vaccines to fight anthrax and other deadly diseases. We'll increase funding to help states and communities train and equip our heroic police and firefighters. We will improve intelligence collection and sharing, expand patrols at our borders, strengthen the security of air travel, and use technology to track the arrivals and departures of visitors to the United States.

Homeland security will make America not only stronger but in many ways better. Knowledge gained from bioterrorism research will improve public health. Stronger police and fire departments will mean safer neighborhoods. Stricter border enforcement will help combat illegal drugs.

And as government works to better secure our homeland, America will continue to depend on the eyes and ears of alert citizens. A few days before Christmas, an airline flight attendant spotted a passenger lighting a match. The crew and passengers quickly subdued the man, who had been trained by al Qaeda and was armed with explosives. The people on that airplane were alert, and as a result likely saved nearly 200 lives. And tonight we wel-

come and thank flight attendants Hermis Moutardier and Christina Jones.

Anticipating a 'Short-Term' Deficit

Once we have funded our national security and our homeland security, the final great priority of my budget is economic security for the American people.

To achieve these great national objectives — to win the war, protect the homeland and revitalize our economy — our budget will run a deficit that will be small and short term so long as Congress restrains spending and acts in a fiscally responsible way.

We have clear priorities, and we must act at home with the same purpose and resolve we have shown overseas. We will prevail in the war, and we will defeat this recession.

Americans who have lost their jobs need our help, and I support extending unemployment benefits and direct assistance for health care coverage. Yet American workers want more than unemployment checks. They want a steady paycheck. When America works, America prospers, so my economic security plan can be summed up in one word: jobs.

Good jobs begin with good schools, and here we've made a fine start. Republicans and Democrats worked together to achieve historic education reform so that no child is left behind. I was proud to work with members of both parties, [House Education Committee] Chairman John Boehner [R-Ohio] and Congressman George Miller [of California, the panel's ranking Democrat], Senator Judd Gregg [of New Hampshire, ranking Republican on the Senate Health, Education, Labor and Pensions (HELP) Committee].

And I was so proud of our work, I even had nice things to say about my friend Ted Kennedy [Edward M. Kennedy, D-Mass., the HELP Committee's chairman]. I know the folks at the Crawford coffee shop couldn't believe I'd say such a thing. But our work on this bill shows what is possible if we set aside posturing and focus on results.

A Call for Permanent Tax Credits

There's more to do. We need to prepare our children to read and succeed in school with improved Head Start and early childhood development pro-

grams. We must upgrade our teacher colleges and teacher training and launch a major recruiting drive with a great goal for America: a quality teacher in every classroom.

Good jobs also depend on reliable and affordable energy. This Congress must act to encourage conservation, promote technology, build infrastructure, and it must act to increase energy production at home so America is less dependent on foreign oil.

Good jobs depend on expanded trade. Selling into new markets creates new jobs, so I ask Congress to finally approve trade promotion authority.

On these two key issues, trade and energy, the House of Representatives has acted to create jobs, and I urge the Senate to pass this legislation.

Good jobs depend on sound tax policy. Last year, some in this hall thought my tax relief plan was too small, some thought it was too big. But when those checks arrived in the mail, most Americans thought tax relief was just about right. Congress listened to the people and responded by reducing tax rates, doubling the child credit and ending the death tax. For the sake of long-term growth, and to help Americans plan for the future, let's make these tax cuts permanent.

The way out of this recession, the way to create jobs, is to grow the economy by encouraging investment in factories and equipment, and by speeding up tax relief so people have more money to spend. For the sake of American workers, let's pass a stimulus package.

Ensuring Retirement Security

Good jobs must be the aim of welfare reform. As we reauthorize these important reforms, we must always remember: The goal is to reduce dependency on government and offer every American the dignity of a job. Americans know economic security can vanish in an instant without health security. I ask Congress to join me this year to enact a patients' bill of rights, to give uninsured workers credits to help buy health coverage, to approve an historic increase in spending for veterans' health and to give seniors a sound and modern Medicare system that includes coverage for prescription drugs.

A good job should lead to security in retirement. I ask Congress to enact

new safeguards for 401(k) and pension plans. Employees who have worked hard and saved all their lives should not have to risk losing everything if their company fails. Through stricter accounting standards and tougher disclosure requirements, corporate America must be made more accountable to employees and shareholders and held to the highest standards of conduct.

Retirement security also depends upon keeping the commitments of Social Security, and we will. We must make Social Security financially stable and allow personal retirement accounts for younger workers who choose them.

Members, you and I will work together in the months ahead on other issues: productive farm policy, a cleaner environment, broader home ownership — especially among minorities — and ways to encourage the good work of charities and faith-based groups.

I ask you to join me on these important domestic issues in the same spirit of cooperation we have applied to our war against terrorism.

During these last few months, I've been humbled and privileged to see the true character of this country in a time of testing. Our enemies believed America was weak and materialistic, that we would splinter in fear and selfishness. They were as wrong as they are evil.

The American people have responded magnificently, with courage and compassion, strength and resolve. As I have met the heroes, hugged the families and looked into the tired faces of rescuers, I have stood in awe of the American people.

And I hope you will join me in expressing thanks to one American for the strength and calm and comfort she brings to our nation in crisis: our first lady, Laura Bush.

Creating a 'Freedom Corps'

None of us would ever wish the evil that was done on September the 11th, yet after America was attacked, it was as if our entire country looked into a mirror and saw our better selves. We were reminded that we are citizens with obligations to each other, to our country, and to history. We began to think less of the goods we can accumulate and more about the

good we can do.

For too long our culture has said, "If it feels good, do it." Now America is embracing a new ethic and a new creed: "Let's roll."

In the sacrifice of soldiers, the fierce brotherhood of firefighters, and the bravery and generosity of ordinary citizens, we have glimpsed what a new culture of responsibility could look like. We want to be a nation that serves goals larger than self. We have been offered a unique opportunity, and we must not let this moment pass. My call tonight is for every American to commit at least two years — 4,000 hours — over the rest of your lifetime to the service of your neighbors and your nation.

Many are already serving, and I thank you. If you aren't sure how to help, I've got a good place to start. To sustain and extend the best that has emerged in America, I invite you to join the new USA Freedom Corps. The Freedom Corps will focus on three areas of need: responding in case of crisis at home, rebuilding our communities and extending American compassion throughout the world.

One purpose of the USA Freedom Corps will be homeland security. America needs retired doctors and nurses who can be mobilized in major emergencies, volunteers to help police and fire departments, transportation and utility workers well trained in spotting danger. Our country also needs citizens working to rebuild our communities. We need mentors to love children, especially children whose parents are in prison. And we need more talented teachers in troubled schools.

USA Freedom Corps will expand and improve the good efforts of AmeriCorps and Senior Corps to recruit more than 200,000 new volunteers.

And America needs citizens to extend the compassion of our country to every part of the world, so we will renew the promise of the Peace Corps, double its volunteers over the next five years and ask it to join a new effort to encourage development and education and opportunity in the Islamic world.

This time of adversity offers a unique moment of opportunity, a moment we must seize to change our culture. Through the gathering momentum of millions of acts of service and decency and kindness, I know we can overcome evil with greater good.

And we have a great opportunity during this time of war to lead the world toward the values that will bring lasting peace. All fathers and mothers, in all societies, want their children to be educated and live free from poverty and violence. No people on Earth yearn to be oppressed or aspire to servitude or eagerly await the midnight knock of the secret police.

If anyone doubts this, let them look to Afghanistan, where the Islamic "street" greeted the fall of tyranny with song and celebration. Let the skeptics look to Islam's own rich history, with its centuries of learning and tolerance and progress.

Defense of 'Human Dignity'

America will lead by defending liberty and justice because they are right and true and unchanging for all people everywhere. No nation owns these aspirations, and no nation is exempt from them. We have no intention of imposing our culture, but America will always stand firm for the non-negotiable demands of human dignity: the rule of law, limits on the power of the state, respect for women, private property, free speech, equal justice and religious tolerance.

America will take the side of brave men and women who advocate these values around the world — including the Islamic world — because we have a greater objective than eliminating threats and containing resentment. We seek a just and peaceful world beyond the war on terror.

In this moment of opportunity, a common danger is erasing old rivalries. America is working with Russia and China and India in ways we never have before to achieve peace and prosperity. In every region, free markets and free trade and free societies are proving their power to lift lives. Together with friends and allies from Europe to Asia, and Africa to Latin America, we will demonstrate that the forces of terror cannot stop the momentum of freedom.

The last time I spoke here, I expressed the hope that life would return to normal. In some ways it has. In others it never will. Those of us who have lived through these challenging times have been changed by them. We've come to know truths that we will never question: Evil is real, and it must be opposed.

Beyond all differences of race or creed, we are one country, mourning together and facing danger together. Deep in the American character there is honor, and it is stronger than cynicism. And many have discovered again that even in tragedy — especially in tragedy — God is near.

In a single instant, we realized that this will be a decisive decade in the history of liberty, that we have been called to a unique role in human events. Rarely has the world faced a choice more clear or consequential.

Our enemies send other people's children on missions of suicide and murder. They embrace tyranny and death as a cause and a creed. We stand for a different choice, made long ago, on the day of our founding. We affirm it again today. We choose freedom and the dignity of every life.

Steadfast in our purpose, we now press on. We have known freedom's price. We have shown freedom's power. And in this great conflict, my fellow Americans, we will see freedom's victory. Thank you all, and may God bless. ◆

Gephardt Urges More Protections For Workers and Pensioners, Pushes for Campaign Finance Overhaul

Following is a transcript of House Minority Leader Richard A. Gephardt of Missouri's response, on behalf of the Democratic Party, to President Bush's State of the Union address Jan. 29, as recorded by eMediaMillWorks Inc.

Good evening. I want to commend the president for his strong and patriotic message tonight, and I can assure you of this: There were two parties tonight in the House Chamber, but one resolve. Like generations that came before us, we will pay any price and bear any burden to make sure that this proud nation wins the first war of the 21st century.

Tonight, we say to our men and women in uniform: Thank you for your bravery, your skill and your sacrifice. When the history of this time is written, your courage will be listed in its proudest pages.

To our friends around the world, we say thank you for your aid and support. True friendship is tested not only in treaties and trade, but in times of trial.

To our enemies, we say with one voice: No act of violence, no threat will drive us apart or steer us from our course to protect America and preserve our democracy. And make no mistake about it: We're going to hunt you down and make you pay.

Now is not a time for finger-pointing or politics as usual. The men and women who are defending our freedom are not fighting for the Democratic Party or the Republican Party. They're fighting for the greatest country that's ever existed on Earth: the United States of America. As Americans, we need to put partisanship aside and work together to solve the problems that face us.

On the day after the attacks, I went to the Oval Office for a meeting with the president. I said, "Mr. President, we have to find a way to work together." I said, "We have to trust you, and you have to trust us."

Since that day, there has been no daylight between us in this war on terrorism. We've met almost every single week and built a bipartisan consensus that is helping America win this war.

Security on the Economic Front

We also know that to defeat terrorism, our economy must be strong. For all the things that have changed in our world over the past four months, the needs of our families have not. While our attention has shifted, our values have not.

We know that real security depends not just on justice abroad, but creating good jobs at home; not just on securing our borders, but strengthening Social Security and Medicare at home; not just on bringing governments together, but creating a government here at home that lives within its means, cuts wasteful spending and invests in the future. Real security depends not just on meeting threats around the world, but living up to our highest values here at home.

Our values call for tax cuts that promote growth and prosperity for all Americans. Our values call for protecting Social Security and not gambling it away on the stock market. Our values call for helping patients and older Americans, not just big HMOs and pharmaceutical companies, ensuring that seniors don't have to choose between food and medicine.

Our values call for helping workers who have lost their 401(k) plans and protecting pensions from corporate mismanagement and abuse. Our values call for helping the unemployed, not just large corporations and the most fortunate.

These same values guide us as we work toward a long-term plan for our nation. We want to roll up our sleeves and work with our president to end America's dependence on foreign oil while preserving our environment, so we don't see gas prices jump every year.

We want to work together to recruit high-quality teachers and invest more in our schools while demanding more from them. We want to say to every student who wants to go to college and every worker who wants to update their skills: The first $10,000 of your education should be tax deductible.

We want to work together to raise the minimum wage, because nobody who works hard and plays by the rules should be forced to live in poverty.

We want to work together to create a universal pension system that follows a worker from job to job through life and protects employees from the next Enron.

We want to work together to build our new economy, creating jobs by investing in technology so America can continue to lead the world in growth and opportunity.

We want to work together to improve homeland security and protect our borders, to keep out those people who want to bring us harm, but also to celebrate our nation's diversity and welcome those hardworking immigrants who pay taxes and keep our country strong.

We want to work together, as we have over the last decade, to continue to build the best-trained, best-equipped fighting force on the face of the planet.

I refuse to accept that while we stand shoulder to shoulder on the war, we should stand toe to toe on the economy. We need to find a way to respect each other, and trust each other, and work together to solve the long-term challenges America faces.

I'm ready to roll up my sleeves and go to work. That's one of the reasons I have proposed that next month a group of leaders from both parties come together at the White House for an economic growth summit to figure out how we're going to help businesses create jobs, reduce the deficit, simplify the tax code and grow our economy.

Call to Revamp Campaign Finance

To accomplish these goals, we need a political system that's worthy of the people of this country. In the next several weeks, the House of Representatives will once again consider campaign finance reform. If the nation's largest bankruptcy, coupled with a clear example of paid political influence, isn't a prime case for reform, I don't know what is.

The forces aligned against this are powerful. So if you've never called or written your member of Congress, now is the time.

I hope the president will stand with us to clean up the political system and get big money out of politics.

Our nation's been through a lot the past four months. If it's even possible to suggest a silver lining in this dark cloud that's fallen over our nation, it's the renewed sense of community that we've seen across America. The more we're able to turn that renewed sense of purpose into a new call for service, to encourage more Americans, young and old, to get involved, join AmeriCorps, the Peace Corps, the military or other endeavors, the more we're going to make our nation a model for all the good things that terrorists hate us for: hope, opportunity and freedom.

It was brought home to me how Americans are already answering that call when I spoke to a friend of mine who's the head of a postal union. Shortly after we learned of the anthrax threat, I asked him how he was doing. "Not well," he said. "We've lost two workers, and some are sick." He said, "I went to New Jersey where they had some of the biggest problems. Because of anthrax, all the workers were working in a tent exposed to the cold, hand-sorting the mail."

He said, "I thought I was going to get an earful, but when I asked for questions, a man stood up and said, 'I've been a postal worker for 30 years. We're here, and we're going to stay here. And if we've got to be outside all winter, we're going to stay here. The mail is going out. The terrorists will not win.' "

As one American said, the terrorists who attacked us wanted to teach us a lesson. They wanted us to know them. But these attacks make clear, they don't know us. They don't know what we'll do to defend freedom, and they don't know what they've started. But they're beginning to find out.

As we look ahead to the future, we do so with the knowledge that we can never fully know what the men and women we lost on that day would have accomplished. We can never know what would have been the full measure of their lives or what they would have contributed to our world if they had lived.

But one thing is certain: It is up to all of us to redeem the lives they would have lived with the lives we live today and to make the most of our time here on earth. Let us be up to that challenge.

Thank you. God bless you, and God bless America. ◆

Bush to U.S. Citizens: Press Congress For Homeland Security Department By Year's End

Following is the statement President Bush made June 6 when he proposed creating a new Department of Homeland Security, the first new Cabinet office since 1989. (Congress subsequently approved the new government office.) The transcript is from the White House.

Good evening. During the next few minutes, I want to update you on the progress we are making in our war against terror, and to propose sweeping changes that will strengthen our homeland against the ongoing threat of terrorist attacks.

Nearly nine months have passed since the day that forever changed our country. Debris from what was once the World Trade Center has been cleared away in a hundred thousand truckloads. The west side of the Pentagon looks almost as it did on Sept. 10th. And as children finish school and families prepare for summer vacations, for many, life seems almost normal.

Yet we are a different nation today: sadder and stronger, less innocent and more courageous, more appreciative of life and, for many who serve our country, more willing to risk life in a great cause. For those who have lost family and friends, the pain will never go away, and neither will the responsibilities that day thrust upon all of us.

America is leading the civilized world in a titanic struggle against terror. Freedom and fear are at war, and freedom is winning.

Tonight, over 60,000 American troops are deployed around the world in the war against terror: more than 7,000 in Afghanistan; others in the Philippines, Yemen, and the Republic of Georgia to train local forces. Next week, Afghanistan will begin selecting a representative government, even as American troops, along with our allies, still continuously raid remote al Qaeda hiding places. Among those we have captured is a man named Abu Zubaida, al Qaeda's chief of operations. From

him, and from hundreds of others, we are learning more about how the terrorists plan and operate — information crucial in anticipating and preventing future attacks.

Our coalition is strong. More than 90 nations have arrested or detained over 2,400 terrorists and their supporters. More than 180 countries have offered or are providing assistance in the war on terrorism. And our military is strong and prepared to oppose any emerging threat to the American people.

Every day in this war will not bring the drama of liberating a country. Yet every day brings new information, a tip or arrest, another step or two or three in a relentless march to bring security to our nation and justice to our enemies.

And every day I review a document called the Threat Assessment. It summarizes what our intelligence services and key law enforcement agencies have picked up about terrorist activity. Sometimes the information is very general, vague talk bragging about future attacks. Sometimes the information is more specific, as in a recent case when an al Qaeda detainee said attacks were planned against financial institutions.

When credible intelligence warrants, appropriate law enforcement and local officials are alerted. These warnings are unfortunately a new reality in American life, and we have recently seen an increase in the volume of general threats. Americans should continue to do what you are doing — go about your lives, but pay attention to your surroundings. Add your eyes and ears to the protection of our homeland.

In protecting our country, we depend on the skill of our people: the troops we send to battle, intelligence operatives who risk their lives for bits of information, law enforcement officers who sift for clues and search for suspects. We are now learning that before Sept. 11, the suspicions and in-

sights of some of our front-line agents did not get enough attention.

My administration supports the important work of the Intelligence committees in Congress to review the activities of law enforcement and intelligence agencies. We need to know when warnings were missed **or signs** unheeded — not to point the finger of blame, but to make sure we correct any problems and prevent them from happening again. Based on everything I have seen, I do not believe anyone could have prevented the horror of Sept. 11. Yet we now know that thousands of trained killers are plotting to attack us, and this terrible knowledge requires us to act differently.

If you are a front-line worker for the FBI, the CIA or some other law enforcement or intelligence agency and you see something that raises suspicions, I want you to report it immediately. I expect your supervisors to treat it with the seriousness it deserves. Information must be fully shared, so we can follow every lead to find the one that may prevent tragedy.

I applaud the leaders and employees at the FBI and CIA for beginning essential reforms. They must continue to think and act differently to defeat the enemy.

The first and best way to secure America's homeland is to attack the enemy where he hides and plans — and we are doing just that. We are also taking significant steps to strengthen our homeland protections — securing cockpits, tightening our borders, stockpiling vaccines, increasing security at water-treatment and nuclear power plants. After Sept. 11, we needed to move quickly, and so I appointed Tom Ridge as my Homeland Security adviser. As Gov. Ridge has worked with all levels of government to prepare a national strategy, and as we have learned more about the plans and capabilities of the terrorist network, we have concluded that our govern-

ment must be reorganized to deal most effectively with the new threats of the 21st century. So tonight, I ask the Congress to join me in creating a single permanent department with an overriding and urgent mission: securing the American homeland and protecting the American people.

Right now, as many as a hundred different government agencies have some responsibilities for homeland security. And no one has final accountability. The Coast Guard has several missions, from search and rescue to maritime treaty enforcement. It reports to the Transportation Department, whose primary responsibilities are roads, rails, bridges and the airways. The Customs Service, among other duties, collects tariffs and prevents smuggling, and it is part of the Treasury Department, whose primary responsibility is fiscal policy, not security.

Tonight, I propose a permanent Cabinet-level Department of Homeland Security to unite essential agencies that must work more closely together, among them the Coast Guard, the Border Patrol, the Customs Service, Immigration officials, the Transportation Security Administration and the Federal Emergency Management Agency. Employees of this new agency will come to work every morning knowing their most important job is to protect their fellow citizens.

The Department of Homeland Secu-rity will be charged with four primary tasks. This new agency will control our borders and prevent terrorists and explosives from entering our country. It will work with state and local authorities to respond quickly and effectively to emergencies. It will bring together our best scientists to develop technologies that detect biological, chemical and nuclear weapons, and to discover the drugs and treatments to best protect our citizens. And this new department will review intelligence and law enforcement information from all agencies of government and produce a single daily picture of threats against our homeland. Analysts will be responsible for imagining the worst and planning to counter it.

The reason to create this department is not to increase the size of government, but to increase its focus and effectiveness. The staff of this new department will be largely drawn from the agencies we are combining. By ending duplication and overlap, we will spend less on overhead, and more on protecting America. This reorganization will give the good people of our government their best opportunity to succeed, by organizing our resources in a way that is thorough and unified.

What I am proposing tonight is the most extensive reorganization of the federal government since the 1940s. During his presidency, Harry Truman recognized that our nation's fragmented defenses had to be reorganized to win the Cold War. He proposed uniting our military forces under a single Department of Defense and creating the National Security Council to bring together defense, intelligence and diplomacy. Truman's reforms are still helping us to fight terror abroad, and now we need similar dramatic reforms to secure our people at home.

Only the United States Congress can create a new department of government.

So tonight I ask for your help in encouraging your representatives to support my plan. We face an urgent need, and we must move quickly, this year, before the end of the congressional session. All in our government have learned a great deal since Sept. 11, and we must act on every lesson. We are stronger and better prepared tonight than we were on that terrible morning — and with your help, and the support of Congress, we will be stronger still.

History has called our nation into action. History has placed a great challenge before us: Will America, with our unique position and power, blink in the face of terror? Or will we lead to a freer, more civilized world?

There is only one answer: This great country will lead the world to safety, security, peace and freedom.

Thank you for listening, good night, and may God bless America. ◆

Bush Urges Peace in Middle East, Sends Secretary of State to Region

Following is the statement President Bush made April 4 when he announced that he would send Secretary of State Colin L. Powell to the Middle East in hopes of working out a peace agreement between the Israelis and the Palestinians. The transcript is from the White House.

Good morning. During the course of one week, the situation in the Middle East has deteriorated dramatically. Last Wednesday, my special envoy, Anthony Zinni, reported to me that we were on the verge of a cease-fire agreement that would have spared Palestinian and Israeli lives. That hope fell away when a terrorist attacked a group of innocent people at a Netanya hotel, killing many men and women in what is a mounting toll of terror.

In the days since, the world has watched with growing concern the horror of bombings and burials and the stark picture of tanks in the street. Across the world, people are grieving for Israelis and Palestinians who have lost their lives.

When an 18-year-old Palestinian girl is induced to blow herself up, and in the process kills a 17-year-old Israeli girl, the future itself is dying, the future of the Palestinian people and the future of the Israeli people.

We mourn the dead, and we mourn the damage done to the hope of peace, the hope of Israel's and the Israelis' desire for a Jewish state at peace with its neighbors; the hope of the Palestinian people to build their own independent state.

Terror must be stopped. No nation can negotiate with terrorists, for there is no way to make peace with those whose only goal is death.

This could be a hopeful moment in the Middle East. The proposal of Crown Prince Abdullah of Saudi Arabia, supported by the Arab League, has put a number of countries in the Arab world closer than ever to recognizing Israel's right to exist.

The United States is on record supporting the legitimate aspirations of the Palestinian people for a Palestinian state. Israel has recognized the goal of a Palestinian state.

The outlines of a just settlement are clear: two states, Israel and Palestine, living side by side in peace and security. This can be a time for hope, but it calls for leadership, not for terror.

Since Sept. 11, I've delivered this message: Everyone must choose. You're either with the civilized world or you're with the terrorists. All in the Middle East also must choose and must move decisively in word and deed against terrorist acts.

The chairman of the Palestinian Authority has not consistently opposed or confronted terrorists.

At Oslo and elsewhere, Chairman Arafat renounced terror as an instrument of his cause, and he agreed to control it. He's not done so.

The situation in which he finds himself today is largely of his own making. He's missed his opportunities and thereby betrayed the hopes of the people he's supposed to lead.

Given his failure, the Israeli government feels it must strike at terrorist networks that are killing its citizens. Yet, Israel must understand that its response to these recent attacks is only a temporary measure. All parties have their own responsibilities, and all parties owe it to their own people to act.

We all know today's situation runs the risk of aggravating long-term bitterness and undermining relationships that are critical to any hope of peace.

I call on the Palestinian people and the Palestinian Authority and our friends in the Arab world to join us in delivering a clear message to terrorists: Blowing yourself up does not help the Palestinian cause. To the contrary, suicide-bombing missions could well blow up the best and only hope for a Palestinian state.

All states must keep their promise, made in a vote in the United Nations, to actively oppose terror in all its forms. No nation can pick and choose its terrorist friends.

I call on the Palestinian Authority and all governments in the region to do everything in their power to stop terrorist activities, to disrupt terrorist financing, and to stop inciting violence by glorifying terror in state-owned media or telling suicide bombers they are martyrs.

They're not martyrs. They're murderers. And they undermine the cause of the Palestinian people.

Those governments, like Iraq, that reward parents for the sacrifice of their children are guilty of soliciting murder of the worst kind.

All who care about the Palestinian people should join in condemning and acting against groups like al Aqsa, Hezbollah, Hamas, Islamic Jihad and all groups which oppose the peace process and seek the destruction of Israel.

The recent Arab League support of Crown Prince Abdullah's initiative for peace is promising, is hopeful because it acknowledges Israel's right to exist. And it raises the hope of sustained, constructive Arab involvement in the search for peace.

This builds on a tradition of visionary leadership begun by President Sadat and King Hussein and carried forward by President Mubarak and King Abdullah. Now other Arab states must rise to this occasion and accept Israel as a nation and as a neighbor.

Peace with Israel is the only avenue to prosperity and success for a new Palestinian state. The Palestinian people deserve peace and an opportunity to better their lives.

They need their closest neighbor, Israel, to be an economic partner, not a mortal enemy. They deserve a government that respects human rights and a government that focuses on their needs, education and health care, rather than feeding their resentments.

It is not enough for Arab nations to defend the Palestinian cause. They must truly help the Palestinian people by seeking peace and fighting terror and promoting development.

Israel faces hard choices of its own. Its government has supported the creation of a Palestinian state that is not a haven for terrorism. Yet, Israel also must recognize that such a state needs to be politically and economically viable.

Consistent with the Mitchell plan, Israeli settlement activity in occupied territories must stop, and the occupation must end through withdrawal to secure and recognized boundaries consistent with United Nations Resolutions 242 and 338. Ultimately, this approach should be the basis of agreements between Israel and Syria, and Israel and Lebanon.

Israel should also show a respect — a respect for and concern about the dignity of the Palestinian people who are and will be their neighbors. It is crucial to distinguish between the terrorists and ordinary Palestinians seeking to provide for their own families. The Israeli government should be compassionate at checkpoints and border crossings, sparing innocent Palestinians daily humiliation.

Israel should take immediate action to ease closures and allow peaceful people to go back to work.

Israel is facing a terrible and serious challenge. For seven days, it has acted to rout out terrorists' nests. America recognizes Israel's right to defend itself from terror.

Yet, to lay the foundations of future peace, I ask Israel to halt incursions into Palestinian-controlled areas and begin the withdrawal from those cities it has recently occupied.

I speak as a committed friend of Israel. I speak out of a concern for its long-term security, the security that will come with a genuine peace.

As Israel steps back, responsible Palestinian leaders and Israel's Arab neighbors must step forward and show the world that they are truly on the side of peace. The choice and the burden will be theirs.

The world expects an immediate cease-fire, immediate resumption of security, cooperation with Israel against terrorism, and an immediate order to crack down on terrorist networks. I expect better leadership, and I expect results.

These are the elements of peace in the Middle East, and now we must build the road to those goals. Decades of bitter experience teach a clear lesson: Progress is impossible when nations emphasize their grievances and ignore their opportunities. The storms of violence cannot go on. Enough is enough.

And to those who would try to use the current crisis as an opportunity to widen the conflict, stay out. Iran's arms shipments and support for terror fuel the fire of conflict in the Middle East, and it must stop. Syria has spoken out against al Qaeda. We expect it to act against Hamas and Hezbollah, as well.

It's time for Iran to focus on meeting its own people's aspirations for freedom and for Syria to decide which side of the war against terror it is on.

The world finds itself at a critical moment. This is a conflict that can widen, or an opportunity we can seize.

And so, I've decided to send Secretary of State Powell to the region next week, to seek broad international support for the vision I've outlayed today.

As a step in this process, he will work to implement United Nations Resolution 1402 — an immediate and meaningful cease-fire, an end to terror and violence and incitement; withdrawal of Israeli troops from Palestinian cities, including Ramallah; implementation of the already agreed-upon Tenet and Mitchell plans, which will lead to a political settlement.

I have no illusions — we have no illusions — about the difficulty of the issues that lay ahead. Yet our nation's resolve is strong. America is committed to ending this conflict and beginning an era of peace.

We know this is possible, because in our lifetimes, we have seen an end to conflicts that no one thought could end. We've seen fierce enemies let go of long histories of strife and anger. America itself counts former adversaries as trusted friends — Germany and Japan and now Russia.

Conflict is not inevitable. Distrust need not be permanent. Peace is possible when we break free of old patterns and habits of hatred.

The violence and grief that trouble the holy land have been among the great tragedies of our time. The Middle East has often been left behind in the political and economic advancement of the world. That is the history of the region, but it need not — and must not — be its fate.

The Middle East could write a new story of trade and development and democracy. And we stand ready to help.

Yet this progress can only come in an atmosphere of peace. And the United States will work for all the children of Abraham to know the benefits of peace.

Thank you very much. ◆

Bush Catalogs Iraq's Offenses, Proposes Future Actions In Address to United Nations

Following is the statement President Bush made Sept. 12 in an appearance before the General Assembly of the United Nations. Bush spoke on the threat that Iraq poses to the United States and the rest of the world. The transcript is from Federal Document Clearinghouse.

Mr. Secretary General, Mr. President, distinguished delegates and ladies and gentlemen. We meet one year and one day after a terrorist attack brought grief to my country and brought grief to many citizens of our world.

Yesterday we remembered the innocent lives taken that terrible morning. Today we turn to the urgent duty of protecting other lives without illusion and without fear.

We've accomplished much in the last year in Afghanistan and beyond. We have much yet to do in Afghanistan and beyond. Many nations represented here have joined in the fight against global terror and the people of the United States are grateful.

The United Nations was born in the hope that survived a world war, the hope of a world moving toward justice, escaping old patterns of conflict and fear. The founding members resolved that the peace of the world must never again be destroyed by the will and wickedness of any man.

We created a United Nations Security Council so that, unlike the League of Nations, our deliberations would be more than talk, our resolutions would be more than wishes. After generations of deceitful dictators and broken treaties and squandered lives, we've dedicated ourselves to standards of human dignity shared by all and to a system of security defended by all.

Today, these standards and this security are challenged.

Our commitment to human dignity is challenged by persistent poverty and raging disease. The suffering is great. And our responsibilities are clear. The United States is joining with the world to supply aid where it reaches people and lifts up lives, to extend trade and the prosperity it brings, and to bring medical care where it is desperately needed. As a symbol of our commitment to human dignity, the United States will return to UNESCO.

This organization has been reformed, and America will participate fully in its mission to advance human rights and tolerance and learning. Our common security is challenged by regional conflicts, ethnic and religious strife that is ancient, but not inevitable.

Peace in the Middle East

In the Middle East there can be no peace for either side without freedom for both sides.

America stands committed to an independent and democratic Palestine, living side by side with Israel in peace and security. Like all other people, Palestinians deserve a government that serves their interests and listens to their voices. My nation will continue to encourage all parties to step up to their responsibilities as we seek a just and comprehensive settlement to the conflict.

Above all, our principles and our security are challenged today by outlaw groups and regimes that accept no law of morality and have no limit to their violent ambitions. In the attacks on America a year ago, we saw the destructive intentions of our enemies. This threat hides within many nations, including my own.

In cells, in camps, terrorists are plotting further destruction and building new bases for their war against civilization. And our greatest fear is that terrorists will find a shortcut to their mad ambitions when an outlaw regime supplies them with the technologies to kill on a massive scale. In one place and one regime, we find all these dangers in their most lethal and aggressive forms, exactly the kind of aggressive threat the United Nations was born to confront.

Twelve years ago, Iraq invaded Kuwait without provocation. And the regime's forces were poised to continue their march to seize other countries and their resources. Had Saddam Hussein been appeased instead of stopped, he would have endangered the peace and stability of the world. Yet this aggression was stopped by the might of coalition forces and the will of the United Nations.

Iraq's Broken Promises

To suspend hostilities, to spare himself, Iraq's dictator accepted a series of commitments. The terms were clear to him and to all, and he agreed to prove he is complying with every one of those obligations. He has proven instead only his contempt for the United Nations and for all his pledges. By breaking every pledge, by his deceptions and by his cruelties, Saddam Hussein has made the case against himself.

In 1991, Security Council Resolution 688 demanded that the Iraqi regime cease at once the repression of its own people, including the systematic repression of minorities, which the council said threatened international peace and security in the region. This demand goes ignored.

Last year, the U.N. Commission on Human Rights found that Iraq continues to commit extremely grave violations of human rights and that the regime's repression is all-pervasive.

Tens of thousands of political opponents and ordinary citizens have been subjected to arbitrary arrest and imprisonment, summary execution and torture by beating and burning, electric shock, starvation, mutilation and rape.

Wives are tortured in front of their husbands; children in the presence of their parents; and all of these horrors

concealed from the world by the apparatus of a totalitarian state.

In 1991, the U.N. Security Council, through Resolutions 686 and 687, demanded that Iraq return all prisoners from Kuwait and other lands. Iraq's regime agreed. It broke this promise.

Last year, the secretary general's high-level coordinator for this issue reported that Kuwaiti, Saudi, Indian, Syrian, Lebanese, Iranian, Egyptian, Bahraini and Omani nationals remain unaccounted for; more than 600 people. One American pilot is among them.

In 1991, the U.N. Security Council, through Resolution 687, demanded that Iraq renounce all involvement with terrorism and permit no terrorist organizations to operate in Iraq.

Iraq's regime agreed. It broke this promise.

In violation of Security Council Resolution 1373, Iraq continues to shelter and support terrorist organizations that direct violence against Iran, Israel and Western governments. Iraqi dissidents abroad are targeted for murder.

In 1993, Iraq attempted to assassinate the emir of Kuwait and a former American president. Iraq's government openly praised the attacks of Sept. 11. And al Qaeda terrorists escaped from Afghanistan and are known to be in Iraq.

In 1991, the Iraqi regime agreed to destroy and stop developing all weapons of mass destruction and long-range missiles and to prove to the world it has done so by complying with rigorous inspections.

Iraq has broken every aspect of this fundamental pledge.

From 1991 to 1995, the Iraqi regime said it had no biological weapons. After a senior official in its weapons program defected and exposed this lie, the regime admitted to producing tens of thousands of liters of anthrax and other deadly biological agents for use with Scud warheads, aerial bombs and aircraft spray tanks.

U.N. inspectors believe Iraq has produced two to four times the amount of biological agents it declared and has failed to account for more than three metric tons of material that could be used to produce biological weapons. Right now, Iraq is expanding and improving facilities that were used for the production of biological weapons.

United Nations' inspections also revealed that Iraq likely maintains stockpiles of VX, mustard and other chemical agents, and that the regime is rebuilding and expanding facilities capable of producing chemical weapons.

And in 1995, after four years of deception, Iraq finally admitted it had a crash nuclear weapons program prior to the Gulf War.

We know now, were it not for that war, the regime in Iraq would likely have possessed a nuclear weapon no later than 1993.

Continued Offenses

Today, Iraq continues to withhold important information about its nuclear program, weapons design, procurement logs, experiment data, and accounting of nuclear materials and documentation of foreign assistance. Iraq employs capable nuclear scientists and technicians. It retains physical infrastructure needed to build a nuclear weapon.

Iraq has made several attempts to buy high-strength aluminum tubes used to enrich uranium for a nuclear weapon. Should Iraq acquire fissile material, it would be able to build a nuclear weapon within a year.

And Iraq's state-controlled media has reported numerous meetings between Saddam Hussein and his nuclear scientists, leaving little doubt about his continued appetite for these weapons.

Iraq also possesses a force of Scud-type missiles with ranges beyond the 150 kilometers permitted by the U.N. Work at testing and production facilities shows that Iraq is building more long-range missiles that can inflict mass death throughout the region.

In 1990, after Iraq's invasion of Kuwait, the world imposed economic sanctions on Iraq. Those sanctions were maintained after the war to compel the regime's compliance with Security Council Resolutions.

In time, Iraq was allowed to use oil revenues to buy food. Saddam Hussein has subverted this program, working around the sanctions to buy missile technology and military materials. He blames the suffering of Iraq's people on the United Nations, even as he uses his oil wealth to build lavish palaces

for himself and to buy arms for his country.

By refusing to comply with his own agreements, he bears full guilt for the hunger and misery of innocent Iraqi citizens. In 1991, Iraq promised U.N. inspectors immediate and unrestricted access to verify Iraq's commitment to rid itself of weapons of mass destruction and long-range missiles. Iraq broke this promise, spending seven years deceiving, evading and harassing U.N. inspectors before ceasing cooperation entirely.

Just months after the 1991 ceasefire, the Security Council twice renewed its demand that the Iraqi regime cooperate fully with inspectors, condemning Iraq's serious violations of its obligation.

The Security Council again renewed that demand in 1994, and twice more in 1996, deploring Iraq's clear violations of its obligation. The Security Council renewed its demand three more times in 1997, citing flagrant violations, and three more times in 1998, calling Iraq's behavior totally unacceptable. And in 1999, the demand was renewed yet again.

As we meet today, it's been almost four years since the last U.N. inspector set foot in Iraq — four years for the Iraqi regime to plan and to build and to test behind the cloak of secrecy. We know that Saddam Hussein pursued weapons of mass murder even when inspectors were in his country. Are we to assume that he stopped when they left?

A 'Gathering Danger'

The history, the logic and the facts lead to one conclusion: Saddam Hussein's regime is a grave and gathering danger.

To suggest otherwise is to hope against the evidence. To assume this regime's good faith is to bet the lives of millions and the peace of the world in a reckless gamble, and this is a risk we must not take.

Delegates to the General Assembly, we have been more than patient. We've tried sanctions. We've tried the carrot of oil for food and the stick of coalition military strikes. But Saddam Hussein has defied all these efforts and continues to develop weapons of mass destruction.

The first time we may be complete-

ly certain he has nuclear weapons is when, God forbid, he uses one. We owe it to all our citizens to do everything in our power to prevent that day from coming.

The conduct of the Iraqi regime is a threat to the authority of the United Nations and a threat to peace. Iraq has answered a decade of U.N. demands with a decade of defiance. All the world now faces a test, and the United Nations a difficult and defining moment.

Are Security Council resolutions to be honored and enforced, or cast aside without consequence?

Will the United Nations serve the purpose of its founding or will it be irrelevant?

The United States helped found the United Nations. We want the United Nations to be effective and respectful and successful. We want the resolutions of the world's most important multilateral body to be enforced. And right now those resolutions are being unilaterally subverted by the Iraqi regime.

Our partnership of nations can meet the test before us by making clear what we now expect of the Iraqi regime.

Iraq Must Take Steps

If the Iraqi regime wishes peace, it will immediately and unconditionally forswear, disclose, and remove or destroy all weapons of mass destruction, long-range missiles and all related material.

If the Iraqi regime wishes peace, it will immediately end all support for terrorism and act to suppress it — as all states are required to do by U.N. Security Council resolutions.

If the Iraqi regime wishes peace, it will cease persecution of its civilian population, including Shi'a, Sunnis, Kurds, Turkomans and others — again, as required by Security Council resolutions.

If the Iraqi regime wishes peace, it will release or account for all Gulf War personnel whose fate is still unknown. It will return the remains of any who are deceased, return stolen property, accept liability for losses resulting from the invasion of Kuwait and fully cooperate with international efforts to resolve these issues as required by Security Council resolutions.

If the Iraqi regime wishes peace, it will immediately end all illicit trade outside the oil-for-food program. It will accept U.N. administration of funds from that program to ensure that the money is used fairly and promptly for the benefit of the Iraqi people.

If all these steps are taken, it will signal a new openness and accountability in Iraq and it could open the prospect of the United Nations helping to build a government that represents all Iraqis, a government based on respect for human rights, economic liberty and internationally supervised elections.

The United States has no quarrel with the Iraqi people. They've suffered too long in silent captivity. Liberty for the Iraqi people is a great moral cause and a great strategic goal.

The people of Iraq deserve it. The security of all nations requires it. Free societies do not intimidate through cruelty and conquest. And open societies do not threaten the world with mass murder. The United States supports political and economic liberty in a unified Iraq.

We can harbor no illusions, and that's important today to remember. Saddam Hussein attacked Iran in 1980 and Kuwait in 1990. He's fired ballistic missiles at Iran and Saudi Arabia, Bahrain and Israel. His regime once ordered the killing of every person between the ages of 15 and 70 in certain Kurdish villages in northern Iraq. He has gassed many Iranians and 40 Iraqi villages.

United States' Involvement

My nation will work with the U.N. Security Council to meet our common challenge. If Iraq's regime defies us again, the world must move deliberately, decisively to hold Iraq to account. We will work with the U.N. Security Council for the necessary resolutions.

But the purposes of the United States should not be doubted. The Security Council resolutions will be enforced, the just demands of peace and security will be met or action will be unavoidable, and a regime that has lost its legitimacy will also lose its power.

Events can turn in one of two ways. If we fail to act in the face of danger, the people of Iraq will continue to live in brutal submission. The regime will have new power to bully and dominate and conquer its neighbors, condemning the Middle East to more years of bloodshed and fear. The regime will remain unstable — the region will remain unstable, with little hope of freedom and isolated from the progress of our times.

With every step the Iraqi regime takes toward gaining and deploying the most terrible weapons, our own options to confront that regime will narrow. And if an emboldened regime were to supply these weapons to terrorist allies, then the attacks of Sept. 11 would be a prelude to far greater horrors.

If we meet our responsibilities, if we overcome this danger, we can arrive at a very different future. The people of Iraq can shake off their captivity. They can one day join a democratic Afghanistan and a democratic Palestine, inspiring reforms throughout the Muslim world. These nations can show by their example that honest government and respect for women and the great Islamic tradition of learning can triumph in the Middle East and beyond. And we will show that the promise of the United Nations can be fulfilled in our time.

Neither of these outcomes is certain. Both have been set before us. We must choose between a world of fear and a world of progress. We cannot stand by and do nothing while dangers gather. We must stand up for our security and for the permanent rights and the hopes of mankind.

By heritage and by choice, the United States of America will make that stand. And, delegates to the United Nations, you have the power to make that stand, as well.

Thank you very much. ◆

Joint Resolution to Authorize Use of Military Force Against Iraq

The following is the text of the legislation (H J Res 114) authorizing President Bush to use military force in Iraq. After debate that stretched over three days, the House voted 296-133 to pass the joint resolution at 3:05 p.m. Oct. 10. The Senate, which had opened debate on its own version (S J Res 45) on Oct. 3, voted 77-23 to clear the House measure 10 hours later, at 1:17 a.m. Oct. 11.

JOINT RESOLUTION to authorize the use of United States Armed Forces against Iraq:

Whereas in 1990 in response to Iraq's war of aggression against and illegal occupation of Kuwait, the United States forged a coalition of nations to liberate Kuwait and its people in order to defend the national security of the United States and enforce United Nations Security Council resolutions relating to Iraq;

Whereas after the liberation of Kuwait in 1991, Iraq entered into a United Nations sponsored cease-fire agreement pursuant to which Iraq unequivocally agreed, among other things, to eliminate its nuclear, biological, and chemical weapons programs and the means to deliver and develop them, and to end its support for international terrorism;

Whereas the efforts of international weapons inspectors, United States intelligence agencies, and Iraqi defectors led to the discovery that Iraq had large stockpiles of chemical weapons and a large scale biological weapons program, and that Iraq had an advanced nuclear weapons development program that was much closer to producing a nuclear weapon than intelligence reporting had previously indicated;

Whereas Iraq, in direct and flagrant violation of the cease-fire, attempted to thwart the efforts of weapons inspectors to identify and destroy Iraq's weapons of mass destruction stockpiles and development capabilities, which finally resulted in the withdrawal of inspectors from Iraq on Oct. 31, 1998;

Whereas in PL 105-235 (Aug. 14, 1998), Congress concluded that Iraq's continuing weapons of mass destruction programs threatened vital United States interests and international peace and security, declared Iraq to be in "material and unacceptable breach of its international obligations" and urged the President "to take appropriate action, in accordance with the Constitution and relevant laws of the United States, to bring Iraq into compliance with its international obligations";

Whereas Iraq both poses a continuing threat to the national security of the United States and international peace and security in the Persian Gulf region and remains in material and unacceptable breach of its international obligations by, among other things, continuing to possess and develop a significant chemical and biological weapons capability, actively seeking a nuclear weapons capability, and supporting and harboring terrorist organizations;

Whereas Iraq persists in violating resolution of the United Nations Security Council by continuing to engage in brutal repression of its civilian population thereby threatening international peace and security in the region, by refusing to release, repatriate, or account for non-Iraqi citizens wrongfully detained by Iraq, including an American serviceman, and by failing to return property wrongfully seized by Iraq from Kuwait;

Whereas the current Iraqi regime has demonstrated its capability and willingness to use weapons of mass destruction against other nations and its own people;

Whereas the current Iraqi regime has demonstrated its continuing hostility toward, and willingness to attack, the United States, including by attempting in 1993 to assassinate former President Bush and by firing on many thousands of occasions on United States and Coalition Armed Forces engaged in enforcing the resolutions of the United Nations Security Council;

Whereas members of al Qaeda, an organization bearing responsibility for attacks on the United States, its citizens, and interests, including the attacks that occurred on Sept. 11, 2001, are known to be in Iraq;

Whereas Iraq continues to aid and harbor other international terrorist organizations, including organizations that threaten the lives and safety of United States citizens;

Whereas the attacks on the United States of Sept. 11, 2001, underscored the gravity of the threat posed by the acquisition of weapons of mass destruction by international terrorist organizations;

Whereas Iraq's demonstrated capability and willingness to use weapons of mass destruction, the risk that the current Iraqi regime will either employ those weapons to launch a surprise attack against the United States or its Armed Forces or provide them to international terrorists who would do so, and the extreme magnitude of harm that would result to the United States and its citizens from such an attack, combine to justify action by the United States to defend itself;

Whereas United Nations Security Council Resolution 678 (1990) authorizes the use of all necessary means to enforce United Nations Security Council Resolution 660 (1990) and subsequent relevant resolutions and to compel Iraq to cease certain activities that threaten international peace and security, including the development of weapons of mass destruction and refusal or obstruction of United Nations weapons inspections in violation of United Nations Security Council Resolution 687 (1991), repression of its civilian population in violation of United Nations Security Council Resolution 688 (1991), and threatening its neighbors or United Nations operations in Iraq in violation of United Nations Security Council Resolution 949 (1994);

Whereas in the Authorization for

Use of Military Force Against Iraq Resolution (PL 102-1), Congress has authorized the President "to use United States Armed Forces pursuant to United Nations Security Council Resolution 678 (1990) in order to achieve implementation of Security Council Resolution 660, 661, 662, 664, 665, 666, 667, 669, 670, 674, and 677";

Whereas in December 1991, Congress expressed its sense that it "supports the use of all necessary means to achieve the goals of United Nations Security Council Resolution 687 as being consistent with the Authorization of Use of Military Force Against Iraq Resolution (PL 102-1)," that Iraq's repression of its civilian population violates United Nations Security Council Resolution 688 and "constitutes a continuing threat to the peace, security, and stability of the Persian Gulf region," and that Congress, "supports the use of all necessary means to achieve the goals of United Nations Security Council Resolution 688";

Whereas the Iraq Liberation Act of 1998 (PL 105-338) expressed the sense of Congress that it should be the policy of the United States to support efforts to remove from power the current Iraqi regime and promote the emergence of a democratic government to replace that regime;

Whereas on Sept. 12, 2002, President Bush committed the United States to "work with the United Nations Security Council to meet our common challenge" posed by Iraq and to "work for the necessary resolutions," while also making clear that "the Security Council resolutions will be enforced, and the just demands of peace and security will be met, or action will be unavoidable";

Whereas the United States is determined to prosecute the war on terrorism and Iraq's ongoing support for international terrorist groups combined with its development of weapons of mass destruction in direct violation of its obligations under the 1991 cease-fire and other United Nations Security Council resolutions make clear that it is in the national security interests of the United States and in furtherance of the war on terrorism that all relevant United Nations Security Council resolutions be enforced, including through the use of force if necessary;

Whereas Congress has taken steps to pursue vigorously the war on terrorism through the provision of authorities and funding requested by the President to take the necessary actions against international terrorists and terrorist organizations, including those nations, organizations, or persons who planned, authorized, committed, or aided the terrorist attacks that occurred on Sept. 11, 2001, or harbored such persons or organizations;

Whereas the President and Congress are determined to continue to take all appropriate actions against international terrorists and terrorist organizations, including those nations, organizations, or persons who planned, authorized, committed, or aided the terrorist attacks that occurred on Sept. 11, 2001, or harbored such persons or organizations;

Whereas the President has authority under the Constitution to take action in order to deter and prevent acts of international terrorism against the United States, as Congress recognized in the joint resolution on Authorization for Use of Military Force (PL 107-40); and

Whereas it is in the national security interests of the United States to restore international peace and security to the Persian Gulf region:

Now, therefore, be it resolved by the Senate and House of Representatives of the United States of America in Congress assembled,

SECTION 1 — SHORT TITLE

This joint resolution may be cited as the "Authorization for Use of Military Force Against Iraq Resolution of 2002."

SECTION 2 — SUPPORT FOR UNITED STATES DIPLOMATIC EFFORTS

The Congress of the United States supports the efforts by the President to —

(1) strictly enforce through the United Nations Security Council all relevant Security Council resolutions regarding Iraq and encourages him in those efforts; and

(2) obtain prompt and decisive action by the Security Council to ensure that Iraq abandons its strategy of delay, evasion and noncompliance and promptly and strictly complies with all relevant Security Council resolutions regarding Iraq.

SECTION 3 — AUTHORIZATION FOR USE OF UNITED STATES ARMED FORCES

(a) Authorization — The President is authorized to use the Armed Forces of the United States as he determines to be necessary and appropriate in order to —

(1) defend the national security of the United States against the continuing threat posed by Iraq; and

(2) enforce all relevant United Nations Security Council resolutions regarding Iraq.

(b) Presidential determination — In connection with the exercise of the authority granted in subsection (a) to use force the President shall, prior to such exercise or as soon thereafter as may be feasible, but no later than 48 hours after exercising such authority, make available to the Speaker of the House of Representatives and the President pro tempore of the Senate his determination that —

(1) reliance by the United States on further diplomatic or other peaceful means alone either (A) will not adequately protect the national security of the United States against the continuing threat posed by Iraq or (B) is not likely to lead to enforcement of all relevant United Nations Security Council resolutions regarding Iraq; and

(2) acting pursuant to this joint resolution is consistent with the United States and other countries continuing to take the necessary actions against international terrorist and terrorist organizations, including those nations, organizations, or persons who planned, authorized, committed or aided the terrorist attacks that occurred on Sept. 11, 2001.

(c) War Powers Resolution Requirements —

(1) Specific statutory authorization —Consistent with section 8(a)(1) of the War Powers Resolution, the Congress declares that this section is intended to constitute specific statutory authorization within the meaning

of section 5(b) of the War Powers Resolution.

(2) Applicability of other requirements — Nothing in this joint resolution supersedes any requirement of the War Powers Resolution.

SECTION 4 — REPORTS TO CONGRESS

(a) Reports — The President shall, at least once every 60 days, submit to the Congress a report on matters relevant to this joint resolution, including actions taken pursuant to the exercise of authority granted in section 3 and the status of planning for efforts that are expected to be required after such actions are completed, including those actions described in section 7 of the Iraq Liberation Act of 1998 (PL 105-338).

(b) Single consolidated report — To the extent that the submission of any report described in subsection (a) coincides with the submission of any other report on matters relevant to this joint resolution otherwise required to be submitted to Congress pursuant to the reporting requirements of the War Powers Resolution (PL 93-148), all such reports may be submitted as a single consolidated report to the Congress.

(c) Rule of construction — To the extent that the information required by section 3 of the Authorization for Use of Military Force Against Iraq Resolution (PL 102-1) is included in the report required by this section, such report shall be considered as meeting the requirements of section 3 of such resolution. ◆

PUBLIC LAWS

Public Laws

Public laws 107-1 through 107-136, enacted in the second session of the 106th Congress, were published in the previous edition of the CQ Almanac. (2001 Almanac, p. E-5)

PL 107-137 (HR 400) Authorize the secretary of the Interior to establish the Ronald Reagan Boyhood Home National Historic Site. Introduced by HASTERT, R-Ill., on Feb. 6, 2001. House Resources reported Nov. 5 (H Rept 107-268). House passed, under suspension of the rules, Nov. 13. Senate passed Jan. 29, 2002. President signed Feb. 6, 2002.

PL 107-138 (HR 1913) Require the valuation of nontribal interest ownership of subsurface rights within the boundaries of the Acoma Indian Reservation. Introduced by SKEEN, R-N.M., on May 17, 2001. House Resources reported, amended, Nov. 13 (H Rept 107-285). House passed, under suspension of the rules, Nov. 27. Senate Indian Affairs discharged Jan. 28, 2002. Senate passed Jan. 28. President signed Feb. 6, 2002.

PL 107-139 (S 1762) Amend the Higher Education Act of 1965 to establish fixed interest rates for student and parent borrowers and extend current law with respect to special allowances for lenders. Introduced by JOHNSON, D-S.D., on Dec. 4, 2001. Senate Health, Education, Labor, and Pensions reported Dec. 12 (no written report). Senate passed Dec. 14. House passed Jan. 24, 2002. President signed Feb. 8, 2002.

PL 107-140 (S 1888) Amend Title 18 of the U.S. Code to correct a technical error in the codification of Title 36 of the U.S. Code. Introduced by STEVENS, R-Alaska, on Dec. 20, 2001. Senate passed Dec. 20. House passed, under suspension of the rules, Feb. 6, 2002. President signed Feb. 8, 2002.

PL 107-141 (HR 700) Reauthorize the Asian Elephant Conservation Act of 1997. Introduced by SAXTON, R-N.J., on Feb. 14, 2001. House Resources reported, amended, June 12 (H Rept 107-94). House passed, under suspension of the rules, June 12. Senate Environment and Public Works reported, amended, Dec. 7 (S Rept 107-113). Senate passed, with amendment, Dec. 18. House agreed to Senate amendment, under suspension of the rules, Jan. 23, 2002. President signed Feb. 12, 2002.

PL 107-142 (HR 1937) Authorize the secretary of the Interior to engage in certain feasibility studies of water resource projects in the state of Washington. Introduced by LARSEN, D-Wash., on May 22, 2001. House Resources reported, amended, July 24 (H Rept 107-155). House passed, under suspension of the rules, Sept. 10. Senate Indian Affairs discharged Jan. 28, 2002. Senate passed Jan. 28. President signed Feb. 12, 2002.

PL 107-143 (H J Res 82) Recognize the 91st birthday of Ronald Reagan. Introduced by COX, R-Calif., on Feb. 5, 2002. House passed, under suspension of the rules, Feb. 6. Senate passed Feb. 6. President signed Feb. 14, 2002.

PL 107-144 (S 737) Designate the facility of the U.S. Postal Service located at 811 South Main St., Yerington, Nev., as the "Joseph E. Dini, Jr. Post Office." Introduced by REID, D-Nev., on April 6, 2001. Senate Governmental Affairs reported Aug. 2 (no written report). Senate passed Aug. 3. House passed, under suspension of the rules, Feb. 5, 2002. President signed Feb. 14, 2002.

PL 107-145 (S 970) Designate the facility of the U.S. Postal Service located at 39 Tremont St., Paris Hill, Maine, as the Horatio King Post Office Building. Introduced by COLLINS, R-Maine, on May 25, 2001. Senate Governmental Affairs reported Aug. 2 (no written report). Senate passed Aug. 3. House passed, under suspension of the rules, Feb. 5, 2002. President signed Feb. 14, 2002.

PL 107-146 (S 1026) Designate the U.S. Post Office located at 60 Third Ave., Long Branch, N.J., as the "Pat King Post Office Building." Introduced by TORRICELLI, D-N.J., on June 13, 2001. Senate Governmental Affairs reported Aug. 2 (no written report). Senate passed Aug. 3. House Government Reform discharged Feb. 6, 2002. House passed Feb. 6. President signed Feb. 14, 2002.

PL 107-147 (HR 3090) Provide tax incentives for economic recovery. Introduced by THOMAS, R-Calif., on Oct. 11, 2001. House Ways and Means reported, amended, Oct. 17 (H Rept 107-251). House passed Oct. 24. Senate Finance reported, with amendments, Nov. 9 (no written report). Senate passed, with amendment, Feb. 14, 2002. House agreed to Senate amendment, with an amendment, March 7. Senate agreed to House amendment March 8. President signed March 9, 2002.

PL 107-148 (HR 2998) Authorize the establishment of Radio Free Afghanistan. Introduced by ROYCE, R-Calif., on Oct. 2, 2001. House International Relations reported, amended, Nov. 1 (no written report). House passed, under suspension of the rules, Nov. 7. Senate passed, with amendment, Feb. 7, 2002. House agreed to Senate amendment, under suspension of the rules, Feb. 12. President signed Mar. 11, 2002.

PL 107-149 (S 1206) Reauthorize the Appalachian Regional Development Act of 1965. Introduced by VOINOVICH, R-Ohio, on July 19, 2001. Senate Environment and Public Works reported, amended, Dec. 20 (S Rept 107-132). Senate passed, amended,

Feb. 8, 2002. House passed, under suspension of the rules, Feb. 26. President signed March 12, 2002.

PL 107-150 (HR 1892) Amend the Immigration and Nationality Act to provide for the acceptance of an affidavit of support from another eligible sponsor if the original sponsor has died and the attorney general has determined for humanitarian reasons that the original sponsor's classification petition should not be revoked. Introduced by CALVERT, R-Calif., on May 17, 2001. House Judiciary reported, amended, July 10 (H Rept 107-127). House passed, under suspension of the rules, July 23. Senate Judiciary reported, with amendment, Dec. 13 (no written report). Senate passed, with amendment, Dec. 20. House agreed to Senate amendment, under suspension of the rules, Feb. 26, 2002. President signed March 13, 2002.

PL 107-151 (HR 3699) Revise certain grants for continuum of care assistance for homeless individuals and families. Introduced by CRENSHAW, R-Fla., on Feb. 7, 2002. House passed, under suspension of the rules, Feb. 12. Senate Banking, Housing, and Urban Affairs discharged Feb. 25. Senate passed Feb. 25. President signed March 13, 2002.

PL 107-152 (S J Res 32) Congratulate the U.S. Military Academy at West Point on its bicentennial anniversary and commend its outstanding contributions to the nation. Introduced by REED, D-R.I., on Feb. 25, 2002. Senate passed Feb. 25. House passed, under suspension of the rules, March 6. President signed March 14, 2002.

PL 107-153 (S 1857) Encourage the negotiated settlement of tribal claims. Introduced by CAMPBELL, R-Colo, on Dec. 19, 2001. Senate Indian Affairs reported, amended, Feb. 13, 2002 (H Rept 107-138). Senate passed, amended, Feb. 26. House passed, under suspension of the rules, March 6. President signed March 19, 2002.

PL 107-154 (HR 3986) Extend the period of availability of unemployment assistance under the Robert T. Stafford Disaster Relief and Emergency Assistance Act in the case of victims of the terrorist attacks of Sept. 11, 2001. Introduced by QUINN, R-N.Y., on March 18, 2002. House passed, under suspension of the rules, March 19. Senate passed March 20. President signed March 25, 2002.

PL 107-155 (HR 2356) Amend the Federal Election Campaign Act of 1971 to provide bipartisan campaign reform. Introduced by SHAYS, R-Conn., on June 28, 2001. House Administration reported July 10 (H Rept 107-131, Part 1). House Energy and Commerce, Judiciary discharged July 10. House passed, amended, Feb. 14, 2002. Senate passed March 20. President signed March 27, 2002.

PL 107-156 (S 2019) Extend the authority of the Export-Import Bank until April 30, 2002. Introduced by SARBANES, D-Md., on March 14, 2002. Senate passed March 14. House passed, under suspension of the rules, March 19. President signed March 31, 2002.

PL 107-157 (HR 1499) Amend the District of Columbia College Access Act of 1999 to permit individuals who enroll in an institution of higher education more than three years after graduating from a secondary school and individuals who attend private historically black colleges and universities nationwide to participate in the tuition assistance programs under the act. Introduced by NORTON, D-D.C., on April 4, 2001. House passed, under suspension of the rules, July 30. Senate Governmental Affairs reported, with amendments, Nov. 29 (S Rept 107-101). Senate passed, with amendments, Dec.12. House agreed to Senate amendments, with an amendment pursuant to H Res 364, on March 12, 2002. Senate agreed to House amendment March 14. President signed April 4, 2002.

PL 107-158 (HR 2739) Amend Public Law 107-10 to require a U.S. plan to endorse and obtain observer status for Taiwan at the annual summit of the World Health Assembly in May 2002 in Geneva, Switzerland. Introduced by BROWN, D-Ohio, on Aug. 2, 2001. House passed, amended, under suspension of the rules, Dec. 19. Senate Foreign Relations reported March 19, 2002 (no written report). Senate passed March 19. President signed April 4, 2002.

PL 107-159 (HR 3985) Amend a 1955 act that authorizes the leasing of restricted Indian lands for public, religious, educational, recreational, residential, business and other purposes requiring the grant of long-term leases, to provide for binding arbitration clauses in leases and contracts related to reservation lands of the Gila River Indian Community. Introduced by HAYWORTH, R-Ariz., on March 18, 2002. House passed, under suspension of the rules, March 19. Senate passed March 21. President signed April 4, 2002.

PL 107-160 (HR 1432) Designate the facility of the U.S. Postal Service located at 3698 Inner Perimeter Rd. in Valdosta, Ga., as the "Major Lyn McIntosh Post Office Building." Introduced by BISHOP, D-Ga., on April 4, 2001. House passed, under suspension of the rules, Dec. 20. Senate passed March 22, 2002. President signed April 18, 2002.

PL 107-161 (HR 1748) Designate the facility of the U.S. Postal Service located at 805 Glen Burnie Rd. in Richmond, Va., as the "Tom Bliley Post Office Building." Introduced by CANTOR, R-Va., on May 8, 2001. House passed, under suspension of the rules, Feb. 12, 2002. Senate Governmental Affairs reported March 21 (no written report). Senate passed March 22. President signed April 18, 2002.

PL 107-162 (HR 1749) Designate the facility of the U.S. Postal Service located at 685 Turnberry Rd. in Newport News, Va., as the "Herbert H. Bateman Post Office Building." Introduced by DAVIS, R-Va., on May 8,

2001. House passed, under suspension of the rules, Oct. 9. Senate Governmental Affairs reported March 21, 2002 (no written report). Senate passed March 22. President signed April 18, 2002.

PL 107-163 (HR 2577) Designate the facility of the U.S. Postal Service located at 310 South State St. in St. Ignace, Mich., as the "Bob Davis Post Office Building." Introduced by STUPAK, D-Mich., on July 19, 2001. House passed, under suspension of the rules, Feb. 12, 2002. Senate Governmental Affairs reported March 21 (no written report). Senate passed March 22. President signed April 18, 2002.

PL 107-164 (HR 2876) Designate the facility of the U.S. Postal Service located in Harlem, Mont., as the "Francis Bardanouve United States Post Office Building." Introduced by REHBERG, R-Mont., on Sept. 10, 2001. House passed, under suspension of the rules, Oct. 16. Senate Governmental Affairs reported March 21, 2002 (no written report). Senate passed March 22. President signed April 18, 2002.

PL 107-165 (HR 2910) Designate the facility of the U.S. Postal Service located at 3131 South Crater Rd. in Petersburg, Va., as the "Norman Sisisky Post Office Building." Introduced by FORBES, R-Va., on Sept. 20, 2001. House passed, under suspension of the rules, Oct. 30. Senate Governmental Affairs reported March 21, 2002 (no written report). Senate passed March 22. President signed April 18, 2002.

PL 107-166 (HR 3072) Designate the facility of the U.S. Postal Service located at 125 Main St. in Forest City, N.C., as the "Vernon Tarlton Post Office Building." Introduced by TAYLOR, R-N.C., on Oct. 9, 2001. House passed, under suspension of the rules, Dec. 18. Senate Governmental Affairs reported March 21, 2002 (no written report). Senate passed March 22. President signed April 18, 2002.

PL 107-167 (HR 3379) Designate the facility of the U.S. Postal Service located at 375 Carlls Path in Deer Park, N.Y., as the "Raymond M. Downey Post Office Building." Introduced by ISRAEL, D-N.Y., on Nov. 29, 2001. House passed, under suspension of the rules, Dec. 18. Senate Governmental Affairs reported March 21, 2002 (no written report). Senate passed March 22. President signed April 18, 2002.

PL 107-168 (S 2248) Extend the authority of the Export-Import Bank until May 31, 2002. Introduced by SARBANES, D-Md., on April 24, 2002. Senate passed April 24. House passed, under suspension of the rules, April 30. President signed May 1, 2002.

PL 107-169 (HR 861) Make technical amendments to section 10 of Title 9, U.S. Code. Introduced by GEKAS, R-Pa., on March 6, 2001. House Judiciary reported March 12 (H Rept 107-16). House passed, under suspension of the rules, March 14. Senate Judi-

ciary reported Dec. 13 (no written report). Senate passed April 18, 2002. President signed May 7, 2002.

PL 107-170 (HR 4167) Extend for eight additional months the period for which Chapter 12 of Title 11, U.S. Code is re-enacted. Introduced by SENSENBRENNER, R-Wis., on April 11, 2002. House passed, under suspension of the rules, April 16, 2002. Senate passed April 23. President signed May 7, 2002.

PL 107-171 (HR 2646) Provide for the continuation of agricultural programs through fiscal 2007. Introduced by COMBEST, R-Texas, on July 26, 2001. House Agriculture reported, amended Aug. 2 (H Rept 107-191, Part 1). House Agriculture filed supplemental report Aug. 31 (Part 2). House International Relations reported, amended, Sept. 10 (Part 3). House passed, amended, Oct. 5. Senate passed, with amendment, Feb. 13, 2002. Conference report filed in the House May 1 (H Rept 107-424). House agreed to conference report May 2. Senate agreed to conference report May 8. President signed May 13, 2002.

PL 107-172 (S 1094) Amend the Public Health Service Act to provide for research, information and education with respect to blood cancer. Introduced by HUTCHISON, R-Texas, on June 22, 2001. Senate Health, Education, Labor and Pensions reported, amended, Nov. 8 (no written report). Senate passed, amended, Nov. 16. House passed, under suspension of the rules, April 30, 2002. President signed May 14, 2002.

PL 107-173 (HR 3525) Enhance the border security of the United States. Introduced by SENSENBRENNER, R-Wis., on Dec. 19, 2001. House passed, amended, under suspension of the rules, Dec. 19. Senate Judiciary discharged. Senate passed, with amendments, April 18, 2002. House agreed to Senate amendments, under suspension of the rules, May 8. President signed May 14, 2002.

PL 107-174 (HR 169) Require that federal agencies be accountable for violations of anti-discrimination and whistleblower protection laws. Introduced by SENSENBRENNER, R-Wis., on Jan. 3, 2001. House Judiciary reported, amended, June 14 (H Rept 107-101, Part 1). House passed, amended, under suspension of the rules, Oct. 2. Senate Governmental Affairs reported, with amendments, April 15, 2002 (S Rept 107-143). Senate passed, amended, April 23. House agreed to Senate amendments, under suspension of the rules, April 30. President signed May 15, 2002.

PL 107-175 (HR 495) Designate the federal building located in Charlotte Amalie, St. Thomas, U.S. Virgin Is., as the "Ron de Lugo Federal Building." Introduced by CHRISTENSEN, D-Virgin Is., on Feb. 7, 2001. House Transportation and Infrastructure reported May 21

(H Rept 107-71). House passed, under suspension of the rules, May 21. Senate Environment and Public Works reported April 25, 2002 (no written report). Senate passed April 30. President signed May 17, 2002.

PL 107-176 (HR 819) Designate the federal building located at 143 West Liberty St., in Medina, Ohio, as the "Donald J. Pease Federal Building." Introduced by BROWN, D-Ohio, on March 1, 2001. House Transportation and Infrastructure reported May 23 (H Rept 107-75). House passed, under suspension of the rules, June 20. Senate Environment and Public Works reported April 25, 2002 (no written report). Senate passed April 30. President signed May 17, 2002.

PL 107-177 (HR 3093) Designate the federal building and U.S. courthouse located at 501 Bell St. in Alton, Ill., as the "William L. Beatty Federal Building and United States Courthouse." Introduced by COSTELLO, D-Ill., on Oct. 11, 2001. House Transportation and Infrastructure Committee discharged. House passed Nov. 16. Senate Environment and Public Works reported April 25, 2002 (no written report). Senate passed April 30. President signed May 17, 2002.

PL 107-178 (HR 3282) Designate the federal building and U.S. courthouse located at 400 North Main St. in Butte, Mont., as the "Mike Mansfield Federal Building and United States Courthouse." Introduced by REHBERG, R-Mont., on Nov. 13, 2001. House passed, under suspension of the rules, Dec. 11. Senate Environment and Public Works reported April 25, 2002 (no written report). Senate passed April 30. President signed May 17, 2002.

PL 107-179 (HR 2048) Require a report on the operations of the State Justice Institute. Introduced by COBLE, R-N.C., on June 5, 2001. House Judiciary reported Aug. 2 (H Rept 107-189). House passed, under suspension of the rules, Sept. 5, 2001. Senate Judiciary reported Dec. 13 (no written report). Senate passed May 7, 2002. President signed May 20, 2002.

PL 107-180 (HR 2305) Require certain federal officials with responsibility for the administration of the criminal justice system of the District of Columbia to serve on and participate in the activities of the District of Columbia Criminal Justice Coordinating Council. Introduced by MORELLA, R-Md., on June 25, 2001. House passed, amended, under suspension of the rules, Dec. 4. Senate Governmental Affairs reported April 29, 2002 (S Rept 107-145). Senate passed May 7. President signed May 20, 2002.

PL 107-181 (HR 4156) Amend the Internal Revenue Code of 1986 to clarify that the parsonage allowance exclusion is limited to the fair rental value of the property. Introduced by RAMSTAD, R-Minn., on April 10, 2002. House passed, amended, under suspension of the rules, April 16. Senate Finance discharged. Senate passed May 2. President signed May 20, 2002.

PL 107-182 (S 378) Redesignate the federal building located at 3348 South Kedzie Ave., in Chicago, Ill., as the "Paul Simon Chicago Job Corps Center." Introduced by DURBIN, D-Ill., on Feb. 15, 2001. Senate Environment and Public Works reported May 23 (no written report). Senate passed May 24. House Transportation and Infrastructure reported May 7, 2002 (H Rept 107-438). House passed, under suspension of the rules, May 7. President signed May 21, 2002.

PL 107-183 (HR 4592) Name the chapel located in the national cemetery in Los Angeles, Calif., as the "Bob Hope Veterans Chapel." Introduced by COX, R-Calif., on April 25, 2002. House passed, under suspension of the rules, May 21. Senate passed May 22. President signed May 29, 2002.

PL 107-184 (HR 4608) Name the Department of Veterans' Affairs medical center in Wichita, Kan., as the "Robert J. Dole Department of Veterans Affairs Medical and Regional Office Center." Introduced by MORAN, R-Kan., on April 25, 2002. House Veterans Affairs reported, amended, May 16 (H Rept 107-474). House passed, amended, under suspension of the rules, May 20. Senate passed May 22. President signed May 29, 2002.

PL 107-185 (HR 1840) Extend eligibility for refugee status of unmarried sons and daughters of certain Vietnamese refugees. Introduced by DAVIS, R-Va., on May 15, 2001. House Judiciary reported, amended, Oct. 29 (H Rept 107-254). House passed, amended, under suspension of the rules, Oct. 30. Senate Judiciary reported Dec. 13 (no written report). Senate passed May 10, 2002. President signed May 30, 2002.

PL 107-186 (HR 4782) Extend the authority of the Export-Import Bank until June 14, 2002. Introduced by OXLEY, R-Ohio, on May 21, 2002. House passed, under suspension of the rules, May 21. Senate passed May 22. President signed May 30, 2002.

PL 107-187 (HR 3167) Endorse the vision of further enlargement of the NATO Alliance articulated by President George W. Bush on June 15, 2001, and by former President Bill Clinton on Oct. 22, 1996. Introduced by BEREUTER, R-Neb., on Oct. 24, 2001. House International Relations reported, amended, Nov. 5 (H Rept 107-266). House passed, amended, Nov. 7. Senate Foreign Relations reported Dec. 12 (no written report). Senate passed May 17, 2002. President signed June 10, 2002.

PL 107-188 (HR 3448) Improve the ability of the United States to prevent, prepare for, and respond to bioterrorism and other public health emergencies. Introduced by TAUZIN, R-La., on Dec. 11, 2001. House passed, under suspension of the rules, Dec. 12. Senate passed, with amendment, Dec. 20. Conference report filed in the House on May 21, 2002 (H Rept 107-481). House agreed to conference report May 22. Senate agreed to conference report May 23. President signed June 12, 2002.

PL 107-189 (S 1372) Reauthorize the Export-Import Bank of the United States. Introduced by SARBANES, D-Md., Aug. 3, 2001. Senate Banking, Housing, and Urban Affairs reported Aug. 3 (S Rept 107-52). Senate passed, amended, March 14, 2002. House passed, with amendment, May 1. Conference report filed in the House on May 24 (H Rept 107-487). House agreed to conference report June 5. Senate agreed to conference report June 6. President signed June 14, 2002.

PL 107-190 (HR 1366) Designate the U.S. Post Office building located at 3101 West Sunflower Ave. in Santa Ana, Calif., as the "Hector G. Godinez Post Office Building." Introduced by SANCHEZ, D-Calif., on April 3, 2001. House Government Reform discharged. House passed April 10, 2002. Senate Governmental Affairs reported May 23 (no written report). Senate passed June 3. President signed June 18, 2002.

PL 107-191 (HR 1374) Designate the facility of the U.S. Postal Service located at 600 Calumet St. in Lake Linden, Mich., as the "Philip E. Ruppe Post Office Building." Introduced by STUPAK, D-Mich., on April 3, 2001. House passed, under suspension of the rules, April 16, 2002. Senate Governmental Affairs reported May 23 (no written report). Senate passed June 3. President signed June 18, 2002.

PL 107-192 (HR 3789) Designate the facility of the U.S. Postal Service located at 2829 Commercial Way in Rock Springs, Wyo., as the "Teno Roncalio Post Office Building." Introduced by CUBIN, R-Wyo., on Feb. 26, 2002. House passed, under suspension of the rules, March 5. Senate Governmental Affairs reported May 23 (no written report). Senate passed June 3. President signed June 18, 2002.

PL 107-193 (HR 3960) Designate the facility of the U.S. Postal Service located at 3719 Highway 4 in Jay, Fla., as the "Joseph W. Westmoreland Post Office Building." Introduced by MILLER, R-Fla., on March 13, 2002. House passed, under suspension of the rules, April 16. Senate Governmental Affairs reported May 23 (no written report). Senate passed June 3. President signed June 18, 2002.

PL 107-194 (HR 4486) Designate the facility of the U.S. Postal Service located at 1590 East Joyce Blvd. in Fayetteville, Ark., as the "Clarence B. Craft Post Office Building." Introduced by BOOZMAN, R-Ark., on April 18, 2002. House passed, under suspension of the rules, May 7. Senate Governmental Affairs reported May 23 (no written report). Senate passed June 3. President signed June 18, 2002.

PL 107-195 (HR 4560) Eliminate the deadlines for spectrum auctions of spectrum previously allocated to television broadcasting. Introduced by TAUZIN, R-La., on April 24, 2002. House Energy and Commerce reported May 7 (H Rept 107-443). House passed, amended, under suspension of the rules, May 7. Sen-

ate passed, with amendment, June 18. House agreed to Senate amendment June 18. President signed June 19, 2002.

PL 107-196 (S 2431) Amend the Omnibus Crime Control and Safe Streets Act of 1968 to ensure that chaplains killed in the line of duty receive public safety officer death benefits. Introduced by LEAHY, D-Vt., on May 1, 2002. Senate Judiciary reported, amended, May 2 (no written report). Senate passed, amended, May 7. House passed June 11. President signed June 24, 2002.

PL 107-197 (HR 3275) Implement the International Convention for the Suppression of Terrorist Bombings to strengthen criminal laws relating to attacks on places of public use, and implement the International Convention of the Suppression of the Financing of Terrorism to combat terrorism and defend the nation against terrorist acts. Introduced by SMITH, R-Texas, on Nov. 9, 2001. House Judiciary reported, amended, Nov. 29 (H Rept 107-307). House passed, amended, under suspension of the rules, Dec. 19. Senate Judiciary discharged. Senate passed, with amendment, June 14, 2002. House agreed to Senate amendment June 18. President signed June 25, 2002.

PL 107-198 (HR 327) Amend Chapter 35 of Title 44, U.S. Code, for the purpose of facilitating compliance by small businesses with certain federal paperwork requirements, and establish a task force to examine information collection and dissemination. Introduced by BURTON, R-Ind., on Jan. 31, 2001. House passed, amended, March 15. Senate Governmental Affairs discharged. Senate passed, with amendments, May 22, 2002. House agreed to Senate amendments June 18. President signed June 28, 2002.

PL 107-199 (S 2578) Amend Title 31 of the U.S. Code to increase the public debt limit. Introduced by DASCHLE, D-S.D., on June 4, 2002. Senate passed June 11. House passed June 27. President signed June 28, 2002.

PL 107-200 (H J Res 87) Approve the site at Yucca Mountain, Nev., for the development of a repository for the disposal of high-level radioactive waste and spent nuclear fuel, pursuant to the Nuclear Waste Policy Act of 1982. Introduced by BARTON, R-Texas, on April 11, 2002. House Energy and Commerce reported May 1 (H Rept 107-425). House passed May 8. Senate passed July 9. President signed July 23, 2002.

PL 107-201 (S 2594) Authorize the secretary of the Treasury to purchase silver on the open market to mint coins when the silver stockpile is depleted. Introduced by REID, D-Nev., on June 6, 2002. Senate Banking, Housing and Urban Affairs discharged June 21. Senate passed June 21. House Financial Services discharged June 28. House passed June 28. President signed July 23, 2002.

PL 107-202 (HR 2362) Establish the Benjamin Franklin

Tercentenary Commission. Introduced by BORSKI, D-Pa., on June 28, 2001. House passed, amended, under suspension of the rules, Oct. 30. Senate passed July 9, 2002. President signed July 24, 2002.

PL 107-203 (HR 3971) Provide for an independent investigation of Forest Service firefighter deaths caused by wildfire entrapment or burnover. Introduced by HASTINGS, R-Wash., on March 14, 2002. House passed, under suspension of the rules, June 24. Senate passed July 10. President signed July 24, 2002.

PL 107-204 (HR 3763) Protect investors by improving the accuracy and reliability of corporate disclosures made pursuant to the securities laws. Introduced by OXLEY, R-Ohio, on Feb. 14, 2002. House Financial Services reported, amended, April 22 (H Rept 107-414). House passed, amended, April 24. Senate Banking, Housing and Urban Affairs discharged July 15. Senate passed, with amendment, July 15. Conference report filed in the House on July 24 (H Rept 107-610). House agreed to conference report July 25. Senate agreed to conference report July 25. President signed July 30, 2002.

PL 107-205 (HR 3487) Amend the Public Health Service Act with respect to health professions programs in the field of nursing. Introduced by BILIRAKIS, R-Fla., on Dec. 13, 2001. House passed, under suspension of the rules, Dec. 20. Senate passed, with amendment, July 22, 2002. House agreed to Senate amendment, under suspension of the rules, July 22. President signed Aug. 1, 2002.

PL 107-206 (HR 4775) Make supplemental appropriations for the fiscal year ending Sept. 30, 2002. Introduced by YOUNG, R-Fla., on May 20, 2002. House Appropriations reported May 20 (H Rept 107-480). House passed, amended, May 24. Senate passed, with amendment, June 7. Conference report filed in the House on July 19 (H Rept 107-593). House agreed to conference report July 23. Senate agreed to conference report July 24. President signed Aug. 2, 2002.

PL 107-207 (HR 2175) Protect infants who are born alive. Introduced by CHABOT, R-Ohio, on June 14, 2001. House Judiciary reported Aug. 2 (H Rept 107-186). House passed, under suspension of the rules, March 12, 2002. Senate passed July 18. President signed Aug. 5, 2002.

PL 107-208 (HR 1209) Amend the Immigration and Nationality Act to determine whether an alien is a child, for purposes of classification as an immediate relative, based on the age of the alien on the date the classification petition with respect to the alien is filed. Introduced by GEKAS, R-Pa., on March 26, 2001. House Judiciary reported April 20 (H Rept 107-45). House passed, amended, under suspension of the rules, June 6. Senate Judiciary reported, with amendment, May 16, 2002 (no written report). Senate passed, with amendment, June 13. House agreed to Senate amendment, un-

der suspension of the rules, July 22. President signed Aug. 6, 2002.

PL 107-209 (S J Res 13) Confer honorary U.S. citizenship on Paul Yves Roch Gilbert du Motier, also known as the Marquis de Lafayette. Introduced by WARNER, R-Va., on April 24, 2001. Senate Judiciary reported Dec. 13 (no written report). Senate passed Dec. 18. House Judiciary reported, with amendments, July 19, 2002 (H Rept 107-595). House passed, with amendments, under suspension of the rules, July 22. Senate agreed to House amendments July 24. President signed Aug. 6, 2002.

PL 107-210 (HR 3009) Extend the Andean Trade Preference Act, grant the president trade promotion authority and expand the Trade Adjustment Assistance program. Introduced by CRANE, R-Ill., on Oct. 3, 2001. House Ways and Means reported, amended, Nov. 14 (H Rept 107-290). House passed, amended, Nov. 16. Senate Finance reported, with amendment, Dec. 14 (S Rept 107-126). Senate passed, with amendment, May 23, 2002. House agreed to Senate amendment with amendment pursuant to H Res 450 on June 26. Conference report filed in the House on July 26 (H Rept 107-624). House agreed to conference report July 27. Senate agreed to conference report Aug. 1. President signed Aug. 6, 2002.

PL 107-211 (HR 223) Amend the Clear Creek County, Colo., Public Lands Transfer Act of 1993 to provide additional time for Clear Creek County to dispose of certain lands transferred to the county under the act. Introduced by UDALL, D-Colo., on Jan. 3, 2001. House passed, under suspension of the rules, March 13. Senate Energy and Natural Resources reported June 28, 2002 (S Rept 107-198). Senate passed Aug. 1. President signed Aug. 21, 2002.

PL 107-212 (HR 309) Allow Guam to tax earnings of foreign investors at the same rates as those applied by the 50 states under U.S. tax treaties with foreign nations. Introduced by UNDERWOOD, D-Guam, on Jan. 30, 2001. House Resources reported April 24 (H Rept 107-48). House passed, under suspension of the rules, May 1. Senate Energy and Natural Resources reported June 24, 2002 (S Rept 107-173). Senate passed Aug. 1. President signed Aug. 21, 2002.

PL 107-213 (HR 601) To redesignate certain lands within the Craters of the Moon National Monument in Idaho pursuant to Presidential Proclamation 7373 of Nov. 9, 2000. Introduced by SIMPSON, R-Idaho, on Feb. 13, 2001. House Resources reported, amended, April 3 (H Rept 107-34). House passed, amended, under suspension of the rules, May 1. Senate Energy and Natural Resources reported June 26, 2002 (S Rept 107-181). Senate passed Aug. 1. President signed Aug. 21, 2002.

PL 107-214 (HR 1384) Designate the route in Arizona and New Mexico on which the Navajo and Mescalero Indian tribes were forced to walk in 1863 and 1864 for possible inclusion in the national trail system. Intro-

duced by UDALL, D- N.M., on April 3, 2001. House Resources reported, amended, Sept. 28 (H Rept 107-222). House passed, amended, under suspension of the rules, Oct. 2. Senate Energy and Natural Resources reported June 27, 2002 (S Rept 107-184). Senate passed Aug. 1. President signed Aug. 21, 2002.

PL 107-215 (HR 1456) Expand the boundary of the Booker T. Washington National Monument. Introduced by GOODE, R-Va., on April 4, 2001. House Resources reported Sept. 28 (H Rept 107-223). House passed, under suspension of the rules, Oct. 2. Senate Energy and Natural Resources reported June 28, 2002 (S Rept 107-199). Senate passed Aug. 1. President signed Aug. 21, 2002.

PL 107-216 (HR 1576) Designate certain lands in the Arapaho and Roosevelt National Forests in Colorado as the James Peak Wilderness and Protection Area. Introduced by UDALL, D-Colo., on April 24, 2001. House Resources reported, amended, Dec. 5 (H Rept 107-316). House passed, amended, under suspension of the rules, Dec. 11. Senate Energy and Resources reported June 28, 2002 (S Rept 107-200). Senate passed Aug. 1. President signed Aug. 21, 2002.

PL 107-217 (HR 2068) Revise, codify and enact without substantive change certain general and permanent laws related to public buildings, property and works, as Title 40, U.S. Code, "Public Buildings, Property, and Works." Introduced by SENSENBRENNER, R-Wis., on June 6, 2001. House Judiciary reported, amended, May 20, 2002 (H Rept 107-479). House passed, under suspension of the rules, June 11. Senate Judiciary reported June 21 (no written report). Senate passed Aug. 1. President signed Aug. 21, 2002.

PL 107-218 (HR 2234) Revise the boundary of the Tumacacori National Historical Park in Arizona. Introduced by PASTOR, D-Ariz., on June 19, 2001. House Resources reported, amended, Dec. 6 (H Rept 107-327). House passed, under suspension of the rules, Jan. 23, 2002. Senate Energy and Natural Resources reported June 27 (S Rept 107-185). Senate passed Aug. 1. President signed Aug. 21, 2002.

PL 107-219 (HR 2440) Rename Wolf Trap Farm Park as "Wolf Trap National Park for the Performing Arts." Introduced by DAVIS, R-Va., on July 10, 2001. House Resources reported, amended, Dec. 11 (H Rept 107-330). House passed, under suspension of the rules, Dec. 11. Senate Energy and Natural Resources reported June 26, 2002 (S Rept 107-182). Senate passed Aug. 1. President signed Aug. 21, 2002.

PL 107-220 (HR 2441) Amend the Public Health Service Act to redesignate a facility as the National Hansen's Disease Programs Center. Introduced by BAKER, R-La., on July 10, 2001. House Energy and Commerce reported July 30 (H Rept 107-174). House passed, under suspension of the rules, Dec. 4. Senate Health, Education, La-

bor and Pensions discharged Aug. 1, 2002. Senate passed Aug. 1. President signed Aug. 21, 2002.

PL 107-221 (HR 2643) Authorize the acquisition of additional lands for inclusion in the Fort Clatsop National Memorial in Oregon. Introduced by WU, D-Ore., on July 25, 2001. House Resources reported, amended, May 14, 2002 (H Rept 107-456). House passed, under suspension of the rules, July 8. Senate passed Aug. 1. President signed Aug. 21, 2002.

PL 107-222 (HR 3343) Amend Title X of the Energy Policy Act of 1992. Introduced by SHIMKUS, R-Ill., on Nov. 19, 2001. House Energy and Commerce reported, amended, Dec. 18 (H Rept 107-341). House passed, amended, under suspension of the rules, Dec. 18. Senate passed Aug. 1, 2002. President signed Aug. 21, 2002.

PL 107-223 (HR 3380) Authorize the secretary of the Interior to issue right-of-way permits for natural gas pipelines within the boundary of Great Smoky Mountains National Park. Introduced by JENKINS, R-Tenn., on Nov. 29, 2001. House Resources reported June 5, 2002 (H Rept 107-491). House passed, under suspension of the rules, July 8. Senate passed Aug. 1. President signed Aug. 21, 2002.

PL 107-224 (HR 5012) Amend the John F. Kennedy Center Act to authorize the secretary of Transportation to carry out a project for construction of a plaza adjacent to the John F. Kennedy Center for the Performing Arts. Introduced by YOUNG, R-Alaska, on June 25, 2002. House Transportation and Infrastructure reported July 26 (H Rept 107-622). House passed, under suspension of the rules, Sept. 4. Senate passed Sept. 5. President signed Sept. 18, 2002.

PL 107-225 (HR 3287) Redesignate the facility of the U.S. Postal Service located at 900 Brentwood Road, NE, in Washington, D.C., as the "Joseph Curseen, Jr. and Thomas Morris, Jr. Processing and Distribution Center." Introduced by WYNN, D-Md., on Nov. 13, 2001. House passed, under suspension of the rules, Sept. 4, 2002. Senate passed Sept. 5. President signed Sept. 24, 2002.

PL 107-226 (HR 3917) Authorize a national memorial to commemorate the passengers and crew of Flight 93 who gave their lives Sept. 11, 2001, thereby thwarting a planned attack on the nation's capital. Introduced by MURTHA, D-Pa., on March 7, 2002. House Resources reported, amended, July 22 (H Rept 107-597). House passed, amended, under suspension of the rules, July 22. Senate Energy and Natural Resources discharged Sept. 10. Senate passed Sept. 10. President signed Sept. 24, 2002.

PL 107-227 (HR 5207) Designate the facility of the U.S. Postal Service located at 6101 West Old Shakopee Road in Bloomington, Minn., as the "Thomas E. Burnett, Jr. Post Office Building." Introduced by RAM-

STAD, R-Minn., on July 24, 2002. House passed, under suspension of the rules, Sept. 4. Senate passed Sept. 5. President signed Sept. 24, 2002.

PL 107-228 (HR 1646) Authorize appropriations for the Department of State for fiscal years 2002 and 2003. Introduced by HYDE, R-Ill., on April 27, 2001. House International Relations reported amended May 4 (H Rept 107-57). House passed, amended, May 16. Senate Foreign Relations discharged May 1, 2002. Senate passed, with amendment, May 1. Conference report filed in the House on Sept. 23 (H Rept 107-671). House agreed to conference report Sept. 25. Senate agreed to conference report Sept. 26. President signed Sept. 30, 2002.

PL 107-229 (H J Res 111) Make continuing appropriations for fiscal 2003. Introduced by YOUNG, R-Fla., on Sept. 25, 2002. House passed Sept. 26. Senate passed Sept. 26. President signed Sept. 30, 2002.

PL 107-230 (HR 3880) Provide a temporary waiver from certain transportation conformity requirements and metropolitan transportation planning requirements under the Clean Air Act and other laws for certain areas in New York where the planning offices and resources have been destroyed by acts of terrorism. Introduced by FOSSELLA, R-N.Y., on March 6, 2002. House Energy and Commerce reported, amended, Sept. 9 (H Rept 107-649, Part 1). House Transportation and Infrastructure discharged Sept. 9. House passed, amended, under suspension of the rules, Sept. 10. Senate passed Sept. 12. President signed Oct. 1, 2002.

PL 107-231 (HR 4687) Provide for the establishment of investigative teams to assess building performance and emergency response and evacuation procedures in the wake of any building failure that has resulted in substantial loss of life or that posed significant potential of substantial loss of life. Introduced by BOEHLERT, R-N.Y., on May 9, 2002. House Science reported, amended, June 25 (H Rept 107-530). House passed, amended, July 12. Senate passed, with amendment, Sept. 9. House agreed to Senate amendment, under suspension of the rules, Sept. 17. President signed Oct. 1, 2002.

PL 107-232 (HR 5157) Amend Section 5307 of Title 49, U.S. Code, to allow transit systems in urbanized areas that exceeded 200,000 in population for the first time in the 2000 census to retain flexibility in using federal transit formula grants in fiscal 2003. Introduced by YOUNG, R-Alaska, on July 18, 2002. House Transportation and Infrastructure reported Sept. 5 (H Rept 107-644). House passed, under suspension of the rules, Sept. 9. Senate passed Sept. 13. President signed Oct. 1, 2002.

PL 107-233 (S 2810) Amend the Communications Satellite Act of 1962 to extend the deadline for the INTELSAT initial public offering. Introduced by HOLLINGS, D-S.C., on July 26, 2002. Senate passed July 26. House passed, under suspension of the rules, Sept. 10. President signed Oct. 1, 2002.

PL 107-234 (HR 4558) Extend the Irish Peace Process Cultural and Training Program. Introduced by WALSH, R-N.Y., on April 23, 2002. House Judiciary reported July 22 (H Rept 107-596, Part 1). House International Relations discharged July 22. House passed, under suspension of the rules, July 22. Senate Foreign Relations reported Aug. 1 (no written report). Senate passed Sept. 18. President signed Oct. 4, 2002.

PL 107-235 (H J Res 112) Make further continuing appropriations for fiscal 2003. Introduced by YOUNG, R-Fla., on Oct. 1, 2002. House passed Oct. 3. Senate passed Oct. 3. President signed Oct. 4, 2002.

PL 107-236 (HR 640) Adjust the boundaries of Santa Monica Mountains National Recreation Area. Introduced by GALLEGLY, R-Calif., on Feb. 14, 2001. House Resources reported, amended, June 6 (H Rept 107-90). House passed, amended, under suspension of the rules, June 6. Senate Energy and Natural Resources reported, with amendment, July 3, 2002 (S Rept 107-204). Senate passed, with amendment, Aug. 1. House agreed to Senate amendment, under suspension of the rules Sept. 24. President signed Oct. 9, 2002.

PL 107-237 (S 238) Authorize the secretary of the Interior to conduct feasibility studies on water optimization in the Burnt River basin, Malheur River basin, Owyhee River basin and Powder River basin in Oregon. Introduced by WYDEN, D-Ore., on Feb. 1, 2001. Senate Energy and Natural Resources reported June 5 (S Rept 107-22). Senate passed Aug. 3. House Resources reported Sept. 4, 2002 (H Rept 107-638). House passed, under suspension of the rules, Sept. 24. President signed Oct. 11, 2002.

PL 107-238 (S 1175) Modify the boundary of Vicksburg National Military Park to include the property known as Pemberton's Headquarters. Introduced by LOTT, R-Miss., on July 12, 2001. Senate Energy and Natural Resources reported, amended, June 27, 2002 (S Rept 107-183). Senate passed, with amendment, July 24. House passed, under suspension of the rules, Sept. 24. President signed Oct. 11, 2002.

PL 107-239 (S 1325) Ratify an agreement between the Aleut Corporation and the United States to exchange land rights received under the Alaska Native Claims Settlement Act for certain land interests on Adak Island. Introduced by MURKOWSKI, R-Alaska, on Aug. 2, 2001. Senate Energy and Natural Resources reported, amended, June 26, 2002 (S Rept 107-180). Senate passed, with amendment, Aug. 1. House passed, under suspension of the rules, Sept. 24. President signed Oct. 11, 2002.

PL 107-240 (H J Res 122) Make further continuing appropriations for fiscal 2003. Introduced by YOUNG, R-Fla., on Oct. 10, 2002. House passed Oct. 10. Senate passed Oct. 11. President signed Oct. 11, 2002.

PL 107-241 (HR 3214) Amend the charter of the AMVETS organization. Introduced by BILIRAKIS, R-Fla., on Nov. 1, 2001. House Judiciary reported July 12, 2002 (H Rept 107-569). House passed, under suspension of the rules, July 15. Senate Judiciary reported Sept. 5 (no written report). Senate passed Oct. 2. President signed Oct. 16, 2002.

PL 107-242 (HR 3838) Amend the charter of the Veterans of Foreign Wars of the United States organization to make members of the armed forces who receive special pay for duty subject to hostile fire or imminent danger eligible for membership. Introduced by SMITH, R-N.J., on March 4, 2002. House Judiciary reported July 12 (H Rept 107-570). House passed, under suspension of the rules, July 15. Senate Judiciary reported Sept. 5 (no written report). Senate passed Oct. 2. President signed Oct. 16, 2002.

PL 107-243 (H J Res 114) Authorize the use of U.S. Armed Forces against Iraq. Introduced by HASTERT, R-Ill., on Oct. 2, 2002. House International Relations reported amended Oct. 7 (H Rept 107-721). House passed, with amendment, Oct. 10. Senate passed Oct. 11. President signed Oct. 16, 2002.

PL 107-244 (H J Res 123) Make further continuing appropriations for fiscal 2003. Introduced by YOUNG, R-Fla., on Oct. 15, 2002. House passed Oct. 16. Senate passed Oct. 16. President signed Oct. 18, 2002.

PL 107-245 (HR 5531) Facilitate famine relief efforts and a comprehensive solution to the war in Sudan. Introduced by TANCREDO, R-Colo., on Oct. 2, 2002. House passed, amended, under suspension of the rules, Oct. 7. Senate passed Oct. 9, 2002. President signed Oct. 21, 2002.

PL 107-246 (HR 2121) Make available funds under the Foreign Assistance Act of 1961 to expand democracy, good governance and anti-corruption programs in the Russian Federation. Introduced by LANTOS, D-Calif., on June 12, 2001. House passed, amended, under suspension of the rules, Dec. 11. Senate Foreign Relations reported, with amendment, Aug. 1, 2002 (no written report). Senate passed, with amendments, Sept. 20. House agreed to Senate amendments, under suspension of the rules, Oct. 7. President signed Oct. 23, 2002.

PL 107-247 (HR 4085) Increase, effective Dec. 1, 2002, rates of compensation for veterans with service-connected disabilities and rates of dependency and indemnity compensation for survivors of certain service-connected disabled veterans. Introduced by SMITH, R-N.J. on April 9, 2002. House Veterans' Affairs reported, amended, May 16 (H Rept 107-472). House passed, amended, under suspension of the rules, May 21. Senate Veterans' Affairs discharged Sept. 26. Senate passed, with amendments, Sept. 26. House agreed to Senate amendments, under

suspension of the rules, Oct. 7, 2002. President signed Oct. 23, 2002.

PL 107-248 (HR 5010) Make appropriations for the Department of Defense for the fiscal year ending Sept. 30, 2003. Introduced by LEWIS, R-Calif., on June 25, 2002. House Appropriations reported June 25 (H Rept 107-532). House passed, amended, June 27. Senate Appropriations reported, with amendment, July 18 (S Rept 107-213). Senate passed, with amendment, Aug. 1. Conference report filed in the House Oct. 9 (H Rept 107-732). House agreed to conference report Oct. 10. Senate agreed to conference report Oct. 16. President signed Oct. 23, 2002.

PL 107-249 (HR 5011) Make appropriations for military construction, family housing and base realignment and closure for the Department of Defense for the fiscal year ending Sept. 30, 2003. Introduced by HOBSON, R-Ohio, on June 25, 2002. House Appropriations reported June 25 (H Rept 107-533). House passed, amended, June 27. Senate passed, with amendment, July 18. Conference report filed in the House Oct. 9 (H Rept 107-731). House agreed to conference report Oct. 10. Senate agreed to conference report Oct. 11. President signed Oct. 23, 2002.

PL 107-250 (HR 5651) Amend the Federal Food, Drug and Cosmetic Act to make improvements in the regulation of medical devices. Introduced by GREENWOOD, R-Pa., on Oct. 16, 2002. House Energy and Commerce discharged. House passed Oct. 16. Senate passed Oct. 17. President signed Oct. 26, 2002.

PL 107-251 (S 1533) Amend the Public Health Service Act to reauthorize and strengthen the health centers program and the National Health Service Corps, and to establish the Healthy Communities Access Program to help coordinate services for the uninsured and underinsured. Introduced by KENNEDY, D-Mass., on Oct. 11, 2001. Senate Health, Education, Labor and Pensions reported Oct. 11 (H Rept 107-83). Senate passed, amended, April 16, 2002. House passed with amendment, under suspension of the rules, Oct. 16. Senate agreed to House amendment Oct. 17. President signed Oct. 26, 2002.

PL 107-252 (HR 3295) Require states and localities to meet uniform and non-discriminatory requirements for federal elections; establish grant programs to assist states and localities in meeting those requirements; improve election technology and the administration of federal elections, and establish the Election Administration Commission. Introduced by NEY, R-Ohio, on Nov. 14, 2001. House Administration reported, amended, Dec. 10 (H Rept 107-329, Part 1). House Judiciary, Science, Government Reform and Armed Services discharged. House passed, amended, Dec. 12. Senate Rules and Administration discharged. Senate passed, with amendments, April 11, 2002. Conference report filed in the House Oct. 8 (H Rept 107-730). House agreed to conference report Oct.

10. Senate agreed to conference report Oct. 16. President signed Oct. 29, 2002.

PL 107-253 (HR 2486) Authorize the National Oceanic and Atmospheric Administration, through the U.S. Weather Service, to conduct research and development, training and outreach activities to improve tropical cyclone inland forecasting. Introduced by ETHERIDGE, D-N.C., on July 12, 2001. House Science reported, amended, June 5, 2002 (H Rept 107-495). House passed, amended, July 11. Senate Commerce, Science and Transportation reported Oct. 10 (S Rept 107-310). Senate passed Oct. 16. President signed Oct. 29, 2002.

PL 107-254 (HR 5647) Authorize the duration of the base Navy-Marine Corps Intranet contract to be more than five years but not more than seven years. Introduced by DAVIS, R-Va., on Oct. 16, 2002. House Armed Services discharged. House passed Oct. 16. Senate passed Oct. 17. President signed Oct. 29, 2002.

PL 107-255 (H J Res 113) Recognize the contributions of Patsy T. Mink. Introduced by MILLER, D-Calif., on Oct. 2, 2002. House passed, amended, under suspension of the rules, Oct. 9. Senate passed Oct. 11. President signed Oct. 29, 2002.

PL 107-256 (S 1227) Authorize the secretary of the Interior to conduct a study of the suitability and feasibility of establishing the Niagara Falls National Heritage Area in the state of New York. Introduced by SCHUMER, D-N.Y., on July 24, 2001. Senate Energy and Natural Resources reported, amended, June 26, 2002 (S Rept 107-179). Senate passed, amended, Aug. 1. House Resources reported Sept. 23 (H Rept 107-668). House passed Oct. 16. President signed Oct. 29, 2002.

PL 107-257 (S 1270) Designate the U.S. courthouse to be constructed at 8th Ave. and Mill St. in Eugene, Ore., as the "Wayne Lyman Morse United States Courthouse." Introduced by WYDEN, D-Ore., on July 30, 2001. Senate Environment and Public Works reported Sept. 25 (no written report). Senate passed Nov. 15. House Transportation and Infrastructure discharged. House passed Oct. 16, 2002. President signed Oct. 29, 2002.

PL 107-258 (S 1339) Amend the Bring Them Home Alive Act of 2000 to provide an asylum program with regard to American Persian Gulf War POW/MIAs. Introduced by CAMPBELL, R-Colo., on Aug. 2, 2001. Senate Judiciary reported, amended, June 27, 2002 (no written report). Senate passed, amended, July 29. House Judiciary reported Oct. 15 (H Rept 107-749, Part 1). House passed, under suspension of the rules, Oct. 15. President signed Oct. 29, 2002.

PL 107-259 (S 1646) Identify certain routes in the states of Texas, Oklahoma, Colorado and New Mexico as part of the Ports-to-Plains Corridor, a high-priority corridor on the National Highway System. Introduced by BINGAMAN, D-N.M., on Nov. 7, 2001. Senate Environment and Public Works reported June 19, 2002 (S Rept 107-165). Senate passed June 26. House Transportation and Infrastructure discharged. House passed Oct. 16. President signed Oct. 29, 2002.

PL 107-260 (S 2558) Amend the Public Health Service Act to provide for the collection of data on benign brain-related tumors through the national program of cancer registries. Introduced by REED, D-R.I., on May 23, 2002. Senate Health, Education, Labor and Pensions discharged. Senate passed Aug. 1. House Energy and Commerce discharged. House passed Oct. 10. President signed Oct. 29, 2002.

PL 107-261 (HR 669) Designate the facility of the U.S. Postal Service located at 127 Social St. in Woonsocket, R.I., as the "Alphonse F. Auclair Post Office Building." Introduced by KENNEDY, D-R.I., on Feb. 14, 2001. House Government Reform discharged. House passed Oct. 10, 2002. Senate passed Oct. 17. President signed Oct. 30, 2002.

PL 107-262 (HR 670) Designate the facility of the U.S. Postal Service located at 7 Commercial St. in Newport, R.I., as the "Bruce F. Cotta Post Office Building." Introduced by KENNEDY, D-R.I., on Feb. 14, 2001. House Government Reform discharged. House passed Oct. 10, 2002. Senate passed Oct. 17. President signed Oct. 30, 2002.

PL 107-263 (HR 3034) Redesignate the facility of the U.S. Postal Service located at 89 River St. in Hoboken, N.J., as the "Frank Sinatra Post Office Building." Introduced by MENENDEZ, D-N.J., on Oct. 4, 2001. House passed, under suspension of the rules, June 27, 2002. Senate Governmental Affairs reported Oct. 15 (no written report). Senate passed Oct. 17. President signed Oct. 30, 2002.

PL 107-264 (HR 3738) Designate the facility of the U.S. Postal Service located at 1299 North 7th St. in Philadelphia as the "Herbert Arlene Post Office Building." Introduced by BRADY, D-Pa., on Feb. 13, 2002. House passed, under suspension of the rules, June 11. Senate Governmental Affairs reported Oct. 15 (no written report). Senate passed Oct. 17. President signed Oct. 30, 2002.

PL 107-265 (HR 3739) Designate the facility of the U.S. Postal Service located at 6150 North Broad St. in Philadelphia as the "Rev. Leon Sullivan Post Office Building." Introduced by BRADY, D-Pa., on Feb. 13, 2002. House passed, under suspension of the rules, June 11. Senate Governmental Affairs reported Oct. 15 (no written report). Senate passed Oct. 17. President signed Oct. 30, 2002.

PL 107-266 (HR 3740) Designate the facility of the U.S. Postal Service located at 925 Dickinson St. in Philadelphia as the "William V. Cibotti Post Office Building." Introduced by BRADY, D-Pa., on Feb. 13, 2002. House passed, amended, under suspension of the rules, June 11. Senate Governmental Affairs reported Oct. 15 (no written report). Senate passed Oct. 17. President signed Oct. 30, 2002.

PL 107-267 (HR 4102) Designate the facility of the U.S. Postal Service located at 120 North Maine St. in Fallon, Nev., as the "Rollan D. Melton Post Office Building." Introduced by GIBBONS, R-Nev., on April 9, 2002. House passed, under suspension of the rules, Sept. 17. Senate Governmental Affairs reported Oct. 15 (no written report). Senate passed Oct. 17. President signed Oct. 30, 2002.

PL 107-268 (HR 4717) Designate the facility of the U.S. Postal Service located at 1199 Pasadena Boulevard in Pasadena, Texas, as the "Jim Fonteno Post Office Building." Introduced by BENTSEN, D-Texas, on May 14, 2002. House passed, under suspension of the rules, June 18. Senate Governmental Affairs reported Oct. 15 (no written report). Senate passed Oct. 17. President signed Oct. 30, 2002.

PL 107-269 (HR 4755) Designate the facility of the U.S. Postal Service located at 204 South Broad St. in Lancaster, Ohio, as the "Clarence Miller Post Office Building." Introduced by HOBSON, R-Ohio, on May 16, 2002. House passed, under suspension of the rules, July 15. Senate Governmental Affairs reported Oct. 15 (no written report). Senate passed Oct. 17. President signed Oct. 30, 2002.

PL 107-270 (HR 4794) Designate the facility of the U.S. Postal Service located at 1895 Avenida Del Oro in Oceanside, Calif., as the "Ronald C. Packard Post Office Building." Introduced by ISSA, R-Calif., on May 22, 2002. House passed, under suspension of the rules, June 18. Senate Governmental Affairs reported Oct. 15 (no written report). Senate passed Oct. 17. President signed Oct. 30, 2002.

PL 107-271 (HR 4797) Redesignate the facility of the U.S. Postal Service located at 265 South Western Ave., Los Angeles, as the "Nat King Cole Post Office." Introduced by BECERRA, D-Calif., on May 22, 2002. House passed, under suspension of the rules, Sept. 9, 2002. Senate Governmental Affairs reported Oct. 15 (no written report). Senate passed Oct. 17. President signed Oct. 30, 2002.

PL 107-272 (HR 4851) Redesignate the facility of the U.S. Postal Service located at 6910 South Yorktown Ave. in Tulsa, Okla., as the "Robert Wayne Jenkins Station." Introduced by SULLIVAN, R-Okla., on May 23, 2002. House passed, under suspension of the rules, Oct. 1. Senate passed Oct. 17. President signed Oct. 30, 2002.

PL 107-273 (HR 2215) Authorize appropriations for the Department of Justice for fiscal 2002-2003. Introduced by SENSENBRENNER, R-Wis., on June 19, 2001. House Judiciary reported, amended, July 10 (H Rept 107-125). House passed, amended, under suspension of the rules, July 23. Senate Judiciary reported, with amendment, Oct. 30 (no written report). Senate passed, with amendment, Dec. 20. Conference report filed in the House Sept. 25, 2002 (H Rept 107-685). House agreed to conference report Sept. 26. Senate agreed to conference report Oct. 3. President signed Nov. 2, 2002.

PL 107-274 (HR 4967) Establish new nonimmigrant classes for border commuter students. Introduced by KOLBE, R-Ariz., on June 19, 2002. House Judiciary reported Oct. 15 (H Rept 107-753). House passed, under suspension of the rules, Oct. 15. Senate passed Oct. 16. President signed Nov. 2, 2002.

PL 107-275 (HR 5542) Consolidate all black lung benefit responsibility under a single official. Introduced by HART, R-Pa., on Oct. 3, 2002. House passed, amended, under suspension of the rules, Oct. 9. Senate passed Oct. 16. President signed Nov. 2, 2002.

PL 107-276 (HR 5596) Amend Section 527 of the Internal Revenue Code of 1986 to eliminate notification and return requirements for state and local party committees and candidate committees, and avoid duplicate reporting by certain state and local political committees of information required to be reported and made publicly available under state law. Introduced by BRADY, R-Texas, on Oct. 10, 2002. House Ways and Means discharged. House passed Oct. 16. Senate passed Oct. 17. President signed Nov. 2, 2002.

PL 107-277 (HR 2733) Authorize the National Institute of Standards and Technology to work with major manufacturing industries on an initiative to develop and implement standards for electronic enterprise integration. Introduced by BARCIA, D-Mich., on Aug. 2, 2001. House Science reported, amended, June 20, 2002 (H Rept 107-520). House passed, amended, July 11. Senate Commerce, Science and Transportation reported Oct. 16 (S Rept 107-319). Senate passed Oct. 17. President signed Nov. 5, 2002.

PL 107-278 (HR 3656) Amend the International Organizations Immunities Act to make it applicable to the European Central Bank. Introduced by LEACH, R-Iowa, on Jan. 29, 2002. House passed, under suspension of the rules, Sept. 24. Senate Foreign Relations reported Oct. 8 (no written report). Senate passed Oct. 17. President signed Nov. 5, 2002.

PL 107-279 (HR 3801) Provide for improvement of federal education research, statistics, evaluation, information and dissemination. Introduced by CASTLE, R-Del., on Feb. 27, 2002. House Education and the Workforce reported, amended, April 11 (H Rept 107-404). House passed, amended, under suspension of the rules, April 30. Senate Health, Education, Labor and Pensions discharged. Senate passed, with amendment, Oct. 15. House agreed to Senate amendment Oct. 16. President signed Nov. 5, 2002.

PL 107-280 (HR 4013) Amend the Public Health Service Act to establish an Office of Rare Diseases at the National Institutes of Health. Introduced by SHIMKUS, R-Ill., on March 20, 2002. House Energy and Commerce reported June 26 (H Rept 107-543). House passed, under suspension of the rules, Oct. 1. Senate passed Oct. 17. President signed Nov. 6, 2002.

PL 107-281 (HR 4014) Amend the Federal Food, Drug, and Cosmetic Act to authorize appropriations for fiscal 2002 through 2006 for grants and contracts for the development of drugs for rare diseases and conditions. Introduced by FOLEY, R-Fla., on March 20, 2002. House Energy and Commerce reported Oct. 1 (H Rept 107-702). House passed, under suspension of the rules, Oct. 1. Senate passed Oct. 17. President signed Nov. 6, 2002.

PL 107-282 (HR 5200) Establish wilderness areas, promote conservation, improve public land and provide for high quality development in Clark County, Nev. Introduced by GIBBONS, R-Nev., on July 24, 2002. House Resources reported, amended, Oct. 15 (H Rept 107-750). House passed, amended, Oct. 16. Senate passed Oct. 17. President signed Nov. 6, 2002.

PL 107-283 (HR 5308) Designate the facility of the U.S. Postal Service located at 301 South Howes St. in Fort Collins, Colo., as the "Barney Apodaca Post Office." Introduced by SCHAFFER, R-Colo., on July 26, 2002. House passed, under suspension of the rules, Sept. 4. Senate Governmental Affairs reported Oct. 15 (no written report). Senate passed Oct. 17. President signed Nov. 6, 2002.

PL 107-284 (HR 5333) Designate the facility of the U.S. Postal Service located at 4 East Central St. in Worcester, Mass., as the "Joseph D. Early Post Office Building." Introduced by McGOVERN, D-Mass., on Sept. 4, 2002. House passed, under suspension of the rules, Sept. 17. Senate Governmental Affairs reported Oct. 15 (no written report). Senate passed Oct. 17. President signed Nov. 6, 2002.

PL 107-285 (HR 5336) Designate the facility of the U.S. Postal Service located at 380 Main St. in Farmingdale, N.Y., as the "Peter J. Ganci Jr. Post Office Building." Introduced by KING, R-N.Y., on Sept. 5, 2002. House passed, under suspension of the rules, Sept. 9. Senate Governmental Affairs reported Oct. 15 (no written report). Senate passed Oct. 17. President signed Nov. 6, 2002.

PL 107-286 (HR 5340) Designate the facility of the U.S. Postal Service located at 5805 White Oak Ave. in Encino, Calif., as the "Francis Dayle 'Chick' Hearn Post Office." Introduced by SHERMAN, D-Calif., on Sept. 5, 2002. House passed, under suspension of the rules, Oct. 7. Senate passed Oct. 17. President signed Nov. 6, 2002.

PL 107-287 (HR 3253) Amend Title 38, U.S. Code, to provide for the establishment of emergency medical preparedness centers in the Department of Veterans Affairs. Introduced by SMITH, R-N.J., on Nov. 8, 2001. House Veterans' Affairs reported, amended, May 16, 2002 (H Rept 107-471). House passed, amended, under suspension of the rules, May 20. Senate Veterans' Affairs discharged. Senate passed, with amendments, Aug. 1. House agreed to Senate amendments with amendment, Sept. 17. Senate agreed to House amendment, with amendment, Oct. 15. House agreed to Senate amendment Oct. 16. President signed Nov. 7, 2002.

PL 107-288 (HR 4015) Amend Title 38, U.S. Code, to revise and improve employment, training and placement services furnished to veterans. Introduced by SIMPSON, R-Idaho, on March 20, 2002. House Veterans' Affairs reported, amended, May 20 (H Rept 107-476). House passed, amended, under suspension of the rules, May 21. Senate Veterans' Affairs discharged. Senate passed, with amendment, Oct. 15. House agreed to Senate amendment Oct. 16. President signed Nov. 7, 2002.

PL 107-289 (HR 4685) Amend Title 31, U.S. Code, to expand the types of federal agencies that are required to prepare audited financial statements. Introduced by TOOMEY, R-Pa., on May 8, 2002. House passed, amended, under suspension of the rules, Oct. 7. Senate passed Oct. 17. President signed Nov. 7, 2002.

PL 107-290 (HR 5205) Amend the District of Columbia Retirement Protection Act of 1997 to permit the secretary of the Treasury to use estimated amounts in determining the service longevity component of the federal benefit payment to certain retirees of the Metropolitan Police Department. Introduced by MORELLA, R-Md., on July 24, 2002. House Government Reform discharged. House passed Oct. 10. Senate passed Oct. 17. President signed Nov. 7, 2002.

PL 107-291 (HR 5574) Designate the facility of the U.S. Postal Service located at 206 South Main St. in Glennville, Ga., as the "Michael Lee Woodcock Post Office." Introduced by KINGSTON, R-Ga., on Oct. 8, 2002. House Government Reform discharged. House passed Oct. 10. Senate passed Oct. 17. President signed Nov. 7, 2002.

PL 107-292 (S 1210) Reauthorize the Native American Housing Assistance and Self-Determination Act of 1996. Introduced by CAMPBELL, R-Colo., on July 20, 2001. Senate Indian Affairs reported, amended, Aug. 28, 2002 (S Rept 107-246). Senate Banking, Housing and Urban Affairs reported amended Sept. 17 (no written report). Senate passed, amended, Oct. 4. House Financial Services discharged. House passed Oct. 16. President signed Nov. 13, 2002.

PL 107-293 (S 2690) Reaffirm the reference to one nation under God in the Pledge of Allegiance. Introduced by HUTCHINSON, R-Ark., on June 27, 2002. Senate passed June 27. House Judiciary reported, with amendment, Sept. 17 (H Rept 107-659). House passed, with amendment, under suspension of the rules, Oct. 8. Senate agreed to House amendment Oct. 17. President signed Nov. 13, 2002.

PL 107-294 (H J Res 124) Make further continuing appropriations for fiscal 2003. Introduced by YOUNG, R-Fla., on Nov. 12, 2002. House passed Nov. 13. Senate passed Nov. 19. President signed Nov. 23, 2002.

PL 107-295 (S 1214) Amend the Merchant Marine Act, 1936, to establish a program to ensure greater security

for U.S. seaports. Introduced by HOLLINGS, D-S.C., on July 20, 2001. Senate Commerce, Science and Transportation reported Sept. 14 (S Rept 107-64). Senate passed, amended, Dec. 20. House passed, with amendment, June 4, 2002. Conference report filed in the House on Nov. 13 (H Rept 107-777). Senate agreed to conference report Nov. 14. House agreed to conference report Nov. 14. President signed Nov. 25, 2002.

PL 107-296 (HR 5005) Establish the Department of Homeland Security. Introduced by ARMEY, R-Texas, on June 24, 2002. House Agriculture, Appropriations, Armed Services, Energy and Commerce, Financial Services, Government Reform, Intelligence, International Relations, Judiciary, Science, Transportation and Infrastructure, and Ways and Means discharge. House Select Homeland Security reported, amended, July 24 (H Rept 107-609, Part 1). House passed, amended, July 26. Senate passed, with amendment, Nov. 19. House agreed to Senate amendment Nov. 22. President signed Nov. 25, 2002.

PL 107-297 (HR 3210) Establish a federal terrorism insurance program to serve as a backstop for commercial property and casualty insurers in the event of cataclysmic terrorist acts. Introduced by OXLEY, R-Ohio, on Nov. 1, 2001. House Financial Services reported, amended, Nov. 19 (H Rept 107-300, Part 1). House Ways and Means reported, amended, Nov. 19 (H Rept 107-300, Part 2). House Budget and Judiciary discharged. House passed, amended, Nov. 29. Senate passed, with amendment, July 25, 2002. Conference report filed in the House on Nov. 13 (H Rept 107-779). House agreed to conference report Nov. 14. Senate agreed to conference report Nov. 19. President signed Nov. 26, 2002.

PL 107-298 (HR 2546) Amend Title 49, U.S. Code, to prohibit states from requiring a license or fee for a motor vehicle that is providing pre-arranged interstate ground transportation service. Introduced by BLUNT, R-Mo., on July 18, 2001. House Transportation and Infrastructure reported, amended, Nov. 13 (H Rept 107-282). House passed, amended, under suspension of the rules, Nov. 13. Senate Commerce, Science and Transportation reported, with amendments, Aug. 1, 2002 (S Rept 107-237). Senate passed, with amendments, Oct. 17. House agreed to Senate amendments, under suspension of the rules, Nov. 12. President signed Nov. 26, 2002.

PL 107-299 (HR 3389) Reauthorize the National Sea Grant College Program Act. Introduced by GILCHREST, R-Md., on Nov. 30, 2001. House Resources reported, amended, March 7, 2002 (H Rept 107-369, Part 1). House Science reported, amended, April 15 (H Rept 107-369, Part 2). House passed, amended, June 19. Senate passed, with amendment, Oct. 11. House agreed to Senate amendment, under suspension of the rules, Nov. 12. President signed Nov. 26, 2002.

PL 107-300 (HR 4878) Provide for reduction of improper payments by federal agencies. Introduced by HORN, R-

Calif., on June 6, 2002. House passed, amended, under suspension of the rules, July 9. Senate Governmental Affairs reported Oct. 15 (S Rept 107-333). Senate passed, with amendment, Oct. 17. House agreed to Senate amendment, under suspension of the rules, Nov. 12. President signed Nov. 26, 2002.

PL 107-301 (HR 5349) Facilitate the use of a portion of the former O'Reilly General Hospital in Springfield, Mo., by the local Boys and Girls Club through the release of the interests retained by the United States in 1955 when the land was conveyed to the state of Missouri. Introduced by BLUNT, R-Mo., on Sept. 9, 2002. House Government Reform discharged. House passed Oct. 10. Senate passed Nov. 13. President signed Nov. 26, 2002.

PL 107-302 (S 3044) Authorize the Court Services and Offender Supervision Agency of the District of Columbia to provide for the interstate supervision of offenders on parole, probation and supervised release. Introduced by DURBIN, D-Ill., on Oct. 3, 2002. Senate Governmental Affairs reported Oct. 15 (S Rept 107-332). Senate passed Nov. 13. House passed Nov. 15. President signed Nov. 26, 2002.

PL 107-303 (HR 1070) Authorize the EPA to make grants for remediation of sediment contamination and authorize assistance for research and development of innovative technologies for such purposes; and modify provisions in the Federal Water Pollution Control Act and the Water Resources Development Act of 2000 relating to the Lake Champlain basin. Introduced by EHLERS, R-Mich., on March 15, 2001. House Transportation and Infrastructure reported July 18, 2002 (H Rept 107-587, Part 1). House Science discharged. House passed, amended, under suspension of the rules, Sept. 4. Senate Environment and Public Works reported, with amendment, Oct. 15 (S Rept 107-312). Senate passed, with amendment, Oct. 17. House agreed to Senate amendment, under suspension of the rules, Nov. 12. President signed Nov. 27, 2002.

PL 107-304 (HR 3340) Amend Title 5, U.S. Code, to allow participants age 50 and over to make certain catch-up contributions to the Thrift Savings Plan. Introduced by MORELLA, R-Md., on Nov. 19, 2001. House Government Reform reported Sept. 25, 2002 (H Rept 107-686). Passed House passed, amended, under suspension of the rules, Oct. 7. Senate passed Nov. 13. President signed Nov. 27, 2002.

PL 107-305 (HR 3394) Authorize funding for computer and network security research and for development and research fellowship programs. Introduced by BOEHLERT, R-N.Y., on Dec. 4, 2001. House Science reported Feb. 4, 2002 (H Rept 107-355, Part 1). House Education and the Workforce discharged. House passed Feb. 7. Senate Commerce, Science and Transportation discharged. Senate passed, with amendment, Oct. 16. House agreed to Senate amendment, under suspension of the rules, Nov. 12. President signed Nov. 27, 2002.

PL 107-306 (HR 4628) Authorize appropriations for fiscal 2003 for intelligence and intelligence-related activities of the U.S. government, the Community Management Account, and the Central Intelligence Agency Retirement and Disability System. Introduced by GOSS, R-Fla., on May 1, 2002. House Intelligence reported, amended, July 18 (H Rept 107-592). House passed, amended, July 25. Senate Intelligence discharged. Senate passed, with amendment, Sept. 25. Conference report filed in the House on Nov. 14 (H Rept 107-789). House agreed to conference report Nov. 15. Senate agreed to conference report Nov. 15. President signed Nov. 27, 2002.

PL 107-307 (HR 2621) Amend Title 18, U.S. Code, to increase consumer product protection against tampering. Introduced by HART, R-Pa., on July 25, 2001. House Judiciary reported, amended, May 23, 2002 (H Rept 107-485). House passed, amended, under suspension of the rules, June 11. Senate passed, with amendment, Oct. 16. House agreed to Senate amendment Nov. 15. President signed Dec. 2, 2002.

PL 107-308 (HR 3908) Reauthorize the North American Wetlands Conservation Act. Introduced by HANSEN, R-Utah, on March 7, 2002. House Resources reported, amended, April 29 (H Rept 107-421). House passed, amended, under suspension of the rules, May 7. Senate Environment and Public Works reported, with amendments, Oct. 8 (H Rept 107-304). Senate passed, with amendments, Nov. 14. House agreed to Senate amendments Nov. 15. President signed Dec. 2, 2002.

PL 107-309 (HR 3988) Amend Title 36, U.S. Code, to clarify the requirements for eligibility in the American Legion. Introduced by GEKAS, R-Pa., on March 18, 2002. House Judiciary reported July 12 (H Rept 107-571). House passed, under suspension of the rules, July 15. Senate Judiciary reported Nov. 14 (no written report). Senate passed Nov. 14. President signed Dec. 2, 2002.

PL 107-310 (HR 4727) Reauthorize the national dam safety program. Introduced by SHUSTER, R-Pa., on May 14, 2002. House Transportation and Infrastructure reported, amended, Sept. 4 (H Rept 107-626). House passed, amended, Sept. 5. Senate Environment and Public Works reported Sept. 26 (no written report). Senate passed Nov. 14. President signed Dec. 2, 2002.

PL 107-311 (HR 5590) Amend Title 10, U.S. Code, to provide for the enforcement and effectiveness of civilian court orders of protection on military installations. Introduced by HAYES, R-N.C., on Oct. 9, 2002. House passed, under suspension of the rules, Oct. 15. Senate passed Nov. 14. President signed Dec. 2, 2002.

PL 107-312 (HR 5708) Reduce existing PAYGO balances. Introduced by NUSSLE, R-Iowa, on Nov. 12, 2002. House passed Nov. 14. Senate passed Nov. 15. President signed Dec. 2, 2002.

PL 107-313 (HR 5716) Amend the Employee Retirement Income Security Act of 1974 and the Public Health Service Act to extend the mental health benefits parity provisions for an additional year. Introduced by BOEHNER, R-Ohio, on Nov. 13, 2002. House Energy and Commerce, and House Education and the Workforce discharged. House passed Nov. 15. Senate passed Nov. 15. President signed Dec. 2, 2002.

PL 107-314 (HR 4546) Authorize appropriations for fiscal 2003 for military activities of the Department of Defense, for military construction, for defense activities of the Department of Energy and to prescribe military personnel strengths for fiscal 2003. Introduced by STUMP, R-Ariz., on April 23, 2002. House Armed Services reported, amended, May 3 (H Rept 107-436). House Armed Services filed supplemental report May 6 (H Rept 107-436, Part 2). House passed, amended, May 10. Senate passed, with amendment, June 27. House agreed to Senate amendment, with amendment, July 25. Conference report filed in the House on Nov. 12 (H Rept 107-772). House agreed to conference report, under suspension of the rules, Nov. 12. Senate agreed to conference report Nov. 13. President signed Dec. 2, 2002.

PL 107-315 (H J Res 117) Approve the location of the commemorative work in the District of Columbia honoring former President John Adams. Introduced by ROEMER, D-Ind., on Oct. 7, 2002. House Resources discharged. House passed Nov. 15. Senate passed Nov. 20. President signed Dec. 2, 2002.

PL 107-316 (S 3156) Provide a grant for the construction of a new community center in St. Paul, Minn., in honor of the late Sen. Paul Wellstone and his wife, Sheila. Introduced by BARKLEY, I-Minn., on Nov. 14, 2002. Senate passed Nov. 14. House passed Nov. 15. President signed Dec. 2, 2002.

PL 107-317 (HR 3833) Facilitate the creation of a new, second-level Internet domain within the U.S. country code domain for material that promotes positive experiences for children and families using the Internet, provides a safe online environment for children and helps to prevent children from being exposed to harmful material on the Internet. Introduced by SHIMKUS, R-Ill., on March 4, 2002. House Energy and Commerce reported, amended, May 8 (H Rept 107-449). House passed, amended, under suspension of the rules, May 21. Senate Commerce, Science and Transportation discharged. Senate passed, with amendment, Nov. 13. House agreed to Senate amendment Nov. 15. President signed Dec. 4, 2002.

PL 107-318 (HR 5504) Provide for the improvement of the safety of child restraints in passenger motor vehicles. Introduced by SHIMKUS, R-Ill., on Oct. 1, 2002. House Energy and Commerce reported, amended, Oct. 7 (H Rept 107-726). House passed, amended, Nov. 15. Senate passed Nov. 18. President signed Dec. 4, 2002.

PL 107-319 (HR 727) Amend the Consumer Product Safety Act to provide that low-speed electric bicycles are consumer products subject to the act. Introduced by STEARNS, R-Fla., on Feb. 27, 2001. House Energy and Commerce reported March 5 (H Rept 107-5). House passed, under suspension of the rules, March 6. Senate Commerce, Science and Transportation discharged. Senate passed Nov. 18, 2002. President signed Dec. 4, 2002.

PL 107-320 (HR 2595) Direct the secretary of the Army to convey a parcel of land to Chatham County, Ga. Introduced by KINGSTON, R-Ga., on July 23, 2001. House passed, amended, under suspension of the rules, Dec. 11. Senate Armed Services discharged. Senate Environment and Public Works reported Sept. 26, 2002 (no written report). Senate passed Nov. 18. President signed Dec. 4, 2002.

PL 107-321 (HR 5469) Suspend for six months the determination of the Librarian of Congress of July 8, 2002, on rates and terms for the digital performance of sound recordings and ephemeral recordings. Introduced by SENSENBRENNER, R-Wis., on Sept. 26, 2002. House passed, amended, under suspension of the rules, Oct. 7. Senate passed, with amendment, Nov. 14. House agreed to Senate amendment Nov. 15. President signed Dec. 4, 2002.

PL 107-322 (S 1010) Extend the deadline for start of construction of a hydroelectric project in North Carolina. Introduced by HELMS, R-N.C., on June 11, 2001. Senate Energy and Natural Resources reported, June 28, 2002 (S Rept 107-192). Senate passed Aug. 1. House Energy and Commerce discharged. House passed, Nov. 15. President signed Dec. 4, 2002.

PL 107-323 (S 1226) Require the display of the POW/MIA flag at the World War II memorial, the Korean War Veterans Memorial and the Vietnam Veterans Memorial. Introduced by CAMPBELL, R-Colo., on July 24, 2001. Senate Judiciary discharged. Senate passed, Oct. 2, 2002. House Resources discharged. House passed Nov. 15. President signed Dec. 4, 2002.

PL 107-324 (S 1907) Direct the secretary of the Interior to convey certain land to the city of Haines, Ore. Introduced by SMITH, R-Ore., on Jan. 29, 2002. Senate Energy and Natural Resources reported, amended, June 28 (S Rept 107-197). Senate passed, amended, Aug. 1. House Resources reported Sept. 24 (H Rept 107-680). House passed Nov. 15. President signed Dec. 4, 2002.

PL 107-325 (S 1946) Amend the National Trails System Act to designate the Old Spanish Trail as a national historic trail. Introduced by CAMPBELL, R-Colo., on Feb. 14, 2002. Senate Energy and Natural Resources reported, amended, July 3 (S Rept 107-203). Senate passed, amended, Aug. 1. House Resources reported Sept. 23 (H Rept 107-670). House passed Nov. 15. President signed Dec. 4, 2002.

PL 107-326 (S 2239) Amend the National Housing Act to simplify the down payment requirements for FHA mortgage insurance for single-family home buyers. Introduced by SARBANES, D-Md., on April 24, 2002. Senate Banking, Housing and Urban Affairs reported, amended, Oct. 15 (no written report). Senate passed, amended, Oct. 17. House Financial Services discharged. House passed Nov. 15. President signed Dec. 4, 2002.

PL 107-327 (S 2712) Authorize economic and democratic development assistance for Afghanistan, and authorize military assistance for Afghanistan and certain other foreign countries. Introduced by HAGEL, R-Neb., on July 9, 2002. Senate Foreign Relations reported, amended, Sept. 12 (S Rept 107-278). Senate passed, amended, Nov. 14. House passed Nov. 15. President signed Dec. 4, 2002.

PL 107-328 (S J Res 53) Resolve that the first session of the 108th Congress will convene at noon on Jan. 7, 2003. Introduced by DASCHLE, D-S.D., on Nov. 14, 2002. Senate passed Nov. 14. House passed Nov. 15. President signed Dec. 4, 2002.

PL 107-329 (S 1240) Provide for the acquisition of land and construction of an interagency administrative and visitor facility at the entrance to American Fork Canyon, Utah. Introduced by BENNETT, R-Utah, on July 25, 2001. Senate Energy and Natural Resources reported, amended, June 25, 2002 (S Rept 107-178). Senate passed, amended, Aug. 1. House Resources reported, Sept. 23 (H Rept 107-669). House passed, with amendment, under suspension of the rules, Sept. 24. Senate agreed to House amendment Nov. 20. President signed Dec. 6, 2002.

PL 107-330 (S 2237) Amend Title 38, U.S. Code, to improve veterans' benefits related to compensation, dependency and indemnity compensation, pensions, education, housing, memorial affairs, life insurance and certain other benefits, and to improve the administration of benefits and the procedures relating to judicial review of veterans' claims. Introduced by ROCKEFELLER, D-W.Va., on April 24, 2002. Senate Veterans' Affairs reported, amended, Aug. 1 (S Rept 107-234). Senate passed, amended, Sept. 26. House passed, with amendments, Nov. 15. Senate agreed to House amendments Nov. 18. President signed Dec. 6, 2002.

PL 107-331 (S 2017) Amend the Indian Financing Act of 1974 to improve the effectiveness of the Indian loan guarantee and insurance program. Introduced by CAMPBELL, R-Colo., on March 14, 2002. Senate Indian Affairs reported, amended, Aug. 28 (S Rept 107-249). Senate passed, amended, Sept. 17. House passed, with amendment, Nov. 15. Senate agreed to House amendment Nov. 20. President signed Dec. 13, 2002.

PL 107-332 (HR 38) Provide for additional lands to be included within the boundaries of the Homestead National Monument of America in Nebraska. Introduced by BEREUTER, R-Neb., on Jan. 3, 2001. House Resources reported, amended, Dec. 6 (H Rept 107-325). House

passed, amended, under suspension of the rules, Dec. 11. Senate Energy and Natural Resources reported Sept. 9, 2002 (S Rept 107-260). Senate passed Nov. 20. President signed Dec. 16, 2002.

PL 107-333 (HR 308) Establish the Guam War Claims Review Commission. Introduced by UNDERWOOD, D-Guam, on Jan. 30, 2001. House passed, amended, under suspension of the rules, March 13. Senate Energy and Natural Resources reported June 24, 2002 (S Rept 107-172). Senate passed Nov. 20. President signed Dec. 16, 2002.

PL 107-334 (HR 451) Make certain adjustments to the boundaries of the Mount Nebo Wilderness Area in Utah. Introduced by HANSEN, R-Utah, on Feb. 6, 2001. House Resources reported, amended, July 23 (H Rept 107-150). House passed, amended, under suspension of the rules, July 23. Senate Energy and Natural Resources reported Oct. 8, 2002 (no written report). Senate passed Nov. 20. President signed Dec. 16, 2002.

PL 107-335 (HR 706) Direct the secretary of the Interior to convey certain properties in the vicinity of the Elephant Butte Reservoir and the Caballo Reservoir in New Mexico. Introduced by SKEEN, R-N.M., on Feb. 14, 2001. House Resources reported, amended, March 7, 2002 (H Rept 107-368). House passed, amended, under suspension of the rules, March 19. Senate Energy and Natural Resources reported Sept. 17 (S Rept 107-287). Senate passed Nov. 20. President signed Dec. 16, 2002.

PL 107-336 (HR 1712) Authorize the secretary of the Interior to make adjustments to the boundary of the National Park of American Samoa to include certain portions of the islands of Ofu and Olosega within the park. Introduced by FALEOMAVAEGA, D-Am. Samoa, on May 3, 2001. House Resources reported, amended, March 12, 2002 (H Rept 107-372). House passed, amended, under suspension of the rules, March 19. Senate Energy and Natural Resources reported Sept. 11 (S Rept 107-270). Senate passed Nov. 20. President signed Dec. 16, 2002.

PL 107-337 (HR 1776) Authorize the secretary of the Interior to study the suitability and feasibility of establishing the Buffalo Bayou National Heritage Area in west Houston, Texas. Introduced by GREEN, D-Texas, on May 9, 2001. House Resources reported, amended, Oct. 30 (H Rept 107-256). House passed, amended, under suspension of the rules, Oct. 30. Senate Energy and Natural Resources reported Sept. 9, 2002 (S Rept 107-262). Senate passed Nov. 20. President signed Dec. 16, 2002.

PL 107-338 (HR 1814) Amend the National Trails System Act to designate the Metacomet-Monadnock-Mattabesett Trail extending through western Massachusetts and central Connecticut for study for potential addition to the National Trails System. Introduced by OLVER, D-Mass., on May 10, 2001. House Resources reported, amended, Sept. 28 (H Rept 107-224). House passed, amended, under suspension of the rules, Oct. 23. Senate Energy and Natural Resources reported Sept. 9, 2002

(S Rept 107-263). Senate passed Nov. 20. President signed Dec. 16, 2002.

PL 107-339 (HR 1870) Provide for the sale of certain real estate property within the Newlands Project to the city of Fallon, Nev. Introduced by GIBBONS, R-Nev., on May 16, 2001. House Resources reported, amended, March 6, 2002 (H Rept 107-366). House passed, amended, under suspension of the rules, March 6. Senate Energy and Natural Resources reported Sept. 11 (S Rept 107-271). Senate passed Nov. 20. President signed Dec. 16, 2002.

PL 107-340 (HR 1906) Amend the act that established the Pu'uhonua O Honaunau National Historical Park to expand the boundaries of that park. Introduced by MINK, D-Hawaii, on May 17, 2001. House Resources reported, amended, May 3, 2002 (H Rept 107-435). House passed, amended, under suspension of the rules, June 17. Senate Energy and Natural Resources reported Sept. 11 (S Rept 107-272). Senate passed Nov. 20. President signed Dec. 16, 2002.

PL 107-341 (HR 1925) Direct the secretary of the Interior to study the suitability and feasibility of designating the Waco Mammoth Site Area in Waco, Texas, as a unit of the National Park System. Introduced by EDWARDS, D-Texas, on May 21, 2001. House Resources reported, amended, Dec. 5 (H Rept 107-317). House passed, amended, under suspension of the rules, May 14, 2002. Senate Energy and Natural Resources reported Sept. 9 (S Rept 107-264). Senate passed Nov. 20. President signed Dec. 16, 2002.

PL 107-342 (HR 2099) Amend the Omnibus Parks and Public Lands Management Act of 1996 to provide adequate funding authorization for the Vancouver National Historic Reserve. Introduced by BAIRD, D-Wash., on June 7, 2001. House Resources reported, amended, Sept. 4, 2002 (H Rept 107-627). House passed, amended, under suspension of the rules, Sept. 24. Senate passed Nov. 20. President signed Dec. 17, 2002.

PL 107-343 (HR 2109) Authorize the secretary of the Interior to conduct a special resource study of Virginia Key Beach Park in Biscayne Bay, Fla., for possible inclusion in the National Park System. Introduced by MEEK, D-Fla., on June 7, 2001. House Resources reported, amended, April 9, 2002 (H Rept 107-390). House passed, amended, under suspension of the rules, April 30. Senate Energy and Natural Resources reported, Sept. 11 (S Rept 107-273). Senate passed, Nov. 20. President signed Dec. 17, 2002.

PL 107-344 (HR 2115) Authorize the secretary of the Interior to participate in the design, planning and construction of a project to reclaim and reuse wastewater within and outside of the service area of the Lakehaven Utility District, Wash. Introduced by SMITH, D-Wash., on June 7, 2001. House Resources reported Nov. 27 (H Rept 107-302). House passed, under suspension of the rules, Dec. 5. Senate Energy and Natural Resources reported Sept. 17, 2002 (S Rept 107-288). Senate passed Nov. 20. President signed Dec. 17, 2002.

PL 107-345 (HR 2187) Amend Title 10, U.S. Code, to make receipts collected from mineral leasing activities on certain naval oil shale reserves available to cover government environmental restoration, waste management and environmental compliance costs incurred with respect to the reserves. Introduced by HEFLEY, R-Colo., on June 14, 2001. House Resources reported, amended, Sept. 10 (H Rept 107-202, Part 1). House Energy and Commerce discharged. House passed, amended, under suspension of the rules, Dec. 18. Senate Armed Services discharged. Senate passed Nov. 20, 2002. President signed Dec. 17, 2002.

PL 107-346 (HR 2385) Convey certain property to the city of St. George, Utah, in order to provide for the protection and preservation of certain rare paleontological resources. Introduced by HANSEN, R-Utah, on June 28, 2001. House Resources reported, amended, Sept. 24 (H Rept 107-215). House passed, amended, under suspension of the rules, Oct. 2. Senate Energy and Natural Resources reported, amended, Sept. 11, 2002 (S Rept 107-274). Senate passed, amended, Nov. 20. President signed Dec. 17, 2002.

PL 107-347 (HR 2458) Establish a federal chief information officer within the Office of Management and Budget, and establish a broad framework of measures that require using Internet-based information technology to enhance citizen access to government information and services. Introduced by TURNER, D-Texas, July 11, 2001. House Government Reform reported, amended, Nov. 14, 2002 (H Rept 107-787, Part 1). House Judiciary discharged. House passed, amended, Nov. 15. Senate passed Nov 15. President signed Dec. 17, 2002.

PL 107-348 (HR 2628) Direct the secretary of the Interior to conduct a study of the suitability and feasibility of establishing the Muscle Shoals National Heritage Area in Alabama. Introduced by CRAMER, D-Ala., on July 25, 2001. House Resources reported April 11, 2002 (H Rept 107-398). House passed, under suspension of the rules, April 30. Senate Energy and Natural Resources reported Oct. 8 (no written report). Senate passed Nov. 20. President signed Dec. 17, 2002.

PL 107-349 (H 2828) Authorize refunds to qualified Klamath Project entities and individual contractors for amounts assessed to them for operation and maintenance of the Klamath Project for 2001. Introduced by WALDEN, R-Ore., on Aug. 2, 2001. House Resources reported, amended, Nov. 13 (H Rept 107-284). House passed, amended, under suspension of the rules, Nov. 13. Senate Energy and Natural Resources reported Sept. 17, 2002 (S Rept 107-289). Senate passed Nov. 20. President signed Dec. 17, 2002.

PL 107-350 (HR 2937) Provide for the conveyance of certain public land in Clark County, Nev., for use as a shooting range. Introduced by GIBBONS, R-Nev., on Sept. 21, 2001. House Resources reported, amended, April 9, 2002 (H Rept 107-387). House passed, amended, under suspension of the rules, April 9. Senate Energy and Natural Resources discharged. Senate passed Nov. 20. President signed Dec. 17, 2002.

PL 107-351 (HR 2990) Amend the Lower Rio Grande Valley Water Resources Conservation and Improvement Act of 2000 to authorize additional projects. Introduced by HINOJOSA, D-Texas, on Oct. 2, 2001. House Resources reported, amended, July 16, 2002 (H Rept 107-580). House passed, amended, under suspension of the rules, July 22. Senate Energy and Natural Resources reported Oct. 8 (no written report). Senate passed Nov. 20. President signed Dec. 17, 2002.

PL 107-352 (HR 3180) Consent to certain amendments to the New Hampshire-Vermont Interstate School Compact. Introduced by BASS, R-N.H., on Oct. 30, 2001. House Judiciary reported May 20, 2002 (H Rept 107-478). House passed, under suspension of the rules, June 26. Senate Judiciary reported Nov. 14 (no written report). Senate passed Nov. 20. President signed Dec. 17, 2002.

PL 107-353 (HR 3401) Provide for the conveyance of Forest Service facilities and lands that make up the Five Mile Regional Learning Center in California to the Clovis Unified School District, and authorize a new special use permit regarding the continued use of unconveyed lands used by the Center. Introduced by RADANOVICH, R-Calif., on Dec. 4, 2001. House Resources reported, amended, July 15, 2002 (H Rept 107-574). House passed, amended, under suspension of the rules, July 22. Senate Energy and Natural Resources reported Oct. 8 (no written report). Senate passed Nov. 20. President signed Dec. 17, 2002.

PL 107-354 (HR 3449) Revise the boundaries of the George Washington Birthplace National Monument. Introduced by DAVIS, R-Va., on Dec. 11, 2001. House Resources reported Sept. 4, 2002 (H Rept 107-631). House passed, under suspension of the rules, Sept. 24. Senate passed Nov. 20. President signed Dec. 17, 2002.

PL 107-355 (HR 3609) Amend Title 49, U.S. Code, to enhance the security and safety of pipelines. Introduced by YOUNG, R-Alaska, on Dec. 20, 2001. House Transportation and Infrastructure reported, amended, July 23, 2002 (H Rept 107-605, Part 1). House Energy and Commerce reported, amended, July 23 (H Rept 107-605, Part 2). House passed, amended, under suspension of the rules, July 23. Senate Commerce, Science and Transportation discharged. Senate passed, with amendment, Nov. 13. House agreed to Senate amendment Nov. 15. President signed Dec. 17, 2002.

PL 107-356 (HR 3858) Modify the boundaries of the New River Gorge National River, W.Va. Introduced by RAHALL, D-W.Va., on March 6, 2002. House Resources reported June 17 (H Rept 107-509). House passed, under suspension of the rules, June 24. Senate Energy and Natural Resources reported Oct. 8 (no written report). Senate passed Nov. 20. President signed Dec. 17, 2002.

PL 107-357 (HR 4692) Amend the act authorizing the establishment of the Andersonville National Historic Site in Georgia to provide for the addition of certain donated lands to the site. Introduced by BISHOP, D-Ga., on May 9, 2002. House Resources reported Oct. 1 (H Rept 107-712). House passed, under suspension of the rules, Oct. 1. Senate passed Nov. 20. President signed Dec. 17, 2002.

PL 107-358 (HR 4823) Repeal the sunset of the Economic Growth and Tax Relief Reconciliation Act of 2001 with respect to the exclusion from federal income tax for restitution received by victims of the Nazi regime. Introduced by SHAW, R-Fla., on May 22, 2002. House passed, under suspension of the rules, June 4. Senate passed Nov. 20. President signed Dec. 17, 2002.

PL 107-359 (HR 5125) Amend the American Battlefield Protection Act of 1996 to authorize the secretary of the Interior to establish a battlefield acquisition grant program. Introduced by MILLER, R-Calif., on July 15, 2002. House Resources reported, amended, Oct. 1 (H Rept 107-710). House passed, amended, under suspension of the rules, Oct. 1. Senate Energy and Natural Resources reported Oct. 8 (no written report). Senate passed Nov. 20. President signed Dec. 17, 2002.

PL 107-360 (HR 5738) Amend the Public Health Service Act with respect to special diabetes programs for Type I diabetes and for Indians. Introduced by SHIMKUS, R-Ill., on Nov. 14, 2002. House Energy and Commerce discharged. House passed Nov. 15. Senate passed Nov. 20. President signed Dec. 17, 2002.

PL 107-361 (HR 2818) Authorize the secretary of the Interior to convey certain public land within the Sand Mountain Wilderness Study Area in Idaho to resolve an occupancy encroachment dating back to 1971. Introduced by SIMPSON, R-Idaho, on Aug. 2, 2001. House Resources reported May 7, 2002 (H Rept 107-440). House passed, under suspension of the rules, May 7. Senate Energy and Natural Resources reported Oct. 8 (no written report). Senate passed Nov. 20. President signed Dec. 17, 2002.

PL 107-362 (HR 3048) Resolve the claims of Cook Inlet Region, Inc., to lands adjacent to the Russian River in Alaska. Introduced by YOUNG, R-Alaska, on Oct. 4, 2001. House Resources reported, amended, July 15, 2002 (H Rept 107-573). House passed, under suspension of the rules, July 22. Senate Energy and Natural Resources reported Sept. 11 (S Rept 107-275). Senate passed Nov. 20. President signed Dec. 19, 2002.

PL 107-363 (HR 3747) Direct the secretary of the Interior to conduct a study of the site commonly known as Eagledale Ferry Dock at Taylor Avenue in Washington for potential inclusion in the National Park System. Introduced by INSLEE, D-Wash., on Feb. 13, 2002. House Resources reported Sept. 25 (H Rept 107-690). House passed Nov. 15. Senate passed Nov. 20. President signed Dec. 19, 2002.

PL 107-364 (HR 3909) Designate certain federal lands in Utah as the Gunn McKay Nature Preserve. Introduced by HANSEN, R-Utah, on March 7, 2002. House Resources reported April 9 (H Rept 107-392). House passed, under suspension of the rules, April 30. Senate Energy and Natural Resources reported Oct. 8 (no written report). Senate passed Nov. 20. President signed Dec. 19, 2002.

PL 107-365 (HR 3954) Designate certain waterways in the Caribbean National Forest in the Commonwealth of Puerto Rico as components of the National Wild and Scenic Rivers System. Introduced by ACEVEDO-VILÁ, D-P.R., on March 13, 2002. House Resources reported, amended, May 7 (H Rept 107-441). House passed, under suspension of the rules, May 7. Senate Energy and Natural Resources reported Oct. 8 (no written report). Senate passed Nov. 20. President signed Dec. 19, 2002.

PL 107-366 (HR 4129) Amend the Central Utah Project Completion Act to clarify the responsibilities of the secretary of the Interior with respect to the Central Utah Project, to redirect unexpended budget authority for wastewater treatment and reuse, to provide for prepayment of repayment contracts for municipal and industrial water delivery facilities and to eliminate a deadline for such prepayment. Introduced by CANNON, R-Utah, on April 10, 2002. House Resources reported, amended, July 8 (H Rept 107-554). House passed, amended, under suspension of the rules, Oct. 1. Senate passed Nov. 20. President signed Dec. 19, 2002.

PL 107-367 (HR 4638) Reauthorize the Mni Wiconi Rural Water Supply Project in South Dakota. Introduced by THUNE, R-S.D., on May 1, 2002. House Resources reported Sept. 4 (H Rept 107-633). House passed, under suspension of the rules, Sept. 24. Senate passed Nov. 20. President signed Dec. 19, 2002.

PL 107-368 (HR 4664) Authorize appropriations for fiscal years 2003 through 2007 for the National Science Foundation. Introduced by SMITH, R-Mich., on May 7, 2002. House Science reported, amended, June 4 (H Rept 107-488). House passed, amended, June 5. Senate Health, Labor and Pensions discharged. Senate passed, with amendments, Nov 14. House agreed to Senate amendments Nov. 15. President signed Dec. 19, 2002.

PL 107-369 (HR 4682) Revise the boundary of the Allegheny Portage Railroad National Historic Site. Introduced by MURTHA, D-Pa., on May 8, 2002. House Resources reported Sept. 4 (H Rept 107-634). House passed, amended, under suspension of the rules, Sept. 24. Senate Energy and Natural Resources reported Oct. 8 (no written report). Senate passed Nov. 20. President signed Dec. 19, 2002.

PL 107-370 (HR 4750) Designate certain lands in California as components of the National Wilderness Preservation System. Introduced by FARR, D-Calif., on May 16,

2002. House Resources discharged. House passed Nov. 15. Senate passed Nov. 20. President signed Dec. 19, 2002.

PL 107-371 (HR 4874) Direct the secretary of the Interior to disclaim any federal interest in lands adjacent to Spirit Lake and Twin Lakes in Idaho resulting from possible omission of lands from an 1880 survey. Introduced by OTTER, R-Idaho, on June 5, 2002. House Resources reported Sept. 24 (H Rept 107-676). House passed, under suspension of the rules, Oct. 1. Senate passed Nov. 20. President signed Dec. 19, 2002.

PL 107-372 (HR 4883) Reauthorize the Hydrographic Services Improvement Act of 1998. Introduced by YOUNG, R-Alaska, on June 6, 2002. House Resources reported, amended, July 26 (H Rept 107-621). House passed, amended, Nov. 15. Senate passed Nov. 20. President signed Dec. 19, 2002.

PL 107-373 (HR 4944) Designate the Cedar Creek and Belle Grove National Historical Park in Virginia as a unit of the National Park System. Introduced by WOLF, R-Va., on June 13, 2002. House Resources reported, amended, Oct. 1 (H Rept 107-713). House passed, amended, under suspension of the rules, Oct. 1. Senate passed Nov. 20. President signed Dec. 19, 2002.

PL 107-374 (HR 4953) Direct the secretary of the Interior to grant to the counties of Deschutes and Crook in Oregon a right-of-way to West Butte Road. Introduced by WALDEN, R-Ore., on June 17, 2002. House Resources reported, amended, Sept. 4 (H Rept 107-637). House passed, amended, under suspension of the rules, Sept. 24. Senate passed Nov. 20. President signed Dec. 19, 2002.

PL 107-375 (HR 5099) Extend the periods of authorization for the secretary of the Interior to implement capital construction projects associated with the endangered fish recovery implementation programs for the Upper Colorado and San Juan River Basins. Introduced by HANSEN, R-Utah, on July 11, 2002. House Resources reported Sept. 24 (H Rept 107-672). House passed, under suspension of the rules, Sept. 24. Senate Energy and Natural Resources reported Oct. 8 (no written report). Senate passed Nov. 20. President signed Dec. 19, 2002.

PL 107-376 (HR 5436) Extend the deadline for commencement of construction of a hydroelectric project in Oregon. Introduced by DeFAZIO, D-Ore., on Sept. 24, 2002. House Energy and Commerce discharged. House passed Nov. 15. Senate passed Nov. 20. President signed Dec. 19, 2002.

PL 107-377 (HR 5472) Extend for six months the period for which Chapter 12 of Title 11, U.S. Code providing bankruptcy relief for family farmers is re-enacted. Introduced by SENSENBRENNER, R-Wis., on Sept. 26, 2002. House passed, under suspension of the rules, Oct. 1. Senate passed Nov. 20. President signed Dec. 19, 2002. ◆

Appendix F

POLITICAL
REPORT

Senate, House, Gubernatorial Results

Following are the results from the 2002 elections, including votes cast on Nov. 5, the Nov. 30 special election in Hawaii, the Dec. 7 runoffs in Louisiana and the Jan. 4, 2003 special election in Hawaii. (The results in Hawaii's 2nd District have not been certified because one of the candidates is challenging the results.) The numbers represent the votes cast for and the percentage won by each candidate.

Symbols: ● Incumbent (Due to redistricting, there may be multiple incumbents listed for one district.)
X Winner without opposition
AL At-large district
\# 2002 newly elected member

ALABAMA

Governor
\# Bob Riley (R)	672,225	49.2
● Donald Siegelman (D)	669,105	49.0
John Peter Sophocleus (LIBERT)	23,272	1.7
write-ins	2,451	.2

Senate
● Jeff Sessions (R)	792,561	58.6
Susan Parker (D)	538,878	39.8
Jeff Allen (LIBERT)	20,234	1.5
write-ins	1,350	.1

House
1	\# Jo Bonner (R)	108,102	60.5
	Judy McCain Belk (D)	67,507	37.8
	Richard M. "Dick" Coffee (LIBERT)	2,957	1.7
	write-ins	121	.1
2	● Terry Everett (R)	129,233	68.8
	Charles Woods (D)	55,495	29.5
	Floyd Shackelford (LIBERT)	2,948	1.6
	write-ins	289	.1
3	\# Mike D. Rogers (R)	91,169	50.3
	Joe Turnham (D)	87,351	48.2
	George Crispin (LIBERT)	2,565	1.4
	write-ins	138	.1
4	● Robert B. Aderholt (R)	139,705	86.7
	Tony Hughes McLendon (LIBERT)	20,858	13.0
	write-ins	538	.3
5	● Robert E. "Bud" Cramer (D)	143,029	73.3
	Stephen P. Engel (R)	48,226	24.7
	Alan Fulton Barksdale (LIBERT)	3,772	1.9
	write-ins	144	.1
6	● Spencer Bachus (R)	178,171	89.8
	J. Holden McAllister (LIBERT)	19,639	9.9
	write-ins	536	.3
7	\# Artur Davis (D)	153,735	92.4
	Lauren Orth McCay (LIBERT)	12,100	7.3
	write-ins	474	.3

ALASKA

Governor
Frank H. Murkowski (R)	129,279	55.9
Fran Ulmer (D)	94,216	40.7
Dian E. Benson (GREEN)	2,926	1.3
Don Wright (AKI)	2,185	.9
Raymond Vinzant Sr. (MOD)	1,506	.7
Billy Toien (LIBERT)	1,109	.5
write-ins	263	.1

Senate
● Ted Stevens (R)	179,438	78.2
Frank Vondersaar (D)	24,133	10.5
Jim Sykes (GREEN)	16,608	7.2
Jim Dore (AKI)	6,724	2.9
Leonard J. "Len" Karpinski (LIBERT)	2,354	1.0
write-ins	291	.1

House
AL	● Don Young (R)	169,685	74.5
	Clifford Mark Greene (D)	39,357	17.3
	Russell deForest (GREEN)	14,435	6.3
	Rob Clift (LIBERT)	3,797	1.7
	write-ins	451	.2

ARIZONA

Governor
\# Janet Napolitano (D)	566,284	46.2
Matt Salmon (R)	554,465	45.2
Richard Mahoney (I)	84,947	6.9
Barry Hess (LIBERT)	20,356	1.7
write-ins	59	—

House
1	\# Rick Renzi (R)	85,967	49.2
	George Cordova (D)	79,730	45.6
	Edwin Porr (LIBERT)	8,990	5.2
2	\# Trent Franks (R)	100,359	59.9
	Randy Camacho (D)	61,217	36.6
	Edward R. Carlson (LIBERT)	5,919	3.5
	write-ins	7	—
3	● John Shadegg (R)	104,847	67.3
	Charles Hill (D)	47,173	30.3
	Mark J. Yannone (LIBERT)	3,731	2.4
4	● Ed Pastor (D)	44,517	67.4
	Jonathan Barnert (R)	18,381	27.8
	Amy Gibbons (LIBERT)	3,167	4.8
5	● J.D. Hayworth (R)	103,870	61.2
	Craig Columbus (D)	61,559	36.3
	Warren Severin (LIBERT)	4,383	2.6
6	● Jeff Flake (R)	103,094	65.9
	Deborah Thomas (D)	49,355	31.6
	Andy Wagner (LIBERT)	3,888	2.5
7	\# Raul M. Grijalva (D)	61,256	59.0
	Ross Hieb (R)	38,474	37.1
	John L. Nemeth (LIBERT)	4,088	3.9
8	● Jim Kolbe (R)	126,930	63.3
	Mary Judge Ryan (D)	67,328	33.6
	Joe Duarte (LIBERT)	6,142	3.1
	write-ins	28	—

ARKANSAS

Governor
● Mike Huckabee (R)	427,189	53.0
Jimmie Lou Fisher (D)	378,303	46.9
Gene Mason — write-in	160	—
Barry Emigh — write-in	154	—
Oscar Stilley — write-in	35	—
Elvis M. Nash — write-in	15	—

Senate
\# Mark Pryor (D)	433,386	53.9
● Tim Hutchinson (R)	370,735	46.1

House
1	● Marion Berry (D)	129,701	66.8
	Tommy F. Robinson (R)	64,357	33.2
2	● Vic Snyder (D)	142,752	92.9
	Ed Garner — write-in	10,874	7.1
3	● John Boozman (R)	141,478	98.9
	George N. Lyne — write-in	1,577	1.1
4	● Mike Ross (D)	119,723	60.6
	Jay Dickey (R)	77,972	39.4

Abbreviations for Party Designations

AC	— American Constitution	GI	— Green Independent	LTI	— Lower Tax Independent	PRO	— Progressive
AKI	— Alaskan Independence	HHD	— Honesty, Humanity, Duty	MML	— Make Marijuana Legal	R	— Republican
AF	— America First	HP	— Homeland Protection	MOD	— Republican Moderate	REF	— Reform
AMI	— American Independent	HUM	— Human Rights	MRF	— Marijuana Reform	RJF	— Restore Justice Freedom
C	— Conservative	I	— Independent	NEB	— Nebraska	RTL	— Right to Life
CC	— Concerned Citizens	IA	— Independent American	NJC	— New Jersey Conservative	S	— Socialist
CNSTP	— Constitution	ICM	— Independent Citizens	NL	— Natural Law	SW	— Socialist Workers
COPP	— Concerns of People		Movement	NNT	— No New Taxes	UC	— United Citizens
D	— Democratic	INDC	— Independence	NON	— Non-Partisan	USTAX	— U.S. Taxpayers
FE	— Free Energy	L	— Liberal	OE	— One Earth	VG	— Vermont Grassroots
GR	— Grassroots	LIBERT	— Libertarian	PAC	— Politicians Are Crooks	WFM	— Working Families
GREEN	— Green	LU	— Liberty Union	PLC	— Pro-Life Conservative	WG	— Wisconsin Greens

CALIFORNIA

Governor

● Gray Davis (D)	3,533,490	47.3
Bill Simon (R)	3,169,801	42.4
Peter Miguel Camejo (GR)	393,036	5.3
Gary D. Copeland (LIBERT)	161,203	2.2
Reinhold Gulke (AMI)	128,035	1.7
Iris Adam (NL)	88,415	1.2
Anselmo A. Chavez	37	—
Will B. King	13	—

House

1 ● Mike Thompson (D)	118,669	64.1
Lawrence Wiesner (R)	60,013	32.4
Kevin Bastian (LIBERT)	6,534	3.5
2 ● Wally Herger (R)	117,747	65.8
Mike Johnson (D)	52,455	29.3
Patrice Thiessen (NL)	4,860	2.7
Charles Martin (LIBERT)	3,923	2.2
3 ● Doug Ose (R)	121,732	62.5
Howard Beeman (D)	67,136	34.4
Douglas Tuma (LIBERT)	6,050	3.1
4 ● John T. Doolittle (R)	147,997	64.8
Mark Norberg (D)	72,860	31.9
Allen M. Roberts (LIBERT)	7,247	3.2
Bill Kirby	401	.2
Philip James Parisius	1	—
5 ● Robert T. Matsui (D)	92,726	70.5
Richard Frankhuizen (R)	34,749	26.4
Timothy E. Roloff (LIBERT)	4,103	3.1
6 ● Lynn Woolsey (D)	139,750	66.7
Paul L. Erickson (R)	62,052	29.6
Richard Barton (LIBERT)	4,936	2.4
Jeff Rainforth (REF)	2,825	1.4
7 ● George Miller (D)	97,849	70.7
Charles R. Hargrave (R)	36,584	26.4
Scott A. Wilson (LIBERT)	3,943	2.9
8 ● Nancy Pelosi (D)	127,684	79.6
G. Michael German (R)	20,063	12.5
Jay Pond (GREEN)	10,033	6.3
Ira Spivack (LIBERT)	2,659	1.7
Deborah Liatos	2	—
9 ● Barbara Lee (D)	135,893	81.4
Jerald Udinsky (R)	25,333	15.2
James M. Eyer (LIBERT)	5,685	3.4
Hector Reyna	6	—
10 ● Ellen O. Tauscher (D)	126,390	75.6
Sonia E. Alonso Harden (LIBERT)	40,807	24.4
11 ● Richard W. Pombo (R)	104,921	60.3
Elaine Dugger Shaw (D)	69,035	39.7
12 ● Tom Lantos (D)	105,597	68.1
Michael Moloney (R)	38,381	24.8
Maad Abu-Ghazalah (LIBERT)	11,006	7.1
13 ● Pete Stark (D)	86,495	71.1
Syed R. Mahmood (R)	26,852	22.1
Mark W. Stroberg (LIBERT)	3,703	3.0
Don Grundmann (AMI)	2,772	2.3
John J. Bambey (REF)	1,901	1.6
14 ● Anna G. Eshoo (D)	117,055	68.2
Joseph H. Nixon (R)	48,346	28.2
Andrew B. Carver (LIBERT)	6,277	3.7
15 ● Michael M. Honda (D)	87,482	65.8
Linda Rae Hermann (R)	41,251	31.0
Jeff Landauer (LIBERT)	4,289	3.2
16 ● Zoe Lofgren (D)	72,370	67.0
Douglas Adams McNea (R)	32,182	29.8
Dennis Michael Umphress (LIBERT)	3,434	3.2
17 ● Sam Farr (D)	101,632	68.1
Clint Engler (R)	40,334	27.0
Ray Glock-Grueneich (GREEN)	4,885	3.3
Jascha Lee (LIBERT)	2,418	1.6
Alan Shugart	27	—
18 # Dennis Cardoza (D)	56,181	51.3
Dick Monteith (R)	47,528	43.4
Kevin H. Cripe (AMI)	3,641	3.3
Linda M. DeGroat (LIBERT)	2,194	2.0
Donna Crowder	49	—
19 ● George P. Radanovich (R)	106,209	67.3
John Veen (D)	47,403	30.0
Patrick Lee McHargue (LIBERT)	4,190	2.7
20 ● Cal Dooley (D)	47,627	63.7
Andre Minuth (R)	25,628	34.3
Varrin Swearingen (LIBERT)	1,515	2.0
21 # Devin Nunes (R)	87,544	70.5
David G. LaPere (D)	32,584	26.2
Jonathan Richter (LIBERT)	4,070	3.3
22 ● Bill Thomas (R)	120,473	73.3
Jaime A. Corvera (D)	38,988	23.7
Frank Coates (LIBERT)	4,824	2.9
23 ● Lois Capps (D)	95,752	59.0
Beth Rogers (R)	62,604	38.6
James E. Hill (LIBERT)	3,866	2.4
24 ● Elton Gallegly (R)	120,585	65.2
Fern Rudin (D)	58,755	31.8
Gary Harber (LIBERT)	5,666	3.1
25 ● Howard P. "Buck" McKeon (R)	80,775	65.0
Robert "Bob" Conaway (D)	38,674	31.1
Frank M. Consolo Jr. (LIBERT)	4,887	3.9
26 ● David Dreier (R)	95,360	63.8
Marjorie Musser Mikels (D)	50,081	33.5
Randall Weissbuch (LIBERT)	4,089	2.7
27 ● Brad Sherman (D)	79,815	62.0
Robert M. Levy (R)	48,996	38.0
28 ● Howard L. Berman (D)	73,771	71.4
David R. Hernandez Jr. (R)	23,926	23.2
Kelley L. Ross (LIBERT)	5,629	5.5
29 ● Adam B. Schiff (D)	76,036	62.6
Jim Scileppi (R)	40,616	33.4
Ted Brown (LIBERT)	4,889	4.0
30 ● Henry A. Waxman (D)	130,604	70.4
Tony Goss (R)	54,989	29.6
31 ● Xavier Becerra (D)	54,569	81.2
Luis Vega (R)	12,674	18.9
32 ● Hilda L. Solis (D)	58,530	68.8
Emma E. Fischbeck (R)	23,366	27.5
Michael McGuire (LIBERT)	3,183	3.7
33 ● Diane Watson (D)	97,779	82.5
Andrew Kim (R)	16,699	14.1
Charles Tate (LIBERT)	3,971	3.4
34 ● Lucille Roybal-Allard (D)	48,734	74.0
Wayne Miller (R)	17,090	26.0
35 ● Maxine Waters (D)	72,401	77.5
Ross Moen (R)	18,094	19.4
Gordon Michael Mego (AMI)	2,912	3.1
36 ● Jane Harman (D)	88,198	61.4
Stuart Johnson (R)	50,328	35.0
Mark McSpadden (LIBERT)	5,225	3.6
37 ● Juanita Millender-McDonald (D)	63,445	72.9
Oscar A. Velasco (R)	20,154	23.2
Herb Peters (LIBERT)	3,413	3.9
38 ● Grace F. Napolitano (D)	62,600	71.1
Alex A. Burrola (R)	23,126	26.3
Al Cuperus (LIBERT)	2,301	2.6
39 # Linda T. Sánchez (D)	52,256	54.8
Tim Escobar (R)	38,925	40.8
Richard G. Newhouse (LIBERT)	4,165	4.4
40 ● Ed Royce (R)	92,422	67.6
Christina Avalos (D)	40,265	29.5
Charles R. "Chuck" McGlawn (LIBERT)	3,955	2.9
41 ● Jerry Lewis (R)	91,326	67.4
Keith A. Johnson (D)	40,155	29.6
Kevin Craig (LIBERT)	4,052	3.0
42 ● Gary G. Miller (R)	98,476	67.8
Richard Waldron (D)	42,090	29.0
Donald Yee (LIBERT)	4,680	3.2
43 ● Joe Baca (D)	45,374	66.4
Wendy C. Neighbor (R)	20,821	30.5
Ethel M. Mohler (LIBERT)	2,145	3.1
44 ● Ken Calvert (R)	76,686	63.7
Louis Vandenberg (D)	38,021	31.6
Phill Courtney (GREEN)	5,756	4.8
45 ● Mary Bono (R)	87,101	65.2
Elle K. Kurpiewski (D)	43,692	32.7
Rod Miller-Boyer (LIBERT)	2,740	2.0
46 ● Dana Rohrabacher (R)	108,807	61.8
Gerrie Schipske (D)	60,890	34.6
Keith Gann (LIBERT)	6,488	3.7
47 ● Loretta Sanchez (D)	42,501	60.9
Jeff Chavez (R)	24,346	34.9
Paul Marsden (LIBERT)	2,944	4.2
48 ● Christopher Cox (R)	122,884	68.4
John L. Graham (D)	51,058	28.4
Joe Cobb (LIBERT)	5,607	3.1
49 ● Darrell Issa (R)	94,594	77.2
Karl W. Dietrich (LIBERT)	26,891	21.9
Michael P. Byron	1,012	.8
50 ● Randy "Duke" Cunningham (R)	111,095	64.3
Del G. Stewart (D)	55,855	32.3
Richard M. Fontanesi (LIBERT)	5,751	3.3
51 ● Bob Filner (D)	59,541	57.9
Maria Guadalupe Garcia (R)	40,430	39.3
Jeffrey S. Keup (LIBERT)	2,816	2.7
52 ● Duncan Hunter (R)	118,561	70.2
Peter Moore-Kochlacs (D)	43,526	25.8
Michael Benoit (LIBERT)	6,923	4.1
53 ● Susan A. Davis (D)	72,252	62.2
Bill VanDeWeghe (R)	43,891	37.8
Jim Dorenkott	37	—

COLORADO

Governor

● Bill Owens (R)	884,583	62.6
Rollie Heath (D)	475,372	33.6
Ron Forthofer (GREEN)	32,099	2.3
Ralph Shnelvar (LIBERT)	20,547	1.5

Senate

● Wayne Allard (R)	717,892	50.7
Tom Strickland (D)	648,129	45.8
Douglas "Dayhorse" Campbell (AC)	21,547	1.5
Rick Stanley (LIBERT)	20,776	1.5
John Heckman (COPP)	7,140	.5
Gary Cooper — write-in	609	—

House

1 ● Diana DeGette (D)	111,718	66.3
Ken Chlouber (R)	49,884	29.6
Ken Seaman (GREEN)	3,209	1.9
Kent Leonard (LIBERT)	2,584	1.5
George C. Lilly (AC)	1,169	.7
2 ● Mark Udall (D)	123,504	60.1
Sandy Hume (R)	75,564	36.8
Norm Olsen (LIBERT)	3,579	1.7
Patrick C. West (NL)	1,617	.8
Erik J. Brauer (AC)	1,258	.6
3 ● Scott McInnis (R)	143,431	65.8
Denis Berckefeldt (D)	68,110	31.3
J. Brent Shroyer (LIBERT)	4,370	2.0
Gary Swing (NL)	1,903	.9
Jason Alessio (SW)	116	—
4 # Marilyn Musgrave (R)	115,359	55.0
Stan Matsunaka (D)	87,499	41.7
John Volz (LIBERT)	7,097	3.4
5 ● Joel Hefley (R)	128,118	69.4
Curtis Imrie (D)	45,587	24.7
Biff Baker (LIBERT)	10,972	5.9

6 ● Tom Tancredo (R)	158,851	66.9
Lance Wright (D)	71,327	30.0
Adam D. Katz (LIBERT)	7,323	3.1
7 # Bob Beauprez (R)	81,789	47.3
Mike Feeley (D)	81,667	47.2
Dave Chandler (GREEN)	3,274	1.9
Victor A. Good (REF)	3,133	1.8
G. T. "Bud" Martin (LIBERT)	2,906	1.7
Stanford Andress — write-in	109	.1
Michael Reigle — write-in	0	—

CONNECTICUT

Governor

● John G. Rowland (R)	573,958	56.1
Bill Curry (D)	448,984	43.9

House

1 ● John B. Larson (D)	134,698	66.8
Phil Steele (R)	66,968	33.2
2 ● Rob Simmons (R)	117,434	54.1
Joseph D. Courtney (D)	99,674	45.9
3 ● Rosa DeLauro (D)	121,557	65.6
Richter Elser (R)	54,757	29.5
Charlie Pillsbury (GREEN)	9,050	4.9
4 ● Christopher Shays (R)	113,197	64.4
Stephanie Sanchez (D)	62,491	35.6
5 ● Nancy L. Johnson (R)	113,626	54.3
● Jim Maloney (D)	90,616	43.3
Joseph A. Zdonczyk (CC)	3,709	1.8
Walter J. Gengarelly (LIBERT)	1,503	.7

DELAWARE

Senate

● Joseph R. Biden Jr. (D)	135,253	58.2
Raymond J. Clatworthy (R)	94,793	40.8
Maurice Barros Bud (I)	996	.4
Raymond T. Buranello (LIBERT)	922	.4
Robert E. "Bob" Mattson (NL)	350	.1

House

AL ● Michael N. Castle (R)	164,605	72.1
Micheal C. Miller Sr. (D)	61,011	26.7
Brad C. Thomas (LIBERT)	2,789	1.2

FLORIDA

Governor

● Jeb Bush (R)	2,856,845	56.0
Bill McBride (D)	2,201,427	43.2
Robert "Bob" Kunst (I)	42,039	.8
John Wayne Smith — write-in	172	—
Nancy Grant — write-in	44	—
Rachele Fruit — write-in	24	—
Terry "Mickee Faust" Galloway — write-in	23	—
C. C. Reed — write-in	7	—

House

1 ● Jeff Miller (R)	152,635	74.6
Bert Oram (D)	51,972	25.4
Tom Wells — write-in	19	—
2 ● Allen Boyd (D)	152,164	66.9
Tom McGurk (R)	75,275	33.1
3 ● Corrine Brown (D)	88,462	59.3
Jennifer Carroll (R)	60,747	40.7
Jon Arnett — write-in	4	—
4 ● Ander Crenshaw (R)	171,152	99.7
Charles S. Knause — write-in	509	.3
5 # Ginny Brown-Waite (R)	121,998	47.9
● Karen L. Thurman (D)	117,758	46.2
Jack "Thro" Gargan (I)	8,639	3.4
Brian Moore (I)	6,223	2.4
Werder	53	—
6 ● Cliff Stearns (R)	141,570	65.4
David E. Bruderly (D)	75,046	34.6

Special Elections

Oklahoma (1)

John Sullivan won 54 percent of the vote Jan. 8 in the special election to succeed fellow Republican Steve Largent, who left in the middle of his fourth term to run for governor of Oklahoma. Largent's resignation took effect Feb. 15, so Sullivan did not take office until the week of Feb. 25, when the House returned from its Presidents' Day recess.

The special election was automatically advanced by five weeks after Cathy Keating, wife of the state's term-limited GOP governor, Frank Keating, withdrew from the scheduled primary runoff. In an upset, Sullivan had bested Keating by 15 percentage points in the initial five-way GOP primary Dec. 11, 2001.

Hawaii (2)

Democrat Ed Case came to Capitol Hill the week of Dec. 2 as representative-elect of Hawaii's 2nd District. But his unique status as the winner of a special election held after Congress had adjourned was underscored when police politely barred him from using members-and-staff-only tunnels under the Capitol.

Case had to endure 25-degree weather outside because he was not an official member. Congress made no provision to swear in the successor to the late Patsy T. Mink (1965-77, 1990-2002).

Case, a 50-year-old lawyer, former state legislator and a cousin of AOL-Time Warner Chairman Steve Case, won the 2nd District seat Nov. 30 in a special election to fill out the last month of Mink's unexpired term in the 107th Congress.

He became a full-fledged member when he won a second special election victory Jan. 4, 2003, to fill the same seat in the 108th Congress. Mink died Sept. 28, 2002, but was re-elected posthumously Nov. 5. Case won the single-ballot, "winner-take-all" contest over 43 other candidates with 43 percent of the vote. He was sworn in Jan. 7, 2003.

7 ● John L. Mica (R)	142,147	59.6
Wayne Hogan (D)	96,444	40.4
8 ● Ric Keller (R)	123,497	65.1
Eddie Diaz (D)	66,099	34.9
9 ● Michael Bilirakis (R)	169,369	71.5
Chuck Kalogianis (D)	67,623	28.5
Andrew Pasayan — write-in	16	—
10 ● C.W. Bill Young (R)	X	X
11 ● Jim Davis (D)	X	X
12 ● Adam H. Putnam (R)	X	X
13 # Katherine Harris (R)	139,048	54.8
Jan Schneider (D)	114,739	45.2
Wayne Genthner — write-in	22	—
14 ● Porter J. Goss (R)	X	X
15 ● Dave Weldon (R)	146,414	63.1
Jim Tso (D)	85,433	36.9
Donald Gibbens — write-in	10	—
16 ● Mark Foley (R)	176,171	78.9
Jack McLain (CNSTP)	47,169	21.1
17 # Kendrick B. Meek (D)	113,749	99.9
Michael Italie — write-in	73	.1
18 ● Ileana Ros-Lehtinen (R)	103,512	69.1
Ray Chote (D)	42,852	28.6
Orin Opperman (I)	3,423	2.3
19 ● Robert Wexler (D)	156,747	72.2
Jack Merkl (R)	60,477	27.8
20 ● Peter Deutsch (D)	X	X
21 ● Lincoln Diaz-Balart (R)	X	X

22 ● E. Clay Shaw Jr. (R)	131,930	60.8
Carol Roberts (D)	83,265	38.4
Juan Xuna (I)	1,902	.9
Stan Smilan — write-in	18	—
23 ● Alcee L. Hastings (D)	96,347	77.5
Charles Laurie (R)	27,986	22.5
write-ins	5	—
24 # Tom Feeney (R)	135,576	61.8
Harry Jacobs (D)	83,667	38.2
25 # Mario Diaz-Balart (R)	81,845	64.7
Annie Betancourt (D)	44,757	35.4

GEORGIA

Governor

# Sonny Perdue (R)	1,042,221	51.4
● Roy Barnes (D)	937,335	46.2
Garrett Michael Hayes (LIBERT)	47,968	2.4

Senate

# Saxby Chambliss (R)	1,071,352	52.7
● Max Cleland (D)	932,422	45.9
Claude "Sandy" Thomas (LIBERT)	27,830	1.4

House

1 ● Jack Kingston (R)	103,661	72.1
Don Smart (D)	40,026	27.9
2 ● Sanford D. Bishop Jr. (D)	102,925	100.0
3 # Jim Marshall (D)	75,394	50.5
Calder Clay (R)	73,866	49.5
4 # Denise L. Majette (D)	118,045	77.0
Cynthia Van Auken (R)	35,202	23.0

5	● John Lewis (D)	116,259	100.0
6	● Johnny Isakson (R)	163,525	79.9
	Jeff Weisberger (D)	41,204	20.1
7	● John Linder (R)	138,997	78.9
	Michael R. Berlon (D)	37,124	21.1
8	● Mac Collins (R)	142,505	78.3
	Angelos Petrakopoulos (D)	39,422	21.7
9	● Charlie Norwood (R)	123,313	72.8
	Barry Gordon Irwin (D)	45,974	27.2
10	● Nathan Deal (R)	129,242	100.0
11	# Phil Gingrey (R)	69,427	51.6
	Roger Kahn (D)	65,007	48.4
12	# Max Burns (R)	77,479	55.2
	Charles "Champ" Walker Jr. (D)	62,904	44.8
13	# David Scott (D)	70,011	59.6
	Clay Cox (R)	47,405	40.4

HAWAII

Governor

	# Linda Lingle (R)	197,009	51.6
	Mazie Hirono (D)	179,647	47.0
	Kau'I "Bu La'ia" Hill (NL)	2,561	.7
	Tracy Ahn Ryan (LIBERT)	1,364	.4
	Jim Brewer (NON)	1,147	.3
	Daniel H. Cunningham (FE)	382	.1

House

1	● Neil Abercrombie (D)	131,673	72.9
	Mark Terry (R)	45,032	24.9
	James H. Bracken (LIBERT)	4,028	2.2
2	● Patsy T. Mink (D)*	100,671	56.2
	Bob McDermott (R)	71,661	40.0

(Nov. 30 special election)

2	# Ed Case (D)	23,576	51.4
	John Mink (D)	16,624	36.3
	John S. Carroll (R)	1,933	4.2
	others	1,233	2.7
	Lloyd Jeffery Mallan (LIBERT)	4,719	2.6
	Whitney T. Anderson (R)	942	2.1
	Nicholas Bedworth (NL)	2,200	1.2
	Mark McNett (NON)	449	1.0
	Kekoa D. Kaapu (D)	269	.6
	Richard H. Haake (R)	229	.5
	Nelson J. Secretario (R)	208	.3
	Whitney T. Anderson (R)	201	.3
	Doug Fairhurst (R)	173	.4
	Kimo Kaloi (R)	149	.3

(Jan. 4, 2003 special election)

2	● Ed Case (D)	33,002	43.7
	Matt Matsunaga (D)	23,050	30.5
	Colleen Hanabusa (D)	6,046	8.0
	Barbara Marumoto (R)	4,497	6.0
	Bob McDermott (R)	4,298	5.7
	others	823	1.1
	Chris Halford (R)	728	1.0
	Kimo Kaloi (R)	642	.8
	John S. Carroll (R)	521	.7
	Frank F. Fasi (R)	483	.6
	Mark McNett (NON)	449	.6
	Jim Rath (R)	414	.6
	Richard H. Haake (R)	212	.3
	Nick Nikhilananda (GREEN)	136	.3
	Solomon Naluai (D)	116	.3

** Patsy T. Mink died Sept. 8, 2002, too late to remove her name from the Nov. 5 ballot.* (Special elections, p. F-5)

IDAHO

Governor

	● Dirk Kempthorne (R)	231,566	56.3
	Jerry M. Brady (D)	171,711	41.7
	Daniel L.J. Adams (LIBERT)	8,187	2.0
	write-ins	13	—

Senate

	● Larry E. Craig (R)	266,215	65.2
	Alan Blinken (D)	132,975	32.5
	Donovan Bramwell (LIBERT)	9,354	2.3

House

1	● C. L. "Butch" Otter (R)	120,743	58.6
	Betty Richardson (D)	80,269	38.9
	Steve Gothard (LIBERT)	5,129	2.5
2	● Mike Simpson (R)	135,605	68.2
	Edward W. Kinghorn (D)	57,769	29.1
	John H. "Jack" Lewis (LIBERT)	5,508	2.8

ILLINOIS

Governor

	# Rod R. Blagojevich (D)	1,847,040	52.2
	Jim Ryan (R)	1,594,960	45.1
	Cal Skinner (LIBERT)	73,794	2.1
	Marisellis Brown (I)	23,089	.7
	write-ins	8	—

Senate

	● Richard J. Durbin (D)	2,103,766	60.3
	Jim Durkin (R)	1,325,703	38.0
	Steven Burgauer (LIBERT)	57,382	1.7

House

1	● Bobby L. Rush (D)	149,068	81.2
	Raymond G. Wardingley (R)	29,776	16.2
	Dorothy G. Tsatsos (LIBERT)	4,812	2.6
2	● Jesse L. Jackson Jr. (D)	151,443	82.3
	Doug Nelson (R)	32,567	17.7
3	● William O. Lipinski (D)	156,042	100.0
4	● Luis V. Gutierrez (D)	67,339	79.7
	Anthony J. "Tony" Lopez-Cisneros (R)	12,778	15.1
	Marjorie Kohls (LIBERT)	4,396	5.2
5	# Rahm Emanuel (D)	106,514	66.8
	Mark A. Augusti (R)	46,008	28.9
	Frank Gonzalez (LIBERT)	6,913	4.3
6	● Henry J. Hyde (R)	113,174	65.1
	Tom Berry (D)	60,698	34.9
7	● Danny K. Davis (D)	137,933	83.2
	Mark Tunney (R)	25,280	15.3
	Martin Pankau (LIBERT)	2,543	1.5
8	● Philip M. Crane (R)	95,275	57.4
	Melissa L. Bean (D)	70,626	42.6
9	● Jan Schakowsky (D)	118,642	70.3
	Nicholas M. Duric (R)	45,307	26.8
	Stephanie "vs. the Machine" Sailor (LIBERT)	4,887	2.9
10	● Mark Steven Kirk (R)	128,611	68.8
	Henry H. "Hank" Perritt Jr. (D)	58,300	31.2
11	● Jerry Weller (R)	124,192	64.3
	Keith S. Van Duyne (D)	68,893	35.7
12	● Jerry F. Costello (D)	131,580	69.3
	David Sadler (R)	58,440	30.8
13	● Judy Biggert (R)	139,546	70.3
	Thomas Mason (D)	59,069	29.7
14	● J. Dennis Hastert (R)	135,198	74.1
	Laurence J. Quick (D)	47,165	25.9
15	● Timothy V. Johnson (R)	134,650	65.2
	Joshua T. Hartke (D)	64,131	31.0
	Carl Estabrook (GREEN)	7,836	3.8
16	● Donald Manzullo (R)	133,339	70.6
	John Kutsch (D)	55,488	29.4
17	● Lane Evans (D)	127,093	62.4
	Peter Calderone (R)	76,519	37.6
18	● Ray LaHood (R)	192,567	100.0
19	● John Shimkus (R)	133,956	54.8
	● David Phelps (D)	110,517	45.2

INDIANA

1	● Peter J. Visclosky (D)	90,443	66.9
	Mark J. Leyva (R)	41,909	31.0
	Timothy P. Brennan (LIBERT)	2,759	2.0
2	# Chris Chocola (R)	95,081	50.5
	Jill Long Thompson (D)	86,253	45.8
	Sharon Metheny (LIBERT)	7,112	3.8
	M. Myer Blatt — write-in	6	—
	James A. Mello — write-in	6	—
3	● Mark Souder (R)	92,566	63.1
	Jay Rigdon (D)	50,509	34.5
	Michael Donlan (LIBERT)	3,531	2.4
4	● Steve Buyer (R)	112,760	71.4
	Bill Abbott (D)	41,314	26.2
	Jerry L. Susong (LIBERT)	3,934	2.5
5	● Dan Burton (R)	129,442	72.0
	Katherine Fox Carr (D)	45,283	25.2
	Christopher Adkins (LIBERT)	5,130	2.9
6	● Mike Pence (R)	118,436	63.8
	Ann Melina Fox (D)	63,871	34.4
	Doris Robertson (LIBERT)	3,346	1.8
7	● Julia Carson (D)	77,478	53.1
	Brose McVey (R)	64,379	44.1
	Andrew Horning (LIBERT)	3,919	2.7
	James Kell "Jim" Jeffries — write-in	64	—
8	● John Hostettler (R)	98,952	51.3
	Bryan L. Hartke (D)	88,763	46.0
	Pam Williams (LIBERT)	5,150	2.7
9	● Baron P. Hill (D)	96,654	51.1
	Mike Sodrel (R)	87,169	46.1
	Jeff Melton (GREEN)	2,745	1.5
	Al Cox (LIBERT)	2,389	1.3

IOWA

Governor

	● Tom Vilsack (D)	540,449	52.7
	Doug Gross (R)	456,612	44.5
	Jay Robinson (GREEN)	14,628	1.4
	Clyde Cleveland (LIBERT)	13,098	1.3
	write-ins	1,015	.1

Senate

	● Tom Harkin (D)	554,278	54.2
	Greg Ganske (R)	447,892	43.8
	Timothy A. Harthan (GREEN)	11,340	1.1
	Richard J. Moore (LIBERT)	8,864	.9
	write-ins	701	.1

House

1	● Jim Nussle (R)	112,280	57.1
	Ann Hutchinson (D)	83,779	42.6
	write-ins	396	.2
2	● Jim Leach (R)	108,130	52.2
	Julie Thomas (D)	94,767	45.7
	Kevin Litten (LIBERT)	4,178	2.0
	write-ins	96	—
3	● Leonard L. Boswell (D)	115,367	53.4
	Sam Thompson (R)	97,285	45.0
	Jeffrey J. Smith (LIBERT)	2,689	1.3
	Edwin B. Fruit (SW)	569	.3
	write-ins	75	—
4	● Tom Latham (R)	115,430	54.8
	John Norris (D)	90,784	43.1
	Terry L. Wilson (LIBERT)	2,952	1.4
	Jim Hennager (EF)	1,544	.7
	write-ins	64	—
5	# Steve King (R)	113,257	62.1
	Paul Shomshor (D)	68,853	37.8
	write-ins	127	.1

KANSAS

Governor

	# Kathleen Sebelius (D)	441,858	52.9
	Tim Shallenburger (R)	376,830	45.1
	Ted Pettibone (REF)	8,907	1.1
	Ira Dennis "Dennis" Hawver (LIBERT)	8,097	1.0

Senate
- ● Pat Roberts (R) — 641,075 — 82.5
- Steven A. Rosile (LIBERT) — 70,725 — 9.1
- George Cook (REF) — 65,050 — 8.4

House
1
- ● Jerry Moran (R) — 189,976 — 91.1
- Jack W. Warner (LIBERT) — 18,585 — 8.9

2
- ● Jim Ryun (R) — 127,477 — 60.4
- Dan Lykins (D) — 79,160 — 37.5
- Arthur L. Clack (LIBERT) — 4,340 — 2.1

3
- ● Dennis Moore (D) — 110,095 — 50.2
- Adam Taff (R) — 102,882 — 46.9
- Dawn Bly (REF) — 5,046 — 2.3
- Douglas Martin (LIBERT) — 1,366 — .6

4
- ● Todd Tiahrt (R) — 115,691 — 60.6
- Carlos Nolla (D) — 70,656 — 37.0
- Maike Warren (LIBERT) — 4,616 — 2.4

KENTUCKY

Senate
- ● Mitch McConnell (R) — 731,679 — 64.7
- Lois Combs Weinberg (D) — 399,634 — 35.3

House
1
- ● Edward Whitfield (R) — 117,600 — 65.3
- Klint Alexander (D) — 62,617 — 34.8

2
- ● Ron Lewis (R) — 122,773 — 69.6
- David L. Williams (D) — 51,431 — 29.2
- Robert Guy Dyer (LIBERT) — 2,084 — 1.2

3
- ● Anne M. Northup (R) — 118,228 — 51.6
- Jack Conway (D) — 110,846 — 48.4

4
- ● Ken Lucas (D) — 87,776 — 51.1
- Geoff Davis (R) — 81,651 — 47.6
- John Grote (LIBERT) — 2,308 — 1.3

5
- ● Harold Rogers (R) — 137,986 — 78.3
- Sidney "Jane" Bailey-Bamer (D) — 38,254 — 21.7

6
- ● Ernie Fletcher (R) — 115,622 — 72.0
- Gatewood Galbraith (I) — 41,753 — 26.0
- Mark Gailey (LIBERT) — 3,313 — 2.1

LOUISIANA

Senate (Nov. 5 general)
- ● Mary L. Landrieu (D) — 573,347 — 46.0
- Suzanne Haik Terrell (R) — 339,506 — 27.2
- John Cooksey (R) — 171,752 — 13.8
- Tony Perkins (R) — 119,776 — 9.6
- Raymond Brown (D) — 23,553 — 1.9
- Patrick E. "Live Wire" Landry (R) — 10,442 — .8
- James Lemann (I) — 3,866 — .3
- Gary D. Robbins (I) — 2,423 — .2
- Ernest Edward Skillman Jr. (R) — 1,668 — .1

Senate (Dec. 7 runoff)
- ● Mary L. Landrieu (D) — 638,654 — 51.7
- Suzanne Haik Terrell (R) — 596,642 — 48.3

House
1
- ● David Vitter (R) — 147,117 — 81.5
- Monica L. Monica (R) — 20,268 — 11.2
- Robert "Bob" Namer (R) — 7,229 — 4.0
- Ian P. Hawkhurst (I) — 5,956 — 3.3

2
- ● William J. Jefferson (D) — 90,310 — 63.5
- Irma Muse Dixon (D) — 28,480 — 20.0
- Silky Sullivan (R) — 15,440 — 10.9
- Clarence "Buddy" Hunt (D) — 4,137 — 2.9
- Wayne E. Clement (I) — 3,789 — 2.7

3
- ● Billy Tauzin (R) — 130,323 — 86.7
- William Beier (I) — 12,964 — 8.6
- David Iwanico (I) — 7,055 — 4.7

4
- ● Jim McCrery (R) — 114,649 — 71.6
- John Milkovich (D) — 42,340 — 26.4
- Bill Jacobs (I) — 3,104 — 1.9

(Nov. 5 general)

5
- Rodney Alexander (D) — 52,952 — 28.7
- Lee Fletcher (R) — 45,278 — 24.5
- Clyde C. Holloway (R) — 42,573 — 23.1
- Robert J. Barham (R) — 34,533 — 18.7
- Sam Houston Melton Jr. (D) — 4,595 — 2.5
- Jack Wright (R) — 3,581 — 1.9
- Vinson Mouser (I) — 1,145 — .6

(Dec. 7 runoff)

5
- # Rodney Alexander (D) — 86,718 — 50.3
- Lee Fletcher (R) — 85,744 — 49.7

6
- ● Richard H. Baker (R) — 146,932 — 84.0
- Rick Moscatello (I) — 27,898 — 16.0

7
- ● Chris John (D) — 138,659 — 86.8
- Roberto Valletta (I) — 21,051 — 13.2

MAINE

Governor
- # John Baldacci (D) — 238,179 — 47.1
- Peter E. Cianchette (R) — 209,496 — 41.5
- Jonathan K. Carter (GI) — 46,903 — 9.3
- John M. Michael (I) — 10,612 — 2.1

Senate
- ● Susan Collins (R) — 295,041 — 58.4
- Chellie Pingree (D) — 209,858 — 41.6

House
1
- ● Tom Allen (D) — 172,646 — 63.8
- Steven Joyce (R) — 97,931 — 36.2

2
- # Michael H. Michaud (D) — 116,868 — 52.0
- Kevin L. Raye (R) — 107,849 — 48.0

MARYLAND

Governor
- # Robert L. Ehrlich Jr. (R) — 879,592 — 51.6
- Kathleen Kennedy Townsend (D) — 813,422 — 47.7
- Spear Lancaster (LIBERT) — 11,546 — .7
- write-ins — 1,357 — .1
- Ralph Jaffe (D) — 201 — —
- James T. Lynch Jr. (D) — 61 — —

House
1
- ● Wayne T. Gilchrest (R) — 192,004 — 76.7
- Ann D. Tamlyn (D) — 57,986 — 23.2
- write-ins — 423 — .2

2
- # C.A. Dutch Ruppersberger (D) — 105,718 — 54.2
- Helen Delich Bentley (R) — 88,954 — 45.6
- write-ins — 530 — .3

3
- ● Benjamin L. Cardin (D) — 145,589 — 65.7
- Scott Alan Conwell (R) — 75,721 — 34.2
- write-ins — 233 — .1

4
- ● Albert R. Wynn (D) — 131,644 — 78.6
- John B. Kimble (R) — 34,890 — 20.8
- write-ins — 826 — .5
- Mignon Bush Davis (D) — 162 — .1
- Floyd W. Anderson Jr. (R) — 33 — —

5
- ● Steny H. Hoyer (D) — 137,903 — 69.3
- Joseph T. Crawford (R) — 60,758 — 30.5
- write-ins — 240 — .1
- B. Auerbach (GREEN) — 186 — .1

6
- ● Roscoe G. Bartlett (R) — 147,825 — 66.1
- Donald M. DeArmon (D) — 75,575 — 33.8
- write-ins — 211 — .1

7
- ● Elijah E. Cummings (D) — 137,047 — 73.5
- Joseph E. Ward (R) — 49,172 — 26.4
- write-ins — 175 — .1

8
- # Chris Van Hollen (D) — 112,788 — 51.7
- ● Constance A. Morella (R) — 103,587 — 47.5
- Stephen Bassett (I) — 1,599 — .7
- write-ins — 139 — .1

MASSACHUSETTS

Governor
- # Mitt Romney (R) — 1,091,988 — 49.8
- Shannon P. O'Brien (D) — 985,981 — 44.9
- Jill Stein (GREEN) — 76,530 — 3.5
- Carla Howell (LIBERT) — 23,044 — 1.1
- Barbara C. Johnson (I) — 15,335 — .7
- write-ins — 1,301 — .1

Senate
- ● John Kerry (D) — 1,605,976 — 80.0
- Michael E. Cloud (LIBERT) — 369,807 — 18.4
- Randall Forsberg — 24,898 — 1.2
- write-ins — 6,077 — .3

House
1
- ● John W. Olver (D) — 137,841 — 67.6
- Matthew W. Kinnaman (R) — 66,061 — 32.4
- write-ins — 117 — .1

2
- ● Richard E. Neal (D) — 153,387 — 99.1
- write-ins — 1,341 — .9

3
- ● Jim McGovern (D) — 155,697 — 98.8
- write-ins — 1,848 — 1.2

4
- ● Barney Frank (D) — 166,125 — 99.0
- write-ins — 1,691 — 1.0

5
- ● Martin T. Meehan (D) — 122,562 — 60.1
- Charles McCarthy (R) — 69,337 — 34.0
- Ilana Freedman (LIBERT) — 11,729 — 5.8
- write-ins — 149 — .1

6
- ● John F. Tierney (D) — 162,900 — 68.3
- Mark C. Smith (R) — 75,462 — 31.6
- write-ins — 253 — .1

7
- ● Edward J. Markey (D) — 170,968 — 98.2
- write-ins — 2,206 — 1.3
- Daniel Melnechuk — 863 — .5

8
- ● Michael E. Capuano (D) — 111,861 — 99.6
- write-ins — 495 — .4

9
- ● Stephen F. Lynch (D) — 168,055 — 99.5
- write-ins — 921 — .6

10
- ● Bill Delahunt (D) — 179,238 — 69.2
- Luiz Gonzaga (R) — 79,624 — 30.7
- write-ins — 140 — —

MICHIGAN

Governor
- # Jennifer M. Granholm (D) — 1,633,796 — 51.4
- Dick Posthumus (R) — 1,506,104 — 47.4
- Douglas Campbell (GREEN) — 25,236 — .8
- Joseph M. Pilchak (USTAX) — 12,411 — .4
- write-ins — 18 — —

Senate
- ● Carl Levin (D) — 1,896,614 — 60.6
- Andrew Raczkowski (R) — 1,185,545 — 37.9
- Eric Borregard (GREEN) — 23,931 — .8
- John Mangopoulos (REF) — 12,831 — .4
- Doug Dern (NL) — 10,366 — .3

House
1
- ● Bart Stupak (D) — 150,701 — 67.7
- Don Hooper (R) — 69,254 — 31.1
- John W. Loosemore (LIBERT) — 2,732 — 1.2

2
- ● Peter Hoekstra (R) — 156,937 — 70.4
- Jeffrey A. Wrisley (D) — 61,749 — 27.7
- Laurie L. Aleck (LIBERT) — 2,680 — 1.2
- Ronald E. Graeser (USTAX) — 1,541 — .7

3
- ● Vernon J. Ehlers (R) — 153,131 — 70.0
- Kathryn D. Lynnes (D) — 61,987 — 28.3
- Tom Quinn (LIBERT) — 2,613 — 1.2
- Richard F. Lucey (REF) — 1,124 — .5

4
- ● Dave Camp (R) — 149,090 — 68.2
- Lawrence D. Hollenbeck (D) — 65,950 — 30.2
- Sterling Johnson (GREEN) — 2,261 — 1.0
- Al Chia Jr. (LIBERT) — 1,272 — .6

5
- ● Dale E. Kildee (D) — 158,709 — 91.6
- Clint Foster (LIBERT) — 9,344 — 5.4
- Harley Mikkelson (GREEN) — 5,188 — 3.0
- write-ins — 98 — .1

District/Office	Candidate	Votes	%
6 ●	Fred Upton (R)	126,936	69.2
	Gary C. Giguere Jr. (D)	53,793	29.3
	Richard M. Overton (REF)	2,788	1.5
7 ●	Nick Smith (R)	121,142	59.7
	Mike Simpson (D)	78,412	38.6
	Kenneth L. Proctor (LIBERT)	3,515	1.7
8 ●	Mike Rogers (R)	156,525	67.9
	Frank McAlpine (D)	70,920	30.8
	Thomas Yeutter (LIBERT)	3,152	1.4
9 ●	Joe Knollenberg (R)	141,102	58.1
	David Fink (D)	96,856	39.9
	Robert Schubring (LIBERT)	4,922	2.0
10 #	Candice S. Miller (R)	137,339	63.3
	Carl J. Marlinga (D)	77,053	35.5
	Renae Coon (LIBERT)	2,536	1.2
11 #	Thaddeus McCotter (R)	126,050	57.2
	Kevin Kelley (D)	87,402	39.7
	William Boyd (GREEN)	4,243	1.9
	Daniel E. Malone (USTAX)	2,710	1.2
12 ●	Sander M. Levin (D)	140,970	68.3
	Harvey R. Dean (R)	61,502	29.8
	Dick Gach (LIBERT)	2,694	1.3
	Steven T. Revis (USTAX)	1,362	.7
13 ●	Carolyn Cheeks Kilpatrick (D)	120,869	91.6
	Raymond H. Warner (LIBERT)	11,072	8.4
14 ●	John Conyers Jr. (D)	145,285	83.2
	Dave Stone (R)	26,544	15.2
	Francis J. Schorr (LIBERT)	1,532	.9
	John D. Litle (GREEN)	1,247	.7
15 ●	John D. Dingell (D)	136,518	72.2
	Martin Kaltenbach (R)	48,626	25.7
	Gregory Stempfle (LIBERT)	3,919	2.1

MINNESOTA

Governor

Candidate	Votes	%
# Tim Pawlenty (R)	999,473	44.4
Roger Moe (D)	821,268	36.5
Timothy J. Penny (INDC)	364,534	16.2
Ken Pentel (GREEN)	50,589	2.3
Booker T. Hodges IV (I)	9,698	.4
Kari J. Sachs (SW)	3,026	.1
Lawrence Michael Aeshliman (CNSTP)	2,537	.1
write-ins	1,340	.1
Richard A. Klatte — write-in	4	—
Bill Dahn — write-in	2	—
Lealand Vettleson — write-in	2	—

Senate

Candidate	Votes	%
# Norm Coleman (R)	1,116,697	49.5
Walter F. Mondale (D)	1,067,246	47.3
Jim Moore (INDC)	45,139	2.0
Paul Wellstone	11,381	.5
Ray Tricomo (GREEN)	10,119	.5
Miro Drago Kovatchevich (CNSTP)	2,254	.1
write-ins	1,803	.1

House

District	Candidate	Votes	%
1 ●	Gil Gutknecht (R)	163,570	61.5
	Steve Andreasen (D)	92,165	34.6
	Greg Mikkelson (GREEN)	9,964	3.8
	write-ins	283	.1
2 #	John Kline (R)	152,970	53.3
●	Bill Luther (D)	121,121	42.2
	Samuel D. Garst (NNT)	12,430	4.3
	write-ins	339	.1
3 ●	Jim Ramstad (R)	213,334	72.0
	Darryl Tyree Stanton (D)	82,575	27.9
	write-ins	309	.1
4 ●	Betty McCollum (D)	164,597	62.2
	Clyde Billington (R)	89,705	33.9
	Scott J. Raskiewicz (GREEN)	9,919	3.8
	write-ins	319	.1
5 ●	Martin Olav Sabo (D)	171,572	67.0
	Daniel Nielsen Mathias (R)	66,271	25.9
	Tim Davis (GR)	17,825	7.0
	write-ins	314	.1
6 ●	Mark Kennedy (R)	164,747	57.3
	Janet Robert (D)	100,738	35.1
	Dan Becker (INDC)	21,484	7.5
	write-ins	343	.1
7 ●	Collin C. Peterson (D)	170,234	65.3
	Dan Stevens (R)	90,342	34.6
	write-ins	237	.1
8 ●	James L. Oberstar (D)	194,909	68.7
	Robert Lemen (R)	88,673	31.2
	write-ins	349	.1

MISSISSIPPI

Senate

Candidate	Votes	%
● Thad Cochran (R)	533,269	84.6
Shawn O'Hara (REF)	97,226	15.4

House

District	Candidate	Votes	%
1 ●	Roger Wicker (R)	95,404	71.4
	Rex N. Weathers (D)	32,318	24.2
	Brenda Blackburn (REF)	3,477	2.6
	Harold M. Taylor (LIBERT)	2,368	1.8
2 ●	Bennie Thompson (D)	89,913	55.1
	Clinton B. LeSueur (R)	69,711	42.8
	Lee F. Dilworth (REF)	3,426	2.1
3 ●	Charles W. "Chip") Pickering Jr. (R)	139,329	63.6
●	Ronnie Shows (D)	76,184	34.8
	Jim Giles (I)	1,431	.7
	Harvey Darden (I)	949	.4
	Brad A. McDonald (LIBERT)	760	.4
	Carroll Grantham (REF)	498	.2
4 ●	Gene Taylor (D)	121,742	75.2
	Karl Mertz (R)	34,373	21.2
	Wayne Parker (LIBERT)	3,311	2.0
	Thomas R. Huffmaster (REF)	2,442	1.5

MISSOURI

Senate

Candidate	Votes	%
# Jim Talent (R)	935,032	49.8
● Jean Carnahan (D)	913,778	48.7
Tamara A. Millay (LIBERT)	18,345	1.0
Daniel "Digger" Romano (GREEN)	10,465	.6

House

District	Candidate	Votes	%
1 ●	William Lacy Clay (D)	133,946	70.1
	Richard Schwadron (R)	51,755	27.1
	James "Jim" Higgins (LIBERT)	5,354	2.8
2 ●	Todd Akin (R)	167,057	67.1
	John Hogan (D)	77,223	31.0
	Darla R. Maloney (LIBERT)	4,548	1.8
3 ●	Richard A. Gephardt (D)	122,181	59.1
	Catherine S. Enz (R)	80,551	38.9
	Daniel "Dan" Byington (LIBERT)	4,146	2.0
4 ●	Ike Skelton (D)	142,204	67.6
	James A. Noland Jr. (R)	64,451	30.7
	Daniel Roy Nelson (LIBERT)	3,583	1.7
5 ●	Karen McCarthy (D)	122,645	65.9
	Steve Gordon (R)	60,245	32.4
	Jeanne F. Bojarski (LIBERT)	3,277	1.8
6 ●	Sam Graves (R)	131,151	63.0
	Cathy Rinehart (D)	73,202	35.2
	Erik Buck (LIBERT)	3,735	1.8
7 ●	Roy Blunt (R)	149,519	74.8
	Ron Lapham (D)	45,964	23.0
	Doug Burlison (LIBERT)	4,378	2.2
	Steven L. Reed (D)	2	—
8 ●	Jo Ann Emerson (R)	135,144	71.8
	Gene Curtis (D)	50,686	26.9
	Eric Van Oostrom (LIBERT)	2,491	1.3
9 ●	Kenny Hulshof (R)	146,032	68.2
	Donald M. "Don" Deichman (D)	61,126	28.6
	Keith Brekhus (GREEN)	4,262	2.0
	John Mruzik (LIBERT)	2,705	1.3

MONTANA

Senate

Candidate	Votes	%
● Max Baucus (D)	204,853	62.7
Mike Taylor (R)	103,611	31.7
Stan Jones (LIBERT)	10,420	3.2
Bob Kelleher (GR)	7,653	2.3

House

District	Candidate	Votes	%
AL ●	Denny Rehberg (R)	214,100	64.6
	Steve Kelly (D)	108,233	32.7
	Mike Fellows (LIBERT)	8,988	2.7

NEBRASKA

Governor

Candidate	Votes	%
● Mike Johanns (R)	330,349	68.7
Stormy Dean (D)	132,348	27.5
Paul A. Rosberg (NEB)	18,294	3.8

Senate

Candidate	Votes	%
● Chuck Hagel (R)	397,438	82.8
Charlie A. Matulka (D)	70,290	14.6
John J. Graziano (LIBERT)	7,423	1.6
Phil Chase (I)	5,066	1.

House

District	Candidate	Votes	%
1 ●	Doug Bereuter (R)	133,013	85.4
	Robert Eckerson (LIBERT)	22,831	14.7
2 ●	Lee Terry (R)	89,917	63.3
	Jim Simon (D)	46,843	33.0
	Doug Paterson (GREEN)	3,236	2.3
	Dave Stock (LIBERT)	2,018	1.4
3 ●	Tom Osborne (R)	163,939	93.2
	Jerry Hickman (LIBERT)	12,017	6.8

NEVADA

Governor

Candidate	Votes	%
● Kenny Guinn (R)	344,001	68.2
Joe Neal (D)	110,935	22.0
None of these candidates	23,674	4.7
Dick Geyer (LIBERT)	8,104	1.6
David G. Holmgren (IA)	7,047	1.4
Jerry L. Norton (I)	5,543	1.1
A. Charles Laws (GREEN)	4,775	1.0

House

District	Candidate	Votes	%
1 ●	Shelley Berkley (D)	64,312	53.7
	Lynette Maria Boggs-McDonald (R)	51,148	42.7
	Steven "Capt. Truth" Dempsey (I)	2,861	2.4
	W. Lane Startin (GR)	1,393	1.2
2 ●	Jim Gibbons (R)	149,574	74.3
	Travis O. Souza (D)	40,189	20.0
	Janine Hansen (IA)	7,240	3.6
	Brendan Trainor (LIBERT)	3,413	1.7
	Robert Winquist (NL)	784	.4
3 #	Jon Porter (R)	100,378	56.1
	Dario Herrera (D)	66,659	37.2
	Pete O'Neil (I)	6,842	3.8
	Neil Scott (LIBERT)	3,421	1.9
	Richard Wayne Odell (IA)	1,694	1.0

NEW HAMPSHIRE

Governor

Candidate	Votes	%
# Craig Benson (R)	259,663	58.6
Mark Fernald (D)	169,277	38.2
John Babiarz (LIBERT)	13,028	2.9
write-ins	1,008	.2

Senate

	Votes	%
# John E. Sununu (R)	227,229	50.8
Jeanne Shaheen (D)	207,478	46.4
Clarence G. Blevens (LIBERT)	9,835	2.2
Robert C. Smith (R)	2,396	.5
write-ins	197	—

House

	Votes	%
1 # Jeb Bradley (R)	128,993	58.1
Martha Fuller Clark (D)	85,426	38.5
Dan Belforti (LIBERT)	7,387	3.3
write-ins	181	.1
2 ● Charles Bass (R)	125,804	56.8
Katrina Swett (D)	90,479	40.9
John Babiarz (LIBERT)	5,051	2.3
write-ins	122	.1

NEW JERSEY

Senate

	Votes	%
# Frank R. Lautenberg (D)	1,138,193	53.9
Doug Forrester (R)	928,439	44.0
Ted Glick (GREEN)	24,308	1.2
Elizabeth Macron (LIBERT)	12,558	.6
Norman E. Wahner (NJC)	6,404	.3
Gregory Pason (S)	2,702	.1

House

	Votes	%
1 ● Robert E. Andrews (D)	121,846	92.7
Timothy Haas (LIBERT)	9,543	7.3
2 ● Frank A. LoBiondo (R)	116,834	69.2
Steven A. Farkas (D)	47,735	28.3
Roger Merle (LIBERT)	1,739	1.0
Michael J. Matthews (GREEN)	1,720	1.0
Constantino Rozzo (S)	771	.5
3 ● H. James Saxton (R)	123,375	65.0
Richard Strada (D)	64,364	33.9
Raymond Byrne (LIBERT)	1,335	.7
Ken Feduniewicz (AF)	665	.4
4 ● Christopher H. Smith (R)	115,293	66.2
Mary Brennan (D)	55,967	32.1
Keith Quarles (LIBERT)	1,211	.7
Hermann Winkelmann (HHD)	1,063	.6
Don Graham (NJC)	767	.4
5 # Scott Garrett (R)	118,881	59.5
Anne Sumers (D)	76,504	38.3
Michael J. Cino (LTI)	4,466	2.2
6 ● Frank Pallone Jr. (D)	91,379	66.5
Ric Medrow (R)	42,479	30.9
Richard D. Strong (GREEN)	1,819	1.3
Barry Allen (LIBERT)	1,206	.9
Mac Dara Francis X. Lyden (HUM)	612	.5
7 ● Mike Ferguson (R)	106,055	58.0
Tim Carden (D)	74,879	40.9
Darren Young (LIBERT)	2,068	1.1
8 ● Bill Pascrell Jr. (D)	88,101	66.8
Jared Silverman (R)	40,318	30.6
Joseph A. Fortunato (GREEN)	3,400	2.6
9 ● Steven R. Rothman (D)	97,108	69.8
Joseph Glass (R)	42,088	30.2
10 ● Donald M. Payne (D)	86,433	84.5
Andrew Wirtz (R)	15,913	15.6
11 ● Rodney Frelinghuysen (R)	132,938	72.4
Vij Pawar (D)	48,477	26.4
Richard S. Roth (LIBERT)	2,263	1.2
12 ● Rush D. Holt (D)	104,806	61.0
DeForest "Buster" Soaries (R)	62,938	36.6
Carl J. Mayer (GREEN)	1,871	1.1
Thomas D. Abrams (LIBERT)	1,259	.7
Karen Anne Zaletel (NJC)	839	.5
13 ● Robert Menendez (D)	72,605	78.3
James Geron (R)	16,852	18.2
Pat Henry Faulkner (GREEN)	1,195	1.3
Esmat Zaklama (I)	774	.8
Richard S. Hester Sr. (PLC)	732	.8
Herbert H. Shaw (PAC)	573	.6

NEW MEXICO

Governor

	Votes	%
# Bill Richardson (D)	268,674	55.5
John A. Sanchez (R)	189,090	39.1
David E. Bacon (GREEN)	26,465	5.5

Senate

	Votes	%
● Pete V. Domenici (R)	314,193	65.0
Gloria Tristani (D)	168,863	35.0

House

	Votes	%
1 ● Heather A. Wilson (R)	95,711	55.3
Richard Romero (D)	77,234	44.7
2 # Steve Pearce (R)	79,631	56.2
John Arthur Smith (D)	61,916	43.7
George L. Dewey (GREEN)	43	—
Padraig Malachy "Paddy" Lynch (R)	39	—
3 ● Tom Udall (D)	122,921	100.0

NEW YORK

Governor

	Votes	%
● George E. Pataki (R, C)	2,262,255	49.4
H. Carl McCall (D, WFM)	1,534,064	33.5
Blase Tom Golisano (INDC)	654,016	14.3
Gerard J. Cronin (RTL)	44,195	1.0
Stanley Aronowitz (GREEN)	41,797	.9
Thomas K. Leighton (MRF)	21,977	.5
Andrew M. Cuomo (L)	15,761	.3
Scott Jeffrey (LIBERT)	5,013	.1

House

	Votes	%
1 # Timothy H. Bishop (D, WFM)	84,276	50.2
● Felix J. Grucci Jr. (R, C, INDC, RTL)	81,524	48.6
Lorna Salzman (GREEN)	1,991	1.2
2 ● Steve Israel (D, INDC, WFM)	85,451	58.5
Joseph P. Finley (R, C, RTL)	59,117	40.5
John Keenan (GREEN)	1,558	1.1
3 ● Peter T. King (R, C, INDC, RTL)	121,537	71.9
Stuart L. Finz (D)	46,022	27.2
Janeen DePrima (L)	1,513	.9
4 ● Carolyn McCarthy (D, INDC, WFM)	94,806	56.3
Marilyn F. O'Grady (R, C, RTL)	72,882	43.2
Tim Derham (GREEN)	852	.5
5 ● Gary L. Ackerman (D, INDC, L, WFM)	68,773	92.3
Perry S. Reich (C)	5,718	7.7
6 ● Gregory W. Meeks (D, L, WFM)	72,799	96.5
Rey Clarke (INDC)	2,632	3.5
7 ● Joseph Crowley (D, WFM)	50,967	73.3
Kevin Brawley (R, C)	18,572	26.7
8 ● Jerrold Nadler (D, L, WFM)	81,002	76.1
Jim Farrin (R, INDC)	19,674	18.5
Alan Jay Gerber (C)	3,361	3.2
Dan Wentzel (GREEN)	1,918	1.8
Joseph Dobrian (LIBERT)	526	.5
9 ● Anthony Weiner (D, L, WFM)	60,737	65.7
Alfred F. Donohue (R, C)	31,698	34.3
10 ● Edolphus Towns (D, L)	73,859	97.8
Herbert F. Ryan (R)	1,639	2.2
11 ● Major R. Owens (D, WFM)	76,917	86.6
Susan Cleary (R, INDC)	11,149	12.6
Alice E. Gaffney (C)	798	.9
12 ● Nydia M. Velazquez (D, WFM)	48,408	95.8
Cesar Estevez (C)	2,119	4.2
13 ● Vito J. Fossella (R, C, RTL)	72,204	69.6
Arne H. Mattsson (D, L, WFM)	29,366	28.3
Anita Lerman (INDC)	1,427	1.4
Henry J. Bardel (GREEN)	696	.7
14 ● Carolyn B. Maloney (D, INDC, L, WFM)	95,931	75.3
Anton Srdanovic (R, C)	31,548	24.8
15 ● Charles B. Rangel (D, WFM)	84,367	88.5
Jessie Fields (R, INDC)	11,008	11.5
16 ● José E. Serrano (D, WFM)	50,716	92.1
Frank Dellavalle (R, C)	4,366	7.9
17 ● Eliot L. Engel (D, L, WFM)	77,535	62.6
C. Scott Vanderhoef (R, C, INDC)	42,634	34.4
Arthur L. Gallagher (RTL)	1,931	1.6
Elizabeth Shanklin (GREEN)	1,743	1.4
18 ● Nita M. Lowey (D, WFM)	98,957	92.0
Michael J. Reynolds (RTL)	8,558	8.0
19 ● Sue W. Kelly (R, C, INDC)	121,129	70.0
Janine M.H. Selendy (D)	44,967	26.0
Christine M. Tighe (RTL)	4,374	2.5
Jonathan M. Wright (GREEN)	2,642	1.5
20 ● John E. Sweeney (R, C)	140,238	73.3
Frank Stoppenbach (D)	45,878	24.0
Margaret Lewis (GREEN)	5,162	2.7
21 ● Michael R. McNulty (D, C, INDC, WFM)	161,329	75.1
Charles B. Rosenstein (R)	53,525	24.9
22 ● Maurice D. Hinchey (D, INDC, L, WFM)	113,280	64.2
Eric Hall (R, C)	58,008	32.9
Steven Greenfield (GREEN)	2,723	1.5
Paul J. Laux (RTL)	2,473	1.4
23 ● John M. McHugh (R, C)	124,682	100.0
24 ● Sherwood Boehlert (R)	108,017	70.7
David L. Walrath (C)	32,991	21.6
Mark Dunau (GREEN)	6,660	4.4
Kathleen M. Peters (RTL)	5,109	3.3
25 ● James T. Walsh (R, C, INDC)	144,610	72.3
Stephanie Aldersley (D)	53,290	26.6
Francis J. Gavin (WFM)	2,131	1.1
26 ● Thomas M. Reynolds (R, C, INDC)	135,089	73.6
Ayesha F. Nariman (D)	41,140	22.4
Shawn Harris (RTL)	4,084	2.2
Paul E. Fallon (GREEN)	3,146	1.7
27 ● Jack Quinn (R, C)	120,117	69.1
Peter Crotty (D, WFM)	47,811	27.5
Thomas Casey (RTL)	3,586	2.1
Albert N. LaBruna (GREEN)	2,405	1.4
28 ● Louise M. Slaughter (D, WFM)	99,057	62.5
Henry F. Wojtaszek (R, C, INDC)	59,547	37.5
29 ● Amo Houghton (R, C)	127,657	73.1
Kisun J. Peters (D)	37,128	21.3
Wendy M. Johnson (RTL)	5,836	3.3
Rachel Treichler (GREEN)	4,010	2.3

NORTH CAROLINA

Senate

	Votes	%
# Elizabeth Dole (R)	1,248,664	53.6
Erskine B. Bowles (D)	1,047,983	45.0
Sean Haugh (LIBERT)	33,807	1.5
Paul G. DeLaney — write-in	727	—

House

	Votes	%
1 # Frank W. Ballance Jr. (D)	93,157	63.7
Greg Dority (R)	50,907	34.8
Mike Ruff (LIBERT)	2,093	1.4
2 ● Bob Etheridge (D)	100,121	65.4
Joseph L. Ellen (R)	50,965	33.3
Gary Minter (LIBERT)	2,098	1.4
3 ● Walter B. Jones (R)	131,448	90.7
Gary Goodson (LIBERT)	13,486	9.3
4 ● David E. Price (D)	132,185	61.2
Tuan A. Nguyen (R)	78,095	36.1
Ken Nelson (LIBERT)	5,766	2.7
5 ● Richard M. Burr (R)	137,879	70.2
David Crawford (D)	58,558	29.8
6 ● Howard Coble (R)	151,430	90.4
Tara Grubb (LIBERT)	16,067	9.6

7 ●	Mike McIntyre (D)	118,543	71.1
	James Adams (R)	45,537	27.3
	David Michael Brooks (LIBERT)	2,574	1.6
8 ●	Robin Hayes (R)	80,298	53.6
	Chris Kouri (D)	66,819	44.6
	Mark Andrew Johnson (LIBERT)	2,619	1.8
9 ●	Sue Myrick (R)	140,095	72.4
	Ed McGuire (D)	49,974	25.8
	Christopher S. Cole (LIBERT)	3,374	1.7
10 ●	Cass Ballenger (R)	102,768	59.3
	Ron Daugherty (D)	65,587	37.9
	Christopher S. Cole (LIBERT)	4,937	2.9
11 ●	Charles H. Taylor (R)	112,335	55.5
	Sam Neill (D)	86,664	42.9
	Eric Henry (LIBERT)	3,261	1.6
12 ●	Melvin Watt (D)	98,821	65.3
	Jeff Kish (R)	49,588	32.8
	Carey Head (LIBERT)	2,830	1.9
13 #	Brad Miller (D)	100,287	54.7
	Carolyn W. Grant (R)	77,688	42.4
	Alex MacDonald (LIBERT)	5,295	2.9

NORTH DAKOTA

AL ●	Earl Pomeroy (D)	121,073	52.4
	Rick Clayburgh (R)	109,957	47.6

OHIO

Governor

●	Bob Taft (R)	1,865,007	57.8
	Tim Hagan (D)	1,236,924	38.3
	John A. Eastman (I)	126,686	3.9
	James G. Whitman (I)	291	—
	Eva Braiman (I)	84	—

House

1 ●	Steve Chabot (R)	110,760	64.8
	Greg Harris (D)	60,168	35.2
2 ●	Rob Portman (R)	139,218	74.0
	Charles W. Sanders (D)	48,785	25.9
	James J. Condit Jr. (I)	13	—
3 #	Michael R. Turner (R)	111,630	58.8
	Rick Carne (D)	78,307	41.2
	Ronald V. Williamitis (I)	14	—
4 ●	Michael G. Oxley (R)	120,001	67.5
	Jim Clark (D)	57,726	32.5
5 ●	Paul E. Gillmor (R)	126,286	67.1
	Roger Anderson (D)	51,872	27.6
	John F. Green (LIBERT)	10,096	5.4
6 ●	Ted Strickland (D)	113,972	59.5
	Mike Halleck (R)	77,643	40.5
7 ●	David L. Hobson (R)	113,252	67.6
	Kara Anastasio (D)	45,568	27.2
	Frank A. Doden (I)	8,812	5.3
8 ●	John A. Boehner (R)	119,947	70.8
	Jeff Hardenbrook (D)	49,444	29.2
9 ●	Marcy Kaptur (D)	132,236	74.0
	Edward Emery (R)	46,481	26.0
10 ●	Dennis J. Kucinich (D)	129,997	74.1
	Jon A. Heben (R)	41,778	23.8
	Judy Locy (I)	3,761	2.1
11 ●	Stephanie Tubbs Jones (D)	116,590	76.3
	Patrick A. Pappano (R)	36,146	23.7
12 ●	Pat Tiberi (R)	116,982	64.4
	Edward S. Brown (D)	64,707	35.6
13 ●	Sherrod Brown (D)	123,025	69.0
	Ed Oliveros (R)	55,357	31.0
14 ●	Steven C. LaTourette (R)	134,413	72.1
	Dale Virgil Blanchard (D)	51,846	27.8
	Sid Stone (LIBERT)	113	.1
15 ●	Deborah Pryce (R)	108,193	66.6
	Mark P. Brown (D)	54,286	33.4

16 ●	Ralph Regula (R)	129,734	68.9
	Jim Rice (D)	58,644	31.1
17 #	Tim Ryan (D)	94,441	51.1
	Ann Womer Benjamin (R)	62,188	33.7
	James A. Traficant Jr. (I)	28,045	15.2
18 ●	Bob Ney (R)	125,546	100.0

OKLAHOMA

Governor

#	Brad Henry (D)	448,143	43.3
	Steve Largent (R)	441,277	42.6
	Gary L. Richardson (I)	146,200	14.1

Senate

●	James M. Inhofe (R)	583,579	57.3
	David L. Walters (D)	369,789	36.3
	James Germalic (I)	65,056	6.4

House

1 ●	John Sullivan (R)	119,566	55.6
	Doug Dodd (D)	90,649	42.2
	Joseph V. Cristiano (LIBERT)	4,740	2.2
2 ●	Brad Carson (D)	146,748	74.1
	Kent Pharaoh (R)	51,234	25.9
3 ●	Frank D. Lucas (R)	148,206	75.6
	Robert T. Murphy (LIBERT)	47,884	24.4
4 #	Tom Cole (R)	106,452	53.8
	Darryl Roberts (D)	91,322	46.2
5 ●	Ernest Istook (R)	121,374	62.2
	Lou Barlow (D)	63,208	32.4
	Donna Davis (I)	10,469	5.4

OREGON

Governor

#	Theodore R. Kulongoski (D)	618,004	49.0
	Kevin L. Mannix (R)	581,785	46.2
	Tom Cox (LIBERT)	57,760	4.6
	write-ins	2,948	.2

Senate

●	Gordon H. Smith (R)	712,287	56.2
	Bill Bradbury (D)	501,898	39.6
	Dan Fitzgerald (LIBERT)	29,979	2.4
	Lon Mabon (CNSTP)	21,703	1.7
	write-ins	1,354	.1

House

1 ●	David Wu (D)	149,215	62.7
	Jim Greenfield (R)	80,917	34.0
	Beth King (LIBERT)	7,639	3.2
	write-ins	265	.1
2 ●	Greg Walden (R)	181,295	71.9
	Peter Buckley (D)	64,991	25.8
	Mike Wood (LIBERT)	5,681	2.3
	write-ins	317	.1
3 ●	Earl Blumenauer (D)	156,851	66.8
	Sarah Seale (R)	62,821	26.7
	Walter F. "Walt" Brown (S)	6,588	2.8
	Kevin Jones (LIBERT)	4,704	2.0
	David Brownlow (CNSTP)	3,495	1.5
	write-ins	518	.2
4 ●	Peter A. DeFazio (D)	168,150	63.8
	Liz VanLeeuwen (R)	90,523	34.4
	Chris Bigelow (LIBERT)	4,602	1.8
	write-ins	206	.1
5 ●	Darlene Hooley (D)	137,713	54.8
	Brian Boquist (R)	113,441	45.1
	write-ins	383	.1

PENNSYLVANIA

Governor

#	Edward G. Rendell (D)	1,899,518	53.6
	Mike Fisher (R)	1,566,567	44.2
	Ken V. Krawchuk (LIBERT)	40,923	1.2
	Michael Morrill (GREEN)	38,423	1.1

House

1 ●	Robert A. Brady (D)	121,076	86.4
	Marie G. Delany (R)	17,444	12.5
	Michael J. "Mike" Ewall (GREEN)	1,570	1.1
2 ●	Chaka Fattah (D)	150,623	87.8
	Thomas G. Dougherty (R)	20,988	12.2
3 ●	Phil English (R)	116,763	77.7
	AnnDrea M. Benson (GREEN)	33,554	22.3
4 ●	Melissa A. Hart (R)	130,534	64.5
	Stevan Drobac Jr. (D)	71,674	35.5
5 ●	John E. Peterson (R)	124,942	87.4
	Thomas A. Martin (LIBERT)	18,078	12.6
6 #	Jim Gerlach (R)	103,648	51.4
	Dan Wofford (D)	98,128	48.6
7 ●	Curt Weldon (R)	146,296	66.1
	Peter A. Lennon (D)	75,055	33.9
8 ●	James C. Greenwood (R)	127,475	62.6
	Timothy T. Reece (D)	76,178	37.4
9 ●	Bill Shuster (R)	124,184	71.1
	John R. Henry (D)	50,558	28.9
10 ●	Don Sherwood (R)	152,017	92.9
	Kurt J. Shotko (GREEN)	11,613	7.1
11 ●	Paul E. Kanjorski (D)	93,758	55.6
	Louis J. Barletta (R)	71,543	42.4
	Thomas J. McLaughlin (REF)	3,304	2.0
12 ●	John P. Murtha (D)	124,201	73.5
	Bill Choby (R)	44,818	26.5
13 ●	Joseph M. Hoeffel (D)	107,945	51.0
	Melissa Brown (R)	100,295	47.3
	John P. McDermott (CNSTP)	3,627	1.7
14 ●	Mike Doyle (D)	123,323	100.0
15 ●	Patrick J. Toomey (R)	98,493	57.4
	Edward J. O'Brien (D)	73,212	42.6
16 ●	Joe Pitts (R)	119,046	88.5
	Will Todd (GREEN)	8,720	6.5
	Kenneth C. Brenneman (CNSTP)	6,766	5.0
17 ●	Tim Holden (D)	103,483	51.4
	● George W. Gekas (R)	97,802	48.6
18 #	Tim Murphy (R)	119,885	60.1
	Jack M. Machek (D)	79,451	39.9
19 ●	Todd R. Platts (R)	143,097	91.1
	Ben G. Price (GREEN)	7,900	5.0
	Michael L. Paoletta (LIBERT)	6,008	3.8

RHODE ISLAND

Governor

#	Donald L. Carcieri (R)	181,687	54.8
	Myrth York (D)	150,147	45.3

Senate

●	Jack Reed (D)	253,774	78.4
	Robert G. Tingle (R)	69,808	21.6

House

1 ●	Patrick J. Kennedy (D)	95,233	60.0
	David W. Rogers (R)	59,316	37.3
	Frank A. Carter (I)	4,314	2.7
2 ●	Jim Langevin (D)	129,312	76.4
	John O. Matson (R)	37,740	22.3
	Dorman J. Hayes Jr. (I)	2,323	1.4

SOUTH CAROLINA

Governor

#	Mark Sanford (R)	580,459	52.8
	● Jim Hodges (D)	518,288	47.1
	write-ins	1,106	.1

Senate

#	Lindsey Graham (R)	595,218	54.4
	Alex Sanders (D)	484,422	44.2
	Ted Adams (CNSTP)	8,202	.8
	Victor Kocher (LIBERT)	6,648	.6
	write-ins	666	.1

House

1 ●	Henry E. Brown Jr. (R)	122,518	89.5
	James E. Dunn (UC)	9,560	7.0
	Joseph F. Innella (NL)	4,775	3.5
	write-ins	57	—
2 ●	Joe Wilson (R)	144,149	84.1
	Mark Whittington (UC)	17,189	10.0
	James R. "Jim" Legg (LIBERT)	9,650	5.6
	write-ins	356	.2
3 #	J. Gresham Barrett (R)	119,644	67.1
	George Brightharp (D)	55,743	31.3
	Mike Boerste (LIBERT)	2,785	1.6
	write-ins	23	—
4 ●	Jim DeMint (R)	122,422	69.0
	Peter J. Ashy (D, UC)	52,635	29.7
	C. Faye Walters (NL)	2,176	1.2
	write-ins	184	.1
5 ●	John M. Spratt Jr. (D)	121,912	85.9
	Doug Kendall (LIBERT)	11,013	7.8
	Steve Lefemine (CNSTP)	8,930	6.3
	write-ins	117	.1
6 ●	James E. Clyburn (D)	115,855	67.0
	Gary McLeod (R)	55,490	32.1
	R. Craig Augenstein (LIBERT)	1,662	1.0
	write-ins	40	—

SOUTH DAKOTA

Governor

#	Michael Rounds (R)	189,920	56.8
	Jim Abbott (D)	140,263	41.9
	James Carlson (I)	2,393	.7
	Nathan A. Barton (LIBERT)	1,983	.6

Senate

●	Tim Johnson (D)	167,481	49.6
	John Thune (R)	166,957	49.5
	Kurt Evans (LIBERT)	3,070	.9

House

AL #	Bill Janklow (R)	180,023	53.5
	Stephanie Herseth (D)	153,656	45.6
	Terry Begay (LIBERT)	3,128	.9

TENNESSEE

Governor

#	Phil Bredesen (D)	837,284	50.6
	Van Hilleary (R)	786,803	47.6
	Edwin C. Sanders (I)	7,749	.5
	Carl Two Feathers Whitaker (I)	5,308	.3
	John Jay Hooker (I)	4,577	.3
	David Gatchell (I)	2,991	.2
	Gabriel Givens (I)	1,591	.1
	Ray Ledford (I)	1,589	.1
	James E. Herren (I)	1,210	.1
	Charles V. Wilhoit Jr. (I)	898	—
	Marivuana Stout Leinoff (I)	645	—
	Francis E. Waldron (I)	635	—
	Ronny Simmons (I)	630	—
	Robert O. Watson (I)	579	—
	write-ins	376	—
	Basil J. Marceaux (I)	302	—

Senate

#	Lamar Alexander (R)	891,420	54.3
	Bob Clement (D)	728,295	44.3
	John Jay Hooker (I)	6,407	.4
	Wesley M. Baker (I)	6,105	.4
	Connie Gammon (I)	5,346	.3
	Karl Stanley Davidson (I)	2,216	.1
	Basil J. Marceaux (I)	1,173	.1
	H. Gary Keplinger (I)	1,103	.1
	write-ins	356	—

House

1 ●	Bill Jenkins (R)	127,300	98.8
	write-ins	1,586	1.2
2 ●	John J. "Jimmy" Duncan Jr. (R)	146,887	79.0
	John Greene (D)	37,035	19.9
	Joshua Williamson (I)	1,110	.6
	George Njezic (I)	940	.5
	write-ins	9	—
3 ●	Zach Wamp (R)	112,254	64.6
	John Wolfe Jr. (D)	58,824	33.9
	William C. Bolen (I)	1,473	.8
	Timothy A. Sevier (I)	947	.6
	write-ins	153	.1
4 #	Lincoln Davis (D)	95,989	52.1
	Janice H. Bowling (R)	85,680	46.5
	William Tharon Chandler (I)	1,073	.6
	John Ray (I)	605	.3
	Bert Mason (I)	504	.3
	Ed Wellmann (I)	399	.2
	write-ins	50	—
5 #	Jim Cooper (D)	108,903	63.7
	Robert Duvall (R)	56,825	33.3
	John Jay Hooker (I)	3,063	1.8
	Johnathan D. Farley (I)	1,205	.7
	Jesse Turner (I)	877	.5
	write-ins	13	—
6 ●	Bart Gordon (D)	117,119	65.9
	Robert L. Garrison (R)	57,397	32.3
	J. Patrick Lyons (I)	3,065	1.7
	write-ins	47	—
7 #	Marsha Blackburn (R)	138,314	70.7
	Tim Barron (D)	51,790	26.5
	Rick Patterson (I)	5,423	2.8
	write-ins	31	—
8 ●	John Tanner (D)	117,811	70.1
	Mat McClain (R)	45,853	27.3
	James L. Hart (I)	4,288	2.6
	write-ins	18	—
9 ●	Harold E. Ford Jr. (D)	120,904	83.8
	Tony Rush (I)	23,208	16.1
	write-ins	148	.1

TEXAS

Governor

●	Rick Perry (R)	2,632,541	57.8
	Tony Sanchez (D)	1,819,843	40.0
	Jeff Daiell (LIBERT)	66,717	1.5
	Rahul Mahajan (GREEN)	32,187	.7
	Elaine Eure Henderson — write-in	1,715	—
	Earl W. "Bill" O'Neil — write-in	976	—

Senate

#	John Cornyn (R)	2,496,243	55.3
	Ron Kirk (D)	1,955,758	43.3
	Scott Lanier Jameson (LIBERT)	35,538	.8
	Roy H. Williams (GREEN)	25,051	.6
	James W. "Jim" Wright — write-in	1,422	—

House

1 ●	Max Sandlin (D)	86,384	56.5
	John Lawrence (R)	66,654	43.6
2 ●	Jim Turner (D)	85,492	60.9
	Van Brookshire (R)	53,656	38.2
	Peter Beach (LIBERT)	1,353	1.0
3 ●	Sam Johnson (R)	113,974	74.0
	Manny Molera (D)	37,503	24.3
	John Davis (LIBERT)	2,656	1.7
4 ●	Ralph M. Hall (D)	97,304	57.8
	John Graves (R)	67,939	40.4
	Barbara L. Robinson (LIBERT)	3,042	1.8
5 #	Jeb Hensarling (R)	81,439	58.2
	Ron Chapman (D)	56,330	40.3
	Dan Michalski (LIBERT)	1,283	.9
	Thomas J. Kemper (GREEN)	856	.6
6 ●	Joe L. Barton (R)	115,396	70.4
	Felix Alvarado (D)	45,404	27.7
	Frank Brady (LIBERT)	1,992	1.2
	B. J. Armstrong (GREEN)	1,245	.8
7 ●	John Culberson (R)	96,795	89.2
	Drew Parks (LIBERT)	11,674	10.8
	John R. Skone-Palmer — write-in	58	—
8 ●	Kevin Brady (R)	140,575	93.1
	Gil Guillory (LIBERT)	10,351	6.9
9 ●	Nick Lampson (D)	86,710	58.6
	Paul Williams (R)	59,635	40.3
	Dean L. Tucker (LIBERT)	1,613	1.1
10 ●	Lloyd Doggett (D)	114,428	84.4
	Michele Messina (LIBERT)	21,196	15.6
11 ●	Chet Edwards (D)	74,678	51.6
	Ramsey W. Farley (R)	68,236	47.1
	Andrew Paul Farris (LIBERT)	1,943	1.3
12 ●	Kay Granger (R)	121,208	91.9
	Edward A. Hanson (LIBERT)	10,723	8.1
13 ●	William M. "Mac" Thornberry (R)	119,401	79.3
	Zane Reese (D)	31,218	20.7
14 ●	Ron Paul (R)	102,905	68.1
	Corby Windham (D)	48,224	31.9
15 ●	Ruben Hinojosa (D)	66,311	100.0
16 ●	Silvestre Reyes (D)	72,383	100.0
17 ●	Charles W. Stenholm (D)	84,136	51.4
	Rob Beckham (R)	77,622	47.4
	Fred Jones (LIBERT)	2,046	1.3
18 ●	Sheila Jackson-Lee (D)	99,161	76.9
	Phillip J. Abbott (R)	27,980	21.7
	Brent Sullivan (LIBERT)	1,785	1.4
19 ●	Larry Combest (R)	117,092	91.6
	Larry Johnson (LIBERT)	10,684	8.4
20 ●	Charlie Gonzalez (D)	68,685	100.0
21 ●	Lamar Smith (R)	161,836	72.9
	John Courage (D)	56,206	25.3
	D G Roberts (LIBERT)	4,051	1.8
22 ●	Tom DeLay (R)	100,499	63.2
	Tim Riley (D)	55,716	35.0
	Gerald W. "Jerry" LaFleur (LIBERT)	1,612	1.0
	Joel West (GREEN)	1,257	.8
23 ●	Henry Bonilla (R)	77,573	51.5
	Henry Cuellar (D)	71,067	47.2
	Jeffrey C. Blunt (LIBERT)	1,106	.7
	Ed Scharf (GREEN)	806	.5
24 ●	Martin Frost (D)	73,002	64.7
	Mike Rivera Ortega (R)	38,332	34.0
	Ken Ashby (LIBERT)	1,560	1.4
25 #	Chris Bell (D)	63,590	54.8
	Tom Reiser (R)	50,041	43.1
	George Reiter (GREEN)	1,399	1.2
	Guy McLendon (LIBERT)	1,096	.9
26 #	Michael C. Burgess (R)	123,195	74.8
	Paul William Lebon (D)	37,485	22.8
	David Wallace Croft (LIBERT)	2,367	1.4
	Gary R. Page (GREEN)	1,631	1.0
27 ●	Solomon P. Ortiz (D)	68,559	61.1
	Pat Ahumada (R)	41,004	36.5
	Christopher J. Claytor (LIBERT)	2,646	2.4
28 ●	Ciro D. Rodriguez (D)	71,393	71.1
	Gabriel Perales Jr. (R)	26,973	26.9
	William A. "Bill" Stallknecht (LIBERT)	2,054	2.0
29 ●	Gene Green (D)	55,760	95.2
	Paul Hansen (LIBERT)	2,833	4.8
30 ●	Eddie Bernice Johnson (D)	88,980	74.3
	Ron Bush (R)	28,981	24.2
	Lance Flores (LIBERT)	1,856	1.6

31 # John Carter (R) — 111,556 — 69.1
David Bagley (D) — 44,183 — 27.4
Clark Simmons (LIBERT) — 2,037 — 1.3
John S. Petersen (GREEN) — 1,992 — 1.2
R.C. Crawford (I) — 1,716 — 1.1
32 ● Pete Sessions (R) — 100,226 — 67.8
Pauline K. Dixon (D) — 44,886 — 30.4
Steve Martin (LIBERT) — 1,582 — 1.1
Carla Hubbell (GREEN) — 1,208 — .8

UTAH

1 # Rob Bishop (R) — 109,265 — 60.9
Dave Thomas (D) — 66,104 — 36.9
Craig Axford (GREEN) — 4,027 — 2.3
write-ins — 16 — —
2 ● Jim Matheson (D) — 110,764 — 49.4
John Swallow (R) — 109,123 — 48.7
Patrick Diehl (GREEN) — 2,589 — 1.2
Ron Copier (LIBERT) — 1,622 — .7
3 ● Chris Cannon (R) — 103,598 — 67.4
Nancy Jane Woodside (D) — 44,533 — 29.0
Kitty K. Burton (LIBERT) — 5,511 — 3.6
write-ins — 1 — —

VERMONT

Governor
Jim Douglas (R) — 103,436 — 44.9
Doug Racine (D) — 97,565 — 42.4
Cornelius "Con" Hogan (I) — 22,353 — 9.7
Cris Ericson (MML) — 1,737 — .8
Michael J. Badamo (PRO) — 1,380 — .6
Joel W. Williams (LIBERT) — 938 — .4
Patricia Hejny (VG) — 771 — .3
Marilynn "Mom" Christian (RJF) — 638 — .3
Peter Diamondstone (LU) — 625 — .3
Brian Pearl (I) — 569 — .3
write-ins — 149 — .1

House
AL ● Bernard Sanders (I) — 144,880 — 64.3
William Meub (R) — 72,813 — 32.3
Jane Newton (PRO) — 3,185 — 1.4
Fawn Skinner (VG) — 2,344 — 1.0
Daniel H. Krymkowski (LIBERT) — 2,033 — .9
write-ins — 221 — .1

VIRGINIA

Senate
● John W. Warner (R) — 1,229,894 — 82.6
Nancy Spannaus (I) — 145,102 — 9.7
Jacob G. Hornberger Jr. (I) — 106,055 — 7.1
write-ins — 8,371 — .6

House
1 ● Jo Ann Davis (R) — 113,168 — 95.9
write-ins — 4,829 — 4.1
2 ● Ed Schrock (R) — 103,807 — 83.2
D. C. Amarasinghe (GREEN) — 20,589 — 16.5
write-ins — 450 — .4
3 ● Robert C. Scott (D) — 87,521 — 96.1
write-ins — 3,552 — 3.9

4 ● J. Randy Forbes (R) — 108,733 — 97.9
write-ins — 2,308 — 2.1
5 ● Virgil H. Goode Jr. (R) — 95,360 — 63.5
Meredith Richards (D) — 54,805 — 36.5
write-ins — 68 — —
6 ● Robert W. Goodlatte (R) — 105,530 — 97.1
write-ins — 3,202 — 3.0
7 ● Eric Cantor (R) — 113,658 — 69.5
Ben L. "Cooter" Jones (D) — 49,854 — 30.5
write-ins — 153 — .1
8 ● James P. Moran (D) — 102,759 — 59.8
Scott C. Tate (R) — 64,121 — 37.3
Ron Crickenberger (I) — 4,558 — 2.6
write-ins — 361 — .2
9 ● Rick Boucher (D) — 100,075 — 65.8
Jay Katzen (R) — 52,076 — 34.2
write-ins — 32 — —
10 ● Frank R. Wolf (R) — 115,917 — 71.7
John B. Stevens Jr. (D) — 45,464 — 28.1
write-ins — 234 — .1
11 ● Thomas M. Davis III (R) — 135,379 — 82.9
Frank W. Creel (CNSTP) — 26,892 — 16.5
write-ins — 1,027 — .6

WASHINGTON

1 ● Jay Inslee (D) — 114,087 — 55.6
Joe Marine (R) — 84,696 — 41.3
Mark B. Wilson (LIBERT) — 6,251 — 3.1
2 ● Rick Larsen (D) — 101,219 — 50.1
Norma Smith (R) — 92,528 — 45.8
Bruce Guthrie (LIBERT) — 4,326 — 2.1
Bernard Patrick "Bern" Haggerty — 4,077 — 2.0
(GREEN)
3 ● Brian Baird (D) — 119,264 — 61.7
Joseph Zarelli (R) — 74,065 — 38.3
4 ● Doc Hastings (R) — 108,257 — 66.9
Craig Mason (D) — 53,572 — 33.1
5 ● George Nethercutt (R) — 126,757 — 62.7
Bart Haggin (D) — 65,146 — 32.2
Rob Chase (LIBERT) — 10,379 — 5.1
6 ● Norm Dicks (D) — 126,116 — 64.2
Bob Lawrence (R) — 61,584 — 31.4
John Bennett (LIBERT) — 8,744 — 4.5
7 ● Jim McDermott (D) — 156,300 — 74.1
Carol Thorne Cassady (R) — 46,256 — 21.9
Stan Lippmann (LIBERT) — 8,447 — 4.0
8 ● Jennifer Dunn (R) — 121,633 — 59.8
Heidi Behrens-Benedict (D) — 75,931 — 37.3
Mark A. Taff (LIBERT) — 5,771 — 2.8
9 ● Adam Smith (D) — 95,805 — 58.5
Sarah Casada (R) — 63,146 — 38.6
J. Mills (LIBERT) — 4,759 — 2.9

WEST VIRGINIA

Senate
● John D. Rockefeller IV (D) — 275,281 — 63.1
Jay Wolfe (R) — 160,902 — 36.9

House
1 ● Alan B. Mollohan (D) — 110,941 — 99.7
Louis 'Lou' Davis — 320 — .3
2 ● Shelley Moore Capito (R) — 98,276 — 60.0
Jim Humphreys (D) — 65,400 — 40.0
3 ● Nick J. Rahall II (D) — 87,783 — 70.2
Paul E. Chapman (R) — 37,229 — 29.8

WISCONSIN

Governor
James E. Doyle (D) — 800,515 — 45.1
● Scott McCallum (R) — 734,779 — 41.4
Ed Thompson (LIBERT) — 185,455 — 10.5
Jim Young (WG) — 44,111 — 2.5
Alan D. Eisenberg (I) — 2,847 — .2
Ty A. Bollerud (I) — 2,637 — .1
write-ins — 2,366 — .1
Michael J. Mangan (I) — 1,710 — .1
Aneb Ja Rasta — 929 — —
Sensas-Utcha Nefer-I

House
1 ● Paul D. Ryan (R) — 140,176 — 67.2
Jeff Thomas (D) — 63,895 — 30.6
George Meyers (LIBERT) — 4,406 — 2.1
write-ins — 136 — .1
2 ● Tammy Baldwin (D) — 163,313 — 66.0
Ron Greer (R) — 83,694 — 33.8
write-ins — 403 — .2
3 ● Ron Kind (D) — 131,038 — 62.8
Bill Arndt (R) — 69,955 — 33.5
Jeff Zastrow (LIBERT) — 6,674 — 3.2
write-ins — 914 — .4
4 ● Gerald D. Kleczka (D) — 122,031 — 86.3
Brian Verdin (WG) — 18,324 — 13.0
write-ins — 1,012 — .7
5 ● F. James Sensenbrenner Jr. (R) — 191,224 — 86.1
Robert R. Raymond (I) — 29,567 — 13.3
write-ins — 1,221 — .6
6 ● Tom Petri (R) — 169,834 — 99.2
write-ins — 1,327 — .8
7 ● David R. Obey (D) — 146,364 — 64.2
Joe Rothbauer (R) — 81,518 — 35.8
write-ins — 73 — —
8 ● Mark Green (R) — 152,745 — 72.6
Andrew M. Becker (D) — 50,284 — 23.9
Dick Kaiser (WG) — 7,338 — 3.5
write-ins — 80 — —

WYOMING

Governor
Dave Freudenthal (D) — 92,662 — 50.0
Eli Bebout (R) — 88,873 — 47.9
Dave Dawson (LIBERT) — 3,924 — 2.1

Senate
● Michael B. Enzi (R) — 133,710 — 73.0
Joyce Jansa Corcoran (D) — 49,570 — 27.1

House
AL ● Barbara Cubin (R) — 110,229 — 60.5
Ron Akin (D) — 65,961 — 36.2
Lewis Stock (LIBERT) — 5,962 — 3.3

Appendix H

HOUSE
ROLL CALL
VOTES

House Roll Call Votes
By Bill Number

Key

Y Voted for (yea).
\# Paired for.
\+ Announced for.
N Voted against (nay).
X Paired against.
– Announced against.
P Voted "present."
C Voted "present" to avoid possible conflict of interest.
? Did not vote or otherwise make a position known.

Democrats   **Republicans**
Independents

1. Quorum Call.* 347 members responded. Jan. 23, 2002.

2. HR 700. Asian Elephants/Concur With Senate Amendment. Gilchrest, R-Md., motion to suspend the rules and concur with the Senate amendment to the bill that would reauthorize through fiscal 2007 the Asian Elephant Conservation Act, which calls for up to $5 million annually in appropriations to the Interior Department's Multi-National Species Conservation Fund to conserve Asian elephants. It also would reauthorize through fiscal 2005 the National Fish and Wildlife Foundation. Motion agreed to 349-23: R 169-22; D 179-0 (ND 131-0, SD 48-0); I 1-1. A two-thirds majority of those present and voting (248 in this case) is required for adoption under suspension of the rules. Jan. 23, 2002.

3. HR 2234. Tumacacori Park Expansion/Passage. Gilchrest, R-Md., motion to suspend the rules and pass the bill that would authorize the Interior Department to expand the Tumacacori National Historic Park through the purchase of 310 acres of adjacent land. Motion agreed to 356-14: R 175-13; D 180-0 (ND 132-0, SD 48-0); I 1-1. A two-thirds majority of those present and voting (247 in this case) is required for passage under suspension of the rules. Jan. 23, 2002.

4. S 1762. Student Loan Formulas/Passage. Passage of the bill that would make permanent the federal government's current formula for determining its contribution to the federal student loan program and prevent a change to the formula scheduled to go into effect July 1, 2003. It also would maintain the current formula for determining loan interest rates until July 1, 2006. After that date, the bill would set a fixed rate of 6.8 percent for students' loans and 7.9 percent for parents' loans. Passed (thus cleared for the president) 372-3: R 190-3; D 180-0 (ND 132-0, SD 48-0); I 2-0. Jan. 24, 2002.

* CQ does not include quorum calls in its vote charts.

	2	3	4
ALABAMA			
1 *Callahan*	?	?	Y
2 *Everett*	?	?	?
3 *Riley*	+	+	+
4 *Aderholt*	Y	Y	Y
5 Cramer	Y	Y	Y
6 *Bachus*	Y	Y	Y
7 Hilliard	Y	Y	Y
ALASKA			
AL *Young*	Y	Y	?
ARIZONA			
1 *Flake*	N	Y	N
2 Pastor	Y	Y	Y
3 *Stump*	N	Y	Y
4 *Shadegg*	N	Y	Y
5 *Kolbe*	Y	Y	Y
6 *Hayworth*	N	Y	Y
ARKANSAS			
1 Berry	Y	Y	Y
2 Snyder	Y	Y	Y
3 *Boozman*	Y	Y	Y
4 Ross	Y	Y	Y
CALIFORNIA			
1 Thompson	Y	Y	Y
2 *Herger*	N	N	Y
3 *Ose*	Y	Y	Y
4 *Doolittle*	Y	Y	Y
5 Matsui	Y	Y	Y
6 Woolsey	?	?	?
7 Miller, George	Y	Y	Y
8 Pelosi	Y	Y	Y
9 Lee	Y	Y	Y
10 Tauscher	Y	Y	Y
11 *Pombo*	Y	Y	Y
12 Lantos	Y	Y	Y
13 Stark	Y	Y	Y
14 Eshoo	Y	Y	Y
15 Honda	Y	Y	Y
16 Lofgren	Y	Y	Y
17 Farr	Y	Y	Y
18 Condit	Y	Y	Y
19 *Radanovich*	?	?	?
20 Dooley	Y	Y	Y
21 *Thomas*	?	+	+
22 Capps	Y	Y	Y
23 *Gallegly*	?	?	?
24 Sherman	Y	Y	Y
25 *McKeon*	Y	Y	Y
26 Berman	?	?	?
27 Schiff	Y	Y	Y
28 *Dreier*	Y	Y	Y
29 Waxman	Y	Y	Y
30 Becerra	?	?	?
31 Solis	+	+	+
32 Watson	Y	Y	Y
33 Roybal-Allard	+	+	+
34 Napolitano	?	?	?
35 Waters	?	?	?
36 Harman	Y	Y	Y
37 Millender-McD.	Y	Y	Y
38 *Horn*	Y	Y	Y

	2	3	4
39 *Royce*	N	N	Y
40 *Lewis*	Y	Y	Y
41 *Miller, Gary*	?	?	?
42 Baca	Y	Y	Y
43 *Calvert*	Y	Y	Y
44 *Bono*	?	?	?
45 *Rohrabacher*	Y	Y	Y
46 Sanchez	Y	Y	Y
47 *Cox*	Y	Y	Y
48 *Issa*	Y	Y	Y
49 Davis	Y	Y	Y
50 Filner	Y	Y	Y
51 *Cunningham*	Y	Y	Y
52 *Hunter*	N	Y	Y
COLORADO			
1 DeGette	?	?	Y
2 Udall	Y	Y	Y
3 *McInnis*	Y	Y	Y
4 *Schaffer*	N	N	Y
5 *Hefley*	Y	Y	Y
6 *Tancredo*	Y	Y	Y
CONNECTICUT			
1 Larson	Y	Y	Y
2 *Simmons*	Y	Y	Y
3 DeLauro	Y	Y	Y
4 *Shays*	Y	Y	Y
5 Maloney	Y	Y	Y
6 *Johnson*	Y	Y	Y
DELAWARE			
AL *Castle*	Y	Y	Y
FLORIDA			
1 *Miller, J.*	Y	Y	Y
2 Boyd	Y	Y	Y
3 Brown	Y	Y	Y
4 *Crenshaw*	Y	Y	Y
5 Thurman	?	?	?
6 *Stearns*	Y	N	Y
7 *Mica*	Y	Y	Y
8 *Keller*	Y	Y	Y
9 *Bilirakis*	Y	Y	Y
10 *Young*	Y	Y	Y
11 Davis	Y	Y	Y
12 *Putnam*	Y	Y	Y
13 *Miller, D.*	Y	Y	Y
14 *Goss*	Y	Y	Y
15 *Weldon*	?	?	?
16 *Foley*	Y	Y	Y
17 Meek	Y	Y	Y
18 *Ros-Lehtinen*	Y	Y	Y
19 Wexler	Y	Y	Y
20 Deutsch	Y	Y	Y
21 *Diaz-Balart*	Y	Y	Y
22 *Shaw*	Y	Y	Y
23 Hastings	Y	Y	Y
GEORGIA			
1 *Kingston*	?	N	Y
2 Bishop	Y	Y	Y
3 *Collins*	N	Y	?
4 McKinney	Y	Y	Y
5 Lewis	Y	Y	Y
6 *Isakson*	Y	Y	Y
7 *Barr*	?	?	Y
8 *Chambliss*	Y	Y	Y
9 *Deal*	Y	Y	Y
10 *Norwood*	Y	Y	Y
11 *Linder*	Y	Y	Y
HAWAII			
1 Abercrombie	Y	Y	Y
2 Mink	?	?	?
IDAHO			
1 *Otter*	Y	Y	Y
2 *Simpson*	Y	Y	Y
ILLINOIS			
1 Rush	Y	Y	Y
2 Jackson	Y	Y	Y
3 Lipinski	Y	Y	Y
4 Gutierrez	?	?	Y
5 Blagojevich	?	?	?
6 *Hyde*	?	?	?
7 Davis	Y	Y	?
8 *Crane*	Y	Y	Y
9 Schakowsky	Y	Y	Y
10 *Kirk*	Y	Y	Y
11 *Weller*	Y	Y	?
12 Costello	Y	Y	Y
13 *Biggert*	Y	Y	Y

ND Northern Democrats   SD Southern Democrats

	2	3	4
14 *Hastert*			
15 *Johnson*	Y	Y	Y
16 *Manzullo*	Y	?	?
17 Evans	Y	Y	Y
18 *LaHood*	Y	Y	Y
19 Phelps	Y	Y	Y
20 *Shimkus*	Y	Y	Y
INDIANA			
1 Visclosky	Y	Y	Y
2 *Pence*	N	Y	Y
3 Roemer	Y	Y	Y
4 *Souder*	Y	Y	Y
5 *Buyer*	Y	Y	Y
6 *Burton*	?	?	?
7 *Kerns*	N	N	Y
8 *Hostettler*	N	N	Y
9 Hill	Y	Y	Y
10 Carson	Y	Y	Y
IOWA			
1 *Leach*	Y	Y	Y
2 *Nussle*	Y	Y	Y
3 Boswell	Y	Y	Y
4 *Ganske*	Y	Y	Y
5 *Latham*	Y	Y	Y
KANSAS			
1 *Moran*	Y	Y	N
2 *Ryun*	N	Y	Y
3 Moore	Y	Y	Y
4 *Tiahrt*	Y	Y	Y
KENTUCKY			
1 *Whitfield*	Y	Y	Y
2 *Lewis*	+	+	?
3 *Northup*	Y	Y	Y
4 Lucas	Y	Y	Y
5 *Rogers*	Y	Y	Y
6 *Fletcher*	Y	Y	?
LOUISIANA			
1 *Vitter*	?	?	?
2 Jefferson	Y	Y	Y
3 *Tauzin*	Y	?	Y
4 *McCrery*	Y	Y	Y
5 *Cooksey*	Y	Y	Y
6 *Baker*	Y	Y	Y
7 John	?	?	Y
MAINE			
1 Allen	Y	Y	Y
2 Baldacci	Y	Y	Y
MARYLAND			
1 *Gilchrest*	Y	Y	Y
2 *Ehrlich*	Y	Y	Y
3 Cardin	Y	Y	Y
4 Wynn	Y	Y	Y
5 Hoyer	Y	Y	Y
6 *Bartlett*	Y	Y	Y
7 Cummings	Y	Y	Y
8 *Morella*	Y	Y	Y
MASSACHUSETTS			
1 Olver	Y	Y	Y
2 Neal	Y	Y	Y
3 McGovern	Y	Y	Y
4 Frank	Y	Y	?
5 Meehan	Y	Y	Y
6 Tierney	Y	Y	Y
7 Markey	Y	Y	Y
8 Capuano	Y	Y	Y
9 Lynch	Y	Y	Y
10 Delahunt	Y	Y	Y
MICHIGAN			
1 Stupak	Y	Y	Y
2 *Hoekstra*	Y	Y	Y
3 *Ehlers*	Y	Y	Y
4 *Camp*	Y	Y	Y
5 Barcia	Y	Y	Y
6 *Upton*	Y	Y	Y
7 *Smith*	Y	N	Y
8 *Rogers*	Y	Y	Y
9 Kildee	Y	Y	Y
10 Bonior	?	?	?
11 *Knollenberg*	Y	Y	Y
12 Levin	Y	Y	Y
13 Rivers	Y	Y	Y
14 Conyers	Y	Y	Y
15 Kilpatrick	+	+	Y
16 Dingell	Y	Y	Y

	2	3	4
MINNESOTA			
1 *Gutknecht*	Y	Y	Y
2 *Kennedy*	Y	Y	Y
3 *Ramstad*	Y	Y	Y
4 McCollum	Y	Y	Y
5 Sabo	Y	Y	Y
6 Luther	?	?	?
7 Peterson	Y	Y	Y
8 Oberstar	Y	Y	Y
MISSISSIPPI			
1 *Wicker*	Y	Y	Y
2 Thompson	Y	Y	Y
3 *Pickering*	Y	Y	Y
4 Shows	Y	Y	Y
5 Taylor	Y	Y	Y
MISSOURI			
1 Clay	Y	Y	?
2 *Akin*	N	Y	Y
3 Gephardt	Y	Y	Y
4 Skelton	Y	Y	Y
5 McCarthy	Y	Y	+
6 *Graves*	Y	Y	Y
7 *Blunt*	Y	Y	Y
8 *Emerson*	Y	Y	Y
9 *Hulshof*	Y	Y	Y
MONTANA			
AL *Rehberg*	Y	Y	Y
NEBRASKA			
1 *Bereuter*	Y	Y	Y
2 *Terry*	Y	Y	Y
3 *Osborne*	Y	Y	Y
NEVADA			
1 Berkley	Y	Y	Y
2 *Gibbons*	?	?	Y
NEW HAMPSHIRE			
1 *Sununu*	Y	Y	Y
2 *Bass*	Y	Y	Y
NEW JERSEY			
1 Andrews	Y	Y	Y
2 *LoBiondo*	Y	Y	Y
3 *Saxton*	Y	Y	Y
4 *Smith*	Y	Y	Y
5 *Roukema*	+	+	+
6 Pallone	Y	Y	Y
7 *Ferguson*	Y	Y	Y
8 Pascrell	Y	Y	Y
9 Rothman	Y	Y	Y
10 Payne	Y	Y	Y
11 *Frelinghuysen*	Y	Y	Y
12 Holt	Y	Y	Y
13 Menendez	Y	Y	Y
NEW MEXICO			
1 *Wilson*	Y	Y	Y
2 *Skeen*	Y	Y	Y
3 Udall	Y	Y	Y
NEW YORK			
1 *Grucci*	Y	Y	Y
2 Israel	Y	Y	Y
3 *King*	Y	Y	Y
4 McCarthy	Y	Y	Y
5 Ackerman	Y	Y	Y
6 Meeks	Y	Y	Y
7 Crowley	Y	Y	Y
8 Nadler	Y	Y	?
9 Weiner	Y	Y	Y
10 Towns	Y	Y	Y
11 Owens	Y	Y	Y
12 Velázquez	Y	Y	Y
13 *Fossella*	Y	Y	Y
14 Maloney	Y	Y	Y
15 Rangel	Y	Y	Y
16 Serrano	Y	Y	Y
17 Engel	Y	Y	Y
18 Lowey	Y	Y	Y
19 *Kelly*	Y	Y	Y
20 *Gilman*	Y	Y	Y
21 McNulty	Y	Y	Y
22 *Sweeney*	Y	Y	Y
23 *Boehlert*	Y	Y	Y
24 *McHugh*	Y	Y	Y
25 *Walsh*	Y	Y	Y
26 Hinchey	?	?	?
27 *Reynolds*	Y	Y	Y
28 Slaughter	+	+	Y
29 LaFalce	Y	Y	Y

	2	3	4
30 *Quinn*	?	?	?
31 *Houghton*	?	?	Y
NORTH CAROLINA			
1 Clayton	Y	Y	Y
2 Etheridge	Y	Y	Y
3 *Jones*	Y	N	?
4 Price	Y	Y	Y
5 *Burr*	Y	Y	Y
6 *Coble*	N	N	Y
7 McIntyre	Y	Y	Y
8 *Hayes*	?	?	Y
9 *Myrick*	Y	+	Y
10 *Ballenger*	?	?	Y
11 *Taylor*	Y	Y	Y
12 Watt	Y	Y	Y
NORTH DAKOTA			
AL Pomeroy	Y	Y	Y
OHIO			
1 *Chabot*	Y	Y	Y
2 *Portman*	Y	Y	Y
3 Hall	?	Y	Y
4 *Oxley*	Y	Y	?
5 *Gillmor*	Y	Y	Y
6 Strickland	Y	Y	Y
7 *Hobson*	Y	Y	Y
8 *Boehner*	Y	Y	Y
9 Kaptur	Y	Y	Y
10 Kucinich	Y	Y	Y
11 Jones	?	?	Y
12 *Tiberi*	Y	Y	Y
13 Brown	Y	Y	Y
14 Sawyer	Y	Y	Y
15 *Pryce*	Y	Y	Y
16 *Regula*	Y	Y	Y
17 Traficant	?	?	Y
18 *Ney*	Y	Y	Y
19 *LaTourette*	Y	Y	Y
OKLAHOMA			
1 *Largent*	?	?	?
2 Carson	?	?	?
3 *Watkins*	?	?	?
4 *Watts*	Y	Y	Y
5 *Istook*	Y	Y	Y
6 *Lucas*	Y	Y	Y
OREGON			
1 Wu	?	?	?
2 *Walden*	Y	Y	Y
3 Blumenauer	?	?	?
4 DeFazio	Y	Y	Y
5 Hooley	?	?	?
PENNSYLVANIA			
1 Brady	Y	Y	Y
2 Fattah	Y	Y	Y
3 Borski	Y	Y	Y
4 *Hart*	Y	Y	Y
5 *Peterson*	Y	Y	Y
6 Holden	Y	Y	Y
7 *Weldon*	Y	Y	Y
8 *Greenwood*	Y	Y	Y
9 *Shuster, Bill*	Y	Y	Y
10 *Sherwood*	Y	Y	?
11 Kanjorski	Y	Y	Y
12 Murtha	Y	Y	?
13 Hoeffel	Y	Y	Y
14 Coyne	Y	Y	Y
15 *Toomey*	N	Y	Y
16 *Pitts*	Y	Y	Y
17 *Gekas*	Y	Y	Y
18 Doyle	?	?	?
19 *Platts*	Y	Y	Y
20 Mascara	Y	Y	Y
21 *English*	?	?	Y
RHODE ISLAND			
1 Kennedy	Y	Y	Y
2 Langevin	Y	Y	Y
SOUTH CAROLINA			
1 *Brown*	Y	Y	Y
2 *Wilson*	Y	Y	Y
3 *Graham*	Y	Y	Y
4 *DeMint*	Y	Y	Y
5 Spratt	Y	Y	Y
6 Clyburn	Y	Y	Y
SOUTH DAKOTA			
AL *Thune*	Y	Y	Y

	2	3	4
TENNESSEE			
1 *Jenkins*	Y	Y	Y
2 *Duncan*	Y	Y	Y
3 *Wamp*	Y	Y	Y
4 *Hilleary*	?	?	Y
5 Clement	Y	Y	Y
6 Gordon	Y	Y	Y
7 *Bryant*	Y	Y	Y
8 Tanner	Y	Y	Y
9 Ford	Y	?	Y
TEXAS			
1 Sandlin	Y	Y	Y
2 Turner	Y	Y	Y
3 *Johnson, Sam*	Y	Y	Y
4 Hall	Y	Y	Y
5 *Sessions*	?	?	?
6 *Barton*	?	?	?
7 *Culberson*	N	Y	Y
8 *Brady*	Y	Y	Y
9 Lampson	Y	Y	Y
10 Doggett	Y	Y	Y
11 Edwards	Y	Y	Y
12 *Granger*	Y	Y	Y
13 *Thornberry*	Y	Y	Y
14 *Paul*	N	N	N
15 Hinojosa	+	+	+
16 Reyes	?	?	Y
17 Stenholm	Y	Y	Y
18 Jackson-Lee	Y	Y	Y
19 *Combest*	Y	Y	Y
20 Gonzalez	Y	Y	Y
21 *Smith*	Y	Y	Y
22 *DeLay*	Y	Y	Y
23 *Bonilla*	?	?	?
24 Frost	Y	Y	Y
25 Bentsen	Y	Y	Y
26 *Armey*	Y	Y	Y
27 Ortiz	?	?	?
28 Rodriguez	Y	Y	Y
29 Green	Y	Y	Y
30 Johnson, E.B.	Y	Y	Y
UTAH			
1 *Hansen*	Y	Y	Y
2 Matheson	Y	Y	Y
3 *Cannon*	Y	Y	Y
VERMONT			
AL *Sanders*	Y	Y	Y
VIRGINIA			
1 *Davis, Jo Ann*	N	Y	Y
2 *Schrock*	Y	Y	Y
3 Scott	Y	Y	Y
4 *Forbes*	Y	Y	Y
5 *Goode*	N	N	Y
6 *Goodlatte*	N	N	Y
7 *Cantor*	N	+	Y
8 Moran	Y	Y	?
9 Boucher	Y	Y	?
10 *Wolf*	Y	Y	Y
11 *Davis, T.*	?	?	Y
WASHINGTON			
1 Inslee	?	?	Y
2 Larsen	Y	Y	Y
3 Baird	Y	Y	Y
4 *Hastings*	Y	Y	Y
5 *Nethercutt*	Y	Y	Y
6 Dicks	?	?	Y
7 McDermott	Y	Y	Y
8 *Dunn*	Y	Y	Y
9 Smith	Y	Y	Y
WEST VIRGINIA			
1 Mollohan	Y	Y	Y
2 *Capito*	Y	Y	Y
3 Rahall	Y	Y	Y
WISCONSIN			
1 *Ryan*	Y	Y	Y
2 Baldwin	Y	Y	Y
3 Kind	+	+	+
4 Kleczka	Y	Y	Y
5 Barrett	Y	Y	Y
6 *Petri*	Y	Y	Y
7 Obey	Y	Y	?
8 *Green*	Y	Y	Y
9 *Sensenbrenner*	N	N	Y
WYOMING			
AL *Cubin*	Y	Y	?

Southern states - Ala., Ark., Fla., Ga., Ky., La., Miss., N.C., Okla., S.C., Tenn., Texas, Va.

5. H Res 335. Catholic Schools/Adoption. Tiberi, R-Ohio, motion to suspend the rules and adopt the resolution that would pay tribute to Catholic schools. Motion agreed to 388-0: R 197-0; D 189-0 (ND 140-0, SD 49-0); I 2-0. A two-thirds majority of those present and voting (259 in this case) is required for adoption under suspension of the rules. Jan. 29, 2002.

	5
ALABAMA	
1 *Callahan*	Y
2 *Everett*	Y
3 *Riley*	?
4 *Aderholt*	Y
5 Cramer	Y
6 *Bachus*	Y
7 Hilliard	Y
ALASKA	
AL *Young*	Y
ARIZONA	
1 *Flake*	Y
2 Pastor	Y
3 *Stump*	Y
4 *Shadegg*	Y
5 *Kolbe*	Y
6 *Hayworth*	?
ARKANSAS	
1 Berry	Y
2 Snyder	Y
3 *Boozman*	Y
4 Ross	Y
CALIFORNIA	
1 Thompson	Y
2 *Herger*	Y
3 *Ose*	Y
4 *Doolittle*	?
5 Matsui	Y
6 Woolsey	Y
7 Miller, George	Y
8 Pelosi	Y
9 Lee	Y
10 Tauscher	Y
11 *Pombo*	Y
12 Lantos	Y
13 Stark	Y
14 Eshoo	Y
15 Honda	Y
16 Lofgren	Y
17 Farr	Y
18 Condit	Y
19 *Radanovich*	?
20 Dooley	Y
21 *Thomas*	Y
22 Capps	Y
23 *Gallegly*	Y
24 Sherman	Y
25 *McKeon*	Y
26 Berman	Y
27 Schiff	Y
28 *Dreier*	Y
29 Waxman	Y
30 Becerra	?
31 Solis	Y
32 Watson	Y
33 Roybal-Allard	?
34 Napolitano	?
35 Waters	?
36 Harman	Y
37 Millender-McD.	Y
38 *Horn*	Y

	5
39 *Royce*	Y
40 *Lewis*	?
41 *Miller, Gary*	Y
42 Baca	Y
43 *Calvert*	?
44 *Bono*	Y
45 *Rohrabacher*	Y
46 Sanchez	Y
47 *Cox*	Y
48 *Issa*	Y
49 Davis	Y
50 Filner	Y
51 *Cunningham*	Y
52 *Hunter*	?
COLORADO	
1 DeGette	Y
2 Udall	Y
3 *McInnis*	Y
4 *Schaffer*	Y
5 *Hefley*	Y
6 *Tancredo*	Y
CONNECTICUT	
1 Larson	Y
2 *Simmons*	Y
3 DeLauro	Y
4 *Shays*	Y
5 Maloney	Y
6 *Johnson*	Y
DELAWARE	
AL *Castle*	Y
FLORIDA	
1 *Miller, J.*	Y
2 Boyd	Y
3 Brown	Y
4 *Crenshaw*	Y
5 Thurman	Y
6 *Stearns*	Y
7 *Mica*	Y
8 *Keller*	Y
9 *Bilirakis*	Y
10 *Young*	Y
11 Davis	Y
12 *Putnam*	Y
13 *Miller, D.*	Y
14 *Goss*	Y
15 *Weldon*	Y
16 *Foley*	Y
17 Meek	Y
18 *Ros-Lehtinen*	Y
19 Wexler	Y
20 Deutsch	Y
21 *Diaz-Balart*	Y
22 *Shaw*	Y
23 Hastings	Y
GEORGIA	
1 *Kingston*	Y
2 Bishop	Y
3 *Collins*	Y
4 McKinney	Y
5 Lewis	Y
6 *Isakson*	?
7 *Barr*	Y
8 *Chambliss*	Y
9 *Deal*	Y
10 *Norwood*	Y
11 *Linder*	Y
HAWAII	
1 Abercrombie	?
2 Mink	Y
IDAHO	
1 *Otter*	Y
2 *Simpson*	?
ILLINOIS	
1 Rush	Y
2 Jackson	Y
3 Lipinski	?
4 Gutierrez	Y
5 Blagojevich	Y
6 *Hyde*	Y
7 Davis	Y
8 *Crane*	Y
9 Schakowsky	Y
10 *Kirk*	Y
11 *Weller*	Y
12 Costello	Y
13 *Biggert*	Y

ND Northern Democrats   SD Southern Democrats

Illinois (cont.)	5
14 Hastert	
15 Johnson	Y
16 Manzullo	?
17 Evans	Y
18 LaHood	Y
19 Phelps	Y
20 Shimkus	Y

INDIANA

	5
1 Visclosky	Y
2 Pence	Y
3 Roemer	Y
4 Souder	Y
5 Buyer	Y
6 Burton	Y
7 Kerns	Y
8 Hostettler	Y
9 Hill	Y
10 Carson	?

IOWA

	5
1 Leach	Y
2 Nussle	Y
3 Boswell	Y
4 Ganske	Y
5 Latham	Y

KANSAS

	5
1 Moran	Y
2 Ryun	Y
3 Moore	Y
4 Tiahrt	?

KENTUCKY

	5
1 Whitfield	?
2 Lewis	Y
3 Northup	Y
4 Lucas	Y
5 Rogers	Y
6 Fletcher	Y

LOUISIANA

	5
1 Vitter	Y
2 Jefferson	?
3 Tauzin	Y
4 McCrery	Y
5 Cooksey	Y
6 Baker	Y
7 John	Y

MAINE

	5
1 Allen	Y
2 Baldacci	Y

MARYLAND

	5
1 Gilchrest	Y
2 Ehrlich	Y
3 Cardin	Y
4 Wynn	Y
5 Hoyer	Y
6 Bartlett	Y
7 Cummings	Y
8 Morella	Y

MASSACHUSETTS

	5
1 Olver	Y
2 Neal	Y
3 McGovern	Y
4 Frank	Y
5 Meehan	Y
6 Tierney	Y
7 Markey	Y
8 Capuano	?
9 Lynch	Y
10 Delahunt	?

MICHIGAN

	5
1 Stupak	Y
2 Hoekstra	Y
3 Ehlers	Y
4 Camp	Y
5 Barcia	Y
6 Upton	Y
7 Smith	?
8 Rogers	Y
9 Kildee	Y
10 Bonior	Y
11 Knollenberg	Y
12 Levin	Y
13 Rivers	Y
14 Conyers	Y
15 Kilpatrick	Y
16 Dingell	Y

MINNESOTA

	5
1 Gutknecht	Y
2 Kennedy	Y
3 Ramstad	Y
4 McCollum	Y
5 Sabo	Y
6 Luther	?
7 Peterson	Y
8 Oberstar	Y

MISSISSIPPI

	5
1 Wicker	Y
2 Thompson	Y
3 Pickering	?
4 Shows	Y
5 Taylor	Y

MISSOURI

	5
1 Clay	Y
2 Akin	Y
3 Gephardt	?
4 Skelton	Y
5 McCarthy	Y
6 Graves	Y
7 Blunt	Y
8 Emerson	Y
9 Hulshof	Y

MONTANA

	5
AL Rehberg	Y

NEBRASKA

	5
1 Bereuter	Y
2 Terry	Y
3 Osborne	Y

NEVADA

	5
1 Berkley	Y
2 Gibbons	?

NEW HAMPSHIRE

	5
1 Sununu	Y
2 Bass	Y

NEW JERSEY

	5
1 Andrews	Y
2 LoBiondo	Y
3 Saxton	Y
4 Smith	Y
5 Roukema	?
6 Pallone	Y
7 Ferguson	Y
8 Pascrell	Y
9 Rothman	Y
10 Payne	Y
11 Frelinghuysen	Y
12 Holt	Y
13 Menendez	Y

NEW MEXICO

	5
1 Wilson	Y
2 Skeen	Y
3 Udall	Y

NEW YORK

	5
1 Grucci	Y
2 Israel	Y
3 King	Y
4 McCarthy	Y
5 Ackerman	Y
6 Meeks	Y
7 Crowley	Y
8 Nadler	Y
9 Weiner	Y
10 Towns	Y
11 Owens	Y
12 Velázquez	Y
13 Fossella	Y
14 Maloney	?
15 Rangel	Y
16 Serrano	Y
17 Engel	Y
18 Lowey	Y
19 Kelly	Y
20 Gilman	Y
21 McNulty	Y
22 Sweeney	Y
23 Boehlert	Y
24 McHugh	Y
25 Walsh	Y
26 Hinchey	?
27 Reynolds	Y
28 Slaughter	Y
29 LaFalce	Y
30 Quinn	Y
31 Houghton	Y

NORTH CAROLINA

	5
1 Clayton	Y
2 Etheridge	Y
3 Jones	Y
4 Price	Y
5 Burr	Y
6 Coble	Y
7 McIntyre	Y
8 Hayes	Y
9 Myrick	Y
10 Ballenger	Y
11 Taylor	Y
12 Watt	Y

NORTH DAKOTA

	5
AL Pomeroy	Y

OHIO

	5
1 Chabot	Y
2 Portman	Y
3 Hall	Y
4 Oxley	Y
5 Gillmor	Y
6 Strickland	Y
7 Hobson	Y
8 Boehner	Y
9 Kaptur	Y
10 Kucinich	Y
11 Jones	Y
12 Tiberi	Y
13 Brown	Y
14 Sawyer	Y
15 Pryce	Y
16 Regula	Y
17 Traficant	?
18 Ney	Y
19 LaTourette	Y

OKLAHOMA

	5
1 Largent	?
2 Carson	Y
3 Watkins	Y
4 Watts	Y
5 Istook	Y
6 Lucas	Y

OREGON

	5
1 Wu	Y
2 Walden	Y
3 Blumenauer	Y
4 DeFazio	?
5 Hooley	Y

PENNSYLVANIA

	5
1 Brady	Y
2 Fattah	Y
3 Borski	Y
4 Hart	Y
5 Peterson	Y
6 Holden	Y
7 Weldon	?
8 Greenwood	Y
9 Shuster, Bill	Y
10 Sherwood	Y
11 Kanjorski	Y
12 Murtha	?
13 Hoeffel	Y
14 Coyne	Y
15 Toomey	?
16 Pitts	Y
17 Gekas	Y
18 Doyle	Y
19 Platts	Y
20 Mascara	Y
21 English	?

RHODE ISLAND

	5
1 Kennedy	Y
2 Langevin	Y

SOUTH CAROLINA

	5
1 Brown	Y
2 Wilson	Y
3 Graham	Y
4 DeMint	Y
5 Spratt	?
6 Clyburn	Y

SOUTH DAKOTA

	5
AL Thune	Y

TENNESSEE

	5
1 Jenkins	Y
2 Duncan	Y
3 Wamp	Y
4 Hilleary	Y
5 Clement	Y
6 Gordon	Y
7 Bryant	?
8 Tanner	Y
9 Ford	Y

TEXAS

	5
1 Sandlin	Y
2 Turner	Y
3 Johnson, Sam	Y
4 Hall	Y
5 Sessions	Y
6 Barton	Y
7 Culberson	Y
8 Brady	Y
9 Lampson	Y
10 Doggett	Y
11 Edwards	Y
12 Granger	Y
13 Thornberry	Y
14 Paul	P
15 Hinojosa	Y
16 Reyes	Y
17 Stenholm	Y
18 Jackson-Lee	Y
19 Combest	Y
20 Gonzalez	?
21 Smith	Y
22 DeLay	Y
23 Bonilla	Y
24 Frost	Y
25 Bentsen	Y
26 Armey	Y
27 Ortiz	?
28 Rodriguez	?
29 Green	Y
30 Johnson, E.B.	Y

UTAH

	5
1 Hansen	?
2 Matheson	Y
3 Cannon	Y

VERMONT

	5
AL Sanders	Y

VIRGINIA

	5
1 Davis, Jo Ann	Y
2 Schrock	Y
3 Scott	Y
4 Forbes	Y
5 Goode	Y
6 Goodlatte	Y
7 Cantor	Y
8 Moran	Y
9 Boucher	Y
10 Wolf	Y
11 Davis, T.	Y

WASHINGTON

	5
1 Inslee	Y
2 Larsen	Y
3 Baird	Y
4 Hastings	Y
5 Nethercutt	?
6 Dicks	Y
7 McDermott	Y
8 Dunn	Y
9 Smith	Y

WEST VIRGINIA

	5
1 Mollohan	Y
2 Capito	Y
3 Rahall	Y

WISCONSIN

	5
1 Ryan	Y
2 Baldwin	Y
3 Kind	Y
4 Kleczka	Y
5 Barrett	Y
6 Petri	Y
7 Obey	Y
8 Green	Y
9 Sensenbrenner	Y

WYOMING

	5
AL Cubin	Y

Southern states - Ala., Ark., Fla., Ga., Ky., La., Miss., N.C., Okla., S.C., Tenn., Texas, Va.

Key

Y	Voted for (yea).
#	Paired for.
+	Announced for.
N	Voted against (nay).
X	Paired against.
–	Announced against.
P	Voted "present."
C	Voted "present" to avoid possible conflict of interest.
?	Did not vote or otherwise make a position known.

• Democrats **Republicans** *Independents*

6. HR 577. Presidential Library Donations/Passage. Horn, R-Calif., motion to suspend the rules and pass the bill that would require annual disclosures to Congress of the amount and source of any donations that exceeded $200 to organizations raising funds for a presidential library. Once the library is under the charge of the National Archives and Records Administration, any donations of more than $5,000 would have to be disclosed. Motion agreed to 392-3: R 203-2; D 187-1 (ND 139-1, SD 48-0); I 2-0. A two-thirds majority of those present and voting (264 in this case) is required for passage under suspension of the rules. Feb. 5, 2002.

7. S 970. Horatio King Building/Passage. Horn, R-Calif., motion to suspend the rules and pass the bill that would name a U.S. Post Office building in Paris Hill, Maine, in honor of the late Horatio King, a former postmaster general. Motion agreed to 394-0: R 202-0; D 190-0 (ND 141-0, SD 49-0); I 2-0. A two-thirds majority of those present and voting (263 in this case) is required for passage under suspension of the rules. Feb. 5, 2002.

8. H Res 342. Suspension Motions/Previous Question. Hastings, R-Wash., motion to order the previous question (thus ending debate and possibility of amendment) on adoption of the rule (H Res 342) to provide for House floor consideration of bills under suspension of the rules on Wednesday, Feb. 6. Motion agreed to 212-204: R 211-0; D 0-203 (ND 0-149, SD 0-54); I 1-1. (Subsequently, the rule was agreed to by voice vote. Feb. 6, 2002.

9. S 1888. Olympic Trademarks/Passage. Sensenbrenner, R-Wis., motion to suspend the rules and pass the bill that would correct an error in title 36 of the U.S. Code to protect Olympic trademarks. A two-thirds majority of those present and voting (276 in this case) is required for adoption under suspension of the rules. Motion agreed to 413-0: R 210-0; D 201-0 (ND 148-0, SD 53-0); I 2-0. Feb. 6, 2002.

10. H Con Res 312. Tax Support/Adoption. Weller, R-Ill., motion to suspend the rules and adopt the concurrent resolution that would express the sense of the House that the $1.35 trillion tax cut package enacted in 2001 should not be suspended or repealed. Motion rejected 235-181: R 208-1; D 26-179 (ND 15-136, SD 11-43); I 1-1. A two-thirds majority of those present and voting (278 in this case) is required for adoption under suspension of the rules. Feb. 6, 2002.

	6	7	8	9	10
ALABAMA					
1 *Callahan*	Y	Y	Y	Y	Y
2 *Everett*	Y	Y	Y	Y	Y
3 *Riley*	+	+	+	+	+
4 *Aderholt*	Y	Y	Y	Y	Y
5 Cramer	Y	Y	N	Y	Y
6 *Bachus*	Y	Y	Y	Y	Y
7 Hilliard	Y	Y	N	Y	N
ALASKA					
AL *Young*	?	?	?	?	?
ARIZONA					
1 *Flake*	N	Y	Y	Y	Y
2 Pastor	Y	Y	N	Y	N
3 *Stump*	?	?	Y	Y	Y
4 *Shadegg*	Y	Y	Y	Y	Y
5 *Kolbe*	Y	Y	Y	Y	Y
6 *Hayworth*	Y	Y	Y	Y	Y
ARKANSAS					
1 Berry	Y	Y	N	Y	N
2 Snyder	Y	Y	N	Y	N
3 *Boozman*	Y	Y	Y	Y	Y
4 Ross	Y	Y	N	Y	Y
CALIFORNIA					
1 Thompson	Y	Y	N	Y	N
2 *Herger*	Y	Y	Y	Y	Y
3 *Ose*	Y	Y	Y	Y	Y
4 *Doolittle*	Y	Y	Y	Y	Y
5 Matsui	Y	Y	N	Y	N
6 Woolsey	Y	Y	N	Y	N
7 Miller, George	?	?	N	Y	N
8 Pelosi	Y	Y	N	Y	N
9 Lee	Y	Y	N	Y	N
10 Tauscher	Y	Y	N	Y	N
11 *Pombo*	Y	Y	N	Y	Y
12 Lantos	Y	Y	N	Y	N
13 Stark	Y	Y	N	Y	N
14 Eshoo	Y	Y	N	Y	N
15 Honda	Y	Y	N	Y	N
16 Lofgren	Y	Y	N	Y	N
17 Farr	Y	Y	N	Y	N
18 Condit	Y	Y	N	Y	Y
19 *Radanovich*	?	?	Y	Y	Y
20 Dooley	Y	Y	N	Y	Y
21 *Thomas*	Y	Y	Y	Y	Y
22 Capps	Y	Y	N	Y	N
23 *Gallegly*	?	?	Y	Y	Y
24 Sherman	Y	Y	N	?	N
25 *McKeon*	Y	Y	Y	Y	Y
26 Berman	Y	Y	N	Y	N
27 Schiff	Y	Y	N	Y	N
28 *Dreier*	Y	Y	Y	Y	Y
29 Waxman	Y	Y	N	Y	N
30 Becerra	Y	Y	N	Y	N
31 Solis	Y	Y	N	Y	N
32 Watson	Y	Y	N	Y	N
33 Roybal-Allard	Y	Y	N	Y	N
34 Napolitano	Y	Y	N	Y	?
35 Waters	?	?	N	Y	N
36 Harman	Y	Y	N	Y	N
37 Millender-McD.	?	?	N	Y	N
38 *Horn*	Y	Y	Y	Y	Y

	6	7	8	9	10
39 *Royce*	Y	Y	Y	Y	Y
40 *Lewis*	Y	Y	Y	Y	Y
41 *Miller, Gary*	Y	Y	Y	Y	Y
42 Baca	?	?	N	Y	N
43 *Calvert*	?	?	Y	Y	Y
44 *Bono*	?	?	?	?	?
45 *Rohrabacher*	Y	Y	Y	Y	Y
46 Sanchez	Y	Y	N	Y	N
47 *Cox*	Y	Y	Y	Y	Y
48 *Issa*	Y	Y	Y	Y	Y
49 Davis	Y	Y	N	Y	N
50 Filner	Y	Y	N	Y	N
51 *Cunningham*	Y	Y	Y	Y	Y
52 *Hunter*	Y	Y	Y	Y	Y
COLORADO					
1 DeGette	Y	Y	N	Y	N
2 Udall	Y	Y	N	Y	N
3 *McInnis*	Y	Y	Y	Y	Y
4 *Schaffer*	Y	Y	Y	Y	Y
5 *Hefley*	Y	Y	Y	Y	Y
6 *Tancredo*	Y	Y	Y	Y	Y
CONNECTICUT					
1 Larson	Y	Y	N	Y	N
2 *Simmons*	Y	Y	Y	Y	Y
3 DeLauro	Y	Y	N	Y	N
4 *Shays*	Y	Y	Y	Y	Y
5 Maloney	Y	Y	N	Y	Y
6 *Johnson*	Y	Y	Y	Y	Y
DELAWARE					
AL *Castle*	Y	Y	Y	Y	Y
FLORIDA					
1 *Miller, J.*	Y	Y	Y	Y	Y
2 Boyd	Y	Y	N	Y	N
3 Brown	?	?	N	Y	N
4 *Crenshaw*	Y	Y	Y	Y	Y
5 Thurman	Y	Y	N	Y	N
6 *Stearns*	Y	Y	Y	Y	Y
7 *Mica*	Y	Y	Y	Y	Y
8 *Keller*	Y	Y	Y	Y	Y
9 *Bilirakis*	Y	Y	Y	Y	Y
10 *Young*	?	?	Y	Y	Y
11 Davis	Y	Y	N	Y	N
12 *Putnam*	Y	Y	Y	Y	Y
13 *Miller, D.*	Y	Y	Y	Y	Y
14 *Goss*	Y	Y	Y	Y	Y
15 *Weldon*	Y	Y	Y	Y	Y
16 *Foley*	Y	Y	Y	Y	Y
17 Meek	Y	Y	N	Y	N
18 *Ros-Lehtinen*	Y	Y	Y	Y	Y
19 Wexler	Y	Y	N	Y	N
20 Deutsch	Y	Y	N	Y	N
21 *Diaz-Balart*	Y	Y	Y	Y	Y
22 *Shaw*	?	?	?	?	?
23 Hastings	Y	Y	N	Y	N
GEORGIA					
1 *Kingston*	Y	Y	Y	Y	Y
2 Bishop	Y	Y	N	Y	Y
3 *Collins*	Y	Y	Y	Y	Y
4 McKinney	Y	Y	N	Y	N
5 Lewis	Y	Y	N	Y	N
6 *Isakson*	Y	Y	Y	Y	Y
7 *Barr*	Y	Y	Y	Y	Y
8 *Chambliss*	Y	Y	Y	Y	Y
9 *Deal*	Y	Y	Y	Y	Y
10 *Norwood*	Y	Y	Y	Y	Y
11 *Linder*	Y	Y	Y	Y	Y
HAWAII					
1 Abercrombie	Y	Y	N	Y	N
2 Mink	N	Y	N	Y	N
IDAHO					
1 *Otter*	Y	Y	Y	Y	Y
2 *Simpson*	Y	Y	Y	Y	Y
ILLINOIS					
1 Rush	Y	Y	N	Y	N
2 Jackson	Y	Y	N	Y	N
3 Lipinski	?	?	N	Y	N
4 Gutierrez	Y	Y	N	Y	N
5 Blagojevich	?	?	?	?	?
6 *Hyde*	Y	Y	Y	Y	Y
7 Davis	Y	Y	N	Y	N
8 *Crane*	Y	Y	Y	Y	Y
9 Schakowsky	Y	Y	N	Y	N
10 *Kirk*	Y	Y	Y	Y	Y
11 *Weller*	Y	Y	Y	Y	Y
12 Costello	Y	Y	N	Y	N
13 *Biggert*	Y	Y	Y	Y	Y

ND Northern Democrats   SD Southern Democrats

	6	7	8	9	10
14 ***Hastert***					
15 ***Johnson***	Y	Y	Y	Y	Y
16 ***Manzullo***	Y	Y	Y	Y	Y
17 Evans	Y	Y	N	Y	N
18 ***LaHood***	Y	Y	Y	Y	Y
19 Phelps	Y	Y	N	Y	N
20 ***Shimkus***	Y	Y	Y	Y	Y
INDIANA					
1 Visclosky	Y	Y	N	Y	N
2 ***Pence***	Y	Y	Y	Y	Y
3 Roemer	Y	Y	N	Y	Y
4 ***Souder***	?	?	Y	Y	Y
5 ***Buyer***	Y	Y	Y	Y	Y
6 ***Burton***	Y	Y	Y	Y	Y
7 ***Kerns***	Y	Y	Y	Y	Y
8 ***Hostettler***	Y	Y	Y	Y	Y
9 Hill	Y	Y	N	Y	N
10 Carson	Y	Y	N	Y	N
IOWA					
1 ***Leach***	Y	Y	Y	Y	Y
2 ***Nussle***	Y	Y	Y	Y	Y
3 Boswell	Y	Y	N	Y	N
4 ***Ganske***	Y	Y	Y	Y	Y
5 ***Latham***	Y	Y	Y	Y	Y
KANSAS					
1 ***Moran***	Y	Y	Y	Y	Y
2 ***Ryun***	Y	Y	Y	Y	Y
3 Moore	Y	Y	N	Y	Y
4 ***Tiahrt***	Y	Y	Y	Y	Y
KENTUCKY					
1 ***Whitfield***	Y	Y	Y	Y	Y
2 ***Lewis***	Y	Y	Y	Y	Y
3 ***Northup***	Y	Y	Y	Y	Y
4 Lucas	Y	Y	N	Y	Y
5 ***Rogers***	Y	Y	Y	Y	Y
6 ***Fletcher***	Y	Y	Y	Y	Y
LOUISIANA					
1 ***Vitter***	Y	Y	Y	Y	Y
2 Jefferson	?	?	N	Y	N
3 ***Tauzin***	Y	Y	Y	Y	Y
4 ***McCrery***	Y	Y	Y	Y	Y
5 ***Cooksey***	?	?	?	?	?
6 ***Baker***	Y	Y	Y	Y	Y
7 John	Y	Y	N	Y	N
MAINE					
1 Allen	?	?	N	Y	N
2 Baldacci	?	?	N	Y	N
MARYLAND					
1 ***Gilchrest***	Y	Y	Y	Y	Y
2 ***Ehrlich***	Y	Y	Y	Y	Y
3 Cardin	Y	Y	N	Y	N
4 Wynn	Y	Y	?	?	N
5 Hoyer	Y	Y	?	?	N
6 ***Bartlett***	Y	Y	Y	Y	Y
7 Cummings	Y	Y	N	Y	N
8 ***Morella***	Y	Y	Y	Y	N
MASSACHUSETTS					
1 Olver	Y	Y	N	Y	N
2 Neal	Y	Y	N	Y	N
3 McGovern	Y	Y	N	Y	N
4 Frank	Y	Y	N	Y	N
5 Meehan	Y	Y	N	Y	N
6 Tierney	Y	Y	N	Y	N
7 Markey	Y	Y	N	Y	N
8 Capuano	Y	Y	N	Y	N
9 Lynch	?	?	N	Y	N
10 Delahunt	Y	Y	N	Y	N
MICHIGAN					
1 Stupak	Y	Y	N	Y	N
2 ***Hoekstra***	Y	Y	Y	Y	Y
3 ***Ehlers***	Y	Y	Y	Y	Y
4 ***Camp***	Y	Y	Y	Y	Y
5 Barcia	Y	Y	N	Y	Y
6 ***Upton***	Y	Y	Y	Y	Y
7 ***Smith***	Y	Y	Y	Y	Y
8 ***Rogers***	Y	Y	Y	Y	Y
9 Kildee	Y	Y	N	Y	N
10 Bonior	?	?	N	Y	N
11 ***Knollenberg***	Y	Y	Y	Y	Y
12 Levin	Y	Y	N	Y	N
13 Rivers	Y	Y	N	Y	N
14 Conyers	?	Y	N	Y	N
15 Kilpatrick	Y	Y	N	Y	N
16 Dingell	Y	Y	N	Y	N

	6	7	8	9	10
MINNESOTA					
1 ***Gutknecht***	Y	Y	Y	Y	Y
2 ***Kennedy***	Y	Y	Y	Y	Y
3 ***Ramstad***	Y	Y	Y	Y	Y
4 McCollum	?	?	N	Y	N
5 Sabo	Y	Y	N	Y	N
6 Luther	?	?	?	?	?
7 Peterson	Y	Y	N	Y	Y
8 Oberstar	Y	Y	N	Y	N
MISSISSIPPI					
1 ***Wicker***	Y	Y	Y	Y	Y
2 Thompson	Y	Y	N	Y	N
3 ***Pickering***	Y	Y	Y	Y	Y
4 Shows	Y	Y	N	Y	Y
5 Taylor	Y	Y	N	Y	N
MISSOURI					
1 Clay	Y	Y	N	Y	N
2 ***Akin***	Y	Y	Y	Y	Y
3 Gephardt	Y	Y	N	Y	N
4 Skelton	Y	Y	N	Y	N
5 McCarthy	Y	Y	N	Y	N
6 ***Graves***	Y	Y	Y	Y	Y
7 ***Blunt***	Y	Y	Y	Y	Y
8 ***Emerson***	Y	Y	Y	Y	Y
9 ***Hulshof***	Y	Y	Y	Y	Y
MONTANA					
AL ***Rehberg***	Y	Y	Y	Y	Y
NEBRASKA					
1 ***Bereuter***	Y	Y	Y	Y	Y
2 ***Terry***	Y	Y	Y	Y	Y
3 ***Osborne***	Y	Y	Y	Y	Y
NEVADA					
1 Berkley	Y	Y	N	Y	N
2 ***Gibbons***	Y	Y	Y	Y	Y
NEW HAMPSHIRE					
1 ***Sununu***	Y	Y	Y	Y	?
2 ***Bass***	Y	Y	Y	Y	Y
NEW JERSEY					
1 Andrews	Y	Y	N	Y	N
2 ***LoBiondo***	Y	Y	Y	Y	Y
3 ***Saxton***	Y	Y	Y	Y	Y
4 ***Smith***	Y	Y	Y	Y	Y
5 ***Roukema***	?	?	?	?	?
6 Pallone	Y	Y	N	Y	N
7 ***Ferguson***	Y	Y	Y	Y	Y
8 Pascrell	Y	Y	N	Y	N
9 Rothman	Y	Y	N	Y	N
10 Payne	Y	Y	N	Y	N
11 ***Frelinghuysen***	?	?	?	?	?
12 Holt	Y	Y	N	Y	N
13 Menendez	Y	Y	N	Y	N
NEW MEXICO					
1 ***Wilson***	Y	Y	Y	Y	Y
2 ***Skeen***	Y	Y	Y	Y	Y
3 Udall	Y	Y	N	Y	N
NEW YORK					
1 ***Grucci***	Y	Y	Y	Y	Y
2 Israel	Y	Y	N	Y	Y
3 ***King***	Y	Y	Y	Y	Y
4 McCarthy	Y	Y	N	Y	Y
5 Ackerman	Y	Y	N	Y	N
6 Meeks	?	?	N	Y	N
7 Crowley	Y	Y	N	Y	N
8 Nadler	Y	Y	N	Y	N
9 Weiner	Y	Y	N	Y	N
10 Towns	Y	Y	N	Y	N
11 Owens	Y	Y	N	Y	N
12 Velázquez	Y	Y	N	?	N
13 ***Fossella***	Y	Y	Y	Y	?
14 Maloney	Y	Y	N	Y	N
15 Rangel	Y	Y	N	Y	N
16 Serrano	Y	Y	N	Y	N
17 Engel	Y	Y	N	Y	N
18 Lowey	Y	Y	N	Y	N
19 ***Kelly***	Y	Y	Y	Y	Y
20 ***Gilman***	Y	Y	Y	Y	Y
21 McNulty	Y	Y	N	Y	N
22 ***Sweeney***	Y	Y	Y	Y	Y
23 ***Boehlert***	Y	Y	Y	Y	Y
24 ***McHugh***	Y	Y	Y	Y	Y
25 ***Walsh***	Y	Y	Y	Y	Y
26 Hinchey	Y	Y	N	Y	N
27 ***Reynolds***	Y	Y	Y	Y	Y
28 Slaughter	+	+	–	+	–
29 LaFalce	?	?	N	Y	N

	6	7	8	9	10
30 ***Quinn***	Y	Y	Y	Y	Y
31 ***Houghton***	Y	Y	Y	Y	Y
NORTH CAROLINA					
1 Clayton	Y	Y	N	Y	N
2 Etheridge	Y	Y	N	Y	N
3 ***Jones***	Y	Y	Y	Y	Y
4 Price	Y	Y	N	Y	N
5 ***Burr***	Y	Y	Y	Y	Y
6 ***Coble***	Y	Y	Y	Y	Y
7 McIntyre	Y	Y	N	Y	Y
8 ***Hayes***	Y	Y	Y	Y	Y
9 ***Myrick***	Y	Y	Y	Y	Y
10 ***Ballenger***	Y	Y	Y	Y	Y
11 ***Taylor***	Y	?	Y	Y	Y
12 Watt	Y	Y	N	Y	N
NORTH DAKOTA					
AL Pomeroy	Y	Y	N	Y	N
OHIO					
1 ***Chabot***	Y	Y	Y	Y	Y
2 ***Portman***	Y	Y	Y	Y	Y
3 Hall	Y	Y	N	Y	Y
4 ***Oxley***	Y	Y	+	+	+
5 ***Gillmor***	Y	Y	Y	Y	Y
6 Strickland	Y	Y	N	Y	N
7 ***Hobson***	Y	Y	Y	Y	Y
8 ***Boehner***	Y	Y	Y	Y	Y
9 Kaptur	Y	Y	N	Y	N
10 Kucinich	Y	Y	N	Y	N
11 Jones	Y	Y	N	Y	N
12 ***Tiberi***	Y	Y	Y	Y	Y
13 Brown	Y	Y	N	Y	N
14 Sawyer	Y	Y	N	Y	N
15 ***Pryce***	?	?	Y	Y	Y
16 ***Regula***	Y	?	Y	Y	Y
17 Traficant	?	?	?	?	?
18 ***Ney***	Y	Y	Y	Y	Y
19 ***LaTourette***	Y	Y	Y	Y	Y
OKLAHOMA					
1 ***Largent***	Y	Y	Y	Y	Y
2 Carson	Y	Y	N	Y	Y
3 ***Watkins***	Y	Y	Y	Y	Y
4 ***Watts***	Y	Y	Y	Y	Y
5 ***Istook***	Y	Y	Y	Y	Y
6 ***Lucas***	?	?	Y	Y	Y
OREGON					
1 Wu	Y	Y	N	Y	N
2 ***Walden***	Y	Y	Y	Y	Y
3 Blumenauer	Y	Y	N	Y	N
4 DeFazio	Y	Y	N	Y	N
5 Hooley	Y	Y	N	Y	Y
PENNSYLVANIA					
1 Brady	Y	Y	N	Y	N
2 Fattah	Y	Y	N	Y	N
3 Borski	Y	Y	N	Y	N
4 ***Hart***	Y	Y	Y	Y	Y
5 ***Peterson***	Y	Y	Y	Y	Y
6 Holden	Y	Y	N	Y	N
7 ***Weldon***	Y	Y	Y	Y	Y
8 ***Greenwood***	Y	Y	Y	Y	Y
9 ***Shuster, Bill***	Y	Y	Y	Y	Y
10 ***Sherwood***	Y	Y	Y	Y	Y
11 Kanjorski	Y	Y	N	Y	N
12 Murtha	Y	Y	N	Y	N
13 Hoeffel	Y	Y	N	Y	N
14 Coyne	Y	Y	N	Y	N
15 ***Toomey***	Y	Y	Y	Y	Y
16 ***Pitts***	Y	Y	Y	Y	Y
17 ***Gekas***	Y	Y	Y	Y	Y
18 Doyle	Y	Y	N	Y	N
19 ***Platts***	Y	Y	Y	Y	Y
20 Mascara	Y	Y	N	Y	N
21 ***English***	Y	Y	Y	Y	Y
RHODE ISLAND					
1 Kennedy	Y	Y	N	Y	N
2 Langevin	Y	Y	N	Y	N
SOUTH CAROLINA					
1 ***Brown***	Y	Y	Y	Y	Y
2 ***Wilson***	Y	Y	Y	Y	Y
3 ***Graham***	Y	Y	Y	Y	Y
4 ***DeMint***	Y	Y	Y	Y	Y
5 Spratt	Y	Y	N	Y	N
6 Clyburn	Y	Y	N	Y	N
SOUTH DAKOTA					
AL ***Thune***	Y	Y	Y	Y	Y

	6	7	8	9	10
TENNESSEE					
1 ***Jenkins***	Y	Y	Y	Y	Y
2 ***Duncan***	Y	Y	Y	Y	Y
3 ***Wamp***	Y	Y	Y	?	Y
4 ***Hilleary***	Y	Y	Y	Y	Y
5 Clement	Y	Y	N	Y	N
6 Gordon	Y	Y	N	Y	Y
7 ***Bryant***	Y	Y	Y	Y	Y
8 Tanner	Y	Y	N	Y	N
9 Ford	Y	Y	N	Y	N
TEXAS					
1 Sandlin	Y	Y	N	Y	Y
2 Turner	Y	Y	N	Y	N
3 ***Johnson, Sam***	Y	Y	Y	Y	Y
4 Hall	?	?	N	Y	Y
5 ***Sessions***	Y	Y	Y	Y	Y
6 ***Barton***	Y	Y	Y	Y	Y
7 ***Culberson***	Y	Y	Y	Y	Y
8 ***Brady***	Y	Y	Y	Y	Y
9 Lampson	?	Y	N	?	N
10 Doggett	Y	Y	N	Y	N
11 Edwards	Y	Y	N	Y	N
12 ***Granger***	?	?	Y	Y	Y
13 ***Thornberry***	Y	Y	Y	Y	Y
14 ***Paul***	N	Y	Y	Y	Y
15 Hinojosa	+	+	N	Y	N
16 Reyes	Y	Y	N	Y	N
17 Stenholm	Y	Y	N	Y	N
18 Jackson-Lee	Y	Y	N	Y	N
19 ***Combest***	Y	Y	Y	Y	Y
20 Gonzalez	Y	Y	N	Y	N
21 ***Smith***	Y	Y	Y	Y	Y
22 ***DeLay***	Y	Y	Y	Y	Y
23 ***Bonilla***	Y	Y	Y	Y	Y
24 Frost	Y	Y	N	Y	N
25 Bentsen	Y	Y	N	Y	N
26 ***Armey***	Y	Y	Y	Y	Y
27 Ortiz	Y	Y	N	Y	N
28 Rodriguez	?	?	N	Y	N
29 Green	Y	Y	N	Y	N
30 Johnson, E.B.	Y	Y	N	Y	N
UTAH					
1 ***Hansen***	Y	Y	Y	Y	Y
2 Matheson	Y	Y	N	Y	Y
3 ***Cannon***	Y	Y	Y	Y	Y
VERMONT					
AL *Sanders*	Y	Y	N	Y	N
VIRGINIA					
1 ***Davis, Jo Ann***	Y	Y	Y	Y	Y
2 ***Schrock***	Y	Y	Y	Y	Y
3 Scott	Y	Y	N	Y	N
4 ***Forbes***	Y	Y	Y	Y	Y
5 *Goode*	Y	Y	Y	Y	Y
6 ***Goodlatte***	Y	Y	Y	Y	Y
7 ***Cantor***	Y	Y	Y	Y	Y
8 Moran	Y	Y	N	Y	N
9 Boucher	Y	Y	N	Y	N
10 ***Wolf***	Y	Y	Y	Y	Y
11 ***Davis, T.***	Y	Y	Y	Y	Y
WASHINGTON					
1 Inslee	Y	Y	N	Y	N
2 Larsen	Y	Y	N	Y	Y
3 Baird	Y	Y	N	Y	N
4 ***Hastings***	Y	Y	Y	Y	Y
5 ***Nethercutt***	Y	Y	Y	Y	Y
6 Dicks	Y	Y	N	Y	N
7 McDermott	Y	Y	?	?	–
8 ***Dunn***	Y	Y	Y	Y	Y
9 Smith	Y	Y	N	Y	N
WEST VIRGINIA					
1 Mollohan	Y	Y	N	Y	N
2 ***Capito***	Y	+	Y	Y	Y
3 Rahall	Y	Y	N	Y	N
WISCONSIN					
1 ***Ryan***	?	?	?	?	?
2 Baldwin	Y	Y	N	Y	N
3 Kind	Y	Y	N	Y	N
4 Kleczka	Y	Y	N	Y	N
5 Barrett	Y	Y	N	Y	N
6 ***Petri***	Y	Y	Y	Y	Y
7 Obey	Y	Y	N	Y	N
8 ***Green***	Y	Y	Y	Y	Y
9 ***Sensenbrenner***	Y	Y	Y	Y	Y
WYOMING					
AL ***Cubin***	Y	Y	?	?	?

Southern states - Ala., Ark., Fla., Ga., Ky., La., Miss., N.C., Okla., S.C., Tenn., Texas, Va.

Key

Y	Voted for (yea).
#	Paired for.
+	Announced for.
N	Voted against (nay).
X	Paired against.
–	Announced against.
P	Voted "present."
C	Voted "present" to avoid possible conflict of interest.
?	Did not vote or otherwise make a position known.

Democrats **Republicans**
Independents

11. H J Res 82. Ronald Reagan's Birthday/Passage. Weldon, R-Pa., motion to suspend the rules and pass the joint resolution that would wish former President Ronald Reagan a happy 91st birthday. Motion agreed to 408-0: R 207-0; D 200-0 (ND 149-0, SD 51-0); I 1-0. A two-thirds majority of those present and voting (272 in this case) is required for passage under suspension of the rules. Feb. 6, 2002.

12. HR 3394. Computer Protection/Rule. Adoption of the rule (H Res 343) to provide for House floor consideration of the bill that would authorize $880 million through fiscal 2007 for the National Science Foundation and the National Institute of Standards and Technology to initiate and operate research programs aimed at protecting federal computer networks. Adopted 392-0: R 198-0; D 193-0 (ND 141-0, SD 52-0); I 1-0. Feb. 7, 2002.

13. HR 3394. Computer Protection/Passage. Passage of the bill that would authorize $880 million through fiscal 2007 for the National Science Foundation and the National Institute of Standards and Technology to initiate and operate research programs aimed at protecting federal computer networks. Passed 400-12: R 198-12; D 200-0 (ND 147-0, SD 53-0); I 2-0. Feb. 7, 2002.

14. Procedural Motion/Journal. Approval of the House Journal of Wednesday, Feb. 6, 2002. Approved 363-33: R 190-10; D 171-23 (ND 126-16, SD 45-7); I 2-0. Feb. 7, 2002.

		11	12	13	14
ALABAMA					
1	*Callahan*	Y	Y	Y	Y
2	*Everett*	Y	Y	Y	?
3	*Riley*	+	+	+	+
4	*Aderholt*	Y	Y	Y	N
5	Cramer	Y	Y	Y	Y
6	*Bachus*	Y	Y	Y	Y
7	Hilliard	Y	Y	Y	Y
ALASKA					
AL	*Young*	?	?	Y	Y
ARIZONA					
1	*Flake*	Y	Y	N	Y
2	Pastor	Y	Y	Y	Y
3	*Stump*	Y	Y	Y	Y
4	*Shadegg*	Y	Y	Y	Y
5	*Kolbe*	Y	Y	Y	Y
6	Hayworth	Y	Y	Y	Y
ARKANSAS					
1	Berry	Y	Y	Y	Y
2	Snyder	Y	Y	Y	Y
3	*Boozman*	Y	Y	Y	Y
4	Ross	Y	Y	Y	Y
CALIFORNIA					
1	Thompson	Y	Y	Y	N
2	*Herger*	Y	Y	Y	Y
3	*Ose*	Y	Y	Y	Y
4	*Doolittle*	Y	Y	Y	Y
5	Matsui	Y	Y	Y	Y
6	Woolsey	Y	Y	Y	Y
7	Miller, George	Y	Y	Y	N
8	Pelosi	Y	Y	Y	Y
9	Lee	P	Y	Y	Y
10	Tauscher	Y	Y	Y	Y
11	*Pombo*	Y	Y	Y	Y
12	Lantos	Y	Y	Y	Y
13	Stark	P	Y	Y	N
14	Eshoo	Y	Y	Y	Y
15	Honda	Y	Y	Y	Y
16	Lofgren	Y	Y	Y	Y
17	Farr	Y	Y	Y	Y
18	Condit	Y	Y	Y	Y
19	*Radanovich*	Y	Y	Y	Y
20	Dooley	Y	Y	Y	Y
21	*Thomas*	Y	Y	Y	Y
22	Capps	Y	Y	Y	Y
23	*Gallegly*	Y	Y	Y	?
24	Sherman	Y	Y	Y	Y
25	*McKeon*	Y	Y	Y	Y
26	Berman	Y	Y	Y	Y
27	Schiff	Y	Y	Y	Y
28	*Dreier*	Y	Y	Y	Y
29	Waxman	Y	Y	Y	Y
30	Becerra	Y	Y	Y	Y
31	Solis	Y	Y	+	Y
32	Watson	P	Y	Y	Y
33	Roybal-Allard	Y	Y	Y	Y
34	Napolitano	Y	Y	Y	Y
35	Waters	Y	?	?	?
36	Harman	Y	Y	Y	Y
37	Millender-McD.	Y	Y	Y	Y
38	*Horn*	Y	Y	Y	Y

		11	12	13	14
39	*Royce*	Y	Y	N	Y
40	*Lewis*	Y	Y	Y	Y
41	*Miller, Gary*	Y	Y	Y	Y
42	Baca	Y	Y	Y	Y
43	*Calvert*	Y	Y	Y	Y
44	*Bono*	?	?	?	?
45	*Rohrabacher*	Y	Y	Y	Y
46	Sanchez	Y	Y	Y	Y
47	*Cox*	Y	Y	Y	Y
48	*Issa*	Y	Y	Y	Y
49	Davis	Y	Y	Y	Y
50	Filner	Y	Y	Y	N
51	*Cunningham*	Y	Y	Y	Y
52	*Hunter*	Y	Y	Y	Y
COLORADO					
1	DeGette	Y	Y	Y	Y
2	Udall	Y	Y	Y	Y
3	*McInnis*	Y	Y	Y	Y
4	*Schaffer*	Y	Y	N	N
5	*Hefley*	Y	Y	N	N
6	*Tancredo*	Y	Y	N	P
CONNECTICUT					
1	Larson	Y	Y	Y	Y
2	*Simmons*	Y	Y	Y	Y
3	DeLauro	Y	Y	Y	Y
4	*Shays*	Y	Y	Y	Y
5	Maloney	Y	Y	Y	Y
6	*Johnson*	Y	Y	Y	Y
DELAWARE					
AL	*Castle*	Y	Y	Y	Y
FLORIDA					
1	*Miller, J.*	Y	Y	Y	Y
2	Boyd	Y	Y	Y	Y
3	Brown	Y	Y	Y	Y
4	*Crenshaw*	Y	Y	Y	Y
5	Thurman	Y	Y	Y	Y
6	*Stearns*	Y	Y	Y	Y
7	*Mica*	Y	Y	Y	Y
8	*Keller*	Y	Y	Y	Y
9	*Bilirakis*	Y	Y	Y	Y
10	*Young*	Y	Y	Y	Y
11	Davis	Y	Y	Y	Y
12	*Putnam*	Y	Y	Y	Y
13	*Miller, D.*	Y	Y	Y	Y
14	*Goss*	Y	Y	Y	Y
15	*Weldon*	Y	?	Y	Y
16	*Foley*	Y	Y	Y	Y
17	Meek	Y	Y	Y	Y
18	*Ros-Lehtinen*	Y	Y	Y	Y
19	Wexler	Y	Y	Y	?
20	Deutsch	Y	Y	Y	Y
21	*Diaz-Balart*	Y	Y	Y	Y
22	*Shaw*	?	?	?	?
23	Hastings	Y	Y	Y	N
GEORGIA					
1	*Kingston*	Y	Y	N	?
2	Bishop	Y	Y	Y	Y
3	*Collins*	Y	Y	N	Y
4	McKinney	Y	?	Y	Y
5	Lewis	Y	Y	Y	Y
6	*Isakson*	Y	Y	Y	Y
7	*Barr*	Y	Y	Y	Y
8	*Chambliss*	Y	Y	Y	Y
9	*Deal*	Y	Y	Y	Y
10	*Norwood*	Y	Y	N	Y
11	*Linder*	Y	?	Y	?
HAWAII					
1	Abercrombie	Y	Y	Y	Y
2	Mink	Y	Y	Y	Y
IDAHO					
1	*Otter*	Y	Y	Y	Y
2	*Simpson*	Y	Y	Y	Y
ILLINOIS					
1	Rush	Y	Y	Y	Y
2	Jackson	Y	Y	Y	Y
3	Lipinski	Y	Y	Y	Y
4	Gutierrez	Y	Y	Y	?
5	Blagojevich	?	?	?	?
6	*Hyde*	Y	?	Y	Y
7	Davis	Y	Y	Y	Y
8	*Crane*	Y	Y	Y	N
9	Schakowsky	Y	Y	Y	?
10	*Kirk*	Y	Y	Y	Y
11	*Weller*	Y	Y	Y	N
12	Costello	Y	Y	Y	N
13	*Biggert*	Y	Y	Y	Y

ND Northern Democrats   SD Southern Democrats

	11	12	13	14
14 Hastert	Y			
15 *Johnson*	Y	Y	Y	Y
16 *Manzullo*	Y	Y	Y	Y
17 Evans	Y	?	Y	Y
18 *LaHood*	Y	Y	Y	Y
19 Phelps	Y	Y	Y	Y
20 *Shimkus*	Y	Y	Y	Y

INDIANA

	11	12	13	14
1 Visclosky	Y	Y	Y	N
2 *Pence*	Y	Y	Y	Y
3 *Roemer*	Y	Y	Y	Y
4 *Souder*	Y	Y	Y	Y
5 *Buyer*	Y	Y	Y	Y
6 *Burton*	Y	+	+	?
7 *Kerns*	Y	Y	Y	Y
8 *Hostettler*	?	Y	Y	Y
9 Hill	Y	Y	Y	Y
10 Carson	Y	Y	Y	Y

IOWA

	11	12	13	14
1 *Leach*	Y	Y	Y	Y
2 *Nussle*	Y	Y	Y	Y
3 Boswell	Y	Y	Y	Y
4 *Ganske*	Y	Y	Y	Y
5 *Latham*	Y	Y	Y	N

KANSAS

	11	12	13	14
1 *Moran*	Y	Y	Y	Y
2 *Ryun*	Y	Y	Y	Y
3 Moore	Y	?	Y	N
4 *Tiahrt*	Y	Y	Y	Y

KENTUCKY

	11	12	13	14
1 *Whitfield*	Y	?	?	?
2 *Lewis*	Y	Y	Y	Y
3 *Northup*	Y	?	Y	Y
4 Lucas	Y	Y	Y	Y
5 *Rogers*	Y	Y	Y	Y
6 *Fletcher*	Y	Y	Y	Y

LOUISIANA

	11	12	13	14
1 *Vitter*	Y	Y	Y	Y
2 Jefferson	?	?	?	?
3 *Tauzin*	Y	?	Y	Y
4 *McCrery*	Y	Y	Y	Y
5 *Cooksey*	Y	Y	Y	Y
6 *Baker*	Y	Y	Y	Y
7 John	Y	Y	Y	Y

MAINE

	11	12	13	14
1 Allen	Y	Y	Y	Y
2 Baldacci	Y	Y	Y	Y

MARYLAND

	11	12	13	14
1 Gilchrest	Y	Y	Y	Y
2 *Ehrlich*	Y	Y	Y	Y
3 Cardin	Y	Y	Y	Y
4 Wynn	Y	Y	Y	Y
5 Hoyer	Y	Y	Y	Y
6 *Bartlett*	Y	Y	Y	Y
7 Cummings	Y	Y	Y	Y
8 *Morella*	Y	Y	Y	Y

MASSACHUSETTS

	11	12	13	14
1 Olver	Y	Y	Y	Y
2 Neal	Y	Y	Y	Y
3 McGovern	Y	Y	Y	Y
4 Frank	Y	Y	Y	Y
5 Meehan	Y	Y	Y	Y
6 Tierney	Y	Y	Y	Y
7 Markey	Y	Y	Y	Y
8 Capuano	Y	?	?	?
9 Lynch	Y	Y	Y	Y
10 Delahunt	Y	Y	Y	Y

MICHIGAN

	11	12	13	14
1 Stupak	Y	Y	Y	Y
2 *Hoekstra*	Y	Y	Y	?
3 *Ehlers*	Y	Y	Y	Y
4 *Camp*	Y	Y	Y	Y
5 Barcia	Y	Y	Y	Y
6 *Upton*	Y	Y	Y	Y
7 *Smith*	Y	Y	Y	?
8 *Rogers*	Y	Y	Y	Y
9 Kildee	Y	Y	Y	Y
10 Bonior	Y	Y	Y	Y
11 *Knollenberg*	Y	Y	Y	Y
12 Levin	Y	Y	Y	Y
13 Rivers	Y	Y	Y	Y
14 Conyers	Y	Y	Y	?
15 Kilpatrick	Y	Y	Y	Y
16 Dingell	Y	Y	Y	Y

MINNESOTA

	11	12	13	14
1 *Gutknecht*	Y	Y	Y	N
2 *Kennedy*	Y	Y	Y	N
3 *Ramstad*	Y	Y	Y	Y
4 McCollum	Y	Y	Y	?
5 Sabo	Y	Y	Y	Y
6 Luther	?	?	?	?
7 Peterson	Y	Y	Y	N
8 Oberstar	Y	Y	Y	N

MISSISSIPPI

	11	12	13	14
1 *Wicker*	Y	Y	Y	Y
2 Thompson	Y	Y	Y	N
3 *Pickering*	Y	Y	Y	Y
4 Shows	Y	Y	Y	Y
5 Taylor	Y	Y	Y	N

MISSOURI

	11	12	13	14
1 Clay	Y	?	Y	Y
2 *Akin*	Y	Y	N	Y
3 Gephardt	Y	Y	Y	Y
4 Skelton	Y	Y	Y	Y
5 McCarthy	Y	Y	Y	+
6 *Graves*	Y	Y	Y	Y
7 *Blunt*	Y	Y	Y	Y
8 *Emerson*	Y	Y	Y	Y
9 *Hulshof*	Y	Y	Y	Y

MONTANA

	11	12	13	14
AL *Rehberg*	Y	Y	Y	Y

NEBRASKA

	11	12	13	14
1 *Bereuter*	Y	Y	Y	Y
2 *Terry*	Y	Y	Y	?
3 *Osborne*	Y	Y	Y	Y

NEVADA

	11	12	13	14
1 Berkley	Y	Y	Y	Y
2 *Gibbons*	Y	Y	Y	Y

NEW HAMPSHIRE

	11	12	13	14
1 *Sununu*	Y	Y	Y	Y
2 *Bass*	Y	Y	Y	Y

NEW JERSEY

	11	12	13	14
1 Andrews	Y	Y	Y	Y
2 *LoBiondo*	Y	Y	Y	N
3 *Saxton*	Y	Y	Y	Y
4 *Smith*	Y	Y	Y	Y
5 *Roukema*	?	?	?	?
6 Pallone	Y	Y	Y	?
7 *Ferguson*	Y	Y	Y	Y
8 Pascrell	Y	Y	Y	Y
9 Rothman	Y	Y	Y	Y
10 Payne	Y	Y	Y	Y
11 *Frelinghuysen*	?	?	?	?
12 Holt	Y	Y	Y	Y
13 Menendez	Y	Y	Y	Y

NEW MEXICO

	11	12	13	14
1 *Wilson*	Y	?	Y	Y
2 *Skeen*	Y	Y	Y	Y
3 Udall	Y	Y	Y	N

NEW YORK

	11	12	13	14
1 *Grucci*	Y	Y	Y	Y
2 Israel	Y	Y	Y	Y
3 *King*	Y	Y	Y	Y
4 McCarthy	Y	Y	Y	Y
5 Ackerman	Y	Y	Y	Y
6 Meeks	Y	Y	Y	Y
7 Crowley	Y	Y	Y	Y
8 Nadler	Y	Y	Y	Y
9 Weiner	Y	Y	Y	Y
10 Towns	Y	Y	Y	Y
11 Owens	Y	Y	Y	Y
12 Velázquez	Y	Y	Y	Y
13 *Fossella*	?	Y	Y	Y
14 Maloney	Y	?	Y	Y
15 Rangel	Y	Y	Y	Y
16 Serrano	Y	Y	Y	Y
17 Engel	Y	Y	Y	Y
18 Lowey	Y	Y	Y	Y
19 *Kelly*	Y	Y	Y	Y
20 *Gilman*	Y	Y	Y	Y
21 McNulty	Y	Y	Y	Y
22 *Sweeney*	Y	Y	Y	Y
23 *Boehlert*	Y	Y	Y	Y
24 *McHugh*	Y	Y	Y	Y
25 *Walsh*	Y	Y	Y	Y
26 Hinchey	Y	Y	Y	Y
27 *Reynolds*	Y	Y	Y	Y
28 Slaughter	+	+	+	+
29 LaFalce	Y	Y	Y	Y
30 *Quinn*	Y	Y	Y	Y
31 Houghton	Y	Y	Y	Y

NORTH CAROLINA

	11	12	13	14
1 Clayton	Y	Y	Y	Y
2 Etheridge	Y	Y	Y	Y
3 *Jones*	Y	Y	N	Y
4 Price	Y	Y	Y	Y
5 *Burr*	Y	?	Y	Y
6 *Coble*	Y	Y	Y	Y
7 McIntyre	Y	Y	Y	Y
8 *Hayes*	Y	Y	Y	Y
9 *Myrick*	Y	Y	Y	Y
10 *Ballenger*	Y	Y	Y	Y
11 *Taylor*	Y	Y	Y	?
12 Watt	Y	Y	Y	Y

NORTH DAKOTA

	11	12	13	14
AL Pomeroy	Y	Y	Y	Y

OHIO

	11	12	13	14
1 *Chabot*	Y	Y	Y	Y
2 *Portman*	Y	Y	Y	Y
3 Hall	Y	?	?	?
4 *Oxley*	+	Y	Y	Y
5 *Gillmor*	Y	Y	Y	Y
6 Strickland	Y	Y	Y	N
7 *Hobson*	Y	Y	Y	Y
8 *Boehner*	?	Y	Y	Y
9 Kaptur	Y	?	Y	Y
10 Kucinich	Y	Y	Y	Y
11 Jones	Y	Y	Y	Y
12 *Tiberi*	Y	Y	Y	Y
13 Brown	Y	Y	Y	Y
14 Sawyer	Y	Y	Y	Y
15 *Pryce*	Y	Y	Y	Y
16 *Regula*	Y	Y	Y	Y
17 Traficant	?	?	?	?
18 *Ney*	Y	Y	Y	Y
19 *LaTourette*	Y	Y	Y	Y

OKLAHOMA

	11	12	13	14
1 *Largent*	Y	?	Y	Y
2 Carson	Y	Y	Y	Y
3 *Watkins*	Y	Y	Y	Y
4 *Watts*	Y	Y	Y	Y
5 *Istook*	Y	Y	Y	Y
6 *Lucas*	Y	?	Y	?

OREGON

	11	12	13	14
1 Wu	Y	Y	Y	N
2 *Walden*	Y	Y	Y	Y
3 Blumenauer	Y	Y	Y	Y
4 DeFazio	Y	Y	Y	N
5 Hooley	Y	Y	Y	Y

PENNSYLVANIA

	11	12	13	14
1 Brady	Y	Y	Y	N
2 Fattah	Y	?	Y	Y
3 Borski	Y	Y	Y	Y
4 *Hart*	Y	Y	Y	Y
5 *Peterson*	Y	Y	Y	Y
6 Holden	Y	Y	Y	Y
7 *Weldon*	?	?	Y	Y
8 *Greenwood*	Y	Y	Y	Y
9 *Shuster, Bill*	Y	Y	Y	Y
10 *Sherwood*	Y	Y	Y	Y
11 Kanjorski	Y	Y	Y	Y
12 Murtha	Y	Y	Y	Y
13 Hoeffel	Y	Y	Y	Y
14 Coyne	Y	Y	Y	Y
15 *Toomey*	Y	Y	Y	Y
16 *Pitts*	Y	?	?	?
17 *Gekas*	Y	Y	Y	Y
18 Doyle	Y	Y	Y	Y
19 *Platts*	Y	Y	Y	Y
20 Mascara	Y	Y	Y	Y
21 *English*	Y	Y	Y	N

RHODE ISLAND

	11	12	13	14
1 Kennedy	Y	Y	Y	Y
2 Langevin	Y	Y	Y	Y

SOUTH CAROLINA

	11	12	13	14
1 *Brown*	Y	Y	Y	Y
2 *Wilson*	+	Y	Y	Y
3 *Graham*	Y	Y	Y	Y
4 *DeMint*	Y	Y	Y	Y
5 Spratt	Y	Y	Y	Y
6 Clyburn	Y	Y	Y	Y

SOUTH DAKOTA

	11	12	13	14
AL *Thune*	Y	Y	Y	Y

TENNESSEE

	11	12	13	14
1 *Jenkins*	Y	Y	Y	Y
2 *Duncan*	Y	Y	N	Y
3 *Wamp*	Y	Y	Y	Y
4 *Hilleary*	Y	?	?	?
5 Clement	Y	Y	Y	Y
6 Gordon	Y	Y	Y	Y
7 *Bryant*	Y	Y	Y	Y
8 Tanner	Y	Y	Y	N
9 Ford	Y	Y	Y	Y

TEXAS

	11	12	13	14
1 Sandlin	Y	Y	Y	Y
2 Turner	Y	Y	Y	Y
3 *Johnson, Sam*	Y	Y	Y	Y
4 Hall	Y	Y	Y	Y
5 *Sessions*	Y	Y	Y	Y
6 *Barton*	Y	+	Y	Y
7 *Culberson*	Y	Y	Y	Y
8 *Brady*	Y	Y	Y	Y
9 Lampson	Y	Y	Y	Y
10 Doggett	Y	Y	Y	Y
11 Edwards	Y	Y	Y	Y
12 *Granger*	Y	Y	Y	Y
13 *Thornberry*	Y	Y	Y	Y
14 *Paul*	Y	Y	N	Y
15 Hinojosa	Y	Y	Y	Y
16 Reyes	Y	Y	Y	Y
17 Stenholm	Y	Y	Y	N
18 Jackson-Lee	Y	Y	Y	Y
19 *Combest*	Y	Y	Y	Y
20 Gonzalez	Y	Y	Y	Y
21 *Smith*	Y	Y	Y	Y
22 *DeLay*	Y	Y	Y	Y
23 *Bonilla*	Y	Y	Y	Y
24 Frost	?	Y	Y	Y
25 Bentsen	Y	Y	Y	Y
26 *Armey*	Y	Y	Y	Y
27 Ortiz	Y	Y	Y	Y
28 Rodriguez	Y	Y	Y	Y
29 Green	Y	Y	Y	Y
30 Johnson, E.B.	P	Y	Y	N

UTAH

	11	12	13	14
1 *Hansen*	Y	Y	Y	Y
2 Matheson	Y	Y	Y	Y
3 *Cannon*	Y	Y	Y	Y

VERMONT

	11	12	13	14
AL *Sanders*	?	Y	Y	Y

VIRGINIA

	11	12	13	14
1 *Davis, Jo Ann*	Y	Y	Y	Y
2 *Schrock*	Y	Y	Y	Y
3 Scott	Y	Y	Y	N
4 *Forbes*	Y	Y	Y	Y
5 *Goode*	Y	?	Y	Y
6 *Goodlatte*	Y	Y	Y	Y
7 *Cantor*	Y	Y	Y	Y
8 Moran	Y	Y	Y	Y
9 Boucher	Y	Y	Y	Y
10 *Wolf*	Y	Y	Y	Y
11 *Davis, T.*	?	Y	Y	Y

WASHINGTON

	11	12	13	14
1 Inslee	Y	Y	Y	Y
2 Larsen	Y	Y	Y	N
3 Baird	Y	Y	Y	N
4 *Hastings*	Y	Y	Y	Y
5 *Nethercutt*	Y	Y	Y	Y
6 Dicks	Y	Y	Y	Y
7 McDermott	+	?	?	?
8 *Dunn*	Y	Y	Y	Y
9 Smith	Y	Y	Y	Y

WEST VIRGINIA

	11	12	13	14
1 Mollohan	Y	Y	Y	Y
2 *Capito*	Y	Y	Y	Y
3 Rahall	Y	Y	Y	Y

WISCONSIN

	11	12	13	14
1 *Ryan*	?	?	?	?
2 Baldwin	Y	Y	Y	Y
3 Kind	Y	Y	Y	Y
4 Kleczka	Y	?	Y	Y
5 Barrett	Y	Y	Y	Y
6 *Petri*	Y	Y	Y	Y
7 Obey	Y	?	?	?
8 *Green*	Y	Y	Y	Y
9 *Sensenbrenner*	Y	Y	Y	Y

WYOMING

	11	12	13	14
AL *Cubin*	?	?	?	?

Southern states - Ala., Ark., Fla., Ga., Ky., La., Miss., N.C., Okla., S.C., Tenn., Texas, Va.

15. HR 2998. Afghan Radio/Concur With Senate Amendment. Hyde, R-Ill., motion to suspend the rules and concur with the Senate amendment to the bill that would authorize $17 million through fiscal 2003 to establish and run Radio Free Afghanistan, which would broadcast programming to Afghans in their native languages. Motion agreed to 421-2: R 212-2; D 207-0 (ND 154-0, SD 53-0); I 2-0. A two-thirds majority of those present and voting (282 in this case) is required for passage under suspension of the rules. Feb. 12, 2002.

16. HR 3699. Liberty Center Funding/Passage. Green, R-Wis., motion to suspend the rules and pass the bill that would limit an award by the Department of Housing and Urban Development to the Liberty Center, a program run in Jacksonville, Fla., by the Continuum of Care Homeless Assistance Programs, to $459,600 and mandate that awarded funds over this amount must be spread among the organization's 10 other programs. Motion agreed to 421-0: R 212-0; D 207-0 (ND 154-0, SD 53-0); I 2-0. A two-thirds majority of those present and voting (281 in this case) is required for passage under suspension of the rules. Feb. 12, 2002.

17. Procedural Motion/Journal. Approval of the House Journal of Tuesday, Feb. 12, 2001. Approved 378-40: R 198-13; D 179-27 (ND 130-23, SD 49-4); I 1-0. Feb. 13, 2002.

18. Procedural Motion/Adjourn. Lewis, D-Ga., motion to adjourn. Motion rejected 13-405: R 11-197; D 2-206 (ND 2-153, SD 0-53); I 0-2. Feb. 13, 2002.

19. HR 2356. Campaign Finance Overhaul/Armey Substitute. Armey, R-Texas, substitute amendment that would ban all "soft money" contributions, including its use for get-out-the-vote and voter registration efforts. Rejected 179-249: R 174-44; D 4-204 (ND 1-153, SD 3-51); I 1-1. Feb. 13, 2002.

20. HR 2356. Campaign Finance Overhaul/Ney Substitute. Ney, R-Ohio, substitute amendment that would ban all "soft money" contributions and restrict issue advocacy communications. It would increase the individual aggregate contribution limit to $30,000 annually and the amount that individuals could give to state political parties to $10,000. House candidates who receive coordinated party contributions could spend only $50,000 of their own money. Rejected 53-377: R 51-169; D 2-206 (ND 1-153, SD 1-53); I 0-2. Feb. 13, 2002.

21. HR 2356. Campaign Finance Overhaul/Shays-Meehan Substitute. Shays, R-Conn., substitute amendment that would ban, beginning Nov. 6, 2002, "soft money" contributions to national political parties but allow up to $10,000 in soft money donations to state and local parties for voter registration and get-out-the vote activity. The bill would prevent issue ads from targeting specific candidates within 60 days of a general election or 30 days of a primary, also effective in 2002. It would maintain the individual contribution limit of $1,000 per election for House candidates but raise it beginning Jan. 1, 2003, to $2,000 for Senate candidates, both of which would be indexed for inflation. Adopted 240-191: R 39-180; D 200-10 (ND 150-6, SD 50-4); I 1-1. Feb. 13, 2002.

22. HR 2356. Campaign Finance Overhaul/Free Speech. Hyde, R-Ill., amendment that would state that no provisions in the bill could violate the First Amendment, including the right to free speech. Rejected 188-237: R 182-33; D 5-203 (ND 2-153, SD 3-50); I 1-1. Feb. 13, 2002.

Key

Y	Voted for (yea).
#	Paired for.
+	Announced for.
N	Voted against (nay).
X	Paired against.
−	Announced against.
P	Voted "present."
C	Voted "present" to avoid possible conflict of interest.
?	Did not vote or otherwise make a position known.

Democrats **Republicans**
Independents

	15	16	17	18	19	20	21	22
ALABAMA								
1 *Callahan*	Y	Y	?	?	Y	N	N	Y
2 *Everett*	Y	Y	N	N	Y	N	N	Y
3 *Riley*	+	+	?	?	?	?	?	?
4 *Aderholt*	Y	Y	N	N	Y	Y	N	+
5 Cramer	Y	Y	Y	N	N	N	Y	N
6 *Bachus*	Y	Y	Y	?	Y	N	Y	Y
7 Hilliard	Y	Y	N	N	N	N	N	N
ALASKA								
AL *Young*	Y	Y	?	?	Y	N	N	Y
ARIZONA								
1 *Flake*	Y	Y	Y	Y	Y	N	N	Y
2 Pastor	Y	Y	Y	N	N	N	Y	N
3 *Stump*	Y	Y	Y	N	Y	N	N	Y
4 *Shadegg*	Y	Y	Y	N	Y	N	N	Y
5 *Kolbe*	Y	Y	Y	N	Y	N	N	Y
6 *Hayworth*	Y	Y	Y	N	Y	N	N	Y
ARKANSAS								
1 Berry	Y	Y	Y	N	N	N	Y	N
2 Snyder	Y	Y	Y	N	N	N	Y	N
3 *Boozman*	Y	Y	Y	N	Y	N	N	Y
4 Ross	Y	Y	Y	N	N	N	Y	N
CALIFORNIA								
1 Thompson	Y	Y	N	N	N	N	Y	N
2 *Herger*	Y	Y	Y	N	Y	N	N	Y
3 *Ose*	Y	Y	Y	N	Y	N	Y	Y
4 *Doolittle*	Y	Y	Y	N	Y	N	Y	Y
5 Matsui	Y	Y	Y	N	N	N	Y	N
6 Woolsey	Y	Y	Y	N	N	N	Y	N
7 Miller, George	Y	Y	Y	N	N	N	Y	N
8 Pelosi	Y	Y	Y	N	N	N	Y	N
9 Lee	Y	Y	Y	N	N	N	Y	N
10 Tauscher	Y	Y	Y	N	N	N	Y	N
11 *Pombo*	Y	Y	Y	N	Y	N	N	Y
12 Lantos	Y	Y	Y	N	N	N	Y	N
13 Stark	Y	Y	Y	N	N	N	Y	N
14 Eshoo	Y	Y	Y	N	N	N	Y	N
15 Honda	Y	Y	Y	N	N	N	Y	N
16 Lofgren	Y	Y	Y	N	N	N	Y	N
17 Farr	Y	Y	Y	N	N	N	Y	N
18 Condit	?	?	Y	N	N	N	Y	N
19 *Radanovich*	Y	Y	Y	N	Y	N	Y	N
20 Dooley	Y	Y	Y	N	N	N	Y	N
21 *Thomas*	Y	Y	Y	N	N	N	N	Y
22 Capps	Y	Y	Y	N	N	N	Y	N
23 *Gallegly*	Y	Y	Y	N	Y	N	Y	Y
24 Sherman	Y	Y	Y	N	N	N	Y	N
25 *McKeon*	Y	Y	Y	N	Y	N	N	Y
26 Berman	Y	Y	Y	N	N	N	Y	N
27 Schiff	Y	Y	Y	N	N	N	Y	N
28 *Dreier*	Y	Y	Y	N	N	N	N	Y
29 Waxman	Y	Y	Y	N	N	N	Y	N
30 Becerra	Y	Y	N	N	N	N	Y	N
31 Solis	Y	Y	Y	N	N	N	Y	N
32 Watson	Y	Y	Y	N	N	N	Y	N
33 Roybal-Allard	Y	Y	Y	N	N	N	Y	N
34 Napolitano	Y	Y	Y	N	N	N	Y	N
35 Waters	Y	Y	N	N	−	N	Y	N
36 Harman	Y	Y	Y	N	N	N	Y	N
37 Millender-McD.	Y	Y	Y	N	N	N	Y	N
38 *Horn*	Y	Y	Y	N	N	N	Y	N

	15	16	17	18	19	20	21	22
39 *Royce*	Y	Y	Y	N	Y	N	N	Y
40 *Lewis*	Y	Y	Y	N	Y	N	N	Y
41 *Miller, Gary*	Y	Y	Y	N	Y	N	N	Y
42 Baca	Y	Y	Y	N	N	N	Y	N
43 *Calvert*	Y	Y	Y	N	Y	N	N	Y
44 *Bono*	Y	Y	Y	N	Y	N	N	Y
45 *Rohrabacher*	Y	Y	Y	N	Y	N	N	Y
46 Sanchez	Y	Y	N	N	N	N	Y	N
47 *Cox*	?	Y	Y	N	Y	N	N	Y
48 *Issa*	Y	Y	Y	N	Y	N	N	Y
49 Davis	Y	Y	Y	N	N	N	Y	N
50 Filner	Y	Y	N	N	N	N	N	N
51 *Cunningham*	Y	Y	Y	?	Y	N	N	Y
52 *Hunter*	Y	Y	Y	?	Y	N	N	Y
COLORADO								
1 DeGette	Y	Y	N	N	N	N	Y	N
2 Udall	Y	Y	N	N	N	N	Y	N
3 *McInnis*	Y	Y	Y	N	Y	N	Y	Y
4 *Schaffer*	Y	Y	N	N	N	N	N	Y
5 *Hefley*	?	Y	N	N	Y	N	N	Y
6 *Tancredo*	Y	Y	?	?	Y	N	N	Y
CONNECTICUT								
1 Larson	Y	Y	N	N	N	N	Y	N
2 *Simmons*	Y	Y	Y	N	N	N	Y	N
3 DeLauro	Y	Y	N	N	N	N	Y	N
4 *Shays*	Y	Y	Y	N	N	N	Y	N
5 Maloney	Y	Y	N	N	N	N	Y	N
6 *Johnson*	Y	Y	Y	N	Y	N	Y	N
DELAWARE								
AL *Castle*	Y	Y	Y	N	N	N	Y	N
FLORIDA								
1 *Miller, J.*	Y	Y	Y	N	Y	N	N	Y
2 Boyd	Y	Y	Y	N	N	N	Y	N
3 Brown	Y	Y	Y	N	N	N	Y	N
4 *Crenshaw*	Y	Y	Y	N	Y	N	N	Y
5 Thurman	Y	Y	Y	N	N	N	Y	N
6 *Stearns*	Y	Y	Y	N	Y	N	N	Y
7 *Mica*	Y	Y	Y	N	Y	N	N	Y
8 *Keller*	Y	Y	Y	N	Y	N	N	Y
9 *Bilirakis*	Y	Y	Y	N	Y	N	N	Y
10 *Young*	Y	Y	?	?	Y	N	N	Y
11 Davis	Y	Y	Y	N	N	N	Y	N
12 *Putnam*	Y	Y	Y	N	Y	N	N	Y
13 *Miller, D.*	Y	Y	Y	N	Y	N	N	Y
14 *Goss*	Y	Y	Y	N	Y	N	N	Y
15 *Weldon*	Y	Y	Y	N	Y	N	N	Y
16 *Foley*	Y	Y	Y	N	Y	N	Y	N
17 Meek	Y	Y	?	?	N	N	Y	N
18 *Ros-Lehtinen*	Y	Y	Y	N	Y	N	Y	N
19 Wexler	Y	Y	Y	N	N	N	Y	N
20 Deutsch	Y	Y	Y	N	N	N	Y	N
21 *Diaz-Balart*	Y	Y	Y	N	Y	N	Y	Y
22 *Shaw*	Y	Y	Y	N	Y	N	N	Y
23 Hastings	Y	Y	Y	N	N	N	Y	N
GEORGIA								
1 *Kingston*	Y	Y	Y	Y	Y	N	N	Y
2 Bishop	Y	Y	Y	N	N	N	Y	N
3 *Collins*	N	Y	Y	N	Y	N	N	Y
4 McKinney	Y	Y	N	N	N	N	Y	N
5 Lewis	Y	Y	Y	N	N	N	Y	N
6 *Isakson*	Y	Y	Y	N	Y	N	N	Y
7 *Barr*	Y	Y	Y	N	Y	N	N	Y
8 *Chambliss*	Y	Y	Y	N	Y	N	N	Y
9 *Deal*	Y	Y	Y	N	Y	N	N	Y
10 *Norwood*	Y	Y	Y	N	Y	N	N	Y
11 *Linder*	Y	Y	N	N	Y	N	N	Y
HAWAII								
1 Abercrombie	Y	Y	Y	N	N	N	Y	N
2 Mink	Y	Y	Y	N	N	N	Y	N
IDAHO								
1 *Otter*	Y	Y	Y	Y	Y	Y	N	Y
2 *Simpson*	Y	Y	Y	N	Y	N	N	Y
ILLINOIS								
1 Rush	Y	Y	Y	N	N	Y	N	N
2 Jackson	Y	Y	Y	N	N	N	Y	N
3 Lipinski	Y	Y	?	N	N	?	N	N
4 Gutierrez	Y	Y	Y	N	N	N	Y	N
5 Blagojevich	Y	Y	Y	N	N	N	Y	N
6 *Hyde*	Y	Y	N	N	Y	N	N	Y
7 Davis	Y	Y	Y	N	N	N	Y	N
8 *Crane*	Y	Y	N	N	Y	N	N	Y
9 Schakowsky	Y	Y	Y	N	N	N	Y	N
10 *Kirk*	Y	Y	Y	N	N	N	Y	N
11 *Weller*	Y	Y	Y	N	Y	N	N	Y
12 Costello	Y	Y	Y	N	N	N	Y	N
13 *Biggert*	Y	Y	Y	N	Y	N	N	Y

ND Northern Democrats   SD Southern Democrats

Member	15	16	17	18	19	20	21	22
14 ***Hastert***								Y
15 ***Johnson***	Y	Y	Y	N	N	N	Y	N
16 ***Manzullo***	Y	Y	Y	N	Y	N	N	Y
17 Evans	Y	Y	Y	N	N	N	Y	N
18 ***LaHood***	Y	Y	Y	N	Y	N	N	Y
19 Phelps	Y	Y	Y	N	N	N	Y	N
20 ***Shimkus***	Y	Y	Y	N	Y	Y	N	Y
INDIANA								
1 Visclosky	Y	Y	N	N	N	N	Y	N
2 ***Pence***	Y	Y	Y	N	Y	N	N	Y
3 Roemer	Y	Y	Y	N	N	N	Y	N
4 ***Souder***	Y	Y	Y	N	Y	Y	N	Y
5 ***Buyer***	Y	Y	Y	N	Y	N	N	Y
6 ***Burton***	Y	Y	Y	N	Y	N	N	Y
7 ***Kerns***	Y	Y	Y	N	Y	N	N	Y
8 ***Hostettler***	Y	Y	Y	N	N	N	N	Y
9 Hill	Y	Y	Y	N	N	N	Y	N
10 Carson	Y	Y	Y	N	N	N	Y	N
IOWA								
1 ***Leach***	Y	Y	Y	N	N	N	Y	N
2 ***Nussle***	Y	Y	Y	N	Y	Y	N	Y
3 Boswell	Y	Y	Y	N	N	N	Y	N
4 ***Ganske***	Y	Y	Y	N	N	N	Y	N
5 ***Latham***	Y	Y	Y	N	Y	N	N	Y
KANSAS								
1 ***Moran***	Y	Y	Y	N	Y	N	N	Y
2 ***Ryun***	Y	Y	Y	Y	Y	N	N	Y
3 Moore	Y	Y	N	N	N	N	Y	N
4 ***Tiahrt***	Y	Y	Y	Y	Y	N	N	Y
KENTUCKY								
1 ***Whitfield***	Y	Y	Y	N	Y	N	N	+
2 ***Lewis***	+	+	Y	N	Y	N	N	Y
3 ***Northup***	Y	Y	Y	N	Y	N	N	Y
4 Lucas	Y	Y	Y	N	N	N	Y	N
5 ***Rogers***	Y	Y	Y	N	Y	N	N	Y
6 ***Fletcher***	Y	Y	Y	N	Y	Y	N	Y
LOUISIANA								
1 ***Vitter***	?	?	Y	N	Y	Y	N	Y
2 Jefferson	?	?	Y	N	N	N	Y	N
3 ***Tauzin***	?	?	Y	N	Y	N	N	Y
4 ***McCrery***	Y	Y	Y	?	N	Y	N	Y
5 ***Cooksey***	?	?	Y	N	Y	N	N	Y
6 ***Baker***	Y	Y	Y	N	Y	N	N	Y
7 John	Y	Y	Y	N	N	N	Y	N
MAINE								
1 Allen	Y	Y	Y	N	N	N	Y	N
2 Baldacci	Y	Y	Y	N	N	N	Y	N
MARYLAND								
1 ***Gilchrest***	Y	Y	Y	N	N	N	Y	Y
2 ***Ehrlich***	Y	Y	?	?	N	N	N	Y
3 Cardin	Y	Y	Y	N	N	N	Y	N
4 Wynn	Y	Y	Y	N	N	N	Y	N
5 Hoyer	Y	Y	Y	N	N	N	Y	N
6 ***Bartlett***	Y	Y	Y	N	Y	N	N	Y
7 Cummings	Y	Y	Y	Y	N	N	Y	N
8 ***Morella***	Y	Y	Y	N	N	N	Y	N
MASSACHUSETTS								
1 Olver	Y	Y	Y	N	N	N	Y	N
2 Neal	Y	Y	Y	N	N	N	Y	N
3 McGovern	Y	Y	Y	N	N	N	Y	N
4 Frank	Y	Y	Y	N	N	N	Y	N
5 Meehan	Y	Y	Y	N	N	N	Y	N
6 Tierney	Y	Y	Y	N	N	N	Y	N
7 Markey	Y	Y	Y	N	N	N	Y	N
8 Capuano	Y	Y	N	N	N	N	Y	N
9 Lynch	Y	Y	Y	N	N	N	Y	N
10 Delahunt	Y	Y	Y	N	N	?	Y	N
MICHIGAN								
1 Stupak	Y	Y	N	N	N	N	Y	N
2 ***Hoekstra***	Y	Y	Y	N	Y	N	N	Y
3 ***Ehlers***	Y	Y	Y	N	Y	N	N	Y
4 ***Camp***	Y	Y	Y	N	Y	N	N	Y
5 Barcia	Y	Y	Y	N	Y	N	Y	N
6 ***Upton***	Y	Y	Y	N	Y	Y	Y	Y
7 ***Smith***	Y	Y	Y	N	Y	Y	Y	Y
8 ***Rogers***	Y	Y	Y	N	Y	Y	N	Y
9 Kildee	Y	Y	Y	N	N	N	Y	N
10 Bonior	Y	Y	Y	N	N	N	Y	N
11 ***Knollenberg***	Y	Y	Y	N	Y	N	N	Y
12 Levin	Y	Y	Y	N	N	N	Y	N
13 Rivers	Y	Y	Y	N	N	N	Y	N
14 Conyers	Y	Y	Y	N	N	N	Y	N
15 Kilpatrick	Y	Y	Y	N	N	N	Y	N
16 Dingell	Y	Y	Y	N	N	N	Y	N

Member	15	16	17	18	19	20	21	22
MINNESOTA								
1 ***Gutknecht***	Y	Y	N	N	Y	N	N	Y
2 ***Kennedy***	Y	Y	N	N	Y	N	N	Y
3 ***Ramstad***	Y	Y	N	N	N	N	Y	N
4 McCollum	Y	Y	Y	N	N	N	Y	N
5 Sabo	Y	Y	N	N	N	N	Y	N
6 Luther	Y	Y	Y	N	N	N	Y	N
7 Peterson	Y	Y	N	N	N	N	N	Y
8 Oberstar	Y	Y	N	N	N	N	Y	N
MISSISSIPPI								
1 ***Wicker***	Y	Y	N	N	Y	N	N	Y
2 Thompson	Y	Y	N	N	N	N	N	N
3 ***Pickering***	Y	Y	Y	?	Y	N	N	Y
4 Shows	Y	Y	Y	N	Y	Y	N	Y
5 Taylor	Y	Y	N	N	Y	N	Y	Y
MISSOURI								
1 Clay	Y	Y	?	?	N	N	Y	N
2 ***Akin***	Y	Y	Y	N	Y	Y	N	Y
3 Gephardt	Y	Y	Y	N	N	N	Y	N
4 Skelton	Y	Y	Y	N	N	N	Y	N
5 McCarthy	Y	Y	Y	N	N	N	Y	N
6 ***Graves***	Y	Y	Y	N	Y	N	N	Y
7 ***Blunt***	Y	Y	Y	N	Y	N	N	Y
8 ***Emerson***	Y	Y	Y	N	Y	Y	N	Y
9 ***Hulshof***	Y	Y	Y	N	N	N	N	Y
MONTANA								
AL ***Rehberg***	Y	Y	Y	N	Y	N	N	Y
NEBRASKA								
1 ***Bereuter***	Y	Y	Y	N	N	N	Y	P
2 ***Terry***	Y	Y	Y	N	Y	N	N	Y
3 ***Osborne***	Y	Y	Y	N	Y	Y	Y	N
NEVADA								
1 Berkley	Y	Y	Y	N	N	N	Y	N
2 ***Gibbons***	Y	Y	Y	N	Y	N	N	Y
NEW HAMPSHIRE								
1 ***Sununu***	Y	Y	Y	N	Y	N	N	Y
2 ***Bass***	Y	Y	Y	?	N	N	Y	N
NEW JERSEY								
1 Andrews	Y	Y	Y	N	N	N	Y	N
2 ***LoBiondo***	Y	Y	N	N	N	N	Y	N
3 ***Saxton***	Y	Y	Y	N	Y	Y	N	Y
4 ***Smith***	Y	Y	Y	N	Y	N	N	?
5 ***Roukema***	Y	Y	Y	N	N	N	Y	N
6 Pallone	Y	Y	N	N	N	N	Y	N
7 ***Ferguson***	Y	Y	Y	N	Y	N	N	N
8 Pascrell	Y	Y	N	N	N	N	Y	N
9 Rothman	Y	Y	Y	N	N	N	Y	N
10 Payne	Y	Y	Y	N	N	N	Y	N
11 ***Frelinghuysen***	Y	Y	Y	N	N	N	Y	N
12 Holt	Y	Y	Y	N	N	N	Y	N
13 Menendez	Y	Y	Y	N	N	N	Y	N
NEW MEXICO								
1 ***Wilson***	Y	Y	Y	N	Y	N	N	Y
2 ***Skeen***	Y	Y	Y	Y	Y	Y	N	Y
3 Udall	Y	Y	N	N	N	N	Y	N
NEW YORK								
1 ***Grucci***	Y	Y	Y	N	N	N	Y	N
2 Israel	Y	Y	Y	N	N	N	Y	N
3 ***King***	Y	Y	Y	N	N	N	N	Y
4 McCarthy	Y	Y	Y	N	N	N	Y	N
5 Ackerman	Y	Y	Y	N	N	N	Y	N
6 Meeks	Y	Y	Y	N	N	N	Y	N
7 Crowley	Y	Y	Y	N	N	N	Y	N
8 Nadler	Y	Y	Y	N	N	N	Y	N
9 Weiner	Y	Y	Y	N	N	N	Y	N
10 Towns	Y	Y	Y	Y	N	N	Y	N
11 Owens	Y	Y	Y	N	–	N	Y	N
12 Velázquez	Y	Y	Y	N	N	N	Y	N
13 ***Fossella***	Y	Y	Y	N	Y	N	N	Y
14 Maloney	Y	Y	Y	N	N	N	Y	N
15 Rangel	Y	Y	Y	N	N	N	Y	?
16 Serrano	Y	Y	Y	N	N	N	Y	N
17 Engel	Y	Y	Y	N	N	N	Y	N
18 Lowey	Y	Y	Y	N	N	N	Y	N
19 ***Kelly***	Y	Y	Y	N	Y	N	N	Y
20 ***Gilman***	Y	Y	Y	Y	N	N	Y	N
21 McNulty	Y	Y	N	N	N	N	Y	N
22 ***Sweeney***	Y	Y	Y	N	Y	N	N	Y
23 ***Boehlert***	Y	Y	Y	N	N	N	Y	N
24 ***McHugh***	Y	Y	Y	N	Y	Y	Y	Y
25 ***Walsh***	Y	Y	Y	N	N	N	Y	N
26 Hinchey	Y	Y	Y	N	N	N	Y	N
27 ***Reynolds***	Y	Y	Y	N	Y	N	N	Y
28 Slaughter	Y	Y	Y	N	N	N	Y	N
29 LaFalce	Y	Y	Y	N	N	N	Y	N

Member	15	16	17	18	19	20	21	22
30 ***Quinn***	Y	Y	Y	N	N	N	Y	N
31 ***Houghton***	Y	Y	?	N	N	N	Y	N
NORTH CAROLINA								
1 Clayton	Y	Y	Y	N	N	N	Y	N
2 Etheridge	Y	Y	N	N	N	N	Y	N
3 ***Jones***	Y	Y	Y	Y	Y	N	N	Y
4 Price	Y	Y	Y	N	N	N	Y	N
5 ***Burr***	Y	Y	Y	N	Y	N	N	Y
6 ***Coble***	Y	Y	Y	N	Y	N	N	Y
7 McIntyre	Y	Y	Y	N	N	N	Y	N
8 ***Hayes***	Y	Y	Y	N	Y	N	N	Y
9 ***Myrick***	Y	Y	Y	N	Y	N	N	Y
10 ***Ballenger***	Y	Y	Y	N	Y	N	N	Y
11 ***Taylor***	Y	Y	Y	N	Y	Y	N	Y
12 Watt	Y	Y	Y	N	N	N	Y	?
NORTH DAKOTA								
AL Pomeroy	Y	Y	Y	N	N	N	Y	N
OHIO								
1 ***Chabot***	Y	Y	Y	N	Y	N	N	Y
2 ***Portman***	Y	Y	Y	N	Y	N	N	Y
3 Hall	?	?	Y	N	N	N	Y	N
4 ***Oxley***	Y	Y	Y	N	Y	N	N	Y
5 ***Gillmor***	Y	Y	Y	N	Y	Y	N	Y
6 Strickland	Y	Y	N	N	N	N	Y	N
7 ***Hobson***	Y	?	Y	N	Y	N	N	Y
8 ***Boehner***	Y	Y	Y	N	N	N	N	Y
9 Kaptur	Y	Y	Y	N	N	N	Y	N
10 Kucinich	Y	Y	N	N	N	N	Y	N
11 Jones	Y	Y	Y	N	N	N	Y	N
12 ***Tiberi***	Y	Y	Y	N	Y	N	N	Y
13 Brown	Y	Y	Y	N	N	N	Y	N
14 Sawyer	Y	Y	Y	N	N	N	Y	N
15 ***Pryce***	Y	Y	Y	N	Y	Y	N	Y
16 ***Regula***	Y	Y	Y	N	Y	Y	N	Y
17 Traficant	?	?	?	?	?	?	?	?
18 ***Ney***	Y	Y	Y	N	Y	N	N	Y
19 ***LaTourette***	Y	Y	Y	N	N	Y	Y	Y
OKLAHOMA								
1 ***Largent***	Y	Y	Y	N	Y	N	N	Y
2 Carson	Y	Y	Y	N	N	N	Y	N
3 ***Watkins***	Y	Y	Y	N	Y	N	N	Y
4 ***Watts***	Y	Y	Y	N	+	N	N	Y
5 ***Istook***	Y	Y	Y	N	Y	N	N	Y
6 ***Lucas***	Y	Y	Y	N	Y	N	N	Y
OREGON								
1 Wu	Y	Y	?	N	N	N	Y	N
2 ***Walden***	Y	Y	Y	N	Y	N	N	Y
3 Blumenauer	Y	Y	Y	N	N	N	Y	N
4 DeFazio	Y	Y	N	N	N	N	Y	N
5 Hooley	Y	Y	Y	N	N	N	Y	N
PENNSYLVANIA								
1 Brady	Y	Y	N	N	N	N	Y	N
2 Fattah	Y	Y	N	N	N	N	Y	N
3 Borski	Y	Y	N	N	N	N	Y	N
4 ***Hart***	Y	Y	Y	N	Y	N	N	Y
5 ***Peterson***	Y	?	Y	N	+	N	N	Y
6 Holden	Y	Y	Y	N	N	N	Y	N
7 ***Weldon***	Y	Y	Y	N	Y	Y	Y	N
8 ***Greenwood***	Y	Y	Y	N	N	N	Y	N
9 ***Shuster, Bill***	Y	Y	Y	N	Y	N	N	Y
10 ***Sherwood***	Y	Y	Y	N	Y	N	N	Y
11 Kanjorski	Y	Y	Y	N	N	N	Y	N
12 Murtha	Y	Y	Y	N	N	N	Y	N
13 Hoeffel	Y	Y	Y	N	N	N	Y	N
14 Coyne	Y	Y	Y	N	N	N	Y	N
15 ***Toomey***	Y	Y	Y	N	Y	N	N	Y
16 ***Pitts***	Y	Y	Y	N	Y	Y	N	Y
17 ***Gekas***	Y	?	Y	N	Y	Y	N	Y
18 Doyle	Y	Y	Y	N	N	N	Y	N
19 ***Platts***	Y	Y	N	N	N	N	Y	N
20 Mascara	Y	Y	Y	N	N	N	Y	N
21 ***English***	Y	Y	N	N	Y	Y	N	Y
RHODE ISLAND								
1 Kennedy	Y	Y	Y	N	N	N	Y	N
2 Langevin	Y	Y	Y	N	N	N	Y	N
SOUTH CAROLINA								
1 ***Brown***	Y	Y	Y	N	Y	N	N	Y
2 ***Wilson***	Y	Y	Y	N	Y	Y	N	Y
3 ***Graham***	Y	Y	Y	N	N	N	Y	N
4 ***DeMint***	Y	Y	Y	N	Y	Y	N	Y
5 Spratt	Y	Y	Y	N	N	N	Y	N
6 Clyburn	Y	Y	Y	N	N	N	Y	N
SOUTH DAKOTA								
AL ***Thune***	Y	Y	Y	N	N	N	Y	N

Member	15	16	17	18	19	20	21	22
TENNESSEE								
1 ***Jenkins***	Y	Y	Y	N	Y	Y	N	Y
2 ***Duncan***	Y	Y	Y	N	Y	Y	N	Y
3 ***Wamp***	Y	Y	Y	N	N	N	Y	N
4 ***Hilleary***	Y	Y	Y	N	Y	N	N	Y
5 Clement	Y	Y	Y	N	N	N	Y	N
6 Gordon	Y	Y	Y	N	N	N	Y	N
7 ***Bryant***	Y	Y	Y	N	Y	N	N	Y
8 Tanner	Y	Y	Y	N	N	N	Y	N
9 Ford	Y	Y	Y	N	N	N	Y	N
TEXAS								
1 Sandlin	Y	Y	Y	N	N	N	Y	N
2 Turner	Y	Y	Y	N	N	N	Y	N
3 ***Johnson, Sam***	Y	Y	Y	Y	Y	Y	N	Y
4 Hall	Y	Y	Y	N	Y	N	N	Y
5 ***Sessions***	Y	Y	Y	Y	Y	N	N	Y
6 ***Barton***	Y	Y	Y	N	Y	Y	N	Y
7 ***Culberson***	Y	Y	Y	N	Y	Y	N	Y
8 ***Brady***	Y	Y	Y	N	Y	N	N	?
9 Lampson	Y	Y	Y	N	N	N	Y	N
10 Doggett	Y	Y	Y	N	N	N	Y	N
11 Edwards	Y	Y	Y	N	N	N	Y	N
12 ***Granger***	Y	Y	Y	N	Y	N	N	Y
13 ***Thornberry***	Y	?	Y	N	Y	N	N	Y
14 ***Paul***	N	Y	Y	N	Y	N	N	Y
15 Hinojosa	Y	Y	Y	N	N	N	Y	N
16 Reyes	Y	Y	Y	N	N	N	Y	N
17 Stenholm	Y	Y	Y	N	N	N	Y	N
18 Jackson-Lee	Y	Y	Y	N	N	N	Y	N
19 ***Combest***	Y	Y	Y	N	Y	Y	N	Y
20 Gonzalez	Y	Y	Y	N	N	N	Y	N
21 ***Smith***	Y	Y	Y	N	N	N	N	Y
22 ***DeLay***	Y	Y	Y	N	Y	N	N	Y
23 ***Bonilla***	Y	Y	Y	N	N	N	N	Y
24 Frost	Y	Y	Y	N	N	N	Y	N
25 Bentsen	Y	Y	Y	N	N	N	Y	N
26 ***Armey***	Y	Y	Y	N	Y	N	N	Y
27 Ortiz	Y	Y	Y	N	N	N	Y	N
28 Rodriguez	Y	Y	Y	N	N	N	Y	N
29 Green	Y	Y	Y	N	N	N	Y	N
30 Johnson, E.B.	Y	Y	Y	N	N	N	Y	N
UTAH								
1 ***Hansen***	Y	Y	Y	N	Y	N	N	Y
2 Matheson	Y	Y	Y	N	N	N	Y	N
3 ***Cannon***	Y	Y	Y	Y	Y	N	N	Y
VERMONT								
AL *Sanders*	Y	Y	?	N	N	N	Y	N
VIRGINIA								
1 ***Davis, Jo Ann***	Y	Y	Y	N	Y	Y	N	Y
2 ***Schrock***	Y	Y	?	?	Y	Y	N	Y
3 Scott	Y	Y	Y	N	N	N	Y	N
4 ***Forbes***	Y	Y	Y	N	Y	Y	N	Y
5 *Goode*	Y	Y	Y	N	Y	N	N	Y
6 ***Goodlatte***	Y	Y	Y	N	Y	N	N	Y
7 ***Cantor***	Y	Y	Y	N	Y	Y	N	Y
8 Moran	Y	Y	Y	N	N	N	Y	N
9 Boucher	Y	Y	Y	N	N	N	Y	N
10 ***Wolf***	Y	Y	Y	N	N	N	Y	N
11 ***Davis, T.***	Y	Y	Y	N	Y	N	N	Y
WASHINGTON								
1 Inslee	Y	Y	N	N	N	N	Y	N
2 Larsen	Y	Y	N	N	N	N	Y	N
3 Baird	Y	Y	Y	N	N	N	Y	N
4 ***Hastings***	Y	Y	Y	N	Y	N	N	Y
5 ***Nethercutt***	Y	Y	Y	N	Y	N	N	Y
6 Dicks	Y	Y	Y	N	N	N	Y	N
7 McDermott	Y	Y	N	N	N	N	Y	N
8 ***Dunn***	Y	Y	Y	N	N	N	N	Y
9 Smith	Y	Y	Y	N	N	N	Y	N
WEST VIRGINIA								
1 Mollohan	Y	Y	Y	N	N	N	N	N
2 ***Capito***	Y	Y	Y	N	Y	Y	Y	Y
3 Rahall	Y	Y	Y	N	N	N	N	N
WISCONSIN								
1 ***Ryan***	Y	Y	Y	N	Y	N	N	Y
2 Baldwin	Y	Y	Y	N	N	N	Y	N
3 Kind	Y	Y	Y	N	N	N	Y	N
4 Kleczka	Y	Y	Y	N	N	N	Y	N
5 Barrett	Y	Y	Y	N	N	N	Y	N
6 ***Petri***	Y	Y	Y	N	N	N	Y	N
7 Obey	Y	Y	Y	N	N	N	Y	N
8 ***Green***	Y	Y	Y	N	N	N	N	Y
9 ***Sensenbrenner***	Y	Y	Y	N	Y	N	N	Y
WYOMING								
AL ***Cubin***	Y	Y	?	?	Y	Y	?	?

Southern states - Ala., Ark., Fla., Ga., Ky., La., Miss., N.C., Okla., S.C., Tenn., Texas, Va.

Key

Y	Voted for (yea).
#	Paired for.
+	Announced for.
N	Voted against (nay).
X	Paired against.
–	Announced against.
P	Voted "present."
C	Voted "present" to avoid possible conflict of interest.
?	Did not vote or otherwise make a position known.

Democrats **Republicans**
Independents

23. HR 2356. Campaign Finance Overhaul/TV Ad Rates. Green, D-Texas, amendment that would remove provisions offering candidates and parties the lowest recent rates charged private customers just before an election for television advertisements. Adopted 327-101: R 207-11; D 119-89 (ND 72-83, SD 47-6); I 1-1. Feb. 13, 2002.

24. HR 2356. Campaign Finance Overhaul/Bearing Arms Advocacy. Pickering, R-Miss., amendment that would exempt advertising restrictions in the bill when the content relates to advocacy on Second Amendment issues. Rejected 209-219: R 187-31; D 21-187 (ND 8-147, SD 13-40); I 1-1. Feb. 13, 2002.

25. HR 2356. Campaign Finance Overhaul/Civil Rights Advocacy. Watts, R-Okla., amendment that would exempt advertising restrictions in the bill when the content relates to advocacy on civil rights issues. Rejected 185-237: R 182-32; D 2-204 (ND 1-151, SD 1-53); I 1-1. Feb. 13, 2002.

26. HR 2356. Campaign Finance Overhaul/Veterans Advocacy. Johnson, R-Texas, amendment that would exempt advertising restrictions in the bill when the content relates to advocacy on issues related to veterans, military personnel, seniors or the families of any of these groups. Rejected 200-228: R 191-26; D 8-201 (ND 3-153, SD 5-48); I 1-1. Feb. 13, 2002.

27. HR 2356. Campaign Finance Overhaul/Workers Advocacy. Combest, R-Texas, amendment that would exempt advertising restrictions in the bill when the content relates to workers, farmers and family issues. Rejected 191-237: R 183-33; D 7-203 (ND 5-151, SD 2-52); I 1-1. Feb. 13, 2002.

28. HR 2356. Campaign Finance Overhaul/Individual Contributions. Wamp, R-Tenn., amendment that would raise the individual contribution limit to House candidates from $1,000 to $2,000 per election. Adopted 218-211: R 201-16; D 17-193 (ND 10-146, SD 7-47); I 0-2. Feb. 13, 2002.

29. HR 2356. Campaign Finance Overhaul/Comprehensive Ban. Emerson, R-Mo., amendment that would ban all forms of "soft money" donations. Rejected 185-244: R 180-38; D 4-205 (ND 2-153, SD 2-52); I 1-1. Feb. 13, 2002.

30. HR 2356. Campaign Finance Overhaul/Non-Citizen Donors. Wicker, R-Miss., amendment that would ban non-U.S. citizens from giving to federal campaigns. Rejected 160-268: R 157-59; D 2-208 (ND 1-155, SD 1-53); I 1-1. Feb. 13, 2002.

	23	24	25	26	27	28	29	30
ALABAMA								
1 *Callahan*	Y	Y	Y	Y	Y	Y	Y	Y
2 *Everett*	Y	Y	Y	Y	Y	Y	Y	Y
3 *Riley*	?	?	?	?	?	?	?	?
4 *Aderholt*	Y	Y	Y	Y	Y	Y	Y	Y
5 Cramer	Y	Y	N	N	N	Y	N	N
6 *Bachus*	Y	Y	Y	Y	Y	Y	N	Y
7 Hilliard	Y	N	N	N	N	N	N	N
ALASKA								
AL *Young*	Y	Y	Y	Y	Y	Y	Y	Y
ARIZONA								
1 *Flake*	Y	Y	Y	Y	Y	Y	Y	Y
2 Pastor	Y	N	N	N	N	N	N	N
3 *Stump*	Y	Y	Y	Y	Y	Y	Y	Y
4 *Shadegg*	Y	Y	Y	Y	Y	Y	Y	Y
5 *Kolbe*	Y	Y	Y	Y	Y	Y	Y	N
6 *Hayworth*	Y	Y	Y	Y	Y	Y	Y	Y
ARKANSAS								
1 Berry	Y	N	N	N	N	N	N	N
2 Snyder	Y	N	N	N	N	N	N	N
3 *Boozman*	Y	Y	Y	Y	Y	Y	Y	Y
4 Ross	Y	Y	N	N	N	N	N	N
CALIFORNIA								
1 Thompson	N	N	N	N	N	N	N	N
2 *Herger*	Y	Y	Y	Y	Y	Y	Y	Y
3 Ose	Y	N	N	N	N	Y	N	N
4 *Doolittle*	Y	Y	Y	Y	Y	Y	Y	Y
5 Matsui	Y	N	N	N	N	N	N	N
6 Woolsey	N	N	N	N	N	N	N	N
7 Miller, George	N	N	N	N	N	N	N	N
8 Pelosi	N	N	N	N	N	N	?	N
9 Lee	N	N	N	N	N	N	N	N
10 Tauscher	N	N	N	N	N	N	N	N
11 *Pombo*	Y	Y	Y	Y	Y	Y	Y	N
12 Lantos	N	N	N	N	N	N	N	N
13 Stark	N	N	?	N	N	N	N	N
14 Eshoo	N	N	N	N	N	N	N	N
15 Honda	N	N	N	N	N	N	N	N
16 Lofgren	N	N	N	N	N	N	N	N
17 Farr	N	N	N	N	N	N	N	N
18 Condit	N	N	N	N	N	N	N	N
19 *Radanovich*	Y	Y	Y	Y	Y	Y	Y	Y
20 Dooley	Y	N	N	N	N	N	N	N
21 *Thomas*	Y	Y	Y	Y	Y	Y	Y	Y
22 Capps	Y	N	N	N	N	N	N	N
23 *Gallegly*	Y	Y	Y	Y	Y	N	Y	Y
24 Sherman	N	N	N	N	N	N	N	N
25 *McKeon*	Y	Y	Y	Y	Y	Y	Y	Y
26 Berman	N	N	N	N	N	N	N	N
27 Schiff	N	N	N	N	N	N	N	N
28 *Dreier*	Y	Y	Y	Y	Y	Y	Y	Y
29 Waxman	N	N	N	N	N	N	N	N
30 Becerra	Y	N	N	N	N	N	N	N
31 Solis	N	N	N	N	N	N	N	N
32 Watson	N	N	N	N	N	N	N	N
33 Roybal-Allard	N	N	N	N	N	N	N	N
34 Napolitano	Y	N	N	N	N	N	N	N
35 Waters	N	N	N	N	N	N	N	N
36 Harman	N	N	N	N	N	N	N	N
37 Millender-McD.	N	N	N	N	N	N	N	N
38 Horn	N	N	N	N	N	N	N	N

	23	24	25	26	27	28	29	30
39 *Royce*	Y	Y	Y	Y	Y	Y	Y	Y
40 *Lewis*	N	Y	Y	Y	Y	Y	Y	Y
41 *Miller, Gary*	Y	Y	Y	Y	Y	Y	Y	Y
42 Baca	Y	N	N	N	N	N	N	N
43 *Calvert*	Y	Y	Y	Y	Y	Y	Y	Y
44 *Bono*	Y	Y	Y	Y	Y	Y	Y	Y
45 *Rohrabacher*	Y	Y	Y	Y	Y	Y	Y	Y
46 Sanchez	Y	N	N	N	N	N	N	N
47 *Cox*	Y	Y	Y	Y	Y	Y	Y	Y
48 *Issa*	Y	Y	Y	Y	Y	Y	Y	Y
49 Davis	N	N	N	N	N	N	N	N
50 Filner	Y	N	N	N	N	N	N	N
51 *Cunningham*	Y	Y	Y	Y	Y	Y	Y	Y
52 *Hunter*	Y	Y	Y	Y	Y	Y	Y	Y
COLORADO								
1 DeGette	Y	N	N	N	N	Y	N	N
2 Udall	Y	N	N	N	N	N	N	N
3 *McInnis*	Y	Y	Y	Y	Y	Y	Y	Y
4 *Schaffer*	Y	Y	Y	Y	Y	Y	Y	Y
5 *Hefley*	Y	Y	Y	Y	Y	N	Y	Y
6 *Tancredo*	Y	Y	Y	Y	Y	Y	Y	Y
CONNECTICUT								
1 Larson	Y	N	N	N	N	Y	N	N
2 *Simmons*	Y	Y	N	N	N	Y	N	N
3 DeLauro	N	N	N	N	N	N	N	N
4 *Shays*	N	N	N	N	N	N	N	N
5 Maloney	Y	N	N	N	N	N	N	N
6 *Johnson*	Y	N	?	N	N	N	Y	N
DELAWARE								
AL *Castle*	Y	N	N	N	N	N	N	N
FLORIDA								
1 *Miller, J.*	Y	Y	Y	Y	Y	Y	Y	Y
2 Boyd	Y	Y	N	?	N	N	N	N
3 Brown	Y	N	N	N	N	N	N	N
4 *Crenshaw*	Y	Y	Y	Y	Y	Y	Y	Y
5 Thurman	Y	N	N	N	N	N	N	N
6 *Stearns*	Y	Y	Y	Y	Y	Y	Y	Y
7 *Mica*	Y	Y	Y	Y	Y	Y	Y	Y
8 *Keller*	Y	Y	Y	Y	Y	Y	Y	Y
9 *Bilirakis*	Y	Y	Y	Y	Y	Y	Y	Y
10 *Young*	Y	Y	Y	Y	Y	Y	Y	?
11 Davis	Y	N	N	N	N	N	N	N
12 *Putnam*	Y	Y	Y	Y	Y	Y	Y	Y
13 *Miller, D.*	Y	Y	Y	Y	Y	Y	Y	Y
14 *Goss*	Y	Y	Y	Y	Y	Y	Y	Y
15 *Weldon*	Y	Y	Y	Y	Y	Y	Y	Y
16 *Foley*	N	N	N	N	Y	N	Y	N
17 Meek	Y	N	N	N	N	N	N	N
18 *Ros-Lehtinen*	Y	Y	Y	Y	Y	Y	Y	Y
19 Wexler	N	N	N	N	N	N	N	N
20 Deutsch	Y	N	N	N	N	N	N	N
21 *Diaz-Balart*	Y	Y	Y	Y	Y	Y	Y	Y
22 *Shaw*	Y	Y	Y	Y	Y	Y	Y	Y
23 Hastings	N	N	N	N	N	N	N	N
GEORGIA								
1 *Kingston*	Y	Y	Y	Y	Y	Y	Y	Y
2 Bishop	Y	Y	N	N	N	Y	N	N
3 *Collins*	Y	Y	Y	Y	Y	Y	Y	Y
4 McKinney	N	N	N	N	N	N	N	N
5 Lewis	N	N	N	N	N	N	N	N
6 *Isakson*	Y	Y	Y	Y	Y	Y	Y	Y
7 *Barr*	Y	Y	Y	Y	Y	N	Y	Y
8 *Chambliss*	Y	Y	Y	Y	Y	Y	Y	Y
9 *Deal*	Y	Y	Y	Y	Y	Y	Y	Y
10 *Norwood*	Y	Y	Y	Y	Y	Y	Y	Y
11 *Linder*	Y	Y	Y	Y	Y	Y	Y	Y
HAWAII								
1 Abercrombie	Y	N	N	N	N	Y	N	N
2 Mink	Y	N	N	N	N	N	N	N
IDAHO								
1 *Otter*	Y	Y	Y	Y	Y	Y	Y	Y
2 *Simpson*	Y	Y	Y	Y	Y	Y	Y	Y
ILLINOIS								
1 Rush	Y	N	?	N	N	N	N	N
2 Jackson	N	N	N	N	N	N	N	N
3 Lipinski	Y	N	N	N	N	N	N	N
4 Gutierrez	?	N	N	N	N	N	N	N
5 Blagojevich	N	N	N	N	N	N	N	N
6 *Hyde*	Y	Y	Y	Y	Y	Y	Y	Y
7 Davis	N	N	N	N	N	N	N	N
8 *Crane*	Y	Y	Y	Y	Y	Y	Y	Y
9 Schakowsky	N	N	N	N	N	N	N	N
10 *Kirk*	Y	N	N	N	N	Y	N	N
11 *Weller*	Y	Y	Y	Y	Y	Y	Y	Y
12 Costello	Y	N	N	N	N	N	N	N
13 *Biggert*	Y	Y	Y	Y	Y	Y	Y	Y

ND Northern Democrats   SD Southern Democrats

	23	24	25	26	27	28	29	30
14 ***Hastert***		Y		Y		Y	Y	
15 ***Johnson***	Y	Y	Y	Y	Y	Y	N	N
16 ***Manzullo***	Y	Y	Y	Y	Y	Y	Y	Y
17 Evans	N	N	N	N	N	N	N	N
18 ***LaHood***	Y	Y	Y	Y	Y	Y	Y	N
19 Phelps	Y	Y	N	N	Y	N	N	N
20 ***Shimkus***	Y	Y	Y	Y	Y	Y	Y	Y
INDIANA								
1 Visclosky	N	N	N	N	N	Y	N	N
2 ***Pence***	Y	Y	Y	Y	Y	Y	Y	Y
3 Roemer	Y	N	N	N	N	N	N	N
4 ***Souder***	Y	Y	Y	Y	Y	Y	Y	N
5 ***Buyer***	Y	Y	Y	Y	Y	Y	Y	Y
6 ***Burton***	Y	Y	Y	Y	Y	Y	Y	N
7 ***Kerns***	Y	Y	Y	Y	Y	Y	N	Y
8 ***Hostettler***	Y	Y	Y	Y	Y	Y	N	Y
9 Hill	Y	N	N	N	N	Y	N	N
10 Carson	Y	N	N	N	N	N	N	N
IOWA								
1 ***Leach***	N	N	N	N	N	N	N	N
2 ***Nussle***	Y	Y	Y	Y	Y	N	Y	Y
3 Boswell	Y	Y	N	N	N	N	N	N
4 ***Ganske***	Y	Y	N	N	N	Y	N	N
5 ***Latham***	Y	Y	Y	Y	Y	Y	Y	Y
KANSAS								
1 ***Moran***	Y	Y	Y	Y	Y	Y	Y	N
2 ***Ryun***	Y	Y	Y	Y	Y	Y	Y	Y
3 Moore	Y	N	N	N	N	N	N	N
4 ***Tiahrt***	Y	Y	?	Y	Y	Y	Y	Y
KENTUCKY								
1 ***Whitfield***	Y	Y	Y	Y	Y	Y	Y	Y
2 ***Lewis***	Y	Y	Y	Y	Y	Y	Y	Y
3 ***Northup***	Y	N	Y	Y	Y	N	Y	Y
4 Lucas	Y	Y	N	N	N	Y	N	N
5 ***Rogers***	Y	Y	Y	Y	Y	Y	Y	Y
6 ***Fletcher***	Y	+	Y	Y	Y	Y	Y	N
LOUISIANA								
1 ***Vitter***	N	Y	Y	Y	Y	Y	Y	Y
2 Jefferson	Y	N	N	N	N	N	N	N
3 ***Tauzin***	Y	Y	Y	Y	Y	Y	Y	Y
4 ***McCrery***	Y	Y	Y	Y	Y	Y	Y	Y
5 ***Cooksey***	Y	Y	Y	Y	Y	Y	Y	Y
6 ***Baker***	Y	Y	Y	Y	Y	Y	Y	Y
7 John	Y	Y	N	N	N	N	N	N
MAINE								
1 Allen	Y	N	N	N	N	N	N	N
2 Baldacci	Y	N	N	N	N	N	N	N
MARYLAND								
1 ***Gilchrest***	Y	N	N	N	N	Y	N	N
2 ***Ehrlich***	Y	Y	Y	Y	Y	Y	Y	Y
3 Cardin	Y	N	N	N	N	N	N	N
4 Wynn	Y	N	N	Y	Y	Y	N	N
5 Hoyer	Y	N	N	N	N	Y	N	N
6 ***Bartlett***	Y	Y	Y	Y	Y	Y	Y	Y
7 Cummings	Y	N	N	N	N	N	N	N
8 ***Morella***	Y	N	N	N	N	Y	N	N
MASSACHUSETTS								
1 Olver	N	N	N	N	N	N	N	N
2 Neal	Y	N	N	N	N	N	N	N
3 McGovern	N	N	N	N	N	N	N	N
4 Frank	N	N	N	N	N	N	N	N
5 Meehan	N	N	N	N	N	N	N	N
6 Tierney	N	N	N	N	N	N	N	N
7 Markey	N	N	N	N	N	N	N	N
8 Capuano	N	N	N	N	N	N	N	N
9 Lynch	Y	N	N	N	N	N	N	N
10 Delahunt	Y	N	N	N	N	N	N	N
MICHIGAN								
1 Stupak	Y	N	N	N	N	N	N	N
2 ***Hoekstra***	Y	Y	Y	Y	Y	Y	Y	Y
3 ***Ehlers***	N	N	Y	Y	Y	Y	Y	N
4 ***Camp***	Y	Y	Y	Y	Y	Y	Y	Y
5 Barcia	Y	Y	N	N	Y	N	N	N
6 ***Upton***	Y	Y	Y	Y	Y	Y	Y	Y
7 ***Smith***	Y	N	N	Y	N	Y	Y	Y
8 ***Rogers***	Y	Y	Y	Y	Y	Y	Y	Y
9 Kildee	N	N	N	N	N	N	N	N
10 Bonior	Y	N	N	N	N	N	N	N
11 ***Knollenberg***	Y	Y	Y	Y	Y	Y	Y	Y
12 Levin	N	N	N	N	N	N	N	N
13 Rivers	N	N	N	N	N	N	N	N
14 Conyers	N	N	N	N	N	N	Y	N
15 Kilpatrick	N	N	N	N	N	N	N	N
16 Dingell	Y	N	N	N	N	N	N	N
MINNESOTA								
1 ***Gutknecht***	Y	Y	Y	Y	Y	Y	Y	Y
2 ***Kennedy***	Y	Y	Y	Y	Y	Y	Y	Y
3 ***Ramstad***	Y	N	N	N	N	Y	N	N
4 McCollum	N	N	N	N	N	N	N	N
5 Sabo	N	N	N	N	N	N	N	N
6 Luther	Y	N	N	N	N	N	N	N
7 Peterson	Y	Y	N	Y	Y	N	Y	N
8 Oberstar	Y	N	N	N	N	N	N	N
MISSISSIPPI								
1 ***Wicker***	Y	Y	Y	Y	Y	Y	Y	Y
2 Thompson	Y	N	N	N	N	N	N	N
3 ***Pickering***	Y	Y	Y	Y	Y	Y	Y	Y
4 Shows	Y	Y	N	Y	Y	N	N	N
5 Taylor	Y	Y	N	Y	N	N	Y	Y
MISSOURI								
1 Clay	Y	N	N	N	N	N	N	N
2 ***Akin***	Y	Y	Y	Y	Y	Y	Y	Y
3 Gephardt	N	N	N	N	N	N	N	N
4 Skelton	Y	N	N	N	N	N	N	N
5 McCarthy	Y	N	N	N	N	N	N	N
6 ***Graves***	Y	Y	Y	Y	Y	Y	Y	Y
7 ***Blunt***	Y	Y	Y	Y	Y	Y	Y	Y
8 ***Emerson***	Y	Y	Y	Y	Y	Y	Y	N
9 ***Hulshof***	Y	Y	Y	Y	Y	Y	N	Y
MONTANA								
AL ***Rehberg***	Y	Y	Y	Y	Y	Y	Y	Y
NEBRASKA								
1 ***Bereuter***	Y	Y	Y	Y	Y	N	Y	Y
2 ***Terry***	Y	Y	Y	Y	Y	Y	Y	N
3 ***Osborne***	Y	Y	N	Y	Y	Y	Y	N
NEVADA								
1 Berkley	Y	N	N	N	N	N	N	N
2 ***Gibbons***	Y	Y	Y	Y	Y	Y	Y	Y
NEW HAMPSHIRE								
1 ***Sununu***	Y	Y	Y	Y	Y	Y	Y	Y
2 ***Bass***	Y	N	N	N	N	Y	N	N
NEW JERSEY								
1 Andrews	Y	N	N	N	N	N	N	N
2 ***LoBiondo***	Y	N	N	N	N	Y	N	N
3 ***Saxton***	Y	N	Y	Y	N	N	Y	Y
4 ***Smith***	Y	Y	Y	Y	Y	Y	Y	Y
5 ***Roukema***	Y	?	?	?	?	?	?	?
6 Pallone	Y	N	N	N	N	N	N	N
7 ***Ferguson***	Y	N	N	N	N	Y	Y	N
8 Pascrell	N	N	N	N	N	N	N	N
9 Rothman	N	N	N	N	N	N	N	N
10 Payne	N	N	?	N	N	N	N	N
11 ***Frelinghuysen***	Y	N	N	N	N	Y	Y	N
12 Holt	N	N	N	N	N	N	N	N
13 Menendez	N	N	N	N	N	N	N	N
NEW MEXICO								
1 ***Wilson***	Y	Y	Y	Y	Y	Y	Y	N
2 ***Skeen***	Y	Y	Y	Y	Y	Y	Y	Y
3 Udall	Y	N	N	N	N	N	N	N
NEW YORK								
1 ***Grucci***	Y	N	N	N	N	Y	N	Y
2 Israel	N	N	N	N	N	N	N	N
3 ***King***	Y	Y	Y	Y	Y	Y	N	N
4 McCarthy	N	N	N	N	N	N	N	N
5 Ackerman	N	N	N	N	N	N	N	N
6 Meeks	Y	N	N	N	N	N	N	N
7 Crowley	N	N	N	N	N	N	N	N
8 Nadler	N	N	N	N	N	N	N	N
9 Weiner	N	N	N	N	N	N	N	N
10 Towns	Y	N	N	N	N	Y	N	N
11 Owens	N	N	N	N	N	N	N	N
12 Velázquez	N	N	N	N	N	N	N	N
13 ***Fossella***	Y	Y	Y	Y	Y	Y	Y	Y
14 Maloney	N	N	N	N	N	N	N	N
15 Rangel	N	N	N	N	N	N	N	N
16 Serrano	Y	N	N	N	N	N	N	N
17 Engel	Y	N	N	N	N	N	N	N
18 Lowey	N	N	N	N	N	N	N	N
19 ***Kelly***	Y	Y	Y	Y	Y	Y	Y	Y
20 ***Gilman***	Y	N	N	Y	N	Y	N	N
21 McNulty	N	N	N	N	N	N	N	N
22 ***Sweeney***	Y	Y	Y	Y	Y	Y	Y	N
23 ***Boehlert***	Y	N	N	N	N	Y	N	N
24 ***McHugh***	Y	Y	Y	Y	Y	Y	Y	Y
25 ***Walsh***	Y	N	N	N	N	Y	N	N
26 Hinchey	N	N	N	N	N	N	N	N
27 ***Reynolds***	Y	Y	Y	Y	Y	Y	Y	Y
28 Slaughter	N	N	N	N	N	N	N	N
29 LaFalce	N	N	N	N	N	N	N	N
30 ***Quinn***	Y	N	N	Y	N	Y	N	N
31 ***Houghton***	N	N	N	N	N	Y	N	N
NORTH CAROLINA								
1 Clayton	Y	N	N	N	N	N	N	N
2 Etheridge	Y	N	N	N	N	N	N	N
3 ***Jones***	Y	Y	Y	Y	Y	Y	Y	Y
4 Price	Y	N	N	N	N	N	N	N
5 ***Burr***	Y	Y	Y	Y	Y	Y	Y	Y
6 ***Coble***	Y	Y	Y	Y	Y	N	Y	Y
7 McIntyre	Y	N	N	N	N	N	N	N
8 ***Hayes***	Y	Y	Y	Y	Y	Y	Y	Y
9 ***Myrick***	Y	Y	Y	Y	Y	Y	Y	Y
10 ***Ballenger***	Y	Y	Y	Y	Y	?	N	Y
11 ***Taylor***	Y	Y	Y	Y	Y	Y	Y	Y
12 Watt	?	N	N	N	N	N	N	N
NORTH DAKOTA								
AL Pomeroy	N	N	N	N	N	N	N	N
OHIO								
1 ***Chabot***	Y	Y	Y	Y	Y	Y	Y	Y
2 ***Portman***	Y	Y	Y	Y	Y	Y	Y	N
3 Hall	N	N	N	N	N	N	N	N
4 ***Oxley***	Y	Y	?	?	?	Y	Y	Y
5 ***Gillmor***	Y	Y	Y	Y	N	Y	Y	Y
6 Strickland	Y	Y	N	N	N	N	N	N
7 ***Hobson***	Y	Y	Y	Y	Y	Y	Y	Y
8 ***Boehner***	Y	Y	Y	Y	Y	Y	Y	Y
9 Kaptur	N	N	N	N	N	N	N	N
10 Kucinich	Y	N	N	N	N	N	N	N
11 Jones	N	N	N	N	N	N	N	N
12 ***Tiberi***	Y	Y	Y	Y	Y	Y	Y	Y
13 Brown	Y	N	N	N	N	N	N	N
14 Sawyer	Y	N	N	N	N	N	N	N
15 ***Pryce***	Y	Y	Y	Y	Y	Y	Y	Y
16 ***Regula***	Y	Y	Y	Y	Y	Y	Y	N
17 Traficant	?	?	?	?	?	?	?	?
18 ***Ney***	Y	Y	Y	Y	Y	Y	Y	Y
19 ***LaTourette***	Y	Y	Y	Y	Y	Y	Y	N
OKLAHOMA								
1 ***Largent***	N	Y	Y	Y	Y	Y	Y	Y
2 Carson	Y	Y	N	Y	N	N	N	N
3 ***Watkins***	Y	Y	Y	Y	Y	Y	Y	Y
4 ***Watts***	Y	Y	Y	Y	Y	Y	Y	Y
5 ***Istook***	Y	Y	Y	Y	Y	Y	Y	Y
6 ***Lucas***	Y	Y	Y	Y	Y	Y	Y	Y
OREGON								
1 Wu	N	N	N	N	N	Y	N	N
2 ***Walden***	Y	Y	Y	Y	Y	N	Y	Y
3 Blumenauer	Y	N	N	N	N	N	N	N
4 DeFazio	N	N	?	N	N	N	N	N
5 Hooley	Y	N	N	N	N	N	N	N
PENNSYLVANIA								
1 Brady	N	N	N	N	N	N	N	N
2 Fattah	Y	N	N	N	N	N	N	N
3 Borski	Y	N	N	N	N	N	N	N
4 ***Hart***	Y	Y	Y	Y	Y	Y	Y	Y
5 ***Peterson***	Y	Y	Y	Y	Y	Y	Y	Y
6 Holden	Y	Y	Y	Y	Y	N	N	Y
7 ***Weldon***	Y	N	N	Y	N	Y	Y	N
8 ***Greenwood***	Y	N	N	N	N	Y	N	N
9 ***Shuster, Bill***	Y	Y	Y	Y	Y	Y	Y	Y
10 ***Sherwood***	N	Y	Y	Y	Y	Y	Y	Y
11 Kanjorski	N	N	N	N	N	N	N	N
12 Murtha	N	N	N	N	N	N	N	N
13 Hoeffel	N	N	N	N	N	Y	N	N
14 Coyne	N	N	N	N	N	N	N	N
15 ***Toomey***	Y	Y	Y	Y	Y	Y	N	Y
16 ***Pitts***	Y	Y	Y	Y	Y	Y	Y	Y
17 ***Gekas***	Y	Y	Y	Y	Y	Y	Y	Y
18 Doyle	Y	N	N	N	N	N	N	N
19 ***Platts***	Y	N	N	N	N	N	N	N
20 Mascara	Y	N	N	N	N	N	N	N
21 ***English***	Y	Y	Y	Y	Y	Y	Y	N
RHODE ISLAND								
1 Kennedy	Y	–	N	N	N	N	N	N
2 Langevin	N	N	N	N	N	N	N	N
SOUTH CAROLINA								
1 ***Brown***	Y	Y	Y	Y	Y	Y	Y	Y
2 ***Wilson***	Y	Y	Y	Y	Y	Y	Y	Y
3 ***Graham***	Y	Y	N	N	Y	Y	N	Y
4 ***DeMint***	Y	Y	Y	Y	Y	Y	Y	Y
5 Spratt	Y	N	N	N	N	N	N	N
6 Clyburn	Y	N	N	N	N	N	N	N
SOUTH DAKOTA								
AL ***Thune***	N	N	N	N	N	N	Y	N
TENNESSEE								
1 ***Jenkins***	Y	Y	Y	Y	Y	N	Y	Y
2 ***Duncan***	Y	Y	Y	Y	Y	Y	Y	Y
3 ***Wamp***	Y	N	N	N	N	Y	N	N
4 ***Hilleary***	Y	Y	Y	Y	Y	Y	Y	Y
5 Clement	Y	N	N	N	N	Y	N	N
6 Gordon	Y	Y	N	N	N	N	N	N
7 ***Bryant***	Y	Y	Y	Y	Y	Y	Y	N
8 Tanner	Y	Y	N	Y	N	N	N	N
9 Ford	Y	N	N	N	N	Y	N	N
TEXAS								
1 Sandlin	Y	N	N	N	N	N	N	N
2 Turner	Y	N	N	N	N	N	N	N
3 ***Johnson, Sam***	Y	Y	Y	Y	Y	Y	Y	Y
4 Hall	Y	Y	Y	Y	Y	N	Y	N
5 ***Sessions***	Y	Y	Y	Y	Y	Y	Y	Y
6 ***Barton***	Y	Y	Y	Y	Y	Y	Y	Y
7 ***Culberson***	Y	Y	Y	Y	Y	Y	Y	Y
8 ***Brady***	?	?	?	?	?	?	?	?
9 Lampson	Y	N	N	N	N	N	N	N
10 Doggett	N	N	N	N	N	N	N	N
11 Edwards	Y	N	N	N	N	N	N	N
12 ***Granger***	Y	Y	Y	Y	Y	Y	Y	N
13 ***Thornberry***	Y	Y	Y	Y	Y	Y	Y	N
14 ***Paul***	Y	Y	Y	Y	Y	Y	N	N
15 Hinojosa	Y	N	N	N	N	N	N	N
16 Reyes	Y	N	N	N	N	N	N	N
17 Stenholm	Y	N	N	N	N	N	N	N
18 Jackson-Lee	Y	N	N	N	N	N	N	N
19 ***Combest***	Y	Y	Y	Y	Y	Y	Y	Y
20 Gonzalez	Y	N	N	N	N	N	N	N
21 ***Smith***	Y	Y	Y	Y	Y	Y	N	Y
22 ***DeLay***	Y	Y	Y	Y	Y	Y	Y	Y
23 ***Bonilla***	Y	Y	Y	Y	Y	Y	Y	N
24 Frost	Y	N	N	N	N	Y	N	N
25 Bentsen	Y	N	N	N	N	N	N	N
26 ***Armey***	Y	Y	Y	Y	Y	Y	Y	Y
27 Ortiz	Y	N	N	N	N	N	N	N
28 Rodriguez	Y	N	N	N	N	N	N	N
29 Green	Y	N	N	N	N	N	N	N
30 Johnson, E.B.	N	N	N	N	N	Y	N	N
UTAH								
1 ***Hansen***	Y	Y	Y	Y	Y	Y	Y	Y
2 Matheson	Y	N	N	N	N	N	N	N
3 ***Cannon***	Y	Y	Y	Y	Y	Y	Y	Y
VERMONT								
AL *Sanders*	N	N	N	N	N	N	N	N
VIRGINIA								
1 ***Davis, Jo Ann***	Y	Y	Y	Y	Y	Y	Y	Y
2 ***Schrock***	Y	Y	Y	Y	Y	Y	Y	Y
3 Scott	Y	N	N	N	N	N	N	N
4 ***Forbes***	Y	Y	Y	Y	Y	Y	Y	Y
5 *Goode*	Y	Y	Y	Y	Y	N	Y	Y
6 ***Goodlatte***	Y	Y	Y	Y	Y	N	Y	Y
7 ***Cantor***	Y	Y	Y	Y	Y	Y	Y	Y
8 Moran	Y	N	N	N	N	N	N	N
9 Boucher	Y	?	N	N	N	N	N	N
10 ***Wolf***	Y	N	N	N	N	Y	N	N
11 ***Davis, T.***	Y	Y	Y	Y	Y	Y	Y	N
WASHINGTON								
1 Inslee	Y	N	N	N	N	N	N	N
2 Larsen	Y	N	N	N	N	N	N	N
3 Baird	Y	N	N	N	N	N	N	N
4 ***Hastings***	Y	Y	Y	Y	Y	Y	Y	Y
5 ***Nethercutt***	Y	Y	Y	Y	Y	Y	Y	Y
6 Dicks	Y	N	N	N	N	N	N	N
7 McDermott	N	N	N	N	N	N	N	N
8 ***Dunn***	Y	Y	Y	Y	Y	Y	N	Y
9 Smith	N	N	N	N	N	N	N	N
WEST VIRGINIA								
1 Mollohan	Y	Y	N	N	N	N	N	N
2 ***Capito***	Y	Y	Y	Y	Y	Y	Y	N
3 Rahall	Y	Y	N	N	N	N	N	N
WISCONSIN								
1 ***Ryan***	Y	Y	Y	Y	Y	Y	Y	N
2 Baldwin	Y	N	N	N	N	N	N	N
3 Kind	Y	N	N	N	N	N	N	N
4 Kleczka	N	N	N	N	N	N	N	N
5 Barrett	N	N	N	N	N	N	N	N
6 ***Petri***	Y	Y	N	Y	N	Y	N	Y
7 Obey	N	N	N	N	N	N	N	N
8 ***Green***	Y	Y	Y	Y	Y	Y	Y	Y
9 ***Sensenbrenner***	Y	Y	Y	Y	Y	Y	Y	Y
WYOMING								
AL ***Cubin***	?	Y	?	?	?	?	?	?

Southern states - Ala., Ark., Fla., Ga., Ky., La., Miss., N.C., Okla., S.C., Tenn., Texas, Va.

31. HR 2356. Campaign Finance Overhaul/Effective Date. Reynolds, R-N.Y., amendment that would make the bill's provisions effective beginning Feb. 14, 2002. Rejected 190-238: R 188-28; D 1-209 (ND 0-156, SD 1-53); I 1-1. Feb. 14, 2002 (in the session that began and the Congressional Record dated Feb. 13, 2002).

32. HR 2356. Campaign Finance Overhaul/Building Funds. Kingston, R-Ga., amendment that would ban the national parties from spending certain funds to defray construction costs for office buildings. Adopted 232-196: R 214-2; D 16-194 (ND 11-145, SD 5-49); I 2-0. Feb. 14, 2002 (in the session that began and the Congressional Record dated Feb. 13, 2002).

33. HR 2356. Campaign Finance Overhaul/Ney and Wynn Substitute. Ney, R-Ohio, substitute amendment that would cap soft money donations at $20,000 per year to national political parties. Soft money expenditures would be limited to certain activities such as voter registration. It would raise the aggregate annual individual limit to candidates, parties and PACs from $25,000 to $37,500. It also would put new disclosure requirements on certain broadcast advertisements. Rejected 181-248: R 172-45; D 8-202 (ND 3-153, SD 5-49); I 1-1. Feb. 14, 2002 (in the session that began and the Congressional Record dated Feb. 13, 2002).

34. HR 2356. Campaign Finance Overhaul/Passage. Passage of the bill that would ban "soft money" donations to national political parties but allow up to $10,000 in soft money donations to state and local parties for voter registration and get-out-the vote activities. The bill would prevent issue ads from targeting specific candidates within 60 days of a general election or 30 days of a primary. The bill also would increase the individual contribution limit from $1,000 to $2,000 per election for House and Senate candidates, both of which would be indexed for inflation. Passed 240-189: R 41-176; D 198-12 (ND 150-6, SD 48-6); I 1-1. Feb. 14, 2002 (in the session that began and the Congressional Record dated Feb. 13, 2002).

35. Procedural Motion/Journal. Approval of the House Journal of Wednesday, Feb. 13, 2002. Approved 342-51: R 179-21; D 162-30 (ND 119-24, SD 43-6); I 1-0. Feb. 14, 2002.

36. HR 622. Unemployment and Tax Benefits/Previous Question. Hastings, R-Wash., motion to order the previous question (thus ending debate and possibility of amendment) on adoption of the rule (H Res 347) to provide for House floor consideration of Senate amendments to the bill that would extend unemployment benefits for 13 more weeks. Motion agreed to 216-207: R 215-0; D 0-206 (ND 0-153, SD 0-53); I 1-1. Feb. 14, 2002.

37. HR 622. Unemployment and Tax Benefits/Rule. Adoption of the rule (H Res 347) to provide for House floor consideration of Senate amendments to the bill that would extend unemployment benefits for 13 more weeks. Adopted 213-206: R 212-0; D 0-205 (ND 0-151, SD 0-54); I 1-1. Feb. 14, 2002.

38. HR 622. Unemployment and Tax Benefits/Concur With Senate Amendments. Thomas, R-Calif., motion to concur in a House amendment to Senate amendments to the bill that would extend unemployment benefits for 13 more weeks and provide additional tax reductions. The House amendment would accelerate a reduction in the 27 percent tax rate for individuals, provide a 30 percent bonus deduction for companies when they purchase equipment, create a refundable health insurance tax credit, and give a tax rebate to individuals who did not receive the total $300 rebate from last year's tax package. Motion agreed to 225-199: R 214-1; D 10-197 (ND 5-149, SD 5-48); I 1-1. Feb. 14, 2002.

Key

Y	Voted for (yea).
#	Paired for.
+	Announced for.
N	Voted against (nay).
X	Paired against.
–	Announced against.
P	Voted "present."
C	Voted "present" to avoid possible conflict of interest.
?	Did not vote or otherwise make a position known.

Democrats **Republicans** *Independents*

	31	32	33	34	35	36	37	38
ALABAMA								
1 *Callahan*	Y	Y	Y	N	Y	Y	Y	Y
2 *Everett*	Y	Y	Y	N	Y	Y	Y	Y
3 *Riley*	?	?	?	?	?	?	?	?
4 *Aderholt*	Y	Y	Y	N	Y	Y	Y	Y
5 Cramer	N	N	N	Y	Y	N	N	Y
6 *Bachus*	N	Y	Y	N	Y	Y	Y	Y
7 Hilliard	N	N	N	N	N	N	N	N
ALASKA								
AL *Young*	Y	Y	Y	N	?	Y	Y	Y
ARIZONA								
1 *Flake*	Y	Y	Y	N	Y	Y	Y	Y
2 Pastor	N	N	N	Y	N	N	N	N
3 *Stump*	Y	Y	Y	N	Y	?	?	?
4 *Shadegg*	Y	Y	Y	N	Y	Y	Y	Y
5 *Kolbe*	Y	Y	Y	N	Y	Y	Y	Y
6 *Hayworth*	Y	Y	Y	N	Y	Y	Y	Y
ARKANSAS								
1 Berry	N	N	N	Y	Y	N	N	N
2 Snyder	N	Y	N	Y	Y	N	N	N
3 *Boozman*	Y	Y	Y	N	Y	Y	Y	Y
4 Ross	N	N	N	Y	Y	N	N	N
CALIFORNIA								
1 Thompson	N	N	N	Y	N	N	N	N
2 *Herger*	Y	Y	Y	N	?	Y	Y	Y
3 *Ose*	Y	Y	Y	N	Y	Y	Y	Y
4 *Doolittle*	Y	Y	Y	N	Y	Y	Y	Y
5 Matsui	N	N	N	Y	N	N	N	N
6 Woolsey	N	N	N	Y	N	N	N	N
7 Miller, George	N	Y	N	Y	N	N	N	N
8 Pelosi	N	N	N	Y	N	N	N	N
9 Lee	N	N	N	Y	N	N	N	N
10 Tauscher	N	N	N	Y	N	N	N	N
11 *Pombo*	Y	Y	Y	N	?	Y	Y	Y
12 Lantos	N	N	N	Y	N	N	N	N
13 Stark	N	N	N	Y	N	N	N	N
14 Eshoo	N	N	N	Y	N	N	N	N
15 Honda	N	N	N	Y	N	N	N	N
16 Lofgren	N	N	N	Y	N	N	N	N
17 Farr	N	N	N	Y	N	N	N	N
18 Condit	N	Y	N	Y	N	N	N	N
19 *Radanovich*	Y	Y	Y	N	Y	Y	Y	Y
20 Dooley	N	N	N	Y	N	N	N	N
21 *Thomas*	Y	Y	Y	N	Y	Y	Y	Y
22 Capps	N	N	N	Y	N	N	N	N
23 *Gallegly*	Y	Y	Y	N	Y	Y	Y	Y
24 Sherman	N	N	N	Y	N	N	N	N
25 *McKeon*	Y	Y	Y	N	Y	Y	Y	Y
26 Berman	N	N	N	Y	?	?	?	?
27 Schiff	N	N	N	Y	N	N	N	N
28 *Dreier*	Y	Y	Y	N	Y	Y	Y	Y
29 Waxman	N	N	N	Y	N	N	N	N
30 Becerra	N	N	N	Y	N	N	N	N
31 Solis	N	N	N	Y	N	N	N	N
32 Watson	N	N	N	Y	Y	N	?	N
33 Roybal-Allard	N	N	N	Y	N	N	N	N
34 Napolitano	N	N	N	Y	N	N	N	N
35 Waters	N	N	N	Y	?	N	N	N
36 Harman	N	N	N	Y	N	N	N	N
37 Millender-McD.	N	N	N	Y	N	N	N	N
38 Horn	N	Y	N	Y	N	N	N	N
39 *Royce*	Y	Y	N	Y	N	Y	Y	Y
40 *Lewis*	Y	Y	N	Y	Y	Y	?	Y
41 *Miller, Gary*	Y	Y	Y	N	Y	Y	Y	Y
42 Baca	N	N	N	Y	N	N	N	N
43 *Calvert*	Y	Y	Y	N	Y	Y	Y	Y
44 *Bono*	Y	Y	Y	N	Y	Y	Y	Y
45 *Rohrabacher*	Y	Y	Y	N	Y	Y	Y	Y
46 Sanchez	N	N	N	Y	N	Y	N	N
47 *Cox*	Y	Y	Y	N	?	Y	Y	Y
48 *Issa*	Y	Y	Y	N	Y	Y	Y	Y
49 Davis	N	N	N	Y	N	N	N	N
50 Filner	N	N	N	Y	N	N	N	N
51 *Cunningham*	Y	Y	Y	N	Y	Y	Y	Y
52 *Hunter*	Y	Y	Y	N	Y	Y	Y	Y
COLORADO								
1 DeGette	N	N	N	Y	N	N	N	N
2 Udall	N	N	N	Y	N	N	N	N
3 *McInnis*	Y	Y	N	Y	Y	Y	Y	Y
4 *Schaffer*	Y	Y	Y	N	Y	Y	Y	Y
5 *Hefley*	?	?	?	N	Y	Y	Y	Y
6 *Tancredo*	Y	Y	Y	N	P	Y	Y	Y
CONNECTICUT								
1 Larson	N	N	N	Y	N	N	N	N
2 *Simmons*	N	Y	N	Y	Y	Y	Y	Y
3 DeLauro	N	N	N	Y	N	N	N	N
4 *Shays*	N	N	N	Y	N	N	N	N
5 Maloney	N	N	N	Y	N	N	N	N
6 *Johnson*	N	Y	N	Y	Y	Y	Y	Y
DELAWARE								
AL *Castle*	N	N	Y	N	Y	Y	Y	Y
FLORIDA								
1 *Miller, J.*	Y	Y	Y	N	Y	Y	Y	Y
2 Boyd	N	N	N	Y	N	N	N	N
3 Brown	N	N	N	Y	N	N	N	N
4 *Crenshaw*	Y	Y	Y	N	Y	Y	Y	Y
5 Thurman	N	N	N	Y	N	N	N	N
6 *Stearns*	Y	Y	Y	N	Y	Y	Y	Y
7 *Mica*	Y	Y	Y	N	Y	Y	Y	Y
8 *Keller*	Y	Y	Y	N	Y	Y	Y	Y
9 *Bilirakis*	Y	Y	Y	N	Y	Y	Y	Y
10 *Young*	Y	Y	Y	N	?	Y	Y	Y
11 Davis	N	N	N	Y	N	N	N	N
12 *Putnam*	Y	Y	Y	N	Y	Y	Y	Y
13 *Miller, D.*	Y	Y	Y	N	Y	Y	Y	?
14 *Goss*	Y	Y	Y	N	Y	Y	Y	Y
15 *Weldon*	Y	Y	Y	N	Y	Y	Y	Y
16 *Foley*	Y	Y	N	Y	N	Y	Y	Y
17 Meek	N	N	N	Y	?	N	N	N
18 *Ros-Lehtinen*	Y	Y	Y	N	Y	Y	Y	Y
19 Wexler	N	N	N	Y	N	N	N	N
20 Deutsch	N	N	N	Y	N	N	N	N
21 *Diaz-Balart*	Y	Y	N	Y	Y	Y	Y	Y
22 *Shaw*	Y	Y	Y	N	Y	Y	Y	Y
23 Hastings	N	N	N	Y	N	N	N	N
GEORGIA								
1 *Kingston*	Y	Y	Y	N	Y	Y	Y	Y
2 Bishop	N	N	N	Y	N	N	N	N
3 *Collins*	Y	Y	Y	N	Y	Y	Y	Y
4 McKinney	N	N	N	Y	N	N	N	N
5 Lewis	N	N	N	Y	N	N	N	N
6 *Isakson*	Y	Y	Y	N	Y	Y	Y	Y
7 *Barr*	Y	Y	N	Y	N	Y	Y	Y
8 *Chambliss*	Y	Y	Y	N	Y	Y	Y	Y
9 *Deal*	Y	Y	Y	N	Y	Y	Y	Y
10 *Norwood*	Y	Y	Y	N	Y	Y	Y	Y
11 *Linder*	Y	Y	Y	N	Y	Y	Y	Y
HAWAII								
1 Abercrombie	N	Y	N	Y	N	N	N	N
2 Mink	N	N	N	Y	N	N	N	N
IDAHO								
1 *Otter*	Y	Y	Y	N	Y	Y	Y	Y
2 *Simpson*	Y	Y	Y	N	Y	Y	Y	Y
ILLINOIS								
1 Rush	N	N	N	Y	N	N	N	N
2 Jackson	N	N	N	Y	N	N	N	N
3 Lipinski	N	Y	N	Y	N	N	N	N
4 Gutierrez	N	N	N	Y	N	N	N	N
5 Blagojevich	N	N	N	Y	N	N	N	N
6 *Hyde*	Y	Y	Y	N	Y	Y	Y	Y
7 Davis	N	N	N	Y	N	N	N	N
8 *Crane*	Y	Y	Y	N	Y	Y	Y	Y
9 Schakowsky	N	N	N	Y	N	N	N	N
10 *Kirk*	N	Y	N	Y	N	Y	Y	Y
11 *Weller*	Y	Y	Y	N	Y	Y	Y	Y
12 Costello	N	Y	N	Y	N	N	N	N
13 *Biggert*	Y	Y	Y	N	Y	Y	Y	Y

ND Northern Democrats   SD Southern Democrats

	31	32	33	34	35	36	37	38
14 ***Hastert***	Y	Y	Y	N	Y			Y
15 ***Johnson***	N	Y	N	Y	Y	Y	Y	Y
16 ***Manzullo***	Y	Y	Y	N	Y	Y	Y	Y
17 Evans	N	N	N	Y	Y	N	N	N
18 ***LaHood***	Y	Y	N	N	Y	Y	Y	Y
19 Phelps	N	N	N	Y	Y	N	N	N
20 ***Shimkus***	Y	Y	Y	N	Y	Y	Y	Y
INDIANA								
1 Visclosky	N	N	N	Y	N	N	N	N
2 ***Pence***	Y	Y	Y	N	Y	Y	Y	Y
3 Roemer	N	Y	N	Y	Y	N	N	N
4 ***Souder***	Y	Y	Y	N	Y	Y	Y	Y
5 ***Buyer***	Y	Y	Y	N	Y	Y	?	Y
6 ***Burton***	Y	Y	Y	N	Y	Y	Y	Y
7 ***Kerns***	Y	Y	Y	N	Y	Y	Y	Y
8 ***Hostettler***	Y	Y	N	N	Y	Y	Y	Y
9 Hill	N	N	N	Y	Y	N	N	N
10 Carson	N	N	N	Y	Y	N	N	N
IOWA								
1 ***Leach***	N	Y	N	Y	Y	Y	Y	Y
2 ***Nussle***	Y	Y	Y	N	Y	Y	Y	Y
3 Boswell	N	N	N	Y	Y	N	N	N
4 ***Ganske***	Y	Y	N	Y	Y	Y	Y	Y
5 ***Latham***	Y	Y	Y	N	Y	Y	Y	Y
KANSAS								
1 ***Moran***	Y	Y	Y	N	N	Y	Y	Y
2 ***Ryun***	Y	Y	Y	N	?	Y	Y	Y
3 Moore	N	Y	N	Y	N	N	N	N
4 ***Tiahrt***	Y	Y	Y	N	Y	Y	Y	Y
KENTUCKY								
1 ***Whitfield***	Y	Y	Y	N	Y	Y	?	Y
2 ***Lewis***	Y	Y	Y	N	Y	Y	Y	Y
3 ***Northup***	Y	Y	Y	N	Y	Y	Y	Y
4 Lucas	N	N	N	Y	Y	N	N	Y
5 ***Rogers***	Y	Y	Y	N	Y	Y	Y	Y
6 ***Fletcher***	Y	Y	Y	N	Y	Y	Y	Y
LOUISIANA								
1 ***Vitter***	Y	Y	Y	N	Y	Y	Y	Y
2 Jefferson	N	N	N	Y	Y	N	N	N
3 ***Tauzin***	Y	Y	Y	N	Y	Y	Y	Y
4 ***McCrery***	Y	Y	Y	N	Y	Y	Y	Y
5 ***Cooksey***	Y	Y	Y	N	Y	Y	Y	Y
6 ***Baker***	Y	Y	Y	N	Y	Y	Y	Y
7 John	N	N	Y	Y	Y	N	N	Y
MAINE								
1 Allen	N	N	N	Y	Y	N	N	N
2 Baldacci	N	N	N	Y	Y	N	N	N
MARYLAND								
1 ***Gilchrest***	N	Y	N	Y	Y	Y	Y	Y
2 ***Ehrlich***	Y	Y	Y	N	?	Y	Y	Y
3 Cardin	N	N	N	Y	Y	N	N	N
4 Wynn	N	N	Y	Y	Y	N	N	N
5 Hoyer	N	N	N	Y	Y	N	N	N
6 ***Bartlett***	Y	Y	Y	N	Y	Y	Y	Y
7 Cummings	N	N	N	Y	Y	N	N	N
8 ***Morella***	N	Y	N	Y	Y	Y	Y	N
MASSACHUSETTS								
1 Olver	N	N	N	Y	Y	N	N	N
2 Neal	N	N	N	Y	?	N	N	N
3 McGovern	N	N	N	Y	Y	N	N	N
4 Frank	N	N	N	Y	Y	N	N	N
5 Meehan	N	N	N	Y	Y	N	N	N
6 Tierney	N	Y	N	Y	Y	N	N	N
7 Markey	N	N	N	Y	Y	N	N	N
8 Capuano	N	N	N	Y	Y	N	N	N
9 Lynch	N	N	N	Y	Y	N	N	N
10 Delahunt	N	N	N	Y	Y	N	N	N
MICHIGAN								
1 Stupak	N	N	N	Y	N	N	N	N
2 ***Hoekstra***	Y	Y	Y	N	Y	Y	Y	Y
3 ***Ehlers***	Y	Y	Y	N	Y	Y	Y	Y
4 ***Camp***	Y	Y	Y	N	Y	Y	Y	Y
5 Barcia	N	N	Y	N	Y	N	N	Y
6 ***Upton***	N	Y	Y	Y	Y	Y	Y	Y
7 ***Smith***	Y	Y	Y	Y	Y	Y	Y	Y
8 ***Rogers***	Y	Y	Y	N	Y	Y	Y	Y
9 Kildee	N	N	N	Y	Y	N	N	N
10 Bonior	N	N	N	Y	Y	N	N	N
11 ***Knollenberg***	Y	Y	Y	N	Y	Y	Y	Y
12 Levin	N	N	N	Y	Y	N	N	N
13 Rivers	N	N	N	Y	Y	N	N	N
14 Conyers	N	N	N	Y	?	N	?	N
15 Kilpatrick	N	N	N	Y	Y	N	N	N
16 Dingell	N	N	N	Y	Y	N	N	N

	31	32	33	34	35	36	37	38
MINNESOTA								
1 ***Gutknecht***	Y	Y	Y	N	N	Y	Y	Y
2 ***Kennedy***	Y	Y	Y	N	N	Y	Y	Y
3 ***Ramstad***	N	Y	N	Y	Y	Y	Y	Y
4 McCollum	N	N	N	Y	Y	N	?	N
5 Sabo	N	N	N	Y	N	N	N	N
6 Luther	N	N	N	Y	Y	N	N	N
7 Peterson	N	N	N	N	N	N	N	N
8 Oberstar	N	N	N	Y	?	N	N	N
MISSISSIPPI								
1 ***Wicker***	Y	Y	Y	N	N	Y	Y	Y
2 Thompson	N	N	N	N	N	N	N	N
3 ***Pickering***	Y	Y	Y	N	Y	Y	Y	Y
4 Shows	N	N	Y	N	Y	N	N	Y
5 Taylor	Y	N	N	Y	N	N	N	N
MISSOURI								
1 Clay	N	N	N	Y	?	N	N	N
2 ***Akin***	Y	Y	Y	N	Y	Y	Y	Y
3 Gephardt	N	N	N	Y	?	N	N	N
4 Skelton	N	N	N	Y	Y	N	N	N
5 McCarthy	N	N	N	Y	Y	N	N	N
6 ***Graves***	Y	Y	Y	N	Y	Y	Y	Y
7 ***Blunt***	Y	Y	Y	N	Y	Y	Y	Y
8 ***Emerson***	Y	Y	N	N	Y	Y	Y	Y
9 ***Hulshof***	N	Y	Y	N	N	Y	Y	Y
MONTANA								
AL ***Rehberg***	Y	Y	Y	N	Y	Y	Y	Y
NEBRASKA								
1 ***Bereuter***	Y	Y	N	Y	Y	Y	Y	Y
2 ***Terry***	Y	Y	Y	N	Y	Y	Y	Y
3 ***Osborne***	Y	Y	N	Y	Y	Y	Y	Y
NEVADA								
1 Berkley	N	Y	N	Y	Y	N	N	N
2 ***Gibbons***	Y	Y	Y	N	Y	Y	Y	Y
NEW HAMPSHIRE								
1 ***Sununu***	Y	Y	Y	N	Y	Y	Y	Y
2 ***Bass***	N	Y	N	Y	Y	Y	Y	Y
NEW JERSEY								
1 Andrews	N	N	N	Y	Y	N	N	N
2 ***LoBiondo***	N	Y	N	Y	N	Y	Y	Y
3 ***Saxton***	Y	Y	N	N	Y	Y	Y	Y
4 ***Smith***	Y	Y	Y	N	?	Y	Y	Y
5 ***Roukema***	?	?	?	?	?	?	?	?
6 Pallone	N	N	N	Y	N	N	N	N
7 ***Ferguson***	Y	Y	Y	Y	N	Y	Y	Y
8 Pascrell	N	N	N	Y	Y	N	N	N
9 Rothman	N	N	N	Y	Y	N	N	N
10 Payne	N	N	N	Y	?	?	?	?
11 ***Frelinghuysen***	Y	Y	N	Y	Y	Y	Y	Y
12 Holt	N	N	N	Y	Y	N	N	N
13 Menendez	N	N	N	Y	N	N	N	N
NEW MEXICO								
1 ***Wilson***	Y	Y	Y	N	Y	Y	Y	Y
2 ***Skeen***	Y	Y	Y	N	Y	Y	Y	Y
3 Udall	N	N	N	Y	?	N	N	N
NEW YORK								
1 ***Grucci***	Y	Y	N	Y	Y	Y	Y	Y
2 Israel	N	N	N	Y	Y	N	N	Y
3 ***King***	Y	Y	Y	N	Y	Y	Y	Y
4 McCarthy	N	N	N	Y	Y	N	N	Y
5 Ackerman	N	N	N	Y	Y	N	N	N
6 Meeks	N	N	N	Y	Y	N	N	N
7 Crowley	N	N	N	Y	Y	N	N	N
8 Nadler	N	N	N	Y	Y	N	N	N
9 Weiner	N	N	N	Y	Y	N	N	N
10 Towns	N	N	N	Y	Y	N	N	N
11 Owens	N	N	N	Y	Y	N	N	N
12 Velázquez	N	N	N	Y	Y	N	N	N
13 ***Fossella***	Y	Y	Y	N	Y	Y	Y	Y
14 Maloney	N	N	N	Y	Y	?	N	N
15 Rangel	N	N	N	Y	Y	N	N	N
16 Serrano	N	N	N	Y	Y	N	N	N
17 Engel	N	N	N	Y	Y	N	N	N
18 Lowey	N	N	N	Y	Y	N	N	N
19 ***Kelly***	Y	Y	Y	N	?	Y	Y	Y
20 ***Gilman***	N	Y	N	Y	Y	Y	Y	Y
21 McNulty	N	N	N	Y	Y	N	N	N
22 ***Sweeney***	Y	Y	Y	N	N	Y	Y	Y
23 ***Boehlert***	N	Y	N	Y	Y	Y	Y	Y
24 ***McHugh***	N	Y	N	Y	Y	Y	Y	Y
25 ***Walsh***	N	Y	N	Y	Y	Y	Y	Y
26 Hinchey	N	N	N	Y	Y	N	N	N
27 ***Reynolds***	Y	Y	Y	N	Y	Y	Y	Y
28 Slaughter	N	N	N	Y	N	N	N	N
29 LaFalce	N	N	N	Y	Y	N	N	N

	31	32	33	34	35	36	37	38
30 ***Quinn***	N	Y	N	Y	Y	Y	Y	Y
31 ***Houghton***	N	Y	N	Y	Y	Y	Y	Y
NORTH CAROLINA								
1 Clayton	N	N	N	Y	Y	N	N	N
2 Etheridge	N	N	N	Y	Y	N	N	N
3 ***Jones***	Y	Y	Y	N	N	Y	Y	Y
4 Price	N	N	N	Y	Y	N	N	N
5 ***Burr***	?	?	Y	N	Y	Y	Y	Y
6 ***Coble***	Y	Y	Y	N	Y	Y	Y	Y
7 McIntyre	N	N	N	Y	Y	N	N	N
8 ***Hayes***	Y	Y	Y	N	Y	Y	Y	Y
9 ***Myrick***	Y	Y	Y	N	+	Y	Y	Y
10 ***Ballenger***	Y	Y	Y	N	Y	Y	Y	Y
11 ***Taylor***	Y	Y	Y	N	Y	Y	?	?
12 Watt	N	N	N	Y	Y	N	N	N
NORTH DAKOTA								
AL Pomeroy	N	N	N	Y	Y	N	N	N
OHIO								
1 ***Chabot***	Y	Y	Y	N	Y	Y	Y	Y
2 ***Portman***	Y	Y	Y	N	Y	Y	Y	Y
3 Hall	N	N	N	Y	?	N	N	N
4 ***Oxley***	Y	Y	Y	N	?	Y	Y	Y
5 ***Gillmor***	Y	Y	Y	N	Y	Y	Y	Y
6 Strickland	N	N	N	Y	Y	N	N	N
7 ***Hobson***	Y	Y	Y	N	N	Y	Y	Y
8 ***Boehner***	Y	Y	Y	N	Y	Y	Y	Y
9 Kaptur	N	N	N	Y	Y	N	N	N
10 Kucinich	N	N	N	Y	N	N	N	N
11 Jones	N	N	N	Y	N	N	N	N
12 ***Tiberi***	Y	Y	Y	N	Y	Y	Y	Y
13 Brown	N	N	N	Y	Y	N	N	N
14 Sawyer	N	N	N	Y	Y	N	N	N
15 ***Pryce***	Y	Y	Y	N	N	Y	Y	Y
16 ***Regula***	Y	Y	Y	N	Y	Y	Y	Y
17 Traficant	?	?	?	?	?	?	?	?
18 ***Ney***	Y	Y	Y	N	N	Y	Y	Y
19 ***LaTourette***	Y	Y	Y	Y	Y	Y	Y	Y
OKLAHOMA								
1 ***Largent***	Y	Y	N	N	Y	Y	Y	Y
2 Carson	N	Y	N	Y	Y	N	N	N
3 ***Watkins***	Y	Y	Y	N	Y	Y	Y	Y
4 ***Watts***	N	Y	Y	N	Y	Y	Y	Y
5 ***Istook***	Y	Y	Y	N	Y	Y	Y	Y
6 ***Lucas***	Y	Y	Y	N	Y	Y	Y	Y
OREGON								
1 Wu	N	N	N	Y	Y	N	N	N
2 ***Walden***	Y	Y	Y	N	Y	Y	Y	Y
3 Blumenauer	N	N	N	Y	Y	N	N	N
4 DeFazio	N	Y	N	Y	Y	N	N	N
5 Hooley	N	N	N	Y	Y	N	N	N
PENNSYLVANIA								
1 Brady	N	N	N	Y	N	N	N	N
2 Fattah	N	N	N	Y	Y	N	N	N
3 Borski	N	N	N	Y	N	N	N	N
4 ***Hart***	Y	Y	Y	N	Y	Y	Y	Y
5 ***Peterson***	Y	Y	Y	N	Y	Y	Y	Y
6 Holden	N	N	N	Y	Y	N	N	N
7 ***Weldon***	Y	Y	N	Y	?	?	?	?
8 ***Greenwood***	N	Y	N	Y	Y	Y	Y	Y
9 ***Shuster, Bill***	Y	Y	Y	N	Y	Y	Y	Y
10 ***Sherwood***	Y	Y	Y	N	Y	Y	Y	Y
11 Kanjorski	N	N	N	Y	Y	N	N	N
12 Murtha	N	N	N	N	?	N	N	N
13 Hoeffel	N	N	N	Y	Y	N	N	N
14 Coyne	N	N	N	Y	?	N	N	N
15 ***Toomey***	Y	Y	Y	N	Y	Y	Y	Y
16 ***Pitts***	Y	Y	Y	N	Y	Y	Y	Y
17 ***Gekas***	Y	Y	Y	N	Y	Y	Y	Y
18 Doyle	N	N	N	Y	Y	N	N	N
19 ***Platts***	N	Y	N	Y	N	Y	Y	Y
20 Mascara	N	N	N	Y	Y	N	N	N
21 ***English***	Y	Y	Y	N	N	Y	Y	Y
RHODE ISLAND								
1 Kennedy	N	N	N	Y	Y	N	N	N
2 Langevin	N	N	N	Y	Y	N	N	N
SOUTH CAROLINA								
1 ***Brown***	Y	Y	Y	N	Y	Y	Y	Y
2 ***Wilson***	Y	Y	Y	N	Y	Y	Y	Y
3 ***Graham***	N	Y	N	Y	Y	Y	Y	Y
4 ***DeMint***	Y	Y	Y	N	Y	Y	Y	Y
5 Spratt	N	N	N	Y	Y	N	N	N
6 Clyburn	N	N	N	Y	Y	N	N	N
SOUTH DAKOTA								
AL ***Thune***	Y	Y	N	Y	Y	Y	Y	Y

	31	32	33	34	35	36	37	38
TENNESSEE								
1 ***Jenkins***	Y	Y	Y	N	Y	Y	Y	Y
2 ***Duncan***	Y	Y	Y	N	Y	Y	Y	Y
3 ***Wamp***	Y	Y	N	Y	Y	Y	Y	Y
4 ***Hilleary***	Y	Y	Y	N	N	Y	Y	Y
5 Clement	N	N	N	Y	Y	N	N	N
6 Gordon	N	N	N	Y	?	N	N	N
7 ***Bryant***	Y	Y	Y	N	Y	Y	Y	Y
8 Tanner	N	N	N	Y	Y	N	N	N
9 Ford	N	N	N	Y	?	N	N	N
TEXAS								
1 Sandlin	N	N	N	Y	Y	N	N	N
2 Turner	N	N	N	Y	Y	N	N	N
3 ***Johnson, Sam***	Y	Y	Y	N	Y	Y	Y	Y
4 Hall	N	Y	Y	N	Y	N	N	Y
5 ***Sessions***	Y	Y	Y	N	?	Y	Y	Y
6 ***Barton***	Y	Y	Y	N	?	Y	Y	Y
7 ***Culberson***	Y	Y	Y	N	Y	Y	Y	Y
8 ***Brady***	?	?	?	?	?	?	?	?
9 Lampson	N	N	N	Y	Y	N	N	N
10 Doggett	N	N	N	Y	N	N	N	N
11 Edwards	N	Y	N	Y	Y	N	N	N
12 ***Granger***	Y	Y	Y	N	Y	Y	Y	Y
13 ***Thornberry***	Y	Y	Y	N	Y	Y	Y	Y
14 ***Paul***	N	N	Y	N	Y	Y	Y	Y
15 Hinojosa	N	N	N	Y	+	N	N	N
16 Reyes	N	N	N	Y	Y	N	N	N
17 Stenholm	N	N	N	Y	Y	N	N	?
18 Jackson-Lee	N	N	Y	N	Y	N	N	N
19 ***Combest***	Y	Y	Y	N	?	Y	Y	Y
20 Gonzalez	N	N	N	Y	Y	N	N	N
21 ***Smith***	Y	Y	N	N	Y	Y	Y	Y
22 ***DeLay***	Y	Y	Y	N	?	Y	Y	Y
23 ***Bonilla***	Y	Y	Y	N	Y	Y	Y	Y
24 Frost	N	N	Y	Y	Y	N	N	N
25 Bentsen	N	N	N	Y	Y	N	N	N
26 ***Armey***	Y	Y	Y	N	Y	Y	Y	Y
27 Ortiz	N	N	N	Y	Y	N	N	N
28 Rodriguez	N	N	N	Y	Y	N	N	N
29 Green	N	N	N	Y	Y	N	N	N
30 Johnson, E.B.	N	N	N	Y	Y	N	N	N
UTAH								
1 ***Hansen***	Y	Y	Y	N	N	Y	Y	Y
2 Matheson	N	Y	N	Y	Y	N	N	N
3 ***Cannon***	Y	Y	Y	N	Y	Y	Y	Y
VERMONT								
AL *Sanders*	N	Y	N	Y	Y	N	N	N
VIRGINIA								
1 ***Davis, Jo Ann***	Y	Y	Y	N	Y	Y	Y	Y
2 ***Schrock***	Y	Y	Y	N	Y	Y	Y	Y
3 Scott	N	N	N	N	N	N	N	N
4 ***Forbes***	Y	Y	Y	N	Y	Y	Y	Y
5 *Goode*	Y	Y	Y	N	?	Y	Y	Y
6 ***Goodlatte***	Y	Y	Y	N	Y	Y	Y	Y
7 ***Cantor***	Y	Y	Y	N	Y	Y	Y	Y
8 Moran	N	N	N	Y	Y	?	N	N
9 Boucher	N	N	Y	N	?	N	N	N
10 ***Wolf***	Y	Y	N	Y	Y	Y	Y	Y
11 ***Davis, T.***	Y	Y	Y	N	Y	Y	Y	Y
WASHINGTON								
1 Inslee	N	N	N	Y	Y	N	N	N
2 Larsen	N	N	N	Y	N	N	N	N
3 Baird	N	N	N	Y	N	N	N	N
4 ***Hastings***	Y	Y	Y	N	Y	Y	Y	Y
5 ***Nethercutt***	Y	Y	Y	N	Y	Y	Y	Y
6 Dicks	N	N	N	Y	Y	N	N	N
7 McDermott	N	N	N	Y	N	N	N	N
8 ***Dunn***	Y	Y	Y	N	Y	Y	Y	Y
9 Smith	N	N	N	Y	Y	N	N	N
WEST VIRGINIA								
1 Mollohan	N	N	N	N	Y	N	N	N
2 ***Capito***	Y	Y	Y	N	Y	Y	Y	Y
3 Rahall	N	N	N	N	Y	N	N	N
WISCONSIN								
1 ***Ryan***	Y	Y	Y	N	Y	Y	Y	Y
2 Baldwin	N	N	N	Y	Y	N	N	N
3 Kind	N	Y	N	Y	Y	N	N	N
4 Kleczka	N	N	N	Y	Y	N	N	N
5 Barrett	N	N	N	Y	Y	N	N	N
6 ***Petri***	N	Y	N	Y	Y	Y	Y	Y
7 Obey	N	N	N	Y	Y	N	N	N
8 ***Green***	Y	Y	N	N	Y	Y	Y	Y
9 ***Sensenbrenner***	Y	Y	Y	N	Y	Y	Y	Y
WYOMING								
AL ***Cubin***	?	?	?	?	?	?	Y	Y

Southern states - Ala., Ark., Fla., Ga., Ky., La., Miss., N.C., Okla., S.C., Tenn., Texas, Va.

39. HR 1892. Immigrant Affidavit/Concur With Senate Amendments. Sensenbrenner, R-Wis., motion to suspend the rules and concur with the Senate amendments to the bill that would authorize close family members of a sponsor of a permanent residency application to sign an affidavit of financial support if the sponsor dies and the attorney general decides the application should not be revoked. Motion agreed to 404-3: R 209-2; D 194-0 (ND 143-0, SD 51-0); I 1-1. A two-thirds majority of those present and voting (272 in this case) is required for adoption under suspension of the rules. Feb. 26, 2002.

40. H Con Res 304. Congo Volcano Victims/Adoption. Royce, R-Calif., motion to suspend the rules and adopt the concurrent resolution that would express the sympathy of Congress for the people affected by the Jan. 17, 2002, eruption of the Nyiragongo volcano in Congo. The measure also would support an increase in U.S. aid to Congo for rebuilding efforts. Motion agreed to 405-1: R 210-1; D 193-0 (ND 142-0, SD 51-0); I 2-0. A two-thirds majority of those present and voting (271 in this case) is required for adoption under suspension of the rules. Feb. 26, 2002.

41. Procedural Motion/Journal. Approval of the House Journal of Tuesday, Feb. 26, 2002. Approved 355-48: R 187-15; D 166-33 (ND 119-29, SD 47-4); I 2-0. Feb. 27, 2002.

42. HR 1542. High-Speed Internet Access/Rule. Adoption of the rule (H Res 350) to provide for House floor consideration of the bill that would permit the four regional Bell telephone companies to enter the high-speed Internet access market through their long distance connections without first having to open up their local phone markets to competition, as otherwise required by the 1996 Telecommunications Act. Adopted 282-142: R 194-20; D 88-120 (ND 51-103, SD 37-17); I 0-2. Feb. 27, 2002.

¹ *Rep. John Sullivan, R-Okla., was sworn in Feb. 27, 2002. The first vote for which he was eligible was Vote 42. Sullivan succeeds Republican Steve Largent, who resigned effective Feb. 15, 2002, to run for governor of Oklahoma. The last vote for which Largent was eligible was Vote 38.*

Key

Y	Voted for (yea).
#	Paired for.
+	Announced for.
N	Voted against (nay).
X	Paired against.
–	Announced against.
P	Voted "present."
C	Voted "present" to avoid possible conflict of interest.
?	Did not vote or otherwise make a position known.

Democrats **Republicans** *Independents*

	39	40	41	42
ALABAMA				
1 *Callahan*	Y	Y	Y	Y
2 *Everett*	Y	Y	Y	Y
3 *Riley*	?	?	Y	Y
4 *Aderholt*	Y	Y	N	Y
5 Cramer	Y	Y	Y	Y
6 *Bachus*	?	?	Y	Y
7 Hilliard	Y	Y	N	Y
ALASKA				
AL *Young*	Y	Y	?	?
ARIZONA				
1 *Flake*	Y	Y	Y	N
2 Pastor	Y	Y	Y	Y
3 *Stump*	N	Y	Y	Y
4 *Shadegg*	Y	Y	N	N
5 *Kolbe*	Y	Y	Y	Y
6 *Hayworth*	Y	Y	Y	Y
ARKANSAS				
1 Berry	Y	Y	Y	Y
2 Snyder	Y	Y	Y	N
3 *Boozman*	Y	Y	Y	Y
4 Ross	Y	Y	Y	Y
CALIFORNIA				
1 Thompson	Y	Y	N	N
2 *Herger*	Y	Y	Y	Y
3 *Ose*	Y	Y	Y	Y
4 *Doolittle*	?	?	Y	Y
5 Matsui	Y	Y	Y	Y
6 Woolsey	Y	Y	Y	N
7 Miller, George	Y	Y	N	N
8 Pelosi	Y	Y	Y	N
9 Lee	Y	Y	Y	N
10 Tauscher	Y	Y	Y	N
11 *Pombo*	Y	Y	Y	Y
12 Lantos	Y	Y	Y	N
13 Stark	Y	Y	N	N
14 Eshoo	Y	Y	Y	N
15 Honda	Y	Y	Y	N
16 Lofgren	Y	Y	Y	N
17 Farr	Y	Y	Y	N
18 Condit	?	?	Y	Y
19 *Radanovich*	Y	Y	Y	Y
20 Dooley	Y	?	Y	N
21 *Thomas*	Y	Y	?	Y
22 Capps	Y	Y	Y	N
23 *Gallegly*	Y	Y	Y	Y
24 Sherman	Y	Y	Y	N
25 *McKeon*	Y	Y	Y	Y
26 Berman	Y	Y	Y	N
27 Schiff	Y	Y	Y	Y
28 *Dreier*	Y	Y	Y	Y
29 Waxman	Y	Y	Y	N
30 Becerra	Y	Y	N	N
31 Solis	Y	Y	Y	N
32 Watson	Y	Y	Y	N
33 Roybal-Allard	Y	Y	Y	N
34 Napolitano	Y	Y	Y	N
35 Waters	?	?	?	N
36 Harman	Y	Y	Y	N
37 Millender-McD.	Y	Y	Y	N
38 *Horn*	Y	Y	Y	Y

	39	40	41	42
39 *Royce*	Y	Y	Y	Y
40 *Lewis*	Y	Y	Y	Y
41 *Miller, Gary*	Y	Y	Y	Y
42 Baca	Y	Y	Y	Y
43 *Calvert*	Y	Y	Y	Y
44 *Bono*	Y	Y	Y	Y
45 *Rohrabacher*	Y	Y	Y	Y
46 Sanchez	Y	Y	Y	N
47 *Cox*	Y	Y	Y	Y
48 *Issa*	Y	Y	Y	Y
49 Davis	Y	Y	Y	N
50 Filner	Y	Y	N	Y
51 *Cunningham*	Y	Y	Y	Y
52 *Hunter*	Y	Y	Y	Y
COLORADO				
1 DeGette	Y	Y	Y	N
2 Udall	Y	Y	N	N
3 *McInnis*	Y	Y	Y	Y
4 *Schaffer*	Y	Y	N	N
5 *Hefley*	Y	Y	N	N
6 *Tancredo*	N	Y	P	Y
CONNECTICUT				
1 Larson	Y	Y	Y	N
2 *Simmons*	Y	Y	Y	Y
3 DeLauro	Y	Y	Y	N
4 *Shays*	Y	Y	Y	N
5 Maloney	Y	Y	Y	Y
6 *Johnson*	Y	Y	Y	Y
DELAWARE				
AL *Castle*	Y	Y	Y	Y
FLORIDA				
1 *Miller, J.*	Y	Y	Y	Y
2 Boyd	Y	Y	Y	Y
3 Brown	?	?	Y	Y
4 *Crenshaw*	Y	Y	Y	Y
5 Thurman	Y	Y	Y	N
6 *Stearns*	Y	Y	Y	Y
7 *Mica*	Y	Y	Y	Y
8 *Keller*	Y	Y	Y	Y
9 *Bilirakis*	Y	Y	Y	Y
10 *Young*	Y	Y	Y	Y
11 Davis	Y	Y	Y	N
12 *Putnam*	Y	Y	Y	Y
13 *Miller, D.*	Y	Y	Y	Y
14 *Goss*	Y	Y	Y	Y
15 *Weldon*	Y	Y	Y	Y
16 *Foley*	Y	Y	Y	Y
17 Meek	Y	Y	?	Y
18 *Ros-Lehtinen*	Y	Y	Y	Y
19 Wexler	Y	Y	Y	N
20 Deutsch	Y	Y	Y	N
21 *Diaz-Balart*	Y	Y	Y	Y
22 *Shaw*	Y	Y	Y	Y
23 Hastings	Y	Y	N	Y
GEORGIA				
1 *Kingston*	Y	Y	Y	Y
2 Bishop	Y	Y	Y	Y
3 *Collins*	Y	Y	?	Y
4 McKinney	Y	Y	?	Y
5 Lewis	Y	Y	Y	Y
6 *Isakson*	Y	Y	Y	Y
7 *Barr*	Y	Y	Y	Y
8 *Chambliss*	Y	Y	Y	Y
9 *Deal*	Y	Y	?	Y
10 *Norwood*	Y	Y	?	Y
11 *Linder*	Y	Y	Y	Y
HAWAII				
1 Abercrombie	Y	Y	Y	N
2 Mink	Y	Y	?	N
IDAHO				
1 *Otter*	Y	Y	Y	Y
2 *Simpson*	Y	Y	Y	Y
ILLINOIS				
1 Rush	?	?	Y	Y
2 Jackson	Y	Y	Y	Y
3 Lipinski	Y	Y	Y	N
4 Gutierrez	Y	Y	Y	Y
5 Blagojevich	?	?	?	Y
6 *Hyde*	Y	Y	Y	Y
7 Davis	Y	Y	Y	Y
8 *Crane*	Y	Y	N	Y
9 Schakowsky	Y	Y	N	N
10 *Kirk*	Y	Y	Y	Y
11 *Weller*	Y	Y	N	Y
12 Costello	?	?	N	N
13 *Biggert*	Y	Y	Y	Y

ND Northern Democrats   SD Southern Democrats

State / District	39	40	41	42
14 Hastert				
15 *Johnson*	Y	Y	Y	Y
16 *Manzullo*	Y	Y	Y	Y
17 Evans	Y	Y	Y	N
18 *LaHood*	Y	Y	Y	Y
19 Phelps	?	?	Y	N
20 *Shimkus*	Y	Y	Y	Y
INDIANA				
1 Visclosky	Y	Y	N	Y
2 *Pence*	Y	Y	Y	Y
3 Roemer	Y	Y	Y	N
4 *Souder*	Y	Y	Y	Y
5 *Buyer*	Y	Y	Y	Y
6 *Burton*	Y	Y	Y	Y
7 *Kerns*	Y	Y	Y	Y
8 *Hostettler*	Y	Y	Y	Y
9 Hill	Y	Y	Y	N
10 Carson	Y	Y	Y	Y
IOWA				
1 *Leach*	Y	Y	Y	N
2 *Nussle*	Y	Y	Y	Y
3 Boswell	Y	Y	Y	N
4 *Ganske*	Y	Y	Y	Y
5 *Latham*	Y	Y	N	Y
KANSAS				
1 *Moran*	Y	Y	N	Y
2 *Ryun*	Y	Y	Y	Y
3 Moore	Y	Y	N	N
4 *Tiahrt*	Y	Y	Y	Y
KENTUCKY				
1 *Whitfield*	Y	Y	Y	Y
2 *Lewis*	Y	Y	Y	Y
3 *Northup*	Y	Y	Y	Y
4 Lucas	Y	Y	Y	Y
5 *Rogers*	Y	Y	Y	Y
6 *Fletcher*	Y	Y	Y	Y
LOUISIANA				
1 *Vitter*	Y	Y	Y	Y
2 Jefferson	Y	Y	Y	Y
3 *Tauzin*	Y	Y	Y	Y
4 *McCrery*	Y	Y	?	Y
5 *Cooksey*	Y	Y	Y	Y
6 *Baker*	Y	Y	Y	Y
7 John	Y	Y	Y	Y
MAINE				
1 Allen	Y	Y	Y	N
2 Baldacci	?	?	?	?
MARYLAND				
1 *Gilchrest*	Y	Y	Y	Y
2 *Ehrlich*	Y	Y	?	N
3 Cardin	Y	Y	Y	Y
4 Wynn	Y	Y	Y	Y
5 Hoyer	Y	Y	Y	Y
6 *Bartlett*	Y	Y	Y	N
7 Cummings	Y	Y	Y	Y
8 *Morella*	Y	Y	Y	N
MASSACHUSETTS				
1 Olver	Y	Y	Y	N
2 Neal	Y	Y	Y	Y
3 McGovern	Y	Y	Y	N
4 Frank	Y	Y	Y	Y
5 Meehan	Y	Y	Y	N
6 Tierney	Y	Y	Y	N
7 Markey	Y	Y	N	N
8 Capuano	Y	Y	N	N
9 Lynch	?	?	Y	N
10 Delahunt	Y	Y	Y	N
MICHIGAN				
1 Stupak	Y	Y	N	N
2 *Hoekstra*	Y	Y	N	N
3 *Ehlers*	Y	Y	Y	Y
4 *Camp*	Y	Y	Y	Y
5 Barcia	Y	Y	Y	Y
6 *Upton*	Y	Y	Y	Y
7 *Smith*	Y	Y	Y	Y
8 *Rogers*	Y	Y	Y	Y
9 Kildee	Y	Y	Y	Y
10 Bonior	?	?	Y	Y
11 *Knollenberg*	Y	Y	Y	Y
12 Levin	Y	Y	Y	Y
13 Rivers	Y	Y	Y	N
14 Conyers	Y	Y	Y	Y
15 Kilpatrick	Y	Y	?	N
16 Dingell	Y	Y	Y	Y

State / District	39	40	41	42
MINNESOTA				
1 *Gutknecht*	Y	Y	N	Y
2 *Kennedy*	Y	Y	N	Y
3 *Ramstad*	Y	Y	N	N
4 McCollum	Y	Y	N	N
5 Sabo	Y	Y	N	N
6 Luther	Y	Y	N	N
7 Peterson	Y	Y	N	N
8 Oberstar	Y	Y	N	N
MISSISSIPPI				
1 *Wicker*	Y	Y	N	Y
2 Thompson	Y	Y	N	N
3 *Pickering*	Y	Y	N	Y
4 Shows	Y	Y	Y	N
5 Taylor	Y	Y	N	N
MISSOURI				
1 Clay	Y	Y	?	Y
2 *Akin*	Y	Y	Y	N
3 Gephardt	Y	Y	Y	N
4 Skelton	Y	Y	Y	N
5 McCarthy	Y	Y	Y	N
6 *Graves*	Y	Y	Y	Y
7 *Blunt*	Y	Y	Y	Y
8 *Emerson*	Y	Y	Y	Y
9 *Hulshof*	Y	Y	Y	Y
MONTANA				
AL *Rehberg*	Y	Y	Y	Y
NEBRASKA				
1 *Bereuter*	Y	Y	Y	Y
2 *Terry*	Y	Y	Y	Y
3 *Osborne*	Y	Y	Y	Y
NEVADA				
1 Berkley	Y	Y	Y	N
2 *Gibbons*	Y	Y	Y	N
NEW HAMPSHIRE				
1 *Sununu*	Y	Y	Y	N
2 *Bass*	Y	Y	Y	Y
NEW JERSEY				
1 Andrews	Y	Y	Y	N
2 *LoBiondo*	Y	Y	N	Y
3 *Saxton*	Y	Y	Y	Y
4 *Smith*	Y	Y	Y	Y
5 Roukema	?	?	?	Y
6 Pallone	Y	Y	N	N
7 *Ferguson*	Y	Y	Y	Y
8 Pascrell	Y	Y	Y	Y
9 Rothman	Y	Y	N	N
10 Payne	?	?	Y	Y
11 *Frelinghuysen*	Y	Y	Y	Y
12 Holt	Y	Y	N	N
13 Menendez	Y	Y	Y	N
NEW MEXICO				
1 *Wilson*	Y	Y	Y	N
2 *Skeen*	Y	Y	Y	Y
3 Udall	Y	Y	N	N
NEW YORK				
1 *Grucci*	Y	Y	Y	Y
2 Israel	Y	Y	Y	N
3 *King*	Y	Y	Y	Y
4 McCarthy	Y	Y	Y	Y
5 Ackerman	?	?	Y	Y
6 Meeks	Y	Y	Y	Y
7 Crowley	Y	Y	Y	Y
8 Nadler	Y	Y	Y	N
9 Weiner	+	+	Y	N
10 Towns	Y	Y	Y	Y
11 Owens	Y	Y	Y	N
12 Velázquez	Y	Y	Y	N
13 *Fossella*	Y	Y	Y	Y
14 Maloney	Y	Y	Y	Y
15 Rangel	Y	Y	Y	N
16 Serrano	Y	Y	Y	Y
17 Engel	Y	Y	Y	Y
18 Lowey	Y	Y	Y	N
19 *Kelly*	Y	Y	Y	Y
20 Gilman	+	+	+	+
21 McNulty	Y	Y	Y	Y
22 *Sweeney*	Y	Y	Y	Y
23 *Boehlert*	Y	Y	Y	Y
24 *McHugh*	Y	Y	Y	Y
25 *Walsh*	Y	Y	Y	Y
26 Hinchey	Y	Y	N	N
27 *Reynolds*	Y	Y	Y	Y
28 Slaughter	Y	Y	Y	N
29 LaFalce	Y	Y	?	N

State / District	39	40	41	42
30 Quinn	Y	Y	Y	Y
31 Houghton	Y	Y	Y	Y
NORTH CAROLINA				
1 Clayton	Y	Y	Y	N
2 Etheridge	Y	Y	Y	N
3 *Jones*	Y	Y	Y	N
4 Price	Y	Y	Y	N
5 *Burr*	Y	Y	?	Y
6 *Coble*	Y	Y	Y	Y
7 McIntyre	Y	Y	Y	N
8 *Hayes*	Y	Y	?	?
9 *Myrick*	Y	Y	+	+
10 *Ballenger*	Y	Y	Y	Y
11 *Taylor*	Y	Y	Y	Y
12 Watt	Y	Y	Y	N
NORTH DAKOTA				
AL Pomeroy	Y	Y	Y	N
OHIO				
1 *Chabot*	Y	Y	Y	Y
2 *Portman*	Y	Y	Y	Y
3 Hall	Y	Y	Y	N
4 *Oxley*	Y	Y	?	Y
5 *Gillmor*	Y	Y	Y	Y
6 Strickland	Y	N	N	N
7 *Hobson*	Y	Y	Y	Y
8 *Boehner*	Y	Y	Y	N
9 Kaptur	Y	Y	N	N
10 Kucinich	Y	Y	N	N
11 Jones	Y	Y	Y	N
12 *Tiberi*	Y	Y	Y	Y
13 Brown	Y	Y	Y	N
14 Sawyer	Y	Y	Y	N
15 *Pryce*	Y	Y	Y	Y
16 *Regula*	Y	Y	Y	Y
17 Traficant	?	?	?	?
18 *Ney*	Y	Y	Y	Y
19 *LaTourette*	Y	Y	Y	Y
OKLAHOMA				
1 *Sullivan* [1]				Y
2 Carson	Y	Y	Y	N
3 *Watkins*	Y	Y	Y	Y
4 *Watts*	+	?	Y	Y
5 *Istook*	Y	Y	Y	Y
6 *Lucas*	Y	Y	Y	Y
OREGON				
1 Wu	Y	Y	Y	N
2 *Walden*	Y	Y	Y	Y
3 Blumenauer	Y	Y	Y	N
4 DeFazio	Y	N	N	N
5 Hooley	Y	Y	Y	N
PENNSYLVANIA				
1 Brady	Y	Y	N	Y
2 Fattah	Y	Y	N	N
3 Borski	Y	Y	N	N
4 *Hart*	Y	Y	Y	Y
5 *Peterson*	Y	Y	Y	?
6 Holden	Y	Y	Y	Y
7 *Weldon*	Y	Y	?	Y
8 *Greenwood*	Y	Y	Y	Y
9 *Shuster, Bill*	Y	Y	Y	Y
10 *Sherwood*	Y	Y	Y	Y
11 Kanjorski	Y	Y	Y	N
12 Murtha	?	?	Y	Y
13 Hoeffel	Y	Y	?	N
14 Coyne	Y	Y	?	Y
15 *Toomey*	Y	Y	Y	Y
16 *Pitts*	Y	Y	Y	Y
17 *Gekas*	Y	Y	Y	Y
18 Doyle	Y	Y	Y	N
19 *Platts*	Y	Y	N	Y
20 Mascara	Y	Y	Y	N
21 *English*	Y	Y	N	Y
RHODE ISLAND				
1 Kennedy	Y	Y	Y	Y
2 Langevin	Y	Y	Y	Y
SOUTH CAROLINA				
1 *Brown*	Y	Y	Y	Y
2 *Wilson*	Y	Y	Y	Y
3 *Graham*	Y	Y	Y	N
4 *DeMint*	Y	Y	Y	N
5 Spratt	Y	Y	Y	N
6 Clyburn	Y	Y	Y	N
SOUTH DAKOTA				
AL *Thune*	Y	Y	Y	Y

State / District	39	40	41	42
TENNESSEE				
1 *Jenkins*	?	?	?	Y
2 *Duncan*	Y	Y	Y	Y
3 *Wamp*	Y	Y	Y	Y
4 *Hilleary*	?	?	?	Y
5 Clement	Y	Y	Y	Y
6 Gordon	Y	Y	Y	Y
7 *Bryant*	Y	Y	Y	Y
8 Tanner	Y	Y	Y	Y
9 Ford	Y	Y	Y	Y
TEXAS				
1 Sandlin	Y	Y	Y	Y
2 Turner	Y	Y	Y	Y
3 *Johnson, Sam*	Y	Y	Y	Y
4 Hall	Y	Y	Y	Y
5 *Sessions*	Y	Y	Y	Y
6 *Barton*	?	?	Y	Y
7 *Culberson*	Y	Y	Y	Y
8 *Brady*	Y	Y	Y	Y
9 Lampson	Y	Y	Y	Y
10 Doggett	Y	Y	Y	Y
11 Edwards	Y	Y	Y	N
12 *Granger*	Y	Y	Y	Y
13 *Thornberry*	Y	Y	Y	Y
14 *Paul*	Y	N	Y	?
15 Hinojosa	Y	Y	Y	Y
16 Reyes	?	?	Y	Y
17 Stenholm	Y	Y	Y	N
18 Jackson-Lee	Y	Y	Y	Y
19 *Combest*	Y	Y	Y	Y
20 Gonzalez	Y	Y	Y	Y
21 *Smith*	Y	Y	Y	Y
22 *DeLay*	Y	Y	Y	Y
23 *Bonilla*	Y	Y	Y	Y
24 Frost	Y	Y	Y	Y
25 Bentsen	?	?	Y	Y
26 *Armey*	Y	Y	Y	Y
27 Ortiz	Y	Y	Y	Y
28 Rodriguez	Y	Y	Y	Y
29 Green	Y	Y	Y	Y
30 Johnson, E.B.	Y	Y	Y	N
UTAH				
1 *Hansen*	Y	Y	Y	Y
2 Matheson	Y	Y	Y	Y
3 *Cannon*	Y	Y	Y	N
VERMONT				
AL *Sanders*	Y	Y	Y	N
VIRGINIA				
1 *Davis, Jo Ann*	Y	Y	Y	Y
2 *Schrock*	Y	Y	Y	Y
3 Scott	Y	Y	Y	N
4 *Forbes*	Y	Y	Y	Y
5 *Goode*	N	Y	Y	Y
6 *Goodlatte*	Y	Y	Y	Y
7 *Cantor*	Y	Y	Y	Y
8 Moran	Y	Y	Y	Y
9 Boucher	Y	Y	?	Y
10 *Wolf*	Y	Y	?	N
11 *Davis, T.*	Y	Y	Y	N
WASHINGTON				
1 Inslee	Y	Y	Y	N
2 Larsen	Y	Y	N	Y
3 Baird	Y	Y	N	N
4 *Hastings*	Y	Y	Y	Y
5 *Nethercutt*	Y	Y	Y	Y
6 Dicks	Y	Y	Y	N
7 McDermott	Y	Y	N	N
8 *Dunn*	Y	Y	Y	Y
9 Smith	Y	Y	Y	Y
WEST VIRGINIA				
1 Mollohan	Y	Y	Y	?
2 *Capito*	Y	Y	Y	Y
3 Rahall	Y	Y	Y	Y
WISCONSIN				
1 *Ryan*	Y	Y	Y	Y
2 Baldwin	Y	Y	Y	Y
3 Kind	Y	Y	Y	Y
4 Kleczka	Y	Y	Y	Y
5 Barrett	Y	Y	Y	N
6 *Petri*	Y	Y	Y	Y
7 Obey	Y	Y	Y	N
8 *Green*	Y	Y	Y	Y
9 *Sensenbrenner*	Y	Y	Y	Y
WYOMING				
AL *Cubin*	Y	Y	?	?

Southern states – Ala., Ark., Fla., Ga., Ky., La., Miss., N.C., Okla., S.C., Tenn., Texas, Va.

Key

Y   Voted for (yea).
\#   Paired for.
+   Announced for.
N   Voted against (nay).
X   Paired against.
–   Announced against.
P   Voted "present."
C   Voted "present" to avoid possible conflict of interest.
?   Did not vote or otherwise make a position known.

Democrats   **Republicans**
Independents

---

43. HR 1542. High-Speed Internet Access/Higher Penalties. Upton, R-Mich., amendment that would raise the amount in penalties the Federal Communications Commission (FCC) could charge the Bells and other telephone companies for violating the 1996 Telecommunications Act. It would raise the maximum fine from $120,000 to $1 million per day per violation and increase the penalty from $1.2 million to $10 million for continuing violations. It also would increase the FCC's ability to enforce the telecommunications law by doubling to two years the statute of limitations and giving the agency "cease and desist" powers. Adopted 421-7: R 211-7; D 208-0 (ND 154-0, SD 54-0); I 2-0. Feb. 27, 2002.

44. HR 1542. High-Speed Internet Access/Previous Question. Motion to order the previous question (thus ending debate and possibility of amendment) on the Markey, D-Mass., motion to recommit the bill to the House Energy and Commerce Committee with instructions to add language that would maintain the ability of the states and the Federal Communications Commission to enforce current telecommunications law regulations over the Bells' entry into the high-speed Internet access market. Motion rejected 173-256: R 62-157; D 109-99 (ND 98-56, SD 11-43); I 2-0.

45. HR 1542. High-Speed Internet Access/Passage. Passage of the bill that would permit the four regional Bell telephone companies to enter the high-speed Internet access market through their long distance connections without first having to open up their local phone markets to competition, as otherwise required by the 1996 Telecommunications Act. It also would establish a new framework under which Bell companies that use fiber lines to provide high-speed (broadband) Internet services to their customers would have to transmit the broadband services of competitors. Passed 273-157: R 156-63; D 117-92 (ND 75-80, SD 42-12); I 0-2. Feb. 27, 2002.

46. HR 3448. Bioterrorism Preparedness/Motion to Instruct. Eshoo, D-Calif., motion to instruct House conferees to work hard to reconcile House and Senate differences, to recognize the importance of maintaining steady funding for bioterrorism and emergency activities, and establishing a national tracking system for biological agents. The motion would stress the need to prioritize resources, to cooperate with President Bush, and to protect drinking water supplies. Motion agreed to 412-0: R 213-0; D 197-0 (ND 146-0, SD 51-0); I 2-0. Feb. 28, 2002.

	43	44	45	46
ALABAMA				
1 *Callahan*	Y	N	Y	Y
2 *Everett*	Y	N	Y	Y
3 *Riley*	Y	N	Y	Y
4 *Aderholt*	Y	N	Y	Y
5 Cramer	Y	N	Y	Y
6 *Bachus*	Y	N	Y	Y
7 Hilliard	Y	N	Y	Y
ALASKA				
AL *Young*	Y	N	N	?
ARIZONA				
1 *Flake*	Y	Y	N	Y
2 Pastor	Y	N	Y	Y
3 *Stump*	Y	N	Y	Y
4 *Shadegg*	Y	Y	N	Y
5 *Kolbe*	Y	Y	N	Y
6 *Hayworth*	Y	Y	N	Y
ARKANSAS				
1 Berry	Y	N	Y	Y
2 Snyder	Y	N	Y	Y
3 *Boozman*	Y	N	Y	Y
4 Ross	Y	N	Y	Y
CALIFORNIA				
1 Thompson	Y	Y	Y	Y
2 *Herger*	Y	N	Y	Y
3 *Ose*	Y	N	Y	Y
4 *Doolittle*	Y	N	Y	Y
5 Matsui	Y	N	Y	Y
6 Woolsey	Y	Y	N	Y
7 Miller, George	Y	Y	N	Y
8 Pelosi	Y	Y	N	Y
9 Lee	Y	Y	N	Y
10 Tauscher	Y	N	Y	Y
11 *Pombo*	Y	Y	Y	Y
12 Lantos	Y	Y	Y	Y
13 Stark	Y	Y	N	Y
14 Eshoo	Y	Y	N	Y
15 Honda	Y	Y	N	Y
16 Lofgren	Y	Y	N	Y
17 Farr	Y	Y	N	Y
18 Condit	Y	Y	Y	?
19 *Radanovich*	Y	N	Y	Y
20 Dooley	Y	N	Y	Y
21 *Thomas*	Y	N	Y	Y
22 Capps	Y	Y	N	Y
23 *Gallegly*	Y	N	Y	?
24 Sherman	Y	Y	Y	Y
25 *McKeon*	Y	N	Y	Y
26 Berman	Y	N	Y	Y
27 Schiff	Y	N	Y	Y
28 *Dreier*	Y	N	N	Y
29 Waxman	Y	Y	N	Y
30 Becerra	Y	Y	Y	Y
31 Solis	Y	Y	N	Y
32 Watson	Y	Y	Y	Y
33 Roybal-Allard	Y	Y	N	Y
34 Napolitano	Y	Y	N	Y
35 Waters	Y	Y	N	Y
36 Harman	Y	Y	Y	Y
37 Millender-McD.	Y	Y	Y	Y
38 *Horn*	Y	N	Y	Y

	43	44	45	46
39 *Royce*	Y	Y	N	Y
40 *Lewis*	Y	N	Y	Y
41 *Miller, Gary*	Y	N	Y	Y
42 Baca	Y	N	Y	Y
43 *Calvert*	Y	N	Y	Y
44 *Bono*	Y	N	Y	Y
45 *Rohrabacher*	Y	Y	N	Y
46 Sanchez	Y	N	Y	Y
47 *Cox*	Y	Y	N	Y
48 *Issa*	Y	N	Y	Y
49 Davis	Y	N	Y	Y
50 Filner	Y	N	Y	Y
51 *Cunningham*	Y	N	Y	Y
52 *Hunter*	Y	N	Y	Y
COLORADO				
1 DeGette	Y	Y	N	Y
2 Udall	Y	Y	N	Y
3 *McInnis*	Y	Y	N	Y
4 *Schaffer*	Y	Y	N	Y
5 *Hefley*	N	Y	N	Y
6 *Tancredo*	Y	N	Y	Y
CONNECTICUT				
1 Larson	Y	N	Y	Y
2 *Simmons*	Y	N	Y	Y
3 DeLauro	Y	Y	Y	Y
4 *Shays*	Y	Y	N	Y
5 Maloney	Y	N	Y	Y
6 *Johnson*	Y	N	Y	Y
DELAWARE				
AL *Castle*	Y	Y	N	Y
FLORIDA				
1 *Miller, J.*	Y	N	N	Y
2 Boyd	Y	N	Y	Y
3 Brown	Y	N	Y	Y
4 *Crenshaw*	Y	N	Y	Y
5 Thurman	Y	Y	Y	Y
6 *Stearns*	Y	N	Y	Y
7 *Mica*	Y	N	Y	Y
8 *Keller*	Y	N	Y	Y
9 *Bilirakis*	Y	N	Y	Y
10 *Young*	Y	Y	N	Y
11 Davis	Y	N	Y	Y
12 *Putnam*	Y	N	Y	Y
13 *Miller, D.*	Y	N	Y	Y
14 *Goss*	Y	N	N	Y
15 *Weldon*	Y	N	Y	Y
16 *Foley*	Y	N	Y	Y
17 Meek	Y	N	Y	Y
18 *Ros-Lehtinen*	Y	N	Y	Y
19 Wexler	Y	N	Y	Y
20 Deutsch	Y	Y	N	Y
21 *Diaz-Balart*	Y	N	Y	Y
22 *Shaw*	Y	N	Y	Y
23 Hastings	Y	N	Y	Y
GEORGIA				
1 *Kingston*	Y	Y	N	Y
2 Bishop	Y	N	Y	Y
3 *Collins*	Y	N	Y	Y
4 McKinney	Y	Y	Y	Y
5 Lewis	Y	N	Y	Y
6 *Isakson*	Y	N	N	Y
7 *Barr*	Y	N	Y	Y
8 *Chambliss*	Y	Y	Y	Y
9 *Deal*	Y	N	Y	Y
10 *Norwood*	Y	Y	Y	?
11 *Linder*	Y	Y	N	?
HAWAII				
1 Abercrombie	Y	Y	N	Y
2 Mink	Y	Y	N	Y
IDAHO				
1 *Otter*	N	N	Y	Y
2 *Simpson*	N	N	Y	Y
ILLINOIS				
1 Rush	Y	N	Y	?
2 Jackson	Y	N	Y	Y
3 Lipinski	Y	Y	N	Y
4 Gutierrez	Y	N	Y	Y
5 Blagojevich	Y	N	Y	?
6 *Hyde*	Y	N	Y	Y
7 Davis	Y	N	Y	Y
8 *Crane*	Y	N	Y	Y
9 Schakowsky	Y	Y	N	Y
10 *Kirk*	Y	N	Y	Y
11 *Weller*	Y	N	Y	Y
12 Costello	Y	Y	N	Y
13 *Biggert*	Y	Y	N	Y

ND Northern Democrats   SD Southern Democrats

	43	44	45	46
14 Hastert				
15 Johnson	Y	N	Y	Y
16 Manzullo	Y	N	Y	Y
17 Evans	Y	?	N	Y
18 LaHood	Y	N	Y	Y
19 Phelps	Y	Y	Y	Y
20 Shimkus	Y	N	Y	Y

INDIANA

	43	44	45	46
1 Visclosky	Y	N	Y	Y
2 Pence	Y	N	Y	Y
3 Roemer	Y	Y	N	Y
4 Souder	Y	N	Y	Y
5 Buyer	Y	N	Y	Y
6 Burton	Y	N	Y	Y
7 Kerns	Y	N	Y	Y
8 Hostettler	Y	N	Y	Y
9 Hill	Y	N	Y	Y
10 Carson	Y	Y	Y	Y

IOWA

	43	44	45	46
1 Leach	Y	N	Y	N
2 Nussle	Y	N	Y	Y
3 Boswell	Y	N	Y	N
4 Ganske	Y	N	Y	Y
5 Latham	Y	N	Y	N

KANSAS

	43	44	45	46
1 Moran	Y	Y	Y	Y
2 Ryun	Y	Y	Y	Y
3 Moore	Y	Y	N	Y
4 Tiahrt	Y	N	Y	Y

KENTUCKY

	43	44	45	46
1 Whitfield	Y	N	Y	Y
2 Lewis	Y	N	Y	Y
3 Northup	Y	N	Y	Y
4 Lucas	Y	N	Y	Y
5 Rogers	Y	N	Y	Y
6 Fletcher	Y	N	Y	Y

LOUISIANA

	43	44	45	46
1 Vitter	Y	N	Y	?
2 Jefferson	Y	N	Y	Y
3 Tauzin	Y	N	Y	Y
4 McCrery	Y	N	Y	Y
5 Cooksey	Y	N	Y	Y
6 Baker	N	N	Y	Y
7 John	Y	N	Y	Y

MAINE

	43	44	45	46
1 Allen	Y	N	Y	Y
2 Baldacci	?	?	?	?

MARYLAND

	43	44	45	46
1 Gilchrest	Y	Y	N	Y
2 Ehrlich	Y	Y	N	Y
3 Cardin	Y	N	Y	Y
4 Wynn	Y	N	Y	Y
5 Hoyer	Y	Y	N	Y
6 Bartlett	Y	Y	N	Y
7 Cummings	Y	N	Y	Y
8 Morella	Y	N	Y	Y

MASSACHUSETTS

	43	44	45	46
1 Olver	Y	Y	Y	Y
2 Neal	Y	N	Y	Y
3 McGovern	Y	N	Y	Y
4 Frank	Y	Y	N	Y
5 Meehan	Y	Y	N	Y
6 Tierney	Y	Y	N	Y
7 Markey	Y	Y	N	Y
8 Capuano	Y	N	Y	Y
9 Lynch	Y	N	Y	?
10 Delahunt	Y	Y	N	Y

MICHIGAN

	43	44	45	46
1 Stupak	Y	Y	N	Y
2 Hoekstra	Y	Y	N	Y
3 Ehlers	Y	N	Y	Y
4 Camp	Y	N	Y	Y
5 Barcia	Y	N	Y	Y
6 Upton	Y	N	Y	Y
7 Smith	Y	N	Y	Y
8 Rogers	Y	N	Y	Y
9 Kildee	Y	N	Y	Y
10 Bonior	Y	N	Y	Y
11 Knollenberg	Y	N	Y	Y
12 Levin	Y	N	Y	Y
13 Rivers	?	Y	N	Y
14 Conyers	Y	N	Y	Y
15 Kilpatrick	Y	Y	N	Y
16 Dingell	Y	N	Y	Y

MINNESOTA

	43	44	45	46
1 Gutknecht	Y	N	Y	Y
2 Kennedy	Y	N	Y	Y
3 Ramstad	Y	Y	N	Y
4 McCollum	Y	Y	N	Y
5 Sabo	Y	Y	N	Y
6 Luther	Y	Y	N	Y
7 Peterson	Y	Y	N	Y
8 Oberstar	Y	Y	N	Y

MISSISSIPPI

	43	44	45	46
1 Wicker	Y	Y	N	Y
2 Thompson	Y	N	Y	Y
3 Pickering	Y	N	Y	Y
4 Shows	Y	N	N	Y
5 Taylor	Y	N	N	Y

MISSOURI

	43	44	45	46
1 Clay	Y	N	Y	?
2 Akin	Y	N	Y	Y
3 Gephardt	Y	Y	Y	Y
4 Skelton	Y	N	Y	Y
5 McCarthy	Y	N	Y	Y
6 Graves	Y	N	Y	Y
7 Blunt	Y	N	Y	Y
8 Emerson	Y	N	Y	Y
9 Hulshof	Y	N	Y	Y

MONTANA

	43	44	45	46
AL Rehberg	Y	N	N	Y

NEBRASKA

	43	44	45	46
1 Bereuter	Y	Y	N	Y
2 Terry	Y	N	Y	Y
3 Osborne	Y	N	N	Y

NEVADA

	43	44	45	46
1 Berkley	Y	Y	N	Y
2 Gibbons	Y	N	Y	Y

NEW HAMPSHIRE

	43	44	45	46
1 Sununu	Y	Y	N	Y
2 Bass	Y	N	Y	Y

NEW JERSEY

	43	44	45	46
1 Andrews	Y	Y	N	Y
2 LoBiondo	Y	N	Y	Y
3 Saxton	Y	N	Y	Y
4 Smith	Y	N	Y	Y
5 Roukema	Y	Y	Y	?
6 Pallone	Y	N	Y	Y
7 Ferguson	Y	N	Y	Y
8 Pascrell	Y	N	Y	Y
9 Rothman	Y	Y	Y	Y
10 Payne	Y	Y	Y	Y
11 Frelinghuysen	Y	N	Y	Y
12 Holt	Y	Y	Y	Y
13 Menendez	Y	N	Y	Y

NEW MEXICO

	43	44	45	46
1 Wilson	Y	Y	N	Y
2 Skeen	N	Y	N	Y
3 Udall	Y	Y	N	Y

NEW YORK

	43	44	45	46
1 Grucci	Y	N	Y	Y
2 Israel	Y	Y	N	Y
3 King	Y	N	Y	Y
4 McCarthy	Y	N	Y	Y
5 Ackerman	Y	N	Y	?
6 Meeks	Y	N	Y	Y
7 Crowley	Y	Y	Y	Y
8 Nadler	Y	Y	N	Y
9 Weiner	Y	Y	N	?
10 Towns	Y	N	Y	Y
11 Owens	Y	Y	Y	Y
12 Velázquez	Y	Y	N	Y
13 Fossella	Y	N	Y	Y
14 Maloney	Y	Y	N	Y
15 Rangel	Y	Y	N	Y
16 Serrano	Y	N	Y	Y
17 Engel	Y	Y	Y	Y
18 Lowey	Y	Y	Y	Y
19 Kelly	Y	N	Y	Y
20 Gilman	+	−	+	+
21 McNulty	Y	N	Y	Y
22 Sweeney	Y	N	Y	Y
23 Boehlert	Y	Y	N	Y
24 McHugh	Y	N	Y	Y
25 Walsh	Y	N	Y	Y
26 Hinchey	Y	Y	N	Y
27 Reynolds	Y	N	Y	Y
28 Slaughter	Y	Y	N	Y
29 LaFalce	Y	Y	N	Y
30 Quinn	Y	N	Y	Y
31 Houghton	Y	N	Y	Y

NORTH CAROLINA

	43	44	45	46
1 Clayton	Y	N	Y	+
2 Etheridge	Y	Y	N	Y
3 Jones	N	Y	Y	Y
4 Price	Y	N	Y	Y
5 Burr	Y	N	Y	Y
6 Coble	Y	N	N	Y
7 McIntyre	Y	N	Y	Y
8 Hayes	Y	N	Y	Y
9 Myrick	Y	N	Y	Y
10 Ballenger	Y	N	Y	Y
11 Taylor	Y	N	Y	Y
12 Watt	Y	Y	N	Y

NORTH DAKOTA

	43	44	45	46
AL Pomeroy	Y	Y	N	Y

OHIO

	43	44	45	46
1 Chabot	Y	Y	N	Y
2 Portman	Y	N	Y	Y
3 Hall	Y	N	Y	Y
4 Oxley	Y	N	Y	Y
5 Gillmor	Y	N	Y	Y
6 Strickland	Y	N	Y	Y
7 Hobson	Y	N	Y	Y
8 Boehner	Y	N	Y	Y
9 Kaptur	Y	N	Y	Y
10 Kucinich	Y	Y	N	Y
11 Jones	Y	N	Y	Y
12 Tiberi	Y	N	Y	Y
13 Brown	Y	Y	N	Y
14 Sawyer	Y	N	Y	Y
15 Pryce	Y	N	Y	Y
16 Regula	Y	N	N	Y
17 Traficant	?	?	?	?
18 Ney	Y	N	Y	Y
19 LaTourette	Y	N	Y	Y

OKLAHOMA

	43	44	45	46
1 Sullivan	Y	N	Y	Y
2 Carson	Y	Y	N	Y
3 Watkins	Y	N	Y	Y
4 Watts	Y	N	Y	Y
5 Istook	Y	N	Y	Y
6 Lucas	Y	N	Y	Y

OREGON

	43	44	45	46
1 Wu	Y	Y	N	Y
2 Walden	Y	Y	N	Y
3 Blumenauer	Y	Y	N	Y
4 DeFazio	Y	Y	N	?
5 Hooley	Y	Y	N	Y

PENNSYLVANIA

	43	44	45	46
1 Brady	Y	N	Y	Y
2 Fattah	Y	N	Y	?
3 Borski	Y	Y	Y	Y
4 Hart	Y	N	Y	Y
5 Peterson	Y	N	Y	Y
6 Holden	Y	N	Y	Y
7 Weldon	Y	N	Y	Y
8 Greenwood	Y	N	Y	Y
9 Shuster, Bill	Y	N	Y	Y
10 Sherwood	?	N	Y	Y
11 Kanjorski	Y	Y	N	Y
12 Murtha	Y	N	Y	Y
13 Hoeffel	Y	Y	N	Y
14 Coyne	Y	N	Y	Y
15 Toomey	Y	N	Y	Y
16 Pitts	Y	N	Y	Y
17 Gekas	Y	N	Y	Y
18 Doyle	Y	N	Y	Y
19 Platts	Y	N	Y	Y
20 Mascara	Y	N	Y	Y
21 English	Y	N	Y	Y

RHODE ISLAND

	43	44	45	46
1 Kennedy	Y	N	Y	Y
2 Langevin	Y	N	Y	Y

SOUTH CAROLINA

	43	44	45	46
1 Brown	Y	N	Y	Y
2 Wilson	Y	N	Y	Y
3 Graham	Y	N	Y	Y
4 DeMint	Y	N	Y	Y
5 Spratt	Y	N	Y	Y
6 Clyburn	Y	N	Y	Y

SOUTH DAKOTA

	43	44	45	46
AL Thune	Y	Y	N	Y

TENNESSEE

	43	44	45	46
1 Jenkins	Y	Y	Y	Y
2 Duncan	Y	Y	N	Y
3 Wamp	Y	N	Y	N
4 Hilleary	Y	N	Y	Y
5 Clement	Y	N	Y	Y
6 Gordon	Y	N	Y	Y
7 Bryant	Y	N	Y	Y
8 Tanner	Y	N	Y	Y
9 Ford	Y	N	Y	Y

TEXAS

	43	44	45	46
1 Sandlin	Y	N	Y	+
2 Turner	Y	N	Y	Y
3 Johnson, Sam	Y	Y	N	Y
4 Hall	Y	N	Y	Y
5 Sessions	Y	N	Y	Y
6 Barton	Y	N	Y	Y
7 Culberson	Y	N	Y	Y
8 Brady	Y	N	Y	Y
9 Lampson	Y	N	Y	Y
10 Doggett	Y	Y	N	Y
11 Edwards	Y	N	Y	Y
12 Granger	Y	N	Y	Y
13 Thornberry	Y	N	Y	Y
14 Paul	N	Y	N	Y
15 Hinojosa	Y	N	Y	?
16 Reyes	Y	N	Y	Y
17 Stenholm	Y	N	Y	Y
18 Jackson-Lee	Y	N	Y	Y
19 Combest	Y	Y	Y	Y
20 Gonzalez	Y	N	Y	Y
21 Smith	Y	N	Y	Y
22 DeLay	Y	N	Y	Y
23 Bonilla	Y	N	Y	Y
24 Frost	Y	N	Y	Y
25 Bentsen	Y	N	Y	Y
26 Armey	Y	N	Y	Y
27 Ortiz	Y	N	Y	Y
28 Rodriguez	Y	N	Y	Y
29 Green	Y	N	Y	Y
30 Johnson, E.B.	Y	Y	N	Y

UTAH

	43	44	45	46
1 Hansen	Y	Y	N	Y
2 Matheson	Y	Y	N	Y
3 Cannon	Y	Y	N	Y

VERMONT

	43	44	45	46
AL Sanders	Y	Y	N	Y

VIRGINIA

	43	44	45	46
1 Davis, Jo Ann	Y	N	Y	Y
2 Schrock	Y	N	Y	Y
3 Scott	Y	N	Y	Y
4 Forbes	Y	N	Y	Y
5 Goode	Y	N	Y	Y
6 Goodlatte	Y	N	Y	Y
7 Cantor	Y	N	Y	Y
8 Moran	Y	N	Y	Y
9 Boucher	Y	N	Y	Y
10 Wolf	Y	N	Y	Y
11 Davis, T.	Y	Y	N	Y

WASHINGTON

	43	44	45	46
1 Inslee	Y	Y	N	Y
2 Larsen	Y	N	Y	Y
3 Baird	Y	N	Y	Y
4 Hastings	Y	N	Y	Y
5 Nethercutt	Y	N	N	Y
6 Dicks	Y	N	Y	Y
7 McDermott	Y	Y	N	Y
8 Dunn	Y	N	Y	Y
9 Smith	Y	N	Y	Y

WEST VIRGINIA

	43	44	45	46
1 Mollohan	Y	N	Y	Y
2 Capito	Y	N	Y	Y
3 Rahall	Y	N	Y	Y

WISCONSIN

	43	44	45	46
1 Ryan	Y	N	Y	Y
2 Baldwin	Y	N	Y	Y
3 Kind	Y	N	Y	Y
4 Kleczka	Y	Y	N	Y
5 Barrett	Y	Y	N	Y
6 Petri	Y	N	Y	Y
7 Obey	Y	N	Y	Y
8 Green	Y	N	Y	Y
9 Sensenbrenner	Y	Y	Y	Y

WYOMING

	43	44	45	46
AL Cubin	?	?	?	?

Southern states - Ala., Ark., Fla., Ga., Ky., La., Miss., N.C., Okla., S.C., Tenn., Texas, Va.

Key

Y	Voted for (yea).
#	Paired for.
+	Announced for.
N	Voted against (nay).
X	Paired against.
−	Announced against.
P	Voted "present."
C	Voted "present" to avoid possible conflict of interest.
?	Did not vote or otherwise make a position known.

Democrats   **Republicans**
Independents

47. H Con Res 305. Reagan Award/Adoption. Linder, R-Ga., motion to suspend the rules and adopt the concurrent resolution that would allow the use of the U.S. Capitol Rotunda for a congressional gold medal awards ceremony for former President Ronald Reagan and Nancy Reagan. Motion agreed to 392-0: R 205-0; D 185-0 (ND 135-0, SD 50-0); I 2-0. A two-thirds majority of those present and voting (262 in this case) is required for adoption under suspension of the rules. March 5, 2002.

48. Procedural Motion/Journal. Approval of the House Journal of Tuesday, March 5, 2002. Approved 352-43: R 193-16; D 157-27 (ND 111-23, SD 46-4); I 2-0. March 6, 2002.

49. H Res 354. Suspension Motions/Previous Question. Sessions, R-Texas, motion to order the previous question (thus ending debate and possibility of amendment) on adoption of the rule (H Res 354) to provide for House floor consideration of bills under suspension of the rules on Wednesday, March 6. Motion agreed to 218-191: R 216-0; D 1-190 (ND 0-139, SD 1-51); I 1-1. Subsequently, the rule was adopted by voice vote. March 6, 2002.

50. S J Res 32. West Point Tribute/Passage. McHugh, R-N.Y., motion to suspend the rules and pass the joint resolution that would pay tribute to the U.S. Military Academy on its 200th birthday. Motion agreed to 407-1: R 214-0; D 192-1 (ND 140-1, SD 52-0); I 1-0. A two-thirds majority of those present and voting (272 in this case) is required for passage under suspension of the rules. March 6, 2002.

51. HR 3090. Economic Stimulus/Previous Question. Pryce, R-Ohio, motion to order the previous question (thus ending debate and possibility of amendment) on adoption of the rule (H Res 360) to provide for House floor consideration of the Senate amendment to the bill that would cost $51.2 billion in fiscal 2002 to extend unemployment benefits for up to 13 additional weeks and give temporary business tax breaks. Motion agreed to 217-192: R 212-0; D 4-191 (ND 2-144, SD 2-47); I 1-1. Subsequently, the rule was adopted by voice vote. March 7, 2002.

52. HR 3090. Economic Stimulus/Concur With Senate Amendment. Thomas, R-Calif., motion to concur in a House amendment to the Senate amendment to the bill that would cost $51.2 billion in fiscal 2002 to extend unemployment benefits for up to 13 additional weeks and give temporary business tax breaks. It would include incentives aimed at rebuilding the area around the World Trade Center in New York, lengthen the net operating loss carryback period by three years, extend a number of expiring tax provisions and reauthorize the Temporary Assistance for Needy Families grant program. Motion agreed to 417-3: R 218-0; D 197-3 (ND 150-0, SD 47-3); I 2-0. March 7, 2002.

	47	48	49	50	51	52
ALABAMA						
1 *Callahan*	?	Y	Y	Y	Y	Y
2 *Everett*	Y	Y	Y	Y	Y	Y
3 *Riley*	Y	Y	Y	Y	Y	Y
4 *Aderholt*	Y	N	Y	Y	Y	Y
5 Cramer	Y	Y	N	Y	N	Y
6 *Bachus*	Y	Y	Y	Y	Y	Y
7 Hilliard	Y	Y	N	Y	N	Y
ALASKA						
AL *Young*	Y	?	Y	Y	?	Y
ARIZONA						
1 *Flake*	Y	Y	Y	Y	Y	Y
2 Pastor	Y	Y	N	Y	N	Y
3 *Stump*	Y	Y	Y	Y	Y	Y
4 *Shadegg*	Y	Y	Y	Y	Y	Y
5 *Kolbe*	Y	Y	Y	Y	Y	Y
6 *Hayworth*	Y	Y	Y	Y	Y	Y
ARKANSAS						
1 Berry	Y	Y	N	Y	N	Y
2 Snyder	Y	Y	N	Y	N	Y
3 *Boozman*	Y	Y	Y	Y	Y	Y
4 Ross	Y	Y	N	Y	?	Y
CALIFORNIA						
1 Thompson	Y	N	N	Y	N	Y
2 *Herger*	Y	Y	Y	Y	Y	Y
3 *Ose*	Y	Y	Y	Y	Y	Y
4 *Doolittle*	?	?	?	?	Y	Y
5 Matsui	Y	Y	N	Y	N	Y
6 Woolsey	+	+	−	+	N	Y
7 Miller, George	Y	?	N	Y	N	Y
8 Pelosi	Y	Y	N	Y	N	Y
9 Lee	+	+	−	+	N	Y
10 Tauscher	Y	Y	N	Y	N	Y
11 *Pombo*	?	Y	Y	Y	Y	Y
12 Lantos	Y	?	?	Y	N	Y
13 Stark	Y	N	N	Y	N	Y
14 Eshoo	Y	N	N	Y	N	Y
15 Honda	Y	N	N	Y	N	Y
16 Lofgren	?	?	?	?	?	?
17 Farr	Y	Y	N	Y	N	Y
18 Condit	?	?	?	?	?	?
19 *Radanovich*	Y	Y	Y	Y	Y	Y
20 Dooley	?	?	?	?	Y	Y
21 *Thomas*	Y	Y	Y	Y	Y	Y
22 Capps	Y	Y	N	Y	N	Y
23 *Gallegly*	Y	Y	Y	Y	?	?
24 Sherman	Y	Y	N	Y	N	Y
25 *McKeon*	?	Y	Y	Y	Y	Y
26 Berman	Y	N	N	Y	N	Y
27 Schiff	Y	Y	N	Y	N	Y
28 *Dreier*	Y	Y	Y	Y	Y	Y
29 Waxman	?	Y	N	Y	N	Y
30 Becerra	+	Y	N	Y	N	Y
31 Solis	+	+	−	+	−	+
32 Watson	+	+	−	+	N	Y
33 Roybal-Allard	+	+	−	+	N	Y
34 Napolitano	?	?	?	?	N	Y
35 Waters	?	?	?	?	N	Y
36 Harman	?	?	?	?	N	Y
37 Millender-McD.	?	?	?	?	N	Y
38 Horn	Y	Y	Y	Y	Y	Y

	47	48	49	50	51	52
39 *Royce*	Y	Y	Y	Y	Y	Y
40 *Lewis*	Y	Y	Y	?	Y	Y
41 *Miller, Gary*	Y	Y	N	Y	N	Y
42 Baca	Y	Y	N	Y	N	Y
43 *Calvert*	?	?	?	?	?	?
44 *Bono*	Y	Y	Y	Y	Y	Y
45 *Rohrabacher*	Y	Y	Y	Y	Y	Y
46 Sanchez	+	+	−	+	−	+
47 *Cox*	Y	?	Y	Y	Y	Y
48 *Issa*	Y	Y	Y	Y	Y	Y
49 Davis	Y	N	N	Y	N	Y
50 Filner	+	−	−	+	N	Y
51 *Cunningham*	Y	Y	Y	Y	Y	Y
52 *Hunter*	?	Y	Y	Y	Y	Y
COLORADO						
1 DeGette	Y	Y	N	Y	N	Y
2 Udall	Y	N	N	Y	N	Y
3 *McInnis*	Y	Y	Y	Y	Y	Y
4 *Schaffer*	Y	N	Y	Y	Y	Y
5 *Hefley*	Y	N	Y	Y	Y	Y
6 *Tancredo*	Y	P	Y	Y	Y	Y
CONNECTICUT						
1 Larson	Y	Y	N	Y	N	Y
2 *Simmons*	Y	Y	Y	Y	?	Y
3 DeLauro	Y	Y	N	Y	N	Y
4 *Shays*	Y	Y	Y	Y	Y	Y
5 Maloney	Y	Y	N	Y	N	Y
6 *Johnson*	Y	Y	Y	Y	Y	Y
DELAWARE						
AL *Castle*	Y	Y	Y	Y	Y	Y
FLORIDA						
1 *Miller, J.*	Y	Y	Y	+	Y	Y
2 Boyd	Y	Y	N	Y	N	N
3 Brown	Y	Y	N	Y	?	Y
4 *Crenshaw*	Y	Y	Y	Y	Y	Y
5 Thurman	Y	Y	N	Y	N	Y
6 *Stearns*	Y	Y	Y	Y	Y	Y
7 *Mica*	Y	Y	Y	Y	Y	Y
8 *Keller*	Y	Y	Y	Y	Y	Y
9 *Bilirakis*	Y	Y	Y	Y	Y	Y
10 *Young*	Y	Y	Y	Y	Y	Y
11 Davis	Y	Y	N	Y	N	Y
12 *Putnam*	Y	Y	Y	Y	Y	Y
13 *Miller, D.*	Y	Y	Y	Y	Y	Y
14 *Goss*	Y	Y	Y	Y	Y	Y
15 *Weldon*	Y	Y	Y	Y	Y	Y
16 *Foley*	Y	Y	Y	Y	Y	Y
17 Meek	Y	Y	N	Y	N	?
18 *Ros-Lehtinen*	?	Y	Y	Y	Y	Y
19 Wexler	?	?	?	?	?	?
20 Deutsch	Y	Y	N	Y	N	Y
21 *Diaz-Balart*	Y	Y	Y	Y	Y	Y
22 *Shaw*	Y	Y	Y	Y	Y	Y
23 Hastings	Y	N	N	Y	N	Y
GEORGIA						
1 *Kingston*	?	Y	Y	Y	Y	Y
2 Bishop	Y	Y	N	Y	N	Y
3 *Collins*	Y	Y	Y	Y	Y	Y
4 McKinney	Y	Y	N	Y	N	Y
5 Lewis	Y	Y	N	Y	N	Y
6 *Isakson*	Y	Y	Y	Y	Y	Y
7 *Barr*	Y	Y	Y	Y	Y	Y
8 *Chambliss*	Y	Y	Y	Y	Y	Y
9 *Deal*	Y	Y	Y	Y	Y	Y
10 *Norwood*	Y	Y	Y	Y	Y	Y
11 *Linder*	Y	?	Y	Y	Y	Y
HAWAII						
1 Abercrombie	Y	+	−	Y	N	Y
2 Mink	Y	Y	N	Y	N	Y
IDAHO						
1 *Otter*	Y	Y	Y	Y	Y	Y
2 *Simpson*	Y	Y	Y	Y	Y	Y
ILLINOIS						
1 Rush	Y	Y	N	Y	N	Y
2 Jackson	Y	Y	N	Y	N	Y
3 Lipinski	Y	Y	N	Y	N	Y
4 Gutierrez	Y	Y	N	Y	N	Y
5 Blagojevich	?	?	?	?	?	?
6 *Hyde*	Y	Y	?	Y	Y	Y
7 Davis	Y	Y	N	Y	?	Y
8 *Crane*	Y	N	Y	Y	Y	Y
9 Schakowsky	Y	Y	N	Y	N	Y
10 *Kirk*	Y	Y	Y	Y	Y	Y
11 *Weller*	Y	N	Y	Y	Y	Y
12 Costello	Y	Y	N	Y	N	Y
13 *Biggert*	Y	Y	Y	Y	Y	Y

ND Northern Democrats   SD Southern Democrats

	47	48	49	50	51	52
14 ***Hastert***						Y
15 ***Johnson***	Y	Y	Y	Y	?	Y
16 ***Manzullo***	Y	Y	Y	Y	Y	Y
17 Evans	Y	Y	N	Y	N	Y
18 ***LaHood***	Y	Y	Y	Y	Y	Y
19 Phelps	Y	Y	N	Y	N	Y
20 ***Shimkus***	Y	Y	Y	Y	Y	Y
INDIANA						
1 Visclosky	Y	N	N	Y	N	Y
2 ***Pence***	Y	Y	Y	Y	Y	Y
3 Roemer	Y	Y	N	Y	N	Y
4 ***Souder***	Y	Y	Y	Y	Y	Y
5 ***Buyer***	Y	Y	?	Y	Y	Y
6 ***Burton***	Y	Y	Y	Y	Y	Y
7 ***Kerns***	Y	Y	Y	Y	Y	Y
8 ***Hostettler***	Y	Y	Y	Y	Y	Y
9 Hill	Y	Y	N	Y	N	Y
10 Carson	Y	Y	N	Y	N	Y
IOWA						
1 ***Leach***	Y	Y	Y	Y	Y	Y
2 ***Nussle***	Y	Y	Y	Y	Y	Y
3 Boswell	Y	Y	N	Y	N	Y
4 ***Ganske***	Y	Y	Y	Y	Y	Y
5 ***Latham***	Y	N	Y	Y	Y	Y
KANSAS						
1 ***Moran***	Y	N	Y	Y	Y	Y
2 ***Ryun***	Y	Y	Y	Y	Y	Y
3 Moore	Y	N	N	Y	N	Y
4 ***Tiahrt***	Y	Y	Y	Y	Y	Y
KENTUCKY						
1 ***Whitfield***	Y	Y	Y	Y	Y	Y
2 ***Lewis***	Y	Y	Y	Y	Y	Y
3 ***Northup***	Y	Y	Y	Y	Y	Y
4 Lucas	Y	Y	N	Y	N	Y
5 ***Rogers***	Y	Y	Y	Y	Y	Y
6 ***Fletcher***	Y	Y	Y	Y	Y	Y
LOUISIANA						
1 ***Vitter***	Y	Y	Y	Y	Y	Y
2 Jefferson	?	Y	N	Y	N	Y
3 ***Tauzin***	Y	Y	Y	Y	Y	Y
4 ***McCrery***	Y	Y	Y	Y	Y	Y
5 ***Cooksey***	Y	Y	Y	Y	Y	Y
6 ***Baker***	Y	Y	Y	Y	Y	Y
7 John	?	?	N	Y	N	Y
MAINE						
1 Allen	Y	Y	N	Y	N	Y
2 Baldacci	Y	N	N	Y	N	Y
MARYLAND						
1 ***Gilchrest***	Y	Y	Y	Y	Y	Y
2 ***Ehrlich***	Y	?	Y	Y	Y	Y
3 Cardin	Y	Y	N	Y	N	Y
4 Wynn	Y	Y	N	Y	N	Y
5 Hoyer	Y	Y	N	Y	N	Y
6 ***Bartlett***	Y	Y	Y	Y	Y	Y
7 Cummings	Y	Y	N	Y	N	Y
8 ***Morella***	Y	Y	Y	Y	?	Y
MASSACHUSETTS						
1 Olver	?	Y	N	Y	N	Y
2 Neal	Y	Y	N	Y	?	?
3 McGovern	Y	Y	N	Y	N	Y
4 Frank	Y	Y	N	Y	N	Y
5 Meehan	Y	Y	N	Y	N	Y
6 Tierney	Y	Y	N	Y	N	Y
7 Markey	Y	Y	N	Y	N	Y
8 Capuano	Y	N	N	Y	N	Y
9 Lynch	Y	Y	N	Y	N	Y
10 Delahunt	Y	Y	N	Y	N	Y
MICHIGAN						
1 Stupak	Y	N	N	Y	N	Y
2 ***Hoekstra***	Y	Y	Y	Y	Y	Y
3 ***Ehlers***	Y	Y	Y	Y	Y	Y
4 ***Camp***	Y	Y	Y	Y	Y	Y
5 Barcia	Y	Y	N	Y	N	Y
6 ***Upton***	Y	Y	Y	Y	Y	Y
7 ***Smith***	Y	Y	Y	Y	Y	Y
8 ***Rogers***	Y	Y	Y	Y	Y	Y
9 Kildee	Y	Y	N	Y	N	Y
10 Bonior	Y	Y	N	Y	N	Y
11 ***Knollenberg***	Y	Y	Y	Y	Y	Y
12 Levin	Y	Y	N	Y	N	Y
13 Rivers	Y	Y	N	Y	N	Y
14 Conyers	Y	Y	N	N	N	Y
15 Kilpatrick	+	+	–	+	N	Y
16 Dingell	Y	Y	N	Y	N	Y
MINNESOTA						
1 ***Gutknecht***	Y	N	Y	Y	Y	Y
2 ***Kennedy***	Y	N	Y	Y	Y	Y
3 ***Ramstad***	Y	N	Y	Y	Y	Y
4 McCollum	Y	Y	N	Y	N	Y
5 Sabo	Y	N	N	Y	N	Y
6 Luther	Y	Y	N	Y	N	Y
7 Peterson	Y	N	N	Y	N	Y
8 Oberstar	Y	?	N	Y	N	Y
MISSISSIPPI						
1 ***Wicker***	Y	N	Y	Y	Y	Y
2 Thompson	Y	N	N	Y	N	Y
3 ***Pickering***	Y	?	Y	Y	Y	Y
4 Shows	Y	Y	N	Y	Y	Y
5 Taylor	Y	N	N	Y	N	N
MISSOURI						
1 Clay	Y	Y	N	Y	N	Y
2 ***Akin***	Y	Y	Y	Y	Y	Y
3 Gephardt	Y	?	N	Y	N	Y
4 Skelton	Y	Y	N	Y	N	Y
5 McCarthy	Y	Y	N	Y	N	Y
6 ***Graves***	Y	Y	Y	Y	Y	Y
7 ***Blunt***	Y	Y	Y	Y	Y	Y
8 ***Emerson***	Y	Y	Y	Y	Y	Y
9 ***Hulshof***	Y	N	Y	Y	Y	Y
MONTANA						
AL ***Rehberg***	Y	Y	Y	Y	Y	Y
NEBRASKA						
1 ***Bereuter***	Y	Y	Y	Y	Y	Y
2 ***Terry***	Y	Y	Y	Y	Y	Y
3 ***Osborne***	Y	Y	Y	Y	Y	Y
NEVADA						
1 Berkley	Y	Y	N	Y	N	Y
2 ***Gibbons***	Y	Y	Y	Y	Y	Y
NEW HAMPSHIRE						
1 ***Sununu***	Y	Y	Y	Y	Y	Y
2 ***Bass***	Y	Y	Y	Y	Y	Y
NEW JERSEY						
1 Andrews	Y	Y	N	Y	N	Y
2 ***LoBiondo***	Y	N	Y	Y	Y	Y
3 ***Saxton***	Y	Y	Y	Y	Y	Y
4 ***Smith***	Y	Y	Y	Y	Y	Y
5 ***Roukema***	Y	Y	Y	Y	Y	Y
6 Pallone	Y	Y	N	Y	N	Y
7 ***Ferguson***	Y	Y	Y	Y	Y	Y
8 Pascrell	Y	Y	N	Y	N	Y
9 Rothman	Y	Y	N	Y	?	Y
10 Payne	Y	Y	N	Y	N	Y
11 ***Frelinghuysen***	Y	Y	Y	Y	Y	Y
12 Holt	Y	Y	N	Y	N	Y
13 Menendez	Y	?	N	Y	N	Y
NEW MEXICO						
1 ***Wilson***	Y	Y	Y	?	Y	Y
2 ***Skeen***	Y	Y	Y	Y	Y	Y
3 Udall	Y	N	N	Y	N	Y
NEW YORK						
1 ***Grucci***	Y	Y	Y	Y	Y	Y
2 Israel	Y	Y	N	Y	N	Y
3 ***King***	Y	Y	Y	Y	Y	Y
4 McCarthy	Y	Y	N	Y	N	Y
5 Ackerman	Y	Y	N	Y	?	Y
6 Meeks	Y	Y	N	Y	N	Y
7 Crowley	Y	Y	N	Y	?	Y
8 Nadler	Y	Y	N	Y	N	Y
9 Weiner	Y	Y	N	Y	N	Y
10 Towns	Y	N	N	Y	N	Y
11 Owens	Y	Y	N	Y	N	Y
12 Velázquez	Y	Y	N	Y	N	Y
13 ***Fossella***	Y	Y	Y	Y	Y	Y
14 Maloney	Y	Y	N	Y	N	Y
15 Rangel	Y	Y	N	Y	N	Y
16 Serrano	Y	Y	N	Y	N	Y
17 Engel	Y	Y	N	Y	N	Y
18 Lowey	Y	Y	N	Y	N	Y
19 ***Kelly***	Y	Y	Y	Y	Y	Y
20 ***Gilman***	Y	Y	Y	Y	Y	Y
21 McNulty	Y	N	N	Y	N	Y
22 ***Sweeney***	Y	N	Y	Y	Y	Y
23 ***Boehlert***	Y	Y	Y	Y	Y	Y
24 ***McHugh***	Y	Y	Y	Y	Y	Y
25 ***Walsh***	Y	Y	Y	Y	Y	Y
26 Hinchey	Y	Y	N	Y	N	Y
27 ***Reynolds***	?	Y	Y	Y	Y	Y
28 Slaughter	Y	Y	N	Y	N	Y
29 LaFalce	Y	Y	N	Y	N	Y
30 ***Quinn***	Y	Y	Y	Y	Y	Y
31 ***Houghton***	Y	Y	Y	Y	Y	Y
NORTH CAROLINA						
1 Clayton	Y	?	N	Y	N	Y
2 Etheridge	Y	Y	N	Y	N	Y
3 ***Jones***	Y	Y	Y	Y	Y	Y
4 Price	Y	Y	N	Y	N	Y
5 ***Burr***	Y	Y	Y	Y	Y	Y
6 ***Coble***	Y	Y	Y	Y	Y	Y
7 McIntyre	Y	Y	N	Y	N	Y
8 ***Hayes***	Y	Y	Y	Y	Y	Y
9 ***Myrick***	Y	Y	Y	Y	Y	Y
10 ***Ballenger***	Y	?	Y	Y	Y	Y
11 ***Taylor***	?	Y	Y	Y	Y	Y
12 Watt	Y	Y	N	Y	N	Y
NORTH DAKOTA						
AL Pomeroy	Y	Y	N	Y	N	Y
OHIO						
1 ***Chabot***	Y	Y	Y	Y	Y	Y
2 ***Portman***	Y	Y	Y	Y	Y	Y
3 Hall	Y	Y	N	Y	N	Y
4 ***Oxley***	Y	Y	Y	Y	Y	Y
5 ***Gillmor***	Y	Y	Y	Y	Y	Y
6 Strickland	Y	N	N	Y	N	Y
7 ***Hobson***	Y	Y	Y	Y	Y	Y
8 ***Boehner***	?	Y	Y	Y	Y	Y
9 Kaptur	Y	Y	N	Y	N	Y
10 Kucinich	Y	N	N	Y	N	Y
11 Jones	Y	N	N	Y	N	Y
12 ***Tiberi***	Y	Y	Y	Y	Y	Y
13 Brown	Y	Y	N	Y	N	Y
14 Sawyer	Y	Y	N	Y	N	Y
15 ***Pryce***	Y	Y	Y	Y	Y	Y
16 ***Regula***	Y	Y	Y	Y	Y	Y
17 Traficant	?	?	?	?	?	?
18 ***Ney***	Y	Y	Y	Y	Y	Y
19 ***LaTourette***	Y	Y	Y	Y	Y	Y
OKLAHOMA						
1 ***Sullivan***	Y	Y	Y	Y	Y	Y
2 Carson	Y	Y	N	Y	N	Y
3 ***Watkins***	Y	Y	Y	Y	Y	Y
4 ***Watts***	?	Y	Y	Y	Y	Y
5 ***Istook***	Y	Y	Y	Y	Y	Y
6 ***Lucas***	Y	Y	Y	Y	Y	Y
OREGON						
1 Wu	Y	N	N	Y	N	Y
2 ***Walden***	Y	Y	Y	Y	Y	Y
3 Blumenauer	Y	Y	N	Y	N	Y
4 DeFazio	Y	N	N	Y	N	Y
5 Hooley	Y	N	N	Y	N	Y
PENNSYLVANIA						
1 Brady	Y	N	N	Y	N	Y
2 Fattah	Y	Y	N	Y	N	Y
3 Borski	?	N	N	Y	N	Y
4 ***Hart***	Y	Y	Y	Y	Y	Y
5 ***Peterson***	Y	Y	Y	Y	Y	Y
6 Holden	Y	Y	N	Y	N	Y
7 ***Weldon***	?	Y	Y	Y	Y	Y
8 ***Greenwood***	Y	Y	Y	Y	Y	Y
9 ***Shuster, Bill***	Y	Y	Y	Y	Y	Y
10 ***Sherwood***	Y	Y	Y	Y	Y	Y
11 Kanjorski	Y	Y	N	Y	N	Y
12 Murtha	?	Y	N	Y	N	Y
13 Hoeffel	Y	Y	N	Y	N	Y
14 Coyne	Y	?	N	Y	N	Y
15 ***Toomey***	Y	?	Y	Y	Y	Y
16 ***Pitts***	Y	Y	Y	Y	Y	Y
17 ***Gekas***	Y	Y	Y	Y	Y	Y
18 Doyle	?	Y	N	Y	N	Y
19 ***Platts***	Y	Y	Y	Y	Y	Y
20 Mascara	Y	Y	N	Y	N	Y
21 ***English***	Y	N	Y	Y	Y	Y
RHODE ISLAND						
1 Kennedy	Y	Y	N	Y	N	Y
2 Langevin	Y	Y	N	Y	N	Y
SOUTH CAROLINA						
1 ***Brown***	Y	Y	Y	Y	Y	Y
2 ***Wilson***	Y	Y	Y	Y	Y	Y
3 ***Graham***	Y	Y	Y	Y	Y	Y
4 ***DeMint***	Y	Y	Y	Y	Y	Y
5 Spratt	Y	Y	N	Y	N	Y
6 Clyburn	Y	Y	N	Y	N	Y
SOUTH DAKOTA						
AL ***Thune***	Y	Y	Y	Y	Y	Y
TENNESSEE						
1 ***Jenkins***	Y	Y	Y	Y	Y	Y
2 ***Duncan***	Y	Y	Y	Y	Y	Y
3 ***Wamp***	Y	Y	Y	Y	Y	Y
4 ***Hilleary***	?	N	Y	Y	Y	Y
5 Clement	Y	Y	N	Y	N	Y
6 Gordon	Y	Y	N	Y	N	Y
7 ***Bryant***	Y	Y	Y	Y	Y	Y
8 Tanner	Y	N	N	Y	N	Y
9 Ford	Y	Y	N	Y	N	Y
TEXAS						
1 Sandlin	Y	Y	N	Y	N	Y
2 Turner	Y	Y	N	Y	N	Y
3 ***Johnson, Sam***	Y	Y	Y	Y	Y	Y
4 Hall	Y	Y	Y	Y	Y	Y
5 ***Sessions***	Y	Y	Y	Y	Y	Y
6 ***Barton***	Y	Y	Y	Y	?	?
7 ***Culberson***	Y	Y	Y	Y	?	Y
8 ***Brady***	Y	Y	Y	Y	Y	Y
9 Lampson	Y	Y	N	Y	N	Y
10 Doggett	Y	Y	N	Y	N	Y
11 Edwards	Y	Y	N	Y	N	Y
12 ***Granger***	Y	Y	Y	Y	Y	Y
13 ***Thornberry***	Y	Y	Y	Y	Y	Y
14 ***Paul***	Y	Y	Y	Y	Y	Y
15 Hinojosa	Y	Y	N	Y	N	Y
16 Reyes	Y	Y	N	Y	N	Y
17 Stenholm	Y	Y	N	Y	N	N
18 Jackson-Lee	Y	Y	N	Y	?	?
19 ***Combest***	Y	Y	Y	Y	Y	Y
20 Gonzalez	Y	Y	N	Y	N	Y
21 ***Smith***	Y	Y	Y	Y	Y	Y
22 ***DeLay***	Y	?	Y	Y	Y	Y
23 ***Bonilla***	Y	Y	Y	Y	Y	Y
24 Frost	Y	Y	N	Y	N	Y
25 Bentsen	?	?	?	?	?	?
26 ***Armey***	Y	Y	Y	Y	Y	Y
27 Ortiz	Y	Y	N	Y	N	Y
28 Rodriguez	Y	Y	N	Y	N	Y
29 Green	Y	Y	N	Y	N	Y
30 Johnson, E.B.	Y	Y	N	Y	N	Y
UTAH						
1 ***Hansen***	Y	Y	Y	Y	Y	Y
2 Matheson	Y	Y	N	Y	N	Y
3 ***Cannon***	Y	Y	Y	Y	Y	Y
VERMONT						
AL *Sanders*	Y	Y	N	?	N	Y
VIRGINIA						
1 ***Davis, Jo Ann***	Y	Y	Y	Y	Y	Y
2 ***Schrock***	Y	Y	Y	Y	Y	Y
3 Scott	Y	Y	N	Y	N	Y
4 ***Forbes***	Y	Y	Y	Y	Y	Y
5 *Goode*	Y	Y	Y	Y	Y	Y
6 ***Goodlatte***	Y	Y	Y	Y	Y	Y
7 ***Cantor***	Y	Y	Y	Y	Y	Y
8 Moran	Y	Y	N	Y	N	Y
9 Boucher	Y	Y	N	Y	N	Y
10 ***Wolf***	Y	Y	Y	Y	Y	Y
11 ***Davis, T.***	?	Y	Y	Y	Y	Y
WASHINGTON						
1 Inslee	Y	Y	N	Y	N	Y
2 Larsen	Y	N	N	Y	N	Y
3 Baird	Y	N	N	Y	N	Y
4 ***Hastings***	Y	Y	Y	Y	Y	Y
5 ***Nethercutt***	Y	Y	Y	Y	Y	Y
6 Dicks	Y	Y	N	Y	Y	Y
7 McDermott	Y	N	N	Y	N	Y
8 ***Dunn***	Y	Y	Y	Y	Y	Y
9 Smith	Y	Y	N	Y	N	Y
WEST VIRGINIA						
1 Mollohan	Y	Y	N	Y	N	Y
2 ***Capito***	Y	Y	Y	Y	Y	Y
3 Rahall	Y	Y	N	Y	N	Y
WISCONSIN						
1 ***Ryan***	Y	Y	Y	Y	Y	Y
2 Baldwin	Y	Y	N	Y	N	Y
3 Kind	Y	Y	N	Y	N	Y
4 Kleczka	Y	Y	N	Y	N	Y
5 Barrett	Y	Y	N	Y	N	Y
6 ***Petri***	Y	Y	Y	Y	Y	Y
7 Obey	Y	Y	N	Y	N	Y
8 ***Green***	Y	Y	Y	Y	Y	Y
9 ***Sensenbrenner***	Y	Y	Y	Y	Y	Y
WYOMING						
AL ***Cubin***	?	?	?	?	?	?

Southern states - Ala., Ark., Fla., Ga., Ky., La., Miss., N.C., Okla., S.C., Tenn., Texas, Va.

Key

Y	Voted for (yea).
#	Paired for.
+	Announced for.
N	Voted against (nay).
X	Paired against.
–	Announced against.
P	Voted "present."
C	Voted "present" to avoid possible conflict of interest.
?	Did not vote or otherwise make a position known.

Democrats **Republicans**
Independents

53. HR 1885. Residency Extension/Concur With Senate Amendment. Sensenbrenner, R-Wis., motion to suspend the rules and adopt the resolution (H Res 365) concurring in House amendments to the Senate amendment to the bill that would extend a law allowing some immigrants to remain in the country while pursuing legal residency. The section 245(i) extension would be through the earlier of Nov. 30, 2002, or four months after the Justice Department issues regulations carrying out the measure. The bill, as amended, also would increase security along U.S. borders. Motion agreed to 275-137: R 92-123; D 182-13 (ND 142-5, SD 40-8); I 1-1. A two-thirds majority of those present and voting (275 in this case) is required for adoption under suspension of the rules. A "yea" was a vote in support of the president's position. March 12, 2002.

54. Procedural Motion/Journal. Approval of the House Journal of Tuesday, March 12, 2002. Approved 355-45: R 187-15; D 166-30 (ND 119-27, SD 47-3); I 2-0. March 13, 2002.

55. HR 2341. Class Action Lawsuits/Previous Question. Pryce, R-Ohio, motion to order the previous question (thus ending debate and possibility of amendment) on adoption of the rule (H Res 367) to provide for House floor consideration of the bill that would give federal courts original jurisdiction over class action lawsuits in which any of the plaintiffs or defendants reside in different states or in another country and the total damages sought are more than $2 million. Motion agreed to 221-198: R 214-0; D 6-197 (ND 1-151, SD 5-46); I 1-1. (Subsequently, the rule was agreed to by voice vote.) March 13, 2002.

56. HR 2341. Class Action Lawsuits/Discovery Documents. Waters, D-Calif., amendment that would mandate that anyone found to have withheld or shredded documents that are required to be handed over through a discovery motion in a class action lawsuit would be found to have admitted to the facts of that motion. Rejected 174-251: R 1-220; D 172-30 (ND 131-19, SD 41-11); I 1-1. March 13, 2002.

57. HR 2341. Class Action Lawsuits/Prosecutors' Suits. Lofgren, D-Calif., amendment that would allow actions brought on behalf of the general public, including civil suits by local prosecutors, to be moved to federal court. It would maintain local prosecutors' authority to enforce consumer and antitrust laws. Rejected 194-231: R 1-220; D 192-10 (ND 147-3, SD 45-7); I 1-1. March 13, 2002.

58. HR 2341. Class Action Lawsuits/Companies' Venues. Conyers, D-Mich., amendment that would prevent a company from being able to move a case from state to federal court by incorporating a new company abroad and acquiring the original company. Rejected 202-223: R 7-213; D 194-9 (ND 149-2, SD 45-7); I 1-1. March 13, 2002.

	53	54	55	56	57	58
ALABAMA						
1 *Callahan*	N	Y	Y	N	N	N
2 *Everett*	N	Y	Y	N	N	N
3 *Riley*	N	Y	Y	N	N	N
4 *Aderholt*	N	N	Y	N	N	N
5 Cramer	Y	Y	N	N	Y	N
6 *Bachus*	N	Y	Y	N	N	N
7 Hilliard	N	N	N	Y	Y	Y
ALASKA						
AL *Young*	N	?	Y	N	N	N
ARIZONA						
1 *Flake*	N	Y	Y	N	N	N
2 Pastor	Y	Y	N	Y	Y	Y
3 *Stump*	N	Y	Y	N	N	N
4 *Shadegg*	N	Y	Y	N	N	N
5 *Kolbe*	Y	Y	Y	N	N	N
6 *Hayworth*	N	Y	Y	N	N	N
ARKANSAS						
1 Berry	Y	Y	N	Y	Y	Y
2 Snyder	Y	Y	N	Y	Y	Y
3 *Boozman*	N	Y	Y	N	N	N
4 Ross	Y	Y	N	Y	Y	Y
CALIFORNIA						
1 Thompson	Y	N	N	Y	Y	Y
2 *Herger*	N	Y	Y	N	N	N
3 *Ose*	Y	Y	Y	N	N	N
4 *Doolittle*	?	Y	Y	N	N	N
5 Matsui	Y	Y	N	Y	Y	Y
6 Woolsey	Y	Y	N	Y	Y	Y
7 Miller, George	Y	N	N	Y	Y	Y
8 Pelosi	Y	Y	N	Y	?	Y
9 Lee	Y	Y	N	Y	Y	Y
10 Tauscher	Y	Y	N	N	Y	Y
11 *Pombo*	N	Y	Y	N	N	N
12 Lantos	Y	Y	N	Y	Y	Y
13 Stark	Y	N	N	Y	Y	Y
14 Eshoo	?	?	?	?	?	?
15 Honda	Y	Y	N	Y	Y	Y
16 Lofgren	Y	Y	N	Y	Y	Y
17 Farr	Y	Y	N	Y	Y	Y
18 Condit	Y	Y	N	N	Y	Y
19 *Radanovich*	Y	Y	?	N	N	N
20 Dooley	Y	Y	N	N	Y	Y
21 *Thomas*	Y	Y	Y	N	N	N
22 Capps	Y	Y	N	Y	Y	Y
23 *Gallegly*	N	Y	Y	N	N	N
24 Sherman	Y	Y	N	Y	Y	Y
25 *McKeon*	Y	Y	Y	N	N	N
26 Berman	Y	Y	N	Y	Y	Y
27 Schiff	Y	Y	N	Y	Y	Y
28 *Dreier*	Y	Y	Y	N	N	N
29 Waxman	Y	Y	N	Y	Y	Y
30 Becerra	Y	Y	N	Y	Y	Y
31 Solis	Y	Y	N	Y	Y	Y
32 Watson	Y	Y	N	Y	Y	Y
33 Roybal-Allard	Y	Y	N	Y	Y	Y
34 Napolitano	Y	Y	N	+	Y	Y
35 Waters	Y	N	N	Y	N	Y
36 Harman	Y	Y	N	Y	Y	Y
37 Millender-McD.	Y	Y	N	Y	Y	Y
38 Horn	N	Y	Y	N	N	N

	53	54	55	56	57	58
39 *Royce*	N	Y	Y	N	N	Y
40 *Lewis*	Y	Y	Y	N	N	N
41 *Miller, Gary*	N	Y	Y	N	N	N
42 Baca	Y	Y	N	Y	Y	Y
43 *Calvert*	Y	Y	Y	N	N	N
44 *Bono*	Y	Y	Y	N	N	N
45 *Rohrabacher*	Y	Y	Y	N	N	N
46 Sanchez	Y	Y	N	Y	Y	Y
47 *Cox*	Y	Y	Y	N	N	N
48 *Issa*	Y	Y	Y	N	N	N
49 Davis	Y	Y	N	Y	Y	Y
50 Filner	Y	N	N	Y	Y	Y
51 *Cunningham*	Y	Y	Y	N	N	N
52 *Hunter*	N	?	Y	N	N	N
COLORADO						
1 DeGette	Y	Y	N	Y	Y	Y
2 Udall	Y	N	N	Y	Y	Y
3 *McInnis*	N	Y	Y	N	N	N
4 *Schaffer*	N	N	Y	N	N	N
5 *Hefley*	N	N	Y	N	N	N
6 *Tancredo*	N	P	Y	N	N	N
CONNECTICUT						
1 Larson	Y	Y	N	Y	Y	Y
2 *Simmons*	Y	Y	Y	N	N	N
3 DeLauro	Y	Y	N	Y	Y	Y
4 *Shays*	Y	Y	Y	N	N	N
5 Maloney	Y	Y	N	Y	Y	Y
6 *Johnson*	Y	Y	Y	N	N	Y
DELAWARE						
AL *Castle*	Y	Y	Y	N	N	Y
FLORIDA						
1 *Miller, J.*	N	Y	Y	N	N	N
2 Boyd	N	Y	Y	N	N	N
3 Brown	Y	Y	N	Y	Y	Y
4 *Crenshaw*	N	Y	Y	N	N	N
5 *Thurman*	N	N	N	Y	Y	Y
6 *Stearns*	N	Y	Y	N	N	N
7 *Mica*	N	Y	Y	N	N	N
8 *Keller*	N	Y	Y	N	N	N
9 *Bilirakis*	N	Y	Y	N	N	N
10 *Young*	N	?	?	N	N	N
11 Davis	N	Y	Y	N	Y	N
12 *Putnam*	N	Y	Y	N	N	N
13 *Miller, D.*	N	Y	Y	N	N	N
14 *Goss*	N	Y	Y	N	N	N
15 *Weldon*	N	Y	Y	N	N	N
16 *Foley*	Y	Y	Y	N	N	N
17 Meek	N	Y	Y	N	Y	Y
18 *Ros-Lehtinen*	Y	Y	Y	N	N	N
19 Wexler	?	N	Y	Y	Y	Y
20 Deutsch	Y	Y	Y	N	Y	N
21 *Diaz-Balart*	Y	Y	Y	N	N	N
22 *Shaw*	Y	?	Y	N	N	N
23 Hastings	Y	Y	N	Y	Y	Y
GEORGIA						
1 *Kingston*	N	Y	Y	N	N	N
2 Bishop	Y	Y	N	Y	N	Y
3 *Collins*	N	Y	Y	N	N	N
4 McKinney	Y	Y	N	Y	Y	Y
5 Lewis	N	Y	N	Y	Y	Y
6 *Isakson*	N	Y	Y	N	N	N
7 *Barr*	N	Y	Y	N	N	N
8 *Chambliss*	N	Y	Y	N	N	N
9 *Deal*	N	Y	Y	N	N	N
10 *Norwood*	N	Y	?	N	N	N
11 *Linder*	N	Y	Y	N	N	N
HAWAII						
1 Abercrombie	Y	Y	N	Y	Y	Y
2 Mink	Y	Y	N	Y	Y	Y
IDAHO						
1 *Otter*	Y	Y	Y	N	N	N
2 *Simpson*	Y	Y	Y	N	N	N
ILLINOIS						
1 Rush	Y	?	N	Y	Y	Y
2 Jackson	Y	Y	N	Y	Y	Y
3 Lipinski	?	Y	N	Y	Y	Y
4 Gutierrez	Y	Y	N	Y	Y	Y
5 Blagojevich	?	?	?	?	?	?
6 *Hyde*	Y	Y	N	N	N	N
7 Davis	?	?	?	?	?	?
8 *Crane*	N	N	Y	N	N	N
9 Schakowsky	Y	N	N	Y	Y	Y
10 *Kirk*	Y	Y	Y	N	N	N
11 *Weller*	N	Y	N	Y	N	N
12 Costello	Y	N	N	Y	Y	Y
13 *Biggert*	Y	Y	Y	N	N	N

ND Northern Democrats   SD Southern Democrats

	53	54	55	56	57	58
14 ***Hastert***						
15 ***Johnson***	Y	Y	Y	N	N	Y
16 ***Manzullo***	N	Y	Y	N	N	N
17 Evans	Y	Y	N	Y	Y	Y
18 ***LaHood***	N	?	Y	N	N	N
19 Phelps	Y	Y	N	Y	Y	Y
20 ***Shimkus***	N	Y	Y	N	N	N
INDIANA						
1 Visclosky	N	N	N	Y	Y	Y
2 ***Pence***	N	Y	Y	N	N	N
3 Roemer	Y	Y	N	Y	Y	Y
4 ***Souder***	Y	Y	Y	N	N	N
5 ***Buyer***	Y	?	Y	N	N	N
6 ***Burton***	?	?	?	N	N	N
7 ***Kerns***	N	Y	Y	N	N	N
8 ***Hostettler***	N	Y	Y	N	N	N
9 Hill	Y	Y	N	N	Y	N
10 Carson	?	Y	N	Y	Y	Y
IOWA						
1 ***Leach***	Y	Y	Y	N	N	N
2 ***Nussle***	Y	Y	Y	N	N	N
3 Boswell	Y	Y	N	Y	Y	Y
4 ***Ganske***	N	Y	Y	N	N	N
5 ***Latham***	Y	N	Y	N	N	N
KANSAS						
1 ***Moran***	N	N	Y	N	N	N
2 ***Ryun***	N	Y	Y	N	N	N
3 Moore	Y	N	N	Y	Y	Y
4 ***Tiahrt***	Y	Y	Y	N	N	N
KENTUCKY						
1 ***Whitfield***	N	Y	Y	N	N	N
2 ***Lewis***	N	Y	Y	N	N	N
3 ***Northup***	Y	Y	Y	N	N	N
4 Lucas	Y	Y	N	N	N	N
5 ***Rogers***	Y	Y	Y	N	N	N
6 ***Fletcher***	Y	Y	Y	N	N	N
LOUISIANA						
1 ***Vitter***	N	Y	Y	N	N	N
2 Jefferson	Y	Y	N	Y	Y	Y
3 ***Tauzin***	Y	Y	Y	N	N	N
4 ***McCrery***	N	Y	Y	N	N	N
5 ***Cooksey***	N	?	Y	N	N	N
6 ***Baker***	N	Y	Y	N	N	N
7 John	Y	Y	N	N	N	N
MAINE						
1 Allen	Y	Y	N	N	Y	Y
2 Baldacci	Y	Y	N	Y	Y	Y
MARYLAND						
1 ***Gilchrest***	Y	Y	Y	N	N	N
2 ***Ehrlich***	Y	?	Y	N	N	N
3 Cardin	Y	Y	N	Y	Y	Y
4 Wynn	Y	Y	N	Y	Y	Y
5 Hoyer	Y	Y	N	Y	Y	Y
6 ***Bartlett***	N	Y	Y	N	N	N
7 Cummings	Y	Y	N	Y	Y	Y
8 ***Morella***	Y	Y	Y	N	N	N
MASSACHUSETTS						
1 Olver	Y	Y	N	Y	Y	Y
2 Neal	?	Y	N	Y	Y	Y
3 McGovern	Y	Y	N	Y	Y	Y
4 Frank	Y	Y	N	N	Y	Y
5 Meehan	Y	Y	N	Y	Y	Y
6 Tierney	Y	Y	N	Y	Y	Y
7 Markey	Y	Y	N	Y	Y	Y
8 Capuano	Y	N	N	Y	Y	Y
9 Lynch	Y	Y	N	Y	Y	Y
10 Delahunt	Y	Y	N	Y	Y	Y
MICHIGAN						
1 Stupak	N	N	N	Y	Y	Y
2 ***Hoekstra***	N	Y	Y	N	N	N
3 ***Ehlers***	Y	Y	Y	N	N	N
4 ***Camp***	N	Y	Y	N	N	N
5 Barcia	N	Y	N	Y	Y	Y
6 ***Upton***	N	Y	Y	N	N	N
7 ***Smith***	N	Y	Y	N	N	N
8 ***Rogers***	N	Y	Y	N	N	N
9 Kildee	Y	Y	N	Y	Y	Y
10 Bonior	Y	Y	N	Y	Y	Y
11 ***Knollenberg***	Y	Y	Y	N	N	N
12 Levin	Y	Y	N	Y	Y	Y
13 Rivers	Y	Y	N	Y	Y	Y
14 Conyers	Y	Y	N	Y	Y	Y
15 Kilpatrick	Y	Y	N	+	?	+
16 Dingell	Y	Y	N	Y	Y	Y
MINNESOTA						
1 ***Gutknecht***	N	N	Y	N	N	N
2 ***Kennedy***	Y	Y	Y	N	N	N
3 ***Ramstad***	N	N	Y	N	N	N
4 McCollum	Y	Y	N	Y	Y	Y
5 Sabo	Y	N	N	N	Y	Y
6 Luther	Y	Y	N	Y	Y	Y
7 Peterson	N	N	N	N	N	Y
8 Oberstar	Y	?	N	N	Y	Y
MISSISSIPPI						
1 ***Wicker***	N	N	Y	N	N	N
2 Thompson	?	N	N	Y	Y	Y
3 ***Pickering***	N	Y	Y	N	N	N
4 Shows	N	Y	N	Y	Y	Y
5 Taylor	N	N	N	N	N	Y
MISSOURI						
1 Clay	Y	Y	N	Y	Y	Y
2 ***Akin***	N	Y	Y	N	N	N
3 Gephardt	Y	Y	N	Y	Y	Y
4 Skelton	Y	Y	N	Y	Y	Y
5 McCarthy	Y	Y	N	Y	Y	Y
6 ***Graves***	N	Y	Y	N	N	N
7 ***Blunt***	N	Y	Y	N	N	N
8 ***Emerson***	N	Y	Y	N	N	N
9 ***Hulshof***	N	N	Y	N	N	N
MONTANA						
AL ***Rehberg***	N	Y	Y	N	N	N
NEBRASKA						
1 ***Bereuter***	N	Y	Y	N	N	N
2 ***Terry***	Y	Y	Y	N	N	N
3 ***Osborne***	Y	Y	Y	N	N	N
NEVADA						
1 Berkley	Y	Y	N	Y	Y	Y
2 ***Gibbons***	Y	Y	Y	N	N	N
NEW HAMPSHIRE						
1 ***Sununu***	Y	Y	Y	N	N	N
2 ***Bass***	N	Y	Y	N	N	N
NEW JERSEY						
1 Andrews	Y	Y	N	Y	Y	Y
2 ***LoBiondo***	N	N	Y	N	N	N
3 ***Saxton***	N	Y	Y	N	N	N
4 ***Smith***	Y	Y	Y	N	N	N
5 ***Roukema***	N	Y	Y	N	N	N
6 Pallone	Y	N	N	Y	Y	Y
7 ***Ferguson***	N	Y	Y	N	N	N
8 Pascrell	Y	Y	N	Y	Y	Y
9 Rothman	Y	?	N	Y	Y	Y
10 Payne	Y	Y	N	Y	Y	Y
11 ***Frelinghuysen***	N	Y	Y	N	N	N
12 Holt	Y	Y	N	Y	Y	Y
13 Menendez	Y	?	N	Y	Y	Y
NEW MEXICO						
1 ***Wilson***	Y	Y	Y	N	N	N
2 ***Skeen***	Y	Y	Y	N	N	N
3 Udall	Y	N	N	Y	Y	Y
NEW YORK						
1 ***Grucci***	Y	Y	Y	N	N	N
2 Israel	Y	Y	N	Y	Y	Y
3 ***King***	Y	?	Y	N	N	N
4 McCarthy	Y	Y	N	Y	Y	Y
5 Ackerman	Y	Y	N	Y	Y	Y
6 Meeks	Y	Y	N	Y	Y	Y
7 Crowley	Y	Y	N	Y	Y	Y
8 Nadler	Y	Y	N	Y	Y	Y
9 Weiner	+	Y	N	Y	Y	Y
10 Towns	Y	Y	N	Y	Y	Y
11 Owens	Y	Y	N	Y	Y	Y
12 Velázquez	Y	Y	N	Y	Y	Y
13 ***Fossella***	Y	Y	Y	N	N	N
14 Maloney	Y	Y	N	Y	Y	Y
15 Rangel	Y	Y	N	Y	Y	Y
16 Serrano	Y	Y	N	Y	Y	Y
17 Engel	Y	Y	N	Y	Y	Y
18 Lowey	?	Y	N	Y	Y	Y
19 ***Kelly***	Y	Y	Y	N	N	N
20 ***Gilman***	Y	Y	Y	Y	Y	Y
21 McNulty	Y	N	N	N	Y	Y
22 ***Sweeney***	?	Y	Y	N	N	N
23 ***Boehlert***	Y	Y	Y	N	N	N
24 ***McHugh***	Y	Y	Y	N	N	N
25 ***Walsh***	Y	Y	Y	N	N	N
26 Hinchey	Y	N	N	Y	Y	Y
27 ***Reynolds***	Y	Y	Y	N	N	N
28 Slaughter	Y	?	N	Y	Y	Y
29 LaFalce	Y	Y	N	Y	Y	Y
30 ***Quinn***	Y	?	Y	N	N	N
31 ***Houghton***	Y	Y	Y	N	N	N
NORTH CAROLINA						
1 Clayton	Y	Y	N	Y	Y	Y
2 Etheridge	Y	Y	N	Y	Y	Y
3 ***Jones***	N	Y	Y	N	N	N
4 Price	Y	Y	N	Y	Y	Y
5 ***Burr***	N	Y	Y	N	N	N
6 ***Coble***	N	Y	Y	N	N	N
7 McIntyre	Y	Y	N	Y	Y	Y
8 ***Hayes***	N	Y	Y	N	N	N
9 ***Myrick***	N	Y	Y	N	N	N
10 ***Ballenger***	N	?	Y	N	N	N
11 ***Taylor***	N	Y	Y	N	N	N
12 Watt	Y	Y	N	Y	Y	Y
NORTH DAKOTA						
AL Pomeroy	Y	Y	N	Y	Y	Y
OHIO						
1 ***Chabot***	Y	Y	Y	N	N	N
2 ***Portman***	Y	Y	Y	N	N	N
3 Hall	Y	Y	Y	Y	Y	Y
4 ***Oxley***	Y	?	Y	N	N	N
5 ***Gillmor***	Y	Y	Y	N	N	N
6 Strickland	Y	N	N	Y	Y	Y
7 ***Hobson***	Y	Y	Y	N	N	N
8 ***Boehner***	Y	Y	Y	N	N	N
9 Kaptur	N	Y	N	Y	Y	Y
10 Kucinich	Y	N	N	Y	Y	Y
11 Jones	Y	Y	N	Y	Y	Y
12 ***Tiberi***	Y	N	Y	N	N	N
13 Brown	Y	Y	N	Y	Y	Y
14 Sawyer	Y	Y	N	Y	Y	Y
15 ***Pryce***	Y	Y	Y	N	N	N
16 ***Regula***	Y	Y	Y	N	N	N
17 Traficant	?	?	?	?	?	?
18 ***Ney***	Y	Y	Y	N	N	N
19 ***LaTourette***	Y	Y	Y	N	N	N
OKLAHOMA						
1 ***Sullivan***	N	?	Y	N	N	N
2 Carson	Y	Y	N	Y	Y	Y
3 ***Watkins***	Y	Y	Y	N	N	N
4 ***Watts***	Y	Y	Y	N	N	N
5 ***Istook***	N	Y	Y	N	N	?
6 ***Lucas***	N	Y	Y	N	N	N
OREGON						
1 Wu	Y	Y	N	N	Y	Y
2 ***Walden***	N	Y	Y	N	N	N
3 Blumenauer	Y	Y	N	N	Y	Y
4 DeFazio	Y	N	N	Y	Y	Y
5 Hooley	Y	Y	N	N	Y	Y
PENNSYLVANIA						
1 Brady	Y	N	N	Y	Y	Y
2 Fattah	Y	Y	N	Y	Y	Y
3 Borski	Y	N	N	Y	Y	Y
4 ***Hart***	Y	Y	Y	N	N	N
5 ***Peterson***	N	Y	Y	N	N	N
6 Holden	Y	Y	N	N	N	Y
7 ***Weldon***	N	Y	Y	N	N	N
8 ***Greenwood***	N	Y	Y	N	N	N
9 ***Shuster, Bill***	N	Y	Y	N	N	N
10 ***Sherwood***	N	Y	Y	N	N	N
11 Kanjorski	Y	Y	N	Y	Y	Y
12 Murtha	Y	Y	N	Y	Y	Y
13 Hoeffel	Y	Y	N	Y	Y	Y
14 Coyne	Y	?	N	Y	Y	Y
15 ***Toomey***	N	Y	Y	N	N	N
16 ***Pitts***	N	Y	Y	N	N	N
17 ***Gekas***	N	Y	Y	N	N	N
18 Doyle	Y	Y	N	Y	Y	Y
19 ***Platts***	N	N	Y	N	N	N
20 Mascara	Y	Y	N	Y	Y	Y
21 ***English***	Y	N	Y	N	N	N
RHODE ISLAND						
1 Kennedy	Y	Y	N	Y	Y	Y
2 Langevin	Y	Y	N	Y	Y	Y
SOUTH CAROLINA						
1 ***Brown***	N	Y	Y	N	N	N
2 ***Wilson***	N	Y	Y	N	N	N
3 ***Graham***	N	Y	?	N	N	N
4 ***DeMint***	N	Y	Y	N	N	N
5 Spratt	Y	Y	N	Y	Y	Y
6 Clyburn	Y	Y	N	Y	Y	Y
SOUTH DAKOTA						
AL ***Thune***	N	Y	Y	N	N	N
TENNESSEE						
1 ***Jenkins***	N	Y	Y	N	N	N
2 ***Duncan***	N	Y	Y	N	N	Y
3 ***Wamp***	N	Y	Y	N	N	N
4 ***Hilleary***	?	Y	Y	N	N	N
5 Clement	N	Y	N	Y	Y	Y
6 Gordon	N	Y	N	Y	Y	Y
7 ***Bryant***	N	Y	Y	N	N	N
8 Tanner	Y	Y	N	Y	Y	Y
9 Ford	Y	Y	N	Y	Y	Y
TEXAS						
1 Sandlin	Y	Y	N	Y	Y	Y
2 Turner	Y	Y	N	Y	Y	Y
3 ***Johnson, Sam***	?	?	Y	N	N	N
4 Hall	N	Y	Y	N	N	N
5 ***Sessions***	N	Y	Y	N	N	N
6 ***Barton***	?	?	?	N	N	N
7 ***Culberson***	N	Y	Y	N	N	N
8 ***Brady***	N	Y	Y	N	N	N
9 Lampson	Y	Y	N	Y	Y	Y
10 Doggett	Y	Y	N	Y	Y	Y
11 Edwards	Y	Y	N	Y	Y	Y
12 ***Granger***	N	Y	Y	N	N	N
13 ***Thornberry***	Y	Y	Y	N	N	N
14 ***Paul***	Y	Y	Y	N	N	N
15 Hinojosa	+	+	–	+	+	+
16 Reyes	Y	Y	N	Y	Y	Y
17 Stenholm	Y	Y	Y	N	N	N
18 Jackson-Lee	+	+	N	Y	Y	Y
19 ***Combest***	N	Y	Y	N	N	N
20 Gonzalez	Y	Y	N	Y	Y	Y
21 ***Smith***	Y	Y	Y	N	N	N
22 ***DeLay***	Y	?	Y	N	N	N
23 ***Bonilla***	Y	Y	Y	N	N	N
24 Frost	Y	Y	N	Y	Y	Y
25 Bentsen	?	?	?	?	?	?
26 ***Armey***	Y	Y	Y	N	N	N
27 Ortiz	+	+	–	Y	Y	Y
28 Rodriguez	Y	Y	N	Y	Y	Y
29 Green	Y	Y	N	Y	Y	Y
30 Johnson, E.B.	Y	Y	N	Y	Y	Y
UTAH						
1 ***Hansen***	N	Y	Y	N	N	N
2 Matheson	Y	N	N	Y	Y	Y
3 ***Cannon***	Y	Y	Y	N	N	N
VERMONT						
AL *Sanders*	Y	Y	N	Y	Y	Y
VIRGINIA						
1 ***Davis, Jo Ann***	N	Y	Y	N	N	N
2 ***Schrock***	N	Y	Y	N	N	N
3 Scott	Y	Y	N	Y	Y	Y
4 ***Forbes***	N	Y	Y	N	N	N
5 *Goode*	N	Y	Y	N	N	N
6 ***Goodlatte***	N	Y	Y	N	N	N
7 ***Cantor***	N	Y	Y	N	N	N
8 Moran	Y	Y	Y	Y	Y	Y
9 Boucher	Y	Y	Y	N	N	N
10 ***Wolf***	N	Y	Y	N	N	N
11 ***Davis, T.***	Y	Y	Y	N	N	N
WASHINGTON						
1 Inslee	Y	Y	N	Y	Y	Y
2 Larsen	Y	N	N	Y	Y	Y
3 Baird	Y	N	N	Y	Y	Y
4 ***Hastings***	Y	Y	Y	N	N	N
5 ***Nethercutt***	Y	Y	Y	N	N	N
6 Dicks	Y	Y	N	Y	Y	N
7 McDermott	Y	N	N	Y	Y	Y
8 ***Dunn***	Y	Y	Y	N	N	N
9 Smith	Y	Y	N	Y	Y	Y
WEST VIRGINIA						
1 Mollohan	Y	Y	N	N	Y	Y
2 ***Capito***	N	Y	Y	N	N	N
3 Rahall	Y	Y	N	Y	Y	Y
WISCONSIN						
1 ***Ryan***	Y	Y	Y	N	N	N
2 Baldwin	Y	Y	N	Y	Y	Y
3 Kind	Y	Y	N	N	Y	Y
4 Kleczka	Y	Y	N	N	Y	Y
5 Barrett	?	?	?	?	?	?
6 ***Petri***	Y	Y	Y	N	N	N
7 Obey	Y	Y	N	Y	Y	Y
8 ***Green***	Y	Y	Y	N	N	N
9 ***Sensenbrenner***	Y	Y	Y	N	N	N
WYOMING						
AL ***Cubin***	N	?	?	N	N	N

Southern states - Ala., Ark., Fla., Ga., Ky., La., Miss., N.C., Okla., S.C., Tenn., Texas, Va.

Key

Y	Voted for (yea).
#	Paired for.
+	Announced for.
N	Voted against (nay).
X	Paired against.
–	Announced against.
P	Voted "present."
C	Voted "present" to avoid possible conflict of interest.
?	Did not vote or otherwise make a position known.

Democrats   **Republicans**
Independents

---

59. HR 2341. Class Action Lawsuits/Evidence Destruction. Jackson-Lee, D-Texas, amendment that would block a party in a class action suit from moving the case's venue to federal court if that party destroys, falsifies or similarly alters material evidence. Rejected 177-248: R 3-218; D 173-29 (ND 135-15, SD 38-14); I 1-1. March 13, 2002.

60. HR 2341. Class Action Lawsuits/Non-Certified Cases. Frank, D-Mass., amendment that would state that suits not certified as class actions subject to a federal court's jurisdiction could then be tried in state court. The case would not later be subject to removal to federal court unless it meets current law party diversity standards. Rejected 191-234: R 3-218; D 187-15 (ND 145-5, SD 42-10); I 1-1. March 13, 2002.

61. HR 2341. Class Action Lawsuits/Recommit. Sandlin, D-Texas, motion to recommit the bill to the House Judiciary Committee with instructions to add language that would block defendants who have knowingly committed a terrorist act from moving a class action suit to federal court. Motion rejected 191-235: R 0-221; D 190-13 (ND 146-4, SD 44-9); I 1-1. March 13, 2002.

62. HR 2341. Class Action Lawsuits/Passage. Passage of the bill that would give federal courts original jurisdiction over class action lawsuits in which any of the plaintiffs or defendants reside in different states or in another country and the total damages sought are more than $2 million. Passed 233-190: R 215-5; D 17-184 (ND 6-142, SD 11-42); I 1-1. A "yea" was a vote in support of the president's position. March 13, 2002.

63. HR 2146. Repeat Child Sex Offenders/Impact Study. Conyers, D-Mich., amendment that would require a federal judge imposing a mandatory life sentence under the law to provide certain information to the Administrative Office of the U.S. Courts, which would then be transmitted to Congress. The reports would include the range of possible sentences that otherwise would have applied, the actual sentence that would have been imposed, and the race, gender, age and ethnicity of both the victim and the defendant in the case. Adopted 259-161: R 64-155; D 194-5 (ND 143-3, SD 51-2); I 1-1. March 14, 2002.

64. HR 2146. Repeat Child Sex Offenders/Passage. Passage of the bill that would impose a mandatory life prison sentence on anyone convicted of repeating any of seven specific sexual offenses against a child on federal property. Passed 382-34: R 218-0; D 162-34 (ND 120-24, SD 42-10); I 2-0. March 14, 2002.

	59	60	61	62	63	64
ALABAMA						
1 *Callahan*	N	N	N	Y	N	Y
2 *Everett*	N	N	N	Y	N	Y
3 *Riley*	N	N	N	Y	N	Y
4 *Aderholt*	N	N	N	Y	N	Y
5 Cramer	N	N	N	Y	Y	Y
6 *Bachus*	N	N	N	Y	N	Y
7 Hilliard	Y	N	Y	N	Y	N
ALASKA						
AL *Young*	N	N	N	Y	N	Y
ARIZONA						
1 *Flake*	N	N	N	Y	N	Y
2 Pastor	Y	Y	Y	N	Y	Y
3 *Stump*	N	N	N	Y	N	Y
4 *Shadegg*	N	N	N	Y	N	Y
5 *Kolbe*	N	N	N	Y	Y	Y
6 *Hayworth*	N	N	N	Y	N	Y
ARKANSAS						
1 Berry	Y	Y	Y	N	Y	Y
2 Snyder	N	Y	Y	N	Y	Y
3 *Boozman*	N	N	N	Y	N	Y
4 Ross	Y	Y	Y	N	Y	Y
CALIFORNIA						
1 Thompson	N	Y	N	Y	Y	Y
2 *Herger*	N	N	N	Y	N	Y
3 *Ose*	N	N	N	Y	N	Y
4 *Doolittle*	N	N	N	Y	N	Y
5 Matsui	Y	Y	Y	N	Y	Y
6 Woolsey	Y	Y	Y	N	Y	Y
7 Miller, George	Y	Y	Y	N	Y	N
8 Pelosi	Y	Y	Y	N	Y	Y
9 Lee	Y	Y	Y	N	Y	N
10 Tauscher	N	Y	N	Y	Y	Y
11 *Pombo*	N	N	N	Y	N	Y
12 Lantos	Y	Y	Y	N	Y	Y
13 Stark	Y	Y	Y	N	Y	N
14 Eshoo	?	?	?	?	?	?
15 Honda	Y	Y	Y	N	Y	Y
16 Lofgren	N	Y	N	Y	N	Y
17 Farr	Y	Y	Y	N	Y	N
18 Condit	N	Y	N	Y	N	Y
19 *Radanovich*	N	N	N	Y	Y	Y
20 Dooley	N	N	N	Y	Y	Y
21 *Thomas*	N	N	N	Y	N	Y
22 Capps	Y	Y	Y	N	Y	Y
23 *Gallegly*	N	N	N	Y	Y	Y
24 Sherman	Y	Y	Y	N	Y	Y
25 *McKeon*	N	N	N	Y	N	Y
26 Berman	Y	Y	Y	N	Y	N
27 Schiff	Y	Y	Y	N	Y	Y
28 *Dreier*	N	N	N	Y	Y	Y
29 Waxman	Y	Y	Y	N	Y	Y
30 Becerra	Y	Y	Y	N	Y	Y
31 Solis	Y	Y	Y	N	+	–
32 Watson	Y	Y	Y	N	Y	Y
33 Roybal-Allard	Y	Y	Y	N	Y	Y
34 Napolitano	Y	Y	Y	N	Y	Y
35 Waters	Y	N	Y	N	Y	N
36 Harman	Y	Y	Y	N	Y	Y
37 Millender-McD.	Y	Y	Y	N	Y	Y
38 Horn	N	N	N	Y	Y	Y

	59	60	61	62	63	64
39 *Royce*	N	N	N	Y	N	Y
40 *Lewis*	N	N	N	Y	N	Y
41 *Miller, Gary*	N	N	N	Y	N	Y
42 Baca	Y	Y	Y	N	Y	Y
43 *Calvert*	N	N	N	Y	N	Y
44 *Bono*	N	N	N	Y	N	Y
45 *Rohrabacher*	N	N	N	Y	N	Y
46 Sanchez	Y	Y	Y	N	Y	Y
47 *Cox*	N	N	N	Y	N	Y
48 *Issa*	N	N	N	Y	N	Y
49 Davis	Y	Y	Y	N	Y	Y
50 Filner	Y	Y	Y	N	Y	N
51 *Cunningham*	N	N	N	Y	N	Y
52 *Hunter*	N	N	N	Y	N	Y
COLORADO						
1 DeGette	Y	Y	Y	N	Y	N
2 Udall	Y	Y	Y	N	Y	+
3 *McInnis*	N	N	N	Y	N	Y
4 *Schaffer*	N	N	N	Y	Y	Y
5 *Hefley*	N	N	N	Y	N	Y
6 *Tancredo*	N	N	N	Y	Y	Y
CONNECTICUT						
1 Larson	Y	Y	Y	Y	Y	Y
2 *Simmons*	Y	Y	Y	N	Y	Y
3 DeLauro	Y	Y	Y	N	Y	Y
4 *Shays*	N	N	N	Y	N	Y
5 Maloney	Y	Y	Y	N	Y	Y
6 *Johnson*	N	N	N	Y	N	Y
DELAWARE						
AL *Castle*	N	N	N	Y	N	Y
FLORIDA						
1 *Miller, J.*	N	N	N	Y	N	Y
2 Boyd	N	N	Y	Y	Y	Y
3 Brown	Y	Y	Y	N	Y	Y
4 *Crenshaw*	N	N	N	Y	N	Y
5 *Thurman*	N	Y	N	Y	N	Y
6 *Stearns*	N	N	N	Y	N	Y
7 *Mica*	N	N	N	Y	N	Y
8 *Keller*	N	N	N	Y	N	Y
9 *Bilirakis*	N	N	N	Y	–	Y
10 *Young*	N	N	N	Y	N	Y
11 Davis	N	Y	N	Y	N	Y
12 *Putnam*	N	N	N	Y	N	Y
13 *Miller, D.*	N	N	N	Y	N	Y
14 *Goss*	N	N	N	Y	N	Y
15 *Weldon*	N	N	N	Y	N	Y
16 *Foley*	N	N	N	Y	N	Y
17 Meek	Y	Y	Y	N	Y	N
18 *Ros-Lehtinen*	N	N	N	Y	N	Y
19 Wexler	Y	Y	Y	N	Y	Y
20 Deutsch	Y	Y	Y	N	Y	Y
21 *Diaz-Balart*	N	N	N	Y	N	Y
22 *Shaw*	N	N	N	Y	N	Y
23 Hastings	Y	Y	Y	N	Y	N
GEORGIA						
1 *Kingston*	N	N	N	Y	N	Y
2 Bishop	Y	Y	Y	N	Y	Y
3 *Collins*	N	N	N	Y	N	Y
4 McKinney	Y	Y	Y	N	Y	N
5 Lewis	Y	Y	Y	N	Y	N
6 *Isakson*	N	N	N	Y	N	Y
7 *Barr*	N	N	N	Y	N	Y
8 *Chambliss*	N	N	N	Y	N	Y
9 *Deal*	N	N	N	Y	N	Y
10 *Norwood*	N	N	N	Y	N	Y
11 *Linder*	N	N	N	Y	N	Y
HAWAII						
1 Abercrombie	Y	Y	Y	N	Y	N
2 Mink	Y	Y	Y	N	Y	N
IDAHO						
1 *Otter*	N	N	N	Y	N	Y
2 *Simpson*	N	N	N	Y	N	Y
ILLINOIS						
1 Rush	Y	Y	Y	?	?	?
2 Jackson	Y	Y	Y	N	Y	N
3 Lipinski	Y	Y	Y	N	N	Y
4 Gutierrez	Y	Y	Y	N	Y	Y
5 Blagojevich	?	?	?	?	?	?
6 *Hyde*	N	N	N	Y	N	Y
7 Davis	?	?	?	?	?	?
8 *Crane*	N	N	N	Y	N	Y
9 Schakowsky	Y	Y	Y	N	Y	N
10 *Kirk*	N	N	N	Y	N	Y
11 *Weller*	N	N	N	Y	N	Y
12 Costello	Y	Y	Y	N	N	Y
13 *Biggert*	N	N	N	Y	Y	Y

ND Northern Democrats   SD Southern Democrats

	59	60	61	62	63	64
14 ***Hastert***						
15 ***Johnson***	N	N	N	Y	N	Y
16 ***Manzullo***	N	N	N	Y	N	Y
17 Evans	Y	Y	Y	N	Y	Y
18 ***LaHood***	N	N	N	Y	N	Y
19 Phelps	Y	Y	Y	N	N	Y
20 ***Shimkus***	N	N	N	Y	N	Y
INDIANA						
1 Visclosky	Y	Y	Y	N	Y	?
2 ***Pence***	N	N	N	Y	N	Y
3 Roemer	N	Y	Y	N	Y	Y
4 ***Souder***	N	N	N	Y	Y	Y
5 ***Buyer***	N	N	N	Y	N	Y
6 ***Burton***	N	N	N	Y	N	Y
7 ***Kerns***	N	N	N	Y	N	Y
8 ***Hostettler***	N	N	N	Y	N	Y
9 Hill	N	Y	Y	N	Y	Y
10 Carson	Y	Y	Y	N	Y	Y
IOWA						
1 ***Leach***	N	N	N	Y	Y	Y
2 ***Nussle***	N	N	N	Y	N	Y
3 Boswell	Y	Y	Y	N	Y	Y
4 ***Ganske***	N	N	N	Y	Y	Y
5 ***Latham***	N	N	N	Y	Y	Y
KANSAS						
1 ***Moran***	N	N	N	Y	Y	Y
2 ***Ryun***	N	N	N	Y	N	Y
3 Moore	Y	Y	Y	N	Y	Y
4 ***Tiahrt***	N	N	N	Y	N	Y
KENTUCKY						
1 ***Whitfield***	N	N	N	Y	N	Y
2 ***Lewis***	N	N	N	Y	N	Y
3 ***Northup***	N	N	N	Y	Y	Y
4 Lucas	N	N	N	Y	N	Y
5 ***Rogers***	N	N	N	Y	N	Y
6 ***Fletcher***	N	N	N	?	N	Y
LOUISIANA						
1 ***Vitter***	N	N	N	Y	N	Y
2 Jefferson	Y	Y	Y	N	Y	Y
3 ***Tauzin***	N	N	N	Y	N	Y
4 ***McCrery***	N	N	N	Y	Y	Y
5 ***Cooksey***	N	N	N	Y	N	Y
6 ***Baker***	N	N	N	Y	N	Y
7 John	N	N	N	Y	Y	Y
MAINE						
1 Allen	N	Y	Y	N	Y	Y
2 Baldacci	Y	Y	Y	N	Y	Y
MARYLAND						
1 ***Gilchrest***	N	N	N	Y	N	Y
2 ***Ehrlich***	N	N	N	Y	?	Y
3 Cardin	Y	Y	Y	N	Y	Y
4 Wynn	Y	Y	Y	N	Y	Y
5 Hoyer	Y	Y	Y	N	Y	Y
6 ***Bartlett***	N	N	N	Y	N	Y
7 Cummings	Y	Y	Y	N	Y	Y
8 ***Morella***	N	N	N	Y	Y	Y
MASSACHUSETTS						
1 Olver	Y	Y	Y	N	Y	N
2 Neal	Y	Y	Y	N	Y	Y
3 McGovern	Y	Y	Y	N	Y	Y
4 Frank	N	Y	Y	N	Y	Y
5 Meehan	Y	Y	Y	N	Y	Y
6 Tierney	Y	Y	Y	N	Y	Y
7 Markey	Y	Y	Y	N	Y	Y
8 Capuano	Y	Y	Y	N	Y	Y
9 Lynch	Y	Y	Y	N	Y	Y
10 Delahunt	Y	Y	Y	N	Y	Y
MICHIGAN						
1 Stupak	Y	Y	Y	N	Y	Y
2 ***Hoekstra***	N	N	N	Y	Y	Y
3 ***Ehlers***	N	N	N	Y	Y	Y
4 ***Camp***	N	N	N	Y	N	Y
5 Barcia	Y	Y	N	Y	Y	Y
6 ***Upton***	N	N	N	Y	Y	Y
7 ***Smith***	N	N	N	Y	N	Y
8 ***Rogers***	N	N	N	Y	Y	Y
9 Kildee	Y	Y	Y	N	Y	Y
10 Bonior	Y	Y	Y	N	Y	Y
11 ***Knollenberg***	N	N	N	Y	N	Y
12 Levin	Y	Y	Y	N	Y	Y
13 Rivers	Y	Y	Y	N	Y	Y
14 Conyers	Y	Y	Y	N	Y	N
15 Kilpatrick	+	+	+	–	+	+
16 Dingell	Y	Y	Y	N	Y	Y

	59	60	61	62	63	64
MINNESOTA						
1 ***Gutknecht***	N	N	N	Y	Y	Y
2 ***Kennedy***	N	N	N	Y	N	Y
3 ***Ramstad***	N	N	N	Y	N	Y
4 McCollum	Y	Y	Y	N	Y	Y
5 Sabo	Y	Y	Y	N	Y	N
6 Luther	Y	Y	Y	N	Y	Y
7 Peterson	N	Y	Y	Y	Y	Y
8 Oberstar	Y	Y	Y	N	Y	N
MISSISSIPPI						
1 ***Wicker***	N	N	N	Y	N	Y
2 Thompson	Y	Y	Y	N	Y	Y
3 ***Pickering***	N	N	N	Y	Y	Y
4 Shows	Y	Y	Y	N	Y	Y
5 Taylor	N	N	N	Y	Y	Y
MISSOURI						
1 Clay	Y	Y	Y	N	Y	Y
2 ***Akin***	N	N	N	Y	N	Y
3 Gephardt	Y	Y	Y	N	Y	Y
4 Skelton	N	Y	Y	N	Y	Y
5 McCarthy	Y	Y	Y	N	Y	Y
6 ***Graves***	N	N	N	Y	N	Y
7 ***Blunt***	N	N	N	Y	N	Y
8 ***Emerson***	N	N	N	Y	Y	Y
9 ***Hulshof***	N	N	N	Y	Y	Y
MONTANA						
AL ***Rehberg***	N	N	N	Y	Y	Y
NEBRASKA						
1 ***Bereuter***	N	N	N	Y	Y	Y
2 ***Terry***	N	N	N	N	N	Y
3 ***Osborne***	N	N	N	Y	N	Y
NEVADA						
1 Berkley	Y	Y	Y	N	Y	Y
2 ***Gibbons***	N	N	N	Y	N	Y
NEW HAMPSHIRE						
1 ***Sununu***	N	N	N	Y	Y	Y
2 ***Bass***	N	N	N	Y	N	Y
NEW JERSEY						
1 Andrews	Y	Y	Y	N	Y	Y
2 ***LoBiondo***	N	N	N	Y	Y	Y
3 ***Saxton***	N	N	N	Y	N	Y
4 ***Smith***	N	N	N	Y	Y	Y
5 ***Roukema***	N	N	N	Y	N	?
6 Pallone	Y	Y	Y	N	Y	Y
7 ***Ferguson***	N	N	N	Y	N	Y
8 Pascrell	Y	Y	Y	N	Y	Y
9 Rothman	Y	Y	Y	N	Y	Y
10 Payne	Y	Y	Y	N	Y	N
11 ***Frelinghuysen***	N	N	N	Y	N	Y
12 Holt	Y	Y	Y	N	Y	Y
13 Menendez	Y	Y	Y	N	Y	Y
NEW MEXICO						
1 ***Wilson***	N	N	N	Y	Y	Y
2 ***Skeen***	N	N	N	Y	N	Y
3 Udall	Y	Y	Y	N	Y	N
NEW YORK						
1 ***Grucci***	N	N	N	Y	N	Y
2 Israel	Y	Y	Y	N	Y	Y
3 ***King***	N	N	N	N	N	Y
4 McCarthy	Y	Y	Y	N	Y	Y
5 Ackerman	Y	Y	Y	N	Y	Y
6 Meeks	Y	Y	Y	N	Y	Y
7 Crowley	Y	Y	Y	N	Y	Y
8 Nadler	Y	Y	Y	N	Y	N
9 Weiner	Y	Y	Y	N	Y	Y
10 Towns	Y	Y	Y	N	?	?
11 Owens	Y	Y	Y	N	Y	Y
12 Velázquez	Y	Y	Y	N	Y	Y
13 ***Fossella***	N	N	N	Y	N	Y
14 Maloney	Y	Y	Y	N	Y	Y
15 Rangel	Y	Y	Y	N	Y	N
16 Serrano	Y	Y	Y	N	Y	Y
17 Engel	Y	Y	Y	N	Y	Y
18 Lowey	Y	Y	Y	N	Y	Y
19 ***Kelly***	N	N	N	Y	Y	Y
20 ***Gilman***	Y	Y	N	N	N	?
21 McNulty	N	Y	Y	N	Y	Y
22 ***Sweeney***	N	N	N	Y	Y	Y
23 ***Boehlert***	N	N	N	Y	N	Y
24 ***McHugh***	N	N	N	Y	N	Y
25 ***Walsh***	N	N	N	Y	N	Y
26 Hinchey	Y	Y	Y	N	Y	N
27 ***Reynolds***	N	N	N	Y	N	Y
28 Slaughter	Y	Y	Y	N	?	?
29 LaFalce	Y	Y	Y	N	Y	Y

	59	60	61	62	63	64
30 ***Quinn***	N	N	N	Y	N	Y
31 ***Houghton***	N	N	N	Y	N	Y
NORTH CAROLINA						
1 Clayton	Y	Y	Y	N	Y	N
2 Etheridge	Y	Y	Y	N	Y	Y
3 ***Jones***	N	N	N	Y	N	Y
4 Price	Y	Y	Y	N	Y	Y
5 ***Burr***	N	N	N	Y	N	Y
6 ***Coble***	N	N	N	Y	Y	Y
7 McIntyre	Y	Y	Y	N	Y	Y
8 ***Hayes***	N	N	N	Y	N	Y
9 ***Myrick***	N	N	N	Y	N	Y
10 ***Ballenger***	N	N	N	Y	N	Y
11 ***Taylor***	N	N	N	Y	N	Y
12 Watt	Y	Y	Y	N	Y	N
NORTH DAKOTA						
AL Pomeroy	Y	Y	Y	N	Y	Y
OHIO						
1 ***Chabot***	N	N	N	Y	N	Y
2 ***Portman***	N	N	N	Y	Y	Y
3 Hall	Y	Y	Y	N	Y	Y
4 ***Oxley***	N	N	N	Y	N	Y
5 ***Gillmor***	N	N	N	Y	Y	Y
6 Strickland	Y	Y	Y	N	Y	Y
7 ***Hobson***	N	N	N	Y	Y	Y
8 ***Boehner***	N	N	N	Y	N	Y
9 Kaptur	Y	Y	Y	N	Y	Y
10 Kucinich	Y	Y	Y	N	Y	Y
11 Jones	Y	Y	Y	N	Y	N
12 ***Tiberi***	N	N	N	Y	N	Y
13 Brown	Y	Y	Y	N	Y	Y
14 Sawyer	Y	Y	Y	N	Y	Y
15 ***Pryce***	N	N	N	Y	N	Y
16 ***Regula***	N	N	N	Y	N	Y
17 Traficant	?	?	?	?	?	?
18 ***Ney***	N	N	N	Y	N	Y
19 ***LaTourette***	N	N	N	Y	N	Y
OKLAHOMA						
1 ***Sullivan***	N	N	N	Y	N	Y
2 Carson	N	Y	Y	N	Y	Y
3 ***Watkins***	N	N	N	Y	N	Y
4 ***Watts***	N	N	N	Y	N	Y
5 ***Istook***	N	Y	N	Y	N	+
6 ***Lucas***	N	N	N	Y	N	Y
OREGON						
1 Wu	Y	Y	Y	N	Y	Y
2 ***Walden***	N	N	N	Y	Y	Y
3 Blumenauer	N	Y	Y	N	Y	Y
4 DeFazio	Y	Y	Y	N	Y	Y
5 Hooley	Y	Y	Y	N	Y	Y
PENNSYLVANIA						
1 Brady	Y	Y	Y	N	Y	Y
2 Fattah	Y	Y	Y	?	Y	Y
3 Borski	Y	Y	Y	N	Y	Y
4 ***Hart***	N	N	N	Y	Y	Y
5 ***Peterson***	N	N	N	Y	N	Y
6 Holden	N	N	N	Y	Y	Y
7 ***Weldon***	N	N	N	Y	Y	Y
8 ***Greenwood***	N	N	N	Y	Y	Y
9 ***Shuster, Bill***	N	N	N	Y	N	Y
10 ***Sherwood***	N	N	N	Y	N	Y
11 Kanjorski	Y	Y	Y	N	Y	Y
12 Murtha	?	?	?	?	Y	Y
13 Hoeffel	Y	Y	Y	N	Y	Y
14 Coyne	Y	Y	Y	N	Y	N
15 ***Toomey***	N	N	N	Y	N	Y
16 ***Pitts***	N	N	N	Y	N	Y
17 ***Gekas***	N	N	N	Y	N	Y
18 Doyle	Y	Y	Y	N	Y	Y
19 ***Platts***	N	N	N	Y	Y	Y
20 Mascara	Y	Y	Y	N	?	?
21 ***English***	N	N	N	Y	N	Y
RHODE ISLAND						
1 Kennedy	Y	Y	Y	N	Y	Y
2 Langevin	Y	Y	Y	N	Y	Y
SOUTH CAROLINA						
1 ***Brown***	N	N	N	Y	N	Y
2 ***Wilson***	N	N	N	Y	N	Y
3 ***Graham***	N	N	N	Y	Y	Y
4 ***DeMint***	N	N	N	Y	N	Y
5 Spratt	Y	Y	Y	N	Y	Y
6 Clyburn	Y	Y	Y	N	Y	N
SOUTH DAKOTA						
AL ***Thune***	N	N	N	Y	N	Y

	59	60	61	62	63	64
TENNESSEE						
1 ***Jenkins***	N	N	N	Y	N	Y
2 ***Duncan***	Y	N	N	Y	N	Y
3 ***Wamp***	N	N	N	Y	N	Y
4 ***Hilleary***	N	N	N	Y	Y	Y
5 Clement	Y	Y	Y	N	Y	Y
6 Gordon	N	Y	Y	Y	Y	Y
7 ***Bryant***	N	N	N	Y	N	Y
8 Tanner	Y	N	N	Y	Y	Y
9 Ford	Y	Y	Y	N	Y	+
TEXAS						
1 Sandlin	Y	Y	Y	N	Y	Y
2 Turner	Y	Y	Y	N	Y	Y
3 ***Johnson, Sam***	N	N	N	Y	N	Y
4 Hall	N	Y	N	Y	Y	Y
5 ***Sessions***	N	N	N	Y	N	Y
6 ***Barton***	N	N	N	Y	N	Y
7 ***Culberson***	N	N	N	Y	N	Y
8 ***Brady***	N	N	N	Y	N	Y
9 Lampson	Y	Y	Y	N	Y	Y
10 Doggett	Y	Y	Y	N	Y	Y
11 Edwards	Y	Y	Y	N	N	Y
12 ***Granger***	N	N	N	Y	Y	Y
13 ***Thornberry***	N	N	N	Y	N	Y
14 ***Paul***	Y	N	N	Y	N	Y
15 Hinojosa	+	+	+	–	+	+
16 Reyes	Y	Y	Y	N	Y	Y
17 Stenholm	N	N	N	Y	Y	Y
18 Jackson-Lee	Y	Y	Y	N	Y	Y
19 ***Combest***	N	N	N	Y	N	Y
20 Gonzalez	Y	Y	Y	N	Y	Y
21 ***Smith***	N	N	N	Y	N	Y
22 ***DeLay***	N	N	N	Y	N	Y
23 ***Bonilla***	N	N	N	Y	N	Y
24 Frost	Y	Y	Y	N	Y	Y
25 Bentsen	?	?	Y	N	Y	Y
26 ***Armey***	N	N	N	Y	N	Y
27 Ortiz	Y	Y	Y	N	Y	Y
28 Rodriguez	Y	Y	Y	N	Y	Y
29 Green	Y	Y	Y	N	Y	Y
30 Johnson, E.B.	Y	Y	Y	N	Y	Y
UTAH						
1 ***Hansen***	N	N	N	Y	N	Y
2 Matheson	Y	Y	Y	N	Y	Y
3 ***Cannon***	N	Y	N	Y	Y	Y
VERMONT						
AL *Sanders*	Y	Y	Y	N	Y	Y
VIRGINIA						
1 ***Davis, Jo Ann***	N	N	N	Y	N	Y
2 ***Schrock***	N	N	N	Y	N	Y
3 Scott	Y	Y	Y	N	Y	N
4 ***Forbes***	N	N	N	Y	N	Y
5 *Goode*	N	N	N	Y	N	Y
6 ***Goodlatte***	N	N	N	Y	N	Y
7 ***Cantor***	N	N	N	Y	N	Y
8 Moran	N	N	N	Y	Y	N
9 Boucher	N	N	N	Y	Y	Y
10 ***Wolf***	N	N	N	Y	N	Y
11 ***Davis, T.***	N	N	N	Y	Y	Y
WASHINGTON						
1 Inslee	Y	Y	Y	N	Y	Y
2 Larsen	Y	Y	Y	N	Y	Y
3 Baird	Y	Y	Y	N	Y	Y
4 ***Hastings***	N	N	N	Y	N	Y
5 ***Nethercutt***	N	N	N	Y	N	Y
6 Dicks	Y	Y	Y	N	Y	Y
7 McDermott	Y	Y	Y	N	Y	N
8 ***Dunn***	N	N	N	Y	Y	Y
9 Smith	Y	N	Y	N	Y	Y
WEST VIRGINIA						
1 Mollohan	Y	Y	Y	N	Y	N
2 ***Capito***	N	N	N	Y	Y	Y
3 Rahall	Y	Y	Y	N	Y	Y
WISCONSIN						
1 ***Ryan***	N	N	N	Y	Y	Y
2 Baldwin	Y	Y	Y	N	Y	Y
3 Kind	N	N	N	N	Y	Y
4 Kleczka	Y	Y	Y	N	Y	Y
5 Barrett	?	?	?	?	?	?
6 ***Petri***	N	N	N	Y	Y	Y
7 Obey	Y	Y	Y	N	Y	Y
8 ***Green***	N	N	N	Y	Y	Y
9 ***Sensenbrenner***	N	N	N	Y	Y	Y
WYOMING						
AL ***Cubin***	N	N	N	Y	N	Y

Southern states - Ala., Ark., Fla., Ga., Ky., La., Miss., N.C., Okla., S.C., Tenn., Texas, Va.

Key

Y	Voted for (yea).
#	Paired for.
+	Announced for.
N	Voted against (nay).
X	Paired against.
−	Announced against.
P	Voted "present."
C	Voted "present" to avoid possible conflict of interest.
?	Did not vote or otherwise make a position known.

Democrats **Republicans**
Independents

65. Procedural Motion/Journal. Approval of the House Journal of Monday, March 18, 2002. Approved 363-44: R 195-14; D 166-30 (ND 118-26, SD 48-4); I 2-0. March 19, 2002.

66. H Res 368. Pentagon Restoration/Adoption. Saxton, R-N.J., motion to suspend the rules and adopt the resolution that would pay tribute to the work being done to restore that part of the Pentagon damaged during the Sept. 11 terrorist attack. Motion agreed to 413-0: R 212-0; D 199-0 (ND 146-0, SD 53-0); I 2-0. A two-thirds majority of those present and voting (276 in this case) is required for adoption under suspension of the rules. March 19, 2002.

67. HR 2509. Foreign Currency Production/Passage. Bereuter, R-Neb., motion to suspend the rules and pass the bill that would allow the Treasury Department to produce another country's currency, stamps and other security documents if that country pays the printing costs and the State Department determines the production is consistent with U.S. foreign policy. Motion agreed to 403-11: R 204-10; D 198-0 (ND 145-0, SD 53-0); I 1-1. A two-thirds majority of those present and voting (276 in this case) is required for passage under suspension of the rules. March 19, 2002.

68. HR 2804. James R. Browning Building/Passage. Cooksey, R-La., motion to suspend the rules and pass the bill that would name a federal building in San Francisco for James R. Browning, a former judge on the Ninth Circuit Court of Appeals. Motion agreed to 403-1: R 209-1; D 192-0 (ND 141-0, SD 51-0); I 2-0. A two-thirds majority of those present and voting (270 in this case) is required for passage under suspension of the rules. March 19, 2002.

69. Procedural Motion/Journal. Approval of the House Journal of Tuesday, March 19, 2002. Approved 351-55: R 195-15; D 154-40 (ND 110-34, SD 44-6); I 2-0. March 20, 2002.

70. H Res 339. Ukrainian Elections/Adoption. Smith, R-N.J., motion to suspend the rules and adopt the resolution that would urge Ukraine to allow fair and open political elections, including the enforcement of a new election law and compliance with international standards for elections as set out in the 1990 Copenhagen Document of the Organization for Security and Cooperation in Europe. Motion agreed to 408-1: R 210-1; D 197-0 (ND 146-0, SD 51-0); I 1-0. A two-thirds majority of those present and voting (273 in this case) is required for adoption under suspension of the rules. March 20, 2002.

71. HR 3924. Working From Home/Passage. Passage of the bill that would allow private contractors working for federal agencies to telecommute from their homes or other off-site areas unless it conflicts with the contracting agency's needs. Passed 421-0: R 216-0; D 203-0 (ND 151-0, SD 52-0); I 2-0. March 20, 2002.

72. H Res 371. Tribute to Women/Adoption. Morella, R-Md., motion to suspend the rules and adopt the resolution that would pay tribute to the contributions of women in honor of Women's History Month. Motion agreed to 423-0: R 217-0; D 204-0 (ND 152-0, SD 52-0); I 2-0. A two-thirds majority of those present and voting (282 in this case) is required for adoption under suspension of the rules. March 20, 2002.

	65	66	67	68	69	70	71	72
ALABAMA								
1 *Callahan*	Y	Y	Y	Y	Y	Y	Y	Y
2 *Everett*	Y	Y	Y	Y	Y	Y	Y	Y
3 *Riley*	+	+	+	Y	Y	Y	Y	Y
4 *Aderholt*	N	Y	Y	Y	N	Y	Y	Y
5 Cramer	Y	Y	Y	Y	Y	Y	Y	Y
6 *Bachus*	Y	Y	Y	Y	Y	Y	Y	Y
7 Hilliard	N	Y	Y	Y	N	Y	Y	Y
ALASKA								
AL *Young*	Y	Y	Y	Y	?	Y	Y	Y
ARIZONA								
1 *Flake*	Y	Y	N	Y	Y	Y	Y	Y
2 Pastor	Y	Y	Y	Y	Y	Y	Y	Y
3 *Stump*	Y	Y	Y	Y	Y	Y	Y	Y
4 *Shadegg*	Y	Y	Y	Y	?	?	?	?
5 *Kolbe*	Y	Y	Y	Y	Y	Y	Y	Y
6 *Hayworth*	Y	Y	Y	Y	Y	Y	Y	Y
ARKANSAS								
1 Berry	Y	Y	Y	Y	Y	Y	Y	Y
2 Snyder	Y	Y	Y	Y	Y	Y	Y	Y
3 *Boozman*	Y	Y	Y	Y	Y	Y	Y	Y
4 Ross	Y	Y	Y	Y	Y	Y	Y	Y
CALIFORNIA								
1 Thompson	Y	Y	Y	Y	N	Y	Y	Y
2 *Herger*	Y	?	Y	Y	Y	Y	Y	Y
3 *Ose*	Y	Y	N	Y	Y	Y	Y	Y
4 *Doolittle*	Y	Y	Y	Y	Y	Y	Y	Y
5 Matsui	Y	Y	Y	Y	Y	Y	Y	Y
6 Woolsey	Y	Y	Y	Y	Y	Y	Y	Y
7 Miller, George	Y	Y	Y	Y	N	Y	Y	Y
8 Pelosi	Y	Y	Y	Y	Y	Y	Y	Y
9 Lee	Y	Y	Y	Y	Y	Y	Y	Y
10 Tauscher	Y	Y	Y	Y	Y	Y	Y	Y
11 *Pombo*	Y	Y	Y	Y	Y	Y	Y	Y
12 Lantos	Y	Y	Y	Y	?	?	Y	Y
13 Stark	N	Y	Y	Y	?	?	Y	Y
14 Eshoo	Y	Y	Y	Y	Y	Y	Y	Y
15 Honda	Y	Y	Y	Y	Y	Y	Y	Y
16 Lofgren	Y	Y	Y	Y	Y	Y	?	Y
17 Farr	Y	Y	Y	Y	Y	Y	Y	Y
18 Condit	?	?	?	?	N	Y	Y	Y
19 *Radanovich*	Y	Y	Y	Y	Y	Y	Y	Y
20 Dooley	Y	Y	Y	Y	Y	Y	Y	Y
21 *Thomas*	Y	Y	Y	Y	Y	?	Y	Y
22 Capps	Y	Y	Y	Y	Y	Y	Y	Y
23 *Gallegly*	Y	Y	Y	Y	Y	Y	Y	Y
24 Sherman	Y	Y	Y	Y	Y	Y	Y	Y
25 *McKeon*	Y	Y	Y	Y	Y	Y	Y	Y
26 Berman	Y	Y	Y	Y	Y	Y	Y	Y
27 Schiff	Y	Y	Y	Y	Y	Y	Y	Y
28 *Dreier*	Y	Y	Y	Y	Y	Y	Y	Y
29 Waxman	Y	Y	Y	Y	Y	Y	Y	Y
30 Becerra	Y	Y	Y	Y	Y	Y	Y	Y
31 Solis	Y	Y	Y	?	Y	Y	Y	Y
32 Watson	Y	Y	Y	Y	Y	Y	Y	Y
33 Roybal-Allard	Y	Y	Y	Y	Y	Y	Y	Y
34 Napolitano	Y	Y	Y	Y	Y	Y	Y	Y
35 Waters	N	Y	Y	N	Y	Y	Y	Y
36 Harman	Y	Y	Y	Y	Y	Y	Y	Y
37 Millender-McD.	Y	Y	Y	Y	Y	Y	Y	Y
38 *Horn*	Y	Y	Y	Y	Y	Y	Y	Y

	65	66	67	68	69	70	71	72
39 *Royce*	Y	Y	Y	Y	Y	Y	Y	Y
40 *Lewis*	?	?	?	?	Y	Y	Y	Y
41 *Miller, Gary*	Y	Y	Y	N	Y	Y	Y	Y
42 Baca	Y	Y	Y	Y	Y	Y	Y	Y
43 *Calvert*	Y	Y	Y	Y	Y	Y	Y	Y
44 *Bono*	Y	Y	Y	Y	Y	Y	Y	Y
45 *Rohrabacher*	Y	Y	N	Y	Y	Y	Y	Y
46 Sanchez	Y	Y	Y	Y	Y	Y	Y	Y
47 *Cox*	Y	Y	Y	Y	?	Y	Y	Y
48 *Issa*	Y	Y	Y	Y	Y	Y	Y	Y
49 Davis	Y	Y	Y	Y	Y	Y	Y	Y
50 Filner	N	Y	N	Y	N	Y	Y	Y
51 *Cunningham*	Y	Y	Y	Y	Y	Y	Y	Y
52 *Hunter*	Y	Y	Y	Y	Y	Y	Y	Y
COLORADO								
1 DeGette	Y	Y	Y	Y	Y	Y	Y	Y
2 Udall	Y	Y	Y	N	Y	Y	Y	Y
3 *McInnis*	Y	Y	Y	Y	Y	Y	Y	Y
4 *Schaffer*	N	Y	Y	N	Y	Y	Y	Y
5 *Hefley*	N	Y	Y	N	Y	Y	Y	Y
6 *Tancredo*	P	Y	N	Y	P	Y	Y	Y
CONNECTICUT								
1 Larson	Y	Y	Y	N	Y	Y	Y	Y
2 *Simmons*	Y	Y	Y	Y	Y	Y	Y	Y
3 DeLauro	Y	Y	Y	Y	Y	Y	Y	Y
4 *Shays*	+	+	+	+	Y	Y	Y	Y
5 Maloney	Y	Y	Y	Y	Y	Y	Y	Y
6 *Johnson*	Y	Y	Y	Y	Y	?	Y	Y
DELAWARE								
AL *Castle*	Y	Y	Y	Y	Y	Y	Y	Y
FLORIDA								
1 *Miller, J.*	Y	Y	N	Y	Y	Y	Y	Y
2 Boyd	Y	Y	Y	Y	Y	Y	Y	Y
3 Brown	Y	Y	Y	Y	Y	Y	Y	Y
4 *Crenshaw*	Y	Y	Y	Y	Y	Y	Y	Y
5 Thurman	Y	Y	Y	Y	Y	Y	Y	Y
6 *Stearns*	Y	Y	Y	Y	Y	Y	Y	Y
7 *Mica*	Y	Y	Y	Y	Y	?	Y	Y
8 *Keller*	Y	Y	Y	Y	Y	Y	Y	Y
9 *Bilirakis*	Y	Y	Y	Y	Y	Y	Y	Y
10 *Young*	?	?	?	?	Y	Y	Y	Y
11 Davis	Y	Y	Y	?	Y	?	?	?
12 *Putnam*	Y	Y	Y	Y	Y	Y	Y	Y
13 *Miller, D.*	Y	Y	Y	Y	Y	Y	Y	Y
14 *Goss*	Y	Y	Y	Y	Y	Y	Y	Y
15 *Weldon*	Y	Y	Y	Y	Y	Y	Y	Y
16 *Foley*	Y	Y	Y	Y	Y	Y	Y	Y
17 Meek	Y	Y	Y	Y	Y	Y	Y	Y
18 *Ros-Lehtinen*	Y	Y	Y	Y	Y	Y	Y	Y
19 Wexler	Y	Y	Y	?	Y	Y	Y	Y
20 Deutsch	Y	Y	Y	?	Y	Y	Y	Y
21 *Diaz-Balart*	Y	Y	Y	Y	Y	Y	Y	Y
22 *Shaw*	Y	Y	Y	Y	Y	Y	Y	Y
23 Hastings	N	Y	Y	N	N	Y	Y	Y
GEORGIA								
1 *Kingston*	Y	Y	N	Y	Y	Y	Y	Y
2 Bishop	Y	Y	Y	Y	Y	Y	Y	Y
3 *Collins*	Y	Y	Y	Y	Y	Y	Y	Y
4 McKinney	Y	Y	Y	Y	Y	Y	Y	Y
5 Lewis	Y	Y	Y	N	Y	Y	Y	Y
6 *Isakson*	Y	Y	Y	Y	Y	Y	Y	Y
7 *Barr*	Y	Y	Y	Y	Y	Y	Y	Y
8 *Chambliss*	Y	Y	Y	Y	Y	Y	Y	Y
9 *Deal*	Y	Y	Y	Y	Y	Y	Y	Y
10 *Norwood*	Y	Y	Y	Y	Y	Y	Y	Y
11 *Linder*	Y	Y	Y	?	Y	Y	Y	Y
HAWAII								
1 Abercrombie	Y	Y	Y	Y	Y	Y	Y	Y
2 Mink	Y	Y	Y	Y	Y	Y	Y	Y
IDAHO								
1 *Otter*	Y	Y	Y	Y	Y	Y	Y	Y
2 *Simpson*	Y	Y	Y	Y	Y	Y	Y	Y
ILLINOIS								
1 Rush	?	?	?	?	?	?	?	?
2 Jackson	Y	Y	Y	Y	Y	Y	Y	Y
3 Lipinski	?	?	?	?	?	?	?	?
4 Gutierrez	?	?	?	?	?	?	?	?
5 Blagojevich	?	?	?	?	?	?	?	?
6 *Hyde*	Y	Y	Y	Y	Y	Y	Y	Y
7 Davis	?	?	?	?	Y	Y	Y	Y
8 *Crane*	N	Y	Y	Y	N	Y	Y	Y
9 Schakowsky	?	?	?	?	N	Y	Y	Y
10 *Kirk*	Y	Y	Y	Y	Y	Y	Y	Y
11 *Weller*	N	Y	Y	Y	N	Y	Y	Y
12 Costello	N	Y	Y	N	N	Y	Y	Y
13 *Biggert*	?	?	?	?	Y	Y	Y	Y

ND Northern Democrats   SD Southern Democrats

	65	66	67	68	69	70	71	72
14 ***Hastert***								
15 ***Johnson***	Y	Y	Y	Y	Y	Y	Y	Y
16 ***Manzullo***	Y	Y	N	Y	Y	Y	Y	Y
17 Evans	Y	Y	Y	Y	Y	Y	Y	Y
18 ***LaHood***	Y	Y	Y	Y	Y	Y	Y	Y
19 Phelps	Y	Y	Y	Y	N	Y	Y	Y
20 ***Shimkus***	Y	Y	Y	Y	Y	Y	Y	Y
INDIANA								
1 Visclosky	N	Y	Y	Y	N	Y	Y	Y
2 ***Pence***	Y	Y	Y	Y	Y	Y	Y	Y
3 Roemer	Y	Y	Y	Y	Y	Y	Y	Y
4 ***Souder***	?	Y	Y	Y	Y	Y	Y	Y
5 ***Buyer***	Y	Y	Y	Y	?	Y	Y	Y
6 ***Burton***	Y	Y	Y	Y	Y	Y	Y	Y
7 ***Kerns***	Y	Y	Y	Y	Y	Y	Y	Y
8 ***Hostettler***	Y	Y	Y	Y	Y	Y	Y	Y
9 Hill	Y	Y	Y	Y	N	Y	Y	Y
10 Carson	Y	Y	Y	Y	Y	Y	Y	Y
IOWA								
1 ***Leach***	Y	Y	Y	Y	Y	Y	Y	Y
2 ***Nussle***	Y	Y	Y	Y	Y	Y	Y	Y
3 Boswell	Y	Y	Y	Y	Y	Y	Y	Y
4 ***Ganske***	Y	Y	Y	Y	Y	Y	Y	Y
5 ***Latham***	N	Y	Y	Y	Y	Y	Y	Y
KANSAS								
1 ***Moran***	Y	Y	Y	Y	Y	Y	Y	Y
2 ***Ryun***	Y	Y	Y	Y	Y	Y	Y	Y
3 Moore	N	Y	Y	Y	N	Y	Y	Y
4 ***Tiahrt***	Y	Y	Y	Y	N	Y	Y	Y
KENTUCKY								
1 ***Whitfield***	Y	Y	Y	Y	Y	Y	Y	Y
2 ***Lewis***	Y	Y	Y	Y	Y	Y	Y	Y
3 ***Northup***	Y	Y	Y	Y	Y	Y	+	Y
4 Lucas	?	Y	Y	Y	Y	Y	Y	Y
5 ***Rogers***	Y	Y	Y	Y	Y	Y	Y	Y
6 ***Fletcher***	Y	Y	Y	Y	Y	Y	Y	Y
LOUISIANA								
1 ***Vitter***	Y	Y	Y	Y	Y	Y	Y	Y
2 Jefferson	Y	Y	Y	Y	Y	Y	Y	Y
3 ***Tauzin***	Y	Y	Y	Y	?	?	Y	Y
4 ***McCrery***	Y	Y	Y	Y	Y	Y	Y	Y
5 ***Cooksey***	Y	Y	Y	Y	Y	Y	Y	Y
6 ***Baker***	Y	Y	Y	Y	Y	Y	Y	Y
7 John	Y	Y	Y	Y	Y	Y	Y	Y
MAINE								
1 Allen	N	Y	Y	Y	Y	Y	Y	Y
2 Baldacci	Y	Y	Y	Y	Y	Y	Y	Y
MARYLAND								
1 ***Gilchrest***	Y	Y	Y	Y	Y	Y	Y	Y
2 ***Ehrlich***	Y	Y	Y	Y	?	?	Y	?
3 Cardin	Y	Y	Y	Y	Y	Y	Y	Y
4 Wynn	Y	Y	Y	Y	Y	Y	Y	Y
5 Hoyer	Y	Y	Y	Y	Y	Y	Y	Y
6 ***Bartlett***	Y	Y	Y	Y	Y	Y	Y	Y
7 Cummings	Y	Y	Y	?	Y	Y	Y	Y
8 ***Morella***	Y	Y	Y	Y	Y	Y	?	?
MASSACHUSETTS								
1 Olver	Y	Y	Y	Y	Y	Y	Y	Y
2 Neal	Y	Y	Y	Y	Y	Y	Y	Y
3 McGovern	Y	Y	Y	Y	Y	Y	Y	Y
4 Frank	Y	Y	Y	Y	Y	Y	Y	Y
5 Meehan	Y	Y	Y	Y	Y	Y	Y	Y
6 Tierney	Y	Y	Y	Y	?	Y	Y	Y
7 Markey	Y	Y	Y	Y	?	Y	Y	Y
8 Capuano	N	Y	Y	Y	N	Y	Y	Y
9 Lynch	Y	Y	Y	Y	Y	Y	Y	Y
10 Delahunt	Y	Y	Y	Y	Y	Y	Y	Y
MICHIGAN								
1 Stupak	N	Y	Y	Y	N	Y	Y	Y
2 ***Hoekstra***	Y	Y	Y	Y	Y	Y	Y	Y
3 ***Ehlers***	Y	Y	Y	Y	Y	Y	Y	Y
4 ***Camp***	Y	Y	Y	Y	Y	Y	Y	Y
5 Barcia	?	?	?	?	Y	Y	Y	Y
6 ***Upton***	Y	Y	Y	Y	Y	Y	Y	Y
7 ***Smith***	Y	Y	Y	Y	Y	Y	Y	Y
8 ***Rogers***	Y	Y	Y	Y	Y	Y	Y	Y
9 Kildee	Y	Y	Y	Y	Y	Y	Y	Y
10 Bonior	Y	Y	Y	Y	Y	Y	Y	Y
11 ***Knollenberg***	Y	Y	Y	Y	Y	Y	Y	Y
12 Levin	Y	Y	Y	Y	Y	Y	Y	Y
13 Rivers	Y	Y	Y	Y	Y	Y	Y	Y
14 Conyers	Y	Y	Y	Y	Y	Y	Y	Y
15 Kilpatrick	Y	Y	Y	Y	Y	Y	Y	Y
16 Dingell	?	?	?	?	?	?	Y	Y
MINNESOTA								
1 ***Gutknecht***	N	Y	Y	Y	N	Y	Y	Y
2 ***Kennedy***	N	Y	Y	Y	N	Y	Y	Y
3 ***Ramstad***	N	Y	Y	Y	N	Y	Y	Y
4 McCollum	Y	Y	Y	Y	Y	Y	Y	Y
5 Sabo	N	Y	Y	Y	N	Y	Y	Y
6 Luther	Y	Y	Y	Y	Y	Y	Y	Y
7 Peterson	N	Y	Y	Y	N	Y	Y	Y
8 Oberstar	Y	Y	Y	Y	N	Y	Y	Y
MISSISSIPPI								
1 ***Wicker***	Y	Y	Y	Y	N	Y	Y	Y
2 Thompson	N	Y	Y	Y	N	Y	Y	Y
3 ***Pickering***	Y	Y	Y	Y	Y	Y	Y	Y
4 Shows	+	+	+	+	+	+	+	+
5 Taylor	N	Y	Y	Y	N	Y	Y	Y
MISSOURI								
1 Clay	Y	Y	Y	Y	?	?	Y	Y
2 ***Akin***	Y	Y	Y	Y	Y	Y	Y	Y
3 Gephardt	Y	Y	Y	Y	Y	Y	Y	Y
4 Skelton	Y	Y	Y	Y	Y	Y	Y	Y
5 McCarthy	Y	Y	Y	Y	Y	Y	Y	Y
6 ***Graves***	Y	Y	Y	Y	Y	Y	Y	Y
7 ***Blunt***	?	Y	Y	Y	Y	Y	Y	Y
8 ***Emerson***	Y	Y	Y	Y	Y	Y	Y	Y
9 ***Hulshof***	N	Y	Y	Y	Y	Y	Y	Y
MONTANA								
AL ***Rehberg***	Y	Y	Y	Y	Y	Y	Y	Y
NEBRASKA								
1 ***Bereuter***	Y	Y	Y	Y	Y	Y	Y	Y
2 ***Terry***	Y	Y	Y	Y	?	Y	Y	Y
3 ***Osborne***	Y	Y	Y	Y	Y	Y	Y	Y
NEVADA								
1 Berkley	?	Y	Y	Y	Y	Y	Y	Y
2 ***Gibbons***	Y	Y	Y	Y	Y	Y	Y	Y
NEW HAMPSHIRE								
1 ***Sununu***	Y	Y	Y	Y	Y	Y	Y	Y
2 ***Bass***	Y	Y	Y	Y	Y	Y	Y	Y
NEW JERSEY								
1 Andrews	Y	Y	Y	Y	Y	Y	Y	Y
2 ***LoBiondo***	N	Y	Y	Y	N	Y	Y	Y
3 ***Saxton***	Y	Y	Y	Y	Y	Y	Y	Y
4 ***Smith***	Y	Y	Y	Y	Y	Y	Y	Y
5 ***Roukema***	Y	Y	Y	?	Y	Y	Y	Y
6 Pallone	Y	Y	Y	Y	Y	Y	Y	Y
7 ***Ferguson***	Y	Y	Y	Y	Y	Y	Y	Y
8 Pascrell	Y	Y	Y	?	Y	Y	Y	Y
9 Rothman	Y	Y	Y	Y	Y	Y	Y	Y
10 Payne	Y	Y	Y	Y	Y	?	Y	Y
11 ***Frelinghuysen***	Y	Y	Y	Y	Y	Y	Y	Y
12 Holt	N	Y	Y	Y	Y	Y	Y	Y
13 Menendez	N	Y	Y	Y	N	Y	Y	Y
NEW MEXICO								
1 ***Wilson***	Y	Y	Y	Y	Y	Y	Y	Y
2 ***Skeen***	Y	Y	Y	Y	Y	Y	Y	Y
3 Udall	N	Y	Y	Y	N	Y	Y	Y
NEW YORK								
1 ***Grucci***	Y	Y	Y	Y	Y	Y	Y	Y
2 Israel	Y	Y	Y	Y	Y	Y	Y	Y
3 ***King***	Y	Y	Y	Y	Y	Y	Y	Y
4 McCarthy	Y	Y	Y	Y	Y	Y	Y	Y
5 Ackerman	Y	Y	Y	Y	Y	Y	Y	Y
6 Meeks	Y	Y	Y	Y	Y	Y	Y	Y
7 Crowley	Y	Y	Y	Y	Y	Y	Y	Y
8 Nadler	Y	Y	Y	Y	Y	Y	Y	Y
9 Weiner	Y	Y	Y	Y	Y	Y	Y	Y
10 Towns	Y	Y	Y	Y	Y	Y	Y	Y
11 Owens	Y	Y	Y	Y	Y	Y	Y	Y
12 Velázquez	Y	Y	Y	?	Y	Y	Y	Y
13 ***Fossella***	N	Y	Y	Y	N	Y	Y	Y
14 Maloney	Y	Y	Y	Y	Y	Y	Y	Y
15 Rangel	Y	Y	Y	Y	Y	Y	Y	Y
16 Serrano	Y	Y	Y	Y	Y	Y	Y	Y
17 Engel	Y	Y	Y	Y	Y	Y	Y	Y
18 Lowey	Y	Y	Y	Y	Y	Y	Y	Y
19 ***Kelly***	Y	Y	Y	Y	Y	Y	Y	Y
20 ***Gilman***	Y	Y	Y	Y	Y	Y	Y	Y
21 McNulty	N	Y	Y	Y	N	Y	Y	Y
22 ***Sweeney***	?	?	?	?	Y	Y	Y	Y
23 ***Boehlert***	Y	Y	Y	Y	Y	Y	Y	Y
24 ***McHugh***	Y	Y	Y	Y	Y	Y	Y	Y
25 ***Walsh***	Y	Y	Y	Y	Y	Y	Y	Y
26 Hinchey	N	Y	Y	Y	N	Y	Y	Y
27 ***Reynolds***	Y	Y	Y	Y	Y	Y	Y	Y
28 Slaughter	Y	Y	Y	Y	Y	Y	Y	Y
29 LaFalce	Y	Y	Y	Y	Y	Y	Y	Y
30 ***Quinn***	Y	Y	Y	Y	Y	Y	Y	Y
31 ***Houghton***	Y	Y	Y	Y	Y	Y	Y	Y
NORTH CAROLINA								
1 Clayton	Y	Y	Y	?	Y	Y	Y	Y
2 Etheridge	Y	Y	Y	Y	Y	Y	Y	Y
3 ***Jones***	Y	Y	Y	Y	Y	Y	Y	Y
4 Price	Y	Y	Y	Y	Y	Y	Y	Y
5 ***Burr***	Y	Y	Y	Y	Y	Y	Y	Y
6 ***Coble***	Y	Y	Y	Y	Y	Y	Y	Y
7 McIntyre	Y	Y	Y	Y	Y	Y	Y	Y
8 ***Hayes***	Y	Y	Y	Y	Y	Y	Y	Y
9 ***Myrick***	Y	Y	Y	Y	Y	Y	Y	Y
10 ***Ballenger***	Y	Y	Y	Y	Y	Y	Y	Y
11 ***Taylor***	Y	Y	Y	Y	Y	Y	Y	Y
12 Watt	Y	Y	Y	Y	Y	Y	Y	Y
NORTH DAKOTA								
AL Pomeroy	Y	Y	Y	Y	N	Y	Y	Y
OHIO								
1 ***Chabot***	Y	Y	Y	Y	Y	Y	Y	Y
2 ***Portman***	Y	Y	Y	Y	Y	Y	Y	Y
3 Hall	N	Y	Y	Y	Y	Y	Y	Y
4 ***Oxley***	Y	Y	Y	Y	Y	Y	Y	Y
5 ***Gillmor***	Y	Y	Y	Y	N	Y	Y	Y
6 Strickland	N	Y	Y	Y	N	Y	Y	Y
7 ***Hobson***	Y	Y	Y	Y	Y	Y	Y	Y
8 ***Boehner***	Y	Y	Y	Y	Y	Y	Y	Y
9 Kaptur	Y	Y	Y	Y	Y	Y	Y	Y
10 Kucinich	N	Y	Y	Y	N	Y	Y	Y
11 Jones	N	Y	Y	Y	N	Y	Y	Y
12 ***Tiberi***	Y	Y	Y	Y	Y	Y	Y	Y
13 Brown	Y	Y	Y	Y	N	Y	Y	Y
14 Sawyer	Y	Y	Y	Y	Y	Y	Y	Y
15 ***Pryce***	Y	Y	Y	Y	Y	Y	Y	Y
16 ***Regula***	Y	Y	Y	Y	Y	Y	Y	Y
17 Traficant	?	?	?	?	?	?	?	?
18 ***Ney***	Y	Y	Y	Y	Y	Y	Y	Y
19 ***LaTourette***	Y	Y	Y	Y	Y	Y	Y	Y
OKLAHOMA								
1 ***Sullivan***	Y	Y	Y	Y	Y	?	Y	Y
2 Carson	Y	Y	Y	Y	Y	Y	Y	Y
3 ***Watkins***	Y	Y	Y	Y	N	Y	Y	Y
4 ***Watts***	?	Y	Y	Y	Y	Y	Y	Y
5 ***Istook***	Y	Y	Y	Y	Y	Y	Y	Y
6 ***Lucas***	?	?	Y	Y	Y	Y	Y	Y
OREGON								
1 Wu	N	Y	Y	Y	Y	Y	Y	Y
2 ***Walden***	Y	Y	Y	Y	Y	Y	Y	Y
3 Blumenauer	Y	Y	Y	Y	Y	Y	Y	Y
4 DeFazio	N	Y	Y	Y	N	Y	Y	Y
5 Hooley	Y	Y	Y	Y	Y	Y	Y	Y
PENNSYLVANIA								
1 Brady	?	?	?	?	N	Y	Y	Y
2 Fattah	?	Y	Y	Y	?	Y	Y	Y
3 Borski	N	Y	Y	Y	N	Y	Y	Y
4 ***Hart***	Y	Y	Y	Y	Y	Y	Y	Y
5 ***Peterson***	Y	Y	Y	Y	Y	Y	?	Y
6 Holden	Y	Y	Y	Y	Y	Y	Y	Y
7 ***Weldon***	Y	Y	Y	Y	?	?	?	?
8 ***Greenwood***	Y	Y	Y	Y	Y	Y	Y	Y
9 ***Shuster, Bill***	Y	Y	Y	Y	Y	Y	Y	Y
10 ***Sherwood***	Y	Y	Y	Y	Y	Y	Y	Y
11 Kanjorski	Y	Y	Y	Y	Y	Y	Y	Y
12 Murtha	Y	Y	Y	Y	Y	?	Y	Y
13 Hoeffel	Y	Y	Y	Y	Y	Y	Y	Y
14 Coyne	Y	Y	Y	Y	Y	Y	Y	Y
15 ***Toomey***	Y	Y	Y	Y	Y	Y	Y	Y
16 ***Pitts***	Y	Y	Y	Y	Y	Y	Y	Y
17 ***Gekas***	Y	Y	Y	Y	Y	Y	Y	Y
18 Doyle	Y	Y	Y	Y	?	Y	Y	Y
19 ***Platts***	Y	Y	Y	Y	?	Y	Y	Y
20 Mascara	Y	Y	Y	Y	Y	Y	Y	Y
21 ***English***	N	Y	Y	Y	N	Y	Y	Y
RHODE ISLAND								
1 Kennedy	Y	Y	Y	Y	Y	Y	Y	Y
2 Langevin	Y	Y	Y	Y	Y	Y	Y	Y
SOUTH CAROLINA								
1 ***Brown***	Y	Y	Y	Y	Y	Y	Y	Y
2 ***Wilson***	Y	Y	Y	Y	Y	Y	Y	Y
3 ***Graham***	Y	Y	Y	Y	Y	Y	Y	Y
4 ***DeMint***	Y	Y	Y	Y	Y	Y	Y	Y
5 Spratt	Y	Y	Y	Y	Y	Y	Y	Y
6 Clyburn	Y	Y	Y	Y	Y	Y	Y	Y
SOUTH DAKOTA								
AL ***Thune***	Y	Y	Y	Y	Y	Y	Y	Y
TENNESSEE								
1 ***Jenkins***	Y	Y	Y	Y	Y	Y	Y	Y
2 ***Duncan***	Y	Y	Y	Y	Y	Y	Y	Y
3 ***Wamp***	Y	Y	Y	Y	Y	Y	Y	Y
4 ***Hilleary***	Y	Y	Y	Y	Y	Y	Y	Y
5 Clement	Y	Y	Y	Y	?	Y	Y	Y
6 Gordon	Y	Y	Y	Y	Y	Y	Y	Y
7 ***Bryant***	Y	Y	Y	Y	Y	Y	Y	Y
8 Tanner	Y	Y	Y	Y	Y	Y	Y	Y
9 Ford	Y	Y	Y	Y	Y	?	Y	Y
TEXAS								
1 Sandlin	Y	Y	Y	Y	Y	Y	Y	Y
2 Turner	Y	Y	Y	Y	Y	Y	Y	Y
3 ***Johnson, Sam***	Y	Y	Y	Y	Y	Y	Y	Y
4 Hall	Y	Y	Y	Y	Y	Y	Y	Y
5 ***Sessions***	Y	Y	Y	Y	?	Y	Y	Y
6 ***Barton***	Y	Y	Y	Y	Y	Y	Y	Y
7 ***Culberson***	Y	Y	Y	Y	Y	Y	Y	Y
8 ***Brady***	Y	Y	Y	Y	Y	Y	Y	Y
9 Lampson	Y	Y	Y	Y	Y	Y	Y	Y
10 Doggett	Y	Y	Y	Y	Y	Y	Y	Y
11 Edwards	Y	Y	Y	Y	Y	Y	Y	Y
12 ***Granger***	Y	Y	Y	Y	Y	Y	Y	Y
13 ***Thornberry***	Y	Y	Y	Y	Y	Y	Y	Y
14 ***Paul***	N	Y	N	Y	Y	N	Y	Y
15 Hinojosa	Y	Y	Y	Y	Y	Y	Y	Y
16 Reyes	Y	Y	Y	Y	Y	Y	Y	Y
17 Stenholm	Y	Y	Y	Y	Y	Y	Y	Y
18 Jackson-Lee	Y	Y	Y	Y	N	Y	Y	Y
19 ***Combest***	Y	Y	Y	Y	Y	Y	Y	Y
20 Gonzalez	Y	Y	Y	Y	Y	Y	Y	Y
21 ***Smith***	Y	Y	Y	?	Y	Y	Y	Y
22 ***DeLay***	Y	Y	Y	Y	Y	Y	Y	Y
23 ***Bonilla***	Y	Y	Y	?	Y	Y	Y	Y
24 Frost	Y	Y	Y	Y	Y	Y	Y	Y
25 Bentsen	Y	Y	Y	Y	Y	Y	Y	Y
26 ***Armey***	?	?	?	?	Y	Y	Y	Y
27 Ortiz	Y	Y	Y	Y	Y	Y	Y	Y
28 Rodriguez	Y	Y	Y	Y	Y	Y	Y	Y
29 Green	Y	Y	Y	Y	Y	Y	Y	Y
30 Johnson, E.B.	Y	Y	Y	Y	Y	Y	Y	Y
UTAH								
1 ***Hansen***	Y	Y	Y	Y	Y	Y	Y	Y
2 Matheson	Y	Y	Y	Y	N	Y	Y	Y
3 ***Cannon***	Y	Y	Y	Y	Y	Y	Y	Y
VERMONT								
AL *Sanders*	Y	Y	Y	Y	Y	?	Y	Y
VIRGINIA								
1 ***Davis, Jo Ann***	Y	Y	Y	Y	Y	Y	Y	Y
2 ***Schrock***	Y	Y	Y	Y	Y	Y	Y	Y
3 Scott	Y	Y	Y	Y	Y	Y	Y	Y
4 ***Forbes***	Y	Y	Y	Y	Y	Y	Y	Y
5 *Goode*	Y	Y	N	Y	Y	Y	Y	Y
6 ***Goodlatte***	Y	Y	N	Y	Y	Y	Y	Y
7 ***Cantor***	Y	Y	Y	Y	Y	Y	Y	Y
8 Moran	Y	Y	Y	Y	Y	Y	Y	Y
9 Boucher	Y	Y	Y	Y	Y	Y	Y	Y
10 ***Wolf***	Y	Y	Y	Y	Y	Y	Y	Y
11 ***Davis, T.***	Y	Y	Y	Y	Y	Y	Y	Y
WASHINGTON								
1 Inslee	Y	Y	Y	Y	Y	Y	Y	Y
2 Larsen	N	Y	Y	Y	N	Y	Y	Y
3 Baird	N	Y	?	?	N	Y	Y	Y
4 ***Hastings***	Y	Y	Y	Y	Y	Y	Y	Y
5 ***Nethercutt***	Y	Y	Y	Y	Y	?	Y	Y
6 Dicks	Y	Y	Y	Y	Y	Y	Y	Y
7 McDermott	N	Y	Y	Y	N	Y	Y	Y
8 ***Dunn***	Y	Y	Y	Y	Y	Y	Y	Y
9 Smith	Y	Y	Y	Y	Y	Y	Y	Y
WEST VIRGINIA								
1 Mollohan	Y	Y	Y	Y	Y	Y	Y	Y
2 ***Capito***	Y	Y	Y	Y	Y	Y	Y	Y
3 Rahall	Y	Y	Y	Y	Y	Y	Y	Y
WISCONSIN								
1 ***Ryan***	Y	Y	Y	Y	Y	Y	Y	Y
2 Baldwin	Y	Y	Y	Y	Y	Y	Y	Y
3 Kind	Y	Y	Y	Y	Y	Y	Y	Y
4 Kleczka	Y	Y	Y	Y	Y	Y	Y	Y
5 Barrett	Y	Y	Y	Y	Y	Y	Y	Y
6 ***Petri***	Y	Y	Y	Y	Y	Y	Y	Y
7 Obey	Y	Y	Y	Y	Y	Y	Y	Y
8 ***Green***	Y	Y	Y	Y	Y	Y	Y	Y
9 ***Sensenbrenner***	Y	Y	Y	Y	Y	Y	Y	Y
WYOMING								
AL ***Cubin***	Y	Y	Y	Y	Y	Y	Y	Y

Southern states - Ala., Ark., Fla., Ga., Ky., La., Miss., N.C., Okla., S.C., Tenn., Texas, Va.

73. Procedural Motion/Adjourn. Sandlin, D-Texas, motion to adjourn. Motion rejected 77-337: R 1-209; D 75-127 (ND 54-95, SD 21-32); I 1-1. March 20, 2002.

74. Procedural Motion/Adjourn. Slaughter, D-N.Y., motion to adjourn. Motion rejected 72-333: R 0-207; D 71-125 (ND 51-93, SD 20-32); I 1-1. March 20, 2002.

75. H Con Res 353. Fiscal 2003 Budget Resolution/Previous Question. Goss, R-Fla., motion to order the previous question (thus ending debate and possibility of amendment) on adoption of the rule (H Res 372) to provide for House floor consideration of the concurrent resolution that would set broad spending and revenue targets over the next five years. Motion agreed to 221-206: R 219-0; D 1-205 (ND 1-152, SD 0-53); I 1-1. March 20, 2002.

76. H Con Res 353. Fiscal 2003 Budget Resolution/Reconsider Vote on Previous Question. Goss, R-Fla., motion to table (kill) the Slaughter, D-N.Y., motion to reconsider the vote on the Goss motion to order the previous question (thus ending debate and possibility of amendment) on adoption of the rule (H Res 372) to provide for House floor consideration of the concurrent resolution that would set broad spending and revenue targets over the next five years. Motion agreed to 222-206: R 219-0; D 2-205 (ND 2-152, SD 0-53); I 1-1. March 20, 2002.

77. H Con Res 353. Fiscal 2003 Budget Resolution/Rule. Adoption of the rule (H Res 372) to provide for House floor consideration of the concurrent resolution that would set broad spending and revenue targets over the next five years. Adopted 222-206: R 221-0; D 0-205 (ND 0-153, SD 0-52); I 1-1. March 20, 2002.

78. H Con Res 353. Fiscal 2003 Budget Resolution/Reconsider Vote on the Rule. Goss, R-Fla., motion to table (kill) the Dreier, R-Calif., motion to reconsider the vote on adoption of the resolution (H Res 372) to provide for House floor consideration of the concurrent resolution that would set broad spending and revenue targets over the next five years. Motion agreed to 213-206: R 212-0; D 0-205 (ND 0-152, SD 0-53); I 1-1. March 20, 2002.

79. H Con Res 353. Fiscal 2003 Budget Resolution/Adoption. Adoption of the concurrent resolution that would set broad spending and revenue targets over the next five years. For fiscal 2003, the resolution would provide $392.8 billion in discretionary defense spending, including a $10 billion anti-terrorism reserve account, and $366.3 billion for non-defense discretionary spending. It also would provide $37.7 billion for homeland security. Adopted (thus sent to the Senate) 221-209: R 219-2; D 1-206 (ND 0-154, SD 1-52); I 1-1. A "yea" was a vote in support of the president's position. March 20, 2002.

Key

Y	Voted for (yea).
#	Paired for.
+	Announced for.
N	Voted against (nay).
X	Paired against.
−	Announced against.
P	Voted "present."
C	Voted "present" to avoid possible conflict of interest.
?	Did not vote or otherwise make a position known.

Democrats **Republicans** *Independents*

	73	74	75	76	77	78	79
ALABAMA							
1 *Callahan*	N	N	Y	Y	Y	?	Y
2 *Everett*	N	N	Y	Y	Y	Y	Y
3 *Riley*	N	?	?	?	Y	Y	Y
4 *Aderholt*	N	N	Y	Y	Y	Y	Y
5 Cramer	N	N	N	N	N	N	N
6 *Bachus*	N	N	Y	Y	Y	Y	Y
7 Hilliard	Y	Y	N	N	N	N	N
ALASKA							
AL *Young*	N	N	Y	Y	Y	Y	Y
ARIZONA							
1 *Flake*	N	N	Y	Y	Y	Y	Y
2 Pastor	Y	Y	N	N	N	N	N
3 *Stump*	N	N	Y	Y	Y	Y	Y
4 *Shadegg*	?	?	Y	Y	Y	?	Y
5 *Kolbe*	N	N	Y	Y	Y	Y	Y
6 *Hayworth*	N	N	Y	Y	Y	Y	Y
ARKANSAS							
1 Berry	Y	N	N	N	N	N	N
2 Snyder	N	N	N	N	N	N	N
3 *Boozman*	N	N	Y	Y	Y	Y	Y
4 Ross	N	N	N	N	N	N	N
CALIFORNIA							
1 Thompson	N	N	N	N	N	N	N
2 *Herger*	N	N	Y	Y	Y	Y	Y
3 *Ose*	N	N	Y	Y	Y	Y	Y
4 *Doolittle*	N	N	Y	Y	Y	?	Y
5 Matsui	N	N	N	N	N	N	N
6 Woolsey	Y	Y	N	N	N	N	N
7 Miller, George	N	?	N	N	N	N	N
8 Pelosi	Y	Y	N	N	N	N	N
9 Lee	Y	Y	N	N	N	N	N
10 Tauscher	N	N	N	N	N	N	N
11 *Pombo*	N	N	Y	Y	Y	Y	Y
12 Lantos	Y	Y	N	N	N	?	N
13 Stark	Y	Y	N	N	N	N	N
14 Eshoo	N	Y	N	N	N	N	N
15 Honda	Y	Y	N	N	N	N	N
16 Lofgren	N	N	N	N	N	N	N
17 Farr	Y	Y	N	N	N	N	N
18 Condit	N	N	N	N	N	N	N
19 *Radanovich*	N	N	Y	Y	Y	Y	Y
20 Dooley	N	?	N	N	N	N	N
21 *Thomas*	N	N	Y	Y	Y	Y	Y
22 Capps	N	N	N	N	N	N	N
23 *Gallegly*	N	N	Y	Y	Y	Y	Y
24 Sherman	N	N	N	N	N	N	N
25 *McKeon*	N	N	Y	Y	Y	Y	Y
26 Berman	N	N	N	N	N	N	N
27 Schiff	N	N	N	N	N	N	N
28 *Dreier*	N	N	Y	Y	Y	Y	Y
29 Waxman	N	N	N	N	N	N	N
30 Becerra	N	N	N	N	N	N	N
31 Solis	Y	N	N	N	N	N	N
32 Watson	Y	Y	N	N	N	N	N
33 Roybal-Allard	Y	Y	N	N	N	N	N
34 Napolitano	N	N	N	N	N	N	N
35 Waters	Y	Y	N	N	N	N	N
36 Harman	N	N	N	?	N	N	N
37 Millender-McD.	?	?	N	N	N	N	N
38 Horn	N	N	Y	Y	Y	Y	Y

	73	74	75	76	77	78	79
39 *Royce*	N	N	Y	Y	Y	Y	Y
40 *Lewis*	N	N	Y	Y	Y	Y	Y
41 *Miller, Gary*	N	N	Y	Y	Y	Y	Y
42 Baca	N	N	N	N	N	N	N
43 *Calvert*	N	N	Y	Y	Y	Y	Y
44 *Bono*	N	N	Y	Y	Y	Y	Y
45 *Rohrabacher*	N	N	Y	Y	Y	Y	Y
46 Sanchez	N	N	N	N	N	N	N
47 *Cox*	N	N	Y	Y	Y	Y	Y
48 *Issa*	N	?	Y	Y	Y	Y	Y
49 Davis	N	N	N	N	N	N	N
50 Filner	Y	N	N	N	N	N	N
51 *Cunningham*	N	N	Y	Y	Y	Y	Y
52 *Hunter*	N	N	Y	Y	Y	Y	Y
COLORADO							
1 DeGette	N	N	N	N	N	N	N
2 Udall	Y	N	N	N	N	N	N
3 *McInnis*	N	N	Y	Y	Y	Y	Y
4 *Schaffer*	N	N	?	Y	Y	Y	Y
5 *Hefley*	N	N	Y	Y	Y	Y	Y
6 *Tancredo*	N	N	Y	Y	Y	Y	Y
CONNECTICUT							
1 Larson	N	N	N	N	N	N	N
2 *Simmons*	N	N	Y	Y	Y	Y	Y
3 DeLauro	N	N	N	N	N	N	N
4 *Shays*	N	N	Y	Y	Y	Y	Y
5 Maloney	N	N	N	N	N	N	N
6 *Johnson*	?	?	Y	Y	Y	Y	Y
DELAWARE							
AL *Castle*	N	N	Y	Y	Y	Y	Y
FLORIDA							
1 *Miller, J.*	N	N	Y	Y	Y	Y	Y
2 Boyd	Y	Y	N	N	?	N	N
3 Brown	Y	Y	N	N	N	N	N
4 *Crenshaw*	N	N	Y	Y	Y	Y	Y
5 Thurman	N	N	N	N	N	N	N
6 *Stearns*	N	N	Y	Y	Y	Y	Y
7 *Mica*	N	N	Y	Y	Y	Y	Y
8 *Keller*	N	N	Y	Y	Y	Y	Y
9 *Bilirakis*	N	N	Y	Y	Y	Y	Y
10 *Young*	N	?	Y	Y	Y	Y	Y
11 Davis	N	N	N	N	N	N	N
12 *Putnam*	N	N	Y	Y	Y	Y	Y
13 *Miller, D.*	N	N	Y	Y	Y	Y	Y
14 *Goss*	N	N	Y	Y	Y	Y	Y
15 *Weldon*	N	N	Y	Y	Y	Y	Y
16 *Foley*	N	N	Y	Y	Y	Y	Y
17 Meek	N	N	N	N	N	N	N
18 *Ros-Lehtinen*	?	?	Y	Y	Y	Y	Y
19 Wexler	Y	N	N	N	N	N	N
20 Deutsch	N	N	N	N	N	N	N
21 *Diaz-Balart*	?	N	Y	Y	Y	Y	Y
22 *Shaw*	N	N	Y	Y	Y	Y	Y
23 Hastings	Y	Y	N	N	N	N	N
GEORGIA							
1 *Kingston*	N	N	Y	Y	Y	Y	Y
2 Bishop	N	N	N	N	N	N	N
3 *Collins*	N	N	Y	Y	Y	Y	Y
4 McKinney	N	N	N	N	N	N	N
5 Lewis	Y	Y	N	N	N	N	N
6 *Isakson*	N	N	Y	Y	Y	Y	Y
7 *Barr*	N	N	Y	Y	Y	Y	Y
8 *Chambliss*	N	N	Y	Y	Y	Y	Y
9 *Deal*	N	N	Y	Y	Y	Y	Y
10 *Norwood*	N	N	Y	Y	Y	Y	Y
11 *Linder*	N	N	Y	Y	Y	Y	Y
HAWAII							
1 Abercrombie	N	N	N	N	N	N	N
2 Mink	Y	Y	N	N	N	N	N
IDAHO							
1 *Otter*	N	N	Y	Y	Y	Y	Y
2 *Simpson*	N	N	Y	Y	Y	Y	Y
ILLINOIS							
1 Rush	?	?	N	N	N	N	N
2 Jackson	Y	Y	N	N	N	N	N
3 Lipinski	?	N	N	N	N	N	N
4 Gutierrez	?	?	?	?	?	?	?
5 Blagojevich	?	?	?	?	?	?	?
6 *Hyde*	N	Y	Y	N	N	N	N
7 Davis	Y	Y	N	N	N	N	N
8 *Crane*	N	N	Y	Y	Y	Y	Y
9 Schakowsky	Y	Y	N	N	N	N	N
10 *Kirk*	N	N	Y	Y	Y	Y	Y
11 *Weller*	N	N	Y	Y	Y	Y	Y
12 Costello	N	N	N	N	N	N	N
13 *Biggert*	N	N	Y	Y	Y	Y	Y

ND Northern Democrats   SD Southern Democrats

Member	73	74	75	76	77	78	79
14 ***Hastert***							Y
15 ***Johnson***	N	N	Y	Y	Y	Y	Y
16 ***Manzullo***	N	N	Y	Y	Y	Y	Y
17 Evans	Y	?	N	N	N	N	N
18 ***LaHood***	N	N	Y	Y	Y	Y	Y
19 Phelps	N	N	N	N	N	N	N
20 ***Shimkus***	N	N	Y	Y	Y	Y	Y
INDIANA							
1 Visclosky	N	N	N	N	N	N	N
2 ***Pence***	N	N	Y	Y	Y	Y	Y
3 Roemer	N	N	N	N	N	N	N
4 ***Souder***	N	N	Y	Y	Y	Y	Y
5 ***Buyer***	N	N	Y	Y	Y	?	Y
6 ***Burton***	N	N	Y	Y	Y	Y	Y
7 ***Kerns***	N	N	Y	Y	Y	Y	Y
8 ***Hostettler***	N	N	Y	Y	Y	Y	Y
9 Hill	N	N	N	N	N	N	N
10 Carson	?	?	N	N	N	N	N
IOWA							
1 ***Leach***	N	N	Y	Y	Y	Y	Y
2 ***Nussle***	N	N	Y	Y	Y	Y	Y
3 Boswell	N	N	N	N	N	N	N
4 ***Ganske***	?	N	Y	Y	Y	Y	Y
5 ***Latham***	N	N	Y	Y	Y	Y	Y
KANSAS							
1 ***Moran***	N	N	Y	Y	Y	Y	Y
2 ***Ryun***	N	?	Y	Y	Y	Y	Y
3 Moore	N	N	N	N	N	N	N
4 ***Tiahrt***	N	N	Y	Y	Y	Y	Y
KENTUCKY							
1 ***Whitfield***	N	N	Y	Y	Y	Y	Y
2 ***Lewis***	N	N	Y	Y	Y	Y	Y
3 ***Northup***	N	N	Y	Y	Y	Y	Y
4 Lucas	N	N	N	N	N	N	Y
5 ***Rogers***	N	N	Y	Y	Y	Y	Y
6 ***Fletcher***	N	N	Y	Y	Y	Y	Y
LOUISIANA							
1 ***Vitter***	N	N	Y	Y	Y	Y	Y
2 Jefferson	Y	Y	N	N	N	N	N
3 ***Tauzin***	N	N	Y	Y	Y	Y	Y
4 ***McCrery***	N	N	Y	Y	Y	Y	Y
5 ***Cooksey***	N	N	Y	Y	Y	Y	Y
6 ***Baker***	N	N	Y	Y	Y	Y	Y
7 John	N	N	N	N	N	N	N
MAINE							
1 Allen	Y	Y	N	N	N	N	N
2 Baldacci	N	N	N	N	N	N	N
MARYLAND							
1 ***Gilchrest***	P	N	Y	Y	Y	Y	Y
2 ***Ehrlich***	N	N	Y	Y	Y	Y	Y
3 Cardin	N	N	N	N	N	N	N
4 Wynn	Y	Y	N	N	N	N	N
5 Hoyer	N	N	N	N	N	N	N
6 ***Bartlett***	N	N	Y	Y	Y	Y	Y
7 Cummings	Y	N	N	N	N	N	N
8 ***Morella***	N	N	Y	Y	Y	Y	Y
MASSACHUSETTS							
1 Olver	Y	Y	N	N	N	N	N
2 Neal	N	N	N	N	N	N	N
3 McGovern	N	N	N	N	N	N	N
4 Frank	Y	Y	N	N	N	N	N
5 Meehan	N	N	N	N	N	N	N
6 Tierney	Y	Y	?	N	N	N	N
7 Markey	Y	Y	N	N	N	N	N
8 Capuano	N	N	N	N	N	N	N
9 Lynch	N	N	N	N	N	N	N
10 Delahunt	N	N	N	N	N	N	N
MICHIGAN							
1 Stupak	N	N	N	N	N	N	N
2 ***Hoekstra***	N	N	Y	Y	Y	Y	Y
3 ***Ehlers***	N	N	Y	Y	Y	Y	+
4 ***Camp***	N	N	Y	Y	Y	Y	Y
5 Barcia	N	N	N	N	N	N	N
6 ***Upton***	N	N	Y	Y	Y	Y	Y
7 ***Smith***	Y	N	Y	Y	Y	Y	Y
8 ***Rogers***	N	N	Y	Y	Y	Y	Y
9 Kildee	N	N	N	N	N	N	N
10 Bonior	N	Y	N	N	N	N	N
11 ***Knollenberg***	N	N	Y	?	Y	Y	Y
12 Levin	N	N	N	N	N	N	N
13 Rivers	N	N	N	N	N	N	N
14 Conyers	Y	Y	N	N	N	N	N
15 Kilpatrick	N	Y	N	N	N	N	N
16 Dingell	N	N	N	N	N	N	N
MINNESOTA							
1 ***Gutknecht***	N	N	Y	Y	Y	Y	Y
2 ***Kennedy***	N	N	Y	Y	Y	+	Y
3 ***Ramstad***	N	N	Y	Y	Y	Y	Y
4 McCollum	N	N	N	N	N	N	N
5 Sabo	Y	N	N	N	N	N	N
6 Luther	N	N	N	N	N	N	N
7 Peterson	N	N	N	N	N	N	N
8 Oberstar	N	N	N	N	N	N	N
MISSISSIPPI							
1 ***Wicker***	N	N	Y	Y	Y	Y	Y
2 Thompson	Y	Y	N	N	N	N	N
3 ***Pickering***	N	N	Y	Y	Y	Y	Y
4 Shows	–	–	–	+	–	–	–
5 Taylor	N	N	N	N	N	N	N
MISSOURI							
1 Clay	Y	Y	N	N	N	N	N
2 ***Akin***	N	N	Y	Y	Y	Y	Y
3 Gephardt	Y	Y	N	N	N	N	N
4 Skelton	N	N	N	N	N	N	N
5 McCarthy	N	N	N	N	N	N	N
6 ***Graves***	N	N	Y	Y	Y	Y	Y
7 ***Blunt***	N	N	Y	Y	Y	Y	Y
8 ***Emerson***	?	?	Y	Y	Y	Y	Y
9 ***Hulshof***	N	N	Y	Y	Y	Y	Y
MONTANA							
AL ***Rehberg***	N	N	Y	Y	Y	Y	Y
NEBRASKA							
1 ***Bereuter***	N	N	Y	Y	Y	Y	Y
2 ***Terry***	N	N	Y	Y	Y	Y	Y
3 ***Osborne***	N	N	Y	Y	Y	Y	Y
NEVADA							
1 Berkley	Y	Y	N	N	N	N	N
2 ***Gibbons***	N	N	Y	Y	Y	Y	Y
NEW HAMPSHIRE							
1 ***Sununu***	N	N	Y	Y	Y	Y	Y
2 ***Bass***	N	N	Y	Y	Y	Y	Y
NEW JERSEY							
1 Andrews	N	N	N	N	N	N	N
2 ***LoBiondo***	N	N	Y	Y	Y	Y	Y
3 ***Saxton***	N	N	Y	Y	Y	?	Y
4 ***Smith***	N	N	Y	Y	Y	Y	Y
5 ***Roukema***	N	N	Y	Y	Y	Y	Y
6 Pallone	N	Y	N	N	N	N	N
7 ***Ferguson***	N	N	Y	Y	Y	Y	Y
8 Pascrell	N	Y	N	N	N	N	N
9 Rothman	?	?	N	N	N	N	N
10 Payne	N	Y	N	N	N	N	N
11 ***Frelinghuysen***	N	N	Y	Y	Y	Y	Y
12 Holt	Y	N	N	N	N	N	N
13 Menendez	N	N	N	N	N	N	N
NEW MEXICO							
1 ***Wilson***	N	N	Y	Y	Y	Y	Y
2 ***Skeen***	N	N	Y	Y	Y	Y	Y
3 Udall	N	N	N	N	N	N	N
NEW YORK							
1 ***Grucci***	N	N	Y	Y	Y	Y	Y
2 Israel	N	N	N	N	N	N	N
3 ***King***	N	N	Y	Y	Y	Y	Y
4 McCarthy	N	N	N	N	N	N	N
5 Ackerman	N	Y	N	N	N	N	N
6 Meeks	N	Y	N	N	N	N	N
7 Crowley	N	N	N	N	N	N	N
8 Nadler	N	N	N	N	N	N	N
9 Weiner	N	N	N	N	N	N	N
10 Towns	Y	Y	N	N	N	N	N
11 Owens	Y	Y	N	N	N	N	N
12 Velázquez	Y	Y	N	N	N	N	N
13 ***Fossella***	N	N	Y	Y	Y	Y	Y
14 Maloney	N	N	N	N	N	N	N
15 Rangel	N	N	N	N	N	N	N
16 Serrano	N	?	N	N	N	N	N
17 Engel	N	N	N	N	N	N	N
18 Lowey	Y	Y	N	N	N	N	N
19 ***Kelly***	N	N	Y	Y	Y	Y	Y
20 ***Gilman***	N	N	Y	Y	Y	Y	Y
21 McNulty	Y	Y	N	N	N	N	N
22 ***Sweeney***	N	N	Y	Y	Y	Y	Y
23 ***Boehlert***	N	N	Y	Y	Y	Y	Y
24 ***McHugh***	N	N	Y	Y	Y	Y	Y
25 ***Walsh***	N	N	Y	Y	Y	Y	Y
26 Hinchey	Y	Y	N	N	N	N	N
27 ***Reynolds***	N	N	Y	Y	Y	Y	Y
28 Slaughter	Y	Y	Y	N	N	N	N
29 LaFalce	Y	Y	N	N	N	N	N
30 ***Quinn***	N	N	Y	Y	Y	Y	Y
31 ***Houghton***	N	N	Y	Y	Y	Y	Y
NORTH CAROLINA							
1 Clayton	N	N	N	N	N	N	N
2 Etheridge	N	N	N	N	N	N	N
3 ***Jones***	N	N	Y	Y	Y	Y	Y
4 Price	Y	Y	N	N	N	N	N
5 ***Burr***	N	N	Y	Y	Y	Y	Y
6 ***Coble***	N	N	Y	Y	Y	Y	Y
7 McIntyre	N	N	N	N	N	N	N
8 ***Hayes***	N	N	Y	Y	Y	Y	Y
9 ***Myrick***	N	N	Y	Y	Y	Y	Y
10 ***Ballenger***	N	N	Y	Y	Y	Y	Y
11 ***Taylor***	N	?	Y	Y	Y	Y	Y
12 Watt	N	N	N	N	N	N	N
NORTH DAKOTA							
AL Pomeroy	Y	Y	N	N	N	N	N
OHIO							
1 ***Chabot***	N	N	Y	Y	Y	Y	Y
2 ***Portman***	N	N	Y	Y	Y	Y	Y
3 Hall	Y	N	N	N	N	N	N
4 ***Oxley***	N	?	Y	Y	Y	Y	Y
5 ***Gillmor***	N	N	Y	Y	Y	Y	Y
6 Strickland	N	N	N	N	N	N	N
7 ***Hobson***	N	N	Y	Y	Y	?	Y
8 ***Boehner***	N	N	Y	Y	Y	Y	Y
9 Kaptur	N	N	N	N	N	N	N
10 Kucinich	N	N	N	N	N	N	N
11 Jones	Y	Y	N	N	N	N	N
12 ***Tiberi***	N	N	Y	Y	Y	Y	Y
13 Brown	N	N	N	N	N	N	N
14 Sawyer	Y	N	N	N	N	N	N
15 ***Pryce***	N	N	Y	Y	Y	Y	Y
16 ***Regula***	N	N	Y	Y	Y	Y	Y
17 Traficant	?	?	?	?	?	?	?
18 ***Ney***	N	N	Y	Y	Y	Y	Y
19 ***LaTourette***	N	N	Y	Y	Y	Y	Y
OKLAHOMA							
1 ***Sullivan***	N	N	Y	Y	Y	Y	Y
2 Carson	Y	Y	N	N	N	N	N
3 ***Watkins***	?	N	Y	Y	Y	Y	Y
4 ***Watts***	N	N	Y	Y	Y	Y	Y
5 ***Istook***	?	N	Y	Y	Y	Y	Y
6 ***Lucas***	N	N	Y	Y	Y	Y	Y
OREGON							
1 Wu	Y	N	N	N	N	N	N
2 ***Walden***	N	N	Y	Y	Y	Y	Y
3 Blumenauer	N	N	N	N	N	N	N
4 DeFazio	Y	Y	N	N	N	N	N
5 Hooley	N	N	N	N	N	N	N
PENNSYLVANIA							
1 Brady	N	N	N	N	N	N	N
2 Fattah	N	N	N	N	N	N	N
3 Borski	N	N	N	N	N	N	N
4 ***Hart***	N	N	Y	Y	Y	Y	Y
5 ***Peterson***	?	N	Y	Y	Y	Y	Y
6 Holden	N	N	N	N	N	N	N
7 ***Weldon***	?	?	Y	Y	Y	Y	N
8 ***Greenwood***	N	N	Y	Y	Y	Y	Y
9 ***Shuster, Bill***	N	N	Y	Y	Y	Y	Y
10 ***Sherwood***	N	?	Y	Y	Y	Y	Y
11 Kanjorski	N	N	N	N	N	N	N
12 Murtha	N	N	N	N	N	N	N
13 Hoeffel	N	N	N	N	N	N	N
14 Coyne	Y	Y	N	N	N	N	N
15 ***Toomey***	N	N	Y	Y	Y	Y	Y
16 ***Pitts***	N	N	Y	Y	Y	Y	Y
17 ***Gekas***	N	N	Y	Y	Y	Y	Y
18 Doyle	N	N	N	N	N	N	N
19 ***Platts***	N	?	Y	Y	Y	Y	Y
20 Mascara	N	N	N	N	N	N	N
21 ***English***	N	N	Y	Y	Y	Y	Y
RHODE ISLAND							
1 Kennedy	Y	Y	N	N	N	N	N
2 Langevin	Y	Y	N	N	N	N	N
SOUTH CAROLINA							
1 ***Brown***	N	N	Y	Y	Y	Y	Y
2 ***Wilson***	N	N	Y	Y	Y	Y	Y
3 ***Graham***	N	N	Y	Y	Y	Y	Y
4 ***DeMint***	N	N	Y	Y	Y	Y	Y
5 Spratt	N	N	N	N	N	N	N
6 Clyburn	Y	Y	N	N	N	N	N
SOUTH DAKOTA							
AL ***Thune***	N	N	Y	Y	Y	Y	Y
TENNESSEE							
1 ***Jenkins***	N	N	Y	Y	Y	?	Y
2 ***Duncan***	N	N	Y	Y	Y	Y	Y
3 ***Wamp***	N	N	Y	Y	Y	Y	Y
4 ***Hilleary***	N	N	Y	Y	Y	?	Y
5 Clement	N	N	N	N	N	N	N
6 Gordon	Y	N	N	N	N	N	N
7 ***Bryant***	N	N	Y	Y	Y	Y	Y
8 Tanner	N	N	N	N	N	N	N
9 Ford	N	N	N	N	N	N	N
TEXAS							
1 Sandlin	Y	Y	N	N	N	N	N
2 Turner	N	N	N	N	N	N	N
3 ***Johnson, Sam***	N	?	Y	Y	Y	Y	Y
4 Hall	N	N	N	N	N	N	N
5 ***Sessions***	N	N	Y	Y	Y	Y	Y
6 ***Barton***	N	N	Y	Y	Y	Y	Y
7 ***Culberson***	N	N	Y	Y	Y	Y	Y
8 ***Brady***	N	N	Y	Y	Y	Y	Y
9 Lampson	N	Y	N	N	N	N	N
10 Doggett	Y	Y	N	N	N	N	N
11 Edwards	N	N	N	N	N	N	N
12 ***Granger***	N	N	Y	Y	Y	Y	Y
13 ***Thornberry***	N	N	Y	Y	Y	Y	Y
14 ***Paul***	N	N	Y	Y	Y	Y	N
15 Hinojosa	N	N	N	N	N	N	N
16 Reyes	N	N	N	N	N	N	N
17 Stenholm	N	N	N	N	N	N	N
18 Jackson-Lee	N	Y	N	N	N	N	N
19 ***Combest***	N	N	Y	Y	Y	Y	Y
20 Gonzalez	N	N	N	N	N	N	N
21 ***Smith***	N	N	Y	Y	Y	Y	Y
22 ***DeLay***	N	N	Y	Y	Y	Y	Y
23 ***Bonilla***	N	N	Y	Y	Y	Y	Y
24 Frost	Y	Y	N	N	N	N	N
25 Bentsen	Y	Y	N	N	N	N	N
26 ***Armey***	N	N	Y	Y	Y	Y	Y
27 Ortiz	N	N	N	N	N	N	N
28 Rodriguez	N	Y	N	N	N	N	N
29 Green	N	N	N	N	N	N	N
30 Johnson, E.B.	Y	Y	N	N	N	N	N
UTAH							
1 ***Hansen***	N	N	Y	Y	Y	Y	Y
2 Matheson	N	N	N	N	N	N	N
3 ***Cannon***	N	N	Y	Y	Y	Y	Y
VERMONT							
AL *Sanders*	Y	Y	N	N	N	N	N
VIRGINIA							
1 ***Davis, Jo Ann***	N	N	Y	Y	Y	Y	Y
2 ***Schrock***	N	N	Y	Y	Y	Y	Y
3 Scott	Y	Y	N	N	N	N	N
4 ***Forbes***	N	N	Y	Y	Y	Y	Y
5 *Goode*	N	N	Y	Y	Y	Y	Y
6 ***Goodlatte***	N	N	Y	Y	Y	Y	Y
7 ***Cantor***	N	N	Y	Y	Y	Y	Y
8 Moran	N	?	N	N	N	N	N
9 Boucher	N	N	N	N	N	N	N
10 ***Wolf***	N	N	Y	Y	Y	Y	Y
11 ***Davis, T.***	N	N	Y	Y	Y	Y	Y
WASHINGTON							
1 Inslee	N	N	N	N	N	N	N
2 Larsen	N	N	N	N	N	N	N
3 Baird	Y	Y	N	N	N	N	N
4 ***Hastings***	N	N	Y	Y	Y	Y	Y
5 ***Nethercutt***	N	N	Y	Y	Y	Y	Y
6 Dicks	Y	Y	N	N	N	N	N
7 McDermott	Y	Y	N	N	N	N	N
8 ***Dunn***	N	N	Y	Y	Y	Y	Y
9 Smith	Y	?	N	Y	N	N	N
WEST VIRGINIA							
1 Mollohan	N	N	N	N	N	N	N
2 ***Capito***	N	N	Y	Y	Y	Y	Y
3 Rahall	N	N	N	N	N	N	N
WISCONSIN							
1 ***Ryan***	N	N	Y	Y	Y	Y	Y
2 Baldwin	Y	Y	N	N	N	N	N
3 Kind	N	N	N	N	N	N	N
4 Kleczka	N	?	N	N	N	?	N
5 Barrett	N	N	N	N	N	N	N
6 ***Petri***	N	N	Y	Y	Y	Y	Y
7 Obey	N	N	N	N	N	N	N
8 ***Green***	N	N	Y	Y	Y	Y	Y
9 ***Sensenbrenner***	N	N	Y	Y	Y	Y	Y
WYOMING							
AL ***Cubin***	N	N	Y	Y	Y	Y	Y

Southern states - Ala., Ark., Fla., Ga., Ky., La., Miss., N.C., Okla., S.C., Tenn., Texas, Va.

80. Procedural Motion/Journal. Approval of the House Journal of Wednesday, March 20, 2002. Approved 361-43: R 187-15; D 172-28 (ND 125-24, SD 47-4); I 2-0. April 9, 2002.

81. H Res 377. Ellis Island Tribute/Adoption. T. Davis, R-Va., motion to suspend the rules and adopt the resolution that would pay tribute to the National Ethnic Coalition of Organizations and recognize the importance of the Ellis Island Medal of Honor, which is awarded to individuals who have preserved their ethnic heritage and distinguished themselves as Americans. Motion agreed to 403-0: R 205-0; D 196-0 (ND 145-0, SD 51-0); I 2-0. A two-thirds majority of those present and voting (269 in this case) is required for adoption under suspension of the rules. April 9, 2002.

82. HR 3958. Bear River Agreement/Passage. Hansen, R-Utah, motion to suspend the rules and pass the bill that would authorize a land claim settlement between the Interior Department and the state of Utah involving the Bear River Migratory Bird Refuge. It would authorize $15 million in federal funding to help protect and improve parts of the wildlife area, require the state to increase the area's water storage capacity, and mandate that the state reimburse the federal government for various expenses if it files and wins a legal action involving the refuge's deed. Motion agreed to 396-6: R 196-6; D 199-0 (ND 149-0, SD 50-0); I 1-0. A two-thirds majority of those present and voting (268 in this case) is required for passage under suspension of the rules. April 9, 2002.

83. HR 3925. Technology Workers Swap/Secrets Protection and Federal Training. Waxman, D-Calif., amendment that would block private employees participating in a government-exchange program from accessing federal agencies' trade secrets and other propriety information and authorize $7 million in fiscal 2003 for an information technology training program for federal employees. Rejected 204-219: R 1-214; D 202-4 (ND 148-4, SD 54-0); I 1-1. April 10, 2002.

84. H Res 363. Olympics Tribute/Adoption. Smith, R-N.J., motion to suspend the rules and adopt the resolution that would pay tribute to those individuals and organizations that helped with and participated in the 2002 Olympic Winter Games in Salt Lake City. Motion agreed to 425-0: R 214-0; D 209-0 (ND 155-0, SD 54-0); I 2-0. A two-thirds majority of those present and voting (284 in this case) is required for adoption under suspension of the rules. April 10, 2002.

85. HR 3991. Tax Code Revisions/Passage. Thomas, R-Calif., motion to suspend the rules and pass the bill that would revise various Internal Revenue Service tax provisions including penalty, interest and collection provisions and eliminate reporting requirements for some groups that file under Section 527. It would change penalties for failure to pay estimated taxes to an interest provision; waive minor, first-time error penalties; exclude interest on unintentional overpayments from taxable income; and give the IRS greater discretion in disciplining employees who violate policies. The bill also would cut reporting provisions for Section 527 organizations who only operate statewide or locally and file state forms "substantially similar" to federal reports. Motion rejected 205-219: R 189-25; D 15-193 (ND 7-147, SD 8-46); I 1-1. A two-thirds majority of those present and voting (283 in this case) is required for passage under suspension of the rules. April 10, 2002.

86. HR 2646. Farm Bill/Motion to Instruct. Phelps, D-Ill., motion to instruct conferees to agree to a Senate provision that would reauthorize the bankruptcy code's family farmer provisions and make them effective as of Oct. 1, 2001. Motion agreed to 424-3: R 216-3; D 206-0 (ND 153-0, SD 53-0); I 2-0. April 10, 2002.

Key

Y	Voted for (yea).
#	Paired for.
+	Announced for.
N	Voted against (nay).
X	Paired against.
−	Announced against.
P	Voted "present."
C	Voted "present" to avoid possible conflict of interest.
?	Did not vote or otherwise make a position known.

Democrats **Republicans**
Independents

	80	81	82	83	84	85	86
ALABAMA							
1 *Callahan*	Y	Y	Y	N	Y	Y	Y
2 *Everett*	N	Y	Y	N	Y	Y	Y
3 *Riley*	+	+	+	N	Y	Y	Y
4 *Aderholt*	N	Y	Y	N	Y	Y	Y
5 Cramer	Y	Y	Y	Y	N	Y	Y
6 *Bachus*	Y	Y	Y	N	Y	Y	Y
7 Hilliard	N	Y	Y	Y	N	Y	Y
ALASKA							
AL *Young*	Y	Y	Y	N	Y	Y	Y
ARIZONA							
1 *Flake*	Y	Y	N	N	Y	Y	N
2 Pastor	Y	Y	Y	Y	N	Y	Y
3 *Stump*	Y	Y	Y	N	Y	Y	Y
4 *Shadegg*	Y	Y	Y	N	Y	Y	Y
5 *Kolbe*	Y	Y	Y	N	Y	Y	Y
6 *Hayworth*	Y	Y	Y	N	Y	Y	Y
ARKANSAS							
1 Berry	Y	Y	Y	Y	Y	N	Y
2 Snyder	Y	Y	Y	Y	Y	N	Y
3 *Boozman*	Y	Y	Y	N	Y	Y	Y
4 Ross	Y	Y	Y	Y	Y	N	Y
CALIFORNIA							
1 Thompson	N	Y	Y	Y	Y	N	Y
2 *Herger*	Y	Y	Y	N	Y	Y	Y
3 *Ose*	Y	Y	Y	N	Y	Y	Y
4 *Doolittle*	Y	Y	Y	N	Y	?	Y
5 Matsui	Y	Y	Y	Y	N	Y	Y
6 Woolsey	Y	Y	Y	Y	N	Y	Y
7 Miller, George	N	Y	Y	Y	Y	N	Y
8 Pelosi	Y	Y	Y	Y	Y	N	Y
9 Lee	Y	Y	Y	Y	Y	N	Y
10 Tauscher	Y	Y	Y	Y	N	Y	Y
11 *Pombo*	N	Y	N	Y	Y	Y	Y
12 Lantos	Y	Y	Y	?	Y	N	Y
13 Stark	Y	Y	Y	Y	Y	N	Y
14 Eshoo	Y	Y	Y	Y	Y	N	Y
15 Honda	Y	Y	Y	Y	Y	N	Y
16 Lofgren	Y	Y	Y	N	Y	N	Y
17 Farr	Y	Y	Y	Y	Y	N	Y
18 Condit	N	Y	Y	Y	Y	N	Y
19 *Radanovich*	?	?	?	N	Y	Y	Y
20 Dooley	Y	Y	Y	Y	Y	N	Y
21 *Thomas*	Y	Y	Y	N	Y	Y	Y
22 Capps	Y	Y	Y	Y	Y	N	Y
23 *Gallegly*	Y	Y	Y	N	Y	Y	Y
24 Sherman	Y	Y	Y	?	Y	N	Y
25 *McKeon*	Y	Y	Y	N	Y	Y	Y
26 Berman	Y	Y	Y	Y	Y	N	Y
27 Schiff	Y	Y	Y	Y	Y	N	Y
28 *Dreier*	Y	Y	Y	N	Y	Y	Y
29 Waxman	Y	Y	Y	Y	Y	N	Y
30 Becerra	+	+	+	Y	Y	N	Y
31 Solis	Y	Y	Y	Y	Y	N	Y
32 Watson	Y	+	Y	Y	Y	N	Y
33 Roybal-Allard	Y	Y	Y	Y	Y	N	Y
34 Napolitano	Y	Y	Y	Y	Y	N	Y
35 Waters	Y	?	Y	Y	Y	N	Y
36 Harman	Y	Y	Y	N	Y	N	Y
37 Millender-McD.	Y	Y	Y	Y	N	Y	Y
38 Horn	Y	Y	Y	N	Y	N	Y

	80	81	82	83	84	85	86
39 *Royce*	Y	Y	Y	?	Y	Y	Y
40 *Lewis*	?	?	?	N	Y	Y	Y
41 *Miller, Gary*	Y	Y	Y	N	Y	Y	Y
42 Baca	Y	Y	Y	Y	Y	N	Y
43 *Calvert*	?	?	?	N	Y	Y	Y
44 *Bono*	Y	Y	Y	N	Y	Y	Y
45 *Rohrabacher*	Y	Y	Y	N	Y	Y	Y
46 Sanchez	Y	Y	Y	Y	Y	N	Y
47 *Cox*	Y	Y	Y	N	Y	Y	Y
48 *Issa*	Y	Y	Y	N	Y	Y	Y
49 Davis	Y	Y	Y	Y	Y	N	Y
50 Filner	N	Y	Y	Y	Y	N	Y
51 *Cunningham*	Y	Y	Y	N	Y	Y	Y
52 *Hunter*	Y	Y	Y	N	Y	Y	Y
COLORADO							
1 DeGette	Y	Y	Y	Y	Y	N	Y
2 Udall	N	Y	Y	Y	Y	N	Y
3 *McInnis*	Y	Y	Y	N	Y	Y	Y
4 *Schaffer*	N	Y	Y	N	Y	Y	Y
5 *Hefley*	N	Y	Y	N	Y	Y	Y
6 *Tancredo*	P	Y	Y	N	Y	Y	Y
CONNECTICUT							
1 Larson	Y	Y	Y	Y	Y	N	Y
2 *Simmons*	Y	Y	Y	N	Y	N	Y
3 DeLauro	Y	Y	Y	Y	Y	N	Y
4 *Shays*	Y	Y	Y	Y	Y	N	Y
5 Maloney	Y	Y	Y	Y	Y	N	Y
6 *Johnson*	Y	Y	Y	Y	Y	N	Y
DELAWARE							
AL *Castle*	Y	Y	Y	N	Y	N	Y
FLORIDA							
1 *Miller, J.*	Y	Y	Y	N	Y	Y	Y
2 Boyd	Y	Y	Y	Y	Y	Y	Y
3 Brown	?	?	?	Y	Y	N	Y
4 *Crenshaw*	Y	Y	Y	N	Y	Y	Y
5 Thurman	Y	Y	Y	Y	N	Y	Y
6 *Stearns*	Y	Y	N	Y	Y	Y	Y
7 *Mica*	?	?	?	N	Y	Y	Y
8 *Keller*	Y	Y	Y	N	Y	Y	Y
9 *Bilirakis*	Y	Y	Y	N	Y	Y	Y
10 *Young*	?	?	?	N	Y	Y	Y
11 Davis	Y	Y	Y	Y	Y	N	Y
12 *Putnam*	Y	Y	Y	N	Y	Y	Y
13 *Miller, D.*	Y	Y	Y	N	Y	Y	Y
14 *Goss*	Y	Y	Y	N	Y	Y	Y
15 *Weldon*	Y	Y	N	?	Y	?	Y
16 *Foley*	Y	Y	Y	N	Y	Y	Y
17 Meek	Y	Y	Y	Y	Y	N	Y
18 *Ros-Lehtinen*	Y	Y	Y	N	Y	Y	Y
19 Wexler	Y	Y	Y	Y	Y	N	Y
20 Deutsch	Y	Y	Y	Y	Y	N	Y
21 *Diaz-Balart*	Y	Y	Y	N	Y	Y	Y
22 *Shaw*	Y	Y	Y	N	Y	Y	Y
23 Hastings	Y	Y	Y	Y	Y	N	Y
GEORGIA							
1 *Kingston*	Y	Y	Y	N	Y	Y	Y
2 Bishop	Y	Y	Y	Y	Y	N	Y
3 *Collins*	?	?	?	N	Y	Y	Y
4 McKinney	?	?	?	Y	Y	N	Y
5 Lewis	Y	Y	Y	Y	Y	N	Y
6 *Isakson*	Y	Y	Y	N	Y	Y	Y
7 *Barr*	Y	Y	Y	N	Y	Y	Y
8 *Chambliss*	Y	Y	Y	N	Y	Y	Y
9 *Deal*	Y	Y	Y	N	Y	Y	Y
10 *Norwood*	Y	Y	Y	N	Y	Y	Y
11 *Linder*	Y	Y	Y	N	Y	Y	Y
HAWAII							
1 Abercrombie	Y	Y	Y	Y	Y	N	Y
2 Mink	Y	Y	Y	Y	Y	N	Y
IDAHO							
1 *Otter*	Y	Y	Y	N	Y	Y	Y
2 *Simpson*	Y	Y	Y	N	Y	Y	Y
ILLINOIS							
1 Rush	Y	Y	Y	Y	Y	N	Y
2 Jackson	Y	Y	Y	Y	Y	N	Y
3 Lipinski	Y	Y	Y	Y	Y	N	Y
4 Gutierrez	?	?	?	Y	Y	N	Y
5 Blagojevich	?	?	?	?	?	?	?
6 *Hyde*	Y	Y	Y	N	Y	Y	Y
7 Davis	Y	Y	Y	Y	Y	N	Y
8 *Crane*	N	Y	Y	N	Y	Y	Y
9 Schakowsky	Y	Y	Y	Y	Y	N	Y
10 *Kirk*	Y	Y	Y	N	Y	Y	Y
11 *Weller*	N	Y	Y	N	Y	Y	Y
12 Costello	N	Y	Y	N	Y	Y	Y
13 *Biggert*	Y	Y	Y	N	Y	Y	Y

ND Northern Democrats   SD Southern Democrats

	80	81	82	83	84	85	86
14 ***Hastert***							
15 ***Johnson***	Y	Y	Y	N	Y	Y	Y
16 ***Manzullo***	Y	Y	Y	N	Y	Y	Y
17 Evans	Y	Y	Y	Y	Y	N	Y
18 ***LaHood***	Y	Y	Y	?	Y	Y	Y
19 Phelps	Y	Y	Y	Y	Y	Y	Y
20 ***Shimkus***	Y	Y	Y	N	Y	Y	Y
INDIANA							
1 Visclosky	N	Y	Y	Y	Y	N	Y
2 ***Pence***	Y	Y	Y	N	Y	Y	Y
3 Roemer	Y	Y	Y	N	Y	N	Y
4 ***Souder***	Y	Y	Y	N	Y	Y	Y
5 ***Buyer***	?	?	?	N	Y	Y	Y
6 ***Burton***	?	?	?	N	Y	Y	Y
7 ***Kerns***	Y	Y	N	N	Y	Y	Y
8 ***Hostettler***	Y	Y	Y	N	Y	Y	Y
9 Hill	Y	Y	Y	Y	Y	N	Y
10 Carson	Y	Y	Y	Y	Y	N	Y
IOWA							
1 ***Leach***	Y	Y	Y	N	Y	N	Y
2 ***Nussle***	Y	Y	Y	N	Y	Y	Y
3 Boswell	Y	Y	Y	Y	Y	N	Y
4 ***Ganske***	Y	Y	Y	N	Y	Y	Y
5 ***Latham***	N	Y	Y	N	Y	Y	Y
KANSAS							
1 ***Moran***	Y	Y	Y	N	Y	Y	Y
2 ***Ryun***	Y	Y	Y	N	Y	Y	Y
3 Moore	N	Y	Y	Y	Y	N	Y
4 ***Tiahrt***	Y	Y	Y	N	Y	Y	Y
KENTUCKY							
1 ***Whitfield***	N	Y	Y	N	Y	Y	Y
2 ***Lewis***	Y	Y	Y	N	Y	Y	Y
3 ***Northup***	Y	Y	Y	N	Y	Y	Y
4 Lucas	Y	Y	Y	Y	Y	Y	Y
5 ***Rogers***	Y	Y	Y	N	Y	Y	Y
6 ***Fletcher***	Y	Y	Y	N	?	Y	Y
LOUISIANA							
1 ***Vitter***	Y	Y	Y	N	Y	Y	Y
2 Jefferson	Y	Y	Y	Y	Y	N	Y
3 ***Tauzin***	Y	Y	Y	N	Y	Y	Y
4 ***McCrery***	Y	Y	Y	N	Y	Y	Y
5 ***Cooksey***	Y	Y	Y	N	Y	Y	Y
6 ***Baker***	Y	Y	Y	N	Y	Y	Y
7 John	Y	Y	Y	Y	Y	Y	Y
MAINE							
1 Allen	Y	Y	Y	Y	Y	N	Y
2 Baldacci	Y	Y	Y	Y	Y	N	Y
MARYLAND							
1 ***Gilchrest***	Y	Y	Y	N	Y	N	Y
2 ***Ehrlich***	Y	Y	Y	N	Y	N	Y
3 Cardin	Y	Y	Y	Y	Y	N	Y
4 Wynn	Y	Y	Y	Y	Y	N	Y
5 Hoyer	Y	?	Y	Y	Y	N	Y
6 ***Bartlett***	Y	Y	Y	N	Y	Y	Y
7 Cummings	Y	Y	Y	Y	Y	N	Y
8 ***Morella***	Y	Y	Y	N	Y	N	Y
MASSACHUSETTS							
1 Olver	N	Y	Y	Y	Y	N	Y
2 Neal	Y	Y	Y	Y	Y	N	Y
3 McGovern	Y	Y	Y	Y	Y	N	Y
4 Frank	Y	Y	Y	Y	Y	N	Y
5 Meehan	Y	Y	Y	Y	Y	N	Y
6 Tierney	Y	Y	Y	Y	Y	N	Y
7 Markey	Y	Y	Y	Y	Y	N	Y
8 Capuano	N	Y	Y	Y	Y	N	Y
9 Lynch	Y	Y	Y	Y	Y	N	Y
10 Delahunt	Y	Y	Y	Y	Y	N	Y
MICHIGAN							
1 Stupak	Y	Y	Y	Y	Y	N	Y
2 ***Hoekstra***	Y	Y	Y	N	Y	Y	Y
3 ***Ehlers***	Y	Y	Y	N	Y	Y	Y
4 ***Camp***	Y	Y	Y	N	Y	Y	Y
5 Barcia	Y	Y	Y	Y	Y	N	Y
6 ***Upton***	Y	Y	Y	N	Y	Y	Y
7 ***Smith***	Y	Y	?	N	Y	Y	Y
8 ***Rogers***	Y	Y	Y	N	Y	Y	Y
9 Kildee	Y	Y	Y	Y	Y	N	Y
10 Bonior	Y	Y	Y	Y	Y	N	Y
11 ***Knollenberg***	Y	Y	Y	N	Y	Y	Y
12 Levin	Y	Y	Y	Y	Y	N	?
13 Rivers	Y	Y	Y	Y	Y	N	Y
14 Conyers	Y	Y	Y	Y	Y	N	Y
15 Kilpatrick	Y	Y	Y	Y	Y	N	Y
16 Dingell	N	Y	Y	Y	Y	?	Y

	80	81	82	83	84	85	86
MINNESOTA							
1 ***Gutknecht***	N	Y	Y	N	Y	Y	Y
2 ***Kennedy***	N	Y	Y	N	Y	Y	Y
3 ***Ramstad***	Y	Y	Y	N	Y	Y	Y
4 McCollum	Y	Y	Y	Y	Y	N	Y
5 Sabo	N	Y	Y	Y	Y	N	Y
6 Luther	Y	Y	Y	Y	Y	N	Y
7 Peterson	N	Y	Y	?	Y	N	Y
8 Oberstar	N	Y	Y	Y	Y	N	Y
MISSISSIPPI							
1 ***Wicker***	N	Y	Y	N	Y	Y	Y
2 Thompson	N	Y	Y	Y	Y	N	Y
3 ***Pickering***	Y	Y	Y	N	Y	Y	Y
4 Shows	Y	Y	Y	Y	Y	Y	Y
5 Taylor	N	Y	Y	Y	Y	N	Y
MISSOURI							
1 Clay	Y	Y	Y	Y	Y	N	Y
2 ***Akin***	Y	Y	Y	N	Y	Y	Y
3 Gephardt	?	?	?	Y	Y	N	Y
4 Skelton	Y	Y	Y	Y	Y	N	Y
5 McCarthy	Y	Y	Y	Y	Y	N	Y
6 ***Graves***	Y	Y	Y	N	Y	Y	Y
7 ***Blunt***	Y	Y	Y	N	Y	Y	Y
8 ***Emerson***	Y	Y	Y	N	Y	Y	Y
9 ***Hulshof***	?	?	?	N	Y	Y	Y
MONTANA							
AL ***Rehberg***	Y	Y	Y	N	Y	Y	Y
NEBRASKA							
1 ***Bereuter***	Y	Y	Y	N	Y	N	Y
2 ***Terry***	Y	Y	Y	N	Y	Y	Y
3 ***Osborne***	Y	Y	Y	N	Y	Y	Y
NEVADA							
1 Berkley	Y	Y	Y	Y	Y	N	Y
2 ***Gibbons***	Y	Y	Y	N	Y	Y	Y
NEW HAMPSHIRE							
1 ***Sununu***	Y	Y	Y	N	Y	Y	Y
2 ***Bass***	Y	Y	Y	N	Y	N	Y
NEW JERSEY							
1 Andrews	Y	Y	Y	Y	Y	N	Y
2 ***LoBiondo***	N	Y	Y	N	Y	N	Y
3 ***Saxton***	Y	Y	Y	N	Y	N	Y
4 ***Smith***	Y	Y	Y	N	Y	N	Y
5 ***Roukema***	Y	Y	?	N	Y	N	Y
6 Pallone	Y	Y	Y	Y	Y	N	Y
7 ***Ferguson***	Y	Y	Y	N	Y	Y	Y
8 Pascrell	Y	Y	Y	Y	Y	N	Y
9 Rothman	Y	Y	Y	Y	Y	N	Y
10 Payne	Y	Y	Y	Y	Y	N	Y
11 ***Frelinghuysen***	Y	Y	Y	N	Y	N	Y
12 Holt	Y	Y	Y	Y	Y	N	Y
13 Menendez	N	Y	Y	Y	Y	N	Y
NEW MEXICO							
1 ***Wilson***	Y	Y	Y	N	Y	Y	Y
2 ***Skeen***	Y	Y	Y	N	Y	Y	Y
3 Udall	N	Y	Y	Y	Y	N	Y
NEW YORK							
1 ***Grucci***	Y	Y	Y	N	Y	Y	Y
2 Israel	Y	Y	Y	Y	Y	Y	Y
3 ***King***	Y	Y	Y	N	Y	Y	Y
4 McCarthy	Y	Y	Y	Y	Y	N	Y
5 Ackerman	Y	Y	Y	Y	Y	N	Y
6 Meeks	Y	Y	Y	Y	Y	N	Y
7 Crowley	Y	Y	Y	Y	Y	N	Y
8 Nadler	Y	Y	Y	Y	Y	N	Y
9 Weiner	Y	Y	Y	Y	Y	N	Y
10 Towns	Y	Y	Y	?	Y	N	Y
11 Owens	Y	Y	Y	Y	Y	N	Y
12 Velázquez	Y	?	Y	Y	Y	N	Y
13 ***Fossella***	?	+	+	N	Y	Y	Y
14 Maloney	Y	Y	Y	Y	Y	N	Y
15 Rangel	Y	Y	Y	Y	Y	N	Y
16 Serrano	Y	Y	Y	Y	Y	N	Y
17 Engel	Y	Y	Y	Y	Y	N	Y
18 Lowey	Y	Y	Y	Y	Y	N	Y
19 ***Kelly***	Y	Y	Y	N	Y	Y	Y
20 ***Gilman***	Y	Y	Y	N	Y	N	Y
21 McNulty	N	Y	Y	Y	Y	N	Y
22 ***Sweeney***	N	Y	Y	N	Y	Y	Y
23 ***Boehlert***	Y	Y	Y	N	Y	N	Y
24 ***McHugh***	Y	Y	Y	N	Y	Y	Y
25 ***Walsh***	Y	Y	Y	N	Y	N	Y
26 Hinchey	Y	Y	Y	Y	Y	N	Y
27 ***Reynolds***	Y	Y	Y	N	?	Y	Y
28 Slaughter	N	Y	Y	Y	Y	N	Y
29 LaFalce	Y	Y	Y	Y	Y	N	Y

	80	81	82	83	84	85	86
30 ***Quinn***	Y	Y	Y	N	Y	Y	Y
31 ***Houghton***	Y	Y	Y	N	Y	Y	Y
NORTH CAROLINA							
1 Clayton	Y	Y	Y	Y	Y	N	Y
2 Etheridge	Y	Y	Y	Y	Y	N	Y
3 ***Jones***	?	?	?	N	Y	Y	Y
4 Price	Y	Y	Y	Y	Y	N	Y
5 ***Burr***	Y	Y	Y	N	Y	Y	Y
6 ***Coble***	Y	Y	N	N	Y	Y	Y
7 McIntyre	Y	Y	Y	Y	Y	Y	Y
8 ***Hayes***	Y	Y	Y	N	Y	Y	Y
9 ***Myrick***	Y	Y	Y	N	Y	Y	Y
10 ***Ballenger***	Y	Y	?	N	Y	Y	Y
11 ***Taylor***	Y	Y	Y	N	Y	Y	Y
12 Watt	Y	Y	Y	Y	Y	N	Y
NORTH DAKOTA							
AL Pomeroy	Y	Y	Y	Y	Y	Y	Y
OHIO							
1 ***Chabot***	Y	Y	Y	N	Y	Y	Y
2 ***Portman***	Y	Y	Y	N	Y	Y	Y
3 Hall	Y	Y	Y	Y	Y	N	Y
4 ***Oxley***	Y	Y	Y	N	?	Y	Y
5 ***Gillmor***	Y	Y	Y	N	Y	Y	Y
6 Strickland	N	Y	Y	Y	Y	N	Y
7 ***Hobson***	Y	Y	Y	N	Y	Y	Y
8 ***Boehner***	Y	Y	Y	N	Y	Y	Y
9 Kaptur	Y	Y	Y	Y	Y	N	Y
10 Kucinich	N	Y	Y	Y	Y	N	Y
11 Jones	Y	Y	Y	Y	Y	N	Y
12 ***Tiberi***	Y	Y	Y	N	Y	Y	Y
13 Brown	Y	Y	Y	Y	Y	N	Y
14 Sawyer	Y	Y	Y	Y	Y	N	Y
15 ***Pryce***	?	?	?	?	?	?	?
16 ***Regula***	Y	Y	Y	N	Y	Y	Y
17 Traficant	?	?	?	?	?	?	?
18 ***Ney***	Y	Y	Y	N	Y	Y	Y
19 ***LaTourette***	Y	Y	Y	N	Y	Y	Y
OKLAHOMA							
1 ***Sullivan***	Y	Y	Y	N	Y	Y	Y
2 Carson	Y	Y	Y	Y	Y	N	Y
3 ***Watkins***	Y	Y	Y	N	Y	Y	Y
4 ***Watts***	Y	Y	Y	N	Y	Y	Y
5 ***Istook***	Y	Y	Y	N	Y	Y	Y
6 ***Lucas***	Y	Y	Y	N	Y	Y	Y
OREGON							
1 Wu	Y	Y	Y	Y	Y	N	Y
2 ***Walden***	Y	Y	Y	N	Y	Y	Y
3 Blumenauer	Y	Y	Y	Y	Y	N	Y
4 DeFazio	N	Y	Y	Y	Y	N	Y
5 Hooley	Y	Y	Y	Y	Y	N	Y
PENNSYLVANIA							
1 Brady	N	Y	Y	Y	Y	N	Y
2 Fattah	Y	Y	Y	Y	Y	N	?
3 Borski	?	?	?	Y	Y	N	Y
4 ***Hart***	Y	Y	Y	N	Y	Y	Y
5 ***Peterson***	Y	Y	Y	N	Y	?	Y
6 Holden	Y	Y	Y	Y	Y	Y	Y
7 ***Weldon***	Y	Y	Y	N	Y	N	Y
8 ***Greenwood***	Y	Y	Y	?	?	?	Y
9 ***Shuster, Bill***	Y	Y	Y	N	Y	Y	Y
10 ***Sherwood***	Y	Y	Y	N	Y	Y	Y
11 Kanjorski	Y	Y	Y	Y	Y	N	Y
12 Murtha	Y	Y	Y	Y	Y	N	Y
13 Hoeffel	Y	Y	Y	Y	Y	N	Y
14 Coyne	Y	Y	Y	Y	Y	N	Y
15 ***Toomey***	Y	Y	Y	N	Y	Y	Y
16 ***Pitts***	Y	Y	Y	N	Y	Y	Y
17 ***Gekas***	Y	Y	Y	N	Y	Y	Y
18 Doyle	?	?	?	Y	Y	N	Y
19 ***Platts***	?	Y	Y	N	Y	N	Y
20 Mascara	Y	Y	Y	Y	Y	N	Y
21 ***English***	N	Y	Y	N	Y	Y	Y
RHODE ISLAND							
1 Kennedy	Y	Y	Y	Y	Y	N	Y
2 Langevin	Y	Y	Y	Y	Y	N	Y
SOUTH CAROLINA							
1 ***Brown***	Y	Y	Y	N	Y	Y	Y
2 ***Wilson***	Y	Y	Y	N	Y	Y	Y
3 ***Graham***	Y	Y	Y	N	Y	Y	Y
4 ***DeMint***	Y	Y	Y	N	Y	Y	Y
5 Spratt	Y	Y	Y	Y	Y	N	Y
6 Clyburn	Y	Y	Y	Y	Y	N	Y
SOUTH DAKOTA							
AL ***Thune***	Y	Y	Y	N	Y	N	Y

	80	81	82	83	84	85	86
TENNESSEE							
1 ***Jenkins***	Y	Y	Y	N	Y	Y	Y
2 ***Duncan***	Y	Y	Y	N	Y	Y	Y
3 ***Wamp***	Y	Y	Y	N	Y	Y	Y
4 ***Hilleary***	Y	Y	Y	N	Y	P	Y
5 Clement	+	+	+	Y	Y	N	Y
6 Gordon	Y	Y	Y	Y	Y	N	?
7 ***Bryant***	Y	Y	Y	N	Y	Y	Y
8 Tanner	Y	Y	Y	Y	Y	N	Y
9 Ford	Y	Y	Y	Y	Y	N	Y
TEXAS							
1 Sandlin	Y	Y	Y	Y	Y	N	Y
2 Turner	Y	Y	Y	Y	Y	N	Y
3 ***Johnson, Sam***	Y	Y	Y	N	Y	Y	Y
4 Hall	Y	Y	Y	Y	Y	Y	Y
5 ***Sessions***	?	?	?	N	Y	Y	Y
6 ***Barton***	Y	Y	Y	N	Y	Y	Y
7 ***Culberson***	Y	Y	Y	N	Y	Y	Y
8 ***Brady***	Y	Y	Y	N	Y	Y	Y
9 Lampson	Y	Y	Y	Y	Y	N	Y
10 Doggett	Y	Y	Y	Y	Y	N	Y
11 Edwards	Y	Y	Y	Y	Y	Y	Y
12 ***Granger***	Y	Y	Y	N	Y	Y	Y
13 ***Thornberry***	Y	Y	Y	N	Y	Y	Y
14 ***Paul***	Y	Y	N	N	Y	Y	N
15 Hinojosa	Y	Y	Y	Y	Y	N	Y
16 Reyes	Y	Y	Y	Y	Y	N	Y
17 Stenholm	Y	Y	Y	Y	Y	N	Y
18 Jackson-Lee	Y	Y	Y	Y	Y	N	Y
19 ***Combest***	Y	Y	Y	N	Y	Y	Y
20 Gonzalez	Y	Y	Y	Y	Y	N	Y
21 ***Smith***	Y	Y	Y	N	Y	Y	Y
22 ***DeLay***	Y	Y	Y	N	Y	Y	Y
23 ***Bonilla***	Y	Y	Y	N	Y	Y	Y
24 Frost	Y	Y	Y	Y	Y	N	Y
25 Bentsen	Y	Y	Y	Y	Y	N	Y
26 ***Armey***	Y	Y	Y	N	Y	Y	Y
27 Ortiz	Y	Y	Y	Y	Y	N	Y
28 Rodriguez	Y	Y	Y	Y	Y	N	Y
29 Green	N	Y	Y	Y	Y	N	Y
30 Johnson, E.B.	Y	Y	Y	Y	Y	N	Y
UTAH							
1 ***Hansen***	Y	Y	Y	N	Y	Y	Y
2 Matheson	Y	Y	Y	Y	Y	Y	Y
3 ***Cannon***	?	?	?	N	Y	Y	Y
VERMONT							
AL *Sanders*	Y	Y	Y	Y	Y	N	Y
VIRGINIA							
1 ***Davis, Jo Ann***	Y	Y	Y	N	Y	Y	Y
2 ***Schrock***	Y	Y	Y	N	Y	Y	Y
3 Scott	Y	Y	?	Y	Y	N	Y
4 ***Forbes***	Y	Y	Y	N	Y	Y	Y
5 *Goode*	Y	Y	?	N	Y	Y	Y
6 ***Goodlatte***	Y	Y	Y	N	Y	Y	Y
7 ***Cantor***	Y	Y	Y	N	Y	Y	Y
8 Moran	Y	Y	Y	Y	Y	N	Y
9 Boucher	Y	Y	Y	Y	Y	N	Y
10 ***Wolf***	Y	Y	Y	N	Y	Y	Y
11 ***Davis, T.***	Y	Y	Y	N	Y	Y	Y
WASHINGTON							
1 Inslee	Y	Y	Y	Y	Y	N	Y
2 Larsen	N	Y	Y	Y	Y	N	Y
3 Baird	Y	Y	Y	Y	Y	N	Y
4 ***Hastings***	Y	Y	Y	N	Y	Y	Y
5 ***Nethercutt***	Y	Y	Y	N	Y	Y	Y
6 Dicks	Y	Y	Y	Y	Y	N	Y
7 McDermott	N	Y	Y	Y	Y	N	Y
8 ***Dunn***	Y	Y	Y	N	Y	Y	Y
9 Smith	Y	Y	Y	Y	Y	N	Y
WEST VIRGINIA							
1 Mollohan	?	?	?	Y	Y	N	Y
2 ***Capito***	Y	Y	Y	N	Y	N	Y
3 Rahall	Y	Y	Y	Y	Y	N	Y
WISCONSIN							
1 ***Ryan***	?	?	?	?	?	?	?
2 Baldwin	Y	Y	Y	Y	Y	N	Y
3 Kind	Y	Y	Y	Y	Y	N	Y
4 Kleczka	Y	Y	Y	Y	Y	N	Y
5 Barrett	Y	Y	Y	Y	Y	N	Y
6 ***Petri***	Y	Y	Y	N	Y	N	Y
7 Obey	Y	Y	Y	Y	Y	N	Y
8 ***Green***	Y	Y	Y	N	Y	N	Y
9 ***Sensenbrenner***	Y	Y	N	N	Y	Y	Y
WYOMING							
AL ***Cubin***	Y	Y	Y	N	Y	Y	Y

Southern states - Ala., Ark., Fla., Ga., Ky., La., Miss., N.C., Okla., S.C., Tenn., Texas, Va.

Key

Y	Voted for (yea).
#	Paired for.
+	Announced for.
N	Voted against (nay).
X	Paired against.
–	Announced against.
P	Voted "present."
C	Voted "present" to avoid possible conflict of interest.
?	Did not vote or otherwise make a position known.

Democrats **Republicans**
Independents

87. HR 3762. Employee Pensions/Previous Question. Linder, R-Ga., motion to order the previous question (thus ending debate and possibility of amendment) on adoption of the rule (H Res 386) to provide for House floor consideration of the bill that would increase employees' control over their pension funds and give them more access to investment information. Motion agreed to 218-208: R 217-0; D 0-207 (ND 0-154, SD 0-53); I 1-1. April 11, 2002.

88. HR 3762. Employee Pensions/Rule. Adoption of the resolution (H Res 386) to provide for House floor consideration of the bill that would increase employees' control over their pension funds and give them more access to investment information. Adopted 215-209: R 214-1; D 0-207 (ND 0-154, SD 0-53); I 1-1. April 11, 2002.

89. Procedural Motion/Journal. Approval of the House Journal of Wednesday, April 10, 2002. Approved 360-56: R 203-8; D 155-48 (ND 112-40, SD 43-8); I 2-0. April 11, 2002.

90. HR 3762. Employee Pensions/Democratic Substitute. Miller, D-Calif., substitute amendment that would allow employees to sell employer-contributed company stock after three years of participation in a pension plan and let them sell stock now held in their pension funds one year after the bill's enactment. Employers that allow employees to invest in company stock would have to provide employees independent investment advice. The bill would require 30-day notice to employees of any limitation on company stock sales and mandate equal employer-employee representation on pension boards. Rejected 187-232: R 1-209; D 185-22 (ND 144-10, SD 41-12); I 1-1. April 11, 2002.

91. HR 3762. Employee Pensions/Recommit. Miller, D-Calif., motion to recommit the bill to the House Education and the Workforce Committee with instructions to add language that would require that deferred compensation be included in an employee's income in the year it was earned, provided the benefit is secured with assets not owned by the employer and not subject to the claims of the creditors. Motion rejected 204-212: R 0-209; D 203-2 (ND 153-0, SD 50-2); I 1-1. April 11, 2002.

92. HR 3762. Employee Pensions/Passage. Passage of the bill that would increase employees' control over their pension funds and give them more access to investment information. It would allow employees to sell company stock three years after employers contribute it and give them the flexibility to sell company stock now held in their pension funds over the next five years. The bill would require 30-day notice to employees of restrictions on stock sales lasting more than three days and make insiders subject to those same limits. It also would allow employers to offer professional investment advice to employees after disclosing potential conflicts of interest and fees. Passed 255-163: R 208-2; D 46-160 (ND 23-131, SD 23-29); I 1-1. A "yea" was a vote in support of the president's position. April 11, 2002.

	87	88	89	90	91	92
ALABAMA						
1 *Callahan*	Y	Y	Y	?	?	?
2 *Everett*	Y	Y	Y	N	N	Y
3 *Riley*	Y	Y	?	N	?	?
4 *Aderholt*	Y	Y	N	N	N	Y
5 Cramer	N	N	Y	N	Y	Y
6 *Bachus*	Y	Y	N	N	N	Y
7 Hilliard	N	N	N	Y	Y	N
ALASKA						
AL *Young*	Y	Y	Y	N	N	Y
ARIZONA						
1 *Flake*	Y	Y	Y	N	N	Y
2 Pastor	N	N	Y	Y	Y	N
3 *Stump*	Y	Y	N	N	N	Y
4 *Shadegg*	Y	Y	Y	N	N	Y
5 *Kolbe*	Y	Y	Y	N	N	Y
6 *Hayworth*	Y	Y	Y	N	N	Y
ARKANSAS						
1 Berry	N	N	N	Y	Y	N
2 Snyder	N	N	Y	N	Y	Y
3 *Boozman*	Y	Y	Y	N	N	Y
4 Ross	N	N	Y	N	Y	Y
CALIFORNIA						
1 Thompson	N	N	N	Y	Y	N
2 *Herger*	Y	Y	Y	N	N	Y
3 *Ose*	Y	Y	Y	N	N	Y
4 *Doolittle*	Y	Y	Y	N	N	Y
5 Matsui	N	N	Y	Y	Y	N
6 Woolsey	N	N	Y	Y	Y	N
7 Miller, George	N	N	Y	Y	Y	N
8 Pelosi	N	N	Y	Y	Y	N
9 Lee	N	N	Y	Y	Y	N
10 Tauscher	N	N	N	Y	Y	N
11 *Pombo*	Y	Y	Y	N	N	Y
12 Lantos	N	N	Y	Y	Y	N
13 Stark	N	N	Y	Y	Y	N
14 Eshoo	N	N	Y	Y	Y	N
15 Honda	N	N	Y	Y	Y	N
16 Lofgren	N	N	Y	Y	Y	N
17 Farr	N	N	Y	Y	Y	N
18 Condit	N	N	N	Y	Y	Y
19 *Radanovich*	Y	Y	Y	N	?	Y
20 Dooley	N	N	N	Y	Y	Y
21 *Thomas*	Y	Y	Y	N	N	Y
22 Capps	N	N	Y	Y	Y	N
23 *Gallegly*	Y	Y	Y	N	N	Y
24 Sherman	N	N	Y	Y	Y	N
25 *McKeon*	Y	Y	Y	N	N	Y
26 Berman	N	N	Y	Y	Y	N
27 Schiff	N	N	Y	Y	Y	N
28 *Dreier*	Y	Y	Y	N	N	Y
29 Waxman	N	N	Y	Y	Y	N
30 Becerra	N	N	Y	Y	Y	N
31 Solis	N	N	Y	Y	Y	N
32 Watson	N	N	Y	Y	Y	N
33 Roybal-Allard	N	N	Y	Y	Y	N
34 Napolitano	N	N	Y	Y	Y	N
35 Waters	N	N	N	Y	Y	N
36 Harman	N	N	Y	Y	Y	N
37 Millender-McD.	N	N	Y	N	Y	N
38 *Horn*	Y	Y	Y	N	N	?

	87	88	89	90	91	92
39 *Royce*	Y	?	Y	N	N	Y
40 *Lewis*	Y	Y	Y	N	N	Y
41 *Miller, Gary*	Y	Y	Y	N	N	Y
42 Baca	N	N	Y	Y	Y	N
43 *Calvert*	Y	Y	Y	N	N	Y
44 *Bono*	Y	Y	Y	N	N	Y
45 *Rohrabacher*	Y	Y	Y	N	N	Y
46 Sanchez	N	N	Y	N	Y	N
47 *Cox*	Y	Y	Y	N	N	Y
48 *Issa*	Y	Y	Y	N	N	Y
49 Davis	N	N	Y	Y	Y	N
50 Filner	N	N	N	Y	Y	N
51 *Cunningham*	Y	Y	Y	N	N	Y
52 *Hunter*	Y	Y	Y	N	N	Y
COLORADO						
1 DeGette	N	N	Y	Y	Y	N
2 Udall	N	N	N	Y	Y	Y
3 *McInnis*	Y	Y	Y	N	N	Y
4 *Schaffer*	Y	Y	?	N	N	Y
5 *Hefley*	Y	Y	N	N	N	Y
6 *Tancredo*	Y	Y	P	N	N	Y
CONNECTICUT						
1 Larson	N	N	N	Y	Y	N
2 *Simmons*	Y	Y	Y	N	N	Y
3 DeLauro	N	N	?	Y	Y	N
4 *Shays*	Y	Y	Y	N	N	Y
5 Maloney	N	N	Y	Y	Y	Y
6 *Johnson*	Y	Y	Y	N	N	Y
DELAWARE						
AL *Castle*	Y	Y	Y	N	N	Y
FLORIDA						
1 *Miller, J.*	Y	Y	Y	N	N	Y
2 Boyd	N	N	Y	N	Y	Y
3 Brown	N	N	?	Y	Y	N
4 *Crenshaw*	Y	Y	Y	N	N	Y
5 Thurman	N	N	Y	Y	Y	N
6 *Stearns*	Y	Y	Y	N	N	Y
7 *Mica*	Y	Y	Y	N	N	Y
8 *Keller*	Y	Y	Y	N	N	Y
9 *Bilirakis*	Y	Y	Y	N	N	Y
10 *Young*	Y	Y	Y	N	?	Y
11 Davis	N	N	Y	N	Y	N
12 *Putnam*	Y	Y	Y	N	N	Y
13 *Miller, D.*	Y	Y	Y	N	N	Y
14 *Goss*	Y	Y	Y	N	N	Y
15 *Weldon*	Y	Y	Y	N	N	Y
16 *Foley*	Y	Y	Y	N	N	Y
17 Meek	N	N	?	Y	?	?
18 *Ros-Lehtinen*	Y	Y	Y	N	N	Y
19 Wexler	N	N	Y	Y	Y	N
20 Deutsch	N	N	Y	Y	Y	N
21 *Diaz-Balart*	Y	Y	Y	?	?	?
22 *Shaw*	Y	Y	Y	N	N	Y
23 Hastings	N	N	N	Y	Y	N
GEORGIA						
1 *Kingston*	Y	Y	Y	N	N	Y
2 Bishop	N	N	Y	Y	Y	Y
3 *Collins*	Y	Y	Y	N	N	Y
4 McKinney	N	N	N	Y	Y	N
5 Lewis	N	N	N	Y	Y	N
6 *Isakson*	Y	Y	Y	N	N	Y
7 *Barr*	Y	Y	Y	N	N	Y
8 *Chambliss*	Y	Y	Y	N	N	Y
9 *Deal*	Y	Y	Y	N	N	Y
10 *Norwood*	Y	Y	Y	N	N	Y
11 *Linder*	Y	Y	Y	N	N	Y
HAWAII						
1 Abercrombie	N	N	Y	Y	Y	N
2 Mink	N	N	Y	Y	Y	N
IDAHO						
1 *Otter*	Y	+	Y	N	N	Y
2 *Simpson*	Y	Y	Y	N	N	Y
ILLINOIS						
1 Rush	N	N	Y	Y	Y	N
2 Jackson	N	N	Y	Y	Y	N
3 Lipinski	N	N	N	Y	Y	N
4 Gutierrez	N	N	N	Y	Y	N
5 Blagojevich	N	N	Y	Y	Y	N
6 *Hyde*	Y	Y	Y	N	N	Y
7 Davis	N	N	Y	Y	Y	N
8 *Crane*	Y	Y	Y	N	N	Y
9 Schakowsky	N	N	N	Y	Y	N
10 *Kirk*	Y	Y	?	N	N	Y
11 *Weller*	Y	Y	N	N	N	Y
12 Costello	N	N	N	Y	Y	N
13 *Biggert*	Y	Y	Y	N	N	Y

ND Northern Democrats   SD Southern Democrats

	87	88	89	90	91	92
14 ***Hastert***					N	Y
15 ***Johnson***	Y	Y	Y	N	N	Y
16 ***Manzullo***	Y	Y	Y	N	N	Y
17 Evans	N	N	N	Y	Y	N
18 ***LaHood***	Y	Y	Y	N	N	Y
19 Phelps	N	N	Y	Y	Y	Y
20 ***Shimkus***	Y	Y	Y	N	N	Y
INDIANA						
1 Visclosky	N	N	N	Y	Y	N
2 ***Pence***	Y	Y	Y	N	N	Y
3 Roemer	N	N	Y	Y	Y	N
4 ***Souder***	Y	Y	Y	N	N	Y
5 ***Buyer***	Y	Y	Y	?	?	?
6 ***Burton***	Y	Y	Y	–	–	+
7 ***Kerns***	Y	Y	Y	N	N	Y
8 ***Hostettler***	Y	Y	Y	N	N	Y
9 Hill	N	N	Y	N	Y	Y
10 Carson	N	N	Y	Y	Y	N
IOWA						
1 ***Leach***	Y	Y	Y	N	N	Y
2 ***Nussle***	Y	Y	Y	N	N	Y
3 Boswell	N	N	Y	Y	Y	N
4 ***Ganske***	Y	Y	Y	N	N	Y
5 ***Latham***	Y	Y	Y	N	N	Y
KANSAS						
1 ***Moran***	Y	Y	N	N	N	Y
2 ***Ryun***	Y	Y	Y	N	N	Y
3 Moore	N	N	Y	N	Y	N
4 ***Tiahrt***	Y	Y	Y	N	–	Y
KENTUCKY						
1 ***Whitfield***	Y	Y	?	N	N	Y
2 ***Lewis***	Y	Y	Y	N	N	Y
3 ***Northup***	Y	Y	Y	N	N	Y
4 Lucas	N	N	Y	N	N	Y
5 ***Rogers***	Y	Y	Y	N	N	Y
6 ***Fletcher***	Y	Y	Y	N	N	Y
LOUISIANA						
1 ***Vitter***	Y	Y	Y	N	N	Y
2 Jefferson	N	N	Y	Y	Y	N
3 ***Tauzin***	Y	Y	Y	N	N	Y
4 ***McCrery***	Y	Y	Y	N	N	Y
5 ***Cooksey***	Y	Y	Y	?	?	?
6 ***Baker***	Y	Y	Y	N	N	Y
7 John	N	N	Y	N	Y	Y
MAINE						
1 Allen	?	?	?	?	?	?
2 Baldacci	N	N	Y	Y	Y	N
MARYLAND						
1 ***Gilchrest***	Y	Y	Y	N	N	Y
2 ***Ehrlich***	Y	Y	Y	N	N	Y
3 Cardin	N	N	Y	N	Y	N
4 Wynn	N	N	Y	Y	Y	N
5 Hoyer	N	N	Y	Y	?	N
6 ***Bartlett***	Y	Y	Y	N	N	Y
7 Cummings	N	N	Y	Y	Y	N
8 ***Morella***	Y	Y	Y	Y	N	Y
MASSACHUSETTS						
1 Olver	N	N	N	Y	Y	N
2 Neal	N	N	N	Y	Y	N
3 McGovern	N	N	N	Y	Y	N
4 Frank	N	N	Y	Y	Y	N
5 Meehan	N	N	Y	?	?	?
6 Tierney	N	N	Y	Y	Y	N
7 Markey	N	N	Y	Y	Y	N
8 Capuano	N	N	N	Y	Y	N
9 Lynch	N	N	Y	Y	Y	N
10 Delahunt	N	N	N	Y	Y	N
MICHIGAN						
1 Stupak	N	N	N	Y	Y	N
2 ***Hoekstra***	Y	Y	Y	N	N	Y
3 ***Ehlers***	Y	Y	Y	N	N	Y
4 ***Camp***	Y	Y	Y	N	N	Y
5 Barcia	N	N	Y	N	Y	Y
6 ***Upton***	Y	Y	Y	N	N	Y
7 ***Smith***	Y	Y	Y	N	N	Y
8 ***Rogers***	Y	Y	Y	N	N	Y
9 Kildee	N	N	Y	Y	Y	N
10 Bonior	N	N	Y	Y	Y	N
11 ***Knollenberg***	Y	Y	Y	N	N	Y
12 Levin	N	N	Y	Y	Y	N
13 Rivers	N	N	?	Y	Y	N
14 Conyers	N	N	Y	Y	Y	N
15 Kilpatrick	N	N	Y	Y	Y	N
16 Dingell	N	N	N	Y	Y	N
MINNESOTA						
1 ***Gutknecht***	Y	N	N	N	N	N
2 ***Kennedy***	Y	Y	Y	N	N	Y
3 ***Ramstad***	Y	Y	Y	N	N	Y
4 McCollum	N	N	Y	Y	Y	N
5 Sabo	N	N	N	Y	Y	N
6 Luther	N	N	Y	Y	Y	Y
7 Peterson	N	N	N	N	Y	Y
8 Oberstar	N	N	N	Y	Y	N
MISSISSIPPI						
1 ***Wicker***	Y	Y	Y	N	N	Y
2 Thompson	N	N	N	Y	Y	N
3 ***Pickering***	Y	Y	Y	N	N	Y
4 Shows	N	N	Y	Y	Y	Y
5 Taylor	N	N	N	Y	Y	Y
MISSOURI						
1 Clay	N	N	Y	Y	Y	N
2 ***Akin***	Y	Y	Y	N	N	Y
3 Gephardt	N	N	Y	Y	Y	N
4 Skelton	N	N	Y	Y	Y	Y
5 McCarthy	N	N	Y	Y	Y	N
6 ***Graves***	Y	Y	Y	N	N	Y
7 ***Blunt***	Y	Y	Y	N	N	Y
8 ***Emerson***	Y	Y	Y	N	N	Y
9 ***Hulshof***	Y	Y	Y	N	N	Y
MONTANA						
AL ***Rehberg***	Y	Y	Y	N	N	Y
NEBRASKA						
1 ***Bereuter***	Y	Y	Y	N	N	Y
2 ***Terry***	Y	Y	Y	N	N	Y
3 ***Osborne***	Y	Y	Y	N	N	Y
NEVADA						
1 Berkley	N	N	Y	Y	Y	N
2 ***Gibbons***	Y	Y	Y	N	N	Y
NEW HAMPSHIRE						
1 ***Sununu***	Y	Y	Y	N	N	Y
2 ***Bass***	Y	Y	Y	N	N	Y
NEW JERSEY						
1 Andrews	N	N	Y	Y	Y	N
2 ***LoBiondo***	Y	Y	N	N	N	Y
3 ***Saxton***	Y	Y	Y	N	N	Y
4 ***Smith***	Y	Y	Y	N	N	Y
5 ***Roukema***	?	?	?	?	?	?
6 Pallone	N	N	Y	Y	Y	N
7 ***Ferguson***	Y	Y	Y	N	N	Y
8 Pascrell	N	N	Y	Y	Y	N
9 Rothman	N	N	Y	Y	Y	N
10 Payne	N	N	Y	Y	Y	N
11 ***Frelinghuysen***	Y	Y	Y	N	N	Y
12 Holt	N	N	N	Y	Y	N
13 Menendez	N	N	N	Y	Y	N
NEW MEXICO						
1 ***Wilson***	Y	Y	Y	N	N	Y
2 ***Skeen***	Y	Y	Y	N	N	Y
3 Udall	N	N	N	Y	Y	N
NEW YORK						
1 ***Grucci***	Y	Y	Y	N	N	Y
2 Israel	N	N	Y	Y	Y	N
3 ***King***	Y	Y	Y	N	N	Y
4 McCarthy	N	N	Y	Y	Y	Y
5 Ackerman	N	N	Y	Y	Y	N
6 Meeks	N	N	Y	Y	Y	N
7 Crowley	N	N	Y	Y	Y	Y
8 Nadler	N	N	Y	Y	Y	N
9 Weiner	N	N	N	Y	Y	N
10 Towns	?	?	?	Y	Y	N
11 Owens	N	N	Y	Y	Y	N
12 Velázquez	N	N	Y	Y	Y	N
13 ***Fossella***	Y	Y	Y	N	N	Y
14 Maloney	N	N	Y	Y	Y	N
15 Rangel	N	N	Y	Y	Y	N
16 Serrano	N	N	Y	Y	Y	N
17 Engel	N	N	Y	Y	Y	N
18 Lowey	N	N	Y	Y	Y	N
19 ***Kelly***	Y	Y	Y	N	N	Y
20 ***Gilman***	Y	Y	Y	N	N	Y
21 McNulty	N	N	N	Y	Y	N
22 ***Sweeney***	Y	Y	Y	N	N	Y
23 ***Boehlert***	Y	Y	Y	N	N	Y
24 ***McHugh***	Y	Y	Y	N	N	Y
25 ***Walsh***	Y	Y	Y	N	N	Y
26 Hinchey	N	N	N	Y	Y	N
27 ***Reynolds***	Y	Y	Y	N	N	Y
28 Slaughter	N	N	N	Y	Y	N
29 LaFalce	N	N	Y	Y	Y	N
30 ***Quinn***	Y	Y	Y	N	N	Y
31 ***Houghton***	Y	Y	Y	N	N	Y
NORTH CAROLINA						
1 Clayton	N	N	Y	Y	Y	N
2 Etheridge	N	N	Y	Y	Y	N
3 ***Jones***	Y	Y	Y	?	N	N
4 Price	N	N	Y	Y	Y	Y
5 ***Burr***	Y	Y	Y	N	N	Y
6 ***Coble***	Y	Y	Y	N	N	Y
7 McIntyre	N	N	Y	Y	Y	Y
8 ***Hayes***	Y	Y	Y	N	N	Y
9 ***Myrick***	Y	Y	Y	N	N	Y
10 ***Ballenger***	Y	Y	?	N	N	Y
11 ***Taylor***	Y	Y	Y	N	N	Y
12 Watt	N	N	Y	Y	Y	N
NORTH DAKOTA						
AL Pomeroy	N	N	Y	N	Y	Y
OHIO						
1 ***Chabot***	Y	Y	Y	N	N	Y
2 ***Portman***	Y	Y	Y	N	N	Y
3 Hall	N	N	Y	Y	Y	Y
4 ***Oxley***	Y	Y	Y	N	N	Y
5 ***Gillmor***	Y	Y	Y	N	N	Y
6 Strickland	N	N	N	Y	Y	N
7 ***Hobson***	Y	Y	Y	N	N	Y
8 ***Boehner***	Y	Y	Y	N	N	Y
9 Kaptur	N	N	Y	Y	Y	N
10 Kucinich	N	N	N	Y	Y	N
11 Jones	N	N	Y	Y	Y	N
12 ***Tiberi***	Y	Y	Y	N	N	Y
13 Brown	N	N	Y	Y	Y	N
14 Sawyer	N	N	Y	Y	Y	N
15 ***Pryce***	?	?	?	?	?	?
16 ***Regula***	Y	Y	Y	N	N	Y
17 Traficant	?	?	?	?	?	?
18 ***Ney***	Y	Y	Y	N	N	Y
19 ***LaTourette***	Y	Y	Y	N	N	Y
OKLAHOMA						
1 ***Sullivan***	Y	Y	Y	N	N	Y
2 Carson	N	N	Y	N	Y	Y
3 ***Watkins***	Y	Y	Y	N	N	Y
4 ***Watts***	Y	Y	Y	N	N	Y
5 ***Istook***	Y	Y	Y	N	N	Y
6 ***Lucas***	Y	Y	Y	N	N	Y
OREGON						
1 Wu	N	N	N	Y	Y	Y
2 ***Walden***	Y	Y	Y	N	N	Y
3 Blumenauer	N	N	Y	Y	Y	N
4 DeFazio	N	N	N	Y	Y	N
5 Hooley	N	N	Y	Y	Y	Y
PENNSYLVANIA						
1 Brady	N	N	N	Y	Y	N
2 Fattah	N	N	Y	Y	Y	N
3 Borski	N	N	Y	Y	Y	N
4 ***Hart***	Y	Y	Y	N	N	Y
5 ***Peterson***	Y	Y	Y	N	N	Y
6 Holden	N	N	Y	Y	Y	Y
7 ***Weldon***	Y	Y	Y	N	N	Y
8 ***Greenwood***	Y	Y	Y	N	N	Y
9 ***Shuster, Bill***	Y	Y	Y	N	N	Y
10 ***Sherwood***	Y	Y	Y	N	N	Y
11 Kanjorski	N	N	Y	Y	Y	N
12 Murtha	N	N	Y	Y	Y	N
13 Hoeffel	N	N	Y	Y	Y	N
14 Coyne	N	N	Y	Y	Y	N
15 ***Toomey***	Y	Y	Y	N	N	Y
16 ***Pitts***	Y	Y	Y	?	N	Y
17 ***Gekas***	Y	Y	Y	N	N	Y
18 Doyle	N	N	Y	Y	Y	N
19 ***Platts***	Y	Y	Y	N	N	Y
20 Mascara	N	N	Y	Y	Y	N
21 ***English***	Y	Y	N	N	N	Y
RHODE ISLAND						
1 Kennedy	N	N	Y	Y	Y	N
2 Langevin	N	N	Y	Y	Y	N
SOUTH CAROLINA						
1 ***Brown***	Y	Y	Y	N	N	Y
2 ***Wilson***	Y	Y	Y	N	N	Y
3 ***Graham***	Y	Y	Y	N	N	Y
4 ***DeMint***	Y	Y	Y	N	N	Y
5 Spratt	N	N	Y	Y	Y	N
6 Clyburn	N	N	Y	Y	Y	N
SOUTH DAKOTA						
AL ***Thune***	Y	Y	Y	N	N	Y
TENNESSEE						
1 ***Jenkins***	Y	Y	Y	N	N	Y
2 ***Duncan***	Y	Y	Y	N	N	Y
3 ***Wamp***	Y	Y	Y	N	N	Y
4 ***Hilleary***	Y	Y	Y	N	N	Y
5 Clement	N	N	Y	Y	Y	Y
6 Gordon	N	N	Y	Y	Y	Y
7 ***Bryant***	Y	Y	Y	N	N	Y
8 Tanner	N	N	Y	N	Y	Y
9 Ford	?	?	?	?	?	?
TEXAS						
1 Sandlin	N	N	Y	Y	Y	N
2 Turner	N	N	Y	N	Y	Y
3 ***Johnson, Sam***	Y	Y	Y	N	N	Y
4 Hall	N	N	Y	N	N	Y
5 ***Sessions***	?	?	?	?	?	?
6 ***Barton***	Y	Y	Y	N	N	Y
7 ***Culberson***	Y	Y	Y	N	N	Y
8 ***Brady***	Y	Y	Y	N	N	Y
9 Lampson	N	N	Y	Y	Y	N
10 Doggett	N	N	Y	Y	Y	N
11 Edwards	N	N	Y	Y	Y	N
12 ***Granger***	Y	Y	Y	N	N	Y
13 ***Thornberry***	Y	Y	Y	N	N	Y
14 ***Paul***	Y	Y	Y	N	N	?
15 Hinojosa	N	N	Y	Y	Y	Y
16 Reyes	N	N	Y	Y	Y	N
17 Stenholm	N	N	Y	N	Y	Y
18 Jackson-Lee	N	N	N	Y	Y	N
19 ***Combest***	Y	Y	Y	N	N	Y
20 Gonzalez	N	N	Y	Y	Y	N
21 ***Smith***	Y	Y	Y	N	N	Y
22 ***DeLay***	Y	Y	Y	N	N	Y
23 ***Bonilla***	Y	Y	Y	N	N	Y
24 Frost	N	N	Y	Y	Y	N
25 Bentsen	N	N	Y	Y	Y	Y
26 ***Armey***	Y	Y	Y	N	N	Y
27 Ortiz	N	N	Y	Y	Y	N
28 Rodriguez	N	N	Y	Y	Y	N
29 Green	N	N	N	Y	Y	N
30 Johnson, E.B.	N	N	Y	Y	Y	N
UTAH						
1 ***Hansen***	Y	Y	Y	N	N	Y
2 Matheson	N	N	N	N	Y	Y
3 ***Cannon***	Y	Y	Y	N	N	Y
VERMONT						
AL *Sanders*	N	N	Y	Y	Y	N
VIRGINIA						
1 ***Davis, Jo Ann***	Y	Y	Y	N	N	Y
2 ***Schrock***	Y	Y	Y	N	N	Y
3 Scott	N	N	Y	Y	Y	N
4 ***Forbes***	Y	Y	Y	N	N	Y
5 *Goode*	Y	Y	Y	N	N	Y
6 ***Goodlatte***	Y	Y	Y	N	N	Y
7 ***Cantor***	Y	Y	Y	N	N	Y
8 Moran	N	N	Y	Y	Y	Y
9 Boucher	N	N	Y	Y	Y	Y
10 ***Wolf***	Y	Y	Y	N	N	Y
11 ***Davis, T.***	Y	Y	Y	N	N	Y
WASHINGTON						
1 Inslee	N	N	Y	Y	Y	N
2 Larsen	N	N	N	Y	Y	Y
3 Baird	N	N	N	Y	Y	N
4 ***Hastings***	Y	Y	Y	N	N	Y
5 ***Nethercutt***	Y	Y	Y	N	N	Y
6 Dicks	N	N	Y	Y	Y	N
7 McDermott	N	N	N	Y	Y	N
8 ***Dunn***	Y	Y	Y	N	N	Y
9 Smith	N	N	Y	N	Y	Y
WEST VIRGINIA						
1 Mollohan	N	N	Y	Y	Y	N
2 ***Capito***	Y	Y	Y	N	N	Y
3 Rahall	N	N	Y	Y	Y	N
WISCONSIN						
1 ***Ryan***	?	?	?	?	?	?
2 Baldwin	N	N	Y	Y	Y	N
3 Kind	N	N	Y	Y	Y	Y
4 Kleczka	N	N	Y	Y	Y	N
5 Barrett	N	N	Y	Y	Y	N
6 ***Petri***	Y	Y	Y	N	N	Y
7 Obey	N	N	N	Y	Y	N
8 ***Green***	Y	Y	Y	N	N	Y
9 ***Sensenbrenner***	Y	Y	Y	N	N	Y
WYOMING						
AL ***Cubin***	Y	Y	Y	N	N	Y

Southern states - Ala., Ark., Fla., Ga., Ky., La., Miss., N.C., Okla., S.C., Tenn., Texas, Va.

Key

Y	Voted for (yea).
#	Paired for.
+	Announced for.
N	Voted against (nay).
X	Paired against.
−	Announced against.
P	Voted "present."
C	Voted "present" to avoid possible conflict of interest.
?	Did not vote or otherwise make a position known.

Democrats **Republicans**
Independents

---

93. HR 1374. Philip Ruppe Building/Passage. J. Davis, R-Va., motion to suspend the rules and pass the bill that would name a U.S. Post Office building in Lake Linden, Mich., after former Rep. Philip Edward Ruppe, R-Mich. Motion agreed to 408-0: R 208-0; D 198-0 (ND 148-0, SD 50-0); I 2-0. A two-thirds majority of those present and voting (272 in this case) is required for passage under suspension of the rules. April 16, 2002.

94. HR 4156. Clergy Housing/Passage. Ramstad, R-Minn., motion to suspend the rules and pass the bill that would clarify an Internal Revenue Service regulation that limits the housing allowance that a clergy member can exclude from taxable income to fair market value. Motion agreed to 408-0: R 207-0; D 199-0 (ND 149-0, SD 50-0); I 2-0. A two-thirds majority of those present and voting (272 in this case) is required for passage under suspension of the rules. April 16, 2002.

95. HR 4167. Family Farmers/Passage. Sensenbrenner, R-Wis., motion to suspend the rules and pass the bill that would extend for eight months Chapter 12 bankruptcy protection for family farmers. Motion agreed to 407-3: R 207-3; D 198-0 (ND 148-0, SD 50-0); I 2-0. A two-thirds majority of those present and voting (274 in this case) is required for passage under suspension of the rules. April 16, 2002.

96. HR 476. Abortion for Minors/Recommit. Jackson-Lee, D-Texas, motion to recommit the bill back to the House Judiciary Committee with instructions that the bill be reported back with an amendment that would exclude a minor's adult siblings, grandparents or religious leaders from transporting the minor across state lines to circumvent parental consent laws. Motion rejected 173-246: R 12-203; D 160-42 (ND 129-24, SD 31-18); I 1-1. April 17, 2002.

97. HR 476. Abortions for Minors/Passage. Passage of the bill to make it a federal crime to transport a minor across state lines with the intent to obtain an abortion and circumvent state parental consent laws unless it is done to protect the life of the minor. The minor would be protected from prosecution under the bill, which carries a punishment of up to one year in jail and a $100,000 fine. Passed 260-161: R 201-14; D 58-146 (ND 33-120, SD 25-26); I 1-1. A "yea" was a vote in support of the president's position. April 17, 2002.

98. Procedural Motion/Journal. Approval of the House Journal of Tuesday, April 16, 2002. Approved 361-51: R 199-12; D 160-39 (ND 120-31, SD 40-8); I 2-0. April 17, 2002.

	93	94	95	96	97	98
ALABAMA						
1 *Callahan*	Y	Y	Y	N	+	Y
2 *Everett*	Y	Y	Y	N	Y	Y
3 *Riley*	?	+	+	N	Y	Y
4 *Aderholt*	Y	Y	Y	N	Y	N
5 Cramer	Y	Y	Y	N	Y	Y
6 *Bachus*	Y	Y	Y	N	Y	Y
7 Hilliard	?	?	?	Y	N	N
ALASKA						
AL *Young*	Y	?	Y	N	Y	Y
ARIZONA						
1 *Flake*	Y	Y	N	N	Y	Y
2 Pastor	Y	Y	Y	Y	N	Y
3 *Stump*	Y	Y	Y	N	Y	Y
4 *Shadegg*	Y	Y	Y	N	Y	Y
5 *Kolbe*	Y	Y	Y	N	Y	Y
6 *Hayworth*	Y	Y	Y	N	Y	Y
ARKANSAS						
1 Berry	Y	Y	Y	N	Y	Y
2 Snyder	Y	Y	Y	N	Y	Y
3 *Boozman*	Y	Y	Y	N	Y	Y
4 Ross	Y	Y	Y	N	Y	Y
CALIFORNIA						
1 Thompson	Y	Y	Y	N	N	N
2 *Herger*	Y	Y	Y	N	Y	Y
3 *Ose*	Y	Y	Y	N	Y	Y
4 *Doolittle*	Y	Y	Y	N	Y	Y
5 Matsui	Y	Y	Y	N	Y	Y
6 Woolsey	Y	Y	Y	Y	N	Y
7 Miller, George	Y	Y	Y	?	N	N
8 Pelosi	Y	Y	Y	Y	N	Y
9 Lee	Y	Y	Y	N	N	Y
10 Tauscher	Y	Y	Y	N	Y	Y
11 *Pombo*	Y	Y	Y	N	Y	Y
12 Lantos	Y	Y	Y	N	Y	Y
13 Stark	Y	Y	Y	N	Y	Y
14 Eshoo	Y	Y	Y	N	Y	Y
15 Honda	Y	Y	Y	N	Y	Y
16 Lofgren	Y	Y	Y	N	Y	Y
17 Farr	Y	Y	Y	N	Y	Y
18 Condit	?	?	?	N	N	N
19 *Radanovich*	Y	Y	Y	N	Y	Y
20 Dooley	Y	Y	Y	N	Y	Y
21 *Thomas*	Y	Y	Y	N	Y	?
22 Capps	Y	Y	Y	N	N	Y
23 *Gallegly*	Y	Y	Y	N	Y	Y
24 Sherman	Y	Y	Y	N	Y	Y
25 *McKeon*	Y	Y	Y	N	Y	Y
26 Berman	?	?	?	N	Y	Y
27 Schiff	Y	Y	Y	N	Y	Y
28 *Dreier*	Y	Y	Y	N	Y	Y
29 Waxman	Y	Y	Y	Y	N	Y
30 Becerra	Y	Y	Y	N	Y	Y
31 Solis	Y	Y	Y	N	Y	?
32 Watson	Y	Y	Y	N	Y	Y
33 Roybal-Allard	Y	Y	Y	N	Y	Y
34 Napolitano	Y	Y	Y	N	Y	Y
35 Waters	Y	Y	Y	N	Y	Y
36 Harman	Y	Y	Y	N	Y	Y
37 Millender-McD.	Y	Y	Y	N	Y	Y
38 *Horn*	Y	Y	Y	N	Y	Y

	93	94	95	96	97	98
39 *Royce*	Y	Y	Y	N	Y	Y
40 *Lewis*	Y	Y	Y	N	Y	Y
41 *Miller, Gary*	Y	Y	Y	N	Y	Y
42 Baca	Y	Y	Y	Y	N	Y
43 *Calvert*	Y	Y	Y	N	Y	Y
44 *Bono*	Y	Y	Y	N	Y	Y
45 *Rohrabacher*	Y	N	N	N	Y	Y
46 Sanchez	Y	Y	Y	Y	N	Y
47 *Cox*	Y	Y	Y	N	Y	Y
48 *Issa*	Y	Y	Y	N	Y	Y
49 Davis	Y	Y	Y	Y	N	Y
50 Filner	+	+	+	Y	N	N
51 *Cunningham*	Y	Y	Y	N	Y	Y
52 *Hunter*	Y	Y	Y	N	Y	Y
COLORADO						
1 DeGette	Y	Y	Y	N	Y	N
2 Udall	Y	Y	Y	N	N	N
3 *McInnis*	Y	Y	Y	N	Y	Y
4 *Schaffer*	Y	Y	Y	N	Y	Y
5 *Hefley*	Y	Y	Y	N	Y	N
6 *Tancredo*	Y	Y	Y	N	Y	Y
CONNECTICUT						
1 Larson	Y	Y	Y	Y	N	Y
2 *Simmons*	Y	Y	Y	N	Y	Y
3 DeLauro	Y	Y	Y	N	Y	Y
4 *Shays*	Y	Y	Y	N	Y	Y
5 Maloney	Y	Y	Y	N	Y	Y
6 *Johnson*	Y	Y	Y	N	Y	Y
DELAWARE						
AL *Castle*	Y	Y	Y	N	Y	Y
FLORIDA						
1 *Miller, J.*	Y	Y	Y	N	Y	Y
2 Boyd	Y	Y	Y	N	Y	Y
3 Brown	Y	Y	Y	N	N	N
4 *Crenshaw*	Y	Y	Y	N	Y	Y
5 Thurman	Y	Y	Y	N	Y	Y
6 *Stearns*	Y	Y	Y	N	Y	Y
7 *Mica*	Y	Y	Y	N	Y	Y
8 *Keller*	Y	Y	Y	N	Y	Y
9 *Bilirakis*	Y	Y	Y	N	Y	Y
10 *Young*	Y	Y	Y	N	Y	Y
11 Davis	Y	Y	Y	N	Y	Y
12 *Putnam*	Y	Y	Y	N	Y	Y
13 *Miller, D.*	Y	Y	Y	N	Y	Y
14 *Goss*	Y	Y	Y	N	Y	Y
15 *Weldon*	Y	Y	Y	N	Y	Y
16 *Foley*	Y	Y	Y	N	N	Y
17 Meek	Y	Y	Y	Y	N	N
18 *Ros-Lehtinen*	Y	Y	Y	N	Y	Y
19 Wexler	Y	Y	Y	N	Y	Y
20 Deutsch	Y	Y	Y	N	Y	Y
21 *Diaz-Balart*	Y	Y	Y	N	Y	Y
22 *Shaw*	Y	Y	Y	N	Y	Y
23 Hastings	?	?	?	?	?	?
GEORGIA						
1 *Kingston*	?	?	?	N	Y	Y
2 Bishop	Y	Y	Y	N	Y	Y
3 *Collins*	Y	Y	Y	N	Y	Y
4 McKinney	Y	Y	Y	N	Y	Y
5 Lewis	Y	Y	Y	N	N	N
6 *Isakson*	Y	Y	Y	N	Y	Y
7 *Barr*	Y	Y	Y	N	Y	Y
8 *Chambliss*	Y	Y	Y	N	Y	Y
9 *Deal*	Y	Y	Y	N	Y	Y
10 *Norwood*	Y	Y	Y	N	Y	Y
11 *Linder*	Y	Y	Y	N	Y	Y
HAWAII						
1 Abercrombie	Y	Y	Y	Y	N	?
2 Mink	Y	Y	Y	Y	N	Y
IDAHO						
1 *Otter*	Y	Y	Y	N	Y	Y
2 *Simpson*	?	Y	Y	N	Y	Y
ILLINOIS						
1 Rush	Y	Y	Y	N	Y	?
2 Jackson	Y	Y	Y	N	Y	Y
3 Lipinski	Y	Y	Y	N	Y	Y
4 Gutierrez	?	?	?	N	Y	Y
5 Blagojevich	?	?	?	Y	N	Y
6 *Hyde*	Y	Y	Y	N	Y	Y
7 Davis	Y	Y	Y	N	Y	Y
8 *Crane*	Y	Y	Y	N	Y	N
9 Schakowsky	Y	Y	Y	N	N	N
10 *Kirk*	Y	Y	Y	N	N	Y
11 *Weller*	Y	Y	Y	N	Y	Y
12 Costello	Y	Y	Y	N	Y	Y
13 *Biggert*	Y	Y	Y	N	Y	Y

ND Northern Democrats   SD Southern Democrats

		93	94	95	96	97	98
14	***Hastert***						
15	***Johnson***	Y	Y	Y	N	Y	Y
16	***Manzullo***	Y	Y	Y	N	Y	Y
17	Evans	Y	Y	Y	Y	N	Y
18	***LaHood***	Y	Y	Y	N	Y	Y
19	Phelps	Y	Y	Y	N	Y	Y
20	***Shimkus***	Y	Y	Y	N	Y	Y
INDIANA							
1	Visclosky	Y	Y	Y	Y	N	N
2	***Pence***	Y	Y	Y	N	Y	Y
3	Roemer	Y	Y	Y	N	Y	Y
4	***Souder***	Y	Y	Y	N	Y	Y
5	***Buyer***	Y	Y	Y	N	Y	Y
6	***Burton***	?	?	?	N	Y	Y
7	***Kerns***	Y	Y	Y	N	Y	Y
8	***Hostettler***	Y	Y	Y	N	Y	Y
9	Hill	Y	Y	Y	N	Y	Y
10	Carson	Y	Y	Y	Y	N	Y
IOWA							
1	***Leach***	Y	Y	Y	N	Y	Y
2	***Nussle***	Y	Y	Y	N	Y	Y
3	Boswell	Y	Y	Y	Y	Y	Y
4	***Ganske***	Y	Y	Y	N	Y	Y
5	***Latham***	Y	Y	Y	N	Y	Y
KANSAS							
1	***Moran***	Y	Y	Y	N	Y	Y
2	***Ryun***	Y	Y	Y	N	Y	Y
3	Moore	Y	Y	Y	Y	N	N
4	***Tiahrt***	Y	Y	Y	N	Y	Y
KENTUCKY							
1	***Whitfield***	Y	Y	Y	N	Y	Y
2	***Lewis***	Y	Y	Y	N	Y	Y
3	***Northup***	Y	Y	Y	N	Y	Y
4	Lucas	Y	Y	Y	N	Y	Y
5	***Rogers***	Y	Y	Y	N	Y	Y
6	***Fletcher***	Y	Y	Y	N	Y	Y
LOUISIANA							
1	***Vitter***	Y	Y	Y	N	Y	Y
2	Jefferson	?	?	?	Y	N	Y
3	***Tauzin***	Y	Y	Y	N	Y	Y
4	***McCrery***	Y	Y	Y	N	Y	Y
5	***Cooksey***	Y	Y	Y	N	Y	Y
6	***Baker***	Y	Y	Y	N	Y	Y
7	John	Y	Y	Y	N	Y	Y
MAINE							
1	Allen	Y	Y	Y	Y	N	Y
2	Baldacci	Y	Y	Y	Y	N	Y
MARYLAND							
1	***Gilchrest***	?	?	?	N	Y	Y
2	***Ehrlich***	Y	Y	Y	N	Y	Y
3	Cardin	Y	Y	Y	Y	N	Y
4	Wynn	Y	Y	Y	Y	N	Y
5	Hoyer	Y	Y	Y	Y	N	Y
6	***Bartlett***	Y	Y	Y	?	Y	Y
7	Cummings	Y	Y	Y	Y	N	Y
8	***Morella***	Y	Y	Y	Y	N	Y
MASSACHUSETTS							
1	Olver	Y	Y	Y	Y	N	N
2	Neal	Y	Y	Y	Y	N	Y
3	McGovern	Y	Y	Y	Y	N	Y
4	Frank	Y	Y	Y	Y	N	Y
5	Meehan	Y	Y	Y	Y	N	Y
6	Tierney	Y	Y	Y	Y	N	Y
7	Markey	Y	Y	Y	Y	N	Y
8	Capuano	Y	Y	Y	Y	N	N
9	Lynch	Y	Y	Y	Y	Y	Y
10	Delahunt	Y	Y	Y	Y	N	N
MICHIGAN							
1	Stupak	Y	Y	Y	N	Y	N
2	***Hoekstra***	Y	Y	Y	N	Y	Y
3	***Ehlers***	Y	?	Y	N	Y	Y
4	***Camp***	Y	Y	Y	N	Y	Y
5	Barcia	Y	Y	Y	N	+	Y
6	***Upton***	Y	Y	Y	N	Y	Y
7	***Smith***	Y	Y	Y	N	Y	?
8	***Rogers***	Y	Y	Y	N	Y	Y
9	Kildee	Y	Y	Y	N	Y	Y
10	Bonior	Y	Y	Y	Y	Y	N
11	***Knollenberg***	Y	Y	Y	N	Y	Y
12	Levin	?	?	+	Y	N	Y
13	Rivers	Y	Y	Y	Y	N	Y
14	Conyers	Y	Y	Y	Y	N	Y
15	Kilpatrick	Y	Y	Y	Y	N	Y
16	Dingell	Y	Y	Y	?	?	?

		93	94	95	96	97	98
MINNESOTA							
1	***Gutknecht***	Y	Y	Y	N	Y	N
2	***Kennedy***	Y	Y	Y	N	Y	N
3	***Ramstad***	Y	Y	Y	N	Y	Y
4	McCollum	Y	Y	Y	Y	N	Y
5	Sabo	Y	Y	Y	Y	N	N
6	Luther	Y	Y	Y	Y	N	Y
7	Peterson	Y	Y	Y	N	Y	N
8	Oberstar	Y	Y	Y	N	Y	N
MISSISSIPPI							
1	***Wicker***	Y	Y	Y	N	Y	N
2	Thompson	Y	Y	Y	Y	N	N
3	***Pickering***	Y	Y	Y	N	Y	Y
4	Shows	Y	Y	Y	N	Y	Y
5	Taylor	Y	Y	Y	?	Y	N
MISSOURI							
1	Clay	Y	Y	Y	Y	N	Y
2	***Akin***	Y	Y	Y	N	Y	Y
3	Gephardt	Y	Y	Y	Y	N	Y
4	Skelton	Y	Y	Y	N	Y	Y
5	McCarthy	Y	Y	Y	Y	N	Y
6	***Graves***	Y	Y	Y	N	Y	Y
7	***Blunt***	Y	Y	Y	N	Y	Y
8	***Emerson***	Y	Y	Y	N	Y	Y
9	***Hulshof***	Y	Y	Y	N	Y	Y
MONTANA							
AL	***Rehberg***	Y	Y	Y	N	Y	Y
NEBRASKA							
1	***Bereuter***	Y	Y	Y	N	Y	Y
2	***Terry***	Y	Y	Y	N	Y	Y
3	***Osborne***	Y	Y	Y	N	Y	Y
NEVADA							
1	Berkley	Y	Y	Y	Y	N	Y
2	***Gibbons***	Y	Y	Y	N	Y	Y
NEW HAMPSHIRE							
1	***Sununu***	Y	Y	Y	N	Y	Y
2	***Bass***	Y	Y	Y	Y	N	Y
NEW JERSEY							
1	Andrews	Y	Y	Y	Y	N	Y
2	***LoBiondo***	Y	Y	Y	N	Y	N
3	***Saxton***	Y	Y	Y	N	Y	Y
4	***Smith***	Y	Y	Y	N	Y	Y
5	***Roukema***	Y	Y	Y	N	Y	Y
6	Pallone	Y	Y	Y	Y	N	N
7	***Ferguson***	Y	Y	Y	N	Y	Y
8	Pascrell	Y	Y	Y	Y	Y	Y
9	Rothman	Y	Y	Y	Y	N	Y
10	Payne	Y	Y	Y	Y	N	Y
11	***Frelinghuysen***	Y	Y	Y	N	Y	?
12	Holt	Y	Y	Y	Y	N	Y
13	Menendez	Y	Y	Y	Y	N	N
NEW MEXICO							
1	***Wilson***	Y	Y	Y	N	Y	Y
2	***Skeen***	Y	Y	Y	N	Y	Y
3	Udall	Y	Y	Y	Y	N	N
NEW YORK							
1	***Grucci***	Y	Y	Y	N	Y	Y
2	Israel	Y	Y	Y	Y	N	Y
3	***King***	Y	Y	Y	N	Y	Y
4	McCarthy	Y	Y	Y	Y	N	Y
5	Ackerman	Y	Y	Y	Y	N	Y
6	Meeks	Y	Y	Y	Y	N	Y
7	Crowley	Y	Y	Y	Y	N	Y
8	Nadler	Y	Y	Y	Y	N	Y
9	Weiner	Y	Y	Y	Y	N	Y
10	Towns	Y	Y	Y	Y	N	Y
11	Owens	Y	Y	Y	Y	N	Y
12	Velázquez	Y	Y	Y	Y	N	Y
13	***Fossella***	Y	Y	Y	N	Y	N
14	Maloney	Y	Y	Y	Y	N	Y
15	Rangel	Y	Y	Y	Y	N	Y
16	Serrano	?	Y	Y	Y	N	Y
17	Engel	Y	Y	Y	Y	N	Y
18	Lowey	Y	Y	Y	Y	N	Y
19	***Kelly***	Y	Y	Y	N	Y	Y
20	***Gilman***	Y	?	Y	Y	N	Y
21	McNulty	Y	Y	Y	N	Y	N
22	***Sweeney***	?	?	?	Y	Y	N
23	***Boehlert***	Y	Y	Y	Y	N	Y
24	***McHugh***	Y	Y	Y	N	Y	Y
25	***Walsh***	Y	Y	Y	N	Y	Y
26	Hinchey	Y	Y	Y	Y	N	Y
27	***Reynolds***	Y	Y	Y	N	Y	Y
28	Slaughter	Y	Y	Y	Y	N	Y
29	LaFalce	Y	Y	Y	Y	Y	Y

		93	94	95	96	97	98
30	***Quinn***	Y	Y	Y	N	Y	Y
31	***Houghton***	Y	Y	Y	Y	N	Y
NORTH CAROLINA							
1	Clayton	Y	Y	Y	Y	N	?
2	Etheridge	Y	Y	Y	Y	Y	Y
3	***Jones***	Y	Y	Y	N	Y	Y
4	Price	Y	Y	Y	Y	N	Y
5	***Burr***	Y	Y	Y	N	Y	Y
6	***Coble***	Y	Y	Y	N	Y	Y
7	McIntyre	Y	Y	Y	N	Y	Y
8	***Hayes***	Y	Y	Y	N	Y	Y
9	***Myrick***	Y	Y	Y	N	Y	Y
10	***Ballenger***	Y	Y	Y	N	Y	?
11	***Taylor***	Y	Y	Y	?	Y	Y
12	Watt	Y	Y	Y	?	N	Y
NORTH DAKOTA							
AL	Pomeroy	Y	Y	Y	N	Y	Y
OHIO							
1	***Chabot***	Y	Y	Y	N	Y	Y
2	***Portman***	Y	Y	Y	N	Y	Y
3	Hall	Y	Y	Y	N	Y	Y
4	***Oxley***	Y	Y	Y	N	Y	Y
5	***Gillmor***	Y	Y	Y	N	Y	Y
6	Strickland	Y	Y	Y	Y	Y	N
7	***Hobson***	Y	Y	Y	N	Y	Y
8	***Boehner***	Y	Y	Y	N	Y	Y
9	Kaptur	Y	Y	Y	Y	N	Y
10	Kucinich	Y	Y	Y	Y	Y	N
11	Jones	+	+	+	+	–	+
12	***Tiberi***	Y	Y	Y	N	Y	Y
13	Brown	Y	Y	Y	Y	N	Y
14	Sawyer	Y	Y	Y	Y	N	Y
15	***Pryce***	+	+	+	–	+	+
16	***Regula***	Y	Y	Y	N	Y	Y
17	Traficant	?	?	?	?	?	?
18	***Ney***	Y	Y	Y	N	Y	Y
19	***LaTourette***	Y	Y	Y	?	?	?
OKLAHOMA							
1	***Sullivan***	Y	Y	Y	N	Y	Y
2	Carson	Y	Y	Y	Y	Y	?
3	***Watkins***	?	Y	Y	N	Y	Y
4	***Watts***	Y	Y	Y	N	+	Y
5	***Istook***	Y	Y	Y	N	Y	Y
6	***Lucas***	Y	Y	Y	N	Y	Y
OREGON							
1	Wu	Y	Y	Y	Y	N	N
2	***Walden***	Y	Y	Y	N	Y	Y
3	Blumenauer	Y	Y	Y	Y	N	Y
4	DeFazio	Y	Y	Y	Y	N	N
5	Hooley	Y	Y	Y	Y	N	Y
PENNSYLVANIA							
1	Brady	Y	Y	Y	Y	N	N
2	Fattah	Y	Y	Y	Y	N	Y
3	Borski	Y	Y	Y	N	Y	N
4	***Hart***	Y	Y	Y	N	Y	Y
5	***Peterson***	Y	Y	Y	N	Y	Y
6	Holden	Y	Y	Y	N	Y	Y
7	***Weldon***	Y	Y	Y	N	Y	Y
8	***Greenwood***	Y	Y	Y	Y	N	?
9	***Shuster, Bill***	Y	Y	Y	N	Y	Y
10	***Sherwood***	Y	Y	Y	N	Y	Y
11	Kanjorski	Y	Y	Y	N	Y	Y
12	Murtha	Y	Y	Y	N	Y	Y
13	Hoeffel	Y	Y	Y	Y	N	Y
14	Coyne	Y	Y	Y	Y	N	Y
15	***Toomey***	Y	Y	Y	N	Y	Y
16	***Pitts***	Y	Y	Y	N	Y	Y
17	***Gekas***	Y	Y	Y	N	Y	Y
18	Doyle	Y	Y	?	N	Y	Y
19	***Platts***	Y	Y	Y	N	Y	Y
20	Mascara	Y	Y	Y	N	Y	Y
21	***English***	Y	Y	Y	N	Y	N
RHODE ISLAND							
1	Kennedy	Y	Y	Y	Y	N	Y
2	Langevin	Y	Y	Y	Y	Y	Y
SOUTH CAROLINA							
1	***Brown***	Y	Y	Y	N	Y	Y
2	***Wilson***	Y	Y	Y	N	Y	Y
3	***Graham***	Y	Y	Y	N	Y	Y
4	***DeMint***	Y	Y	Y	N	Y	Y
5	Spratt	Y	Y	Y	Y	Y	Y
6	Clyburn	Y	Y	Y	?	?	?
SOUTH DAKOTA							
AL	***Thune***	Y	Y	Y	N	Y	Y

		93	94	95	96	97	98
TENNESSEE							
1	***Jenkins***	+	+	+	N	Y	Y
2	***Duncan***	Y	Y	Y	N	Y	Y
3	***Wamp***	Y	Y	Y	N	Y	Y
4	***Hilleary***	?	?	?	N	Y	Y
5	Clement	+	+	+	?	?	?
6	Gordon	Y	Y	Y	N	Y	Y
7	***Bryant***	Y	Y	Y	N	Y	Y
8	Tanner	Y	Y	Y	N	Y	Y
9	Ford	Y	Y	Y	Y	Y	Y
TEXAS							
1	Sandlin	Y	Y	Y	Y	Y	Y
2	Turner	Y	Y	Y	N	Y	Y
3	***Johnson, Sam***	Y	Y	Y	N	Y	Y
4	Hall	Y	Y	Y	N	Y	Y
5	***Sessions***	Y	Y	Y	N	Y	Y
6	***Barton***	Y	Y	Y	N	Y	Y
7	***Culberson***	Y	Y	Y	N	Y	Y
8	***Brady***	Y	Y	Y	N	Y	Y
9	Lampson	Y	Y	Y	Y	N	Y
10	Doggett	Y	Y	Y	Y	N	?
11	Edwards	Y	Y	Y	N	Y	Y
12	***Granger***	Y	Y	Y	N	Y	Y
13	***Thornberry***	?	?	?	?	?	?
14	***Paul***	Y	Y	N	N	N	Y
15	Hinojosa	Y	Y	Y	Y	N	Y
16	Reyes	Y	Y	Y	N	Y	Y
17	Stenholm	Y	Y	Y	N	Y	Y
18	Jackson-Lee	Y	Y	Y	Y	N	N
19	***Combest***	Y	Y	Y	N	Y	Y
20	Gonzalez	Y	Y	Y	Y	N	Y
21	***Smith***	Y	Y	Y	N	Y	Y
22	***DeLay***	Y	Y	Y	N	Y	?
23	***Bonilla***	Y	Y	Y	N	Y	Y
24	Frost	Y	Y	Y	Y	N	Y
25	Bentsen	Y	Y	Y	Y	N	Y
26	***Armey***	Y	Y	Y	N	Y	Y
27	Ortiz	Y	Y	Y	N	Y	Y
28	Rodriguez	Y	Y	Y	Y	N	Y
29	Green	Y	Y	Y	Y	N	N
30	Johnson, E.B.	Y	Y	Y	Y	N	Y
UTAH							
1	***Hansen***	?	?	?	N	Y	Y
2	Matheson	Y	Y	Y	Y	Y	Y
3	***Cannon***	?	?	?	N	Y	Y
VERMONT							
AL	*Sanders*	Y	Y	Y	Y	N	Y
VIRGINIA							
1	***Davis, Jo Ann***	Y	Y	Y	N	Y	Y
2	***Schrock***	Y	Y	Y	N	Y	Y
3	Scott	Y	Y	Y	Y	N	Y
4	***Forbes***	Y	Y	Y	N	Y	Y
5	*Goode*	Y	Y	Y	N	Y	Y
6	***Goodlatte***	Y	Y	Y	N	Y	Y
7	***Cantor***	Y	Y	Y	N	Y	Y
8	Moran	Y	Y	Y	Y	N	Y
9	Boucher	Y	Y	Y	Y	N	Y
10	***Wolf***	Y	Y	Y	N	Y	Y
11	***Davis, T.***	Y	Y	Y	N	Y	Y
WASHINGTON							
1	Inslee	Y	Y	Y	Y	N	Y
2	Larsen	Y	Y	Y	Y	N	N
3	Baird	Y	Y	Y	Y	N	N
4	***Hastings***	Y	Y	Y	N	Y	Y
5	***Nethercutt***	Y	Y	Y	N	Y	?
6	Dicks	Y	Y	Y	Y	N	Y
7	McDermott	Y	Y	Y	Y	N	N
8	***Dunn***	Y	Y	Y	N	?	Y
9	Smith	Y	Y	Y	Y	N	Y
WEST VIRGINIA							
1	Mollohan	Y	Y	Y	N	Y	Y
2	***Capito***	Y	Y	Y	N	Y	Y
3	Rahall	Y	Y	Y	N	Y	Y
WISCONSIN							
1	***Ryan***	Y	Y	Y	?	Y	Y
2	Baldwin	Y	Y	Y	Y	N	Y
3	Kind	Y	Y	Y	Y	N	Y
4	Kleczka	Y	Y	Y	N	Y	Y
5	Barrett	Y	Y	Y	Y	N	Y
6	***Petri***	Y	Y	Y	N	Y	Y
7	Obey	Y	Y	Y	N	Y	Y
8	***Green***	Y	Y	Y	N	Y	Y
9	***Sensenbrenner***	Y	Y	Y	N	Y	Y
WYOMING							
AL	***Cubin***	Y	Y	Y	N	Y	Y

Southern states - Ala., Ark., Fla., Ga., Ky., La., Miss., N.C., Okla., S.C., Tenn., Texas, Va.

Key

Y   Voted for (yea).
\#   Paired for.
\+   Announced for.
N   Voted against (nay).
X   Paired against.
–   Announced against.
P   Voted "present."
C   Voted "present" to avoid possible conflict of interest.
?   Did not vote or otherwise make a position known.

•

Democrats   **Republicans**
Independents

---

99. Procedural Motion/Journal. Approval of the House Journal of Wednesday, April 17, 2002. Approved 369-52: R 199-17; D 168-35 (ND 127-25, SD 41-10); I 2-0. April 18, 2002.

100. HR 2646. Farm Bill/Motion to Instruct. Smith, R-Mich., motion to instruct conferees to agree to Senate provisions that would limit commodity price support payments and mandate additional conservation and agricultural research funding. Motion agreed to 265-158: R 113-103; D 151-54 (ND 135-19, SD 16-35); I 1-1. April 18, 2002.

101. HR 586. Permanent Tax Cuts/Previous Question. Hastings, R-Wash., motion to order the previous question (thus ending debate and possibility of amendment) on adoption of the rule (H Res 390) to provide for House floor consideration of the Senate amendments to the bill that would extend permanently the cuts in last year's $1.35 trillion tax reduction package, many of which are set to expire in 2010. Motion agreed to 219-206: R 218-0; D 0-205 (ND 0-153, SD 0-52); I 1-1. April 18, 2002.

102. HR 586. Permanent Tax Cuts/Rule. Adoption of the rule (H Res 390) to provide for House floor consideration of the Senate amendments to the bill that would extend permanently the cuts in last year's $1.35 trillion tax reduction package, many of which are set to expire in 2010. Adopted 218-205: R 217-0; D 0-204 (ND 0-152, SD 0-52); I 1-1. April 18, 2002.

103. HR 586. Permanent Tax Cuts/Concur With Senate Amendments. Thomas, R-Calif., motion to concur in a House amendment to Senate amendments to the bill that would extend permanently the cuts in last year's $1.35 trillion tax reduction package, which are set to expire in 2010. It would extend reductions in income tax rates, relief of the marriage penalty, elimination of the estate tax, doubling of the child tax credit, and expansion of pension and education savings provisions. The bill also would revise various Internal Revenue Service tax provisions, including penalty, interest and collection provisions. It would change penalties for failure to pay estimated taxes; waive minor, first-time error penalties; exclude interest on unintentional overpayments from taxable income; and allow the IRS greater discretion in disciplining employees who violate policies. Motion agreed to 229-198: R 219-1; D 9-196 (ND 3-150, SD 6-46); I 1-1. A "yea" was a vote in support of the president's position. April 18, 2002.

	99	100	101	102	103
ALABAMA					
1 *Callahan*	Y	N	Y	Y	Y
2 *Everett*	Y	N	Y	Y	Y
3 *Riley*	N	N	Y	Y	Y
4 *Aderholt*	N	N	Y	Y	Y
5 Cramer	Y	N	N	N	Y
6 *Bachus*	Y	N	Y	Y	Y
7 Hilliard	N	N	N	N	N
ALASKA					
AL *Young*	?	?	Y	Y	Y
ARIZONA					
1 *Flake*	Y	Y	Y	Y	Y
2 Pastor	Y	N	N	N	N
3 *Stump*	Y	N	Y	Y	Y
4 *Shadegg*	Y	N	Y	Y	Y
5 *Kolbe*	Y	N	Y	Y	Y
6 *Hayworth*	Y	N	Y	Y	Y
ARKANSAS					
1 Berry	N	N	N	N	N
2 Snyder	Y	N	N	N	N
3 *Boozman*	Y	N	Y	Y	Y
4 Ross	Y	N	N	N	N
CALIFORNIA					
1 Thompson	N	N	N	N	N
2 *Herger*	Y	N	Y	Y	Y
3 *Ose*	Y	N	Y	Y	Y
4 *Doolittle*	Y	N	Y	Y	Y
5 Matsui	Y	N	N	N	N
6 Woolsey	Y	N	N	N	N
7 Miller, George	Y	Y	N	N	N
8 Pelosi	Y	Y	N	N	N
9 Lee	Y	Y	N	N	N
10 Tauscher	Y	Y	N	N	N
11 *Pombo*	Y	N	Y	Y	Y
12 Lantos	Y	Y	N	N	N
13 Stark	?	Y	N	N	N
14 Eshoo	Y	Y	N	N	N
15 Honda	Y	Y	N	N	N
16 Lofgren	Y	Y	N	N	N
17 Farr	Y	Y	N	N	N
18 Condit	Y	N	N	N	Y
19 *Radanovich*	Y	N	Y	Y	Y
20 Dooley	Y	N	N	N	N
21 *Thomas*	Y	N	Y	Y	Y
22 Capps	Y	Y	N	N	N
23 *Gallegly*	Y	N	Y	Y	Y
24 Sherman	Y	Y	N	N	N
25 *McKeon*	Y	N	Y	Y	Y
26 Berman	Y	Y	N	N	N
27 Schiff	Y	Y	N	N	N
28 *Dreier*	Y	N	Y	Y	Y
29 Waxman	Y	Y	N	N	N
30 Becerra	+	Y	N	N	N
31 Solis	Y	Y	N	N	N
32 Watson	Y	Y	N	N	N
33 Roybal-Allard	Y	Y	N	N	N
34 Napolitano	Y	Y	N	N	N
35 Waters	N	Y	N	N	N
36 Harman	Y	Y	N	N	N
37 Millender-McD.	Y	Y	N	N	N
38 *Horn*	Y	Y	?	Y	Y

	99	100	101	102	103
39 *Royce*	Y	Y	Y	Y	Y
40 *Lewis*	Y	Y	Y	Y	Y
41 *Miller, Gary*	Y	Y	Y	Y	Y
42 Baca	Y	N	N	N	N
43 *Calvert*	Y	Y	Y	Y	Y
44 *Bono*	Y	Y	Y	Y	Y
45 *Rohrabacher*	Y	Y	Y	Y	Y
46 Sanchez	Y	Y	N	N	N
47 *Cox*	Y	Y	Y	Y	Y
48 *Issa*	Y	+	Y	Y	Y
49 Davis	Y	N	N	N	N
50 Filner	N	N	N	N	N
51 *Cunningham*	Y	N	Y	Y	Y
52 *Hunter*	Y	Y	Y	Y	Y
COLORADO					
1 DeGette	Y	N	N	N	N
2 Udall	N	N	N	N	N
3 *McInnis*	Y	Y	Y	Y	Y
4 *Schaffer*	?	?	Y	Y	Y
5 *Hefley*	N	Y	Y	Y	Y
6 *Tancredo*	Y	Y	Y	Y	Y
CONNECTICUT					
1 Larson	Y	N	N	N	N
2 *Simmons*	Y	Y	Y	Y	Y
3 DeLauro	Y	N	N	N	N
4 *Shays*	Y	Y	Y	Y	Y
5 Maloney	Y	N	N	N	N
6 *Johnson*	Y	Y	Y	Y	Y
DELAWARE					
AL *Castle*	Y	Y	Y	Y	Y
FLORIDA					
1 *Miller, J.*	Y	Y	Y	Y	Y
2 Boyd	Y	N	N	N	N
3 Brown	N	N	N	N	N
4 *Crenshaw*	Y	N	Y	Y	Y
5 Thurman	Y	N	N	N	N
6 *Stearns*	Y	Y	Y	Y	Y
7 *Mica*	Y	Y	Y	Y	Y
8 *Keller*	Y	Y	Y	Y	Y
9 *Bilirakis*	Y	Y	Y	Y	Y
10 *Young*	Y	Y	Y	Y	Y
11 Davis	Y	Y	N	N	N
12 *Putnam*	Y	N	Y	Y	Y
13 *Miller, D.*	Y	Y	Y	Y	Y
14 *Goss*	Y	Y	Y	Y	Y
15 *Weldon*	Y	Y	Y	Y	Y
16 *Foley*	Y	N	Y	Y	Y
17 Meek	Y	Y	N	N	N
18 *Ros-Lehtinen*	Y	Y	Y	Y	Y
19 Wexler	Y	N	N	N	N
20 Deutsch	Y	Y	N	N	N
21 *Diaz-Balart*	Y	Y	Y	Y	Y
22 *Shaw*	Y	Y	Y	Y	Y
23 Hastings	?	?	?	?	?
GEORGIA					
1 *Kingston*	Y	N	Y	Y	Y
2 Bishop	Y	N	N	N	N
3 *Collins*	Y	Y	Y	Y	Y
4 McKinney	Y	Y	N	N	N
5 Lewis	Y	N	N	N	N
6 *Isakson*	Y	Y	Y	Y	Y
7 *Barr*	Y	Y	Y	Y	Y
8 *Chambliss*	Y	N	Y	Y	Y
9 *Deal*	Y	Y	Y	Y	Y
10 *Norwood*	Y	N	Y	Y	Y
11 *Linder*	Y	Y	Y	Y	Y
HAWAII					
1 Abercrombie	Y	N	N	N	N
2 Mink	Y	N	N	N	N
IDAHO					
1 *Otter*	Y	N	Y	Y	Y
2 *Simpson*	?	?	Y	Y	Y
ILLINOIS					
1 Rush	Y	Y	N	N	N
2 Jackson	Y	Y	N	N	N
3 Lipinski	Y	Y	N	N	N
4 Gutierrez	Y	Y	N	N	N
5 Blagojevich	Y	Y	N	N	N
6 *Hyde*	Y	Y	Y	Y	Y
7 Davis	Y	Y	N	N	N
8 *Crane*	N	Y	Y	Y	Y
9 Schakowsky	Y	Y	N	N	N
10 *Kirk*	Y	Y	Y	Y	Y
11 *Weller*	N	N	Y	Y	Y
12 Costello	N	N	N	N	N
13 *Biggert*	Y	Y	Y	Y	Y

ND Northern Democrats   SD Southern Democrats

	99	100	101	102	103
14 ***Hastert***					Y
15 ***Johnson***	Y	N	Y	Y	Y
16 ***Manzullo***	Y	N	Y	Y	Y
17 Evans	Y	Y	N	N	N
18 ***LaHood***	Y	N	Y	Y	Y
19 Phelps	Y	N	N	N	N
20 ***Shimkus***	Y	N	Y	Y	Y
INDIANA					
1 Visclosky	N	N	N	N	Y
2 ***Pence***	Y	N	Y	Y	Y
3 Roemer	Y	Y	N	N	Y
4 ***Souder***	Y	N	Y	Y	Y
5 ***Buyer***	Y	N	Y	Y	Y
6 ***Burton***	Y	N	Y	Y	Y
7 ***Kerns***	Y	Y	Y	Y	Y
8 ***Hostettler***	Y	Y	Y	Y	Y
9 Hill	Y	N	N	N	N
10 Carson	Y	Y	N	N	N
IOWA					
1 ***Leach***	Y	Y	Y	Y	Y
2 ***Nussle***	Y	Y	Y	Y	Y
3 Boswell	Y	Y	N	N	N
4 ***Ganske***	Y	Y	Y	Y	Y
5 ***Latham***	Y	Y	Y	Y	Y
KANSAS					
1 ***Moran***	N	N	Y	Y	Y
2 ***Ryun***	Y	N	Y	Y	Y
3 Moore	Y	Y	N	N	N
4 ***Tiahrt***	Y	N	Y	Y	Y
KENTUCKY					
1 ***Whitfield***	Y	N	Y	?	Y
2 ***Lewis***	Y	N	Y	Y	Y
3 ***Northup***	Y	Y	Y	Y	Y
4 Lucas	Y	N	N	N	Y
5 ***Rogers***	?	?	?	?	?
6 ***Fletcher***	N	N	Y	Y	Y
LOUISIANA					
1 ***Vitter***	Y	N	Y	Y	Y
2 Jefferson	Y	N	N	N	N
3 ***Tauzin***	Y	N	Y	Y	Y
4 ***McCrery***	Y	N	Y	Y	Y
5 ***Cooksey***	Y	N	Y	Y	Y
6 ***Baker***	Y	N	Y	Y	Y
7 John	Y	N	N	N	N
MAINE					
1 Allen	Y	Y	N	N	N
2 Baldacci	Y	Y	N	N	N
MARYLAND					
1 ***Gilchrest***	Y	N	Y	Y	Y
2 ***Ehrlich***	Y	Y	Y	Y	Y
3 Cardin	Y	Y	N	N	N
4 Wynn	Y	Y	N	N	N
5 Hoyer	Y	Y	N	N	N
6 ***Bartlett***	Y	Y	Y	Y	Y
7 Cummings	Y	Y	N	N	N
8 ***Morella***	Y	Y	Y	Y	N
MASSACHUSETTS					
1 Olver	N	Y	N	N	N
2 Neal	Y	Y	N	N	N
3 McGovern	Y	Y	N	N	N
4 Frank	Y	Y	N	N	N
5 Meehan	Y	Y	N	N	N
6 Tierney	Y	Y	N	N	N
7 Markey	Y	?	N	N	N
8 Capuano	N	Y	N	N	N
9 Lynch	Y	Y	N	N	N
10 Delahunt	Y	N	N	N	?
MICHIGAN					
1 Stupak	N	Y	N	N	N
2 ***Hoekstra***	Y	Y	Y	Y	Y
3 ***Ehlers***	Y	Y	Y	Y	Y
4 ***Camp***	Y	N	Y	Y	Y
5 Barcia	Y	Y	N	N	Y
6 ***Upton***	Y	Y	Y	Y	Y
7 ***Smith***	Y	Y	Y	Y	Y
8 ***Rogers***	Y	N	Y	Y	Y
9 Kildee	Y	Y	N	N	N
10 Bonior	Y	Y	N	N	N
11 ***Knollenberg***	Y	N	Y	Y	Y
12 Levin	Y	Y	N	N	N
13 Rivers	Y	Y	N	N	N
14 Conyers	Y	Y	N	N	N
15 Kilpatrick	Y	Y	N	N	N
16 Dingell	Y	Y	N	N	N

	99	100	101	102	103
MINNESOTA					
1 ***Gutknecht***	N	N	Y	Y	Y
2 ***Kennedy***	N	Y	Y	Y	Y
3 ***Ramstad***	N	Y	Y	Y	Y
4 McCollum	Y	Y	N	N	N
5 Sabo	N	Y	N	N	N
6 Luther	Y	Y	N	N	N
7 Peterson	N	N	N	N	N
8 Oberstar	N	Y	N	N	–
MISSISSIPPI					
1 ***Wicker***	Y	N	Y	Y	Y
2 Thompson	N	N	N	N	N
3 ***Pickering***	Y	N	Y	Y	Y
4 Shows	Y	N	N	N	N
5 Taylor	N	Y	N	N	N
MISSOURI					
1 Clay	?	Y	N	N	N
2 ***Akin***	Y	N	Y	Y	Y
3 Gephardt	Y	Y	N	N	N
4 Skelton	Y	N	N	N	N
5 McCarthy	Y	Y	N	N	N
6 ***Graves***	Y	N	Y	Y	Y
7 ***Blunt***	Y	N	Y	Y	Y
8 ***Emerson***	N	N	Y	Y	Y
9 ***Hulshof***	Y	N	Y	Y	Y
MONTANA					
AL ***Rehberg***	Y	N	Y	Y	Y
NEBRASKA					
1 ***Bereuter***	Y	Y	Y	Y	Y
2 ***Terry***	Y	N	Y	Y	Y
3 ***Osborne***	Y	N	Y	Y	Y
NEVADA					
1 Berkley	Y	Y	N	N	N
2 ***Gibbons***	Y	Y	Y	Y	Y
NEW HAMPSHIRE					
1 ***Sununu***	Y	Y	Y	Y	Y
2 ***Bass***	Y	Y	Y	Y	Y
NEW JERSEY					
1 Andrews	Y	Y	N	N	N
2 ***LoBiondo***	N	Y	Y	Y	Y
3 ***Saxton***	Y	Y	Y	Y	Y
4 ***Smith***	Y	Y	Y	Y	Y
5 ***Roukema***	Y	Y	Y	Y	?
6 Pallone	N	Y	N	N	N
7 ***Ferguson***	Y	Y	Y	Y	Y
8 Pascrell	Y	Y	N	N	N
9 Rothman	Y	Y	N	N	N
10 Payne	Y	Y	N	N	N
11 ***Frelinghuysen***	Y	Y	Y	+	Y
12 Holt	Y	Y	N	N	N
13 Menendez	N	Y	N	N	N
NEW MEXICO					
1 ***Wilson***	Y	Y	Y	Y	Y
2 ***Skeen***	Y	N	Y	Y	Y
3 Udall	N	Y	N	N	N
NEW YORK					
1 ***Grucci***	Y	N	Y	Y	Y
2 Israel	Y	Y	N	N	N
3 ***King***	Y	Y	Y	Y	Y
4 McCarthy	Y	Y	N	N	N
5 Ackerman	Y	Y	N	N	N
6 Meeks	Y	Y	N	N	N
7 Crowley	Y	Y	N	N	N
8 Nadler	Y	Y	N	N	N
9 Weiner	Y	Y	N	N	N
10 Towns	Y	Y	N	N	N
11 Owens	Y	Y	N	N	N
12 Velázquez	Y	Y	N	N	N
13 ***Fossella***	Y	Y	Y	Y	Y
14 Maloney	Y	Y	N	N	N
15 Rangel	Y	Y	N	N	N
16 Serrano	Y	Y	N	N	N
17 Engel	Y	Y	N	N	N
18 Lowey	Y	Y	N	N	N
19 ***Kelly***	Y	Y	Y	Y	Y
20 ***Gilman***	Y	Y	Y	Y	Y
21 McNulty	N	Y	N	N	N
22 ***Sweeney***	N	Y	Y	Y	Y
23 ***Boehlert***	Y	Y	Y	Y	Y
24 ***McHugh***	Y	Y	Y	Y	Y
25 ***Walsh***	Y	Y	Y	Y	Y
26 Hinchey	N	Y	N	N	N
27 ***Reynolds***	Y	Y	Y	Y	Y
28 Slaughter	Y	Y	N	N	N
29 LaFalce	Y	Y	N	N	N

	99	100	101	102	103
30 ***Quinn***	Y	Y	Y	Y	Y
31 ***Houghton***	Y	Y	Y	Y	Y
NORTH CAROLINA					
1 Clayton	Y	Y	N	N	N
2 Etheridge	Y	N	N	N	N
3 ***Jones***	Y	N	Y	Y	Y
4 Price	Y	N	N	N	N
5 ***Burr***	Y	N	Y	Y	Y
6 ***Coble***	Y	N	Y	Y	Y
7 McIntyre	Y	N	N	N	Y
8 ***Hayes***	Y	N	Y	Y	Y
9 ***Myrick***	Y	N	Y	Y	Y
10 ***Ballenger***	Y	N	Y	Y	Y
11 ***Taylor***	Y	N	Y	Y	Y
12 Watt	Y	Y	N	N	N
NORTH DAKOTA					
AL Pomeroy	Y	Y	N	N	N
OHIO					
1 ***Chabot***	Y	Y	Y	Y	Y
2 ***Portman***	Y	Y	Y	Y	Y
3 Hall	Y	Y	?	?	N
4 ***Oxley***	Y	Y	Y	Y	Y
5 ***Gillmor***	N	Y	Y	Y	Y
6 Strickland	N	Y	N	N	N
7 ***Hobson***	Y	Y	Y	Y	Y
8 ***Boehner***	Y	N	Y	Y	Y
9 Kaptur	Y	Y	N	?	N
10 Kucinich	N	Y	N	N	N
11 Jones	?	?	?	?	?
12 ***Tiberi***	Y	Y	Y	Y	Y
13 Brown	Y	Y	?	?	N
14 Sawyer	Y	Y	N	N	N
15 ***Pryce***	Y	Y	Y	Y	Y
16 ***Regula***	Y	Y	Y	Y	Y
17 Traficant	?	?	?	?	?
18 ***Ney***	Y	Y	Y	Y	Y
19 ***LaTourette***	Y	N	Y	Y	Y
OKLAHOMA					
1 ***Sullivan***	Y	N	Y	Y	Y
2 Carson	Y	N	N	N	N
3 ***Watkins***	Y	N	Y	Y	Y
4 ***Watts***	Y	N	Y	Y	Y
5 ***Istook***	Y	Y	Y	Y	Y
6 ***Lucas***	Y	N	Y	Y	Y
OREGON					
1 Wu	N	Y	N	N	N
2 ***Walden***	N	N	Y	Y	Y
3 Blumenauer	Y	Y	N	N	N
4 DeFazio	Y	Y	N	N	N
5 Hooley	Y	Y	N	N	N
PENNSYLVANIA					
1 Brady	N	Y	N	N	N
2 Fattah	Y	Y	N	N	N
3 Borski	N	Y	N	N	N
4 ***Hart***	Y	Y	Y	Y	Y
5 ***Peterson***	Y	Y	Y	Y	Y
6 Holden	Y	Y	N	N	N
7 ***Weldon***	Y	Y	Y	Y	Y
8 ***Greenwood***	Y	Y	Y	Y	Y
9 ***Shuster, Bill***	Y	Y	Y	Y	Y
10 ***Sherwood***	Y	Y	Y	Y	Y
11 Kanjorski	Y	Y	N	N	N
12 Murtha	Y	Y	N	N	N
13 Hoeffel	Y	Y	N	N	N
14 Coyne	Y	Y	N	N	N
15 ***Toomey***	Y	Y	Y	Y	Y
16 ***Pitts***	Y	Y	Y	Y	Y
17 ***Gekas***	Y	Y	Y	Y	Y
18 Doyle	Y	Y	N	N	N
19 ***Platts***	Y	Y	Y	Y	Y
20 Mascara	Y	Y	N	N	N
21 ***English***	N	Y	Y	Y	Y
RHODE ISLAND					
1 Kennedy	Y	Y	N	N	N
2 Langevin	Y	Y	N	N	N
SOUTH CAROLINA					
1 ***Brown***	Y	N	Y	Y	Y
2 ***Wilson***	Y	Y	Y	Y	Y
3 ***Graham***	Y	Y	Y	Y	Y
4 ***DeMint***	Y	Y	Y	Y	Y
5 Spratt	Y	Y	N	N	N
6 Clyburn	Y	Y	N	N	N
SOUTH DAKOTA					
AL ***Thune***	Y	Y	Y	Y	Y

	99	100	101	102	103
TENNESSEE					
1 ***Jenkins***	Y	N	Y	Y	Y
2 ***Duncan***	Y	Y	?	?	Y
3 ***Wamp***	?	Y	Y	Y	Y
4 ***Hilleary***	Y	N	Y	Y	Y
5 Clement	?	?	?	?	?
6 Gordon	Y	N	N	N	Y
7 ***Bryant***	Y	N	Y	Y	Y
8 Tanner	Y	N	N	N	N
9 Ford	N	Y	N	N	N
TEXAS					
1 Sandlin	Y	N	N	N	Y
2 Turner	Y	N	N	N	N
3 ***Johnson, Sam***	Y	N	Y	Y	Y
4 Hall	Y	N	N	N	Y
5 ***Sessions***	Y	N	Y	Y	Y
6 ***Barton***	Y	N	Y	Y	Y
7 ***Culberson***	Y	Y	Y	Y	Y
8 ***Brady***	Y	N	Y	Y	Y
9 Lampson	N	N	N	N	N
10 Doggett	Y	Y	N	N	N
11 Edwards	Y	N	N	N	N
12 ***Granger***	Y	N	Y	Y	Y
13 ***Thornberry***	Y	N	Y	Y	Y
14 ***Paul***	N	N	Y	Y	Y
15 Hinojosa	Y	Y	N	N	N
16 Reyes	?	?	N	N	N
17 Stenholm	Y	N	N	N	N
18 Jackson-Lee	N	N	N	N	N
19 ***Combest***	Y	N	Y	Y	Y
20 Gonzalez	Y	N	N	N	N
21 ***Smith***	Y	N	Y	Y	Y
22 ***DeLay***	Y	N	Y	Y	Y
23 ***Bonilla***	Y	N	Y	Y	Y
24 Frost	Y	N	N	N	N
25 Bentsen	Y	N	N	N	N
26 ***Armey***	Y	N	Y	Y	Y
27 Ortiz	Y	N	N	N	N
28 Rodriguez	Y	N	N	N	N
29 Green	Y	Y	N	N	N
30 Johnson, E.B.	N	N	N	N	N
UTAH					
1 ***Hansen***	Y	N	Y	Y	Y
2 Matheson	N	Y	N	N	N
3 ***Cannon***	Y	Y	Y	Y	Y
VERMONT					
AL *Sanders*	Y	Y	N	N	N
VIRGINIA					
1 ***Davis, Jo Ann***	Y	N	Y	Y	Y
2 ***Schrock***	Y	N	Y	Y	Y
3 Scott	N	N	N	N	N
4 ***Forbes***	Y	N	Y	Y	Y
5 *Goode*	Y	N	Y	Y	Y
6 ***Goodlatte***	Y	N	Y	Y	Y
7 ***Cantor***	Y	N	Y	Y	Y
8 Moran	Y	Y	N	N	N
9 Boucher	Y	Y	N	N	N
10 ***Wolf***	Y	Y	Y	Y	Y
11 ***Davis, T.***	Y	Y	Y	Y	Y
WASHINGTON					
1 Inslee	Y	Y	N	N	N
2 Larsen	N	N	N	N	N
3 Baird	Y	Y	N	N	N
4 ***Hastings***	Y	N	Y	Y	Y
5 ***Nethercutt***	Y	N	Y	Y	Y
6 Dicks	Y	Y	N	N	N
7 McDermott	N	Y	N	N	N
8 ***Dunn***	Y	N	Y	Y	Y
9 Smith	Y	Y	N	N	N
WEST VIRGINIA					
1 Mollohan	Y	Y	N	N	N
2 ***Capito***	Y	Y	Y	Y	Y
3 Rahall	Y	Y	N	N	N
WISCONSIN					
1 ***Ryan***	Y	Y	Y	Y	Y
2 Baldwin	Y	Y	N	N	N
3 Kind	Y	Y	N	N	N
4 Kleczka	Y	Y	N	N	N
5 Barrett	Y	Y	N	N	N
6 ***Petri***	Y	Y	Y	Y	Y
7 Obey	Y	Y	N	N	N
8 ***Green***	Y	Y	Y	Y	Y
9 ***Sensenbrenner***	Y	Y	Y	Y	Y
WYOMING					
AL ***Cubin***	Y	Y	Y	Y	Y

Southern states - Ala., Ark., Fla., Ga., Ky., La., Miss., N.C., Okla., S.C., Tenn., Texas, Va.

Key

Y Voted for (yea).
\# Paired for.
\+ Announced for.
N Voted against (nay).
X Paired against.
− Announced against.
P Voted "present."
C Voted "present" to avoid possible conflict of interest.
? Did not vote or otherwise make a position known.

•
Democrats   **Republicans**
Independents

104. HR 3839. Child Protection/Passage. Hoekstra, R-Mich., motion to suspend the rules and pass the bill that would authorize $312 million in fiscal 2003 and other amounts as needed through fiscal 2007 to renew various child abuse prevention, family support and child adoption programs. It would extend funding and reauthorize state grants to improve child protection efforts, family support programs aimed at preventing child abuse and neglect, adoption promotion programs and programs to help children and domestic violence victims secure housing. Motion agreed to 411-5: R 208-5; D 201-0 (ND 148-0, SD 53-0); I 2-0. A two-thirds majority of those present and voting (278 in this case) is required for passage under suspension of the rules. April 23, 2002.

105. HR 2646. Farm Bill/Motion to Instruct. Dooley, D-Calif., motion to instruct conferees to agree to Senate provisions that would lift a ban on private financing of agricultural sales to Cuba. Motion agreed to 273-143: R 92-121; D 180-21 (ND 134-14, SD 46-7); I 1-1. April 23, 2002.

106. HR 2646. Farm Bill/Motion to Instruct. Baca, D-Calif., motion to instruct conferees to agree to Senate provisions that would give food stamps to recently arrived immigrant children, the disabled, refugees and legal permanent residents who have lived in the United States for at least five years or worked here for a total of 16 quarters or more. Motion agreed to 244-171: R 47-165; D 196-5 (ND 149-0, SD 47-5); I 1-1. April 23, 2002.

107. HR 3763. Auditing Safeguards/Federal Bureau of Audits. Kucinich, D-Ohio, substitute amendment that would establish the Federal Bureau of Audits within the Securities and Exchange Commission (SEC) to audit annually all publicly traded companies' financial statements. The SEC would set auditing standards. The bureau would have independence and full powers of investigation, and its employees would be subject to conflict-of-interest restrictions. Rejected 39-381: R 0-213; D 38-167 (ND 29-123, SD 9-44); I 1-1. April 24, 2002.

108. HR 3763. Auditing Safeguards/Public Regulator. LaFalce, D-N.Y., substitute amendment that would create a public regulator to oversee auditors, with authority to set auditing standards and rules and conduct more thorough investigations. It also would require company executives to certify the truthfulness of their financial statements and set up additional restrictions on companies and auditing firms, including stronger penalties for false information. Rejected 202-219: R 1-214; D 200-4 (ND 149-2, SD 51-2); I 1-1. April 24, 2002.

109. HR 3763. Auditing Safeguards/Recommit. LaFalce, D-N.Y., motion to recommit the bill to the House Financial Services Committee with instructions that it be reported back with language similar to that contained in the LaFalce substitute amendment related to the establishment of a public regulator and executive accountability provisions. Motion rejected 205-222: R 0-218; D 204-3 (ND 153-1, SD 51-2); I 1-1. April 24, 2002.

	104	105	106	107	108	109
ALABAMA						
1 *Callahan*	Y	Y	N	N	N	N
2 *Everett*	Y	N	N	N	N	N
3 *Riley*	?	?	?	?	N	N
4 *Aderholt*	Y	N	N	N	N	N
5 Cramer	Y	Y	N	N	Y	Y
6 *Bachus*	Y	N	N	N	N	N
7 Hilliard	Y	Y	Y	Y	Y	Y
ALASKA						
AL *Young*	Y	N	N	N	N	N
ARIZONA						
1 *Flake*	N	Y	N	N	N	N
2 Pastor	Y	Y	Y	Y	Y	Y
3 *Stump*	Y	Y	N	N	N	N
4 *Shadegg*	Y	N	N	N	N	N
5 *Kolbe*	Y	Y	Y	N	N	N
6 *Hayworth*	Y	N	N	N	N	N
ARKANSAS						
1 Berry	Y	Y	Y	N	Y	Y
2 Snyder	Y	Y	Y	N	Y	Y
3 *Boozman*	Y	Y	N	N	N	N
4 Ross	Y	Y	N	Y	Y	Y
CALIFORNIA						
1 Thompson	Y	Y	Y	N	Y	Y
2 *Herger*	Y	Y	N	N	N	N
3 *Ose*	Y	Y	Y	N	N	N
4 *Doolittle*	Y	N	N	N	N	N
5 Matsui	Y	Y	Y	N	Y	Y
6 Woolsey	Y	Y	Y	Y	Y	Y
7 Miller, George	Y	Y	Y	N	Y	Y
8 Pelosi	Y	Y	Y	N	Y	Y
9 Lee	Y	Y	Y	Y	Y	Y
10 Tauscher	Y	Y	Y	N	Y	Y
11 *Pombo*	Y	N	N	N	N	N
12 Lantos	Y	Y	Y	N	Y	Y
13 Stark	Y	Y	Y	Y	?	Y
14 Eshoo	Y	Y	Y	N	Y	Y
15 Honda	Y	Y	Y	N	Y	Y
16 Lofgren	Y	Y	Y	N	Y	Y
17 Farr	Y	Y	Y	N	Y	Y
18 Condit	?	?	?	N	Y	N
19 *Radanovich*	?	?	?	N	N	N
20 Dooley	Y	Y	Y	N	Y	Y
21 *Thomas*	Y	N	N	N	N	N
22 Capps	Y	Y	Y	N	Y	Y
23 *Gallegly*	Y	Y	N	N	N	N
24 Sherman	Y	Y	Y	N	Y	Y
25 *McKeon*	Y	N	N	N	N	N
26 Berman	Y	Y	Y	N	Y	Y
27 Schiff	Y	Y	Y	N	Y	Y
28 *Dreier*	Y	N	N	N	N	N
29 Waxman	Y	Y	Y	N	Y	Y
30 Becerra	Y	Y	Y	N	Y	Y
31 Solis	Y	Y	Y	Y	Y	Y
32 Watson	Y	Y	Y	Y	Y	Y
33 Roybal-Allard	Y	Y	Y	Y	Y	Y
34 Napolitano	Y	Y	Y	N	Y	Y
35 Waters	Y	Y	Y	Y	Y	Y
36 Harman	Y	Y	Y	N	Y	Y
37 Millender-McD.	Y	Y	Y	N	Y	Y
38 *Horn*	Y	Y	Y	N	N	N
39 *Royce*	Y	N	N	N	N	N
40 *Lewis*	Y	N	N	N	N	N
41 *Miller, Gary*	Y	N	N	N	N	N
42 Baca	Y	Y	Y	N	Y	Y
43 *Calvert*	Y	N	N	N	N	N
44 *Bono*	Y	Y	N	N	N	N
45 *Rohrabacher*	N	N	N	N	N	N
46 Sanchez	Y	Y	Y	N	Y	N
47 *Cox*	Y	N	N	N	N	N
48 *Issa*	Y	N	N	N	N	N
49 Davis	Y	Y	Y	N	Y	Y
50 Filner	Y	Y	Y	Y	Y	Y
51 *Cunningham*	Y	N	N	N	N	N
52 *Hunter*	Y	N	N	N	N	N
COLORADO						
1 DeGette	?	?	?	?	?	Y
2 Udall	Y	Y	Y	N	Y	Y
3 *McInnis*	Y	N	N	N	Y	N
4 *Schaffer*	N	N	N	N	N	N
5 *Hefley*	Y	N	N	N	N	N
6 *Tancredo*	N	N	N	N	N	N
CONNECTICUT						
1 Larson	Y	Y	Y	N	Y	Y
2 *Simmons*	Y	Y	Y	N	Y	Y
3 DeLauro	Y	Y	Y	N	Y	Y
4 *Shays*	Y	Y	Y	N	N	N
5 Maloney	Y	Y	Y	N	Y	Y
6 *Johnson*	Y	Y	Y	N	N	N
DELAWARE						
AL *Castle*	Y	Y	Y	N	N	N
FLORIDA						
1 *Miller, J.*	Y	N	N	N	N	N
2 Boyd	Y	Y	Y	N	Y	Y
3 Brown	Y	Y	Y	N	Y	Y
4 *Crenshaw*	Y	N	N	N	N	N
5 Thurman	Y	Y	Y	N	Y	Y
6 *Stearns*	Y	N	N	N	N	N
7 *Mica*	Y	N	N	N	N	N
8 *Keller*	Y	N	N	N	N	N
9 *Bilirakis*	Y	N	N	N	N	N
10 *Young*	Y	N	N	N	N	N
11 Davis	Y	Y	Y	N	Y	Y
12 *Putnam*	Y	N	N	N	N	N
13 *Miller, D.*	Y	N	N	N	N	N
14 *Goss*	Y	N	N	N	N	N
15 *Weldon*	Y	N	N	N	N	N
16 *Foley*	Y	N	N	N	N	N
17 Meek	Y	N	Y	N	Y	Y
18 *Ros-Lehtinen*	Y	N	N	N	N	N
19 Wexler	Y	N	Y	N	Y	Y
20 Deutsch	Y	N	N	N	Y	Y
21 *Diaz-Balart*	Y	N	N	N	N	N
22 *Shaw*	Y	N	Y	N	N	N
23 Hastings	Y	Y	Y	N	Y	Y
GEORGIA						
1 *Kingston*	Y	N	N	N	N	N
2 Bishop	Y	Y	Y	N	Y	Y
3 *Collins*	Y	Y	N	N	N	N
4 McKinney	Y	Y	Y	Y	Y	Y
5 Lewis	Y	Y	Y	Y	Y	Y
6 *Isakson*	Y	Y	N	N	N	N
7 *Barr*	N	N	N	N	N	N
8 *Chambliss*	Y	N	N	N	N	N
9 *Deal*	Y	N	N	N	N	N
10 *Norwood*	Y	N	N	N	N	N
11 *Linder*	Y	N	N	N	N	N
HAWAII						
1 Abercrombie	Y	Y	Y	Y	Y	Y
2 Mink	Y	Y	Y	Y	Y	Y
IDAHO						
1 *Otter*	Y	Y	N	N	N	N
2 *Simpson*	Y	Y	N	N	N	N
ILLINOIS						
1 Rush	Y	Y	Y	N	Y	Y
2 Jackson	Y	Y	Y	Y	Y	Y
3 Lipinski	Y	N	Y	N	Y	Y
4 Gutierrez	Y	N	Y	Y	Y	Y
5 Blagojevich	?	?	?	?	?	?
6 *Hyde*	Y	N	N	N	N	N
7 Davis	Y	Y	Y	Y	Y	Y
8 *Crane*	?	?	?	N	N	N
9 Schakowsky	Y	Y	Y	Y	Y	Y
10 *Kirk*	Y	N	Y	N	N	N
11 *Weller*	Y	Y	N	N	N	N
12 Costello	Y	Y	Y	N	Y	Y
13 *Biggert*	Y	Y	Y	N	N	N

ND Northern Democrats   SD Southern Democrats

	104	105	106	107	108	109
14 ***Hastert***						
15 ***Johnson***	Y	Y	Y	N	N	N
16 ***Manzullo***	Y	Y	N	N	N	N
17 Evans	Y	Y	Y	Y	Y	Y
18 ***LaHood***	Y	Y	N	N	N	N
19 Phelps	Y	Y	Y	N	Y	Y
20 ***Shimkus***	Y	Y	N	N	N	N
INDIANA						
1 Visclosky	Y	Y	Y	N	Y	Y
2 ***Pence***	Y	N	N	N	N	N
3 Roemer	Y	Y	Y	N	N	Y
4 ***Souder***	Y	N	Y	N	N	N
5 ***Buyer***	Y	N	N	N	N	N
6 ***Burton***	Y	N	N	N	N	N
7 ***Kerns***	Y	N	N	N	N	N
8 ***Hostettler***	Y	Y	N	N	N	N
9 Hill	Y	Y	Y	N	Y	Y
10 Carson	Y	Y	Y	N	Y	Y
IOWA						
1 ***Leach***	Y	Y	Y	N	N	N
2 ***Nussle***	Y	Y	N	N	N	N
3 Boswell	Y	Y	Y	N	Y	Y
4 ***Ganske***	?	?	?	N	N	N
5 ***Latham***	Y	Y	Y	N	N	N
KANSAS						
1 ***Moran***	Y	Y	Y	N	N	N
2 ***Ryun***	Y	Y	N	N	N	N
3 Moore	Y	?	Y	N	Y	Y
4 ***Tiahrt***	Y	Y	Y	N	N	N
KENTUCKY						
1 ***Whitfield***	Y	Y	N	N	N	N
2 ***Lewis***	Y	N	N	N	N	N
3 ***Northup***	Y	N	N	N	N	N
4 Lucas	Y	N	N	N	N	N
5 ***Rogers***	Y	N	N	N	N	N
6 ***Fletcher***	Y	N	N	N	N	N
LOUISIANA						
1 ***Vitter***	Y	N	N	N	N	N
2 Jefferson	Y	Y	Y	N	Y	Y
3 ***Tauzin***	Y	N	N	N	N	N
4 ***McCrery***	Y	N	N	N	N	N
5 ***Cooksey***	Y	N	N	N	N	N
6 ***Baker***	Y	N	N	N	N	N
7 John	Y	Y	Y	N	Y	Y
MAINE						
1 Allen	Y	Y	Y	N	Y	Y
2 Baldacci	Y	Y	Y	N	Y	Y
MARYLAND						
1 ***Gilchrest***	?	?	?	?	?	?
2 ***Ehrlich***	Y	Y	N	N	N	N
3 Cardin	Y	Y	Y	N	Y	Y
4 Wynn	Y	Y	Y	N	Y	Y
5 Hoyer	Y	Y	Y	N	Y	Y
6 ***Bartlett***	Y	N	N	N	N	N
7 Cummings	Y	Y	Y	N	Y	Y
8 ***Morella***	Y	Y	Y	N	N	N
MASSACHUSETTS						
1 Olver	Y	Y	Y	Y	Y	Y
2 Neal	Y	Y	Y	N	Y	Y
3 McGovern	Y	Y	Y	N	Y	Y
4 Frank	Y	Y	Y	Y	Y	Y
5 Meehan	Y	Y	Y	N	Y	Y
6 Tierney	Y	Y	Y	N	Y	Y
7 Markey	Y	Y	Y	N	Y	Y
8 Capuano	Y	Y	Y	N	Y	Y
9 Lynch	Y	Y	Y	N	Y	Y
10 Delahunt	Y	Y	Y	N	Y	Y
MICHIGAN						
1 Stupak	Y	Y	Y	N	Y	Y
2 ***Hoekstra***	Y	N	N	N	N	N
3 ***Ehlers***	Y	Y	Y	N	N	N
4 ***Camp***	Y	Y	N	N	N	N
5 Barcia	Y	Y	Y	N	Y	Y
6 ***Upton***	Y	Y	N	N	N	N
7 ***Smith***	Y	Y	N	N	N	N
8 ***Rogers***	Y	N	N	N	N	N
9 Kildee	Y	Y	Y	N	Y	Y
10 Bonior	+	+	+	Y	Y	Y
11 ***Knollenberg***	Y	N	N	N	N	N
12 Levin	?	Y	Y	N	Y	Y
13 Rivers	Y	Y	Y	N	Y	Y
14 Conyers	Y	Y	Y	Y	Y	Y
15 Kilpatrick	+	+	+	N	Y	Y
16 Dingell	Y	Y	Y	N	Y	Y
MINNESOTA						
1 ***Gutknecht***	Y	N	N	N	N	N
2 ***Kennedy***	Y	Y	N	N	N	N
3 ***Ramstad***	Y	Y	Y	N	N	N
4 McCollum	Y	Y	Y	N	Y	Y
5 Sabo	Y	Y	Y	N	Y	Y
6 Luther	Y	Y	Y	N	Y	Y
7 Peterson	Y	Y	Y	N	N	N
8 Oberstar	Y	Y	Y	N	Y	Y
MISSISSIPPI						
1 ***Wicker***	Y	N	N	N	N	N
2 Thompson	Y	Y	Y	Y	Y	Y
3 ***Pickering***	Y	Y	N	N	N	N
4 Shows	Y	Y	N	N	N	N
5 Taylor	Y	Y	N	N	Y	Y
MISSOURI						
1 Clay	Y	Y	Y	N	Y	Y
2 ***Akin***	Y	Y	N	N	N	N
3 Gephardt	Y	N	Y	N	Y	Y
4 Skelton	Y	Y	Y	N	Y	Y
5 McCarthy	Y	Y	Y	N	Y	Y
6 ***Graves***	Y	Y	N	N	N	N
7 ***Blunt***	Y	N	N	N	N	N
8 ***Emerson***	Y	Y	?	N	N	N
9 ***Hulshof***	Y	Y	Y	N	N	N
MONTANA						
AL ***Rehberg***	Y	Y	N	N	N	N
NEBRASKA						
1 ***Bereuter***	Y	Y	N	N	N	N
2 ***Terry***	Y	Y	N	N	N	N
3 ***Osborne***	Y	Y	Y	N	N	N
NEVADA						
1 Berkley	Y	N	Y	Y	Y	Y
2 ***Gibbons***	Y	N	N	N	N	N
NEW HAMPSHIRE						
1 ***Sununu***	Y	Y	N	N	N	N
2 ***Bass***	Y	Y	N	N	N	N
NEW JERSEY						
1 Andrews	Y	N	Y	N	Y	Y
2 ***LoBiondo***	Y	N	Y	N	N	N
3 ***Saxton***	Y	N	N	N	N	N
4 ***Smith***	Y	N	Y	N	N	N
5 ***Roukema***	Y	N	N	N	N	N
6 Pallone	Y	N	Y	N	Y	Y
7 ***Ferguson***	Y	N	Y	N	–	N
8 Pascrell	Y	N	Y	Y	Y	Y
9 Rothman	Y	N	Y	N	Y	Y
10 Payne	Y	Y	Y	Y	Y	Y
11 ***Frelinghuysen***	Y	N	N	N	N	N
12 Holt	Y	Y	Y	N	Y	Y
13 Menendez	Y	N	Y	N	Y	Y
NEW MEXICO						
1 ***Wilson***	Y	Y	Y	N	N	N
2 ***Skeen***	Y	N	Y	N	N	N
3 Udall	Y	Y	Y	N	Y	Y
NEW YORK						
1 ***Grucci***	Y	N	Y	N	N	N
2 Israel	Y	Y	Y	N	Y	Y
3 ***King***	Y	N	Y	N	N	N
4 McCarthy	Y	Y	Y	N	Y	Y
5 Ackerman	Y	N	Y	N	Y	Y
6 Meeks	Y	Y	?	N	Y	Y
7 Crowley	Y	N	Y	N	Y	Y
8 Nadler	Y	Y	Y	N	Y	Y
9 Weiner	Y	Y	Y	–	Y	Y
10 Towns	Y	Y	Y	N	Y	Y
11 Owens	Y	Y	Y	Y	Y	Y
12 Velázquez	Y	Y	Y	N	Y	Y
13 ***Fossella***	Y	N	N	N	N	N
14 Maloney	Y	Y	Y	N	Y	Y
15 Rangel	Y	Y	Y	N	Y	Y
16 Serrano	Y	Y	Y	N	Y	Y
17 Engel	Y	N	Y	N	Y	Y
18 Lowey	Y	Y	Y	N	Y	Y
19 ***Kelly***	Y	N	Y	N	N	N
20 ***Gilman***	Y	N	Y	N	N	N
21 McNulty	Y	Y	Y	N	Y	Y
22 ***Sweeney***	Y	Y	Y	N	N	N
23 ***Boehlert***	Y	Y	Y	N	N	N
24 ***McHugh***	Y	Y	Y	N	N	N
25 ***Walsh***	Y	Y	Y	N	N	N
26 Hinchey	?	+	Y	N	Y	Y
27 ***Reynolds***	Y	N	N	N	N	N
28 Slaughter	Y	Y	Y	N	Y	Y
29 LaFalce	Y	Y	Y	N	Y	Y
30 ***Quinn***	Y	Y	Y	N	N	N
31 ***Houghton***	?	?	?	?	?	?
NORTH CAROLINA						
1 Clayton	Y	Y	Y	Y	Y	Y
2 Etheridge	Y	Y	Y	N	Y	Y
3 ***Jones***	Y	N	N	N	N	N
4 Price	Y	Y	Y	N	Y	Y
5 ***Burr***	Y	N	N	N	N	N
6 ***Coble***	Y	N	N	N	N	N
7 McIntyre	Y	Y	N	N	Y	Y
8 ***Hayes***	Y	N	N	N	N	N
9 ***Myrick***	Y	N	N	N	N	N
10 ***Ballenger***	Y	N	N	N	N	N
11 ***Taylor***	Y	N	N	N	N	N
12 Watt	Y	Y	Y	N	Y	Y
NORTH DAKOTA						
AL Pomeroy	Y	Y	Y	N	Y	Y
OHIO						
1 ***Chabot***	Y	N	N	N	N	N
2 ***Portman***	Y	Y	N	N	N	N
3 Hall	Y	Y	Y	N	Y	Y
4 ***Oxley***	Y	Y	N	N	N	N
5 ***Gillmor***	Y	Y	Y	N	N	N
6 Strickland	Y	Y	Y	N	Y	Y
7 ***Hobson***	Y	Y	N	N	N	N
8 ***Boehner***	Y	N	N	N	N	N
9 Kaptur	Y	Y	Y	Y	Y	Y
10 Kucinich	Y	Y	Y	Y	Y	Y
11 Jones	Y	Y	Y	N	Y	Y
12 ***Tiberi***	Y	Y	N	N	N	N
13 Brown	Y	Y	Y	N	Y	Y
14 Sawyer	Y	Y	Y	N	Y	Y
15 ***Pryce***	?	?	?	?	N	N
16 ***Regula***	Y	Y	N	?	N	N
17 Traficant	?	?	?	?	?	?
18 ***Ney***	Y	Y	N	N	N	N
19 ***LaTourette***	?	?	?	N	N	N
OKLAHOMA						
1 ***Sullivan***	Y	N	N	N	N	N
2 Carson	Y	Y	Y	N	Y	Y
3 ***Watkins***	Y	Y	N	N	N	N
4 ***Watts***	Y	N	N	N	–	N
5 ***Istook***	Y	Y	N	N	N	N
6 ***Lucas***	Y	N	N	N	N	N
OREGON						
1 Wu	Y	N	Y	N	Y	Y
2 ***Walden***	Y	Y	N	N	N	N
3 Blumenauer	Y	Y	Y	N	Y	Y
4 DeFazio	Y	Y	Y	N	Y	Y
5 Hooley	Y	Y	Y	N	Y	Y
PENNSYLVANIA						
1 Brady	Y	Y	Y	N	Y	Y
2 Fattah	Y	Y	Y	N	Y	Y
3 Borski	Y	Y	Y	N	Y	Y
4 ***Hart***	Y	N	N	?	N	N
5 ***Peterson***	Y	Y	N	N	N	N
6 Holden	Y	Y	Y	N	Y	Y
7 ***Weldon***	Y	Y	N	N	N	N
8 ***Greenwood***	Y	Y	N	N	N	N
9 ***Shuster, Bill***	Y	N	N	N	N	N
10 ***Sherwood***	Y	Y	N	N	N	N
11 Kanjorski	Y	Y	Y	N	Y	Y
12 Murtha	Y	Y	Y	N	Y	Y
13 Hoeffel	Y	Y	Y	N	Y	Y
14 Coyne	Y	Y	Y	N	Y	Y
15 ***Toomey***	Y	Y	N	N	N	N
16 ***Pitts***	Y	N	N	N	N	N
17 ***Gekas***	Y	Y	Y	N	N	N
18 Doyle	Y	Y	Y	N	Y	Y
19 ***Platts***	Y	Y	N	N	N	N
20 Mascara	Y	Y	Y	N	Y	Y
21 ***English***	Y	Y	N	–	N	N
RHODE ISLAND						
1 Kennedy	Y	N	Y	Y	Y	Y
2 Langevin	Y	Y	Y	N	Y	Y
SOUTH CAROLINA						
1 ***Brown***	Y	Y	N	N	N	N
2 ***Wilson***	Y	N	N	N	N	N
3 ***Graham***	Y	N	N	N	N	N
4 ***DeMint***	Y	Y	N	N	N	N
5 Spratt	Y	Y	?	N	Y	Y
6 Clyburn	Y	Y	Y	Y	Y	Y
SOUTH DAKOTA						
AL ***Thune***	Y	Y	Y	?	?	?
TENNESSEE						
1 ***Jenkins***	Y	N	N	N	N	N
2 ***Duncan***	Y	N	N	N	N	N
3 ***Wamp***	Y	Y	N	N	N	N
4 ***Hilleary***	Y	Y	N	N	N	N
5 Clement	Y	Y	Y	N	Y	Y
6 Gordon	Y	Y	Y	N	Y	Y
7 ***Bryant***	Y	N	N	N	N	N
8 Tanner	Y	Y	Y	N	Y	Y
9 Ford	Y	Y	Y	N	Y	Y
TEXAS						
1 Sandlin	Y	Y	Y	N	Y	Y
2 Turner	Y	Y	Y	N	Y	Y
3 ***Johnson, Sam***	Y	N	N	N	N	N
4 Hall	Y	Y	Y	N	Y	Y
5 ***Sessions***	Y	N	N	N	N	N
6 ***Barton***	Y	N	N	N	N	N
7 ***Culberson***	Y	N	N	N	N	N
8 ***Brady***	Y	Y	N	N	N	N
9 Lampson	Y	Y	Y	N	Y	Y
10 Doggett	Y	Y	Y	N	Y	Y
11 Edwards	Y	Y	Y	N	Y	Y
12 ***Granger***	Y	N	N	N	N	N
13 ***Thornberry***	Y	Y	N	N	N	N
14 ***Paul***	N	Y	N	N	N	N
15 Hinojosa	Y	Y	Y	N	Y	Y
16 Reyes	Y	N	Y	N	Y	Y
17 Stenholm	Y	Y	Y	N	Y	Y
18 Jackson-Lee	Y	Y	Y	Y	Y	Y
19 ***Combest***	Y	N	N	N	N	N
20 Gonzalez	Y	Y	Y	N	Y	Y
21 ***Smith***	Y	N	N	N	N	N
22 ***DeLay***	Y	N	N	N	N	N
23 ***Bonilla***	Y	N	N	N	N	N
24 Frost	Y	Y	Y	N	Y	Y
25 Bentsen	Y	Y	Y	N	Y	Y
26 ***Armey***	Y	N	N	N	N	N
27 Ortiz	Y	N	Y	N	Y	Y
28 Rodriguez	?	?	?	?	?	?
29 Green	Y	N	Y	Y	Y	Y
30 Johnson, E.B.	Y	Y	Y	N	Y	Y
UTAH						
1 ***Hansen***	Y	Y	N	N	N	N
2 Matheson	Y	Y	Y	N	Y	Y
3 ***Cannon***	Y	N	N	N	N	N
VERMONT						
AL *Sanders*	Y	Y	Y	Y	Y	Y
VIRGINIA						
1 ***Davis, Jo Ann***	Y	N	N	N	N	N
2 ***Schrock***	Y	N	N	N	N	N
3 Scott	Y	Y	Y	N	Y	Y
4 ***Forbes***	Y	N	N	N	N	N
5 *Goode*	Y	N	N	N	N	N
6 ***Goodlatte***	Y	N	N	N	N	N
7 ***Cantor***	Y	N	N	N	N	N
8 Moran	Y	Y	Y	N	Y	Y
9 Boucher	Y	Y	Y	N	Y	Y
10 ***Wolf***	Y	N	N	N	N	N
11 ***Davis, T.***	Y	N	Y	N	?	N
WASHINGTON						
1 Inslee	Y	Y	Y	N	Y	Y
2 Larsen	Y	Y	Y	N	Y	Y
3 Baird	Y	Y	Y	N	Y	Y
4 ***Hastings***	Y	N	N	N	N	N
5 ***Nethercutt***	Y	Y	N	N	N	N
6 Dicks	Y	Y	Y	N	Y	Y
7 McDermott	Y	Y	Y	Y	Y	Y
8 ***Dunn***	Y	N	N	N	N	N
9 Smith	?	?	?	?	?	?
WEST VIRGINIA						
1 Mollohan	Y	Y	Y	N	Y	Y
2 ***Capito***	Y	N	N	N	N	N
3 Rahall	Y	Y	Y	N	Y	Y
WISCONSIN						
1 ***Ryan***	Y	Y	N	N	N	N
2 Baldwin	Y	Y	Y	Y	Y	Y
3 Kind	Y	Y	Y	N	Y	Y
4 Kleczka	Y	Y	Y	N	Y	Y
5 Barrett	Y	Y	Y	N	Y	Y
6 ***Petri***	Y	Y	N	N	N	N
7 Obey	Y	Y	Y	N	?	Y
8 ***Green***	Y	Y	N	N	N	N
9 ***Sensenbrenner***	Y	Y	N	N	N	N
WYOMING						
AL ***Cubin***	Y	Y	N	N	N	N

Southern states - Ala., Ark., Fla., Ga., Ky., La., Miss., N.C., Okla., S.C., Tenn., Texas, Va.

110. HR 3763. Auditing Safeguards/Passage. Passage of the bill that would increase federal regulation over firms that audit publicly traded companies and impose new corporate accounting and reporting requirements. It would direct the SEC to establish an oversight board to set and impose standards for accounting firms and order the agency to promulgate rules banning outside firms from both compiling financial reports and auditing the same company. It would order a corporation to promptly report to the SEC circumstances currently not required in financial statements that could affect its financial condition and report promptly and electronically "insider" sales and purchases. The bill also would ban corporate executives from engaging in company stock transactions when employees were prevented from doing so with their pension investments. Passed 334-90: R 214-2; D 119-87 (ND 77-77, SD 42-10); I 1-1. April 24, 2002.

111. HR 3231. Immigration Agency Overhaul/Previous Question. Hastings, D-Fla., motion to order the previous question (thus ending debate and possibility of amendment) on adoption of the rule (H Res 396) to provide for House floor consideration of the bill that would eliminate the Immigration and Naturalization Service and transfer its responsibilities to a new Agency for Immigration Affairs divided into two separate bureaus. Motion agreed to 384-36: R 219-0; D 164-36 (ND 119-30, SD 45-6); I 1-0. April 25, 2002.

112. HR 3231. Immigration Agency Overhaul/Rule. Adoption of the rule (H Res 396) to provide for House floor consideration of the bill that would eliminate the Immigration and Naturalization Service and transfer its responsibilities to a new Agency for Immigration Affairs divided into two separate bureaus. Adopted 388-34: R 212-5; D 175-28 (ND 131-20, SD 44-8); I 1-1. April 25, 2002.

113. Procedural Motion/Journal. Approval of the House Journal of Wednesday, April 24, 2002. Approved 372-47: R 202-12; D 168-35 (ND 122-29, SD 46-6); I 2-0. April 25, 2002.

114. HR 3231. Immigration Agency Overhaul/Excepted Service Employees. Issa, R-Calif., amendment that would make employees of the new Agency for Immigration Affairs "excepted service" employees, who have limited protections and recourse for certain disciplinary measures. Rejected 145-272: R 141-75; D 3-196 (ND 1-147, SD 2-49); I 1-1. April 25, 2002.

115. HR 3231. Immigration Agency Overhaul/Technology Goods. Lofgren, D-Calif., amendment that would expedite through fiscal 2004 the procurement process for information technology goods and services. Rejected 105-312: R 82-133; D 23-177 (ND 17-132, SD 6-45); I 0-2. April 25, 2002.

116. HR 3231. Immigration Agency Overhaul/Passage. Passage of the bill that would eliminate the Immigration and Naturalization Service and transfer its responsibilities to a new Agency for Immigration Affairs divided into two separate bureaus, one responsible for providing immigration services, the other for enforcing immigration laws, and headed by an associate attorney general in the Justice Department. The Bureau of Citizenship and Immigration Services and the Bureau of Immigration Enforcement each would have its own directors, budgets, staffs and policies. The Office of the Associate Attorney General for Immigration Affairs would be responsible for coordinating overall immigration policy and overseeing and supervising the two bureaus. The associate attorney general would rank just under the U.S. attorney general and deputy attorney general. Passed 405-9: R 215-1; D 189-7 (ND 142-5, SD 47-2); I 1-1. April 25, 2002.

Key

Y	Voted for (yea).
#	Paired for.
+	Announced for.
N	Voted against (nay).
X	Paired against.
–	Announced against.
P	Voted "present."
C	Voted "present" to avoid possible conflict of interest.
?	Did not vote or otherwise make a position known.

• Democrats   **Republicans**   *Independents*

	110	111	112	113	114	115	116
ALABAMA							
1 *Callahan*	Y	Y	Y	Y	Y	N	Y
2 *Everett*	Y	Y	Y	Y	Y	N	Y
3 *Riley*	Y	Y	Y	Y	Y	N	Y
4 *Aderholt*	Y	Y	Y	N	Y	Y	Y
5 Cramer	Y	Y	Y	N	Y	N	Y
6 *Bachus*	Y	Y	Y	Y	Y	N	Y
7 Hilliard	Y	Y	N	N	N	N	Y
ALASKA							
AL *Young*	Y	Y	Y	N	N	N	Y
ARIZONA							
1 *Flake*	N	Y	Y	Y	Y	Y	Y
2 Pastor	Y	Y	Y	N	N	N	Y
3 *Stump*	Y	Y	Y	Y	Y	N	Y
4 *Shadegg*	Y	Y	Y	Y	Y	Y	Y
5 *Kolbe*	?	Y	N	Y	Y	Y	N
6 *Hayworth*	Y	Y	Y	Y	Y	Y	Y
ARKANSAS							
1 Berry	Y	Y	Y	N	N	N	Y
2 Snyder	Y	Y	Y	N	N	N	Y
3 *Boozman*	Y	Y	Y	Y	Y	N	Y
4 Ross	Y	Y	Y	N	N	N	Y
CALIFORNIA							
1 Thompson	Y	Y	Y	N	N	N	Y
2 *Herger*	Y	Y	Y	Y	Y	N	Y
3 *Ose*	Y	Y	Y	N	N	N	Y
4 *Doolittle*	Y	Y	Y	Y	Y	Y	Y
5 Matsui	Y	Y	Y	?	N	Y	Y
6 Woolsey	N	N	Y	N	N	N	Y
7 Miller, George	N	N	N	N	N	N	Y
8 Pelosi	N	Y	Y	N	N	N	Y
9 Lee	N	N	N	Y	N	N	Y
10 Tauscher	Y	Y	Y	N	N	N	Y
11 *Pombo*	Y	Y	Y	Y	Y	Y	Y
12 Lantos	Y	Y	Y	N	N	N	?
13 Stark	N	N	Y	N	N	N	Y
14 Eshoo	Y	Y	Y	N	N	N	Y
15 Honda	N	?	N	Y	N	Y	N
16 Lofgren	Y	N	N	Y	N	Y	N
17 Farr	Y	N	Y	N	N	Y	Y
18 Condit	Y	Y	N	Y	N	N	Y
19 *Radanovich*	Y	Y	Y	Y	Y	N	Y
20 Dooley	Y	Y	Y	N	Y	N	Y
21 *Thomas*	Y	Y	Y	N	Y	N	Y
22 Capps	Y	Y	Y	N	N	N	Y
23 *Gallegly*	Y	Y	Y	Y	Y	N	Y
24 Sherman	Y	Y	Y	N	N	N	Y
25 *McKeon*	Y	Y	Y	Y	Y	Y	Y
26 Berman	N	Y	Y	N	N	Y	Y
27 Schiff	Y	Y	Y	N	N	N	Y
28 *Dreier*	Y	Y	Y	Y	Y	N	Y
29 Waxman	N	Y	Y	?	?	?	?
30 Becerra	N	N	Y	N	N	N	Y
31 Solis	N	Y	Y	N	N	N	Y
32 Watson	N	Y	N	N	N	N	Y
33 Roybal-Allard	N	Y	Y	N	N	N	Y
34 Napolitano	Y	Y	Y	N	N	N	Y
35 Waters	N	N	N	N	N	N	Y
36 Harman	Y	Y	Y	Y	?	Y	Y
37 Millender-McD.	Y	Y	Y	N	N	N	Y
38 *Horn*	Y	Y	Y	Y	N	Y	Y

	110	111	112	113	114	115	116
39 *Royce*	Y	Y	Y	Y	N	N	Y
40 *Lewis*	Y	Y	Y	Y	Y	N	Y
41 *Miller, Gary*	Y	Y	Y	Y	Y	N	Y
42 Baca	Y	Y	Y	N	N	N	Y
43 *Calvert*	Y	Y	Y	Y	Y	N	Y
44 *Bono*	Y	Y	Y	Y	Y	N	Y
45 *Rohrabacher*	Y	N	N	N	N	N	Y
46 Sanchez	N	N	N	N	N	N	Y
47 *Cox*	Y	Y	Y	Y	Y	Y	Y
48 *Issa*	Y	Y	Y	Y	Y	N	Y
49 Davis	Y	Y	Y	N	N	N	Y
50 Filner	N	N	N	N	N	N	Y
51 *Cunningham*	Y	Y	Y	Y	Y	Y	Y
52 *Hunter*	Y	Y	Y	Y	Y	Y	Y
COLORADO							
1 DeGette	N	Y	Y	N	Y	Y	Y
2 Udall	Y	Y	Y	Y	N	N	Y
3 *McInnis*	Y	Y	Y	Y	Y	Y	Y
4 *Schaffer*	Y	Y	N	N	?	?	+
5 *Hefley*	Y	Y	N	Y	Y	Y	Y
6 *Tancredo*	Y	Y	N	P	Y	N	Y
CONNECTICUT							
1 Larson	N	Y	Y	Y	N	N	Y
2 *Simmons*	Y	Y	Y	Y	N	N	Y
3 DeLauro	N	Y	Y	Y	N	N	Y
4 *Shays*	Y	Y	Y	Y	N	N	Y
5 Maloney	Y	Y	Y	Y	N	N	Y
6 *Johnson*	Y	Y	Y	Y	N	N	Y
DELAWARE							
AL *Castle*	Y	Y	Y	Y	N	N	Y
FLORIDA							
1 *Miller, J.*	Y	Y	Y	Y	N	N	Y
2 Boyd	Y	Y	Y	Y	N	Y	Y
3 Brown	Y	Y	N	N	N	N	Y
4 *Crenshaw*	Y	Y	Y	Y	N	N	Y
5 Thurman	Y	Y	Y	Y	Y	Y	Y
6 *Stearns*	Y	Y	Y	Y	Y	Y	Y
7 *Mica*	Y	Y	Y	Y	Y	Y	Y
8 *Keller*	Y	Y	Y	Y	N	N	Y
9 *Bilirakis*	Y	Y	Y	Y	N	N	Y
10 *Young*	Y	Y	Y	N	N	N	Y
11 Davis	Y	?	Y	N	N	N	Y
12 *Putnam*	Y	Y	Y	Y	Y	N	Y
13 *Miller, D.*	Y	Y	Y	Y	Y	N	Y
14 *Goss*	Y	Y	Y	Y	N	N	Y
15 *Weldon*	Y	Y	Y	Y	N	N	Y
16 *Foley*	Y	Y	Y	N	N	N	Y
17 Meek	N	N	N	N	N	N	Y
18 *Ros-Lehtinen*	Y	Y	Y	N	N	N	Y
19 Wexler	N	Y	N	N	N	N	Y
20 Deutsch	Y	N	Y	N	N	N	Y
21 *Diaz-Balart*	Y	Y	Y	N	N	N	Y
22 *Shaw*	Y	Y	Y	N	N	N	Y
23 Hastings	N	N	N	Y	N	Y	Y
GEORGIA							
1 *Kingston*	Y	Y	Y	Y	N	N	Y
2 Bishop	Y	Y	Y	Y	N	N	Y
3 *Collins*	Y	Y	Y	Y	N	N	Y
4 McKinney	N	N	N	Y	N	N	Y
5 Lewis	N	Y	Y	N	N	N	Y
6 *Isakson*	Y	Y	Y	Y	N	N	Y
7 *Barr*	Y	Y	Y	N	N	N	Y
8 *Chambliss*	Y	Y	Y	Y	N	N	Y
9 *Deal*	Y	Y	Y	Y	N	N	Y
10 *Norwood*	Y	Y	Y	N	N	N	Y
11 *Linder*	Y	Y	Y	?	Y	Y	Y
HAWAII							
1 Abercrombie	N	N	Y	Y	N	N	N
2 Mink	N	N	Y	Y	N	N	N
IDAHO							
1 *Otter*	Y	Y	Y	Y	Y	N	Y
2 *Simpson*	Y	Y	Y	Y	Y	N	Y
ILLINOIS							
1 Rush	N	Y	Y	Y	N	N	Y
2 Jackson	N	Y	Y	N	N	N	Y
3 Lipinski	Y	Y	Y	Y	N	N	Y
4 Gutierrez	Y	N	N	N	N	N	Y
5 Blagojevich	?	?	?	?	?	?	?
6 *Hyde*	Y	Y	Y	Y	Y	N	Y
7 Davis	N	N	Y	N	N	N	Y
8 *Crane*	Y	Y	N	Y	Y	Y	Y
9 Schakowsky	N	N	N	Y	N	N	Y
10 *Kirk*	Y	Y	Y	Y	Y	Y	Y
11 *Weller*	Y	Y	?	Y	Y	N	Y
12 Costello	Y	Y	Y	N	N	N	Y
13 *Biggert*	Y	Y	Y	N	N	N	Y

ND Northern Democrats   SD Southern Democrats

	110	111	112	113	114	115	116
14 ***Hastert***							Y
15 ***Johnson***	Y	Y	Y	Y	N	N	Y
16 ***Manzullo***	Y	Y	Y	Y	Y	N	Y
17 Evans	N	Y	Y	Y	N	N	Y
18 ***LaHood***	Y	Y	Y	Y	N	N	Y
19 Phelps	Y	Y	Y	Y	N	N	Y
20 ***Shimkus***	Y	Y	Y	Y	N	Y	Y
INDIANA							
1 Visclosky	N	Y	Y	N	N	N	Y
2 ***Pence***	Y	Y	Y	Y	Y	N	Y
3 Roemer	Y	Y	Y	Y	N	N	Y
4 ***Souder***	Y	Y	Y	Y	Y	Y	Y
5 ***Buyer***	Y	Y	Y	Y	Y	N	Y
6 ***Burton***	Y	Y	Y	Y	N	Y	Y
7 ***Kerns***	Y	Y	Y	Y	Y	N	Y
8 ***Hostettler***	Y	Y	Y	Y	N	N	Y
9 Hill	Y	Y	Y	Y	N	Y	Y
10 Carson	N	N	Y	Y	N	N	Y
IOWA							
1 ***Leach***	Y	?	?	?	?	?	Y
2 ***Nussle***	Y	Y	Y	Y	N	Y	Y
3 Boswell	Y	Y	Y	Y	N	N	Y
4 ***Ganske***	Y	Y	Y	Y	N	Y	Y
5 ***Latham***	Y	Y	Y	Y	N	N	Y
KANSAS							
1 ***Moran***	Y	Y	Y	N	Y	Y	Y
2 ***Ryun***	Y	Y	Y	Y	Y	Y	Y
3 Moore	Y	Y	Y	N	N	Y	Y
4 ***Tiahrt***	Y	Y	Y	Y	Y	N	Y
KENTUCKY							
1 ***Whitfield***	Y	Y	Y	Y	Y	N	Y
2 ***Lewis***	Y	Y	Y	Y	Y	N	Y
3 ***Northup***	Y	Y	Y	Y	Y	N	Y
4 Lucas	Y	Y	Y	Y	N	N	Y
5 ***Rogers***	Y	Y	Y	Y	Y	N	Y
6 ***Fletcher***	Y	Y	Y	Y	N	N	Y
LOUISIANA							
1 ***Vitter***	Y	Y	Y	Y	Y	Y	Y
2 Jefferson	Y	Y	Y	Y	N	N	Y
3 ***Tauzin***	Y	Y	Y	Y	Y	N	Y
4 ***McCrery***	Y	Y	Y	Y	Y	N	Y
5 ***Cooksey***	Y	Y	Y	Y	?	?	?
6 ***Baker***	Y	Y	Y	Y	Y	Y	Y
7 John	Y	Y	Y	Y	N	N	?
MAINE							
1 Allen	Y	Y	Y	Y	N	N	Y
2 Baldacci	Y	?	?	?	?	?	?
MARYLAND							
1 ***Gilchrest***	?	Y	Y	Y	N	N	Y
2 ***Ehrlich***	Y	Y	Y	Y	Y	N	Y
3 Cardin	Y	Y	Y	Y	N	N	Y
4 Wynn	Y	Y	Y	Y	N	N	Y
5 Hoyer	Y	Y	Y	Y	N	N	Y
6 ***Bartlett***	Y	Y	Y	Y	Y	Y	Y
7 Cummings	Y	Y	Y	Y	N	N	Y
8 ***Morella***	Y	Y	Y	Y	N	Y	Y
MASSACHUSETTS							
1 Olver	N	N	N	N	N	Y	Y
2 Neal	N	Y	Y	Y	N	N	Y
3 McGovern	N	N	N	Y	N	N	Y
4 Frank	N	Y	N	Y	N	Y	Y
5 Meehan	N	Y	Y	Y	N	N	Y
6 Tierney	N	Y	Y	Y	N	N	Y
7 Markey	N	Y	Y	Y	N	N	Y
8 Capuano	Y	Y	Y	N	N	N	Y
9 Lynch	N	N	Y	Y	N	N	Y
10 Delahunt	N	Y	Y	Y	N	Y	Y
MICHIGAN							
1 Stupak	Y	Y	Y	N	N	N	Y
2 ***Hoekstra***	Y	Y	Y	Y	N	N	Y
3 ***Ehlers***	Y	Y	Y	Y	Y	Y	Y
4 ***Camp***	Y	Y	Y	Y	Y	N	Y
5 Barcia	Y	Y	Y	Y	N	N	Y
6 ***Upton***	Y	Y	Y	Y	Y	N	Y
7 ***Smith***	?	Y	Y	Y	N	N	Y
8 ***Rogers***	Y	Y	Y	Y	Y	N	Y
9 Kildee	N	Y	Y	Y	N	N	Y
10 Bonior	N	Y	Y	Y	N	N	Y
11 ***Knollenberg***	Y	Y	Y	Y	N	N	Y
12 Levin	N	Y	Y	Y	N	N	Y
13 Rivers	N	Y	Y	Y	N	N	Y
14 Conyers	N	N	Y	Y	N	N	Y
15 Kilpatrick	N	Y	N	Y	N	N	Y
16 Dingell	N	N	Y	Y	N	N	Y

	110	111	112	113	114	115	116
MINNESOTA							
1 ***Gutknecht***	Y	Y	Y	N	Y	Y	Y
2 ***Kennedy***	Y	Y	Y	N	Y	Y	Y
3 ***Ramstad***	Y	Y	Y	N	Y	Y	Y
4 McCollum	Y	Y	Y	Y	N	N	Y
5 Sabo	N	Y	Y	N	N	N	Y
6 Luther	Y	Y	Y	Y	N	N	Y
7 Peterson	Y	Y	Y	N	N	N	Y
8 Oberstar	N	Y	Y	N	N	N	Y
MISSISSIPPI							
1 ***Wicker***	Y	Y	Y	N	Y	Y	Y
2 Thompson	Y	Y	Y	N	N	N	Y
3 ***Pickering***	Y	Y	Y	Y	Y	Y	Y
4 Shows	?	Y	Y	Y	N	N	Y
5 Taylor	Y	Y	N	N	Y	N	Y
MISSOURI							
1 Clay	Y	Y	Y	Y	N	N	Y
2 ***Akin***	Y	Y	Y	Y	Y	Y	Y
3 Gephardt	N	N	Y	Y	N	N	Y
4 Skelton	Y	Y	Y	Y	N	N	Y
5 McCarthy	Y	Y	Y	Y	N	N	Y
6 ***Graves***	Y	Y	Y	Y	Y	N	Y
7 ***Blunt***	Y	Y	Y	Y	Y	N	Y
8 ***Emerson***	Y	Y	Y	Y	Y	N	Y
9 ***Hulshof***	Y	?	?	?	?	?	?
MONTANA							
AL ***Rehberg***	Y	Y	Y	Y	Y	N	Y
NEBRASKA							
1 ***Bereuter***	Y	Y	Y	Y	N	N	Y
2 ***Terry***	Y	Y	Y	Y	Y	N	Y
3 ***Osborne***	Y	Y	Y	Y	Y	Y	Y
NEVADA							
1 Berkley	Y	Y	Y	Y	N	N	Y
2 ***Gibbons***	Y	Y	Y	Y	Y	Y	Y
NEW HAMPSHIRE							
1 ***Sununu***	Y	Y	Y	Y	Y	Y	Y
2 ***Bass***	Y	Y	Y	Y	Y	Y	Y
NEW JERSEY							
1 Andrews	Y	Y	Y	Y	N	N	Y
2 ***LoBiondo***	Y	Y	Y	Y	N	N	Y
3 ***Saxton***	Y	Y	Y	Y	N	N	Y
4 ***Smith***	Y	Y	Y	Y	N	Y	Y
5 ***Roukema***	Y	Y	Y	Y	N	N	Y
6 Pallone	Y	N	Y	N	N	N	Y
7 ***Ferguson***	Y	Y	Y	Y	N	N	Y
8 Pascrell	Y	Y	Y	Y	N	N	Y
9 Rothman	Y	Y	Y	Y	N	N	Y
10 Payne	N	N	Y	Y	N	N	Y
11 ***Frelinghuysen***	Y	Y	Y	Y	N	N	Y
12 Holt	Y	?	?	?	?	?	?
13 Menendez	Y	Y	Y	Y	N	N	Y
NEW MEXICO							
1 ***Wilson***	Y	Y	Y	Y	N	Y	Y
2 ***Skeen***	Y	Y	Y	Y	N	N	Y
3 Udall	N	Y	Y	N	N	N	Y
NEW YORK							
1 ***Grucci***	Y	Y	Y	Y	N	N	Y
2 Israel	Y	Y	Y	Y	N	N	Y
3 ***King***	Y	Y	Y	Y	N	N	Y
4 McCarthy	Y	Y	Y	Y	N	N	Y
5 Ackerman	N	Y	Y	Y	N	N	Y
6 Meeks	Y	Y	Y	Y	N	N	?
7 Crowley	Y	?	Y	Y	N	N	Y
8 Nadler	N	Y	Y	Y	N	N	Y
9 Weiner	Y	Y	Y	Y	N	N	Y
10 Towns	Y	Y	Y	Y	N	N	Y
11 Owens	N	N	Y	Y	N	N	Y
12 Velázquez	Y	Y	Y	N	N	N	Y
13 ***Fossella***	Y	Y	Y	Y	N	Y	Y
14 Maloney	N	Y	Y	Y	N	N	Y
15 Rangel	N	?	?	?	?	?	?
16 Serrano	N	N	Y	Y	N	N	Y
17 Engel	N	Y	Y	Y	N	N	Y
18 Lowey	N	Y	Y	Y	N	N	Y
19 ***Kelly***	Y	Y	Y	Y	Y	N	Y
20 ***Gilman***	Y	Y	Y	Y	N	N	Y
21 McNulty	N	N	N	N	N	N	Y
22 ***Sweeney***	Y	Y	Y	Y	N	N	Y
23 ***Boehlert***	Y	Y	Y	Y	N	N	Y
24 ***McHugh***	Y	Y	Y	Y	N	N	Y
25 ***Walsh***	Y	Y	Y	Y	Y	N	Y
26 Hinchey	N	N	N	Y	N	N	Y
27 ***Reynolds***	Y	Y	Y	Y	N	N	Y
28 Slaughter	N	N	Y	Y	N	N	Y
29 LaFalce	N	N	Y	Y	N	N	Y

	110	111	112	113	114	115	116
30 ***Quinn***	Y	Y	Y	Y	N	N	Y
31 ***Houghton***	?	Y	Y	Y	Y	N	Y
NORTH CAROLINA							
1 Clayton	N	N	Y	?	N	N	N
2 Etheridge	Y	Y	Y	Y	N	N	Y
3 ***Jones***	Y	Y	Y	Y	?	?	?
4 Price	Y	Y	Y	Y	N	N	Y
5 ***Burr***	Y	Y	Y	Y	N	Y	Y
6 ***Coble***	Y	Y	Y	Y	Y	Y	Y
7 McIntyre	Y	Y	Y	Y	N	N	Y
8 ***Hayes***	Y	Y	Y	Y	N	N	Y
9 ***Myrick***	Y	Y	Y	Y	N	Y	Y
10 ***Ballenger***	Y	Y	Y	?	Y	Y	Y
11 ***Taylor***	Y	Y	Y	Y	Y	N	Y
12 Watt	Y	N	N	N	N	N	N
NORTH DAKOTA							
AL Pomeroy	Y	Y	Y	Y	N	N	N
OHIO							
1 ***Chabot***	Y	Y	Y	Y	Y	N	Y
2 ***Portman***	Y	Y	+	Y	Y	N	Y
3 Hall	Y	Y	Y	Y	N	N	Y
4 ***Oxley***	Y	Y	Y	Y	Y	Y	Y
5 ***Gillmor***	Y	Y	Y	N	N	N	Y
6 Strickland	Y	Y	Y	Y	N	N	Y
7 ***Hobson***	Y	Y	Y	Y	N	N	Y
8 ***Boehner***	Y	Y	Y	Y	N	N	Y
9 Kaptur	N	Y	Y	Y	N	N	Y
10 Kucinich	N	N	N	N	N	N	Y
11 Jones	N	Y	Y	Y	N	N	Y
12 ***Tiberi***	Y	Y	Y	Y	N	N	Y
13 Brown	N	Y	Y	Y	N	N	Y
14 Sawyer	N	Y	Y	Y	N	N	Y
15 ***Pryce***	Y	Y	Y	Y	N	N	Y
16 ***Regula***	Y	Y	Y	Y	N	N	Y
17 Traficant	?	?	?	?	?	?	?
18 ***Ney***	Y	Y	Y	Y	N	N	Y
19 ***LaTourette***	Y	Y	Y	Y	N	N	Y
OKLAHOMA							
1 ***Sullivan***	Y	Y	Y	Y	Y	N	Y
2 Carson	Y	Y	Y	Y	N	N	Y
3 ***Watkins***	Y	Y	Y	Y	Y	N	Y
4 ***Watts***	Y	Y	Y	Y	N	N	Y
5 ***Istook***	Y	Y	Y	Y	Y	N	Y
6 ***Lucas***	Y	Y	Y	Y	Y	N	Y
OREGON							
1 Wu	Y	Y	Y	N	N	Y	Y
2 ***Walden***	Y	Y	Y	Y	Y	Y	Y
3 Blumenauer	Y	Y	Y	Y	N	N	Y
4 DeFazio	N	Y	Y	N	N	N	Y
5 Hooley	Y	Y	Y	Y	N	N	Y
PENNSYLVANIA							
1 Brady	N	Y	Y	N	N	N	Y
2 Fattah	N	N	Y	Y	N	N	Y
3 Borski	N	Y	Y	N	N	N	Y
4 ***Hart***	Y	Y	Y	Y	N	N	Y
5 ***Peterson***	Y	Y	Y	Y	Y	N	Y
6 Holden	Y	Y	Y	Y	N	N	Y
7 ***Weldon***	Y	Y	Y	Y	Y	N	Y
8 ***Greenwood***	Y	Y	N	Y	Y	N	Y
9 ***Shuster, Bill***	Y	Y	Y	Y	Y	N	Y
10 ***Sherwood***	Y	Y	Y	Y	N	N	Y
11 Kanjorski	N	Y	Y	Y	N	N	Y
12 Murtha	N	Y	Y	Y	N	?	?
13 Hoeffel	Y	Y	Y	Y	N	N	Y
14 Coyne	N	Y	Y	Y	N	N	Y
15 ***Toomey***	Y	Y	Y	Y	Y	N	Y
16 ***Pitts***	Y	Y	Y	Y	Y	N	Y
17 ***Gekas***	Y	Y	Y	Y	N	N	Y
18 Doyle	Y	Y	Y	Y	N	N	Y
19 ***Platts***	Y	Y	Y	Y	Y	N	Y
20 Mascara	Y	Y	Y	Y	N	N	Y
21 ***English***	Y	Y	Y	?	N	N	Y
RHODE ISLAND							
1 Kennedy	Y	Y	Y	Y	N	Y	Y
2 Langevin	Y	Y	Y	Y	N	N	Y
SOUTH CAROLINA							
1 ***Brown***	Y	Y	Y	Y	Y	N	Y
2 ***Wilson***	Y	Y	Y	Y	Y	Y	Y
3 ***Graham***	Y	Y	Y	Y	Y	Y	Y
4 ***DeMint***	Y	Y	Y	Y	Y	Y	Y
5 Spratt	Y	?	?	Y	N	N	Y
6 Clyburn	N	Y	Y	Y	N	N	Y
SOUTH DAKOTA							
AL ***Thune***	?	Y	Y	Y	Y	N	Y

	110	111	112	113	114	115	116
TENNESSEE							
1 ***Jenkins***	Y	Y	Y	Y	N	N	Y
2 ***Duncan***	Y	Y	Y	Y	Y	Y	Y
3 ***Wamp***	Y	Y	Y	Y	Y	Y	Y
4 ***Hilleary***	Y	Y	Y	Y	Y	Y	Y
5 Clement	Y	Y	Y	Y	N	N	Y
6 Gordon	Y	Y	Y	Y	N	N	Y
7 ***Bryant***	Y	Y	Y	Y	Y	Y	Y
8 Tanner	Y	Y	Y	Y	?	?	?
9 Ford	Y	Y	Y	Y	N	N	Y
TEXAS							
1 Sandlin	Y	Y	Y	Y	N	N	?
2 Turner	Y	Y	Y	Y	N	N	Y
3 ***Johnson, Sam***	Y	Y	Y	Y	Y	Y	Y
4 Hall	Y	Y	Y	Y	Y	Y	Y
5 ***Sessions***	Y	Y	Y	Y	Y	Y	Y
6 ***Barton***	Y	Y	Y	Y	Y	N	Y
7 ***Culberson***	Y	Y	Y	Y	Y	N	Y
8 ***Brady***	Y	Y	Y	Y	Y	Y	Y
9 Lampson	Y	Y	Y	Y	N	N	Y
10 Doggett	N	N	Y	Y	N	N	Y
11 Edwards	Y	Y	Y	Y	N	N	Y
12 ***Granger***	Y	Y	Y	Y	Y	N	Y
13 ***Thornberry***	Y	Y	N	Y	Y	Y	Y
14 ***Paul***	N	Y	Y	Y	Y	Y	Y
15 Hinojosa	Y	Y	Y	Y	?	?	?
16 Reyes	Y	Y	Y	Y	N	N	Y
17 Stenholm	Y	Y	N	Y	N	N	Y
18 Jackson-Lee	N	Y	Y	Y	N	N	Y
19 ***Combest***	Y	Y	Y	Y	Y	Y	Y
20 Gonzalez	Y	Y	Y	Y	N	N	Y
21 ***Smith***	Y	Y	Y	Y	N	N	Y
22 ***DeLay***	Y	Y	Y	Y	Y	N	Y
23 ***Bonilla***	Y	Y	Y	?	Y	Y	Y
24 Frost	Y	Y	Y	Y	N	N	Y
25 Bentsen	Y	Y	Y	Y	N	N	Y
26 ***Armey***	Y	Y	Y	Y	Y	Y	Y
27 Ortiz	Y	Y	Y	Y	N	N	Y
28 Rodriguez	?	?	?	?	?	?	?
29 Green	Y	Y	Y	Y	N	N	Y
30 Johnson, E.B.	Y	Y	Y	N	N	N	Y
UTAH							
1 ***Hansen***	Y	Y	Y	Y	Y	N	Y
2 Matheson	Y	Y	Y	Y	N	N	Y
3 ***Cannon***	Y	Y	Y	Y	Y	Y	Y
VERMONT							
AL *Sanders*	N	?	N	Y	N	N	N
VIRGINIA							
1 ***Davis, Jo Ann***	Y	Y	Y	Y	N	Y	Y
2 ***Schrock***	Y	Y	Y	Y	Y	N	Y
3 Scott	N	Y	Y	Y	N	N	Y
4 ***Forbes***	Y	Y	Y	Y	Y	N	Y
5 *Goode*	Y	Y	Y	Y	Y	N	Y
6 ***Goodlatte***	Y	Y	Y	Y	Y	Y	Y
7 ***Cantor***	Y	Y	Y	Y	Y	Y	Y
8 Moran	Y	Y	Y	Y	N	Y	Y
9 Boucher	Y	Y	Y	Y	N	N	Y
10 ***Wolf***	Y	Y	Y	Y	Y	N	Y
11 ***Davis, T.***	Y	Y	Y	Y	N	Y	?
WASHINGTON							
1 Inslee	Y	Y	Y	Y	N	N	Y
2 Larsen	Y	Y	Y	Y	N	N	Y
3 Baird	Y	Y	Y	N	N	N	Y
4 ***Hastings***	Y	Y	Y	Y	Y	Y	Y
5 ***Nethercutt***	Y	Y	Y	Y	Y	Y	?
6 Dicks	Y	Y	Y	Y	N	N	Y
7 McDermott	N	Y	Y	N	N	N	Y
8 ***Dunn***	Y	Y	Y	Y	N	?	Y
9 Smith	?	?	?	?	?	?	?
WEST VIRGINIA							
1 Mollohan	N	Y	Y	Y	N	N	Y
2 ***Capito***	Y	Y	Y	Y	N	N	Y
3 Rahall	N	Y	Y	Y	N	N	Y
WISCONSIN							
1 ***Ryan***	Y	Y	Y	Y	Y	Y	Y
2 Baldwin	N	Y	Y	N	N	N	Y
3 Kind	Y	Y	Y	Y	N	Y	Y
4 Kleczka	Y	Y	Y	Y	N	N	Y
5 Barrett	N	Y	Y	Y	N	N	Y
6 ***Petri***	Y	Y	Y	Y	N	N	Y
7 Obey	N	Y	Y	Y	N	N	Y
8 ***Green***	Y	Y	Y	Y	Y	N	Y
9 ***Sensenbrenner***	Y	Y	Y	Y	N	N	Y
WYOMING							
AL ***Cubin***	Y	Y	Y	Y	Y	N	Y

Southern states - Ala., Ark., Fla., Ga., Ky., La., Miss., N.C., Okla., S.C., Tenn., Texas, Va.

Key

Y	Voted for (yea).
#	Paired for.
+	Announced for.
N	Voted against (nay).
X	Paired against.
–	Announced against.
P	Voted "present."
C	Voted "present" to avoid possible conflict of interest.
?	Did not vote or otherwise make a position known.

Democrats **Republicans**
Independents

117. HR 169. Federal Employees' Protection/Concur With Senate Amendments. Sensenbrenner, R-Wis., motion to suspend the rules and concur with Senate amendments to the bill that would increase federal agencies' requirements under anti-discrimination and whistle-blower protection laws by requiring them to pay for judgments against them out of their own budgets, better notify employees about relevant laws and mandate detailed annual reports to Congress on actions filed against them. Motion agreed to (thus cleared for the president) 412-0: R 210-0; D 200-0 (ND 148-0, SD 52-0); I 2-0. A two-thirds majority of those present and voting (275 in this case) is required for passage under suspension of the rules. April 30, 2002.

118. S 2248. Export-Import Extension/Passage. Bereuter, R-Neb., motion to suspend the rules and pass the bill that would reauthorize the Export-Import Bank through May 31, 2002. Motion agreed to (thus cleared for the president) 318-92: R 167-42; D 151-48 (ND 104-44, SD 47-4); I 0-2. A two-thirds majority of those present and voting (274 in this case) is required for passage under suspension of the rules. April 30, 2002.

119. H Con Res 386. Charter Schools Tribute/Adoption. Castle, R-Del., motion to suspend the rules and adopt the concurrent resolution that would honor charter schools on their 10th anniversary and support National Charter Schools Week. Motion agreed to 404-3: R 208-0; D 194-3 (ND 142-3, SD 52-0); I 2-0. A two-thirds majority of those present and voting (272 in this case) is required for adoption under suspension of the rules. April 30, 2002.

120. HR 2871. Export-Import Reauthorization/Domestic Layoffs. Sanders, I-Vt., amendment that would ban companies that lay off a greater percentage of U.S. employees than overseas employees from receiving assistance through the Export-Import Bank. Rejected 135-283: R 22-192; D 111-91 (ND 91-59, SD 20-32); I 2-0. May 1, 2002.

121. HR 2215. Justice Department Reauthorization/Motion to Instruct. DeGette, D-Colo., motion to instruct conferees to agree to a provision that would establish a Violence Against Women Office and another provision in section 402 of the House-passed bill that would establish duties for the director of that office. Motion agreed to 416-3: R 212-3; D 202-0 (ND 152-0, SD 50-0); I 2-0. May 1, 2002.

	117	118	119	120	121
ALABAMA					
1 *Callahan*	Y	Y	Y	N	Y
2 *Everett*	Y	Y	Y	N	Y
3 *Riley*	+	+	+	N	Y
4 *Aderholt*	Y	Y	Y	N	Y
5 Cramer	Y	Y	Y	N	Y
6 *Bachus*	Y	Y	Y	N	Y
7 Hilliard	Y	Y	Y	Y	Y
ALASKA					
AL *Young*	Y	Y	Y	N	Y
ARIZONA					
1 *Flake*	Y	N	Y	N	N
2 Pastor	Y	Y	Y	Y	Y
3 *Stump*	Y	Y	Y	N	Y
4 *Shadegg*	Y	N	Y	N	Y
5 *Kolbe*	Y	Y	Y	N	Y
6 *Hayworth*	Y	N	Y	N	Y
ARKANSAS					
1 Berry	Y	Y	Y	Y	Y
2 Snyder	Y	Y	Y	N	Y
3 *Boozman*	Y	Y	Y	N	Y
4 Ross	Y	Y	Y	Y	Y
CALIFORNIA					
1 Thompson	Y	N	Y	Y	Y
2 *Herger*	Y	Y	Y	N	Y
3 *Ose*	Y	Y	Y	N	Y
4 *Doolittle*	Y	N	Y	?	Y
5 Matsui	Y	Y	Y	N	Y
6 Woolsey	Y	Y	Y	Y	Y
7 Miller, George	Y	N	Y	Y	Y
8 Pelosi	Y	Y	Y	N	Y
9 Lee	Y	N	Y	Y	Y
10 Tauscher	Y	Y	Y	N	Y
11 *Pombo*	?	?	?	N	Y
12 Lantos	Y	Y	Y	N	Y
13 Stark	Y	N	Y	Y	Y
14 Eshoo	Y	Y	Y	N	Y
15 Honda	Y	Y	Y	–	Y
16 Lofgren	Y	Y	Y	N	Y
17 Farr	Y	Y	Y	Y	Y
18 Condit	Y	N	Y	?	Y
19 *Radanovich*	Y	Y	Y	N	Y
20 Dooley	Y	Y	Y	N	Y
21 *Thomas*	Y	Y	Y	N	Y
22 Capps	Y	Y	?	N	Y
23 *Gallegly*	Y	Y	Y	N	Y
24 Sherman	Y	Y	Y	Y	Y
25 *McKeon*	Y	Y	Y	N	Y
26 Berman	Y	Y	Y	N	Y
27 Schiff	Y	Y	Y	N	Y
28 *Dreier*	Y	Y	Y	N	Y
29 Waxman	Y	Y	Y	N	Y
30 Becerra	Y	Y	Y	Y	Y
31 Solis	Y	N	Y	Y	Y
32 Watson	Y	Y	Y	Y	Y
33 Roybal-Allard	Y	Y	Y	Y	Y
34 Napolitano	Y	Y	Y	Y	Y
35 Waters	Y	N	Y	Y	Y
36 Harman	Y	Y	Y	Y	Y
37 Millender-McD.	?	?	?	?	?
38 *Horn*	Y	Y	Y	N	Y
39 *Royce*	Y	N	Y	N	Y
40 *Lewis*	Y	Y	Y	Y	Y
41 *Miller, Gary*	Y	Y	Y	Y	Y
42 Baca	Y	Y	Y	Y	Y
43 *Calvert*	Y	Y	Y	N	Y
44 *Bono*	Y	Y	Y	N	Y
45 *Rohrabacher*	Y	N	Y	N	Y
46 Sanchez	Y	Y	Y	N	Y
47 *Cox*	Y	N	Y	?	Y
48 *Issa*	Y	Y	Y	N	Y
49 Davis	Y	Y	Y	N	Y
50 Filner	Y	Y	Y	Y	Y
51 *Cunningham*	Y	Y	Y	N	Y
52 *Hunter*	Y	N	Y	N	Y
COLORADO					
1 DeGette	Y	Y	Y	Y	Y
2 Udall	Y	Y	Y	?	Y
3 *McInnis*	Y	N	N	Y	N
4 *Schaffer*	?	?	?	N	Y
5 *Hefley*	Y	N	Y	N	Y
6 *Tancredo*	Y	N	Y	Y	Y
CONNECTICUT					
1 Larson	Y	Y	Y	N	Y
2 *Simmons*	Y	Y	Y	N	Y
3 DeLauro	Y	Y	Y	N	Y
4 *Shays*	Y	Y	Y	N	Y
5 Maloney	Y	Y	Y	N	Y
6 *Johnson*	Y	Y	Y	N	Y
DELAWARE					
AL *Castle*	Y	Y	Y	N	Y
FLORIDA					
1 *Miller, J.*	Y	N	Y	N	Y
2 Boyd	Y	Y	Y	N	Y
3 Brown	Y	Y	Y	Y	Y
4 *Crenshaw*	Y	Y	Y	N	Y
5 Thurman	Y	Y	Y	Y	Y
6 *Stearns*	Y	Y	Y	N	Y
7 *Mica*	Y	Y	Y	N	Y
8 *Keller*	Y	Y	Y	N	Y
9 *Bilirakis*	Y	N	Y	N	Y
10 *Young*	Y	?	?	?	Y
11 Davis	Y	Y	Y	N	Y
12 *Putnam*	Y	Y	Y	N	Y
13 *Miller, D.*	Y	Y	Y	N	Y
14 *Goss*	Y	Y	Y	N	Y
15 *Weldon*	?	?	?	N	Y
16 *Foley*	Y	Y	Y	N	Y
17 Meek	Y	N	Y	Y	?
18 *Ros-Lehtinen*	Y	Y	Y	N	Y
19 Wexler	Y	Y	Y	N	Y
20 Deutsch	Y	Y	Y	N	Y
21 *Diaz-Balart*	Y	Y	Y	N	Y
22 *Shaw*	Y	Y	Y	N	Y
23 Hastings	Y	N	Y	Y	Y
GEORGIA					
1 *Kingston*	Y	Y	Y	N	Y
2 Bishop	Y	Y	Y	Y	Y
3 *Collins*	Y	Y	Y	N	Y
4 McKinney	Y	N	Y	Y	Y
5 Lewis	Y	N	Y	Y	?
6 *Isakson*	Y	Y	Y	N	Y
7 *Barr*	Y	Y	Y	N	Y
8 *Chambliss*	Y	Y	Y	N	Y
9 *Deal*	Y	Y	Y	N	Y
10 *Norwood*	Y	Y	Y	N	Y
11 *Linder*	Y	Y	Y	N	Y
HAWAII					
1 Abercrombie	Y	N	Y	Y	Y
2 Mink	Y	N	Y	Y	Y
IDAHO					
1 *Otter*	Y	N	Y	N	Y
2 *Simpson*	Y	Y	Y	N	Y
ILLINOIS					
1 Rush	Y	Y	Y	N	Y
2 Jackson	Y	N	Y	Y	Y
3 Lipinski	Y	Y	Y	Y	Y
4 Gutierrez	?	?	?	Y	Y
5 Blagojevich	?	?	?	Y	Y
6 *Hyde*	Y	Y	Y	N	Y
7 Davis	Y	Y	Y	N	Y
8 *Crane*	?	?	?	?	?
9 Schakowsky	Y	Y	Y	Y	Y
10 *Kirk*	Y	Y	Y	N	Y
11 *Weller*	Y	Y	Y	N	?
12 Costello	Y	N	Y	N	Y
13 *Biggert*	Y	Y	Y	N	Y

ND Northern Democrats   SD Southern Democrats

	117	118	119	120	121
14 ***Hastert***					
15 ***Johnson***	Y	Y	Y	N	Y
16 ***Manzullo***	Y	Y	Y	N	Y
17 Evans	Y	N	Y	Y	Y
18 ***LaHood***	Y	Y	Y	N	Y
19 Phelps	Y	Y	Y	Y	Y
20 ***Shimkus***	Y	Y	Y	N	Y
INDIANA					
1 Visclosky	Y	N	Y	Y	Y
2 ***Pence***	Y	N	Y	N	Y
3 Roemer	Y	Y	Y	Y	Y
4 ***Souder***	?	?	?	N	Y
5 ***Buyer***	?	?	?	N	Y
6 ***Burton***	Y	Y	Y	N	Y
7 ***Kerns***	Y	N	Y	Y	Y
8 ***Hostettler***	Y	N	Y	Y	N
9 Hill	Y	Y	Y	N	Y
10 Carson	Y	Y	Y	Y	Y
IOWA					
1 ***Leach***	Y	Y	Y	N	Y
2 ***Nussle***	Y	Y	Y	N	Y
3 Boswell	Y	Y	Y	Y	Y
4 ***Ganske***	Y	Y	Y	N	Y
5 ***Latham***	Y	Y	Y	N	Y
KANSAS					
1 ***Moran***	Y	Y	Y	N	Y
2 ***Ryun***	Y	Y	Y	N	Y
3 Moore	Y	Y	Y	N	Y
4 ***Tiahrt***	Y	Y	Y	N	Y
KENTUCKY					
1 ***Whitfield***	Y	Y	Y	N	Y
2 ***Lewis***	Y	Y	Y	N	Y
3 ***Northup***	Y	Y	Y	N	Y
4 Lucas	Y	Y	Y	N	Y
5 ***Rogers***	Y	Y	Y	N	Y
6 ***Fletcher***	Y	Y	Y	N	Y
LOUISIANA					
1 ***Vitter***	Y	Y	Y	N	Y
2 Jefferson	Y	Y	Y	N	Y
3 ***Tauzin***	?	?	?	N	Y
4 ***McCrery***	Y	Y	Y	N	?
5 ***Cooksey***	Y	Y	Y	N	Y
6 ***Baker***	Y	Y	Y	N	Y
7 John	Y	Y	Y	N	Y
MAINE					
1 Allen	Y	Y	Y	Y	Y
2 Baldacci	Y	Y	Y	Y	Y
MARYLAND					
1 ***Gilchrest***	Y	Y	Y	N	Y
2 ***Ehrlich***	Y	Y	Y	–	Y
3 Cardin	Y	Y	Y	Y	Y
4 Wynn	?	?	?	Y	Y
5 Hoyer	Y	Y	Y	N	Y
6 ***Bartlett***	Y	N	Y	Y	Y
7 Cummings	Y	Y	Y	Y	Y
8 ***Morella***	Y	Y	Y	N	Y
MASSACHUSETTS					
1 Olver	Y	N	Y	Y	Y
2 Neal	Y	Y	Y	N	Y
3 McGovern	Y	Y	Y	Y	Y
4 Frank	?	?	?	N	Y
5 Meehan	Y	Y	Y	N	Y
6 Tierney	Y	Y	Y	Y	Y
7 Markey	Y	Y	Y	N	Y
8 Capuano	Y	Y	P	Y	Y
9 Lynch	Y	Y	Y	Y	Y
10 Delahunt	Y	Y	Y	N	?
MICHIGAN					
1 Stupak	Y	N	Y	Y	Y
2 ***Hoekstra***	Y	N	Y	N	Y
3 ***Ehlers***	Y	Y	Y	N	Y
4 ***Camp***	Y	Y	Y	N	Y
5 Barcia	Y	N	Y	Y	Y
6 ***Upton***	Y	Y	Y	N	Y
7 ***Smith***	Y	N	Y	N	Y
8 ***Rogers***	Y	Y	Y	N	Y
9 Kildee	Y	N	Y	Y	Y
10 Bonior	Y	N	Y	Y	Y
11 ***Knollenberg***	Y	Y	Y	N	Y
12 Levin	Y	Y	Y	N	Y
13 Rivers	Y	N	N	Y	Y
14 Conyers	Y	N	Y	Y	Y
15 Kilpatrick	Y	Y	Y	Y	Y
16 Dingell	Y	Y	Y	Y	Y

	117	118	119	120	121
MINNESOTA					
1 ***Gutknecht***	Y	N	Y	N	Y
2 ***Kennedy***	Y	Y	Y	N	Y
3 ***Ramstad***	Y	Y	Y	N	Y
4 McCollum	Y	Y	Y	Y	Y
5 Sabo	Y	Y	Y	N	Y
6 Luther	Y	Y	Y	Y	Y
7 Peterson	Y	N	Y	N	Y
8 Oberstar	Y	N	Y	Y	Y
MISSISSIPPI					
1 ***Wicker***	Y	Y	Y	N	Y
2 Thompson	Y	Y	Y	N	Y
3 ***Pickering***	Y	Y	Y	N	Y
4 Shows	Y	Y	Y	N	Y
5 Taylor	Y	Y	Y	Y	Y
MISSOURI					
1 Clay	Y	N	Y	Y	Y
2 ***Akin***	Y	N	Y	N	Y
3 Gephardt	Y	Y	Y	N	Y
4 Skelton	Y	Y	Y	N	Y
5 McCarthy	Y	Y	Y	N	Y
6 ***Graves***	Y	Y	Y	N	Y
7 ***Blunt***	Y	Y	Y	N	Y
8 ***Emerson***	Y	Y	Y	N	Y
9 ***Hulshof***	Y	Y	Y	N	Y
MONTANA					
AL ***Rehberg***	Y	Y	Y	N	Y
NEBRASKA					
1 ***Bereuter***	Y	Y	Y	N	Y
2 ***Terry***	Y	Y	Y	N	Y
3 ***Osborne***	Y	Y	Y	N	Y
NEVADA					
1 Berkley	Y	Y	Y	Y	Y
2 ***Gibbons***	Y	Y	Y	N	Y
NEW HAMPSHIRE					
1 ***Sununu***	Y	N	Y	N	Y
2 ***Bass***	Y	N	Y	N	Y
NEW JERSEY					
1 Andrews	Y	N	Y	Y	Y
2 ***LoBiondo***	Y	Y	Y	N	Y
3 ***Saxton***	Y	Y	Y	N	Y
4 ***Smith***	Y	Y	Y	Y	Y
5 ***Roukema***	Y	Y	?	N	Y
6 Pallone	Y	N	Y	Y	Y
7 ***Ferguson***	Y	Y	Y	N	Y
8 Pascrell	Y	N	Y	Y	Y
9 Rothman	Y	Y	Y	N	Y
10 Payne	Y	N	Y	Y	Y
11 ***Frelinghuysen***	Y	Y	Y	N	Y
12 Holt	Y	Y	Y	N	Y
13 Menendez	Y	Y	Y	N	Y
NEW MEXICO					
1 ***Wilson***	Y	Y	Y	N	Y
2 ***Skeen***	Y	Y	Y	N	Y
3 Udall	Y	N	Y	Y	Y
NEW YORK					
1 ***Grucci***	Y	Y	Y	N	Y
2 Israel	Y	Y	Y	N	Y
3 ***King***	Y	Y	Y	N	Y
4 McCarthy	Y	Y	Y	N	Y
5 Ackerman	Y	Y	Y	N	Y
6 Meeks	Y	Y	Y	N	Y
7 Crowley	Y	Y	Y	N	Y
8 Nadler	Y	Y	Y	Y	Y
9 Weiner	Y	Y	Y	Y	Y
10 Towns	Y	N	Y	N	Y
11 Owens	Y	N	Y	Y	Y
12 Velázquez	Y	Y	Y	N	Y
13 ***Fossella***	Y	Y	Y	N	Y
14 Maloney	Y	Y	Y	N	Y
15 Rangel	Y	Y	Y	N	Y
16 Serrano	Y	Y	Y	Y	Y
17 Engel	Y	Y	Y	Y	Y
18 Lowey	Y	Y	Y	N	Y
19 ***Kelly***	Y	Y	Y	N	Y
20 ***Gilman***	Y	Y	Y	N	Y
21 McNulty	Y	Y	Y	Y	Y
22 ***Sweeney***	Y	N	Y	N	Y
23 ***Boehlert***	Y	Y	Y	N	Y
24 ***McHugh***	Y	N	Y	N	Y
25 ***Walsh***	Y	Y	Y	N	Y
26 Hinchey	Y	N	N	Y	Y
27 ***Reynolds***	Y	Y	Y	N	Y
28 Slaughter	Y	Y	Y	Y	Y
29 LaFalce	Y	Y	Y	N	Y

	117	118	119	120	121
30 ***Quinn***	Y	Y	Y	N	Y
31 ***Houghton***	Y	Y	Y	N	Y
NORTH CAROLINA					
1 Clayton	+	+	+	?	?
2 Etheridge	Y	Y	Y	N	Y
3 ***Jones***	Y	N	Y	Y	Y
4 Price	Y	Y	Y	N	Y
5 ***Burr***	Y	Y	Y	Y	Y
6 ***Coble***	Y	N	Y	Y	Y
7 McIntyre	Y	Y	Y	Y	Y
8 ***Hayes***	Y	N	Y	N	Y
9 ***Myrick***	Y	Y	Y	N	Y
10 ***Ballenger***	Y	Y	Y	N	Y
11 ***Taylor***	Y	N	Y	Y	Y
12 Watt	Y	Y	Y	Y	Y
NORTH DAKOTA					
AL Pomeroy	Y	Y	Y	N	Y
OHIO					
1 ***Chabot***	Y	N	Y	Y	Y
2 ***Portman***	Y	Y	Y	N	Y
3 Hall	Y	Y	Y	Y	Y
4 ***Oxley***	Y	Y	Y	N	Y
5 ***Gillmor***	Y	Y	Y	N	Y
6 Strickland	Y	N	Y	Y	Y
7 ***Hobson***	Y	Y	Y	N	Y
8 ***Boehner***	Y	Y	Y	N	Y
9 Kaptur	Y	Y	Y	Y	Y
10 Kucinich	Y	N	P	Y	Y
11 Jones	Y	N	N	Y	Y
12 ***Tiberi***	Y	Y	Y	N	Y
13 Brown	Y	N	Y	Y	Y
14 Sawyer	Y	Y	Y	Y	Y
15 ***Pryce***	Y	Y	Y	N	Y
16 ***Regula***	Y	Y	Y	Y	Y
17 Traficant	?	?	?	?	?
18 ***Ney***	Y	Y	Y	N	Y
19 ***LaTourette***	Y	Y	Y	N	Y
OKLAHOMA					
1 ***Sullivan***	Y	Y	Y	N	Y
2 Carson	Y	Y	Y	N	Y
3 ***Watkins***	?	?	?	N	Y
4 ***Watts***	Y	Y	Y	N	Y
5 ***Istook***	Y	Y	Y	N	Y
6 ***Lucas***	Y	Y	Y	N	Y
OREGON					
1 Wu	Y	Y	Y	N	Y
2 ***Walden***	Y	Y	Y	N	Y
3 Blumenauer	Y	Y	Y	N	Y
4 DeFazio	Y	N	Y	Y	Y
5 Hooley	Y	Y	Y	N	Y
PENNSYLVANIA					
1 Brady	Y	N	Y	Y	Y
2 Fattah	Y	N	Y	Y	Y
3 Borski	Y	Y	Y	Y	Y
4 ***Hart***	Y	Y	Y	N	Y
5 ***Peterson***	Y	Y	Y	Y	Y
6 Holden	Y	N	Y	Y	Y
7 ***Weldon***	Y	Y	Y	?	Y
8 ***Greenwood***	Y	Y	Y	N	Y
9 ***Shuster, Bill***	Y	Y	Y	N	Y
10 ***Sherwood***	Y	Y	Y	Y	Y
11 Kanjorski	Y	Y	Y	N	Y
12 Murtha	?	?	?	?	?
13 Hoeffel	Y	Y	Y	Y	Y
14 Coyne	Y	N	Y	Y	Y
15 ***Toomey***	Y	Y	Y	N	Y
16 ***Pitts***	Y	Y	Y	N	Y
17 ***Gekas***	Y	N	Y	N	Y
18 Doyle	Y	Y	Y	Y	Y
19 ***Platts***	Y	N	Y	Y	Y
20 Mascara	+	–	+	?	?
21 ***English***	Y	Y	Y	N	Y
RHODE ISLAND					
1 Kennedy	Y	Y	Y	Y	Y
2 Langevin	Y	Y	Y	Y	Y
SOUTH CAROLINA					
1 ***Brown***	Y	Y	Y	N	Y
2 ***Wilson***	Y	Y	Y	N	Y
3 ***Graham***	Y	Y	Y	Y	Y
4 ***DeMint***	?	?	?	N	Y
5 Spratt	Y	Y	Y	Y	Y
6 Clyburn	Y	Y	Y	Y	Y
SOUTH DAKOTA					
AL ***Thune***	Y	Y	Y	N	Y

	117	118	119	120	121
TENNESSEE					
1 ***Jenkins***	Y	Y	Y	N	Y
2 ***Duncan***	Y	N	Y	Y	Y
3 ***Wamp***	Y	N	Y	Y	Y
4 ***Hilleary***	Y	N	Y	N	Y
5 Clement	Y	?	Y	N	Y
6 Gordon	Y	Y	Y	N	Y
7 ***Bryant***	Y	Y	Y	N	Y
8 Tanner	?	?	?	Y	Y
9 Ford	Y	Y	Y	N	Y
TEXAS					
1 Sandlin	Y	Y	Y	N	Y
2 Turner	Y	Y	Y	N	Y
3 ***Johnson, Sam***	Y	Y	Y	N	Y
4 Hall	Y	Y	Y	N	Y
5 ***Sessions***	Y	Y	Y	N	Y
6 ***Barton***	Y	Y	Y	N	Y
7 ***Culberson***	Y	N	Y	N	Y
8 ***Brady***	Y	Y	Y	N	Y
9 Lampson	Y	Y	Y	Y	Y
10 Doggett	Y	Y	Y	N	Y
11 Edwards	Y	Y	Y	N	Y
12 ***Granger***	Y	Y	Y	N	Y
13 ***Thornberry***	Y	Y	Y	N	Y
14 ***Paul***	Y	N	Y	Y	N
15 Hinojosa	Y	Y	Y	N	Y
16 Reyes	Y	Y	Y	N	Y
17 Stenholm	Y	Y	Y	N	Y
18 Jackson-Lee	Y	Y	Y	Y	Y
19 ***Combest***	Y	Y	Y	N	Y
20 Gonzalez	Y	Y	Y	N	Y
21 ***Smith***	Y	Y	Y	N	Y
22 ***DeLay***	Y	N	Y	N	Y
23 ***Bonilla***	Y	Y	Y	N	Y
24 Frost	Y	Y	Y	N	Y
25 Bentsen	Y	Y	Y	N	Y
26 ***Armey***	Y	N	Y	N	Y
27 Ortiz	Y	Y	Y	N	Y
28 Rodriguez	Y	Y	Y	Y	Y
29 Green	Y	Y	Y	?	?
30 Johnson, E.B.	Y	Y	Y	N	Y
UTAH					
1 ***Hansen***	Y	Y	Y	N	Y
2 Matheson	Y	N	Y	Y	Y
3 ***Cannon***	?	?	?	?	?
VERMONT					
AL *Sanders*	Y	N	Y	Y	Y
VIRGINIA					
1 ***Davis, Jo Ann***	Y	N	Y	N	Y
2 ***Schrock***	Y	Y	Y	N	Y
3 Scott	Y	Y	Y	N	Y
4 ***Forbes***	Y	Y	Y	N	Y
5 *Goode*	Y	N	Y	Y	Y
6 ***Goodlatte***	Y	Y	Y	N	Y
7 ***Cantor***	Y	Y	Y	N	Y
8 Moran	Y	Y	Y	N	Y
9 Boucher	Y	Y	Y	Y	Y
10 ***Wolf***	Y	Y	Y	N	Y
11 ***Davis, T.***	Y	Y	Y	N	?
WASHINGTON					
1 Inslee	Y	Y	Y	N	Y
2 Larsen	Y	Y	Y	N	Y
3 Baird	Y	Y	Y	N	Y
4 ***Hastings***	Y	Y	Y	N	Y
5 ***Nethercutt***	Y	Y	Y	N	Y
6 Dicks	Y	Y	Y	N	Y
7 McDermott	Y	Y	Y	N	Y
8 ***Dunn***	Y	Y	Y	N	Y
9 Smith	?	?	?	N	Y
WEST VIRGINIA					
1 Mollohan	Y	N	Y	Y	Y
2 ***Capito***	Y	Y	Y	N	Y
3 Rahall	Y	N	Y	Y	Y
WISCONSIN					
1 ***Ryan***	Y	Y	Y	N	Y
2 Baldwin	Y	N	Y	Y	Y
3 Kind	Y	Y	Y	N	Y
4 Kleczka	Y	Y	Y	Y	Y
5 Barrett	Y	Y	Y	Y	Y
6 ***Petri***	Y	N	Y	N	Y
7 Obey	Y	Y	Y	Y	Y
8 ***Green***	Y	Y	Y	N	Y
9 ***Sensenbrenner***	Y	N	Y	N	Y
WYOMING					
AL ***Cubin***	Y	Y	Y	N	Y

Southern states - Ala., Ark., Fla., Ga., Ky., La., Miss., N.C., Okla., S.C., Tenn., Texas, Va.

Key

Y	Voted for (yea).
#	Paired for.
+	Announced for.
N	Voted against (nay).
X	Paired against.
−	Announced against.
P	Voted "present."
C	Voted "present" to avoid possible conflict of interest.
?	Did not vote or otherwise make a position known.

•

Democrats   **Republicans**
Independents

122. HR 2646. Farm Bill/Recommit. Kind, D-Wis., motion to recommit the conference report to the conference committee with instructions to add language that would lower payment limitations for commodity payments, eliminate provisions to evade the limits and increase funding for conservation, nutrition, rural development and energy programs. Motion rejected 172-251: R 51-164; D 121-85 (ND 112-41, SD 9-44); I 0-2. May 2, 2002.

123. HR 2646. Farm Bill/Conference Report. Adoption of the conference report on the bill that would reauthorize federal agriculture programs for six years. The agreement would re-establish programs that supply payments to farmers when commodity prices fall below a specified level. It would raise mandatory and direct farm program spending by $73.5 billion over 10 years, provide $243 billion for food stamps and restore benefits for legal immigrants, and increase conservation spending to $17.1 billion. After two years, the agreement would require certain goods to be labeled by country origin. It would lower the total limit on payments to individual farmers to $360,000 and authorize a new $1 billion dairy program for three-and-a-half years. Adopted (thus sent to the Senate) 280-141: R 141-73; D 137-68 (ND 89-63, SD 48-5); I 2-0. May 2, 2002.

124. H Res 392. Israel Support/Previous Question. Diaz-Balart, R-Fla., motion to order the previous question (thus ending debate and possibility of amendment) on the rule (H Res 404) to provide for House floor consideration of a motion to suspend the rules and adopt the resolution that would support Israel's efforts to fight terrorism in Palestinian areas and condemn Yasser Arafat's support of terror. Motion agreed to 328-82: R 202-3; D 125-78 (ND 88-65, SD 37-13); I 1-1. May 2, 2002.

125. H Res 392. Israel Support/Rule. Adoption of the rule (H Res 404) to provide for House floor consideration of a motion to suspend the rules and adopt the resolution that would support Israel's efforts to fight terrorism in Palestinian areas and condemn Yasser Arafat's support of terror. Adopted 329-76: R 199-2; D 129-73 (ND 92-60, SD 37-13); I 1-1. May 2, 2002.

126. H Res 392. Israel Support/Adoption. Hyde, R-Ill., motion to suspend the rules and adopt the resolution that would support Israel's efforts to fight terrorism in Palestinian areas and condemn Yasser Arafat's support of terror. It also would express support for international humanitarian efforts for Palestinians. Motion agreed to 352-21: R 194-4; D 157-17 (ND 116-14, SD 41-3); I 1-0. A two-thirds majority of those present and voting (249 in this case) is required for adoption under suspension of the rules. May 2, 2002.

	122	123	124	125	126
ALABAMA					
1 *Callahan*	N	Y	?	?	?
2 *Everett*	N	Y	+	+	+
3 *Riley*	N	Y	?	?	?
4 *Aderholt*	N	Y	Y	Y	Y
5 Cramer	N	Y	Y	Y	Y
6 *Bachus*	N	Y	Y	Y	Y
7 Hilliard	N	Y	N	N	N
ALASKA					
AL *Young*	N	Y	Y	Y	Y
ARIZONA					
1 *Flake*	Y	N	Y	Y	Y
2 Pastor	Y	Y	N	Y	Y
3 *Stump*	N	Y	Y	Y	Y
4 *Shadegg*	N	N	Y	Y	Y
5 *Kolbe*	N	N	Y	Y	Y
6 *Hayworth*	N	N	Y	Y	Y
ARKANSAS					
1 Berry	N	Y	Y	Y	Y
2 Snyder	N	Y	N	N	Y
3 *Boozman*	N	Y	Y	Y	Y
4 Ross	N	Y	Y	Y	Y
CALIFORNIA					
1 Thompson	N	Y	N	N	P
2 *Herger*	N	Y	Y	Y	Y
3 *Ose*	N	Y	Y	Y	Y
4 *Doolittle*	N	N	Y	Y	Y
5 Matsui	Y	N	Y	Y	Y
6 Woolsey	Y	Y	N	N	P
7 Miller, George	Y	N	N	N	N
8 Pelosi	Y	N	Y	Y	Y
9 Lee	Y	N	N	N	N
10 Tauscher	Y	N	Y	Y	Y
11 *Pombo*	N	Y	Y	Y	Y
12 Lantos	Y	N	Y	Y	Y
13 Stark	Y	N	N	N	N
14 Eshoo	Y	N	N	N	Y
15 Honda	Y	N	N	N	Y
16 Lofgren	Y	N	N	N	Y
17 Farr	Y	N	N	N	P
18 Condit	N	Y	N	N	N
19 *Radanovich*	N	Y	Y	Y	Y
20 Dooley	N	N	Y	?	+
21 *Thomas*	N	Y	Y	Y	Y
22 Capps	Y	N	N	Y	Y
23 Gallegly	Y	N	Y	Y	Y
24 Sherman	Y	N	Y	Y	Y
25 *McKeon*	N	N	Y	Y	Y
26 Berman	Y	N	Y	Y	Y
27 Schiff	Y	N	Y	Y	Y
28 *Dreier*	N	N	Y	Y	Y
29 Waxman	Y	N	Y	Y	Y
30 Becerra	Y	N	N	N	P
31 Solis	Y	Y	N	N	P
32 Watson	Y	N	Y	Y	Y
33 Roybal-Allard	Y	Y	N	N	Y
34 Napolitano	N	Y	Y	Y	Y
35 Waters	Y	N	N	N	Y
36 Harman	Y	N	Y	Y	Y
37 Millender-McD.	?	?	?	?	?
38 *Horn*	N	Y	Y	Y	Y

	122	123	124	125	126
39 *Royce*	Y	N	Y	Y	Y
40 *Lewis*	N	N	Y	Y	Y
41 *Miller, Gary*	N	N	Y	Y	Y
42 Baca	N	Y	Y	Y	Y
43 *Calvert*	N	N	Y	Y	Y
44 *Bono*	N	Y	Y	Y	Y
45 *Rohrabacher*	N	N	Y	Y	N
46 Sanchez	Y	N	N	Y	Y
47 *Cox*	Y	N	Y	Y	Y
48 *Issa*	N	N	Y	?	Y
49 Davis	Y	N	Y	Y	Y
50 Filner	Y	Y	N	N	Y
51 *Cunningham*	N	Y	Y	Y	Y
52 *Hunter*	N	Y	Y	Y	Y
COLORADO					
1 DeGette	Y	N	N	N	Y
2 Udall	Y	N	N	N	Y
3 *McInnis*	Y	N	Y	Y	Y
4 *Schaffer*	N	Y	Y	Y	Y
5 *Hefley*	Y	N	Y	Y	Y
6 *Tancredo*	Y	N	Y	Y	Y
CONNECTICUT					
1 Larson	Y	N	Y	Y	Y
2 *Simmons*	N	Y	Y	Y	Y
3 DeLauro	N	Y	Y	Y	Y
4 *Shays*	Y	N	Y	Y	Y
5 Maloney	Y	N	Y	Y	Y
6 *Johnson*	Y	N	Y	Y	Y
DELAWARE					
AL *Castle*	Y	N	Y	Y	Y
FLORIDA					
1 *Miller, J.*	N	N	Y	Y	Y
2 Boyd	N	Y	Y	Y	Y
3 Brown	N	Y	?	?	?
4 *Crenshaw*	N	Y	Y	Y	Y
5 Thurman	N	Y	Y	Y	P
6 *Stearns*	Y	N	Y	Y	Y
7 *Mica*	N	N	Y	Y	Y
8 *Keller*	N	Y	Y	Y	Y
9 *Bilirakis*	Y	N	?	?	?
10 *Young*	Y	N	Y	?	?
11 Davis	Y	N	Y	Y	Y
12 *Putnam*	N	Y	Y	Y	Y
13 *Miller, D.*	Y	N	Y	Y	Y
14 *Goss*	Y	Y	Y	Y	Y
15 *Weldon*	Y	Y	Y	Y	Y
16 *Foley*	N	Y	Y	Y	Y
17 Meek	N	Y	Y	Y	Y
18 *Ros-Lehtinen*	?	?	?	?	?
19 Wexler	Y	Y	Y	Y	Y
20 Deutsch	Y	N	Y	Y	Y
21 *Diaz-Balart*	N	Y	Y	Y	Y
22 *Shaw*	Y	N	Y	Y	Y
23 Hastings	N	Y	Y	Y	Y
GEORGIA					
1 *Kingston*	N	Y	Y	Y	Y
2 Bishop	N	Y	Y	Y	P
3 *Collins*	Y	N	Y	Y	Y
4 McKinney	Y	N	N	N	N
5 Lewis	Y	Y	Y	Y	Y
6 *Isakson*	N	Y	Y	Y	Y
7 *Barr*	N	N	Y	Y	P
8 *Chambliss*	N	Y	Y	Y	Y
9 *Deal*	N	Y	Y	Y	Y
10 *Norwood*	N	Y	Y	Y	Y
11 *Linder*	N	N	Y	?	Y
HAWAII					
1 Abercrombie	N	Y	N	N	N
2 Mink	N	Y	N	N	P
IDAHO					
1 *Otter*	N	Y	Y	Y	Y
2 *Simpson*	N	Y	Y	Y	Y
ILLINOIS					
1 Rush	N	Y	N	N	Y
2 Jackson	Y	Y	N	N	N
3 Lipinski	N	Y	N	N	Y
4 Gutierrez	N	Y	Y	Y	Y
5 Blagojevich	N	Y	Y	Y	Y
6 *Hyde*	N	Y	Y	Y	Y
7 Davis	Y	N	Y	Y	Y
8 *Crane*	?	?	?	?	?
9 Schakowsky	N	Y	Y	Y	Y
10 *Kirk*	N	N	Y	Y	Y
11 *Weller*	N	Y	Y	Y	Y
12 Costello	N	Y	Y	N	Y
13 *Biggert*	Y	N	Y	Y	Y

ND Northern Democrats   SD Southern Democrats

	122	123	124	125	126
14 Hastert					
15 *Johnson*	N	Y	Y	Y	Y
16 *Manzullo*	N	Y	Y	Y	Y
17 Evans	N	Y	Y	Y	Y
18 *LaHood*	N	Y	Y	Y	Y
19 Phelps	N	Y	Y	Y	Y
20 *Shimkus*	N	Y	Y	Y	Y
INDIANA					
1 Visclosky	N	Y	Y	Y	Y
2 *Pence*	N	Y	Y	Y	Y
3 Roemer	Y	Y	Y	Y	Y
4 *Souder*	N	Y	Y	Y	Y
5 *Buyer*	N	Y	Y	Y	Y
6 *Burton*	N	+	?	?	?
7 *Kerns*	Y	Y	Y	Y	Y
8 *Hostettler*	Y	Y	Y	Y	P
9 Hill	N	Y	Y	Y	Y
10 Carson	N	Y	Y	Y	Y
IOWA					
1 *Leach*	Y	Y	Y	Y	Y
2 *Nussle*	Y	Y	Y	Y	Y
3 Boswell	N	Y	Y	Y	Y
4 *Ganske*	Y	N	Y	Y	Y
5 *Latham*	Y	N	Y	Y	Y
KANSAS					
1 *Moran*	N	Y	Y	Y	Y
2 *Ryun*	N	N	Y	Y	Y
3 Moore	Y	Y	Y	Y	Y
4 *Tiahrt*	N	Y	Y	Y	Y
KENTUCKY					
1 *Whitfield*	N	Y	Y	Y	Y
2 *Lewis*	N	Y	Y	Y	Y
3 *Northup*	N	N	Y	Y	Y
4 Lucas	N	Y	Y	Y	Y
5 *Rogers*	N	Y	Y	Y	Y
6 *Fletcher*	N	Y	Y	Y	Y
LOUISIANA					
1 *Vitter*	N	Y	Y	Y	Y
2 Jefferson	?	?	?	?	?
3 *Tauzin*	N	Y	Y	Y	Y
4 *McCrery*	N	Y	Y	Y	Y
5 *Cooksey*	N	Y	?	?	?
6 *Baker*	N	Y	Y	Y	Y
7 John	N	Y	?	?	?
MAINE					
1 Allen	Y	N	N	Y	Y
2 Baldacci	Y	Y	Y	Y	Y
MARYLAND					
1 *Gilchrest*	N	Y	Y	Y	Y
2 *Ehrlich*	N	Y	Y	Y	Y
3 Cardin	Y	N	Y	Y	Y
4 Wynn	N	Y	Y	Y	Y
5 Hoyer	Y	Y	Y	Y	Y
6 *Bartlett*	N	Y	Y	Y	Y
7 Cummings	N	Y	Y	Y	Y
8 *Morella*	Y	N	Y	Y	Y
MASSACHUSETTS					
1 Olver	Y	Y	N	N	Y
2 Neal	Y	Y	Y	N	Y
3 McGovern	Y	Y	N	N	Y
4 Frank	Y	N	N	N	Y
5 Meehan	Y	Y	Y	N	Y
6 Tierney	Y	N	N	N	Y
7 Markey	Y	N	Y	N	Y
8 Capuano	Y	N	N	N	P
9 Lynch	Y	Y	N	Y	Y
10 Delahunt	Y	N	N	N	Y
MICHIGAN					
1 Stupak	Y	Y	Y	Y	Y
2 *Hoekstra*	Y	N	?	?	?
3 *Ehlers*	Y	Y	Y	Y	Y
4 *Camp*	N	Y	Y	Y	Y
5 Barcia	N	Y	Y	Y	Y
6 *Upton*	Y	Y	Y	Y	Y
7 *Smith*	Y	Y	Y	Y	N
8 *Rogers*	N	Y	Y	Y	Y
9 Kildee	Y	Y	N	N	Y
10 Bonior	Y	N	N	N	N
11 *Knollenberg*	N	Y	Y	Y	Y
12 Levin	Y	Y	N	N	Y
13 Rivers	Y	N	N	N	P
14 Conyers	Y	Y	N	N	Y
15 Kilpatrick	Y	Y	N	N	P
16 Dingell	Y	Y	N	N	N

	122	123	124	125	126
MINNESOTA					
1 *Gutknecht*	N	Y	Y	Y	Y
2 *Kennedy*	N	Y	Y	Y	Y
3 *Ramstad*	Y	N	Y	Y	Y
4 McCollum	Y	Y	Y	Y	Y
5 Sabo	N	Y	N	N	P
6 Luther	Y	Y	Y	Y	Y
7 Peterson	N	Y	N	N	P
8 Oberstar	N	Y	N	N	P
MISSISSIPPI					
1 *Wicker*	N	Y	Y	Y	Y
2 Thompson	N	Y	?	?	?
3 *Pickering*	N	Y	Y	Y	Y
4 Shows	N	Y	Y	Y	Y
5 Taylor	N	Y	N	N	Y
MISSOURI					
1 Clay	N	Y	N	N	Y
2 *Akin*	N	N	Y	Y	Y
3 Gephardt	N	Y	Y	Y	Y
4 Skelton	N	Y	Y	Y	Y
5 McCarthy	Y	N	Y	Y	Y
6 *Graves*	N	Y	Y	Y	Y
7 *Blunt*	N	Y	Y	Y	Y
8 *Emerson*	N	Y	Y	Y	Y
9 *Hulshof*	N	Y	Y	Y	Y
MONTANA					
AL *Rehberg*	N	Y	Y	Y	Y
NEBRASKA					
1 *Bereuter*	Y	Y	N	N	?
2 *Terry*	N	Y	Y	Y	Y
3 *Osborne*	N	Y	Y	Y	Y
NEVADA					
1 *Berkley*	Y	Y	Y	Y	Y
2 *Gibbons*	N	N	Y	Y	Y
NEW HAMPSHIRE					
1 *Sununu*	Y	N	Y	Y	Y
2 *Bass*	Y	N	Y	Y	Y
NEW JERSEY					
1 Andrews	Y	N	Y	Y	Y
2 *LoBiondo*	Y	N	Y	Y	Y
3 *Saxton*	N	N	Y	Y	Y
4 *Smith*	N	Y	Y	Y	Y
5 *Roukema*	?	?	?	?	?
6 Pallone	Y	N	Y	Y	Y
7 *Ferguson*	N	N	Y	Y	Y
8 Pascrell	Y	Y	N	Y	Y
9 Rothman	Y	Y	Y	Y	Y
10 Payne	Y	N	N	N	P
11 *Frelinghuysen*	N	N	Y	Y	Y
12 Holt	Y	N	Y	N	Y
13 Menendez	Y	Y	Y	Y	Y
NEW MEXICO					
1 *Wilson*	N	Y	Y	Y	Y
2 *Skeen*	N	Y	Y	Y	Y
3 Udall	Y	Y	Y	Y	Y
NEW YORK					
1 *Grucci*	N	Y	Y	Y	Y
2 Israel	Y	N	Y	Y	Y
3 *King*	N	Y	Y	Y	Y
4 McCarthy	N	Y	Y	Y	Y
5 Ackerman	Y	N	Y	Y	Y
6 Meeks	Y	Y	Y	Y	Y
7 Crowley	Y	N	Y	Y	Y
8 Nadler	Y	Y	Y	Y	Y
9 Weiner	Y	Y	Y	Y	Y
10 Towns	N	Y	Y	Y	Y
11 Owens	Y	Y	Y	Y	Y
12 Velázquez	Y	Y	Y	Y	Y
13 *Fossella*	N	N	Y	Y	Y
14 Maloney	Y	N	Y	Y	Y
15 Rangel	Y	N	Y	Y	Y
16 Serrano	Y	Y	N	N	Y
17 Engel	Y	Y	Y	Y	Y
18 Lowey	Y	Y	Y	Y	Y
19 *Kelly*	N	Y	Y	Y	Y
20 Gilman	N	Y	Y	Y	Y
21 McNulty	Y	Y	Y	Y	Y
22 *Sweeney*	N	Y	Y	Y	Y
23 *Boehlert*	N	Y	Y	Y	Y
24 *McHugh*	N	Y	?	?	?
25 *Walsh*	N	Y	Y	Y	Y
26 Hinchey	Y	Y	N	N	Y
27 *Reynolds*	N	Y	Y	Y	Y
28 Slaughter	Y	Y	Y	Y	Y
29 LaFalce	Y	Y	Y	Y	Y

	122	123	124	125	126
30 *Quinn*	N	Y	Y	Y	Y
31 Houghton	Y	Y	Y	Y	Y
NORTH CAROLINA					
1 Clayton	N	Y	N	N	P
2 Etheridge	N	Y	Y	Y	Y
3 *Jones*	N	Y	Y	Y	Y
4 Price	N	Y	Y	Y	Y
5 *Burr*	N	Y	N	N	Y
6 *Coble*	N	Y	Y	Y	Y
7 McIntyre	N	Y	Y	Y	Y
8 *Hayes*	N	Y	Y	Y	Y
9 *Myrick*	Y	N	Y	Y	Y
10 *Ballenger*	N	Y	Y	Y	Y
11 *Taylor*	N	Y	Y	Y	?
12 Watt	N	Y	N	N	P
NORTH DAKOTA					
AL Pomeroy	N	Y	N	Y	Y
OHIO					
1 *Chabot*	Y	N	Y	Y	Y
2 *Portman*	N	N	Y	Y	Y
3 Hall	N	Y	N	N	Y
4 *Oxley*	N	N	Y	Y	?
5 *Gillmor*	N	Y	Y	Y	Y
6 Strickland	Y	Y	Y	Y	Y
7 *Hobson*	Y	N	Y	Y	Y
8 *Boehner*	N	N	Y	Y	Y
9 Kaptur	Y	Y	N	N	P
10 Kucinich	Y	N	N	N	P
11 Jones	N	Y	N	N	P
12 *Tiberi*	Y	N	Y	Y	Y
13 Brown	Y	N	N	N	P
14 Sawyer	Y	Y	N	N	Y
15 *Pryce*	N	N	Y	Y	Y
16 *Regula*	N	Y	Y	Y	Y
17 Traficant	?	?	?	?	?
18 *Ney*	N	Y	Y	Y	Y
19 *LaTourette*	N	Y	Y	Y	Y
OKLAHOMA					
1 *Sullivan*	−	+	?	?	?
2 Carson	N	Y	Y	Y	Y
3 *Watkins*	N	Y	Y	Y	Y
4 *Watts*	N	Y	Y	Y	Y
5 *Istook*	?	?	?	?	?
6 *Lucas*	N	Y	Y	Y	Y
OREGON					
1 Wu	Y	Y	Y	Y	Y
2 *Walden*	N	Y	Y	Y	Y
3 Blumenauer	Y	N	N	N	Y
4 DeFazio	Y	N	N	N	N
5 Hooley	N	Y	Y	Y	?
PENNSYLVANIA					
1 Brady	Y	Y	Y	Y	Y
2 Fattah	?	?	?	?	?
3 Borski	Y	Y	Y	Y	Y
4 *Hart*	N	Y	Y	Y	Y
5 *Peterson*	N	Y	Y	Y	Y
6 Holden	N	Y	Y	Y	Y
7 *Weldon*	N	Y	Y	Y	Y
8 *Greenwood*	Y	Y	Y	Y	Y
9 *Shuster, Bill*	N	Y	Y	Y	Y
10 *Sherwood*	N	Y	Y	Y	Y
11 Kanjorski	Y	Y	Y	Y	Y
12 Murtha	?	?	?	?	?
13 Hoeffel	Y	N	Y	Y	Y
14 Coyne	Y	N	Y	Y	Y
15 *Toomey*	N	Y	Y	Y	Y
16 *Pitts*	N	Y	Y	Y	Y
17 *Gekas*	N	Y	Y	Y	Y
18 Doyle	Y	N	Y	Y	Y
19 *Platts*	N	Y	Y	Y	Y
20 Mascara	N	Y	Y	Y	Y
21 *English*	N	Y	Y	Y	Y
RHODE ISLAND					
1 Kennedy	Y	N	Y	Y	Y
2 Langevin	Y	N	Y	Y	Y
SOUTH CAROLINA					
1 *Brown*	N	Y	Y	Y	Y
2 *Wilson*	N	Y	Y	Y	Y
3 *Graham*	N	Y	Y	Y	Y
4 *DeMint*	Y	Y	Y	Y	Y
5 Spratt	N	Y	Y	Y	Y
6 Clyburn	N	Y	N	N	Y
SOUTH DAKOTA					
AL *Thune*	Y	Y	Y	Y	Y

	122	123	124	125	126
TENNESSEE					
1 *Jenkins*	N	Y	?	?	?
2 *Duncan*	N	N	Y	Y	Y
3 *Wamp*	N	N	?	?	?
4 *Hilleary*	N	Y	Y	Y	Y
5 Clement	N	Y	Y	Y	Y
6 Gordon	N	Y	Y	Y	Y
7 *Bryant*	N	Y	Y	Y	Y
8 Tanner	N	Y	Y	Y	Y
9 Ford	N	Y	Y	Y	Y
TEXAS					
1 Sandlin	N	Y	Y	Y	Y
2 Turner	N	Y	Y	Y	Y
3 *Johnson, Sam*	N	N	Y	Y	Y
4 Hall	N	Y	Y	Y	Y
5 *Sessions*	N	Y	Y	Y	Y
6 *Barton*	N	Y	Y	Y	Y
7 *Culberson*	N	Y	Y	Y	Y
8 *Brady*	N	Y	Y	Y	Y
9 Lampson	N	Y	Y	Y	Y
10 Doggett	Y	N	N	N	Y
11 Edwards	N	Y	Y	Y	Y
12 *Granger*	N	Y	Y	Y	Y
13 *Thornberry*	N	Y	Y	Y	Y
14 *Paul*	N	N	Y	Y	N
15 Hinojosa	N	Y	Y	Y	Y
16 Reyes	N	Y	Y	Y	Y
17 Stenholm	N	Y	Y	N	?
18 Jackson-Lee	Y	Y	Y	Y	Y
19 *Combest*	N	Y	Y	Y	Y
20 Gonzalez	N	Y	Y	Y	Y
21 *Smith*	N	Y	Y	Y	Y
22 *DeLay*	N	Y	Y	Y	Y
23 *Bonilla*	N	Y	Y	Y	Y
24 Frost	N	Y	Y	Y	Y
25 Bentsen	N	Y	Y	Y	Y
26 *Armey*	N	N	Y	Y	Y
27 Ortiz	N	Y	Y	Y	Y
28 Rodriguez	N	Y	Y	Y	Y
29 Green	Y	Y	Y	Y	Y
30 Johnson, E.B.	N	Y	N	N	Y
UTAH					
1 *Hansen*	N	Y	Y	Y	Y
2 Matheson	Y	Y	Y	Y	Y
3 *Cannon*	?	?	?	?	?
VERMONT					
AL *Sanders*	N	Y	N	N	P
VIRGINIA					
1 *Davis, Jo Ann*	N	Y	Y	Y	Y
2 *Schrock*	N	N	Y	Y	Y
3 Scott	Y	Y	Y	Y	Y
4 *Forbes*	N	N	Y	Y	Y
5 *Goode*	N	Y	Y	Y	Y
6 *Goodlatte*	N	Y	Y	Y	Y
7 *Cantor*	N	Y	Y	Y	Y
8 Moran	Y	N	N	N	P
9 Boucher	Y	Y	N	N	N
10 *Wolf*	Y	N	Y	Y	Y
11 *Davis, T.*	Y	N	Y	Y	Y
WASHINGTON					
1 Inslee	Y	N	N	N	Y
2 Larsen	N	Y	Y	Y	Y
3 Baird	N	Y	Y	Y	Y
4 *Hastings*	N	Y	Y	Y	Y
5 *Nethercutt*	N	Y	Y	Y	Y
6 Dicks	Y	Y	Y	Y	Y
7 McDermott	N	N	N	N	P
8 *Dunn*	N	N	Y	Y	Y
9 Smith	Y	N	Y	Y	Y
WEST VIRGINIA					
1 Mollohan	Y	?	N	N	P
2 *Capito*	Y	Y	Y	Y	Y
3 Rahall	Y	Y	N	N	N
WISCONSIN					
1 *Ryan*	N	Y	Y	Y	Y
2 Baldwin	Y	N	N	N	P
3 Kind	Y	N	N	N	P
4 Kleczka	Y	N	N	N	N
5 Barrett	Y	N	Y	N	Y
6 *Petri*	Y	Y	N	N	N
7 Obey	Y	N	N	N	N
8 *Green*	N	Y	N	Y	Y
9 *Sensenbrenner*	Y	N	Y	Y	Y
WYOMING					
AL *Cubin*	N	Y	Y	Y	Y

Southern states - Ala., Ark., Fla., Ga., Ky., La., Miss., N.C., Okla., S.C., Tenn., Texas, Va.

House Votes 127, 128, 129, 130, 131, 132, 133, 134

127. HR 2911. Harvey W. Wiley Building/Passage. Boozman, R-Ark., motion to suspend the rules and pass the bill that would name a federal building in College Park, Md., after the late Harvey W. Wiley, a chemist whose work helped lead to food and drug legislation. Motion agreed to 402-0: R 208-0; D 192-0 (ND 140-0, SD 52-0); I 2-0. A two-thirds majority of those present and voting (268 in this case) is required for passage under suspension of the rules. May 7, 2002.

128. H Con Res 271. Importance of Health Care/Adoption. Wilson, R-N.M., motion to suspend the rules and adopt the concurrent resolution that would express the sense of Congress that it is important to increase individuals' awareness of available health care coverage options and to establish a National Importance of Health Care Coverage Month. Motion agreed to 402-1: R 207-1; D 193-0 (ND 141-0, SD 52-0); I 2-0. A two-thirds majority of those present and voting (269 in this case) is required for adoption under suspension of the rules. May 7, 2002.

129. H J Res 84. Steel Tariffs/Previous Question. Reynolds, R-N.Y., motion to order the previous question (thus ending debate and possibility of amendment) on the rule (H Res 414) that would table (kill) the joint resolution that states that Congress does not approve of President Bush's March 5 decision to impose tariffs of up to 30 percent on steel imports. Motion agreed to 355-62: R 214-2; D 140-59 (ND 101-44, SD 39-15); I 1-1. May 8, 2002.

130. H J Res 84. Steel Tariffs/Rule. Adoption of the rule (H Res 414) that would table (kill) the joint resolution that would state that Congress does not approve of President Bush's March 5 decision to impose tariffs of up to 30 percent on steel imports. Adopted 386-30: R 202-12; D 182-18 (ND 134-12, SD 48-6); I 2-0. A "yea" was a vote in support of the president's position. May 8, 2002.

131. HR 3525. Border Security/Concur With Senate Amendments. Sensenbrenner, R-Wis., motion to suspend the rules and concur with Senate amendments to the bill that would authorize the hiring of additional border inspectors. Planes and passenger ships traveling from other countries would be required to provide immigration officials with lists of passengers and crew members before arriving. The bill would create a database of suspected terrorists that federal agencies could use to screen visa applicants, and require schools to tell government officials if foreign students do not report for class. The bill would ban residents of terrorist-sponsoring countries from receiving temporary visas. All visas, passports and other travel documents would have to contain biometric data. Motion agreed to 411-0: R 212-0; D 198-0 (ND 144-0, SD 54-0); I 1-0. A two-thirds majority of those present and voting (274 in this case) is required for adoption under suspension of the rules. May 8, 2002.

132. H J Res 87. Nuclear Waste/Motion to Consider. Tauzin, R-La., motion to consider under section 115 of the Nuclear Waste Policy Act of 1982 the joint resolution that would approve a site at Yucca Mountain, Nev., as a repository for the nation's spent nuclear fuel and high-level radioactive waste. (Gibbons, R-Nev., raised a point of order that the joint resolution would impose an unfunded mandate in violation of the Congressional Budget Act.) Motion agreed to 308-105: R 201-12; D 106-92 (ND 62-83, SD 44-9); I 1-1. May 8, 2002.

133. H J Res 87. Nuclear Waste/Passage. Passage of the joint resolution that would approve a site at Yucca Mountain, Nev., as a repository for the nation's spent nuclear fuel and high-level radioactive waste. Passed 306-117: R 203-13; D 102-103 (ND 60-92, SD 42-11); I 1-1. A "yea" was a vote in support of the president's position. May 8, 2002.

134. Procedural Motion/Adjourn. Taylor, D-Miss., motion to adjourn. Motion rejected 44-366: R 1-209; D 43-155 (ND 32-115, SD 11-40); I 0-2. May 9, 2002.

Key

Y	Voted for (yea).
#	Paired for.
+	Announced for.
N	Voted against (nay).
X	Paired against.
–	Announced against.
P	Voted "present."
C	Voted "present" to avoid possible conflict of interest.
?	Did not vote or otherwise make a position known.

• Democrats   **Republicans**   *Independents*

	127	128	129	130	131	132	133	134
ALABAMA								
1 *Callahan*	Y	Y	Y	Y	Y	Y	Y	N
2 *Everett*	Y	Y	Y	Y	Y	Y	Y	N
3 *Riley*	?	?	?	?	?	?	?	?
4 *Aderholt*	Y	Y	Y	Y	Y	Y	Y	N
5 Cramer	Y	Y	Y	Y	Y	Y	Y	N
6 *Bachus*	Y	Y	Y	Y	Y	Y	Y	N
7 Hilliard	Y	Y	Y	Y	Y	Y	Y	N
ALASKA								
AL *Young*	Y	Y	Y	Y	Y	N	N	?
ARIZONA								
1 *Flake*	Y	Y	Y	N	Y	Y	Y	N
2 Pastor	Y	Y	N	Y	Y	Y	Y	N
3 *Stump*	Y	Y	Y	Y	Y	Y	Y	N
4 *Shadegg*	Y	Y	Y	Y	Y	Y	Y	N
5 *Kolbe*	Y	Y	Y	N	Y	Y	Y	N
6 *Hayworth*	Y	Y	Y	Y	Y	Y	Y	N
ARKANSAS								
1 Berry	Y	Y	Y	Y	Y	Y	Y	Y
2 Snyder	Y	Y	Y	Y	Y	Y	Y	N
3 *Boozman*	Y	Y	Y	Y	Y	Y	Y	N
4 Ross	Y	Y	Y	Y	Y	Y	Y	N
CALIFORNIA								
1 Thompson	Y	Y	Y	Y	Y	N	N	N
2 *Herger*	Y	Y	Y	N	Y	Y	Y	N
3 *Ose*	?	?	?	?	?	?	?	?
4 *Doolittle*	Y	Y	Y	Y	Y	Y	Y	N
5 Matsui	Y	Y	Y	Y	Y	N	N	N
6 Woolsey	Y	Y	N	Y	?	N	N	Y
7 Miller, George	Y	Y	?	Y	Y	N	N	Y
8 Pelosi	Y	Y	N	Y	N	N	N	Y
9 Lee	Y	Y	N	Y	N	N	N	Y
10 Tauscher	Y	Y	Y	Y	Y	Y	Y	N
11 *Pombo*	Y	Y	Y	?	Y	N	N	N
12 Lantos	Y	Y	N	Y	Y	N	N	N
13 Stark	Y	Y	Y	Y	Y	N	N	Y
14 Eshoo	Y	Y	Y	Y	Y	N	N	N
15 Honda	Y	Y	?	?	Y	N	N	Y
16 Lofgren	Y	Y	N	N	Y	N	N	N
17 Farr	Y	Y	Y	Y	N	N	N	N
18 Condit	Y	Y	Y	Y	Y	N	N	N
19 *Radanovich*	Y	Y	Y	Y	Y	N	N	N
20 Dooley	Y	Y	N	N	Y	N	Y	N
21 *Thomas*	Y	Y	Y	Y	Y	Y	Y	N
22 Capps	Y	Y	Y	Y	Y	N	N	N
23 *Gallegly*	Y	Y	Y	Y	Y	N	N	N
24 Sherman	Y	Y	Y	Y	Y	N	N	N
25 *McKeon*	Y	Y	Y	Y	Y	N	N	N
26 Berman	Y	Y	N	N	Y	N	N	N
27 Schiff	Y	Y	Y	Y	Y	N	N	N
28 *Dreier*	Y	Y	Y	Y	Y	Y	N	N
29 Waxman	?	?	?	?	?	?	?	?
30 Becerra	Y	Y	N	Y	Y	N	N	N
31 Solis	Y	Y	N	N	Y	N	N	N
32 Watson	Y	Y	N	N	Y	N	N	?
33 Roybal-Allard	Y	Y	Y	Y	Y	N	N	N
34 Napolitano	Y	Y	N	N	Y	N	N	?
35 Waters	Y	Y	N	N	Y	N	N	Y
36 Harman	Y	Y	N	N	Y	N	N	N
37 Millender-McD.	Y	Y	Y	Y	Y	N	N	N
38 *Horn*	Y	Y	Y	Y	Y	Y	Y	N

	127	128	129	130	131	132	133	134
39 *Royce*	Y	Y	Y	Y	Y	Y	N	N
40 *Lewis*	Y	Y	Y	Y	Y	Y	N	N
41 *Miller, Gary*	Y	Y	Y	Y	Y	Y	Y	N
42 Baca	Y	Y	Y	Y	Y	N	N	N
43 *Calvert*	Y	Y	Y	Y	Y	Y	Y	N
44 *Bono*	Y	Y	Y	Y	Y	Y	Y	N
45 *Rohrabacher*	Y	Y	Y	Y	Y	Y	Y	N
46 Sanchez	Y	Y	Y	Y	Y	N	N	N
47 *Cox*	Y	Y	Y	Y	+	Y	Y	N
48 *Issa*	Y	Y	Y	Y	Y	Y	Y	N
49 Davis	Y	Y	N	N	Y	N	N	N
50 Filner	Y	Y	Y	Y	Y	N	N	Y
51 *Cunningham*	Y	Y	Y	Y	Y	Y	Y	N
52 *Hunter*	?	?	Y	Y	Y	Y	Y	N
COLORADO								
1 DeGette	Y	Y	N	N	Y	N	N	N
2 Udall	?	?	?	?	?	N	N	N
3 *McInnis*	Y	Y	Y	Y	Y	Y	Y	N
4 *Schaffer*	Y	Y	Y	Y	Y	Y	Y	?
5 *Hefley*	Y	Y	Y	Y	Y	Y	Y	N
6 *Tancredo*	Y	Y	Y	P	P	Y	Y	N
CONNECTICUT								
1 Larson	Y	Y	Y	Y	Y	Y	Y	Y
2 *Simmons*	Y	Y	Y	Y	Y	Y	Y	N
3 DeLauro	Y	Y	N	Y	Y	N	N	N
4 *Shays*	Y	Y	Y	Y	Y	Y	Y	N
5 Maloney	Y	Y	Y	Y	Y	Y	Y	–
6 *Johnson*	Y	Y	Y	Y	Y	Y	Y	N
DELAWARE								
AL *Castle*	Y	Y	N	N	Y	Y	Y	N
FLORIDA								
1 *Miller, J.*	Y	Y	Y	Y	Y	Y	Y	N
2 Boyd	Y	Y	Y	Y	Y	Y	Y	N
3 Brown	Y	Y	Y	Y	Y	Y	Y	N
4 *Crenshaw*	Y	Y	Y	Y	Y	Y	Y	N
5 Thurman	Y	Y	Y	Y	Y	Y	Y	N
6 *Stearns*	Y	Y	Y	Y	Y	Y	Y	N
7 *Mica*	Y	Y	Y	Y	Y	Y	Y	N
8 *Keller*	Y	Y	Y	Y	Y	Y	Y	N
9 *Bilirakis*	Y	Y	Y	Y	Y	Y	Y	N
10 *Young*	Y	Y	Y	Y	Y	Y	Y	N
11 Davis	?	?	N	N	Y	Y	Y	N
12 *Putnam*	Y	Y	Y	Y	Y	Y	Y	N
13 *Miller, D.*	Y	Y	Y	Y	Y	Y	Y	N
14 *Goss*	Y	Y	Y	Y	Y	Y	Y	N
15 *Weldon*	Y	Y	Y	Y	Y	Y	Y	N
16 *Foley*	Y	Y	Y	Y	Y	Y	Y	N
17 Meek	Y	Y	N	Y	Y	Y	N	N
18 *Ros-Lehtinen*	Y	Y	Y	Y	Y	Y	Y	N
19 Wexler	Y	Y	Y	Y	Y	Y	N	N
20 Deutsch	Y	Y	Y	Y	Y	Y	N	N
21 *Diaz-Balart*	Y	Y	Y	Y	Y	N	N	N
22 *Shaw*	Y	Y	Y	Y	Y	Y	Y	N
23 Hastings	Y	Y	N	N	Y	Y	Y	N
GEORGIA								
1 *Kingston*	?	?	Y	Y	Y	Y	Y	N
2 Bishop	Y	Y	Y	Y	Y	Y	Y	?
3 *Collins*	Y	Y	Y	Y	Y	Y	Y	N
4 McKinney	Y	N	Y	N	Y	N	N	N
5 Lewis	Y	Y	N	Y	Y	N	N	Y
6 *Isakson*	Y	Y	Y	Y	Y	Y	Y	N
7 *Barr*	Y	Y	Y	Y	Y	Y	Y	N
8 *Chambliss*	Y	Y	Y	Y	Y	Y	Y	N
9 *Deal*	Y	Y	Y	Y	Y	Y	Y	N
10 *Norwood*	Y	Y	Y	Y	Y	Y	Y	?
11 *Linder*	Y	Y	Y	Y	Y	Y	Y	N
HAWAII								
1 Abercrombie	Y	Y	Y	Y	P	N	N	?
2 Mink	Y	Y	Y	Y	Y	N	N	Y
IDAHO								
1 *Otter*	Y	Y	Y	Y	Y	Y	Y	N
2 *Simpson*	Y	Y	Y	Y	Y	?	Y	N
ILLINOIS								
1 Rush	Y	Y	Y	Y	Y	Y	Y	N
2 Jackson	Y	Y	Y	Y	Y	N	N	N
3 Lipinski	Y	Y	Y	Y	Y	Y	Y	N
4 Gutierrez	?	?	Y	Y	Y	N	N	N
5 Blagojevich	?	?	Y	Y	Y	N	N	N
6 *Hyde*	Y	Y	Y	Y	Y	?	N	N
7 Davis	Y	Y	Y	Y	Y	N	N	N
8 *Crane*	?	?	?	?	?	?	?	?
9 Schakowsky	Y	Y	Y	Y	N	Y	N	Y
10 *Kirk*	Y	Y	Y	Y	Y	Y	Y	N
11 *Weller*	Y	Y	Y	Y	Y	Y	Y	N
12 Costello	?	?	Y	Y	Y	Y	Y	N
13 *Biggert*	Y	Y	Y	Y	Y	Y	Y	N

ND Northern Democrats   SD Southern Democrats

	127	128	129	130	131	132	133	134
14 ***Hastert***							Y	
15 ***Johnson***	Y	Y	Y	Y	Y	Y	Y	N
16 ***Manzullo***	Y	Y	Y	Y	Y	Y	Y	N
17 Evans	Y	Y	Y	Y	Y	Y	N	N
18 ***LaHood***	Y	Y	Y	Y	Y	Y	Y	N
19 Phelps	Y	Y	Y	Y	Y	Y	Y	N
20 ***Shimkus***	Y	Y	Y	Y	Y	Y	Y	N
INDIANA								
1 Visclosky	+	+	Y	Y	Y	Y	Y	N
2 ***Pence***	Y	Y	Y	Y	Y	N	N	N
3 Roemer	Y	Y	Y	Y	Y	N	N	N
4 ***Souder***	?	?	Y	Y	Y	N	N	N
5 ***Buyer***	?	?	?	?	?	?	Y	N
6 ***Burton***	?	?	?	?	?	?	?	?
7 ***Kerns***	Y	P	Y	Y	Y	Y	Y	N
8 ***Hostettler***	Y	Y	Y	Y	Y	Y	Y	N
9 Hill	Y	Y	Y	Y	Y	Y	Y	N
10 Carson	?	?	?	?	?	?	N	N
IOWA								
1 ***Leach***	Y	Y	Y	Y	Y	Y	Y	N
2 ***Nussle***	Y	Y	Y	Y	Y	Y	Y	N
3 Boswell	Y	Y	Y	Y	Y	N	N	N
4 ***Ganske***	Y	Y	Y	Y	Y	Y	Y	N
5 ***Latham***	Y	Y	Y	Y	Y	Y	Y	N
KANSAS								
1 ***Moran***	Y	Y	Y	Y	Y	Y	Y	N
2 ***Ryun***	Y	Y	Y	Y	Y	Y	Y	N
3 Moore	Y	Y	Y	Y	Y	N	N	N
4 ***Tiahrt***	Y	Y	Y	Y	Y	Y	Y	N
KENTUCKY								
1 ***Whitfield***	Y	Y	Y	Y	Y	Y	Y	N
2 ***Lewis***	Y	Y	Y	Y	Y	Y	Y	N
3 ***Northup***	Y	Y	Y	Y	Y	Y	Y	N
4 Lucas	Y	Y	Y	Y	Y	Y	Y	N
5 ***Rogers***	Y	Y	Y	Y	Y	Y	Y	N
6 ***Fletcher***	Y	Y	Y	Y	Y	Y	Y	N
LOUISIANA								
1 ***Vitter***	Y	Y	N	N	Y	Y	Y	N
2 Jefferson	Y	Y	N	N	Y	Y	Y	Y
3 ***Tauzin***	Y	Y	Y	N	Y	Y	Y	N
4 ***McCrery***	Y	Y	Y	N	Y	Y	Y	N
5 ***Cooksey***	Y	Y	Y	N	Y	Y	Y	N
6 ***Baker***	?	Y	Y	N	Y	Y	Y	N
7 John	Y	Y	Y	N	Y	Y	Y	N
MAINE								
1 Allen	Y	Y	Y	Y	Y	Y	Y	Y
2 Baldacci	Y	Y	Y	Y	Y	Y	Y	N
MARYLAND								
1 ***Gilchrest***	Y	Y	Y	Y	Y	N	Y	N
2 ***Ehrlich***	Y	Y	Y	Y	Y	Y	Y	N
3 Cardin	Y	Y	Y	Y	Y	Y	Y	N
4 Wynn	Y	Y	Y	Y	Y	Y	Y	N
5 Hoyer	Y	Y	Y	Y	Y	Y	Y	N
6 ***Bartlett***	Y	Y	Y	Y	Y	Y	Y	N
7 Cummings	Y	Y	Y	Y	Y	Y	Y	N
8 ***Morella***	Y	Y	Y	Y	Y	Y	Y	N
MASSACHUSETTS								
1 Olver	Y	Y	N	Y	Y	Y	Y	N
2 Neal	Y	Y	N	Y	Y	Y	Y	N
3 McGovern	Y	Y	N	Y	Y	N	N	Y
4 Frank	Y	Y	N	Y	Y	Y	N	Y
5 Meehan	Y	Y	Y	Y	Y	N	N	?
6 Tierney	Y	Y	N	Y	Y	N	N	N
7 Markey	Y	Y	N	Y	Y	N	N	N
8 Capuano	Y	Y	N	Y	Y	N	N	Y
9 Lynch	Y	Y	N	Y	Y	N	N	N
10 Delahunt	Y	Y	N	Y	Y	Y	Y	N
MICHIGAN								
1 Stupak	Y	Y	Y	Y	Y	?	Y	N
2 ***Hoekstra***	Y	Y	Y	Y	Y	Y	Y	N
3 ***Ehlers***	Y	Y	Y	N	Y	Y	Y	N
4 ***Camp***	Y	Y	Y	Y	Y	Y	Y	N
5 Barcia	Y	Y	Y	Y	Y	Y	Y	N
6 ***Upton***	Y	Y	Y	Y	Y	Y	Y	N
7 ***Smith***	Y	Y	Y	Y	Y	Y	Y	N
8 ***Rogers***	Y	Y	Y	Y	Y	Y	Y	N
9 Kildee	Y	Y	Y	Y	Y	Y	Y	N
10 Bonior	?	?	Y	Y	Y	N	N	N
11 ***Knollenberg***	Y	Y	Y	Y	Y	Y	Y	N
12 Levin	Y	Y	Y	Y	Y	Y	Y	N
13 Rivers	Y	Y	Y	Y	Y	N	N	N
14 Conyers	Y	Y	N	Y	Y	N	N	Y
15 Kilpatrick	Y	Y	Y	Y	Y	Y	Y	N
16 Dingell	Y	Y	Y	Y	Y	Y	Y	Y

	127	128	129	130	131	132	133	134
MINNESOTA								
1 ***Gutknecht***	Y	Y	Y	Y	?	Y	Y	N
2 ***Kennedy***	Y	Y	Y	Y	Y	Y	Y	N
3 ***Ramstad***	Y	Y	Y	Y	Y	Y	Y	N
4 McCollum	Y	Y	Y	Y	Y	N	N	N
5 Sabo	Y	Y	N	Y	Y	N	N	N
6 Luther	Y	Y	Y	Y	Y	N	N	N
7 Peterson	Y	Y	N	Y	Y	Y	Y	N
8 Oberstar	Y	Y	N	Y	Y	N	N	N
MISSISSIPPI								
1 ***Wicker***	Y	Y	Y	Y	Y	Y	Y	N
2 Thompson	Y	Y	Y	Y	Y	N	Y	N
3 ***Pickering***	Y	Y	Y	Y	Y	Y	Y	N
4 Shows	Y	Y	Y	Y	Y	Y	Y	Y
5 Taylor	Y	Y	Y	Y	Y	Y	Y	Y
MISSOURI								
1 Clay	Y	Y	?	?	Y	Y	Y	?
2 ***Akin***	Y	Y	Y	Y	Y	Y	Y	N
3 Gephardt	Y	Y	Y	Y	Y	N	N	N
4 Skelton	Y	Y	N	Y	Y	Y	Y	N
5 McCarthy	Y	Y	N	Y	Y	N	N	N
6 ***Graves***	Y	Y	Y	Y	Y	Y	Y	N
7 ***Blunt***	Y	Y	Y	Y	Y	Y	Y	N
8 ***Emerson***	Y	Y	Y	Y	Y	Y	Y	N
9 ***Hulshof***	Y	Y	Y	Y	Y	Y	Y	N
MONTANA								
AL ***Rehberg***	Y	Y	Y	Y	Y	Y	Y	N
NEBRASKA								
1 ***Bereuter***	Y	+	Y	Y	Y	Y	Y	N
2 ***Terry***	Y	Y	Y	Y	Y	Y	Y	N
3 ***Osborne***	Y	Y	Y	Y	Y	Y	Y	N
NEVADA								
1 Berkley	Y	Y	Y	Y	Y	N	N	N
2 ***Gibbons***	Y	Y	Y	Y	Y	N	N	N
NEW HAMPSHIRE								
1 ***Sununu***	Y	Y	Y	Y	Y	Y	Y	N
2 ***Bass***	Y	Y	Y	Y	Y	Y	Y	N
NEW JERSEY								
1 Andrews	Y	Y	Y	Y	Y	Y	Y	Y
2 ***LoBiondo***	Y	Y	Y	Y	Y	Y	Y	N
3 ***Saxton***	Y	Y	Y	Y	Y	Y	Y	N
4 ***Smith***	Y	Y	Y	Y	Y	Y	Y	?
5 ***Roukema***	Y	Y	Y	Y	Y	Y	Y	N
6 Pallone	Y	Y	Y	Y	Y	N	N	Y
7 ***Ferguson***	Y	Y	Y	Y	Y	Y	Y	N
8 Pascrell	Y	Y	Y	Y	Y	Y	Y	Y
9 Rothman	?	?	Y	Y	Y	N	N	N
10 Payne	Y	Y	N	N	Y	Y	Y	Y
11 ***Frelinghuysen***	Y	Y	Y	Y	Y	Y	Y	N
12 Holt	Y	Y	N	Y	Y	N	N	Y
13 Menendez	Y	Y	N	Y	Y	N	N	N
NEW MEXICO								
1 ***Wilson***	Y	Y	Y	Y	Y	Y	Y	N
2 ***Skeen***	Y	Y	Y	Y	Y	Y	Y	?
3 Udall	Y	Y	Y	Y	Y	N	N	N
NEW YORK								
1 ***Grucci***	Y	Y	Y	Y	Y	Y	Y	N
2 Israel	Y	Y	N	Y	Y	N	N	N
3 ***King***	Y	Y	Y	Y	Y	Y	Y	N
4 McCarthy	Y	Y	Y	Y	Y	Y	Y	N
5 Ackerman	?	?	Y	Y	Y	N	N	N
6 Meeks	Y	Y	N	Y	Y	Y	Y	N
7 Crowley	Y	Y	Y	Y	Y	Y	N	Y
8 Nadler	Y	Y	?	?	?	?	?	N
9 Weiner	?	Y	Y	Y	Y	N	N	N
10 Towns	Y	Y	Y	Y	Y	Y	Y	Y
11 Owens	Y	Y	Y	Y	Y	N	N	Y
12 Velázquez	Y	Y	Y	Y	Y	N	N	N
13 ***Fossella***	+	Y	Y	Y	Y	Y	Y	N
14 Maloney	Y	Y	Y	Y	Y	N	N	N
15 Rangel	Y	Y	Y	Y	Y	N	N	N
16 Serrano	Y	Y	Y	Y	Y	N	N	N
17 Engel	Y	Y	Y	Y	Y	Y	Y	N
18 Lowey	Y	Y	Y	Y	Y	N	N	N
19 ***Kelly***	Y	Y	Y	Y	Y	N	N	N
20 ***Gilman***	Y	Y	Y	Y	Y	Y	Y	N
21 McNulty	Y	Y	Y	Y	Y	N	N	N
22 ***Sweeney***	Y	Y	Y	Y	Y	Y	Y	N
23 ***Boehlert***	Y	Y	Y	Y	Y	Y	Y	N
24 ***McHugh***	Y	Y	Y	Y	Y	Y	Y	N
25 ***Walsh***	Y	Y	Y	Y	Y	Y	Y	N
26 Hinchey	Y	Y	Y	Y	Y	N	N	Y
27 ***Reynolds***	Y	Y	Y	Y	Y	Y	Y	N
28 Slaughter	Y	Y	Y	Y	Y	N	N	Y
29 LaFalce	Y	Y	Y	Y	Y	Y	N	N

	127	128	129	130	131	132	133	134
30 ***Quinn***	Y	Y	Y	Y	Y	Y	Y	N
31 ***Houghton***	Y	Y	Y	Y	Y	Y	Y	N
NORTH CAROLINA								
1 Clayton	Y	Y	N	Y	Y	Y	Y	N
2 Etheridge	Y	Y	Y	Y	Y	Y	Y	N
3 ***Jones***	Y	Y	Y	Y	Y	N	Y	N
4 Price	?	?	N	Y	Y	Y	Y	N
5 ***Burr***	Y	Y	Y	Y	Y	Y	Y	N
6 ***Coble***	Y	Y	Y	Y	Y	Y	Y	N
7 McIntyre	Y	Y	Y	Y	Y	Y	Y	N
8 ***Hayes***	Y	Y	Y	Y	Y	Y	Y	N
9 ***Myrick***	Y	Y	Y	Y	Y	Y	Y	N
10 ***Ballenger***	Y	Y	Y	Y	Y	Y	Y	N
11 ***Taylor***	?	Y	Y	Y	Y	Y	Y	N
12 Watt	Y	Y	N	Y	Y	Y	Y	N
NORTH DAKOTA								
AL Pomeroy	Y	Y	Y	Y	Y	Y	Y	N
OHIO								
1 ***Chabot***	Y	Y	Y	Y	Y	Y	Y	N
2 ***Portman***	Y	Y	Y	Y	Y	Y	Y	N
3 Hall	Y	Y	?	?	?	?	?	?
4 ***Oxley***	Y	Y	Y	Y	Y	Y	Y	N
5 ***Gillmor***	Y	Y	Y	Y	Y	Y	Y	N
6 Strickland	Y	Y	Y	Y	Y	Y	Y	N
7 ***Hobson***	Y	Y	Y	Y	Y	Y	Y	N
8 ***Boehner***	Y	Y	Y	N	Y	?	Y	N
9 Kaptur	Y	Y	Y	Y	Y	Y	N	?
10 Kucinich	Y	Y	N	Y	Y	N	N	N
11 Jones	?	?	?	?	?	?	Y	N
12 ***Tiberi***	Y	Y	Y	Y	Y	Y	Y	N
13 Brown	?	?	Y	Y	Y	Y	Y	N
14 Sawyer	?	?	?	?	?	?	Y	N
15 ***Pryce***	?	?	Y	Y	?	Y	Y	N
16 ***Regula***	Y	Y	Y	Y	Y	Y	Y	N
17 Traficant	?	?	?	?	?	?	?	?
18 ***Ney***	Y	Y	Y	Y	Y	Y	Y	N
19 ***LaTourette***	Y	Y	Y	Y	Y	Y	Y	N
OKLAHOMA								
1 ***Sullivan***	Y	Y	Y	Y	Y	Y	Y	N
2 Carson	Y	Y	Y	Y	Y	Y	Y	N
3 ***Watkins***	?	?	Y	Y	Y	Y	N	N
4 ***Watts***	Y	Y	Y	Y	Y	Y	Y	N
5 ***Istook***	Y	Y	Y	Y	Y	Y	Y	N
6 ***Lucas***	Y	Y	Y	Y	Y	Y	Y	N
OREGON								
1 Wu	Y	Y	N	Y	Y	Y	N	Y
2 ***Walden***	Y	Y	Y	Y	Y	Y	Y	N
3 Blumenauer	Y	Y	Y	Y	Y	N	N	N
4 DeFazio	Y	Y	N	Y	Y	N	N	Y
5 Hooley	Y	Y	Y	Y	Y	N	N	N
PENNSYLVANIA								
1 Brady	Y	Y	Y	Y	Y	Y	Y	Y
2 Fattah	Y	Y	Y	Y	Y	Y	Y	N
3 Borski	Y	Y	Y	Y	Y	Y	Y	N
4 ***Hart***	Y	Y	Y	Y	Y	Y	Y	N
5 ***Peterson***	Y	Y	Y	Y	Y	Y	Y	?
6 Holden	Y	Y	Y	Y	Y	Y	Y	N
7 ***Weldon***	Y	Y	Y	Y	Y	Y	?	N
8 ***Greenwood***	Y	Y	Y	Y	Y	Y	Y	N
9 ***Shuster, Bill***	Y	Y	Y	Y	Y	Y	Y	N
10 ***Sherwood***	Y	Y	Y	Y	Y	Y	Y	N
11 Kanjorski	Y	Y	Y	Y	?	Y	Y	N
12 Murtha	Y	Y	Y	Y	Y	Y	Y	N
13 Hoeffel	Y	Y	Y	Y	Y	Y	Y	N
14 Coyne	Y	Y	Y	Y	Y	?	N	N
15 ***Toomey***	Y	Y	Y	Y	Y	Y	Y	N
16 ***Pitts***	Y	Y	Y	Y	Y	Y	Y	N
17 ***Gekas***	Y	Y	Y	Y	Y	Y	Y	N
18 Doyle	Y	Y	Y	Y	Y	Y	Y	N
19 ***Platts***	Y	Y	Y	Y	Y	Y	Y	N
20 Mascara	Y	Y	Y	Y	Y	Y	Y	N
21 ***English***	Y	Y	Y	Y	Y	Y	Y	N
RHODE ISLAND								
1 Kennedy	Y	Y	Y	Y	Y	N	N	N
2 Langevin	Y	Y	Y	Y	Y	N	N	Y
SOUTH CAROLINA								
1 ***Brown***	Y	Y	Y	Y	Y	Y	Y	N
2 ***Wilson***	Y	Y	Y	Y	Y	Y	Y	N
3 ***Graham***	Y	Y	Y	Y	Y	Y	Y	N
4 ***DeMint***	Y	Y	Y	Y	Y	Y	Y	N
5 Spratt	Y	Y	Y	Y	Y	Y	Y	Y
6 Clyburn	Y	Y	Y	Y	Y	Y	Y	N
SOUTH DAKOTA								
AL ***Thune***	Y	Y	Y	Y	Y	Y	Y	N

	127	128	129	130	131	132	133	134
TENNESSEE								
1 ***Jenkins***	Y	Y	Y	Y	Y	Y	Y	N
2 ***Duncan***	Y	Y	Y	Y	Y	Y	Y	N
3 ***Wamp***	Y	Y	Y	Y	Y	Y	Y	N
4 ***Hilleary***	Y	Y	Y	Y	Y	Y	Y	N
5 Clement	Y	Y	Y	Y	Y	Y	Y	N
6 Gordon	Y	Y	Y	Y	Y	Y	Y	N
7 ***Bryant***	Y	Y	Y	Y	Y	Y	Y	N
8 Tanner	Y	Y	Y	Y	Y	Y	Y	Y
9 Ford	Y	Y	N	Y	Y	Y	Y	N
TEXAS								
1 Sandlin	Y	Y	Y	Y	Y	Y	Y	Y
2 Turner	Y	Y	Y	Y	Y	Y	Y	N
3 ***Johnson, Sam***	Y	Y	Y	Y	Y	Y	Y	N
4 Hall	Y	Y	Y	Y	Y	Y	Y	N
5 ***Sessions***	Y	Y	Y	Y	Y	Y	Y	N
6 ***Barton***	Y	Y	Y	Y	Y	Y	Y	Y
7 ***Culberson***	Y	Y	Y	Y	Y	Y	Y	N
8 ***Brady***	Y	Y	Y	Y	Y	Y	Y	N
9 Lampson	Y	Y	Y	Y	Y	Y	Y	Y
10 Doggett	Y	Y	Y	Y	Y	N	N	Y
11 Edwards	Y	Y	Y	Y	Y	Y	Y	N
12 ***Granger***	Y	Y	Y	Y	Y	Y	Y	N
13 ***Thornberry***	Y	Y	Y	Y	Y	Y	Y	N
14 ***Paul***	Y	N	Y	Y	Y	Y	N	N
15 Hinojosa	Y	Y	Y	Y	Y	Y	N	N
16 Reyes	Y	Y	N	Y	Y	N	N	N
17 Stenholm	Y	Y	N	N	Y	Y	Y	N
18 Jackson-Lee	Y	Y	Y	Y	Y	N	N	?
19 ***Combest***	Y	Y	Y	Y	Y	Y	Y	N
20 Gonzalez	Y	Y	Y	Y	Y	N	N	N
21 ***Smith***	Y	Y	Y	Y	Y	?	Y	N
22 ***DeLay***	Y	Y	Y	Y	Y	Y	Y	N
23 ***Bonilla***	Y	Y	Y	Y	Y	Y	Y	N
24 Frost	Y	Y	Y	Y	Y	Y	N	N
25 Bentsen	Y	Y	N	Y	Y	Y	Y	N
26 ***Armey***	Y	Y	Y	Y	Y	Y	Y	N
27 Ortiz	Y	Y	Y	Y	Y	N	N	N
28 Rodriguez	Y	Y	Y	Y	Y	N	N	N
29 Green	Y	Y	Y	Y	Y	Y	Y	N
30 Johnson, E.B.	Y	Y	Y	Y	Y	Y	Y	N
UTAH								
1 ***Hansen***	Y	Y	Y	Y	Y	Y	Y	N
2 Matheson	Y	Y	Y	Y	Y	N	N	N
3 ***Cannon***	Y	Y	Y	Y	Y	Y	Y	N
VERMONT								
AL *Sanders*	Y	Y	N	Y	Y	N	N	N
VIRGINIA								
1 ***Davis, Jo Ann***	Y	Y	Y	Y	Y	Y	Y	N
2 ***Schrock***	Y	Y	Y	Y	Y	Y	Y	N
3 Scott	Y	Y	Y	Y	Y	Y	?	N
4 ***Forbes***	Y	Y	Y	Y	Y	Y	Y	N
5 *Goode*	Y	Y	Y	Y	?	Y	Y	N
6 ***Goodlatte***	Y	+	Y	Y	Y	Y	Y	N
7 ***Cantor***	Y	Y	Y	Y	Y	Y	Y	N
8 Moran	Y	Y	N	N	Y	?	Y	?
9 Boucher	Y	Y	N	Y	Y	Y	Y	N
10 ***Wolf***	Y	Y	Y	Y	Y	Y	Y	N
11 ***Davis, T.***	Y	Y	Y	N	Y	N	N	N
WASHINGTON								
1 Inslee	Y	Y	Y	Y	Y	N	Y	N
2 Larsen	Y	Y	Y	N	Y	Y	Y	N
3 Baird	Y	Y	Y	Y	Y	Y	Y	N
4 ***Hastings***	Y	Y	Y	Y	Y	Y	Y	N
5 ***Nethercutt***	Y	Y	Y	Y	Y	Y	Y	N
6 Dicks	Y	Y	Y	N	Y	Y	Y	N
7 McDermott	Y	Y	N	N	Y	N	N	Y
8 ***Dunn***	Y	Y	Y	Y	Y	Y	Y	N
9 Smith	Y	Y	N	N	Y	N	N	N
WEST VIRGINIA								
1 Mollohan	?	?	Y	Y	Y	Y	Y	N
2 ***Capito***	Y	Y	Y	Y	Y	Y	Y	N
3 Rahall	Y	Y	Y	Y	Y	N	N	N
WISCONSIN								
1 ***Ryan***	Y	Y	Y	Y	Y	Y	Y	N
2 Baldwin	Y	Y	N	Y	Y	N	N	N
3 Kind	?	?	?	?	?	?	?	N
4 Kleczka	Y	Y	Y	Y	Y	?	N	N
5 Barrett	Y	Y	Y	Y	Y	Y	Y	N
6 ***Petri***	Y	Y	Y	Y	Y	Y	Y	N
7 Obey	Y	Y	N	Y	Y	Y	Y	N
8 ***Green***	Y	Y	Y	Y	Y	Y	Y	N
9 ***Sensenbrenner***	Y	Y	Y	Y	Y	Y	Y	N
WYOMING								
AL ***Cubin***	Y	Y	Y	Y	Y	Y	Y	?

Southern states - Ala., Ark., Fla., Ga., Ky., La., Miss., N.C., Okla., S.C., Tenn., Texas, Va.

Key

Y	Voted for (yea).
#	Paired for.
+	Announced for.
N	Voted against (nay).
X	Paired against.
–	Announced against.
P	Voted "present."
C	Voted "present" to avoid possible conflict of interest.
?	Did not vote or otherwise make a position known.

Democrats   ***Republicans***
Independents

135. HR 4546. Fiscal 2003 Defense Authorization/Previous Question. Myrick, R-N.C., motion to order the previous question (thus ending debate and possibility of amendment) on the rule (H Res 415) to provide for House floor consideration of the bill that would authorize $383.4 billion for defense programs for fiscal 2003. Motion agreed to 215-202: R 214-1; D 0-200 (ND 0-150, SD 0-50); I 1-1. May 9, 2002.

136. HR 4546. Fiscal 2003 Defense Authorization/Rule. Adoption of the rule (H Res 415) to provide for House floor consideration of the bill that would authorize $383.4 billion for defense programs for fiscal 2003. Adopted 216-200: R 209-6; D 6-193 (ND 4-146, SD 2-47); I 1-1. May 9, 2002.

137. Procedural Motion/Adjourn. Taylor, D-Miss., motion to adjourn. Motion rejected 35-375: R 1-211; D 34-162 (ND 26-121, SD 8-41); I 0-2. May 9, 2002.

138. HR 4546. Fiscal 2003 Defense Authorization/Motion to Rise. Taylor, D-Miss., motion to rise from the Committee of the Whole. Motion rejected 51-356: R 1-206; D 50-148 (ND 42-105, SD 8-43); I 0-2. May 9, 2002.

139. HR 4546. Fiscal 2003 Defense Authorization/Motion to Rise. Taylor, D-Miss., motion to rise from the Committee of the Whole. Motion rejected 49-352: R 3-200; D 46-150 (ND 38-109, SD 8-41); I 0-2. May 9, 2002.

140. HR 4546. Fiscal 2003 Defense Authorization/Motion to Rise. Taylor, D-Miss., motion to rise from the Committee of the Whole. Motion rejected 51-360: R 0-210; D 51-148 (ND 41-108, SD 10-40); I 0-2. May 9, 2002.

141. HR 4546. Fiscal 2003 Defense Authorization/Nuclear Penetrator Weapons. Markey, D-Mass., amendment that would block fiscal 2003 funding for a study on the nuclear earth-penetrator weapon and prohibit any future funding for such a program. Rejected 172-243: R 4-207; D 167-35 (ND 138-13, SD 29-22); I 1-1. May 9, 2002.

142. HR 4546. Fiscal 2003 Defense Authorization/Nuclear Weapons Development. Weldon, R-Pa., amendment that would state that U.S. policy toward Russia on nuclear weapons matters is to pursue cooperation and transparency. It also would repeal the ban on designing and developing low-yield nuclear weapons under certain conditions, including that another nation is conducting nuclear tests or developing nuclear weapons. Adopted 362-53: R 209-1; D 152-51 (ND 107-45, SD 45-6); I 1-1. May 9, 2002.

	135	136	137	138	139	140	141	142
ALABAMA								
1 Callahan	Y	Y	N	N	N	N	N	Y
2 Everett	Y	Y	N	N	N	N	N	Y
3 Riley	?	?	?	?	?	?	?	?
4 Aderholt	Y	Y	N	N	N	N	N	?
5 Cramer	N	N	N	N	N	N	N	Y
6 Bachus	Y	Y	N	N	N	N	N	Y
7 Hilliard	N	N	N	N	N	N	Y	Y
ALASKA								
AL *Young*	Y	Y	N	N	N	N	?	?
ARIZONA								
1 *Flake*	Y	Y	N	N	N	N	N	Y
2 Pastor	N	N	N	N	N	N	N	Y
3 *Stump*	Y	Y	N	N	N	N	N	Y
4 *Shadegg*	Y	Y	N	N	N	N	N	Y
5 *Kolbe*	Y	Y	N	N	N	N	N	Y
6 *Hayworth*	Y	Y	N	N	N	N	N	Y
ARKANSAS								
1 Berry	N	N	Y	Y	Y	Y	N	Y
2 Snyder	N	N	N	N	N	N	Y	Y
3 *Boozman*	Y	Y	N	N	N	N	N	Y
4 Ross	N	N	N	N	N	N	Y	Y
CALIFORNIA								
1 Thompson	N	N	N	N	N	N	Y	Y
2 *Herger*	Y	Y	N	N	N	N	N	Y
3 *Ose*	?	?	?	?	?	?	?	?
4 *Doolittle*	Y	Y	N	?	N	N	N	Y
5 Matsui	N	N	N	N	N	N	Y	Y
6 Woolsey	N	N	N	N	N	N	Y	N
7 Miller, George	N	N	Y	Y	Y	Y	Y	N
8 Pelosi	N	N	?	Y	Y	Y	Y	N
9 Lee	N	N	Y	Y	Y	Y	Y	N
10 Tauscher	N	N	N	N	N	N	Y	Y
11 *Pombo*	Y	Y	N	N	N	N	N	Y
12 Lantos	N	N	N	N	N	N	Y	Y
13 Stark	N	N	Y	Y	?	Y	Y	N
14 Eshoo	N	N	N	N	N	N	Y	Y
15 Honda	N	N	N	Y	Y	Y	Y	N
16 Lofgren	N	N	N	N	N	N	Y	N
17 Farr	N	N	N	N	N	N	Y	Y
18 Condit	N	N	Y	Y	Y	Y	N	Y
19 *Radanovich*	Y	Y	N	N	Y	N	N	Y
20 Dooley	N	N	N	?	N	?	Y	Y
21 *Thomas*	Y	Y	N	N	N	N	N	Y
22 Capps	N	N	N	N	N	N	Y	Y
23 *Gallegly*	Y	Y	N	N	N	N	N	Y
24 Sherman	N	N	N	N	N	N	Y	Y
25 *McKeon*	Y	Y	N	N	N	N	N	Y
26 Berman	N	N	?	N	N	N	Y	Y
27 Schiff	N	N	N	N	N	N	Y	Y
28 *Dreier*	Y	Y	N	N	N	N	N	Y
29 Waxman	?	?	?	?	?	?	?	?
30 Becerra	N	N	N	Y	N	N	Y	N
31 Solis	N	N	N	Y	Y	Y	Y	N
32 Watson	?	?	?	?	?	?	?	?
33 Roybal-Allard	N	N	N	N	N	N	Y	N
34 Napolitano	N	N	N	Y	N	N	Y	N
35 Waters	N	N	Y	Y	Y	Y	Y	N
36 Harman	N	N	?	N	N	N	Y	Y
37 Millender-McD.	N	N	N	N	?	?	?	?
38 Horn	Y	Y	N	N	N	N	N	Y
39 *Royce*	Y	Y	N	N	N	N	N	Y
40 *Lewis*	Y	Y	N	N	N	N	N	Y
41 *Miller, Gary*	Y	Y	N	N	N	N	N	Y
42 Baca	N	N	N	N	N	N	Y	Y
43 *Calvert*	Y	Y	N	N	N	N	N	Y
44 *Bono*	Y	Y	N	N	N	N	N	Y
45 *Rohrabacher*	Y	Y	N	N	N	N	N	Y
46 Sanchez	N	N	N	N	N	N	Y	Y
47 *Cox*	Y	Y	N	N	N	?	N	Y
48 *Issa*	Y	Y	N	N	N	N	N	Y
49 Davis	N	N	N	N	N	N	Y	Y
50 Filner	N	N	Y	Y	Y	Y	Y	N
51 *Cunningham*	Y	Y	N	N	N	N	N	Y
52 *Hunter*	Y	Y	N	N	N	N	N	Y
COLORADO								
1 DeGette	N	N	N	Y	Y	Y	Y	N
2 Udall	N	N	N	N	N	N	Y	N
3 *McInnis*	Y	Y	N	N	N	N	N	Y
4 *Schaffer*	Y	Y	N	?	N	N	N	Y
5 *Hefley*	Y	Y	N	N	N	N	N	Y
6 *Tancredo*	N	N	N	N	N	N	N	Y
CONNECTICUT								
1 Larson	N	N	N	Y	Y	Y	Y	Y
2 *Simmons*	Y	Y	N	N	N	N	N	Y
3 DeLauro	N	N	N	N	N	N	Y	Y
4 *Shays*	Y	Y	N	N	N	N	N	Y
5 Maloney	–	–	–	–	N	N	Y	Y
6 *Johnson*	Y	Y	N	N	N	N	N	Y
DELAWARE								
AL *Castle*	Y	N	N	N	N	N	N	Y
FLORIDA								
1 *Miller, J.*	Y	Y	N	N	N	N	N	Y
2 Boyd	N	N	N	N	Y	Y	N	Y
3 Brown	N	N	N	N	N	N	Y	Y
4 *Crenshaw*	Y	Y	N	N	N	N	N	Y
5 Thurman	N	N	N	N	N	N	Y	Y
6 *Stearns*	Y	Y	N	N	N	N	N	Y
7 *Mica*	Y	Y	N	N	N	N	N	Y
8 *Keller*	Y	Y	N	N	N	N	N	Y
9 *Bilirakis*	Y	Y	N	N	N	N	N	Y
10 *Young*	Y	Y	N	?	N	N	N	Y
11 Davis	N	?	N	N	N	N	N	Y
12 *Putnam*	Y	Y	N	N	N	N	N	Y
13 *Miller, D.*	Y	Y	N	N	N	N	N	Y
14 *Goss*	Y	Y	?	N	N	N	N	Y
15 *Weldon*	Y	Y	N	N	N	N	N	Y
16 *Foley*	Y	Y	N	N	N	N	N	Y
17 Meek	N	N	N	N	?	N	Y	Y
18 *Ros-Lehtinen*	Y	Y	N	N	N	N	N	Y
19 Wexler	N	N	N	N	N	N	Y	Y
20 Deutsch	N	N	N	N	N	N	Y	Y
21 *Diaz-Balart*	Y	Y	N	N	N	N	N	Y
22 *Shaw*	Y	Y	N	N	N	N	N	Y
23 Hastings	N	N	Y	N	N	N	Y	Y
GEORGIA								
1 *Kingston*	Y	Y	N	N	N	N	N	Y
2 Bishop	?	?	?	N	N	N	N	Y
3 *Collins*	Y	Y	N	N	N	N	N	Y
4 McKinney	N	N	N	N	N	N	N	Y
5 Lewis	N	N	N	?	?	?	?	?
6 *Isakson*	Y	Y	N	N	N	N	N	Y
7 *Barr*	Y	Y	N	N	N	N	N	Y
8 *Chambliss*	Y	Y	N	N	N	N	N	Y
9 *Deal*	Y	Y	N	N	N	N	N	Y
10 *Norwood*	Y	Y	N	N	?	N	N	Y
11 *Linder*	Y	Y	N	N	N	N	N	Y
HAWAII								
1 Abercrombie	N	N	Y	Y	Y	Y	Y	N
2 Mink	N	N	Y	Y	Y	Y	Y	N
IDAHO								
1 *Otter*	Y	Y	N	N	N	N	N	Y
2 *Simpson*	Y	Y	N	N	N	N	N	Y
ILLINOIS								
1 Rush	N	N	N	N	N	N	Y	Y
2 Jackson	N	N	N	N	N	N	Y	Y
3 Lipinski	N	N	N	N	N	N	Y	Y
4 Gutierrez	N	N	N	?	?	?	Y	Y
5 Blagojevich	N	N	N	N	N	N	Y	Y
6 *Hyde*	Y	Y	N	?	?	N	N	Y
7 Davis	N	N	N	N	?	?	?	Y
8 *Crane*	?	?	?	?	?	?	?	?
9 Schakowsky	N	N	Y	N	Y	Y	Y	N
10 *Kirk*	Y	Y	N	N	N	N	N	Y
11 *Weller*	Y	Y	N	N	N	N	N	Y
12 Costello	N	N	N	N	N	N	Y	Y
13 *Biggert*	Y	Y	N	N	N	N	N	Y

ND Northern Democrats   SD Southern Democrats

	135	136	137	138	139	140	141	142
14 ***Hastert***								
15 ***Johnson***	Y	Y	N	N	N	N	N	Y
16 ***Manzullo***	Y	Y	N	N	N	N	N	Y
17 Evans	N	N	N	N	Y	N	Y	Y
18 ***LaHood***	Y	Y	N	N	N	N	N	Y
19 Phelps	N	N	N	N	N	N	N	Y
20 ***Shimkus***	Y	Y	N	N	N	N	N	Y
INDIANA								
1 Visclosky	N	N	N	Y	N	N	Y	Y
2 ***Pence***	Y	Y	N	N	N	N	N	Y
3 Roemer	N	N	N	N	N	Y	Y	Y
4 ***Souder***	Y	Y	N	?	N	N	N	Y
5 ***Buyer***	Y	Y	N	N	N	N	N	Y
6 ***Burton***	?	?	?	?	?	?	?	?
7 ***Kerns***	Y	Y	N	N	N	N	N	Y
8 ***Hostettler***	Y	N	N	N	N	N	N	Y
9 Hill	N	Y	N	N	N	N	Y	Y
10 Carson	N	N	N	N	N	N	Y	N
IOWA								
1 ***Leach***	Y	Y	N	N	N	N	Y	Y
2 ***Nussle***	Y	Y	N	N	?	?	N	Y
3 Boswell	N	N	N	N	N	N	Y	Y
4 ***Ganske***	Y	Y	N	N	N	N	N	Y
5 ***Latham***	Y	Y	N	N	N	N	N	Y
KANSAS								
1 ***Moran***	Y	Y	N	N	N	N	N	Y
2 ***Ryun***	Y	Y	N	N	N	N	N	Y
3 Moore	N	N	N	N	N	N	Y	Y
4 ***Tiahrt***	Y	Y	N	N	N	N	N	Y
KENTUCKY								
1 ***Whitfield***	Y	Y	N	N	N	N	N	Y
2 ***Lewis***	Y	Y	N	N	N	N	N	Y
3 ***Northup***	Y	Y	N	N	N	N	N	Y
4 Lucas	N	N	N	N	N	N	N	Y
5 ***Rogers***	Y	Y	N	N	N	N	N	Y
6 ***Fletcher***	Y	Y	N	N	N	N	N	Y
LOUISIANA								
1 ***Vitter***	Y	Y	N	N	N	N	N	Y
2 Jefferson	N	N	N	Y	Y	Y	Y	Y
3 ***Tauzin***	Y	Y	N	N	N	N	N	Y
4 ***McCrery***	Y	Y	N	N	?	N	N	Y
5 ***Cooksey***	Y	Y	N	N	N	N	N	Y
6 ***Baker***	Y	Y	N	N	N	N	N	Y
7 John	N	N	N	N	N	N	N	Y
MAINE								
1 Allen	N	N	Y	N	N	N	Y	Y
2 Baldacci	N	N	N	N	N	N	Y	Y
MARYLAND								
1 ***Gilchrest***	Y	Y	N	N	N	N	N	Y
2 ***Ehrlich***	Y	Y	N	N	N	N	N	Y
3 Cardin	N	N	N	N	N	N	Y	Y
4 Wynn	N	N	N	N	Y	N	Y	Y
5 Hoyer	N	N	?	N	N	N	Y	Y
6 ***Bartlett***	Y	Y	N	N	Y	N	N	Y
7 Cummings	N	N	N	N	Y	N	Y	Y
8 ***Morella***	Y	N	N	N	N	N	Y	Y
MASSACHUSETTS								
1 Olver	N	N	Y	N	N	Y	Y	N
2 Neal	N	N	N	N	N	N	Y	N
3 McGovern	N	N	Y	Y	Y	Y	Y	N
4 Frank	N	N	Y	Y	Y	Y	Y	N
5 Meehan	?	?	?	N	N	N	Y	N
6 Tierney	N	N	N	Y	N	N	Y	N
7 Markey	N	N	N	Y	Y	Y	Y	N
8 Capuano	N	N	Y	Y	Y	Y	Y	N
9 Lynch	N	N	N	N	Y	Y	Y	Y
10 Delahunt	N	N	Y	Y	N	Y	Y	Y
MICHIGAN								
1 Stupak	N	N	N	Y	Y	Y	Y	Y
2 ***Hoekstra***	Y	Y	N	N	N	N	N	Y
3 ***Ehlers***	N	N	N	N	N	N	N	Y
4 ***Camp***	Y	Y	N	N	N	N	N	Y
5 Barcia	N	N	N	N	N	N	N	Y
6 ***Upton***	Y	Y	N	N	N	N	N	Y
7 ***Smith***	Y	Y	N	N	?	?	?	?
8 ***Rogers***	Y	Y	N	N	N	N	N	Y
9 Kildee	N	N	N	N	N	N	Y	Y
10 Bonior	N	N	N	Y	N	Y	Y	N
11 ***Knollenberg***	Y	Y	N	N	N	N	N	Y
12 Levin	N	N	N	N	N	N	Y	Y
13 Rivers	N	N	N	N	N	N	Y	Y
14 Conyers	N	N	N	Y	Y	Y	Y	N
15 Kilpatrick	N	N	N	N	N	N	Y	Y
16 Dingell	N	N	Y	Y	Y	Y	Y	N

	135	136	137	138	139	140	141	142
MINNESOTA								
1 ***Gutknecht***	Y	Y	N	N	N	N	N	Y
2 ***Kennedy***	Y	Y	N	?	?	?	?	?
3 ***Ramstad***	Y	Y	N	N	N	N	N	Y
4 McCollum	N	N	N	N	N	N	Y	Y
5 Sabo	N	N	N	N	N	N	Y	Y
6 Luther	N	N	N	N	N	N	Y	Y
7 Peterson	N	Y	N	N	N	N	Y	Y
8 Oberstar	N	N	N	N	N	Y	Y	Y
MISSISSIPPI								
1 ***Wicker***	Y	Y	N	N	N	N	N	Y
2 Thompson	N	N	N	N	N	N	Y	Y
3 ***Pickering***	Y	Y	N	N	N	N	N	Y
4 Shows	N	N	Y	Y	Y	Y	N	Y
5 Taylor	N	N	Y	Y	Y	Y	N	Y
MISSOURI								
1 Clay	N	N	N	N	Y	Y	Y	N
2 ***Akin***	Y	Y	N	N	N	N	N	Y
3 Gephardt	N	N	N	N	N	N	Y	Y
4 Skelton	N	Y	N	N	N	N	Y	Y
5 McCarthy	N	N	N	N	N	N	Y	Y
6 ***Graves***	Y	Y	N	N	N	N	N	Y
7 ***Blunt***	Y	Y	N	N	N	N	N	Y
8 ***Emerson***	Y	Y	N	N	N	N	N	Y
9 ***Hulshof***	Y	Y	N	N	?	N	N	Y
MONTANA								
AL ***Rehberg***	Y	Y	N	N	N	N	N	Y
NEBRASKA								
1 ***Bereuter***	Y	Y	N	N	N	N	N	Y
2 ***Terry***	Y	Y	N	N	N	N	N	Y
3 ***Osborne***	Y	Y	N	N	N	N	N	Y
NEVADA								
1 Berkley	N	N	N	N	N	N	Y	Y
2 ***Gibbons***	Y	Y	N	N	N	N	N	Y
NEW HAMPSHIRE								
1 ***Sununu***	Y	Y	N	N	N	N	N	Y
2 ***Bass***	Y	Y	N	N	N	N	N	Y
NEW JERSEY								
1 Andrews	N	N	N	N	N	N	Y	Y
2 ***LoBiondo***	Y	Y	N	N	N	N	N	Y
3 ***Saxton***	Y	Y	N	N	N	N	N	Y
4 ***Smith***	?	?	?	N	N	N	Y	Y
5 ***Roukema***	?	?	?	?	?	?	?	?
6 Pallone	N	N	Y	N	Y	Y	Y	Y
7 ***Ferguson***	Y	Y	N	N	N	N	N	Y
8 Pascrell	N	N	N	N	N	N	Y	Y
9 Rothman	N	N	N	N	N	N	N	Y
10 Payne	N	N	N	N	N	N	Y	N
11 ***Frelinghuysen***	Y	Y	N	N	N	N	N	Y
12 Holt	N	N	Y	Y	Y	N	Y	N
13 Menendez	N	N	N	N	N	N	Y	Y
NEW MEXICO								
1 ***Wilson***	Y	Y	N	N	N	N	N	Y
2 ***Skeen***	Y	Y	N	N	N	N	N	Y
3 Udall	N	N	N	N	N	N	Y	Y
NEW YORK								
1 ***Grucci***	Y	Y	N	N	N	N	N	Y
2 Israel	N	Y	N	N	N	N	N	Y
3 ***King***	Y	Y	N	N	N	N	N	Y
4 McCarthy	N	N	N	N	N	N	N	Y
5 Ackerman	N	N	N	N	Y	Y	Y	N
6 Meeks	N	N	N	N	N	N	N	Y
7 Crowley	N	N	N	N	N	N	Y	Y
8 Nadler	N	N	N	N	N	N	Y	N
9 Weiner	N	N	N	N	N	N	N	Y
10 Towns	N	N	N	N	Y	Y	Y	Y
11 Owens	N	N	Y	Y	N	N	Y	N
12 Velázquez	N	N	N	N	N	N	Y	Y
13 ***Fossella***	Y	Y	N	N	N	N	N	Y
14 Maloney	N	N	N	N	?	N	Y	Y
15 Rangel	N	N	N	N	N	N	Y	N
16 Serrano	N	N	N	N	N	N	Y	Y
17 Engel	N	N	N	N	N	N	Y	Y
18 Lowey	N	N	N	N	N	N	Y	Y
19 ***Kelly***	Y	Y	N	N	N	N	N	Y
20 ***Gilman***	Y	Y	N	N	N	N	N	Y
21 McNulty	N	N	N	N	N	N	Y	N
22 ***Sweeney***	Y	Y	N	N	N	N	N	Y
23 ***Boehlert***	Y	Y	N	N	?	N	N	Y
24 ***McHugh***	Y	Y	N	N	N	N	N	Y
25 ***Walsh***	Y	Y	N	N	N	N	N	Y
26 Hinchey	N	N	Y	Y	Y	Y	Y	N
27 ***Reynolds***	Y	Y	N	N	N	N	N	Y
28 Slaughter	N	N	Y	Y	?	Y	Y	N
29 LaFalce	?	?	N	?	N	N	Y	Y

	135	136	137	138	139	140	141	142
30 ***Quinn***	Y	Y	N	N	N	N	N	Y
31 ***Houghton***	Y	Y	N	N	N	N	N	Y
NORTH CAROLINA								
1 Clayton	N	N	N	N	N	N	Y	N
2 Etheridge	N	N	N	N	N	N	Y	Y
3 ***Jones***	Y	Y	N	N	N	N	N	Y
4 Price	N	N	N	N	N	N	Y	Y
5 ***Burr***	Y	Y	N	N	N	N	N	Y
6 ***Coble***	Y	Y	N	N	N	N	N	Y
7 McIntyre	N	N	Y	Y	Y	Y	N	Y
8 ***Hayes***	Y	Y	N	N	N	N	N	Y
9 ***Myrick***	Y	Y	N	N	N	N	N	Y
10 ***Ballenger***	Y	Y	N	N	N	N	N	Y
11 ***Taylor***	Y	Y	N	N	N	N	N	Y
12 Watt	N	N	N	N	N	N	Y	N
NORTH DAKOTA								
AL Pomeroy	N	N	N	Y	N	N	Y	Y
OHIO								
1 ***Chabot***	Y	Y	N	N	N	N	N	Y
2 ***Portman***	Y	Y	N	N	N	N	N	Y
3 Hall	?	?	?	?	?	?	?	?
4 ***Oxley***	Y	Y	N	N	?	N	N	Y
5 ***Gillmor***	Y	Y	N	N	N	N	N	Y
6 Strickland	N	N	N	N	N	N	Y	Y
7 ***Hobson***	Y	Y	N	N	N	N	N	Y
8 ***Boehner***	Y	Y	N	N	N	N	N	Y
9 Kaptur	N	N	N	N	N	N	Y	Y
10 Kucinich	N	N	N	Y	N	N	Y	N
11 Jones	N	N	Y	Y	Y	Y	Y	N
12 ***Tiberi***	Y	Y	N	N	Y	N	N	Y
13 Brown	N	N	N	Y	N	Y	Y	Y
14 Sawyer	N	N	N	N	N	N	Y	Y
15 ***Pryce***	Y	Y	N	N	?	N	N	Y
16 ***Regula***	Y	Y	N	N	N	N	N	Y
17 Traficant	?	?	?	?	?	?	?	?
18 ***Ney***	Y	Y	N	N	N	N	N	Y
19 ***LaTourette***	Y	Y	N	N	N	N	N	Y
OKLAHOMA								
1 ***Sullivan***	Y	Y	N	N	N	N	N	Y
2 Carson	N	N	N	N	N	N	N	Y
3 ***Watkins***	Y	Y	N	N	N	N	N	Y
4 ***Watts***	Y	Y	?	N	N	N	N	Y
5 ***Istook***	Y	Y	N	N	N	N	N	Y
6 ***Lucas***	Y	Y	N	N	N	N	N	Y
OREGON								
1 Wu	N	N	N	Y	Y	Y	Y	Y
2 ***Walden***	Y	Y	N	N	N	N	N	Y
3 Blumenauer	N	N	N	N	Y	Y	Y	Y
4 DeFazio	N	N	Y	Y	Y	Y	Y	N
5 Hooley	N	N	N	N	N	N	Y	Y
PENNSYLVANIA								
1 Brady	N	N	Y	Y	Y	Y	Y	Y
2 Fattah	N	N	N	N	N	N	Y	N
3 Borski	N	N	N	N	N	N	Y	Y
4 ***Hart***	Y	Y	N	N	N	N	N	Y
5 ***Peterson***	Y	Y	N	N	N	N	N	Y
6 Holden	N	N	N	N	N	N	N	Y
7 ***Weldon***	Y	Y	N	N	N	N	N	Y
8 ***Greenwood***	Y	Y	Y	N	N	N	N	Y
9 ***Shuster, Bill***	Y	Y	N	N	N	N	N	Y
10 ***Sherwood***	Y	Y	N	N	N	N	N	Y
11 Kanjorski	N	N	N	N	N	N	N	Y
12 Murtha	N	N	N	N	N	N	N	Y
13 Hoeffel	N	N	N	N	N	N	Y	Y
14 Coyne	N	N	N	N	N	N	Y	Y
15 ***Toomey***	Y	Y	N	N	N	N	N	Y
16 ***Pitts***	Y	Y	N	N	N	N	N	Y
17 ***Gekas***	Y	Y	N	N	N	N	N	Y
18 Doyle	N	N	N	?	N	N	N	Y
19 ***Platts***	Y	Y	N	N	N	N	N	Y
20 Mascara	N	N	N	N	N	N	N	Y
21 ***English***	Y	Y	N	N	N	N	N	Y
RHODE ISLAND								
1 Kennedy	N	N	N	N	N	N	Y	Y
2 Langevin	N	N	Y	N	N	N	Y	Y
SOUTH CAROLINA								
1 ***Brown***	Y	Y	N	N	N	N	N	Y
2 ***Wilson***	Y	Y	N	N	N	N	N	Y
3 ***Graham***	Y	Y	N	N	N	N	N	Y
4 ***DeMint***	Y	Y	N	N	N	N	N	Y
5 Spratt	N	N	N	N	N	N	Y	Y
6 Clyburn	N	N	N	N	N	N	Y	Y
SOUTH DAKOTA								
AL ***Thune***	Y	Y	N	N	N	N	N	Y

	135	136	137	138	139	140	141	142
TENNESSEE								
1 ***Jenkins***	Y	Y	N	N	N	N	N	Y
2 ***Duncan***	Y	Y	N	N	N	N	N	Y
3 ***Wamp***	Y	Y	N	N	N	N	N	Y
4 ***Hilleary***	Y	Y	N	?	N	N	N	Y
5 Clement	N	N	N	N	N	N	N	Y
6 Gordon	N	N	N	N	N	N	N	Y
7 ***Bryant***	Y	Y	N	N	N	N	N	Y
8 Tanner	N	N	Y	Y	Y	Y	N	Y
9 Ford	N	N	N	N	?	N	Y	Y
TEXAS								
1 Sandlin	N	N	N	N	N	N	N	N
2 Turner	N	N	N	N	N	N	N	Y
3 ***Johnson, Sam***	Y	Y	N	?	N	N	N	Y
4 Hall	N	Y	N	N	N	N	N	Y
5 ***Sessions***	Y	Y	N	N	N	N	N	Y
6 ***Barton***	Y	Y	N	N	N	N	N	Y
7 ***Culberson***	Y	Y	N	N	N	N	N	Y
8 ***Brady***	Y	Y	?	N	N	N	N	Y
9 Lampson	N	N	N	N	N	N	Y	Y
10 Doggett	N	N	Y	Y	Y	Y	Y	N
11 Edwards	N	N	N	N	N	N	Y	Y
12 ***Granger***	Y	Y	N	N	N	N	N	Y
13 ***Thornberry***	Y	Y	N	N	N	N	N	Y
14 ***Paul***	Y	Y	N	N	N	N	N	N
15 Hinojosa	N	N	N	N	N	N	N	Y
16 Reyes	N	Y	?	?	?	?	?	?
17 Stenholm	N	N	N	N	N	Y	N	Y
18 Jackson-Lee	?	?	?	?	?	?	?	?
19 ***Combest***	Y	Y	N	N	N	N	N	Y
20 Gonzalez	N	N	N	N	N	N	Y	Y
21 ***Smith***	Y	Y	N	N	N	N	N	Y
22 ***DeLay***	Y	Y	N	N	?	N	N	Y
23 ***Bonilla***	Y	Y	N	N	N	N	N	Y
24 Frost	N	N	N	N	N	N	Y	Y
25 Bentsen	?	?	?	N	N	N	Y	Y
26 ***Armey***	Y	Y	N	N	N	N	N	Y
27 Ortiz	N	N	N	N	N	N	N	Y
28 Rodriguez	N	N	N	N	N	N	Y	Y
29 Green	N	N	N	N	N	N	N	Y
30 Johnson, E.B.	N	N	Y	Y	N	Y	Y	N
UTAH								
1 ***Hansen***	Y	Y	N	N	N	N	N	Y
2 Matheson	N	N	N	N	N	N	Y	Y
3 ***Cannon***	Y	Y	N	?	N	?	?	?
VERMONT								
AL *Sanders*	N	N	N	N	N	N	Y	N
VIRGINIA								
1 ***Davis, Jo Ann***	Y	Y	N	N	N	N	N	Y
2 ***Schrock***	Y	Y	N	N	N	N	N	Y
3 Scott	N	N	N	N	N	N	Y	Y
4 ***Forbes***	Y	Y	N	N	N	N	N	Y
5 *Goode*	Y	Y	N	N	N	N	N	Y
6 ***Goodlatte***	Y	Y	N	N	N	N	N	Y
7 ***Cantor***	Y	Y	N	N	N	N	N	Y
8 Moran	N	N	N	N	N	N	Y	Y
9 Boucher	?	?	?	N	N	?	Y	Y
10 ***Wolf***	Y	Y	N	N	N	N	N	Y
11 ***Davis, T.***	Y	Y	N	N	N	N	N	Y
WASHINGTON								
1 Inslee	N	N	N	N	N	N	Y	N
2 Larsen	N	N	N	N	N	N	Y	Y
3 Baird	N	N	N	N	N	N	Y	Y
4 ***Hastings***	Y	Y	N	N	N	N	N	Y
5 ***Nethercutt***	Y	Y	N	?	?	?	?	?
6 Dicks	N	N	?	N	N	N	Y	Y
7 McDermott	N	N	Y	Y	Y	Y	Y	N
8 ***Dunn***	Y	Y	N	N	N	N	N	Y
9 Smith	N	N	N	N	N	N	Y	Y
WEST VIRGINIA								
1 Mollohan	N	N	N	?	N	N	N	Y
2 ***Capito***	Y	Y	N	N	N	N	N	Y
3 Rahall	N	N	N	N	N	N	Y	Y
WISCONSIN								
1 ***Ryan***	Y	Y	N	N	N	N	N	Y
2 Baldwin	N	N	N	Y	Y	Y	Y	N
3 Kind	N	N	N	N	N	N	Y	Y
4 Kleczka	N	N	N	Y	N	N	Y	Y
5 Barrett	N	N	N	N	N	N	Y	Y
6 ***Petri***	Y	Y	N	N	N	N	N	Y
7 Obey	N	N	N	N	Y	Y	Y	Y
8 ***Green***	Y	Y	N	N	N	N	N	Y
9 ***Sensenbrenner***	Y	Y	N	N	N	N	N	Y
WYOMING								
AL ***Cubin***	Y	Y	N	N	N	N	N	Y

Southern states - Ala., Ark., Fla., Ga., Ky., La., Miss., N.C., Okla., S.C., Tenn., Texas, Va.

Key

Y	Voted for (yea).
#	Paired for.
+	Announced for.
N	Voted against (nay).
X	Paired against.
−	Announced against.
P	Voted "present."
C	Voted "present" to avoid possible conflict of interest.
?	Did not vote or otherwise make a position known.

Democrats **Republicans**
Independents

143. HR 4546. Fiscal 2003 Defense Authorization/Motion to Rise. Taylor, D-Miss., motion to rise from the Committee of the Whole. Motion rejected 46-356: R 0-204; D 46-151 (ND 37-111, SD 9-40); I 0-1. May 9, 2002.

144. HR 4546. Fiscal 2003 Defense Authorization/Motion to Rise. Taylor, D-Miss., motion to rise from the Committee of the Whole. Motion rejected 48-356: R 0-205; D 48-149 (ND 37-110, SD 11-39); I 0-2. May 9, 2002.

145. HR 4546. Fiscal 2003 Defense Authorization/Space-Based Missiles. Tierney, D-Mass., amendment that would block fiscal 2003 funding for space-based missile defense programs. Rejected 159-253: R 2-206; D 156-46 (ND 128-24, SD 28-22); I 1-1. A "nay" was a vote in support of the president's position. May 9, 2002.

146. HR 4546. Fiscal 2003 Defense Authorization/Motion to Rise. Taylor, D-Miss., motion to rise from the Committee of the Whole. Motion rejected 55-336: R 0-194; D 55-140 (ND 40-106, SD 15-34); I 0-2. May 9, 2002.

147. HR 4546. Fiscal 2003 Defense Authorization/Motion to Rise. Taylor, D-Miss., motion to rise from the Committee of the Whole. Motion rejected 56-339: R 0-199; D 56-138 (ND 42-105, SD 14-33); I 0-2. May 9, 2002.

148. HR 4546. Fiscal 2003 Defense Authorization/Motion to Rise. Taylor, D-Miss., motion to rise from the Committee of the Whole. Motion rejected 58-325: R 0-190; D 58-134 (ND 45-98, SD 13-36); I 0-1. May 9, 2002.

149. HR 4546. Fiscal 2003 Defense Authorization/Motion to Rise. Taylor, D-Miss., motion to rise from the Committee of the Whole. Motion rejected 75-319: R 0-195; D 74-123 (ND 56-91, SD 18-32); I 1-1. May 9, 2002.

150. HR 4546. Fiscal 2003 Defense Authorization/Motion to Rise. Taylor, D-Miss., motion to rise from the Committee of the Whole. Motion rejected 83-312: R 0-198; D 82-113 (ND 61-85, SD 21-28); I 1-1. May 9, 2002.

	143	144	145	146	147	148	149	150
ALABAMA								
1 *Callahan*	N	N	N	N	N	N	N
2 *Everett*	N	N	N	?	N	?	?
3 *Riley*	?	?	?	?	?	?	?
4 *Aderholt*	N	N	N	N	N	N	N
5 Cramer	N	N	N	N	N	N	N
6 *Bachus*	N	N	N	N	N	N	N
7 Hilliard	N	N	Y	N	N	Y	Y
ALASKA								
AL *Young*	N	N	N	N	N	N	N
ARIZONA								
1 *Flake*	N	N	N	N	N	N	N
2 Pastor	N	N	Y	N	N	N	N
3 *Stump*	?	N	N	N	N	N	N
4 *Shadegg*	N	N	N	N	N	N	N
5 *Kolbe*	N	N	N	N	N	N	N
6 *Hayworth*	N	N	N	N	N	N	N
ARKANSAS								
1 Berry	Y	Y	N	Y	Y	Y	Y
2 Snyder	N	N	N	N	N	N	N
3 *Boozman*	N	N	N	N	N	N	N
4 Ross	N	N	N	N	N	N	N
CALIFORNIA								
1 Thompson	N	N	Y	N	N	N	Y
2 *Herger*	N	N	N	N	N	N	N
3 *Ose*	?	?	?	?	?	?	?
4 *Doolittle*	N	N	N	N	N	N	N
5 Matsui	N	N	Y	N	N	N	N
6 Woolsey	N	N	Y	N	?	N	Y
7 Miller, George	Y	Y	Y	Y	Y	Y	Y
8 Pelosi	Y	Y	Y	Y	Y	Y	Y
9 Lee	Y	Y	Y	Y	Y	Y	Y
10 Tauscher	N	N	N	N	N	N	N
11 *Pombo*	N	N	N	N	N	N	N
12 Lantos	N	N	Y	N	N	Y	Y
13 Stark	Y	Y	Y	Y	?	?	Y
14 Eshoo	N	N	Y	N	N	N	N
15 Honda	Y	Y	Y	Y	Y	Y	Y
16 Lofgren	N	N	Y	N	Y	Y	Y
17 Farr	N	N	Y	N	N	N	N
18 Condit	Y	Y	N	Y	Y	Y	Y
19 *Radanovich*	N	N	?	N	?	N	?
20 Dooley	N	?	N	?	N	N	?	Y
21 *Thomas*	N	?	?	N	N	N	N
22 Capps	N	N	Y	N	N	N	Y
23 *Gallegly*	N	?	?	N	N	N	N
24 Sherman	N	N	Y	N	N	N	N
25 *McKeon*	N	N	N	N	N	N	N
26 Berman	?	N	Y	?	N	?	N	?
27 Schiff	N	N	Y	N	N	N	N
28 *Dreier*	N	N	N	N	N	N	N
29 Waxman	?	?	?	?	?	?	?
30 Becerra	N	N	Y	N	N	N	Y	Y
31 Solis	Y	Y	Y	Y	Y	Y	Y
32 Watson	?	?	?	?	?	?	?
33 Roybal-Allard	N	N	Y	N	N	N	Y
34 Napolitano	N	?	Y	Y	Y	Y	Y
35 Waters	Y	Y	Y	Y	Y	Y	Y
36 Harman	N	N	N	N	N	N	N
37 Millender-McD.	?	?	?	?	?	?	?
38 *Horn*	N	N	N	N	N	N	N

	143	144	145	146	147	148	149	150
39 *Royce*	N	N	N	?	N	N	N
40 *Lewis*	N	N	N	N	N	N	N
41 *Miller, Gary*	N	N	N	N	N	N	N
42 Baca	N	N	Y	N	N	N	N
43 *Calvert*	N	N	N	N	N	N	?
44 *Bono*	N	N	N	N	N	N	N
45 *Rohrabacher*	N	N	Y	N	Y	Y	Y
46 Sanchez	N	N	Y	N	Y	Y	Y
47 *Cox*	N	N	N	N	N	N	N
48 *Issa*	N	N	N	N	N	N	N
49 Davis	N	N	Y	N	N	N	N
50 Filner	Y	Y	Y	Y	Y	Y	Y
51 *Cunningham*	N	N	N	N	N	N	N
52 *Hunter*	N	N	N	N	N	?	N
COLORADO								
1 DeGette	Y	Y	Y	Y	Y	Y	Y
2 Udall	N	N	Y	N	N	N	N
3 *McInnis*	N	N	N	N	N	N	N
4 *Schaffer*	N	N	N	N	?	?	N
5 *Hefley*	N	N	N	N	N	N	N
6 *Tancredo*	N	N	N	N	N	N	N
CONNECTICUT								
1 Larson	Y	Y	Y	Y	Y	Y	Y
2 *Simmons*	N	N	N	N	N	N	N
3 DeLauro	N	N	N	N	N	N	N
4 *Shays*	N	N	N	N	N	N	N
5 Maloney	N	N	N	N	N	N	N
6 *Johnson*	N	N	N	N	N	N	N
DELAWARE								
AL *Castle*	N	N	N	N	N	N	N
FLORIDA								
1 *Miller, J.*	N	N	N	N	N	N	N
2 Boyd	Y	Y	N	Y	Y	Y	Y
3 Brown	N	N	Y	N	N	N	N
4 *Crenshaw*	N	N	N	N	N	N	N
5 Thurman	N	N	Y	N	N	Y	Y
6 *Stearns*	N	N	N	N	N	N	N
7 *Mica*	N	N	N	N	N	N	N
8 *Keller*	N	N	N	N	N	N	N
9 *Bilirakis*	N	N	N	N	N	N	N
10 *Young*	?	N	N	N	N	N	N
11 Davis	N	N	Y	N	Y	N	Y
12 *Putnam*	N	N	N	N	N	N	N
13 *Miller, D.*	N	N	N	N	N	N	N
14 *Goss*	N	N	N	N	?	N	N
15 *Weldon*	N	N	N	N	N	N	N
16 *Foley*	N	N	N	?	N	?	N
17 Meek	?	N	Y	N	N	N	N
18 *Ros-Lehtinen*	N	N	N	N	N	N	N
19 Wexler	N	N	Y	N	N	N	Y
20 Deutsch	N	N	N	N	N	N	N
21 *Diaz-Balart*	?	N	N	N	?	N	N
22 *Shaw*	N	N	N	N	N	N	N
23 Hastings	N	Y	Y	N	N	Y	N
GEORGIA								
1 *Kingston*	N	N	N	N	N	N	N
2 Bishop	N	N	N	N	N	N	N
3 *Collins*	N	N	N	N	N	N	N
4 McKinney	N	N	N	N	N	N	N
5 Lewis	?	?	?	?	?	?	?
6 *Isakson*	N	N	N	N	N	N	N
7 *Barr*	N	N	N	?	?	?	?
8 *Chambliss*	N	N	N	N	N	N	N
9 *Deal*	N	N	N	N	N	N	N
10 *Norwood*	N	N	N	?	?	?	N
11 *Linder*	N	N	N	N	N	N	?
HAWAII								
1 Abercrombie	Y	Y	Y	Y	Y	Y	Y
2 Mink	Y	Y	Y	Y	Y	?	Y	?
IDAHO								
1 *Otter*	N	N	N	N	N	N	N
2 *Simpson*	?	N	N	?	?	?	N
ILLINOIS								
1 Rush	Y	N	Y	N	N	N	N
2 Jackson	N	N	Y	N	N	N	N
3 Lipinski	?	N	N	N	N	N	N
4 Gutierrez	N	N	Y	N	N	N	N
5 Blagojevich	N	N	N	N	N	N	N
6 *Hyde*	N	N	N	N	N	N	N
7 Davis	Y	N	Y	N	N	N	N
8 *Crane*	?	?	?	?	?	?	?
9 Schakowsky	N	Y	Y	Y	Y	N	Y
10 *Kirk*	N	N	N	N	N	N	N
11 *Weller*	N	N	N	N	N	N	N
12 Costello	N	N	N	N	Y	Y	Y
13 *Biggert*	N	N	N	N	N	N	N

ND Northern Democrats   SD Southern Democrats

	143	144	145	146	147	148	149	150
14 ***Hastert***								
15 ***Johnson***	N	N	N	N	N	N	N	N
16 ***Manzullo***	N	N	N	N	N	N	N	N
17 Evans	N	N	Y	Y	N	N	Y	Y
18 ***LaHood***	N	N	N	N	N	N	N	N
19 Phelps	N	N	N	N	N	N	N	N
20 ***Shimkus***	N	N	N	N	N	N	N	?
INDIANA								
1 Visclosky	N	N	Y	N	N	Y	N	N
2 ***Pence***	N	N	N	N	N	?	N	N
3 Roemer	N	N	Y	N	N	N	N	N
4 ***Souder***	?	N	N	N	N	?	N	?
5 ***Buyer***	N	N	N	N	N	N	N	N
6 ***Burton***	?	?	?	?	?	?	?	?
7 ***Kerns***	N	N	N	N	N	N	N	N
8 ***Hostettler***	N	N	N	N	N	N	N	N
9 Hill	Y	Y	Y	Y	Y	Y	Y	Y
10 Carson	N	N	Y	N	N	N	N	N
IOWA								
1 ***Leach***	N	N	Y	N	N	N	N	N
2 ***Nussle***	N	N	N	N	N	N	?	?
3 Boswell	N	N	Y	N	N	N	N	N
4 ***Ganske***	N	N	N	?	N	N	?	N
5 ***Latham***	N	N	N	N	N	N	N	N
KANSAS								
1 ***Moran***	N	N	N	N	N	N	N	N
2 ***Ryun***	N	N	N	N	N	N	N	N
3 Moore	N	N	Y	N	N	N	Y	Y
4 ***Tiahrt***	N	N	N	N	N	N	N	N
KENTUCKY								
1 ***Whitfield***	N	N	N	N	N	N	N	N
2 ***Lewis***	N	N	N	N	N	N	N	N
3 ***Northup***	N	N	N	N	N	N	N	N
4 Lucas	N	N	N	N	N	Y	N	N
5 ***Rogers***	N	N	N	N	N	N	N	N
6 ***Fletcher***	N	N	N	N	N	N	N	N
LOUISIANA								
1 ***Vitter***	N	N	N	N	N	N	N	N
2 Jefferson	Y	Y	Y	Y	Y	Y	Y	Y
3 ***Tauzin***	N	N	N	N	N	N	N	N
4 ***McCrery***	N	?	?	?	N	N	N	N
5 ***Cooksey***	N	N	N	?	N	N	N	?
6 ***Baker***	N	N	N	N	N	N	N	N
7 John	N	?	?	?	?	?	?	?
MAINE								
1 Allen	N	N	Y	N	N	N	N	N
2 Baldacci	N	N	Y	N	N	N	N	Y
MARYLAND								
1 ***Gilchrest***	N	N	N	N	N	N	N	N
2 ***Ehrlich***	N	N	N	N	N	N	N	N
3 Cardin	N	N	Y	N	N	N	N	N
4 Wynn	N	N	Y	N	N	N	N	N
5 Hoyer	N	N	Y	N	?	N	N	N
6 ***Bartlett***	N	?	N	N	N	N	N	N
7 Cummings	N	N	Y	N	N	N	Y	Y
8 ***Morella***	N	N	N	N	N	N	?	N
MASSACHUSETTS								
1 Olver	Y	Y	Y	Y	Y	Y	Y	N
2 Neal	N	N	Y	N	N	N	N	N
3 McGovern	Y	Y	Y	Y	Y	Y	Y	Y
4 Frank	Y	Y	Y	Y	Y	Y	Y	Y
5 Meehan	N	N	Y	N	N	N	N	N
6 Tierney	N	?	Y	N	Y	N	N	N
7 Markey	Y	Y	Y	Y	Y	Y	Y	Y
8 Capuano	Y	Y	Y	Y	Y	Y	Y	Y
9 Lynch	Y	Y	Y	Y	Y	Y	Y	Y
10 Delahunt	?	Y	Y	Y	Y	Y	Y	?
MICHIGAN								
1 Stupak	N	?	Y	N	N	N	N	Y
2 ***Hoekstra***	N	N	N	N	N	N	N	N
3 ***Ehlers***	N	N	N	N	N	N	N	N
4 ***Camp***	N	N	N	N	N	N	N	N
5 Barcia	N	N	N	N	N	?	N	N
6 ***Upton***	N	N	N	N	N	N	N	N
7 ***Smith***	N	N	N	N	N	N	N	N
8 ***Rogers***	N	N	N	N	N	N	N	N
9 Kildee	N	N	N	N	N	N	N	N
10 Bonior	Y	Y	Y	Y	Y	Y	Y	Y
11 ***Knollenberg***	N	N	N	N	N	N	N	N
12 Levin	N	N	Y	N	N	N	N	N
13 Rivers	N	N	Y	N	N	N	N	N
14 Conyers	Y	Y	Y	Y	Y	Y	Y	Y
15 Kilpatrick	N	N	Y	N	N	N	N	N
16 Dingell	Y	Y	Y	Y	N	N	N	N

	143	144	145	146	147	148	149	150
MINNESOTA								
1 ***Gutknecht***	N	N	N	N	N	N	N	N
2 ***Kennedy***	?	?	?	?	?	?	?	?
3 ***Ramstad***	N	N	N	N	N	N	N	N
4 McCollum	N	N	Y	N	N	N	N	N
5 Sabo	N	N	Y	N	N	N	N	N
6 Luther	N	N	Y	N	N	N	N	N
7 Peterson	N	N	N	N	Y	Y	Y	N
8 Oberstar	Y	Y	Y	Y	Y	Y	Y	Y
MISSISSIPPI								
1 ***Wicker***	N	N	N	N	N	N	N	N
2 Thompson	N	N	Y	N	N	N	N	Y
3 ***Pickering***	N	N	N	N	N	N	N	N
4 Shows	Y	Y	N	Y	Y	Y	Y	Y
5 Taylor	Y	Y	N	Y	Y	Y	Y	Y
MISSOURI								
1 Clay	N	Y	Y	?	?	?	?	?
2 ***Akin***	N	N	N	N	N	N	N	N
3 Gephardt	N	N	Y	N	N	N	?	N
4 Skelton	N	N	Y	N	N	N	Y	N
5 McCarthy	N	N	Y	N	N	N	N	N
6 ***Graves***	N	N	N	N	N	N	N	N
7 ***Blunt***	N	N	N	?	N	N	N	N
8 ***Emerson***	N	N	N	N	N	N	N	N
9 ***Hulshof***	N	N	N	N	N	?	?	N
MONTANA								
AL ***Rehberg***	N	N	N	N	N	N	N	N
NEBRASKA								
1 ***Bereuter***	N	N	N	N	N	N	N	N
2 ***Terry***	N	N	N	N	N	N	N	N
3 ***Osborne***	N	N	N	N	N	N	N	N
NEVADA								
1 Berkley	N	N	Y	N	N	N	N	N
2 ***Gibbons***	N	N	N	N	N	N	N	N
NEW HAMPSHIRE								
1 ***Sununu***	N	N	N	N	N	N	N	N
2 ***Bass***	N	N	N	N	N	N	N	N
NEW JERSEY								
1 Andrews	N	N	N	N	N	N	N	N
2 ***LoBiondo***	N	N	N	N	N	N	N	N
3 ***Saxton***	N	N	N	N	N	N	N	?
4 ***Smith***	N	N	N	N	N	N	N	N
5 ***Roukema***	?	?	?	?	?	?	?	?
6 Pallone	N	N	Y	N	N	N	N	N
7 ***Ferguson***	N	N	N	N	N	N	N	N
8 Pascrell	N	N	Y	N	N	Y	Y	Y
9 Rothman	N	N	Y	N	N	N	N	?
10 Payne	N	N	Y	N	N	N	N	N
11 ***Frelinghuysen***	N	N	N	N	N	N	N	N
12 Holt	Y	Y	Y	Y	Y	Y	Y	Y
13 Menendez	N	N	Y	N	N	?	N	N
NEW MEXICO								
1 ***Wilson***	N	N	N	N	N	N	N	N
2 ***Skeen***	N	N	N	N	N	N	N	N
3 Udall	N	N	Y	N	N	Y	Y	Y
NEW YORK								
1 ***Grucci***	N	N	N	N	?	N	N	N
2 Israel	N	N	N	N	N	N	Y	N
3 ***King***	N	N	N	N	N	N	N	N
4 McCarthy	N	N	N	N	N	N	N	N
5 Ackerman	N	N	N	N	Y	?	Y	N
6 Meeks	N	N	Y	N	Y	N	Y	Y
7 Crowley	N	N	Y	N	N	N	N	Y
8 Nadler	N	?	Y	N	N	Y	N	N
9 Weiner	Y	N	Y	N	N	N	N	N
10 Towns	Y	Y	Y	Y	Y	Y	Y	Y
11 Owens	N	N	Y	N	N	Y	N	N
12 Velázquez	N	N	Y	N	N	N	N	Y
13 ***Fossella***	N	N	N	N	N	N	N	N
14 Maloney	N	Y	Y	N	N	N	N	N
15 Rangel	N	N	Y	N	N	N	N	Y
16 Serrano	N	N	Y	N	N	N	N	N
17 Engel	N	N	Y	N	N	N	N	N
18 Lowey	N	N	Y	N	N	N	N	N
19 ***Kelly***	N	N	N	N	N	N	N	N
20 ***Gilman***	N	N	N	N	N	N	N	N
21 McNulty	N	N	Y	N	N	N	N	N
22 ***Sweeney***	N	N	N	N	N	N	N	N
23 ***Boehlert***	N	N	N	N	N	N	N	N
24 ***McHugh***	N	N	N	N	N	N	N	N
25 ***Walsh***	N	N	N	N	N	N	N	N
26 Hinchey	N	Y	Y	?	Y	N	N	Y
27 ***Reynolds***	N	N	N	N	N	?	N	N
28 Slaughter	Y	Y	Y	Y	N	Y	Y	Y
29 LaFalce	N	N	Y	?	?	N	N	N

	143	144	145	146	147	148	149	150
30 ***Quinn***	N	N	N	N	N	N	N	N
31 ***Houghton***	N	N	N	N	N	N	N	N
NORTH CAROLINA								
1 Clayton	N	N	Y	N	?	?	?	?
2 Etheridge	N	N	Y	Y	N	N	N	N
3 ***Jones***	N	N	N	N	N	N	N	N
4 Price	N	N	Y	N	N	N	N	N
5 ***Burr***	N	N	N	N	N	N	N	N
6 ***Coble***	N	N	N	N	N	N	N	N
7 McIntyre	Y	Y	N	Y	Y	Y	Y	Y
8 ***Hayes***	N	N	N	N	N	N	N	N
9 ***Myrick***	N	N	N	N	N	N	N	N
10 ***Ballenger***	?	N	N	?	?	?	?	N
11 ***Taylor***	N	N	N	N	N	N	N	N
12 Watt	N	Y	Y	Y	Y	N	N	N
NORTH DAKOTA								
AL Pomeroy	N	N	N	N	N	N	N	N
OHIO								
1 ***Chabot***	N	N	N	N	N	N	N	N
2 ***Portman***	N	N	N	N	N	N	N	N
3 Hall	?	?	?	?	?	?	?	?
4 ***Oxley***	N	?	N	?	?	?	?	N
5 ***Gillmor***	N	N	N	?	?	?	?	N
6 Strickland	N	N	Y	N	N	N	N	N
7 ***Hobson***	N	N	N	N	N	N	N	N
8 ***Boehner***	N	?	?	?	?	?	?	N
9 Kaptur	N	N	Y	N	Y	Y	Y	N
10 Kucinich	N	N	Y	N	Y	N	N	N
11 Jones	Y	N	Y	N	N	N	Y	N
12 ***Tiberi***	N	N	N	N	N	N	N	N
13 Brown	N	N	Y	N	N	N	N	N
14 Sawyer	N	N	Y	N	N	N	N	N
15 ***Pryce***	N	N	?	?	?	?	?	N
16 ***Regula***	N	N	N	N	N	N	N	N
17 Traficant	?	?	?	?	?	?	?	?
18 ***Ney***	?	N	N	N	N	N	N	N
19 ***LaTourette***	N	N	N	?	?	?	N	N
OKLAHOMA								
1 ***Sullivan***	N	N	N	N	N	N	N	N
2 Carson	N	N	N	N	N	N	N	N
3 ***Watkins***	N	N	N	N	N	N	N	?
4 ***Watts***	N	N	N	N	?	N	N	N
5 ***Istook***	N	N	N	N	N	N	N	N
6 ***Lucas***	N	N	N	N	N	N	N	N
OREGON								
1 Wu	Y	Y	Y	Y	Y	Y	Y	Y
2 ***Walden***	N	N	N	N	N	N	N	N
3 Blumenauer	Y	Y	Y	Y	Y	Y	Y	Y
4 DeFazio	N	N	Y	P	?	P	P	N
5 Hooley	N	N	Y	Y	N	N	N	N
PENNSYLVANIA								
1 Brady	Y	Y	Y	Y	Y	Y	Y	Y
2 Fattah	N	N	Y	N	N	N	N	N
3 Borski	N	N	Y	N	N	N	N	N
4 ***Hart***	N	N	N	N	N	N	N	N
5 ***Peterson***	N	N	N	N	N	N	N	N
6 Holden	N	N	N	N	N	N	N	N
7 ***Weldon***	N	N	N	N	N	N	N	N
8 ***Greenwood***	?	N	N	N	N	N	N	N
9 ***Shuster, Bill***	N	N	N	N	N	N	N	N
10 ***Sherwood***	N	N	?	N	N	N	N	N
11 Kanjorski	N	N	Y	N	N	N	N	N
12 Murtha	?	N	N	N	N	N	N	N
13 Hoeffel	N	N	Y	N	N	N	N	Y
14 Coyne	N	N	Y	N	N	N	N	N
15 ***Toomey***	N	N	N	N	N	N	?	N
16 ***Pitts***	N	N	N	N	N	N	N	N
17 ***Gekas***	N	N	N	N	N	N	N	N
18 Doyle	N	N	Y	N	N	N	N	N
19 ***Platts***	N	N	N	N	N	?	N	N
20 Mascara	N	N	N	N	N	N	N	N
21 ***English***	N	?	N	N	N	N	N	?
RHODE ISLAND								
1 Kennedy	N	N	N	N	N	N	N	N
2 Langevin	N	N	Y	N	Y	Y	Y	Y
SOUTH CAROLINA								
1 ***Brown***	N	N	N	N	N	N	N	N
2 ***Wilson***	N	N	N	N	N	N	N	N
3 ***Graham***	N	N	N	N	N	N	N	N
4 ***DeMint***	N	N	N	N	N	N	N	N
5 Spratt	N	N	Y	N	N	N	N	N
6 Clyburn	N	N	Y	N	N	N	N	N
SOUTH DAKOTA								
AL ***Thune***	N	N	N	N	N	N	N	N

	143	144	145	146	147	148	149	150
TENNESSEE								
1 ***Jenkins***	N	N	N	N	N	N	N	N
2 ***Duncan***	N	N	Y	N	N	N	N	N
3 ***Wamp***	N	N	N	N	N	N	N	N
4 ***Hilleary***	N	?	N	N	N	?	N	N
5 Clement	N	N	N	N	N	N	N	N
6 Gordon	N	N	N	?	?	?	N	Y
7 ***Bryant***	N	N	N	N	N	N	N	N
8 Tanner	Y	Y	N	Y	Y	Y	Y	Y
9 Ford	N	N	N	N	Y	N	Y	Y
TEXAS								
1 Sandlin	N	N	N	N	N	N	N	N
2 Turner	N	N	N	N	N	N	N	N
3 ***Johnson, Sam***	N	N	N	?	N	N	N	N
4 Hall	N	N	N	N	N	N	N	N
5 ***Sessions***	N	N	N	N	N	N	N	N
6 ***Barton***	N	N	N	N	N	N	N	N
7 ***Culberson***	N	N	N	N	N	?	N	N
8 ***Brady***	N	N	N	N	N	N	N	?
9 Lampson	N	N	Y	N	N	N	N	N
10 Doggett	Y	Y	Y	Y	Y	Y	Y	Y
11 Edwards	N	N	?	N	?	N	N	N
12 ***Granger***	N	N	N	N	N	N	N	N
13 ***Thornberry***	N	N	N	N	N	N	N	N
14 ***Paul***	N	N	N	N	N	N	N	N
15 Hinojosa	N	?	Y	N	N	N	N	Y
16 Reyes	?	?	?	?	?	?	?	?
17 Stenholm	N	N	N	Y	Y	Y	Y	Y
18 Jackson-Lee	N	N	Y	Y	Y	N	Y	Y
19 ***Combest***	N	N	N	?	?	?	N	?
20 Gonzalez	N	N	Y	N	N	N	N	N
21 ***Smith***	N	N	N	N	N	N	N	N
22 ***DeLay***	N	N	N	N	N	N	?	?
23 ***Bonilla***	N	N	N	N	N	N	N	N
24 Frost	N	N	Y	N	N	N	N	N
25 Bentsen	?	N	Y	N	N	N	N	N
26 ***Armey***	N	N	N	N	N	N	N	N
27 Ortiz	N	N	N	N	N	Y	Y	Y
28 Rodriguez	N	N	Y	Y	Y	Y	Y	Y
29 Green	N	N	Y	N	N	N	N	N
30 Johnson, E.B.	Y	Y	Y	N	Y	Y	Y	Y
UTAH								
1 ***Hansen***	?	N	N	N	?	N	?	N
2 Matheson	N	N	Y	N	N	N	N	N
3 ***Cannon***	?	?	?	?	?	?	?	?
VERMONT								
AL *Sanders*	?	N	Y	N	N	?	Y	Y
VIRGINIA								
1 ***Davis, Jo Ann***	N	N	N	N	N	N	N	N
2 ***Schrock***	N	N	N	N	N	N	N	N
3 Scott	N	N	Y	N	N	N	N	N
4 ***Forbes***	N	N	N	N	N	N	N	N
5 *Goode*	N	N	N	N	N	N	N	N
6 ***Goodlatte***	N	N	N	N	N	N	N	N
7 ***Cantor***	N	N	N	N	N	N	N	N
8 Moran	N	N	N	N	N	N	N	N
9 Boucher	?	N	Y	?	?	N	N	?
10 ***Wolf***	N	N	N	N	N	N	N	N
11 ***Davis, T.***	N	N	N	N	N	N	N	N
WASHINGTON								
1 Inslee	N	N	Y	N	N	N	N	N
2 Larsen	N	N	N	N	N	N	N	N
3 Baird	N	N	Y	N	N	N	?	Y
4 ***Hastings***	N	N	N	N	N	N	N	N
5 ***Nethercutt***	?	?	?	?	?	?	?	?
6 Dicks	Y	N	N	N	N	N	N	Y
7 McDermott	Y	Y	Y	Y	Y	Y	Y	Y
8 ***Dunn***	N	N	N	N	N	N	N	N
9 Smith	N	N	N	N	N	N	N	N
WEST VIRGINIA								
1 Mollohan	N	N	N	N	N	N	N	N
2 ***Capito***	N	N	N	N	N	N	N	N
3 Rahall	N	N	Y	N	N	N	Y	Y
WISCONSIN								
1 ***Ryan***	N	N	N	N	N	?	?	N
2 Baldwin	Y	Y	Y	Y	Y	Y	Y	Y
3 Kind	N	N	Y	N	N	N	N	N
4 Kleczka	N	N	Y	N	N	N	N	N
5 Barrett	N	N	Y	N	N	Y	Y	Y
6 ***Petri***	N	N	N	N	N	N	N	N
7 Obey	N	N	Y	Y	Y	N	N	N
8 ***Green***	N	N	N	N	N	N	N	N
9 ***Sensenbrenner***	N	N	N	N	N	N	N	N
WYOMING								
AL ***Cubin***	N	N	N	N	N	N	N	N

Southern states - Ala., Ark., Fla., Ga., Ky., La., Miss., N.C., Okla., S.C., Tenn., Texas, Va.

Key

Y	Voted for (yea).
#	Paired for.
+	Announced for.
N	Voted against (nay).
X	Paired against.
−	Announced against.
P	Voted "present."
C	Voted "present" to avoid possible conflict of interest.
?	Did not vote or otherwise make a position known.

Democrats **Republicans** *Independents*

151. HR 4546. Fiscal 2003 Defense Authorization/Motion to Rise. Taylor, D-Miss., motion to rise from the Committee of the Whole. Motion rejected 154-249: R 0-204; D 153-44 (ND 113-34, SD 40-10); I 1-1. May 9, 2002.

152. HR 4546. Fiscal 2003 Defense Authorization/Motion to Rise. Taylor, D-Miss., motion to rise from the Committee of the Whole. Motion rejected 168-241: R 0-210; D 167-30 (ND 125-22, SD 42-8); I 1-1. May 10, 2002 (in the session that began and the Congressional Record dated May 9, 2002).

153. HR 4546. Fiscal 2003 Defense Authorization/Abortions Overseas. Sanchez, D-Calif., amendment that would allow abortions at U.S. military medical facilities abroad if a doctor agrees to perform the procedure and it is paid for by the patient. Rejected 202-215: R 30-183; D 171-31 (ND 129-22, SD 42-9); I 1-1. May 10, 2002 (in the session that began and the Congressional Record dated May 9, 2002).

154. HR 4546. Fiscal 2003 Defense Authorization/Border Security. Goode, I-Va., amendment that would allow the military to help the Immigration and Naturalization Service and the U.S. Customs Service if requested by either the attorney general or the secretary of the Treasury. Adopted 232-183: R 192-19; D 39-163 (ND 23-128, SD 16-35); I 1-1. May 10, 2002 (in the session that began and the Congressional Record dated May 9, 2002).

155. HR 4546. Fiscal 2003 Defense Authorization/International Tribunals. Paul, R-Texas, amendment that would ban funds to provide any support for the International Criminal Court. Adopted 264-152: R 204-8; D 59-143 (ND 36-115, SD 23-28); I 1-1. May 10, 2002 (in the session that began and the Congressional Record dated May 9, 2002).

156. HR 4546. Fiscal 2003 Defense Authorization/Military Athletes. Bereuter, R-Neb., amendment that would authorize the National Guard to use funds to pay the costs of competing in military-related athletic events and training. Adopted 412-2: R 210-1; D 200-1 (ND 149-1, SD 51-0); I 2-0. May 10, 2002 (in the session that began and the Congressional Record dated May 9, 2002).

157. HR 4546. Fiscal 2003 Defense Authorization/Motion to Recommit. Spratt, D-S.C., motion to recommit the bill to the House Armed Services Committee with instructions to report the bill back with language that would ban any funds from being spent to develop nuclear-tipped ballistic missile interceptors. Motion rejected 193-223: R 2-210; D 190-12 (ND 148-3, SD 42-9); I 1-1. May 10, 2002 (in the session that began and the Congressional Record dated May 9, 2002).

158. HR 4546. Fiscal 2003 Defense Authorization/Passage. Passage of the bill that would authorize $383.4 billion for defense programs for fiscal 2003. It would include the president's request of $7.8 billion for missile defense systems and $7.3 billion for counterterrorism programs. It would provide $475 million for the Crusader artillery system. The bill also would exempt military activities from certain environmental regulations and include an average 4.7 percent pay increase for military personnel. Passed 359-58: R 212-1; D 146-56 (ND 100-51, SD 46-5); I 1-1. May 10, 2002 (in the session that began and the Congressional Record dated May 9, 2002).

	151	152	153	154	155	156	157	158
ALABAMA								
1 *Callahan*	N	N	N	Y	Y	Y	N	Y
2 *Everett*	N	N	N	Y	Y	Y	N	Y
3 *Riley*	?	?	?	?	?	?	?	?
4 *Aderholt*	N	N	N	Y	Y	Y	N	Y
5 Cramer	N	N	Y	Y	Y	Y	Y	Y
6 *Bachus*	N	N	N	Y	Y	Y	N	Y
7 Hilliard	Y	Y	Y	N	N	Y	Y	Y
ALASKA								
AL *Young*	N	N	N	Y	Y	Y	N	Y
ARIZONA								
1 *Flake*	N	N	N	Y	Y	N	Y	Y
2 Pastor	N	N	Y	N	N	Y	Y	Y
3 *Stump*	N	N	N	Y	Y	Y	N	Y
4 *Shadegg*	N	N	N	Y	Y	Y	N	Y
5 *Kolbe*	N	N	Y	N	Y	Y	N	Y
6 *Hayworth*	N	N	N	Y	Y	Y	N	Y
ARKANSAS								
1 Berry	Y	Y	N	N	Y	Y	Y	Y
2 Snyder	Y	Y	N	N	N	Y	Y	Y
3 *Boozman*	N	N	N	Y	Y	Y	N	Y
4 Ross	Y	Y	N	N	Y	Y	Y	Y
CALIFORNIA								
1 Thompson	Y	Y	Y	N	N	Y	Y	Y
2 *Herger*	N	N	N	Y	Y	Y	N	Y
3 *Ose*	?	?	?	?	?	?	?	?
4 *Doolittle*	N	N	N	Y	Y	Y	N	Y
5 Matsui	Y	Y	N	N	N	Y	Y	Y
6 Woolsey	Y	Y	Y	N	N	Y	Y	N
7 Miller, George	Y	Y	N	N	N	Y	Y	N
8 Pelosi	Y	Y	Y	N	N	Y	Y	N
9 Lee	Y	Y	Y	N	N	Y	Y	N
10 Tauscher	Y	Y	Y	N	N	Y	Y	Y
11 *Pombo*	N	N	N	Y	Y	Y	N	Y
12 Lantos	Y	Y	Y	N	N	Y	Y	Y
13 Stark	Y	Y	Y	N	N	N	Y	N
14 Eshoo	Y	Y	Y	N	N	Y	Y	N
15 Honda	Y	Y	Y	N	N	Y	Y	N
16 Lofgren	Y	Y	Y	N	N	Y	Y	N
17 Farr	Y	Y	Y	N	N	Y	Y	Y
18 Condit	Y	Y	Y	N	N	Y	Y	Y
19 *Radanovich*	N	N	N	Y	Y	Y	N	Y
20 Dooley	?	?	N	N	Y	Y	Y	Y
21 *Thomas*	N	N	N	Y	Y	Y	N	Y
22 Capps	Y	Y	Y	N	N	Y	Y	Y
23 *Gallegly*	N	N	N	Y	Y	Y	N	Y
24 Sherman	Y	Y	Y	N	Y	Y	Y	Y
25 *McKeon*	N	N	N	Y	Y	Y	N	Y
26 Berman	?	Y	Y	N	Y	Y	Y	Y
27 Schiff	Y	Y	Y	N	Y	Y	Y	Y
28 *Dreier*	N	N	N	Y	Y	Y	N	Y
29 Waxman	?	?	?	?	?	?	?	?
30 Becerra	Y	Y	Y	N	N	Y	Y	N
31 Solis	Y	Y	Y	N	N	Y	Y	Y
32 Watson	?	?	?	?	?	?	?	?
33 Roybal-Allard	Y	Y	Y	N	N	Y	Y	Y
34 Napolitano	Y	Y	Y	N	N	Y	Y	Y
35 Waters	Y	Y	Y	N	N	Y	Y	N
36 Harman	Y	Y	Y	N	Y	Y	N	Y
37 Millender-McD.	?	?	?	?	?	?	?	?
38 *Horn*	N	N	Y	Y	Y	Y	N	Y

	151	152	153	154	155	156	157	158
39 *Royce*	N	N	N	Y	Y	Y	N	Y
40 *Lewis*	N	N	N	Y	Y	Y	N	Y
41 *Miller, Gary*	N	N	N	Y	Y	Y	N	Y
42 Baca	Y	Y	Y	N	Y	Y	Y	Y
43 *Calvert*	N	N	N	Y	Y	Y	N	Y
44 *Bono*	N	N	Y	Y	Y	Y	N	Y
45 *Rohrabacher*	N	N	N	Y	Y	Y	N	Y
46 Sanchez	Y	Y	Y	N	N	Y	Y	Y
47 *Cox*	N	N	N	Y	Y	Y	N	Y
48 *Issa*	N	N	N	Y	Y	Y	N	Y
49 Davis	Y	Y	Y	N	N	Y	Y	Y
50 Filner	Y	Y	Y	N	N	Y	Y	N
51 *Cunningham*	N	N	N	Y	Y	Y	N	Y
52 *Hunter*	N	N	N	Y	Y	Y	N	Y
COLORADO								
1 DeGette	Y	Y	Y	N	N	Y	Y	N
2 Udall	Y	Y	Y	N	Y	Y	Y	Y
3 *McInnis*	N	N	N	Y	Y	Y	N	Y
4 *Schaffer*	N	N	N	Y	Y	Y	N	Y
5 *Hefley*	N	N	N	Y	Y	Y	N	Y
6 *Tancredo*	N	N	N	Y	Y	Y	N	Y
CONNECTICUT								
1 Larson	Y	Y	Y	N	N	Y	Y	Y
2 *Simmons*	N	N	Y	N	Y	Y	N	Y
3 DeLauro	Y	Y	Y	N	N	Y	Y	Y
4 *Shays*	N	N	Y	N	Y	Y	N	Y
5 Maloney	Y	Y	Y	N	Y	Y	Y	Y
6 *Johnson*	N	N	Y	N	Y	N	Y	Y
DELAWARE								
AL *Castle*	N	N	Y	Y	Y	Y	N	Y
FLORIDA								
1 *Miller, J.*	N	N	N	Y	Y	Y	N	Y
2 Boyd	Y	Y	Y	Y	Y	Y	Y	Y
3 Brown	Y	Y	Y	N	N	Y	Y	Y
4 *Crenshaw*	N	N	N	Y	Y	Y	N	Y
5 Thurman	Y	Y	Y	Y	Y	Y	Y	Y
6 *Stearns*	N	N	N	Y	Y	Y	N	Y
7 *Mica*	N	N	N	Y	Y	Y	N	Y
8 *Keller*	N	N	N	Y	Y	Y	N	Y
9 *Bilirakis*	N	N	N	Y	Y	Y	N	Y
10 *Young*	N	N	N	Y	Y	Y	N	Y
11 Davis	Y	Y	Y	N	N	Y	Y	Y
12 *Putnam*	N	N	N	Y	Y	Y	N	Y
13 *Miller, D.*	N	N	N	Y	Y	Y	N	Y
14 *Goss*	N	N	N	Y	Y	Y	N	Y
15 *Weldon*	N	N	N	Y	Y	Y	N	Y
16 *Foley*	N	N	N	Y	Y	Y	N	Y
17 Meek	N	Y	N	N	Y	Y	Y	Y
18 *Ros-Lehtinen*	N	N	N	Y	Y	Y	N	Y
19 Wexler	Y	Y	Y	N	N	Y	Y	Y
20 Deutsch	Y	Y	Y	N	N	Y	Y	Y
21 *Diaz-Balart*	N	N	N	Y	Y	Y	N	Y
22 *Shaw*	N	N	N	Y	Y	Y	N	Y
23 Hastings	Y	Y	Y	N	Y	Y	Y	Y
GEORGIA								
1 *Kingston*	N	N	N	Y	Y	Y	N	Y
2 Bishop	Y	Y	Y	N	Y	Y	Y	Y
3 *Collins*	N	N	N	Y	Y	Y	N	Y
4 McKinney	N	N	Y	N	N	Y	Y	N
5 Lewis	?	?	?	?	?	?	?	?
6 *Isakson*	N	N	N	Y	Y	Y	N	Y
7 *Barr*	N	N	N	Y	Y	Y	N	Y
8 *Chambliss*	N	N	N	Y	Y	Y	N	Y
9 *Deal*	N	N	N	Y	Y	Y	N	Y
10 Norwood	N	N	N	Y	Y	Y	N	Y
11 *Linder*	?	N	N	Y	Y	Y	N	Y
HAWAII								
1 Abercrombie	Y	Y	Y	N	N	Y	Y	Y
2 Mink	Y	Y	Y	N	Y	Y	Y	Y
IDAHO								
1 *Otter*	N	N	N	Y	Y	Y	N	Y
2 *Simpson*	N	N	N	Y	Y	Y	N	Y
ILLINOIS								
1 Rush	Y	Y	Y	N	N	Y	Y	Y
2 Jackson	N	Y	Y	N	N	Y	Y	N
3 Lipinski	Y	Y	N	Y	Y	Y	Y	Y
4 Gutierrez	Y	?	N	Y	N	Y	Y	Y
5 Blagojevich	N	N	N	Y	Y	Y	Y	Y
6 *Hyde*	N	N	N	Y	Y	Y	N	Y
7 Davis	Y	N	Y	N	N	Y	Y	Y
8 *Crane*	?	?	?	?	?	?	?	?
9 Schakowsky	Y	Y	Y	N	N	Y	Y	N
10 *Kirk*	N	N	Y	Y	Y	Y	N	Y
11 *Weller*	N	N	N	Y	Y	Y	N	Y
12 Costello	Y	Y	N	Y	Y	Y	Y	Y
13 *Biggert*	N	N	Y	Y	Y	Y	N	Y

ND Northern Democrats   SD Southern Democrats

	151	152	153	154	155	156	157	158
14 ***Hastert***			N					Y
15 ***Johnson***	N	N	N	Y	Y	Y	N	Y
16 ***Manzullo***	N	N	N	Y	Y	Y	N	Y
17 Evans	Y	Y	Y	N	N	Y	Y	Y
18 ***LaHood***	N	N	N	Y	Y	Y	N	Y
19 Phelps	Y	Y	N	Y	Y	Y	N	Y
20 ***Shimkus***	?	?	N	Y	Y	Y	N	Y
INDIANA								
1 Visclosky	N	N	Y	N	Y	Y	Y	Y
2 ***Pence***	N	N	N	Y	Y	Y	N	Y
3 Roemer	N	Y	N	Y	Y	Y	Y	Y
4 ***Souder***	?	N	N	N	Y	Y	N	Y
5 ***Buyer***	N	N	N	N	Y	Y	N	Y
6 ***Burton***	?	?	?	?	?	?	?	?
7 ***Kerns***	N	N	N	Y	Y	Y	N	Y
8 ***Hostettler***	N	N	N	Y	Y	Y	N	Y
9 Hill	Y	?	Y	N	Y	Y	Y	Y
10 Carson	N	N	Y	N	N	Y	Y	Y
IOWA								
1 ***Leach***	N	N	Y	N	N	Y	Y	Y
2 ***Nussle***	N	N	N	Y	Y	Y	N	Y
3 Boswell	Y	Y	Y	Y	Y	Y	Y	Y
4 ***Ganske***	N	N	N	N	Y	Y	N	Y
5 ***Latham***	N	N	N	Y	Y	Y	N	Y
KANSAS								
1 ***Moran***	N	N	N	Y	Y	Y	N	Y
2 ***Ryun***	N	N	N	Y	Y	Y	N	Y
3 Moore	Y	Y	Y	Y	N	Y	Y	Y
4 ***Tiahrt***	N	N	N	Y	Y	Y	N	Y
KENTUCKY								
1 ***Whitfield***	N	N	N	N	Y	Y	N	Y
2 ***Lewis***	N	N	N	Y	Y	Y	N	Y
3 ***Northup***	N	N	N	?	Y	Y	N	Y
4 Lucas	N	Y	N	Y	Y	Y	N	Y
5 ***Rogers***	N	N	N	Y	Y	Y	N	Y
6 ***Fletcher***	N	?	N	Y	Y	Y	N	Y
LOUISIANA								
1 ***Vitter***	N	N	N	Y	Y	Y	N	Y
2 Jefferson	Y	Y	Y	N	N	Y	Y	Y
3 ***Tauzin***	N	N	N	Y	Y	Y	N	Y
4 ***McCrery***	N	N	N	Y	Y	Y	N	Y
5 ***Cooksey***	N	N	N	Y	Y	Y	N	Y
6 ***Baker***	N	N	N	Y	Y	Y	N	Y
7 John	?	?	?	?	?	?	?	?
MAINE								
1 Allen	Y	Y	Y	N	N	Y	Y	Y
2 Baldacci	Y	Y	Y	N	N	Y	Y	Y
MARYLAND								
1 ***Gilchrest***	N	N	Y	Y	Y	Y	N	Y
2 ***Ehrlich***	N	N	Y	N	Y	Y	N	Y
3 Cardin	N	Y	Y	N	N	Y	Y	Y
4 Wynn	Y	Y	Y	N	N	Y	Y	Y
5 Hoyer	Y	Y	Y	N	N	Y	Y	Y
6 ***Bartlett***	N	N	N	Y	Y	Y	N	Y
7 Cummings	Y	Y	Y	N	N	Y	Y	Y
8 ***Morella***	N	N	Y	N	N	Y	N	Y
MASSACHUSETTS								
1 Olver	Y	Y	Y	N	N	Y	Y	N
2 Neal	Y	Y	Y	N	N	Y	Y	Y
3 McGovern	Y	Y	Y	N	N	Y	Y	N
4 Frank	Y	Y	Y	N	N	Y	Y	N
5 Meehan	Y	Y	Y	N	N	Y	Y	Y
6 Tierney	Y	Y	Y	N	N	Y	Y	N
7 Markey	Y	Y	Y	N	N	Y	Y	N
8 Capuano	Y	Y	Y	N	N	Y	Y	N
9 Lynch	Y	Y	N	N	Y	Y	Y	Y
10 Delahunt	Y	Y	Y	N	N	Y	Y	N
MICHIGAN								
1 Stupak	Y	Y	N	N	Y	Y	Y	Y
2 ***Hoekstra***	N	N	N	Y	Y	Y	N	Y
3 ***Ehlers***	N	N	N	N	N	Y	Y	Y
4 ***Camp***	N	N	N	Y	Y	Y	N	Y
5 Barcia	N	N	N	Y	Y	Y	Y	Y
6 ***Upton***	N	N	N	Y	Y	Y	N	Y
7 ***Smith***	N	N	N	Y	Y	Y	N	Y
8 ***Rogers***	N	N	N	Y	Y	Y	N	Y
9 Kildee	Y	Y	N	N	Y	Y	Y	Y
10 Bonior	Y	Y	Y	N	N	Y	Y	N
11 ***Knollenberg***	N	N	N	Y	Y	Y	N	Y
12 Levin	Y	Y	Y	Y	N	Y	Y	Y
13 Rivers	N	N	Y	N	N	Y	Y	N
14 Conyers	?	Y	Y	N	N	Y	Y	N
15 Kilpatrick	Y	Y	Y	N	N	Y	Y	N
16 Dingell	N	Y	Y	N	N	Y	Y	Y
MINNESOTA								
1 ***Gutknecht***	N	N	N	Y	Y	Y	N	Y
2 ***Kennedy***	?	?	?	?	?	?	?	?
3 ***Ramstad***	N	N	Y	Y	Y	Y	N	Y
4 McCollum	Y	Y	Y	N	N	Y	Y	Y
5 Sabo	N	Y	Y	N	N	Y	Y	Y
6 Luther	N	N	Y	Y	N	Y	Y	Y
7 Peterson	N	Y	N	Y	Y	Y	N	Y
8 Oberstar	Y	Y	N	N	N	Y	Y	N
MISSISSIPPI								
1 ***Wicker***	N	N	N	Y	Y	Y	N	Y
2 Thompson	Y	Y	Y	N	N	Y	Y	Y
3 ***Pickering***	N	N	N	Y	Y	Y	N	Y
4 Shows	Y	Y	N	Y	Y	Y	N	Y
5 Taylor	Y	Y	N	Y	Y	Y	N	Y
MISSOURI								
1 Clay	?	?	?	?	?	?	?	?
2 ***Akin***	N	N	N	Y	Y	Y	N	Y
3 Gephardt	N	Y	Y	N	N	Y	Y	Y
4 Skelton	Y	N	N	N	Y	Y	Y	Y
5 McCarthy	N	Y	Y	N	N	?	Y	Y
6 ***Graves***	N	N	N	Y	Y	Y	N	Y
7 ***Blunt***	N	N	N	Y	Y	Y	N	Y
8 ***Emerson***	N	N	N	Y	Y	Y	N	Y
9 ***Hulshof***	?	N	N	Y	Y	Y	N	Y
MONTANA								
AL ***Rehberg***	N	N	N	Y	Y	Y	N	Y
NEBRASKA								
1 ***Bereuter***	N	N	N	Y	Y	Y	N	Y
2 ***Terry***	N	N	N	N	Y	Y	N	Y
3 ***Osborne***	N	N	N	Y	Y	Y	N	Y
NEVADA								
1 Berkley	Y	Y	Y	N	N	Y	Y	Y
2 ***Gibbons***	N	N	N	Y	Y	Y	N	Y
NEW HAMPSHIRE								
1 ***Sununu***	N	N	N	Y	Y	Y	N	Y
2 ***Bass***	N	N	Y	Y	Y	Y	N	Y
NEW JERSEY								
1 Andrews	Y	Y	Y	N	N	Y	Y	Y
2 ***LoBiondo***	N	N	N	Y	Y	Y	N	Y
3 ***Saxton***	N	N	N	Y	Y	Y	N	Y
4 ***Smith***	N	N	N	Y	Y	Y	N	Y
5 ***Roukema***	?	?	?	?	?	?	?	?
6 Pallone	Y	Y	Y	N	N	Y	Y	Y
7 ***Ferguson***	N	N	N	Y	Y	Y	N	Y
8 Pascrell	Y	Y	Y	N	Y	Y	Y	Y
9 Rothman	N	N	Y	N	Y	Y	Y	Y
10 Payne	Y	Y	Y	N	N	Y	Y	N
11 ***Frelinghuysen***	N	N	Y	Y	Y	Y	N	Y
12 Holt	Y	Y	Y	N	N	Y	Y	N
13 Menendez	N	N	Y	N	Y	Y	Y	Y
NEW MEXICO								
1 ***Wilson***	N	N	N	N	Y	Y	N	Y
2 ***Skeen***	N	N	N	N	Y	Y	N	Y
3 Udall	Y	Y	Y	Y	N	Y	Y	Y
NEW YORK								
1 ***Grucci***	N	N	N	Y	Y	Y	N	Y
2 Israel	Y	N	Y	Y	N	Y	Y	Y
3 ***King***	N	N	N	Y	Y	Y	N	Y
4 McCarthy	Y	Y	Y	Y	Y	Y	Y	Y
5 Ackerman	Y	Y	Y	N	N	Y	Y	Y
6 Meeks	Y	Y	Y	N	N	Y	Y	N
7 Crowley	Y	Y	Y	N	N	Y	Y	Y
8 Nadler	N	Y	Y	N	N	Y	Y	N
9 Weiner	Y	Y	Y	N	N	Y	Y	N
10 Towns	Y	Y	Y	N	N	Y	Y	N
11 Owens	Y	Y	Y	N	N	Y	Y	N
12 Velázquez	Y	Y	Y	N	N	Y	Y	N
13 ***Fossella***	N	N	N	Y	Y	Y	N	Y
14 Maloney	N	N	Y	N	N	Y	Y	Y
15 Rangel	Y	Y	Y	N	N	Y	Y	N
16 Serrano	N	N	Y	N	N	Y	Y	N
17 Engel	N	Y	Y	N	N	Y	Y	Y
18 Lowey	N	N	Y	Y	N	Y	Y	Y
19 ***Kelly***	N	N	Y	Y	Y	Y	N	Y
20 ***Gilman***	N	N	Y	Y	Y	Y	N	Y
21 McNulty	N	Y	N	N	N	Y	Y	Y
22 ***Sweeney***	N	N	N	Y	Y	Y	N	Y
23 ***Boehlert***	N	N	Y	Y	Y	Y	N	Y
24 ***McHugh***	N	N	N	Y	Y	Y	N	Y
25 ***Walsh***	N	N	N	Y	Y	Y	N	Y
26 Hinchey	Y	Y	Y	N	N	Y	Y	N
27 ***Reynolds***	N	N	N	Y	Y	Y	N	Y
28 Slaughter	Y	Y	Y	N	N	Y	Y	Y
29 LaFalce	Y	Y	N	N	N	Y	Y	Y
30 ***Quinn***	N	N	N	Y	Y	Y	N	Y
31 ***Houghton***	N	N	Y	N	N	Y	N	Y
NORTH CAROLINA								
1 Clayton	?	?	Y	N	N	Y	Y	N
2 Etheridge	Y	Y	Y	Y	Y	Y	Y	Y
3 ***Jones***	N	N	N	Y	Y	Y	N	Y
4 Price	N	N	Y	N	N	Y	Y	Y
5 ***Burr***	N	N	N	Y	Y	Y	N	Y
6 ***Coble***	N	N	N	Y	Y	Y	N	Y
7 McIntyre	Y	Y	N	Y	Y	Y	Y	Y
8 ***Hayes***	N	N	N	Y	Y	Y	N	Y
9 ***Myrick***	N	N	N	Y	Y	Y	N	Y
10 ***Ballenger***	N	N	N	Y	Y	Y	N	Y
11 ***Taylor***	N	N	N	Y	Y	Y	N	Y
12 Watt	Y	N	Y	N	N	Y	Y	N
NORTH DAKOTA								
AL Pomeroy	Y	Y	Y	Y	Y	Y	Y	Y
OHIO								
1 ***Chabot***	N	N	N	Y	Y	Y	N	Y
2 ***Portman***	N	N	N	Y	Y	Y	N	Y
3 Hall	?	?	?	?	?	?	?	?
4 ***Oxley***	?	N	N	Y	Y	Y	N	Y
5 ***Gillmor***	N	N	N	Y	Y	Y	N	Y
6 Strickland	Y	Y	Y	Y	Y	Y	Y	Y
7 ***Hobson***	N	N	N	Y	Y	Y	N	Y
8 ***Boehner***	N	N	N	Y	Y	?	N	Y
9 Kaptur	Y	N	Y	Y	Y	Y	Y	Y
10 Kucinich	Y	Y	Y	N	N	Y	Y	N
11 Jones	Y	Y	Y	N	N	Y	Y	N
12 ***Tiberi***	N	N	N	Y	Y	Y	N	Y
13 Brown	Y	Y	Y	N	N	Y	Y	N
14 Sawyer	Y	Y	Y	N	N	Y	Y	Y
15 ***Pryce***	N	N	Y	Y	Y	Y	N	Y
16 ***Regula***	N	N	N	Y	Y	Y	N	Y
17 Traficant	?	?	?	?	?	?	?	?
18 ***Ney***	N	N	N	Y	Y	Y	N	Y
19 ***LaTourette***	N	N	N	Y	Y	Y	N	Y
OKLAHOMA								
1 ***Sullivan***	N	N	N	Y	Y	Y	N	Y
2 Carson	Y	Y	Y	N	Y	Y	N	Y
3 ***Watkins***	N	N	N	Y	Y	Y	N	Y
4 ***Watts***	N	N	N	Y	Y	Y	N	Y
5 ***Istook***	N	N	N	Y	Y	Y	N	Y
6 ***Lucas***	N	N	N	Y	Y	Y	N	Y
OREGON								
1 Wu	Y	Y	Y	N	N	Y	Y	N
2 ***Walden***	N	N	Y	Y	Y	Y	N	Y
3 Blumenauer	Y	Y	Y	N	N	Y	Y	N
4 DeFazio	Y	Y	Y	Y	Y	Y	Y	N
5 Hooley	N	N	Y	N	N	Y	Y	Y
PENNSYLVANIA								
1 Brady	Y	Y	Y	N	Y	Y	Y	Y
2 Fattah	N	N	Y	N	N	Y	Y	N
3 Borski	N	Y	N	N	N	Y	Y	Y
4 ***Hart***	N	N	N	Y	Y	Y	N	Y
5 ***Peterson***	N	N	N	Y	Y	Y	N	Y
6 Holden	Y	Y	N	Y	Y	Y	Y	Y
7 ***Weldon***	?	N	N	Y	Y	Y	N	Y
8 ***Greenwood***	N	N	Y	Y	Y	Y	N	Y
9 ***Shuster, Bill***	N	N	N	Y	Y	Y	N	Y
10 ***Sherwood***	N	N	N	Y	Y	Y	N	Y
11 Kanjorski	N	N	N	N	Y	Y	Y	Y
12 Murtha	N	Y	N	N	Y	Y	Y	Y
13 Hoeffel	Y	Y	Y	N	N	Y	Y	Y
14 Coyne	?	?	Y	N	N	Y	Y	N
15 ***Toomey***	N	N	N	Y	Y	Y	N	Y
16 ***Pitts***	N	N	N	Y	Y	Y	N	Y
17 ***Gekas***	N	N	N	Y	Y	Y	N	Y
18 Doyle	Y	Y	N	N	N	Y	Y	Y
19 ***Platts***	N	N	N	Y	Y	Y	N	Y
20 Mascara	N	N	N	N	Y	Y	Y	Y
21 ***English***	N	N	N	Y	Y	Y	N	Y
RHODE ISLAND								
1 Kennedy	N	Y	Y	N	N	Y	Y	Y
2 Langevin	Y	Y	N	N	Y	Y	Y	Y
SOUTH CAROLINA								
1 ***Brown***	N	N	N	Y	Y	Y	N	Y
2 ***Wilson***	N	N	N	Y	Y	Y	N	Y
3 ***Graham***	N	N	N	Y	Y	Y	N	Y
4 ***DeMint***	N	N	N	Y	Y	Y	N	Y
5 Spratt	Y	Y	Y	Y	Y	Y	Y	Y
6 Clyburn	Y	Y	Y	N	N	Y	Y	Y
SOUTH DAKOTA								
AL ***Thune***	N	N	N	Y	Y	Y	N	Y
TENNESSEE								
1 ***Jenkins***	N	N	N	Y	Y	Y	N	Y
2 ***Duncan***	N	N	N	Y	Y	Y	N	Y
3 ***Wamp***	N	N	N	Y	Y	Y	N	Y
4 ***Hilleary***	N	N	N	Y	Y	Y	N	Y
5 Clement	N	N	Y	N	N	Y	Y	Y
6 Gordon	Y	Y	Y	Y	Y	Y	Y	Y
7 ***Bryant***	N	N	N	Y	Y	Y	N	Y
8 Tanner	Y	Y	Y	Y	Y	Y	Y	Y
9 Ford	Y	Y	Y	N	N	Y	Y	Y
TEXAS								
1 Sandlin	Y	Y	Y	N	Y	Y	N	Y
2 Turner	Y	Y	Y	N	Y	Y	N	Y
3 ***Johnson, Sam***	N	N	N	Y	Y	Y	N	Y
4 Hall	Y	Y	N	Y	Y	Y	N	Y
5 ***Sessions***	N	N	N	Y	Y	Y	N	Y
6 ***Barton***	N	N	N	Y	N	Y	N	Y
7 ***Culberson***	?	N	N	Y	Y	Y	N	Y
8 ***Brady***	?	?	N	Y	Y	Y	N	Y
9 Lampson	Y	Y	Y	N	Y	Y	Y	Y
10 Doggett	Y	Y	Y	N	N	Y	Y	N
11 Edwards	N	N	Y	N	Y	Y	Y	Y
12 ***Granger***	N	N	N	Y	Y	Y	N	Y
13 ***Thornberry***	N	N	N	N	Y	Y	N	Y
14 ***Paul***	N	N	N	N	Y	Y	N	N
15 Hinojosa	Y	Y	Y	N	N	Y	Y	Y
16 Reyes	?	?	?	?	?	?	?	?
17 Stenholm	Y	Y	N	Y	Y	Y	N	Y
18 Jackson-Lee	Y	Y	Y	N	N	Y	Y	N
19 ***Combest***	?	N	?	?	?	?	?	?
20 Gonzalez	Y	Y	Y	N	N	Y	Y	Y
21 ***Smith***	N	N	N	Y	Y	Y	N	Y
22 ***DeLay***	N	N	N	Y	Y	Y	N	Y
23 ***Bonilla***	N	N	N	Y	Y	Y	N	Y
24 Frost	N	N	Y	N	N	Y	Y	Y
25 Bentsen	Y	Y	Y	N	N	Y	Y	Y
26 ***Armey***	N	N	N	Y	Y	Y	N	Y
27 Ortiz	Y	Y	N	N	Y	Y	Y	Y
28 Rodriguez	Y	Y	Y	N	N	Y	Y	Y
29 Green	Y	Y	Y	N	Y	Y	Y	Y
30 Johnson, E.B.	Y	Y	Y	N	N	Y	Y	Y
UTAH								
1 ***Hansen***	N	N	N	Y	Y	Y	N	Y
2 Matheson	N	Y	Y	N	N	Y	Y	Y
3 ***Cannon***	?	?	?	?	?	?	?	?
VERMONT								
AL *Sanders*	Y	Y	Y	N	N	Y	Y	N
VIRGINIA								
1 ***Davis, Jo Ann***	N	N	N	Y	Y	Y	N	Y
2 ***Schrock***	N	N	N	Y	Y	Y	N	Y
3 Scott	N	Y	Y	N	N	Y	Y	Y
4 ***Forbes***	N	N	N	Y	Y	Y	N	Y
5 *Goode*	N	N	N	Y	Y	Y	N	Y
6 ***Goodlatte***	N	N	N	Y	Y	Y	N	Y
7 ***Cantor***	N	N	N	Y	Y	Y	N	Y
8 Moran	N	N	Y	N	N	Y	Y	Y
9 Boucher	Y	Y	Y	N	N	Y	Y	Y
10 ***Wolf***	N	N	N	Y	Y	Y	N	Y
11 ***Davis, T.***	N	N	N	Y	Y	Y	N	Y
WASHINGTON								
1 Inslee	Y	Y	Y	N	Y	Y	Y	Y
2 Larsen	Y	Y	Y	N	Y	Y	Y	Y
3 Baird	Y	Y	Y	N	N	Y	Y	Y
4 ***Hastings***	N	N	N	Y	Y	Y	N	Y
5 ***Nethercutt***	?	?	?	?	?	?	?	?
6 Dicks	Y	Y	Y	N	Y	Y	Y	Y
7 McDermott	Y	Y	Y	N	N	Y	Y	N
8 ***Dunn***	N	N	Y	Y	Y	Y	N	Y
9 Smith	N	N	Y	N	Y	Y	Y	Y
WEST VIRGINIA								
1 Mollohan	N	N	N	N	Y	Y	Y	Y
2 ***Capito***	N	N	Y	Y	Y	Y	N	Y
3 Rahall	Y	Y	N	N	Y	Y	Y	Y
WISCONSIN								
1 ***Ryan***	N	N	N	Y	Y	Y	N	Y
2 Baldwin	Y	Y	Y	N	N	Y	Y	N
3 Kind	Y	Y	Y	N	N	Y	Y	N
4 Kleczka	N	Y	Y	N	N	Y	Y	N
5 Barrett	Y	Y	Y	N	N	Y	Y	N
6 ***Petri***	N	N	N	Y	Y	Y	N	Y
7 Obey	Y	Y	Y	N	N	Y	Y	N
8 ***Green***	N	N	N	Y	Y	Y	N	Y
9 ***Sensenbrenner***	N	N	N	Y	Y	Y	N	Y
WYOMING								
AL ***Cubin***	N	N	N	Y	Y	Y	N	Y

Southern states - Ala., Ark., Fla., Ga., Ky., La., Miss., N.C., Okla., S.C., Tenn., Texas, Va.

Key

Y	Voted for (yea).
#	Paired for.
+	Announced for.
N	Voted against (nay).
X	Paired against.
–	Announced against.
P	Voted "present."
C	Voted "present" to avoid possible conflict of interest.
?	Did not vote or otherwise make a position known.

Democrats **Republicans**
Independents

159. HR3694. Increased Highway Fund/Passage. Young, R-Alaska, motion to suspend the rules and pass the bill to increase funding for the 1998 surface transportation law TEA-21 (PL 105-178) by $4.4 billion to a $27.7 billion base level for fiscal 2003. The change would make up for a shortfall in gasoline revenues, which pay for the transportation improvements. Motion agreed to 410-5: R 208-5; D 200-0 (ND 147-0, SD 53-0); I 2-0. A two-thirds majority of those present and voting (277 in this case) is required for passage under suspension of the rules. May 14, 2002.

160. HR 4069. Social Security Benefit Expansion for Widows/Passage. Shaw, R-Fla., motion to suspend the rules and pass the bill that would expand Social Security benefits for widows, including easing penalties on those whose spouses retire early, with reduced Social Security benefits, then die, leaving their spouses with reduced benefits for life. Passed 418-0: R 214-0; D 202-0 (ND 149-0, SD 53-0); I 2-0. A two-thirds majority of those present and voting (279 in this case) is required for passage under suspension of the rules. May 14, 2002.

161. Procedural Motion/Journal. Approval of the House Journal of Monday, May 13, 2002. Approved 371-40: R 199-10; D 170-30 (ND 121-27, SD 49-3); I 2-0. May 14, 2002.

162. HR 3994. Afghan Aid/Rule. Adoption of the rule (H Res 419) to provide for House floor consideration of the bill that would authorize $1.05 billion in aid to Afghanistan over the next four years to support humanitarian programs, counternarcotics efforts, democracy building, reconstruction and other security activities. Adopted 415-0: R 211-0; D 202-0 (ND 150-0, SD 52-0); I 2-0. May 15, 2002.

163. Procedural Motion/Journal. Approval of the House Journal of Tuesday, May 14, 2002. Approved 352-55: R 190-15; D 160-40 (ND 114-34, SD 46-6); I 2-0. May 15, 2002.

164. HR 4737. Welfare Renewal/Consideration of Rule. Adoption of the resolution (H Res 420) that would waive the two-thirds vote requirement for same-day consideration of the rule (H Res 422) to provide for House floor consideration of the bill that would authorize $16.5 billion to renew the Temporary Assistance for Needy Families block grant program through fiscal 2007 and require new welfare aid conditions. Adopted 219-200: R 216-0; D 2-199 (ND 1-148, SD 1-51); I 1-1. May 15, 2002.

	159	160	161	162	163	164
ALABAMA						
1 *Callahan*	Y	Y	Y	Y	Y	Y
2 *Everett*	Y	Y	Y	Y	Y	Y
3 *Riley*	+	+	Y	Y	?	Y
4 *Aderholt*	Y	Y	N	Y	N	Y
5 Cramer	Y	Y	Y	Y	Y	N
6 *Bachus*	Y	Y	Y	Y	Y	Y
7 Hilliard	Y	Y	N	Y	N	N
ALASKA						
AL *Young*	Y	Y	Y	Y	Y	Y
ARIZONA						
1 *Flake*	N	Y	Y	Y	Y	Y
2 Pastor	Y	Y	Y	Y	Y	N
3 *Stump*	?	Y	Y	Y	Y	Y
4 *Shadegg*	N	Y	Y	Y	N	Y
5 *Kolbe*	Y	Y	Y	Y	Y	?
6 *Hayworth*	Y	Y	Y	Y	Y	Y
ARKANSAS						
1 Berry	Y	Y	Y	Y	Y	N
2 Snyder	Y	Y	Y	Y	Y	N
3 *Boozman*	Y	Y	Y	Y	Y	Y
4 Ross	Y	Y	Y	Y	Y	N
CALIFORNIA						
1 Thompson	Y	Y	N	N	N	N
2 *Herger*	Y	Y	Y	Y	Y	Y
3 *Ose*	Y	Y	Y	Y	Y	Y
4 *Doolittle*	Y	Y	Y	Y	Y	Y
5 Matsui	Y	Y	Y	Y	Y	N
6 Woolsey	Y	Y	Y	Y	Y	N
7 Miller, George	Y	Y	N	?	?	?
8 Pelosi	Y	Y	Y	Y	Y	N
9 Lee	+	Y	Y	Y	Y	N
10 Tauscher	Y	Y	Y	Y	Y	N
11 *Pombo*	Y	Y	Y	Y	Y	Y
12 Lantos	Y	Y	Y	Y	Y	N
13 Stark	Y	Y	Y	Y	N	?
14 Eshoo	Y	Y	Y	Y	Y	N
15 Honda	Y	Y	Y	?	Y	N
16 Lofgren	Y	Y	Y	Y	Y	N
17 Farr	Y	Y	Y	Y	Y	N
18 Condit	Y	Y	N	Y	Y	N
19 *Radanovich*	Y	Y	Y	Y	Y	Y
20 Dooley	Y	Y	Y	Y	Y	N
21 *Thomas*	Y	Y	Y	Y	Y	Y
22 Capps	Y	Y	Y	Y	Y	N
23 *Gallegly*	Y	Y	Y	Y	Y	Y
24 Sherman	Y	Y	Y	Y	Y	N
25 *McKeon*	Y	Y	Y	Y	Y	Y
26 Berman	Y	Y	Y	Y	Y	N
27 Schiff	Y	Y	Y	Y	Y	N
28 *Dreier*	Y	Y	Y	Y	Y	Y
29 Waxman	Y	Y	Y	Y	Y	N
30 Becerra	Y	Y	Y	Y	Y	N
31 Solis	Y	Y	Y	Y	Y	N
32 Watson	Y	Y	Y	Y	Y	N
33 Roybal-Allard	Y	Y	Y	Y	Y	N
34 Napolitano	Y	Y	Y	Y	?	?
35 Waters	Y	Y	Y	Y	N	N
36 Harman	Y	Y	Y	Y	Y	N
37 Millender-McD.	Y	Y	Y	Y	Y	N
38 *Horn*	Y	Y	Y	Y	Y	Y

	159	160	161	162	163	164
39 *Royce*	N	Y	Y	Y	Y	Y
40 *Lewis*	Y	Y	Y	Y	Y	Y
41 *Miller, Gary*	Y	Y	Y	Y	Y	Y
42 Baca	Y	Y	Y	Y	Y	N
43 *Calvert*	Y	Y	Y	Y	Y	Y
44 *Bono*	Y	Y	Y	Y	Y	Y
45 *Rohrabacher*	Y	Y	Y	Y	Y	Y
46 Sanchez	Y	Y	Y	Y	Y	N
47 *Cox*	Y	Y	Y	Y	Y	Y
48 *Issa*	Y	Y	Y	Y	Y	Y
49 Davis	Y	Y	Y	Y	Y	N
50 Filner	Y	Y	N	Y	N	N
51 *Cunningham*	Y	Y	?	Y	?	Y
52 *Hunter*	Y	Y	Y	Y	Y	Y
COLORADO						
1 DeGette	Y	Y	Y	Y	Y	N
2 Udall	Y	Y	Y	Y	Y	N
3 *McInnis*	Y	Y	Y	Y	Y	Y
4 *Schaffer*	?	?	Y	Y	?	Y
5 *Hefley*	Y	Y	N	Y	N	Y
6 *Tancredo*	Y	Y	P	Y	P	Y
CONNECTICUT						
1 Larson	Y	Y	Y	Y	Y	N
2 *Simmons*	Y	Y	Y	Y	Y	Y
3 DeLauro	Y	Y	Y	Y	Y	N
4 *Shays*	Y	Y	Y	Y	Y	Y
5 Maloney	Y	Y	Y	Y	Y	N
6 *Johnson*	Y	Y	Y	Y	Y	Y
DELAWARE						
AL *Castle*	Y	Y	Y	Y	Y	Y
FLORIDA						
1 *Miller, J.*	Y	Y	Y	Y	Y	Y
2 Boyd	Y	Y	Y	Y	Y	N
3 Brown	Y	Y	Y	Y	Y	N
4 *Crenshaw*	Y	Y	Y	Y	Y	Y
5 Thurman	Y	Y	Y	Y	Y	N
6 *Stearns*	Y	Y	Y	Y	Y	Y
7 *Mica*	Y	Y	?	Y	Y	Y
8 *Keller*	Y	Y	Y	?	Y	Y
9 *Bilirakis*	Y	Y	Y	Y	Y	Y
10 *Young*	Y	Y	Y	Y	Y	Y
11 Davis	Y	Y	Y	Y	Y	N
12 *Putnam*	Y	Y	Y	Y	Y	Y
13 *Miller, D.*	Y	Y	Y	Y	Y	Y
14 *Goss*	Y	Y	Y	Y	Y	Y
15 *Weldon*	Y	Y	Y	Y	Y	Y
16 *Foley*	Y	Y	Y	Y	Y	Y
17 Meek	Y	Y	Y	Y	N	N
18 *Ros-Lehtinen*	Y	Y	Y	Y	Y	Y
19 Wexler	Y	Y	Y	Y	Y	N
20 Deutsch	Y	Y	Y	Y	Y	N
21 *Diaz-Balart*	+	+	Y	Y	Y	Y
22 *Shaw*	Y	Y	Y	Y	Y	Y
23 Hastings	Y	Y	Y	Y	N	N
GEORGIA						
1 *Kingston*	Y	Y	Y	Y	Y	Y
2 Bishop	Y	Y	Y	Y	Y	N
3 *Collins*	Y	Y	Y	Y	Y	Y
4 McKinney	Y	Y	Y	?	Y	N
5 Lewis	Y	Y	Y	Y	Y	N
6 *Isakson*	Y	Y	Y	Y	Y	Y
7 *Barr*	Y	Y	Y	Y	Y	Y
8 *Chambliss*	Y	Y	Y	Y	Y	Y
9 *Deal*	Y	Y	Y	?	Y	Y
10 *Norwood*	Y	Y	Y	Y	Y	Y
11 *Linder*	Y	Y	Y	Y	Y	Y
HAWAII						
1 Abercrombie	Y	Y	Y	Y	Y	Y
2 Mink	Y	Y	Y	Y	Y	N
IDAHO						
1 *Otter*	Y	Y	Y	Y	Y	Y
2 *Simpson*	Y	Y	Y	Y	Y	Y
ILLINOIS						
1 Rush	Y	Y	Y	Y	Y	N
2 Jackson	Y	Y	Y	Y	Y	N
3 Lipinski	Y	Y	Y	Y	Y	N
4 Gutierrez	Y	Y	Y	Y	Y	N
5 Blagojevich	?	?	?	Y	Y	Y
6 *Hyde*	Y	Y	Y	Y	Y	Y
7 Davis	Y	Y	Y	Y	Y	N
8 *Crane*	Y	Y	N	Y	N	Y
9 Schakowsky	Y	Y	Y	Y	Y	N
10 *Kirk*	Y	Y	Y	Y	Y	Y
11 *Weller*	Y	Y	N	Y	N	Y
12 Costello	Y	Y	N	N	N	N
13 *Biggert*	Y	Y	Y	Y	Y	Y

ND Northern Democrats   SD Southern Democrats

	159	160	161	162	163	164
14 ***Hastert***						
15 ***Johnson***	Y	Y	Y	Y	Y	Y
16 ***Manzullo***	Y	Y	Y	Y	Y	Y
17 Evans	Y	Y	Y	Y	Y	N
18 ***LaHood***	Y	Y	Y	Y	Y	Y
19 Phelps	Y	Y	Y	Y	Y	N
20 ***Shimkus***	Y	Y	Y	Y	Y	Y
INDIANA						
1 Visclosky	Y	Y	N	Y	N	N
2 ***Pence***	Y	Y	Y	Y	Y	Y
3 Roemer	Y	Y	Y	Y	Y	N
4 ***Souder***	Y	Y	?	Y	Y	Y
5 ***Buyer***	Y	Y	Y	Y	Y	Y
6 ***Burton***	?	?	?	?	?	?
7 ***Kerns***	Y	Y	Y	Y	Y	Y
8 ***Hostettler***	Y	Y	Y	Y	Y	Y
9 Hill	Y	Y	Y	Y	Y	N
10 Carson	Y	Y	Y	Y	Y	N
IOWA						
1 ***Leach***	Y	Y	Y	Y	Y	Y
2 ***Nussle***	Y	Y	Y	Y	Y	Y
3 Boswell	Y	Y	Y	Y	Y	N
4 ***Ganske***	Y	Y	Y	Y	Y	Y
5 ***Latham***	Y	Y	Y	Y	N	Y
KANSAS						
1 ***Moran***	Y	Y	N	Y	N	Y
2 ***Ryun***	Y	Y	Y	Y	Y	Y
3 Moore	Y	Y	N	Y	N	N
4 ***Tiahrt***	Y	Y	Y	Y	Y	Y
KENTUCKY						
1 ***Whitfield***	Y	Y	Y	Y	Y	Y
2 ***Lewis***	Y	Y	Y	Y	Y	Y
3 ***Northup***	Y	Y	Y	Y	Y	Y
4 Lucas	Y	Y	Y	Y	Y	N
5 ***Rogers***	Y	Y	Y	Y	Y	Y
6 ***Fletcher***	Y	Y	Y	Y	?	Y
LOUISIANA						
1 ***Vitter***	Y	Y	Y	Y	Y	Y
2 Jefferson	Y	Y	Y	Y	Y	N
3 ***Tauzin***	Y	Y	Y	Y	Y	Y
4 ***McCrery***	Y	Y	Y	Y	Y	Y
5 ***Cooksey***	Y	Y	Y	Y	Y	Y
6 ***Baker***	Y	Y	Y	Y	Y	Y
7 John	Y	Y	Y	Y	Y	N
MAINE						
1 Allen	Y	Y	Y	Y	Y	N
2 Baldacci	Y	Y	Y	Y	Y	N
MARYLAND						
1 ***Gilchrest***	Y	Y	Y	Y	Y	Y
2 ***Ehrlich***	Y	Y	Y	Y	Y	Y
3 Cardin	Y	Y	Y	Y	Y	N
4 Wynn	Y	Y	Y	Y	Y	N
5 Hoyer	Y	Y	Y	Y	Y	N
6 ***Bartlett***	Y	Y	Y	Y	Y	Y
7 Cummings	Y	Y	Y	Y	Y	N
8 ***Morella***	Y	Y	Y	Y	Y	Y
MASSACHUSETTS						
1 Olver	Y	Y	N	Y	N	N
2 Neal	Y	Y	Y	Y	Y	N
3 McGovern	Y	Y	Y	Y	Y	N
4 Frank	Y	Y	Y	Y	Y	N
5 Meehan	Y	Y	Y	Y	Y	N
6 Tierney	Y	Y	Y	Y	Y	N
7 Markey	Y	Y	N	Y	N	N
8 Capuano	Y	Y	N	Y	N	N
9 Lynch	Y	Y	Y	Y	Y	N
10 Delahunt	Y	Y	Y	Y	Y	N
MICHIGAN						
1 Stupak	Y	Y	N	?	?	?
2 ***Hoekstra***	Y	Y	Y	Y	Y	Y
3 ***Ehlers***	Y	Y	Y	Y	Y	Y
4 ***Camp***	Y	Y	Y	Y	Y	Y
5 Barcia	Y	Y	Y	Y	Y	N
6 ***Upton***	Y	Y	Y	Y	Y	Y
7 ***Smith***	Y	Y	?	Y	Y	Y
8 ***Rogers***	Y	Y	Y	Y	Y	Y
9 Kildee	Y	Y	Y	Y	Y	N
10 Bonior	Y	Y	Y	Y	Y	N
11 ***Knollenberg***	Y	Y	Y	Y	Y	Y
12 Levin	Y	Y	Y	Y	Y	N
13 Rivers	Y	Y	Y	Y	Y	N
14 Conyers	Y	Y	Y	Y	Y	N
15 Kilpatrick	Y	Y	Y	Y	Y	N
16 Dingell	Y	Y	Y	Y	Y	N
MINNESOTA						
1 ***Gutknecht***	Y	Y	Y	Y	N	Y
2 ***Kennedy***	Y	Y	Y	Y	N	Y
3 ***Ramstad***	Y	Y	N	Y	N	Y
4 McCollum	Y	Y	Y	Y	Y	N
5 Sabo	Y	Y	N	?	?	N
6 Luther	Y	Y	Y	Y	Y	N
7 Peterson	?	Y	N	Y	N	N
8 Oberstar	Y	Y	N	Y	N	N
MISSISSIPPI						
1 ***Wicker***	Y	Y	N	?	Y	Y
2 Thompson	Y	Y	Y	Y	N	N
3 ***Pickering***	Y	Y	Y	?	?	Y
4 Shows	Y	Y	Y	Y	Y	N
5 Taylor	Y	Y	N	Y	N	N
MISSOURI						
1 Clay	Y	Y	Y	Y	Y	N
2 ***Akin***	Y	Y	Y	Y	Y	Y
3 Gephardt	Y	Y	Y	Y	N	N
4 Skelton	Y	Y	Y	Y	Y	N
5 McCarthy	Y	Y	Y	Y	Y	N
6 ***Graves***	Y	Y	Y	Y	Y	Y
7 ***Blunt***	Y	Y	Y	?	?	Y
8 ***Emerson***	Y	Y	Y	Y	?	Y
9 ***Hulshof***	Y	Y	Y	Y	Y	Y
MONTANA						
AL ***Rehberg***	Y	Y	?	Y	Y	Y
NEBRASKA						
1 ***Bereuter***	Y	Y	Y	Y	Y	Y
2 ***Terry***	?	?	?	Y	Y	Y
3 ***Osborne***	Y	Y	Y	Y	Y	Y
NEVADA						
1 Berkley	Y	Y	Y	Y	Y	N
2 ***Gibbons***	Y	Y	Y	Y	Y	?
NEW HAMPSHIRE						
1 ***Sununu***	Y	Y	Y	Y	Y	Y
2 ***Bass***	Y	Y	Y	Y	Y	Y
NEW JERSEY						
1 Andrews	Y	Y	Y	Y	Y	N
2 ***LoBiondo***	Y	Y	N	Y	N	Y
3 ***Saxton***	Y	Y	Y	Y	Y	Y
4 ***Smith***	Y	Y	Y	Y	Y	Y
5 ***Roukema***	Y	Y	Y	Y	Y	Y
6 Pallone	Y	Y	Y	Y	N	N
7 ***Ferguson***	Y	Y	Y	Y	Y	Y
8 Pascrell	Y	Y	Y	Y	Y	N
9 Rothman	?	?	Y	Y	Y	N
10 Payne	?	?	?	Y	Y	N
11 ***Frelinghuysen***	Y	Y	Y	Y	Y	Y
12 Holt	Y	Y	Y	Y	N	N
13 Menendez	Y	Y	Y	Y	N	N
NEW MEXICO						
1 ***Wilson***	Y	Y	Y	Y	Y	Y
2 ***Skeen***	Y	Y	Y	Y	Y	Y
3 Udall	Y	Y	N	Y	N	N
NEW YORK						
1 ***Grucci***	Y	Y	Y	Y	Y	Y
2 Israel	Y	Y	Y	Y	Y	N
3 ***King***	Y	Y	Y	Y	Y	Y
4 McCarthy	Y	Y	Y	Y	Y	N
5 Ackerman	?	?	?	Y	Y	N
6 Meeks	Y	Y	Y	Y	N	N
7 Crowley	Y	Y	Y	Y	Y	N
8 Nadler	Y	Y	Y	Y	Y	N
9 Weiner	Y	Y	Y	Y	Y	N
10 Towns	Y	Y	?	Y	Y	N
11 Owens	Y	Y	Y	Y	Y	N
12 Velázquez	Y	Y	Y	Y	N	N
13 ***Fossella***	Y	Y	Y	Y	Y	Y
14 Maloney	Y	Y	Y	Y	Y	N
15 Rangel	Y	Y	Y	?	?	N
16 Serrano	Y	Y	Y	Y	Y	N
17 Engel	Y	Y	Y	Y	Y	N
18 Lowey	Y	Y	Y	Y	Y	N
19 ***Kelly***	Y	Y	Y	Y	Y	Y
20 ***Gilman***	Y	Y	Y	Y	Y	Y
21 McNulty	Y	Y	Y	Y	N	N
22 ***Sweeney***	?	?	?	Y	N	Y
23 ***Boehlert***	Y	Y	Y	Y	Y	Y
24 ***McHugh***	Y	Y	Y	Y	Y	Y
25 ***Walsh***	Y	Y	Y	Y	Y	Y
26 Hinchey	Y	Y	Y	Y	N	N
27 ***Reynolds***	Y	Y	Y	Y	Y	Y
28 Slaughter	Y	Y	Y	Y	N	N
29 LaFalce	Y	Y	Y	Y	N	N
30 ***Quinn***	Y	Y	Y	?	?	Y
31 ***Houghton***	Y	Y	Y	Y	Y	Y
NORTH CAROLINA						
1 Clayton	Y	Y	Y	Y	Y	N
2 Etheridge	Y	Y	Y	Y	Y	N
3 ***Jones***	Y	Y	Y	Y	Y	Y
4 Price	Y	Y	Y	Y	Y	N
5 ***Burr***	Y	Y	Y	Y	Y	Y
6 ***Coble***	Y	Y	Y	Y	Y	Y
7 McIntyre	+	+	+	Y	Y	N
8 ***Hayes***	Y	Y	Y	Y	Y	Y
9 ***Myrick***	Y	Y	Y	Y	Y	Y
10 ***Ballenger***	Y	Y	Y	Y	Y	Y
11 ***Taylor***	Y	Y	Y	Y	Y	Y
12 Watt	Y	Y	Y	Y	Y	N
NORTH DAKOTA						
AL Pomeroy	Y	Y	Y	Y	Y	N
OHIO						
1 ***Chabot***	Y	Y	Y	Y	Y	Y
2 ***Portman***	Y	Y	Y	Y	Y	Y
3 Hall	Y	Y	Y	?	?	?
4 ***Oxley***	Y	Y	Y	Y	Y	Y
5 ***Gillmor***	Y	Y	N	Y	N	Y
6 Strickland	Y	Y	N	Y	Y	N
7 ***Hobson***	Y	Y	Y	Y	Y	Y
8 ***Boehner***	Y	Y	Y	Y	Y	Y
9 Kaptur	Y	Y	Y	Y	Y	N
10 Kucinich	Y	Y	N	Y	N	N
11 Jones	Y	Y	Y	Y	N	N
12 ***Tiberi***	Y	Y	Y	Y	Y	Y
13 Brown	Y	Y	N	Y	Y	N
14 Sawyer	Y	Y	Y	Y	Y	N
15 ***Pryce***	Y	Y	Y	Y	Y	Y
16 ***Regula***	Y	Y	Y	Y	Y	Y
17 Traficant	?	?	?	?	?	?
18 ***Ney***	Y	Y	Y	Y	Y	Y
19 ***LaTourette***	Y	Y	Y	Y	Y	Y
OKLAHOMA						
1 ***Sullivan***	Y	Y	Y	Y	Y	Y
2 Carson	Y	Y	Y	Y	Y	N
3 ***Watkins***	Y	Y	Y	Y	Y	Y
4 ***Watts***	Y	Y	Y	Y	N	Y
5 ***Istook***	Y	Y	Y	Y	Y	Y
6 ***Lucas***	Y	Y	Y	Y	Y	Y
OREGON						
1 Wu	Y	Y	N	Y	Y	N
2 ***Walden***	Y	Y	Y	Y	Y	Y
3 Blumenauer	Y	Y	Y	Y	Y	N
4 DeFazio	Y	Y	N	Y	N	N
5 Hooley	Y	Y	Y	Y	N	N
PENNSYLVANIA						
1 Brady	+	+	+	Y	N	N
2 Fattah	Y	Y	N	Y	Y	N
3 Borski	Y	Y	N	Y	N	N
4 ***Hart***	Y	Y	Y	Y	Y	Y
5 ***Peterson***	Y	Y	Y	Y	Y	?
6 Holden	Y	Y	Y	Y	Y	N
7 ***Weldon***	Y	Y	Y	Y	Y	Y
8 ***Greenwood***	Y	Y	Y	Y	Y	Y
9 ***Shuster, Bill***	Y	Y	Y	Y	Y	Y
10 ***Sherwood***	Y	Y	Y	?	?	Y
11 Kanjorski	Y	Y	Y	Y	Y	N
12 Murtha	?	?	?	?	?	?
13 Hoeffel	Y	Y	Y	Y	Y	N
14 Coyne	Y	Y	Y	Y	Y	N
15 ***Toomey***	Y	Y	Y	?	Y	Y
16 ***Pitts***	Y	Y	Y	Y	?	Y
17 ***Gekas***	Y	Y	Y	Y	Y	Y
18 Doyle	Y	Y	Y	Y	Y	N
19 ***Platts***	Y	Y	Y	Y	Y	Y
20 Mascara	?	?	?	Y	Y	?
21 ***English***	Y	Y	N	Y	N	Y
RHODE ISLAND						
1 Kennedy	Y	Y	Y	Y	Y	N
2 Langevin	Y	Y	Y	Y	Y	N
SOUTH CAROLINA						
1 ***Brown***	Y	Y	Y	Y	Y	Y
2 ***Wilson***	Y	Y	Y	Y	Y	Y
3 ***Graham***	Y	Y	Y	Y	Y	Y
4 ***DeMint***	Y	Y	Y	Y	Y	Y
5 Spratt	Y	Y	Y	Y	Y	N
6 Clyburn	Y	Y	Y	Y	Y	N
SOUTH DAKOTA						
AL ***Thune***	Y	Y	Y	Y	Y	Y
TENNESSEE						
1 ***Jenkins***	Y	Y	Y	Y	Y	Y
2 ***Duncan***	Y	Y	Y	Y	Y	Y
3 ***Wamp***	Y	Y	Y	Y	Y	Y
4 ***Hilleary***	Y	Y	Y	Y	Y	Y
5 Clement	Y	Y	Y	?	?	N
6 Gordon	Y	Y	Y	Y	Y	N
7 ***Bryant***	Y	Y	Y	Y	Y	Y
8 Tanner	Y	Y	Y	Y	Y	N
9 Ford	Y	Y	Y	Y	Y	N
TEXAS						
1 Sandlin	Y	Y	Y	Y	Y	N
2 Turner	Y	Y	Y	Y	Y	Y
3 ***Johnson, Sam***	Y	Y	Y	Y	Y	Y
4 Hall	Y	Y	Y	Y	Y	N
5 ***Sessions***	N	Y	Y	Y	Y	Y
6 ***Barton***	Y	Y	Y	Y	Y	Y
7 ***Culberson***	Y	Y	Y	Y	Y	Y
8 ***Brady***	Y	Y	Y	Y	Y	Y
9 Lampson	Y	Y	?	Y	Y	N
10 Doggett	Y	Y	Y	Y	Y	N
11 Edwards	Y	Y	Y	Y	Y	N
12 ***Granger***	Y	Y	Y	Y	Y	Y
13 ***Thornberry***	Y	Y	Y	Y	?	?
14 ***Paul***	N	Y	Y	Y	Y	Y
15 Hinojosa	Y	Y	Y	Y	Y	N
16 Reyes	Y	Y	Y	Y	?	?
17 Stenholm	Y	Y	N	Y	N	N
18 Jackson-Lee	Y	Y	Y	Y	Y	N
19 ***Combest***	Y	Y	Y	Y	Y	Y
20 Gonzalez	Y	Y	Y	Y	Y	N
21 ***Smith***	Y	Y	Y	Y	Y	Y
22 ***DeLay***	Y	Y	Y	Y	Y	Y
23 ***Bonilla***	Y	Y	Y	Y	Y	Y
24 Frost	Y	Y	Y	Y	Y	N
25 Bentsen	Y	Y	Y	Y	Y	N
26 ***Armey***	Y	Y	Y	Y	Y	Y
27 Ortiz	Y	Y	Y	Y	Y	N
28 Rodriguez	Y	Y	Y	Y	Y	N
29 Green	Y	Y	Y	Y	Y	N
30 Johnson, E.B.	Y	Y	Y	Y	Y	N
UTAH						
1 ***Hansen***	Y	Y	Y	Y	Y	Y
2 Matheson	Y	Y	N	Y	?	N
3 ***Cannon***	?	?	?	?	?	Y
VERMONT						
AL *Sanders*	Y	Y	Y	Y	Y	N
VIRGINIA						
1 ***Davis, Jo Ann***	Y	Y	Y	Y	Y	Y
2 ***Schrock***	Y	Y	Y	Y	Y	Y
3 Scott	Y	Y	Y	Y	Y	N
4 ***Forbes***	Y	Y	Y	Y	Y	Y
5 *Goode*	Y	Y	Y	Y	Y	Y
6 ***Goodlatte***	Y	Y	Y	Y	Y	Y
7 ***Cantor***	Y	Y	Y	Y	Y	Y
8 Moran	Y	Y	Y	Y	Y	N
9 Boucher	Y	Y	Y	Y	Y	?
10 ***Wolf***	Y	Y	Y	Y	Y	Y
11 ***Davis, T.***	Y	Y	Y	Y	Y	Y
WASHINGTON						
1 Inslee	Y	Y	Y	Y	Y	N
2 Larsen	Y	Y	N	Y	N	N
3 Baird	Y	Y	N	Y	N	N
4 ***Hastings***	Y	Y	Y	Y	Y	Y
5 ***Nethercutt***	Y	Y	Y	Y	Y	Y
6 Dicks	Y	Y	?	Y	Y	N
7 McDermott	Y	Y	N	Y	N	N
8 ***Dunn***	Y	Y	Y	Y	Y	Y
9 Smith	Y	Y	Y	Y	Y	N
WEST VIRGINIA						
1 Mollohan	Y	Y	Y	Y	Y	N
2 ***Capito***	Y	Y	Y	Y	Y	Y
3 Rahall	Y	Y	Y	Y	Y	N
WISCONSIN						
1 ***Ryan***	Y	Y	Y	Y	Y	Y
2 Baldwin	Y	Y	N	Y	N	N
3 Kind	Y	Y	Y	Y	Y	N
4 Kleczka	Y	Y	Y	Y	Y	N
5 Barrett	Y	Y	Y	Y	Y	N
6 ***Petri***	Y	Y	Y	Y	?	Y
7 Obey	Y	Y	Y	Y	N	N
8 ***Green***	Y	Y	Y	Y	Y	Y
9 ***Sensenbrenner***	Y	Y	Y	Y	Y	Y
WYOMING						
AL ***Cubin***	Y	Y	Y	Y	Y	Y

Southern states - Ala., Ark., Fla., Ga., Ky., La., Miss., N.C., Okla., S.C., Tenn., Texas, Va.

Key

Y	Voted for (yea).
#	Paired for.
+	Announced for.
N	Voted against (nay).
X	Paired against.
–	Announced against.
P	Voted "present."
C	Voted "present" to avoid possible conflict of interest.
?	Did not vote or otherwise make a position known.

Democrats **Republicans** *Independents*

---

165. HR 4737. Welfare Renewal/Previous Question. Motion to order the previous question (thus ending debate and possibility of amendment) on the rule (H Res 422) to provide for House floor consideration of the bill that would authorize $16.5 billion to renew the Temporary Assistance for Needy Families block grant program through fiscal 2007 and require new welfare aid conditions. Motion agreed to 213-204: R 212-0; D 0-203 (ND 0-151, SD 0-52); I 1-1. May 15, 2002.

166. HR 4737. Welfare Renewal/Rule. Adoption of the rule (H Res 422) to provide for House floor consideration of the bill that would authorize $16.5 billion to renew the Temporary Assistance for Needy Families block grant program through fiscal 2007 and require new welfare aid conditions. Adopted 214-205: R 213-1; D 0-203 (ND 0-151, SD 0-52); I 1-1. May 15, 2002.

167. Procedural Motion/Journal. Approval of the House Journal of Wednesday, May 15, 2002. Approved 330-63: R 191-14; D 138-49 (ND 101-39, SD 37-10); I 1-0. May 16, 2002.

168. HR 4737. Welfare Renewal/Cardin Substitute. Cardin, D-Md., amendment that would increase child care funding by $11 billion over the next five years, maintain the 30-hour-per-week work requirement on individual beneficiaries, and allow legal immigrants to receive benefits. Block grant funding would be increased annually to keep up with inflation and education and training programs could count toward a state's participation rate. Rejected 198-222: R 4-210; D 194-10 (ND 146-7, SD 48-3); I 0-2. May 16, 2002.

169. HR 4737. Welfare Renewal/Recommit. Maloney, D-Conn., motion to recommit to the House Ways and Means Committee with instructions that it be reported back with language to strike the existing section 208 of the bill and to insert a new section 208 setting new levels for entitlement funding. Motion rejected 207-219: R 0-218; D 206-0 (ND 154-0, SD 52-0); I 1-1. May 16, 2002.

170. HR 4737. Welfare Renewal/Passage. Passage of the bill that would authorize $16.5 billion to renew the Temporary Assistance for Needy Families block grant program through fiscal 2007 and require new welfare aid conditions. The bill would require individuals to work 40 hours per week to be eligible for assistance and require states to have 70 percent or more of their families working by 2007. It would authorize additional funding for child care and marriage promotion activities. The bill also would allow states to combine different types of block grants but bar them from using a waiver to transfer funds from one welfare account to another. Motion agreed to 229-197: R 214-4; D 14-192 (ND 7-147, SD 7-45); I 1-1. A two-thirds majority of those present and voting (282 in this case) is required for passage under suspension of the rules. A "yea" was a vote in support of the president's position. May 16, 2002.

	165	166	167	168	169	170
ALABAMA						
1 *Callahan*	Y	Y	Y	N	N	Y
2 *Everett*	Y	Y	Y	N	N	Y
3 *Riley*	Y	Y	Y	N	N	Y
4 *Aderholt*	Y	Y	Y	N	N	Y
5 Cramer	N	N	Y	Y	Y	Y
6 *Bachus*	?	?	Y	N	N	Y
7 Hilliard	N	N	N	Y	Y	N
ALASKA						
AL *Young*	Y	Y	?	N	N	Y
ARIZONA						
1 *Flake*	Y	Y	Y	N	N	Y
2 Pastor	N	N	?	Y	Y	N
3 *Stump*	?	?	Y	N	N	Y
4 *Shadegg*	Y	Y	Y	N	N	Y
5 *Kolbe*	?	?	Y	N	N	Y
6 *Hayworth*	Y	Y	Y	N	N	Y
ARKANSAS						
1 Berry	N	N	Y	Y	Y	N
2 Snyder	N	N	N	Y	Y	N
3 *Boozman*	Y	Y	Y	N	N	Y
4 Ross	N	N	Y	Y	Y	N
CALIFORNIA						
1 Thompson	N	N	N	Y	Y	N
2 *Herger*	Y	Y	Y	N	N	Y
3 *Ose*	Y	Y	Y	N	N	Y
4 *Doolittle*	Y	Y	Y	N	N	Y
5 Matsui	N	N	Y	Y	Y	N
6 Woolsey	N	N	Y	Y	Y	N
7 Miller, George	?	N	N	Y	Y	N
8 Pelosi	N	N	Y	Y	Y	N
9 Lee	N	N	Y	Y	Y	N
10 Tauscher	N	N	N	Y	Y	N
11 *Pombo*	Y	Y	?	?	?	?
12 Lantos	N	N	Y	Y	Y	N
13 Stark	N	N	?	Y	Y	N
14 Eshoo	N	N	Y	Y	Y	N
15 Honda	N	N	Y	Y	Y	N
16 Lofgren	N	N	Y	Y	Y	N
17 Farr	N	N	Y	Y	Y	N
18 Condit	N	N	?	Y	Y	N
19 *Radanovich*	Y	Y	Y	N	N	Y
20 Dooley	N	N	Y	Y	Y	N
21 *Thomas*	Y	Y	Y	N	N	Y
22 Capps	N	N	Y	Y	Y	N
23 *Gallegly*	Y	Y	Y	N	N	Y
24 Sherman	N	N	Y	Y	Y	N
25 *McKeon*	Y	Y	Y	N	N	Y
26 Berman	N	N	Y	Y	Y	N
27 Schiff	N	N	Y	Y	Y	N
28 *Dreier*	Y	Y	Y	N	N	Y
29 Waxman	N	N	Y	Y	Y	N
30 Becerra	N	N	Y	Y	Y	N
31 Solis	N	N	Y	Y	Y	N
32 Watson	N	N	Y	Y	Y	N
33 Roybal-Allard	N	N	Y	Y	Y	N
34 Napolitano	N	N	Y	Y	Y	N
35 Waters	N	N	N	N	N	N
36 Harman	N	–	Y	Y	Y	N
37 Millender-McD.	N	N	Y	?	Y	N
38 Horn	Y	Y	Y	N	N	Y

	165	166	167	168	169	170
39 *Royce*	Y	Y	Y	N	N	Y
40 *Lewis*	Y	Y	Y	N	N	Y
41 *Miller, Gary*	Y	Y	Y	N	N	Y
42 Baca	N	N	Y	Y	Y	N
43 *Calvert*	Y	Y	Y	N	N	Y
44 *Bono*	Y	Y	Y	N	N	Y
45 *Rohrabacher*	Y	Y	Y	N	N	Y
46 Sanchez	N	N	Y	Y	Y	N
47 *Cox*	Y	Y	Y	N	N	Y
48 *Issa*	Y	Y	Y	N	N	Y
49 Davis	N	N	Y	Y	Y	N
50 Filner	N	N	N	Y	Y	N
51 *Cunningham*	?	Y	Y	N	N	Y
52 *Hunter*	Y	Y	?	N	N	Y
COLORADO						
1 DeGette	N	N	Y	Y	Y	N
2 Udall	N	N	N	Y	Y	N
3 *McInnis*	Y	Y	Y	N	N	Y
4 *Schaffer*	Y	Y	Y	N	N	Y
5 *Hefley*	Y	N	N	N	N	Y
6 *Tancredo*	Y	Y	P	N	N	Y
CONNECTICUT						
1 Larson	N	N	Y	Y	Y	N
2 *Simmons*	Y	Y	Y	N	N	Y
3 DeLauro	N	N	Y	Y	Y	N
4 *Shays*	Y	Y	Y	N	N	Y
5 Maloney	N	N	?	N	Y	N
6 *Johnson*	Y	Y	Y	N	N	Y
DELAWARE						
AL *Castle*	Y	Y	Y	N	N	Y
FLORIDA						
1 *Miller, J.*	Y	Y	Y	N	N	Y
2 Boyd	N	N	Y	Y	Y	Y
3 Brown	N	N	?	Y	Y	N
4 *Crenshaw*	Y	Y	Y	N	N	Y
5 Thurman	N	N	Y	Y	Y	N
6 *Stearns*	Y	?	Y	N	N	Y
7 *Mica*	Y	Y	Y	N	N	Y
8 *Keller*	Y	Y	Y	N	N	Y
9 *Bilirakis*	Y	Y	Y	N	N	Y
10 *Young*	Y	Y	Y	N	N	Y
11 Davis	N	N	Y	Y	Y	N
12 *Putnam*	Y	Y	Y	N	N	Y
13 *Miller, D.*	Y	Y	Y	N	N	Y
14 *Goss*	Y	Y	Y	N	N	Y
15 *Weldon*	Y	Y	Y	N	N	Y
16 *Foley*	Y	Y	Y	N	N	Y
17 Meek	N	N	?	Y	Y	N
18 *Ros-Lehtinen*	Y	Y	Y	N	N	Y
19 Wexler	N	N	Y	Y	Y	N
20 Deutsch	N	N	?	Y	Y	N
21 *Diaz-Balart*	Y	Y	Y	N	N	Y
22 *Shaw*	Y	Y	Y	N	N	Y
23 Hastings	N	N	N	Y	Y	N
GEORGIA						
1 *Kingston*	Y	Y	Y	N	N	Y
2 Bishop	N	N	Y	Y	Y	N
3 *Collins*	Y	Y	Y	N	N	Y
4 McKinney	N	N	?	N	Y	N
5 Lewis	N	N	Y	Y	Y	N
6 *Isakson*	Y	Y	Y	N	N	Y
7 *Barr*	Y	Y	Y	N	N	Y
8 *Chambliss*	Y	Y	Y	N	N	Y
9 *Deal*	Y	Y	Y	N	N	Y
10 *Norwood*	Y	Y	Y	?	N	Y
11 *Linder*	Y	Y	Y	N	N	Y
HAWAII						
1 Abercrombie	N	N	Y	Y	Y	N
2 Mink	N	N	?	N	Y	N
IDAHO						
1 *Otter*	Y	Y	Y	N	N	Y
2 *Simpson*	Y	Y	Y	N	N	Y
ILLINOIS						
1 Rush	N	N	N	Y	N	N
2 Jackson	N	N	N	Y	N	N
3 Lipinski	N	N	N	Y	Y	N
4 Gutierrez	N	N	?	Y	Y	N
5 Blagojevich	N	N	?	Y	Y	N
6 *Hyde*	Y	Y	Y	N	N	Y
7 Davis	N	N	Y	Y	Y	N
8 *Crane*	Y	Y	?	N	N	Y
9 Schakowsky	N	N	N	Y	Y	N
10 *Kirk*	Y	Y	Y	N	N	Y
11 *Weller*	Y	Y	Y	N	N	Y
12 Costello	N	N	N	Y	Y	N
13 *Biggert*	Y	Y	Y	N	N	Y

ND Northern Democrats   SD Southern Democrats

	165	166	167	168	169	170
14 ***Hastert***					N	Y
15 ***Johnson***	Y	Y	Y	N	N	Y
16 ***Manzullo***	Y	Y	Y	N	N	Y
17 Evans	N	N	Y	Y	Y	N
18 ***LaHood***	Y	Y	Y	N	N	Y
19 Phelps	N	N	N	Y	Y	Y
20 ***Shimkus***	Y	Y	Y	N	N	Y
INDIANA						
1 Visclosky	N	N	N	Y	Y	N
2 ***Pence***	Y	Y	Y	N	N	Y
3 Roemer	N	N	Y	Y	Y	N
4 ***Souder***	Y	Y	Y	N	N	Y
5 ***Buyer***	Y	Y	Y	?	?	?
6 ***Burton***	?	?	?	N	N	Y
7 ***Kerns***	Y	Y	Y	N	N	N
8 ***Hostettler***	Y	Y	Y	N	N	N
9 Hill	N	N	Y	Y	Y	N
10 Carson	N	N	Y	Y	Y	N
IOWA						
1 ***Leach***	Y	Y	?	N	N	Y
2 ***Nussle***	Y	Y	Y	N	N	Y
3 Boswell	N	N	Y	Y	Y	N
4 ***Ganske***	Y	Y	Y	N	N	Y
5 ***Latham***	Y	Y	N	N	N	Y
KANSAS						
1 ***Moran***	Y	Y	N	N	N	Y
2 ***Ryun***	Y	Y	Y	N	N	Y
3 Moore	N	N	N	Y	Y	N
4 ***Tiahrt***	Y	Y	Y	N	N	Y
KENTUCKY						
1 ***Whitfield***	Y	Y	Y	N	N	Y
2 ***Lewis***	Y	Y	Y	N	N	Y
3 ***Northup***	Y	Y	Y	N	N	Y
4 Lucas	N	N	Y	N	Y	Y
5 ***Rogers***	Y	Y	Y	N	N	Y
6 ***Fletcher***	Y	Y	N	N	N	Y
LOUISIANA						
1 ***Vitter***	Y	Y	?	N	N	Y
2 Jefferson	N	N	Y	Y	Y	N
3 ***Tauzin***	?	Y	Y	N	N	Y
4 ***McCrery***	Y	Y	Y	N	N	Y
5 ***Cooksey***	Y	Y	Y	N	N	Y
6 ***Baker***	Y	Y	Y	N	N	Y
7 John	N	N	Y	Y	Y	N
MAINE						
1 Allen	N	N	Y	Y	Y	N
2 Baldacci	N	N	Y	Y	Y	N
MARYLAND						
1 ***Gilchrest***	Y	Y	Y	N	N	Y
2 ***Ehrlich***	Y	Y	?	N	N	Y
3 Cardin	N	N	Y	Y	Y	N
4 Wynn	N	N	Y	Y	Y	N
5 Hoyer	N	N	Y	Y	Y	N
6 ***Bartlett***	Y	Y	Y	N	N	Y
7 Cummings	N	N	Y	Y	Y	N
8 ***Morella***	Y	N	Y	Y	N	N
MASSACHUSETTS						
1 Olver	N	N	N	Y	Y	N
2 Neal	N	N	Y	Y	Y	N
3 McGovern	N	N	N	Y	Y	N
4 Frank	N	N	Y	Y	Y	N
5 Meehan	N	N	Y	Y	Y	N
6 Tierney	N	N	Y	Y	Y	N
7 Markey	N	N	N	Y	Y	N
8 Capuano	N	N	N	Y	Y	N
9 Lynch	N	N	Y	Y	Y	N
10 Delahunt	N	N	Y	Y	Y	N
MICHIGAN						
1 Stupak	?	?	N	Y	Y	N
2 ***Hoekstra***	Y	Y	Y	N	N	Y
3 ***Ehlers***	Y	Y	Y	N	N	Y
4 ***Camp***	Y	Y	Y	N	N	Y
5 Barcia	N	N	Y	Y	Y	Y
6 ***Upton***	Y	Y	Y	N	N	Y
7 ***Smith***	Y	Y	Y	N	N	Y
8 ***Rogers***	Y	Y	Y	N	N	Y
9 Kildee	N	N	Y	Y	Y	N
10 Bonior	N	N	N	Y	Y	N
11 ***Knollenberg***	Y	Y	Y	N	N	Y
12 Levin	N	N	Y	Y	Y	N
13 Rivers	N	N	Y	Y	Y	N
14 Conyers	N	N	Y	Y	Y	N
15 Kilpatrick	N	N	Y	Y	Y	N
16 Dingell	N	N	Y	Y	Y	N

	165	166	167	168	169	170
MINNESOTA						
1 ***Gutknecht***	?	Y	N	N	N	Y
2 ***Kennedy***	Y	Y	N	N	N	Y
3 ***Ramstad***	Y	Y	N	N	N	Y
4 McCollum	N	N	Y	Y	Y	N
5 Sabo	N	N	N	Y	Y	N
6 Luther	N	N	Y	Y	Y	Y
7 Peterson	N	N	N	Y	Y	Y
8 Oberstar	N	N	N	Y	Y	N
MISSISSIPPI						
1 ***Wicker***	Y	Y	N	N	N	Y
2 Thompson	N	N	N	Y	Y	N
3 ***Pickering***	Y	Y	Y	N	N	Y
4 Shows	N	N	Y	+	Y	Y
5 Taylor	N	N	N	Y	Y	Y
MISSOURI						
1 Clay	N	N	?	Y	Y	N
2 ***Akin***	Y	Y	Y	N	N	Y
3 Gephardt	N	N	Y	Y	Y	N
4 Skelton	N	N	Y	Y	Y	N
5 McCarthy	N	N	Y	Y	Y	N
6 ***Graves***	Y	Y	Y	N	N	Y
7 ***Blunt***	Y	Y	Y	N	N	Y
8 ***Emerson***	Y	Y	Y	N	N	Y
9 ***Hulshof***	Y	Y	?	N	N	Y
MONTANA						
AL ***Rehberg***	Y	Y	Y	N	N	Y
NEBRASKA						
1 ***Bereuter***	Y	Y	Y	N	N	Y
2 ***Terry***	Y	Y	Y	N	N	Y
3 ***Osborne***	Y	Y	Y	N	N	Y
NEVADA						
1 Berkley	N	N	Y	Y	Y	N
2 ***Gibbons***	?	Y	Y	N	N	Y
NEW HAMPSHIRE						
1 ***Sununu***	Y	Y	Y	N	N	Y
2 ***Bass***	Y	Y	Y	N	N	Y
NEW JERSEY						
1 Andrews	N	N	Y	Y	Y	N
2 ***LoBiondo***	Y	Y	N	N	N	Y
3 ***Saxton***	Y	Y	Y	N	N	Y
4 ***Smith***	Y	Y	Y	N	N	Y
5 ***Roukema***	Y	Y	Y	N	N	Y
6 Pallone	N	N	N	Y	Y	N
7 ***Ferguson***	Y	Y	Y	N	N	Y
8 Pascrell	N	N	Y	Y	Y	N
9 Rothman	N	N	Y	Y	Y	N
10 Payne	N	N	Y	Y	Y	N
11 ***Frelinghuysen***	Y	Y	Y	N	N	Y
12 Holt	N	N	N	Y	Y	N
13 Menendez	N	N	N	Y	Y	N
NEW MEXICO						
1 ***Wilson***	Y	Y	Y	N	N	Y
2 ***Skeen***	Y	Y	Y	N	N	Y
3 Udall	N	N	N	Y	Y	N
NEW YORK						
1 ***Grucci***	Y	Y	Y	N	N	Y
2 Israel	N	N	Y	Y	Y	N
3 ***King***	Y	Y	Y	?	?	?
4 McCarthy	N	N	Y	Y	Y	N
5 Ackerman	N	N	Y	Y	Y	N
6 Meeks	N	N	Y	Y	Y	N
7 Crowley	N	N	Y	Y	Y	N
8 Nadler	N	N	Y	Y	Y	N
9 Weiner	N	N	Y	Y	Y	N
10 Towns	N	N	Y	Y	Y	N
11 Owens	N	N	Y	Y	Y	N
12 Velázquez	N	N	Y	Y	Y	N
13 ***Fossella***	Y	Y	?	N	N	Y
14 Maloney	N	N	Y	Y	Y	N
15 Rangel	N	N	?	Y	Y	N
16 Serrano	N	N	Y	Y	Y	N
17 Engel	N	N	?	Y	Y	N
18 Lowey	N	N	Y	Y	Y	N
19 ***Kelly***	Y	Y	Y	N	N	Y
20 ***Gilman***	Y	Y	Y	Y	N	Y
21 McNulty	N	N	N	Y	Y	N
22 ***Sweeney***	Y	Y	Y	N	N	Y
23 ***Boehlert***	Y	Y	Y	N	N	Y
24 ***McHugh***	Y	Y	Y	N	N	Y
25 ***Walsh***	Y	Y	Y	N	N	Y
26 Hinchey	N	N	N	Y	Y	N
27 ***Reynolds***	Y	Y	Y	N	N	Y
28 Slaughter	N	N	?	Y	Y	N
29 LaFalce	N	N	?	Y	Y	N

	165	166	167	168	169	170
30 ***Quinn***	Y	Y	Y	N	N	Y
31 ***Houghton***	Y	Y	Y	N	N	Y
NORTH CAROLINA						
1 Clayton	N	N	Y	Y	Y	N
2 Etheridge	N	N	Y	Y	Y	N
3 ***Jones***	Y	Y	Y	N	N	Y
4 Price	N	N	Y	Y	Y	N
5 ***Burr***	Y	Y	Y	N	N	Y
6 ***Coble***	Y	Y	Y	N	N	Y
7 McIntyre	N	N	Y	Y	Y	N
8 ***Hayes***	Y	Y	Y	N	N	Y
9 ***Myrick***	Y	Y	Y	N	N	Y
10 ***Ballenger***	Y	Y	Y	N	N	Y
11 ***Taylor***	Y	Y	?	N	N	Y
12 Watt	N	N	Y	N	Y	N
NORTH DAKOTA						
AL Pomeroy	N	N	Y	Y	Y	Y
OHIO						
1 ***Chabot***	Y	Y	Y	N	N	Y
2 ***Portman***	Y	Y	Y	N	N	Y
3 Hall	?	?	?	Y	Y	N
4 ***Oxley***	Y	Y	?	N	N	Y
5 ***Gillmor***	Y	Y	Y	N	N	Y
6 Strickland	N	N	N	Y	Y	N
7 ***Hobson***	Y	Y	Y	N	N	Y
8 ***Boehner***	Y	Y	Y	N	N	Y
9 Kaptur	N	N	Y	Y	Y	N
10 Kucinich	N	N	N	N	Y	N
11 Jones	N	N	N	Y	Y	N
12 ***Tiberi***	Y	Y	Y	N	N	Y
13 Brown	N	N	Y	Y	Y	N
14 Sawyer	N	N	Y	Y	Y	N
15 ***Pryce***	Y	Y	Y	N	N	Y
16 ***Regula***	Y	Y	Y	N	N	Y
17 Traficant	?	?	?	?	?	?
18 ***Ney***	Y	Y	Y	N	N	Y
19 ***LaTourette***	Y	Y	Y	N	N	Y
OKLAHOMA						
1 ***Sullivan***	Y	Y	Y	N	N	Y
2 Carson	N	N	N	Y	Y	N
3 ***Watkins***	Y	Y	Y	N	N	Y
4 ***Watts***	Y	Y	N	N	N	Y
5 ***Istook***	Y	Y	Y	N	N	Y
6 ***Lucas***	Y	Y	Y	N	N	Y
OREGON						
1 Wu	N	N	N	Y	Y	Y
2 ***Walden***	Y	Y	Y	N	N	Y
3 Blumenauer	N	N	Y	Y	Y	N
4 DeFazio	N	N	N	Y	Y	N
5 Hooley	N	N	Y	Y	Y	N
PENNSYLVANIA						
1 Brady	N	N	N	Y	Y	N
2 Fattah	N	N	N	Y	Y	N
3 Borski	N	N	N	Y	Y	N
4 ***Hart***	Y	Y	Y	N	N	Y
5 ***Peterson***	Y	Y	Y	N	N	Y
6 Holden	N	N	Y	Y	Y	Y
7 ***Weldon***	Y	Y	Y	N	N	Y
8 ***Greenwood***	Y	Y	Y	N	N	Y
9 ***Shuster, Bill***	Y	Y	Y	N	N	Y
10 ***Sherwood***	Y	Y	Y	N	N	Y
11 Kanjorski	N	N	Y	Y	Y	N
12 Murtha	?	?	?	?	?	?
13 Hoeffel	N	N	Y	Y	Y	N
14 Coyne	N	N	Y	Y	Y	N
15 ***Toomey***	Y	Y	Y	N	N	Y
16 ***Pitts***	Y	Y	Y	N	N	Y
17 ***Gekas***	Y	Y	Y	N	N	Y
18 Doyle	N	N	?	Y	Y	N
19 ***Platts***	Y	Y	?	N	N	Y
20 Mascara	?	?	?	?	?	?
21 ***English***	Y	Y	N	N	N	Y
RHODE ISLAND						
1 Kennedy	N	N	Y	Y	Y	N
2 Langevin	N	N	Y	Y	Y	N
SOUTH CAROLINA						
1 ***Brown***	Y	Y	Y	N	N	Y
2 ***Wilson***	Y	Y	Y	N	N	Y
3 ***Graham***	Y	Y	Y	N	N	Y
4 ***DeMint***	Y	Y	Y	N	N	Y
5 Spratt	N	N	Y	Y	Y	N
6 Clyburn	N	N	Y	Y	Y	N
SOUTH DAKOTA						
AL ***Thune***	Y	Y	Y	N	N	Y

	165	166	167	168	169	170
TENNESSEE						
1 ***Jenkins***	Y	Y	Y	N	N	Y
2 ***Duncan***	Y	Y	Y	N	N	Y
3 ***Wamp***	Y	Y	Y	N	N	Y
4 ***Hilleary***	Y	Y	Y	N	N	Y
5 Clement	N	N	Y	Y	Y	N
6 Gordon	?	?	?	Y	Y	N
7 ***Bryant***	Y	Y	Y	N	N	Y
8 Tanner	N	N	N	?	?	?
9 Ford	N	N	Y	Y	Y	N
TEXAS						
1 Sandlin	N	N	Y	Y	Y	N
2 Turner	N	N	Y	Y	Y	N
3 ***Johnson, Sam***	Y	Y	Y	N	N	Y
4 Hall	N	N	Y	Y	Y	Y
5 ***Sessions***	Y	Y	Y	N	N	Y
6 ***Barton***	Y	Y	Y	?	N	Y
7 ***Culberson***	Y	Y	?	N	N	Y
8 ***Brady***	Y	Y	Y	N	N	Y
9 Lampson	N	N	?	?	?	?
10 Doggett	N	N	N	Y	Y	N
11 Edwards	N	N	?	Y	Y	Y
12 ***Granger***	Y	Y	Y	N	N	Y
13 ***Thornberry***	?	?	Y	N	N	Y
14 ***Paul***	Y	Y	Y	N	N	N
15 Hinojosa	N	N	Y	Y	Y	N
16 Reyes	?	?	Y	Y	Y	N
17 Stenholm	N	N	Y	Y	Y	N
18 Jackson-Lee	N	N	Y	Y	Y	N
19 ***Combest***	Y	Y	Y	?	?	?
20 Gonzalez	N	N	Y	Y	Y	N
21 ***Smith***	Y	Y	Y	N	N	Y
22 ***DeLay***	Y	Y	Y	N	N	Y
23 ***Bonilla***	Y	Y	Y	N	N	Y
24 Frost	N	N	N	Y	Y	N
25 Bentsen	N	N	Y	Y	Y	N
26 ***Armey***	Y	Y	Y	N	N	Y
27 Ortiz	N	N	Y	Y	Y	N
28 Rodriguez	N	N	Y	Y	Y	N
29 Green	N	N	Y	Y	Y	N
30 Johnson, E.B.	N	N	N	Y	Y	N
UTAH						
1 ***Hansen***	Y	Y	Y	N	N	Y
2 Matheson	N	N	Y	Y	Y	N
3 ***Cannon***	Y	Y	Y	N	N	Y
VERMONT						
AL *Sanders*	N	N	?	N	Y	N
VIRGINIA						
1 ***Davis, Jo Ann***	Y	Y	Y	N	N	Y
2 ***Schrock***	Y	Y	Y	N	N	Y
3 Scott	N	N	Y	Y	Y	N
4 ***Forbes***	Y	Y	Y	N	N	Y
5 *Goode*	Y	Y	Y	N	N	Y
6 ***Goodlatte***	Y	Y	Y	N	N	Y
7 ***Cantor***	Y	Y	Y	N	N	Y
8 Moran	N	N	Y	Y	Y	N
9 Boucher	N	N	Y	Y	Y	N
10 ***Wolf***	Y	Y	Y	N	N	Y
11 ***Davis, T.***	Y	Y	?	?	N	Y
WASHINGTON						
1 Inslee	N	N	Y	Y	Y	N
2 Larsen	N	N	N	Y	Y	N
3 Baird	N	N	N	Y	Y	N
4 ***Hastings***	Y	Y	Y	N	N	Y
5 ***Nethercutt***	Y	Y	Y	N	N	Y
6 Dicks	N	N	Y	Y	Y	N
7 McDermott	N	N	N	Y	Y	N
8 ***Dunn***	Y	Y	Y	N	N	Y
9 Smith	N	N	Y	Y	Y	N
WEST VIRGINIA						
1 Mollohan	N	N	Y	Y	Y	N
2 ***Capito***	Y	Y	Y	N	N	Y
3 Rahall	N	N	Y	Y	Y	N
WISCONSIN						
1 ***Ryan***	Y	P	Y	N	N	Y
2 Baldwin	N	N	N	Y	Y	N
3 Kind	N	N	Y	Y	Y	N
4 Kleczka	N	N	Y	Y	Y	N
5 Barrett	N	N	Y	Y	Y	N
6 ***Petri***	Y	Y	Y	N	N	Y
7 Obey	N	N	N	Y	Y	N
8 ***Green***	Y	Y	Y	N	N	Y
9 ***Sensenbrenner***	Y	Y	Y	N	N	Y
WYOMING						
AL ***Cubin***	Y	Y	Y	N	N	Y

Southern states - Ala., Ark., Fla., Ga., Ky., La., Miss., N.C., Okla., S.C., Tenn., Texas, Va.

Key

Y	Voted for (yea).
#	Paired for.
+	Announced for.
N	Voted against (nay).
X	Paired against.
–	Announced against.
P	Voted "present."
C	Voted "present" to avoid possible conflict of interest.
?	Did not vote or otherwise make a position known.

Democrats **Republicans**
Independents

171. H Con Res 314. Veterans Tribute/Adoption. Smith, R-N.J., motion to suspend the rules and adopt the concurrent resolution that would pay tribute to AmVets, an organization open to anyone who is currently serving or has honorably served in the U.S. armed forces since Sept. 15, 1940. Motion agreed to 360-0: R 184-0; D 175-0 (ND 129-0, SD 46-0); I 1-0. A two-thirds majority of those present and voting (240 in this case) is required for adoption under suspension of the rules. May 20, 2002.

172. H Con Res 165. Fibroids Awareness/Adoption. Bilirakis, R-Fla., motion to suspend the rules and adopt the concurrent resolution that would support additional research into, education on, and awareness of fibroids, the most frequently diagnosed tumors in the female pelvis. Motion agreed to 363-0: R 186-0; D 175-0 (ND 129-0, SD 46-0); I 2-0. A two-thirds majority of those present and voting (242 in this case) is required for adoption under suspension of the rules. May 20, 2002.

173. H Con Res 309. Cervical Health Awareness/Adoption. Bilirakis, R-Fla., motion to suspend the rules and adopt the concurrent resolution that would recognize the importance of good cervical health and support additional awareness of cervical cancer. Motion agreed to 361-0: R 186-0; D 173-0 (ND 127-0, SD 46-0); I 2-0. A two-thirds majority of those present and voting (241 in this case) is required for adoption under suspension of the rules. May 20, 2002.

174. HR 3833. Internet for Children/Passage. Upton, R-Mich., motion to suspend the rules and pass the bill that would establish a separate Internet domain that would carry only Web sites 'suitable for minors' and 'not harmful to minors' under 13 years old. The 'kids.us' domain would be set up by the Commerce Department and maintained by NeuStar Inc. Motion agreed to 406-2: R 209-1; D 195-1 (ND 144-1, SD 51-0); I 2-0. A two-thirds majority of those present and voting (272 in this case) is required for passage under suspension of the rules. May 21, 2002.

175. HR 1877. Expansion of Wiretaps/Passage. Sensenbrenner, R-Wis., motion to suspend the rules and pass the bill that would allow federal law enforcement agents to obtain wiretaps to aid in investigation of child pornography, the buying and selling of children for sexual exploitation, inducing or coercing someone to cross state lines to engage in illegal sexual activities, and transporting minors for illegal sexual activity. Motion agreed to 396-11: R 210-1; D 184-10 (ND 137-7, SD 47-3); I 2-0. A two-thirds majority of those present and voting (272 in this case) is required for passage under suspension of the rules. May 21, 2002.

176. HR 3375. East Africa Embassy Bombings/Passage. Sensenbrenner, R-Wis., motion to suspend the rules and pass the bill that would extend to victims of the 1998 U.S. embassy bombings in East Africa the same compensation offered to victims of the Sept. 11, 2001, terrorist attacks. Victims would have to give up rights to sue in civil court to receive compensation. The compensation fund would be run by the special master in charge of the Sept. 11 fund. Motion agreed to 391-18: R 194-17; D 196-0 (ND 145-0, SD 51-0); I 1-1. A two-thirds majority of those present and voting (273 in this case) is required for passage under suspension of the rules. A "nay" was a vote in support of the president's position. May 21, 2002.

	171	172	173	174	175	176
ALABAMA						
1 *Callahan*	?	?	?	?	?	Y
2 *Everett*	Y	Y	Y	Y	Y	N
3 *Riley*	+	+	+	+	+	+
4 *Aderholt*	Y	Y	Y	Y	Y	Y
5 Cramer	Y	Y	Y	Y	Y	Y
6 *Bachus*	Y	Y	Y	Y	Y	Y
7 Hilliard	?	?	?	Y	Y	Y
ALASKA						
AL *Young*	Y	Y	Y	Y	Y	Y
ARIZONA						
1 *Flake*	+	+	+	Y	Y	N
2 Pastor	Y	Y	Y	Y	Y	Y
3 *Stump*	?	?	?	?	?	?
4 *Shadegg*	Y	Y	Y	Y	Y	Y
5 *Kolbe*	Y	Y	Y	Y	Y	Y
6 *Hayworth*	?	?	?	Y	Y	Y
ARKANSAS						
1 Berry	Y	Y	Y	Y	Y	Y
2 Snyder	?	?	?	?	?	?
3 *Boozman*	Y	Y	Y	Y	Y	Y
4 Ross	Y	Y	Y	Y	Y	Y
CALIFORNIA						
1 Thompson	Y	Y	Y	Y	Y	Y
2 *Herger*	?	?	?	Y	Y	Y
3 *Ose*	Y	Y	Y	Y	Y	Y
4 *Doolittle*	Y	Y	Y	Y	Y	Y
5 Matsui	?	?	?	?	?	?
6 Woolsey	Y	Y	Y	Y	Y	Y
7 Miller, George	Y	Y	Y	Y	Y	Y
8 Pelosi	Y	Y	Y	Y	Y	Y
9 Lee	Y	Y	Y	Y	Y	Y
10 Tauscher	Y	Y	Y	Y	Y	Y
11 *Pombo*	?	?	?	?	?	?
12 Lantos	?	?	?	Y	Y	Y
13 Stark	Y	Y	Y	Y	N	N
14 Eshoo	Y	Y	Y	Y	Y	Y
15 Honda	Y	Y	Y	Y	Y	Y
16 Lofgren	Y	Y	Y	Y	Y	Y
17 Farr	Y	Y	Y	Y	?	Y
18 Condit	Y	Y	Y	Y	Y	Y
19 *Radanovich*	Y	Y	Y	Y	Y	Y
20 Dooley	Y	Y	Y	Y	Y	Y
21 *Thomas*	Y	Y	Y	Y	Y	Y
22 Capps	Y	Y	Y	Y	Y	Y
23 *Gallegly*	Y	Y	Y	Y	Y	Y
24 Sherman	Y	Y	Y	Y	Y	Y
25 *McKeon*	Y	Y	Y	Y	Y	Y
26 Berman	Y	Y	Y	Y	Y	Y
27 Schiff	Y	Y	Y	Y	Y	Y
28 *Dreier*	Y	Y	Y	Y	Y	Y
29 Waxman	Y	Y	Y	Y	Y	Y
30 Becerra	+	+	+	Y	Y	Y
31 Solis	Y	Y	Y	Y	Y	Y
32 Watson	Y	Y	Y	Y	Y	Y
33 Roybal-Allard	Y	Y	Y	Y	Y	Y
34 Napolitano	Y	Y	Y	Y	Y	Y
35 Waters	Y	Y	Y	Y	Y	Y
36 Harman	?	?	?	Y	Y	Y
37 Millender-McD.	Y	Y	Y	Y	Y	Y
38 *Horn*	Y	Y	Y	Y	Y	Y

	171	172	173	174	175	176
39 *Royce*	Y	Y	Y	Y	Y	Y
40 *Lewis*	Y	Y	Y	Y	Y	Y
41 *Miller, Gary*	Y	Y	Y	Y	Y	Y
42 Baca	Y	Y	Y	Y	Y	Y
43 *Calvert*	Y	Y	Y	Y	Y	Y
44 *Bono*	Y	Y	Y	Y	Y	Y
45 *Rohrabacher*	Y	Y	Y	Y	Y	Y
46 Sanchez	Y	Y	Y	Y	Y	Y
47 *Cox*	?	?	?	?	?	?
48 *Issa*	Y	Y	Y	Y	Y	Y
49 Davis	Y	Y	Y	Y	Y	Y
50 Filner	Y	Y	Y	N	Y	Y
51 *Cunningham*	Y	Y	Y	Y	Y	Y
52 *Hunter*	Y	Y	Y	Y	Y	Y
COLORADO						
1 DeGette	Y	Y	Y	Y	Y	Y
2 Udall	Y	Y	Y	Y	Y	Y
3 *McInnis*	Y	Y	Y	Y	Y	N
4 *Schaffer*	?	?	?	Y	Y	Y
5 *Hefley*	Y	Y	Y	Y	Y	Y
6 *Tancredo*	Y	Y	Y	Y	Y	Y
CONNECTICUT						
1 Larson	Y	Y	Y	Y	Y	Y
2 *Simmons*	?	Y	Y	Y	Y	Y
3 DeLauro	Y	Y	Y	Y	Y	Y
4 *Shays*	Y	Y	Y	Y	Y	Y
5 Maloney	Y	Y	Y	Y	Y	Y
6 *Johnson*	Y	Y	Y	Y	Y	Y
DELAWARE						
AL *Castle*	Y	Y	Y	Y	Y	Y
FLORIDA						
1 *Miller, J.*	Y	Y	Y	Y	Y	Y
2 Boyd	Y	Y	Y	Y	Y	Y
3 Brown	?	?	?	Y	Y	Y
4 *Crenshaw*	Y	Y	Y	Y	Y	Y
5 Thurman	Y	Y	Y	Y	Y	Y
6 *Stearns*	Y	Y	Y	Y	Y	Y
7 *Mica*	Y	Y	Y	Y	Y	Y
8 *Keller*	?	?	?	Y	Y	Y
9 *Bilirakis*	Y	Y	Y	Y	Y	Y
10 *Young*	?	?	?	Y	Y	Y
11 Davis	Y	Y	Y	Y	Y	Y
12 *Putnam*	Y	Y	Y	Y	Y	Y
13 *Miller, D.*	Y	Y	Y	Y	Y	Y
14 *Goss*	Y	Y	Y	Y	Y	Y
15 *Weldon*	Y	Y	Y	Y	Y	Y
16 *Foley*	Y	Y	Y	Y	Y	Y
17 Meek	Y	Y	Y	Y	Y	Y
18 *Ros-Lehtinen*	?	?	?	Y	Y	Y
19 Wexler	Y	Y	Y	Y	Y	Y
20 Deutsch	?	?	?	?	?	?
21 *Diaz-Balart*	?	?	?	Y	Y	Y
22 *Shaw*	Y	Y	Y	Y	Y	Y
23 Hastings	Y	Y	Y	Y	N	Y
GEORGIA						
1 *Kingston*	Y	Y	Y	Y	Y	N
2 Bishop	Y	Y	Y	Y	Y	Y
3 *Collins*	Y	Y	Y	Y	Y	N
4 McKinney	Y	Y	Y	Y	Y	Y
5 Lewis	?	?	?	?	?	?
6 *Isakson*	Y	Y	Y	Y	Y	Y
7 *Barr*	Y	Y	Y	Y	Y	Y
8 *Chambliss*	Y	Y	Y	Y	Y	Y
9 *Deal*	Y	Y	Y	Y	Y	N
10 *Norwood*	Y	Y	Y	Y	Y	N
11 *Linder*	Y	Y	Y	Y	Y	Y
HAWAII						
1 Abercrombie	Y	Y	Y	Y	Y	Y
2 Mink	Y	Y	Y	Y	Y	Y
IDAHO						
1 *Otter*	Y	Y	Y	Y	Y	Y
2 *Simpson*	Y	Y	Y	Y	Y	Y
ILLINOIS						
1 Rush	Y	Y	Y	Y	Y	Y
2 Jackson	Y	Y	Y	N	Y	Y
3 Lipinski	?	?	?	?	?	?
4 Gutierrez	Y	Y	Y	Y	Y	Y
5 Blagojevich	?	?	?	?	?	?
6 *Hyde*	Y	Y	Y	Y	Y	Y
7 Davis	?	?	?	Y	Y	Y
8 *Crane*	Y	Y	Y	Y	Y	Y
9 Schakowsky	Y	Y	Y	Y	Y	Y
10 *Kirk*	Y	Y	Y	Y	Y	Y
11 *Weller*	Y	Y	Y	Y	Y	Y
12 Costello	Y	Y	Y	Y	Y	Y
13 *Biggert*	Y	Y	Y	Y	Y	Y

ND Northern Democrats   SD Southern Democrats

	171	172	173	174	175	176
14 ***Hastert***						
15 ***Johnson***	Y	Y	Y	Y	Y	Y
16 ***Manzullo***	Y	Y	Y	Y	Y	N
17 Evans	Y	Y	Y	Y	Y	Y
18 ***LaHood***	?	?	?	Y	Y	Y
19 Phelps	Y	Y	Y	Y	Y	Y
20 ***Shimkus***	Y	Y	Y	Y	Y	Y
INDIANA						
1 Visclosky	Y	Y	Y	Y	Y	Y
2 ***Pence***	Y	Y	Y	Y	Y	Y
3 Roemer	Y	Y	Y	Y	Y	Y
4 ***Souder***	Y	Y	Y	Y	Y	Y
5 ***Buyer***	Y	Y	Y	Y	Y	Y
6 ***Burton***	?	?	?	?	?	?
7 ***Kerns***	Y	Y	Y	Y	Y	Y
8 ***Hostettler***	Y	Y	Y	Y	Y	Y
9 Hill	Y	Y	Y	Y	Y	Y
10 Carson	Y	Y	Y	Y	Y	Y
IOWA						
1 ***Leach***	Y	Y	Y	Y	Y	Y
2 ***Nussle***	Y	Y	Y	Y	Y	Y
3 Boswell	Y	Y	Y	Y	Y	Y
4 ***Ganske***	Y	Y	Y	Y	Y	Y
5 ***Latham***	Y	Y	Y	Y	Y	Y
KANSAS						
1 ***Moran***	Y	Y	Y	Y	Y	Y
2 ***Ryun***	Y	Y	Y	Y	Y	Y
3 Moore	Y	Y	Y	Y	Y	Y
4 ***Tiahrt***	Y	Y	Y	Y	Y	Y
KENTUCKY						
1 ***Whitfield***	Y	Y	Y	Y	Y	Y
2 ***Lewis***	Y	Y	Y	Y	Y	Y
3 ***Northup***	Y	Y	Y	Y	Y	Y
4 Lucas	Y	Y	Y	Y	Y	Y
5 ***Rogers***	Y	Y	Y	Y	Y	Y
6 ***Fletcher***	Y	Y	Y	Y	Y	Y
LOUISIANA						
1 ***Vitter***	Y	Y	Y	Y	Y	Y
2 Jefferson	?	?	?	Y	Y	Y
3 ***Tauzin***	?	?	?	Y	Y	Y
4 ***McCrery***	Y	Y	Y	Y	Y	Y
5 ***Cooksey***	?	?	?	Y	Y	Y
6 ***Baker***	?	?	?	Y	Y	Y
7 John	?	?	?	Y	Y	Y
MAINE						
1 Allen	Y	Y	Y	Y	Y	Y
2 Baldacci	Y	Y	Y	Y	Y	Y
MARYLAND						
1 ***Gilchrest***	Y	Y	Y	Y	Y	Y
2 ***Ehrlich***	Y	Y	Y	Y	Y	Y
3 Cardin	Y	Y	Y	Y	Y	Y
4 Wynn	Y	Y	Y	Y	Y	Y
5 Hoyer	Y	Y	Y	Y	Y	Y
6 ***Bartlett***	Y	Y	Y	Y	Y	N
7 Cummings	Y	Y	Y	Y	Y	Y
8 ***Morella***	Y	Y	Y	?	Y	Y
MASSACHUSETTS						
1 Olver	?	?	?	Y	N	Y
2 Neal	?	?	?	Y	Y	Y
3 McGovern	Y	Y	Y	Y	Y	Y
4 Frank	Y	Y	Y	?	?	?
5 Meehan	Y	Y	Y	Y	Y	Y
6 Tierney	Y	Y	Y	Y	Y	Y
7 Markey	Y	Y	Y	Y	Y	Y
8 Capuano	Y	Y	Y	Y	Y	Y
9 Lynch	Y	Y	Y	Y	Y	Y
10 Delahunt	Y	Y	Y	Y	Y	Y
MICHIGAN						
1 Stupak	Y	Y	Y	Y	Y	Y
2 ***Hoekstra***	Y	Y	Y	Y	Y	Y
3 ***Ehlers***	Y	Y	Y	Y	Y	Y
4 ***Camp***	Y	Y	Y	Y	Y	Y
5 Barcia	Y	Y	Y	Y	Y	Y
6 ***Upton***	Y	Y	Y	Y	Y	Y
7 ***Smith***	Y	Y	Y	Y	Y	N
8 ***Rogers***	Y	Y	Y	Y	Y	Y
9 Kildee	Y	Y	Y	Y	Y	Y
10 Bonior	Y	Y	Y	+	+	+
11 ***Knollenberg***	?	?	?	Y	Y	Y
12 Levin	Y	Y	Y	Y	Y	Y
13 Rivers	Y	Y	Y	Y	Y	Y
14 Conyers	?	?	?	?	?	?
15 Kilpatrick	+	+	+	Y	N	Y
16 Dingell	Y	Y	Y	Y	N	Y
MINNESOTA						
1 ***Gutknecht***	Y	Y	Y	Y	Y	N
2 ***Kennedy***	Y	Y	Y	Y	Y	Y
3 ***Ramstad***	Y	Y	Y	Y	Y	Y
4 McCollum	Y	Y	Y	Y	Y	Y
5 Sabo	Y	Y	Y	Y	Y	Y
6 Luther	Y	Y	Y	Y	Y	Y
7 Peterson	Y	Y	Y	Y	Y	Y
8 Oberstar	Y	Y	Y	Y	Y	Y
MISSISSIPPI						
1 ***Wicker***	Y	Y	Y	Y	Y	Y
2 Thompson	Y	Y	Y	Y	Y	Y
3 ***Pickering***	Y	Y	Y	Y	Y	Y
4 Shows	Y	Y	Y	Y	Y	Y
5 Taylor	Y	Y	Y	Y	Y	Y
MISSOURI						
1 Clay	?	?	?	Y	Y	Y
2 ***Akin***	Y	Y	Y	Y	Y	Y
3 Gephardt	Y	Y	Y	Y	Y	Y
4 Skelton	Y	Y	Y	Y	Y	Y
5 McCarthy	Y	Y	Y	Y	Y	Y
6 ***Graves***	Y	Y	Y	Y	Y	Y
7 ***Blunt***	Y	Y	Y	Y	Y	Y
8 ***Emerson***	?	?	?	?	?	?
9 ***Hulshof***	?	?	?	Y	Y	Y
MONTANA						
AL ***Rehberg***	Y	Y	Y	Y	Y	Y
NEBRASKA						
1 ***Bereuter***	Y	Y	Y	Y	Y	Y
2 ***Terry***	?	?	?	Y	Y	N
3 ***Osborne***	Y	Y	Y	Y	Y	Y
NEVADA						
1 Berkley	Y	Y	Y	Y	Y	Y
2 ***Gibbons***	Y	Y	Y	Y	Y	Y
NEW HAMPSHIRE						
1 ***Sununu***	Y	Y	Y	Y	Y	Y
2 ***Bass***	Y	Y	Y	Y	Y	Y
NEW JERSEY						
1 Andrews	Y	Y	Y	Y	Y	Y
2 ***LoBiondo***	Y	Y	Y	Y	Y	Y
3 ***Saxton***	Y	Y	Y	Y	Y	Y
4 ***Smith***	Y	Y	Y	Y	Y	Y
5 ***Roukema***	Y	Y	Y	Y	Y	Y
6 Pallone	Y	Y	Y	Y	Y	Y
7 ***Ferguson***	Y	Y	Y	Y	Y	Y
8 Pascrell	Y	Y	Y	Y	Y	Y
9 Rothman	Y	Y	Y	Y	Y	Y
10 Payne	?	?	?	Y	Y	Y
11 ***Frelinghuysen***	Y	Y	Y	Y	Y	Y
12 Holt	Y	Y	Y	Y	Y	Y
13 Menendez	Y	Y	Y	?	?	?
NEW MEXICO						
1 ***Wilson***	Y	Y	Y	Y	Y	Y
2 ***Skeen***	Y	Y	Y	Y	Y	Y
3 Udall	Y	Y	Y	Y	Y	Y
NEW YORK						
1 ***Grucci***	Y	Y	Y	Y	Y	Y
2 Israel	Y	Y	Y	Y	Y	Y
3 ***King***	?	?	?	Y	Y	Y
4 McCarthy	Y	Y	Y	Y	Y	Y
5 Ackerman	Y	Y	Y	Y	Y	Y
6 Meeks	Y	Y	Y	Y	Y	Y
7 Crowley	Y	Y	Y	Y	Y	Y
8 Nadler	Y	Y	Y	Y	Y	Y
9 Weiner	+	+	+	Y	Y	Y
10 Towns	?	?	?	Y	Y	Y
11 Owens	+	+	+	Y	N	Y
12 Velázquez	Y	Y	Y	Y	Y	Y
13 ***Fossella***	Y	Y	Y	Y	Y	Y
14 Maloney	Y	Y	Y	Y	Y	Y
15 Rangel	Y	Y	Y	Y	Y	Y
16 Serrano	Y	Y	Y	Y	Y	Y
17 Engel	Y	Y	Y	Y	Y	Y
18 Lowey	Y	Y	Y	Y	Y	Y
19 ***Kelly***	Y	Y	Y	Y	Y	Y
20 ***Gilman***	Y	Y	Y	Y	Y	Y
21 McNulty	Y	Y	Y	Y	Y	Y
22 ***Sweeney***	Y	Y	Y	Y	Y	Y
23 ***Boehlert***	Y	Y	Y	Y	Y	Y
24 ***McHugh***	Y	Y	Y	Y	Y	Y
25 ***Walsh***	Y	Y	Y	Y	Y	Y
26 Hinchey	+	+	+	Y	Y	Y
27 ***Reynolds***	Y	Y	Y	Y	Y	Y
28 Slaughter	Y	Y	Y	Y	Y	Y
29 LaFalce	Y	Y	Y	Y	Y	Y
30 ***Quinn***	Y	Y	Y	Y	Y	Y
31 ***Houghton***	Y	Y	Y	Y	Y	Y
NORTH CAROLINA						
1 Clayton	Y	Y	Y	Y	Y	Y
2 Etheridge	Y	Y	Y	Y	Y	Y
3 ***Jones***	Y	Y	Y	Y	Y	N
4 Price	Y	Y	Y	Y	Y	Y
5 ***Burr***	Y	Y	Y	Y	Y	Y
6 ***Coble***	Y	Y	Y	Y	Y	N
7 McIntyre	Y	Y	Y	Y	Y	Y
8 ***Hayes***	Y	Y	Y	Y	Y	Y
9 ***Myrick***	Y	Y	Y	Y	Y	Y
10 ***Ballenger***	Y	Y	Y	Y	Y	N
11 ***Taylor***	?	?	?	Y	Y	Y
12 Watt	Y	Y	Y	Y	N	Y
NORTH DAKOTA						
AL Pomeroy	Y	Y	Y	Y	Y	Y
OHIO						
1 ***Chabot***	Y	Y	Y	Y	Y	Y
2 ***Portman***	Y	Y	Y	Y	Y	Y
3 Hall	Y	Y	Y	Y	Y	Y
4 ***Oxley***	Y	Y	Y	Y	Y	Y
5 ***Gillmor***	Y	Y	Y	Y	Y	Y
6 Strickland	Y	Y	Y	Y	Y	Y
7 ***Hobson***	Y	Y	Y	Y	Y	Y
8 ***Boehner***	Y	Y	Y	Y	Y	Y
9 Kaptur	Y	Y	Y	Y	Y	Y
10 Kucinich	Y	Y	?	Y	Y	Y
11 Jones	Y	Y	Y	Y	Y	Y
12 ***Tiberi***	Y	Y	Y	Y	Y	Y
13 Brown	Y	Y	Y	Y	Y	Y
14 Sawyer	Y	Y	Y	Y	Y	Y
15 ***Pryce***	?	?	?	Y	Y	Y
16 ***Regula***	Y	Y	Y	Y	Y	Y
17 Traficant	?	?	?	?	?	?
18 ***Ney***	Y	Y	Y	Y	Y	Y
19 ***LaTourette***	Y	Y	Y	Y	Y	Y
OKLAHOMA						
1 ***Sullivan***	Y	Y	Y	Y	Y	Y
2 Carson	Y	Y	Y	Y	Y	Y
3 ***Watkins***	?	?	?	?	?	?
4 ***Watts***	+	+	?	Y	Y	Y
5 ***Istook***	Y	Y	Y	Y	Y	Y
6 ***Lucas***	Y	Y	Y	Y	Y	Y
OREGON						
1 Wu	Y	Y	Y	Y	Y	Y
2 ***Walden***	Y	Y	Y	Y	Y	Y
3 Blumenauer	Y	Y	Y	Y	Y	Y
4 DeFazio	Y	Y	Y	Y	Y	Y
5 Hooley	Y	Y	Y	Y	Y	Y
PENNSYLVANIA						
1 Brady	?	?	?	?	?	?
2 Fattah	?	?	?	Y	Y	Y
3 Borski	?	?	?	?	?	?
4 ***Hart***	Y	Y	Y	Y	Y	Y
5 ***Peterson***	Y	Y	Y	Y	Y	Y
6 Holden	?	?	?	Y	Y	Y
7 ***Weldon***	?	?	?	Y	Y	Y
8 ***Greenwood***	?	?	?	?	?	?
9 ***Shuster, Bill***	Y	Y	Y	Y	Y	Y
10 ***Sherwood***	Y	Y	Y	Y	Y	Y
11 Kanjorski	?	?	?	Y	Y	Y
12 Murtha	?	?	?	?	?	?
13 Hoeffel	Y	Y	?	Y	Y	Y
14 Coyne	?	?	?	Y	Y	Y
15 ***Toomey***	Y	Y	Y	Y	Y	Y
16 ***Pitts***	Y	Y	Y	Y	Y	Y
17 ***Gekas***	Y	Y	Y	Y	Y	Y
18 Doyle	?	?	?	Y	Y	Y
19 ***Platts***	Y	Y	Y	Y	Y	Y
20 Mascara	?	?	?	?	?	?
21 ***English***	Y	Y	Y	Y	Y	Y
RHODE ISLAND						
1 Kennedy	Y	Y	Y	Y	Y	Y
2 Langevin	Y	Y	Y	Y	Y	Y
SOUTH CAROLINA						
1 ***Brown***	Y	Y	Y	Y	Y	Y
2 ***Wilson***	Y	Y	Y	Y	Y	Y
3 ***Graham***	Y	Y	Y	Y	Y	Y
4 ***DeMint***	Y	Y	Y	Y	Y	Y
5 Spratt	Y	Y	Y	Y	Y	Y
6 Clyburn	Y	Y	Y	Y	Y	Y
SOUTH DAKOTA						
AL ***Thune***	Y	Y	Y	Y	Y	Y
TENNESSEE						
1 ***Jenkins***	?	?	?	Y	Y	Y
2 ***Duncan***	Y	Y	Y	Y	Y	Y
3 ***Wamp***	Y	Y	Y	Y	Y	Y
4 ***Hilleary***	?	Y	Y	Y	Y	Y
5 Clement	?	?	?	Y	Y	Y
6 Gordon	Y	Y	Y	Y	Y	Y
7 ***Bryant***	?	?	?	Y	Y	Y
8 Tanner	Y	Y	Y	Y	Y	Y
9 Ford	Y	Y	Y	Y	Y	Y
TEXAS						
1 Sandlin	Y	Y	Y	Y	?	Y
2 Turner	Y	Y	Y	Y	Y	Y
3 ***Johnson, Sam***	?	?	?	?	?	?
4 Hall	Y	Y	Y	Y	Y	Y
5 ***Sessions***	?	?	?	Y	Y	Y
6 ***Barton***	Y	Y	Y	Y	Y	Y
7 ***Culberson***	Y	Y	Y	Y	Y	Y
8 ***Brady***	Y	Y	Y	Y	Y	Y
9 Lampson	Y	Y	Y	Y	Y	Y
10 Doggett	Y	Y	Y	Y	Y	Y
11 Edwards	Y	Y	Y	Y	Y	Y
12 ***Granger***	Y	Y	Y	Y	Y	Y
13 ***Thornberry***	Y	Y	Y	Y	Y	N
14 ***Paul***	Y	Y	Y	N	N	N
15 Hinojosa	Y	Y	Y	Y	Y	Y
16 Reyes	Y	Y	Y	Y	Y	Y
17 Stenholm	Y	Y	Y	Y	Y	Y
18 Jackson-Lee	Y	Y	Y	Y	Y	Y
19 ***Combest***	Y	Y	Y	Y	Y	Y
20 Gonzalez	Y	Y	Y	Y	Y	Y
21 ***Smith***	Y	Y	Y	Y	Y	Y
22 ***DeLay***	Y	Y	Y	Y	Y	Y
23 ***Bonilla***	Y	Y	Y	Y	Y	Y
24 Frost	Y	Y	Y	Y	Y	Y
25 Bentsen	Y	Y	Y	Y	Y	Y
26 ***Armey***	Y	Y	Y	Y	Y	Y
27 Ortiz	Y	Y	Y	Y	Y	Y
28 Rodriguez	Y	Y	Y	Y	Y	Y
29 Green	Y	Y	Y	Y	Y	Y
30 Johnson, E.B.	Y	Y	Y	Y	Y	Y
UTAH						
1 ***Hansen***	Y	Y	Y	Y	Y	Y
2 Matheson	Y	Y	Y	Y	Y	Y
3 ***Cannon***	?	?	?	Y	Y	Y
VERMONT						
AL *Sanders*	?	Y	Y	Y	Y	Y
VIRGINIA						
1 ***Davis, Jo Ann***	Y	Y	Y	Y	Y	Y
2 ***Schrock***	Y	Y	Y	Y	Y	?
3 Scott	Y	Y	Y	Y	N	Y
4 ***Forbes***	Y	Y	Y	Y	Y	Y
5 *Goode*	Y	Y	Y	Y	Y	N
6 ***Goodlatte***	Y	Y	Y	Y	Y	Y
7 ***Cantor***	Y	Y	Y	Y	Y	Y
8 Moran	Y	Y	Y	Y	Y	Y
9 Boucher	Y	Y	Y	Y	Y	Y
10 ***Wolf***	Y	Y	Y	Y	Y	Y
11 ***Davis, T.***	Y	Y	Y	Y	Y	Y
WASHINGTON						
1 Inslee	Y	Y	Y	Y	Y	Y
2 Larsen	Y	Y	Y	Y	Y	Y
3 Baird	Y	Y	Y	Y	Y	Y
4 ***Hastings***	Y	Y	Y	Y	Y	Y
5 ***Nethercutt***	?	?	?	Y	Y	Y
6 Dicks	Y	Y	Y	Y	Y	Y
7 McDermott	Y	Y	Y	Y	N	Y
8 ***Dunn***	Y	Y	Y	Y	Y	Y
9 Smith	Y	Y	Y	Y	Y	Y
WEST VIRGINIA						
1 Mollohan	Y	Y	Y	Y	Y	Y
2 ***Capito***	Y	Y	Y	Y	Y	Y
3 Rahall	?	?	?	Y	Y	Y
WISCONSIN						
1 ***Ryan***	Y	Y	Y	Y	Y	Y
2 Baldwin	Y	Y	Y	Y	Y	Y
3 Kind	Y	Y	Y	Y	Y	Y
4 Kleczka	Y	Y	Y	Y	Y	Y
5 Barrett	Y	Y	Y	Y	Y	Y
6 ***Petri***	Y	Y	Y	Y	Y	Y
7 Obey	Y	Y	Y	Y	Y	Y
8 ***Green***	Y	Y	Y	Y	Y	Y
9 ***Sensenbrenner***	Y	Y	Y	Y	Y	Y
WYOMING						
AL ***Cubin***	Y	Y	Y	Y	Y	Y

Southern states - Ala., Ark., Fla., Ga., Ky., La., Miss., N.C., Okla., S.C., Tenn., Texas, Va.

177. HR 4626. Marriage and Job Tax Credits/Passage. Weller, R-Ill., motion to suspend the rules and pass the bill that would move up the start date of the phase-in of the doubling of the standard deduction for married couples from 2005 to 2003. The bill also would combine the work opportunity and welfare-to-work tax credits. Motion agreed to 409-1: R 211-0; D 196-1 (ND 145-1, SD 51-0); I 2-0. A two-thirds majority of those present and voting (274 in this case) is required for passage under suspension of the rules. May 21, 2002.

178. H Con Res 405. East Timor Sovereignty/Adoption. Smith, R-N.J., motion to suspend the rules and adopt the concurrent resolution that would recognize the sovereignty of East Timor. Motion agreed to 405-1: R 209-1; D 194-0 (ND 144-0, SD 50-0); I 2-0. A two-thirds majority of those present and voting (271 in this case) is required for adoption under suspension of the rules. May 21, 2002.

179. HR 3994. Afghan Aid/Security Assistance. Lantos, D-Calif., amendment that would support U.S. policies to meet the immediate security needs of Afghanistan, including protecting humanitarian assistance, upholding the rule of law, and supporting a representative government. It also would require the president to report to Congress within 45 days on a security strategy for the country. Adopted 407-4: R 208-3; D 198-0 (ND 147-0, SD 51-0); I 1-1. May 21, 2002.

180. HR 3994. Afghan Aid/Child Soldiers. Jackson-Lee, D-Texas, amendment that would express the sense of Congress that the Afghan army should not use children as soldiers. Adopted 413-0: R 213-0; D 198-0 (ND 147-0, SD 51-0); I 2-0. May 21, 2002.

181. HR 3994. Afghan Aid/Drug Trafficking. Waters, D-Calif., amendment that would prohibit the intelligence community from engaging in any drug trafficking activities and require reports on narcotics trafficking and drug eradication efforts. Adopted 412-0: R 212-0; D 198-0 (ND 147-0, SD 51-0); I 2-0. May 21, 2002.

182. HR 3994. Afghan Aid/Passage. Passage of the bill that would authorize $1.05 billion in aid to Afghanistan over the next four years to support humanitarian programs, counternarcotics efforts, democracy building, reconstruction and other security activities. It would allow the president to use up to $300 million for military assistance and urge him to appoint a coordinator for policy and aid to Afghanistan. Passed 390-22: R 194-18; D 195-3 (ND 146-1, SD 49-2); I 1-1. May 21, 2002.

183. HR 4514. Veterans Medical Centers/Passage. Smith, R-N.J., motion to suspend the rules and pass the bill that would authorize $285 million in fiscal 2003 to upgrade patient care medical facilities at Veterans Affairs centers. Half of those renovations would address earthquake concerns in California. Motion agreed to 411-0: R 212-0; D 197-0 (ND 147-0, SD 50-0); I 2-0. A two-thirds majority of those present and voting (274 in this case) is required for passage under suspension of the rules. May 21, 2002.

184. HR 4015. Veterans Employment/Passage. Smith, R-N.J., motion to suspend the rules and pass the bill that would authorize $260 million from fiscal 2004 through fiscal 2008 for an awards program to encourage states to improve employment placement programs for veterans. Awards would consist of contracts for new employment-related activities. Motion agreed to 409-0: R 209-0; D 198-0 (ND 147-0, SD 51-0); I 2-0. A two-thirds majority of those present and voting (273 in this case) is required for passage under suspension of the rules. May 21, 2002.

Key

Y	Voted for (yea).
#	Paired for.
+	Announced for.
N	Voted against (nay).
X	Paired against.
–	Announced against.
P	Voted "present."
C	Voted "present" to avoid possible conflict of interest.
?	Did not vote or otherwise make a position known.

Democrats **Republicans**
Independents

	177	178	179	180	181	182	183	184
ALABAMA								
1 *Callahan*	Y	Y	Y	Y	Y	Y	Y	Y
2 *Everett*	Y	Y	Y	Y	Y	N	Y	Y
3 *Riley*	+	+	+	+	+	+	+	+
4 *Aderholt*	Y	Y	Y	Y	Y	Y	Y	Y
5 Cramer	Y	Y	Y	Y	Y	Y	Y	Y
6 *Bachus*	Y	Y	Y	Y	Y	Y	Y	Y
7 Hilliard	Y	Y	Y	Y	Y	Y	Y	Y
ALASKA								
AL *Young*	Y	Y	Y	Y	Y	Y	Y	Y
ARIZONA								
1 *Flake*	Y	Y	Y	Y	Y	N	Y	Y
2 Pastor	Y	Y	Y	Y	Y	Y	Y	Y
3 *Stump*	?	?	Y	Y	Y	Y	Y	Y
4 *Shadegg*	Y	Y	Y	Y	Y	Y	Y	Y
5 *Kolbe*	Y	Y	Y	Y	Y	Y	Y	Y
6 *Hayworth*	Y	Y	Y	Y	Y	Y	Y	Y
ARKANSAS								
1 Berry	Y	Y	Y	Y	Y	N	Y	Y
2 Snyder	?	?	?	?	?	?	?	?
3 *Boozman*	Y	Y	Y	Y	Y	Y	Y	Y
4 Ross	Y	Y	Y	Y	Y	Y	Y	Y
CALIFORNIA								
1 Thompson	Y	Y	Y	Y	Y	Y	Y	Y
2 *Herger*	Y	Y	Y	Y	Y	Y	Y	Y
3 *Ose*	Y	Y	Y	Y	Y	Y	Y	Y
4 *Doolittle*	Y	Y	Y	Y	Y	Y	Y	Y
5 Matsui	?	?	Y	Y	Y	Y	Y	Y
6 Woolsey	Y	Y	Y	Y	Y	Y	Y	Y
7 Miller, George	Y	Y	Y	Y	Y	Y	Y	Y
8 Pelosi	Y	Y	Y	Y	Y	Y	Y	Y
9 Lee	Y	Y	Y	Y	Y	Y	Y	Y
10 Tauscher	Y	Y	Y	Y	Y	Y	Y	Y
11 *Pombo*	?	?	?	?	?	?	?	?
12 Lantos	Y	Y	Y	Y	Y	Y	Y	Y
13 Stark	Y	Y	Y	Y	Y	Y	Y	Y
14 Eshoo	Y	Y	Y	Y	Y	Y	Y	Y
15 Honda	Y	Y	Y	Y	Y	Y	Y	Y
16 Lofgren	Y	Y	Y	Y	Y	Y	Y	Y
17 Farr	Y	Y	Y	Y	Y	Y	Y	Y
18 Condit	Y	Y	Y	Y	Y	N	Y	Y
19 *Radanovich*	Y	Y	Y	Y	Y	Y	Y	Y
20 Dooley	Y	Y	Y	Y	Y	Y	Y	Y
21 *Thomas*	Y	Y	Y	Y	Y	Y	Y	Y
22 Capps	Y	Y	Y	Y	Y	Y	Y	Y
23 *Gallegly*	Y	Y	Y	Y	Y	Y	Y	Y
24 Sherman	Y	Y	Y	Y	Y	Y	Y	Y
25 *McKeon*	Y	Y	Y	Y	Y	Y	Y	Y
26 Berman	Y	Y	Y	Y	Y	Y	Y	Y
27 Schiff	Y	Y	Y	Y	Y	Y	Y	Y
28 *Dreier*	Y	Y	Y	Y	Y	Y	Y	Y
29 Waxman	Y	Y	Y	Y	Y	Y	Y	Y
30 Becerra	Y	Y	Y	Y	Y	Y	Y	Y
31 Solis	Y	Y	Y	Y	Y	Y	Y	Y
32 Watson	Y	Y	Y	Y	Y	Y	Y	Y
33 Roybal-Allard	Y	Y	Y	Y	Y	Y	Y	Y
34 Napolitano	Y	Y	Y	Y	Y	Y	Y	Y
35 Waters	Y	Y	Y	Y	Y	Y	Y	Y
36 Harman	Y	Y	Y	Y	Y	Y	Y	Y
37 Millender-McD.	Y	Y	Y	Y	Y	Y	Y	Y
38 *Horn*	Y	Y	Y	Y	Y	Y	Y	Y

	177	178	179	180	181	182	183	184
39 *Royce*	Y	Y	Y	Y	Y	Y	Y	Y
40 *Lewis*	Y	Y	Y	Y	Y	Y	Y	Y
41 *Miller, Gary*	Y	Y	Y	Y	Y	Y	Y	Y
42 Baca	Y	Y	Y	Y	Y	Y	Y	Y
43 *Calvert*	Y	Y	Y	Y	Y	Y	Y	Y
44 *Bono*	Y	Y	Y	Y	Y	Y	Y	Y
45 *Rohrabacher*	Y	Y	Y	Y	Y	Y	Y	Y
46 Sanchez	Y	Y	Y	Y	Y	Y	Y	Y
47 *Cox*	?	?	Y	Y	Y	Y	Y	?
48 *Issa*	Y	Y	Y	Y	Y	Y	Y	Y
49 Davis	Y	Y	Y	Y	Y	Y	Y	Y
50 Filner	Y	Y	Y	Y	Y	Y	Y	Y
51 *Cunningham*	Y	Y	Y	Y	Y	Y	Y	Y
52 *Hunter*	Y	Y	Y	Y	Y	Y	Y	Y
COLORADO								
1 DeGette	Y	Y	Y	Y	Y	Y	Y	Y
2 Udall	Y	Y	Y	Y	Y	Y	Y	Y
3 *McInnis*	Y	Y	Y	Y	Y	Y	Y	Y
4 *Schaffer*	Y	Y	Y	Y	Y	Y	Y	Y
5 *Hefley*	Y	Y	Y	Y	Y	Y	Y	Y
6 *Tancredo*	Y	Y	Y	Y	Y	Y	Y	Y
CONNECTICUT								
1 Larson	Y	Y	Y	Y	Y	Y	Y	Y
2 *Simmons*	Y	Y	Y	Y	Y	Y	Y	Y
3 DeLauro	Y	Y	Y	Y	Y	Y	Y	Y
4 *Shays*	Y	Y	Y	Y	Y	Y	Y	Y
5 Maloney	Y	Y	Y	Y	Y	Y	Y	Y
6 *Johnson*	Y	Y	Y	Y	Y	Y	Y	Y
DELAWARE								
AL *Castle*	Y	Y	Y	Y	Y	Y	Y	Y
FLORIDA								
1 *Miller, J.*	Y	Y	Y	Y	N	Y	Y	Y
2 Boyd	Y	Y	Y	Y	Y	Y	Y	Y
3 Brown	Y	Y	Y	Y	Y	Y	Y	Y
4 *Crenshaw*	Y	Y	Y	Y	Y	Y	Y	Y
5 Thurman	Y	Y	Y	Y	Y	Y	Y	Y
6 *Stearns*	Y	Y	Y	Y	N	Y	Y	Y
7 *Mica*	Y	Y	Y	Y	Y	Y	Y	Y
8 *Keller*	Y	Y	Y	Y	Y	Y	Y	Y
9 *Bilirakis*	Y	Y	Y	Y	Y	Y	Y	Y
10 *Young*	Y	Y	Y	Y	Y	Y	Y	Y
11 Davis	Y	Y	Y	Y	Y	+	Y	Y
12 *Putnam*	Y	Y	Y	Y	Y	Y	Y	Y
13 *Miller, D.*	Y	Y	Y	Y	Y	Y	Y	Y
14 *Goss*	Y	Y	Y	Y	Y	Y	Y	Y
15 *Weldon*	Y	Y	Y	Y	Y	Y	Y	Y
16 *Foley*	Y	Y	Y	Y	Y	Y	Y	Y
17 Meek	Y	Y	Y	Y	Y	Y	Y	Y
18 *Ros-Lehtinen*	Y	Y	Y	Y	Y	Y	Y	Y
19 Wexler	Y	Y	Y	Y	Y	Y	Y	Y
20 Deutsch	?	?	?	?	?	?	?	?
21 *Diaz-Balart*	Y	Y	Y	Y	Y	Y	Y	Y
22 *Shaw*	Y	Y	Y	Y	Y	Y	Y	Y
23 Hastings	Y	Y	Y	Y	Y	Y	Y	Y
GEORGIA								
1 *Kingston*	Y	Y	Y	Y	Y	Y	Y	Y
2 Bishop	Y	Y	Y	Y	Y	Y	Y	Y
3 *Collins*	Y	?	Y	Y	Y	N	Y	Y
4 McKinney	Y	Y	Y	Y	Y	Y	Y	Y
5 Lewis	?	?	?	?	?	?	?	?
6 *Isakson*	Y	Y	Y	Y	Y	Y	Y	Y
7 *Barr*	Y	Y	Y	Y	Y	Y	Y	Y
8 *Chambliss*	Y	Y	Y	Y	Y	Y	Y	Y
9 *Deal*	Y	Y	Y	Y	Y	N	Y	Y
10 *Norwood*	Y	Y	Y	Y	Y	N	Y	Y
11 *Linder*	Y	Y	Y	Y	Y	Y	Y	Y
HAWAII								
1 Abercrombie	Y	Y	Y	Y	Y	Y	Y	Y
2 Mink	Y	Y	Y	Y	Y	Y	Y	Y
IDAHO								
1 *Otter*	Y	Y	Y	Y	Y	Y	Y	Y
2 *Simpson*	Y	Y	Y	Y	Y	Y	Y	Y
ILLINOIS								
1 Rush	Y	Y	Y	Y	Y	Y	Y	Y
2 Jackson	Y	Y	Y	Y	Y	Y	Y	Y
3 Lipinski	Y	Y	Y	Y	Y	Y	Y	Y
4 Gutierrez	Y	Y	Y	Y	Y	Y	Y	Y
5 Blagojevich	?	?	?	?	?	?	?	?
6 *Hyde*	Y	Y	Y	Y	Y	Y	Y	Y
7 Davis	Y	Y	Y	Y	Y	Y	Y	Y
8 *Crane*	Y	Y	Y	Y	Y	Y	Y	Y
9 Schakowsky	Y	Y	Y	Y	Y	Y	Y	Y
10 *Kirk*	Y	Y	?	Y	Y	Y	Y	Y
11 *Weller*	Y	Y	Y	Y	Y	Y	Y	Y
12 Costello	Y	Y	Y	Y	Y	Y	Y	Y
13 *Biggert*	Y	Y	Y	Y	Y	Y	Y	Y

ND Northern Democrats   SD Southern Democrats

Illinois (cont.)	177	178	179	180	181	182	183	184
14 Hastert								
15 *Johnson*	Y	Y	Y	Y	Y	Y	Y	Y
16 *Manzullo*	Y	Y	Y	Y	Y	Y	Y	Y
17 Evans	Y	Y	Y	Y	Y	Y	Y	Y
18 *LaHood*	Y	Y	Y	Y	Y	Y	Y	Y
19 Phelps	Y	Y	Y	Y	Y	Y	Y	Y
20 *Shimkus*	Y	Y	Y	Y	Y	Y	Y	Y

INDIANA

	177	178	179	180	181	182	183	184
1 Visclosky	Y	Y	Y	Y	Y	Y	Y	Y
2 *Pence*	Y	Y	Y	Y	Y	Y	Y	Y
3 Roemer	Y	Y	Y	Y	Y	Y	Y	Y
4 *Souder*	Y	Y	Y	Y	Y	Y	Y	Y
5 *Buyer*	Y	Y	Y	Y	Y	Y	Y	Y
6 Burton	?	?	?	?	?	?	?	?
7 *Kerns*	Y	Y	Y	Y	Y	N	Y	Y
8 *Hostettler*	Y	Y	N	Y	N	Y	Y	Y
9 Hill								
10 Carson	Y	Y	Y	Y	Y	Y	Y	Y

IOWA

	177	178	179	180	181	182	183	184
1 *Leach*	Y	Y	Y	Y	Y	Y	Y	Y
2 *Nussle*	Y	Y	Y	Y	Y	Y	Y	Y
3 Boswell	Y	Y	Y	Y	Y	Y	Y	Y
4 *Ganske*	Y	Y	Y	Y	Y	Y	Y	Y
5 *Latham*	Y	Y	Y	Y	Y	Y	Y	Y

KANSAS

	177	178	179	180	181	182	183	184
1 *Moran*	Y	Y	Y	Y	Y	Y	Y	Y
2 *Ryun*	Y	Y	Y	Y	Y	Y	Y	Y
3 Moore	Y	Y	Y	Y	Y	Y	Y	Y
4 *Tiahrt*	Y	Y	Y	Y	Y	Y	Y	Y

KENTUCKY

	177	178	179	180	181	182	183	184
1 *Whitfield*	Y	Y	Y	Y	Y	Y	Y	Y
2 *Lewis*	Y	Y	Y	Y	Y	Y	Y	Y
3 *Northup*	Y	Y	Y	Y	Y	Y	Y	Y
4 Lucas	Y	Y	Y	Y	Y	Y	Y	Y
5 *Rogers*	Y	Y	Y	Y	Y	Y	Y	Y
6 *Fletcher*	Y	Y	Y	Y	Y	Y	Y	Y

LOUISIANA

	177	178	179	180	181	182	183	184
1 *Vitter*	Y	Y	Y	Y	Y	Y	Y	Y
2 Jefferson	Y	Y	Y	Y	Y	Y	Y	Y
3 *Tauzin*	Y	Y	Y	Y	Y	Y	Y	Y
4 *McCrery*	Y	Y	Y	Y	Y	Y	Y	Y
5 *Cooksey*	Y	Y	Y	Y	Y	Y	Y	Y
6 *Baker*	Y	Y	Y	Y	Y	Y	Y	Y
7 John	Y	Y	Y	Y	Y	Y	Y	Y

MAINE

	177	178	179	180	181	182	183	184
1 Allen	Y	Y	Y	Y	Y	Y	Y	Y
2 Baldacci	Y	Y	Y	Y	Y	Y	Y	Y

MARYLAND

	177	178	179	180	181	182	183	184
1 *Gilchrest*	Y	Y	Y	Y	Y	Y	Y	Y
2 *Ehrlich*	Y	Y	Y	Y	Y	Y	Y	Y
3 Cardin	Y	Y	Y	Y	Y	Y	Y	Y
4 Wynn	Y	Y	Y	Y	Y	Y	Y	Y
5 Hoyer	Y	Y	Y	Y	Y	Y	Y	Y
6 *Bartlett*	Y	Y	Y	Y	N	Y	Y	Y
7 Cummings	Y	Y	Y	Y	Y	Y	Y	Y
8 *Morella*	Y	Y	Y	Y	Y	Y	Y	Y

MASSACHUSETTS

	177	178	179	180	181	182	183	184
1 Olver	Y	?	Y	Y	Y	Y	Y	Y
2 Neal	Y	Y	Y	Y	Y	Y	Y	Y
3 McGovern	Y	Y	Y	Y	Y	Y	Y	Y
4 Frank	?	Y	Y	Y	Y	Y	Y	Y
5 Meehan	Y	Y	Y	Y	Y	Y	Y	Y
6 Tierney	Y	Y	Y	Y	Y	Y	Y	Y
7 Markey	Y	Y	Y	Y	Y	Y	Y	Y
8 Capuano	Y	Y	Y	Y	Y	Y	Y	Y
9 Lynch	Y	Y	Y	Y	Y	Y	Y	Y
10 Delahunt	Y	?	Y	Y	Y	Y	Y	Y

MICHIGAN

	177	178	179	180	181	182	183	184
1 Stupak	Y	Y	Y	Y	Y	Y	Y	Y
2 *Hoekstra*	Y	Y	Y	Y	Y	Y	Y	Y
3 *Ehlers*	Y	Y	Y	Y	Y	Y	Y	Y
4 *Camp*	Y	Y	Y	Y	Y	Y	Y	Y
5 Barcia	Y	Y	Y	Y	Y	Y	Y	Y
6 *Upton*	Y	Y	Y	Y	Y	Y	Y	Y
7 *Smith*	Y	Y	?	Y	Y	Y	Y	Y
8 *Rogers*	Y	Y	Y	Y	Y	Y	Y	Y
9 Kildee	Y	Y	Y	Y	Y	Y	Y	Y
10 Bonior	+	+	+	+	+	+	+	+
11 *Knollenberg*	Y	Y	Y	Y	Y	Y	Y	Y
12 Levin	Y	Y	Y	Y	Y	Y	Y	Y
13 Rivers	Y	Y	Y	Y	Y	Y	Y	Y
14 Conyers	?	?	?	?	?	?	?	?
15 Kilpatrick	Y	Y	Y	Y	Y	Y	Y	Y
16 Dingell	Y	Y	Y	Y	Y	Y	Y	Y

MINNESOTA

	177	178	179	180	181	182	183	184
1 *Gutknecht*	Y	Y	Y	Y	Y	Y	Y	Y
2 *Kennedy*	Y	Y	Y	Y	Y	Y	Y	Y
3 *Ramstad*	Y	Y	Y	Y	Y	Y	Y	Y
4 McCollum	Y	Y	Y	Y	Y	Y	Y	Y
5 Sabo	Y	Y	Y	Y	Y	Y	Y	Y
6 Luther	Y	Y	Y	Y	Y	Y	Y	Y
7 Peterson	Y	Y	Y	Y	Y	Y	Y	Y
8 Oberstar	Y	Y	Y	Y	Y	Y	Y	Y

MISSISSIPPI

	177	178	179	180	181	182	183	184
1 *Wicker*	Y	Y	Y	Y	Y	Y	Y	Y
2 Thompson	Y	Y	Y	Y	Y	Y	Y	Y
3 *Pickering*	Y	Y	Y	Y	Y	Y	Y	Y
4 Shows	Y	Y	Y	Y	Y	Y	Y	Y
5 Taylor	Y	Y	Y	Y	Y	Y	Y	Y

MISSOURI

	177	178	179	180	181	182	183	184
1 Clay	Y	Y	Y	Y	Y	Y	Y	Y
2 *Akin*	Y	Y	Y	Y	Y	Y	Y	Y
3 Gephardt	Y	Y	Y	Y	Y	Y	Y	Y
4 Skelton	Y	Y	Y	Y	Y	Y	Y	Y
5 McCarthy	Y	Y	Y	Y	Y	Y	Y	Y
6 *Graves*	Y	Y	Y	Y	Y	Y	Y	Y
7 *Blunt*	Y	Y	Y	Y	Y	Y	Y	Y
8 *Emerson*	?	?	?	?	?	?	?	?
9 *Hulshof*	Y	Y	Y	Y	Y	Y	Y	Y

MONTANA

	177	178	179	180	181	182	183	184
AL *Rehberg*	Y	Y	Y	Y	Y	Y	Y	Y

NEBRASKA

	177	178	179	180	181	182	183	184
1 *Bereuter*	Y	Y	Y	Y	Y	Y	Y	Y
2 *Terry*	Y	Y	Y	Y	Y	N	Y	Y
3 *Osborne*	Y	Y	Y	Y	Y	Y	Y	Y

NEVADA

	177	178	179	180	181	182	183	184
1 Berkley	Y	Y	Y	Y	Y	Y	Y	Y
2 *Gibbons*	Y	Y	Y	Y	Y	Y	Y	Y

NEW HAMPSHIRE

	177	178	179	180	181	182	183	184
1 *Sununu*	Y	Y	Y	Y	Y	Y	Y	Y
2 *Bass*	Y	Y	Y	Y	Y	Y	Y	Y

NEW JERSEY

	177	178	179	180	181	182	183	184
1 Andrews	Y	Y	Y	Y	Y	Y	Y	Y
2 *LoBiondo*	Y	Y	Y	Y	Y	Y	Y	Y
3 *Saxton*	Y	Y	Y	Y	Y	Y	Y	Y
4 *Smith*	Y	Y	Y	Y	Y	Y	Y	Y
5 *Roukema*	Y	Y	Y	Y	Y	Y	Y	Y
6 Pallone	Y	Y	Y	Y	Y	Y	Y	Y
7 *Ferguson*	Y	Y	Y	Y	Y	Y	Y	Y
8 Pascrell	Y	Y	Y	Y	Y	Y	Y	Y
9 Rothman	Y	Y	Y	Y	Y	Y	Y	Y
10 Payne	Y	Y	Y	Y	Y	Y	Y	Y
11 *Frelinghuysen*	Y	Y	Y	Y	Y	Y	Y	Y
12 Holt	Y	Y	Y	Y	Y	Y	Y	Y
13 Menendez	?	?	?	?	?	?	?	?

NEW MEXICO

	177	178	179	180	181	182	183	184
1 *Wilson*	Y	Y	Y	Y	Y	Y	Y	Y
2 *Skeen*	Y	Y	Y	Y	Y	Y	Y	Y
3 Udall	Y	Y	Y	Y	Y	Y	Y	Y

NEW YORK

	177	178	179	180	181	182	183	184
1 *Grucci*	Y	Y	Y	Y	Y	Y	Y	Y
2 Israel	Y	Y	Y	Y	Y	Y	Y	Y
3 *King*	Y	Y	Y	Y	Y	Y	Y	Y
4 McCarthy	Y	Y	Y	Y	Y	Y	Y	Y
5 Ackerman	Y	Y	Y	Y	Y	Y	Y	Y
6 Meeks	Y	Y	Y	Y	Y	Y	Y	Y
7 Crowley	Y	Y	Y	Y	Y	Y	Y	Y
8 Nadler	Y	Y	?	?	?	?	?	?
9 Weiner	Y	Y	Y	Y	Y	Y	Y	Y
10 Towns	Y	Y	Y	Y	Y	Y	Y	Y
11 Owens	Y	Y	Y	Y	Y	Y	Y	Y
12 Velázquez	Y	Y	Y	Y	Y	Y	Y	Y
13 *Fossella*	Y	Y	Y	Y	Y	Y	Y	Y
14 Maloney	Y	Y	Y	Y	Y	Y	Y	Y
15 Rangel	Y	Y	Y	Y	Y	Y	Y	Y
16 Serrano	Y	Y	Y	Y	Y	Y	Y	Y
17 Engel	Y	Y	Y	Y	Y	Y	Y	Y
18 Lowey	Y	Y	Y	Y	Y	Y	Y	Y
19 *Kelly*	Y	Y	Y	Y	Y	Y	Y	Y
20 *Gilman*	Y	Y	Y	Y	Y	Y	Y	Y
21 McNulty	Y	Y	Y	Y	Y	Y	Y	Y
22 *Sweeney*	Y	Y	Y	Y	Y	Y	Y	Y
23 *Boehlert*	Y	Y	Y	Y	Y	Y	Y	Y
24 *McHugh*	Y	Y	Y	Y	Y	Y	Y	Y
25 *Walsh*	Y	Y	Y	Y	Y	Y	Y	Y
26 Hinchey	Y	Y	Y	Y	Y	Y	Y	Y
27 *Reynolds*	Y	Y	Y	Y	?	?	?	?
28 Slaughter	Y	Y	Y	Y	Y	Y	Y	Y
29 LaFalce	Y	Y	Y	Y	Y	Y	Y	Y

OHIO (cont.)

	177	178	179	180	181	182	183	184
30 *Quinn*	Y	Y	Y	Y	Y	Y	Y	Y
31 *Houghton*	Y	Y	Y	Y	Y	Y	Y	Y

NORTH CAROLINA

	177	178	179	180	181	182	183	184
1 Clayton	Y	Y	Y	Y	Y	Y	Y	Y
2 Etheridge	Y	Y	Y	Y	Y	Y	Y	Y
3 *Jones*	Y	Y	N	Y	N	Y	Y	Y
4 Price	Y	Y	Y	Y	Y	Y	Y	Y
5 *Burr*	Y	Y	Y	Y	Y	Y	Y	Y
6 *Coble*	Y	Y	Y	Y	Y	N	Y	Y
7 McIntyre	Y	Y	Y	Y	Y	Y	Y	Y
8 *Hayes*	Y	Y	Y	Y	Y	Y	Y	Y
9 *Myrick*	Y	Y	Y	Y	Y	Y	Y	Y
10 *Ballenger*	Y	Y	Y	Y	Y	Y	Y	Y
11 *Taylor*	Y	Y	Y	Y	Y	N	Y	Y
12 Watt	Y	Y	Y	Y	Y	Y	Y	Y

NORTH DAKOTA

	177	178	179	180	181	182	183	184
AL Pomeroy	Y	Y	Y	Y	Y	Y	Y	Y

OHIO

	177	178	179	180	181	182	183	184
1 *Chabot*	Y	Y	Y	Y	Y	Y	Y	Y
2 *Portman*	Y	Y	Y	Y	Y	Y	Y	Y
3 Hall	Y	Y	Y	Y	Y	Y	Y	Y
4 *Oxley*	Y	Y	Y	Y	Y	Y	Y	Y
5 *Gillmor*	Y	Y	Y	Y	Y	Y	Y	?
6 Strickland	Y	Y	Y	Y	Y	Y	Y	Y
7 *Hobson*	Y	Y	Y	Y	Y	Y	Y	Y
8 *Boehner*	Y	Y	Y	Y	Y	Y	Y	Y
9 Kaptur	Y	Y	Y	Y	Y	Y	Y	Y
10 Kucinich	Y	Y	Y	Y	Y	Y	Y	Y
11 Jones	Y	Y	Y	Y	Y	Y	Y	Y
12 *Tiberi*	Y	Y	Y	Y	Y	Y	Y	Y
13 Brown	Y	Y	Y	Y	Y	Y	Y	Y
14 Sawyer	Y	Y	Y	Y	Y	Y	Y	Y
15 *Pryce*	Y	Y	Y	Y	Y	Y	Y	Y
16 *Regula*	Y	Y	Y	Y	Y	Y	Y	Y
17 Traficant	?	?	?	?	?	?	?	?
18 *Ney*	Y	Y	Y	Y	Y	Y	Y	Y
19 *LaTourette*	Y	Y	Y	Y	Y	Y	Y	Y

OKLAHOMA

	177	178	179	180	181	182	183	184
1 *Sullivan*	Y	Y	Y	Y	Y	Y	Y	Y
2 Carson	Y	Y	Y	Y	Y	Y	Y	Y
3 *Watkins*	?	?	?	?	?	?	?	?
4 *Watts*	Y	Y	+	+	+	+	+	+
5 *Istook*	Y	Y	Y	Y	Y	Y	Y	Y
6 *Lucas*	Y	Y	Y	Y	Y	Y	Y	Y

OREGON

	177	178	179	180	181	182	183	184
1 Wu	Y	Y	Y	Y	Y	Y	Y	Y
2 *Walden*	Y	Y	Y	Y	Y	Y	Y	Y
3 Blumenauer	Y	Y	Y	Y	Y	Y	Y	Y
4 DeFazio	Y	Y	Y	Y	Y	Y	Y	Y
5 Hooley	Y	Y	Y	Y	Y	Y	Y	Y

PENNSYLVANIA

	177	178	179	180	181	182	183	184
1 Brady	?	?	?	?	?	?	?	?
2 Fattah	Y	Y	Y	Y	Y	Y	Y	Y
3 Borski	?	?	?	?	?	?	?	?
4 *Hart*	Y	Y	Y	Y	Y	Y	Y	+
5 Peterson	Y	Y	Y	Y	Y	Y	Y	Y
6 Holden	Y	Y	Y	Y	Y	Y	Y	Y
7 *Weldon*	Y	Y	Y	Y	Y	Y	Y	Y
8 *Greenwood*	?	?	?	?	?	?	?	?
9 *Shuster, Bill*	Y	Y	Y	Y	Y	Y	Y	Y
10 *Sherwood*	Y	Y	Y	Y	Y	Y	Y	Y
11 Kanjorski	Y	Y	Y	Y	Y	Y	Y	Y
12 Murtha	?	?	?	?	?	?	?	?
13 Hoeffel	Y	Y	Y	Y	Y	Y	Y	Y
14 Coyne	Y	Y	Y	Y	Y	Y	Y	Y
15 *Toomey*	Y	Y	Y	Y	Y	Y	Y	Y
16 *Pitts*	Y	Y	Y	Y	Y	Y	Y	Y
17 *Gekas*	Y	Y	Y	Y	Y	Y	Y	Y
18 Doyle	Y	Y	Y	Y	Y	Y	Y	Y
19 *Platts*	Y	Y	Y	Y	Y	Y	Y	Y
20 Mascara	?	?	?	?	?	?	?	?
21 *English*	Y	Y	Y	Y	Y	Y	Y	Y

RHODE ISLAND

	177	178	179	180	181	182	183	184
1 Kennedy	Y	Y	Y	Y	Y	Y	Y	Y
2 Langevin	Y	Y	Y	Y	Y	Y	Y	Y

SOUTH CAROLINA

	177	178	179	180	181	182	183	184
1 *Brown*	Y	Y	Y	Y	Y	Y	Y	Y
2 *Wilson*	Y	Y	Y	Y	Y	Y	Y	Y
3 *Graham*	Y	Y	Y	Y	Y	Y	Y	Y
4 *DeMint*	Y	Y	Y	Y	Y	Y	Y	Y
5 Spratt	Y	?	Y	Y	Y	Y	Y	Y
6 Clyburn	Y	Y	Y	Y	Y	Y	Y	Y

SOUTH DAKOTA

	177	178	179	180	181	182	183	184
AL *Thune*	Y	Y	Y	Y	Y	Y	Y	Y

TENNESSEE

	177	178	179	180	181	182	183	184
1 *Jenkins*	Y	Y	Y	Y	Y	Y	Y	Y
2 *Duncan*	Y	Y	Y	Y	N	Y	Y	
3 *Wamp*	Y	Y	Y	Y	Y	Y	Y	Y
4 *Hilleary*	Y	Y	Y	Y	Y	Y	Y	Y
5 Clement	Y	Y	Y	Y	Y	Y	Y	Y
6 Gordon	Y	Y	Y	Y	Y	Y	Y	Y
7 *Bryant*	Y	Y	Y	Y	Y	Y	Y	Y
8 Tanner	Y	Y	Y	Y	Y	Y	Y	Y
9 Ford	Y	Y	Y	Y	Y	Y	Y	Y

TEXAS

	177	178	179	180	181	182	183	184
1 Sandlin	Y	Y	Y	Y	Y	Y	Y	Y
2 Turner	Y	Y	Y	Y	Y	Y	Y	Y
3 *Johnson, Sam*	?	?	Y	Y	Y	N	Y	Y
4 Hall	Y	Y	Y	Y	N	Y	Y	Y
5 *Sessions*	Y	Y	Y	Y	Y	Y	Y	Y
6 *Barton*	Y	Y	Y	Y	Y	Y	Y	Y
7 *Culberson*	Y	Y	Y	Y	Y	Y	Y	Y
8 *Brady*	Y	Y	Y	Y	Y	Y	Y	Y
9 Lampson	Y	Y	Y	Y	Y	Y	Y	Y
10 Doggett	Y	Y	Y	Y	Y	Y	Y	Y
11 Edwards	Y	Y	Y	Y	Y	Y	Y	Y
12 *Granger*	Y	Y	Y	Y	Y	Y	Y	Y
13 *Thornberry*	Y	Y	Y	Y	Y	Y	Y	Y
14 *Paul*	Y	N	N	Y	N	N	Y	Y
15 Hinojosa	Y	Y	Y	Y	Y	Y	Y	Y
16 Reyes	Y	Y	Y	Y	Y	Y	Y	Y
17 Stenholm	Y	Y	Y	Y	Y	Y	Y	Y
18 Jackson-Lee	Y	Y	Y	Y	Y	Y	Y	Y
19 *Combest*	Y	Y	Y	Y	Y	Y	Y	Y
20 Gonzalez	Y	Y	Y	Y	Y	Y	Y	Y
21 *Smith*	Y	Y	Y	Y	Y	Y	Y	Y
22 *DeLay*	Y	Y	Y	Y	Y	Y	Y	Y
23 *Bonilla*	Y	Y	Y	Y	Y	Y	Y	Y
24 Frost	Y	Y	Y	Y	Y	Y	Y	Y
25 Bentsen	Y	Y	Y	Y	Y	Y	Y	Y
26 *Armey*	Y	Y	Y	Y	Y	Y	Y	Y
27 Ortiz	Y	Y	Y	Y	Y	Y	Y	Y
28 Rodriguez	Y	Y	Y	Y	Y	Y	Y	Y
29 Green	Y	Y	Y	Y	Y	Y	Y	Y
30 Johnson, E.B.	Y	Y	Y	Y	Y	Y	Y	Y

UTAH

	177	178	179	180	181	182	183	184
1 *Hansen*	Y	Y	Y	Y	Y	Y	Y	Y
2 Matheson	Y	Y	Y	Y	Y	Y	Y	Y
3 *Cannon*	?	?	?	?	?	?	?	?

VERMONT

	177	178	179	180	181	182	183	184
AL *Sanders*	Y	Y	Y	Y	Y	Y	Y	Y

VIRGINIA

	177	178	179	180	181	182	183	184
1 *Davis, Jo Ann*	Y	Y	Y	Y	Y	Y	Y	Y
2 *Schrock*	Y	Y	Y	Y	Y	Y	Y	Y
3 Scott	Y	Y	Y	Y	Y	Y	Y	Y
4 *Forbes*	Y	Y	Y	Y	Y	Y	Y	Y
5 *Goode*	Y	Y	N	Y	N	Y	Y	Y
6 *Goodlatte*	Y	Y	Y	Y	Y	Y	Y	Y
7 *Cantor*	Y	Y	Y	Y	Y	Y	Y	Y
8 Moran	Y	Y	Y	Y	Y	Y	Y	Y
9 Boucher	Y	Y	Y	Y	Y	Y	Y	Y
10 *Wolf*	Y	Y	Y	Y	Y	Y	Y	Y
11 *Davis, T.*	Y	Y	Y	Y	Y	Y	Y	Y

WASHINGTON

	177	178	179	180	181	182	183	184
1 Inslee	Y	Y	Y	Y	Y	Y	Y	Y
2 Larsen	Y	Y	Y	Y	Y	Y	Y	Y
3 Baird	Y	Y	Y	Y	Y	Y	Y	Y
4 *Hastings*	Y	Y	Y	Y	Y	Y	Y	Y
5 *Nethercutt*	Y	Y	Y	Y	Y	Y	Y	Y
6 Dicks	Y	Y	Y	Y	Y	Y	Y	Y
7 McDermott	Y	Y	Y	Y	Y	Y	Y	Y
8 *Dunn*	Y	Y	Y	Y	Y	Y	Y	Y
9 Smith	Y	Y	Y	Y	Y	Y	Y	Y

WEST VIRGINIA

	177	178	179	180	181	182	183	184
1 Mollohan	N	Y	Y	Y	Y	Y	Y	Y
2 *Capito*	Y	Y	Y	Y	Y	Y	Y	Y
3 Rahall	Y	Y	Y	Y	Y	Y	Y	Y

WISCONSIN

	177	178	179	180	181	182	183	184
1 *Ryan*	Y	Y	Y	Y	Y	Y	Y	Y
2 Baldwin	Y	Y	Y	Y	Y	Y	Y	Y
3 Kind	Y	Y	Y	Y	Y	Y	Y	Y
4 Kleczka	Y	Y	Y	Y	Y	Y	Y	Y
5 Barrett	Y	Y	Y	Y	Y	Y	Y	Y
6 *Petri*	Y	Y	Y	Y	Y	Y	Y	Y
7 Obey	Y	Y	Y	Y	Y	Y	Y	Y
8 *Green*	Y	Y	Y	Y	Y	Y	Y	Y
9 *Sensenbrenner*	Y	Y	Y	Y	N	Y	Y	Y

WYOMING

	177	178	179	180	181	182	183	184
AL *Cubin*	Y	Y	Y	Y	Y	Y	Y	Y

Southern states - Ala., Ark., Fla., Ga., Ky., La., Miss., N.C., Okla., S.C., Tenn., Texas, Va.

Key

Y	Voted for (yea).
#	Paired for.
+	Announced for.
N	Voted against (nay).
X	Paired against.
−	Announced against.
P	Voted "present."
C	Voted "present" to avoid possible conflict of interest.
?	Did not vote or otherwise make a position known.

Democrats **Republicans**
Independents

185. HR 4085. Veterans Benefits/Passage. Smith, R-N.J., motion to suspend the rules and pass the bill that would increase various benefit programs for veterans. It would include an annual cost of living adjustment and allow surviving spouses of veterans over 65 years old to remarry and retain benefits. Motion agreed to 410-0: R 212-0; D 196-0 (ND 146-0, SD 50-0); I 2-0. A two-thirds majority of those present and voting (274 in this case) is required for passage under suspension of the rules. May 21, 2002.

186. HR 3448. Bioterrorism Preparedness/Rule. Adoption of the rule (H Res 427) to provide for House floor consideration of the conference report on the bill that would authorize federal, state and local governments to spend up to $4.2 billion in fiscal 2003, and additional amounts in future years, to prepare and respond to acts of bioterrorism. Adopted 403-19: R 215-0; D 187-18 (ND 137-17, SD 50-1); I 1-1. May 22, 2002.

187. Procedural Motion/Journal. Approval of the House Journal of Tuesday, May 21, 2002. Approved 361-57: R 198-15; D 161-42 (ND 117-36, SD 44-6); I 2-0. May 22, 2002.

188. HR 3129. Customs Service Authorization/Rule. Adoption of the rule (H Res 426) that would provide for House floor consideration of the bill that would authorize $9.1 billion through fiscal 2004 for the activities of the U.S. Customs Service. Adopted 386-32: R 213-1; D 171-31 (ND 125-27, SD 46-4); I 2-0. May 22, 2002.

189. HR 3448. Bioterrorism Preparedness/Conference Report. Adoption of the conference report on the bill that would authorize federal, state and local governments to spend up to $4.2 billion in fiscal 2003, and additional amounts in future years, to prepare for and respond to acts of bioterrorism. The bill includes funds to increase medicine and vaccine stockpiles, expand facilities and laboratories run by the Centers for Disease Control and Prevention and safeguard the nation's food and water supplies. It also would mandate new requirements on biological agents, and reauthorize through fiscal 2007 the Food and Drug Administration user fee system that supports drug approval reviews. Adopted (thus sent to the Senate) 425-1: R 215-1; D 208-0 (ND 155-0, SD 53-0); I 2-0. May 22, 2002.

190. HR 3717. Federal Deposit Protection/Passage. Oxley, R-Ohio, motion to suspend the rules and pass the bill that would combine two Federal Deposit Insurance Corporation insurance funds into one, raise the individual coverage limit for federally insured deposits from $100,000 to $130,000 and index it for inflation, and change the formula used to collect premiums from banks. Motion agreed to 408-18: R 209-8; D 198-9 (ND 146-8, SD 52-1); I 1-1. A two-thirds majority of those present and voting (284 in this case) is required for passage under suspension of the rules. May 22, 2002.

191. H Res 424. New York Recovery Workers/Adoption. Ose, R-Calif., motion to suspend the rules and adopt the resolution that would pay tribute to individuals working on recovery efforts at the site of the Sept. 11, 2001, terrorist attacks in New York City. Motion agreed to 416-0: R 214-0; D 200-0 (ND 147-0, SD 53-0); I 2-0. A two-thirds majority of those present and voting (284 in this case) is required for adoption under suspension of the rules. May 22, 2002.

	185	186	187	188	189	190	191
ALABAMA							
1 *Callahan*	Y	Y	Y	Y	Y	Y	Y
2 *Everett*	Y	Y	Y	Y	Y	Y	Y
3 *Riley*	+	?	?	?	?	?	?
4 *Aderholt*	Y	Y	N	Y	Y	Y	Y
5 Cramer	Y	Y	Y	Y	Y	Y	Y
6 *Bachus*	Y	Y	Y	Y	Y	Y	Y
7 Hilliard	Y	Y	N	Y	Y	Y	Y
ALASKA							
AL *Young*	Y	Y	Y	Y	Y	Y	Y
ARIZONA							
1 *Flake*	Y	Y	Y	Y	Y	N	Y
2 Pastor	Y	Y	Y	N	Y	Y	Y
3 *Stump*	Y	Y	Y	Y	Y	Y	Y
4 *Shadegg*	Y	Y	Y	Y	Y	Y	Y
5 *Kolbe*	Y	Y	Y	Y	Y	Y	Y
6 *Hayworth*	Y	Y	Y	Y	Y	Y	Y
ARKANSAS							
1 Berry	Y	Y	Y	Y	Y	Y	Y
2 Snyder	?	?	?	?	Y	Y	Y
3 *Boozman*	Y	Y	Y	Y	Y	Y	Y
4 Ross	Y	Y	Y	Y	Y	Y	Y
CALIFORNIA							
1 Thompson	Y	Y	Y	Y	Y	Y	Y
2 *Herger*	Y	Y	Y	Y	Y	Y	Y
3 *Ose*	Y	Y	Y	Y	Y	N	Y
4 *Doolittle*	Y	Y	Y	Y	Y	Y	Y
5 Matsui	Y	Y	Y	Y	Y	Y	Y
6 Woolsey	Y	Y	Y	Y	Y	Y	?
7 Miller, George	Y	N	N	N	Y	?	?
8 Pelosi	Y	Y	Y	Y	Y	Y	Y
9 Lee	Y	N	Y	N	Y	Y	Y
10 Tauscher	Y	Y	Y	Y	Y	Y	Y
11 *Pombo*	?	Y	Y	Y	Y	Y	Y
12 Lantos	Y	Y	Y	Y	Y	Y	Y
13 Stark	Y	N	Y	Y	Y	N	Y
14 Eshoo	Y	Y	Y	Y	Y	Y	Y
15 Honda	Y	Y	Y	Y	Y	Y	Y
16 Lofgren	Y	Y	Y	Y	Y	Y	Y
17 Farr	Y	Y	Y	Y	Y	Y	Y
18 Condit	Y	Y	N	Y	Y	Y	Y
19 *Radanovich*	Y	Y	Y	Y	Y	Y	Y
20 Dooley	Y	Y	Y	Y	Y	Y	Y
21 *Thomas*	Y	Y	Y	Y	Y	Y	Y
22 Capps	Y	Y	Y	Y	Y	Y	Y
23 *Gallegly*	Y	Y	Y	Y	Y	Y	Y
24 Sherman	Y	Y	Y	Y	Y	Y	Y
25 *McKeon*	Y	Y	Y	Y	Y	Y	Y
26 Berman	Y	Y	Y	?	Y	Y	Y
27 Schiff	Y	Y	Y	Y	Y	Y	Y
28 *Dreier*	Y	Y	Y	Y	Y	Y	Y
29 Waxman	Y	Y	Y	Y	Y	Y	Y
30 Becerra	Y	Y	N	Y	Y	Y	Y
31 Solis	Y	Y	Y	−	Y	Y	Y
32 Watson	Y	Y	Y	Y	Y	Y	Y
33 Roybal-Allard	Y	Y	Y	Y	Y	Y	?
34 Napolitano	Y	Y	Y	Y	Y	Y	Y
35 Waters	Y	N	N	N	Y	Y	Y
36 Harman	Y	Y	Y	Y	Y	Y	Y
37 Millender-McD.	Y	Y	Y	Y	Y	Y	Y
38 *Horn*	Y	Y	Y	Y	Y	Y	Y

	185	186	187	188	189	190	191
39 *Royce*	Y	Y	Y	Y	Y	N	Y
40 *Lewis*	Y	Y	Y	Y	Y	Y	Y
41 *Miller, Gary*	Y	Y	Y	Y	Y	Y	Y
42 Baca	Y	Y	Y	Y	Y	Y	Y
43 *Calvert*	Y	Y	Y	Y	Y	Y	Y
44 *Bono*	Y	Y	Y	Y	Y	Y	Y
45 *Rohrabacher*	Y	Y	Y	Y	Y	Y	Y
46 Sanchez	Y	Y	N	Y	Y	Y	Y
47 *Cox*	Y	Y	Y	Y	Y	Y	Y
48 *Issa*	Y	Y	Y	Y	Y	Y	Y
49 Davis	Y	Y	Y	Y	Y	Y	Y
50 Filner	Y	N	N	N	Y	Y	Y
51 *Cunningham*	Y	Y	Y	Y	Y	Y	Y
52 *Hunter*	Y	Y	Y	Y	Y	Y	Y
COLORADO							
1 DeGette	Y	Y	Y	N	Y	Y	Y
2 Udall	Y	Y	N	Y	Y	Y	Y
3 *McInnis*	Y	Y	Y	Y	Y	Y	Y
4 *Schaffer*	Y	?	?	?	Y	Y	Y
5 *Hefley*	Y	Y	N	Y	Y	Y	Y
6 *Tancredo*	Y	Y	Y	Y	Y	Y	Y
CONNECTICUT							
1 Larson	Y	Y	Y	Y	Y	Y	Y
2 *Simmons*	Y	Y	Y	Y	Y	Y	Y
3 DeLauro	Y	Y	Y	Y	Y	Y	Y
4 *Shays*	Y	Y	Y	Y	Y	Y	Y
5 Maloney	Y	Y	Y	Y	Y	Y	Y
6 *Johnson*	Y	Y	Y	Y	Y	Y	?
DELAWARE							
AL *Castle*	Y	Y	Y	Y	Y	Y	Y
FLORIDA							
1 *Miller, J.*	Y	Y	Y	Y	Y	Y	Y
2 Boyd	Y	Y	Y	Y	Y	Y	Y
3 Brown	Y	Y	Y	Y	Y	Y	Y
4 *Crenshaw*	Y	Y	Y	Y	Y	Y	Y
5 Thurman	Y	Y	Y	Y	Y	Y	Y
6 *Stearns*	Y	Y	Y	Y	Y	Y	Y
7 *Mica*	Y	Y	Y	Y	Y	Y	Y
8 *Keller*	Y	Y	Y	Y	Y	Y	Y
9 *Bilirakis*	Y	Y	Y	N	Y	Y	Y
10 *Young*	Y	Y	Y	Y	Y	Y	Y
11 Davis	Y	Y	Y	Y	Y	Y	Y
12 *Putnam*	Y	Y	Y	Y	Y	Y	Y
13 *Miller, D.*	Y	Y	Y	Y	Y	Y	Y
14 *Goss*	Y	Y	Y	Y	Y	Y	Y
15 *Weldon*	Y	Y	Y	Y	Y	Y	Y
16 *Foley*	Y	Y	Y	Y	Y	Y	Y
17 Meek	Y	?	?	?	Y	Y	Y
18 *Ros-Lehtinen*	Y	Y	Y	Y	Y	Y	Y
19 Wexler	Y	Y	Y	Y	Y	Y	Y
20 Deutsch	?	?	?	?	?	?	?
21 *Diaz-Balart*	Y	Y	Y	Y	Y	Y	Y
22 *Shaw*	Y	Y	Y	Y	Y	Y	Y
23 Hastings	Y	Y	N	Y	Y	Y	Y
GEORGIA							
1 *Kingston*	Y	Y	Y	Y	Y	Y	Y
2 Bishop	Y	Y	Y	Y	Y	Y	Y
3 *Collins*	Y	Y	Y	Y	Y	Y	Y
4 McKinney	Y	Y	Y	?	Y	Y	Y
5 Lewis	?	Y	Y	N	Y	Y	Y
6 *Isakson*	Y	Y	Y	Y	Y	Y	Y
7 *Barr*	Y	Y	Y	Y	Y	Y	Y
8 *Chambliss*	Y	Y	Y	Y	Y	Y	Y
9 *Deal*	Y	Y	Y	Y	Y	Y	Y
10 *Norwood*	Y	Y	Y	Y	Y	Y	Y
11 *Linder*	?	Y	Y	?	Y	Y	Y
HAWAII							
1 Abercrombie	Y	Y	Y	Y	Y	Y	Y
2 Mink	Y	Y	Y	Y	Y	Y	Y
IDAHO							
1 *Otter*	Y	Y	Y	Y	Y	Y	Y
2 *Simpson*	Y	Y	Y	Y	Y	N	Y
ILLINOIS							
1 Rush	Y	Y	Y	Y	Y	Y	Y
2 Jackson	Y	Y	Y	Y	Y	Y	Y
3 Lipinski	Y	Y	Y	Y	Y	Y	Y
4 Gutierrez	Y	Y	Y	Y	Y	Y	Y
5 Blagojevich	?	Y	Y	Y	Y	Y	Y
6 *Hyde*	Y	Y	Y	Y	Y	Y	Y
7 Davis	Y	Y	Y	Y	Y	Y	Y
8 *Crane*	Y	N	N	Y	Y	Y	Y
9 Schakowsky	Y	N	N	N	Y	Y	Y
10 *Kirk*	Y	Y	Y	Y	Y	Y	Y
11 *Weller*	Y	Y	N	Y	Y	Y	Y
12 Costello	Y	Y	N	Y	Y	Y	?
13 *Biggert*	Y	Y	Y	Y	Y	Y	Y

ND Northern Democrats   SD Southern Democrats

	185	186	187	188	189	190	191
14 ***Hastert***							
15 ***Johnson***	Y	Y	Y	Y	Y	Y	Y
16 ***Manzullo***	Y	Y	?	Y	Y	Y	Y
17 Evans	Y	Y	Y	Y	Y	Y	Y
18 ***LaHood***	Y	Y	Y	Y	Y	Y	Y
19 Phelps	Y	Y	Y	Y	Y	Y	?
20 ***Shimkus***	Y	Y	Y	Y	Y	Y	Y
INDIANA							
1 Visclosky	Y	Y	N	Y	Y	Y	Y
2 ***Pence***	Y	Y	Y	Y	Y	Y	Y
3 Roemer	Y	Y	Y	Y	Y	Y	Y
4 ***Souder***	Y	Y	Y	Y	Y	Y	Y
5 ***Buyer***	Y	Y	Y	Y	Y	Y	Y
6 ***Burton***	?	?	?	?	?	?	?
7 ***Kerns***	Y	Y	Y	Y	Y	Y	Y
8 ***Hostettler***	Y	Y	Y	Y	Y	Y	Y
9 Hill	Y	Y	Y	Y	Y	Y	Y
10 Carson	Y	Y	Y	Y	Y	Y	Y
IOWA							
1 ***Leach***	Y	Y	Y	Y	Y	Y	Y
2 ***Nussle***	Y	Y	Y	Y	Y	Y	Y
3 Boswell	Y	Y	Y	Y	Y	Y	Y
4 ***Ganske***	Y	Y	Y	Y	Y	Y	Y
5 ***Latham***	Y	Y	N	Y	Y	Y	Y
KANSAS							
1 ***Moran***	Y	Y	Y	Y	Y	Y	Y
2 ***Ryun***	Y	Y	Y	Y	Y	Y	Y
3 Moore	Y	Y	N	Y	Y	Y	Y
4 ***Tiahrt***	Y	Y	Y	Y	Y	Y	Y
KENTUCKY							
1 ***Whitfield***	Y	Y	Y	Y	Y	Y	Y
2 ***Lewis***	Y	Y	Y	Y	Y	Y	Y
3 ***Northup***	Y	Y	Y	Y	Y	Y	Y
4 Lucas	Y	Y	Y	Y	Y	Y	Y
5 ***Rogers***	Y	Y	Y	Y	Y	Y	Y
6 ***Fletcher***	Y	Y	N	Y	Y	Y	Y
LOUISIANA							
1 ***Vitter***	Y	Y	?	Y	Y	Y	Y
2 Jefferson	Y	Y	Y	Y	Y	Y	Y
3 ***Tauzin***	Y	Y	Y	Y	Y	Y	Y
4 ***McCrery***	Y	Y	Y	Y	Y	Y	Y
5 ***Cooksey***	Y	Y	Y	Y	?	Y	Y
6 ***Baker***	Y	Y	Y	Y	Y	Y	Y
7 John	Y	Y	Y	Y	Y	Y	Y
MAINE							
1 Allen	Y	Y	Y	Y	Y	Y	Y
2 Baldacci	Y	Y	Y	Y	Y	Y	Y
MARYLAND							
1 ***Gilchrest***	Y	Y	Y	Y	Y	Y	Y
2 ***Ehrlich***	Y	+	Y	Y	Y	Y	Y
3 Cardin	Y	Y	Y	Y	Y	Y	Y
4 Wynn	Y	Y	Y	Y	Y	Y	?
5 Hoyer	Y	Y	Y	Y	Y	Y	Y
6 ***Bartlett***	Y	Y	Y	Y	Y	Y	Y
7 Cummings	Y	Y	Y	Y	Y	Y	Y
8 ***Morella***	Y	Y	Y	Y	Y	Y	Y
MASSACHUSETTS							
1 Olver	Y	Y	N	N	Y	N	Y
2 Neal	Y	Y	Y	N	Y	Y	Y
3 McGovern	Y	Y	Y	Y	Y	N	Y
4 Frank	Y	Y	Y	N	Y	N	Y
5 Meehan	Y	Y	Y	N	Y	Y	Y
6 Tierney	Y	Y	Y	N	Y	N	Y
7 Markey	Y	Y	N	N	Y	N	Y
8 Capuano	Y	Y	N	N	Y	N	Y
9 Lynch	Y	Y	Y	Y	Y	Y	Y
10 Delahunt	Y	Y	Y	N	Y	Y	Y
MICHIGAN							
1 Stupak	Y	N	N	N	Y	Y	Y
2 ***Hoekstra***	Y	Y	Y	Y	Y	Y	Y
3 ***Ehlers***	Y	Y	Y	Y	Y	Y	Y
4 ***Camp***	Y	Y	Y	Y	Y	Y	Y
5 Barcia	Y	Y	Y	Y	Y	Y	Y
6 ***Upton***	Y	Y	Y	Y	Y	Y	Y
7 ***Smith***	Y	Y	Y	Y	Y	Y	Y
8 ***Rogers***	Y	Y	Y	Y	Y	Y	Y
9 Kildee	Y	Y	Y	Y	Y	Y	Y
10 Bonior	+	Y	?	Y	Y	Y	Y
11 ***Knollenberg***	Y	Y	Y	Y	Y	Y	Y
12 Levin	Y	Y	Y	Y	Y	Y	Y
13 Rivers	Y	Y	Y	Y	Y	Y	Y
14 Conyers	?	N	Y	Y	Y	Y	Y
15 Kilpatrick	Y	Y	Y	Y	Y	Y	?
16 Dingell	Y	Y	Y	Y	Y	Y	Y
MINNESOTA							
1 ***Gutknecht***	Y	Y	N	Y	Y	Y	Y
2 ***Kennedy***	Y	Y	N	Y	Y	Y	Y
3 ***Ramstad***	Y	Y	N	Y	Y	Y	Y
4 McCollum	Y	Y	Y	Y	Y	Y	Y
5 Sabo	Y	Y	N	N	Y	Y	Y
6 Luther	Y	Y	Y	Y	Y	Y	Y
7 Peterson	Y	Y	N	Y	Y	Y	Y
8 Oberstar	Y	Y	N	Y	Y	Y	Y
MISSISSIPPI							
1 ***Wicker***	Y	Y	N	Y	Y	Y	Y
2 Thompson	Y	Y	N	Y	Y	Y	Y
3 ***Pickering***	Y	Y	Y	Y	Y	Y	Y
4 Shows	Y	Y	Y	Y	Y	Y	Y
5 Taylor	Y	Y	N	Y	Y	N	Y
MISSOURI							
1 Clay	Y	Y	Y	N	Y	Y	Y
2 ***Akin***	Y	Y	Y	Y	Y	Y	Y
3 Gephardt	Y	Y	N	Y	Y	Y	Y
4 Skelton	Y	Y	Y	Y	Y	Y	Y
5 McCarthy	Y	Y	Y	Y	Y	Y	Y
6 ***Graves***	Y	Y	Y	Y	Y	Y	Y
7 ***Blunt***	Y	Y	Y	Y	Y	Y	Y
8 ***Emerson***	?	?	?	?	?	?	?
9 ***Hulshof***	Y	Y	N	Y	Y	Y	Y
MONTANA							
AL ***Rehberg***	Y	Y	Y	Y	Y	Y	Y
NEBRASKA							
1 ***Bereuter***	Y	Y	Y	Y	Y	Y	Y
2 ***Terry***	Y	Y	Y	Y	Y	Y	Y
3 ***Osborne***	Y	Y	Y	Y	Y	Y	Y
NEVADA							
1 Berkley	Y	Y	Y	Y	Y	Y	Y
2 ***Gibbons***	Y	Y	Y	Y	Y	Y	Y
NEW HAMPSHIRE							
1 ***Sununu***	Y	Y	Y	Y	Y	Y	Y
2 ***Bass***	Y	Y	Y	Y	Y	Y	Y
NEW JERSEY							
1 Andrews	Y	Y	Y	Y	Y	Y	Y
2 ***LoBiondo***	Y	Y	N	Y	Y	Y	Y
3 ***Saxton***	Y	Y	?	Y	Y	Y	Y
4 ***Smith***	Y	Y	Y	Y	Y	Y	Y
5 ***Roukema***	Y	Y	Y	Y	Y	Y	Y
6 Pallone	Y	Y	N	Y	Y	Y	Y
7 ***Ferguson***	Y	Y	Y	Y	Y	Y	Y
8 Pascrell	Y	Y	Y	Y	Y	Y	Y
9 Rothman	Y	Y	Y	Y	Y	Y	Y
10 Payne	Y	N	Y	N	Y	Y	Y
11 ***Frelinghuysen***	Y	Y	Y	Y	Y	Y	Y
12 Holt	Y	Y	N	Y	Y	Y	Y
13 Menendez	?	Y	Y	Y	Y	Y	Y
NEW MEXICO							
1 ***Wilson***	Y	Y	Y	Y	Y	Y	Y
2 ***Skeen***	Y	Y	Y	Y	Y	Y	Y
3 Udall	Y	Y	N	Y	Y	Y	Y
NEW YORK							
1 ***Grucci***	Y	Y	Y	Y	Y	Y	Y
2 Israel	Y	Y	Y	Y	Y	Y	Y
3 ***King***	Y	Y	Y	Y	Y	Y	Y
4 McCarthy	Y	Y	Y	Y	Y	Y	Y
5 Ackerman	Y	Y	Y	Y	Y	Y	Y
6 Meeks	Y	Y	Y	Y	Y	Y	Y
7 Crowley	Y	Y	Y	Y	Y	Y	Y
8 Nadler	?	Y	Y	Y	Y	Y	Y
9 Weiner	Y	Y	Y	Y	Y	Y	Y
10 Towns	Y	N	Y	Y	Y	Y	Y
11 Owens	Y	N	Y	Y	Y	Y	Y
12 Velázquez	Y	Y	Y	Y	Y	Y	Y
13 ***Fossella***	Y	Y	Y	Y	Y	Y	Y
14 Maloney	Y	Y	Y	Y	Y	Y	Y
15 Rangel	Y	N	Y	N	Y	Y	Y
16 Serrano	Y	Y	Y	Y	Y	Y	Y
17 Engel	Y	Y	Y	Y	Y	Y	Y
18 Lowey	Y	Y	Y	Y	Y	Y	Y
19 ***Kelly***	Y	Y	Y	Y	Y	Y	Y
20 ***Gilman***	Y	Y	Y	Y	Y	Y	Y
21 McNulty	Y	Y	N	Y	Y	Y	Y
22 ***Sweeney***	Y	Y	Y	Y	Y	Y	Y
23 ***Boehlert***	Y	Y	Y	Y	Y	Y	Y
24 ***McHugh***	Y	Y	Y	Y	Y	Y	Y
25 ***Walsh***	Y	Y	Y	Y	Y	Y	Y
26 Hinchey	Y	N	N	N	Y	Y	Y
27 ***Reynolds***	?	Y	Y	Y	Y	Y	Y
28 Slaughter	Y	Y	N	Y	Y	Y	Y
29 LaFalce	Y	Y	Y	Y	Y	Y	Y
30 ***Quinn***	Y	Y	Y	Y	Y	Y	Y
31 ***Houghton***	Y	Y	Y	Y	Y	Y	Y
NORTH CAROLINA							
1 Clayton	Y	Y	Y	Y	Y	Y	Y
2 Etheridge	Y	Y	Y	Y	Y	Y	Y
3 ***Jones***	Y	Y	Y	Y	Y	Y	Y
4 Price	Y	Y	Y	Y	Y	Y	Y
5 ***Burr***	Y	Y	Y	Y	Y	Y	Y
6 ***Coble***	Y	Y	Y	Y	Y	Y	Y
7 McIntyre	Y	Y	Y	Y	Y	Y	Y
8 ***Hayes***	Y	Y	Y	Y	Y	Y	Y
9 ***Myrick***	Y	Y	Y	Y	Y	Y	?
10 ***Ballenger***	Y	Y	Y	Y	Y	Y	Y
11 ***Taylor***	Y	Y	Y	Y	Y	Y	Y
12 Watt	Y	N	Y	N	Y	Y	Y
NORTH DAKOTA							
AL Pomeroy	Y	Y	Y	Y	Y	Y	Y
OHIO							
1 ***Chabot***	Y	Y	Y	Y	Y	Y	Y
2 ***Portman***	Y	Y	Y	Y	Y	Y	Y
3 Hall	Y	Y	Y	?	Y	Y	Y
4 ***Oxley***	Y	Y	Y	Y	Y	Y	Y
5 ***Gillmor***	Y	Y	Y	Y	Y	Y	Y
6 Strickland	Y	N	Y	Y	Y	Y	Y
7 ***Hobson***	Y	Y	Y	Y	Y	Y	Y
8 ***Boehner***	Y	Y	Y	Y	Y	Y	Y
9 Kaptur	Y	Y	Y	Y	Y	Y	Y
10 Kucinich	Y	N	N	N	Y	Y	Y
11 Jones	Y	Y	Y	N	Y	Y	Y
12 ***Tiberi***	Y	Y	Y	Y	Y	Y	Y
13 Brown	Y	Y	N	Y	Y	Y	Y
14 Sawyer	Y	Y	Y	Y	Y	Y	Y
15 ***Pryce***	Y	Y	Y	Y	Y	Y	Y
16 ***Regula***	Y	Y	Y	Y	Y	Y	Y
17 Traficant	?	?	?	?	?	?	?
18 ***Ney***	Y	Y	Y	Y	Y	Y	Y
19 ***LaTourette***	Y	Y	Y	Y	Y	Y	Y
OKLAHOMA							
1 ***Sullivan***	Y	Y	Y	Y	Y	Y	Y
2 Carson	Y	Y	N	Y	Y	Y	Y
3 ***Watkins***	?	Y	Y	Y	Y	Y	Y
4 ***Watts***	+	+	+	+	+	+	+
5 ***Istook***	Y	Y	Y	Y	Y	Y	Y
6 ***Lucas***	Y	Y	Y	Y	Y	Y	Y
OREGON							
1 Wu	Y	Y	Y	Y	Y	Y	Y
2 ***Walden***	Y	Y	Y	Y	Y	Y	Y
3 Blumenauer	Y	Y	Y	Y	Y	Y	?
4 DeFazio	Y	N	N	N	Y	N	Y
5 Hooley	Y	Y	Y	Y	Y	Y	Y
PENNSYLVANIA							
1 Brady	?	Y	N	Y	Y	Y	Y
2 Fattah	Y	Y	N	Y	Y	Y	Y
3 Borski	?	Y	N	Y	Y	Y	Y
4 ***Hart***	Y	Y	N	Y	Y	Y	Y
5 ***Peterson***	Y	Y	Y	?	Y	Y	Y
6 Holden	Y	Y	Y	Y	Y	Y	Y
7 ***Weldon***	Y	Y	Y	Y	Y	Y	Y
8 ***Greenwood***	?	Y	Y	Y	Y	Y	Y
9 ***Shuster, Bill***	Y	Y	Y	Y	Y	Y	Y
10 ***Sherwood***	Y	Y	Y	Y	Y	Y	Y
11 Kanjorski	Y	Y	Y	Y	Y	Y	Y
12 Murtha	?	?	Y	Y	Y	Y	Y
13 Hoeffel	Y	Y	Y	Y	Y	Y	Y
14 Coyne	Y	Y	Y	Y	Y	Y	Y
15 ***Toomey***	Y	Y	Y	Y	Y	Y	Y
16 ***Pitts***	Y	Y	Y	Y	Y	Y	Y
17 ***Gekas***	Y	Y	Y	Y	Y	Y	Y
18 Doyle	Y	Y	Y	Y	Y	Y	Y
19 ***Platts***	Y	Y	Y	Y	Y	Y	?
20 Mascara	?	?	?	?	?	?	?
21 ***English***	Y	Y	N	Y	Y	Y	Y
RHODE ISLAND							
1 Kennedy	Y	Y	Y	Y	Y	Y	Y
2 Langevin	Y	Y	Y	Y	Y	Y	Y
SOUTH CAROLINA							
1 ***Brown***	Y	Y	Y	Y	Y	Y	Y
2 ***Wilson***	Y	Y	Y	Y	Y	Y	Y
3 ***Graham***	Y	Y	Y	Y	Y	Y	Y
4 ***DeMint***	Y	Y	Y	Y	Y	Y	Y
5 Spratt	Y	Y	Y	Y	Y	Y	Y
6 Clyburn	Y	Y	Y	Y	Y	Y	Y
SOUTH DAKOTA							
AL ***Thune***	Y	Y	Y	Y	Y	Y	Y
TENNESSEE							
1 ***Jenkins***	Y	Y	Y	Y	Y	Y	Y
2 ***Duncan***	Y	Y	Y	Y	Y	Y	Y
3 ***Wamp***	Y	Y	N	Y	Y	Y	Y
4 ***Hilleary***	Y	Y	Y	Y	Y	Y	Y
5 Clement	Y	Y	Y	Y	Y	Y	Y
6 Gordon	Y	Y	Y	Y	Y	Y	Y
7 ***Bryant***	Y	Y	Y	Y	Y	Y	Y
8 Tanner	Y	Y	Y	Y	Y	Y	Y
9 Ford	Y	Y	Y	N	Y	Y	Y
TEXAS							
1 Sandlin	Y	Y	?	Y	Y	Y	Y
2 Turner	Y	Y	Y	Y	Y	Y	Y
3 ***Johnson, Sam***	Y	Y	Y	Y	Y	Y	Y
4 Hall	Y	Y	Y	Y	Y	Y	Y
5 ***Sessions***	Y	Y	Y	Y	Y	Y	Y
6 ***Barton***	Y	Y	Y	Y	Y	Y	Y
7 ***Culberson***	Y	Y	Y	Y	Y	Y	Y
8 ***Brady***	Y	Y	Y	Y	Y	Y	Y
9 Lampson	Y	Y	Y	Y	Y	Y	Y
10 Doggett	Y	Y	Y	Y	Y	Y	Y
11 Edwards	Y	Y	Y	Y	Y	Y	Y
12 ***Granger***	Y	Y	Y	Y	Y	Y	Y
13 ***Thornberry***	Y	Y	Y	Y	Y	Y	Y
14 ***Paul***	Y	Y	Y	Y	N	N	Y
15 Hinojosa	Y	Y	Y	Y	Y	Y	Y
16 Reyes	Y	Y	Y	Y	Y	Y	Y
17 Stenholm	Y	Y	N	Y	Y	Y	Y
18 Jackson-Lee	Y	Y	Y	N	Y	Y	Y
19 ***Combest***	Y	Y	Y	Y	Y	Y	Y
20 Gonzalez	Y	Y	Y	Y	Y	Y	Y
21 ***Smith***	Y	Y	Y	Y	Y	Y	Y
22 ***DeLay***	Y	Y	Y	Y	Y	Y	Y
23 ***Bonilla***	Y	Y	Y	Y	Y	Y	Y
24 Frost	Y	Y	Y	Y	Y	Y	Y
25 Bentsen	Y	Y	Y	Y	Y	Y	Y
26 ***Armey***	Y	Y	Y	Y	Y	Y	Y
27 Ortiz	Y	Y	Y	Y	Y	Y	Y
28 Rodriguez	Y	Y	Y	Y	Y	Y	Y
29 Green	Y	Y	Y	Y	Y	Y	Y
30 Johnson, E.B.	Y	Y	Y	Y	Y	Y	Y
UTAH							
1 ***Hansen***	Y	Y	Y	Y	Y	Y	Y
2 Matheson	Y	Y	N	Y	Y	Y	Y
3 ***Cannon***	?	Y	Y	Y	Y	Y	Y
VERMONT							
AL *Sanders*	Y	N	Y	Y	Y	Y	Y
VIRGINIA							
1 ***Davis, Jo Ann***	Y	Y	Y	Y	Y	N	Y
2 ***Schrock***	Y	Y	Y	Y	Y	Y	Y
3 Scott	Y	Y	Y	Y	Y	Y	Y
4 ***Forbes***	Y	Y	Y	Y	Y	N	Y
5 *Goode*	Y	Y	Y	Y	Y	N	Y
6 ***Goodlatte***	Y	Y	Y	Y	Y	Y	Y
7 ***Cantor***	Y	Y	Y	Y	Y	Y	Y
8 Moran	?	Y	Y	Y	Y	Y	Y
9 Boucher	Y	Y	Y	Y	Y	Y	Y
10 ***Wolf***	Y	Y	Y	Y	Y	Y	Y
11 ***Davis, T.***	Y	Y	Y	Y	Y	Y	Y
WASHINGTON							
1 Inslee	Y	Y	Y	Y	Y	Y	Y
2 Larsen	Y	Y	N	Y	Y	Y	Y
3 Baird	Y	Y	N	Y	Y	Y	Y
4 ***Hastings***	Y	Y	Y	Y	Y	Y	Y
5 ***Nethercutt***	Y	Y	Y	Y	Y	Y	Y
6 Dicks	Y	Y	Y	Y	Y	Y	Y
7 McDermott	Y	N	N	N	Y	Y	Y
8 ***Dunn***	Y	Y	Y	Y	Y	Y	Y
9 Smith	Y	Y	Y	Y	Y	Y	Y
WEST VIRGINIA							
1 Mollohan	Y	Y	Y	Y	Y	Y	Y
2 ***Capito***	Y	Y	Y	Y	Y	Y	Y
3 Rahall	Y	Y	Y	Y	Y	Y	Y
WISCONSIN							
1 ***Ryan***	Y	Y	Y	Y	Y	Y	Y
2 Baldwin	Y	Y	N	Y	Y	Y	Y
3 Kind	Y	Y	?	Y	Y	Y	Y
4 Kleczka	Y	Y	Y	Y	Y	Y	Y
5 Barrett	Y	Y	Y	Y	Y	Y	Y
6 ***Petri***	Y	Y	Y	Y	Y	Y	Y
7 Obey	Y	Y	N	N	Y	Y	Y
8 ***Green***	Y	Y	Y	Y	Y	Y	Y
9 ***Sensenbrenner***	Y	Y	Y	Y	Y	Y	Y
WYOMING							
AL ***Cubin***	Y	Y	Y	Y	Y	Y	Y

Southern states - Ala., Ark., Fla., Ga., Ky., La., Miss., N.C., Okla., S.C., Tenn., Texas, Va.

Key

Y	Voted for (yea).
#	Paired for.
+	Announced for.
N	Voted against (nay).
X	Paired against.
–	Announced against.
P	Voted "present."
C	Voted "present" to avoid possible conflict of interest.
?	Did not vote or otherwise make a position known.

Democrats **Republicans**
Independents

192. HR 3129. Customs Service Authorization/Democratic Substitute. Waters, D-Calif., amendment that would protect U.S. Customs Service officers from liability for wrongful personal searches but allow the government to be held liable for resulting damages in civil court. It also would ban expanded searches of outbound mail. Rejected 197-231: R 5-213; D 191-17 (ND 147-8, SD 44-9); I 1-1. May 22, 2002.

193. HR 3129. Customs Service Authorization/Passage. Passage of the bill that would authorize $9.1 billion through fiscal 2004 for the activities of the U.S. Customs Service. Passed 327-101: R 215-4; D 110-97 (ND 72-82, SD 38-15); I 2-0. May 22, 2002.

194. HR 4775. Fiscal 2002 Supplemental Appropriations/Rule. Adoption of the rule (H Res 428) that would provide for House floor consideration of the bill that would provide $28.8 billion in supplemental appropriations for fiscal 2002, more than half of which would go toward military operations. Adopted 216-209: R 214-3; D 1-205 (ND 1-153, SD 0-52); I 1-1. May 22, 2002.

195. Procedural Motion/Adjourn. Obey, D-Wis., motion to adjourn. Motion rejected 94-300: R 3-203; D 91-96 (ND 65-75, SD 26-21); I 0-1. May 22, 2002.

196. HR 4775. Fiscal 2002 Supplemental Appropriations/Motion to Rise. Obey, D-Wis., motion to rise from the Committee of the Whole. Motion rejected 134-250: R 1-198; D 132-51 (ND 100-38, SD 32-13); I 1-1. May 22, 2002.

197. HR 4775. Fiscal 2002 Supplemental Appropriations/Motion to Rise. Obey, D-Wis., motion to rise from the Committee of the Whole. Motion rejected 99-289: R 0-203; D 98-85 (ND 78-61, SD 20-24); I 1-1. May 23, 2002.

198. HR 4775. Fiscal 2002 Supplemental Appropriations/Ruling of the Chair. On sustaining the ruling of the chair upholding the Young, R-Fla., point of order against the Gephardt, D-Mo., amendment. The Gephardt amendment would strike language stating that all necessary steps be taken to guarantee the full faith and credit of the government. The Young point of order stated that the Gephardt amendment would strike an amendment previously adopted, in violation of House rules. Ruling of the chair upheld 215-203: R 214-0; D 0-202 (ND 0-151, SD 0-51); I 1-1. May 23, 2002.

	192	193	194	195	196	197	198
ALABAMA							
1 Callahan	N	Y	N	N	N	N	Y
2 Everett	N	Y	Y	N	N	N	Y
3 Riley	N	Y	Y	N	N	N	Y
4 Aderholt	N	Y	Y	N	N	N	Y
5 Cramer	N	Y	N	N	N	N	N
6 Bachus	N	Y	Y	N	N	N	Y
7 Hilliard	Y	N	N	N	Y	Y	N
ALASKA							
AL *Young*	N	Y	Y	N	N	?	Y
ARIZONA							
1 *Flake*	Y	N	Y	N	N	N	Y
2 Pastor	Y	N	N	N	N	N	N
3 *Stump*	N	Y	Y	N	N	N	Y
4 *Shadegg*	N	Y	Y	N	N	N	Y
5 *Kolbe*	N	Y	N	N	N	N	Y
6 *Hayworth*	N	Y	Y	N	N	N	Y
ARKANSAS							
1 Berry	Y	Y	N	Y	Y	Y	N
2 Snyder	Y	Y	N	Y	Y	Y	N
3 *Boozman*	N	Y	Y	N	N	N	Y
4 Ross	Y	Y	N	N	N	N	N
CALIFORNIA							
1 Thompson	Y	Y	N	N	Y	N	N
2 *Herger*	N	Y	Y	N	N	?	Y
3 *Ose*	N	Y	Y	N	N	N	N
4 *Doolittle*	N	Y	Y	N	?	N	Y
5 Matsui	Y	Y	N	Y	Y	Y	N
6 Woolsey	Y	N	N	?	Y	N	N
7 Miller, George	Y	N	N	Y	?	Y	N
8 Pelosi	Y	N	N	Y	Y	Y	N
9 Lee	Y	N	N	Y	Y	Y	N
10 Tauscher	Y	Y	N	N	N	N	N
11 *Pombo*	N	Y	Y	N	N	N	Y
12 Lantos	Y	N	N	N	N	N	N
13 Stark	Y	N	Y	?	?	N	N
14 Eshoo	Y	Y	N	Y	Y	N	N
15 Honda	Y	N	N	Y	Y	Y	N
16 Lofgren	Y	N	N	Y	Y	N	N
17 Farr	Y	N	N	Y	Y	N	N
18 Condit	N	Y	N	N	Y	?	?
19 *Radanovich*	N	Y	Y	?	N	N	Y
20 Dooley	Y	Y	N	?	N	N	N
21 *Thomas*	N	Y	N	N	N	N	Y
22 Capps	Y	N	N	Y	N	Y	N
23 *Gallegly*	N	Y	Y	N	N	N	Y
24 Sherman	Y	Y	N	Y	Y	N	N
25 *McKeon*	N	Y	Y	N	N	N	Y
26 Berman	Y	Y	N	Y	Y	Y	N
27 Schiff	Y	Y	N	Y	Y	Y	N
28 *Dreier*	N	Y	Y	N	N	N	Y
29 Waxman	Y	Y	N	Y	Y	Y	N
30 Becerra	Y	N	N	Y	?	?	N
31 Solis	Y	N	N	Y	Y	Y	N
32 Watson	Y	N	Y	N	Y	N	N
33 Roybal-Allard	Y	N	N	Y	Y	Y	N
34 Napolitano	Y	N	N	Y	Y	Y	N
35 Waters	Y	N	N	Y	?	Y	N
36 Harman	Y	N	N	Y	?	Y	N
37 Millender-McD.	Y	N	Y	N	Y	N	N
38 *Horn*	N	Y	Y	N	?	N	Y

	192	193	194	195	196	197	198
39 *Royce*	N	Y	Y	N	N	N	Y
40 *Lewis*	N	Y	Y	N	N	N	Y
41 *Miller, Gary*	N	Y	Y	?	N	N	Y
42 Baca	Y	N	N	N	Y	N	N
43 *Calvert*	N	Y	Y	N	N	N	Y
44 *Bono*	N	Y	Y	N	N	N	Y
45 *Rohrabacher*	Y	Y	Y	N	N	N	N
46 Sanchez	Y	N	Y	N	Y	Y	N
47 *Cox*	N	Y	Y	?	N	?	Y
48 *Issa*	N	Y	Y	N	N	N	Y
49 Davis	Y	N	N	N	N	N	N
50 Filner	Y	N	N	Y	N	Y	N
51 *Cunningham*	N	Y	Y	N	N	N	Y
52 *Hunter*	N	Y	Y	N	N	N	Y
COLORADO							
1 DeGette	Y	N	N	N	Y	N	N
2 Udall	Y	Y	N	N	N	Y	N
3 *McInnis*	N	Y	Y	N	N	N	Y
4 *Schaffer*	N	Y	Y	N	N	N	Y
5 *Hefley*	N	Y	Y	Y	Y	N	Y
6 *Tancredo*	N	Y	Y	N	N	N	Y
CONNECTICUT							
1 Larson	Y	N	N	N	Y	Y	N
2 *Simmons*	N	Y	Y	N	N	N	Y
3 DeLauro	Y	N	N	N	N	N	N
4 *Shays*	N	Y	Y	N	N	N	Y
5 Maloney	N	Y	N	N	N	N	N
6 *Johnson*	N	Y	Y	N	N	N	Y
DELAWARE							
AL *Castle*	N	Y	Y	N	N	N	Y
FLORIDA							
1 *Miller, J.*	N	Y	Y	N	N	N	Y
2 Boyd	N	Y	N	Y	Y	–	N
3 Brown	Y	Y	N	Y	Y	?	N
4 *Crenshaw*	N	Y	Y	N	N	N	Y
5 *Thurman*	Y	Y	N	Y	Y	Y	N
6 *Stearns*	N	Y	Y	N	N	N	Y
7 *Mica*	N	Y	Y	N	N	N	Y
8 *Keller*	N	Y	Y	N	N	N	Y
9 *Bilirakis*	N	Y	Y	N	?	N	Y
10 *Young*	N	Y	Y	N	N	N	Y
11 Davis	Y	Y	N	N	N	N	N
12 *Putnam*	N	Y	Y	N	N	N	Y
13 *Miller, D.*	N	Y	Y	N	N	N	Y
14 *Goss*	N	Y	Y	N	N	N	Y
15 *Weldon*	N	Y	Y	N	N	N	Y
16 *Foley*	N	Y	Y	?	?	N	Y
17 Meek	Y	Y	N	Y	?	N	Y
18 *Ros-Lehtinen*	N	Y	N	N	N	N	Y
19 Wexler	Y	Y	?	?	N	N	N
20 Deutsch	?	?	?	?	?	?	?
21 *Diaz-Balart*	N	Y	Y	N	N	N	Y
22 *Shaw*	N	Y	Y	N	N	N	Y
23 Hastings	Y	N	N	Y	Y	Y	N
GEORGIA							
1 *Kingston*	N	Y	Y	N	N	N	Y
2 Bishop	Y	Y	N	Y	Y	Y	N
3 *Collins*	N	Y	Y	N	N	N	Y
4 McKinney	Y	N	N	N	N	?	N
5 Lewis	Y	N	N	Y	Y	N	N
6 *Isakson*	N	Y	Y	N	N	?	Y
7 *Barr*	N	Y	Y	N	?	N	Y
8 *Chambliss*	N	Y	Y	N	N	N	Y
9 *Deal*	N	Y	Y	N	N	N	Y
10 *Norwood*	N	Y	Y	N	?	N	Y
11 *Linder*	N	Y	Y	N	N	?	?
HAWAII							
1 Abercrombie	Y	N	N	N	?	N	N
2 Mink	Y	N	N	Y	Y	Y	N
IDAHO							
1 *Otter*	Y	N	Y	N	N	N	Y
2 *Simpson*	N	Y	Y	?	N	N	Y
ILLINOIS							
1 Rush	Y	N	N	Y	Y	Y	?
2 Jackson	Y	N	N	Y	N	N	N
3 Lipinski	N	Y	?	?	?	?	?
4 Gutierrez	Y	N	N	N	?	?	?
5 Blagojevich	Y	Y	N	N	Y	N	N
6 *Hyde*	N	Y	Y	N	N	N	Y
7 Davis	Y	N	N	N	N	?	N
8 *Crane*	N	Y	Y	N	N	?	Y
9 Schakowsky	Y	N	N	?	Y	Y	N
10 *Kirk*	N	Y	Y	N	N	N	Y
11 *Weller*	N	Y	Y	N	N	N	Y
12 Costello	Y	Y	N	N	N	N	N
13 *Biggert*	N	Y	Y	N	N	N	Y

ND Northern Democrats   SD Southern Democrats

	192	193	194	195	196	197	198
14 ***Hastert***			Y	N			
15 ***Johnson***	N	Y	Y	N	N	N	Y
16 ***Manzullo***	N	Y	Y	N	N	N	Y
17 Evans	Y	N	N	Y	Y	Y	N
18 ***LaHood***	N	Y	Y	N	N	N	Y
19 Phelps	N	Y	N	N	N	N	N
20 ***Shimkus***	N	Y	Y	N	N	N	Y
INDIANA							
1 Visclosky	Y	N	N	N	Y	Y	N
2 ***Pence***	N	Y	Y	N	?	N	Y
3 Roemer	N	Y	N	N	N	N	N
4 ***Souder***	N	Y	Y	N	N	?	Y
5 ***Buyer***	N	Y	Y	N	?	N	Y
6 ***Burton***	?	?	?	?	?	?	?
7 ***Kerns***	N	Y	Y	N	N	N	Y
8 ***Hostettler***	N	Y	Y	N	N	N	Y
9 Hill	Y	N	N	Y	Y	Y	N
10 Carson	Y	N	N	N	Y	N	N
IOWA							
1 ***Leach***	N	Y	Y	N	N	?	Y
2 ***Nussle***	N	Y	Y	N	N	N	Y
3 Boswell	Y	Y	N	N	N	N	N
4 ***Ganske***	N	Y	Y	N	N	N	Y
5 ***Latham***	N	Y	Y	N	N	N	Y
KANSAS							
1 ***Moran***	N	Y	Y	N	N	N	Y
2 ***Ryun***	N	Y	Y	N	N	N	Y
3 Moore	Y	Y	N	N	N	N	N
4 ***Tiahrt***	N	Y	Y	N	N	?	Y
KENTUCKY							
1 ***Whitfield***	N	Y	Y	N	N	N	Y
2 ***Lewis***	N	Y	Y	N	N	N	Y
3 ***Northup***	N	Y	Y	N	N	N	Y
4 Lucas	N	Y	N	N	N	N	N
5 ***Rogers***	N	Y	Y	N	N	N	Y
6 ***Fletcher***	N	Y	Y	?	N	N	Y
LOUISIANA							
1 ***Vitter***	N	Y	Y	N	N	N	?
2 Jefferson	Y	N	N	Y	Y	Y	?
3 ***Tauzin***	N	Y	Y	N	?	N	Y
4 ***McCrery***	N	Y	Y	N	N	N	Y
5 ***Cooksey***	N	Y	Y	N	N	?	Y
6 ***Baker***	N	Y	Y	N	N	N	Y
7 John	Y	Y	N	N	N	Y	N
MAINE							
1 Allen	Y	Y	N	Y	Y	Y	N
2 Baldacci	Y	Y	N	N	N	?	N
MARYLAND							
1 ***Gilchrest***	N	Y	Y	N	N	N	Y
2 ***Ehrlich***	N	Y	Y	?	?	?	Y
3 Cardin	Y	Y	N	N	Y	Y	N
4 Wynn	Y	N	N	Y	Y	?	N
5 Hoyer	Y	Y	N	N	?	N	N
6 ***Bartlett***	N	Y	Y	N	N	N	Y
7 Cummings	Y	N	N	N	Y	?	N
8 ***Morella***	Y	Y	Y	N	N	N	Y
MASSACHUSETTS							
1 Olver	Y	N	N	Y	Y	Y	N
2 Neal	Y	N	N	Y	?	Y	N
3 McGovern	Y	N	N	Y	Y	Y	N
4 Frank	Y	N	N	Y	Y	Y	N
5 Meehan	Y	N	N	Y	Y	Y	N
6 Tierney	Y	N	N	Y	Y	N	N
7 Markey	Y	N	N	Y	Y	?	N
8 Capuano	Y	N	N	Y	Y	Y	N
9 Lynch	Y	Y	N	Y	Y	Y	N
10 Delahunt	Y	N	N	Y	Y	Y	N
MICHIGAN							
1 Stupak	Y	Y	N	Y	Y	Y	N
2 ***Hoekstra***	N	Y	Y	Y	N	N	Y
3 ***Ehlers***	N	Y	Y	N	N	–	Y
4 ***Camp***	N	Y	Y	N	N	N	Y
5 Barcia	N	Y	N	N	N	N	N
6 ***Upton***	N	Y	Y	N	N	N	Y
7 ***Smith***	N	Y	Y	N	N	N	Y
8 ***Rogers***	N	Y	Y	N	N	N	Y
9 Kildee	Y	Y	N	N	N	N	N
10 Bonior	Y	Y	N	?	Y	Y	N
11 ***Knollenberg***	N	Y	Y	N	N	N	Y
12 Levin	Y	Y	N	N	N	N	N
13 Rivers	Y	N	N	?	N	N	N
14 Conyers	Y	N	N	?	Y	Y	N
15 Kilpatrick	Y	N	N	Y	Y	Y	N
16 Dingell	Y	Y	N	?	Y	Y	N
MINNESOTA							
1 ***Gutknecht***	N	Y	Y	N	?	N	Y
2 ***Kennedy***	N	Y	Y	N	N	N	Y
3 ***Ramstad***	N	Y	Y	N	N	N	Y
4 McCollum	Y	Y	N	N	N	N	N
5 Sabo	Y	N	N	N	Y	Y	N
6 Luther	N	Y	N	N	N	N	N
7 Peterson	N	Y	N	N	Y	Y	N
8 Oberstar	Y	N	N	Y	Y	Y	N
MISSISSIPPI							
1 ***Wicker***	N	Y	N	N	N	N	Y
2 Thompson	Y	N	N	Y	Y	?	?
3 ***Pickering***	N	Y	Y	N	?	N	Y
4 Shows	N	Y	N	Y	N	Y	N
5 Taylor	N	Y	N	Y	Y	Y	N
MISSOURI							
1 Clay	Y	N	N	?	?	?	?
2 ***Akin***	N	Y	Y	N	N	N	Y
3 Gephardt	Y	N	N	Y	Y	Y	N
4 Skelton	Y	Y	N	N	N	N	N
5 McCarthy	Y	Y	N	N	N	N	N
6 ***Graves***	N	Y	Y	N	N	N	Y
7 ***Blunt***	N	Y	Y	N	N	N	Y
8 ***Emerson***	?	?	?	?	?	N	Y
9 ***Hulshof***	N	Y	Y	N	?	N	Y
MONTANA							
AL ***Rehberg***	N	Y	Y	N	N	N	Y
NEBRASKA							
1 ***Bereuter***	N	Y	Y	N	N	N	Y
2 ***Terry***	N	Y	Y	N	N	N	Y
3 ***Osborne***	N	Y	Y	N	N	N	Y
NEVADA							
1 Berkley	Y	Y	N	N	Y	Y	N
2 ***Gibbons***	N	Y	Y	N	N	N	Y
NEW HAMPSHIRE							
1 ***Sununu***	N	Y	Y	N	N	N	Y
2 ***Bass***	N	Y	Y	N	N	N	Y
NEW JERSEY							
1 Andrews	Y	Y	N	Y	Y	Y	N
2 ***LoBiondo***	N	Y	Y	N	N	N	Y
3 ***Saxton***	N	Y	Y	N	N	N	Y
4 ***Smith***	N	Y	Y	N	N	N	Y
5 ***Roukema***	N	Y	Y	N	N	N	?
6 Pallone	Y	N	N	N	Y	Y	N
7 ***Ferguson***	N	Y	Y	N	N	N	Y
8 Pascrell	Y	N	N	Y	Y	Y	N
9 Rothman	Y	Y	N	N	N	?	N
10 Payne	Y	N	N	N	N	N	N
11 ***Frelinghuysen***	N	Y	Y	N	N	N	Y
12 Holt	Y	N	N	Y	Y	Y	N
13 Menendez	Y	N	N	N	N	N	N
NEW MEXICO							
1 ***Wilson***	N	Y	Y	N	N	N	Y
2 ***Skeen***	N	Y	Y	N	N	N	Y
3 Udall	Y	N	N	Y	Y	Y	N
NEW YORK							
1 ***Grucci***	N	Y	Y	N	N	N	Y
2 Israel	Y	Y	N	N	Y	N	N
3 ***King***	N	Y	Y	N	N	N	Y
4 McCarthy	Y	Y	N	Y	Y	Y	N
5 Ackerman	Y	Y	N	Y	Y	Y	N
6 Meeks	Y	N	N	?	Y	N	N
7 Crowley	Y	Y	N	N	Y	N	N
8 Nadler	Y	N	N	N	Y	?	N
9 Weiner	Y	Y	N	N	N	N	N
10 Towns	Y	N	N	Y	Y	Y	N
11 Owens	Y	N	N	Y	Y	N	N
12 Velázquez	Y	N	N	Y	Y	Y	N
13 ***Fossella***	N	Y	Y	N	N	N	Y
14 Maloney	Y	N	N	Y	Y	Y	N
15 Rangel	Y	N	N	Y	Y	Y	N
16 Serrano	Y	N	N	N	Y	N	N
17 Engel	Y	N	N	N	Y	?	N
18 Lowey	Y	Y	N	Y	Y	Y	N
19 ***Kelly***	N	Y	Y	Y	N	N	Y
20 ***Gilman***	N	Y	Y	N	N	N	Y
21 McNulty	Y	Y	N	Y	Y	Y	N
22 ***Sweeney***	N	Y	Y	N	N	N	Y
23 ***Boehlert***	N	Y	Y	N	N	N	Y
24 ***McHugh***	N	Y	Y	N	N	N	Y
25 ***Walsh***	N	Y	Y	N	N	N	Y
26 Hinchey	Y	Y	N	Y	Y	?	N
27 ***Reynolds***	N	Y	Y	N	N	N	Y
28 Slaughter	Y	Y	N	Y	?	Y	N
29 LaFalce	Y	Y	N	N	?	N	N
30 ***Quinn***	N	Y	Y	N	N	N	?
31 ***Houghton***	N	Y	Y	N	N	N	Y
NORTH CAROLINA							
1 Clayton	Y	N	N	Y	?	Y	N
2 Etheridge	Y	Y	N	N	Y	N	N
3 ***Jones***	N	Y	Y	N	N	N	Y
4 Price	Y	Y	N	N	Y	Y	N
5 ***Burr***	N	Y	Y	N	N	N	Y
6 ***Coble***	N	Y	Y	?	N	N	Y
7 McIntyre	Y	Y	N	?	?	N	N
8 ***Hayes***	N	Y	Y	N	N	N	Y
9 ***Myrick***	N	Y	Y	N	N	N	Y
10 ***Ballenger***	N	Y	Y	N	N	N	Y
11 ***Taylor***	N	Y	Y	N	N	N	Y
12 Watt	Y	N	N	N	Y	?	N
NORTH DAKOTA							
AL Pomeroy	Y	Y	N	Y	Y	Y	N
OHIO							
1 ***Chabot***	N	Y	Y	N	N	N	Y
2 ***Portman***	N	Y	Y	N	N	N	Y
3 Hall	Y	Y	N	?	Y	N	N
4 ***Oxley***	N	Y	Y	N	?	N	Y
5 ***Gillmor***	N	Y	Y	N	N	N	Y
6 Strickland	Y	N	N	N	Y	N	N
7 ***Hobson***	N	Y	Y	N	N	N	Y
8 ***Boehner***	N	Y	Y	N	?	N	Y
9 Kaptur	Y	Y	N	Y	Y	Y	N
10 Kucinich	Y	N	N	N	Y	N	N
11 Jones	Y	N	N	Y	Y	Y	N
12 ***Tiberi***	N	Y	Y	N	N	N	Y
13 Brown	Y	N	N	N	Y	Y	N
14 Sawyer	Y	N	N	?	?	N	N
15 ***Pryce***	N	Y	Y	N	N	N	Y
16 ***Regula***	N	Y	Y	N	N	N	Y
17 Traficant	?	?	?	?	?	?	?
18 ***Ney***	N	Y	Y	N	N	N	Y
19 ***LaTourette***	N	Y	Y	N	N	N	Y
OKLAHOMA							
1 ***Sullivan***	N	Y	Y	N	N	N	Y
2 Carson	N	Y	N	?	Y	N	N
3 ***Watkins***	N	Y	Y	?	N	?	Y
4 ***Watts***	–	Y	Y	N	N	N	Y
5 ***Istook***	N	Y	Y	N	N	N	Y
6 ***Lucas***	N	Y	Y	N	N	N	Y
OREGON							
1 Wu	Y	Y	N	N	Y	Y	N
2 ***Walden***	N	Y	Y	N	N	N	Y
3 Blumenauer	Y	N	N	N	N	Y	N
4 DeFazio	Y	Y	N	Y	Y	Y	N
5 Hooley	Y	Y	N	N	Y	N	N
PENNSYLVANIA							
1 Brady	Y	N	N	Y	Y	Y	N
2 Fattah	Y	N	N	?	?	?	N
3 Borski	Y	Y	N	Y	N	N	N
4 ***Hart***	N	Y	Y	N	N	N	Y
5 ***Peterson***	N	Y	Y	N	?	N	Y
6 Holden	N	Y	N	N	N	N	N
7 ***Weldon***	N	Y	Y	N	N	?	Y
8 ***Greenwood***	N	Y	Y	?	N	N	Y
9 ***Shuster, Bill***	N	Y	Y	N	N	N	Y
10 ***Sherwood***	N	Y	Y	N	N	N	Y
11 Kanjorski	Y	Y	Y	N	N	N	N
12 Murtha	Y	Y	N	N	N	?	N
13 Hoeffel	Y	Y	N	N	Y	Y	N
14 Coyne	Y	N	N	?	N	N	N
15 ***Toomey***	N	Y	Y	N	N	N	Y
16 ***Pitts***	N	Y	Y	N	N	N	Y
17 ***Gekas***	N	Y	Y	N	N	N	Y
18 Doyle	Y	Y	N	N	N	N	N
19 ***Platts***	N	Y	Y	?	N	N	Y
20 Mascara	?	?	?	?	?	N	N
21 ***English***	N	Y	Y	N	N	?	Y
RHODE ISLAND							
1 Kennedy	Y	Y	N	N	Y	N	N
2 Langevin	Y	Y	N	Y	N	N	N
SOUTH CAROLINA							
1 ***Brown***	N	Y	Y	N	N	N	Y
2 ***Wilson***	N	Y	Y	N	N	N	Y
3 ***Graham***	N	Y	Y	?	?	N	Y
4 ***DeMint***	N	Y	Y	N	N	N	Y
5 Spratt	Y	Y	N	Y	Y	N	N
6 Clyburn	Y	N	N	Y	Y	Y	N
SOUTH DAKOTA							
AL ***Thune***	N	Y	Y	N	N	N	Y
TENNESSEE							
1 ***Jenkins***	N	Y	Y	N	N	N	Y
2 ***Duncan***	N	N	Y	N	N	N	Y
3 ***Wamp***	N	Y	P	N	N	N	Y
4 ***Hilleary***	N	Y	Y	?	?	N	Y
5 Clement	Y	Y	N	Y	Y	N	N
6 Gordon	Y	Y	N	Y	?	N	N
7 ***Bryant***	N	Y	Y	N	N	N	Y
8 Tanner	Y	Y	N	N	Y	Y	N
9 Ford	Y	N	N	Y	Y	Y	N
TEXAS							
1 Sandlin	Y	Y	N	Y	Y	?	N
2 Turner	N	Y	N	Y	N	N	N
3 ***Johnson, Sam***	N	Y	Y	N	?	N	Y
4 Hall	N	Y	N	N	N	N	N
5 ***Sessions***	N	Y	Y	N	N	N	Y
6 ***Barton***	N	Y	Y	N	N	?	Y
7 ***Culberson***	N	Y	Y	N	?	N	Y
8 ***Brady***	N	Y	Y	N	N	N	Y
9 Lampson	Y	Y	N	?	?	N	N
10 Doggett	Y	N	N	Y	Y	Y	N
11 Edwards	Y	Y	N	Y	N	N	N
12 ***Granger***	N	Y	Y	N	N	N	Y
13 ***Thornberry***	N	Y	Y	N	N	N	Y
14 ***Paul***	Y	N	Y	N	N	N	?
15 Hinojosa	Y	Y	N	?	Y	?	N
16 Reyes	Y	Y	N	N	Y	N	N
17 Stenholm	N	Y	N	N	?	Y	N
18 Jackson-Lee	Y	N	N	Y	Y	Y	N
19 ***Combest***	N	Y	Y	N	N	?	?
20 Gonzalez	Y	N	N	N	Y	N	N
21 ***Smith***	N	Y	Y	N	N	N	Y
22 ***DeLay***	N	Y	Y	N	N	N	Y
23 ***Bonilla***	N	Y	P	N	N	N	Y
24 Frost	Y	Y	N	N	?	N	N
25 Bentsen	Y	Y	N	N	Y	N	N
26 ***Armey***	N	Y	Y	N	N	N	Y
27 Ortiz	Y	Y	N	?	N	N	N
28 Rodriguez	Y	N	N	Y	Y	Y	N
29 Green	Y	Y	N	N	N	N	N
30 Johnson, E.B.	Y	Y	N	Y	Y	?	N
UTAH							
1 ***Hansen***	N	Y	Y	N	N	N	Y
2 Matheson	Y	Y	N	N	Y	N	N
3 ***Cannon***	N	Y	Y	?	N	N	Y
VERMONT							
AL *Sanders*	Y	Y	N	?	Y	Y	N
VIRGINIA							
1 ***Davis, Jo Ann***	N	Y	Y	N	N	N	Y
2 ***Schrock***	N	Y	Y	N	N	N	Y
3 Scott	Y	N	N	N	?	N	N
4 ***Forbes***	N	Y	Y	N	N	N	Y
5 *Goode*	N	Y	Y	N	N	N	Y
6 ***Goodlatte***	N	Y	Y	N	N	N	Y
7 ***Cantor***	N	Y	Y	N	N	N	Y
8 Moran	Y	Y	N	N	N	N	N
9 Boucher	Y	Y	N	Y	Y	Y	N
10 ***Wolf***	N	Y	Y	N	N	N	Y
11 ***Davis, T.***	N	Y	Y	N	N	N	Y
WASHINGTON							
1 Inslee	Y	N	N	N	Y	Y	N
2 Larsen	Y	Y	N	N	Y	Y	N
3 Baird	Y	Y	N	Y	Y	Y	N
4 ***Hastings***	N	Y	Y	N	N	N	Y
5 ***Nethercutt***	N	Y	P	N	N	N	Y
6 Dicks	Y	Y	N	N	Y	N	N
7 McDermott	Y	?	N	Y	?	Y	N
8 ***Dunn***	N	Y	Y	N	N	N	Y
9 Smith	Y	Y	N	N	N	Y	N
WEST VIRGINIA							
1 Mollohan	Y	N	N	N	N	N	N
2 ***Capito***	N	Y	Y	N	N	N	Y
3 Rahall	Y	N	N	N	N	N	N
WISCONSIN							
1 ***Ryan***	N	Y	Y	N	N	N	Y
2 Baldwin	Y	N	N	?	Y	Y	N
3 Kind	Y	Y	N	N	Y	Y	N
4 Kleczka	Y	N	N	N	Y	Y	N
5 Barrett	Y	N	N	Y	Y	Y	N
6 ***Petri***	N	Y	Y	N	N	N	Y
7 Obey	Y	Y	N	Y	Y	Y	N
8 ***Green***	N	Y	Y	N	N	N	Y
9 ***Sensenbrenner***	N	Y	Y	N	N	N	Y
WYOMING							
AL ***Cubin***	N	Y	Y	N	N	N	Y

Southern states - Ala., Ark., Fla., Ga., Ky., La., Miss., N.C., Okla., S.C., Tenn., Texas, Va.

Key

Y	Voted for (yea).
#	Paired for.
+	Announced for.
N	Voted against (nay).
X	Paired against.
−	Announced against.
P	Voted "present."
C	Voted "present" to avoid possible conflict of interest.
?	Did not vote or otherwise make a position known.

Democrats **Republicans**
Independents

199. HR 4775. Fiscal 2002 Supplemental Appropriations/Motion to Rise. Obey, D-Wis., motion to rise from the Committee of the Whole. Motion rejected 144-252: R 2-198; D 141-53 (ND 108-38, SD 33-15); I 1-1. May 23, 2002.

200. HR 4775. Fiscal 2002 Supplemental Appropriations/Law Enforcement Operations. Obey, D-Wis., amendment that would strike language designating FBI salaries and expenses as emergency funds that are subject to specific budget requests. Rejected 199-213: R 1-212; D 197-0 (ND 148-0, SD 49-0); I 1-1. May 23, 2002.

201. HR 4775. Fiscal 2002 Supplemental Appropriations/National Guard Activities. Obey, D-Wis., amendment that would reduce from $1.4 billion to $604 million the amount of funds for National Guard activities that are subject to emergency designation. Rejected 197-216: R 0-214; D 196-1 (ND 148-0, SD 48-1); I 1-1. May 23, 2002.

202. HR 4775. Fiscal 2002 Supplemental Appropriations/Colombian Anti-Drug Activities. McGovern, D-Mass., amendment that would strike a provision that would allow Colombian counternarcotics funds to be used for a broader anti-terrorism campaign. Rejected 192-225: R 20-195 (ND 131-19, SD 39-11); I 2-0. May 23, 2002.

203. Procedural Motion/Adjourn to Time Certain. Armey, R-Texas, motion to adjourn until 1:00 a.m. May 24. Motion agreed to 211-189: R 204-1; D 6-187 (ND 2-143, SD 4-44); I 1-1. May 24, 2002 (in the session that began and the Congressional Record dated May 23, 2002).

204. HR 4775. Fiscal 2002 Supplemental Appropriations/Rule. Adoption of the rule (H Res 431) that would provide for further House floor consideration of the bill that would provide $28.8 billion in supplemental appropriations available for fiscal 2002, more than half of which would go toward military operations. Adopted 213-201: R 212-1; D 0-199 (ND 0-149, SD 0-50); I 1-1. May 24, 2002.

205. HR 4775. Fiscal 2002 Supplemental Appropriations/Recommit. Obey, D-Wis., motion to recommit the bill to the House Appropriations Committee with instructions that it be reported back after striking language that would state that all necessary steps be taken to guarantee the full faith and credit of the government. Motion rejected 201-215: R 0-214; D 200-0 (ND 150-0, SD 50-0); I 1-1. May 24, 2002.

206. HR 4775. Fiscal 2002 Supplemental Appropriations/Passage. Passage of the bill that would provide $28.8 billion in supplemental appropriations for fiscal 2002, more than half of which would go toward military operations. It would deem the House-passed budget resolution (H Con Res 353) the blueprint for fiscal 2003 appropriations and include language stating that all necessary steps will be taken to guarantee the full faith and credit of the government. Passed 280-138: R 196-20; D 84-116 (ND 59-91, SD 25-25); I 0-2. A "yea" was a vote in support of the president's position. May 24, 2002.

	199	200	201	202	203	204	205	206
ALABAMA								
1 *Callahan*	N	N	N	Y	N	Y	N	Y
2 *Everett*	N	N	N	Y	N	Y	N	Y
3 *Riley*	?	?	?	N	?	Y	N	Y
4 *Aderholt*	?	N	N	Y	N	Y	N	Y
5 Cramer	N	Y	Y	N	N	?	?	?
6 *Bachus*	N	N	N	Y	N	Y	N	Y
7 Hilliard	Y	Y	Y	N	N	N	Y	N
ALASKA								
AL *Young*	N	N	N	Y	N	Y	N	Y
ARIZONA								
1 *Flake*	N	N	N	Y	Y	Y	N	N
2 Pastor	?	Y	Y	Y	N	N	Y	Y
3 *Stump*	N	N	N	Y	N	Y	N	Y
4 *Shadegg*	N	N	N	Y	N	Y	N	Y
5 *Kolbe*	N	N	N	Y	N	Y	N	Y
6 *Hayworth*	N	N	N	Y	N	Y	N	Y
ARKANSAS								
1 Berry	Y	Y	Y	N	N	N	Y	N
2 Snyder	Y	Y	Y	N	N	N	Y	N
3 *Boozman*	N	N	N	Y	N	Y	N	Y
4 Ross	N	Y	Y	Y	N	N	Y	Y
CALIFORNIA								
1 Thompson	?	?	?	?	?	?	?	?
2 *Herger*	N	N	N	Y	N	Y	N	Y
3 Ose	N	N	N	Y	N	Y	N	Y
4 *Doolittle*	N	N	N	Y	N	Y	N	Y
5 Matsui	Y	Y	Y	Y	N	N	Y	N
6 Woolsey	N	Y	Y	Y	N	N	Y	N
7 Miller, George	Y	Y	Y	Y	N	N	Y	N
8 Pelosi	Y	Y	Y	Y	N	N	Y	N
9 Lee	Y	Y	Y	Y	N	N	Y	N
10 Tauscher	N	Y	Y	N	N	N	Y	N
11 *Pombo*	N	N	N	Y	N	Y	N	Y
12 Lantos	Y	Y	Y	N	N	N	Y	N
13 Stark	Y	Y	Y	?	N	N	Y	N
14 Eshoo	N	Y	Y	Y	N	N	Y	N
15 Honda	Y	Y	Y	Y	N	N	Y	N
16 Lofgren	N	Y	Y	Y	N	N	Y	N
17 Farr	Y	Y	Y	Y	N	N	Y	N
18 Condit	?	?	?	?	?	?	?	?
19 *Radanovich*	?	?	?	?	?	?	?	?
20 Dooley	?	Y	Y	N	?	N	Y	N
21 *Thomas*	N	N	N	N	N	Y	N	Y
22 Capps	N	Y	Y	Y	N	N	Y	N
23 *Gallegly*	N	N	N	Y	N	Y	N	Y
24 Sherman	N	Y	Y	Y	N	N	Y	N
25 *McKeon*	N	N	N	Y	N	Y	N	Y
26 Berman	Y	Y	Y	Y	N	N	Y	Y
27 Schiff	Y	Y	Y	Y	N	N	Y	Y
28 *Dreier*	N	N	N	Y	N	Y	N	Y
29 Waxman	Y	Y	Y	Y	N	N	Y	N
30 Becerra	Y	Y	Y	Y	N	N	Y	N
31 Solis	Y	Y	Y	Y	N	N	Y	N
32 Watson	Y	Y	Y	Y	N	N	Y	N
33 Roybal-Allard	N	Y	Y	Y	N	N	Y	N
34 Napolitano	Y	Y	Y	Y	N	N	Y	N
35 Waters	Y	Y	Y	Y	N	N	Y	N
36 Harman	Y	Y	Y	N	N	N	Y	N
37 Millender-McD.	Y	Y	Y	Y	N	N	Y	N
38 *Horn*	N	N	N	N	N	Y	N	Y

	199	200	201	202	203	204	205	206
39 *Royce*	N	N	N	Y	N	Y	N	Y
40 *Lewis*	N	N	N	Y	N	Y	N	Y
41 *Miller, Gary*	N	N	N	Y	N	Y	N	Y
42 Baca	Y	Y	Y	Y	N	N	Y	Y
43 *Calvert*	N	N	N	Y	N	Y	N	Y
44 *Bono*	N	N	N	Y	Y	Y	N	N
45 *Rohrabacher*	N	N	N	Y	Y	Y	N	N
46 Sanchez	Y	Y	Y	Y	N	N	Y	Y
47 *Cox*	N	N	N	?	N	Y	N	N
48 *Issa*	N	N	N	Y	N	Y	N	Y
49 Davis	N	Y	Y	N	N	Y	N	Y
50 Filner	Y	Y	Y	Y	N	N	Y	N
51 *Cunningham*	N	N	N	?	N	Y	N	Y
52 *Hunter*	N	N	N	Y	N	Y	N	Y
COLORADO								
1 DeGette	N	Y	Y	Y	N	N	Y	N
2 Udall	N	Y	Y	Y	N	N	Y	N
3 *McInnis*	N	N	N	Y	Y	Y	N	Y
4 *Schaffer*	N	N	N	Y	N	Y	N	Y
5 *Hefley*	Y	N	N	N	N	N	N	Y
6 *Tancredo*	N	N	N	Y	Y	Y	N	Y
CONNECTICUT								
1 Larson	Y	Y	Y	Y	N	N	Y	N
2 *Simmons*	N	N	N	Y	Y	Y	N	Y
3 DeLauro	Y	Y	Y	Y	N	N	Y	N
4 *Shays*	N	N	N	Y	N	Y	N	Y
5 Maloney	Y	Y	Y	Y	N	Y	Y	Y
6 *Johnson*	N	N	N	Y	N	Y	N	Y
DELAWARE								
AL *Castle*	N	N	N	Y	N	Y	N	Y
FLORIDA								
1 *Miller, J.*	N	N	N	Y	N	Y	N	Y
2 Boyd	Y	Y	Y	N	N	N	Y	N
3 Brown	Y	Y	Y	Y	N	N	Y	N
4 *Crenshaw*	N	N	N	Y	N	Y	N	Y
5 Thurman	Y	Y	Y	N	N	N	Y	N
6 *Stearns*	N	N	N	?	N	Y	N	Y
7 *Mica*	N	N	N	Y	N	Y	N	Y
8 *Keller*	N	N	N	Y	N	Y	N	Y
9 *Bilirakis*	N	N	N	Y	N	Y	N	Y
10 *Young*	N	N	N	Y	N	Y	N	Y
11 Davis	N	Y	Y	N	N	N	Y	N
12 *Putnam*	N	N	N	Y	N	Y	N	Y
13 *Miller, D.*	N	N	N	Y	N	Y	N	Y
14 *Goss*	N	N	N	Y	N	Y	N	Y
15 *Weldon*	N	N	N	Y	N	Y	N	Y
16 *Foley*	N	N	N	Y	N	Y	N	Y
17 *Meek*	Y	Y	Y	Y	N	N	Y	N
18 *Ros-Lehtinen*	N	N	N	Y	N	Y	N	Y
19 Wexler	Y	?	?	?	N	N	Y	N
20 Deutsch	?	?	?	?	?	?	?	?
21 *Diaz-Balart*	N	N	N	Y	N	Y	N	Y
22 *Shaw*	N	N	N	Y	N	Y	N	Y
23 Hastings	Y	Y	Y	Y	N	N	Y	N
GEORGIA								
1 *Kingston*	N	N	N	Y	N	Y	N	Y
2 Bishop	Y	Y	Y	N	N	N	Y	N
3 *Collins*	N	N	N	Y	N	Y	N	Y
4 McKinney	Y	Y	Y	Y	N	N	Y	N
5 Lewis	N	Y	Y	Y	N	N	Y	N
6 *Isakson*	N	N	N	Y	N	Y	N	Y
7 *Barr*	N	N	N	Y	N	Y	N	Y
8 *Chambliss*	N	N	N	Y	N	Y	N	Y
9 *Deal*	N	N	N	Y	N	Y	N	Y
10 *Norwood*	N	N	N	Y	N	Y	N	Y
11 *Linder*	?	?	?	?	?	?	?	?
HAWAII								
1 Abercrombie	?	Y	Y	Y	N	N	Y	Y
2 Mink	Y	Y	Y	Y	N	N	Y	N
IDAHO								
1 *Otter*	N	N	Y	Y	Y	Y	N	Y
2 *Simpson*	N	N	N	Y	Y	Y	N	Y
ILLINOIS								
1 Rush	Y	Y	Y	Y	N	N	Y	N
2 Jackson	Y	Y	Y	Y	N	N	Y	N
3 Lipinski	?	?	?	?	?	?	?	?
4 Gutierrez	?	?	?	?	?	?	?	?
5 Blagojevich	N	Y	Y	Y	N	N	Y	N
6 *Hyde*	?	N	N	N	N	Y	N	Y
7 Davis	Y	Y	Y	Y	N	N	Y	N
8 *Crane*	N	N	N	Y	N	Y	N	Y
9 Schakowsky	Y	Y	Y	Y	N	N	Y	N
10 *Kirk*	N	N	N	Y	N	Y	N	Y
11 *Weller*	N	N	N	Y	N	Y	N	Y
12 Costello	N	Y	Y	N	N	N	Y	N
13 *Biggert*	N	N	N	Y	N	Y	N	Y

ND Northern Democrats SD Southern Democrats

	199	200	201	202	203	204	205	206
14 ***Hastert***		N	N	N	Y	Y	N	Y
15 ***Johnson***	N	N	N	N	Y	Y	N	Y
16 ***Manzullo***	N	N	N	N	Y	Y	N	N
17 Evans	Y	Y	Y	Y	N	N	Y	Y
18 ***LaHood***	N	N	N	N	Y	Y	N	Y
19 Phelps	N	Y	Y	N	N	N	Y	Y
20 ***Shimkus***	N	N	N	N	Y	Y	N	Y
INDIANA								
1 Visclosky	Y	Y	Y	Y	N	N	Y	N
2 ***Pence***	N	N	N	N	Y	Y	N	Y
3 Roemer	N	Y	Y	Y	N	N	Y	Y
4 ***Souder***	N	N	N	N	Y	Y	N	Y
5 ***Buyer***	N	N	N	N	Y	Y	N	Y
6 ***Burton***	?	?	?	?	?	?	?	?
7 ***Kerns***	N	N	N	N	Y	Y	N	Y
8 ***Hostettler***	N	N	N	Y	Y	Y	N	Y
9 Hill	Y	Y	Y	Y	N	N	Y	N
10 Carson	N	Y	Y	Y	N	N	Y	N
IOWA								
1 ***Leach***	N	N	N	Y	Y	Y	Y	N
2 ***Nussle***	?	N	N	N	Y	Y	?	Y
3 Boswell	N	Y	Y	Y	N	N	Y	N
4 ***Ganske***	N	N	N	N	Y	Y	N	Y
5 ***Latham***	N	N	N	N	Y	Y	N	Y
KANSAS								
1 ***Moran***	N	N	N	Y	Y	Y	N	N
2 ***Ryun***	N	N	N	N	Y	Y	N	Y
3 Moore	N	Y	Y	Y	N	N	Y	Y
4 ***Tiahrt***	N	N	N	N	Y	Y	N	Y
KENTUCKY								
1 ***Whitfield***	?	N	N	N	Y	?	N	Y
2 ***Lewis***	N	N	N	N	Y	Y	N	Y
3 ***Northup***	N	N	N	N	Y	Y	N	Y
4 Lucas	N	Y	Y	N	N	N	Y	Y
5 ***Rogers***	N	N	N	N	Y	Y	N	Y
6 ***Fletcher***	N	N	N	N	Y	Y	N	Y
LOUISIANA								
1 ***Vitter***	?	?	?	?	?	?	?	?
2 Jefferson	Y	Y	Y	Y	N	N	Y	N
3 ***Tauzin***	N	N	N	N	Y	Y	N	Y
4 ***McCrery***	N	N	N	N	Y	Y	N	Y
5 ***Cooksey***	N	N	N	N	Y	Y	N	Y
6 ***Baker***	N	N	N	N	Y	Y	N	Y
7 John	N	Y	Y	N	Y	N	Y	Y
MAINE								
1 Allen	Y	Y	Y	Y	N	N	Y	Y
2 Baldacci	Y	Y	Y	Y	N	N	Y	Y
MARYLAND								
1 ***Gilchrest***	N	N	N	N	Y	Y	N	Y
2 ***Ehrlich***	N	N	N	N	Y	Y	N	Y
3 Cardin	Y	Y	Y	Y	N	N	Y	Y
4 Wynn	Y	Y	Y	Y	N	N	Y	Y
5 Hoyer	Y	Y	Y	Y	N	N	Y	Y
6 ***Bartlett***	N	N	N	N	Y	Y	N	Y
7 Cummings	Y	Y	Y	Y	N	N	Y	N
8 ***Morella***	N	N	N	Y	Y	Y	N	Y
MASSACHUSETTS								
1 Olver	Y	Y	Y	Y	N	N	Y	N
2 Neal	Y	Y	Y	Y	N	N	Y	N
3 McGovern	Y	Y	Y	Y	N	N	Y	N
4 Frank	Y	Y	Y	N	N	N	Y	N
5 Meehan	Y	Y	Y	Y	N	N	Y	N
6 Tierney	Y	Y	Y	Y	N	N	Y	N
7 Markey	Y	Y	Y	Y	N	N	Y	N
8 Capuano	Y	Y	Y	Y	N	N	Y	N
9 Lynch	Y	?	?	Y	Y	N	Y	N
10 Delahunt	Y	Y	Y	Y	N	N	Y	N
MICHIGAN								
1 Stupak	Y	Y	Y	Y	N	N	Y	N
2 ***Hoekstra***	N	N	N	Y	Y	Y	N	Y
3 ***Ehlers***	N	N	N	Y	Y	Y	N	Y
4 ***Camp***	N	N	N	N	Y	Y	N	Y
5 Barcia	N	Y	Y	N	N	N	Y	Y
6 ***Upton***	N	N	N	N	Y	Y	N	Y
7 ***Smith***	N	N	N	N	Y	Y	N	N
8 ***Rogers***	N	N	N	N	Y	Y	N	Y
9 Kildee	Y	Y	Y	Y	N	N	Y	Y
10 Bonior	?	?	?	?	?	?	?	?
11 ***Knollenberg***	N	N	N	N	Y	Y	N	Y
12 Levin	Y	Y	Y	Y	N	N	Y	Y
13 Rivers	N	Y	Y	Y	N	N	Y	N
14 Conyers	Y	Y	Y	Y	N	N	Y	N
15 Kilpatrick	Y	Y	Y	Y	N	N	Y	N
16 Dingell	Y	Y	Y	Y	N	N	Y	N

	199	200	201	202	203	204	205	206
MINNESOTA								
1 ***Gutknecht***	N	N	N	Y	Y	Y	N	N
2 ***Kennedy***	N	N	N	N	Y	Y	N	Y
3 ***Ramstad***	N	N	N	N	Y	Y	N	Y
4 McCollum	N	Y	Y	Y	N	N	Y	N
5 Sabo	Y	Y	Y	Y	N	N	Y	Y
6 Luther	N	Y	Y	N	N	N	Y	Y
7 Peterson	Y	Y	Y	N	N	N	Y	N
8 Oberstar	Y	Y	Y	Y	N	N	Y	N
MISSISSIPPI								
1 ***Wicker***	?	N	N	N	Y	Y	N	Y
2 Thompson	?	?	?	?	?	?	?	?
3 ***Pickering***	N	N	N	N	Y	Y	N	Y
4 Shows	Y	Y	Y	Y	N	N	Y	Y
5 Taylor	Y	Y	Y	Y	Y	N	Y	N
MISSOURI								
1 Clay	Y	Y	Y	Y	N	?	Y	N
2 ***Akin***	N	N	N	N	Y	Y	N	Y
3 Gephardt	Y	Y	Y	Y	N	N	Y	N
4 Skelton	N	Y	Y	Y	N	N	Y	Y
5 McCarthy	N	Y	Y	Y	N	N	Y	N
6 ***Graves***	N	N	N	N	Y	Y	N	Y
7 ***Blunt***	N	N	N	N	Y	Y	N	Y
8 ***Emerson***	N	N	N	N	Y	Y	N	Y
9 ***Hulshof***	N	N	N	Y	?	Y	N	Y
MONTANA								
AL ***Rehberg***	N	N	N	N	Y	Y	N	Y
NEBRASKA								
1 ***Bereuter***	N	N	N	N	Y	Y	N	Y
2 ***Terry***	N	N	N	N	Y	Y	N	Y
3 ***Osborne***	N	N	N	N	Y	Y	N	Y
NEVADA								
1 Berkley	Y	Y	Y	N	N	N	Y	Y
2 ***Gibbons***	N	N	N	N	Y	Y	N	Y
NEW HAMPSHIRE								
1 ***Sununu***	N	N	N	N	Y	Y	N	Y
2 ***Bass***	N	N	N	N	Y	Y	N	Y
NEW JERSEY								
1 Andrews	Y	Y	Y	Y	N	N	Y	Y
2 ***LoBiondo***	N	N	N	N	Y	Y	N	Y
3 ***Saxton***	N	N	N	N	Y	Y	N	Y
4 ***Smith***	N	N	N	N	Y	Y	N	Y
5 ***Roukema***	?	?	?	?	?	?	?	?
6 Pallone	Y	Y	Y	Y	N	N	Y	N
7 ***Ferguson***	N	N	N	N	Y	Y	N	Y
8 Pascrell	Y	Y	Y	Y	N	N	Y	Y
9 Rothman	Y	Y	Y	N	N	N	Y	Y
10 Payne	N	Y	Y	Y	N	N	Y	N
11 ***Frelinghuysen***	N	N	N	N	Y	Y	N	Y
12 Holt	Y	Y	Y	Y	N	N	Y	Y
13 Menendez	N	Y	Y	N	N	N	Y	N
NEW MEXICO								
1 ***Wilson***	N	N	N	N	Y	Y	N	Y
2 ***Skeen***	N	N	N	N	Y	Y	N	Y
3 Udall	N	Y	Y	Y	N	N	Y	N
NEW YORK								
1 ***Grucci***	N	N	N	N	Y	Y	N	Y
2 Israel	N	Y	Y	N	N	N	Y	Y
3 ***King***	N	N	N	N	Y	Y	N	Y
4 McCarthy	Y	Y	Y	N	N	N	Y	Y
5 Ackerman	Y	Y	Y	Y	N	N	Y	N
6 Meeks	Y	Y	Y	Y	N	N	Y	N
7 Crowley	?	?	?	?	?	?	?	?
8 Nadler	Y	Y	Y	Y	N	N	Y	Y
9 Weiner	N	Y	Y	Y	N	N	Y	Y
10 Towns	Y	Y	Y	Y	N	N	Y	N
11 Owens	Y	Y	Y	Y	N	N	Y	N
12 Velázquez	Y	Y	Y	Y	N	N	Y	N
13 ***Fossella***	N	N	N	N	Y	Y	N	Y
14 Maloney	N	Y	Y	Y	N	N	Y	Y
15 Rangel	Y	Y	Y	Y	N	N	Y	N
16 Serrano	N	Y	Y	Y	N	N	Y	N
17 Engel	N	Y	Y	Y	N	N	Y	Y
18 Lowey	Y	Y	Y	Y	N	N	Y	Y
19 ***Kelly***	N	N	N	N	Y	Y	N	Y
20 ***Gilman***	N	N	N	N	Y	Y	N	Y
21 McNulty	Y	Y	Y	Y	N	N	Y	Y
22 ***Sweeney***	N	N	N	N	Y	Y	N	Y
23 ***Boehlert***	N	N	N	N	Y	Y	N	Y
24 ***McHugh***	N	N	N	N	Y	Y	N	Y
25 ***Walsh***	N	N	N	N	Y	Y	N	Y
26 Hinchey	Y	Y	Y	Y	N	N	Y	N
27 ***Reynolds***	N	?	N	N	Y	Y	N	Y
28 Slaughter	Y	Y	Y	Y	N	N	Y	N
29 LaFalce	Y	Y	Y	Y	N	N	Y	N

	199	200	201	202	203	204	205	206
30 ***Quinn***	N	N	N	N	Y	Y	N	Y
31 ***Houghton***	?	N	N	N	Y	Y	N	Y
NORTH CAROLINA								
1 Clayton	Y	Y	Y	Y	N	N	Y	N
2 Etheridge	Y	Y	Y	Y	N	N	Y	Y
3 ***Jones***	Y	N	N	Y	Y	Y	N	N
4 Price	Y	Y	Y	Y	N	N	Y	Y
5 ***Burr***	?	N	N	N	Y	Y	N	Y
6 ***Coble***	N	N	N	N	Y	Y	N	Y
7 McIntyre	?	?	?	?	?	?	?	?
8 ***Hayes***	N	N	N	N	Y	Y	N	Y
9 ***Myrick***	N	N	N	N	Y	Y	N	Y
10 ***Ballenger***	N	N	N	N	Y	Y	N	Y
11 ***Taylor***	N	N	N	N	Y	Y	N	Y
12 Watt	Y	Y	Y	Y	N	N	Y	N
NORTH DAKOTA								
AL Pomeroy	Y	Y	Y	Y	N	N	Y	Y
OHIO								
1 ***Chabot***	N	N	N	N	Y	Y	N	N
2 ***Portman***	N	N	N	N	Y	Y	N	Y
3 Hall	N	Y	Y	Y	?	N	Y	Y
4 ***Oxley***	?	N	N	N	Y	Y	N	Y
5 ***Gillmor***	N	N	N	N	Y	Y	N	Y
6 Strickland	N	Y	Y	Y	N	N	Y	Y
7 ***Hobson***	N	N	N	N	Y	Y	N	Y
8 ***Boehner***	?	N	N	N	?	Y	N	Y
9 Kaptur	Y	Y	Y	Y	N	N	Y	N
10 Kucinich	Y	Y	Y	Y	N	N	Y	N
11 Jones	Y	Y	Y	Y	N	N	Y	N
12 ***Tiberi***	N	N	N	N	Y	Y	N	Y
13 Brown	Y	Y	Y	Y	N	N	Y	N
14 Sawyer	?	Y	Y	Y	N	N	Y	N
15 ***Pryce***	?	N	N	N	Y	Y	N	Y
16 ***Regula***	N	N	N	N	Y	Y	N	Y
17 Traficant	?	?	?	?	?	?	?	?
18 ***Ney***	N	N	N	N	Y	Y	N	Y
19 ***LaTourette***	N	N	N	N	Y	?	N	Y
OKLAHOMA								
1 ***Sullivan***	N	N	N	N	Y	Y	N	Y
2 Carson	N	Y	Y	N	Y	N	Y	Y
3 ***Watkins***	N	N	N	N	Y	Y	N	Y
4 ***Watts***	N	N	N	N	?	Y	N	Y
5 ***Istook***	N	N	N	N	Y	Y	N	Y
6 ***Lucas***	N	N	N	N	Y	Y	N	Y
OREGON								
1 Wu	Y	Y	Y	Y	N	N	Y	Y
2 ***Walden***	N	N	N	N	Y	Y	N	Y
3 Blumenauer	N	Y	Y	Y	N	N	Y	N
4 DeFazio	Y	Y	Y	Y	?	N	Y	N
5 Hooley	Y	Y	Y	Y	N	N	Y	Y
PENNSYLVANIA								
1 Brady	Y	Y	Y	Y	N	N	Y	Y
2 Fattah	Y	Y	Y	Y	N	N	Y	Y
3 Borski	Y	Y	Y	Y	N	N	Y	Y
4 ***Hart***	N	N	N	N	Y	Y	N	Y
5 ***Peterson***	N	N	N	N	?	Y	N	Y
6 Holden	Y	Y	Y	Y	N	N	Y	Y
7 ***Weldon***	N	N	N	N	Y	?	N	Y
8 ***Greenwood***	N	N	N	N	Y	Y	N	Y
9 ***Shuster, Bill***	N	N	N	N	Y	Y	N	Y
10 ***Sherwood***	N	N	N	N	Y	Y	N	Y
11 Kanjorski	N	Y	Y	Y	N	N	Y	Y
12 Murtha	Y	Y	Y	Y	N	N	Y	Y
13 Hoeffel	Y	Y	Y	Y	N	N	Y	Y
14 Coyne	Y	Y	Y	Y	N	N	Y	N
15 ***Toomey***	?	N	N	Y	Y	Y	N	Y
16 ***Pitts***	N	N	N	Y	Y	Y	N	Y
17 ***Gekas***	N	N	N	N	Y	Y	N	Y
18 Doyle	Y	Y	Y	Y	?	N	Y	Y
19 ***Platts***	N	N	N	N	Y	Y	N	Y
20 Mascara	Y	Y	Y	Y	N	N	Y	Y
21 ***English***	N	N	N	N	Y	Y	N	Y
RHODE ISLAND								
1 Kennedy	Y	Y	Y	N	N	N	Y	Y
2 Langevin	Y	?	?	Y	N	N	Y	N
SOUTH CAROLINA								
1 ***Brown***	N	N	N	N	Y	Y	N	Y
2 ***Wilson***	N	N	N	N	Y	Y	N	Y
3 ***Graham***	N	N	N	N	Y	Y	N	Y
4 ***DeMint***	N	N	N	N	Y	Y	N	Y
5 Spratt	Y	Y	Y	Y	N	N	Y	N
6 Clyburn	Y	Y	Y	Y	N	N	Y	N
SOUTH DAKOTA								
AL ***Thune***	N	N	N	Y	Y	Y	N	Y

	199	200	201	202	203	204	205	206
TENNESSEE								
1 ***Jenkins***	N	N	N	N	Y	Y	N	Y
2 ***Duncan***	N	N	N	N	Y	Y	N	N
3 ***Wamp***	N	N	N	N	Y	Y	N	Y
4 ***Hilleary***	N	N	N	N	Y	Y	N	Y
5 Clement	Y	Y	Y	N	N	N	Y	Y
6 Gordon	N	Y	N	Y	N	N	Y	N
7 ***Bryant***	N	N	N	N	Y	Y	N	Y
8 Tanner	Y	Y	Y	Y	N	N	Y	N
9 Ford	Y	Y	Y	Y	N	N	Y	N
TEXAS								
1 Sandlin	Y	Y	Y	Y	N	N	Y	Y
2 Turner	N	Y	Y	Y	N	N	Y	Y
3 ***Johnson, Sam***	N	N	N	N	Y	Y	N	Y
4 Hall	N	Y	Y	N	N	N	Y	Y
5 ***Sessions***	N	N	N	N	Y	Y	N	Y
6 ***Barton***	N	N	N	N	Y	Y	N	Y
7 ***Culberson***	N	N	N	N	?	Y	N	Y
8 ***Brady***	?	N	N	N	Y	Y	N	Y
9 Lampson	N	Y	Y	Y	N	N	Y	Y
10 Doggett	Y	Y	Y	Y	N	N	Y	N
11 Edwards	N	Y	Y	N	?	N	Y	Y
12 ***Granger***	?	?	?	?	?	Y	N	Y
13 ***Thornberry***	N	N	N	N	Y	Y	N	Y
14 ***Paul***	N	N	N	Y	Y	Y	N	N
15 Hinojosa	Y	?	?	Y	?	N	Y	Y
16 Reyes	?	Y	Y	Y	N	N	Y	Y
17 Stenholm	Y	Y	Y	N	N	N	Y	N
18 Jackson-Lee	Y	Y	Y	Y	N	N	Y	N
19 ***Combest***	?	?	?	?	?	?	?	?
20 Gonzalez	Y	Y	Y	Y	N	N	Y	Y
21 ***Smith***	N	N	N	N	Y	Y	N	Y
22 ***DeLay***	N	N	N	N	Y	Y	N	Y
23 ***Bonilla***	N	N	N	N	?	Y	N	Y
24 Frost	Y	Y	Y	Y	N	N	Y	Y
25 Bentsen	?	Y	Y	Y	?	N	Y	Y
26 ***Armey***	N	N	N	N	Y	Y	N	Y
27 Ortiz	?	Y	Y	Y	N	N	Y	Y
28 Rodriguez	Y	Y	Y	Y	N	N	Y	Y
29 Green	N	Y	Y	Y	N	N	Y	Y
30 Johnson, E.B.	Y	Y	Y	Y	Y	N	Y	N
UTAH								
1 ***Hansen***	N	N	N	N	Y	Y	N	Y
2 Matheson	N	Y	Y	Y	N	N	Y	Y
3 ***Cannon***	N	N	N	N	Y	Y	?	Y
VERMONT								
AL *Sanders*	Y	Y	Y	Y	N	N	Y	N
VIRGINIA								
1 ***Davis, Jo Ann***	N	N	N	N	Y	Y	N	Y
2 ***Schrock***	N	N	N	N	Y	Y	N	Y
3 Scott	N	Y	Y	Y	N	N	Y	Y
4 ***Forbes***	N	N	N	N	Y	Y	N	Y
5 *Goode*	N	N	N	Y	Y	Y	N	N
6 ***Goodlatte***	N	N	N	N	Y	Y	N	Y
7 ***Cantor***	N	N	N	N	Y	Y	N	Y
8 Moran	Y	Y	Y	Y	N	N	Y	N
9 Boucher	Y	Y	Y	Y	N	N	Y	Y
10 ***Wolf***	N	Y	N	N	Y	Y	N	Y
11 ***Davis, T.***	N	N	N	N	Y	Y	N	Y
WASHINGTON								
1 Inslee	Y	Y	Y	Y	N	N	Y	N
2 Larsen	Y	Y	Y	Y	N	N	Y	Y
3 Baird	Y	Y	Y	Y	N	N	Y	N
4 ***Hastings***	N	N	N	N	Y	Y	N	Y
5 ***Nethercutt***	N	N	N	N	Y	Y	N	Y
6 Dicks	N	Y	Y	Y	N	N	Y	Y
7 McDermott	Y	Y	Y	Y	N	N	Y	N
8 ***Dunn***	N	N	N	N	Y	Y	N	Y
9 Smith	Y	Y	Y	Y	N	N	Y	N
WEST VIRGINIA								
1 Mollohan	Y	Y	Y	Y	N	N	Y	Y
2 ***Capito***	N	N	N	N	Y	Y	N	Y
3 Rahall	N	Y	Y	Y	N	N	Y	N
WISCONSIN								
1 ***Ryan***	N	N	N	N	Y	Y	N	N
2 Baldwin	Y	Y	Y	Y	N	N	Y	N
3 Kind	Y	Y	Y	Y	N	N	Y	N
4 Kleczka	Y	Y	Y	Y	N	N	Y	N
5 Barrett	Y	Y	Y	Y	N	N	Y	N
6 ***Petri***	?	N	N	Y	Y	Y	N	Y
7 Obey	Y	Y	Y	N	N	N	Y	N
8 ***Green***	N	N	N	N	Y	Y	N	Y
9 ***Sensenbrenner***	N	N	N	Y	Y	Y	N	N
WYOMING								
AL ***Cubin***	N	N	N	N	Y	Y	N	Y

Southern states - Ala., Ark., Fla., Ga., Ky., La., Miss., N.C., Okla., S.C., Tenn., Texas, Va.

Key

Y	Voted for (yea).
#	Paired for.
+	Announced for.
N	Voted against (nay).
X	Paired against.
–	Announced against.
P	Voted "present."
C	Voted "present" to avoid possible conflict of interest.
?	Did not vote or otherwise make a position known.

Democrats **Republicans** *Independents*

207. HR 4823. Holocaust Payments/Passage. Shaw, R-Fla., motion to suspend the rules and pass the bill that would permanently extend a provision in last year's $1.35 trillion tax cut package exempting from taxable income restitution payments to Holocaust victims. Motion agreed to 392-1: R 205-0; D 186-1 (ND 136-0, SD 50-1); I 1-0. A two-thirds majority of those present and voting (262 in this case) is required for passage under suspension of the rules. A "yea" was a vote in support of the president's position. June 4, 2002.

208. HR 4800. Adoption Tax Credit/Passage. Camp, R-Mich., motion to suspend the rules and pass the bill that would permanently extend a provision in last year's $1.35 trillion tax cut package increasing the adoption tax credit from $5,000 ($6,000 for children with special needs) to $10,000. It would double to $10,000 the amount an employer may deduct for employee-adoption assistance. Motion agreed to 391-1: R 204-0; D 185-1 (ND 137-0, SD 48-1); I 2-0. A two-thirds majority of those present and voting (262 in this case) is required for passage under suspension of the rules. A "yea" was a vote in support of the president's position. June 4, 2002.

209. Procedural Motion/Journal. Approval of the House Journal of Tuesday, June 4, 2002. Approved 363-40: R 191-13; D 170-27 (ND 119-26, SD 51-1); I 2-0. June 5, 2002.

210. S 1372. Export-Import Bank/Conference Report. Adoption of the conference report on the bill that would reauthorize the Export-Import Bank through fiscal 2006. The agreement would increase the bank's aggregate loan limit from $75 billion to $100 billion over the next four years and increase small business related activities including doubling, to 20 percent, loans assisting those businesses. Adopted (thus sent to the Senate) 344-78: R 164-50; D 180-26 (ND 129-25, SD 51-1); I 0-2. June 5, 2002.

211. HR 4664. National Science Foundation/Biosafety Research. Woolsey, D-Calif., amendment that would authorize $35 million to establish a Biosafety Research program that would study the impact on biological systems of new variations of plant and other species. Rejected 165-259: R 1-216; D 163-42 (ND 128-24, SD 35-18); I 1-1. June 5, 2002.

212. HR 4664. National Science Foundation/Passage. Passage of the bill that would reauthorize the National Science Foundation (NSF) through fiscal 2005. It would authorize $5.5 billion for the agency for fiscal 2003 and increase that amount by 15 percent annually over the next two years. The bill would set specific allocation levels among the NSF's research, education and other accounts. Passed 397-25: R 194-22; D 201-3 (ND 150-2, SD 51-1); I 2-0. June 5, 2002.

	207	208	209	210	211	212
ALABAMA						
1 *Callahan*	?	?	?	Y	N	?
2 *Everett*	Y	Y	Y	N	N	Y
3 *Riley*	?	?	?	?	?	?
4 *Aderholt*	Y	Y	Y	N	N	Y
5 Cramer	Y	Y	Y	Y	N	Y
6 *Bachus*	+	+	+	+	N	Y
7 Hilliard	?	?	?	?	?	?
ALASKA						
AL *Young*	Y	Y	?	Y	N	Y
ARIZONA						
1 *Flake*	Y	Y	Y	N	N	N
2 Pastor	Y	Y	Y	Y	Y	Y
3 *Stump*	Y	Y	Y	N	N	N
4 *Shadegg*	Y	Y	Y	N	N	N
5 *Kolbe*	Y	Y	Y	N	N	Y
6 *Hayworth*	Y	Y	Y	N	N	Y
ARKANSAS						
1 Berry	Y	Y	Y	Y	N	Y
2 Snyder	Y	Y	Y	Y	N	Y
3 *Boozman*	Y	Y	Y	N	N	Y
4 Ross	Y	Y	Y	Y	N	Y
CALIFORNIA						
1 Thompson	Y	Y	N	Y	Y	Y
2 *Herger*	Y	Y	?	Y	N	N
3 *Ose*	Y	Y	Y	N	N	Y
4 *Doolittle*	?	?	Y	N	N	Y
5 Matsui	Y	Y	Y	Y	Y	Y
6 Woolsey	Y	Y	Y	Y	Y	Y
7 Miller, George	Y	Y	Y	Y	Y	Y
8 Pelosi	Y	Y	Y	Y	Y	Y
9 Lee	Y	Y	Y	Y	Y	Y
10 Tauscher	Y	Y	Y	Y	Y	Y
11 *Pombo*	Y	Y	Y	N	N	Y
12 Lantos	Y	Y	Y	Y	Y	Y
13 Stark	Y	Y	N	N	Y	Y
14 Eshoo	Y	Y	Y	Y	Y	Y
15 Honda	Y	Y	Y	Y	Y	Y
16 Lofgren	Y	Y	Y	Y	Y	Y
17 Farr	Y	Y	Y	Y	Y	Y
18 Condit	Y	Y	N	N	N	Y
19 *Radanovich*	Y	Y	Y	N	N	Y
20 Dooley	Y	Y	Y	Y	N	Y
21 *Thomas*	Y	Y	Y	N	N	Y
22 Capps	Y	Y	Y	Y	Y	Y
23 *Gallegly*	Y	Y	Y	N	N	Y
24 Sherman	Y	Y	Y	Y	Y	Y
25 *McKeon*	Y	Y	Y	N	N	Y
26 Berman	Y	Y	Y	Y	Y	Y
27 Schiff	?	?	Y	Y	Y	Y
28 *Dreier*	Y	Y	Y	N	N	Y
29 Waxman	Y	Y	Y	Y	Y	Y
30 Becerra	Y	Y	Y	Y	Y	Y
31 Solis	+	+	Y	Y	Y	Y
32 Watson	+	+	Y	Y	Y	Y
33 Roybal-Allard	Y	Y	Y	Y	Y	Y
34 Napolitano	Y	Y	Y	Y	Y	Y
35 Waters	Y	Y	N	N	Y	Y
36 Harman	Y	Y	Y	Y	Y	Y
37 Millender-McD.	?	?	Y	Y	Y	Y
38 *Horn*	Y	Y	Y	Y	N	Y

	207	208	209	210	211	212
39 *Royce*	Y	Y	Y	N	N	N
40 *Lewis*	?	?	Y	Y	N	Y
41 *Miller, Gary*	Y	Y	Y	Y	N	N
42 Baca	Y	Y	Y	Y	Y	Y
43 *Calvert*	?	?	Y	Y	N	Y
44 *Bono*	Y	Y	Y	N	N	Y
45 *Rohrabacher*	Y	Y	Y	N	N	N
46 Sanchez	Y	Y	?	Y	Y	Y
47 *Cox*	Y	Y	Y	N	N	Y
48 *Issa*	Y	Y	Y	Y	Y	Y
49 Davis	Y	Y	Y	Y	Y	Y
50 Filner	Y	Y	N	N	Y	Y
51 *Cunningham*	Y	Y	Y	N	N	Y
52 *Hunter*	Y	Y	?	N	N	Y
COLORADO						
1 DeGette	Y	Y	Y	Y	Y	Y
2 Udall	Y	Y	N	Y	Y	Y
3 *McInnis*	Y	Y	Y	N	N	Y
4 *Schaffer*	Y	Y	N	N	N	Y
5 *Hefley*	Y	Y	N	N	N	Y
6 *Tancredo*	Y	Y	P	N	N	N
CONNECTICUT						
1 Larson	Y	Y	?	Y	Y	Y
2 *Simmons*	Y	Y	Y	Y	N	Y
3 DeLauro	Y	Y	Y	Y	Y	Y
4 *Shays*	Y	Y	Y	Y	Y	Y
5 Maloney	Y	Y	Y	Y	Y	Y
6 *Johnson*	Y	Y	Y	Y	N	Y
DELAWARE						
AL *Castle*	Y	Y	Y	N	N	Y
FLORIDA						
1 *Miller, J.*	Y	Y	Y	N	N	N
2 Boyd	Y	Y	Y	N	N	Y
3 Brown	Y	Y	Y	Y	Y	Y
4 *Crenshaw*	Y	Y	Y	N	N	Y
5 Thurman	Y	Y	Y	N	N	Y
6 *Stearns*	Y	Y	Y	N	N	N
7 *Mica*	Y	Y	Y	N	N	Y
8 *Keller*	Y	Y	Y	N	N	Y
9 *Bilirakis*	Y	Y	Y	N	N	Y
10 *Young*	Y	Y	Y	N	N	Y
11 Davis	Y	Y	Y	Y	N	Y
12 *Putnam*	Y	Y	Y	N	N	Y
13 *Miller, D.*	Y	Y	?	?	N	Y
14 *Goss*	Y	Y	Y	N	N	Y
15 *Weldon*	Y	Y	Y	N	N	N
16 *Foley*	Y	Y	Y	N	N	Y
17 Meek	Y	Y	Y	Y	Y	Y
18 *Ros-Lehtinen*	Y	Y	Y	Y	N	Y
19 Wexler	Y	Y	Y	Y	Y	Y
20 Deutsch	Y	Y	Y	Y	Y	Y
21 *Diaz-Balart*	Y	Y	Y	Y	N	Y
22 *Shaw*	Y	Y	Y	Y	N	Y
23 Hastings	Y	Y	Y	Y	Y	Y
GEORGIA						
1 *Kingston*	Y	Y	Y	N	N	N
2 Bishop	Y	Y	Y	Y	Y	Y
3 *Collins*	Y	Y	Y	N	N	N
4 McKinney	?	?	N	Y	Y	Y
5 Lewis	Y	Y	Y	Y	Y	Y
6 *Isakson*	Y	Y	Y	N	N	Y
7 *Barr*	Y	Y	N	N	N	Y
8 *Chambliss*	Y	Y	Y	N	N	Y
9 *Deal*	+	+	?	N	N	N
10 *Norwood*	Y	Y	Y	N	N	N
11 *Linder*	Y	Y	Y	N	N	Y
HAWAII						
1 Abercrombie	+	+	Y	Y	Y	Y
2 Mink	Y	Y	Y	N	Y	Y
IDAHO						
1 *Otter*	Y	Y	Y	N	N	Y
2 *Simpson*	Y	Y	Y	Y	N	Y
ILLINOIS						
1 Rush	?	?	?	Y	Y	Y
2 Jackson	Y	Y	Y	N	Y	Y
3 Lipinski	?	?	P	Y	N	Y
4 Gutierrez	Y	Y	?	Y	Y	Y
5 Blagojevich	?	?	?	?	?	?
6 *Hyde*	Y	Y	Y	Y	N	N
7 Davis	Y	Y	Y	Y	Y	Y
8 *Crane*	Y	N	N	N	N	Y
9 Schakowsky	Y	Y	Y	Y	Y	Y
10 *Kirk*	Y	Y	Y	Y	N	Y
11 *Weller*	Y	N	N	Y	N	Y
12 Costello	Y	Y	Y	N	N	Y
13 *Biggert*	Y	Y	Y	Y	N	Y

ND Northern Democrats   SD Southern Democrats

Member	207	208	209	210	211	212
14 ***Hastert***						
15 ***Johnson***	Y	Y	Y	Y	N	Y
16 ***Manzullo***	Y	Y	Y	Y	N	Y
17 Evans	?	?	Y	Y	Y	Y
18 ***LaHood***	Y	Y	Y	Y	N	Y
19 Phelps	Y	Y	Y	Y	N	Y
20 ***Shimkus***	Y	Y	Y	Y	N	Y
INDIANA						
1 Visclosky	Y	Y	N	Y	Y	Y
2 ***Pence***	Y	Y	Y	N	N	Y
3 Roemer	Y	Y	Y	Y	Y	Y
4 ***Souder***	?	?	Y	Y	N	Y
5 ***Buyer***	Y	Y	Y	Y	N	Y
6 ***Burton***	Y	Y	Y	N	N	Y
7 ***Kerns***	Y	Y	Y	N	N	N
8 ***Hostettler***	Y	Y	Y	N	N	N
9 Hill	Y	Y	Y	Y	N	Y
10 Carson	Y	Y	Y	Y	Y	Y
IOWA						
1 ***Leach***	Y	Y	Y	Y	N	Y
2 ***Nussle***	Y	Y	Y	Y	N	Y
3 Boswell	Y	Y	Y	Y	N	Y
4 ***Ganske***	?	?	?	?	N	Y
5 ***Latham***	Y	Y	N	Y	N	Y
KANSAS						
1 ***Moran***	Y	Y	Y	Y	N	Y
2 ***Ryun***	Y	Y	Y	Y	N	Y
3 Moore	Y	Y	Y	Y	N	Y
4 ***Tiahrt***	Y	Y	Y	Y	N	Y
KENTUCKY						
1 ***Whitfield***	Y	Y	Y	Y	N	Y
2 ***Lewis***	Y	Y	Y	Y	N	Y
3 ***Northup***	Y	Y	Y	Y	N	Y
4 Lucas	Y	Y	Y	Y	N	Y
5 ***Rogers***	Y	?	Y	Y	N	Y
6 ***Fletcher***	Y	Y	N	Y	N	Y
LOUISIANA						
1 ***Vitter***	Y	Y	Y	Y	N	Y
2 Jefferson	Y	Y	Y	Y	N	Y
3 ***Tauzin***	Y	Y	Y	Y	N	Y
4 ***McCrery***	Y	Y	Y	Y	N	Y
5 ***Cooksey***	Y	Y	Y	Y	N	Y
6 ***Baker***	Y	Y	Y	Y	N	Y
7 John	Y	Y	Y	Y	N	Y
MAINE						
1 Allen	Y	Y	Y	Y	Y	Y
2 Baldacci	Y	Y	Y	Y	Y	Y
MARYLAND						
1 ***Gilchrest***	?	?	?	?	?	?
2 ***Ehrlich***	Y	Y	Y	Y	N	Y
3 Cardin	Y	Y	Y	Y	Y	Y
4 Wynn	Y	Y	Y	Y	N	Y
5 Hoyer	Y	Y	Y	Y	Y	Y
6 ***Bartlett***	Y	Y	Y	N	N	Y
7 Cummings	Y	Y	N	Y	Y	Y
8 ***Morella***	Y	Y	Y	Y	?	?
MASSACHUSETTS						
1 Olver	Y	Y	N	Y	Y	Y
2 Neal	Y	Y	Y	Y	Y	Y
3 McGovern	Y	Y	N	Y	Y	Y
4 Frank	Y	Y	Y	Y	Y	Y
5 Meehan	Y	Y	Y	Y	Y	Y
6 Tierney	Y	Y	Y	Y	Y	Y
7 Markey	Y	Y	Y	Y	Y	Y
8 Capuano	Y	Y	N	Y	N	Y
9 Lynch	Y	Y	Y	Y	Y	Y
10 Delahunt	Y	Y	Y	Y	Y	Y
MICHIGAN						
1 Stupak	Y	Y	Y	N	Y	Y
2 ***Hoekstra***	Y	Y	Y	N	N	Y
3 ***Ehlers***	Y	Y	Y	Y	N	Y
4 ***Camp***	Y	Y	Y	Y	N	Y
5 Barcia	Y	Y	Y	N	N	Y
6 ***Upton***	Y	Y	Y	Y	N	Y
7 ***Smith***	Y	Y	Y	N	N	Y
8 ***Rogers***	Y	Y	Y	Y	N	Y
9 Kildee	Y	Y	Y	Y	Y	Y
10 Bonior	?	?	Y	N	Y	Y
11 ***Knollenberg***	Y	Y	Y	Y	N	Y
12 Levin	Y	Y	Y	Y	Y	Y
13 Rivers	Y	Y	Y	N	Y	Y
14 Conyers	Y	Y	Y	N	Y	Y
15 Kilpatrick	?	?	Y	Y	Y	Y
16 Dingell	Y	Y	Y	Y	Y	Y

Member	207	208	209	210	211	212
MINNESOTA						
1 ***Gutknecht***	Y	Y	N	Y	N	Y
2 ***Kennedy***	Y	Y	N	Y	N	Y
3 ***Ramstad***	Y	Y	N	Y	N	Y
4 McCollum	Y	Y	Y	Y	Y	Y
5 Sabo	Y	Y	N	Y	Y	Y
6 Luther	Y	Y	Y	Y	Y	Y
7 Peterson	Y	Y	N	N	N	N
8 Oberstar	Y	Y	Y	N	N	Y
MISSISSIPPI						
1 ***Wicker***	Y	Y	Y	Y	N	Y
2 Thompson	?	?	?	Y	Y	Y
3 ***Pickering***	Y	Y	Y	Y	N	Y
4 Shows	Y	Y	Y	Y	N	Y
5 Taylor	Y	Y	N	Y	N	N
MISSOURI						
1 Clay	Y	Y	Y	Y	Y	Y
2 ***Akin***	Y	Y	Y	N	N	Y
3 Gephardt	Y	Y	?	Y	N	Y
4 Skelton	Y	Y	Y	Y	N	Y
5 McCarthy	Y	Y	Y	Y	Y	Y
6 ***Graves***	?	?	Y	Y	N	Y
7 ***Blunt***	Y	Y	Y	Y	N	Y
8 ***Emerson***	Y	Y	Y	Y	N	Y
9 ***Hulshof***	Y	Y	Y	Y	N	Y
MONTANA						
AL ***Rehberg***	Y	Y	Y	Y	N	Y
NEBRASKA						
1 ***Bereuter***	Y	Y	Y	Y	N	Y
2 ***Terry***	?	?	Y	Y	N	N
3 ***Osborne***	Y	Y	Y	Y	N	Y
NEVADA						
1 Berkley	Y	Y	Y	Y	Y	Y
2 ***Gibbons***	Y	Y	Y	Y	N	Y
NEW HAMPSHIRE						
1 ***Sununu***	Y	Y	Y	N	N	Y
2 ***Bass***	Y	Y	Y	N	N	Y
NEW JERSEY						
1 Andrews	Y	Y	Y	N	Y	Y
2 ***LoBiondo***	Y	Y	N	Y	N	Y
3 ***Saxton***	?	?	?	Y	N	Y
4 ***Smith***	Y	Y	Y	Y	N	Y
5 ***Roukema***	?	?	?	?	N	Y
6 Pallone	Y	Y	Y	N	Y	Y
7 ***Ferguson***	Y	Y	Y	Y	N	Y
8 Pascrell	Y	Y	Y	Y	Y	Y
9 Rothman	?	?	Y	Y	Y	Y
10 Payne	?	?	Y	Y	Y	Y
11 ***Frelinghuysen***	Y	Y	Y	Y	N	Y
12 Holt	Y	Y	Y	Y	Y	Y
13 Menendez	+	+	N	Y	N	Y
NEW MEXICO						
1 ***Wilson***	Y	Y	Y	Y	N	Y
2 ***Skeen***	Y	Y	Y	Y	N	Y
3 Udall	Y	Y	Y	Y	Y	Y
NEW YORK						
1 ***Grucci***	Y	Y	Y	Y	N	Y
2 Israel	Y	Y	Y	Y	Y	Y
3 ***King***	Y	Y	Y	Y	N	Y
4 McCarthy	Y	Y	Y	Y	Y	Y
5 Ackerman	Y	Y	Y	Y	Y	Y
6 Meeks	Y	Y	Y	Y	?	?
7 Crowley	Y	Y	Y	Y	Y	Y
8 Nadler	Y	Y	Y	N	Y	Y
9 Weiner	Y	Y	Y	Y	Y	Y
10 Towns	Y	Y	Y	Y	Y	Y
11 Owens	Y	Y	Y	N	Y	Y
12 Velázquez	?	Y	Y	Y	Y	Y
13 ***Fossella***	Y	Y	Y	Y	N	Y
14 Maloney	Y	Y	Y	Y	Y	Y
15 Rangel	Y	Y	Y	Y	Y	Y
16 Serrano	Y	Y	Y	Y	Y	Y
17 Engel	Y	Y	Y	Y	Y	Y
18 Lowey	Y	Y	Y	Y	Y	Y
19 ***Kelly***	Y	Y	Y	Y	N	Y
20 ***Gilman***	Y	Y	Y	Y	N	Y
21 McNulty	Y	Y	Y	Y	Y	Y
22 ***Sweeney***	Y	Y	Y	Y	N	Y
23 ***Boehlert***	Y	Y	Y	Y	N	Y
24 ***McHugh***	Y	Y	Y	Y	N	Y
25 ***Walsh***	Y	Y	Y	Y	N	Y
26 Hinchey	Y	Y	?	Y	Y	Y
27 ***Reynolds***	Y	Y	Y	Y	N	Y
28 Slaughter	?	?	?	+	+	+
29 LaFalce	Y	Y	Y	Y	?	?

Member	207	208	209	210	211	212
30 ***Quinn***	Y	Y	Y	Y	N	Y
31 ***Houghton***	Y	Y	Y	Y	Y	Y
NORTH CAROLINA						
1 Clayton	Y	Y	Y	Y	Y	Y
2 Etheridge	Y	Y	Y	Y	Y	Y
3 ***Jones***	Y	Y	Y	N	N	N
4 Price	Y	Y	Y	Y	Y	Y
5 ***Burr***	Y	Y	Y	Y	N	Y
6 ***Coble***	Y	Y	Y	N	N	Y
7 McIntyre	Y	Y	Y	Y	N	Y
8 ***Hayes***	Y	Y	Y	N	N	Y
9 ***Myrick***	Y	Y	Y	Y	N	Y
10 ***Ballenger***	Y	Y	?	Y	N	Y
11 ***Taylor***	Y	Y	Y	Y	N	Y
12 Watt	Y	Y	Y	Y	Y	Y
NORTH DAKOTA						
AL Pomeroy	Y	Y	Y	Y	Y	Y
OHIO						
1 ***Chabot***	Y	Y	Y	N	N	Y
2 ***Portman***	Y	Y	Y	Y	N	Y
3 Hall	Y	Y	?	Y	N	Y
4 ***Oxley***	Y	Y	Y	Y	N	Y
5 ***Gillmor***	Y	Y	Y	Y	N	Y
6 Strickland	Y	Y	N	N	Y	Y
7 ***Hobson***	Y	Y	Y	Y	N	Y
8 ***Boehner***	Y	Y	Y	Y	N	Y
9 Kaptur	Y	Y	Y	N	Y	Y
10 Kucinich	Y	Y	N	N	Y	Y
11 Jones	Y	Y	Y	Y	Y	Y
12 ***Tiberi***	Y	Y	Y	Y	N	Y
13 Brown	Y	Y	Y	N	Y	Y
14 Sawyer	Y	Y	Y	Y	Y	Y
15 ***Pryce***	Y	Y	Y	Y	N	Y
16 ***Regula***	Y	Y	Y	Y	N	Y
17 Traficant	?	?	?	?	?	?
18 ***Ney***	Y	Y	Y	Y	N	Y
19 ***LaTourette***	Y	Y	Y	Y	N	Y
OKLAHOMA						
1 ***Sullivan***	Y	Y	Y	N	N	Y
2 Carson	Y	Y	Y	Y	Y	Y
3 ***Watkins***	Y	Y	Y	Y	N	Y
4 ***Watts***	Y	Y	N	Y	N	Y
5 ***Istook***	Y	Y	Y	Y	N	Y
6 ***Lucas***	Y	Y	Y	Y	N	Y
OREGON						
1 Wu	Y	Y	N	Y	Y	Y
2 ***Walden***	Y	Y	Y	Y	N	Y
3 Blumenauer	Y	Y	Y	Y	Y	Y
4 DeFazio	Y	Y	N	N	Y	Y
5 Hooley	Y	Y	Y	Y	Y	Y
PENNSYLVANIA						
1 Brady	Y	Y	N	Y	Y	Y
2 Fattah	Y	Y	N	Y	Y	Y
3 Borski	Y	Y	N	Y	Y	Y
4 ***Hart***	Y	Y	N	Y	N	Y
5 ***Peterson***	?	?	?	?	?	?
6 Holden	Y	Y	Y	Y	N	Y
7 ***Weldon***	Y	Y	?	Y	N	Y
8 ***Greenwood***	Y	Y	Y	Y	N	Y
9 ***Shuster, Bill***	Y	Y	Y	Y	N	Y
10 ***Sherwood***	Y	Y	Y	Y	N	Y
11 Kanjorski	Y	Y	Y	Y	Y	Y
12 Murtha	?	?	?	Y	N	Y
13 Hoeffel	Y	Y	Y	Y	Y	Y
14 Coyne	?	?	Y	Y	Y	Y
15 ***Toomey***	Y	Y	Y	Y	N	Y
16 ***Pitts***	Y	Y	Y	Y	N	Y
17 ***Gekas***	Y	Y	Y	Y	N	Y
18 Doyle	Y	Y	Y	Y	Y	Y
19 ***Platts***	Y	Y	Y	N	N	Y
20 Mascara	Y	Y	Y	Y	Y	Y
21 ***English***	Y	Y	N	Y	N	Y
RHODE ISLAND						
1 Kennedy	Y	Y	Y	Y	Y	Y
2 Langevin	Y	Y	Y	Y	Y	Y
SOUTH CAROLINA						
1 ***Brown***	Y	Y	Y	Y	N	Y
2 ***Wilson***	Y	Y	Y	Y	N	Y
3 ***Graham***	Y	Y	Y	Y	N	Y
4 ***DeMint***	Y	Y	Y	N	N	Y
5 Spratt	Y	Y	Y	Y	Y	Y
6 Clyburn	Y	Y	Y	Y	Y	Y
SOUTH DAKOTA						
AL ***Thune***	Y	Y	Y	Y	N	Y

Member	207	208	209	210	211	212
TENNESSEE						
1 ***Jenkins***	Y	Y	Y	Y	N	Y
2 ***Duncan***	Y	Y	Y	N	N	Y
3 ***Wamp***	Y	Y	Y	N	N	Y
4 ***Hilleary***	Y	Y	Y	N	N	Y
5 Clement	Y	Y	Y	Y	Y	Y
6 Gordon	Y	Y	Y	Y	Y	Y
7 ***Bryant***	Y	Y	Y	Y	N	Y
8 Tanner	Y	Y	Y	Y	N	Y
9 Ford	Y	Y	Y	Y	N	Y
TEXAS						
1 Sandlin	Y	Y	Y	Y	Y	Y
2 Turner	Y	Y	Y	Y	N	Y
3 ***Johnson, Sam***	Y	Y	Y	Y	N	Y
4 Hall	Y	Y	Y	Y	Y	Y
5 ***Sessions***	Y	Y	Y	Y	N	Y
6 ***Barton***	Y	Y	Y	Y	N	Y
7 ***Culberson***	Y	Y	Y	N	N	Y
8 ***Brady***	Y	Y	Y	Y	N	Y
9 Lampson	Y	Y	Y	Y	Y	Y
10 Doggett	Y	Y	Y	Y	Y	Y
11 Edwards	Y	?	Y	Y	N	Y
12 ***Granger***	Y	Y	Y	Y	N	Y
13 ***Thornberry***	Y	Y	Y	Y	N	Y
14 ***Paul***	Y	Y	Y	N	N	N
15 Hinojosa	Y	Y	Y	Y	Y	Y
16 Reyes	Y	Y	Y	Y	Y	Y
17 Stenholm	N	N	Y	Y	N	Y
18 Jackson-Lee	Y	Y	Y	Y	Y	Y
19 ***Combest***	Y	Y	Y	Y	N	Y
20 Gonzalez	Y	Y	Y	Y	Y	Y
21 ***Smith***	Y	Y	Y	Y	N	Y
22 ***DeLay***	Y	Y	Y	N	N	Y
23 ***Bonilla***	Y	Y	?	Y	N	Y
24 Frost	Y	Y	Y	Y	Y	Y
25 Bentsen	Y	Y	Y	?	Y	Y
26 ***Armey***	Y	Y	Y	N	N	Y
27 Ortiz	Y	Y	Y	Y	Y	+
28 Rodriguez	Y	Y	Y	Y	Y	Y
29 Green	Y	?	Y	Y	Y	Y
30 Johnson, E.B.	Y	Y	Y	Y	Y	Y
UTAH						
1 ***Hansen***	?	?	Y	Y	N	Y
2 Matheson	Y	Y	N	N	Y	Y
3 ***Cannon***	Y	Y	Y	Y	N	Y
VERMONT						
AL *Sanders*	Y	Y	Y	N	Y	Y
VIRGINIA						
1 ***Davis, Jo Ann***	Y	Y	Y	N	N	Y
2 ***Schrock***	Y	Y	Y	Y	N	Y
3 Scott	Y	Y	Y	Y	Y	Y
4 ***Forbes***	Y	Y	Y	N	N	Y
5 *Goode*	?	Y	Y	N	N	Y
6 ***Goodlatte***	Y	Y	Y	Y	N	Y
7 ***Cantor***	Y	Y	Y	Y	N	Y
8 Moran	Y	Y	Y	Y	Y	Y
9 Boucher	Y	Y	Y	Y	N	Y
10 ***Wolf***	Y	Y	Y	Y	N	Y
11 ***Davis, T.***	Y	Y	Y	Y	N	Y
WASHINGTON						
1 Inslee	Y	Y	Y	Y	Y	Y
2 Larsen	Y	Y	N	Y	Y	Y
3 Baird	Y	Y	Y	Y	Y	Y
4 ***Hastings***	Y	Y	Y	Y	N	Y
5 ***Nethercutt***	Y	Y	Y	Y	N	Y
6 Dicks	Y	Y	Y	Y	Y	Y
7 McDermott	+	+	N	Y	Y	Y
8 ***Dunn***	Y	Y	Y	Y	N	Y
9 Smith	Y	Y	Y	Y	Y	Y
WEST VIRGINIA						
1 Mollohan	?	?	Y	N	Y	N
2 ***Capito***	Y	Y	Y	Y	N	Y
3 Rahall	Y	Y	Y	Y	Y	Y
WISCONSIN						
1 ***Ryan***	Y	Y	Y	Y	N	Y
2 Baldwin	Y	Y	N	N	N	Y
3 Kind	Y	Y	Y	Y	N	Y
4 Kleczka	Y	Y	Y	Y	Y	Y
5 Barrett	Y	Y	Y	Y	N	Y
6 ***Petri***	Y	Y	Y	N	N	N
7 Obey	Y	Y	N	Y	N	Y
8 ***Green***	Y	Y	Y	Y	N	Y
9 ***Sensenbrenner***	Y	Y	Y	N	N	N
WYOMING						
AL ***Cubin***	Y	Y	Y	N	N	Y

Southern states - Ala., Ark., Fla., Ga., Ky., La., Miss., N.C., Okla., S.C., Tenn., Texas, Va.

Key

Y	Voted for (yea).
#	Paired for.
+	Announced for.
N	Voted against (nay).
X	Paired against.
–	Announced against.
P	Voted "present."
C	Voted "present" to avoid possible conflict of interest.
?	Did not vote or otherwise make a position known.

Democrats **Republicans**
Independents

213. Procedural Motion/Adjourn. Kucinich, D-Ohio, motion to adjourn. Motion rejected 37-363: R 2-199; D 34-163 (ND 28-120, SD 6-43); I 1-1. June 6, 2002.

214. Question of Privilege/Ruling of the Chair. Hyde, R-Ill., motion to table (kill) the Kucinich, D-Ohio, appeal of the ruling of the chair that the Kucinich resolution does not constitute a point of privilege under Rule IX of the House. The Kucinich resolution would call for congressional approval before the president's withdrawal of the United States from the 1972 Anti-Ballistic Missile Treaty. Motion agreed to 254-169: R 215-0; D 38-168 (ND 20-134, SD 18-34); I 1-1. June 6, 2002.

215. HR 2143. Estate Tax Repeal/Previous Question. Hastings, R-Wash., motion to order the previous question (thus ending debate and possibility of amendment) on the rule (H Res 435) to provide for House floor consideration of the bill that would permanently extend the repeal of the estate and gift tax contained in the 2001 tax cut law (PL 107-16). Motion agreed to 223-201: R 216-0; D 6-200 (ND 1-153, SD 5-47); I 1-1. June 6, 2002.

216. HR 2143. Estate Tax Repeal/Rule. Adoption of the rule (H Res 435) to provide for House floor consideration of the bill that would permanently extend the repeal of the estate and gift tax contained in the 2001 tax cut law. Adopted 227-195: R 216-0; D 10-194 (ND 5-148, SD 5-46); I 1-1. June 6, 2002.

217. HR 2143. Estate Tax Repeal/Democratic Substitute. Pomeroy, D-N.D., substitute amendment that would strike the bill's permanent repeal language and replace it with provisions that would cap the maximum estate tax rate at 50 percent and permanently raise from $1 million to $3 million the value of an estate exempt from taxation. It also would reimpose a 5 percent surtax on estates worth more than $10 million. Rejected 197-231: R 6-212; D 190-18 (ND 139-16, SD 51-2); I 1-1. A "nay" was a vote in support of the president's position. June 6, 2002.

218. HR 2143. Estate Tax Repeal/Recommit. Stenholm, D-Texas, motion to recommit the bill to the House Ways and Means Committee with instructions that it be reported back with a new section that would make the bill's tax reductions contingent on preserving Social Security. Motion rejected 205-223: R 1-217; D 203-5 (ND 154-1, SD 49-4); I 1-1. June 6, 2002.

219. HR 2143. Estate Tax Repeal/Passage. Passage of the bill that would permanently extend the repeal of the estate and gift tax contained in the 2001 tax cut law (PL 107-16). Passed 256-171: R 214-4; D 41-166 (ND 21-133, SD 20-33); I 1-1. A "yea" was a vote in support of the president's position. June 6, 2002.

	213	214	215	216	217	218	219
ALABAMA							
1 *Callahan*	?	Y	Y	Y	N	N	Y
2 *Everett*	N	Y	Y	Y	N	N	Y
3 *Riley*	?	?	Y	Y	N	N	Y
4 *Aderholt*	N	Y	Y	Y	N	N	Y
5 Cramer	N	Y	N	N	Y	Y	Y
6 *Bachus*	N	Y	Y	Y	N	N	Y
7 Hilliard	N	N	N	N	Y	Y	N
ALASKA							
AL *Young*	?	Y	Y	Y	N	N	Y
ARIZONA							
1 *Flake*	N	Y	Y	Y	N	N	Y
2 Pastor	N	N	N	N	Y	Y	N
3 *Stump*	N	Y	Y	Y	N	N	Y
4 *Shadegg*	N	Y	Y	Y	N	N	Y
5 *Kolbe*	?	Y	Y	Y	N	N	Y
6 *Hayworth*	N	Y	Y	Y	N	N	Y
ARKANSAS							
1 Berry	N	N	N	N	Y	Y	Y
2 Snyder	N	Y	N	N	Y	Y	N
3 *Boozman*	N	Y	Y	Y	N	N	Y
4 Ross	N	N	N	N	Y	Y	Y
CALIFORNIA							
1 Thompson	N	N	N	N	Y	Y	Y
2 *Herger*	N	Y	Y	Y	N	N	Y
3 *Ose*	N	Y	Y	Y	N	N	Y
4 *Doolittle*	N	Y	Y	Y	N	N	Y
5 Matsui	Y	N	N	N	Y	Y	N
6 Woolsey	Y	N	N	N	Y	Y	N
7 Miller, George	N	N	N	N	Y	Y	N
8 Pelosi	N	N	N	N	Y	Y	N
9 Lee	Y	N	N	N	Y	Y	N
10 Tauscher	N	N	N	N	Y	Y	N
11 *Pombo*	N	Y	Y	Y	N	N	Y
12 Lantos	?	N	N	N	Y	Y	N
13 Stark	N	N	N	N	Y	Y	N
14 Eshoo	N	N	N	N	Y	Y	N
15 Honda	Y	N	N	N	Y	Y	N
16 Lofgren	N	N	N	N	Y	Y	N
17 Farr	N	N	N	N	Y	Y	N
18 Condit	N	N	Y	Y	Y	Y	Y
19 *Radanovich*	N	Y	Y	Y	N	N	Y
20 Dooley	N	N	N	N	Y	Y	Y
21 *Thomas*	N	Y	Y	Y	N	N	Y
22 Capps	N	N	N	N	Y	Y	N
23 *Gallegly*	N	Y	Y	Y	N	N	Y
24 Sherman	N	N	N	N	Y	Y	N
25 *McKeon*	N	Y	Y	Y	N	N	Y
26 Berman	N	Y	N	N	Y	Y	N
27 Schiff	N	N	Y	N	Y	Y	N
28 *Dreier*	N	Y	Y	Y	N	N	Y
29 Waxman	N	N	N	N	Y	Y	N
30 Becerra	Y	N	N	N	Y	Y	N
31 Solis	N	N	N	N	Y	Y	N
32 Watson	N	N	N	N	Y	Y	N
33 Roybal-Allard	N	N	N	N	Y	Y	N
34 Napolitano	N	N	?	N	Y	Y	N
35 Waters	Y	N	N	N	Y	Y	N
36 Harman	N	N	N	?	Y	Y	Y
37 Millender-McD.	N	N	N	N	Y	Y	N
38 *Horn*	N	Y	Y	Y	N	N	Y

	213	214	215	216	217	218	219
39 *Royce*	N	Y	Y	Y	N	N	Y
40 *Lewis*	N	Y	Y	Y	N	N	Y
41 *Miller, Gary*	N	Y	Y	Y	N	N	Y
42 Baca	N	N	N	N	Y	Y	N
43 *Calvert*	N	Y	Y	Y	N	N	Y
44 *Bono*	N	Y	Y	Y	N	N	Y
45 *Rohrabacher*	N	Y	Y	Y	N	N	Y
46 Sanchez	N	N	N	N	Y	Y	N
47 *Cox*	N	Y	Y	Y	N	N	Y
48 *Issa*	N	Y	Y	Y	N	N	Y
49 Davis	N	N	N	N	Y	Y	N
50 Filner	Y	N	N	N	Y	Y	N
51 *Cunningham*	N	Y	Y	Y	N	N	Y
52 *Hunter*	N	Y	Y	Y	N	N	Y
COLORADO							
1 DeGette	N	N	N	N	Y	Y	N
2 Udall	N	N	N	N	Y	Y	N
3 *McInnis*	N	Y	Y	Y	N	N	Y
4 *Schaffer*	N	Y	Y	Y	N	N	Y
5 *Hefley*	N	Y	Y	Y	N	N	Y
6 *Tancredo*	N	Y	Y	Y	N	N	Y
CONNECTICUT							
1 Larson	N	N	N	N	Y	Y	N
2 *Simmons*	Y	Y	Y	Y	N	N	Y
3 DeLauro	N	N	N	N	Y	Y	N
4 *Shays*	N	Y	Y	Y	N	N	Y
5 Maloney	N	N	N	N	Y	Y	Y
6 *Johnson*	N	Y	Y	Y	N	N	Y
DELAWARE							
AL *Castle*	N	Y	Y	Y	N	N	Y
FLORIDA							
1 *Miller, J.*	N	Y	Y	Y	N	N	Y
2 Boyd	N	N	N	N	Y	Y	Y
3 Brown	N	N	?	N	Y	Y	N
4 *Crenshaw*	N	Y	Y	Y	N	N	Y
5 Thurman	N	N	N	N	Y	Y	N
6 *Stearns*	N	Y	Y	Y	N	N	Y
7 *Mica*	N	Y	Y	Y	N	N	Y
8 *Keller*	N	Y	Y	Y	N	N	Y
9 *Bilirakis*	N	Y	Y	Y	N	N	Y
10 *Young*	N	Y	Y	Y	N	N	Y
11 Davis	N	N	N	N	Y	Y	N
12 *Putnam*	N	Y	Y	Y	N	N	Y
13 *Miller, D.*	N	Y	Y	Y	N	N	Y
14 *Goss*	?	Y	Y	Y	N	N	Y
15 *Weldon*	N	Y	Y	Y	N	N	Y
16 *Foley*	N	Y	Y	Y	N	N	Y
17 Meek	?	N	N	N	Y	Y	N
18 *Ros-Lehtinen*	N	Y	Y	Y	N	N	Y
19 Wexler	?	N	N	N	Y	Y	N
20 Deutsch	N	N	N	N	Y	Y	N
21 *Diaz-Balart*	N	Y	Y	Y	N	N	Y
22 *Shaw*	N	Y	Y	Y	N	N	Y
23 Hastings	Y	N	N	N	Y	Y	N
GEORGIA							
1 *Kingston*	N	?	Y	Y	N	N	Y
2 Bishop	Y	Y	Y	Y	Y	Y	Y
3 *Collins*	N	Y	Y	Y	N	N	Y
4 McKinney	N	N	N	N	Y	Y	N
5 Lewis	?	?	?	?	?	?	?
6 *Isakson*	N	Y	Y	Y	N	N	Y
7 *Barr*	N	Y	Y	Y	N	N	Y
8 *Chambliss*	N	Y	?	?	N	N	Y
9 *Deal*	N	Y	Y	Y	N	N	Y
10 *Norwood*	N	Y	Y	Y	N	N	Y
11 *Linder*	N	Y	Y	Y	N	N	Y
HAWAII							
1 Abercrombie	N	N	N	N	N	Y	Y
2 Mink	Y	N	N	N	Y	Y	N
IDAHO							
1 *Otter*	N	Y	Y	Y	N	N	Y
2 *Simpson*	N	Y	?	Y	N	N	Y
ILLINOIS							
1 Rush	N	N	N	N	Y	Y	N
2 Jackson	N	N	N	N	Y	Y	N
3 Lipinski	N	N	N	N	Y	Y	N
4 Gutierrez	?	N	N	N	Y	Y	N
5 Blagojevich	N	N	N	N	Y	Y	N
6 *Hyde*	N	Y	Y	Y	N	N	Y
7 Davis	N	N	N	N	Y	Y	N
8 *Crane*	N	Y	Y	Y	N	N	Y
9 Schakowsky	N	N	N	N	Y	Y	N
10 *Kirk*	?	Y	Y	Y	N	N	Y
11 *Weller*	N	Y	Y	Y	N	N	Y
12 Costello	N	N	N	N	Y	Y	N
13 *Biggert*	N	Y	Y	Y	N	N	Y

ND Northern Democrats SD Southern Democrats

Member	213	214	215	216	217	218	219
14 ***Hastert***					N	N	Y
15 ***Johnson***	N	Y	Y	Y	N	N	Y
16 ***Manzullo***	N	Y	Y	Y	N	N	Y
17 Evans	Y	N	N	N	Y	Y	N
18 ***LaHood***	N	Y	Y	Y	N	N	Y
19 Phelps	N	N	N	N	Y	Y	Y
20 ***Shimkus***	N	Y	Y	Y	N	N	Y
INDIANA							
1 Visclosky	N	N	N	N	Y	Y	N
2 ***Pence***	N	Y	Y	Y	N	N	Y
3 Roemer	N	Y	N	Y	Y	Y	N
4 ***Souder***	N	Y	Y	Y	N	N	Y
5 ***Buyer***	N	Y	Y	Y	Y	N	Y
6 ***Burton***	N	Y	Y	Y	N	N	Y
7 ***Kerns***	N	Y	Y	Y	N	N	Y
8 ***Hostettler***	N	Y	Y	Y	N	N	Y
9 Hill	N	N	N	N	Y	Y	N
10 Carson	Y	N	N	N	Y	Y	N
IOWA							
1 ***Leach***	N	Y	Y	Y	Y	Y	N
2 ***Nussle***	N	Y	Y	Y	N	N	Y
3 Boswell	N	N	N	N	Y	Y	Y
4 ***Ganske***	N	Y	Y	Y	N	N	Y
5 ***Latham***	N	Y	Y	Y	Y	N	Y
KANSAS							
1 ***Moran***	N	Y	Y	Y	N	N	Y
2 ***Ryun***	N	Y	Y	Y	N	N	Y
3 Moore	N	Y	N	N	N	Y	N
4 ***Tiahrt***	N	Y	Y	Y	N	N	Y
KENTUCKY							
1 ***Whitfield***	N	Y	Y	Y	N	N	Y
2 ***Lewis***	N	Y	Y	Y	N	N	Y
3 ***Northup***	N	Y	Y	Y	N	N	Y
4 Lucas	N	Y	Y	Y	Y	N	Y
5 ***Rogers***	N	Y	Y	Y	N	N	Y
6 ***Fletcher***	N	Y	Y	Y	N	N	Y
LOUISIANA							
1 ***Vitter***	N	Y	Y	Y	N	N	Y
2 Jefferson	Y	N	N	N	Y	Y	Y
3 ***Tauzin***	N	Y	Y	Y	N	N	Y
4 ***McCrery***	N	Y	Y	Y	N	N	Y
5 ***Cooksey***	?	Y	Y	Y	N	N	Y
6 ***Baker***	N	Y	Y	Y	N	N	Y
7 John	N	Y	N	N	Y	Y	Y
MAINE							
1 Allen	N	N	N	N	Y	Y	N
2 Baldacci	N	N	N	N	Y	Y	N
MARYLAND							
1 ***Gilchrest***	?	?	?	?	?	?	?
2 ***Ehrlich***	?	Y	Y	Y	N	N	Y
3 Cardin	N	N	N	N	Y	Y	N
4 Wynn	N	N	N	N	Y	Y	N
5 Hoyer	N	N	N	N	Y	Y	N
6 ***Bartlett***	N	Y	Y	Y	N	N	Y
7 Cummings	N	N	N	N	Y	Y	N
8 ***Morella***	N	Y	Y	Y	Y	N	N
MASSACHUSETTS							
1 Olver	Y	N	N	N	N	Y	N
2 Neal	N	N	N	N	Y	Y	N
3 McGovern	N	N	N	N	Y	Y	N
4 Frank	N	Y	N	N	Y	Y	N
5 Meehan	N	Y	N	N	Y	Y	N
6 Tierney	Y	N	N	N	Y	Y	N
7 Markey	Y	N	N	N	Y	Y	N
8 Capuano	Y	Y	N	N	Y	Y	?
9 Lynch	N	N	N	?	Y	Y	N
10 Delahunt	Y	N	N	N	Y	Y	N
MICHIGAN							
1 Stupak	Y	N	N	N	Y	Y	N
2 ***Hoekstra***	N	Y	Y	Y	N	N	Y
3 ***Ehlers***	N	Y	Y	Y	N	N	Y
4 ***Camp***	N	Y	Y	Y	N	N	Y
5 Barcia	N	N	Y	Y	Y	N	Y
6 ***Upton***	N	Y	Y	Y	N	N	Y
7 ***Smith***	N	Y	Y	?	N	N	Y
8 ***Rogers***	N	Y	Y	Y	N	N	Y
9 Kildee	N	N	N	N	Y	Y	N
10 Bonior	N	N	N	N	Y	Y	N
11 ***Knollenberg***	N	Y	Y	Y	N	N	Y
12 Levin	N	N	N	N	Y	Y	N
13 Rivers	N	N	N	N	Y	Y	N
14 Conyers	Y	N	N	N	Y	Y	N
15 Kilpatrick	N	N	N	N	Y	Y	N
16 Dingell	N	N	N	N	Y	Y	N
MINNESOTA							
1 ***Gutknecht***	N	Y	Y	Y	N	N	Y
2 ***Kennedy***	N	Y	Y	Y	N	N	Y
3 ***Ramstad***	N	Y	Y	Y	N	N	Y
4 McCollum	N	N	N	N	Y	Y	N
5 Sabo	N	N	N	N	Y	Y	N
6 Luther	N	N	N	N	Y	Y	N
7 Peterson	N	N	N	Y	Y	Y	Y
8 Oberstar	N	N	N	N	Y	Y	N
MISSISSIPPI							
1 ***Wicker***	N	Y	Y	Y	N	N	Y
2 Thompson	N	N	N	N	Y	Y	N
3 ***Pickering***	N	Y	Y	Y	N	N	Y
4 Shows	N	N	N	N	Y	N	Y
5 Taylor	N	N	N	N	Y	Y	N
MISSOURI							
1 Clay	Y	N	N	N	Y	Y	Y
2 ***Akin***	N	Y	Y	Y	N	N	Y
3 Gephardt	N	N	N	N	Y	Y	N
4 Skelton	N	N	N	N	Y	Y	Y
5 McCarthy	N	N	N	N	Y	Y	N
6 ***Graves***	N	Y	Y	Y	N	N	Y
7 ***Blunt***	?	Y	Y	Y	N	N	Y
8 ***Emerson***	N	Y	Y	Y	?	?	?
9 ***Hulshof***	N	Y	Y	Y	N	N	Y
MONTANA							
AL ***Rehberg***	N	Y	Y	Y	N	N	Y
NEBRASKA							
1 ***Bereuter***	N	Y	Y	Y	Y	N	N
2 ***Terry***	N	Y	Y	Y	N	N	Y
3 ***Osborne***	N	Y	Y	Y	N	N	Y
NEVADA							
1 Berkley	N	N	N	N	Y	Y	Y
2 ***Gibbons***	N	Y	Y	Y	N	N	Y
NEW HAMPSHIRE							
1 ***Sununu***	N	Y	Y	Y	N	N	Y
2 ***Bass***	N	Y	Y	Y	N	N	Y
NEW JERSEY							
1 Andrews	?	N	N	N	N	Y	N
2 ***LoBiondo***	N	Y	Y	Y	N	N	Y
3 ***Saxton***	N	Y	Y	Y	N	N	Y
4 ***Smith***	N	Y	Y	Y	N	N	Y
5 ***Roukema***	N	Y	Y	Y	?	?	?
6 Pallone	N	N	N	N	Y	Y	N
7 ***Ferguson***	N	Y	Y	Y	N	N	Y
8 Pascrell	N	N	N	N	Y	Y	N
9 Rothman	N	N	N	N	Y	Y	N
10 Payne	N	N	N	N	Y	Y	N
11 ***Frelinghuysen***	N	Y	Y	Y	N	N	Y
12 Holt	N	N	N	N	Y	Y	Y
13 Menendez	N	Y	N	N	Y	Y	N
NEW MEXICO							
1 ***Wilson***	N	Y	Y	Y	N	N	Y
2 ***Skeen***	N	Y	Y	Y	N	N	Y
3 Udall	N	N	N	N	Y	Y	N
NEW YORK							
1 ***Grucci***	N	Y	Y	Y	N	N	Y
2 Israel	N	N	N	N	Y	Y	Y
3 ***King***	N	Y	Y	Y	N	N	Y
4 McCarthy	N	Y	N	N	Y	Y	Y
5 Ackerman	N	N	N	N	Y	Y	N
6 Meeks	N	N	N	N	Y	Y	N
7 Crowley	N	N	N	N	Y	Y	N
8 Nadler	N	N	N	N	Y	Y	N
9 Weiner	N	Y	N	N	Y	Y	N
10 Towns	?	N	N	N	Y	Y	N
11 Owens	N	N	N	N	Y	Y	N
12 Velázquez	Y	N	N	N	Y	Y	N
13 ***Fossella***	N	Y	Y	Y	N	N	Y
14 Maloney	N	N	N	N	Y	Y	N
15 Rangel	Y	N	N	N	Y	Y	N
16 Serrano	N	?	?	?	?	?	?
17 Engel	?	N	N	N	Y	Y	N
18 Lowey	?	N	N	N	Y	Y	N
19 ***Kelly***	N	Y	Y	Y	N	N	Y
20 ***Gilman***	N	Y	Y	Y	N	N	Y
21 McNulty	Y	N	N	N	Y	Y	N
22 ***Sweeney***	N	Y	Y	Y	N	N	Y
23 ***Boehlert***	N	Y	Y	Y	N	N	Y
24 ***McHugh***	N	Y	Y	Y	N	N	Y
25 ***Walsh***	?	Y	Y	Y	N	N	Y
26 Hinchey	Y	N	N	N	Y	Y	N
27 ***Reynolds***	?	Y	Y	Y	N	N	Y
28 Slaughter	N	N	N	N	Y	Y	N
29 LaFalce	N	N	N	N	Y	Y	N
30 ***Quinn***	N	Y	Y	Y	N	N	Y
31 ***Houghton***	?	?	?	?	N	N	N
NORTH CAROLINA							
1 Clayton	N	N	N	N	Y	Y	N
2 Etheridge	N	N	N	N	Y	Y	N
3 ***Jones***	N	Y	Y	Y	N	N	Y
4 Price	N	N	N	N	Y	Y	N
5 ***Burr***	N	Y	Y	Y	N	N	Y
6 ***Coble***	N	Y	Y	Y	N	N	Y
7 McIntyre	N	Y	N	N	Y	Y	Y
8 ***Hayes***	N	Y	Y	Y	N	N	Y
9 ***Myrick***	N	Y	Y	Y	N	N	Y
10 ***Ballenger***	N	Y	Y	Y	N	N	Y
11 ***Taylor***	N	Y	Y	Y	N	N	Y
12 Watt	N	Y	N	N	Y	Y	N
NORTH DAKOTA							
AL Pomeroy	N	N	N	N	Y	Y	N
OHIO							
1 ***Chabot***	N	Y	Y	Y	N	N	Y
2 ***Portman***	N	Y	Y	Y	N	N	Y
3 Hall	N	N	N	N	Y	Y	N
4 ***Oxley***	N	Y	Y	Y	N	N	Y
5 ***Gillmor***	N	Y	Y	Y	N	N	Y
6 Strickland	N	N	N	N	Y	Y	N
7 ***Hobson***	N	Y	Y	Y	N	N	Y
8 ***Boehner***	N	Y	Y	Y	N	N	Y
9 Kaptur	?	N	N	N	Y	Y	N
10 Kucinich	Y	N	N	N	N	Y	N
11 Jones	Y	N	N	N	Y	Y	N
12 ***Tiberi***	N	Y	Y	Y	N	N	Y
13 Brown	N	N	N	N	N	Y	N
14 Sawyer	N	N	N	N	Y	Y	N
15 ***Pryce***	N	Y	Y	Y	N	N	Y
16 ***Regula***	N	Y	Y	Y	N	N	Y
17 Traficant	?	?	?	?	?	?	?
18 ***Ney***	N	Y	Y	Y	N	N	Y
19 ***LaTourette***	N	Y	Y	Y	N	N	Y
OKLAHOMA							
1 ***Sullivan***	N	Y	Y	Y	N	N	Y
2 Carson	N	Y	Y	?	Y	Y	Y
3 ***Watkins***	N	Y	Y	Y	N	N	Y
4 ***Watts***	?	Y	Y	Y	N	N	Y
5 ***Istook***	N	Y	Y	Y	N	N	Y
6 ***Lucas***	N	Y	Y	Y	N	N	Y
OREGON							
1 Wu	N	N	N	N	Y	Y	N
2 ***Walden***	N	Y	Y	Y	N	N	Y
3 Blumenauer	N	Y	N	N	Y	Y	N
4 DeFazio	N	N	N	N	Y	Y	N
5 Hooley	N	N	N	N	Y	Y	Y
PENNSYLVANIA							
1 Brady	N	N	N	N	Y	Y	N
2 Fattah	N	N	N	N	Y	Y	N
3 Borski	N	N	N	N	Y	Y	N
4 ***Hart***	N	Y	Y	Y	N	N	Y
5 ***Peterson***	N	Y	Y	Y	N	N	Y
6 Holden	N	Y	N	N	Y	Y	N
7 ***Weldon***	N	Y	Y	Y	N	N	Y
8 ***Greenwood***	N	?	Y	Y	N	N	Y
9 ***Shuster, Bill***	N	Y	Y	Y	N	N	Y
10 ***Sherwood***	N	Y	Y	Y	N	N	Y
11 Kanjorski	N	Y	N	N	Y	Y	N
12 Murtha	N	Y	N	N	Y	Y	N
13 Hoeffel	N	N	N	N	Y	Y	N
14 Coyne	N	N	N	N	Y	Y	N
15 ***Toomey***	N	Y	Y	Y	N	N	Y
16 ***Pitts***	N	Y	Y	Y	N	N	Y
17 ***Gekas***	N	Y	Y	Y	N	N	Y
18 Doyle	N	N	N	N	Y	Y	N
19 ***Platts***	N	Y	Y	Y	N	N	Y
20 Mascara	N	N	N	N	Y	Y	N
21 ***English***	Y	Y	Y	Y	N	N	Y
RHODE ISLAND							
1 Kennedy	Y	N	N	N	Y	Y	N
2 Langevin	Y	N	N	N	Y	Y	N
SOUTH CAROLINA							
1 ***Brown***	N	Y	Y	Y	N	N	Y
2 ***Wilson***	N	Y	Y	Y	N	N	Y
3 ***Graham***	N	Y	Y	Y	N	N	Y
4 ***DeMint***	N	Y	Y	Y	N	N	Y
5 Spratt	N	Y	N	N	Y	Y	N
6 Clyburn	N	N	N	N	Y	Y	N
SOUTH DAKOTA							
AL ***Thune***	N	Y	Y	Y	N	N	Y
TENNESSEE							
1 ***Jenkins***	N	Y	Y	Y	N	N	Y
2 ***Duncan***	N	Y	Y	Y	N	N	Y
3 ***Wamp***	N	Y	Y	Y	N	N	Y
4 ***Hilleary***	?	Y	Y	Y	N	N	Y
5 Clement	N	N	N	N	Y	Y	Y
6 Gordon	?	N	N	N	Y	Y	Y
7 ***Bryant***	N	Y	Y	Y	N	N	Y
8 Tanner	N	N	N	Y	Y	Y	Y
9 Ford	N	N	N	N	Y	Y	Y
TEXAS							
1 Sandlin	N	Y	N	?	Y	Y	Y
2 Turner	N	Y	N	N	Y	Y	N
3 ***Johnson, Sam***	N	Y	Y	Y	N	N	Y
4 Hall	N	Y	Y	Y	Y	N	Y
5 ***Sessions***	N	Y	Y	Y	N	N	Y
6 ***Barton***	?	Y	Y	Y	N	N	Y
7 ***Culberson***	N	Y	Y	Y	N	N	Y
8 ***Brady***	N	Y	Y	Y	N	N	Y
9 Lampson	N	N	N	N	Y	Y	Y
10 Doggett	Y	N	N	N	Y	Y	N
11 Edwards	N	Y	N	N	Y	Y	Y
12 ***Granger***	N	Y	Y	Y	N	N	Y
13 ***Thornberry***	N	Y	Y	Y	N	N	Y
14 ***Paul***	N	Y	Y	Y	N	N	Y
15 Hinojosa	N	N	N	N	Y	Y	Y
16 Reyes	N	Y	N	N	Y	Y	N
17 Stenholm	N	Y	N	N	Y	Y	N
18 Jackson-Lee	N	N	N	N	Y	Y	N
19 ***Combest***	?	?	?	?	?	?	?
20 Gonzalez	N	N	N	N	Y	Y	N
21 ***Smith***	N	Y	Y	Y	N	N	Y
22 ***DeLay***	?	Y	Y	Y	N	N	Y
23 ***Bonilla***	N	Y	Y	Y	N	N	Y
24 Frost	N	N	N	N	Y	Y	N
25 Bentsen	N	N	N	N	Y	Y	N
26 ***Armey***	?	Y	Y	Y	N	N	Y
27 Ortiz	N	Y	N	N	Y	Y	N
28 Rodriguez	Y	N	N	N	Y	Y	N
29 Green	N	N	N	N	Y	Y	N
30 Johnson, E.B.	Y	N	N	N	Y	Y	N
UTAH							
1 ***Hansen***	N	Y	Y	Y	N	N	Y
2 Matheson	N	Y	N	Y	Y	Y	Y
3 ***Cannon***	N	Y	Y	Y	N	N	Y
VERMONT							
AL *Sanders*	Y	N	N	N	Y	Y	N
VIRGINIA							
1 ***Davis, Jo Ann***	N	Y	Y	Y	N	N	Y
2 ***Schrock***	N	Y	Y	Y	N	N	Y
3 Scott	N	N	N	N	Y	Y	N
4 ***Forbes***	N	Y	Y	Y	N	N	Y
5 *Goode*	N	Y	Y	Y	N	N	Y
6 ***Goodlatte***	N	Y	Y	Y	N	N	Y
7 ***Cantor***	N	Y	Y	Y	N	N	Y
8 Moran	?	Y	N	N	Y	Y	N
9 Boucher	N	?	Y	Y	N	N	Y
10 ***Wolf***	N	Y	Y	Y	N	N	Y
11 ***Davis, T.***	N	Y	Y	Y	N	N	Y
WASHINGTON							
1 Inslee	N	N	N	N	Y	Y	N
2 Larsen	N	N	N	N	Y	Y	Y
3 Baird	N	Y	N	N	Y	Y	N
4 ***Hastings***	N	Y	Y	Y	N	N	Y
5 ***Nethercutt***	N	Y	Y	Y	N	N	Y
6 Dicks	N	N	N	N	Y	Y	N
7 McDermott	Y	N	N	N	Y	Y	N
8 ***Dunn***	N	Y	Y	Y	N	N	Y
9 Smith	N	?	N	N	N	Y	N
WEST VIRGINIA							
1 Mollohan	N	Y	N	N	N	Y	N
2 ***Capito***	N	Y	Y	Y	N	N	Y
3 Rahall	?	Y	N	N	Y	Y	N
WISCONSIN							
1 ***Ryan***	N	Y	Y	Y	N	N	Y
2 Baldwin	N	N	N	N	Y	Y	N
3 Kind	N	N	N	N	Y	Y	N
4 Kleczka	N	N	N	N	Y	Y	N
5 Barrett	N	N	N	N	Y	Y	N
6 ***Petri***	N	Y	Y	Y	N	N	Y
7 Obey	N	Y	N	N	N	Y	N
8 ***Green***	N	Y	Y	Y	N	N	Y
9 ***Sensenbrenner***	N	Y	Y	Y	N	N	Y
WYOMING							
AL ***Cubin***	?	Y	Y	Y	N	N	Y

Southern states - Ala., Ark., Fla., Ga., Ky., La., Miss., N.C., Okla., S.C., Tenn., Texas, Va.

Key

Y Voted for (yea).
\# Paired for.
\+ Announced for.
N Voted against (nay).
X Paired against.
− Announced against.
P Voted "present."
C Voted "present" to avoid possible conflict of interest.
? Did not vote or otherwise make a position known.

Democrats   **Republicans**
Independents

---

220. H Res 438. Impact of Obesity/Adoption. Fossella, R-N.Y., motion to suspend the rules and adopt the resolution that would express the sense of the House that obesity is a major health problem and urge efforts to combat it. Motion agreed to 400-2: R 204-2; D 194-0 (ND 142-0, SD 52-0); I 2-0. A two-thirds majority of those present and voting (268 in this case) is required for adoption under suspension of the rules. June 11, 2002.

221. H Con Res 394. World Cup Hosts/Adoption. Royce, R-Calif., motion to suspend the rules and adopt the concurrent resolution that would pay tribute to the Republic of Korea and Japan as hosts of the 2002 World Cup soccer tournament and recognize the importance of those two countries' relationship with the United States. Motion agreed to 402-1: R 205-1; D 195-0 (ND 144-0, SD 51-0); I 2-0. A two-thirds majority of those present and voting (269 in this case) is required for adoption under suspension of the rules. June 11, 2002.

222. H Con Res 213. North Korean Refugees/Adoption. Leach, R-Iowa, motion to suspend the rules and adopt the concurrent resolution that would urge China to respect rights of asylum for North Korean refugees and meet the requirements of the 1951 U.N. Convention on the Status of Refugees. Motion agreed to 406-0: R 207-0; D 197-0 (ND 146-0, SD 51-0); I 2-0. A two-thirds majority of those present and voting (271 in this case) is required for adoption under suspension of the rules. June 11, 2002.

223. HR 4. Energy Plan/Motion to Instruct. Markey, D-Mass., motion to instruct House conferees to insist that no provisions in the bill create a net annual deficit in the non-Social Security portion of the budget during the 10-year estimating period. Motion agreed to 412-1: R 212-0; D 198-1 (ND 145-1, SD 53-0); I 2-0. June 12, 2002.

224. HR 4775. Fiscal 2002 Supplemental Appropriations/Motion to Instruct. Obey, D-Wis., motion to instruct House conferees to insist that the conference report include the higher dollar amount of the House or Senate-passed version of the bill for items related to homeland security and the war on terrorism and include no additional funds earmarked for items unrelated to those efforts. Motion rejected 181-235: R 2-213; D 178-21 (ND 134-12, SD 44-9); I 1-1. June 12, 2002.

	220	221	222	223	224
ALABAMA					
1 *Callahan*	Y	Y	Y	Y	N
2 *Everett*	Y	Y	Y	Y	N
3 *Riley*	+	+	+	Y	N
4 *Aderholt*	Y	Y	Y	Y	N
5 Cramer	Y	Y	Y	Y	N
6 *Bachus*	Y	Y	Y	Y	N
7 Hilliard	Y	Y	Y	Y	Y
ALASKA					
AL *Young*	Y	Y	Y	Y	N
ARIZONA					
1 *Flake*	N	Y	Y	Y	N
2 Pastor	Y	Y	Y	Y	Y
3 *Stump*	Y	Y	Y	Y	N
4 *Shadegg*	Y	N	Y	Y	N
5 *Kolbe*	Y	Y	Y	Y	N
6 *Hayworth*	Y	Y	Y	Y	N
ARKANSAS					
1 Berry	Y	Y	Y	Y	Y
2 Snyder	Y	Y	Y	Y	Y
3 *Boozman*	Y	Y	Y	Y	N
4 Ross	Y	Y	Y	Y	Y
CALIFORNIA					
1 Thompson	Y	Y	Y	Y	Y
2 *Herger*	Y	Y	Y	Y	N
3 *Ose*	Y	Y	Y	Y	N
4 *Doolittle*	Y	Y	Y	Y	N
5 Matsui	Y	Y	Y	Y	Y
6 Woolsey	Y	Y	Y	Y	Y
7 Miller, George	Y	Y	Y	Y	Y
8 Pelosi	Y	Y	Y	?	?
9 Lee	Y	Y	Y	Y	Y
10 Tauscher	Y	Y	Y	Y	Y
11 *Pombo*	Y	Y	Y	Y	N
12 Lantos	Y	Y	Y	Y	Y
13 Stark	Y	Y	Y	Y	Y
14 Eshoo	Y	Y	Y	Y	Y
15 Honda	Y	Y	Y	Y	Y
16 Lofgren	Y	Y	Y	Y	Y
17 Farr	Y	Y	Y	Y	Y
18 Condit	Y	Y	Y	Y	Y
19 *Radanovich*	?	?	?	Y	N
20 Dooley	Y	Y	Y	Y	N
21 *Thomas*	Y	Y	Y	P	N
22 Capps	Y	Y	Y	Y	Y
23 *Gallegly*	Y	Y	Y	Y	N
24 Sherman	Y	Y	Y	Y	Y
25 *McKeon*	Y	Y	Y	Y	N
26 Berman	Y	Y	Y	Y	Y
27 Schiff	Y	Y	Y	Y	Y
28 *Dreier*	?	?	?	Y	N
29 Waxman	Y	Y	Y	Y	Y
30 Becerra	Y	Y	Y	Y	Y
31 Solis	Y	Y	Y	Y	Y
32 Watson	Y	Y	Y	Y	Y
33 Roybal-Allard	Y	Y	Y	Y	Y
34 Napolitano	+	Y	Y	Y	Y
35 Waters	Y	Y	Y	Y	Y
36 Harman	Y	Y	Y	Y	Y
37 Millender-McD.	Y	Y	Y	Y	Y
38 *Horn*	Y	Y	Y	Y	Y

	220	221	222	223	224
39 *Royce*	Y	Y	Y	Y	N
40 *Lewis*	Y	Y	Y	Y	N
41 *Miller, Gary*	Y	Y	Y	Y	N
42 Baca	Y	Y	Y	Y	Y
43 *Calvert*	Y	Y	Y	Y	N
44 *Bono*	?	?	?	?	?
45 *Rohrabacher*	Y	Y	Y	Y	N
46 Sanchez	Y	Y	Y	Y	Y
47 *Cox*	Y	?	Y	Y	N
48 *Issa*	Y	Y	Y	Y	N
49 Davis	Y	Y	Y	Y	N
50 Filner	Y	Y	Y	Y	Y
51 *Cunningham*	Y	Y	Y	Y	N
52 *Hunter*	Y	Y	Y	?	N
COLORADO					
1 DeGette	Y	Y	Y	Y	Y
2 Udall	Y	Y	Y	Y	Y
3 *McInnis*	Y	Y	Y	Y	N
4 *Schaffer*	Y	Y	Y	Y	N
5 *Hefley*	Y	Y	Y	Y	N
6 *Tancredo*	Y	Y	Y	Y	N
CONNECTICUT					
1 Larson	Y	Y	Y	Y	Y
2 *Simmons*	Y	Y	Y	Y	N
3 DeLauro	Y	Y	Y	Y	Y
4 *Shays*	Y	Y	Y	Y	N
5 Maloney	Y	Y	Y	Y	Y
6 *Johnson*	Y	Y	Y	Y	N
DELAWARE					
AL *Castle*	Y	Y	Y	Y	N
FLORIDA					
1 *Miller, J.*	Y	Y	Y	Y	N
2 Boyd	Y	Y	Y	Y	Y
3 Brown	Y	Y	Y	Y	Y
4 *Crenshaw*	Y	Y	Y	Y	N
5 Thurman	Y	Y	Y	Y	Y
6 *Stearns*	Y	Y	Y	Y	N
7 *Mica*	Y	Y	Y	Y	N
8 *Keller*	Y	Y	Y	Y	N
9 *Bilirakis*	Y	Y	Y	Y	N
10 *Young*	Y	Y	Y	Y	N
11 Davis	Y	Y	Y	Y	Y
12 *Putnam*	Y	Y	Y	Y	N
13 *Miller, D.*	Y	Y	Y	Y	N
14 *Goss*	Y	Y	Y	+	−
15 *Weldon*	Y	Y	Y	Y	N
16 *Foley*	Y	Y	Y	Y	N
17 Meek	Y	Y	Y	Y	Y
18 *Ros-Lehtinen*	Y	Y	Y	Y	N
19 Wexler	Y	Y	Y	Y	Y
20 Deutsch	Y	Y	Y	Y	Y
21 *Diaz-Balart*	Y	Y	Y	Y	N
22 *Shaw*	Y	Y	Y	Y	N
23 Hastings	Y	Y	Y	Y	Y
GEORGIA					
1 *Kingston*	Y	Y	Y	Y	N
2 Bishop	Y	Y	Y	Y	Y
3 *Collins*	Y	Y	Y	Y	N
4 McKinney	Y	Y	Y	Y	Y
5 Lewis	Y	Y	Y	Y	Y
6 *Isakson*	Y	Y	Y	Y	N
7 *Barr*	Y	Y	Y	Y	N
8 *Chambliss*	?	?	?	Y	N
9 *Deal*	Y	Y	Y	Y	N
10 *Norwood*	Y	Y	Y	Y	N
11 *Linder*	Y	Y	Y	Y	N
HAWAII					
1 Abercrombie	Y	Y	Y	Y	Y
2 Mink	Y	Y	Y	Y	Y
IDAHO					
1 *Otter*	Y	Y	Y	Y	N
2 *Simpson*	Y	Y	Y	Y	N
ILLINOIS					
1 Rush	Y	Y	Y	Y	Y
2 Jackson	Y	Y	Y	Y	Y
3 Lipinski	?	?	?	Y	Y
4 Gutierrez	?	?	?	Y	Y
5 Blagojevich	?	?	?	?	?
6 *Hyde*	Y	Y	Y	Y	N
7 Davis	Y	Y	Y	Y	Y
8 *Crane*	Y	Y	Y	Y	N
9 Schakowsky	Y	Y	Y	Y	Y
10 *Kirk*	Y	Y	Y	Y	N
11 *Weller*	Y	Y	Y	Y	N
12 Costello	?	?	?	Y	Y
13 *Biggert*	Y	Y	Y	Y	N

ND Northern Democrats   SD Southern Democrats

	220	221	222	223	224
14 Hastert					
15 Johnson	Y	Y	Y	Y	N
16 Manzullo	Y	Y	Y	Y	N
17 Evans	Y	Y	Y	Y	Y
18 LaHood	Y	Y	Y	Y	N
19 Phelps	Y	Y	Y	Y	N
20 Shimkus	Y	Y	Y	Y	N
INDIANA					
1 Visclosky	Y	Y	Y	Y	N
2 Pence	Y	Y	Y	Y	N
3 Roemer	Y	Y	Y	Y	Y
4 Souder	Y	Y	Y	Y	N
5 Buyer	Y	Y	Y	Y	N
6 Burton	Y	Y	Y	Y	N
7 Kerns	Y	Y	Y	Y	N
8 Hostettler	Y	Y	Y	Y	N
9 Hill	Y	Y	Y	Y	N
10 Carson	Y	Y	Y	Y	Y
IOWA					
1 Leach	Y	Y	Y	Y	Y
2 Nussle	Y	Y	Y	Y	N
3 Boswell	Y	Y	Y	Y	N
4 Ganske	Y	Y	Y	Y	N
5 Latham	Y	Y	Y	Y	N
KANSAS					
1 Moran	?	?	?	Y	N
2 Ryun	Y	Y	Y	Y	N
3 Moore	Y	Y	Y	Y	N
4 Tiahrt	Y	Y	Y	Y	N
KENTUCKY					
1 Whitfield	Y	Y	Y	Y	N
2 Lewis	Y	Y	Y	Y	N
3 Northup	Y	Y	Y	Y	N
4 Lucas	Y	Y	Y	Y	Y
5 Rogers	Y	Y	Y	Y	N
6 Fletcher	Y	Y	Y	Y	N
LOUISIANA					
1 Vitter	Y	Y	Y	Y	N
2 Jefferson	Y	Y	Y	Y	Y
3 Tauzin	Y	Y	Y	Y	N
4 McCrery	Y	Y	Y	P	N
5 Cooksey	Y	Y	Y	Y	N
6 Baker	Y	Y	Y	Y	N
7 John	Y	Y	Y	Y	N
MAINE					
1 Allen	Y	Y	Y	Y	Y
2 Baldacci	?	?	?	Y	Y
MARYLAND					
1 Gilchrest	Y	Y	Y	Y	N
2 Ehrlich	Y	Y	Y	Y	N
3 Cardin	Y	Y	Y	Y	N
4 Wynn	Y	Y	Y	Y	N
5 Hoyer	?	Y	Y	Y	N
6 Bartlett	Y	Y	Y	Y	N
7 Cummings	Y	Y	Y	Y	N
8 Morella	Y	Y	Y	Y	N
MASSACHUSETTS					
1 Olver	?	Y	Y	Y	Y
2 Neal	Y	Y	Y	Y	Y
3 McGovern	Y	Y	Y	Y	Y
4 Frank	Y	Y	Y	Y	Y
5 Meehan	Y	Y	Y	Y	Y
6 Tierney	Y	Y	Y	Y	Y
7 Markey	Y	Y	Y	Y	Y
8 Capuano	Y	Y	Y	Y	Y
9 Lynch	?	?	?	?	?
10 Delahunt	Y	Y	Y	Y	Y
MICHIGAN					
1 Stupak	Y	Y	Y	Y	Y
2 Hoekstra	Y	Y	Y	Y	N
3 Ehlers	Y	Y	Y	Y	N
4 Camp	Y	Y	Y	Y	N
5 Barcia	Y	Y	Y	Y	Y
6 Upton	Y	Y	Y	Y	N
7 Smith	Y	Y	Y	Y	N
8 Rogers	Y	Y	Y	Y	N
9 Kildee	Y	Y	Y	Y	Y
10 Bonior	?	?	?	Y	Y
11 Knollenberg	Y	Y	Y	Y	N
12 Levin	Y	Y	Y	Y	Y
13 Rivers	?	?	?	?	Y
14 Conyers	?	?	?	?	Y
15 Kilpatrick	Y	Y	Y	Y	Y
16 Dingell	Y	Y	Y	Y	Y

	220	221	222	223	224
MINNESOTA					
1 Gutknecht	Y	Y	Y	Y	N
2 Kennedy	Y	Y	Y	Y	N
3 Ramstad	Y	Y	Y	Y	N
4 McCollum	Y	Y	Y	Y	Y
5 Sabo	Y	Y	Y	N	Y
6 Luther	Y	Y	Y	Y	Y
7 Peterson	Y	Y	Y	?	?
8 Oberstar	Y	Y	Y	Y	Y
MISSISSIPPI					
1 Wicker	Y	Y	Y	Y	N
2 Thompson	Y	Y	Y	Y	Y
3 Pickering	Y	Y	Y	Y	N
4 Shows	Y	Y	Y	Y	N
5 Taylor	Y	Y	Y	Y	Y
MISSOURI					
1 Clay	Y	Y	Y	Y	Y
2 Akin	Y	Y	Y	Y	N
3 Gephardt	Y	Y	Y	Y	N
4 Skelton	Y	Y	Y	Y	N
5 McCarthy	Y	Y	Y	Y	N
6 Graves	?	?	?	Y	N
7 Blunt	Y	Y	Y	Y	N
8 Emerson	Y	Y	Y	Y	N
9 Hulshof	?	?	?	Y	N
MONTANA					
AL Rehberg	Y	Y	Y	Y	N
NEBRASKA					
1 Bereuter	Y	Y	Y	Y	N
2 Terry	Y	Y	Y	Y	N
3 Osborne	Y	Y	Y	Y	N
NEVADA					
1 Berkley	Y	Y	Y	Y	Y
2 Gibbons	Y	Y	Y	Y	N
NEW HAMPSHIRE					
1 Sununu	Y	Y	Y	Y	N
2 Bass	Y	Y	Y	Y	N
NEW JERSEY					
1 Andrews	Y	Y	Y	Y	Y
2 LoBiondo	Y	Y	Y	Y	N
3 Saxton	Y	Y	Y	Y	N
4 Smith	Y	Y	Y	Y	N
5 Roukema	Y	Y	Y	Y	N
6 Pallone	Y	Y	Y	Y	Y
7 Ferguson	?	?	?	Y	N
8 Pascrell	Y	Y	Y	Y	Y
9 Rothman	Y	Y	Y	Y	Y
10 Payne	Y	Y	Y	?	?
11 Frelinghuysen	Y	Y	Y	Y	N
12 Holt	Y	Y	Y	Y	Y
13 Menendez	Y	Y	Y	?	?
NEW MEXICO					
1 Wilson	Y	Y	Y	Y	N
2 Skeen	Y	Y	Y	Y	N
3 Udall	Y	Y	Y	Y	N
NEW YORK					
1 Grucci	Y	Y	Y	Y	Y
2 Israel	Y	Y	Y	Y	Y
3 King	Y	Y	Y	Y	Y
4 McCarthy	Y	Y	Y	Y	Y
5 Ackerman	Y	Y	Y	Y	Y
6 Meeks	Y	Y	Y	Y	Y
7 Crowley	Y	Y	Y	Y	Y
8 Nadler	Y	Y	Y	Y	Y
9 Weiner	Y	Y	Y	Y	Y
10 Towns	Y	Y	Y	Y	Y
11 Owens	Y	Y	Y	?	?
12 Velázquez	Y	Y	Y	Y	Y
13 Fossella	Y	Y	Y	Y	N
14 Maloney	Y	Y	Y	?	?
15 Rangel	?	?	?	Y	Y
16 Serrano	Y	Y	Y	Y	Y
17 Engel	Y	Y	Y	Y	Y
18 Lowey	Y	Y	Y	Y	Y
19 Kelly	Y	Y	Y	Y	N
20 Gilman	Y	Y	Y	Y	N
21 McNulty	Y	Y	Y	Y	Y
22 Sweeney	?	?	?	?	N
23 Boehlert	Y	Y	Y	Y	N
24 McHugh	Y	Y	Y	Y	N
25 Walsh	Y	Y	Y	Y	N
26 Hinchey	Y	Y	Y	Y	Y
27 Reynolds	Y	Y	Y	Y	N
28 Slaughter	Y	Y	Y	Y	Y
29 LaFalce	Y	Y	Y	Y	Y

	220	221	222	223	224
30 Quinn	Y	Y	Y	?	?
31 Houghton	Y	Y	Y	?	?
NORTH CAROLINA					
1 Clayton	?	?	?	?	?
2 Etheridge	Y	Y	Y	Y	N
3 Jones	Y	Y	Y	Y	N
4 Price	Y	Y	Y	Y	N
5 Burr	Y	Y	Y	Y	N
6 Coble	Y	Y	Y	Y	N
7 McIntyre	Y	Y	Y	Y	N
8 Hayes	Y	Y	Y	Y	N
9 Myrick	Y	Y	Y	Y	N
10 Ballenger	Y	Y	Y	Y	N
11 Taylor	Y	Y	Y	Y	N
12 Watt	Y	Y	Y	Y	Y
NORTH DAKOTA					
AL Pomeroy	Y	Y	Y	Y	Y
OHIO					
1 Chabot	Y	Y	Y	Y	N
2 Portman	Y	Y	Y	Y	N
3 Hall	?	?	?	?	?
4 Oxley	Y	Y	Y	Y	N
5 Gillmor	Y	Y	Y	Y	N
6 Strickland	Y	Y	Y	Y	N
7 Hobson	Y	Y	Y	Y	N
8 Boehner	Y	Y	Y	Y	N
9 Kaptur	Y	Y	Y	Y	Y
10 Kucinich	Y	Y	Y	Y	Y
11 Jones	Y	Y	Y	Y	?
12 Tiberi	Y	Y	Y	Y	N
13 Brown	Y	Y	Y	Y	Y
14 Sawyer	Y	Y	Y	Y	Y
15 Pryce	Y	Y	Y	Y	N
16 Regula	Y	Y	Y	Y	N
17 Traficant	?	?	?	?	?
18 Ney	Y	Y	Y	Y	N
19 LaTourette	Y	Y	Y	Y	N
OKLAHOMA					
1 Sullivan	Y	Y	Y	Y	N
2 Carson	Y	Y	Y	Y	N
3 Watkins	Y	Y	Y	Y	N
4 Watts	+	Y	Y	Y	N
5 Istook	Y	Y	Y	Y	N
6 Lucas	Y	Y	Y	Y	N
OREGON					
1 Wu	Y	Y	Y	Y	Y
2 Walden	Y	Y	Y	Y	N
3 Blumenauer	Y	Y	Y	Y	Y
4 DeFazio	Y	Y	Y	Y	Y
5 Hooley	Y	Y	Y	Y	Y
PENNSYLVANIA					
1 Brady	Y	Y	Y	Y	Y
2 Fattah	Y	Y	Y	Y	Y
3 Borski	Y	Y	Y	Y	Y
4 Hart	Y	Y	Y	Y	N
5 Peterson	Y	Y	Y	Y	N
6 Holden	Y	Y	Y	Y	Y
7 Weldon	Y	Y	Y	Y	N
8 Greenwood	Y	Y	Y	Y	N
9 Shuster, Bill	Y	Y	Y	Y	N
10 Sherwood	Y	Y	Y	Y	N
11 Kanjorski	Y	Y	Y	Y	Y
12 Murtha	Y	Y	Y	Y	Y
13 Hoeffel	Y	Y	Y	Y	Y
14 Coyne	Y	Y	Y	Y	Y
15 Toomey	Y	Y	Y	Y	N
16 Pitts	Y	Y	Y	Y	N
17 Gekas	Y	Y	Y	Y	N
18 Doyle	Y	Y	Y	Y	Y
19 Platts	Y	Y	Y	Y	N
20 Mascara	Y	Y	Y	Y	Y
21 English	Y	Y	Y	Y	N
RHODE ISLAND					
1 Kennedy	Y	?	Y	Y	Y
2 Langevin	Y	Y	Y	Y	Y
SOUTH CAROLINA					
1 Brown	Y	Y	Y	Y	N
2 Wilson	Y	Y	Y	Y	N
3 Graham	Y	Y	Y	Y	N
4 DeMint	+	+	+	Y	N
5 Spratt	Y	Y	Y	Y	N
6 Clyburn	?	?	?	Y	Y
SOUTH DAKOTA					
AL Thune	Y	Y	Y	Y	N

	220	221	222	223	224
TENNESSEE					
1 Jenkins	Y	Y	Y	Y	N
2 Duncan	Y	Y	Y	Y	N
3 Wamp	Y	Y	Y	Y	N
4 Hilleary	Y	Y	Y	Y	Y
5 Clement	Y	Y	Y	Y	Y
6 Gordon	Y	Y	Y	Y	N
7 Bryant	Y	Y	Y	Y	N
8 Tanner	Y	Y	Y	Y	N
9 Ford	Y	Y	Y	Y	Y
TEXAS					
1 Sandlin	Y	?	Y	Y	Y
2 Turner	Y	Y	Y	Y	N
3 Johnson, Sam	Y	Y	Y	Y	N
4 Hall	Y	Y	Y	Y	Y
5 Sessions	Y	Y	Y	Y	N
6 Barton	Y	Y	Y	Y	N
7 Culberson	Y	Y	Y	Y	N
8 Brady	Y	Y	Y	Y	N
9 Lampson	Y	Y	Y	Y	Y
10 Doggett	Y	Y	Y	Y	Y
11 Edwards	Y	Y	Y	Y	Y
12 Granger	Y	Y	Y	Y	N
13 Thornberry	Y	Y	Y	Y	N
14 Paul	N	Y	Y	Y	N
15 Hinojosa	Y	Y	Y	Y	Y
16 Reyes	Y	Y	Y	Y	Y
17 Stenholm	Y	Y	Y	Y	Y
18 Jackson-Lee	Y	Y	Y	Y	Y
19 Combest	?	?	?	?	?
20 Gonzalez	Y	Y	Y	Y	Y
21 Smith	?	?	?	?	?
22 DeLay	Y	Y	Y	Y	N
23 Bonilla	Y	Y	Y	Y	N
24 Frost	Y	Y	Y	Y	Y
25 Bentsen	Y	Y	Y	Y	Y
26 Armey	Y	Y	Y	Y	N
27 Ortiz	Y	Y	?	Y	Y
28 Rodriguez	Y	Y	Y	Y	Y
29 Green	Y	Y	Y	Y	Y
30 Johnson, E.B.	Y	Y	Y	Y	Y
UTAH					
1 Hansen	Y	Y	Y	Y	N
2 Matheson	Y	Y	Y	Y	Y
3 Cannon	Y	Y	Y	Y	N
VERMONT					
AL Sanders	Y	Y	Y	Y	Y
VIRGINIA					
1 Davis, Jo Ann	Y	Y	Y	Y	N
2 Schrock	Y	Y	Y	Y	N
3 Scott	Y	Y	Y	Y	Y
4 Forbes	Y	Y	Y	Y	N
5 Goode	Y	Y	Y	Y	Y
6 Goodlatte	Y	Y	Y	Y	N
7 Cantor	Y	Y	Y	Y	N
8 Moran	Y	Y	Y	Y	Y
9 Boucher	Y	Y	Y	Y	Y
10 Wolf	Y	Y	Y	Y	N
11 Davis, T.	Y	Y	Y	Y	N
WASHINGTON					
1 Inslee	Y	Y	Y	Y	Y
2 Larsen	Y	Y	Y	Y	Y
3 Baird	Y	Y	Y	Y	Y
4 Hastings	Y	Y	Y	Y	N
5 Nethercutt	Y	Y	Y	Y	N
6 Dicks	Y	Y	Y	Y	Y
7 McDermott	Y	Y	Y	Y	Y
8 Dunn	Y	Y	Y	Y	N
9 Smith	Y	Y	Y	Y	Y
WEST VIRGINIA					
1 Mollohan	Y	Y	Y	Y	N
2 Capito	Y	Y	Y	Y	N
3 Rahall	Y	Y	Y	Y	N
WISCONSIN					
1 Ryan	Y	Y	Y	Y	N
2 Baldwin	Y	Y	Y	Y	Y
3 Kind	Y	Y	Y	Y	Y
4 Kleczka	Y	Y	Y	Y	Y
5 Barrett	Y	Y	Y	Y	Y
6 Petri	Y	Y	Y	Y	N
7 Obey	Y	Y	Y	Y	Y
8 Green	Y	Y	Y	Y	N
9 Sensenbrenner	Y	Y	Y	Y	N
WYOMING					
AL Cubin	?	?	?	Y	N

Southern states - Ala., Ark., Fla., Ga., Ky., La., Miss., N.C., Okla., S.C., Tenn., Texas, Va.

Key

Y	Voted for (yea).	
#	Paired for.	
+	Announced for.	
N	Voted against (nay).	
X	Paired against.	
–	Announced against.	
P	Voted "present."	
C	Voted "present" to avoid possible conflict of interest.	
?	Did not vote or otherwise make a position known.	

Democrats   **Republicans**
Independents

225. H J Res 96. Tax Limitation Constitutional Amendment/Passage. Passage of the joint resolution that would propose a constitutional amendment to require a two-thirds majority vote of both the House and Senate to pass legislation that raises federal revenues by more than a "de minimus" amount, except in times of war or military conflict threatening national security. Rejected 227-178: R 201-11; D 25-166 (ND 13-128, SD 12-38); I 1-1. A two-thirds majority vote of those present and voting (270 in this case) is required to pass a joint resolution proposing an amendment to the Constitution. June 12, 2002.

226. HR 4019. Married Couples Tax Relief/Rule. Adoption of the rule (H Res 440) to provide for House floor consideration of the bill that would extend beyond 2010 breaks for married couples contained in last year's $1.35 trillion tax cut law (PL 107-16). Adopted 385-22: R 207-0; D 177-21 (ND 129-19, SD 48-2); I 1-1. June 13, 2002.

227. Procedural Motion/Journal. Approval of the House Journal of Wednesday, June 12, 2002. Approved 344-56: R 187-17; D 155-39 (ND 115-31, SD 40-8); I 2-0. June 13, 2002.

228. HR 4019. Married Couples Tax Relief/Democratic Substitute. Matsui, D-Calif., substitute amendment that would extend beyond 2010 breaks for married couples contained in last year's $1.35 trillion tax cut law, but only if the Office of Management and Budget certifies that none of the funds to pay for the tax breaks would come from the Social Security trust fund during the 10-year period beginning in fiscal 2011. Rejected 198-213: R 1-207; D 196-5 (ND 145-4, SD 51-1); I 1-1. June 13, 2002.

229. HR 4019. Married Couples Tax Relief/Passage. Passage of the bill that would extend beyond 2010 breaks for married couples contained in last year's $1.35 trillion tax cut law. Passed 271-142: R 210-0; D 60-141 (ND 36-113, SD 24-28); I 1-1. A "yea" was a vote in support of the president's position. June 13, 2002.

230. Procedural Motion/Journal. Approval of the House Journal of Friday, June 14, 2002. Approved 307-45: R 172-16; D 134-29 (ND 94-25, SD 40-4); I 1-0. June 17, 2002.

	225	226	227	228	229	230
ALABAMA						
1 *Callahan*	Y	Y	Y	N	Y	?
2 *Everett*	Y	Y	Y	N	Y	Y
3 *Riley*	Y	Y	Y	N	Y	+
4 *Aderholt*	Y	Y	N	N	Y	N
5 Cramer	Y	Y	Y	Y	Y	Y
6 *Bachus*	Y	Y	Y	N	Y	+
7 Hilliard	N	N	N	Y	Y	?
ALASKA						
AL *Young*	Y	?	?	N	Y	Y
ARIZONA						
1 *Flake*	Y	Y	Y	N	Y	Y
2 Pastor	N	N	Y	Y	N	Y
3 *Stump*	Y	Y	?	N	Y	Y
4 *Shadegg*	Y	Y	Y	N	Y	?
5 *Kolbe*	Y	Y	Y	N	Y	Y
6 *Hayworth*	Y	Y	Y	N	Y	Y
ARKANSAS						
1 Berry	Y	Y	Y	Y	N	Y
2 Snyder	N	Y	Y	Y	Y	Y
3 *Boozman*	Y	Y	Y	N	Y	Y
4 Ross	Y	Y	Y	Y	Y	Y
CALIFORNIA						
1 Thompson	N	Y	N	Y	N	N
2 *Herger*	Y	Y	Y	?	Y	?
3 *Ose*	Y	Y	Y	N	Y	Y
4 *Doolittle*	Y	Y	Y	N	Y	Y
5 Matsui	N	Y	Y	Y	N	?
6 Woolsey	N	Y	Y	Y	N	Y
7 Miller, George	N	Y	N	Y	N	N
8 Pelosi	N	Y	Y	Y	N	?
9 Lee	N	N	Y	Y	N	Y
10 Tauscher	N	Y	Y	Y	N	Y
11 *Pombo*	Y	Y	Y	N	Y	N
12 Lantos	N	Y	Y	Y	N	Y
13 Stark	N	N	?	Y	N	Y
14 Eshoo	N	Y	Y	Y	N	Y
15 Honda	–	Y	Y	Y	N	+
16 Lofgren	N	Y	Y	Y	N	Y
17 Farr	N	Y	Y	Y	N	Y
18 Condit	Y	Y	Y	Y	N	Y
19 *Radanovich*	Y	Y	Y	N	Y	Y
20 Dooley	N	Y	Y	Y	N	?
21 *Thomas*	N	Y	Y	N	Y	Y
22 Capps	N	Y	Y	Y	Y	Y
23 *Gallegly*	Y	Y	Y	N	Y	?
24 Sherman	N	N	Y	Y	N	Y
25 *McKeon*	Y	Y	Y	N	Y	?
26 Berman	?	Y	Y	Y	N	?
27 Schiff	N	Y	Y	Y	N	Y
28 *Dreier*	N	Y	Y	N	Y	Y
29 Waxman	?	Y	Y	Y	N	Y
30 Becerra	N	Y	Y	Y	N	+
31 Solis	N	Y	Y	Y	N	Y
32 Watson	?	Y	Y	Y	N	Y
33 Roybal-Allard	N	Y	Y	Y	N	Y
34 Napolitano	N	Y	Y	Y	N	Y
35 Waters	N	N	N	Y	N	N
36 Harman	Y	Y	Y	Y	Y	Y
37 Millender-McD.	N	Y	Y	Y	N	?
38 Horn	Y	Y	Y	N	Y	Y

	225	226	227	228	229	230
39 *Royce*	Y	Y	Y	N	Y	Y
40 *Lewis*	Y	Y	Y	N	Y	Y
41 *Miller, Gary*	Y	Y	Y	N	Y	Y
42 Baca	N	Y	Y	Y	Y	Y
43 *Calvert*	Y	Y	Y	N	Y	Y
44 *Bono*	?	?	?	?	?	Y
45 *Rohrabacher*	Y	Y	Y	N	Y	Y
46 Sanchez	Y	Y	Y	N	N	N
47 *Cox*	Y	Y	Y	?	Y	Y
48 *Issa*	Y	Y	Y	N	Y	Y
49 Davis	N	Y	Y	Y	Y	Y
50 Filner	N	N	N	P	N	N
51 *Cunningham*	Y	Y	Y	N	Y	Y
52 *Hunter*	Y	Y	Y	N	Y	Y
COLORADO						
1 DeGette	N	Y	Y	Y	N	Y
2 Udall	N	Y	N	Y	Y	N
3 *McInnis*	Y	?	?	?	?	?
4 *Schaffer*	Y	Y	N	N	Y	Y
5 *Hefley*	Y	Y	N	N	Y	Y
6 *Tancredo*	Y	Y	P	N	Y	Y
CONNECTICUT						
1 Larson	N	Y	Y	Y	N	?
2 *Simmons*	Y	Y	Y	N	Y	Y
3 DeLauro	N	Y	Y	Y	N	Y
4 *Shays*	Y	Y	Y	N	Y	+
5 Maloney	Y	Y	Y	Y	Y	Y
6 *Johnson*	N	Y	Y	N	Y	?
DELAWARE						
AL *Castle*	Y	Y	Y	N	Y	Y
FLORIDA						
1 *Miller, J.*	Y	Y	Y	N	Y	Y
2 Boyd	N	Y	Y	Y	N	Y
3 Brown	N	Y	Y	Y	N	?
4 *Crenshaw*	Y	Y	Y	N	Y	Y
5 Thurman	N	Y	Y	Y	N	Y
6 *Stearns*	Y	Y	Y	N	Y	Y
7 *Mica*	Y	Y	Y	N	Y	Y
8 *Keller*	Y	Y	Y	N	Y	Y
9 *Bilirakis*	Y	Y	Y	N	Y	Y
10 *Young*	Y	Y	Y	N	Y	Y
11 Davis	N	Y	Y	N	Y	Y
12 *Putnam*	Y	Y	Y	N	Y	+
13 *Miller, D.*	Y	Y	Y	N	Y	Y
14 *Goss*	Y	Y	Y	N	Y	Y
15 *Weldon*	Y	Y	Y	N	Y	Y
16 *Foley*	Y	Y	Y	N	Y	Y
17 Meek	N	Y	Y	Y	N	Y
18 *Ros-Lehtinen*	Y	Y	Y	N	Y	Y
19 Wexler	?	Y	Y	Y	N	?
20 Deutsch	N	+	+	+	+	Y
21 *Diaz-Balart*	Y	Y	Y	N	Y	Y
22 *Shaw*	N	Y	Y	N	Y	Y
23 Hastings	N	Y	N	Y	N	N
GEORGIA						
1 *Kingston*	Y	Y	Y	N	Y	?
2 Bishop	Y	Y	Y	N	Y	?
3 *Collins*	Y	Y	Y	N	Y	?
4 McKinney	N	Y	Y	Y	N	Y
5 Lewis	N	Y	N	Y	N	Y
6 *Isakson*	Y	Y	Y	N	Y	Y
7 *Barr*	Y	Y	Y	N	Y	Y
8 *Chambliss*	+	Y	Y	N	Y	Y
9 *Deal*	Y	Y	Y	N	Y	Y
10 *Norwood*	Y	Y	Y	N	Y	Y
11 *Linder*	Y	Y	Y	N	Y	Y
HAWAII						
1 Abercrombie	N	N	Y	Y	Y	Y
2 Mink	N	Y	Y	Y	Y	Y
IDAHO						
1 *Otter*	Y	Y	Y	N	Y	Y
2 *Simpson*	Y	Y	Y	N	Y	Y
ILLINOIS						
1 Rush	N	Y	Y	Y	N	?
2 Jackson	N	N	Y	N	Y	Y
3 Lipinski	N	Y	Y	Y	Y	Y
4 Gutierrez	N	Y	Y	Y	N	+
5 Blagojevich	?	?	?	?	?	?
6 *Hyde*	N	Y	Y	N	Y	Y
7 Davis	N	Y	Y	Y	N	Y
8 *Crane*	Y	?	N	N	Y	N
9 Schakowsky	N	N	N	Y	N	Y
10 *Kirk*	Y	Y	Y	N	Y	Y
11 *Weller*	Y	Y	N	N	Y	Y
12 Costello	N	Y	Y	Y	Y	Y
13 *Biggert*	Y	Y	Y	N	Y	Y

ND Northern Democrats   SD Southern Democrats

	225	226	227	228	229	230
14 ***Hastert***						
15 ***Johnson***	Y	Y	Y	N	Y	Y
16 ***Manzullo***	Y	Y	N	N	Y	Y
17 Evans	N	Y	Y	Y	N	Y
18 ***LaHood***	Y	Y	Y	N	Y	Y
19 Phelps	Y	Y	Y	Y	Y	?
20 ***Shimkus***	Y	Y	Y	N	Y	Y
INDIANA						
1 Visclosky	N	Y	N	Y	N	N
2 ***Pence***	Y	Y	Y	?	?	Y
3 Roemer	Y	Y	Y	Y	Y	Y
4 ***Souder***	Y	Y	Y	N	Y	Y
5 ***Buyer***	Y	Y	Y	N	Y	Y
6 ***Burton***	?	+	+	–	+	Y
7 ***Kerns***	Y	Y	Y	N	Y	Y
8 ***Hostettler***	N	Y	Y	N	Y	Y
9 Hill	N	Y	Y	Y	N	Y
10 Carson	N	Y	Y	Y	N	Y
IOWA						
1 ***Leach***	Y	Y	Y	N	Y	Y
2 ***Nussle***	Y	+	Y	N	Y	Y
3 Boswell	Y	Y	Y	Y	Y	Y
4 ***Ganske***	Y	Y	Y	N	Y	Y
5 ***Latham***	Y	Y	N	N	Y	N
KANSAS						
1 ***Moran***	Y	Y	N	N	Y	N
2 ***Ryun***	Y	Y	Y	N	Y	?
3 Moore	N	Y	Y	Y	Y	Y
4 ***Tiahrt***	Y	Y	Y	N	Y	Y
KENTUCKY						
1 ***Whitfield***	Y	Y	Y	N	Y	Y
2 ***Lewis***	Y	Y	Y	N	Y	Y
3 ***Northup***	Y	Y	Y	N	Y	Y
4 Lucas	Y	Y	Y	Y	Y	Y
5 ***Rogers***	Y	Y	Y	N	Y	Y
6 ***Fletcher***	Y	Y	N	N	Y	N
LOUISIANA						
1 ***Vitter***	Y	Y	Y	N	Y	?
2 Jefferson	N	Y	Y	Y	Y	Y
3 ***Tauzin***	Y	Y	Y	N	Y	Y
4 ***McCrery***	Y	Y	Y	N	Y	Y
5 ***Cooksey***	Y	Y	Y	N	Y	?
6 ***Baker***	Y	Y	Y	N	Y	?
7 John	N	Y	Y	Y	Y	Y
MAINE						
1 Allen	N	Y	Y	Y	N	Y
2 Baldacci	N	Y	Y	Y	N	Y
MARYLAND						
1 ***Gilchrest***	Y	Y	Y	N	Y	Y
2 ***Ehrlich***	Y	?	Y	N	Y	Y
3 Cardin	?	N	Y	Y	N	Y
4 Wynn	N	Y	Y	Y	Y	Y
5 Hoyer	N	Y	Y	Y	N	Y
6 ***Bartlett***	Y	Y	Y	N	Y	Y
7 Cummings	N	N	Y	Y	N	Y
8 ***Morella***	N	Y	Y	N	Y	Y
MASSACHUSETTS						
1 Olver	N	Y	N	Y	N	N
2 Neal	N	Y	Y	Y	N	?
3 McGovern	N	Y	N	Y	N	Y
4 Frank	N	Y	Y	Y	N	Y
5 Meehan	N	Y	Y	Y	N	Y
6 Tierney	N	N	Y	Y	N	Y
7 Markey	N	Y	N	Y	N	Y
8 Capuano	N	Y	N	Y	N	N
9 Lynch	?	Y	Y	Y	N	?
10 Delahunt	N	Y	Y	Y	N	Y
MICHIGAN						
1 Stupak	N	Y	N	Y	N	N
2 ***Hoekstra***	Y	Y	Y	N	Y	Y
3 ***Ehlers***	Y	Y	Y	N	Y	Y
4 ***Camp***	Y	Y	Y	N	Y	Y
5 Barcia	Y	Y	Y	N	Y	Y
6 ***Upton***	Y	Y	Y	N	Y	Y
7 ***Smith***	Y	Y	Y	N	Y	Y
8 ***Rogers***	Y	Y	Y	N	Y	Y
9 Kildee	N	Y	Y	Y	N	Y
10 Bonior	N	Y	Y	Y	Y	+
11 ***Knollenberg***	Y	Y	Y	N	Y	Y
12 Levin	N	Y	Y	Y	N	Y
13 Rivers	N	Y	Y	Y	N	Y
14 Conyers	N	N	Y	Y	N	?
15 Kilpatrick	N	Y	Y	Y	N	+
16 Dingell	N	Y	Y	Y	N	Y

	225	226	227	228	229	230
MINNESOTA						
1 ***Gutknecht***	Y	Y	N	N	Y	N
2 ***Kennedy***	Y	Y	N	N	Y	N
3 ***Ramstad***	Y	Y	N	N	Y	N
4 McCollum	Y	Y	Y	Y	N	Y
5 Sabo	N	N	N	Y	N	N
6 Luther	N	Y	Y	Y	Y	Y
7 Peterson	?	?	?	?	?	N
8 Oberstar	N	Y	N	Y	N	N
MISSISSIPPI						
1 ***Wicker***	Y	Y	N	N	Y	Y
2 Thompson	N	Y	N	Y	N	N
3 ***Pickering***	Y	Y	Y	N	Y	Y
4 Shows	Y	Y	Y	Y	Y	Y
5 Taylor	Y	Y	N	Y	N	N
MISSOURI						
1 Clay	N	Y	Y	Y	N	Y
2 ***Akin***	Y	Y	Y	N	Y	Y
3 Gephardt	N	Y	Y	Y	N	?
4 Skelton	N	Y	Y	Y	Y	Y
5 McCarthy	N	Y	Y	Y	?	Y
6 ***Graves***	Y	Y	Y	N	Y	Y
7 ***Blunt***	Y	Y	Y	N	Y	Y
8 ***Emerson***	Y	Y	Y	N	Y	Y
9 ***Hulshof***	Y	Y	N	N	Y	N
MONTANA						
AL ***Rehberg***	Y	Y	Y	N	Y	Y
NEBRASKA						
1 ***Bereuter***	N	Y	Y	N	Y	Y
2 ***Terry***	Y	Y	Y	N	Y	Y
3 ***Osborne***	Y	Y	Y	N	Y	Y
NEVADA						
1 Berkley	Y	Y	Y	Y	Y	Y
2 ***Gibbons***	Y	Y	Y	N	Y	Y
NEW HAMPSHIRE						
1 ***Sununu***	Y	Y	Y	N	Y	Y
2 ***Bass***	Y	Y	Y	N	Y	Y
NEW JERSEY						
1 Andrews	Y	Y	Y	Y	N	Y
2 ***LoBiondo***	Y	Y	N	N	Y	N
3 ***Saxton***	Y	Y	Y	N	Y	Y
4 ***Smith***	Y	Y	Y	N	Y	Y
5 ***Roukema***	N	Y	Y	N	Y	?
6 Pallone	Y	Y	N	Y	N	Y
7 ***Ferguson***	Y	Y	Y	N	Y	?
8 Pascrell	N	Y	Y	Y	N	Y
9 Rothman	N	Y	Y	Y	N	?
10 Payne	?	Y	N	Y	N	?
11 ***Frelinghuysen***	Y	Y	Y	N	Y	Y
12 Holt	N	Y	Y	Y	Y	Y
13 Menendez	–	Y	N	Y	N	N
NEW MEXICO						
1 ***Wilson***	Y	Y	Y	Y	Y	?
2 ***Skeen***	Y	Y	Y	N	Y	Y
3 Udall	N	Y	N	Y	N	N
NEW YORK						
1 ***Grucci***	Y	Y	Y	N	Y	Y
2 Israel	N	Y	Y	Y	Y	+
3 ***King***	Y	Y	Y	N	Y	?
4 McCarthy	Y	Y	Y	Y	Y	Y
5 Ackerman	N	Y	Y	Y	N	Y
6 Meeks	N	Y	Y	Y	Y	Y
7 Crowley	N	Y	Y	Y	N	+
8 Nadler	N	N	Y	Y	N	?
9 Weiner	N	Y	Y	Y	N	Y
10 Towns	N	?	?	Y	Y	?
11 Owens	?	?	?	?	?	Y
12 Velázquez	N	Y	Y	Y	N	?
13 ***Fossella***	Y	Y	Y	N	Y	Y
14 Maloney	–	Y	Y	Y	N	Y
15 Rangel	N	Y	Y	Y	N	?
16 Serrano	N	Y	Y	Y	N	?
17 Engel	N	Y	Y	Y	Y	Y
18 Lowey	N	Y	Y	Y	?	Y
19 ***Kelly***	Y	Y	Y	N	Y	Y
20 ***Gilman***	Y	Y	Y	N	Y	+
21 McNulty	N	Y	N	Y	N	N
22 ***Sweeney***	Y	Y	N	N	Y	Y
23 ***Boehlert***	N	Y	Y	N	Y	?
24 ***McHugh***	Y	Y	Y	N	Y	Y
25 ***Walsh***	Y	Y	Y	N	Y	Y
26 Hinchey	N	N	N	Y	N	?
27 ***Reynolds***	Y	Y	Y	N	Y	Y
28 Slaughter	N	Y	Y	Y	N	Y
29 LaFalce	N	Y	Y	Y	N	?

	225	226	227	228	229	230
30 ***Quinn***	?	?	?	?	?	?
31 ***Houghton***	?	?	?	?	?	Y
NORTH CAROLINA						
1 Clayton	?	?	?	?	?	Y
2 Etheridge	Y	Y	Y	Y	Y	Y
3 ***Jones***	Y	Y	Y	N	Y	Y
4 Price	N	?	?	Y	N	Y
5 ***Burr***	Y	Y	Y	N	Y	Y
6 ***Coble***	Y	Y	Y	N	Y	Y
7 McIntyre	Y	Y	Y	Y	Y	Y
8 ***Hayes***	Y	Y	Y	N	Y	Y
9 ***Myrick***	Y	Y	Y	N	Y	Y
10 ***Ballenger***	Y	Y	Y	N	Y	Y
11 ***Taylor***	Y	Y	Y	N	Y	?
12 Watt	N	N	Y	Y	N	Y
NORTH DAKOTA						
AL Pomeroy	N	Y	Y	Y	Y	Y
OHIO						
1 ***Chabot***	Y	Y	Y	N	Y	Y
2 ***Portman***	Y	Y	Y	N	Y	+
3 Hall	?	?	?	?	?	Y
4 ***Oxley***	Y	Y	Y	N	Y	Y
5 ***Gillmor***	N	Y	Y	N	Y	N
6 Strickland	N	Y	N	Y	N	N
7 ***Hobson***	Y	Y	Y	N	Y	Y
8 ***Boehner***	Y	Y	Y	N	Y	Y
9 Kaptur	N	Y	?	?	N	?
10 Kucinich	N	N	N	Y	N	N
11 Jones	?	–	+	+	–	?
12 ***Tiberi***	Y	Y	Y	N	Y	Y
13 Brown	N	Y	N	Y	N	Y
14 Sawyer	N	Y	Y	Y	N	Y
15 ***Pryce***	Y	Y	Y	N	Y	?
16 ***Regula***	Y	Y	Y	N	Y	Y
17 Traficant	?	?	?	?	?	?
18 ***Ney***	Y	Y	Y	N	Y	Y
19 ***LaTourette***	Y	Y	Y	N	Y	Y
OKLAHOMA						
1 ***Sullivan***	Y	Y	Y	N	Y	Y
2 Carson	N	Y	Y	Y	Y	?
3 ***Watkins***	Y	Y	Y	N	Y	?
4 ***Watts***	Y	Y	Y	N	Y	Y
5 ***Istook***	Y	Y	Y	N	Y	Y
6 ***Lucas***	Y	Y	Y	N	Y	Y
OREGON						
1 Wu	N	Y	N	Y	Y	N
2 ***Walden***	Y	Y	Y	N	Y	Y
3 Blumenauer	N	Y	Y	Y	N	Y
4 DeFazio	N	N	N	Y	Y	N
5 Hooley	N	Y	Y	Y	Y	Y
PENNSYLVANIA						
1 Brady	N	Y	N	Y	N	?
2 Fattah	N	Y	Y	Y	N	?
3 Borski	N	Y	N	Y	N	?
4 ***Hart***	Y	Y	N	N	Y	Y
5 ***Peterson***	+	Y	Y	N	Y	Y
6 Holden	N	Y	Y	Y	Y	Y
7 ***Weldon***	Y	Y	Y	N	Y	Y
8 ***Greenwood***	Y	Y	Y	N	Y	Y
9 ***Shuster, Bill***	Y	Y	Y	N	Y	Y
10 ***Sherwood***	Y	Y	Y	N	Y	Y
11 Kanjorski	N	Y	Y	N	N	Y
12 Murtha	N	Y	Y	N	N	Y
13 Hoeffel	N	Y	Y	Y	N	Y
14 Coyne	N	Y	Y	Y	N	Y
15 ***Toomey***	Y	Y	Y	N	Y	Y
16 ***Pitts***	Y	Y	?	N	Y	Y
17 ***Gekas***	Y	Y	Y	N	Y	Y
18 Doyle	N	Y	Y	Y	N	Y
19 ***Platts***	Y	Y	Y	N	Y	Y
20 Mascara	N	Y	Y	Y	Y	Y
21 ***English***	Y	?	?	N	?	N
RHODE ISLAND						
1 Kennedy	N	+	+	Y	N	Y
2 Langevin	N	Y	Y	Y	N	Y
SOUTH CAROLINA						
1 ***Brown***	Y	Y	Y	N	Y	Y
2 ***Wilson***	Y	Y	Y	N	Y	Y
3 ***Graham***	Y	Y	Y	N	Y	Y
4 ***DeMint***	Y	Y	Y	N	Y	Y
5 Spratt	N	Y	Y	Y	N	Y
6 Clyburn	N	Y	Y	Y	N	Y
SOUTH DAKOTA						
AL ***Thune***	Y	Y	Y	N	Y	Y

	225	226	227	228	229	230
TENNESSEE						
1 ***Jenkins***	Y	Y	Y	N	Y	+
2 ***Duncan***	Y	Y	Y	N	Y	Y
3 ***Wamp***	Y	Y	Y	N	Y	Y
4 ***Hilleary***	Y	?	?	?	?	?
5 Clement	N	Y	Y	Y	Y	?
6 Gordon	Y	Y	Y	Y	Y	Y
7 ***Bryant***	Y	Y	Y	N	Y	Y
8 Tanner	N	Y	N	Y	N	Y
9 Ford	–	Y	?	Y	Y	?
TEXAS						
1 Sandlin	Y	Y	Y	Y	Y	?
2 Turner	N	Y	Y	Y	N	Y
3 ***Johnson, Sam***	Y	Y	Y	N	Y	Y
4 Hall	Y	Y	Y	Y	Y	Y
5 ***Sessions***	Y	Y	Y	N	Y	?
6 ***Barton***	Y	Y	Y	N	Y	?
7 ***Culberson***	Y	Y	Y	N	Y	Y
8 ***Brady***	Y	Y	Y	N	Y	Y
9 Lampson	N	Y	Y	Y	N	Y
10 Doggett	N	Y	Y	N	N	Y
11 Edwards	N	Y	Y	Y	Y	Y
12 ***Granger***	Y	Y	Y	N	Y	Y
13 ***Thornberry***	Y	Y	Y	N	Y	Y
14 ***Paul***	Y	Y	Y	N	Y	Y
15 Hinojosa	N	Y	Y	Y	Y	Y
16 Reyes	?	Y	Y	Y	Y	Y
17 Stenholm	N	Y	?	Y	N	?
18 Jackson-Lee	N	Y	Y	Y	N	Y
19 ***Combest***	?	?	?	?	?	Y
20 Gonzalez	N	Y	Y	Y	N	Y
21 ***Smith***	?	?	?	?	?	Y
22 ***DeLay***	?	Y	?	N	Y	Y
23 ***Bonilla***	Y	Y	Y	?	Y	Y
24 Frost	N	Y	Y	Y	N	Y
25 Bentsen	N	Y	Y	Y	N	Y
26 ***Armey***	Y	Y	?	N	Y	Y
27 Ortiz	N	Y	Y	Y	N	Y
28 Rodriguez	N	Y	Y	Y	N	Y
29 Green	N	Y	N	Y	N	Y
30 Johnson, E.B.	N	?	?	Y	N	N
UTAH						
1 ***Hansen***	Y	Y	Y	N	Y	Y
2 Matheson	N	Y	Y	Y	Y	Y
3 ***Cannon***	Y	Y	Y	N	Y	?
VERMONT						
AL *Sanders*	N	N	Y	Y	N	?
VIRGINIA						
1 ***Davis, Jo Ann***	Y	Y	Y	N	Y	Y
2 ***Schrock***	Y	Y	Y	N	Y	Y
3 Scott	N	Y	N	Y	N	Y
4 ***Forbes***	Y	+	+	–	+	Y
5 *Goode*	Y	Y	Y	N	Y	Y
6 ***Goodlatte***	Y	Y	Y	N	Y	Y
7 ***Cantor***	Y	Y	Y	N	Y	Y
8 Moran	N	Y	Y	Y	Y	Y
9 Boucher	N	Y	Y	Y	Y	?
10 ***Wolf***	Y	Y	Y	N	Y	Y
11 ***Davis, T.***	Y	Y	Y	N	Y	Y
WASHINGTON						
1 Inslee	N	Y	Y	Y	N	Y
2 Larsen	N	Y	N	Y	N	N
3 Baird	N	Y	N	Y	Y	Y
4 ***Hastings***	Y	Y	Y	N	Y	Y
5 ***Nethercutt***	Y	Y	Y	N	Y	Y
6 Dicks	?	Y	Y	Y	N	Y
7 McDermott	N	?	?	Y	N	N
8 ***Dunn***	Y	Y	Y	N	Y	Y
9 Smith	N	Y	Y	Y	N	Y
WEST VIRGINIA						
1 Mollohan	N	Y	Y	N	N	Y
2 ***Capito***	Y	Y	Y	N	Y	Y
3 Rahall	N	Y	Y	Y	N	Y
WISCONSIN						
1 ***Ryan***	Y	Y	Y	N	Y	Y
2 Baldwin	N	Y	N	Y	N	N
3 Kind	N	Y	Y	Y	N	Y
4 Kleczka	N	N	Y	Y	N	Y
5 Barrett	N	Y	Y	Y	Y	Y
6 ***Petri***	Y	Y	Y	N	Y	Y
7 Obey	N	Y	Y	Y	N	Y
8 ***Green***	Y	Y	?	N	Y	Y
9 ***Sensenbrenner***	Y	Y	Y	N	Y	Y
WYOMING						
AL ***Cubin***	Y	Y	Y	N	Y	Y

Southern states - Ala., Ark., Fla., Ga., Ky., La., Miss., N.C., Okla., S.C., Tenn., Texas, Va.

Key

Y	Voted for (yea).
#	Paired for.
+	Announced for.
N	Voted against (nay).
X	Paired against.
–	Announced against.
P	Voted "present."
C	Voted "present" to avoid possible conflict of interest.
?	Did not vote or otherwise make a position known.

Democrats • **Republicans**
Independents

231. H Con Res 415. Importance of Homeownership/Adoption. Miller, R-Calif., motion to suspend the rules and adopt the concurrent resolution that would recognize June as National Homeownership Month. Motion agreed to 358-0: R 186-0; D 171-0 (ND 125-0, SD 46-0); I 1-0. A two-thirds majority of those present and voting (239 in this case) is required for adoption under suspension of the rules. June 17, 2002.

232. H Con Res 340. Awareness of Meningitis/Adoption. Mica, R-Fla., motion to suspend the rules and adopt the concurrent resolution that would express the support of Congress for Meningitis Awareness Month. Motion agreed to 360-0: R 189-0; D 170-0 (ND 124-0, SD 46-0); I 1-0. A two-thirds majority of those present and voting (240 in this case) is required for adoption under suspension of the rules. June 17, 2002.

233. HR 327. Small Business Paperwork Reduction/Concur With Senate Amendments. Ose, R-Calif., motion to concur with Senate amendments to the bill that would require federal agencies to further reduce paperwork requirements for businesses with fewer than 25 employees. It would order the Office of Management and Budget to publish reporting and other paperwork regulations in the Federal Register and on its Web site, require the appointment of single-point-of-contact liaisons within agencies, and establish an interagency task force to study other means of streamlining requirements for small businesses. Motion agreed to 418-0: R 216-0; D 201-0 (ND 150-0, SD 51-0); I 1-0. June 18, 2002.

234. HR 4794. Ronald Packard Tribute/Passage. Ose, R-Calif., motion to suspend the rules and pass the bill that would name an Oceanside, Calif., post office building after former Rep. Ronald C. Packard, R-Calif. (1983-2001). Motion agreed to 418-0: R 216-0; D 201-0 (ND 150-0, SD 51-0); I 1-0. A two-thirds majority of those present and voting (279 in this case) is required for passage under suspension of the rules. June 18, 2002.

235. HR 4717. Jim Fonteno Tribute/Passage. Ose, R-Calif., motion to suspend the rules and pass the bill that would name a Pasadena, Texas, post office building after Jim Fonteno, a county commissioner and former municipal court judge. Motion agreed to 415-0: R 214-0; D 200-0 (ND 150-0, SD 50-0); I 1-0. A two-thirds majority of those present and voting (277 in this case) is required for passage under suspension of the rules. June 18, 2002.

236. Procedural Motion/Journal. Approval of the House Journal of Tuesday, June 18, 2002. Approved 353-42: R 188-11; D 164-31 (ND 118-28, SD 46-3); I 1-0. June 19, 2002.

237. HR 3389. Marine Grants/Passage. Passage of the bill that would reauthorize the National Sea Grant College Program through fiscal 2008. It would authorize $60 million for the marine conservation and resource management programs in fiscal 2003 and gradually increase the funding to a high of $85 million in fiscal 2008. The bill also would authorize $15 million annually for research on zebra mussels, algae blooms and oysters. Passed 407-2: R 205-2; D 201-0 (ND 150-0, SD 51-0); I 1-0. June 19, 2002.

	231	232	233	234	235	236	237
ALABAMA							
1 *Callahan*	?	?	Y	Y	Y	Y	Y
2 *Everett*	Y	Y	Y	Y	Y	Y	Y
3 *Riley*	+	+	?	?	?	Y	Y
4 *Aderholt*	Y	Y	Y	Y	Y	N	Y
5 Cramer	Y	Y	Y	Y	Y	Y	Y
6 *Bachus*	?	?	?	?	?	?	Y
7 Hilliard	?	?	?	?	?	?	?
ALASKA							
AL *Young*	Y	Y	Y	Y	Y	?	Y
ARIZONA							
1 *Flake*	Y	Y	Y	Y	Y	Y	N
2 Pastor	Y	Y	Y	Y	Y	Y	Y
3 *Stump*	Y	Y	Y	Y	Y	Y	Y
4 *Shadegg*	?	?	Y	Y	Y	Y	Y
5 *Kolbe*	Y	Y	Y	Y	Y	Y	Y
6 *Hayworth*	Y	Y	Y	Y	Y	Y	Y
ARKANSAS							
1 Berry	Y	Y	Y	Y	Y	Y	Y
2 Snyder	Y	Y	Y	Y	Y	Y	Y
3 *Boozman*	Y	Y	Y	Y	Y	Y	Y
4 Ross	Y	Y	Y	Y	Y	Y	Y
CALIFORNIA							
1 Thompson	Y	Y	Y	Y	Y	N	Y
2 *Herger*	?	?	Y	Y	Y	?	Y
3 *Ose*	Y	Y	Y	Y	Y	Y	Y
4 *Doolittle*	Y	Y	Y	Y	Y	Y	Y
5 Matsui	?	?	Y	Y	Y	Y	Y
6 Woolsey	Y	Y	Y	Y	Y	Y	Y
7 Miller, George	Y	Y	Y	Y	Y	Y	Y
8 Pelosi	Y	Y	Y	Y	Y	Y	Y
9 Lee	Y	Y	Y	Y	Y	Y	Y
10 Tauscher	Y	Y	Y	Y	Y	Y	Y
11 *Pombo*	Y	Y	Y	Y	Y	Y	Y
12 Lantos	?	?	Y	Y	Y	Y	Y
13 Stark	Y	Y	Y	Y	Y	?	Y
14 Eshoo	Y	Y	Y	Y	Y	Y	Y
15 Honda	+	+	Y	Y	Y	Y	Y
16 Lofgren	Y	Y	Y	Y	Y	Y	Y
17 Farr	Y	Y	Y	Y	Y	Y	Y
18 Condit	Y	Y	Y	Y	Y	Y	Y
19 *Radanovich*	Y	Y	Y	Y	Y	Y	Y
20 Dooley	?	?	Y	Y	Y	Y	Y
21 *Thomas*	Y	Y	Y	Y	Y	Y	Y
22 Capps	Y	Y	Y	Y	Y	Y	Y
23 *Gallegly*	?	?	Y	Y	Y	Y	Y
24 Sherman	Y	Y	Y	Y	Y	Y	Y
25 *McKeon*	?	?	Y	Y	Y	Y	Y
26 Berman	?	?	Y	Y	Y	Y	Y
27 Schiff	Y	Y	Y	Y	Y	Y	Y
28 *Dreier*	Y	Y	Y	Y	Y	Y	Y
29 Waxman	Y	Y	Y	Y	Y	Y	Y
30 Becerra	+	+	Y	Y	Y	Y	Y
31 Solis	Y	Y	Y	Y	Y	Y	Y
32 Watson	Y	Y	Y	Y	Y	Y	Y
33 Roybal-Allard	Y	Y	Y	Y	Y	Y	Y
34 Napolitano	Y	Y	Y	Y	Y	Y	+
35 Waters	Y	Y	?	?	?	N	Y
36 Harman	Y	Y	Y	Y	Y	Y	Y
37 Millender-McD.	?	?	?	?	?	Y	Y
38 *Horn*	Y	?	Y	Y	Y	Y	Y

	231	232	233	234	235	236	237
39 *Royce*	Y	Y	Y	Y	Y	Y	Y
40 *Lewis*	Y	Y	Y	Y	Y	Y	Y
41 *Miller, Gary*	Y	Y	Y	Y	Y	Y	Y
42 Baca	Y	Y	Y	Y	Y	Y	Y
43 *Calvert*	Y	Y	Y	Y	Y	Y	Y
44 *Bono*	Y	Y	Y	Y	Y	Y	Y
45 *Rohrabacher*	Y	Y	Y	Y	Y	Y	Y
46 Sanchez	Y	Y	Y	Y	Y	N	Y
47 *Cox*	Y	Y	Y	Y	Y	Y	Y
48 *Issa*	Y	Y	Y	Y	Y	Y	Y
49 Davis	Y	Y	Y	Y	Y	Y	Y
50 Filner	Y	Y	Y	Y	Y	Y	Y
51 *Cunningham*	Y	Y	Y	Y	Y	Y	Y
52 *Hunter*	Y	Y	Y	Y	Y	Y	Y
COLORADO							
1 DeGette	Y	Y	Y	Y	Y	Y	Y
2 Udall	Y	Y	Y	Y	Y	Y	Y
3 *McInnis*	?	?	Y	Y	Y	Y	Y
4 *Schaffer*	Y	Y	Y	Y	Y	N	Y
5 *Hefley*	Y	Y	Y	Y	Y	N	Y
6 *Tancredo*	Y	Y	Y	Y	Y	P	Y
CONNECTICUT							
1 Larson	Y	Y	Y	Y	Y	Y	Y
2 *Simmons*	Y	Y	Y	Y	Y	Y	Y
3 DeLauro	?	?	Y	Y	Y	Y	Y
4 *Shays*	?	?	?	?	?	?	?
5 Maloney	Y	Y	Y	Y	Y	Y	Y
6 *Johnson*	?	Y	Y	Y	Y	Y	Y
DELAWARE							
AL *Castle*	Y	Y	Y	Y	Y	Y	Y
FLORIDA							
1 *Miller, J.*	Y	Y	Y	Y	Y	Y	Y
2 Boyd	Y	Y	Y	Y	Y	Y	Y
3 Brown	?	?	Y	Y	Y	Y	Y
4 *Crenshaw*	Y	Y	Y	Y	Y	Y	Y
5 Thurman	Y	Y	Y	Y	Y	Y	Y
6 *Stearns*	Y	Y	Y	Y	Y	Y	Y
7 *Mica*	Y	Y	Y	Y	Y	Y	Y
8 *Keller*	Y	Y	Y	Y	Y	Y	Y
9 *Bilirakis*	Y	Y	Y	Y	Y	Y	Y
10 *Young*	Y	Y	Y	Y	Y	Y	Y
11 Davis	Y	Y	Y	Y	Y	Y	Y
12 *Putnam*	?	?	?	?	?	?	?
13 *Miller, D.*	?	?	?	?	?	?	?
14 *Goss*	Y	Y	Y	Y	Y	Y	Y
15 *Weldon*	Y	Y	Y	Y	Y	Y	Y
16 *Foley*	Y	Y	Y	Y	Y	?	Y
17 Meek	Y	Y	Y	Y	Y	?	Y
18 *Ros-Lehtinen*	Y	Y	Y	Y	Y	Y	Y
19 Wexler	?	?	Y	Y	Y	Y	Y
20 Deutsch	Y	Y	Y	Y	Y	Y	Y
21 *Diaz-Balart*	Y	Y	Y	Y	Y	Y	Y
22 *Shaw*	Y	Y	Y	Y	Y	Y	Y
23 Hastings	Y	Y	Y	Y	Y	Y	Y
GEORGIA							
1 *Kingston*	?	?	Y	Y	Y	Y	Y
2 Bishop	Y	Y	Y	Y	Y	?	?
3 *Collins*	?	?	Y	Y	Y	?	?
4 McKinney	Y	Y	Y	Y	Y	?	?
5 Lewis	Y	Y	Y	Y	Y	?	?
6 *Isakson*	Y	Y	Y	Y	Y	?	?
7 *Barr*	Y	Y	Y	Y	Y	?	Y
8 *Chambliss*	Y	Y	Y	Y	Y	Y	Y
9 *Deal*	Y	Y	Y	Y	Y	?	Y
10 *Norwood*	Y	Y	Y	Y	Y	?	?
11 *Linder*	Y	Y	Y	Y	Y	?	?
HAWAII							
1 Abercrombie	Y	Y	Y	Y	Y	Y	Y
2 Mink	Y	Y	Y	Y	Y	Y	Y
IDAHO							
1 *Otter*	Y	Y	Y	Y	Y	Y	Y
2 *Simpson*	Y	Y	Y	Y	Y	Y	Y
ILLINOIS							
1 Rush	?	?	Y	Y	Y	Y	Y
2 Jackson	Y	Y	Y	Y	Y	Y	Y
3 Lipinski	?	?	Y	Y	Y	Y	Y
4 Gutierrez	+	+	Y	Y	Y	Y	?
5 Blagojevich	?	?	?	?	?	?	?
6 *Hyde*	Y	Y	Y	Y	Y	?	Y
7 Davis	Y	Y	Y	Y	Y	Y	Y
8 *Crane*	Y	Y	Y	Y	Y	N	Y
9 Schakowsky	Y	Y	Y	Y	Y	Y	+
10 *Kirk*	Y	Y	Y	Y	Y	Y	Y
11 *Weller*	Y	Y	Y	Y	Y	N	Y
12 Costello	Y	Y	Y	Y	Y	N	Y
13 *Biggert*	Y	Y	Y	Y	Y	Y	Y

ND *Northern Democrats*   SD *Southern Democrats*

	231	232	233	234	235	236	237
14 ***Hastert***							
15 ***Johnson***	Y	Y	Y	Y	Y	Y	Y
16 ***Manzullo***	Y	Y	Y	Y	Y	Y	Y
17 Evans	Y	Y	Y	Y	Y	Y	Y
18 ***LaHood***	Y	Y	Y	Y	Y	Y	Y
19 Phelps	?	?	Y	Y	Y	Y	Y
20 ***Shimkus***	Y	Y	Y	Y	Y	Y	Y
INDIANA							
1 Visclosky	Y	Y	Y	Y	Y	N	Y
2 ***Pence***	Y	Y	Y	Y	Y	Y	Y
3 Roemer	Y	Y	Y	Y	Y	Y	Y
4 ***Souder***	Y	Y	Y	Y	Y	Y	Y
5 ***Buyer***	Y	Y	Y	Y	Y	Y	Y
6 ***Burton***	Y	Y	Y	Y	Y	Y	Y
7 ***Kerns***	Y	Y	Y	Y	Y	Y	Y
8 ***Hostettler***	Y	Y	Y	Y	Y	Y	Y
9 Hill	Y	Y	Y	Y	Y	Y	Y
10 Carson	Y	Y	Y	Y	Y	Y	Y
IOWA							
1 ***Leach***	Y	Y	Y	Y	Y	?	Y
2 ***Nussle***	Y	Y	Y	Y	Y	Y	Y
3 Boswell	Y	?	Y	Y	Y	Y	Y
4 ***Ganske***	Y	Y	Y	Y	Y	Y	Y
5 ***Latham***	Y	Y	Y	Y	Y	Y	Y
KANSAS							
1 ***Moran***	Y	Y	Y	Y	Y	Y	Y
2 ***Ryun***	?	?	Y	Y	Y	Y	Y
3 Moore	Y	Y	Y	Y	Y	N	Y
4 ***Tiahrt***	Y	Y	Y	Y	Y	Y	Y
KENTUCKY							
1 ***Whitfield***	Y	Y	Y	Y	Y	Y	Y
2 ***Lewis***	Y	Y	Y	Y	Y	Y	Y
3 ***Northup***	Y	Y	Y	Y	Y	Y	Y
4 Lucas	Y	Y	Y	Y	Y	Y	Y
5 ***Rogers***	Y	Y	Y	Y	Y	Y	Y
6 ***Fletcher***	Y	Y	Y	Y	Y	Y	Y
LOUISIANA							
1 ***Vitter***	?	?	Y	Y	Y	Y	Y
2 Jefferson	Y	Y	Y	Y	Y	Y	Y
3 ***Tauzin***	Y	Y	Y	Y	Y	Y	Y
4 ***McCrery***	Y	Y	Y	Y	Y	Y	Y
5 ***Cooksey***	?	?	Y	Y	?	Y	?
6 ***Baker***	?	?	Y	Y	Y	Y	?
7 John	Y	Y	Y	Y	Y	Y	Y
MAINE							
1 Allen	Y	Y	Y	Y	Y	Y	Y
2 Baldacci	Y	Y	Y	Y	Y	Y	Y
MARYLAND							
1 ***Gilchrest***	Y	Y	Y	Y	Y	Y	Y
2 ***Ehrlich***	Y	Y	Y	Y	Y	?	Y
3 Cardin	Y	Y	Y	Y	Y	Y	Y
4 Wynn	Y	Y	Y	Y	Y	?	Y
5 Hoyer	Y	Y	?	?	?	Y	Y
6 ***Bartlett***	Y	Y	Y	Y	Y	Y	Y
7 Cummings	Y	Y	Y	Y	Y	?	Y
8 ***Morella***	Y	Y	Y	Y	Y	?	Y
MASSACHUSETTS							
1 Olver	Y	Y	Y	Y	Y	N	Y
2 Neal	Y	Y	Y	Y	Y	N	Y
3 McGovern	Y	Y	Y	Y	Y	Y	Y
4 Frank	Y	Y	Y	Y	Y	Y	Y
5 Meehan	Y	Y	Y	Y	Y	Y	Y
6 Tierney	Y	Y	Y	Y	Y	Y	Y
7 Markey	Y	Y	Y	Y	Y	N	Y
8 Capuano	Y	Y	Y	Y	Y	N	Y
9 Lynch	Y	Y	Y	Y	Y	Y	Y
10 Delahunt	Y	Y	Y	Y	Y	?	Y
MICHIGAN							
1 Stupak	Y	Y	Y	Y	Y	N	Y
2 ***Hoekstra***	Y	Y	Y	Y	Y	Y	Y
3 ***Ehlers***	Y	Y	Y	Y	Y	Y	Y
4 ***Camp***	Y	Y	Y	Y	Y	Y	Y
5 Barcia	Y	Y	Y	Y	Y	Y	Y
6 ***Upton***	Y	Y	Y	Y	Y	Y	Y
7 ***Smith***	Y	Y	Y	Y	Y	Y	Y
8 ***Rogers***	Y	Y	Y	Y	Y	Y	Y
9 Kildee	Y	Y	Y	Y	Y	Y	Y
10 Bonior	+	+	Y	Y	Y	Y	Y
11 ***Knollenberg***	Y	Y	Y	Y	Y	Y	Y
12 Levin	Y	Y	Y	Y	Y	Y	Y
13 Rivers	Y	Y	Y	Y	Y	Y	Y
14 Conyers	?	?	?	?	?	?	?
15 Kilpatrick	+	+	Y	Y	Y	Y	Y
16 Dingell	Y	Y	Y	Y	Y	Y	Y
MINNESOTA							
1 ***Gutknecht***	Y	Y	Y	Y	Y	N	Y
2 ***Kennedy***	Y	Y	Y	Y	Y	N	Y
3 ***Ramstad***	Y	Y	Y	Y	Y	N	Y
4 McCollum	Y	Y	Y	Y	Y	Y	Y
5 Sabo	Y	Y	Y	Y	Y	N	Y
6 Luther	Y	Y	Y	Y	Y	Y	Y
7 Peterson	Y	Y	Y	Y	Y	N	Y
8 Oberstar	Y	Y	Y	Y	Y	N	Y
MISSISSIPPI							
1 ***Wicker***	Y	Y	Y	Y	Y	Y	Y
2 Thompson	Y	Y	Y	Y	Y	N	Y
3 ***Pickering***	Y	Y	Y	Y	Y	Y	Y
4 Shows	Y	Y	Y	Y	Y	Y	Y
5 Taylor	Y	Y	Y	Y	Y	N	Y
MISSOURI							
1 Clay	Y	Y	Y	Y	Y	?	Y
2 ***Akin***	Y	Y	Y	Y	Y	Y	Y
3 Gephardt	Y	Y	Y	Y	Y	Y	Y
4 Skelton	Y	Y	Y	Y	Y	Y	Y
5 McCarthy	Y	Y	Y	Y	Y	Y	Y
6 ***Graves***	Y	Y	Y	Y	Y	Y	Y
7 ***Blunt***	Y	Y	Y	Y	Y	Y	?
8 ***Emerson***	Y	Y	Y	Y	Y	Y	Y
9 ***Hulshof***	Y	Y	Y	Y	Y	?	Y
MONTANA							
AL ***Rehberg***	Y	Y	Y	Y	Y	Y	Y
NEBRASKA							
1 ***Bereuter***	Y	Y	Y	Y	Y	Y	Y
2 ***Terry***	Y	Y	Y	Y	Y	Y	Y
3 ***Osborne***	Y	Y	Y	Y	Y	Y	Y
NEVADA							
1 Berkley	Y	Y	Y	Y	Y	Y	Y
2 ***Gibbons***	Y	Y	Y	Y	Y	Y	Y
NEW HAMPSHIRE							
1 ***Sununu***	Y	Y	Y	Y	Y	Y	Y
2 ***Bass***	Y	Y	Y	Y	Y	Y	Y
NEW JERSEY							
1 Andrews	Y	Y	Y	Y	Y	Y	Y
2 ***LoBiondo***	Y	Y	Y	Y	Y	N	Y
3 ***Saxton***	?	Y	Y	Y	Y	Y	Y
4 ***Smith***	Y	Y	Y	Y	Y	?	Y
5 ***Roukema***	?	?	?	?	?	?	?
6 Pallone	Y	Y	Y	Y	Y	Y	Y
7 ***Ferguson***	?	?	Y	Y	Y	Y	Y
8 Pascrell	Y	Y	Y	Y	Y	Y	Y
9 Rothman	?	?	?	?	?	Y	Y
10 Payne	?	?	Y	Y	Y	Y	Y
11 ***Frelinghuysen***	Y	Y	Y	Y	Y	Y	Y
12 Holt	Y	Y	Y	Y	Y	N	Y
13 Menendez	Y	Y	Y	Y	Y	Y	Y
NEW MEXICO							
1 ***Wilson***	?	?	Y	Y	Y	Y	Y
2 ***Skeen***	Y	Y	Y	Y	Y	Y	Y
3 Udall	Y	Y	Y	Y	Y	N	Y
NEW YORK							
1 ***Grucci***	Y	Y	Y	Y	Y	Y	Y
2 Israel	+	+	Y	Y	Y	Y	Y
3 ***King***	?	?	Y	Y	Y	Y	Y
4 McCarthy	Y	Y	Y	Y	Y	Y	Y
5 Ackerman	Y	Y	Y	Y	Y	Y	Y
6 Meeks	Y	Y	Y	Y	Y	Y	Y
7 Crowley	?	?	Y	Y	Y	Y	Y
8 Nadler	?	?	Y	Y	Y	Y	Y
9 Weiner	Y	Y	Y	Y	Y	Y	Y
10 Towns	?	?	Y	Y	Y	?	Y
11 Owens	Y	Y	Y	Y	Y	Y	Y
12 Velázquez	?	?	Y	Y	Y	Y	Y
13 ***Fossella***	Y	Y	Y	Y	Y	?	Y
14 Maloney	Y	Y	Y	Y	Y	Y	Y
15 Rangel	?	?	Y	Y	Y	Y	Y
16 Serrano	?	?	Y	Y	Y	?	Y
17 Engel	Y	Y	Y	Y	Y	Y	Y
18 Lowey	Y	Y	Y	Y	Y	Y	Y
19 ***Kelly***	Y	Y	Y	Y	Y	Y	Y
20 ***Gilman***	+	+	Y	Y	Y	Y	Y
21 McNulty	Y	Y	Y	Y	Y	N	Y
22 ***Sweeney***	Y	Y	Y	Y	Y	?	?
23 ***Boehlert***	?	Y	Y	Y	Y	Y	Y
24 ***McHugh***	Y	Y	Y	Y	Y	?	?
25 ***Walsh***	Y	Y	Y	Y	Y	Y	Y
26 Hinchey	?	?	Y	Y	Y	Y	Y
27 ***Reynolds***	Y	Y	Y	Y	Y	Y	Y
28 Slaughter	Y	Y	Y	Y	Y	Y	Y
29 LaFalce	Y	Y	Y	Y	Y	Y	Y
30 ***Quinn***	?	?	Y	Y	Y	Y	Y
31 ***Houghton***	Y	Y	Y	Y	Y	Y	Y
NORTH CAROLINA							
1 Clayton	Y	Y	Y	Y	Y	Y	Y
2 Etheridge	Y	Y	Y	Y	Y	N	Y
3 ***Jones***	Y	Y	Y	Y	Y	Y	Y
4 Price	Y	Y	Y	Y	Y	Y	Y
5 ***Burr***	Y	Y	Y	Y	Y	Y	Y
6 ***Coble***	Y	Y	Y	Y	Y	Y	Y
7 McIntyre	Y	Y	?	?	?	Y	Y
8 ***Hayes***	Y	Y	Y	Y	Y	Y	Y
9 ***Myrick***	Y	Y	Y	Y	Y	Y	Y
10 ***Ballenger***	Y	Y	Y	Y	Y	Y	Y
11 ***Taylor***	?	?	Y	Y	Y	Y	?
12 Watt	Y	Y	Y	Y	Y	Y	Y
NORTH DAKOTA							
AL Pomeroy	Y	Y	Y	Y	Y	Y	Y
OHIO							
1 ***Chabot***	Y	Y	Y	Y	Y	Y	Y
2 ***Portman***	+	+	Y	Y	Y	?	Y
3 Hall	Y	Y	Y	Y	Y	Y	Y
4 ***Oxley***	Y	Y	Y	Y	Y	Y	Y
5 ***Gillmor***	Y	Y	Y	Y	Y	Y	Y
6 Strickland	Y	Y	Y	Y	Y	N	Y
7 ***Hobson***	Y	Y	Y	Y	Y	Y	Y
8 ***Boehner***	Y	Y	Y	Y	Y	Y	Y
9 Kaptur	?	?	Y	Y	Y	?	Y
10 Kucinich	Y	Y	Y	Y	Y	N	Y
11 Jones	?	?	Y	Y	Y	Y	Y
12 ***Tiberi***	Y	Y	Y	Y	Y	Y	Y
13 Brown	Y	Y	Y	Y	Y	Y	Y
14 Sawyer	Y	Y	Y	Y	Y	Y	Y
15 ***Pryce***	?	?	Y	Y	Y	Y	Y
16 ***Regula***	Y	Y	Y	Y	Y	Y	Y
17 Traficant	?	?	?	?	?	?	?
18 ***Ney***	Y	Y	Y	Y	Y	Y	Y
19 ***LaTourette***	Y	Y	Y	Y	Y	Y	Y
OKLAHOMA							
1 ***Sullivan***	Y	Y	Y	Y	Y	Y	Y
2 Carson	?	?	Y	Y	Y	Y	Y
3 ***Watkins***	?	?	Y	Y	Y	Y	Y
4 ***Watts***	Y	Y	Y	Y	Y	Y	Y
5 ***Istook***	Y	Y	Y	Y	Y	Y	Y
6 ***Lucas***	Y	Y	Y	Y	Y	Y	Y
OREGON							
1 Wu	Y	Y	Y	Y	Y	N	Y
2 ***Walden***	Y	Y	Y	Y	Y	Y	Y
3 Blumenauer	Y	Y	Y	Y	Y	Y	Y
4 DeFazio	Y	Y	Y	Y	Y	N	Y
5 Hooley	Y	Y	Y	Y	Y	Y	Y
PENNSYLVANIA							
1 Brady	?	?	Y	Y	Y	N	Y
2 Fattah	?	?	Y	Y	Y	Y	Y
3 Borski	?	?	Y	Y	Y	N	Y
4 ***Hart***	?	Y	Y	Y	Y	Y	Y
5 ***Peterson***	Y	Y	Y	Y	Y	Y	Y
6 Holden	Y	Y	Y	Y	Y	Y	Y
7 ***Weldon***	Y	Y	Y	Y	Y	Y	Y
8 ***Greenwood***	Y	Y	Y	Y	Y	Y	Y
9 ***Shuster, Bill***	Y	Y	Y	Y	Y	Y	Y
10 ***Sherwood***	Y	Y	Y	Y	Y	Y	Y
11 Kanjorski	Y	Y	Y	Y	Y	Y	Y
12 Murtha	Y	Y	Y	Y	Y	Y	Y
13 Hoeffel	Y	Y	Y	Y	Y	Y	Y
14 Coyne	Y	Y	Y	Y	Y	Y	Y
15 ***Toomey***	Y	Y	Y	Y	Y	Y	Y
16 ***Pitts***	Y	Y	Y	Y	Y	Y	Y
17 ***Gekas***	Y	Y	Y	Y	Y	Y	Y
18 Doyle	Y	Y	Y	Y	Y	Y	Y
19 ***Platts***	Y	Y	Y	Y	Y	N	Y
20 Mascara	Y	Y	Y	Y	Y	Y	Y
21 ***English***	Y	Y	Y	Y	Y	N	Y
RHODE ISLAND							
1 Kennedy	Y	Y	Y	Y	Y	Y	Y
2 Langevin	Y	Y	Y	Y	Y	Y	Y
SOUTH CAROLINA							
1 ***Brown***	Y	Y	Y	Y	Y	Y	Y
2 ***Wilson***	Y	Y	Y	Y	Y	Y	Y
3 ***Graham***	Y	Y	Y	Y	Y	Y	Y
4 ***DeMint***	Y	Y	Y	Y	Y	Y	Y
5 Spratt	Y	Y	Y	Y	Y	Y	Y
6 Clyburn	Y	Y	Y	Y	Y	Y	Y
SOUTH DAKOTA							
AL ***Thune***	Y	Y	Y	Y	Y	Y	Y
TENNESSEE							
1 ***Jenkins***	+	+	Y	Y	Y	Y	Y
2 ***Duncan***	Y	Y	Y	Y	?	Y	Y
3 ***Wamp***	Y	Y	Y	Y	Y	Y	Y
4 ***Hilleary***	?	?	Y	Y	Y	Y	Y
5 Clement	?	?	Y	Y	Y	Y	Y
6 Gordon	Y	Y	Y	Y	Y	Y	Y
7 ***Bryant***	Y	Y	Y	Y	Y	Y	Y
8 Tanner	Y	Y	Y	Y	Y	Y	Y
9 Ford	?	?	Y	Y	Y	Y	Y
TEXAS							
1 Sandlin	?	?	Y	Y	Y	Y	Y
2 Turner	Y	Y	Y	Y	Y	Y	Y
3 ***Johnson, Sam***	Y	Y	Y	Y	Y	Y	Y
4 Hall	Y	Y	Y	Y	Y	Y	Y
5 ***Sessions***	?	?	Y	Y	Y	Y	Y
6 ***Barton***	?	?	Y	Y	Y	Y	Y
7 ***Culberson***	Y	Y	Y	Y	Y	Y	Y
8 ***Brady***	Y	Y	Y	Y	Y	Y	Y
9 Lampson	Y	Y	Y	Y	Y	Y	Y
10 Doggett	Y	Y	Y	Y	?	Y	Y
11 Edwards	Y	Y	Y	Y	Y	Y	Y
12 ***Granger***	Y	Y	Y	Y	Y	Y	Y
13 ***Thornberry***	Y	Y	Y	Y	Y	Y	Y
14 ***Paul***	Y	Y	Y	Y	Y	Y	N
15 Hinojosa	Y	Y	Y	Y	Y	?	Y
16 Reyes	Y	Y	Y	Y	Y	Y	Y
17 Stenholm	?	?	Y	Y	Y	Y	Y
18 Jackson-Lee	Y	Y	Y	Y	Y	Y	Y
19 ***Combest***	Y	Y	Y	Y	Y	Y	Y
20 Gonzalez	Y	Y	Y	Y	Y	Y	Y
21 ***Smith***	Y	Y	Y	Y	Y	Y	Y
22 ***DeLay***	Y	Y	Y	Y	Y	Y	Y
23 ***Bonilla***	Y	Y	Y	Y	Y	Y	Y
24 Frost	Y	Y	Y	Y	Y	Y	Y
25 Bentsen	Y	Y	Y	Y	Y	Y	Y
26 ***Armey***	Y	Y	Y	Y	Y	Y	?
27 Ortiz	Y	Y	Y	Y	Y	Y	Y
28 Rodriguez	Y	Y	Y	Y	Y	Y	Y
29 Green	Y	Y	Y	Y	Y	Y	Y
30 Johnson, E.B.	Y	Y	Y	Y	Y	Y	Y
UTAH							
1 ***Hansen***	Y	Y	Y	Y	Y	Y	Y
2 Matheson	Y	Y	Y	Y	Y	Y	Y
3 ***Cannon***	?	?	Y	Y	Y	Y	Y
VERMONT							
AL *Sanders*	?	?	?	?	?	?	?
VIRGINIA							
1 ***Davis, Jo Ann***	Y	Y	Y	Y	Y	Y	Y
2 ***Schrock***	Y	Y	Y	Y	Y	Y	Y
3 Scott	Y	Y	Y	Y	Y	Y	Y
4 ***Forbes***	Y	Y	Y	Y	Y	Y	Y
5 *Goode*	Y	Y	Y	Y	Y	Y	Y
6 ***Goodlatte***	Y	Y	Y	Y	Y	Y	Y
7 ***Cantor***	Y	Y	Y	Y	Y	Y	Y
8 Moran	Y	Y	?	?	?	Y	Y
9 Boucher	Y	Y	Y	Y	Y	Y	Y
10 ***Wolf***	Y	Y	Y	Y	Y	Y	Y
11 ***Davis, T.***	Y	Y	Y	Y	Y	Y	Y
WASHINGTON							
1 Inslee	Y	Y	Y	Y	Y	Y	Y
2 Larsen	Y	Y	Y	Y	Y	N	Y
3 Baird	Y	Y	Y	Y	Y	N	Y
4 ***Hastings***	Y	Y	Y	Y	Y	Y	Y
5 ***Nethercutt***	Y	Y	Y	Y	Y	Y	Y
6 Dicks	Y	Y	Y	Y	Y	Y	Y
7 McDermott	Y	Y	Y	Y	Y	N	Y
8 ***Dunn***	Y	Y	Y	Y	Y	Y	Y
9 Smith	Y	Y	Y	Y	Y	Y	Y
WEST VIRGINIA							
1 Mollohan	Y	Y	Y	Y	Y	Y	Y
2 ***Capito***	Y	Y	Y	Y	Y	Y	Y
3 Rahall	Y	Y	Y	Y	Y	Y	Y
WISCONSIN							
1 ***Ryan***	Y	Y	Y	Y	Y	Y	Y
2 Baldwin	Y	Y	Y	Y	Y	N	Y
3 Kind	Y	Y	Y	Y	Y	Y	Y
4 Kleczka	Y	Y	Y	Y	Y	Y	?
5 Barrett	Y	Y	Y	Y	Y	Y	Y
6 ***Petri***	Y	Y	Y	Y	Y	Y	Y
7 Obey	Y	Y	Y	Y	Y	Y	Y
8 ***Green***	Y	Y	Y	Y	Y	Y	Y
9 ***Sensenbrenner***	Y	Y	Y	Y	Y	Y	Y
WYOMING							
AL ***Cubin***	Y	Y	Y	Y	Y	Y	Y

Southern states - Ala., Ark., Fla., Ga., Ky., La., Miss., N.C., Okla., S.C., Tenn., Texas, Va.

Key

Y	Voted for (yea).
#	Paired for.
+	Announced for.
N	Voted against (nay).
X	Paired against.
–	Announced against.
P	Voted "present."
C	Voted "present" to avoid possible conflict of interest.
?	Did not vote or otherwise make a position known.

Democrats ***Republicans***
Independents

238. HR 3295. Election Overhaul/Motion to Instruct. Hastings, D-Fla., motion to instruct House conferees to insist on provisions in the House-passed bill that would require states to implement federal minimum election standards no later than November 2004. It also would instruct conferees to oppose a Senate provision that would allow states that receive funds under the bill a "safe harbor" from Justice Department enforcement provisions until 2010. Motion rejected 206-210: R 5-208; D 201-1 (ND 150-1, SD 51-0); I 0-1. June 19, 2002.

239. Procedural Motion/Journal. Approval of the House Journal of Wednesday, June 19, 2002. Approved 352-50: R 189-13; D 161-37 (ND 114-34, SD 47-3); I 2-0. June 20, 2002.

240. HR 1979. Airport Control Towers/Rule. Adoption of the rule (H Res 447) to provide for House floor consideration of the bill that would allow small airports to use funds from the federal Airport Improvement Program to pay for the construction and equipment costs of control towers operated by private companies under the contract control tower program. Adopted 419-0: R 211-0; D 206-0 (ND 155-0, SD 51-0); I 2-0. June 20, 2002.

241. HR 1979. Airport Control Towers/Reimbursement Funds. Oberstar, D-Minn., amendment that would cut provisions that would allow small airports to use funds to reimburse themselves for the costs of already-constructed towers. Rejected 202-223: R 3-213; D 198-9 (ND 152-3, SD 46-6); I 1-1. June 20, 2002.

242. HR 1979. Airport Control Towers/Cost Share Study. Nethercutt, R-Wash., amendment that would require a study of the impact of allowing airports to use 10 percent of their Airport Improvement Program funds to offset a reduction in the mandatory local cost share portion of operating control towers. Adopted 415-12: R 217-1; D 196-11 (ND 149-6, SD 47-5); I 2-0. June 20, 2002.

243. HR 1979. Airport Control Towers/Passage. Passage of the bill that would allow small airports to use funds from the federal Airport Improvement Program to pay for the construction and equipment costs of control towers operated by private companies under the contract control tower program. Small airports could use funds to reimburse themselves for the costs of towers built before Oct. 1, 1996. Passed 284-143: R 217-1; D 66-141 (ND 46-109, SD 20-32); I 1-1. June 20, 2002.

	238	239	240	241	242	243
ALABAMA						
1 *Callahan*	N	Y	Y	N	Y	Y
2 *Everett*	N	Y	Y	N	Y	Y
3 *Riley*	N	Y	Y	N	Y	Y
4 *Aderholt*	N	N	Y	N	Y	Y
5 Cramer	Y	Y	Y	Y	Y	Y
6 *Bachus*	N	Y	Y	N	Y	Y
7 Hilliard	?	?	?	?	?	?
ALASKA						
AL *Young*	N	?	Y	N	Y	Y
ARIZONA						
1 *Flake*	N	Y	Y	N	Y	Y
2 Pastor	Y	Y	Y	Y	Y	N
3 *Stump*	N	?	Y	N	Y	Y
4 *Shadegg*	N	Y	Y	N	Y	Y
5 *Kolbe*	N	Y	Y	N	Y	Y
6 *Hayworth*	N	Y	Y	N	Y	Y
ARKANSAS						
1 Berry	Y	Y	Y	Y	Y	Y
2 Snyder	Y	Y	Y	Y	Y	Y
3 *Boozman*	N	Y	Y	N	Y	Y
4 Ross	Y	Y	Y	Y	Y	Y
CALIFORNIA						
1 Thompson	Y	N	Y	Y	Y	Y
2 *Herger*	N	Y	Y	N	Y	Y
3 *Ose*	N	Y	Y	N	Y	Y
4 *Doolittle*	N	Y	Y	N	Y	Y
5 Matsui	Y	Y	Y	Y	Y	N
6 Woolsey	Y	Y	Y	Y	Y	Y
7 Miller, George	Y	Y	Y	?	?	N
8 Pelosi	Y	Y	Y	Y	Y	N
9 Lee	Y	Y	Y	Y	Y	N
10 Tauscher	Y	Y	Y	Y	Y	N
11 *Pombo*	N	Y	Y	N	Y	Y
12 Lantos	Y	Y	Y	Y	Y	N
13 Stark	Y	N	Y	N	N	N
14 Eshoo	Y	Y	Y	Y	Y	N
15 Honda	Y	Y	Y	Y	Y	N
16 Lofgren	Y	Y	Y	Y	Y	N
17 Farr	Y	Y	Y	Y	Y	N
18 Condit	Y	Y	Y	Y	Y	Y
19 *Radanovich*	N	Y	Y	N	Y	Y
20 Dooley	Y	Y	Y	Y	Y	Y
21 *Thomas*	N	Y	Y	N	Y	Y
22 Capps	Y	Y	Y	Y	Y	Y
23 *Gallegly*	N	Y	Y	N	Y	Y
24 Sherman	Y	Y	Y	Y	Y	N
25 *McKeon*	N	Y	Y	N	Y	Y
26 Berman	Y	Y	Y	Y	Y	Y
27 Schiff	Y	Y	Y	Y	Y	Y
28 *Dreier*	N	Y	Y	N	Y	Y
29 Waxman	Y	Y	Y	Y	Y	N
30 Becerra	Y	Y	Y	Y	Y	N
31 Solis	Y	Y	Y	Y	Y	N
32 Watson	Y	Y	Y	Y	Y	N
33 Roybal-Allard	Y	Y	Y	Y	Y	N
34 Napolitano	Y	Y	Y	Y	Y	N
35 Waters	Y	Y	Y	Y	Y	N
36 Harman	Y	Y	Y	Y	Y	N
37 Millender-McD.	Y	Y	Y	Y	Y	N
38 *Horn*	Y	Y	Y	N	Y	Y

	238	239	240	241	242	243
39 *Royce*	N	?	Y	N	Y	Y
40 *Lewis*	N	Y	Y	N	?	Y
41 *Miller, Gary*	N	Y	Y	N	Y	Y
42 Baca	Y	Y	Y	Y	Y	Y
43 *Calvert*	N	Y	Y	N	Y	Y
44 *Bono*	N	Y	Y	N	Y	Y
45 *Rohrabacher*	N	Y	Y	N	Y	N
46 Sanchez	Y	N	Y	Y	Y	Y
47 *Cox*	N	?	?	N	Y	Y
48 *Issa*	N	Y	Y	N	Y	Y
49 Davis	Y	Y	Y	Y	Y	N
50 Filner	Y	N	Y	Y	Y	Y
51 *Cunningham*	N	Y	Y	N	Y	Y
52 *Hunter*	N	Y	Y	N	Y	Y
COLORADO						
1 DeGette	Y	Y	Y	Y	Y	N
2 Udall	Y	N	Y	Y	Y	Y
3 *McInnis*	N	?	?	?	?	?
4 *Schaffer*	N	N	Y	N	Y	Y
5 *Hefley*	N	N	?	Y	Y	Y
6 *Tancredo*	N	?	Y	N	Y	Y
CONNECTICUT						
1 Larson	Y	Y	Y	Y	Y	N
2 *Simmons*	N	Y	Y	N	Y	Y
3 DeLauro	Y	Y	Y	Y	Y	N
4 *Shays*	?	?	Y	N	Y	Y
5 Maloney	Y	Y	Y	N	N	Y
6 *Johnson*	N	Y	Y	N	Y	Y
DELAWARE						
AL *Castle*	N	Y	Y	N	Y	Y
FLORIDA						
1 *Miller, J.*	N	Y	Y	N	Y	Y
2 Boyd	Y	Y	Y	Y	Y	N
3 Brown	Y	Y	Y	Y	Y	N
4 *Crenshaw*	N	Y	Y	N	Y	Y
5 Thurman	Y	Y	Y	Y	Y	N
6 *Stearns*	N	Y	Y	N	Y	Y
7 *Mica*	N	Y	Y	N	Y	Y
8 *Keller*	N	Y	Y	N	Y	Y
9 *Bilirakis*	N	Y	Y	N	Y	Y
10 *Young*	N	Y	Y	N	Y	Y
11 Davis	Y	Y	Y	Y	N	N
12 *Putnam*	?	Y	Y	N	Y	Y
13 *Miller, D.*	N	Y	Y	N	Y	Y
14 *Goss*	N	Y	Y	N	Y	Y
15 *Weldon*	N	Y	Y	N	Y	Y
16 *Foley*	N	Y	Y	N	Y	Y
17 Meek	Y	Y	Y	Y	Y	N
18 *Ros-Lehtinen*	N	Y	Y	N	Y	Y
19 Wexler	Y	?	Y	N	Y	Y
20 Deutsch	Y	Y	Y	Y	Y	N
21 *Diaz-Balart*	N	Y	Y	N	Y	Y
22 *Shaw*	N	Y	Y	N	Y	Y
23 Hastings	Y	Y	Y	N	Y	Y
GEORGIA						
1 *Kingston*	N	?	?	N	Y	Y
2 Bishop	Y	Y	Y	Y	Y	Y
3 *Collins*	N	Y	Y	?	Y	Y
4 McKinney	Y	Y	Y	Y	Y	Y
5 Lewis	?	?	?	?	?	?
6 *Isakson*	N	?	?	N	Y	Y
7 *Barr*	N	Y	Y	N	Y	Y
8 *Chambliss*	N	?	?	N	Y	Y
9 *Deal*	?	Y	Y	N	Y	Y
10 *Norwood*	?	Y	Y	N	Y	Y
11 *Linder*	?	Y	Y	N	Y	Y
HAWAII						
1 Abercrombie	Y	Y	Y	N	Y	Y
2 Mink	Y	Y	Y	Y	Y	Y
IDAHO						
1 *Otter*	N	N	Y	N	Y	Y
2 *Simpson*	N	?	Y	N	Y	Y
ILLINOIS						
1 Rush	Y	?	Y	Y	Y	?
2 Jackson	Y	Y	Y	Y	Y	N
3 Lipinski	Y	Y	Y	Y	Y	N
4 Gutierrez	?	Y	Y	Y	Y	N
5 Blagojevich	?	Y	Y	Y	Y	Y
6 *Hyde*	N	?	Y	N	Y	Y
7 Davis	Y	Y	Y	Y	Y	N
8 *Crane*	N	?	Y	N	Y	Y
9 Schakowsky	Y	Y	Y	Y	Y	N
10 *Kirk*	N	Y	Y	N	Y	Y
11 *Weller*	N	N	Y	N	Y	Y
12 Costello	Y	N	Y	N	N	Y
13 *Biggert*	N	Y	Y	N	Y	Y

ND Northern Democrats   SD Southern Democrats

	238	239	240	241	242	243
14 ***Hastert***	N					
15 ***Johnson***	N	Y	Y	N	Y	Y
16 ***Manzullo***	N	Y	Y	N	Y	Y
17 Evans	Y	Y	Y	Y	Y	Y
18 ***LaHood***	N	Y	Y	N	Y	Y
19 Phelps	Y	Y	Y	Y	Y	N
20 ***Shimkus***	N	Y	Y	N	Y	Y
INDIANA						
1 Visclosky	Y	N	Y	Y	Y	N
2 ***Pence***	N	Y	Y	N	Y	Y
3 Roemer	Y	Y	Y	Y	N	Y
4 ***Souder***	N	Y	Y	N	Y	?
5 ***Buyer***	N	Y	Y	N	Y	Y
6 ***Burton***	N	Y	Y	N	Y	Y
7 ***Kerns***	N	Y	Y	N	Y	Y
8 ***Hostettler***	N	Y	Y	N	Y	Y
9 Hill	Y	Y	Y	N	Y	Y
10 Carson	Y	Y	Y	Y	Y	N
IOWA						
1 ***Leach***	N	Y	Y	N	Y	Y
2 ***Nussle***	N	Y	Y	N	Y	Y
3 Boswell	Y	Y	Y	Y	Y	N
4 ***Ganske***	N	Y	Y	N	Y	Y
5 ***Latham***	N	Y	Y	N	Y	Y
KANSAS						
1 ***Moran***	N	N	Y	N	Y	Y
2 ***Ryun***	N	?	Y	N	Y	Y
3 Moore	+	Y	Y	Y	Y	Y
4 ***Tiahrt***	N	Y	Y	N	Y	Y
KENTUCKY						
1 ***Whitfield***	N	Y	Y	N	Y	Y
2 ***Lewis***	N	Y	Y	N	Y	Y
3 ***Northup***	N	Y	Y	N	Y	Y
4 Lucas	Y	Y	Y	Y	Y	Y
5 ***Rogers***	N	Y	Y	N	Y	Y
6 ***Fletcher***	N	Y	Y	N	Y	Y
LOUISIANA						
1 ***Vitter***	N	Y	Y	N	Y	Y
2 Jefferson	Y	Y	Y	Y	Y	N
3 ***Tauzin***	N	Y	Y	N	Y	Y
4 ***McCrery***	N	Y	Y	N	Y	Y
5 ***Cooksey***	?	Y	Y	N	Y	Y
6 ***Baker***	N	Y	Y	N	Y	Y
7 John	Y	Y	Y	Y	N	Y
MAINE						
1 Allen	Y	Y	Y	Y	N	N
2 Baldacci	Y	?	Y	Y	Y	N
MARYLAND						
1 ***Gilchrest***	N	Y	Y	N	Y	Y
2 ***Ehrlich***	Y	?	Y	N	Y	Y
3 Cardin	Y	Y	Y	Y	Y	Y
4 Wynn	Y	?	Y	Y	Y	Y
5 Hoyer	Y	Y	Y	Y	Y	Y
6 ***Bartlett***	N	Y	Y	N	Y	Y
7 Cummings	Y	?	Y	Y	Y	Y
8 ***Morella***	Y	Y	Y	N	Y	Y
MASSACHUSETTS						
1 Olver	Y	N	Y	Y	Y	N
2 Neal	Y	N	Y	Y	Y	N
3 McGovern	Y	Y	Y	Y	Y	N
4 Frank	Y	Y	Y	Y	Y	Y
5 Meehan	Y	Y	Y	Y	Y	N
6 Tierney	Y	Y	Y	Y	Y	N
7 Markey	Y	Y	Y	Y	Y	N
8 Capuano	Y	N	Y	Y	Y	N
9 Lynch	Y	Y	Y	Y	Y	N
10 Delahunt	Y	Y	Y	Y	Y	N
MICHIGAN						
1 Stupak	Y	N	Y	Y	Y	Y
2 ***Hoekstra***	N	Y	Y	N	Y	Y
3 ***Ehlers***	N	Y	Y	N	Y	Y
4 ***Camp***	N	Y	Y	N	Y	Y
5 Barcia	?	Y	Y	Y	Y	Y
6 ***Upton***	N	Y	Y	N	Y	Y
7 ***Smith***	N	Y	Y	N	Y	Y
8 ***Rogers***	N	Y	Y	N	Y	Y
9 Kildee	Y	Y	Y	Y	Y	N
10 Bonior	Y	Y	Y	Y	Y	N
11 ***Knollenberg***	N	Y	Y	N	Y	Y
12 Levin	Y	Y	Y	Y	Y	N
13 Rivers	Y	Y	Y	Y	Y	N
14 Conyers	?	?	Y	Y	Y	N
15 Kilpatrick	Y	Y	Y	Y	Y	N
16 Dingell	Y	Y	Y	Y	Y	N

	238	239	240	241	242	243
MINNESOTA						
1 ***Gutknecht***	N	N	Y	N	Y	Y
2 ***Kennedy***	N	N	Y	N	Y	Y
3 ***Ramstad***	N	N	Y	Y	Y	Y
4 McCollum	Y	Y	Y	Y	Y	N
5 Sabo	Y	N	Y	Y	Y	Y
6 Luther	Y	Y	Y	Y	Y	Y
7 Peterson	N	N	Y	Y	Y	N
8 Oberstar	Y	N	Y	Y	Y	N
MISSISSIPPI						
1 ***Wicker***	N	Y	Y	N	Y	Y
2 Thompson	Y	N	Y	Y	Y	Y
3 ***Pickering***	N	Y	Y	–	Y	Y
4 Shows	Y	Y	Y	N	Y	Y
5 Taylor	Y	N	Y	N	Y	Y
MISSOURI						
1 Clay	Y	Y	Y	Y	Y	N
2 ***Akin***	N	Y	Y	N	Y	Y
3 Gephardt	Y	Y	Y	Y	Y	N
4 Skelton	Y	Y	Y	Y	Y	Y
5 McCarthy	Y	Y	Y	Y	Y	N
6 ***Graves***	N	Y	Y	N	Y	Y
7 ***Blunt***	N	Y	Y	N	Y	Y
8 ***Emerson***	N	Y	Y	N	Y	Y
9 ***Hulshof***	N	Y	Y	N	Y	Y
MONTANA						
AL ***Rehberg***	N	Y	Y	N	Y	Y
NEBRASKA						
1 ***Bereuter***	N	Y	Y	N	Y	Y
2 ***Terry***	N	Y	Y	N	Y	Y
3 ***Osborne***	N	Y	Y	N	Y	Y
NEVADA						
1 Berkley	Y	Y	Y	Y	Y	N
2 ***Gibbons***	N	Y	Y	N	Y	Y
NEW HAMPSHIRE						
1 ***Sununu***	N	Y	Y	N	Y	Y
2 ***Bass***	N	Y	Y	N	Y	Y
NEW JERSEY						
1 Andrews	Y	Y	Y	Y	Y	N
2 ***LoBiondo***	N	N	Y	N	Y	Y
3 ***Saxton***	N	Y	Y	N	Y	Y
4 ***Smith***	N	?	Y	N	Y	Y
5 ***Roukema***	?	?	?	?	?	?
6 Pallone	Y	Y	Y	Y	Y	N
7 ***Ferguson***	N	Y	Y	N	Y	Y
8 Pascrell	Y	Y	Y	Y	Y	N
9 Rothman	Y	Y	Y	Y	Y	N
10 Payne	Y	Y	Y	Y	Y	N
11 ***Frelinghuysen***	N	Y	Y	N	Y	Y
12 Holt	Y	N	Y	Y	Y	N
13 Menendez	Y	N	Y	Y	Y	N
NEW MEXICO						
1 ***Wilson***	N	Y	Y	N	Y	Y
2 ***Skeen***	N	Y	Y	N	Y	Y
3 Udall	Y	N	Y	Y	Y	N
NEW YORK						
1 ***Grucci***	N	Y	+	N	Y	Y
2 Israel	Y	N	Y	Y	Y	Y
3 ***King***	N	Y	Y	N	Y	Y
4 McCarthy	Y	Y	Y	Y	Y	N
5 Ackerman	Y	Y	Y	Y	Y	N
6 Meeks	Y	Y	Y	Y	Y	N
7 Crowley	Y	Y	Y	Y	Y	N
8 Nadler	Y	Y	Y	Y	Y	N
9 Weiner	Y	?	?	Y	Y	N
10 Towns	Y	Y	Y	Y	Y	N
11 Owens	Y	Y	Y	Y	Y	N
12 Velázquez	Y	Y	Y	Y	Y	N
13 ***Fossella***	N	Y	Y	N	Y	Y
14 Maloney	Y	Y	Y	Y	Y	N
15 Rangel	Y	Y	Y	Y	Y	N
16 Serrano	Y	Y	Y	Y	Y	N
17 Engel	Y	Y	Y	Y	Y	N
18 Lowey	Y	Y	Y	Y	Y	N
19 ***Kelly***	N	Y	Y	N	Y	Y
20 ***Gilman***	Y	Y	Y	N	Y	Y
21 McNulty	Y	N	Y	Y	Y	N
22 ***Sweeney***	?	N	Y	N	Y	Y
23 ***Boehlert***	N	Y	Y	N	Y	Y
24 ***McHugh***	?	Y	Y	N	Y	Y
25 ***Walsh***	N	Y	Y	N	Y	Y
26 Hinchey	Y	N	Y	Y	Y	N
27 ***Reynolds***	N	Y	Y	N	Y	Y
28 Slaughter	Y	N	Y	Y	Y	Y
29 LaFalce	Y	Y	Y	Y	Y	N

	238	239	240	241	242	243
30 ***Quinn***	Y	Y	Y	N	Y	Y
31 ***Houghton***	N	Y	Y	?	Y	Y
NORTH CAROLINA						
1 Clayton	Y	Y	Y	N	Y	Y
2 Etheridge	Y	Y	Y	Y	Y	Y
3 ***Jones***	N	Y	Y	N	Y	Y
4 Price	Y	Y	Y	Y	Y	N
5 ***Burr***	N	Y	Y	N	Y	Y
6 ***Coble***	N	Y	Y	N	Y	Y
7 McIntyre	Y	Y	Y	Y	Y	Y
8 ***Hayes***	N	Y	Y	N	Y	Y
9 ***Myrick***	N	Y	Y	N	Y	Y
10 ***Ballenger***	N	Y	Y	N	Y	Y
11 ***Taylor***	N	Y	Y	N	Y	Y
12 Watt	Y	Y	Y	Y	Y	N
NORTH DAKOTA						
AL Pomeroy	Y	?	Y	Y	Y	Y
OHIO						
1 ***Chabot***	N	Y	Y	N	Y	Y
2 ***Portman***	N	Y	Y	N	Y	Y
3 Hall	Y	Y	Y	Y	Y	Y
4 ***Oxley***	N	Y	Y	N	Y	Y
5 ***Gillmor***	N	Y	Y	N	Y	Y
6 Strickland	Y	N	Y	Y	Y	Y
7 ***Hobson***	N	Y	Y	N	Y	Y
8 ***Boehner***	N	Y	Y	N	Y	Y
9 Kaptur	Y	Y	Y	Y	Y	N
10 Kucinich	Y	N	Y	Y	Y	N
11 Jones	Y	N	Y	Y	Y	Y
12 ***Tiberi***	N	Y	Y	N	Y	Y
13 Brown	Y	N	Y	Y	Y	N
14 Sawyer	Y	Y	Y	Y	Y	N
15 ***Pryce***	N	Y	Y	N	Y	Y
16 ***Regula***	N	Y	Y	N	Y	Y
17 Traficant	?	?	?	?	?	?
18 ***Ney***	N	Y	Y	N	Y	Y
19 ***LaTourette***	N	Y	Y	N	Y	Y
OKLAHOMA						
1 ***Sullivan***	N	Y	Y	N	Y	Y
2 Carson	Y	Y	Y	Y	N	N
3 ***Watkins***	N	Y	Y	N	Y	Y
4 ***Watts***	N	Y	Y	N	Y	Y
5 ***Istook***	N	Y	Y	N	Y	Y
6 ***Lucas***	N	Y	Y	N	Y	Y
OREGON						
1 Wu	Y	N	Y	Y	Y	Y
2 ***Walden***	N	Y	Y	N	Y	Y
3 Blumenauer	Y	Y	Y	Y	Y	Y
4 DeFazio	Y	N	Y	Y	Y	Y
5 Hooley	Y	Y	Y	Y	Y	Y
PENNSYLVANIA						
1 Brady	Y	N	Y	Y	Y	N
2 Fattah	Y	Y	Y	Y	Y	N
3 Borski	Y	N	Y	Y	Y	N
4 ***Hart***	N	N	Y	N	Y	Y
5 ***Peterson***	N	Y	?	N	Y	Y
6 Holden	Y	Y	Y	Y	Y	Y
7 ***Weldon***	N	?	Y	N	Y	Y
8 ***Greenwood***	N	Y	Y	N	Y	Y
9 ***Shuster, Bill***	N	Y	Y	N	Y	Y
10 ***Sherwood***	N	Y	Y	N	Y	Y
11 Kanjorski	Y	Y	Y	Y	Y	Y
12 Murtha	Y	Y	Y	Y	Y	Y
13 Hoeffel	Y	Y	Y	Y	Y	N
14 Coyne	Y	Y	Y	Y	Y	N
15 ***Toomey***	N	Y	Y	N	Y	Y
16 ***Pitts***	N	Y	Y	N	Y	Y
17 ***Gekas***	N	Y	Y	N	Y	Y
18 Doyle	Y	?	Y	Y	Y	Y
19 ***Platts***	N	Y	Y	N	Y	Y
20 Mascara	Y	Y	Y	Y	Y	Y
21 ***English***	N	N	Y	N	Y	Y
RHODE ISLAND						
1 Kennedy	Y	Y	Y	Y	Y	N
2 Langevin	Y	Y	Y	Y	Y	N
SOUTH CAROLINA						
1 ***Brown***	N	Y	Y	N	Y	Y
2 ***Wilson***	N	Y	Y	N	Y	Y
3 ***Graham***	N	Y	Y	N	Y	Y
4 ***DeMint***	N	Y	Y	N	Y	Y
5 Spratt	Y	Y	Y	Y	Y	N
6 Clyburn	Y	Y	Y	Y	Y	N
SOUTH DAKOTA						
AL ***Thune***	N	Y	Y	N	Y	Y

	238	239	240	241	242	243
TENNESSEE						
1 ***Jenkins***	N	Y	Y	N	Y	Y
2 ***Duncan***	N	Y	Y	N	Y	Y
3 ***Wamp***	N	Y	Y	N	Y	Y
4 ***Hilleary***	N	Y	Y	N	Y	Y
5 Clement	Y	Y	Y	Y	Y	N
6 Gordon	Y	?	Y	Y	Y	N
7 ***Bryant***	N	Y	Y	N	Y	Y
8 Tanner	Y	Y	?	Y	Y	N
9 Ford	Y	Y	Y	Y	N	N
TEXAS						
1 Sandlin	Y	Y	Y	Y	Y	N
2 Turner	Y	Y	Y	Y	Y	Y
3 ***Johnson, Sam***	N	Y	Y	N	N	Y
4 Hall	Y	Y	Y	N	Y	Y
5 ***Sessions***	N	Y	Y	N	Y	Y
6 ***Barton***	N	Y	Y	N	Y	Y
7 ***Culberson***	N	Y	Y	N	Y	Y
8 ***Brady***	N	Y	Y	N	Y	Y
9 Lampson	Y	Y	Y	Y	Y	N
10 Doggett	Y	Y	Y	Y	Y	Y
11 Edwards	?	Y	Y	Y	Y	N
12 ***Granger***	N	Y	Y	N	Y	Y
13 ***Thornberry***	N	Y	Y	N	Y	Y
14 ***Paul***	N	Y	Y	Y	Y	N
15 Hinojosa	Y	Y	Y	Y	Y	N
16 Reyes	Y	Y	Y	Y	Y	N
17 Stenholm	Y	Y	Y	Y	Y	Y
18 Jackson-Lee	Y	Y	Y	Y	Y	N
19 ***Combest***	N	Y	Y	N	Y	Y
20 Gonzalez	Y	Y	Y	Y	N	N
21 ***Smith***	N	?	Y	N	Y	Y
22 ***DeLay***	N	Y	Y	N	Y	Y
23 ***Bonilla***	N	Y	?	N	Y	Y
24 Frost	Y	Y	Y	Y	Y	N
25 Bentsen	Y	Y	Y	Y	Y	N
26 ***Armey***	N	Y	Y	N	Y	Y
27 Ortiz	Y	Y	Y	Y	Y	N
28 Rodriguez	Y	Y	Y	Y	Y	N
29 Green	Y	Y	Y	Y	Y	N
30 Johnson, E.B.	Y	N	Y	Y	Y	N
UTAH						
1 ***Hansen***	N	Y	Y	N	Y	Y
2 Matheson	Y	Y	Y	Y	Y	N
3 ***Cannon***	N	Y	Y	N	Y	Y
VERMONT						
AL *Sanders*	?	Y	Y	Y	Y	N
VIRGINIA						
1 ***Davis, Jo Ann***	N	Y	Y	N	Y	Y
2 ***Schrock***	N	Y	Y	N	Y	Y
3 Scott	Y	Y	Y	Y	Y	N
4 ***Forbes***	N	Y	Y	N	Y	Y
5 *Goode*	N	Y	Y	N	Y	Y
6 ***Goodlatte***	N	Y	Y	N	Y	Y
7 ***Cantor***	N	Y	Y	N	Y	Y
8 Moran	Y	Y	Y	Y	Y	N
9 Boucher	Y	Y	Y	Y	Y	N
10 ***Wolf***	N	Y	Y	N	Y	Y
11 ***Davis, T.***	N	Y	Y	N	Y	Y
WASHINGTON						
1 Inslee	Y	Y	Y	Y	Y	N
2 Larsen	Y	N	Y	Y	Y	N
3 Baird	Y	N	Y	Y	Y	N
4 ***Hastings***	N	Y	Y	N	Y	Y
5 ***Nethercutt***	N	Y	Y	N	Y	Y
6 Dicks	Y	Y	Y	Y	Y	Y
7 McDermott	Y	N	Y	Y	Y	Y
8 ***Dunn***	N	Y	Y	N	Y	Y
9 Smith	Y	Y	Y	Y	Y	Y
WEST VIRGINIA						
1 Mollohan	Y	Y	Y	Y	Y	Y
2 ***Capito***	N	Y	Y	N	Y	Y
3 Rahall	Y	Y	Y	Y	Y	N
WISCONSIN						
1 ***Ryan***	N	Y	Y	N	Y	Y
2 Baldwin	Y	N	Y	Y	Y	N
3 Kind	Y	Y	Y	Y	Y	N
4 Kleczka	Y	Y	Y	Y	Y	Y
5 Barrett	Y	Y	Y	Y	Y	Y
6 ***Petri***	N	Y	Y	N	Y	Y
7 Obey	Y	Y	Y	Y	Y	Y
8 ***Green***	N	Y	Y	N	Y	Y
9 ***Sensenbrenner***	N	Y	Y	N	Y	Y
WYOMING						
AL ***Cubin***	N	Y	Y	N	Y	Y

Southern states - Ala., Ark., Fla., Ga., Ky., La., Miss., N.C., Okla., S.C., Tenn., Texas, Va.

244. Procedural Motion/Journal. Approval of the House Journal of Thursday, June 20, 2002. Approved 318-45: R 181-12; D 136-33 (ND 101-27, SD 35-6); I 1-0. June 21, 2002.

245. HR 4931. Pension Benefits/Rule. Adoption of the rule (H Res 451) to provide for House floor consideration of the bill that would make permanent the additional incentives for pension and retirement contributions contained in last year's $1.35 trillion tax cut law (PL 107-16). Adopted 344-52: R 204-0; D 139-51 (ND 101-40, SD 38-11); I 1-1. June 21, 2002.

246. HR 4931. Pension Benefits/Democratic Substitute. Neal, D-Mass., amendment that would add benefits for lower-level employees and place additional constraints on top executives. It would extend a non-refundable tax credit for retirement plan contributions by middle- and low-income employees set to expire in 2006, allow the $200,000 maximum compensation limit in determining employee pension benefits only if it does not result in lower benefits to lower-paid employees, and alter "top heavy" requirements so that employer matching contributions are not considered when determining whether the minimum benefit requirement has been met for non-key employees. Rejected 182-204: R 2-195; D 179-8 (ND 138-1, SD 41-7); I 1-1. June 21, 2002.

247. HR 4931. Pension Benefits/Recommit. Neal, D-Mass., motion to recommit the bill to the House Ways and Means Committee with instructions that it be reported back with language that would prevent the practice of "corporate inversion," under which a U.S. company inverts its corporate structure so that the parent firm is technically located in a tax-free nation and only a subsidiary is located in the United States, for the purpose of escaping federal taxes. Motion rejected 186-192: R 2-191; D 183-0 (ND 136-0, SD 47-0); I 1-1. June 21, 2002.

248. HR 4931. Pension Benefits/Passage. Passage of the bill that would make permanent the additional incentives for pension and retirement contributions contained in last year's $1.35 trillion tax cut law, including the increase in annual limits for individual retirement account and 401(k) contributions, catch-up contributions for individuals age 50 and older, and quicker vesting and easier rollovers of pension plans. Passed 308-70: R 192-0; D 115-69 (ND 82-54, SD 33-15); I 1-1. A "yea" was a vote in support of the president's position. June 21, 2002.

249. HR 3937. Cibola National Wildlife Refuge/Passage. Cannon, R-Utah, motion to suspend the rules and pass the bill that would revoke refuge designation for the 140-acre parcel of land making up "Walter's Camp" in California's Cibola National Wildlife Refuge. Motion agreed to 375-0: R 197-0; D 177-0 (ND 132-0, SD 45-0); I 1-0. A two-thirds majority of those present and voting (250 in this case) is required for passage under suspension of the rules. June 24, 2002.

250. HR 3786. Glen Canyon Recreation Area/Passage. Cannon, R-Utah, motion to suspend the rules and pass the bill that would allow the Interior Department to exchange 370 acres in Arizona's Glen Canyon National Recreation Area for 152 acres located nearby and owned by Page One Corp. Motion agreed to 374-0: R 197-0; D 176-0 (ND 129-0, SD 47-0); I 1-0. A two-thirds majority of those present and voting (250 in this case) is required for passage under suspension of the rules. June 24, 2002.

251. HR 3971. Wildfire Fatalities/Passage. Goodlatte, R-Va., motion to suspend the rules and pass the bill that would require the Agriculture Department's inspector general to independently investigate any death of a National Forest Service employee caused by wildfire entrapment or burnover. Motion agreed to 377-0: R 199-0; D 177-0 (ND 130-0, SD 47-0); I 1-0. A two-thirds majority of those present and voting (252 in this case) is required for passage under suspension of the rules. June 24, 2002.

Key

Y	Voted for (yea).
#	Paired for.
+	Announced for.
N	Voted against (nay).
X	Paired against.
–	Announced against.
P	Voted "present."
C	Voted "present" to avoid possible conflict of interest.
?	Did not vote or otherwise make a position known.

Democrats **Republicans**
Independents

	244	245	246	247	248	249	250	251
ALABAMA								
1 *Callahan*	?	?	?	?	?	?	?	?
2 *Everett*	+	+	–	–	+	+	+	+
3 *Riley*	+	+	–	?	?	+	+	+
4 *Aderholt*	N	Y	N	N	Y	Y	Y	Y
5 Cramer	Y	Y	N	Y	Y	Y	Y	Y
6 *Bachus*	Y	Y	N	N	Y	Y	Y	Y
7 Hilliard	?	?	?	?	?	?	?	?
ALASKA								
AL *Young*	?	Y	N	N	Y	Y	Y	Y
ARIZONA								
1 *Flake*	Y	Y	N	N	Y	+	+	+
2 Pastor	N	N	Y	Y	N	Y	Y	Y
3 *Stump*	?	Y	N	N	Y	Y	Y	Y
4 *Shadegg*	Y	Y	N	N	Y	Y	Y	Y
5 *Kolbe*	Y	Y	N	N	Y	Y	Y	Y
6 *Hayworth*	Y	Y	N	N	Y	?	?	?
ARKANSAS								
1 Berry	N	Y	N	Y	N	Y	Y	Y
2 Snyder	Y	Y	Y	Y	N	Y	Y	Y
3 *Boozman*	Y	Y	N	N	Y	Y	Y	Y
4 Ross	Y	Y	Y	Y	Y	Y	Y	Y
CALIFORNIA								
1 Thompson	N	Y	Y	Y	Y	Y	Y	Y
2 *Herger*	Y	Y	N	N	Y	Y	Y	Y
3 *Ose*	Y	Y	N	N	Y	Y	Y	Y
4 *Doolittle*	?	Y	N	N	Y	Y	Y	Y
5 Matsui	Y	Y	Y	Y	N	Y	Y	Y
6 Woolsey	Y	N	Y	Y	N	Y	Y	Y
7 Miller, George	N	N	Y	Y	N	?	?	?
8 Pelosi	Y	Y	Y	Y	N	Y	Y	Y
9 Lee	Y	N	Y	Y	N	Y	Y	Y
10 Tauscher	?	Y	Y	Y	Y	Y	Y	Y
11 *Pombo*	Y	Y	N	N	Y	Y	Y	Y
12 Lantos	Y	Y	Y	Y	N	Y	Y	Y
13 Stark	?	N	Y	Y	N	Y	Y	Y
14 Eshoo	Y	Y	Y	Y	Y	Y	Y	Y
15 Honda	Y	Y	Y	Y	Y	?	?	?
16 Lofgren	Y	Y	Y	Y	Y	Y	Y	Y
17 Farr	Y	Y	Y	Y	Y	Y	Y	Y
18 Condit	Y	Y	Y	Y	Y	?	?	?
19 *Radanovich*	Y	Y	N	N	+	Y	Y	Y
20 Dooley	Y	Y	Y	Y	Y	Y	Y	Y
21 *Thomas*	?	Y	N	N	Y	Y	Y	Y
22 Capps	Y	Y	Y	Y	Y	Y	Y	Y
23 *Gallegly*	Y	Y	N	N	Y	Y	Y	Y
24 Sherman	Y	N	Y	N	Y	Y	Y	Y
25 *McKeon*	Y	Y	N	N	Y	Y	Y	Y
26 Berman	?	?	?	?	?	Y	Y	Y
27 Schiff	Y	Y	Y	Y	Y	Y	Y	Y
28 *Dreier*	Y	Y	N	N	Y	Y	Y	Y
29 Waxman	Y	Y	Y	N	Y	Y	Y	Y
30 Becerra	Y	Y	+	+	–	+	+	Y
31 Solis	Y	Y	Y	Y	N	Y	Y	Y
32 Watson	Y	N	Y	Y	N	Y	Y	Y
33 Roybal-Allard	Y	Y	Y	Y	N	Y	Y	Y
34 Napolitano	Y	Y	Y	?	Y	Y	Y	Y
35 Waters	N	N	?	N	Y	N	?	Y
36 Harman	Y	Y	Y	Y	Y	Y	Y	Y
37 Millender-McD.	Y	N	Y	Y	Y	Y	Y	?
38 *Horn*	Y	Y	N	N	Y	Y	Y	Y

	244	245	246	247	248	249	250	251
39 *Royce*	Y	Y	N	N	Y	Y	Y	Y
40 *Lewis*	Y	Y	N	N	Y	Y	Y	Y
41 *Miller, Gary*	Y	Y	Y	?	?	Y	Y	Y
42 Baca	Y	Y	Y	Y	N	Y	Y	Y
43 *Calvert*	Y	Y	N	N	Y	Y	Y	Y
44 *Bono*	Y	Y	N	N	Y	Y	Y	Y
45 *Rohrabacher*	Y	Y	N	N	Y	Y	Y	Y
46 Sanchez	N	Y	Y	Y	+	+	+	+
47 *Cox*	?	?	?	N	Y	Y	Y	Y
48 *Issa*	Y	Y	N	N	Y	Y	Y	Y
49 Davis	Y	Y	Y	Y	Y	Y	Y	Y
50 Filner	N	N	Y	Y	N	Y	Y	Y
51 *Cunningham*	Y	Y	N	N	?	Y	Y	Y
52 *Hunter*	Y	Y	N	N	Y	Y	Y	Y
COLORADO								
1 DeGette	Y	?	Y	Y	Y	?	?	?
2 Udall	?	Y	Y	Y	Y	Y	Y	Y
3 *McInnis*	?	?	?	?	?	Y	Y	Y
4 *Schaffer*	N	Y	N	N	Y	Y	Y	Y
5 *Hefley*	Y	Y	N	N	Y	Y	Y	Y
6 *Tancredo*	P	Y	N	N	Y	Y	Y	Y
CONNECTICUT								
1 Larson	Y	Y	Y	Y	Y	Y	Y	Y
2 *Simmons*	Y	Y	N	N	Y	?	?	?
3 DeLauro	Y	Y	Y	Y	N	Y	Y	Y
4 *Shays*	Y	Y	N	N	Y	Y	Y	Y
5 Maloney	Y	Y	Y	Y	Y	Y	Y	Y
6 *Johnson*	Y	Y	Y	Y	Y	Y	Y	Y
DELAWARE								
AL *Castle*	Y	Y	N	N	Y	Y	Y	Y
FLORIDA								
1 *Miller, J.*	Y	Y	N	N	Y	Y	Y	Y
2 Boyd	Y	Y	N	Y	N	Y	Y	Y
3 Brown	?	?	?	?	?	?	?	?
4 *Crenshaw*	Y	Y	N	N	Y	Y	Y	Y
5 Thurman	Y	Y	Y	Y	Y	Y	Y	Y
6 *Stearns*	Y	Y	N	N	Y	Y	Y	Y
7 *Mica*	Y	Y	N	–	+	Y	Y	Y
8 *Keller*	?	?	?	?	?	Y	Y	Y
9 *Bilirakis*	Y	Y	–	–	+	Y	Y	Y
10 *Young*	Y	Y	N	N	Y	Y	Y	Y
11 Davis	?	Y	Y	Y	N	Y	Y	Y
12 *Putnam*	Y	Y	N	N	Y	Y	Y	Y
13 *Miller, D.*	?	?	?	?	?	Y	Y	Y
14 *Goss*	Y	Y	N	N	Y	Y	Y	Y
15 *Weldon*	Y	Y	N	N	Y	Y	Y	Y
16 *Foley*	Y	Y	N	N	Y	Y	Y	Y
17 Meek	?	Y	Y	N	Y	Y	Y	Y
18 *Ros-Lehtinen*	Y	Y	N	N	Y	Y	Y	Y
19 Wexler	Y	Y	Y	Y	N	?	?	?
20 Deutsch	Y	Y	Y	Y	N	Y	Y	Y
21 *Diaz-Balart*	Y	Y	N	N	Y	Y	Y	Y
22 *Shaw*	Y	Y	N	N	Y	Y	Y	Y
23 Hastings	Y	Y	Y	Y	N	Y	Y	Y
GEORGIA								
1 *Kingston*	Y	Y	N	N	Y	Y	Y	Y
2 Bishop	Y	Y	Y	Y	N	Y	Y	Y
3 *Collins*	Y	Y	N	N	Y	Y	Y	Y
4 McKinney	?	?	?	?	?	Y	Y	Y
5 Lewis	?	?	?	?	?	Y	Y	Y
6 *Isakson*	Y	Y	N	N	Y	Y	Y	Y
7 *Barr*	Y	Y	N	N	Y	Y	Y	Y
8 *Chambliss*	Y	Y	N	N	Y	Y	Y	Y
9 *Deal*	Y	Y	N	N	Y	Y	Y	Y
10 *Norwood*	?	?	?	?	?	Y	Y	Y
11 *Linder*	Y	Y	N	N	Y	Y	Y	Y
HAWAII								
1 Abercrombie	Y	Y	Y	Y	Y	+	+	+
2 Mink	Y	N	Y	Y	Y	Y	Y	Y
IDAHO								
1 *Otter*	Y	Y	N	N	Y	Y	Y	Y
2 *Simpson*	Y	Y	N	N	Y	Y	Y	Y
ILLINOIS								
1 Rush	Y	Y	Y	Y	Y	Y	?	Y
2 Jackson	Y	Y	Y	Y	N	Y	Y	Y
3 Lipinski	?	?	?	?	?	Y	Y	Y
4 Gutierrez	?	?	?	?	?	Y	Y	Y
5 Blagojevich	?	?	?	?	?	?	?	?
6 *Hyde*	Y	Y	Y	Y	Y	Y	Y	Y
7 Davis	Y	Y	Y	N	Y	Y	Y	Y
8 *Crane*	?	Y	N	N	Y	Y	Y	Y
9 Schakowsky	N	N	Y	N	Y	Y	Y	Y
10 *Kirk*	Y	Y	N	N	Y	Y	Y	Y
11 *Weller*	N	Y	N	N	Y	Y	Y	Y
12 Costello	N	Y	Y	Y	Y	?	?	Y
13 *Biggert*	Y	Y	N	N	Y	Y	Y	Y

ND Northern Democrats   SD Southern Democrats

	244	245	246	247	248	249	250	251
14 ***Hastert***				N	Y			
15 ***Johnson***	Y	Y	N	N	Y	Y	+	Y
16 ***Manzullo***	?	?	?	?	?	?	?	?
17 Evans	Y	Y	Y	Y	Y	Y	Y	Y
18 ***LaHood***	?	?	?	?	?	Y	Y	Y
19 Phelps	Y	Y	Y	Y	Y	Y	Y	Y
20 ***Shimkus***	Y	Y	N	N	Y	Y	Y	Y
INDIANA								
1 Visclosky	N	Y	Y	Y	N	Y	Y	Y
2 ***Pence***	Y	Y	?	?	?	Y	Y	Y
3 Roemer	Y	Y	Y	Y	Y	Y	Y	Y
4 ***Souder***	Y	Y	N	N	Y	Y	Y	Y
5 ***Buyer***	Y	Y	?	?	?	?	?	?
6 ***Burton***	Y	Y	–	–	+	?	?	?
7 ***Kerns***	Y	Y	N	N	Y	Y	Y	Y
8 ***Hostettler***	Y	Y	N	N	Y	Y	Y	Y
9 Hill	Y	Y	Y	Y	Y	?	?	?
10 Carson	?	?	?	?	?	?	?	?
IOWA								
1 ***Leach***	Y	Y	Y	Y	Y	Y	Y	Y
2 ***Nussle***	Y	Y	N	N	Y	Y	Y	Y
3 Boswell	Y	Y	Y	Y	Y	Y	Y	Y
4 ***Ganske***	?	?	?	?	?	Y	Y	Y
5 ***Latham***	Y	Y	N	N	Y	Y	Y	Y
KANSAS								
1 ***Moran***	Y	Y	N	N	Y	Y	Y	Y
2 ***Ryun***	Y	Y	?	N	Y	Y	Y	Y
3 Moore	N	Y	Y	Y	Y	Y	Y	Y
4 ***Tiahrt***	Y	Y	N	N	Y	Y	Y	Y
KENTUCKY								
1 ***Whitfield***	N	Y	N	?	?	Y	Y	Y
2 ***Lewis***	Y	Y	N	N	Y	Y	Y	Y
3 ***Northup***	?	?	?	?	?	Y	Y	Y
4 Lucas	Y	Y	N	Y	Y	Y	Y	Y
5 ***Rogers***	Y	Y	N	N	Y	Y	Y	Y
6 ***Fletcher***	N	Y	N	N	Y	Y	Y	Y
LOUISIANA								
1 ***Vitter***	Y	Y	N	N	Y	Y	Y	Y
2 Jefferson	Y	Y	Y	Y	Y	?	?	?
3 ***Tauzin***	Y	Y	N	N	Y	Y	Y	Y
4 ***McCrery***	Y	Y	N	N	?	Y	?	Y
5 ***Cooksey***	Y	Y	N	N	Y	Y	Y	Y
6 ***Baker***	?	?	?	?	?	Y	Y	Y
7 John	Y	Y	Y	Y	Y	Y	Y	Y
MAINE								
1 Allen	Y	?	Y	Y	Y	Y	Y	Y
2 Baldacci	Y	Y	Y	Y	Y	Y	Y	Y
MARYLAND								
1 ***Gilchrest***	Y	Y	N	N	Y	Y	Y	Y
2 ***Ehrlich***	Y	Y	N	N	Y	Y	Y	Y
3 Cardin	Y	Y	Y	Y	Y	Y	Y	Y
4 Wynn	?	Y	Y	Y	Y	Y	Y	Y
5 Hoyer	Y	Y	Y	Y	Y	Y	Y	Y
6 ***Bartlett***	Y	Y	N	N	Y	Y	Y	Y
7 Cummings	?	Y	Y	Y	Y	Y	Y	Y
8 ***Morella***	Y	Y	N	N	Y	Y	Y	Y
MASSACHUSETTS								
1 Olver	N	N	Y	Y	?	Y	Y	Y
2 Neal	N	Y	Y	Y	N	Y	Y	Y
3 McGovern	Y	Y	Y	Y	N	Y	Y	Y
4 Frank	Y	Y	Y	Y	N	Y	Y	Y
5 Meehan	Y	Y	Y	Y	Y	Y	Y	Y
6 Tierney	Y	N	Y	?	?	Y	Y	Y
7 Markey	N	Y	Y	Y	N	Y	Y	Y
8 Capuano	N	N	Y	Y	N	Y	Y	Y
9 Lynch	Y	Y	Y	Y	Y	Y	Y	Y
10 Delahunt	?	N	Y	Y	N	Y	Y	Y
MICHIGAN								
1 Stupak	?	Y	Y	Y	Y	Y	Y	Y
2 ***Hoekstra***	Y	Y	N	N	Y	Y	Y	Y
3 ***Ehlers***	Y	Y	N	N	Y	Y	Y	Y
4 ***Camp***	Y	Y	N	N	Y	?	?	?
5 Barcia	Y	Y	?	?	?	Y	Y	Y
6 ***Upton***	Y	Y	N	N	Y	Y	Y	Y
7 ***Smith***	?	Y	N	N	Y	Y	Y	Y
8 ***Rogers***	Y	Y	N	N	Y	Y	Y	Y
9 Kildee	Y	Y	Y	Y	N	Y	Y	Y
10 Bonior	?	?	?	?	?	+	+	+
11 ***Knollenberg***	Y	Y	N	N	Y	Y	Y	Y
12 Levin	Y	Y	Y	Y	N	Y	Y	Y
13 Rivers	Y	N	Y	Y	N	Y	?	Y
14 Conyers	?	N	Y	Y	N	?	?	?
15 Kilpatrick	Y	N	Y	Y	Y	+	+	?
16 Dingell	?	?	?	?	?	Y	Y	Y
MINNESOTA								
1 ***Gutknecht***	N	Y	N	N	Y	Y	Y	Y
2 ***Kennedy***	N	Y	N	N	Y	Y	Y	Y
3 ***Ramstad***	N	Y	N	N	Y	Y	Y	Y
4 McCollum	Y	N	Y	Y	Y	Y	Y	Y
5 Sabo	N	Y	Y	Y	N	Y	Y	Y
6 Luther	Y	Y	Y	Y	Y	Y	Y	Y
7 Peterson	N	Y	Y	Y	Y	?	?	?
8 Oberstar	N	N	Y	Y	N	Y	Y	Y
MISSISSIPPI								
1 ***Wicker***	Y	Y	N	N	Y	Y	Y	Y
2 Thompson	N	N	Y	Y	Y	Y	Y	Y
3 ***Pickering***	Y	Y	N	N	Y	Y	Y	Y
4 Shows	Y	N	Y	Y	Y	Y	Y	Y
5 Taylor	N	N	N	Y	N	Y	Y	Y
MISSOURI								
1 Clay	?	Y	Y	Y	N	Y	Y	Y
2 ***Akin***	Y	Y	N	N	Y	Y	Y	Y
3 Gephardt	Y	N	Y	Y	N	Y	Y	Y
4 Skelton	Y	Y	Y	Y	Y	Y	Y	Y
5 McCarthy	Y	Y	Y	Y	Y	Y	Y	Y
6 ***Graves***	Y	Y	N	N	Y	Y	Y	Y
7 ***Blunt***	Y	Y	N	N	Y	Y	Y	Y
8 ***Emerson***	Y	Y	N	N	Y	Y	Y	Y
9 ***Hulshof***	Y	Y	N	N	Y	Y	Y	Y
MONTANA								
AL ***Rehberg***	Y	Y	N	N	Y	Y	Y	Y
NEBRASKA								
1 ***Bereuter***	Y	Y	N	N	Y	Y	Y	Y
2 ***Terry***	Y	Y	N	N	Y	Y	Y	Y
3 ***Osborne***	Y	Y	N	N	Y	Y	Y	Y
NEVADA								
1 Berkley	Y	Y	Y	Y	Y	Y	Y	Y
2 ***Gibbons***	?	Y	N	N	Y	Y	Y	Y
NEW HAMPSHIRE								
1 ***Sununu***	?	Y	N	N	Y	Y	Y	Y
2 ***Bass***	Y	Y	N	+	Y	Y	Y	Y
NEW JERSEY								
1 Andrews	Y	N	Y	Y	N	Y	Y	Y
2 ***LoBiondo***	N	Y	N	N	Y	Y	Y	Y
3 ***Saxton***	Y	Y	N	N	Y	Y	Y	Y
4 ***Smith***	Y	Y	N	N	Y	?	Y	Y
5 ***Roukema***	?	?	?	?	?	Y	Y	Y
6 Pallone	Y	Y	Y	Y	Y	Y	Y	Y
7 ***Ferguson***	Y	Y	N	N	Y	Y	Y	Y
8 Pascrell	Y	Y	Y	Y	Y	Y	Y	Y
9 Rothman	Y	Y	Y	Y	Y	Y	Y	Y
10 Payne	Y	Y	Y	Y	N	Y	Y	Y
11 ***Frelinghuysen***	Y	Y	N	N	Y	Y	Y	Y
12 Holt	Y	Y	Y	Y	Y	Y	Y	Y
13 Menendez	Y	Y	Y	+	Y	Y	Y	
NEW MEXICO								
1 ***Wilson***	Y	Y	N	N	Y	Y	Y	Y
2 ***Skeen***	Y	Y	N	N	Y	Y	Y	Y
3 Udall	N	Y	Y	Y	N	Y	Y	Y
NEW YORK								
1 ***Grucci***	Y	Y	N	N	Y	Y	Y	Y
2 Israel	Y	Y	Y	Y	Y	+	+	+
3 ***King***	Y	Y	N	N	Y	Y	Y	Y
4 McCarthy	Y	Y	Y	Y	Y	Y	Y	Y
5 Ackerman	?	?	?	?	?	Y	Y	Y
6 Meeks	?	Y	Y	Y	Y	?	?	?
7 Crowley	Y	Y	Y	Y	Y	Y	Y	Y
8 Nadler	?	Y	Y	Y	N	?	?	?
9 Weiner	?	?	?	?	?	?	?	?
10 Towns	Y	N	Y	Y	Y	Y	Y	Y
11 Owens	?	N	Y	Y	N	+	+	+
12 Velázquez	Y	Y	Y	Y	Y	?	Y	Y
13 ***Fossella***	Y	Y	N	N	Y	+	+	+
14 Maloney	Y	Y	Y	Y	Y	Y	Y	Y
15 Rangel	Y	N	Y	Y	N	Y	Y	?
16 Serrano	Y	Y	Y	Y	Y	Y	Y	Y
17 Engel	Y	Y	Y	Y	Y	Y	Y	Y
18 Lowey	Y	Y	Y	Y	Y	Y	Y	Y
19 ***Kelly***	Y	Y	N	N	Y	Y	Y	Y
20 ***Gilman***	Y	Y	?	N	Y	Y	Y	Y
21 McNulty	N	N	Y	Y	N	Y	Y	Y
22 ***Sweeney***	N	Y	N	N	Y	Y	Y	Y
23 ***Boehlert***	Y	Y	N	N	Y	Y	Y	Y
24 ***McHugh***	Y	Y	N	N	Y	Y	Y	Y
25 ***Walsh***	Y	Y	N	?	?	Y	Y	Y
26 Hinchey	?	N	Y	Y	N	Y	Y	Y
27 ***Reynolds***	Y	Y	N	N	Y	Y	Y	Y
28 Slaughter	Y	Y	Y	Y	N	Y	Y	Y
29 LaFalce	Y	N	?	?	?	Y	Y	Y
30 ***Quinn***	Y	Y	?	?	?	Y	Y	Y
31 ***Houghton***	?	?	?	?	?	?	?	?
NORTH CAROLINA								
1 Clayton	Y	Y	Y	Y	Y	Y	Y	Y
2 Etheridge	Y	Y	Y	Y	Y	Y	Y	Y
3 ***Jones***	Y	Y	N	N	Y	Y	Y	Y
4 Price	Y	Y	Y	Y	Y	Y	Y	Y
5 ***Burr***	Y	Y	N	N	Y	Y	Y	Y
6 ***Coble***	Y	Y	N	N	Y	Y	Y	Y
7 McIntyre	Y	Y	Y	Y	Y	Y	Y	Y
8 ***Hayes***	Y	Y	N	N	Y	Y	Y	Y
9 ***Myrick***	Y	Y	N	N	Y	Y	Y	Y
10 ***Ballenger***	Y	Y	N	N	Y	Y	Y	Y
11 ***Taylor***	Y	Y	N	N	Y	Y	Y	Y
12 Watt	?	N	Y	Y	Y	Y	Y	Y
NORTH DAKOTA								
AL Pomeroy	Y	Y	Y	Y	Y	+	+	+
OHIO								
1 ***Chabot***	Y	Y	N	N	Y	Y	Y	Y
2 ***Portman***	Y	Y	N	N	Y	Y	Y	Y
3 Hall	Y	Y	Y	Y	Y	Y	Y	Y
4 ***Oxley***	?	Y	N	N	Y	Y	Y	Y
5 ***Gillmor***	Y	?	?	?	?	Y	Y	Y
6 Strickland	N	Y	Y	Y	N	Y	Y	Y
7 ***Hobson***	Y	Y	N	N	Y	Y	Y	Y
8 ***Boehner***	Y	Y	N	N	Y	?	?	?
9 Kaptur	Y	Y	Y	Y	N	Y	Y	Y
10 Kucinich	N	N	Y	Y	N	Y	Y	Y
11 Jones	Y	N	Y	Y	Y	?	?	?
12 ***Tiberi***	Y	Y	N	N	Y	Y	Y	Y
13 Brown	?	N	Y	Y	N	Y	Y	Y
14 Sawyer	Y	Y	Y	Y	Y	Y	Y	Y
15 ***Pryce***	Y	Y	N	N	Y	?	?	?
16 ***Regula***	Y	Y	N	N	Y	Y	Y	Y
17 Traficant	?	?	?	?	?	?	?	?
18 ***Ney***	Y	Y	N	N	Y	Y	Y	Y
19 ***LaTourette***	Y	Y	N	N	Y	Y	Y	Y
OKLAHOMA								
1 ***Sullivan***	Y	Y	N	N	Y	Y	Y	Y
2 Carson	N	Y	Y	Y	Y	Y	Y	Y
3 ***Watkins***	Y	Y	N	N	Y	Y	Y	Y
4 ***Watts***	Y	Y	N	N	Y	+	+	+
5 ***Istook***	Y	Y	N	N	Y	Y	Y	Y
6 ***Lucas***	Y	Y	N	N	Y	Y	Y	Y
OREGON								
1 Wu	N	Y	Y	Y	Y	Y	Y	Y
2 ***Walden***	Y	Y	N	N	Y	Y	Y	Y
3 Blumenauer	Y	Y	Y	Y	Y	Y	Y	Y
4 DeFazio	N	N	Y	Y	Y	Y	Y	Y
5 Hooley	Y	Y	Y	Y	Y	Y	Y	Y
PENNSYLVANIA								
1 Brady	N	N	Y	Y	Y	Y	Y	Y
2 Fattah	Y	N	Y	Y	N	Y	Y	Y
3 Borski	?	?	?	?	?	?	?	?
4 ***Hart***	N	Y	N	N	Y	Y	Y	Y
5 ***Peterson***	Y	Y	N	N	Y	?	?	?
6 Holden	Y	Y	Y	Y	Y	Y	Y	Y
7 ***Weldon***	Y	Y	N	N	Y	Y	Y	Y
8 ***Greenwood***	Y	Y	N	N	Y	Y	Y	Y
9 ***Shuster, Bill***	Y	Y	N	N	Y	Y	Y	Y
10 ***Sherwood***	Y	Y	N	N	Y	Y	Y	Y
11 Kanjorski	Y	Y	Y	Y	Y	Y	Y	Y
12 Murtha	?	?	?	?	?	Y	Y	Y
13 Hoeffel	Y	Y	Y	Y	Y	Y	Y	Y
14 Coyne	?	?	?	?	?	Y	Y	Y
15 ***Toomey***	Y	Y	N	N	Y	Y	Y	Y
16 ***Pitts***	?	Y	N	N	Y	Y	Y	Y
17 ***Gekas***	Y	Y	N	N	Y	Y	Y	Y
18 Doyle	?	Y	Y	Y	Y	Y	Y	Y
19 ***Platts***	Y	Y	N	?	Y	?	Y	Y
20 Mascara	Y	N	Y	Y	Y	Y	Y	Y
21 ***English***	N	Y	N	N	Y	Y	Y	Y
RHODE ISLAND								
1 Kennedy	Y	Y	Y	Y	Y	Y	Y	Y
2 Langevin	Y	Y	Y	Y	Y	Y	Y	Y
SOUTH CAROLINA								
1 ***Brown***	Y	Y	N	N	Y	Y	Y	Y
2 ***Wilson***	Y	Y	N	N	Y	Y	Y	Y
3 ***Graham***	Y	Y	N	N	Y	Y	Y	Y
4 ***DeMint***	Y	Y	N	N	Y	Y	Y	Y
5 Spratt	Y	Y	Y	Y	Y	Y	Y	Y
6 Clyburn	Y	N	Y	Y	Y	Y	Y	Y
SOUTH DAKOTA								
AL ***Thune***	Y	Y	N	N	Y	Y	Y	Y
TENNESSEE								
1 ***Jenkins***	Y	Y	N	?	?	?	?	?
2 ***Duncan***	Y	Y	N	N	Y	Y	Y	Y
3 ***Wamp***	Y	Y	N	N	Y	Y	Y	Y
4 ***Hilleary***	?	Y	N	?	?	?	?	?
5 Clement	?	Y	Y	Y	Y	+	+	+
6 Gordon	?	Y	Y	Y	Y	?	?	?
7 ***Bryant***	Y	Y	N	N	Y	?	?	?
8 Tanner	N	Y	Y	Y	Y	Y	Y	Y
9 Ford	Y	N	Y	Y	N	Y	Y	Y
TEXAS								
1 Sandlin	Y	Y	Y	Y	Y	Y	Y	Y
2 Turner	Y	N	N	Y	N	Y	Y	Y
3 ***Johnson, Sam***	Y	Y	N	N	Y	Y	Y	Y
4 Hall	Y	Y	Y	Y	Y	Y	Y	Y
5 ***Sessions***	Y	Y	N	N	Y	Y	Y	Y
6 ***Barton***	Y	Y	N	N	Y	Y	Y	Y
7 ***Culberson***	Y	Y	N	N	Y	Y	Y	Y
8 ***Brady***	Y	Y	N	N	Y	Y	Y	Y
9 Lampson	?	Y	Y	Y	Y	Y	Y	Y
10 Doggett	Y	Y	Y	Y	N	Y	Y	Y
11 Edwards	Y	Y	Y	Y	Y	Y	Y	Y
12 ***Granger***	Y	Y	N	N	Y	Y	Y	Y
13 ***Thornberry***	Y	Y	N	N	Y	Y	Y	Y
14 ***Paul***	Y	Y	N	N	Y	Y	Y	Y
15 Hinojosa	Y	Y	Y	Y	N	?	?	?
16 Reyes	?	Y	?	?	?	Y	Y	Y
17 Stenholm	Y	N	N	Y	N	Y	Y	Y
18 Jackson-Lee	Y	Y	Y	Y	Y	Y	Y	Y
19 ***Combest***	Y	Y	N	N	Y	Y	Y	Y
20 Gonzalez	Y	Y	Y	Y	Y	Y	Y	Y
21 ***Smith***	Y	Y	N	N	?	Y	Y	Y
22 ***DeLay***	Y	Y	N	N	Y	Y	Y	Y
23 ***Bonilla***	Y	Y	N	N	Y	Y	Y	Y
24 Frost	Y	Y	Y	Y	Y	Y	Y	Y
25 Bentsen	Y	Y	Y	Y	Y	Y	Y	Y
26 ***Armey***	Y	Y	N	N	Y	Y	Y	Y
27 Ortiz	?	?	?	?	?	Y	Y	Y
28 Rodriguez	Y	Y	Y	Y	Y	Y	Y	Y
29 Green	Y	N	Y	Y	N	Y	Y	Y
30 Johnson, E.B.	N	N	Y	Y	N	Y	Y	Y
UTAH								
1 ***Hansen***	?	?	?	?	?	?	?	?
2 Matheson	Y	Y	Y	Y	Y	Y	Y	Y
3 ***Cannon***	Y	Y	N	?	Y	Y	Y	Y
VERMONT								
AL *Sanders*	?	N	Y	Y	N	?	?	?
VIRGINIA								
1 ***Davis, Jo Ann***	Y	Y	N	N	Y	Y	Y	Y
2 ***Schrock***	Y	Y	N	N	Y	Y	Y	Y
3 Scott	Y	N	Y	Y	N	Y	Y	Y
4 ***Forbes***	Y	Y	N	N	Y	Y	Y	Y
5 *Goode*	Y	Y	N	N	Y	Y	Y	Y
6 ***Goodlatte***	Y	Y	N	N	Y	Y	Y	Y
7 ***Cantor***	Y	Y	N	N	Y	Y	Y	Y
8 Moran	Y	Y	Y	?	Y	Y	Y	Y
9 Boucher	?	Y	Y	Y	Y	Y	Y	Y
10 ***Wolf***	Y	Y	N	N	Y	Y	Y	Y
11 ***Davis, T.***	?	Y	N	N	Y	Y	Y	Y
WASHINGTON								
1 Inslee	Y	Y	Y	Y	N	Y	Y	Y
2 Larsen	?	Y	Y	Y	Y	Y	Y	Y
3 Baird	N	Y	Y	Y	Y	Y	Y	Y
4 ***Hastings***	Y	Y	N	N	Y	Y	Y	Y
5 ***Nethercutt***	Y	Y	N	N	Y	?	?	?
6 Dicks	Y	Y	Y	Y	N	Y	Y	Y
7 McDermott	N	Y	Y	Y	N	Y	Y	Y
8 ***Dunn***	Y	Y	N	N	Y	Y	Y	Y
9 Smith	Y	?	?	?	?	Y	Y	Y
WEST VIRGINIA								
1 Mollohan	Y	N	Y	Y	N	Y	Y	Y
2 ***Capito***	Y	Y	N	N	Y	Y	Y	Y
3 Rahall	Y	N	Y	Y	N	Y	Y	Y
WISCONSIN								
1 ***Ryan***	Y	Y	N	N	Y	Y	Y	Y
2 Baldwin	N	N	Y	Y	N	Y	Y	Y
3 Kind	Y	Y	Y	Y	Y	Y	Y	Y
4 Kleczka	Y	Y	Y	Y	Y	+	+	?
5 Barrett	Y	Y	Y	Y	Y	Y	Y	Y
6 ***Petri***	Y	Y	N	N	Y	Y	Y	Y
7 Obey	Y	Y	Y	Y	N	Y	Y	Y
8 ***Green***	Y	Y	N	N	Y	Y	Y	Y
9 ***Sensenbrenner***	Y	Y	N	N	Y	Y	Y	Y
WYOMING								
AL ***Cubin***	Y	Y	N	N	Y	Y	Y	Y

Southern states - Ala., Ark., Fla., Ga., Ky., La., Miss., N.C., Okla., S.C., Tenn., Texas, Va.

252. H J Res 95. Medal of Honor Flag/Passage. Schrock, R-Va., motion to suspend the rules and pass the resolution that would designate an official Medal of Honor flag to be presented to medal recipients. Motion agreed to 380-0: R 199-0; D 180-0 (ND 133-0, SD 47-0); I 1-0. A two-thirds majority of those present and voting (254 in this case) is required for passage under suspension of the rules. June 24, 2002.

253. Procedural Motion/Journal. Approval of the House Journal of Monday, June 24, 2002. Approved 371-40: R 200-10; D 169-30 (ND 122-26, SD 47-4); I 2-0. June 25, 2002.

254. HR 4858. Doctor Visas/Passage. Sensenbrenner, R-Wis., motion to suspend the rules and pass the bill that would extend for two years, retroactive to May 31, 2002, a visa waiver program that allows foreign doctors serving medically underserved areas in the United States to remain in the country without going home after finishing medical training. It also would raise the maximum number of such waivers in each state from 20 to 30. Motion agreed to 407-7: R 206-6; D 200-0 (ND 148-0, SD 52-0); I 1-1. A two-thirds majority of those present and voting (276 in this case) is required for passage under suspension of the rules. June 25, 2002.

255. HR 4679. Sex Offender Supervision/Passage. Sensenbrenner, R-Wis., motion to suspend the rules and pass the bill that would increase from five years to up to life the maximum amount of post-imprisonment supervision time a judge may impose on an individual convicted of a sex offense. Motion agreed to 409-3: R 211-0; D 196-3 (ND 147-1, SD 49-2); I 2-0. A two-thirds majority of those present and voting (275 in this case) is required for passage under suspension of the rules. June 25, 2002.

256. HR 4623. Virtual Pornography/Passage. Sensenbrenner, R-Wis., motion to suspend the rules and pass the bill that would forbid producing, trafficking in, or possessing computer images and computer-generated images of minors, or images virtually indistinguishable from minors, engaged in sexually explicit conduct. Motion agreed to 413-8: R 215-1; D 196-7 (ND 146-5, SD 50-2); I 2-0. A two-thirds majority of those present and voting (281 in this case) is required for passage under suspension of the rules. A "yea" was a vote in support of the president's position. June 25, 2002.

257. HR 4846. Silver Coins/Passage. Oxley, R-Ohio, motion to suspend the rules and pass the bill that would allow the U.S. Mint to continue to produce Silver Eagle coins by authorizing the purchase of silver on the open market. It also would require annual and audited reports on the mint's financial position. Motion agreed to 417-1: R 212-1; D 203-0 (ND 152-0, SD 51-0); I 2-0. A two-thirds majority of those present and voting (279 in this case) is required for passage under suspension of the rules. June 25, 2002.

258. HR 4598. Homeland Security Information/Passage. Passage of the bill that would give federal agencies six months to develop procedures for sharing both classified and non-classified information on homeland security threats with law enforcement and other state and local officials. Agencies also would have to share information with the House and Senate Intelligence and Judiciary committees. The bill also would lift prohibitions on the sharing of grand jury, wiretap and foreign intelligence information. Passed 422-2: R 213-0; D 207-2 (ND 154-2, SD 53-0); I 2-0. June 26, 2002.

259. HR 4477. Illicit Sexual Activity/Passage. Sensenbrenner, R-Wis., motion to suspend the rules and pass the bill that would criminalize traveling to the United States or to a foreign country to engage in illicit sexual conduct with a minor. Intent would not have to be proved for individuals traveling abroad and engaging in illicit activity. The bill also would criminalize facilitating or conspiring in such activity. Violations would be punishable for up to 15 years in prison. Motion agreed to 418-8: R 213-1; D 203-7 (ND 152-4, SD 51-3); I 2-0. A two-thirds majority of those present and voting (284 in this case) is required for passage under suspension of the rules. June 26, 2002.

Key

Y	Voted for (yea).	
#	Paired for.	
+	Announced for.	
N	Voted against (nay).	
X	Paired against.	
−	Announced against.	
P	Voted "present."	
C	Voted "present" to avoid possible conflict of interest.	
?	Did not vote or otherwise make a position known.	

Democrats **Republicans**
Independents

	252	253	254	255	256	257	258	259
ALABAMA								
1 *Callahan*	?	?	?	?	?	?	Y	Y
2 *Everett*	+	+	+	Y	Y	Y	Y	Y
3 *Riley*	+	+	+	+	+	Y	Y	Y
4 *Aderholt*	Y	Y	Y	Y	Y	Y	Y	Y
5 Cramer	Y	Y	Y	Y	Y	Y	Y	Y
6 *Bachus*	Y	Y	Y	Y	Y	Y	Y	Y
7 Hilliard	?	?	?	?	?	?	Y	Y
ALASKA								
AL *Young*	Y	Y	Y	Y	Y	Y	Y	Y
ARIZONA								
1 *Flake*	+	Y	Y	Y	Y	Y	Y	Y
2 Pastor	Y	Y	Y	Y	Y	Y	Y	Y
3 *Stump*	Y	Y	Y	Y	Y	Y	Y	Y
4 *Shadegg*	Y	Y	Y	Y	Y	Y	Y	Y
5 *Kolbe*	Y	+	Y	Y	Y	Y	Y	Y
6 *Hayworth*	?	?	?	?	?	?	Y	Y
ARKANSAS								
1 Berry	Y	Y	Y	Y	Y	Y	Y	Y
2 Snyder	Y	Y	Y	Y	Y	Y	Y	Y
3 *Boozman*	Y	Y	Y	Y	Y	Y	Y	Y
4 Ross	Y	Y	Y	Y	Y	Y	Y	Y
CALIFORNIA								
1 Thompson	Y	N	Y	Y	Y	Y	Y	Y
2 *Herger*	Y	Y	Y	Y	Y	Y	Y	Y
3 *Ose*	Y	Y	Y	Y	Y	Y	Y	Y
4 *Doolittle*	Y	Y	Y	Y	Y	Y	Y	Y
5 Matsui	Y	Y	Y	Y	Y	Y	Y	Y
6 Woolsey	Y	Y	Y	Y	Y	Y	Y	Y
7 Miller, George	?	N	Y	Y	Y	Y	Y	Y
8 Pelosi	Y	Y	Y	Y	Y	Y	Y	Y
9 Lee	Y	Y	Y	Y	Y	Y	Y	Y
10 Tauscher	Y	Y	Y	Y	Y	Y	Y	Y
11 *Pombo*	Y	Y	Y	Y	Y	Y	Y	Y
12 Lantos	Y	Y	Y	Y	Y	Y	Y	Y
13 Stark	Y	Y	Y	Y	Y	Y	Y	Y
14 Eshoo	Y	Y	Y	Y	Y	Y	Y	Y
15 Honda	?	Y	Y	Y	Y	Y	Y	Y
16 Lofgren	Y	Y	Y	Y	Y	Y	Y	Y
17 Farr	Y	Y	Y	Y	Y	Y	Y	Y
18 Condit	?	N	Y	Y	Y	Y	Y	Y
19 *Radanovich*	Y	Y	Y	Y	Y	Y	Y	Y
20 Dooley	Y	Y	Y	Y	Y	Y	Y	Y
21 *Thomas*	Y	Y	Y	Y	Y	Y	Y	Y
22 Capps	Y	Y	Y	Y	Y	Y	Y	Y
23 *Gallegly*	Y	Y	Y	Y	Y	Y	Y	Y
24 Sherman	Y	Y	Y	Y	Y	Y	Y	Y
25 *McKeon*	Y	Y	Y	Y	Y	Y	Y	Y
26 Berman	Y	Y	Y	Y	N	Y	Y	Y
27 Schiff	Y	Y	Y	Y	Y	Y	Y	Y
28 *Dreier*	Y	Y	Y	Y	Y	Y	Y	Y
29 Waxman	Y	Y	Y	Y	N	Y	Y	Y
30 Becerra	+	Y	Y	Y	Y	Y	Y	Y
31 Solis	Y	Y	Y	Y	Y	Y	Y	Y
32 Watson	Y	Y	Y	Y	Y	Y	Y	Y
33 Roybal-Allard	Y	Y	Y	Y	Y	Y	Y	Y
34 Napolitano	Y	Y	Y	Y	+	Y	Y	Y
35 Waters	Y	N	Y	Y	Y	Y	Y	Y
36 Harman	Y	Y	Y	Y	Y	Y	Y	Y
37 Millender-McD.	Y	Y	Y	Y	Y	Y	Y	Y
38 Horn	Y	Y	Y	?	Y	Y	Y	Y

	252	253	254	255	256	257	258	259
39 *Royce*	Y	Y	Y	Y	Y	Y	Y	Y
40 *Lewis*	Y	Y	?	Y	Y	Y	Y	Y
41 *Miller, Gary*	Y	Y	Y	Y	Y	Y	Y	Y
42 Baca	Y	Y	Y	Y	Y	Y	Y	Y
43 *Calvert*	Y	Y	Y	Y	Y	Y	Y	Y
44 *Bono*	Y	Y	Y	Y	Y	Y	Y	Y
45 *Rohrabacher*	Y	Y	Y	Y	Y	Y	Y	Y
46 Sanchez	+	+	+	+	+	+	Y	Y
47 *Cox*	Y	Y	Y	Y	Y	Y	Y	Y
48 *Issa*	Y	Y	Y	Y	Y	Y	Y	Y
49 Davis	Y	Y	Y	Y	Y	Y	Y	Y
50 Filner	Y	N	Y	Y	Y	Y	Y	Y
51 *Cunningham*	Y	Y	Y	Y	Y	Y	Y	Y
52 *Hunter*	Y	Y	Y	Y	Y	Y	?	Y
COLORADO								
1 DeGette	?	Y	Y	Y	Y	Y	Y	Y
2 Udall	Y	Y	Y	?	Y	Y	Y	Y
3 *McInnis*	Y	Y	Y	Y	Y	Y	Y	Y
4 *Schaffer*	Y	?	Y	Y	Y	Y	Y	Y
5 *Hefley*	Y	N	N	Y	Y	Y	Y	Y
6 *Tancredo*	Y	P	N	Y	Y	Y	Y	Y
CONNECTICUT								
1 Larson	Y	+	+	Y	Y	Y	Y	Y
2 *Simmons*	?	Y	Y	Y	Y	Y	Y	Y
3 DeLauro	Y	Y	Y	Y	Y	Y	Y	Y
4 *Shays*	Y	Y	Y	Y	Y	Y	Y	Y
5 Maloney	Y	Y	Y	Y	Y	Y	Y	Y
6 *Johnson*	Y	Y	Y	Y	Y	Y	Y	Y
DELAWARE								
AL *Castle*	Y	Y	Y	Y	Y	Y	Y	Y
FLORIDA								
1 *Miller, J.*	Y	Y	Y	Y	Y	Y	Y	Y
2 Boyd	Y	Y	Y	Y	Y	Y	Y	Y
3 Brown	?	Y	Y	Y	Y	Y	Y	Y
4 *Crenshaw*	Y	Y	Y	Y	Y	Y	Y	Y
5 Thurman	Y	Y	Y	Y	Y	Y	Y	Y
6 *Stearns*	Y	Y	N	Y	Y	Y	Y	Y
7 *Mica*	Y	Y	Y	Y	Y	Y	Y	Y
8 *Keller*	Y	Y	Y	Y	Y	Y	Y	Y
9 *Bilirakis*	Y	Y	N	Y	Y	Y	Y	Y
10 *Young*	Y	Y	Y	Y	Y	Y	Y	Y
11 Davis	Y	Y	Y	Y	Y	Y	Y	Y
12 *Putnam*	Y	Y	Y	Y	Y	Y	Y	Y
13 *Miller, D.*	Y	Y	Y	Y	Y	Y	Y	Y
14 *Goss*	Y	Y	Y	Y	Y	Y	Y	Y
15 *Weldon*	Y	Y	Y	Y	Y	Y	Y	Y
16 *Foley*	Y	Y	Y	Y	Y	Y	Y	Y
17 Meek	Y	?	Y	Y	Y	Y	Y	Y
18 *Ros-Lehtinen*	Y	Y	Y	Y	Y	Y	Y	Y
19 Wexler	?	Y	Y	Y	Y	Y	Y	Y
20 Deutsch	Y	Y	Y	Y	Y	Y	Y	Y
21 *Diaz-Balart*	Y	Y	Y	Y	Y	Y	Y	Y
22 *Shaw*	Y	Y	Y	Y	Y	Y	Y	Y
23 Hastings	Y	N	Y	Y	Y	Y	Y	N
GEORGIA								
1 *Kingston*	Y	Y	Y	Y	Y	Y	Y	Y
2 Bishop	Y	Y	Y	Y	Y	Y	Y	Y
3 *Collins*	Y	Y	Y	Y	Y	Y	Y	Y
4 McKinney	Y	Y	Y	Y	Y	Y	Y	Y
5 Lewis	Y	N	Y	Y	Y	Y	Y	Y
6 *Isakson*	Y	Y	Y	Y	Y	Y	Y	Y
7 *Barr*	Y	Y	Y	Y	Y	Y	Y	Y
8 *Chambliss*	Y	Y	Y	Y	Y	Y	Y	Y
9 *Deal*	Y	Y	Y	Y	Y	Y	Y	Y
10 *Norwood*	Y	Y	Y	Y	Y	Y	Y	Y
11 *Linder*	Y	Y	Y	Y	Y	Y	Y	Y
HAWAII								
1 Abercrombie	+	Y	Y	Y	Y	Y	Y	Y
2 Mink	Y	Y	Y	Y	Y	Y	Y	Y
IDAHO								
1 *Otter*	Y	Y	Y	Y	Y	Y	+	Y
2 *Simpson*	Y	Y	Y	Y	Y	Y	Y	Y
ILLINOIS								
1 Rush	Y	Y	Y	Y	Y	Y	Y	Y
2 Jackson	Y	Y	Y	Y	Y	Y	Y	Y
3 Lipinski	Y	Y	Y	Y	Y	Y	Y	Y
4 Gutierrez	Y	Y	Y	Y	Y	Y	Y	Y
5 Blagojevich	?	?	?	?	?	?	Y	Y
6 *Hyde*	?	Y	Y	Y	Y	Y	Y	Y
7 Davis	Y	Y	Y	Y	Y	Y	Y	Y
8 *Crane*	Y	N	Y	Y	Y	Y	Y	Y
9 Schakowsky	Y	Y	Y	Y	Y	Y	Y	Y
10 *Kirk*	Y	Y	Y	Y	Y	Y	Y	Y
11 *Weller*	Y	N	Y	Y	Y	Y	Y	Y
12 Costello	?	N	Y	Y	Y	Y	Y	Y
13 *Biggert*	Y	Y	Y	Y	Y	Y	Y	Y

ND Northern Democrats   SD Southern Democrats

	252	253	254	255	256	257	258	259
14 ***Hastert***								
15 ***Johnson***	Y	Y	Y	Y	Y	Y	Y	Y
16 ***Manzullo***	?	Y	Y	Y	Y	Y	Y	Y
17 Evans	Y	Y	Y	Y	Y	Y	Y	Y
18 ***LaHood***	Y	Y	Y	Y	Y	Y	Y	Y
19 Phelps	Y	Y	Y	Y	Y	Y	Y	Y
20 ***Shimkus***	Y	Y	Y	Y	Y	Y	Y	Y
INDIANA								
1 Visclosky	Y	N	Y	Y	Y	Y	Y	Y
2 ***Pence***	Y	Y	Y	Y	Y	Y	Y	Y
3 Roemer	Y	Y	Y	Y	Y	Y	Y	Y
4 ***Souder***	Y	Y	Y	Y	Y	Y	Y	Y
5 ***Buyer***	?	Y	Y	Y	Y	Y	Y	Y
6 ***Burton***	Y	Y	Y	Y	Y	Y	Y	Y
7 ***Kerns***	Y	Y	Y	Y	Y	Y	Y	Y
8 ***Hostettler***	Y	Y	Y	Y	Y	Y	Y	Y
9 Hill	Y	Y	Y	Y	Y	Y	Y	Y
10 Carson	?	P	Y	Y	Y	Y	Y	Y
IOWA								
1 ***Leach***	Y	Y	Y	Y	Y	Y	Y	?
2 ***Nussle***	Y	Y	Y	Y	Y	Y	Y	Y
3 Boswell	Y	Y	Y	Y	Y	Y	Y	Y
4 ***Ganske***	Y	Y	Y	Y	Y	Y	Y	Y
5 ***Latham***	Y	Y	Y	Y	Y	Y	Y	Y
KANSAS								
1 ***Moran***	Y	Y	Y	Y	Y	Y	Y	Y
2 ***Ryun***	Y	Y	Y	Y	Y	Y	Y	Y
3 Moore	Y	N	Y	Y	Y	Y	Y	Y
4 ***Tiahrt***	Y	Y	Y	Y	Y	Y	Y	Y
KENTUCKY								
1 ***Whitfield***	Y	Y	Y	Y	Y	Y	Y	Y
2 ***Lewis***	Y	Y	Y	Y	Y	Y	Y	Y
3 ***Northup***	Y	Y	Y	Y	Y	Y	?	?
4 Lucas	Y	Y	Y	Y	Y	Y	Y	Y
5 ***Rogers***	Y	Y	Y	Y	Y	Y	Y	Y
6 ***Fletcher***	Y	Y	Y	Y	Y	Y	Y	Y
LOUISIANA								
1 ***Vitter***	Y	Y	Y	Y	Y	Y	Y	Y
2 Jefferson	?	Y	Y	Y	Y	Y	Y	Y
3 ***Tauzin***	Y	Y	Y	Y	Y	Y	Y	Y
4 ***McCrery***	Y	Y	Y	Y	Y	Y	Y	Y
5 ***Cooksey***	Y	Y	Y	Y	Y	Y	Y	Y
6 ***Baker***	Y	Y	Y	Y	Y	Y	Y	Y
7 John	Y	Y	Y	Y	Y	Y	Y	Y
MAINE								
1 Allen	Y	Y	Y	Y	Y	Y	Y	Y
2 Baldacci	Y	Y	Y	Y	Y	Y	Y	Y
MARYLAND								
1 ***Gilchrest***	Y	Y	Y	Y	Y	Y	Y	Y
2 ***Ehrlich***	Y	Y	Y	Y	Y	Y	Y	Y
3 Cardin	Y	Y	Y	Y	Y	Y	Y	Y
4 Wynn	Y	Y	Y	Y	Y	Y	Y	Y
5 Hoyer	Y	Y	Y	Y	Y	Y	Y	Y
6 ***Bartlett***	Y	Y	Y	Y	Y	Y	Y	Y
7 Cummings	Y	Y	Y	Y	Y	Y	Y	Y
8 ***Morella***	Y	Y	Y	Y	Y	Y	Y	Y
MASSACHUSETTS								
1 Olver	Y	N	Y	Y	Y	Y	Y	N
2 Neal	Y	Y	Y	Y	Y	Y	Y	Y
3 McGovern	Y	Y	Y	Y	Y	Y	Y	Y
4 Frank	Y	Y	Y	Y	N	Y	Y	N
5 Meehan	Y	Y	Y	Y	Y	Y	Y	Y
6 Tierney	Y	Y	Y	Y	Y	Y	Y	Y
7 Markey	Y	Y	Y	Y	Y	Y	Y	Y
8 Capuano	Y	Y	Y	Y	Y	Y	Y	Y
9 Lynch	Y	Y	Y	Y	Y	Y	Y	Y
10 Delahunt	Y	Y	Y	Y	Y	Y	N	Y
MICHIGAN								
1 Stupak	Y	N	Y	Y	Y	Y	Y	Y
2 ***Hoekstra***	Y	Y	Y	Y	Y	Y	Y	Y
3 ***Ehlers***	Y	Y	Y	Y	Y	Y	Y	Y
4 ***Camp***	?	Y	Y	Y	Y	Y	Y	Y
5 Barcia	Y	Y	Y	Y	Y	Y	Y	Y
6 ***Upton***	Y	Y	Y	Y	Y	Y	Y	Y
7 ***Smith***	Y	Y	Y	Y	Y	?	?	?
8 ***Rogers***	Y	Y	Y	Y	Y	Y	Y	Y
9 Kildee	Y	Y	Y	Y	Y	Y	Y	Y
10 Bonior	+	?	?	Y	Y	Y	Y	Y
11 ***Knollenberg***	Y	Y	Y	Y	Y	Y	Y	Y
12 Levin	Y	Y	Y	Y	Y	Y	Y	Y
13 Rivers	Y	Y	Y	Y	Y	Y	Y	Y
14 Conyers	?	?	?	Y	N	Y	Y	Y
15 Kilpatrick	+	Y	Y	Y	Y	Y	Y	Y
16 Dingell	Y	Y	Y	Y	Y	Y	Y	Y

	252	253	254	255	256	257	258	259
MINNESOTA								
1 ***Gutknecht***	Y	N	Y	Y	Y	Y	Y	Y
2 ***Kennedy***	Y	N	Y	Y	Y	Y	Y	Y
3 ***Ramstad***	Y	N	Y	Y	Y	Y	Y	Y
4 McCollum	Y	Y	Y	Y	Y	Y	Y	Y
5 Sabo	Y	N	Y	Y	Y	Y	Y	Y
6 Luther	Y	Y	Y	Y	Y	Y	Y	Y
7 Peterson	?	?	?	?	Y	Y	Y	Y
8 Oberstar	Y	N	Y	Y	Y	Y	Y	Y
MISSISSIPPI								
1 ***Wicker***	Y	Y	Y	Y	Y	Y	Y	Y
2 Thompson	Y	N	Y	Y	Y	Y	Y	Y
3 ***Pickering***	Y	Y	Y	Y	Y	Y	Y	Y
4 Shows	Y	Y	Y	Y	Y	Y	Y	Y
5 Taylor	Y	N	Y	Y	Y	Y	Y	Y
MISSOURI								
1 Clay	Y	N	Y	Y	Y	Y	Y	Y
2 ***Akin***	Y	Y	Y	Y	Y	Y	Y	Y
3 Gephardt	Y	Y	Y	Y	Y	Y	Y	Y
4 Skelton	Y	Y	Y	Y	Y	Y	Y	Y
5 McCarthy	Y	Y	Y	Y	Y	Y	Y	Y
6 ***Graves***	Y	Y	Y	Y	Y	Y	Y	Y
7 ***Blunt***	Y	Y	Y	Y	Y	Y	Y	Y
8 ***Emerson***	Y	Y	Y	Y	Y	Y	Y	Y
9 ***Hulshof***	Y	Y	Y	Y	Y	Y	Y	Y
MONTANA								
AL ***Rehberg***	Y	Y	Y	Y	Y	Y	Y	Y
NEBRASKA								
1 ***Bereuter***	Y	Y	Y	Y	Y	Y	Y	Y
2 ***Terry***	Y	Y	Y	Y	Y	Y	Y	Y
3 ***Osborne***	Y	Y	Y	Y	Y	Y	Y	Y
NEVADA								
1 Berkley	Y	Y	Y	Y	Y	Y	Y	Y
2 ***Gibbons***	Y	Y	Y	Y	Y	Y	Y	Y
NEW HAMPSHIRE								
1 ***Sununu***	Y	Y	Y	Y	Y	Y	Y	Y
2 ***Bass***	Y	Y	Y	Y	Y	Y	Y	Y
NEW JERSEY								
1 Andrews	Y	Y	Y	Y	Y	Y	Y	Y
2 ***LoBiondo***	Y	N	Y	Y	Y	Y	Y	Y
3 ***Saxton***	Y	Y	Y	Y	Y	Y	Y	Y
4 ***Smith***	Y	Y	Y	Y	Y	Y	Y	Y
5 ***Roukema***	?	Y	Y	Y	Y	Y	?	?
6 Pallone	Y	Y	Y	Y	Y	Y	Y	Y
7 ***Ferguson***	Y	Y	Y	Y	Y	Y	Y	Y
8 Pascrell	Y	Y	Y	Y	Y	Y	Y	Y
9 Rothman	Y	Y	Y	Y	Y	Y	Y	Y
10 Payne	Y	Y	Y	Y	Y	Y	Y	Y
11 ***Frelinghuysen***	Y	Y	Y	Y	Y	Y	Y	Y
12 Holt	Y	N	Y	Y	Y	Y	Y	Y
13 Menendez	Y	Y	Y	Y	Y	Y	Y	Y
NEW MEXICO								
1 ***Wilson***	Y	Y	Y	Y	Y	Y	Y	Y
2 ***Skeen***	Y	Y	Y	Y	Y	Y	Y	Y
3 Udall	Y	N	Y	Y	Y	Y	Y	Y
NEW YORK								
1 ***Grucci***	Y	Y	Y	Y	Y	Y	Y	Y
2 Israel	+	Y	Y	Y	Y	Y	Y	Y
3 ***King***	Y	Y	Y	Y	Y	Y	Y	Y
4 McCarthy	Y	Y	Y	?	Y	Y	Y	Y
5 Ackerman	Y	Y	Y	Y	P	Y	Y	Y
6 Meeks	?	?	?	?	?	?	Y	Y
7 Crowley	Y	Y	Y	Y	Y	Y	Y	Y
8 Nadler	?	Y	Y	N	N	Y	Y	N
9 Weiner	?	Y	Y	Y	Y	?	Y	Y
10 Towns	Y	Y	Y	Y	Y	Y	Y	Y
11 Owens	+	Y	Y	Y	Y	Y	Y	Y
12 Velázquez	Y	Y	Y	Y	Y	Y	Y	Y
13 ***Fossella***	+	?	?	?	Y	Y	Y	Y
14 Maloney	Y	Y	Y	Y	Y	Y	Y	Y
15 Rangel	Y	Y	Y	Y	Y	Y	Y	N
16 Serrano	Y	Y	Y	Y	Y	Y	Y	Y
17 Engel	Y	Y	Y	Y	Y	Y	Y	Y
18 Lowey	Y	Y	Y	Y	Y	Y	Y	Y
19 ***Kelly***	Y	Y	Y	Y	Y	Y	Y	Y
20 ***Gilman***	Y	Y	Y	Y	Y	Y	Y	Y
21 McNulty	Y	N	Y	Y	Y	Y	Y	Y
22 ***Sweeney***	Y	N	Y	Y	Y	Y	+	?
23 ***Boehlert***	Y	Y	Y	Y	Y	Y	Y	Y
24 ***McHugh***	Y	Y	Y	Y	Y	Y	Y	Y
25 ***Walsh***	Y	Y	Y	Y	Y	Y	Y	Y
26 Hinchey	Y	Y	Y	Y	Y	Y	Y	Y
27 ***Reynolds***	Y	Y	Y	Y	Y	Y	Y	Y
28 Slaughter	Y	Y	Y	Y	Y	Y	Y	Y
29 LaFalce	Y	Y	Y	?	Y	Y	Y	Y

	252	253	254	255	256	257	258	259
30 ***Quinn***	Y	Y	Y	Y	Y	Y	Y	Y
31 ***Houghton***	?	Y	Y	Y	Y	Y	Y	Y
NORTH CAROLINA								
1 Clayton	Y	Y	Y	Y	Y	Y	Y	Y
2 Etheridge	Y	Y	Y	Y	Y	Y	Y	Y
3 ***Jones***	Y	Y	Y	Y	Y	Y	Y	Y
4 Price	Y	Y	Y	Y	Y	Y	Y	Y
5 ***Burr***	Y	Y	Y	Y	Y	Y	Y	Y
6 ***Coble***	Y	Y	Y	Y	Y	Y	Y	Y
7 McIntyre	Y	Y	Y	Y	Y	Y	Y	Y
8 ***Hayes***	Y	Y	Y	Y	Y	Y	Y	Y
9 ***Myrick***	Y	Y	Y	Y	Y	Y	Y	Y
10 ***Ballenger***	Y	Y	Y	Y	Y	Y	Y	Y
11 ***Taylor***	Y	Y	Y	Y	Y	Y	Y	Y
12 Watt	Y	Y	Y	N	N	Y	Y	N
NORTH DAKOTA								
AL Pomeroy	+	Y	Y	Y	Y	Y	Y	Y
OHIO								
1 ***Chabot***	Y	Y	Y	Y	Y	Y	Y	Y
2 ***Portman***	Y	Y	Y	Y	Y	Y	Y	Y
3 Hall	Y	Y	Y	Y	Y	Y	Y	Y
4 ***Oxley***	Y	Y	Y	Y	Y	Y	Y	Y
5 ***Gillmor***	Y	Y	Y	Y	Y	Y	Y	Y
6 Strickland	Y	N	Y	Y	Y	Y	Y	Y
7 ***Hobson***	Y	Y	Y	Y	Y	Y	Y	Y
8 ***Boehner***	?	Y	Y	Y	Y	Y	Y	Y
9 Kaptur	Y	Y	Y	Y	Y	Y	Y	Y
10 Kucinich	Y	N	Y	Y	Y	Y	N	Y
11 Jones	?	Y	Y	Y	Y	Y	Y	Y
12 ***Tiberi***	Y	Y	Y	Y	Y	Y	Y	Y
13 Brown	Y	Y	Y	Y	Y	Y	Y	Y
14 Sawyer	Y	Y	Y	Y	Y	Y	Y	Y
15 ***Pryce***	?	?	?	?	Y	Y	Y	Y
16 ***Regula***	Y	Y	Y	Y	Y	Y	Y	Y
17 Traficant	?	?	?	?	?	?	?	?
18 ***Ney***	Y	Y	Y	Y	Y	Y	Y	Y
19 ***LaTourette***	Y	Y	Y	Y	Y	Y	Y	Y
OKLAHOMA								
1 ***Sullivan***	Y	Y	Y	Y	Y	Y	Y	Y
2 Carson	Y	Y	Y	Y	Y	?	Y	Y
3 ***Watkins***	Y	Y	Y	Y	Y	Y	Y	Y
4 ***Watts***	+	?	?	?	?	?	+	+
5 ***Istook***	Y	Y	Y	Y	Y	Y	Y	Y
6 ***Lucas***	Y	Y	Y	?	Y	Y	Y	Y
OREGON								
1 Wu	Y	N	Y	Y	Y	Y	Y	Y
2 ***Walden***	Y	Y	Y	Y	Y	Y	Y	Y
3 Blumenauer	Y	Y	Y	Y	Y	Y	Y	Y
4 DeFazio	Y	N	Y	Y	Y	Y	Y	Y
5 Hooley	Y	Y	Y	Y	Y	Y	Y	Y
PENNSYLVANIA								
1 Brady	Y	N	Y	Y	Y	Y	Y	Y
2 Fattah	Y	Y	Y	Y	Y	Y	Y	Y
3 Borski	?	N	Y	Y	Y	Y	Y	Y
4 ***Hart***	Y	N	Y	Y	Y	Y	Y	Y
5 ***Peterson***	?	Y	Y	Y	Y	Y	Y	Y
6 Holden	Y	Y	Y	Y	Y	Y	Y	Y
7 ***Weldon***	Y	Y	Y	Y	Y	Y	Y	Y
8 ***Greenwood***	Y	Y	Y	Y	Y	Y	Y	+
9 ***Shuster, Bill***	Y	Y	Y	Y	Y	Y	Y	Y
10 ***Sherwood***	Y	Y	Y	Y	Y	Y	Y	Y
11 Kanjorski	Y	Y	Y	Y	Y	Y	Y	Y
12 Murtha	Y	Y	Y	Y	Y	Y	Y	Y
13 Hoeffel	Y	Y	Y	Y	Y	Y	Y	Y
14 Coyne	Y	Y	Y	Y	Y	Y	Y	Y
15 ***Toomey***	Y	Y	Y	Y	Y	Y	Y	Y
16 ***Pitts***	Y	Y	Y	Y	Y	Y	Y	Y
17 ***Gekas***	Y	Y	Y	Y	Y	?	Y	Y
18 Doyle	Y	Y	Y	Y	Y	Y	Y	Y
19 ***Platts***	Y	Y	Y	Y	Y	Y	Y	Y
20 Mascara	Y	Y	Y	Y	Y	Y	Y	Y
21 ***English***	Y	N	Y	Y	Y	Y	Y	Y
RHODE ISLAND								
1 Kennedy	Y	Y	?	?	Y	Y	Y	Y
2 Langevin	Y	Y	Y	Y	Y	Y	Y	Y
SOUTH CAROLINA								
1 ***Brown***	Y	Y	Y	Y	Y	Y	Y	Y
2 ***Wilson***	Y	Y	Y	Y	Y	Y	Y	Y
3 ***Graham***	Y	Y	Y	Y	Y	Y	Y	Y
4 ***DeMint***	Y	Y	Y	Y	Y	Y	Y	Y
5 Spratt	Y	Y	Y	Y	Y	Y	Y	Y
6 Clyburn	Y	Y	Y	?	Y	Y	Y	Y
SOUTH DAKOTA								
AL ***Thune***	Y	Y	Y	Y	Y	Y	Y	Y

	252	253	254	255	256	257	258	259
TENNESSEE								
1 ***Jenkins***	?	?	?	?	?	?	Y	Y
2 ***Duncan***	Y	Y	N	Y	Y	Y	Y	Y
3 ***Wamp***	Y	Y	Y	Y	Y	Y	Y	Y
4 ***Hilleary***	?	Y	Y	Y	Y	Y	Y	Y
5 Clement	+	Y	Y	Y	Y	Y	Y	Y
6 Gordon	?	Y	Y	Y	Y	Y	Y	Y
7 ***Bryant***	?	Y	Y	Y	Y	Y	Y	Y
8 Tanner	Y	Y	Y	Y	Y	Y	Y	Y
9 Ford	Y	Y	Y	Y	Y	Y	Y	Y
TEXAS								
1 Sandlin	Y	Y	Y	Y	Y	Y	Y	Y
2 Turner	Y	Y	Y	Y	Y	Y	Y	Y
3 ***Johnson, Sam***	Y	Y	Y	Y	Y	Y	Y	Y
4 Hall	Y	Y	Y	Y	Y	Y	Y	Y
5 ***Sessions***	Y	Y	Y	Y	Y	Y	Y	Y
6 ***Barton***	Y	Y	Y	Y	Y	Y	Y	Y
7 ***Culberson***	Y	Y	Y	Y	Y	Y	Y	Y
8 ***Brady***	Y	Y	Y	Y	Y	Y	Y	Y
9 Lampson	Y	Y	Y	Y	Y	Y	Y	Y
10 Doggett	Y	Y	Y	Y	Y	Y	Y	Y
11 Edwards	Y	Y	Y	Y	Y	Y	Y	Y
12 ***Granger***	Y	Y	Y	Y	Y	N	Y	Y
13 ***Thornberry***	Y	Y	Y	Y	Y	Y	Y	Y
14 ***Paul***	Y	Y	Y	Y	N	Y	Y	N
15 Hinojosa	?	?	?	?	?	?	Y	Y
16 Reyes	Y	Y	Y	Y	Y	Y	?	Y
17 Stenholm	Y	Y	Y	Y	Y	Y	Y	Y
18 Jackson-Lee	Y	Y	Y	Y	Y	Y	Y	Y
19 ***Combest***	Y	Y	Y	Y	Y	Y	Y	Y
20 Gonzalez	Y	Y	Y	Y	Y	Y	Y	Y
21 ***Smith***	Y	Y	Y	Y	Y	Y	Y	Y
22 ***DeLay***	Y	Y	Y	Y	Y	Y	Y	Y
23 ***Bonilla***	Y	Y	Y	Y	Y	Y	Y	Y
24 Frost	Y	Y	Y	Y	Y	Y	Y	Y
25 Bentsen	Y	Y	Y	Y	Y	Y	Y	Y
26 ***Armey***	Y	Y	Y	Y	Y	Y	Y	Y
27 Ortiz	Y	Y	Y	Y	Y	Y	Y	Y
28 Rodriguez	Y	Y	Y	Y	Y	Y	Y	Y
29 Green	Y	Y	Y	Y	Y	Y	Y	Y
30 Johnson, E.B.	Y	Y	Y	Y	Y	Y	Y	Y
UTAH								
1 ***Hansen***	?	Y	Y	Y	Y	Y	Y	Y
2 Matheson	Y	Y	Y	Y	Y	Y	Y	Y
3 ***Cannon***	Y	Y	Y	Y	Y	Y	Y	Y
VERMONT								
AL *Sanders*	?	Y	Y	Y	Y	Y	Y	Y
VIRGINIA								
1 ***Davis, Jo Ann***	Y	Y	N	Y	Y	Y	Y	Y
2 ***Schrock***	Y	Y	Y	Y	Y	Y	Y	Y
3 Scott	Y	Y	Y	N	N	Y	Y	N
4 ***Forbes***	Y	Y	Y	Y	Y	Y	Y	Y
5 *Goode*	Y	Y	N	Y	Y	Y	Y	Y
6 ***Goodlatte***	Y	Y	Y	Y	Y	Y	Y	Y
7 ***Cantor***	Y	Y	Y	Y	Y	Y	Y	Y
8 Moran	Y	Y	Y	Y	Y	Y	Y	Y
9 Boucher	Y	Y	Y	Y	Y	Y	Y	Y
10 ***Wolf***	Y	Y	Y	Y	Y	Y	Y	Y
11 ***Davis, T.***	Y	Y	Y	Y	Y	Y	Y	Y
WASHINGTON								
1 Inslee	Y	Y	Y	Y	Y	Y	Y	Y
2 Larsen	Y	N	Y	Y	Y	Y	Y	Y
3 Baird	Y	N	Y	Y	Y	Y	Y	Y
4 ***Hastings***	Y	Y	Y	Y	Y	Y	Y	Y
5 ***Nethercutt***	?	Y	Y	Y	Y	Y	Y	Y
6 Dicks	Y	Y	Y	Y	Y	Y	Y	Y
7 McDermott	Y	N	Y	Y	Y	Y	Y	Y
8 ***Dunn***	Y	Y	Y	Y	Y	Y	Y	Y
9 Smith	Y	Y	Y	Y	Y	Y	Y	Y
WEST VIRGINIA								
1 Mollohan	Y	Y	Y	Y	Y	Y	Y	Y
2 ***Capito***	Y	Y	Y	Y	Y	Y	Y	Y
3 Rahall	Y	Y	Y	Y	Y	Y	Y	Y
WISCONSIN								
1 ***Ryan***	Y	Y	Y	Y	Y	Y	Y	Y
2 Baldwin	Y	N	Y	Y	Y	Y	Y	Y
3 Kind	Y	Y	Y	Y	Y	Y	Y	Y
4 Kleczka	+	Y	Y	Y	Y	Y	Y	Y
5 Barrett	Y	Y	Y	Y	Y	Y	Y	Y
6 ***Petri***	Y	Y	Y	Y	Y	Y	Y	Y
7 Obey	Y	Y	Y	Y	Y	Y	Y	Y
8 ***Green***	Y	Y	Y	Y	Y	Y	Y	Y
9 ***Sensenbrenner***	Y	Y	Y	Y	Y	Y	Y	Y
WYOMING								
AL ***Cubin***	Y	Y	Y	Y	Y	Y	Y	Y

Southern states - Ala., Ark., Fla., Ga., Ky., La., Miss., N.C., Okla., S.C., Tenn., Texas, Va.

Key

Y	Voted for (yea).
#	Paired for.
+	Announced for.
N	Voted against (nay).
X	Paired against.
−	Announced against.
P	Voted "present."
C	Voted "present" to avoid possible conflict of interest.
?	Did not vote or otherwise make a position known.

Democrats ● **Republicans**
Independents

260. HR 4070. Social Security Fraud/Passage. Shaw, R-Fla., motion to suspend the rules and pass the bill that would require the Social Security Administration to reissue benefits when a "representative payee," either an individual or an organization, misuses those funds. Non-governmental organizations serving as representative payees would have to be bonded and licensed if possible in their state of residence; convicted felons would be barred from serving as representatives. A representative payee misusing benefits would be liable for the funds and subject to a $5,000 fine per violation plus twice the amount of misused benefits. Other anti-fraud provisions include fines for individuals who fail to notify the Social Security Administration of circumstances that could affect the amount of benefits received. Motion agreed to 425-0: R 214-0; D 209-0 (ND 156-0, SD 53-0); I 2-0. A two-thirds majority of those present and voting (284 in this case) is required for passage under suspension of the rules. June 26, 2002.

261. Procedural Motion/Journal. Approval of the House Journal of Tuesday, June 25, 2002. Approved 369-41: R 191-13; D 176-28 (ND 128-23, SD 48-5); I 2-0. June 26, 2002.

262. Procedural Motion/Adjourn. Hastings, D-Fla., motion to adjourn. Motion rejected 45-378: R 3-212; D 41-165 (ND 30-123, SD 11-42); I 1-1. June 26, 2002.

263. Procedural Motion/Adjourn. Hastings, D-Fla., motion to adjourn. Motion rejected 40-384: R 1-217; D 38-166 (ND 25-126, SD 13-40); I 1-1. June 26, 2002.

264. HR 3009. Andean Trade/Expanded Conference. Adoption of the rule (H Res 450) that would request a conference with the Senate on the bill that would extend through 2006 the Andean Trade Preference Act. The rule would expand the scope of the conference to include amended House positions on fast-track trade authority, extension of Trade Adjustment Assistance and other trade legislation. Adopted 216-215: R 205-14; D 11-199 (ND 3-153, SD 8-46); I 0-2. June 26, 2002.

265. HR 3764. Securities and Exchange Commission/Passage. Oxley, R-Ohio, motion to suspend the rules and pass the bill that would authorize $776 million for fiscal 2003 activities of the Securities and Exchange Commission, including at least $134 million for the commission's corporate finance division and chief accountant, $326 million for its enforcement division, and $76 million to raise employee compensation. Motion agreed to 422-4: R 213-3; D 207-1 (ND 153-1, SD 54-0); I 2-0. A two-thirds majority of those present and voting (284 in this case) is required for passage under suspension of the rules. June 26, 2002.

266. HR 3180. School Compact Consent/Passage. Sensenbrenner, R-Wis., motion to suspend the rules and pass the bill that would give congressional consent to two school districts in the New Hampshire-Vermont Interstate School Compact to change the way they vote on bond initiatives. Motion agreed to 425-0: R 216-0; D 207-0 (ND 154-0, SD 53-0); I 2-0. A two-thirds majority of those present and voting (284 in this case) is required for passage under suspension of the rules. June 26, 2002.

	260	261	262	263	264	265	266
ALABAMA							
1 *Callahan*	Y	Y	N	N	Y	Y	Y
2 *Everett*	Y	Y	N	N	Y	Y	Y
3 *Riley*	Y	Y	?	N	Y	Y	Y
4 *Aderholt*	Y	N	N	N	Y	Y	Y
5 Cramer	Y	Y	N	N	Y	Y	Y
6 *Bachus*	Y	Y	N	N	Y	Y	Y
7 Hilliard	Y	N	Y	N	N	Y	Y
ALASKA							
AL *Young*	Y	Y	?	N	Y	Y	Y
ARIZONA							
1 *Flake*	Y	Y	N	N	Y	N	Y
2 Pastor	Y	Y	N	?	N	Y	Y
3 *Stump*	Y	Y	N	N	Y	Y	Y
4 *Shadegg*	Y	Y	N	N	Y	Y	Y
5 *Kolbe*	Y	Y	N	N	Y	Y	Y
6 *Hayworth*	Y	Y	N	N	Y	Y	Y
ARKANSAS							
1 Berry	Y	Y	Y	Y	N	Y	Y
2 Snyder	Y	Y	N	N	Y	Y	Y
3 *Boozman*	Y	Y	N	N	Y	Y	Y
4 Ross	Y	Y	N	N	N	Y	Y
CALIFORNIA							
1 Thompson	Y	N	N	N	N	Y	Y
2 *Herger*	Y	Y	N	N	Y	Y	?
3 *Ose*	Y	Y	N	N	Y	Y	Y
4 *Doolittle*	Y	Y	N	N	Y	Y	Y
5 Matsui	Y	Y	N	N	N	Y	Y
6 Woolsey	Y	Y	N	N	N	Y	Y
7 Miller, George	Y	N	N	N	N	Y	Y
8 Pelosi	Y	Y	Y	N	Y	N	Y
9 Lee	Y	Y	N	N	N	Y	Y
10 Tauscher	Y	Y	N	N	N	Y	Y
11 *Pombo*	Y	Y	N	Y	Y	Y	Y
12 Lantos	Y	Y	N	N	N	Y	Y
13 Stark	Y	Y	N	?	N	Y	Y
14 Eshoo	Y	Y	N	N	N	Y	Y
15 Honda	Y	Y	N	N	N	Y	Y
16 Lofgren	Y	Y	N	N	N	Y	Y
17 Farr	Y	Y	Y	N	Y	N	Y
18 Condit	Y	Y	N	N	N	Y	Y
19 *Radanovich*	Y	?	N	N	Y	Y	Y
20 Dooley	Y	Y	N	N	N	Y	Y
21 *Thomas*	Y	Y	N	N	Y	Y	Y
22 Capps	Y	Y	N	N	N	Y	Y
23 *Gallegly*	Y	?	N	N	Y	Y	Y
24 Sherman	Y	Y	N	N	N	Y	Y
25 *McKeon*	Y	Y	N	N	Y	Y	Y
26 Berman	Y	Y	N	N	N	Y	Y
27 Schiff	Y	Y	N	N	N	Y	Y
28 *Dreier*	Y	Y	N	N	Y	Y	Y
29 Waxman	Y	Y	Y	N	N	?	?
30 Becerra	Y	Y	N	N	N	Y	Y
31 Solis	Y	Y	N	N	N	Y	Y
32 Watson	Y	Y	Y	N	N	Y	Y
33 Roybal-Allard	Y	Y	N	N	N	Y	Y
34 Napolitano	Y	Y	N	N	N	Y	Y
35 Waters	Y	N	Y	N	N	Y	Y
36 Harman	Y	Y	N	N	N	Y	Y
37 Millender-McD.	Y	Y	N	N	N	Y	Y
38 *Horn*	Y	Y	N	N	Y	Y	Y
39 *Royce*	Y	Y	N	N	Y	Y	Y
40 *Lewis*	Y	Y	N	N	Y	Y	Y
41 *Miller, Gary*	Y	Y	N	N	Y	Y	Y
42 Baca	Y	Y	N	N	N	Y	Y
43 *Calvert*	Y	Y	N	N	Y	Y	Y
44 *Bono*	Y	Y	N	N	Y	Y	Y
45 *Rohrabacher*	Y	Y	N	N	Y	Y	Y
46 Sanchez	Y	Y	Y	N	N	N	Y
47 *Cox*	Y	Y	N	N	Y	Y	Y
48 *Issa*	Y	Y	N	N	Y	Y	Y
49 Davis	Y	Y	N	N	N	Y	Y
50 Filner	Y	N	N	Y	N	Y	Y
51 *Cunningham*	Y	Y	N	N	Y	Y	Y
52 *Hunter*	Y	Y	N	N	Y	Y	Y
COLORADO							
1 DeGette	Y	Y	N	N	N	Y	Y
2 Udall	Y	N	N	N	N	Y	Y
3 *McInnis*	Y	N	N	N	Y	Y	Y
4 *Schaffer*	Y	N	N	N	Y	Y	Y
5 *Hefley*	Y	N	N	N	Y	Y	Y
6 *Tancredo*	Y	P	N	N	Y	Y	Y
CONNECTICUT							
1 Larson	Y	Y	N	N	N	Y	Y
2 *Simmons*	Y	Y	Y	N	N	?	Y
3 DeLauro	Y	Y	N	N	N	Y	Y
4 *Shays*	Y	Y	N	Y	?	?	Y
5 Maloney	Y	Y	N	N	N	Y	Y
6 *Johnson*	Y	Y	N	N	Y	Y	Y
DELAWARE							
AL *Castle*	Y	Y	N	N	Y	Y	Y
FLORIDA							
1 *Miller, J.*	Y	Y	N	N	Y	Y	Y
2 Boyd	Y	Y	N	N	N	Y	Y
3 Brown	Y	Y	Y	N	N	Y	Y
4 *Crenshaw*	Y	Y	N	N	Y	Y	Y
5 Thurman	Y	Y	N	N	N	Y	Y
6 *Stearns*	Y	Y	N	N	Y	Y	Y
7 *Mica*	Y	Y	N	N	Y	Y	Y
8 *Keller*	Y	Y	N	N	Y	Y	Y
9 *Bilirakis*	Y	Y	N	N	Y	Y	Y
10 *Young*	Y	Y	N	N	Y	Y	Y
11 Davis	Y	Y	N	N	N	Y	Y
12 *Putnam*	Y	Y	N	N	Y	Y	Y
13 *Miller, D.*	Y	Y	N	N	Y	Y	Y
14 *Goss*	Y	Y	N	N	Y	Y	Y
15 *Weldon*	Y	Y	N	N	Y	Y	Y
16 *Foley*	Y	Y	N	N	Y	Y	Y
17 Meek	Y	?	Y	Y	N	Y	Y
18 *Ros-Lehtinen*	Y	Y	N	N	Y	Y	Y
19 Wexler	Y	Y	N	N	N	Y	Y
20 Deutsch	Y	Y	N	N	N	Y	Y
21 *Diaz-Balart*	Y	Y	N	N	Y	Y	Y
22 *Shaw*	Y	Y	N	N	Y	Y	Y
23 Hastings	Y	Y	Y	Y	N	Y	Y
GEORGIA							
1 *Kingston*	Y	Y	N	N	Y	Y	Y
2 Bishop	Y	Y	Y	N	Y	Y	Y
3 *Collins*	Y	Y	N	N	Y	Y	Y
4 McKinney	Y	Y	N	N	N	Y	Y
5 Lewis	Y	Y	N	N	N	Y	Y
6 *Isakson*	Y	Y	N	N	Y	Y	Y
7 *Barr*	Y	Y	N	N	Y	Y	Y
8 *Chambliss*	Y	Y	N	N	Y	Y	Y
9 *Deal*	Y	Y	N	N	Y	Y	Y
10 *Norwood*	Y	Y	N	N	N	Y	Y
11 *Linder*	Y	Y	N	N	Y	Y	Y
HAWAII							
1 Abercrombie	Y	Y	N	N	N	Y	Y
2 Mink	Y	Y	Y	N	N	Y	Y
IDAHO							
1 *Otter*	Y	Y	N	N	Y	Y	Y
2 *Simpson*	Y	Y	N	N	Y	Y	Y
ILLINOIS							
1 Rush	Y	Y	N	N	N	Y	Y
2 Jackson	Y	Y	Y	N	N	Y	Y
3 Lipinski	Y	Y	N	N	N	Y	Y
4 Gutierrez	Y	?	N	N	N	Y	Y
5 Blagojevich	Y	Y	N	N	N	Y	Y
6 *Hyde*	Y	Y	N	N	Y	Y	Y
7 Davis	Y	Y	N	N	N	Y	Y
8 *Crane*	Y	N	N	N	Y	Y	Y
9 Schakowsky	Y	Y	N	N	N	Y	Y
10 *Kirk*	Y	Y	N	N	Y	Y	Y
11 *Weller*	Y	N	N	N	Y	Y	Y
12 Costello	Y	Y	N	N	N	Y	Y
13 *Biggert*	Y	Y	N	N	Y	Y	Y

ND Northern Democrats   SD Southern Democrats

	260	261	262	263	264	265	266
14 ***Hastert***					Y		
15 ***Johnson***	Y	Y	N	N	Y	Y	Y
16 ***Manzullo***	Y	Y	N	N	Y	Y	Y
17 Evans	Y	Y	Y	Y	N	Y	?
18 ***LaHood***	Y	Y	N	N	Y	Y	Y
19 Phelps	Y	Y	N	N	N	Y	Y
20 ***Shimkus***	Y	Y	N	N	Y	Y	Y
INDIANA							
1 Visclosky	Y	Y	N	N	N	Y	Y
2 ***Pence***	Y	Y	N	N	Y	Y	Y
3 Roemer	Y	Y	N	N	N	Y	Y
4 ***Souder***	Y	Y	N	N	Y	N	Y
5 ***Buyer***	Y	?	N	N	Y	Y	Y
6 ***Burton***	Y	Y	N	N	Y	Y	Y
7 ***Kerns***	Y	Y	N	N	Y	Y	Y
8 ***Hostettler***	Y	Y	N	N	Y	Y	Y
9 Hill	Y	Y	N	N	Y	Y	Y
10 Carson	Y	?	N	Y	N	Y	Y
IOWA							
1 ***Leach***	?	Y	N	N	Y	Y	Y
2 ***Nussle***	Y	Y	N	?	Y	Y	Y
3 Boswell	Y	Y	N	N	N	Y	Y
4 ***Ganske***	Y	Y	N	N	Y	Y	Y
5 ***Latham***	Y	N	N	N	Y	Y	Y
KANSAS							
1 ***Moran***	Y	Y	N	N	Y	Y	Y
2 ***Ryun***	Y	Y	N	N	Y	Y	Y
3 Moore	Y	N	N	N	N	Y	Y
4 ***Tiahrt***	Y	?	N	N	Y	Y	Y
KENTUCKY							
1 ***Whitfield***	Y	Y	N	N	Y	Y	Y
2 ***Lewis***	Y	Y	N	N	Y	Y	Y
3 ***Northup***	?	?	N	N	Y	Y	Y
4 Lucas	Y	Y	N	N	Y	Y	Y
5 ***Rogers***	Y	Y	N	N	Y	Y	Y
6 ***Fletcher***	Y	Y	N	N	Y	Y	Y
LOUISIANA							
1 ***Vitter***	Y	Y	N	N	Y	Y	Y
2 Jefferson	Y	Y	N	?	N	Y	Y
3 ***Tauzin***	Y	?	N	N	Y	Y	Y
4 ***McCrery***	Y	Y	N	N	Y	Y	Y
5 ***Cooksey***	Y	Y	N	N	Y	Y	Y
6 ***Baker***	Y	Y	N	N	Y	Y	Y
7 John	Y	Y	N	N	Y	Y	Y
MAINE							
1 Allen	Y	Y	N	N	N	Y	Y
2 Baldacci	Y	Y	N	N	N	Y	Y
MARYLAND							
1 ***Gilchrest***	Y	Y	N	N	Y	Y	Y
2 ***Ehrlich***	Y	Y	N	N	Y	Y	Y
3 Cardin	Y	Y	N	N	N	Y	Y
4 Wynn	Y	Y	Y	Y	N	Y	Y
5 Hoyer	Y	Y	Y	Y	N	Y	Y
6 ***Bartlett***	Y	Y	N	N	Y	Y	Y
7 Cummings	Y	?	Y	N	N	Y	Y
8 ***Morella***	Y	Y	N	N	Y	Y	Y
MASSACHUSETTS							
1 Olver	Y	?	Y	Y	N	Y	Y
2 Neal	Y	Y	N	N	N	Y	Y
3 McGovern	Y	N	Y	Y	N	Y	Y
4 Frank	Y	Y	N	N	N	Y	Y
5 Meehan	Y	Y	N	N	N	Y	Y
6 Tierney	Y	Y	N	N	N	?	Y
7 Markey	Y	Y	N	N	N	Y	Y
8 Capuano	Y	N	Y	Y	N	Y	Y
9 Lynch	Y	Y	N	Y	N	Y	Y
10 Delahunt	Y	Y	N	?	N	Y	Y
MICHIGAN							
1 Stupak	Y	N	Y	Y	N	Y	Y
2 ***Hoekstra***	Y	Y	N	Y	Y	Y	Y
3 ***Ehlers***	Y	Y	N	N	Y	Y	Y
4 ***Camp***	Y	Y	N	N	Y	Y	Y
5 Barcia	Y	Y	N	N	N	Y	Y
6 ***Upton***	Y	Y	N	N	Y	Y	Y
7 ***Smith***	?	?	?	?	?	?	?
8 ***Rogers***	Y	Y	N	N	Y	Y	Y
9 Kildee	Y	Y	N	N	N	Y	Y
10 Bonior	Y	Y	Y	N	N	Y	Y
11 ***Knollenberg***	Y	Y	N	N	Y	Y	Y
12 Levin	Y	Y	N	N	N	Y	Y
13 Rivers	Y	Y	N	N	N	Y	Y
14 Conyers	Y	Y	Y	Y	N	N	Y
15 Kilpatrick	Y	Y	N	N	N	Y	Y
16 Dingell	Y	Y	Y	Y	N	Y	Y
MINNESOTA							
1 ***Gutknecht***	Y	N	N	N	Y	Y	Y
2 ***Kennedy***	Y	Y	N	N	Y	Y	Y
3 ***Ramstad***	Y	N	N	N	Y	Y	Y
4 McCollum	Y	Y	N	N	N	Y	Y
5 Sabo	Y	Y	N	N	N	Y	Y
6 Luther	Y	Y	N	N	N	Y	Y
7 Peterson	Y	N	N	N	N	Y	Y
8 Oberstar	Y	Y	N	N	N	Y	Y
MISSISSIPPI							
1 ***Wicker***	Y	Y	N	N	Y	Y	Y
2 Thompson	Y	N	Y	Y	N	Y	Y
3 ***Pickering***	Y	Y	N	N	Y	Y	Y
4 Shows	Y	Y	N	N	N	Y	Y
5 Taylor	Y	N	N	Y	N	Y	Y
MISSOURI							
1 Clay	Y	Y	Y	Y	N	Y	Y
2 ***Akin***	Y	Y	N	N	Y	Y	Y
3 Gephardt	Y	?	N	N	N	Y	Y
4 Skelton	Y	Y	N	N	N	Y	Y
5 McCarthy	Y	Y	N	N	N	Y	Y
6 ***Graves***	Y	Y	N	N	Y	Y	Y
7 ***Blunt***	Y	Y	N	N	Y	Y	Y
8 ***Emerson***	Y	Y	N	N	Y	Y	Y
9 ***Hulshof***	Y	Y	N	N	Y	Y	Y
MONTANA							
AL ***Rehberg***	Y	Y	N	N	Y	Y	Y
NEBRASKA							
1 ***Bereuter***	Y	Y	N	N	Y	Y	Y
2 ***Terry***	Y	Y	N	N	Y	Y	Y
3 ***Osborne***	Y	Y	N	N	Y	Y	Y
NEVADA							
1 Berkley	Y	Y	N	N	N	Y	Y
2 ***Gibbons***	Y	Y	N	N	Y	Y	Y
NEW HAMPSHIRE							
1 ***Sununu***	Y	Y	N	N	Y	Y	Y
2 ***Bass***	Y	Y	N	N	Y	Y	Y
NEW JERSEY							
1 Andrews	Y	Y	N	N	N	Y	Y
2 ***LoBiondo***	Y	N	N	N	N	Y	Y
3 ***Saxton***	Y	N	N	N	Y	Y	Y
4 ***Smith***	Y	Y	N	N	N	Y	Y
5 ***Roukema***	?	?	?	?	?	?	?
6 Pallone	Y	Y	N	N	N	Y	Y
7 ***Ferguson***	Y	Y	N	N	Y	Y	Y
8 Pascrell	Y	N	N	N	N	Y	Y
9 Rothman	Y	Y	N	N	N	Y	Y
10 Payne	Y	Y	N	N	N	Y	Y
11 ***Frelinghuysen***	Y	Y	N	N	Y	Y	Y
12 Holt	Y	Y	N	N	N	Y	Y
13 Menendez	Y	Y	N	N	N	Y	Y
NEW MEXICO							
1 ***Wilson***	Y	Y	N	N	Y	Y	Y
2 ***Skeen***	Y	Y	N	N	Y	Y	Y
3 Udall	Y	N	N	N	N	Y	Y
NEW YORK							
1 ***Grucci***	Y	Y	N	N	Y	Y	Y
2 Israel	Y	Y	N	N	N	Y	Y
3 ***King***	Y	Y	N	N	Y	Y	Y
4 McCarthy	Y	Y	N	N	N	Y	Y
5 Ackerman	Y	Y	Y	N	N	Y	Y
6 Meeks	Y	Y	N	N	N	Y	Y
7 Crowley	Y	Y	N	N	N	Y	Y
8 Nadler	Y	Y	N	N	N	Y	Y
9 Weiner	Y	Y	N	N	N	Y	Y
10 Towns	Y	Y	Y	Y	N	Y	Y
11 Owens	Y	Y	N	?	N	Y	Y
12 Velázquez	Y	Y	Y	Y	N	Y	Y
13 ***Fossella***	Y	Y	N	N	Y	Y	Y
14 Maloney	Y	Y	N	N	N	Y	Y
15 Rangel	Y	Y	N	N	N	Y	Y
16 Serrano	Y	Y	N	N	N	Y	Y
17 Engel	Y	Y	N	N	N	Y	Y
18 Lowey	Y	Y	N	N	N	Y	Y
19 ***Kelly***	Y	Y	N	N	Y	Y	Y
20 ***Gilman***	Y	Y	N	N	Y	Y	Y
21 McNulty	Y	N	N	N	N	Y	Y
22 ***Sweeney***	?	?	N	N	Y	Y	Y
23 ***Boehlert***	Y	Y	N	N	Y	Y	Y
24 ***McHugh***	Y	Y	N	N	N	Y	Y
25 ***Walsh***	Y	Y	N	N	Y	Y	Y
26 Hinchey	Y	Y	Y	N	N	Y	Y
27 ***Reynolds***	Y	Y	N	N	Y	Y	Y
28 Slaughter	Y	Y	N	N	N	Y	Y
29 LaFalce	Y	Y	?	?	N	Y	Y
30 ***Quinn***	Y	Y	N	N	N	Y	Y
31 ***Houghton***	Y	Y	N	N	Y	Y	Y
NORTH CAROLINA							
1 Clayton	Y	Y	?	N	N	Y	Y
2 Etheridge	Y	Y	N	N	N	Y	Y
3 ***Jones***	Y	Y	N	N	Y	Y	Y
4 Price	Y	Y	N	N	N	Y	Y
5 ***Burr***	Y	Y	N	N	Y	Y	Y
6 ***Coble***	Y	Y	N	N	N	Y	Y
7 McIntyre	Y	Y	N	N	N	Y	Y
8 ***Hayes***	Y	Y	N	N	N	Y	Y
9 ***Myrick***	Y	Y	N	N	Y	Y	Y
10 ***Ballenger***	Y	Y	N	N	N	Y	Y
11 ***Taylor***	Y	Y	N	N	Y	Y	Y
12 Watt	Y	Y	N	N	N	Y	Y
NORTH DAKOTA							
AL Pomeroy	Y	Y	N	N	N	Y	Y
OHIO							
1 ***Chabot***	Y	Y	N	N	Y	Y	Y
2 ***Portman***	Y	Y	N	N	Y	Y	Y
3 Hall	Y	Y	N	N	N	Y	Y
4 ***Oxley***	Y	Y	N	N	Y	Y	Y
5 ***Gillmor***	Y	N	N	N	Y	Y	Y
6 Strickland	Y	N	N	N	N	Y	Y
7 ***Hobson***	Y	Y	N	N	Y	Y	Y
8 ***Boehner***	Y	Y	N	N	Y	Y	Y
9 Kaptur	Y	Y	N	Y	N	Y	Y
10 Kucinich	Y	N	N	N	N	Y	Y
11 Jones	Y	Y	Y	Y	N	Y	Y
12 ***Tiberi***	Y	Y	N	N	Y	Y	Y
13 Brown	Y	Y	N	N	N	Y	Y
14 Sawyer	Y	Y	N	N	N	Y	Y
15 ***Pryce***	Y	?	N	N	Y	Y	Y
16 ***Regula***	Y	Y	N	N	Y	Y	Y
17 Traficant	?	?	?	?	?	?	?
18 ***Ney***	Y	Y	N	N	Y	Y	Y
19 ***LaTourette***	Y	Y	N	N	Y	Y	Y
OKLAHOMA							
1 ***Sullivan***	Y	Y	N	N	Y	Y	Y
2 Carson	Y	Y	N	N	Y	Y	Y
3 ***Watkins***	Y	Y	N	N	Y	Y	Y
4 ***Watts***	+	+	?	N	Y	Y	Y
5 ***Istook***	Y	Y	Y	N	Y	Y	?
6 ***Lucas***	Y	Y	N	N	Y	Y	Y
OREGON							
1 Wu	Y	N	N	N	N	Y	Y
2 ***Walden***	Y	Y	N	N	Y	Y	Y
3 Blumenauer	Y	Y	N	N	N	Y	Y
4 DeFazio	Y	N	Y	Y	N	Y	Y
5 Hooley	Y	Y	N	N	N	Y	Y
PENNSYLVANIA							
1 Brady	Y	N	N	N	N	Y	Y
2 Fattah	Y	Y	N	N	N	Y	Y
3 Borski	Y	N	N	N	N	Y	Y
4 ***Hart***	Y	Y	N	N	Y	Y	Y
5 ***Peterson***	Y	Y	N	N	Y	?	Y
6 Holden	Y	Y	N	N	N	Y	Y
7 ***Weldon***	Y	Y	N	N	N	Y	Y
8 ***Greenwood***	+	+	N	N	Y	Y	Y
9 ***Shuster, Bill***	Y	Y	N	N	Y	Y	Y
10 ***Sherwood***	Y	Y	N	N	Y	Y	Y
11 Kanjorski	Y	Y	N	N	N	Y	Y
12 Murtha	Y	Y	N	N	N	Y	Y
13 Hoeffel	Y	Y	N	N	N	Y	Y
14 Coyne	Y	Y	N	N	N	Y	Y
15 ***Toomey***	Y	Y	N	N	Y	Y	Y
16 ***Pitts***	Y	Y	N	N	Y	Y	Y
17 ***Gekas***	Y	Y	N	N	Y	Y	Y
18 Doyle	Y	Y	?	N	N	Y	Y
19 ***Platts***	Y	Y	N	N	Y	Y	Y
20 Mascara	Y	Y	N	N	N	Y	Y
21 ***English***	Y	N	N	N	Y	Y	Y
RHODE ISLAND							
1 Kennedy	Y	Y	N	N	N	Y	Y
2 Langevin	Y	Y	N	N	N	Y	Y
SOUTH CAROLINA							
1 ***Brown***	Y	Y	N	N	Y	Y	Y
2 ***Wilson***	Y	Y	N	N	N	Y	Y
3 ***Graham***	Y	Y	N	N	N	Y	Y
4 ***DeMint***	Y	Y	N	N	N	Y	Y
5 Spratt	Y	Y	N	N	N	Y	Y
6 Clyburn	Y	Y	N	N	N	Y	Y
SOUTH DAKOTA							
AL ***Thune***	Y	Y	Y	N	Y	Y	Y
TENNESSEE							
1 ***Jenkins***	Y	Y	N	N	Y	Y	Y
2 ***Duncan***	Y	Y	N	N	Y	Y	Y
3 ***Wamp***	Y	N	N	N	Y	Y	Y
4 ***Hilleary***	Y	Y	N	N	Y	Y	Y
5 Clement	Y	Y	N	N	N	Y	Y
6 Gordon	Y	Y	N	N	N	Y	Y
7 ***Bryant***	Y	Y	N	N	Y	Y	Y
8 Tanner	Y	Y	N	N	Y	Y	Y
9 Ford	Y	Y	N	N	N	Y	Y
TEXAS							
1 Sandlin	Y	Y	Y	Y	N	Y	Y
2 Turner	Y	Y	N	N	N	Y	Y
3 ***Johnson, Sam***	Y	Y	N	N	Y	Y	Y
4 Hall	Y	Y	N	N	Y	Y	Y
5 ***Sessions***	Y	Y	N	N	Y	Y	Y
6 ***Barton***	Y	Y	N	N	Y	Y	Y
7 ***Culberson***	Y	Y	N	N	Y	Y	Y
8 ***Brady***	Y	Y	N	N	Y	Y	Y
9 Lampson	Y	Y	N	N	N	Y	?
10 Doggett	Y	Y	Y	Y	N	Y	Y
11 Edwards	+	Y	N	N	N	Y	Y
12 ***Granger***	Y	Y	N	N	Y	Y	Y
13 ***Thornberry***	Y	Y	N	N	Y	Y	Y
14 ***Paul***	Y	Y	N	N	P	N	Y
15 Hinojosa	Y	Y	N	N	N	Y	Y
16 Reyes	Y	Y	N	N	N	Y	Y
17 Stenholm	Y	Y	N	N	Y	Y	Y
18 Jackson-Lee	Y	Y	N	Y	N	Y	Y
19 ***Combest***	Y	Y	N	N	Y	Y	Y
20 Gonzalez	Y	Y	N	Y	N	Y	Y
21 ***Smith***	Y	Y	N	N	Y	Y	Y
22 ***DeLay***	Y	Y	N	N	Y	Y	Y
23 ***Bonilla***	Y	Y	N	N	Y	Y	Y
24 Frost	Y	Y	N	N	N	Y	Y
25 Bentsen	Y	Y	N	N	N	Y	Y
26 ***Armey***	Y	Y	N	N	Y	Y	Y
27 Ortiz	Y	Y	N	N	N	Y	Y
28 Rodriguez	Y	Y	N	N	N	Y	Y
29 Green	Y	Y	N	N	N	Y	Y
30 Johnson, E.B.	Y	N	Y	Y	N	Y	Y
UTAH							
1 ***Hansen***	Y	Y	N	N	Y	Y	Y
2 Matheson	Y	Y	N	N	Y	Y	Y
3 ***Cannon***	Y	Y	N	N	Y	Y	Y
VERMONT							
AL *Sanders*	Y	Y	Y	Y	N	Y	Y
VIRGINIA							
1 ***Davis, Jo Ann***	Y	?	N	N	Y	Y	Y
2 ***Schrock***	Y	Y	N	N	Y	Y	Y
3 Scott	Y	N	N	N	N	Y	Y
4 ***Forbes***	Y	Y	N	N	Y	Y	Y
5 *Goode*	Y	Y	N	N	N	Y	Y
6 ***Goodlatte***	Y	?	N	N	Y	Y	Y
7 ***Cantor***	Y	Y	N	N	Y	Y	Y
8 Moran	Y	Y	Y	N	N	Y	Y
9 Boucher	Y	Y	N	Y	N	Y	Y
10 ***Wolf***	Y	Y	?	N	Y	Y	Y
11 ***Davis, T.***	Y	Y	N	N	Y	Y	Y
WASHINGTON							
1 Inslee	Y	Y	N	N	N	Y	Y
2 Larsen	Y	N	N	N	N	Y	Y
3 Baird	Y	Y	N	N	N	Y	Y
4 ***Hastings***	Y	Y	N	N	Y	Y	Y
5 ***Nethercutt***	Y	?	N	N	Y	Y	Y
6 Dicks	Y	Y	Y	N	N	Y	Y
7 McDermott	Y	N	Y	Y	N	Y	Y
8 ***Dunn***	Y	Y	N	N	Y	Y	Y
9 Smith	Y	Y	N	N	N	Y	Y
WEST VIRGINIA							
1 Mollohan	Y	Y	N	N	N	Y	Y
2 ***Capito***	Y	Y	N	N	N	Y	Y
3 Rahall	Y	Y	N	N	N	Y	Y
WISCONSIN							
1 ***Ryan***	Y	Y	N	N	Y	Y	Y
2 Baldwin	Y	N	N	N	N	Y	Y
3 Kind	Y	Y	N	N	N	Y	Y
4 Kleczka	Y	Y	N	N	N	Y	Y
5 Barrett	Y	Y	N	N	N	Y	Y
6 ***Petri***	Y	Y	N	N	Y	Y	Y
7 Obey	Y	Y	?	Y	N	Y	Y
8 ***Green***	Y	?	N	N	Y	Y	Y
9 ***Sensenbrenner***	Y	Y	N	N	Y	Y	?
WYOMING							
AL ***Cubin***	Y	Y	N	N	Y	Y	Y

Southern states - Ala., Ark., Fla., Ga., Ky., La., Miss., N.C., Okla., S.C., Tenn., Texas, Va.

267. Procedural Motion/Journal. Approval of the House Journal of Wednesday, June 26, 2002. Approved 348-59: R 202-9; D 144-50 (ND 104-37, SD 40-13); I 2-0. June 26, 2002.

268. Procedural Motion/Adjourn. McNulty, D-N.Y., motion to adjourn. Motion rejected 70-332: R 5-202; D 64-129 (ND 48-94, SD 16-35); I 1-1. June 26, 2002.

269. HR 5010. Fiscal 2003 Defense Appropriations/Fort Greely Silos. Tierney, D-Mass., amendment that would cut $122 million for construction of silos at Fort Greely, Alaska. Rejected 112-314: R 5-212; D 106-101 (ND 93-60, SD 13-41); I 1-1. June 27, 2002.

270. HR 5010. Fiscal 2003 Defense Appropriations/Passage. Passage of the bill that would provide $354.7 billion for the Defense Department for fiscal 2003, about 10 percent more than fiscal 2002. The bill would include $7.4 billion for ballistic missile defense, meet the president's request for several aircraft programs including funding for the new Joint Strike Fighter and 23 F-22 fighters and increase funding for counter-terrorism activities. The bill also would fund several shipbuilding programs and increase pay for military personnel by 4.1 percent. Passed 413-18: R 218-1; D 194-16 (ND 141-15, SD 53-1); I 1-1. June 27, 2002.

271. H Con Res 424. Pentagon Volunteer Roofers Tribute/Adoption. Sullivan, R-Okla., motion to suspend the rules and adopt the concurrent resolution that would pay tribute to the professional roofing contractors who volunteered their time and worked to repair the Pentagon after it was damaged in the Sept. 11 terrorist attacks. Motion agreed to 428-0: R 219-0; D 207-0 (ND 154-0, SD 53-0); I 2-0. A two-thirds majority of those present and voting (286 in this case) is required for adoption under suspension of the rules. June 27, 2002.

272. HR 3034. Frank Sinatra Building/Passage. Sullivan, R-Okla., motion to suspend the rules and pass the bill that would name a post office in Hoboken, N.J., after the late singer and entertainer Frank Sinatra. Motion agreed to 427-0: R 216-0; D 209-0 (ND 155-0, SD 54-0); I 2-0. A two-thirds majority of those present and voting (285 in this case) is required for passage under suspension of the rules. June 27, 2002.

273. H Res 459. Pledge of Allegiance/Adoption. Sensenbrenner, R-Wis., motion to suspend the rules and adopt the resolution that would express the sense of the House that the Ninth Circuit Court of Appeals erred in holding in *Newdow v. U.S. Congress* that having the Pledge of Allegiance read in public schools is an unconstitutional endorsement of religion because of the words "one nation, under God." It also supports the current wording of the pledge and urges the court to reverse its decision in the case. Motion agreed to 416-3: R 220-0; D 194-3 (ND 143-2, SD 51-1); I 2-0. A two-thirds majority of those present and voting (280 in this case) is required for adoption under suspension of the rules. June 27, 2002.

274. HR 5011. Fiscal 2003 Military Construction Appropriations/Previous Question. Motion to order the previous question (thus ending debate and possibility of amendment) on the amendment to the rule (H Res 462) to provide for House floor consideration of the bill that would provide $10.1 billion in fiscal 2003 for military construction projects. The amendment also would provide for House floor consideration of the bill (S 2578) that would increase the public debt limit by approximately $450 billion. Motion agreed to 221-210: R 220-0; D 0-209 (ND 0-155, SD 0-54); I 1-1. June 27, 2002.

Key

Y	Voted for (yea).
#	Paired for.
+	Announced for.
N	Voted against (nay).
X	Paired against.
−	Announced against.
P	Voted "present."
C	Voted "present" to avoid possible conflict of interest.
?	Did not vote or otherwise make a position known.

Democrats **Republicans** *Independents*

	267	268	269	270	271	272	273	274
ALABAMA								
1 *Callahan*	Y	N	N	Y	Y	Y	Y	Y
2 *Everett*	Y	N	N	Y	Y	Y	Y	Y
3 *Riley*	?	?	N	Y	Y	Y	Y	Y
4 *Aderholt*	N	N	N	Y	Y	Y	Y	Y
5 Cramer	Y	N	N	Y	Y	Y	Y	Y
6 *Bachus*	Y	N	N	Y	Y	Y	Y	Y
7 Hilliard	N	N	Y	Y	Y	Y	Y	N
ALASKA								
AL *Young*	?	?	N	Y	Y	Y	Y	Y
ARIZONA								
1 *Flake*	Y	N	N	Y	Y	Y	Y	Y
2 Pastor	N	N	N	Y	Y	Y	Y	N
3 *Stump*	Y	N	N	Y	Y	Y	Y	N
4 *Shadegg*	Y	N	N	Y	Y	Y	Y	Y
5 *Kolbe*	Y	Y	N	Y	Y	Y	Y	Y
6 *Hayworth*	Y	N	N	Y	Y	Y	Y	Y
ARKANSAS								
1 Berry	N	Y	N	Y	Y	Y	Y	N
2 Snyder	Y	N	N	Y	Y	Y	Y	N
3 *Boozman*	Y	N	N	Y	Y	Y	Y	Y
4 Ross	Y	N	N	Y	Y	Y	Y	N
CALIFORNIA								
1 Thompson	N	Y	Y	Y	Y	Y	Y	N
2 *Herger*	Y	N	N	Y	Y	Y	Y	Y
3 *Ose*	Y	N	N	Y	Y	Y	Y	Y
4 *Doolittle*	Y	N	N	Y	Y	Y	Y	Y
5 Matsui	Y	N	N	Y	Y	Y	Y	N
6 Woolsey	Y	Y	Y	N	Y	Y	Y	N
7 Miller, George	N	Y	Y	N	Y	Y	Y	N
8 Pelosi	Y	Y	Y	Y	Y	Y	Y	N
9 Lee	Y	Y	Y	N	Y	Y	Y	N
10 Tauscher	Y	N	N	Y	Y	Y	Y	N
11 *Pombo*	Y	N	N	Y	Y	Y	Y	Y
12 Lantos	Y	Y	Y	Y	Y	Y	Y	N
13 Stark	?	Y	Y	N	Y	N	N	N
14 Eshoo	Y	N	Y	Y	Y	Y	Y	N
15 Honda	Y	Y	Y	Y	Y	Y	N	N
16 Lofgren	Y	N	Y	Y	Y	Y	Y	N
17 Farr	Y	N	Y	N	Y	Y	Y	N
18 Condit	N	N	N	Y	Y	Y	Y	N
19 *Radanovich*	Y	N	N	Y	Y	Y	Y	Y
20 Dooley	Y	N	N	Y	Y	Y	Y	N
21 *Thomas*	Y	N	N	Y	Y	Y	Y	Y
22 Capps	Y	N	Y	Y	Y	Y	Y	N
23 *Gallegly*	Y	N	N	Y	Y	Y	Y	Y
24 Sherman	Y	N	N	Y	Y	Y	Y	N
25 *McKeon*	Y	N	N	Y	Y	Y	Y	Y
26 Berman	Y	N	N	Y	Y	Y	?	N
27 Schiff	Y	Y	N	Y	Y	Y	Y	N
28 *Dreier*	Y	N	N	Y	Y	Y	Y	Y
29 Waxman	?	N	Y	Y	Y	Y	Y	N
30 Becerra	Y	N	Y	Y	Y	Y	Y	N
31 Solis	Y	Y	Y	Y	Y	Y	Y	N
32 Watson	Y	Y	Y	N	Y	Y	Y	N
33 Roybal-Allard	Y	N	Y	Y	Y	Y	Y	N
34 Napolitano	Y	N	N	Y	Y	Y	Y	N
35 Waters	N	Y	Y	N	Y	Y	Y	N
36 Harman	Y	N	N	Y	Y	?	Y	N
37 Millender-McD.	Y	N	N	Y	Y	Y	Y	N
38 *Horn*	Y	N	N	Y	Y	Y	Y	Y

	267	268	269	270	271	272	273	274
39 *Royce*	Y	N	N	Y	Y	Y	Y	Y
40 *Lewis*	Y	N	N	Y	Y	Y	Y	Y
41 *Miller, Gary*	Y	N	N	Y	Y	Y	Y	Y
42 Baca	Y	N	N	Y	Y	Y	Y	N
43 *Calvert*	Y	N	N	Y	Y	Y	Y	Y
44 *Bono*	Y	N	N	Y	Y	Y	Y	Y
45 *Rohrabacher*	?	N	N	Y	Y	Y	Y	Y
46 Sanchez	N	N	N	Y	Y	Y	Y	N
47 *Cox*	Y	N	N	Y	Y	Y	Y	Y
48 *Issa*	Y	N	N	Y	Y	Y	Y	Y
49 Davis	Y	N	N	Y	Y	Y	Y	N
50 Filner	N	Y	N	Y	Y	Y	Y	N
51 *Cunningham*	Y	N	N	Y	Y	Y	Y	Y
52 *Hunter*	Y	?	N	Y	Y	Y	Y	Y
COLORADO								
1 DeGette	Y	N	Y	Y	Y	Y	Y	N
2 Udall	N	N	Y	Y	Y	Y	Y	N
3 *McInnis*	Y	N	N	Y	Y	Y	Y	Y
4 *Schaffer*	N	N	N	Y	Y	Y	Y	Y
5 *Hefley*	N	N	N	Y	Y	Y	Y	Y
6 *Tancredo*	P	N	N	Y	Y	Y	Y	Y
CONNECTICUT								
1 Larson	Y	N	N	Y	Y	Y	Y	N
2 *Simmons*	Y	N	N	Y	Y	Y	Y	Y
3 DeLauro	Y	N	N	Y	Y	Y	Y	N
4 *Shays*	Y	N	Y	Y	Y	Y	Y	Y
5 Maloney	?	N	N	Y	Y	Y	Y	N
6 *Johnson*	Y	N	N	Y	Y	Y	Y	Y
DELAWARE								
AL *Castle*	Y	N	N	Y	Y	Y	Y	Y
FLORIDA								
1 *Miller, J.*	Y	N	N	Y	Y	Y	Y	Y
2 Boyd	Y	N	N	Y	Y	Y	Y	N
3 Brown	N	Y	N	Y	Y	Y	Y	N
4 *Crenshaw*	Y	N	N	Y	Y	Y	Y	Y
5 Thurman	Y	N	N	Y	Y	Y	Y	N
6 *Stearns*	Y	N	N	Y	Y	Y	Y	Y
7 *Mica*	Y	N	N	Y	Y	Y	Y	Y
8 *Keller*	Y	?	N	Y	Y	Y	Y	Y
9 *Bilirakis*	Y	N	N	Y	Y	Y	Y	Y
10 *Young*	Y	N	N	Y	Y	Y	Y	Y
11 Davis	Y	N	N	Y	Y	Y	Y	N
12 *Putnam*	Y	N	N	Y	Y	Y	Y	Y
13 *Miller, D.*	Y	N	N	Y	Y	Y	Y	Y
14 *Goss*	Y	N	N	Y	Y	Y	Y	Y
15 *Weldon*	Y	N	N	Y	Y	Y	Y	Y
16 *Foley*	Y	N	N	Y	Y	Y	Y	Y
17 Meek	?	?	Y	Y	Y	Y	Y	N
18 *Ros-Lehtinen*	Y	N	N	Y	Y	Y	Y	Y
19 Wexler	Y	N	N	Y	Y	Y	Y	N
20 Deutsch	Y	N	N	Y	Y	Y	Y	N
21 *Diaz-Balart*	Y	N	N	Y	Y	Y	Y	Y
22 *Shaw*	Y	N	N	Y	Y	Y	Y	Y
23 Hastings	N	?	Y	Y	Y	Y	P	N
GEORGIA								
1 *Kingston*	Y	N	N	Y	Y	Y	Y	Y
2 Bishop	Y	Y	N	Y	Y	Y	Y	N
3 *Collins*	Y	N	N	Y	Y	Y	Y	Y
4 McKinney	Y	N	Y	N	Y	Y	Y	N
5 Lewis	Y	Y	Y	N	Y	Y	Y	N
6 *Isakson*	Y	N	N	Y	Y	Y	Y	Y
7 *Barr*	Y	N	N	Y	Y	Y	Y	Y
8 *Chambliss*	Y	N	N	Y	Y	Y	Y	Y
9 *Deal*	Y	N	N	Y	Y	Y	Y	Y
10 *Norwood*	Y	N	N	Y	Y	Y	Y	Y
11 *Linder*	Y	N	N	Y	Y	Y	Y	Y
HAWAII								
1 Abercrombie	Y	N	Y	Y	Y	Y	Y	N
2 Mink	Y	N	Y	Y	Y	Y	Y	N
IDAHO								
1 *Otter*	Y	N	Y	Y	Y	Y	Y	Y
2 *Simpson*	Y	N	N	Y	Y	Y	Y	Y
ILLINOIS								
1 Rush	Y	?	Y	Y	Y	Y	Y	N
2 Jackson	Y	N	Y	N	Y	Y	Y	N
3 Lipinski	Y	N	N	Y	Y	Y	Y	N
4 Gutierrez	Y	N	N	Y	Y	P	Y	N
5 Blagojevich	Y	N	N	Y	Y	Y	Y	N
6 *Hyde*	Y	?	N	Y	Y	Y	Y	Y
7 Davis	N	N	Y	N	Y	Y	Y	N
8 *Crane*	N	N	N	Y	Y	Y	Y	Y
9 Schakowsky	N	N	Y	N	Y	Y	Y	N
10 *Kirk*	Y	N	N	Y	Y	Y	Y	Y
11 *Weller*	N	N	N	Y	Y	Y	Y	Y
12 Costello	N	N	N	Y	Y	Y	Y	N
13 *Biggert*	Y	N	N	Y	Y	Y	Y	Y

ND Northern Democrats   SD Southern Democrats

	267	268	269	270	271	272	273	274
14 ***Hastert***							Y	
15 ***Johnson***	Y	N	N	Y	Y	Y	Y	Y
16 ***Manzullo***	Y	N	N	Y	Y	Y	Y	Y
17 Evans	Y	Y	Y	Y	Y	Y	Y	N
18 ***LaHood***	Y	N	N	Y	Y	Y	Y	Y
19 Phelps	Y	N	N	Y	Y	Y	Y	N
20 ***Shimkus***	Y	N	N	Y	Y	Y	Y	Y
INDIANA								
1 Visclosky	N	N	N	Y	Y	Y	Y	N
2 ***Pence***	Y	N	N	Y	Y	Y	Y	Y
3 Roemer	Y	N	N	Y	Y	Y	Y	N
4 ***Souder***	Y	N	N	Y	Y	Y	Y	Y
5 ***Buyer***	Y	N	N	Y	Y	?	Y	Y
6 ***Burton***	Y	N	N	Y	Y	Y	Y	Y
7 ***Kerns***	Y	N	N	Y	Y	Y	Y	Y
8 ***Hostettler***	Y	N	N	Y	Y	Y	Y	Y
9 Hill	Y	N	N	Y	Y	Y	Y	N
10 Carson	N	N	Y	Y	Y	Y	Y	N
IOWA								
1 ***Leach***	Y	N	Y	Y	Y	Y	Y	Y
2 ***Nussle***	?	N	N	Y	Y	Y	Y	Y
3 Boswell	Y	N	N	Y	Y	Y	Y	N
4 ***Ganske***	Y	N	N	Y	Y	Y	Y	Y
5 ***Latham***	Y	N	N	Y	Y	Y	Y	Y
KANSAS								
1 ***Moran***	Y	N	N	Y	Y	Y	Y	Y
2 ***Ryun***	Y	N	N	Y	Y	Y	Y	Y
3 Moore	N	?	N	Y	Y	Y	Y	N
4 ***Tiahrt***	Y	N	N	Y	Y	Y	Y	Y
KENTUCKY								
1 ***Whitfield***	Y	N	N	Y	Y	Y	Y	Y
2 ***Lewis***	Y	N	N	Y	Y	Y	Y	Y
3 ***Northup***	?	?	?	?	?	?	Y	Y
4 Lucas	Y	N	N	Y	Y	Y	Y	N
5 ***Rogers***	Y	N	N	Y	Y	Y	Y	Y
6 ***Fletcher***	Y	?	N	Y	Y	Y	Y	Y
LOUISIANA								
1 ***Vitter***	Y	?	N	Y	Y	Y	Y	Y
2 Jefferson	Y	Y	Y	Y	Y	Y	Y	N
3 ***Tauzin***	?	?	N	Y	Y	Y	Y	Y
4 ***McCrery***	Y	N	N	Y	Y	Y	Y	Y
5 ***Cooksey***	Y	N	N	Y	Y	Y	Y	Y
6 ***Baker***	Y	N	N	Y	Y	Y	Y	Y
7 John	Y	N	N	Y	Y	Y	Y	N
MAINE								
1 Allen	N	Y	?	Y	Y	Y	Y	N
2 Baldacci	Y	N	N	Y	Y	Y	Y	N
MARYLAND								
1 ***Gilchrest***	Y	N	N	Y	Y	Y	Y	Y
2 ***Ehrlich***	?	?	N	Y	Y	Y	Y	Y
3 Cardin	Y	N	Y	Y	Y	Y	Y	N
4 Wynn	N	?	Y	Y	Y	Y	Y	N
5 Hoyer	Y	N	N	Y	Y	Y	Y	N
6 ***Bartlett***	Y	N	N	Y	Y	Y	Y	Y
7 Cummings	Y	N	N	Y	Y	Y	Y	N
8 ***Morella***	Y	N	Y	Y	Y	Y	Y	Y
MASSACHUSETTS								
1 Olver	N	Y	Y	Y	Y	Y	Y	N
2 Neal	Y	Y	Y	Y	Y	Y	Y	N
3 McGovern	N	Y	Y	Y	Y	Y	Y	N
4 Frank	Y	N	Y	N	Y	Y	P	N
5 Meehan	Y	Y	Y	Y	Y	Y	Y	N
6 Tierney	Y	Y	Y	Y	Y	Y	Y	N
7 Markey	Y	Y	Y	Y	Y	Y	Y	N
8 Capuano	N	N	N	Y	Y	Y	P	N
9 Lynch	Y	Y	Y	Y	Y	Y	Y	N
10 Delahunt	Y	Y	Y	Y	Y	Y	Y	N
MICHIGAN								
1 Stupak	N	Y	Y	Y	Y	Y	Y	N
2 ***Hoekstra***	Y	?	N	Y	Y	Y	Y	Y
3 ***Ehlers***	Y	N	Y	Y	Y	Y	Y	Y
4 ***Camp***	Y	N	N	Y	Y	Y	Y	Y
5 Barcia	Y	?	N	Y	Y	Y	Y	N
6 ***Upton***	Y	N	N	Y	Y	Y	Y	Y
7 ***Smith***	Y	N	N	Y	Y	Y	Y	Y
8 ***Rogers***	Y	N	N	Y	Y	Y	Y	Y
9 Kildee	Y	N	N	Y	Y	Y	Y	N
10 Bonior	Y	Y	Y	Y	Y	Y	Y	N
11 ***Knollenberg***	Y	N	N	Y	Y	Y	Y	Y
12 Levin	Y	N	Y	Y	Y	Y	Y	N
13 Rivers	Y	N	Y	Y	Y	Y	Y	N
14 Conyers	?	Y	Y	N	Y	Y	Y	N
15 Kilpatrick	Y	N	N	Y	Y	Y	Y	N
16 Dingell	Y	Y	N	Y	Y	Y	Y	N

	267	268	269	270	271	272	273	274
MINNESOTA								
1 ***Gutknecht***	Y	N	N	Y	Y	Y	Y	Y
2 ***Kennedy***	N	N	N	Y	Y	Y	Y	Y
3 ***Ramstad***	N	N	N	Y	Y	Y	Y	Y
4 McCollum	Y	N	Y	Y	Y	Y	Y	N
5 Sabo	N	N	?	Y	Y	Y	Y	N
6 Luther	Y	N	Y	Y	Y	Y	Y	N
7 Peterson	N	N	N	Y	Y	Y	Y	N
8 Oberstar	?	?	Y	Y	Y	Y	P	N
MISSISSIPPI								
1 ***Wicker***	Y	N	N	Y	Y	?	Y	Y
2 Thompson	N	N	N	Y	Y	Y	Y	N
3 ***Pickering***	Y	N	N	Y	Y	Y	Y	Y
4 Shows	Y	N	N	Y	Y	Y	Y	N
5 Taylor	N	N	N	Y	Y	Y	Y	N
MISSOURI								
1 Clay	?	?	Y	Y	Y	Y	Y	N
2 ***Akin***	Y	N	N	Y	Y	Y	Y	Y
3 Gephardt	Y	?	Y	Y	Y	Y	Y	N
4 Skelton	Y	N	N	Y	Y	Y	Y	N
5 McCarthy	Y	N	Y	Y	Y	Y	Y	N
6 ***Graves***	Y	N	N	Y	Y	Y	Y	Y
7 ***Blunt***	Y	N	N	Y	Y	Y	Y	Y
8 ***Emerson***	Y	N	N	Y	Y	Y	Y	Y
9 ***Hulshof***	Y	N	N	Y	Y	Y	Y	Y
MONTANA								
AL ***Rehberg***	Y	N	N	Y	Y	Y	Y	Y
NEBRASKA								
1 ***Bereuter***	Y	N	N	Y	Y	Y	Y	Y
2 ***Terry***	Y	N	N	Y	Y	Y	Y	Y
3 ***Osborne***	Y	Y	N	Y	Y	Y	Y	Y
NEVADA								
1 Berkley	Y	N	Y	Y	Y	Y	Y	N
2 ***Gibbons***	Y	N	N	Y	Y	Y	Y	Y
NEW HAMPSHIRE								
1 ***Sununu***	Y	N	N	Y	Y	Y	Y	Y
2 ***Bass***	Y	N	N	Y	Y	Y	Y	Y
NEW JERSEY								
1 Andrews	Y	N	N	Y	Y	Y	Y	N
2 ***LoBiondo***	N	N	N	Y	Y	Y	Y	Y
3 ***Saxton***	Y	N	N	Y	Y	Y	Y	Y
4 ***Smith***	Y	N	N	Y	Y	Y	Y	Y
5 ***Roukema***	?	?	?	?	?	?	?	?
6 Pallone	Y	N	N	Y	Y	Y	Y	N
7 ***Ferguson***	Y	N	N	Y	Y	Y	Y	Y
8 Pascrell	Y	N	N	Y	Y	Y	Y	N
9 Rothman	Y	N	N	Y	Y	Y	Y	N
10 Payne	Y	N	Y	N	Y	Y	Y	N
11 ***Frelinghuysen***	Y	N	N	Y	Y	Y	Y	Y
12 Holt	Y	N	Y	Y	Y	Y	Y	N
13 Menendez	Y	N	N	Y	Y	Y	Y	N
NEW MEXICO								
1 ***Wilson***	Y	N	N	Y	Y	Y	Y	Y
2 ***Skeen***	Y	N	N	Y	Y	Y	Y	Y
3 Udall	N	N	Y	Y	Y	Y	Y	N
NEW YORK								
1 ***Grucci***	Y	N	N	Y	Y	Y	Y	Y
2 Israel	+	−	N	Y	Y	Y	Y	N
3 ***King***	Y	N	N	Y	Y	Y	Y	Y
4 McCarthy	Y	Y	?	Y	Y	Y	Y	N
5 Ackerman	Y	Y	Y	Y	Y	Y	P	N
6 Meeks	Y	Y	Y	Y	Y	Y	Y	N
7 Crowley	Y	N	Y	Y	Y	Y	Y	N
8 Nadler	Y	N	Y	Y	Y	Y	P	N
9 Weiner	Y	N	Y	Y	Y	Y	Y	N
10 Towns	?	Y	Y	Y	Y	Y	Y	N
11 Owens	?	Y	Y	Y	Y	Y	Y	N
12 Velázquez	Y	Y	Y	Y	Y	Y	P	N
13 ***Fossella***	Y	N	N	Y	Y	Y	Y	Y
14 Maloney	Y	N	Y	Y	Y	Y	Y	N
15 Rangel	Y	Y	Y	Y	Y	Y	Y	N
16 Serrano	Y	N	Y	Y	Y	Y	Y	N
17 Engel	Y	N	Y	Y	Y	Y	Y	?
18 Lowey	Y	N	Y	Y	Y	Y	Y	N
19 ***Kelly***	Y	N	N	Y	Y	Y	Y	Y
20 ***Gilman***	Y	N	N	Y	Y	Y	Y	Y
21 McNulty	N	Y	Y	Y	Y	Y	Y	N
22 ***Sweeney***	Y	N	N	Y	Y	Y	Y	Y
23 ***Boehlert***	Y	N	N	Y	Y	Y	Y	Y
24 ***McHugh***	Y	N	N	Y	Y	Y	Y	Y
25 ***Walsh***	Y	N	N	Y	Y	Y	Y	Y
26 Hinchey	?	?	Y	Y	Y	Y	Y	N
27 ***Reynolds***	Y	N	N	Y	Y	Y	Y	Y
28 Slaughter	N	Y	N	Y	?	Y	Y	N
29 LaFalce	?	?	Y	Y	Y	Y	?	N

	267	268	269	270	271	272	273	274
30 ***Quinn***	Y	N	N	Y	Y	Y	Y	Y
31 ***Houghton***	Y	N	N	Y	Y	Y	Y	Y
NORTH CAROLINA								
1 Clayton	Y	N	Y	Y	Y	Y	Y	N
2 Etheridge	Y	Y	N	Y	Y	Y	Y	N
3 ***Jones***	Y	N	N	Y	Y	Y	Y	Y
4 Price	N	N	Y	Y	Y	Y	Y	N
5 ***Burr***	Y	N	?	Y	Y	Y	Y	Y
6 ***Coble***	Y	N	N	Y	Y	Y	Y	Y
7 McIntyre	Y	N	N	Y	Y	Y	Y	N
8 ***Hayes***	Y	N	N	Y	Y	Y	Y	Y
9 ***Myrick***	Y	N	N	Y	Y	Y	Y	Y
10 ***Ballenger***	Y	N	N	Y	Y	Y	Y	Y
11 ***Taylor***	Y	N	N	Y	Y	Y	Y	Y
12 Watt	Y	N	Y	Y	Y	Y	P	N
NORTH DAKOTA								
AL Pomeroy	Y	Y	N	Y	Y	Y	Y	N
OHIO								
1 ***Chabot***	Y	N	N	Y	Y	Y	Y	Y
2 ***Portman***	Y	N	N	Y	Y	Y	Y	Y
3 Hall	Y	N	N	Y	Y	Y	Y	N
4 ***Oxley***	?	N	N	Y	Y	Y	Y	Y
5 ***Gillmor***	Y	N	N	Y	Y	Y	Y	Y
6 Strickland	N	N	Y	Y	Y	Y	Y	N
7 ***Hobson***	Y	N	N	Y	Y	Y	Y	Y
8 ***Boehner***	Y	N	?	Y	Y	Y	Y	Y
9 Kaptur	Y	Y	N	Y	Y	Y	Y	N
10 Kucinich	N	N	Y	N	Y	Y	Y	N
11 Jones	Y	Y	Y	Y	Y	Y	Y	N
12 ***Tiberi***	Y	N	N	Y	Y	Y	Y	Y
13 Brown	N	Y	Y	N	?	Y	Y	N
14 Sawyer	Y	N	Y	Y	Y	Y	Y	N
15 ***Pryce***	Y	N	N	Y	Y	Y	Y	Y
16 ***Regula***	Y	N	N	Y	Y	Y	Y	Y
17 Traficant	?	?	?	?	?	?	?	?
18 ***Ney***	Y	N	N	Y	Y	Y	Y	Y
19 ***LaTourette***	Y	N	N	Y	Y	Y	Y	Y
OKLAHOMA								
1 ***Sullivan***	Y	N	N	Y	Y	Y	Y	Y
2 Carson	N	Y	N	Y	Y	Y	Y	N
3 ***Watkins***	Y	?	N	Y	Y	Y	Y	Y
4 ***Watts***	Y	N	N	Y	Y	Y	Y	Y
5 ***Istook***	Y	N	N	Y	Y	Y	Y	Y
6 ***Lucas***	Y	N	N	Y	Y	Y	Y	Y
OREGON								
1 Wu	N	?	Y	Y	Y	Y	Y	N
2 ***Walden***	Y	N	N	Y	Y	Y	Y	Y
3 Blumenauer	Y	N	Y	Y	Y	Y	P	N
4 DeFazio	N	Y	Y	N	Y	Y	Y	N
5 Hooley	Y	?	Y	Y	Y	Y	Y	N
PENNSYLVANIA								
1 Brady	N	N	N	Y	Y	Y	Y	N
2 Fattah	?	?	Y	Y	Y	Y	Y	N
3 Borski	N	N	N	Y	Y	Y	Y	N
4 ***Hart***	Y	N	N	Y	Y	Y	Y	Y
5 ***Peterson***	Y	N	N	Y	Y	Y	Y	Y
6 Holden	Y	N	N	Y	Y	Y	Y	N
7 ***Weldon***	Y	N	N	Y	Y	Y	Y	Y
8 ***Greenwood***	Y	N	N	Y	Y	Y	?	Y
9 ***Shuster, Bill***	Y	N	N	Y	Y	Y	Y	Y
10 ***Sherwood***	Y	N	N	Y	Y	Y	Y	Y
11 Kanjorski	Y	?	N	Y	Y	Y	Y	N
12 Murtha	Y	N	N	Y	Y	Y	Y	N
13 Hoeffel	Y	N	Y	Y	Y	Y	Y	N
14 Coyne	?	N	Y	Y	Y	Y	Y	N
15 ***Toomey***	Y	N	N	Y	Y	Y	Y	Y
16 ***Pitts***	Y	N	N	Y	Y	Y	Y	Y
17 ***Gekas***	Y	N	N	Y	Y	Y	Y	Y
18 Doyle	Y	N	N	Y	Y	Y	Y	N
19 ***Platts***	Y	?	N	Y	Y	Y	Y	Y
20 Mascara	Y	N	N	Y	Y	Y	Y	N
21 ***English***	N	N	N	Y	Y	Y	Y	Y
RHODE ISLAND								
1 Kennedy	Y	Y	N	Y	Y	Y	Y	N
2 Langevin	Y	Y	N	Y	Y	Y	Y	N
SOUTH CAROLINA								
1 ***Brown***	Y	N	N	Y	Y	Y	Y	Y
2 ***Wilson***	Y	N	N	Y	Y	Y	Y	Y
3 ***Graham***	Y	N	N	Y	Y	Y	Y	Y
4 ***DeMint***	Y	N	N	Y	Y	Y	Y	Y
5 Spratt	Y	N	N	Y	Y	Y	Y	N
6 Clyburn	N	Y	Y	Y	Y	Y	Y	N
SOUTH DAKOTA								
AL ***Thune***	Y	N	N	Y	Y	Y	Y	Y

	267	268	269	270	271	272	273	274
TENNESSEE								
1 ***Jenkins***	Y	N	N	Y	Y	Y	Y	Y
2 ***Duncan***	Y	N	Y	Y	Y	Y	Y	Y
3 ***Wamp***	Y	N	N	Y	Y	Y	Y	Y
4 ***Hilleary***	Y	N	N	Y	Y	Y	Y	Y
5 Clement	Y	N	N	Y	Y	Y	Y	N
6 Gordon	Y	N	N	Y	Y	Y	Y	N
7 ***Bryant***	Y	N	N	Y	Y	Y	Y	Y
8 Tanner	Y	N	N	Y	Y	Y	Y	N
9 Ford	Y	N	N	Y	Y	Y	Y	N
TEXAS								
1 Sandlin	N	Y	N	Y	Y	Y	Y	N
2 Turner	Y	N	N	Y	Y	Y	Y	N
3 ***Johnson, Sam***	Y	N	N	Y	Y	Y	Y	Y
4 Hall	Y	N	N	Y	Y	Y	Y	N
5 ***Sessions***	Y	N	N	Y	Y	Y	Y	Y
6 ***Barton***	Y	N	N	Y	Y	Y	Y	Y
7 ***Culberson***	Y	N	N	Y	Y	?	Y	Y
8 ***Brady***	Y	N	N	Y	Y	Y	Y	Y
9 Lampson	Y	Y	N	Y	Y	Y	Y	N
10 Doggett	Y	Y	Y	Y	Y	Y	Y	N
11 Edwards	Y	N	N	Y	Y	Y	Y	N
12 ***Granger***	Y	N	N	Y	Y	Y	Y	Y
13 ***Thornberry***	Y	N	N	Y	Y	Y	Y	Y
14 ***Paul***	Y	N	Y	N	Y	Y	Y	Y
15 Hinojosa	Y	N	N	Y	Y	Y	Y	N
16 Reyes	Y	?	N	Y	Y	Y	Y	N
17 Stenholm	Y	N	N	Y	Y	Y	Y	N
18 Jackson-Lee	N	N	Y	Y	Y	Y	Y	N
19 ***Combest***	Y	N	N	Y	Y	Y	Y	Y
20 Gonzalez	Y	N	N	Y	Y	Y	Y	N
21 ***Smith***	Y	N	N	Y	Y	Y	Y	Y
22 ***DeLay***	Y	N	N	Y	Y	Y	Y	Y
23 ***Bonilla***	Y	N	N	Y	Y	Y	Y	Y
24 Frost	Y	N	N	Y	Y	Y	Y	N
25 Bentsen	Y	Y	N	Y	?	Y	Y	N
26 ***Armey***	Y	N	N	Y	Y	Y	Y	Y
27 Ortiz	Y	N	N	Y	Y	Y	Y	N
28 Rodriguez	Y	N	N	Y	Y	Y	Y	N
29 Green	N	N	N	Y	Y	Y	Y	N
30 Johnson, E.B.	N	Y	N	Y	Y	Y	Y	N
UTAH								
1 ***Hansen***	Y	N	N	Y	Y	Y	Y	Y
2 Matheson	Y	N	N	Y	Y	Y	Y	N
3 ***Cannon***	Y	N	N	Y	Y	Y	Y	Y
VERMONT								
AL *Sanders*	Y	Y	Y	N	Y	Y	Y	N
VIRGINIA								
1 ***Davis, Jo Ann***	Y	N	N	Y	Y	Y	Y	Y
2 ***Schrock***	Y	N	N	Y	Y	Y	Y	Y
3 Scott	Y	N	N	Y	Y	Y	N	N
4 ***Forbes***	Y	N	N	Y	Y	Y	Y	Y
5 *Goode*	Y	N	N	Y	Y	Y	Y	Y
6 ***Goodlatte***	Y	N	N	Y	Y	Y	Y	Y
7 ***Cantor***	Y	N	N	Y	Y	Y	Y	Y
8 Moran	Y	Y	N	Y	Y	Y	Y	N
9 Boucher	Y	N	N	Y	Y	Y	Y	N
10 ***Wolf***	Y	N	N	Y	Y	Y	Y	Y
11 ***Davis, T.***	Y	N	N	Y	Y	Y	Y	Y
WASHINGTON								
1 Inslee	Y	N	Y	Y	Y	Y	Y	N
2 Larsen	N	Y	Y	Y	Y	Y	Y	N
3 Baird	N	Y	Y	Y	Y	Y	Y	N
4 ***Hastings***	Y	N	N	Y	Y	Y	Y	Y
5 ***Nethercutt***	Y	N	N	Y	Y	Y	Y	Y
6 Dicks	?	Y	N	Y	Y	Y	Y	N
7 McDermott	N	Y	Y	N	Y	Y	P	N
8 ***Dunn***	Y	N	N	Y	Y	Y	Y	Y
9 Smith	?	N	Y	Y	Y	Y	Y	N
WEST VIRGINIA								
1 Mollohan	Y	N	N	Y	Y	Y	Y	N
2 ***Capito***	Y	Y	N	Y	Y	Y	Y	Y
3 Rahall	Y	N	Y	Y	Y	Y	Y	N
WISCONSIN								
1 ***Ryan***	Y	N	N	Y	Y	Y	Y	Y
2 Baldwin	N	Y	Y	N	Y	Y	Y	N
3 Kind	Y	N	Y	Y	Y	Y	Y	N
4 Kleczka	Y	N	Y	Y	Y	Y	Y	N
5 Barrett	Y	N	Y	Y	Y	Y	Y	N
6 ***Petri***	Y	N	N	Y	Y	Y	Y	Y
7 Obey	N	Y	Y	Y	Y	Y	Y	N
8 ***Green***	Y	N	N	Y	Y	Y	Y	Y
9 ***Sensenbrenner***	Y	N	N	Y	Y	Y	Y	Y
WYOMING								
AL ***Cubin***	Y	Y	N	Y	Y	Y	Y	Y

Southern states - Ala., Ark., Fla., Ga., Ky., La., Miss., N.C., Okla., S.C., Tenn., Texas, Va.

275. HR 5011. Fiscal 2003 Military Construction Appropriations/ Amendment to the Rule. Myrick, R-N.C., amendment to the rule (H Res 462) that would provide for House floor consideration of the bill that would provide $10.1 billion in fiscal 2003 for military construction projects. The amendment would provide for House floor consideration of the bill (S 2578) that would increase the public debt limit by approximately $450 billion. Approved 219-211: R 218-1; D 0-209 (ND 0-155, SD 0-54); I 1-1. June 27, 2002.

276. HR 5011. Fiscal 2003 Military Construction Appropriations/Rule. Adoption of the rule (H Res 462) to provide for House floor consideration of the bill that would provide $10.1 billion in fiscal 2003 for military construction projects and of the bill (S 2578) that would increase the public debt limit by approximately $450 billion. Adopted 269-160: R 220-0; D 48-159 (ND 27-126, SD 21-33); I 1-1. June 27, 2002.

277. HR 5011. Fiscal 2003 Military Construction Appropriations/Passage. Passage of the bill that would provide $10.1 billion in fiscal 2003 for military construction projects including the building of barracks, family housing, and medical facilities, $522 million less than the current level. The bill includes $545 million to cover costs of prior base closures and $673 million for anti-terrorism activities. It also includes funds for child care centers, environmental clean up at closed military facilities, and the U.S. contribution to North Atlantic Treaty Organization security efforts. Passed 426-1: R 218-1; D 206-0 (ND 153-0, SD 53-0); I 2-0. June 27, 2002.

278. S 2578. Debt Limit/Recommit. Moore, D-Kansas, motion to recommit the bill to the House Ways and Means Committee with instructions that it be reported back with language that would increase the public debt limit by approximately $150 billion. Motion rejected 207-222: R 0-218; D 206-3 (ND 153-2, SD 53-1); I 1-1. June 27, 2002.

279. S 2578. Debt Limit/Passage. Passage of the bill that would increase the public debt limit by approximately $450 billion. Passed (thus cleared for the president) 215-214: R 212-6; D 3-206 (ND 2-153, SD 1-53); I 0-2. A "yea" was a vote in support of the president's position. June 27, 2002.

280. HR 4954. Prescription Drug Coverage/Rule. Adoption of the rule (H Res 465) to provide for House floor consideration of the bill that would allow Medicare recipients to cover prescription drug costs through private insurance policies beginning in 2005. Adopted 218-213: R 217-4; D 0-208 (ND 0-154, SD 0-54); I 1-1. June 27, 2002.

281. HR4954. Prescription Drug Coverage/Recommit. Gephardt, D-Mo., motion to recommit the bill to the House Ways and Means Committee and the Energy and Commerce Committee with instructions that it be reported back promptly with language that would set up a prescription drug program through Medicare. Patients would pay a $25 monthly premium, with a $100 deductible. Patients would be required to pay 20 percent of drug costs up to $2,000; Medicare would cover all costs above $2,000. Motion rejected 204-223: R 0-220; D 203-2 (ND 152-1, SD 51-1); I 1-1. June 28, 2002 (in the session that began and the Congressional Record that is dated June 27, 2002).

282. HR 4954. Prescription Drug Coverage/Passage. Passage of the bill that would allow Medicare recipients to cover prescription drug costs through private insurance policies beginning in 2005. The bill would cost $350 billion over 10 years. Patients would pay a $33 monthly premium, with a $250 annual deductible. Patients would pay 20 percent of drug costs from $251 to $1,000 and 50 percent of the next $1,000. They would pay all costs from $2,001 to $3,700, after which insurers would pay the entire cost. Subsidies would reduce premiums and co-payments for low-income patients. Passed 221-208: R 212-8; D 8-199 (ND 6-148, SD 2-51); I 1-1. June 28, 2002 (in the session that began and the Congressional Record that is dated June 27, 2002).

Key

Y	Voted for (yea).
#	Paired for.
+	Announced for.
N	Voted against (nay).
X	Paired against.
−	Announced against.
P	Voted "present."
C	Voted "present" to avoid possible conflict of interest.
?	Did not vote or otherwise make a position known.

Democrats **Republicans**
Independents

		275	276	277	278	279	280	281	282
ALABAMA									
1	*Callahan*	Y	Y	Y	N	Y	Y	N	Y
2	*Everett*	Y	Y	Y	N	Y	Y	N	Y
3	*Riley*	Y	Y	Y	N	Y	Y	N	Y
4	*Aderholt*	Y	Y	Y	N	Y	Y	N	Y
5	Cramer	N	N	Y	Y	N	N	Y	N
6	*Bachus*	Y	Y	Y	N	Y	Y	N	Y
7	Hilliard	N	N	Y	Y	N	N	Y	N
ALASKA									
AL	*Young*	Y	Y	Y	N	Y	Y	N	Y
ARIZONA									
1	*Flake*	Y	Y	Y	N	Y	Y	N	N
2	Pastor	N	Y	Y	Y	N	N	Y	N
3	*Stump*	Y	Y	Y	N	Y	Y	N	Y
4	*Shadegg*	Y	Y	Y	N	Y	Y	N	Y
5	*Kolbe*	Y	Y	Y	N	Y	Y	N	Y
6	*Hayworth*	Y	Y	Y	N	Y	Y	N	Y
ARKANSAS									
1	Berry	N	N	Y	Y	N	N	N	N
2	Snyder	N	N	Y	Y	N	N	Y	N
3	*Boozman*	Y	Y	Y	N	Y	Y	N	Y
4	Ross	N	N	Y	Y	N	N	Y	N
CALIFORNIA									
1	Thompson	N	N	Y	N	N	N	Y	N
2	*Herger*	Y	Y	Y	N	Y	Y	N	Y
3	*Ose*	Y	Y	Y	N	Y	Y	N	Y
4	*Doolittle*	Y	Y	Y	N	Y	Y	N	Y
5	Matsui	N	N	Y	Y	N	N	Y	N
6	Woolsey	N	N	Y	Y	N	N	Y	N
7	Miller, George	N	N	?	Y	N	N	Y	N
8	Pelosi	N	Y	Y	Y	N	N	Y	N
9	Lee	N	N	Y	Y	N	N	Y	N
10	Tauscher	N	N	Y	Y	N	N	Y	N
11	*Pombo*	Y	Y	Y	N	Y	Y	N	Y
12	Lantos	N	Y	Y	Y	N	N	Y	N
13	Stark	N	N	Y	Y	N	N	Y	N
14	Eshoo	N	N	Y	Y	N	N	Y	N
15	Honda	N	N	Y	Y	N	N	Y	N
16	Lofgren	N	N	Y	Y	N	N	Y	N
17	Farr	N	N	Y	Y	N	N	Y	N
18	Condit	N	N	Y	Y	N	N	N	Y
19	*Radanovich*	Y	Y	Y	N	Y	Y	N	Y
20	Dooley	N	N	Y	Y	N	N	Y	N
21	*Thomas*	Y	Y	Y	N	Y	Y	N	Y
22	Capps	N	Y	Y	Y	N	N	Y	N
23	*Gallegly*	Y	Y	Y	N	Y	Y	N	Y
24	Sherman	N	N	Y	Y	N	N	Y	N
25	*McKeon*	Y	Y	Y	N	Y	Y	N	Y
26	Berman	N	N	Y	Y	N	N	Y	N
27	Schiff	N	Y	Y	Y	N	N	Y	N
28	*Dreier*	Y	Y	Y	N	Y	Y	N	Y
29	Waxman	N	N	Y	Y	N	N	Y	N
30	Becerra	N	N	Y	Y	N	N	Y	N
31	Solis	N	N	Y	Y	N	N	Y	N
32	Watson	N	N	Y	Y	N	N	Y	N
33	Roybal-Allard	N	N	Y	Y	N	N	Y	N
34	Napolitano	N	N	Y	Y	N	N	Y	N
35	Waters	N	N	Y	Y	N	N	Y	N
36	Harman	N	N	Y	Y	N	N	Y	N
37	Millender-McD.	N	N	Y	Y	N	N	Y	N
38	*Horn*	Y	Y	Y	N	Y	Y	N	Y

		275	276	277	278	279	280	281	282
39	*Royce*	Y	Y	Y	N	Y	Y	N	Y
40	*Lewis*	Y	Y	Y	N	Y	Y	N	Y
41	*Miller, Gary*	Y	Y	Y	N	Y	Y	N	Y
42	Baca	N	?	Y	Y	N	N	Y	N
43	*Calvert*	Y	Y	Y	N	Y	Y	N	Y
44	*Bono*	Y	Y	Y	N	Y	Y	N	Y
45	*Rohrabacher*	Y	Y	Y	N	Y	Y	N	Y
46	Sanchez	N	N	Y	Y	N	N	Y	N
47	*Cox*	Y	Y	Y	N	Y	Y	N	Y
48	*Issa*	Y	Y	Y	N	Y	Y	N	Y
49	Davis	N	Y	Y	Y	N	N	Y	N
50	Filner	N	N	Y	Y	N	N	Y	N
51	*Cunningham*	Y	Y	Y	N	Y	Y	N	Y
52	*Hunter*	Y	Y	Y	N	Y	Y	N	Y
COLORADO									
1	DeGette	N	N	Y	Y	N	N	Y	N
2	Udall	N	N	Y	Y	N	N	Y	N
3	*McInnis*	Y	Y	Y	N	Y	Y	N	Y
4	*Schaffer*	Y	Y	Y	N	Y	Y	N	Y
5	*Hefley*	Y	Y	Y	N	Y	Y	N	Y
6	*Tancredo*	Y	Y	Y	N	Y	Y	N	Y
CONNECTICUT									
1	Larson	N	Y	Y	Y	N	N	Y	N
2	*Simmons*	Y	Y	Y	N	Y	Y	N	Y
3	DeLauro	N	N	Y	Y	N	N	Y	N
4	*Shays*	Y	Y	Y	N	Y	Y	N	Y
5	Maloney	N	Y	Y	Y	N	N	Y	N
6	*Johnson*	Y	Y	Y	N	Y	Y	N	Y
DELAWARE									
AL	*Castle*	Y	Y	Y	N	Y	Y	N	Y
FLORIDA									
1	*Miller, J.*	N	N	Y	N	Y	Y	N	Y
2	Boyd	N	N	Y	N	N	N	N	N
3	Brown	N	N	Y	Y	N	N	Y	N
4	*Crenshaw*	Y	Y	Y	N	Y	Y	N	Y
5	Thurman	N	N	Y	Y	N	N	Y	N
6	*Stearns*	Y	Y	Y	N	Y	Y	N	Y
7	*Mica*	Y	Y	Y	N	Y	Y	N	Y
8	*Keller*	Y	Y	Y	N	Y	Y	N	Y
9	*Bilirakis*	Y	Y	Y	N	Y	Y	N	Y
10	*Young*	Y	Y	Y	N	Y	Y	N	Y
11	Davis	N	N	Y	Y	N	N	Y	N
12	*Putnam*	Y	Y	Y	N	Y	Y	N	Y
13	*Miller, D.*	Y	Y	Y	N	Y	Y	N	Y
14	*Goss*	Y	Y	Y	N	Y	Y	N	Y
15	*Weldon*	Y	Y	Y	N	Y	Y	N	Y
16	*Foley*	Y	Y	Y	N	Y	Y	N	Y
17	Meek	N	N	Y	Y	N	N	Y	N
18	*Ros-Lehtinen*	Y	Y	Y	N	Y	Y	N	Y
19	Wexler	N	N	Y	Y	N	N	Y	N
20	Deutsch	N	N	Y	Y	N	N	Y	N
21	*Diaz-Balart*	Y	Y	Y	N	Y	Y	N	Y
22	*Shaw*	Y	Y	Y	N	Y	Y	N	Y
23	Hastings	N	N	Y	Y	N	N	Y	N
GEORGIA									
1	*Kingston*	Y	Y	Y	N	Y	Y	N	Y
2	Bishop	N	Y	Y	N	N	N	Y	N
3	*Collins*	Y	Y	Y	N	Y	Y	N	Y
4	McKinney	N	Y	Y	Y	N	N	Y	N
5	Lewis	N	N	Y	Y	N	N	Y	N
6	*Isakson*	Y	Y	Y	N	Y	Y	N	Y
7	*Barr*	Y	Y	Y	N	Y	Y	N	Y
8	*Chambliss*	Y	Y	Y	N	Y	Y	N	Y
9	*Deal*	Y	Y	Y	N	Y	Y	N	Y
10	*Norwood*	Y	Y	Y	N	Y	Y	N	Y
11	*Linder*	Y	Y	Y	N	Y	Y	N	Y
HAWAII									
1	Abercrombie	N	N	Y	Y	N	N	Y	N
2	Mink	N	N	Y	Y	N	N	Y	N
IDAHO									
1	*Otter*	Y	Y	Y	N	Y	Y	N	Y
2	*Simpson*	Y	Y	Y	N	Y	Y	N	Y
ILLINOIS									
1	Rush	N	N	Y	N	N	N	Y	N
2	Jackson	N	N	Y	Y	N	N	Y	N
3	Lipinski	N	N	Y	Y	N	N	Y	N
4	Gutierrez	N	N	Y	N	N	N	?	N
5	Blagojevich	N	N	Y	Y	N	N	Y	N
6	*Hyde*	Y	Y	Y	N	Y	Y	N	Y
7	Davis	N	N	Y	N	N	N	Y	N
8	*Crane*	Y	Y	Y	N	Y	Y	N	Y
9	Schakowsky	N	N	Y	Y	N	N	Y	N
10	*Kirk*	Y	Y	Y	N	Y	Y	N	Y
11	*Weller*	Y	Y	Y	N	Y	Y	N	Y
12	Costello	N	N	Y	Y	N	N	Y	N
13	*Biggert*	Y	Y	Y	N	Y	Y	N	Y

ND Northern Democrats SD Southern Democrats

	275	276	277	278	279	280	281	282
14 ***Hastert***				N	Y	Y	N	Y
15 ***Johnson***	Y	Y	Y	N	Y	Y	N	Y
16 ***Manzullo***	Y	Y	Y	N	Y	Y	N	N
17 Evans	N	N	Y	Y	N	N	Y	N
18 ***LaHood***	Y	Y	Y	N	Y	Y	N	Y
19 Phelps	N	N	Y	Y	N	N	Y	N
20 ***Shimkus***	Y	Y	Y	N	Y	Y	N	Y
INDIANA								
1 Visclosky	N	N	Y	Y	N	N	Y	N
2 ***Pence***	Y	Y	Y	N	Y	Y	N	Y
3 Roemer	N	N	Y	Y	N	N	N	N
4 ***Souder***	Y	Y	Y	N	Y	Y	N	Y
5 ***Buyer***	Y	Y	Y	N	Y	Y	N	Y
6 ***Burton***	Y	Y	Y	N	Y	Y	N	Y
7 ***Kerns***	Y	Y	Y	N	Y	Y	N	Y
8 ***Hostettler***	Y	Y	Y	N	Y	Y	N	N
9 Hill	N	N	Y	Y	N	N	Y	N
10 Carson	N	N	Y	Y	N	N	Y	N
IOWA								
1 ***Leach***	Y	Y	Y	N	Y	Y	N	Y
2 ***Nussle***	Y	Y	Y	N	Y	Y	N	Y
3 Boswell	N	N	Y	Y	N	N	Y	Y
4 ***Ganske***	Y	Y	Y	N	Y	Y	N	Y
5 ***Latham***	Y	Y	Y	N	Y	Y	N	Y
KANSAS								
1 ***Moran***	Y	Y	Y	N	N	Y	N	Y
2 ***Ryun***	Y	Y	Y	N	Y	Y	N	Y
3 Moore	N	N	Y	Y	N	N	Y	N
4 ***Tiahrt***	Y	Y	Y	N	Y	Y	N	Y
KENTUCKY								
1 ***Whitfield***	Y	Y	Y	N	Y	Y	N	Y
2 ***Lewis***	Y	Y	Y	N	Y	Y	N	Y
3 ***Northup***	Y	Y	Y	N	Y	Y	N	Y
4 Lucas	N	Y	Y	Y	N	N	Y	Y
5 ***Rogers***	Y	Y	Y	N	Y	Y	N	Y
6 ***Fletcher***	Y	Y	Y	N	Y	Y	N	Y
LOUISIANA								
1 ***Vitter***	Y	Y	Y	N	Y	Y	N	Y
2 Jefferson	N	N	Y	Y	N	N	?	?
3 ***Tauzin***	Y	Y	Y	N	Y	Y	N	Y
4 ***McCrery***	Y	Y	Y	N	Y	Y	N	Y
5 ***Cooksey***	Y	Y	Y	N	Y	Y	N	Y
6 ***Baker***	Y	Y	Y	N	Y	Y	N	Y
7 John	N	N	Y	Y	N	N	Y	N
MAINE								
1 Allen	N	N	Y	Y	N	N	Y	N
2 Baldacci	N	N	Y	Y	N	N	Y	N
MARYLAND								
1 ***Gilchrest***	Y	Y	Y	N	Y	Y	N	Y
2 ***Ehrlich***	Y	Y	Y	N	Y	Y	N	Y
3 Cardin	N	Y	Y	Y	N	N	Y	N
4 Wynn	N	Y	Y	Y	N	N	Y	N
5 Hoyer	N	Y	Y	Y	N	N	Y	N
6 ***Bartlett***	Y	Y	Y	N	P	Y	N	Y
7 Cummings	N	Y	Y	Y	N	N	Y	N
8 ***Morella***	Y	Y	Y	N	Y	N	N	Y
MASSACHUSETTS								
1 Olver	N	N	Y	Y	N	N	Y	N
2 Neal	N	N	Y	Y	N	N	Y	N
3 McGovern	N	N	Y	Y	N	N	Y	N
4 Frank	N	N	Y	Y	N	N	Y	N
5 Meehan	N	N	Y	Y	N	N	Y	N
6 Tierney	N	N	?	Y	N	N	Y	N
7 Markey	N	N	Y	Y	N	N	Y	N
8 Capuano	N	N	Y	Y	N	N	Y	N
9 Lynch	N	N	Y	Y	N	N	Y	N
10 Delahunt	N	N	Y	Y	N	N	Y	N
MICHIGAN								
1 Stupak	N	N	Y	Y	N	N	Y	N
2 ***Hoekstra***	Y	Y	Y	N	Y	Y	N	Y
3 ***Ehlers***	Y	Y	Y	N	Y	Y	N	Y
4 ***Camp***	Y	Y	Y	N	Y	Y	N	Y
5 Barcia	N	N	Y	Y	N	N	Y	N
6 ***Upton***	Y	Y	Y	N	Y	Y	N	Y
7 ***Smith***	Y	Y	Y	N	Y	Y	N	N
8 ***Rogers***	Y	Y	Y	N	Y	Y	N	Y
9 Kildee	N	N	Y	Y	N	N	Y	N
10 Bonior	N	N	Y	Y	N	N	Y	N
11 ***Knollenberg***	Y	Y	Y	N	Y	Y	N	Y
12 Levin	N	N	Y	Y	N	N	Y	N
13 Rivers	N	N	Y	Y	N	N	Y	N
14 Conyers	N	N	Y	Y	N	N	Y	N
15 Kilpatrick	N	Y	Y	Y	N	N	Y	N
16 Dingell	N	N	Y	Y	N	N	Y	N
MINNESOTA								
1 ***Gutknecht***	Y	Y	Y	N	Y	N	N	N
2 ***Kennedy***	Y	Y	Y	N	Y	Y	N	Y
3 ***Ramstad***	Y	Y	Y	N	Y	Y	N	Y
4 McCollum	N	N	Y	Y	N	N	Y	N
5 Sabo	N	Y	Y	Y	N	N	Y	N
6 Luther	N	N	Y	Y	N	N	Y	N
7 Peterson	N	N	Y	Y	N	N	Y	Y
8 Oberstar	N	N	Y	Y	N	N	Y	N
MISSISSIPPI								
1 ***Wicker***	Y	Y	Y	N	Y	Y	N	Y
2 Thompson	N	N	Y	Y	N	N	?	N
3 ***Pickering***	Y	Y	Y	N	Y	Y	N	Y
4 Shows	N	N	Y	Y	N	N	Y	N
5 Taylor	N	N	Y	N	N	N	N	N
MISSOURI								
1 Clay	N	N	Y	Y	N	?	?	?
2 ***Akin***	Y	Y	Y	N	Y	Y	N	Y
3 Gephardt	N	N	Y	Y	N	N	Y	N
4 Skelton	N	N	Y	Y	N	N	Y	N
5 McCarthy	N	Y	Y	Y	N	N	Y	N
6 ***Graves***	Y	Y	Y	N	Y	Y	N	Y
7 ***Blunt***	Y	Y	Y	N	Y	Y	N	Y
8 ***Emerson***	Y	Y	Y	N	Y	Y	N	N
9 ***Hulshof***	Y	Y	Y	N	Y	Y	N	Y
MONTANA								
AL ***Rehberg***	Y	Y	Y	N	Y	Y	N	Y
NEBRASKA								
1 ***Bereuter***	Y	Y	Y	N	Y	Y	N	Y
2 ***Terry***	Y	Y	Y	N	Y	Y	N	Y
3 ***Osborne***	Y	Y	Y	N	Y	Y	N	Y
NEVADA								
1 Berkley	N	Y	Y	Y	N	N	Y	N
2 ***Gibbons***	Y	Y	Y	N	Y	Y	N	Y
NEW HAMPSHIRE								
1 ***Sununu***	Y	Y	Y	N	Y	Y	N	Y
2 ***Bass***	Y	Y	Y	N	Y	Y	N	Y
NEW JERSEY								
1 Andrews	N	N	Y	Y	N	N	Y	N
2 ***LoBiondo***	Y	Y	Y	N	Y	Y	N	Y
3 ***Saxton***	Y	Y	Y	N	Y	Y	N	Y
4 ***Smith***	Y	Y	Y	N	Y	Y	N	Y
5 ***Roukema***	?	?	?	?	?	?	?	?
6 Pallone	N	N	Y	Y	N	N	Y	N
7 ***Ferguson***	Y	Y	Y	N	Y	Y	N	Y
8 Pascrell	N	N	Y	Y	N	N	Y	N
9 Rothman	N	N	Y	Y	N	N	Y	N
10 Payne	N	N	Y	Y	N	N	Y	N
11 ***Frelinghuysen***	Y	Y	Y	N	Y	Y	N	Y
12 Holt	N	N	Y	Y	N	N	Y	N
13 Menendez	N	N	Y	Y	N	N	Y	N
NEW MEXICO								
1 ***Wilson***	Y	Y	Y	N	Y	Y	N	Y
2 ***Skeen***	Y	Y	Y	N	Y	Y	N	Y
3 Udall	N	Y	Y	Y	N	N	Y	N
NEW YORK								
1 ***Grucci***	Y	Y	Y	N	Y	Y	N	Y
2 Israel	N	N	Y	Y	N	N	Y	Y
3 ***King***	Y	Y	Y	N	Y	Y	N	Y
4 McCarthy	N	N	Y	Y	N	N	Y	N
5 Ackerman	N	N	Y	Y	N	N	Y	N
6 Meeks	N	N	Y	Y	N	N	Y	N
7 Crowley	N	N	Y	Y	N	N	Y	N
8 Nadler	N	Y	Y	Y	N	N	Y	N
9 Weiner	N	Y	Y	Y	N	N	Y	N
10 Towns	N	N	Y	Y	N	N	?	?
11 Owens	N	N	Y	Y	N	N	Y	N
12 Velázquez	N	N	Y	Y	N	N	Y	N
13 ***Fossella***	?	Y	Y	N	Y	Y	N	Y
14 Maloney	N	Y	Y	Y	N	N	Y	N
15 Rangel	N	N	Y	Y	N	N	Y	N
16 Serrano	N	N	Y	Y	N	N	Y	N
17 Engel	?	?	?	?	?	?	Y	N
18 Lowey	N	N	Y	Y	N	N	Y	N
19 ***Kelly***	Y	Y	Y	N	Y	Y	N	Y
20 ***Gilman***	Y	Y	Y	N	Y	Y	N	Y
21 McNulty	N	N	Y	Y	N	N	Y	N
22 ***Sweeney***	Y	Y	Y	N	Y	Y	N	Y
23 ***Boehlert***	Y	Y	Y	N	Y	Y	N	Y
24 ***McHugh***	Y	Y	Y	N	Y	Y	N	Y
25 ***Walsh***	Y	Y	Y	N	Y	Y	N	Y
26 Hinchey	N	N	Y	Y	N	N	Y	N
27 ***Reynolds***	Y	Y	Y	N	Y	Y	N	Y
28 Slaughter	N	Y	Y	Y	N	N	Y	N
29 LaFalce	N	N	Y	Y	N	N	Y	N
30 ***Quinn***	Y	Y	Y	N	Y	Y	N	Y
31 ***Houghton***	Y	Y	Y	N	Y	Y	N	Y
NORTH CAROLINA								
1 Clayton	N	N	Y	Y	N	N	Y	N
2 Etheridge	N	Y	Y	Y	N	N	Y	N
3 ***Jones***	Y	Y	Y	N	N	N	N	Y
4 Price	N	Y	Y	Y	N	N	Y	N
5 ***Burr***	Y	Y	Y	N	Y	Y	N	Y
6 ***Coble***	Y	Y	Y	N	Y	Y	N	Y
7 McIntyre	N	N	Y	Y	N	N	Y	N
8 ***Hayes***	Y	Y	Y	N	?	Y	N	Y
9 ***Myrick***	Y	Y	Y	N	Y	Y	N	Y
10 ***Ballenger***	Y	Y	Y	N	Y	Y	N	Y
11 ***Taylor***	Y	Y	Y	N	Y	Y	N	Y
12 Watt	N	N	Y	Y	N	N	Y	N
NORTH DAKOTA								
AL Pomeroy	N	Y	Y	Y	N	N	Y	N
OHIO								
1 ***Chabot***	Y	Y	Y	N	Y	Y	N	Y
2 ***Portman***	Y	Y	Y	N	Y	Y	N	Y
3 Hall	N	N	Y	Y	N	N	Y	N
4 ***Oxley***	Y	Y	Y	?	?	Y	N	Y
5 ***Gillmor***	Y	Y	Y	N	Y	Y	N	Y
6 Strickland	N	N	Y	Y	N	N	Y	N
7 ***Hobson***	Y	Y	Y	N	Y	Y	N	Y
8 ***Boehner***	Y	Y	Y	N	Y	Y	N	Y
9 Kaptur	N	N	Y	Y	N	N	Y	N
10 Kucinich	N	N	Y	Y	Y	N	Y	N
11 Jones	N	N	Y	Y	N	N	Y	N
12 ***Tiberi***	Y	Y	Y	N	Y	Y	N	Y
13 Brown	N	N	Y	Y	N	N	Y	N
14 Sawyer	N	N	Y	Y	N	N	Y	N
15 ***Pryce***	Y	Y	Y	N	Y	Y	N	Y
16 ***Regula***	Y	Y	Y	N	Y	Y	N	Y
17 Traficant	?	?	?	?	?	?	?	?
18 ***Ney***	Y	Y	Y	N	Y	Y	N	Y
19 ***LaTourette***	Y	Y	Y	N	Y	Y	N	Y
OKLAHOMA								
1 ***Sullivan***	Y	Y	Y	N	Y	Y	N	Y
2 Carson	N	N	Y	Y	N	N	Y	N
3 ***Watkins***	Y	Y	Y	N	Y	Y	N	Y
4 ***Watts***	Y	Y	Y	N	Y	Y	N	Y
5 ***Istook***	Y	Y	Y	N	Y	N	N	N
6 ***Lucas***	Y	Y	Y	N	Y	Y	N	Y
OREGON								
1 Wu	N	N	Y	N	N	N	Y	N
2 ***Walden***	Y	Y	Y	N	Y	Y	N	Y
3 Blumenauer	N	N	Y	Y	N	N	Y	N
4 DeFazio	N	N	Y	Y	N	N	Y	N
5 Hooley	N	N	Y	Y	N	N	Y	N
PENNSYLVANIA								
1 Brady	N	N	Y	Y	N	N	Y	N
2 Fattah	N	?	Y	Y	N	N	Y	N
3 Borski	N	N	Y	Y	N	N	Y	N
4 ***Hart***	Y	Y	Y	N	Y	Y	N	Y
5 ***Peterson***	Y	Y	Y	N	Y	Y	N	Y
6 Holden	N	N	Y	Y	N	N	Y	N
7 ***Weldon***	Y	Y	Y	?	Y	Y	N	Y
8 ***Greenwood***	Y	Y	Y	N	Y	Y	N	Y
9 ***Shuster, Bill***	Y	Y	Y	N	Y	Y	N	Y
10 ***Sherwood***	Y	Y	Y	N	Y	Y	N	Y
11 Kanjorski	N	N	Y	Y	N	N	Y	N
12 Murtha	N	Y	Y	Y	N	N	Y	N
13 Hoeffel	N	N	Y	Y	N	N	Y	N
14 Coyne	N	N	Y	Y	N	N	Y	N
15 ***Toomey***	Y	Y	Y	N	Y	Y	N	Y
16 ***Pitts***	Y	Y	Y	N	Y	Y	N	Y
17 ***Gekas***	Y	Y	Y	N	Y	Y	N	Y
18 Doyle	N	N	Y	Y	N	N	Y	N
19 ***Platts***	Y	Y	Y	N	Y	Y	N	Y
20 Mascara	N	N	Y	Y	N	N	Y	N
21 ***English***	Y	Y	Y	N	Y	Y	N	Y
RHODE ISLAND								
1 Kennedy	N	N	Y	Y	N	N	Y	N
2 Langevin	N	N	Y	Y	N	N	Y	N
SOUTH CAROLINA								
1 ***Brown***	Y	Y	?	N	Y	Y	N	Y
2 ***Wilson***	Y	Y	Y	?	Y	Y	N	Y
3 ***Graham***	Y	Y	Y	N	Y	Y	N	Y
4 ***DeMint***	Y	Y	Y	N	Y	Y	N	Y
5 Spratt	N	Y	Y	Y	N	N	Y	N
6 Clyburn	N	N	Y	Y	N	N	Y	N
SOUTH DAKOTA								
AL ***Thune***	Y	Y	Y	N	Y	Y	N	Y
TENNESSEE								
1 ***Jenkins***	Y	Y	Y	N	Y	Y	N	Y
2 ***Duncan***	Y	Y	Y	N	N	Y	N	Y
3 ***Wamp***	Y	Y	Y	N	N	Y	N	Y
4 ***Hilleary***	Y	Y	Y	N	Y	Y	N	Y
5 Clement	N	Y	Y	Y	N	N	Y	N
6 Gordon	N	Y	?	Y	N	N	Y	N
7 ***Bryant***	Y	Y	Y	N	Y	Y	N	Y
8 Tanner	N	Y	Y	Y	N	N	Y	N
9 Ford	N	N	Y	Y	N	N	Y	N
TEXAS								
1 Sandlin	N	Y	Y	Y	N	N	Y	N
2 Turner	N	N	Y	Y	N	N	Y	N
3 ***Johnson, Sam***	Y	Y	Y	N	Y	Y	N	Y
4 Hall	N	Y	Y	Y	Y	N	Y	Y
5 ***Sessions***	Y	Y	Y	N	Y	Y	N	Y
6 ***Barton***	Y	Y	Y	N	Y	Y	N	Y
7 ***Culberson***	Y	Y	Y	N	Y	Y	N	Y
8 ***Brady***	Y	Y	Y	N	Y	Y	N	Y
9 Lampson	N	N	Y	Y	N	N	Y	N
10 Doggett	N	N	Y	Y	N	N	Y	N
11 Edwards	N	N	Y	Y	N	N	Y	N
12 ***Granger***	Y	Y	Y	N	Y	Y	N	Y
13 ***Thornberry***	Y	Y	Y	N	Y	Y	N	Y
14 ***Paul***	Y	Y	N	N	N	Y	?	?
15 Hinojosa	N	N	Y	Y	N	N	Y	N
16 Reyes	N	Y	Y	Y	N	N	Y	N
17 Stenholm	N	Y	Y	Y	N	N	Y	N
18 Jackson-Lee	N	N	Y	Y	N	N	Y	N
19 ***Combest***	Y	Y	Y	N	Y	Y	N	Y
20 Gonzalez	N	N	Y	Y	N	N	Y	N
21 ***Smith***	Y	Y	Y	N	Y	Y	N	Y
22 ***DeLay***	Y	Y	Y	N	Y	Y	N	Y
23 ***Bonilla***	Y	Y	Y	N	Y	Y	N	Y
24 Frost	N	Y	Y	Y	N	N	Y	N
25 Bentsen	N	N	Y	Y	N	N	Y	N
26 ***Armey***	Y	Y	Y	N	Y	Y	N	Y
27 Ortiz	N	Y	Y	Y	N	N	Y	N
28 Rodriguez	N	Y	Y	Y	N	N	Y	N
29 Green	N	N	Y	Y	N	N	Y	N
30 Johnson, E.B.	N	Y	Y	Y	N	N	Y	N
UTAH								
1 ***Hansen***	Y	Y	Y	N	Y	Y	N	Y
2 Matheson	N	N	Y	Y	N	N	Y	Y
3 ***Cannon***	Y	Y	Y	N	Y	Y	N	Y
VERMONT								
AL *Sanders*	N	N	Y	Y	N	N	Y	N
VIRGINIA								
1 ***Davis, Jo Ann***	Y	Y	Y	N	Y	Y	N	Y
2 ***Schrock***	Y	Y	Y	N	Y	Y	N	Y
3 Scott	N	Y	Y	Y	N	N	Y	N
4 ***Forbes***	Y	Y	Y	N	Y	Y	N	Y
5 *Goode*	Y	Y	Y	N	N	Y	N	Y
6 ***Goodlatte***	Y	Y	Y	N	Y	Y	N	Y
7 ***Cantor***	Y	Y	Y	N	Y	Y	N	Y
8 Moran	N	N	Y	Y	N	N	Y	N
9 Boucher	N	N	Y	Y	N	N	Y	N
10 ***Wolf***	Y	Y	Y	N	Y	Y	N	Y
11 ***Davis, T.***	Y	Y	Y	N	Y	Y	N	Y
WASHINGTON								
1 Inslee	N	N	Y	Y	N	N	Y	N
2 Larsen	N	N	Y	Y	N	N	Y	N
3 Baird	N	N	Y	Y	N	N	Y	N
4 ***Hastings***	Y	Y	Y	N	Y	Y	N	Y
5 ***Nethercutt***	Y	Y	Y	N	Y	Y	N	Y
6 Dicks	N	Y	Y	Y	N	N	Y	N
7 McDermott	N	N	Y	Y	N	N	Y	N
8 ***Dunn***	Y	Y	Y	N	Y	Y	N	Y
9 Smith	N	N	Y	Y	Y	N	Y	N
WEST VIRGINIA								
1 Mollohan	N	Y	Y	Y	N	N	Y	N
2 ***Capito***	Y	Y	Y	N	Y	Y	N	Y
3 Rahall	N	N	Y	Y	N	N	Y	N
WISCONSIN								
1 ***Ryan***	Y	Y	Y	N	Y	Y	N	Y
2 Baldwin	N	N	Y	Y	N	N	Y	N
3 Kind	N	N	Y	Y	N	N	Y	N
4 Kleczka	N	N	Y	Y	N	N	Y	N
5 Barrett	N	N	Y	Y	N	N	Y	N
6 ***Petri***	Y	Y	Y	N	Y	Y	N	Y
7 Obey	N	N	Y	Y	N	N	Y	N
8 ***Green***	Y	Y	Y	N	Y	Y	N	Y
9 ***Sensenbrenner***	Y	Y	Y	N	Y	Y	N	Y
WYOMING								
AL ***Cubin***	Y	Y	Y	N	Y	Y	N	Y

Southern states - Ala., Ark., Fla., Ga., Ky., La., Miss., N.C., Okla., S.C., Tenn., Texas, Va.

Key

Y	Voted for (yea).
#	Paired for.
+	Announced for.
N	Voted against (nay).
X	Paired against.
−	Announced against.
P	Voted "present."
C	Voted "present" to avoid possible conflict of interest.
?	Did not vote or otherwise make a position known.

Democrats   **Republicans**
Independents

---

283. HR 4609. Aquifer Study/Passage. Osborne, R-Neb., motion to suspend the rules and pass the bill that would direct the Interior Department to conduct a comprehensive study of the Rathdrum Prairie/Spokane Valley Aquifer in consultation with the states of Washington and Idaho. Motion agreed to 340-9: R 177-9; D 161-0 (ND 117-0, SD 44-0); I 2-0. A two-thirds majority of those present and voting (233 in this case) is required for passage under suspension of the rules. July 8, 2002.

284. HR 2643. Fort Clatsop National Memorial Expansion/Passage. Osborne, R-Neb., motion to suspend the rules and pass the bill that would authorize the acquisition of additional lands for the Fort Clatsop National Memorial, specifically the trail between Fort Clatsop and the Pacific Ocean and approximately 1,375 acres in Oregon. Motion agreed to 331-18: R 169-16; D 160-2 (ND 117-1, SD 43-1); I 2-0. A two-thirds majority of those present and voting (233 in this case) is required for passage under suspension of the rules. July 8, 2002.

285. HR 3295. Election Overhaul/Motion to Instruct. Langevin, D-R.I., motion to instruct House conferees to insist on Senate provisions that would require voting systems to be as accessible to voters with disabilities, including those with vision and reading impairments, as other voters. The accessibility requirement could be met by providing at least one electronic voting system, or other system equipped for voters with disabilities, at each polling place. Motion agreed to 410-2: R 212-0; D 197-0 (ND 146-0, SD 51-0); I 1-0. July 9, 2002.

286. HR 5063. Military Tax Breaks/Passage. Houghton, R-N.Y., motion to suspend the rules and pass the bill that would exempt from taxable income the full $6,000 cash payment given to the survivors of military members killed in the line of duty, to help offset funeral expenses. It also would ease for military members the requirement that a person live in a principal residence at least two of the last five years to qualify for a capital gains exclusion on the sale of the residence. Motion agreed to 413-0: R 214-0; D 197-0 (ND 146-0, SD 51-0); I 2-0. A two-thirds majority of those present and voting (276 in this case) is required for passage under suspension of the rules. July 9, 2002.

287. H Res 393. European Anti-Semitism/Adoption. Gilman, R-N.Y., motion to suspend the rules and adopt the resolution that would express the sense of the House that European governments should take steps to protect Jewish communities and make a concerted push to create a cooperative atmosphere among Jewish and non-Jewish residents. Motion agreed to 412-0: R 214-0; D 196-0 (ND 145-0, SD 51-0); I 2-0. A two-thirds majority of those present and voting (275 in this case) is required for adoption under suspension of the rules. July 9, 2002.

288. HR 4635. Armed Commercial Pilots/Permanent Program. DeFazio, D-Ore., amendment that would eliminate the bill's 2 percent cap on the number of pilots allowed to participate in the program, make the program permanent, and require that weapons training for pilots volunteering for the program begin within two months of enactment. Adopted 250-175: R 188-31; D 61-143 (ND 34-117, SD 27-26); I 1-1. July 10, 2002.

	283	284	285	286	287	288
ALABAMA						
1 *Callahan*	?	?	Y	Y	Y	Y
2 *Everett*	Y	N	Y	Y	Y	Y
3 *Riley*	+	+	+	+	+	Y
4 *Aderholt*	?	?	Y	Y	Y	Y
5 Cramer	Y	Y	Y	Y	Y	Y
6 *Bachus*	Y	Y	Y	Y	Y	Y
7 Hilliard	Y	Y	Y	Y	Y	Y
ALASKA						
AL *Young*	?	?	Y	Y	Y	N
ARIZONA						
1 *Flake*	N	N	N	Y	Y	Y
2 Pastor	Y	Y	Y	Y	Y	N
3 *Stump*	?	?	Y	Y	Y	Y
4 *Shadegg*	Y	N	Y	Y	Y	Y
5 *Kolbe*	Y	Y	Y	Y	Y	Y
6 *Hayworth*	Y	Y	Y	Y	Y	Y
ARKANSAS						
1 Berry	Y	Y	Y	Y	Y	Y
2 Snyder	Y	Y	Y	Y	Y	N
3 *Boozman*	Y	Y	Y	Y	Y	Y
4 Ross	Y	Y	Y	Y	Y	Y
CALIFORNIA						
1 Thompson	Y	Y	Y	Y	Y	Y
2 *Herger*	Y	Y	Y	Y	Y	Y
3 *Ose*	Y	N	Y	Y	Y	Y
4 *Doolittle*	Y	Y	Y	Y	Y	Y
5 Matsui	?	?	Y	Y	Y	N
6 Woolsey	+	+	Y	Y	Y	N
7 Miller, George	?	?	Y	Y	Y	N
8 Pelosi	Y	Y	?	?	?	N
9 Lee	Y	Y	Y	Y	Y	N
10 Tauscher	Y	Y	Y	Y	Y	N
11 *Pombo*	Y	Y	Y	Y	Y	Y
12 Lantos	?	?	Y	Y	?	N
13 Stark	Y	Y	Y	Y	Y	N
14 Eshoo	Y	Y	Y	Y	Y	N
15 Honda	Y	Y	Y	Y	Y	N
16 Lofgren	Y	Y	Y	Y	Y	N
17 Farr	Y	Y	Y	Y	Y	N
18 Condit	Y	N	Y	Y	Y	Y
19 *Radanovich*	?	?	Y	Y	Y	N
20 Dooley	Y	Y	Y	Y	Y	Y
21 *Thomas*	Y	Y	Y	Y	Y	Y
22 Capps	Y	Y	Y	Y	Y	N
23 *Gallegly*	?	?	Y	Y	Y	N
24 Sherman	Y	Y	Y	Y	Y	Y
25 *McKeon*	Y	Y	Y	Y	Y	Y
26 Berman	?	?	Y	Y	Y	N
27 Schiff	Y	Y	Y	Y	Y	N
28 *Dreier*	Y	Y	?	?	?	Y
29 Waxman	Y	Y	Y	Y	Y	N
30 Becerra	+	+	Y	Y	Y	N
31 Solis	Y	Y	Y	Y	Y	N
32 Watson	Y	Y	Y	Y	Y	N
33 Roybal-Allard	Y	Y	Y	Y	Y	N
34 Napolitano	Y	Y	Y	Y	Y	N
35 Waters	Y	Y	Y	Y	Y	N
36 Harman	Y	Y	Y	Y	Y	Y
37 Millender-McD.	Y	Y	Y	Y	Y	N
38 *Horn*	Y	Y	Y	Y	Y	N

	283	284	285	286	287	288
39 *Royce*	N	N	Y	Y	Y	Y
40 *Lewis*	?	?	Y	Y	Y	Y
41 *Miller, Gary*	Y	Y	Y	Y	Y	Y
42 Baca	Y	Y	Y	Y	Y	N
43 *Calvert*	Y	Y	Y	Y	Y	Y
44 *Bono*	Y	Y	Y	Y	Y	Y
45 *Rohrabacher*	Y	Y	Y	Y	Y	Y
46 Sanchez	Y	Y	Y	Y	Y	N
47 *Cox*	Y	Y	Y	Y	Y	Y
48 *Issa*	Y	Y	Y	Y	Y	Y
49 Davis	Y	Y	Y	Y	Y	N
50 Filner	+	+	Y	Y	Y	N
51 *Cunningham*	Y	Y	Y	Y	Y	Y
52 *Hunter*	Y	Y	Y	Y	Y	Y
COLORADO						
1 DeGette	Y	Y	Y	Y	Y	N
2 Udall	Y	Y	Y	Y	Y	N
3 *McInnis*	Y	Y	Y	Y	Y	Y
4 *Schaffer*	?	?	?	?	?	Y
5 *Hefley*	Y	Y	Y	Y	Y	Y
6 *Tancredo*	?	?	Y	Y	Y	Y
CONNECTICUT						
1 Larson	Y	Y	Y	Y	Y	N
2 *Simmons*	Y	Y	Y	Y	Y	N
3 DeLauro	Y	Y	Y	Y	Y	N
4 *Shays*	Y	Y	Y	Y	Y	Y
5 Maloney	Y	Y	Y	Y	Y	N
6 *Johnson*	Y	Y	Y	Y	Y	N
DELAWARE						
AL *Castle*	Y	Y	Y	Y	Y	N
FLORIDA						
1 *Miller, J.*	Y	Y	Y	Y	Y	Y
2 Boyd	Y	Y	Y	Y	Y	Y
3 Brown	?	?	Y	Y	Y	N
4 *Crenshaw*	Y	Y	Y	Y	Y	Y
5 Thurman	Y	Y	Y	Y	Y	Y
6 *Stearns*	Y	N	Y	Y	Y	Y
7 *Mica*	Y	Y	Y	Y	Y	Y
8 *Keller*	Y	Y	Y	Y	Y	Y
9 *Bilirakis*	Y	Y	Y	Y	Y	Y
10 *Young*	Y	Y	Y	Y	Y	Y
11 Davis	Y	Y	Y	Y	Y	N
12 *Putnam*	Y	Y	Y	Y	Y	Y
13 *Miller, D.*	?	?	Y	Y	Y	Y
14 *Goss*	Y	Y	Y	Y	Y	Y
15 *Weldon*	Y	Y	Y	Y	Y	Y
16 *Foley*	Y	Y	Y	Y	Y	Y
17 Meek	?	?	Y	Y	Y	N
18 *Ros-Lehtinen*	Y	Y	Y	Y	Y	Y
19 Wexler	Y	Y	Y	Y	Y	N
20 Deutsch	Y	Y	Y	Y	Y	Y
21 *Diaz-Balart*	Y	Y	Y	Y	Y	Y
22 *Shaw*	Y	Y	Y	Y	Y	Y
23 Hastings	?	?	?	?	?	?
GEORGIA						
1 *Kingston*	?	?	Y	Y	Y	Y
2 Bishop	?	?	Y	Y	Y	N
3 *Collins*	Y	N	Y	Y	Y	Y
4 McKinney	Y	Y	Y	Y	Y	N
5 Lewis	?	?	Y	Y	Y	N
6 *Isakson*	Y	Y	Y	Y	Y	Y
7 *Barr*	Y	Y	Y	Y	Y	Y
8 *Chambliss*	Y	Y	Y	Y	Y	Y
9 *Deal*	Y	Y	Y	Y	Y	Y
10 *Norwood*	Y	Y	Y	Y	Y	?
11 *Linder*	Y	Y	Y	Y	Y	Y
HAWAII						
1 Abercrombie	Y	Y	Y	Y	Y	Y
2 Mink	Y	Y	Y	Y	Y	N
IDAHO						
1 *Otter*	Y	Y	Y	Y	Y	Y
2 *Simpson*	Y	Y	Y	Y	Y	Y
ILLINOIS						
1 Rush	Y	Y	Y	Y	Y	N
2 Jackson	Y	Y	Y	Y	Y	N
3 Lipinski	?	?	Y	Y	Y	N
4 Gutierrez	?	?	Y	Y	Y	N
5 Blagojevich	?	?	?	?	?	Y
6 *Hyde*	Y	Y	Y	Y	Y	Y
7 Davis	?	?	Y	Y	Y	N
8 *Crane*	Y	Y	Y	Y	Y	Y
9 Schakowsky	+	+	Y	Y	Y	N
10 *Kirk*	Y	Y	Y	Y	Y	N
11 *Weller*	Y	Y	Y	Y	Y	N
12 Costello	Y	Y	Y	Y	Y	N
13 *Biggert*	Y	Y	Y	Y	Y	Y

ND Northern Democrats   SD Southern Democrats

	283	284	285	286	287	288
14 ***Hastert***						
15 ***Johnson***	Y	Y	Y	Y	Y	Y
16 ***Manzullo***	Y	Y	Y	Y	Y	Y
17 Evans	Y	Y	Y	Y	Y	N
18 ***LaHood***	?	?	Y	Y	Y	Y
19 Phelps	Y	Y	Y	Y	Y	Y
20 ***Shimkus***	Y	Y	Y	Y	Y	Y
INDIANA						
1 Visclosky	Y	Y	Y	Y	Y	N
2 ***Pence***	Y	Y	Y	Y	Y	Y
3 Roemer	Y	Y	Y	Y	Y	N
4 ***Souder***	?	?	?	?	?	N
5 ***Buyer***	Y	Y	Y	Y	Y	Y
6 ***Burton***	Y	Y	Y	Y	Y	Y
7 ***Kerns***	N	N	Y	Y	Y	Y
8 ***Hostettler***	Y	N	Y	Y	Y	Y
9 Hill	Y	Y	Y	Y	Y	Y
10 Carson	?	?	Y	Y	Y	N
IOWA						
1 ***Leach***	Y	Y	Y	Y	Y	Y
2 ***Nussle***	Y	Y	Y	Y	Y	Y
3 Boswell	Y	Y	Y	Y	Y	Y
4 ***Ganske***	Y	Y	Y	Y	Y	Y
5 ***Latham***	Y	Y	Y	Y	Y	Y
KANSAS						
1 ***Moran***	Y	Y	Y	Y	Y	Y
2 ***Ryun***	Y	Y	Y	Y	Y	Y
3 Moore	Y	Y	Y	Y	Y	N
4 ***Tiahrt***	Y	Y	Y	Y	Y	Y
KENTUCKY						
1 ***Whitfield***	?	?	Y	Y	Y	Y
2 ***Lewis***	Y	Y	Y	Y	Y	Y
3 ***Northup***	Y	Y	Y	Y	Y	Y
4 Lucas	Y	Y	Y	Y	Y	Y
5 ***Rogers***	Y	Y	Y	Y	Y	N
6 ***Fletcher***	Y	Y	Y	Y	Y	Y
LOUISIANA						
1 ***Vitter***	Y	Y	Y	Y	Y	Y
2 Jefferson	Y	Y	Y	Y	Y	N
3 ***Tauzin***	Y	Y	Y	Y	Y	Y
4 ***McCrery***	Y	Y	Y	Y	Y	N
5 ***Cooksey***	?	?	Y	Y	Y	Y
6 ***Baker***	Y	Y	Y	Y	Y	Y
7 John	Y	Y	Y	Y	Y	N
MAINE						
1 Allen	Y	Y	Y	Y	Y	N
2 Baldacci	Y	Y	Y	Y	Y	N
MARYLAND						
1 ***Gilchrest***	Y	Y	Y	Y	Y	Y
2 ***Ehrlich***	Y	Y	Y	Y	Y	Y
3 Cardin	?	?	Y	Y	Y	N
4 Wynn	Y	Y	Y	Y	Y	N
5 Hoyer	?	?	Y	Y	Y	N
6 ***Bartlett***	Y	Y	Y	Y	Y	Y
7 Cummings	Y	Y	?	?	?	N
8 ***Morella***	Y	Y	Y	Y	Y	N
MASSACHUSETTS						
1 Olver	?	?	?	?	?	?
2 Neal	Y	Y	Y	Y	Y	N
3 McGovern	Y	Y	Y	Y	Y	N
4 Frank	Y	Y	Y	Y	Y	Y
5 Meehan	Y	Y	Y	Y	Y	N
6 Tierney	Y	Y	Y	Y	Y	N
7 Markey	Y	Y	Y	Y	Y	N
8 Capuano	Y	Y	Y	Y	Y	N
9 Lynch	Y	Y	Y	Y	Y	N
10 Delahunt	Y	Y	?	?	?	?
MICHIGAN						
1 Stupak	Y	Y	Y	Y	Y	Y
2 ***Hoekstra***	Y	Y	Y	Y	Y	N
3 ***Ehlers***	Y	Y	Y	Y	Y	N
4 ***Camp***	?	?	Y	Y	Y	Y
5 Barcia	?	?	Y	Y	Y	Y
6 ***Upton***	Y	Y	Y	Y	Y	Y
7 ***Smith***	?	?	Y	Y	Y	N
8 ***Rogers***	Y	Y	Y	Y	Y	Y
9 Kildee	Y	Y	Y	Y	Y	N
10 Bonior	?	?	?	?	?	?
11 ***Knollenberg***	Y	Y	Y	Y	Y	Y
12 Levin	Y	Y	Y	Y	Y	N
13 Rivers	?	?	Y	Y	Y	N
14 Conyers	?	?	Y	Y	Y	N
15 Kilpatrick	+	+	Y	Y	Y	N
16 Dingell	?	?	Y	Y	Y	N
MINNESOTA						
1 ***Gutknecht***	Y	Y	Y	Y	Y	Y
2 ***Kennedy***	Y	Y	Y	Y	Y	Y
3 ***Ramstad***	Y	Y	Y	Y	Y	Y
4 McCollum	Y	Y	Y	Y	Y	N
5 Sabo	Y	Y	Y	Y	Y	N
6 Luther	?	?	Y	Y	Y	Y
7 Peterson	Y	Y	Y	Y	Y	Y
8 Oberstar	Y	Y	Y	Y	Y	N
MISSISSIPPI						
1 ***Wicker***	Y	Y	Y	Y	Y	Y
2 Thompson	Y	Y	Y	Y	Y	Y
3 ***Pickering***	Y	Y	Y	Y	Y	Y
4 Shows	Y	Y	Y	Y	Y	Y
5 Taylor	Y	Y	Y	Y	Y	Y
MISSOURI						
1 Clay	Y	Y	Y	Y	Y	N
2 ***Akin***	Y	Y	Y	Y	Y	Y
3 Gephardt	?	?	Y	Y	Y	N
4 Skelton	Y	Y	Y	Y	Y	Y
5 McCarthy	Y	Y	Y	Y	Y	N
6 ***Graves***	Y	Y	Y	Y	Y	Y
7 ***Blunt***	?	?	Y	Y	Y	Y
8 ***Emerson***	Y	Y	Y	Y	Y	Y
9 ***Hulshof***	?	?	?	?	?	Y
MONTANA						
AL ***Rehberg***	Y	Y	Y	Y	Y	Y
NEBRASKA						
1 ***Bereuter***	Y	Y	Y	Y	Y	N
2 ***Terry***	Y	Y	Y	Y	Y	Y
3 ***Osborne***	Y	Y	Y	Y	Y	N
NEVADA						
1 Berkley	Y	Y	Y	Y	Y	N
2 ***Gibbons***	Y	Y	Y	Y	Y	N
NEW HAMPSHIRE						
1 ***Sununu***	Y	Y	Y	Y	Y	Y
2 ***Bass***	Y	Y	Y	Y	Y	Y
NEW JERSEY						
1 Andrews	Y	Y	Y	Y	Y	?
2 ***LoBiondo***	Y	Y	Y	Y	Y	Y
3 ***Saxton***	Y	Y	Y	Y	Y	Y
4 ***Smith***	?	?	Y	Y	Y	Y
5 ***Roukema***	?	?	?	?	?	?
6 Pallone	Y	Y	Y	Y	Y	N
7 ***Ferguson***	Y	Y	Y	Y	Y	N
8 Pascrell	Y	Y	Y	Y	Y	N
9 Rothman	Y	Y	Y	Y	Y	N
10 Payne	?	?	Y	Y	Y	N
11 ***Frelinghuysen***	Y	Y	Y	Y	Y	N
12 Holt	Y	Y	?	?	?	N
13 Menendez	Y	Y	Y	Y	Y	N
NEW MEXICO						
1 ***Wilson***	Y	Y	Y	Y	Y	N
2 ***Skeen***	Y	Y	Y	Y	Y	N
3 Udall	Y	Y	Y	Y	Y	N
NEW YORK						
1 ***Grucci***	Y	Y	Y	Y	Y	Y
2 Israel	Y	Y	Y	Y	Y	N
3 ***King***	Y	Y	Y	Y	Y	N
4 McCarthy	Y	Y	Y	Y	Y	N
5 Ackerman	Y	Y	?	?	?	N
6 Meeks	Y	Y	?	?	?	N
7 Crowley	Y	Y	Y	Y	Y	N
8 Nadler	?	?	Y	Y	Y	N
9 Weiner	?	?	Y	Y	Y	N
10 Towns	Y	Y	Y	Y	Y	N
11 Owens	+	+	Y	Y	Y	Y
12 Velázquez	Y	Y	Y	Y	Y	N
13 ***Fossella***	Y	Y	Y	Y	Y	Y
14 Maloney	Y	Y	Y	Y	Y	N
15 Rangel	?	?	Y	Y	Y	N
16 Serrano	Y	Y	Y	Y	Y	N
17 Engel	Y	Y	Y	Y	Y	Y
18 Lowey	?	?	Y	Y	Y	N
19 ***Kelly***	Y	Y	Y	Y	Y	Y
20 ***Gilman***	Y	Y	Y	Y	Y	Y
21 McNulty	Y	Y	Y	Y	Y	Y
22 ***Sweeney***	?	?	Y	Y	Y	Y
23 ***Boehlert***	Y	Y	Y	Y	Y	Y
24 ***McHugh***	Y	Y	Y	Y	Y	Y
25 ***Walsh***	?	?	?	?	?	Y
26 Hinchey	Y	Y	Y	Y	Y	Y
27 ***Reynolds***	Y	Y	Y	Y	Y	Y
28 Slaughter	+	+	Y	Y	Y	N
29 LaFalce	Y	Y	Y	Y	Y	N
30 ***Quinn***	Y	Y	Y	Y	Y	N
31 ***Houghton***	Y	Y	Y	Y	Y	Y
NORTH CAROLINA						
1 Clayton	Y	Y	Y	Y	Y	N
2 Etheridge	Y	Y	Y	Y	Y	N
3 ***Jones***	N	N	Y	Y	Y	Y
4 Price	Y	Y	Y	Y	Y	N
5 ***Burr***	Y	Y	Y	Y	Y	N
6 ***Coble***	N	N	Y	Y	Y	Y
7 McIntyre	Y	Y	Y	Y	Y	Y
8 ***Hayes***	Y	Y	Y	Y	Y	Y
9 ***Myrick***	Y	Y	Y	Y	Y	N
10 ***Ballenger***	Y	Y	Y	Y	Y	Y
11 ***Taylor***	?	?	Y	Y	Y	Y
12 Watt	Y	Y	Y	Y	Y	N
NORTH DAKOTA						
AL Pomeroy	?	?	Y	Y	Y	Y
OHIO						
1 ***Chabot***	Y	Y	Y	Y	Y	Y
2 ***Portman***	Y	Y	Y	Y	Y	Y
3 Hall	?	?	Y	Y	Y	Y
4 ***Oxley***	Y	?	Y	Y	Y	Y
5 ***Gillmor***	Y	Y	Y	Y	Y	Y
6 Strickland	Y	Y	Y	Y	Y	Y
7 ***Hobson***	Y	Y	Y	Y	Y	Y
8 ***Boehner***	Y	Y	Y	Y	Y	Y
9 Kaptur	?	?	Y	Y	Y	N
10 Kucinich	Y	Y	Y	Y	Y	N
11 Jones	Y	Y	Y	Y	Y	N
12 ***Tiberi***	Y	Y	Y	Y	Y	Y
13 Brown	Y	Y	Y	Y	Y	Y
14 Sawyer	Y	Y	Y	Y	Y	N
15 ***Pryce***	?	?	Y	Y	Y	Y
16 ***Regula***	Y	Y	Y	Y	Y	Y
17 Traficant	?	?	?	?	?	?
18 ***Ney***	Y	Y	Y	Y	Y	Y
19 ***LaTourette***	Y	Y	Y	Y	Y	Y
OKLAHOMA						
1 ***Sullivan***	Y	Y	Y	Y	Y	Y
2 Carson	?	?	Y	Y	Y	Y
3 ***Watkins***	Y	Y	Y	Y	Y	Y
4 ***Watts***	+	+	Y	Y	Y	Y
5 ***Istook***	?	?	Y	Y	Y	Y
6 ***Lucas***	Y	Y	Y	Y	Y	Y
OREGON						
1 Wu	Y	Y	Y	Y	Y	Y
2 ***Walden***	Y	Y	Y	Y	Y	Y
3 Blumenauer	Y	Y	Y	Y	Y	N
4 DeFazio	Y	Y	Y	Y	Y	Y
5 Hooley	Y	Y	Y	Y	Y	N
PENNSYLVANIA						
1 Brady	Y	Y	Y	Y	Y	N
2 Fattah	Y	Y	Y	Y	Y	N
3 Borski	?	?	Y	Y	Y	N
4 ***Hart***	Y	Y	Y	Y	Y	Y
5 ***Peterson***	Y	Y	Y	Y	Y	Y
6 Holden	Y	Y	Y	Y	Y	Y
7 ***Weldon***	Y	Y	Y	Y	Y	Y
8 ***Greenwood***	Y	Y	Y	Y	Y	Y
9 ***Shuster, Bill***	Y	Y	Y	Y	Y	Y
10 ***Sherwood***	Y	Y	Y	Y	Y	Y
11 Kanjorski	Y	Y	Y	Y	Y	Y
12 Murtha	Y	Y	Y	Y	Y	N
13 Hoeffel	+	+	Y	Y	Y	N
14 Coyne	?	?	Y	Y	Y	N
15 ***Toomey***	N	N	Y	Y	Y	Y
16 ***Pitts***	?	?	Y	Y	Y	Y
17 ***Gekas***	Y	Y	Y	Y	Y	Y
18 Doyle	Y	Y	Y	Y	Y	N
19 ***Platts***	Y	Y	Y	Y	Y	Y
20 Mascara	Y	Y	Y	Y	Y	N
21 ***English***	Y	Y	Y	Y	Y	Y
RHODE ISLAND						
1 Kennedy	Y	Y	Y	Y	Y	N
2 Langevin	Y	Y	Y	Y	Y	N
SOUTH CAROLINA						
1 ***Brown***	Y	Y	Y	Y	Y	Y
2 ***Wilson***	Y	Y	Y	Y	Y	Y
3 ***Graham***	Y	Y	Y	Y	Y	Y
4 ***DeMint***	Y	Y	Y	Y	Y	Y
5 Spratt	?	?	?	?	?	N
6 Clyburn	Y	Y	Y	Y	Y	N
SOUTH DAKOTA						
AL ***Thune***	Y	Y	Y	Y	Y	Y
TENNESSEE						
1 ***Jenkins***	Y	Y	Y	Y	Y	Y
2 ***Duncan***	N	N	Y	Y	Y	Y
3 ***Wamp***	Y	Y	Y	Y	Y	Y
4 ***Hilleary***	?	?	Y	Y	Y	Y
5 Clement	+	+	Y	Y	Y	Y
6 Gordon	Y	Y	Y	Y	Y	Y
7 ***Bryant***	?	?	Y	Y	Y	Y
8 Tanner	Y	Y	Y	Y	Y	Y
9 Ford	Y	Y	Y	Y	Y	Y
TEXAS						
1 Sandlin	Y	Y	Y	Y	Y	Y
2 Turner	Y	Y	Y	Y	Y	Y
3 ***Johnson, Sam***	Y	Y	Y	Y	Y	Y
4 Hall	Y	N	Y	Y	Y	Y
5 ***Sessions***	Y	Y	Y	Y	Y	Y
6 ***Barton***	Y	Y	Y	Y	Y	Y
7 ***Culberson***	?	?	Y	Y	Y	Y
8 ***Brady***	Y	Y	Y	Y	Y	Y
9 Lampson	Y	Y	Y	Y	Y	Y
10 Doggett	Y	Y	Y	Y	Y	N
11 Edwards	Y	Y	Y	Y	Y	Y
12 ***Granger***	Y	Y	Y	Y	Y	Y
13 ***Thornberry***	Y	Y	Y	Y	Y	N
14 ***Paul***	N	N	N	Y	Y	Y
15 Hinojosa	Y	Y	Y	Y	Y	N
16 Reyes	Y	Y	Y	Y	Y	Y
17 Stenholm	Y	Y	Y	Y	Y	Y
18 Jackson-Lee	?	?	Y	Y	Y	N
19 ***Combest***	Y	Y	Y	Y	Y	Y
20 Gonzalez	Y	Y	Y	Y	Y	N
21 ***Smith***	?	?	Y	Y	Y	Y
22 ***DeLay***	Y	Y	Y	Y	Y	Y
23 ***Bonilla***	Y	Y	Y	Y	Y	Y
24 Frost	Y	Y	Y	Y	Y	N
25 Bentsen	Y	Y	Y	Y	Y	N
26 ***Armey***	Y	Y	Y	Y	Y	Y
27 Ortiz	Y	Y	Y	Y	Y	Y
28 Rodriguez	Y	Y	Y	Y	Y	N
29 Green	Y	Y	Y	Y	Y	Y
30 Johnson, E.B.	Y	Y	Y	Y	Y	N
UTAH						
1 ***Hansen***	?	?	Y	Y	Y	Y
2 Matheson	Y	Y	Y	Y	Y	Y
3 ***Cannon***	Y	Y	Y	Y	Y	Y
VERMONT						
AL *Sanders*	Y	Y	Y	Y	Y	N
VIRGINIA						
1 ***Davis, Jo Ann***	?	?	Y	Y	Y	Y
2 ***Schrock***	Y	Y	Y	Y	Y	Y
3 Scott	?	?	Y	Y	Y	N
4 ***Forbes***	Y	Y	Y	Y	Y	Y
5 *Goode*	Y	Y	?	Y	Y	Y
6 ***Goodlatte***	Y	Y	Y	Y	Y	Y
7 ***Cantor***	Y	N	Y	Y	Y	Y
8 Moran	Y	Y	Y	Y	Y	N
9 Boucher	Y	Y	?	?	?	Y
10 ***Wolf***	Y	Y	Y	Y	Y	Y
11 ***Davis, T.***	Y	Y	Y	Y	Y	Y
WASHINGTON						
1 Inslee	Y	Y	Y	Y	Y	N
2 Larsen	Y	Y	Y	Y	Y	N
3 Baird	Y	Y	Y	Y	Y	Y
4 ***Hastings***	Y	Y	Y	Y	Y	Y
5 ***Nethercutt***	Y	Y	Y	Y	Y	Y
6 Dicks	Y	Y	Y	Y	Y	N
7 McDermott	Y	Y	Y	Y	Y	N
8 ***Dunn***	Y	Y	Y	Y	Y	Y
9 Smith	Y	Y	Y	Y	Y	Y
WEST VIRGINIA						
1 Mollohan	Y	Y	Y	Y	Y	Y
2 ***Capito***	Y	Y	Y	Y	Y	Y
3 Rahall	Y	Y	Y	Y	Y	Y
WISCONSIN						
1 ***Ryan***	Y	Y	Y	Y	Y	Y
2 Baldwin	Y	Y	Y	Y	Y	N
3 Kind	Y	Y	Y	Y	Y	Y
4 Kleczka	Y	Y	Y	Y	Y	N
5 Barrett	?	?	?	?	?	?
6 ***Petri***	Y	Y	Y	Y	Y	Y
7 Obey	?	Y	Y	Y	Y	N
8 ***Green***	Y	Y	Y	Y	Y	Y
9 ***Sensenbrenner***	N	N	Y	Y	Y	Y
WYOMING						
AL ***Cubin***	Y	Y	Y	Y	Y	Y

Southern states - Ala., Ark., Fla., Ga., Ky., La., Miss., N.C., Okla., S.C., Tenn., Texas, Va.

Key

Y	Voted for (yea).
#	Paired for.
+	Announced for.
N	Voted against (nay).
X	Paired against.
–	Announced against.
P	Voted "present."
C	Voted "present" to avoid possible conflict of interest.
?	Did not vote or otherwise make a position known.

Democrats • **Republicans**
Independents

289. HR 4635. Armed Commercial Pilots/Participant Cap. Hostettler, R-Ind., amendment that would eliminate the bill's 2 percent cap and require 20 percent of all pilots who volunteer during the first month to be trained and deputized as federal flight deck officers within 180 days of enactment. Eighty percent of all pilots who volunteer would have to be trained and deputized within the program's two-year test period. Rejected 169-256: R 126-93; D 42-162 (ND 23-128, SD 19-34); I 1-1. July 10, 2002.

290. HR 4635. Armed Commercial Pilots/Pilot Preference. Hostettler, R-Ind., amendment that would eliminate the bill's preference for pilots with prior military or law enforcement experience. Rejected 49-376: R 43-176; D 5-199 (ND 3-148, SD 2-51); I 1-1. July 10, 2002.

291. HR 4635. Armed Commercial Pilots/Permanent Program. DeFazio, D-Ore., amendment that would eliminate the 2 percent cap on the number of pilots allowed to participate in the program, make the program permanent and require that weapons training for pilots volunteering for the program begin within two months of enactment. Adopted 251-172: R 188-30; D 62-141 (ND 33-117, SD 29-24); I 1-1. July 10, 2002.

292. HR 4635. Armed Commercial Pilots/Passage. Passage of the bill that would establish a program that would deputize commercial pilots as federal law enforcement officers and allow them to carry guns aboard airlines. At least 250 commercial pilots would undergo specialized training to participate in the program. The Transportation Security Agency (TSA) would be required to begin weapons training for pilot volunteers within two months of enactment. Pilots and airlines generally would be exempt from liability resulting from defending planes from terrorist acts. The TSA could suspend the program temporarily if a pilot's gun accidentally discharges and causes injury to a passenger or crew member. Passed 310-113: R 206-11; D 102-102 (ND 70-81, SD 32-21); I 2-0. A "nay" was a vote in support of the president's position. July 10, 2002.

293. HR 2733. Coordinated Information Exchange/Passage. Passage of the bill that would authorize $47 million through fiscal 2005 to establish a new division within the National Institute of Standards and Technology to develop standards for coordinating information exchange among different levels and types of businesses. The new Enterprise Integration Initiative also would provide technical and financial aid to small businesses that create pilot projects in enterprise integration. Passed 397-22: R 194-22; D 201-0 (ND 150-0, SD 51-0); I 2-0. July 11, 2002.

294. HR 2486. Flood Warning Systems/Passage. Passage of the bill that would require the U.S. Weather Research Program to improve its capabilities to forecast inland flooding. It would require development of a new warning scale and require personnel training on that model and other new forecasting methods. It also would require public outreach and educational initiatives. Passed 413-3: R 211-3; D 200-0 (ND 148-0, SD 52-0); I 2-0. July 11, 2002.

	289	290	291	292	293	294
ALABAMA						
1 *Callahan*	N	N	Y	Y	Y	Y
2 *Everett*	Y	N	Y	Y	Y	Y
3 *Riley*	Y	N	Y	Y	Y	Y
4 *Aderholt*	N	N	Y	Y	Y	Y
5 Cramer	Y	N	Y	Y	Y	Y
6 *Bachus*	Y	N	Y	Y	Y	Y
7 Hilliard	Y	N	Y	Y	Y	Y
ALASKA						
AL *Young*	N	N	N	Y	Y	Y
ARIZONA						
1 *Flake*	Y	Y	Y	N	N	N
2 Pastor	N	N	N	N	Y	Y
3 *Stump*	Y	N	Y	Y	Y	Y
4 *Shadegg*	Y	Y	Y	Y	Y	Y
5 *Kolbe*	Y	N	Y	Y	Y	Y
6 *Hayworth*	Y	N	Y	Y	Y	Y
ARKANSAS						
1 Berry	Y	N	Y	Y	Y	Y
2 Snyder	N	N	N	N	Y	Y
3 *Boozman*	N	N	Y	Y	Y	Y
4 Ross	Y	N	Y	Y	Y	Y
CALIFORNIA						
1 Thompson	N	N	N	Y	Y	Y
2 *Herger*	Y	N	Y	Y	Y	Y
3 *Ose*	Y	N	Y	Y	Y	Y
4 *Doolittle*	Y	Y	Y	Y	Y	Y
5 Matsui	N	N	N	N	Y	Y
6 Woolsey	N	N	N	N	Y	Y
7 Miller, George	Y	N	Y	Y	Y	?
8 Pelosi	N	N	N	N	Y	Y
9 Lee	N	N	N	N	Y	Y
10 Tauscher	N	N	N	Y	Y	Y
11 *Pombo*	Y	Y	Y	Y	Y	Y
12 Lantos	N	N	N	Y	Y	Y
13 Stark	N	N	N	N	Y	Y
14 Eshoo	N	N	N	N	Y	Y
15 Honda	N	N	N	N	Y	Y
16 Lofgren	N	N	N	Y	Y	Y
17 Condit	Y	Y	Y	Y	Y	Y
18 Condit	Y	Y	Y	Y	Y	Y
19 *Radanovich*	Y	N	?	Y	Y	Y
20 Dooley	N	N	N	Y	Y	Y
21 *Thomas*	N	N	N	Y	Y	Y
22 Capps	N	N	N	Y	Y	Y
23 *Gallegly*	Y	N	Y	Y	Y	Y
24 Sherman	N	N	N	Y	Y	Y
25 *McKeon*	Y	N	Y	Y	Y	Y
26 Berman	N	N	N	N	Y	Y
27 Schiff	N	N	N	Y	Y	Y
28 *Dreier*	N	N	Y	Y	Y	Y
29 Waxman	N	N	N	N	Y	Y
30 Becerra	N	N	N	N	?	Y
31 Solis	N	N	N	N	Y	Y
32 Watson	N	N	N	N	Y	Y
33 Roybal-Allard	N	N	N	N	Y	Y
34 Napolitano	N	N	N	N	Y	Y
35 Waters	N	N	?	N	Y	Y
36 Harman	Y	N	N	Y	Y	Y
37 Millender-McD.	N	N	N	N	Y	Y
38 *Horn*	N	N	N	Y	Y	Y

	289	290	291	292	293	294
39 *Royce*	Y	Y	Y	Y	N	Y
40 *Lewis*	N	N	N	Y	Y	Y
41 *Miller, Gary*	Y	Y	Y	Y	Y	Y
42 Baca	Y	N	Y	Y	Y	Y
43 *Calvert*	N	N	Y	Y	Y	Y
44 *Bono*	Y	N	Y	Y	Y	Y
45 *Rohrabacher*	Y	N	Y	N	Y	Y
46 Sanchez	N	N	Y	Y	Y	Y
47 *Cox*	Y	N	Y	Y	Y	?
48 *Issa*	N	N	Y	Y	Y	Y
49 Davis	N	N	N	Y	Y	Y
50 Filner	N	N	N	N	Y	Y
51 *Cunningham*	N	N	Y	Y	Y	Y
52 *Hunter*	Y	N	Y	Y	Y	Y
COLORADO						
1 DeGette	N	N	N	Y	Y	Y
2 Udall	N	N	N	Y	Y	Y
3 *McInnis*	N	N	N	Y	Y	Y
4 *Schaffer*	N	Y	Y	Y	N	Y
5 *Hefley*	N	N	Y	Y	N	Y
6 *Tancredo*	Y	Y	Y	Y	N	Y
CONNECTICUT						
1 Larson	N	N	N	N	Y	Y
2 *Simmons*	N	N	Y	Y	Y	Y
3 DeLauro	N	N	N	N	Y	Y
4 *Shays*	Y	N	Y	Y	Y	Y
5 Maloney	N	N	N	Y	Y	Y
6 *Johnson*	N	N	N	Y	Y	Y
DELAWARE						
AL *Castle*	N	N	N	Y	Y	Y
FLORIDA						
1 *Miller, J.*	Y	Y	Y	Y	N	Y
2 Boyd	Y	N	Y	Y	Y	Y
3 Brown	N	N	N	N	Y	Y
4 *Crenshaw*	N	N	Y	Y	Y	Y
5 Thurman	N	N	Y	Y	Y	Y
6 *Stearns*	N	N	Y	Y	N	Y
7 *Mica*	N	N	N	Y	Y	Y
8 *Keller*	Y	Y	Y	Y	Y	Y
9 *Bilirakis*	N	N	Y	Y	Y	Y
10 *Young*	N	N	Y	Y	Y	Y
11 Davis	N	N	N	N	Y	Y
12 *Putnam*	N	N	Y	Y	Y	Y
13 *Miller, D.*	N	N	N	Y	Y	Y
14 *Goss*	N	N	N	Y	Y	Y
15 *Weldon*	N	N	Y	Y	Y	Y
16 *Foley*	Y	N	Y	Y	Y	Y
17 Meek	N	N	N	N	Y	Y
18 *Ros-Lehtinen*	Y	Y	Y	Y	Y	Y
19 Wexler	N	N	N	Y	Y	Y
20 Deutsch	N	N	Y	Y	Y	Y
21 *Diaz-Balart*	Y	Y	Y	Y	Y	Y
22 *Shaw*	N	Y	Y	Y	Y	Y
23 Hastings	?	?	?	?	?	?
GEORGIA						
1 *Kingston*	Y	N	Y	Y	Y	Y
2 Bishop	N	N	N	Y	Y	Y
3 *Collins*	Y	N	Y	Y	?	?
4 McKinney	N	N	N	N	Y	Y
5 Lewis	N	N	N	N	?	?
6 *Isakson*	N	N	Y	Y	Y	Y
7 *Barr*	N	N	Y	Y	Y	Y
8 *Chambliss*	Y	N	+	Y	Y	Y
9 *Deal*	N	N	Y	Y	Y	Y
10 *Norwood*	?	?	?	?	Y	Y
11 *Linder*	Y	Y	Y	Y	Y	Y
HAWAII						
1 Abercrombie	N	N	N	N	Y	Y
2 Mink	N	N	N	N	Y	Y
IDAHO						
1 *Otter*	Y	N	Y	Y	N	Y
2 *Simpson*	N	N	Y	Y	Y	Y
ILLINOIS						
1 Rush	N	N	N	N	Y	Y
2 Jackson	N	N	N	N	Y	Y
3 Lipinski	N	N	N	N	Y	Y
4 Gutierrez	N	N	N	N	Y	Y
5 Blagojevich	Y	N	Y	Y	?	?
6 *Hyde*	N	N	N	N	Y	Y
7 Davis	N	N	N	N	Y	Y
8 *Crane*	Y	N	Y	Y	Y	Y
9 Schakowsky	N	N	N	N	Y	Y
10 *Kirk*	N	N	Y	Y	Y	Y
11 *Weller*	Y	N	Y	Y	Y	Y
12 Costello	Y	N	Y	Y	Y	Y
13 *Biggert*	Y	N	Y	Y	Y	Y

ND Northern Democrats   SD Southern Democrats

	289	290	291	292	293	294
14 *Hastert*						
15 *Johnson*	Y	N	Y	Y	Y	Y
16 *Manzullo*	Y	N	Y	Y	Y	Y
17 Evans	N	N	N	N	Y	?
18 *LaHood*	Y	Y	Y	Y	Y	Y
19 Phelps	Y	N	Y	Y	Y	Y
20 *Shimkus*	Y	Y	Y	Y	Y	Y
INDIANA						
1 Visclosky	N	N	N	N	Y	Y
2 *Pence*	Y	Y	Y	Y	N	Y
3 Roemer	N	N	N	Y	Y	Y
4 *Souder*	N	N	N	N	Y	Y
5 *Buyer*	Y	N	Y	Y	Y	Y
6 *Burton*	Y	N	Y	Y	N	?
7 *Kerns*	Y	Y	Y	Y	N	N
8 *Hostettler*	Y	Y	Y	Y	N	Y
9 Hill	Y	N	Y	Y	Y	Y
10 Carson	N	N	N	N	Y	Y
IOWA						
1 *Leach*	Y	N	Y	Y	Y	Y
2 *Nussle*	Y	N	Y	Y	Y	Y
3 Boswell	Y	N	Y	Y	Y	Y
4 *Ganske*	N	N	Y	Y	Y	Y
5 *Latham*	Y	N	Y	Y	Y	Y
KANSAS						
1 *Moran*	Y	N	Y	Y	Y	Y
2 *Ryun*	Y	N	Y	Y	N	Y
3 Moore	N	N	N	Y	Y	Y
4 *Tiahrt*	N	N	Y	Y	Y	Y
KENTUCKY						
1 *Whitfield*	N	N	Y	Y	Y	Y
2 *Lewis*	Y	N	Y	Y	Y	Y
3 *Northup*	N	N	Y	Y	Y	Y
4 Lucas	Y	N	Y	Y	Y	Y
5 *Rogers*	Y	N	N	Y	Y	Y
6 *Fletcher*	Y	N	Y	Y	Y	Y
LOUISIANA						
1 *Vitter*	Y	Y	Y	Y	Y	Y
2 Jefferson	N	N	Y	Y	Y	Y
3 *Tauzin*	N	N	Y	Y	Y	Y
4 *McCrery*	Y	N	N	Y	Y	Y
5 *Cooksey*	Y	Y	Y	Y	Y	Y
6 *Baker*	N	N	Y	Y	Y	Y
7 John	N	N	Y	Y	Y	Y
MAINE						
1 Allen	N	N	N	N	Y	Y
2 Baldacci	N	N	N	N	Y	+
MARYLAND						
1 *Gilchrest*	Y	N	Y	Y	Y	Y
2 *Ehrlich*	Y	N	Y	Y	Y	Y
3 Cardin	N	N	N	Y	Y	Y
4 Wynn	N	N	N	Y	Y	Y
5 Hoyer	N	N	N	N	Y	Y
6 *Bartlett*	Y	N	Y	Y	Y	Y
7 Cummings	N	N	N	Y	Y	Y
8 *Morella*	N	N	N	N	Y	Y
MASSACHUSETTS						
1 Olver	?	?	?	?	Y	Y
2 Neal	N	N	N	N	Y	Y
3 McGovern	N	N	N	N	Y	Y
4 Frank	N	N	N	Y	Y	Y
5 Meehan	N	N	N	Y	?	?
6 Tierney	N	N	N	N	Y	Y
7 Markey	N	N	N	N	Y	Y
8 Capuano	N	N	N	N	Y	Y
9 Lynch	N	N	N	Y	Y	Y
10 Delahunt	?	?	?	?	Y	Y
MICHIGAN						
1 Stupak	N	N	Y	Y	Y	Y
2 *Hoekstra*	N	N	N	N	Y	Y
3 *Ehlers*	N	N	N	N	Y	Y
4 *Camp*	N	N	Y	Y	Y	Y
5 Barcia	Y	N	Y	Y	Y	Y
6 *Upton*	Y	N	Y	Y	Y	Y
7 *Smith*	N	N	N	N	Y	Y
8 *Rogers*	N	Y	Y	Y	Y	Y
9 Kildee	N	N	N	Y	Y	Y
10 Bonior	?	?	?	?	?	?
11 *Knollenberg*	Y	N	Y	Y	Y	Y
12 Levin	N	N	N	N	Y	Y
13 Rivers	N	N	N	N	Y	Y
14 Conyers	N	N	N	N	Y	Y
15 Kilpatrick	N	N	N	N	Y	Y
16 Dingell	N	N	N	Y	Y	Y

	289	290	291	292	293	294
MINNESOTA						
1 *Gutknecht*	Y	Y	Y	Y	Y	Y
2 *Kennedy*	Y	Y	Y	Y	Y	Y
3 *Ramstad*	Y	N	Y	Y	Y	Y
4 McCollum	N	N	N	N	Y	Y
5 Sabo	N	N	N	N	Y	Y
6 Luther	Y	N	Y	Y	Y	Y
7 Peterson	Y	Y	Y	Y	Y	Y
8 Oberstar	N	N	N	N	Y	Y
MISSISSIPPI						
1 *Wicker*	Y	N	Y	Y	Y	Y
2 Thompson	N	N	Y	Y	Y	Y
3 *Pickering*	Y	N	Y	Y	Y	Y
4 Shows	Y	N	Y	Y	Y	Y
5 Taylor	Y	N	Y	Y	Y	Y
MISSOURI						
1 Clay	N	N	N	N	Y	Y
2 *Akin*	Y	Y	Y	Y	N	Y
3 Gephardt	N	N	N	N	Y	Y
4 Skelton	Y	N	Y	Y	Y	Y
5 McCarthy	N	N	N	N	Y	Y
6 *Graves*	Y	Y	Y	Y	Y	Y
7 *Blunt*	Y	N	Y	Y	Y	Y
8 *Emerson*	N	N	Y	Y	Y	Y
9 *Hulshof*	Y	Y	Y	Y	Y	Y
MONTANA						
AL *Rehberg*	N	Y	Y	Y	Y	Y
NEBRASKA						
1 *Bereuter*	N	N	N	N	Y	Y
2 *Terry*	N	N	Y	Y	Y	Y
3 *Osborne*	N	N	N	Y	Y	?
NEVADA						
1 Berkley	N	N	N	Y	Y	Y
2 *Gibbons*	N	N	N	N	Y	Y
NEW HAMPSHIRE						
1 *Sununu*	Y	N	Y	Y	Y	Y
2 *Bass*	Y	N	Y	Y	Y	Y
NEW JERSEY						
1 Andrews	?	?	?	+	Y	Y
2 *LoBiondo*	N	N	Y	Y	Y	Y
3 *Saxton*	N	N	Y	Y	Y	Y
4 *Smith*	N	N	Y	Y	Y	Y
5 *Roukema*	?	?	?	?	?	?
6 Pallone	N	N	N	N	Y	Y
7 *Ferguson*	N	N	N	N	Y	Y
8 Pascrell	N	N	N	N	Y	Y
9 Rothman	N	N	N	Y	Y	Y
10 Payne	N	N	N	N	Y	Y
11 *Frelinghuysen*	N	N	N	Y	Y	Y
12 Holt	N	N	N	Y	Y	Y
13 Menendez	N	N	N	N	Y	Y
NEW MEXICO						
1 *Wilson*	Y	N	N	Y	Y	Y
2 *Skeen*	N	N	N	N	Y	Y
3 Udall	N	N	N	Y	Y	Y
NEW YORK						
1 *Grucci*	Y	N	Y	Y	Y	Y
2 Israel	N	N	N	Y	Y	Y
3 *King*	N	N	N	Y	Y	Y
4 McCarthy	N	N	N	Y	Y	Y
5 Ackerman	N	N	N	Y	Y	Y
6 Meeks	N	N	N	Y	Y	Y
7 Crowley	N	N	N	N	Y	Y
8 Nadler	N	N	N	Y	Y	Y
9 Weiner	N	N	N	N	Y	Y
10 Towns	N	N	N	N	Y	Y
11 Owens	N	N	N	Y	Y	Y
12 Velázquez	N	N	N	N	?	Y
13 *Fossella*	N	N	Y	Y	Y	Y
14 Maloney	N	N	N	Y	Y	Y
15 Rangel	N	N	N	N	Y	Y
16 Serrano	N	N	N	N	Y	Y
17 Engel	N	N	Y	Y	Y	Y
18 Lowey	N	N	N	Y	Y	?
19 *Kelly*	N	N	Y	Y	Y	Y
20 *Gilman*	N	N	Y	Y	Y	Y
21 McNulty	Y	N	Y	Y	Y	Y
22 *Sweeney*	Y	N	Y	Y	Y	Y
23 *Boehlert*	N	N	Y	Y	Y	Y
24 *McHugh*	N	N	Y	Y	Y	Y
25 *Walsh*	Y	N	Y	Y	Y	Y
26 Hinchey	Y	N	Y	Y	Y	Y
27 *Reynolds*	N	N	Y	Y	Y	Y
28 Slaughter	N	N	N	N	Y	Y
29 LaFalce	N	N	N	N	Y	Y

	289	290	291	292	293	294
30 *Quinn*	N	N	N	Y	Y	Y
31 *Houghton*	N	N	Y	Y	Y	Y
NORTH CAROLINA						
1 Clayton	N	N	N	N	Y	Y
2 Etheridge	N	N	N	N	Y	Y
3 *Jones*	Y	Y	Y	Y	Y	Y
4 Price	N	N	N	N	Y	Y
5 *Burr*	N	N	N	N	Y	Y
6 *Coble*	Y	N	Y	Y	N	Y
7 McIntyre	Y	N	Y	Y	Y	Y
8 *Hayes*	Y	Y	Y	Y	Y	Y
9 *Myrick*	N	N	N	Y	Y	Y
10 *Ballenger*	N	N	Y	Y	Y	Y
11 *Taylor*	Y	N	Y	Y	Y	Y
12 Watt	N	N	N	N	Y	Y
NORTH DAKOTA						
AL Pomeroy	Y	N	Y	Y	Y	Y
OHIO						
1 *Chabot*	Y	N	Y	Y	Y	Y
2 *Portman*	Y	N	Y	Y	Y	Y
3 Hall	Y	N	Y	Y	Y	Y
4 *Oxley*	N	N	Y	Y	Y	Y
5 *Gillmor*	N	N	Y	Y	Y	Y
6 Strickland	Y	N	Y	Y	Y	Y
7 *Hobson*	Y	N	Y	Y	Y	Y
8 *Boehner*	Y	N	Y	Y	Y	Y
9 Kaptur	N	N	N	N	Y	Y
10 Kucinich	N	N	N	N	Y	Y
11 Jones	N	N	N	N	Y	Y
12 *Tiberi*	Y	N	Y	Y	Y	Y
13 Brown	N	N	Y	Y	Y	Y
14 Sawyer	N	N	N	N	Y	Y
15 *Pryce*	Y	N	Y	Y	Y	Y
16 *Regula*	Y	N	Y	Y	Y	Y
17 Traficant	?	?	?	?	?	?
18 *Ney*	N	Y	Y	Y	Y	Y
19 *LaTourette*	N	N	Y	Y	Y	Y
OKLAHOMA						
1 *Sullivan*	Y	N	Y	Y	Y	Y
2 Carson	Y	N	Y	Y	Y	Y
3 *Watkins*	Y	N	Y	Y	?	Y
4 *Watts*	Y	N	Y	Y	Y	Y
5 *Istook*	N	N	Y	Y	Y	Y
6 *Lucas*	Y	Y	Y	Y	Y	Y
OREGON						
1 Wu	N	N	Y	Y	Y	Y
2 *Walden*	Y	N	Y	Y	Y	Y
3 Blumenauer	N	N	N	N	Y	Y
4 DeFazio	Y	N	Y	Y	Y	Y
5 Hooley	N	N	N	Y	Y	Y
PENNSYLVANIA						
1 Brady	N	N	N	N	Y	Y
2 Fattah	N	N	N	N	Y	Y
3 Borski	N	N	N	N	Y	Y
4 *Hart*	N	N	Y	+	Y	Y
5 *Peterson*	N	N	Y	Y	Y	Y
6 Holden	Y	N	Y	Y	Y	Y
7 *Weldon*	Y	N	Y	Y	Y	Y
8 *Greenwood*	N	N	Y	Y	Y	Y
9 *Shuster, Bill*	N	N	Y	Y	Y	Y
10 *Sherwood*	N	N	Y	Y	Y	Y
11 Kanjorski	N	N	Y	Y	Y	Y
12 Murtha	N	N	N	Y	Y	Y
13 Hoeffel	N	N	N	N	Y	Y
14 Coyne	N	N	N	N	Y	Y
15 *Toomey*	Y	Y	Y	Y	N	Y
16 *Pitts*	Y	N	Y	Y	Y	Y
17 *Gekas*	N	N	Y	Y	Y	Y
18 Doyle	N	N	N	N	Y	Y
19 *Platts*	Y	Y	Y	Y	Y	Y
20 Mascara	N	N	N	N	Y	Y
21 *English*	Y	N	Y	Y	Y	Y
RHODE ISLAND						
1 Kennedy	N	N	N	Y	Y	Y
2 Langevin	N	N	N	Y	Y	Y
SOUTH CAROLINA						
1 *Brown*	N	N	Y	Y	Y	Y
2 *Wilson*	Y	Y	Y	Y	Y	Y
3 *Graham*	Y	N	Y	Y	Y	Y
4 *DeMint*	Y	Y	Y	Y	Y	Y
5 Spratt	N	N	N	N	Y	Y
6 Clyburn	N	N	N	N	Y	Y
SOUTH DAKOTA						
AL *Thune*	Y	N	Y	Y	Y	Y

	289	290	291	292	293	294
TENNESSEE						
1 *Jenkins*	N	N	Y	Y	Y	Y
2 *Duncan*	Y	N	Y	Y	N	Y
3 *Wamp*	Y	N	Y	Y	Y	Y
4 *Hilleary*	Y	N	Y	Y	Y	Y
5 Clement	Y	N	Y	Y	Y	Y
6 Gordon	Y	Y	Y	Y	Y	Y
7 *Bryant*	Y	N	Y	Y	Y	Y
8 Tanner	Y	N	Y	Y	Y	Y
9 Ford	N	N	Y	Y	Y	Y
TEXAS						
1 Sandlin	Y	N	Y	Y	Y	Y
2 Turner	Y	N	Y	Y	Y	Y
3 *Johnson, Sam*	Y	Y	Y	Y	Y	Y
4 Hall	N	N	Y	Y	Y	Y
5 *Sessions*	Y	Y	Y	Y	Y	Y
6 *Barton*	N	N	Y	Y	Y	Y
7 *Culberson*	Y	N	Y	Y	N	Y
8 *Brady*	Y	N	Y	Y	Y	Y
9 Lampson	Y	N	Y	Y	Y	Y
10 Doggett	N	N	N	N	Y	Y
11 Edwards	N	N	Y	Y	Y	Y
12 *Granger*	Y	N	Y	Y	Y	Y
13 *Thornberry*	N	N	N	Y	Y	Y
14 *Paul*	Y	Y	Y	Y	N	Y
15 Hinojosa	N	N	N	N	Y	Y
16 Reyes	N	N	Y	Y	?	Y
17 Stenholm	N	N	Y	Y	Y	Y
18 Jackson-Lee	N	N	N	N	Y	Y
19 *Combest*	N	Y	Y	Y	Y	Y
20 Gonzalez	N	N	N	N	Y	Y
21 *Smith*	N	N	Y	Y	Y	Y
22 *DeLay*	Y	Y	Y	Y	Y	Y
23 *Bonilla*	Y	Y	Y	Y	Y	Y
24 Frost	N	N	N	N	Y	Y
25 Bentsen	N	N	N	N	Y	Y
26 *Armey*	Y	N	Y	Y	Y	Y
27 Ortiz	Y	N	Y	Y	Y	Y
28 Rodriguez	N	N	N	Y	Y	Y
29 Green	Y	N	Y	Y	Y	Y
30 Johnson, E.B.	N	N	N	N	Y	Y
UTAH						
1 *Hansen*	Y	N	Y	Y	Y	Y
2 Matheson	Y	N	Y	Y	Y	Y
3 *Cannon*	Y	Y	Y	Y	Y	Y
VERMONT						
AL *Sanders*	N	N	N	Y	Y	Y
VIRGINIA						
1 *Davis, Jo Ann*	Y	N	Y	Y	Y	Y
2 *Schrock*	N	N	Y	Y	Y	Y
3 Scott	N	N	N	N	Y	Y
4 *Forbes*	Y	N	Y	Y	Y	Y
5 *Goode*	Y	Y	Y	Y	Y	Y
6 *Goodlatte*	Y	Y	Y	Y	?	?
7 *Cantor*	Y	N	Y	Y	Y	Y
8 Moran	N	N	N	N	Y	Y
9 Boucher	Y	Y	Y	Y	Y	Y
10 *Wolf*	Y	N	Y	Y	Y	Y
11 *Davis, T.*	N	N	Y	Y	Y	Y
WASHINGTON						
1 Inslee	N	N	N	N	Y	Y
2 Larsen	N	N	N	Y	Y	Y
3 Baird	N	Y	Y	Y	Y	Y
4 *Hastings*	N	N	Y	Y	Y	Y
5 *Nethercutt*	N	N	Y	Y	Y	Y
6 Dicks	N	N	N	Y	Y	Y
7 McDermott	N	N	N	N	Y	Y
8 *Dunn*	N	N	Y	Y	+	+
9 Smith	N	N	Y	Y	Y	Y
WEST VIRGINIA						
1 Mollohan	Y	N	Y	Y	Y	Y
2 *Capito*	Y	N	Y	Y	Y	Y
3 Rahall	N	N	Y	Y	Y	Y
WISCONSIN						
1 *Ryan*	Y	N	Y	Y	Y	Y
2 Baldwin	N	N	N	N	Y	Y
3 Kind	Y	N	Y	Y	Y	Y
4 Kleczka	N	N	N	N	Y	Y
5 Barrett	?	?	?	?	?	?
6 *Petri*	N	N	Y	Y	Y	Y
7 Obey	N	N	N	N	Y	Y
8 *Green*	Y	N	Y	Y	Y	Y
9 *Sensenbrenner*	Y	N	Y	Y	N	N
WYOMING						
AL *Cubin*	Y	N	Y	Y	N	Y

Southern states - Ala., Ark., Fla., Ga., Ky., La., Miss., N.C., Okla., S.C., Tenn., Texas, Va.

295. HR 4687. Building Investigations/Passage. Passage of the bill that would authorize $75 million through fiscal 2005 for the National Institute of Standards and Technology to set up and operate rapid response teams to investigate fatal and near-fatal building collapses and recommend changes to building standards and emergency procedures based on their findings. Passed 338-23: R 167-22; D 170-0 (ND 123-0, SD 47-0); I 1-1. July 12, 2002.

296. HR 3482. Technology Crime Enforcement/Passage. Smith, R-Texas, motion to suspend the rules and pass the bill that would stiffen penalties for computer-related crimes and increase law enforcement's capacity to track down and prosecute technology crimes. Motion agreed to 385-3: R 203-2; D 181-1 (ND 130-1, SD 51-0); I 1-0. A two-thirds majority of those present and voting (259 in this case) is required for passage under suspension of the rules. July 15, 2002.

297. HR 4755. Clarence Miller Post Office/Passage. Hobson, R-Ohio, motion to suspend the rules and pass the bill that would designate the U.S. Postal Service facility at 204 S. Broad St., Lancaster, Ohio, as the "Clarence Miller Post Office Building." Motion agreed to 389-0: R 206-0; D 182-0 (ND 132-0, SD 50-0); I 1-0. A two-thirds majority of those present and voting (260 in this case) is required for passage under suspension of the rules. July 15, 2002.

298. HR 3479. O'Hare Airport Expansion/Passage. Lipinski, D-Ill., motion to suspend the rules and pass the bill that would fund and expedite an expansion of Chicago O'Hare International Airport. Motion rejected 247-143: R 111-96; D 136-46 (ND 104-28, SD 32-18); I 0-1. A two-thirds majority of those present and voting (260 in this case) is required for passage under suspension of the rules. July 15, 2002.

299. HR 5118. Corporate Fraud Penalties/Passage. Sensenbrenner, R-Wis., motion to suspend the rules and pass the bill that would create a criminal penalty for securities fraud punishable with a 25-year prison sentence, require top corporate executives to certify company financial statements, and impose penalties of up to $5 million in fines and up to 20 years in prison for violations. Motion agreed to 391-28: R 214-1; D 176-26 (ND 127-24, SD 49-2); I 1-1. A two-thirds majority of those present (280 in this case) is required for passage under suspension of the rules. July 16, 2002.

300. H Res 482. Ted Williams Tribute/Adoption. Markey, D-Mass., motion to suspend the rules and adopt the resolution that would honor Ted Williams and extend the condolences of the House of Representatives on his death. Motion agreed to 418-0: R 214-0; D 202-0 (ND 151-0, SD 51-0); I 2-0. A two-thirds majority of those present and voting (279 in this case) is required for adoption under suspension of the rules. July 16, 2002.

301. H Res 452. Detroit Red Wings Tribute/Adoption. Kilpatrick, D-Mich., motion to suspend the rules and adopt the resolution that would congratulate the Detroit Red Wings for winning the 2002 Stanley Cup. Motion agreed to 410-1: R 209-0; D 200-0 (ND 149-0, SD 51-0); I 1-0. A two-thirds majority of those present and voting (274 in this case) is required for adoption under suspension of the rules. July 16, 2002.

302. HR 5093. Fiscal 2003 Interior Department Appropriations/Rule. Adoption of the rule (H Res 483) to provide for House floor consideration of the bill that would appropriate $19.8 billion for the Interior Department for fiscal 2003. Adopted 322-101: R 192-26; D 130-73 (ND 86-64, SD 44-9); I 0-2. July 16, 2002.

Key

Y	Voted for (yea).
#	Paired for.
+	Announced for.
N	Voted against (nay).
X	Paired against.
−	Announced against.
P	Voted "present."
C	Voted "present" to avoid possible conflict of interest.
?	Did not vote or otherwise make a position known.

• Democrats **Republicans** Independents

	295	296	297	298	299	300	301	302
ALABAMA								
1 Callahan	Y	Y	Y	Y	Y	Y	Y	Y
2 Everett	Y	Y	Y	N	Y	Y	Y	Y
3 Riley	+	?	?	?	?	?	?	?
4 Aderholt	Y	Y	Y	N	Y	Y	Y	Y
5 Cramer	Y	Y	Y	Y	Y	Y	Y	Y
6 Bachus	Y	?	?	?	Y	Y	Y	Y
7 Hilliard	Y	Y	Y	N	Y	Y	Y	Y
ALASKA								
AL Young	?	Y	Y	Y	Y	Y	Y	N
ARIZONA								
1 Flake	N	Y	N	Y	N	Y	Y	N
2 Pastor	Y	Y	Y	Y	Y	Y	Y	Y
3 Stump	Y	Y	Y	N	Y	Y	Y	Y
4 Shadegg	N	Y	N	Y	N	Y	Y	N
5 Kolbe	Y	Y	Y	Y	Y	Y	Y	Y
6 Hayworth	Y	Y	Y	N	Y	Y	Y	Y
ARKANSAS								
1 Berry	Y	Y	Y	Y	Y	Y	Y	Y
2 Snyder	Y	Y	Y	N	Y	Y	Y	Y
3 Boozman	Y	Y	Y	Y	Y	Y	Y	Y
4 Ross	Y	Y	Y	Y	Y	Y	Y	Y
CALIFORNIA								
1 Thompson	Y	Y	Y	Y	Y	Y	Y	N
2 Herger	Y	Y	Y	N	Y	Y	Y	Y
3 Ose	Y	Y	Y	N	Y	Y	Y	Y
4 Doolittle	Y	Y	Y	N	Y	Y	Y	Y
5 Matsui	Y	Y	Y	Y	Y	Y	Y	Y
6 Woolsey	Y	Y	Y	Y	Y	Y	Y	N
7 Miller, George	?	?	?	?	Y	Y	Y	Y
8 Pelosi	Y	?	?	?	Y	Y	Y	Y
9 Lee	Y	Y	Y	N	N	Y	Y	N
10 Tauscher	Y	Y	Y	Y	Y	Y	Y	Y
11 Pombo	Y	?	?	?	Y	Y	Y	Y
12 Lantos	?	?	?	?	Y	Y	Y	Y
13 Stark	Y	?	?	?	N	Y	Y	N
14 Eshoo	Y	Y	Y	Y	Y	Y	Y	Y
15 Honda	Y	Y	Y	N	Y	Y	Y	N
16 Lofgren	?	Y	Y	Y	Y	Y	Y	N
17 Farr	Y	Y	Y	Y	Y	Y	Y	Y
18 Condit	Y	Y	Y	Y	Y	Y	Y	Y
19 Radanovich	?	Y	Y	N	Y	Y	Y	Y
20 Dooley	Y	?	?	?	Y	Y	Y	Y
21 Thomas	Y	Y	Y	Y	Y	Y	?	Y
22 Capps	Y	Y	Y	Y	Y	Y	Y	Y
23 Gallegly	?	Y	Y	N	Y	Y	Y	Y
24 Sherman	Y	Y	Y	N	Y	Y	Y	Y
25 McKeon	Y	Y	Y	N	Y	Y	Y	Y
26 Berman	?	Y	Y	Y	Y	Y	Y	Y
27 Schiff	Y	Y	Y	N	Y	Y	Y	Y
28 Dreier	Y	Y	Y	Y	Y	Y	Y	Y
29 Waxman	Y	?	?	?	Y	Y	Y	N
30 Becerra	+	+	+	−	Y	Y	Y	N
31 Solis	Y	Y	Y	Y	Y	Y	Y	N
32 Watson	Y	Y	Y	N	Y	Y	Y	Y
33 Roybal-Allard	Y	Y	Y	Y	Y	Y	Y	Y
34 Napolitano	Y	Y	Y	Y	Y	Y	Y	Y
35 Waters	Y	Y	Y	N	N	Y	Y	Y
36 Harman	Y	?	?	?	Y	Y	Y	Y
37 Millender-McD.	Y	Y	Y	N	Y	Y	Y	Y
38 Horn	Y	Y	Y	N	Y	Y	Y	Y
39 Royce	N	Y	Y	N	Y	Y	?	Y
40 Lewis	Y	Y	Y	N	Y	Y	Y	Y
41 Miller, Gary	?	Y	Y	Y	Y	Y	Y	Y
42 Baca	Y	Y	Y	Y	Y	Y	Y	N
43 Calvert	?	Y	Y	N	Y	Y	?	Y
44 Bono	Y	Y	Y	N	Y	Y	Y	Y
45 Rohrabacher	Y	Y	Y	N	Y	Y	Y	Y
46 Sanchez	Y	Y	Y	Y	Y	Y	Y	N
47 Cox	Y	Y	Y	Y	Y	Y	Y	Y
48 Issa	?	Y	Y	N	Y	Y	Y	Y
49 Davis	Y	Y	Y	Y	Y	Y	Y	Y
50 Filner	Y	?	+	+	N	Y	Y	N
51 Cunningham	Y	Y	Y	Y	Y	Y	Y	Y
52 Hunter	?	Y	Y	N	Y	Y	Y	Y
COLORADO								
1 DeGette	Y	Y	Y	Y	N	Y	Y	N
2 Udall	Y	?	+	+	Y	Y	Y	N
3 McInnis	Y	Y	Y	N	Y	Y	Y	Y
4 Schaffer	?	?	?	?	?	?	?	?
5 Hefley	Y	Y	Y	N	Y	Y	Y	Y
6 Tancredo	?	Y	Y	N	Y	Y	P	Y
CONNECTICUT								
1 Larson	Y	Y	Y	Y	Y	Y	Y	Y
2 Simmons	Y	Y	Y	Y	Y	Y	Y	Y
3 DeLauro	Y	Y	Y	Y	Y	Y	Y	Y
4 Shays	Y	Y	Y	N	Y	Y	Y	Y
5 Maloney	Y	?	+	+	Y	Y	Y	N
6 Johnson	Y	Y	Y	Y	Y	Y	Y	Y
DELAWARE								
AL Castle	Y	Y	Y	N	Y	Y	Y	Y
FLORIDA								
1 Miller, J.	Y	N	Y	N	Y	Y	Y	Y
2 Boyd	Y	Y	Y	Y	Y	Y	Y	Y
3 Brown	Y	Y	Y	Y	Y	Y	Y	Y
4 Crenshaw	Y	Y	Y	N	Y	Y	Y	Y
5 Thurman	Y	Y	Y	N	Y	Y	Y	N
6 Stearns	Y	Y	Y	N	Y	Y	Y	Y
7 Mica	Y	Y	Y	Y	Y	Y	Y	Y
8 Keller	Y	Y	Y	N	Y	Y	Y	Y
9 Bilirakis	Y	Y	Y	N	Y	Y	Y	Y
10 Young	Y	Y	Y	Y	Y	Y	Y	Y
11 Davis	Y	Y	Y	Y	Y	Y	Y	N
12 Putnam	Y	Y	Y	Y	Y	Y	Y	Y
13 Miller, D.	Y	Y	Y	Y	Y	Y	Y	Y
14 Goss	Y	Y	Y	Y	Y	Y	Y	Y
15 Weldon	Y	Y	Y	N	Y	Y	Y	Y
16 Foley	Y	Y	Y	N	Y	Y	Y	Y
17 Meek	Y	Y	Y	Y	Y	Y	Y	N
18 Ros-Lehtinen	Y	Y	Y	N	Y	Y	Y	Y
19 Wexler	?	Y	?	?	Y	Y	Y	N
20 Deutsch	Y	Y	Y	Y	Y	Y	Y	Y
21 Diaz-Balart	?	Y	Y	N	Y	Y	Y	Y
22 Shaw	Y	Y	Y	N	Y	Y	Y	Y
23 Hastings	?	?	?	?	?	?	?	?
GEORGIA								
1 Kingston	N	Y	Y	N	Y	Y	Y	Y
2 Bishop	Y	Y	Y	N	Y	Y	Y	Y
3 Collins	Y	Y	Y	N	Y	Y	Y	Y
4 McKinney	Y	Y	Y	N	N	Y	Y	N
5 Lewis	?	Y	Y	Y	?	?	?	Y
6 Isakson	N	Y	Y	N	Y	Y	Y	Y
7 Barr	Y	Y	Y	N	Y	Y	Y	Y
8 Chambliss	N	?	?	?	Y	Y	Y	Y
9 Deal	?	Y	Y	N	Y	Y	Y	Y
10 Norwood	N	Y	Y	N	Y	Y	Y	Y
11 Linder	Y	Y	Y	N	Y	Y	Y	Y
HAWAII								
1 Abercrombie	Y	Y	Y	N	Y	N	Y	N
2 Mink	Y	Y	Y	Y	Y	Y	Y	Y
IDAHO								
1 Otter	N	Y	Y	N	Y	Y	Y	Y
2 Simpson	Y	Y	Y	Y	Y	Y	Y	Y
ILLINOIS								
1 Rush	Y	Y	Y	Y	Y	Y	Y	N
2 Jackson	Y	Y	Y	N	Y	Y	Y	N
3 Lipinski	?	Y	Y	Y	Y	Y	Y	?
4 Gutierrez	?	?	?	?	Y	Y	Y	Y
5 Blagojevich	?	Y	Y	Y	?	?	?	?
6 Hyde	Y	Y	Y	N	Y	Y	Y	Y
7 Davis	Y	Y	Y	N	Y	Y	Y	N
8 Crane	?	Y	Y	N	Y	Y	Y	Y
9 Schakowsky	Y	Y	Y	N	Y	Y	Y	N
10 Kirk	Y	Y	Y	Y	Y	Y	Y	Y
11 Weller	Y	Y	Y	N	Y	Y	Y	Y
12 Costello	Y	Y	Y	Y	Y	Y	Y	Y
13 Biggert	Y	Y	Y	Y	Y	Y	Y	Y

ND Northern Democrats   SD Southern Democrats

	295	296	297	298	299	300	301	302
14 ***Hastert***								
15 ***Johnson***	Y	Y	Y	Y	Y	Y	Y	Y
16 ***Manzullo***	?	Y	Y	Y	Y	Y	Y	Y
17 Evans	Y	Y	Y	Y	Y	Y	Y	Y
18 ***LaHood***	Y	Y	Y	N	Y	Y	Y	Y
19 Phelps	Y	Y	Y	Y	Y	Y	Y	N
20 ***Shimkus***	Y	Y	Y	Y	Y	Y	Y	Y
INDIANA								
1 Visclosky	Y	Y	Y	Y	Y	Y	Y	Y
2 ***Pence***	N	Y	Y	Y	Y	Y	Y	N
3 Roemer	Y	Y	Y	Y	Y	Y	Y	Y
4 ***Souder***	Y	Y	Y	Y	Y	Y	Y	Y
5 ***Buyer***	Y	Y	Y	N	Y	Y	Y	Y
6 ***Burton***	Y	Y	Y	N	Y	Y	Y	Y
7 ***Kerns***	Y	Y	Y	N	Y	Y	Y	Y
8 ***Hostettler***	N	Y	Y	N	Y	Y	Y	N
9 Hill	Y	Y	Y	Y	Y	Y	Y	Y
10 Carson	Y	Y	Y	Y	Y	Y	Y	Y
IOWA								
1 ***Leach***	Y	Y	Y	Y	Y	Y	Y	Y
2 ***Nussle***	Y	Y	Y	Y	Y	Y	Y	Y
3 Boswell	Y	Y	Y	Y	Y	Y	Y	Y
4 ***Ganske***	?	Y	Y	Y	Y	Y	Y	Y
5 ***Latham***	Y	Y	Y	Y	Y	Y	Y	Y
KANSAS								
1 ***Moran***	Y	Y	Y	Y	Y	Y	Y	Y
2 ***Ryun***	N	+	+	–	Y	Y	Y	N
3 Moore	Y	Y	Y	Y	Y	Y	Y	Y
4 ***Tiahrt***	+	Y	Y	Y	Y	Y	Y	Y
KENTUCKY								
1 ***Whitfield***	Y	Y	Y	Y	Y	Y	Y	Y
2 ***Lewis***	Y	Y	Y	Y	Y	Y	Y	Y
3 ***Northup***	Y	Y	Y	Y	Y	Y	Y	Y
4 Lucas	Y	Y	Y	Y	Y	Y	Y	Y
5 ***Rogers***	Y	Y	Y	Y	Y	Y	Y	Y
6 ***Fletcher***	Y	Y	Y	Y	Y	Y	Y	Y
LOUISIANA								
1 ***Vitter***	Y	?	?	Y	Y	Y	Y	Y
2 Jefferson	Y	Y	Y	Y	Y	Y	Y	Y
3 ***Tauzin***	Y	Y	Y	Y	Y	Y	Y	Y
4 ***McCrery***	Y	Y	Y	Y	Y	?	?	Y
5 ***Cooksey***	Y	Y	Y	Y	Y	Y	Y	Y
6 ***Baker***	?	Y	Y	Y	Y	Y	Y	Y
7 John	?	?	?	?	?	?	?	Y
MAINE								
1 Allen	Y	Y	Y	Y	+	+	+	N
2 Baldacci	Y	Y	Y	Y	Y	Y	Y	N
MARYLAND								
1 ***Gilchrest***	Y	Y	Y	N	Y	Y	Y	Y
2 ***Ehrlich***	?	Y	Y	N	Y	Y	Y	Y
3 Cardin	Y	Y	Y	Y	Y	Y	Y	Y
4 Wynn	Y	Y	Y	N	Y	Y	Y	Y
5 Hoyer	Y	Y	Y	Y	Y	Y	Y	Y
6 ***Bartlett***	Y	Y	Y	N	Y	Y	Y	N
7 Cummings	Y	Y	Y	N	Y	Y	Y	Y
8 ***Morella***	Y	Y	Y	N	+	?	?	Y
MASSACHUSETTS								
1 Olver	Y	Y	Y	Y	N	Y	Y	Y
2 Neal	Y	Y	Y	Y	Y	Y	Y	Y
3 McGovern	Y	Y	Y	Y	N	Y	Y	Y
4 Frank	Y	Y	Y	Y	Y	Y	Y	Y
5 Meehan	?	Y	Y	Y	Y	Y	Y	Y
6 Tierney	?	Y	Y	Y	Y	Y	Y	Y
7 Markey	?	Y	Y	Y	N	Y	Y	Y
8 Capuano	?	Y	Y	Y	Y	Y	Y	Y
9 Lynch	Y	Y	Y	Y	Y	Y	Y	Y
10 Delahunt	Y	Y	Y	Y	Y	Y	Y	Y
MICHIGAN								
1 Stupak	Y	Y	Y	N	Y	Y	Y	Y
2 ***Hoekstra***	Y	Y	Y	Y	Y	Y	Y	N
3 ***Ehlers***	Y	Y	Y	Y	Y	Y	Y	Y
4 ***Camp***	Y	Y	Y	N	Y	Y	Y	N
5 Barcia	Y	Y	Y	Y	Y	Y	Y	N
6 ***Upton***	Y	Y	Y	Y	Y	Y	Y	Y
7 ***Smith***	Y	?	Y	N	Y	Y	Y	N
8 ***Rogers***	Y	Y	Y	Y	Y	Y	Y	Y
9 Kildee	Y	Y	Y	N	Y	Y	Y	N
10 Bonior	?	?	?	?	?	?	?	?
11 ***Knollenberg***	Y	Y	Y	Y	Y	Y	Y	Y
12 Levin	Y	Y	Y	N	Y	Y	Y	Y
13 Rivers	Y	Y	Y	N	Y	Y	Y	N
14 Conyers	?	?	?	?	N	Y	Y	N
15 Kilpatrick	Y	+	+	+	Y	Y	Y	N
16 Dingell	Y	Y	Y	N	Y	Y	Y	N
MINNESOTA								
1 ***Gutknecht***	Y	Y	Y	N	Y	Y	Y	N
2 ***Kennedy***	Y	Y	Y	Y	Y	Y	Y	Y
3 ***Ramstad***	Y	Y	Y	N	Y	Y	Y	Y
4 McCollum	Y	Y	Y	Y	Y	Y	Y	N
5 Sabo	Y	Y	Y	N	N	Y	Y	Y
6 Luther	Y	Y	Y	Y	Y	Y	Y	N
7 Peterson	Y	Y	Y	Y	Y	Y	Y	Y
8 Oberstar	?	Y	Y	Y	N	Y	Y	Y
MISSISSIPPI								
1 ***Wicker***	Y	Y	Y	Y	Y	Y	Y	Y
2 Thompson	Y	Y	Y	N	Y	Y	Y	Y
3 ***Pickering***	?	Y	Y	N	Y	Y	Y	Y
4 Shows	Y	Y	Y	N	Y	Y	Y	Y
5 Taylor	Y	Y	Y	Y	Y	Y	Y	Y
MISSOURI								
1 Clay	+	Y	Y	N	N	Y	P	Y
2 ***Akin***	N	Y	Y	N	Y	Y	Y	N
3 Gephardt	Y	?	?	?	Y	Y	Y	Y
4 Skelton	Y	Y	Y	Y	Y	Y	Y	Y
5 McCarthy	?	Y	Y	N	Y	Y	Y	Y
6 ***Graves***	Y	Y	Y	Y	Y	Y	Y	Y
7 ***Blunt***	Y	Y	Y	N	Y	Y	Y	Y
8 ***Emerson***	?	Y	Y	N	Y	Y	Y	Y
9 ***Hulshof***	Y	Y	Y	Y	Y	Y	P	Y
MONTANA								
AL ***Rehberg***	Y	Y	Y	Y	Y	Y	Y	Y
NEBRASKA								
1 ***Bereuter***	Y	Y	Y	Y	Y	Y	Y	N
2 ***Terry***	Y	Y	Y	N	Y	Y	Y	N
3 ***Osborne***	Y	Y	Y	Y	Y	Y	Y	Y
NEVADA								
1 Berkley	Y	Y	Y	Y	Y	Y	Y	Y
2 ***Gibbons***	Y	Y	Y	Y	+	Y	Y	Y
NEW HAMPSHIRE								
1 ***Sununu***	Y	Y	Y	N	Y	Y	Y	Y
2 ***Bass***	Y	Y	Y	Y	Y	Y	Y	Y
NEW JERSEY								
1 Andrews	Y	Y	Y	Y	Y	Y	Y	N
2 ***LoBiondo***	Y	Y	Y	N	Y	Y	Y	Y
3 ***Saxton***	Y	Y	Y	Y	Y	Y	Y	Y
4 ***Smith***	Y	Y	Y	Y	Y	Y	Y	Y
5 ***Roukema***	?	?	?	?	?	?	?	Y
6 Pallone	Y	Y	Y	Y	Y	Y	Y	N
7 ***Ferguson***	Y	Y	Y	Y	Y	Y	Y	Y
8 Pascrell	?	Y	Y	Y	Y	Y	Y	+
9 Rothman	Y	Y	Y	N	Y	Y	Y	Y
10 Payne	Y	Y	Y	N	Y	Y	Y	N
11 ***Frelinghuysen***	Y	Y	Y	Y	Y	Y	Y	Y
12 Holt	Y	Y	Y	N	Y	Y	Y	N
13 Menendez	Y	Y	Y	Y	Y	Y	Y	N
NEW MEXICO								
1 ***Wilson***	Y	Y	Y	Y	Y	Y	Y	Y
2 ***Skeen***	Y	Y	Y	Y	Y	Y	Y	Y
3 Udall	Y	Y	Y	Y	Y	Y	Y	N
NEW YORK								
1 ***Grucci***	Y	Y	Y	Y	Y	Y	Y	Y
2 Israel	Y	Y	Y	Y	Y	Y	Y	Y
3 ***King***	Y	?	?	?	Y	Y	Y	Y
4 McCarthy	Y	Y	Y	Y	Y	Y	Y	Y
5 Ackerman	?	Y	Y	Y	Y	Y	Y	Y
6 Meeks	Y	?	?	?	Y	Y	Y	Y
7 Crowley	Y	?	?	?	Y	Y	Y	Y
8 Nadler	Y	+	+	+	+	+	+	–
9 Weiner	Y	Y	Y	Y	Y	Y	Y	Y
10 Towns	Y	Y	Y	Y	Y	Y	Y	Y
11 Owens	?	Y	Y	N	Y	Y	Y	Y
12 Velázquez	?	Y	Y	Y	Y	Y	Y	N
13 ***Fossella***	?	?	?	?	Y	Y	Y	Y
14 Maloney	Y	Y	Y	Y	Y	Y	Y	N
15 Rangel	Y	Y	Y	Y	Y	Y	Y	Y
16 Serrano	Y	Y	Y	Y	Y	Y	Y	Y
17 Engel	?	Y	Y	Y	Y	Y	Y	Y
18 Lowey	Y	Y	Y	Y	Y	Y	Y	Y
19 ***Kelly***	Y	Y	Y	Y	Y	Y	Y	Y
20 ***Gilman***	Y	Y	Y	Y	Y	Y	Y	Y
21 McNulty	Y	Y	Y	Y	Y	Y	Y	N
22 ***Sweeney***	?	?	?	?	Y	Y	Y	Y
23 ***Boehlert***	Y	Y	Y	Y	Y	Y	Y	Y
24 ***McHugh***	?	Y	Y	Y	Y	Y	Y	Y
25 ***Walsh***	Y	Y	Y	N	Y	Y	Y	Y
26 Hinchey	Y	+	+	–	N	Y	Y	N
27 ***Reynolds***	Y	Y	Y	Y	Y	Y	Y	Y
28 Slaughter	Y	Y	Y	Y	Y	Y	Y	Y
29 LaFalce	Y	Y	Y	Y	Y	Y	Y	Y
30 ***Quinn***	Y	Y	Y	Y	Y	Y	Y	Y
31 ***Houghton***	Y	Y	Y	N	Y	Y	Y	Y
NORTH CAROLINA								
1 Clayton	Y	Y	Y	N	Y	Y	Y	N
2 Etheridge	Y	Y	Y	Y	Y	Y	Y	Y
3 ***Jones***	N	Y	Y	N	Y	Y	Y	N
4 Price	Y	Y	Y	Y	Y	Y	Y	Y
5 ***Burr***	Y	Y	Y	N	Y	Y	Y	Y
6 ***Coble***	N	Y	Y	N	Y	Y	Y	Y
7 McIntyre	Y	Y	Y	Y	Y	Y	Y	Y
8 ***Hayes***	Y	Y	Y	Y	Y	Y	Y	Y
9 ***Myrick***	Y	Y	Y	N	Y	Y	Y	N
10 ***Ballenger***	Y	Y	Y	N	Y	Y	Y	Y
11 ***Taylor***	N	?	?	?	Y	Y	Y	Y
12 Watt	Y	Y	Y	N	Y	Y	Y	Y
NORTH DAKOTA								
AL Pomeroy	Y	Y	Y	Y	Y	Y	Y	N
OHIO								
1 ***Chabot***	Y	Y	Y	N	Y	Y	Y	N
2 ***Portman***	Y	Y	Y	Y	Y	Y	Y	Y
3 Hall	Y	Y	Y	Y	Y	Y	Y	Y
4 ***Oxley***	Y	Y	Y	N	Y	Y	Y	Y
5 ***Gillmor***	?	Y	Y	Y	Y	Y	Y	Y
6 Strickland	Y	Y	Y	Y	Y	Y	Y	Y
7 ***Hobson***	Y	Y	Y	Y	Y	Y	Y	Y
8 ***Boehner***	Y	Y	Y	Y	Y	Y	Y	Y
9 Kaptur	Y	Y	Y	Y	Y	Y	?	Y
10 Kucinich	Y	N	Y	N	N	Y	Y	N
11 Jones	?	Y	Y	N	N	Y	Y	Y
12 ***Tiberi***	Y	Y	Y	Y	Y	Y	Y	Y
13 Brown	Y	Y	Y	N	Y	Y	Y	N
14 Sawyer	Y	Y	Y	Y	Y	Y	Y	Y
15 ***Pryce***	Y	Y	Y	N	Y	Y	Y	Y
16 ***Regula***	Y	Y	Y	N	Y	Y	Y	N
17 Traficant	?	?	?	?	?	?	?	?
18 ***Ney***	Y	Y	Y	Y	Y	Y	Y	Y
19 ***LaTourette***	Y	Y	Y	Y	Y	Y	Y	Y
OKLAHOMA								
1 ***Sullivan***	Y	Y	Y	Y	Y	Y	Y	Y
2 Carson	Y	Y	Y	Y	Y	Y	Y	N
3 ***Watkins***	Y	Y	Y	Y	Y	Y	Y	Y
4 ***Watts***	Y	Y	Y	Y	Y	Y	Y	Y
5 ***Istook***	Y	Y	Y	Y	Y	Y	Y	Y
6 ***Lucas***	Y	Y	Y	Y	Y	Y	?	Y
OREGON								
1 Wu	Y	Y	Y	Y	Y	Y	Y	N
2 ***Walden***	?	Y	Y	Y	Y	Y	Y	Y
3 Blumenauer	?	Y	Y	Y	N	Y	Y	N
4 DeFazio	?	Y	Y	Y	Y	Y	Y	N
5 Hooley	Y	Y	Y	Y	Y	Y	Y	N
PENNSYLVANIA								
1 Brady	?	Y	Y	Y	N	Y	Y	N
2 Fattah	?	Y	Y	Y	N	Y	Y	N
3 Borski	?	Y	Y	Y	Y	Y	Y	N
4 ***Hart***	Y	Y	Y	Y	Y	Y	Y	Y
5 ***Peterson***	Y	Y	Y	N	Y	Y	Y	Y
6 Holden	Y	Y	Y	Y	Y	Y	Y	Y
7 ***Weldon***	Y	Y	Y	Y	Y	Y	Y	Y
8 ***Greenwood***	Y	Y	Y	N	Y	Y	Y	Y
9 ***Shuster, Bill***	Y	Y	Y	Y	Y	Y	Y	Y
10 ***Sherwood***	Y	Y	Y	Y	Y	Y	Y	Y
11 Kanjorski	Y	Y	Y	Y	Y	Y	Y	Y
12 Murtha	Y	Y	Y	Y	Y	Y	Y	Y
13 Hoeffel	Y	Y	Y	Y	Y	Y	Y	Y
14 Coyne	Y	?	?	?	Y	Y	Y	Y
15 ***Toomey***	N	Y	Y	N	Y	Y	Y	N
16 ***Pitts***	Y	Y	Y	N	Y	Y	Y	N
17 ***Gekas***	Y	Y	Y	Y	Y	Y	Y	Y
18 Doyle	Y	?	Y	Y	Y	Y	Y	Y
19 ***Platts***	Y	Y	Y	Y	Y	Y	Y	Y
20 Mascara	Y	?	?	?	?	?	?	?
21 ***English***	Y	Y	Y	N	Y	Y	Y	Y
RHODE ISLAND								
1 Kennedy	Y	Y	Y	Y	Y	Y	Y	N
2 Langevin	Y	Y	Y	Y	Y	Y	Y	Y
SOUTH CAROLINA								
1 ***Brown***	Y	Y	Y	Y	Y	Y	Y	Y
2 ***Wilson***	Y	Y	Y	Y	Y	Y	Y	Y
3 ***Graham***	Y	Y	Y	N	Y	Y	Y	Y
4 ***DeMint***	Y	Y	Y	Y	Y	Y	Y	N
5 Spratt	Y	Y	Y	Y	Y	Y	Y	Y
6 Clyburn	Y	Y	Y	N	Y	Y	Y	Y
SOUTH DAKOTA								
AL ***Thune***	Y	Y	Y	Y	Y	Y	Y	Y
TENNESSEE								
1 ***Jenkins***	?	Y	Y	N	Y	Y	Y	Y
2 ***Duncan***	N	Y	Y	Y	Y	Y	Y	Y
3 ***Wamp***	Y	Y	Y	N	Y	Y	Y	Y
4 ***Hilleary***	?	?	?	?	?	?	?	?
5 Clement	+	Y	Y	Y	Y	Y	Y	Y
6 Gordon	?	Y	Y	Y	Y	Y	Y	Y
7 ***Bryant***	?	?	?	?	Y	Y	Y	Y
8 Tanner	Y	Y	Y	Y	Y	Y	Y	Y
9 Ford	Y	Y	Y	Y	Y	Y	Y	Y
TEXAS								
1 Sandlin	Y	Y	Y	Y	Y	Y	Y	Y
2 Turner	Y	Y	Y	Y	Y	Y	Y	Y
3 ***Johnson, Sam***	Y	Y	Y	Y	Y	Y	Y	N
4 Hall	Y	Y	Y	N	Y	Y	Y	Y
5 ***Sessions***	Y	Y	Y	Y	Y	Y	Y	Y
6 ***Barton***	?	Y	Y	Y	Y	Y	Y	Y
7 ***Culberson***	N	Y	Y	N	Y	Y	Y	Y
8 ***Brady***	Y	Y	Y	Y	Y	Y	Y	Y
9 Lampson	Y	Y	Y	Y	Y	Y	Y	Y
10 Doggett	Y	Y	Y	Y	Y	Y	Y	N
11 Edwards	Y	Y	Y	N	Y	Y	Y	Y
12 ***Granger***	Y	?	?	?	Y	Y	Y	Y
13 ***Thornberry***	Y	Y	Y	Y	Y	Y	Y	Y
14 ***Paul***	N	N	Y	N	N	Y	Y	Y
15 Hinojosa	Y	Y	Y	Y	Y	Y	Y	Y
16 Reyes	Y	Y	Y	Y	Y	Y	Y	Y
17 Stenholm	Y	Y	Y	Y	Y	Y	Y	Y
18 Jackson-Lee	Y	Y	Y	N	Y	Y	Y	Y
19 ***Combest***	Y	Y	Y	Y	Y	Y	Y	Y
20 Gonzalez	Y	Y	Y	Y	Y	Y	Y	Y
21 ***Smith***	Y	Y	Y	Y	Y	Y	Y	Y
22 ***DeLay***	Y	Y	Y	Y	Y	Y	Y	Y
23 ***Bonilla***	Y	Y	Y	Y	Y	Y	Y	Y
24 Frost	Y	Y	Y	Y	Y	Y	Y	Y
25 Bentsen	Y	Y	Y	Y	Y	Y	Y	Y
26 ***Armey***	Y	Y	Y	Y	Y	Y	Y	Y
27 Ortiz	Y	Y	Y	Y	Y	Y	Y	Y
28 Rodriguez	Y	Y	Y	Y	Y	Y	Y	Y
29 Green	Y	Y	Y	Y	Y	Y	Y	Y
30 Johnson, E.B.	Y	Y	Y	Y	Y	Y	Y	Y
UTAH								
1 ***Hansen***	?	Y	Y	N	Y	Y	Y	Y
2 Matheson	Y	Y	Y	Y	Y	Y	Y	Y
3 ***Cannon***	N	Y	Y	N	Y	Y	Y	Y
VERMONT								
AL *Sanders*	Y	?	?	?	N	Y	P	N
VIRGINIA								
1 ***Davis, Jo Ann***	Y	Y	Y	N	Y	Y	Y	Y
2 ***Schrock***	Y	Y	Y	Y	Y	Y	Y	Y
3 Scott	Y	Y	Y	N	N	Y	Y	Y
4 ***Forbes***	Y	Y	Y	N	Y	Y	Y	Y
5 *Goode*	N	Y	Y	N	Y	Y	Y	N
6 ***Goodlatte***	N	Y	Y	N	Y	Y	Y	Y
7 ***Cantor***	N	Y	Y	Y	Y	Y	Y	Y
8 Moran	Y	Y	Y	N	Y	Y	Y	Y
9 Boucher	?	?	?	?	Y	Y	Y	Y
10 ***Wolf***	Y	Y	Y	N	Y	Y	Y	Y
11 ***Davis, T.***	Y	Y	Y	Y	Y	Y	Y	Y
WASHINGTON								
1 Inslee	Y	Y	Y	N	Y	Y	Y	N
2 Larsen	?	Y	Y	Y	Y	Y	Y	Y
3 Baird	Y	Y	Y	Y	Y	Y	Y	N
4 ***Hastings***	Y	Y	Y	N	Y	Y	Y	Y
5 ***Nethercutt***	Y	Y	Y	N	Y	Y	Y	Y
6 Dicks	?	Y	Y	Y	Y	Y	Y	Y
7 McDermott	+	+	+	+	N	Y	Y	N
8 ***Dunn***	Y	Y	Y	N	Y	Y	Y	Y
9 Smith	?	Y	Y	N	Y	Y	Y	Y
WEST VIRGINIA								
1 Mollohan	Y	Y	Y	Y	Y	Y	Y	Y
2 ***Capito***	Y	Y	Y	Y	Y	Y	Y	Y
3 Rahall	Y	Y	Y	Y	Y	Y	Y	N
WISCONSIN								
1 ***Ryan***	Y	Y	Y	Y	Y	Y	Y	N
2 Baldwin	Y	Y	Y	N	N	Y	Y	N
3 Kind	Y	Y	Y	Y	Y	Y	Y	N
4 Kleczka	Y	Y	Y	Y	Y	Y	Y	N
5 Barrett	+	+	+	–	Y	Y	Y	N
6 ***Petri***	Y	Y	Y	Y	Y	Y	Y	Y
7 Obey	Y	Y	Y	N	Y	Y	Y	Y
8 ***Green***	Y	Y	Y	Y	Y	Y	Y	N
9 ***Sensenbrenner***	Y	Y	Y	N	Y	Y	Y	Y
WYOMING								
AL ***Cubin***	+	Y	Y	N	Y	Y	Y	Y

Southern states - Ala., Ark., Fla., Ga., Ky., La., Miss., N.C., Okla., S.C., Tenn., Texas, Va.

Key

Y	Voted for (yea).
#	Paired for.
+	Announced for.
N	Voted against (nay).
X	Paired against.
−	Announced against.
P	Voted "present."
C	Voted "present" to avoid possible conflict of interest.
?	Did not vote or otherwise make a position known.

Democrats **Republicans**
Independents

---

303. HR 4866. Amendments to Higher Education Act/Adoption. Boehner, R-Ohio, motion to suspend the rules and adopt the resolution that would make technical changes to the Higher Education Act (PL 105-244). Motion rejected 246-177: R 218-0; D 27-176 (ND 13-137, SD 14-39); I 1-1. A two-thirds majority of those present and voting (282 in this case) is required for adoption under suspension of the rules. July 16, 2002.

304. H Con Res 395. Puerto Rico 50th Anniversary/Adoption. Gilchrest, R-Md., motion to suspend the rules and adopt the resolution that would celebrate the 50th anniversary of the constitution of the Commonwealth of Puerto Rico. Motion agreed to 389-32: R 211-6; D 177-25 (ND 126-23, SD 51-2); I 1-1. A two-thirds majority of those present and voting (281 in this case) is required for adoption under suspension of the rules. July 16, 2002.

305. HR 5093. Fiscal 2003 Interior Department Appropriations/ Bureau of Land Management. Toomey, R-Pa., amendment that would reduce appropriations for the Bureau of Land Management's lands and resources management by $162.3 million to $664.7 million. Rejected 84-332: R 75-140; D 8-191 (ND 1-146, SD 7-45); I 1-1. July 16, 2002.

306. HR 5093. Fiscal 2003 Interior Department Appropriations/ Motion to Limit Debate. Nethercutt, R-Wash., motion to limit debate to 10 minutes on the Flake amendment that would reduce the appropriation for the Bureau of Land Management by $51.3 million. Motion agreed to 324-79: R 152-53; D 170-26 (ND 126-21, SD 44-5); I 2-0. July 16, 2002.

307. HR 5093. Fiscal 2003 Interior Department Appropriations/ Bureau of Land Management Reduction. Flake, R-Ariz., amendment that would reduce the appropriation for the Bureau of Land Management by $51.3 million. Rejected 85-337: R 75-142; D 10-193 (ND 5-146, SD 5-47); I 0-2. July 16, 2002.

308. HR 5093. Fiscal 2003 Interior Department Appropriations/ Motion to Rise. Dicks, D-Wash., motion to rise to the Committee of the Whole. Motion rejected 209-210: R 9-207; D 199-2 (ND 149-1, SD 50-1); I 1-1. July 16, 2002.

309. Procedural Motion/Journal. Approval of the House Journal of Tuesday, July 16, 2002. Approved 361-50: R 197-16; D 162-34 (ND 116-30, SD 46-4); I 2-0. July 17, 2002.

310. HR 5093. Fiscal 2003 Interior Department Appropriations/Challenge America Grants. Slaughter, D-N.Y., amendment that would increase funding for Challenge America Grants and the National Endowment for the Humanities, offset by reductions in administrative funds for the Interior Department and the Forest Service. Adopted 234-192: R 42-177; D 191-14 (ND 147-4, SD 44-10); I 1-1. July 17, 2002.

	303	304	305	306	307	308	309	310
ALABAMA								
1 *Callahan*	Y	Y	N	Y	N	N	Y	N
2 *Everett*	Y	Y	N	Y	N	N	Y	N
3 *Riley*	?	?	?	?	?	?	Y	N
4 *Aderholt*	Y	Y	N	Y	N	N	N	N
5 Cramer	N	Y	N	Y	N	Y	Y	Y
6 *Bachus*	Y	Y	N	N	N	N	Y	N
7 Hilliard	N	Y	N	Y	N	Y	N	Y
ALASKA								
AL *Young*	Y	Y	N	Y	N	N	Y	N
ARIZONA								
1 *Flake*	Y	Y	Y	N	Y	N	Y	N
2 Pastor	N	Y	N	Y	N	Y	Y	Y
3 *Stump*	Y	Y	N	N	N	N	?	N
4 *Shadegg*	Y	Y	Y	N	Y	N	Y	N
5 *Kolbe*	Y	Y	N	Y	N	N	Y	Y
6 *Hayworth*	Y	Y	N	N	N	N	Y	N
ARKANSAS								
1 Berry	Y	Y	Y	Y	Y	Y	Y	Y
2 Snyder	N	Y	N	Y	N	Y	Y	Y
3 *Boozman*	Y	Y	Y	Y	N	N	Y	N
4 Ross	Y	Y	N	Y	N	Y	Y	Y
CALIFORNIA								
1 Thompson	N	N	Y	N	Y	N	Y	Y
2 *Herger*	Y	Y	N	N	N	N	Y	N
3 *Ose*	Y	Y	N	Y	N	N	Y	N
4 *Doolittle*	Y	Y	N	N	N	N	Y	N
5 Matsui	N	N	N	Y	N	Y	Y	Y
6 Woolsey	N	Y	N	Y	N	Y	Y	Y
7 Miller, George	N	Y	N	Y	N	Y	N	Y
8 Pelosi	N	Y	N	Y	N	Y	Y	Y
9 Lee	N	N	N	Y	N	Y	Y	Y
10 Tauscher	N	Y	N	Y	N	Y	Y	Y
11 *Pombo*	Y	Y	N	N	N	N	Y	N
12 Lantos	N	Y	N	Y	N	Y	Y	Y
13 Stark	N	N	N	N	Y	?	Y	Y
14 Eshoo	N	Y	N	Y	N	Y	Y	Y
15 Honda	N	Y	N	Y	N	Y	Y	Y
16 Lofgren	N	Y	N	Y	N	Y	Y	Y
17 Farr	N	N	N	Y	N	Y	Y	Y
18 Condit	N	N	N	Y	N	Y	Y	N
19 *Radanovich*	Y	Y	N	N	N	N	Y	N
20 Dooley	N	Y	?	?	?	?	Y	Y
21 *Thomas*	Y	Y	N	Y	N	N	Y	N
22 Capps	N	Y	N	Y	N	Y	Y	Y
23 *Gallegly*	Y	Y	N	N	N	N	Y	N
24 Sherman	N	Y	N	Y	N	Y	Y	Y
25 *McKeon*	Y	Y	N	Y	N	N	Y	Y
26 Berman	N	Y	N	Y	N	Y	Y	Y
27 Schiff	N	Y	N	Y	N	Y	Y	Y
28 *Dreier*	Y	Y	N	Y	N	N	Y	N
29 Waxman	N	Y	N	Y	N	Y	Y	Y
30 Becerra	N	Y	N	Y	N	Y	Y	Y
31 Solis	N	Y	N	Y	N	Y	?	Y
32 Watson	N	Y	N	Y	N	Y	Y	Y
33 Roybal-Allard	N	Y	N	Y	N	Y	Y	Y
34 Napolitano	N	Y	N	Y	N	Y	Y	Y
35 Waters	N	N	N	N	Y	N	Y	Y
36 Harman	N	Y	?	Y	N	Y	Y	Y
37 Millender-McD.	N	Y	N	Y	N	Y	Y	Y
38 *Horn*	Y	Y	N	Y	N	N	Y	N

	303	304	305	306	307	308	309	310
39 *Royce*	Y	Y	Y	N	Y	N	Y	N
40 *Lewis*	Y	Y	N	Y	N	N	Y	N
41 *Miller, Gary*	Y	Y	N	Y	N	Y	Y	N
42 Baca	N	Y	N	Y	N	Y	Y	Y
43 *Calvert*	Y	Y	N	Y	N	N	Y	N
44 *Bono*	Y	Y	N	Y	N	N	Y	N
45 *Rohrabacher*	Y	N	Y	N	Y	N	Y	Y
46 Sanchez	N	N	N	Y	N	Y	Y	Y
47 *Cox*	Y	Y	N	Y	N	N	Y	N
48 *Issa*	Y	Y	N	Y	N	N	Y	N
49 Davis	N	Y	N	Y	N	Y	Y	Y
50 Filner	N	N	N	N	Y	−	Y
51 *Cunningham*	Y	Y	N	Y	N	N	?	N
52 *Hunter*	Y	Y	N	N	N	N	Y	N
COLORADO								
1 DeGette	N	Y	N	Y	N	Y	Y	Y
2 Udall	N	Y	N	Y	N	Y	N	Y
3 *McInnis*	Y	Y	N	Y	N	Y	Y	N
4 *Schaffer*	Y	Y	Y	N	Y	N	Y	N
5 *Hefley*	Y	Y	Y	Y	Y	Y	N	N
6 *Tancredo*	Y	N	Y	N	Y	N	P	N
CONNECTICUT								
1 Larson	N	N	N	Y	N	Y	Y	Y
2 *Simmons*	Y	Y	N	Y	N	N	Y	Y
3 DeLauro	N	Y	N	Y	N	Y	Y	Y
4 *Shays*	Y	Y	N	Y	N	N	Y	Y
5 Maloney	Y	Y	N	Y	N	Y	Y	Y
6 *Johnson*	Y	Y	N	Y	N	N	Y	Y
DELAWARE								
AL *Castle*	Y	Y	N	Y	N	N	Y	Y
FLORIDA								
1 *Miller, J.*	Y	P	Y	Y	Y	N	Y	N
2 Boyd	Y	Y	N	Y	N	Y	Y	Y
3 Brown	N	Y	N	Y	N	Y	Y	Y
4 *Crenshaw*	Y	Y	N	Y	N	N	Y	N
5 Thurman	N	Y	N	Y	N	Y	Y	Y
6 *Stearns*	Y	Y	Y	Y	Y	N	Y	N
7 *Mica*	Y	Y	Y	N	N	N	Y	N
8 *Keller*	Y	Y	Y	N	Y	N	Y	N
9 *Bilirakis*	Y	Y	N	Y	N	N	Y	N
10 *Young*	Y	Y	N	Y	N	N	Y	N
11 Davis	N	Y	N	Y	N	Y	Y	Y
12 *Putnam*	Y	Y	N	Y	N	N	Y	N
13 *Miller, D.*	Y	Y	N	Y	N	N	Y	N
14 *Goss*	Y	Y	N	Y	N	N	Y	N
15 *Weldon*	Y	Y	Y	Y	Y	N	Y	N
16 *Foley*	Y	Y	N	Y	N	N	Y	N
17 Meek	N	Y	N	Y	N	Y	?	Y
18 *Ros-Lehtinen*	Y	Y	N	Y	N	N	Y	N
19 Wexler	N	Y	N	Y	N	Y	Y	Y
20 Deutsch	N	N	N	Y	N	Y	Y	Y
21 *Diaz-Balart*	Y	Y	N	Y	N	N	Y	N
22 *Shaw*	Y	Y	N	Y	N	N	Y	N
23 Hastings	?	?	?	?	?	?	?	?
GEORGIA								
1 *Kingston*	Y	Y	N	Y	N	N	Y	N
2 Bishop	N	Y	N	Y	N	Y	Y	Y
3 *Collins*	Y	Y	Y	Y	Y	Y	Y	N
4 McKinney	N	N	N	N	Y	N	Y	Y
5 Lewis	N	Y	N	N	N	Y	Y	Y
6 *Isakson*	Y	Y	N	?	N	N	Y	N
7 *Barr*	Y	Y	Y	Y	N	Y	Y	N
8 *Chambliss*	Y	Y	N	Y	N	N	Y	N
9 *Deal*	Y	Y	N	Y	N	N	Y	N
10 *Norwood*	Y	Y	Y	Y	N	Y	Y	N
11 *Linder*	Y	Y	N	Y	N	N	Y	N
HAWAII								
1 Abercrombie	Y	Y	N	Y	N	Y	Y	Y
2 Mink	Y	Y	N	Y	N	Y	Y	Y
IDAHO								
1 *Otter*	Y	Y	N	N	Y	N	Y	N
2 *Simpson*	Y	Y	N	Y	N	N	Y	N
ILLINOIS								
1 Rush	N	Y	N	Y	N	Y	Y	Y
2 Jackson	N	Y	N	Y	N	Y	Y	Y
3 Lipinski	?	Y	N	Y	N	Y	Y	Y
4 Gutierrez	N	P	N	Y	N	Y	Y	Y
5 Blagojevich	?	?	?	?	?	?	?	?
6 *Hyde*	Y	?	N	Y	N	N	?	N
7 Davis	N	Y	N	Y	N	Y	Y	Y
8 *Crane*	Y	Y	N	Y	N	N	N	N
9 Schakowsky	N	Y	N	Y	N	Y	N	Y
10 *Kirk*	Y	Y	Y	?	Y	N	Y	Y
11 *Weller*	Y	Y	N	Y	N	N	Y	N
12 Costello	N	Y	N	Y	N	Y	N	Y
13 *Biggert*	Y	Y	N	Y	N	N	Y	Y

ND Northern Democrats   SD Southern Democrats

	303	304	305	306	307	308	309	310
14 ***Hastert***								
15 Johnson	Y	Y	N	Y	N	N	Y	Y
16 ***Manzullo***	Y	Y	Y	Y	Y	N	?	N
17 Evans	N	Y	N	Y	N	Y	Y	Y
18 ***LaHood***	Y	Y	N	Y	N	N	Y	Y
19 Phelps	Y	Y	N	Y	N	Y	Y	N
20 ***Shimkus***	Y	Y	Y	N	Y	N	Y	N
INDIANA								
1 Visclosky	N	Y	N	Y	N	Y	N	Y
2 ***Pence***	Y	Y	Y	N	Y	N	Y	N
3 Roemer	N	Y	N	Y	N	Y	N	Y
4 ***Souder***	Y	Y	Y	N	Y	N	Y	N
5 ***Buyer***	Y	Y	N	?	?	N	Y	N
6 ***Burton***	Y	N	Y	N	Y	N	Y	N
7 ***Kerns***	Y	Y	Y	Y	Y	Y	Y	N
8 ***Hostettler***	Y	Y	Y	N	Y	N	Y	N
9 Hill	N	Y	Y	Y	Y	Y	Y	Y
10 Carson	N	Y	N	N	N	Y	Y	Y
IOWA								
1 ***Leach***	Y	Y	N	Y	N	N	Y	Y
2 ***Nussle***	Y	Y	Y	?	Y	N	Y	N
3 Boswell	Y	Y	N	Y	Y	N	Y	Y
4 ***Ganske***	Y	Y	N	Y	N	N	N	N
5 ***Latham***	Y	Y	N	Y	N	N	Y	N
KANSAS								
1 ***Moran***	Y	Y	N	N	N	N	Y	Y
2 ***Ryun***	Y	Y	Y	N	Y	N	Y	N
3 Moore	N	Y	N	Y	N	Y	N	Y
4 ***Tiahrt***	Y	Y	N	Y	N	N	Y	N
KENTUCKY								
1 ***Whitfield***	Y	Y	N	Y	N	N	Y	N
2 ***Lewis***	Y	Y	N	Y	N	N	Y	N
3 ***Northup***	Y	Y	N	Y	N	N	Y	Y
4 Lucas	Y	Y	Y	Y	N	Y	Y	N
5 ***Rogers***	Y	Y	N	Y	N	N	Y	N
6 ***Fletcher***	Y	Y	N	Y	N	N	N	N
LOUISIANA								
1 ***Vitter***	Y	Y	N	Y	N	N	Y	N
2 Jefferson	N	Y	N	Y	N	Y	?	Y
3 ***Tauzin***	Y	Y	N	?	N	N	Y	N
4 ***McCrery***	Y	Y	N	Y	N	N	Y	N
5 ***Cooksey***	Y	Y	N	?	?	N	Y	N
6 ***Baker***	Y	Y	N	Y	N	Y	Y	N
7 John	N	Y	N	Y	N	Y	Y	N
MAINE								
1 Allen	Y	Y	N	Y	N	Y	Y	Y
2 Baldacci	Y	Y	N	Y	N	Y	Y	Y
MARYLAND								
1 ***Gilchrest***	Y	Y	N	N	Y	N	Y	N
2 ***Ehrlich***	Y	Y	?	Y	N	N	Y	?
3 Cardin	N	Y	N	Y	N	Y	Y	Y
4 Wynn	N	Y	N	Y	N	Y	Y	Y
5 Hoyer	N	Y	N	Y	N	Y	Y	Y
6 ***Bartlett***	Y	Y	Y	N	Y	N	Y	N
7 Cummings	N	Y	N	Y	N	Y	Y	Y
8 ***Morella***	Y	Y	N	Y	N	N	Y	Y
MASSACHUSETTS								
1 Olver	N	N	N	Y	N	Y	N	Y
2 Neal	N	Y	N	Y	N	Y	N	Y
3 McGovern	N	N	N	N	N	Y	N	Y
4 Frank	N	Y	N	N	N	Y	Y	Y
5 Meehan	N	Y	N	Y	N	Y	Y	Y
6 Tierney	N	Y	N	Y	N	Y	N	Y
7 Markey	N	Y	N	Y	N	Y	Y	Y
8 Capuano	N	N	N	N	N	Y	?	Y
9 Lynch	N	Y	?	?	N	Y	Y	Y
10 Delahunt	N	N	N	N	N	Y	Y	Y
MICHIGAN								
1 Stupak	N	Y	N	Y	N	Y	N	Y
2 ***Hoekstra***	Y	Y	Y	N	Y	Y	Y	N
3 ***Ehlers***	Y	Y	N	Y	N	N	Y	Y
4 ***Camp***	Y	Y	N	Y	N	N	Y	N
5 Barcia	N	Y	N	Y	N	Y	Y	N
6 ***Upton***	Y	Y	Y	Y	Y	N	Y	N
7 ***Smith***	Y	Y	Y	N	Y	Y	Y	N
8 ***Rogers***	Y	Y	Y	N	Y	N	Y	Y
9 Kildee	N	Y	N	Y	N	Y	Y	Y
10 Bonior	?	?	?	?	?	?	?	?
11 ***Knollenberg***	Y	Y	N	Y	N	N	Y	N
12 Levin	N	Y	N	Y	N	Y	Y	Y
13 Rivers	N	Y	N	Y	N	Y	Y	Y
14 Conyers	N	N	N	Y	N	Y	Y	Y
15 Kilpatrick	N	Y	N	Y	N	Y	Y	Y
16 Dingell	N	Y	N	Y	N	Y	Y	Y

	303	304	305	306	307	308	309	310
MINNESOTA								
1 ***Gutknecht***	Y	Y	Y	N	Y	N	N	N
2 ***Kennedy***	Y	Y	Y	Y	Y	N	N	N
3 ***Ramstad***	Y	Y	N	Y	N	N	N	Y
4 McCollum	N	Y	N	N	N	Y	Y	Y
5 Sabo	N	Y	N	Y	N	?	N	Y
6 Luther	Y	Y	N	N	Y	Y	Y	Y
7 Peterson	Y	Y	N	Y	N	Y	N	Y
8 Oberstar	N	Y	N	Y	N	Y	N	Y
MISSISSIPPI								
1 ***Wicker***	Y	Y	N	?	N	N	N	N
2 Thompson	N	Y	N	Y	N	Y	N	Y
3 ***Pickering***	Y	Y	N	Y	N	N	Y	N
4 Shows	Y	Y	Y	Y	N	Y	Y	N
5 Taylor	N	Y	Y	Y	Y	Y	N	N
MISSOURI								
1 Clay	N	Y	?	N	Y	Y	?	Y
2 ***Akin***	Y	Y	Y	N	Y	N	Y	N
3 Gephardt	N	Y	N	Y	N	Y	Y	Y
4 Skelton	N	Y	N	Y	N	Y	Y	Y
5 McCarthy	N	N	N	Y	N	Y	Y	Y
6 ***Graves***	Y	Y	Y	N	Y	N	Y	N
7 ***Blunt***	Y	Y	N	N	N	?	Y	N
8 ***Emerson***	Y	Y	N	Y	N	N	Y	N
9 ***Hulshof***	Y	Y	N	Y	N	N	N	N
MONTANA								
AL ***Rehberg***	Y	Y	N	Y	N	N	Y	N
NEBRASKA								
1 ***Bereuter***	Y	Y	N	Y	N	N	Y	Y
2 ***Terry***	Y	Y	Y	N	Y	N	Y	N
3 ***Osborne***	Y	Y	N	Y	N	N	Y	N
NEVADA								
1 Berkley	N	Y	N	Y	N	Y	Y	Y
2 ***Gibbons***	Y	Y	N	Y	N	N	Y	N
NEW HAMPSHIRE								
1 ***Sununu***	Y	Y	?	N	Y	N	Y	N
2 ***Bass***	Y	Y	Y	Y	N	N	Y	N
NEW JERSEY								
1 Andrews	N	Y	N	Y	N	Y	Y	Y
2 ***LoBiondo***	Y	Y	N	Y	N	N	N	Y
3 ***Saxton***	Y	Y	N	Y	N	N	Y	N
4 ***Smith***	Y	Y	N	Y	N	N	Y	N
5 ***Roukema***	Y	Y	N	?	?	?	Y	Y
6 Pallone	N	N	N	Y	N	Y	N	Y
7 ***Ferguson***	Y	Y	N	Y	N	N	Y	N
8 Pascrell	+	+	N	Y	N	Y	Y	Y
9 Rothman	N	Y	N	Y	N	Y	Y	Y
10 Payne	N	Y	N	Y	N	Y	Y	Y
11 ***Frelinghuysen***	Y	Y	N	Y	N	N	Y	Y
12 Holt	N	Y	N	Y	N	Y	Y	Y
13 Menendez	N	Y	N	Y	N	Y	Y	Y
NEW MEXICO								
1 ***Wilson***	Y	Y	N	Y	N	N	Y	N
2 ***Skeen***	Y	Y	N	Y	N	N	Y	N
3 Udall	N	N	N	Y	N	Y	Y	Y
NEW YORK								
1 ***Grucci***	Y	Y	N	Y	N	N	Y	Y
2 Israel	N	Y	N	Y	N	Y	Y	Y
3 ***King***	Y	Y	N	Y	N	N	Y	N
4 McCarthy	N	Y	N	Y	N	Y	Y	Y
5 Ackerman	N	Y	N	Y	N	Y	Y	Y
6 Meeks	N	N	N	Y	N	Y	Y	Y
7 Crowley	N	N	N	Y	N	Y	Y	Y
8 Nadler	–	+	–	–	–	+	+	+
9 Weiner	N	N	N	Y	N	Y	Y	Y
10 Towns	N	Y	N	Y	N	Y	Y	Y
11 Owens	N	Y	N	Y	N	Y	Y	Y
12 Velázquez	N	Y	N	Y	N	Y	Y	Y
13 ***Fossella***	Y	Y	Y	N	Y	N	Y	Y
14 Maloney	N	Y	N	Y	N	Y	Y	Y
15 Rangel	N	Y	N	Y	N	Y	?	Y
16 Serrano	N	N	N	N	N	Y	Y	Y
17 Engel	N	P	N	Y	N	Y	Y	Y
18 Lowey	N	Y	N	Y	N	Y	Y	Y
19 ***Kelly***	Y	Y	N	Y	N	N	Y	Y
20 ***Gilman***	Y	N	?	Y	N	N	Y	Y
21 McNulty	N	Y	N	Y	N	Y	N	Y
22 ***Sweeney***	Y	Y	N	Y	N	N	Y	Y
23 ***Boehlert***	Y	Y	N	Y	N	N	Y	Y
24 ***McHugh***	Y	Y	N	Y	N	N	Y	?
25 ***Walsh***	Y	Y	N	Y	N	N	Y	Y
26 Hinchey	N	Y	N	N	N	Y	Y	Y
27 ***Reynolds***	Y	Y	N	Y	N	?	Y	Y
28 Slaughter	N	Y	N	Y	N	Y	Y	Y
29 LaFalce	N	Y	N	Y	N	Y	N	Y

	303	304	305	306	307	308	309	310
30 ***Quinn***	Y	Y	?	?	N	N	Y	Y
31 ***Houghton***	Y	N	N	Y	N	N	Y	Y
NORTH CAROLINA								
1 Clayton	N	Y	N	?	N	Y	?	Y
2 Etheridge	N	Y	N	Y	N	Y	Y	Y
3 ***Jones***	Y	Y	Y	N	Y	Y	Y	N
4 Price	N	Y	N	Y	N	Y	Y	Y
5 ***Burr***	Y	Y	Y	?	Y	N	Y	N
6 ***Coble***	Y	Y	Y	Y	Y	N	Y	N
7 McIntyre	N	Y	N	Y	N	Y	Y	N
8 ***Hayes***	Y	Y	N	Y	N	N	Y	N
9 ***Myrick***	Y	Y	Y	N	Y	N	Y	N
10 ***Ballenger***	Y	Y	N	Y	N	N	Y	Y
11 ***Taylor***	Y	Y	N	Y	N	N	Y	N
12 Watt	N	Y	N	Y	N	Y	Y	Y
NORTH DAKOTA								
AL Pomeroy	Y	Y	N	Y	N	Y	Y	Y
OHIO								
1 ***Chabot***	Y	Y	Y	N	Y	N	Y	N
2 ***Portman***	Y	Y	Y	Y	Y	N	Y	N
3 Hall	N	Y	N	?	N	Y	Y	Y
4 ***Oxley***	Y	Y	N	Y	N	N	Y	N
5 ***Gillmor***	Y	Y	N	Y	N	N	N	N
6 Strickland	N	Y	N	Y	N	Y	N	Y
7 ***Hobson***	Y	Y	N	Y	N	N	Y	N
8 ***Boehner***	Y	Y	Y	?	Y	N	Y	N
9 Kaptur	N	Y	N	Y	N	Y	Y	?
10 Kucinich	N	Y	N	Y	N	Y	N	Y
11 Jones	N	Y	N	Y	N	Y	Y	Y
12 ***Tiberi***	Y	Y	Y	Y	Y	N	Y	N
13 Brown	N	Y	N	Y	N	Y	Y	Y
14 Sawyer	N	Y	N	Y	N	Y	Y	Y
15 ***Pryce***	Y	Y	N	Y	N	N	Y	N
16 ***Regula***	Y	Y	N	Y	N	N	Y	N
17 Traficant	?	?	?	?	?	?	?	?
18 ***Ney***	Y	Y	N	Y	N	?	Y	N
19 ***LaTourette***	Y	Y	N	?	N	N	Y	Y
OKLAHOMA								
1 ***Sullivan***	Y	Y	Y	N	Y	N	Y	N
2 Carson	Y	Y	N	Y	N	Y	Y	Y
3 ***Watkins***	Y	Y	N	Y	N	N	Y	N
4 ***Watts***	Y	Y	N	?	N	N	Y	N
5 ***Istook***	Y	Y	?	Y	N	N	Y	N
6 ***Lucas***	Y	Y	N	Y	N	N	Y	N
OREGON								
1 Wu	N	Y	N	N	N	Y	N	Y
2 ***Walden***	Y	Y	N	Y	N	N	Y	N
3 Blumenauer	N	Y	N	Y	N	Y	Y	Y
4 DeFazio	N	Y	N	Y	N	Y	N	Y
5 Hooley	N	Y	N	Y	N	Y	Y	Y
PENNSYLVANIA								
1 Brady	N	Y	N	Y	N	Y	N	Y
2 Fattah	N	N	N	Y	N	Y	Y	Y
3 Borski	N	Y	N	Y	N	Y	N	Y
4 ***Hart***	Y	Y	Y	N	Y	N	N	N
5 ***Peterson***	Y	Y	N	Y	N	N	Y	N
6 Holden	Y	Y	N	Y	N	Y	Y	Y
7 ***Weldon***	Y	Y	N	Y	N	N	Y	Y
8 ***Greenwood***	Y	Y	N	Y	N	N	Y	Y
9 ***Shuster, Bill***	Y	Y	N	Y	Y	N	Y	N
10 ***Sherwood***	Y	Y	N	Y	N	N	Y	N
11 Kanjorski	N	Y	N	Y	N	Y	Y	Y
12 Murtha	N	Y	N	Y	N	Y	Y	Y
13 Hoeffel	N	Y	N	Y	N	Y	Y	Y
14 Coyne	N	Y	N	?	N	Y	Y	Y
15 ***Toomey***	Y	Y	Y	N	Y	N	Y	N
16 ***Pitts***	Y	Y	Y	N	Y	N	Y	N
17 ***Gekas***	Y	Y	N	Y	N	N	Y	N
18 Doyle	N	Y	N	Y	N	Y	Y	Y
19 ***Platts***	Y	Y	Y	N	Y	N	?	N
20 Mascara	?	?	?	?	?	?	?	?
21 ***English***	Y	Y	N	Y	N	N	N	Y
RHODE ISLAND								
1 Kennedy	N	N	N	Y	N	Y	Y	Y
2 Langevin	N	Y	N	Y	N	Y	Y	Y
SOUTH CAROLINA								
1 ***Brown***	Y	Y	N	Y	N	N	Y	N
2 ***Wilson***	Y	Y	Y	N	Y	N	Y	N
3 ***Graham***	Y	Y	Y	N	Y	N	Y	Y
4 ***DeMint***	Y	Y	Y	N	Y	N	Y	N
5 Spratt	N	Y	?	?	N	Y	Y	Y
6 Clyburn	N	Y	N	Y	N	Y	Y	Y
SOUTH DAKOTA								
AL ***Thune***	Y	Y	N	Y	N	N	Y	N

	303	304	305	306	307	308	309	310
TENNESSEE								
1 ***Jenkins***	Y	Y	N	N	N	N	Y	N
2 ***Duncan***	Y	Y	Y	Y	Y	N	Y	N
3 ***Wamp***	Y	Y	N	Y	N	N	Y	N
4 ***Hilleary***	?	?	Y	N	Y	N	?	N
5 Clement	Y	Y	N	Y	N	Y	Y	N
6 Gordon	Y	Y	N	?	N	Y	Y	Y
7 ***Bryant***	Y	Y	N	Y	N	N	Y	N
8 Tanner	Y	Y	N	Y	N	Y	Y	N
9 Ford	N	Y	N	Y	N	Y	Y	Y
TEXAS								
1 Sandlin	N	Y	N	Y	N	Y	Y	Y
2 Turner	Y	Y	Y	Y	Y	Y	Y	N
3 ***Johnson, Sam***	Y	Y	Y	N	Y	N	Y	N
4 Hall	Y	Y	N	Y	N	N	Y	N
5 ***Sessions***	Y	Y	Y	N	Y	N	Y	N
6 ***Barton***	Y	Y	Y	N	Y	N	Y	N
7 ***Culberson***	Y	Y	Y	Y	Y	N	?	N
8 ***Brady***	Y	Y	Y	N	Y	N	Y	N
9 Lampson	N	Y	N	Y	N	Y	Y	Y
10 Doggett	N	Y	N	Y	Y	Y	Y	Y
11 Edwards	Y	Y	N	Y	N	Y	Y	Y
12 ***Granger***	Y	Y	N	Y	N	N	Y	N
13 ***Thornberry***	Y	Y	Y	Y	N	N	Y	N
14 ***Paul***	Y	Y	Y	?	Y	Y	Y	N
15 Hinojosa	N	Y	N	?	?	Y	Y	Y
16 Reyes	N	Y	N	Y	N	Y	Y	Y
17 Stenholm	Y	Y	Y	N	Y	Y	Y	N
18 Jackson-Lee	N	Y	N	N	N	Y	Y	Y
19 ***Combest***	Y	Y	N	Y	N	N	Y	N
20 Gonzalez	N	Y	N	Y	N	Y	Y	Y
21 ***Smith***	Y	Y	N	Y	N	N	Y	N
22 ***DeLay***	?	Y	Y	N	Y	N	Y	N
23 ***Bonilla***	Y	N	N	Y	N	N	Y	N
24 Frost	N	Y	N	Y	N	Y	Y	Y
25 Bentsen	N	Y	N	Y	N	Y	Y	Y
26 ***Armey***	Y	Y	Y	Y	Y	N	Y	N
27 Ortiz	N	Y	N	Y	N	Y	Y	Y
28 Rodriguez	Y	Y	N	Y	N	Y	Y	Y
29 Green	N	Y	N	Y	N	Y	N	Y
30 Johnson, E.B.	N	Y	N	Y	N	Y	Y	Y
UTAH								
1 ***Hansen***	Y	Y	N	Y	N	N	Y	N
2 Matheson	N	Y	N	N	N	Y	Y	N
3 ***Cannon***	Y	Y	N	?	N	N	Y	N
VERMONT								
AL *Sanders*	N	Y	N	Y	N	Y	Y	Y
VIRGINIA								
1 ***Davis, Jo Ann***	Y	Y	Y	Y	Y	N	Y	N
2 ***Schrock***	Y	Y	N	Y	N	N	Y	N
3 Scott	N	Y	N	Y	N	Y	Y	Y
4 ***Forbes***	Y	Y	Y	Y	N	N	Y	N
5 *Goode*	Y	N	Y	Y	N	N	Y	N
6 ***Goodlatte***	Y	Y	Y	Y	Y	N	Y	N
7 ***Cantor***	Y	Y	Y	N	N	N	Y	N
8 Moran	N	Y	N	Y	N	?	Y	Y
9 Boucher	N	Y	N	Y	N	?	Y	Y
10 ***Wolf***	Y	Y	N	Y	N	N	Y	N
11 ***Davis, T.***	Y	Y	N	Y	N	N	Y	Y
WASHINGTON								
1 Inslee	N	Y	N	Y	N	Y	Y	Y
2 Larsen	N	Y	N	Y	N	Y	N	Y
3 Baird	N	Y	N	N	N	Y	N	Y
4 ***Hastings***	Y	Y	N	Y	N	N	Y	N
5 ***Nethercutt***	Y	Y	N	Y	N	N	Y	N
6 Dicks	N	Y	N	Y	N	Y	Y	Y
7 McDermott	N	Y	N	N	N	Y	N	Y
8 ***Dunn***	Y	Y	N	Y	N	N	Y	N
9 Smith	N	N	?	?	N	Y	Y	Y
WEST VIRGINIA								
1 Mollohan	Y	Y	N	Y	N	Y	Y	Y
2 ***Capito***	Y	Y	N	Y	N	N	Y	Y
3 Rahall	N	Y	N	Y	N	Y	Y	Y
WISCONSIN								
1 ***Ryan***	Y	Y	Y	N	Y	N	Y	N
2 Baldwin	N	Y	N	Y	N	Y	Y	Y
3 Kind	Y	Y	N	Y	N	Y	Y	Y
4 Kleczka	N	Y	N	Y	N	Y	Y	Y
5 Barrett	N	Y	N	Y	Y	Y	Y	Y
6 ***Petri***	Y	Y	Y	Y	Y	N	Y	N
7 Obey	N	Y	N	Y	N	Y	N	Y
8 ***Green***	Y	Y	Y	Y	Y	N	Y	N
9 ***Sensenbrenner***	Y	Y	Y	Y	Y	N	Y	N
WYOMING								
AL ***Cubin***	Y	Y	N	N	N	N	Y	N

Southern states - Ala., Ark., Fla., Ga., Ky., La., Miss., N.C., Okla., S.C., Tenn., Texas, Va.

Key

Y	Voted for (yea).
#	Paired for.
+	Announced for.
N	Voted against (nay).
X	Paired against.
−	Announced against.
P	Voted "present."
C	Voted "present" to avoid possible conflict of interest.
?	Did not vote or otherwise make a position known.

Democrats **Republicans**
Independents

311. HR 5093. Fiscal 2003 Interior Department Appropriations/Indian Account Review. Rahall, D-W.Va., amendment that would strike a $15 million "historical accounting" of each Individual Indian Money Account. Adopted 281-144: R 88-131; D 192-12 (ND 144-6, SD 48-6); I 1-1. July 17, 2002.

312. HR 5093. Fiscal 2003 Interior Department Appropriations/Indian Gaming Study. Hayworth, R-Ariz., amendment that would strike a requirement to establish a commission to study Indian gaming. Adopted 273-151: R 90-128; D 182-22 (ND 135-15, SD 47-7); I 1-1. July 17, 2002.

313. HR 3763. Corporate Fraud Penalties/Motion to Instruct. Conyers, D-Mich., motion to instruct House conferees to accept changes included in the Senate version of the bill, including whistleblower protections for corporate employees, extending statute of limitations for securities fraud claims, requiring auditors to retain records for at least five years, and increasing fraud prison sentences in cases of extreme consequences. Motion rejected 207-218: R 3-216; D 203-1 (ND 150-0, SD 53-1); I 1-1. July 17, 2002.

314. HR 5093. Fiscal 2003 Interior Department Appropriations/NEA Funds to Forest Service. Tancredo, R-Colo., amendment that would transfer $50 million from the National Endowment for the Arts to the U.S. Forest Service. Rejected 123-300: R 117-101; D 5-198 (ND 1-148, SD 4-50); I 1-1. July 17, 2002.

315. HR 5093. Fiscal 2003 Interior Department Appropriations/Coastal California Drilling Prohibition. Capps, D-Calif., amendment that would prohibit funds from being used to allow new drilling in any of 36 leases off the coast of California. Adopted 252-172: R 67-151; D 184-20 (ND 149-1, SD 35-19); I 1-1. July 17, 2002.

316. HR 5093. Fiscal 2003 Interior Department Appropriations/Western Irrigation Prohibition. Blumenauer, D-Ore., amendment that would prohibit the Fish and Wildlife Services from issuing new commercial agricultural leases for row crops or alfalfa on the Lower Klamath and Tule Lake National Wildlife refuges in Oregon and California. Rejected 201-223: R 23-195; D 177-27 (ND 137-13, SD 40-14); I 1-1. July 17, 2002.

317. HR 5093. Fiscal 2003 Interior Department Appropriations/Firefighting Funding. Shadegg, R-Ariz., amendment that would cut $36 million from the Bureau of Land Management land acquisition program and increase by $23.1 million the BLM firefighting program. Rejected 153-269: R 146-71; D 6-197 (ND 3-146, SD 3-51); I 1-1. July 17, 2002.

	311	312	313	314	315	316	317
ALABAMA							
1 *Callahan*	N	N	Y	Y	N	N	N
2 *Everett*	N	N	Y	Y	N	Y	Y
3 *Riley*	N	N	Y	Y	Y	Y	Y
4 *Aderholt*	Y	N	Y	N	N	N	N
5 Cramer	Y	Y	Y	Y	Y	Y	N
6 *Bachus*	N	N	Y	N	N	Y	Y
7 Hilliard	Y	Y	Y	Y	Y	N	N
ALASKA							
AL *Young*	N	N	Y	?	N	N	N
ARIZONA							
1 *Flake*	Y	Y	N	Y	N	Y	Y
2 Pastor	Y	Y	Y	Y	Y	N	N
3 *Stump*	N	N	Y	N	N	Y	Y
4 *Shadegg*	N	N	Y	N	N	Y	Y
5 *Kolbe*	Y	N	Y	N	N	N	N
6 *Hayworth*	N	N	Y	N	N	Y	Y
ARKANSAS							
1 Berry	Y	Y	Y	Y	Y	Y	Y
2 Snyder	Y	Y	Y	Y	Y	N	N
3 *Boozman*	Y	Y	Y	Y	Y	N	N
4 Ross	Y	Y	Y	Y	Y	N	N
CALIFORNIA							
1 Thompson	Y	Y	Y	Y	Y	N	N
2 *Herger*	N	Y	Y	N	Y	N	Y
3 *Ose*	N	N	Y	Y	N	N	N
4 *Doolittle*	N	N	Y	N	Y	N	Y
5 Matsui	Y	Y	Y	Y	Y	N	N
6 Woolsey	Y	Y	Y	Y	Y	N	N
7 Miller, George	Y	Y	Y	Y	Y	N	N
8 Pelosi	Y	Y	Y	Y	Y	N	N
9 Lee	Y	Y	Y	N	Y	N	N
10 Tauscher	Y	Y	Y	Y	Y	N	N
11 *Pombo*	N	N	Y	N	N	N	N
12 Lantos	Y	Y	Y	Y	Y	N	N
13 Stark	Y	Y	Y	Y	Y	N	N
14 Eshoo	Y	Y	Y	Y	Y	N	N
15 Honda	Y	Y	Y	Y	Y	N	N
16 Lofgren	Y	Y	Y	Y	Y	N	N
17 Farr	Y	Y	Y	Y	Y	N	N
18 Condit	Y	Y	?	Y	N	N	N
19 *Radanovich*	N	N	Y	N	Y	N	Y
20 Dooley	Y	Y	Y	Y	Y	N	N
21 *Thomas*	N	N	Y	N	N	N	N
22 Capps	Y	Y	Y	Y	Y	N	N
23 *Gallegly*	N	N	Y	N	Y	N	Y
24 Sherman	Y	N	Y	Y	Y	N	N
25 *McKeon*	N	N	Y	N	N	N	N
26 Berman	Y	Y	Y	Y	Y	N	N
27 Schiff	Y	N	Y	Y	Y	N	N
28 *Dreier*	N	N	Y	N	Y	N	N
29 Waxman	Y	Y	Y	Y	Y	N	N
30 Becerra	Y	Y	Y	Y	Y	N	N
31 Solis	Y	Y	Y	Y	Y	N	N
32 Watson	Y	Y	Y	Y	Y	N	N
33 Roybal-Allard	Y	Y	Y	Y	Y	N	N
34 Napolitano	Y	Y	Y	Y	Y	N	N
35 Waters	Y	Y	N	Y	N	N	N
36 Harman	Y	Y	Y	Y	Y	Y	Y
37 Millender-McD.	Y	Y	Y	Y	N	N	N
38 *Horn*	Y	Y	Y	N	N	N	N

	311	312	313	314	315	316	317
39 *Royce*	N	N	Y	N	Y	N	Y
40 *Lewis*	N	N	Y	N	N	N	N
41 *Miller, Gary*	N	N	Y	N	Y	N	Y
42 Baca	Y	Y	Y	Y	Y	Y	N
43 *Calvert*	N	N	Y	N	N	N	N
44 *Bono*	Y	Y	Y	N	N	N	N
45 *Rohrabacher*	N	N	Y	N	N	Y	Y
46 Sanchez	Y	Y	Y	Y	Y	N	N
47 *Cox*	N	N	Y	Y	?	N	Y
48 *Issa*	Y	N	Y	N	N	N	N
49 Davis	Y	Y	Y	Y	Y	N	N
50 Filner	Y	Y	Y	Y	Y	N	N
51 *Cunningham*	N	N	Y	N	N	N	N
52 *Hunter*	N	N	Y	Y	N	N	N
COLORADO							
1 DeGette	Y	Y	Y	Y	Y	N	N
2 Udall	Y	Y	Y	Y	Y	N	N
3 *McInnis*	N	N	Y	N	Y	N	Y
4 *Schaffer*	N	N	Y	N	Y	N	Y
5 *Hefley*	N	N	Y	N	N	N	N
6 *Tancredo*	N	N	Y	Y	?	?	?
CONNECTICUT							
1 Larson	Y	Y	Y	Y	Y	N	N
2 *Simmons*	Y	N	Y	N	Y	N	N
3 DeLauro	Y	Y	Y	Y	Y	N	N
4 *Shays*	Y	Y	Y	N	Y	N	Y
5 Maloney	N	Y	Y	Y	Y	N	N
6 *Johnson*	Y	Y	Y	Y	Y	N	N
DELAWARE							
AL *Castle*	Y	N	Y	Y	N	Y	Y
FLORIDA							
1 *Miller, J.*	N	N	N	Y	N	Y	Y
2 Boyd	Y	Y	Y	Y	Y	N	N
3 Brown	Y	N	Y	Y	Y	N	N
4 *Crenshaw*	N	N	Y	N	N	N	N
5 Thurman	Y	Y	Y	Y	Y	N	N
6 *Stearns*	?	?	?	?	?	?	?
7 *Mica*	N	N	Y	N	Y	N	Y
8 *Keller*	N	N	Y	N	Y	Y	Y
9 *Bilirakis*	N	N	Y	N	N	Y	Y
10 *Young*	N	N	?	N	N	N	N
11 Davis	Y	N	Y	Y	N	N	N
12 *Putnam*	N	N	Y	N	N	N	N
13 *Miller, D.*	N	N	Y	N	N	N	N
14 *Goss*	N	N	Y	N	N	N	N
15 *Weldon*	N	N	Y	N	N	Y	Y
16 *Foley*	N	N	Y	N	Y	Y	Y
17 Meek	N	N	?	Y	N	N	N
18 *Ros-Lehtinen*	N	N	Y	Y	Y	Y	Y
19 Wexler	N	N	Y	Y	Y	N	N
20 Deutsch	Y	N	Y	Y	Y	N	N
21 *Diaz-Balart*	N	N	Y	Y	Y	Y	Y
22 *Shaw*	N	N	Y	N	N	N	N
23 Hastings	N	N	Y	Y	N	N	N
GEORGIA							
1 *Kingston*	N	N	Y	Y	N	N	N
2 Bishop	Y	Y	?	Y	N	N	N
3 *Collins*	N	N	Y	N	Y	Y	Y
4 McKinney	Y	Y	Y	N	Y	N	N
5 Lewis	Y	Y	Y	Y	N	N	N
6 *Isakson*	N	N	Y	N	N	N	N
7 *Barr*	N	N	Y	N	Y	Y	Y
8 *Chambliss*	N	N	Y	Y	Y	N	Y
9 *Deal*	N	N	Y	N	Y	N	N
10 *Norwood*	N	N	Y	N	Y	Y	Y
11 *Linder*	N	N	Y	Y	Y	Y	Y
HAWAII							
1 Abercrombie	Y	Y	Y	Y	Y	N	N
2 Mink	Y	Y	Y	Y	Y	N	N
IDAHO							
1 *Otter*	Y	Y	Y	N	Y	N	Y
2 *Simpson*	N	N	Y	N	N	N	N
ILLINOIS							
1 Rush	Y	Y	Y	Y	N	N	N
2 Jackson	Y	Y	Y	Y	N	N	N
3 Lipinski	N	N	Y	?	N	N	N
4 Gutierrez	Y	N	Y	Y	N	N	N
5 Blagojevich	Y	Y	Y	Y	N	N	N
6 *Hyde*	N	N	Y	N	Y	N	Y
7 Davis	Y	Y	Y	Y	N	N	N
8 *Crane*	N	N	Y	N	Y	N	Y
9 Schakowsky	Y	Y	Y	Y	N	N	N
10 *Kirk*	Y	N	Y	N	Y	N	Y
11 *Weller*	Y	N	Y	Y	Y	Y	Y
12 Costello	Y	Y	Y	Y	N	N	N
13 *Biggert*	Y	Y	Y	N	Y	N	N

ND Northern Democrats   SD Southern Democrats

	311	312	313	314	315	316	317
14 ***Hastert***							
15 ***Johnson***	Y	Y	Y	Y	N	Y	N
16 ***Manzullo***	Y	Y	Y	Y	N	Y	Y
17 Evans	Y	Y	Y	Y	Y	Y	N
18 ***LaHood***	Y	Y	Y	Y	Y	N	N
19 Phelps	Y	Y	Y	Y	Y	Y	Y
20 ***Shimkus***	Y	Y	Y	Y	Y	Y	Y
INDIANA							
1 Visclosky	Y	Y	Y	Y	Y	N	N
2 ***Pence***	N	N	Y	Y	N	Y	Y
3 Roemer	Y	Y	Y	Y	Y	N	Y
4 ***Souder***	N	N	Y	Y	N	Y	N
5 ***Buyer***	N	N	Y	Y	N	Y	Y
6 ***Burton***	N	N	Y	?	N	Y	Y
7 ***Kerns***	N	N	Y	Y	N	N	Y
8 ***Hostettler***	Y	N	Y	Y	N	Y	Y
9 Hill	Y	Y	?	Y	Y	Y	Y
10 Carson	Y	Y	Y	Y	Y	N	N
IOWA							
1 ***Leach***	Y	Y	Y	Y	Y	N	N
2 ***Nussle***	Y	Y	Y	Y	N	N	Y
3 Boswell	Y	Y	Y	Y	Y	Y	Y
4 ***Ganske***	Y	Y	Y	Y	Y	Y	N
5 ***Latham***	Y	Y	Y	Y	N	N	N
KANSAS							
1 ***Moran***	Y	Y	Y	Y	N	Y	Y
2 ***Ryun***	N	N	Y	Y	N	Y	Y
3 Moore	Y	Y	Y	Y	Y	Y	N
4 ***Tiahrt***	Y	N	Y	Y	N	Y	Y
KENTUCKY							
1 ***Whitfield***	Y	N	Y	Y	N	Y	Y
2 ***Lewis***	N	N	Y	Y	Y	Y	N
3 ***Northup***	N	N	Y	Y	N	N	N
4 Lucas	N	N	Y	Y	Y	Y	Y
5 ***Rogers***	N	N	Y	Y	N	Y	N
6 ***Fletcher***	N	N	Y	Y	Y	Y	N
LOUISIANA							
1 ***Vitter***	N	N	Y	Y	N	Y	Y
2 Jefferson	Y	Y	Y	Y	Y	N	N
3 ***Tauzin***	N	N	Y	Y	N	N	Y
4 ***McCrery***	N	N	Y	Y	N	N	N
5 ***Cooksey***	Y	N	Y	Y	N	Y	Y
6 ***Baker***	N	N	Y	Y	Y	N	Y
7 John	Y	Y	Y	Y	Y	Y	N
MAINE							
1 Allen	Y	Y	Y	Y	Y	N	N
2 Baldacci	Y	Y	Y	Y	Y	N	N
MARYLAND							
1 ***Gilchrest***	Y	N	Y	Y	N	N	N
2 ***Ehrlich***	N	N	Y	?	Y	Y	Y
3 Cardin	Y	N	Y	Y	Y	N	N
4 Wynn	Y	Y	Y	Y	Y	N	N
5 Hoyer	Y	Y	Y	Y	Y	N	N
6 ***Bartlett***	Y	N	Y	Y	N	Y	Y
7 Cummings	Y	Y	Y	Y	Y	N	N
8 ***Morella***	Y	Y	Y	Y	Y	N	N
MASSACHUSETTS							
1 Olver	Y	Y	Y	Y	Y	N	N
2 Neal	Y	Y	Y	Y	Y	N	N
3 McGovern	Y	Y	Y	Y	Y	N	N
4 Frank	Y	Y	Y	Y	Y	N	N
5 Meehan	Y	Y	Y	Y	Y	N	N
6 Tierney	Y	Y	Y	Y	Y	N	N
7 Markey	Y	Y	Y	Y	Y	N	N
8 Capuano	Y	Y	Y	Y	Y	N	N
9 Lynch	Y	Y	Y	Y	Y	N	N
10 Delahunt	Y	Y	Y	Y	?	N	N
MICHIGAN							
1 Stupak	Y	Y	Y	Y	Y	N	N
2 ***Hoekstra***	N	N	Y	Y	N	Y	Y
3 ***Ehlers***	Y	N	Y	Y	N	N	N
4 ***Camp***	Y	N	Y	Y	N	Y	N
5 Barcia	Y	Y	Y	Y	Y	Y	Y
6 ***Upton***	Y	Y	Y	Y	N	Y	Y
7 ***Smith***	Y	N	Y	Y	Y	Y	Y
8 ***Rogers***	N	N	Y	Y	N	Y	N
9 Kildee	Y	Y	Y	Y	Y	N	N
10 Bonior	?	?	?	?	?	?	?
11 ***Knollenberg***	N	N	Y	Y	N	N	N
12 Levin	Y	Y	Y	Y	Y	N	N
13 Rivers	Y	Y	Y	Y	Y	N	N
14 Conyers	Y	Y	Y	Y	Y	N	N
15 Kilpatrick	Y	Y	Y	Y	Y	N	N
16 Dingell	N	Y	Y	Y	Y	N	N

	311	312	313	314	315	316	317
MINNESOTA							
1 ***Gutknecht***	N	N	Y	Y	Y	Y	Y
2 ***Kennedy***	N	N	Y	Y	N	Y	Y
3 ***Ramstad***	Y	Y	Y	Y	N	Y	Y
4 McCollum	Y	Y	Y	Y	Y	N	N
5 Sabo	Y	Y	Y	Y	Y	N	N
6 Luther	Y	Y	Y	Y	Y	Y	Y
7 Peterson	Y	Y	Y	Y	Y	N	Y
8 Oberstar	Y	Y	Y	Y	Y	N	N
MISSISSIPPI							
1 ***Wicker***	N	N	Y	Y	N	Y	Y
2 Thompson	Y	Y	Y	Y	Y	N	N
3 ***Pickering***	N	N	Y	Y	N	Y	Y
4 Shows	Y	Y	Y	Y	Y	Y	Y
5 Taylor	Y	Y	Y	Y	Y	Y	Y
MISSOURI							
1 Clay	Y	Y	?	?	Y	N	N
2 ***Akin***	N	N	Y	Y	N	Y	Y
3 Gephardt	N	N	Y	Y	Y	N	N
4 Skelton	N	N	Y	Y	Y	N	N
5 McCarthy	Y	Y	Y	Y	Y	N	N
6 ***Graves***	Y	Y	Y	Y	Y	N	Y
7 ***Blunt***	N	N	Y	Y	N	N	Y
8 ***Emerson***	Y	Y	Y	Y	Y	N	N
9 ***Hulshof***	N	N	Y	Y	N	Y	N
MONTANA							
AL ***Rehberg***	Y	Y	Y	Y	N	Y	Y
NEBRASKA							
1 ***Bereuter***	Y	N	Y	Y	N	Y	Y
2 ***Terry***	Y	N	Y	Y	N	Y	Y
3 ***Osborne***	Y	Y	Y	Y	N	Y	N
NEVADA							
1 Berkley	N	N	Y	Y	Y	N	N
2 ***Gibbons***	N	N	Y	Y	N	Y	Y
NEW HAMPSHIRE							
1 ***Sununu***	Y	N	Y	Y	N	Y	N
2 ***Bass***	Y	N	Y	Y	N	Y	N
NEW JERSEY							
1 Andrews	N	N	Y	Y	Y	N	N
2 ***LoBiondo***	N	N	Y	Y	Y	Y	N
3 ***Saxton***	N	N	Y	Y	Y	Y	N
4 ***Smith***	N	N	Y	Y	Y	Y	N
5 ***Roukema***	N	N	Y	Y	Y	Y	Y
6 Pallone	N	N	Y	Y	Y	N	N
7 ***Ferguson***	N	N	Y	Y	Y	Y	N
8 Pascrell	N	N	Y	Y	Y	N	N
9 Rothman	N	N	Y	Y	Y	N	N
10 Payne	Y	Y	Y	Y	Y	N	N
11 ***Frelinghuysen***	N	N	Y	Y	N	N	N
12 Holt	Y	Y	Y	Y	Y	N	N
13 Menendez	N	N	Y	Y	Y	N	N
NEW MEXICO							
1 ***Wilson***	N	N	Y	Y	N	N	N
2 ***Skeen***	N	N	Y	Y	N	N	N
3 Udall	Y	Y	Y	Y	Y	N	N
NEW YORK							
1 ***Grucci***	Y	N	Y	Y	Y	N	N
2 Israel	Y	Y	Y	Y	Y	N	N
3 ***King***	N	N	Y	Y	Y	N	N
4 McCarthy	Y	Y	Y	Y	Y	N	N
5 Ackerman	N	N	Y	Y	Y	N	N
6 Meeks	Y	Y	Y	Y	Y	N	N
7 Crowley	Y	Y	Y	Y	Y	N	N
8 Nadler	Y	Y	Y	Y	Y	N	N
9 Weiner	Y	Y	Y	Y	Y	N	N
10 Towns	Y	Y	Y	Y	Y	N	N
11 Owens	Y	Y	Y	Y	Y	N	N
12 Velázquez	Y	Y	Y	Y	Y	N	N
13 ***Fossella***	N	N	Y	Y	Y	N	Y
14 Maloney	Y	Y	Y	Y	Y	N	N
15 Rangel	Y	Y	Y	Y	Y	N	N
16 Serrano	Y	Y	Y	Y	Y	N	N
17 Engel	N	N	Y	?	Y	N	N
18 Lowey	Y	Y	Y	Y	Y	N	N
19 ***Kelly***	N	N	Y	Y	Y	Y	N
20 ***Gilman***	N	N	Y	Y	Y	N	N
21 McNulty	Y	Y	Y	Y	Y	N	N
22 ***Sweeney***	N	N	Y	Y	Y	N	N
23 ***Boehlert***	Y	N	Y	Y	Y	N	N
24 ***McHugh***	Y	N	Y	Y	Y	N	N
25 ***Walsh***	N	N	Y	Y	Y	N	N
26 Hinchey	Y	Y	Y	Y	Y	N	N
27 ***Reynolds***	N	N	Y	Y	N	N	Y
28 Slaughter	Y	Y	Y	Y	Y	N	?
29 LaFalce	Y	Y	Y	Y	Y	N	N
30 ***Quinn***	N	N	Y	Y	Y	N	N

	311	312	313	314	315	316	317
31 ***Houghton***	Y	N	Y	Y	N	N	N
NORTH CAROLINA							
1 Clayton	Y	Y	Y	Y	Y	N	N
2 Etheridge	Y	N	Y	Y	Y	N	N
3 ***Jones***	N	N	Y	Y	Y	Y	Y
4 Price	Y	Y	Y	Y	Y	N	N
5 ***Burr***	N	N	Y	Y	N	Y	Y
6 ***Coble***	N	N	Y	Y	N	Y	Y
7 McIntyre	Y	N	Y	Y	Y	Y	N
8 ***Hayes***	N	N	Y	Y	Y	Y	Y
9 ***Myrick***	N	N	Y	Y	N	Y	Y
10 ***Ballenger***	N	N	Y	Y	N	Y	Y
11 ***Taylor***	N	N	Y	Y	N	Y	Y
12 Watt	Y	Y	Y	Y	Y	N	N
NORTH DAKOTA							
AL Pomeroy	Y	Y	Y	Y	Y	N	N
OHIO							
1 ***Chabot***	N	N	Y	Y	N	Y	Y
2 ***Portman***	N	N	Y	Y	N	N	N
3 Hall	Y	Y	Y	?	Y	N	N
4 ***Oxley***	N	N	Y	Y	N	Y	Y
5 ***Gillmor***	N	N	Y	Y	N	N	N
6 Strickland	Y	Y	Y	Y	Y	N	N
7 ***Hobson***	N	N	Y	Y	N	N	N
8 ***Boehner***	N	N	Y	Y	N	N	N
9 Kaptur	Y	Y	Y	?	Y	N	N
10 Kucinich	Y	Y	Y	N	Y	N	N
11 Jones	Y	Y	Y	Y	Y	N	N
12 ***Tiberi***	Y	Y	Y	Y	N	Y	Y
13 Brown	Y	Y	Y	Y	Y	N	N
14 Sawyer	Y	Y	Y	Y	Y	N	N
15 ***Pryce***	N	N	Y	Y	N	N	N
16 ***Regula***	N	N	Y	Y	N	N	N
17 Traficant	?	?	?	?	?	?	?
18 ***Ney***	Y	N	Y	Y	N	N	N
19 ***LaTourette***	N	N	Y	Y	Y	N	N
OKLAHOMA							
1 ***Sullivan***	N	N	Y	Y	N	Y	Y
2 Carson	Y	Y	Y	Y	Y	N	N
3 ***Watkins***	N	N	Y	Y	N	N	N
4 ***Watts***	N	N	Y	Y	N	Y	Y
5 ***Istook***	N	N	Y	Y	N	N	N
6 ***Lucas***	N	N	Y	Y	N	N	N
OREGON							
1 Wu	N	N	Y	Y	Y	N	N
2 ***Walden***	N	N	Y	Y	N	Y	Y
3 Blumenauer	Y	Y	Y	Y	Y	N	N
4 DeFazio	+	+	+	Y	Y	Y	N
5 Hooley	Y	Y	Y	Y	Y	N	N
PENNSYLVANIA							
1 Brady	Y	Y	Y	Y	Y	N	N
2 Fattah	Y	Y	Y	Y	Y	N	N
3 Borski	Y	Y	Y	Y	Y	N	N
4 ***Hart***	N	N	Y	Y	Y	Y	Y
5 ***Peterson***	Y	Y	Y	Y	N	N	Y
6 Holden	Y	N	Y	Y	Y	N	N
7 ***Weldon***	Y	N	Y	Y	Y	Y	Y
8 ***Greenwood***	Y	N	Y	Y	N	N	N
9 ***Shuster, Bill***	N	N	Y	Y	N	Y	N
10 ***Sherwood***	N	N	Y	Y	N	N	N
11 Kanjorski	Y	N	Y	Y	Y	N	N
12 Murtha	Y	N	Y	Y	Y	N	N
13 Hoeffel	Y	Y	Y	Y	Y	N	N
14 Coyne	Y	Y	Y	Y	Y	N	N
15 ***Toomey***	N	N	Y	Y	N	Y	Y
16 ***Pitts***	N	N	Y	Y	N	Y	Y
17 ***Gekas***	N	N	Y	Y	Y	N	N
18 Doyle	Y	Y	Y	Y	Y	N	N
19 ***Platts***	Y	N	Y	?	Y	Y	Y
20 Mascara	Y	Y	Y	Y	Y	N	N
21 ***English***	Y	N	Y	Y	Y	N	Y
RHODE ISLAND							
1 Kennedy	N	N	Y	Y	Y	N	N
2 Langevin	Y	Y	Y	Y	Y	N	N
SOUTH CAROLINA							
1 ***Brown***	Y	N	Y	Y	N	N	N
2 ***Wilson***	N	N	Y	Y	N	Y	Y
3 ***Graham***	N	N	Y	Y	N	Y	Y
4 ***DeMint***	N	N	Y	Y	N	Y	Y
5 Spratt	Y	N	Y	Y	Y	N	N
6 Clyburn	Y	Y	Y	Y	Y	N	N
SOUTH DAKOTA							
AL ***Thune***	Y	Y	Y	Y	N	Y	N

	311	312	313	314	315	316	317
TENNESSEE							
1 ***Jenkins***	N	N	Y	Y	N	Y	Y
2 ***Duncan***	N	N	Y	Y	N	Y	Y
3 ***Wamp***	N	N	Y	Y	N	Y	Y
4 ***Hilleary***	N	N	Y	Y	N	Y	Y
5 Clement	Y	Y	Y	Y	Y	Y	Y
6 Gordon	Y	Y	Y	Y	Y	Y	N
7 ***Bryant***	N	N	Y	Y	N	Y	Y
8 Tanner	Y	Y	Y	Y	Y	Y	Y
9 Ford	Y	Y	Y	Y	Y	N	N
TEXAS							
1 Sandlin	Y	Y	Y	Y	Y	N	N
2 Turner	Y	Y	Y	Y	Y	Y	Y
3 ***Johnson, Sam***	N	N	Y	?	N	Y	Y
4 Hall	Y	Y	Y	Y	Y	Y	Y
5 ***Sessions***	N	N	Y	Y	N	Y	Y
6 ***Barton***	N	N	Y	Y	N	N	Y
7 ***Culberson***	N	N	Y	Y	N	N	Y
8 ***Brady***	Y	N	Y	Y	N	N	Y
9 Lampson	Y	Y	Y	Y	Y	N	N
10 Doggett	Y	Y	Y	Y	Y	Y	Y
11 Edwards	Y	Y	Y	Y	Y	N	N
12 ***Granger***	N	N	Y	Y	Y	N	N
13 ***Thornberry***	Y	N	Y	Y	N	N	Y
14 ***Paul***	Y	Y	N	?	N	Y	Y
15 Hinojosa	Y	Y	Y	Y	Y	N	N
16 Reyes	Y	N	Y	Y	Y	N	N
17 Stenholm	Y	Y	Y	Y	Y	Y	Y
18 Jackson-Lee	Y	Y	Y	Y	Y	N	N
19 ***Combest***	Y	N	Y	Y	N	Y	N
20 Gonzalez	Y	Y	Y	Y	Y	N	N
21 ***Smith***	N	N	Y	Y	N	Y	Y
22 ***DeLay***	N	N	Y	Y	N	N	N
23 ***Bonilla***	N	N	Y	Y	N	N	N
24 Frost	Y	Y	Y	Y	Y	N	N
25 Bentsen	Y	Y	Y	Y	Y	N	N
26 ***Armey***	N	N	Y	Y	N	Y	Y
27 Ortiz	Y	N	Y	Y	Y	N	N
28 Rodriguez	Y	Y	Y	Y	Y	N	N
29 Green	N	N	Y	Y	Y	Y	N
30 Johnson, E.B.	Y	Y	Y	Y	Y	N	N
UTAH							
1 ***Hansen***	?	N	Y	Y	Y	Y	Y
2 Matheson	Y	Y	Y	Y	Y	Y	Y
3 ***Cannon***	N	N	Y	Y	?	Y	Y
VERMONT							
AL *Sanders*	Y	Y	Y	Y	Y	N	N
VIRGINIA							
1 ***Davis, Jo Ann***	N	N	Y	Y	Y	Y	Y
2 ***Schrock***	N	N	Y	Y	N	N	Y
3 Scott	Y	Y	Y	Y	Y	N	N
4 ***Forbes***	N	N	Y	Y	Y	Y	Y
5 *Goode*	N	N	Y	Y	N	Y	Y
6 ***Goodlatte***	N	Y	Y	N	Y	Y	
7 ***Cantor***	N	N	Y	Y	N	N	Y
8 Moran	Y	Y	Y	Y	Y	N	N
9 Boucher	Y	Y	Y	Y	Y	N	N
10 ***Wolf***	N	N	Y	Y	Y	N	N
11 ***Davis, T.***	N	N	Y	Y	Y	N	N
WASHINGTON							
1 Inslee	Y	Y	Y	Y	Y	N	N
2 Larsen	Y	Y	Y	Y	Y	N	N
3 Baird	Y	Y	Y	Y	Y	N	N
4 ***Hastings***	N	N	Y	Y	N	Y	N
5 ***Nethercutt***	Y	N	Y	Y	N	Y	N
6 Dicks	Y	Y	Y	Y	Y	N	N
7 McDermott	Y	Y	Y	Y	Y	N	N
8 ***Dunn***	N	N	Y	Y	N	N	N
9 Smith	Y	Y	Y	Y	Y	Y	Y
WEST VIRGINIA							
1 Mollohan	Y	Y	Y	Y	Y	N	N
2 ***Capito***	N	N	Y	Y	Y	N	N
3 Rahall	Y	Y	Y	Y	Y	N	N
WISCONSIN							
1 ***Ryan***	Y	Y	Y	Y	N	Y	Y
2 Baldwin	Y	Y	Y	Y	Y	N	N
3 Kind	Y	Y	Y	Y	Y	Y	N
4 Kleczka	Y	Y	?	Y	Y	N	N
5 Barrett	Y	Y	Y	Y	Y	Y	N
6 ***Petri***	N	N	Y	Y	Y	Y	Y
7 Obey	Y	Y	Y	Y	Y	N	N
8 ***Green***	N	N	Y	Y	N	Y	N
9 ***Sensenbrenner***	N	N	Y	Y	N	Y	Y
WYOMING							
AL ***Cubin***	N	N	Y	Y	N	Y	Y

Southern states - Ala., Ark., Fla., Ga., Ky., La., Miss., N.C., Okla., S.C., Tenn., Texas, Va.

Key

Y	Voted for (yea).
#	Paired for.
+	Announced for.
N	Voted against (nay).
X	Paired against.
–	Announced against.
P	Voted "present."
C	Voted "present" to avoid possible conflict of interest.
?	Did not vote or otherwise make a position known.

Democrats **Republicans** *Independents*

318. HR 5093. Fiscal 2003 Interior Department Appropriations/ Passage. Passage of the bill that would appropriate $19.8 billion in fiscal 2003 and $700 million in emergency supplemental spending for fiscal 2002, which is not subject to spending caps. It would provide $1.4 billion for conservation, $4.6 billion for the Forest Service, $2.4 billion for the National Park Service, $2.1 billion for the Bureau of Land Management, $1.4 billion for the Fish and Wildlife Service, $1.9 billion for energy-related services, $99 million for the National Endowment for the Arts, $2.9 billion for the Indian Health Service, and $2.3 billion for the Bureau of Indian Affairs. Passed 377-46: R 178-41; D 198-4 (ND 146-2, SD 52-2); I 1-1. July 17, 2002.

319. HR 5121. Fiscal 2003 Legislative Branch Appropriations/Rule. Adoption of the rule (H Res 489) to provide for House floor consideration of the bill that would appropriate $2.7 billion for legislative branch operations for fiscal 2003. Adopted 219-206: R 218-0; D 0-205 (ND 0-152, SD 0-53); I 1-1. July 18, 2002.

320. HR 5121. Fiscal 2003 Legislative Branch Appropriations/Tax Committee Funding. Moran, D-Va., amendment that would decrease funding for the Joint Committee on Taxation by $590,000. Rejected 206-213: R 5-211; D 200-1 (ND 148-1, SD 52-0); I 1-1. July 18, 2002.

321. HR 5121. Fiscal 2003 Legislative Branch Appropriations/Passage. Passage of the bill that would appropriate $2.7 billion in fiscal 2003, including $960 million for congressional operations and $1.7 billion for other legislative branch agencies that do not provide primary support to Congress, such as the Library of Congress, General Accounting Office and Government Printing Office. Passed 365-49: R 183-32; D 181-16 (ND 137-10, SD 44-6); I 1-1. July 18, 2002.

322. HR 5120. Fiscal 2003 Treasury-Postal Service Appropriations/ Previous Question. Linder, R-Ga., motion to order the previous question (thus ending debate and possibility of amendment) on adoption of the rule (H Res 488) to provide for House floor consideration of the bill that would allocate $35.1 billion in fiscal 2003 for the Treasury Department, Postal Service, Executive Office of the President and other federal agencies. Motion agreed to 258-156: R 128-84; D 129-71 (ND 101-48, SD 28-23); I 1-1. July 18, 2002.

323. HR 5120. Fiscal 2003 Treasury-Postal Appropriations/Rule. Adoption of the rule (H Res 488) to provide for House floor consideration of the bill that would provide $35.1 billion in fiscal 2003 for the Treasury Department, Postal Service, Executive Office of the President and other federal agencies. Adopted 224-188: R 194-19; D 29-168 (ND 25-121, SD 4-47); I 1-1. July 18, 2002.

	318	319	320	321	322	323
ALABAMA						
1 *Callahan*	N	N	Y	Y	N	N
2 *Everett*	N	N	Y	Y	N	Y
3 *Riley*	N	N	Y	Y	Y	Y
4 *Aderholt*	Y	N	Y	N	N	N
5 Cramer	Y	Y	Y	Y	Y	N
6 *Bachus*	N	N	Y	N	Y	Y
7 Hilliard	Y	Y	Y	Y	N	N
ALASKA						
AL *Young*	N	N	Y	?	N	N
ARIZONA						
1 *Flake*	Y	N	N	Y	N	Y
2 Pastor	Y	Y	Y	Y	N	N
3 *Stump*	N	N	Y	N	Y	Y
4 *Shadegg*	N	N	Y	N	Y	Y
5 *Kolbe*	Y	N	Y	N	N	N
6 *Hayworth*	N	N	Y	N	Y	Y
ARKANSAS						
1 Berry	Y	Y	Y	Y	Y	Y
2 Snyder	Y	Y	Y	Y	N	N
3 *Boozman*	Y	Y	Y	N	Y	N
4 Ross	Y	Y	Y	Y	N	N
CALIFORNIA						
1 Thompson	Y	Y	Y	Y	N	N
2 *Herger*	N	N	Y	N	Y	Y
3 *Ose*	N	N	Y	N	N	N
4 *Doolittle*	N	N	Y	N	Y	Y
5 Matsui	Y	Y	Y	Y	N	N
6 Woolsey	Y	Y	Y	Y	N	N
7 Miller, George	Y	Y	Y	Y	Y	N
8 Pelosi	Y	Y	Y	Y	N	N
9 Lee	Y	Y	N	Y	N	N
10 Tauscher	Y	Y	Y	Y	N	N
11 *Pombo*	N	N	Y	N	N	N
12 Lantos	Y	Y	Y	Y	N	N
13 Stark	Y	Y	Y	Y	N	N
14 Eshoo	Y	Y	Y	Y	N	N
15 Honda	Y	Y	Y	Y	N	N
16 Lofgren	Y	Y	Y	Y	N	N
17 Farr	Y	Y	Y	Y	N	N
18 Condit	Y	Y	Y	?	N	N
19 *Radanovich*	N	N	Y	N	Y	N
20 Dooley	Y	Y	Y	Y	N	N
21 *Thomas*	N	N	Y	N	N	N
22 Capps	Y	Y	Y	Y	N	N
23 *Gallegly*	N	N	Y	N	Y	Y
24 Sherman	Y	N	Y	Y	N	N
25 *McKeon*	N	N	Y	N	N	N
26 Berman	Y	Y	Y	Y	N	N
27 Schiff	Y	N	Y	Y	N	N
28 *Dreier*	N	N	Y	N	N	N
29 Waxman	Y	Y	Y	Y	N	N
30 Becerra	Y	Y	Y	Y	N	N
31 Solis	Y	Y	Y	Y	N	N
32 Watson	Y	Y	Y	Y	N	N
33 Roybal-Allard	Y	Y	Y	Y	N	N
34 Napolitano	Y	Y	Y	Y	N	N
35 Waters	Y	Y	N	Y	N	N
36 Harman	Y	Y	Y	Y	Y	Y
37 Millender-McD.	Y	Y	Y	Y	N	N
38 *Horn*	Y	Y	Y	Y	N	N

	318	319	320	321	322	323
39 *Royce*	N	N	Y	Y	N	Y
40 *Lewis*	N	N	Y	N	Y	Y
41 *Miller, Gary*	N	N	Y	N	Y	Y
42 Baca	Y	Y	Y	Y	N	N
43 *Calvert*	N	N	Y	N	N	N
44 *Bono*	Y	Y	Y	N	N	N
45 *Rohrabacher*	N	N	Y	N	Y	Y
46 Sanchez	Y	Y	Y	Y	N	N
47 *Cox*	N	N	Y	?	N	Y
48 *Issa*	Y	N	Y	N	N	N
49 Davis	Y	Y	Y	Y	N	N
50 Filner	Y	Y	Y	Y	N	N
51 *Cunningham*	N	N	Y	N	Y	Y
52 *Hunter*	N	N	Y	Y	N	N
COLORADO						
1 DeGette	Y	Y	Y	Y	N	N
2 Udall	Y	Y	Y	Y	N	N
3 *McInnis*	N	N	Y	N	Y	Y
4 *Schaffer*	N	N	Y	N	Y	Y
5 *Hefley*	N	N	Y	N	Y	Y
6 *Tancredo*	N	N	Y	?	?	?
CONNECTICUT						
1 Larson	Y	Y	Y	Y	N	N
2 *Simmons*	Y	N	Y	N	Y	Y
3 DeLauro	Y	Y	Y	Y	N	N
4 *Shays*	Y	Y	Y	N	N	Y
5 Maloney	N	N	Y	Y	N	N
6 *Johnson*	Y	Y	Y	Y	N	N
DELAWARE						
AL *Castle*	Y	N	Y	N	Y	Y
FLORIDA						
1 *Miller, J.*	N	N	N	Y	N	Y
2 Boyd	Y	Y	Y	Y	N	N
3 Brown	Y	N	Y	Y	N	N
4 *Crenshaw*	N	N	Y	N	N	N
5 Thurman	Y	Y	Y	Y	N	N
6 *Stearns*	?	?	?	?	?	?
7 *Mica*	N	N	Y	N	Y	Y
8 *Keller*	N	N	Y	N	Y	Y
9 *Bilirakis*	N	N	Y	N	Y	Y
10 *Young*	N	N	Y	?	N	N
11 Davis	Y	N	Y	N	N	N
12 *Putnam*	N	N	Y	N	N	N
13 *Miller, D.*	N	N	Y	N	Y	N
14 *Goss*	N	N	Y	N	N	N
15 *Weldon*	N	N	Y	N	N	N
16 *Foley*	N	N	Y	N	Y	N
17 Meek	N	N	Y	?	Y	N
18 *Ros-Lehtinen*	N	N	Y	N	Y	Y
19 Wexler	N	N	Y	Y	N	N
20 Deutsch	N	N	Y	Y	N	N
21 *Diaz-Balart*	N	N	Y	N	N	Y
22 *Shaw*	N	N	Y	N	N	N
23 Hastings	N	N	Y	Y	N	N
GEORGIA						
1 *Kingston*	N	N	Y	?	N	N
2 Bishop	Y	Y	Y	Y	N	N
3 *Collins*	N	N	Y	N	Y	Y
4 McKinney	Y	Y	Y	N	N	N
5 Lewis	Y	Y	Y	Y	N	N
6 *Isakson*	N	N	Y	N	N	N
7 *Barr*	N	N	Y	N	Y	Y
8 *Chambliss*	N	N	Y	N	N	N
9 *Deal*	N	N	Y	N	N	N
10 *Norwood*	N	N	Y	N	N	N
11 *Linder*	N	N	Y	N	Y	Y
HAWAII						
1 Abercrombie	Y	Y	Y	Y	N	N
2 Mink	Y	Y	Y	Y	N	N
IDAHO						
1 *Otter*	Y	Y	Y	N	Y	Y
2 *Simpson*	N	N	Y	N	N	N
ILLINOIS						
1 Rush	Y	Y	Y	Y	N	N
2 Jackson	Y	Y	Y	Y	N	N
3 Lipinski	N	N	Y	?	N	N
4 Gutierrez	Y	N	Y	Y	N	N
5 Blagojevich	Y	N	Y	Y	N	N
6 *Hyde*	N	N	Y	N	Y	Y
7 Davis	Y	Y	Y	Y	N	N
8 *Crane*	N	N	Y	N	Y	Y
9 Schakowsky	Y	Y	Y	Y	N	N
10 *Kirk*	Y	N	Y	N	Y	Y
11 *Weller*	Y	N	Y	Y	Y	Y
12 Costello	Y	Y	Y	Y	N	N
13 *Biggert*	Y	Y	Y	N	Y	N

ND Northern Democrats   SD Southern Democrats

	318	319	320	321	322	323	
14 ***Hastert***							
15 ***Johnson***	Y	Y	Y	Y	N	Y	N
16 ***Manzullo***	Y	Y	Y	Y	N	Y	Y
17 Evans	Y	Y	Y	Y	Y	Y	N
18 ***LaHood***	Y	Y	Y	Y	Y	N	N
19 Phelps	Y	Y	Y	Y	Y	Y	Y
20 ***Shimkus***	Y	Y	Y	Y	Y	Y	Y
INDIANA							
1 Visclosky	Y	Y	Y	Y	Y	N	N
2 ***Pence***	N	N	Y	Y	N	Y	Y
3 Roemer	Y	Y	Y	Y	Y	N	Y
4 ***Souder***	N	N	Y	Y	N	Y	N
5 ***Buyer***	N	N	Y	Y	N	Y	Y
6 ***Burton***	N	N	Y	?	N	Y	Y
7 ***Kerns***	N	N	Y	Y	N	N	Y
8 ***Hostettler***	Y	N	Y	Y	N	Y	Y
9 Hill	Y	Y	?	Y	Y	Y	Y
10 Carson	Y	Y	Y	Y	Y	N	N
IOWA							
1 ***Leach***	Y	Y	Y	Y	Y	N	N
2 ***Nussle***	Y	Y	Y	Y	N	N	Y
3 Boswell	Y	Y	Y	Y	Y	Y	Y
4 ***Ganske***	Y	Y	Y	Y	Y	Y	N
5 ***Latham***	Y	Y	Y	Y	N	N	N
KANSAS							
1 ***Moran***	Y	Y	Y	Y	N	Y	Y
2 ***Ryun***	N	N	Y	Y	N	Y	Y
3 Moore	Y	Y	Y	Y	Y	Y	N
4 ***Tiahrt***	Y	N	Y	Y	N	Y	Y
KENTUCKY							
1 ***Whitfield***	Y	N	Y	Y	N	Y	Y
2 ***Lewis***	N	N	Y	Y	N	Y	N
3 ***Northup***	N	N	Y	Y	N	N	N
4 Lucas	N	N	Y	Y	Y	Y	Y
5 ***Rogers***	N	N	Y	Y	N	Y	N
6 ***Fletcher***	N	N	Y	Y	Y	Y	N
LOUISIANA							
1 ***Vitter***	N	N	Y	Y	N	Y	Y
2 Jefferson	Y	Y	Y	Y	Y	N	N
3 ***Tauzin***	N	N	Y	Y	N	N	Y
4 ***McCrery***	N	N	Y	Y	N	N	N
5 ***Cooksey***	Y	N	Y	Y	N	Y	Y
6 ***Baker***	N	N	Y	Y	Y	N	Y
7 John	Y	Y	Y	Y	Y	Y	N
MAINE							
1 Allen	Y	Y	Y	Y	Y	N	N
2 Baldacci	Y	Y	Y	Y	Y	N	N
MARYLAND							
1 ***Gilchrest***	Y	N	Y	Y	N	N	N
2 ***Ehrlich***	N	N	Y	?	Y	Y	Y
3 Cardin	Y	N	Y	Y	Y	N	N
4 Wynn	Y	Y	Y	Y	Y	N	N
5 Hoyer	Y	Y	Y	Y	Y	N	N
6 ***Bartlett***	Y	N	Y	Y	N	Y	Y
7 Cummings	Y	Y	Y	Y	Y	N	N
8 ***Morella***	Y	Y	Y	Y	Y	N	N
MASSACHUSETTS							
1 Olver	Y	Y	Y	Y	Y	N	N
2 Neal	Y	Y	Y	Y	Y	N	N
3 McGovern	Y	Y	Y	Y	Y	N	N
4 Frank	Y	Y	Y	Y	Y	N	N
5 Meehan	Y	Y	Y	Y	Y	N	N
6 Tierney	Y	Y	Y	Y	Y	N	N
7 Markey	Y	Y	Y	Y	Y	N	N
8 Capuano	Y	Y	Y	Y	Y	N	N
9 Lynch	Y	Y	Y	Y	Y	N	N
10 Delahunt	Y	Y	Y	Y	?	N	N
MICHIGAN							
1 Stupak	Y	Y	Y	Y	Y	N	N
2 ***Hoekstra***	N	N	Y	Y	N	Y	Y
3 ***Ehlers***	Y	N	Y	Y	N	N	N
4 ***Camp***	Y	N	Y	Y	N	Y	N
5 Barcia	Y	Y	Y	Y	Y	Y	Y
6 ***Upton***	Y	Y	Y	Y	N	Y	Y
7 ***Smith***	Y	N	Y	Y	Y	Y	Y
8 ***Rogers***	N	N	Y	Y	N	Y	N
9 Kildee	Y	Y	Y	Y	Y	N	N
10 Bonior	?	?	?	?	?	?	?
11 ***Knollenberg***	N	N	Y	Y	N	N	N
12 Levin	Y	Y	Y	Y	Y	N	N
13 Rivers	Y	Y	Y	Y	Y	N	N
14 Conyers	Y	Y	Y	Y	Y	N	N
15 Kilpatrick	Y	Y	Y	Y	Y	N	N
16 Dingell	N	Y	Y	Y	Y	N	N

	318	319	320	321	322	323	
MINNESOTA							
1 ***Gutknecht***	N	N	Y	Y	Y	Y	Y
2 ***Kennedy***	N	N	Y	Y	N	Y	Y
3 ***Ramstad***	Y	Y	Y	Y	N	Y	Y
4 McCollum	Y	Y	Y	Y	Y	N	N
5 Sabo	Y	Y	Y	Y	Y	N	N
6 Luther	Y	Y	Y	Y	Y	Y	Y
7 Peterson	Y	Y	Y	Y	Y	N	Y
8 Oberstar	Y	Y	Y	Y	Y	N	N
MISSISSIPPI							
1 ***Wicker***	N	N	Y	Y	N	Y	Y
2 Thompson	Y	Y	Y	Y	Y	N	N
3 ***Pickering***	N	N	Y	Y	N	Y	Y
4 Shows	Y	Y	Y	Y	Y	Y	Y
5 Taylor	Y	Y	Y	Y	Y	Y	Y
MISSOURI							
1 Clay	Y	Y	?	?	Y	N	N
2 ***Akin***	N	N	Y	Y	N	Y	Y
3 Gephardt	N	N	Y	Y	Y	N	N
4 Skelton	N	N	Y	Y	Y	N	N
5 McCarthy	Y	Y	Y	Y	Y	N	N
6 ***Graves***	Y	Y	Y	Y	Y	N	Y
7 ***Blunt***	N	N	Y	Y	N	N	Y
8 ***Emerson***	Y	Y	Y	Y	Y	N	N
9 ***Hulshof***	N	N	Y	Y	N	Y	N
MONTANA							
AL ***Rehberg***	Y	Y	Y	Y	N	Y	Y
NEBRASKA							
1 ***Bereuter***	Y	N	Y	Y	N	Y	Y
2 ***Terry***	Y	N	Y	Y	N	Y	Y
3 ***Osborne***	Y	Y	Y	Y	N	Y	N
NEVADA							
1 Berkley	N	N	Y	Y	Y	N	N
2 ***Gibbons***	N	N	Y	Y	N	Y	Y
NEW HAMPSHIRE							
1 ***Sununu***	Y	N	Y	Y	N	Y	N
2 ***Bass***	Y	N	Y	Y	N	Y	N
NEW JERSEY							
1 Andrews	N	N	Y	Y	Y	N	N
2 ***LoBiondo***	N	N	Y	Y	Y	Y	N
3 ***Saxton***	N	N	Y	Y	Y	Y	N
4 ***Smith***	N	N	Y	Y	Y	Y	N
5 ***Roukema***	N	N	Y	Y	Y	Y	Y
6 Pallone	N	N	Y	Y	Y	N	N
7 ***Ferguson***	N	N	Y	Y	Y	Y	N
8 Pascrell	N	N	Y	Y	Y	N	N
9 Rothman	N	N	Y	Y	Y	N	N
10 Payne	Y	Y	Y	Y	Y	N	N
11 ***Frelinghuysen***	N	N	Y	Y	N	N	N
12 Holt	Y	Y	Y	Y	Y	N	N
13 Menendez	N	N	Y	Y	Y	N	N
NEW MEXICO							
1 ***Wilson***	N	N	Y	Y	N	N	N
2 ***Skeen***	N	N	Y	Y	N	N	N
3 Udall	Y	Y	Y	Y	Y	N	N
NEW YORK							
1 ***Grucci***	Y	N	Y	Y	Y	N	N
2 Israel	Y	Y	Y	Y	Y	N	N
3 ***King***	N	N	Y	Y	Y	N	N
4 McCarthy	Y	Y	Y	Y	Y	N	N
5 Ackerman	N	N	Y	Y	Y	N	N
6 Meeks	Y	Y	Y	Y	Y	N	N
7 Crowley	Y	Y	Y	Y	Y	N	N
8 Nadler	Y	Y	Y	Y	Y	N	N
9 Weiner	Y	Y	Y	Y	Y	N	N
10 Towns	Y	Y	Y	Y	Y	N	N
11 Owens	Y	Y	Y	Y	Y	N	N
12 Velázquez	Y	Y	Y	Y	Y	N	N
13 ***Fossella***	N	N	Y	Y	Y	N	Y
14 Maloney	Y	Y	Y	Y	Y	N	N
15 Rangel	Y	Y	Y	Y	Y	N	N
16 Serrano	Y	Y	Y	Y	Y	N	N
17 Engel	N	N	Y	?	Y	N	N
18 Lowey	Y	Y	Y	Y	Y	N	N
19 ***Kelly***	N	N	Y	Y	Y	Y	N
20 ***Gilman***	N	N	Y	Y	Y	Y	N
21 McNulty	Y	Y	Y	Y	Y	N	N
22 ***Sweeney***	N	N	Y	Y	Y	N	N
23 ***Boehlert***	Y	N	Y	Y	Y	N	N
24 ***McHugh***	Y	N	Y	Y	Y	N	N
25 ***Walsh***	N	N	Y	Y	Y	N	N
26 Hinchey	Y	Y	Y	Y	Y	N	N
27 ***Reynolds***	N	N	Y	Y	N	N	Y
28 Slaughter	Y	Y	Y	Y	Y	N	?
29 LaFalce	Y	Y	Y	Y	Y	N	N
30 ***Quinn***	N	N	Y	Y	Y	N	N

	318	319	320	321	322	323	
31 ***Houghton***	Y	N	Y	Y	N	N	N
NORTH CAROLINA							
1 Clayton	Y	Y	Y	Y	Y	N	N
2 Etheridge	Y	N	Y	Y	Y	N	N
3 ***Jones***	N	N	Y	Y	Y	Y	Y
4 Price	Y	Y	Y	Y	Y	N	N
5 ***Burr***	N	N	Y	Y	N	Y	Y
6 ***Coble***	N	N	Y	Y	N	Y	Y
7 McIntyre	Y	N	Y	Y	Y	Y	N
8 ***Hayes***	N	N	Y	Y	Y	Y	Y
9 ***Myrick***	N	N	Y	Y	N	Y	Y
10 ***Ballenger***	N	N	Y	Y	N	Y	Y
11 ***Taylor***	N	N	Y	Y	N	Y	Y
12 Watt	Y	Y	Y	Y	Y	N	N
NORTH DAKOTA							
AL Pomeroy	Y	Y	Y	Y	Y	N	N
OHIO							
1 ***Chabot***	N	N	Y	Y	N	Y	Y
2 ***Portman***	N	N	Y	Y	N	N	N
3 Hall	Y	Y	Y	?	Y	N	N
4 ***Oxley***	N	N	Y	Y	N	Y	Y
5 ***Gillmor***	N	N	Y	Y	N	N	N
6 Strickland	Y	Y	Y	Y	Y	N	N
7 ***Hobson***	N	N	Y	Y	N	N	N
8 ***Boehner***	N	N	Y	Y	N	N	N
9 Kaptur	Y	Y	Y	?	Y	N	N
10 Kucinich	Y	Y	Y	N	Y	N	N
11 Jones	Y	Y	Y	Y	Y	N	N
12 ***Tiberi***	Y	Y	Y	Y	N	Y	Y
13 Brown	Y	Y	Y	Y	Y	N	N
14 Sawyer	Y	Y	Y	Y	Y	N	N
15 ***Pryce***	N	N	Y	Y	N	N	N
16 ***Regula***	N	N	Y	Y	N	N	N
17 Traficant	?	?	?	?	?	?	?
18 ***Ney***	Y	N	Y	Y	N	Y	N
19 ***LaTourette***	N	N	Y	Y	Y	N	N
OKLAHOMA							
1 ***Sullivan***	N	N	Y	Y	N	Y	Y
2 Carson	Y	Y	Y	Y	Y	N	N
3 ***Watkins***	N	N	Y	Y	N	N	N
4 ***Watts***	N	N	Y	Y	N	Y	Y
5 ***Istook***	N	N	Y	Y	N	N	N
6 ***Lucas***	N	N	Y	Y	N	N	N
OREGON							
1 Wu	N	N	Y	Y	Y	N	N
2 ***Walden***	N	N	Y	Y	N	Y	Y
3 Blumenauer	Y	Y	Y	Y	Y	N	N
4 DeFazio	+	+	+	Y	Y	Y	N
5 Hooley	Y	Y	Y	Y	Y	N	N
PENNSYLVANIA							
1 Brady	Y	Y	Y	Y	Y	N	N
2 Fattah	Y	Y	Y	Y	Y	N	N
3 Borski	Y	Y	Y	Y	Y	N	N
4 ***Hart***	N	N	Y	Y	Y	Y	Y
5 ***Peterson***	Y	Y	Y	Y	N	N	Y
6 Holden	Y	N	Y	Y	Y	N	N
7 ***Weldon***	Y	N	Y	Y	Y	Y	Y
8 ***Greenwood***	Y	N	Y	Y	N	N	N
9 ***Shuster, Bill***	N	N	Y	Y	N	Y	N
10 ***Sherwood***	N	N	Y	Y	N	N	N
11 Kanjorski	Y	N	Y	Y	Y	N	N
12 Murtha	Y	N	Y	Y	Y	N	N
13 Hoeffel	Y	Y	Y	Y	Y	N	N
14 Coyne	Y	Y	Y	Y	Y	N	N
15 ***Toomey***	N	N	Y	Y	N	Y	Y
16 ***Pitts***	N	N	Y	Y	N	Y	Y
17 ***Gekas***	N	N	Y	Y	Y	N	N
18 Doyle	Y	Y	Y	Y	Y	N	N
19 ***Platts***	Y	N	Y	?	Y	Y	Y
20 Mascara	Y	Y	Y	Y	Y	N	N
21 ***English***	Y	N	Y	Y	Y	N	Y
RHODE ISLAND							
1 Kennedy	N	N	Y	Y	Y	N	N
2 Langevin	Y	Y	Y	Y	Y	N	N
SOUTH CAROLINA							
1 ***Brown***	Y	N	Y	Y	N	N	N
2 ***Wilson***	N	N	Y	Y	N	Y	Y
3 ***Graham***	N	N	Y	Y	N	Y	Y
4 ***DeMint***	N	N	Y	Y	N	Y	Y
5 Spratt	Y	N	Y	Y	Y	N	N
6 Clyburn	Y	Y	Y	Y	Y	N	N
SOUTH DAKOTA							
AL ***Thune***	Y	Y	Y	Y	N	Y	N

	318	319	320	321	322	323	
TENNESSEE							
1 ***Jenkins***	N	N	Y	Y	N	Y	Y
2 ***Duncan***	N	N	Y	Y	N	Y	Y
3 ***Wamp***	N	N	Y	Y	N	Y	Y
4 ***Hilleary***	N	N	Y	Y	N	Y	Y
5 Clement	Y	Y	Y	Y	Y	Y	Y
6 Gordon	Y	Y	Y	Y	Y	Y	N
7 ***Bryant***	N	N	Y	Y	N	Y	Y
8 Tanner	Y	Y	Y	Y	Y	Y	Y
9 Ford	Y	Y	Y	Y	Y	N	N
TEXAS							
1 Sandlin	Y	Y	Y	Y	Y	N	N
2 Turner	Y	Y	Y	Y	Y	Y	Y
3 ***Johnson, Sam***	N	N	Y	?	N	Y	Y
4 Hall	Y	Y	Y	Y	Y	Y	Y
5 ***Sessions***	N	N	Y	Y	N	Y	Y
6 ***Barton***	N	N	Y	Y	N	N	Y
7 ***Culberson***	N	N	Y	Y	N	N	Y
8 ***Brady***	Y	N	Y	Y	N	N	Y
9 Lampson	Y	Y	Y	Y	Y	N	N
10 Doggett	Y	Y	Y	Y	Y	Y	Y
11 Edwards	Y	Y	Y	Y	Y	N	N
12 ***Granger***	N	N	Y	Y	N	N	N
13 ***Thornberry***	Y	N	Y	Y	N	N	Y
14 ***Paul***	Y	Y	N	?	N	Y	Y
15 Hinojosa	Y	Y	Y	Y	Y	N	N
16 Reyes	Y	N	Y	Y	Y	N	N
17 Stenholm	Y	Y	Y	Y	Y	Y	Y
18 Jackson-Lee	Y	Y	Y	Y	Y	N	N
19 ***Combest***	Y	N	Y	Y	N	Y	N
20 Gonzalez	Y	Y	Y	Y	Y	N	N
21 ***Smith***	N	N	Y	Y	N	Y	Y
22 ***DeLay***	N	N	Y	Y	N	N	N
23 ***Bonilla***	N	N	Y	Y	N	N	N
24 Frost	Y	Y	Y	Y	Y	N	N
25 Bentsen	Y	Y	Y	Y	Y	N	N
26 ***Armey***	N	N	Y	Y	N	Y	Y
27 Ortiz	Y	N	Y	Y	Y	N	N
28 Rodriguez	Y	Y	Y	Y	Y	N	N
29 Green	N	N	Y	Y	Y	Y	N
30 Johnson, E.B.	Y	Y	Y	Y	Y	N	N
UTAH							
1 ***Hansen***	?	N	Y	Y	Y	Y	Y
2 Matheson	Y	Y	Y	Y	Y	Y	Y
3 ***Cannon***	N	N	Y	Y	?	Y	Y
VERMONT							
AL *Sanders*	Y	Y	Y	Y	Y	N	N
VIRGINIA							
1 ***Davis, Jo Ann***	N	N	Y	Y	Y	Y	Y
2 ***Schrock***	N	N	Y	Y	N	N	Y
3 Scott	Y	Y	Y	Y	Y	N	N
4 ***Forbes***	N	N	Y	Y	Y	Y	Y
5 *Goode*	N	N	Y	Y	N	Y	Y
6 ***Goodlatte***	N	Y	Y	N	Y	Y	
7 ***Cantor***	N	N	Y	Y	N	N	Y
8 Moran	Y	Y	Y	Y	Y	N	N
9 Boucher	Y	Y	Y	Y	Y	N	N
10 ***Wolf***	N	N	Y	Y	Y	N	N
11 ***Davis, T.***	N	N	Y	Y	Y	N	N
WASHINGTON							
1 Inslee	Y	Y	Y	Y	Y	N	N
2 Larsen	Y	Y	Y	Y	Y	N	N
3 Baird	Y	Y	Y	Y	Y	N	N
4 ***Hastings***	N	N	Y	Y	N	Y	N
5 ***Nethercutt***	Y	N	Y	Y	N	Y	N
6 Dicks	Y	Y	Y	Y	Y	N	N
7 McDermott	Y	Y	Y	Y	Y	N	N
8 ***Dunn***	N	N	Y	Y	N	N	N
9 Smith	Y	Y	Y	Y	Y	Y	Y
WEST VIRGINIA							
1 Mollohan	Y	Y	Y	Y	Y	N	N
2 ***Capito***	N	N	Y	Y	Y	N	N
3 Rahall	Y	Y	Y	Y	Y	N	N
WISCONSIN							
1 ***Ryan***	Y	Y	Y	Y	N	Y	Y
2 Baldwin	Y	Y	Y	Y	Y	N	N
3 Kind	Y	Y	Y	Y	Y	Y	N
4 Kleczka	Y	Y	?	Y	Y	N	N
5 Barrett	Y	Y	Y	Y	Y	Y	N
6 ***Petri***	N	N	Y	Y	Y	Y	Y
7 Obey	Y	Y	Y	Y	Y	N	N
8 ***Green***	N	N	Y	Y	N	Y	N
9 ***Sensenbrenner***	N	N	Y	Y	N	Y	Y
WYOMING							
AL ***Cubin***	N	N	Y	Y	N	Y	Y

Southern states - Ala., Ark., Fla., Ga., Ky., La., Miss., N.C., Okla., S.C., Tenn., Texas, Va.

324. H Con Res 439. Corinne "Lindy" Boggs Tribute/Adoption. Linder, R-Ga., motion to suspend the rules and adopt the concurrent resolution that would pay tribute to former Rep. Corinne "Lindy" Boggs, D-La. (1973-91), who helped found the Congressional Women's Caucus. Motion agreed to 378-0: R 193-0; D 183-0 (ND 136-0, SD 47-0); I 2-0. A two-thirds majority of those present and voting (252 in this case) is required for adoption under suspension of the rules. July 22, 2002.

325. H Res 492. New York Landfill Workers Tribute/Adoption. Putnam, R-Fla., motion to suspend the rules and adopt the resolution that would pay tribute to workers at the Fresh Kills landfill in Staten Island, N.Y., where debris and remains from the Sept. 11, 2001, attacks in New York were taken. Motion agreed to 375-0: R 192-0; D 181-0 (ND 135-0, SD 46-0); I 2-0. A two-thirds majority of those present and voting (250 in this case) is required for adoption under suspension of the rules. July 22, 2002.

326. Procedural Motion/Journal. Approval of the House Journal of Monday, July 22, 2002. Approved 339-45: R 184-11; D 153-34 (ND 112-30, SD 41-4); I 2-0. July 23, 2002.

327. HR 3479. O'Hare Airport Expansion/Passage. Mica, R-Fla., motion to suspend the rules and pass the bill that would fund and expedite an expansion of Chicago's O'Hare International Airport. Motion agreed to 343-87: R 169-51; D 173-35 (ND 131-24, SD 42-11); I 1-1. A two-thirds majority of those present and voting (287 in this case) is required for passage under suspension of the rules. July 23, 2002.

328. HR 4775. Fiscal 2002 Supplemental Appropriations/Conference Report. Adoption of the conference report on the bill that would provide approximately $28.9 billion in supplemental appropriations for fiscal 2002. The agreement includes $14.4 billion for the Defense Department, $6.7 billion for homeland security programs and $5.5 billion for post-Sept. 11 recovery efforts in New York. It also would provide $2.1 billion for foreign aid, including funds to rebuild Afghanistan, fight international terrorism and provide U.S. embassy security. Adopted (thus sent to the Senate) 397-32: R 201-18; D 195-13 (ND 145-10, SD 50-3); I 1-1. A "yea" was a vote in support of the president's position. July 23, 2002.

329. H J Res 101. Vietnam Trade/Passage. Passage of the joint resolution that would disapprove President Bush's June 3, 2002, decision to allow the United States to continue normal trade relations with Vietnam. Rejected 91-338: R 62-158; D 27-180 (ND 19-135, SD 8-45); I 2-0. A "nay" was a vote in support of the president's position. July 23, 2002.

330. HR 5120. Fiscal 2003 Treasury-Postal Service Appropriations/Cuba Travel. Goss, R-Fla., amendment that would require that before any provision in the bill limiting the use of funds to enforce a ban on travel to Cuba could take effect, the president would have to certify that the Cuban government does not possess and is not developing biological weapons that could threaten the United States, is not aiding terrorist states or organizations on such weapons, and is not providing support or sanctuary to terrorists. Rejected 182-247: R 156-64; D 25-182 (ND 14-139, SD 11-43); I 1-1. July 23, 2002.

331. HR 5120. Fiscal 2003 Treasury-Postal Service Appropriations/Cuba Travel. Flake, R-Ariz., amendment that would ban the expenditure of funds to enforce the ban on travel to Cuba. Adopted 262-167: R 73-147; D 188-19 (ND 142-12, SD 46-7); I 1-1. A "nay" was a vote in support of the president's position. July 23, 2002.

Key

Y	Voted for (yea).
#	Paired for.
+	Announced for.
N	Voted against (nay).
X	Paired against.
–	Announced against.
P	Voted "present."
C	Voted "present" to avoid possible conflict of interest.
?	Did not vote or otherwise make a position known.

Democrats   **Republicans**
Independents

	324	325	326	327	328	329	330	331
ALABAMA								
1 *Callahan*	?	?	?	Y	Y	N	N	Y
2 *Everett*	Y	Y	Y	Y	Y	Y	N	Y
3 *Riley*	+	+	?	N	Y	Y	Y	N
4 *Aderholt*	Y	Y	N	N	Y	Y	Y	Y
5 Cramer	?	?	Y	Y	N	Y	N	N
6 *Bachus*	?	?	Y	Y	Y	N	N	Y
7 Hilliard	Y	Y	N	N	Y	N	N	Y
ALASKA								
AL *Young*	Y	Y	?	Y	Y	N	Y	N
ARIZONA								
1 *Flake*	Y	Y	Y	N	N	Y	N	Y
2 Pastor	Y	Y	Y	Y	N	N	N	Y
3 *Stump*	?	?	?	N	Y	Y	Y	N
4 *Shadegg*	Y	Y	Y	N	N	Y	N	Y
5 *Kolbe*	Y	Y	Y	Y	Y	N	N	Y
6 *Hayworth*	Y	Y	Y	Y	Y	Y	Y	N
ARKANSAS								
1 Berry	Y	Y	Y	Y	Y	Y	N	Y
2 Snyder	Y	Y	Y	N	Y	N	N	Y
3 *Boozman*	Y	Y	Y	Y	N	N	N	Y
4 Ross	Y	Y	Y	Y	Y	Y	N	Y
CALIFORNIA								
1 Thompson	Y	Y	N	Y	N	Y	N	Y
2 *Herger*	Y	Y	Y	Y	Y	N	N	Y
3 *Ose*	Y	Y	Y	Y	Y	N	N	Y
4 *Doolittle*	Y	Y	Y	Y	Y	Y	N	Y
5 Matsui	Y	Y	Y	Y	Y	N	N	Y
6 Woolsey	Y	?	Y	Y	Y	N	N	Y
7 Miller, George	Y	N	Y	Y	N	N	N	Y
8 Pelosi	Y	Y	Y	Y	Y	?	N	Y
9 Lee	Y	Y	Y	N	Y	N	N	Y
10 Tauscher	Y	Y	Y	Y	Y	N	N	Y
11 *Pombo*	Y	Y	Y	Y	Y	Y	Y	N
12 Lantos	Y	Y	Y	Y	Y	N	N	Y
13 Stark	Y	Y	N	Y	N	N	N	Y
14 Eshoo	Y	Y	Y	Y	Y	N	N	Y
15 Honda	Y	Y	Y	Y	Y	N	N	Y
16 Lofgren	Y	Y	Y	Y	Y	N	N	Y
17 Farr	Y	Y	Y	Y	N	N	N	Y
18 Condit	Y	Y	Y	Y	N	Y	N	Y
19 *Radanovich*	Y	Y	N	Y	N	Y	N	Y
20 Dooley	?	?	Y	Y	Y	N	N	Y
21 *Thomas*	Y	Y	Y	Y	Y	N	Y	N
22 Capps	Y	Y	Y	Y	Y	N	N	Y
23 *Gallegly*	Y	Y	Y	N	Y	N	N	Y
24 Sherman	Y	Y	Y	N	N	N	N	Y
25 *McKeon*	?	?	Y	Y	N	Y	N	Y
26 Berman	Y	Y	Y	N	Y	N	N	Y
27 Schiff	Y	Y	Y	N	Y	N	N	Y
28 *Dreier*	Y	Y	Y	Y	Y	N	N	Y
29 Waxman	Y	Y	Y	Y	N	N	N	Y
30 Becerra	+	+	Y	Y	Y	N	N	Y
31 Solis	Y	Y	Y	Y	N	N	N	Y
32 Watson	Y	Y	Y	Y	N	N	N	Y
33 Roybal-Allard	Y	Y	Y	Y	N	N	N	Y
34 Napolitano	Y	N	Y	Y	N	N	N	Y
35 Waters	Y	N	N	N	N	N	N	Y
36 Harman	Y	Y	Y	Y	N	Y	N	Y
37 Millender-McD.	?	?	Y	Y	N	Y	N	Y
38 *Horn*	Y	Y	Y	Y	N	Y	N	Y

	324	325	326	327	328	329	330	331
39 *Royce*	Y	Y	Y	N	N	Y	Y	N
40 *Lewis*	Y	Y	Y	Y	Y	N	Y	N
41 *Miller, Gary*	Y	Y	Y	Y	Y	N	Y	N
42 Baca	Y	Y	Y	Y	Y	N	N	Y
43 *Calvert*	?	?	Y	Y	Y	N	Y	N
44 *Bono*	Y	Y	?	Y	N	Y	Y	N
45 *Rohrabacher*	Y	Y	N	Y	N	Y	Y	N
46 Sanchez	Y	Y	Y	Y	Y	N	N	Y
47 *Cox*	?	Y	Y	Y	Y	Y	Y	Y
48 *Issa*	Y	Y	Y	N	N	Y	N	Y
49 Davis	Y	Y	Y	Y	N	N	N	Y
50 Filner	Y	Y	N	Y	N	N	N	Y
51 *Cunningham*	Y	Y	N	Y	N	Y	Y	N
52 *Hunter*	Y	?	N	Y	N	Y	Y	N
COLORADO								
1 DeGette	Y	Y	Y	Y	Y	N	?	Y
2 Udall	Y	Y	N	Y	N	Y	N	Y
3 *McInnis*	Y	Y	Y	Y	N	Y	N	N
4 *Schaffer*	?	?	N	N	Y	Y	N	N
5 *Hefley*	Y	Y	N	N	Y	Y	N	N
6 *Tancredo*	?	?	P	N	N	Y	Y	N
CONNECTICUT								
1 Larson	Y	Y	Y	Y	Y	N	N	Y
2 *Simmons*	Y	Y	Y	Y	Y	N	N	Y
3 DeLauro	Y	Y	Y	Y	Y	N	N	Y
4 *Shays*	Y	Y	Y	Y	Y	N	N	Y
5 Maloney	+	+	+	Y	N	Y	N	Y
6 *Johnson*	Y	Y	Y	Y	Y	N	N	Y
DELAWARE								
AL *Castle*	Y	Y	Y	Y	Y	N	N	Y
FLORIDA								
1 *Miller, J.*	Y	Y	Y	N	Y	Y	N	Y
2 Boyd	Y	Y	Y	Y	Y	N	N	Y
3 Brown	Y	Y	Y	N	N	N	N	P
4 *Crenshaw*	Y	Y	Y	Y	Y	N	N	Y
5 Thurman	Y	Y	N	Y	N	Y	N	Y
6 *Stearns*	Y	Y	?	?	?	?	?	Y
7 *Mica*	Y	Y	Y	N	Y	N	N	Y
8 *Keller*	Y	Y	Y	N	Y	N	N	Y
9 *Bilirakis*	Y	Y	N	Y	N	N	N	Y
10 *Young*	?	?	?	Y	Y	Y	Y	N
11 Davis	?	?	Y	Y	N	N	N	Y
12 *Putnam*	Y	Y	Y	Y	N	Y	N	Y
13 *Miller, D.*	?	?	?	Y	Y	N	N	Y
14 *Goss*	Y	Y	Y	+	+	N	Y	N
15 *Weldon*	Y	Y	Y	N	Y	N	N	Y
16 *Foley*	+	Y	Y	Y	Y	N	N	Y
17 Meek	?	?	Y	N	Y	N	N	Y
18 *Ros-Lehtinen*	Y	Y	Y	N	Y	N	N	Y
19 Wexler	Y	Y	Y	Y	N	N	N	Y
20 Deutsch	Y	Y	?	Y	Y	N	N	Y
21 *Diaz-Balart*	Y	Y	Y	N	Y	N	N	Y
22 *Shaw*	Y	Y	Y	Y	N	Y	N	Y
23 Hastings	?	?	?	Y	Y	N	N	N
GEORGIA								
1 *Kingston*	Y	Y	Y	Y	Y	Y	N	Y
2 Bishop	Y	Y	Y	Y	Y	N	N	Y
3 *Collins*	Y	Y	Y	N	N	Y	N	Y
4 McKinney	Y	Y	Y	N	N	N	N	Y
5 Lewis	?	?	?	?	?	?	N	Y
6 *Isakson*	Y	Y	Y	Y	Y	N	N	Y
7 *Barr*	Y	Y	Y	N	Y	N	N	N
8 *Chambliss*	Y	Y	Y	Y	Y	N	N	N
9 *Deal*	Y	Y	Y	N	N	Y	N	Y
10 *Norwood*	Y	Y	Y	Y	N	Y	N	N
11 *Linder*	Y	Y	N	N	Y	Y	N	N
HAWAII								
1 Abercrombie	+	+	+	Y	N	N	N	Y
2 Mink	Y	Y	Y	Y	Y	N	N	Y
IDAHO								
1 *Otter*	Y	Y	Y	Y	N	N	N	Y
2 *Simpson*	Y	Y	Y	Y	N	N	N	N
ILLINOIS								
1 Rush	?	?	Y	Y	Y	N	N	Y
2 Jackson	Y	Y	N	Y	N	N	N	Y
3 Lipinski	Y	Y	Y	N	Y	N	N	Y
4 Gutierrez	?	?	Y	Y	N	N	N	Y
5 Blagojevich	?	?	Y	Y	Y	N	N	Y
6 *Hyde*	Y	Y	?	N	Y	N	N	Y
7 Davis	Y	Y	?	Y	N	N	N	Y
8 *Crane*	?	?	N	N	Y	Y	N	N
9 Schakowsky	Y	Y	Y	N	N	N	N	Y
10 *Kirk*	Y	Y	Y	Y	Y	N	N	Y
11 *Weller*	Y	N	Y	N	Y	N	N	Y
12 Costello	Y	Y	Y	N	Y	N	N	Y
13 *Biggert*	Y	Y	Y	Y	Y	N	N	Y

ND Northern Democrats   SD Southern Democrats

	324	325	326	327	328	329	330	331
14 ***Hastert***				Y				
15 ***Johnson***	Y	Y	Y	Y	Y	N	N	Y
16 ***Manzullo***	Y	Y	Y	Y	N	N	N	Y
17 Evans	Y	Y	Y	Y	Y	N	N	Y
18 ***LaHood***	Y	Y	Y	N	Y	N	N	Y
19 Phelps	?	?	?	Y	Y	N	N	Y
20 ***Shimkus***	Y	Y	Y	Y	Y	N	N	Y
INDIANA								
1 Visclosky	Y	Y	N	Y	Y	Y	N	Y
2 ***Pence***	Y	Y	Y	N	Y	N	N	N
3 Roemer	Y	Y	Y	Y	Y	N	N	Y
4 ***Souder***	Y	Y	Y	Y	Y	Y	Y	N
5 ***Buyer***	Y	Y	Y	N	Y	Y	Y	N
6 ***Burton***	Y	Y	Y	N	Y	Y	Y	N
7 ***Kerns***	Y	Y	Y	N	N	N	Y	N
8 ***Hostettler***	Y	Y	Y	N	Y	N	N	Y
9 Hill	Y	Y	Y	Y	Y	N	N	Y
10 Carson	Y	Y	Y	Y	Y	N	N	Y
IOWA								
1 ***Leach***	Y	Y	Y	Y	Y	N	N	Y
2 ***Nussle***	Y	Y	Y	Y	Y	N	N	Y
3 Boswell	Y	Y	Y	Y	Y	N	N	Y
4 ***Ganske***	Y	Y	Y	Y	Y	N	N	Y
5 ***Latham***	Y	Y	N	Y	Y	N	N	Y
KANSAS								
1 ***Moran***	Y	Y	Y	Y	Y	N	N	Y
2 ***Ryun***	Y	Y	?	N	Y	N	Y	N
3 Moore	Y	Y	N	Y	Y	N	N	Y
4 ***Tiahrt***	Y	Y	Y	Y	Y	N	Y	Y
KENTUCKY								
1 ***Whitfield***	Y	?	Y	Y	Y	N	N	Y
2 ***Lewis***	Y	Y	Y	Y	Y	N	Y	N
3 ***Northup***	Y	Y	Y	Y	Y	N	Y	N
4 Lucas	Y	Y	Y	Y	Y	N	Y	N
5 ***Rogers***	Y	Y	Y	Y	Y	N	Y	Y
6 ***Fletcher***	?	?	Y	Y	Y	N	Y	N
LOUISIANA								
1 ***Vitter***	Y	Y	Y	Y	Y	N	Y	N
2 Jefferson	Y	Y	?	Y	Y	N	N	Y
3 ***Tauzin***	Y	Y	Y	Y	Y	N	Y	N
4 ***McCrery***	?	?	?	Y	Y	N	Y	N
5 ***Cooksey***	Y	Y	Y	Y	Y	N	N	Y
6 ***Baker***	Y	Y	Y	Y	Y	N	Y	N
7 John	Y	Y	Y	Y	Y	N	N	Y
MAINE								
1 Allen	Y	Y	Y	Y	Y	N	N	Y
2 Baldacci	Y	Y	Y	Y	Y	N	N	Y
MARYLAND								
1 ***Gilchrest***	Y	Y	Y	Y	Y	N	N	Y
2 ***Ehrlich***	Y	Y	?	Y	Y	Y	Y	N
3 Cardin	Y	Y	Y	Y	Y	N	N	Y
4 Wynn	Y	Y	Y	Y	Y	N	N	Y
5 Hoyer	Y	Y	Y	Y	Y	N	N	Y
6 ***Bartlett***	Y	Y	Y	N	Y	Y	Y	Y
7 Cummings	Y	Y	?	N	Y	N	N	Y
8 ***Morella***	Y	Y	?	N	Y	N	N	Y
MASSACHUSETTS								
1 Olver	Y	Y	N	Y	Y	N	N	Y
2 Neal	Y	Y	Y	Y	Y	N	N	Y
3 McGovern	Y	Y	Y	Y	Y	N	N	Y
4 Frank	Y	Y	Y	Y	N	Y	N	Y
5 Meehan	Y	Y	Y	Y	Y	N	N	Y
6 Tierney	?	Y	N	Y	Y	N	N	Y
7 Markey	Y	Y	Y	Y	Y	N	N	Y
8 Capuano	Y	Y	?	Y	N	N	N	Y
9 Lynch	Y	Y	?	Y	Y	N	N	Y
10 Delahunt	Y	Y	Y	N	N	N	N	Y
MICHIGAN								
1 Stupak	Y	Y	N	Y	Y	N	N	Y
2 ***Hoekstra***	Y	Y	Y	Y	Y	N	N	Y
3 ***Ehlers***	Y	Y	Y	Y	Y	N	N	Y
4 ***Camp***	Y	Y	Y	Y	Y	N	N	Y
5 Barcia	Y	Y	Y	Y	Y	N	N	Y
6 ***Upton***	Y	Y	Y	Y	Y	N	N	Y
7 ***Smith***	Y	Y	Y	Y	Y	N	N	Y
8 ***Rogers***	Y	Y	Y	Y	Y	Y	Y	N
9 Kildee	Y	Y	Y	Y	Y	N	N	Y
10 Bonior	?	?	?	Y	Y	Y	?	?
11 ***Knollenberg***	Y	Y	Y	Y	Y	N	Y	N
12 Levin	Y	Y	Y	Y	Y	N	N	Y
13 Rivers	Y	Y	Y	N	Y	Y	N	Y
14 Conyers	?	?	Y	N	Y	N	N	Y
15 Kilpatrick	+	+	Y	N	Y	N	N	Y
16 Dingell	Y	Y	Y	N	Y	N	N	Y
MINNESOTA								
1 ***Gutknecht***	Y	Y	N	N	Y	Y	Y	N
2 ***Kennedy***	Y	Y	N	Y	Y	N	Y	N
3 ***Ramstad***	Y	Y	N	Y	Y	N	N	Y
4 McCollum	Y	Y	Y	Y	Y	N	N	Y
5 Sabo	Y	Y	N	N	Y	N	N	Y
6 Luther	Y	Y	Y	Y	Y	N	N	Y
7 Peterson	Y	Y	N	Y	Y	N	N	Y
8 Oberstar	Y	Y	N	Y	N	N	N	Y
MISSISSIPPI								
1 ***Wicker***	Y	Y	Y	Y	Y	Y	Y	N
2 Thompson	Y	Y	N	Y	Y	N	N	Y
3 ***Pickering***	Y	Y	Y	Y	Y	Y	Y	N
4 Shows	Y	Y	Y	N	Y	Y	Y	Y
5 Taylor	Y	Y	N	Y	Y	Y	N	Y
MISSOURI								
1 Clay	Y	Y	?	Y	Y	N	N	Y
2 ***Akin***	Y	Y	Y	N	Y	N	N	N
3 Gephardt	Y	Y	Y	Y	Y	N	Y	N
4 Skelton	Y	Y	Y	Y	Y	N	Y	N
5 McCarthy	Y	Y	?	N	Y	N	N	Y
6 ***Graves***	Y	Y	Y	Y	Y	N	N	Y
7 ***Blunt***	?	?	Y	Y	Y	N	Y	N
8 ***Emerson***	?	?	?	Y	Y	N	N	Y
9 ***Hulshof***	Y	Y	Y	Y	Y	N	Y	N
MONTANA								
AL ***Rehberg***	Y	Y	Y	Y	Y	N	N	Y
NEBRASKA								
1 ***Bereuter***	Y	Y	Y	Y	Y	N	N	Y
2 ***Terry***	Y	Y	Y	Y	N	N	Y	Y
3 ***Osborne***	Y	Y	Y	Y	Y	N	N	Y
NEVADA								
1 Berkley	Y	Y	Y	Y	Y	N	Y	N
2 ***Gibbons***	Y	Y	Y	Y	Y	Y	Y	N
NEW HAMPSHIRE								
1 ***Sununu***	Y	Y	Y	N	Y	N	Y	Y
2 ***Bass***	Y	Y	Y	Y	Y	N	Y	Y
NEW JERSEY								
1 Andrews	Y	Y	Y	Y	Y	Y	Y	N
2 ***LoBiondo***	Y	Y	N	Y	Y	Y	Y	N
3 ***Saxton***	Y	Y	Y	Y	Y	N	N	N
4 ***Smith***	Y	Y	Y	Y	Y	Y	Y	N
5 ***Roukema***	Y	Y	Y	Y	Y	N	Y	N
6 Pallone	Y	Y	Y	Y	Y	N	Y	N
7 ***Ferguson***	Y	Y	Y	Y	Y	N	Y	N
8 Pascrell	Y	Y	Y	Y	Y	N	Y	N
9 Rothman	Y	Y	Y	N	Y	Y	Y	N
10 Payne	Y	Y	Y	N	Y	Y	N	Y
11 ***Frelinghuysen***	?	?	?	Y	Y	N	Y	N
12 Holt	Y	Y	Y	Y	Y	N	N	Y
13 Menendez	Y	Y	Y	Y	Y	N	Y	N
NEW MEXICO								
1 ***Wilson***	Y	Y	Y	Y	Y	N	Y	Y
2 ***Skeen***	Y	Y	Y	Y	Y	N	Y	N
3 Udall	Y	Y	N	Y	Y	N	N	Y
NEW YORK								
1 ***Grucci***	Y	Y	Y	Y	Y	N	Y	Y
2 Israel	Y	Y	Y	Y	Y	N	N	Y
3 ***King***	Y	Y	Y	Y	Y	N	Y	N
4 McCarthy	Y	Y	Y	Y	Y	N	N	Y
5 Ackerman	Y	Y	Y	Y	Y	N	Y	N
6 Meeks	Y	Y	Y	Y	Y	N	N	Y
7 Crowley	Y	Y	Y	Y	Y	N	N	Y
8 Nadler	Y	Y	Y	Y	Y	N	N	Y
9 Weiner	Y	Y	Y	Y	Y	N	N	Y
10 Towns	Y	Y	Y	Y	Y	N	N	Y
11 Owens	Y	Y	Y	Y	Y	N	N	Y
12 Velázquez	Y	Y	N	Y	Y	N	N	Y
13 ***Fossella***	Y	Y	Y	Y	Y	N	Y	N
14 Maloney	Y	Y	Y	Y	Y	N	N	Y
15 Rangel	Y	Y	Y	Y	Y	N	N	Y
16 Serrano	Y	Y	Y	Y	Y	N	N	Y
17 Engel	Y	Y	?	Y	Y	N	Y	N
18 Lowey	Y	Y	Y	Y	Y	N	N	Y
19 ***Kelly***	Y	Y	Y	Y	Y	Y	Y	N
20 ***Gilman***	Y	Y	Y	Y	Y	Y	Y	N
21 McNulty	Y	Y	N	Y	Y	Y	N	Y
22 ***Sweeney***	Y	Y	Y	Y	Y	N	Y	N
23 ***Boehlert***	Y	Y	Y	Y	Y	N	N	Y
24 ***McHugh***	Y	Y	Y	Y	Y	N	Y	N
25 ***Walsh***	Y	Y	Y	Y	Y	N	Y	N
26 Hinchey	?	?	Y	Y	Y	N	N	Y
27 ***Reynolds***	Y	Y	Y	Y	Y	N	Y	N
28 Slaughter	Y	Y	Y	Y	Y	Y	N	Y
29 LaFalce	Y	Y	Y	Y	Y	N	N	Y
30 ***Quinn***	Y	Y	Y	Y	Y	N	Y	N
31 ***Houghton***	Y	Y	Y	N	Y	Y	N	Y
NORTH CAROLINA								
1 Clayton	Y	Y	Y	Y	Y	N	N	Y
2 Etheridge	Y	Y	Y	Y	Y	N	Y	Y
3 ***Jones***	Y	Y	?	N	Y	Y	N	N
4 Price	Y	Y	Y	Y	Y	N	N	Y
5 ***Burr***	Y	Y	Y	Y	Y	N	Y	N
6 ***Coble***	Y	Y	Y	N	Y	Y	Y	N
7 McIntyre	Y	Y	Y	Y	Y	Y	Y	Y
8 ***Hayes***	Y	Y	Y	Y	Y	Y	Y	N
9 ***Myrick***	+	+	Y	Y	Y	N	Y	N
10 ***Ballenger***	Y	Y	Y	N	Y	Y	Y	N
11 ***Taylor***	?	?	?	Y	Y	Y	Y	N
12 Watt	Y	Y	Y	N	Y	N	N	Y
NORTH DAKOTA								
AL Pomeroy	Y	Y	Y	Y	Y	N	N	Y
OHIO								
1 ***Chabot***	Y	Y	Y	N	N	Y	Y	N
2 ***Portman***	Y	Y	Y	Y	Y	N	Y	N
3 Hall	?	?	Y	Y	Y	N	N	Y
4 ***Oxley***	Y	Y	Y	Y	Y	N	Y	N
5 ***Gillmor***	Y	Y	Y	N	Y	N	Y	N
6 Strickland	Y	Y	N	Y	Y	Y	N	Y
7 ***Hobson***	Y	Y	Y	Y	Y	N	Y	N
8 ***Boehner***	Y	Y	Y	Y	Y	N	Y	N
9 Kaptur	Y	Y	Y	Y	Y	N	N	Y
10 Kucinich	Y	Y	N	N	N	Y	N	Y
11 Jones	+	+	?	?	?	?	N	Y
12 ***Tiberi***	Y	Y	Y	Y	Y	N	N	Y
13 Brown	Y	Y	Y	N	Y	Y	N	Y
14 Sawyer	Y	Y	Y	Y	Y	N	N	Y
15 ***Pryce***	Y	Y	?	Y	Y	N	Y	N
16 ***Regula***	Y	Y	Y	Y	Y	N	Y	N
17 Traficant	?	?	?	?	?	?	?	?
18 ***Ney***	Y	Y	Y	Y	Y	N	N	Y
19 ***LaTourette***	Y	Y	Y	Y	Y	N	Y	Y
OKLAHOMA								
1 ***Sullivan***	Y	Y	Y	Y	Y	N	Y	N
2 Carson	?	?	?	Y	Y	N	N	Y
3 ***Watkins***	Y	Y	Y	Y	Y	N	Y	N
4 ***Watts***	Y	Y	Y	Y	Y	N	Y	N
5 ***Istook***	Y	Y	Y	Y	Y	N	Y	N
6 ***Lucas***	Y	Y	Y	Y	Y	N	Y	N
OREGON								
1 Wu	Y	Y	Y	Y	Y	N	Y	Y
2 ***Walden***	Y	Y	Y	Y	Y	N	Y	N
3 Blumenauer	Y	Y	Y	Y	Y	N	N	Y
4 DeFazio	Y	Y	N	Y	Y	N	+	
5 Hooley	Y	Y	Y	Y	Y	N	N	Y
PENNSYLVANIA								
1 Brady	Y	Y	N	Y	Y	N	N	Y
2 Fattah	Y	Y	N	N	Y	N	N	Y
3 Borski	?	?	N	Y	N	N	N	Y
4 ***Hart***	Y	Y	Y	Y	Y	N	Y	N
5 ***Peterson***	Y	Y	Y	Y	Y	N	N	Y
6 Holden	Y	Y	Y	Y	Y	N	N	Y
7 ***Weldon***	Y	?	Y	Y	Y	N	N	Y
8 ***Greenwood***	Y	Y	Y	Y	Y	N	N	Y
9 ***Shuster, Bill***	Y	Y	Y	Y	Y	N	Y	N
10 ***Sherwood***	Y	Y	Y	Y	Y	N	N	N
11 Kanjorski	Y	Y	Y	Y	Y	N	N	Y
12 Murtha	?	?	Y	Y	Y	N	N	Y
13 Hoeffel	Y	Y	Y	Y	Y	N	N	Y
14 Coyne	?	?	Y	Y	Y	N	N	Y
15 ***Toomey***	Y	Y	Y	N	Y	N	N	Y
16 ***Pitts***	Y	Y	Y	Y	Y	N	Y	N
17 ***Gekas***	Y	Y	Y	Y	Y	N	Y	N
18 Doyle	Y	?	Y	Y	Y	N	N	Y
19 ***Platts***	Y	Y	?	Y	Y	N	Y	Y
20 Mascara	Y	Y	Y	Y	Y	N	N	Y
21 ***English***	Y	Y	N	Y	Y	N	Y	Y
RHODE ISLAND								
1 Kennedy	Y	Y	Y	N	Y	Y	Y	N
2 Langevin	Y	Y	Y	Y	Y	N	N	Y
SOUTH CAROLINA								
1 ***Brown***	Y	Y	Y	Y	Y	Y	Y	Y
2 ***Wilson***	Y	Y	Y	Y	Y	N	Y	N
3 ***Graham***	Y	Y	Y	N	Y	Y	Y	N
4 ***DeMint***	Y	Y	Y	Y	Y	N	Y	Y
5 Spratt	Y	Y	Y	Y	Y	N	N	Y
6 Clyburn	Y	Y	Y	Y	Y	N	N	Y
SOUTH DAKOTA								
AL ***Thune***	Y	Y	Y	Y	Y	N	N	Y
TENNESSEE								
1 ***Jenkins***	Y	Y	Y	N	Y	Y	Y	N
2 ***Duncan***	Y	Y	Y	Y	N	Y	Y	N
3 ***Wamp***	Y	Y	Y	Y	Y	Y	Y	N
4 ***Hilleary***	?	?	Y	N	Y	Y	Y	N
5 Clement	+	+	Y	Y	Y	N	N	Y
6 Gordon	Y	Y	Y	Y	Y	N	N	Y
7 ***Bryant***	?	?	Y	Y	Y	N	Y	N
8 Tanner	Y	Y	Y	Y	Y	N	N	Y
9 Ford	Y	Y	Y	Y	Y	N	N	Y
TEXAS								
1 Sandlin	Y	Y	Y	Y	Y	N	N	Y
2 Turner	Y	Y	Y	Y	Y	N	N	Y
3 ***Johnson, Sam***	?	?	?	Y	Y	Y	Y	N
4 Hall	Y	Y	Y	N	Y	Y	N	Y
5 ***Sessions***	?	?	Y	Y	Y	N	Y	N
6 ***Barton***	?	?	Y	Y	Y	N	Y	N
7 ***Culberson***	Y	Y	Y	Y	Y	Y	Y	N
8 ***Brady***	?	?	Y	Y	Y	N	N	Y
9 Lampson	Y	Y	Y	Y	Y	N	N	Y
10 Doggett	Y	Y	Y	Y	N	N	N	Y
11 Edwards	Y	Y	Y	Y	Y	N	Y	Y
12 ***Granger***	Y	Y	?	Y	Y	N	Y	N
13 ***Thornberry***	Y	Y	Y	Y	Y	N	Y	Y
14 ***Paul***	Y	Y	Y	N	N	Y	N	Y
15 Hinojosa	Y	Y	Y	Y	Y	N	N	Y
16 Reyes	Y	Y	Y	Y	Y	N	N	Y
17 Stenholm	Y	Y	Y	Y	Y	N	N	Y
18 Jackson-Lee	Y	Y	Y	Y	Y	Y	N	Y
19 ***Combest***	Y	Y	Y	Y	Y	N	N	Y
20 Gonzalez	Y	?	Y	Y	Y	N	N	Y
21 ***Smith***	Y	Y	Y	Y	Y	N	Y	N
22 ***DeLay***	Y	Y	?	Y	Y	N	Y	N
23 ***Bonilla***	?	?	?	Y	Y	Y	Y	N
24 Frost	Y	Y	Y	Y	Y	N	N	Y
25 Bentsen	Y	Y	?	Y	Y	N	N	Y
26 ***Armey***	Y	Y	Y	Y	Y	N	Y	N
27 Ortiz	Y	Y	Y	Y	Y	N	Y	Y
28 Rodriguez	Y	Y	Y	Y	Y	N	N	Y
29 Green	Y	Y	N	Y	Y	Y	Y	N
30 Johnson, E.B.	Y	Y	?	Y	N	N	N	Y
UTAH								
1 ***Hansen***	?	?	Y	Y	Y	N	N	N
2 Matheson	Y	Y	Y	Y	Y	N	N	Y
3 ***Cannon***	Y	Y	Y	Y	Y	N	Y	N
VERMONT								
AL *Sanders*	Y	Y	Y	Y	Y	Y	N	Y
VIRGINIA								
1 ***Davis, Jo Ann***	Y	Y	Y	N	Y	Y	Y	N
2 ***Schrock***	Y	Y	Y	Y	Y	N	Y	N
3 Scott	Y	Y	Y	N	Y	N	N	Y
4 ***Forbes***	Y	Y	Y	Y	Y	N	Y	N
5 *Goode*	Y	Y	Y	N	N	Y	Y	N
6 ***Goodlatte***	Y	Y	Y	N	Y	N	Y	N
7 ***Cantor***	Y	Y	Y	Y	Y	N	Y	N
8 Moran	Y	Y	?	N	Y	N	N	Y
9 Boucher	Y	Y	Y	Y	Y	N	N	Y
10 ***Wolf***	Y	Y	Y	N	Y	Y	Y	N
11 ***Davis, T.***	Y	Y	Y	Y	Y	Y	Y	N
WASHINGTON								
1 Inslee	Y	Y	Y	Y	Y	N	N	Y
2 Larsen	Y	Y	N	Y	Y	N	N	Y
3 Baird	Y	Y	N	Y	Y	N	N	Y
4 ***Hastings***	Y	Y	Y	Y	Y	N	Y	N
5 ***Nethercutt***	Y	Y	Y	Y	Y	N	N	Y
6 Dicks	Y	Y	Y	Y	Y	N	N	Y
7 McDermott	Y	Y	N	Y	N	N	N	Y
8 ***Dunn***	Y	Y	Y	Y	Y	N	Y	N
9 Smith	Y	Y	Y	N	N	N	N	Y
WEST VIRGINIA								
1 Mollohan	Y	Y	Y	Y	Y	N	N	Y
2 ***Capito***	Y	Y	Y	Y	Y	N	Y	N
3 Rahall	Y	Y	Y	Y	Y	N	N	Y
WISCONSIN								
1 ***Ryan***	Y	Y	Y	Y	N	N	N	Y
2 Baldwin	Y	Y	N	Y	Y	N	N	Y
3 Kind	Y	Y	Y	Y	N	N	N	Y
4 Kleczka	Y	Y	Y	Y	Y	N	N	Y
5 Barrett	+	+	+	Y	Y	N	N	Y
6 ***Petri***	Y	Y	Y	Y	N	N	Y	N
7 Obey	Y	Y	Y	N	Y	Y	N	Y
8 ***Green***	Y	Y	Y	Y	N	Y	Y	N
9 ***Sensenbrenner***	Y	Y	Y	N	N	N	Y	N
WYOMING								
AL ***Cubin***	Y	Y	?	N	N	N	Y	N

Southern states - Ala., Ark., Fla., Ga., Ky., La., Miss., N.C., Okla., S.C., Tenn., Texas, Va.

Key

Y	Voted for (yea).
#	Paired for.
+	Announced for.
N	Voted against (nay).
X	Paired against.
–	Announced against.
P	Voted "present."
C	Voted "present" to avoid possible conflict of interest.
?	Did not vote or otherwise make a position known.

Democrats **Republicans**
Independents

332. HR 5120. Fiscal 2003 Treasury-Postal Service Appropriations/ Cuban Nationals. Flake, R-Ariz., amendment that would ban the expenditure of funds to enforce any restriction on remittances to nationals of Cuba. Adopted 251-177: R 63-155; D 187-21 (ND 139-15, SD 48-6); I 1-1. July 23, 2002.

333. HR 5120. Fiscal 2003 Treasury-Postal Service Appropriations/ Cuba Embargo. Rangel, D-N.Y., amendment that would ban the expenditure of funds to operate and enforce the Cuban economic embargo. Rejected 204-226: R 30-190; D 173-35 (ND 132-22, SD 41-13); I 1-1. A "nay" was a vote in support of the president's position. July 23, 2002.

334. HR 3609. Pipeline Safety/Passage. Young, R-Alaska, motion to suspend the rules and pass the bill that would require the Transportation Department to develop specific criteria for inspections of high-risk natural gas pipelines and impose new qualification requirements for pipeline workers. The bill would increase civil penalties for safety violations and require operator-written plans for employee qualifications. Motion agreed to 423-4: R 217-3; D 204-1 (ND 150-1, SD 54-0); I 2-0. A two-thirds majority of those present and voting (285 in this case) is required for passage under suspension of the rules. July 23, 2002.

335. HR 4547. Fiscal 2003 War Funds Authorization/Passage. Hunter, R-Calif., motion to suspend the rules and pass the bill that would authorize $10 billion for operations conducted as part of the war on terrorism in fiscal 2003, and add that to the fiscal 2003 Defense Department authorization bill. The authorization would include $3.5 billion for operations associated with the war, $1 billion to replace equipment lost during operations, $3.1 billion for a variety of procurement, research and development, and operations and maintenance programs, and almost $2 billion for classified activities. Motion agreed to 413-3: R 213-0; D 198-3 (ND 147-2, SD 51-1); I 2-0. A two-thirds majority of those present and voting (278 in this case) is required for passage under suspension of the rules. July 24, 2002.

336. HR 5120. Fiscal 2003 Treasury-Postal Service Appropriations/ Private Contractor Quotas. Moran, D-Va., amendment that would prohibit the Office of Management and Budget, or any other federal agency, from using numerical quotas, targets and goals for the outsourcing of federal jobs to private contractors. Adopted 261-166: R 52-165; D 208-0 (ND 154-0, SD 54-0); I 1-1. A "nay" was a vote in support of the president's position. July 24, 2002.

337. HR 5120. Fiscal 2003 Treasury-Postal Service Appropriations/ Presidential Allowances. Hefley, R-Colo., amendment that would mandate a 10 percent cut in the $3.3 million allowance for former presidents. Rejected 165-265: R 135-84; D 29-180 (ND 14-141, SD 15-39); I 1-1. July 24, 2002.

338. HR 5120. Fiscal 2003 Treasury-Postal Service Appropriations/ Across-the-Board Cut. Hefley, R-Colo., amendment that would mandate a 1 percent cut in the total discretionary funding for the departments and agencies funded in the bill. Rejected 147-282: R 125-94; D 21-187 (ND 11-143, SD 10-44); I 1-1. July 24, 2002.

	332	333	334	335	336	337	338
ALABAMA							
1 *Callahan*	N	N	Y	Y	N	N	N
2 *Everett*	N	N	Y	N	Y	Y	Y
3 *Riley*	N	N	Y	Y	Y	Y	Y
4 *Aderholt*	Y	N	Y	N	N	N	N
5 Cramer	Y	Y	Y	Y	Y	N	N
6 *Bachus*	N	N	Y	Y	N	Y	Y
7 Hilliard	Y	Y	Y	Y	Y	N	N
ALASKA							
AL *Young*	N	N	Y	?	N	N	N
ARIZONA							
1 *Flake*	Y	Y	N	Y	N	Y	Y
2 Pastor	Y	Y	Y	Y	Y	N	N
3 *Stump*	N	N	Y	N	Y	Y	Y
4 *Shadegg*	N	N	Y	Y	N	Y	Y
5 *Kolbe*	Y	N	Y	N	N	N	N
6 *Hayworth*	N	N	Y	N	Y	Y	Y
ARKANSAS							
1 Berry	Y	Y	Y	Y	Y	Y	Y
2 Snyder	Y	Y	Y	Y	Y	N	N
3 *Boozman*	Y	Y	Y	N	Y	N	N
4 Ross	Y	Y	Y	Y	Y	N	N
CALIFORNIA							
1 Thompson	Y	Y	Y	Y	Y	N	N
2 *Herger*	N	Y	Y	Y	N	Y	Y
3 *Ose*	N	N	Y	Y	N	N	N
4 *Doolittle*	N	N	Y	Y	N	Y	Y
5 Matsui	Y	Y	Y	Y	Y	N	N
6 Woolsey	Y	Y	Y	Y	Y	N	N
7 Miller, George	Y	Y	Y	Y	Y	N	N
8 Pelosi	Y	Y	Y	Y	Y	N	N
9 Lee	Y	Y	Y	N	Y	N	N
10 Tauscher	Y	Y	Y	Y	Y	N	N
11 *Pombo*	N	N	Y	N	N	N	N
12 Lantos	Y	Y	Y	Y	Y	N	N
13 Stark	Y	Y	Y	Y	Y	N	N
14 Eshoo	Y	Y	Y	Y	Y	N	N
15 Honda	Y	Y	Y	Y	Y	N	N
16 Lofgren	Y	Y	Y	Y	Y	N	N
17 Farr	Y	Y	Y	Y	Y	N	N
18 Condit	Y	Y	?	Y	Y	N	N
19 *Radanovich*	N	N	Y	N	Y	N	N
20 Dooley	Y	Y	Y	Y	Y	N	N
21 *Thomas*	N	N	Y	N	N	N	N
22 Capps	Y	Y	Y	Y	Y	N	N
23 *Gallegly*	N	N	Y	N	Y	Y	Y
24 Sherman	Y	Y	Y	Y	Y	N	N
25 *McKeon*	N	N	Y	N	N	N	N
26 Berman	Y	Y	Y	Y	Y	N	N
27 Schiff	Y	Y	Y	Y	Y	N	N
28 *Dreier*	N	N	Y	N	N	N	N
29 Waxman	Y	Y	Y	Y	Y	N	N
30 Becerra	Y	Y	Y	Y	Y	N	N
31 Solis	Y	Y	Y	Y	Y	N	N
32 Watson	Y	Y	Y	Y	Y	N	N
33 Roybal-Allard	Y	Y	Y	Y	Y	N	N
34 Napolitano	Y	Y	Y	Y	Y	N	N
35 Waters	Y	Y	N	Y	Y	N	N
36 Harman	Y	Y	Y	Y	Y	Y	Y
37 Millender-McD.	Y	Y	Y	Y	Y	N	N
38 *Horn*	Y	Y	Y	Y	N	N	N

	332	333	334	335	336	337	338
39 *Royce*	N	N	Y	Y	N	Y	Y
40 *Lewis*	N	N	Y	N	N	N	N
41 *Miller, Gary*	N	N	Y	Y	N	N	Y
42 Baca	Y	Y	Y	Y	Y	N	N
43 *Calvert*	N	N	Y	N	N	N	N
44 *Bono*	Y	Y	Y	N	N	N	N
45 *Rohrabacher*	N	N	Y	Y	N	Y	Y
46 Sanchez	Y	Y	Y	Y	Y	N	N
47 *Cox*	N	N	Y	Y	?	N	Y
48 *Issa*	Y	N	Y	N	N	N	Y
49 Davis	Y	Y	Y	Y	Y	N	N
50 Filner	Y	Y	Y	Y	Y	N	N
51 *Cunningham*	N	N	Y	N	Y	Y	Y
52 *Hunter*	N	N	Y	Y	N	N	N
COLORADO							
1 DeGette	Y	Y	Y	Y	Y	N	N
2 Udall	Y	Y	Y	Y	Y	N	N
3 *McInnis*	N	N	Y	N	Y	Y	Y
4 *Schaffer*	N	N	Y	N	N	Y	Y
5 *Hefley*	N	N	Y	N	Y	Y	Y
6 *Tancredo*	N	N	Y	?	?	?	?
CONNECTICUT							
1 Larson	Y	Y	Y	Y	Y	N	N
2 *Simmons*	Y	N	Y	Y	N	Y	Y
3 DeLauro	Y	Y	Y	Y	Y	N	N
4 *Shays*	Y	Y	Y	Y	N	N	Y
5 Maloney	N	N	Y	Y	Y	N	N
6 *Johnson*	Y	Y	Y	Y	Y	N	N
DELAWARE							
AL *Castle*	Y	N	Y	N	Y	Y	Y
FLORIDA							
1 *Miller, J.*	N	N	N	Y	N	Y	Y
2 Boyd	Y	Y	Y	Y	Y	N	N
3 Brown	Y	N	Y	Y	Y	N	N
4 *Crenshaw*	N	N	Y	Y	Y	N	N
5 Thurman	Y	Y	Y	Y	Y	N	N
6 *Stearns*	?	?	?	?	?	?	?
7 *Mica*	N	N	Y	N	N	N	N
8 *Keller*	N	N	Y	N	N	Y	Y
9 *Bilirakis*	N	N	Y	N	Y	N	N
10 *Young*	N	N	Y	?	N	N	N
11 Davis	N	N	Y	N	N	N	N
12 *Putnam*	N	N	Y	N	N	N	N
13 *Miller, D.*	N	N	Y	N	Y	Y	Y
14 *Goss*	N	N	Y	N	N	N	N
15 *Weldon*	N	N	Y	N	N	Y	Y
16 *Foley*	N	N	Y	N	Y	Y	Y
17 Meek	N	N	?	Y	N	N	N
18 *Ros-Lehtinen*	N	N	Y	Y	Y	N	N
19 Wexler	N	N	Y	Y	Y	N	N
20 Deutsch	N	N	Y	Y	Y	N	N
21 *Diaz-Balart*	N	N	Y	N	N	N	N
22 *Shaw*	N	N	Y	N	N	N	N
23 Hastings	N	N	Y	N	Y	N	N
GEORGIA							
1 *Kingston*	N	N	Y	Y	N	N	N
2 Bishop	Y	Y	Y	?	Y	N	N
3 *Collins*	N	N	Y	N	Y	Y	Y
4 McKinney	Y	Y	Y	N	Y	N	N
5 Lewis	Y	Y	Y	Y	Y	N	N
6 *Isakson*	N	N	Y	N	N	N	N
7 *Barr*	N	N	Y	N	Y	Y	Y
8 *Chambliss*	N	N	Y	Y	Y	Y	Y
9 *Deal*	N	N	Y	N	N	Y	Y
10 *Norwood*	N	N	Y	N	N	Y	Y
11 *Linder*	N	N	Y	N	Y	Y	Y
HAWAII							
1 Abercrombie	Y	Y	Y	Y	Y	N	N
2 Mink	Y	Y	Y	Y	Y	N	N
IDAHO							
1 *Otter*	Y	Y	Y	Y	N	Y	Y
2 *Simpson*	N	N	Y	Y	N	N	N
ILLINOIS							
1 Rush	Y	Y	Y	Y	Y	N	N
2 Jackson	Y	Y	Y	Y	Y	N	N
3 Lipinski	N	N	Y	?	Y	N	N
4 Gutierrez	Y	N	Y	Y	Y	N	N
5 Blagojevich	Y	N	Y	Y	Y	N	N
6 *Hyde*	N	N	Y	N	Y	Y	Y
7 Davis	Y	Y	Y	Y	Y	N	N
8 *Crane*	N	N	Y	N	Y	Y	Y
9 Schakowsky	Y	Y	Y	N	Y	N	N
10 *Kirk*	Y	N	Y	N	Y	Y	Y
11 *Weller*	N	Y	Y	Y	Y	Y	Y
12 Costello	Y	Y	Y	Y	Y	N	N
13 *Biggert*	Y	Y	Y	Y	N	Y	N

ND Northern Democrats   SD Southern Democrats

	332	333	334	335	336	337	338
14 ***Hastert***							
15 Johnson	Y	Y	Y	Y	N	Y	N
16 ***Manzullo***	Y	Y	Y	Y	N	Y	Y
17 Evans	Y	Y	Y	Y	Y	Y	N
18 ***LaHood***	Y	Y	Y	Y	Y	N	N
19 Phelps	Y	Y	Y	Y	Y	Y	Y
20 ***Shimkus***	Y	Y	Y	Y	Y	Y	Y
INDIANA							
1 Visclosky	Y	Y	Y	Y	Y	N	N
2 ***Pence***	N	N	Y	Y	N	Y	Y
3 Roemer	Y	Y	Y	Y	Y	N	Y
4 ***Souder***	N	N	Y	Y	N	Y	N
5 ***Buyer***	N	N	Y	Y	N	Y	Y
6 ***Burton***	N	N	Y	?	N	Y	Y
7 ***Kerns***	N	N	Y	Y	N	N	Y
8 ***Hostettler***	Y	N	Y	Y	N	Y	Y
9 Hill	Y	Y	?	Y	Y	Y	Y
10 Carson	Y	Y	Y	Y	Y	N	N
IOWA							
1 ***Leach***	Y	Y	Y	Y	Y	N	N
2 ***Nussle***	Y	Y	Y	Y	N	N	Y
3 Boswell	Y	Y	Y	Y	Y	Y	Y
4 ***Ganske***	Y	Y	Y	Y	Y	Y	N
5 ***Latham***	Y	Y	Y	Y	N	N	N
KANSAS							
1 ***Moran***	Y	Y	Y	Y	N	Y	Y
2 ***Ryun***	N	N	Y	Y	N	Y	Y
3 Moore	Y	Y	Y	Y	Y	Y	N
4 ***Tiahrt***	Y	N	Y	Y	N	Y	Y
KENTUCKY							
1 ***Whitfield***	Y	N	Y	Y	N	Y	Y
2 ***Lewis***	N	N	Y	Y	Y	Y	N
3 ***Northup***	N	N	Y	Y	N	N	N
4 Lucas	N	N	Y	Y	Y	Y	Y
5 ***Rogers***	N	N	Y	Y	N	Y	N
6 ***Fletcher***	N	N	Y	Y	Y	Y	N
LOUISIANA							
1 ***Vitter***	N	N	Y	Y	N	Y	Y
2 Jefferson	Y	Y	Y	Y	Y	N	N
3 ***Tauzin***	N	N	Y	Y	N	N	Y
4 ***McCrery***	N	N	Y	Y	N	N	N
5 ***Cooksey***	Y	N	Y	Y	N	Y	Y
6 ***Baker***	N	N	Y	Y	Y	N	Y
7 John	Y	Y	Y	Y	Y	Y	N
MAINE							
1 Allen	Y	Y	Y	Y	Y	N	N
2 Baldacci	Y	Y	Y	Y	Y	N	N
MARYLAND							
1 ***Gilchrest***	Y	N	Y	Y	N	N	N
2 ***Ehrlich***	N	N	Y	?	Y	Y	Y
3 Cardin	Y	N	Y	Y	Y	N	N
4 Wynn	Y	Y	Y	Y	Y	N	N
5 Hoyer	Y	Y	Y	Y	Y	N	N
6 ***Bartlett***	Y	N	Y	Y	N	Y	Y
7 Cummings	Y	Y	Y	Y	Y	N	N
8 ***Morella***	Y	Y	Y	Y	Y	N	N
MASSACHUSETTS							
1 Olver	Y	Y	Y	Y	Y	N	N
2 Neal	Y	Y	Y	Y	Y	N	N
3 McGovern	Y	Y	Y	Y	Y	N	N
4 Frank	Y	Y	Y	Y	Y	N	N
5 Meehan	Y	Y	Y	Y	Y	N	N
6 Tierney	Y	Y	Y	Y	Y	N	N
7 Markey	Y	Y	Y	Y	Y	N	N
8 Capuano	Y	Y	Y	Y	Y	N	N
9 Lynch	Y	Y	Y	Y	Y	N	N
10 Delahunt	Y	Y	Y	Y	?	N	N
MICHIGAN							
1 Stupak	Y	Y	Y	Y	Y	N	N
2 ***Hoekstra***	N	N	Y	Y	N	Y	Y
3 ***Ehlers***	Y	N	Y	Y	N	N	N
4 ***Camp***	Y	N	Y	Y	N	Y	N
5 Barcia	Y	Y	Y	Y	Y	Y	Y
6 ***Upton***	Y	Y	Y	Y	N	Y	Y
7 ***Smith***	Y	N	Y	Y	Y	Y	Y
8 ***Rogers***	N	N	Y	Y	N	Y	N
9 Kildee	Y	Y	Y	Y	Y	N	N
10 Bonior	?	?	?	?	?	?	?
11 ***Knollenberg***	N	N	Y	Y	N	N	N
12 Levin	Y	Y	Y	Y	Y	N	N
13 Rivers	Y	Y	Y	Y	Y	N	N
14 Conyers	Y	Y	Y	Y	Y	N	N
15 Kilpatrick	Y	Y	Y	Y	Y	N	N
16 Dingell	N	Y	Y	Y	Y	N	N

	332	333	334	335	336	337	338
MINNESOTA							
1 ***Gutknecht***	N	N	Y	Y	Y	Y	Y
2 ***Kennedy***	N	N	Y	Y	N	Y	Y
3 ***Ramstad***	Y	Y	Y	Y	N	Y	Y
4 McCollum	Y	Y	Y	Y	Y	N	N
5 Sabo	Y	Y	Y	Y	Y	N	N
6 Luther	Y	Y	Y	Y	Y	Y	Y
7 Peterson	Y	Y	Y	Y	Y	N	Y
8 Oberstar	Y	Y	Y	Y	Y	N	N
MISSISSIPPI							
1 ***Wicker***	N	N	Y	Y	N	Y	Y
2 Thompson	Y	Y	Y	Y	Y	N	N
3 ***Pickering***	N	N	Y	Y	N	Y	Y
4 Shows	Y	Y	Y	Y	Y	Y	Y
5 Taylor	Y	Y	Y	Y	Y	Y	Y
MISSOURI							
1 Clay	Y	Y	?	?	Y	N	N
2 ***Akin***	N	N	Y	Y	N	Y	Y
3 Gephardt	N	N	Y	Y	Y	N	N
4 Skelton	N	N	Y	Y	Y	N	N
5 McCarthy	Y	Y	Y	Y	Y	N	N
6 ***Graves***	Y	Y	Y	Y	Y	N	Y
7 ***Blunt***	N	N	Y	Y	N	N	Y
8 ***Emerson***	Y	Y	Y	Y	Y	N	N
9 ***Hulshof***	N	N	Y	Y	N	Y	N
MONTANA							
AL ***Rehberg***	Y	Y	Y	Y	N	Y	Y
NEBRASKA							
1 ***Bereuter***	Y	N	Y	Y	N	Y	Y
2 ***Terry***	Y	N	Y	Y	N	Y	Y
3 ***Osborne***	Y	Y	Y	Y	N	Y	N
NEVADA							
1 Berkley	N	N	Y	Y	Y	N	N
2 ***Gibbons***	N	N	Y	Y	N	Y	Y
NEW HAMPSHIRE							
1 ***Sununu***	Y	N	Y	Y	N	Y	N
2 ***Bass***	Y	N	Y	Y	N	Y	N
NEW JERSEY							
1 Andrews	N	N	Y	Y	Y	N	N
2 ***LoBiondo***	N	N	Y	Y	Y	Y	N
3 ***Saxton***	N	N	Y	Y	Y	Y	N
4 ***Smith***	N	N	Y	Y	Y	Y	N
5 ***Roukema***	N	N	Y	Y	Y	Y	Y
6 Pallone	N	N	Y	Y	Y	N	N
7 ***Ferguson***	N	N	Y	Y	Y	Y	N
8 Pascrell	N	N	Y	Y	Y	N	N
9 Rothman	N	N	Y	Y	Y	N	N
10 Payne	Y	Y	Y	Y	Y	N	N
11 ***Frelinghuysen***	N	N	Y	Y	N	N	N
12 Holt	Y	Y	Y	Y	Y	N	N
13 Menendez	N	N	Y	Y	Y	N	N
NEW MEXICO							
1 ***Wilson***	N	N	Y	Y	N	N	N
2 ***Skeen***	N	N	Y	Y	N	N	N
3 Udall	Y	Y	Y	Y	Y	N	N
NEW YORK							
1 ***Grucci***	Y	N	Y	Y	Y	N	N
2 Israel	Y	Y	Y	Y	Y	N	N
3 ***King***	N	N	Y	Y	Y	N	N
4 McCarthy	Y	Y	Y	Y	Y	N	N
5 Ackerman	N	N	Y	Y	Y	N	N
6 Meeks	Y	Y	Y	Y	Y	N	N
7 Crowley	Y	Y	Y	Y	Y	N	N
8 Nadler	Y	Y	Y	Y	Y	N	N
9 Weiner	Y	Y	Y	Y	Y	N	N
10 Towns	Y	Y	Y	Y	Y	N	N
11 Owens	Y	Y	Y	Y	Y	N	N
12 Velázquez	Y	Y	Y	Y	Y	N	N
13 ***Fossella***	N	N	Y	Y	Y	N	Y
14 Maloney	Y	Y	Y	Y	Y	N	N
15 Rangel	Y	Y	Y	Y	Y	N	N
16 Serrano	Y	Y	Y	Y	Y	N	N
17 Engel	N	N	Y	?	Y	N	N
18 Lowey	Y	Y	Y	Y	Y	N	N
19 ***Kelly***	N	N	Y	Y	Y	Y	N
20 ***Gilman***	N	N	Y	Y	Y	Y	N
21 McNulty	Y	Y	Y	Y	Y	N	N
22 ***Sweeney***	N	N	Y	Y	Y	N	N
23 ***Boehlert***	Y	N	Y	Y	Y	N	N
24 ***McHugh***	Y	N	Y	Y	Y	N	N
25 ***Walsh***	N	N	Y	Y	Y	N	N
26 Hinchey	Y	Y	Y	Y	Y	N	N
27 ***Reynolds***	N	N	Y	Y	N	N	Y
28 Slaughter	Y	Y	Y	Y	Y	N	?
29 LaFalce	Y	Y	Y	Y	Y	N	N

	332	333	334	335	336	337	338
30 ***Quinn***	N	N	Y	Y	Y	N	N
31 ***Houghton***	Y	N	Y	Y	N	N	N
NORTH CAROLINA							
1 Clayton	Y	Y	Y	Y	Y	N	N
2 Etheridge	Y	N	Y	Y	Y	N	N
3 ***Jones***	N	N	Y	Y	Y	Y	Y
4 Price	Y	Y	Y	Y	Y	N	N
5 ***Burr***	N	N	Y	Y	N	Y	Y
6 ***Coble***	N	N	Y	Y	N	Y	Y
7 McIntyre	Y	N	Y	Y	Y	Y	N
8 ***Hayes***	N	N	Y	Y	Y	Y	Y
9 ***Myrick***	N	N	Y	Y	N	Y	Y
10 ***Ballenger***	N	N	Y	Y	N	Y	Y
11 ***Taylor***	N	N	Y	Y	N	Y	Y
12 Watt	Y	Y	Y	Y	Y	N	N
NORTH DAKOTA							
AL Pomeroy	Y	Y	Y	Y	Y	N	N
OHIO							
1 ***Chabot***	N	N	Y	Y	N	Y	Y
2 ***Portman***	N	N	Y	Y	N	N	N
3 Hall	Y	Y	Y	?	Y	N	N
4 ***Oxley***	N	N	Y	Y	N	Y	Y
5 ***Gillmor***	N	N	Y	Y	N	N	N
6 Strickland	Y	Y	Y	Y	Y	N	N
7 ***Hobson***	N	N	Y	Y	N	N	N
8 ***Boehner***	N	N	Y	Y	N	N	N
9 Kaptur	Y	Y	Y	?	Y	N	N
10 Kucinich	Y	Y	Y	N	Y	N	N
11 Jones	Y	Y	Y	Y	Y	N	N
12 ***Tiberi***	Y	Y	Y	Y	N	Y	Y
13 Brown	Y	Y	Y	Y	Y	N	N
14 Sawyer	Y	Y	Y	Y	Y	N	N
15 ***Pryce***	N	N	Y	Y	N	N	N
16 ***Regula***	N	N	Y	Y	N	N	N
17 Traficant	?	?	?	?	?	?	?
18 ***Ney***	Y	N	Y	Y	N	Y	N
19 ***LaTourette***	N	N	Y	Y	Y	N	N
OKLAHOMA							
1 ***Sullivan***	N	N	Y	Y	N	Y	Y
2 Carson	Y	Y	Y	Y	Y	N	N
3 ***Watkins***	N	N	Y	Y	N	N	N
4 ***Watts***	N	N	Y	Y	N	Y	Y
5 ***Istook***	N	N	Y	Y	N	N	N
6 ***Lucas***	N	N	Y	Y	N	N	N
OREGON							
1 Wu	N	N	Y	Y	Y	N	N
2 ***Walden***	N	N	Y	Y	N	Y	Y
3 Blumenauer	Y	Y	Y	Y	Y	N	N
4 DeFazio	+	+	+	Y	Y	Y	N
5 Hooley	Y	Y	Y	Y	Y	N	N
PENNSYLVANIA							
1 Brady	Y	Y	Y	Y	Y	N	N
2 Fattah	Y	Y	Y	Y	Y	N	N
3 Borski	Y	Y	Y	Y	Y	N	N
4 ***Hart***	N	N	Y	Y	Y	Y	Y
5 ***Peterson***	Y	Y	Y	Y	N	N	Y
6 Holden	Y	N	Y	Y	Y	N	N
7 ***Weldon***	Y	N	Y	Y	Y	Y	Y
8 ***Greenwood***	Y	N	Y	Y	N	N	N
9 ***Shuster, Bill***	N	N	Y	Y	N	Y	N
10 ***Sherwood***	N	N	Y	Y	N	N	N
11 Kanjorski	Y	N	Y	Y	Y	N	N
12 Murtha	Y	N	Y	Y	Y	N	N
13 Hoeffel	Y	Y	Y	Y	Y	N	N
14 Coyne	Y	Y	Y	Y	Y	N	N
15 ***Toomey***	N	N	Y	Y	N	Y	Y
16 ***Pitts***	N	N	Y	Y	N	Y	Y
17 ***Gekas***	N	N	Y	Y	Y	N	N
18 Doyle	Y	Y	Y	Y	Y	N	N
19 ***Platts***	Y	N	Y	?	Y	Y	Y
20 Mascara	Y	Y	Y	Y	Y	N	N
21 ***English***	Y	N	Y	Y	Y	N	Y
RHODE ISLAND							
1 Kennedy	N	N	Y	Y	Y	N	N
2 Langevin	Y	Y	Y	Y	Y	N	N
SOUTH CAROLINA							
1 ***Brown***	Y	N	Y	Y	N	N	N
2 ***Wilson***	N	N	Y	Y	N	Y	Y
3 ***Graham***	N	N	Y	Y	N	Y	Y
4 ***DeMint***	N	N	Y	Y	N	Y	Y
5 Spratt	Y	N	Y	Y	Y	N	N
6 Clyburn	Y	Y	Y	Y	Y	N	N
SOUTH DAKOTA							
AL ***Thune***	Y	Y	Y	Y	N	Y	N

	332	333	334	335	336	337	338
TENNESSEE							
1 ***Jenkins***	N	N	Y	Y	N	Y	Y
2 ***Duncan***	N	N	Y	Y	N	Y	Y
3 ***Wamp***	N	N	Y	Y	N	Y	Y
4 ***Hilleary***	N	N	Y	Y	N	Y	Y
5 Clement	Y	Y	Y	Y	Y	Y	Y
6 Gordon	Y	Y	Y	Y	Y	Y	N
7 ***Bryant***	N	N	Y	Y	N	Y	Y
8 Tanner	Y	Y	Y	Y	Y	Y	Y
9 Ford	Y	Y	Y	Y	Y	N	N
TEXAS							
1 Sandlin	Y	Y	Y	Y	Y	N	N
2 Turner	Y	Y	Y	Y	Y	Y	Y
3 ***Johnson, Sam***	N	N	Y	?	N	Y	Y
4 Hall	Y	Y	Y	Y	Y	Y	Y
5 ***Sessions***	N	N	Y	Y	N	Y	Y
6 ***Barton***	N	N	Y	Y	N	N	Y
7 ***Culberson***	N	N	Y	Y	N	N	Y
8 ***Brady***	Y	N	Y	Y	N	N	Y
9 Lampson	Y	Y	Y	Y	Y	N	N
10 Doggett	Y	Y	Y	Y	Y	Y	Y
11 Edwards	Y	Y	Y	Y	Y	N	N
12 ***Granger***	N	N	Y	Y	Y	N	N
13 ***Thornberry***	Y	N	Y	Y	N	N	Y
14 ***Paul***	Y	Y	N	?	N	Y	Y
15 Hinojosa	Y	Y	Y	Y	Y	N	N
16 Reyes	Y	N	Y	Y	Y	N	N
17 Stenholm	Y	Y	Y	Y	Y	Y	Y
18 Jackson-Lee	Y	Y	Y	Y	Y	N	N
19 ***Combest***	Y	N	Y	Y	N	Y	N
20 Gonzalez	Y	Y	Y	Y	Y	N	N
21 ***Smith***	N	N	Y	Y	N	Y	Y
22 ***DeLay***	N	N	Y	Y	N	N	N
23 ***Bonilla***	N	N	Y	Y	N	N	N
24 Frost	Y	Y	Y	Y	Y	N	N
25 Bentsen	Y	Y	Y	Y	Y	N	N
26 ***Armey***	N	N	Y	Y	N	Y	Y
27 Ortiz	Y	N	Y	Y	Y	N	N
28 Rodriguez	Y	Y	Y	Y	Y	N	N
29 Green	N	N	Y	Y	Y	Y	N
30 Johnson, E.B.	Y	Y	Y	Y	Y	N	N
UTAH							
1 ***Hansen***	?	N	Y	Y	Y	Y	Y
2 Matheson	Y	Y	Y	Y	Y	Y	Y
3 ***Cannon***	N	N	Y	Y	?	Y	Y
VERMONT							
AL *Sanders*	Y	Y	Y	Y	Y	N	N
VIRGINIA							
1 ***Davis, Jo Ann***	N	N	Y	Y	Y	Y	Y
2 ***Schrock***	N	N	Y	Y	N	N	Y
3 Scott	Y	Y	Y	Y	Y	Y	N
4 ***Forbes***	N	N	Y	Y	Y	Y	Y
5 *Goode*	N	N	Y	Y	N	Y	Y
6 ***Goodlatte***	–	N	Y	Y	N	Y	Y
7 ***Cantor***	N	N	Y	Y	N	N	Y
8 Moran	Y	Y	Y	Y	Y	N	N
9 Boucher	Y	Y	Y	Y	Y	N	N
10 ***Wolf***	N	N	Y	Y	Y	N	N
11 ***Davis, T.***	N	N	Y	Y	Y	N	N
WASHINGTON							
1 Inslee	Y	Y	Y	Y	Y	N	N
2 Larsen	Y	Y	Y	Y	Y	N	N
3 Baird	Y	Y	Y	Y	Y	N	N
4 ***Hastings***	N	N	Y	Y	N	Y	N
5 ***Nethercutt***	Y	N	Y	Y	N	Y	N
6 Dicks	Y	Y	Y	Y	Y	N	N
7 McDermott	Y	Y	Y	Y	Y	N	N
8 ***Dunn***	N	N	Y	Y	N	N	N
9 Smith	Y	Y	Y	Y	Y	Y	Y
WEST VIRGINIA							
1 Mollohan	Y	Y	Y	Y	Y	N	N
2 ***Capito***	N	N	Y	Y	Y	N	N
3 Rahall	Y	Y	Y	Y	Y	N	N
WISCONSIN							
1 ***Ryan***	Y	Y	Y	Y	N	Y	Y
2 Baldwin	Y	Y	Y	Y	Y	N	N
3 Kind	Y	Y	Y	Y	Y	Y	N
4 Kleczka	Y	Y	?	Y	Y	N	N
5 Barrett	Y	Y	Y	Y	Y	Y	N
6 ***Petri***	N	N	Y	Y	Y	Y	Y
7 Obey	Y	Y	Y	Y	Y	N	N
8 ***Green***	N	N	Y	Y	Y	Y	N
9 ***Sensenbrenner***	N	N	Y	Y	N	Y	Y
WYOMING							
AL ***Cubin***	N	N	Y	Y	N	Y	Y

Southern states - Ala., Ark., Fla., Ga., Ky., La., Miss., N.C., Okla., S.C., Tenn., Texas, Va.

Key

Y	Voted for (yea).
#	Paired for.
+	Announced for.
N	Voted against (nay).
X	Paired against.
–	Announced against.
P	Voted "present."
C	Voted "present" to avoid possible conflict of interest.
?	Did not vote or otherwise make a position known.

Democrats   **Republicans**
Independents

339. HR 5120. Fiscal 2003 Treasury-Postal Service Appropriations/ Pension Protection. Sanders, I-Vt., amendment that would prohibit the IRS from using funds in the bill to implement tax laws that provide benefits to private companies if those companies' pension plans violate federal pension, age discrimination and other tax laws. Adopted 308-121: R 102-116; D 204-5 (ND 152-3, SD 52-2); I 2-0. July 24, 2002.

340. HR 4965. "Partial Birth" Abortion Ban/Rule. Adoption of the resolution (H Res 498) to provide for House floor consideration of the bill that would ban the medical procedure described by opponents as "partial birth" abortion. Adopted 248-177: R 207-8; D 40-168 (ND 24-130, SD 16-38); I 1-1. July 24, 2002.

341. HR 5120. Fiscal 2003 Treasury-Postal Service Appropriations/ Passage. Passage of the bill that would provide $35.1 billion in fiscal 2003 for the Treasury Department, U.S. Postal Service, various offices of the Executive Office of the President and certain independent agencies, a $1.1 billion increase over fiscal 2002 spending. The total includes $9.9 billion for the IRS and $3.1 billion for the Customs Service. The measure provides that all federal employees would receive a 4.1 percent pay raise. Passed 308-121: R 148-71; D 159-49 (ND 123-31, SD 36-18); I 1-1. July 24, 2002.

342. HR 4965. "Partial Birth" Abortion Ban/Recommit. Baldwin, D-Wis., motion to recommit the bill to the House Judiciary Committee with instructions that it be reported back promptly with language that would allow for consideration of the health of the woman. Motion rejected 187-241: R 19-199; D 167-41 (ND 129-25, SD 38-16); I 1-1. July 24, 2002.

343. HR 4965. "Partial Birth" Abortion Ban/Passage. Passage of the bill that would ban a procedure described by opponents as "partial birth" abortion. It would allow the procedure only when necessary to save a woman's life. Those who perform the procedure for other reasons would face fines and up to two years in prison; the woman would not be criminally liable. The bill includes congressional findings in support of the constitutionality of the measure. Passed 274-151: R 208-9; D 65-141 (ND 37-115, SD 28-26); I 1-1. A "yea" was a vote in support of the president's position. July 24, 2002.

344. H Con Res 188. Falun Gong Persecution/Adoption. Ros-Lehtinen, R-Fla., motion to suspend the rules and adopt the resolution that would urge the government of the People's Republic of China to cease persecution of Falun Gong practitioners. Motion agreed to 420-0: R 214-0; D 204-0 (ND 150-0, SD 54-0); I 2-0. A two-thirds majority of those present and voting (280 in this case) is required for adoption under suspension of the rules. July 24, 2002.

345. H Res 495. Traficant Expulsion/Motion to Postpone. LaTourette, R-Ohio, motion to postpone consideration until Sept. 4, 2002, of the resolution that would expel Rep. James A. Traficant Jr., D-Ohio. Motion rejected 146-285: R 98-121; D 47-163 (ND 32-124, SD 15-39); I 1-1. July 24, 2002.

346. H Res 495. Traficant Expulsion/Adoption. Adoption of the resolution that would expel Rep. James A. Traficant Jr., D-Ohio, from the House of Representatives. Adopted 420-1: R 211-0; D 207-1 (ND 154-1, SD 53-0); I 2-0. July 24, 2002.

	339	340	341	342	343	344	345	346
ALABAMA								
1 *Callahan*	N	Y	Y	N	Y	Y	Y	P
2 *Everett*	N	Y	N	N	Y	Y	Y	Y
3 *Riley*	N	Y	N	N	Y	Y	Y	Y
4 *Aderholt*	N	Y	Y	N	Y	Y	Y	Y
5 Cramer	Y	Y	Y	N	Y	Y	N	Y
6 *Bachus*	Y	Y	N	N	Y	?	Y	Y
7 Hilliard	Y	N	Y	N	Y	Y	N	Y
ALASKA								
AL *Young*	Y	Y	Y	N	Y	Y	Y	P
ARIZONA								
1 *Flake*	N	Y	N	N	Y	Y	N	Y
2 Pastor	Y	N	Y	Y	N	Y	N	Y
3 *Stump*	Y	Y	N	N	Y	Y	N	Y
4 *Shadegg*	Y	Y	N	N	Y	Y	N	Y
5 *Kolbe*	N	Y	Y	N	Y	Y	N	Y
6 *Hayworth*	N	Y	N	N	Y	Y	N	Y
ARKANSAS								
1 Berry	Y	Y	N	N	Y	Y	N	Y
2 Snyder	Y	N	Y	N	N	Y	N	Y
3 *Boozman*	N	Y	Y	N	Y	Y	N	Y
4 Ross	Y	Y	N	N	Y	Y	N	Y
CALIFORNIA								
1 Thompson	Y	N	Y	N	Y	Y	N	Y
2 *Herger*	N	Y	N	N	Y	Y	Y	Y
3 *Ose*	Y	N	Y	N	Y	Y	Y	Y
4 *Doolittle*	N	Y	N	N	Y	Y	Y	Y
5 Matsui	Y	N	Y	N	Y	Y	N	Y
6 Woolsey	Y	N	Y	N	Y	Y	N	Y
7 Miller, George	Y	N	Y	N	Y	Y	N	Y
8 Pelosi	Y	N	Y	Y	N	Y	N	Y
9 Lee	Y	N	Y	N	Y	Y	N	Y
10 Tauscher	Y	N	Y	N	Y	Y	N	Y
11 *Pombo*	N	Y	N	Y	N	Y	N	Y
12 Lantos	Y	N	Y	N	Y	Y	N	Y
13 Stark	Y	N	Y	N	Y	Y	N	Y
14 Eshoo	Y	N	Y	N	Y	Y	N	Y
15 Honda	Y	N	Y	N	Y	Y	N	Y
16 Lofgren	Y	N	Y	N	Y	Y	N	Y
17 Farr	Y	N	Y	N	Y	Y	N	Y
18 Condit	Y	?	?	?	?	?	Y	N
19 *Radanovich*	Y	Y	N	Y	N	Y	N	Y
20 Dooley	N	N	Y	N	Y	N	N	Y
21 *Thomas*	N	Y	Y	Y	Y	Y	N	Y
22 Capps	Y	N	Y	N	Y	Y	N	Y
23 *Gallegly*	N	Y	Y	N	Y	Y	Y	Y
24 Sherman	Y	N	Y	N	Y	Y	N	Y
25 *McKeon*	N	Y	Y	N	Y	Y	Y	Y
26 Berman	Y	N	Y	N	Y	Y	N	Y
27 Schiff	Y	N	N	Y	N	Y	N	Y
28 *Dreier*	N	Y	Y	N	Y	Y	Y	Y
29 Waxman	Y	N	Y	N	Y	Y	N	Y
30 Becerra	Y	N	Y	N	Y	Y	N	Y
31 Solis	Y	N	Y	N	Y	Y	N	Y
32 Watson	Y	N	Y	N	Y	Y	N	Y
33 Roybal-Allard	Y	N	Y	N	Y	Y	N	Y
34 Napolitano	Y	N	N	Y	N	Y	N	Y
35 Waters	Y	N	Y	N	Y	Y	Y	Y
36 Harman	Y	N	Y	N	Y	Y	N	Y
37 Millender-McD.	Y	N	Y	N	Y	Y	N	Y
38 *Horn*	Y	N	Y	N	Y	Y	Y	Y

	339	340	341	342	343	344	345	346
39 *Royce*	Y	Y	N	N	Y	Y	N	Y
40 *Lewis*	Y	Y	N	Y	Y	Y	Y	Y
41 *Miller, Gary*	N	Y	Y	N	Y	Y	Y	Y
42 Baca	Y	N	Y	N	Y	N	Y	Y
43 *Calvert*	N	Y	N	Y	Y	Y	Y	Y
44 *Bono*	N	Y	Y	N	Y	Y	Y	N
45 *Rohrabacher*	Y	Y	N	Y	N	Y	Y	N
46 Sanchez	Y	N	Y	N	Y	Y	N	Y
47 *Cox*	Y	Y	N	Y	Y	Y	N	Y
48 *Issa*	N	Y	N	Y	?	Y	Y	Y
49 Davis	Y	N	N	Y	N	Y	N	Y
50 Filner	Y	N	Y	N	Y	N	Y	Y
51 *Cunningham*	Y	Y	N	+	Y	Y	Y	Y
52 *Hunter*	Y	Y	N	N	Y	Y	Y	Y
COLORADO								
1 DeGette	Y	N	Y	N	Y	N	Y	Y
2 Udall	Y	N	Y	N	Y	N	Y	Y
3 *McInnis*	Y	N	N	N	Y	Y	N	Y
4 *Schaffer*	Y	N	N	Y	Y	Y	Y	Y
5 *Hefley*	Y	N	N	N	Y	Y	N	Y
6 *Tancredo*	?	Y	N	N	Y	Y	Y	Y
CONNECTICUT								
1 Larson	Y	N	Y	N	Y	N	Y	Y
2 *Simmons*	Y	N	Y	N	Y	N	Y	Y
3 DeLauro	Y	N	Y	N	Y	N	Y	Y
4 *Shays*	N	Y	Y	Y	N	Y	N	Y
5 Maloney	Y	N	Y	N	Y	Y	N	Y
6 *Johnson*	N	N	Y	Y	N	Y	N	Y
DELAWARE								
AL *Castle*	Y	Y	Y	Y	Y	Y	N	Y
FLORIDA								
1 *Miller, J.*	N	Y	N	N	Y	Y	N	Y
2 Boyd	Y	N	Y	Y	Y	Y	N	Y
3 Brown	Y	N	Y	N	Y	Y	Y	Y
4 *Crenshaw*	N	Y	N	N	Y	Y	N	Y
5 Thurman	Y	N	N	Y	N	Y	N	Y
6 *Stearns*	?	?	?	?	?	?	?	?
7 *Mica*	N	Y	N	N	Y	Y	N	Y
8 *Keller*	N	Y	Y	N	Y	Y	N	Y
9 *Bilirakis*	Y	Y	N	Y	N	Y	Y	P
10 *Young*	Y	Y	Y	N	Y	Y	Y	Y
11 Davis	Y	N	Y	N	Y	Y	N	Y
12 *Putnam*	N	Y	Y	Y	Y	Y	Y	Y
13 *Miller, D.*	Y	Y	N	Y	Y	Y	Y	Y
14 *Goss*	Y	Y	N	N	Y	Y	Y	Y
15 *Weldon*	N	Y	N	N	Y	Y	Y	Y
16 *Foley*	Y	Y	N	N	Y	?	Y	Y
17 Meek	Y	N	Y	N	Y	Y	N	Y
18 *Ros-Lehtinen*	Y	Y	N	N	Y	Y	N	Y
19 Wexler	Y	N	Y	N	Y	Y	N	Y
20 Deutsch	Y	N	N	Y	N	Y	N	Y
21 *Diaz-Balart*	N	N	N	Y	Y	Y	Y	Y
22 *Shaw*	Y	Y	N	Y	Y	Y	Y	Y
23 Hastings	Y	N	Y	N	Y	Y	Y	Y
GEORGIA								
1 *Kingston*	Y	Y	N	Y	Y	Y	Y	Y
2 Bishop	Y	N	Y	Y	Y	Y	N	Y
3 *Collins*	N	Y	N	N	Y	Y	Y	Y
4 McKinney	Y	N	Y	N	Y	N	Y	Y
5 Lewis	Y	N	Y	N	Y	Y	N	Y
6 *Isakson*	N	Y	Y	N	Y	Y	N	Y
7 *Barr*	N	Y	N	N	Y	Y	Y	Y
8 *Chambliss*	N	Y	Y	N	Y	Y	Y	Y
9 *Deal*	N	Y	N	N	Y	Y	Y	Y
10 *Norwood*	N	Y	N	N	Y	Y	Y	Y
11 *Linder*	N	Y	Y	N	Y	Y	N	Y
HAWAII								
1 Abercrombie	Y	N	Y	N	Y	N	Y	Y
2 Mink	Y	N	Y	N	Y	Y	Y	Y
IDAHO								
1 *Otter*	N	Y	N	N	Y	Y	Y	P
2 *Simpson*	N	Y	Y	N	Y	Y	Y	P
ILLINOIS								
1 Rush	Y	N	Y	N	Y	Y	Y	Y
2 Jackson	Y	N	Y	N	Y	Y	Y	Y
3 Lipinski	Y	Y	Y	N	Y	N	Y	Y
4 Gutierrez	Y	N	Y	N	Y	N	N	Y
5 Blagojevich	Y	N	Y	N	Y	N	N	Y
6 *Hyde*	N	Y	N	Y	Y	Y	Y	Y
7 Davis	Y	N	Y	N	Y	Y	N	Y
8 *Crane*	N	N	N	Y	Y	Y	Y	Y
9 Schakowsky	Y	N	Y	N	Y	Y	N	Y
10 *Kirk*	N	Y	Y	Y	N	Y	N	Y
11 *Weller*	N	Y	Y	N	Y	Y	Y	Y
12 Costello	Y	Y	N	Y	N	Y	N	Y
13 *Biggert*	N	Y	Y	Y	Y	Y	N	Y

ND Northern Democrats   SD Southern Democrats

	339	340	341	342	343	344	345	346
14 ***Hastert***								
15 ***Johnson***	N	Y	N	N	Y	Y	N	Y
16 ***Manzullo***	Y	Y	Y	N	Y	Y	N	Y
17 Evans	Y	N	Y	Y	N	Y	N	Y
18 ***LaHood***	Y	Y	Y	N	Y	Y	N	Y
19 Phelps	Y	Y	N	N	?	Y	N	Y
20 ***Shimkus***	Y	Y	N	N	Y	Y	N	Y
INDIANA								
1 Visclosky	Y	N	Y	Y	Y	Y	N	Y
2 ***Pence***	N	Y	N	N	Y	Y	N	Y
3 Roemer	Y	Y	N	N	Y	Y	N	Y
4 ***Souder***	Y	Y	Y	N	Y	Y	N	Y
5 ***Buyer***	N	Y	Y	N	Y	Y	Y	Y
6 ***Burton***	N	Y	Y	N	Y	Y	Y	Y
7 ***Kerns***	N	Y	N	N	Y	Y	Y	Y
8 ***Hostettler***	N	Y	N	N	Y	Y	N	P
9 Hill	Y	N	N	Y	Y	Y	N	Y
10 Carson	Y	N	N	Y	N	Y	Y	Y
IOWA								
1 ***Leach***	Y	Y	Y	N	Y	Y	N	Y
2 ***Nussle***	Y	Y	Y	N	Y	Y	N	Y
3 Boswell	N	N	N	N	Y	Y	Y	Y
4 ***Ganske***	Y	Y	Y	N	Y	Y	N	Y
5 ***Latham***	Y	Y	Y	N	Y	Y	N	Y
KANSAS								
1 ***Moran***	N	Y	N	N	Y	Y	N	Y
2 ***Ryun***	Y	Y	N	N	Y	Y	Y	Y
3 Moore	Y	N	N	Y	N	Y	N	Y
4 ***Tiahrt***	N	Y	Y	N	Y	Y	Y	Y
KENTUCKY								
1 ***Whitfield***	Y	?	Y	N	Y	Y	Y	Y
2 ***Lewis***	Y	Y	Y	N	Y	Y	Y	Y
3 ***Northup***	N	?	Y	N	Y	Y	N	Y
4 Lucas	N	Y	N	N	Y	Y	N	Y
5 ***Rogers***	Y	Y	Y	N	Y	Y	N	Y
6 ***Fletcher***	Y	Y	Y	N	Y	Y	N	Y
LOUISIANA								
1 ***Vitter***	N	Y	Y	N	Y	Y	N	Y
2 Jefferson	Y	N	Y	Y	Y	Y	N	Y
3 ***Tauzin***	N	Y	Y	N	Y	Y	Y	Y
4 ***McCrery***	N	Y	Y	N	Y	Y	N	Y
5 ***Cooksey***	Y	Y	Y	N	Y	Y	Y	Y
6 ***Baker***	Y	Y	N	N	Y	Y	N	Y
7 John	Y	Y	Y	N	Y	Y	N	Y
MAINE								
1 Allen	Y	N	Y	Y	N	Y	N	Y
2 Baldacci	Y	N	Y	Y	N	Y	N	Y
MARYLAND								
1 ***Gilchrest***	Y	Y	Y	Y	Y	Y	N	Y
2 ***Ehrlich***	Y	Y	Y	N	Y	Y	N	Y
3 Cardin	Y	N	Y	Y	N	Y	N	Y
4 Wynn	Y	N	Y	Y	N	Y	N	Y
5 Hoyer	Y	N	Y	Y	N	Y	N	Y
6 ***Bartlett***	Y	Y	Y	N	Y	Y	Y	P
7 Cummings	Y	N	Y	Y	N	Y	Y	Y
8 ***Morella***	Y	N	Y	Y	N	Y	N	Y
MASSACHUSETTS								
1 Olver	Y	N	Y	Y	N	Y	N	Y
2 Neal	Y	N	Y	Y	Y	Y	Y	Y
3 McGovern	Y	N	Y	Y	N	Y	Y	Y
4 Frank	Y	N	Y	Y	N	Y	N	Y
5 Meehan	Y	N	Y	Y	N	Y	N	Y
6 Tierney	Y	N	Y	Y	N	Y	N	Y
7 Markey	Y	N	Y	Y	N	Y	N	Y
8 Capuano	Y	N	N	Y	N	Y	N	Y
9 Lynch	Y	Y	Y	Y	Y	Y	N	Y
10 Delahunt	Y	N	Y	Y	N	Y	Y	Y
MICHIGAN								
1 Stupak	Y	Y	N	N	Y	Y	N	Y
2 ***Hoekstra***	Y	Y	N	N	Y	Y	N	Y
3 ***Ehlers***	N	Y	Y	N	Y	Y	N	Y
4 ***Camp***	N	Y	Y	N	Y	Y	N	Y
5 Barcia	Y	Y	N	N	Y	?	N	Y
6 ***Upton***	Y	Y	Y	N	Y	Y	N	Y
7 ***Smith***	Y	Y	Y	N	Y	Y	Y	Y
8 ***Rogers***	N	Y	Y	N	Y	Y	N	Y
9 Kildee	Y	Y	Y	N	Y	Y	N	Y
10 Bonior	?	?	?	?	?	?	?	?
11 ***Knollenberg***	?	?	?	?	?	?	?	?
12 Levin	Y	N	Y	Y	N	Y	N	Y
13 Rivers	Y	N	Y	Y	N	Y	N	Y
14 Conyers	Y	N	N	Y	N	?	N	Y
15 Kilpatrick	Y	N	Y	Y	N	Y	N	Y
16 Dingell	Y	N	Y	Y	Y	Y	N	Y

	339	340	341	342	343	344	345	346
MINNESOTA								
1 ***Gutknecht***	Y	Y	N	N	Y	Y	Y	Y
2 ***Kennedy***	N	Y	Y	N	Y	Y	N	Y
3 ***Ramstad***	N	Y	N	N	Y	Y	N	Y
4 McCollum	Y	N	Y	Y	N	Y	N	Y
5 Sabo	Y	N	Y	Y	N	Y	N	Y
6 Luther	Y	N	N	Y	N	Y	N	Y
7 Peterson	Y	Y	N	N	Y	Y	Y	Y
8 Oberstar	Y	Y	Y	N	Y	Y	Y	Y
MISSISSIPPI								
1 ***Wicker***	N	Y	Y	N	Y	Y	Y	Y
2 Thompson	Y	N	Y	Y	N	Y	Y	Y
3 ***Pickering***	Y	Y	Y	N	Y	Y	N	Y
4 Shows	Y	Y	N	N	Y	Y	N	Y
5 Taylor	Y	Y	N	N	Y	Y	N	Y
MISSOURI								
1 Clay	Y	N	Y	Y	N	Y	Y	Y
2 ***Akin***	N	Y	N	N	Y	Y	N	Y
3 Gephardt	Y	N	Y	Y	Y	?	N	Y
4 Skelton	Y	Y	Y	N	Y	Y	N	Y
5 McCarthy	Y	N	Y	Y	N	Y	N	Y
6 ***Graves***	N	Y	N	N	Y	Y	N	Y
7 ***Blunt***	N	Y	Y	N	Y	Y	N	Y
8 ***Emerson***	N	Y	Y	N	Y	Y	N	Y
9 ***Hulshof***	N	Y	Y	N	Y	Y	N	Y
MONTANA								
AL ***Rehberg***	N	Y	Y	N	Y	Y	N	Y
NEBRASKA								
1 ***Bereuter***	N	Y	Y	N	Y	Y	N	Y
2 ***Terry***	Y	Y	N	N	Y	Y	N	Y
3 ***Osborne***	N	Y	Y	N	Y	Y	Y	Y
NEVADA								
1 Berkley	Y	N	Y	Y	N	Y	N	Y
2 ***Gibbons***	N	Y	Y	N	Y	Y	Y	Y
NEW HAMPSHIRE								
1 ***Sununu***	Y	Y	Y	N	Y	Y	N	Y
2 ***Bass***	Y	Y	Y	Y	Y	Y	N	Y
NEW JERSEY								
1 Andrews	Y	N	Y	Y	N	Y	N	Y
2 ***LoBiondo***	Y	Y	Y	N	Y	Y	N	Y
3 ***Saxton***	Y	Y	Y	N	Y	Y	N	Y
4 ***Smith***	Y	Y	Y	N	Y	Y	Y	Y
5 ***Roukema***	Y	Y	Y	N	Y	Y	N	Y
6 Pallone	Y	N	Y	Y	N	Y	N	Y
7 ***Ferguson***	Y	Y	Y	N	Y	Y	N	Y
8 Pascrell	Y	N	Y	N	Y	Y	N	Y
9 Rothman	Y	N	Y	Y	N	Y	Y	Y
10 Payne	Y	N	Y	Y	N	Y	Y	Y
11 ***Frelinghuysen***	Y	Y	Y	Y	Y	Y	N	Y
12 Holt	Y	N	Y	Y	N	Y	N	Y
13 Menendez	Y	N	N	Y	N	Y	N	Y
NEW MEXICO								
1 ***Wilson***	Y	Y	Y	N	Y	Y	N	Y
2 ***Skeen***	N	Y	Y	N	Y	Y	Y	Y
3 Udall	Y	N	Y	Y	N	Y	N	Y
NEW YORK								
1 ***Grucci***	Y	Y	Y	N	Y	Y	Y	Y
2 Israel	Y	N	N	Y	N	Y	N	Y
3 ***King***	Y	Y	Y	N	Y	Y	Y	Y
4 McCarthy	Y	N	Y	Y	N	Y	N	Y
5 Ackerman	Y	N	Y	Y	N	Y	N	Y
6 Meeks	Y	N	Y	Y	N	Y	N	Y
7 Crowley	Y	N	Y	Y	Y	Y	N	Y
8 Nadler	Y	N	Y	Y	N	Y	N	Y
9 Weiner	Y	N	Y	Y	N	Y	N	Y
10 Towns	Y	N	Y	Y	N	Y	Y	Y
11 Owens	Y	N	Y	Y	N	Y	N	Y
12 Velázquez	Y	N	Y	Y	N	Y	N	Y
13 ***Fossella***	Y	Y	N	N	Y	Y	Y	Y
14 Maloney	Y	N	N	Y	N	Y	N	Y
15 Rangel	Y	N	Y	Y	N	Y	N	Y
16 Serrano	Y	N	Y	Y	N	Y	Y	Y
17 Engel	Y	N	Y	Y	N	Y	N	Y
18 Lowey	Y	N	Y	Y	N	Y	N	Y
19 ***Kelly***	Y	Y	Y	Y	Y	Y	N	Y
20 ***Gilman***	Y	N	Y	Y	N	Y	Y	Y
21 McNulty	Y	Y	Y	N	Y	Y	N	Y
22 ***Sweeney***	Y	Y	Y	N	Y	Y	Y	Y
23 ***Boehlert***	Y	N	Y	Y	N	Y	N	Y
24 ***McHugh***	Y	Y	Y	N	Y	Y	N	Y
25 ***Walsh***	Y	Y	Y	N	Y	Y	N	Y
26 Hinchey	Y	N	Y	Y	N	Y	Y	Y
27 ***Reynolds***	Y	Y	Y	N	Y	Y	N	Y
28 Slaughter	Y	N	N	Y	N	Y	N	Y
29 LaFalce	Y	Y	Y	N	Y	Y	Y	Y

	339	340	341	342	343	344	345	346
30 ***Quinn***	Y	Y	Y	N	Y	Y	N	Y
31 ***Houghton***	N	Y	Y	Y	Y	Y	N	Y
NORTH CAROLINA								
1 Clayton	Y	N	Y	Y	N	Y	Y	Y
2 Etheridge	Y	N	N	Y	Y	Y	N	Y
3 ***Jones***	Y	Y	N	N	Y	Y	Y	Y
4 Price	Y	N	Y	Y	N	Y	N	Y
5 ***Burr***	N	Y	Y	N	Y	Y	Y	Y
6 ***Coble***	Y	Y	N	N	Y	Y	Y	Y
7 McIntyre	Y	Y	Y	N	Y	Y	N	Y
8 ***Hayes***	Y	Y	Y	N	Y	Y	N	Y
9 ***Myrick***	N	Y	Y	N	Y	Y	N	Y
10 ***Ballenger***	N	Y	Y	N	Y	Y	Y	Y
11 ***Taylor***	Y	Y	Y	N	Y	Y	Y	Y
12 Watt	Y	N	Y	Y	N	Y	Y	Y
NORTH DAKOTA								
AL Pomeroy	N	Y	N	Y	Y	Y	N	Y
OHIO								
1 ***Chabot***	N	Y	N	N	Y	Y	Y	Y
2 ***Portman***	N	Y	Y	N	Y	Y	Y	Y
3 Hall	Y	Y	Y	N	Y	Y	N	Y
4 ***Oxley***	N	Y	N	N	Y	Y	Y	Y
5 ***Gillmor***	Y	Y	Y	N	Y	Y	Y	Y
6 Strickland	Y	N	N	Y	Y	Y	N	Y
7 ***Hobson***	Y	Y	Y	N	Y	Y	Y	Y
8 ***Boehner***	N	Y	Y	N	Y	Y	Y	Y
9 Kaptur	Y	N	Y	N	Y	Y	Y	Y
10 Kucinich	Y	N	N	Y	P	Y	Y	Y
11 Jones	Y	N	Y	Y	N	Y	N	Y
12 ***Tiberi***	N	Y	N	N	Y	Y	Y	Y
13 Brown	Y	N	Y	Y	N	Y	N	Y
14 Sawyer	Y	N	Y	Y	N	Y	N	Y
15 ***Pryce***	Y	?	Y	N	Y	Y	Y	Y
16 ***Regula***	Y	Y	Y	N	Y	Y	Y	Y
17 Traficant	?	?	?	?	?	?	Y	?
18 ***Ney***	Y	Y	Y	N	Y	Y	Y	Y
19 ***LaTourette***	Y	Y	Y	N	Y	Y	Y	Y
OKLAHOMA								
1 ***Sullivan***	Y	Y	N	N	Y	Y	N	Y
2 Carson	Y	N	N	Y	Y	Y	N	Y
3 ***Watkins***	N	Y	Y	N	Y	Y	Y	Y
4 ***Watts***	N	Y	Y	N	Y	Y	Y	Y
5 ***Istook***	N	Y	Y	N	Y	?	N	Y
6 ***Lucas***	N	Y	Y	N	Y	Y	Y	Y
OREGON								
1 Wu	Y	N	Y	Y	N	Y	N	Y
2 ***Walden***	Y	Y	Y	N	Y	Y	N	Y
3 Blumenauer	Y	N	Y	Y	N	Y	N	Y
4 DeFazio	Y	N	Y	Y	N	Y	N	Y
5 Hooley	Y	N	Y	Y	N	Y	N	Y
PENNSYLVANIA								
1 Brady	Y	N	Y	Y	N	Y	N	Y
2 Fattah	Y	N	Y	Y	N	Y	N	Y
3 Borski	Y	Y	Y	N	Y	Y	N	Y
4 ***Hart***	N	Y	Y	N	Y	Y	Y	Y
5 ***Peterson***	Y	Y	Y	N	Y	Y	Y	Y
6 Holden	Y	Y	Y	N	Y	Y	N	Y
7 ***Weldon***	Y	Y	Y	?	?	?	Y	Y
8 ***Greenwood***	N	N	Y	Y	N	Y	N	Y
9 ***Shuster, Bill***	Y	Y	Y	N	Y	Y	Y	Y
10 ***Sherwood***	Y	Y	Y	N	Y	Y	Y	Y
11 Kanjorski	Y	Y	Y	N	Y	Y	N	Y
12 Murtha	Y	Y	Y	N	Y	Y	N	Y
13 Hoeffel	Y	N	Y	Y	N	Y	N	Y
14 Coyne	Y	N	Y	Y	N	Y	Y	Y
15 ***Toomey***	Y	Y	N	N	Y	Y	N	Y
16 ***Pitts***	N	Y	N	N	Y	Y	Y	Y
17 ***Gekas***	Y	Y	Y	N	Y	Y	Y	Y
18 Doyle	Y	Y	Y	N	Y	Y	N	Y
19 ***Platts***	Y	Y	N	N	Y	Y	N	Y
20 Mascara	Y	Y	Y	N	Y	Y	N	Y
21 ***English***	N	Y	Y	N	Y	Y	Y	Y
RHODE ISLAND								
1 Kennedy	Y	N	Y	Y	Y	Y	N	Y
2 Langevin	Y	Y	Y	N	Y	Y	N	Y
SOUTH CAROLINA								
1 ***Brown***	Y	Y	Y	N	Y	Y	N	Y
2 ***Wilson***	N	Y	N	N	Y	Y	N	Y
3 ***Graham***	Y	Y	N	N	Y	Y	N	Y
4 ***DeMint***	N	Y	N	N	Y	Y	N	Y
5 Spratt	Y	N	Y	Y	Y	Y	N	Y
6 Clyburn	Y	N	Y	Y	N	Y	Y	Y
SOUTH DAKOTA								
AL ***Thune***	Y	Y	N	N	Y	Y	N	Y

	339	340	341	342	343	344	345	346
TENNESSEE								
1 ***Jenkins***	Y	Y	N	N	Y	Y	Y	Y
2 ***Duncan***	N	Y	N	N	Y	Y	Y	Y
3 ***Wamp***	N	Y	Y	N	Y	Y	Y	Y
4 ***Hilleary***	Y	Y	N	N	Y	Y	Y	Y
5 Clement	Y	Y	N	N	Y	Y	N	Y
6 Gordon	Y	N	Y	Y	Y	Y	Y	Y
7 ***Bryant***	Y	Y	N	N	Y	Y	Y	Y
8 Tanner	Y	Y	N	Y	Y	Y	N	Y
9 Ford	Y	N	N	Y	Y	Y	N	P
TEXAS								
1 Sandlin	Y	Y	N	Y	Y	Y	Y	Y
2 Turner	Y	Y	N	Y	Y	Y	N	Y
3 ***Johnson, Sam***	N	Y	Y	N	Y	Y	N	Y
4 Hall	Y	Y	N	N	Y	Y	Y	Y
5 ***Sessions***	N	Y	N	N	Y	Y	Y	Y
6 ***Barton***	N	Y	N	N	Y	Y	N	Y
7 ***Culberson***	N	Y	N	N	Y	Y	N	Y
8 ***Brady***	N	Y	N	N	Y	Y	N	Y
9 Lampson	Y	N	Y	N	Y	Y	N	Y
10 Doggett	Y	N	N	N	N	Y	N	Y
11 Edwards	Y	N	Y	Y	N	Y	Y	Y
12 ***Granger***	N	Y	Y	N	Y	Y	N	Y
13 ***Thornberry***	N	Y	Y	N	Y	Y	N	Y
14 ***Paul***	N	Y	N	N	Y	Y	Y	P
15 Hinojosa	Y	N	Y	Y	Y	Y	N	Y
16 Reyes	Y	Y	Y	N	Y	Y	N	Y
17 Stenholm	N	Y	Y	N	Y	Y	N	Y
18 Jackson-Lee	Y	N	Y	Y	N	Y	Y	Y
19 ***Combest***	N	Y	Y	N	Y	Y	N	Y
20 Gonzalez	Y	N	Y	Y	N	Y	N	Y
21 ***Smith***	N	Y	Y	N	Y	Y	N	Y
22 ***DeLay***	N	Y	Y	N	Y	Y	N	Y
23 ***Bonilla***	N	Y	Y	N	Y	Y	Y	Y
24 Frost	Y	N	Y	Y	N	Y	N	Y
25 Bentsen	Y	N	Y	Y	N	Y	N	Y
26 ***Armey***	N	?	Y	N	Y	Y	N	Y
27 Ortiz	Y	Y	Y	N	Y	Y	N	Y
28 Rodriguez	Y	N	Y	Y	N	Y	N	Y
29 Green	Y	N	N	Y	N	Y	N	Y
30 Johnson, E.B.	Y	N	Y	Y	N	Y	Y	Y
UTAH								
1 ***Hansen***	Y	Y	Y	N	Y	Y	N	Y
2 Matheson	Y	N	N	Y	N	Y	N	Y
3 ***Cannon***	N	Y	Y	N	Y	Y	Y	Y
VERMONT								
AL *Sanders*	Y	N	Y	Y	N	Y	N	Y
VIRGINIA								
1 ***Davis, Jo Ann***	Y	Y	N	N	Y	Y	N	Y
2 ***Schrock***	Y	Y	N	N	Y	Y	N	Y
3 Scott	Y	N	Y	Y	N	Y	Y	Y
4 ***Forbes***	Y	Y	N	N	Y	Y	N	Y
5 *Goode*	Y	Y	N	N	Y	Y	Y	Y
6 ***Goodlatte***	Y	Y	N	N	Y	Y	N	Y
7 ***Cantor***	N	Y	Y	N	Y	Y	N	Y
8 Moran	Y	N	Y	Y	Y	Y	N	Y
9 Boucher	Y	N	Y	Y	N	Y	N	Y
10 ***Wolf***	N	Y	Y	N	Y	Y	N	Y
11 ***Davis, T.***	N	Y	Y	N	Y	Y	N	Y
WASHINGTON								
1 Inslee	Y	N	N	Y	N	Y	Y	Y
2 Larsen	Y	N	Y	Y	N	Y	N	Y
3 Baird	Y	N	Y	Y	N	Y	N	Y
4 ***Hastings***	N	Y	Y	N	Y	Y	N	Y
5 ***Nethercutt***	N	Y	Y	N	Y	Y	N	Y
6 Dicks	Y	N	Y	Y	N	?	N	Y
7 McDermott	Y	N	Y	Y	N	Y	Y	Y
8 ***Dunn***	N	Y	Y	N	Y	Y	N	Y
9 Smith	Y	N	N	Y	N	Y	N	Y
WEST VIRGINIA								
1 Mollohan	Y	Y	Y	N	Y	Y	N	Y
2 ***Capito***	Y	Y	N	N	Y	Y	N	Y
3 Rahall	Y	Y	Y	N	Y	Y	N	Y
WISCONSIN								
1 ***Ryan***	N	Y	N	N	Y	Y	N	Y
2 Baldwin	Y	N	N	Y	N	Y	N	Y
3 Kind	Y	N	N	Y	N	Y	N	Y
4 Kleczka	Y	N	N	Y	Y	Y	N	Y
5 Barrett	Y	N	N	Y	N	Y	N	Y
6 ***Petri***	Y	Y	N	N	Y	Y	Y	Y
7 Obey	Y	N	Y	Y	Y	Y	N	Y
8 ***Green***	N	Y	Y	N	Y	Y	Y	Y
9 ***Sensenbrenner***	N	Y	N	N	Y	Y	N	Y
WYOMING								
AL ***Cubin***	N	Y	N	N	Y	Y	Y	Y

Southern states - Ala., Ark., Fla., Ga., Ky., La., Miss., N.C., Okla., S.C., Tenn., Texas, Va.

347. HR 4628. Fiscal 2003 Intelligence Authorization/Sept. 11 Task Force. Roemer, D-Ind., amendment that would establish a National Commission on Terrorist Attacks Upon the United States. The commission would review the implementation by the intelligence agencies of the recommendations of a joint House-Senate intelligence investigation and other inquiries into the Sept. 11, 2001, terrorist attacks. Adopted 219-188: R 25-183; D 193-4 (ND 145-1, SD 48-3); I 1-1. (Subsequently, the House passed the bill by voice vote.) A "nay" was a vote in support of the president's position. July 25, 2002 (in the session that began and the Congressional Record that is dated July 24, 2002).

348. HR 3763. Accounting Industry Overhaul/Conference Report. Adoption of the conference report on the bill that would overhaul regulation of the accounting industry. A new Public Company Accounting Oversight Board, funded by fees on publicly traded companies, would police the industry. Accounting firms would be barred from performing several services, including investment banking and management consulting, for companies they audit. The bill would create a new securities fraud penalty with a maximum prison sentence of up to 25 years, and new criminal penalties of up to 20 years imprisonment for shareholder fraud and document shredding. Top corporate executives would have to certify company financial statements. Executives engaged in financial misconduct would be required to pay back bonuses and profits. Civil penalties would be placed in a fund for defrauded investors. Adopted (thus sent to the Senate) 423-3: R 215-3; D 206-0 (ND 153-0, SD 53-0); I 2-0. July 25, 2002.

349. HR 4546. Fiscal 2003 Defense Authorization/Motion to Instruct. Taylor, D-Miss., motion to instruct conferees to insist on House-passed language that would direct the Pentagon to create 23 additional Weapons of Mass Destruction Civil Support Teams, ensuring one for each state and territory. Motion agreed to 419-2: R 213-2; D 204-0 (ND 154-0, SD 50-0); I 2-0. July 25, 2002.

350. HR 4546. Fiscal 2003 Defense Authorization/Motion to Close Conference. Stump, R-Ariz., motion to close portions of the conference on the bill that would authorize defense funding for fiscal 2003. Motion agreed to 420-3: R 214-0; D 204-3 (ND 152-2, SD 52-1); I 2-0. July 25, 2002.

351. HR 4946. Long-Term Health Care/Passage. Hayworth, R-Ariz., motion to suspend the rules and pass the bill that would grant tax breaks to purchase long-term health care insurance. Buyers of long-term coverage who pay at least half the cost of their premiums would be allowed to deduct a portion of those premiums, beginning in 2003. The deduction would rise to up to 50 percent of qualified premiums by 2012. It would be phased out for individuals with modified adjusted gross income between $20,000 and $40,000, and for couples with double that range. It also would grant an additional personal exemption, which would gradually rise to $3,000 by 2012, for each dependent family member with long-term care needs. Motion agreed to 362-61: R 217-0; D 144-60 (ND 106-46, SD 38-14); I 1-1. A two-thirds majority of those present and voting (282 in this case) is required for passage under suspension of the rules. July 25, 2002.

Rep. James A. Traficant Jr., D-Ohio, was expelled from the House of Representatives July 24, 2002. The last vote for which he was eligible was vote 346.

Key

Y	Voted for (yea).
#	Paired for.
+	Announced for.
N	Voted against (nay).
X	Paired against.
–	Announced against.
P	Voted "present."
C	Voted "present" to avoid possible conflict of interest.
?	Did not vote or otherwise make a position known.

Democrats **Republicans**
Independents

	347	348	349	350	351
ALABAMA					
1 *Callahan*	?	Y	Y	Y	Y
2 *Everett*	N	Y	Y	Y	Y
3 *Riley*	N	Y	Y	Y	Y
4 *Aderholt*	N	Y	Y	Y	Y
5 Cramer	Y	Y	Y	Y	Y
6 *Bachus*	N	Y	Y	Y	Y
7 Hilliard	Y	Y	Y	Y	Y
ALASKA					
AL *Young*	?	Y	?	?	Y
ARIZONA					
1 *Flake*	N	N	N	Y	Y
2 Pastor	Y	Y	Y	Y	Y
3 *Stump*	?	Y	Y	Y	Y
4 *Shadegg*	N	Y	Y	Y	Y
5 *Kolbe*	N	Y	Y	Y	Y
6 *Hayworth*	N	Y	Y	Y	Y
ARKANSAS					
1 Berry	Y	Y	Y	Y	N
2 Snyder	Y	Y	Y	Y	Y
3 *Boozman*	N	Y	Y	Y	Y
4 Ross	Y	Y	Y	Y	Y
CALIFORNIA					
1 Thompson	Y	Y	Y	Y	Y
2 *Herger*	N	Y	Y	?	Y
3 *Ose*	N	Y	+	Y	Y
4 *Doolittle*	N	Y	Y	Y	Y
5 Matsui	Y	Y	Y	Y	N
6 Woolsey	Y	Y	Y	Y	N
7 Miller, George	Y	Y	Y	Y	N
8 Pelosi	Y	Y	Y	Y	Y
9 Lee	Y	Y	Y	Y	Y
10 Tauscher	Y	Y	Y	Y	Y
11 *Pombo*	N	Y	Y	Y	Y
12 Lantos	Y	Y	Y	Y	Y
13 Stark	Y	Y	Y	Y	N
14 Eshoo	Y	Y	Y	Y	N
15 Honda	Y	Y	Y	Y	N
16 Lofgren	Y	Y	Y	Y	Y
17 Farr	Y	Y	Y	Y	Y
18 Condit	?	Y	Y	Y	Y
19 *Radanovich*	N	Y	Y	Y	Y
20 Dooley	Y	Y	Y	Y	Y
21 *Thomas*	N	Y	Y	Y	Y
22 Capps	Y	Y	Y	Y	Y
23 *Gallegly*	N	Y	Y	Y	Y
24 Sherman	Y	Y	Y	Y	Y
25 *McKeon*	N	Y	Y	Y	Y
26 Berman	Y	Y	Y	Y	N
27 Schiff	Y	Y	Y	Y	Y
28 *Dreier*	N	Y	Y	Y	Y
29 Waxman	Y	Y	Y	Y	Y
30 Becerra	Y	Y	Y	Y	N
31 Solis	Y	Y	Y	Y	Y
32 Watson	Y	Y	Y	Y	Y
33 Roybal-Allard	Y	Y	Y	Y	N
34 Napolitano	Y	Y	Y	Y	Y
35 Waters	Y	Y	Y	Y	N
36 Harman	Y	Y	Y	Y	Y
37 Millender-McD.	Y	Y	Y	Y	Y
38 *Horn*	N	Y	Y	Y	Y

	347	348	349	350	351
39 *Royce*	N	Y	N	Y	Y
40 *Lewis*	N	Y	Y	Y	Y
41 *Miller, Gary*	N	Y	Y	Y	Y
42 Baca	Y	Y	Y	Y	Y
43 *Calvert*	N	Y	Y	Y	Y
44 *Bono*	N	Y	Y	Y	Y
45 *Rohrabacher*	N	Y	Y	Y	Y
46 Sanchez	Y	Y	Y	Y	N
47 *Cox*	?	Y	Y	Y	Y
48 *Issa*	?	Y	Y	Y	Y
49 Davis	Y	Y	Y	Y	Y
50 Filner	Y	Y	Y	Y	N
51 *Cunningham*	N	Y	Y	Y	Y
52 *Hunter*	N	Y	Y	Y	Y
COLORADO					
1 DeGette	Y	Y	Y	Y	Y
2 Udall	Y	Y	Y	Y	Y
3 *McInnis*	N	Y	Y	Y	Y
4 *Schaffer*	N	Y	Y	Y	Y
5 *Hefley*	N	Y	Y	Y	Y
6 *Tancredo*	Y	Y	Y	Y	Y
CONNECTICUT					
1 Larson	Y	Y	Y	Y	Y
2 *Simmons*	N	Y	Y	Y	Y
3 DeLauro	Y	Y	Y	Y	Y
4 *Shays*	N	Y	Y	Y	Y
5 Maloney	Y	Y	Y	Y	Y
6 *Johnson*	Y	Y	Y	Y	Y
DELAWARE					
AL *Castle*	N	Y	Y	Y	Y
FLORIDA					
1 *Miller, J.*	N	+	Y	Y	Y
2 Boyd	N	Y	Y	Y	N
3 Brown	Y	Y	Y	Y	Y
4 *Crenshaw*	N	Y	Y	Y	Y
5 Thurman	Y	Y	Y	Y	Y
6 *Stearns*	?	?	?	?	?
7 *Mica*	N	Y	Y	Y	Y
8 *Keller*	N	Y	Y	Y	Y
9 *Bilirakis*	N	Y	Y	Y	Y
10 *Young*	N	Y	Y	Y	Y
11 Davis	Y	Y	?	Y	Y
12 *Putnam*	N	Y	Y	Y	Y
13 *Miller, D.*	N	Y	Y	Y	Y
14 *Goss*	N	Y	Y	Y	Y
15 *Weldon*	N	Y	Y	Y	Y
16 *Foley*	N	Y	Y	Y	Y
17 Meek	N	Y	Y	Y	Y
18 *Ros-Lehtinen*	N	Y	Y	Y	Y
19 Wexler	Y	Y	?	?	Y
20 Deutsch	Y	Y	Y	Y	N
21 *Diaz-Balart*	N	Y	Y	Y	Y
22 *Shaw*	N	Y	Y	Y	Y
23 Hastings	Y	Y	Y	Y	Y
GEORGIA					
1 *Kingston*	N	Y	Y	Y	Y
2 Bishop	Y	Y	Y	Y	Y
3 *Collins*	N	N	Y	Y	Y
4 McKinney	Y	Y	Y	N	Y
5 Lewis	Y	Y	Y	Y	Y
6 *Isakson*	N	Y	Y	Y	Y
7 *Barr*	Y	Y	Y	Y	Y
8 *Chambliss*	N	Y	Y	Y	Y
9 *Deal*	N	Y	Y	Y	Y
10 *Norwood*	N	Y	Y	Y	Y
11 *Linder*	N	Y	Y	Y	Y
HAWAII					
1 Abercrombie	Y	Y	Y	Y	N
2 Mink	Y	Y	Y	Y	Y
IDAHO					
1 *Otter*	?	Y	Y	Y	Y
2 *Simpson*	N	Y	Y	Y	Y
ILLINOIS					
1 Rush	Y	Y	Y	Y	Y
2 Jackson	Y	Y	Y	Y	N
3 Lipinski	Y	Y	Y	Y	Y
4 Gutierrez	?	Y	Y	Y	Y
5 Blagojevich	Y	Y	Y	Y	Y
6 *Hyde*	N	Y	Y	Y	Y
7 Davis	Y	Y	Y	Y	Y
8 *Crane*	N	Y	Y	Y	Y
9 Schakowsky	Y	Y	Y	Y	Y
10 *Kirk*	N	Y	Y	Y	Y
11 *Weller*	N	Y	Y	Y	Y
12 Costello	Y	Y	Y	Y	Y
13 *Biggert*	N	Y	Y	Y	Y

ND Northern Democrats   SD Southern Democrats

	347	348	349	350	351
14 ***Hastert***	N	Y			
15 ***Johnson***	N	Y	Y	Y	Y
16 ***Manzullo***	N	Y	Y	Y	Y
17 Evans	Y	Y	Y	Y	Y
18 ***LaHood***	N	Y	Y	Y	Y
19 Phelps	Y	Y	Y	Y	Y
20 ***Shimkus***	N	Y	Y	Y	Y
INDIANA					
1 Visclosky	Y	Y	Y	Y	Y
2 ***Pence***	N	Y	Y	Y	Y
3 Roemer	Y	Y	Y	Y	Y
4 ***Souder***	N	Y	Y	Y	Y
5 ***Buyer***	N	Y	Y	Y	Y
6 ***Burton***	Y	Y	Y	Y	?
7 ***Kerns***	N	Y	Y	Y	Y
8 ***Hostettler***	N	Y	Y	Y	Y
9 Hill	Y	Y	Y	Y	Y
10 Carson	Y	Y	Y	Y	Y
IOWA					
1 ***Leach***	Y	Y	Y	Y	Y
2 ***Nussle***	N	Y	Y	Y	Y
3 Boswell	Y	Y	Y	Y	Y
4 ***Ganske***	Y	Y	Y	Y	Y
5 ***Latham***	N	Y	Y	Y	Y
KANSAS					
1 ***Moran***	N	Y	Y	Y	Y
2 ***Ryun***	N	Y	Y	Y	Y
3 Moore	Y	Y	Y	Y	Y
4 ***Tiahrt***	N	Y	Y	Y	Y
KENTUCKY					
1 ***Whitfield***	N	Y	Y	Y	Y
2 ***Lewis***	N	Y	Y	Y	Y
3 ***Northup***	N	Y	Y	Y	Y
4 Lucas	Y	Y	Y	Y	Y
5 ***Rogers***	N	Y	Y	Y	Y
6 ***Fletcher***	N	Y	Y	Y	Y
LOUISIANA					
1 ***Vitter***	N	Y	Y	Y	Y
2 Jefferson	Y	Y	Y	Y	Y
3 ***Tauzin***	N	Y	Y	Y	Y
4 ***McCrery***	N	Y	Y	Y	Y
5 ***Cooksey***	N	Y	Y	Y	Y
6 ***Baker***	N	Y	Y	Y	Y
7 John	Y	Y	+	Y	Y
MAINE					
1 Allen	Y	Y	Y	Y	Y
2 Baldacci	Y	Y	Y	Y	Y
MARYLAND					
1 ***Gilchrest***	Y	Y	Y	Y	Y
2 ***Ehrlich***	Y	Y	Y	Y	Y
3 Cardin	Y	Y	Y	Y	Y
4 Wynn	Y	Y	Y	Y	Y
5 Hoyer	Y	Y	Y	Y	Y
6 ***Bartlett***	Y	Y	Y	Y	Y
7 Cummings	Y	Y	Y	Y	Y
8 ***Morella***	Y	Y	Y	Y	Y
MASSACHUSETTS					
1 Olver	Y	Y	Y	Y	N
2 Neal	Y	Y	Y	Y	N
3 McGovern	Y	Y	Y	Y	N
4 Frank	Y	Y	Y	Y	N
5 Meehan	Y	?	?	?	?
6 Tierney	Y	Y	Y	Y	N
7 Markey	Y	Y	Y	Y	N
8 Capuano	Y	Y	Y	Y	Y
9 Lynch	Y	Y	Y	Y	Y
10 Delahunt	Y	Y	Y	Y	N
MICHIGAN					
1 Stupak	Y	Y	Y	Y	N
2 ***Hoekstra***	N	Y	Y	Y	Y
3 ***Ehlers***	N	Y	Y	Y	Y
4 ***Camp***	N	Y	Y	Y	Y
5 Barcia	Y	Y	Y	Y	Y
6 ***Upton***	N	Y	Y	Y	Y
7 ***Smith***	N	Y	Y	Y	Y
8 ***Rogers***	N	Y	Y	Y	Y
9 Kildee	Y	Y	Y	Y	Y
10 Bonior	?	Y	Y	Y	Y
11 ***Knollenberg***	?	?	?	?	?
12 Levin	Y	Y	Y	Y	Y
13 Rivers	Y	Y	Y	Y	Y
14 Conyers	Y	Y	Y	Y	N
15 Kilpatrick	Y	Y	Y	Y	Y
16 Dingell	Y	Y	Y	Y	N

	347	348	349	350	351
MINNESOTA					
1 ***Gutknecht***	Y	Y	Y	Y	Y
2 ***Kennedy***	N	Y	?	Y	Y
3 ***Ramstad***	N	Y	Y	Y	Y
4 McCollum	Y	Y	Y	Y	N
5 Sabo	Y	Y	Y	Y	N
6 Luther	Y	Y	Y	Y	Y
7 Peterson	Y	Y	Y	Y	Y
8 Oberstar	Y	Y	Y	Y	Y
MISSISSIPPI					
1 ***Wicker***	N	Y	Y	Y	Y
2 Thompson	Y	Y	Y	Y	Y
3 ***Pickering***	N	Y	Y	Y	Y
4 Shows	Y	Y	Y	Y	Y
5 Taylor	Y	Y	Y	Y	N
MISSOURI					
1 Clay	?	+	Y	Y	Y
2 ***Akin***	N	Y	Y	Y	Y
3 Gephardt	Y	Y	Y	Y	N
4 Skelton	Y	Y	Y	Y	Y
5 McCarthy	+	Y	Y	Y	N
6 ***Graves***	N	Y	Y	Y	Y
7 ***Blunt***	?	Y	Y	Y	Y
8 ***Emerson***	N	Y	Y	Y	Y
9 ***Hulshof***	N	Y	Y	Y	Y
MONTANA					
AL ***Rehberg***	N	Y	Y	Y	Y
NEBRASKA					
1 ***Bereuter***	N	Y	Y	Y	Y
2 ***Terry***	N	Y	Y	Y	Y
3 ***Osborne***	N	Y	Y	Y	Y
NEVADA					
1 Berkley	Y	Y	Y	Y	Y
2 ***Gibbons***	N	Y	Y	Y	Y
NEW HAMPSHIRE					
1 ***Sununu***	N	Y	Y	Y	Y
2 ***Bass***	N	Y	Y	Y	Y
NEW JERSEY					
1 Andrews	Y	+	+	+	+
2 ***LoBiondo***	Y	Y	Y	Y	Y
3 ***Saxton***	N	Y	Y	Y	Y
4 ***Smith***	Y	Y	Y	Y	Y
5 ***Roukema***	?	Y	Y	Y	Y
6 Pallone	Y	Y	Y	Y	N
7 ***Ferguson***	Y	Y	Y	Y	Y
8 Pascrell	Y	Y	Y	Y	N
9 Rothman	Y	Y	Y	Y	Y
10 Payne	Y	Y	Y	Y	N
11 ***Frelinghuysen***	Y	Y	Y	Y	Y
12 Holt	Y	Y	Y	Y	Y
13 Menendez	Y	Y	Y	Y	Y
NEW MEXICO					
1 ***Wilson***	N	Y	Y	Y	Y
2 ***Skeen***	N	Y	Y	Y	Y
3 Udall	Y	Y	Y	Y	Y
NEW YORK					
1 ***Grucci***	N	Y	Y	Y	Y
2 Israel	Y	Y	Y	Y	Y
3 ***King***	N	Y	Y	Y	Y
4 McCarthy	Y	Y	Y	Y	Y
5 Ackerman	Y	Y	Y	Y	Y
6 Meeks	Y	Y	Y	Y	Y
7 Crowley	Y	Y	Y	Y	Y
8 Nadler	Y	Y	Y	Y	?
9 Weiner	Y	Y	Y	Y	Y
10 Towns	Y	Y	Y	Y	Y
11 Owens	Y	Y	Y	Y	Y
12 Velázquez	Y	Y	Y	Y	N
13 ***Fossella***	N	Y	Y	Y	Y
14 Maloney	Y	Y	Y	Y	Y
15 Rangel	Y	Y	Y	Y	Y
16 Serrano	Y	Y	Y	Y	Y
17 Engel	Y	Y	Y	Y	Y
18 Lowey	Y	Y	Y	Y	Y
19 ***Kelly***	N	Y	Y	Y	Y
20 ***Gilman***	Y	Y	Y	Y	Y
21 McNulty	Y	Y	Y	Y	Y
22 ***Sweeney***	N	Y	Y	Y	Y
23 ***Boehlert***	N	Y	Y	?	Y
24 ***McHugh***	N	Y	Y	Y	Y
25 ***Walsh***	N	Y	Y	Y	Y
26 Hinchey	Y	Y	Y	Y	N
27 ***Reynolds***	N	Y	Y	Y	Y
28 Slaughter	?	Y	Y	Y	Y
29 LaFalce	?	Y	Y	Y	N

	347	348	349	350	351
30 ***Quinn***	N	Y	?	?	Y
31 ***Houghton***	N	Y	Y	Y	Y
NORTH CAROLINA					
1 Clayton	Y	Y	Y	Y	Y
2 Etheridge	Y	Y	Y	Y	Y
3 ***Jones***	Y	Y	Y	Y	Y
4 Price	Y	Y	Y	Y	Y
5 ***Burr***	N	Y	Y	Y	Y
6 ***Coble***	N	Y	N	Y	Y
7 McIntyre	Y	Y	Y	Y	Y
8 ***Hayes***	N	Y	Y	Y	Y
9 ***Myrick***	N	Y	Y	Y	Y
10 ***Ballenger***	N	Y	Y	Y	Y
11 ***Taylor***	N	Y	Y	Y	Y
12 Watt	Y	Y	Y	Y	Y
NORTH DAKOTA					
AL Pomeroy	N	Y	Y	Y	Y
OHIO					
1 ***Chabot***	N	Y	Y	Y	Y
2 ***Portman***	N	Y	Y	Y	Y
3 Hall	?	Y	Y	Y	Y
4 ***Oxley***	N	Y	Y	Y	Y
5 ***Gillmor***	N	Y	Y	Y	Y
6 Strickland	Y	Y	Y	Y	Y
7 ***Hobson***	N	Y	Y	Y	Y
8 ***Boehner***	?	Y	Y	Y	Y
9 Kaptur	Y	Y	Y	Y	Y
10 Kucinich	Y	Y	Y	Y	N
11 Jones	Y	Y	Y	Y	Y
12 ***Tiberi***	N	Y	Y	Y	Y
13 Brown	Y	Y	Y	Y	N
14 Sawyer	Y	Y	Y	Y	Y
15 ***Pryce***	N	Y	Y	Y	Y
16 ***Regula***	N	Y	Y	Y	Y
17 Vacant *					
18 ***Ney***	N	Y	Y	Y	Y
19 ***LaTourette***	Y	Y	Y	Y	Y
OKLAHOMA					
1 ***Sullivan***	N	Y	Y	Y	Y
2 Carson	Y	Y	Y	Y	Y
3 ***Watkins***	N	?	Y	Y	Y
4 ***Watts***	N	Y	Y	Y	Y
5 ***Istook***	N	Y	Y	Y	Y
6 ***Lucas***	N	Y	Y	Y	Y
OREGON					
1 Wu	Y	Y	Y	Y	Y
2 ***Walden***	N	Y	Y	Y	Y
3 Blumenauer	Y	Y	Y	N	Y
4 DeFazio	Y	Y	Y	N	?
5 Hooley	Y	Y	Y	Y	Y
PENNSYLVANIA					
1 Brady	Y	Y	Y	Y	Y
2 Fattah	Y	Y	Y	Y	Y
3 Borski	Y	Y	Y	Y	Y
4 ***Hart***	N	Y	Y	Y	Y
5 ***Peterson***	N	Y	Y	Y	Y
6 Holden	Y	Y	Y	Y	Y
7 ***Weldon***	Y	Y	Y	Y	Y
8 ***Greenwood***	N	Y	Y	Y	Y
9 ***Shuster, Bill***	N	Y	Y	Y	Y
10 ***Sherwood***	N	Y	Y	Y	Y
11 Kanjorski	Y	Y	Y	Y	Y
12 Murtha	?	Y	Y	Y	Y
13 Hoeffel	Y	Y	Y	Y	Y
14 Coyne	Y	Y	Y	Y	N
15 ***Toomey***	N	Y	Y	Y	Y
16 ***Pitts***	N	Y	Y	Y	Y
17 ***Gekas***	N	Y	Y	Y	Y
18 Doyle	Y	Y	Y	Y	Y
19 ***Platts***	N	Y	Y	Y	Y
20 Mascara	Y	Y	Y	Y	Y
21 ***English***	N	Y	Y	Y	Y
RHODE ISLAND					
1 Kennedy	Y	Y	Y	Y	N
2 Langevin	Y	Y	Y	Y	N
SOUTH CAROLINA					
1 ***Brown***	N	Y	Y	Y	Y
2 ***Wilson***	N	Y	Y	Y	Y
3 ***Graham***	N	Y	Y	Y	Y
4 ***DeMint***	N	Y	Y	Y	Y
5 Spratt	Y	Y	Y	Y	Y
6 Clyburn	Y	Y	Y	Y	Y
SOUTH DAKOTA					
AL ***Thune***	N	Y	Y	Y	Y

	347	348	349	350	351
TENNESSEE					
1 ***Jenkins***	N	Y	Y	Y	Y
2 ***Duncan***	Y	Y	Y	Y	Y
3 ***Wamp***	N	Y	Y	Y	Y
4 ***Hilleary***	Y	Y	Y	Y	Y
5 Clement	Y	Y	Y	Y	?
6 Gordon	?	?	Y	Y	Y
7 ***Bryant***	N	Y	Y	Y	Y
8 Tanner	N	Y	Y	Y	Y
9 Ford	Y	Y	Y	Y	Y
TEXAS					
1 Sandlin	Y	Y	Y	Y	N
2 Turner	?	Y	Y	Y	N
3 ***Johnson, Sam***	N	Y	Y	Y	Y
4 Hall	N	Y	Y	Y	Y
5 ***Sessions***	N	Y	Y	Y	Y
6 ***Barton***	N	Y	Y	Y	Y
7 ***Culberson***	N	Y	Y	Y	Y
8 ***Brady***	N	Y	Y	Y	Y
9 Lampson	Y	Y	Y	Y	Y
10 Doggett	Y	Y	Y	Y	N
11 Edwards	Y	Y	Y	Y	Y
12 ***Granger***	N	Y	Y	Y	Y
13 ***Thornberry***	N	Y	Y	Y	Y
14 ***Paul***	N	N	Y	Y	Y
15 Hinojosa	Y	Y	Y	Y	Y
16 Reyes	Y	Y	Y	Y	Y
17 Stenholm	Y	Y	Y	Y	N
18 Jackson-Lee	Y	Y	Y	Y	Y
19 ***Combest***	?	Y	Y	Y	Y
20 Gonzalez	Y	Y	Y	Y	N
21 ***Smith***	N	Y	Y	Y	Y
22 ***DeLay***	N	Y	Y	Y	Y
23 ***Bonilla***	N	Y	Y	Y	Y
24 Frost	Y	Y	Y	Y	Y
25 Bentsen	Y	Y	Y	Y	Y
26 ***Armey***	N	Y	Y	Y	Y
27 Ortiz	Y	Y	?	Y	Y
28 Rodriguez	Y	Y	Y	Y	N
29 Green	Y	Y	Y	Y	Y
30 Johnson, E.B.	Y	Y	Y	Y	N
UTAH					
1 ***Hansen***	?	Y	Y	?	?
2 Matheson	Y	Y	Y	Y	Y
3 ***Cannon***	N	Y	Y	Y	Y
VERMONT					
AL *Sanders*	Y	Y	Y	Y	N
VIRGINIA					
1 ***Davis, Jo Ann***	N	Y	Y	Y	Y
2 ***Schrock***	N	Y	Y	Y	Y
3 Scott	Y	Y	Y	Y	N
4 ***Forbes***	N	Y	Y	Y	Y
5 *Goode*	N	Y	Y	Y	Y
6 ***Goodlatte***	N	Y	Y	Y	Y
7 ***Cantor***	N	Y	Y	Y	Y
8 Moran	Y	Y	Y	Y	Y
9 Boucher	?	Y	Y	Y	N
10 ***Wolf***	Y	Y	Y	Y	Y
11 ***Davis, T.***	?	Y	Y	Y	Y
WASHINGTON					
1 Inslee	Y	Y	Y	Y	Y
2 Larsen	Y	Y	Y	Y	Y
3 Baird	Y	Y	Y	Y	Y
4 ***Hastings***	N	Y	Y	Y	Y
5 ***Nethercutt***	Y	Y	Y	Y	Y
6 Dicks	Y	Y	Y	Y	Y
7 McDermott	Y	Y	Y	Y	N
8 ***Dunn***	N	Y	Y	Y	Y
9 Smith	?	Y	Y	Y	Y
WEST VIRGINIA					
1 Mollohan	Y	Y	Y	Y	N
2 ***Capito***	Y	Y	Y	Y	Y
3 Rahall	Y	Y	Y	Y	N
WISCONSIN					
1 ***Ryan***	N	Y	Y	Y	Y
2 Baldwin	Y	Y	Y	Y	N
3 Kind	Y	Y	Y	Y	Y
4 Kleczka	Y	Y	Y	Y	Y
5 Barrett	Y	Y	Y	Y	Y
6 ***Petri***	N	Y	Y	Y	Y
7 Obey	Y	Y	Y	Y	Y
8 ***Green***	N	Y	Y	Y	Y
9 ***Sensenbrenner***	N	Y	Y	Y	Y
WYOMING					
AL ***Cubin***	N	Y	Y	Y	Y

Southern states - Ala., Ark., Fla., Ga., Ky., La., Miss., N.C., Okla., S.C., Tenn., Texas, Va.

Key

Y	Voted for (yea).
#	Paired for.
+	Announced for.
N	Voted against (nay).
X	Paired against.
–	Announced against.
P	Voted "present."
C	Voted "present" to avoid possible conflict of interest.
?	Did not vote or otherwise make a position known.

Democrats **Republicans**
Independents

---

352. HR 5005. Homeland Security/Congressional Oversight. Waxman, D-Calif., amendment that would tighten congressional oversight of the White House Office of Homeland Security. It would create the office in statute. It would give the director, who would be confirmed by the Senate, review and de-certification authority over the budgets of all agencies in the Homeland Security Department. Rejected 175-248: R 0-216; D 174-31 (ND 136-15, SD 38-16); I 1-1. July 26, 2002.

353. HR 5005. Homeland Security/FEMA. Oberstar, D-Minn., amendment that would maintain the Federal Emergency Management Agency (FEMA) as an independent agency. Rejected 165-261: R 10-207; D 154-53 (ND 119-34, SD 35-19); I 1-1. July 26, 2002.

354. HR 5005. Homeland Security/Customs Service. Cardin, D-Md., amendment that would preserve the Customs Service as a distinct entity within the Homeland Security Department. Rejected 177-245: R 6-206; D 170-38 (ND 128-26, SD 42-12); I 1-1. July 26, 2002.

355. HR 5005. Homeland Security/Joint Task Force. Rogers, R-Ky., amendment that would authorize the secretary of the Homeland Security Department to establish a Joint Interagency Homeland Security Task Force. Adopted 240-188: R 206-11; D 33-176 (ND 21-134, SD 12-42); I 1-1. July 26, 2002.

356. HR 5005. Homeland Security/Union Membership. Shays, R-Conn., amendment that would give federal employees who transfer into the Homeland Security Department the right to join a union. The president could deny employees the right to unionize when he certified in writing that membership would hurt national security. Adopted 229-201: R 217-2; D 11-198 (ND 5-150, SD 6-48); I 1-1. July 26, 2002.

357. HR 5005. Homeland Security/Union Membership. Morella, R-Md., amendment that would give federal employees who transfer into the Homeland Security Department the right to join a union if they were under union protection before the transfer. The president could exempt employees from union membership when duties are directly related to the war on terrorism. Rejected 208-222: R 5-214; D 202-7 (ND 153-2, SD 49-5); I 1-1. A "nay" was a vote in support of the president's position. July 26, 2002.

358. HR 5005. Homeland Security/Collective Bargaining. Quinn, R-N.Y., amendment that would allow only the president to exclude for security reasons individual employees from the right to collective bargaining. Adopted 227-202: R 218-1; D 8-200 (ND 3-151, SD 5-49); I 1-1. July 26, 2002.

359. HR 5005. Homeland Security/Indemnification. Turner, D-Texas, amendment that would indemnify companies that sell anti-terrorism technologies to federal, state and local governments similar to protections under PL 85-804 for contractors with unusually hazardous risks. Rejected 214-215: R 5-213; D 208-1 (ND 155-0, SD 53-1); I 1-1. A "nay" was a vote in support of the president's position. July 26, 2002.

	352	353	354	355	356	357	358	359
ALABAMA								
1 *Callahan*	N	N	N	Y	Y	N	Y	N
2 *Everett*	N	N	N	Y	Y	N	Y	N
3 *Riley*	N	N	N	Y	Y	N	Y	N
4 *Aderholt*	N	N	N	Y	Y	N	Y	N
5 Cramer	N	N	Y	Y	Y	Y	Y	N
6 *Bachus*	N	N	N	Y	Y	N	Y	N
7 Hilliard	Y	Y	Y	N	N	Y	N	Y
ALASKA								
AL *Young*	?	?	?	?	Y	N	Y	N
ARIZONA								
1 *Flake*	N	N	N	Y	N	N	Y	N
2 Pastor	Y	Y	Y	N	N	Y	N	Y
3 *Stump*	N	N	N	Y	?	N	Y	N
4 *Shadegg*	N	N	N	Y	Y	N	Y	N
5 *Kolbe*	N	N	N	Y	Y	N	Y	N
6 *Hayworth*	N	N	N	Y	N	N	Y	N
ARKANSAS								
1 Berry	N	Y	N	N	N	Y	N	Y
2 Snyder	N	Y	N	N	N	Y	N	Y
3 *Boozman*	N	Y	N	Y	Y	N	Y	N
4 Ross	Y	Y	N	N	N	Y	N	Y
CALIFORNIA								
1 Thompson	Y	N	N	N	N	Y	N	Y
2 *Herger*	N	N	N	Y	Y	N	Y	N
3 *Ose*	N	N	N	Y	Y	N	Y	N
4 *Doolittle*	?	?	?	?	Y	N	Y	N
5 Matsui	Y	Y	Y	N	N	Y	N	Y
6 Woolsey	Y	Y	Y	N	N	Y	N	Y
7 Miller, George	Y	Y	Y	N	N	Y	N	Y
8 Pelosi	Y	Y	Y	N	N	Y	N	Y
9 Lee	Y	Y	Y	N	N	Y	N	Y
10 Tauscher	N	N	N	Y	Y	Y	Y	Y
11 *Pombo*	?	?	?	Y	Y	N	Y	N
12 Lantos	Y	Y	Y	N	N	Y	N	Y
13 Stark	?	?	Y	N	N	Y	N	Y
14 Eshoo	Y	Y	Y	N	N	Y	N	Y
15 Honda	Y	Y	Y	N	N	Y	N	Y
16 Lofgren	Y	N	Y	N	N	Y	N	Y
17 Farr	Y	Y	Y	N	N	Y	N	Y
18 Condit	?	?	?	N	N	Y	N	Y
19 *Radanovich*	N	N	N	Y	Y	N	?	N
20 Dooley	N	N	N	N	N	Y	N	Y
21 *Thomas*	N	N	N	Y	Y	N	Y	N
22 Capps	Y	Y	Y	N	N	Y	N	Y
23 *Gallegly*	N	N	N	Y	Y	N	Y	N
24 Sherman	Y	Y	Y	N	N	Y	N	Y
25 *McKeon*	N	N	N	Y	Y	N	Y	N
26 Berman	Y	Y	Y	N	N	Y	N	Y
27 Schiff	N	N	N	Y	Y	Y	N	Y
28 *Dreier*	N	N	N	Y	Y	N	Y	N
29 Waxman	Y	Y	Y	N	N	Y	N	Y
30 Becerra	Y	Y	Y	N	N	Y	N	Y
31 Solis	Y	Y	Y	N	N	Y	N	Y
32 Watson	Y	Y	Y	N	N	Y	N	Y
33 Roybal-Allard	Y	Y	Y	N	N	Y	N	Y
34 Napolitano	Y	Y	Y	N	N	Y	N	Y
35 Waters	?	Y	Y	N	N	Y	N	Y
36 Harman	N	N	N	Y	Y	N	Y	N
37 Millender-McD.	N	Y	N	N	N	Y	N	Y
38 Horn	N	N	N	Y	Y	N	Y	N

	352	353	354	355	356	357	358	359
39 *Royce*	N	N	N	Y	Y	N	Y	N
40 *Lewis*	N	N	N	Y	Y	N	Y	N
41 *Miller, Gary*	N	N	N	Y	Y	N	Y	N
42 Baca	Y	Y	Y	N	N	Y	N	Y
43 *Calvert*	N	N	N	Y	Y	N	Y	N
44 *Bono*	N	N	N	Y	Y	N	Y	N
45 *Rohrabacher*	N	N	N	Y	Y	N	Y	N
46 Sanchez	Y	Y	N	N	N	Y	N	Y
47 *Cox*	N	N	N	Y	Y	N	Y	N
48 *Issa*	N	N	N	Y	Y	N	Y	N
49 Davis	Y	Y	N	N	N	Y	N	Y
50 Filner	Y	Y	Y	N	N	Y	N	Y
51 *Cunningham*	N	N	N	Y	Y	N	Y	?
52 *Hunter*	N	N	N	Y	N	Y	N	N
COLORADO								
1 DeGette	Y	N	Y	N	N	Y	N	Y
2 Udall	Y	Y	Y	N	N	Y	N	Y
3 *McInnis*	N	N	N	Y	Y	N	Y	N
4 *Schaffer*	N	N	N	Y	Y	N	Y	N
5 *Hefley*	N	N	N	Y	N	N	Y	N
6 *Tancredo*	N	N	N	Y	Y	N	Y	N
CONNECTICUT								
1 Larson	Y	N	Y	N	N	Y	N	Y
2 *Simmons*	N	N	N	Y	Y	Y	Y	N
3 DeLauro	Y	Y	Y	N	N	Y	N	Y
4 *Shays*	N	N	N	Y	Y	N	Y	N
5 Maloney	N	N	N	N	N	Y	N	Y
6 *Johnson*	N	N	N	Y	Y	N	Y	N
DELAWARE								
AL *Castle*	N	N	N	Y	Y	N	Y	N
FLORIDA								
1 *Miller, J.*	N	N	N	Y	Y	N	Y	N
2 Boyd	N	N	Y	Y	Y	Y	N	Y
3 Brown	N	Y	N	N	N	Y	N	Y
4 *Crenshaw*	N	N	N	Y	Y	N	Y	N
5 Thurman	Y	Y	N	N	N	Y	N	Y
6 *Stearns*	N	N	N	Y	Y	N	Y	N
7 *Mica*	N	Y	N	Y	Y	N	Y	N
8 *Keller*	N	N	N	Y	Y	N	Y	N
9 *Bilirakis*	N	N	N	Y	Y	N	Y	N
10 *Young*	N	N	N	Y	Y	N	Y	N
11 Davis	Y	Y	Y	N	N	Y	N	Y
12 *Putnam*	N	N	N	Y	Y	N	Y	N
13 *Miller, D.*	N	N	N	Y	Y	N	Y	N
14 *Goss*	N	N	N	Y	N	N	Y	N
15 *Weldon*	N	N	?	Y	Y	N	Y	N
16 *Foley*	N	N	N	Y	Y	N	Y	N
17 Meek	Y	Y	Y	N	N	Y	N	Y
18 *Ros-Lehtinen*	N	N	N	Y	Y	N	Y	N
19 Wexler	Y	N	N	N	N	Y	N	Y
20 Deutsch	N	N	N	N	Y	Y	N	Y
21 *Diaz-Balart*	N	N	N	Y	Y	N	Y	N
22 *Shaw*	N	N	N	Y	Y	N	Y	N
23 Hastings	Y	Y	Y	N	N	Y	N	Y
GEORGIA								
1 *Kingston*	N	N	N	Y	Y	N	Y	N
2 Bishop	N	Y	Y	N	N	Y	N	Y
3 *Collins*	N	N	N	Y	?	N	Y	N
4 McKinney	Y	Y	Y	N	N	Y	N	Y
5 Lewis	Y	Y	Y	N	N	Y	N	Y
6 *Isakson*	N	Y	N	Y	Y	N	Y	N
7 *Barr*	N	N	N	Y	N	N	Y	N
8 *Chambliss*	N	N	N	Y	Y	N	Y	N
9 *Deal*	N	N	N	Y	Y	N	Y	N
10 *Norwood*	N	N	N	Y	Y	N	Y	N
11 *Linder*	N	N	N	Y	Y	N	Y	N
HAWAII								
1 Abercrombie	Y	N	Y	N	N	Y	N	Y
2 Mink	Y	Y	Y	N	N	Y	N	Y
IDAHO								
1 *Otter*	N	N	N	Y	N	Y	N	N
2 *Simpson*	N	N	N	Y	Y	N	Y	N
ILLINOIS								
1 Rush	Y	Y	Y	N	N	Y	N	Y
2 Jackson	Y	Y	Y	N	N	Y	N	Y
3 Lipinski	Y	Y	Y	N	N	Y	N	Y
4 Gutierrez	Y	Y	Y	N	N	Y	N	Y
5 Blagojevich	N	Y	N	N	N	Y	N	Y
6 *Hyde*	N	N	N	Y	Y	N	Y	N
7 Davis	Y	Y	Y	N	N	Y	N	Y
8 *Crane*	N	N	Y	Y	Y	N	Y	N
9 Schakowsky	Y	Y	Y	N	N	Y	N	Y
10 *Kirk*	N	N	N	Y	Y	N	Y	N
11 *Weller*	N	N	N	Y	Y	N	Y	N
12 Costello	Y	Y	Y	N	N	Y	N	Y
13 *Biggert*	N	N	N	Y	Y	N	Y	N

ND Northern Democrats   SD Southern Democrats

	352	353	354	355	356	357	358	359
14 ***Hastert***	N	N						N
15 ***Johnson***	N	N	N	Y	Y	N	Y	Y
16 ***Manzullo***	N	N	N	Y	Y	N	Y	N
17 Evans	Y	Y	Y	N	N	Y	N	Y
18 ***LaHood***	N	N	N	Y	Y	N	Y	N
19 Phelps	N	N	N	Y	N	Y	N	Y
20 ***Shimkus***	N	N	N	Y	Y	N	Y	N
INDIANA								
1 Visclosky	Y	Y	Y	N	N	Y	N	Y
2 ***Pence***	N	N	N	Y	Y	N	Y	N
3 Roemer	Y	Y	N	N	N	Y	N	Y
4 ***Souder***	N	N	N	Y	Y	N	Y	N
5 ***Buyer***	N	N	N	Y	Y	N	Y	N
6 ***Burton***	N	N	N	Y	Y	N	Y	N
7 ***Kerns***	N	N	N	Y	Y	N	Y	N
8 ***Hostettler***	N	Y	N	N	Y	N	Y	N
9 Hill	N	N	N	Y	Y	N	Y	Y
10 Carson	Y	Y	Y	N	N	Y	N	Y
IOWA								
1 ***Leach***	N	N	N	Y	Y	N	Y	N
2 ***Nussle***	N	N	N	Y	Y	N	Y	N
3 Boswell	Y	Y	Y	Y	N	Y	N	Y
4 ***Ganske***	N	N	N	Y	Y	N	Y	N
5 ***Latham***	N	N	N	Y	Y	N	Y	N
KANSAS								
1 ***Moran***	N	N	N	Y	Y	N	Y	N
2 ***Ryun***	N	N	N	Y	Y	N	Y	N
3 Moore	N	Y	Y	N	N	Y	N	Y
4 ***Tiahrt***	N	N	N	Y	Y	N	Y	N
KENTUCKY								
1 ***Whitfield***	N	N	N	Y	Y	N	Y	N
2 ***Lewis***	N	N	N	Y	Y	N	Y	N
3 ***Northup***	N	N	N	Y	Y	N	Y	N
4 Lucas	N	N	N	Y	Y	N	Y	Y
5 ***Rogers***	N	N	N	Y	Y	N	Y	N
6 ***Fletcher***	N	N	?	Y	Y	N	Y	N
LOUISIANA								
1 ***Vitter***	N	N	N	Y	Y	N	Y	N
2 Jefferson	Y	Y	Y	N	N	Y	N	Y
3 ***Tauzin***	N	N	N	Y	Y	N	Y	N
4 ***McCrery***	N	N	N	Y	Y	N	Y	N
5 ***Cooksey***	N	N	N	Y	Y	N	Y	N
6 ***Baker***	N	N	N	Y	Y	N	Y	N
7 John	Y	N	N	Y	N	Y	N	Y
MAINE								
1 Allen	Y	Y	Y	N	N	Y	N	Y
2 Baldacci	Y	Y	Y	N	N	Y	N	Y
MARYLAND								
1 ***Gilchrest***	N	N	N	Y	Y	N	Y	?
2 ***Ehrlich***	N	N	N	Y	Y	N	Y	N
3 Cardin	Y	Y	Y	N	N	Y	N	Y
4 Wynn	Y	Y	Y	N	N	Y	N	Y
5 Hoyer	Y	N	Y	N	N	Y	N	Y
6 ***Bartlett***	N	N	N	Y	Y	N	Y	N
7 Cummings	Y	Y	Y	N	N	Y	N	Y
8 ***Morella***	N	N	?	Y	N	Y	N	Y
MASSACHUSETTS								
1 Olver	Y	Y	Y	N	N	Y	N	Y
2 Neal	Y	Y	Y	N	N	Y	N	Y
3 McGovern	Y	N	Y	N	N	Y	N	Y
4 Frank	Y	Y	Y	N	N	Y	N	Y
5 Meehan	?	?	?	?	?	?	?	?
6 Tierney	Y	Y	Y	N	N	Y	N	Y
7 Markey	Y	Y	Y	N	N	Y	N	Y
8 Capuano	Y	Y	Y	N	N	Y	N	Y
9 Lynch	Y	Y	N	Y	N	Y	N	Y
10 Delahunt	N	N	Y	N	N	Y	N	Y
MICHIGAN								
1 Stupak	Y	Y	Y	N	N	Y	N	Y
2 ***Hoekstra***	N	N	N	Y	Y	N	Y	N
3 ***Ehlers***	N	N	N	Y	Y	N	Y	N
4 ***Camp***	N	N	N	Y	Y	N	Y	N
5 Barcia	Y	Y	Y	N	N	Y	N	Y
6 ***Upton***	N	N	N	Y	Y	N	Y	N
7 ***Smith***	N	N	N	Y	Y	N	Y	N
8 ***Rogers***	N	N	N	Y	Y	N	Y	N
9 Kildee	Y	N	Y	N	N	Y	N	Y
10 Bonior	Y	N	Y	Y	N	Y	N	Y
11 ***Knollenberg***	N	N	N	Y	Y	N	Y	N
12 Levin	Y	N	Y	N	N	Y	N	Y
13 Rivers	Y	Y	Y	N	N	Y	N	Y
14 Conyers	Y	Y	Y	N	N	Y	N	Y
15 Kilpatrick	Y	Y	Y	N	N	Y	N	Y
16 Dingell	Y	Y	Y	N	N	Y	N	Y
MINNESOTA								
1 ***Gutknecht***	N	N	N	Y	Y	N	Y	N
2 ***Kennedy***	N	N	N	Y	Y	N	Y	N
3 ***Ramstad***	N	N	N	Y	Y	N	Y	N
4 McCollum	Y	Y	Y	N	N	Y	N	Y
5 Sabo	Y	Y	Y	N	N	Y	N	Y
6 Luther	Y	N	N	N	N	Y	N	Y
7 Peterson	Y	Y	N	Y	N	Y	N	Y
8 Oberstar	Y	Y	Y	N	N	Y	N	Y
MISSISSIPPI								
1 ***Wicker***	N	N	N	Y	Y	N	Y	N
2 Thompson	Y	Y	Y	N	N	Y	N	Y
3 ***Pickering***	–	N	N	Y	Y	N	Y	N
4 Shows	Y	Y	N	N	N	Y	N	Y
5 Taylor	Y	N	N	N	Y	N	Y	Y
MISSOURI								
1 Clay	?	Y	N	N	N	Y	N	Y
2 ***Akin***	N	N	N	N	Y	N	Y	N
3 Gephardt	Y	Y	Y	Y	N	Y	N	Y
4 Skelton	Y	Y	N	N	N	Y	N	Y
5 McCarthy	Y	Y	Y	N	N	Y	N	Y
6 ***Graves***	N	N	N	Y	Y	N	Y	N
7 ***Blunt***	?	?	?	?	?	?	?	?
8 ***Emerson***	N	N	N	Y	Y	N	Y	N
9 ***Hulshof***	N	N	N	Y	Y	N	Y	N
MONTANA								
AL ***Rehberg***	N	N	N	Y	Y	N	Y	N
NEBRASKA								
1 ***Bereuter***	N	N	N	Y	Y	N	Y	N
2 ***Terry***	N	N	N	Y	Y	N	Y	N
3 ***Osborne***	N	N	N	Y	Y	N	Y	N
NEVADA								
1 Berkley	Y	Y	Y	N	N	Y	N	Y
2 ***Gibbons***	N	N	N	Y	Y	N	Y	N
NEW HAMPSHIRE								
1 ***Sununu***	N	N	N	Y	Y	N	Y	N
2 ***Bass***	N	N	N	Y	Y	N	Y	N
NEW JERSEY								
1 Andrews	Y	N	N	N	N	Y	N	Y
2 ***LoBiondo***	N	N	N	Y	Y	N	Y	N
3 ***Saxton***	N	N	N	Y	Y	N	Y	N
4 ***Smith***	N	N	N	Y	Y	N	Y	N
5 ***Roukema***	N	N	N	Y	Y	N	Y	N
6 Pallone	Y	Y	Y	N	N	Y	N	Y
7 ***Ferguson***	N	N	N	Y	Y	N	Y	N
8 Pascrell	N	N	N	N	N	Y	N	Y
9 Rothman	Y	N	Y	N	N	Y	N	Y
10 Payne	Y	Y	Y	N	N	Y	N	Y
11 ***Frelinghuysen***	N	N	N	Y	Y	N	Y	N
12 Holt	Y	N	Y	N	N	Y	N	Y
13 Menendez	Y	N	Y	N	N	Y	N	Y
NEW MEXICO								
1 ***Wilson***	N	N	N	Y	Y	N	Y	N
2 ***Skeen***	N	N	N	Y	Y	N	Y	N
3 Udall	Y	Y	N	N	N	Y	N	Y
NEW YORK								
1 ***Grucci***	N	N	N	Y	Y	N	Y	N
2 Israel	Y	N	Y	Y	N	Y	N	Y
3 ***King***	N	N	N	Y	Y	N	Y	N
4 McCarthy	Y	Y	N	N	N	Y	N	Y
5 Ackerman	Y	Y	Y	N	N	Y	N	Y
6 Meeks	Y	Y	Y	N	N	Y	N	Y
7 Crowley	N	Y	Y	N	N	Y	N	Y
8 Nadler	Y	Y	Y	N	N	Y	N	Y
9 Weiner	Y	Y	Y	N	N	Y	N	Y
10 Towns	Y	Y	Y	N	N	Y	N	Y
11 Owens	Y	Y	Y	N	N	Y	N	Y
12 Velázquez	Y	Y	Y	N	N	Y	N	Y
13 ***Fossella***	N	N	N	Y	Y	N	Y	N
14 Maloney	Y	Y	Y	Y	N	Y	N	Y
15 Rangel	Y	Y	Y	N	N	Y	N	Y
16 Serrano	Y	Y	Y	N	N	Y	N	Y
17 Engel	Y	Y	Y	N	N	Y	N	Y
18 Lowey	Y	Y	Y	N	N	Y	N	Y
19 ***Kelly***	N	N	N	Y	Y	N	Y	N
20 ***Gilman***	N	N	N	Y	Y	N	Y	Y
21 McNulty	Y	Y	Y	N	N	Y	N	Y
22 ***Sweeney***	N	N	N	Y	Y	N	Y	N
23 ***Boehlert***	N	N	N	Y	Y	N	Y	N
24 ***McHugh***	N	N	Y	Y	Y	N	Y	N
25 ***Walsh***	N	N	N	Y	Y	N	Y	N
26 Hinchey	Y	Y	Y	N	N	Y	N	Y
27 ***Reynolds***	N	N	N	Y	Y	N	Y	N
28 Slaughter	Y	Y	Y	N	N	Y	N	Y
29 LaFalce	Y	Y	N	Y	N	Y	N	Y
30 ***Quinn***	N	N	N	Y	Y	N	Y	N
31 ***Houghton***	N	N	Y	Y	Y	N	Y	N
NORTH CAROLINA								
1 Clayton	Y	Y	Y	N	N	Y	N	Y
2 Etheridge	Y	Y	Y	N	N	Y	N	Y
3 ***Jones***	N	N	N	N	Y	N	Y	N
4 Price	Y	Y	Y	N	N	Y	N	Y
5 ***Burr***	N	N	N	Y	Y	N	Y	N
6 ***Coble***	N	N	N	Y	Y	N	Y	N
7 McIntyre	N	Y	Y	Y	N	Y	N	Y
8 ***Hayes***	N	N	N	Y	Y	N	Y	N
9 ***Myrick***	N	N	N	Y	Y	N	Y	N
10 ***Ballenger***	N	N	N	Y	Y	N	Y	N
11 ***Taylor***	N	N	N	N	Y	N	Y	N
12 Watt	Y	Y	Y	N	N	Y	N	Y
NORTH DAKOTA								
AL Pomeroy	Y	N	Y	N	N	Y	N	Y
OHIO								
1 ***Chabot***	N	N	N	Y	Y	N	Y	N
2 ***Portman***	N	N	N	Y	Y	N	Y	N
3 Hall	Y	Y	Y	N	N	Y	N	Y
4 ***Oxley***	N	N	N	Y	Y	N	Y	N
5 ***Gillmor***	N	N	N	Y	Y	N	Y	N
6 Strickland	Y	Y	Y	N	N	Y	N	Y
7 ***Hobson***	N	N	N	Y	Y	N	Y	N
8 ***Boehner***	N	N	N	Y	Y	N	Y	N
9 Kaptur	Y	Y	Y	N	N	Y	?	Y
10 Kucinich	Y	Y	Y	N	N	Y	N	Y
11 Jones	Y	Y	Y	N	N	Y	N	Y
12 ***Tiberi***	N	N	N	Y	Y	N	Y	N
13 Brown	Y	Y	Y	N	N	Y	N	Y
14 Sawyer	Y	Y	Y	N	N	Y	N	Y
15 ***Pryce***	N	N	–	Y	Y	N	Y	N
16 ***Regula***	N	N	N	Y	Y	N	Y	N
17 Vacant								
18 ***Ney***	N	N	N	Y	Y	N	Y	N
19 ***LaTourette***	N	Y	N	Y	Y	N	Y	N
OKLAHOMA								
1 ***Sullivan***	N	N	N	Y	Y	N	Y	N
2 Carson	N	Y	Y	N	N	Y	N	Y
3 ***Watkins***	N	N	N	Y	Y	N	Y	N
4 ***Watts***	N	N	N	Y	Y	N	Y	N
5 ***Istook***	N	Y	Y	Y	Y	N	Y	N
6 ***Lucas***	N	N	N	Y	Y	N	Y	N
OREGON								
1 Wu	Y	Y	Y	Y	N	Y	N	Y
2 ***Walden***	N	N	N	Y	Y	N	Y	N
3 Blumenauer	Y	Y	Y	N	N	Y	N	Y
4 DeFazio	Y	Y	Y	N	N	Y	N	Y
5 Hooley	Y	Y	N	N	N	Y	N	Y
PENNSYLVANIA								
1 Brady	Y	N	Y	N	N	Y	N	Y
2 Fattah	Y	Y	Y	N	N	Y	N	Y
3 Borski	Y	Y	Y	Y	N	Y	N	Y
4 ***Hart***	N	N	N	Y	Y	N	Y	N
5 ***Peterson***	N	N	N	Y	Y	N	Y	N
6 Holden	Y	N	N	N	N	Y	N	Y
7 ***Weldon***	N	N	N	Y	Y	N	Y	Y
8 ***Greenwood***	N	N	N	Y	Y	N	Y	N
9 ***Shuster, Bill***	N	N	N	Y	Y	N	Y	N
10 ***Sherwood***	N	N	N	Y	Y	N	Y	N
11 Kanjorski	Y	Y	Y	N	N	Y	N	Y
12 Murtha	Y	N	N	N	N	Y	N	Y
13 Hoeffel	Y	N	Y	N	N	Y	N	Y
14 Coyne	Y	Y	Y	N	N	Y	N	Y
15 ***Toomey***	N	N	N	Y	Y	N	Y	N
16 ***Pitts***	N	N	N	Y	Y	N	Y	N
17 ***Gekas***	N	N	N	Y	Y	N	Y	N
18 Doyle	Y	Y	Y	N	N	Y	N	Y
19 ***Platts***	N	N	N	Y	Y	N	Y	N
20 Mascara	Y	Y	Y	N	N	Y	N	Y
21 ***English***	N	N	N	Y	Y	N	Y	N
RHODE ISLAND								
1 Kennedy	Y	Y	Y	N	N	Y	N	Y
2 Langevin	Y	N	Y	N	N	Y	N	Y
SOUTH CAROLINA								
1 ***Brown***	N	N	N	Y	Y	N	Y	N
2 ***Wilson***	N	N	N	Y	Y	N	Y	N
3 ***Graham***	N	N	N	Y	Y	N	Y	N
4 ***DeMint***	N	N	N	Y	Y	N	Y	N
5 Spratt	N	Y	Y	N	N	Y	N	Y
6 Clyburn	Y	Y	Y	N	N	Y	N	Y
SOUTH DAKOTA								
AL ***Thune***	N	N	N	Y	Y	N	Y	N
TENNESSEE								
1 ***Jenkins***	N	N	N	Y	Y	N	Y	N
2 ***Duncan***	N	Y	N	Y	Y	N	Y	N
3 ***Wamp***	N	N	N	Y	Y	N	Y	N
4 ***Hilleary***	N	N	N	Y	Y	N	Y	N
5 Clement	N	Y	Y	Y	N	Y	N	Y
6 Gordon	Y	Y	Y	Y	N	Y	N	Y
7 ***Bryant***	N	N	N	Y	Y	N	Y	N
8 Tanner	Y	N	Y	Y	N	Y	N	Y
9 Ford	N	N	Y	N	N	Y	N	Y
TEXAS								
1 Sandlin	Y	Y	Y	N	N	Y	N	Y
2 Turner	Y	N	Y	Y	N	Y	N	Y
3 ***Johnson, Sam***	N	N	N	N	Y	N	Y	N
4 Hall	N	N	N	N	Y	N	Y	N
5 ***Sessions***	N	N	N	Y	Y	N	Y	N
6 ***Barton***	N	N	N	Y	Y	N	Y	N
7 ***Culberson***	N	N	N	Y	Y	N	Y	N
8 ***Brady***	N	N	N	Y	Y	N	Y	N
9 Lampson	Y	Y	Y	N	N	Y	N	Y
10 Doggett	Y	N	Y	N	N	Y	N	Y
11 Edwards	Y	N	N	Y	N	Y	N	Y
12 ***Granger***	N	N	N	N	Y	N	Y	N
13 ***Thornberry***	N	N	N	N	Y	N	Y	N
14 ***Paul***	N	Y	Y	N	Y	N	Y	N
15 Hinojosa	Y	Y	Y	N	N	Y	N	Y
16 Reyes	Y	Y	Y	N	N	Y	N	Y
17 Stenholm	N	N	N	Y	Y	N	Y	Y
18 Jackson-Lee	Y	N	Y	N	N	Y	N	Y
19 ***Combest***	N	N	N	Y	Y	N	Y	?
20 Gonzalez	Y	Y	Y	N	N	Y	N	Y
21 ***Smith***	?	?	?	?	Y	N	Y	N
22 ***DeLay***	N	N	N	Y	Y	N	Y	N
23 ***Bonilla***	N	N	N	Y	Y	N	Y	N
24 Frost	Y	Y	Y	N	N	Y	N	Y
25 Bentsen	Y	N	Y	N	N	Y	N	Y
26 ***Armey***	N	N	N	Y	Y	N	Y	N
27 Ortiz	Y	Y	Y	N	N	Y	N	Y
28 Rodriguez	Y	Y	Y	N	N	Y	N	Y
29 Green	Y	N	Y	N	N	Y	N	Y
30 Johnson, E.B.	Y	N	Y	N	N	Y	N	Y
UTAH								
1 ***Hansen***	N	N	N	Y	Y	N	Y	N
2 Matheson	Y	Y	Y	N	N	Y	N	Y
3 ***Cannon***	N	N	N	Y	Y	N	Y	N
VERMONT								
AL *Sanders*	Y	Y	Y	N	N	Y	N	Y
VIRGINIA								
1 ***Davis, Jo Ann***	N	Y	N	Y	Y	N	Y	N
2 ***Schrock***	N	N	N	Y	Y	N	Y	N
3 Scott	Y	Y	Y	N	N	Y	N	Y
4 ***Forbes***	N	N	N	Y	Y	N	Y	N
5 *Goode*	N	N	N	Y	Y	N	Y	N
6 ***Goodlatte***	N	N	N	Y	Y	N	Y	N
7 ***Cantor***	N	N	N	Y	Y	N	Y	N
8 Moran	N	N	Y	N	N	Y	N	Y
9 Boucher	Y	Y	Y	Y	N	Y	N	Y
10 ***Wolf***	N	N	N	Y	Y	N	Y	N
11 ***Davis, T.***	N	N	Y	Y	Y	N	Y	N
WASHINGTON								
1 Inslee	Y	Y	Y	N	N	Y	N	Y
2 Larsen	Y	Y	Y	N	N	Y	N	Y
3 Baird	N	Y	Y	N	N	Y	N	Y
4 ***Hastings***	N	N	N	Y	Y	N	Y	N
5 ***Nethercutt***	N	N	N	Y	Y	N	Y	N
6 Dicks	Y	Y	Y	Y	N	Y	N	Y
7 McDermott	Y	Y	Y	N	N	Y	N	Y
8 ***Dunn***	N	N	N	Y	Y	N	Y	N
9 Smith	N	N	Y	Y	N	Y	N	Y
WEST VIRGINIA								
1 Mollohan	Y	N	Y	Y	N	Y	N	Y
2 ***Capito***	N	N	N	Y	Y	Y	Y	N
3 Rahall	Y	Y	Y	N	N	Y	N	Y
WISCONSIN								
1 ***Ryan***	N	N	N	N	Y	N	Y	N
2 Baldwin	Y	Y	Y	N	N	Y	N	Y
3 Kind	N	Y	N	Y	N	Y	N	Y
4 Kleczka	Y	Y	Y	N	N	Y	N	Y
5 Barrett	Y	Y	N	N	N	Y	N	Y
6 ***Petri***	N	Y	Y	Y	Y	Y	Y	N
7 Obey	Y	Y	Y	N	N	Y	N	Y
8 ***Green***	N	N	N	Y	Y	N	Y	N
9 ***Sensenbrenner***	N	N	N	Y	Y	N	Y	N
WYOMING								
AL ***Cubin***	N	N	N	Y	Y	N	Y	N

Southern states - Ala., Ark., Fla., Ga., Ky., La., Miss., N.C., Okla., S.C., Tenn., Texas, Va.

360. HR 5005. Homeland Security/Civil Service Employment Regulations. Waxman, D-Calif., amendment that would bar Homeland Security Department employee exemptions from Title 5 civil service employment rules and provide certain salary and other employment protections, including a bar on pay reductions, for federal employees who transfer into the new department. Rejected 208-220: R 1-216; D 206-3 (ND 155-0, SD 51-3); I 1-1. July 26, 2002.

361. HR 5005. Homeland Security/Manager's Amendment. Armey, R-Texas, amendment that would make various changes, including creating a reward program for businesses that work on anti-terrorism technologies. It would cut the Office of Management and Budget (OMB) director's authority over certain incidental transfers of personnel and assets. It would clarify that generally there are no state and local law pre-emptions and express the sense of Congress in favor of the Posse Comitatus law, which prohibits soldiers from assuming police powers within the United States. It would require federal agencies to adhere to information security standards and centralize the enforcement of those standards in OMB. It also would clarify liability protections, including the reimposition of certain protections for aviation screening contractors, and clarify the department's responsibilities regarding narcotics interdiction and other activities. Adopted 222-204: R 214-1; D 7-202 (ND 4-151, SD 3-51); I 1-1. July 26, 2002.

362. HR 5005. Homeland Security/Airport Bomb Detectors. Oberstar, D-Minn., amendment that would strike a provision extending airports' deadline for installing bomb detection equipment by one year, to Dec. 31, 2003. Rejected 211-217: R 23-194; D 187-22 (ND 146-9, SD 41-13); I 1-1. July 26, 2002.

363. HR 5005. Homeland Security/FOIA and Whistleblower Protection. Schakowsky, D-Ill., amendment that would delete a provision containing Freedom of Information Act (FOIA) exemptions. It also would replace a provision to establish advisory committees with a provision to allow remedies for retaliation against whistleblowers. Rejected 188-240: R 6-211; D 181-28 (ND 145-10, SD 36-18); I 1-1. July 26, 2002.

364. HR 5005. Homeland Security/FOIA. Davis, R-Va., amendment that would extend FOIA exemptions to other agencies as determined by the Homeland Security secretary. Rejected 195-233: R 179-39; D 15-193 (ND 5-149, SD 10-44); I 1-1. July 26, 2002.

365. HR 5005. Homeland Security/Visas. Weldon, R-Fla., amendment that would change certain visa provisions, including transferring the visa office from the State Department to the Homeland Security Department, allowing Foreign Service Officers to remain in posts issuing visas until the new department hires and trains its own employees, and maintaining the secretary of State's ability to deny visas when in the national interest. Rejected 118-309: R 108-110; D 9-198 (ND 6-147, SD 3-51); I 1-1. A "nay" was a vote in support of the president's position. July 26, 2002.

366. HR 5005. Homeland Security/Recommit. DeLauro, D-Conn., motion to recommit the bill to the Select Committee on Homeland Security with instructions that it be reported back with language that would ban contracts with corporate expatriates. Motion agreed to 318-110: R 109-109; D 207-1 (ND 153-1, SD 54-0); I 2-0. July 26, 2002.

Key

Y Voted for (yea).
Paired for.
+ Announced for.
N Voted against (nay).
X Paired against.
– Announced against.
P Voted "present."
C Voted "present" to avoid possible conflict of interest.
? Did not vote or otherwise make a position known.

Democrats   *Republicans*   *Independents*

	360	361	362	363	364	365	366
ALABAMA							
1 *Callahan*	N	Y	N	N	Y	N	N
2 *Everett*	N	Y	N	N	Y	Y	Y
3 *Riley*	N	Y	N	N	Y	Y	Y
4 *Aderholt*	N	Y	N	N	Y	Y	Y
5 Cramer	Y	N	Y	N	Y	N	Y
6 *Bachus*	N	Y	N	N	N	N	Y
7 Hilliard	Y	N	Y	Y	N	N	Y
ALASKA							
AL *Young*	N	Y	N	N	Y	N	N
ARIZONA							
1 *Flake*	N	Y	N	N	N	N	N
2 Pastor	Y	Y	N	Y	N	N	Y
3 *Stump*	N	Y	N	N	Y	N	N
4 *Shadegg*	N	Y	N	N	Y	Y	N
5 *Kolbe*	N	Y	Y	N	Y	Y	N
6 *Hayworth*	N	Y	N	N	Y	Y	N
ARKANSAS							
1 Berry	Y	N	Y	N	N	N	Y
2 Snyder	Y	N	Y	N	N	N	Y
3 *Boozman*	N	Y	N	N	Y	N	Y
4 Ross	Y	N	Y	Y	N	N	Y
CALIFORNIA							
1 Thompson	Y	N	Y	N	Y	N	Y
2 *Herger*	N	Y	N	N	Y	N	N
3 *Ose*	N	Y	N	Y	Y	Y	Y
4 *Doolittle*	N	Y	N	N	Y	N	N
5 Matsui	Y	N	Y	N	Y	N	Y
6 Woolsey	Y	N	Y	Y	N	N	Y
7 Miller, George	Y	N	Y	Y	N	N	Y
8 Pelosi	Y	N	Y	Y	N	N	Y
9 Lee	Y	N	Y	Y	N	N	Y
10 Tauscher	Y	N	N	N	N	N	Y
11 *Pombo*	N	Y	N	N	Y	Y	N
12 Lantos	Y	N	Y	N	N	N	Y
13 Stark	Y	N	Y	Y	N	N	Y
14 Eshoo	Y	N	Y	Y	N	N	Y
15 Honda	Y	N	Y	Y	N	N	Y
16 Lofgren	Y	N	Y	Y	N	N	Y
17 Farr	Y	N	Y	Y	N	N	Y
18 Condit	Y	N	Y	Y	N	N	Y
19 *Radanovich*	N	N	N	N	Y	Y	N
20 Dooley	Y	Y	N	Y	N	N	Y
21 *Thomas*	N	Y	N	N	N	N	N
22 Capps	Y	N	Y	Y	N	N	Y
23 *Gallegly*	N	Y	N	N	Y	Y	Y
24 Sherman	Y	N	Y	Y	N	N	Y
25 *McKeon*	N	Y	N	N	Y	N	N
26 Berman	Y	N	Y	N	N	N	Y
27 Schiff	Y	N	Y	N	N	N	Y
28 *Dreier*	N	Y	N	N	Y	N	N
29 Waxman	Y	N	Y	Y	N	N	Y
30 Becerra	Y	N	Y	N	N	N	Y
31 Solis	Y	N	Y	Y	N	N	Y
32 Watson	Y	N	Y	N	N	N	Y
33 Roybal-Allard	Y	N	Y	N	N	N	Y
34 Napolitano	Y	N	Y	Y	N	N	Y
35 Waters	Y	N	Y	Y	N	N	?
36 Harman	Y	Y	N	Y	N	N	Y
37 Millender-McD.	Y	N	Y	N	N	N	Y
38 *Horn*	N	Y	N	Y	N	N	N

	360	361	362	363	364	365	366
39 *Royce*	N	Y	N	N	Y	N	Y
40 *Lewis*	N	Y	N	N	Y	N	N
41 *Miller, Gary*	N	Y	N	N	Y	N	N
42 Baca	Y	N	Y	N	N	N	N
43 *Calvert*	N	Y	N	N	Y	N	N
44 *Bono*	N	Y	N	N	Y	Y	N
45 *Rohrabacher*	N	Y	N	N	Y	Y	N
46 Sanchez	Y	N	Y	Y	N	N	Y
47 *Cox*	N	Y	?	N	Y	N	N
48 *Issa*	N	Y	N	N	Y	N	N
49 Davis	Y	N	Y	N	N	N	Y
50 Filner	Y	N	Y	N	N	N	Y
51 *Cunningham*	?	Y	N	N	Y	Y	Y
52 *Hunter*	N	Y	N	N	Y	Y	N
COLORADO							
1 DeGette	Y	N	N	Y	N	N	Y
2 Udall	Y	N	Y	N	N	N	Y
3 *McInnis*	N	Y	N	N	Y	Y	N
4 *Schaffer*	N	Y	N	N	Y	Y	N
5 *Hefley*	N	Y	N	N	Y	Y	Y
6 *Tancredo*	N	Y	N	N	Y	Y	Y
CONNECTICUT							
1 Larson	Y	N	Y	N	N	N	Y
2 *Simmons*	N	Y	Y	N	Y	N	Y
3 DeLauro	Y	N	Y	N	N	N	Y
4 *Shays*	N	Y	Y	N	Y	N	Y
5 Maloney	Y	N	Y	N	Y	N	Y
6 *Johnson*	N	Y	Y	N	Y	N	Y
DELAWARE							
AL *Castle*	N	Y	N	N	Y	Y	Y
FLORIDA							
1 *Miller, J.*	N	Y	N	N	N	Y	N
2 Boyd	Y	N	Y	N	N	N	Y
3 Brown	Y	N	Y	N	Y	N	Y
4 *Crenshaw*	N	Y	N	N	Y	N	N
5 Thurman	Y	N	Y	N	N	N	Y
6 *Stearns*	N	Y	N	N	Y	N	Y
7 *Mica*	N	Y	N	N	Y	N	Y
8 *Keller*	N	Y	N	N	Y	Y	Y
9 *Bilirakis*	N	Y	N	N	Y	Y	Y
10 *Young*	N	Y	N	N	Y	N	Y
11 Davis	Y	N	N	Y	N	N	Y
12 *Putnam*	N	Y	N	N	Y	Y	N
13 *Miller, D.*	N	Y	N	N	Y	N	N
14 *Goss*	N	Y	N	N	Y	N	N
15 *Weldon*	N	Y	N	N	Y	Y	Y
16 *Foley*	N	Y	N	N	Y	Y	Y
17 Meek	Y	N	N	Y	N	N	Y
18 *Ros-Lehtinen*	N	Y	N	N	Y	N	N
19 Wexler	Y	N	Y	N	N	N	Y
20 Deutsch	Y	N	Y	N	N	N	Y
21 *Diaz-Balart*	N	Y	N	N	N	N	N
22 *Shaw*	N	Y	N	N	Y	N	N
23 Hastings	Y	N	N	Y	N	N	Y
GEORGIA							
1 *Kingston*	N	Y	N	N	Y	Y	Y
2 Bishop	Y	N	N	N	N	N	Y
3 *Collins*	N	Y	N	N	Y	N	N
4 McKinney	Y	N	Y	N	N	N	Y
5 Lewis	Y	N	Y	N	N	N	Y
6 *Isakson*	N	Y	N	N	Y	N	Y
7 *Barr*	N	Y	N	N	Y	N	N
8 *Chambliss*	N	Y	N	N	Y	N	Y
9 *Deal*	N	Y	N	N	Y	N	N
10 *Norwood*	N	Y	N	N	Y	Y	Y
11 *Linder*	N	Y	N	N	N	N	N
HAWAII							
1 Abercrombie	Y	N	Y	Y	N	N	Y
2 Mink	Y	N	Y	N	N	N	Y
IDAHO							
1 *Otter*	N	Y	N	N	Y	N	N
2 *Simpson*	N	Y	N	N	Y	N	N
ILLINOIS							
1 Rush	Y	N	Y	Y	N	N	Y
2 Jackson	Y	N	Y	Y	N	N	Y
3 Lipinski	Y	N	Y	Y	N	?	?
4 Gutierrez	Y	N	Y	Y	N	N	Y
5 Blagojevich	Y	N	Y	Y	N	N	Y
6 *Hyde*	N	Y	N	N	N	N	Y
7 Davis	Y	N	Y	Y	N	N	Y
8 *Crane*	N	Y	N	N	Y	Y	N
9 Schakowsky	Y	N	Y	Y	N	N	Y
10 *Kirk*	N	Y	N	N	Y	Y	N
11 *Weller*	N	Y	N	N	Y	Y	Y
12 Costello	Y	N	Y	Y	N	N	Y
13 *Biggert*	N	Y	N	N	Y	N	N

ND Northern Democrats   SD Southern Democrats

	360	361	362	363	364	365	366
14 ***Hastert***							
15 ***Johnson***	N	N	N	N	Y	Y	Y
16 ***Manzullo***	N	Y	N	Y	Y	Y	Y
17 Evans	Y	N	Y	Y	N	N	Y
18 ***LaHood***	N	Y	N	N	Y	N	N
19 Phelps	Y	N	Y	Y	N	N	Y
20 ***Shimkus***	N	Y	Y	N	Y	Y	Y
INDIANA							
1 Visclosky	Y	N	Y	Y	N	N	Y
2 ***Pence***	N	Y	N	N	Y	Y	Y
3 Roemer	Y	N	Y	N	N	N	Y
4 ***Souder***	N	Y	N	N	Y	N	N
5 ***Buyer***	N	Y	N	N	Y	Y	Y
6 ***Burton***	N	Y	N	N	Y	Y	Y
7 ***Kerns***	N	Y	N	N	N	Y	Y
8 ***Hostettler***	N	Y	N	Y	N	Y	N
9 Hill	Y	N	Y	N	N	N	Y
10 Carson	Y	N	Y	Y	N	N	Y
IOWA							
1 ***Leach***	N	Y	Y	N	N	N	Y
2 ***Nussle***	N	Y	N	N	Y	N	Y
3 Boswell	Y	N	Y	Y	N	N	Y
4 ***Ganske***	N	Y	Y	N	N	N	Y
5 ***Latham***	N	Y	N	N	Y	N	Y
KANSAS							
1 ***Moran***	N	Y	Y	N	N	Y	Y
2 ***Ryun***	N	Y	N	N	N	Y	N
3 Moore	Y	N	Y	Y	N	N	Y
4 ***Tiahrt***	N	Y	N	N	Y	Y	Y
KENTUCKY							
1 ***Whitfield***	N	Y	N	N	Y	N	Y
2 ***Lewis***	N	Y	N	N	Y	Y	N
3 ***Northup***	N	Y	N	N	Y	Y	Y
4 Lucas	N	Y	N	N	Y	N	Y
5 ***Rogers***	N	Y	N	N	Y	Y	Y
6 ***Fletcher***	N	Y	N	N	N	Y	Y
LOUISIANA							
1 ***Vitter***	N	Y	Y	N	Y	Y	N
2 Jefferson	Y	N	Y	Y	N	N	Y
3 ***Tauzin***	N	Y	N	N	N	Y	N
4 ***McCrery***	N	Y	N	N	Y	N	N
5 ***Cooksey***	N	Y	N	N	Y	Y	Y
6 ***Baker***	N	Y	N	N	Y	Y	N
7 John	Y	N	Y	N	Y	N	Y
MAINE							
1 Allen	Y	N	Y	Y	N	N	Y
2 Baldacci	Y	N	Y	Y	N	N	Y
MARYLAND							
1 ***Gilchrest***	?	?	N	N	Y	Y	Y
2 ***Ehrlich***	N	Y	N	N	Y	Y	Y
3 Cardin	Y	N	Y	Y	N	N	Y
4 Wynn	Y	N	Y	Y	N	N	Y
5 Hoyer	Y	N	Y	Y	N	N	Y
6 ***Bartlett***	N	Y	N	N	Y	Y	Y
7 Cummings	Y	N	Y	Y	N	N	Y
8 ***Morella***	Y	Y	N	Y	N	N	Y
MASSACHUSETTS							
1 Olver	Y	N	Y	Y	N	N	Y
2 Neal	Y	N	Y	Y	N	N	Y
3 McGovern	Y	N	Y	Y	N	N	Y
4 Frank	Y	N	Y	Y	N	N	Y
5 Meehan	?	?	?	?	?	?	?
6 Tierney	Y	N	Y	Y	N	N	Y
7 Markey	Y	N	Y	Y	N	N	Y
8 Capuano	Y	N	Y	Y	N	N	Y
9 Lynch	Y	N	Y	Y	N	N	Y
10 Delahunt	Y	N	Y	Y	N	N	Y
MICHIGAN							
1 Stupak	Y	N	Y	Y	N	N	Y
2 ***Hoekstra***	N	Y	N	N	N	N	N
3 ***Ehlers***	N	Y	N	N	Y	Y	N
4 ***Camp***	N	Y	N	N	Y	Y	N
5 Barcia	Y	N	Y	Y	N	N	Y
6 ***Upton***	N	Y	Y	N	Y	Y	Y
7 ***Smith***	N	Y	N	N	Y	N	N
8 ***Rogers***	N	Y	N	N	Y	Y	Y
9 Kildee	Y	N	Y	Y	N	N	Y
10 Bonior	Y	N	Y	Y	N	N	Y
11 ***Knollenberg***	N	Y	N	N	Y	N	N
12 Levin	Y	N	Y	Y	N	N	Y
13 Rivers	Y	N	Y	Y	N	N	Y
14 Conyers	Y	N	Y	Y	N	N	Y
15 Kilpatrick	Y	N	Y	Y	N	N	Y
16 Dingell	Y	N	Y	Y	N	N	Y

	360	361	362	363	364	365	366
MINNESOTA							
1 ***Gutknecht***	N	Y	N	N	N	Y	Y
2 ***Kennedy***	N	Y	N	N	Y	Y	Y
3 ***Ramstad***	N	Y	Y	N	Y	Y	Y
4 McCollum	Y	N	Y	Y	N	N	Y
5 Sabo	Y	N	Y	Y	N	N	Y
6 Luther	Y	N	Y	Y	N	N	Y
7 Peterson	Y	N	Y	N	Y	N	Y
8 Oberstar	Y	N	Y	Y	N	N	Y
MISSISSIPPI							
1 ***Wicker***	N	?	N	N	Y	Y	Y
2 Thompson	Y	N	Y	Y	N	N	Y
3 ***Pickering***	N	Y	N	N	Y	Y	Y
4 Shows	Y	N	Y	N	N	Y	Y
5 Taylor	Y	N	Y	N	N	Y	Y
MISSOURI							
1 Clay	Y	N	Y	Y	N	N	Y
2 ***Akin***	N	Y	N	N	Y	N	N
3 Gephardt	Y	N	Y	Y	N	N	Y
4 Skelton	Y	N	Y	Y	Y	N	Y
5 McCarthy	Y	N	Y	Y	N	N	Y
6 ***Graves***	N	Y	Y	N	Y	Y	Y
7 ***Blunt***	?	?	?	?	?	?	?
8 ***Emerson***	N	Y	N	N	Y	Y	Y
9 ***Hulshof***	N	Y	N	N	Y	Y	N
MONTANA							
AL ***Rehberg***	N	Y	N	N	Y	N	N
NEBRASKA							
1 ***Bereuter***	N	Y	N	N	Y	N	N
2 ***Terry***	N	Y	N	?	Y	N	N
3 ***Osborne***	N	Y	N	N	Y	N	N
NEVADA							
1 Berkley	Y	N	N	Y	N	N	Y
2 ***Gibbons***	N	Y	N	N	Y	N	N
NEW HAMPSHIRE							
1 ***Sununu***	N	Y	N	N	Y	N	Y
2 ***Bass***	N	Y	N	N	Y	N	Y
NEW JERSEY							
1 Andrews	Y	N	Y	Y	N	N	Y
2 ***LoBiondo***	N	Y	N	N	Y	N	Y
3 ***Saxton***	N	Y	N	N	Y	N	Y
4 ***Smith***	N	Y	N	N	N	N	Y
5 ***Roukema***	N	Y	?	?	?	?	?
6 Pallone	Y	N	Y	Y	N	N	Y
7 ***Ferguson***	N	Y	N	N	N	N	Y
8 Pascrell	Y	N	Y	Y	N	N	Y
9 Rothman	Y	N	Y	Y	N	N	Y
10 Payne	Y	N	Y	Y	N	N	Y
11 ***Frelinghuysen***	N	?	Y	N	Y	N	N
12 Holt	Y	N	Y	Y	N	N	Y
13 Menendez	Y	N	Y	N	N	N	Y
NEW MEXICO							
1 ***Wilson***	N	Y	Y	N	Y	N	Y
2 ***Skeen***	N	Y	N	N	Y	N	Y
3 Udall	Y	N	Y	Y	N	N	Y
NEW YORK							
1 ***Grucci***	N	Y	Y	N	Y	Y	Y
2 Israel	Y	N	Y	Y	N	N	Y
3 ***King***	N	Y	Y	N	Y	Y	Y
4 McCarthy	Y	N	Y	Y	N	N	Y
5 Ackerman	Y	N	Y	Y	N	N	Y
6 Meeks	Y	N	Y	Y	N	N	Y
7 Crowley	Y	N	Y	Y	N	N	Y
8 Nadler	Y	N	Y	Y	N	N	Y
9 Weiner	Y	N	Y	Y	N	Y	Y
10 Towns	Y	N	Y	Y	N	N	Y
11 Owens	Y	N	Y	Y	N	N	Y
12 Velázquez	Y	N	Y	Y	N	N	Y
13 ***Fossella***	N	Y	Y	N	N	Y	Y
14 Maloney	Y	N	Y	Y	N	N	Y
15 Rangel	Y	N	Y	Y	?	N	Y
16 Serrano	Y	N	Y	Y	N	N	Y
17 Engel	Y	N	Y	Y	N	N	Y
18 Lowey	Y	N	Y	Y	N	N	Y
19 ***Kelly***	N	Y	Y	N	Y	Y	Y
20 ***Gilman***	N	Y	N	N	Y	N	Y
21 McNulty	Y	N	Y	Y	N	N	Y
22 ***Sweeney***	N	Y	N	N	Y	Y	Y
23 ***Boehlert***	N	Y	N	N	Y	N	Y
24 ***McHugh***	N	Y	N	N	Y	N	Y
25 ***Walsh***	N	Y	N	N	Y	N	Y
26 Hinchey	Y	N	Y	Y	N	N	Y
27 ***Reynolds***	N	Y	N	N	Y	N	N
28 Slaughter	Y	N	Y	Y	N	N	Y
29 LaFalce	Y	N	Y	Y	N	N	Y

	360	361	362	363	364	365	366
30 ***Quinn***	N	Y	N	N	Y	N	Y
31 ***Houghton***	N	Y	N	N	Y	N	N
NORTH CAROLINA							
1 Clayton	Y	N	Y	Y	N	N	Y
2 Etheridge	Y	N	Y	Y	N	N	Y
3 ***Jones***	N	Y	N	N	N	Y	Y
4 Price	Y	N	Y	Y	N	N	Y
5 ***Burr***	N	Y	N	N	N	N	N
6 ***Coble***	N	Y	N	N	Y	Y	N
7 McIntyre	Y	N	Y	N	Y	N	Y
8 ***Hayes***	N	Y	N	N	Y	N	Y
9 ***Myrick***	N	Y	N	N	Y	Y	Y
10 ***Ballenger***	N	Y	N	N	Y	N	Y
11 ***Taylor***	N	Y	N	N	N	N	N
12 Watt	Y	N	Y	Y	N	N	Y
NORTH DAKOTA							
AL Pomeroy	Y	N	Y	Y	N	N	Y
OHIO							
1 ***Chabot***	N	Y	N	N	N	N	Y
2 ***Portman***	N	Y	N	N	Y	N	N
3 Hall	Y	N	Y	Y	N	N	Y
4 ***Oxley***	N	Y	N	N	Y	N	N
5 ***Gillmor***	N	Y	N	N	Y	Y	N
6 Strickland	Y	N	Y	Y	N	N	Y
7 ***Hobson***	N	Y	N	N	Y	Y	N
8 ***Boehner***	N	Y	N	N	Y	N	N
9 Kaptur	Y	N	Y	Y	N	N	Y
10 Kucinich	Y	N	Y	Y	N	N	Y
11 Jones	Y	N	Y	Y	N	N	Y
12 ***Tiberi***	N	Y	N	N	Y	N	N
13 Brown	Y	N	Y	Y	N	N	Y
14 Sawyer	Y	N	Y	Y	N	N	Y
15 ***Pryce***	N	Y	N	N	N	N	N
16 ***Regula***	N	Y	N	N	Y	N	N
17 Vacant							
18 ***Ney***	N	Y	N	N	Y	N	N
19 ***LaTourette***	N	Y	N	N	Y	N	N
OKLAHOMA							
1 ***Sullivan***	N	Y	N	N	Y	Y	Y
2 Carson	Y	N	Y	Y	N	N	Y
3 ***Watkins***	N	Y	N	N	Y	Y	N
4 ***Watts***	N	Y	N	N	Y	N	N
5 ***Istook***	N	?	N	N	Y	Y	N
6 ***Lucas***	N	Y	N	N	Y	Y	N
OREGON							
1 Wu	Y	N	Y	Y	N	N	Y
2 ***Walden***	N	Y	N	N	Y	N	N
3 Blumenauer	Y	N	Y	Y	N	N	N
4 DeFazio	Y	N	Y	Y	N	Y	Y
5 Hooley	Y	N	Y	Y	N	N	Y
PENNSYLVANIA							
1 Brady	Y	N	Y	Y	N	N	Y
2 Fattah	Y	N	Y	Y	N	N	Y
3 Borski	Y	N	Y	Y	N	N	Y
4 ***Hart***	N	Y	N	N	Y	N	N
5 ***Peterson***	N	Y	N	N	Y	N	N
6 Holden	Y	N	Y	Y	N	N	Y
7 ***Weldon***	N	Y	N	N	N	Y	Y
8 ***Greenwood***	N	Y	N	N	Y	N	Y
9 ***Shuster, Bill***	N	Y	N	N	Y	Y	Y
10 ***Sherwood***	N	Y	N	N	Y	N	N
11 Kanjorski	Y	N	Y	Y	N	N	Y
12 Murtha	Y	N	Y	N	N	N	Y
13 Hoeffel	Y	N	Y	Y	N	N	Y
14 Coyne	Y	N	Y	Y	N	N	Y
15 ***Toomey***	N	Y	N	N	N	N	Y
16 ***Pitts***	N	Y	N	N	Y	Y	N
17 ***Gekas***	N	Y	N	N	Y	N	Y
18 Doyle	Y	N	Y	Y	N	N	Y
19 ***Platts***	N	Y	N	N	N	Y	Y
20 Mascara	Y	N	Y	Y	N	N	Y
21 ***English***	N	Y	N	N	Y	N	N
RHODE ISLAND							
1 Kennedy	Y	N	Y	Y	N	N	Y
2 Langevin	Y	N	Y	Y	N	N	Y
SOUTH CAROLINA							
1 ***Brown***	N	Y	N	N	Y	Y	Y
2 ***Wilson***	N	Y	N	N	Y	Y	N
3 ***Graham***	N	Y	N	N	Y	N	Y
4 ***DeMint***	N	Y	N	N	Y	Y	N
5 Spratt	Y	N	Y	N	N	N	Y
6 Clyburn	Y	N	Y	Y	N	N	Y
SOUTH DAKOTA							
AL ***Thune***	N	Y	Y	N	N	Y	Y

	360	361	362	363	364	365	366
TENNESSEE							
1 ***Jenkins***	N	Y	N	N	Y	Y	Y
2 ***Duncan***	N	Y	N	N	Y	Y	Y
3 ***Wamp***	N	Y	N	N	Y	Y	Y
4 ***Hilleary***	N	Y	N	N	N	Y	Y
5 Clement	Y	N	Y	Y	N	N	Y
6 Gordon	Y	N	Y	Y	N	N	Y
7 ***Bryant***	N	Y	N	N	N	Y	Y
8 Tanner	Y	N	Y	N	N	N	Y
9 Ford	Y	N	Y	N	N	N	Y
TEXAS							
1 Sandlin	Y	N	Y	Y	N	N	Y
2 Turner	Y	N	Y	N	Y	N	Y
3 ***Johnson, Sam***	N	Y	N	N	Y	Y	N
4 Hall	N	Y	N	N	Y	Y	Y
5 ***Sessions***	N	Y	N	N	Y	Y	N
6 ***Barton***	N	Y	N	N	Y	Y	N
7 ***Culberson***	N	Y	N	N	Y	Y	N
8 ***Brady***	N	Y	N	N	Y	Y	N
9 Lampson	Y	N	Y	N	N	N	Y
10 Doggett	Y	N	Y	Y	N	N	Y
11 Edwards	Y	N	Y	Y	N	N	Y
12 ***Granger***	N	Y	N	N	N	Y	Y
13 ***Thornberry***	N	Y	N	N	Y	N	N
14 ***Paul***	N	Y	N	Y	N	Y	N
15 Hinojosa	Y	N	Y	Y	N	N	Y
16 Reyes	Y	N	Y	Y	N	N	Y
17 Stenholm	N	Y	N	N	Y	N	Y
18 Jackson-Lee	Y	N	Y	Y	N	N	Y
19 ***Combest***	?	?	?	?	?	?	?
20 Gonzalez	Y	N	Y	Y	N	N	Y
21 ***Smith***	N	Y	N	N	Y	Y	N
22 ***DeLay***	N	Y	N	N	Y	Y	N
23 ***Bonilla***	N	Y	N	N	Y	Y	Y
24 Frost	Y	N	N	Y	N	N	Y
25 Bentsen	Y	N	N	Y	N	N	Y
26 ***Armey***	N	Y	N	N	Y	N	N
27 Ortiz	Y	N	Y	Y	N	N	Y
28 Rodriguez	Y	N	Y	Y	N	N	Y
29 Green	Y	N	N	Y	N	N	Y
30 Johnson, E.B.	Y	N	N	Y	N	N	Y
UTAH							
1 ***Hansen***	N	Y	N	N	Y	Y	N
2 Matheson	Y	N	N	Y	N	N	Y
3 ***Cannon***	N	Y	N	N	Y	N	N
VERMONT							
AL *Sanders*	Y	N	Y	Y	N	N	Y
VIRGINIA							
1 ***Davis, Jo Ann***	N	Y	N	N	Y	N	Y
2 ***Schrock***	N	Y	N	N	Y	N	N
3 Scott	Y	N	Y	Y	N	N	Y
4 ***Forbes***	N	Y	N	N	Y	Y	Y
5 *Goode*	N	Y	N	N	Y	Y	Y
6 ***Goodlatte***	N	Y	N	N	Y	Y	Y
7 ***Cantor***	N	Y	N	N	Y	N	Y
8 Moran	Y	N	N	N	Y	N	Y
9 Boucher	Y	N	Y	Y	Y	N	Y
10 ***Wolf***	N	Y	N	N	Y	N	N
11 ***Davis, T.***	N	Y	N	N	Y	N	N
WASHINGTON							
1 Inslee	Y	N	Y	Y	N	N	Y
2 Larsen	Y	N	Y	Y	N	N	Y
3 Baird	Y	N	Y	Y	N	N	Y
4 ***Hastings***	N	Y	N	N	Y	N	N
5 ***Nethercutt***	N	Y	N	N	Y	N	N
6 Dicks	Y	N	Y	N	N	N	Y
7 McDermott	Y	N	Y	Y	N	N	Y
8 ***Dunn***	N	Y	N	N	Y	N	N
9 Smith	Y	N	N	N	N	N	Y
WEST VIRGINIA							
1 Mollohan	Y	N	Y	Y	N	N	Y
2 ***Capito***	N	Y	Y	N	N	N	Y
3 Rahall	Y	N	Y	Y	N	N	Y
WISCONSIN							
1 ***Ryan***	N	Y	N	N	N	N	Y
2 Baldwin	Y	N	Y	Y	N	N	Y
3 Kind	Y	N	Y	N	Y	N	Y
4 Kleczka	Y	N	N	Y	N	N	Y
5 Barrett	Y	N	Y	Y	N	N	Y
6 ***Petri***	N	Y	N	Y	N	N	Y
7 Obey	Y	N	Y	Y	N	N	Y
8 ***Green***	N	Y	Y	N	N	Y	Y
9 ***Sensenbrenner***	N	Y	N	N	Y	Y	N
WYOMING							
AL ***Cubin***	N	Y	N	N	Y	Y	Y

Southern states - Ala., Ark., Fla., Ga., Ky., La., Miss., N.C., Okla., S.C., Tenn., Texas, Va.

	367	368	369	370

Key

Y	Voted for (yea).
#	Paired for.
+	Announced for.
N	Voted against (nay).
X	Paired against.
−	Announced against.
P	Voted "present."
C	Voted "present" to avoid possible conflict of interest.
?	Did not vote or otherwise make a position known.

•

Democrats   **Republicans**
Independents

---

367. HR 5005. Homeland Security/Passage. Passage of the bill that would consolidate 22 agencies into a new Cabinet-level Homeland Security Department charged with protecting domestic security. It would have a $37.5 billion budget and nearly 170,000 employees. Merged agencies would include the Coast Guard, the Federal Emergency Management Agency, the Customs Service, the Secret Service and the Transportation Security Administration. It would split the Immigration and Naturalization Service and include only its enforcement and border protection services in the new department. It would give the president considerable leeway in hiring for the department and authority to set personnel policies. Passed 295-132: R 207-10; D 88-120 (ND 54-100, SD 34-20); I 0-2. A "yea" was a vote in support of the president's position. July 26, 2002.

368. H Res 507. Rules/Same-Day Waiver. Adoption of the resolution (H Res 507) that would waive the two-thirds majority vote requirement for same-day consideration of rules reported by the House Rules Committee on July 26, 2002, on the conference reports for the bills on Trade Promotion Authority (HR 3009), bankruptcy overhaul (HR 333) and election overhaul (HR 3295). Adopted 217-207: R 209-5; D 8-200 (ND 3-151, SD 5-49); I 0-2. July 27, 2002 (in the session that began and the Congressional Record dated July 26, 2002).

369. HR 3009. Trade Promotion Authority/Rule. Adoption of the rule (H Res 509) to provide for House floor consideration of the conference report on the bill that would allow special trade promotion authority for congressional consideration of trade agreements reached prior to June 1, 2005, and extend duty-free status to certain products from Bolivia, Colombia, Ecuador and Peru. Adopted 220-200: R 206-7; D 14-191 (ND 6-146, SD 8-45); I 0-2. July 27, 2002 (in the session that began and the Congressional Record dated July 26, 2002).

370. HR 3009. Trade Promotion Authority/Conference Report. Adoption of the conference report on the bill that would allow special trade promotion authority for congressional consideration of trade agreements reached prior to June 1, 2005, and extend duty-free status to certain products from Bolivia, Colombia, Ecuador and Peru. It also would reauthorize and expand a program to provide retraining assistance to U.S. workers hurt by trade agreements, create a 65 percent tax credit for health insurance costs for displaced workers, and authorize a five-year extension of the Generalized System of Preferences. Adopted (thus sent to the Senate) 215-212: R 190-27; D 25-183 (ND 11-143, SD 14-40); I 0-2. A "yea" was a vote in support of the president's position. July 27, 2002 (in the session that began and the Congressional Record dated July 26, 2002).

	367	368	369	370
ALABAMA				
1 *Callahan*	Y	Y	Y	Y
2 *Everett*	Y	Y	Y	Y
3 *Riley*	Y	?	Y	Y
4 *Aderholt*	Y	Y	Y	Y
5 Cramer	Y	N	N	N
6 *Bachus*	Y	Y	Y	Y
7 Hilliard	N	N	N	N
ALASKA				
AL *Young*	Y	Y	Y	N
ARIZONA				
1 *Flake*	N	Y	Y	Y
2 Pastor	N	N	N	N
3 *Stump*	Y	?	?	?
4 *Shadegg*	Y	Y	Y	Y
5 *Kolbe*	Y	Y	Y	Y
6 *Hayworth*	Y	Y	Y	Y
ARKANSAS				
1 Berry	Y	N	N	N
2 Snyder	N	N	N	N
3 *Boozman*	Y	Y	Y	Y
4 Ross	Y	N	N	N
CALIFORNIA				
1 Thompson	N	N	N	N
2 *Herger*	Y	Y	Y	Y
3 *Ose*	Y	Y	Y	Y
4 *Doolittle*	Y	Y	Y	Y
5 Matsui	N	N	N	N
6 Woolsey	N	N	N	N
7 Miller, George	N	N	N	N
8 Pelosi	N	N	N	N
9 Lee	N	N	N	N
10 Tauscher	Y	N	Y	Y
11 *Pombo*	Y	Y	Y	Y
12 Lantos	N	N	N	N
13 Stark	N	N	?	N
14 Eshoo	N	N	N	N
15 Honda	N	N	N	N
16 Lofgren	N	N	N	N
17 Farr	N	N	N	N
18 Condit	Y	N	N	N
19 *Radanovich*	Y	Y	Y	Y
20 Dooley	Y	Y	Y	Y
21 *Thomas*	N	Y	Y	Y
22 Capps	Y	N	N	N
23 *Gallegly*	Y	Y	Y	Y
24 Sherman	N	N	N	N
25 *McKeon*	Y	Y	Y	Y
26 Berman	N	N	N	N
27 Schiff	Y	N	N	N
28 *Dreier*	Y	Y	Y	Y
29 Waxman	N	N	N	N
30 Becerra	N	N	N	N
31 Solis	N	N	N	N
32 Watson	N	N	N	N
33 Roybal-Allard	N	N	N	N
34 Napolitano	N	N	N	N
35 Waters	N	N	N	N
36 Harman	Y	N	N	N
37 Millender-McD.	Y	N	N	N
38 *Horn*	Y	Y	Y	Y

	367	368	369	370
39 *Royce*	Y	Y	Y	Y
40 *Lewis*	Y	Y	?	Y
41 *Miller, Gary*	Y	Y	Y	Y
42 Baca	N	N	N	N
43 *Calvert*	Y	Y	Y	Y
44 *Bono*	Y	Y	Y	Y
45 *Rohrabacher*	Y	Y	Y	N
46 Sanchez	Y	N	N	N
47 *Cox*	Y	Y	Y	Y
48 *Issa*	Y	Y	Y	Y
49 Davis	Y	N	N	Y
50 Filner	N	N	N	N
51 *Cunningham*	Y	Y	Y	Y
52 *Hunter*	Y	Y	Y	N
COLORADO				
1 DeGette	N	N	N	N
2 Udall	Y	N	N	N
3 *McInnis*	Y	Y	Y	Y
4 *Schaffer*	Y	Y	Y	Y
5 *Hefley*	Y	N	?	Y
6 *Tancredo*	N	Y	Y	Y
CONNECTICUT				
1 Larson	N	N	N	N
2 *Simmons*	Y	Y	Y	N
3 DeLauro	N	N	N	N
4 *Shays*	Y	Y	Y	Y
5 Maloney	Y	N	N	N
6 *Johnson*	Y	Y	Y	Y
DELAWARE				
AL *Castle*	Y	Y	Y	Y
FLORIDA				
1 *Miller, J.*	Y	Y	Y	Y
2 Boyd	Y	N	N	N
3 Brown	N	N	N	N
4 *Crenshaw*	Y	Y	Y	Y
5 Thurman	Y	N	N	N
6 *Stearns*	Y	Y	Y	N
7 *Mica*	Y	Y	Y	Y
8 *Keller*	Y	Y	Y	Y
9 *Bilirakis*	Y	Y	Y	Y
10 *Young*	Y	Y	N	Y
11 Davis	Y	N	N	Y
12 *Putnam*	Y	Y	Y	Y
13 *Miller, D.*	Y	Y	Y	Y
14 *Goss*	Y	Y	Y	Y
15 *Weldon*	Y	Y	Y	Y
16 *Foley*	Y	Y	Y	Y
17 Meek	N	N	N	N
18 *Ros-Lehtinen*	Y	Y	Y	Y
19 Wexler	Y	N	N	N
20 Deutsch	Y	N	N	N
21 *Diaz-Balart*	Y	Y	Y	Y
22 *Shaw*	Y	Y	Y	Y
23 Hastings	N	N	N	N
GEORGIA				
1 *Kingston*	Y	Y	Y	Y
2 Bishop	Y	N	N	N
3 *Collins*	Y	Y	Y	Y
4 McKinney	N	N	N	N
5 Lewis	N	N	N	N
6 *Isakson*	Y	Y	Y	Y
7 *Barr*	Y	Y	Y	Y
8 *Chambliss*	Y	Y	Y	Y
9 *Deal*	Y	Y	Y	Y
10 *Norwood*	Y	N	N	N
11 *Linder*	Y	Y	Y	Y
HAWAII				
1 Abercrombie	N	N	N	N
2 Mink	N	N	N	N
IDAHO				
1 *Otter*	Y	Y	Y	Y
2 *Simpson*	Y	Y	Y	Y
ILLINOIS				
1 Rush	Y	N	N	N
2 Jackson	Y	N	N	N
3 Lipinski	?	?	?	?
4 Gutierrez	N	N	N	N
5 Blagojevich	Y	N	N	N
6 *Hyde*	Y	Y	Y	Y
7 Davis	N	N	N	N
8 *Crane*	Y	Y	Y	Y
9 Schakowsky	N	N	N	N
10 *Kirk*	Y	Y	Y	Y
11 *Weller*	Y	Y	Y	Y
12 Costello	N	N	N	N
13 *Biggert*	Y	Y	Y	Y

ND Northern Democrats   SD Southern Democrats

	367	368	369	370
14 Hastert			Y	Y
15 Johnson	Y	Y	Y	Y
16 Manzullo	Y	Y	Y	Y
17 Evans	N	N	N	N
18 LaHood	Y	Y	Y	Y
19 Phelps	Y	N	N	N
20 Shimkus	Y	Y	Y	Y
INDIANA				
1 Visclosky	N	N	N	N
2 Pence	Y	Y	Y	Y
3 Roemer	N	N	N	N
4 Souder	Y	Y	Y	Y
5 Buyer	Y	Y	Y	Y
6 Burton	Y	Y	Y	Y
7 Kerns	Y	Y	Y	Y
8 Hostettler	N	Y	Y	N
9 Hill	Y	N	N	Y
10 Carson	N	N	N	N
IOWA				
1 Leach	Y	Y	Y	Y
2 Nussle	Y	?	Y	Y
3 Boswell	Y	N	N	N
4 Ganske	Y	Y	Y	Y
5 Latham	Y	Y	Y	Y
KANSAS				
1 Moran	N	Y	Y	Y
2 Ryun	Y	Y	Y	Y
3 Moore	Y	N	N	Y
4 Tiahrt	Y	Y	Y	Y
KENTUCKY				
1 Whitfield	Y	Y	?	Y
2 Lewis	Y	Y	Y	Y
3 Northup	Y	Y	Y	Y
4 Lucas	Y	Y	Y	Y
5 Rogers	Y	Y	Y	Y
6 Fletcher	Y	Y	Y	Y
LOUISIANA				
1 Vitter	Y	Y	Y	Y
2 Jefferson	Y	N	N	Y
3 Tauzin	Y	Y	Y	Y
4 McCrery	Y	Y	Y	Y
5 Cooksey	Y	Y	Y	Y
6 Baker	Y	Y	Y	Y
7 John	Y	N	Y	Y
MAINE				
1 Allen	Y	N	N	N
2 Baldacci	Y	N	N	N
MARYLAND				
1 Gilchrest	Y	Y	Y	Y
2 Ehrlich	+	Y	Y	Y
3 Cardin	Y	N	N	N
4 Wynn	N	N	N	N
5 Hoyer	N	N	N	N
6 Bartlett	Y	Y	Y	Y
7 Cummings	N	N	N	N
8 Morella	Y	Y	Y	Y
MASSACHUSETTS				
1 Olver	N	N	N	N
2 Neal	N	N	N	N
3 McGovern	N	N	N	N
4 Frank	N	N	N	N
5 Meehan	?	?	?	?
6 Tierney	N	N	N	N
7 Markey	N	N	N	N
8 Capuano	N	N	N	N
9 Lynch	N	N	N	N
10 Delahunt	Y	N	N	N
MICHIGAN				
1 Stupak	N	N	N	N
2 Hoekstra	Y	Y	Y	N
3 Ehlers	Y	Y	Y	Y
4 Camp	Y	Y	Y	Y
5 Barcia	Y	N	N	Y
6 Upton	Y	Y	Y	Y
7 Smith	Y	?	Y	Y
8 Rogers	Y	Y	Y	Y
9 Kildee	Y	N	N	N
10 Bonior	N	N	N	N
11 Knollenberg	Y	Y	Y	Y
12 Levin	N	N	N	N
13 Rivers	N	N	N	N
14 Conyers	N	N	N	N
15 Kilpatrick	N	N	N	N
16 Dingell	N	N	N	N

	367	368	369	370
MINNESOTA				
1 Gutknecht	Y	Y	Y	Y
2 Kennedy	Y	Y	Y	Y
3 Ramstad	Y	Y	Y	Y
4 McCollum	N	N	N	N
5 Sabo	N	N	N	N
6 Luther	Y	N	N	N
7 Peterson	Y	N	N	N
8 Oberstar	N	N	N	N
MISSISSIPPI				
1 Wicker	Y	Y	Y	Y
2 Thompson	N	N	N	N
3 Pickering	Y	Y	Y	Y
4 Shows	Y	N	N	N
5 Taylor	Y	N	N	N
MISSOURI				
1 Clay	Y	N	N	N
2 Akin	Y	Y	Y	Y
3 Gephardt	N	N	N	N
4 Skelton	Y	N	Y	N
5 McCarthy	Y	N	N	N
6 Graves	Y	Y	Y	Y
7 Blunt	?	?	?	?
8 Emerson	Y	Y	Y	Y
9 Hulshof	Y	Y	Y	Y
MONTANA				
AL Rehberg	Y	Y	Y	Y
NEBRASKA				
1 Bereuter	Y	Y	Y	Y
2 Terry	Y	Y	Y	Y
3 Osborne	Y	Y	Y	Y
NEVADA				
1 Berkley	Y	N	N	N
2 Gibbons	Y	Y	Y	Y
NEW HAMPSHIRE				
1 Sununu	Y	Y	Y	Y
2 Bass	Y	Y	Y	Y
NEW JERSEY				
1 Andrews	Y	N	N	N
2 LoBiondo	Y	Y	Y	Y
3 Saxton	Y	Y	Y	Y
4 Smith	Y	Y	Y	N
5 Roukema	?	?	?	?
6 Pallone	N	N	N	N
7 Ferguson	Y	Y	Y	Y
8 Pascrell	Y	N	N	N
9 Rothman	Y	N	N	N
10 Payne	N	N	N	N
11 Frelinghuysen	Y	Y	Y	Y
12 Holt	Y	N	N	N
13 Menendez	N	N	N	N
NEW MEXICO				
1 Wilson	Y	Y	Y	Y
2 Skeen	Y	Y	N	Y
3 Udall	N	N	N	N
NEW YORK				
1 Grucci	Y	Y	Y	Y
2 Israel	Y	N	N	N
3 King	Y	Y	Y	Y
4 McCarthy	Y	N	N	N
5 Ackerman	N	N	N	N
6 Meeks	Y	N	N	N
7 Crowley	Y	N	N	N
8 Nadler	N	N	N	N
9 Weiner	Y	N	N	N
10 Towns	N	N	N	N
11 Owens	N	N	N	N
12 Velázquez	N	N	N	N
13 Fossella	Y	Y	Y	Y
14 Maloney	Y	N	N	N
15 Rangel	N	N	N	N
16 Serrano	N	N	N	N
17 Engel	Y	N	N	N
18 Lowey	N	N	N	N
19 Kelly	Y	Y	Y	Y
20 Gilman	Y	Y	Y	Y
21 McNulty	N	N	N	N
22 Sweeney	Y	Y	Y	Y
23 Boehlert	Y	Y	Y	Y
24 McHugh	Y	Y	Y	N
25 Walsh	Y	Y	Y	N
26 Hinchey	N	N	N	N
27 Reynolds	Y	Y	Y	Y
28 Slaughter	N	N	N	N
29 LaFalce	N	N	N	N

	367	368	369	370
30 Quinn	Y	Y	Y	N
31 Houghton	Y	Y	Y	Y
NORTH CAROLINA				
1 Clayton	N	N	N	N
2 Etheridge	Y	N	N	N
3 Jones	Y	N	N	N
4 Price	Y	N	N	N
5 Burr	Y	Y	Y	Y
6 Coble	Y	Y	Y	Y
7 McIntyre	Y	N	N	N
8 Hayes	Y	Y	Y	Y
9 Myrick	Y	Y	Y	Y
10 Ballenger	Y	Y	Y	Y
11 Taylor	N	Y	Y	Y
12 Watt	N	N	N	N
NORTH DAKOTA				
AL Pomeroy	Y	N	N	N
OHIO				
1 Chabot	Y	Y	Y	Y
2 Portman	Y	Y	Y	Y
3 Hall	Y	N	N	N
4 Oxley	Y	Y	Y	Y
5 Gillmor	Y	Y	?	Y
6 Strickland	Y	N	N	N
7 Hobson	Y	Y	Y	Y
8 Boehner	Y	Y	Y	Y
9 Kaptur	N	N	N	N
10 Kucinich	N	N	N	N
11 Jones	N	N	N	N
12 Tiberi	Y	Y	Y	Y
13 Brown	N	N	N	N
14 Sawyer	N	N	N	N
15 Pryce	Y	Y	Y	Y
16 Regula	Y	Y	Y	N
17 Vacant				
18 Ney	Y	Y	?	N
19 LaTourette	Y	Y	Y	N
OKLAHOMA				
1 Sullivan	Y	Y	Y	Y
2 Carson	Y	Y	Y	Y
3 Watkins	Y	Y	Y	Y
4 Watts	Y	Y	Y	Y
5 Istook	Y	Y	Y	Y
6 Lucas	Y	Y	Y	Y
OREGON				
1 Wu	Y	N	N	N
2 Walden	Y	Y	Y	Y
3 Blumenauer	N	N	N	N
4 DeFazio	N	N	N	N
5 Hooley	Y	N	N	N
PENNSYLVANIA				
1 Brady	N	N	N	N
2 Fattah	N	N	N	N
3 Borski	N	N	N	N
4 Hart	Y	Y	Y	Y
5 Peterson	Y	Y	Y	Y
6 Holden	Y	N	N	N
7 Weldon	Y	Y	Y	Y
8 Greenwood	Y	Y	Y	Y
9 Shuster, Bill	Y	Y	Y	Y
10 Sherwood	Y	Y	Y	Y
11 Kanjorski	N	N	N	N
12 Murtha	N	N	N	N
13 Hoeffel	Y	N	N	N
14 Coyne	N	N	N	N
15 Toomey	Y	Y	Y	Y
16 Pitts	Y	Y	Y	Y
17 Gekas	Y	Y	Y	Y
18 Doyle	N	N	N	N
19 Platts	Y	Y	Y	Y
20 Mascara	Y	N	N	N
21 English	Y	Y	Y	Y
RHODE ISLAND				
1 Kennedy	Y	N	N	N
2 Langevin	Y	N	N	N
SOUTH CAROLINA				
1 Brown	Y	Y	Y	Y
2 Wilson	Y	N	N	N
3 Graham	N	N	N	N
4 DeMint	Y	Y	Y	Y
5 Spratt	Y	N	N	N
6 Clyburn	N	N	N	N
SOUTH DAKOTA				
AL Thune	Y	Y	Y	Y

	367	368	369	370
TENNESSEE				
1 Jenkins	Y	Y	Y	Y
2 Duncan	N	Y	Y	N
3 Wamp	Y	Y	Y	Y
4 Hilleary	Y	Y	Y	Y
5 Clement	Y	N	Y	N
6 Gordon	Y	N	N	N
7 Bryant	Y	Y	Y	Y
8 Tanner	Y	Y	Y	Y
9 Ford	Y	N	N	Y
TEXAS				
1 Sandlin	Y	N	N	N
2 Turner	Y	N	N	N
3 Johnson, Sam	Y	Y	Y	Y
4 Hall	Y	Y	Y	Y
5 Sessions	Y	Y	Y	Y
6 Barton	Y	Y	Y	Y
7 Culberson	Y	Y	Y	Y
8 Brady	Y	Y	Y	Y
9 Lampson	N	N	N	N
10 Doggett	N	N	N	N
11 Edwards	Y	N	N	N
12 Granger	Y	Y	Y	Y
13 Thornberry	Y	Y	Y	Y
14 Paul	N	Y	N	N
15 Hinojosa	Y	N	?	Y
16 Reyes	Y	N	N	N
17 Stenholm	Y	N	N	N
18 Jackson-Lee	N	N	N	N
19 Combest	?	?	?	?
20 Gonzalez	N	N	N	N
21 Smith	Y	Y	Y	Y
22 DeLay	Y	Y	Y	Y
23 Bonilla	Y	Y	Y	Y
24 Frost	Y	N	N	N
25 Bentsen	N	N	Y	Y
26 Armey	Y	Y	Y	Y
27 Ortiz	Y	N	N	N
28 Rodriguez	N	N	N	N
29 Green	Y	N	N	N
30 Johnson, E.B.	N	N	N	N
UTAH				
1 Hansen	Y	Y	Y	?
2 Matheson	Y	Y	Y	Y
3 Cannon	N	Y	Y	Y
VERMONT				
AL Sanders	N	N	N	N
VIRGINIA				
1 Davis, Jo Ann	Y	Y	Y	N
2 Schrock	Y	Y	Y	Y
3 Scott	N	N	N	N
4 Forbes	Y	Y	Y	Y
5 Goode	N	N	N	N
6 Goodlatte	Y	Y	Y	Y
7 Cantor	Y	Y	Y	Y
8 Moran	N	N	Y	N
9 Boucher	Y	N	N	N
10 Wolf	Y	Y	Y	Y
11 Davis, T.	Y	Y	Y	Y
WASHINGTON				
1 Inslee	N	N	N	N
2 Larsen	N	N	N	Y
3 Baird	Y	N	?	N
4 Hastings	Y	Y	Y	Y
5 Nethercutt	Y	Y	Y	Y
6 Dicks	Y	Y	Y	Y
7 McDermott	N	N	N	N
8 Dunn	Y	Y	Y	Y
9 Smith	Y	N	Y	Y
WEST VIRGINIA				
1 Mollohan	N	N	N	N
2 Capito	Y	Y	Y	N
3 Rahall	N	N	N	N
WISCONSIN				
1 Ryan	Y	Y	Y	Y
2 Baldwin	N	N	N	N
3 Kind	Y	N	N	N
4 Kleczka	N	N	N	N
5 Barrett	Y	N	N	N
6 Petri	N	Y	Y	Y
7 Obey	N	N	N	N
8 Green	Y	Y	Y	Y
9 Sensenbrenner	Y	Y	Y	Y
WYOMING				
AL Cubin	Y	Y	Y	Y

Southern states - Ala., Ark., Fla., Ga., Ky., La., Miss., N.C., Okla., S.C., Tenn., Texas, Va.

Key

Y	Voted for (yea).
#	Paired for.
+	Announced for.
N	Voted against (nay).
X	Paired against.
–	Announced against.
P	Voted "present."
C	Voted "present" to avoid possible conflict of interest.
?	Did not vote or otherwise make a position known.

• Democrats **Republicans** *Independents*

371. HR 5203. Education Tax Break/Passage. Hulshof, R-Mo., motion to suspend the rules and pass the bill that would permanently extend a provision in last year's $1.35 trillion tax cut package increasing to $2,000 the contribution limits for education savings accounts and allowing tax-free withdrawals to pay qualified expenses for elementary and secondary public, private or religious schools. The bill also would extend indefinitely an exclusion from gross income for employer-provided aid for higher education; an increase in the phase-out income range for deducting student loan interest; and a repeal of the 60-month limit on the amount of time a taxpayer can claim the interest deduction. Motion rejected 213-188: R 203-4; D 10-183 (ND 5-135, SD 5-48); I 0-1. A two-thirds majority of those present and voting (268 in this case) is required for passage under suspension of the rules. A "yea" was a vote in support of the president's position. Sept. 4, 2002.

372. HR 3287. Brentwood Post Office/Passage. Morella, R-Md., motion to suspend the rules and pass the bill that would name a U.S. Post Office building in Washington, D.C., after Joseph Curseen Jr. and Thomas Morris Jr., two postal employees who died after anthrax inhalation. Motion agreed to 401-0: R 207-0; D 193-0 (ND 140-0, SD 53-0); I 1-0. A two-thirds majority of those present and voting (268 in this case) is required for passage under suspension of the rules. Sept. 4, 2002.

373. HR 4727. Dam Safety/Passage. Passage of the bill that would reauthorize the national dam safety program through fiscal 2006 at $8.6 million per year. The program provides state grants, training and other assistance aimed at preventing dam failure. The bill would establish a National Dam Safety Review Board, which would have broad authority to monitor dam safety and would require the Federal Emergency Management Agency to draw up an overall safety plan. Passed 401-2: R 207-2; D 193-0 (ND 142-0, SD 51-0); I 1-0. Sept. 5, 2002.

374. H Res 94. Williams Tribute/Adoption. Morella, R-Md., motion to suspend the rules and adopt the resolution that would pay tribute to champion tennis players and sisters Venus Williams and Serena Williams. Motion agreed to 398-0: R 202-0; D 195-0 (ND 143-0, SD 52-0); I 1-0. A two-thirds majority of those present and voting (266 in this case) is required for adoption under suspension of the rules. Sept. 5, 2002.

* Rep. Virgil H. Goode Jr. of Virginia switched his party affiliation from independent to Republican, effective Aug. 1, 2002.

		371	372	373	374
ALABAMA					
1	*Callahan*	Y	Y	Y	Y
2	*Everett*	Y	Y	Y	Y
3	*Riley*	Y	Y	Y	Y
4	*Aderholt*	Y	Y	Y	Y
5	Cramer	N	Y	Y	Y
6	*Bachus*	Y	Y	Y	Y
7	Hilliard	N	Y	Y	Y
ALASKA					
AL	*Young*	?	?	?	?
ARIZONA					
1	*Flake*	Y	Y	N	Y
2	Pastor	N	Y	Y	Y
3	*Stump*	?	?	?	?
4	*Shadegg*	Y	Y	Y	Y
5	*Kolbe*	Y	Y	Y	Y
6	*Hayworth*	Y	Y	Y	Y
ARKANSAS					
1	Berry	N	Y	Y	Y
2	Snyder	N	Y	Y	Y
3	*Boozman*	Y	Y	Y	Y
4	Ross	N	Y	Y	Y
CALIFORNIA					
1	Thompson	N	Y	Y	Y
2	*Herger*	Y	Y	Y	Y
3	*Ose*	Y	Y	Y	Y
4	*Doolittle*	Y	Y	Y	Y
5	Matsui	N	Y	Y	Y
6	Woolsey	N	Y	Y	Y
7	Miller, George	N	Y	Y	Y
8	Pelosi	N	Y	Y	Y
9	Lee	N	Y	Y	Y
10	Tauscher	N	Y	Y	Y
11	*Pombo*	Y	Y	Y	Y
12	Lantos	N	Y	?	?
13	Stark	N	Y	Y	Y
14	Eshoo	N	Y	Y	Y
15	Honda	N	Y	Y	Y
16	Lofgren	N	Y	Y	Y
17	Farr	N	Y	Y	Y
18	Condit	?	?	?	?
19	*Radanovich*	Y	Y	Y	Y
20	Dooley	N	Y	Y	Y
21	*Thomas*	Y	Y	+	+
22	Capps	N	Y	Y	Y
23	*Gallegly*	Y	Y	Y	Y
24	Sherman	N	Y	Y	Y
25	*McKeon*	Y	Y	Y	Y
26	Berman	?	?	?	?
27	Schiff	N	Y	Y	Y
28	*Dreier*	Y	Y	Y	Y
29	Waxman	N	Y	Y	Y
30	Becerra	N	Y	Y	Y
31	Solis	N	Y	Y	Y
32	Watson	N	Y	Y	Y
33	Roybal-Allard	N	Y	Y	Y
34	Napolitano	N	Y	Y	Y
35	Waters	N	Y	Y	Y
36	Harman	N	Y	Y	Y
37	Millender-McD.	N	Y	Y	Y
38	*Horn*	Y	Y	Y	Y

		371	372	373	374
39	*Royce*	Y	Y	Y	Y
40	*Lewis*	Y	Y	Y	Y
41	*Miller, Gary*	?	?	?	?
42	Baca	N	Y	Y	Y
43	*Calvert*	Y	Y	Y	Y
44	*Bono*	?	?	?	?
45	*Rohrabacher*	?	?	?	?
46	Sanchez	–	+	+	+
47	*Cox*	Y	Y	Y	?
48	*Issa*	Y	Y	Y	Y
49	Davis	N	Y	Y	Y
50	Filner	N	Y	Y	Y
51	*Cunningham*	Y	Y	Y	Y
52	*Hunter*	Y	Y	Y	Y
COLORADO					
1	DeGette	N	Y	Y	Y
2	Udall	N	Y	Y	Y
3	*McInnis*	Y	Y	Y	Y
4	*Schaffer*	Y	Y	Y	Y
5	*Hefley*	Y	Y	Y	Y
6	*Tancredo*	Y	Y	Y	Y
CONNECTICUT					
1	Larson	N	Y	Y	Y
2	*Simmons*	Y	Y	Y	Y
3	DeLauro	N	Y	Y	Y
4	*Shays*	Y	Y	Y	Y
5	Maloney	N	Y	Y	Y
6	*Johnson*	Y	Y	Y	Y
DELAWARE					
AL	*Castle*	Y	Y	Y	Y
FLORIDA					
1	*Miller, J.*	Y	Y	Y	Y
2	Boyd	N	Y	Y	Y
3	Brown	N	Y	Y	Y
4	*Crenshaw*	Y	Y	Y	Y
5	Thurman	N	Y	Y	Y
6	*Stearns*	Y	Y	Y	Y
7	*Mica*	Y	Y	Y	Y
8	*Keller*	Y	Y	Y	Y
9	*Bilirakis*	Y	Y	Y	Y
10	*Young*	Y	Y	Y	Y
11	Davis	N	Y	Y	Y
12	*Putnam*	Y	Y	Y	Y
13	*Miller, D.*	Y	Y	Y	Y
14	*Goss*	Y	Y	Y	Y
15	*Weldon*	Y	Y	Y	Y
16	*Foley*	Y	Y	Y	Y
17	Meek	N	Y	Y	Y
18	*Ros-Lehtinen*	Y	Y	Y	Y
19	Wexler	?	?	Y	Y
20	Deutsch	N	Y	Y	Y
21	*Diaz-Balart*	Y	Y	Y	Y
22	*Shaw*	Y	Y	Y	Y
23	Hastings	N	Y	Y	Y
GEORGIA					
1	*Kingston*	Y	Y	Y	Y
2	Bishop	Y	Y	Y	Y
3	*Collins*	Y	Y	Y	Y
4	McKinney	N	Y	?	?
5	Lewis	N	Y	Y	Y
6	*Isakson*	Y	Y	Y	Y
7	*Barr*	?	?	?	?
8	*Chambliss*	Y	Y	Y	Y
9	*Deal*	Y	Y	Y	Y
10	*Norwood*	Y	Y	Y	Y
11	*Linder*	Y	Y	Y	Y
HAWAII					
1	Abercrombie	N	Y	Y	Y
2	Mink	?	?	?	?
IDAHO					
1	*Otter*	Y	Y	Y	Y
2	*Simpson*	Y	Y	Y	Y
ILLINOIS					
1	Rush	N	Y	Y	Y
2	Jackson	N	Y	Y	Y
3	Lipinski	N	Y	Y	Y
4	Gutierrez	N	Y	Y	Y
5	Blagojevich	N	Y	Y	Y
6	*Hyde*	Y	Y	Y	Y
7	Davis	N	Y	Y	Y
8	*Crane*	Y	Y	Y	Y
9	Schakowsky	N	Y	Y	Y
10	*Kirk*	Y	Y	Y	Y
11	*Weller*	Y	Y	Y	Y
12	Costello	N	Y	Y	Y
13	*Biggert*	Y	Y	Y	Y

ND Northern Democrats   SD Southern Democrats

	371	372	373	374
14 Hastert				
15 *Johnson*	Y	Y	Y	Y
16 *Manzullo*	Y	Y	Y	Y
17 Evans	?	?	Y	Y
18 *LaHood*	Y	Y	Y	Y
19 Phelps	N	Y	Y	Y
20 *Shimkus*	Y	Y	Y	Y

INDIANA

	371	372	373	374
1 Visclosky	N	Y	Y	Y
2 *Pence*	Y	Y	Y	Y
3 Roemer	N	Y	Y	Y
4 *Souder*	Y	Y	Y	Y
5 *Buyer*	?	?	?	?
6 *Burton*	Y	Y	Y	Y
7 *Kerns*	Y	Y	Y	Y
8 *Hostettler*	Y	Y	Y	?
9 Hill	N	Y	Y	Y
10 Carson	?	?	?	?

IOWA

	371	372	373	374
1 *Leach*	Y	Y	Y	Y
2 *Nussle*	Y	Y	Y	Y
3 Boswell	N	Y	Y	Y
4 *Ganske*	Y	Y	Y	Y
5 *Latham*	Y	Y	Y	Y

KANSAS

	371	372	373	374
1 *Moran*	Y	Y	Y	Y
2 *Ryun*	Y	Y	Y	Y
3 Moore	N	Y	Y	Y
4 *Tiahrt*	Y	Y	Y	Y

KENTUCKY

	371	372	373	374
1 *Whitfield*	Y	Y	Y	Y
2 *Lewis*	Y	Y	Y	Y
3 *Northup*	Y	Y	?	?
4 Lucas	Y	Y	?	?
5 *Rogers*	Y	Y	Y	Y
6 *Fletcher*	Y	Y	Y	Y

LOUISIANA

	371	372	373	374
1 *Vitter*	Y	Y	Y	Y
2 Jefferson	N	Y	Y	Y
3 *Tauzin*	Y	Y	Y	Y
4 *McCrery*	Y	Y	Y	Y
5 *Cooksey*	?	?	Y	Y
6 *Baker*	Y	Y	Y	Y
7 John	Y	Y	Y	Y

MAINE

	371	372	373	374
1 Allen	N	Y	Y	Y
2 Baldacci	N	Y	Y	Y

MARYLAND

	371	372	373	374
1 *Gilchrest*	Y	Y	Y	Y
2 *Ehrlich*	?	?	Y	Y
3 Cardin	N	Y	Y	Y
4 Wynn	N	Y	Y	Y
5 Hoyer	N	Y	Y	Y
6 *Bartlett*	Y	Y	Y	Y
7 Cummings	N	Y	Y	Y
8 *Morella*	N	Y	Y	Y

MASSACHUSETTS

	371	372	373	374
1 Olver	N	Y	Y	Y
2 Neal	N	Y	Y	Y
3 McGovern	N	Y	Y	Y
4 Frank	N	Y	Y	Y
5 Meehan	N	Y	Y	Y
6 Tierney	N	Y	Y	Y
7 Markey	N	Y	Y	Y
8 Capuano	N	Y	Y	Y
9 Lynch	N	Y	Y	Y
10 Delahunt	N	Y	Y	Y

MICHIGAN

	371	372	373	374
1 Stupak	N	Y	Y	Y
2 *Hoekstra*	Y	Y	Y	Y
3 *Ehlers*	Y	Y	Y	Y
4 *Camp*	Y	Y	Y	Y
5 Barcia	Y	Y	Y	Y
6 *Upton*	Y	Y	Y	Y
7 *Smith*	Y	Y	Y	Y
8 *Rogers*	Y	Y	Y	Y
9 Kildee	N	Y	Y	Y
10 Bonior	N	Y	Y	Y
11 *Knollenberg*	Y	Y	Y	Y
12 Levin	N	Y	Y	Y
13 Rivers	?	?	Y	Y
14 Conyers	N	Y	?	?
15 Kilpatrick	N	Y	Y	Y
16 Dingell	N	Y	Y	Y

MINNESOTA

	371	372	373	374
1 *Gutknecht*	Y	Y	Y	Y
2 *Kennedy*	Y	Y	Y	Y
3 *Ramstad*	Y	Y	Y	Y
4 McCollum	N	Y	Y	Y
5 Sabo	N	Y	Y	Y
6 Luther	N	Y	Y	Y
7 Peterson	N	Y	Y	Y
8 Oberstar	N	Y	Y	Y

MISSISSIPPI

	371	372	373	374
1 *Wicker*	Y	Y	Y	Y
2 Thompson	N	Y	Y	Y
3 *Pickering*	Y	Y	Y	Y
4 Shows	N	Y	Y	Y
5 Taylor	N	Y	Y	Y

MISSOURI

	371	372	373	374
1 Clay	N	Y	?	?
2 *Akin*	Y	Y	Y	Y
3 Gephardt	N	Y	Y	Y
4 Skelton	N	Y	Y	Y
5 McCarthy	N	Y	Y	Y
6 *Graves*	Y	Y	Y	Y
7 *Blunt*	Y	Y	Y	Y
8 *Emerson*	Y	Y	Y	Y
9 *Hulshof*	Y	Y	Y	Y

MONTANA

	371	372	373	374
AL *Rehberg*	Y	Y	Y	Y

NEBRASKA

	371	372	373	374
1 *Bereuter*	Y	Y	Y	Y
2 *Terry*	Y	Y	Y	Y
3 *Osborne*	Y	Y	Y	Y

NEVADA

	371	372	373	374
1 Berkley	N	Y	Y	Y
2 *Gibbons*	Y	Y	Y	Y

NEW HAMPSHIRE

	371	372	373	374
1 *Sununu*	Y	Y	Y	Y
2 *Bass*	Y	Y	Y	Y

NEW JERSEY

	371	372	373	374
1 Andrews	N	Y	?	?
2 *LoBiondo*	Y	Y	Y	Y
3 *Saxton*	Y	Y	Y	Y
4 *Smith*	Y	Y	Y	Y
5 *Roukema*	?	?	?	?
6 Pallone	N	Y	Y	Y
7 *Ferguson*	Y	Y	Y	Y
8 Pascrell	N	Y	Y	Y
9 Rothman	N	Y	Y	Y
10 Payne	N	Y	Y	Y
11 *Frelinghuysen*	Y	Y	Y	Y
12 Holt	N	Y	Y	Y
13 Menendez	N	Y	Y	Y

NEW MEXICO

	371	372	373	374
1 *Wilson*	Y	Y	Y	Y
2 *Skeen*	Y	Y	Y	Y
3 Udall	N	Y	Y	Y

NEW YORK

	371	372	373	374
1 *Grucci*	Y	Y	Y	Y
2 Israel	Y	Y	Y	Y
3 *King*	Y	Y	Y	Y
4 McCarthy	N	Y	Y	Y
5 Ackerman	N	Y	Y	Y
6 Meeks	N	Y	Y	Y
7 Crowley	?	?	?	Y
8 Nadler	N	Y	Y	Y
9 Weiner	N	Y	Y	Y
10 Towns	?	?	?	?
11 Owens	N	Y	Y	Y
12 Velázquez	?	?	?	?
13 *Fossella*	Y	Y	Y	Y
14 Maloney	N	Y	Y	Y
15 Rangel	N	Y	Y	Y
16 Serrano	N	Y	Y	Y
17 Engel	N	Y	?	Y
18 Lowey	N	Y	Y	Y
19 *Kelly*	Y	Y	Y	Y
20 Gilman	?	Y	Y	Y
21 McNulty	N	Y	Y	Y
22 *Sweeney*	Y	Y	Y	Y
23 *Boehlert*	N	Y	Y	Y
24 *McHugh*	N	Y	Y	Y
25 *Walsh*	Y	Y	Y	Y
26 Hinchey	N	Y	Y	Y
27 *Reynolds*	Y	Y	Y	Y
28 Slaughter	N	Y	Y	Y
29 LaFalce	N	Y	Y	Y
30 *Quinn*	N	Y	Y	Y
31 Houghton	Y	Y	Y	?

NORTH CAROLINA

	371	372	373	374
1 Clayton	N	Y	Y	Y
2 Etheridge	N	Y	Y	Y
3 *Jones*	Y	Y	Y	Y
4 Price	N	Y	Y	Y
5 *Burr*	Y	Y	Y	Y
6 *Coble*	Y	Y	Y	Y
7 McIntyre	Y	Y	Y	Y
8 *Hayes*	Y	Y	Y	Y
9 *Myrick*	Y	Y	Y	Y
10 *Ballenger*	Y	Y	Y	Y
11 *Taylor*	Y	Y	Y	Y
12 Watt	N	Y	Y	Y

NORTH DAKOTA

	371	372	373	374
AL Pomeroy	N	Y	Y	Y

OHIO

	371	372	373	374
1 *Chabot*	Y	Y	Y	Y
2 *Portman*	Y	Y	Y	Y
3 Hall	?	?	Y	Y
4 *Oxley*	Y	Y	Y	Y
5 *Gillmor*	Y	Y	Y	Y
6 Strickland	N	Y	Y	Y
7 *Hobson*	Y	Y	Y	Y
8 *Boehner*	Y	Y	Y	Y
9 Kaptur	?	?	Y	Y
10 Kucinich	N	Y	Y	Y
11 Jones	N	Y	Y	Y
12 *Tiberi*	Y	Y	Y	Y
13 Brown	N	Y	Y	Y
14 Sawyer	N	Y	Y	Y
15 *Pryce*	Y	Y	Y	Y
16 *Regula*	Y	Y	Y	Y
17 Vacant				
18 *Ney*	Y	Y	Y	Y
19 *LaTourette*	Y	Y	Y	Y

OKLAHOMA

	371	372	373	374
1 *Sullivan*	Y	Y	Y	Y
2 Carson	N	Y	Y	Y
3 *Watkins*	Y	Y	Y	Y
4 *Watts*	Y	Y	Y	Y
5 *Istook*	Y	Y	Y	Y
6 *Lucas*	Y	Y	Y	Y

OREGON

	371	372	373	374
1 Wu	Y	Y	Y	Y
2 *Walden*	Y	Y	Y	Y
3 Blumenauer	N	Y	Y	Y
4 DeFazio	N	Y	Y	Y
5 Hooley	N	Y	Y	Y

PENNSYLVANIA

	371	372	373	374
1 Brady	N	Y	Y	Y
2 Fattah	N	Y	Y	Y
3 Borski	N	Y	Y	Y
4 *Hart*	Y	Y	Y	Y
5 *Peterson*	Y	Y	Y	Y
6 Holden	N	Y	Y	Y
7 *Weldon*	Y	Y	Y	Y
8 *Greenwood*	Y	Y	Y	Y
9 *Shuster, Bill*	Y	Y	Y	Y
10 *Sherwood*	Y	Y	Y	Y
11 Kanjorski	N	Y	Y	Y
12 Murtha	?	?	Y	Y
13 Hoeffel	N	Y	Y	Y
14 Coyne	N	Y	Y	Y
15 *Toomey*	Y	Y	Y	Y
16 *Pitts*	Y	Y	Y	Y
17 *Gekas*	Y	Y	Y	Y
18 Doyle	N	Y	Y	Y
19 *Platts*	Y	Y	Y	Y
20 Mascara	N	Y	Y	Y
21 *English*	Y	Y	Y	Y

RHODE ISLAND

	371	372	373	374
1 Kennedy	N	Y	Y	Y
2 Langevin	N	Y	Y	Y

SOUTH CAROLINA

	371	372	373	374
1 *Brown*	Y	Y	Y	Y
2 *Wilson*	Y	Y	Y	Y
3 *Graham*	?	?	Y	Y
4 *DeMint*	Y	Y	Y	Y
5 Spratt	N	Y	Y	Y
6 Clyburn	N	Y	Y	Y

SOUTH DAKOTA

	371	372	373	374
AL *Thune*	Y	Y	Y	Y

TENNESSEE

	371	372	373	374
1 *Jenkins*	Y	Y	Y	Y
2 *Duncan*	Y	Y	Y	Y
3 *Wamp*	Y	Y	Y	?
4 *Hilleary*	Y	Y	Y	Y
5 Clement	Y	Y	Y	Y
6 Gordon	N	Y	Y	Y
7 *Bryant*	Y	Y	Y	Y
8 Tanner	N	Y	Y	Y
9 Ford	N	Y	Y	Y

TEXAS

	371	372	373	374
1 Sandlin	N	Y	Y	Y
2 Turner	N	Y	Y	Y
3 *Johnson, Sam*	Y	Y	Y	?
4 Hall	Y	Y	Y	Y
5 *Sessions*	Y	Y	Y	Y
6 *Barton*	Y	Y	Y	Y
7 *Culberson*	Y	Y	Y	Y
8 *Brady*	Y	?	Y	Y
9 Lampson	N	Y	Y	Y
10 Doggett	N	Y	Y	Y
11 Edwards	N	Y	Y	Y
12 *Granger*	Y	Y	Y	Y
13 *Thornberry*	Y	Y	Y	Y
14 *Paul*	Y	Y	N	Y
15 Hinojosa	N	Y	Y	Y
16 Reyes	N	Y	Y	Y
17 Stenholm	N	Y	Y	Y
18 Jackson-Lee	N	Y	Y	Y
19 *Combest*	Y	Y	Y	Y
20 Gonzalez	N	Y	Y	Y
21 *Smith*	Y	Y	Y	Y
22 *DeLay*	Y	Y	Y	Y
23 *Bonilla*	Y	Y	Y	Y
24 Frost	N	Y	Y	Y
25 Bentsen	N	Y	Y	Y
26 *Armey*	Y	Y	Y	Y
27 Ortiz	N	Y	Y	Y
28 Rodriguez	N	Y	Y	Y
29 Green	N	Y	Y	Y
30 Johnson, E.B.	N	Y	Y	Y

UTAH

	371	372	373	374
1 *Hansen*	Y	Y	Y	Y
2 Matheson	Y	Y	Y	Y
3 *Cannon*	Y	Y	Y	Y

VERMONT

	371	372	373	374
AL *Sanders*	N	Y	Y	Y

VIRGINIA

	371	372	373	374
1 *Davis, Jo Ann*	Y	Y	Y	?
2 *Schrock*	?	?	?	?
3 Scott	N	Y	Y	Y
4 *Forbes*	Y	Y	Y	Y
5 *Goode* *	Y	Y	Y	Y
6 *Goodlatte*	Y	Y	Y	Y
7 *Cantor*	Y	Y	Y	Y
8 Moran	N	Y	?	Y
9 Boucher	N	Y	Y	Y
10 *Wolf*	Y	Y	Y	Y
11 *Davis, T.*	?	?	Y	Y

WASHINGTON

	371	372	373	374
1 Inslee	N	Y	Y	Y
2 Larsen	Y	Y	Y	Y
3 Baird	N	Y	Y	Y
4 *Hastings*	?	?	?	?
5 *Nethercutt*	Y	Y	Y	Y
6 Dicks	N	Y	Y	Y
7 McDermott	N	Y	Y	Y
8 *Dunn*	Y	Y	Y	?
9 Smith	?	?	?	?

WEST VIRGINIA

	371	372	373	374
1 Mollohan	N	Y	Y	Y
2 *Capito*	Y	Y	Y	Y
3 Rahall	N	Y	Y	Y

WISCONSIN

	371	372	373	374
1 *Ryan*	Y	Y	Y	Y
2 Baldwin	?	?	Y	Y
3 Kind	N	Y	Y	Y
4 Kleczka	N	Y	Y	Y
5 Barrett	?	?	?	?
6 *Petri*	Y	Y	Y	Y
7 Obey	N	Y	Y	Y
8 *Green*	Y	Y	Y	Y
9 *Sensenbrenner*	Y	Y	Y	Y

WYOMING

	371	372	373	374
AL *Cubin*	Y	Y	?	?

Southern states - Ala., Ark., Fla., Ga., Ky., La., Miss., N.C., Okla., S.C., Tenn., Texas, Va.

Key

Y	Voted for (yea).
#	Paired for.
+	Announced for.
N	Voted against (nay).
X	Paired against.
–	Announced against.
P	Voted "present."
C	Voted "present" to avoid possible conflict of interest.
?	Did not vote or otherwise make a position known.

Democrats **Republicans**
Independents

---

375. HR 5157. Transit Grants/Passage. Petri, R-Wis., motion to suspend the rules and pass the bill that would allow transit systems in 52 communities that surpassed 200,000 people, according to a 2000 Census survey, to continue to use federal transit formula grants for fiscal 2003 operating expenses. Motion agreed to 350-0: R 182-0; D 168-0 (ND 122-0, SD 46-0); I 0-0. A two-thirds majority of those present and voting (234 in this case) is required for passage under suspension of the rules. Sept. 9, 2002.

376. H Con Res 401. Flight Attendant Tribute/Adoption. Petri, R-Wis., motion to suspend the rules and adopt the resolution that would thank flight attendants for their contributions to air safety and pay tribute to attendants who acted heroically during the Sept. 11 terrorist attacks. Motion agreed to 351-0: R 182-0; D 169-0 (ND 122-0, SD 47-0); I 0-0. A two-thirds majority of those present and voting (234 in this case) is required for adoption under suspension of the rules. Sept. 9, 2002.

377. H Res 516. Little League Champions Tribute/Adoption. Jo Ann Davis, R-Va., motion to suspend the rules and adopt the resolution that would honor the Valley Sports American Little League from Louisville, Ky., for winning the 2002 Little League World Series. Motion agreed to 344-0: R 178-0; D 166-0 (ND 119-0, SD 47-0); I 0-0. A two-thirds majority of those present and voting (230 in this case) is required for adoption under suspension of the rules. Sept. 9, 2002.

378. HR 5010. Fiscal 2003 Defense Appropriations/Motion to Close Conference. Lewis, R-Calif., motion to close portions of the conference on the bill that would appropriate funding for the Defense Department for fiscal 2003. Motion agreed to 365-0: R 189-0; D 176-0 (ND 126-0, SD 50-0); I 0-0. Sept. 10, 2002.

379. HR 3210. Terrorism Insurance/Motion to Instruct. Fossella, R-N.Y., motion to instruct House conferees to agree to Section 11 of the Senate-passed bill that would require that seized assets of terrorists and their sponsors go toward compensating U.S. victims who win monetary damages in federal court stemming from terrorist activity. Motion agreed to 373-0: R 191-0; D 182-0 (ND 131-0, SD 51-0); I 0-0. Sept. 10, 2002.

380. Procedural Motion/Journal. Approval of the House Journal of Monday, Sept. 9, 2002. Approved 335-35: R 183-9; D 152-26 (ND 108-21, SD 44-5); I 0-0. Sept. 10, 2002.

381. H Res 513. Irish Economic Development/Adoption. Smith, R-N.J., motion to suspend the rules and adopt the resolution that would recognize the importance of the United States-Ireland Business Summit and the benefit of economic development to building peace in Northern Ireland. Motion agreed to 372-0: R 188-0; D 184-0 (ND 132-0, SD 52-0); I 0-0. A two-thirds majority of those present and voting (248 in this case) is required for adoption under suspension of the rules. Sept. 10, 2002.

* Rep. Tony P. Hall, D-Ohio, resigned effective Sept. 9, 2002. The last vote for which he was eligible was vote 377.

	375	376	377	378	379	380	381
ALABAMA							
1 *Callahan*	?	?	?	?	?	?	?
2 *Everett*	?	?	?	Y	Y	Y	Y
3 *Riley*	?	?	?	+	+	+	+
4 *Aderholt*	Y	Y	Y	Y	Y	Y	Y
5 *Cramer*	Y	Y	Y	Y	Y	Y	Y
6 *Bachus*	Y	Y	Y	Y	Y	Y	Y
7 Hilliard	Y	Y	Y	Y	Y	N	Y
ALASKA							
AL *Young*	Y	Y	Y	?	?	?	Y
ARIZONA							
1 *Flake*	Y	Y	Y	Y	Y	Y	Y
2 Pastor	Y	Y	Y	Y	Y	Y	Y
3 *Stump*	?	?	?	?	?	?	?
4 *Shadegg*	Y	Y	Y	Y	Y	Y	Y
5 *Kolbe*	Y	Y	Y	Y	Y	Y	Y
6 *Hayworth*	Y	Y	Y	Y	Y	Y	Y
ARKANSAS							
1 Berry	Y	Y	Y	Y	Y	Y	Y
2 Snyder	Y	Y	Y	Y	Y	Y	Y
3 *Boozman*	Y	Y	Y	Y	Y	Y	Y
4 Ross	Y	Y	Y	Y	Y	Y	Y
CALIFORNIA							
1 Thompson	Y	Y	Y	Y	Y	N	Y
2 *Herger*	Y	Y	Y	+	+	Y	Y
3 *Ose*	Y	Y	Y	Y	Y	Y	Y
4 *Doolittle*	Y	Y	Y	Y	Y	Y	?
5 Matsui	Y	Y	Y	Y	Y	Y	Y
6 Woolsey	Y	Y	Y	Y	Y	Y	Y
7 Miller, George	?	?	?	?	?	?	?
8 Pelosi	Y	Y	Y	Y	Y	Y	Y
9 Lee	Y	Y	Y	Y	Y	Y	Y
10 Tauscher	Y	Y	Y	Y	Y	Y	Y
11 *Pombo*	Y	Y	Y	Y	Y	Y	Y
12 Lantos	Y	Y	Y	Y	?	Y	Y
13 Stark	Y	Y	Y	Y	Y	Y	Y
14 Eshoo	Y	Y	Y	Y	Y	Y	Y
15 Honda	Y	Y	Y	Y	Y	Y	Y
16 Lofgren	Y	Y	Y	Y	Y	Y	Y
17 Farr	Y	Y	Y	Y	Y	Y	Y
18 Condit	?	?	?	?	Y	N	Y
19 *Radanovich*	Y	Y	Y	Y	Y	Y	Y
20 Dooley	Y	Y	Y	Y	Y	Y	?
21 *Thomas*	Y	Y	Y	Y	Y	Y	Y
22 Capps	Y	Y	Y	Y	Y	Y	Y
23 *Gallegly*	?	?	?	Y	Y	Y	Y
24 Sherman	Y	Y	Y	Y	Y	Y	Y
25 *McKeon*	Y	Y	Y	Y	Y	Y	Y
26 Berman	Y	Y	Y	Y	Y	Y	Y
27 Schiff	Y	Y	Y	Y	Y	Y	Y
28 *Dreier*	Y	Y	Y	Y	Y	Y	Y
29 Waxman	Y	Y	Y	Y	Y	Y	Y
30 Becerra	Y	Y	Y	Y	Y	Y	Y
31 Solis	Y	Y	Y	Y	Y	Y	Y
32 Watson	Y	Y	Y	Y	Y	Y	Y
33 Roybal-Allard	Y	Y	Y	Y	Y	Y	Y
34 Napolitano	Y	Y	Y	+	+	Y	Y
35 Waters	?	?	?	?	?	?	?
36 Harman	Y	Y	Y	Y	Y	Y	Y
37 Millender-McD.	?	?	?	Y	Y	Y	Y
38 *Horn*	Y	Y	?	Y	Y	Y	Y

	375	376	377	378	379	380	381
39 *Royce*	Y	Y	Y	Y	Y	Y	Y
40 *Lewis*	Y	Y	Y	Y	Y	Y	Y
41 *Miller, Gary*	Y	Y	Y	Y	Y	Y	Y
42 Baca	Y	Y	Y	Y	Y	Y	Y
43 *Calvert*	Y	Y	?	Y	Y	Y	Y
44 *Bono*	Y	Y	Y	Y	Y	Y	Y
45 *Rohrabacher*	Y	Y	Y	Y	Y	Y	Y
46 Sanchez	Y	Y	Y	Y	Y	Y	Y
47 *Cox*	Y	Y	Y	Y	Y	Y	?
48 *Issa*	Y	Y	Y	Y	Y	Y	Y
49 Davis	Y	Y	Y	Y	Y	Y	Y
50 Filner	Y	Y	Y	Y	Y	N	Y
51 *Cunningham*	Y	Y	Y	Y	Y	Y	?
52 *Hunter*	Y	Y	Y	Y	Y	Y	Y
COLORADO							
1 DeGette	Y	Y	Y	Y	Y	Y	Y
2 Udall	Y	Y	Y	Y	Y	Y	Y
3 *McInnis*	Y	Y	Y	Y	Y	Y	Y
4 *Schaffer*	?	?	?	?	?	?	?
5 *Hefley*	Y	Y	Y	Y	Y	N	Y
6 *Tancredo*	Y	Y	Y	Y	Y	P	Y
CONNECTICUT							
1 Larson	Y	Y	Y	Y	Y	Y	Y
2 *Simmons*	Y	Y	Y	Y	Y	Y	Y
3 DeLauro	Y	Y	?	Y	Y	Y	Y
4 *Shays*	Y	Y	Y	Y	Y	Y	Y
5 Maloney	+	+	+	Y	Y	Y	Y
6 *Johnson*	Y	Y	?	Y	Y	Y	Y
DELAWARE							
AL *Castle*	Y	Y	Y	Y	Y	Y	Y
FLORIDA							
1 *Miller, J.*	?	?	?	?	?	?	?
2 Boyd	Y	Y	Y	Y	Y	Y	Y
3 Brown	?	?	?	?	?	?	?
4 *Crenshaw*	Y	Y	Y	Y	Y	Y	Y
5 Thurman	?	?	?	?	Y	?	Y
6 *Stearns*	Y	Y	Y	Y	Y	Y	Y
7 *Mica*	Y	Y	Y	Y	Y	Y	Y
8 *Keller*	Y	Y	Y	Y	Y	Y	Y
9 *Bilirakis*	Y	Y	Y	Y	Y	Y	Y
10 *Young*	?	?	?	?	Y	Y	Y
11 Davis	Y	Y	Y	Y	Y	Y	Y
12 *Putnam*	Y	Y	Y	Y	Y	Y	Y
13 *Miller, D.*	Y	Y	Y	Y	Y	Y	Y
14 *Goss*	Y	Y	Y	Y	Y	Y	Y
15 *Weldon*	Y	Y	Y	Y	Y	Y	Y
16 *Foley*	Y	Y	Y	Y	Y	Y	Y
17 Meek	?	Y	Y	Y	Y	Y	Y
18 *Ros-Lehtinen*	?	?	?	?	?	?	?
19 Wexler	Y	Y	Y	Y	Y	Y	Y
20 Deutsch	Y	Y	Y	Y	Y	Y	Y
21 *Diaz-Balart*	?	?	?	?	?	?	?
22 *Shaw*	Y	+	Y	Y	Y	Y	Y
23 Hastings	Y	Y	Y	Y	Y	Y	Y
GEORGIA							
1 *Kingston*	Y	Y	Y	Y	Y	Y	Y
2 Bishop	?	?	?	Y	Y	Y	Y
3 *Collins*	?	?	?	?	?	?	?
4 McKinney	?	Y	Y	Y	Y	Y	Y
5 Lewis	Y	Y	Y	Y	Y	Y	Y
6 *Isakson*	Y	Y	Y	Y	Y	Y	Y
7 *Barr*	?	?	?	Y	?	Y	Y
8 *Chambliss*	?	?	?	Y	Y	Y	Y
9 *Deal*	Y	Y	Y	Y	Y	Y	Y
10 *Norwood*	Y	Y	Y	Y	Y	Y	Y
11 *Linder*	Y	Y	Y	?	Y	Y	?
HAWAII							
1 Abercrombie	Y	Y	Y	Y	Y	Y	Y
2 Mink	?	?	?	?	?	?	?
IDAHO							
1 *Otter*	Y	Y	Y	Y	Y	Y	Y
2 *Simpson*	Y	Y	Y	Y	Y	Y	Y
ILLINOIS							
1 Rush	?	?	?	?	Y	Y	Y
2 Jackson	Y	Y	Y	Y	Y	Y	Y
3 Lipinski	?	?	?	?	Y	Y	Y
4 Gutierrez	?	?	?	?	Y	Y	Y
5 Blagojevich	?	?	?	?	Y	Y	Y
6 *Hyde*	Y	Y	Y	Y	Y	Y	Y
7 Davis	Y	Y	Y	Y	Y	Y	Y
8 *Crane*	Y	Y	Y	Y	Y	N	Y
9 Schakowsky	Y	Y	Y	Y	Y	Y	Y
10 *Kirk*	Y	Y	Y	Y	Y	Y	Y
11 *Weller*	+	+	+	+	+	Y	Y
12 Costello	Y	Y	Y	Y	Y	N	Y
13 *Biggert*	Y	Y	Y	Y	Y	Y	Y

ND Northern Democrats SD Southern Democrats

	375	376	377	378	379	380	381
14 ***Hastert***							
15 ***Johnson***	Y	Y	Y	Y	Y	Y	Y
16 ***Manzullo***	Y	Y	Y	Y	Y	Y	Y
17 Evans	Y	Y	Y	Y	Y	Y	Y
18 ***LaHood***	?	?	?	Y	Y	Y	Y
19 Phelps	Y	Y	Y	Y	Y	Y	Y
20 ***Shimkus***	Y	Y	Y	Y	Y	Y	Y
INDIANA							
1 Visclosky	Y	Y	Y	Y	Y	N	Y
2 ***Pence***	Y	Y	Y	Y	Y	Y	Y
3 Roemer	Y	Y	Y	Y	Y	Y	Y
4 ***Souder***	Y	Y	Y	?	?	?	?
5 ***Buyer***	Y	Y	Y	Y	Y	Y	Y
6 ***Burton***	Y	Y	Y	Y	Y	Y	Y
7 ***Kerns***	Y	Y	Y	Y	Y	Y	Y
8 ***Hostettler***	Y	Y	Y	Y	Y	Y	Y
9 Hill	Y	Y	Y	Y	Y	Y	Y
10 Carson	Y	Y	Y	Y	Y	Y	Y
IOWA							
1 ***Leach***	Y	Y	Y	Y	Y	Y	Y
2 ***Nussle***	Y	Y	Y	Y	Y	Y	Y
3 Boswell	Y	Y	Y	Y	Y	Y	Y
4 ***Ganske***	Y	Y	Y	Y	Y	Y	Y
5 ***Latham***	Y	Y	Y	Y	Y	N	Y
KANSAS							
1 ***Moran***	Y	Y	Y	Y	Y	N	Y
2 ***Ryun***	Y	Y	Y	Y	Y	Y	Y
3 Moore	Y	Y	Y	Y	Y	N	Y
4 ***Tiahrt***	Y	Y	Y	Y	Y	Y	Y
KENTUCKY							
1 ***Whitfield***	Y	Y	Y	Y	Y	Y	Y
2 ***Lewis***	Y	Y	Y	Y	Y	Y	Y
3 ***Northup***	Y	Y	Y	Y	Y	Y	Y
4 Lucas	Y	Y	Y	Y	Y	Y	Y
5 ***Rogers***	Y	Y	Y	Y	Y	Y	Y
6 ***Fletcher***	Y	Y	Y	Y	Y	Y	Y
LOUISIANA							
1 ***Vitter***	Y	Y	Y	Y	Y	Y	Y
2 Jefferson	Y	Y	Y	Y	Y	?	Y
3 ***Tauzin***	Y	Y	Y	Y	Y	Y	Y
4 ***McCrery***	Y	Y	Y	Y	Y	Y	?
5 ***Cooksey***	?	?	?	Y	Y	Y	Y
6 ***Baker***	Y	Y	Y	Y	Y	Y	Y
7 John	Y	?	?	Y	Y	Y	Y
MAINE							
1 Allen	Y	Y	Y	Y	Y	Y	Y
2 Baldacci	?	?	?	Y	Y	Y	Y
MARYLAND							
1 ***Gilchrest***	?	?	?	?	?	Y	Y
2 ***Ehrlich***	?	?	?	?	?	?	?
3 Cardin	Y	Y	Y	?	?	?	?
4 Wynn	Y	Y	Y	?	?	?	?
5 Hoyer	Y	Y	Y	+	+	+	Y
6 ***Bartlett***	Y	Y	Y	?	?	?	Y
7 Cummings	Y	Y	Y	Y	Y	Y	Y
8 ***Morella***	Y	Y	Y	+	+	+	+
MASSACHUSETTS							
1 Olver	Y	Y	Y	Y	Y	N	Y
2 Neal	?	?	?	?	Y	Y	Y
3 McGovern	Y	Y	Y	Y	Y	Y	Y
4 Frank	Y	Y	Y	Y	Y	Y	Y
5 Meehan	?	?	?	Y	Y	Y	Y
6 Tierney	Y	Y	Y	Y	Y	Y	Y
7 Markey	Y	Y	Y	Y	Y	Y	Y
8 Capuano	Y	Y	Y	Y	Y	N	Y
9 Lynch	?	?	?	?	?	?	?
10 Delahunt	?	?	?	?	?	?	?
MICHIGAN							
1 Stupak	Y	Y	Y	Y	Y	N	Y
2 ***Hoekstra***	?	?	?	Y	Y	Y	Y
3 ***Ehlers***	Y	Y	Y	Y	Y	Y	Y
4 ***Camp***	Y	Y	Y	Y	Y	Y	Y
5 Barcia	Y	Y	Y	Y	Y	Y	Y
6 ***Upton***	Y	Y	Y	Y	Y	Y	Y
7 ***Smith***	Y	Y	Y	Y	Y	Y	?
8 ***Rogers***	Y	Y	Y	Y	Y	Y	Y
9 Kildee	Y	Y	Y	Y	Y	Y	Y
10 Bonior	Y	Y	Y	Y	Y	Y	?
11 ***Knollenberg***	Y	Y	Y	Y	Y	Y	Y
12 Levin	Y	Y	Y	Y	Y	Y	Y
13 Rivers	Y	Y	Y	Y	Y	Y	Y
14 Conyers	Y	Y	Y	Y	Y	Y	Y
15 Kilpatrick	Y	Y	Y	Y	Y	Y	Y
16 Dingell	?	?	?	Y	Y	Y	Y
MINNESOTA							
1 ***Gutknecht***	Y	Y	Y	Y	Y	N	?
2 ***Kennedy***	Y	Y	Y	Y	Y	N	Y
3 ***Ramstad***	Y	Y	Y	Y	Y	N	Y
4 McCollum	Y	Y	Y	Y	Y	Y	Y
5 Sabo	Y	Y	Y	Y	Y	N	Y
6 Luther	Y	Y	Y	Y	Y	Y	Y
7 Peterson	Y	Y	Y	Y	Y	N	Y
8 Oberstar	Y	Y	Y	Y	Y	N	Y
MISSISSIPPI							
1 ***Wicker***	Y	Y	Y	Y	Y	Y	Y
2 Thompson	Y	Y	Y	Y	Y	N	Y
3 ***Pickering***	Y	Y	Y	Y	Y	Y	Y
4 Shows	Y	Y	Y	Y	Y	Y	Y
5 Taylor	Y	Y	Y	Y	Y	N	Y
MISSOURI							
1 Clay	Y	Y	Y	Y	Y	Y	Y
2 ***Akin***	Y	Y	Y	Y	Y	Y	?
3 Gephardt	Y	Y	Y	Y	Y	Y	Y
4 Skelton	Y	Y	Y	Y	Y	Y	Y
5 McCarthy	Y	Y	Y	Y	Y	?	Y
6 ***Graves***	Y	Y	Y	Y	Y	Y	Y
7 ***Blunt***	Y	Y	Y	Y	Y	Y	Y
8 ***Emerson***	Y	Y	Y	Y	Y	Y	Y
9 ***Hulshof***	Y	Y	Y	Y	Y	Y	Y
MONTANA							
AL ***Rehberg***	Y	Y	Y	Y	Y	Y	Y
NEBRASKA							
1 ***Bereuter***	Y	Y	Y	Y	Y	Y	Y
2 ***Terry***	Y	Y	Y	Y	Y	Y	Y
3 ***Osborne***	Y	Y	Y	Y	Y	Y	Y
NEVADA							
1 Berkley	Y	Y	Y	Y	Y	Y	Y
2 ***Gibbons***	Y	Y	Y	Y	Y	Y	?
NEW HAMPSHIRE							
1 ***Sununu***	?	?	?	?	?	?	?
2 ***Bass***	Y	Y	Y	Y	Y	Y	Y
NEW JERSEY							
1 Andrews	Y	Y	Y	Y	Y	Y	Y
2 ***LoBiondo***	Y	Y	Y	Y	Y	Y	Y
3 ***Saxton***	+	+	+	Y	Y	Y	?
4 ***Smith***	Y	?	Y	Y	Y	Y	Y
5 ***Roukema***	?	?	?	?	?	?	?
6 Pallone	Y	Y	Y	Y	Y	Y	Y
7 ***Ferguson***	Y	Y	Y	Y	Y	Y	Y
8 Pascrell	?	?	?	Y	Y	Y	Y
9 Rothman	Y	Y	Y	Y	Y	Y	Y
10 Payne	Y	Y	Y	Y	Y	Y	Y
11 ***Frelinghuysen***	Y	Y	Y	Y	Y	Y	Y
12 Holt	Y	Y	?	Y	Y	Y	Y
13 Menendez	Y	Y	Y	Y	Y	Y	Y
NEW MEXICO							
1 ***Wilson***	Y	Y	Y	Y	Y	Y	Y
2 ***Skeen***	Y	Y	Y	Y	Y	Y	Y
3 Udall	Y	Y	Y	Y	Y	N	Y
NEW YORK							
1 ***Grucci***	Y	Y	Y	Y	Y	Y	Y
2 Israel	Y	Y	Y	Y	Y	Y	Y
3 ***King***	Y	Y	Y	?	?	?	?
4 McCarthy	Y	Y	Y	Y	Y	Y	Y
5 Ackerman	Y	Y	Y	Y	Y	Y	Y
6 Meeks	?	?	?	?	?	?	?
7 Crowley	?	?	?	?	?	?	?
8 Nadler	?	?	?	Y	Y	Y	Y
9 Weiner	Y	Y	Y	+	+	+	Y
10 Towns	?	?	?	?	?	?	?
11 Owens	+	+	+	+	+	+	+
12 Velázquez	?	?	?	?	?	?	?
13 ***Fossella***	+	Y	Y	Y	Y	Y	Y
14 Maloney	+	+	+	+	+	+	+
15 Rangel	Y	Y	Y	Y	Y	Y	Y
16 Serrano	?	?	?	?	?	?	?
17 Engel	Y	Y	Y	Y	Y	Y	Y
18 Lowey	+	+	+	Y	Y	Y	Y
19 ***Kelly***	Y	Y	Y	Y	Y	Y	Y
20 ***Gilman***	Y	Y	Y	Y	Y	Y	Y
21 McNulty	Y	Y	Y	Y	Y	Y	Y
22 ***Sweeney***	?	?	?	?	?	?	?
23 ***Boehlert***	?	?	?	?	?	?	?
24 ***McHugh***	Y	Y	Y	Y	Y	Y	Y
25 ***Walsh***	?	?	?	?	?	?	?
26 Hinchey	Y	Y	Y	Y	Y	N	Y
27 ***Reynolds***	Y	Y	Y	Y	Y	Y	Y
28 Slaughter	Y	Y	Y	Y	Y	Y	Y
29 LaFalce	Y	Y	Y	Y	Y	Y	Y
30 ***Quinn***	Y	Y	Y	Y	Y	Y	Y
31 ***Houghton***	Y	Y	Y	Y	Y	Y	Y
NORTH CAROLINA							
1 Clayton	Y	Y	Y	Y	Y	Y	Y
2 Etheridge	Y	Y	Y	Y	Y	Y	Y
3 ***Jones***	Y	Y	Y	Y	Y	Y	?
4 Price	Y	Y	Y	Y	Y	Y	Y
5 ***Burr***	Y	Y	Y	Y	Y	Y	Y
6 ***Coble***	Y	Y	Y	Y	Y	Y	Y
7 McIntyre	Y	Y	Y	Y	Y	Y	Y
8 ***Hayes***	Y	Y	Y	Y	Y	Y	Y
9 ***Myrick***	Y	Y	Y	Y	Y	Y	Y
10 ***Ballenger***	Y	Y	Y	Y	Y	Y	Y
11 ***Taylor***	?	?	?	?	?	?	?
12 Watt	Y	Y	Y	Y	Y	Y	Y
NORTH DAKOTA							
AL Pomeroy	Y	Y	Y	Y	Y	Y	Y
OHIO							
1 ***Chabot***	Y	Y	Y	Y	Y	Y	Y
2 ***Portman***	Y	Y	Y	Y	Y	Y	Y
3 Hall *	?	?	?				
4 ***Oxley***	Y	Y	?	Y	Y	Y	Y
5 ***Gillmor***	Y	Y	Y	Y	Y	Y	Y
6 Strickland	Y	Y	Y	Y	Y	Y	Y
7 ***Hobson***	Y	Y	Y	Y	Y	Y	Y
8 ***Boehner***	Y	Y	Y	Y	Y	Y	Y
9 Kaptur	?	?	?	?	?	?	?
10 Kucinich	Y	Y	Y	Y	Y	N	Y
11 Jones	Y	Y	Y	Y	Y	Y	Y
12 ***Tiberi***	Y	Y	Y	Y	Y	Y	Y
13 Brown	Y	Y	Y	Y	Y	Y	Y
14 Sawyer	Y	Y	Y	Y	Y	Y	Y
15 ***Pryce***	?	?	?	?	?	?	Y
16 ***Regula***	Y	Y	Y	Y	Y	Y	Y
17 Vacant							
18 ***Ney***	Y	Y	?	Y	Y	Y	Y
19 ***LaTourette***	?	?	?	?	?	?	?
OKLAHOMA							
1 ***Sullivan***	Y	Y	Y	Y	Y	Y	Y
2 Carson	Y	Y	Y	Y	Y	Y	Y
3 ***Watkins***	+	+	+	Y	Y	Y	Y
4 ***Watts***	+	+	+	Y	Y	Y	Y
5 ***Istook***	Y	Y	Y	?	?	?	Y
6 ***Lucas***	Y	Y	Y	Y	Y	Y	Y
OREGON							
1 Wu	Y	Y	Y	Y	Y	N	Y
2 ***Walden***	Y	Y	Y	Y	Y	Y	Y
3 Blumenauer	Y	Y	Y	Y	Y	Y	Y
4 DeFazio	Y	Y	Y	Y	Y	N	Y
5 Hooley	Y	Y	Y	Y	Y	Y	Y
PENNSYLVANIA							
1 Brady	Y	Y	Y	Y	Y	N	Y
2 Fattah	Y	Y	Y	?	?	?	Y
3 Borski	?	?	?	?	?	?	?
4 ***Hart***	Y	Y	Y	Y	Y	N	Y
5 ***Peterson***	Y	Y	Y	Y	Y	Y	Y
6 Holden	Y	Y	Y	Y	Y	Y	Y
7 ***Weldon***	Y	Y	Y	Y	Y	Y	Y
8 ***Greenwood***	?	?	Y	Y	Y	Y	Y
9 ***Shuster, Bill***	Y	Y	Y	Y	Y	Y	Y
10 ***Sherwood***	Y	Y	Y	Y	Y	Y	Y
11 Kanjorski	Y	Y	Y	Y	Y	Y	Y
12 Murtha	Y	Y	Y	?	Y	Y	Y
13 Hoeffel	Y	Y	Y	Y	Y	Y	Y
14 Coyne	Y	Y	Y	Y	Y	Y	Y
15 ***Toomey***	?	Y	Y	Y	Y	Y	Y
16 ***Pitts***	Y	Y	Y	Y	Y	Y	Y
17 ***Gekas***	Y	Y	Y	Y	Y	Y	Y
18 Doyle	?	?	?	Y	Y	Y	Y
19 ***Platts***	Y	Y	Y	?	?	?	Y
20 Mascara	+	+	+	+	+	+	+
21 ***English***	Y	Y	Y	Y	Y	N	Y
RHODE ISLAND							
1 Kennedy	+	+	+	+	+	+	+
2 Langevin	Y	Y	Y	Y	Y	Y	Y
SOUTH CAROLINA							
1 ***Brown***	Y	Y	Y	Y	Y	Y	Y
2 ***Wilson***	Y	Y	Y	Y	Y	Y	Y
3 ***Graham***	Y	Y	Y	Y	Y	Y	Y
4 ***DeMint***	Y	Y	Y	Y	Y	Y	Y
5 Spratt	Y	Y	Y	Y	Y	Y	Y
6 Clyburn	Y	Y	Y	Y	Y	Y	Y
SOUTH DAKOTA							
AL ***Thune***	Y	Y	Y	Y	Y	Y	Y
TENNESSEE							
1 ***Jenkins***	Y	Y	Y	Y	Y	Y	Y
2 ***Duncan***	Y	Y	Y	Y	Y	Y	Y
3 ***Wamp***	?	?	?	Y	Y	Y	Y
4 ***Hilleary***	?	?	?	?	?	?	?
5 Clement	+	+	+	+	+	+	+
6 Gordon	Y	Y	Y	Y	Y	Y	Y
7 ***Bryant***	?	?	?	?	?	?	Y
8 Tanner	Y	Y	Y	Y	Y	Y	Y
9 Ford	Y	Y	Y	Y	Y	Y	Y
TEXAS							
1 Sandlin	Y	Y	Y	Y	Y	Y	Y
2 Turner	Y	Y	Y	Y	Y	Y	Y
3 ***Johnson, Sam***	Y	Y	Y	Y	Y	Y	Y
4 Hall	?	?	?	Y	Y	Y	Y
5 ***Sessions***	?	?	?	Y	Y	Y	Y
6 ***Barton***	Y	Y	Y	?	Y	Y	Y
7 ***Culberson***	Y	Y	Y	Y	Y	Y	Y
8 ***Brady***	Y	Y	Y	Y	Y	Y	Y
9 Lampson	Y	Y	Y	Y	Y	Y	Y
10 Doggett	Y	Y	Y	Y	Y	Y	Y
11 Edwards	Y	Y	Y	Y	Y	Y	Y
12 ***Granger***	Y	Y	Y	Y	Y	Y	Y
13 ***Thornberry***	Y	Y	Y	Y	Y	Y	Y
14 ***Paul***	Y	Y	Y	Y	Y	Y	Y
15 Hinojosa	Y	Y	Y	Y	Y	Y	Y
16 Reyes	Y	Y	Y	Y	Y	Y	Y
17 Stenholm	Y	Y	Y	Y	Y	N	Y
18 Jackson-Lee	Y	Y	Y	+	+	+	Y
19 ***Combest***	Y	Y	Y	Y	Y	Y	Y
20 Gonzalez	Y	Y	Y	Y	Y	Y	Y
21 ***Smith***	Y	Y	?	Y	Y	Y	Y
22 ***DeLay***	Y	Y	Y	Y	Y	Y	Y
23 ***Bonilla***	Y	Y	Y	Y	Y	Y	Y
24 Frost	?	?	?	Y	Y	Y	Y
25 Bentsen	Y	Y	Y	Y	Y	Y	Y
26 ***Armey***	Y	Y	Y	Y	Y	Y	Y
27 Ortiz	Y	Y	Y	Y	Y	Y	Y
28 Rodriguez	Y	Y	Y	Y	Y	Y	Y
29 Green	Y	Y	Y	Y	Y	N	Y
30 Johnson, E.B.	Y	Y	Y	Y	Y	Y	Y
UTAH							
1 ***Hansen***	?	?	?	Y	Y	Y	Y
2 Matheson	Y	Y	Y	Y	Y	Y	Y
3 ***Cannon***	?	?	?	Y	Y	Y	Y
VERMONT							
AL *Sanders*	?	?	?	?	?	?	?
VIRGINIA							
1 ***Davis, Jo Ann***	Y	Y	Y	Y	Y	Y	Y
2 ***Schrock***	Y	Y	Y	Y	Y	Y	Y
3 Scott	Y	Y	Y	Y	Y	Y	Y
4 ***Forbes***	Y	Y	Y	Y	Y	Y	Y
5 ***Goode***	Y	Y	Y	Y	Y	Y	Y
6 ***Goodlatte***	Y	Y	Y	Y	Y	Y	Y
7 ***Cantor***	Y	Y	?	Y	Y	Y	Y
8 Moran	Y	Y	Y	?	Y	Y	Y
9 Boucher	Y	Y	Y	Y	Y	Y	Y
10 ***Wolf***	Y	Y	Y	Y	Y	Y	Y
11 ***Davis, T.***	Y	Y	Y	Y	Y	Y	?
WASHINGTON							
1 Inslee	Y	Y	Y	Y	Y	Y	Y
2 Larsen	Y	Y	Y	Y	Y	N	Y
3 Baird	Y	Y	Y	Y	Y	N	Y
4 ***Hastings***	?	?	?	?	?	?	?
5 ***Nethercutt***	Y	Y	Y	?	?	Y	Y
6 Dicks	Y	Y	Y	Y	Y	Y	Y
7 McDermott	Y	Y	Y	Y	Y	?	Y
8 ***Dunn***	Y	Y	Y	Y	Y	Y	Y
9 Smith	Y	Y	Y	Y	Y	Y	Y
WEST VIRGINIA							
1 Mollohan	Y	Y	Y	Y	Y	Y	Y
2 ***Capito***	Y	Y	Y	Y	Y	Y	Y
3 Rahall	Y	Y	Y	?	Y	Y	Y
WISCONSIN							
1 ***Ryan***	Y	Y	Y	Y	Y	Y	Y
2 Baldwin	Y	Y	Y	Y	Y	N	Y
3 Kind	Y	Y	Y	Y	Y	Y	Y
4 Kleczka	+	+	+	+	+	+	+
5 Barrett	?	?	?	?	?	?	?
6 ***Petri***	Y	Y	Y	Y	Y	Y	Y
7 Obey	Y	Y	Y	Y	Y	Y	?
8 ***Green***	Y	Y	Y	Y	Y	Y	Y
9 ***Sensenbrenner***	Y	Y	Y	Y	Y	Y	Y
WYOMING							
AL ***Cubin***	Y	Y	Y	Y	Y	Y	Y

Southern states - Ala., Ark., Fla., Ga., Ky., La., Miss., N.C., Okla., S.C., Tenn., Texas, Va.

Key

Y	Voted for (yea).
#	Paired for.
+	Announced for.
N	Voted against (nay).
X	Paired against.
–	Announced against.
P	Voted "present."
C	Voted "present" to avoid possible conflict of interest.
?	Did not vote or otherwise make a position known.

Democrats **Republicans** *Independents*

382. HR 3880. New York Clean Air/Passage. Upton, R-Mich., motion to suspend the rules and pass the bill that would give several counties and cities in the New York City metropolitan area until Sept. 30, 2005, to file reports detailing how federally funded transportation projects will help to meet the Clean Air Act's National Ambient Air Quality Standards. Motion agreed to 377-0: R 191-0; D 185-0 (ND 133-0, SD 52-0); I 1-0. A two-thirds majority of those present and voting (252 in this case) is required for passage under suspension of the rules. Sept. 10, 2002.

383. H Con Res 320. Scleroderma Awareness/Adoption. Fossella, R-N.Y., motion to suspend the rules and adopt the resolution that would express the sense of Congress in support of efforts to combat the debilitating autoimmune disease scleroderma. Motion agreed to 369-2: R 190-2; D 178-0 (ND 126-0, SD 52-0); I 1-0. A two-thirds majority of those present and voting (248 in this case) is required for adoption under suspension of the rules. Sept. 10, 2002.

384. H Con Res 464. Sept. 11 Remembrance/Adoption. Adoption of the resolution that would express the sense of Congress that Sept. 11 should be a day of remembrance for those killed in terrorist attacks at the World Trade Center, the Pentagon, and aboard a hijacked plane that crashed in Pennsylvania. The resolution expresses sympathy for the terrorist victims, honors passengers who downed the plane in Pennsylvania, and gives tribute to emergency workers who responded to the attacks. It also commends the work of the president and the military in removing the Taliban from power. Adopted 370-0: R 197-0; D 172-0 (ND 123-0, SD 49-0); I 1-0. Sept. 11, 2002.

385. HR 1646. State Department Authorization/Agree to Conference. Hyde, R-Ill., motion that the House disagree to the Senate amendment and agree to a conference on the bill that would authorize appropriations for fiscal years 2002 and 2003 for the Department of State and foreign broadcasting operations. The bill would authorize payment of the third $244 million installment in a $926 million plan to pay U.S. dues to the United Nations, and lift restrictions imposed in 1994 capping U.S. contributions to 25 percent of the U.N. peacekeeping budget. Motion agreed to 382-0: R 197-0; D 184-0 (ND 137-0, SD 47-0); I 1-0. Sept. 12, 2002.

386. Procedural Motion/Journal. Approval of the House Journal of Wednesday, Sept. 11, 2002. Approved 342-42: R 185-13; D 156-29 (ND 113-24, SD 43-5); I 1-0. Sept. 12, 2002.

387. HR 5193. Education Tax Deduction/Rule. Adoption of the resolution (H Res 521) to provide for House floor consideration of the bill that would broaden the tax deduction for higher education costs to allow middle- and low-income families to deduct up to $3,000 in expenses associated with having their children in grades K-12. Adopted 208-201: R 208-2; D 0-198 (ND 0-147, SD 0-51); I 0-1. Sept. 12, 2002.

		382	383	384	385	386	387
ALABAMA							
1	*Callahan*	?	?	Y	Y	Y	Y
2	*Everett*	Y	Y	Y	Y	Y	Y
3	*Riley*	+	+	Y	Y	Y	Y
4	*Aderholt*	Y	Y	Y	Y	N	Y
5	Cramer	Y	Y	Y	?	?	N
6	*Bachus*	Y	Y	Y	Y	N	Y
7	Hilliard	Y	Y	Y	N	N	N
ALASKA							
AL	*Young*	Y	Y	Y	Y	Y	Y
ARIZONA							
1	*Flake*	Y	N	Y	Y	Y	Y
2	Pastor	Y	Y	Y	Y	Y	N
3	*Stump*	?	?	?	?	?	?
4	*Shadegg*	Y	Y	Y	Y	Y	Y
5	*Kolbe*	Y	Y	Y	Y	Y	Y
6	*Hayworth*	Y	Y	Y	Y	Y	Y
ARKANSAS							
1	Berry	Y	Y	Y	Y	Y	N
2	Snyder	Y	Y	Y	Y	?	N
3	*Boozman*	Y	Y	Y	Y	Y	Y
4	Ross	Y	Y	Y	Y	Y	N
CALIFORNIA							
1	Thompson	Y	Y	Y	Y	N	N
2	*Herger*	Y	Y	Y	Y	Y	Y
3	*Ose*	Y	Y	Y	Y	Y	Y
4	*Doolittle*	?	?	Y	Y	Y	Y
5	Matsui	Y	Y	Y	Y	Y	N
6	Woolsey	Y	Y	Y	Y	Y	N
7	Miller, George	?	?	?	?	?	?
8	Pelosi	Y	Y	Y	Y	?	N
9	Lee	Y	Y	Y	Y	Y	N
10	Tauscher	Y	Y	Y	Y	Y	N
11	*Pombo*	Y	Y	Y	Y	Y	Y
12	Lantos	Y	Y	Y	Y	Y	N
13	Stark	Y	Y	Y	Y	Y	N
14	Eshoo	Y	Y	Y	Y	Y	N
15	Honda	Y	Y	Y	Y	Y	N
16	Lofgren	Y	Y	Y	Y	Y	N
17	Farr	Y	Y	Y	Y	Y	N
18	Condit	Y	Y	Y	?	Y	N
19	*Radanovich*	Y	Y	Y	Y	Y	Y
20	Dooley	?	?	Y	Y	Y	N
21	*Thomas*	Y	Y	Y	Y	Y	Y
22	Capps	Y	Y	Y	Y	N	N
23	*Gallegly*	Y	Y	?	?	?	?
24	Sherman	Y	Y	Y	Y	Y	N
25	*McKeon*	Y	Y	Y	Y	Y	Y
26	Berman	Y	Y	Y	?	?	N
27	Schiff	Y	Y	Y	Y	Y	N
28	*Dreier*	Y	Y	Y	Y	Y	Y
29	Waxman	Y	Y	Y	Y	Y	N
30	Becerra	Y	Y	Y	Y	Y	N
31	Solis	Y	Y	Y	Y	Y	N
32	Watson	Y	?	Y	?	Y	N
33	Roybal-Allard	Y	?	Y	Y	Y	N
34	Napolitano	Y	Y	Y	Y	Y	N
35	Waters	?	?	?	Y	N	N
36	Harman	Y	Y	Y	Y	Y	N
37	Millender-McD.	Y	Y	Y	Y	Y	N
38	*Horn*	Y	+	Y	Y	Y	Y

		382	383	384	385	386	387
39	*Royce*	Y	Y	Y	Y	Y	Y
40	*Lewis*	Y	Y	Y	Y	Y	Y
41	*Miller, Gary*	Y	Y	?	?	?	Y
42	Baca	Y	Y	Y	Y	Y	N
43	*Calvert*	Y	Y	Y	Y	Y	Y
44	*Bono*	Y	Y	Y	Y	Y	Y
45	*Rohrabacher*	Y	Y	Y	Y	Y	Y
46	Sanchez	Y	Y	Y	Y	Y	N
47	*Cox*	?	?	Y	Y	Y	Y
48	*Issa*	Y	Y	Y	?	?	Y
49	Davis	Y	Y	Y	Y	Y	N
50	Filner	Y	Y	Y	N	N	N
51	*Cunningham*	?	?	Y	Y	Y	Y
52	*Hunter*	Y	?	Y	Y	Y	Y
COLORADO							
1	DeGette	Y	Y	Y	Y	Y	N
2	Udall	Y	Y	Y	Y	N	N
3	*McInnis*	Y	Y	Y	Y	Y	Y
4	*Schaffer*	?	?	Y	Y	N	Y
5	*Hefley*	Y	Y	Y	Y	N	Y
6	*Tancredo*	Y	Y	Y	Y	P	Y
CONNECTICUT							
1	Larson	Y	Y	Y	Y	Y	N
2	*Simmons*	Y	Y	Y	Y	Y	Y
3	DeLauro	Y	Y	Y	Y	Y	N
4	*Shays*	Y	Y	?	Y	Y	Y
5	Maloney	Y	Y	Y	Y	Y	N
6	*Johnson*	Y	Y	Y	Y	Y	Y
DELAWARE							
AL	*Castle*	Y	Y	Y	Y	Y	N
FLORIDA							
1	*Miller, J.*	?	?	Y	Y	Y	Y
2	Boyd	Y	Y	Y	Y	Y	N
3	Brown	?	?	?	?	?	N
4	*Crenshaw*	Y	Y	Y	Y	Y	Y
5	Thurman	Y	Y	Y	Y	Y	N
6	*Stearns*	Y	Y	Y	Y	Y	+
7	*Mica*	Y	Y	Y	Y	Y	Y
8	*Keller*	Y	Y	Y	Y	Y	Y
9	*Bilirakis*	Y	Y	Y	Y	Y	Y
10	*Young*	Y	Y	Y	Y	Y	Y
11	Davis	Y	Y	?	Y	Y	N
12	*Putnam*	Y	Y	Y	Y	Y	Y
13	*Miller, D.*	Y	Y	Y	Y	Y	Y
14	*Goss*	Y	Y	Y	Y	Y	Y
15	*Weldon*	Y	Y	Y	Y	Y	Y
16	*Foley*	Y	Y	Y	Y	Y	Y
17	Meek	Y	Y	Y	?	?	?
18	*Ros-Lehtinen*	?	?	Y	Y	Y	Y
19	Wexler	Y	Y	Y	?	Y	N
20	Deutsch	Y	Y	Y	Y	Y	N
21	*Diaz-Balart*	?	?	Y	Y	Y	Y
22	*Shaw*	Y	Y	Y	Y	Y	Y
23	Hastings	Y	Y	Y	Y	N	N
GEORGIA							
1	*Kingston*	Y	Y	?	Y	Y	Y
2	Bishop	Y	Y	Y	Y	Y	N
3	*Collins*	?	?	Y	Y	Y	Y
4	McKinney	Y	Y	?	Y	Y	N
5	Lewis	Y	Y	Y	Y	Y	N
6	*Isakson*	Y	Y	Y	Y	Y	Y
7	*Barr*	Y	Y	?	?	?	Y
8	*Chambliss*	Y	Y	Y	Y	Y	Y
9	*Deal*	Y	Y	Y	Y	Y	Y
10	*Norwood*	Y	Y	Y	Y	Y	Y
11	*Linder*	Y	Y	Y	Y	Y	Y
HAWAII							
1	Abercrombie	Y	Y	Y	Y	Y	N
2	Mink	?	?	?	?	?	?
IDAHO							
1	*Otter*	Y	Y	Y	Y	Y	Y
2	*Simpson*	Y	Y	Y	Y	Y	Y
ILLINOIS							
1	Rush	Y	Y	Y	Y	Y	N
2	Jackson	Y	Y	Y	Y	Y	N
3	Lipinski	Y	Y	Y	Y	Y	N
4	Gutierrez	Y	?	Y	Y	Y	N
5	Blagojevich	Y	Y	Y	Y	Y	N
6	*Hyde*	Y	Y	Y	Y	Y	Y
7	Davis	Y	Y	Y	Y	Y	N
8	*Crane*	Y	Y	?	?	?	Y
9	Schakowsky	Y	Y	Y	Y	Y	N
10	*Kirk*	Y	Y	Y	?	?	Y
11	*Weller*	Y	Y	Y	Y	Y	Y
12	Costello	Y	Y	Y	Y	N	N
13	*Biggert*	Y	Y	Y	Y	Y	Y

ND Northern Democrats   SD Southern Democrats

	382	383	384	385	386	387
14 ***Hastert***			Y			
15 ***Johnson***	Y	Y	Y	Y	Y	Y
16 ***Manzullo***	Y	Y	Y	Y	Y	Y
17 Evans	Y	?	Y	Y	Y	N
18 ***LaHood***	Y	Y	Y	Y	Y	Y
19 Phelps	Y	Y	Y	Y	Y	N
20 ***Shimkus***	Y	Y	Y	Y	Y	Y
INDIANA						
1 Visclosky	Y	Y	Y	Y	N	N
2 ***Pence***	Y	Y	+	Y	Y	Y
3 Roemer	Y	Y	Y	Y	Y	N
4 ***Souder***	?	?	?	?	?	Y
5 ***Buyer***	Y	Y	Y	Y	Y	Y
6 ***Burton***	Y	Y	Y	Y	Y	Y
7 ***Kerns***	Y	Y	Y	Y	Y	Y
8 ***Hostettler***	Y	Y	Y	Y	Y	Y
9 Hill	Y	Y	Y	Y	Y	N
10 Carson	Y	Y	Y	Y	Y	N
IOWA						
1 ***Leach***	Y	Y	Y	Y	Y	Y
2 ***Nussle***	Y	Y	Y	Y	Y	Y
3 Boswell	Y	Y	?	Y	Y	N
4 ***Ganske***	Y	Y	Y	Y	Y	Y
5 ***Latham***	Y	Y	Y	Y	N	Y
KANSAS						
1 ***Moran***	Y	Y	Y	Y	Y	Y
2 ***Ryun***	Y	Y	Y	Y	Y	Y
3 Moore	Y	Y	Y	Y	N	N
4 ***Tiahrt***	Y	Y	Y	Y	Y	Y
KENTUCKY						
1 ***Whitfield***	Y	Y	Y	Y	Y	Y
2 ***Lewis***	Y	Y	Y	Y	Y	Y
3 ***Northup***	Y	Y	Y	Y	Y	Y
4 Lucas	Y	Y	Y	Y	Y	N
5 ***Rogers***	Y	Y	Y	Y	Y	Y
6 ***Fletcher***	Y	Y	?	Y	Y	Y
LOUISIANA						
1 ***Vitter***	Y	Y	Y	Y	Y	Y
2 Jefferson	Y	Y	Y	Y	Y	N
3 ***Tauzin***	Y	Y	Y	Y	Y	Y
4 ***McCrery***	?	?	Y	Y	Y	Y
5 ***Cooksey***	Y	Y	Y	?	?	?
6 ***Baker***	Y	Y	Y	Y	Y	Y
7 John	Y	Y	Y	Y	Y	N
MAINE						
1 Allen	Y	Y	Y	Y	Y	N
2 Baldacci	Y	Y	Y	Y	Y	N
MARYLAND						
1 ***Gilchrest***	Y	Y	Y	Y	Y	Y
2 ***Ehrlich***	?	?	Y	?	?	Y
3 Cardin	?	?	Y	Y	Y	N
4 Wynn	?	?	Y	Y	Y	N
5 Hoyer	Y	Y	Y	Y	Y	N
6 ***Bartlett***	Y	Y	Y	Y	Y	Y
7 Cummings	Y	Y	?	Y	Y	N
8 ***Morella***	+	Y	Y	Y	Y	N
MASSACHUSETTS						
1 Olver	Y	Y	Y	Y	N	N
2 Neal	Y	Y	?	?	?	?
3 McGovern	Y	Y	Y	Y	Y	N
4 Frank	Y	Y	Y	Y	Y	N
5 Meehan	Y	Y	?	Y	Y	N
6 Tierney	Y	Y	?	Y	Y	N
7 Markey	Y	Y	Y	Y	Y	N
8 Capuano	Y	Y	+	+	+	N
9 Lynch	?	?	Y	Y	Y	?
10 Delahunt	?	?	Y	Y	Y	N
MICHIGAN						
1 Stupak	Y	Y	+	+	N	N
2 ***Hoekstra***	Y	Y	?	Y	Y	Y
3 ***Ehlers***	Y	Y	Y	Y	Y	Y
4 ***Camp***	Y	Y	Y	Y	Y	Y
5 Barcia	Y	Y	Y	Y	Y	N
6 ***Upton***	Y	Y	Y	Y	Y	Y
7 ***Smith***	?	?	?	?	Y	Y
8 ***Rogers***	Y	Y	Y	Y	Y	Y
9 Kildee	Y	Y	Y	Y	Y	N
10 Bonior	?	?	Y	Y	Y	N
11 ***Knollenberg***	Y	Y	Y	Y	Y	Y
12 Levin	Y	Y	+	Y	Y	N
13 Rivers	Y	Y	Y	Y	Y	N
14 Conyers	Y	Y	?	?	?	N
15 Kilpatrick	Y	Y	Y	Y	Y	N
16 Dingell	Y	Y	Y	Y	Y	N

	382	383	384	385	386	387
MINNESOTA						
1 ***Gutknecht***	?	?	Y	Y	Y	Y
2 ***Kennedy***	Y	Y	Y	Y	N	Y
3 ***Ramstad***	Y	Y	?	?	?	Y
4 McCollum	Y	Y	Y	Y	Y	N
5 Sabo	Y	Y	Y	Y	N	N
6 Luther	Y	Y	Y	Y	Y	N
7 Peterson	Y	Y	Y	Y	N	N
8 Oberstar	Y	Y	Y	Y	N	N
MISSISSIPPI						
1 ***Wicker***	Y	Y	Y	Y	N	Y
2 Thompson	Y	Y	Y	Y	N	N
3 ***Pickering***	Y	Y	Y	Y	Y	Y
4 Shows	Y	Y	Y	Y	Y	N
5 Taylor	Y	Y	Y	Y	N	N
MISSOURI						
1 Clay	Y	Y	Y	?	?	N
2 ***Akin***	?	Y	Y	Y	Y	Y
3 Gephardt	Y	Y	Y	Y	?	N
4 Skelton	Y	Y	Y	Y	Y	N
5 McCarthy	Y	Y	Y	Y	Y	N
6 ***Graves***	Y	Y	Y	Y	Y	Y
7 ***Blunt***	Y	Y	Y	Y	Y	Y
8 ***Emerson***	Y	Y	Y	Y	Y	Y
9 ***Hulshof***	Y	Y	Y	Y	Y	Y
MONTANA						
AL ***Rehberg***	Y	Y	Y	Y	Y	Y
NEBRASKA						
1 ***Bereuter***	Y	Y	Y	+	+	Y
2 ***Terry***	Y	Y	Y	Y	Y	Y
3 ***Osborne***	Y	Y	Y	Y	Y	Y
NEVADA						
1 Berkley	Y	?	Y	Y	Y	N
2 ***Gibbons***	?	?	Y	Y	Y	Y
NEW HAMPSHIRE						
1 ***Sununu***	?	?	Y	?	?	Y
2 ***Bass***	Y	Y	Y	Y	Y	Y
NEW JERSEY						
1 Andrews	Y	Y	Y	Y	Y	N
2 ***LoBiondo***	Y	Y	Y	Y	N	Y
3 ***Saxton***	Y	Y	Y	Y	Y	Y
4 ***Smith***	Y	Y	Y	Y	Y	Y
5 ***Roukema***	?	?	?	?	?	?
6 Pallone	Y	Y	Y	Y	Y	N
7 ***Ferguson***	Y	Y	+	Y	Y	Y
8 Pascrell	Y	Y	?	Y	Y	N
9 Rothman	Y	Y	?	Y	Y	N
10 Payne	Y	Y	Y	Y	Y	N
11 ***Frelinghuysen***	Y	Y	Y	Y	Y	Y
12 Holt	Y	Y	Y	Y	Y	N
13 Menendez	Y	Y	?	Y	Y	N
NEW MEXICO						
1 ***Wilson***	Y	Y	?	Y	Y	Y
2 ***Skeen***	Y	Y	Y	Y	Y	Y
3 Udall	Y	Y	Y	Y	N	N
NEW YORK						
1 ***Grucci***	Y	Y	+	Y	Y	Y
2 Israel	Y	Y	?	Y	Y	N
3 ***King***	?	?	?	Y	Y	Y
4 McCarthy	Y	?	Y	Y	Y	N
5 Ackerman	Y	Y	?	?	?	?
6 Meeks	?	?	Y	Y	Y	N
7 Crowley	?	?	?	Y	Y	N
8 Nadler	Y	Y	?	Y	Y	N
9 Weiner	Y	Y	?	Y	Y	N
10 Towns	?	?	?	?	?	?
11 Owens	+	+	Y	Y	Y	N
12 Velázquez	?	?	?	?	?	?
13 ***Fossella***	Y	Y	+	Y	Y	Y
14 Maloney	+	+	Y	Y	Y	N
15 Rangel	Y	Y	Y	Y	Y	N
16 Serrano	?	?	?	Y	?	N
17 Engel	Y	Y	Y	Y	Y	N
18 Lowey	Y	Y	?	Y	Y	N
19 ***Kelly***	Y	Y	?	Y	Y	Y
20 ***Gilman***	Y	Y	?	?	?	?
21 McNulty	Y	Y	Y	Y	Y	N
22 ***Sweeney***	?	?	Y	Y	N	Y
23 ***Boehlert***	?	?	Y	Y	Y	Y
24 ***McHugh***	Y	Y	Y	?	?	Y
25 ***Walsh***	?	?	Y	Y	Y	Y
26 Hinchey	Y	Y	Y	Y	N	N
27 ***Reynolds***	Y	Y	Y	Y	Y	Y
28 Slaughter	Y	?	Y	Y	N	N
29 LaFalce	Y	Y	Y	Y	Y	N

	382	383	384	385	386	387
30 ***Quinn***	Y	Y	Y	Y	Y	Y
31 ***Houghton***	Y	Y	Y	Y	Y	Y
NORTH CAROLINA						
1 Clayton	Y	Y	Y	Y	Y	N
2 Etheridge	Y	Y	Y	Y	Y	N
3 ***Jones***	?	?	?	Y	Y	Y
4 Price	Y	Y	Y	Y	Y	N
5 ***Burr***	Y	Y	Y	Y	Y	Y
6 ***Coble***	Y	Y	Y	Y	Y	Y
7 McIntyre	Y	Y	Y	Y	Y	N
8 ***Hayes***	Y	Y	Y	Y	Y	Y
9 ***Myrick***	Y	Y	Y	?	?	Y
10 ***Ballenger***	Y	Y	Y	Y	Y	Y
11 ***Taylor***	?	?	Y	Y	Y	Y
12 Watt	Y	Y	Y	Y	Y	N
NORTH DAKOTA						
AL Pomeroy	Y	Y	Y	Y	Y	N
OHIO						
1 ***Chabot***	Y	Y	Y	Y	Y	Y
2 ***Portman***	Y	Y	Y	?	Y	Y
3 Vacant						
4 ***Oxley***	Y	Y	Y	Y	?	Y
5 ***Gillmor***	Y	Y	Y	Y	N	Y
6 Strickland	Y	Y	Y	Y	N	N
7 ***Hobson***	Y	Y	Y	Y	Y	Y
8 ***Boehner***	Y	Y	Y	Y	Y	Y
9 Kaptur	?	?	Y	Y	Y	N
10 Kucinich	Y	Y	Y	Y	N	N
11 Jones	Y	Y	Y	Y	Y	N
12 ***Tiberi***	Y	Y	Y	Y	Y	Y
13 Brown	Y	Y	Y	Y	Y	N
14 Sawyer	Y	Y	Y	Y	Y	N
15 ***Pryce***	Y	Y	Y	Y	Y	Y
16 ***Regula***	Y	Y	Y	Y	Y	Y
17 Vacant						
18 ***Ney***	Y	Y	Y	Y	Y	Y
19 ***LaTourette***	Y	Y	Y	Y	Y	Y
OKLAHOMA						
1 ***Sullivan***	Y	Y	Y	Y	Y	Y
2 Carson	Y	Y	Y	Y	Y	N
3 ***Watkins***	?	Y	Y	Y	Y	Y
4 ***Watts***	Y	Y	Y	Y	Y	Y
5 ***Istook***	Y	Y	Y	Y	Y	Y
6 ***Lucas***	Y	Y	Y	Y	Y	Y
OREGON						
1 Wu	Y	Y	Y	Y	N	N
2 ***Walden***	Y	Y	Y	Y	Y	Y
3 Blumenauer	Y	Y	Y	Y	Y	N
4 DeFazio	Y	Y	Y	Y	N	N
5 Hooley	Y	Y	Y	Y	?	N
PENNSYLVANIA						
1 Brady	Y	Y	?	Y	N	N
2 Fattah	Y	Y	?	?	Y	N
3 Borski	?	?	Y	Y	N	N
4 ***Hart***	Y	Y	Y	Y	N	Y
5 ***Peterson***	Y	Y	Y	Y	Y	Y
6 Holden	Y	Y	Y	Y	Y	N
7 ***Weldon***	Y	Y	Y	Y	Y	Y
8 ***Greenwood***	Y	Y	Y	Y	Y	Y
9 ***Shuster, Bill***	Y	?	?	Y	Y	Y
10 ***Sherwood***	Y	Y	Y	Y	Y	Y
11 Kanjorski	Y	Y	Y	Y	Y	N
12 Murtha	Y	Y	?	Y	Y	N
13 Hoeffel	Y	Y	?	Y	Y	N
14 Coyne	Y	Y	Y	Y	Y	N
15 ***Toomey***	Y	Y	Y	Y	Y	Y
16 ***Pitts***	Y	Y	Y	Y	Y	Y
17 ***Gekas***	Y	Y	Y	Y	Y	Y
18 Doyle	Y	Y	Y	Y	Y	N
19 ***Platts***	Y	Y	Y	Y	Y	Y
20 Mascara	+	+	Y	Y	Y	N
21 ***English***	Y	Y	Y	Y	N	Y
RHODE ISLAND						
1 Kennedy	+	+	+	?	?	N
2 Langevin	Y	Y	Y	Y	Y	N
SOUTH CAROLINA						
1 ***Brown***	Y	Y	Y	Y	Y	Y
2 ***Wilson***	Y	Y	Y	Y	Y	Y
3 ***Graham***	Y	Y	Y	Y	Y	Y
4 ***DeMint***	Y	Y	Y	Y	Y	Y
5 Spratt	Y	Y	Y	Y	Y	N
6 Clyburn	Y	Y	Y	Y	Y	N
SOUTH DAKOTA						
AL ***Thune***	Y	Y	Y	Y	Y	Y

	382	383	384	385	386	387
TENNESSEE						
1 ***Jenkins***	Y	Y	Y	Y	Y	Y
2 ***Duncan***	Y	Y	Y	Y	Y	Y
3 ***Wamp***	Y	Y	Y	Y	Y	Y
4 ***Hilleary***	?	?	?	?	?	?
5 Clement	+	+	+	?	?	?
6 Gordon	Y	Y	Y	Y	Y	N
7 ***Bryant***	Y	Y	Y	Y	Y	Y
8 Tanner	Y	Y	Y	Y	Y	N
9 Ford	Y	Y	Y	+	Y	N
TEXAS						
1 Sandlin	Y	Y	Y	Y	Y	N
2 Turner	Y	Y	Y	Y	Y	N
3 ***Johnson, Sam***	Y	Y	Y	Y	Y	Y
4 Hall	Y	Y	Y	Y	Y	N
5 ***Sessions***	Y	Y	Y	Y	Y	Y
6 ***Barton***	Y	Y	Y	Y	Y	Y
7 ***Culberson***	Y	Y	Y	Y	Y	Y
8 ***Brady***	Y	Y	Y	Y	Y	Y
9 Lampson	Y	Y	Y	Y	Y	N
10 Doggett	Y	Y	Y	Y	Y	N
11 Edwards	Y	Y	Y	Y	Y	N
12 ***Granger***	Y	Y	Y	Y	Y	Y
13 ***Thornberry***	Y	Y	Y	Y	Y	Y
14 ***Paul***	Y	N	?	Y	Y	Y
15 Hinojosa	Y	Y	Y	Y	Y	N
16 Reyes	Y	Y	Y	Y	Y	N
17 Stenholm	Y	Y	Y	Y	Y	N
18 Jackson-Lee	Y	Y	Y	Y	Y	N
19 ***Combest***	Y	Y	Y	?	?	?
20 Gonzalez	Y	Y	?	?	?	?
21 ***Smith***	Y	Y	Y	Y	Y	Y
22 ***DeLay***	Y	Y	Y	Y	Y	Y
23 ***Bonilla***	Y	Y	Y	?	?	?
24 Frost	Y	Y	Y	Y	Y	N
25 Bentsen	Y	Y	Y	Y	Y	N
26 ***Armey***	Y	Y	Y	?	Y	Y
27 Ortiz	Y	Y	Y	Y	Y	N
28 Rodriguez	Y	Y	Y	Y	Y	N
29 Green	Y	Y	Y	Y	N	N
30 Johnson, E.B.	Y	Y	Y	Y	Y	N
UTAH						
1 ***Hansen***	Y	Y	Y	Y	Y	Y
2 Matheson	Y	Y	Y	Y	Y	N
3 ***Cannon***	Y	Y	Y	Y	Y	Y
VERMONT						
AL *Sanders*	Y	Y	Y	Y	Y	N
VIRGINIA						
1 ***Davis, Jo Ann***	Y	Y	Y	Y	Y	Y
2 ***Schrock***	Y	Y	Y	Y	Y	Y
3 Scott	Y	Y	Y	Y	Y	N
4 ***Forbes***	Y	Y	Y	Y	Y	Y
5 ***Goode***	Y	Y	Y	Y	Y	Y
6 ***Goodlatte***	Y	Y	Y	Y	Y	Y
7 ***Cantor***	Y	Y	Y	Y	Y	Y
8 Moran	Y	Y	Y	Y	Y	N
9 Boucher	Y	Y	Y	Y	Y	N
10 ***Wolf***	Y	Y	Y	Y	Y	Y
11 ***Davis, T.***	?	?	Y	Y	Y	Y
WASHINGTON						
1 Inslee	Y	Y	Y	Y	Y	N
2 Larsen	Y	Y	Y	Y	N	N
3 Baird	Y	Y	Y	Y	Y	N
4 ***Hastings***	?	?	?	?	?	?
5 ***Nethercutt***	Y	Y	Y	Y	Y	Y
6 Dicks	Y	Y	Y	?	Y	N
7 McDermott	Y	Y	Y	Y	N	N
8 ***Dunn***	Y	Y	Y	Y	Y	Y
9 Smith	Y	Y	Y	Y	Y	N
WEST VIRGINIA						
1 Mollohan	Y	Y	Y	Y	Y	N
2 ***Capito***	Y	Y	Y	Y	Y	Y
3 Rahall	Y	Y	?	?	?	?
WISCONSIN						
1 ***Ryan***	Y	Y	Y	?	?	Y
2 Baldwin	Y	Y	Y	Y	N	N
3 Kind	Y	Y	Y	Y	Y	N
4 Kleczka	+	+	+	Y	Y	N
5 Barrett	?	?	?	?	?	N
6 ***Petri***	Y	Y	Y	Y	Y	Y
7 Obey	Y	Y	Y	Y	Y	N
8 ***Green***	Y	Y	Y	Y	Y	Y
9 ***Sensenbrenner***	Y	Y	Y	Y	Y	Y
WYOMING						
AL ***Cubin***	Y	Y	Y	Y	Y	Y

Southern states - Ala., Ark., Fla., Ga., Ky., La., Miss., N.C., Okla., S.C., Tenn., Texas, Va.

388. H Con Res 435. Rebirthing/Adoption. Bilirakis, R-Fla., motion to suspend the rules and adopt the concurrent resolution that would express the sense of Congress that rebirthing, the therapeutic process that re-enacts the birthing process, is dangerous. It also would encourage states to pass laws banning the technique. Motion agreed to 397-0: R 202-0; D 194-0 (ND 143-0, SD 51-0); I 1-0. A two-thirds majority of those present and voting (265 in this case) is required for adoption under suspension of the rules. Sept. 17, 2002.

389. HR 4102. Rollan Melton Tribute/Passage. Cannon, R-Utah, motion to suspend the rules and pass the bill that would name a post office in Fallon, Nev., after the late journalist Rollan Doyle Melton. Motion agreed to 398-0: R 205-0; D 192-0 (ND 140-0, SD 52-0); I 1-0. A two-thirds majority of those present and voting (266 in this case) is required for passage under suspension of the rules. Sept. 17, 2002.

390. HR 5333. Joseph Early Tribute/Passage. Cannon, R-Utah, motion to suspend the rules and pass the bill that would name a post office in Worcester, Mass., after former Rep. Joseph Daniel Early, D-Mass. (1975-93). Motion agreed to 397-0: R 206-0; D 190-0 (ND 139-0, SD 51-0); I 1-0. A two-thirds majority of those present and voting (266 in this case) is required for passage under suspension of the rules. Sept. 17, 2002.

391. HR 1701. Rent-to-Own Contracts/Rule. Adoption of the rule (H Res 528) to provide for House floor consideration of the bill that would set federal standards for rent-to-own contracts, including requiring merchants to provide certain types of information about such transactions and classifying contracts as renewable leases and not as "credit sales." Adopted 238-178: R 213-0; D 25-177 (ND 10-139, SD 15-38); I 0-1. Sept. 18, 2002.

392. HR 1701. Rent-to-Own Contracts/Total Cost Limit. LaFalce, D-N.Y., amendment that would limit the total cost of a product bought through a rent-to-own contract to twice its cash price. At least half of every periodic payment made by a customer would go toward ownership of the product. The formula for determining a product's cash price would be derived by the Federal Reserve and would be based on the approximate standard retail price adjusted by special costs related to rent-to-own transactions. Rejected 184-232: R 2-211; D 181-21 (ND 138-11, SD 43-10); I 1-0. Sept. 18, 2002.

393. HR 1701. Rent-to-Own Contracts/Loss and Damage Liability. Waters, D-Calif., amendment that would prohibit merchants from making consumers liable for loss, damage or destruction of property in rent-to-own contracts except in cases of intentional or negligent conduct. Rejected 157-255: R 3-207; D 153-48 (ND 118-30, SD 35-18); I 1-0. Sept. 18, 2002.

394. HR 1701. Rent-to-Own Contracts/Recommit. Waters, D-Calif., motion to recommit the bill to the House Financial Services Committee with instructions that it be reported back after striking provisions that would pre-empt more stringent state laws on rent-to-own contracts, including those that would treat such agreements as credit transactions subject to Truth in Lending Act requirements. Motion rejected 190-227: R 18-195; D 171-32 (ND 135-16, SD 36-16); I 1-0. Sept. 18, 2002.

395. HR 1701. Rent-to-Own Contracts/Passage. Passage of the bill that would set federal standards for rent-to-own contracts. Merchants would have to disclose certain information, including details about a rental property's description; the amount of the initial payment; the amount and timing of subsequent payments; and the total number of payments needed to purchase the goods. The contracts would be classified as renewable leases, not as "credit sales." The bill would pre-empt certain state laws regarding rent-to-own contracts. Passed 215-201: R 169-43; D 46-157 (ND 22-128, SD 24-29); I 0-1. Sept. 18, 2002.

Key

Y	Voted for (yea).
#	Paired for.
+	Announced for.
N	Voted against (nay).
X	Paired against.
–	Announced against.
P	Voted "present."
C	Voted "present" to avoid possible conflict of interest.
?	Did not vote or otherwise make a position known.

Democrats   ***Republicans***
Independents

	388	389	390	391	392	393	394	395
ALABAMA								
1 *Callahan*	Y	Y	Y	Y	N	N	N	P
2 *Everett*	Y	Y	Y	Y	N	N	N	Y
3 *Riley*	?	Y	Y	Y	N	N	N	Y
4 *Aderholt*	Y	Y	Y	Y	N	N	N	Y
5 Cramer	Y	Y	Y	N	N	N	N	Y
6 *Bachus*	Y	Y	Y	Y	N	N	N	Y
7 Hilliard	Y	Y	Y	N	Y	Y	Y	N
ALASKA								
AL *Young*	Y	Y	Y	Y	N	N	N	Y
ARIZONA								
1 *Flake*	Y	Y	Y	Y	N	N	N	N
2 Pastor	Y	Y	Y	N	Y	Y	Y	N
3 *Stump*	?	?	?	?	?	?	?	?
4 *Shadegg*	Y	Y	Y	Y	N	N	N	Y
5 *Kolbe*	Y	Y	Y	Y	N	N	N	Y
6 *Hayworth*	Y	Y	Y	Y	N	N	N	Y
ARKANSAS								
1 Berry	Y	Y	Y	N	Y	N	Y	N
2 Snyder	Y	Y	Y	N	Y	N	Y	N
3 *Boozman*	Y	Y	Y	Y	N	N	N	Y
4 Ross	Y	Y	Y	Y	N	N	N	Y
CALIFORNIA								
1 Thompson	Y	Y	Y	N	N	N	Y	N
2 *Herger*	Y	Y	Y	Y	N	N	N	Y
3 *Ose*	Y	Y	Y	Y	N	N	N	Y
4 *Doolittle*	Y	Y	Y	Y	N	N	N	Y
5 Matsui	Y	Y	Y	N	Y	Y	Y	N
6 Woolsey	Y	Y	Y	N	Y	Y	Y	N
7 Miller, George	?	?	?	?	?	?	?	?
8 Pelosi	Y	?	?	N	Y	Y	Y	N
9 Lee	Y	Y	Y	N	Y	Y	Y	N
10 Tauscher	Y	Y	Y	N	N	N	Y	N
11 *Pombo*	Y	Y	Y	Y	N	N	N	Y
12 Lantos	Y	Y	Y	N	Y	Y	Y	N
13 Stark	?	?	?	N	Y	Y	Y	N
14 Eshoo	Y	Y	Y	N	Y	Y	Y	N
15 Honda	Y	Y	Y	N	Y	Y	Y	N
16 Lofgren	Y	Y	Y	N	Y	Y	Y	N
17 Farr	Y	Y	Y	N	Y	Y	Y	N
18 Condit	Y	Y	Y	N	Y	Y	Y	N
19 *Radanovich*	Y	Y	Y	Y	N	N	N	Y
20 Dooley	?	?	?	N	Y	N	N	Y
21 *Thomas*	Y	Y	Y	Y	N	N	N	Y
22 Capps	Y	Y	Y	N	Y	Y	Y	N
23 *Gallegly*	Y	Y	Y	Y	N	N	N	Y
24 Sherman	Y	Y	Y	N	Y	N	Y	N
25 *McKeon*	Y	Y	Y	Y	N	N	N	Y
26 Berman	Y	Y	Y	N	Y	Y	Y	N
27 Schiff	Y	Y	Y	N	Y	Y	Y	N
28 *Dreier*	Y	Y	Y	Y	N	N	N	Y
29 Waxman	Y	Y	Y	N	Y	Y	Y	N
30 Becerra	Y	Y	Y	N	Y	Y	Y	N
31 Solis	Y	Y	Y	N	Y	Y	Y	N
32 Watson	?	?	?	N	Y	Y	Y	N
33 Roybal-Allard	Y	Y	Y	N	Y	Y	Y	N
34 Napolitano	Y	Y	Y	N	Y	Y	Y	N
35 Waters	Y	Y	Y	N	Y	Y	Y	N
36 Harman	Y	Y	Y	N	Y	Y	Y	N
37 Millender-McD.	Y	Y	Y	N	Y	Y	Y	N
38 *Horn*	Y	Y	Y	Y	N	Y	N	Y

	388	389	390	391	392	393	394	395
39 *Royce*	?	Y	Y	Y	N	N	?	Y
40 *Lewis*	Y	Y	Y	Y	N	?	N	Y
41 *Miller, Gary*	Y	Y	Y	Y	N	N	N	Y
42 Baca	Y	Y	Y	N	Y	Y	N	Y
43 *Calvert*	Y	Y	Y	Y	N	N	N	Y
44 *Bono*	Y	Y	Y	Y	N	N	N	Y
45 *Rohrabacher*	Y	Y	Y	Y	N	N	N	N
46 Sanchez	Y	Y	Y	N	Y	Y	Y	N
47 *Cox*	Y	Y	Y	N	N	N	N	Y
48 *Issa*	Y	Y	Y	Y	N	N	N	Y
49 Davis	Y	Y	Y	N	Y	N	Y	N
50 Filner	Y	Y	Y	N	Y	Y	Y	N
51 *Cunningham*	Y	Y	Y	Y	N	N	N	Y
52 *Hunter*	Y	Y	Y	Y	N	N	N	Y
COLORADO								
1 DeGette	Y	Y	Y	N	Y	Y	Y	N
2 Udall	Y	Y	Y	N	N	Y	Y	N
3 *McInnis*	Y	Y	Y	Y	N	N	N	Y
4 *Schaffer*	?	?	?	Y	N	N	N	N
5 *Hefley*	Y	Y	Y	Y	N	N	N	Y
6 *Tancredo*	Y	Y	Y	Y	N	N	Y	Y
CONNECTICUT								
1 Larson	Y	Y	Y	N	Y	Y	Y	Y
2 *Simmons*	Y	Y	Y	?	?	?	?	?
3 DeLauro	Y	Y	Y	N	Y	Y	Y	N
4 *Shays*	Y	Y	Y	Y	N	N	N	Y
5 Maloney	Y	Y	Y	N	N	N	N	Y
6 *Johnson*	Y	Y	Y	Y	N	N	N	Y
DELAWARE								
AL *Castle*	Y	Y	Y	Y	N	N	N	Y
FLORIDA								
1 *Miller, J.*	Y	Y	Y	Y	N	N	N	N
2 Boyd	Y	Y	Y	N	N	Y	N	Y
3 Brown	?	?	?	?	?	?	?	?
4 *Crenshaw*	Y	Y	Y	Y	N	N	N	Y
5 Thurman	Y	Y	Y	N	Y	Y	Y	N
6 *Stearns*	Y	Y	Y	Y	N	N	N	Y
7 *Mica*	Y	Y	Y	Y	N	N	N	Y
8 *Keller*	Y	Y	Y	Y	N	?	N	Y
9 *Bilirakis*	Y	Y	Y	Y	N	N	N	Y
10 *Young*	Y	Y	Y	?	N	N	N	Y
11 Davis	?	Y	Y	N	N	N	N	Y
12 *Putnam*	Y	Y	Y	Y	N	N	N	Y
13 *Miller, D.*	Y	Y	Y	Y	N	N	N	Y
14 *Goss*	Y	Y	Y	Y	N	N	N	Y
15 *Weldon*	Y	Y	Y	Y	N	N	N	Y
16 *Foley*	Y	Y	Y	Y	N	N	N	Y
17 Meek	Y	Y	Y	N	Y	Y	Y	N
18 *Ros-Lehtinen*	Y	Y	Y	Y	N	N	N	Y
19 Wexler	Y	Y	Y	N	Y	Y	Y	N
20 Deutsch	Y	Y	Y	N	Y	N	Y	N
21 *Diaz-Balart*	Y	Y	Y	Y	N	N	N	Y
22 *Shaw*	Y	Y	Y	Y	N	N	N	Y
23 Hastings	Y	Y	Y	N	Y	Y	Y	N
GEORGIA								
1 *Kingston*	Y	Y	Y	?	?	?	?	?
2 Bishop	Y	Y	Y	N	Y	Y	Y	N
3 *Collins*	?	?	?	Y	N	N	N	Y
4 McKinney	?	?	?	N	Y	Y	?	N
5 Lewis	Y	Y	Y	N	Y	Y	Y	N
6 *Isakson*	Y	Y	Y	Y	N	N	N	Y
7 *Barr*	?	?	?	Y	N	N	N	Y
8 *Chambliss*	Y	Y	Y	Y	N	N	N	Y
9 *Deal*	Y	Y	Y	N	N	N	N	Y
10 *Norwood*	Y	Y	Y	Y	N	N	N	Y
11 *Linder*	Y	Y	Y	Y	N	N	N	Y
HAWAII								
1 Abercrombie	Y	Y	Y	N	Y	Y	Y	N
2 Mink	?	?	?	?	?	?	?	?
IDAHO								
1 *Otter*	Y	Y	Y	Y	N	N	N	Y
2 *Simpson*	Y	Y	Y	Y	N	N	N	Y
ILLINOIS								
1 Rush	Y	Y	Y	N	?	Y	Y	N
2 Jackson	Y	Y	Y	N	Y	Y	Y	N
3 Lipinski	?	?	?	N	Y	N	Y	N
4 Gutierrez	Y	Y	Y	N	Y	Y	Y	N
5 Blagojevich	?	?	?	?	?	?	?	?
6 *Hyde*	Y	Y	Y	Y	N	N	N	Y
7 Davis	Y	Y	Y	N	Y	Y	Y	N
8 *Crane*	Y	Y	Y	N	N	N	N	Y
9 Schakowsky	Y	Y	Y	N	Y	Y	Y	N
10 *Kirk*	Y	Y	Y	Y	N	N	N	Y
11 *Weller*	Y	Y	Y	Y	N	–	N	?
12 Costello	Y	Y	Y	N	Y	N	Y	N
13 *Biggert*	Y	Y	Y	Y	N	N	N	Y

ND Northern Democrats   SD Southern Democrats

	388	389	390	391	392	393	394	395
14 ***Hastert***								
15 ***Johnson***	Y	Y	Y	Y	N	N	N	Y
16 ***Manzullo***	Y	Y	Y	Y	N	N	N	Y
17 Evans	Y	Y	Y	Y	Y	Y	Y	?
18 ***LaHood***	Y	Y	Y	Y	N	N	N	Y
19 Phelps	?	?	?	N	Y	N	N	Y
20 ***Shimkus***	Y	Y	Y	Y	N	N	N	Y
INDIANA								
1 Visclosky	Y	Y	Y	N	Y	N	Y	N
2 ***Pence***	Y	Y	Y	Y	N	N	N	Y
3 Roemer	Y	+	+	N	Y	N	Y	N
4 ***Souder***	Y	Y	Y	Y	N	N	N	N
5 ***Buyer***	Y	Y	Y	Y	N	N	N	Y
6 ***Burton***	Y	Y	Y	Y	N	N	N	Y
7 ***Kerns***	Y	Y	Y	Y	N	N	N	N
8 ***Hostettler***	Y	Y	Y	Y	N	N	N	Y
9 Hill	Y	Y	Y	N	Y	N	Y	N
10 Carson	Y	Y	Y	N	Y	Y	Y	N
IOWA								
1 ***Leach***	Y	Y	Y	?	N	N	N	Y
2 ***Nussle***	Y	Y	Y	Y	N	N	N	Y
3 Boswell	Y	Y	Y	N	Y	N	Y	N
4 ***Ganske***	?	?	?	Y	N	N	N	Y
5 ***Latham***	Y	Y	Y	Y	N	N	N	Y
KANSAS								
1 ***Moran***	Y	Y	Y	Y	N	N	N	Y
2 ***Ryun***	Y	Y	Y	Y	N	N	N	Y
3 Moore	Y	Y	Y	N	N	Y	N	Y
4 ***Tiahrt***	Y	Y	Y	Y	N	N	N	Y
KENTUCKY								
1 ***Whitfield***	Y	Y	Y	Y	N	N	N	Y
2 ***Lewis***	Y	Y	Y	Y	N	N	N	Y
3 ***Northup***	Y	Y	Y	Y	N	N	N	Y
4 Lucas	Y	Y	Y	Y	N	N	N	Y
5 ***Rogers***	Y	Y	Y	Y	N	N	N	Y
6 ***Fletcher***	Y	Y	Y	Y	N	N	N	Y
LOUISIANA								
1 ***Vitter***	Y	Y	Y	Y	N	N	N	Y
2 Jefferson	Y	Y	Y	N	Y	Y	Y	N
3 ***Tauzin***	Y	Y	Y	Y	N	N	N	Y
4 ***McCrery***	Y	Y	Y	Y	N	N	N	Y
5 ***Cooksey***	Y	Y	Y	Y	N	?	?	?
6 ***Baker***	Y	Y	Y	Y	N	N	N	Y
7 John	Y	Y	?	Y	N	N	N	Y
MAINE								
1 Allen	Y	Y	Y	N	Y	Y	Y	N
2 Baldacci	Y	Y	Y	N	Y	Y	Y	N
MARYLAND								
1 ***Gilchrest***	Y	Y	Y	Y	N	N	N	Y
2 ***Ehrlich***	?	?	?	Y	N	N	Y	N
3 Cardin	Y	Y	Y	N	Y	N	Y	N
4 Wynn	Y	Y	Y	N	Y	Y	N	Y
5 Hoyer	Y	Y	Y	Y	Y	N	N	Y
6 ***Bartlett***	Y	Y	Y	Y	N	N	N	Y
7 Cummings	Y	Y	?	N	Y	Y	Y	N
8 ***Morella***	Y	Y	Y	Y	Y	N	Y	N
MASSACHUSETTS								
1 Olver	Y	Y	Y	N	Y	Y	Y	N
2 Neal	Y	Y	Y	N	Y	Y	Y	N
3 McGovern	Y	Y	Y	N	Y	Y	Y	N
4 Frank	Y	Y	Y	N	Y	Y	Y	N
5 Meehan	Y	Y	Y	N	Y	Y	Y	N
6 Tierney	Y	Y	Y	N	Y	Y	Y	N
7 Markey	Y	Y	Y	N	Y	Y	Y	N
8 Capuano	Y	Y	Y	N	Y	Y	Y	N
9 Lynch	?	?	?	N	Y	N	Y	N
10 Delahunt	Y	Y	Y	N	Y	Y	Y	N
MICHIGAN								
1 Stupak	Y	Y	Y	N	Y	Y	Y	N
2 ***Hoekstra***	Y	Y	Y	Y	N	N	N	N
3 ***Ehlers***	Y	Y	Y	Y	N	N	Y	N
4 ***Camp***	Y	Y	Y	Y	N	N	N	Y
5 Barcia	Y	Y	Y	Y	Y	Y	Y	N
6 ***Upton***	Y	Y	Y	Y	N	N	Y	N
7 ***Smith***	Y	Y	Y	Y	N	N	N	N
8 ***Rogers***	Y	Y	Y	Y	N	N	N	N
9 Kildee	Y	Y	Y	Y	Y	Y	Y	N
10 Bonior	Y	Y	Y	?	Y	Y	Y	N
11 ***Knollenberg***	Y	Y	Y	Y	N	N	N	Y
12 Levin	Y	Y	Y	N	Y	Y	Y	N
13 Rivers	Y	Y	Y	N	Y	Y	Y	N
14 Conyers	Y	Y	Y	N	?	?	?	?
15 Kilpatrick	Y	Y	Y	N	Y	Y	Y	N
16 Dingell	Y	Y	Y	N	Y	Y	Y	N
MINNESOTA								
1 ***Gutknecht***	Y	Y	Y	Y	N	N	N	Y
2 ***Kennedy***	Y	Y	Y	Y	N	N	N	N
3 ***Ramstad***	Y	Y	Y	Y	N	N	Y	N
4 McCollum	Y	Y	Y	N	Y	Y	Y	N
5 Sabo	Y	Y	Y	N	Y	Y	Y	N
6 Luther	Y	Y	Y	N	Y	Y	Y	N
7 Peterson	Y	Y	Y	Y	N	N	N	Y
8 Oberstar	Y	Y	Y	N	Y	Y	Y	N
MISSISSIPPI								
1 ***Wicker***	Y	Y	Y	Y	N	N	N	Y
2 Thompson	Y	Y	Y	N	Y	Y	Y	N
3 ***Pickering***	Y	Y	Y	Y	N	N	N	Y
4 Shows	Y	Y	Y	Y	N	N	N	Y
5 Taylor	Y	Y	Y	N	N	N	N	Y
MISSOURI								
1 Clay	Y	Y	Y	?	Y	Y	Y	Y
2 ***Akin***	Y	Y	Y	Y	N	N	N	Y
3 Gephardt	Y	Y	Y	N	Y	Y	Y	N
4 Skelton	Y	Y	Y	N	Y	N	N	Y
5 McCarthy	Y	Y	Y	N	Y	Y	Y	N
6 ***Graves***	Y	Y	Y	Y	N	N	N	Y
7 ***Blunt***	Y	Y	Y	Y	N	N	N	N
8 ***Emerson***	Y	Y	Y	Y	N	N	N	Y
9 ***Hulshof***	?	?	?	Y	N	N	N	Y
MONTANA								
AL ***Rehberg***	Y	Y	Y	Y	N	N	N	Y
NEBRASKA								
1 ***Bereuter***	Y	Y	Y	Y	N	N	N	Y
2 ***Terry***	Y	Y	Y	Y	N	N	N	Y
3 ***Osborne***	Y	Y	Y	Y	N	N	N	Y
NEVADA								
1 Berkley	Y	Y	Y	N	Y	Y	Y	Y
2 ***Gibbons***	Y	Y	Y	Y	N	N	N	Y
NEW HAMPSHIRE								
1 ***Sununu***	Y	Y	Y	Y	N	N	N	Y
2 ***Bass***	Y	Y	Y	Y	N	N	Y	N
NEW JERSEY								
1 Andrews	Y	Y	Y	N	Y	Y	Y	N
2 ***LoBiondo***	Y	Y	Y	Y	N	N	Y	N
3 ***Saxton***	Y	Y	Y	Y	N	N	Y	N
4 ***Smith***	Y	Y	Y	Y	N	N	N	N
5 ***Roukema***	?	?	?	?	?	?	?	?
6 Pallone	Y	Y	Y	N	Y	Y	Y	N
7 ***Ferguson***	Y	Y	Y	Y	N	N	Y	N
8 Pascrell	Y	Y	Y	N	Y	Y	Y	N
9 Rothman	Y	Y	Y	N	Y	Y	Y	N
10 Payne	Y	Y	Y	N	Y	Y	Y	N
11 ***Frelinghuysen***	Y	Y	Y	Y	N	N	Y	N
12 Holt	Y	Y	Y	N	Y	Y	Y	N
13 Menendez	Y	Y	Y	N	Y	Y	Y	N
NEW MEXICO								
1 ***Wilson***	Y	Y	Y	Y	N	N	N	Y
2 ***Skeen***	Y	Y	Y	Y	N	N	N	N
3 Udall	Y	Y	Y	N	Y	Y	Y	N
NEW YORK								
1 ***Grucci***	Y	Y	Y	Y	N	N	N	Y
2 Israel	Y	Y	Y	N	Y	Y	Y	N
3 ***King***	Y	Y	Y	Y	N	N	N	Y
4 McCarthy	Y	Y	Y	N	Y	Y	Y	N
5 Ackerman	Y	Y	Y	N	Y	Y	Y	Y
6 Meeks	Y	Y	Y	N	Y	Y	N	Y
7 Crowley	Y	Y	Y	N	Y	Y	Y	N
8 Nadler	?	?	?	N	Y	Y	Y	N
9 Weiner	Y	Y	Y	N	Y	?	Y	N
10 Towns	Y	Y	Y	Y	N	Y	Y	Y
11 Owens	Y	Y	Y	N	Y	Y	Y	N
12 Velázquez	Y	Y	Y	?	Y	?	Y	N
13 ***Fossella***	Y	Y	Y	Y	N	N	N	Y
14 Maloney	Y	Y	Y	N	Y	Y	Y	N
15 Rangel	Y	Y	Y	N	?	?	Y	N
16 Serrano	Y	?	Y	N	Y	Y	Y	N
17 Engel	Y	Y	Y	N	Y	Y	Y	N
18 Lowey	Y	Y	Y	N	Y	Y	Y	N
19 ***Kelly***	Y	Y	Y	Y	N	N	N	Y
20 ***Gilman***	Y	Y	Y	Y	N	N	N	N
21 McNulty	Y	Y	Y	N	Y	Y	Y	N
22 ***Sweeney***	Y	Y	Y	Y	N	N	N	Y
23 ***Boehlert***	Y	Y	Y	Y	N	N	N	Y
24 ***McHugh***	Y	Y	Y	Y	N	Y	N	Y
25 ***Walsh***	Y	Y	Y	Y	N	N	N	Y
26 Hinchey	Y	Y	Y	N	Y	Y	Y	N
27 ***Reynolds***	Y	Y	Y	Y	N	N	N	Y
28 Slaughter	Y	Y	Y	N	Y	Y	Y	N
29 LaFalce	Y	Y	Y	N	Y	Y	Y	N
30 ***Quinn***	Y	Y	Y	Y	N	N	N	Y
31 ***Houghton***	Y	Y	Y	Y	N	N	?	Y
NORTH CAROLINA								
1 Clayton	Y	Y	Y	N	Y	Y	Y	N
2 Etheridge	Y	Y	Y	Y	Y	Y	Y	N
3 ***Jones***	Y	Y	Y	Y	N	N	N	Y
4 Price	Y	Y	Y	N	Y	Y	Y	N
5 ***Burr***	?	?	?	Y	N	N	N	Y
6 ***Coble***	Y	Y	Y	Y	N	N	N	Y
7 McIntyre	Y	Y	Y	Y	Y	N	N	Y
8 ***Hayes***	Y	Y	Y	Y	N	N	N	Y
9 ***Myrick***	Y	Y	Y	+	N	N	N	Y
10 ***Ballenger***	Y	Y	Y	Y	N	N	N	Y
11 ***Taylor***	Y	Y	Y	Y	N	N	N	Y
12 Watt	Y	Y	Y	N	Y	Y	Y	N
NORTH DAKOTA								
AL Pomeroy	Y	Y	Y	N	Y	Y	Y	N
OHIO								
1 ***Chabot***	Y	Y	Y	Y	N	N	N	Y
2 ***Portman***	Y	Y	Y	Y	?	N	N	Y
3 Vacant								
4 ***Oxley***	Y	Y	Y	Y	N	N	N	Y
5 ***Gillmor***	Y	Y	Y	Y	N	N	N	Y
6 Strickland	Y	Y	Y	N	Y	Y	Y	N
7 ***Hobson***	Y	Y	Y	Y	N	N	N	Y
8 ***Boehner***	Y	Y	Y	Y	N	N	N	Y
9 Kaptur	Y	Y	Y	N	Y	Y	Y	N
10 Kucinich	Y	Y	Y	N	Y	Y	Y	N
11 Jones	Y	Y	Y	N	Y	Y	Y	N
12 ***Tiberi***	Y	Y	Y	Y	N	N	N	Y
13 Brown	Y	Y	Y	N	Y	Y	Y	N
14 Sawyer	Y	Y	Y	N	Y	Y	Y	N
15 ***Pryce***	Y	Y	Y	Y	N	N	N	Y
16 ***Regula***	Y	Y	Y	Y	N	N	N	Y
17 Vacant								
18 ***Ney***	?	Y	Y	Y	N	N	N	Y
19 ***LaTourette***	?	?	?	Y	N	N	N	Y
OKLAHOMA								
1 ***Sullivan***	Y	Y	Y	Y	N	N	N	Y
2 Carson	Y	Y	Y	N	Y	N	Y	Y
3 ***Watkins***	Y	Y	Y	Y	N	N	N	+
4 ***Watts***	+	+	+	Y	?	?	N	Y
5 ***Istook***	Y	Y	Y	Y	N	N	N	N
6 ***Lucas***	Y	Y	Y	Y	N	N	N	Y
OREGON								
1 Wu	Y	Y	Y	N	Y	Y	Y	Y
2 ***Walden***	Y	Y	Y	Y	N	N	N	N
3 Blumenauer	Y	Y	Y	N	Y	N	Y	N
4 DeFazio	Y	Y	Y	N	Y	Y	Y	N
5 Hooley	Y	Y	Y	Y	N	N	N	Y
PENNSYLVANIA								
1 Brady	Y	Y	Y	N	Y	Y	Y	N
2 Fattah	Y	Y	Y	N	Y	Y	Y	N
3 Borski	Y	Y	Y	N	Y	Y	Y	N
4 ***Hart***	Y	Y	Y	Y	N	N	N	Y
5 ***Peterson***	Y	Y	Y	Y	N	N	N	Y
6 Holden	Y	Y	Y	Y	N	N	N	Y
7 ***Weldon***	Y	Y	Y	Y	N	N	N	Y
8 ***Greenwood***	Y	Y	Y	Y	N	N	N	Y
9 ***Shuster, Bill***	Y	Y	Y	Y	N	N	N	Y
10 ***Sherwood***	Y	Y	Y	Y	N	N	N	Y
11 Kanjorski	Y	Y	Y	Y	N	N	N	Y
12 Murtha	Y	Y	Y	N	Y	N	N	Y
13 Hoeffel	Y	Y	Y	N	Y	Y	Y	N
14 Coyne	Y	Y	Y	N	Y	Y	Y	N
15 ***Toomey***	Y	Y	Y	Y	N	N	N	Y
16 ***Pitts***	Y	Y	Y	Y	N	N	N	Y
17 ***Gekas***	?	?	Y	Y	N	N	N	Y
18 Doyle	Y	Y	?	N	Y	Y	Y	N
19 ***Platts***	Y	Y	Y	Y	Y	N	N	N
20 Mascara	+	+	+	N	Y	Y	Y	N
21 ***English***	Y	Y	Y	Y	N	N	N	Y
RHODE ISLAND								
1 Kennedy	Y	Y	Y	N	Y	Y	Y	N
2 Langevin	Y	Y	Y	N	Y	Y	Y	N
SOUTH CAROLINA								
1 ***Brown***	Y	Y	Y	Y	N	N	N	Y
2 ***Wilson***	Y	Y	Y	Y	N	N	N	Y
3 ***Graham***	Y	Y	Y	Y	N	N	Y	N
4 ***DeMint***	Y	Y	Y	Y	N	N	N	Y
5 Spratt	Y	Y	Y	Y	Y	Y	Y	Y
6 Clyburn	Y	Y	Y	N	Y	Y	Y	Y
SOUTH DAKOTA								
AL ***Thune***	Y	Y	Y	Y	N	N	N	Y
TENNESSEE								
1 ***Jenkins***	Y	Y	Y	Y	N	N	N	Y
2 ***Duncan***	Y	Y	Y	Y	N	N	N	Y
3 ***Wamp***	Y	Y	Y	Y	N	N	N	Y
4 ***Hilleary***	?	?	?	?	?	?	?	?
5 Clement	Y	Y	Y	Y	Y	N	N	Y
6 Gordon	Y	Y	Y	N	Y	N	N	Y
7 ***Bryant***	Y	Y	Y	?	?	?	?	?
8 Tanner	Y	Y	Y	Y	Y	N	N	Y
9 Ford	Y	Y	Y	N	Y	Y	Y	Y
TEXAS								
1 Sandlin	Y	Y	Y	Y	Y	Y	Y	Y
2 Turner	Y	Y	Y	Y	Y	Y	N	Y
3 ***Johnson, Sam***	Y	Y	Y	Y	N	N	N	Y
4 Hall	Y	Y	Y	Y	N	N	N	Y
5 ***Sessions***	Y	Y	Y	Y	N	N	N	Y
6 ***Barton***	Y	Y	Y	Y	N	N	N	N
7 ***Culberson***	Y	Y	Y	Y	N	N	N	N
8 ***Brady***	Y	Y	Y	Y	N	N	N	Y
9 Lampson	Y	Y	Y	Y	Y	Y	N	Y
10 Doggett	Y	Y	Y	N	Y	Y	Y	N
11 Edwards	Y	Y	Y	N	Y	Y	Y	N
12 ***Granger***	Y	Y	Y	Y	N	N	N	Y
13 ***Thornberry***	Y	Y	Y	Y	N	N	N	Y
14 ***Paul***	Y	Y	Y	Y	N	N	Y	N
15 Hinojosa	Y	Y	Y	N	Y	Y	Y	N
16 Reyes	Y	Y	Y	N	Y	Y	N	Y
17 Stenholm	Y	Y	Y	N	N	N	N	Y
18 Jackson-Lee	Y	Y	Y	N	Y	Y	Y	N
19 ***Combest***	?	?	?	Y	N	N	N	Y
20 Gonzalez	Y	Y	Y	N	Y	Y	Y	Y
21 ***Smith***	Y	Y	Y	Y	N	N	N	Y
22 ***DeLay***	?	?	?	Y	?	N	N	Y
23 ***Bonilla***	Y	Y	Y	Y	N	N	N	Y
24 Frost	Y	Y	Y	Y	Y	N	N	Y
25 Bentsen	Y	Y	Y	N	Y	Y	Y	Y
26 ***Armey***	Y	Y	Y	Y	N	N	N	Y
27 Ortiz	Y	Y	Y	N	Y	Y	Y	Y
28 Rodriguez	Y	Y	Y	N	Y	Y	Y	N
29 Green	Y	Y	Y	N	Y	Y	Y	N
30 Johnson, E.B.	Y	Y	Y	N	Y	Y	Y	N
UTAH								
1 ***Hansen***	?	?	?	Y	N	N	N	Y
2 Matheson	Y	Y	Y	Y	N	N	Y	Y
3 ***Cannon***	Y	Y	Y	Y	N	N	N	N
VERMONT								
AL *Sanders*	Y	Y	Y	N	Y	Y	Y	N
VIRGINIA								
1 ***Davis, Jo Ann***	Y	Y	Y	Y	N	N	Y	Y
2 ***Schrock***	Y	Y	Y	Y	N	N	N	Y
3 Scott	Y	Y	Y	N	Y	Y	Y	N
4 ***Forbes***	Y	Y	Y	Y	N	N	N	Y
5 ***Goode***	Y	Y	Y	Y	N	N	N	Y
6 ***Goodlatte***	Y	Y	Y	Y	N	N	N	Y
7 ***Cantor***	Y	Y	Y	Y	N	N	N	Y
8 Moran	Y	Y	Y	N	Y	Y	Y	N
9 Boucher	Y	Y	Y	N	Y	Y	Y	N
10 ***Wolf***	Y	Y	Y	Y	N	N	N	N
11 ***Davis, T.***	Y	Y	Y	Y	N	N	N	N
WASHINGTON								
1 Inslee	Y	Y	Y	N	Y	N	Y	Y
2 Larsen	Y	Y	Y	N	Y	Y	Y	N
3 Baird	+	+	+	N	Y	N	Y	N
4 ***Hastings***	Y	Y	Y	Y	N	N	N	Y
5 ***Nethercutt***	?	?	?	Y	N	N	N	Y
6 Dicks	Y	Y	Y	N	Y	Y	Y	N
7 McDermott	Y	Y	Y	N	Y	Y	Y	N
8 ***Dunn***	Y	Y	Y	Y	N	N	N	Y
9 Smith	Y	Y	Y	N	Y	N	Y	N
WEST VIRGINIA								
1 Mollohan	Y	Y	Y	N	Y	N	Y	N
2 ***Capito***	Y	Y	Y	Y	N	N	N	Y
3 Rahall	Y	Y	Y	N	Y	Y	Y	N
WISCONSIN								
1 ***Ryan***	Y	Y	Y	Y	N	N	Y	N
2 Baldwin	Y	Y	Y	N	Y	Y	Y	N
3 Kind	Y	Y	Y	N	Y	N	Y	N
4 Kleczka	Y	Y	Y	N	Y	Y	Y	N
5 Barrett	Y	Y	Y	N	Y	Y	Y	N
6 ***Petri***	Y	Y	Y	Y	N	N	Y	N
7 Obey	Y	Y	Y	N	Y	Y	Y	N
8 ***Green***	Y	Y	Y	Y	N	N	Y	N
9 ***Sensenbrenner***	Y	Y	Y	Y	N	N	Y	N
WYOMING								
AL ***Cubin***	Y	Y	Y	Y	N	?	N	N

Southern states - Ala., Ark., Fla., Ga., Ky., La., Miss., N.C., Okla., S.C., Tenn., Texas, Va.

Key

Y	Voted for (yea).	
#	Paired for.	
+	Announced for.	
N	Voted against (nay).	
X	Paired against.	
–	Announced against.	
P	Voted "present."	
C	Voted "present" to avoid possible conflict of interest.	
?	Did not vote or otherwise make a position known.	

●

Democrats ***Republicans***
Independents

396. Procedural Motion/Journal. Approval of the House Journal of Wednesday, Sept. 18, 2002. Approved 329-53: R 178-15; D 150-38 (ND 109-32, SD 41-6); I 1-0. Sept. 19, 2002.

397. H Res 524, H Res 525. Welfare Overhaul, Estate Tax Repeal/Previous Question. Motion to order the previous question (thus ending debate and possibility of amendment) on adoption of the rule (H Res 527) to provide for House floor consideration of resolutions that would express the sense of the House that Congress should clear the bills permanently extending the estate tax repeal (HR 2143) and reauthorizing welfare programs (HR 4737). Motion agreed to 214-202: R 213-0; D 1-201 (ND 1-148, SD 0-53); I 0-1. Sept. 19, 2002.

398. H Res 524, H Res 525. Welfare Overhaul, Estate Tax Repeal/Rule. Adoption of the rule (H Res 527) to provide for House floor consideration of resolutions that would express the sense of the House that Congress should clear bills permanently extending the estate tax repeal (HR 2143) and reauthorizing welfare programs (HR 4737). Adopted 213-200: R 212-0; D 1-199 (ND 1-145, SD 0-54); I 0-1. Sept. 19, 2002.

399. H Res 523. Black Colleges Tribute/Adoption. Boehner, R-Ohio, motion to suspend the rules and adopt the resolution that would pay tribute to the nation's black colleges and universities. Motion agreed to 413-0: R 210-0; D 202-0 (ND 149-0, SD 53-0); I 1-0. A two-thirds majority of those present and voting (276 in this case) is required for adoption under suspension of the rules. Sept. 19, 2002.

400. H Res 525. House Support for Welfare Overhaul/Adoption. Adoption of the resolution that would express the sense of the House that Congress should clear for the president's signature before Sept. 30, 2002, legislation (HR 4737) that would reauthorize through fiscal 2007 the Temporary Assistance for Needy Families block grant program and make other changes to the nation's welfare program. Adopted 280-123: R 203-2; D 77-120 (ND 51-94, SD 26-26); I 0-1. Sept. 19, 2002.

401. H Res 524. House Support for Estate Tax Repeal/Adoption. Adoption of the resolution that would express the sense of the House that Congress should, before it adjourns, clear for the president's signature legislation (HR 2143) that would make permanent the estate tax repeal and gift tax reduction in last year's $1.35 trillion tax cut law. Adopted 242-158: R 200-3; D 42-155 (ND 23-121, SD 19-34); I 0-0. Sept. 19, 2002.

402. H Con Res 337. Negro Baseball Leagues Tribute/Adoption. LaTourette, R-Ohio, motion to suspend the rules and adopt the concurrent resolution that would pay tribute to the Negro baseball leagues, which operated between 1920 and 1960. Motion agreed to 394-0: R 200-0; D 193-0 (ND 141-0, SD 52-0); I 1-0. A two-thirds majority of those present and voting (263 in this case) is required for adoption under suspension of the rules. Sept. 19, 2002.

403. HR 3295. Election Overhaul/Motion to Instruct. Waters, D-Calif., motion to instruct House conferees to take appropriate actions to ensure that a conference report on the bill is filed before Oct. 1, 2002. Motion agreed to 365-26: R 173-25; D 191-1 (ND 140-0, SD 51-1); I 1-0. Sept. 19, 2002.

	396	397	398	399	400	401	402	403
ALABAMA								
1 *Callahan*	Y	Y	Y	Y	?	?	?	?
2 *Everett*	Y	Y	Y	Y	?	?	?	?
3 *Riley*	N	Y	Y	Y	Y	Y	Y	Y
4 *Aderholt*	N	Y	Y	Y	Y	Y	Y	Y
5 Cramer	Y	N	N	Y	Y	Y	Y	Y
6 *Bachus*	+	+	+	Y	Y	Y	Y	Y
7 Hilliard	N	N	N	Y	N	N	Y	Y
ALASKA								
AL *Young*	?	Y	Y	Y	Y	Y	Y	N
ARIZONA								
1 *Flake*	Y	Y	Y	Y	Y	Y	Y	Y
2 Pastor	Y	N	N	Y	N	Y	Y	Y
3 *Stump*	?	?	?	?	?	?	?	?
4 *Shadegg*	Y	Y	Y	Y	Y	Y	?	N
5 *Kolbe*	Y	Y	Y	Y	Y	Y	Y	Y
6 *Hayworth*	Y	Y	Y	Y	Y	Y	Y	Y
ARKANSAS								
1 Berry	N	N	N	Y	N	Y	Y	Y
2 Snyder	Y	N	N	Y	Y	N	Y	Y
3 *Boozman*	Y	Y	Y	Y	Y	Y	Y	Y
4 Ross	Y	N	N	Y	Y	Y	Y	Y
CALIFORNIA								
1 Thompson	N	N	N	Y	N	Y	Y	Y
2 *Herger*	Y	Y	Y	Y	Y	Y	Y	Y
3 *Ose*	Y	Y	Y	Y	Y	Y	Y	Y
4 *Doolittle*	Y	Y	Y	Y	Y	Y	Y	Y
5 Matsui	?	N	N	Y	N	N	Y	Y
6 Woolsey	Y	N	N	Y	N	N	Y	Y
7 Miller, George	?	?	?	?	?	?	?	?
8 Pelosi	Y	N	N	Y	N	N	Y	Y
9 Lee	Y	N	N	Y	N	N	Y	Y
10 Tauscher	Y	N	N	Y	Y	N	Y	Y
11 *Pombo*	Y	Y	Y	Y	Y	Y	Y	Y
12 Lantos	Y	N	N	Y	N	N	Y	Y
13 Stark	Y	N	?	Y	N	N	Y	Y
14 Eshoo	Y	N	N	Y	N	N	Y	Y
15 Honda	Y	N	N	Y	N	N	Y	Y
16 Lofgren	Y	N	N	Y	N	N	Y	Y
17 Farr	Y	N	N	Y	N	N	Y	Y
18 Condit	Y	Y	Y	Y	Y	Y	Y	Y
19 *Radanovich*	Y	Y	Y	Y	Y	Y	Y	Y
20 Dooley	Y	N	N	Y	Y	Y	Y	Y
21 *Thomas*	Y	Y	Y	Y	Y	Y	?	?
22 Capps	Y	N	N	Y	N	N	Y	Y
23 *Gallegly*	Y	Y	Y	Y	Y	Y	Y	Y
24 Sherman	Y	N	N	Y	Y	N	Y	Y
25 *McKeon*	Y	Y	Y	Y	Y	Y	Y	Y
26 Berman	?	N	N	Y	N	N	Y	Y
27 Schiff	Y	N	N	Y	Y	N	Y	Y
28 *Dreier*	Y	Y	Y	Y	Y	Y	Y	Y
29 Waxman	Y	N	N	Y	N	N	Y	Y
30 Becerra	Y	N	N	Y	N	N	Y	Y
31 Solis	Y	N	N	Y	N	N	Y	Y
32 Watson	Y	N	N	Y	N	N	Y	Y
33 Roybal-Allard	Y	N	N	Y	N	N	Y	Y
34 Napolitano	Y	N	N	Y	N	N	Y	Y
35 Waters	N	?	N	Y	N	N	Y	Y
36 Harman	Y	N	Y	Y	Y	N	Y	Y
37 Millender-McD.	Y	N	N	Y	N	N	Y	Y
38 *Horn*	Y	Y	Y	Y	Y	Y	Y	Y
39 *Royce*	Y	Y	Y	Y	Y	Y	Y	Y
40 *Lewis*	?	Y	Y	Y	Y	Y	Y	Y
41 *Miller, Gary*	Y	Y	Y	Y	Y	Y	Y	Y
42 Baca	Y	N	N	Y	N	N	Y	Y
43 *Calvert*	Y	Y	Y	Y	Y	Y	Y	Y
44 *Bono*	Y	Y	Y	Y	Y	+	Y	Y
45 *Rohrabacher*	Y	Y	Y	Y	Y	Y	Y	Y
46 Sanchez	N	N	N	Y	N	Y	Y	Y
47 *Cox*	Y	Y	Y	Y	Y	Y	Y	Y
48 *Issa*	Y	Y	Y	Y	Y	+	Y	Y
49 Davis	Y	N	N	Y	N	N	Y	Y
50 Filner	N	N	N	Y	N	N	Y	Y
51 *Cunningham*	Y	Y	Y	Y	N	Y	Y	Y
52 *Hunter*	Y	Y	?	?	Y	Y	Y	Y
COLORADO								
1 DeGette	Y	N	N	Y	N	N	Y	Y
2 Udall	N	N	N	Y	N	N	Y	Y
3 *McInnis*	Y	Y	Y	Y	Y	Y	Y	Y
4 *Schaffer*	?	Y	Y	Y	Y	Y	Y	Y
5 *Hefley*	N	Y	Y	Y	Y	Y	Y	Y
6 *Tancredo*	P	Y	Y	Y	Y	Y	Y	N
CONNECTICUT								
1 Larson	Y	N	N	Y	–	?	+	+
2 *Simmons*	Y	Y	Y	Y	Y	Y	Y	Y
3 DeLauro	Y	N	N	Y	N	N	Y	Y
4 *Shays*	?	Y	?	Y	Y	Y	Y	Y
5 Maloney	Y	N	N	Y	N	Y	Y	Y
6 *Johnson*	Y	Y	Y	Y	Y	Y	Y	Y
DELAWARE								
AL *Castle*	Y	Y	Y	Y	Y	Y	Y	Y
FLORIDA								
1 *Miller, J.*	Y	Y	Y	Y	Y	Y	Y	N
2 Boyd	Y	N	N	Y	Y	Y	Y	Y
3 Brown	Y	N	N	Y	N	N	Y	Y
4 *Crenshaw*	Y	Y	Y	Y	Y	Y	Y	Y
5 Thurman	Y	N	N	Y	Y	N	Y	Y
6 *Stearns*	Y	Y	Y	Y	Y	Y	Y	Y
7 *Mica*	Y	Y	Y	Y	Y	Y	Y	Y
8 *Keller*	?	Y	Y	Y	Y	Y	Y	Y
9 *Bilirakis*	Y	Y	Y	Y	Y	Y	Y	Y
10 *Young*	Y	Y	Y	Y	Y	Y	Y	Y
11 Davis	Y	N	N	Y	N	Y	Y	Y
12 *Putnam*	Y	Y	Y	Y	Y	Y	Y	Y
13 *Miller, D.*	Y	Y	Y	Y	Y	Y	Y	Y
14 *Goss*	Y	Y	Y	Y	Y	Y	Y	Y
15 *Weldon*	Y	Y	Y	Y	Y	Y	Y	Y
16 *Foley*	Y	Y	Y	Y	Y	Y	Y	Y
17 Meek	?	N	N	Y	N	N	Y	Y
18 *Ros-Lehtinen*	Y	Y	Y	Y	?	?	?	?
19 Wexler	Y	N	N	Y	N	N	Y	Y
20 Deutsch	Y	N	N	Y	N	N	Y	Y
21 *Diaz-Balart*	Y	Y	Y	Y	?	Y	Y	Y
22 *Shaw*	Y	Y	Y	Y	Y	Y	Y	Y
23 Hastings	Y	N	N	Y	N	N	Y	Y
GEORGIA								
1 *Kingston*	Y	Y	Y	Y	Y	Y	Y	Y
2 Bishop	Y	N	N	Y	N	N	Y	Y
3 *Collins*	Y	Y	Y	Y	Y	Y	Y	N
4 McKinney	Y	?	N	Y	N	N	?	Y
5 Lewis	Y	N	N	Y	N	N	Y	Y
6 *Isakson*	Y	Y	Y	Y	Y	Y	Y	Y
7 *Barr*	Y	Y	Y	Y	Y	Y	Y	N
8 *Chambliss*	Y	Y	Y	Y	Y	Y	+	Y
9 *Deal*	Y	Y	Y	Y	?	?	?	?
10 *Norwood*	Y	Y	Y	Y	Y	Y	Y	N
11 *Linder*	Y	Y	Y	Y	Y	Y	Y	Y
HAWAII								
1 Abercrombie	Y	N	N	Y	Y	Y	Y	Y
2 Mink	?	?	?	?	?	?	?	?
IDAHO								
1 *Otter*	Y	Y	Y	Y	Y	Y	Y	Y
2 *Simpson*	?	Y	Y	Y	Y	Y	Y	Y
ILLINOIS								
1 Rush	Y	N	?	Y	N	N	Y	Y
2 Jackson	Y	N	N	Y	N	N	Y	Y
3 Lipinski	N	N	N	Y	Y	N	Y	Y
4 Gutierrez	Y	N	N	Y	N	N	Y	Y
5 Blagojevich	?	?	?	?	?	?	?	?
6 *Hyde*	Y	Y	Y	Y	Y	Y	Y	Y
7 Davis	Y	N	N	Y	N	N	Y	Y
8 *Crane*	N	Y	Y	Y	Y	Y	Y	Y
9 Schakowsky	N	N	N	Y	N	N	Y	Y
10 *Kirk*	?	Y	Y	Y	Y	Y	Y	Y
11 *Weller*	N	Y	Y	+	Y	Y	Y	Y
12 Costello	Y	N	N	Y	Y	Y	Y	Y
13 *Biggert*	Y	Y	Y	Y	Y	Y	Y	Y

ND Northern Democrats   SD Southern Democrats

	396	397	398	399	400	401	402	403
14 ***Hastert***								
15 ***Johnson***	Y	Y	Y	Y	Y	Y	Y	Y
16 ***Manzullo***	Y	Y	Y	Y	Y	Y	Y	Y
17 Evans	Y	N	N	Y	N	N	Y	Y
18 ***LaHood***	Y	Y	Y	Y	Y	Y	Y	Y
19 Phelps	Y	N	N	Y	Y	Y	Y	Y
20 ***Shimkus***	Y	Y	Y	Y	Y	Y	Y	Y
INDIANA								
1 Visclosky	N	N	N	Y	N	N	Y	Y
2 ***Pence***	Y	Y	Y	Y	Y	Y	Y	Y
3 Roemer	Y	N	N	Y	Y	N	Y	Y
4 ***Souder***	Y	Y	Y	Y	Y	Y	Y	Y
5 ***Buyer***	?	Y	Y	Y	?	?	?	?
6 ***Burton***	Y	Y	Y	Y	Y	Y	Y	Y
7 ***Kerns***	Y	Y	Y	Y	Y	Y	Y	N
8 ***Hostettler***	Y	Y	Y	Y	Y	Y	Y	N
9 Hill	Y	N	N	Y	Y	N	Y	Y
10 Carson	?	?	?	?	?	–	?	?
IOWA								
1 ***Leach***	Y	Y	Y	Y	Y	N	Y	Y
2 ***Nussle***	Y	Y	Y	Y	Y	Y	Y	Y
3 Boswell	Y	N	N	Y	Y	Y	Y	Y
4 ***Ganske***	Y	Y	Y	Y	Y	Y	?	Y
5 ***Latham***	N	Y	Y	Y	Y	Y	Y	Y
KANSAS								
1 ***Moran***	Y	Y	Y	Y	Y	Y	Y	Y
2 ***Ryun***	Y	Y	Y	Y	Y	Y	Y	Y
3 Moore	N	N	N	Y	Y	N	Y	Y
4 ***Tiahrt***	Y	Y	Y	Y	Y	Y	Y	Y
KENTUCKY								
1 ***Whitfield***	Y	Y	Y	Y	Y	Y	Y	Y
2 ***Lewis***	Y	Y	Y	Y	Y	Y	Y	Y
3 ***Northup***	Y	Y	Y	Y	Y	Y	Y	Y
4 Lucas	Y	N	N	Y	Y	Y	Y	Y
5 ***Rogers***	Y	Y	Y	Y	Y	Y	Y	Y
6 ***Fletcher***	Y	Y	Y	Y	Y	Y	Y	Y
LOUISIANA								
1 ***Vitter***	?	Y	Y	Y	Y	Y	Y	Y
2 Jefferson	?	N	N	Y	?	N	Y	Y
3 ***Tauzin***	?	Y	Y	Y	Y	Y	Y	Y
4 ***McCrery***	Y	Y	Y	Y	Y	Y	Y	Y
5 ***Cooksey***	?	?	?	?	?	?	?	?
6 ***Baker***	Y	Y	Y	Y	Y	Y	Y	Y
7 John	Y	N	N	Y	Y	Y	Y	Y
MAINE								
1 Allen	Y	N	N	Y	Y	N	Y	Y
2 Baldacci	Y	N	N	Y	Y	N	Y	Y
MARYLAND								
1 ***Gilchrest***	Y	Y	Y	Y	Y	Y	Y	Y
2 ***Ehrlich***	?	Y	Y	Y	Y	Y	Y	Y
3 Cardin	Y	N	N	Y	Y	N	Y	Y
4 Wynn	Y	N	N	Y	Y	N	Y	Y
5 Hoyer	Y	N	N	Y	Y	N	Y	Y
6 ***Bartlett***	Y	Y	Y	Y	Y	Y	Y	Y
7 Cummings	Y	N	N	Y	Y	N	Y	Y
8 ***Morella***	Y	Y	Y	Y	N	N	Y	Y
MASSACHUSETTS								
1 Olver	N	N	N	Y	N	N	Y	Y
2 Neal	Y	N	N	Y	?	?	?	?
3 McGovern	Y	N	N	Y	N	N	Y	Y
4 Frank	Y	N	N	Y	N	N	Y	Y
5 Meehan	Y	N	N	Y	N	N	Y	Y
6 Tierney	Y	N	N	Y	N	N	Y	Y
7 Markey	N	N	N	Y	N	N	Y	?
8 Capuano	N	N	N	Y	N	N	Y	Y
9 Lynch	Y	N	N	Y	N	N	?	Y
10 Delahunt	?	N	N	Y	N	N	Y	Y
MICHIGAN								
1 Stupak	N	N	N	Y	Y	N	Y	Y
2 ***Hoekstra***	Y	Y	Y	Y	Y	Y	Y	Y
3 ***Ehlers***	Y	Y	Y	Y	Y	Y	Y	Y
4 ***Camp***	Y	Y	Y	Y	Y	Y	Y	Y
5 Barcia	Y	N	N	Y	Y	Y	Y	Y
6 ***Upton***	Y	Y	Y	Y	Y	Y	Y	Y
7 ***Smith***	Y	Y	Y	Y	Y	Y	Y	Y
8 ***Rogers***	Y	Y	Y	Y	Y	Y	Y	Y
9 Kildee	Y	N	N	Y	N	N	Y	Y
10 Bonior	Y	N	N	Y	N	N	Y	Y
11 ***Knollenberg***	Y	Y	Y	Y	Y	Y	Y	Y
12 Levin	Y	N	N	Y	Y	N	Y	Y
13 Rivers	Y	N	N	Y	N	N	Y	Y
14 Conyers	N	N	N	Y	N	N	Y	Y
15 Kilpatrick	Y	N	N	Y	N	N	Y	Y
16 Dingell	Y	N	N	Y	N	N	Y	Y
MINNESOTA								
1 ***Gutknecht***	N	Y	Y	Y	Y	Y	Y	Y
2 ***Kennedy***	N	Y	Y	Y	Y	Y	Y	Y
3 ***Ramstad***	N	Y	Y	Y	Y	Y	Y	Y
4 McCollum	Y	N	N	Y	N	N	Y	Y
5 Sabo	?	N	N	Y	N	N	Y	Y
6 Luther	Y	N	N	Y	Y	N	Y	Y
7 Peterson	N	N	N	Y	Y	Y	Y	Y
8 Oberstar	N	N	N	Y	N	N	Y	Y
MISSISSIPPI								
1 ***Wicker***	Y	Y	Y	Y	Y	Y	Y	Y
2 Thompson	N	N	N	Y	N	N	Y	Y
3 ***Pickering***	Y	Y	Y	Y	Y	Y	Y	Y
4 Shows	Y	N	N	Y	Y	Y	Y	Y
5 Taylor	N	N	N	Y	Y	N	Y	Y
MISSOURI								
1 Clay	Y	N	N	Y	N	Y	Y	Y
2 ***Akin***	Y	Y	Y	Y	Y	Y	Y	Y
3 Gephardt	?	?	?	?	?	?	?	?
4 Skelton	Y	N	N	Y	Y	Y	Y	Y
5 McCarthy	Y	N	N	Y	Y	N	Y	?
6 ***Graves***	Y	Y	Y	Y	Y	Y	Y	Y
7 ***Blunt***	?	Y	Y	Y	Y	Y	Y	Y
8 ***Emerson***	Y	Y	Y	Y	Y	Y	Y	Y
9 ***Hulshof***	N	Y	Y	Y	Y	Y	Y	Y
MONTANA								
AL ***Rehberg***	Y	Y	Y	Y	Y	Y	Y	Y
NEBRASKA								
1 ***Bereuter***	Y	Y	Y	Y	Y	N	Y	Y
2 ***Terry***	Y	Y	Y	Y	Y	Y	Y	Y
3 ***Osborne***	Y	Y	Y	Y	Y	Y	Y	?
NEVADA								
1 Berkley	Y	N	N	Y	N	Y	Y	Y
2 ***Gibbons***	Y	Y	Y	?	Y	Y	Y	Y
NEW HAMPSHIRE								
1 ***Sununu***	Y	Y	Y	Y	Y	Y	Y	Y
2 ***Bass***	Y	Y	Y	Y	Y	Y	Y	Y
NEW JERSEY								
1 Andrews	?	N	N	Y	Y	N	Y	Y
2 ***LoBiondo***	N	Y	Y	Y	Y	Y	Y	Y
3 ***Saxton***	Y	Y	Y	Y	Y	Y	Y	Y
4 ***Smith***	Y	Y	Y	Y	Y	Y	Y	Y
5 ***Roukema***	?	?	?	?	?	?	?	?
6 Pallone	Y	N	N	Y	N	N	Y	Y
7 ***Ferguson***	Y	Y	Y	Y	Y	Y	Y	Y
8 Pascrell	Y	N	N	Y	N	N	Y	Y
9 Rothman	Y	N	N	Y	N	N	Y	Y
10 Payne	Y	N	?	Y	N	N	Y	Y
11 ***Frelinghuysen***	Y	Y	Y	Y	Y	Y	Y	Y
12 Holt	N	Y	N	Y	Y	Y	Y	Y
13 Menendez	Y	N	N	Y	N	N	Y	Y
NEW MEXICO								
1 ***Wilson***	Y	Y	Y	Y	Y	Y	Y	Y
2 ***Skeen***	Y	Y	Y	Y	Y	Y	Y	Y
3 Udall	N	N	N	Y	N	N	Y	Y
NEW YORK								
1 ***Grucci***	Y	Y	Y	Y	Y	Y	Y	Y
2 Israel	Y	N	N	Y	Y	Y	Y	Y
3 ***King***	Y	Y	Y	Y	Y	Y	Y	Y
4 McCarthy	Y	N	N	Y	Y	Y	Y	Y
5 Ackerman	Y	N	N	Y	N	N	Y	Y
6 Meeks	Y	N	N	Y	N	N	Y	Y
7 Crowley	Y	N	N	Y	N	N	Y	Y
8 Nadler	Y	N	N	Y	N	N	Y	Y
9 Weiner	Y	N	N	Y	Y	N	Y	Y
10 Towns	Y	N	N	Y	N	N	Y	Y
11 Owens	Y	N	N	Y	N	N	Y	Y
12 Velázquez	Y	N	N	Y	N	N	Y	Y
13 ***Fossella***	N	Y	Y	Y	?	?	?	?
14 Maloney	Y	N	N	Y	N	N	Y	Y
15 Rangel	Y	N	N	Y	N	N	Y	Y
16 Serrano	Y	N	N	Y	N	N	Y	Y
17 Engel	Y	N	N	Y	N	N	Y	Y
18 Lowey	Y	N	N	Y	Y	N	Y	Y
19 ***Kelly***	Y	Y	Y	Y	Y	Y	Y	Y
20 ***Gilman***	Y	Y	Y	Y	Y	Y	Y	Y
21 McNulty	N	N	N	Y	N	N	Y	Y
22 ***Sweeney***	N	Y	Y	Y	Y	Y	Y	Y
23 ***Boehlert***	Y	Y	Y	Y	Y	Y	Y	Y
24 ***McHugh***	?	Y	Y	Y	Y	Y	Y	Y
25 ***Walsh***	Y	Y	Y	Y	Y	Y	Y	Y
26 Hinchey	N	N	N	Y	N	N	Y	Y
27 ***Reynolds***	Y	Y	Y	Y	Y	Y	Y	Y
28 Slaughter	N	N	N	Y	N	N	?	?
29 LaFalce	?	N	N	?	N	N	Y	Y
30 ***Quinn***	Y	Y	Y	Y	Y	Y	Y	Y
31 ***Houghton***	Y	Y	Y	Y	Y	Y	Y	Y
NORTH CAROLINA								
1 Clayton	Y	N	N	Y	N	N	Y	Y
2 Etheridge	Y	N	N	Y	Y	N	Y	Y
3 ***Jones***	Y	Y	Y	Y	Y	Y	Y	N
4 Price	Y	N	N	Y	Y	N	Y	Y
5 ***Burr***	?	Y	Y	Y	Y	Y	Y	Y
6 ***Coble***	Y	Y	Y	Y	Y	Y	Y	Y
7 McIntyre	Y	N	N	Y	N	Y	Y	Y
8 ***Hayes***	Y	Y	Y	Y	Y	Y	Y	Y
9 ***Myrick***	+	Y	Y	Y	Y	Y	Y	N
10 ***Ballenger***	Y	Y	Y	Y	Y	Y	Y	Y
11 ***Taylor***	Y	Y	Y	Y	?	?	?	?
12 Watt	Y	N	N	Y	N	N	Y	Y
NORTH DAKOTA								
AL Pomeroy	Y	N	N	Y	Y	N	Y	Y
OHIO								
1 ***Chabot***	?	Y	Y	Y	Y	Y	Y	Y
2 ***Portman***	Y	Y	Y	Y	Y	Y	Y	Y
3 Vacant								
4 ***Oxley***	?	?	?	?	Y	Y	Y	Y
5 ***Gillmor***	?	?	?	?	?	?	?	?
6 Strickland	N	N	N	Y	Y	N	Y	Y
7 ***Hobson***	Y	Y	Y	Y	Y	Y	Y	Y
8 ***Boehner***	Y	Y	Y	Y	Y	Y	Y	Y
9 Kaptur	Y	N	N	Y	N	N	Y	Y
10 Kucinich	Y	N	N	Y	N	N	Y	Y
11 Jones	Y	N	N	Y	N	N	Y	Y
12 ***Tiberi***	Y	Y	Y	Y	Y	Y	Y	Y
13 Brown	Y	N	N	Y	N	N	Y	Y
14 Sawyer	Y	N	N	Y	?	?	?	?
15 ***Pryce***	Y	Y	Y	Y	Y	Y	Y	Y
16 ***Regula***	Y	Y	Y	Y	Y	Y	Y	Y
17 Vacant								
18 ***Ney***	Y	Y	Y	Y	Y	Y	Y	Y
19 ***LaTourette***	Y	Y	Y	Y	Y	Y	Y	Y
OKLAHOMA								
1 ***Sullivan***	Y	Y	Y	Y	Y	Y	Y	Y
2 Carson	Y	N	N	Y	Y	Y	Y	Y
3 ***Watkins***	Y	Y	Y	Y	Y	Y	Y	Y
4 ***Watts***	Y	Y	Y	Y	Y	Y	Y	Y
5 ***Istook***	Y	Y	Y	Y	Y	Y	Y	Y
6 ***Lucas***	Y	Y	Y	Y	Y	Y	Y	Y
OREGON								
1 Wu	N	N	N	Y	Y	N	Y	Y
2 ***Walden***	Y	Y	Y	Y	Y	Y	Y	Y
3 Blumenauer	Y	N	N	Y	N	N	Y	Y
4 DeFazio	N	N	N	Y	Y	N	Y	Y
5 Hooley	N	N	N	Y	Y	Y	Y	Y
PENNSYLVANIA								
1 Brady	N	N	N	Y	N	N	Y	Y
2 Fattah	Y	N	N	Y	N	N	Y	Y
3 Borski	N	N	N	Y	N	N	Y	Y
4 ***Hart***	N	Y	Y	Y	Y	Y	Y	Y
5 ***Peterson***	Y	Y	Y	Y	Y	Y	?	?
6 Holden	Y	N	N	Y	Y	N	Y	Y
7 ***Weldon***	Y	Y	Y	Y	Y	Y	Y	Y
8 ***Greenwood***	Y	Y	Y	Y	Y	Y	Y	Y
9 ***Shuster, Bill***	Y	Y	Y	Y	Y	Y	Y	Y
10 ***Sherwood***	Y	Y	Y	Y	Y	Y	Y	Y
11 Kanjorski	Y	N	N	Y	N	N	Y	Y
12 Murtha	?	N	N	Y	N	N	Y	Y
13 Hoeffel	Y	N	N	Y	Y	N	Y	Y
14 Coyne	?	N	N	Y	N	N	Y	Y
15 ***Toomey***	Y	Y	Y	Y	Y	Y	Y	N
16 ***Pitts***	Y	Y	Y	Y	Y	Y	Y	Y
17 ***Gekas***	Y	Y	Y	Y	Y	Y	Y	Y
18 Doyle	Y	N	N	Y	N	?	?	?
19 ***Platts***	Y	Y	Y	Y	Y	Y	Y	Y
20 Mascara	Y	N	N	Y	Y	Y	Y	Y
21 ***English***	N	Y	Y	Y	Y	Y	Y	Y
RHODE ISLAND								
1 Kennedy	Y	N	N	Y	N	N	Y	Y
2 Langevin	Y	N	N	Y	N	N	Y	Y
SOUTH CAROLINA								
1 ***Brown***	Y	Y	Y	Y	+	+	+	+
2 ***Wilson***	Y	Y	Y	Y	Y	Y	Y	Y
3 ***Graham***	Y	Y	Y	Y	Y	Y	Y	Y
4 ***DeMint***	Y	Y	Y	Y	Y	Y	Y	Y
5 Spratt	Y	N	N	Y	Y	N	Y	Y
6 Clyburn	Y	N	N	Y	N	N	Y	Y
SOUTH DAKOTA								
AL ***Thune***	Y	Y	Y	Y	Y	Y	Y	?
TENNESSEE								
1 ***Jenkins***	?	?	?	?	?	?	?	?
2 ***Duncan***	Y	Y	Y	Y	Y	Y	Y	N
3 ***Wamp***	Y	Y	Y	Y	Y	Y	Y	?
4 ***Hilleary***	?	?	?	?	?	?	?	?
5 Clement	Y	N	N	Y	Y	Y	Y	?
6 Gordon	?	N	N	Y	Y	Y	Y	Y
7 ***Bryant***	?	?	?	?	?	?	?	?
8 Tanner	N	N	N	Y	Y	Y	Y	Y
9 Ford	?	N	N	Y	N	N	Y	Y
TEXAS								
1 Sandlin	?	N	N	Y	Y	Y	Y	Y
2 Turner	Y	N	N	Y	Y	Y	Y	Y
3 ***Johnson, Sam***	Y	Y	Y	Y	Y	Y	Y	N
4 Hall	Y	N	N	Y	Y	Y	Y	N
5 ***Sessions***	Y	Y	Y	Y	Y	?	Y	N
6 ***Barton***	Y	Y	Y	Y	Y	Y	Y	N
7 ***Culberson***	Y	Y	Y	Y	Y	Y	Y	N
8 ***Brady***	Y	Y	Y	Y	Y	Y	Y	N
9 Lampson	Y	N	N	Y	Y	Y	Y	Y
10 Doggett	Y	N	N	Y	N	N	Y	Y
11 Edwards	Y	N	N	Y	Y	Y	Y	Y
12 ***Granger***	Y	Y	Y	Y	Y	Y	Y	Y
13 ***Thornberry***	Y	Y	Y	Y	Y	Y	Y	N
14 ***Paul***	Y	Y	Y	Y	N	Y	Y	N
15 Hinojosa	Y	N	N	Y	Y	Y	Y	Y
16 Reyes	?	N	N	Y	N	N	Y	Y
17 Stenholm	Y	N	N	Y	Y	N	Y	Y
18 Jackson-Lee	Y	N	N	Y	N	N	Y	Y
19 ***Combest***	Y	Y	Y	Y	Y	Y	Y	?
20 Gonzalez	Y	N	N	Y	N	N	Y	Y
21 ***Smith***	Y	Y	Y	Y	Y	Y	Y	Y
22 ***DeLay***	Y	Y	Y	Y	Y	Y	Y	Y
23 ***Bonilla***	Y	Y	Y	Y	Y	Y	Y	N
24 Frost	Y	N	N	+	Y	N	Y	Y
25 Bentsen	?	N	N	Y	N	N	Y	Y
26 ***Armey***	?	Y	Y	Y	Y	Y	Y	Y
27 Ortiz	Y	N	N	Y	?	?	?	?
28 Rodriguez	Y	N	N	Y	N	N	Y	Y
29 Green	N	N	N	Y	N	N	Y	Y
30 Johnson, E.B.	Y	N	N	Y	N	N	Y	Y
UTAH								
1 ***Hansen***	Y	Y	Y	Y	Y	Y	Y	N
2 Matheson	Y	N	N	Y	Y	Y	Y	Y
3 ***Cannon***	Y	Y	Y	Y	Y	Y	Y	N
VERMONT								
AL *Sanders*	Y	N	N	Y	N	?	Y	Y
VIRGINIA								
1 ***Davis, Jo Ann***	Y	Y	Y	Y	Y	Y	Y	Y
2 ***Schrock***	Y	Y	Y	Y	?	?	?	?
3 Scott	Y	N	N	Y	N	N	Y	Y
4 ***Forbes***	Y	Y	Y	Y	Y	Y	Y	Y
5 ***Goode***	Y	Y	Y	Y	Y	Y	Y	N
6 ***Goodlatte***	Y	Y	Y	Y	Y	Y	Y	Y
7 ***Cantor***	Y	Y	Y	Y	Y	Y	Y	Y
8 Moran	Y	N	N	Y	N	N	Y	Y
9 Boucher	Y	N	N	Y	N	Y	Y	Y
10 ***Wolf***	Y	Y	Y	Y	Y	Y	Y	Y
11 ***Davis, T.***	Y	Y	Y	Y	Y	Y	Y	Y
WASHINGTON								
1 Inslee	Y	N	?	Y	N	N	Y	Y
2 Larsen	N	N	N	Y	Y	Y	Y	Y
3 Baird	N	N	N	Y	N	N	Y	Y
4 ***Hastings***	Y	Y	Y	Y	Y	Y	Y	Y
5 ***Nethercutt***	Y	Y	Y	Y	Y	Y	Y	Y
6 Dicks	?	N	N	Y	N	N	Y	Y
7 McDermott	N	N	N	Y	N	N	Y	Y
8 ***Dunn***	Y	Y	Y	Y	Y	Y	+	+
9 Smith	Y	N	N	Y	Y	N	?	?
WEST VIRGINIA								
1 Mollohan	Y	N	N	Y	N	N	Y	Y
2 ***Capito***	Y	Y	Y	Y	Y	Y	Y	Y
3 Rahall	Y	N	N	Y	N	N	Y	Y
WISCONSIN								
1 ***Ryan***	?	Y	Y	Y	Y	Y	Y	Y
2 Baldwin	N	N	N	Y	N	N	Y	Y
3 Kind	Y	N	N	Y	Y	N	Y	Y
4 Kleczka	Y	N	N	Y	Y	N	Y	Y
5 Barrett	Y	N	N	Y	?	?	?	?
6 ***Petri***	Y	Y	Y	Y	Y	Y	Y	Y
7 Obey	Y	N	N	Y	?	?	?	?
8 ***Green***	Y	Y	Y	Y	Y	Y	Y	Y
9 ***Sensenbrenner***	Y	Y	Y	Y	Y	Y	Y	Y
WYOMING								
AL ***Cubin***	Y	Y	Y	Y	Y	Y	Y	?

Southern states - Ala., Ark., Fla., Ga., Ky., La., Miss., N.C., Okla., S.C., Tenn., Texas, Va.

404. H Con Res 472. Tribute to 4-H/Adoption. Isakson, R-Ga., motion to suspend the rules and adopt the concurrent resolution that would pay tribute to the 4-H Youth Development Program on its 100th anniversary. Motion agreed to 407-0: R 213-0; D 193-0 (ND 142-0, SD 51-0); I 1-0. A two-thirds majority of those present and voting (272 in this case) is required for adoption under suspension of the rules. Sept. 24, 2002.

405. H Con Res 301. Gold and Blue Star Mothers Tribute/Adoption. Watts, R-Okla., motion to suspend the rules and adopt the concurrent resolution that would express the sense of Congress in support of the patriotism of American Gold Star Mothers Inc. and Blue Star Mothers of America Inc. It would encourage family members of U.S. military personnel to renew the World War II tradition of displaying a service flag or special lapel button during the war against terrorism. Motion agreed to 411-0: R 214-0; D 196-0 (ND 143-0, SD 53-0); I 1-0. A two-thirds majority of those present and voting (274 in this case) is required for adoption under suspension of the rules. Sept. 24, 2002.

406. H Res 533. Taiwan First Lady Tribute/Adoption. Rohrabacher, R-Calif., motion to suspend the rules and adopt the resolution that would welcome Chen Wu-Sue-jen, the wife of Taiwan President Chen Shui-bian, to Washington and pay tribute to her humanitarian and democratic efforts. Motion agreed to 410-0: R 212-0; D 197-0 (ND 144-0, SD 53-0); I 1-0. A two-thirds majority of those present and voting (274 in this case) is required for adoption under suspension of the rules. Sept. 24, 2002.

407. Procedural Motion/Journal. Approval of the House Journal of Tuesday, Sept. 24, 2002. Approved 366-48: R 200-14; D 165-34 (ND 119-29, SD 46-5); I 1-0. Sept. 25, 2002.

408. HR 2982. Terrorism Victims Memorial/Passage. Hansen, R-Utah, motion to suspend the rules and pass the bill that would authorize a memorial in Washington, D.C., to honor U.S. citizens killed in terrorist attacks. A 13-member panel would be charged with raising funds for the memorial's construction and maintenance as well as determining its design and location. The panel would work with the National Capital Memorial Commission and the secretary of the Interior on the memorial. Construction would begin one year after the bill's enactment. Motion agreed to 418-0: R 216-0; D 201-0 (ND 149-0, SD 52-0); I 1-0. A two-thirds majority of those present and voting (279 in this case) is required for passage under suspension of the rules. Sept. 25, 2002.

409. H Con Res 297. Korean-American Tribute/Adoption. Davis, R-Va., motion to suspend the rules and adopt the concurrent resolution that would honor the 100th anniversary of Koreans' arrival in the United States. It also would honor Korean-Americans for their contributions and achievements. Motion agreed to 417-0: R 215-0; D 201-0 (ND 149-0, SD 52-0); I 1-0. A two-thirds majority of those present and voting (278 in this case) is required for adoption under suspension of the rules. Sept. 25, 2002.

410. HR 4691. Abortion Service Refusals/Rule. Adoption of the rule (H Res 546) to provide for House floor consideration of the bill that would prohibit the federal government, and state and local governments that receive federal funding, from discriminating against health care providers, health maintenance organizations, health insurers, and "any other kind of health care facility, organization or plan," that refuse to perform, pay for, or provide referrals for abortion services. Adopted 229-194: R 201-18; D 28-175 (ND 18-133, SD 10-42); I 0-1. Sept. 25, 2002.

Key

Y	Voted for (yea).
#	Paired for.
+	Announced for.
N	Voted against (nay).
X	Paired against.
–	Announced against.
P	Voted "present."
C	Voted "present" to avoid possible conflict of interest.
?	Did not vote or otherwise make a position known.

Democrats   **Republicans**
Independents

		404	405	406	407	408	409	410
ALABAMA								
1	*Callahan*	Y	Y	Y	?	?	?	?
2	*Everett*	Y	Y	?	Y	Y	Y	Y
3	*Riley*	?	Y	Y	Y	Y	Y	Y
4	*Aderholt*	Y	Y	Y	N	Y	Y	Y
5	Cramer	Y	Y	Y	Y	Y	Y	N
6	*Bachus*	Y	Y	Y	Y	Y	Y	Y
7	Hilliard	Y	Y	N	Y	N	Y	N
ALASKA								
AL	*Young*	Y	Y	Y	?	?	?	Y
ARIZONA								
1	*Flake*	Y	Y	Y	Y	Y	Y	Y
2	Pastor	Y	Y	Y	Y	Y	Y	N
3	*Stump*	?	?	?	?	?	?	?
4	*Shadegg*	Y	Y	Y	Y	Y	Y	Y
5	*Kolbe*	Y	Y	Y	Y	Y	Y	Y
6	*Hayworth*	Y	Y	Y	Y	Y	Y	Y
ARKANSAS								
1	Berry	Y	Y	Y	Y	Y	Y	Y
2	Snyder	Y	Y	Y	Y	Y	Y	N
3	*Boozman*	Y	Y	Y	Y	Y	Y	Y
4	Ross	Y	Y	Y	Y	Y	Y	N
CALIFORNIA								
1	Thompson	Y	Y	Y	N	Y	Y	N
2	*Herger*	Y	Y	Y	Y	Y	Y	Y
3	*Ose*	Y	Y	Y	Y	Y	Y	Y
4	*Doolittle*	?	?	?	Y	Y	Y	Y
5	Matsui	Y	Y	Y	?	Y	Y	N
6	Woolsey	?	Y	Y	Y	Y	Y	N
7	Miller, George	Y	Y	N	Y	N	Y	N
8	Pelosi	Y	Y	Y	Y	Y	Y	N
9	Lee	Y	Y	Y	Y	Y	Y	N
10	Tauscher	Y	Y	Y	Y	Y	Y	N
11	*Pombo*	Y	Y	Y	Y	Y	Y	Y
12	Lantos	Y	Y	Y	Y	Y	Y	N
13	Stark	?	?	Y	Y	Y	Y	N
14	Eshoo	Y	Y	Y	Y	Y	Y	N
15	Honda	Y	Y	Y	Y	Y	Y	N
16	Lofgren	Y	Y	Y	Y	Y	Y	N
17	Farr	Y	Y	Y	Y	Y	Y	N
18	Condit	?	?	?	Y	Y	Y	N
19	*Radanovich*	Y	Y	Y	Y	Y	Y	Y
20	Dooley	Y	Y	Y	Y	Y	Y	N
21	*Thomas*	Y	Y	Y	Y	Y	Y	Y
22	Capps	Y	Y	Y	Y	Y	Y	N
23	*Gallegly*	Y	Y	Y	Y	Y	Y	Y
24	Sherman	Y	Y	Y	Y	Y	Y	N
25	*McKeon*	Y	Y	Y	Y	Y	Y	Y
26	Berman	Y	Y	Y	Y	Y	Y	N
27	Schiff	Y	Y	Y	Y	Y	Y	N
28	*Dreier*	Y	Y	Y	Y	Y	Y	Y
29	Waxman	Y	Y	Y	Y	Y	Y	N
30	Becerra	Y	Y	Y	Y	Y	Y	N
31	Solis	Y	Y	Y	Y	Y	Y	N
32	Watson	Y	Y	Y	Y	Y	Y	N
33	Roybal-Allard	Y	Y	Y	Y	Y	Y	N
34	Napolitano	Y	Y	Y	Y	Y	Y	N
35	Waters	Y	Y	Y	N	Y	N	N
36	Harman	Y	Y	Y	Y	Y	Y	N
37	Millender-McD.	Y	Y	Y	Y	Y	Y	N
38	*Horn*	Y	Y	Y	Y	Y	Y	Y

		404	405	406	407	408	409	410
39	*Royce*	Y	Y	Y	Y	Y	Y	Y
40	*Lewis*	?	?	?	Y	Y	Y	Y
41	*Miller, Gary*	Y	Y	Y	Y	Y	Y	Y
42	Baca	Y	Y	Y	Y	Y	Y	N
43	*Calvert*	Y	Y	Y	Y	Y	Y	Y
44	*Bono*	Y	Y	Y	Y	Y	Y	Y
45	*Rohrabacher*	Y	Y	Y	Y	Y	Y	Y
46	Sanchez	Y	Y	N	N	Y	N	N
47	*Cox*	Y	Y	Y	Y	Y	Y	Y
48	*Issa*	Y	Y	Y	Y	Y	Y	Y
49	Davis	Y	Y	Y	Y	Y	Y	N
50	Filner	Y	Y	N	Y	N	Y	N
51	*Cunningham*	Y	Y	Y	Y	Y	Y	Y
52	*Hunter*	Y	Y	Y	Y	?	?	Y
COLORADO								
1	DeGette	Y	Y	Y	Y	Y	Y	N
2	Udall	Y	Y	N	Y	Y	Y	N
3	*McInnis*	Y	Y	Y	Y	Y	Y	Y
4	*Schaffer*	Y	Y	N	Y	Y	Y	Y
5	*Hefley*	Y	Y	Y	Y	Y	Y	Y
6	*Tancredo*	Y	Y	Y	P	Y	Y	Y
CONNECTICUT								
1	Larson	Y	Y	Y	Y	Y	Y	N
2	*Simmons*	Y	Y	Y	Y	Y	Y	N
3	DeLauro	Y	Y	Y	Y	Y	Y	N
4	*Shays*	Y	Y	Y	Y	Y	Y	N
5	Maloney	Y	Y	Y	Y	Y	Y	N
6	*Johnson*	Y	Y	Y	Y	Y	Y	N
DELAWARE								
AL	*Castle*	Y	Y	Y	Y	Y	Y	N
FLORIDA								
1	*Miller, J.*	Y	Y	Y	Y	Y	Y	Y
2	Boyd	Y	Y	Y	Y	Y	Y	N
3	Brown	Y	Y	Y	Y	Y	Y	N
4	*Crenshaw*	Y	Y	Y	Y	Y	Y	Y
5	Thurman	?	?	?	?	?	?	?
6	*Stearns*	Y	Y	Y	Y	Y	Y	Y
7	*Mica*	Y	Y	Y	Y	Y	Y	Y
8	*Keller*	Y	Y	Y	Y	Y	Y	Y
9	*Bilirakis*	Y	Y	Y	Y	Y	Y	Y
10	*Young*	Y	Y	Y	Y	Y	Y	Y
11	Davis	Y	Y	Y	Y	Y	Y	N
12	*Putnam*	Y	Y	Y	Y	Y	Y	Y
13	*Miller, D.*	Y	Y	Y	Y	Y	Y	Y
14	*Goss*	Y	Y	Y	Y	Y	Y	Y
15	*Weldon*	Y	Y	Y	Y	Y	Y	Y
16	*Foley*	Y	Y	Y	Y	Y	Y	N
17	Meek	Y	Y	Y	?	?	?	N
18	*Ros-Lehtinen*	Y	Y	Y	Y	Y	Y	Y
19	Wexler	Y	Y	Y	Y	Y	Y	N
20	Deutsch	Y	Y	Y	Y	Y	Y	N
21	*Diaz-Balart*	Y	Y	Y	Y	Y	Y	Y
22	*Shaw*	Y	Y	Y	Y	Y	Y	Y
23	Hastings	Y	Y	Y	N	Y	N	N
GEORGIA								
1	*Kingston*	Y	Y	Y	Y	Y	Y	Y
2	Bishop	Y	Y	Y	Y	Y	Y	N
3	*Collins*	Y	Y	Y	Y	Y	Y	Y
4	McKinney	?	Y	?	Y	Y	Y	?
5	Lewis	?	Y	Y	Y	Y	Y	N
6	*Isakson*	Y	Y	Y	Y	Y	Y	Y
7	*Barr*	Y	Y	Y	Y	Y	Y	Y
8	*Chambliss*	Y	Y	Y	Y	Y	Y	Y
9	*Deal*	Y	Y	Y	Y	Y	Y	Y
10	*Norwood*	Y	Y	Y	Y	Y	Y	Y
11	*Linder*	Y	Y	Y	Y	Y	Y	Y
HAWAII								
1	Abercrombie	Y	Y	Y	Y	Y	Y	N
2	Mink	?	?	?	?	?	?	?
IDAHO								
1	*Otter*	Y	Y	Y	Y	Y	Y	Y
2	*Simpson*	Y	Y	Y	Y	Y	Y	Y
ILLINOIS								
1	Rush	Y	Y	Y	Y	Y	Y	N
2	Jackson	Y	Y	Y	Y	Y	Y	N
3	Lipinski	Y	Y	Y	Y	Y	Y	N
4	Gutierrez	Y	Y	Y	Y	Y	Y	N
5	Blagojevich	?	?	?	Y	Y	Y	N
6	*Hyde*	Y	Y	Y	Y	Y	Y	Y
7	Davis	Y	Y	Y	Y	Y	Y	N
8	*Crane*	Y	Y	N	Y	Y	Y	Y
9	Schakowsky	Y	Y	Y	N	Y	N	N
10	*Kirk*	Y	Y	Y	Y	Y	Y	N
11	*Weller*	Y	Y	N	Y	N	Y	Y
12	Costello	Y	Y	Y	Y	Y	Y	Y
13	*Biggert*	Y	Y	Y	Y	Y	Y	N

ND Northern Democrats   SD Southern Democrats

	404	405	406	407	408	409	410
14 ***Hastert***							
15 ***Johnson***	Y	Y	Y	Y	Y	Y	Y
16 ***Manzullo***	Y	Y	Y	Y	Y	Y	Y
17 Evans	Y	Y	Y	Y	Y	Y	N
18 ***LaHood***	?	?	?	Y	Y	Y	Y
19 Phelps	Y	Y	Y	N	Y	Y	Y
20 ***Shimkus***	Y	Y	Y	Y	Y	Y	Y
INDIANA							
1 Visclosky	Y	Y	Y	Y	Y	Y	N
2 ***Pence***	Y	Y	Y	Y	Y	Y	Y
3 Roemer	Y	Y	Y	Y	Y	Y	Y
4 ***Souder***	Y	Y	Y	Y	Y	Y	Y
5 ***Buyer***	Y	Y	Y	Y	Y	Y	Y
6 ***Burton***	Y	Y	Y	Y	Y	Y	Y
7 ***Kerns***	Y	Y	Y	Y	Y	Y	Y
8 ***Hostettler***	Y	Y	Y	Y	Y	Y	Y
9 Hill	Y	Y	Y	Y	Y	Y	N
10 Carson	Y	Y	Y	Y	Y	Y	N
IOWA							
1 ***Leach***	Y	Y	Y	Y	Y	Y	N
2 ***Nussle***	Y	Y	Y	Y	Y	Y	Y
3 Boswell	Y	Y	Y	Y	Y	Y	N
4 ***Ganske***	Y	Y	?	Y	Y	Y	Y
5 ***Latham***	Y	Y	Y	N	Y	Y	Y
KANSAS							
1 ***Moran***	Y	Y	Y	Y	Y	Y	Y
2 ***Ryun***	Y	Y	Y	Y	Y	Y	Y
3 Moore	Y	Y	Y	N	Y	Y	N
4 ***Tiahrt***	Y	Y	Y	Y	Y	Y	Y
KENTUCKY							
1 ***Whitfield***	Y	Y	Y	?	Y	Y	Y
2 ***Lewis***	Y	Y	Y	Y	Y	Y	Y
3 ***Northup***	Y	Y	Y	Y	Y	Y	Y
4 Lucas	Y	Y	Y	Y	Y	Y	Y
5 ***Rogers***	Y	Y	Y	Y	Y	Y	Y
6 ***Fletcher***	Y	Y	Y	Y	Y	Y	Y
LOUISIANA							
1 ***Vitter***	Y	Y	Y	Y	Y	Y	Y
2 Jefferson	Y	Y	Y	Y	Y	Y	N
3 ***Tauzin***	Y	Y	Y	Y	Y	Y	Y
4 ***McCrery***	Y	Y	Y	Y	Y	Y	Y
5 ***Cooksey***	Y	Y	Y	Y	Y	Y	Y
6 ***Baker***	Y	Y	Y	Y	Y	Y	Y
7 John	Y	Y	Y	Y	Y	Y	Y
MAINE							
1 Allen	Y	Y	Y	Y	Y	Y	N
2 Baldacci	Y	Y	Y	Y	Y	Y	N
MARYLAND							
1 ***Gilchrest***	?	?	?	Y	Y	Y	Y
2 ***Ehrlich***	?	?	?	?	Y	Y	Y
3 Cardin	Y	Y	Y	Y	Y	Y	N
4 Wynn	Y	Y	Y	Y	Y	Y	N
5 Hoyer	Y	Y	Y	Y	Y	Y	N
6 ***Bartlett***	Y	Y	Y	Y	Y	Y	Y
7 Cummings	Y	Y	Y	Y	Y	Y	N
8 ***Morella***	Y	Y	Y	Y	Y	Y	N
MASSACHUSETTS							
1 Olver	Y	Y	Y	N	Y	Y	N
2 Neal	Y	Y	Y	Y	Y	Y	N
3 McGovern	Y	Y	Y	Y	Y	Y	N
4 Frank	Y	Y	Y	Y	Y	Y	N
5 Meehan	Y	Y	Y	Y	Y	Y	N
6 Tierney	Y	Y	Y	N	Y	Y	N
7 Markey	Y	Y	Y	Y	Y	Y	N
8 Capuano	Y	Y	Y	N	Y	Y	N
9 Lynch	Y	Y	Y	Y	Y	Y	N
10 Delahunt	Y	Y	Y	Y	Y	Y	N
MICHIGAN							
1 Stupak	Y	Y	Y	N	Y	Y	Y
2 ***Hoekstra***	Y	Y	Y	Y	Y	Y	Y
3 ***Ehlers***	Y	Y	Y	Y	Y	Y	Y
4 ***Camp***	Y	Y	Y	Y	Y	Y	Y
5 Barcia	Y	Y	Y	Y	Y	Y	Y
6 ***Upton***	Y	Y	Y	Y	Y	Y	Y
7 ***Smith***	Y	Y	Y	Y	Y	Y	Y
8 ***Rogers***	Y	Y	Y	Y	Y	Y	Y
9 Kildee	Y	Y	Y	Y	Y	Y	Y
10 Bonior	Y	Y	Y	Y	Y	Y	N
11 ***Knollenberg***	Y	Y	Y	Y	Y	Y	Y
12 Levin	Y	Y	Y	Y	Y	Y	N
13 Rivers	Y	Y	Y	Y	Y	Y	N
14 Conyers	Y	Y	Y	Y	Y	Y	N
15 Kilpatrick	Y	Y	Y	Y	Y	Y	N
16 Dingell	Y	Y	Y	Y	Y	Y	N
MINNESOTA							
1 ***Gutknecht***	Y	Y	Y	N	Y	Y	Y
2 ***Kennedy***	Y	Y	Y	N	Y	Y	Y
3 ***Ramstad***	Y	Y	Y	N	Y	Y	Y
4 McCollum	Y	Y	Y	Y	Y	Y	N
5 Sabo	?	Y	Y	N	Y	Y	N
6 Luther	Y	Y	Y	Y	Y	Y	N
7 Peterson	Y	Y	Y	N	Y	Y	Y
8 Oberstar	Y	Y	Y	N	Y	Y	Y
MISSISSIPPI							
1 ***Wicker***	Y	Y	Y	N	Y	Y	Y
2 Thompson	Y	Y	Y	N	Y	Y	N
3 ***Pickering***	Y	Y	Y	Y	Y	Y	Y
4 Shows	Y	Y	Y	Y	Y	Y	Y
5 Taylor	Y	Y	Y	N	Y	Y	Y
MISSOURI							
1 Clay	Y	Y	Y	?	?	?	N
2 ***Akin***	Y	Y	Y	Y	Y	Y	Y
3 Gephardt	Y	Y	Y	Y	Y	Y	N
4 Skelton	Y	Y	Y	Y	Y	Y	Y
5 McCarthy	Y	Y	Y	Y	Y	Y	N
6 ***Graves***	Y	Y	Y	Y	Y	Y	Y
7 ***Blunt***	Y	Y	Y	Y	Y	Y	Y
8 ***Emerson***	Y	Y	Y	Y	Y	Y	Y
9 ***Hulshof***	Y	Y	Y	N	Y	Y	Y
MONTANA							
AL ***Rehberg***	Y	Y	Y	Y	Y	Y	Y
NEBRASKA							
1 ***Bereuter***	Y	Y	Y	Y	Y	Y	Y
2 ***Terry***	Y	Y	Y	Y	Y	Y	Y
3 ***Osborne***	Y	Y	Y	Y	Y	Y	Y
NEVADA							
1 Berkley	Y	Y	Y	Y	Y	Y	N
2 ***Gibbons***	Y	Y	Y	Y	Y	Y	Y
NEW HAMPSHIRE							
1 ***Sununu***	Y	Y	Y	Y	Y	Y	Y
2 ***Bass***	Y	Y	Y	Y	Y	Y	N
NEW JERSEY							
1 Andrews	Y	Y	Y	Y	Y	Y	N
2 ***LoBiondo***	Y	Y	Y	N	Y	Y	Y
3 ***Saxton***	Y	Y	Y	Y	Y	Y	Y
4 ***Smith***	Y	Y	Y	Y	Y	Y	Y
5 ***Roukema***	?	?	?	?	?	?	?
6 Pallone	Y	Y	Y	N	Y	Y	N
7 ***Ferguson***	Y	Y	Y	Y	Y	Y	Y
8 Pascrell	Y	Y	Y	Y	Y	Y	N
9 Rothman	Y	Y	Y	Y	Y	Y	N
10 Payne	Y	Y	Y	Y	Y	Y	N
11 ***Frelinghuysen***	Y	Y	Y	Y	Y	Y	N
12 Holt	Y	Y	Y	N	Y	Y	N
13 Menendez	Y	Y	Y	Y	Y	Y	N
NEW MEXICO							
1 ***Wilson***	Y	Y	Y	Y	Y	Y	Y
2 ***Skeen***	Y	Y	Y	Y	Y	Y	Y
3 Udall	Y	Y	Y	N	Y	Y	N
NEW YORK							
1 ***Grucci***	Y	Y	Y	Y	Y	Y	Y
2 Israel	Y	Y	Y	Y	Y	Y	N
3 ***King***	Y	Y	Y	Y	Y	Y	Y
4 McCarthy	Y	Y	Y	Y	Y	Y	N
5 Ackerman	Y	Y	Y	Y	Y	Y	N
6 Meeks	Y	Y	Y	Y	Y	Y	N
7 Crowley	Y	Y	Y	Y	Y	Y	N
8 Nadler	Y	Y	Y	Y	Y	Y	N
9 Weiner	Y	Y	Y	Y	Y	Y	N
10 Towns	?	?	?	?	?	?	?
11 Owens	Y	Y	Y	Y	Y	Y	N
12 Velázquez	Y	Y	Y	Y	Y	Y	N
13 ***Fossella***	Y	Y	Y	N	Y	Y	Y
14 Maloney	?	?	?	?	?	?	?
15 Rangel	Y	Y	Y	Y	Y	Y	N
16 Serrano	Y	Y	Y	Y	Y	Y	N
17 Engel	Y	Y	Y	Y	Y	Y	N
18 Lowey	Y	Y	Y	Y	Y	Y	N
19 ***Kelly***	Y	Y	Y	Y	Y	Y	Y
20 ***Gilman***	Y	Y	Y	Y	Y	Y	N
21 McNulty	Y	Y	Y	Y	Y	Y	N
22 ***Sweeney***	Y	Y	Y	N	Y	Y	Y
23 ***Boehlert***	Y	Y	Y	Y	Y	Y	N
24 ***McHugh***	Y	Y	Y	Y	Y	Y	Y
25 ***Walsh***	Y	Y	Y	Y	Y	Y	Y
26 Hinchey	Y	Y	Y	N	Y	Y	N
27 ***Reynolds***	Y	Y	Y	Y	Y	Y	Y
28 Slaughter	Y	Y	Y	Y	Y	Y	N
29 LaFalce	?	?	?	Y	Y	Y	Y
30 ***Quinn***	Y	Y	Y	Y	Y	Y	Y
31 ***Houghton***	Y	Y	Y	Y	Y	Y	N
NORTH CAROLINA							
1 Clayton	Y	Y	Y	Y	Y	Y	N
2 Etheridge	Y	Y	Y	Y	Y	Y	N
3 ***Jones***	Y	Y	Y	Y	Y	Y	Y
4 Price	Y	Y	Y	Y	Y	Y	N
5 ***Burr***	Y	Y	Y	Y	Y	Y	Y
6 ***Coble***	Y	Y	Y	Y	Y	Y	Y
7 McIntyre	Y	Y	Y	Y	Y	Y	Y
8 ***Hayes***	Y	Y	Y	Y	Y	Y	Y
9 ***Myrick***	Y	Y	Y	Y	Y	Y	Y
10 ***Ballenger***	Y	Y	Y	Y	Y	Y	Y
11 ***Taylor***	Y	Y	Y	Y	Y	Y	Y
12 Watt	Y	Y	Y	Y	Y	Y	N
NORTH DAKOTA							
AL Pomeroy	Y	Y	Y	Y	Y	Y	N
OHIO							
1 ***Chabot***	Y	Y	Y	Y	Y	Y	Y
2 ***Portman***	Y	Y	Y	Y	Y	Y	Y
3 Vacant							
4 ***Oxley***	Y	Y	Y	Y	Y	Y	Y
5 ***Gillmor***	Y	Y	Y	Y	Y	Y	Y
6 Strickland	Y	Y	Y	N	Y	Y	N
7 ***Hobson***	Y	Y	Y	Y	Y	Y	Y
8 ***Boehner***	Y	Y	Y	Y	Y	Y	Y
9 Kaptur	Y	Y	Y	Y	Y	Y	N
10 Kucinich	Y	Y	Y	Y	Y	Y	N
11 Jones	Y	Y	Y	N	Y	Y	N
12 ***Tiberi***	Y	Y	Y	Y	Y	Y	Y
13 Brown	Y	?	Y	Y	Y	Y	N
14 Sawyer	Y	Y	Y	Y	Y	Y	N
15 ***Pryce***	Y	Y	Y	Y	Y	Y	Y
16 ***Regula***	Y	Y	Y	Y	Y	Y	Y
17 Vacant							
18 ***Ney***	Y	Y	Y	Y	Y	Y	Y
19 ***LaTourette***	Y	Y	Y	Y	Y	Y	Y
OKLAHOMA							
1 ***Sullivan***	Y	Y	Y	Y	Y	Y	Y
2 Carson	Y	Y	Y	Y	Y	Y	N
3 ***Watkins***	Y	Y	Y	Y	Y	?	Y
4 ***Watts***	Y	Y	Y	Y	Y	Y	Y
5 ***Istook***	Y	Y	Y	Y	Y	Y	Y
6 ***Lucas***	Y	Y	Y	Y	Y	Y	Y
OREGON							
1 Wu	Y	Y	Y	N	Y	Y	N
2 ***Walden***	Y	Y	Y	Y	Y	Y	Y
3 Blumenauer	Y	Y	Y	Y	Y	Y	N
4 DeFazio	Y	Y	Y	N	Y	Y	N
5 Hooley	Y	Y	Y	Y	Y	Y	N
PENNSYLVANIA							
1 Brady	Y	Y	Y	Y	Y	Y	N
2 Fattah	Y	Y	Y	Y	Y	Y	N
3 Borski	?	?	?	N	Y	Y	N
4 ***Hart***	Y	Y	Y	Y	Y	Y	Y
5 ***Peterson***	Y	Y	Y	Y	Y	Y	Y
6 Holden	Y	Y	Y	Y	Y	Y	Y
7 ***Weldon***	Y	Y	Y	Y	Y	Y	Y
8 ***Greenwood***	Y	Y	Y	Y	Y	Y	N
9 ***Shuster, Bill***	Y	Y	Y	Y	Y	Y	Y
10 ***Sherwood***	Y	Y	Y	Y	Y	Y	Y
11 Kanjorski	Y	Y	Y	Y	Y	Y	Y
12 Murtha	Y	Y	Y	Y	Y	Y	Y
13 Hoeffel	Y	Y	Y	Y	Y	Y	N
14 Coyne	Y	Y	Y	Y	Y	Y	N
15 ***Toomey***	Y	Y	Y	Y	Y	Y	Y
16 ***Pitts***	Y	Y	Y	Y	Y	Y	Y
17 ***Gekas***	Y	Y	Y	Y	Y	Y	Y
18 Doyle	Y	Y	Y	Y	Y	Y	Y
19 ***Platts***	Y	Y	Y	Y	Y	Y	Y
20 Mascara	?	?	?	?	?	?	?
21 ***English***	Y	Y	Y	N	Y	Y	Y
RHODE ISLAND							
1 Kennedy	Y	Y	Y	Y	Y	Y	N
2 Langevin	Y	Y	Y	Y	Y	Y	N
SOUTH CAROLINA							
1 ***Brown***	Y	Y	Y	Y	Y	Y	Y
2 ***Wilson***	Y	Y	Y	Y	Y	Y	Y
3 ***Graham***	Y	Y	Y	Y	Y	Y	Y
4 ***DeMint***	Y	Y	Y	Y	Y	Y	Y
5 Spratt	Y	Y	Y	Y	Y	Y	N
6 Clyburn	Y	Y	Y	Y	Y	Y	N
SOUTH DAKOTA							
AL ***Thune***	Y	Y	Y	Y	Y	Y	Y
TENNESSEE							
1 ***Jenkins***	Y	Y	Y	Y	Y	Y	Y
2 ***Duncan***	Y	Y	Y	Y	Y	Y	Y
3 ***Wamp***	Y	Y	Y	Y	Y	Y	Y
4 ***Hilleary***	?	?	?	Y	Y	Y	Y
5 Clement	Y	Y	Y	Y	Y	Y	N
6 Gordon	Y	Y	Y	Y	Y	Y	N
7 ***Bryant***	Y	Y	Y	Y	Y	Y	Y
8 Tanner	Y	Y	Y	Y	Y	Y	N
9 Ford	Y	Y	Y	Y	Y	Y	N
TEXAS							
1 Sandlin	Y	Y	Y	Y	Y	Y	N
2 Turner	Y	Y	Y	Y	Y	Y	N
3 ***Johnson, Sam***	Y	Y	Y	Y	Y	Y	Y
4 Hall	Y	Y	Y	Y	Y	Y	Y
5 ***Sessions***	Y	Y	Y	Y	Y	Y	Y
6 ***Barton***	Y	Y	Y	Y	Y	Y	Y
7 ***Culberson***	Y	Y	Y	Y	Y	Y	Y
8 ***Brady***	Y	Y	Y	Y	Y	Y	Y
9 Lampson	Y	Y	Y	Y	Y	Y	N
10 Doggett	Y	Y	Y	Y	Y	Y	N
11 Edwards	Y	Y	Y	Y	Y	Y	N
12 ***Granger***	Y	Y	Y	Y	Y	Y	Y
13 ***Thornberry***	Y	Y	Y	Y	Y	Y	Y
14 ***Paul***	Y	Y	Y	?	?	?	Y
15 Hinojosa	Y	Y	Y	Y	Y	Y	N
16 Reyes	Y	Y	Y	Y	Y	Y	N
17 Stenholm	Y	Y	Y	Y	Y	Y	Y
18 Jackson-Lee	Y	Y	Y	Y	Y	Y	N
19 ***Combest***	Y	Y	Y	Y	Y	Y	Y
20 Gonzalez	Y	Y	Y	Y	Y	Y	N
21 ***Smith***	Y	Y	Y	Y	Y	Y	Y
22 ***DeLay***	Y	Y	Y	Y	Y	Y	Y
23 ***Bonilla***	Y	Y	Y	Y	Y	Y	Y
24 Frost	Y	Y	Y	Y	Y	Y	N
25 Bentsen	Y	Y	Y	Y	Y	Y	N
26 ***Armey***	Y	Y	Y	Y	Y	Y	Y
27 Ortiz	Y	Y	Y	Y	Y	Y	Y
28 Rodriguez	Y	Y	Y	Y	Y	Y	N
29 Green	Y	Y	Y	Y	Y	Y	N
30 Johnson, E.B.	Y	Y	Y	N	Y	Y	N
UTAH							
1 ***Hansen***	Y	Y	Y	Y	Y	Y	Y
2 Matheson	Y	Y	Y	Y	Y	Y	N
3 ***Cannon***	Y	Y	Y	Y	Y	Y	Y
VERMONT							
AL *Sanders*	Y	Y	Y	Y	Y	Y	N
VIRGINIA							
1 ***Davis, Jo Ann***	Y	Y	Y	Y	Y	Y	Y
2 ***Schrock***	Y	Y	Y	Y	Y	Y	Y
3 Scott	Y	Y	Y	Y	Y	Y	N
4 ***Forbes***	Y	Y	Y	Y	Y	Y	Y
5 ***Goode***	Y	Y	Y	Y	Y	Y	Y
6 ***Goodlatte***	Y	Y	Y	Y	Y	Y	Y
7 ***Cantor***	Y	Y	Y	Y	Y	Y	Y
8 Moran	Y	Y	Y	Y	Y	Y	N
9 Boucher	Y	Y	Y	Y	Y	Y	N
10 ***Wolf***	Y	Y	Y	Y	Y	Y	Y
11 ***Davis, T.***	Y	Y	Y	Y	Y	Y	Y
WASHINGTON							
1 Inslee	Y	Y	Y	Y	Y	Y	N
2 Larsen	Y	Y	Y	N	Y	Y	N
3 Baird	Y	Y	Y	N	Y	Y	N
4 ***Hastings***	Y	Y	Y	Y	Y	Y	Y
5 ***Nethercutt***	Y	Y	Y	Y	Y	Y	Y
6 Dicks	Y	Y	Y	Y	Y	Y	N
7 McDermott	Y	Y	Y	N	Y	Y	N
8 ***Dunn***	Y	Y	Y	Y	Y	Y	Y
9 Smith	?	?	?	Y	Y	Y	N
WEST VIRGINIA							
1 Mollohan	?	?	?	?	?	?	Y
2 ***Capito***	Y	Y	Y	Y	Y	Y	Y
3 Rahall	Y	Y	Y	Y	Y	Y	Y
WISCONSIN							
1 ***Ryan***	Y	Y	Y	Y	Y	Y	Y
2 Baldwin	Y	Y	Y	N	Y	Y	N
3 Kind	Y	Y	Y	Y	Y	Y	N
4 Kleczka	Y	Y	Y	Y	Y	Y	N
5 Barrett	Y	Y	Y	Y	Y	Y	N
6 ***Petri***	Y	Y	Y	Y	Y	Y	Y
7 Obey	Y	Y	Y	Y	Y	Y	N
8 ***Green***	Y	Y	Y	Y	Y	Y	Y
9 ***Sensenbrenner***	Y	Y	Y	Y	Y	Y	Y
WYOMING							
AL ***Cubin***	Y	Y	Y	Y	Y	Y	Y

Southern states - Ala., Ark., Fla., Ga., Ky., La., Miss., N.C., Okla., S.C., Tenn., Texas, Va.

411. HR 4691. Abortion Service Refusals/Recommit. Brown, D-Ohio, motion to recommit the bill to the House Energy and Commerce Committee with instructions that it be reported back with language that would clarify that none of the bill's provisions would authorize a medical institution to withhold from patients medically appropriate information or services, allow an institution to bar its health care providers from discussing or providing all medically appropriate information or services, or pre-empt state enforcement of state laws and regulations. Motion rejected 191-230: R 18-199; D 172-31 (ND 130-21, SD 42-10); I 1-0. Sept. 25, 2002.

412. HR 4691. Abortion Service Refusals/Passage. Passage of the bill that would prohibit the federal government and state and local governments that receive federal funding from discriminating against health care providers, health maintenance organizations, health insurers, and "any other kind of health care facility, organization or plan," that refuse to perform, pay for or provide referrals for abortion services. The bill would rewrite a current law "conscience clause" that provides protection for physician training programs that refuse to provide abortion training. Passed 229-189: R 192-24; D 37-164 (ND 23-125, SD 14-39); I 0-1. A "yea" was a vote in support of the president's position. Sept. 25, 2002.

413. H Res 547. Employee Pensions, Married Couples Tax Relief, Pension Benefits/Previous Question. Sessions, R-Texas, motion to order the previous question (thus ending debate and possibility of amendment) on adoption of the rule (H Res 547) to provide for House floor consideration of resolutions (H Res 540, H Res 543, H Res 544) that would express the sense of the House that Congress should clear bills that would increase employees' control over their pension funds (HR 3762), permanently extend breaks for married couples (HR 4019) and provide additional incentives for pension and retirement contributions (HR 4931). Motion agreed to 217-200: R 216-0; D 1-199 (ND 0-148, SD 1-51); I 0-1. (Subsequently, the rule was adopted by voice vote.) Sept. 25, 2002.

414. H Res 540. House Support for Employee Pensions/Adoption. Adoption of the resolution that would express the sense of the House that Congress should, before it adjourns, clear for the president's signature legislation (HR 3762) that would increase employees' control over their pension funds and give them more access to investment information. Adopted 258-152: R 216-1; D 42-150 (ND 22-120, SD 20-30); I 0-1. Sept. 25, 2002.

415. H Res 544. House Support for Pension Benefits/Adoption. Adoption of the resolution that would express the sense of the House that Congress should, before it adjourns, clear for the president's signature legislation (HR 4931) that would permanently extend the additional incentives for pension and retirement contributions contained in last year's $1.35 trillion tax cut law. Adopted 291-118: R 215-0; D 76-117 (ND 53-90, SD 23-27); I 0-1. Sept. 25, 2002.

416. HR 2215. Justice Department Reauthorization/Previous Question. Motion to order the previous question (thus ending debate and possibility of amendment) on adoption of the resolution (H Res 552) to provide for House floor consideration of the conference report on the bill that would authorize $17.6 billion in fiscal 2002 and $20.5 billion in fiscal 2003 for Justice Department operations. Motion agreed to 208-199: R 208-2; D 0-196 (ND 0-144, SD 0-52); I 0-1. (Subsequently, the resolution was adopted by voice vote.) Sept. 26, 2002.

417. Procedural Motion/Journal. Approval of the House Journal of Wednesday, Sept. 25, 2002. Approved 346-58: R 194-14; D 151-44 (ND 105-38, SD 46-6); I 1-0. Sept. 26, 2002.

Key

Y	Voted for (yea).
#	Paired for.
+	Announced for.
N	Voted against (nay).
X	Paired against.
–	Announced against.
P	Voted "present."
C	Voted "present" to avoid possible conflict of interest.
?	Did not vote or otherwise make a position known.

Democrats   **Republicans**
Independents

	411	412	413	414	415	416	417
ALABAMA							
1 *Callahan*	?	?	?	?	?	?	?
2 *Everett*	N	Y	Y	Y	Y	Y	Y
3 *Riley*	N	Y	Y	Y	Y	Y	Y
4 *Aderholt*	N	Y	Y	Y	Y	Y	N
5 Cramer	Y	Y	N	Y	Y	N	Y
6 *Bachus*	?	?	?	?	?	?	?
7 Hilliard	?	N	N	N	N	N	N
ALASKA							
AL *Young*	N	Y	?	Y	Y	Y	Y
ARIZONA							
1 *Flake*	N	Y	Y	Y	Y	Y	Y
2 Pastor	Y	N	N	N	N	N	Y
3 *Stump*	?	?	?	?	?	?	?
4 *Shadegg*	N	Y	Y	Y	Y	Y	Y
5 *Kolbe*	Y	N	Y	Y	Y	Y	Y
6 *Hayworth*	N	Y	Y	Y	Y	Y	Y
ARKANSAS							
1 Berry	N	Y	N	Y	N	N	Y
2 Snyder	Y	N	N	Y	Y	N	Y
3 *Boozman*	N	Y	Y	Y	Y	Y	Y
4 Ross	N	Y	N	Y	N	N	Y
CALIFORNIA							
1 Thompson	Y	N	?	?	?	?	?
2 *Herger*	N	Y	Y	Y	Y	Y	Y
3 *Ose*	Y	N	Y	Y	Y	Y	Y
4 *Doolittle*	N	Y	Y	Y	Y	Y	Y
5 Matsui	Y	N	N	N	N	N	Y
6 Woolsey	Y	N	N	N	N	N	Y
7 Miller, George	Y	N	N	N	N	N	N
8 Pelosi	Y	N	N	N	N	N	Y
9 Lee	Y	N	N	N	N	N	Y
10 Tauscher	Y	N	N	Y	Y	N	Y
11 *Pombo*	N	Y	Y	Y	Y	Y	Y
12 Lantos	Y	N	N	N	N	N	Y
13 Stark	Y	N	N	N	N	N	Y
14 Eshoo	Y	N	N	N	N	N	Y
15 Honda	Y	N	N	N	N	N	Y
16 Lofgren	Y	N	N	N	N	N	Y
17 Farr	Y	N	N	N	N	N	Y
18 Condit	Y	N	N	Y	N	Y	Y
19 *Radanovich*	N	Y	?	Y	Y	Y	Y
20 Dooley	Y	N	N	Y	N	N	Y
21 *Thomas*	Y	N	Y	Y	Y	Y	Y
22 Capps	Y	N	N	N	N	N	Y
23 *Gallegly*	N	Y	Y	Y	Y	Y	Y
24 Sherman	Y	N	N	N	N	N	Y
25 *McKeon*	N	Y	Y	Y	Y	Y	Y
26 Berman	Y	N	N	N	N	N	Y
27 Schiff	Y	N	N	N	N	N	Y
28 *Dreier*	N	Y	Y	Y	Y	Y	Y
29 Waxman	Y	N	N	?	?	N	Y
30 Becerra	Y	N	N	N	N	N	Y
31 Solis	Y	N	N	N	N	N	Y
32 Watson	Y	N	N	N	N	N	Y
33 Roybal-Allard	Y	N	N	N	N	N	Y
34 Napolitano	Y	N	N	N	N	N	Y
35 Waters	Y	N	N	N	N	N	Y
36 Harman	Y	N	N	Y	N	N	Y
37 Millender-McD.	Y	N	N	N	N	N	Y
38 *Horn*	Y	N	Y	Y	Y	Y	Y

	411	412	413	414	415	416	417
39 *Royce*	N	Y	Y	Y	Y	Y	Y
40 *Lewis*	N	Y	Y	Y	Y	Y	Y
41 *Miller, Gary*	N	Y	Y	Y	Y	Y	Y
42 Baca	Y	N	N	N	N	N	Y
43 *Calvert*	N	Y	Y	Y	Y	Y	Y
44 *Bono*	N	Y	Y	Y	Y	Y	Y
45 *Rohrabacher*	N	Y	Y	Y	Y	Y	Y
46 Sanchez	Y	N	N	N	N	N	N
47 *Cox*	N	Y	Y	Y	Y	Y	Y
48 *Issa*	N	Y	Y	Y	Y	Y	Y
49 Davis	Y	N	N	N	Y	N	Y
50 Filner	N	N	N	N	N	N	N
51 *Cunningham*	N	Y	Y	Y	Y	Y	Y
52 *Hunter*	N	Y	Y	Y	Y	Y	?
COLORADO							
1 DeGette	Y	N	N	N	Y	N	Y
2 Udall	Y	N	N	Y	N	N	N
3 *McInnis*	N	Y	Y	Y	Y	Y	Y
4 *Schaffer*	N	Y	Y	Y	Y	?	?
5 *Hefley*	N	Y	Y	Y	Y	Y	Y
6 *Tancredo*	N	Y	Y	Y	Y	Y	Y
CONNECTICUT							
1 Larson	Y	N	N	N	Y	N	Y
2 *Simmons*	Y	N	Y	Y	Y	Y	Y
3 DeLauro	Y	N	N	N	N	N	Y
4 *Shays*	Y	N	Y	Y	Y	Y	Y
5 Maloney	Y	N	N	Y	N	Y	Y
6 *Johnson*	Y	N	Y	Y	Y	Y	Y
DELAWARE							
AL *Castle*	Y	N	Y	Y	Y	Y	Y
FLORIDA							
1 *Miller, J.*	N	Y	Y	Y	Y	Y	Y
2 Boyd	Y	N	N	Y	N	N	Y
3 Brown	Y	N	N	N	N	N	Y
4 *Crenshaw*	N	Y	Y	Y	Y	Y	Y
5 Thurman	?	?	?	?	?	?	?
6 *Stearns*	N	Y	Y	Y	Y	Y	Y
7 *Mica*	N	Y	Y	Y	Y	Y	Y
8 *Keller*	N	Y	Y	Y	Y	Y	?
9 *Bilirakis*	N	Y	Y	Y	Y	Y	Y
10 *Young*	N	Y	Y	Y	Y	Y	Y
11 Davis	Y	N	N	Y	N	N	Y
12 *Putnam*	N	Y	Y	Y	Y	Y	Y
13 *Miller, D.*	N	N	Y	Y	Y	Y	Y
14 *Goss*	N	Y	Y	Y	Y	Y	Y
15 *Weldon*	N	Y	Y	Y	Y	Y	Y
16 *Foley*	N	Y	Y	Y	Y	Y	Y
17 Meek	Y	N	N	N	N	N	Y
18 *Ros-Lehtinen*	N	Y	Y	Y	Y	Y	Y
19 Wexler	Y	N	N	N	N	N	Y
20 Deutsch	Y	N	N	N	N	N	Y
21 *Diaz-Balart*	N	Y	Y	Y	Y	Y	Y
22 *Shaw*	N	Y	Y	Y	Y	Y	Y
23 Hastings	Y	N	N	N	N	N	N
GEORGIA							
1 *Kingston*	N	Y	Y	Y	Y	Y	Y
2 Bishop	Y	N	N	?	?	N	Y
3 *Collins*	N	Y	Y	Y	Y	Y	Y
4 McKinney	Y	N	?	?	?	N	Y
5 Lewis	Y	N	N	N	N	N	N
6 *Isakson*	N	Y	Y	Y	Y	Y	Y
7 *Barr*	N	Y	Y	Y	Y	Y	Y
8 *Chambliss*	N	Y	Y	Y	Y	Y	Y
9 *Deal*	N	Y	Y	Y	Y	Y	Y
10 *Norwood*	N	Y	Y	Y	Y	Y	Y
11 *Linder*	N	Y	Y	Y	Y	Y	Y
HAWAII							
1 Abercrombie	Y	N	N	N	N	N	Y
2 Mink	?	?	?	?	?	?	?
IDAHO							
1 *Otter*	N	Y	Y	Y	Y	Y	Y
2 *Simpson*	N	Y	Y	Y	Y	Y	Y
ILLINOIS							
1 Rush	Y	N	N	N	N	N	Y
2 Jackson	Y	N	N	N	N	N	Y
3 Lipinski	N	N	N	N	N	N	Y
4 Gutierrez	Y	N	N	?	N	N	Y
5 Blagojevich	Y	N	N	N	N	N	Y
6 *Hyde*	N	Y	Y	Y	Y	Y	Y
7 Davis	Y	N	N	N	N	N	N
8 *Crane*	N	Y	Y	Y	Y	Y	N
9 Schakowsky	Y	N	N	N	N	N	N
10 *Kirk*	N	Y	Y	Y	Y	Y	Y
11 *Weller*	N	Y	Y	Y	Y	Y	N
12 Costello	N	N	N	N	N	N	N
13 *Biggert*	Y	N	Y	Y	Y	Y	Y

ND Northern Democrats   SD Southern Democrats

	411	412	413	414	415	416	417
14 ***Hastert***							
15 ***Johnson***	N	Y	Y	Y	Y	Y	Y
16 ***Manzullo***	N	Y	Y	Y	Y	Y	Y
17 Evans	Y	N	N	N	N	N	N
18 ***LaHood***	N	Y	Y	Y	Y	Y	Y
19 Phelps	N	Y	N	Y	Y	N	Y
20 ***Shimkus***	N	Y	Y	Y	Y	Y	Y
INDIANA							
1 Visclosky	Y	N	N	N	N	N	N
2 ***Pence***	N	Y	Y	Y	Y	Y	Y
3 Roemer	N	Y	N	N	Y	N	Y
4 ***Souder***	N	Y	Y	Y	Y	Y	Y
5 ***Buyer***	N	Y	Y	Y	Y	Y	Y
6 ***Burton***	N	Y	Y	Y	Y	Y	Y
7 ***Kerns***	N	Y	Y	Y	Y	Y	Y
8 ***Hostettler***	N	Y	Y	Y	Y	Y	Y
9 Hill	Y	N	N	Y	Y	N	Y
10 Carson	Y	N	N	Y	Y	N	N
IOWA							
1 ***Leach***	Y	N	Y	Y	Y	Y	Y
2 ***Nussle***	N	Y	Y	Y	Y	Y	Y
3 Boswell	Y	N	N	Y	Y	N	Y
4 ***Ganske***	?	Y	Y	Y	Y	Y	Y
5 ***Latham***	N	Y	Y	Y	Y	Y	Y
KANSAS							
1 ***Moran***	N	Y	Y	Y	Y	Y	N
2 ***Ryun***	N	Y	Y	Y	Y	Y	Y
3 Moore	Y	N	N	Y	Y	N	N
4 ***Tiahrt***	N	Y	Y	Y	Y	Y	Y
KENTUCKY							
1 ***Whitfield***	N	Y	Y	Y	Y	?	?
2 ***Lewis***	N	Y	Y	Y	Y	Y	Y
3 ***Northup***	N	Y	Y	Y	Y	Y	Y
4 Lucas	N	Y	N	Y	Y	N	Y
5 ***Rogers***	N	Y	Y	Y	Y	Y	Y
6 ***Fletcher***	N	Y	Y	Y	Y	Y	N
LOUISIANA							
1 ***Vitter***	N	Y	Y	Y	Y	Y	Y
2 Jefferson	Y	N	N	N	Y	N	Y
3 ***Tauzin***	N	Y	Y	Y	Y	Y	Y
4 ***McCrery***	N	Y	Y	Y	Y	Y	Y
5 ***Cooksey***	N	Y	Y	Y	Y	Y	Y
6 ***Baker***	N	Y	Y	Y	Y	Y	Y
7 John	N	Y	N	Y	Y	?	?
MAINE							
1 Allen	Y	N	N	N	N	N	Y
2 Baldacci	Y	N	N	N	Y	N	Y
MARYLAND							
1 ***Gilchrest***	N	N	Y	Y	Y	Y	Y
2 ***Ehrlich***	N	Y	Y	?	?	Y	Y
3 Cardin	Y	N	N	N	Y	N	Y
4 Wynn	Y	N	N	N	Y	?	?
5 Hoyer	Y	N	N	N	Y	N	Y
6 ***Bartlett***	N	Y	Y	Y	Y	Y	Y
7 Cummings	Y	N	N	N	Y	N	Y
8 ***Morella***	Y	N	Y	Y	Y	Y	Y
MASSACHUSETTS							
1 Olver	Y	?	N	N	N	N	N
2 Neal	Y	Y	N	N	N	N	N
3 McGovern	Y	N	N	N	N	N	N
4 Frank	Y	N	N	N	N	N	Y
5 Meehan	Y	N	N	N	N	N	Y
6 Tierney	Y	N	N	N	N	N	N
7 Markey	Y	N	N	N	N	N	N
8 Capuano	Y	N	N	N	Y	?	?
9 Lynch	Y	Y	N	N	N	N	Y
10 Delahunt	Y	N	N	N	N	N	Y
MICHIGAN							
1 Stupak	N	Y	N	N	N	N	N
2 ***Hoekstra***	N	Y	Y	Y	Y	Y	N
3 ***Ehlers***	N	Y	Y	Y	Y	Y	Y
4 ***Camp***	N	Y	Y	Y	Y	Y	Y
5 Barcia	N	Y	N	Y	Y	?	?
6 ***Upton***	N	Y	Y	Y	Y	Y	Y
7 ***Smith***	N	Y	Y	Y	Y	?	?
8 ***Rogers***	N	Y	Y	Y	Y	Y	Y
9 Kildee	N	Y	N	N	N	N	Y
10 Bonior	Y	N	?	?	?	?	?
11 ***Knollenberg***	N	Y	Y	Y	Y	Y	Y
12 Levin	Y	N	N	N	N	N	Y
13 Rivers	Y	N	N	N	N	N	Y
14 Conyers	Y	N	N	N	N	N	Y
15 Kilpatrick	Y	N	N	N	N	N	Y
16 Dingell	Y	N	N	N	N	N	Y

	411	412	413	414	415	416	417
MINNESOTA							
1 ***Gutknecht***	N	Y	Y	Y	Y	Y	Y
2 ***Kennedy***	N	Y	Y	Y	Y	Y	N
3 ***Ramstad***	N	Y	Y	Y	Y	Y	N
4 McCollum	Y	N	N	N	N	N	Y
5 Sabo	Y	N	N	N	N	N	N
6 Luther	Y	N	N	Y	Y	N	Y
7 Peterson	N	Y	N	Y	Y	N	N
8 Oberstar	N	Y	N	N	N	N	N
MISSISSIPPI							
1 ***Wicker***	N	Y	Y	Y	Y	Y	N
2 Thompson	Y	N	N	N	N	N	N
3 ***Pickering***	N	Y	Y	Y	Y	Y	Y
4 Shows	N	Y	Y	Y	Y	N	Y
5 Taylor	N	Y	N	Y	N	N	N
MISSOURI							
1 Clay	Y	N	N	N	N	?	?
2 ***Akin***	N	Y	Y	Y	Y	Y	Y
3 Gephardt	Y	N	N	N	N	N	N
4 Skelton	N	Y	N	Y	Y	N	Y
5 McCarthy	Y	N	N	N	Y	N	Y
6 ***Graves***	N	Y	Y	Y	Y	Y	N
7 ***Blunt***	N	Y	Y	Y	Y	Y	Y
8 ***Emerson***	N	Y	Y	Y	Y	Y	Y
9 ***Hulshof***	N	Y	Y	Y	Y	?	?
MONTANA							
AL ***Rehberg***	N	Y	Y	Y	Y	Y	Y
NEBRASKA							
1 ***Bereuter***	N	Y	Y	Y	Y	N	Y
2 ***Terry***	N	Y	Y	Y	Y	Y	Y
3 ***Osborne***	N	Y	Y	Y	Y	Y	Y
NEVADA							
1 Berkley	Y	N	N	Y	Y	N	Y
2 ***Gibbons***	N	N	Y	Y	Y	Y	Y
NEW HAMPSHIRE							
1 ***Sununu***	N	Y	Y	Y	Y	Y	Y
2 ***Bass***	Y	N	Y	Y	Y	Y	Y
NEW JERSEY							
1 Andrews	Y	N	N	N	N	N	Y
2 ***LoBiondo***	N	Y	Y	Y	Y	Y	N
3 ***Saxton***	N	Y	Y	Y	Y	Y	Y
4 ***Smith***	N	Y	Y	Y	Y	Y	Y
5 ***Roukema***	?	?	?	?	?	?	?
6 Pallone	Y	N	N	N	Y	N	N
7 ***Ferguson***	N	Y	Y	Y	Y	Y	Y
8 Pascrell	Y	N	N	N	Y	N	N
9 Rothman	Y	N	N	N	Y	N	Y
10 Payne	Y	N	N	N	N	N	N
11 ***Frelinghuysen***	Y	N	Y	Y	Y	Y	Y
12 Holt	Y	N	N	N	Y	N	N
13 Menendez	Y	N	N	N	N	N	Y
NEW MEXICO							
1 ***Wilson***	N	Y	Y	Y	Y	Y	Y
2 ***Skeen***	N	Y	Y	Y	Y	Y	Y
3 Udall	Y	N	N	N	N	N	N
NEW YORK							
1 ***Grucci***	N	Y	Y	Y	Y	Y	Y
2 Israel	Y	N	N	N	Y	N	Y
3 ***King***	N	Y	Y	Y	Y	Y	Y
4 McCarthy	Y	N	N	Y	Y	N	Y
5 Ackerman	Y	N	N	N	N	N	Y
6 Meeks	Y	N	N	N	Y	N	Y
7 Crowley	Y	N	N	N	N	N	Y
8 Nadler	Y	N	N	N	N	N	Y
9 Weiner	Y	N	N	N	N	N	Y
10 Towns	?	?	N	N	N	N	N
11 Owens	Y	N	N	N	N	N	N
12 Velázquez	Y	N	N	N	N	N	N
13 ***Fossella***	N	Y	Y	Y	Y	?	?
14 Maloney	?	?	?	?	?	?	?
15 Rangel	Y	N	N	N	N	N	Y
16 Serrano	Y	N	N	N	N	N	Y
17 Engel	Y	N	N	N	N	N	Y
18 Lowey	Y	N	N	N	N	N	Y
19 ***Kelly***	Y	N	Y	Y	Y	Y	Y
20 ***Gilman***	Y	N	Y	Y	Y	Y	Y
21 McNulty	Y	N	N	N	N	N	N
22 ***Sweeney***	N	N	Y	Y	Y	Y	N
23 ***Boehlert***	Y	N	Y	Y	Y	Y	Y
24 ***McHugh***	N	Y	Y	Y	Y	Y	Y
25 ***Walsh***	N	Y	Y	Y	Y	Y	Y
26 Hinchey	Y	N	N	N	N	N	N
27 ***Reynolds***	N	Y	Y	Y	Y	Y	Y
28 Slaughter	Y	N	N	?	?	N	N
29 LaFalce	N	Y	N	?	?	N	Y

	411	412	413	414	415	416	417
30 ***Quinn***	N	Y	Y	Y	Y	Y	Y
31 ***Houghton***	Y	N	Y	Y	Y	Y	Y
NORTH CAROLINA							
1 Clayton	Y	N	N	N	N	N	Y
2 Etheridge	Y	N	N	N	Y	N	Y
3 ***Jones***	N	Y	Y	Y	Y	+	+
4 Price	Y	N	N	N	Y	N	Y
5 ***Burr***	N	Y	Y	Y	Y	Y	Y
6 ***Coble***	N	Y	Y	Y	Y	Y	Y
7 McIntyre	N	Y	N	Y	Y	N	Y
8 ***Hayes***	N	Y	Y	Y	Y	Y	Y
9 ***Myrick***	N	Y	Y	Y	Y	Y	Y
10 ***Ballenger***	N	Y	Y	Y	Y	Y	Y
11 ***Taylor***	N	Y	Y	Y	Y	Y	Y
12 Watt	Y	N	N	N	N	N	Y
NORTH DAKOTA							
AL Pomeroy	N	Y	N	Y	Y	N	Y
OHIO							
1 ***Chabot***	N	Y	Y	Y	Y	Y	Y
2 ***Portman***	N	Y	Y	Y	Y	Y	Y
3 Vacant							
4 ***Oxley***	N	Y	Y	Y	?	Y	Y
5 ***Gillmor***	N	Y	Y	Y	Y	Y	N
6 Strickland	Y	N	N	N	N	N	N
7 ***Hobson***	N	Y	Y	Y	Y	Y	Y
8 ***Boehner***	N	Y	Y	Y	Y	Y	Y
9 Kaptur	Y	P	N	N	N	N	Y
10 Kucinich	N	P	N	N	N	N	N
11 Jones	Y	N	N	N	N	N	Y
12 ***Tiberi***	N	Y	Y	Y	Y	Y	Y
13 Brown	Y	N	N	N	N	N	Y
14 Sawyer	Y	N	N	N	N	N	Y
15 ***Pryce***	N	Y	Y	Y	Y	Y	Y
16 ***Regula***	N	Y	Y	Y	Y	Y	Y
17 Vacant							
18 ***Ney***	N	Y	Y	Y	Y	Y	Y
19 ***LaTourette***	N	Y	Y	Y	Y	Y	Y
OKLAHOMA							
1 ***Sullivan***	N	Y	Y	Y	Y	Y	Y
2 Carson	Y	N	N	Y	Y	N	Y
3 ***Watkins***	N	Y	Y	Y	Y	Y	Y
4 ***Watts***	N	Y	Y	Y	Y	Y	Y
5 ***Istook***	N	Y	Y	Y	Y	Y	Y
6 ***Lucas***	N	Y	Y	Y	Y	Y	Y
OREGON							
1 Wu	Y	N	N	Y	Y	?	?
2 ***Walden***	N	Y	Y	Y	Y	Y	Y
3 Blumenauer	Y	N	N	N	Y	N	Y
4 DeFazio	Y	N	N	N	N	N	N
5 Hooley	Y	N	N	Y	Y	N	Y
PENNSYLVANIA							
1 Brady	Y	N	N	N	Y	N	N
2 Fattah	Y	N	N	N	Y	N	Y
3 Borski	N	Y	?	?	?	N	N
4 ***Hart***	N	Y	Y	Y	Y	Y	Y
5 ***Peterson***	N	Y	Y	Y	Y	Y	Y
6 Holden	N	Y	N	Y	Y	N	Y
7 ***Weldon***	N	Y	Y	Y	Y	Y	Y
8 ***Greenwood***	Y	N	Y	Y	?	Y	Y
9 ***Shuster, Bill***	N	Y	Y	Y	Y	Y	Y
10 ***Sherwood***	N	?	Y	Y	Y	Y	Y
11 Kanjorski	N	Y	N	Y	Y	N	Y
12 Murtha	N	Y	N	?	?	N	?
13 Hoeffel	Y	N	N	N	Y	N	Y
14 Coyne	Y	N	N	N	N	N	Y
15 ***Toomey***	N	Y	Y	Y	Y	Y	Y
16 ***Pitts***	N	Y	Y	Y	Y	Y	Y
17 ***Gekas***	N	Y	Y	Y	Y	Y	Y
18 Doyle	N	Y	N	N	Y	N	Y
19 ***Platts***	N	Y	Y	Y	Y	Y	N
20 Mascara	?	?	?	?	?	N	Y
21 ***English***	N	Y	Y	Y	Y	?	–
RHODE ISLAND							
1 Kennedy	Y	N	N	N	Y	?	?
2 Langevin	N	Y	N	N	Y	N	Y
SOUTH CAROLINA							
1 ***Brown***	N	Y	Y	Y	Y	Y	Y
2 ***Wilson***	N	Y	Y	Y	Y	Y	Y
3 ***Graham***	N	Y	Y	Y	Y	Y	Y
4 ***DeMint***	N	Y	Y	Y	Y	Y	Y
5 Spratt	Y	N	N	N	Y	N	Y
6 Clyburn	Y	N	N	N	N	N	Y
SOUTH DAKOTA							
AL ***Thune***	N	Y	Y	Y	Y	N	Y

	411	412	413	414	415	416	417
TENNESSEE							
1 ***Jenkins***	N	Y	Y	Y	Y	Y	Y
2 ***Duncan***	N	Y	Y	Y	Y	Y	Y
3 ***Wamp***	N	Y	Y	Y	Y	Y	Y
4 ***Hilleary***	N	Y	Y	Y	Y	Y	Y
5 Clement	Y	Y	N	Y	Y	N	Y
6 Gordon	Y	Y	N	Y	Y	N	Y
7 ***Bryant***	N	Y	Y	Y	Y	Y	Y
8 Tanner	Y	Y	N	Y	N	N	Y
9 Ford	Y	N	N	Y	N	N	Y
TEXAS							
1 Sandlin	Y	N	N	N	Y	N	Y
2 Turner	Y	N	N	Y	N	N	Y
3 ***Johnson, Sam***	N	Y	Y	Y	Y	Y	Y
4 Hall	N	Y	N	Y	Y	N	Y
5 ***Sessions***	N	Y	Y	Y	Y	Y	Y
6 ***Barton***	N	Y	Y	Y	Y	Y	Y
7 ***Culberson***	N	Y	Y	Y	Y	Y	Y
8 ***Brady***	N	Y	Y	Y	Y	Y	Y
9 Lampson	Y	N	N	N	N	N	Y
10 Doggett	Y	N	N	N	N	N	N
11 Edwards	Y	N	N	Y	Y	N	Y
12 ***Granger***	N	Y	Y	Y	Y	Y	Y
13 ***Thornberry***	N	Y	Y	Y	Y	Y	Y
14 ***Paul***	N	Y	Y	N	Y	Y	Y
15 Hinojosa	Y	N	N	?	Y	N	Y
16 Reyes	Y	N	N	N	N	N	Y
17 Stenholm	N	Y	N	Y	N	N	Y
18 Jackson-Lee	Y	N	N	N	N	N	Y
19 ***Combest***	N	Y	Y	Y	Y	Y	Y
20 Gonzalez	Y	N	N	N	N	N	Y
21 ***Smith***	N	Y	Y	Y	Y	Y	Y
22 ***DeLay***	N	Y	Y	Y	Y	Y	Y
23 ***Bonilla***	N	Y	Y	Y	Y	Y	Y
24 Frost	Y	N	N	N	Y	N	Y
25 Bentsen	Y	N	N	N	Y	N	Y
26 ***Armey***	N	Y	Y	Y	Y	Y	Y
27 Ortiz	N	Y	N	N	N	N	Y
28 Rodriguez	Y	N	N	N	N	N	Y
29 Green	Y	N	N	Y	Y	N	Y
30 Johnson, E.B.	Y	N	N	N	N	N	Y
UTAH							
1 ***Hansen***	N	Y	Y	Y	Y	Y	Y
2 Matheson	Y	N	N	Y	Y	N	Y
3 ***Cannon***	N	Y	Y	Y	Y	Y	Y
VERMONT							
AL *Sanders*	Y	N	N	N	N	N	Y
VIRGINIA							
1 ***Davis, Jo Ann***	N	Y	Y	Y	Y	Y	Y
2 ***Schrock***	N	Y	Y	Y	Y	Y	Y
3 Scott	Y	N	N	N	N	N	Y
4 ***Forbes***	N	Y	Y	Y	Y	Y	Y
5 ***Goode***	N	Y	Y	Y	Y	Y	Y
6 ***Goodlatte***	N	Y	Y	Y	Y	Y	Y
7 ***Cantor***	N	Y	Y	Y	Y	Y	Y
8 Moran	Y	N	N	N	?	N	Y
9 Boucher	Y	N	N	N	Y	N	Y
10 ***Wolf***	N	Y	Y	Y	Y	Y	Y
11 ***Davis, T.***	N	Y	Y	Y	Y	Y	Y
WASHINGTON							
1 Inslee	Y	N	N	N	N	N	Y
2 Larsen	Y	N	N	Y	Y	N	N
3 Baird	Y	N	N	N	Y	N	N
4 ***Hastings***	N	Y	Y	Y	Y	?	?
5 ***Nethercutt***	N	Y	Y	Y	Y	Y	Y
6 Dicks	Y	N	N	N	N	N	Y
7 McDermott	Y	N	?	?	?	?	?
8 ***Dunn***	N	Y	Y	Y	Y	Y	Y
9 Smith	Y	N	N	Y	N	N	Y
WEST VIRGINIA							
1 Mollohan	N	Y	N	N	N	N	Y
2 ***Capito***	N	Y	Y	Y	Y	Y	Y
3 Rahall	N	Y	N	N	N	N	Y
WISCONSIN							
1 ***Ryan***	N	Y	Y	Y	Y	Y	Y
2 Baldwin	Y	N	N	N	N	N	N
3 Kind	Y	N	N	N	N	N	Y
4 Kleczka	Y	N	N	N	N	N	Y
5 Barrett	Y	N	N	N	N	N	Y
6 ***Petri***	N	Y	Y	Y	Y	Y	Y
7 Obey	Y	Y	N	?	?	N	N
8 ***Green***	N	Y	Y	Y	Y	Y	Y
9 ***Sensenbrenner***	N	Y	Y	Y	Y	Y	Y
WYOMING							
AL ***Cubin***	N	?	Y	Y	Y	Y	Y

Southern states - Ala., Ark., Fla., Ga., Ky., La., Miss., N.C., Okla., S.C., Tenn., Texas, Va.

Key

Y Voted for (yea).
Paired for.
+ Announced for.
N Voted against (nay).
X Paired against.
− Announced against.
P Voted "present."
C Voted "present" to avoid possible conflict of interest.
? Did not vote or otherwise make a position known.

Democrats   **Republicans**   *Independents*

418. HR 3295. Election Overhaul/Motion to Instruct. Johnson, D-Texas, motion to instruct House conferees to take appropriate actions to ensure that a conference report on the bill that would overhaul the nation's election procedures is filed before Oct. 1, 2002. Motion agreed to 385-16: R 191-16; D 193-0 (ND 141-0, SD 52-0); I 1-0. Sept. 26, 2002.

419. HR 4600. Medical Malpractice Awards/Rule. Adoption of the rule (H Res 553) to provide for House floor consideration of the bill that would cap the amount plaintiffs and their attorneys could receive in successful medical malpractice cases. Adopted 221-197: R 214-1; D 7-195 (ND 3-147, SD 4-48); I 0-1. Sept. 26, 2002.

420. HR 4600. Medical Malpractice Awards/Recommit. Conyers, D-Mich., motion to recommit the bill to the House Judiciary Committee and House Energy and Commerce Committee with instructions that it be reported back with language stating that no provisions would pre-empt state laws related to the liability of health maintenance organizations. Motion rejected 193-225: R 6-212; D 186-13 (ND 142-5, SD 44-8); I 1-0. Sept. 26, 2002.

421. HR 4600. Medical Malpractice Awards/Passage. Passage of the bill that would cap the amount plaintiffs and their attorneys could receive in successful medical malpractice cases. The bill would limit punitive damages to the greater of $250,000 or double economic damages, and cap attorneys' contingency fees. It would require malpractice suits to be filed within three years of an injury or one year of its discovery, whichever is earlier. No punitive damages could be assessed against drug and medical device manufacturers if their products were approved by the Food and Drug Administration or are generally considered safe. Passed 217-203: R 203-15; D 14-187 (ND 6-142, SD 8-45); I 0-1. A "yea" was a vote in support of the president's position. Sept. 26, 2002.

422. HR 2215. Justice Department Reauthorization/Conference Report. Adoption of the conference report on the bill that would authorize $17.6 billion in fiscal 2002 and $20.5 billion in fiscal 2003 for Justice Department operations. Adopted (thus sent to the Senate) 400-4: R 206-4; D 193-0 (ND 143-0, SD 50-0); I 1-0. Sept. 26, 2002.

423. H J Res 111. Fiscal 2003 Continuing Appropriations/Passage. Passage of the joint resolution to provide continuing appropriations through Oct. 4 for all federal departments and programs. The continuing resolution would set spending at fiscal 2002 levels. Passed 370-1: R 186-0; D 183-1 (ND 135-1, SD 48-0); I 1-0. Sept. 26, 2002.

	418	419	420	421	422	423
ALABAMA						
1 *Callahan*	?	?	?	?	?	?
2 *Everett*	Y	Y	N	Y	Y	?
3 *Riley*	Y	Y	N	Y	Y	Y
4 *Aderholt*	Y	Y	N	Y	Y	Y
5 Cramer	Y	N	N	Y	Y	Y
6 *Bachus*	?	?	?	?	?	?
7 Hilliard	Y	N	?	N	Y	Y
ALASKA						
AL *Young*	N	Y	N	Y	?	?
ARIZONA						
1 *Flake*	N	Y	N	N	N	Y
2 Pastor	Y	N	Y	N	Y	Y
3 *Stump*	?	?	?	?	?	?
4 *Shadegg*	Y	Y	N	Y	?	?
5 *Kolbe*	Y	Y	N	Y	Y	Y
6 *Hayworth*	Y	Y	N	Y	Y	Y
ARKANSAS						
1 Berry	Y	N	Y	N	Y	Y
2 Snyder	Y	N	Y	N	Y	Y
3 *Boozman*	Y	Y	N	Y	Y	Y
4 Ross	Y	N	Y	N	Y	Y
CALIFORNIA						
1 Thompson	?	?	?	?	?	?
2 *Herger*	Y	Y	N	Y	Y	Y
3 *Ose*	Y	Y	N	Y	Y	Y
4 *Doolittle*	Y	Y	N	Y	Y	Y
5 Matsui	Y	N	Y	N	Y	Y
6 Woolsey	Y	N	Y	N	Y	Y
7 Miller, George	Y	N	Y	N	Y	Y
8 Pelosi	Y	N	Y	N	Y	Y
9 Lee	Y	N	Y	N	Y	Y
10 Tauscher	Y	N	Y	N	Y	Y
11 *Pombo*	Y	Y	N	Y	Y	Y
12 Lantos	Y	N	Y	N	Y	Y
13 Stark	Y	N	Y	N	Y	Y
14 Eshoo	Y	N	Y	N	Y	Y
15 Honda	Y	N	Y	N	Y	Y
16 Lofgren	Y	N	Y	N	Y	Y
17 Farr	Y	N	Y	N	Y	Y
18 Condit	Y	N	Y	N	?	?
19 *Radanovich*	Y	Y	N	Y	Y	Y
20 Dooley	Y	N	Y	?	?	?
21 *Thomas*	Y	Y	N	Y	Y	Y
22 Capps	Y	N	Y	N	Y	Y
23 *Gallegly*	Y	Y	N	Y	Y	?
24 Sherman	Y	N	Y	N	Y	Y
25 *McKeon*	Y	Y	N	Y	Y	Y
26 Berman	Y	N	Y	N	Y	?
27 Schiff	Y	N	Y	N	Y	Y
28 *Dreier*	Y	Y	N	Y	Y	Y
29 Waxman	Y	N	Y	N	?	Y
30 Becerra	Y	N	Y	N	Y	Y
31 Solis	Y	N	Y	N	Y	Y
32 Watson	Y	N	Y	N	Y	Y
33 Roybal-Allard	Y	N	Y	N	Y	Y
34 Napolitano	Y	N	Y	N	Y	Y
35 Waters	Y	N	Y	N	Y	Y
36 Harman	Y	N	Y	N	Y	Y
37 Millender-McD.	Y	N	Y	N	Y	Y
38 *Horn*	Y	Y	N	Y	Y	Y

	418	419	420	421	422	423
39 *Royce*	Y	Y	N	Y	Y	Y
40 *Lewis*	Y	Y	N	Y	Y	Y
41 *Miller, Gary*	Y	Y	N	Y	Y	?
42 Baca	Y	N	Y	N	Y	Y
43 *Calvert*	Y	Y	N	Y	Y	Y
44 *Bono*	Y	Y	N	Y	Y	Y
45 *Rohrabacher*	Y	Y	N	Y	Y	Y
46 Sanchez	Y	N	Y	N	Y	Y
47 *Cox*	Y	Y	N	Y	Y	Y
48 *Issa*	Y	Y	N	Y	Y	?
49 Davis	Y	N	Y	N	Y	Y
50 Filner	Y	N	Y	N	Y	Y
51 *Cunningham*	Y	Y	N	Y	Y	Y
52 *Hunter*	?	Y	N	Y	Y	Y
COLORADO						
1 DeGette	Y	N	Y	N	Y	Y
2 Udall	Y	N	Y	N	Y	Y
3 *McInnis*	Y	Y	N	Y	Y	?
4 *Schaffer*	?	Y	N	Y	Y	Y
5 *Hefley*	Y	Y	N	Y	Y	Y
6 *Tancredo*	Y	Y	N	Y	Y	Y
CONNECTICUT						
1 Larson	?	N	Y	N	Y	Y
2 *Simmons*	Y	Y	N	Y	Y	Y
3 DeLauro	Y	N	Y	N	Y	Y
4 *Shays*	Y	Y	N	Y	Y	Y
5 Maloney	Y	N	Y	N	Y	Y
6 *Johnson*	Y	Y	N	Y	Y	Y
DELAWARE						
AL *Castle*	Y	Y	N	Y	Y	Y
FLORIDA						
1 *Miller, J.*	N	Y	N	Y	Y	Y
2 Boyd	Y	N	N	Y	Y	Y
3 Brown	Y	N	Y	N	Y	Y
4 *Crenshaw*	Y	Y	N	Y	Y	Y
5 Thurman	?	?	?	?	?	?
6 *Stearns*	Y	Y	N	Y	Y	Y
7 *Mica*	Y	Y	N	Y	Y	Y
8 *Keller*	Y	Y	N	Y	Y	Y
9 *Bilirakis*	Y	Y	N	Y	Y	?
10 *Young*	?	Y	N	Y	Y	Y
11 Davis	Y	N	Y	N	Y	Y
12 *Putnam*	Y	Y	N	Y	Y	Y
13 *Miller, D.*	Y	Y	N	Y	Y	Y
14 *Goss*	Y	Y	N	Y	Y	Y
15 *Weldon*	Y	Y	N	Y	Y	Y
16 *Foley*	Y	Y	N	Y	Y	Y
17 Meek	Y	?	Y	N	?	?
18 *Ros-Lehtinen*	Y	Y	N	Y	Y	Y
19 Wexler	Y	N	Y	N	Y	Y
20 Deutsch	Y	N	Y	N	Y	Y
21 *Diaz-Balart*	Y	Y	N	Y	Y	Y
22 *Shaw*	Y	Y	N	Y	Y	Y
23 Hastings	Y	N	Y	N	Y	Y
GEORGIA						
1 *Kingston*	Y	Y	N	Y	Y	Y
2 Bishop	Y	N	Y	N	Y	Y
3 *Collins*	N	N	N	Y	Y	Y
4 McKinney	Y	N	N	N	?	?
5 Lewis	Y	N	Y	N	Y	Y
6 *Isakson*	Y	Y	N	Y	Y	Y
7 *Barr*	N	?	Y	Y	Y	Y
8 *Chambliss*	Y	Y	N	Y	Y	Y
9 *Deal*	Y	Y	N	Y	Y	?
10 *Norwood*	N	Y	N	Y	Y	Y
11 *Linder*	Y	Y	N	Y	Y	Y
HAWAII						
1 Abercrombie	Y	N	Y	N	Y	Y
2 Mink	?	?	?	?	?	?
IDAHO						
1 *Otter*	Y	Y	N	Y	Y	?
2 *Simpson*	Y	Y	N	Y	?	?
ILLINOIS						
1 Rush	Y	N	Y	N	Y	Y
2 Jackson	Y	N	Y	N	Y	Y
3 Lipinski	Y	N	Y	N	Y	Y
4 Gutierrez	Y	N	Y	N	Y	Y
5 Blagojevich	Y	N	Y	N	Y	Y
6 *Hyde*	Y	Y	N	Y	Y	Y
7 Davis	Y	N	Y	N	Y	Y
8 *Crane*	Y	Y	N	Y	Y	Y
9 Schakowsky	Y	N	Y	N	Y	Y
10 *Kirk*	Y	Y	N	Y	Y	Y
11 *Weller*	Y	Y	N	Y	Y	Y
12 Costello	Y	N	Y	N	Y	Y
13 *Biggert*	Y	Y	N	Y	Y	Y

ND Northern Democrats   SD Southern Democrats

	418	419	420	421	422	423
14 ***Hastert***						
15 ***Johnson***	Y	Y	Y	N	Y	Y
16 ***Manzullo***	Y	Y	N	Y	Y	Y
17 Evans	Y	N	Y	N	Y	Y
18 ***LaHood***	Y	Y	N	Y	Y	?
19 Phelps	Y	N	Y	N	Y	Y
20 ***Shimkus***	Y	Y	N	Y	Y	Y
INDIANA						
1 Visclosky	Y	N	N	N	Y	?
2 ***Pence***	Y	Y	N	Y	Y	Y
3 Roemer	Y	N	Y	N	Y	Y
4 ***Souder***	Y	Y	N	Y	Y	Y
5 ***Buyer***	Y	?	N	Y	Y	?
6 ***Burton***	Y	Y	N	Y	Y	?
7 ***Kerns***	N	Y	N	Y	N	Y
8 ***Hostettler***	N	Y	N	Y	Y	Y
9 Hill	Y	N	Y	N	Y	Y
10 Carson	Y	N	Y	N	Y	Y
IOWA						
1 ***Leach***	Y	Y	N	Y	Y	Y
2 ***Nussle***	Y	Y	N	Y	Y	Y
3 Boswell	Y	N	Y	N	Y	Y
4 ***Ganske***	Y	Y	Y	Y	Y	Y
5 ***Latham***	Y	Y	N	Y	Y	Y
KANSAS						
1 ***Moran***	Y	Y	N	Y	Y	Y
2 ***Ryun***	Y	Y	N	Y	Y	Y
3 Moore	Y	N	Y	N	Y	Y
4 ***Tiahrt***	Y	Y	N	Y	Y	Y
KENTUCKY						
1 ***Whitfield***	?	Y	N	Y	Y	Y
2 ***Lewis***	Y	Y	N	Y	Y	Y
3 ***Northup***	Y	Y	N	Y	Y	Y
4 Lucas	Y	Y	N	Y	Y	Y
5 ***Rogers***	Y	Y	N	Y	Y	Y
6 ***Fletcher***	?	Y	N	Y	Y	Y
LOUISIANA						
1 ***Vitter***	Y	Y	N	Y	Y	Y
2 Jefferson	Y	N	Y	N	Y	Y
3 ***Tauzin***	Y	Y	N	Y	Y	Y
4 ***McCrery***	?	Y	N	Y	Y	?
5 ***Cooksey***	Y	Y	N	Y	Y	?
6 ***Baker***	Y	Y	N	Y	Y	?
7 John	?	N	Y	N	Y	Y
MAINE						
1 Allen	Y	N	Y	N	Y	Y
2 Baldacci	Y	N	Y	N	Y	Y
MARYLAND						
1 ***Gilchrest***	Y	Y	N	Y	+	Y
2 ***Ehrlich***	Y	Y	N	N	?	?
3 Cardin	Y	N	Y	N	Y	?
4 Wynn	?	N	Y	N	Y	Y
5 Hoyer	Y	N	Y	N	Y	Y
6 ***Bartlett***	Y	Y	N	Y	Y	Y
7 Cummings	Y	N	Y	N	Y	Y
8 ***Morella***	Y	Y	N	N	Y	Y
MASSACHUSETTS						
1 Olver	Y	N	Y	N	Y	Y
2 Neal	Y	N	Y	N	Y	Y
3 McGovern	Y	N	Y	N	Y	Y
4 Frank	Y	N	Y	N	Y	Y
5 Meehan	Y	N	Y	N	Y	Y
6 Tierney	Y	N	Y	N	Y	Y
7 Markey	Y	N	Y	N	Y	Y
8 Capuano	?	N	Y	N	Y	Y
9 Lynch	Y	N	Y	N	Y	Y
10 Delahunt	Y	N	Y	N	Y	?
MICHIGAN						
1 Stupak	Y	N	Y	N	Y	Y
2 ***Hoekstra***	Y	Y	N	Y	Y	?
3 ***Ehlers***	Y	Y	N	Y	Y	Y
4 ***Camp***	Y	Y	N	Y	Y	Y
5 Barcia	?	Y	?	?	?	?
6 ***Upton***	Y	Y	N	Y	Y	Y
7 ***Smith***	Y	Y	N	Y	?	Y
8 ***Rogers***	Y	Y	N	Y	Y	Y
9 Kildee	Y	N	Y	N	Y	Y
10 Bonior	?	?	?	?	?	?
11 ***Knollenberg***	Y	Y	N	Y	Y	Y
12 Levin	Y	N	Y	N	Y	Y
13 Rivers	Y	N	Y	N	Y	Y
14 Conyers	Y	N	Y	N	?	?
15 Kilpatrick	Y	N	Y	N	Y	Y
16 Dingell	Y	N	Y	N	Y	Y

	418	419	420	421	422	423
MINNESOTA						
1 ***Gutknecht***	Y	Y	N	Y	Y	Y
2 ***Kennedy***	Y	Y	N	Y	Y	Y
3 ***Ramstad***	Y	Y	N	Y	Y	Y
4 McCollum	Y	N	Y	N	Y	Y
5 Sabo	Y	N	Y	N	Y	Y
6 Luther	Y	N	Y	N	Y	Y
7 Peterson	Y	Y	N	Y	Y	Y
8 Oberstar	Y	N	Y	N	Y	Y
MISSISSIPPI						
1 ***Wicker***	Y	Y	N	Y	Y	Y
2 Thompson	Y	N	Y	N	Y	Y
3 ***Pickering***	Y	Y	N	Y	Y	Y
4 Shows	Y	N	Y	N	Y	Y
5 Taylor	Y	Y	N	Y	Y	Y
MISSOURI						
1 Clay	?	N	Y	N	Y	Y
2 ***Akin***	Y	Y	N	Y	Y	Y
3 Gephardt	Y	N	Y	N	Y	Y
4 Skelton	Y	N	Y	N	Y	Y
5 McCarthy	Y	N	Y	N	Y	+
6 ***Graves***	Y	Y	N	Y	Y	Y
7 ***Blunt***	Y	Y	N	Y	Y	Y
8 ***Emerson***	Y	Y	N	Y	Y	Y
9 ***Hulshof***	?	Y	N	Y	Y	Y
MONTANA						
AL ***Rehberg***	Y	Y	N	Y	Y	Y
NEBRASKA						
1 ***Bereuter***	Y	Y	N	Y	Y	?
2 ***Terry***	Y	Y	N	N	Y	Y
3 ***Osborne***	Y	Y	N	Y	Y	Y
NEVADA						
1 Berkley	Y	N	Y	N	Y	Y
2 ***Gibbons***	Y	Y	N	Y	Y	Y
NEW HAMPSHIRE						
1 ***Sununu***	Y	Y	N	Y	Y	Y
2 ***Bass***	Y	Y	N	Y	Y	Y
NEW JERSEY						
1 Andrews	Y	N	Y	N	Y	Y
2 ***LoBiondo***	Y	Y	N	Y	Y	Y
3 ***Saxton***	Y	Y	N	Y	Y	Y
4 ***Smith***	Y	Y	N	Y	Y	Y
5 ***Roukema***	?	?	?	?	?	?
6 Pallone	Y	N	Y	N	Y	Y
7 ***Ferguson***	Y	Y	N	Y	Y	Y
8 Pascrell	Y	N	Y	N	Y	Y
9 Rothman	Y	N	Y	N	Y	Y
10 Payne	Y	N	Y	N	Y	Y
11 ***Frelinghuysen***	Y	Y	N	Y	Y	Y
12 Holt	Y	N	Y	N	Y	Y
13 Menendez	Y	N	Y	N	Y	Y
NEW MEXICO						
1 ***Wilson***	Y	Y	N	Y	Y	Y
2 ***Skeen***	Y	Y	N	Y	Y	Y
3 Udall	Y	N	Y	N	Y	Y
NEW YORK						
1 ***Grucci***	Y	Y	N	N	Y	Y
2 Israel	Y	N	+	–	+	+
3 ***King***	Y	Y	N	N	Y	?
4 McCarthy	Y	N	Y	N	Y	Y
5 Ackerman	Y	N	Y	N	Y	Y
6 Meeks	Y	N	Y	N	Y	Y
7 Crowley	Y	N	Y	N	Y	Y
8 Nadler	Y	N	Y	N	Y	Y
9 Weiner	Y	N	Y	N	Y	Y
10 Towns	Y	N	Y	N	Y	Y
11 Owens	Y	N	Y	N	Y	Y
12 Velázquez	Y	N	Y	N	Y	Y
13 ***Fossella***	?	Y	N	Y	Y	Y
14 Maloney	?	?	?	?	?	?
15 Rangel	Y	N	Y	N	Y	Y
16 Serrano	Y	N	Y	N	Y	Y
17 Engel	Y	N	Y	N	Y	Y
18 Lowey	Y	N	Y	N	Y	Y
19 ***Kelly***	Y	Y	N	Y	Y	Y
20 ***Gilman***	Y	Y	N	N	Y	Y
21 McNulty	Y	N	Y	N	Y	Y
22 ***Sweeney***	Y	Y	N	Y	Y	Y
23 ***Boehlert***	Y	Y	N	Y	Y	?
24 ***McHugh***	Y	Y	N	Y	Y	Y
25 ***Walsh***	Y	Y	N	Y	Y	Y
26 Hinchey	Y	N	Y	N	Y	Y
27 ***Reynolds***	Y	Y	N	Y	Y	Y
28 Slaughter	Y	N	?	N	Y	?
29 LaFalce	Y	N	Y	N	Y	Y

	418	419	420	421	422	423
30 ***Quinn***	Y	Y	N	Y	Y	?
31 ***Houghton***	Y	Y	N	Y	Y	?
NORTH CAROLINA						
1 Clayton	Y	N	Y	N	?	Y
2 Etheridge	Y	N	Y	N	Y	Y
3 ***Jones***	–	Y	N	Y	Y	Y
4 Price	Y	N	Y	N	Y	Y
5 ***Burr***	Y	Y	N	Y	Y	Y
6 ***Coble***	Y	Y	Y	N	Y	Y
7 McIntyre	Y	N	Y	N	Y	Y
8 ***Hayes***	Y	Y	N	Y	Y	Y
9 ***Myrick***	N	Y	N	Y	Y	Y
10 ***Ballenger***	Y	Y	N	Y	Y	Y
11 ***Taylor***	Y	Y	N	Y	Y	Y
12 Watt	Y	N	Y	N	Y	Y
NORTH DAKOTA						
AL Pomeroy	Y	Y	N	Y	Y	Y
OHIO						
1 ***Chabot***	Y	Y	N	Y	Y	Y
2 ***Portman***	Y	Y	N	Y	Y	Y
3 Vacant						
4 ***Oxley***	Y	Y	N	Y	Y	Y
5 ***Gillmor***	Y	Y	N	Y	Y	Y
6 Strickland	Y	N	Y	N	Y	Y
7 ***Hobson***	Y	Y	N	Y	Y	Y
8 ***Boehner***	Y	Y	N	Y	Y	Y
9 Kaptur	Y	N	Y	N	Y	Y
10 Kucinich	Y	N	Y	N	Y	Y
11 Jones	Y	N	Y	N	Y	Y
12 ***Tiberi***	Y	Y	N	Y	Y	Y
13 Brown	Y	N	Y	N	Y	Y
14 Sawyer	Y	N	Y	N	Y	?
15 ***Pryce***	Y	Y	N	Y	Y	Y
16 ***Regula***	Y	Y	N	Y	Y	Y
17 Vacant						
18 ***Ney***	Y	Y	N	Y	Y	Y
19 ***LaTourette***	Y	Y	N	Y	Y	?
OKLAHOMA						
1 ***Sullivan***	Y	Y	N	Y	Y	Y
2 Carson	Y	N	Y	N	Y	Y
3 ***Watkins***	Y	Y	N	Y	Y	Y
4 ***Watts***	Y	Y	N	Y	Y	Y
5 ***Istook***	Y	Y	N	N	Y	?
6 ***Lucas***	Y	Y	N	Y	Y	Y
OREGON						
1 Wu	?	N	Y	N	Y	Y
2 ***Walden***	Y	Y	N	Y	Y	Y
3 Blumenauer	Y	N	Y	N	?	Y
4 DeFazio	Y	N	Y	N	Y	N
5 Hooley	Y	N	Y	N	Y	Y
PENNSYLVANIA						
1 Brady	Y	N	Y	N	Y	Y
2 Fattah	Y	N	Y	N	Y	Y
3 Borski	Y	N	Y	N	Y	Y
4 ***Hart***	Y	Y	N	Y	Y	Y
5 ***Peterson***	Y	Y	N	Y	Y	Y
6 Holden	Y	N	N	Y	Y	Y
7 ***Weldon***	Y	Y	N	Y	Y	Y
8 ***Greenwood***	Y	Y	N	Y	Y	Y
9 ***Shuster, Bill***	Y	Y	N	Y	Y	Y
10 ***Sherwood***	Y	Y	N	Y	Y	Y
11 Kanjorski	Y	N	Y	N	Y	Y
12 Murtha	?	N	N	Y	Y	?
13 Hoeffel	Y	N	Y	N	Y	Y
14 Coyne	Y	N	Y	N	Y	Y
15 ***Toomey***	N	Y	N	Y	Y	Y
16 ***Pitts***	Y	Y	N	Y	Y	Y
17 ***Gekas***	Y	Y	N	Y	Y	Y
18 Doyle	Y	N	Y	N	Y	Y
19 ***Platts***	Y	Y	N	Y	Y	Y
20 Mascara	Y	N	Y	N	Y	Y
21 ***English***	+	Y	Y	Y	Y	Y
RHODE ISLAND						
1 Kennedy	?	N	Y	N	Y	Y
2 Langevin	Y	N	Y	N	Y	Y
SOUTH CAROLINA						
1 ***Brown***	Y	Y	N	Y	Y	Y
2 ***Wilson***	Y	Y	N	N	Y	Y
3 ***Graham***	Y	Y	Y	N	Y	Y
4 ***DeMint***	Y	Y	N	Y	Y	Y
5 Spratt	Y	N	Y	N	Y	Y
6 Clyburn	Y	N	Y	N	Y	Y
SOUTH DAKOTA						
AL ***Thune***	Y	Y	N	Y	Y	Y

	418	419	420	421	422	423
TENNESSEE						
1 ***Jenkins***	Y	Y	N	Y	Y	Y
2 ***Duncan***	N	N	Y	Y	N	Y
3 ***Wamp***	Y	Y	N	Y	Y	Y
4 ***Hilleary***	Y	Y	N	Y	Y	?
5 Clement	Y	N	Y	N	Y	Y
6 Gordon	Y	N	Y	N	Y	Y
7 ***Bryant***	Y	Y	N	Y	Y	Y
8 Tanner	Y	N	Y	N	Y	Y
9 Ford	Y	N	Y	N	Y	Y
TEXAS						
1 Sandlin	Y	N	Y	N	Y	?
2 Turner	Y	N	Y	N	Y	Y
3 ***Johnson, Sam***	Y	Y	N	Y	Y	Y
4 Hall	Y	Y	N	Y	Y	Y
5 ***Sessions***	Y	Y	N	Y	Y	Y
6 ***Barton***	Y	Y	N	Y	Y	Y
7 ***Culberson***	N	Y	N	Y	Y	Y
8 ***Brady***	Y	Y	N	Y	Y	Y
9 Lampson	Y	N	Y	N	Y	Y
10 Doggett	Y	N	Y	N	Y	Y
11 Edwards	Y	N	Y	Y	Y	Y
12 ***Granger***	Y	Y	N	Y	Y	Y
13 ***Thornberry***	N	Y	N	Y	Y	Y
14 ***Paul***	N	?	N	N	N	?
15 Hinojosa	Y	N	Y	N	Y	?
16 Reyes	Y	N	Y	N	Y	Y
17 Stenholm	Y	N	N	Y	Y	Y
18 Jackson-Lee	Y	N	Y	N	Y	Y
19 ***Combest***	Y	Y	N	Y	Y	Y
20 Gonzalez	Y	N	Y	N	Y	Y
21 ***Smith***	Y	Y	N	Y	Y	Y
22 ***DeLay***	Y	Y	N	Y	Y	Y
23 ***Bonilla***	N	Y	N	Y	Y	Y
24 Frost	Y	N	Y	N	Y	Y
25 Bentsen	Y	N	Y	N	Y	Y
26 ***Armey***	Y	Y	N	Y	Y	?
27 Ortiz	Y	N	Y	N	Y	?
28 Rodriguez	Y	N	Y	N	Y	Y
29 Green	Y	N	Y	N	Y	?
30 Johnson, E.B.	Y	N	Y	N	Y	Y
UTAH						
1 ***Hansen***	Y	Y	N	Y	Y	Y
2 Matheson	Y	N	Y	N	Y	Y
3 ***Cannon***	Y	Y	N	Y	Y	Y
VERMONT						
AL *Sanders*	Y	N	Y	N	Y	Y
VIRGINIA						
1 ***Davis, Jo Ann***	Y	Y	N	Y	Y	Y
2 ***Schrock***	Y	Y	N	Y	Y	Y
3 Scott	Y	N	Y	N	Y	Y
4 ***Forbes***	Y	Y	N	Y	Y	Y
5 ***Goode***	N	Y	N	Y	Y	Y
6 ***Goodlatte***	Y	Y	N	Y	Y	Y
7 ***Cantor***	Y	Y	N	Y	Y	Y
8 Moran	Y	Y	N	Y	Y	Y
9 Boucher	Y	N	Y	N	Y	Y
10 ***Wolf***	Y	Y	N	Y	Y	Y
11 ***Davis, T.***	Y	Y	N	Y	Y	Y
WASHINGTON						
1 Inslee	Y	N	Y	N	Y	Y
2 Larsen	Y	N	Y	N	Y	Y
3 Baird	Y	N	Y	N	Y	Y
4 ***Hastings***	?	Y	N	Y	Y	Y
5 ***Nethercutt***	Y	Y	N	Y	Y	Y
6 Dicks	Y	N	Y	N	Y	Y
7 McDermott	?	?	?	?	?	?
8 ***Dunn***	Y	Y	N	Y	Y	Y
9 Smith	Y	N	Y	N	Y	Y
WEST VIRGINIA						
1 Mollohan	Y	N	Y	N	Y	Y
2 ***Capito***	Y	Y	N	Y	Y	Y
3 Rahall	Y	N	Y	N	Y	Y
WISCONSIN						
1 ***Ryan***	Y	Y	N	Y	Y	Y
2 Baldwin	+	N	Y	N	Y	Y
3 Kind	Y	N	Y	N	Y	?
4 Kleczka	Y	N	Y	N	Y	Y
5 Barrett	Y	N	Y	N	Y	Y
6 ***Petri***	Y	Y	N	Y	Y	Y
7 Obey	Y	N	Y	N	Y	Y
8 ***Green***	Y	Y	N	Y	Y	Y
9 ***Sensenbrenner***	Y	Y	N	Y	Y	Y
WYOMING						
AL ***Cubin***	Y	Y	N	Y	Y	Y

Southern states - Ala., Ark., Fla., Ga., Ky., La., Miss., N.C., Okla., S.C., Tenn., Texas, Va.

Key

424. S 434. Indian Compensation and Mormon Grant/Passage. Hansen, R-Utah, motion to suspend the rules and pass the bill that would compensate Indian tribes for land flooded along the Missouri River because of dam construction in 1944 and, as amended, require the government to sell 940 acres of federal land in Wyoming to the Church of Jesus Christ of Latter-day Saints. Motion agreed to 357-37: R 180-30; D 176-7 (ND 133-4, SD 43-3); I 1-0. A two-thirds majority of those present and voting (263 in this case) is required for passage under suspension of the rules. Oct. 1, 2002.

425. HR 4125. Federal Court Administration/Passage. Sensenbrenner, R-Wis., motion to suspend the rules and pass the bill that would make a variety of administrative changes to the federal court system, including striking current provisions that exempt from jury service military members, emergency response personnel, and federal and state government officers. It also would make it a crime to file a false lien or civil claim against a federal judge; allow judges to file yearly summary reports on wiretap orders; and strike a requirement that district courts have original jurisdiction over cases involving citizens and certain foreigners who have permanent resident status living in the same state. Motion agreed to 370-21: R 207-2; D 163-18 (ND 118-17, SD 45-1); I 0-1. A two-thirds majority of those present and voting (261 in this case) is required for passage under suspension of the rules. Oct. 1, 2002.

426. H Res 538. Johnny Unitas Tribute/Adoption. Sullivan, R-Okla., motion to suspend the rules and adopt the resolution that would pay tribute to the late football player Johnny Unitas. Motion agreed to 389-0: R 208-0; D 180-0 (ND 134-0, SD 46-0); I 1-0. A two-thirds majority of those present and voting (260 in this case) is required for adoption under suspension of the rules. Oct. 1, 2002.

427. Procedural Motion/Journal. Approval of the House Journal of Tuesday, Oct. 1, 2002. Approved 343-55: R 191-13; D 151-42 (ND 109-36, SD 42-6); I 1-0. Oct. 2, 2002.

428. H Con Res 476. Firefighter Tribute/Adoption. Smith, R-Mich., motion to suspend the rules and adopt the concurrent resolution that would support the idea of a day of tribute to firefighters killed in the line of duty. Motion agreed to 407-0: R 211-0; D 195-0 (ND 145-0, SD 50-0); I 1-0. A two-thirds majority of those and present (272 in this case) is required for adoption under suspension of the rules. Oct. 2, 2002.

429. HR 2357. Churches and Campaign Activities/Passage. Herger, R-Calif., motion to suspend the rules and pass the bill that would amend the tax code to allow a religiously affiliated organization to carry out political campaign activities and still maintain its 501(c)(3) tax exempt status so long as such efforts are not a "substantial part" of its work. Motion rejected 178-239: R 168-46; D 10-192 (ND 5-146, SD 5-46); I 0-1. A two-thirds majority of those present and voting (278 in this case) is required for passage under suspension of the rules. Oct. 2, 2002.

* Rep. Patsy T. Mink, D-Hawaii, died Sept. 28, 2002. The last vote for which she was eligible was vote 423.

	424	425	426	427	428	429
ALABAMA						
1 *Callahan*	N	Y	Y	Y	Y	Y
2 *Everett*	N	Y	Y	Y	Y	Y
3 *Riley*	N	Y	Y	Y	Y	Y
4 *Aderholt*	N	Y	Y	N	Y	N
5 Cramer	Y	Y	Y	Y	Y	N
6 *Bachus*	Y	Y	Y	Y	Y	Y
7 Hilliard	Y	Y	Y	N	Y	N
ALASKA						
AL *Young*	Y	Y	Y	?	?	Y
ARIZONA						
1 *Flake*	Y	Y	Y	Y	Y	Y
2 Pastor	Y	Y	Y	Y	Y	N
3 *Stump*	?	?	?	?	?	?
4 *Shadegg*	Y	Y	Y	Y	Y	Y
5 *Kolbe*	Y	Y	Y	Y	Y	N
6 *Hayworth*	Y	Y	Y	Y	Y	Y
ARKANSAS						
1 Berry	Y	Y	Y	Y	Y	N
2 Snyder	N	Y	Y	Y	Y	N
3 *Boozman*	Y	Y	Y	Y	Y	Y
4 Ross	Y	Y	Y	Y	Y	N
CALIFORNIA						
1 Thompson	+	+	+	N	Y	N
2 *Herger*	Y	Y	Y	Y	Y	Y
3 *Ose*	Y	Y	Y	Y	Y	N
4 *Doolittle*	Y	Y	Y	Y	Y	Y
5 Matsui	Y	Y	Y	Y	Y	N
6 Woolsey	Y	N	Y	Y	Y	N
7 Miller, George	Y	Y	Y	Y	Y	N
8 Pelosi	Y	Y	Y	Y	Y	N
9 Lee	Y	Y	Y	N	Y	N
10 Tauscher	?	?	?	Y	Y	N
11 *Pombo*	Y	Y	Y	Y	Y	Y
12 Lantos	Y	Y	Y	Y	Y	N
13 Stark	Y	N	Y	Y	Y	N
14 Eshoo	Y	Y	Y	Y	Y	N
15 Honda	Y	Y	Y	Y	Y	N
16 Lofgren	Y	Y	Y	Y	Y	N
17 Farr	Y	Y	Y	Y	Y	N
18 Condit	?	?	?	N	Y	N
19 *Radanovich*	Y	Y	Y	Y	Y	Y
20 Dooley	Y	Y	Y	Y	Y	N
21 *Thomas*	N	Y	Y	Y	Y	N
22 Capps	Y	Y	Y	Y	Y	N
23 *Gallegly*	?	?	?	Y	Y	Y
24 Sherman	Y	Y	Y	N	Y	N
25 *McKeon*	Y	Y	Y	Y	Y	Y
26 Berman	Y	Y	Y	Y	Y	N
27 Schiff	Y	Y	Y	Y	Y	N
28 *Dreier*	Y	Y	Y	Y	Y	Y
29 Waxman	Y	Y	Y	Y	Y	N
30 Becerra	+	+	+	Y	Y	N
31 Solis	Y	Y	Y	Y	Y	N
32 Watson	Y	N	Y	Y	Y	N
33 Roybal-Allard	Y	Y	Y	Y	Y	N
34 Napolitano	Y	Y	Y	Y	Y	N
35 Waters	Y	N	Y	N	Y	N
36 Harman	?	?	?	Y	Y	N
37 Millender-McD.	Y	Y	Y	Y	Y	N
38 *Horn*	Y	Y	?	Y	Y	N

	424	425	426	427	428	429
39 *Royce*	?	Y	Y	Y	Y	Y
40 *Lewis*	Y	Y	Y	Y	Y	N
41 *Miller, Gary*	Y	Y	Y	Y	Y	Y
42 Baca	Y	Y	Y	Y	Y	N
43 *Calvert*	Y	Y	Y	Y	Y	Y
44 *Bono*	Y	Y	Y	Y	Y	N
45 *Rohrabacher*	Y	Y	Y	Y	Y	Y
46 Sanchez	Y	Y	Y	?	?	N
47 *Cox*	?	?	?	?	?	?
48 *Issa*	Y	Y	Y	Y	Y	Y
49 Davis	Y	Y	Y	Y	Y	N
50 Filner	Y	N	Y	N	Y	N
51 *Cunningham*	Y	Y	Y	Y	Y	Y
52 *Hunter*	Y	Y	Y	Y	Y	?
COLORADO						
1 DeGette	Y	N	Y	Y	Y	N
2 Udall	Y	Y	Y	N	Y	N
3 *McInnis*	Y	Y	Y	Y	Y	Y
4 *Schaffer*	N	Y	Y	N	Y	Y
5 *Hefley*	N	Y	Y	N	Y	Y
6 *Tancredo*	Y	Y	Y	P	Y	Y
CONNECTICUT						
1 Larson	Y	Y	Y	Y	+	N
2 *Simmons*	Y	Y	Y	Y	Y	N
3 DeLauro	Y	Y	Y	Y	Y	N
4 *Shays*	Y	Y	Y	Y	Y	N
5 Maloney	Y	Y	Y	Y	Y	N
6 *Johnson*	Y	Y	Y	Y	Y	N
DELAWARE						
AL *Castle*	Y	Y	Y	Y	Y	N
FLORIDA						
1 *Miller, J.*	N	Y	Y	Y	Y	Y
2 Boyd	Y	Y	Y	Y	Y	N
3 Brown	Y	Y	Y	Y	Y	N
4 *Crenshaw*	Y	Y	Y	Y	Y	Y
5 Thurman	Y	Y	Y	Y	Y	N
6 *Stearns*	N	Y	Y	Y	Y	Y
7 *Mica*	Y	Y	Y	Y	Y	Y
8 *Keller*	Y	Y	Y	Y	Y	Y
9 *Bilirakis*	Y	Y	Y	Y	Y	Y
10 *Young*	N	Y	Y	Y	Y	Y
11 Davis	Y	Y	Y	?	?	N
12 *Putnam*	Y	Y	Y	Y	Y	Y
13 *Miller, D.*	Y	Y	Y	Y	Y	Y
14 *Goss*	Y	Y	Y	Y	Y	N
15 *Weldon*	Y	Y	Y	Y	Y	Y
16 *Foley*	Y	Y	Y	Y	Y	Y
17 Meek	Y	Y	Y	?	Y	N
18 *Ros-Lehtinen*	Y	?	?	Y	Y	Y
19 Wexler	?	?	?	Y	Y	N
20 Deutsch	Y	Y	Y	?	?	?
21 *Diaz-Balart*	?	?	?	Y	Y	Y
22 *Shaw*	Y	Y	Y	Y	Y	Y
23 Hastings	?	?	?	?	?	?
GEORGIA						
1 *Kingston*	Y	Y	Y	Y	Y	Y
2 Bishop	Y	Y	Y	Y	Y	N
3 *Collins*	N	Y	Y	Y	Y	Y
4 *McKinney*	?	?	?	?	Y	N
5 Lewis	Y	N	Y	Y	Y	N
6 *Isakson*	Y	Y	Y	Y	Y	Y
7 *Barr*	Y	Y	Y	Y	Y	Y
8 *Chambliss*	N	Y	Y	Y	Y	Y
9 *Deal*	?	?	?	?	?	?
10 *Norwood*	N	Y	Y	Y	Y	Y
11 *Linder*	Y	Y	Y	Y	Y	Y
HAWAII						
1 Abercrombie	Y	Y	Y	Y	Y	N
2 Vacant *						
IDAHO						
1 *Otter*	Y	Y	Y	Y	Y	Y
2 *Simpson*	Y	Y	Y	Y	Y	Y
ILLINOIS						
1 Rush	Y	?	Y	Y	Y	N
2 Jackson	Y	N	Y	Y	Y	N
3 Lipinski	Y	Y	Y	Y	Y	N
4 Gutierrez	Y	Y	Y	N	Y	N
5 Blagojevich	?	?	?	Y	Y	N
6 *Hyde*	Y	Y	Y	?	Y	N
7 Davis	Y	Y	Y	Y	Y	N
8 *Crane*	Y	Y	Y	?	Y	Y
9 Schakowsky	Y	Y	Y	N	Y	N
10 *Kirk*	Y	Y	Y	Y	Y	N
11 *Weller*	N	Y	Y	N	Y	N
12 Costello	Y	Y	Y	N	Y	N
13 *Biggert*	Y	Y	Y	Y	Y	N

	424	425	426	427	428	429
14 ***Hastert***						
15 ***Johnson***	Y	Y	Y	Y	Y	N
16 ***Manzullo***	Y	Y	Y	Y	Y	Y
17 Evans	Y	Y	Y	Y	Y	N
18 ***LaHood***	?	?	?	Y	Y	Y
19 Phelps	Y	Y	?	Y	Y	Y
20 ***Shimkus***	Y	Y	Y	Y	Y	Y
INDIANA						
1 Visclosky	Y	Y	Y	N	Y	N
2 ***Pence***	Y	Y	Y	Y	Y	Y
3 Roemer	Y	Y	Y	Y	Y	N
4 ***Souder***	Y	Y	Y	Y	Y	Y
5 ***Buyer***	Y	Y	Y	Y	Y	N
6 ***Burton***	Y	Y	Y	Y	Y	Y
7 ***Kerns***	N	N	Y	Y	Y	Y
8 ***Hostettler***	Y	Y	Y	Y	Y	Y
9 Hill	Y	Y	Y	Y	Y	N
10 Carson	Y	Y	Y	Y	Y	N
IOWA						
1 ***Leach***	Y	Y	Y	Y	Y	N
2 ***Nussle***	Y	Y	Y	N	Y	N
3 Boswell	Y	Y	Y	Y	Y	N
4 ***Ganske***	Y	Y	Y	Y	Y	N
5 ***Latham***	Y	Y	Y	N	Y	N
KANSAS						
1 ***Moran***	Y	Y	Y	Y	Y	Y
2 ***Ryun***	Y	Y	Y	Y	+	Y
3 Moore	Y	Y	Y	N	Y	N
4 ***Tiahrt***	Y	Y	Y	Y	Y	Y
KENTUCKY						
1 ***Whitfield***	N	Y	Y	Y	Y	Y
2 ***Lewis***	Y	Y	Y	Y	Y	Y
3 ***Northup***	Y	Y	Y	Y	Y	Y
4 Lucas	Y	Y	Y	Y	Y	Y
5 ***Rogers***	Y	Y	Y	Y	Y	Y
6 ***Fletcher***	Y	Y	Y	Y	Y	Y
LOUISIANA						
1 ***Vitter***	N	Y	Y	Y	Y	Y
2 Jefferson	Y	Y	Y	Y	Y	N
3 ***Tauzin***	Y	Y	Y	Y	Y	Y
4 ***McCrery***	Y	Y	?	Y	Y	Y
5 ***Cooksey***	Y	Y	Y	?	Y	Y
6 ***Baker***	Y	Y	Y	Y	Y	Y
7 John	?	?	?	Y	Y	N
MAINE						
1 Allen	Y	Y	Y	Y	Y	N
2 Baldacci	Y	Y	Y	Y	Y	N
MARYLAND						
1 ***Gilchrest***	Y	Y	Y	Y	Y	N
2 ***Ehrlich***	Y	Y	Y	?	?	?
3 Cardin	Y	Y	Y	Y	Y	N
4 Wynn	Y	Y	Y	Y	Y	N
5 Hoyer	Y	Y	Y	Y	Y	N
6 ***Bartlett***	Y	Y	Y	Y	Y	Y
7 Cummings	?	?	?	Y	Y	N
8 ***Morella***	Y	Y	Y	Y	Y	N
MASSACHUSETTS						
1 Olver	Y	Y	Y	N	Y	N
2 Neal	Y	Y	Y	Y	Y	N
3 McGovern	Y	Y	Y	N	Y	N
4 Frank	Y	Y	?	Y	Y	N
5 Meehan	Y	Y	Y	Y	Y	N
6 Tierney	Y	Y	Y	Y	Y	N
7 Markey	Y	Y	Y	N	Y	N
8 Capuano	Y	N	Y	N	Y	N
9 Lynch	Y	Y	Y	Y	Y	N
10 Delahunt	Y	Y	Y	Y	Y	N
MICHIGAN						
1 Stupak	Y	Y	Y	N	Y	N
2 ***Hoekstra***	Y	Y	Y	Y	Y	Y
3 ***Ehlers***	Y	Y	Y	Y	Y	Y
4 ***Camp***	Y	Y	Y	Y	Y	Y
5 Barcia	?	?	?	Y	Y	Y
6 ***Upton***	Y	Y	Y	Y	Y	N
7 ***Smith***	Y	Y	Y	Y	Y	Y
8 ***Rogers***	Y	Y	Y	Y	Y	Y
9 Kildee	Y	Y	Y	Y	Y	N
10 Bonior	?	?	?	?	?	N
11 ***Knollenberg***	Y	Y	Y	Y	Y	N
12 Levin	Y	Y	Y	?	?	N
13 Rivers	Y	N	Y	Y	Y	N
14 Conyers	Y	N	Y	?	?	N
15 Kilpatrick	Y	Y	Y	Y	Y	N
16 Dingell	Y	N	Y	Y	Y	N

	424	425	426	427	428	429
MINNESOTA						
1 ***Gutknecht***	Y	Y	Y	N	Y	Y
2 ***Kennedy***	Y	Y	Y	N	Y	Y
3 ***Ramstad***	Y	Y	Y	N	Y	Y
4 McCollum	Y	Y	Y	Y	Y	N
5 Sabo	Y	N	Y	N	Y	N
6 Luther	Y	Y	Y	Y	Y	N
7 Peterson	Y	Y	Y	N	Y	N
8 Oberstar	Y	Y	Y	N	Y	N
MISSISSIPPI						
1 ***Wicker***	Y	Y	Y	Y	Y	Y
2 Thompson	Y	Y	Y	N	Y	N
3 ***Pickering***	Y	Y	Y	Y	Y	Y
4 Shows	Y	Y	Y	Y	Y	Y
5 Taylor	Y	Y	Y	N	Y	N
MISSOURI						
1 Clay	Y	Y	Y	?	?	?
2 ***Akin***	Y	Y	Y	Y	Y	Y
3 Gephardt	Y	Y	Y	?	Y	N
4 Skelton	Y	Y	Y	Y	Y	N
5 McCarthy	Y	Y	Y	Y	Y	N
6 ***Graves***	Y	Y	Y	Y	Y	Y
7 ***Blunt***	N	Y	Y	?	Y	Y
8 ***Emerson***	Y	Y	Y	Y	Y	Y
9 ***Hulshof***	Y	Y	Y	N	Y	Y
MONTANA						
AL ***Rehberg***	Y	Y	Y	Y	Y	Y
NEBRASKA						
1 ***Bereuter***	Y	Y	Y	+	+	N
2 ***Terry***	Y	Y	Y	Y	Y	N
3 ***Osborne***	Y	Y	Y	Y	Y	N
NEVADA						
1 Berkley	Y	Y	Y	Y	Y	N
2 ***Gibbons***	Y	Y	Y	Y	Y	Y
NEW HAMPSHIRE						
1 ***Sununu***	Y	Y	Y	Y	Y	Y
2 ***Bass***	Y	Y	Y	Y	Y	N
NEW JERSEY						
1 Andrews	Y	Y	Y	Y	Y	N
2 ***LoBiondo***	Y	Y	Y	N	Y	Y
3 ***Saxton***	N	?	Y	Y	Y	Y
4 ***Smith***	Y	Y	Y	Y	Y	Y
5 ***Roukema***	?	?	?	?	?	?
6 Pallone	?	?	?	N	Y	N
7 ***Ferguson***	Y	Y	Y	N	Y	Y
8 Pascrell	Y	Y	Y	Y	Y	N
9 Rothman	?	?	?	Y	Y	N
10 Payne	?	?	?	Y	Y	N
11 ***Frelinghuysen***	Y	Y	Y	Y	Y	Y
12 Holt	Y	Y	Y	N	Y	N
13 Menendez	?	?	?	Y	Y	N
NEW MEXICO						
1 ***Wilson***	Y	Y	Y	Y	Y	N
2 ***Skeen***	Y	Y	Y	Y	Y	N
3 Udall	Y	Y	Y	N	Y	N
NEW YORK						
1 ***Grucci***	Y	Y	Y	Y	Y	Y
2 Israel	Y	Y	Y	Y	Y	N
3 ***King***	Y	Y	Y	Y	Y	Y
4 McCarthy	Y	Y	Y	Y	Y	N
5 Ackerman	Y	Y	Y	Y	Y	N
6 Meeks	Y	Y	Y	Y	Y	N
7 Crowley	Y	Y	Y	Y	Y	N
8 Nadler	Y	Y	Y	Y	Y	N
9 Weiner	Y	Y	Y	Y	Y	N
10 Towns	Y	Y	Y	Y	Y	N
11 Owens	Y	Y	Y	Y	Y	N
12 Velázquez	Y	Y	Y	Y	Y	N
13 ***Fossella***	N	Y	Y	Y	Y	Y
14 Maloney	Y	Y	Y	Y	Y	N
15 Rangel	Y	Y	Y	Y	Y	N
16 Serrano	Y	Y	Y	Y	Y	N
17 Engel	Y	Y	Y	Y	Y	N
18 Lowey	Y	Y	Y	Y	Y	N
19 ***Kelly***	Y	Y	Y	Y	Y	Y
20 ***Gilman***	Y	Y	Y	Y	Y	N
21 McNulty	Y	Y	Y	N	Y	N
22 ***Sweeney***	Y	Y	Y	Y	Y	N
23 ***Boehlert***	Y	Y	Y	Y	Y	N
24 ***McHugh***	Y	Y	Y	Y	Y	Y
25 ***Walsh***	Y	Y	Y	Y	Y	Y
26 Hinchey	Y	Y	Y	N	Y	N
27 ***Reynolds***	Y	Y	Y	Y	Y	Y
28 Slaughter	N	Y	Y	N	Y	N
29 LaFalce	Y	Y	Y	Y	Y	N

	424	425	426	427	428	429
30 ***Quinn***	Y	Y	Y	Y	Y	N
31 ***Houghton***	Y	Y	Y	Y	Y	N
NORTH CAROLINA						
1 Clayton	Y	Y	Y	Y	Y	N
2 Etheridge	Y	Y	Y	N	Y	N
3 ***Jones***	N	Y	Y	Y	Y	Y
4 Price	?	?	?	Y	Y	N
5 ***Burr***	Y	Y	Y	Y	?	Y
6 ***Coble***	N	Y	Y	Y	Y	Y
7 McIntyre	Y	Y	Y	Y	Y	N
8 ***Hayes***	Y	Y	Y	Y	Y	Y
9 ***Myrick***	Y	Y	Y	Y	Y	Y
10 ***Ballenger***	Y	Y	Y	Y	Y	Y
11 ***Taylor***	N	Y	Y	Y	Y	Y
12 Watt	Y	Y	Y	Y	Y	N
NORTH DAKOTA						
AL Pomeroy	Y	Y	Y	Y	Y	N
OHIO						
1 ***Chabot***	N	Y	Y	Y	Y	Y
2 ***Portman***	?	Y	Y	Y	Y	Y
3 Vacant						
4 ***Oxley***	Y	Y	Y	Y	Y	Y
5 ***Gillmor***	Y	Y	Y	?	Y	Y
6 Strickland	N	Y	Y	N	Y	N
7 ***Hobson***	N	Y	Y	Y	Y	N
8 ***Boehner***	Y	Y	Y	Y	Y	N
9 Kaptur	Y	Y	Y	Y	Y	N
10 Kucinich	Y	N	Y	Y	Y	N
11 Jones	?	?	?	Y	Y	N
12 ***Tiberi***	Y	Y	Y	Y	Y	Y
13 Brown	N	Y	Y	?	?	N
14 Sawyer	Y	N	Y	Y	Y	N
15 ***Pryce***	Y	Y	Y	Y	Y	N
16 ***Regula***	Y	Y	Y	Y	Y	Y
17 Vacant						
18 ***Ney***	Y	Y	Y	Y	Y	Y
19 ***LaTourette***	Y	Y	Y	Y	Y	N
OKLAHOMA						
1 ***Sullivan***	?	Y	Y	Y	Y	Y
2 Carson	Y	Y	Y	Y	Y	N
3 ***Watkins***	Y	Y	Y	Y	Y	Y
4 ***Watts***	Y	Y	Y	Y	Y	Y
5 ***Istook***	Y	Y	Y	Y	Y	Y
6 ***Lucas***	Y	Y	Y	Y	Y	Y
OREGON						
1 Wu	Y	Y	Y	N	Y	N
2 ***Walden***	Y	Y	Y	Y	Y	N
3 Blumenauer	Y	Y	Y	Y	Y	N
4 DeFazio	Y	N	Y	N	Y	N
5 Hooley	Y	Y	Y	N	Y	N
PENNSYLVANIA						
1 Brady	Y	Y	Y	N	Y	N
2 Fattah	N	Y	Y	Y	Y	N
3 Borski	?	?	?	N	Y	N
4 ***Hart***	Y	Y	Y	Y	Y	Y
5 ***Peterson***	Y	Y	Y	Y	Y	Y
6 Holden	Y	Y	Y	Y	Y	N
7 ***Weldon***	Y	Y	Y	Y	Y	Y
8 ***Greenwood***	Y	Y	Y	Y	Y	N
9 ***Shuster, Bill***	Y	Y	Y	Y	Y	Y
10 ***Sherwood***	Y	Y	Y	Y	Y	Y
11 Kanjorski	Y	Y	Y	Y	Y	N
12 Murtha	Y	?	?	Y	Y	N
13 Hoeffel	Y	Y	Y	Y	Y	N
14 Coyne	Y	Y	Y	Y	Y	N
15 ***Toomey***	Y	Y	Y	Y	Y	Y
16 ***Pitts***	Y	Y	Y	Y	Y	Y
17 ***Gekas***	Y	Y	Y	Y	Y	N
18 Doyle	Y	Y	Y	Y	Y	N
19 ***Platts***	Y	Y	Y	?	Y	N
20 Mascara	+	+	+	?	?	?
21 ***English***	Y	Y	Y	N	Y	Y
RHODE ISLAND						
1 Kennedy	Y	Y	Y	Y	Y	N
2 Langevin	Y	Y	Y	Y	Y	N
SOUTH CAROLINA						
1 ***Brown***	Y	Y	Y	Y	Y	Y
2 ***Wilson***	Y	Y	Y	Y	Y	Y
3 ***Graham***	Y	Y	Y	Y	Y	Y
4 ***DeMint***	Y	Y	Y	Y	Y	Y
5 Spratt	Y	Y	Y	Y	Y	N
6 Clyburn	Y	Y	Y	Y	Y	N
SOUTH DAKOTA						
AL ***Thune***	Y	Y	Y	Y	Y	Y

	424	425	426	427	428	429
TENNESSEE						
1 ***Jenkins***	N	Y	Y	Y	Y	Y
2 ***Duncan***	Y	Y	Y	Y	Y	Y
3 ***Wamp***	Y	Y	Y	Y	Y	Y
4 ***Hilleary***	?	?	?	?	?	?
5 Clement	Y	Y	Y	Y	Y	Y
6 Gordon	Y	Y	Y	Y	Y	N
7 ***Bryant***	Y	Y	Y	Y	Y	Y
8 Tanner	?	?	?	?	?	?
9 Ford	Y	Y	Y	N	Y	N
TEXAS						
1 Sandlin	Y	Y	Y	Y	Y	N
2 Turner	Y	Y	Y	Y	Y	N
3 ***Johnson, Sam***	Y	Y	Y	?	Y	Y
4 Hall	N	Y	Y	Y	Y	Y
5 ***Sessions***	Y	Y	Y	Y	Y	Y
6 ***Barton***	N	Y	Y	?	Y	Y
7 ***Culberson***	Y	Y	Y	Y	Y	Y
8 ***Brady***	Y	Y	Y	Y	Y	Y
9 Lampson	Y	Y	Y	Y	Y	N
10 Doggett	Y	Y	Y	Y	Y	N
11 Edwards	Y	Y	Y	Y	Y	N
12 ***Granger***	Y	Y	Y	Y	Y	Y
13 ***Thornberry***	Y	Y	Y	Y	Y	Y
14 ***Paul***	N	N	Y	Y	Y	Y
15 Hinojosa	Y	Y	Y	Y	Y	N
16 Reyes	?	?	?	Y	Y	N
17 Stenholm	N	Y	Y	Y	Y	Y
18 Jackson-Lee	Y	Y	Y	Y	Y	N
19 ***Combest***	?	?	?	Y	Y	Y
20 Gonzalez	Y	Y	Y	Y	Y	N
21 ***Smith***	Y	Y	Y	Y	Y	Y
22 ***DeLay***	Y	Y	Y	Y	Y	Y
23 ***Bonilla***	Y	Y	Y	Y	Y	Y
24 Frost	Y	Y	Y	Y	Y	N
25 Bentsen	Y	Y	Y	Y	Y	N
26 ***Armey***	Y	?	?	Y	Y	Y
27 Ortiz	Y	Y	Y	Y	Y	N
28 Rodriguez	Y	Y	Y	Y	Y	N
29 Green	Y	Y	Y	N	Y	N
30 Johnson, E.B.	Y	Y	Y	Y	Y	N
UTAH						
1 ***Hansen***	Y	?	?	Y	Y	Y
2 Matheson	Y	Y	Y	Y	Y	N
3 ***Cannon***	Y	Y	Y	Y	Y	Y
VERMONT						
AL *Sanders*	Y	N	Y	Y	Y	N
VIRGINIA						
1 ***Davis, Jo Ann***	Y	Y	Y	Y	Y	Y
2 ***Schrock***	Y	Y	Y	?	?	?
3 Scott	Y	Y	Y	Y	Y	N
4 ***Forbes***	Y	Y	Y	Y	Y	Y
5 ***Goode***	Y	Y	Y	Y	Y	Y
6 ***Goodlatte***	Y	Y	Y	Y	Y	Y
7 ***Cantor***	Y	Y	Y	Y	Y	Y
8 Moran	?	?	?	Y	Y	N
9 Boucher	Y	Y	Y	Y	Y	N
10 ***Wolf***	Y	Y	Y	Y	Y	Y
11 ***Davis, T.***	Y	Y	Y	Y	Y	Y
WASHINGTON						
1 Inslee	Y	Y	Y	Y	Y	N
2 Larsen	Y	Y	Y	N	Y	N
3 Baird	Y	Y	Y	N	Y	N
4 ***Hastings***	Y	Y	Y	Y	Y	Y
5 ***Nethercutt***	Y	Y	Y	Y	Y	Y
6 Dicks	Y	Y	Y	Y	Y	N
7 McDermott	?	+	+	?	?	N
8 ***Dunn***	Y	Y	Y	Y	Y	Y
9 Smith	Y	Y	Y	Y	Y	N
WEST VIRGINIA						
1 Mollohan	Y	N	Y	Y	Y	N
2 ***Capito***	Y	Y	Y	Y	Y	Y
3 Rahall	Y	Y	Y	Y	Y	Y
WISCONSIN						
1 ***Ryan***	Y	Y	Y	Y	Y	Y
2 Baldwin	Y	Y	Y	N	Y	N
3 Kind	Y	Y	Y	Y	Y	N
4 Kleczka	Y	Y	Y	Y	Y	N
5 Barrett	Y	Y	Y	Y	Y	N
6 ***Petri***	Y	Y	Y	Y	Y	N
7 Obey	Y	N	Y	N	Y	N
8 ***Green***	Y	Y	Y	Y	Y	Y
9 ***Sensenbrenner***	N	Y	Y	Y	Y	N
WYOMING						
AL ***Cubin***	N	Y	Y	Y	Y	Y

Southern states - Ala., Ark., Fla., Ga., Ky., La., Miss., N.C., Okla., S.C., Tenn., Texas, Va.

Key

Y	Voted for (yea).
#	Paired for.
+	Announced for.
N	Voted against (nay).
X	Paired against.
–	Announced against.
P	Voted "present."
C	Voted "present" to avoid possible conflict of interest.
?	Did not vote or otherwise make a position known.

Democrats   **Republicans**   *Independents*

430. H Res 543. Support for Married Couples Tax Relief/Adoption. Adoption of the resolution that would express the sense of the House that Congress should, before it adjourns, clear for the president's signature legislation (HR 4019) that would permanently extend breaks for married couples contained in last year's $1.35 trillion tax cut law. Adopted 285-130: R 212-0; D 72-130 (ND 47-104, SD 25-26); I 1-0. Oct. 2, 2002.

431. H Res 559. House Special Elections/Adoption. Adoption of the resolution that would urge state governments to review their policies on special elections for House members to expedite those procedures so vacancies caused by a catastrophe could be filled in a timely fashion. Adopted 414-0: R 212-0; D 201-0 (ND 151-0, SD 50-0); I 1-0. Oct. 2, 2002.

432. HR 3295. Election Overhaul/Motion to Instruct. Meek, D-Fla., motion to instruct House conferees on the election overhaul bill to take appropriate actions to convene a public meeting of House and Senate conferees and to ensure that a conference report is filed before Oct. 4, 2002. Motion agreed to 400-14: R 197-14; D 202-0 (ND 152-0, SD 50-0); I 1-0. Oct. 2, 2002.

433. Question of Privilege/Ruling of the Chair. Miller, R-Fla., motion to table (kill) the Visclosky, D-Ind., appeal of the ruling of the chair that the Visclosky resolution does not constitute a point of privilege under Rule IX of the House. The Visclosky resolution would express the sense of the House that Congress should give states the resources necessary to implement last year's education overhaul legislation (PL 107-110) through completion of the fiscal 2003 Labor, Health, and Human Services spending bill (HR 5320) because failure to do so would impugn the integrity of the House. Motion agreed to 210-200: R 210-0; D 0-199 (ND 0-149, SD 0-50); I 0-1. Oct. 2, 2002.

434. Question of Privilege/Ruling of the Chair. Burr, R-N.C., motion to table (kill) the Brown, D-Ohio, appeal of the ruling of the chair that the Brown resolution does not constitute a point of privilege under Rule IX of the House. The Brown resolution would express the sense of the House that it should consider pending legislation that would speed up the approval process of generic drugs. Motion agreed to 212-204: R 212-2; D 0-201 (ND 0-151, SD 0-50); I 0-1. Oct. 2, 2002.

435. Question of Privilege/Ruling of the Chair. Sensenbrenner, R-Wis., motion to table (kill) the Holden, D-Pa., appeal of the ruling of the chair that the Holden resolution does not constitute a point of privilege under Rule IX of the House. The Holden resolution would express the sense of the House that the Speaker should immediately bring to the floor a bill (HR 5348) that would permanently extend the Chapter 12 farm bankruptcy program and expand it to include family fishermen because failure to do so would impugn the integrity of the House. Motion agreed to 214-202: R 214-0; D 0-201 (ND 0-151, SD 0-50); I 0-1. Oct. 2, 2002.

	430	431	432	433	434	435
ALABAMA						
1 *Callahan*	Y	Y	Y	?	Y	Y
2 *Everett*	Y	Y	N	Y	Y	Y
3 *Riley*	Y	Y	Y	Y	Y	Y
4 *Aderholt*	Y	Y	Y	Y	Y	Y
5 Cramer	Y	Y	N	N	N	N
6 *Bachus*	Y	Y	Y	Y	Y	Y
7 Hilliard	N	Y	N	N	N	N
ALASKA						
AL *Young*	Y	Y	Y	Y	Y	Y
ARIZONA						
1 *Flake*	Y	Y	N	Y	Y	Y
2 Pastor	N	Y	Y	N	N	N
3 *Stump*	?	?	?	?	?	?
4 *Shadegg*	Y	Y	Y	Y	Y	Y
5 *Kolbe*	Y	Y	Y	Y	Y	Y
6 *Hayworth*	Y	Y	Y	Y	Y	Y
ARKANSAS						
1 Berry	N	Y	Y	N	N	N
2 Snyder	Y	Y	Y	N	N	N
3 *Boozman*	Y	Y	Y	Y	Y	Y
4 Ross	Y	Y	Y	N	N	N
CALIFORNIA						
1 Thompson	N	Y	Y	N	N	N
2 *Herger*	?	?	?	Y	Y	Y
3 *Ose*	Y	Y	Y	Y	Y	Y
4 *Doolittle*	Y	Y	Y	Y	Y	Y
5 Matsui	N	Y	Y	N	N	N
6 Woolsey	N	Y	Y	N	N	N
7 Miller, George	N	Y	Y	N	N	N
8 Pelosi	N	Y	Y	N	N	N
9 Lee	N	Y	Y	N	N	N
10 Tauscher	N	Y	Y	N	N	N
11 *Pombo*	Y	Y	Y	Y	Y	Y
12 Lantos	Y	Y	Y	N	N	N
13 Stark	N	Y	Y	N	N	N
14 Eshoo	N	Y	Y	N	N	N
15 Honda	N	Y	Y	N	N	N
16 Lofgren	N	Y	Y	N	N	N
17 Farr	N	Y	Y	N	N	N
18 Condit	Y	Y	Y	N	N	N
19 *Radanovich*	Y	Y	Y	Y	Y	Y
20 Dooley	Y	Y	Y	N	N	N
21 *Thomas*	Y	Y	Y	Y	Y	Y
22 Capps	Y	Y	Y	N	N	N
23 *Gallegly*	Y	Y	Y	Y	Y	Y
24 Sherman	N	Y	Y	N	N	N
25 *McKeon*	Y	Y	Y	Y	Y	Y
26 Berman	N	Y	Y	N	N	N
27 Schiff	N	Y	Y	N	N	N
28 *Dreier*	Y	Y	Y	Y	Y	Y
29 Waxman	N	Y	Y	N	N	N
30 Becerra	N	Y	Y	N	N	N
31 Solis	N	Y	Y	N	N	N
32 Watson	N	Y	Y	N	N	N
33 Roybal-Allard	N	Y	Y	N	N	N
34 Napolitano	N	Y	Y	N	N	N
35 Waters	N	Y	Y	N	N	N
36 Harman	Y	Y	Y	N	N	N
37 Millender-McD.	N	Y	Y	N	N	N
38 *Horn*	Y	Y	Y	Y	Y	Y
39 *Royce*	Y	Y	Y	Y	Y	Y
40 *Lewis*	Y	Y	Y	Y	Y	Y
41 *Miller, Gary*	Y	Y	Y	Y	Y	Y
42 Baca	N	Y	Y	N	N	N
43 *Calvert*	Y	Y	Y	Y	Y	Y
44 *Bono*	Y	Y	Y	Y	Y	Y
45 *Rohrabacher*	Y	Y	Y	Y	Y	Y
46 Sanchez	?	?	?	?	?	N
47 *Cox*	Y	Y	Y	Y	Y	Y
48 *Issa*	Y	Y	Y	Y	Y	Y
49 Davis	Y	Y	Y	N	N	N
50 Filner	N	Y	Y	N	N	N
51 *Cunningham*	Y	Y	Y	Y	Y	Y
52 *Hunter*	Y	Y	Y	Y	Y	?
COLORADO						
1 DeGette	N	Y	Y	N	N	N
2 Udall	Y	Y	Y	N	N	N
3 *McInnis*	Y	Y	Y	Y	Y	Y
4 *Schaffer*	Y	Y	Y	Y	Y	Y
5 *Hefley*	Y	Y	Y	Y	Y	Y
6 *Tancredo*	Y	Y	Y	Y	Y	Y
CONNECTICUT						
1 Larson	N	Y	Y	N	N	N
2 *Simmons*	Y	Y	Y	Y	Y	Y
3 DeLauro	N	Y	Y	N	N	N
4 *Shays*	Y	Y	Y	Y	Y	Y
5 Maloney	Y	Y	Y	N	N	N
6 *Johnson*	Y	Y	Y	Y	Y	Y
DELAWARE						
AL *Castle*	Y	Y	Y	Y	Y	Y
FLORIDA						
1 *Miller, J.*	Y	Y	N	Y	Y	Y
2 Boyd	N	Y	Y	N	N	N
3 Brown	N	Y	Y	N	N	N
4 *Crenshaw*	Y	Y	Y	Y	Y	Y
5 Thurman	N	Y	Y	N	N	N
6 *Stearns*	Y	Y	Y	Y	Y	Y
7 *Mica*	Y	Y	Y	Y	Y	Y
8 *Keller*	Y	Y	Y	Y	Y	Y
9 *Bilirakis*	Y	Y	Y	Y	Y	Y
10 *Young*	Y	Y	Y	Y	Y	Y
11 Davis	Y	Y	Y	N	N	N
12 *Putnam*	Y	Y	Y	Y	Y	Y
13 *Miller, D.*	Y	Y	Y	Y	Y	Y
14 *Goss*	Y	Y	Y	Y	Y	Y
15 *Weldon*	Y	Y	Y	Y	Y	Y
16 *Foley*	Y	Y	Y	Y	Y	Y
17 Meek	N	Y	Y	N	N	N
18 *Ros-Lehtinen*	Y	Y	Y	Y	Y	Y
19 Wexler	N	Y	Y	N	N	N
20 Deutsch	Y	Y	Y	N	N	N
21 *Diaz-Balart*	Y	Y	Y	Y	Y	Y
22 *Shaw*	Y	Y	Y	Y	Y	Y
23 Hastings	?	?	?	?	?	?
GEORGIA						
1 *Kingston*	Y	Y	N	Y	Y	Y
2 Bishop	Y	Y	Y	N	N	N
3 *Collins*	Y	Y	N	Y	Y	Y
4 McKinney	Y	Y	Y	?	?	?
5 Lewis	N	Y	Y	N	N	N
6 *Isakson*	Y	Y	Y	Y	Y	Y
7 *Barr*	Y	Y	N	?	?	?
8 *Chambliss*	Y	Y	Y	Y	Y	Y
9 *Deal*	?	?	?	?	?	?
10 *Norwood*	Y	Y	Y	Y	Y	Y
11 *Linder*	Y	Y	Y	Y	Y	Y
HAWAII						
1 Abercrombie	Y	Y	Y	?	N	?
2 Vacant						
IDAHO						
1 *Otter*	Y	Y	Y	Y	Y	Y
2 *Simpson*	Y	Y	Y	Y	Y	Y
ILLINOIS						
1 Rush	N	Y	N	N	N	N
2 Jackson	N	Y	N	N	N	N
3 Lipinski	Y	Y	Y	N	N	N
4 Gutierrez	N	Y	?	N	N	N
5 Blagojevich	N	Y	Y	N	N	N
6 *Hyde*	Y	Y	Y	Y	Y	Y
7 Davis	N	Y	N	N	N	N
8 *Crane*	Y	Y	Y	Y	Y	Y
9 Schakowsky	N	Y	N	N	N	N
10 *Kirk*	Y	Y	Y	Y	Y	Y
11 *Weller*	Y	Y	Y	Y	Y	Y
12 Costello	Y	Y	Y	N	N	N
13 *Biggert*	Y	Y	Y	Y	Y	Y

ND Northern Democrats   SD Southern Democrats

	430	431	432	433	434	435
14 ***Hastert***						
15 ***Johnson***	Y	Y	Y	Y	Y	Y
16 ***Manzullo***	Y	Y	Y	Y	Y	Y
17 Evans	N	Y	Y	N	N	N
18 ***LaHood***	Y	Y	Y	Y	Y	Y
19 Phelps	Y	Y	Y	N	N	N
20 ***Shimkus***	Y	Y	Y	Y	Y	Y
INDIANA						
1 Visclosky	N	Y	Y	N	N	N
2 ***Pence***	Y	Y	Y	Y	Y	Y
3 Roemer	Y	Y	Y	N	N	N
4 ***Souder***	Y	Y	Y	Y	Y	Y
5 ***Buyer***	Y	Y	Y	Y	Y	Y
6 ***Burton***	Y	Y	Y	Y	Y	Y
7 ***Kerns***	Y	Y	N	Y	Y	Y
8 ***Hostettler***	Y	Y	N	Y	Y	Y
9 Hill	N	Y	Y	N	N	N
10 Carson	N	Y	Y	N	N	N
IOWA						
1 ***Leach***	Y	Y	Y	Y	Y	Y
2 ***Nussle***	Y	Y	Y	Y	Y	Y
3 Boswell	Y	Y	Y	N	N	N
4 ***Ganske***	Y	Y	Y	?	?	Y
5 ***Latham***	Y	Y	Y	Y	Y	Y
KANSAS						
1 ***Moran***	Y	Y	Y	Y	Y	Y
2 ***Ryun***	Y	Y	Y	Y	Y	Y
3 Moore	Y	Y	Y	N	N	N
4 ***Tiahrt***	Y	Y	Y	Y	Y	Y
KENTUCKY						
1 ***Whitfield***	Y	Y	Y	Y	Y	Y
2 ***Lewis***	Y	Y	Y	Y	Y	Y
3 ***Northup***	Y	Y	Y	Y	N	Y
4 Lucas	Y	Y	Y	N	N	N
5 ***Rogers***	Y	Y	Y	Y	Y	Y
6 ***Fletcher***	Y	Y	Y	Y	Y	Y
LOUISIANA						
1 ***Vitter***	Y	Y	Y	Y	Y	Y
2 Jefferson	Y	Y	Y	N	N	N
3 ***Tauzin***	Y	Y	Y	Y	Y	Y
4 ***McCrery***	Y	Y	Y	Y	Y	Y
5 ***Cooksey***	?	?	?	?	Y	Y
6 ***Baker***	Y	Y	Y	Y	Y	?
7 John	Y	Y	Y	N	N	N
MAINE						
1 Allen	Y	Y	Y	N	N	N
2 Baldacci	Y	Y	Y	N	N	N
MARYLAND						
1 ***Gilchrest***	Y	Y	Y	Y	Y	Y
2 ***Ehrlich***	?	?	?	?	?	?
3 Cardin	N	Y	Y	N	N	N
4 Wynn	Y	Y	Y	N	N	N
5 Hoyer	N	Y	Y	N	N	N
6 ***Bartlett***	Y	Y	Y	Y	Y	Y
7 Cummings	N	Y	Y	N	N	N
8 ***Morella***	Y	Y	Y	Y	N	Y
MASSACHUSETTS						
1 Olver	N	Y	Y	N	N	N
2 Neal	N	Y	Y	N	N	N
3 McGovern	N	Y	Y	N	N	N
4 Frank	N	Y	Y	N	N	N
5 Meehan	N	Y	Y	N	N	N
6 Tierney	N	Y	Y	N	N	N
7 Markey	N	Y	Y	N	N	N
8 Capuano	N	Y	Y	N	N	N
9 Lynch	N	Y	Y	N	N	N
10 Delahunt	N	Y	Y	N	N	N
MICHIGAN						
1 Stupak	Y	Y	Y	N	N	N
2 ***Hoekstra***	Y	Y	Y	Y	Y	Y
3 ***Ehlers***	Y	Y	Y	Y	Y	Y
4 ***Camp***	Y	Y	Y	Y	Y	Y
5 Barcia	Y	Y	Y	N	N	N
6 ***Upton***	Y	Y	Y	Y	Y	Y
7 ***Smith***	Y	Y	Y	Y	Y	Y
8 ***Rogers***	Y	Y	Y	Y	Y	Y
9 Kildee	N	Y	Y	N	N	N
10 Bonior	N	Y	Y	N	N	N
11 ***Knollenberg***	Y	Y	Y	Y	Y	Y
12 Levin	N	Y	Y	N	N	N
13 Rivers	N	Y	Y	N	N	N
14 Conyers	N	Y	Y	N	N	N
15 Kilpatrick	N	Y	Y	N	N	N
16 Dingell	N	Y	Y	N	N	N

	430	431	432	433	434	435
MINNESOTA						
1 ***Gutknecht***	Y	Y	Y	Y	Y	Y
2 ***Kennedy***	Y	Y	Y	Y	Y	Y
3 ***Ramstad***	Y	Y	Y	Y	Y	Y
4 McCollum	N	Y	Y	N	N	N
5 Sabo	N	Y	Y	N	N	?
6 Luther	Y	Y	Y	N	N	N
7 Peterson	Y	Y	Y	N	N	N
8 Oberstar	N	Y	Y	N	N	N
MISSISSIPPI						
1 ***Wicker***	Y	Y	Y	Y	Y	Y
2 Thompson	Y	Y	Y	N	N	N
3 ***Pickering***	Y	Y	Y	Y	Y	Y
4 Shows	Y	Y	Y	N	N	N
5 Taylor	N	Y	Y	N	N	N
MISSOURI						
1 Clay	Y	Y	Y	N	N	N
2 ***Akin***	Y	Y	Y	Y	Y	Y
3 Gephardt	N	Y	Y	N	N	N
4 Skelton	Y	Y	Y	N	?	N
5 McCarthy	N	Y	Y	N	N	N
6 ***Graves***	Y	Y	Y	Y	Y	Y
7 ***Blunt***	Y	Y	Y	Y	Y	Y
8 ***Emerson***	Y	Y	Y	Y	Y	Y
9 ***Hulshof***	Y	Y	Y	Y	Y	Y
MONTANA						
AL ***Rehberg***	Y	Y	Y	Y	Y	Y
NEBRASKA						
1 ***Bereuter***	Y	Y	Y	Y	Y	Y
2 ***Terry***	Y	Y	Y	Y	Y	Y
3 ***Osborne***	Y	Y	Y	Y	Y	Y
NEVADA						
1 Berkley	Y	Y	Y	N	N	N
2 ***Gibbons***	Y	Y	Y	Y	Y	Y
NEW HAMPSHIRE						
1 ***Sununu***	Y	Y	Y	Y	Y	Y
2 ***Bass***	Y	Y	?	Y	Y	Y
NEW JERSEY						
1 Andrews	N	Y	Y	N	N	N
2 ***LoBiondo***	Y	Y	Y	Y	Y	Y
3 ***Saxton***	Y	Y	Y	Y	Y	Y
4 ***Smith***	Y	Y	Y	Y	Y	Y
5 ***Roukema***	?	?	?	?	?	?
6 Pallone	N	Y	Y	N	N	N
7 ***Ferguson***	Y	Y	Y	Y	Y	Y
8 Pascrell	N	Y	Y	N	N	N
9 Rothman	N	Y	Y	N	N	N
10 Payne	N	Y	Y	N	N	N
11 ***Frelinghuysen***	Y	Y	Y	Y	Y	Y
12 Holt	Y	Y	Y	N	N	N
13 Menendez	N	Y	Y	N	N	N
NEW MEXICO						
1 ***Wilson***	Y	Y	Y	Y	Y	Y
2 ***Skeen***	Y	Y	Y	Y	Y	Y
3 Udall	N	Y	Y	N	N	N
NEW YORK						
1 ***Grucci***	Y	Y	Y	Y	Y	Y
2 Israel	Y	Y	Y	N	N	N
3 ***King***	Y	Y	Y	Y	Y	Y
4 McCarthy	Y	Y	Y	N	N	N
5 Ackerman	N	Y	Y	N	N	N
6 Meeks	Y	Y	Y	N	N	N
7 Crowley	N	Y	Y	N	N	N
8 Nadler	N	Y	Y	N	N	N
9 Weiner	N	Y	Y	N	N	N
10 Towns	Y	Y	Y	N	N	N
11 Owens	N	Y	Y	N	N	N
12 Velázquez	N	Y	Y	N	N	N
13 ***Fossella***	Y	Y	Y	Y	Y	Y
14 Maloney	Y	Y	Y	N	N	N
15 Rangel	N	Y	Y	N	N	N
16 Serrano	N	Y	Y	N	N	N
17 Engel	Y	Y	Y	N	N	N
18 Lowey	N	Y	Y	N	N	N
19 ***Kelly***	Y	Y	Y	Y	Y	Y
20 ***Gilman***	?	Y	Y	Y	Y	Y
21 McNulty	Y	Y	Y	N	N	N
22 ***Sweeney***	Y	Y	Y	Y	Y	Y
23 ***Boehlert***	Y	Y	Y	Y	Y	Y
24 ***McHugh***	Y	Y	Y	Y	Y	Y
25 ***Walsh***	Y	Y	Y	Y	Y	Y
26 Hinchey	N	Y	Y	N	N	N
27 ***Reynolds***	Y	Y	Y	Y	Y	Y
28 Slaughter	N	Y	Y	N	N	N
29 LaFalce	N	Y	Y	?	N	N

	430	431	432	433	434	435
30 ***Quinn***	Y	Y	Y	Y	Y	Y
31 ***Houghton***	Y	?	?	Y	Y	Y
NORTH CAROLINA						
1 Clayton	N	?	?	N	N	N
2 Etheridge	Y	Y	Y	N	N	N
3 ***Jones***	Y	Y	Y	Y	Y	Y
4 Price	N	Y	Y	N	N	N
5 ***Burr***	Y	Y	Y	Y	Y	Y
6 ***Coble***	Y	Y	Y	Y	Y	Y
7 McIntyre	Y	Y	Y	N	N	N
8 ***Hayes***	Y	Y	Y	Y	Y	Y
9 ***Myrick***	Y	Y	Y	Y	Y	Y
10 ***Ballenger***	Y	Y	Y	Y	Y	Y
11 ***Taylor***	Y	Y	Y	Y	Y	Y
12 Watt	N	Y	Y	N	N	N
NORTH DAKOTA						
AL Pomeroy	Y	Y	Y	N	N	N
OHIO						
1 ***Chabot***	Y	Y	Y	Y	Y	Y
2 ***Portman***	Y	Y	Y	Y	Y	Y
3 Vacant						
4 ***Oxley***	Y	Y	Y	Y	Y	Y
5 ***Gillmor***	Y	Y	Y	Y	Y	Y
6 Strickland	N	Y	Y	N	N	N
7 ***Hobson***	Y	Y	Y	Y	Y	Y
8 ***Boehner***	Y	Y	Y	Y	Y	Y
9 Kaptur	N	Y	Y	N	N	N
10 Kucinich	N	Y	Y	N	N	N
11 Jones	N	Y	Y	N	N	N
12 ***Tiberi***	Y	Y	Y	Y	Y	Y
13 Brown	N	Y	Y	N	N	N
14 Sawyer	N	Y	Y	N	N	N
15 ***Pryce***	Y	Y	Y	Y	Y	Y
16 ***Regula***	Y	Y	Y	Y	Y	Y
17 Vacant						
18 ***Ney***	Y	Y	Y	Y	Y	Y
19 ***LaTourette***	Y	Y	Y	Y	Y	Y
OKLAHOMA						
1 ***Sullivan***	Y	Y	Y	Y	Y	Y
2 Carson	Y	Y	Y	N	N	N
3 ***Watkins***	Y	Y	Y	?	Y	Y
4 ***Watts***	Y	Y	Y	Y	Y	Y
5 ***Istook***	Y	Y	Y	Y	Y	Y
6 ***Lucas***	Y	Y	Y	Y	Y	Y
OREGON						
1 Wu	Y	Y	Y	N	N	N
2 ***Walden***	Y	Y	Y	Y	Y	Y
3 Blumenauer	N	Y	Y	N	N	N
4 DeFazio	Y	Y	Y	N	N	N
5 Hooley	Y	Y	Y	N	N	N
PENNSYLVANIA						
1 Brady	N	Y	Y	N	N	N
2 Fattah	N	Y	Y	N	N	N
3 Borski	N	Y	Y	N	N	N
4 ***Hart***	Y	Y	Y	Y	Y	Y
5 ***Peterson***	Y	Y	Y	Y	Y	Y
6 Holden	Y	Y	Y	N	N	N
7 ***Weldon***	Y	Y	Y	Y	Y	Y
8 ***Greenwood***	Y	Y	Y	Y	Y	Y
9 ***Shuster, Bill***	Y	Y	Y	Y	Y	Y
10 ***Sherwood***	Y	Y	Y	Y	Y	Y
11 Kanjorski	N	Y	Y	N	N	N
12 Murtha	N	Y	Y	N	N	N
13 Hoeffel	N	Y	Y	N	N	N
14 Coyne	N	Y	Y	N	N	N
15 ***Toomey***	Y	Y	N	Y	Y	Y
16 ***Pitts***	?	?	?	?	?	?
17 ***Gekas***	Y	Y	Y	Y	Y	Y
18 Doyle	Y	Y	Y	N	N	N
19 ***Platts***	Y	Y	Y	Y	Y	Y
20 Mascara	?	?	?	?	?	?
21 ***English***	Y	Y	Y	Y	Y	Y
RHODE ISLAND						
1 Kennedy	Y	Y	Y	N	N	N
2 Langevin	N	Y	Y	N	N	N
SOUTH CAROLINA						
1 ***Brown***	Y	Y	Y	Y	Y	Y
2 ***Wilson***	Y	Y	Y	Y	Y	Y
3 ***Graham***	Y	Y	Y	Y	Y	Y
4 ***DeMint***	Y	Y	Y	Y	Y	Y
5 Spratt	N	Y	Y	N	N	N
6 Clyburn	Y	Y	Y	N	N	N
SOUTH DAKOTA						
AL ***Thune***	Y	Y	Y	Y	Y	Y

	430	431	432	433	434	435
TENNESSEE						
1 ***Jenkins***	Y	Y	Y	Y	Y	Y
2 ***Duncan***	Y	Y	Y	Y	Y	Y
3 ***Wamp***	Y	Y	Y	Y	Y	Y
4 ***Hilleary***	?	?	?	?	?	?
5 Clement	Y	Y	Y	N	N	N
6 Gordon	Y	Y	Y	N	N	N
7 ***Bryant***	Y	Y	Y	Y	Y	Y
8 Tanner	?	?	?	?	?	?
9 Ford	Y	Y	Y	N	N	N
TEXAS						
1 Sandlin	Y	Y	Y	N	N	N
2 Turner	N	Y	Y	N	N	N
3 ***Johnson, Sam***	?	?	?	Y	Y	Y
4 Hall	Y	Y	Y	N	N	N
5 ***Sessions***	Y	Y	Y	Y	Y	Y
6 ***Barton***	Y	Y	Y	Y	Y	Y
7 ***Culberson***	Y	Y	N	Y	Y	Y
8 ***Brady***	Y	Y	Y	Y	Y	Y
9 Lampson	?	?	?	?	?	?
10 Doggett	N	Y	Y	N	N	N
11 Edwards	Y	Y	Y	N	N	N
12 ***Granger***	Y	Y	Y	Y	Y	Y
13 ***Thornberry***	Y	Y	N	Y	Y	Y
14 ***Paul***	Y	Y	N	Y	Y	Y
15 Hinojosa	Y	Y	Y	N	N	N
16 Reyes	N	Y	Y	N	N	N
17 Stenholm	N	Y	Y	N	N	N
18 Jackson-Lee	N	Y	Y	N	N	N
19 ***Combest***	Y	Y	Y	Y	Y	Y
20 Gonzalez	N	Y	Y	N	N	N
21 ***Smith***	Y	Y	Y	Y	Y	Y
22 ***DeLay***	Y	Y	Y	Y	Y	Y
23 ***Bonilla***	Y	Y	N	Y	Y	Y
24 Frost	N	Y	Y	N	N	N
25 Bentsen	N	Y	Y	N	N	N
26 ***Armey***	Y	Y	Y	Y	Y	Y
27 Ortiz	N	Y	Y	N	N	N
28 Rodriguez	N	Y	Y	N	N	N
29 Green	N	Y	Y	N	N	N
30 Johnson, E.B.	N	Y	Y	N	N	N
UTAH						
1 ***Hansen***	Y	Y	Y	Y	Y	Y
2 Matheson	Y	Y	Y	N	N	N
3 ***Cannon***	Y	Y	Y	Y	Y	Y
VERMONT						
AL *Sanders*	Y	Y	Y	N	N	N
VIRGINIA						
1 ***Davis, Jo Ann***	Y	Y	Y	Y	Y	Y
2 ***Schrock***	Y	Y	Y	Y	Y	Y
3 Scott	N	Y	Y	N	N	N
4 ***Forbes***	Y	Y	Y	Y	Y	Y
5 ***Goode***	Y	Y	N	Y	Y	Y
6 ***Goodlatte***	Y	Y	Y	Y	Y	Y
7 ***Cantor***	Y	Y	Y	Y	Y	Y
8 Moran	N	Y	Y	N	N	N
9 Boucher	Y	Y	Y	N	N	N
10 ***Wolf***	Y	Y	Y	Y	Y	Y
11 ***Davis, T.***	Y	Y	Y	?	Y	Y
WASHINGTON						
1 Inslee	N	Y	Y	N	N	N
2 Larsen	N	Y	Y	N	N	N
3 Baird	Y	Y	Y	N	N	N
4 ***Hastings***	Y	Y	Y	Y	Y	Y
5 ***Nethercutt***	Y	Y	Y	Y	Y	Y
6 Dicks	Y	Y	Y	N	N	N
7 McDermott	N	Y	Y	N	N	N
8 ***Dunn***	Y	Y	Y	Y	Y	Y
9 Smith	Y	Y	Y	N	N	N
WEST VIRGINIA						
1 Mollohan	N	Y	Y	N	N	N
2 ***Capito***	Y	Y	Y	Y	Y	Y
3 Rahall	?	?	Y	N	N	N
WISCONSIN						
1 ***Ryan***	Y	Y	Y	Y	Y	Y
2 Baldwin	N	Y	Y	N	N	N
3 Kind	Y	Y	Y	N	N	N
4 Kleczka	N	Y	Y	N	N	N
5 Barrett	Y	Y	Y	N	N	N
6 ***Petri***	Y	Y	Y	Y	Y	Y
7 Obey	N	Y	Y	N	N	N
8 ***Green***	Y	Y	Y	Y	Y	Y
9 ***Sensenbrenner***	Y	Y	Y	Y	Y	Y
WYOMING						
AL ***Cubin***	Y	Y	Y	Y	Y	Y

Southern states - Ala., Ark., Fla., Ga., Ky., La., Miss., N.C., Okla., S.C., Tenn., Texas, Va.

Key

Y	Voted for (yea).
#	Paired for.
+	Announced for.
N	Voted against (nay).
X	Paired against.
−	Announced against.
P	Voted "present."
C	Voted "present" to avoid possible conflict of interest.
?	Did not vote or otherwise make a position known.

Democrats   **Republicans**
Independents

436. Question of Privilege/Ruling of the Chair. LaHood, R-Ill., motion to table (kill) the Obey, D-Wis., appeal of the ruling of the chair that the Obey resolution does not constitute a point of privilege under Rule IX of the House. The Obey resolution would express the sense of the House that Congress should complete the fiscal 2003 Labor, Health, and Human Services spending bill (HR 5320) before adjournment and fund last year's education overhaul legislation (PL 107-110) at promised levels because failure to do so would discredit the institution. Motion agreed to 212-202: R 212-0; D 0-201 (ND 0-151, SD 0-50); I 0-1. Oct. 2, 2002.

437. Procedural Motion/Journal. Approval of the House Journal of Wednesday, Oct. 2, 2002. Approved 327-53: R 176-14; D 150-39 (ND 112-33, SD 38-6); I 1-0. Oct. 3, 2002.

438. H J Res 112. Fiscal 2003 Continuing Appropriations/Previous Question. Hastings, R-Wash., motion to order the previous question (thus ending debate and possibility of amendment) on adoption of the rule (H Res 568) to provide for House floor consideration of the joint resolution to provide continuing appropriations through Oct. 11 for all federal departments and programs. Motion agreed to 206-198: R 206-0; D 0-197 (ND 0-149, SD 0-48); I 0-1. Subsequently, the rule was adopted by voice vote. Oct. 3, 2002.

439. H J Res 112. Fiscal 2003 Continuing Appropriations/Passage. Passage of the joint resolution to provide continuing appropriations through Oct. 11 for all federal departments and programs at fiscal 2002 levels, including that year's supplemental appropriations. Passed 404-7: R 210-2; D 193-5 (ND 144-5, SD 49-0); I 1-0. Oct. 3, 2002.

440. Question of Privilege/Ruling of the Chair. Hulshof, R-Mo., motion to table (kill) the Farr, D-Calif., appeal of the ruling of the chair that the Farr resolution does not constitute a point of privilege under Rule IX of the House. The Farr resolution would express the sense of the House that Congress should complete work on a bill (HR 854) that would repeal cuts in payments to hospitals that serve low-income patients or other reimbursement legislation and ensure necessary Medicare and Medicaid funding. Motion agreed to 206-192: R 206-0; D 0-191 (ND 0-143, SD 0-48); I 0-1. Oct. 3, 2002.

441. Question of Privilege/Ruling of the Chair. Rogers, R-Mich., motion to table (kill) the Carson, D-Ind., appeal of the ruling of the chair that the Carson resolution does not constitute a point of privilege under Rule IX of the House. The Carson resolution would express the sense of the House that Congress should complete work on the fiscal 2003 Transportation Department appropriations bill, with $1.2 billion in spending for Amtrak. Motion agreed to 203-192: R 203-0; D 0-191 (ND 0-144, SD 0-47); I 0-1. Oct. 3, 2002.

	436	437	438	439	440	441
ALABAMA						
1 *Callahan*	Y	?	?	?	?	?
2 *Everett*	Y	Y	Y	Y	Y	Y
3 *Riley*	Y	Y	Y	Y	Y	Y
4 *Aderholt*	?	?	+	Y	Y	Y
5 Cramer	N	Y	N	Y	N	N
6 *Bachus*	Y	Y	Y	Y	Y	Y
7 Hilliard	N	N	N	Y	N	N
ALASKA						
AL *Young*	Y	?	Y	Y	Y	Y
ARIZONA						
1 *Flake*	Y	Y	Y	Y	Y	Y
2 Pastor	N	N	N	Y	N	N
3 *Stump*	?	?	?	?	?	?
4 *Shadegg*	Y	Y	Y	Y	Y	Y
5 *Kolbe*	Y	Y	Y	Y	Y	Y
6 *Hayworth*	Y	Y	Y	Y	Y	Y
ARKANSAS						
1 Berry	N	Y	N	Y	N	N
2 Snyder	N	Y	N	Y	N	N
3 *Boozman*	Y	Y	Y	Y	Y	Y
4 Ross	N	Y	N	Y	N	N
CALIFORNIA						
1 Thompson	N	N	N	Y	N	N
2 *Herger*	Y	?	Y	Y	Y	Y
3 *Ose*	Y	Y	Y	Y	Y	Y
4 *Doolittle*	Y	Y	Y	Y	Y	Y
5 Matsui	N	Y	N	Y	N	N
6 Woolsey	N	Y	N	Y	N	N
7 Miller, George	N	N	N	N	N	N
8 Pelosi	N	Y	N	Y	N	N
9 Lee	N	Y	N	Y	N	N
10 Tauscher	Y	Y	Y	Y	Y	Y
11 Pombo	Y	Y	Y	Y	Y	Y
12 Lantos	N	?	N	Y	N	N
13 Stark	N	Y	N	Y	N	?
14 Eshoo	N	Y	N	Y	N	N
15 Honda	N	Y	N	Y	N	N
16 Lofgren	N	Y	N	Y	N	N
17 Farr	N	Y	N	Y	N	N
18 Condit	N	Y	N	Y	N	N
19 *Radanovich*	Y	Y	Y	Y	Y	Y
20 Dooley	N	N	N	Y	N	N
21 *Thomas*	N	?	Y	Y	Y	Y
22 Capps	N	Y	N	Y	N	N
23 *Gallegly*	Y	Y	Y	Y	Y	Y
24 Sherman	N	?	N	Y	N	N
25 *McKeon*	Y	Y	Y	Y	Y	Y
26 Berman	N	Y	N	Y	N	N
27 Schiff	N	Y	N	Y	N	N
28 *Dreier*	Y	Y	Y	Y	Y	Y
29 Waxman	N	Y	?	Y	N	N
30 Becerra	N	Y	N	Y	N	N
31 Solis	N	Y	N	Y	N	N
32 Watson	N	Y	N	Y	N	N
33 Roybal-Allard	N	Y	?	Y	N	N
34 Napolitano	N	Y	?	Y	N	N
35 Waters	N	N	N	Y	N	N
36 Harman	N	Y	N	Y	N	N
37 Millender-McD.	N	Y	N	Y	N	N
38 *Horn*	Y	Y	Y	Y	Y	Y

	436	437	438	439	440	441
39 *Royce*	Y	Y	Y	Y	Y	Y
40 *Lewis*	Y	Y	Y	?	?	?
41 *Miller, Gary*	Y	Y	Y	Y	Y	Y
42 Baca	N	Y	N	Y	N	N
43 *Calvert*	Y	Y	Y	Y	Y	Y
44 *Bono*	Y	Y	Y	Y	Y	Y
45 *Rohrabacher*	Y	Y	Y	Y	Y	Y
46 Sanchez	N	Y	N	Y	N	N
47 *Cox*	Y	Y	Y	Y	?	Y
48 *Issa*	Y	Y	Y	Y	Y	Y
49 Davis	N	Y	N	Y	N	N
50 Filner	N	N	N	Y	N	N
51 *Cunningham*	Y	Y	Y	Y	Y	Y
52 *Hunter*	Y	Y	Y	Y	Y	Y
COLORADO						
1 DeGette	N	Y	N	Y	?	?
2 Udall	N	Y	N	Y	N	N
3 *McInnis*	Y	Y	Y	Y	?	?
4 *Schaffer*	Y	N	Y	Y	Y	Y
5 *Hefley*	Y	N	Y	Y	?	?
6 *Tancredo*	Y	?	Y	Y	Y	Y
CONNECTICUT						
1 Larson	N	Y	N	Y	N	N
2 *Simmons*	Y	Y	Y	Y	Y	Y
3 DeLauro	N	Y	N	Y	N	N
4 *Shays*	Y	Y	Y	Y	Y	Y
5 Maloney	N	Y	N	Y	−	−
6 *Johnson*	Y	Y	Y	Y	Y	Y
DELAWARE						
AL *Castle*	Y	Y	Y	Y	Y	Y
FLORIDA						
1 *Miller, J.*	Y	Y	Y	Y	Y	Y
2 Boyd	N	Y	N	Y	N	N
3 Brown	N	N	N	Y	N	N
4 *Crenshaw*	Y	Y	Y	Y	Y	Y
5 Thurman	N	Y	N	Y	N	?
6 *Stearns*	Y	Y	Y	Y	Y	Y
7 *Mica*	Y	Y	Y	Y	Y	Y
8 *Keller*	Y	Y	Y	Y	?	?
9 *Bilirakis*	Y	Y	Y	Y	Y	Y
10 *Young*	Y	Y	Y	Y	Y	Y
11 Davis	N	Y	N	Y	N	N
12 *Putnam*	Y	Y	Y	Y	Y	Y
13 *Miller, D.*	Y	Y	Y	Y	Y	Y
14 *Goss*	Y	?	Y	Y	Y	Y
15 *Weldon*	Y	Y	Y	Y	Y	Y
16 *Foley*	Y	Y	Y	Y	Y	Y
17 Meek	N	?	N	Y	N	N
18 *Ros-Lehtinen*	Y	?	Y	Y	Y	Y
19 Wexler	N	Y	N	Y	N	N
20 Deutsch	N	Y	N	Y	N	N
21 *Diaz-Balart*	Y	?	Y	Y	Y	Y
22 *Shaw*	Y	Y	Y	Y	Y	Y
23 Hastings	?	?	?	?	?	?
GEORGIA						
1 *Kingston*	Y	Y	Y	Y	Y	Y
2 Bishop	N	Y	N	Y	N	N
3 *Collins*	Y	Y	Y	Y	Y	Y
4 *McKinney*	?	?	?	Y	?	?
5 Lewis	N	Y	N	Y	N	N
6 *Isakson*	Y	Y	Y	Y	Y	Y
7 *Barr*	Y	Y	Y	Y	Y	Y
8 *Chambliss*	Y	Y	Y	Y	Y	Y
9 *Deal*	?	?	?	?	?	?
10 *Norwood*	Y	Y	Y	Y	Y	Y
11 *Linder*	Y	Y	Y	Y	?	?
HAWAII						
1 Abercrombie	N	Y	N	Y	N	N
2 Vacant						
IDAHO						
1 *Otter*	Y	N	Y	Y	Y	Y
2 *Simpson*	Y	Y	Y	Y	Y	Y
ILLINOIS						
1 Rush	N	N	N	Y	N	N
2 Jackson	N	Y	N	Y	N	N
3 Lipinski	N	Y	N	Y	N	N
4 Gutierrez	N	Y	N	Y	N	N
5 Blagojevich	N	Y	N	Y	N	N
6 *Hyde*	Y	?	Y	Y	Y	Y
7 Davis	N	Y	N	Y	N	N
8 *Crane*	Y	N	Y	Y	Y	Y
9 Schakowsky	N	N	N	Y	N	N
10 *Kirk*	Y	?	Y	Y	Y	Y
11 *Weller*	Y	Y	Y	Y	Y	Y
12 Costello	N	N	N	Y	N	N
13 *Biggert*	Y	Y	Y	Y	Y	Y

ND Northern Democrats   SD Southern Democrats

	436	437	438	439	440	441
14 *Hastert*					Y	
15 *Johnson*	Y	Y	Y	Y	Y	Y
16 *Manzullo*	Y	Y	Y	Y	Y	Y
17 Evans	N	Y	N	Y	N	N
18 *LaHood*	Y	Y	Y	Y	Y	Y
19 Phelps	N	Y	N	Y	N	N
20 *Shimkus*	Y	Y	Y	Y	Y	Y
INDIANA						
1 Visclosky	N	N	N	Y	N	N
2 *Pence*	Y	Y	Y	Y	Y	Y
3 Roemer	N	Y	N	Y	N	N
4 *Souder*	Y	?	?	Y	Y	Y
5 *Buyer*	Y	Y	Y	Y	Y	Y
6 *Burton*	Y	Y	Y	Y	Y	Y
7 *Kerns*	Y	Y	Y	Y	Y	Y
8 *Hostettler*	Y	Y	Y	Y	Y	Y
9 Hill	N	Y	N	Y	N	N
10 Carson	N	Y	N	Y	N	N
IOWA						
1 *Leach*	Y	Y	Y	Y	Y	Y
2 *Nussle*	Y	N	Y	N	Y	Y
3 Boswell	N	Y	N	Y	N	N
4 *Ganske*	Y	Y	Y	Y	?	?
5 *Latham*	Y	Y	Y	Y	Y	Y
KANSAS						
1 *Moran*	Y	Y	Y	Y	Y	Y
2 *Ryun*	Y	Y	Y	Y	Y	Y
3 Moore	N	N	N	Y	N	N
4 *Tiahrt*	Y	Y	Y	Y	Y	Y
KENTUCKY						
1 *Whitfield*	Y	?	Y	Y	Y	?
2 *Lewis*	Y	Y	Y	Y	Y	Y
3 *Northup*	Y	?	Y	Y	Y	Y
4 Lucas	N	Y	N	Y	N	N
5 *Rogers*	Y	Y	Y	Y	Y	Y
6 *Fletcher*	Y	Y	Y	Y	Y	Y
LOUISIANA						
1 *Vitter*	Y	Y	Y	Y	Y	Y
2 Jefferson	N	Y	N	Y	N	N
3 *Tauzin*	Y	Y	?	Y	Y	Y
4 *McCrery*	Y	Y	Y	Y	Y	Y
5 *Cooksey*	Y	?	?	?	?	?
6 *Baker*	?	?	?	?	?	?
7 John	N	Y	N	Y	N	N
MAINE						
1 Allen	N	Y	N	Y	N	N
2 Baldacci	N	?	N	Y	N	N
MARYLAND						
1 *Gilchrest*	Y	Y	Y	Y	Y	Y
2 *Ehrlich*	?	?	Y	Y	Y	Y
3 Cardin	N	Y	N	Y	N	N
4 Wynn	N	Y	N	Y	N	N
5 Hoyer	N	Y	N	Y	N	N
6 *Bartlett*	Y	Y	Y	Y	Y	Y
7 Cummings	N	Y	N	Y	N	N
8 *Morella*	Y	Y	Y	Y	Y	Y
MASSACHUSETTS						
1 Olver	N	N	N	Y	N	N
2 Neal	N	Y	N	Y	N	N
3 McGovern	N	N	N	Y	N	N
4 Frank	N	Y	N	Y	N	N
5 Meehan	N	Y	N	Y	N	N
6 Tierney	N	Y	N	?	N	N
7 Markey	N	N	N	Y	N	N
8 Capuano	N	N	N	Y	N	N
9 Lynch	N	Y	N	Y	N	N
10 Delahunt	N	?	N	Y	N	N
MICHIGAN						
1 Stupak	N	N	N	Y	?	?
2 *Hoekstra*	Y	Y	Y	Y	?	Y
3 *Ehlers*	Y	Y	+	Y	Y	Y
4 *Camp*	Y	Y	Y	Y	Y	Y
5 Barcia	N	Y	N	Y	?	?
6 *Upton*	Y	Y	Y	Y	Y	Y
7 *Smith*	Y	Y	Y	Y	Y	Y
8 *Rogers*	Y	Y	Y	Y	Y	Y
9 Kildee	N	Y	N	Y	N	N
10 Bonior	N	Y	N	?	N	N
11 *Knollenberg*	Y	Y	Y	Y	Y	Y
12 Levin	N	Y	N	Y	N	N
13 Rivers	N	Y	N	Y	N	N
14 Conyers	?	Y	N	Y	N	N
15 Kilpatrick	N	Y	N	Y	N	N
16 Dingell	N	Y	N	Y	N	N

	436	437	438	439	440	441
MINNESOTA						
1 *Gutknecht*	Y	N	Y	Y	?	Y
2 *Kennedy*	Y	N	+	Y	Y	Y
3 *Ramstad*	Y	N	Y	Y	Y	Y
4 McCollum	N	Y	N	Y	N	N
5 Sabo	N	N	N	Y	N	N
6 Luther	N	Y	N	Y	N	N
7 Peterson	N	N	N	Y	N	N
8 Oberstar	N	N	N	N	N	N
MISSISSIPPI						
1 *Wicker*	Y	Y	Y	Y	Y	Y
2 Thompson	N	N	N	Y	N	N
3 *Pickering*	?	Y	Y	Y	Y	Y
4 Shows	N	Y	N	Y	N	N
5 Taylor	N	N	N	Y	N	N
MISSOURI						
1 Clay	N	?	N	Y	N	N
2 *Akin*	Y	Y	Y	Y	Y	Y
3 Gephardt	N	Y	N	Y	N	N
4 Skelton	N	Y	N	Y	N	N
5 McCarthy	N	Y	N	Y	N	N
6 *Graves*	Y	Y	Y	Y	Y	Y
7 *Blunt*	Y	Y	Y	Y	Y	Y
8 *Emerson*	Y	Y	Y	Y	Y	Y
9 *Hulshof*	Y	N	Y	Y	Y	Y
MONTANA						
AL *Rehberg*	Y	Y	Y	Y	Y	Y
NEBRASKA						
1 *Bereuter*	Y	Y	Y	Y	Y	Y
2 *Terry*	Y	Y	Y	Y	Y	Y
3 *Osborne*	Y	Y	Y	Y	Y	Y
NEVADA						
1 Berkley	N	Y	N	Y	N	N
2 *Gibbons*	Y	Y	Y	Y	Y	Y
NEW HAMPSHIRE						
1 *Sununu*	Y	Y	Y	Y	Y	Y
2 *Bass*	Y	Y	Y	Y	Y	Y
NEW JERSEY						
1 Andrews	N	Y	N	Y	N	N
2 *LoBiondo*	Y	N	Y	Y	Y	Y
3 *Saxton*	Y	Y	Y	Y	Y	Y
4 *Smith*	Y	Y	Y	Y	Y	Y
5 *Roukema*	?	?	?	?	?	?
6 Pallone	N	N	N	Y	N	N
7 *Ferguson*	Y	Y	Y	Y	Y	Y
8 Pascrell	N	Y	N	Y	N	N
9 Rothman	N	Y	N	Y	N	N
10 Payne	N	Y	N	Y	N	N
11 *Frelinghuysen*	Y	Y	Y	Y	Y	Y
12 Holt	N	Y	N	Y	N	N
13 Menendez	N	Y	N	Y	N	N
NEW MEXICO						
1 *Wilson*	Y	Y	Y	Y	Y	Y
2 *Skeen*	Y	Y	Y	Y	Y	Y
3 Udall	N	N	N	Y	N	N
NEW YORK						
1 *Grucci*	Y	Y	Y	Y	Y	Y
2 Israel	N	Y	N	Y	N	N
3 *King*	Y	Y	Y	Y	Y	Y
4 McCarthy	N	Y	N	Y	N	N
5 Ackerman	N	Y	N	Y	N	N
6 Meeks	N	Y	N	Y	N	N
7 Crowley	N	Y	N	Y	N	N
8 Nadler	N	Y	N	Y	N	N
9 Weiner	N	Y	N	Y	N	N
10 Towns	N	N	N	Y	?	?
11 Owens	N	Y	N	N	N	N
12 Velázquez	N	N	N	Y	N	N
13 *Fossella*	Y	Y	Y	Y	Y	Y
14 Maloney	N	Y	N	Y	N	N
15 Rangel	N	Y	N	Y	N	N
16 Serrano	N	Y	N	Y	N	N
17 Engel	N	Y	N	Y	N	N
18 Lowey	N	Y	N	Y	N	N
19 *Kelly*	Y	Y	Y	Y	Y	Y
20 *Gilman*	?	Y	Y	Y	Y	Y
21 McNulty	N	N	N	Y	N	N
22 *Sweeney*	Y	N	Y	Y	Y	Y
23 *Boehlert*	Y	Y	Y	?	Y	Y
24 *McHugh*	Y	Y	Y	Y	Y	Y
25 *Walsh*	Y	Y	Y	Y	Y	Y
26 Hinchey	N	Y	N	Y	N	N
27 *Reynolds*	Y	Y	Y	Y	Y	?
28 Slaughter	N	Y	N	Y	?	?
29 LaFalce	N	Y	N	Y	?	N

	436	437	438	439	440	441
30 *Quinn*	Y	Y	Y	Y	Y	Y
31 *Houghton*	Y	?	Y	Y	Y	Y
NORTH CAROLINA						
1 Clayton	N	?	?	Y	N	N
2 Etheridge	N	N	N	Y	N	N
3 *Jones*	Y	Y	Y	Y	Y	Y
4 Price	N	Y	N	Y	N	N
5 *Burr*	Y	Y	Y	Y	Y	Y
6 *Coble*	Y	Y	Y	Y	Y	Y
7 McIntyre	N	Y	N	Y	N	N
8 *Hayes*	Y	Y	Y	Y	Y	Y
9 *Myrick*	Y	?	?	Y	Y	Y
10 *Ballenger*	Y	Y	Y	Y	Y	Y
11 *Taylor*	Y	Y	Y	Y	Y	Y
12 Watt	N	Y	N	Y	N	N
NORTH DAKOTA						
AL Pomeroy	N	Y	N	Y	N	N
OHIO						
1 *Chabot*	Y	Y	Y	Y	Y	Y
2 *Portman*	Y	Y	Y	Y	Y	Y
3 Vacant						
4 *Oxley*	Y	Y	Y	Y	Y	?
5 *Gillmor*	Y	N	Y	Y	Y	Y
6 Strickland	N	N	N	Y	N	N
7 *Hobson*	Y	Y	Y	Y	Y	Y
8 *Boehner*	Y	Y	Y	Y	Y	?
9 Kaptur	N	Y	N	Y	N	N
10 Kucinich	N	N	N	Y	N	N
11 Jones	N	Y	N	Y	N	N
12 *Tiberi*	Y	Y	Y	Y	Y	Y
13 Brown	N	Y	N	Y	N	N
14 Sawyer	N	Y	N	Y	?	?
15 *Pryce*	Y	Y	Y	Y	Y	Y
16 *Regula*	Y	Y	Y	Y	Y	Y
17 Vacant						
18 *Ney*	Y	Y	Y	Y	Y	Y
19 *LaTourette*	Y	Y	Y	Y	Y	Y
OKLAHOMA						
1 *Sullivan*	Y	Y	+	Y	Y	Y
2 Carson	N	Y	N	Y	N	N
3 *Watkins*	Y	Y	Y	Y	Y	Y
4 *Watts*	Y	Y	Y	Y	Y	Y
5 *Istook*	Y	Y	Y	Y	Y	Y
6 *Lucas*	Y	Y	Y	Y	Y	Y
OREGON						
1 Wu	N	N	N	Y	N	N
2 *Walden*	Y	Y	Y	Y	Y	Y
3 Blumenauer	N	?	N	Y	N	N
4 DeFazio	N	N	N	N	N	N
5 Hooley	N	Y	N	Y	N	N
PENNSYLVANIA						
1 Brady	N	N	N	Y	N	N
2 Fattah	N	?	?	?	?	?
3 Borski	N	N	N	Y	N	N
4 *Hart*	Y	Y	Y	Y	Y	Y
5 *Peterson*	Y	Y	Y	Y	Y	Y
6 Holden	N	Y	N	Y	N	N
7 *Weldon*	Y	Y	Y	Y	Y	Y
8 *Greenwood*	Y	Y	Y	Y	Y	Y
9 *Shuster, Bill*	Y	Y	Y	Y	Y	Y
10 *Sherwood*	Y	Y	Y	Y	Y	Y
11 Kanjorski	N	Y	N	Y	N	N
12 Murtha	?	Y	N	Y	N	N
13 Hoeffel	N	Y	N	Y	N	N
14 Coyne	N	Y	N	Y	N	N
15 *Toomey*	Y	Y	Y	Y	Y	Y
16 *Pitts*	?	?	Y	Y	Y	Y
17 *Gekas*	Y	?	Y	Y	Y	Y
18 Doyle	N	Y	N	Y	N	N
19 *Platts*	Y	?	+	Y	Y	Y
20 Mascara	?	?	?	?	?	?
21 *English*	Y	N	Y	Y	Y	Y
RHODE ISLAND						
1 Kennedy	N	Y	N	Y	N	N
2 Langevin	N	Y	N	Y	N	N
SOUTH CAROLINA						
1 *Brown*	Y	Y	Y	Y	Y	Y
2 *Wilson*	Y	?	Y	Y	Y	Y
3 *Graham*	Y	Y	Y	Y	Y	Y
4 *DeMint*	Y	Y	Y	Y	Y	Y
5 Spratt	N	Y	N	Y	N	N
6 Clyburn	N	Y	N	Y	N	N
SOUTH DAKOTA						
AL *Thune*	Y	Y	Y	Y	Y	Y

	436	437	438	439	440	441
TENNESSEE						
1 *Jenkins*	Y	Y	Y	Y	Y	?
2 *Duncan*	Y	Y	Y	Y	Y	Y
3 *Wamp*	Y	Y	Y	Y	Y	Y
4 *Hilleary*	?	?	?	?	?	?
5 Clement	N	Y	N	?	?	?
6 Gordon	N	Y	N	Y	N	N
7 *Bryant*	Y	Y	Y	Y	Y	Y
8 Tanner	?	?	?	?	?	?
9 Ford	N	N	N	Y	N	N
TEXAS						
1 Sandlin	N	Y	N	Y	N	N
2 Turner	N	Y	N	Y	N	N
3 *Johnson, Sam*	Y	Y	Y	Y	Y	Y
4 Hall	N	Y	N	Y	N	N
5 *Sessions*	Y	Y	Y	Y	Y	Y
6 *Barton*	Y	Y	Y	Y	Y	Y
7 *Culberson*	Y	Y	Y	Y	Y	Y
8 *Brady*	Y	Y	Y	Y	Y	Y
9 Lampson	?	?	?	?	?	?
10 Doggett	N	Y	N	Y	N	N
11 Edwards	N	Y	N	Y	N	N
12 *Granger*	Y	Y	Y	Y	Y	?
13 *Thornberry*	Y	Y	Y	Y	Y	Y
14 *Paul*	Y	Y	Y	N	Y	Y
15 Hinojosa	N	Y	N	Y	N	N
16 Reyes	N	?	N	Y	N	N
17 Stenholm	N	Y	N	Y	N	N
18 Jackson-Lee	N	Y	N	Y	N	N
19 *Combest*	Y	Y	Y	Y	Y	Y
20 Gonzalez	N	Y	N	Y	N	N
21 *Smith*	Y	Y	Y	Y	Y	Y
22 *DeLay*	Y	?	Y	Y	Y	Y
23 *Bonilla*	Y	?	Y	Y	Y	Y
24 Frost	N	Y	N	Y	N	N
25 Bentsen	N	Y	N	Y	N	N
26 *Armey*	Y	Y	Y	Y	Y	Y
27 Ortiz	N	Y	N	Y	N	N
28 Rodriguez	N	Y	N	Y	N	N
29 Green	N	?	?	?	?	?
30 Johnson, E.B.	N	N	N	Y	N	N
UTAH						
1 *Hansen*	Y	Y	Y	Y	Y	Y
2 Matheson	N	Y	N	Y	N	N
3 *Cannon*	Y	Y	Y	Y	Y	Y
VERMONT						
AL *Sanders*	N	Y	N	Y	N	N
VIRGINIA						
1 *Davis, Jo Ann*	Y	Y	Y	Y	Y	Y
2 *Schrock*	Y	?	?	?	?	?
3 Scott	N	?	N	Y	N	N
4 *Forbes*	Y	Y	Y	Y	Y	Y
5 *Goode*	Y	Y	Y	Y	Y	Y
6 *Goodlatte*	Y	Y	Y	Y	Y	Y
7 *Cantor*	Y	Y	Y	Y	Y	Y
8 Moran	N	Y	N	Y	N	N
9 Boucher	N	?	N	Y	N	N
10 *Wolf*	Y	Y	Y	Y	Y	Y
11 *Davis, T.*	Y	Y	?	Y	Y	Y
WASHINGTON						
1 Inslee	N	Y	N	Y	N	N
2 Larsen	N	N	N	?	N	N
3 Baird	N	N	N	Y	N	N
4 *Hastings*	Y	Y	Y	Y	Y	Y
5 *Nethercutt*	Y	Y	Y	Y	Y	Y
6 Dicks	N	Y	N	Y	N	N
7 McDermott	N	N	N	N	N	N
8 *Dunn*	Y	Y	Y	Y	Y	Y
9 Smith	N	?	N	Y	N	N
WEST VIRGINIA						
1 Mollohan	N	Y	N	Y	N	N
2 *Capito*	Y	Y	Y	Y	Y	Y
3 Rahall	N	Y	N	Y	N	N
WISCONSIN						
1 *Ryan*	Y	Y	Y	Y	Y	Y
2 Baldwin	N	N	N	Y	N	N
3 Kind	N	Y	N	Y	N	N
4 Kleczka	N	Y	N	Y	?	N
5 Barrett	N	Y	N	Y	N	N
6 *Petri*	Y	Y	Y	Y	Y	Y
7 Obey	N	N	N	Y	N	N
8 *Green*	Y	Y	Y	Y	Y	Y
9 *Sensenbrenner*	Y	Y	Y	Y	Y	Y
WYOMING						
AL *Cubin*	Y	Y	Y	Y	Y	Y

Southern states - Ala., Ark., Fla., Ga., Ky., La., Miss., N.C., Okla., S.C., Tenn., Texas, Va.

442. HR 3340. Federal Retiree Contributions/Passage. Morella, R-Md., motion to suspend the rules and pass the bill that would allow federal employees 50 and older to make "catch-up" contributions to their tax-deferred, employer-sponsored retirement saving plans. Their contribution limit would increase annually until 2006, after which it would remain at $5,000 above the limit for younger employees. Motion agreed to 372-0: R 193-0; D 178-0 (ND 131-0, SD 47-0); I 1-0. A two-thirds majority of those present and voting (248 in this case) is required for passage under suspension of the rules. Oct. 7, 2002.

443. HR 5531. Sudan Aid/Passage. Smith, R-N.J., motion to suspend the rules and pass the bill that would authorize $100 million annually through fiscal 2005 for aid to areas of Sudan not controlled by the government. It also contains provisions aimed at supporting an internationally sanctioned peace process in Sudan. Motion agreed to 359-8: R 186-6; D 172-2 (ND 126-0, SD 46-2); I 1-0. A two-thirds majority of those present and voting (245 in this case) is required for passage under suspension of the rules. Oct. 7, 2002.

444. H Res 468. NATO Expansion/Adoption. Gallegly, R-Calif., motion to suspend the rules and adopt the resolution that would reaffirm U.S. support for the North Atlantic Treaty Organization (NATO) and support its expansion. It also would urge NATO to increase its cooperation with Russia and upgrade its military capabilities. Motion agreed to 358-9: R 187-4; D 170-5 (ND 122-5, SD 48-0); I 1-0. A two-thirds majority of those present and voting (246 in this case) is required for adoption under suspension of the rules. Oct. 7, 2002.

445. S 2690. Pledge of Allegiance Reaffirmation/Passage. Sensenbrenner, R-Wis., motion to suspend the rules and pass the bill that would reaffirm the Pledge of Allegiance and the reference to "one nation under God" as well as the national motto of "In God We Trust." Motion agreed to 401-5: R 212-0; D 188-5 (ND 140-4, SD 48-1); I 1-0. A two-thirds majority of those present and voting (274 in this case) is required for passage under suspension of the rules. Oct. 8, 2002.

446. HR 5422. Protection of Minors/Passage. Sensenbrenner, R-Wis., motion to suspend the rules and pass the bill that would increase the federal role in an alert system on missing children; increase penalties and post-imprisonment supervision time for those convicted of specific crimes against children; and criminalize traveling into the United States or to a foreign country to engage in illicit sexual conduct with a minor. It also would allow federal law enforcement agents to obtain wiretaps in their investigation of certain crimes against children. Motion agreed to 390-24: R 211-1; D 178-23 (ND 131-18, SD 47-5); I 1-0. A two-thirds majority of those present and voting (276 in this case) is required for passage under suspension of the rules. Oct. 8, 2002.

447. H Res 549. Great Britain Tribute/Adoption. Gilman, R-N.Y., motion to suspend the rules and adopt the resolution that would express the thanks of the House for the leadership of British Prime Minister Tony Blair in the war against terrorism, commend British intelligence and law enforcement anti-terrorism efforts, and express sympathy for British victims of the Sept. 11, 2001, terrorist attacks. Motion agreed to 408-1: R 209-0; D 198-1 (ND 147-0, SD 51-1); I 1-0. A two-thirds majority of those present and voting (274 in this case) is required for adoption under suspension of the rules. Oct. 8, 2002.

448. HR 5542. Black Lung Claims/Passage. Biggert, R-Ill., motion to suspend the rules and pass the bill that would transfer from the Social Security Administration to the Labor Department the administration of all federal claims for compensation related to black lung disease. Motion agreed to 404-0: R 206-0; D 197-0 (ND 145-0, SD 52-0); I 1-0. A two-thirds majority of those present and voting (270 in this case) is required for passage under suspension of the rules. Oct. 9, 2002.

Key

Y	Voted for (yea).
#	Paired for.
+	Announced for.
N	Voted against (nay).
X	Paired against.
–	Announced against.
P	Voted "present."
C	Voted "present" to avoid possible conflict of interest.
?	Did not vote or otherwise make a position known.

Democrats   **Republicans**
Independents

	442	443	444	445	446	447	448
ALABAMA							
1 *Callahan*	?	?	?	Y	Y	Y	Y
2 *Everett*	?	?	?	Y	Y	Y	Y
3 *Riley*	+	+	+	Y	Y	Y	Y
4 *Aderholt*	Y	Y	Y	Y	Y	Y	Y
5 Cramer	Y	Y	Y	Y	Y	Y	Y
6 *Bachus*	Y	Y	Y	Y	Y	Y	Y
7 Hilliard	Y	Y	Y	Y	Y	Y	Y
ALASKA							
AL *Young*	Y	Y	Y	Y	Y	Y	?
ARIZONA							
1 *Flake*	Y	N	Y	Y	Y	Y	Y
2 Pastor	Y	Y	Y	Y	Y	Y	Y
3 *Stump*	?	?	?	?	?	?	?
4 *Shadegg*	Y	Y	Y	Y	Y	Y	Y
5 *Kolbe*	Y	Y	Y	Y	Y	Y	Y
6 *Hayworth*	Y	Y	Y	Y	Y	Y	Y
ARKANSAS							
1 Berry	Y	N	Y	Y	Y	Y	Y
2 Snyder	Y	Y	Y	Y	Y	Y	Y
3 *Boozman*	Y	Y	Y	Y	Y	Y	Y
4 Ross	Y	Y	Y	Y	Y	Y	Y
CALIFORNIA							
1 Thompson	Y	Y	Y	Y	Y	Y	Y
2 *Herger*	Y	Y	Y	Y	Y	Y	Y
3 *Ose*	Y	Y	Y	Y	Y	Y	Y
4 *Doolittle*	Y	Y	Y	Y	Y	Y	?
5 Matsui	Y	Y	Y	Y	Y	Y	Y
6 Woolsey	Y	Y	Y	N	Y	Y	Y
7 Miller, George	?	?	Y	Y	Y	Y	Y
8 Pelosi	Y	Y	Y	Y	Y	Y	Y
9 Lee	Y	Y	Y	N	Y	Y	Y
10 Tauscher	Y	Y	Y	Y	Y	Y	Y
11 *Pombo*	Y	Y	Y	Y	Y	Y	Y
12 Lantos	?	?	Y	Y	Y	Y	Y
13 Stark	Y	Y	Y	N	N	Y	Y
14 Eshoo	Y	Y	Y	Y	Y	Y	Y
15 Honda	Y	Y	Y	N	N	Y	Y
16 Lofgren	Y	Y	Y	Y	Y	Y	?
17 Farr	Y	Y	Y	Y	Y	Y	Y
18 Condit	Y	Y	Y	Y	Y	Y	Y
19 *Radanovich*	Y	Y	Y	Y	Y	Y	Y
20 Dooley	Y	Y	Y	Y	Y	Y	Y
21 *Thomas*	Y	Y	?	Y	Y	Y	Y
22 Capps	Y	Y	Y	Y	Y	Y	Y
23 *Gallegly*	Y	Y	Y	Y	Y	Y	Y
24 Sherman	Y	Y	P	Y	Y	Y	Y
25 *McKeon*	Y	Y	Y	Y	Y	Y	Y
26 Berman	Y	Y	Y	Y	Y	Y	Y
27 Schiff	Y	Y	Y	Y	Y	Y	Y
28 *Dreier*	Y	Y	Y	Y	Y	Y	Y
29 Waxman	Y	Y	N	Y	N	Y	Y
30 Becerra	Y	Y	Y	Y	Y	Y	Y
31 Solis	+	+	+	+	+	+	Y
32 Watson	Y	Y	Y	Y	Y	Y	Y
33 Roybal-Allard	Y	Y	Y	Y	Y	Y	Y
34 Napolitano	Y	Y	Y	Y	Y	Y	Y
35 Waters	Y	Y	Y	Y	Y	Y	Y
36 Harman	Y	Y	Y	Y	Y	Y	Y
37 Millender-McD.	Y	Y	Y	Y	Y	Y	Y
38 *Horn*	Y	Y	Y	Y	Y	Y	Y

	442	443	444	445	446	447	448
39 *Royce*	Y	Y	Y	Y	Y	Y	Y
40 *Lewis*	?	?	?	?	?	?	Y
41 *Miller, Gary*	Y	Y	Y	Y	Y	Y	Y
42 Baca	Y	Y	Y	Y	Y	Y	Y
43 *Calvert*	Y	Y	Y	Y	Y	Y	Y
44 *Bono*	Y	Y	Y	Y	Y	Y	?
45 *Rohrabacher*	Y	Y	N	Y	Y	Y	Y
46 Sanchez	Y	Y	Y	Y	Y	Y	Y
47 *Cox*	Y	Y	Y	Y	Y	?	Y
48 *Issa*	Y	Y	Y	Y	Y	Y	Y
49 Davis	Y	Y	Y	Y	Y	Y	Y
50 Filner	Y	?	?	Y	N	Y	Y
51 *Cunningham*	Y	Y	Y	Y	Y	Y	Y
52 *Hunter*	Y	Y	Y	Y	Y	Y	Y
COLORADO							
1 DeGette	Y	Y	Y	Y	Y	Y	Y
2 Udall	Y	Y	Y	Y	Y	Y	Y
3 *McInnis*	Y	Y	Y	Y	Y	Y	Y
4 *Schaffer*	?	?	?	Y	Y	?	Y
5 *Hefley*	Y	Y	Y	Y	Y	Y	Y
6 *Tancredo*	Y	Y	Y	Y	Y	Y	Y
CONNECTICUT							
1 Larson	Y	Y	Y	Y	Y	Y	Y
2 *Simmons*	Y	Y	Y	Y	Y	Y	Y
3 DeLauro	Y	Y	Y	Y	Y	Y	Y
4 *Shays*	Y	Y	Y	Y	Y	Y	Y
5 Maloney	Y	Y	Y	Y	Y	Y	Y
6 *Johnson*	Y	Y	Y	Y	Y	Y	Y
DELAWARE							
AL *Castle*	Y	Y	Y	Y	Y	Y	Y
FLORIDA							
1 *Miller, J.*	Y	N	Y	Y	Y	Y	Y
2 Boyd	Y	Y	Y	Y	Y	Y	Y
3 Brown	Y	Y	Y	Y	Y	Y	Y
4 *Crenshaw*	Y	Y	Y	Y	Y	Y	Y
5 *Thurman*	Y	Y	Y	Y	Y	Y	Y
6 *Stearns*	Y	Y	Y	Y	Y	Y	Y
7 *Mica*	Y	Y	Y	Y	Y	Y	Y
8 *Keller*	Y	Y	Y	Y	Y	Y	Y
9 *Bilirakis*	+	+	+	+	+	+	Y
10 *Young*	?	?	?	Y	Y	Y	Y
11 Davis	Y	Y	Y	Y	Y	Y	Y
12 *Putnam*	Y	Y	Y	Y	Y	Y	Y
13 *Miller, D.*	Y	Y	Y	Y	Y	Y	Y
14 *Goss*	Y	Y	Y	Y	Y	Y	Y
15 *Weldon*	Y	Y	Y	Y	Y	Y	Y
16 *Foley*	Y	?	?	Y	Y	Y	Y
17 Meek	?	Y	Y	?	N	Y	Y
18 *Ros-Lehtinen*	Y	Y	Y	Y	Y	Y	Y
19 Wexler	Y	Y	Y	Y	Y	Y	Y
20 Deutsch	Y	Y	Y	Y	Y	Y	Y
21 *Diaz-Balart*	Y	Y	Y	Y	Y	Y	?
22 *Shaw*	Y	Y	Y	Y	Y	Y	Y
23 Hastings	+	+	+	+	–	+	Y
GEORGIA							
1 *Kingston*	Y	Y	Y	Y	Y	Y	Y
2 Bishop	Y	Y	Y	Y	Y	Y	Y
3 *Collins*	Y	Y	Y	Y	Y	Y	Y
4 *McKinney*	?	?	?	?	Y	N	Y
5 Lewis	Y	Y	Y	?	?	?	Y
6 *Isakson*	Y	Y	Y	Y	Y	Y	Y
7 *Barr*	?	?	?	Y	Y	Y	Y
8 *Chambliss*	Y	Y	Y	Y	Y	Y	Y
9 *Deal*	Y	Y	Y	Y	Y	Y	Y
10 *Norwood*	Y	Y	Y	Y	Y	Y	Y
11 *Linder*	Y	Y	Y	Y	Y	Y	Y
HAWAII							
1 Abercrombie	Y	Y	Y	Y	N	Y	Y
2 Vacant							
IDAHO							
1 *Otter*	Y	Y	Y	Y	Y	Y	Y
2 *Simpson*	Y	Y	Y	Y	Y	Y	Y
ILLINOIS							
1 Rush	?	?	?	Y	Y	Y	Y
2 Jackson	?	?	?	Y	Y	Y	Y
3 Lipinski	?	?	?	Y	Y	Y	Y
4 Gutierrez	?	?	?	Y	Y	Y	Y
5 Blagojevich	?	?	?	Y	Y	Y	Y
6 *Hyde*	Y	Y	Y	Y	Y	Y	Y
7 Davis	Y	Y	Y	Y	Y	Y	Y
8 *Crane*	Y	Y	Y	Y	Y	Y	Y
9 Schakowsky	Y	Y	Y	Y	N	Y	Y
10 *Kirk*	Y	Y	Y	Y	Y	Y	Y
11 *Weller*	Y	Y	Y	Y	Y	Y	Y
12 Costello	?	?	?	Y	Y	Y	Y
13 *Biggert*	Y	Y	Y	Y	Y	Y	Y

ND Northern Democrats   SD Southern Democrats

	442	443	444	445	446	447	448
14 ***Hastert***							
15 ***Johnson***	Y	Y	Y	Y	Y	Y	Y
16 ***Manzullo***	Y	Y	Y	Y	Y	Y	+
17 Evans	Y	Y	Y	Y	Y	Y	Y
18 ***LaHood***	Y	Y	Y	Y	Y	Y	Y
19 Phelps	Y	Y	Y	Y	Y	Y	Y
20 ***Shimkus***	Y	Y	Y	Y	Y	Y	Y
INDIANA							
1 Visclosky	Y	Y	Y	Y	Y	Y	Y
2 ***Pence***	?	?	?	Y	Y	Y	Y
3 Roemer	Y	Y	Y	Y	Y	Y	Y
4 ***Souder***	Y	Y	Y	Y	Y	Y	Y
5 ***Buyer***	Y	Y	Y	Y	Y	Y	Y
6 ***Burton***	Y	Y	Y	Y	Y	Y	Y
7 ***Kerns***	Y	Y	Y	Y	Y	Y	Y
8 ***Hostettler***	Y	N	Y	Y	Y	Y	Y
9 Hill	Y	Y	Y	Y	Y	Y	Y
10 Carson	?	?	?	Y	Y	Y	Y
IOWA							
1 ***Leach***	Y	Y	Y	Y	Y	Y	Y
2 ***Nussle***	Y	Y	Y	Y	Y	Y	Y
3 Boswell	Y	Y	Y	Y	Y	Y	Y
4 ***Ganske***	Y	Y	Y	Y	Y	Y	Y
5 ***Latham***	Y	Y	Y	Y	Y	Y	Y
KANSAS							
1 ***Moran***	Y	Y	Y	Y	Y	Y	Y
2 ***Ryun***	Y	Y	Y	Y	Y	Y	Y
3 Moore	Y	Y	Y	Y	Y	Y	Y
4 ***Tiahrt***	+	+	+	Y	Y	Y	Y
KENTUCKY							
1 ***Whitfield***	Y	Y	Y	Y	Y	Y	Y
2 ***Lewis***	Y	Y	Y	Y	Y	Y	Y
3 ***Northup***	Y	Y	Y	Y	Y	Y	Y
4 Lucas	Y	Y	Y	Y	Y	Y	Y
5 ***Rogers***	Y	Y	Y	Y	Y	Y	Y
6 ***Fletcher***	Y	Y	Y	Y	Y	Y	Y
LOUISIANA							
1 ***Vitter***	Y	Y	Y	Y	Y	Y	Y
2 Jefferson	Y	Y	Y	Y	Y	Y	Y
3 ***Tauzin***	?	?	?	Y	Y	Y	Y
4 ***McCrery***	Y	Y	Y	Y	Y	Y	Y
5 ***Cooksey***	?	?	?	?	?	?	?
6 ***Baker***	Y	Y	Y	Y	Y	Y	Y
7 John	Y	Y	Y	Y	Y	Y	Y
MAINE							
1 Allen	Y	Y	Y	Y	Y	Y	Y
2 Baldacci	Y	Y	Y	Y	Y	Y	Y
MARYLAND							
1 ***Gilchrest***	Y	Y	Y	Y	Y	Y	Y
2 ***Ehrlich***	?	?	?	Y	Y	Y	?
3 Cardin	Y	Y	Y	Y	Y	Y	Y
4 Wynn	Y	Y	Y	Y	Y	Y	Y
5 Hoyer	Y	Y	Y	Y	Y	Y	Y
6 ***Bartlett***	Y	Y	Y	Y	Y	Y	Y
7 Cummings	Y	Y	Y	Y	Y	Y	?
8 ***Morella***	Y	Y	Y	Y	Y	Y	Y
MASSACHUSETTS							
1 Olver	Y	Y	Y	Y	Y	Y	Y
2 Neal	?	?	?	?	?	?	Y
3 McGovern	Y	Y	Y	Y	Y	Y	Y
4 Frank	Y	Y	Y	N	N	Y	Y
5 Meehan	Y	Y	Y	Y	Y	Y	Y
6 Tierney	Y	Y	Y	Y	N	Y	Y
7 Markey	Y	Y	Y	Y	Y	Y	Y
8 Capuano	Y	Y	Y	Y	Y	Y	Y
9 Lynch	Y	Y	Y	Y	Y	Y	Y
10 Delahunt	Y	Y	Y	Y	Y	Y	Y
MICHIGAN							
1 Stupak	Y	Y	Y	Y	Y	Y	Y
2 ***Hoekstra***	?	?	?	Y	Y	Y	Y
3 ***Ehlers***	Y	Y	Y	Y	Y	Y	Y
4 ***Camp***	Y	Y	Y	Y	Y	Y	Y
5 Barcia	Y	Y	Y	Y	Y	Y	Y
6 ***Upton***	Y	Y	Y	Y	Y	Y	Y
7 ***Smith***	Y	Y	Y	Y	Y	Y	Y
8 ***Rogers***	Y	Y	Y	Y	Y	Y	Y
9 Kildee	Y	Y	Y	Y	Y	Y	Y
10 Bonior	Y	Y	Y	Y	N	Y	Y
11 ***Knollenberg***	+	+	+	Y	Y	Y	Y
12 Levin	Y	?	Y	Y	Y	Y	Y
13 Rivers	Y	Y	Y	Y	Y	Y	Y
14 Conyers	?	?	?	Y	N	?	?
15 Kilpatrick	+	+	+	Y	Y	Y	Y
16 Dingell	Y	Y	Y	Y	Y	Y	Y
MINNESOTA							
1 ***Gutknecht***	Y	Y	N	Y	Y	Y	Y
2 ***Kennedy***	Y	Y	Y	Y	Y	Y	Y
3 ***Ramstad***	Y	Y	Y	Y	Y	Y	Y
4 McCollum	Y	Y	Y	Y	Y	Y	Y
5 Sabo	Y	Y	N	Y	N	Y	Y
6 Luther	Y	Y	Y	Y	Y	Y	Y
7 Peterson	Y	Y	Y	Y	Y	Y	Y
8 Oberstar	Y	Y	Y	Y	N	Y	Y
MISSISSIPPI							
1 ***Wicker***	Y	Y	Y	Y	Y	Y	Y
2 Thompson	Y	Y	Y	Y	Y	Y	Y
3 ***Pickering***	Y	Y	Y	Y	Y	Y	Y
4 Shows	Y	Y	Y	Y	Y	Y	Y
5 Taylor	?	?	?	Y	Y	Y	Y
MISSOURI							
1 Clay	?	?	?	?	Y	Y	Y
2 ***Akin***	Y	Y	Y	Y	Y	Y	?
3 Gephardt	Y	Y	Y	Y	Y	Y	Y
4 Skelton	Y	Y	Y	Y	Y	Y	Y
5 McCarthy	Y	Y	Y	Y	Y	Y	Y
6 ***Graves***	Y	Y	Y	Y	Y	Y	Y
7 ***Blunt***	Y	Y	Y	Y	Y	Y	Y
8 ***Emerson***	Y	Y	Y	Y	Y	Y	Y
9 ***Hulshof***	Y	Y	Y	Y	Y	Y	Y
MONTANA							
AL ***Rehberg***	Y	Y	Y	Y	Y	Y	Y
NEBRASKA							
1 ***Bereuter***	Y	Y	Y	Y	Y	?	Y
2 ***Terry***	Y	Y	Y	Y	Y	Y	Y
3 ***Osborne***	Y	Y	Y	Y	Y	Y	Y
NEVADA							
1 Berkley	Y	Y	Y	Y	Y	Y	Y
2 ***Gibbons***	Y	Y	Y	Y	Y	Y	Y
NEW HAMPSHIRE							
1 ***Sununu***	?	?	?	?	?	?	Y
2 ***Bass***	Y	Y	Y	Y	Y	Y	Y
NEW JERSEY							
1 Andrews	Y	Y	Y	Y	Y	Y	?
2 ***LoBiondo***	Y	Y	Y	Y	Y	Y	Y
3 ***Saxton***	Y	Y	Y	Y	Y	Y	Y
4 ***Smith***	Y	Y	Y	Y	Y	Y	Y
5 ***Roukema***	?	?	?	?	?	?	?
6 Pallone	Y	Y	Y	Y	Y	Y	Y
7 ***Ferguson***	Y	Y	Y	?	?	?	Y
8 Pascrell	?	?	?	Y	Y	Y	Y
9 Rothman	?	?	?	Y	Y	Y	Y
10 Payne	Y	Y	Y	Y	Y	Y	Y
11 ***Frelinghuysen***	Y	Y	Y	Y	Y	Y	Y
12 Holt	Y	Y	Y	Y	N	Y	Y
13 Menendez	Y	Y	Y	Y	Y	Y	Y
NEW MEXICO							
1 ***Wilson***	Y	Y	Y	Y	Y	Y	Y
2 ***Skeen***	Y	Y	Y	Y	Y	Y	Y
3 Udall	Y	Y	Y	Y	Y	Y	Y
NEW YORK							
1 ***Grucci***	Y	Y	Y	Y	Y	Y	Y
2 Israel	Y	Y	Y	Y	Y	Y	Y
3 ***King***	Y	Y	Y	Y	Y	Y	Y
4 McCarthy	Y	Y	Y	Y	Y	Y	Y
5 Ackerman	Y	Y	Y	P	Y	Y	Y
6 Meeks	?	?	?	Y	Y	Y	Y
7 Crowley	Y	Y	Y	Y	Y	Y	Y
8 Nadler	Y	Y	Y	Y	Y	Y	Y
9 Weiner	Y	Y	Y	Y	Y	Y	Y
10 Towns	?	?	?	?	?	?	Y
11 Owens	+	+	+	Y	Y	P	Y
12 Velázquez	Y	Y	Y	P	Y	Y	Y
13 ***Fossella***	Y	Y	Y	Y	Y	Y	Y
14 Maloney	Y	Y	Y	Y	Y	Y	Y
15 Rangel	Y	?	?	Y	Y	Y	Y
16 Serrano	Y	?	Y	Y	Y	Y	Y
17 Engel	Y	Y	Y	Y	Y	Y	Y
18 Lowey	Y	Y	Y	Y	Y	Y	Y
19 ***Kelly***	Y	Y	Y	Y	Y	Y	Y
20 ***Gilman***	Y	Y	Y	Y	Y	Y	Y
21 McNulty	Y	Y	Y	Y	Y	Y	Y
22 ***Sweeney***	?	?	?	Y	Y	Y	Y
23 ***Boehlert***	Y	Y	Y	Y	Y	Y	Y
24 ***McHugh***	Y	Y	Y	Y	Y	Y	Y
25 ***Walsh***	Y	Y	Y	Y	Y	Y	Y
26 Hinchey	Y	Y	Y	Y	Y	Y	Y
27 ***Reynolds***	Y	Y	Y	Y	Y	Y	Y
28 Slaughter	Y	Y	Y	Y	Y	Y	Y
29 LaFalce	Y	Y	Y	Y	Y	Y	?
30 ***Quinn***	Y	Y	Y	Y	Y	Y	?
31 ***Houghton***	Y	Y	Y	Y	Y	Y	?
NORTH CAROLINA							
1 Clayton	Y	Y	Y	Y	N	Y	Y
2 Etheridge	Y	Y	Y	Y	Y	Y	Y
3 ***Jones***	Y	Y	Y	Y	Y	Y	Y
4 Price	Y	Y	Y	Y	Y	Y	Y
5 ***Burr***	Y	Y	Y	Y	Y	Y	Y
6 ***Coble***	Y	N	Y	Y	Y	Y	Y
7 McIntyre	Y	Y	Y	Y	Y	Y	Y
8 ***Hayes***	Y	Y	Y	Y	Y	Y	Y
9 ***Myrick***	Y	Y	Y	Y	Y	Y	Y
10 ***Ballenger***	Y	Y	Y	Y	Y	Y	Y
11 ***Taylor***	?	?	?	Y	Y	Y	Y
12 Watt	Y	Y	Y	P	N	Y	Y
NORTH DAKOTA							
AL Pomeroy	Y	Y	Y	Y	Y	Y	Y
OHIO							
1 ***Chabot***	?	?	?	Y	Y	Y	Y
2 ***Portman***	+	+	+	Y	Y	Y	Y
3 Vacant							
4 ***Oxley***	Y	Y	Y	Y	Y	Y	Y
5 ***Gillmor***	Y	Y	Y	Y	Y	Y	Y
6 Strickland	Y	Y	Y	Y	Y	Y	Y
7 ***Hobson***	Y	Y	Y	Y	Y	Y	Y
8 ***Boehner***	?	?	?	Y	Y	Y	Y
9 Kaptur	Y	Y	Y	Y	Y	Y	?
10 Kucinich	Y	Y	Y	Y	Y	Y	Y
11 Jones	Y	Y	Y	?	Y	Y	Y
12 ***Tiberi***	Y	Y	Y	Y	Y	Y	Y
13 Brown	Y	Y	Y	Y	Y	Y	Y
14 Sawyer	Y	Y	Y	Y	Y	Y	?
15 ***Pryce***	Y	Y	Y	Y	Y	Y	Y
16 ***Regula***	Y	Y	Y	Y	Y	Y	Y
17 Vacant							
18 ***Ney***	Y	Y	Y	Y	Y	Y	Y
19 ***LaTourette***	Y	Y	Y	Y	Y	Y	Y
OKLAHOMA							
1 ***Sullivan***	Y	Y	Y	Y	Y	Y	Y
2 Carson	Y	Y	Y	Y	Y	Y	Y
3 ***Watkins***	Y	Y	Y	Y	Y	Y	Y
4 ***Watts***	Y	Y	Y	Y	Y	Y	Y
5 ***Istook***	?	?	?	?	?	?	?
6 ***Lucas***	Y	Y	Y	Y	Y	Y	Y
OREGON							
1 Wu	Y	Y	Y	Y	Y	Y	Y
2 ***Walden***	Y	Y	Y	Y	Y	Y	Y
3 Blumenauer	Y	Y	N	P	N	Y	Y
4 DeFazio	Y	Y	N	Y	Y	Y	Y
5 Hooley	Y	Y	Y	Y	Y	Y	Y
PENNSYLVANIA							
1 Brady	Y	Y	Y	Y	Y	Y	Y
2 Fattah	?	?	?	Y	Y	Y	Y
3 Borski	?	?	?	Y	Y	Y	Y
4 ***Hart***	Y	Y	Y	Y	Y	Y	Y
5 ***Peterson***	Y	Y	Y	Y	Y	Y	Y
6 Holden	Y	Y	Y	Y	Y	Y	Y
7 ***Weldon***	?	?	?	?	?	?	Y
8 ***Greenwood***	Y	Y	Y	Y	Y	Y	Y
9 ***Shuster, Bill***	Y	Y	Y	Y	Y	Y	Y
10 ***Sherwood***	Y	Y	Y	Y	Y	Y	Y
11 Kanjorski	?	?	?	?	?	?	Y
12 Murtha	Y	?	?	Y	Y	Y	Y
13 Hoeffel	Y	Y	Y	Y	Y	Y	Y
14 Coyne	Y	Y	Y	Y	Y	Y	Y
15 ***Toomey***	Y	Y	Y	Y	Y	Y	Y
16 ***Pitts***	Y	Y	Y	Y	Y	Y	Y
17 ***Gekas***	Y	Y	Y	Y	Y	Y	Y
18 Doyle	Y	Y	Y	Y	Y	Y	Y
19 ***Platts***	Y	Y	Y	Y	Y	Y	Y
20 Mascara	+	+	+	?	?	?	?
21 ***English***	Y	Y	Y	Y	Y	Y	Y
RHODE ISLAND							
1 Kennedy	Y	Y	Y	Y	Y	Y	Y
2 Langevin	Y	Y	Y	Y	Y	Y	Y
SOUTH CAROLINA							
1 ***Brown***	Y	Y	Y	Y	Y	Y	Y
2 ***Wilson***	Y	Y	Y	Y	Y	Y	Y
3 ***Graham***	Y	Y	Y	Y	Y	Y	Y
4 ***DeMint***	Y	Y	Y	Y	Y	Y	Y
5 Spratt	?	?	?	Y	Y	Y	Y
6 Clyburn	Y	Y	Y	Y	Y	Y	Y
SOUTH DAKOTA							
AL ***Thune***	Y	Y	Y	Y	Y	Y	Y
TENNESSEE							
1 ***Jenkins***	Y	Y	Y	Y	Y	Y	Y
2 ***Duncan***	Y	N	N	Y	Y	Y	Y
3 ***Wamp***	Y	Y	Y	Y	Y	Y	Y
4 ***Hilleary***	?	?	?	?	?	?	?
5 Clement	+	+	+	Y	Y	Y	Y
6 Gordon	Y	Y	Y	Y	Y	Y	?
7 ***Bryant***	?	?	?	Y	Y	Y	Y
8 Tanner	Y	N	Y	Y	Y	Y	Y
9 Ford	?	?	?	Y	Y	Y	Y
TEXAS							
1 Sandlin	Y	Y	Y	Y	Y	Y	Y
2 Turner	Y	Y	Y	Y	Y	Y	Y
3 ***Johnson, Sam***	Y	?	Y	Y	Y	Y	Y
4 Hall	Y	Y	Y	Y	Y	Y	Y
5 ***Sessions***	Y	Y	Y	Y	Y	Y	?
6 ***Barton***	Y	Y	Y	Y	Y	Y	Y
7 ***Culberson***	Y	Y	Y	Y	Y	Y	Y
8 ***Brady***	Y	Y	Y	Y	Y	Y	Y
9 Lampson	Y	Y	Y	Y	Y	Y	Y
10 Doggett	Y	Y	Y	Y	Y	Y	?
11 Edwards	Y	Y	Y	Y	Y	Y	Y
12 ***Granger***	Y	Y	Y	Y	Y	Y	Y
13 ***Thornberry***	Y	Y	Y	Y	Y	Y	Y
14 ***Paul***	Y	N	N	Y	N	Y	Y
15 Hinojosa	Y	Y	Y	Y	Y	Y	Y
16 Reyes	Y	Y	Y	Y	Y	Y	Y
17 Stenholm	Y	Y	Y	Y	Y	Y	Y
18 Jackson-Lee	Y	Y	Y	Y	Y	Y	Y
19 ***Combest***	Y	Y	Y	Y	Y	Y	Y
20 Gonzalez	Y	Y	Y	Y	Y	Y	Y
21 ***Smith***	Y	Y	Y	Y	Y	Y	Y
22 ***DeLay***	Y	Y	Y	Y	Y	Y	Y
23 ***Bonilla***	Y	Y	Y	Y	Y	Y	Y
24 Frost	Y	Y	Y	Y	Y	Y	Y
25 Bentsen	Y	Y	Y	Y	Y	Y	Y
26 ***Armey***	Y	Y	Y	Y	Y	Y	Y
27 Ortiz	Y	Y	Y	Y	Y	Y	Y
28 Rodriguez	Y	Y	Y	Y	Y	Y	Y
29 Green	Y	Y	Y	Y	Y	Y	Y
30 Johnson, E.B.	Y	Y	Y	Y	Y	Y	Y
UTAH							
1 ***Hansen***	Y	Y	Y	Y	Y	Y	Y
2 Matheson	Y	Y	Y	Y	Y	Y	Y
3 ***Cannon***	Y	Y	Y	Y	Y	Y	?
VERMONT							
AL *Sanders*	Y	Y	Y	Y	Y	Y	Y
VIRGINIA							
1 ***Davis, Jo Ann***	Y	Y	Y	Y	Y	Y	Y
2 ***Schrock***	Y	Y	Y	Y	Y	Y	Y
3 Scott	Y	Y	Y	N	N	Y	Y
4 ***Forbes***	Y	Y	Y	Y	Y	Y	Y
5 ***Goode***	Y	Y	Y	Y	Y	Y	Y
6 ***Goodlatte***	Y	Y	Y	Y	Y	Y	Y
7 ***Cantor***	Y	Y	Y	Y	Y	Y	Y
8 Moran	Y	Y	Y	Y	N	Y	Y
9 Boucher	Y	Y	Y	Y	Y	Y	Y
10 ***Wolf***	Y	Y	Y	Y	Y	Y	Y
11 ***Davis, T.***	Y	Y	Y	Y	Y	Y	Y
WASHINGTON							
1 Inslee	Y	Y	Y	Y	Y	Y	Y
2 Larsen	?	?	?	Y	Y	Y	Y
3 Baird	Y	Y	Y	Y	Y	Y	Y
4 ***Hastings***	Y	Y	Y	Y	Y	Y	Y
5 ***Nethercutt***	Y	Y	Y	Y	Y	Y	Y
6 Dicks	Y	Y	Y	Y	Y	Y	Y
7 McDermott	Y	Y	Y	N	N	Y	Y
8 ***Dunn***	Y	Y	Y	Y	Y	Y	Y
9 Smith	Y	Y	Y	Y	Y	Y	Y
WEST VIRGINIA							
1 Mollohan	Y	Y	Y	Y	N	Y	Y
2 ***Capito***	Y	Y	Y	Y	Y	Y	Y
3 Rahall	Y	Y	Y	Y	Y	Y	Y
WISCONSIN							
1 ***Ryan***	Y	Y	Y	Y	Y	Y	Y
2 Baldwin	Y	Y	Y	Y	Y	Y	Y
3 Kind	Y	Y	Y	Y	Y	Y	Y
4 Kleczka	Y	Y	Y	Y	Y	Y	Y
5 Barrett	Y	Y	Y	Y	Y	Y	Y
6 ***Petri***	Y	Y	Y	Y	Y	Y	Y
7 Obey	Y	Y	N	Y	Y	Y	Y
8 ***Green***	Y	Y	Y	Y	Y	Y	Y
9 ***Sensenbrenner***	Y	Y	Y	Y	Y	Y	Y
WYOMING							
AL ***Cubin***	?	?	?	Y	Y	Y	Y

Southern states - Ala., Ark., Fla., Ga., Ky., La., Miss., N.C., Okla., S.C., Tenn., Texas, Va.

Key

Y	Voted for (yea).
#	Paired for.
+	Announced for.
N	Voted against (nay).
X	Paired against.
–	Announced against.
P	Voted "present."
C	Voted "present" to avoid possible conflict of interest.
?	Did not vote or otherwise make a position known.

Democrats **Republicans** *Independents*

449. H J Res 113. Patsy T. Mink Tribute/Passage. Isakson, R-Ga., motion to suspend the rules and pass the joint resolution that would pay tribute to the late Rep. Patsy T. Mink, D-Hawaii, by renaming Title IX of the Education Amendments of 1972 (PL 92-318) as the Patsy T. Mink Equal Opportunity in Education Act. Motion agreed to 410-0: R 206-0; D 203-0 (ND 149-0, SD 54-0); I 1-0. A two-thirds majority of those present and voting (274 in this case) is required for passage under suspension of the rules. Oct. 9, 2002.

450. HR 3580. New Medical Devices/Passage. Burr, R-N.C., motion to suspend the rules and pass the bill that would authorize the Food and Drug Administration (FDA) to collect user fees from companies seeking FDA product approvals for new medical devices. The FDA would be required to use the added funds to meet performance goals aimed at speeding the review and approval process. Motion agreed to 406-3: R 204-3; D 201-0 (ND 148-0, SD 53-0); I 1-0. A two-thirds majority of those present and voting (273 in this case) is required for passage under suspension of the rules. Oct. 9, 2002.

451. HR 5557. Military Tax Breaks/Passage. Weller, R-Ill., motion to suspend the rules and pass the bill that would exempt from taxable income the full $6,000 cash payment given to survivors of military members killed in the line of duty, ease capital gains rules on home sales by military personnel and provide flexibility in filing tax returns for those participating in contingency operations. Motion agreed to 412-0: R 208-0; D 203-0 (ND 149-0, SD 54-0); I 1-0. A two-thirds majority of those present and voting (275 in this case) is required for passage under suspension of the rules. Oct. 9, 2002.

452. H J Res 114. Use of Force/U.N. Involvement. Lee, D-Calif., amendment that would urge the president to work through the United Nations to ensure that Iraq is not developing weapons of mass destruction, and urge the use of peaceful means to resolve the issue, including the resumption of weapons inspections. Rejected 72-355: R 1-219; D 70-136 (ND 56-97, SD 14-39); I 1-0. Oct. 10, 2002.

453. H J Res 114. Use of Force/Military Support for U.N. Resolution. Spratt, D-S.C., amendment that would authorize the U.S. military to support any new U.N. Security Council resolution that orders the elimination, by force if required, of Iraq's weapons of mass destruction, long-range missiles, and the means of producing such weapons. The president would be required to seek congressional authority before using military force against Iraq without such a U.N. resolution. Rejected 155-270: R 7-210; D 147-60 (ND 112-42, SD 35-18); I 1-0. Oct. 11, 2002.

454. H J Res 114. Use of Force/Recommit. Kucinich, D-Ohio, motion to recommit the bill to the House International Relations Committee with instructions that it be reported back with language that would require the president prior to the use of force to report to Congress on the effect of war with Iraq, including estimates of its impact on the U.S. economy, Iraqi citizens and international stability. Motion rejected 101-325: R 1-219; D 99-106 (ND 80-73, SD 19-33); I 1-0. Oct. 10, 2002.

455. H J Res 114. Use of Force/Passage. Passage of the joint resolution that would authorize the use of force against Iraq and require the administration to report to Congress that diplomatic options have been exhausted no later than 48 hours after military action has begun. The president also would be required to submit a progress report to Congress at least every 60 days. Passed 296-133: R 215-6; D 81-126 (ND 49-105, SD 32-21); I 0-1. A "yea" was a vote in support of the president's position. Oct. 10, 2002.

	449	450	451	452	453	454	455
ALABAMA							
1 *Callahan*	Y	Y	Y	N	N	N	Y
2 *Everett*	Y	Y	Y	N	N	N	Y
3 *Riley*	Y	Y	Y	N	N	N	Y
4 *Aderholt*	Y	Y	Y	N	N	N	Y
5 Cramer	Y	Y	Y	N	N	N	Y
6 *Bachus*	Y	Y	Y	N	N	N	Y
7 Hilliard	Y	Y	Y	Y	Y	Y	N
ALASKA							
AL *Young*	?	?	?	N	N	N	Y
ARIZONA							
1 *Flake*	Y	N	N	N	N	N	Y
2 Pastor	Y	Y	Y	N	Y	Y	N
3 *Stump*	?	?	?	?	?	?	?
4 *Shadegg*	Y	Y	Y	N	N	N	Y
5 *Kolbe*	Y	Y	Y	N	N	N	Y
6 *Hayworth*	Y	Y	Y	N	N	N	Y
ARKANSAS							
1 Berry	Y	Y	Y	N	Y	N	Y
2 Snyder	Y	Y	Y	N	Y	N	N
3 *Boozman*	Y	Y	Y	N	N	N	Y
4 Ross	Y	Y	Y	N	N	N	Y
CALIFORNIA							
1 Thompson	Y	Y	Y	N	Y	Y	N
2 *Herger*	?	Y	Y	N	N	N	Y
3 *Ose*	Y	Y	Y	N	N	N	Y
4 *Doolittle*	Y	Y	Y	N	N	N	Y
5 Matsui	Y	Y	Y	N	N	Y	N
6 Woolsey	Y	Y	Y	Y	Y	Y	N
7 Miller, George	Y	Y	Y	Y	N	Y	N
8 Pelosi	Y	Y	Y	Y	N	Y	N
9 Lee	Y	Y	Y	Y	Y	Y	N
10 Tauscher	Y	Y	Y	N	Y	Y	Y
11 *Pombo*	Y	Y	Y	N	N	N	Y
12 Lantos	Y	Y	Y	N	N	N	Y
13 Stark	Y	Y	Y	Y	N	Y	N
14 Eshoo	Y	Y	Y	N	N	Y	N
15 Honda	Y	Y	Y	Y	N	Y	N
16 Lofgren	?	?	?	N	Y	N	N
17 Farr	Y	Y	Y	Y	N	Y	N
18 Condit	Y	Y	Y	Y	N	Y	N
19 *Radanovich*	Y	Y	Y	N	N	N	Y
20 Dooley	Y	Y	Y	N	N	N	Y
21 *Thomas*	Y	Y	Y	Y	N	N	Y
22 Capps	Y	Y	Y	Y	N	Y	N
23 *Gallegly*	Y	Y	Y	N	N	N	Y
24 Sherman	Y	Y	Y	N	N	N	Y
25 *McKeon*	Y	Y	Y	N	N	N	Y
26 Berman	Y	Y	Y	N	N	N	Y
27 Schiff	Y	Y	Y	N	N	N	Y
28 *Dreier*	Y	Y	Y	N	N	N	Y
29 Waxman	Y	Y	Y	N	Y	Y	Y
30 Becerra	Y	Y	Y	Y	Y	Y	N
31 Solis	Y	Y	Y	Y	Y	Y	N
32 Watson	Y	Y	Y	Y	N	Y	N
33 Roybal-Allard	Y	Y	Y	Y	N	Y	N
34 Napolitano	Y	Y	Y	Y	Y	Y	N
35 Waters	Y	Y	Y	Y	N	Y	N
36 Harman	Y	Y	Y	N	N	N	Y
37 Millender-McD.	Y	Y	Y	Y	Y	Y	N
38 Horn	Y	Y	Y	N	N	N	Y

	449	450	451	452	453	454	455
39 *Royce*	Y	Y	Y	N	N	N	Y
40 *Lewis*	Y	Y	Y	N	N	N	Y
41 *Miller, Gary*	Y	Y	Y	N	N	N	Y
42 Baca	Y	Y	Y	N	N	N	N
43 *Calvert*	Y	Y	Y	N	N	N	Y
44 *Bono*	?	?	Y	N	N	N	Y
45 *Rohrabacher*	Y	Y	Y	N	N	N	Y
46 Sanchez	Y	Y	Y	Y	Y	Y	N
47 *Cox*	Y	?	Y	N	N	N	Y
48 *Issa*	Y	Y	Y	N	N	N	Y
49 Davis	Y	Y	Y	N	Y	N	Y
50 Filner	Y	Y	Y	Y	Y	Y	N
51 *Cunningham*	Y	Y	Y	N	N	N	Y
52 *Hunter*	Y	Y	Y	N	N	N	Y
COLORADO							
1 DeGette	Y	Y	Y	N	Y	Y	N
2 Udall	Y	Y	Y	N	Y	N	N
3 *McInnis*	Y	Y	Y	N	N	N	Y
4 *Schaffer*	Y	Y	Y	N	N	N	Y
5 *Hefley*	Y	Y	Y	N	N	N	Y
6 *Tancredo*	Y	Y	Y	N	N	N	Y
CONNECTICUT							
1 Larson	Y	+	Y	N	Y	N	N
2 *Simmons*	Y	Y	Y	N	Y	N	Y
3 DeLauro	Y	Y	Y	N	Y	N	N
4 *Shays*	Y	Y	Y	N	N	N	Y
5 Maloney	Y	Y	Y	N	Y	N	N
6 *Johnson*	Y	Y	Y	N	N	N	Y
DELAWARE							
AL *Castle*	Y	Y	Y	N	N	N	Y
FLORIDA							
1 *Miller, J.*	Y	Y	Y	N	N	N	Y
2 Boyd	Y	Y	Y	N	Y	N	Y
3 Brown	Y	Y	Y	Y	Y	Y	N
4 *Crenshaw*	Y	Y	Y	N	N	N	Y
5 Thurman	Y	Y	Y	N	Y	N	Y
6 *Stearns*	Y	Y	Y	N	N	N	Y
7 *Mica*	Y	Y	Y	N	N	N	Y
8 *Keller*	Y	Y	Y	N	N	N	Y
9 *Bilirakis*	Y	Y	Y	N	N	N	Y
10 *Young*	Y	Y	Y	N	N	N	Y
11 Davis	Y	Y	Y	N	Y	N	Y
12 *Putnam*	Y	Y	Y	N	N	N	Y
13 *Miller, D.*	Y	Y	Y	N	N	N	Y
14 *Goss*	Y	Y	Y	N	N	N	Y
15 *Weldon*	Y	Y	Y	N	N	N	Y
16 *Foley*	Y	Y	Y	N	N	N	Y
17 Meek	Y	Y	Y	Y	Y	Y	N
18 *Ros-Lehtinen*	Y	Y	Y	N	N	N	Y
19 Wexler	Y	Y	Y	N	Y	Y	Y
20 Deutsch	Y	Y	Y	N	N	N	Y
21 *Diaz-Balart*	?	?	?	N	N	N	Y
22 *Shaw*	Y	Y	Y	N	N	N	Y
23 Hastings	Y	Y	Y	Y	Y	Y	N
GEORGIA							
1 *Kingston*	Y	Y	Y	N	N	N	Y
2 Bishop	Y	Y	Y	N	Y	N	Y
3 *Collins*	Y	Y	Y	N	N	N	Y
4 McKinney	Y	?	Y	N	?	N	?
5 Lewis	Y	Y	Y	N	Y	N	N
6 *Isakson*	Y	Y	Y	N	N	N	Y
7 *Barr*	Y	Y	Y	N	?	N	Y
8 *Chambliss*	Y	Y	Y	N	N	N	Y
9 *Deal*	Y	Y	Y	N	N	N	Y
10 *Norwood*	Y	Y	Y	N	N	N	Y
11 *Linder*	Y	Y	Y	N	N	N	Y
HAWAII							
1 Abercrombie	Y	Y	Y	Y	N	N	N
2 Vacant							
IDAHO							
1 *Otter*	Y	Y	Y	N	N	N	Y
2 *Simpson*	Y	Y	Y	N	N	N	Y
ILLINOIS							
1 Rush	Y	Y	Y	N	Y	N	N
2 Jackson	Y	Y	Y	N	Y	N	N
3 Lipinski	Y	Y	Y	N	N	N	N
4 Gutierrez	Y	Y	Y	Y	Y	?	N
5 Blagojevich	?	?	?	N	Y	N	Y
6 *Hyde*	Y	Y	Y	N	N	N	Y
7 Davis	Y	Y	Y	N	Y	N	N
8 *Crane*	Y	Y	Y	N	N	N	Y
9 Schakowsky	Y	Y	Y	Y	Y	Y	N
10 *Kirk*	Y	Y	Y	N	N	N	Y
11 *Weller*	Y	Y	Y	N	N	N	Y
12 Costello	Y	Y	Y	N	N	N	Y
13 *Biggert*	Y	Y	Y	N	N	N	Y

ND Northern Democrats   SD Southern Democrats

	449	450	451	452	453	454	455
14 ***Hastert***							Y
15 ***Johnson***	Y	Y	Y	N	N	N	Y
16 ***Manzullo***	+	+	+	N	N	N	Y
17 Evans	Y	Y	Y	N	Y	Y	N
18 ***LaHood***	Y	Y	Y	N	N	N	Y
19 Phelps	Y	Y	Y	N	N	N	Y
20 ***Shimkus***	Y	Y	Y	N	N	N	Y
INDIANA							
1 Visclosky	Y	Y	Y	N	Y	N	N
2 ***Pence***	Y	Y	Y	N	N	N	Y
3 Roemer	Y	Y	Y	N	N	N	Y
4 ***Souder***	Y	Y	Y	N	N	N	Y
5 ***Buyer***	Y	Y	Y	N	N	N	Y
6 ***Burton***	Y	Y	Y	N	N	N	Y
7 ***Kerns***	Y	Y	Y	N	N	N	Y
8 ***Hostettler***	Y	Y	Y	N	N	N	N
9 Hill	Y	Y	Y	N	Y	N	Y
10 Carson	Y	Y	Y	Y	Y	Y	N
IOWA							
1 ***Leach***	?	Y	Y	N	N	N	N
2 ***Nussle***	Y	Y	Y	N	N	N	Y
3 Boswell	Y	Y	Y	N	N	N	Y
4 ***Ganske***	Y	Y	Y	N	N	N	Y
5 ***Latham***	Y	Y	Y	N	N	N	Y
KANSAS							
1 ***Moran***	Y	Y	Y	N	N	N	Y
2 ***Ryun***	Y	Y	Y	N	N	N	Y
3 Moore	Y	Y	Y	N	N	N	Y
4 ***Tiahrt***	?	Y	Y	N	N	N	Y
KENTUCKY							
1 ***Whitfield***	Y	Y	Y	N	N	N	Y
2 ***Lewis***	Y	Y	Y	N	N	N	Y
3 ***Northup***	Y	Y	Y	N	N	N	Y
4 Lucas	Y	Y	Y	N	N	N	Y
5 ***Rogers***	Y	Y	Y	N	N	N	Y
6 ***Fletcher***	Y	Y	Y	N	?	N	Y
LOUISIANA							
1 ***Vitter***	Y	Y	Y	N	N	N	Y
2 Jefferson	Y	Y	Y	N	Y	Y	Y
3 ***Tauzin***	Y	Y	Y	N	N	N	Y
4 ***McCrery***	Y	Y	Y	N	N	N	Y
5 ***Cooksey***	?	?	?	N	?	N	Y
6 ***Baker***	Y	Y	Y	N	N	N	Y
7 John	Y	Y	Y	N	N	N	Y
MAINE							
1 Allen	Y	Y	Y	N	Y	Y	N
2 Baldacci	Y	Y	Y	N	Y	N	N
MARYLAND							
1 ***Gilchrest***	Y	Y	Y	N	N	N	Y
2 ***Ehrlich***	?	?	?	N	N	N	Y
3 Cardin	Y	Y	Y	N	Y	N	N
4 Wynn	Y	Y	Y	Y	Y	N	Y
5 Hoyer	Y	Y	Y	N	Y	N	Y
6 ***Bartlett***	Y	Y	Y	N	Y	N	Y
7 Cummings	Y	Y	Y	Y	Y	Y	N
8 ***Morella***	Y	Y	Y	Y	Y	N	N
MASSACHUSETTS							
1 Olver	Y	Y	Y	N	Y	Y	N
2 Neal	Y	Y	Y	N	Y	Y	N
3 McGovern	Y	Y	Y	Y	Y	Y	N
4 Frank	Y	Y	Y	N	Y	Y	N
5 Meehan	Y	Y	Y	N	Y	Y	Y
6 Tierney	Y	Y	Y	N	Y	Y	N
7 Markey	Y	Y	Y	N	Y	Y	Y
8 Capuano	Y	Y	Y	Y	Y	Y	N
9 Lynch	Y	Y	Y	N	Y	N	Y
10 Delahunt	Y	Y	Y	Y	Y	Y	N
MICHIGAN							
1 Stupak	Y	Y	Y	N	Y	N	N
2 ***Hoekstra***	Y	Y	Y	N	N	N	Y
3 ***Ehlers***	Y	Y	Y	N	N	N	Y
4 ***Camp***	Y	Y	Y	N	N	N	Y
5 Barcia	Y	Y	Y	N	Y	N	Y
6 ***Upton***	Y	Y	Y	N	N	N	Y
7 ***Smith***	Y	Y	Y	N	N	N	Y
8 ***Rogers***	Y	Y	Y	N	N	N	Y
9 Kildee	Y	Y	Y	N	Y	N	N
10 Bonior	Y	Y	Y	Y	N	Y	N
11 ***Knollenberg***	Y	Y	Y	N	N	N	Y
12 Levin	Y	Y	Y	N	Y	N	N
13 Rivers	Y	Y	Y	Y	N	N	N
14 Conyers	Y	Y	Y	Y	Y	Y	N
15 Kilpatrick	Y	Y	Y	Y	Y	Y	N
16 Dingell	Y	Y	Y	N	Y	Y	N
MINNESOTA							
1 ***Gutknecht***	Y	Y	Y	N	N	N	Y
2 ***Kennedy***	Y	Y	Y	N	N	N	Y
3 ***Ramstad***	Y	Y	Y	N	N	N	Y
4 McCollum	Y	Y	Y	N	Y	Y	N
5 Sabo	Y	Y	Y	Y	Y	Y	N
6 Luther	Y	Y	Y	N	Y	N	Y
7 Peterson	Y	Y	Y	N	Y	N	Y
8 Oberstar	Y	Y	Y	Y	N	Y	N
MISSISSIPPI							
1 ***Wicker***	?	Y	Y	N	N	N	Y
2 Thompson	Y	Y	Y	Y	Y	Y	N
3 ***Pickering***	Y	Y	Y	N	N	N	Y
4 Shows	Y	Y	Y	N	N	N	Y
5 Taylor	Y	Y	Y	N	N	N	Y
MISSOURI							
1 Clay	Y	Y	Y	?	Y	Y	N
2 ***Akin***	Y	Y	Y	N	N	N	Y
3 Gephardt	Y	Y	Y	N	N	N	Y
4 Skelton	Y	Y	Y	N	Y	N	Y
5 McCarthy	Y	Y	Y	N	Y	N	N
6 ***Graves***	Y	Y	Y	N	N	N	Y
7 ***Blunt***	Y	Y	Y	N	N	N	Y
8 ***Emerson***	Y	Y	Y	N	N	N	Y
9 ***Hulshof***	Y	Y	Y	N	Y	N	Y
MONTANA							
AL ***Rehberg***	Y	Y	Y	N	N	N	Y
NEBRASKA							
1 ***Bereuter***	Y	Y	Y	N	N	N	Y
2 ***Terry***	Y	Y	Y	N	N	N	Y
3 ***Osborne***	Y	Y	Y	N	N	N	Y
NEVADA							
1 Berkley	Y	Y	Y	N	N	N	Y
2 ***Gibbons***	Y	Y	Y	N	N	N	Y
NEW HAMPSHIRE							
1 ***Sununu***	Y	Y	Y	N	N	N	Y
2 ***Bass***	Y	Y	Y	N	N	N	Y
NEW JERSEY							
1 Andrews	+	+	Y	N	N	N	Y
2 ***LoBiondo***	Y	Y	Y	N	N	N	Y
3 ***Saxton***	Y	Y	Y	N	N	N	Y
4 ***Smith***	Y	Y	Y	N	N	N	Y
5 ***Roukema***	?	?	?	?	?	?	?
6 Pallone	Y	Y	Y	N	Y	N	N
7 ***Ferguson***	Y	Y	Y	N	N	N	Y
8 Pascrell	Y	Y	Y	N	Y	Y	Y
9 Rothman	Y	Y	Y	N	N	N	Y
10 Payne	Y	Y	Y	Y	Y	Y	N
11 ***Frelinghuysen***	Y	Y	Y	N	N	N	Y
12 Holt	Y	Y	Y	N	Y	Y	N
13 Menendez	Y	Y	Y	N	Y	N	N
NEW MEXICO							
1 ***Wilson***	Y	Y	Y	N	N	N	Y
2 ***Skeen***	Y	Y	Y	N	N	N	Y
3 Udall	Y	Y	Y	Y	Y	Y	N
NEW YORK							
1 ***Grucci***	Y	Y	Y	N	N	N	Y
2 Israel	Y	Y	Y	N	N	N	Y
3 ***King***	Y	Y	Y	N	N	N	Y
4 McCarthy	Y	Y	Y	N	Y	N	Y
5 Ackerman	Y	Y	Y	N	Y	N	Y
6 Meeks	Y	Y	Y	Y	Y	Y	N
7 Crowley	Y	Y	Y	N	Y	Y	Y
8 Nadler	Y	Y	Y	N	Y	N	N
9 Weiner	Y	Y	Y	N	Y	N	Y
10 Towns	Y	Y	Y	Y	N	Y	N
11 Owens	Y	Y	Y	N	Y	Y	N
12 Velázquez	Y	Y	?	Y	N	Y	N
13 ***Fossella***	Y	Y	Y	N	N	N	Y
14 Maloney	Y	Y	Y	N	Y	Y	Y
15 Rangel	Y	Y	Y	Y	N	Y	N
16 Serrano	Y	Y	Y	Y	N	N	N
17 Engel	Y	Y	Y	N	Y	N	Y
18 Lowey	Y	Y	Y	N	N	N	Y
19 ***Kelly***	Y	Y	Y	N	N	N	Y
20 ***Gilman***	Y	Y	Y	N	N	N	Y
21 McNulty	Y	Y	Y	N	N	N	Y
22 ***Sweeney***	Y	Y	Y	N	N	N	Y
23 ***Boehlert***	Y	Y	Y	N	N	N	Y
24 ***McHugh***	Y	Y	Y	N	N	N	Y
25 ***Walsh***	Y	Y	Y	N	N	N	Y
26 Hinchey	Y	Y	Y	Y	Y	Y	N
27 ***Reynolds***	Y	Y	Y	N	N	N	Y
28 Slaughter	Y	Y	Y	N	Y	Y	N
29 LaFalce	?	?	?	N	Y	N	N
30 ***Quinn***	?	?	?	N	N	N	Y
31 ***Houghton***	?	?	?	N	N	N	N
NORTH CAROLINA							
1 Clayton	Y	Y	Y	Y	Y	Y	N
2 Etheridge	Y	Y	Y	N	Y	N	Y
3 ***Jones***	Y	Y	Y	N	N	N	Y
4 Price	Y	Y	Y	N	Y	N	N
5 ***Burr***	Y	Y	Y	N	N	N	Y
6 ***Coble***	Y	Y	Y	N	N	N	Y
7 McIntyre	Y	Y	Y	N	Y	N	Y
8 ***Hayes***	Y	Y	Y	N	N	N	Y
9 ***Myrick***	Y	Y	Y	N	N	N	Y
10 ***Ballenger***	Y	Y	Y	N	N	N	Y
11 ***Taylor***	Y	Y	Y	N	N	N	Y
12 Watt	Y	Y	Y	Y	Y	Y	N
NORTH DAKOTA							
AL Pomeroy	Y	Y	Y	N	N	N	Y
OHIO							
1 ***Chabot***	Y	Y	Y	N	N	N	Y
2 ***Portman***	Y	Y	Y	N	N	N	Y
3 Vacant							
4 ***Oxley***	Y	Y	Y	N	N	N	Y
5 ***Gillmor***	Y	Y	Y	N	N	N	Y
6 Strickland	Y	Y	Y	N	Y	N	N
7 ***Hobson***	Y	Y	Y	N	N	N	Y
8 ***Boehner***	Y	Y	Y	N	N	N	Y
9 Kaptur	Y	Y	Y	N	Y	Y	N
10 Kucinich	Y	Y	Y	Y	N	Y	N
11 Jones	Y	Y	Y	Y	N	Y	N
12 ***Tiberi***	Y	Y	Y	N	N	N	Y
13 Brown	Y	Y	Y	Y	Y	Y	N
14 Sawyer	Y	Y	Y	N	Y	Y	N
15 ***Pryce***	Y	Y	Y	N	N	N	Y
16 ***Regula***	Y	Y	Y	N	N	N	Y
17 Vacant							
18 ***Ney***	Y	Y	Y	N	N	N	Y
19 ***LaTourette***	Y	Y	Y	N	Y	N	Y
OKLAHOMA							
1 ***Sullivan***	Y	Y	Y	N	N	N	Y
2 Carson	Y	Y	Y	N	N	N	Y
3 ***Watkins***	Y	Y	Y	N	N	N	Y
4 ***Watts***	Y	Y	Y	N	N	N	Y
5 ***Istook***	?	?	?	N	N	N	Y
6 ***Lucas***	Y	Y	Y	N	N	N	Y
OREGON							
1 Wu	Y	Y	Y	N	Y	Y	N
2 ***Walden***	Y	Y	Y	N	N	N	Y
3 Blumenauer	Y	Y	Y	Y	Y	Y	N
4 DeFazio	Y	Y	Y	Y	Y	Y	N
5 Hooley	Y	Y	Y	N	Y	Y	N
PENNSYLVANIA							
1 Brady	Y	Y	Y	N	Y	N	N
2 Fattah	Y	Y	Y	Y	Y	Y	N
3 Borski	Y	Y	Y	N	Y	N	Y
4 ***Hart***	Y	Y	Y	N	N	N	Y
5 ***Peterson***	Y	Y	Y	N	N	N	Y
6 Holden	Y	Y	Y	N	N	N	Y
7 ***Weldon***	Y	Y	Y	N	N	N	Y
8 ***Greenwood***	Y	Y	Y	N	N	N	Y
9 ***Shuster, Bill***	Y	Y	Y	N	N	N	Y
10 ***Sherwood***	Y	Y	Y	N	N	N	Y
11 Kanjorski	Y	Y	Y	N	N	N	Y
12 Murtha	Y	Y	Y	N	N	N	Y
13 Hoeffel	Y	Y	Y	N	Y	N	Y
14 Coyne	Y	Y	Y	Y	Y	Y	N
15 ***Toomey***	Y	Y	Y	N	N	N	Y
16 ***Pitts***	Y	Y	Y	N	N	N	Y
17 ***Gekas***	Y	Y	Y	N	N	N	Y
18 Doyle	Y	Y	Y	N	Y	N	N
19 ***Platts***	Y	Y	Y	N	N	N	Y
20 Mascara	?	?	?	N	Y	N	Y
21 ***English***	Y	Y	Y	N	N	N	Y
RHODE ISLAND							
1 Kennedy	Y	Y	Y	N	N	N	Y
2 Langevin	Y	Y	Y	N	Y	N	N
SOUTH CAROLINA							
1 ***Brown***	Y	Y	Y	N	N	N	Y
2 ***Wilson***	Y	Y	Y	N	N	N	Y
3 ***Graham***	Y	Y	Y	N	N	N	Y
4 ***DeMint***	Y	Y	Y	N	N	N	Y
5 Spratt	Y	Y	Y	N	Y	N	Y
6 Clyburn	Y	Y	Y	Y	Y	Y	N
SOUTH DAKOTA							
AL ***Thune***	Y	Y	Y	N	N	N	Y
TENNESSEE							
1 ***Jenkins***	Y	Y	Y	N	N	N	Y
2 ***Duncan***	Y	Y	Y	N	N	N	N
3 ***Wamp***	Y	Y	Y	N	N	N	Y
4 ***Hilleary***	?	?	?	N	N	N	Y
5 Clement	Y	Y	Y	N	N	N	Y
6 Gordon	Y	Y	Y	N	N	N	Y
7 ***Bryant***	Y	Y	Y	N	N	N	Y
8 Tanner	Y	Y	Y	N	Y	N	Y
9 Ford	Y	Y	Y	N	Y	N	Y
TEXAS							
1 Sandlin	Y	Y	Y	?	Y	N	Y
2 Turner	Y	Y	Y	N	N	N	Y
3 ***Johnson, Sam***	Y	Y	Y	N	N	N	Y
4 Hall	Y	Y	Y	N	N	N	Y
5 ***Sessions***	Y	Y	Y	N	N	N	Y
6 ***Barton***	Y	Y	Y	N	N	N	Y
7 ***Culberson***	Y	Y	Y	N	N	N	Y
8 ***Brady***	Y	Y	Y	N	N	N	Y
9 Lampson	Y	Y	Y	N	Y	N	Y
10 Doggett	Y	Y	Y	Y	Y	Y	N
11 Edwards	Y	Y	Y	N	N	N	Y
12 ***Granger***	Y	Y	Y	N	N	N	Y
13 ***Thornberry***	Y	Y	Y	N	N	N	Y
14 ***Paul***	Y	N	Y	N	Y	Y	N
15 Hinojosa	Y	Y	Y	N	Y	Y	N
16 Reyes	Y	Y	Y	N	Y	N	N
17 Stenholm	Y	Y	Y	N	N	N	Y
18 Jackson-Lee	Y	Y	Y	Y	Y	Y	N
19 ***Combest***	Y	Y	Y	N	N	N	Y
20 Gonzalez	Y	Y	Y	N	Y	N	N
21 ***Smith***	Y	Y	Y	N	N	N	Y
22 ***DeLay***	Y	Y	Y	N	N	N	Y
23 ***Bonilla***	Y	Y	Y	N	N	N	Y
24 Frost	Y	Y	Y	N	N	N	Y
25 Bentsen	Y	Y	Y	N	Y	N	Y
26 ***Armey***	Y	?	?	N	N	N	Y
27 Ortiz	Y	Y	Y	N	?	?	?
28 Rodriguez	Y	Y	Y	N	Y	Y	N
29 Green	Y	Y	Y	N	N	Y	Y
30 Johnson, E.B.	Y	Y	Y	Y	Y	Y	N
UTAH							
1 ***Hansen***	Y	Y	Y	N	N	N	Y
2 Matheson	Y	Y	Y	N	N	N	Y
3 ***Cannon***	Y	Y	Y	N	N	N	Y
VERMONT							
AL *Sanders*	Y	Y	Y	Y	Y	Y	N
VIRGINIA							
1 ***Davis, Jo Ann***	Y	Y	Y	N	N	N	Y
2 ***Schrock***	Y	Y	Y	N	N	N	Y
3 Scott	Y	Y	Y	Y	Y	Y	N
4 ***Forbes***	Y	Y	Y	N	N	N	Y
5 ***Goode***	Y	Y	Y	N	N	N	Y
6 ***Goodlatte***	Y	Y	Y	N	N	N	Y
7 ***Cantor***	Y	Y	Y	N	N	N	Y
8 Moran	Y	Y	Y	N	Y	Y	N
9 Boucher	Y	Y	Y	N	Y	N	Y
10 ***Wolf***	Y	Y	Y	N	N	N	Y
11 ***Davis, T.***	Y	?	?	N	N	N	Y
WASHINGTON							
1 Inslee	Y	Y	Y	N	Y	Y	N
2 Larsen	Y	Y	Y	N	Y	N	N
3 Baird	Y	Y	Y	N	Y	N	N
4 ***Hastings***	Y	Y	Y	N	N	N	Y
5 ***Nethercutt***	Y	Y	Y	N	N	N	Y
6 Dicks	Y	Y	Y	N	N	N	Y
7 McDermott	Y	Y	Y	Y	N	Y	N
8 ***Dunn***	Y	Y	Y	N	N	N	Y
9 Smith	Y	Y	Y	N	Y	N	Y
WEST VIRGINIA							
1 Mollohan	Y	Y	Y	N	Y	N	N
2 ***Capito***	Y	Y	Y	N	N	N	Y
3 Rahall	Y	Y	Y	Y	Y	N	N
WISCONSIN							
1 ***Ryan***	Y	Y	Y	N	N	N	Y
2 Baldwin	Y	Y	Y	Y	Y	Y	N
3 Kind	Y	Y	Y	N	Y	N	Y
4 Kleczka	Y	Y	Y	N	Y	Y	N
5 Barrett	Y	Y	Y	N	Y	Y	N
6 ***Petri***	Y	Y	Y	N	N	N	Y
7 Obey	Y	Y	Y	N	Y	Y	N
8 ***Green***	Y	Y	Y	N	N	N	Y
9 ***Sensenbrenner***	Y	N	Y	N	N	N	Y
WYOMING							
AL ***Cubin***	Y	Y	Y	N	N	N	Y

Southern states - Ala., Ark., Fla., Ga., Ky., La., Miss., N.C., Okla., S.C., Tenn., Texas, Va.

456. HR 5010. Fiscal 2003 Defense Appropriations/Rule. Adoption of the rule (H Res 579) to provide for House floor consideration of the conference report on the bill that would provide $355.1 billion for the Defense Department for fiscal 2003. Adopted 374-37: R 210-0; D 163-37 (ND 117-32, SD 46-5); I 1-0. Oct. 10, 2002.

457. HR 5010. Fiscal 2003 Defense Appropriations/Conference Report. Adoption of the conference report on the bill that would provide $355.1 billion for the Defense Department for fiscal 2003, an increase of $21 billion over fiscal 2002 regular and supplemental funds. The agreement include $71.5 billion for procurement programs and $7.4 billion for ballistic missile defense. It includes $4 billion for the Air Force's F-22 fighter jet program and also would fund a 4.1 percent pay increase for military personnel. Adopted (thus sent to the Senate) 409-14: R 218-1; D 190-13 (ND 140-11, SD 50-2); I 1-0. Oct. 10, 2002.

458. HR 5011. Fiscal 2003 Military Construction Appropriations/Conference Report. Adoption of the conference report on the bill that would provide $10.5 billion in fiscal 2003, $105 million less than the current level, for military construction projects, including the building of barracks, family housing and medical facilities. The bill includes $561 million to cover costs of prior base closures and $799 million for anti-terrorism activities. Adopted (thus sent to the Senate) 419-0: R 217-0; D 201-0 (ND 149-0, SD 52-0); I 1-0. Oct. 10, 2002.

459. H J Res 122. Fiscal 2003 Continuing Appropriations/Rule. Adoption of the rule (H Res 580) to provide for House floor consideration of the joint resolution that would provide continuing appropriations through Oct. 18 for all federal departments and programs. Adopted 225-193: R 216-0; D 9-192 (ND 7-143, SD 2-49); I 0-1. Oct. 10, 2002.

460. H J Res 122. Fiscal 2003 Continuing Appropriations/Recommit. Obey, D-Wis., motion to recommit the joint resolution to the House Appropriations Committee with instructions that it be reported back with language that would provide for continuing appropriations through Oct. 12. Motion rejected 202-214: R 0-214; D 201-0 (ND 151-0, SD 50-0); I 1-0. Oct. 10, 2002.

461. H J Res 122. Fiscal 2003 Continuing Appropriations/Passage. Passage of the joint resolution that would provide continuing appropriations through Oct. 18 for all federal departments and programs. The joint resolution would set spending at fiscal 2002 levels, including that year's supplemental appropriations. It would continue federal highway spending at $31.8 billion, the fiscal 2002 level, but cap total funds allowed for the program through continuing resolutions at $27.7 billion. Entitlements and mandatory spending would be kept at a level necessary to maintain program levels under current law. Passed 272-144: R 211-2; D 61-141 (ND 39-112, SD 22-29); I 0-1. Oct. 10, 2002.

462. HR 3295. Election Overhaul/Conference Report. Adoption of the conference report on the bill that would overhaul the nation's election procedures by authorizing $3.9 billion in federal funds to states over three years to improve the administration of elections and help states meet nationwide voting standards. Adopted (thus sent to the Senate) 357-48: R 172-37; D 184-11 (ND 135-8, SD 49-3); I 1-0. Oct. 10, 2002.

463. HR 4546. Fiscal 2003 Defense Authorization/Motion to Instruct. Taylor, D-Miss., motion to instruct conferees to insist on language that would allow armed forces retirees to concurrently receive both pension payments and disability pay. Motion agreed to 391-0: R 201-0; D 189-0 (ND 138-0, SD 51-0); I 1-0. Oct. 10, 2002.

Key

Y	Voted for (yea).
#	Paired for.
+	Announced for.
N	Voted against (nay).
X	Paired against.
−	Announced against.
P	Voted "present."
C	Voted "present" to avoid possible conflict of interest.
?	Did not vote or otherwise make a position known.

•
Democrats **Republicans**
Independents

	456	457	458	459	460	461	462	463
ALABAMA								
1 *Callahan*	Y	Y	Y	Y	N	Y	N	Y
2 *Everett*	Y	Y	Y	Y	N	Y	N	Y
3 *Riley*	Y	Y	Y	Y	N	Y	N	Y
4 *Aderholt*	Y	Y	Y	Y	N	Y	Y	Y
5 Cramer	Y	Y	Y	N	Y	Y	Y	Y
6 *Bachus*	Y	Y	Y	Y	N	Y	Y	Y
7 Hilliard	N	Y	Y	N	Y	N	Y	Y
ALASKA								
AL *Young*	?	Y	Y	Y	N	Y	?	?
ARIZONA								
1 *Flake*	Y	Y	Y	Y	N	Y	N	Y
2 Pastor	Y	Y	Y	N	Y	N	N	Y
3 *Stump*	?	?	?	?	?	?	?	?
4 *Shadegg*	Y	Y	Y	Y	N	Y	N	Y
5 *Kolbe*	Y	Y	Y	Y	N	Y	Y	Y
6 *Hayworth*	Y	Y	Y	Y	N	Y	Y	Y
ARKANSAS								
1 Berry	Y	Y	Y	N	Y	N	Y	Y
2 Snyder	Y	Y	Y	N	Y	N	Y	Y
3 *Boozman*	Y	Y	Y	Y	N	Y	Y	Y
4 Ross	Y	Y	Y	Y	Y	Y	Y	Y
CALIFORNIA								
1 Thompson	Y	Y	Y	N	Y	N	Y	Y
2 *Herger*	Y	Y	Y	Y	N	Y	Y	Y
3 *Ose*	Y	Y	Y	Y	N	Y	Y	Y
4 *Doolittle*	Y	Y	Y	Y	N	Y	Y	Y
5 Matsui	Y	Y	Y	N	Y	N	?	?
6 Woolsey	N	N	Y	N	Y	N	Y	Y
7 Miller, George	N	N	Y	N	Y	N	Y	Y
8 Pelosi	Y	Y	Y	N	Y	N	Y	Y
9 Lee	N	N	Y	N	Y	N	Y	Y
10 Tauscher	Y	Y	Y	N	Y	N	Y	Y
11 *Pombo*	Y	Y	Y	Y	N	Y	Y	Y
12 Lantos	Y	Y	Y	N	Y	N	Y	Y
13 Stark	N	N	Y	N	Y	N	Y	?
14 Eshoo	Y	Y	Y	N	Y	N	Y	Y
15 Honda	Y	Y	Y	N	Y	N	Y	Y
16 Lofgren	Y	Y	Y	N	Y	N	Y	Y
17 Farr	Y	Y	Y	N	Y	N	Y	Y
18 Condit	Y	Y	Y	N	Y	N	Y	Y
19 *Radanovich*	Y	Y	Y	Y	N	Y	Y	Y
20 Dooley	Y	Y	Y	N	Y	N	Y	?
21 *Thomas*	Y	Y	Y	N	Y	N	N	Y
22 Capps	Y	Y	Y	N	Y	N	Y	Y
23 *Gallegly*	Y	Y	Y	Y	N	Y	Y	Y
24 Sherman	Y	Y	Y	N	Y	N	Y	Y
25 *McKeon*	Y	Y	Y	Y	N	Y	Y	Y
26 Berman	?	Y	?	?	?	?	?	?
27 Schiff	Y	Y	Y	N	Y	N	Y	Y
28 *Dreier*	Y	Y	Y	Y	N	Y	Y	Y
29 Waxman	Y	Y	Y	N	Y	N	?	?
30 Becerra	Y	Y	Y	N	Y	N	N	Y
31 Solis	Y	Y	Y	N	Y	N	Y	Y
32 Watson	Y	Y	Y	N	Y	N	Y	Y
33 Roybal-Allard	Y	Y	Y	N	Y	N	Y	Y
34 Napolitano	Y	Y	Y	N	Y	N	Y	Y
35 Waters	N	N	Y	N	Y	N	Y	Y
36 Harman	Y	Y	Y	N	Y	N	Y	Y
37 Millender-McD.	Y	Y	Y	N	Y	N	Y	Y
38 *Horn*	Y	Y	Y	Y	N	Y	Y	Y

	456	457	458	459	460	461	462	463
39 *Royce*	Y	Y	Y	Y	N	Y	Y	Y
40 *Lewis*	Y	Y	Y	?	N	Y	Y	Y
41 *Miller, Gary*	Y	Y	Y	Y	N	Y	?	Y
42 Baca	Y	Y	Y	N	Y	N	Y	Y
43 *Calvert*	Y	Y	Y	Y	N	Y	Y	Y
44 *Bono*	Y	Y	Y	Y	N	Y	Y	Y
45 *Rohrabacher*	Y	Y	Y	Y	N	Y	Y	Y
46 Sanchez	Y	Y	N	Y	N	Y	Y	Y
47 *Cox*	Y	Y	Y	Y	N	Y	Y	Y
48 *Issa*	Y	Y	Y	Y	N	Y	Y	Y
49 Davis	Y	Y	Y	N	Y	N	Y	Y
50 Filner	N	N	Y	N	Y	N	N	Y
51 *Cunningham*	Y	Y	Y	Y	N	Y	Y	Y
52 *Hunter*	Y	Y	Y	Y	N	Y	Y	Y
COLORADO								
1 DeGette	N	N	Y	N	Y	N	Y	Y
2 Udall	N	Y	Y	N	Y	N	Y	Y
3 *McInnis*	Y	Y	Y	Y	N	Y	Y	Y
4 *Schaffer*	Y	Y	Y	Y	N	Y	N	Y
5 *Hefley*	Y	Y	Y	Y	N	Y	N	Y
6 *Tancredo*	Y	Y	Y	Y	N	Y	Y	Y
CONNECTICUT								
1 Larson	Y	Y	Y	N	Y	N	Y	Y
2 *Simmons*	Y	Y	Y	N	Y	N	Y	Y
3 DeLauro	Y	Y	Y	N	Y	N	Y	Y
4 *Shays*	Y	Y	Y	Y	N	Y	Y	Y
5 Maloney	Y	Y	Y	N	Y	N	Y	Y
6 *Johnson*	Y	Y	Y	Y	N	Y	Y	Y
DELAWARE								
AL *Castle*	Y	Y	Y	Y	N	Y	Y	Y
FLORIDA								
1 *Miller, J.*	Y	Y	Y	Y	N	Y	N	Y
2 Boyd	Y	Y	Y	N	Y	Y	Y	Y
3 Brown	Y	Y	Y	N	Y	N	Y	Y
4 *Crenshaw*	Y	Y	Y	Y	N	Y	Y	Y
5 Thurman	Y	Y	Y	N	Y	N	Y	Y
6 *Stearns*	Y	Y	Y	Y	N	Y	N	Y
7 *Mica*	Y	Y	Y	Y	N	Y	N	Y
8 *Keller*	Y	Y	Y	Y	N	Y	Y	Y
9 *Bilirakis*	Y	Y	Y	Y	N	Y	Y	Y
10 *Young*	Y	Y	Y	Y	N	Y	Y	Y
11 Davis	Y	Y	Y	N	Y	N	Y	Y
12 *Putnam*	Y	Y	Y	Y	N	Y	N	Y
13 *Miller, D.*	Y	Y	Y	Y	N	Y	Y	Y
14 *Goss*	Y	Y	Y	Y	N	Y	Y	Y
15 *Weldon*	?	Y	Y	Y	N	Y	Y	Y
16 *Foley*	Y	Y	Y	N	Y	N	Y	Y
17 Meek	Y	Y	?	?	?	?	Y	Y
18 *Ros-Lehtinen*	Y	Y	Y	Y	N	Y	Y	Y
19 Wexler	Y	Y	Y	N	Y	N	Y	Y
20 Deutsch	Y	Y	Y	N	Y	N	Y	Y
21 *Diaz-Balart*	Y	Y	?	Y	N	Y	Y	?
22 *Shaw*	Y	Y	Y	Y	N	Y	Y	Y
23 Hastings	Y	Y	Y	N	Y	N	Y	Y
GEORGIA								
1 *Kingston*	Y	Y	Y	Y	N	Y	N	Y
2 Bishop	Y	Y	Y	N	Y	Y	Y	Y
3 *Collins*	Y	Y	Y	Y	N	Y	N	Y
4 *McKinney*	?	?	Y	Y	?	Y	Y	?
5 Lewis	N	N	N	N	Y	N	Y	Y
6 *Isakson*	Y	Y	Y	Y	N	Y	Y	Y
7 *Barr*	?	Y	Y	N	Y	N	N	Y
8 *Chambliss*	Y	Y	Y	Y	N	Y	N	Y
9 *Deal*	Y	Y	Y	Y	N	Y	Y	Y
10 *Norwood*	Y	Y	Y	Y	N	Y	N	Y
11 *Linder*	Y	Y	Y	Y	N	Y	N	Y
HAWAII								
1 Abercrombie	Y	Y	Y	N	Y	Y	Y	Y
2 Vacant								
IDAHO								
1 *Otter*	Y	Y	Y	Y	N	Y	N	Y
2 *Simpson*	Y	Y	Y	Y	N	Y	Y	Y
ILLINOIS								
1 Rush	Y	Y	Y	N	Y	N	Y	Y
2 Jackson	Y	N	Y	N	Y	N	Y	Y
3 Lipinski	Y	Y	Y	N	Y	N	?	?
4 Gutierrez	Y	Y	Y	?	Y	N	?	?
5 Blagojevich	Y	Y	Y	N	Y	Y	?	?
6 *Hyde*	Y	Y	Y	Y	N	Y	Y	Y
7 Davis	Y	Y	Y	N	Y	N	Y	Y
8 *Crane*	Y	Y	Y	Y	N	Y	Y	Y
9 Schakowsky	N	N	Y	N	Y	N	Y	Y
10 *Kirk*	Y	Y	Y	Y	N	Y	Y	Y
11 *Weller*	Y	Y	Y	Y	N	Y	Y	Y
12 Costello	Y	Y	Y	N	Y	N	Y	Y
13 *Biggert*	Y	Y	Y	Y	N	Y	Y	Y

ND Northern Democrats   SD Southern Democrats

	456	457	458	459	460	461	462	463
14 ***Hastert***								
15 ***Johnson***	Y	Y	Y	Y	N	Y	Y	Y
16 ***Manzullo***	Y	Y	Y	Y	N	Y	?	?
17 Evans	Y	Y	Y	N	Y	N	Y	Y
18 ***LaHood***	Y	Y	Y	Y	N	Y	Y	Y
19 Phelps	Y	Y	Y	N	Y	Y	Y	Y
20 ***Shimkus***	Y	Y	Y	Y	N	Y	Y	Y
INDIANA								
1 Visclosky	Y	Y	Y	N	Y	N	Y	Y
2 ***Pence***	Y	Y	Y	Y	N	Y	Y	Y
3 Roemer	Y	Y	Y	N	Y	N	Y	Y
4 ***Souder***	Y	Y	Y	Y	N	Y	N	Y
5 ***Buyer***	Y	Y	Y	Y	N	Y	Y	Y
6 ***Burton***	Y	Y	Y	Y	N	?	Y	Y
7 ***Kerns***	Y	Y	Y	Y	N	Y	N	Y
8 ***Hostettler***	Y	Y	Y	Y	N	Y	N	Y
9 Hill	Y	Y	Y	N	Y	Y	Y	Y
10 Carson	Y	Y	Y	N	Y	Y	Y	Y
IOWA								
1 ***Leach***	Y	Y	Y	Y	N	Y	Y	Y
2 ***Nussle***	Y	Y	Y	Y	N	Y	Y	Y
3 Boswell	Y	Y	Y	N	Y	Y	Y	Y
4 ***Ganske***	Y	Y	Y	?	?	?	?	?
5 ***Latham***	Y	Y	Y	Y	N	Y	Y	Y
KANSAS								
1 ***Moran***	Y	Y	Y	Y	N	N	N	Y
2 ***Ryun***	Y	Y	Y	Y	N	Y	Y	Y
3 Moore	Y	Y	Y	N	Y	Y	Y	Y
4 ***Tiahrt***	Y	Y	Y	Y	N	Y	Y	Y
KENTUCKY								
1 ***Whitfield***	Y	Y	Y	Y	N	Y	N	Y
2 ***Lewis***	Y	Y	Y	Y	N	Y	Y	Y
3 ***Northup***	Y	Y	Y	Y	N	Y	Y	Y
4 Lucas	Y	Y	Y	N	Y	Y	Y	Y
5 ***Rogers***	Y	Y	Y	Y	N	Y	Y	Y
6 ***Fletcher***	Y	Y	Y	Y	N	Y	Y	Y
LOUISIANA								
1 ***Vitter***	Y	Y	Y	Y	N	Y	Y	Y
2 Jefferson	Y	Y	Y	N	Y	N	Y	Y
3 ***Tauzin***	Y	Y	Y	Y	N	Y	Y	Y
4 ***McCrery***	Y	Y	Y	Y	N	Y	Y	Y
5 ***Cooksey***	?	?	?	?	?	?	?	?
6 ***Baker***	Y	Y	Y	?	N	Y	Y	Y
7 John	Y	Y	Y	N	Y	Y	Y	Y
MAINE								
1 Allen	Y	Y	Y	N	Y	N	Y	Y
2 Baldacci	?	?	Y	Y	Y	Y	Y	Y
MARYLAND								
1 ***Gilchrest***	Y	Y	Y	Y	N	Y	Y	Y
2 ***Ehrlich***	Y	Y	Y	Y	N	?	?	?
3 Cardin	Y	Y	Y	N	Y	Y	Y	Y
4 Wynn	Y	Y	Y	N	Y	N	Y	Y
5 Hoyer	Y	Y	Y	N	Y	N	Y	Y
6 ***Bartlett***	Y	Y	Y	Y	N	Y	Y	Y
7 Cummings	Y	Y	Y	N	Y	N	Y	Y
8 ***Morella***	Y	Y	Y	Y	N	Y	Y	Y
MASSACHUSETTS								
1 Olver	Y	Y	Y	N	Y	N	Y	Y
2 Neal	Y	Y	Y	N	Y	N	?	Y
3 McGovern	Y	Y	Y	N	Y	N	Y	Y
4 Frank	?	N	Y	N	Y	N	Y	Y
5 Meehan	Y	Y	Y	N	Y	N	Y	Y
6 Tierney	N	Y	Y	N	Y	N	Y	Y
7 Markey	Y	Y	Y	N	Y	N	Y	Y
8 Capuano	Y	Y	Y	N	Y	N	N	Y
9 Lynch	Y	Y	Y	N	Y	N	Y	Y
10 Delahunt	N	Y	Y	N	Y	N	Y	Y
MICHIGAN								
1 Stupak	Y	Y	Y	N	Y	N	Y	Y
2 ***Hoekstra***	Y	Y	Y	Y	N	Y	N	Y
3 ***Ehlers***	Y	Y	Y	Y	N	Y	Y	Y
4 ***Camp***	Y	Y	Y	Y	N	Y	Y	Y
5 Barcia	Y	Y	Y	N	Y	Y	Y	Y
6 ***Upton***	Y	Y	Y	Y	N	Y	Y	Y
7 ***Smith***	Y	Y	Y	Y	N	Y	N	?
8 ***Rogers***	Y	Y	Y	Y	N	Y	Y	Y
9 Kildee	Y	Y	Y	N	Y	N	Y	Y
10 Bonior	?	?	?	?	?	?	?	?
11 ***Knollenberg***	Y	Y	Y	Y	N	Y	Y	Y
12 Levin	Y	Y	Y	N	Y	N	Y	Y
13 Rivers	N	Y	Y	N	Y	N	Y	Y
14 Conyers	N	Y	Y	N	Y	N	Y	Y
15 Kilpatrick	Y	Y	Y	N	Y	N	Y	Y
16 Dingell	Y	Y	Y	N	Y	N	Y	Y
MINNESOTA								
1 ***Gutknecht***	Y	Y	Y	Y	N	Y	N	Y
2 ***Kennedy***	Y	Y	Y	Y	N	Y	Y	Y
3 ***Ramstad***	Y	Y	Y	Y	N	Y	Y	Y
4 McCollum	Y	Y	Y	N	Y	N	Y	Y
5 Sabo	Y	Y	Y	N	Y	N	N	Y
6 Luther	Y	Y	Y	N	Y	Y	Y	Y
7 Peterson	Y	Y	Y	N	Y	Y	Y	Y
8 Oberstar	N	N	Y	N	Y	N	Y	Y
MISSISSIPPI								
1 ***Wicker***	Y	Y	Y	Y	N	Y	Y	Y
2 Thompson	Y	Y	Y	N	Y	N	Y	Y
3 ***Pickering***	Y	Y	Y	Y	N	Y	Y	Y
4 Shows	Y	Y	Y	N	Y	Y	Y	Y
5 Taylor	Y	Y	Y	N	Y	Y	Y	Y
MISSOURI								
1 Clay	Y	Y	Y	N	Y	N	Y	?
2 ***Akin***	Y	Y	Y	Y	N	Y	Y	Y
3 Gephardt	N	Y	Y	N	Y	N	Y	?
4 Skelton	Y	Y	Y	N	Y	Y	Y	Y
5 McCarthy	Y	Y	Y	N	Y	Y	Y	Y
6 ***Graves***	Y	Y	Y	Y	N	Y	Y	Y
7 ***Blunt***	Y	Y	Y	Y	N	Y	Y	?
8 ***Emerson***	Y	Y	Y	Y	N	Y	Y	Y
9 ***Hulshof***	Y	Y	Y	Y	?	Y	Y	Y
MONTANA								
AL ***Rehberg***	Y	Y	Y	Y	N	Y	Y	Y
NEBRASKA								
1 ***Bereuter***	Y	Y	Y	Y	N	Y	Y	Y
2 ***Terry***	Y	Y	Y	Y	N	Y	Y	Y
3 ***Osborne***	?	Y	Y	Y	N	Y	Y	Y
NEVADA								
1 Berkley	Y	Y	Y	N	Y	N	Y	Y
2 ***Gibbons***	Y	Y	Y	Y	N	Y	Y	Y
NEW HAMPSHIRE								
1 ***Sununu***	Y	Y	Y	Y	?	?	?	?
2 ***Bass***	Y	Y	Y	Y	N	Y	Y	Y
NEW JERSEY								
1 Andrews	Y	Y	Y	N	Y	N	Y	Y
2 ***LoBiondo***	Y	Y	Y	Y	N	Y	Y	Y
3 ***Saxton***	Y	Y	Y	Y	N	Y	Y	Y
4 ***Smith***	Y	Y	Y	Y	N	Y	Y	Y
5 ***Roukema***	?	?	?	?	?	?	?	?
6 Pallone	Y	Y	Y	N	Y	N	Y	Y
7 ***Ferguson***	Y	Y	Y	Y	N	Y	Y	Y
8 Pascrell	Y	Y	Y	N	Y	Y	Y	Y
9 Rothman	Y	Y	Y	N	Y	Y	Y	Y
10 Payne	N	N	Y	N	Y	N	Y	Y
11 ***Frelinghuysen***	Y	Y	Y	Y	N	Y	Y	Y
12 Holt	N	Y	Y	N	Y	Y	Y	Y
13 Menendez	Y	Y	Y	N	Y	Y	Y	Y
NEW MEXICO								
1 ***Wilson***	Y	Y	Y	Y	N	Y	Y	Y
2 ***Skeen***	Y	Y	Y	Y	N	Y	Y	Y
3 Udall	N	Y	Y	N	Y	N	N	Y
NEW YORK								
1 ***Grucci***	Y	Y	Y	Y	N	Y	Y	Y
2 Israel	Y	Y	Y	N	Y	Y	Y	Y
3 ***King***	Y	Y	Y	Y	N	Y	?	?
4 McCarthy	Y	Y	Y	N	Y	N	Y	Y
5 Ackerman	Y	Y	Y	N	Y	N	Y	Y
6 Meeks	Y	Y	Y	N	Y	N	Y	Y
7 Crowley	Y	Y	Y	N	Y	N	Y	Y
8 Nadler	Y	Y	Y	N	Y	N	Y	Y
9 Weiner	Y	Y	Y	N	Y	N	Y	Y
10 Towns	Y	Y	?	N	Y	N	Y	Y
11 Owens	N	Y	Y	N	Y	N	Y	Y
12 Velázquez	Y	Y	Y	N	Y	N	N	Y
13 ***Fossella***	Y	Y	Y	Y	N	Y	Y	?
14 Maloney	Y	Y	Y	N	Y	N	Y	Y
15 Rangel	N	Y	Y	N	Y	N	Y	Y
16 Serrano	Y	Y	Y	N	Y	N	Y	Y
17 Engel	Y	Y	Y	N	Y	N	Y	Y
18 Lowey	Y	Y	Y	N	Y	N	Y	Y
19 ***Kelly***	Y	Y	Y	Y	N	Y	Y	Y
20 ***Gilman***	Y	Y	Y	Y	N	Y	Y	Y
21 McNulty	Y	Y	Y	N	Y	N	Y	Y
22 ***Sweeney***	Y	Y	Y	Y	N	Y	Y	Y
23 ***Boehlert***	Y	Y	Y	Y	N	Y	Y	Y
24 ***McHugh***	Y	Y	Y	Y	N	Y	Y	Y
25 ***Walsh***	Y	Y	Y	Y	N	Y	Y	Y
26 Hinchey	N	Y	Y	N	Y	N	Y	Y
27 ***Reynolds***	Y	Y	Y	Y	N	Y	Y	Y
28 Slaughter	N	Y	?	N	Y	N	Y	Y
29 LaFalce	Y	Y	Y	N	Y	N	Y	?
30 ***Quinn***	Y	Y	Y	Y	N	Y	Y	Y
31 ***Houghton***	Y	Y	Y	Y	N	Y	?	?
NORTH CAROLINA								
1 Clayton	N	Y	Y	N	Y	N	Y	Y
2 Etheridge	Y	Y	Y	N	Y	N	Y	Y
3 ***Jones***	Y	Y	Y	Y	N	Y	N	Y
4 Price	Y	Y	Y	N	Y	N	Y	Y
5 ***Burr***	?	Y	Y	Y	N	Y	Y	Y
6 ***Coble***	Y	Y	Y	Y	N	Y	N	Y
7 McIntyre	Y	Y	Y	N	Y	N	Y	Y
8 ***Hayes***	Y	Y	Y	Y	N	Y	Y	Y
9 ***Myrick***	Y	Y	Y	Y	N	Y	Y	Y
10 ***Ballenger***	Y	Y	Y	Y	N	Y	Y	Y
11 ***Taylor***	Y	Y	Y	Y	?	?	?	?
12 Watt	N	N	Y	N	Y	N	N	Y
NORTH DAKOTA								
AL Pomeroy	Y	Y	Y	N	Y	Y	Y	Y
OHIO								
1 ***Chabot***	Y	Y	Y	Y	N	Y	Y	Y
2 ***Portman***	?	Y	Y	Y	N	Y	Y	Y
3 Vacant								
4 ***Oxley***	Y	Y	Y	Y	N	Y	Y	?
5 ***Gillmor***	Y	Y	Y	Y	N	Y	Y	?
6 Strickland	N	Y	Y	N	Y	N	Y	Y
7 ***Hobson***	Y	Y	Y	Y	N	Y	Y	Y
8 ***Boehner***	Y	Y	Y	Y	N	Y	Y	?
9 Kaptur	Y	Y	Y	N	Y	N	Y	Y
10 Kucinich	N	N	Y	N	Y	N	Y	Y
11 Jones	N	Y	Y	N	Y	N	Y	Y
12 ***Tiberi***	Y	Y	Y	Y	N	Y	Y	Y
13 Brown	N	Y	Y	N	Y	N	Y	Y
14 Sawyer	N	Y	Y	N	Y	N	Y	Y
15 ***Pryce***	Y	Y	Y	Y	N	Y	Y	Y
16 ***Regula***	Y	Y	Y	Y	N	Y	Y	Y
17 Vacant								
18 ***Ney***	Y	Y	Y	Y	N	Y	Y	Y
19 ***LaTourette***	Y	Y	Y	Y	N	Y	Y	Y
OKLAHOMA								
1 ***Sullivan***	Y	Y	Y	Y	N	Y	Y	Y
2 Carson	Y	Y	Y	N	Y	Y	Y	Y
3 ***Watkins***	Y	Y	Y	Y	N	Y	Y	Y
4 ***Watts***	Y	Y	Y	Y	N	Y	N	Y
5 ***Istook***	Y	Y	Y	Y	N	Y	N	Y
6 ***Lucas***	Y	Y	Y	Y	N	Y	N	Y
OREGON								
1 Wu	Y	Y	Y	N	Y	N	Y	Y
2 ***Walden***	Y	Y	Y	Y	N	Y	Y	Y
3 Blumenauer	Y	N	Y	N	Y	N	Y	Y
4 DeFazio	N	Y	Y	N	Y	N	Y	Y
5 Hooley	Y	Y	Y	N	Y	N	Y	Y
PENNSYLVANIA								
1 Brady	Y	Y	Y	Y	Y	Y	Y	Y
2 Fattah	Y	Y	Y	N	Y	N	Y	Y
3 Borski	Y	Y	Y	N	Y	N	Y	Y
4 ***Hart***	Y	Y	Y	Y	N	Y	Y	Y
5 ***Peterson***	Y	Y	Y	Y	N	Y	Y	Y
6 Holden	Y	Y	Y	N	Y	Y	Y	Y
7 ***Weldon***	Y	Y	Y	Y	N	Y	Y	Y
8 ***Greenwood***	?	Y	Y	Y	N	Y	Y	Y
9 ***Shuster, Bill***	Y	Y	Y	Y	N	Y	Y	Y
10 ***Sherwood***	Y	Y	Y	Y	N	Y	Y	Y
11 Kanjorski	Y	Y	Y	Y	Y	Y	Y	Y
12 Murtha	Y	Y	Y	Y	Y	Y	?	?
13 Hoeffel	Y	Y	Y	N	Y	Y	Y	?
14 Coyne	?	?	?	?	?	?	?	?
15 ***Toomey***	Y	Y	Y	Y	N	Y	N	Y
16 ***Pitts***	Y	Y	Y	Y	N	Y	Y	Y
17 ***Gekas***	Y	Y	Y	Y	N	Y	Y	Y
18 Doyle	Y	Y	Y	N	Y	Y	Y	Y
19 ***Platts***	Y	Y	Y	Y	N	Y	Y	Y
20 Mascara	Y	Y	Y	N	Y	Y	Y	Y
21 ***English***	Y	Y	Y	Y	N	Y	Y	Y
RHODE ISLAND								
1 Kennedy	Y	Y	Y	N	Y	Y	Y	Y
2 Langevin	Y	Y	Y	N	Y	N	Y	Y
SOUTH CAROLINA								
1 ***Brown***	Y	Y	Y	Y	N	Y	Y	Y
2 ***Wilson***	Y	Y	Y	Y	N	Y	Y	Y
3 ***Graham***	Y	Y	Y	Y	N	Y	Y	Y
4 ***DeMint***	Y	Y	Y	Y	N	Y	Y	Y
5 Spratt	Y	Y	Y	N	Y	N	Y	Y
6 Clyburn	Y	Y	Y	N	Y	N	Y	Y
SOUTH DAKOTA								
AL ***Thune***	Y	Y	Y	Y	N	Y	Y	Y
TENNESSEE								
1 ***Jenkins***	Y	Y	Y	Y	?	?	?	?
2 ***Duncan***	Y	Y	Y	Y	N	Y	N	Y
3 ***Wamp***	Y	Y	Y	Y	N	Y	N	Y
4 ***Hilleary***	?	Y	Y	Y	N	Y	Y	Y
5 Clement	Y	Y	Y	N	Y	Y	Y	Y
6 Gordon	Y	Y	Y	N	Y	Y	Y	Y
7 ***Bryant***	Y	Y	Y	Y	N	Y	Y	Y
8 Tanner	?	Y	Y	N	Y	Y	Y	Y
9 Ford	Y	Y	Y	N	Y	N	Y	Y
TEXAS								
1 Sandlin	Y	Y	Y	N	Y	N	Y	Y
2 Turner	Y	Y	Y	N	Y	N	Y	Y
3 ***Johnson, Sam***	Y	Y	Y	Y	N	Y	Y	Y
4 Hall	Y	Y	Y	N	Y	Y	Y	Y
5 ***Sessions***	Y	Y	Y	Y	N	Y	N	Y
6 ***Barton***	Y	Y	Y	Y	N	Y	Y	Y
7 ***Culberson***	Y	Y	Y	Y	N	Y	Y	Y
8 ***Brady***	?	Y	Y	Y	N	Y	Y	Y
9 Lampson	Y	Y	Y	N	Y	N	Y	Y
10 Doggett	N	Y	Y	N	Y	N	Y	Y
11 Edwards	Y	Y	Y	N	Y	Y	Y	Y
12 ***Granger***	Y	Y	Y	Y	N	Y	Y	Y
13 ***Thornberry***	Y	Y	Y	Y	N	Y	N	Y
14 ***Paul***	Y	N	?	Y	N	N	N	Y
15 Hinojosa	Y	Y	Y	N	Y	N	Y	Y
16 Reyes	Y	Y	?	?	?	?	?	?
17 Stenholm	Y	Y	Y	N	Y	N	Y	Y
18 Jackson-Lee	Y	Y	Y	N	Y	N	Y	Y
19 ***Combest***	Y	Y	Y	Y	N	Y	Y	?
20 Gonzalez	Y	Y	Y	N	Y	N	N	Y
21 ***Smith***	Y	Y	Y	Y	N	Y	Y	Y
22 ***DeLay***	Y	Y	Y	Y	N	Y	Y	?
23 ***Bonilla***	Y	Y	Y	Y	N	Y	N	Y
24 Frost	Y	Y	Y	N	Y	N	Y	Y
25 Bentsen	Y	Y	Y	N	Y	N	Y	Y
26 ***Armey***	Y	Y	Y	Y	N	Y	Y	Y
27 Ortiz	?	?	?	?	?	?	?	?
28 Rodriguez	Y	Y	Y	N	Y	N	N	Y
29 Green	Y	Y	Y	N	Y	Y	Y	Y
30 Johnson, E.B.	Y	Y	Y	N	Y	N	Y	Y
UTAH								
1 ***Hansen***	Y	Y	Y	Y	N	Y	Y	Y
2 Matheson	Y	Y	Y	N	Y	Y	Y	Y
3 ***Cannon***	Y	Y	Y	Y	N	Y	N	Y
VERMONT								
AL *Sanders*	Y	Y	Y	N	Y	N	Y	Y
VIRGINIA								
1 ***Davis, Jo Ann***	Y	Y	Y	Y	N	Y	Y	Y
2 ***Schrock***	Y	Y	Y	Y	N	Y	Y	Y
3 Scott	Y	Y	Y	N	Y	N	Y	Y
4 ***Forbes***	Y	Y	Y	Y	N	Y	Y	Y
5 ***Goode***	Y	Y	Y	Y	N	Y	N	Y
6 ***Goodlatte***	Y	Y	Y	Y	N	Y	N	Y
7 ***Cantor***	Y	Y	Y	Y	N	Y	Y	Y
8 Moran	Y	Y	Y	N	Y	Y	Y	Y
9 Boucher	Y	Y	Y	N	Y	Y	Y	Y
10 ***Wolf***	Y	Y	Y	Y	N	Y	Y	Y
11 ***Davis, T.***	Y	Y	Y	Y	N	Y	Y	Y
WASHINGTON								
1 Inslee	Y	Y	Y	N	Y	N	Y	Y
2 Larsen	Y	Y	Y	N	Y	N	Y	Y
3 Baird	Y	Y	Y	N	Y	N	Y	Y
4 ***Hastings***	Y	Y	Y	Y	N	Y	Y	Y
5 ***Nethercutt***	Y	Y	Y	Y	N	Y	Y	Y
6 Dicks	Y	Y	Y	Y	Y	Y	?	?
7 McDermott	N	N	Y	N	Y	N	Y	Y
8 ***Dunn***	Y	Y	Y	Y	N	Y	Y	Y
9 Smith	Y	Y	Y	N	Y	Y	Y	Y
WEST VIRGINIA								
1 Mollohan	Y	Y	Y	Y	Y	Y	Y	Y
2 ***Capito***	Y	Y	Y	Y	N	Y	Y	Y
3 Rahall	Y	Y	Y	N	Y	N	Y	Y
WISCONSIN								
1 ***Ryan***	Y	Y	Y	Y	N	Y	Y	Y
2 Baldwin	N	Y	Y	N	Y	N	Y	Y
3 Kind	Y	Y	Y	N	Y	N	Y	Y
4 Kleczka	Y	Y	Y	N	Y	N	Y	Y
5 Barrett	N	Y	Y	N	Y	N	Y	Y
6 ***Petri***	Y	Y	Y	Y	N	Y	Y	Y
7 Obey	N	Y	Y	N	Y	N	Y	Y
8 ***Green***	Y	Y	Y	Y	N	Y	Y	Y
9 ***Sensenbrenner***	Y	Y	Y	Y	N	Y	N	Y
WYOMING								
AL ***Cubin***	Y	Y	Y	Y	N	Y	N	Y

Southern states - Ala., Ark., Fla., Ga., Ky., La., Miss., N.C., Okla., S.C., Tenn., Texas, Va.

Key

Y	Voted for (yea).
#	Paired for.
+	Announced for.
N	Voted against (nay).
X	Paired against.
−	Announced against.
P	Voted "present."
C	Voted "present" to avoid possible conflict of interest.
?	Did not vote or otherwise make a position known.

Democrats   **Republicans**
Independents

464. Procedural Motion/Journal. Approval of the House Journal of Tuesday, Oct. 15, 2002. Approved 330-52: R 182-17; D 147-35 (ND 106-28, SD 41-7); I 1-0. Oct. 16, 2002.

465. HR 2155. Drunken Driving at U.S. Borders/Passage. Sensenbrenner, R-Wis., motion to suspend the rules and pass the bill that would make it a federal crime to operate a motor vehicle at any of the nation's border entry points while under the influence of alcohol or drugs. INS agents would have authority to take offenders into custody. Motion agreed to 296-94: R 202-0; D 94-93 (ND 68-71, SD 26-22); I 0-1. A two-thirds majority of those present and voting (260 in this case) is required for passage under suspension of the rules. Oct. 16, 2002.

466. S 1533. Community and Rural Health Care/Passage. Stearns, R-Fla., motion to suspend the rules and pass the bill that would authorize funds through fiscal 2006 for community health centers, the National Health Service Corps and rural health care providers. The bill would authorize $1.3 billion in fiscal 2002 and such funds as are necessary through fiscal 2006 for community health centers. Motion agreed to 392-5: R 201-5; D 190-0 (ND 141-0, SD 49-0); I 1-0. A two-thirds majority of those present and voting (265 in this case) is required for passage under suspension of the rules. Oct. 16, 2002.

467. H J Res 123. Fiscal 2003 Continuing Appropriations/Previous Question. Hastings, R-Wash., motion to order the previous question (thus ending debate and possibility of amendment) on adoption of the rule (H Res 585) to provide for House floor consideration of the joint resolution to provide continuing appropriations through Nov. 22 for all federal departments and programs. Motion agreed to 209-193: R 209-0; D 0-192 (ND 0-144, SD 0-48); I 0-1. Oct. 16, 2002.

468. H J Res 123. Fiscal 2003 Continuing Appropriations/Rule. Adoption of the rule (H Res 585) to provide for House floor consideration of the joint resolution to provide continuing appropriations through Nov. 22 for all federal departments and programs. Adopted 206-193: R 201-7; D 5-185 (ND 5-137, SD 0-48); I 0-1. Oct. 16, 2002.

469. H J Res 123. Fiscal 2003 Continuing Appropriations/Recommit. Obey, D-Wis., motion to recommit the joint resolution to the House Appropriations Committee with instructions that it be reported back with language that would provide for continuing appropriations through Oct. 21. Motion rejected 194-210: R 1-208; D 192-2 (ND 143-1, SD 49-1); I 1-0. Oct. 16, 2002.

470. H J Res 123. Fiscal 2003 Continuing Appropriations/Passage. Passage of the joint resolution to provide continuing appropriations through Nov. 22 for all federal departments and programs. The continuing resolution would set spending at fiscal 2002 levels, including that year's supplemental appropriations. Passed 228-172: R 202-6; D 26-165 (ND 21-121, SD 5-44); I 0-1. Oct. 16, 2002.

	464	465	466	467	468	469	470
ALABAMA							
1 *Callahan*	?	?	?	Y	N	Y	Y
2 *Everett*	Y	Y	Y	Y	Y	N	Y
3 *Riley*	?	?	?	?	?	?	?
4 *Aderholt*	N	Y	Y	Y	Y	N	Y
5 Cramer	Y	Y	Y	N	N	Y	N
6 *Bachus*	Y	Y	Y	Y	Y	N	Y
7 Hilliard	N	N	Y	N	N	Y	N
ALASKA							
AL *Young*	Y	Y	Y	Y	Y	N	Y
ARIZONA							
1 *Flake*	Y	Y	N	Y	Y	N	Y
2 Pastor	N	N	Y	N	N	Y	N
3 *Stump*	?	?	?	?	?	?	?
4 *Shadegg*	Y	Y	Y	Y	Y	N	Y
5 *Kolbe*	Y	Y	Y	Y	Y	N	Y
6 *Hayworth*	Y	Y	Y	Y	Y	N	Y
ARKANSAS							
1 Berry	Y	Y	Y	N	N	Y	N
2 Snyder	Y	Y	Y	N	N	Y	N
3 *Boozman*	Y	Y	Y	Y	Y	N	Y
4 Ross	Y	Y	Y	N	N	Y	Y
CALIFORNIA							
1 Thompson	N	N	Y	N	N	Y	N
2 *Herger*	Y	Y	Y	Y	Y	N	Y
3 *Ose*	Y	Y	Y	Y	Y	N	Y
4 *Doolittle*	Y	Y	Y	Y	Y	N	Y
5 Matsui	Y	Y	Y	N	N	Y	N
6 Woolsey	Y	N	Y	N	N	Y	N
7 Miller, George	N	Y	N	N	N	Y	N
8 Pelosi	Y	N	Y	N	N	Y	N
9 Lee	Y	N	Y	N	N	Y	N
10 Tauscher	Y	Y	Y	N	N	Y	N
11 *Pombo*	Y	Y	Y	Y	Y	N	Y
12 Lantos	Y	Y	Y	N	N	Y	N
13 Stark	Y	N	Y	N	N	Y	N
14 Eshoo	Y	Y	Y	N	N	Y	N
15 Honda	Y	N	Y	N	N	Y	N
16 Lofgren	Y	Y	Y	N	N	Y	N
17 Farr	Y	Y	Y	N	N	Y	N
18 Condit	N	Y	N	N	N	N	N
19 *Radanovich*	Y	Y	Y	Y	Y	N	Y
20 Dooley	?	?	?	?	?	?	?
21 *Thomas*	Y	Y	Y	Y	Y	N	Y
22 Capps	Y	N	Y	N	N	Y	N
23 *Gallegly*	Y	Y	Y	Y	Y	N	Y
24 Sherman	N	N	Y	N	N	Y	N
25 *McKeon*	Y	Y	Y	Y	Y	N	Y
26 Berman	Y	Y	Y	N	N	Y	N
27 Schiff	Y	Y	Y	N	N	Y	N
28 *Dreier*	Y	Y	Y	Y	Y	N	Y
29 Waxman	Y	Y	Y	N	N	Y	?
30 Becerra	Y	Y	Y	N	N	Y	N
31 Solis	Y	N	Y	N	N	Y	N
32 Watson	Y	N	Y	N	N	Y	N
33 Roybal-Allard	Y	N	Y	N	N	Y	N
34 Napolitano	Y	N	Y	N	N	Y	N
35 Waters	?	?	?	?	?	?	?
36 Harman	Y	Y	Y	N	N	Y	N
37 Millender-McD.	Y	N	Y	N	N	Y	N
38 Horn	Y	Y	Y	Y	Y	N	Y

	464	465	466	467	468	469	470
39 *Royce*	Y	Y	Y	Y	Y	N	Y
40 *Lewis*	Y	Y	Y	Y	Y	N	Y
41 *Miller, Gary*	?	?	?	?	?	?	?
42 Baca	Y	Y	N	N	N	Y	N
43 *Calvert*	Y	Y	Y	Y	Y	N	Y
44 *Bono*	Y	Y	Y	Y	Y	N	Y
45 *Rohrabacher*	Y	Y	Y	Y	Y	N	Y
46 Sanchez	Y	N	N	N	N	Y	N
47 *Cox*	Y	Y	Y	Y	Y	N	Y
48 *Issa*	Y	Y	Y	Y	Y	N	Y
49 Davis	Y	Y	Y	N	N	Y	N
50 Filner	−	−	+	−	−	+	−
51 *Cunningham*	Y	Y	Y	Y	Y	N	Y
52 *Hunter*	Y	Y	Y	Y	Y	N	Y
COLORADO							
1 DeGette	?	?	?	N	N	Y	N
2 Udall	Y	Y	Y	N	N	Y	N
3 *McInnis*	?	?	?	Y	Y	N	Y
4 *Schaffer*	N	Y	Y	Y	Y	N	Y
5 *Hefley*	N	Y	Y	Y	Y	N	Y
6 *Tancredo*	P	Y	Y	Y	Y	N	Y
CONNECTICUT							
1 Larson	Y	N	Y	N	N	Y	N
2 *Simmons*	Y	Y	Y	Y	Y	N	Y
3 DeLauro	Y	N	Y	N	N	Y	N
4 *Shays*	Y	Y	Y	Y	Y	N	Y
5 Maloney	?	?	?	?	?	?	?
6 *Johnson*	Y	Y	Y	Y	Y	N	Y
DELAWARE							
AL *Castle*	Y	Y	Y	Y	Y	N	Y
FLORIDA							
1 *Miller, J.*	Y	Y	Y	Y	Y	N	Y
2 Boyd	Y	Y	Y	N	N	Y	N
3 Brown	Y	N	Y	N	Y	N	N
4 *Crenshaw*	Y	Y	Y	Y	Y	N	Y
5 Thurman	Y	Y	Y	N	N	Y	N
6 *Stearns*	+	Y	Y	Y	Y	N	Y
7 *Mica*	?	?	?	?	?	?	?
8 *Keller*	Y	Y	Y	Y	Y	N	Y
9 *Bilirakis*	Y	Y	Y	Y	Y	N	Y
10 *Young*	Y	Y	Y	Y	Y	N	Y
11 Davis	Y	Y	Y	N	N	Y	N
12 *Putnam*	Y	Y	Y	Y	Y	N	Y
13 *Miller, D.*	Y	Y	Y	Y	Y	N	Y
14 *Goss*	Y	Y	Y	Y	Y	N	Y
15 *Weldon*	Y	Y	Y	Y	Y	N	Y
16 *Foley*	Y	Y	Y	Y	Y	N	Y
17 Meek	Y	N	Y	?	?	Y	N
18 *Ros-Lehtinen*	Y	Y	Y	Y	Y	N	Y
19 Wexler	Y	Y	Y	N	N	Y	N
20 Deutsch	Y	Y	Y	N	N	Y	N
21 *Diaz-Balart*	Y	Y	Y	Y	Y	N	Y
22 *Shaw*	Y	Y	Y	Y	Y	N	Y
23 Hastings	N	N	Y	N	N	Y	N
GEORGIA							
1 *Kingston*	Y	Y	Y	Y	Y	N	Y
2 Bishop	Y	N	Y	N	N	Y	N
3 *Collins*	Y	Y	Y	Y	Y	N	Y
4 McKinney	?	?	?	?	?	?	?
5 Lewis	?	N	Y	N	N	Y	N
6 *Isakson*	Y	Y	Y	Y	Y	N	Y
7 *Barr*	Y	Y	Y	Y	Y	N	Y
8 *Chambliss*	Y	Y	Y	Y	Y	N	Y
9 *Deal*	Y	Y	Y	Y	Y	N	Y
10 *Norwood*	Y	Y	Y	Y	Y	N	Y
11 *Linder*	Y	Y	Y	Y	?	N	Y
HAWAII							
1 Abercrombie	Y	N	Y	N	N	Y	N
2 Vacant							
IDAHO							
1 *Otter*	Y	Y	Y	Y	Y	N	Y
2 *Simpson*	Y	Y	Y	Y	Y	N	Y
ILLINOIS							
1 Rush	?	?	?	?	?	?	?
2 Jackson	Y	N	Y	N	N	Y	N
3 Lipinski	Y	Y	Y	N	N	Y	N
4 Gutierrez	Y	N	Y	N	Y	Y	N
5 Blagojevich	?	Y	Y	N	Y	Y	Y
6 *Hyde*	Y	Y	Y	Y	Y	N	Y
7 Davis	Y	N	Y	N	N	Y	N
8 *Crane*	N	Y	Y	Y	Y	N	Y
9 Schakowsky	N	N	Y	N	N	Y	N
10 *Kirk*	Y	Y	Y	Y	Y	N	Y
11 *Weller*	N	Y	Y	Y	Y	N	Y
12 Costello	N	Y	Y	N	N	Y	N
13 *Biggert*	Y	Y	Y	Y	Y	N	Y

ND Northern Democrats   SD Southern Democrats

	464	465	466	467	468	469	470
14 ***Hastert***					Y	N	Y
15 ***Johnson***	Y	Y	Y	Y	Y	N	Y
16 ***Manzullo***	?	?	?	?	?	?	?
17 Evans	Y	N	Y	N	N	Y	N
18 ***LaHood***	?	?	?	?	?	?	?
19 Phelps	Y	Y	Y	N	N	Y	N
20 ***Shimkus***	Y	Y	Y	Y	N	N	N
INDIANA							
1 Visclosky	N	Y	Y	N	N	Y	N
2 ***Pence***	Y	Y	Y	Y	Y	N	Y
3 Roemer	Y	Y	Y	N	N	Y	N
4 ***Souder***	Y	Y	Y	Y	Y	N	Y
5 ***Buyer***	Y	Y	Y	Y	Y	N	Y
6 ***Burton***	Y	Y	Y	Y	Y	N	Y
7 ***Kerns***	Y	Y	N	Y	Y	N	Y
8 ***Hostettler***	Y	Y	N	Y	Y	N	Y
9 Hill	Y	Y	Y	N	N	Y	Y
10 Carson	Y	N	Y	N	N	Y	N
IOWA							
1 ***Leach***	Y	Y	Y	Y	Y	N	Y
2 ***Nussle***	Y	Y	Y	Y	Y	N	Y
3 Boswell	Y	Y	Y	N	N	Y	N
4 ***Ganske***	?	?	?	?	?	?	?
5 ***Latham***	N	Y	Y	Y	Y	N	Y
KANSAS							
1 ***Moran***	Y	Y	Y	Y	N	N	N
2 ***Ryun***	Y	Y	Y	Y	Y	N	Y
3 Moore	N	Y	Y	N	N	Y	Y
4 ***Tiahrt***	Y	Y	Y	Y	?	N	Y
KENTUCKY							
1 ***Whitfield***	Y	Y	Y	Y	Y	N	Y
2 ***Lewis***	Y	Y	Y	Y	Y	N	Y
3 ***Northup***	Y	Y	Y	Y	Y	N	Y
4 Lucas	Y	Y	Y	N	N	Y	Y
5 ***Rogers***	Y	Y	Y	Y	Y	N	Y
6 ***Fletcher***	Y	Y	Y	Y	Y	N	Y
LOUISIANA							
1 ***Vitter***	Y	Y	Y	Y	Y	N	Y
2 Jefferson	Y	Y	Y	N	N	Y	N
3 ***Tauzin***	Y	Y	Y	Y	Y	N	Y
4 ***McCrery***	Y	Y	Y	Y	Y	N	Y
5 ***Cooksey***	?	?	?	?	?	?	?
6 ***Baker***	Y	Y	Y	Y	Y	N	Y
7 John	Y	Y	Y	N	N	Y	N
MAINE							
1 Allen	Y	Y	Y	N	N	Y	N
2 Baldacci	?	?	?	?	?	?	?
MARYLAND							
1 ***Gilchrest***	Y	Y	Y	Y	Y	N	Y
2 ***Ehrlich***	?	?	?	Y	Y	?	?
3 Cardin	Y	Y	Y	N	N	Y	N
4 Wynn	Y	N	Y	N	N	Y	Y
5 Hoyer	Y	Y	Y	N	N	Y	Y
6 ***Bartlett***	Y	Y	Y	Y	Y	N	Y
7 Cummings	Y	N	Y	N	N	Y	N
8 ***Morella***	Y	Y	Y	Y	Y	N	Y
MASSACHUSETTS							
1 Olver	N	Y	Y	N	N	Y	N
2 Neal	Y	Y	Y	N	N	Y	N
3 McGovern	N	Y	Y	N	N	Y	N
4 Frank	Y	Y	Y	N	N	Y	?
5 Meehan	Y	Y	Y	N	N	Y	N
6 Tierney	Y	N	Y	N	N	Y	N
7 Markey	Y	N	Y	N	N	Y	N
8 Capuano	N	N	Y	N	N	Y	N
9 Lynch	Y	N	Y	N	N	Y	N
10 Delahunt	?	?	?	?	?	?	?
MICHIGAN							
1 Stupak	N	N	Y	N	N	Y	N
2 ***Hoekstra***	Y	Y	Y	Y	Y	N	Y
3 ***Ehlers***	Y	Y	Y	Y	Y	N	Y
4 ***Camp***	Y	Y	Y	Y	Y	N	Y
5 Barcia	Y	Y	Y	N	N	Y	N
6 ***Upton***	Y	Y	Y	Y	Y	N	Y
7 ***Smith***	Y	Y	Y	Y	Y	N	Y
8 ***Rogers***	Y	Y	Y	Y	Y	N	Y
9 Kildee	Y	N	Y	N	N	Y	N
10 Bonior	Y	N	Y	N	N	Y	N
11 ***Knollenberg***	Y	Y	Y	Y	Y	N	Y
12 Levin	Y	Y	Y	N	N	Y	N
13 Rivers	Y	N	Y	N	N	Y	N
14 Conyers	?	N	Y	N	N	Y	N
15 Kilpatrick	Y	N	Y	N	N	Y	N
16 Dingell	Y	Y	Y	N	N	Y	N
MINNESOTA							
1 ***Gutknecht***	N	Y	Y	Y	Y	N	Y
2 ***Kennedy***	N	Y	Y	Y	Y	N	Y
3 ***Ramstad***	N	Y	Y	Y	Y	N	Y
4 McCollum	Y	N	Y	N	N	Y	N
5 Sabo	?	?	Y	N	N	Y	N
6 Luther	?	?	?	N	N	Y	Y
7 Peterson	?	?	Y	N	N	Y	N
8 Oberstar	N	N	Y	N	N	Y	N
MISSISSIPPI							
1 ***Wicker***	N	Y	Y	Y	Y	N	Y
2 Thompson	N	Y	Y	N	N	Y	N
3 ***Pickering***	Y	Y	Y	Y	Y	N	Y
4 Shows	Y	?	Y	N	N	Y	Y
5 Taylor	N	Y	Y	N	N	Y	N
MISSOURI							
1 Clay	N	N	Y	N	N	Y	N
2 ***Akin***	Y	Y	Y	Y	Y	N	Y
3 Gephardt	?	?	?	N	N	Y	N
4 Skelton	Y	Y	Y	N	N	Y	N
5 McCarthy	Y	N	Y	N	N	Y	N
6 ***Graves***	Y	Y	Y	Y	Y	N	+
7 ***Blunt***	Y	Y	Y	Y	Y	N	Y
8 ***Emerson***	Y	Y	Y	Y	N	N	Y
9 ***Hulshof***	Y	Y	Y	Y	Y	N	Y
MONTANA							
AL ***Rehberg***	Y	Y	Y	Y	Y	N	Y
NEBRASKA							
1 ***Bereuter***	Y	Y	Y	Y	N	N	N
2 ***Terry***	Y	Y	Y	Y	N	N	Y
3 ***Osborne***	Y	Y	Y	Y	N	N	N
NEVADA							
1 Berkley	Y	Y	Y	N	N	Y	Y
2 ***Gibbons***	Y	Y	Y	Y	Y	N	Y
NEW HAMPSHIRE							
1 ***Sununu***	Y	Y	Y	Y	Y	N	Y
2 ***Bass***	Y	Y	Y	Y	Y	N	Y
NEW JERSEY							
1 Andrews	Y	N	Y	N	N	Y	N
2 ***LoBiondo***	N	Y	Y	Y	Y	N	Y
3 ***Saxton***	Y	Y	Y	Y	Y	N	Y
4 ***Smith***	Y	Y	Y	Y	Y	N	Y
5 ***Roukema***	?	?	?	?	?	?	?
6 Pallone	N	N	Y	N	N	Y	N
7 ***Ferguson***	Y	Y	Y	Y	Y	N	Y
8 Pascrell	Y	Y	Y	N	N	Y	N
9 Rothman	Y	N	Y	N	N	Y	N
10 Payne	?	N	Y	N	N	Y	N
11 ***Frelinghuysen***	Y	Y	Y	Y	Y	N	Y
12 Holt	Y	Y	Y	N	N	Y	Y
13 Menendez	Y	N	Y	N	N	Y	N
NEW MEXICO							
1 ***Wilson***	Y	Y	Y	Y	Y	N	Y
2 ***Skeen***	Y	Y	Y	Y	Y	N	Y
3 Udall	N	N	Y	N	N	Y	N
NEW YORK							
1 ***Grucci***	Y	Y	Y	Y	Y	N	Y
2 Israel	Y	Y	Y	N	N	Y	Y
3 ***King***	Y	Y	Y	Y	Y	N	Y
4 McCarthy	?	Y	Y	N	N	Y	Y
5 Ackerman	Y	Y	Y	N	N	Y	N
6 Meeks	Y	N	Y	N	N	Y	N
7 Crowley	Y	N	Y	N	N	Y	N
8 Nadler	Y	Y	Y	N	N	Y	N
9 Weiner	Y	N	Y	N	N	Y	N
10 Towns	Y	N	Y	N	N	Y	N
11 Owens	Y	N	Y	N	N	Y	N
12 Velázquez	Y	N	Y	N	?	Y	N
13 ***Fossella***	N	Y	Y	Y	Y	N	Y
14 Maloney	Y	Y	Y	N	N	Y	N
15 Rangel	Y	N	Y	N	N	Y	N
16 Serrano	Y	N	Y	N	N	Y	N
17 Engel	Y	Y	Y	N	N	Y	Y
18 Lowey	Y	N	Y	N	N	Y	N
19 ***Kelly***	Y	Y	Y	Y	Y	N	Y
20 ***Gilman***	Y	Y	Y	Y	Y	N	Y
21 McNulty	N	Y	Y	N	N	Y	N
22 ***Sweeney***	N	Y	Y	Y	Y	N	Y
23 ***Boehlert***	Y	Y	Y	Y	Y	N	Y
24 ***McHugh***	Y	Y	Y	Y	Y	N	Y
25 ***Walsh***	Y	Y	Y	Y	Y	N	Y
26 Hinchey	?	–	+	N	N	Y	N
27 ***Reynolds***	Y	Y	Y	Y	Y	N	Y
28 Slaughter	+	?	+	+	–	+	–
29 LaFalce	Y	Y	Y	N	N	Y	N
30 ***Quinn***	Y	Y	Y	Y	Y	N	Y
31 ***Houghton***	Y	Y	Y	Y	Y	N	Y
NORTH CAROLINA							
1 Clayton	?	?	?	?	?	?	?
2 Etheridge	Y	Y	Y	N	N	Y	N
3 ***Jones***	Y	Y	Y	Y	Y	N	Y
4 Price	Y	Y	Y	N	N	Y	N
5 ***Burr***	Y	Y	Y	Y	Y	N	Y
6 ***Coble***	Y	Y	N	Y	Y	N	Y
7 McIntyre	Y	Y	Y	N	N	Y	N
8 ***Hayes***	Y	Y	Y	Y	Y	N	Y
9 ***Myrick***	Y	Y	Y	Y	Y	N	Y
10 ***Ballenger***	Y	Y	Y	Y	Y	N	Y
11 ***Taylor***	?	?	Y	Y	Y	N	Y
12 Watt	Y	N	Y	N	N	Y	N
NORTH DAKOTA							
AL Pomeroy	Y	Y	Y	N	N	Y	N
OHIO							
1 ***Chabot***	Y	Y	Y	Y	Y	N	Y
2 ***Portman***	Y	Y	Y	Y	Y	N	Y
3 Vacant							
4 ***Oxley***	Y	Y	Y	Y	Y	N	Y
5 ***Gillmor***	N	Y	Y	Y	Y	N	Y
6 Strickland	Y	Y	Y	N	N	Y	N
7 ***Hobson***	Y	Y	Y	Y	Y	N	Y
8 ***Boehner***	Y	Y	Y	Y	Y	N	Y
9 Kaptur	Y	Y	Y	N	N	Y	N
10 Kucinich	N	N	Y	N	N	Y	N
11 Jones	N	N	Y	N	N	Y	N
12 ***Tiberi***	Y	Y	Y	Y	Y	N	Y
13 Brown	Y	N	Y	N	N	Y	N
14 Sawyer	Y	N	Y	N	N	Y	N
15 ***Pryce***	Y	Y	Y	Y	Y	N	Y
16 ***Regula***	Y	Y	Y	Y	Y	N	Y
17 Vacant							
18 ***Ney***	Y	Y	Y	Y	Y	N	Y
19 ***LaTourette***	Y	Y	Y	Y	Y	N	Y
OKLAHOMA							
1 ***Sullivan***	Y	Y	Y	Y	Y	N	Y
2 Carson	?	?	?	?	?	?	?
3 ***Watkins***	Y	Y	Y	Y	Y	N	Y
4 ***Watts***	Y	Y	Y	Y	Y	N	Y
5 ***Istook***	Y	Y	Y	Y	Y	N	Y
6 ***Lucas***	Y	Y	Y	Y	Y	N	Y
OREGON							
1 Wu	Y	Y	Y	N	N	Y	N
2 ***Walden***	Y	Y	Y	Y	Y	N	Y
3 Blumenauer	Y	Y	Y	N	N	Y	N
4 DeFazio	N	Y	Y	N	N	Y	N
5 Hooley	Y	Y	Y	N	N	Y	N
PENNSYLVANIA							
1 Brady	N	N	Y	N	N	Y	N
2 Fattah	N	N	Y	N	N	Y	N
3 Borski	N	Y	Y	?	?	?	?
4 ***Hart***	N	Y	Y	Y	Y	N	Y
5 ***Peterson***	?	?	?	Y	Y	N	Y
6 Holden	Y	Y	Y	N	N	Y	Y
7 ***Weldon***	Y	Y	Y	Y	Y	N	Y
8 ***Greenwood***	Y	Y	Y	Y	Y	N	Y
9 ***Shuster, Bill***	Y	Y	Y	Y	Y	N	Y
10 ***Sherwood***	Y	Y	Y	Y	Y	N	Y
11 Kanjorski	Y	Y	Y	N	N	Y	Y
12 Murtha	Y	Y	Y	N	N	Y	Y
13 Hoeffel	Y	Y	Y	N	N	Y	Y
14 Coyne	?	?	?	N	N	Y	N
15 ***Toomey***	Y	Y	Y	Y	Y	N	Y
16 ***Pitts***	Y	Y	Y	Y	Y	N	Y
17 ***Gekas***	Y	Y	Y	Y	Y	N	Y
18 Doyle	Y	Y	Y	N	N	Y	N
19 ***Platts***	N	Y	Y	Y	Y	N	Y
20 Mascara	Y	Y	Y	N	N	Y	Y
21 ***English***	N	Y	Y	Y	Y	N	Y
RHODE ISLAND							
1 Kennedy	Y	N	Y	N	?	Y	N
2 Langevin	Y	Y	Y	N	N	Y	N
SOUTH CAROLINA							
1 ***Brown***	Y	Y	Y	Y	Y	N	Y
2 ***Wilson***	Y	Y	Y	Y	Y	N	Y
3 ***Graham***	Y	Y	Y	?	?	?	?
4 ***DeMint***	Y	Y	Y	Y	Y	N	Y
5 Spratt	Y	Y	Y	N	N	Y	N
6 Clyburn	Y	N	Y	N	N	Y	N
SOUTH DAKOTA							
AL ***Thune***	Y	Y	Y	Y	N	Y	N
TENNESSEE							
1 ***Jenkins***	Y	Y	Y	Y	Y	N	Y
2 ***Duncan***	Y	Y	Y	Y	Y	N	Y
3 ***Wamp***	Y	Y	Y	Y	Y	N	Y
4 ***Hilleary***	?	?	?	?	?	?	?
5 Clement	?	?	?	?	?	?	?
6 Gordon	Y	Y	Y	N	N	Y	N
7 ***Bryant***	?	?	Y	Y	Y	N	Y
8 Tanner	Y	Y	Y	N	N	Y	N
9 Ford	Y	N	Y	N	N	Y	N
TEXAS							
1 Sandlin	Y	N	Y	N	N	Y	N
2 Turner	Y	Y	Y	N	N	Y	N
3 ***Johnson, Sam***	Y	Y	Y	Y	Y	N	Y
4 Hall	Y	Y	Y	N	N	N	?
5 ***Sessions***	Y	Y	Y	Y	Y	N	Y
6 ***Barton***	Y	Y	Y	Y	Y	N	Y
7 ***Culberson***	Y	Y	Y	Y	Y	N	Y
8 ***Brady***	Y	Y	Y	Y	Y	N	Y
9 Lampson	Y	N	Y	N	N	Y	N
10 Doggett	Y	N	Y	N	N	Y	N
11 Edwards	Y	Y	Y	N	N	Y	N
12 ***Granger***	Y	Y	Y	Y	Y	N	Y
13 ***Thornberry***	Y	Y	Y	Y	Y	N	Y
14 ***Paul***	Y	Y	N	Y	Y	N	Y
15 Hinojosa	+	–	+	+	–	+	–
16 Reyes	N	N	Y	N	N	Y	N
17 Stenholm	N	Y	Y	N	N	Y	N
18 Jackson-Lee	Y	N	Y	N	N	Y	N
19 ***Combest***	?	?	?	?	?	?	?
20 Gonzalez	Y	N	Y	N	N	Y	N
21 ***Smith***	Y	Y	Y	Y	Y	N	Y
22 ***DeLay***	Y	Y	Y	Y	Y	N	Y
23 ***Bonilla***	Y	Y	Y	Y	Y	N	Y
24 Frost	Y	N	Y	N	N	Y	N
25 Bentsen	Y	N	Y	N	N	Y	N
26 ***Armey***	?	Y	Y	Y	Y	N	Y
27 Ortiz	Y	N	Y	N	N	Y	N
28 Rodriguez	Y	N	Y	N	N	Y	N
29 Green	Y	N	Y	N	N	Y	N
30 Johnson, E.B.	N	N	Y	N	N	Y	N
UTAH							
1 ***Hansen***	Y	Y	Y	Y	Y	N	Y
2 Matheson	Y	Y	Y	N	N	Y	Y
3 ***Cannon***	Y	Y	Y	Y	Y	N	Y
VERMONT							
AL *Sanders*	Y	N	Y	N	N	Y	N
VIRGINIA							
1 ***Davis, Jo Ann***	Y	Y	Y	Y	Y	N	Y
2 ***Schrock***	Y	Y	Y	Y	Y	N	Y
3 Scott	Y	N	Y	N	N	Y	N
4 ***Forbes***	Y	Y	Y	Y	Y	N	Y
5 ***Goode***	?	?	Y	Y	Y	N	Y
6 ***Goodlatte***	Y	Y	Y	Y	Y	N	Y
7 ***Cantor***	Y	Y	Y	Y	Y	N	Y
8 Moran	Y	Y	Y	N	N	Y	Y
9 Boucher	Y	Y	Y	N	N	Y	N
10 ***Wolf***	Y	Y	Y	Y	Y	N	Y
11 ***Davis, T.***	?	?	Y	Y	Y	N	Y
WASHINGTON							
1 Inslee	Y	Y	Y	N	N	Y	N
2 Larsen	N	Y	Y	?	?	?	?
3 Baird	N	Y	Y	N	N	Y	N
4 ***Hastings***	Y	Y	Y	Y	Y	N	Y
5 ***Nethercutt***	Y	Y	Y	Y	Y	N	Y
6 Dicks	Y	N	Y	N	N	Y	Y
7 McDermott	N	N	Y	N	N	Y	N
8 ***Dunn***	Y	Y	Y	Y	Y	N	Y
9 Smith	Y	Y	Y	N	N	Y	N
WEST VIRGINIA							
1 Mollohan	Y	N	Y	N	N	Y	Y
2 ***Capito***	Y	Y	Y	Y	Y	N	Y
3 Rahall	Y	N	Y	N	N	Y	N
WISCONSIN							
1 ***Ryan***	Y	Y	Y	Y	Y	N	Y
2 Baldwin	N	N	Y	N	N	Y	N
3 Kind	Y	Y	Y	N	N	Y	N
4 Kleczka	Y	N	Y	N	N	Y	N
5 Barrett	Y	N	Y	N	N	Y	N
6 ***Petri***	Y	Y	Y	Y	Y	N	Y
7 Obey	?	N	Y	N	N	Y	N
8 ***Green***	Y	Y	Y	Y	Y	N	Y
9 ***Sensenbrenner***	Y	Y	Y	Y	Y	N	Y
WYOMING							
AL ***Cubin***	?	?	?	?	?	?	?

Southern states - Ala., Ark., Fla., Ga., Ky., La., Miss., N.C., Okla., S.C., Tenn., Texas, Va.

471. Procedural Motion/Adjourn. Obey, D-Wis., motion to adjourn. Motion rejected 24-338: R 0-191; D 24-146 (ND 17-104, SD 7-42); I 0-1. Nov. 13, 2002.

472. H J Res 124, HR 5708. Fiscal 2003 Continuing Appropriations and PAYGO Reduction /Rule. Adoption of the rule (H Res 602) to provide for House floor consideration of the joint resolution (H J Res 124) to provide continuing appropriations through Jan. 11, 2003, and a bill (HR 5708) that would reduce to zero any balances in the pay-as-you-go account. Adopted 215-189: R 215-0; D 0-188 (ND 0-137, SD 0-51); I 0-1. Nov. 13, 2002.

473. H J Res 124. Fiscal 2003 Continuing Appropriations/Recommit. Obey, D-Wis., motion to recommit the joint resolution to the House Appropriations Committee with instructions that it be reported back with additional funding for veterans' health care, National Institutes of Health bioterrorism and research programs, the Federal Emergency Management Agency and first responders, and corporate oversight activities of the Securities and Exchange Commission. Motion rejected 196-216: R 1-214; D 194-2 (ND 142-1, SD 52-1); I 1-0. Nov. 13, 2002.

474. H J Res 124. Fiscal 2003 Continuing Appropriations/Passage. Passage of the joint resolution to provide continuing appropriations through Jan. 11, 2003, for all federal departments and programs not covered by enacted fiscal 2003 spending bills. The resolution would set spending at fiscal 2002 levels, including fiscal 2002 supplemental appropriations. Passed 270-143: R 208-6; D 62-136 (ND 39-105, SD 23-31); I 0-1. Nov. 13, 2002.

475. HR 5710. Homeland Security/Rule. Adoption of the rule (H Res 600) to provide for House floor consideration of the bill that would consolidate 22 agencies into a new Cabinet-level Homeland Security Department charged with protecting domestic security. Adopted 237-177: R 216-1; D 21-175 (ND 10-134, SD 11-41); I 0-1. Nov. 13, 2002.

476. HR 5710. Homeland Security/Recommit. Roemer, D-Ind., motion to recommit the bill to the Select Committee on Homeland Security with instructions that it be reported back with language that would establish a National Commission on Terrorist Attacks Upon the United States to examine and report on the facts and circumstances relating to the Sept. 11, 2001, terrorist attacks. Motion rejected 203-215: R 2-215; D 200-0 (ND 148-0, SD 52-0); I 1-0. A "nay" was a vote in support of the president's position. Nov. 13, 2002.

477. HR 5710. Homeland Security/Passage. Passage of the bill that would consolidate 22 agencies into a new cabinet-level Homeland Security Department charged with protecting domestic security. Agencies moved to the new department would include the Coast Guard, the Federal Emergency Management Agency, the Customs Service, the Secret Service and the Transportation Security Administration. The Immigration and Naturalization Service would be split into separate agencies for immigration enforcement and citizen services, both of which would be in the new department. The president could exempt some employees from collective bargaining units for national security reasons. The department could make changes to personnel rules, but unions could object to and negotiate those changes. Passed 299-121: R 212-6; D 87-114 (ND 52-95, SD 35-19); I 0-1. A "yea" was a vote in support of the president's position. Nov. 13, 2002.

Key

Y	Voted for (yea).
#	Paired for.
+	Announced for.
N	Voted against (nay).
–	Paired against.
–	Announced against.
P	Voted "present."
C	Voted "present" to avoid possible conflict of interest.
?	Did not vote or otherwise make a position known.

Democrats **Republicans**
Independents

	471	472	473	474	475	476	477
ALABAMA							
1 *Callahan*	?	Y	N	Y	Y	N	Y
2 *Everett*	N	Y	N	Y	Y	N	Y
3 *Riley*	N	Y	N	Y	Y	N	Y
4 *Aderholt*	N	Y	N	Y	Y	N	Y
5 Cramer	N	N	Y	Y	Y	Y	Y
6 *Bachus*	N	Y	N	Y	Y	N	Y
7 Hilliard	Y	N	Y	Y	N	Y	N
ALASKA							
AL *Young*	N	Y	N	Y	Y	N	Y
ARIZONA							
1 *Flake*	N	Y	N	Y	Y	N	N
2 Pastor	N	N	Y	Y	N	Y	Y
3 *Stump*	?	?	?	?	?	?	?
4 *Shadegg*	N	Y	N	Y	Y	?	Y
5 *Kolbe*	N	Y	N	N	Y	N	Y
6 *Hayworth*	N	Y	N	Y	Y	N	Y
ARKANSAS							
1 Berry	Y	N	Y	N	N	Y	Y
2 Snyder	N	N	Y	N	N	Y	N
3 *Boozman*	N	Y	N	Y	Y	N	Y
4 Ross	N	N	Y	N	N	Y	Y
CALIFORNIA							
1 Thompson	N	N	Y	N	N	Y	N
2 *Herger*	N	Y	N	?	Y	N	Y
3 *Ose*	N	Y	N	Y	Y	N	Y
4 *Doolittle*	N	Y	N	Y	Y	N	Y
5 Matsui	N	N	Y	N	Y	N	Y
6 Woolsey	Y	N	N	N	N	Y	N
7 *Miller, George*	?	?	?	?	?	Y	N
8 Pelosi	N	N	N	N	N	Y	N
9 Lee	N	N	N	N	N	Y	N
10 Tauscher	N	N	Y	Y	Y	Y	Y
11 *Pombo*	N	Y	N	Y	Y	N	Y
12 Lantos	N	N	N	N	N	Y	N
13 Stark	Y	N	N	?	Y	N	N
14 Eshoo	N	N	Y	N	N	Y	Y
15 Honda	Y	N	N	N	N	Y	N
16 Lofgren	N	N	Y	N	N	Y	N
17 Farr	N	N	N	–	Y	N	N
18 Condit	?	?	?	?	?	?	?
19 *Radanovich*	?	Y	N	Y	Y	N	Y
20 Dooley	N	N	Y	N	Y	N	Y
21 *Thomas*	N	Y	N	Y	Y	N	Y
22 Capps	N	N	Y	N	N	Y	Y
23 *Gallegly*	N	Y	N	Y	Y	N	Y
24 Sherman	N	N	Y	N	N	Y	N
25 *McKeon*	N	Y	N	Y	Y	N	Y
26 Berman	?	N	Y	N	N	Y	Y
27 Schiff	N	N	Y	N	N	Y	Y
28 *Dreier*	N	Y	N	Y	Y	N	Y
29 Waxman	N	N	Y	N	N	Y	N
30 Becerra	N	N	Y	N	N	Y	N
31 Solis	N	N	Y	N	N	Y	N
32 Watson	N	N	Y	N	N	Y	N
33 Roybal-Allard	N	N	Y	N	N	Y	N
34 Napolitano	N	N	N	N	N	Y	N
35 Waters	?	N	Y	N	N	Y	Y
36 Harman	N	N	Y	Y	Y	Y	Y
37 Millender-McD.	N	N	Y	Y	N	Y	Y
38 *Horn*	?	Y	N	Y	Y	N	Y

	471	472	473	474	475	476	477
39 *Royce*	N	Y	N	?	Y	N	Y
40 *Lewis*	N	Y	N	Y	Y	N	Y
41 *Miller, Gary*	N	Y	N	Y	Y	Y	Y
42 Baca	N	N	Y	N	Y	N	Y
43 *Calvert*	N	Y	N	Y	Y	N	Y
44 *Bono*	N	Y	N	Y	Y	N	Y
45 *Rohrabacher*	N	Y	N	Y	Y	N	Y
46 Sanchez	N	N	N	N	N	Y	N
47 *Cox*	N	Y	N	Y	Y	N	Y
48 *Issa*	N	Y	N	Y	Y	N	Y
49 Davis	N	N	N	N	N	Y	Y
50 Filner	Y	N	N	N	N	Y	N
51 *Cunningham*	N	Y	N	Y	Y	N	Y
52 *Hunter*	N	Y	N	Y	Y	N	Y
COLORADO							
1 DeGette	N	N	Y	N	N	Y	N
2 Udall	N	N	Y	N	N	Y	Y
3 *McInnis*	N	Y	N	Y	Y	N	Y
4 *Schaffer*	?	Y	N	Y	Y	N	Y
5 *Hefley*	N	Y	N	Y	Y	N	Y
6 *Tancredo*	?	Y	N	Y	Y	N	Y
CONNECTICUT							
1 Larson	N	N	Y	N	N	N	Y
2 *Simmons*	N	Y	N	?	N	Y	Y
3 DeLauro	N	N	Y	N	N	Y	N
4 *Shays*	N	Y	N	Y	N	Y	Y
5 *Maloney*	?	N	Y	Y	Y	Y	Y
6 *Johnson*	N	Y	N	Y	Y	N	Y
DELAWARE							
AL *Castle*	N	Y	N	Y	Y	N	Y
FLORIDA							
1 *Miller, J.*	N	Y	N	Y	Y	N	Y
2 Boyd	N	N	Y	N	Y	Y	Y
3 Brown	N	N	Y	N	N	Y	N
4 *Crenshaw*	N	Y	N	Y	Y	N	Y
5 Thurman	N	N	Y	N	Y	Y	Y
6 *Stearns*	?	Y	N	Y	Y	N	Y
7 *Mica*	N	Y	N	Y	Y	N	Y
8 *Keller*	N	Y	N	Y	Y	N	Y
9 *Bilirakis*	N	Y	N	Y	Y	N	Y
10 *Young*	N	Y	N	Y	Y	N	Y
11 Davis	N	N	Y	N	N	Y	Y
12 *Putnam*	N	Y	N	Y	Y	N	Y
13 *Miller, D.*	N	Y	N	Y	Y	N	Y
14 *Goss*	N	Y	N	Y	Y	N	Y
15 *Weldon*	N	Y	N	Y	Y	N	Y
16 *Foley*	N	Y	N	Y	Y	N	Y
17 Meek	?	N	Y	N	?	Y	N
18 *Ros-Lehtinen*	N	Y	N	Y	Y	N	Y
19 Wexler	?	N	Y	N	Y	N	Y
20 Deutsch	N	N	Y	N	N	Y	Y
21 *Diaz-Balart*	N	Y	N	Y	Y	N	Y
22 *Shaw*	N	Y	N	Y	Y	N	Y
23 Hastings	Y	N	Y	N	N	Y	N
GEORGIA							
1 *Kingston*	N	Y	N	Y	Y	N	Y
2 Bishop	N	N	Y	N	Y	Y	Y
3 *Collins*	N	Y	N	Y	Y	N	Y
4 McKinney	?	?	?	Y	?	Y	N
5 Lewis	N	N	Y	N	N	Y	N
6 *Isakson*	N	Y	N	Y	Y	N	Y
7 *Barr*	?	Y	N	?	Y	N	Y
8 *Chambliss*	N	Y	N	Y	Y	N	Y
9 *Deal*	N	Y	N	Y	Y	N	Y
10 *Norwood*	N	Y	N	Y	Y	N	Y
11 *Linder*	N	Y	N	Y	Y	N	Y
HAWAII							
1 Abercrombie	?	N	Y	Y	N	Y	N
2 Vacant							
IDAHO							
1 *Otter*	N	Y	N	Y	Y	N	Y
2 *Simpson*	N	Y	N	Y	Y	N	Y
ILLINOIS							
1 Rush	N	N	Y	N	Y	N	?
2 Jackson	N	N	Y	N	N	Y	N
3 Lipinski	?	?	Y	N	N	Y	N
4 Gutierrez	?	?	Y	N	N	Y	N
5 Blagojevich	?	?	?	?	?	?	?
6 *Hyde*	N	Y	N	Y	Y	N	Y
7 Davis	N	N	Y	N	N	Y	N
8 *Crane*	N	Y	N	Y	Y	N	Y
9 Schakowsky	N	N	Y	N	N	Y	N
10 *Kirk*	N	Y	N	Y	Y	N	Y
11 *Weller*	N	Y	N	Y	Y	N	Y
12 Costello	N	N	Y	N	N	Y	N
13 *Biggert*	N	Y	N	Y	Y	N	Y

ND Northern Democrats   SD Southern Democrats

	471	472	473	474	475	476	477
14 ***Hastert***							
15 ***Johnson***	N	Y	N	Y	Y	N	Y
16 ***Manzullo***	–	+	N	Y	Y	N	Y
17 Evans	N	N	Y	N	N	Y	N
18 ***LaHood***	N	Y	N	Y	Y	N	Y
19 Phelps	N	N	Y	N	N	Y	Y
20 ***Shimkus***	N	Y	N	Y	Y	N	Y
INDIANA							
1 Visclosky	N	N	?	N	N	Y	N
2 ***Pence***	N	Y	N	Y	Y	N	Y
3 Roemer	N	N	Y	N	N	Y	N
4 ***Souder***	N	Y	N	Y	Y	N	Y
5 ***Buyer***	N	Y	N	Y	Y	N	Y
6 ***Burton***	N	Y	N	Y	Y	N	Y
7 ***Kerns***	N	Y	N	Y	Y	N	Y
8 ***Hostettler***	N	Y	N	Y	Y	N	N
9 Hill	?	N	?	N	Y	Y	Y
10 Carson	N	N	Y	N	N	Y	N
IOWA							
1 ***Leach***	N	Y	Y	Y	Y	N	Y
2 ***Nussle***	N	Y	N	Y	Y	N	Y
3 Boswell	N	N	Y	N	N	Y	Y
4 ***Ganske***	N	Y	N	Y	Y	N	Y
5 ***Latham***	N	Y	N	Y	Y	N	Y
KANSAS							
1 ***Moran***	N	Y	N	N	Y	N	N
2 ***Ryun***	N	Y	N	Y	Y	N	Y
3 Moore	N	N	Y	Y	N	Y	Y
4 ***Tiahrt***	N	Y	N	Y	Y	N	Y
KENTUCKY							
1 ***Whitfield***	N	Y	N	Y	Y	N	Y
2 ***Lewis***	N	Y	N	Y	Y	N	Y
3 ***Northup***	?	Y	N	Y	Y	N	Y
4 Lucas	N	N	Y	Y	Y	Y	Y
5 ***Rogers***	N	Y	N	Y	Y	N	Y
6 ***Fletcher***	N	Y	N	Y	Y	N	Y
LOUISIANA							
1 ***Vitter***	N	Y	N	Y	Y	N	Y
2 Jefferson	Y	N	Y	N	N	Y	Y
3 ***Tauzin***	N	Y	N	Y	Y	N	Y
4 ***McCrery***	N	Y	N	Y	Y	N	Y
5 ***Cooksey***	?	Y	N	Y	Y	N	Y
6 ***Baker***	N	Y	N	Y	Y	N	Y
7 John	N	N	Y	Y	Y	?	Y
MAINE							
1 Allen	N	N	Y	N	N	Y	Y
2 Baldacci	?	N	Y	N	N	Y	Y
MARYLAND							
1 ***Gilchrest***	?	Y	N	Y	Y	N	Y
2 ***Ehrlich***	N	Y	?	Y	Y	N	Y
3 Cardin	N	N	Y	Y	N	Y	Y
4 Wynn	N	N	Y	Y	N	Y	N
5 Hoyer	N	N	Y	Y	N	Y	N
6 ***Bartlett***	N	Y	N	Y	Y	N	Y
7 Cummings	N	N	Y	Y	N	Y	N
8 ***Morella***	N	Y	N	Y	Y	?	?
MASSACHUSETTS							
1 Olver	Y	N	Y	N	N	Y	N
2 Neal	?	?	?	?	N	Y	N
3 McGovern	?	N	Y	N	N	Y	N
4 Frank	Y	N	Y	N	N	?	?
5 Meehan	?	N	Y	N	N	Y	N
6 Tierney	N	N	Y	N	N	Y	N
7 Markey	?	N	Y	N	N	Y	N
8 Capuano	Y	N	Y	N	N	Y	N
9 Lynch	?	N	Y	N	N	Y	N
10 Delahunt	Y	N	N	N	N	Y	N
MICHIGAN							
1 Stupak	N	N	Y	N	Y	Y	Y
2 ***Hoekstra***	N	Y	N	Y	Y	N	Y
3 ***Ehlers***	N	Y	N	Y	Y	N	Y
4 ***Camp***	N	Y	N	Y	Y	N	Y
5 Barcia	N	N	Y	Y	N	Y	Y
6 ***Upton***	N	Y	N	Y	Y	N	Y
7 ***Smith***	N	Y	N	Y	Y	N	Y
8 ***Rogers***	N	Y	N	Y	Y	N	Y
9 Kildee	N	N	Y	N	N	Y	N
10 Bonior	?	N	Y	N	N	Y	N
11 ***Knollenberg***	N	Y	N	Y	Y	N	Y
12 Levin	N	N	Y	N	N	Y	N
13 Rivers	N	N	Y	N	N	Y	N
14 Conyers	Y	N	Y	N	N	Y	N
15 Kilpatrick	N	N	Y	N	N	Y	N
16 Dingell	?	?	Y	N	N	Y	N

	471	472	473	474	475	476	477
MINNESOTA							
1 ***Gutknecht***	N	Y	N	Y	Y	N	Y
2 ***Kennedy***	N	Y	N	Y	Y	N	Y
3 ***Ramstad***	N	Y	N	Y	Y	N	Y
4 McCollum	N	N	Y	N	N	Y	N
5 Sabo	N	N	Y	N	N	Y	N
6 Luther	N	N	Y	N	N	Y	Y
7 Peterson	N	N	Y	N	N	Y	Y
8 Oberstar	N	N	Y	N	N	Y	N
MISSISSIPPI							
1 ***Wicker***	N	Y	N	Y	Y	N	Y
2 Thompson	N	N	Y	N	N	Y	Y
3 ***Pickering***	N	Y	N	Y	Y	N	Y
4 Shows	N	N	Y	Y	N	Y	Y
5 Taylor	N	N	Y	Y	N	Y	Y
MISSOURI							
1 Clay	?	N	Y	N	N	Y	Y
2 ***Akin***	N	Y	N	Y	Y	N	Y
3 Gephardt	N	N	Y	Y	N	Y	N
4 Skelton	N	N	Y	Y	N	Y	Y
5 McCarthy	N	N	Y	?	N	Y	N
6 ***Graves***	N	Y	N	Y	Y	N	Y
7 ***Blunt***	N	Y	N	Y	Y	N	Y
8 ***Emerson***	N	Y	N	Y	Y	N	Y
9 ***Hulshof***	?	Y	N	Y	?	N	Y
MONTANA							
AL ***Rehberg***	N	Y	N	Y	Y	N	Y
NEBRASKA							
1 ***Bereuter***	N	Y	N	Y	Y	N	Y
2 ***Terry***	N	Y	N	Y	Y	N	Y
3 ***Osborne***	N	Y	N	Y	Y	N	Y
NEVADA							
1 Berkley	N	N	Y	Y	N	Y	Y
2 ***Gibbons***	N	Y	N	Y	Y	N	Y
NEW HAMPSHIRE							
1 ***Sununu***	N	Y	N	Y	Y	N	Y
2 ***Bass***	N	Y	N	Y	Y	N	Y
NEW JERSEY							
1 Andrews	N	N	Y	Y	N	Y	Y
2 ***LoBiondo***	N	Y	N	Y	Y	N	Y
3 ***Saxton***	?	Y	N	Y	Y	N	Y
4 ***Smith***	N	Y	N	Y	Y	Y	Y
5 ***Roukema***	?	?	?	?	?	?	?
6 Pallone	Y	N	Y	N	N	Y	N
7 ***Ferguson***	N	Y	N	Y	Y	N	Y
8 Pascrell	N	N	Y	N	N	Y	Y
9 Rothman	N	N	Y	N	N	Y	Y
10 Payne	?	?	?	N	N	Y	N
11 ***Frelinghuysen***	N	Y	N	Y	Y	N	Y
12 Holt	N	N	Y	N	N	Y	N
13 Menendez	N	N	Y	N	N	Y	Y
NEW MEXICO							
1 ***Wilson***	N	Y	N	Y	Y	N	Y
2 ***Skeen***	N	Y	N	Y	Y	N	Y
3 Udall	N	N	Y	N	N	Y	N
NEW YORK							
1 ***Grucci***	?	?	?	Y	Y	N	Y
2 Israel	N	N	Y	Y	N	Y	Y
3 ***King***	N	Y	N	Y	Y	N	Y
4 McCarthy	N	N	Y	Y	?	Y	Y
5 Ackerman	N	N	Y	N	N	Y	N
6 Meeks	N	N	Y	N	N	Y	N
7 Crowley	N	N	Y	N	Y	Y	Y
8 Nadler	?	N	Y	N	N	Y	N
9 Weiner	?	?	Y	Y	N	Y	N
10 Towns	Y	N	Y	N	N	Y	N
11 Owens	?	N	Y	N	N	Y	N
12 Velázquez	Y	N	Y	N	N	Y	N
13 ***Fossella***	?	Y	N	Y	Y	Y	Y
14 Maloney	N	N	Y	N	N	Y	Y
15 Rangel	?	?	?	?	?	?	?
16 Serrano	N	N	Y	N	N	Y	N
17 Engel	?	N	Y	Y	N	Y	Y
18 Lowey	N	N	Y	Y	Y	Y	N
19 ***Kelly***	N	Y	N	Y	Y	N	Y
20 ***Gilman***	N	Y	N	Y	Y	N	Y
21 McNulty	N	N	Y	Y	N	Y	N
22 ***Sweeney***	N	Y	N	Y	Y	N	Y
23 ***Boehlert***	N	Y	N	Y	Y	N	Y
24 ***McHugh***	N	Y	N	Y	Y	N	Y
25 ***Walsh***	N	Y	N	Y	Y	N	Y
26 Hinchey	?	?	?	?	?	Y	N
27 ***Reynolds***	N	Y	N	Y	Y	N	Y
28 Slaughter	Y	N	Y	N	N	Y	N
29 LaFalce	N	N	Y	N	N	Y	N

	471	472	473	474	475	476	477
30 ***Quinn***	N	Y	N	Y	Y	N	Y
31 ***Houghton***	?	?	?	?	?	?	?
NORTH CAROLINA							
1 Clayton	N	N	Y	N	N	Y	N
2 Etheridge	N	N	Y	N	N	Y	Y
3 ***Jones***	N	Y	N	Y	Y	N	Y
4 Price	N	N	Y	N	N	Y	Y
5 ***Burr***	?	Y	N	Y	Y	N	Y
6 ***Coble***	N	Y	N	Y	Y	N	Y
7 McIntyre	N	N	Y	N	Y	Y	Y
8 ***Hayes***	N	Y	N	Y	Y	N	Y
9 ***Myrick***	N	Y	N	Y	Y	N	Y
10 ***Ballenger***	N	Y	N	Y	Y	N	Y
11 ***Taylor***	?	Y	N	Y	Y	N	Y
12 Watt	N	N	Y	N	N	Y	N
NORTH DAKOTA							
AL Pomeroy	N	N	Y	Y	Y	Y	Y
OHIO							
1 ***Chabot***	N	Y	N	Y	Y	N	Y
2 ***Portman***	N	Y	N	Y	Y	N	Y
3 Vacant							
4 ***Oxley***	?	?	?	?	Y	N	Y
5 ***Gillmor***	N	Y	N	Y	Y	N	Y
6 Strickland	N	?	Y	Y	N	Y	Y
7 ***Hobson***	N	Y	N	Y	Y	N	Y
8 ***Boehner***	?	Y	N	Y	Y	N	Y
9 Kaptur	N	N	Y	N	N	Y	N
10 Kucinich	N	N	Y	N	N	Y	N
11 Jones	N	N	Y	?	N	Y	N
12 ***Tiberi***	N	Y	N	Y	Y	N	Y
13 Brown	?	N	Y	N	N	Y	N
14 Sawyer	?	?	Y	N	N	Y	Y
15 ***Pryce***	?	Y	N	Y	Y	N	Y
16 ***Regula***	N	Y	N	Y	Y	N	Y
17 Vacant							
18 ***Ney***	N	Y	N	Y	Y	N	Y
19 ***LaTourette***	N	Y	N	Y	Y	N	Y
OKLAHOMA							
1 ***Sullivan***	N	Y	N	Y	Y	N	Y
2 Carson	N	N	Y	Y	N	Y	Y
3 ***Watkins***	?	Y	N	Y	Y	N	Y
4 ***Watts***	N	Y	N	Y	Y	N	Y
5 ***Istook***	N	Y	N	Y	Y	N	Y
6 ***Lucas***	N	Y	N	Y	Y	N	Y
OREGON							
1 Wu	N	N	Y	N	N	Y	Y
2 ***Walden***	N	Y	N	Y	Y	N	Y
3 Blumenauer	N	N	Y	N	N	Y	N
4 DeFazio	N	N	Y	N	N	Y	N
5 Hooley	?	?	?	?	?	?	?
PENNSYLVANIA							
1 Brady	N	N	Y	Y	N	Y	N
2 Fattah	?	?	?	?	N	Y	N
3 Borski	N	N	Y	N	N	?	?
4 ***Hart***	N	Y	N	Y	Y	N	Y
5 ***Peterson***	N	Y	N	Y	Y	N	Y
6 Holden	N	N	Y	Y	N	Y	Y
7 ***Weldon***	N	Y	N	Y	Y	N	Y
8 ***Greenwood***	N	Y	N	Y	Y	N	Y
9 ***Shuster, Bill***	N	Y	N	Y	Y	N	Y
10 ***Sherwood***	N	Y	N	Y	Y	N	Y
11 Kanjorski	N	N	Y	Y	N	Y	Y
12 Murtha	?	?	Y	Y	N	Y	Y
13 Hoeffel	N	N	Y	Y	N	Y	Y
14 Coyne	Y	N	Y	N	N	Y	N
15 ***Toomey***	N	Y	N	Y	Y	N	Y
16 ***Pitts***	N	Y	N	Y	Y	N	Y
17 ***Gekas***	N	Y	N	Y	Y	N	Y
18 Doyle	?	?	Y	Y	N	Y	N
19 ***Platts***	N	Y	N	N	Y	N	Y
20 Mascara	N	N	Y	N	N	Y	Y
21 ***English***	N	Y	N	Y	Y	N	Y
RHODE ISLAND							
1 Kennedy	Y	N	Y	N	N	Y	Y
2 Langevin	N	N	Y	N	N	Y	Y
SOUTH CAROLINA							
1 ***Brown***	N	Y	N	Y	Y	N	Y
2 ***Wilson***	N	Y	N	Y	Y	N	Y
3 ***Graham***	N	Y	N	Y	Y	N	Y
4 ***DeMint***	N	Y	N	Y	Y	N	Y
5 Spratt	N	N	Y	N	N	Y	Y
6 Clyburn	N	N	Y	N	N	Y	Y
SOUTH DAKOTA							
AL ***Thune***	N	Y	N	N	Y	N	Y

	471	472	473	474	475	476	477
TENNESSEE							
1 ***Jenkins***	N	Y	N	Y	Y	N	Y
2 ***Duncan***	N	Y	N	Y	Y	N	N
3 ***Wamp***	N	Y	N	N	Y	N	Y
4 ***Hilleary***	?	Y	N	Y	Y	N	Y
5 Clement	?	?	Y	Y	N	Y	Y
6 Gordon	?	?	Y	Y	N	Y	Y
7 ***Bryant***	N	Y	N	Y	Y	N	Y
8 Tanner	N	N	Y	Y	N	Y	Y
9 Ford	N	N	Y	N	N	Y	Y
TEXAS							
1 Sandlin	N	N	Y	N	N	Y	Y
2 Turner	N	N	Y	N	N	Y	Y
3 ***Johnson, Sam***	?	Y	N	Y	Y	N	Y
4 Hall	N	N	Y	N	Y	Y	Y
5 ***Sessions***	N	Y	N	Y	Y	N	Y
6 ***Barton***	N	Y	N	Y	Y	N	Y
7 ***Culberson***	N	Y	N	Y	Y	N	Y
8 ***Brady***	N	Y	N	Y	Y	N	Y
9 Lampson	N	N	Y	N	N	Y	N
10 Doggett	N	N	Y	N	N	Y	N
11 Edwards	N	N	Y	Y	Y	Y	Y
12 ***Granger***	?	Y	N	Y	Y	N	Y
13 ***Thornberry***	N	Y	N	Y	Y	N	Y
14 ***Paul***	N	Y	N	N	N	N	N
15 Hinojosa	N	N	Y	N	N	Y	Y
16 Reyes	N	N	Y	Y	N	Y	Y
17 Stenholm	N	N	N	Y	Y	Y	Y
18 Jackson-Lee	N	N	Y	N	N	Y	N
19 ***Combest***	N	Y	N	Y	Y	N	Y
20 Gonzalez	N	N	Y	Y	N	Y	N
21 ***Smith***	N	Y	N	Y	Y	N	Y
22 ***DeLay***	N	Y	N	Y	Y	N	Y
23 ***Bonilla***	N	Y	N	Y	Y	N	Y
24 Frost	Y	N	Y	Y	Y	Y	Y
25 Bentsen	Y	N	Y	N	N	Y	Y
26 ***Armey***	N	Y	N	Y	Y	N	Y
27 Ortiz	N	N	Y	Y	N	Y	Y
28 Rodriguez	N	N	Y	N	N	Y	N
29 Green	N	N	Y	Y	N	Y	N
30 Johnson, E.B.	Y	N	Y	Y	N	Y	N
UTAH							
1 ***Hansen***	?	Y	N	Y	Y	N	Y
2 Matheson	N	N	Y	Y	N	Y	Y
3 ***Cannon***	N	Y	N	Y	Y	N	N
VERMONT							
AL *Sanders*	N	N	Y	N	N	Y	N
VIRGINIA							
1 ***Davis, Jo Ann***	N	Y	N	Y	Y	N	Y
2 ***Schrock***	N	Y	N	Y	Y	N	Y
3 Scott	N	N	Y	N	N	Y	N
4 ***Forbes***	N	Y	N	Y	Y	N	Y
5 ***Goode***	N	Y	N	Y	Y	N	Y
6 ***Goodlatte***	N	Y	N	Y	Y	N	Y
7 ***Cantor***	N	Y	N	Y	Y	N	Y
8 Moran	N	N	Y	N	N	Y	N
9 Boucher	N	N	Y	Y	N	Y	Y
10 ***Wolf***	N	Y	N	Y	Y	N	Y
11 ***Davis, T.***	?	Y	N	Y	Y	N	Y
WASHINGTON							
1 Inslee	N	N	Y	Y	N	Y	Y
2 Larsen	N	N	Y	Y	Y	Y	N
3 Baird	N	N	Y	N	N	Y	Y
4 ***Hastings***	N	Y	N	Y	Y	N	Y
5 ***Nethercutt***	N	Y	N	Y	Y	N	Y
6 Dicks	N	N	Y	Y	N	Y	Y
7 McDermott	Y	N	Y	N	?	Y	N
8 ***Dunn***	?	Y	N	Y	Y	N	Y
9 Smith	N	N	Y	N	Y	Y	Y
WEST VIRGINIA							
1 Mollohan	N	N	Y	Y	N	Y	N
2 ***Capito***	N	Y	N	Y	Y	N	Y
3 Rahall	N	N	Y	N	N	Y	N
WISCONSIN							
1 ***Ryan***	N	Y	N	Y	Y	N	Y
2 Baldwin	N	N	Y	N	N	Y	N
3 Kind	N	N	Y	N	N	Y	Y
4 Kleczka	?	N	Y	N	N	Y	N
5 Barrett	N	N	Y	N	N	Y	Y
6 ***Petri***	N	Y	N	Y	Y	N	Y
7 Obey	Y	N	Y	N	N	Y	N
8 ***Green***	N	Y	N	Y	Y	N	Y
9 ***Sensenbrenner***	N	Y	N	Y	Y	N	Y
WYOMING							
AL ***Cubin***	?	?	?	?	Y	N	Y

Southern states - Ala., Ark., Fla., Ga., Ky., La., Miss., N.C., Okla., S.C., Tenn., Texas, Va.

478. HR 333. Bankruptcy Overhaul/Rule. Adoption of the rule (H Res 606) to provide for House floor consideration of the conference report on the bill that would require debtors able to repay $10,000 or 25 percent of their debts over five years to file under Chapter 13, which requires a reorganization of debts under a repayment plan, instead of seeking to discharge their debts under Chapter 7. It also would block abortion and other protesters from declaring bankruptcy to avoid paying court-ordered fines and judgments. Rejected 172-243: R 124-87; D 48-155 (ND 24-127, SD 24-28); I 0-1. Nov. 14, 2002.

479. HR 5063. Welfare and Unemployment Benefits/Previous Question. Motion to order the previous question (thus ending debate and possibility of amendment) on adoption of the rule (H Res 609) to provide for House floor consideration of the bill, which would be amended by the rule to extend funding for Temporary Assistance for Needy Families, the national welfare block grant program, through March 31, 2003, and extend current recipients' unemployment benefits through January 2003. Motion agreed to 207-198: R 207-0; D 0-197 (ND 0-146, SD 0-51); I 0-1. Nov. 14, 2002.

480. HR 5063. Welfare and Unemployment Benefits/Rule. Adoption of the rule (H Res 609) to provide for House floor consideration of the bill, which would be amended by the rule to extend funding for Temporary Assistance for Needy Families, the national welfare block grant program, through March 31, 2003, and extend current recipients' unemployment benefits through January 2003. Adopted 245-137: R 191-2; D 54-134 (ND 28-110, SD 26-24); I 0-1. (Subsequently, the amended bill was passed by voice vote.) Nov. 14, 2002.

481. HR 5708. PAYGO Reduction/Recommit. Moore, D-Kan., motion to recommit the bill to the House Budget Committee with instructions that it be reported back with language that would reduce balances in the pay-as-you-go account to zero for fiscal 2002 and 2003 only. Motion rejected 187-201: R 0-200; D 186-1 (ND 138-1, SD 48-0); I 1-0. Nov. 14, 2002.

482. HR 5708. PAYGO Reduction/Passage. Passage of the bill that would reduce balances in the pay-as-you-go account to zero to avoid automatic cuts in mandatory spending programs. Passed 366-19: R 197-0; D 168-19 (ND 122-17, SD 46-2); I 1-0. Nov. 14, 2002.

483. HR 4628. Fiscal 2003 Intelligence Authorization/Conference Report. Adoption of the conference report on the bill that would authorize classified amounts in fiscal 2003 for U.S. intelligence agencies and intelligence-related activities of the U.S. government, including the Central Intelligence Agency, the National Security Agency, the Defense Department, the Federal Bureau of Investigation, the State Department and other agencies. The agreement also would establish a National Commission on Terrorist Attacks Upon the United States that would examine and report on the facts and circumstances relating to the Sept. 11, 2001, attacks. Adopted (thus sent to the Senate) 366-3: R 188-3; D 177-0 (ND 131-0, SD 46-0); I 1-0. Nov. 15, 2002 (in the session that began and the Congressional Record that is dated Nov. 14, 2002).

484. HR 333. Bankruptcy Overhaul/Concur with Senate Amendment. Gekas, R-Pa., motion to concur in a House amendment to the Senate amendment to the bill that would require debtors able to repay $10,000 or 25 percent of their debts over five years to file under Chapter 13, which requires a reorganization of debts under a repayment plan, instead of seeking to discharge their debts under Chapter 7. (The amendment was identical to the conference report on the bill, except that it omitted provisions on anti-abortion protesters and on certain bankruptcy judgeships.) Motion agreed to 244-116: R 189-0; D 55-115 (ND 33-93, SD 22-22); I 0-1. Nov. 15, 2002 (in the session that began and the Congressional Record that is dated Nov. 14, 2002).

Key

Y	Voted for (yea).
#	Paired for.
+	Announced for.
N	Voted against (nay).
X	Paired against.
–	Announced against.
P	Voted "present."
C	Voted "present" to avoid possible conflict of interest.
?	Did not vote or otherwise make a position known.

Democrats **Republicans**
Independents

	478	479	480	481	482	483	484
ALABAMA							
1 *Callahan*	?	?	?	?	?	?	?
2 *Everett*	N	Y	Y	N	Y	Y	Y
3 *Riley*	Y	Y	Y	N	Y	Y	Y
4 *Aderholt*	N	Y	Y	N	Y	Y	Y
5 Cramer	Y	N	Y	Y	Y	Y	Y
6 *Bachus*	Y	Y	Y	N	Y	Y	Y
7 Hilliard	N	N	?	?	?	Y	N
ALASKA							
AL *Young*	Y	Y	Y	N	Y	Y	Y
ARIZONA							
1 *Flake*	N	Y	Y	N	Y	Y	Y
2 Pastor	N	N	Y	Y	Y	Y	N
3 *Stump*	?	?	?	?	?	?	?
4 *Shadegg*	N	Y	Y	N	Y	Y	Y
5 *Kolbe*	Y	Y	Y	N	Y	Y	Y
6 *Hayworth*	N	Y	Y	N	Y	Y	Y
ARKANSAS							
1 Berry	Y	N	Y	Y	Y	Y	Y
2 Snyder	Y	N	N	Y	Y	Y	Y
3 *Boozman*	N	Y	Y	N	Y	Y	Y
4 Ross	N	N	Y	Y	Y	Y	Y
CALIFORNIA							
1 Thompson	Y	N	N	Y	Y	Y	N
2 *Herger*	Y	Y	?	N	Y	Y	Y
3 *Ose*	Y	Y	Y	N	Y	Y	Y
4 *Doolittle*	?	?	?	?	?	?	?
5 Matsui	N	N	N	Y	Y	Y	N
6 Woolsey	N	N	N	Y	Y	Y	N
7 Miller, George	N	N	N	Y	Y	Y	N
8 Pelosi	N	N	N	Y	Y	Y	N
9 Lee	N	N	N	Y	N	Y	N
10 Tauscher	Y	N	N	Y	Y	Y	N
11 *Pombo*	N	Y	Y	N	Y	Y	Y
12 Lantos	N	N	N	Y	Y	?	?
13 Stark	N	N	N	Y	N	?	?
14 Eshoo	N	N	Y	Y	Y	Y	N
15 Honda	N	N	N	Y	Y	Y	N
16 Lofgren	N	N	N	Y	Y	Y	N
17 Farr	N	N	N	Y	Y	Y	N
18 Condit	?	?	?	?	?	?	?
19 *Radanovich*	Y	Y	?	N	Y	Y	Y
20 Dooley	Y	N	Y	N	Y	N	Y
21 *Thomas*	Y	Y	Y	N	Y	Y	Y
22 Capps	N	N	N	Y	Y	Y	Y
23 *Gallegly*	Y	Y	Y	N	Y	Y	Y
24 Sherman	N	N	N	Y	Y	Y	Y
25 *McKeon*	N	Y	Y	N	Y	Y	Y
26 Berman	N	N	N	Y	Y	Y	N
27 Schiff	N	N	Y	Y	Y	Y	N
28 *Dreier*	Y	Y	Y	N	Y	Y	Y
29 Waxman	N	N	N	Y	Y	?	?
30 Becerra	N	N	N	?	?	?	?
31 Solis	N	N	N	Y	Y	Y	N
32 Watson	N	N	?	Y	Y	Y	N
33 Roybal-Allard	N	N	N	Y	Y	Y	N
34 Napolitano	N	N	N	Y	Y	Y	Y
35 Waters	N	N	N	Y	N	Y	N
36 Harman	N	N	Y	Y	Y	Y	?
37 Millender-McD.	N	N	N	Y	Y	Y	N
38 *Horn*	Y	Y	Y	N	Y	Y	Y

	478	479	480	481	482	483	484
39 *Royce*	Y	Y	Y	N	Y	Y	Y
40 *Lewis*	N	Y	Y	N	Y	Y	Y
41 *Miller, Gary*	N	Y	?	N	?	?	?
42 Baca	N	N	Y	Y	Y	Y	Y
43 *Calvert*	Y	Y	Y	N	Y	Y	Y
44 *Bono*	Y	Y	Y	N	Y	Y	Y
45 *Rohrabacher*	Y	Y	Y	N	Y	Y	Y
46 Sanchez	N	N	N	Y	Y	Y	Y
47 *Cox*	Y	Y	Y	N	Y	Y	Y
48 *Issa*	Y	Y	Y	N	Y	?	?
49 Davis	N	N	N	Y	Y	Y	N
50 Filner	N	N	N	Y	Y	Y	N
51 *Cunningham*	N	Y	Y	N	Y	Y	Y
52 *Hunter*	Y	Y	Y	N	Y	Y	Y
COLORADO							
1 DeGette	N	N	N	Y	N	Y	N
2 Udall	N	N	Y	Y	Y	Y	N
3 *McInnis*	Y	Y	?	?	?	?	?
4 *Schaffer*	N	Y	Y	N	Y	Y	Y
5 *Hefley*	N	Y	Y	N	Y	Y	?
6 *Tancredo*	N	Y	Y	?	?	Y	Y
CONNECTICUT							
1 Larson	N	N	Y	Y	Y	Y	N
2 *Simmons*	Y	Y	Y	N	Y	Y	Y
3 DeLauro	N	N	N	Y	Y	Y	N
4 *Shays*	Y	Y	Y	N	Y	Y	Y
5 Maloney	Y	N	Y	Y	Y	Y	Y
6 *Johnson*	Y	Y	Y	N	Y	Y	Y
DELAWARE							
AL *Castle*	Y	Y	Y	N	Y	Y	Y
FLORIDA							
1 *Miller, J.*	N	Y	Y	N	Y	Y	Y
2 Boyd	?	?	?	?	?	?	?
3 Brown	N	N	Y	Y	Y	Y	N
4 *Crenshaw*	Y	Y	Y	N	Y	Y	Y
5 Thurman	N	N	Y	Y	Y	Y	Y
6 *Stearns*	N	Y	Y	N	Y	?	Y
7 *Mica*	N	Y	Y	N	Y	Y	Y
8 *Keller*	Y	Y	?	N	Y	?	Y
9 *Bilirakis*	Y	Y	Y	N	Y	Y	Y
10 *Young*	N	Y	Y	?	?	?	?
11 Davis	Y	N	N	Y	Y	Y	N
12 *Putnam*	N	Y	Y	N	Y	Y	Y
13 *Miller, D.*	Y	Y	Y	N	Y	Y	Y
14 *Goss*	Y	Y	Y	N	Y	Y	Y
15 *Weldon*	N	Y	Y	N	Y	Y	Y
16 *Foley*	Y	Y	Y	N	Y	Y	Y
17 Meek	N	N	N	Y	Y	?	?
18 *Ros-Lehtinen*	N	Y	Y	N	Y	Y	Y
19 Wexler	N	N	Y	Y	Y	Y	Y
20 Deutsch	N	N	?	Y	Y	Y	Y
21 *Diaz-Balart*	?	?	?	?	?	?	?
22 *Shaw*	N	Y	Y	N	Y	Y	Y
23 Hastings	N	N	N	Y	?	Y	N
GEORGIA							
1 *Kingston*	Y	Y	Y	N	Y	Y	Y
2 Bishop	N	N	Y	Y	Y	Y	Y
3 *Collins*	Y	Y	Y	N	Y	Y	Y
4 McKinney	?	?	?	?	?	?	?
5 Lewis	N	?	N	Y	Y	Y	N
6 *Isakson*	Y	Y	Y	N	Y	Y	Y
7 *Barr*	N	Y	Y	?	?	?	?
8 *Chambliss*	N	Y	Y	N	Y	Y	Y
9 *Deal*	Y	Y	Y	N	Y	Y	Y
10 *Norwood*	N	Y	Y	N	Y	Y	Y
11 *Linder*	Y	Y	Y	N	Y	Y	Y
HAWAII							
1 Abercrombie	N	N	N	Y	Y	Y	N
2 Vacant							
IDAHO							
1 *Otter*	N	Y	?	N	Y	Y	Y
2 *Simpson*	Y	Y	?	N	Y	Y	Y
ILLINOIS							
1 Rush	N	N	N	Y	Y	Y	N
2 Jackson	N	N	N	Y	Y	Y	N
3 Lipinski	N	?	?	?	?	?	?
4 Gutierrez	N	N	N	Y	Y	Y	N
5 Blagojevich	?	?	?	?	?	?	?
6 *Hyde*	Y	Y	Y	N	Y	Y	Y
7 Davis	N	N	N	Y	Y	Y	N
8 *Crane*	Y	Y	?	N	Y	Y	Y
9 Schakowsky	N	N	N	Y	Y	Y	N
10 *Kirk*	Y	Y	Y	N	Y	Y	Y
11 *Weller*	Y	Y	Y	N	Y	Y	Y
12 Costello	N	N	Y	Y	N	Y	N
13 *Biggert*	Y	Y	Y	N	Y	Y	Y

ND Northern Democrats   SD Southern Democrats

	478	479	480	481	482	483	484
14 *Hastert*	Y						Y
15 *Johnson*	N	Y	Y	N	Y	Y	Y
16 *Manzullo*	N	Y	Y	N	Y	Y	Y
17 Evans	N	N	Y	Y	Y	Y	N
18 *LaHood*	N	Y	Y	N	Y	N	Y
19 Phelps	N	N	Y	Y	Y	Y	Y
20 *Shimkus*	N	Y	Y	N	Y	Y	Y
INDIANA							
1 Visclosky	N	N	N	Y	N	Y	N
2 *Pence*	N	Y	Y	N	Y	Y	Y
3 Roemer	N	N	N	Y	Y	Y	Y
4 *Souder*	N	Y	Y	N	Y	Y	Y
5 *Buyer*	Y	Y	Y	N	Y	Y	Y
6 *Burton*	N	Y	Y	N	Y	Y	Y
7 *Kerns*	N	Y	Y	N	Y	N	Y
8 *Hostettler*	N	Y	N	N	Y	Y	Y
9 Hill	Y	N	Y	Y	N	Y	Y
10 Carson	N	N	N	Y	Y	Y	?
IOWA							
1 *Leach*	Y	Y	Y	N	Y	Y	Y
2 *Nussle*	Y	Y	N	N	Y	Y	Y
3 Boswell	Y	N	N	Y	Y	Y	Y
4 *Ganske*	Y	Y	Y	N	Y	?	?
5 *Latham*	Y	Y	Y	N	Y	Y	Y
KANSAS							
1 *Moran*	N	Y	Y	N	Y	Y	Y
2 *Ryun*	N	Y	Y	N	Y	Y	Y
3 Moore	Y	N	Y	Y	Y	Y	Y
4 *Tiahrt*	N	+	+	N	Y	Y	Y
KENTUCKY							
1 *Whitfield*	N	Y	Y	N	Y	Y	Y
2 *Lewis*	N	Y	Y	N	Y	Y	Y
3 *Northup*	Y	Y	Y	N	Y	Y	Y
4 Lucas	Y	N	Y	Y	Y	Y	Y
5 *Rogers*	Y	Y	Y	N	Y	Y	Y
6 *Fletcher*	Y	Y	Y	N	Y	Y	Y
LOUISIANA							
1 *Vitter*	N	Y	Y	N	Y	Y	Y
2 Jefferson	N	N	Y	Y	Y	Y	?
3 *Tauzin*	N	Y	Y	N	Y	Y	Y
4 *McCrery*	Y	Y	Y	N	Y	Y	?
5 *Cooksey*	?	?	?	?	?	?	?
6 *Baker*	Y	Y	?	N	Y	Y	Y
7 John	N	N	Y	Y	Y	Y	N
MAINE							
1 Allen	N	N	N	Y	Y	Y	N
2 Baldacci	N	?	?	?	?	?	?
MARYLAND							
1 *Gilchrest*	Y	Y	Y	N	Y	Y	Y
2 *Ehrlich*	?	?	?	?	?	?	?
3 Cardin	N	N	Y	Y	Y	Y	N
4 Wynn	Y	N	N	?	?	?	?
5 Hoyer	N	N	Y	Y	Y	Y	N
6 *Bartlett*	N	Y	Y	N	Y	Y	Y
7 Cummings	N	N	N	Y	Y	Y	N
8 *Morella*	Y	Y	Y	N	Y	Y	Y
MASSACHUSETTS							
1 Olver	N	N	N	Y	N	Y	N
2 Neal	N	N	N	Y	Y	Y	Y
3 McGovern	N	N	N	Y	Y	Y	N
4 Frank	N	N	N	Y	Y	Y	N
5 Meehan	N	N	N	Y	Y	Y	N
6 Tierney	N	N	N	Y	Y	Y	N
7 Markey	N	N	N	Y	Y	?	?
8 Capuano	N	N	N	Y	N	Y	N
9 Lynch	N	N	N	Y	Y	Y	N
10 Delahunt	N	N	N	Y	N	Y	N
MICHIGAN							
1 Stupak	N	N	Y	Y	Y	Y	N
2 *Hoekstra*	N	Y	Y	N	Y	Y	Y
3 *Ehlers*	N	Y	Y	N	Y	Y	Y
4 *Camp*	Y	Y	Y	N	Y	Y	Y
5 Barcia	N	?	?	?	?	?	?
6 *Upton*	Y	Y	Y	N	Y	Y	Y
7 *Smith*	Y	Y	Y	?	Y	Y	Y
8 *Rogers*	N	Y	Y	N	Y	Y	Y
9 Kildee	N	N	N	Y	Y	Y	N
10 Bonior	N	N	?	?	?	?	?
11 *Knollenberg*	Y	Y	Y	N	Y	Y	Y
12 Levin	N	N	N	Y	Y	Y	N
13 Rivers	Y	N	N	Y	Y	Y	Y
14 Conyers	N	N	N	?	?	?	N
15 Kilpatrick	N	N	N	Y	Y	Y	N
16 Dingell	N	N	Y	Y	Y	Y	N
MINNESOTA							
1 *Gutknecht*	N	Y	Y	N	Y	Y	Y
2 *Kennedy*	N	Y	Y	N	Y	Y	Y
3 *Ramstad*	Y	Y	Y	N	Y	Y	Y
4 McCollum	N	N	N	Y	Y	Y	N
5 Sabo	N	N	N	Y	Y	Y	Y
6 Luther	N	N	?	Y	Y	Y	N
7 Peterson	N	N	N	Y	Y	Y	Y
8 Oberstar	N	?	?	?	?	?	?
MISSISSIPPI							
1 *Wicker*	N	Y	Y	N	Y	Y	Y
2 Thompson	N	N	N	Y	Y	Y	N
3 *Pickering*	N	Y	Y	N	Y	Y	Y
4 Shows	N	N	Y	Y	Y	Y	Y
5 Taylor	N	N	Y	Y	N	Y	Y
MISSOURI							
1 Clay	N	N	N	?	?	?	?
2 *Akin*	N	Y	Y	N	Y	Y	Y
3 Gephardt	N	N	?	Y	Y	Y	?
4 Skelton	Y	N	Y	Y	Y	Y	Y
5 McCarthy	N	N	N	Y	Y	Y	?
6 *Graves*	Y	Y	Y	N	Y	Y	Y
7 *Blunt*	Y	Y	Y	N	Y	Y	Y
8 *Emerson*	Y	Y	Y	N	Y	Y	Y
9 *Hulshof*	Y	Y	Y	N	Y	Y	Y
MONTANA							
AL *Rehberg*	N	Y	Y	N	Y	Y	Y
NEBRASKA							
1 *Bereuter*	Y	Y	Y	?	?	Y	Y
2 *Terry*	N	Y	Y	N	Y	Y	Y
3 *Osborne*	N	Y	Y	N	Y	Y	Y
NEVADA							
1 Berkley	N	N	Y	Y	Y	Y	Y
2 *Gibbons*	Y	Y	Y	N	Y	Y	Y
NEW HAMPSHIRE							
1 *Sununu*	N	Y	Y	N	Y	?	?
2 *Bass*	Y	Y	Y	N	Y	Y	Y
NEW JERSEY							
1 Andrews	N	N	Y	Y	Y	Y	Y
2 *LoBiondo*	N	Y	Y	N	Y	Y	Y
3 *Saxton*	N	Y	Y	N	?	Y	?
4 *Smith*	N	Y	Y	N	Y	Y	Y
5 *Roukema*	?	?	?	?	?	?	?
6 Pallone	N	N	N	Y	Y	Y	Y
7 *Ferguson*	N	Y	Y	N	Y	Y	Y
8 Pascrell	N	N	N	Y	Y	?	?
9 Rothman	Y	N	Y	Y	Y	Y	Y
10 Payne	N	N	N	Y	Y	Y	N
11 *Frelinghuysen*	Y	Y	Y	N	Y	Y	Y
12 Holt	N	N	Y	Y	Y	Y	N
13 Menendez	N	N	Y	Y	Y	Y	Y
NEW MEXICO							
1 *Wilson*	Y	Y	Y	N	Y	Y	Y
2 *Skeen*	Y	Y	Y	N	Y	Y	Y
3 Udall	N	N	N	Y	Y	Y	N
NEW YORK							
1 *Grucci*	?	?	?	?	?	?	?
2 Israel	Y	N	Y	Y	Y	Y	Y
3 *King*	Y	Y	Y	N	Y	?	?
4 McCarthy	Y	N	Y	Y	Y	Y	Y
5 Ackerman	N	N	N	Y	Y	Y	N
6 Meeks	Y	N	N	Y	Y	Y	Y
7 Crowley	Y	N	N	Y	Y	Y	Y
8 Nadler	N	N	?	N	Y	Y	N
9 Weiner	N	N	N	Y	Y	Y	N
10 Towns	N	N	N	Y	Y	Y	N
11 Owens	N	N	N	Y	Y	Y	N
12 Velázquez	N	N	N	Y	Y	Y	N
13 *Fossella*	Y	Y	Y	N	Y	Y	Y
14 Maloney	Y	N	N	Y	Y	Y	Y
15 Rangel	N	N	N	Y	Y	?	?
16 Serrano	N	N	N	Y	Y	Y	N
17 Engel	N	N	N	Y	Y	Y	N
18 Lowey	N	N	N	Y	Y	Y	N
19 *Kelly*	Y	Y	Y	N	Y	Y	Y
20 *Gilman*	Y	Y	Y	N	Y	?	?
21 McNulty	N	N	N	Y	Y	Y	N
22 *Sweeney*	Y	Y	Y	N	Y	Y	Y
23 *Boehlert*	Y	Y	Y	N	Y	Y	Y
24 *McHugh*	Y	Y	Y	N	Y	Y	Y
25 *Walsh*	Y	Y	Y	N	Y	Y	Y
26 Hinchey	N	N	N	Y	N	Y	N
27 *Reynolds*	Y	Y	Y	N	Y	Y	Y
28 Slaughter	N	N	N	Y	Y	?	?
29 LaFalce	N	N	N	?	?	Y	?
30 *Quinn*	Y	Y	Y	N	Y	Y	Y
31 *Houghton*	?	?	?	?	?	?	?
NORTH CAROLINA							
1 Clayton	N	N	Y	Y	Y	Y	N
2 Etheridge	Y	N	N	Y	Y	Y	Y
3 *Jones*	N	Y	Y	N	Y	Y	Y
4 Price	Y	N	N	Y	Y	Y	Y
5 *Burr*	Y	Y	Y	N	Y	Y	Y
6 *Coble*	Y	Y	Y	N	Y	Y	Y
7 McIntyre	N	N	Y	Y	Y	Y	Y
8 *Hayes*	N	Y	Y	N	Y	Y	Y
9 *Myrick*	Y	Y	Y	N	Y	Y	Y
10 *Ballenger*	N	Y	Y	?	?	?	?
11 *Taylor*	Y	Y	Y	N	Y	Y	Y
12 Watt	N	N	N	Y	Y	?	?
NORTH DAKOTA							
AL Pomeroy	N	N	Y	Y	Y	Y	Y
OHIO							
1 *Chabot*	Y	Y	Y	N	Y	Y	Y
2 *Portman*	N	Y	Y	N	Y	Y	Y
3 Vacant							
4 *Oxley*	Y	Y	Y	N	Y	?	?
5 *Gillmor*	Y	Y	?	?	Y	?	?
6 Strickland	Y	N	N	Y	Y	Y	Y
7 *Hobson*	Y	Y	Y	N	Y	Y	Y
8 *Boehner*	Y	Y	Y	N	Y	?	Y
9 Kaptur	N	N	N	Y	Y	Y	N
10 Kucinich	N	N	N	Y	Y	Y	N
11 Jones	N	N	N	Y	Y	Y	N
12 *Tiberi*	Y	Y	Y	N	Y	Y	Y
13 Brown	N	N	N	Y	Y	Y	N
14 Sawyer	N	N	N	Y	?	?	?
15 *Pryce*	Y	Y	Y	N	Y	Y	Y
16 *Regula*	Y	Y	Y	N	Y	Y	Y
17 Vacant							
18 *Ney*	Y	Y	Y	N	Y	Y	Y
19 *LaTourette*	Y	Y	Y	?	?	Y	Y
OKLAHOMA							
1 *Sullivan*	N	Y	Y	N	Y	Y	Y
2 Carson	Y	N	N	Y	Y	Y	Y
3 *Watkins*	Y	Y	Y	N	Y	Y	Y
4 *Watts*	N	Y	Y	N	Y	Y	Y
5 *Istook*	N	Y	Y	N	Y	Y	Y
6 *Lucas*	Y	Y	Y	N	Y	Y	Y
OREGON							
1 Wu	Y	N	N	Y	Y	Y	N
2 *Walden*	Y	Y	Y	N	Y	Y	Y
3 Blumenauer	N	N	N	Y	N	Y	N
4 DeFazio	N	N	Y	Y	N	Y	N
5 Hooley	?	?	?	?	?	?	?
PENNSYLVANIA							
1 Brady	N	N	N	Y	Y	Y	N
2 Fattah	N	N	N	Y	Y	Y	N
3 Borski	N	N	?	?	?	?	?
4 *Hart*	Y	Y	Y	N	Y	Y	Y
5 *Peterson*	Y	Y	Y	?	?	?	?
6 Holden	N	N	Y	Y	Y	Y	N
7 *Weldon*	N	?	?	N	Y	Y	Y
8 *Greenwood*	Y	Y	Y	N	?	?	?
9 *Shuster, Bill*	N	Y	Y	N	Y	Y	Y
10 *Sherwood*	Y	Y	Y	N	Y	Y	Y
11 Kanjorski	N	N	N	Y	Y	Y	N
12 Murtha	N	N	N	Y	Y	?	?
13 Hoeffel	N	N	N	Y	Y	Y	N
14 Coyne	N	N	N	Y	N	Y	N
15 *Toomey*	?	?	?	?	?	?	?
16 *Pitts*	N	Y	Y	N	Y	Y	Y
17 *Gekas*	Y	Y	Y	N	Y	Y	Y
18 Doyle	N	N	N	Y	Y	Y	N
19 *Platts*	Y	Y	Y	N	Y	Y	Y
20 Mascara	N	N	N	Y	Y	Y	?
21 *English*	Y	Y	Y	N	Y	Y	Y
RHODE ISLAND							
1 Kennedy	N	N	N	Y	Y	Y	N
2 Langevin	N	N	N	Y	N	Y	N
SOUTH CAROLINA							
1 *Brown*	Y	Y	Y	N	Y	Y	Y
2 *Wilson*	N	Y	Y	N	Y	Y	Y
3 *Graham*	N	Y	Y	N	?	Y	Y
4 *DeMint*	N	Y	Y	N	Y	Y	Y
5 Spratt	Y	N	N	Y	Y	Y	N
6 Clyburn	N	N	N	?	?	Y	N
SOUTH DAKOTA							
AL *Thune*	N	Y	Y	N	Y	Y	Y
TENNESSEE							
1 *Jenkins*	Y	Y	Y	N	?	Y	Y
2 *Duncan*	Y	Y	Y	N	Y	Y	Y
3 *Wamp*	N	Y	Y	N	Y	Y	Y
4 *Hilleary*	N	Y	Y	N	Y	Y	Y
5 Clement	Y	N	Y	Y	Y	?	?
6 Gordon	Y	N	Y	Y	Y	?	?
7 *Bryant*	N	Y	Y	N	Y	Y	Y
8 Tanner	Y	N	N	Y	Y	Y	Y
9 Ford	Y	N	N	Y	Y	?	?
TEXAS							
1 Sandlin	N	N	N	Y	Y	Y	Y
2 Turner	Y	N	Y	Y	Y	Y	Y
3 *Johnson, Sam*	N	Y	Y	N	Y	Y	?
4 Hall	N	N	Y	Y	Y	Y	Y
5 *Sessions*	Y	Y	Y	N	Y	Y	Y
6 *Barton*	Y	Y	Y	N	Y	Y	?
7 *Culberson*	Y	Y	Y	N	Y	Y	Y
8 *Brady*	Y	Y	Y	N	Y	Y	Y
9 Lampson	Y	N	N	Y	Y	Y	Y
10 Doggett	N	N	N	Y	Y	Y	N
11 Edwards	Y	N	Y	Y	Y	Y	Y
12 *Granger*	Y	Y	Y	N	Y	Y	Y
13 *Thornberry*	N	Y	Y	N	Y	Y	Y
14 *Paul*	N	Y	Y	?	?	N	Y
15 Hinojosa	Y	N	N	Y	Y	Y	?
16 Reyes	N	N	Y	Y	Y	Y	N
17 Stenholm	Y	N	Y	Y	N	Y	Y
18 Jackson-Lee	N	N	Y	Y	Y	Y	N
19 *Combest*	?	?	?	?	?	?	?
20 Gonzalez	Y	N	Y	Y	Y	Y	N
21 *Smith*	Y	Y	Y	N	Y	?	?
22 *DeLay*	Y	Y	Y	N	Y	Y	Y
23 *Bonilla*	Y	Y	Y	N	Y	Y	Y
24 Frost	Y	N	Y	?	?	Y	N
25 Bentsen	Y	N	N	Y	Y	Y	N
26 *Armey*	Y	Y	?	N	Y	Y	Y
27 Ortiz	N	N	Y	Y	Y	Y	Y
28 Rodriguez	N	N	Y	Y	Y	Y	N
29 Green	N	N	N	Y	Y	Y	N
30 Johnson, E.B.	Y	N	N	Y	Y	Y	N
UTAH							
1 *Hansen*	Y	Y	?	N	Y	Y	Y
2 Matheson	Y	N	Y	Y	Y	Y	Y
3 *Cannon*	Y	Y	Y	N	Y	Y	Y
VERMONT							
AL *Sanders*	N	N	N	Y	Y	Y	N
VIRGINIA							
1 *Davis, Jo Ann*	N	Y	Y	N	Y	Y	?
2 *Schrock*	Y	Y	Y	N	Y	Y	Y
3 Scott	N	N	N	Y	Y	Y	N
4 *Forbes*	N	Y	Y	N	Y	Y	Y
5 *Goode*	N	Y	Y	N	Y	Y	Y
6 *Goodlatte*	N	Y	+	N	Y	Y	Y
7 *Cantor*	Y	Y	Y	N	Y	Y	Y
8 Moran	Y	N	N	?	?	Y	Y
9 Boucher	Y	N	N	Y	Y	Y	N
10 *Wolf*	N	Y	Y	N	Y	Y	Y
11 *Davis, T.*	?	Y	Y	N	Y	Y	Y
WASHINGTON							
1 Inslee	N	N	N	Y	Y	Y	Y
2 Larsen	Y	N	?	Y	Y	Y	Y
3 Baird	Y	N	N	Y	Y	Y	N
4 *Hastings*	Y	Y	Y	N	Y	Y	Y
5 *Nethercutt*	Y	?	Y	N	Y	Y	Y
6 Dicks	Y	N	Y	Y	Y	Y	N
7 McDermott	N	N	N	Y	Y	Y	N
8 *Dunn*	Y	Y	Y	N	Y	Y	Y
9 Smith	Y	N	N	Y	Y	?	Y
WEST VIRGINIA							
1 Mollohan	N	N	?	Y	Y	Y	Y
2 *Capito*	Y	Y	Y	N	Y	Y	Y
3 Rahall	N	N	Y	Y	Y	Y	N
WISCONSIN							
1 *Ryan*	Y	Y	?	N	Y	Y	Y
2 Baldwin	N	N	N	Y	Y	Y	N
3 Kind	Y	N	N	Y	Y	Y	Y
4 Kleczka	N	?	?	Y	N	Y	N
5 Barrett	N	N	N	Y	Y	Y	N
6 *Petri*	Y	Y	Y	N	Y	Y	Y
7 Obey	N	N	N	?	Y	Y	N
8 *Green*	Y	Y	Y	N	Y	Y	Y
9 *Sensenbrenner*	Y	?	?	N	Y	?	?
WYOMING							
AL *Cubin*	N	Y	Y	N	Y	Y	Y

Southern states - Ala., Ark., Fla., Ga., Ky., La., Miss., N.C., Okla., S.C., Tenn., Texas, Va.

House Roll Call Votes
By Subject

House Votes

SENATE ROLL CALL VOTES

Senate Roll Call Votes
By Bill Number

Senate Bills

S 517, S-12, S-13, S-14, S-15, S-16,
    S-17, S-18, S-19, S-20, S-21
S 565, S-10, S-11, S-12, S-16, S-17
S 625, S-31
S 812, S-36, S-37, S-38, S-39, S-40,
    S-41
S 1214, S-50
S 1731, S-7, S-8, S-9, S-10
S 2514, S-33, S-34
S 2578, S-31
S 2600, S-32, S-33
S 2673, S-35, S-36
S 2690, S-34

S J Res 34, S-35
S J Res 45, S-48

S Res 272, S-31
S Res 292, S-34

House Bills

H J Res 114, S-48
H J Res 124, S-52

HR 4, S-21
HR 8, S-31, S-32
HR 622, S-4, S-5, S-6, S-7
HR 2215, S-47
HR 2356, S-14
HR 2646, S-10, S-23
HR 3090, S-13, S-22, S-24, S-25, S-26,
    S-27, S-28, S-40, S-41
HR 3167, S-26
HR 3210, S-52
HR 3275, S-33
HR 3295, S-49
HR 3448, S-27
HR 3525, S-18
HR 3763, S-39
HR 4775, S-29, S-30, S-38
HR 5005, S-42, S-43, S-44, S-45, S-46,
    S-47, S-50, S-51
HR 5010, S-41, S-49
HR 5011, S-37
HR 5093, S-43, S-44, S-45, S-46
HR 5121, S-39

Key

Y	Voted for (yea).
#	Paired for.
+	Announced for.
N	Voted against (nay).
X	Paired against.
−	Announced against.
P	Voted "present."
C	Voted "present" to avoid possible conflict of interest.
?	Did not vote or otherwise make a position known.

Democrats **Republicans**
Independents

	1	2
ALABAMA		
Shelby	?	?
Sessions	?	N
ALASKA		
Stevens	Y	N
Murkowski	?	?
ARIZONA		
McCain	N	?
Kyl	Y	N
ARKANSAS		
Hutchinson	Y	Y
Lincoln	Y	Y
CALIFORNIA		
Feinstein	Y	+
Boxer	Y	Y
COLORADO		
Campbell	Y	Y
Allard	Y	Y
CONNECTICUT		
Dodd	Y	?
Lieberman	?	Y
DELAWARE		
Carper	Y	Y
Biden	Y	?
FLORIDA		
Graham	Y	Y
Nelson	Y	N
GEORGIA		
Miller	?	?
Cleland	Y	Y
HAWAII		
Inouye	Y	Y
Akaka	?	?
IDAHO		
Craig	Y	Y
Crapo	Y	Y
ILLINOIS		
Durbin	Y	Y
Fitzgerald	Y	N
INDIANA		
Lugar	Y	N
Bayh	Y	Y

	1	2
IOWA		
Grassley	Y	N
Harkin	Y	Y
KANSAS		
Brownback	Y	N
Roberts	Y	N
KENTUCKY		
McConnell	Y	N
Bunning	Y	N
LOUISIANA		
Breaux	N	Y
Landrieu	Y	Y
MAINE		
Snowe	Y	N
Collins	Y	N
MARYLAND		
Sarbanes	Y	Y
Mikulski	Y	Y
MASSACHUSETTS		
Kennedy	Y	Y
Kerry	Y	Y
MICHIGAN		
Levin	Y	Y
Stabenow	Y	Y
MINNESOTA		
Wellstone	Y	Y
Dayton	Y	Y
MISSISSIPPI		
Cochran	Y	Y
Lott	Y	N
MISSOURI		
Bond	N	Y
Carnahan	Y	Y
MONTANA		
Baucus	Y	Y
Burns	Y	Y
NEBRASKA		
Nelson	Y	Y
Hagel	Y	N
NEVADA		
Reid	Y	Y
Ensign	Y	N

	1	2
NEW HAMPSHIRE		
Smith	Y	N
Gregg	N	N
NEW JERSEY		
Corzine	Y	Y
Torricelli	Y	Y
NEW MEXICO		
Domenici	Y	?
Bingaman	Y	Y
NEW YORK		
Clinton	Y	Y
Schumer	Y	Y
NORTH CAROLINA		
Helms	Y	N
Edwards	Y	Y
NORTH DAKOTA		
Conrad	Y	Y
Dorgan	Y	Y
OHIO		
DeWine	Y	N
Voinovich	Y	N
OKLAHOMA		
Nickles	Y	N
Inhofe	N	+
OREGON		
Wyden	Y	Y
Smith	Y	Y
PENNSYLVANIA		
Specter	Y	N
Santorum	Y	N
RHODE ISLAND		
Reed	Y	Y
Chafee	Y	N
SOUTH CAROLINA		
Thurmond	Y	N
Hollings	Y	Y
SOUTH DAKOTA		
Daschle	Y	Y
Johnson	Y	Y
TENNESSEE		
Thompson	Y	N
Frist	Y	N

	1	2
TEXAS		
Gramm	Y	N
Hutchison	Y	Y
UTAH		
Hatch	Y	Y
Bennett	Y	Y
VERMONT		
Leahy	Y	Y
Jeffords	Y	Y
VIRGINIA		
Warner	Y	N
Allen	N	N
WASHINGTON		
Cantwell	Y	Y
Murray	Y	Y
WEST VIRGINIA		
Byrd	Y	N
Rockefeller	Y	Y
WISCONSIN		
Kohl	Y	Y
Feingold	Y	N
WYOMING		
Thomas	Y	Y
Enzi	Y	Y

ND Northern Democrats   SD Southern Democrats

Southern states - Ala., Ark., Fla., Ga., Ky., La., Miss., N.C., Okla., S.C., Tenn., Texas, Va.

1. Procedural Motion/Require Attendance. Daschle, D-S.D., motion to instruct the sergeant-at-arms to request the attendance of absent senators. Motion agreed to 88-6: R 41-5; D 46-1 (ND 39-0, SD 7-1); I 1-0. Jan. 23, 2002.

2. HR 622. Adoption Tax Credit/Agriculture Assistance. Baucus, D-Mont., motion to waive the Budget Act with respect to the Nickles, R-Okla., point of order against the emergency designation of the Baucus amendment to the Daschle, D-S.D., substitute amendment. The Baucus amendment would provide $2.35 billion in emergency agriculture assistance. The Daschle amendment would strike the text of the underlying bill and insert an economic stimulus measure that would extend unemployment benefits to displaced workers for 13 weeks, allow for a $300 rebate to the working poor who did not receive tax rebates last year, allow for a tax cut for businesses that buy equipment this year and provide $5 billion in Medicaid assistance to states. Motion rejected 57-33: R 14-30; D 42-3 (ND 35-2, SD 7-1); I 1-0. A three-fifths majority vote (60) of the total Senate is required to waive the Budget Act. (Subsequently, the chair upheld the point of order and the emergency designation was stricken. Nickles then raised another point of order against the Baucus amendment and the amendment fell.) Jan. 24, 2002.

	3	4	5	6
ALABAMA				
Shelby	?	?	?	N
Sessions	?	?	?	N
ALASKA				
Stevens	Y	Y	Y	N
Murkowski	?	?	?	N
ARIZONA				
McCain	?	?	?	Y
Kyl	?	+	+	N
ARKANSAS				
Hutchinson	Y	Y	?	N
Lincoln	N	Y	Y	Y
CALIFORNIA				
Feinstein	N	Y	Y	Y
Boxer	N	?	?	?
COLORADO				
Campbell	Y	Y	Y	Y
Allard	Y	Y	Y	N
CONNECTICUT				
Dodd	?	?	?	?
Lieberman	N	Y	Y	Y
DELAWARE				
Carper	N	Y	Y	Y
Biden	N	Y	Y	Y
FLORIDA				
Graham	N	Y	Y	Y
Nelson	?	?	?	Y
GEORGIA				
Miller	?	?	?	N
Cleland	N	Y	Y	Y
HAWAII				
Inouye	N	Y	Y	Y
Akaka	?	?	?	?
IDAHO				
Craig	Y	Y	Y	N
Crapo	Y	Y	Y	N
ILLINOIS				
Durbin	N	Y	Y	Y
Fitzgerald	Y	Y	Y	N
INDIANA				
Lugar	Y	Y	Y	N
Bayh	N	Y	Y	Y

	3	4	5	6
IOWA				
Grassley	Y	Y	Y	N
Harkin	N	Y	Y	Y
KANSAS				
Brownback	Y	Y	Y	N
Roberts	?	?	?	N
KENTUCKY				
McConnell	Y	Y	Y	N
Bunning	Y	Y	Y	N
LOUISIANA				
Breaux	N	Y	Y	Y
Landrieu	N	Y	Y	Y
MAINE				
Snowe	Y	Y	Y	N
Collins	Y	Y	Y	Y
MARYLAND				
Sarbanes	N	Y	Y	Y
Mikulski	N	Y	Y	Y
MASSACHUSETTS				
Kennedy	?	?	?	Y
Kerry	N	Y	Y	Y
MICHIGAN				
Levin	N	Y	Y	Y
Stabenow	N	Y	Y	Y
MINNESOTA				
Wellstone	N	Y	Y	Y
Dayton	N	Y	Y	Y
MISSISSIPPI				
Cochran	Y	Y	Y	Y
Lott	Y	Y	Y	N
MISSOURI				
Bond	Y	Y	Y	N
Carnahan	N	Y	?	Y
MONTANA				
Baucus	N	Y	Y	Y
Burns	Y	Y	Y	–
NEBRASKA				
Nelson	N	Y	Y	Y
Hagel	Y	Y	Y	N
NEVADA				
Reid	N	Y	Y	Y
Ensign	Y	Y	Y	?

	3	4	5	6
NEW HAMPSHIRE				
Smith	Y	Y	Y	N
Gregg	Y	Y	Y	?
NEW JERSEY				
Corzine	N	Y	Y	Y
Torricelli	N	Y	Y	Y
NEW MEXICO				
Domenici	?	?	?	N
Bingaman	N	Y	Y	Y
NEW YORK				
Clinton	–	Y	Y	Y
Schumer	N	Y	Y	Y
NORTH CAROLINA				
Helms	Y	Y	Y	N
Edwards	N	Y	Y	Y
NORTH DAKOTA				
Conrad	N	Y	Y	Y
Dorgan	–	+	+	Y
OHIO				
DeWine	Y	Y	Y	N
Voinovich	?	?	?	Y
OKLAHOMA				
Nickles	Y	Y	Y	N
Inhofe	+	+	+	+
OREGON				
Wyden	N	Y	Y	Y
Smith	Y	Y	Y	Y
PENNSYLVANIA				
Specter	Y	Y	Y	N
Santorum	Y	Y	Y	N
RHODE ISLAND				
Reed	N	Y	Y	Y
Chafee	N	Y	Y	N
SOUTH CAROLINA				
Thurmond	Y	Y	Y	N
Hollings	N	Y	Y	Y
SOUTH DAKOTA				
Daschle	N	Y	Y	Y
Johnson	N	Y	Y	Y
TENNESSEE				
Thompson	Y	?	?	?
Frist	Y	Y	Y	N

	3	4	5	6
TEXAS				
Gramm	Y	Y	Y	N
Hutchison	Y	Y	Y	N
UTAH				
Hatch	Y	Y	Y	N
Bennett	Y	Y	Y	N
VERMONT				
Leahy	N	Y	Y	Y
Jeffords	N	Y	Y	Y
VIRGINIA				
Warner	Y	Y	Y	N
Allen	Y	Y	Y	N
WASHINGTON				
Cantwell	N	Y	Y	Y
Murray	N	Y	Y	Y
WEST VIRGINIA				
Byrd	N	Y	Y	Y
Rockefeller	N	Y	Y	Y
WISCONSIN				
Kohl	N	Y	Y	Y
Feingold	N	Y	Y	Y
WYOMING				
Thomas	Y	Y	Y	N
Enzi	Y	Y	Y	N

Key

Y	Voted for (yea).
#	Paired for.
+	Announced for.
N	Voted against (nay).
X	Paired against.
–	Announced against.
P	Voted "present."
C	Voted "present" to avoid possible conflict of interest.
?	Did not vote or otherwise make a position known.

Democrats   ***Republicans***
Independents

ND Northern Democrats   SD Southern Democrats

Southern states - Ala., Ark., Fla., Ga., Ky., La., Miss., N.C., Okla., S.C., Tenn., Texas, Va.

3. HR 622. Adoption Tax Credit/Bonus Depreciation. Smith, R-Ore., motion to waive the Budget Act with respect to the Conrad, D-N.D., point of order against the Smith amendment to the Daschle, D-S.D., substitute amendment. The Smith amendment would provide a 30 percent bonus depreciation through Sept. 11, 2004. The Daschle amendment would extend unemployment benefits to displaced workers for 13 weeks, allow for a $300 rebate to taxpayers who did not receive rebates in 2001, allow for a tax cut for businesses that buy equipment this year and provide $5 billion in Medicaid assistance to states. Motion rejected 39-45: R 39-1; D 0-43 (ND 0-36, SD 0-7); I 0-1. A three-fifths majority vote (60) of the total Senate is required to waive the Budget Act. (Subsequently, the chair upheld the point of order and the amendment fell.) Jan. 25, 2002.

4. Krieger Nomination/Confirmation. Confirmation of President Bush's nomination of Marcia S. Krieger of Colorado to be U.S. District judge for the District of Colorado. Confirmed 83-0: R 39-0; D 43-0 (ND 36-0, SD 7-0); I 1-0. A "yea" was a vote in support of the president's position. Jan. 25, 2002.

5. Mahan Nomination/Confirmation. Confirmation of President Bush's nomination of James C. Mahan of Nevada to be U.S. District judge for the District of Nevada. Confirmed 81-0: R 38-0; D 42-0 (ND 35-0, SD 7-0); I 1-0. A "yea" was a vote in support of the president's position. Jan. 25, 2002.

6. HR 622. Adoption Tax Credit/Unemployment Benefits. Durbin, D-Ill., motion to waive the Budget Act with respect to the Nickles, R-Okla., point of order against the Durbin amendment to the Daschle, D-S.D., substitute amendment. The Durbin amendment would provide a temporary supplement to unemployment insurance benefits of 15 percent or $25 per week, whichever is greater, and would require states to provide temporary unemployment benefits to former part-time workers who are seeking another part-time job. Motion rejected 57-35: R 10-34; D 46-1 (ND 38-0, SD 8-1); I 1-0. A three-fifths majority vote (60) of the total Senate is required to waive the Budget Act. (Subsequently, the chair upheld the point of order and the amendment fell.) Jan. 29, 2002.

	7	8	9	10
ALABAMA				
Shelby	Y	Y	Y	Y
Sessions	Y	Y	Y	Y
ALASKA				
Stevens	Y	N	Y	Y
Murkowski	Y	Y	Y	Y
ARIZONA				
McCain	Y	N	Y	Y
Kyl	Y	N	Y	N
ARKANSAS				
Hutchinson	Y	Y	Y	Y
Lincoln	Y	Y	Y	Y
CALIFORNIA				
Feinstein	Y	Y	Y	Y
Boxer	?	Y	Y	N
COLORADO				
Campbell	Y	Y	Y	N
Allard	Y	N	Y	N
CONNECTICUT				
Dodd	?	?	?	?
Lieberman	Y	Y	Y	N
DELAWARE				
Carper	Y	Y	Y	Y
Biden	Y	Y	Y	Y
FLORIDA				
Graham	Y	Y	Y	N
Nelson	Y	Y	Y	Y
GEORGIA				
Miller	Y	Y	Y	Y
Cleland	Y	Y	Y	Y
HAWAII				
Inouye	Y	Y	Y	Y
Akaka	?	?	?	?
IDAHO				
Craig	Y	N	Y	Y
Crapo	Y	N	Y	Y
ILLINOIS				
Durbin	Y	Y	Y	Y
Fitzgerald	Y	N	Y	Y
INDIANA				
Lugar	Y	N	Y	Y
Bayh	Y	Y	Y	Y

	7	8	9	10
IOWA				
Grassley	Y	N	Y	Y
Harkin	Y	Y	Y	Y
KANSAS				
Brownback	Y	N	Y	Y
Roberts	Y	N	Y	Y
KENTUCKY				
McConnell	Y	N	Y	N
Bunning	Y	N	Y	N
LOUISIANA				
Breaux	Y	Y	Y	Y
Landrieu	Y	Y	Y	Y
MAINE				
Snowe	Y	Y	Y	Y
Collins	Y	Y	Y	Y
MARYLAND				
Sarbanes	Y	Y	Y	N
Mikulski	Y	Y	Y	Y
MASSACHUSETTS				
Kennedy	Y	Y	Y	N
Kerry	Y	Y	Y	Y
MICHIGAN				
Levin	Y	Y	Y	N
Stabenow	Y	Y	Y	Y
MINNESOTA				
Wellstone	Y	Y	Y	Y
Dayton	Y	Y	Y	N
MISSISSIPPI				
Cochran	Y	N	Y	Y
Lott	Y	N	Y	N
MISSOURI				
Bond	Y	N	Y	N
Carnahan	Y	Y	Y	Y
MONTANA				
Baucus	Y	Y	Y	Y
Burns	+	–	+	Y
NEBRASKA				
Nelson	Y	N	Y	Y
Hagel	Y	N	Y	?
NEVADA				
Reid	Y	Y	Y	Y
Ensign	?	?	?	?

	7	8	9	10
NEW HAMPSHIRE				
Smith	Y	N	Y	N
Gregg	?	?	?	?
NEW JERSEY				
Corzine	Y	Y	Y	Y
Torricelli	Y	Y	?	Y
NEW MEXICO				
Domenici	Y	N	Y	Y
Bingaman	Y	Y	Y	N
NEW YORK				
Clinton	Y	Y	Y	Y
Schumer	Y	Y	Y	Y
NORTH CAROLINA				
Helms	Y	N	Y	N
Edwards	Y	Y	Y	Y
NORTH DAKOTA				
Conrad	Y	N	Y	N
Dorgan	Y	Y	Y	N
OHIO				
DeWine	Y	N	Y	N
Voinovich	Y	N	Y	N
OKLAHOMA				
Nickles	Y	N	Y	N
Inhofe	+	N	Y	N
OREGON				
Wyden	Y	Y	Y	Y
Smith	Y	N	Y	Y
PENNSYLVANIA				
Specter	Y	N	Y	N
Santorum	Y	N	Y	N
RHODE ISLAND				
Reed	Y	Y	Y	N
Chafee	N	N	N	N
SOUTH CAROLINA				
Thurmond	Y	N	Y	N
Hollings	Y	Y	Y	Y
SOUTH DAKOTA				
Daschle	Y	Y	Y	Y
Johnson	Y	Y	Y	Y
TENNESSEE				
Thompson	?	N	N	N
Frist	Y	N	Y	N

Key

Y	Voted for (yea).
#	Paired for.
+	Announced for.
N	Voted against (nay).
X	Paired against.
–	Announced against.
P	Voted "present."
C	Voted "present" to avoid possible conflict of interest.
?	Did not vote or otherwise make a position known.

Democrats **Republicans**
Independents

	7	8	9	10
TEXAS				
Gramm	Y	N	Y	N
Hutchison	Y	N	Y	Y
UTAH				
Hatch	Y	N	Y	Y
Bennett	Y	N	Y	Y
VERMONT				
Leahy	Y	Y	Y	N
Jeffords	Y	Y	Y	Y
VIRGINIA				
Warner	Y	Y	Y	N
Allen	Y	N	Y	Y
WASHINGTON				
Cantwell	Y	Y	Y	Y
Murray	Y	Y	Y	Y
WEST VIRGINIA				
Byrd	Y	Y	Y	N
Rockefeller	Y	Y	Y	Y
WISCONSIN				
Kohl	Y	Y	Y	Y
Feingold	N	N	Y	N
WYOMING				
Thomas	Y	N	Y	N
Enzi	Y	N	Y	N

ND Northern Democrats   SD Southern Democrats

Southern states - Ala., Ark., Fla., Ga., Ky., La., Miss., N.C., Okla., S.C., Tenn., Texas, Va.

7. HR 622. Adoption Tax Credit/Small Business Expensing. Bond, R-Mo., amendment that would provide for a two-year increase in small business expensing, from $24,000 to $40,000, and temporarily increase the size of businesses that are eligible to take advantage of the expensing provision. Adopted 90-2: R 43-1; D 46-1 (ND 37-1, SD 9-0); I 1-0. Jan. 29, 2002.

8. HR 622. Adoption Tax Credit/Federal Medicaid Matching Rate. Baucus, D-Mont., motion to waive the Budget Act with respect to the Grassley, R-Iowa, point of order against the Harkin, D-Iowa, amendment to the Daschle, D-S.D., substitute amendment. The Harkin amendment would increase the federal Medicaid matching rate for fiscal 2002 by 3 percentage points for all states and by a total of 4.5 percentage points for states with high unemployment rates. Motion rejected 54-41: R 8-38; D 45-3 (ND 36-3, SD 9-0); I 1-0. A three-fifths majority vote (60) of the total Senate is required to waive the Budget Act. (Subsequently, the chair upheld the point of order and the amendment fell.) Jan. 29, 2002.

9. HR 622. Adoption Tax Credit/Terrorist Response Tax Exemption. Allen, R-Va., amendment to the Daschle, D-S.D., substitute amendment. The Allen amendment would exclude from gross income any compensation received by a civilian uniformed employee for any month during which the employee provides security, safety, fire management or medical services during the initial response in a terrorist attack zone. Adopted 92-2: R 44-2; D 47-0 (ND 38-0, SD 9-0); I 1-0. Jan. 29, 2002.

10. HR 622. Adoption Tax Credit/Bonus Depreciation. Baucus, D-Mont., motion to waive the Budget Act with respect to the Conrad, D-N.D., point of order against the Baucus amendment to the Daschle, D-S.D., substitute amendment. The Baucus amendment would provide 30 percent bonus depreciation for the cost for certain capital purchases by businesses in 2002 and 2003. It also would provide for a two-year increase in the federal match of state Medicaid payments. Motion agreed to 62-33: R 27-19; D 34-14 (ND 26-13, SD 8-1); I 1-0. A three-fifths majority vote (60) of the total Senate is required to waive the Budget Act. (Subsequently, the amendment was adopted by voice vote.) Jan. 29, 2002.

	11	12	13	14	15
ALABAMA					
Shelby	Y	Y	N	N	N
Sessions	Y	Y	N	Y	N
ALASKA					
Stevens	?	Y	N	Y	Y
Murkowski	Y	Y	N	Y	N
ARIZONA					
McCain	?	?	?	?	?
Kyl	Y	Y	N	Y	N
ARKANSAS					
Hutchinson	Y	Y	Y	Y	N
Lincoln	Y	Y	Y	N	N
CALIFORNIA					
Feinstein	Y	Y	Y	N	N
Boxer	Y	Y	Y	N	N
COLORADO					
Campbell	Y	Y	N	Y	N
Allard	Y	Y	N	Y	N
CONNECTICUT					
Dodd	Y	Y	Y	N	Y
Lieberman	Y	Y	Y	N	Y
DELAWARE					
Carper	Y	Y	Y	N	Y
Biden	Y	Y	Y	N	Y
FLORIDA					
Graham	Y	Y	Y	N	N
Nelson	Y	Y	Y	N	N
GEORGIA					
Miller	?	?	Y	Y	N
Cleland	Y	Y	Y	Y	Y
HAWAII					
Inouye	?	Y	Y	N	Y
Akaka	Y	Y	Y	N	Y
IDAHO					
Craig	Y	Y	N	Y	N
Crapo	Y	Y	N	Y	N
ILLINOIS					
Durbin	Y	Y	Y	N	Y
Fitzgerald	Y	Y	N	Y	N
INDIANA					
Lugar	Y	Y	N	Y	Y
Bayh	Y	Y	Y	N	N

	11	12	13	14	15
IOWA					
Grassley	Y	Y	N	Y	N
Harkin	?	Y	Y	N	Y
KANSAS					
Brownback	?	Y	N	Y	N
Roberts	Y	Y	N	Y	N
KENTUCKY					
McConnell	?	Y	N	Y	N
Bunning	Y	Y	N	Y	N
LOUISIANA					
Breaux	Y	Y	Y	Y	N
Landrieu	Y	Y	Y	Y	N
MAINE					
Snowe	Y	Y	Y	Y	Y
Collins	Y	Y	Y	Y	Y
MARYLAND					
Sarbanes	Y	Y	Y	N	Y
Mikulski	Y	Y	Y	N	Y
MASSACHUSETTS					
Kennedy	Y	Y	Y	N	Y
Kerry	?	?	Y	N	Y
MICHIGAN					
Levin	Y	Y	Y	N	Y
Stabenow	Y	Y	Y	N	Y
MINNESOTA					
Wellstone	+	Y	Y	N	Y
Dayton	Y	Y	Y	N	Y
MISSISSIPPI					
Cochran	?	?	N	Y	N
Lott	?	?	N	Y	N
MISSOURI					
Bond	?	Y	N	Y	N
Carnahan	Y	Y	Y	N	Y
MONTANA					
Baucus	Y	Y	Y	N	N
Burns	Y	Y	N	Y	N
NEBRASKA					
Nelson	Y	Y	Y	Y	N
Hagel	Y	Y	N	Y	N
NEVADA					
Reid	Y	Y	Y	N	Y
Ensign	Y	Y	N	Y	Y

	11	12	13	14	15
NEW HAMPSHIRE					
Smith	Y	Y	N	Y	Y
Gregg	Y	Y	N	Y	Y
NEW JERSEY					
Corzine	?	Y	Y	N	Y
Torricelli	?	Y	Y	N	Y
NEW MEXICO					
Domenici	Y	Y	?	?	?
Bingaman	Y	Y	Y	N	N
NEW YORK					
Clinton	Y	Y	Y	N	Y
Schumer	?	Y	Y	N	Y
NORTH CAROLINA					
Helms	Y	Y	?	?	N
Edwards	Y	Y	Y	N	N
NORTH DAKOTA					
Conrad	Y	Y	Y	N	Y
Dorgan	Y	Y	Y	N	Y
OHIO					
DeWine	Y	Y	N	Y	N
Voinovich	Y	Y	Y	N	N
OKLAHOMA					
Nickles	?	Y	N	Y	N
Inhofe	Y	Y	N	Y	N
OREGON					
Wyden	Y	Y	Y	N	N
Smith	Y	Y	Y	Y	N
PENNSYLVANIA					
Specter	+	?	Y	Y	Y
Santorum	?	Y	N	Y	Y
RHODE ISLAND					
Reed	Y	Y	Y	N	Y
Chafee	Y	Y	N	N	Y
SOUTH CAROLINA					
Thurmond	Y	Y	N	Y	N
Hollings	Y	Y	Y	N	Y
SOUTH DAKOTA					
Daschle	Y	Y	Y	N	Y
Johnson	Y	Y	Y	N	Y
TENNESSEE					
Thompson	?	?	?	?	?
Frist	?	Y	N	Y	N

ND Northern Democrats   SD Southern Democrats

Southern states - Ala., Ark., Fla., Ga., Ky., La., Miss., N.C., Okla., S.C., Tenn., Texas, Va.

Key

Y	Voted for (yea).
#	Paired for.
+	Announced for.
N	Voted against (nay).
X	Paired against.
−	Announced against.
P	Voted "present."
C	Voted "present" to avoid possible conflict of interest.
?	Did not vote or otherwise make a position known.

Democrats **Republicans** *Independents*

	11	12	13	14	15
TEXAS					
Gramm	?	Y	N	Y	N
Hutchison	?	Y	N	Y	N
UTAH					
Hatch	?	Y	N	Y	N
Bennett	Y	Y	N	Y	N
VERMONT					
Leahy	Y	Y	Y	N	Y
Jeffords	Y	Y	?	?	?
VIRGINIA					
Warner	?	Y	Y	N	Y
Allen	Y	Y	N	Y	N
WASHINGTON					
Cantwell	Y	Y	N	N	N
Murray	Y	Y	N	N	N
WEST VIRGINIA					
Byrd	Y	Y	N	N	Y
Rockefeller	Y	Y	Y	N	Y
WISCONSIN					
Kohl	Y	Y	Y	N	Y
Feingold	Y	Y	Y	N	Y
WYOMING					
Thomas	Y	Y	N	Y	N
Enzi	?	Y	N	Y	N

11. Granade Nomination/Confirmation. Confirmation of President Bush's nomination of Callie V. Granade of Alabama to be U.S. district judge for the Southern District of Alabama. Confirmed 75-0; R 32-0; D 42-0 (ND 34-0, SD 8-0); I 1-0. A "yea" was a vote in support of the president's position. Feb. 4, 2002.

12. Martinez Nomination/Confirmation. Confirmation of President Bush's nomination of Philip R. Martinez of Texas to be U.S. district judge for the Western District of Texas. Confirmed 93-0: R 44-0; D 48-0 (ND 40-0, SD 8-0); I 1-0. A "yea" was a vote in support of the president's position. Feb. 5, 2002.

13. HR 622. Adoption Tax Credit/Cloture. Motion to invoke cloture (thus limiting debate) on the Daschle, D-S.D., substitute amendment that would strike the text of the underlying bill and insert an economic stimulus measure that would extend unemployment benefits to displaced workers for 13 weeks, allow for a $300 payment to taxpayers who did not receive rebates last year, allow for a tax cut for businesses that buy equipment this year and provide $5 billion in Medicaid assistance to states. Motion rejected 56-39: R 7-38; D 49-1 (ND 40-1, SD 9-0); I 0-0. Three-fifths of the total Senate (60) is required to invoke cloture. Feb. 6, 2002.

14. HR 622. Adoption Tax Credit/Cloture. Motion to invoke cloture (thus limiting debate) on the Grassley, R-Iowa, substitute amendment that would add an economic stimulus measure that would reduce individual and business taxes, extend unemployment benefits to displaced workers for 13 weeks, allow for a $300 payment to taxpayers who did not receive rebates last year, and increase the amount of income exempt from the alternative minimum tax. Motion rejected 48-47: R 43-2; D 5-45 (ND 1-40, SD 4-5); I 0-0. Three-fifths of the total Senate (60) is required to invoke cloture. Feb. 6, 2002.

15. S 1731. Farm Bill/EQIP Funds. Wellstone, D-Minn., amendment to the Daschle, D-S.D., substitute amendment that would restrict certain new or expanding large animal feeding operations from receiving Environmental Quality Incentives Program funds for animal waste facilities. The substitute amendment would reauthorize federal agriculture programs for five years, including a dairy provision that would authorize $2 billion in direct federal subsidies to milk producers. It also would re-establish programs that supply payments to farmers when commodity prices fall below a specified level. Rejected 44-52: R 10-36; D 34-16 (ND 32-9, SD 2-7); I 0-0. Feb. 6, 2002.

	16	17	18	19	20
ALABAMA					
Shelby	Y	Y	Y	N	Y
Sessions	Y	N	Y	N	Y
ALASKA					
Stevens	N	Y	N	N	Y
Murkowski	Y	Y	N	N	Y
ARIZONA					
McCain	?	?	?	?	?
Kyl	N	Y	Y	Y	Y
ARKANSAS					
Hutchinson	Y	Y	Y	N	Y
Lincoln	Y	Y	Y	N	Y
CALIFORNIA					
Feinstein	Y	Y	N	N	Y
Boxer	Y	Y	N	N	Y
COLORADO					
Campbell	N	Y	N	N	Y
Allard	Y	Y	N	N	Y
CONNECTICUT					
Dodd	Y	Y	Y	N	Y
Lieberman	Y	Y	Y	N	Y
DELAWARE					
Carper	N	Y	N	N	Y
Biden	N	Y	N	N	Y
FLORIDA					
Graham	Y	Y	Y	N	Y
Nelson	Y	Y	Y	N	Y
GEORGIA					
Miller	Y	Y	Y	N	Y
Cleland	Y	Y	Y	N	Y
HAWAII					
Inouye	Y	Y	N	N	Y
Akaka	Y	Y	Y	N	Y
IDAHO					
Craig	N	Y	N	N	Y
Crapo	Y	Y	N	N	Y
ILLINOIS					
Durbin	Y	Y	N	N	Y
Fitzgerald	Y	Y	N	N	C
INDIANA					
Lugar	N	Y	N	Y	Y
Bayh	Y	Y	N	N	Y

	16	17	18	19	20
IOWA					
Grassley	Y	Y	N	N	Y
Harkin	Y	Y	N	N	Y
KANSAS					
Brownback	Y	Y	N	N	Y
Roberts	Y	Y	N	N	Y
KENTUCKY					
McConnell	Y	Y	N	N	Y
Bunning	Y	Y	N	N	+
LOUISIANA					
Breaux	Y	Y	Y	N	Y
Landrieu	Y	Y	Y	N	Y
MAINE					
Snowe	Y	Y	N	N	Y
Collins	Y	Y	N	N	Y
MARYLAND					
Sarbanes	Y	Y	N	N	Y
Mikulski	Y	Y	N	N	Y
MASSACHUSETTS					
Kennedy	Y	Y	N	N	Y
Kerry	Y	Y	N	N	Y
MICHIGAN					
Levin	Y	Y	N	N	Y
Stabenow	Y	Y	N	N	Y
MINNESOTA					
Wellstone	Y	Y	N	N	Y
Dayton	Y	Y	N	N	Y
MISSISSIPPI					
Cochran	N	Y	N	N	Y
Lott	Y	Y	Y	N	+
MISSOURI					
Bond	Y	Y	Y	N	Y
Carnahan	Y	Y	Y	N	Y
MONTANA					
Baucus	Y	Y	Y	N	Y
Burns	Y	Y	Y	N	Y
NEBRASKA					
Nelson	Y	Y	N	N	Y
Hagel	Y	Y	N	N	Y
NEVADA					
Reid	Y	Y	N	N	Y
Ensign	Y	Y	N	Y	Y

	16	17	18	19	20
NEW HAMPSHIRE					
Smith	N	Y	N	Y	Y
Gregg	Y	Y	N	Y	Y
NEW JERSEY					
Corzine	Y	Y	N	Y	Y
Torricelli	Y	Y	N	N	Y
NEW MEXICO					
Domenici	?	?	?	?	?
Bingaman	Y	Y	Y	N	Y
NEW YORK					
Clinton	Y	Y	N	N	Y
Schumer	Y	Y	N	N	Y
NORTH CAROLINA					
Helms	N	Y	Y	N	Y
Edwards	Y	Y	Y	N	Y
NORTH DAKOTA					
Conrad	Y	Y	N	N	Y
Dorgan	Y	Y	N	N	Y
OHIO					
DeWine	Y	Y	N	N	Y
Voinovich	Y	Y	N	Y	Y
OKLAHOMA					
Nickles	Y	Y	N	N	Y
Inhofe	Y	Y	Y	N	Y
OREGON					
Wyden	Y	Y	N	N	Y
Smith	N	Y	N	N	Y
PENNSYLVANIA					
Specter	Y	Y	N	N	Y
Santorum	Y	Y	N	Y	Y
RHODE ISLAND					
Reed	Y	Y	N	N	Y
Chafee	Y	Y	N	Y	Y
SOUTH CAROLINA					
Thurmond	N	Y	Y	N	Y
Hollings	Y	Y	Y	N	Y
SOUTH DAKOTA					
Daschle	Y	Y	N	N	Y
Johnson	Y	Y	N	N	Y
TENNESSEE					
Thompson	?	?	?	?	?
Frist	Y	Y	Y	N	Y

Key

Y	Voted for (yea).
#	Paired for.
+	Announced for.
N	Voted against (nay).
X	Paired against.
−	Announced against.
P	Voted "present."
C	Voted "present" to avoid possible conflict of interest.
?	Did not vote or otherwise make a position known.

Democrats **Republicans**
Independents

	16	17	18	19	20
TEXAS					
Gramm	Y	Y	N	?	?
Hutchison	N	Y	Y	N	Y
UTAH					
Hatch	Y	Y	N	N	Y
Bennett	Y	Y	N	N	Y
VERMONT					
Leahy	Y	Y	Y	N	Y
Jeffords	?	Y	Y	N	?
VIRGINIA					
Warner	Y	Y	N	N	Y
Allen	N	Y	Y	N	Y
WASHINGTON					
Cantwell	Y	Y	N	N	Y
Murray	Y	Y	N	N	Y
WEST VIRGINIA					
Byrd	Y	Y	N	N	Y
Rockefeller	Y	Y	N	N	Y
WISCONSIN					
Kohl	Y	Y	N	N	Y
Feingold	Y	Y	N	N	Y
WYOMING					
Thomas	Y	Y	N	N	Y
Enzi	Y	Y	N	N	Y

ND Northern Democrats   SD Southern Democrats

Southern states - Ala., Ark., Fla., Ga., Ky., La., Miss., N.C., Okla., S.C., Tenn., Texas, Va.

16. S 1731. Farm Bill/Livestock Producers. Harkin, D-Iowa, amendment to the Daschle, D-S.D., substitute amendment that would give livestock producers the right to discuss their contracts with certain people, including their attorney, banker, accountant and landlord. Adopted 82-14: R 34-12; D 48-2 (ND 39-2, SD 9-0); I 0-0. Feb. 6, 2002.

17. S 1731. Farm Bill/Food Stamp Eligibility. Durbin, D-Ill., amendment to the Daschle, D-S.D., substitute amendment. The Durbin amendment would restore food stamp eligibility to legal immigrants who have lived in the United States for at least five years. The cost would be offset by prohibiting support payments for crops grown on land that has not been used in one of the past five years or three of the past 10 years. The amendment also would prohibit illegal aliens in the United States from participating in the program, regardless of their current status. Adopted 96-1: R 45-1; D 50-0 (ND 41-0, SD 9-0); I 1-0. Feb. 7, 2002.

18. S 1731. Farm Bill/Commodity Payments. Lincoln, D-Ark., motion to table (kill) the Dorgan, D-N.D., amendment to the Daschle, D-S.D., substitute amendment. The Dorgan amendment would limit direct and counter-cyclical payments to individual farmers to $75,000, and marketing loan gains and loan deficiency payments to $150,000. Motion rejected 31-66: R 14-32; D 16-34 (ND 7-34, SD 9-0); I 1-0. (Subsequently the Dorgan amendment was adopted by voice vote.) Feb. 7, 2002.

19. S 1731. Farm Bill/Commodity Payments. Lugar, R-Ind., amendment to the Daschle, D-S.D., substitute amendment. The Lugar amendment would strike the commodity section of the bill and insert language to provide $7,000 in equity payments to producers of all agricultural commodities for each of the 2003 through 2006 crop years. Rejected 11-85: R 10-35; D 1-49 (ND 1-40, SD 0-9); I 0-1. Feb. 7, 2002.

20. S 1731. Farm Bill/Bankruptcy. Carnahan, D-Mo., amendment to the Daschle, D-S.D., substitute amendment. The Carnahan amendment would make permanent Chapter 12 of the bankruptcy code, which provides expedited procedures that enable individuals to reorganize their family farms without having to liquidate their assets. Adopted 93-0: R 43-0; D 50-0 (ND 41-0, SD 9-0); I 0-0. Feb. 7, 2002.

	21	22	23	24	25	26	27
ALABAMA							
Shelby	Y	Y	N	N	N	N	Y
Sessions	Y	Y	N	N	N	?	Y
ALASKA							
Stevens	Y	Y	Y	N	N	N	Y
Murkowski	Y	Y	Y	N	N	N	Y
ARIZONA							
McCain	Y	Y	Y	N	N	N	Y
Kyl	Y	Y	Y	N	N	N	Y
ARKANSAS							
Hutchinson	?	?	Y	N	Y	N	Y
Lincoln	Y	Y	Y	Y	Y	N	Y
CALIFORNIA							
Feinstein	Y	Y	Y	Y	Y	N	Y
Boxer	Y	Y	Y	Y	Y	N	Y
COLORADO							
Campbell	Y	Y	N	N	N	N	Y
Allard	Y	Y	Y	N	Y	N	Y
CONNECTICUT							
Dodd	Y	Y	N	Y	Y	N	Y
Lieberman	Y	Y	N	Y	Y	N	Y
DELAWARE							
Carper	Y	Y	N	Y	N	N	Y
Biden	Y	Y	N	Y	Y	N	Y
FLORIDA							
Graham	Y	Y	N	Y	Y	Y	Y
Nelson	Y	Y	N	Y	Y	Y	Y
GEORGIA							
Miller	?	?	Y	Y	Y	N	Y
Cleland	Y	Y	Y	Y	Y	N	Y
HAWAII							
Inouye	Y	Y	Y	Y	Y	N	Y
Akaka	Y	Y	Y	Y	Y	Y	Y
IDAHO							
Craig	?	?	Y	N	Y	N	Y
Crapo	Y	Y	Y	N	Y	N	Y
ILLINOIS							
Durbin	Y	Y	N	Y	Y	N	Y
Fitzgerald	Y	Y	Y	Y	N	N	Y
INDIANA							
Lugar	Y	Y	Y	N	N	N	Y
Bayh	Y	Y	Y	Y	Y	N	Y

	21	22	23	24	25	26	27
IOWA							
Grassley	Y	Y	N	N	Y	Y	Y
Harkin	Y	Y	N	Y	Y	Y	Y
KANSAS							
Brownback	Y	Y	Y	N	N	Y	Y
Roberts	Y	Y	Y	N	N	Y	Y
KENTUCKY							
McConnell	Y	Y	Y	N	N	N	Y
Bunning	Y	Y	Y	N	N	N	Y
LOUISIANA							
Breaux	Y	Y	N	Y	N	Y	Y
Landrieu	Y	Y	N	Y	Y	N	Y
MAINE							
Snowe	Y	Y	N	Y	Y	N	Y
Collins	Y	Y	N	Y	Y	N	Y
MARYLAND							
Sarbanes	Y	Y	N	Y	Y	Y	Y
Mikulski	Y	Y	N	Y	Y	Y	Y
MASSACHUSETTS							
Kennedy	Y	Y	N	Y	Y	N	Y
Kerry	Y	Y	N	Y	Y	N	Y
MICHIGAN							
Levin	Y	Y	N	Y	Y	N	Y
Stabenow	Y	Y	N	Y	Y	N	Y
MINNESOTA							
Wellstone	Y	Y	N	Y	Y	N	Y
Dayton	Y	Y	N	Y	Y	N	Y
MISSISSIPPI							
Cochran	Y	Y	N	N	N	N	Y
Lott	Y	Y	Y	N	N	N	Y
MISSOURI							
Bond	Y	Y	Y	N	N	N	Y
Carnahan	Y	Y	N	Y	Y	Y	Y
MONTANA							
Baucus	Y	Y	N	N	N	N	Y
Burns	+	Y	N	N	Y	N	Y
NEBRASKA							
Nelson	Y	Y	N	N	N	N	Y
Hagel	Y	Y	N	N	Y	Y	Y
NEVADA							
Reid	Y	Y	N	Y	Y	Y	Y
Ensign	Y	Y	Y	N	N	N	Y

	21	22	23	24	25	26	27
NEW HAMPSHIRE							
Smith	Y	Y	N	Y	N	N	Y
Gregg	Y	Y	Y	N	N	N	Y
NEW JERSEY							
Corzine	Y	Y	N	Y	Y	N	Y
Torricelli	Y	Y	N	Y	Y	N	Y
NEW MEXICO							
Domenici	Y	Y	N	N	?	?	?
Bingaman	Y	Y	N	Y	N	N	Y
NEW YORK							
Clinton	Y	Y	N	Y	Y	N	Y
Schumer	Y	Y	Y	Y	Y	N	Y
NORTH CAROLINA							
Helms	Y	Y	N	N	N	N	Y
Edwards	Y	Y	Y	Y	Y	N	Y
NORTH DAKOTA							
Conrad	Y	Y	N	N	N	N	Y
Dorgan	Y	Y	N	N	N	N	Y
OHIO							
DeWine	Y	Y	N	N	N	N	Y
Voinovich	?	?	Y	N	Y	Y	Y
OKLAHOMA							
Nickles	Y	Y	N	N	N	N	Y
Inhofe	Y	Y	Y	N	N	N	Y
OREGON							
Wyden	Y	Y	N	Y	Y	N	Y
Smith	?	?	Y	N	Y	N	Y
PENNSYLVANIA							
Specter	Y	Y	N	N	N	N	Y
Santorum	Y	Y	Y	N	N	N	Y
RHODE ISLAND							
Reed	+	+	N	Y	Y	N	Y
Chafee	Y	Y	N	N	N	N	Y
SOUTH CAROLINA							
Thurmond	Y	Y	N	N	N	N	Y
Hollings	Y	Y	N	Y	Y	Y	Y
SOUTH DAKOTA							
Daschle	Y	Y	N	Y	Y	N	Y
Johnson	Y	Y	N	Y	Y	N	Y
TENNESSEE							
Thompson	Y	Y	Y	N	N	N	Y
Frist	Y	Y	Y	N	N	N	Y

Key

Y	Voted for (yea).
#	Paired for.
+	Announced for.
N	Voted against (nay).
X	Paired against.
−	Announced against.
P	Voted "present."
C	Voted "present" to avoid possible conflict of interest.
?	Did not vote or otherwise make a position known.

Democrats   ***Republicans***

Independents

	21	22	23	24	25	26	27
TEXAS							
Gramm	Y	Y	Y	N	N	N	Y
Hutchison	Y	Y	Y	N	N	Y	Y
UTAH							
Hatch	Y	Y	Y	N	Y	N	Y
Bennett	?	?	Y	N	Y	?	?
VERMONT							
Leahy	Y	Y	N	Y	Y	N	Y
Jeffords	Y	Y	N	Y	Y	N	Y
VIRGINIA							
Warner	?	?	Y	Y	Y	Y	Y
Allen	Y	Y	Y	N	N	N	Y
WASHINGTON							
Cantwell	Y	Y	N	Y	Y	N	Y
Murray	Y	Y	N	Y	Y	N	Y
WEST VIRGINIA							
Byrd	Y	Y	?	Y	Y	N	Y
Rockefeller	Y	Y	N	Y	Y	N	Y
WISCONSIN							
Kohl	Y	Y	N	Y	Y	Y	Y
Feingold	Y	Y	N	Y	N	N	Y
WYOMING							
Thomas	Y	Y	N	N	Y	N	Y
Enzi	Y	Y	N	N	Y	N	Y

ND Northern Democrats   SD Southern Democrats

Southern states - Ala., Ark., Fla., Ga., Ky., La., Miss., N.C., Okla., S.C., Tenn., Texas, Va.

21. Melloy Nomination/Confirmation. Confirmation of President Bush's nomination of Michael J. Melloy of Iowa to be a judge for the 8th U.S. Circuit Court of Appeals. Confirmed 91-0: R 42-0; D 48-0 (ND 40-0, SD 8-0); I 1-0. A "yea" was a vote in support of the president's position. Feb. 11, 2002.

22. Zainey Nomination/Confirmation. Confirmation of President Bush's nomination of Jay C. Zainey of Louisiana to be a U.S. district judge for the Eastern District of Louisiana. Confirmed 92-0: R 43-0; D 48-0 (ND 40-0, SD 8-0); I 1-0. A "yea" was a vote in support of the president's position. Feb. 11, 2002.

23. S 1731. Farm Bill/Meat Packers. Craig, R-Idaho, motion to table (kill) the Grassley, R-Iowa, amendment to the Craig amendment to the Daschle, D-S.D., substitute amendment. The Grassley amendment would prohibit meatpackers from owning, feeding or controlling livestock for more than 14 days prior to slaughter. The Craig amendment would provide for a study of a proposal to prohibit certain packers from owning, feeding or controlling livestock. The Daschle substitute amendment would reauthorize federal agriculture programs for five years, including a dairy provision that would authorize $2 billion in direct federal subsidies to milk producers. It also would re-establish programs that supply payments to farmers when commodity prices fall below a specified level. Motion rejected 46-53: R 36-13; D 10-39 (ND 6-34, SD 4-5); I 0-1. (Subsequently the amendment was adopted by voice vote.) Feb. 12, 2002.

24. S 1731. Farm Bill/Water Conservation. Reid, D-Nev., motion to table (kill) the Crapo, R-Idaho, amendment to the Daschle, D-S.D., substitute amendment. The Crapo amendment would strike the water conservation program provision in the substitute amendment. Motion agreed to 55-45: R 8-41;

D 46-4 (ND 37-4, SD 9-0); I 1-0. Feb. 12, 2002.

25. S 1731. Farm Bill/Agriculture Emergency Assistance. Baucus, D-Mont., motion to waive the Budget Act with respect to the Lugar, R-Ind., point of order against the Baucus amendment to the Daschle, D-S.D., substitute amendment. The Baucus amendment would provide $2.4 billion for agriculture assistance. It also would provide $1.8 billion of the funds of the Commodity Credit Corporation to make emergency financial assistance available to producers on a farm that has qualified income losses in calendar year 2001. Motion agreed to 69-30: R 20-28; D 48-2 (ND 39-2, SD 9-0); I 1-0. A three-fifths majority vote (60) of the total Senate is required to waive the Budget Act. (Subsequently the amendment was adopted by voice vote.) Feb. 12, 2002.

26. S 1731. Farm Bill/Farm Savings Accounts. Harkin, D-Iowa, amendment to the McConnell, R-Ky., amendment to the Daschle, D-S.D., substitute amendment. The Harkin amendment would decrease the income protection prices and loan rate for marketing assistance for certain commodities. It also would establish a four-year pilot program for countercyclical farm savings accounts in 10 states. The McConnell amendment would decrease the income protection prices and loan rate for marketing assistance for certain commodities and shift the funding to nutrition programs. Rejected 17-80: R 6-40; D 11-39 (ND 8-33, SD 3-6); I 0-1. Feb. 12, 2002.

27. S 1731. Farm Bill/Social Security Surplus. Conrad, D-N.D., amendment to the Daschle, D-S.D., substitute amendment. The Conrad amendment would express the sense of the Senate that no Social Security surplus funds should be used to pay for making currently scheduled tax cuts permanent. Adopted 98-0: R 47-0; D 50-0 (ND 41-0, SD 9-0); I 1-0. Feb. 13, 2002.

	28	29	30	31	32	33	34
ALABAMA							
Shelby	Y	N	Y	N	N	N	Y
Sessions	Y	N	Y	N	N	N	Y
ALASKA							
Stevens	Y	N	N	?	N	N	Y
Murkowski	Y	N	N	N	N	N	Y
ARIZONA							
McCain	N	N	N	N	N	N	N
Kyl	Y	N	N	N	N	N	Y
ARKANSAS							
Hutchinson	Y	N	N	N	N	N	Y
Lincoln	Y	Y	N	Y	N	N	Y
CALIFORNIA							
Feinstein	Y	Y	Y	N	Y	Y	N
Boxer	N	Y	Y	Y	Y	Y	N
COLORADO							
Campbell	Y	N	N	?	?	?	?
Allard	Y	N	N	N	N	N	Y
CONNECTICUT							
Dodd	N	Y	Y	N	Y	N	Y
Lieberman	N	Y	Y	Y	Y	Y	N
DELAWARE							
Carper	N	Y	Y	N	Y	Y	N
Biden	N	Y	Y	N	Y	Y	N
FLORIDA							
Graham	N	N	N	Y	N	Y	N
Nelson	Y	N	N	Y	N	Y	N
GEORGIA							
Miller	Y	Y	Y	Y	Y	Y	N
Cleland	Y	Y	Y	Y	Y	Y	N
HAWAII							
Inouye	N	Y	Y	Y	N	Y	N
Akaka	N	Y	Y	Y	?	Y	N
IDAHO							
Craig	Y	N	N	N	N	N	Y
Crapo	Y	N	N	N	N	N	Y
ILLINOIS							
Durbin	N	Y	Y	Y	Y	Y	N
Fitzgerald	Y	N	Y	N	N	N	Y
INDIANA							
Lugar	Y	N	N	N	N	N	Y
Bayh	Y	N	Y	N	Y	Y	N

	28	29	30	31	32	33	34
IOWA							
Grassley	Y	Y	Y	N	N	N	Y
Harkin	N	Y	Y	N	Y	Y	N
KANSAS							
Brownback	Y	N	N	N	N	N	Y
Roberts	Y	N	N	N	N	N	Y
KENTUCKY							
McConnell	Y	N	N	N	N	N	Y
Bunning	Y	N	N	N	N	N	Y
LOUISIANA							
Breaux	N	Y	Y	N	Y	Y	N
Landrieu	Y	Y	Y	N	Y	Y	N
MAINE							
Snowe	Y	Y	Y	N	N	N	Y
Collins	Y	Y	Y	N	N	N	N
MARYLAND							
Sarbanes	N	Y	Y	Y	Y	Y	N
Mikulski	N	Y	Y	Y	Y	Y	N
MASSACHUSETTS							
Kennedy	N	Y	Y	Y	Y	Y	N
Kerry	N	Y	Y	Y	Y	Y	N
MICHIGAN							
Levin	N	Y	Y	Y	Y	Y	N
Stabenow	N	Y	Y	N	Y	Y	N
MINNESOTA							
Wellstone	N	Y	Y	Y	Y	Y	N
Dayton	N	Y	Y	Y	Y	Y	N
MISSISSIPPI							
Cochran	Y	N	N	N	N	N	Y
Lott	Y	N	N	N	N	N	Y
MISSOURI							
Bond	Y	N	N	N	N	N	N
Carnahan	N	Y	Y	N	Y	N	N
MONTANA							
Baucus	Y	Y	Y	N	?	?	?
Burns	Y	N	N	N	N	N	Y
NEBRASKA							
Nelson	Y	Y	Y	N	N	N	N
Hagel	Y	N	N	N	N	N	Y
NEVADA							
Reid	N	Y	Y	Y	Y	Y	N
Ensign	Y	N	N	N	N	N	Y

	28	29	30	31	32	33	34
NEW HAMPSHIRE							
Smith	Y	Y	N	N	N	N	Y
Gregg	Y	Y	N	N	N	N	Y
NEW JERSEY							
Corzine	N	Y	N	Y	Y	Y	N
Torricelli	N	Y	Y	N	Y	Y	N
NEW MEXICO							
Domenici	?	?	?	?	?	?	?
Bingaman	N	N	Y	Y	Y	Y	N
NEW YORK							
Clinton	N	Y	Y	Y	Y	Y	N
Schumer	N	Y	Y	N	Y	Y	N
NORTH CAROLINA							
Helms	Y	N	N	N	N	N	Y
Edwards	N	Y	Y	N	Y	Y	N
NORTH DAKOTA							
Conrad	N	Y	Y	N	N	N	N
Dorgan	N	Y	Y	N	Y	N	N
OHIO							
DeWine	Y	N	N	Y	N	N	Y
Voinovich	Y	N	N	N	N	N	N
OKLAHOMA							
Nickles	Y	N	N	N	N	N	Y
Inhofe	Y	N	N	N	N	N	Y
OREGON							
Wyden	Y	Y	Y	N	Y	Y	N
Smith	Y	N	N	?	N	N	Y
PENNSYLVANIA							
Specter	Y	Y	N	Y	N	N	Y
Santorum	Y	Y	N	Y	N	N	Y
RHODE ISLAND							
Reed	N	Y	Y	Y	Y	Y	N
Chafee	N	Y	N	N	N	N	N
SOUTH CAROLINA							
Thurmond	Y	N	N	N	N	N	Y
Hollings	N	Y	Y	Y	Y	Y	N
SOUTH DAKOTA							
Daschle	N	Y	Y	Y	Y	Y	N
Johnson	Y	Y	Y	N	N	Y	N
TENNESSEE							
Thompson	Y	N	N	N	N	N	Y
Frist	Y	N	N	N	N	N	Y

Key

Y	Voted for (yea).
#	Paired for.
+	Announced for.
N	Voted against (nay).
X	Paired against.
−	Announced against.
P	Voted "present."
C	Voted "present" to avoid possible conflict of interest.
?	Did not vote or otherwise make a position known.

Democrats **Republicans**
Independents

	28	29	30	31	32	33	34
TEXAS							
Gramm	Y	N	N	N	N	N	Y
Hutchison	Y	N	N	N	N	N	Y
UTAH							
Hatch	Y	N	N	?	?	?	?
Bennett	?	?	?	?	?	?	?
VERMONT							
Leahy	N	Y	Y	Y	Y	Y	N
Jeffords	N	Y	Y	Y	Y	Y	N
VIRGINIA							
Warner	Y	N	N	Y	N	N	Y
Allen	Y	N	Y	N	N	N	Y
WASHINGTON							
Cantwell	N	Y	Y	Y	Y	Y	N
Murray	N	Y	Y	Y	Y	Y	N
WEST VIRGINIA							
Byrd	N	Y	N	Y	N	N	N
Rockefeller	N	Y	Y	N	N	N	N
WISCONSIN							
Kohl	N	Y	Y	Y	N	N	N
Feingold	N	Y	Y	Y	Y	N	N
WYOMING							
Thomas	Y	N	N	N	N	N	Y
Enzi	Y	N	N	N	N	N	Y

ND Northern Democrats SD Southern Democrats

Southern states - Ala., Ark., Fla., Ga., Ky., La., Miss., N.C., Okla., S.C., Tenn., Texas, Va.

28. S 1731. Farm Bill/Estate Tax. Kyl, R-Ariz., amendment to the Daschle, D-S.D., substitute amendment. The Kyl amendment would express the sense of the Senate that the repeal of the estate tax should be made permanent. Adopted 56-42: R 45-2; D 11-39 (ND 6-35, SD 5-4); I 0-1. Feb. 13, 2002.

29. S 1731. Farm Bill/Dairy Program. Daschle, D-S.D., motion to table (kill) the Domenici, R-N.M., amendment to the Daschle substitute amendment. The Domenici amendment would strike the dairy provision in the substitute and insert language that would provide for a new program that would make direct fixed payments to dairy producers equal to 31.5 cents per hundred pounds of milk produced annually. Motion agreed to 56-42: R 9-38; D 46-4 (ND 39-2, SD 7-2); I 1-0. Feb. 13, 2002.

30. HR 2646. Farm Bill/Passage. Passage of the bill that would reauthorize federal agriculture programs for five years, including a dairy provision that would authorize $2 billion in direct federal subsidies to milk producers. It also would re-establish programs that supply payments to farmers when commodity prices fall below a specified level. Passed 58-40: R 9-38; D 48-2 (ND 40-1, SD 8-1); I 1-0. (Before passage, the Senate struck all after the enacting clause, and inserted the text of S 1731, as amended, into the bill.) A "nay" was a vote in support of the president's position. Feb. 13, 2002.

31. S 565. Election Overhaul/Voting Rights. Reid, D-Nev., amendment that would authorize previously convicted felons who have fully served their prison sentences the right to vote in federal elections. Rejected 31-63: R 3-40; D 27-23 (ND 23-18, SD 4-5); I 1-0. Feb. 14, 2002.

32. S 565. Election Overhaul/Punch-Card Voting. Durbin, D-Ill., amendment that would require purchased voting systems to notify a voter of an over-vote, and permit all voters, including punch-card voters, to verify their votes and provide an opportunity to correct any errors before the ballot is cast and counted. Rejected 44-50: R 0-45; D 43-5 (ND 35-4, SD 8-1); I 1-0. Feb. 14, 2002.

33. S 565. Election Overhaul/Poll Workers. Lieberman, D-Conn., amendment that would allow federal employees to use administrative leave to work as non-partisan poll workers in federal elections. Rejected 46-49: R 0-45; D 45-4 (ND 36-4, SD 9-0); I 1-0. Feb. 14, 2002.

34. S 565. Election Overhaul/Voter List Removal. Burns, R-Mont., amendment that would allow election officials to purge official voter lists every four years. They would remove voters who have not voted in two or more consecutive federal elections, and have not notified the registrar or responded to a notice that they intend to remain registered in the jurisdiction. Rejected 40-55: R 40-5; D 0-49 (ND 0-40, SD 0-9); I 0-1. Feb. 14, 2002.

	35	36	37	38
ALABAMA				
Shelby	Y	Y	Y	Y
Sessions	Y	Y	Y	Y
ALASKA				
Stevens	Y	Y	Y	Y
Murkowski	Y	Y	Y	Y
ARIZONA				
McCain	Y	Y	Y	Y
Kyl	Y	Y	Y	Y
ARKANSAS				
Hutchinson	Y	Y	Y	Y
Lincoln	Y	Y	Y	N
CALIFORNIA				
Feinstein	Y	Y	Y	N
Boxer	Y	Y	Y	N
COLORADO				
Campbell	Y	Y	Y	N
Allard	Y	Y	Y	Y
CONNECTICUT				
Dodd	Y	Y	Y	N
Lieberman	Y	Y	Y	N
DELAWARE				
Carper	Y	Y	Y	N
Biden	Y	Y	Y	N
FLORIDA				
Graham	Y	Y	Y	N
Nelson	Y	Y	Y	N
GEORGIA				
Miller	Y	Y	Y	N
Cleland	Y	Y	Y	N
HAWAII				
Inouye	Y	Y	Y	N
Akaka	Y	Y	Y	N
IDAHO				
Craig	Y	Y	Y	Y
Crapo	Y	Y	Y	Y
ILLINOIS				
Durbin	Y	Y	Y	N
Fitzgerald	Y	Y	Y	Y
INDIANA				
Lugar	Y	Y	Y	Y
Bayh	Y	Y	Y	N

	35	36	37	38
IOWA				
Grassley	Y	Y	Y	Y
Harkin	Y	Y	Y	N
KANSAS				
Brownback	Y	Y	Y	Y
Roberts	Y	Y	Y	Y
KENTUCKY				
McConnell	Y	Y	Y	Y
Bunning	Y	Y	Y	Y
LOUISIANA				
Breaux	Y	Y	Y	N
Landrieu	Y	Y	Y	N
MAINE				
Snowe	Y	Y	Y	Y
Collins	Y	Y	Y	Y
MARYLAND				
Sarbanes	Y	Y	Y	N
Mikulski	Y	Y	Y	N
MASSACHUSETTS				
Kennedy	Y	Y	Y	N
Kerry	Y	Y	Y	N
MICHIGAN				
Levin	Y	Y	Y	N
Stabenow	Y	Y	Y	N
MINNESOTA				
Wellstone	Y	Y	Y	N
Dayton	Y	Y	Y	N
MISSISSIPPI				
Cochran	Y	Y	Y	Y
Lott	Y	Y	Y	Y
MISSOURI				
Bond	Y	Y	Y	Y
Carnahan	Y	Y	Y	N
MONTANA				
Baucus	Y	Y	Y	N
Burns	Y	Y	Y	Y
NEBRASKA				
Nelson	Y	Y	Y	N
Hagel	Y	Y	Y	Y
NEVADA				
Reid	Y	Y	Y	X
Ensign	?	?	?	#

	35	36	37	38
NEW HAMPSHIRE				
Smith	Y	Y	Y	Y
Gregg	Y	Y	Y	Y
NEW JERSEY				
Corzine	Y	Y	Y	N
Torricelli	Y	Y	Y	N
NEW MEXICO				
Domenici	Y	Y	Y	Y
Bingaman	Y	Y	Y	N
NEW YORK				
Clinton	Y	Y	Y	N
Schumer	Y	Y	Y	N
NORTH CAROLINA				
Helms	Y	Y	Y	N
Edwards	Y	Y	Y	N
NORTH DAKOTA				
Conrad	Y	Y	Y	N
Dorgan	Y	Y	Y	N
OHIO				
DeWine	Y	Y	Y	Y
Voinovich	Y	Y	Y	Y
OKLAHOMA				
Nickles	Y	Y	Y	Y
Inhofe	?	Y	Y	Y
OREGON				
Wyden	Y	Y	Y	N
Smith	Y	Y	Y	N
PENNSYLVANIA				
Specter	Y	Y	Y	Y
Santorum	Y	Y	Y	Y
RHODE ISLAND				
Reed	Y	Y	Y	N
Chafee	Y	Y	Y	N
SOUTH CAROLINA				
Thurmond	Y	?	?	Y
Hollings	Y	Y	Y	N
SOUTH DAKOTA				
Daschle	Y	Y	Y	N
Johnson	Y	Y	Y	N
TENNESSEE				
Thompson	Y	Y	Y	Y
Frist	Y	Y	Y	Y

	35	36	37	38
TEXAS				
Gramm	Y	Y	Y	Y
Hutchison	Y	Y	Y	Y
UTAH				
Hatch	Y	Y	Y	?
Bennett	Y	Y	Y	Y
VERMONT				
Leahy	Y	Y	Y	N
Jeffords	Y	?	Y	N
VIRGINIA				
Warner	Y	Y	Y	Y
Allen	Y	Y	Y	Y
WASHINGTON				
Cantwell	Y	Y	Y	N
Murray	Y	Y	Y	N
WEST VIRGINIA				
Byrd	Y	Y	Y	N
Rockefeller	Y	Y	Y	N
WISCONSIN				
Kohl	Y	Y	Y	N
Feingold	Y	Y	Y	N
WYOMING				
Thomas	Y	Y	Y	Y
Enzi	Y	Y	Y	Y

ND Northern Democrats SD Southern Democrats

Southern states - Ala., Ark., Fla., Ga., Ky., La., Miss., N.C., Okla., S.C., Tenn., Texas, Va.

35. Blackburn Nomination/Confirmation. Confirmation of President Bush's nomination of Robert E. Blackburn of Colorado to be U.S. district judge for the District of Colorado. Confirmed 98-0: R 47-0; D 50-0 (ND 41-0, SD 9-0); I 1-0. A "yea" was a vote in support of the president's position. Feb. 26, 2002.

36. S 565. Election Overhaul/Title Change. Cleland, D-Ga., amendment that would change the title of the bill to be the Martin Luther King Jr. Equal Protection of Voting Rights Act of 2001. Adopted 97-0: R 47-0; D 50-0 (ND 41-0, SD 9-0); I 0-0. Feb. 26, 2002.

37. Jorgenson Nomination/Confirmation. Confirmation of President Bush's nomination of Cindy K. Jorgenson of Arizona to be U.S. district judge for the District of Arizona. Confirmed 98-0: R 47-0; D 50-0 (ND 41-0, SD 9-0); I 1-0. A "yea" was a vote in support of the president's position. Feb. 26, 2002.

38. S 565. Election Overhaul/Voter Identification. Bond, R-Mo., motion to table (kill) the Schumer, D-N.Y., amendment that would strike the provision in the bill that would require first-time voters who register by mail to present photo identification or other proof of residence before being allowed to vote, and insert language that would permit the use of a signature or personal mark in identifying voters who register by mail. Motion rejected 46-51: R 46-1; D 0-49 (ND 0-40, SD 0-9); I 0-1. Feb. 27, 2002.

	39	40	41	42	43
ALABAMA					
Shelby	N	N	Y	Y	Y
Sessions	N	N	Y	Y	Y
ALASKA					
Stevens	N	?	Y	Y	Y
Murkowski	N	N	Y	Y	Y
ARIZONA					
McCain	N	N	N	Y	Y
Kyl	N	N	N	Y	Y
ARKANSAS					
Hutchinson	N	?	Y	Y	Y
Lincoln	Y	Y	Y	Y	Y
CALIFORNIA					
Feinstein	Y	Y	Y	N	N
Boxer	Y	Y	Y	N	N
COLORADO					
Campbell	N	N	Y	Y	Y
Allard	N	N	Y	Y	Y
CONNECTICUT					
Dodd	Y	Y	Y	Y	Y
Lieberman	Y	Y	Y	Y	N
DELAWARE					
Carper	Y	Y	Y	Y	Y
Biden	Y	Y	Y	N	N
FLORIDA					
Graham	Y	Y	Y	Y	Y
Nelson	Y	Y	Y	Y	Y
GEORGIA					
Miller	?	Y	Y	Y	Y
Cleland	Y	Y	Y	Y	Y
HAWAII					
Inouye	Y	Y	Y	N	Y
Akaka	Y	Y	Y	Y	Y
IDAHO					
Craig	?	N	Y	Y	Y
Crapo	N	N	Y	Y	Y
ILLINOIS					
Durbin	Y	Y	Y	Y	N
Fitzgerald	N	N	Y	Y	N
INDIANA					
Lugar	N	N	Y	Y	Y
Bayh	Y	Y	Y	Y	Y

	39	40	41	42	43
IOWA					
Grassley	N	N	Y	Y	Y
Harkin	Y	Y	Y	N	Y
KANSAS					
Brownback	?	N	Y	Y	Y
Roberts	N	N	?	Y	Y
KENTUCKY					
McConnell	N	N	Y	Y	Y
Bunning	N	N	Y	Y	Y
LOUISIANA					
Breaux	Y	Y	Y	Y	Y
Landrieu	Y	Y	Y	Y	Y
MAINE					
Snowe	N	N	Y	N	Y
Collins	N	N	Y	N	Y
MARYLAND					
Sarbanes	Y	Y	Y	Y	N
Mikulski	Y	Y	Y	Y	N
MASSACHUSETTS					
Kennedy	Y	Y	Y	?	?
Kerry	Y	Y	Y	N	N
MICHIGAN					
Levin	Y	Y	Y	Y	Y
Stabenow	Y	Y	Y	Y	N
MINNESOTA					
Wellstone	Y	Y	Y	N	Y
Dayton	Y	Y	Y	N	N
MISSISSIPPI					
Cochran	N	N	Y	Y	Y
Lott	N	N	Y	Y	Y
MISSOURI					
Bond	N	N	Y	Y	Y
Carnahan	Y	Y	Y	Y	Y
MONTANA					
Baucus	Y	Y	Y	N	Y
Burns	–	N	Y	Y	Y
NEBRASKA					
Nelson	Y	Y	Y	N	Y
Hagel	N	N	Y	Y	Y
NEVADA					
Reid	#	Y	Y	N	Y
Ensign	X	N	Y	N	Y

	39	40	41	42	43
NEW HAMPSHIRE					
Smith	N	N	Y	Y	Y
Gregg	N	N	Y	Y	Y
NEW JERSEY					
Corzine	Y	Y	Y	Y	N
Torricelli	Y	?	Y	Y	Y
NEW MEXICO					
Domenici	N	N	Y	Y	Y
Bingaman	Y	Y	Y	Y	Y
NEW YORK					
Clinton	Y	Y	Y	N	N
Schumer	Y	Y	Y	N	N
NORTH CAROLINA					
Helms	?	N	Y	Y	Y
Edwards	Y	Y	Y	Y	Y
NORTH DAKOTA					
Conrad	Y	Y	Y	Y	Y
Dorgan	Y	Y	Y	Y	Y
OHIO					
DeWine	N	N	Y	Y	Y
Voinovich	N	N	Y	Y	Y
OKLAHOMA					
Nickles	?	N	N	Y	Y
Inhofe	?	N	Y	Y	Y
OREGON					
Wyden	Y	Y	Y	N	Y
Smith	Y	Y	Y	Y	Y
PENNSYLVANIA					
Specter	N	N	Y	Y	Y
Santorum	N	N	Y	Y	Y
RHODE ISLAND					
Reed	Y	Y	Y	N	N
Chafee	N	N	Y	Y	Y
SOUTH CAROLINA					
Thurmond	N	N	Y	Y	Y
Hollings	Y	Y	Y	Y	Y
SOUTH DAKOTA					
Daschle	N	Y	Y	Y	Y
Johnson	Y	Y	Y	Y	Y
TENNESSEE					
Thompson	N	N	Y	Y	Y
Frist	N	N	Y	Y	Y

Key

Y	Voted for (yea).
#	Paired for.
+	Announced for.
N	Voted against (nay).
X	Paired against.
–	Announced against.
P	Voted "present."
C	Voted "present" to avoid possible conflict of interest.
?	Did not vote or otherwise make a position known.

Democrats **Republicans**
Independents

	39	40	41	42	43
TEXAS					
Gramm	?	N	N	Y	Y
Hutchison	?	N	N	Y	Y
UTAH					
Hatch	N	N	Y	Y	Y
Bennett	N	N	Y	Y	Y
VERMONT					
Leahy	Y	Y	Y	N	N
Jeffords	Y	Y	Y	N	N
VIRGINIA					
Warner	N	?	?	Y	Y
Allen	N	?	Y	Y	Y
WASHINGTON					
Cantwell	Y	Y	Y	Y	N
Murray	Y	Y	Y	Y	N
WEST VIRGINIA					
Byrd	Y	Y	Y	Y	Y
Rockefeller	Y	Y	Y	Y	N
WISCONSIN					
Kohl	Y	Y	Y	Y	N
Feingold	Y	Y	Y	N	N
WYOMING					
Thomas	N	N	Y	Y	Y
Enzi	?	N	Y	Y	Y

ND Northern Democrats   SD Southern Democrats

Southern states - Ala., Ark., Fla., Ga., Ky., La., Miss., N.C., Okla., S.C., Tenn., Texas, Va.

39. S 565. Election Overhaul/Cloture. Motion to invoke cloture (thus limiting debate) on the bill that would impose detailed voting-procedure requirements on states. Motion rejected 49-39: R 1-38; D 47-1 (ND 39-1, SD 8-0); I 1-0. Three-fifths of the total Senate (60) is required to invoke cloture. March 1, 2002.

40. S 565. Election Overhaul/Cloture. Motion to invoke cloture (thus limiting debate) on the bill that would impose detailed voting-procedure requirements on states. Motion rejected 51-44: R 1-44; D 49-0 (ND 40-0, SD 9-0); I 1-0. Three-fifths of the total Senate (60) is required to invoke cloture. March 4, 2002.

41. S 517. Energy Policy/Alaska Pipeline. Daschle, D-S.D., amendment to the Daschle substitute amendment. The amendment would prohibit the issuance of a permit for the development of a gas pipeline to transport Alaskan North Slope natural gas from running offshore in the Beaufort Sea between Alaska and Canada. The substitute amendment would overhaul the nation's energy policies, including a restructuring of the nation's electricity system, pro-viding $16.04 billion in energy-related tax incentives and increasing the corporate average fuel economy (CAFE) standards for passenger cars and light trucks to 35 miles per gallon by 2013. Adopted 93-5: R 42-5; D 50-0 (ND 41-0, SD 9-0); I 1-0. March 6, 2002.

42. S 517. Energy Policy/Nuclear Accident Liability. Voinovich, R-Ohio, amendment to the Daschle, D-S.D., substitute amendment. The Voinovich amendment would insert language that would provide a 10-year authorization for the Nuclear Regulatory Commission to indemnify its licensees against liability for a nuclear accident. Adopted 78-21: R 46-3; D 32-17 (ND 23-17, SD 9-0); I 0-1. March 7, 2002.

43. S 517. Energy Policy/Hydraulic Fracture Study. Bingaman, D-N.M., amendment to the Daschle, D-S.D., substitute amendment. The Bingaman amendment would require the EPA to study the effects of hydraulic fracturing on underground sources of drinking water within two years. Adopted 78-21: R 48-1; D 30-19 (ND 21-19, SD 9-0); I 0-1. March 7, 2002.

	44	45	46	47	48	49	50
ALABAMA							
Shelby	Y	Y	Y	Y	Y	Y	N
Sessions	Y	Y	Y	Y	Y	Y	N
ALASKA							
Stevens	Y	Y	Y	Y	Y	Y	N
Murkowski	Y	Y	Y	Y	Y	Y	N
ARIZONA							
McCain	Y	Y	Y	N	N	N	N
Kyl	Y	Y	Y	Y	Y	Y	N
ARKANSAS							
Hutchinson	Y	Y	Y	Y	Y	Y	N
Lincoln	Y	Y	Y	Y	Y	Y	N
CALIFORNIA							
Feinstein	Y	Y	Y	N	N	Y	Y
Boxer	Y	Y	Y	N	N	Y	Y
COLORADO							
Campbell	Y	Y	Y	N	Y	N	N
Allard	Y	Y	Y	Y	Y	Y	N
CONNECTICUT							
Dodd	N	Y	Y	N	N	N	Y
Lieberman	Y	Y	Y	N	N	N	Y
DELAWARE							
Carper	N	Y	Y	Y	N	N	N
Biden	Y	Y	Y	N	N	N	N
FLORIDA							
Graham	Y	Y	Y	N	N	N	N
Nelson	Y	Y	Y	N	N	N	N
GEORGIA							
Miller	?	?	Y	Y	Y	Y	N
Cleland	Y	Y	Y	Y	Y	N	N
HAWAII							
Inouye	?	?	Y	N	N	N	N
Akaka	Y	Y	Y	N	N	N	N
IDAHO							
Craig	Y	Y	Y	Y	Y	Y	N
Crapo	Y	Y	Y	Y	Y	Y	N
ILLINOIS							
Durbin	Y	Y	Y	N	N	N	Y
Fitzgerald	Y	Y	Y	Y	N	N	Y
INDIANA							
Lugar	Y	Y	Y	Y	Y	N	N
Bayh	Y	Y	Y	N	N	N	N
IOWA							
Grassley	Y	Y	Y	Y	Y	Y	N
Harkin	Y	Y	Y	N	Y	N	Y
KANSAS							
Brownback	Y	Y	Y	Y	Y	Y	N
Roberts	Y	Y	Y	Y	Y	Y	N
KENTUCKY							
McConnell	Y	Y	Y	Y	Y	Y	N
Bunning	Y	Y	Y	Y	Y	Y	N
LOUISIANA							
Breaux	?	?	Y	Y	Y	N	N
Landrieu	Y	Y	Y	Y	Y	N	N
MAINE							
Snowe	Y	Y	Y	N	N	Y	Y
Collins	Y	Y	Y	N	N	Y	Y
MARYLAND							
Sarbanes	Y	Y	Y	N	N	N	Y
Mikulski	?	?	Y	Y	N	N	Y
MASSACHUSETTS							
Kennedy	?	?	Y	N	N	N	Y
Kerry	Y	Y	Y	N	N	N	Y
MICHIGAN							
Levin	N	Y	Y	N	N	N	N
Stabenow	Y	Y	Y	N	N	N	N
MINNESOTA							
Wellstone	Y	Y	Y	N	N	N	N
Dayton	N	Y	Y	N	N	N	N
MISSISSIPPI							
Cochran	Y	Y	Y	Y	Y	Y	N
Lott	Y	Y	Y	Y	Y	Y	N
MISSOURI							
Bond	Y	Y	Y	Y	N	N	N
Carnahan	Y	Y	Y	Y	Y	N	N
MONTANA							
Baucus	Y	Y	Y	Y	Y	Y	Y
Burns	Y	Y	Y	Y	Y	Y	N
NEBRASKA							
Nelson	Y	Y	Y	Y	Y	Y	N
Hagel	Y	Y	Y	Y	Y	Y	N
NEVADA							
Reid	Y	Y	Y	N	N	N	Y
Ensign	Y	Y	Y	N	Y	N	Y
NEW HAMPSHIRE							
Smith	Y	Y	Y	Y	Y	Y	N
Gregg	Y	Y	Y	N	N	Y	N
NEW JERSEY							
Corzine	Y	Y	Y	N	N	N	Y
Torricelli	Y	Y	Y	N	N	N	?
NEW MEXICO							
Domenici	Y	Y	Y	Y	Y	Y	N
Bingaman	Y	Y	Y	N	N	N	N
NEW YORK							
Clinton	Y	Y	Y	N	N	N	Y
Schumer	Y	Y	Y	N	N	N	Y
NORTH CAROLINA							
Helms	Y	Y	Y	N	Y	N	N
Edwards	Y	Y	Y	N	N	N	N
NORTH DAKOTA							
Conrad	N	Y	Y	Y	Y	Y	N
Dorgan	Y	Y	Y	Y	Y	Y	N
OHIO							
DeWine	Y	Y	Y	Y	Y	Y	N
Voinovich	Y	Y	Y	Y	Y	Y	N
OKLAHOMA							
Nickles	Y	Y	Y	Y	Y	Y	N
Inhofe	Y	Y	Y	Y	Y	Y	N
OREGON							
Wyden	Y	Y	Y	N	N	Y	N
Smith	Y	Y	Y	N	N	Y	N
PENNSYLVANIA							
Specter	Y	Y	?	Y	N	N	Y
Santorum	Y	Y	?	Y	Y	N	N
RHODE ISLAND							
Reed	Y	Y	Y	N	N	N	Y
Chafee	N	Y	N	N	N	N	Y
SOUTH CAROLINA							
Thurmond	Y	Y	Y	Y	Y	Y	N
Hollings	Y	Y	Y	N	Y	N	N
SOUTH DAKOTA							
Daschle	Y	Y	Y	N	Y	N	N
Johnson	Y	Y	Y	Y	Y	Y	N
TENNESSEE							
Thompson	Y	Y	Y	Y	Y	Y	N
Frist	Y	Y	Y	Y	Y	Y	N
TEXAS							
Gramm	Y	Y	Y	Y	Y	Y	N
Hutchison	Y	Y	Y	Y	Y	Y	N
UTAH							
Hatch	Y	Y	Y	Y	Y	Y	N
Bennett	Y	Y	Y	Y	Y	Y	N
VERMONT							
Leahy	Y	Y	Y	N	N	N	Y
Jeffords	Y	Y	Y	N	N	Y	Y
VIRGINIA							
Warner	Y	Y	Y	Y	Y	Y	N
Allen	Y	Y	Y	Y	Y	Y	N
WASHINGTON							
Cantwell	Y	Y	Y	N	N	Y	Y
Murray	Y	Y	Y	N	N	Y	Y
WEST VIRGINIA							
Byrd	N	Y	Y	Y	Y	N	N
Rockefeller	N	Y	Y	Y	N	N	N
WISCONSIN							
Kohl	Y	Y	Y	N	N	Y	N
Feingold	N	Y	Y	N	N	N	Y
WYOMING							
Thomas	Y	Y	Y	Y	Y	Y	N
Enzi	?	?	Y	Y	Y	Y	N

Key

Y	Voted for (yea).
#	Paired for.
+	Announced for.
N	Voted against (nay).
X	Paired against.
–	Announced against.
P	Voted "present."
C	Voted "present" to avoid possible conflict of interest.
?	Did not vote or otherwise make a position known.

Democrats ***Republicans***
Independents

ND Northern Democrats   SD Southern Democrats

Southern states - Ala., Ark., Fla., Ga., Ky., La., Miss., N.C., Okla., S.C., Tenn., Texas, Va.

44. HR 3090. Economic Stimulus/Concur With House Amendment. Daschle, D-S.D., motion to concur with the House amendment to the Senate amendment to the bill that would extend unemployment benefits for up to 13 weeks and give temporary business tax breaks at a cost of $51.2 billion in fiscal 2002. It would provide incentives aimed at rebuilding the area around the World Trade Center in New York City, lengthen the net operating loss carry-back period by three years, extend a number of expiring tax provisions and reauthorize the Temporary Assistance for Needy Families grant program. Motion agreed to (thus cleared for the president) 85-9: R 47-1; D 37-8 (ND 30-8, SD 7-0); I 1-0. March 8, 2002.

45. S 517. Energy Plan/Pipeline Safety. McCain, R-Ariz., amendment to the Daschle, D-S.D., substitute amendment. The McCain amendment would reauthorize and strengthen pipeline safety programs for fiscal 2003 through 2005 at $64 million annually. The substitute amendment would overhaul the nation's energy policies, including a restructuring of the nation's electricity system, and provide $16.04 billion in energy-related tax incentives. It also would increase corporate average fuel economy (CAFE) standards for passenger cars and light trucks to 35 miles per gallon by 2013. Adopted 94-0: R 48-0; D 45-0 (ND 38-0, SD 7-0); I 1-0. March 8, 2002.

46. Beistline Nomination/Confirmation. Confirmation of President Bush's nomination of Ralph R. Beistline of Alaska to be U.S. district judge for the District of Alaska. Confirmed 98-0: R 47-0; D 50-0 (ND 41-0, SD 9-0); I 1-0. A "yea" was a vote in support of the president's position. March 12, 2002.

47. S 517. Energy Plan/CAFE Standards. Levin, D-Mich., amendment to the Daschle, D-S.D., substitute amendment. The Levin amendment would strike the CAFE standard in the substitute and replace it with language directing the National Highway Traffic Safety Administration (NHTSA) to set a new standard in 15 months. Congress would be permitted to raise the standard if NHTSA did not act within the 15-month time period. Adopted 62-38: R 43-6; D 19-31 (ND 14-27, SD 5-4); I 0-1. March 13, 2002.

48. S 517. Energy Plan/Pickup Trucks. Miller, D-Ga., amendment to the Daschle, D-S.D., substitute amendment. The Miller amendment would require any CAFE standard to be no higher than 20.7 miles per gallon for pickup trucks manufactured after model year 2004. Adopted 56-44: R 40-9; D 16-34 (ND 10-31, SD 6-3); I 0-1. March 13, 2002.

49. S 517. Energy Plan/Reliability Standards. Thomas, R-Wyo., motion to waive the Budget Act with respect to the Bingaman, D-N.M., point of order against the Thomas amendment to the Daschle substitute amendment. The Thomas amendment would strike the provision in the substitute that directs the Federal Energy Regulatory Commission (FERC) to establish and enforce national or regional reliability standards for interstate electric transmission systems and replace it with language that would require the FERC to certify non-governmental electric reliability organizations with authority to establish and enforce electric reliability standards. Motion agreed to 60-40: R 45-4; D 14-36 (ND 11-30, SD 3-6); I 1-0. A three-fifths majority vote (60) of the total Senate is required to waive the Budget Act. (Subsequently, the Bingaman point of order failed and the amendment was adopted by voice vote.) March 14, 2002.

50. S 517. Energy Plan/Renewable Resources. Jeffords, I-Vt., amendment to the Bingaman, D-N.M., amendment to the Daschle, D-S.D., substitute amendment. The Jeffords amendment would require utilities to generate 20 percent of their electricity from renewable energy facilities by 2020. The Bingaman amendment would replace the renewable energy provision in the underlying amendment with language that would require utilities to generate 10 percent of electricity from renewable energy facilities by 2020. Rejected 29-70: R 5-44; D 23-26 (ND 23-17, SD 0-9); I 1-0. March 14, 2002.

	51	52	53	54	55
ALABAMA					
Shelby	Y	Y	N	N	?
Sessions	Y	Y	N	N	Y
ALASKA					
Stevens	Y	Y	Y	N	Y
Murkowski	Y	Y	N	N	Y
ARIZONA					
McCain	+	?	Y	Y	Y
Kyl	Y	?	Y	N	Y
ARKANSAS					
Hutchinson	Y	Y	N	N	Y
Lincoln	?	Y	Y	Y	N
CALIFORNIA					
Feinstein	Y	Y	Y	Y	N
Boxer	Y	Y	Y	Y	N
COLORADO					
Campbell	Y	Y	N	N	Y
Allard	Y	Y	N	N	Y
CONNECTICUT					
Dodd	Y	Y	Y	Y	N
Lieberman	Y	Y	Y	Y	N
DELAWARE					
Carper	Y	Y	Y	Y	N
Biden	Y	Y	Y	Y	N
FLORIDA					
Graham	Y	Y	Y	Y	N
Nelson	Y	Y	Y	Y	N
GEORGIA					
Miller	?	Y	Y	Y	Y
Cleland	Y	Y	Y	Y	Y
HAWAII					
Inouye	Y	Y	Y	Y	N
Akaka	Y	Y	Y	Y	N
IDAHO					
Craig	?	Y	N	N	Y
Crapo	Y	Y	N	N	Y
ILLINOIS					
Durbin	Y	Y	Y	Y	N
Fitzgerald	Y	Y	Y	Y	N
INDIANA					
Lugar	Y	Y	Y	Y	Y
Bayh	Y	Y	Y	Y	N

	51	52	53	54	55
IOWA					
Grassley	Y	Y	Y	N	N
Harkin	Y	?	Y	Y	N
KANSAS					
Brownback	?	Y	N	N	N
Roberts	Y	Y	N	N	Y
KENTUCKY					
McConnell	?	Y	N	N	N
Bunning	Y	Y	N	N	Y
LOUISIANA					
Breaux	Y	Y	Y	Y	N
Landrieu	Y	?	Y	Y	N
MAINE					
Snowe	Y	Y	Y	Y	N
Collins	Y	Y	Y	Y	N
MARYLAND					
Sarbanes	Y	Y	Y	Y	N
Mikulski	Y	Y	Y	Y	N
MASSACHUSETTS					
Kennedy	Y	Y	Y	Y	N
Kerry	Y	Y	Y	Y	N
MICHIGAN					
Levin	Y	Y	Y	Y	N
Stabenow	Y	Y	Y	Y	N
MINNESOTA					
Wellstone	Y	Y	Y	Y	N
Dayton	Y	Y	Y	Y	N
MISSISSIPPI					
Cochran	Y	Y	Y	Y	Y
Lott	Y	Y	N	N	Y
MISSOURI					
Bond	Y	?	N	N	Y
Carnahan	Y	Y	Y	Y	N
MONTANA					
Baucus	Y	Y	Y	Y	N
Burns	+	Y	N	N	Y
NEBRASKA					
Nelson	Y	Y	Y	N	N
Hagel	Y	Y	Y	N	Y
NEVADA					
Reid	Y	Y	Y	Y	N
Ensign	Y	Y	N	N	N

	51	52	53	54	55
NEW HAMPSHIRE					
Smith	Y	Y	N	N	Y
Gregg	Y	Y	N	N	N
NEW JERSEY					
Corzine	Y	Y	Y	Y	N
Torricelli	Y	?	Y	Y	N
NEW MEXICO					
Domenici	Y	Y	Y	Y	Y
Bingaman	Y	Y	Y	Y	N
NEW YORK					
Clinton	Y	Y	Y	Y	N
Schumer	Y	?	Y	Y	N
NORTH CAROLINA					
Helms	?	+	N	N	Y
Edwards	Y	Y	Y	Y	N
NORTH DAKOTA					
Conrad	Y	Y	Y	Y	N
Dorgan	Y	Y	Y	Y	N
OHIO					
DeWine	Y	Y	N	N	Y
Voinovich	Y	Y	N	N	Y
OKLAHOMA					
Nickles	Y	Y	N	N	Y
Inhofe	Y	Y	N	N	Y
OREGON					
Wyden	Y	Y	Y	Y	N
Smith	Y	Y	Y	N	N
PENNSYLVANIA					
Specter	Y	Y	Y	Y	N
Santorum	Y	Y	N	N	Y
RHODE ISLAND					
Reed	Y	Y	Y	Y	N
Chafee	Y	Y	Y	Y	N
SOUTH CAROLINA					
Thurmond	Y	Y	N	N	Y
Hollings	Y	Y	Y	Y	N
SOUTH DAKOTA					
Daschle	Y	Y	Y	Y	N
Johnson	Y	?	Y	Y	N
TENNESSEE					
Thompson	Y	Y	Y	Y	Y
Frist	?	Y	Y	N	Y

Key

Y	Voted for (yea).	
#	Paired for.	
+	Announced for.	
N	Voted against (nay).	
X	Paired against.	
–	Announced against.	
P	Voted "present."	
C	Voted "present" to avoid possible conflict of interest.	
?	Did not vote or otherwise make a position known.	

Democrats   **Republicans**
Independents

	51	52	53	54	55
TEXAS					
Gramm	Y	Y	N	N	Y
Hutchison	?	Y	N	N	Y
UTAH					
Hatch	Y	Y	N	N	Y
Bennett	Y	Y	N	N	Y
VERMONT					
Leahy	Y	Y	Y	Y	N
Jeffords	Y	Y	Y	Y	N
VIRGINIA					
Warner	Y	Y	Y	Y	+
Allen	Y	Y	N	N	Y
WASHINGTON					
Cantwell	Y	Y	Y	Y	N
Murray	Y	Y	Y	Y	N
WEST VIRGINIA					
Byrd	Y	Y	Y	Y	Y
Rockefeller	Y	Y	Y	Y	N
WISCONSIN					
Kohl	Y	Y	Y	Y	N
Feingold	Y	Y	Y	Y	N
WYOMING					
Thomas	Y	Y	N	N	Y
Enzi	Y	Y	N	N	Y

ND Northern Democrats   SD Southern Democrats

Southern states - Ala., Ark., Fla., Ga., Ky., La., Miss., N.C., Okla., S.C., Tenn., Texas, Va.

51. Bury Nomination/Confirmation. Confirmation of President Bush's nomination of David C. Bury of Arizona to be U.S. district judge for the District of Arizona. Confirmed 90-0: R 41-0; D 48-0 (ND 41-0, SD 7-0); I 1-0. A "yea" was a vote in support of the president's position. March 15, 2002.

52. Crane Nomination/Confirmation. Confirmation of President Bush's nomination of Randy Crane of Texas to be U.S. district judge for the Southern District of Texas. Confirmed 91-0: R 45-0; D 45-0 (ND 37-0, SD 8-0); I 1-0. A "yea" was a vote in support of the president's position. March 18, 2002.

53. HR 2356. Campaign Finance Overhaul/Cloture. Motion to invoke cloture (thus limiting debate) on the bill that would ban "soft money" donations to national political parties but allow up to $10,000 in soft-money donations to state and local parties for voter registration and get-out-the-vote activity. The bill would prevent issue ads from targeting specific candidates within 60 days of a general election or 30 days of a primary. The bill also would increase the individual contribution limit from $1,000 to $2,000 per election for House and Senate candidates, both of which would be indexed for inflation. Motion agreed to 68-32: R 17-32; D 50-0 (ND 41-0, SD 9-0); I 1-0. Three-fifths of the total Senate (60) is required to invoke cloture. March 20, 2002.

54. HR 2356. Campaign Finance Overhaul/Passage. Passage of the bill that would ban "soft money" donations to national political parties but allow

up to $10,000 in soft-money donations to state and local parties for voter registration and get-out-the-vote activity. The bill would prevent issue ads from targeting specific candidates within 60 days of a general election or 30 days of a primary. The bill also would increase the individual contribution limit from $1,000 to $2,000 per election for House and Senate candidates, both of which would be indexed for inflation. Passed (thus cleared for the president) 60-40: R 11-38; D 48-2 (ND 40-1, SD 8-1); I 1-0. March 20, 2002.

55. S 517. Energy Plan/Renewable Resources. Kyl, R-Ariz., amendment to the Bingaman, D-N.M., amendment to the Daschle, D-S.D., substitute amendment. The Kyl amendment would strike the text of the Bingaman amendment and replace it with language that would require utilities to offer consumers electricity produced from renewable resources to the extent available. The Bingaman amendment would replace the renewable energy provision in the underlying amendment with language that would require utilities to generate 10 percent of electricity from renewable energy facilities by 2020. The substitute amendment would overhaul the nation's energy policies, restructure the electricity system and provide for $16.04 billion in energy-related tax incentives. It also would give the National Highway Traffic Safety Administration (NHTSA) 15 months to two years to set new CAFE standards. Rejected 40-58: R 37-10; D 3-47 (ND 1-40, SD 2-7); I 0-1. March 21, 2002.

	56	57	58	59
ALABAMA				
Shelby	Y	Y	Y	Y
Sessions	Y	Y	Y	Y
ALASKA				
Stevens	?	?	?	?
Murkowski	Y	Y	Y	Y
ARIZONA				
McCain	Y	Y	Y	Y
Kyl	Y	Y	Y	Y
ARKANSAS				
Hutchinson	Y	Y	Y	Y
Lincoln	Y	N	N	N
CALIFORNIA				
Feinstein	Y	N	N	N
Boxer	Y	N	N	N
COLORADO				
Campbell	Y	Y	Y	Y
Allard	Y	Y	Y	Y
CONNECTICUT				
Dodd	Y	N	N	N
Lieberman	Y	N	N	N
DELAWARE				
Carper	Y	N	N	N
Biden	Y	N	N	N
FLORIDA				
Graham	Y	N	N	N
Nelson	Y	N	N	N
GEORGIA				
Miller	Y	N	Y	Y
Cleland	Y	N	N	Y
HAWAII				
Inouye	Y	N	Y	N
Akaka	Y	N	Y	N
IDAHO				
Craig	Y	Y	Y	Y
Crapo	Y	Y	Y	Y
ILLINOIS				
Durbin	Y	N	N	N
Fitzgerald	Y	Y	N	N
INDIANA				
Lugar	Y	Y	Y	Y
Bayh	Y	N	N	N

	56	57	58	59
IOWA				
Grassley	Y	Y	N	N
Harkin	Y	N	N	N
KANSAS				
Brownback	Y	Y	N	N
Roberts	Y	Y	Y	Y
KENTUCKY				
McConnell	Y	Y	Y	Y
Bunning	Y	Y	Y	Y
LOUISIANA				
Breaux	Y	N	N	N
Landrieu	Y	N	N	N
MAINE				
Snowe	Y	Y	N	N
Collins	Y	Y	N	N
MARYLAND				
Sarbanes	Y	N	N	N
Mikulski	Y	N	N	N
MASSACHUSETTS				
Kennedy	Y	N	N	N
Kerry	Y	N	N	N
MICHIGAN				
Levin	Y	N	N	N
Stabenow	Y	N	N	N
MINNESOTA				
Wellstone	Y	N	N	N
Dayton	Y	N	N	N
MISSISSIPPI				
Cochran	Y	Y	Y	Y
Lott	Y	Y	Y	Y
MISSOURI				
Bond	Y	Y	Y	Y
Carnahan	Y	N	N	N
MONTANA				
Baucus	Y	N	N	N
Burns	Y	Y	Y	Y
NEBRASKA				
Nelson	N	N	N	N
Hagel	Y	Y	Y	Y
NEVADA				
Reid	Y	N	N	N
Ensign	Y	Y	N	N

	56	57	58	59
NEW HAMPSHIRE				
Smith	Y	Y	Y	Y
Gregg	Y	Y	N	N
NEW JERSEY				
Corzine	Y	N	N	N
Torricelli	Y	N	N	N
NEW MEXICO				
Domenici	Y	Y	Y	Y
Bingaman	Y	N	N	N
NEW YORK				
Clinton	Y	N	N	N
Schumer	Y	N	N	N
NORTH CAROLINA				
Helms	Y	Y	Y	Y
Edwards	Y	N	N	N
NORTH DAKOTA				
Conrad	Y	N	N	N
Dorgan	Y	N	N	N
OHIO				
DeWine	Y	Y	Y	Y
Voinovich	Y	Y	N	?
OKLAHOMA				
Nickles	Y	Y	Y	Y
Inhofe	Y	Y	Y	Y
OREGON				
Wyden	Y	N	N	N
Smith	Y	Y	N	N
PENNSYLVANIA				
Specter	Y	Y	?	N
Santorum	Y	Y	Y	Y
RHODE ISLAND				
Reed	Y	N	N	N
Chafee	Y	Y	N	N
SOUTH CAROLINA				
Thurmond	Y	Y	?	?
Hollings	Y	N	Y	Y
SOUTH DAKOTA				
Daschle	Y	N	N	N
Johnson	Y	N	N	N
TENNESSEE				
Thompson	Y	Y	Y	Y
Frist	Y	Y	Y	Y

Key

Y	Voted for (yea).
#	Paired for.
+	Announced for.
N	Voted against (nay).
X	Paired against.
–	Announced against.
P	Voted "present."
C	Voted "present" to avoid possible conflict of interest.
?	Did not vote or otherwise make a position known.

Democrats   **Republicans**
Independents

	56	57	58	59
TEXAS				
Gramm	Y	Y	Y	Y
Hutchison	Y	Y	Y	?
UTAH				
Hatch	Y	Y	Y	Y
Bennett	Y	Y	Y	Y
VERMONT				
Leahy	Y	N	N	N
Jeffords	Y	N	N	N
VIRGINIA				
Warner	Y	Y	Y	Y
Allen	Y	Y	Y	Y
WASHINGTON				
Cantwell	Y	N	N	N
Murray	Y	N	N	N
WEST VIRGINIA				
Byrd	Y	N	N	N
Rockefeller	Y	N	N	N
WISCONSIN				
Kohl	Y	N	N	N
Feingold	Y	N	N	N
WYOMING				
Thomas	Y	Y	Y	Y
Enzi	?	?	?	?

ND Northern Democrats   SD Southern Democrats

Southern states - Ala., Ark., Fla., Ga., Ky., La., Miss., N.C., Okla., S.C., Tenn., Texas, Va.

56. S 517. Energy Plan/Judicial Nominations. Reid, D-Nev., amendment to the Daschle, D-S.D., substitute amendment. The Reid amendment would express the sense of the Senate that the Senate Judiciary Committee should continue to hold regular hearings on judicial nominees. Adopted 97-1: R 47-0; D 49-1 (ND 40-1, SD 9-0); I 1-0. March 21, 2002.

57. S 517. Energy Plan/Judicial Nominations. Lott, R-Miss., amendment to the Daschle, D-S.D., substitute amendment. The Lott amendment would express the sense of the Senate that the Senate Judiciary Committee should hold hearings by May 9, 2002, on judicial nominees submitted by the president on May 9, 2001. Rejected 47-51: R 47-0; D 0-50 (ND 0-41, SD 0-9); I 0-1. March 21, 2002.

58. S 517. Energy Plan/Renewable Resources. Murkowski, R-Alaska, amendment to the Bingaman, D-N.M., amendment to the Daschle, D-S.D., substitute amendment. The Murkowski amendment would exempt retail electric suppliers in states that have state renewable energy standards from the federal renewable standard in the underlying amendment. Rejected 39-57: R 35-10; D 4-46 (ND 2-39, SD 2-7); I 0-1. March 21, 2002.

59. S 517. Energy Plan/Renewable Resources. Kyl, R-Ariz., amendment to the Bingaman, D-N.M., amendment to the Daschle, D-S.D., substitute amendment. The Kyl amendment would allow governors to opt out of the federal renewable standard if the standard would adversely affect consumers in the state. Rejected 37-58: R 34-10; D 3-47 (ND 0-41, SD 3-6); I 0-1. March 21, 2002.

	60	61	62	63
ALABAMA				
Shelby	N	N	Y	Y
Sessions	N	N	Y	Y
ALASKA				
Stevens	N	N	N	Y
Murkowski	N	N	N	Y
ARIZONA				
McCain	N	Y	Y	Y
Kyl	N	N	Y	Y
ARKANSAS				
Hutchinson	N	N	N	Y
Lincoln	N	N	N	Y
CALIFORNIA				
Feinstein	Y	Y	Y	Y
Boxer	Y	Y	Y	Y
COLORADO				
Campbell	N	N	Y	Y
Allard	N	N	Y	Y
CONNECTICUT				
Dodd	Y	Y	N	N
Lieberman	Y	Y	N	N
DELAWARE				
Carper	N	Y	N	N
Biden	Y	Y	N	N
FLORIDA				
Graham	Y	Y	N	N
Nelson	Y	Y	N	N
GEORGIA				
Miller	Y	N	Y	Y
Cleland	N	Y	Y	Y
HAWAII				
Inouye	Y	Y	N	N
Akaka	Y	Y	N	N
IDAHO				
Craig	N	N	Y	Y
Crapo	N	N	Y	Y
ILLINOIS				
Durbin	Y	Y	N	N
Fitzgerald	Y	Y	N	N
INDIANA				
Lugar	Y	N	N	Y
Bayh	N	Y	N	?

	60	61	62	63
IOWA				
Grassley	N	N	N	Y
Harkin	Y	Y	N	N
KANSAS				
Brownback	N	N	N	Y
Roberts	N	N	Y	Y
KENTUCKY				
McConnell	N	N	N	Y
Bunning	N	N	N	Y
LOUISIANA				
Breaux	Y	Y	Y	Y
Landrieu	N	N	N	N
MAINE				
Snowe	N	N	N	Y
Collins	N	N	N	Y
MARYLAND				
Sarbanes	Y	Y	N	N
Mikulski	N	Y	N	N
MASSACHUSETTS				
Kennedy	Y	Y	N	N
Kerry	Y	Y	N	N
MICHIGAN				
Levin	Y	Y	Y	Y
Stabenow	Y	Y	Y	Y
MINNESOTA				
Wellstone	Y	Y	N	N
Dayton	Y	Y	Y	N
MISSISSIPPI				
Cochran	N	N	N	Y
Lott	N	N	N	Y
MISSOURI				
Bond	N	N	Y	N
Carnahan	Y	Y	N	N
MONTANA				
Baucus	?	?	?	N
Burns	N	N	Y	Y
NEBRASKA				
Nelson	N	N	N	N
Hagel	N	N	N	Y
NEVADA				
Reid	N	Y	N	Y
Ensign	N	N	N	Y

	60	61	62	63
NEW HAMPSHIRE				
Smith	N	N	N	Y
Gregg	N	N	N	Y
NEW JERSEY				
Corzine	Y	Y	N	N
Torricelli	N	Y	N	N
NEW MEXICO				
Domenici	N	N	N	Y
Bingaman	N	Y	N	N
NEW YORK				
Clinton	Y	Y	N	N
Schumer	Y	Y	N	N
NORTH CAROLINA				
Helms	N	N	Y	Y
Edwards	Y	Y	N	N
NORTH DAKOTA				
Conrad	Y	Y	N	N
Dorgan	Y	Y	N	N
OHIO				
DeWine	N	N	Y	Y
Voinovich	N	N	Y	Y
OKLAHOMA				
Nickles	N	N	N	Y
Inhofe	N	N	N	Y
OREGON				
Wyden	Y	Y	N	N
Smith	N	N	N	Y
PENNSYLVANIA				
Specter	N	?	N	Y
Santorum	N	N	N	Y
RHODE ISLAND				
Reed	Y	Y	N	N
Chafee	Y	N	Y	N
SOUTH CAROLINA				
Thurmond	N	N	Y	Y
Hollings	Y	Y	Y	N
SOUTH DAKOTA				
Daschle	Y	Y	N	N
Johnson	N	Y	N	Y
TENNESSEE				
Thompson	N	N	N	Y
Frist	N	N	N	Y

	60	61	62	63
TEXAS				
Gramm	N	N	N	Y
Hutchison	N	N	N	Y
UTAH				
Hatch	N	N	Y	Y
Bennett	N	N	Y	Y
VERMONT				
Leahy	Y	Y	N	N
Jeffords	N	Y	N	N
VIRGINIA				
Warner	N	N	N	Y
Allen	N	N	N	Y
WASHINGTON				
Cantwell	Y	Y	Y	N
Murray	Y	Y	Y	N
WEST VIRGINIA				
Byrd	Y	Y	N	N
Rockefeller	N	Y	N	N
WISCONSIN				
Kohl	Y	Y	N	N
Feingold	Y	Y	Y	N
WYOMING				
Thomas	N	N	N	Y
Enzi	N	N	N	Y

Key

Y	Voted for (yea).
#	Paired for.
+	Announced for.
N	Voted against (nay).
X	Paired against.
−	Announced against.
P	Voted "present."
C	Voted "present" to avoid possible conflict of interest.
?	Did not vote or otherwise make a position known.

Democrats **Republicans**
Independents

ND Northern Democrats SD Southern Democrats

Southern states - Ala., Ark., Fla., Ga., Ky., La., Miss., N.C., Okla., S.C., Tenn., Texas, Va.

60. S 517. Energy Plan/Energy Derivatives. Feinstein, D-Calif., motion to table (kill) the Reid, D-Nev., amendment to the Feinstein, D-Calif., amendment to the Daschle, D-S.D., substitute amendment. The Reid amendment would exempt metals derivatives from the Feinstein amendment. The Feinstein amendment would provide the Commodity Futures Trading Commission with regulatory oversight of derivative transactions of energy commodities. It also would require entities running online trading forums to maintain capital commensurate with risk to carry out their operations. The substitute amendment would overhaul the nation's energy policies, restructure the electricity system and provide for $16.04 billion in energy-related tax incentives. It also would give the National Highway Traffic Safety Administration 15 months to two years to set new Corporate Average Fuel Economy standards. Motion rejected 40-59: R 3-46; D 37-12 (ND 31-9, SD 6-3); I 0-1. (Subsequently, the Feinstein amendment was withdrawn.) April 9, 2002.

61. S 517. Energy Plan/Cloture. Motion to invoke cloture (thus limiting debate) on the Feinstein, D-Calif., amendment to the Daschle, D-S.D., substi-

tute amendment. Motion rejected 48-50: R 2-46; D 45-4 (ND 39-1, SD 6-3); I 1-0. Three-fifths of the total Senate (60) is required to invoke cloture. April 10, 2002.

62. S 517. Energy Plan/Electric Deregulation. Craig, R-Idaho, amendment to the Daschle, D-S.D., substitute amendment. The Craig amendment would remove language in the bill that would deregulate the electric utility industry and replace it with original Title II provisions related to consumer protection and reliability. Rejected 32-67: R 20-29; D 12-37 (ND 8-32, SD 4-5); I 0-1. A "nay" was a vote in support of the president's position. April 10, 2002.

63. S 565. Election Overhaul/Notice Requirement. Roberts, R-Kan., amendment that would eliminate a provision that would require election officials to send a notice to all provisional ballot voters within 30 days to notify them whether their vote was counted. Adopted 56-43: R 46-3; D 10-39 (ND 6-34, SD 4-5); I 0-1. April 11, 2002.

	64	65	66	67
ALABAMA				
Shelby	N	Y	N	N
Sessions	N	Y	Y	N
ALASKA				
Stevens	N	Y	N	Y
Murkowski	N	Y	N	Y
ARIZONA				
McCain	N	Y	Y	N
Kyl	N	Y	N	N
ARKANSAS				
Hutchinson	N	Y	N	Y
Lincoln	Y	Y	Y	Y
CALIFORNIA				
Feinstein	Y	Y	Y	N
Boxer	Y	Y	Y	N
COLORADO				
Campbell	N	Y	N	N
Allard	N	Y	Y	N
CONNECTICUT				
Dodd	N	Y	N	Y
Lieberman	Y	Y	Y	Y
DELAWARE				
Carper	Y	Y	Y	Y
Biden	Y	Y	Y	N
FLORIDA				
Graham	Y	Y	Y	Y
Nelson	Y	Y	Y	Y
GEORGIA				
Miller	Y	Y	Y	?
Cleland	Y	Y	Y	Y
HAWAII				
Inouye	Y	Y	Y	N
Akaka	Y	Y	Y	Y
IDAHO				
Craig	N	Y	N	Y
Crapo	N	Y	N	Y
ILLINOIS				
Durbin	Y	Y	Y	Y
Fitzgerald	N	Y	N	Y
INDIANA				
Lugar	N	Y	N	Y
Bayh	Y	Y	Y	Y

	64	65	66	67
IOWA				
Grassley	N	Y	Y	Y
Harkin	Y	Y	Y	Y
KANSAS				
Brownback	N	Y	N	Y
Roberts	N	Y	N	Y
KENTUCKY				
McConnell	N	Y	N	Y
Bunning	N	Y	N	Y
LOUISIANA				
Breaux	Y	Y	Y	Y
Landrieu	Y	Y	Y	Y
MAINE				
Snowe	N	Y	Y	N
Collins	N	Y	Y	N
MARYLAND				
Sarbanes	Y	Y	Y	Y
Mikulski	Y	Y	Y	Y
MASSACHUSETTS				
Kennedy	Y	Y	Y	N
Kerry	Y	Y	Y	Y
MICHIGAN				
Levin	Y	Y	Y	Y
Stabenow	Y	Y	Y	Y
MINNESOTA				
Wellstone	Y	Y	Y	Y
Dayton	Y	Y	Y	Y
MISSISSIPPI				
Cochran	N	Y	N	Y
Lott	N	Y	N	Y
MISSOURI				
Bond	N	Y	N	Y
Carnahan	N	Y	Y	Y
MONTANA				
Baucus	N	Y	Y	Y
Burns	N	N	N	Y
NEBRASKA				
Nelson	Y	Y	Y	Y
Hagel	N	Y	N	Y
NEVADA				
Reid	Y	Y	Y	Y
Ensign	N	Y	N	Y

	64	65	66	67
NEW HAMPSHIRE				
Smith	N	Y	N	Y
Gregg	N	Y	Y	?
NEW JERSEY				
Corzine	Y	Y	Y	N
Torricelli	Y	Y	Y	N
NEW MEXICO				
Domenici	N	Y	Y	N
Bingaman	Y	Y	Y	Y
NEW YORK				
Clinton	Y	Y	Y	N
Schumer	Y	Y	Y	N
NORTH CAROLINA				
Helms	N	Y	N	Y
Edwards	Y	Y	Y	Y
NORTH DAKOTA				
Conrad	Y	Y	Y	Y
Dorgan	Y	Y	Y	Y
OHIO				
DeWine	N	Y	Y	N
Voinovich	N	Y	Y	N
OKLAHOMA				
Nickles	N	Y	N	N
Inhofe	N	Y	N	Y
OREGON				
Wyden	Y	Y	Y	N
Smith	N	Y	Y	N
PENNSYLVANIA				
Specter	N	Y	N	Y
Santorum	N	Y	N	N
RHODE ISLAND				
Reed	Y	Y	Y	N
Chafee	N	Y	Y	Y
SOUTH CAROLINA				
Thurmond	N	Y	N	Y
Hollings	Y	Y	Y	Y
SOUTH DAKOTA				
Daschle	Y	Y	Y	Y
Johnson	Y	Y	Y	Y
TENNESSEE				
Thompson	N	Y	N	Y
Frist	N	Y	N	Y

Key

Y	Voted for (yea).
#	Paired for.
+	Announced for.
N	Voted against (nay).
X	Paired against.
−	Announced against.
P	Voted "present."
C	Voted "present" to avoid possible conflict of interest.
?	Did not vote or otherwise make a position known.

Democrats **Republicans**
Independents

	64	65	66	67
TEXAS				
Gramm	N	Y	?	?
Hutchison	N	Y	Y	N
UTAH				
Hatch	N	Y	Y	Y
Bennett	N	Y	N	N
VERMONT				
Leahy	Y	Y	Y	N
Jeffords	Y	Y	Y	Y
VIRGINIA				
Warner	N	Y	N	Y
Allen	N	Y	Y	N
WASHINGTON				
Cantwell	Y	Y	Y	N
Murray	Y	Y	Y	N
WEST VIRGINIA				
Byrd	Y	Y	Y	Y
Rockefeller	Y	Y	Y	Y
WISCONSIN				
Kohl	Y	Y	Y	N
Feingold	Y	Y	Y	Y
WYOMING				
Thomas	N	Y	N	Y
Enzi	N	Y	N	N

ND Northern Democrats   SD Southern Democrats

Southern states - Ala., Ark., Fla., Ga., Ky., La., Miss., N.C., Okla., S.C., Tenn., Texas, Va.

64. S 565. Election Overhaul/Vote Error Rate. Clinton, D-N.Y., amendment that would establish a "residual vote error rate" by the director of the Office of Election Administration and give the office authority to waive the standards for areas with historically high rates of intentional undervoting. Rejected 48-52: R 0-49; D 47-3 (ND 38-3, SD 9-0); I 1-0. April 11, 2002.

65. S 565. Election Overhaul/Passage. Passage of the bill that would impose detailed voting-procedure requirements on states. It would require states to let voters verify their votes before casting a ballot, allow voters to change their ballots before submitting their vote and notify voters if they vote for more than one candidate for an office. A first-time voter who registers by mail would be required to include a copy of his driver's license, a utility bill, a government check or some other proof of residence, except in Oregon and Washington, where voters would be permitted to write their driver's license numbers or the last four digits of their Social Security numbers on their registration forms. Passed 99-1: R 48-1; D 50-0 (ND 41-0, SD 9-0); I 1-0. April 11, 2002.

66. S 517. Energy Plan/Energy Commission. Durbin, D-Ill., amendment to the Daschle, D-S.D., substitute amendment. The Durbin amendment would establish an 11-member Consumer Energy Commission that would be required to conduct a study on energy price spikes. Adopted 69-30: R 18-30; D 50-0 (ND 41-0, SD 9-0); I 1-0. April 11, 2002.

67. S 517. Energy Plan/Ethanol. Reid, D-Nev., motion to table (kill) the Feinstein, D-Calif., amendment to the Daschle, D-S.D., substitute amendment. The Feinstein amendment would reduce to 30 days the time the EPA may act on a state's request for a waiver regarding ethanol. Adopted 61-36: R 27-20; D 33-16 (ND 25-16, SD 8-0); I 1-0. April 11, 2002.

Member	68	69	70	71	72	73	74	75
ALABAMA								
Shelby	Y	Y	Y	Y	Y	Y	Y	Y
Sessions	?	Y	Y	Y	Y	Y	Y	Y
ALASKA								
Stevens	Y	Y	Y	Y	Y	Y	Y	Y
Murkowski	Y	Y	Y	Y	Y	Y	Y	Y
ARIZONA								
McCain	Y	Y	N	N	Y	Y	Y	Y
Kyl	Y	Y	N	Y	Y	Y	Y	Y
ARKANSAS								
Hutchinson	Y	Y	Y	Y	Y	Y	Y	Y
Lincoln	Y	Y	N	N	Y	Y	Y	Y
CALIFORNIA								
Feinstein	Y	Y	N	N	Y	Y	Y	Y
Boxer	Y	Y	N	N	Y	Y	Y	Y
COLORADO								
Campbell	Y	Y	Y	Y	Y	Y	Y	Y
Allard	Y	Y	Y	Y	Y	Y	Y	Y
CONNECTICUT								
Dodd	Y	Y	N	N	Y	Y	Y	Y
Lieberman	Y	Y	N	N	Y	Y	Y	Y
DELAWARE								
Carper	Y	Y	N	N	N	Y	Y	Y
Biden	Y	Y	N	N	N	Y	Y	Y
FLORIDA								
Graham	Y	Y	N	N	Y	Y	Y	Y
Nelson	Y	Y	N	N	Y	Y	Y	Y
GEORGIA								
Miller	Y	Y	Y	Y	Y	Y	Y	Y
Cleland	Y	Y	N	N	Y	Y	Y	Y
HAWAII								
Inouye	Y	Y	Y	Y	?	?	?	?
Akaka	Y	Y	Y	Y	Y	Y	Y	Y
IDAHO								
Craig	Y	Y	Y	Y	Y	Y	Y	Y
Crapo	Y	Y	Y	Y	Y	Y	Y	Y
ILLINOIS								
Durbin	Y	Y	N	N	Y	Y	Y	Y
Fitzgerald	Y	Y	N	N	N	Y	Y	Y
INDIANA								
Lugar	Y	Y	Y	Y	N	Y	Y	Y
Bayh	Y	Y	N	N	Y	Y	Y	Y
IOWA								
Grassley	Y	Y	Y	Y	Y	Y	Y	Y
Harkin	Y	Y	N	N	Y	Y	Y	Y
KANSAS								
Brownback	Y	Y	N	Y	Y	Y	Y	Y
Roberts	Y	Y	N	Y	Y	Y	Y	Y
KENTUCKY								
McConnell	Y	Y	Y	Y	Y	Y	Y	Y
Bunning	Y	Y	Y	Y	Y	Y	Y	Y
LOUISIANA								
Breaux	Y	Y	Y	Y	Y	Y	Y	Y
Landrieu	Y	Y	Y	Y	Y	Y	Y	Y
MAINE								
Snowe	Y	Y	N	N	Y	Y	Y	Y
Collins	Y	Y	N	N	Y	Y	Y	Y
MARYLAND								
Sarbanes	Y	Y	N	N	Y	Y	Y	Y
Mikulski	Y	Y	N	N	Y	Y	Y	Y
MASSACHUSETTS								
Kennedy	Y	Y	N	N	Y	Y	Y	Y
Kerry	Y	Y	N	N	Y	Y	Y	Y
MICHIGAN								
Levin	Y	Y	N	N	Y	Y	Y	Y
Stabenow	Y	Y	N	N	Y	Y	Y	Y
MINNESOTA								
Wellstone	Y	Y	N	N	Y	Y	Y	Y
Dayton	Y	+	N	N	Y	Y	Y	Y
MISSISSIPPI								
Cochran	Y	Y	Y	Y	Y	Y	Y	Y
Lott	Y	Y	Y	Y	Y	Y	Y	Y
MISSOURI								
Bond	Y	Y	Y	Y	Y	Y	Y	Y
Carnahan	Y	Y	N	N	Y	Y	Y	Y
MONTANA								
Baucus	Y	Y	N	N	Y	Y	Y	Y
Burns	Y	Y	Y	Y	Y	Y	Y	Y
NEBRASKA								
Nelson	Y	Y	N	N	N	?	?	?
Hagel	Y	Y	Y	N	Y	Y	Y	Y
NEVADA								
Reid	Y	Y	N	N	Y	Y	Y	Y
Ensign	Y	Y	N	Y	Y	Y	Y	Y
NEW HAMPSHIRE								
Smith	Y	Y	N	N	Y	Y	Y	Y
Gregg	Y	Y	N	Y	Y	Y	Y	Y
NEW JERSEY								
Corzine	Y	Y	N	N	Y	Y	Y	Y
Torricelli	?	Y	N	N	Y	Y	Y	Y
NEW MEXICO								
Domenici	Y	Y	Y	Y	Y	Y	Y	Y
Bingaman	Y	Y	N	N	N	Y	Y	Y
NEW YORK								
Clinton	Y	Y	N	N	Y	Y	Y	Y
Schumer	Y	Y	N	N	Y	Y	Y	Y
NORTH CAROLINA								
Helms	Y	Y	Y	Y	Y	Y	Y	Y
Edwards	Y	Y	N	N	Y	Y	Y	Y
NORTH DAKOTA								
Conrad	Y	Y	N	N	Y	Y	Y	Y
Dorgan	Y	Y	N	N	Y	Y	Y	Y
OHIO								
DeWine	Y	Y	N	N	Y	Y	Y	Y
Voinovich	Y	Y	Y	Y	Y	Y	Y	Y
OKLAHOMA								
Nickles	Y	Y	N	Y	?	?	?	?
Inhofe	Y	Y	Y	Y	Y	Y	Y	Y
OREGON								
Wyden	Y	Y	N	N	Y	Y	Y	Y
Smith	Y	Y	N	N	Y	Y	Y	Y
PENNSYLVANIA								
Specter	Y	Y	Y	Y	Y	Y	Y	Y
Santorum	Y	Y	Y	Y	Y	Y	Y	Y
RHODE ISLAND								
Reed	Y	Y	N	N	Y	Y	Y	Y
Chafee	Y	Y	N	N	N	Y	Y	Y
SOUTH CAROLINA								
Thurmond	Y	Y	Y	Y	Y	Y	Y	Y
Hollings	Y	Y	N	N	Y	Y	Y	Y
SOUTH DAKOTA								
Daschle	Y	Y	N	N	Y	Y	Y	Y
Johnson	Y	Y	N	N	Y	Y	Y	Y
TENNESSEE								
Thompson	Y	?	Y	Y	Y	Y	Y	Y
Frist	Y	Y	Y	Y	Y	Y	Y	Y
TEXAS								
Gramm	Y	Y	N	Y	Y	Y	Y	Y
Hutchison	Y	Y	N	Y	Y	Y	Y	Y
UTAH								
Hatch	Y	Y	Y	Y	Y	Y	Y	Y
Bennett	Y	Y	N	Y	Y	Y	Y	Y
VERMONT								
Leahy	Y	Y	N	N	Y	Y	Y	Y
Jeffords	Y	Y	N	N	Y	Y	Y	Y
VIRGINIA								
Warner	Y	Y	Y	Y	Y	Y	Y	Y
Allen	Y	Y	Y	Y	Y	Y	Y	Y
WASHINGTON								
Cantwell	Y	Y	N	N	Y	Y	Y	Y
Murray	Y	Y	N	N	Y	Y	Y	Y
WEST VIRGINIA								
Byrd	Y	?	Y	N	N	Y	Y	Y
Rockefeller	Y	Y	N	N	Y	Y	Y	Y
WISCONSIN								
Kohl	Y	Y	N	N	Y	Y	Y	Y
Feingold	Y	Y	N	N	Y	Y	Y	Y
WYOMING								
Thomas	Y	Y	N	Y	Y	Y	Y	Y
Enzi	Y	Y	N	Y	Y	Y	Y	Y

Key

Y	Voted for (yea).
#	Paired for.
+	Announced for.
N	Voted against (nay).
X	Paired against.
−	Announced against.
P	Voted "present."
C	Voted "present" to avoid possible conflict of interest.
?	Did not vote or otherwise make a position known.

Democrats **Republicans**
Independents

ND Northern Democrats   SD Southern Democrats

Southern states - Ala., Ark., Fla., Ga., Ky., La., Miss., N.C., Okla., S.C., Tenn., Texas, Va.

68. O'Brien Nomination/Confirmation. Confirmation of President Bush's nomination of Terrence L. O'Brien of Wyoming to be a judge for the 10th U. S. Circuit Court of Appeals. Confirmed 98-0: R 48-0; D 49-0 (ND 40-0, SD 9-0); I 1-0. A "yea" was a vote in support of the president's position. April 15, 2002.

69. Africk Nomination/Confirmation. Confirmation of President Bush's nomination of Lance M. Africk of Louisiana to be a U.S. district judge for the Eastern District of Louisiana. Confirmed 97-0: R 48-0; D 48-0 (ND 39-0, SD 9-0); I 1-0. A "yea" was a vote in support of the president's position. April 17, 2002.

70. S 517. Energy Plan/Cloture. Motion to invoke cloture (thus limiting debate) on the Stevens, R-Alaska, amendment to the Murkowski, R-Alaska, amendment to the Daschle, D-S.D., substitute amendment. The Stevens amendment would allow oil and gas development in a portion of the Arctic National Wildlife Refuge and establish a trust fund to help finance a "steel legacy" benefits program, coal miner health benefits and other programs. The Murkowski amendment would allow for oil and gas development in a portion of the refuge if the president certifies to Congress that production in the area is in the nation's economic and security interests. It would limit the amount of surface disturbances to 2,000 acres, impose an export ban (with the exception of exports to Israel) on the oil produced from the refuge, and designate an additional 1.5 million acres as wilderness in exchange for opening to drilling approximately 1.5 million acres of non-wilderness in the coastal plain region of the refuge. The substitute amendment would overhaul the nation's energy policies, restructure the electricity system and provide for $16.04 billion in energy-related tax incentives. It also would give the National Highway Traffic Safety Administration 15 months to two years to set new CAFE standards. Motion rejected 36-64: R 30-19; D 6-44 (ND 3-38, SD 3-6); I 0-1. Three-fifths of the total Senate (60) is required to invoke cloture. April 18, 2002.

71. S 517. Energy Plan/Cloture. Motion to invoke cloture (thus limiting debate) on the Murkowski, R-Alaska, amendment to the Daschle, D-S.D., substitute amendment. Motion rejected 46-54: R 41-8; D 5-45 (ND 2-39, SD 3-6); I 0-1. Three-fifths of the total Senate (60) is required to invoke cloture. April 18, 2002.

72. S 517. Energy Plan/Iraqi Oil Imports. Murkowski, R-Alaska, amendment to the Daschle, D-S.D., substitute amendment. The Murkowski amendment would set conditions for the importation of Iraqi oil. Adopted 88-10: R 43-5; D 44-5 (ND 35-5, SD 9-0); I 1-0. April 18, 2002.

73. HR 3525. Border Security/INS Review. Byrd, D-W.Va., amendment that would require the Immigration and Naturalization Service to review educational and other institutions certified to receive foreign students and exchange visitors every two years. Adopted 97-0: R 48-0; D 48-0 (ND 39-0, SD 9-0); I 1-0. April 18, 2002.

74. HR 3525. Border Security/Visa Waiver Program. Byrd, D-W.Va., amendment that would require the attorney general to consult with the secretary of State and evaluate the effect of each country's participation in the Visa Waiver Program, and stipulate that countries participating in the program report to U.S. government officials on the thefts of blank passports. Adopted 97-0: R 48-0; D 48-0 (ND 39-0, SD 9-0); I 1-0. April 18, 2002.

75. HR 3525. Border Security/Passage. Passage of a bill that would require planes and passenger ships traveling from other countries to give immigration officials lists of passengers and crew members before arriving. It also would create a database of suspected terrorists that federal agencies could use to screen visa applicants, and require schools to tell government officials if foreign students do not report for class. All visas, passports and other travel documents would be required to contain biometric data. Passed 97-0: R 48-0; D 48-0 (ND 39-0, SD 9-0); I 1-0. April 18, 2002.

Senate Votes 76, 77, 78, 79, 80, 81, 82

	76	77	78	79	80	81	82
ALABAMA							
Shelby	Y	Y	N	Y	Y	Y	Y
Sessions	Y	Y	N	Y	Y	Y	Y
ALASKA							
Stevens	Y	Y	Y	Y	Y	Y	Y
Murkowski	Y	Y	Y	Y	Y	Y	Y
ARIZONA							
McCain	Y	N	N	Y	Y	Y	Y
Kyl	Y	N	N	Y	Y	Y	Y
ARKANSAS							
Hutchinson	Y	Y	Y	Y	Y	Y	N
Lincoln	Y	Y	Y	Y	Y	Y	N
CALIFORNIA							
Feinstein	Y	N	N	Y	N	N	N
Boxer	?	N	N	Y	N	N	N
COLORADO							
Campbell	Y	Y	Y	Y	Y	Y	Y
Allard	Y	Y	N	Y	Y	Y	Y
CONNECTICUT							
Dodd	Y	Y	Y	Y	N	Y	N
Lieberman	Y	Y	Y	Y	N	N	N
DELAWARE							
Carper	Y	Y	Y	Y	Y	Y	Y
Biden	Y	Y	Y	Y	Y	Y	N
FLORIDA							
Graham	Y	N	Y	Y	N	N	Y
Nelson	Y	Y	Y	Y	N	N	Y
GEORGIA							
Miller	Y	Y	Y	Y	Y	Y	Y
Cleland	Y	Y	N	Y	Y	Y	N
HAWAII							
Inouye	?	Y	N	Y	N	N	N
Akaka	Y	Y	N	Y	Y	N	N
IDAHO							
Craig	Y	Y	Y	Y	Y	Y	Y
Crapo	Y	Y	Y	Y	Y	Y	Y
ILLINOIS							
Durbin	Y	Y	Y	Y	N	N	N
Fitzgerald	Y	Y	Y	Y	Y	Y	N
INDIANA							
Lugar	Y	Y	Y	Y	Y	Y	Y
Bayh	Y	Y	Y	Y	Y	N	N

	76	77	78	79	80	81	82
IOWA							
Grassley	Y	Y	Y	Y	Y	Y	Y
Harkin	Y	Y	Y	Y	N	N	N
KANSAS							
Brownback	Y	Y	Y	Y	Y	Y	N
Roberts	?	Y	Y	Y	Y	Y	Y
KENTUCKY							
McConnell	Y	Y	Y	Y	Y	Y	Y
Bunning	Y	Y	Y	Y	Y	Y	Y
LOUISIANA							
Breaux	Y	Y	Y	Y	Y	Y	N
Landrieu	Y	Y	Y	Y	Y	Y	N
MAINE							
Snowe	Y	Y	Y	Y	N	N	N
Collins	Y	Y	Y	Y	N	Y	N
MARYLAND							
Sarbanes	Y	Y	Y	Y	N	N	N
Mikulski	Y	Y	Y	Y	N	N	N
MASSACHUSETTS							
Kennedy	Y	Y	N	Y	N	N	N
Kerry	Y	Y	Y	N	N	N	N
MICHIGAN							
Levin	Y	Y	Y	Y	N	N	N
Stabenow	Y	N	Y	N	N	N	N
MINNESOTA							
Wellstone	Y	Y	Y	Y	N	N	N
Dayton	Y	Y	Y	Y	N	N	N
MISSISSIPPI							
Cochran	Y	Y	Y	Y	Y	Y	Y
Lott	Y	Y	Y	Y	Y	Y	Y
MISSOURI							
Bond	?	Y	Y	Y	Y	Y	N
Carnahan	Y	Y	Y	Y	N	N	N
MONTANA							
Baucus	Y	Y	Y	Y	N	N	N
Burns	Y	Y	Y	Y	Y	Y	Y
NEBRASKA							
Nelson	?	Y	Y	Y	Y	Y	N
Hagel	Y	Y	Y	Y	Y	Y	Y
NEVADA							
Reid	Y	Y	Y	Y	N	N	N
Ensign	Y	Y	N	Y	Y	Y	Y

	76	77	78	79	80	81	82
NEW HAMPSHIRE							
Smith	Y	Y	Y	Y	Y	Y	N
Gregg	Y	Y	Y	Y	Y	N	N
NEW JERSEY							
Corzine	Y	Y	N	Y	N	N	N
Torricelli	Y	Y	Y	Y	Y	N	N
NEW MEXICO							
Domenici	Y	Y	Y	Y	Y	Y	Y
Bingaman	Y	Y	Y	Y	Y	N	Y
NEW YORK							
Clinton	Y	N	N	Y	N	N	N
Schumer	Y	N	N	Y	N	N	N
NORTH CAROLINA							
Helms	Y	?	?	?	?	?	?
Edwards	Y	Y	Y	Y	N	N	N
NORTH DAKOTA							
Conrad	Y	Y	Y	Y	N	N	N
Dorgan	Y	Y	Y	Y	N	N	N
OHIO							
DeWine	Y	Y	Y	Y	Y	Y	N
Voinovich	Y	Y	Y	Y	Y	Y	N
OKLAHOMA							
Nickles	?	Y	N	Y	Y	Y	Y
Inhofe	Y	Y	Y	Y	Y	Y	Y
OREGON							
Wyden	Y	N	N	Y	N	N	N
Smith	Y	N	Y	N	Y	N	Y
PENNSYLVANIA							
Specter	Y	Y	N	Y	Y	Y	N
Santorum	Y	Y	N	Y	Y	Y	N
RHODE ISLAND							
Reed	Y	N	N	Y	N	N	N
Chafee	Y	Y	Y	Y	N	N	N
SOUTH CAROLINA							
Thurmond	Y	Y	Y	Y	Y	Y	Y
Hollings	Y	Y	N	Y	N	Y	N
SOUTH DAKOTA							
Daschle	Y	Y	Y	Y	?	?	?
Johnson	Y	Y	Y	Y	?	?	?
TENNESSEE							
Thompson	Y	Y	N	Y	Y	Y	N
Frist	Y	Y	Y	Y	Y	Y	N

	76	77	78	79	80	81	82
TEXAS							
Gramm	Y	Y	N	Y	Y	Y	Y
Hutchison	Y	Y	N	Y	Y	Y	Y
UTAH							
Hatch	Y	Y	Y	Y	Y	Y	Y
Bennett	Y	Y	Y	Y	Y	Y	Y
VERMONT							
Leahy	Y	Y	N	Y	N	N	N
Jeffords	Y	Y	Y	Y	N	N	N
VIRGINIA							
Warner	Y	Y	N	Y	Y	Y	Y
Allen	Y	Y	N	Y	Y	Y	Y
WASHINGTON							
Cantwell	Y	N	Y	Y	N	N	Y
Murray	Y	N	Y	Y	N	N	Y
WEST VIRGINIA							
Byrd	Y	Y	Y	Y	N	N	N
Rockefeller	Y	Y	Y	Y	Y	N	N
WISCONSIN							
Kohl	Y	Y	Y	Y	N	N	N
Feingold	Y	N	Y	Y	N	N	N
WYOMING							
Thomas	Y	Y	N	Y	Y	Y	Y
Enzi	Y	Y	N	Y	Y	Y	Y

ND Northern Democrats   SD Southern Democrats

Southern states - Ala., Ark., Fla., Ga., Ky., La., Miss., N.C., Okla., S.C., Tenn., Texas, Va.

76. Davis Nomination/Confirmation. Confirmation of President Bush's nomination of Legrome D. Davis of Pennsylvania to be U.S. district judge for the Eastern District of Pennsylvania. Confirmed 94-0: R 46-0; D 47-0 (ND 38-0, SD 9-0); I 1-0. A "yea" was a vote in support of the president's position. April 18, 2002.

77. S 517. Energy Plan/Cloture. Motion to invoke cloture (thus limiting debate) on the Daschle, D-S.D., substitute amendment that would overhaul the nation's energy policies, restructure the electricity system and provide for $14.1 billion in energy-related tax incentives. It also would give the National Highway Traffic Safety Administration (NHTSA) 15 months to two years to set new CAFE standards. Motion agreed to 86-13: R 46-2; D 39-11 (ND 31-10, SD 8-1); I 1-0. Three-fifths of the total Senate (60) is required to invoke cloture. April 23, 2002.

78. S 517. Energy Plan/Renewable Fuel. Bingaman, D-N.M., motion to table (kill) the Schumer, D-N.Y., amendment to the Daschle, D-S.D., substitute amendment. The Schumer amendment would strike the section in the underlying measure that would establish a renewable fuel content requirement for motor vehicle fuel. Motion agreed to 69-30: R 31-17; D 37-13 (ND 30-11, SD 7-2); I 1-0. April 23, 2002.

79. Howard Nomination/Confirmation. Confirmation of President Bush's nomination of Jeffrey R. Howard of New Hampshire to be a judge for the 1st U.S. Circuit Court of Appeals. Confirmed 99-0: R 48-0; D 50-0 (ND 41-0, SD 9-0); I 1-0. A "yea" was a vote in support of the president's position. April 23, 2002.

80. S 517. Energy Plan/Electricity. Bingaman, D-N.M., motion to table (kill) the Cantwell, D-Wash., amendment to the Daschle, D-S.D., substitute amendment. The Cantwell amendment would repeal the Public Utility Holding Company Act and require the Federal Energy Regulatory Commission (FERC) to ensure that the proposal would "advance the public interest" before approving electric utility mergers. It also would change the standard the FERC uses to review asset sales and direct the commission to establish rules and procedures for market monitoring. Motion agreed to 58-39: R 44-4; D 14-34 (ND 9-30, SD 5-4); I 0-1. April 24, 2002.

81. S 517. Energy Plan/Hydro Power. Nelson, D-Neb., motion to table (kill) the Bingaman, D-N.M., amendment to the Nelson amendment to the Daschle, D-S.D., substitute amendment. The Bingaman amendment would require the FERC and administration officials to consult affected states and tribes before reviewing a process that allows license applicants and third parties to propose alternative mandatory conditions and "alternative mandatory fishway prescriptions" for licenses. The Nelson amendment would allow energy producers to propose alternative conditions for license requirements for projects and fishways. Motion agreed to 54-43: R 44-4; D 10-38 (ND 4-35, SD 6-3); I 0-1. April 24, 2002.

82. S 517. Energy Plan/Electricity Regulation. Murkowski, R-Alaska, motion to table (kill) the Carper, D-Del., amendment to the Daschle, D-S.D., substitute amendment. The Carper amendment would terminate mandatory electric purchase and sale requirements under the Public Utility Regulatory Policies Act if the FERC finds that an energy facility has access to electricity sales through independently administered auction-based and real-time markets. Motion rejected 37-60: R 31-17; D 6-42 (ND 3-36, SD 3-6); I 0-1. Subsequently, the bill was adopted by voice vote. April 24, 2002.

	83	84	85	86	87	88	89
ALABAMA							
Shelby	N	Y	Y	Y	Y	N	Y
Sessions	N	Y	Y	Y	Y	Y	Y
ALASKA							
Stevens	N	Y	Y	Y	Y	Y	Y
Murkowski	N	Y	Y	Y	Y	Y	Y
ARIZONA							
McCain	N	N	Y	Y	N	N	Y
Kyl	N	N	Y	Y	N	N	Y
ARKANSAS							
Hutchinson	N	Y	Y	Y	Y	Y	Y
Lincoln	N	Y	Y	Y	Y	Y	Y
CALIFORNIA							
Feinstein	N	Y	Y	Y	N	N	N
Boxer	Y	N	Y	Y	N	N	N
COLORADO							
Campbell	N	Y	Y	Y	Y	Y	Y
Allard	N	N	Y	Y	Y	N	Y
CONNECTICUT							
Dodd	Y	Y	Y	Y	N	Y	N
Lieberman	Y	Y	Y	Y	N	N	N
DELAWARE							
Carper	Y	Y	Y	Y	N	Y	N
Biden	Y	N	Y	Y	N	N	N
FLORIDA							
Graham	N	Y	Y	Y	N	Y	N
Nelson	N	Y	Y	Y	N	Y	N
GEORGIA							
Miller	N	Y	Y	Y	Y	Y	Y
Cleland	N	Y	Y	Y	Y	N	Y
HAWAII							
Inouye	Y	Y	Y	Y	N	Y	N
Akaka	N	Y	Y	Y	N	N	N
IDAHO							
Craig	N	N	Y	Y	Y	Y	Y
Crapo	N	N	Y	Y	Y	Y	Y
ILLINOIS							
Durbin	Y	N	Y	Y	N	Y	N
Fitzgerald	N	N	Y	Y	N	Y	N
INDIANA							
Lugar	N	Y	Y	Y	Y	Y	Y
Bayh	N	Y	Y	Y	Y	Y	Y

	83	84	85	86	87	88	89
IOWA							
Grassley	N	Y	Y	Y	Y	Y	Y
Harkin	Y	N	Y	Y	Y	Y	Y
KANSAS							
Brownback	N	Y	Y	Y	Y	Y	Y
Roberts	N	Y	Y	Y	Y	Y	Y
KENTUCKY							
McConnell	N	N	Y	Y	Y	Y	Y
Bunning	N	Y	Y	Y	Y	Y	Y
LOUISIANA							
Breaux	N	Y	Y	Y	Y	Y	Y
Landrieu	N	Y	Y	Y	Y	Y	Y
MAINE							
Snowe	Y	N	Y	Y	N	N	N
Collins	Y	N	Y	Y	N	N	N
MARYLAND							
Sarbanes	Y	N	Y	Y	N	Y	N
Mikulski	Y	N	Y	Y	N	Y	N
MASSACHUSETTS							
Kennedy	Y	N	Y	Y	N	N	N
Kerry	Y	N	Y	Y	N	N	N
MICHIGAN							
Levin	Y	N	Y	Y	N	Y	N
Stabenow	Y	N	Y	Y	N	Y	N
MINNESOTA							
Wellstone	Y	N	Y	Y	N	Y	N
Dayton	Y	N	Y	Y	N	Y	N
MISSISSIPPI							
Cochran	N	N	Y	Y	Y	Y	Y
Lott	N	Y	Y	Y	Y	Y	Y
MISSOURI							
Bond	N	N	Y	Y	Y	Y	Y
Carnahan	Y	N	Y	Y	Y	Y	N
MONTANA							
Baucus	Y	Y	Y	Y	Y	Y	N
Burns	N	N	Y	Y	Y	Y	Y
NEBRASKA							
Nelson	Y	Y	Y	Y	Y	Y	N
Hagel	N	Y	Y	Y	Y	Y	Y
NEVADA							
Reid	Y	N	Y	Y	N	N	N
Ensign	N	N	Y	Y	N	N	Y

	83	84	85	86	87	88	89
NEW HAMPSHIRE							
Smith	N	N	Y	Y	Y	Y	N
Gregg	N	N	Y	Y	Y	Y	N
NEW JERSEY							
Corzine	N	N	Y	N	N	N	N
Torricelli	Y	Y	Y	N	N	Y	N
NEW MEXICO							
Domenici	N	N	Y	Y	Y	Y	Y
Bingaman	Y	Y	Y	N	N	N	N
NEW YORK							
Clinton	Y	Y	Y	N	N	N	Y
Schumer	N	N	Y	N	N	N	Y
NORTH CAROLINA							
Helms	?	?	?	?	?	?	?
Edwards	Y	N	Y	Y	N	Y	N
NORTH DAKOTA							
Conrad	Y	N	Y	Y	N	Y	N
Dorgan	Y	Y	Y	Y	Y	Y	N
OHIO							
DeWine	N	Y	Y	Y	Y	Y	Y
Voinovich	N	Y	Y	Y	Y	Y	Y
OKLAHOMA							
Nickles	N	Y	Y	Y	Y	N	Y
Inhofe	N	Y	Y	Y	Y	Y	Y
OREGON							
Wyden	Y	Y	Y	Y	N	N	N
Smith	N	Y	Y	Y	N	N	N
PENNSYLVANIA							
Specter	N	N	Y	Y	N	N	N
Santorum	N	Y	Y	Y	N	Y	N
RHODE ISLAND							
Reed	Y	N	Y	Y	N	Y	N
Chafee	Y	N	Y	Y	N	Y	N
SOUTH CAROLINA							
Thurmond	N	Y	Y	Y	Y	N	Y
Hollings	N	N	Y	Y	N	N	Y
SOUTH DAKOTA							
Daschle	?	?	Y	Y	Y	Y	N
Johnson	?	?	Y	Y	Y	Y	N
TENNESSEE							
Thompson	N	Y	Y	Y	Y	N	Y
Frist	N	Y	Y	Y	Y	Y	Y

Key

Y	Voted for (yea).
#	Paired for.
+	Announced for.
N	Voted against (nay).
X	Paired against.
−	Announced against.
P	Voted "present."
C	Voted "present" to avoid possible conflict of interest.
?	Did not vote or otherwise make a position known.

Democrats **Republicans**
Independents

	83	84	85	86	87	88	89
TEXAS							
Gramm	N	N	Y	Y	N	N	Y
Hutchison	N	N	Y	Y	N	Y	N
UTAH							
Hatch	N	Y	Y	Y	Y	N	N
Bennett	N	N	Y	Y	Y	N	Y
VERMONT							
Leahy	Y	N	Y	Y	N	N	N
Jeffords	Y	?	Y	Y	Y	Y	N
VIRGINIA							
Warner	N	Y	Y	Y	Y	N	Y
Allen	N	Y	Y	Y	Y	N	Y
WASHINGTON							
Cantwell	Y	N	Y	Y	N	N	N
Murray	Y	N	Y	Y	N	N	N
WEST VIRGINIA							
Byrd	N	Y	Y	Y	Y	N	Y
Rockefeller	Y	Y	Y	Y	N	N	Y
WISCONSIN							
Kohl	Y	N	Y	Y	N	Y	N
Feingold	Y	N	Y	Y	N	Y	N
WYOMING							
Thomas	N	Y	Y	Y	Y	N	Y
Enzi	N	Y	Y	Y	Y	N	Y

ND Northern Democrats   SD Southern Democrats

Southern states - Ala., Ark., Fla., Ga., Ky., La., Miss., N.C., Okla., S.C., Tenn., Texas, Va.

83. S 517. Energy Plan/Penalties. Bingaman, D-N.M., motion to table (kill) the Nickles, R-Okla., amendment to the Daschle, D-S.D., substitute amendment. The Nickles amendment would reduce the penalty from 3 cents per kilowatt hour to 1.5 cents per kilowatt hour for utilities that do not meet the 10 percent renewable standard by using alternative sources of energy by 2019. Motion rejected 38-59: R 3-45; D 34-14 (ND 33-6, SD 1-8); I 1-0. Subsequently, the amendment was adopted by voice vote. April 24, 2002.

84. S 517. Energy Plan/Municipal Waste. Bingaman, D-N.M., motion to table (kill) the Fitzgerald, D-Ill., amendment to the Daschle, D-S.D., substitute amendment. The Fitzgerald amendment would modify the definition of "biomass" and "renewable energy" to exclude municipal waste. Motion agreed to 50-46: R 27-21; D 23-25 (ND 16-23, SD 7-2); I 0-0. April 24, 2002.

85. Anderson Nomination/Confirmation. Confirmation of Percy Anderson of California to be U.S. district judge for the Central District of California. Confirmed 99-0: R 48-0; D 50-0 (ND 41-0, SD 9-0); I 1-0. A "yea" was a vote in support of the president's position. April 25, 2002.

86. Walter Nomination/Confirmation. Confirmation of John F. Walter of California to be U.S. district judge for the Central District of California. Confirmed 99-0: R 48-0; D 50-0 (ND 41-0, SD 9-0); I 1-0. A "yea" was a vote in support of the president's position. April 25, 2002.

87. S 517. Energy Plan/Liability Standards. Reid, D-Nev., motion to table (kill) the Boxer, D-Calif., amendment to the Boxer amendment to the Daschle, D-S.D., substitute amendment. The Boxer amendment would provide equal liability standards for vehicle fuels, renewable fuels and fuel additives, with an effective date one day after the bill's enactment. The underlying Boxer amendment specified no enactment date. Motion agreed to 57-42: R 38-10; D 18-32 (ND 12-29, SD 6-3); I 1-0. April 25, 2002.

88. S 517. Energy Plan/Ethanol Requirement Date. Reid, D-Nev., motion to table (kill) the Feinstein, D-Calif., amendment to the Daschle, D-S.D. substitute amendment. The Feinstein amendment would delay the implementation of the ethanol requirement in motor vehicle fuel from calendar year 2004 to 2005. Motion agreed to 60-39: R 28-20; D 31-19 (ND 23-18, SD 8-1); I 1-0. April 25, 2002.

89. S 517. Energy Plan/Seasonal Energy Efficiency Standard. Harkin, D-Iowa, amendment to the Daschle, D-S.D., substitute amendment. The Harkin amendment would strike the provision that requires a 30 percent increase in the minimum seasonal energy efficiency standards for central air conditioners and air conditioning pumps by 2006 and insert language in the underlying measure to direct the Energy secretary to revise the standard. Adopted 52-47: R 41-7; D 11-39 (ND 5-36, SD 6-3); I 0-1. April 25, 2002.

Senate Votes 90, 91, 92, 93, 94, 95, 96

	90	91	92	93	94	95	96
ALABAMA							
Shelby	Y	Y	Y	Y	Y	Y	Y
Sessions	Y	Y	Y	Y	Y	Y	Y
ALASKA							
Stevens	Y	Y	Y	Y	Y	Y	Y
Murkowski	Y	Y	Y	Y	Y	Y	Y
ARIZONA							
McCain	N	N	Y	N	N	Y	Y
Kyl	Y	N	Y	Y	N	Y	Y
ARKANSAS							
Hutchinson	Y	Y	Y	Y	Y	Y	Y
Lincoln	Y	Y	Y	Y	Y	Y	Y
CALIFORNIA							
Feinstein	N	Y	N	Y	N	Y	Y
Boxer	N	Y	N	N	N	Y	Y
COLORADO							
Campbell	Y	Y	Y	Y	Y	Y	Y
Allard	Y	Y	Y	Y	Y	Y	Y
CONNECTICUT							
Dodd	N	Y	N	N	Y	Y	Y
Lieberman	N	Y	N	Y	Y	Y	Y
DELAWARE							
Carper	N	Y	N	Y	Y	Y	Y
Biden	N	Y	Y	N	Y	Y	Y
FLORIDA							
Graham	N	Y	N	N	N	Y	Y
Nelson	N	Y	N	N	Y	Y	Y
GEORGIA							
Miller	Y	Y	Y	Y	Y	Y	Y
Cleland	N	Y	Y	Y	Y	Y	Y
HAWAII							
Inouye	N	Y	N	Y	Y	Y	Y
Akaka	N	Y	N	Y	Y	Y	Y
IDAHO							
Craig	Y	Y	Y	Y	Y	Y	Y
Crapo	Y	Y	Y	Y	Y	Y	Y
ILLINOIS							
Durbin	N	Y	Y	N	Y	Y	Y
Fitzgerald	Y	N	Y	Y	Y	Y	Y
INDIANA							
Lugar	N	Y	Y	Y	Y	Y	Y
Bayh	Y	Y	Y	Y	Y	Y	Y

	90	91	92	93	94	95	96
IOWA							
Grassley	Y	Y	Y	Y	Y	Y	Y
Harkin	N	Y	Y	N	Y	Y	Y
KANSAS							
Brownback	Y	Y	Y	Y	Y	Y	?
Roberts	Y	Y	Y	Y	Y	Y	Y
KENTUCKY							
McConnell	Y	Y	Y	Y	Y	Y	Y
Bunning	Y	Y	Y	Y	Y	Y	Y
LOUISIANA							
Breaux	Y	Y	Y	Y	Y	Y	Y
Landrieu	Y	Y	Y	Y	Y	Y	Y
MAINE							
Snowe	N	Y	N	Y	Y	Y	Y
Collins	N	Y	N	Y	Y	Y	Y
MARYLAND							
Sarbanes	N	Y	N	Y	Y	Y	Y
Mikulski	Y	Y	N	N	Y	Y	Y
MASSACHUSETTS							
Kennedy	Y	Y	N	N	N	Y	Y
Kerry	N	Y	N	N	N	Y	Y
MICHIGAN							
Levin	Y	Y	Y	N	Y	Y	Y
Stabenow	Y	Y	Y	Y	Y	Y	Y
MINNESOTA							
Wellstone	N	Y	N	N	N	Y	Y
Dayton	Y	Y	N	N	Y	Y	Y
MISSISSIPPI							
Cochran	Y	Y	Y	Y	Y	Y	Y
Lott	Y	N	Y	Y	Y	Y	Y
MISSOURI							
Bond	Y	Y	Y	Y	Y	Y	Y
Carnahan	Y	Y	N	Y	Y	Y	Y
MONTANA							
Baucus	Y	Y	Y	Y	Y	Y	Y
Burns	Y	N	Y	Y	Y	Y	Y
NEBRASKA							
Nelson	Y	Y	Y	Y	Y	Y	Y
Hagel	Y	Y	Y	Y	Y	Y	Y
NEVADA							
Reid	N	Y	Y	Y	Y	Y	Y
Ensign	Y	Y	Y	Y	Y	Y	Y

	90	91	92	93	94	95	96
NEW HAMPSHIRE							
Smith	Y	Y	Y	Y	Y	Y	Y
Gregg	N	Y	N	Y	Y	Y	Y
NEW JERSEY							
Corzine	N	Y	N	N	Y	Y	Y
Torricelli	N	Y	N	Y	Y	Y	Y
NEW MEXICO							
Domenici	Y	Y	Y	Y	Y	Y	Y
Bingaman	N	Y	Y	Y	Y	Y	Y
NEW YORK							
Clinton	N	Y	N	N	N	Y	Y
Schumer	N	Y	N	N	N	Y	Y
NORTH CAROLINA							
Helms	?	?	?	?	?	?	?
Edwards	N	Y	N	Y	Y	Y	Y
NORTH DAKOTA							
Conrad	N	Y	N	Y	Y	Y	Y
Dorgan	Y	Y	Y	Y	Y	Y	Y
OHIO							
DeWine	Y	Y	Y	Y	Y	Y	Y
Voinovich	Y	Y	Y	Y	Y	Y	Y
OKLAHOMA							
Nickles	Y	N	Y	Y	Y	Y	Y
Inhofe	Y	Y	Y	Y	Y	Y	?
OREGON							
Wyden	N	Y	N	Y	Y	Y	Y
Smith	N	Y	Y	Y	Y	Y	Y
PENNSYLVANIA							
Specter	N	Y	N	Y	Y	Y	Y
Santorum	Y	Y	Y	Y	Y	Y	Y
RHODE ISLAND							
Reed	N	Y	N	N	N	Y	Y
Chafee	N	Y	N	Y	N	Y	Y
SOUTH CAROLINA							
Thurmond	Y	Y	Y	Y	Y	Y	Y
Hollings	N	Y	N	N	N	Y	Y
SOUTH DAKOTA							
Daschle	N	Y	Y	Y	Y	Y	Y
Johnson	Y	Y	Y	Y	Y	Y	Y
TENNESSEE							
Thompson	N	Y	Y	Y	Y	Y	Y
Frist	Y	Y	Y	Y	Y	Y	Y

	90	91	92	93	94	95	96
TEXAS							
Gramm	Y	N	Y	N	N	Y	Y
Hutchison	Y	Y	Y	Y	Y	Y	Y
UTAH							
Hatch	Y	Y	Y	Y	Y	Y	Y
Bennett	Y	Y	Y	Y	Y	Y	Y
VERMONT							
Leahy	N	Y	N	Y	Y	Y	Y
Jeffords	N	Y	N	Y	Y	Y	Y
VIRGINIA							
Warner	Y	Y	Y	Y	Y	Y	Y
Allen	Y	Y	Y	Y	Y	Y	Y
WASHINGTON							
Cantwell	N	Y	N	Y	Y	Y	Y
Murray	N	Y	N	Y	Y	Y	Y
WEST VIRGINIA							
Byrd	Y	Y	Y	Y	Y	Y	Y
Rockefeller	N	Y	Y	Y	Y	Y	Y
WISCONSIN							
Kohl	Y	Y	Y	Y	Y	Y	Y
Feingold	Y	N	N	N	N	Y	Y
WYOMING							
Thomas	Y	Y	Y	Y	Y	Y	Y
Enzi	Y	Y	Y	Y	Y	Y	Y

ND Northern Democrats   SD Southern Democrats

Southern states - Ala., Ark., Fla., Ga., Ky., La., Miss., N.C., Okla., S.C., Tenn., Texas, Va.

90. S 517. Energy Plan/Fuel Consumption. Levin, D-Mich., motion to table (kill) the Carper, D-Del., amendment to the Daschle, D-S.D., substitute amendment. The Carper amendment would require new regulations for automobiles manufactured after the model year 2006 to reduce the amount of oil consumed by at least 1 million barrels per day by 2015. Motion agreed to 57-42: R 39-9; D 18-32 (ND 14-27, SD 4-5); I 0-1. April 25, 2002.

91. S 517. Energy Plan/Alternative Vehicles. Hatch, R-Utah, motion to table (kill) the Kyl, R-Ariz., amendment to the Daschle, D-S.D., substitute amendment. The Kyl amendment would strike provisions in the underlying measure related to alternative vehicles and fuel incentives. Motion agreed to 91-8: R 41-7; D 49-1 (ND 40-1, SD 9-0); I 1-0. April 25, 2002.

92. S 517. Energy Plan/Delayed Rental Payments. Nickles, R-Okla., motion to table (kill) the Graham, D-Fla., amendment to the Daschle, D-S.D., substitute amendment. The Graham amendment would strike the provision in the underlying bill that would allow delayed rental payments to be deducted over two years. Motion agreed to 73-26: R 45-3; D 27-23 (ND 22-19, SD 5-4); I 1-0. April 25, 2002.

93. S 517. Energy Plan/Tax Conditions. Nickles, R-Okla., motion to table (kill) the Graham, D-Fla., amendment to the Daschle, D-S.D., substitute amendment. The Graham amendment would place certain conditions on the implementation of the tax provisions in the measure. It would require legislation to be enacted that would raise federal revenues or reduce federal spending sufficient to offset the cost of the tax provisions. Motion agreed to 70-29: R 44-4; D 25-25 (ND 19-22, SD 6-3); I 1-0. April 25, 2002.

94. HR 4. Energy Plan/Passage. Passage of the bill that would overhaul the nation's energy policies, restructure the electricity system and provide for approximately $15 billion in energy-related tax incentives. It also would direct the NHTSA to set a new CAFE standard within 15 months to two years. It would encourage the use of alternative energy and require utilities to increase their reliance on renewable fuels. Passed 88-11: R 45-3; D 42-8 (ND 34-7, SD 8-1); I 1-0. Before passage, the Senate struck all after the enacting clause and inserted the text of S 517 as amended. April 25, 2002.

95. Lancaster Nomination/Confirmation. Confirmation of Joan E. Lancaster of Minnesota to be U.S. district judge for the District of Minnesota. Confirmed 99-0: R 48-0; D 50-0 (ND 41-0, SD 9-0); I 1-0. A "yea" was a vote in support of the president's position. April 25, 2002.

96. Griesbach Nomination/Confirmation. Confirmation of William C. Griesbach of Wisconsin to be U.S. district judge for the Eastern District of Wisconsin. Confirmed 97-0: R 46-0; D 50-0 (ND 41-0, SD 9-0); I 1-0. A "yea" was a vote in support of the president's position. April 25, 2002.

	97	98	99	100	101	102
ALABAMA						
Shelby	N	Y	Y	N	N	Y
Sessions	N	Y	Y	N	N	Y
ALASKA						
Stevens	Y	Y	Y	Y	Y	Y
Murkowski	?	Y	Y	Y	N	Y
ARIZONA						
McCain	Y	Y	Y	Y	Y	Y
Kyl	Y	Y	Y	Y	Y	Y
ARKANSAS						
Hutchinson	?	Y	Y	Y	N	Y
Lincoln	Y	Y	Y	Y	N	Y
CALIFORNIA						
Feinstein	Y	Y	Y	Y	N	Y
Boxer	Y	Y	Y	Y	N	Y
COLORADO						
Campbell	Y	Y	Y	Y	N	Y
Allard	Y	Y	Y	Y	N	Y
CONNECTICUT						
Dodd	?	?	?	?	N	Y
Lieberman	Y	Y	Y	Y	N	Y
DELAWARE						
Carper	Y	Y	Y	Y	N	Y
Biden	Y	Y	Y	Y	N	Y
FLORIDA						
Graham	Y	Y	Y	Y	N	Y
Nelson	Y	Y	Y	Y	N	Y
GEORGIA						
Miller	Y	Y	Y	Y	Y	Y
Cleland	Y	Y	Y	Y	N	Y
HAWAII						
Inouye	N	Y	Y	N	N	Y
Akaka	Y	Y	Y	Y	N	Y
IDAHO						
Craig	?	Y	Y	Y	N	Y
Crapo	Y	Y	Y	Y	N	Y
ILLINOIS						
Durbin	Y	Y	Y	Y	N	Y
Fitzgerald	Y	Y	Y	Y	Y	Y
INDIANA						
Lugar	Y	Y	Y	Y	Y	Y
Bayh	Y	Y	Y	Y	N	Y

	97	98	99	100	101	102
IOWA						
Grassley	Y	Y	Y	Y	Y	Y
Harkin	Y	Y	Y	Y	N	Y
KANSAS						
Brownback	Y	Y	Y	Y	Y	Y
Roberts	Y	Y	Y	Y	N	Y
KENTUCKY						
McConnell	Y	Y	Y	Y	Y	Y
Bunning	N	Y	Y	N	+	+
LOUISIANA						
Breaux	Y	Y	Y	Y	Y	Y
Landrieu	Y	Y	Y	Y	N	Y
MAINE						
Snowe	N	Y	Y	N	N	Y
Collins	Y	Y	Y	Y	N	Y
MARYLAND						
Sarbanes	N	Y	Y	N	N	Y
Mikulski	N	Y	Y	N	N	Y
MASSACHUSETTS						
Kennedy	N	Y	Y	N	N	Y
Kerry	Y	Y	Y	Y	N	Y
MICHIGAN						
Levin	N	Y	Y	N	N	Y
Stabenow	Y	Y	Y	Y	N	Y
MINNESOTA						
Wellstone	N	Y	Y	N	N	Y
Dayton	N	Y	Y	N	N	Y
MISSISSIPPI						
Cochran	Y	Y	Y	Y	Y	Y
Lott	Y	Y	Y	Y	Y	Y
MISSOURI						
Bond	Y	Y	Y	Y	Y	Y
Carnahan	?	Y	Y	Y	N	Y
MONTANA						
Baucus	Y	Y	Y	Y	N	Y
Burns	N	Y	Y	N	N	Y
NEBRASKA						
Nelson	Y	Y	Y	Y	N	Y
Hagel	Y	Y	Y	Y	Y	Y
NEVADA						
Reid	Y	Y	Y	Y	N	Y
Ensign	Y	Y	Y	Y	N	Y

	97	98	99	100	101	102
NEW HAMPSHIRE						
Smith	Y	Y	Y	Y	N	Y
Gregg	Y	Y	Y	N	Y	Y
NEW JERSEY						
Corzine	?	Y	Y	N	N	Y
Torricelli	?	Y	Y	Y	?	?
NEW MEXICO						
Domenici	?	Y	Y	Y	Y	Y
Bingaman	Y	Y	Y	Y	N	Y
NEW YORK						
Clinton	Y	Y	Y	Y	N	Y
Schumer	?	Y	Y	Y	N	Y
NORTH CAROLINA						
Helms	–	+	+	–	–	+
Edwards	Y	Y	Y	Y	N	Y
NORTH DAKOTA						
Conrad	Y	Y	Y	Y	N	Y
Dorgan	N	Y	Y	N	N	Y
OHIO						
DeWine	Y	Y	Y	Y	Y	Y
Voinovich	Y	Y	Y	Y	Y	Y
OKLAHOMA						
Nickles	Y	Y	Y	Y	Y	Y
Inhofe	Y	Y	Y	Y	N	Y
OREGON						
Wyden	Y	Y	Y	Y	N	Y
Smith	Y	Y	Y	Y	N	Y
PENNSYLVANIA						
Specter	Y	Y	Y	Y	N	Y
Santorum	Y	Y	Y	Y	Y	Y
RHODE ISLAND						
Reed	N	Y	Y	N	N	Y
Chafee	Y	Y	Y	Y	Y	Y
SOUTH CAROLINA						
Thurmond	N	Y	Y	N	N	Y
Hollings	N	Y	Y	N	N	N
SOUTH DAKOTA						
Daschle	Y	Y	Y	Y	N	Y
Johnson	Y	Y	Y	Y	N	Y
TENNESSEE						
Thompson	Y	Y	Y	Y	Y	Y
Frist	Y	Y	Y	Y	Y	Y

Key

Y	Voted for (yea).
#	Paired for.
+	Announced for.
N	Voted against (nay).
X	Paired against.
–	Announced against.
P	Voted "present."
C	Voted "present" to avoid possible conflict of interest.
?	Did not vote or otherwise make a position known.

Democrats **Republicans**
Independents

	97	98	99	100	101	102
TEXAS						
Gramm	Y	Y	Y	Y	Y	Y
Hutchison	Y	Y	Y	Y	Y	Y
UTAH						
Hatch	Y	Y	Y	Y	Y	Y
Bennett	Y	Y	Y	Y	?	?
VERMONT						
Leahy	Y	Y	Y	Y	N	Y
Jeffords	Y	Y	Y	Y	N	Y
VIRGINIA						
Warner	N	Y	Y	Y	Y	Y
Allen	N	Y	Y	Y	Y	Y
WASHINGTON						
Cantwell	Y	Y	Y	Y	N	Y
Murray	Y	Y	Y	Y	N	Y
WEST VIRGINIA						
Byrd	N	Y	Y	N	N	N
Rockefeller	N	Y	Y	N	N	Y
WISCONSIN						
Kohl	Y	Y	Y	Y	N	Y
Feingold	N	Y	Y	N	N	Y
WYOMING						
Thomas	Y	Y	Y	Y	N	Y
Enzi	Y	Y	Y	Y	Y	Y

ND Northern Democrats   SD Southern Democrats

Southern states - Ala., Ark., Fla., Ga., Ky., La., Miss., N.C., Okla., S.C., Tenn., Texas, Va.

97. HR 3009. Andean Trade/Cloture. Motion to invoke cloture (thus limiting debate) on the motion to proceed to the bill that would extend duty-free status to certain products from Bolivia, Colombia, Ecuador and Peru. Motion agreed to 69-21: R 36-8; D 32-13 (ND 24-12, SD 8-1); I 1-0. Three-fifths of the total Senate (60) is required to invoke cloture. April 29, 2002.

98. Baylson Nomination/Confirmation. Confirmation of President Bush's nomination of Michael M. Baylson of Pennsylvania to be U.S. district judge for the Eastern District of Pennsylvania. Confirmed 98-0: R 48-0; D 49-0 (ND 40-0, SD 9-0); I 1-0. A "yea" was a vote in support of the president's position. April 30, 2002.

99. Rufe Nomination/Confirmation. Confirmation of President Bush's nomination of Cynthia M. Rufe of Pennsylvania to be U.S. district judge for the Eastern District of Pennsylvania. Confirmed 98-0: R 48-0; D 49-0 (ND 40-0, SD 9-0); I 1-0. A "yea" was a vote in support of the president's position. April 30, 2002.

100. HR 3009. Andean Trade/Motion to Proceed. Motion to proceed to the bill that would extend duty-free status to certain products from Bolivia, Colombia, Ecuador and Peru. Motion agreed to 77-21: R 41-7; D 35-14 (ND 27-13, SD 8-1); I 1-0. May 1, 2002.

101. HR 3009. Andean Trade/NAFTA Tribunals. Reid, D-Nev., motion to table (kill) the Dorgan, D-N.D., amendment to the Daschle, D-S.D., substitute amendment. The Dorgan amendment would require the president to negotiate an amendment to the North American Free Trade Agreement (NAFTA) with Canada and Mexico that would increase transparency regarding NAFTA tribunal settlements. The Daschle amendment would extend duty-free status to certain products from Bolivia, Colombia, Ecuador and Peru, renew the president's fast-track authority, and reauthorize and expand a program to provide retraining and relocation assistance to U.S. workers hurt by trade agreements. It also would create a refundable 73 percent tax credit for health insurance costs for displaced workers. Motion rejected 29-67: R 27-19; D 2-47 (ND 0-40, SD 2-7); I 0-1. May 2, 2002.

102. HR 3009. Andean Trade/Israel Support. Lieberman, D-Conn., amendment to the Dorgan, D-N.D., amendment to the Daschle, D-S.D., substitute amendment. The Lieberman amendment would express that Congress stands in solidarity with Israel, condemns Palestinian suicide bombings and urges all Arab states to oppose all forms of terrorism. Adopted 94-2: R 46-0; D 47-2 (ND 39-1, SD 8-1); I 1-0. May 2, 2002.

ALABAMA	103	104	105	106	107
Shelby	Y	Y	Y	Y	Y
Sessions	Y	Y	Y	Y	Y
ALASKA					
Stevens	Y	Y	Y	Y	Y
Murkowski	Y	Y	Y	Y	Y
ARIZONA					
McCain	N	Y	Y	Y	Y
Kyl	N	Y	Y	Y	Y
ARKANSAS					
Hutchinson	Y	Y	Y	Y	Y
Lincoln	Y	Y	Y	Y	Y
CALIFORNIA					
Feinstein	Y	Y	Y	Y	Y
Boxer	Y	Y	Y	Y	Y
COLORADO					
Campbell	Y	Y	Y	Y	Y
Allard	Y	Y	Y	Y	Y
CONNECTICUT					
Dodd	Y	Y	Y	Y	Y
Lieberman	Y	Y	Y	Y	Y
DELAWARE					
Carper	N	Y	Y	Y	Y
Biden	Y	Y	Y	Y	Y
FLORIDA					
Graham	N	Y	Y	Y	Y
Nelson	N	Y	Y	Y	Y
GEORGIA					
Miller	Y	Y	Y	Y	Y
Cleland	Y	Y	Y	Y	Y
HAWAII					
Inouye	Y	Y	Y	Y	Y
Akaka	Y	Y	Y	Y	Y
IDAHO					
Craig	Y	Y	Y	Y	Y
Crapo	Y	Y	Y	Y	Y
ILLINOIS					
Durbin	Y	Y	Y	Y	Y
Fitzgerald	Y	Y	Y	Y	Y
INDIANA					
Lugar	N	Y	Y	Y	Y
Bayh	Y	Y	Y	Y	Y

IOWA	103	104	105	106	107
Grassley	N	Y	Y	Y	Y
Harkin	Y	Y	Y	Y	Y
KANSAS					
Brownback	N	Y	Y	Y	Y
Roberts	N	Y	Y	Y	Y
KENTUCKY					
McConnell	N	Y	Y	Y	Y
Bunning	N	Y	Y	Y	Y
LOUISIANA					
Breaux	Y	Y	Y	Y	Y
Landrieu	Y	Y	Y	Y	?
MAINE					
Snowe	Y	Y	Y	Y	Y
Collins	N	Y	Y	Y	Y
MARYLAND					
Sarbanes	Y	Y	Y	Y	Y
Mikulski	Y	Y	Y	Y	Y
MASSACHUSETTS					
Kennedy	Y	Y	Y	Y	Y
Kerry	Y	Y	Y	Y	Y
MICHIGAN					
Levin	Y	Y	Y	Y	Y
Stabenow	Y	Y	Y	Y	Y
MINNESOTA					
Wellstone	Y	Y	Y	Y	Y
Dayton	Y	Y	Y	Y	Y
MISSISSIPPI					
Cochran	Y	Y	Y	Y	Y
Lott	Y	Y	Y	Y	Y
MISSOURI					
Bond	Y	Y	Y	Y	Y
Carnahan	Y	Y	Y	Y	Y
MONTANA					
Baucus	Y	Y	Y	Y	Y
Burns	Y	Y	Y	Y	Y
NEBRASKA					
Nelson	Y	Y	Y	Y	Y
Hagel	N	Y	Y	Y	Y
NEVADA					
Reid	Y	Y	Y	Y	Y
Ensign	N	Y	Y	Y	Y

NEW HAMPSHIRE	103	104	105	106	107
Smith	N	Y	Y	Y	Y
Gregg	N	Y	Y	Y	Y
NEW JERSEY					
Corzine	N	?	?	?	?
Torricelli	Y	?	?	?	?
NEW MEXICO					
Domenici	N	Y	Y	Y	Y
Bingaman	N	Y	Y	Y	Y
NEW YORK					
Clinton	Y	Y	Y	Y	Y
Schumer	Y	Y	Y	Y	Y
NORTH CAROLINA					
Helms	–	+	+	+	+
Edwards	Y	Y	Y	Y	Y
NORTH DAKOTA					
Conrad	Y	Y	Y	Y	Y
Dorgan	Y	Y	Y	Y	Y
OHIO					
DeWine	N	Y	Y	Y	Y
Voinovich	N	Y	Y	Y	Y
OKLAHOMA					
Nickles	N	Y	Y	Y	Y
Inhofe	Y	Y	Y	Y	Y
OREGON					
Wyden	Y	?	Y	Y	Y
Smith	Y	Y	Y	Y	Y
PENNSYLVANIA					
Specter	N	Y	Y	Y	Y
Santorum	N	Y	Y	Y	Y
RHODE ISLAND					
Reed	N	Y	Y	Y	Y
Chafee	N	Y	Y	Y	Y
SOUTH CAROLINA					
Thurmond	Y	Y	Y	Y	Y
Hollings	Y	Y	Y	Y	Y
SOUTH DAKOTA					
Daschle	Y	Y	Y	Y	Y
Johnson	Y	Y	Y	Y	Y
TENNESSEE					
Thompson	N	Y	Y	Y	Y
Frist	Y	Y	Y	Y	Y

TEXAS	103	104	105	106	107
Gramm	N	Y	Y	Y	Y
Hutchison	Y	Y	Y	Y	Y
UTAH					
Hatch	N	Y	Y	Y	Y
Bennett	N	Y	Y	Y	Y
VERMONT					
Leahy	Y	Y	Y	Y	Y
Jeffords	Y	Y	Y	Y	?
VIRGINIA					
Warner	N	Y	Y	Y	Y
Allen	N	Y	Y	Y	Y
WASHINGTON					
Cantwell	Y	Y	Y	Y	Y
Murray	Y	Y	Y	Y	Y
WEST VIRGINIA					
Byrd	Y	Y	Y	Y	Y
Rockefeller	Y	Y	Y	Y	Y
WISCONSIN					
Kohl	Y	Y	Y	Y	Y
Feingold	N	Y	Y	Y	Y
WYOMING					
Thomas	N	?	?	?	?
Enzi	N	Y	Y	Y	Y

ND Northern Democrats   SD Southern Democrats

Southern states - Ala., Ark., Fla., Ga., Ky., La., Miss., N.C., Okla., S.C., Tenn., Texas, Va.

103. HR 2646. Farm Bill/Conference Report. Adoption of the conference report on the bill that would reauthorize federal agriculture programs for six years. The agreement would re-establish programs that supply payments to farmers when commodity prices fall below a specified level. It would raise mandatory and direct farm program spending by $73.5 billion over 10 years, provide $243 billion for food stamps and restore benefits for legal immigrants, and increase conservation spending to $17.1 billion. After two years, the agreement would require certain goods to be labeled by country origin. It would lower the total limit on payments to individual farmers to $360,000 and authorize a new $1 billion dairy program for three and a half years. Adopted (thus cleared for the president) 64-35: R 20-28; D 43-7 (ND 36-5, SD 7-2); I 1-0. May 8, 2002.

104. Davis Nomination/Confirmation. Confirmation of President Bush's nomination of Leonard E. Davis of Texas to be U.S. district judge for the Eastern District of Texas. Confirmed 97-0: R 47-0; D 49-0 (ND 40-0, SD 9-0); I 1-0. A "yea" was a vote in support of the president's position. May 9, 2002.

105. Hanen Nomination/Confirmation. Confirmation of President Bush's nomination of Andrew S. Hanen of Texas to be U.S. district judge for the Southern District of Texas. Confirmed 97-0: R 47-0; D 49-0 (ND 40-0, SD 9-0); I 1-0. A "yea" was a vote in support of the president's position. May 9, 2002.

106. Mays Nomination/Confirmation. Confirmation of President Bush's nomination of Samuel H. Mays Jr. of Tennessee to be U.S. district judge for the Western District of Tennessee. Confirmed 97-0: R 47-0; D 49-0 (ND 40-0, SD 9-0); I 1-0. A "yea" was a vote in support of the president's position. May 9, 2002.

107. Rose Nomination/Confirmation. Confirmation of President Bush's nomination of Thomas M. Rose of Ohio to be U.S. district judge for the Southern District of Ohio. Confirmed 95-0: R 47-0; D 48-0 (ND 40-0, SD 8-0); I 0-0. A "yea" was a vote in support of the president's position. May 9, 2002.

	108	109	110	111
ALABAMA				
Shelby	Y	Y	N	Y
Sessions	?	Y	N	Y
ALASKA				
Stevens	Y	Y	Y	Y
Murkowski	Y	Y	Y	N
ARIZONA				
McCain	Y	Y	Y	N
Kyl	Y	Y	Y	N
ARKANSAS				
Hutchinson	Y	Y	Y	N
Lincoln	Y	Y	Y	Y
CALIFORNIA				
Feinstein	Y	Y	N	Y
Boxer	N	Y	N	Y
COLORADO				
Campbell	Y	Y	N	Y
Allard	Y	Y	Y	N
CONNECTICUT				
Dodd	Y	Y	N	Y
Lieberman	?	Y	Y	Y
DELAWARE				
Carper	Y	Y	N	Y
Biden	?	Y	N	Y
FLORIDA				
Graham	Y	Y	N	Y
Nelson	Y	Y	N	Y
GEORGIA				
Miller	?	?	Y	Y
Cleland	Y	Y	N	Y
HAWAII				
Inouye	?	Y	N	Y
Akaka	N	Y	N	Y
IDAHO				
Craig	Y	Y	N	N
Crapo	Y	Y	N	N
ILLINOIS				
Durbin	N	Y	N	Y
Fitzgerald	Y	Y	Y	N
INDIANA				
Lugar	Y	Y	Y	N
Bayh	Y	Y	N	Y

	108	109	110	111
IOWA				
Grassley	Y	Y	Y	Y
Harkin	?	Y	N	Y
KANSAS				
Brownback	Y	Y	Y	N
Roberts	Y	Y	Y	N
KENTUCKY				
McConnell	Y	Y	Y	N
Bunning	Y	Y	N	N
LOUISIANA				
Breaux	Y	Y	Y	Y
Landrieu	?	Y	Y	Y
MAINE				
Snowe	Y	Y	N	Y
Collins	Y	Y	N	Y
MARYLAND				
Sarbanes	N	Y	N	Y
Mikulski	?	Y	N	Y
MASSACHUSETTS				
Kennedy	N	Y	N	Y
Kerry	?	Y	N	Y
MICHIGAN				
Levin	N	Y	N	Y
Stabenow	N	Y	N	Y
MINNESOTA				
Wellstone	N	Y	N	Y
Dayton	N	Y	N	Y
MISSISSIPPI				
Cochran	Y	Y	Y	Y
Lott	Y	Y	Y	N
MISSOURI				
Bond	Y	Y	Y	N
Carnahan	Y	Y	N	Y
MONTANA				
Baucus	Y	Y	Y	Y
Burns	Y	Y	N	N
NEBRASKA				
Nelson	?	Y	N	Y
Hagel	Y	Y	Y	N
NEVADA				
Reid	Y	Y	N	Y
Ensign	Y	Y	Y	N

	108	109	110	111
NEW HAMPSHIRE				
Smith	Y	Y	N	N
Gregg	Y	Y	Y	N
NEW JERSEY				
Corzine	N	Y	N	Y
Torricelli	?	Y	N	Y
NEW MEXICO				
Domenici	Y	Y	Y	N
Bingaman	N	Y	N	Y
NEW YORK				
Clinton	N	Y	N	Y
Schumer	N	Y	N	Y
NORTH CAROLINA				
Helms	+	+	–	+
Edwards	Y	Y	N	Y
NORTH DAKOTA				
Conrad	N	Y	N	Y
Dorgan	Y	Y	N	Y
OHIO				
DeWine	Y	Y	Y	N
Voinovich	Y	Y	Y	N
OKLAHOMA				
Nickles	Y	Y	Y	N
Inhofe	Y	Y	Y	N
OREGON				
Wyden	N	Y	N	Y
Smith	Y	Y	N	Y
PENNSYLVANIA				
Specter	Y	Y	N	N
Santorum	Y	Y	Y	N
RHODE ISLAND				
Reed	N	Y	N	Y
Chafee	Y	Y	Y	Y
SOUTH CAROLINA				
Thurmond	Y	Y	N	Y
Hollings	Y	Y	N	Y
SOUTH DAKOTA				
Daschle	N	Y	N	Y
Johnson	N	Y	N	Y
TENNESSEE				
Thompson	Y	Y	Y	N
Frist	Y	Y	Y	N

	108	109	110	111
TEXAS				
Gramm	Y	Y	Y	N
Hutchison	Y	Y	Y	Y
UTAH				
Hatch	Y	Y	Y	N
Bennett	Y	Y	Y	N
VERMONT				
Leahy	N	Y	N	Y
Jeffords	?	Y	N	Y
VIRGINIA				
Warner	Y	Y	N	Y
Allen	Y	Y	N	Y
WASHINGTON				
Cantwell	Y	Y	N	Y
Murray	Y	Y	N	Y
WEST VIRGINIA				
Byrd	Y	Y	N	Y
Rockefeller	Y	Y	N	Y
WISCONSIN				
Kohl	Y	Y	N	Y
Feingold	N	Y	N	Y
WYOMING				
Thomas	Y	Y	Y	N
Enzi	Y	Y	N	N

Key

Y	Voted for (yea).
#	Paired for.
+	Announced for.
N	Voted against (nay).
X	Paired against.
–	Announced against.
P	Voted "present."
C	Voted "present" to avoid possible conflict of interest.
?	Did not vote or otherwise make a position known.

Democrats   **Republicans**
Independents

ND Northern Democrats   SD Southern Democrats

Southern states - Ala., Ark., Fla., Ga., Ky., La., Miss., N.C., Okla., S.C., Tenn., Texas, Va.

108. Cassell Nomination/Confirmation. Confirmation of President Bush's nomination of Paul G. Cassell of Utah to be U.S. district judge for the District of Utah. Confirmed 67-20: R 47-0; D 20-20 (ND 13-20, SD 7-0); I 0-0. A "yea" was a vote in support of the president's position. May 13, 2002.

109. HR 3009. Andean Trade/Investor Protection. Baucus, D-Mont., amendment to the Baucus substitute amendment. The Baucus amendment would clarify that foreign investors would not be accorded greater legal protection than U.S. investors under the investment provisions of trade agreements. The Baucus substitute would extend duty-free status to certain products from Bolivia, Colombia, Ecuador and Peru, renew the president's fast-track authority and reauthorize and expand a program to provide retraining and relocation assistance to U.S. workers hurt by trade agreements. It also would create a refundable 70 percent tax credit for health insurance costs for displaced workers. Adopted 98-0: R 48-0; D 49-0 (ND 41-0, SD 8-0); I 1-0. May 14, 2002.

110. HR 3009. Andean Trade/Fast-Track Procedures. Reid, D-Nev., motion to table (kill) the Dayton, D-Minn., amendment to the Baucus substitute amendment. The Dayton amendment would establish a point of order in the Senate against any portion of trade agreements that would modify U.S. trade remedy laws. A point of order could be waived with a majority vote. If the point of order was sustained, the portion of the bill would proceed under normal legislative procedure, while the remainder of the agreement would proceed under the expedited procedures set up under fast track. Motion rejected 38-61: R 32-16; D 6-44 (ND 2-39, SD 4-5); I 0-1. (Subsequently, the Dayton amendment was adopted by voice vote.) A "yea" was a vote in support of the president's position. May 14, 2002.

111. HR 3009. Andean Trade/Textile Trading Authority. Edwards, D-N.C., amendment to the Baucus, D-Mont., substitute amendment. The Edwards amendment would outline additional trade negotiating objectives regarding textiles and establish a grant program for community colleges that provide training programs for displaced workers. Adopted 66-33: R 15-33; D 50-0 (ND 41-0, SD 9-0); I 1-0. May 15, 2002.

Key

Y	Voted for (yea).
#	Paired for.
+	Announced for.
N	Voted against (nay).
X	Paired against.
–	Announced against.
P	Voted "present."
C	Voted "present" to avoid possible conflict of interest.
?	Did not vote or otherwise make a position known.

Democrats   **Republicans**
Independents

	112	113	114	115
ALABAMA				
Shelby	Y	Y	Y	Y
Sessions	Y	Y	N	Y
ALASKA				
Stevens	Y	Y	N	Y
Murkowski	Y	Y	?	?
ARIZONA				
McCain	Y	Y	N	Y
Kyl	Y	Y	N	Y
ARKANSAS				
Hutchinson	Y	Y	N	Y
Lincoln	Y	Y	Y	N
CALIFORNIA				
Feinstein	N	N	Y	N
Boxer	N	N	Y	N
COLORADO				
Campbell	Y	Y	N	Y
Allard	Y	Y	N	Y
CONNECTICUT				
Dodd	N	N	Y	N
Lieberman	N	Y	Y	N
DELAWARE				
Carper	N	Y	Y	N
Biden	N	Y	Y	N
FLORIDA				
Graham	Y	Y	Y	N
Nelson	N	Y	Y	N
GEORGIA				
Miller	Y	Y	Y	Y
Cleland	N	Y	Y	N
HAWAII				
Inouye	Y	Y	Y	N
Akaka	N	N	Y	N
IDAHO				
Craig	Y	Y	N	Y
Crapo	Y	Y	N	Y
ILLINOIS				
Durbin	N	N	Y	N
Fitzgerald	Y	Y	N	Y
INDIANA				
Lugar	Y	Y	N	Y
Bayh	N	Y	Y	N

	112	113	114	115
IOWA				
Grassley	Y	Y	Y	Y
Harkin	N	N	Y	N
KANSAS				
Brownback	Y	Y	N	Y
Roberts	Y	Y	N	Y
KENTUCKY				
McConnell	Y	Y	N	Y
Bunning	Y	Y	N	Y
LOUISIANA				
Breaux	Y	Y	Y	Y
Landrieu	N	Y	Y	N
MAINE				
Snowe	Y	Y	Y	Y
Collins	Y	Y	N	Y
MARYLAND				
Sarbanes	N	N	Y	N
Mikulski	N	N	Y	N
MASSACHUSETTS				
Kennedy	N	N	Y	N
Kerry	N	N	Y	N
MICHIGAN				
Levin	N	N	Y	N
Stabenow	N	N	Y	N
MINNESOTA				
Wellstone	N	N	Y	N
Dayton	N	N	Y	N
MISSISSIPPI				
Cochran	Y	Y	N	Y
Lott	Y	Y	?	Y
MISSOURI				
Bond	Y	Y	N	Y
Carnahan	N	N	Y	N
MONTANA				
Baucus	Y	Y	Y	Y
Burns	Y	Y	N	Y
NEBRASKA				
Nelson	Y	Y	Y	Y
Hagel	Y	Y	N	Y
NEVADA				
Reid	N	N	Y	N
Ensign	Y	Y	N	Y

	112	113	114	115
NEW HAMPSHIRE				
Smith	Y	Y	N	Y
Gregg	Y	Y	N	Y
NEW JERSEY				
Corzine	N	N	Y	N
Torricelli	N	N	Y	N
NEW MEXICO				
Domenici	Y	Y	N	Y
Bingaman	N	Y	Y	N
NEW YORK				
Clinton	N	N	Y	N
Schumer	N	N	Y	N
NORTH CAROLINA				
Helms	+	+	?	?
Edwards	N	Y	Y	N
NORTH DAKOTA				
Conrad	N	N	N	N
Dorgan	N	N	Y	N
OHIO				
DeWine	Y	Y	Y	Y
Voinovich	Y	Y	Y	Y
OKLAHOMA				
Nickles	Y	Y	N	Y
Inhofe	Y	Y	N	Y
OREGON				
Wyden	N	Y	Y	N
Smith	Y	Y	Y	Y
PENNSYLVANIA				
Specter	Y	Y	Y	Y
Santorum	Y	Y	N	Y
RHODE ISLAND				
Reed	N	N	Y	N
Chafee	Y	Y	Y	Y
SOUTH CAROLINA				
Thurmond	Y	Y	N	Y
Hollings	N	N	Y	N
SOUTH DAKOTA				
Daschle	N	N	Y	N
Johnson	N	N	Y	N
TENNESSEE				
Thompson	Y	Y	N	Y
Frist	Y	Y	N	Y

	112	113	114	115
TEXAS				
Gramm	Y	Y	Y	Y
Hutchison	Y	Y	N	Y
UTAH				
Hatch	Y	Y	N	Y
Bennett	Y	Y	N	Y
VERMONT				
Leahy	N	N	Y	N
Jeffords	N	Y	Y	N
VIRGINIA				
Warner	?	Y	–	Y
Allen	Y	Y	N	Y
WASHINGTON				
Cantwell	N	Y	N	Y
Murray	N	Y	Y	N
WEST VIRGINIA				
Byrd	N	N	Y	N
Rockefeller	N	N	Y	N
WISCONSIN				
Kohl	N	Y	Y	N
Feingold	N	N	Y	N
WYOMING				
Thomas	Y	Y	N	Y
Enzi	Y	Y	N	Y

ND Northern Democrats   SD Southern Democrats

Southern states - Ala., Ark., Fla., Ga., Ky., La., Miss., N.C., Okla., S.C., Tenn., Texas, Va.

112. HR 3009. Andean Trade/Retaliatory Action. Baucus, D-Mont., motion to table (kill) the Lieberman, D-Conn., amendment to the Baucus substitute amendment. The Lieberman amendment would strike a provision in the underlying substitute that would prohibit legal retaliatory action based on a decision by a government that does not comply with domestic labor standards and environmental protection provisions agreed to in trade agreements. Motion agreed to 54-44: R 47-0; D 7-43 (ND 3-38, SD 4-5); I 0-1. A "yea" was a vote in support of the president's position. May 15, 2002.

113. HR 3009. Andean Trade/Trade Negotiating Authority. Baucus, D-Mont., motion to table (kill) the Durbin, D-Ill., amendment to the Baucus substitute amendment. The Durbin amendment would change the trade negotiating authority in the underlying substitute. The amendment would require that preserving trade laws be the principal objective of U.S. negotiations. It also would provide equal status to the enforcement of labor and environmental provisions compared to all other provisions in the agreement, provide for a biennial review of negotiations and allow for an opportunity for a disapproval resolution once each Congress. Motion agreed to 69-30: R 48-0; D 20-30 (ND 12-29, SD 8-1); I 1-0. A "yea" was a vote in support of the president's position. May 15, 2002.

114. HR 3009. Andean Trade/Wage Insurance. Baucus, D-Mont., motion to table (kill) the Gregg, R-N.H., amendment to the Baucus substitute amendment. The Gregg amendment would strike the wage insurance provisions in the underlying substitute that would require the Labor Secretary to establish a wage insurance pilot program for older workers within one year. Motion agreed to 58-38: R 9-36; D 48-2 (ND 39-2, SD 9-0); I 1-0. May 16, 2002.

115. HR 3009. Andean Trade/Labor and Environmental Standards. Grassley, R-Iowa, motion to table (kill) the Dodd, D-Conn., amendment to the Baucus, D-Mont., substitute amendment. The Dodd amendment would clarify the principal negotiating objectives with respect to labor and the environmental standards. Motion agreed to 52-46: R 47-0; D 5-45 (ND 3-38, SD 2-7); I 0-1. A "yea" was a vote in support of the president's position. May 16, 2002.

	116	117	118	119	120
ALABAMA					
Shelby	Y	Y	N	N	Y
Sessions	Y	N	N	N	Y
ALASKA					
Stevens	N	N	N	Y	Y
Murkowski	?	N	N	Y	Y
ARIZONA					
McCain	?	N	N	Y	Y
Kyl	Y	N	N	Y	Y
ARKANSAS					
Hutchinson	?	?	?	?	?
Lincoln	Y	Y	Y	Y	Y
CALIFORNIA					
Feinstein	Y	Y	Y	N	Y
Boxer	Y	Y	Y	N	Y
COLORADO					
Campbell	Y	Y	N	Y	Y
Allard	Y	N	N	Y	Y
CONNECTICUT					
Dodd	Y	Y	Y	N	Y
Lieberman	Y	Y	Y	N	Y
DELAWARE					
Carper	Y	Y	Y	N	Y
Biden	Y	Y	Y	N	Y
FLORIDA					
Graham	Y	Y	Y	N	Y
Nelson	Y	Y	Y	Y	Y
GEORGIA					
Miller	?	?	Y	N	Y
Cleland	Y	Y	Y	N	Y
HAWAII					
Inouye	Y	Y	Y	Y	Y
Akaka	Y	Y	Y	N	Y
IDAHO					
Craig	N	N	N	Y	Y
Crapo	Y	N	N	Y	Y
ILLINOIS					
Durbin	Y	Y	Y	N	Y
Fitzgerald	Y	N	N	N	Y
INDIANA					
Lugar	Y	Y	N	Y	Y
Bayh	Y	Y	Y	N	Y

	116	117	118	119	120
IOWA					
Grassley	Y	N	Y	Y	Y
Harkin	Y	Y	?	N	Y
KANSAS					
Brownback	Y	N	Y	Y	Y
Roberts	N	N	N	Y	Y
KENTUCKY					
McConnell	Y	N	N	Y	Y
Bunning	Y	Y	N	N	Y
LOUISIANA					
Breaux	Y	Y	N	Y	Y
Landrieu	Y	Y	Y	N	Y
MAINE					
Snowe	Y	N	Y	N	Y
Collins	Y	N	N	N	Y
MARYLAND					
Sarbanes	Y	Y	Y	N	Y
Mikulski	Y	Y	Y	N	Y
MASSACHUSETTS					
Kennedy	Y	Y	Y	N	Y
Kerry	Y	Y	?	N	Y
MICHIGAN					
Levin	Y	Y	Y	N	Y
Stabenow	Y	Y	Y	N	Y
MINNESOTA					
Wellstone	Y	Y	Y	N	Y
Dayton	Y	Y	Y	N	Y
MISSISSIPPI					
Cochran	Y	N	Y	Y	Y
Lott	Y	N	N	Y	Y
MISSOURI					
Bond	Y	N	N	Y	Y
Carnahan	Y	Y	Y	N	Y
MONTANA					
Baucus	Y	Y	Y	Y	Y
Burns	Y	N	N	Y	Y
NEBRASKA					
Nelson	Y	N	Y	Y	Y
Hagel	Y	N	Y	Y	Y
NEVADA					
Reid	Y	Y	Y	Y	Y
Ensign	Y	N	N	Y	Y

	116	117	118	119	120
NEW HAMPSHIRE					
Smith	N	N	N	Y	Y
Gregg	?	N	Y	Y	?
NEW JERSEY					
Corzine	Y	Y	Y	N	Y
Torricelli	Y	Y	Y	Y	Y
NEW MEXICO					
Domenici	?	N	Y	Y	Y
Bingaman	Y	Y	Y	N	Y
NEW YORK					
Clinton	Y	Y	Y	N	Y
Schumer	Y	Y	Y	N	Y
NORTH CAROLINA					
Helms	?	?	?	?	?
Edwards	Y	Y	Y	N	Y
NORTH DAKOTA					
Conrad	–	Y	Y	Y	Y
Dorgan	Y	Y	Y	N	Y
OHIO					
DeWine	Y	Y	N	N	Y
Voinovich	Y	Y	Y	Y	Y
OKLAHOMA					
Nickles	Y	N	N	Y	Y
Inhofe	N	?	?	Y	Y
OREGON					
Wyden	Y	Y	Y	Y	Y
Smith	Y	N	N	Y	Y
PENNSYLVANIA					
Specter	Y	Y	N	N	Y
Santorum	Y	N	N	Y	Y
RHODE ISLAND					
Reed	Y	Y	?	N	Y
Chafee	Y	N	Y	Y	Y
SOUTH CAROLINA					
Thurmond	Y	N	N	N	Y
Hollings	Y	Y	Y	N	Y
SOUTH DAKOTA					
Daschle	Y	Y	Y	Y	Y
Johnson	Y	Y	Y	N	Y
TENNESSEE					
Thompson	Y	N	?	Y	?
Frist	Y	N	N	Y	Y

Key

Y	Voted for (yea).
#	Paired for.
+	Announced for.
N	Voted against (nay).
X	Paired against.
–	Announced against.
P	Voted "present."
C	Voted "present" to avoid possible conflict of interest.
?	Did not vote or otherwise make a position known.

Democrats **Republicans**
Independents

	116	117	118	119	120
TEXAS					
Gramm	Y	N	Y	Y	Y
Hutchison	Y	N	N	Y	Y
UTAH					
Hatch	Y	N	Y	Y	Y
Bennett	Y	N	N	Y	Y
VERMONT					
Leahy	Y	Y	Y	N	Y
Jeffords	Y	Y	Y	Y	Y
VIRGINIA					
Warner	N	N	N	Y	Y
Allen	Y	N	N	N	Y
WASHINGTON					
Cantwell	Y	Y	Y	N	Y
Murray	Y	Y	Y	N	Y
WEST VIRGINIA					
Byrd	Y	Y	Y	Y	Y
Rockefeller	Y	Y	Y	N	Y
WISCONSIN					
Kohl	Y	Y	Y	N	Y
Feingold	Y	Y	Y	N	Y
WYOMING					
Thomas	Y	N	N	Y	Y
Enzi	?	N	N	Y	Y

ND Northern Democrats   SD Southern Democrats

Southern states - Ala., Ark., Fla., Ga., Ky., La., Miss., N.C., Okla., S.C., Tenn., Texas, Va.

116. HR 3167. NATO Expansion/Passage. Passage of the bill that would support further expansion of the North Atlantic Treaty Organization, authorize military assistance to several eastern European countries and lift assistance restrictions on Slovakia. Passed 85-6: R 36-6; D 48-0 (ND 40-0, SD 8-0); I 1-0. May 17, 2002.

117. HR 3009. Andean Trade/Cloture. Motion to invoke cloture (thus limiting debate) on the Rockefeller, D-W.Va., amendment to the Baucus, D-Mont., substitute amendment. The Rockefeller amendment would allow retired steelworkers and certain beneficiaries to be eligible for a 70 percent tax credit for assistance with health insurance costs for one year. The Baucus substitute would extend duty-free status to certain products from Bolivia, Colombia, Ecuador and Peru, renew the president's fast-track authority, and reauthorize and expand a program to provide retraining and relocation assistance to U.S. workers hurt by trade agreements. It also would create a refundable 70 percent tax credit for health insurance costs for displaced workers. Motion rejected 56-40: R 7-39; D 48-1 (ND 40-1, SD 8-0); I 1-0. Three-fifths of the total Senate (60) is required to invoke cloture. May 21, 2002.

118. Procedural Motion/Require Attendance. Reid, D-Nev., motion to instruct the sergeant at arms to request the attendance of absent senators. Motion agreed to 58-35: R 11-34; D 46-1 (ND 38-0, SD 8-1); I 1-0. May 21, 2002.

119. HR 3009. Andean Trade/Mortgage Assistance. Baucus, D-Mont., motion to table (kill) the Allen, R-Va., amendment to the Baucus substitute amendment. The Allen amendment would require the Labor Department to establish a pilot program that would provide low-interest loans to displaced workers to enable them to make monthly mortgage payments on their primary residence. Motion agreed to, with Vice President Cheney casting a "yea" vote, 49-49: R 36-11; D 12-38 (ND 9-32, SD 3-6); I 1-0. A "yea" was a vote in support of the president's position. May 21, 2002.

120. HR 3009. Andean Trade/Anti-Terrorism Support. Hutchison, R-Texas, amendment to the Baucus, D-Mont., substitute amendment. The Hutchison amendment would specify that to be eligible for U.S. trade preferences, a country must support U.S. efforts to combat terrorism. Adopted 96-0: R 45-0; D 50-0 (ND 41-0, SD 9-0); I 1-0. May 21, 2002.

	121	122	123	124	125
ALABAMA					
Shelby	Y	N	Y	Y	Y
Sessions	Y	N	Y	Y	Y
ALASKA					
Stevens	Y	Y	Y	Y	Y
Murkowski	Y	Y	Y	Y	Y
ARIZONA					
McCain	Y	Y	Y	Y	Y
Kyl	Y	Y	Y	Y	Y
ARKANSAS					
Hutchinson	?	Y	Y	Y	Y
Lincoln	Y	Y	Y	Y	Y
CALIFORNIA					
Feinstein	Y	Y	N	Y	N
Boxer	N	N	N	Y	N
COLORADO					
Campbell	Y	Y	Y	Y	Y
Allard	Y	Y	Y	Y	Y
CONNECTICUT					
Dodd	N	N	N	Y	N
Lieberman	N	Y	N	Y	Y
DELAWARE					
Carper	Y	Y	Y	Y	Y
Biden	N	Y	Y	Y	Y
FLORIDA					
Graham	Y	Y	N	Y	Y
Nelson	N	Y	N	Y	N
GEORGIA					
Miller	Y	Y	Y	Y	Y
Cleland	N	Y	N	Y	N
HAWAII					
Inouye	N	?	?	?	?
Akaka	N	Y	N	Y	Y
IDAHO					
Craig	Y	Y	Y	Y	Y
Crapo	Y	Y	Y	Y	Y
ILLINOIS					
Durbin	N	N	N	Y	Y
Fitzgerald	Y	Y	Y	Y	Y
INDIANA					
Lugar	Y	Y	Y	Y	Y
Bayh	N	Y	N	Y	Y

	121	122	123	124	125
IOWA					
Grassley	Y	Y	Y	Y	Y
Harkin	N	N	N	Y	N
KANSAS					
Brownback	Y	Y	Y	Y	Y
Roberts	Y	Y	Y	Y	Y
KENTUCKY					
McConnell	Y	Y	Y	Y	Y
Bunning	Y	Y	Y	Y	Y
LOUISIANA					
Breaux	Y	Y	Y	Y	Y
Landrieu	Y	Y	Y	Y	N
MAINE					
Snowe	Y	Y	Y	Y	Y
Collins	N	Y	Y	Y	Y
MARYLAND					
Sarbanes	N	N	N	Y	N
Mikulski	N	N	N	Y	N
MASSACHUSETTS					
Kennedy	N	N	N	Y	N
Kerry	N	N	N	Y	N
MICHIGAN					
Levin	N	N	N	Y	N
Stabenow	N	N	N	Y	N
MINNESOTA					
Wellstone	N	N	N	Y	N
Dayton	N	N	N	Y	N
MISSISSIPPI					
Cochran	Y	Y	Y	Y	Y
Lott	Y	Y	Y	Y	Y
MISSOURI					
Bond	Y	Y	Y	Y	Y
Carnahan	N	N	N	Y	N
MONTANA					
Baucus	Y	Y	Y	Y	Y
Burns	Y	Y	Y	Y	Y
NEBRASKA					
Nelson	Y	Y	Y	Y	Y
Hagel	Y	Y	Y	Y	Y
NEVADA					
Reid	N	N	N	Y	N
Ensign	Y	N	Y	Y	Y

	121	122	123	124	125
NEW HAMPSHIRE					
Smith	Y	Y	Y	Y	Y
Gregg	?	Y	Y	Y	Y
NEW JERSEY					
Corzine	N	N	N	Y	N
Torricelli	N	–	N	Y	N
NEW MEXICO					
Domenici	?	Y	Y	Y	Y
Bingaman	Y	Y	Y	Y	Y
NEW YORK					
Clinton	N	N	N	Y	N
Schumer	N	N	N	Y	N
NORTH CAROLINA					
Helms	?	–	?	?	?
Edwards	N	Y	N	Y	N
NORTH DAKOTA					
Conrad	N	N	N	Y	N
Dorgan	N	N	N	Y	N
OHIO					
DeWine	Y	Y	Y	Y	Y
Voinovich	Y	Y	Y	Y	Y
OKLAHOMA					
Nickles	Y	Y	Y	Y	Y
Inhofe	Y	Y	Y	Y	Y
OREGON					
Wyden	N	Y	N	Y	N
Smith	Y	Y	Y	Y	Y
PENNSYLVANIA					
Specter	Y	N	Y	Y	Y
Santorum	Y	Y	Y	Y	Y
RHODE ISLAND					
Reed	N	N	N	Y	N
Chafee	Y	Y	Y	Y	Y
SOUTH CAROLINA					
Thurmond	Y	N	Y	Y	Y
Hollings	N	N	N	Y	N
SOUTH DAKOTA					
Daschle	N	Y	N	Y	N
Johnson	N	Y	N	Y	N
TENNESSEE					
Thompson	Y	Y	Y	Y	Y
Frist	Y	Y	Y	Y	Y

	121	122	123	124	125
TEXAS					
Gramm	Y	Y	Y	Y	Y
Hutchison	Y	Y	Y	Y	Y
UTAH					
Hatch	Y	Y	Y	Y	Y
Bennett	Y	Y	Y	Y	Y
VERMONT					
Leahy	N	N	N	Y	N
Jeffords	N	Y	N	Y	Y
VIRGINIA					
Warner	Y	Y	Y	Y	Y
Allen	Y	Y	Y	Y	Y
WASHINGTON					
Cantwell	Y	Y	Y	Y	Y
Murray	N	Y	N	Y	Y
WEST VIRGINIA					
Byrd	N	N	N	Y	N
Rockefeller	N	N	N	Y	Y
WISCONSIN					
Kohl	N	Y	Y	Y	Y
Feingold	N	N	N	Y	N
WYOMING					
Thomas	Y	Y	Y	Y	Y
Enzi	Y	Y	Y	Y	Y

Key

Y	Voted for (yea).
#	Paired for.
+	Announced for.
N	Voted against (nay).
X	Paired against.
–	Announced against.
P	Voted "present."
C	Voted "present" to avoid possible conflict of interest.
?	Did not vote or otherwise make a position known.

Democrats **Republicans**
Independents

ND Northern Democrats   SD Southern Democrats

Southern states - Ala., Ark., Fla., Ga., Ky., La., Miss., N.C., Okla., S.C., Tenn., Texas, Va.

121. HR 3009. Andean Trade/Foreign Investment. Baucus, D-Mont., motion to table (kill) the Kerry, D-Mass., amendment to the Baucus substitute amendment. The Kerry amendment would make it more difficult for foreign trading partners to win trade disputes claiming compensation for U.S. laws they consider trade barriers. Motion agreed to 55-41: R 44-1; D 11-39 (ND 6-35, SD 5-4); I 0-1. A "yea" was a vote in support of the president's position. May 21, 2002.

122. HR 3009. Andean Trade/Cloture. Motion to invoke cloture (thus limiting debate) on the Baucus, D-Mont., substitute amendment. Motion agreed to 68-29: R 43-5; D 24-24 (ND 16-23, SD 8-1); I 1-0. Three-fifths of the total Senate (60) is required to invoke cloture. May 22, 2002.

123. HR 3009. Andean Trade/Tariff Reduction. Baucus, D-Mont., motion to table (kill) the Nelson, D-Fla., amendment to the Baucus substitute amendment. The Nelson amendment would prohibit the reduction of tariffs on commodities that are the subject of an anti-dumping order or a countervailing duty order. Motion agreed to 60-38: R 48-0; D 12-37 (ND 8-32, SD 4-5); I 0-1. A "yea" was a vote in support of the president's position. May 22, 2002.

124. HR 3448. Bioterrorism Preparedness/Conference Report. Adoption of the conference report on the bill that would authorize federal, state and local governments to spend up to $4.2 billion in fiscal 2003, and additional amounts in future years, to prepare for and respond to acts of bioterrorism. The bill includes funds to increase medicine and vaccine stockpiles, expand facilities and laboratories run by the Centers for Disease Control and Prevention and safeguard the nation's food and water supplies. It also would mandate new requirements on biological agents and reauthorize through fiscal 2007 the Food and Drug Administration user fee system that supports drug approval reviews. Adopted (thus cleared for the president) 98-0: R 48-0; D 49-0 (ND 40-0; SD 9-0); I 1-0. May 23, 2002.

125. HR 3009. Andean Trade/Congressional Oversight Group. Nickles, R-Okla., motion to table (kill) the Byrd, D-W.Va., amendment to the Baucus, D-Mont., substitute amendment. The Byrd amendment would alter the composition of the proposed congressional oversight group to include 11 members from each chamber who are not on the Senate Finance or House Ways and Means committees. Motion agreed to 66-32: R 48-0; D 17-32 (ND 13-27, SD 4-5); I 1-0. May 23, 2002.

	126	127	128	129	130
ALABAMA					
Shelby	Y	?	?	?	?
Sessions	Y	Y	N	Y	N
ALASKA					
Stevens	Y	Y	N	Y	Y
Murkowski	Y	Y	N	Y	Y
ARIZONA					
McCain	Y	Y	N	Y	Y
Kyl	Y	Y	N	Y	Y
ARKANSAS					
Hutchinson	Y	Y	N	N	Y
Lincoln	Y	Y	Y	N	Y
CALIFORNIA					
Feinstein	Y	N	Y	N	Y
Boxer	N	N	Y	N	N
COLORADO					
Campbell	Y	Y	N	Y	N
Allard	Y	Y	N	Y	Y
CONNECTICUT					
Dodd	N	N	Y	N	N
Lieberman	Y	N	Y	?	Y
DELAWARE					
Carper	N	N	Y	N	Y
Biden	N	N	Y	N	Y
FLORIDA					
Graham	Y	N	Y	N	Y
Nelson	N	N	Y	N	Y
GEORGIA					
Miller	Y	Y	N	Y	Y
Cleland	Y	Y	N	Y	Y
HAWAII					
Inouye	?	?	?	?	?
Akaka	N	N	Y	N	N
IDAHO					
Craig	Y	Y	N	Y	Y
Crapo	Y	Y	N	Y	Y
ILLINOIS					
Durbin	N	N	Y	N	N
Fitzgerald	Y	Y	N	N	Y
INDIANA					
Lugar	Y	Y	N	Y	Y
Bayh	N	N	Y	N	Y
IOWA					
Grassley	Y	Y	N	Y	Y
Harkin	Y	N	Y	N	Y
KANSAS					
Brownback	Y	?	?	?	?
Roberts	Y	Y	N	Y	Y
KENTUCKY					
McConnell	Y	Y	N	Y	Y
Bunning	Y	Y	N	Y	Y
LOUISIANA					
Breaux	Y	Y	Y	Y	Y
Landrieu	N	N	Y	N	Y
MAINE					
Snowe	Y	N	Y	N	Y
Collins	Y	N	N	N	Y
MARYLAND					
Sarbanes	N	N	Y	N	N
Mikulski	N	N	Y	N	N
MASSACHUSETTS					
Kennedy	N	N	Y	N	N
Kerry	N	N	Y	N	N
MICHIGAN					
Levin	N	N	Y	N	N
Stabenow	N	N	Y	N	N
MINNESOTA					
Wellstone	N	N	Y	N	N
Dayton	N	N	Y	N	Y
MISSISSIPPI					
Cochran	Y	Y	N	Y	Y
Lott	Y	Y	N	Y	Y
MISSOURI					
Bond	Y	Y	N	Y	Y
Carnahan	N	N	Y	N	N
MONTANA					
Baucus	Y	Y	Y	Y	Y
Burns	Y	Y	N	Y	Y
NEBRASKA					
Nelson	Y	Y	N	Y	Y
Hagel	Y	Y	N	Y	Y
NEVADA					
Reid	N	N	Y	N	N
Ensign	Y	Y	N	Y	N
NEW HAMPSHIRE					
Smith	Y	Y	N	Y	Y
Gregg	Y	Y	N	Y	N
NEW JERSEY					
Corzine	N	N	Y	N	N
Torricelli	Y	N	Y	N	N
NEW MEXICO					
Domenici	Y	Y	N	Y	Y
Bingaman	Y	Y	Y	Y	Y
NEW YORK					
Clinton	N	N	Y	N	N
Schumer	N	N	Y	N	N
NORTH CAROLINA					
Helms	?	?	?	?	?
Edwards	N	N	Y	N	Y
NORTH DAKOTA					
Conrad	N	N	Y	N	N
Dorgan	N	N	Y	N	N
OHIO					
DeWine	Y	Y	N	Y	Y
Voinovich	Y	Y	N	Y	Y
OKLAHOMA					
Nickles	Y	Y	N	Y	Y
Inhofe	Y	Y	N	Y	Y
OREGON					
Wyden	Y	N	Y	N	Y
Smith	Y	N	N	N	Y
PENNSYLVANIA					
Specter	Y	Y	N	Y	N
Santorum	Y	Y	Y	Y	Y
RHODE ISLAND					
Reed	N	N	Y	N	N
Chafee	Y	Y	N	Y	Y
SOUTH CAROLINA					
Thurmond	Y	Y	N	Y	N
Hollings	N	N	Y	N	N
SOUTH DAKOTA					
Daschle	Y	N	N	N	Y
Johnson	N	N	Y	N	N
TENNESSEE					
Thompson	Y	Y	N	Y	Y
Frist	Y	Y	N	Y	Y
TEXAS					
Gramm	Y	Y	N	Y	N
Hutchison	Y	Y	Y	Y	Y
UTAH					
Hatch	Y	Y	N	Y	Y
Bennett	Y	Y	N	Y	Y
VERMONT					
Leahy	N	N	Y	N	N
Jeffords	Y	N	Y	N	Y
VIRGINIA					
Warner	Y	Y	N	Y	Y
Allen	Y	Y	N	Y	Y
WASHINGTON					
Cantwell	Y	N	Y	N	Y
Murray	Y	N	Y	N	Y
WEST VIRGINIA					
Byrd	N	N	Y	N	N
Rockefeller	N	N	Y	N	N
WISCONSIN					
Kohl	Y	N	Y	N	Y
Feingold	N	N	N	N	N
WYOMING					
Thomas	Y	Y	N	Y	Y
Enzi	Y	Y	N	Y	Y

Key

Y Voted for (yea).
Paired for.
+ Announced for.
N Voted against (nay).
X Paired against.
– Announced against.
P Voted "present."
C Voted "present" to avoid possible conflict of interest.
? Did not vote or otherwise make a position known.

Democrats **Republicans**
Independents

ND Northern Democrats   SD Southern Democrats

Southern states - Ala., Ark., Fla., Ga., Ky., La., Miss., N.C., Okla., S.C., Tenn., Texas, Va.

126. HR 3009. Andean Trade/Disapproval Resolution. Grassley, R-Iowa, motion to table (kill) the Byrd, D-W.Va., amendment to the Baucus, D-Mont., substitute amendment. The Byrd amendment would create procedures under which any resolution of disapproval against a trade agreement introduced in the Senate would come to the floor for a vote. Motion agreed to 66-32: R 48-0; D 18-31 (ND 13-27, SD 5-4); I 0-1. May 23, 2002.

127. HR 3009. Andean Trade/Privatization. Grassley, R-Iowa, motion to table (kill) the Corzine, D-N.J., amendment to the Baucus, D-Mont., substitute amendment. The Corzine amendment would provide that trade agreements should not include a commitment to privatize significant government services. Motion agreed to 49-47: R 43-3; D 6-43 (ND 3-37, SD 3-6); I 0-1. A "yea" was a vote in support of the president's position. May 23, 2002.

128. HR 3009. Andean Trade/Maritime Workers. Landrieu, D-La., motion to waive the Budget Act with respect to the Gramm, R-Texas, point of order against the Landrieu amendment to the Baucus, D-Mont., substitute amendment. The Landrieu amendment would require the Labor secretary to establish a program to provide assistance to certain maritime workers displaced as a result of tariffs imposed on steel imports. Motion rejected 50-46: R 4-42; D 45-4 (ND 37-3, SD 8-1); I 1-0. A three-fifths majority vote (60) of the total

Senate is required to waive the Budget Act. A "nay" was a vote in support of the president's position. May 23, 2002.

129. HR 3009. Andean Trade/Human Rights. Baucus, D-Mont., motion to table (kill) the Wellstone, D-Minn., amendment to the Baucus substitute amendment. The Wellstone amendment would insert a provision that states that the principal negotiating objective regarding human rights and democracy is to require trading partners to strive to protect internationally recognized civil, political and human rights. Motion rejected 42-53: R 39-7; D 3-45 (ND 1-38, SD 2-7); I 0-1. (Subsequently, the Wellstone amendment was adopted by voice vote.) May 23, 2002.

130. HR 3009. Andean Trade/Passage. Passage of the bill that would extend duty-free status to certain products from Bolivia, Colombia, Ecuador and Peru, renew the president's fast-track authority and reauthorize and expand a program to provide retraining and relocation assistance to U.S. workers hurt by trade agreements. It also would create a refundable 70 percent tax credit for health insurance costs for displaced workers, and authorize a five-year extension of the Generalized System of Preferences. Passed 66-30: R 41-5; D 24-25 (ND 16-24, SD 8-1); I 1-0. (Before passage, the Senate adopted the Baucus substitute amendment, as amended, by voice vote.) A "yea" was a vote in support of the president's position. May 23, 2002.

	131	132	133	134	135	136	137	138
ALABAMA								
Shelby	Y	N	Y	Y	Y	Y	Y	Y
Sessions	Y	N	Y	Y	N	N	N	N
ALASKA								
Stevens	Y	N	N	Y	Y	Y	Y	Y
Murkowski	?	N	Y	Y	Y	Y	Y	Y
ARIZONA								
McCain	Y	N	Y	Y	N	N	N	N
Kyl	Y	N	Y	Y	N	N	N	N
ARKANSAS								
Hutchinson	Y	N	Y	Y	Y	N	N	N
Lincoln	Y	Y	N	Y	Y	Y	Y	Y
CALIFORNIA								
Feinstein	Y	Y	N	Y	Y	Y	Y	Y
Boxer	Y	Y	N	Y	Y	Y	Y	Y
COLORADO								
Campbell	Y	N	N	Y	Y	Y	Y	Y
Allard	Y	N	Y	Y	Y	N	N	Y
CONNECTICUT								
Dodd	Y	Y	N	Y	Y	Y	Y	Y
Lieberman	Y	Y	Y	Y	Y	Y	Y	Y
DELAWARE								
Carper	Y	N	Y	Y	Y	Y	Y	Y
Biden	Y	Y	N	Y	Y	Y	Y	Y
FLORIDA								
Graham	Y	N	Y	Y	Y	Y	Y	Y
Nelson	Y	Y	N	Y	Y	Y	Y	Y
GEORGIA								
Miller	Y	N	Y	Y	Y	Y	Y	Y
Cleland	Y	N	Y	Y	Y	Y	Y	Y
HAWAII								
Inouye	?	N	N	Y	Y	Y	Y	Y
Akaka	Y	Y	N	Y	Y	Y	Y	Y
IDAHO								
Craig	Y	N	Y	Y	Y	N	N	Y
Crapo	Y	N	Y	Y	Y	Y	N	N
ILLINOIS								
Durbin	Y	Y	N	Y	Y	Y	Y	Y
Fitzgerald	N	N	Y	Y	N	N	N	N
INDIANA								
Lugar	Y	N	Y	Y	Y	N	N	Y
Bayh	Y	Y	Y	Y	Y	N	N	Y

	131	132	133	134	135	136	137	138
IOWA								
Grassley	Y	N	Y	Y	N	N	N	Y
Harkin	Y	Y	N	Y	Y	Y	Y	Y
KANSAS								
Brownback	Y	N	Y	Y	N	N	N	Y
Roberts	Y	N	Y	Y	Y	Y	Y	Y
KENTUCKY								
McConnell	Y	N	Y	Y	Y	Y	Y	Y
Bunning	Y	N	Y	Y	N	N	N	N
LOUISIANA								
Breaux	Y	Y	N	Y	Y	Y	Y	Y
Landrieu	Y	Y	N	Y	Y	Y	Y	Y
MAINE								
Snowe	Y	N	Y	Y	Y	Y	Y	Y
Collins	Y	N	Y	Y	Y	Y	Y	Y
MARYLAND								
Sarbanes	Y	Y	N	Y	Y	Y	Y	Y
Mikulski	Y	Y	N	Y	Y	Y	Y	Y
MASSACHUSETTS								
Kennedy	Y	Y	N	Y	Y	Y	Y	Y
Kerry	Y	Y	Y	Y	Y	Y	Y	Y
MICHIGAN								
Levin	Y	Y	N	Y	Y	Y	Y	Y
Stabenow	Y	Y	N	Y	Y	Y	Y	Y
MINNESOTA								
Wellstone	Y	N	N	Y	Y	Y	Y	Y
Dayton	Y	N	N	Y	Y	?	?	?
MISSISSIPPI								
Cochran	Y	N	N	Y	Y	Y	Y	Y
Lott	Y	N	Y	Y	N	N	N	N
MISSOURI								
Bond	Y	N	N	Y	Y	Y	Y	Y
Carnahan	Y	N	N	Y	Y	Y	Y	Y
MONTANA								
Baucus	Y	N	N	Y	Y	Y	Y	Y
Burns	Y	N	Y	Y	Y	Y	Y	Y
NEBRASKA								
Nelson	Y	Y	N	Y	Y	Y	Y	Y
Hagel	Y	N	N	Y	Y	N	N	N
NEVADA								
Reid	Y	Y	N	Y	Y	Y	Y	Y
Ensign	Y	N	Y	Y	Y	N	N	N

	131	132	133	134	135	136	137	138
NEW HAMPSHIRE								
Smith	Y	N	Y	Y	N	N	N	N
Gregg	Y	N	Y	Y	Y	Y	Y	Y
NEW JERSEY								
Corzine	Y	Y	N	Y	Y	Y	Y	Y
Torricelli	Y	?	?	?	Y	Y	Y	Y
NEW MEXICO								
Domenici	?	N	N	Y	Y	Y	Y	Y
Bingaman	Y	Y	N	?	?	?	?	?
NEW YORK								
Clinton	Y	N	N	Y	Y	Y	Y	Y
Schumer	Y	Y	N	Y	Y	Y	Y	Y
NORTH CAROLINA								
Helms	+	-	+	?	?	?	?	?
Edwards	Y	Y	Y	Y	Y	Y	Y	Y
NORTH DAKOTA								
Conrad	Y	N	N	Y	Y	Y	N	N
Dorgan	Y	Y	N	Y	Y	Y	Y	Y
OHIO								
DeWine	Y	N	Y	Y	Y	Y	Y	Y
Voinovich	Y	N	Y	Y	Y	Y	Y	N
OKLAHOMA								
Nickles	Y	N	Y	Y	Y	N	N	N
Inhofe	Y	N	Y	Y	Y	N	N	N
OREGON								
Wyden	Y	Y	N	Y	Y	Y	Y	Y
Smith	Y	Y	Y	Y	Y	Y	Y	N
PENNSYLVANIA								
Specter	Y	Y	N	Y	Y	Y	Y	Y
Santorum	Y	N	Y	Y	N	N	N	N
RHODE ISLAND								
Reed	Y	Y	N	Y	Y	Y	Y	Y
Chafee	Y	N	Y	Y	Y	N	N	Y
SOUTH CAROLINA								
Thurmond	Y	N	N	Y	Y	Y	Y	Y
Hollings	Y	Y	N	Y	Y	Y	Y	Y
SOUTH DAKOTA								
Daschle	Y	Y	N	Y	?	?	?	?
Johnson	Y	Y	N	Y	Y	Y	Y	Y
TENNESSEE								
Thompson	Y	N	Y	Y	Y	N	N	N
Frist	Y	N	Y	Y	Y	N	N	Y

ND Northern Democrats   SD Southern Democrats

Key

Y	Voted for (yea).
#	Paired for.
+	Announced for.
N	Voted against (nay).
X	Paired against.
–	Announced against.
P	Voted "present."
C	Voted "present" to avoid possible conflict of interest.
?	Did not vote or otherwise make a position known.

Democrats   ***Republicans***
Independents

	131	132	133	134	135	136	137	138
TEXAS								
Gramm	N	N	Y	Y	Y	N	N	N
Hutchison	Y	N	Y	Y	Y	Y	Y	N
UTAH								
Hatch	Y	N	Y	Y	Y	Y	N	Y
Bennett	Y	N	Y	Y	Y	Y	N	N
VERMONT								
Leahy	Y	N	N	Y	Y	Y	Y	Y
Jeffords	Y	Y	N	Y	Y	Y	Y	Y
VIRGINIA								
Warner	Y	N	N	Y	Y	Y	Y	Y
Allen	Y	N	N	Y	N	N	N	N
WASHINGTON								
Cantwell	Y	Y	Y	Y	Y	Y	N	N
Murray	Y	Y	N	Y	Y	Y	Y	Y
WEST VIRGINIA								
Byrd	Y	N	N	Y	Y	Y	Y	Y
Rockefeller	?	Y	N	?	Y	Y	Y	Y
WISCONSIN								
Kohl	Y	Y	N	Y	Y	Y	Y	Y
Feingold	Y	N	Y	Y	N	N	N	Y
WYOMING								
Thomas	N	N	Y	Y	Y	N	N	Y
Enzi	N	N	Y	Y	Y	N	N	Y

Southern states - Ala., Ark., Fla., Ga., Ky., La., Miss., N.C., Okla., S.C., Tenn., Texas, Va.

131. HR 4775. Fiscal 2002 Supplemental Appropriations/Airline Loan Guarantees. Byrd, D-W.Va., amendment that would strike the provision of the bill that would cap the amount of loan guarantees available to airlines for the remainder of the current fiscal year. Adopted 91-4: R 42-4; D 48-0 (ND 39-0, SD 9-0); I 1-0. June 4, 2002.

132. HR 4775. Fiscal 2002 Supplemental Appropriations/Summer School Programs. Kennedy, D-Mass., motion to waive the Budget Act with respect to the Byrd, D-W.Va., point of order against the Kennedy amendment. The Kennedy amendment would provide $150 million in emergency funds in fiscal 2002 for summer school programs. Motion rejected 38-60: R 2-46; D 35-14 (ND 30-10, SD 5-4); I 1-0. A three-fifths majority vote (60) of the total Senate is required to waive the Budget Act. June 5, 2002.

133. HR 4775. Fiscal 2002 Supplemental Appropriations/Budget Enforcement. Gregg, R-N.H., motion to waive the Budget Act with respect to the Conrad, D-N.D., point of order against the Gregg amendment. The Gregg amendment would establish and extend for five years caps on discretionary spending based on the levels in the budget resolution reported by the Senate Budget Committee. It would establish and extend pay-as-you-go rules that control entitlement spending and tax law changes. Motion rejected 49-49: R 38-10; D 11-38 (ND 7-33, SD 4-5); I 0-1. A three-fifths majority vote (60) of the total Senate is required to waive the Budget Act. (Subsequently the chair upheld the point of order and the amendment fell.) June 5, 2002.

134. HR 4775. Fiscal 2002 Supplemental Appropriations/Budget Resolution. Daschle, D-S.D., motion to table (kill) the Santorum, R-Pa., amendment to the Daschle amendment. The Santorum amendment would replace the text of the Daschle amendment with the text of the committee-approved budget resolution that would set total discretionary spending at $768 billion for fiscal 2003. The Daschle amendment would extend through fiscal 2007

discretionary spending caps and pay-as-you-go rules. Motion agreed to 96-0: R 48-0; D 47-0 (ND 38-0, SD 9-0); I 1-0. June 5, 2002.

135. HR 4775. Fiscal 2002 Supplemental Appropriations/Cloture. Motion to invoke cloture (thus limiting debate) on the bill that would provide $31 billion in supplemental appropriations available for fiscal 2002. Motion agreed to 87-10: R 39-9; D 47-1 (ND 38-1, SD 9-0); I 1-0. Three-fifths of the total Senate (60) is required to invoke cloture. June 6, 2002.

136. HR 4775. Fiscal 2002 Supplemental Appropriations/Smithsonian Construction Funds. Stevens, R-Alaska, motion to table (kill) the McCain, R-Ariz., amendment that would strike a provision in the bill that would provide $2 million in construction funds for a Smithsonian Institution storage facility for specimens stored in alcohol. Motion agreed to 67-29: R 25-23; D 41-6 (ND 33-5, SD 8-1); I 1-0. June 6, 2002.

137. HR 4775. Fiscal 2002 Supplemental Appropriations/Coral Reef Mapping. Inouye, D-Hawaii, motion to table (kill) the McCain, R-Ariz., amendment that would strike provisions that would designate $2.5 million for coral reef mapping of the waters off the coast of Hawaii. Motion agreed to 65-31: R 20-28; D 44-3 (ND 35-3, SD 9-0); I 1-0. June 6, 2002.

138. HR 4775. Fiscal 2002 Supplemental Appropriations/Agricultural Research Service. Harkin, D-Iowa, motion to table (kill) the McCain, R-Ariz., amendment that would strike a provision in the bill that would provide $50 million to the Agricultural Research Service for the construction and renovation of facilities at the National Animal Disease Laboratory in Ames, Iowa. Motion agreed to 72-24: R 25-23; D 46-1 (ND 37-1, SD 9-0); I 1-0. June 6, 2002.

	139	140	141	142	143	144	145
ALABAMA							
Shelby	Y	Y	N	Y	Y	Y	Y
Sessions	Y	Y	N	Y	N	N	N
ALASKA							
Stevens	Y	Y	N	Y	Y	Y	Y
Murkowski	Y	Y	N	Y	Y	Y	Y
ARIZONA							
McCain	Y	Y	N	N	N	N	N
Kyl	Y	Y	N	N	N	N	N
ARKANSAS							
Hutchinson	Y	Y	N	Y	Y	Y	Y
Lincoln	Y	Y	Y	Y	Y	Y	Y
CALIFORNIA							
Feinstein	N	Y	Y	Y	Y	Y	Y
Boxer	N	N	Y	Y	Y	Y	Y
COLORADO							
Campbell	?	?	?	?	?	?	?
Allard	Y	Y	N	N	N	N	N
CONNECTICUT							
Dodd	N	N	Y	Y	Y	Y	Y
Lieberman	N	N	Y	?	Y	Y	Y
DELAWARE							
Carper	N	N	N	Y	Y	Y	Y
Biden	N	N	Y	Y	Y	Y	Y
FLORIDA							
Graham	N	N	Y	Y	Y	Y	Y
Nelson	Y	Y	Y	Y	Y	Y	Y
GEORGIA							
Miller	Y	Y	N	Y	Y	Y	Y
Cleland	Y	Y	Y	Y	Y	Y	Y
HAWAII							
Inouye	N	Y	Y	Y	Y	Y	Y
Akaka	N	N	Y	Y	Y	Y	Y
IDAHO							
Craig	Y	Y	N	N	N	Y	Y
Crapo	Y	Y	N	Y	N	N	Y
ILLINOIS							
Durbin	N	N	Y	Y	Y	Y	Y
Fitzgerald	Y	Y	N	Y	N	N	N
INDIANA							
Lugar	Y	Y	N	Y	Y	Y	Y
Bayh	N	Y	Y	Y	N	Y	N

	139	140	141	142	143	144	145
IOWA							
Grassley	Y	Y	N	Y	N	N	N
Harkin	N	Y	Y	Y	Y	Y	Y
KANSAS							
Brownback	Y	Y	N	Y	N	N	N
Roberts	Y	Y	N	Y	Y	Y	Y
KENTUCKY							
McConnell	Y	Y	N	Y	N	Y	Y
Bunning	Y	Y	N	Y	N	N	N
LOUISIANA							
Breaux	N	Y	Y	Y	Y	Y	Y
Landrieu	Y	Y	Y	Y	Y	Y	Y
MAINE							
Snowe	Y	Y	N	Y	Y	Y	Y
Collins	Y	Y	Y	Y	Y	Y	Y
MARYLAND							
Sarbanes	N	N	Y	Y	Y	Y	Y
Mikulski	N	Y	Y	Y	Y	Y	Y
MASSACHUSETTS							
Kennedy	N	N	Y	Y	Y	Y	?
Kerry	N	Y	Y	Y	Y	Y	Y
MICHIGAN							
Levin	N	Y	Y	Y	Y	Y	Y
Stabenow	N	Y	Y	Y	Y	Y	Y
MINNESOTA							
Wellstone	N	N	Y	Y	Y	Y	Y
Dayton	?	?	?	?	?	?	?
MISSISSIPPI							
Cochran	Y	Y	N	Y	Y	Y	Y
Lott	Y	Y	N	?	N	N	N
MISSOURI							
Bond	Y	Y	N	Y	N	Y	Y
Carnahan	N	Y	Y	Y	Y	Y	Y
MONTANA							
Baucus	Y	Y	N	Y	Y	Y	Y
Burns	Y	Y	N	Y	Y	Y	Y
NEBRASKA							
Nelson	Y	Y	N	Y	Y	Y	Y
Hagel	Y	Y	N	N	N	N	N
NEVADA							
Reid	N	Y	Y	Y	Y	Y	Y
Ensign	Y	Y	N	Y	N	N	N

	139	140	141	142	143	144	145
NEW HAMPSHIRE							
Smith	Y	Y	N	N	N	N	N
Gregg	Y	Y	N	N	N	N	Y
NEW JERSEY							
Corzine	N	Y	Y	Y	Y	Y	Y
Torricelli	N	Y	Y	Y	Y	Y	Y
NEW MEXICO							
Domenici	Y	Y	N	Y	N	Y	Y
Bingaman	?	?	?	?	?	?	?
NEW YORK							
Clinton	Y	Y	Y	Y	Y	Y	Y
Schumer	N	Y	Y	Y	Y	Y	Y
NORTH CAROLINA							
Helms	?	?	?	?	?	?	?
Edwards	N	Y	Y	Y	Y	Y	Y
NORTH DAKOTA							
Conrad	Y	Y	Y	Y	Y	Y	Y
Dorgan	Y	Y	Y	Y	Y	Y	Y
OHIO							
DeWine	Y	Y	Y	N	Y	Y	Y
Voinovich	Y	+	N	N	N	N	N
OKLAHOMA							
Nickles	Y	Y	N	Y	N	N	N
Inhofe	Y	Y	N	N	N	N	Y
OREGON							
Wyden	N	Y	Y	Y	Y	Y	Y
Smith	Y	Y	Y	Y	Y	Y	Y
PENNSYLVANIA							
Specter	N	N	Y	Y	Y	Y	Y
Santorum	Y	Y	N	Y	N	N	N
RHODE ISLAND							
Reed	N	N	Y	Y	Y	Y	Y
Chafee	N	Y	N	Y	N	N	Y
SOUTH CAROLINA							
Thurmond	Y	Y	N	Y	?	?	?
Hollings	Y	Y	N	Y	Y	Y	Y
SOUTH DAKOTA							
Daschle	?	?	?	?	?	?	?
Johnson	N	Y	N	Y	Y	Y	Y
TENNESSEE							
Thompson	Y	Y	N	Y	N	N	N
Frist	Y	Y	N	Y	N	N	Y

	139	140	141	142	143	144	145
TEXAS							
Gramm	Y	Y	N	N	N	N	N
Hutchison	Y	Y	N	N	N	N	Y
UTAH							
Hatch	Y	Y	Y	N	Y	N	Y
Bennett	Y	Y	N	Y	N	Y	Y
VERMONT							
Leahy	N	N	Y	Y	Y	Y	Y
Jeffords	N	N	Y	Y	Y	Y	Y
VIRGINIA							
Warner	Y	Y	N	Y	Y	Y	Y
Allen	Y	Y	N	Y	N	Y	Y
WASHINGTON							
Cantwell	N	N	Y	Y	Y	Y	Y
Murray	N	N	Y	Y	Y	Y	Y
WEST VIRGINIA							
Byrd	N	N	N	Y	Y	Y	Y
Rockefeller	N	Y	Y	Y	Y	Y	Y
WISCONSIN							
Kohl	N	N	Y	Y	Y	Y	Y
Feingold	N	N	Y	Y	N	N	N
WYOMING							
Thomas	Y	Y	N	N	N	N	N
Enzi	Y	Y	N	N	N	N	N

ND Northern Democrats   SD Southern Democrats

Southern states - Ala., Ark., Fla., Ga., Ky., La., Miss., N.C., Okla., S.C., Tenn., Texas, Va.

139. HR 4775. Fiscal 2002 Supplemental Appropriations/International Criminal Court. Warner, R-Va., motion to table (kill) the Dodd, D-Conn., amendment to the Warner amendment. The Dodd amendment would add language to the underlying amendment that would allow the United States to assist the International Criminal Court through Sept. 30, 2002, in cases involving Saddam Hussein, Slobodan Milosevic, Osama bin Laden, Islamic Jihad, the al Qaeda terrorist network or any nationals accused of genocide, war crimes or crimes against humanity. The Warner amendment would prohibit U.S. assistance to, or cooperation with, the international court, except to assist or defend U.S. or allied citizens. Motion agreed to 55-40: R 45-2; D 10-37 (ND 4-34, SD 6-3); I 0-1. June 6, 2002.

140. HR 4775. Fiscal 2002 Supplemental Appropriations/International Criminal Court. Warner, R-Va., amendment that would prohibit U.S. assistance to, or cooperation with, the International Criminal Court, except to assist or defend U.S. or allied citizens. It would authorize the president to use "all means necessary and appropriate" to free any U.S. personnel or personnel of NATO and major non-NATO allies detained by the international court. Adopted 75-19: R 45-1; D 30-17 (ND 21-17, SD 9-0); I 0-1. June 6, 2002.

141. HR 4775. Fiscal 2002 Supplemental Appropriations/AIDS Fund. Durbin, D-Ill., motion to waive the Budget Act with respect to the Byrd, D-W.Va., point of order against the Durbin amendment that would increase the amount of emergency supplemental appropriations in the bill from $100 million to $500 million for funds available as a U.S. contribution to the Global Fund to Combat AIDS, tuberculosis and malaria. Motion rejected 46-49: R 5-42; D 40-7 (ND 34-4, SD 6-3); I 1-0. A three-fifths majority vote (60) of the total Senate is required to waive the Budget Act. (Subsequently the chair upheld the point of order and the amendment fell.) June 6, 2002.

142. HR 4775. Fiscal 2002 Supplemental Appropriations/AIDS Fund. Helms, R-N.C., amendment that would increase the amount of emergency supplemental appropriations in the bill from $100 million to $200 million for funds available as a U.S. contribution to the Global Fund to Combat AIDS, tuberculosis and malaria. Adopted 79-14: R 32-14; D 46-0 (ND 37-0, SD 9-0); I 1-0. June 6, 2002.

143. HR 4775. Fiscal 2002 Supplemental Appropriations/Non-Defense Funds. Stevens, R-Alaska, motion to table (kill) the Nickles, R-Okla., amendment that would strike a provision in the bill that would require the president to designate all emergency non-defense funds before making any of those funds available. Motion agreed to 58-36: R 12-34; D 45-2 (ND 36-2, SD 9-0); I 1-0. A "nay" was a vote in support of the president's position. June 6, 2002.

144. HR 4775. Fiscal 2002 Supplemental Appropriations/Non-Defense Emergency Designation. Byrd, D-W.Va., motion to waive the Gramm, R-Texas, point of order against all non-defense emergency designations in the bill. Motion agreed to 69-25: R 22-24; D 46-1 (ND 37-1, SD 9-0); I 1-0. Three-fifths of the total Senate (60) is required to waive the point of order. June 6, 2002.

145. HR 4775. Fiscal 2002 Supplemental Appropriations/Passage. Passage of the bill that would provide $31.5 billion in supplemental appropriations available for fiscal 2002, including $14 billion for the Defense Department, $5.8 billion for homeland security programs and $5.5 billion for post-Sept. 11 recovery efforts in New York. Passed 71-22: R 26-20; D 44-2 (ND 35-2, SD 9-0); I 1-0. June 7, 2002 (in the session that began and the Congressional Record that is dated June 6, 2002).

	146	147	148	149
ALABAMA				
Shelby	Y	N	N	N
Sessions	Y	N	N	N
ALASKA				
Stevens	Y	N	Y	N
Murkowski	Y	N	Y	N
ARIZONA				
McCain	?	N	N	Y
Kyl	Y	N	N	N
ARKANSAS				
Hutchinson	?	N	Y	N
Lincoln	Y	Y	N	N
CALIFORNIA				
Feinstein	Y	Y	Y	Y
Boxer	Y	Y	Y	Y
COLORADO				
Campbell	Y	N	N	N
Allard	Y	N	N	N
CONNECTICUT				
Dodd	Y	Y	Y	Y
Lieberman	+	Y	Y	Y
DELAWARE				
Carper	Y	Y	N	N
Biden	?	Y	Y	Y
FLORIDA				
Graham	Y	Y	N	Y
Nelson	Y	Y	Y	Y
GEORGIA				
Miller	Y	Y	Y	N
Cleland	Y	Y	Y	N
HAWAII				
Inouye	Y	Y	Y	Y
Akaka	Y	Y	Y	Y
IDAHO				
Craig	Y	N	Y	N
Crapo	?	?	?	?
ILLINOIS				
Durbin	Y	Y	Y	Y
Fitzgerald	Y	N	N	N
INDIANA				
Lugar	Y	N	Y	N
Bayh	Y	Y	N	Y

	146	147	148	149
IOWA				
Grassley	Y	N	Y	N
Harkin	?	Y	N	Y
KANSAS				
Brownback	Y	N	Y	N
Roberts	Y	N	Y	N
KENTUCKY				
McConnell	Y	N	Y	N
Bunning	Y	N	Y	N
LOUISIANA				
Breaux	Y	Y	Y	Y
Landrieu	Y	Y	Y	Y
MAINE				
Snowe	Y	Y	Y	Y
Collins	Y	Y	Y	Y
MARYLAND				
Sarbanes	Y	Y	Y	Y
Mikulski	?	Y	Y	Y
MASSACHUSETTS				
Kennedy	?	Y	Y	Y
Kerry	Y	Y	Y	Y
MICHIGAN				
Levin	Y	Y	Y	Y
Stabenow	Y	Y	N	Y
MINNESOTA				
Wellstone	Y	Y	Y	Y
Dayton	Y	Y	N	Y
MISSISSIPPI				
Cochran	Y	N	Y	N
Lott	Y	N	Y	N
MISSOURI				
Bond	Y	?	?	N
Carnahan	Y	Y	Y	Y
MONTANA				
Baucus	Y	Y	Y	N
Burns	Y	N	Y	N
NEBRASKA				
Nelson	?	Y	Y	N
Hagel	Y	N	Y	N
NEVADA				
Reid	Y	Y	Y	Y
Ensign	Y	N	N	N

	146	147	148	149
NEW HAMPSHIRE				
Smith	Y	N	N	N
Gregg	Y	N	Y	N
NEW JERSEY				
Corzine	?	Y	N	Y
Torricelli	+	Y	N	Y
NEW MEXICO				
Domenici	Y	N	Y	N
Bingaman	Y	Y	Y	N
NEW YORK				
Clinton	Y	Y	N	N
Schumer	Y	Y	Y	Y
NORTH CAROLINA				
Helms	+	–	?	–
Edwards	Y	Y	Y	Y
NORTH DAKOTA				
Conrad	Y	Y	N	N
Dorgan	Y	Y	N	Y
OHIO				
DeWine	Y	N	Y	N
Voinovich	?	N	Y	N
OKLAHOMA				
Nickles	Y	N	Y	N
Inhofe	Y	N	N	N
OREGON				
Wyden	Y	Y	Y	N
Smith	Y	Y	N	N
PENNSYLVANIA				
Specter	Y	N	Y	Y
Santorum	Y	N	Y	N
RHODE ISLAND				
Reed	Y	Y	Y	Y
Chafee	Y	Y	N	N
SOUTH CAROLINA				
Thurmond	Y	N	Y	N
Hollings	Y	Y	N	Y
SOUTH DAKOTA				
Daschle	Y	N	Y	Y
Johnson	Y	Y	Y	Y
TENNESSEE				
Thompson	Y	N	Y	N
Frist	Y	N	Y	N

Key

Y	Voted for (yea).
#	Paired for.
+	Announced for.
N	Voted against (nay).
X	Paired against.
–	Announced against.
P	Voted "present."
C	Voted "present" to avoid possible conflict of interest.
?	Did not vote or otherwise make a position known.

Democrats **Republicans**
Independents

	146	147	148	149
TEXAS				
Gramm	Y	N	N	N
Hutchison	Y	N	Y	N
UTAH				
Hatch	Y	N	Y	N
Bennett	Y	N	Y	N
VERMONT				
Leahy	Y	Y	Y	Y
Jeffords	Y	Y	Y	Y
VIRGINIA				
Warner	Y	N	N	N
Allen	Y	N	Y	N
WASHINGTON				
Cantwell	Y	Y	Y	Y
Murray	Y	Y	Y	N
WEST VIRGINIA				
Byrd	Y	Y	Y	Y
Rockefeller	Y	Y	Y	Y
WISCONSIN				
Kohl	Y	Y	Y	Y
Feingold	Y	Y	N	N
WYOMING				
Thomas	Y	N	Y	N
Enzi	Y	N	N	N

ND Northern Democrats   SD Southern Democrats

Southern states - Ala., Ark., Fla., Ga., Ky., La., Miss., N.C., Okla., S.C., Tenn., Texas, Va.

146. S Res 272. Varela Project/Adoption. Adoption of the resolution that would express the sense of the Senate that the Cuban government should give serious consideration to the Varela Project, a petition drive that has resulted in more than 10,000 certified signatures in support of a national referendum on civil liberties. Adopted 87-0: R 44-0; D 42-0 (ND 33-0, SD 9-0); I 1-0. June 10, 2002.

147. S 625. Hate Crimes/Cloture. Motion to invoke cloture (thus limiting debate) on the bill that would broaden the definition of hate crimes to include acts committed because of the victim's sex, sexual orientation or disability and allow the federal government to help states prosecute hate crimes even if no federally protected activity was involved. Motion rejected 54-43: R 4-42; D 49-1 (ND 40-1, SD 9-0); I 1-0. Three-fifths of the total Senate (60) is required to invoke cloture. June 11, 2002.

148. S 2578. Debt Limit/Passage. Passage of the bill that would increase the public debt limit by approximately $450 billion to $6.4 trillion.

Passed 68-29: R 31-15; D 36-14 (ND 30-11, SD 6-3); I 1-0. A "yea" was a vote in support of the president's position. June 11, 2002.

149. HR 8. Estate Tax/Family Business Exemption. Dorgan, D-N.D., motion to waive the Budget Act with respect to the Gramm, R-Texas, point of order against the Dorgan amendment to the Conrad, D-N.D., substitute amendment. The Dorgan amendment would increase the estate tax exemption to $4 million in 2009 and provide a full deduction for family-owned businesses beginning in 2003. The Conrad amendment would increase the exemption from estate taxes to $3 million in fiscal 2003 through 2008, and $3.5 million in 2009 and beyond. It would cap the maximum tax rate at 50 percent for estates under $10 million and repeal the sunset provision in current law as it applies to estates, gifts and transfers. Motion rejected 44-54: R 4-43; D 39-11 (ND 33-8, SD 6-3); I 1-0. A three-fifths majority vote (60) of the total Senate is required to waive the Budget Act. (Subsequently the point of order was sustained and the Dorgan amendment fell.) June 12, 2002.

	150	151	152	153
ALABAMA				
Shelby	N	Y	N	Y
Sessions	N	Y	N	Y
ALASKA				
Stevens	N	Y	N	Y
Murkowski	N	Y	N	Y
ARIZONA				
McCain	N	N	N	Y
Kyl	N	Y	N	Y
ARKANSAS				
Hutchinson	N	Y	N	Y
Lincoln	N	Y	Y	N
CALIFORNIA				
Feinstein	Y	N	Y	Y
Boxer	Y	N	Y	–
COLORADO				
Campbell	N	Y	N	Y
Allard	N	Y	N	Y
CONNECTICUT				
Dodd	Y	N	Y	Y
Lieberman	Y	N	Y	Y
DELAWARE				
Carper	N	N	Y	Y
Biden	Y	N	Y	N
FLORIDA				
Graham	Y	N	Y	N
Nelson	Y	Y	Y	N
GEORGIA				
Miller	N	Y	Y	Y
Cleland	N	Y	Y	N
HAWAII				
Inouye	Y	N	Y	?
Akaka	Y	N	Y	N
IDAHO				
Craig	N	Y	N	Y
Crapo	?	?	?	?
ILLINOIS				
Durbin	Y	N	Y	N
Fitzgerald	N	Y	N	Y
INDIANA				
Lugar	N	Y	N	Y
Bayh	Y	Y	Y	Y

	150	151	152	153
IOWA				
Grassley	N	Y	N	Y
Harkin	Y	N	Y	Y
KANSAS				
Brownback	N	Y	N	Y
Roberts	N	Y	N	Y
KENTUCKY				
McConnell	N	Y	N	Y
Bunning	N	Y	N	Y
LOUISIANA				
Breaux	Y	N	Y	Y
Landrieu	N	Y	Y	N
MAINE				
Snowe	N	Y	N	Y
Collins	N	Y	N	Y
MARYLAND				
Sarbanes	Y	N	Y	Y
Mikulski	Y	N	Y	N
MASSACHUSETTS				
Kennedy	Y	N	Y	N
Kerry	Y	N	Y	Y
MICHIGAN				
Levin	Y	N	Y	N
Stabenow	Y	N	Y	N
MINNESOTA				
Wellstone	Y	N	Y	N
Dayton	Y	N	Y	N
MISSISSIPPI				
Cochran	N	Y	N	Y
Lott	N	Y	N	Y
MISSOURI				
Bond	N	Y	N	Y
Carnahan	N	N	Y	Y
MONTANA				
Baucus	N	Y	Y	N
Burns	N	Y	N	Y
NEBRASKA				
Nelson	N	Y	Y	Y
Hagel	N	Y	N	Y
NEVADA				
Reid	Y	N	Y	Y
Ensign	N	Y	N	Y

	150	151	152	153
NEW HAMPSHIRE				
Smith	N	Y	N	Y
Gregg	N	Y	N	Y
NEW JERSEY				
Corzine	Y	N	Y	Y
Torricelli	Y	N	Y	N
NEW MEXICO				
Domenici	N	Y	N	Y
Bingaman	Y	N	Y	N
NEW YORK				
Clinton	Y	N	Y	N
Schumer	Y	N	Y	Y
NORTH CAROLINA				
Helms	–	+	–	?
Edwards	Y	N	Y	Y
NORTH DAKOTA				
Conrad	Y	N	Y	Y
Dorgan	Y	N	Y	Y
OHIO				
DeWine	N	Y	N	Y
Voinovich	N	Y	N	Y
OKLAHOMA				
Nickles	N	Y	N	Y
Inhofe	N	Y	N	Y
OREGON				
Wyden	N	Y	Y	Y
Smith	N	Y	N	Y
PENNSYLVANIA				
Specter	N	Y	N	Y
Santorum	N	Y	N	Y
RHODE ISLAND				
Reed	Y	N	Y	Y
Chafee	N	N	?	Y
SOUTH CAROLINA				
Thurmond	N	Y	N	Y
Hollings	N	N	Y	N
SOUTH DAKOTA				
Daschle	Y	N	Y	Y
Johnson	Y	N	Y	N
TENNESSEE				
Thompson	N	Y	N	Y
Frist	N	Y	N	Y

	150	151	152	153
TEXAS				
Gramm	N	Y	N	Y
Hutchison	N	Y	N	Y
UTAH				
Hatch	N	Y	N	Y
Bennett	N	Y	N	Y
VERMONT				
Leahy	Y	N	Y	N
Jeffords	Y	N	?	?
VIRGINIA				
Warner	N	Y	N	Y
Allen	N	Y	N	?
WASHINGTON				
Cantwell	N	N	Y	Y
Murray	N	N	Y	Y
WEST VIRGINIA				
Byrd	Y	N	Y	Y
Rockefeller	Y	N	Y	N
WISCONSIN				
Kohl	Y	N	Y	N
Feingold	N	N	Y	N
WYOMING				
Thomas	N	Y	N	Y
Enzi	N	Y	N	Y

Key

Y	Voted for (yea).
#	Paired for.
+	Announced for.
N	Voted against (nay).
X	Paired against.
–	Announced against.
P	Voted "present."
C	Voted "present" to avoid possible conflict of interest.
?	Did not vote or otherwise make a position known.

Democrats **Republicans**
Independents

ND Northern Democrats   SD Southern Democrats

Southern states - Ala., Ark., Fla., Ga., Ky., La., Miss., N.C., Okla., S.C., Tenn., Texas, Va.

150. HR 8. Estate Tax/Exemption Increase. Conrad, D-N.D., motion to waive the Budget Act with respect to the Gramm, R-Texas, point of order against the Conrad substitute amendment. Motion rejected 38-60: R 0-47; D 37-13 (ND 33-8, SD 4-5); I 1-0. A three-fifths majority vote (60) of the total Senate is required to waive the Budget Act. (Subsequently the point of order was sustained and the Conrad amendment fell.) June 12, 2002.

151. HR 8. Estate Tax/Permanent Repeal. Gramm, R-Texas, motion to waive the Budget Act with respect to the Conrad, D-N.D., point of order against the Gramm amendment that would permanently extend the repeal of the estate tax contained in last year's $1.35 trillion tax cut law. Motion rejected 54-44: R 45-2; D 9-41 (ND 4-37, SD 5-4); I 0-1. A three-fifths majority vote (60) of the total Senate is required to waive the Budget Act. (Subsequently the point of order was sustained and the Gramm amendment fell.) A "yea" was a vote in support of the president's position. June 12, 2002.

152. S 2600. Terrorism Insurance/Punitive Damages. Reid, D-Nev., mo-

tion to table (kill) the McConnell, R-Ky., amendment that would prohibit punitive damages unless the defendant is convicted of a criminal offense related to the plaintiff's injury. It also would require the secretary of the Treasury to approve any lawsuit settlements. Motion agreed to 50-46: R 0-46; D 50-0 (ND 41-0, SD 9-0); I 0-0. June 13, 2002.

153. S 2600. Terrorism Insurance/Premiums. Reid, D-Nev., motion to table (kill) the Nelson, D-Fla., amendment that would require insurance companies to identify the portion of the total premium charged that can be attributed to terrorism risk and establish a separate account for that portion. It also would direct the Treasury secretary to establish guidelines for terrorism insurance premiums. Insurance companies would be required to charge terrorism insurance premiums no higher than the rate set by the Treasury secretary and refund premiums attributed to terrorism risk already collected in excess of that amount. Motion agreed to 70-24: R 46-0; D 24-24 (ND 21-18, SD 3-6); I 0-0. June 13, 2002.

	154	155	156	157	158	159
ALABAMA						
Shelby	Y	Y	N	Y	Y	Y
Sessions	Y	Y	N	N	Y	N
ALASKA						
Stevens	Y	Y	Y	Y	Y	Y
Murkowski	?	?	N	Y	Y	N
ARIZONA						
McCain	Y	Y	Y	Y	Y	Y
Kyl	Y	Y	N	N	Y	N
ARKANSAS						
Hutchinson	Y	Y	N	N	Y	N
Lincoln	Y	Y	Y	Y	Y	Y
CALIFORNIA						
Feinstein	Y	Y	Y	Y	Y	Y
Boxer	?	?	?	Y	Y	Y
COLORADO						
Campbell	Y	Y	N	N	Y	N
Allard	?	?	N	Y	Y	N
CONNECTICUT						
Dodd	Y	Y	Y	Y	Y	Y
Lieberman	Y	Y	Y	Y	Y	Y
DELAWARE						
Carper	Y	Y	Y	Y	Y	Y
Biden	Y	Y	Y	Y	Y	Y
FLORIDA						
Graham	Y	Y	Y	Y	Y	Y
Nelson	Y	Y	N	Y	Y	Y
GEORGIA						
Miller	Y	Y	Y	Y	Y	Y
Cleland	Y	Y	Y	Y	Y	Y
HAWAII						
Inouye	?	?	Y	Y	Y	Y
Akaka	Y	Y	Y	Y	Y	Y
IDAHO						
Craig	Y	Y	N	N	Y	N
Crapo	?	?	N	Y	Y	N
ILLINOIS						
Durbin	Y	Y	Y	Y	Y	Y
Fitzgerald	Y	Y	Y	Y	Y	N
INDIANA						
Lugar	Y	N	Y	Y	Y	N
Bayh	Y	Y	Y	Y	Y	Y

	154	155	156	157	158	159
IOWA						
Grassley	Y	Y	N	N	Y	N
Harkin	Y	Y	Y	Y	Y	Y
KANSAS						
Brownback	?	?	N	Y	Y	N
Roberts	?	?	N	Y	Y	N
KENTUCKY						
McConnell	Y	Y	N	N	Y	N
Bunning	+	+	N	Y	Y	N
LOUISIANA						
Breaux	Y	Y	Y	Y	Y	Y
Landrieu	Y	Y	Y	Y	Y	Y
MAINE						
Snowe	Y	Y	Y	Y	Y	Y
Collins	Y	Y	Y	Y	Y	Y
MARYLAND						
Sarbanes	Y	Y	Y	Y	Y	Y
Mikulski	Y	Y	Y	Y	Y	Y
MASSACHUSETTS						
Kennedy	Y	Y	Y	Y	Y	Y
Kerry	Y	Y	+	+	Y	Y
MICHIGAN						
Levin	Y	Y	Y	Y	Y	Y
Stabenow	Y	Y	Y	Y	Y	Y
MINNESOTA						
Wellstone	Y	Y	Y	Y	Y	Y
Dayton	Y	Y	Y	Y	Y	Y
MISSISSIPPI						
Cochran	Y	Y	Y	Y	Y	Y
Lott	Y	Y	N	Y	Y	N
MISSOURI						
Bond	Y	Y	N	Y	Y	N
Carnahan	Y	Y	Y	Y	Y	Y
MONTANA						
Baucus	Y	Y	Y	Y	Y	Y
Burns	?	?	N	N	Y	N
NEBRASKA						
Nelson	Y	Y	Y	Y	Y	Y
Hagel	Y	N	N	Y	Y	N
NEVADA						
Reid	Y	Y	Y	Y	Y	Y
Ensign	Y	Y	N	Y	Y	N

	154	155	156	157	158	159
NEW HAMPSHIRE						
Smith	Y	Y	N	N	Y	N
Gregg	Y	Y	N	Y	Y	Y
NEW JERSEY						
Corzine	Y	Y	Y	Y	Y	Y
Torricelli	+	+	Y	Y	Y	Y
NEW MEXICO						
Domenici	Y	Y	Y	Y	Y	Y
Bingaman	Y	Y	Y	Y	Y	Y
NEW YORK						
Clinton	Y	Y	Y	Y	N	Y
Schumer	Y	Y	Y	Y	N	Y
NORTH CAROLINA						
Helms	?	?	?	?	?	?
Edwards	Y	Y	Y	Y	Y	Y
NORTH DAKOTA						
Conrad	+	+	Y	Y	Y	Y
Dorgan	?	?	Y	Y	Y	Y
OHIO						
DeWine	Y	Y	N	Y	Y	N
Voinovich	Y	Y	N	Y	N	N
OKLAHOMA						
Nickles	Y	Y	N	N	Y	N
Inhofe	Y	Y	N	Y	Y	N
OREGON						
Wyden	Y	Y	Y	Y	Y	Y
Smith	Y	Y	Y	Y	Y	N
PENNSYLVANIA						
Specter	Y	Y	Y	Y	Y	Y
Santorum	Y	Y	N	N	Y	N
RHODE ISLAND						
Reed	Y	Y	Y	Y	Y	Y
Chafee	Y	N	Y	Y	Y	Y
SOUTH CAROLINA						
Thurmond	Y	Y	N	Y	Y	N
Hollings	Y	Y	Y	Y	Y	Y
SOUTH DAKOTA						
Daschle	Y	Y	Y	Y	Y	Y
Johnson	Y	Y	Y	Y	Y	Y
TENNESSEE						
Thompson	Y	Y	N	Y	Y	N
Frist	Y	Y	N	Y	Y	N

	154	155	156	157	158	159
TEXAS						
Gramm	Y	Y	N	N	Y	N
Hutchison	Y	Y	?	N	Y	N
UTAH						
Hatch	+	?	Y	Y	Y	N
Bennett	?	?	Y	Y	Y	N
VERMONT						
Leahy	Y	Y	Y	Y	Y	Y
Jeffords	?	?	Y	Y	Y	Y
VIRGINIA						
Warner	Y	Y	Y	Y	Y	Y
Allen	Y	Y	Y	Y	Y	N
WASHINGTON						
Cantwell	Y	Y	Y	Y	Y	Y
Murray	Y	Y	Y	Y	Y	Y
WEST VIRGINIA						
Byrd	Y	Y	Y	Y	Y	Y
Rockefeller	Y	Y	Y	Y	Y	Y
WISCONSIN						
Kohl	Y	Y	Y	Y	Y	Y
Feingold	N	Y	Y	Y	Y	Y
WYOMING						
Thomas	Y	Y	N	N	Y	N
Enzi	Y	Y	N	N	Y	N

Key

Y	Voted for (yea).
#	Paired for.
+	Announced for.
N	Voted against (nay).
X	Paired against.
−	Announced against.
P	Voted "present."
C	Voted "present" to avoid possible conflict of interest.
?	Did not vote or otherwise make a position known.

Democrats **Republicans**
Independents

ND Northern Democrats   SD Southern Democrats

Southern states - Ala., Ark., Fla., Ga., Ky., La., Miss., N.C., Okla., S.C., Tenn., Texas, Va.

154. HR 3275. Anti-Terrorism Accords/Passage. Passage of the bill that would implement the International Convention of the Suppression of Terrorist Bombings and the International Convention of the Suppression of the Financing of Terrorism by making it a federal crime to place or detonate an explosive in certain public places or to engage in financial transactions related to those acts. Passed 83-1: R 39-0; D 44-1 (ND 35-1, SD 9-0); I 0-0. June 14, 2002.

155. S 2600. Terrorism Insurance/Frozen Assets. Allen, R-Va., amendment that would allow victims of terrorism to recover damages from the frozen assets of terrorists, terrorist organizations or state sponsors of terrorist acts. Adopted 81-3: R 36-3; D 45-0 (ND 36-0, SD 9-0); I 0-0. June 14, 2002.

156. S 2600. Terrorism Insurance/Cloture. Motion to invoke cloture (thus limiting debate) on the bill that would require the federal government to reimburse insurance companies for 90 percent of catastrophic losses related to terrorism between $10 billion and $100 billion in 2002, with an option to renew the program the following year to cover 90 percent of claims between $15 billion and $100 billion. Motion agreed to 65-31: R 17-30; D 47-1 (ND 39-0, SD 8-1); I 1-0. Three-fifths of the total Senate (60) is required to invoke cloture. June 18, 2002.

157. S 2600. Terrorism Insurance/Passage. Passage of the bill that would require the federal government to reimburse insurance companies for 90 per-

cent of catastrophic losses related to terrorism between $10 billion and $100 billion in 2002, with an option to renew the program the following year to cover 90 percent of claims between $15 billion and $100 billion. Passed 84-14: R 34-14; D 49-0 (ND 40-0, SD 9-0); I 1-0. June 18, 2002.

158. S 2514. Defense Authorization/Crusader. Levin, D-Mich., amendment that would set aside $476 million designated for the Crusader howitzer and allocate the funding to the Army's Future Combat System. The Army would be required to complete a review within 30 days of the bill's enactment of artillery programs that could improve the Army over the next 20 years. The funds could be spent after the Defense secretary submits his recommendations and the required report to the congressional defense committees. Adopted 96-3: R 47-1; D 48-2 (ND 39-2, SD 9-0); I 1-0. June 19, 2002.

159. S 2514. Defense Authorization/Budgetary Caps. Feingold, D-Wis., motion to waive the Budget Act with respect to the Gramm, R-Texas, point of order against the Feingold amendment that would create a discretionary spending cap of $768.1 billion in fiscal 2003 and $786.5 billion in fiscal 2004, extend the budget enforcement points of order and sequestration for five years, establish a one-year defense firewall in the Senate, and extend the pay-go rule. Motion rejected 59-40: R 8-40; D 50-0 (ND 41-0, SD 9-0); I 1-0. A three-fifths majority vote (60) of the total Senate is required to waive the Budget Act. (Subsequently, the chair upheld the point of order and the amendment fell.) A "nay" was a vote in support of the president's position. June 20, 2002.

	160	161	162	163	164	165	166
ALABAMA							
Shelby	N	Y	Y	Y	Y	Y	Y
Sessions	N	Y	Y	Y	Y	Y	Y
ALASKA							
Stevens	Y	Y	Y	Y	Y	Y	Y
Murkowski	N	?	Y	Y	Y	Y	Y
ARIZONA							
McCain	N	Y	Y	Y	Y	Y	Y
Kyl	N	Y	Y	Y	Y	Y	Y
ARKANSAS							
Hutchinson	N	?	Y	Y	Y	Y	Y
Lincoln	Y	Y	N	Y	Y	Y	Y
CALIFORNIA							
Feinstein	Y	Y	N	Y	Y	Y	Y
Boxer	Y	Y	Y	Y	Y	Y	Y
COLORADO							
Campbell	N	Y	Y	Y	Y	Y	Y
Allard	N	Y	Y	Y	Y	Y	Y
CONNECTICUT							
Dodd	Y	Y	N	Y	Y	Y	Y
Lieberman	Y	Y	N	Y	Y	Y	Y
DELAWARE							
Carper	Y	Y	N	Y	Y	Y	Y
Biden	Y	Y	N	Y	Y	Y	Y
FLORIDA							
Graham	Y	Y	N	Y	Y	Y	Y
Nelson	Y	Y	N	Y	Y	Y	Y
GEORGIA							
Miller	?	Y	N	Y	Y	Y	Y
Cleland	Y	Y	N	Y	Y	Y	Y
HAWAII							
Inouye	Y	Y	N	Y	Y	Y	Y
Akaka	Y	Y	N	Y	Y	Y	Y
IDAHO							
Craig	?	Y	Y	Y	Y	Y	Y
Crapo	N	Y	Y	Y	Y	Y	Y
ILLINOIS							
Durbin	Y	+	N	Y	Y	Y	Y
Fitzgerald	N	Y	Y	Y	Y	Y	Y
INDIANA							
Lugar	N	Y	Y	Y	Y	Y	Y
Bayh	Y	Y	N	Y	Y	Y	Y

	160	161	162	163	164	165	166
IOWA							
Grassley	N	Y	Y	Y	Y	Y	Y
Harkin	Y	Y	N	Y	Y	Y	Y
KANSAS							
Brownback	N	Y	Y	Y	Y	Y	Y
Roberts	N	Y	Y	Y	Y	Y	Y
KENTUCKY							
McConnell	N	Y	Y	Y	Y	Y	Y
Bunning	N	Y	Y	Y	Y	Y	Y
LOUISIANA							
Breaux	?	Y	Y	Y	Y	Y	Y
Landrieu	Y	Y	N	Y	Y	Y	Y
MAINE							
Snowe	Y	Y	Y	Y	Y	Y	Y
Collins	Y	Y	Y	Y	Y	Y	Y
MARYLAND							
Sarbanes	Y	Y	N	Y	Y	Y	Y
Mikulski	Y	+	N	Y	Y	Y	Y
MASSACHUSETTS							
Kennedy	Y	Y	N	Y	Y	Y	Y
Kerry	Y	Y	N	Y	Y	Y	Y
MICHIGAN							
Levin	Y	Y	N	Y	Y	Y	Y
Stabenow	Y	Y	N	Y	Y	Y	Y
MINNESOTA							
Wellstone	Y	Y	N	Y	Y	Y	Y
Dayton	Y	Y	N	Y	Y	Y	Y
MISSISSIPPI							
Cochran	N	Y	Y	Y	Y	Y	Y
Lott	N	Y	Y	Y	Y	Y	Y
MISSOURI							
Bond	N	Y	Y	Y	Y	Y	Y
Carnahan	Y	Y	N	Y	Y	Y	Y
MONTANA							
Baucus	Y	Y	N	Y	Y	Y	Y
Burns	N	Y	Y	Y	Y	Y	Y
NEBRASKA							
Nelson	N	Y	N	Y	Y	Y	Y
Hagel	N	Y	Y	Y	Y	Y	Y
NEVADA							
Reid	N	Y	N	Y	Y	Y	Y
Ensign	N	Y	Y	Y	Y	Y	Y

	160	161	162	163	164	165	166
NEW HAMPSHIRE							
Smith	N	Y	Y	Y	Y	Y	Y
Gregg	N	Y	Y	Y	Y	Y	Y
NEW JERSEY							
Corzine	Y	Y	N	Y	Y	Y	Y
Torricelli	Y	?	N	Y	Y	Y	Y
NEW MEXICO							
Domenici	N	Y	Y	Y	Y	Y	Y
Bingaman	Y	Y	N	Y	Y	Y	Y
NEW YORK							
Clinton	Y	Y	N	Y	Y	Y	Y
Schumer	Y	Y	N	Y	?	Y	Y
NORTH CAROLINA							
Helms	–	?	?	+	?	?	?
Edwards	Y	Y	N	Y	Y	Y	Y
NORTH DAKOTA							
Conrad	Y	Y	N	Y	Y	Y	Y
Dorgan	Y	Y	N	Y	Y	Y	Y
OHIO							
DeWine	N	Y	Y	Y	Y	Y	Y
Voinovich	N	Y	Y	Y	Y	Y	Y
OKLAHOMA							
Nickles	N	Y	Y	Y	Y	Y	Y
Inhofe	N	Y	Y	Y	Y	Y	Y
OREGON							
Wyden	Y	Y	N	Y	Y	Y	Y
Smith	N	Y	Y	Y	Y	Y	Y
PENNSYLVANIA							
Specter	Y	Y	N	Y	Y	Y	Y
Santorum	–	?	Y	Y	Y	Y	Y
RHODE ISLAND							
Reed	Y	Y	N	Y	Y	Y	Y
Chafee	Y	Y	Y	Y	Y	Y	Y
SOUTH CAROLINA							
Thurmond	N	Y	Y	Y	Y	Y	Y
Hollings	Y	Y	N	Y	Y	Y	Y
SOUTH DAKOTA							
Daschle	Y	Y	N	Y	Y	Y	Y
Johnson	Y	Y	N	Y	Y	Y	Y
TENNESSEE							
Thompson	N	Y	Y	Y	Y	Y	Y
Frist	N	Y	Y	Y	Y	Y	Y

Key

Y	Voted for (yea).
#	Paired for.
+	Announced for.
N	Voted against (nay).
X	Paired against.
–	Announced against.
P	Voted "present."
C	Voted "present" to avoid possible conflict of interest.
?	Did not vote or otherwise make a position known.

Democrats   ***Republicans***
Independents

	160	161	162	163	164	165	166
TEXAS							
Gramm	?	Y	Y	Y	Y	Y	Y
Hutchison	?	Y	Y	Y	Y	Y	Y
UTAH							
Hatch	N	Y	Y	Y	Y	Y	Y
Bennett	N	Y	Y	Y	Y	Y	Y
VERMONT							
Leahy	Y	Y	N	Y	Y	Y	Y
Jeffords	Y	Y	N	Y	Y	Y	Y
VIRGINIA							
Warner	N	Y	Y	Y	Y	Y	Y
Allen	N	Y	Y	Y	Y	Y	Y
WASHINGTON							
Cantwell	Y	Y	N	Y	Y	Y	Y
Murray	Y	Y	N	Y	Y	Y	Y
WEST VIRGINIA							
Byrd	Y	Y	N	Y	Y	N	Y
Rockefeller	Y	Y	N	Y	Y	Y	Y
WISCONSIN							
Kohl	Y	Y	N	Y	Y	Y	Y
Feingold	Y	Y	N	Y	Y	N	Y
WYOMING							
Thomas	?	Y	Y	Y	Y	Y	Y
Enzi	N	Y	Y	Y	Y	Y	Y

ND Northern Democrats   SD Southern Democrats

Southern states - Ala., Ark., Fla., Ga., Ky., La., Miss., N.C., Okla., S.C., Tenn., Texas, Va.

160. S 2514. Defense Authorization/Military Abortions. Murray, D-Wash., amendment that would give military women and dependents of military personnel stationed overseas access to abortion services. Adopted 52-40: R 5-38; D 46-2 (ND 39-2, SD 7-0); I 1-0. June 21, 2002.

161. S 2514. Defense Authorization/Abaya. Smith, R-N.H., amendment that would prohibit the Defense Department from imposing a policy to require or encourage military members to wear an abaya, a garment worn by women in Middle Eastern nations that covers the face and body. It also would prohibit the use of any funds made available to the Defense Department for the procurement of abayas. Adopted 93-0: R 45-0; D 47-0 (ND 38-0, SD 9-0); I 1-0. June 24, 2002.

162. S 2514. Defense Authorization/Defense Contracts. Warner, R-Va., motion to table (kill) the Kennedy, D-Mass., amendment that would allow private and public agencies to compete for new Defense Department contracts based on current department standards. It also would codify a contracting prohibition on work currently performed in the public sector unless the agency can show a savings of at least 10 percent in fiscal 2004. Motion agreed to 50-49: R 48-0; D 2-48 (ND 1-40, SD 1-8); I 0-1. June 25, 2002.

163. S Res 292. Pledge of Allegiance Support/Adoption. Adoption of a resolution expressing support for the Pledge of Allegiance and authorizing the Senate legal counsel to defend the constitutionality of the Pledge of Allegiance. Adopted 99-0: R 48-0; D 50-0 (ND 41-0, SD 9-0); I 1-0. June 26, 2002.

164. S 2514. Defense Authorization/Cloture. Motion to invoke cloture (thus limiting debate) on the bill that would authorize $393.3 billion for defense-related programs for fiscal 2003. Motion agreed to 98-0: R 48-0; D 49-0 (ND 40-0, SD 9-0); I 1-0. Three-fifths of the total Senate (60) is required to invoke cloture. June 26, 2002.

165. S 2514. Defense Authorization/Passage. Passage of the bill that would authorize $393.3 billion for defense-related programs for fiscal 2003, including $9.3 billion for shipbuilding, up to $7.8 billion for ballistic missile defense and a military pay raise of 4.1 percent. It also would set aside $10 billion to fund operating costs for the war on terrorism and would allow the president to decide whether $814 million is designated for missile defense or counter-terrorism. It would allow the Pentagon to redirect funding for the Crusader howitzer to study new artillery systems. Passed 97-2: R 48-0; D 48-2 (ND 39-2, SD 9-0); I 1-0. (Subsequently, the Senate incorporated the text into HR 4546.) June 27, 2002.

166. S 2690. Pledge of Allegiance Reaffirmation/Passage. Passage of the bill that would reaffirm the Pledge of Allegiance and the reference to "one nation under God" as well as the national motto of "In God We Trust." Passed 99-0: R 48-0; D 50-0 (ND 41-0, SD 9-0); I 1-0. June 27, 2002.

	167	168	169	170	171	172
ALABAMA						
Shelby	Y	N	Y	Y	Y	Y
Sessions	Y	N	Y	Y	Y	N
ALASKA						
Stevens	Y	N	Y	Y	Y	N
Murkowski	Y	Y	Y	Y	Y	N
ARIZONA						
McCain	Y	N	Y	Y	Y	Y
Kyl	Y	N	Y	Y	Y	N
ARKANSAS						
Hutchinson	Y	N	Y	Y	Y	N
Lincoln	Y	Y	Y	Y	Y	Y
CALIFORNIA						
Feinstein	N	Y	Y	Y	Y	Y
Boxer	N	Y	Y	Y	Y	Y
COLORADO						
Campbell	N	N	Y	Y	Y	N
Allard	Y	N	Y	Y	Y	N
CONNECTICUT						
Dodd	N	Y	Y	Y	Y	Y
Lieberman	N	Y	Y	Y	Y	Y
DELAWARE						
Carper	N	Y	Y	Y	Y	Y
Biden	N	Y	Y	Y	Y	Y
FLORIDA						
Graham	Y	Y	Y	Y	Y	Y
Nelson	Y	Y	Y	Y	Y	Y
GEORGIA						
Miller	Y	Y	Y	Y	Y	Y
Cleland	Y	Y	Y	Y	Y	Y
HAWAII						
Inouye	N	Y	Y	Y	Y	Y
Akaka	N	Y	Y	Y	Y	Y
IDAHO						
Craig	Y	N	Y	Y	Y	N
Crapo	Y	N	?	?	?	?
ILLINOIS						
Durbin	Y	Y	Y	Y	Y	Y
Fitzgerald	Y	N	Y	Y	Y	N
INDIANA						
Lugar	Y	N	Y	Y	Y	N
Bayh	N	Y	Y	Y	Y	Y

	167	168	169	170	171	172
IOWA						
Grassley	Y	N	Y	Y	Y	N
Harkin	N	Y	Y	Y	Y	Y
KANSAS						
Brownback	Y	N	Y	Y	Y	N
Roberts	Y	N	Y	Y	Y	N
KENTUCKY						
McConnell	Y	N	Y	Y	Y	N
Bunning	Y	N	Y	Y	Y	N
LOUISIANA						
Breaux	N	Y	Y	Y	Y	Y
Landrieu	Y	Y	Y	Y	Y	Y
MAINE						
Snowe	Y	N	Y	Y	Y	Y
Collins	Y	N	Y	Y	Y	Y
MARYLAND						
Sarbanes	N	Y	Y	Y	Y	Y
Mikulski	N	Y	Y	Y	Y	Y
MASSACHUSETTS						
Kennedy	N	Y	Y	Y	Y	Y
Kerry	N	Y	Y	Y	Y	Y
MICHIGAN						
Levin	Y	Y	Y	Y	Y	Y
Stabenow	N	Y	Y	Y	Y	Y
MINNESOTA						
Wellstone	N	Y	Y	Y	Y	Y
Dayton	N	Y	Y	Y	Y	Y
MISSISSIPPI						
Cochran	Y	N	Y	Y	Y	N
Lott	Y	N	Y	Y	Y	N
MISSOURI						
Bond	Y	N	Y	Y	Y	N
Carnahan	N	Y	Y	Y	Y	Y
MONTANA						
Baucus	N	Y	Y	Y	Y	Y
Burns	Y	N	Y	Y	Y	N
NEBRASKA						
Nelson	Y	Y	Y	Y	Y	Y
Hagel	Y	N	Y	Y	Y	Y
NEVADA						
Reid	N	Y	Y	Y	Y	Y
Ensign	N	N	Y	Y	Y	N

	167	168	169	170	171	172
NEW HAMPSHIRE						
Smith	Y	N	Y	Y	Y	N
Gregg	Y	N	Y	Y	Y	N
NEW JERSEY						
Corzine	N	Y	Y	+	Y	Y
Torricelli	N	Y	Y	Y	Y	Y
NEW MEXICO						
Domenici	Y	N	Y	Y	Y	N
Bingaman	Y	Y	Y	Y	Y	Y
NEW YORK						
Clinton	N	Y	Y	Y	Y	Y
Schumer	N	Y	Y	Y	Y	Y
NORTH CAROLINA						
Helms	+	–	+	+	+	–
Edwards	Y	Y	Y	Y	Y	Y
NORTH DAKOTA						
Conrad	N	Y	Y	Y	Y	Y
Dorgan	N	Y	Y	Y	Y	Y
OHIO						
DeWine	Y	N	Y	Y	Y	N
Voinovich	Y	?	?	?	?	?
OKLAHOMA						
Nickles	Y	N	Y	Y	Y	N
Inhofe	Y	N	Y	Y	Y	N
OREGON						
Wyden	N	Y	Y	Y	Y	Y
Smith	Y	Y	Y	Y	Y	N
PENNSYLVANIA						
Specter	Y	Y	Y	Y	Y	Y
Santorum	Y	N	Y	Y	Y	N
RHODE ISLAND						
Reed	N	Y	Y	Y	Y	Y
Chafee	N	Y	Y	Y	Y	Y
SOUTH CAROLINA						
Thurmond	Y	N	Y	Y	Y	N
Hollings	Y	Y	Y	Y	Y	Y
SOUTH DAKOTA						
Daschle	N	Y	Y	Y	Y	Y
Johnson	N	Y	Y	Y	Y	Y
TENNESSEE						
Thompson	Y	N	Y	Y	Y	N
Frist	Y	N	Y	Y	Y	N

Key

Y	Voted for (yea).
#	Paired for.
+	Announced for.
N	Voted against (nay).
X	Paired against.
–	Announced against.
P	Voted "present."
C	Voted "present" to avoid possible conflict of interest.
?	Did not vote or otherwise make a position known.

Democrats **Republicans**
Independents

	167	168	169	170	171	172
TEXAS						
Gramm	Y	N	Y	Y	Y	N
Hutchison	Y	N	Y	Y	Y	N
UTAH						
Hatch	Y	N	Y	Y	Y	N
Bennett	Y	N	Y	Y	Y	N
VERMONT						
Leahy	Y	Y	Y	Y	Y	Y
Jeffords	N	Y	Y	Y	Y	Y
VIRGINIA						
Warner	Y	N	Y	Y	Y	Y
Allen	Y	N	Y	Y	Y	Y
WASHINGTON						
Cantwell	N	Y	Y	Y	Y	Y
Murray	Y	Y	Y	Y	Y	Y
WEST VIRGINIA						
Byrd	N	Y	Y	Y	Y	Y
Rockefeller	N	Y	Y	Y	Y	Y
WISCONSIN						
Kohl	Y	Y	Y	Y	Y	Y
Feingold	N	Y	Y	Y	Y	Y
WYOMING						
Thomas	Y	N	Y	Y	Y	N
Enzi	Y	N	Y	Y	Y	Y

ND Northern Democrats   SD Southern Democrats

Southern states - Ala., Ark., Fla., Ga., Ky., La., Miss., N.C., Okla., S.C., Tenn., Texas, Va.

167. S J Res 34. Nuclear Waste Storage/Motion to Proceed. Murkowski, R-Alaska, motion to proceed to the joint resolution that would approve a site at Yucca Mountain, Nev., as a repository for the nation's spent nuclear and high-level radioactive waste. Motion agreed to 60-39: R 45-3; D 15-35 (ND 7-34, SD 8-1); I 0-1. (Subsequently, the Senate passed the House version (H J Res 87) by voice vote.) July 9, 2002.

168. S 2673. Accounting Industry Overhaul/Labor Organizations. Sarbanes, D-Md., motion to table (kill) the McConnell, R-Ky., amendment to the Leahy, D-Vt., amendment. The McConnell amendment would require labor organizations with gross annual receipts of $200,000 or more to use financial reporting procedures comparable to those required of publicly traded corporations under the Securities and Exchange Act. It also would provide civil monetary penalties, as established under the securities law, for violations of reporting and auditing requirements. Motion agreed to 55-43: R 4-43; D 50-0 (ND 41-0, SD 9-0); I 1-0. July 10, 2002.

169. S 2673. Accounting Industry Overhaul/Securities Fraud Felony. Leahy, D-Vt., amendment that would create a 10-year felony for anyone who knowingly defrauds shareholders, create a 10-year felony for the destruction of evidence when records are under subpoena, and direct the U.S. Sentencing Commission to raise penalties in obstruction-of-justice cases where evidence is destroyed. It also would require the preservation of key financial audits for five years and create a five-year felony for intentionally destroying such documents. Adopted 97-0: R 46-0; D 50-0 (ND 41-0, SD 9-0); I 1-0. July 10, 2002.

170. S 2673. Accounting Industry Overhaul/Criminal Penalties. Biden, D-Del., amendment that would raise the maximum penalties for mail and wire fraud from five years to 10 years, raise the penalty for federal pension law violations from one year to 10 years, and provide the same penalties for conspiracy as for the underlying crime. Corporate officials of regulated companies would be required to certify that financial reports accurately reflect the financial condition of the company, with criminal penalties of up to five years for recklessly failing to certify and up to 10 years for willfully failing to do so. Adopted 96-0: R 46-0; D 49-0 (ND 40-0, SD 9-0); I 1-0. July 10, 2002.

171. S 2673. Accounting Industry Overhaul/Corporate Fraud Penalties. Lott, R-Miss., amendment that would increase the maximum sentence for mail and wire fraud from five years to 10 years. It also would allow the government to charge obstruction against individuals who acted alone, even if tampering took place before a grand jury subpoena issuance. It would allow the Securities and Exchange Commission (SEC) to seek an order in federal court imposing a 45-day freeze on "extraordinary" payments to corporate executives and request the Sentencing Commission to adopt stronger penalties for fraud when the crime is committed by a corporate officer or a corporate director. Adopted 97-0: R 46-0; D 50-0 (ND 41-0, SD 9-0); I 1-0. July 10, 2002.

172. S 2673. Accounting Industry Overhaul/Attorney Disclosures. Enzi, R-Wyo., motion to table (kill) the McConnell, R-Ky., amendment to the Edwards, D-N.C., amendment. The McConnell amendment would require attorneys to make a written disclosure of potential fees and other matters before retention by a client. It also would prohibit unsolicited communications concerning a potential civil action for personal injury or wrongful death until 45 days following the incident. Violators would be subject to a maximum penalty of $5,000 for each violation. The Edwards amendment would require the Securities and Exchange Commission (SEC) to establish new rules setting professional standards of conduct for attorneys representing public companies who appear before the SEC, including a rule requiring an attorney to report evidence of a material violation of securities law to the company's chief legal counsel or chief executive officer, or to the board of directors if necessary. Motion agreed to 62-35: R 11-35; D 50-0 (ND 41-0, SD 9-0); I 1-0. July 11, 2002.

Senate Votes 173, 174, 175, 176, 177, 178

State / Senator	173	174	175	176	177	178
ALABAMA						
Shelby	Y	Y	Y	Y	Y	Y
Sessions	Y	Y	Y	Y	Y	Y
ALASKA						
Stevens	Y	Y	Y	Y	Y	Y
Murkowski	Y	Y	Y	Y	Y	Y
ARIZONA						
McCain	N	Y	Y	Y	Y	Y
Kyl	Y	Y	Y	Y	Y	Y
ARKANSAS						
Hutchinson	Y	Y	Y	Y	Y	Y
Lincoln	Y	Y	Y	Y	Y	Y
CALIFORNIA						
Feinstein	Y	Y	Y	Y	Y	Y
Boxer	Y	Y	Y	Y	Y	Y
COLORADO						
Campbell	Y	Y	Y	Y	Y	Y
Allard	Y	Y	Y	Y	Y	Y
CONNECTICUT						
Dodd	Y	Y	Y	Y	Y	Y
Lieberman	Y	Y	Y	Y	Y	Y
DELAWARE						
Carper	Y	Y	Y	Y	Y	Y
Biden	Y	Y	Y	Y	Y	Y
FLORIDA						
Graham	Y	Y	Y	Y	Y	Y
Nelson	Y	Y	Y	Y	Y	Y
GEORGIA						
Miller	Y	Y	Y	Y	Y	Y
Cleland	Y	Y	Y	Y	Y	Y
HAWAII						
Inouye	?	Y	Y	Y	Y	Y
Akaka	Y	Y	Y	Y	Y	Y
IDAHO						
Craig	Y	?	?	+	?	Y
Crapo	+	+	+	+	+	Y
ILLINOIS						
Durbin	Y	Y	Y	Y	Y	Y
Fitzgerald	Y	Y	Y	Y	Y	Y
INDIANA						
Lugar	Y	Y	Y	Y	Y	Y
Bayh	Y	Y	Y	Y	Y	Y
IOWA						
Grassley	Y	Y	Y	Y	Y	Y
Harkin	Y	Y	Y	Y	Y	Y
KANSAS						
Brownback	Y	Y	Y	Y	Y	Y
Roberts	Y	Y	Y	Y	Y	Y
KENTUCKY						
McConnell	Y	Y	Y	Y	Y	Y
Bunning	Y	Y	Y	Y	Y	Y
LOUISIANA						
Breaux	Y	Y	Y	Y	Y	Y
Landrieu	?	Y	Y	Y	Y	Y
MAINE						
Snowe	Y	Y	Y	Y	Y	Y
Collins	Y	Y	Y	Y	Y	Y
MARYLAND						
Sarbanes	Y	Y	Y	Y	Y	Y
Mikulski	Y	Y	Y	Y	Y	Y
MASSACHUSETTS						
Kennedy	Y	Y	Y	Y	Y	Y
Kerry	+	Y	Y	Y	Y	Y
MICHIGAN						
Levin	N	Y	Y	Y	Y	Y
Stabenow	Y	Y	Y	Y	Y	Y
MINNESOTA						
Wellstone	Y	Y	Y	Y	N	Y
Dayton	Y	Y	Y	Y	N	Y
MISSISSIPPI						
Cochran	Y	Y	Y	Y	Y	Y
Lott	Y	Y	Y	Y	Y	Y
MISSOURI						
Bond	Y	Y	Y	Y	Y	Y
Carnahan	Y	Y	Y	Y	Y	Y
MONTANA						
Baucus	Y	Y	Y	Y	Y	Y
Burns	Y	Y	Y	Y	Y	Y
NEBRASKA						
Nelson	Y	Y	Y	Y	Y	Y
Hagel	Y	Y	Y	Y	Y	Y
NEVADA						
Reid	Y	Y	Y	Y	Y	Y
Ensign	Y	Y	Y	Y	Y	Y
NEW HAMPSHIRE						
Smith	Y	Y	Y	Y	Y	Y
Gregg	Y	Y	Y	Y	Y	Y
NEW JERSEY						
Corzine	Y	Y	Y	Y	Y	Y
Torricelli	Y	Y	Y	Y	Y	Y
NEW MEXICO						
Domenici	Y	Y	Y	Y	Y	Y
Bingaman	Y	Y	Y	Y	Y	Y
NEW YORK						
Clinton	Y	Y	Y	Y	Y	Y
Schumer	Y	Y	Y	Y	Y	Y
NORTH CAROLINA						
Helms	?	?	?	+	?	?
Edwards	Y	Y	Y	Y	Y	Y
NORTH DAKOTA						
Conrad	Y	Y	Y	Y	Y	Y
Dorgan	Y	Y	Y	Y	Y	Y
OHIO						
DeWine	Y	Y	Y	Y	Y	Y
Voinovich	?	Y	Y	Y	Y	Y
OKLAHOMA						
Nickles	Y	Y	Y	Y	Y	Y
Inhofe	Y	Y	Y	Y	Y	Y
OREGON						
Wyden	Y	Y	Y	Y	Y	Y
Smith	Y	Y	Y	Y	Y	Y
PENNSYLVANIA						
Specter	Y	Y	Y	Y	Y	Y
Santorum	Y	Y	Y	Y	Y	Y
RHODE ISLAND						
Reed	Y	Y	Y	Y	Y	Y
Chafee	Y	Y	Y	Y	Y	Y
SOUTH CAROLINA						
Thurmond	Y	Y	Y	Y	Y	Y
Hollings	Y	Y	Y	Y	Y	Y
SOUTH DAKOTA						
Daschle	Y	Y	Y	Y	Y	Y
Johnson	Y	Y	Y	Y	Y	Y
TENNESSEE						
Thompson	Y	Y	Y	Y	Y	Y
Frist	Y	Y	Y	Y	Y	Y
TEXAS						
Gramm	Y	Y	Y	Y	Y	Y
Hutchison	Y	Y	Y	Y	Y	Y
UTAH						
Hatch	Y	Y	Y	Y	Y	Y
Bennett	Y	Y	Y	Y	Y	Y
VERMONT						
Leahy	Y	Y	Y	Y	Y	Y
Jeffords	Y	Y	Y	Y	Y	Y
VIRGINIA						
Warner	?	Y	Y	Y	Y	Y
Allen	Y	Y	Y	Y	Y	Y
WASHINGTON						
Cantwell	Y	Y	Y	Y	Y	Y
Murray	Y	Y	Y	Y	Y	Y
WEST VIRGINIA						
Byrd	Y	Y	Y	Y	Y	Y
Rockefeller	Y	Y	Y	Y	Y	Y
WISCONSIN						
Kohl	Y	Y	Y	Y	Y	Y
Feingold	Y	Y	Y	Y	N	Y
WYOMING						
Thomas	Y	Y	Y	Y	Y	Y
Enzi	Y	Y	Y	Y	Y	Y

Key

Y Voted for (yea).
Paired for.
+ Announced for.
N Voted against (nay).
X Paired against.
– Announced against.
P Voted "present."
C Voted "present" to avoid possible conflict of interest.
? Did not vote or otherwise make a position known.

Democrats **Republicans**
Independents

ND Northern Democrats SD Southern Democrats

Southern states - Ala., Ark., Fla., Ga., Ky., La., Miss., N.C., Okla., S.C., Tenn., Texas, Va.

173. S 2673. Accounting Industry Overhaul/Cloture. Motion to invoke cloture (thus limiting debate) on the bill that would require more complete disclosure of corporate finances and overhaul regulation of the accounting industry. Motion agreed to 91-2: R 44-1; D 46-1 (ND 38-1, SD 8-0); I 1-0. Three-fifths of the total Senate (60) is required to invoke cloture. July 12, 2002.

174. S 2673. Accounting Industry Overhaul/Electronic Filing. Carnahan, D-Mo., amendment to the Edwards, D-N.C., amendment. The Carnahan amendment would require corporate executives or directors who have purchased or sold securities in their firm to file an electronic statement with the Securities and Exchange Commission (SEC) before the end of the second business day following the transaction. The SEC would be required to provide the statement on a publicly accessible Internet site at the end of the second business day following that filing. Adopted 97-0: R 46-0; D 50-0 (ND 41-0, SD 9-0); I 1-0. July 15, 2002.

175. S 2673. Accounting Industry Overhaul/Conduct Standards. Edwards, D-N.C., amendment that would require the SEC to establish new rules setting professional standards of conduct for attorneys representing public companies who appear before the SEC, including a rule requiring an attorney to report evidence of a material violation of securities law to the company's chief legal counsel or chief executive officer, or to the board of directors if necessary. Adopted 97-0: R 46-0; D 50-0 (ND 41-0, SD 9-0); I 1-0. July 15, 2002.

176. S 2673. Accounting Industry Overhaul/Passage. Passage of the bill that would require more complete disclosure of corporate finances and overhaul regulation of the accounting industry. The bill would establish a new oversight board to police accounting firms, and forbid firms from providing investment banking, management consulting and other services for publicly traded companies. It would create new criminal penalties for shareholder fraud and obstruction of justice involving document shredding and require chief executive officers and chief financial officers to attest to the accuracy of financial statements included in SEC filings. Passed 97-0: R 46-0; D 50-0 (ND 41-0, SD 9-0); I 1-0. July 15, 2002.

177. Smith Nomination/Cloture. Motion to invoke cloture (thus limiting debate) on President Bush's nomination of Lavenski R. Smith of Arkansas to be a judge for the 8th Circuit Court of Appeals. Motion agreed to 94-3: R 46-0; D 47-3 (ND 38-3, SD 9-0); I 1-0. Three-fifths of the total Senate (60) is required to invoke cloture. July 15, 2002.

178. S 812. Drug Patents/Cloture. Motion to invoke cloture (thus limiting debate) on the motion to proceed to the bill that would allow for a single 30-month stay against Food and Drug Administration approval of a generic drug patent when a brand-name company's patent is challenged. Motion agreed to 99-0: R 48-0; D 50-0 (ND 41-0, SD 9-0); I 1-0. Three-fifths of the total Senate (60) is required to invoke cloture. July 17, 2002.

	179	180	181	182	183	184
ALABAMA						
Shelby	N	Y	Y	N	Y	Y
Sessions	Y	Y	Y	N	Y	Y
ALASKA						
Stevens	Y	Y	Y	N	Y	Y
Murkowski	Y	Y	Y	N	Y	Y
ARIZONA						
McCain	Y	Y	N	N	N	Y
Kyl	N	Y	N	N	Y	Y
ARKANSAS						
Hutchinson	N	Y	Y	N	Y	Y
Lincoln	Y	Y	Y	Y	Y	Y
CALIFORNIA						
Feinstein	Y	Y	Y	Y	Y	Y
Boxer	Y	Y	Y	Y	Y	Y
COLORADO						
Campbell	N	Y	Y	N	Y	Y
Allard	Y	Y	Y	N	Y	Y
CONNECTICUT						
Dodd	Y	Y	Y	Y	Y	Y
Lieberman	Y	Y	Y	Y	Y	Y
DELAWARE						
Carper	N	Y	Y	Y	Y	Y
Biden	Y	Y	Y	Y	Y	Y
FLORIDA						
Graham	Y	Y	Y	Y	Y	Y
Nelson	Y	Y	Y	Y	Y	Y
GEORGIA						
Miller	Y	Y	Y	Y	Y	Y
Cleland	Y	Y	Y	Y	Y	Y
HAWAII						
Inouye	Y	Y	Y	Y	Y	Y
Akaka	Y	Y	Y	Y	Y	Y
IDAHO						
Craig	Y	Y	Y	N	Y	Y
Crapo	Y	Y	Y	N	Y	Y
ILLINOIS						
Durbin	Y	Y	Y	Y	Y	Y
Fitzgerald	Y	Y	Y	N	Y	Y
INDIANA						
Lugar	Y	Y	Y	N	Y	Y
Bayh	N	Y	Y	Y	Y	Y

	179	180	181	182	183	184
IOWA						
Grassley	Y	Y	Y	N	Y	Y
Harkin	Y	Y	Y	Y	?	Y
KANSAS						
Brownback	Y	Y	Y	N	Y	Y
Roberts	N	Y	Y	N	Y	Y
KENTUCKY						
McConnell	Y	Y	Y	N	Y	Y
Bunning	Y	Y	Y	N	Y	Y
LOUISIANA						
Breaux	N	Y	Y	N	Y	Y
Landrieu	Y	Y	Y	Y	Y	Y
MAINE						
Snowe	Y	Y	Y	Y	Y	Y
Collins	Y	Y	Y	Y	Y	Y
MARYLAND						
Sarbanes	Y	Y	Y	Y	Y	Y
Mikulski	Y	Y	Y	Y	Y	Y
MASSACHUSETTS						
Kennedy	Y	Y	Y	Y	Y	Y
Kerry	Y	Y	Y	Y	Y	Y
MICHIGAN						
Levin	Y	Y	Y	Y	Y	Y
Stabenow	Y	Y	Y	Y	Y	Y
MINNESOTA						
Wellstone	Y	Y	Y	Y	Y	Y
Dayton	Y	Y	Y	Y	Y	Y
MISSISSIPPI						
Cochran	Y	Y	Y	N	Y	Y
Lott	Y	Y	Y	N	Y	Y
MISSOURI						
Bond	Y	Y	Y	N	Y	Y
Carnahan	Y	Y	Y	Y	Y	Y
MONTANA						
Baucus	Y	Y	Y	Y	Y	Y
Burns	Y	Y	Y	N	Y	Y
NEBRASKA						
Nelson	Y	Y	Y	N	Y	Y
Hagel	N	Y	Y	N	Y	Y
NEVADA						
Reid	Y	Y	Y	Y	Y	Y
Ensign	N	Y	Y	N	Y	Y

	179	180	181	182	183	184
NEW HAMPSHIRE						
Smith	Y	Y	Y	N	Y	Y
Gregg	Y	Y	Y	N	Y	Y
NEW JERSEY						
Corzine	N	Y	Y	Y	Y	Y
Torricelli	N	Y	Y	Y	Y	Y
NEW MEXICO						
Domenici	N	Y	Y	N	Y	Y
Bingaman	Y	Y	Y	Y	Y	Y
NEW YORK						
Clinton	Y	Y	Y	Y	Y	Y
Schumer	Y	Y	Y	Y	Y	Y
NORTH CAROLINA						
Helms	–	?	+	?	?	?
Edwards	Y	Y	Y	Y	Y	Y
NORTH DAKOTA						
Conrad	Y	Y	Y	Y	Y	Y
Dorgan	Y	Y	Y	Y	Y	Y
OHIO						
DeWine	N	Y	Y	N	Y	Y
Voinovich	N	Y	Y	Y	Y	?
OKLAHOMA						
Nickles	N	Y	Y	N	Y	Y
Inhofe	N	Y	Y	N	Y	Y
OREGON						
Wyden	Y	Y	Y	Y	Y	Y
Smith	Y	Y	Y	Y	Y	Y
PENNSYLVANIA						
Specter	Y	Y	Y	Y	Y	Y
Santorum	N	Y	Y	N	Y	Y
RHODE ISLAND						
Reed	Y	Y	Y	Y	Y	Y
Chafee	Y	Y	Y	Y	Y	Y
SOUTH CAROLINA						
Thurmond	N	Y	Y	N	Y	Y
Hollings	Y	Y	Y	Y	Y	Y
SOUTH DAKOTA						
Daschle	Y	Y	Y	Y	Y	Y
Johnson	Y	Y	Y	Y	Y	Y
TENNESSEE						
Thompson	N	Y	Y	N	Y	Y
Frist	N	Y	Y	N	Y	Y

Key

Y	Voted for (yea).
#	Paired for.
+	Announced for.
N	Voted against (nay).
X	Paired against.
–	Announced against.
P	Voted "present."
C	Voted "present" to avoid possible conflict of interest.
?	Did not vote or otherwise make a position known.

Democrats **Republicans**
Independents

	179	180	181	182	183	184
TEXAS						
Gramm	N	Y	Y	N	Y	Y
Hutchison	N	Y	Y	N	Y	Y
UTAH						
Hatch	N	Y	Y	N	Y	Y
Bennett	N	Y	Y	N	Y	Y
VERMONT						
Leahy	Y	Y	Y	Y	Y	Y
Jeffords	Y	Y	Y	Y	Y	Y
VIRGINIA						
Warner	N	Y	Y	N	Y	Y
Allen	N	Y	Y	N	Y	Y
WASHINGTON						
Cantwell	Y	Y	Y	Y	Y	Y
Murray	Y	Y	Y	Y	Y	Y
WEST VIRGINIA						
Byrd	Y	Y	Y	Y	Y	Y
Rockefeller	Y	Y	Y	Y	Y	Y
WISCONSIN						
Kohl	Y	Y	Y	Y	Y	Y
Feingold	Y	Y	N	Y	Y	Y
WYOMING						
Thomas	N	Y	Y	N	Y	Y
Enzi	N	Y	Y	N	Y	Y

ND Northern Democrats   SD Southern Democrats

Southern states - Ala., Ark., Fla., Ga., Ky., La., Miss., N.C., Okla., S.C., Tenn., Texas, Va.

179. S 812. Drug Patents/Drug Reimportation. Dorgan, D-N.D., amendment to the Dorgan amendment. The Dorgan amendment would add language that would provide for an import suspension of any covered products found to be counterfeit or in violation of current law. The underlying Dorgan amendment would authorize the Secretary of Health and Human Services (HHS) to promulgate regulations permitting pharmacists and wholesalers to import prescription drugs from Canada into the United States. It also would require Canadian pharmacies and wholesalers that provide drugs for importation to register with HHS and allow individuals to import prescription drugs from Canada if the medication is for personal use and is less than a 90-day supply. Adopted 69-30: R 23-25; D 45-5 (ND 37-4, SD 8-1); I 1-0. July 17, 2002.

180. S 812. Drug Patents/Reimportation Certification. Cochran, R-Miss., amendment to the Dorgan, D-N.D., amendment. The Cochran amendment would require the HHS secretary to certify to Congress that the implementation of the provisions pose no risk to the public's health and safety and would result in a significant cost reduction of prescription drugs for consumers before the provisions of the Dorgan amendment can go into effect. Adopted 99-0: R 48-0; D 50-0 (ND 41-0, SD 9-0); I 1-0. July 17, 2002.

181. HR 5011. Fiscal 2003 Military Construction Appropriations/Passage. Passage of the bill that would provide $10.6 billion in fiscal 2003 for military construction projects, including $1.1 billion for the building and modern-ization of barracks, $4.2 billion for family housing, and $645 million to cover costs of prior base closures. It also includes funds for medical facilities, child care centers, environmental clean up at closed military facilities and the U.S. contribution to North Atlantic Treaty Organization security efforts. Passed 96-3: R 46-2; D 49-1 (ND 40-1, SD 9-0); I 1-0. July 18, 2002.

182. S 812. Drug Patents/State Authority. Stabenow, D-Mich., amendment to the Dorgan, D-N.D., amendment. The Stabenow amendment would codify state authority to set up programs designed to force pharmaceutical companies to offer discounted Medicaid drug prices for other groups. Adopted 56-43: R 7-41; D 48-2 (ND 40-1, SD 8-1); I 1-0. July 18, 2002.

183. Clifton Nomination/Cloture. Motion to invoke cloture (thus limiting debate) on President Bush's nomination of Richard R. Clifton of Hawaii to be a judge for the 9th Circuit Court of Appeals. Motion agreed to 97-1: R 47-1; D 49-0 (ND 40-0, SD 9-0); I 1-0. Three-fifths of the total Senate (60) is required to invoke cloture. July 18, 2002.

184. Clifton Nomination/Confirmation. Confirmation of President Bush's nomination of Richard R. Clifton of Hawaii to be a judge for the 9th Circuit Court of Appeals. Confirmed 98-0: R 47-0; D 50-0 (ND 41-0, SD 9-0); I 1-0. A "yea" was a vote in support of the president's position. July 18, 2002.

	185	186	187	188	189
ALABAMA					
Shelby	Y	N	Y	Y	Y
Sessions	Y	N	Y	Y	Y
ALASKA					
Stevens	Y	N	Y	Y	Y
Murkowski	Y	N	Y	Y	Y
ARIZONA					
McCain	Y	N	Y	N	Y
Kyl	Y	N	Y	Y	Y
ARKANSAS					
Hutchinson	Y	N	Y	Y	N
Lincoln	Y	Y	N	Y	N
CALIFORNIA					
Feinstein	Y	Y	N	Y	N
Boxer	Y	Y	N	Y	N
COLORADO					
Campbell	Y	N	Y	Y	Y
Allard	Y	N	Y	Y	Y
CONNECTICUT					
Dodd	Y	Y	N	Y	N
Lieberman	Y	Y	N	Y	N
DELAWARE					
Carper	Y	Y	N	Y	Y
Biden	Y	Y	N	Y	N
FLORIDA					
Graham	Y	Y	N	Y	N
Nelson	Y	Y	N	Y	N
GEORGIA					
Miller	Y	Y	N	Y	N
Cleland	Y	Y	N	Y	N
HAWAII					
Inouye	Y	Y	N	Y	N
Akaka	Y	Y	N	Y	N
IDAHO					
Craig	Y	N	Y	Y	Y
Crapo	Y	N	Y	Y	Y
ILLINOIS					
Durbin	Y	Y	N	Y	N
Fitzgerald	Y	Y	Y	N	Y
INDIANA					
Lugar	Y	N	N	Y	Y
Bayh	Y	Y	N	Y	N

	185	186	187	188	189
IOWA					
Grassley	Y	N	Y	Y	Y
Harkin	Y	Y	N	Y	N
KANSAS					
Brownback	Y	N	Y	Y	Y
Roberts	Y	N	Y	Y	Y
KENTUCKY					
McConnell	Y	N	Y	Y	Y
Bunning	Y	N	Y	Y	Y
LOUISIANA					
Breaux	Y	Y	Y	Y	Y
Landrieu	Y	Y	Y	Y	N
MAINE					
Snowe	Y	N	Y	Y	Y
Collins	Y	N	Y	Y	Y
MARYLAND					
Sarbanes	Y	Y	N	Y	N
Mikulski	Y	Y	N	Y	N
MASSACHUSETTS					
Kennedy	Y	Y	N	Y	N
Kerry	Y	Y	N	Y	N
MICHIGAN					
Levin	Y	Y	N	Y	N
Stabenow	Y	Y	N	Y	N
MINNESOTA					
Wellstone	Y	Y	N	Y	N
Dayton	Y	Y	N	Y	N
MISSISSIPPI					
Cochran	Y	N	Y	Y	Y
Lott	Y	N	Y	Y	Y
MISSOURI					
Bond	Y	N	Y	Y	Y
Carnahan	Y	Y	N	Y	N
MONTANA					
Baucus	Y	Y	N	Y	N
Burns	Y	N	Y	Y	Y
NEBRASKA					
Nelson	Y	Y	N	Y	N
Hagel	Y	N	N	Y	Y
NEVADA					
Reid	Y	Y	N	Y	N
Ensign	Y	N	Y	Y	Y

	185	186	187	188	189
NEW HAMPSHIRE					
Smith	Y	N	Y	Y	Y
Gregg	Y	N	Y	Y	Y
NEW JERSEY					
Corzine	Y	Y	N	Y	N
Torricelli	Y	Y	N	Y	N
NEW MEXICO					
Domenici	Y	N	Y	Y	Y
Bingaman	Y	Y	N	Y	N
NEW YORK					
Clinton	Y	Y	N	Y	N
Schumer	Y	Y	N	Y	N
NORTH CAROLINA					
Helms	?	?	?	?	?
Edwards	Y	Y	N	Y	N
NORTH DAKOTA					
Conrad	Y	Y	N	Y	N
Dorgan	Y	Y	N	Y	N
OHIO					
DeWine	Y	N	Y	Y	Y
Voinovich	Y	N	Y	N	Y
OKLAHOMA					
Nickles	Y	N	Y	Y	Y
Inhofe	Y	N	Y	Y	Y
OREGON					
Wyden	Y	Y	N	Y	N
Smith	Y	N	Y	Y	Y
PENNSYLVANIA					
Specter	?	N	Y	N	Y
Santorum	Y	N	Y	N	Y
RHODE ISLAND					
Reed	Y	Y	N	Y	N
Chafee	Y	N	N	Y	Y
SOUTH CAROLINA					
Thurmond	Y	N	Y	Y	Y
Hollings	Y	Y	N	Y	N
SOUTH DAKOTA					
Daschle	Y	Y	N	Y	N
Johnson	Y	Y	N	Y	N
TENNESSEE					
Thompson	Y	N	Y	Y	Y
Frist	Y	N	Y	Y	Y

	185	186	187	188	189
TEXAS					
Gramm	Y	N	Y	Y	Y
Hutchison	Y	N	Y	Y	Y
UTAH					
Hatch	Y	N	Y	Y	Y
Bennett	Y	N	Y	Y	Y
VERMONT					
Leahy	Y	Y	N	Y	N
Jeffords	Y	Y	Y	Y	N
VIRGINIA					
Warner	Y	N	Y	Y	Y
Allen	Y	N	Y	Y	Y
WASHINGTON					
Cantwell	Y	Y	N	Y	N
Murray	Y	Y	N	Y	N
WEST VIRGINIA					
Byrd	Y	Y	N	Y	Y
Rockefeller	Y	Y	N	Y	N
WISCONSIN					
Kohl	Y	Y	N	Y	N
Feingold	Y	Y	N	N	N
WYOMING					
Thomas	Y	N	Y	N	Y
Enzi	Y	N	Y	Y	Y

ND Northern Democrats   SD Southern Democrats

Southern states - Ala., Ark., Fla., Ga., Ky., La., Miss., N.C., Okla., S.C., Tenn., Texas, Va.

185. Carmona Nomination/Cloture. Motion to invoke cloture (thus limiting debate) on the nomination of Richard Carmona to be surgeon general. Motion agreed to 98-0: R 47-0; D 50-0 (ND 41-0, SD 9-0); I 1-0. Three-fifths of the total Senate (60) is required to invoke cloture. (Subsequently, the nomination was confirmed by voice vote.) July 23, 2002.

186. S 812. Drug Patents/Prescription Drugs. Kennedy, D-Mass., motion to waive the Budget Act with respect to the Grassley, R-Iowa, point of order against the Graham, D-Fla., amendment that would provide a new voluntary prescription drug benefit for eligible Medicare beneficiaries. It would limit monthly premiums to $25 and the co-payment for all drugs to between $10 and $60. Catastrophic coverage would begin at $4,000. Motion rejected 52-47: R 1-47; D 50-0 (ND 41-0, SD 9-0); I 1-0. A three-fifths majority vote (60) of the total Senate is required to waive the Budget Act. (Subsequently, the chair upheld the point of order, and the amendment fell.) July 23, 2002.

187. S 812. Drug Patents/Prescription Drugs. Grassley, R-Iowa., motion to waive the Budget Act with respect to the Daschle, D-S.D., point of order against the Grassley amendment that would provide a new voluntary prescription drug benefit for eligible Medicare beneficiaries. It would limit monthly premiums to $24, establish a $250 deductible and a 50 percent cost share between $251 and $3,450, and set a catastrophic limit of $3,700 for out-of-pocket expenses. It would provide beneficiaries a choice of at least two competing plans. Motion rejected 48-51: R 45-3; D 2-48 (ND 0-41, SD 2-7); I 1-0. A three-fifths majority vote (60) of the total Senate is required to waive the Budget Act. (Subsequently, the chair upheld the point of order, and the amendment fell.) July 23, 2002.

188. HR 4775. Fiscal 2002 Supplemental Appropriations/Conference Report. Adoption of the conference report on the bill that would provide approximately $28.9 billion in supplemental appropriations for fiscal 2002. The agreement includes $14.4 billion for the Defense Department, $6.7 billion for homeland security programs and $5.5 billion for post-Sept. 11 recovery efforts in New York. It also would provide $2.1 billion for foreign aid, including funds to rebuild Afghanistan, fight international terrorism and provide U.S. embassy security. Adopted (thus cleared for the president) 92-7: R 42-6; D 49-1 (ND 40-1, SD 9-0); I 1-0. A "yea" was a vote in support of the president's position. July 24, 2002.

189. S 812. Drug Patents/Prescription Drugs. Hagel, R-Neb., motion to waive the Budget Act with respect to the Kennedy, D-Mass., point of order against the Hagel amendment to the Dorgan, D-N.D., amendment. The Hagel amendment would establish a voluntary prescription drug discount card for Medicare participants and set sliding scale limits on out-of-pocket expenses based on income levels. It also would create a Medicare Prescription Drug Advisory Board to advise the secretary of Health and Human Services (HHS) and establish a Center for Medicare Prescription Drugs to administer the program. The Dorgan amendment would authorize the HHS secretary to promulgate regulations permitting pharmacists and wholesalers to import prescription drugs from Canada into the United States. It also would require Canadian pharmacies and wholesalers that provide drugs for importation to register with HHS and allow individuals to import prescription drugs from Canada if the medication is for personal use and is less than a 90-day supply. Motion rejected 51-48: R 47-1; D 4-46 (ND 3-38, SD 1-8); I 0-1. A three-fifths majority vote (60) of the total Senate is required to waive the Budget Act. (Subsequently, the chair upheld the point of order, and the amendment fell.) July 24, 2002.

	190	191	192
ALABAMA			
Shelby	Y	Y	Y
Sessions	Y	Y	Y
ALASKA			
Stevens	Y	Y	Y
Murkowski	Y	Y	Y
ARIZONA			
McCain	Y	Y	Y
Kyl	N	Y	Y
ARKANSAS			
Hutchinson	Y	Y	Y
Lincoln	Y	Y	Y
CALIFORNIA			
Feinstein	Y	Y	Y
Boxer	Y	Y	Y
COLORADO			
Campbell	Y	Y	Y
Allard	Y	N	Y
CONNECTICUT			
Dodd	Y	Y	Y
Lieberman	Y	Y	Y
DELAWARE			
Carper	N	Y	Y
Biden	Y	Y	Y
FLORIDA			
Graham	Y	Y	Y
Nelson	Y	Y	Y
GEORGIA			
Miller	Y	Y	Y
Cleland	Y	Y	Y
HAWAII			
Inouye	Y	Y	Y
Akaka	Y	Y	Y
IDAHO			
Craig	N	Y	Y
Crapo	N	Y	Y
ILLINOIS			
Durbin	Y	Y	Y
Fitzgerald	Y	N	Y
INDIANA			
Lugar	Y	Y	Y
Bayh	Y	N	Y

	190	191	192
IOWA			
Grassley	N	Y	Y
Harkin	Y	Y	Y
KANSAS			
Brownback	N	N	Y
Roberts	N	N	Y
KENTUCKY			
McConnell	Y	Y	Y
Bunning	Y	N	Y
LOUISIANA			
Breaux	Y	Y	Y
Landrieu	Y	Y	Y
MAINE			
Snowe	Y	Y	Y
Collins	Y	Y	Y
MARYLAND			
Sarbanes	Y	Y	Y
Mikulski	Y	Y	Y
MASSACHUSETTS			
Kennedy	Y	Y	Y
Kerry	Y	Y	Y
MICHIGAN			
Levin	Y	Y	Y
Stabenow	Y	Y	Y
MINNESOTA			
Wellstone	Y	Y	Y
Dayton	Y	Y	Y
MISSISSIPPI			
Cochran	Y	Y	Y
Lott	N	Y	Y
MISSOURI			
Bond	N	Y	Y
Carnahan	N	Y	Y
MONTANA			
Baucus	Y	Y	Y
Burns	Y	Y	Y
NEBRASKA			
Nelson	Y	Y	Y
Hagel	Y	Y	Y
NEVADA			
Reid	Y	Y	Y
Ensign	N	N	Y

	190	191	192
NEW HAMPSHIRE			
Smith	N	N	Y
Gregg	N	Y	Y
NEW JERSEY			
Corzine	Y	Y	Y
Torricelli	Y	Y	Y
NEW MEXICO			
Domenici	Y	Y	Y
Bingaman	Y	Y	Y
NEW YORK			
Clinton	Y	Y	Y
Schumer	Y	Y	Y
NORTH CAROLINA			
Helms	?	?	+
Edwards	Y	Y	Y
NORTH DAKOTA			
Conrad	Y	N	Y
Dorgan	Y	Y	Y
OHIO			
DeWine	N	Y	Y
Voinovich	N	N	Y
OKLAHOMA			
Nickles	N	Y	Y
Inhofe	N	N	Y
OREGON			
Wyden	Y	Y	Y
Smith	Y	Y	Y
PENNSYLVANIA			
Specter	Y	Y	Y
Santorum	N	Y	Y
RHODE ISLAND			
Reed	Y	Y	Y
Chafee	Y	Y	Y
SOUTH CAROLINA			
Thurmond	N	Y	Y
Hollings	Y	Y	Y
SOUTH DAKOTA			
Daschle	Y	Y	Y
Johnson	Y	Y	Y
TENNESSEE			
Thompson	N	Y	Y
Frist	N	Y	Y

Key

Y	Voted for (yea).
#	Paired for.
+	Announced for.
N	Voted against (nay).
X	Paired against.
−	Announced against.
P	Voted "present."
C	Voted "present" to avoid possible conflict of interest.
?	Did not vote or otherwise make a position known.

Democrats **Republicans**
Independents

	190	191	192
TEXAS			
Gramm	N	N	Y
Hutchison	Y	Y	Y
UTAH			
Hatch	Y	Y	Y
Bennett	Y	Y	Y
VERMONT			
Leahy	Y	Y	Y
Jeffords	Y	Y	Y
VIRGINIA			
Warner	Y	Y	Y
Allen	Y	Y	Y
WASHINGTON			
Cantwell	Y	Y	Y
Murray	Y	Y	Y
WEST VIRGINIA			
Byrd	Y	Y	Y
Rockefeller	Y	Y	Y
WISCONSIN			
Kohl	Y	Y	Y
Feingold	N	Y	Y
WYOMING			
Thomas	N	N	Y
Enzi	Y	N	Y

ND Northern Democrats　　SD Southern Democrats

Southern states - Ala., Ark., Fla., Ga., Ky., La., Miss., N.C., Okla., S.C., Tenn., Texas, Va.

190. S 812. Drug Patents/Federal Medical Assistance Percentage Program. Reid, D-Nev., motion to waive the Budget Act with respect to the Gramm, R-Texas, point of order against the Rockefeller, D-W.Va., amendment to the Dorgan, D-N.D., amendment. The Rockefeller amendment would provide approximately $6 billion in temporary financial assistance to states through an increase in the Federal Medical Assistance Percentage program. It also would provide $3 billion to states in fiscal relief grants that could be used for social service programs. Motion agreed to 75-24: R 27-21; D 47-3 (ND 38-3, SD 9-0); I 1-0. A three-fifths majority vote (60) of the total Senate is required to waive the Budget Act. July 25, 2002.

191. HR 5121. Fiscal 2003 Legislative Branch Appropriations/Passage. Passage of the bill that would appropriate approximately $2.42 billion in fiscal 2003 for legislative activities, including $1.46 billion for congressional operations, $497 million for the Library of Congress, $122.4 million for the Government Printing Office and $454.5 million for the General Accounting Office. Passed 85-14: R 36-12; D 48-2 (ND 39-2, SD 9-0); I 1-0. (Before passage the Senate struck all after the enacting clause and inserted the text of S 2720 as amended). July 25, 2002.

192. HR 3763. Accounting Industry Overhaul/Conference Report. Adoption of the conference report on the bill that would overhaul regulation of the accounting industry. A new Public Company Accounting Oversight Board, funded by fees on publicly traded companies, would police the industry. Accounting firms would be barred from performing several services, including investment banking and management consulting, for companies they audit. The bill would create a new securities fraud penalty with a maximum prison sentence of up to 25 years, and new criminal penalties of up to 20 years imprisonment for shareholder fraud and document shredding. Top corporate executives would have to certify company financial statements. Executives engaged in financial misconduct would be required to pay back bonuses and profits. Civil penalties would be placed in a fund for defrauded investors. Adopted (thus cleared for the president) 99-0: R 48-0; D 50-0 (ND 41-0, SD 9-0); I 1-0. July 25, 2002.

	193	194	195	196	197	198	199	200
ALABAMA								
Shelby	Y	Y	Y	Y	Y	N	N	Y
Sessions	Y	Y	Y	Y	N	N	N	Y
ALASKA								
Stevens	Y	Y	Y	Y	N	N	N	N
Murkowski	Y	Y	Y	Y	N	N	N	N
ARIZONA								
McCain	Y	Y	Y	Y	N	Y	N	Y
Kyl	Y	Y	Y	Y	N	Y	N	N
ARKANSAS								
Hutchinson	?	?	?	?	N	Y	Y	Y
Lincoln	Y	Y	Y	Y	Y	Y	Y	Y
CALIFORNIA								
Feinstein	Y	Y	Y	Y	Y	N	Y	Y
Boxer	?	Y	Y	Y	Y	N	Y	Y
COLORADO								
Campbell	Y	Y	Y	Y	N	N	N	N
Allard	Y	Y	Y	Y	N	Y	N	N
CONNECTICUT								
Dodd	Y	Y	Y	Y	Y	N	Y	Y
Lieberman	Y	Y	Y	Y	Y	Y	Y	Y
DELAWARE								
Carper	Y	Y	Y	Y	Y	Y	Y	Y
Biden	+	Y	Y	Y	Y	Y	Y	Y
FLORIDA								
Graham	Y	Y	Y	Y	Y	Y	Y	Y
Nelson	Y	+	Y	Y	Y	Y	Y	Y
GEORGIA								
Miller	?	Y	Y	Y	Y	Y	Y	Y
Cleland	Y	Y	Y	Y	Y	Y	Y	Y
HAWAII								
Inouye	?	Y	Y	Y	Y	Y	Y	Y
Akaka	Y	Y	Y	Y	Y	N	Y	Y
IDAHO								
Craig	Y	Y	Y	Y	N	N	N	N
Crapo	Y	Y	Y	Y	Y	N	N	N
ILLINOIS								
Durbin	Y	Y	Y	Y	N	Y	N	Y
Fitzgerald	Y	Y	Y	Y	N	Y	N	Y
INDIANA								
Lugar	Y	Y	Y	Y	Y	N	N	N
Bayh	Y	Y	Y	Y	Y	Y	Y	Y

	193	194	195	196	197	198	199	200
IOWA								
Grassley	Y	Y	Y	Y	N	Y	N	Y
Harkin	Y	Y	Y	Y	N	Y	N	Y
KANSAS								
Brownback	Y	Y	Y	Y	N	Y	N	N
Roberts	Y	Y	Y	Y	N	Y	N	N
KENTUCKY								
McConnell	Y	?	?	?	N	Y	N	N
Bunning	Y	Y	Y	Y	N	Y	N	N
LOUISIANA								
Breaux	Y	Y	Y	Y	Y	Y	N	Y
Landrieu	Y	Y	Y	Y	Y	Y	Y	Y
MAINE								
Snowe	Y	Y	Y	Y	N	N	N	Y
Collins	Y	Y	Y	Y	N	Y	Y	Y
MARYLAND								
Sarbanes	Y	Y	Y	Y	Y	N	Y	Y
Mikulski	Y	Y	Y	Y	Y	N	Y	Y
MASSACHUSETTS								
Kennedy	Y	Y	Y	Y	Y	Y	Y	Y
Kerry	Y	Y	Y	Y	Y	Y	Y	Y
MICHIGAN								
Levin	Y	Y	Y	Y	Y	Y	Y	Y
Stabenow	Y	Y	Y	Y	Y	N	Y	Y
MINNESOTA								
Wellstone	Y	Y	Y	Y	Y	Y	Y	Y
Dayton	Y	Y	Y	Y	Y	N	Y	Y
MISSISSIPPI								
Cochran	Y	Y	Y	Y	N	Y	N	N
Lott	Y	Y	Y	Y	N	Y	N	N
MISSOURI								
Bond	?	Y	Y	Y	N	Y	N	N
Carnahan	Y	Y	Y	Y	N	Y	N	Y
MONTANA								
Baucus	Y	Y	Y	Y	Y	Y	Y	Y
Burns	Y	Y	Y	Y	N	Y	N	N
NEBRASKA								
Nelson	Y	Y	Y	Y	N	Y	N	Y
Hagel	Y	Y	Y	Y	N	Y	N	N
NEVADA								
Reid	Y	Y	Y	Y	N	Y	N	Y
Ensign	Y	Y	Y	Y	N	N	N	N

	193	194	195	196	197	198	199	200
NEW HAMPSHIRE								
Smith	Y	Y	Y	Y	N	Y	N	Y
Gregg	Y	Y	Y	Y	N	Y	N	Y
NEW JERSEY								
Corzine	Y	Y	Y	Y	Y	N	Y	Y
Torricelli	Y	Y	Y	Y	Y	N	Y	Y
NEW MEXICO								
Domenici	Y	Y	Y	Y	N	Y	N	Y
Bingaman	Y	Y	Y	Y	Y	Y	Y	Y
NEW YORK								
Clinton	Y	Y	Y	Y	Y	N	Y	Y
Schumer	Y	Y	Y	Y	Y	N	Y	Y
NORTH CAROLINA								
Helms	?	?	?	?	–	–	–	–
Edwards	Y	Y	Y	Y	Y	Y	Y	Y
NORTH DAKOTA								
Conrad	Y	Y	Y	Y	Y	N	Y	Y
Dorgan	Y	Y	Y	Y	Y	N	Y	Y
OHIO								
DeWine	Y	?	?	?	N	Y	N	Y
Voinovich	Y	Y	Y	Y	N	Y	N	Y
OKLAHOMA								
Nickles	Y	Y	Y	Y	N	Y	N	N
Inhofe	Y	Y	Y	Y	N	Y	N	N
OREGON								
Wyden	Y	Y	Y	Y	Y	Y	Y	Y
Smith	Y	Y	Y	Y	Y	Y	Y	Y
PENNSYLVANIA								
Specter	Y	Y	Y	Y	Y	Y	N	N
Santorum	Y	Y	Y	Y	Y	Y	N	N
RHODE ISLAND								
Reed	Y	Y	Y	Y	N	Y	Y	Y
Chafee	Y	Y	Y	Y	N	Y	Y	Y
SOUTH CAROLINA								
Thurmond	Y	Y	Y	Y	N	N	N	N
Hollings	Y	Y	Y	Y	N	N	N	Y
SOUTH DAKOTA								
Daschle	Y	Y	Y	Y	Y	N	Y	Y
Johnson	Y	Y	Y	Y	Y	Y	Y	Y
TENNESSEE								
Thompson	Y	Y	Y	Y	N	Y	N	N
Frist	Y	Y	Y	Y	N	Y	N	N

	193	194	195	196	197	198	199	200
TEXAS								
Gramm	?	Y	Y	Y	N	Y	N	N
Hutchison	?	Y	Y	Y	N	Y	N	N
UTAH								
Hatch	Y	Y	Y	Y	N	Y	N	N
Bennett	Y	Y	Y	Y	N	Y	N	N
VERMONT								
Leahy	Y	Y	Y	Y	Y	N	Y	Y
Jeffords	Y	Y	Y	Y	Y	Y	N	Y
VIRGINIA								
Warner	Y	Y	Y	Y	N	Y	N	N
Allen	Y	Y	Y	Y	N	Y	N	N
WASHINGTON								
Cantwell	Y	Y	Y	Y	Y	Y	Y	Y
Murray	?	Y	Y	Y	Y	Y	Y	Y
WEST VIRGINIA								
Byrd	Y	Y	Y	Y	N	Y	N	Y
Rockefeller	Y	Y	Y	Y	N	Y	N	Y
WISCONSIN								
Kohl	Y	Y	Y	Y	Y	Y	Y	Y
Feingold	Y	Y	Y	Y	Y	N	N	Y
WYOMING								
Thomas	?	Y	Y	Y	N	Y	N	N
Enzi	Y	Y	Y	Y	N	Y	N	N

ND Northern Democrats   SD Southern Democrats

Southern states - Ala., Ark., Fla., Ga., Ky., La., Miss., N.C., Okla., S.C., Tenn., Texas, Va.

193. Gibbons Nomination/Cloture. Motion to invoke cloture (thus limiting debate) on the nomination of Julia Smith Gibbons of Tennessee to be a judge for the 6th Circuit Court of Appeals. Motion agreed to 89-0: R 43-0; D 45-0 (ND 37-0, SD 8-0); I 1-0. Three-fifths of the total Senate (60) is required to invoke cloture. July 26, 2002.

194. Gibbons Nomination/Confirmation. Confirmation of President Bush's nomination of Julia Smith Gibbons of Tennessee to be a judge for the 6th Circuit Court of Appeals. Confirmed 95-0: R 45-0; D 49-0 (ND 41-0, SD 8-0); I 1-0. A "yea" was a vote in support of the president's position. July 29, 2002.

195. Conti Nomination/Confirmation. Confirmation of President Bush's nomination of Joy Flowers Conti of Pennsylvania to be U.S. district judge for the Western District of Pennsylvania. Confirmed 96-0: R 45-0; D 50-0 (ND 41-0, SD 9-0); I 1-0. A "yea" was a vote in support of the president's position. July 29, 2002.

196. Jones Nomination/Confirmation. Confirmation of President Bush's nomination of John E. Jones III of Pennsylvania to be U.S. district judge for the Middle District of Pennsylvania. Confirmed 96-0: R 45-0; D 50-0 (ND 41-0, SD 9-0); I 1-0. A "yea" was a vote in support of the president's position. July 29, 2002.

197. S 812. Drug Patents/Medical Malpractice. Reid, D-Nev., motion to table (kill) the McConnell R-Ky., amendment to the Dorgan, D-N.D., amendment. The McConnell amendment would limit punitive damages to twice the sum of compensatory damages. It would place limits on attorneys' fees and require lawsuits to be filed within two years of the discovery of an injury. The Dorgan amendment would authorize the secretary of Health and Human Services (HHS) to promulgate regulations permitting pharmacists and wholesalers to import prescription drugs from Canada into the United States. It also would require Canadian pharmacies and wholesalers that provide drugs for importation to register with HHS and allow individuals to import prescription drugs from Canada if the medication is for personal use and is less than a 90-day supply. Motion agreed to 57-42: R 6-42; D 50-0 (ND 41-0, SD 9-0); I 1-0. July 30, 2002.

198. HR 3009. Trade Promotion Authority/Motion to Proceed. Reid, D-Nev., motion to proceed to the conference report on the bill that would allow special trade promotion authority for congressional consideration of trade agreements reached before June 1, 2005, and extend duty-free status to certain products from Bolivia, Colombia, Ecuador and Peru. Motion agreed to 66-33: R 40-8; D 25-25 (ND 17-24, SD 8-1); I 1-0. July 30, 2002.

199. S 812. Drug Patents/Prescription Drugs. Graham, D-Fla., motion to waive the Budget Act with respect to the Frist, R-Tenn., point of order against the Graham amendment to the Dorgan, D-N.D., amendment. The Graham amendment would provide prescription drug coverage for Medicare recipients with incomes of up to 200 percent of the poverty level. It also would provide catastrophic coverage for drug costs over $3,300 per year for an annual payment of $25 per year. All recipients would be eligible for a discount of 5 percent or more on prescription drugs. Motion rejected 49-50: R 4-44; D 45-5 (ND 38-3, SD 7-2); I 0-1. A three-fifths majority vote (60) of the total Senate is required to waive the Budget Act. (Subsequently, the chair upheld the point of order, and the amendment fell.) July 31, 2002.

200. S 812. Drug Patents/Cloture. Motion to invoke cloture (thus limiting debate) on the bill that would allow for a single 30-month stay against Food and Drug Administration approval of a generic drug patent when a brand-name company's patent is challenged. Motion agreed to 66-33: R 15-33; D 50-0 (ND 41-0, SD 9-0); I 1-0. Three-fifths of the total Senate (60) is required to invoke cloture. July 31, 2002.

ALABAMA	201	202	203	204	205	206	207
Shelby	Y	Y	N	Y	Y	N	N
Sessions	Y	Y	N	Y	Y	N	N
ALASKA							
Stevens	Y	Y	Y	Y	Y	Y	Y
Murkowski	Y	Y	Y	Y	Y	Y	Y
ARIZONA							
McCain	Y	Y	Y	N	Y	Y	Y
Kyl	N	Y	Y	Y	Y	Y	Y
ARKANSAS							
Hutchinson	Y	Y	Y	Y	Y	Y	Y
Lincoln	Y	Y	Y	Y	Y	Y	Y
CALIFORNIA							
Feinstein	Y	N	Y	Y	Y	Y	Y
Boxer	Y	N	N	Y	Y	N	N
COLORADO							
Campbell	Y	Y	N	Y	Y	N	N
Allard	Y	Y	Y	Y	Y	Y	Y
CONNECTICUT							
Dodd	Y	N	N	Y	Y	N	N
Lieberman	Y	N	Y	Y	Y	Y	Y
DELAWARE							
Carper	Y	Y	Y	Y	Y	Y	Y
Biden	Y	Y	Y	Y	Y	Y	N
FLORIDA							
Graham	Y	Y	Y	Y	Y	Y	Y
Nelson	Y	Y	Y	Y	Y	Y	Y
GEORGIA							
Miller	Y	Y	Y	Y	Y	Y	Y
Cleland	Y	N	Y	Y	Y	Y	Y
HAWAII							
Inouye	Y	N	N	Y	Y	N	N
Akaka	Y	N	?	?	?	?	?
IDAHO							
Craig	Y	Y	Y	Y	Y	Y	Y
Crapo	Y	Y	Y	Y	Y	Y	Y
ILLINOIS							
Durbin	Y	N	N	Y	Y	N	N
Fitzgerald	Y	Y	Y	Y	Y	Y	Y
INDIANA							
Lugar	N	Y	Y	Y	Y	Y	Y
Bayh	Y	Y	Y	Y	Y	Y	Y

IOWA	201	202	203	204	205	206	207
Grassley	Y	Y	Y	Y	Y	Y	Y
Harkin	Y	N	N	Y	Y	Y	N
KANSAS							
Brownback	N	Y	Y	Y	Y	Y	Y
Roberts	N	Y	Y	Y	Y	Y	Y
KENTUCKY							
McConnell	Y	Y	Y	Y	Y	Y	Y
Bunning	Y	Y	Y	Y	Y	Y	Y
LOUISIANA							
Breaux	N	Y	Y	Y	Y	Y	Y
Landrieu	Y	Y	Y	Y	Y	Y	Y
MAINE							
Snowe	Y	Y	Y	Y	Y	Y	Y
Collins	Y	Y	Y	Y	Y	Y	Y
MARYLAND							
Sarbanes	Y	N	N	Y	Y	N	N
Mikulski	Y	N	N	Y	Y	N	N
MASSACHUSETTS							
Kennedy	Y	N	N	Y	Y	N	N
Kerry	Y	N	Y	Y	Y	Y	Y
MICHIGAN							
Levin	Y	N	N	Y	Y	N	N
Stabenow	Y	N	N	Y	Y	N	N
MINNESOTA							
Wellstone	Y	N	N	Y	Y	N	N
Dayton	Y	N	N	Y	Y	N	N
MISSISSIPPI							
Cochran	Y	Y	Y	Y	Y	Y	Y
Lott	N	Y	Y	Y	Y	Y	Y
MISSOURI							
Bond	N	Y	Y	Y	Y	Y	Y
Carnahan	Y	Y	N	Y	Y	N	N
MONTANA							
Baucus	Y	N	Y	Y	Y	Y	Y
Burns	Y	Y	N	Y	Y	N	N
NEBRASKA							
Nelson	Y	Y	Y	Y	Y	Y	Y
Hagel	N	Y	Y	Y	Y	Y	Y
NEVADA							
Reid	Y	N	N	Y	Y	N	N
Ensign	Y	Y	Y	Y	Y	Y	Y

NEW HAMPSHIRE	201	202	203	204	205	206	207
Smith	Y	Y	Y	Y	Y	Y	Y
Gregg	N	Y	Y	Y	Y	Y	Y
NEW JERSEY							
Corzine	Y	N	N	Y	Y	N	N
Torricelli	Y	N	N	Y	Y	N	N
NEW MEXICO							
Domenici	Y	Y	Y	Y	Y	Y	Y
Bingaman	Y	N	Y	Y	Y	Y	Y
NEW YORK							
Clinton	Y	N	N	Y	Y	N	N
Schumer	Y	N	N	Y	Y	N	N
NORTH CAROLINA							
Helms	–	+	?	+	?	–	–
Edwards	Y	Y	Y	Y	Y	N	N
NORTH DAKOTA							
Conrad	Y	N	N	Y	Y	N	N
Dorgan	Y	Y	N	Y	Y	N	N
OHIO							
DeWine	N	Y	Y	Y	Y	Y	Y
Voinovich	N	Y	N	Y	Y	Y	Y
OKLAHOMA							
Nickles	N	Y	Y	Y	Y	Y	Y
Inhofe	Y	Y	Y	Y	Y	Y	Y
OREGON							
Wyden	Y	N	Y	Y	Y	Y	Y
Smith	Y	Y	Y	Y	Y	Y	Y
PENNSYLVANIA							
Specter	Y	Y	Y	Y	Y	Y	Y
Santorum	N	Y	Y	Y	Y	Y	Y
RHODE ISLAND							
Reed	Y	N	N	Y	Y	N	N
Chafee	Y	Y	Y	Y	Y	Y	Y
SOUTH CAROLINA							
Thurmond	N	Y	N	Y	Y	N	N
Hollings	Y	Y	Y	Y	Y	N	N
SOUTH DAKOTA							
Daschle	Y	N	Y	Y	Y	N	N
Johnson	Y	N	N	Y	Y	N	N
TENNESSEE							
Thompson	N	Y	Y	Y	Y	Y	Y
Frist	N	Y	Y	Y	Y	Y	Y

TEXAS	201	202	203	204	205	206	207
Gramm	N	Y	Y	Y	Y	Y	Y
Hutchison	N	Y	Y	Y	Y	Y	Y
UTAH							
Hatch	N	Y	Y	Y	Y	Y	Y
Bennett	N	Y	Y	Y	Y	Y	Y
VERMONT							
Leahy	Y	N	?	Y	Y	N	N
Jeffords	Y	N	?	Y	Y	Y	Y
VIRGINIA							
Warner	Y	Y	Y	Y	Y	Y	Y
Allen	Y	Y	Y	Y	Y	Y	Y
WASHINGTON							
Cantwell	Y	N	Y	Y	Y	N	N
Murray	Y	N	Y	Y	Y	N	N
WEST VIRGINIA							
Byrd	Y	Y	N	Y	Y	N	N
Rockefeller	Y	N	N	Y	Y	N	N
WISCONSIN							
Kohl	Y	Y	Y	Y	Y	Y	Y
Feingold	Y	N	N	N	Y	N	N
WYOMING							
Thomas	Y	Y	Y	Y	Y	Y	Y
Enzi	N	Y	Y	Y	Y	Y	Y

ND Northern Democrats   SD Southern Democrats

Southern states - Ala., Ark., Fla., Ga., Ky., La., Miss., N.C., Okla., S.C., Tenn., Texas, Va.

201. S 812. Drug Patents/Passage. Passage of the bill that would allow for a single 30-month stay against Food and Drug Administration approval of a generic drug patent when a brand-name company's patent is challenged. The bill, as amended, would authorize the secretary of Health and Human Services to promulgate regulations permitting pharmacists and wholesalers to import prescription drugs from Canada into the United States. Canadian pharmacies and wholesalers that provide drugs for importation would be required to register with HHS. Individuals would be allowed to import prescription drugs from Canada if the medication is for personal use and is less than a 90-day supply. Passed 78-21: R 28-20; D 49-1 (ND 41-0, SD 8-1); I 1-0. July 31, 2002.

202. Smith Nomination/Confirmation. Confirmation of President Bush's nomination of D. Brooks Smith of Pennsylvania to be a judge for the 3rd U.S. Circuit Court of Appeals. Confirmed 64-35: R 48-0; D 16-34 (ND 8-33, SD 8-1); I 0-1. A "yea" was a vote in support of the president's position. July 31, 2002.

203. HR 3009. Trade Promotion Authority/Cloture. Motion to invoke cloture (thus limiting debate) on the conference report on the bill that would allow special trade promotion authority for congressional consideration of trade agreements reached before June 1, 2005, and extend duty-free status to certain products from Bolivia, Colombia, Ecuador and Peru. Motion agreed to 64-32: R 43-5; D 21-27 (ND 14-25, SD 7-2); I 0-0. Three-fifths of the total Senate (60) is required to invoke cloture. Aug. 1, 2002.

204. HR 5010. Fiscal 2003 Defense Appropriations/Passage. Passage of the bill that would provide $355.4 billion for the Defense Department for fiscal 2003, an increase of $34.4 billion over fiscal 2002. The bill would include $71.5 billion for procurement programs and $6.9 billion for ballistic missile defense, with the option of using $814 million of that for counterterrorism pro-

grams. It also would fund a 4.1 percent pay increase for military personnel and shift funds for the Crusader howitzer to the Future Combat System. Passed 95-3: R 46-2; D 48-1 (ND 39-1, SD 9-0); I 1-0. Aug. 1, 2002.

205. Autrey Nomination/Confirmation. Confirmation of President Bush's nomination of Henry E. Autrey of Missouri to be a U.S. district judge for the Eastern District of Missouri. Confirmed 98-0: R 48-0; D 49-0 (ND 40-0, SD 9-0); I 1-0. A "yea" was a vote in support of the president's position. Aug. 1, 2002.

206. HR 3009. Trade Promotion Authority/Budget Act Waiver. Daschle, D-S.D., motion to waive the Budget Act with respect to the Byrd, D-W.Va., point of order against the conference report on the bill that would allow special trade promotion authority for congressional consideration of trade agreements reached prior to June 1, 2005, and extend duty-free status to certain products from Bolivia, Colombia, Ecuador and Peru. Motion agreed to 67-31: R 44-4; D 22-27 (ND 15-25, SD 7-2); I 1-0. A three-fifths majority vote (60) of the total Senate is required to waive the Budget Act. Aug. 1, 2002.

207. HR 3009. Trade Promotion Authority/Conference Report. Adoption of the conference report on the bill that would allow special trade promotion authority for congressional consideration of trade agreements reached prior to June 1, 2005, and extend duty-free status to certain products from Bolivia, Colombia, Ecuador and Peru. It also would reauthorize and expand a program to provide retraining assistance to U.S. workers hurt by trade agreements, create a 65 percent tax credit for health insurance costs for displaced workers, and authorize a five-year extension of the Generalized System of Preferences. Adopted (thus cleared for the president) 64-34: R 43-5; D 20-29 (ND 13-27, SD 7-2); I 1-0. A "yea" was a vote in support of the president's position. Aug. 1, 2002.

	208	209	210
ALABAMA			
Shelby	Y	Y	Y
Sessions	Y	Y	Y
ALASKA			
Stevens	Y	Y	Y
Murkowski	?	?	Y
ARIZONA			
McCain	Y	Y	Y
Kyl	Y	Y	Y
ARKANSAS			
Hutchinson	Y	Y	Y
Lincoln	Y	Y	Y
CALIFORNIA			
Feinstein	Y	Y	Y
Boxer	Y	Y	Y
COLORADO			
Campbell	Y	Y	Y
Allard	Y	Y	Y
CONNECTICUT			
Dodd	Y	Y	Y
Lieberman	Y	Y	Y
DELAWARE			
Carper	Y	Y	Y
Biden	?	?	?
FLORIDA			
Graham	Y	Y	Y
Nelson	Y	Y	Y
GEORGIA			
Miller	Y	Y	Y
Cleland	Y	Y	Y
HAWAII			
Inouye	Y	Y	Y
Akaka	?	?	?
IDAHO			
Craig	Y	Y	Y
Crapo	Y	Y	Y
ILLINOIS			
Durbin	Y	Y	Y
Fitzgerald	Y	Y	Y
INDIANA			
Lugar	Y	Y	Y
Bayh	Y	Y	Y

	208	209	210
IOWA			
Grassley	Y	Y	Y
Harkin	Y	Y	?
KANSAS			
Brownback	Y	Y	Y
Roberts	Y	Y	Y
KENTUCKY			
McConnell	Y	Y	Y
Bunning	Y	Y	+
LOUISIANA			
Breaux	Y	Y	Y
Landrieu	Y	Y	Y
MAINE			
Snowe	Y	Y	Y
Collins	Y	Y	Y
MARYLAND			
Sarbanes	Y	Y	Y
Mikulski	Y	Y	Y
MASSACHUSETTS			
Kennedy	Y	Y	N
Kerry	Y	Y	Y
MICHIGAN			
Levin	Y	Y	Y
Stabenow	Y	Y	Y
MINNESOTA			
Wellstone	Y	Y	Y
Dayton	Y	Y	Y
MISSISSIPPI			
Cochran	Y	Y	Y
Lott	Y	Y	Y
MISSOURI			
Bond	Y	Y	Y
Carnahan	Y	Y	Y
MONTANA			
Baucus	Y	Y	Y
Burns	Y	Y	Y
NEBRASKA			
Nelson	Y	Y	Y
Hagel	Y	Y	Y
NEVADA			
Reid	Y	Y	Y
Ensign	Y	Y	?

	208	209	210
NEW HAMPSHIRE			
Smith	Y	Y	Y
Gregg	Y	Y	Y
NEW JERSEY			
Corzine	Y	Y	N
Torricelli	?	Y	?
NEW MEXICO			
Domenici	+	Y	Y
Bingaman	Y	Y	Y
NEW YORK			
Clinton	Y	Y	Y
Schumer	Y	Y	Y
NORTH CAROLINA			
Helms	+	?	?
Edwards	Y	Y	Y
NORTH DAKOTA			
Conrad	Y	Y	Y
Dorgan	Y	Y	Y
OHIO			
DeWine	Y	Y	Y
Voinovich	Y	Y	Y
OKLAHOMA			
Nickles	Y	Y	Y
Inhofe	Y	Y	Y
OREGON			
Wyden	Y	Y	Y
Smith	Y	Y	Y
PENNSYLVANIA			
Specter	?	Y	N
Santorum	?	?	Y
RHODE ISLAND			
Reed	Y	Y	N
Chafee	Y	Y	N
SOUTH CAROLINA			
Thurmond	Y	Y	Y
Hollings	Y	Y	Y
SOUTH DAKOTA			
Daschle	Y	Y	Y
Johnson	Y	Y	Y
TENNESSEE			
Thompson	Y	Y	Y
Frist	Y	Y	Y

	208	209	210
TEXAS			
Gramm	?	?	Y
Hutchison	?	Y	Y
UTAH			
Hatch	Y	Y	Y
Bennett	Y	Y	Y
VERMONT			
Leahy	?	Y	Y
Jeffords	?	Y	N
VIRGINIA			
Warner	Y	Y	Y
Allen	Y	Y	Y
WASHINGTON			
Cantwell	Y	Y	Y
Murray	Y	Y	Y
WEST VIRGINIA			
Byrd	Y	Y	Y
Rockefeller	Y	Y	Y
WISCONSIN			
Kohl	Y	Y	Y
Feingold	Y	Y	Y
WYOMING			
Thomas	Y	Y	Y
Enzi	Y	Y	Y

ND Northern Democrats   SD Southern Democrats

Southern states - Ala., Ark., Fla., Ga., Ky., La., Miss., N.C., Okla., S.C., Tenn., Texas, Va.

208. McVerry Nomination/Confirmation. Confirmation of President Bush's nomination of Terrence F. McVerry of Pennsylvania to be U.S. district judge for the Western District of Pennsylvania. Confirmed 88-0: R 42-0; D 46-0 (ND 37-0, SD 9-0); I 0-0. A "yea" was a vote in support of the president's position. Sept. 3, 2002.

209. HR 5005. Homeland Security/Motion to Proceed. Motion to proceed to the bill that would consolidate 22 agencies into a new Cabinet-level homeland security department charged with protecting domestic security. Motion agreed to 94-0: R 45-0; D 48-0 (ND 39-0, SD 9-0); I 1-0. Sept. 3, 2002.

210. HR 5005. Homeland Security/Armed Pilots. Boxer, D-Calif., amendment to the Smith, R-N.H., amendment to the Lieberman, D-Conn., substitute amendment. The Boxer amendment would add language requiring that deputized pilots receive the same training as federal law enforcement officers. The provisions of the amendment would take effect on the day after the bill's enactment. The Smith amendment would require the undersecretary of Transportation for security to establish a program within 90 days of enactment to deputize qualified pilots of commercial passenger and cargo planes as federal law enforcement officers, and authorize those officers to carry firearms and use lethal force against individuals in defense of an aircraft if security is at risk. The substitute amendment would create a new Cabinet-level Homeland Security Department charged with protecting domestic security. Adopted 87-6: R 44-2; D 43-3 (ND 34-3, SD 9-0); I 0-1. (Subsequently, the Smith amendment was adopted by voice vote.) Sept. 5, 2002.

ALABAMA	211	212	213	214	215
Shelby	?	N	Y	?	N
Sessions	?	N	?	N	N
ALASKA					
Stevens	Y	Y	Y	N	N
Murkowski	Y	Y	Y	N	N
ARIZONA					
McCain	Y	Y	Y	N	N
Kyl	Y	N	Y	N	N
ARKANSAS					
Hutchinson	?	Y	?	N	N
Lincoln	Y	Y	Y	Y	Y
CALIFORNIA					
Feinstein	Y	Y	Y	Y	Y
Boxer	Y	Y	Y	Y	Y
COLORADO					
Campbell	?	Y	Y	N	Y
Allard	?	Y	Y	N	N
CONNECTICUT					
Dodd	Y	Y	?	Y	Y
Lieberman	?	Y	Y	Y	Y
DELAWARE					
Carper	Y	Y	?	Y	Y
Biden	Y	Y	Y	Y	Y
FLORIDA					
Graham	Y	Y	Y	Y	Y
Nelson	Y	Y	Y	Y	Y
GEORGIA					
Miller	Y	Y	Y	N	N
Cleland	Y	Y	Y	Y	Y
HAWAII					
Inouye	Y	Y	Y	Y	Y
Akaka	?	?	?	?	?
IDAHO					
Craig	Y	Y	Y	N	N
Crapo	Y	Y	Y	N	N
ILLINOIS					
Durbin	?	Y	Y	Y	Y
Fitzgerald	Y	N	Y	N	N
INDIANA					
Lugar	Y	N	Y	N	N
Bayh	Y	Y	Y	N	Y

IOWA	211	212	213	214	215
Grassley	Y	Y	Y	N	N
Harkin	?	Y	Y	N	Y
KANSAS					
Brownback	Y	Y	Y	N	N
Roberts	Y	Y	Y	N	N
KENTUCKY					
McConnell	Y	Y	Y	N	N
Bunning	?	Y	Y	N	N
LOUISIANA					
Breaux	Y	Y	Y	N	Y
Landrieu	Y	Y	Y	Y	Y
MAINE					
Snowe	Y	N	Y	N	N
Collins	Y	Y	Y	N	N
MARYLAND					
Sarbanes	Y	Y	Y	Y	Y
Mikulski	?	Y	Y	Y	Y
MASSACHUSETTS					
Kennedy	Y	Y	Y	Y	Y
Kerry	Y	Y	Y	Y	Y
MICHIGAN					
Levin	Y	Y	Y	Y	Y
Stabenow	Y	Y	Y	Y	Y
MINNESOTA					
Wellstone	Y	Y	+	Y	Y
Dayton	Y	Y	Y	Y	Y
MISSISSIPPI					
Cochran	Y	Y	Y	N	N
Lott	Y	N	Y	N	N
MISSOURI					
Bond	?	Y	Y	N	N
Carnahan	Y	Y	Y	Y	Y
MONTANA					
Baucus	Y	Y	Y	Y	Y
Burns	Y	Y	Y	N	N
NEBRASKA					
Nelson	Y	Y	Y	N	Y
Hagel	Y	Y	Y	N	N
NEVADA					
Reid	Y	Y	Y	Y	Y
Ensign	Y	N	Y	N	N

NEW HAMPSHIRE	211	212	213	214	215
Smith	?	?	?	?	?
Gregg	?	?	?	N	N
NEW JERSEY					
Corzine	Y	Y	Y	Y	Y
Torricelli	Y	?	?	?	?
NEW MEXICO					
Domenici	Y	Y	Y	N	N
Bingaman	Y	Y	Y	Y	Y
NEW YORK					
Clinton	Y	Y	?	N	Y
Schumer	Y	Y	Y	Y	Y
NORTH CAROLINA					
Helms	?	?	?	N	N
Edwards	Y	Y	Y	Y	Y
NORTH DAKOTA					
Conrad	Y	Y	Y	Y	Y
Dorgan	Y	Y	Y	Y	Y
OHIO					
DeWine	Y	Y	Y	N	N
Voinovich	Y	Y	Y	N	N
OKLAHOMA					
Nickles	Y	N	Y	N	N
Inhofe	Y	Y	Y	N	N
OREGON					
Wyden	Y	Y	Y	Y	Y
Smith	Y	Y	Y	N	N
PENNSYLVANIA					
Specter	?	Y	Y	N	N
Santorum	?	N	Y	N	N
RHODE ISLAND					
Reed	Y	Y	Y	Y	Y
Chafee	Y	N	Y	N	N
SOUTH CAROLINA					
Thurmond	Y	Y	Y	N	N
Hollings	Y	Y	Y	Y	Y
SOUTH DAKOTA					
Daschle	Y	Y	Y	Y	Y
Johnson	Y	Y	Y	Y	Y
TENNESSEE					
Thompson	Y	N	Y	N	N
Frist	Y	N	Y	N	N

TEXAS	211	212	213	214	215
Gramm	Y	N	Y	N	N
Hutchison	Y	N	Y	N	N
UTAH					
Hatch	Y	Y	Y	N	N
Bennett	Y	Y	Y	N	N
VERMONT					
Leahy	Y	Y	Y	Y	Y
Jeffords	Y	Y	Y	N	Y
VIRGINIA					
Warner	Y	Y	Y	N	N
Allen	Y	Y	Y	N	N
WASHINGTON					
Cantwell	Y	Y	Y	N	Y
Murray	?	Y	Y	Y	Y
WEST VIRGINIA					
Byrd	Y	Y	Y	Y	N
Rockefeller	Y	Y	Y	Y	Y
WISCONSIN					
Kohl	Y	Y	Y	Y	Y
Feingold	Y	N	Y	Y	Y
WYOMING					
Thomas	Y	Y	Y	N	N
Enzi	Y	Y	?	N	N

Key

Y	Voted for (yea).
#	Paired for.
+	Announced for.
N	Voted against (nay).
X	Paired against.
–	Announced against.
P	Voted "present."
C	Voted "present" to avoid possible conflict of interest.
?	Did not vote or otherwise make a position known.

Democrats **Republicans**
Independents

ND Northern Democrats   SD Southern Democrats

Southern states - Ala., Ark., Fla., Ga., Ky., La., Miss., N.C., Okla., S.C., Tenn., Texas, Va.

211. Marra Nomination/Confirmation. Confirmation of President Bush's nomination of Kenneth A. Marra of Florida to be U.S. district judge for the Southern District of Florida. Confirmed 82-0: R 37-0; D 44-0 (ND 35-0, SD 9-0); I 1-0. A "yea" was a vote in support of the president's position. Sept. 9, 2002.

212. HR 5093. Fiscal 2003 Interior Appropriations/Agriculture Disaster Aid. Daschle, D-S.D., motion to waive the Budget Act with respect to the Gramm, R-Texas, point of order against the Daschle amendment to the Byrd, D-W.Va., amendment to the Byrd substitute amendment. The Daschle amendment would provide nearly $6 billion in emergency disaster aid for farmers. The Byrd amendment would provide $825 million to replace funds that previously were taken out for emergency wildfire suppression expenses. The substitute would appropriate $19.3 billion in fiscal 2003 for the Interior Department, related agencies and programs. Motion agreed to 79-16: R 31-15; D 47-1 (ND 38-1, SD 9-0); I 1-0. A three-fifths majority vote (60) of the total Senate is required to waive the Budget Act. (Subsequently, the amendment was agreed to by voice vote.) Sept. 10, 2002.

213. Corrigan Nomination/Confirmation. Confirmation of President Bush's nomination of Timothy J. Corrigan of Florida to be U.S. district judge for the Middle District of Florida. Confirmed 88-0: R 43-0; D 44-0 (ND 35-0, SD 9-0); I 1-0. A "yea" was a vote in support of the president's position. Sept. 12, 2002.

214. HR 5005. Homeland Security/White House Anti-Terrorism Office. Lieberman, D-Conn., motion to table (kill) the Thompson, R-Tenn., amendment to the Lieberman substitute amendment. The Thompson amendment would remove provisions that would establish the White House anti-terrorism office by statute and require that its director be confirmed by the Senate. The substitute amendment would create a new Cabinet-level homeland security department charged with protecting domestic security. Motion rejected 41-55: R 0-47; D 41-7 (ND 34-5, SD 7-2); I 0-1. Sept. 12, 2002.

215. HR 5005. Homeland Security/National Security Council Membership. Hollings, D-S.C., amendment to the Lieberman, D-Conn., substitute amendment. The Hollings amendment would make the attorney general and the secretary of a new department of homeland security full statutory members of the National Security Council. It also would make the director of the FBI an advisory member of the council. Rejected 48-49: R 1-47; D 46-2 (ND 38-1, SD 8-1); I 1-0. Sept. 12, 2002.

	216	217	218
ALABAMA			
Shelby	Y	N	N
Sessions	Y	N	N
ALASKA			
Stevens	Y	N	N
Murkowski	?	N	N
ARIZONA			
McCain	Y	N	N
Kyl	Y	N	N
ARKANSAS			
Hutchinson	Y	N	N
Lincoln	Y	Y	Y
CALIFORNIA			
Feinstein	Y	Y	Y
Boxer	Y	Y	Y
COLORADO			
Campbell	Y	N	N
Allard	Y	Y	N
CONNECTICUT			
Dodd	Y	Y	Y
Lieberman	Y	Y	Y
DELAWARE			
Carper	Y	Y	Y
Biden	Y	Y	Y
FLORIDA			
Graham	Y	Y	Y
Nelson	Y	Y	Y
GEORGIA			
Miller	?	Y	Y
Cleland	Y	Y	Y
HAWAII			
Inouye	Y	Y	Y
Akaka	?	Y	Y
IDAHO			
Craig	Y	N	N
Crapo	Y	N	?
ILLINOIS			
Durbin	Y	Y	Y
Fitzgerald	Y	N	N
INDIANA			
Lugar	Y	N	N
Bayh	Y	Y	Y
IOWA			
Grassley	Y	N	N
Harkin	Y	Y	Y
KANSAS			
Brownback	Y	N	N
Roberts	?	N	N
KENTUCKY			
McConnell	Y	N	N
Bunning	Y	N	N
LOUISIANA			
Breaux	Y	Y	Y
Landrieu	Y	Y	Y
MAINE			
Snowe	Y	N	N
Collins	Y	N	N
MARYLAND			
Sarbanes	Y	Y	Y
Mikulski	Y	Y	Y
MASSACHUSETTS			
Kennedy	Y	Y	Y
Kerry	Y	Y	Y
MICHIGAN			
Levin	Y	Y	Y
Stabenow	Y	Y	Y
MINNESOTA			
Wellstone	Y	Y	Y
Dayton	Y	Y	Y
MISSISSIPPI			
Cochran	?	N	N
Lott	Y	N	N
MISSOURI			
Bond	Y	N	N
Carnahan	Y	Y	Y
MONTANA			
Baucus	Y	Y	Y
Burns	Y	N	N
NEBRASKA			
Nelson	Y	Y	Y
Hagel	Y	N	N
NEVADA			
Reid	Y	Y	Y
Ensign	Y	N	N
NEW HAMPSHIRE			
Smith	?	N	N
Gregg	Y	N	N
NEW JERSEY			
Corzine	Y	Y	Y
Torricelli	Y	Y	Y
NEW MEXICO			
Domenici	Y	N	N
Bingaman	Y	Y	Y
NEW YORK			
Clinton	Y	Y	Y
Schumer	Y	?	Y
NORTH CAROLINA			
Helms	?	N	N
Edwards	Y	Y	Y
NORTH DAKOTA			
Conrad	Y	Y	Y
Dorgan	Y	Y	Y
OHIO			
DeWine	Y	N	N
Voinovich	Y	N	N
OKLAHOMA			
Nickles	Y	N	N
Inhofe	Y	N	N
OREGON			
Wyden	Y	Y	Y
Smith	?	N	N
PENNSYLVANIA			
Specter	Y	N	N
Santorum	Y	N	N
RHODE ISLAND			
Reed	Y	Y	Y
Chafee	Y	N	N
SOUTH CAROLINA			
Thurmond	Y	N	N
Hollings	Y	Y	Y
SOUTH DAKOTA			
Daschle	Y	N	Y
Johnson	Y	Y	Y
TENNESSEE			
Thompson	Y	N	N
Frist	Y	N	N
TEXAS			
Gramm	Y	N	N
Hutchison	Y	N	N
UTAH			
Hatch	Y	N	N
Bennett	Y	N	N
VERMONT			
Leahy	Y	Y	Y
Jeffords	Y	Y	Y
VIRGINIA			
Warner	Y	N	N
Allen	Y	N	N
WASHINGTON			
Cantwell	Y	Y	Y
Murray	Y	Y	Y
WEST VIRGINIA			
Byrd	Y	Y	Y
Rockefeller	Y	Y	Y
WISCONSIN			
Kohl	Y	Y	Y
Feingold	Y	Y	Y
WYOMING			
Thomas	Y	N	N
Enzi	Y	N	N

ND Northern Democrats   SD Southern Democrats

Southern states - Ala., Ark., Fla., Ga., Ky., La., Miss., N.C., Okla., S.C., Tenn., Texas, Va.

Key

Y	Voted for (yea).
#	Paired for.
+	Announced for.
N	Voted against (nay).
X	Paired against.
–	Announced against.
P	Voted "present."
C	Voted "present" to avoid possible conflict of interest.
?	Did not vote or otherwise make a position known.

Democrats   **Republicans**
Independents

216. Schwab Nomination/Confirmation. Confirmation of President Bush's nomination of Arthur J. Schwab of Pennsylvania to be U.S. district judge for the Western District of Pennsylvania. Confirmed 92-0: R 43-0; D 48-0 (ND 40-0, SD 8-0); I 1-0. A "yea" was a vote in support of the president's position. Sept. 13, 2002.

217. HR 5093. Fiscal 2002 Interior Appropriations/Cloture. Motion to invoke cloture (thus limiting debate) on the Byrd, D-W.Va., amendment to the Byrd substitute amendment. The Byrd amendment would provide $825 million to replace funds that previously were taken out for emergency wildfire suppression expenses. As amended, it also would provide nearly $6 billion in disaster aid for farmers. The substitute would appropriate $19.3 billion in fiscal 2003 for the Interior Department and related agencies and programs. Motion rejected 50-49: R 1-48; D 48-1 (ND 39-1, SD 9-0); I 1-0. Three-fifths of the total Senate (60) is required to invoke cloture. Sept. 17, 2002.

218. HR 5005. Homeland Security/Cloture. Motion to invoke cloture (thus limiting debate) on the Lieberman, D-Conn., substitute amendment that would create a new cabinet-level Homeland Security Department charged with protecting domestic security. Motion rejected 50-49: R 0-48; D 49-1 (ND 41-0, SD 8-1); I 1-0. Three-fifths of the total Senate (60) is required to invoke cloture. Sept. 19, 2002.

	219	220	221	222	223
ALABAMA					
Shelby	Y	Y	N	N	Y
Sessions	?	N	N	N	Y
ALASKA					
Stevens	Y	Y	N	N	Y
Murkowski	?	?	?	N	Y
ARIZONA					
McCain	Y	Y	N	N	Y
Kyl	Y	N	N	N	Y
ARKANSAS					
Hutchinson	Y	?	?	N	Y
Lincoln	Y	Y	Y	N	Y
CALIFORNIA					
Feinstein	Y	Y	Y	Y	Y
Boxer	?	Y	Y	Y	Y
COLORADO					
Campbell	Y	Y	N	N	Y
Allard	Y	Y	Y	N	Y
CONNECTICUT					
Dodd	Y	N	Y	N	Y
Lieberman	Y	N	Y	N	Y
DELAWARE					
Carper	Y	Y	Y	N	Y
Biden	Y	Y	Y	Y	Y
FLORIDA					
Graham	Y	Y	Y	Y	Y
Nelson	Y	Y	Y	Y	Y
GEORGIA					
Miller	Y	Y	Y	Y	Y
Cleland	Y	N	Y	N	Y
HAWAII					
Inouye	Y	Y	Y	?	?
Akaka	Y	Y	Y	N	Y
IDAHO					
Craig	Y	Y	N	N	Y
Crapo	Y	Y	N	N	Y
ILLINOIS					
Durbin	Y	Y	Y	N	Y
Fitzgerald	Y	Y	N	N	Y
INDIANA					
Lugar	Y	N	N	N	N
Bayh	Y	Y	Y	N	Y

	219	220	221	222	223
IOWA					
Grassley	Y	Y	N	N	Y
Harkin	Y	Y	Y	Y	Y
KANSAS					
Brownback	Y	Y	N	N	Y
Roberts	?	Y	N	N	Y
KENTUCKY					
McConnell	Y	Y	N	N	Y
Bunning	Y	Y	N	N	Y
LOUISIANA					
Breaux	Y	Y	Y	N	Y
Landrieu	Y	N	Y	N	Y
MAINE					
Snowe	Y	Y	N	N	Y
Collins	Y	Y	N	N	Y
MARYLAND					
Sarbanes	?	Y	Y	Y	Y
Mikulski	Y	Y	Y	Y	Y
MASSACHUSETTS					
Kennedy	?	Y	Y	Y	Y
Kerry	?	+	?	N	Y
MICHIGAN					
Levin	Y	Y	Y	N	Y
Stabenow	Y	Y	Y	Y	Y
MINNESOTA					
Wellstone	+	Y	Y	Y	Y
Dayton	Y	Y	Y	Y	Y
MISSISSIPPI					
Cochran	Y	Y	N	N	N
Lott	Y	Y	N	N	N
MISSOURI					
Bond	Y	Y	N	N	N
Carnahan	Y	N	Y	N	Y
MONTANA					
Baucus	Y	?	?	?	?
Burns	Y	Y	N	N	Y
NEBRASKA					
Nelson	Y	Y	Y	N	Y
Hagel	Y	Y	N	N	Y
NEVADA					
Reid	Y	N	Y	Y	Y
Ensign	?	N	N	N	Y

	219	220	221	222	223
NEW HAMPSHIRE					
Smith	Y	Y	N	N	Y
Gregg	Y	Y	N	N	N
NEW JERSEY					
Corzine	Y	N	Y	N	Y
Torricelli	?	?	?	N	Y
NEW MEXICO					
Domenici	Y	Y	N	N	Y
Bingaman	Y	Y	Y	N	Y
NEW YORK					
Clinton	Y	Y	Y	Y	Y
Schumer	Y	Y	Y	Y	Y
NORTH CAROLINA					
Helms	?	N	N	N	Y
Edwards	Y	Y	Y	N	Y
NORTH DAKOTA					
Conrad	Y	Y	Y	Y	Y
Dorgan	Y	Y	Y	Y	Y
OHIO					
DeWine	Y	Y	N	N	Y
Voinovich	Y	Y	N	N	Y
OKLAHOMA					
Nickles	Y	N	N	N	Y
Inhofe	Y	N	N	N	Y
OREGON					
Wyden	Y	Y	Y	Y	Y
Smith	?	Y	N	N	Y
PENNSYLVANIA					
Specter	Y	Y	N	N	Y
Santorum	Y	Y	N	N	Y
RHODE ISLAND					
Reed	Y	Y	Y	Y	Y
Chafee	Y	Y	N	N	Y
SOUTH CAROLINA					
Thurmond	Y	Y	N	N	Y
Hollings	Y	Y	Y	Y	Y
SOUTH DAKOTA					
Daschle	Y	Y	Y	N	Y
Johnson	Y	Y	Y	Y	Y
TENNESSEE					
Thompson	?	Y	N	N	Y
Frist	Y	Y	N	N	Y

Key

Y	Voted for (yea).
#	Paired for.
+	Announced for.
N	Voted against (nay).
X	Paired against.
–	Announced against.
P	Voted "present."
C	Voted "present" to avoid possible conflict of interest.
?	Did not vote or otherwise make a position known.

Democrats   *Republicans*
Independents

	219	220	221	222	223
TEXAS					
Gramm	Y	Y	N	N	N
Hutchison	Y	Y	N	N	Y
UTAH					
Hatch	Y	Y	N	N	Y
Bennett	Y	Y	N	N	Y
VERMONT					
Leahy	Y	Y	Y	Y	Y
Jeffords	Y	N	Y	Y	Y
VIRGINIA					
Warner	Y	Y	N	N	Y
Allen	Y	Y	N	N	Y
WASHINGTON					
Cantwell	Y	Y	Y	Y	Y
Murray	Y	Y	Y	Y	Y
WEST VIRGINIA					
Byrd	Y	Y	Y	Y	Y
Rockefeller	Y	Y	Y	N	Y
WISCONSIN					
Kohl	Y	Y	Y	Y	Y
Feingold	Y	Y	Y	Y	Y
WYOMING					
Thomas	?	Y	N	N	N
Enzi	?	Y	N	N	Y

ND Northern Democrats   SD Southern Democrats

Southern states - Ala., Ark., Fla., Ga., Ky., La., Miss., N.C., Okla., S.C., Tenn., Texas, Va.

219. Raggi Nomination/Confirmation. Confirmation of President Bush's nomination of Reena Raggi of New York to be a judge for the 2nd U.S. Circuit Court of Appeals. Confirmed 85-0: R 40-0; D 44-0 (ND 35-0, SD 9-0); I 1-0. A "yea" was a vote in support of the president's position. Sept. 20, 2002.

220. HR 5093. Fiscal 2003 Interior Appropriations/Tribe Recognition. Inouye, D-Hawaii, motion to table (kill) the Dodd, D-Conn., amendment to the Byrd, D-W.Va., substitute amendment. The Dodd amendment would prohibit the use of any funds made available in the bill for the approval or denial of a petition to be federally recognized as an Indian tribe or a tribal nation until the Interior secretary certifies to Congress that certain administrative procedures have been implemented. It also would permit the use of up to $1.9 million for the Bureau of Indian Affairs Branch of Acknowledgement and Research. The substitute would appropriate $19.3 billion in fiscal 2003 for the Interior Department and related agencies and programs. Motion agreed to 80-15: R 40-7; D 40-7 (ND 33-5, SD 7-2); I 0-1. Sept. 23, 2002.

221. HR 5093. Fiscal 2002 Interior Appropriations/Cloture. Motion to invoke cloture (thus limiting debate) on the Byrd, D-W.Va., amendment to the Byrd substitute amendment. The Byrd amendment would provide $825 million to replace funds that previously were taken out for emergency wildfire suppression expenses. As amended, it also would provide nearly $6 billion in disaster aid for farmers. The substitute would appropriate $19.3 billion in fiscal 2003 for the Interior Department and related agencies and programs. Motion rejected 49-46: R 1-46; D 47-0 (ND 38-0, SD 9-0); I 1-0. Three-fifths of the total Senate (60) is required to invoke cloture. Sept. 23, 2002.

222. HR 5005. Homeland Security/Congressional Involvement. Byrd, D-W.Va., amendment to the Lieberman, D-Conn., substitute amendment. The Byrd amendment would establish a superstructure for a new homeland security department with six directorates and a Senate-confirmed secretary of homeland security. The administration would be required to submit legislative recommendations in 120-day intervals for the transfer of agencies, functions and employees to the new department. The substitute amendment would create a new Cabinet-level homeland security department charged with protecting domestic security. Rejected 28-70: R 0-49; D 27-21 (ND 24-15, SD 3-6); I 1-0. Sept. 24, 2002.

223. HR 5005. Homeland Security/Independent Commission. Lieberman, D-Conn., amendment to the Lieberman substitute amendment. The amendment would establish the National Commission on Terrorist Attacks Upon the United States to investigate the facts and circumstances relating to the Sept. 11 terrorist attacks. The commission would be required to report its initial findings and recommendations to the president and to Congress within six months of its first meeting, followed by a second report within one year. Adopted 90-8: R 41-8; D 48-0 (ND 39-0, SD 9-0); I 1-0. Sept. 24, 2002.

	224	225	226	227
ALABAMA				
Shelby	N	N	N	N
Sessions	N	N	N	N
ALASKA				
Stevens	N	N	N	N
Murkowski	N	N	N	N
ARIZONA				
McCain	N	N	N	N
Kyl	N	N	N	N
ARKANSAS				
Hutchinson	N	N	N	N
Lincoln	Y	Y	Y	Y
CALIFORNIA				
Feinstein	Y	Y	Y	Y
Boxer	Y	Y	Y	Y
COLORADO				
Campbell	Y	N	N	N
Allard	Y	N	N	N
CONNECTICUT				
Dodd	Y	Y	Y	Y
Lieberman	Y	Y	Y	Y
DELAWARE				
Carper	Y	Y	Y	Y
Biden	Y	Y	Y	Y
FLORIDA				
Graham	Y	Y	Y	Y
Nelson	Y	Y	Y	Y
GEORGIA				
Miller	Y	N	N	N
Cleland	Y	Y	Y	Y
HAWAII				
Inouye	Y	Y	Y	Y
Akaka	Y	Y	Y	Y
IDAHO				
Craig	N	N	N	N
Crapo	N	N	N	N
ILLINOIS				
Durbin	Y	Y	Y	Y
Fitzgerald	N	N	N	N
INDIANA				
Lugar	N	N	N	N
Bayh	Y	Y	Y	Y

	224	225	226	227
IOWA				
Grassley	N	N	N	N
Harkin	Y	Y	Y	Y
KANSAS				
Brownback	N	N	N	N
Roberts	N	N	N	N
KENTUCKY				
McConnell	N	N	N	N
Bunning	N	N	N	N
LOUISIANA				
Breaux	Y	Y	Y	Y
Landrieu	Y	Y	?	?
MAINE				
Snowe	N	N	N	N
Collins	N	N	N	N
MARYLAND				
Sarbanes	Y	Y	Y	N
Mikulski	Y	Y	Y	Y
MASSACHUSETTS				
Kennedy	Y	Y	Y	N
Kerry	Y	Y	Y	Y
MICHIGAN				
Levin	Y	Y	Y	Y
Stabenow	Y	Y	Y	Y
MINNESOTA				
Wellstone	Y	Y	Y	Y
Dayton	Y	Y	Y	Y
MISSISSIPPI				
Cochran	N	N	N	N
Lott	N	N	N	N
MISSOURI				
Bond	N	N	N	N
Carnahan	Y	Y	Y	Y
MONTANA				
Baucus	Y	Y	Y	Y
Burns	N	N	N	N
NEBRASKA				
Nelson	Y	Y	Y	Y
Hagel	N	N	N	N
NEVADA				
Reid	Y	Y	Y	Y
Ensign	N	N	N	N

	224	225	226	227
NEW HAMPSHIRE				
Smith	N	N	N	N
Gregg	N	N	N	N
NEW JERSEY				
Corzine	Y	Y	Y	Y
Torricelli	?	?	Y	Y
NEW MEXICO				
Domenici	N	N	N	?
Bingaman	Y	Y	Y	Y
NEW YORK				
Clinton	Y	Y	Y	Y
Schumer	Y	Y	Y	Y
NORTH CAROLINA				
Helms	?	?	N	?
Edwards	Y	Y	Y	Y
NORTH DAKOTA				
Conrad	Y	Y	Y	Y
Dorgan	Y	Y	Y	Y
OHIO				
DeWine	N	N	N	N
Voinovich	N	N	N	N
OKLAHOMA				
Nickles	N	N	N	N
Inhofe	N	N	N	N
OREGON				
Wyden	Y	Y	Y	Y
Smith	N	N	N	N
PENNSYLVANIA				
Specter	N	N	N	N
Santorum	N	N	N	N
RHODE ISLAND				
Reed	Y	Y	Y	Y
Chafee	N	Y	Y	Y
SOUTH CAROLINA				
Thurmond	N	N	N	N
Hollings	Y	Y	Y	Y
SOUTH DAKOTA				
Daschle	N	N	Y	N
Johnson	Y	Y	Y	Y
TENNESSEE				
Thompson	N	N	N	N
Frist	N	N	N	N

	224	225	226	227
TEXAS				
Gramm	N	N	N	N
Hutchison	N	N	N	N
UTAH				
Hatch	N	N	N	N
Bennett	N	N	N	N
VERMONT				
Leahy	Y	Y	Y	Y
Jeffords	Y	Y	Y	Y
VIRGINIA				
Warner	N	N	N	N
Allen	N	N	N	N
WASHINGTON				
Cantwell	Y	Y	Y	Y
Murray	Y	Y	Y	Y
WEST VIRGINIA				
Byrd	Y	Y	Y	N
Rockefeller	Y	Y	Y	Y
WISCONSIN				
Kohl	Y	Y	Y	N
Feingold	Y	Y	Y	N
WYOMING				
Thomas	N	N	N	N
Enzi	N	N	N	N

Key

Y	Voted for (yea).
#	Paired for.
+	Announced for.
N	Voted against (nay).
X	Paired against.
–	Announced against.
P	Voted "present."
C	Voted "present" to avoid possible conflict of interest.
?	Did not vote or otherwise make a position known.

Democrats **Republicans**
Independents

ND Northern Democrats   SD Southern Democrats

Southern states - Ala., Ark., Fla., Ga., Ky., La., Miss., N.C., Okla., S.C., Tenn., Texas, Va.

224. HR 5093. Fiscal 2002 Interior Appropriations/Cloture. Motion to invoke cloture (thus limiting debate) on the Byrd, D-W.Va., amendment to the Byrd substitute amendment. The Byrd amendment would provide $825 million to replace funds that previously were taken out for emergency wildfire suppression expenses. As amended, it also would provide nearly $6 billion in disaster aid for farmers. The substitute would appropriate $19.3 billion in fiscal 2003 for the Interior Department and related agencies and programs. Motion rejected 51-47: R 2-46; D 48-1 (ND 39-1, SD 9-0); I 1-0. Three-fifths of the total Senate (60) is required to invoke cloture. Sept. 25, 2002.

225. HR 5005. Homeland Security/Cloture. Motion to invoke cloture (thus limiting debate) on the Lieberman, D-Conn., substitute amendment that would create a Cabinet-level Homeland Security Department charged with protecting domestic security. Motion rejected 49-49: R 1-47; D 47-2 (ND 39-1, SD 8-1); I 1-0. Three-fifths of the total Senate (60) is required to invoke cloture. Sept. 25, 2002.

226. HR 5005. Homeland Security/Cloture. Motion to invoke cloture (thus limiting debate) on the Lieberman, D-Conn., substitute amendment that would create a Cabinet-level Homeland Security Department charged with protecting domestic security. Motion rejected 50-49: R 1-48; D 48-1 (ND 41-0, SD 7-1); I 1-0. Three-fifths of the total Senate (60) is required to invoke cloture. Sept. 26, 2002.

227. HR 5005. Homeland Security/Cloture. Motion to invoke cloture (thus limiting debate) on the Daschle, D-S.D. (for Gramm, R-Texas) substitute amendment, to the Daschle motion to commit the bill to the Governmental Affairs Committee with instructions that it be reported back to the Senate with the Lieberman, D-Conn., substitute amendment. The Gramm amendment would create a Cabinet-level Homeland Security Department charged with protecting domestic security. It would also allow the president to exclude workers from union representation for national security reasons, but require the president to certify his reasons in writing. Motion rejected 44-53: R 1-46; D 42-7 (ND 35-6, SD 7-1); I 1-0. Three-fifths of the total Senate (60) is required to invoke cloture. Sept. 26, 2002.

	228	229	230
ALABAMA			
Shelby	N	Y	Y
Sessions	N	Y	Y
ALASKA			
Stevens	N	Y	Y
Murkowski	N	Y	Y
ARIZONA			
McCain	N	Y	Y
Kyl	N	Y	Y
ARKANSAS			
Hutchinson	N	Y	Y
Lincoln	Y	Y	Y
CALIFORNIA			
Feinstein	Y	Y	Y
Boxer	N	Y	Y
COLORADO			
Campbell	N	Y	Y
Allard	?	Y	Y
CONNECTICUT			
Dodd	Y	Y	Y
Lieberman	Y	Y	Y
DELAWARE			
Carper	Y	Y	Y
Biden	Y	Y	Y
FLORIDA			
Graham	Y	Y	Y
Nelson	Y	Y	Y
GEORGIA			
Miller	N	Y	Y
Cleland	Y	Y	Y
HAWAII			
Inouye	Y	Y	?
Akaka	Y	Y	?
IDAHO			
Craig	N	Y	Y
Crapo	N	Y	Y
ILLINOIS			
Durbin	Y	Y	Y
Fitzgerald	N	Y	Y
INDIANA			
Lugar	N	N	Y
Bayh	Y	Y	Y

	228	229	230
IOWA			
Grassley	N	Y	Y
Harkin	Y	Y	Y
KANSAS			
Brownback	N	Y	Y
Roberts	N	Y	Y
KENTUCKY			
McConnell	N	Y	Y
Bunning	N	Y	Y
LOUISIANA			
Breaux	Y	Y	Y
Landrieu	Y	Y	Y
MAINE			
Snowe	N	Y	Y
Collins	N	Y	Y
MARYLAND			
Sarbanes	N	Y	Y
Mikulski	Y	Y	Y
MASSACHUSETTS			
Kennedy	N	Y	Y
Kerry	Y	Y	Y
MICHIGAN			
Levin	Y	Y	Y
Stabenow	Y	Y	Y
MINNESOTA			
Wellstone	Y	Y	Y
Dayton	Y	Y	Y
MISSISSIPPI			
Cochran	N	Y	Y
Lott	N	N	Y
MISSOURI			
Bond	N	Y	Y
Carnahan	Y	Y	Y
MONTANA			
Baucus	Y	Y	Y
Burns	N	Y	Y
NEBRASKA			
Nelson	Y	Y	Y
Hagel	N	Y	Y
NEVADA			
Reid	Y	Y	Y
Ensign	N	Y	Y

	228	229	230
NEW HAMPSHIRE			
Smith	N	N	Y
Gregg	N	Y	Y
NEW JERSEY			
Corzine	+	Y	Y
Torricelli	?	Y	Y
NEW MEXICO			
Domenici	N	Y	Y
Bingaman	Y	Y	Y
NEW YORK			
Clinton	Y	Y	Y
Schumer	Y	Y	Y
NORTH CAROLINA			
Helms	N	?	?
Edwards	Y	Y	Y
NORTH DAKOTA			
Conrad	Y	Y	Y
Dorgan	Y	Y	Y
OHIO			
DeWine	N	Y	Y
Voinovich	N	Y	Y
OKLAHOMA			
Nickles	N	Y	Y
Inhofe	N	Y	Y
OREGON			
Wyden	Y	Y	Y
Smith	N	Y	Y
PENNSYLVANIA			
Specter	Y	Y	Y
Santorum	N	N	Y
RHODE ISLAND			
Reed	Y	Y	Y
Chafee	Y	Y	Y
SOUTH CAROLINA			
Thurmond	N	Y	Y
Hollings	Y	Y	Y
SOUTH DAKOTA			
Daschle	Y	Y	Y
Johnson	Y	Y	Y
TENNESSEE			
Thompson	N	Y	Y
Frist	N	Y	Y

Key

Y	Voted for (yea).
#	Paired for.
+	Announced for.
N	Voted against (nay).
X	Paired against.
−	Announced against.
P	Voted "present."
C	Voted "present" to avoid possible conflict of interest.
?	Did not vote or otherwise make a position known.

Democrats **Republicans**
Independents

	228	229	230
TEXAS			
Gramm	N	N	Y
Hutchison	N	Y	Y
UTAH			
Hatch	N	+	?
Bennett	N	Y	Y
VERMONT			
Leahy	Y	Y	Y
Jeffords	Y	Y	Y
VIRGINIA			
Warner	N	Y	Y
Allen	N	Y	Y
WASHINGTON			
Cantwell	Y	Y	Y
Murray	Y	Y	Y
WEST VIRGINIA			
Byrd	N	Y	N
Rockefeller	Y	Y	Y
WISCONSIN			
Kohl	Y	Y	Y
Feingold	N	Y	Y
WYOMING			
Thomas	N	Y	Y
Enzi	N	Y	Y

ND Northern Democrats   SD Southern Democrats

Southern states - Ala., Ark., Fla., Ga., Ky., La., Miss., N.C., Okla., S.C., Tenn., Texas, Va.

228. HR 5005. Homeland Security/Cloture. Motion to invoke cloture (thus limiting debate) on the Daschle, D-S.D. (for Gramm, R-Texas), substitute amendment, to the Daschle motion to commit the bill to the Governmental Affairs Committee with instructions that it be reported back to the Senate with the Lieberman, D-Conn., substitute amendment. The Gramm amendment would create a Cabinet-level homeland security department charged with protecting domestic security. It also would allow the president to exclude workers from union representation for national security reasons, but require the president to certify his reasons in writing. The Lieberman substitute amendment would create a Cabinet-level homeland security department charged with protecting domestic security. Motion rejected 45-52: R 2-46; D 42-6 (ND 34-5, SD 8-1); I 1-0. Three-fifths of the total Senate (60) is required to invoke cloture. Oct. 1, 2002.

229. HR 2215. Justice Department Reauthorization/Cloture. Motion to invoke cloture (thus limiting debate) on the conference report on the bill that would authorize $17.6 billion in fiscal 2002 and $20.5 billion in fiscal 2003 for Justice Department operations. Motion agreed to 93-5: R 42-5; D 50-0 (ND 41-0, SD 9-0); I 1-0. Three-fifths of the total Senate (60) is required to invoke cloture. (Subsequently, the conference report was adopted by voice voice, thus clearing the bill for the president.) Oct. 3, 2002.

230. S J Res 45. Use of Force/Cloture. Motion to invoke cloture (thus limiting debate) on the motion to proceed to the joint resolution that would authorize the use of force against Iraq. Motion agreed to 95-1: R 47-0; D 47-1 (ND 38-1, SD 9-0); I 1-0. Three-fifths of the total Senate (60) is required to invoke cloture. Oct. 3, 2002.

Senate Votes 231, 232, 233, 234, 235, 236, 237

	231	232	233	234	235	236	237
ALABAMA							
Shelby	Y	N	Y	N	N	N	N
Sessions	Y	N	Y	N	N	N	N
ALASKA							
Stevens	Y	N	Y	N	N	N	Y
Murkowski	Y	N	Y	N	N	N	Y
ARIZONA							
McCain	Y	N	Y	N	N	N	Y
Kyl	Y	N	Y	N	N	N	Y
ARKANSAS							
Hutchinson	Y	N	Y	N	N	N	Y
Lincoln	N	?	Y	N	N	N	Y
CALIFORNIA							
Feinstein	Y	N	Y	N	Y	N	Y
Boxer	Y	Y	N	Y	Y	Y	N
COLORADO							
Campbell	Y	N	Y	N	N	N	Y
Allard	Y	N	Y	N	N	N	Y
CONNECTICUT							
Dodd	Y	Y	N	N	N	Y	Y
Lieberman	Y	N	Y	N	N	N	N
DELAWARE							
Carper	Y	N	N	N	N	Y	Y
Biden	Y	Y	Y	N	N	N	Y
FLORIDA							
Graham	N	N	Y	N	N	N	N
Nelson	N	N	Y	N	N	N	Y
GEORGIA							
Miller	Y	N	Y	N	N	N	Y
Cleland	Y	N	Y	N	N	N	Y
HAWAII							
Inouye	Y	Y	N	Y	Y	Y	N
Akaka	Y	Y	N	Y	N	N	N
IDAHO							
Craig	Y	N	Y	N	N	N	Y
Crapo	Y	N	Y	N	N	N	Y
ILLINOIS							
Durbin	Y	Y	N	Y	N	N	Y
Fitzgerald	Y	N	Y	N	N	N	Y
INDIANA							
Lugar	Y	N	Y	N	N	N	Y
Bayh	Y	N	Y	N	N	N	Y
IOWA							
Grassley	Y	N	Y	N	N	N	Y
Harkin	Y	Y	Y	N	Y	Y	Y
KANSAS							
Brownback	Y	N	Y	N	N	N	Y
Roberts	Y	N	Y	N	N	N	Y
KENTUCKY							
McConnell	Y	N	Y	N	N	N	Y
Bunning	Y	N	Y	N	N	N	Y
LOUISIANA							
Breaux	N	N	Y	N	N	N	Y
Landrieu	?	N	Y	N	N	N	Y
MAINE							
Snowe	Y	N	Y	N	N	N	Y
Collins	Y	N	Y	N	N	N	Y
MARYLAND							
Sarbanes	Y	Y	N	Y	Y	Y	N
Mikulski	Y	?	Y	Y	Y	Y	N
MASSACHUSETTS							
Kennedy	Y	Y	N	Y	Y	Y	N
Kerry	Y	Y	Y	N	Y	Y	Y
MICHIGAN							
Levin	Y	Y	N	Y	Y	Y	N
Stabenow	Y	Y	N	Y	Y	Y	N
MINNESOTA							
Wellstone	Y	Y	N	Y	Y	Y	N
Dayton	N	Y	N	Y	Y	Y	N
MISSISSIPPI							
Cochran	Y	N	Y	N	N	N	Y
Lott	Y	N	Y	N	N	N	Y
MISSOURI							
Bond	Y	N	Y	N	N	N	Y
Carnahan	Y	N	Y	N	N	N	Y
MONTANA							
Baucus	N	N	Y	N	N	N	Y
Burns	Y	N	Y	N	N	N	Y
NEBRASKA							
Nelson	Y	N	Y	N	N	Y	Y
Hagel	Y	N	Y	N	N	N	Y
NEVADA							
Reid	Y	N	Y	N	N	N	Y
Ensign	?	N	Y	N	N	N	Y
NEW HAMPSHIRE							
Smith	Y	N	Y	N	N	N	Y
Gregg	Y	N	Y	N	N	N	Y
NEW JERSEY							
Corzine	N	Y	N	N	Y	Y	N
Torricelli	N	Y	Y	N	Y	Y	Y
NEW MEXICO							
Domenici	Y	N	Y	N	N	N	Y
Bingaman	Y	Y	Y	N	N	Y	N
NEW YORK							
Clinton	Y	Y	Y	N	N	N	Y
Schumer	Y	Y	Y	N	N	Y	Y
NORTH CAROLINA							
Helms	Y	?	Y	N	N	N	Y
Edwards	Y	N	Y	N	N	N	Y
NORTH DAKOTA							
Conrad	Y	Y	N	Y	N	Y	N
Dorgan	Y	Y	Y	N	Y	Y	Y
OHIO							
DeWine	Y	N	Y	N	N	N	Y
Voinovich	Y	N	Y	N	N	N	Y
OKLAHOMA							
Nickles	Y	N	Y	N	N	N	Y
Inhofe	Y	N	Y	N	N	N	Y
OREGON							
Wyden	Y	Y	N	Y	N	Y	N
Smith	Y	N	Y	N	N	N	Y
PENNSYLVANIA							
Specter	Y	N	Y	N	N	N	Y
Santorum	Y	N	Y	N	N	N	Y
RHODE ISLAND							
Reed	Y	N	Y	N	N	Y	Y
Chafee	Y	Y	N	N	Y	N	N
SOUTH CAROLINA							
Thurmond	Y	N	Y	N	N	N	Y
Hollings	Y	Y	N	Y	N	N	Y
SOUTH DAKOTA							
Daschle	Y	N	Y	N	N	N	Y
Johnson	Y	N	Y	N	N	N	Y
TENNESSEE							
Thompson	Y	N	Y	N	N	N	Y
Frist	Y	N	Y	N	N	N	Y
TEXAS							
Gramm	Y	N	Y	N	N	N	Y
Hutchison	Y	N	Y	N	N	N	Y
UTAH							
Hatch	Y	N	Y	N	N	N	Y
Bennett	Y	N	Y	N	?	N	Y
VERMONT							
Leahy	Y	Y	N	Y	Y	Y	N
Jeffords	Y	Y	N	Y	Y	Y	N
VIRGINIA							
Warner	Y	N	Y	N	N	N	Y
Allen	Y	N	Y	N	N	N	Y
WASHINGTON							
Cantwell	Y	Y	N	Y	N	Y	Y
Murray	Y	N	N	Y	N	Y	N
WEST VIRGINIA							
Byrd	N	Y	N	Y	Y	Y	N
Rockefeller	N	Y	Y	N	Y	Y	N
WISCONSIN							
Kohl	Y	Y	N	Y	N	N	Y
Feingold	Y	Y	N	Y	N	Y	N
WYOMING							
Thomas	Y	N	Y	N	N	N	Y
Enzi	Y	N	Y	N	N	N	Y

Key

- **Y** Voted for (yea).
- **#** Paired for.
- **+** Announced for.
- **N** Voted against (nay).
- **X** Paired against.
- **–** Announced against.
- **P** Voted "present."
- **C** Voted "present" to avoid possible conflict of interest.
- **?** Did not vote or otherwise make a position known.

Democrats   ***Republicans***
Independents

ND Northern Democrats   SD Southern Democrats

Southern states - Ala., Ark., Fla., Ga., Ky., La., Miss., N.C., Okla., S.C., Tenn., Texas, Va.

231. S J Res 45. Use of Force/Terrorist Organizations. McCain, R-Ariz., motion to table (kill) the Graham, D-Fla., amendment to the Lieberman, D-Conn., substitute amendment. The Graham amendment would authorize the use of force against Iraq and five terrorist organizations. It would require the administration to report to Congress that diplomatic options have been exhausted no later than 48 hours after action has begun. The president would be required to report to Congress at least every 60 days. Motion agreed to 88-10: R 48-0; D 39-10 (ND 35-6, SD 4-4); I 1-0. Oct. 9, 2002.

232. S J Res 45. Use of Force/Termination. Byrd, D-W.Va., amendment to the Lieberman, D-Conn., substitute amendment. The Byrd amendment would provide for the termination of congressional authorization of the use of force 12 months after the resolution's enactment, unless the president certifies that an extension is necessary and Congress does not pass a joint resolution disapproving of the extension. Rejected 31-66: R 1-47; D 29-19 (ND 28-12, SD 1-7); I 1-0. Oct. 10, 2002.

233. S J Res 45. Use of Force/Cloture. Motion to invoke cloture (thus limiting debate) on the Lieberman, D-Conn., substitute amendment that would authorize the use of force against Iraq and require the administration to report to Congress that diplomatic options have been exhausted no later than 48 hours after military action has begun. The president also would be required to submit a progress report to Congress at least every 60 days. Motion agreed to 75-25: R 47-2; D 28-22 (ND 20-21, SD 8-1); I 0-1. Three-fifths of the total Senate (60) is required to invoke cloture. Oct. 10, 2002.

234. S J Res 45. Use of Force/Congressional Authority. Byrd, D-W.Va., amendment to the Lieberman, D-Conn., substitute amendment. The Byrd amendment would clarify that any authorization of the use of force against Iraq would not alter the constitutional authority of Congress to declare war. It also would clarify that no additional authority not directly related to a clear threat of imminent, sudden and direct attack on the United States be granted to the president unless Congress authorizes it. Rejected 14-86: R 1-48; D 12-38 (ND 12-29, SD 0-9); I 1-0. Oct. 10, 2002.

235. S J Res 45 Use of Force/U.N. Resolution. Levin, D-Mich., amendment to the Lieberman, D-Conn., substitute amendment. The Levin amendment would authorize the use of force against Iraq if it failed to comply with a new U.N. resolution that demanded unrestricted access for U.N. weapons inspectors in Iraq and authorized the use of military force by U.N. members to enforce the resolution. Congress could return to session at any time to promptly consider proposals related to Iraq if the U.N. failed to adopt such a resolution. Rejected 24-75: R 1-47; D 22-28 (ND 22-19, SD 0-9); I 1-0. Oct. 10, 2002.

236. S J Res 45. Use of Force/Imminent Threat. Durbin, D-Ill., amendment to the Lieberman, D-Conn., substitute amendment. The Durbin amendment would authorize the use of military force to cover an "imminent threat" by Iraq's weapons of mass destruction rather than a "continuing threat" by Iraq. Rejected 30-70: R 0-49; D 29-21 (ND 29-12, SD 0-9); I 1-0. Oct. 10, 2002.

237. H J Res 114. Use of Force/Passage. Passage of the joint resolution that would authorize the use of force against Iraq and require the administration to report to Congress that diplomatic options have been exhausted no later than 48 hours after military action has begun. The president also would be required to submit a progress report to Congress at least every 60 days. Passed (thus cleared for the president) 77-23: R 48-1; D 29-21 (ND 21-20, SD 8-1); I 0-1. A "yea" was a vote in support of the president's position. Oct. 11, 2002 (in the session that began and the Congressional Record dated Oct. 10, 2002).

	238	239
ALABAMA		
Shelby	Y	Y
Sessions	?	?
ALASKA		
Stevens	Y	Y
Murkowski	Y	Y
ARIZONA		
McCain	Y	?
Kyl	Y	Y
ARKANSAS		
Hutchinson	?	?
Lincoln	Y	Y
CALIFORNIA		
Feinstein	Y	Y
Boxer	Y	Y
COLORADO		
Campbell	Y	Y
Allard	?	?
CONNECTICUT		
Dodd	Y	Y
Lieberman	Y	Y
DELAWARE		
Carper	Y	Y
Biden	Y	Y
FLORIDA		
Graham	Y	Y
Nelson	Y	Y
GEORGIA		
Miller	Y	Y
Cleland	Y	Y
HAWAII		
Inouye	Y	Y
Akaka	Y	Y
IDAHO		
Craig	Y	Y
Crapo	Y	Y
ILLINOIS		
Durbin	Y	Y
Fitzgerald	Y	Y
INDIANA		
Lugar	Y	Y
Bayh	Y	Y

	238	239
IOWA		
Grassley	Y	Y
Harkin	Y	Y
KANSAS		
Brownback	Y	Y
Roberts	Y	Y
KENTUCKY		
McConnell	Y	Y
Bunning	Y	Y
LOUISIANA		
Breaux	Y	Y
Landrieu	Y	Y
MAINE		
Snowe	Y	Y
Collins	Y	Y
MARYLAND		
Sarbanes	Y	Y
Mikulski	Y	Y
MASSACHUSETTS		
Kennedy	Y	Y
Kerry	Y	Y
MICHIGAN		
Levin	Y	Y
Stabenow	Y	Y
MINNESOTA		
Wellstone	Y	Y
Dayton	Y	Y
MISSISSIPPI		
Cochran	Y	Y
Lott	Y	Y
MISSOURI		
Bond	Y	Y
Carnahan	Y	Y
MONTANA		
Baucus	Y	Y
Burns	Y	Y
NEBRASKA		
Nelson	Y	Y
Hagel	Y	Y
NEVADA		
Reid	Y	Y
Ensign	Y	Y

	238	239
NEW HAMPSHIRE		
Smith	Y	Y
Gregg	Y	Y
NEW JERSEY		
Corzine	Y	Y
Torricelli	?	?
NEW MEXICO		
Domenici	Y	Y
Bingaman	Y	Y
NEW YORK		
Clinton	N	Y
Schumer	N	Y
NORTH CAROLINA		
Helms	Y	Y
Edwards	Y	Y
NORTH DAKOTA		
Conrad	Y	Y
Dorgan	Y	Y
OHIO		
DeWine	Y	Y
Voinovich	Y	Y
OKLAHOMA		
Nickles	Y	Y
Inhofe	Y	Y
OREGON		
Wyden	Y	Y
Smith	Y	Y
PENNSYLVANIA		
Specter	Y	Y
Santorum	Y	Y
RHODE ISLAND		
Reed	Y	Y
Chafee	Y	Y
SOUTH CAROLINA		
Thurmond	Y	Y
Hollings	Y	Y
SOUTH DAKOTA		
Daschle	Y	Y
Johnson	Y	Y
TENNESSEE		
Thompson	Y	Y
Frist	Y	Y

Key

Y	Voted for (yea).
#	Paired for.
+	Announced for.
N	Voted against (nay).
X	Paired against.
−	Announced against.
P	Voted "present."
C	Voted "present" to avoid possible conflict of interest.
?	Did not vote or otherwise make a position known.

Democrats   **Republicans**
Independents

	238	239
TEXAS		
Gramm	?	Y
Hutchison	Y	Y
UTAH		
Hatch	Y	Y
Bennett	Y	Y
VERMONT		
Leahy	Y	Y
Jeffords	Y	Y
VIRGINIA		
Warner	Y	Y
Allen	Y	Y
WASHINGTON		
Cantwell	Y	Y
Murray	Y	Y
WEST VIRGINIA		
Byrd	Y	Y
Rockefeller	Y	Y
WISCONSIN		
Kohl	Y	Y
Feingold	Y	N
WYOMING		
Thomas	Y	Y
Enzi	?	?

ND Northern Democrats   SD Southern Democrats

Southern states - Ala., Ark., Fla., Ga., Ky., La., Miss., N.C., Okla., S.C., Tenn., Texas, Va.

238. HR 3295. Election Overhaul/Conference Report. Adoption of the conference report on the bill that would overhaul the nation's election procedures by authorizing $3.9 billion in federal funds to states over three years to improve the administration of elections and help states meet nationwide voting standards. Adopted (thus cleared for the president) 92-2: R 44-0; D 47-2 (ND 38-2, SD 9-0); I 1-0. Oct. 16, 2002.

239. HR 5010. Fiscal 2003 Defense Appropriations/Conference Report. Adoption of the conference report on the bill that would provide $355.1 billion for the Defense Department for fiscal 2003, an increase of $21 billion over fiscal 2002 regular and supplemental funds. The agreement includes $71.5 billion for procurement programs and $7.4 billion for ballistic missile defense. It includes $4 billion for the Air Force's F-22 fighter jet program and would fund a 4.1 percent pay increase for military personnel. Adopted (thus cleared for the president) 93-1: R 44-0; D 48-1 (ND 39-1, SD 9-0); I 1-0. Oct. 16, 2002.

	240	241	242	243
ALABAMA				
Shelby	Y	Y	Y	Y
Sessions	Y	Y	N	Y
ALASKA				
Stevens	Y	Y	Y	Y
Murkowski	Y	Y	Y	Y
ARIZONA				
McCain	Y	Y	N	Y
Kyl	Y	Y	Y	Y
ARKANSAS				
Hutchinson	Y	Y	N	Y
Lincoln	Y	N	N	Y
CALIFORNIA				
Feinstein	Y	N	Y	Y
Boxer	N	N	Y	Y
COLORADO				
Campbell	Y	Y	Y	Y
Allard	Y	Y	N	Y
CONNECTICUT				
Dodd	Y	N	Y	Y
Lieberman	Y	N	Y	Y
DELAWARE				
Carper	Y	N	Y	Y
Biden	Y	N	Y	Y
FLORIDA				
Graham	Y	N	Y	Y
Nelson	Y	N	N	Y
GEORGIA				
Miller	Y	Y	N	Y
Cleland	Y	N	N	Y
HAWAII				
Inouye	Y	N	Y	?
Akaka	Y	N	Y	Y
IDAHO				
Craig	Y	Y	?	Y
Crapo	Y	Y	Y	Y
ILLINOIS				
Durbin	Y	N	Y	Y
Fitzgerald	Y	Y	N	Y
INDIANA				
Lugar	Y	Y	Y	Y
Bayh	Y	N	N	Y

	240	241	242	243
IOWA				
Grassley	Y	Y	N	Y
Harkin	?	?	?	Y
KANSAS				
Brownback	Y	Y	N	Y
Roberts	Y	Y	N	Y
KENTUCKY				
McConnell	Y	Y	Y	Y
Bunning	Y	Y	N	Y
LOUISIANA				
Breaux	Y	N	Y	Y
Landrieu	Y	N	N	?
MAINE				
Snowe	Y	Y	N	Y
Collins	Y	Y	N	Y
MARYLAND				
Sarbanes	N	N	Y	Y
Mikulski	Y	N	Y	Y
MASSACHUSETTS				
Kennedy	N	N	?	?
Kerry	Y	N	N	Y
MICHIGAN				
Levin	Y	N	Y	Y
Stabenow	Y	N	N	Y
MINNESOTA				
Dayton	Y	N	Y	Y
Barkley *	Y	Y	Y	Y
MISSISSIPPI				
Cochran	Y	Y	Y	Y
Lott	Y	Y	Y	Y
MISSOURI				
Bond	Y	Y	Y	Y
Carnahan	Y	N	?	Y
MONTANA				
Baucus	Y	N	N	Y
Burns	Y	Y	Y	Y
NEBRASKA				
Nelson	Y	N	Y	Y
Hagel	Y	Y	Y	Y
NEVADA				
Reid	Y	N	Y	Y
Ensign	Y	Y	N	Y

	240	241	242	243
NEW HAMPSHIRE				
Smith	Y	Y	N	Y
Gregg	Y	Y	Y	Y
NEW JERSEY				
Corzine	N	N	N	Y
Torricelli	?	?	?	?
NEW MEXICO				
Domenici	Y	Y	Y	Y
Bingaman	Y	N	Y	Y
NEW YORK				
Clinton	Y	N	N	Y
Schumer	Y	N	N	Y
NORTH CAROLINA				
Helms	?	?	?	?
Edwards	Y	N	N	Y
NORTH DAKOTA				
Conrad	Y	N	Y	Y
Dorgan	Y	N	N	Y
OHIO				
DeWine	Y	Y	N	Y
Voinovich	Y	Y	Y	Y
OKLAHOMA				
Nickles	Y	Y	Y	Y
Inhofe	Y	Y	Y	Y
OREGON				
Wyden	Y	N	N	Y
Smith	Y	Y	N	Y
PENNSYLVANIA				
Specter	Y	Y	N	Y
Santorum	Y	Y	Y	Y
RHODE ISLAND				
Reed	N	N	Y	Y
Chafee	Y	Y	Y	Y
SOUTH CAROLINA				
Thurmond	Y	Y	Y	Y
Hollings	Y	N	Y	Y
SOUTH DAKOTA				
Daschle	Y	N	Y	Y
Johnson	Y	N	N	Y
TENNESSEE				
Thompson	Y	Y	Y	Y
Frist	Y	Y	Y	Y

	240	241	242	243
TEXAS				
Gramm	Y	Y	Y	Y
Hutchison	Y	Y	N	Y
UTAH				
Hatch	Y	Y	Y	Y
Bennett	Y	Y	Y	Y
VERMONT				
Leahy	Y	N	N	Y
Jeffords	N	N	Y	Y
VIRGINIA				
Warner	Y	Y	Y	Y
Allen	Y	Y	Y	Y
WASHINGTON				
Cantwell	Y	N	Y	Y
Murray	Y	N	N	Y
WEST VIRGINIA				
Byrd	N	N	Y	Y
Rockefeller	Y	N	Y	Y
WISCONSIN				
Kohl	Y	N	Y	Y
Feingold	N	N	N	Y
WYOMING				
Thomas	Y	Y	Y	Y
Enzi	Y	Y	Y	Y

ND Northern Democrats   SD Southern Democrats

Southern states - Ala., Ark., Fla., Ga., Ky., La., Miss., N.C., Okla., S.C., Tenn., Texas, Va.

240. HR 5005. Homeland Security/Cloture. Motion to invoke cloture (thus limiting debate) on the Daschle, D-S.D. (for Gramm, R-Texas), substitute amendment that would create a Cabinet-level Homeland Security Department charged with protecting domestic security. It also would allow the president to exclude workers from union representation for national security reasons, but require the president to certify his reasons in writing. Motion agreed to 89-8: R 48-0; D 40-7 (ND 31-7, SD 9-0); I 0-1. Three-fifths of the total Senate (60) is required to invoke cloture. Nov. 13, 2002.

241. HR 5005. Homeland Security/Democratic Substitute. Thompson, R-Tenn., motion to table (kill) the Lieberman, D-Conn., substitute amendment that would create a Cabinet-level Homeland Security Department charged with protecting domestic security. It would establish the position of Secretary of Homeland Security, to be appointed by the president and subject to confirmation by the Senate. It also would allow employees in agencies transferred to the new department to retain their collective bargaining rights unless their primary jobs change to consist of intelligence, counterintelligence, or terrorism investigation and it is demonstrated that collective bargaining would adversely affect national security. Motion agreed to 50-47: R 48-0; D 1-46 (ND 0-38, SD 1-8); I 0-1. Nov. 13, 2002.

242. HR 5005. Homeland Security/COLA Increase. Reid, D-Nev., motion to table (kill) the Feingold, D-Wis., amendment that would bar members of Congress from receiving a cost of living increase in fiscal 2003. Motion agreed to 58-36: R 30-17; D 26-19 (ND 23-13, SD 3-6); I 1-0. Nov. 13, 2002.

243. S 1214. Port Security/Conference Report. Adoption of the conference report on the bill that would require the Transportation Department to develop a comprehensive national maritime security plan to prevent or deter terrorist attacks. It also would authorize $6 billion in fiscal 2003 for the Coast Guard, establish a new matching grant program to help ports and facilities improve security and authorize an armed Sea Marshal program. The Transportation Department would be required to develop and issue a new, national transportation security card to eligible port workers that would allow them to work in "secure" areas of ports, port facilities and other transportation facilities. Adopted 95-0: R 48-0; D 45-0 (ND 37-0, SD 8-0); I 1-0. Nov. 14, 2002.

* Sen. Dean Barkley, I-Minn., was sworn in Nov. 12, 2002, to replace Sen. Paul Wellstone, D-Minn., who died Oct. 25, 2002. The last vote for which Wellstone was eligible was vote 239. The first vote for which Barkley was eligible was vote 240.

	244	245	246	247	248	249
ALABAMA						
Shelby	Y	N	Y	Y	Y	Y
Sessions	Y	N	Y	Y	Y	Y
ALASKA						
Stevens	Y	N	Y	Y	Y	Y
Murkowski	Y	N	Y	Y	Y	?
ARIZONA						
McCain	Y	Y	Y	Y	Y	Y
Kyl	Y	N	Y	Y	Y	Y
ARKANSAS						
Hutchinson	Y	N	Y	Y	Y	Y
Lincoln	Y	Y	Y	Y	Y	Y
CALIFORNIA						
Feinstein	Y	Y	Y	Y	Y	Y
Boxer	N	Y	N	N	N	Y
COLORADO						
Campbell	?	N	Y	Y	Y	Y
Allard	Y	N	Y	Y	Y	Y
CONNECTICUT						
Dodd	N	Y	N	N	N	Y
Lieberman	Y	Y	Y	Y	Y	Y
DELAWARE						
Carper	N	Y	Y	Y	Y	Y
Biden	N	Y	N	N	Y	Y
FLORIDA						
Graham	Y	Y	N	Y	Y	Y
Nelson	N	Y	Y	Y	Y	Y
GEORGIA						
Miller	Y	N	Y	Y	Y	Y
Cleland	Y	Y	Y	Y	Y	Y
HAWAII						
Inouye	?	Y	N	N	Y	N
Akaka	N	Y	N	N	N	N
IDAHO						
Craig	Y	N	Y	Y	Y	Y
Crapo	Y	N	Y	Y	Y	Y
ILLINOIS						
Durbin	N	Y	N	N	N	Y
Fitzgerald	Y	N	Y	Y	Y	Y
INDIANA						
Lugar	Y	N	Y	Y	Y	Y
Bayh	Y	Y	Y	Y	Y	Y

	244	245	246	247	248	249
IOWA						
Grassley	Y	N	Y	Y	Y	Y
Harkin	N	Y	N	N	N	Y
KANSAS						
Brownback	Y	N	Y	Y	Y	Y
Roberts	Y	N	Y	Y	Y	Y
KENTUCKY						
McConnell	Y	N	Y	Y	Y	Y
Bunning	Y	N	Y	Y	Y	Y
LOUISIANA						
Breaux	Y	Y	Y	Y	Y	Y
Landrieu	Y	N	Y	Y	Y	Y
MAINE						
Snowe	Y	N	Y	Y	Y	Y
Collins	Y	N	Y	Y	Y	Y
MARYLAND						
Sarbanes	N	Y	N	N	N	N
Mikulski	N	Y	N	N	N	Y
MASSACHUSETTS						
Kennedy	?	?	?	?	?	N
Kerry	?	Y	Y	Y	Y	Y
MICHIGAN						
Levin	N	Y	N	N	N	N
Stabenow	N	Y	N	N	N	Y
MINNESOTA						
Barkley	Y	N	Y	Y	Y	Y
Dayton	N	Y	N	Y	Y	Y
MISSISSIPPI						
Cochran	Y	N	Y	Y	Y	Y
Lott	Y	N	Y	Y	Y	Y
MISSOURI						
Bond	Y	N	Y	Y	Y	Y
Carnahan	Y	Y	Y	Y	Y	Y
MONTANA						
Baucus	N	Y	Y	Y	Y	Y
Burns	Y	N	Y	Y	Y	Y
NEBRASKA						
Nelson	Y	N	Y	Y	Y	Y
Hagel	Y	N	Y	Y	Y	Y
NEVADA						
Reid	N	Y	N	N	N	Y
Ensign	Y	N	Y	Y	Y	Y

	244	245	246	247	248	249
NEW HAMPSHIRE						
Smith	Y	N	Y	Y	Y	Y
Gregg	Y	N	Y	Y	Y	Y
NEW JERSEY						
Corzine	N	Y	N	N	N	Y
Torricelli	?	Y	N	N	N	Y
NEW MEXICO						
Domenici	Y	N	Y	Y	Y	Y
Bingaman	Y	Y	Y	Y	Y	Y
NEW YORK						
Clinton	N	Y	N	N	Y	Y
Schumer	N	Y	N	Y	Y	Y
NORTH CAROLINA						
Helms	?	N	Y	Y	Y	Y
Edwards	Y	Y	Y	Y	Y	Y
NORTH DAKOTA						
Conrad	N	Y	N	N	N	Y
Dorgan	N	Y	N	Y	Y	Y
OHIO						
DeWine	Y	N	Y	Y	Y	Y
Voinovich	Y	N	Y	Y	Y	Y
OKLAHOMA						
Nickles	Y	N	Y	Y	Y	Y
Inhofe	Y	N	Y	Y	Y	Y
OREGON						
Wyden	N	Y	N	N	Y	Y
Smith	Y	N	Y	Y	Y	Y
PENNSYLVANIA						
Specter	Y	N	Y	Y	Y	Y
Santorum	Y	N	Y	Y	Y	Y
RHODE ISLAND						
Reed	N	Y	N	N	N	Y
Chafee	Y	N	Y	Y	Y	Y
SOUTH CAROLINA						
Thurmond	Y	N	Y	Y	Y	Y
Hollings	Y	Y	N	N	Y	N
SOUTH DAKOTA						
Daschle	Y	Y	N	N	Y	Y
Johnson	Y	Y	N	N	Y	Y
TENNESSEE						
Thompson	Y	N	Y	Y	Y	Y
Frist	Y	N	Y	Y	Y	Y

Key

Y	Voted for (yea).
#	Paired for.
+	Announced for.
N	Voted against (nay).
X	Paired against.
−	Announced against.
P	Voted "present."
C	Voted "present" to avoid possible conflict of interest.
?	Did not vote or otherwise make a position known.

Democrats **Republicans**
Independents

	244	245	246	247	248	249
TEXAS						
Gramm	Y	N	Y	Y	Y	Y
Hutchison	Y	N	Y	Y	Y	Y
UTAH						
Hatch	Y	N	Y	Y	Y	Y
Bennett	Y	N	Y	Y	Y	Y
VERMONT						
Leahy	N	Y	N	Y	Y	Y
Jeffords	N	Y	N	N	N	N
VIRGINIA						
Warner	Y	N	Y	Y	Y	Y
Allen	Y	N	Y	Y	Y	Y
WASHINGTON						
Cantwell	Y	Y	Y	Y	Y	Y
Murray	N	Y	N	N	N	Y
WEST VIRGINIA						
Byrd	N	Y	N	N	N	N
Rockefeller	N	Y	N	Y	Y	Y
WISCONSIN						
Kohl	N	Y	Y	Y	Y	Y
Feingold	N	Y	N	N	N	N
WYOMING						
Thomas	Y	N	Y	Y	Y	Y
Enzi	Y	N	Y	Y	Y	Y

ND Northern Democrats   SD Southern Democrats

Southern states - Ala., Ark., Fla., Ga., Ky., La., Miss., N.C., Okla., S.C., Tenn., Texas, Va.

244. HR 5005. Homeland Security/Cloture. Motion to invoke cloture (thus limiting debate) on the Thompson, R-Tenn., substitute amendment that would create a Cabinet-level Homeland Security Department charged with protecting domestic security. Three-fifths of the total Senate (60) is required to invoke cloture. Motion agreed to 65-29: R 47-0; D 17-28 (ND 9-27, SD 8-1); I 1-1. Nov. 15, 2002.

245. HR 5005. Homeland Security/Democratic Changes. Daschle, D-S.D., amendment to the Daschle amendment to the Thompson, R-Tenn., substitute amendment. The Daschle amendment would strike seven provisions in the Thompson substitute, effective one day after the bill's enactment. One of the seven would allow the new agency to contract with companies that have reincorporated abroad to avoid paying U.S. taxes. Others would limit liability for manufacturers of certain anti-terrorism technologies, for pharmaceutical companies that produce vaccine preservative, and for companies that provide airport screening. The underlying Daschle amendment is identical, except that it does not include an effective date. Rejected 47-52: R 1-48; D 45-3 (ND 38-1, SD 7-2); I 1-1. (Subsequently, the underlying Daschle amendment was rejected by voice vote.) Nov. 19, 2002.

246. HR 5005. Homeland Security/Republican Substitute. Gramm, R-Texas, motion to waive the Budget Act with respect to the Byrd, D-W.Va., point of order against the Thompson, R-Tenn., substitute amendment. A three-fifths majority vote (60) of the total Senate is required to waive the Budget Act. Motion agreed to 69-30: R 49-0; D 19-29 (ND 12-27, SD 7-2); I 1-1. (Subsequently, the Byrd point of order failed.) Nov. 19, 2002.

247. HR 5005. Homeland Security/Republican Substitute. Thompson, R-Tenn., substitute amendment that would create a Cabinet-level Homeland Security Department charged with protecting domestic security. It would give the president the ability to exempt some employees from collective bargaining units for national security reasons and allow the department to make changes to personnel rules but would establish a process for unions to object to and negotiate those changes. Adopted 73-26: R 49-0; D 23-25 (ND 15-24, SD 8-1); I 1-1. Nov. 19, 2002.

248. HR 5005. Homeland Security/Cloture. Motion to invoke cloture (thus limiting debate) on the bill that would create a Cabinet-level Homeland Security Department charged with protecting domestic security. Three-fifths of the total Senate (60) is required to invoke cloture. Motion agreed to 83-16: R 49-0; D 33-15 (ND 24-15, SD 9-0); I 1-1. Nov. 19, 2002.

249. HR 5005. Homeland Security/Passage. Passage of the bill that would consolidate 22 agencies into a new Cabinet-level Homeland Security Department charged with protecting domestic security. Agencies moved to the new department would include the Coast Guard, the Federal Emergency Management Agency, the Customs Service, the Secret Service and the Transportation Security Administration. The Immigration and Naturalization Service would be split into separate agencies for immigration enforcement and citizen services, both of which would be in the new department. It would give the president the ability to exempt some employees from collective bargaining units for national security reasons and allow the department to make changes to personnel rules but would establish a process for unions to object to and negotiate those changes. Passed 90-9: R 48-0; D 41-8 (ND 33-7, SD 8-1); I 1-1. A "yea" was a vote in support of the president's position. Nov. 19, 2002.

	250	251	252	253
ALABAMA				
Shelby	Y	N	N	Y
Sessions	Y	N	N	Y
ALASKA				
Stevens	Y	Y	Y	Y
Murkowski	?	?	?	?
ARIZONA				
McCain	Y	Y	Y	Y
Kyl	Y	N	N	Y
ARKANSAS				
Hutchinson	Y	?	?	?
Lincoln	Y	Y	Y	N
CALIFORNIA				
Feinstein	N	Y	Y	Y
Boxer	N	Y	Y	Y
COLORADO				
Campbell	Y	Y	Y	Y
Allard	Y	Y	Y	Y
CONNECTICUT				
Dodd	N	Y	Y	Y
Lieberman	N	Y	Y	Y
DELAWARE				
Carper	N	Y	Y	Y
Biden	N	Y	Y	Y
FLORIDA				
Graham	Y	Y	Y	Y
Nelson	N	Y	Y	Y
GEORGIA				
Miller	Y	Y	Y	Y
Cleland	N	Y	Y	?
HAWAII				
Inouye	Y	Y	Y	Y
Akaka	N	Y	Y	Y
IDAHO				
Craig	Y	N	N	Y
Crapo	Y	Y	Y	Y
ILLINOIS				
Durbin	N	Y	Y	Y
Fitzgerald	Y	Y	Y	Y
INDIANA				
Lugar	Y	Y	Y	Y
Bayh	N	Y	Y	Y

	250	251	252	253
IOWA				
Grassley	Y	N	N	Y
Harkin	N	Y	Y	Y
KANSAS				
Brownback	Y	Y	Y	Y
Roberts	Y	Y	Y	Y
KENTUCKY				
McConnell	Y	Y	N	Y
Bunning	Y	Y	Y	Y
LOUISIANA				
Breaux	N	Y	Y	Y
Landrieu	N	Y	Y	Y
MAINE				
Snowe	Y	Y	Y	Y
Collins	Y	Y	Y	Y
MARYLAND				
Sarbanes	N	Y	Y	Y
Mikulski	N	Y	Y	Y
MASSACHUSETTS				
Kennedy	N	Y	Y	Y
Kerry	N	Y	Y	N
MICHIGAN				
Levin	N	Y	Y	Y
Stabenow	N	Y	Y	Y
MINNESOTA				
Barkley	N	Y	Y	Y
Dayton	N	Y	Y	Y
MISSISSIPPI				
Cochran	Y	Y	Y	Y
Lott	Y	Y	Y	Y
MISSOURI				
Bond	Y	Y	Y	Y
Carnahan	N	Y	Y	?
MONTANA				
Baucus	N	Y	Y	Y
Burns	Y	Y	Y	Y
NEBRASKA				
Nelson	Y	Y	Y	Y
Hagel	Y	Y	Y	Y
NEVADA				
Reid	N	Y	Y	Y
Ensign	Y	N	Y	Y

	250	251	252	253
NEW HAMPSHIRE				
Smith	Y	Y	Y	Y
Gregg	Y	Y	Y	Y
NEW JERSEY				
Corzine	N	Y	Y	Y
Torricelli	N	Y	Y	Y
NEW MEXICO				
Domenici	Y	Y	Y	Y
Bingaman	N	Y	Y	Y
NEW YORK				
Clinton	N	Y	Y	Y
Schumer	N	Y	Y	?
NORTH CAROLINA				
Helms	Y	?	?	?
Edwards	N	Y	Y	Y
NORTH DAKOTA				
Conrad	N	Y	Y	Y
Dorgan	N	Y	Y	Y
OHIO				
DeWine	Y	Y	Y	Y
Voinovich	Y	Y	Y	Y
OKLAHOMA				
Nickles	Y	N	N	Y
Inhofe	Y	Y	Y	Y
OREGON				
Wyden	N	Y	Y	Y
Smith	Y	Y	Y	Y
PENNSYLVANIA				
Specter	Y	Y	Y	Y
Santorum	Y	N	Y	Y
RHODE ISLAND				
Reed	N	Y	Y	Y
Chafee	Y	Y	Y	Y
SOUTH CAROLINA				
Thurmond	Y	Y	Y	Y
Hollings	Y	Y	Y	Y
SOUTH DAKOTA				
Daschle	N	Y	Y	Y
Johnson	N	Y	Y	Y
TENNESSEE				
Thompson	Y	Y	Y	Y
Frist	Y	Y	Y	Y

Key

Y	Voted for (yea).
#	Paired for.
+	Announced for.
N	Voted against (nay).
X	Paired against.
−	Announced against.
P	Voted "present."
C	Voted "present" to avoid possible conflict of interest.
?	Did not vote or otherwise make a position known.

Democrats **Republicans**
Independents

	250	251	252	253
TEXAS				
Gramm	Y	N	N	Y
Hutchison	Y	N	N	Y
UTAH				
Hatch	Y	Y	Y	Y
Bennett	Y	Y	Y	Y
VERMONT				
Leahy	N	Y	Y	Y
Jeffords	N	Y	Y	Y
VIRGINIA				
Warner	Y	Y	Y	Y
Allen	Y	Y	Y	Y
WASHINGTON				
Cantwell	N	Y	Y	Y
Murray	N	Y	Y	Y
WEST VIRGINIA				
Byrd	Y	Y	Y	Y
Rockefeller	N	Y	Y	Y
WISCONSIN				
Kohl	N	Y	Y	Y
Feingold	N	Y	Y	Y
WYOMING				
Thomas	Y	N	N	Y
Enzi	Y	N	N	Y

ND Northern Democrats   SD Southern Democrats

Southern states - Ala., Ark., Fla., Ga., Ky., La., Miss., N.C., Okla., S.C., Tenn., Texas, Va.

250. Shedd Nomination/Confirmation. Confirmation of President Bush's nomination of Dennis W. Shedd of South Carolina to be a judge for the 4th U.S. Circuit Court of Appeals. Confirmed 55-44: R 48-0; D 7-42 (ND 3-37, SD 4-5); I 0-2. A "yea" was a vote in support of the president's position. Nov. 19, 2002.

251. HR 3210. Terrorism Insurance/Cloture. Motion to invoke cloture (thus limiting debate) on the conference report on the bill that would authorize a federal loan program through the end of 2005 to help the commercial casualty and property insurance industry cover claims related to future terrorism-related losses. Three-fifths of the total Senate (60) is required to invoke cloture. Motion agreed to 85-12: R 34-12; D 49-0 (ND 40-0, SD 9-0); I 2-0. Nov. 19, 2002.

252. HR 3210. Terrorism Insurance/Conference Report. Adoption of the conference report on the bill that would authorize a federal loan program through the end of 2005 to help the commercial casualty and property insurance industry cover claims related to future terrorism-related losses. The federal aid would cover 90 percent of industrywide losses that exceed $10 billion before the end of 2003, $12.5 billion in 2004, and $15 billion in 2005. Losses covered by the program would be capped at $100 billion each year, and a certain amount of the federal aid would have to be repaid. The measure also would limit terrorism-related lawsuits to federal courts. Adopted (thus cleared for the president) 86-11: R 35-11; D 49-0 (ND 40-0, SD 9-0); I 2-0. A "yea" was a vote in support of the president's position. Nov. 19, 2002.

253. H J Res 124 Continuing Appropriations/Passage. Passage of the joint resolution to provide continuing appropriations through Jan. 11, 2003, for all federal departments and programs. The continuing resolution would set spending at fiscal 2002 levels. Passed (thus cleared for the president) 92-2: R 46-0; D 44-2 (ND 37-1, SD 7-1); I 2-0. Nov. 19, 2002.

Senate Roll Call Votes By Subject

Appendix I

GENERAL INDEX

General Index

General Index

Flood aid
Supplemental appropriations, 2-43
Flood control
Appropriations, 2-16
Florida
Bankruptcy overhaul, 5-5
District court judgeship, 13-4
Everglades restoration, 2-23
Oil and gas drilling, 2-22
Presidential election of 2000, 14-3
FOIA. See Freedom of Information Act
Foley, Mark, R-Fla. (16)
Corporate fraud bill, 11-6
Food and Drug Administration (FDA)
Bioterrorism preparedness, 10-10–10-11
Medical malpractice caps, 10-13, 10-14, 10-15
Prescription drug patents, 10-8–10-9
User fees, 10-11, 10-12–10-13
Food and nutrition. See also Food stamps
Bioterrorism preparedness, 10-10, 10-11
Food sales to Cuba, 2-5, 2-6, 4-7
Labeling, 4-3, 4-7, 18-5
Women, Infants and Children food program, 2-5
Food for Peace program
Agriculture appropriations, 2-5
Food stamps
Agriculture appropriations, 2-5
Farm bill, 4-3, 4-4, 4-5
Welfare overhaul, 15-5
Ford, Harold E. Jr., D-Tenn. (9)
House leadership and organization, 1-9
Foreign affairs. See also Foreign aid; Foreign trade; Homeland security; Intelligence; Terrorism; War; specific countries
Bush's "axis of evil," 1-3, 9-3
Intelligence information requests, 7-19
Sex tourism ban, 13-6
U.S. outreach and media programs, 9-6, 9-7, 9-8
Foreign aid. See also specific countries
Appropriations, 2-18–2-20
Debt relief, 9-7, 9-8
Economic assistance, 2-19
Food aid, 2-5
HIV/AIDS, 2-18–2-19, 2-40, 2-41, 2-43, 6-8, 9-8
Humanitarian aid, 2-19, 2-20, 6-8
Military aid, 2-18–2-19, 6-8, 9-6, 9-7
Foreign investment
Trade negotiating authority, 18-6
Foreign Relations Committee (Senate)
HIV/AIDS program funding, 9-8
State Department reauthorization, 9-6
Foreign trade. See also Trade negotiating authority; specific countries
Agriculture appropriations, 2-5, 2-6
Andean trade, C-22
Bioterrorism preparedness, 10-10
Dual-use technology exports, 18-11
Export-Import Bank reauthorization, 18-10–18-11
Farm bill, 4-3, 4-4, 4-7
Port security, 19-5–19-7
Prescription drug reimportation, 10-8, 10-9
Supplemental appropriations, 2-42, 2-43, 2-44
Forest management
Forest thinning and wildfire control, 2-23
Interior appropriations, 2-21, 2-22
Forest Service. See National Forest Service
Forrester, Douglas
Torricelli campaign fundraising, 1-14
Fort Bragg
Domestic violence in the military, 2-12
Fort Greeley
Missile defense, 2-11
Frank, Barney, D-Mass. (4)
Class action suit limits, 13-10
Freedom of information
Bioterrorism preparedness bill, 10-10, 10-11
Energy task force records, 1-15–1-16
Homeland security FOIA exemption, 7-4, 7-7
Intelligence information requests, 7-19
Freedom of Information Act (FOIA)
Bioterrorism preparedness bill, 10-10
Homeland Security Department exemption, 7-4, 7-7
Intelligence information requests, 7-19
Frelinghuysen, Rodney, R-N.J. (11)
Defense appropriations, 2-10
Frist, Bill, R-Tenn.
Lott controversy, 1-11
Senate leadership and organization, 1-10, 1-11
Supplemental appropriations, 2-43

Frost, Martin, D-Texas (24)
House leadership and organization, 1-9, 1-10
Fruits. See also specific fruits
Labeling, 4-3, 4-7
Fuel. See Energy
Future Combat Systems
Defense appropriations, 2-11
Defense authorization, 7-16

G

GAO. See General Accounting Office
Gas industry. See Oil and gas industry
Gasoline. See also Energy
Ethanol as additive, 8-5–8-7
Fuel economy standards, 8-4, 8-7, C-11–C-12, C-22
Gas tax revenues, 2-32, 8-5
Seasonal price spikes, 8-5
GATT. See General Agreement on Tariffs and Trade
General Accounting Office (GAO)
Amtrak reauthorization, 19-7, 19-8
Appropriations, 2-27
Army Corps of Engineers spending, 2-16
Energy task force records, 1-15–1-16
Government credit card use, 2-12
Medical malpractice insurance costs, 10-15
General Agreement on Tariffs and Trade (GATT)
Trade negotiating authority, 13-4
General Dynamics
Navy shipbuilding, 2-12
Genetics
Human cloning, 17-5–17-6
Gephardt, Richard A., D-Mo. (3)
Debt limit, 6-11
Homeland security, 1-7
House leadership and organization, 1-9, 1-10
Iraq war authorization resolution, 1-8, 1-10, 9-3, 9-4
Prescription drug coverage, 1-7, 10-9
State of the Union response, D-7–D-8
Tax cuts, 16-6
Global Fund to Fight AIDS, Tuberculosis and Malaria
Funding, 9-8
Global warming
Energy bill, 8-5, 8-6, 8-7
Glover, Gregory J.
Prescription drug patents, 10-8
Goldwater, former Sen. Barry, R-Ariz. (1953-65; 1969-87)
Thurmond's profile, 1-13
Gonzales, Alberto R.
Judicial nominations, 13-12
Goode, Virgil H. Jr., R-Va. (5)
Defense authorization, 7-15
Goodlatte, Robert W., R-Va. (6)
Class action suit limits, 13-9
Gore, former Vice President Al
Presidential election of 2000, 14-3
Gorelick, Jamie
Intelligence commission, 7-21
Gorton, former Sen. Slade, R-Wash. (1981-87; 1989-2001)
Intelligence commission, 7-21
Goss, Porter J., R-Fla. (14)
Cuba travel ban, 2-37
Intelligence authorization, 7-19
Intelligence failure investigation, 7-20
Government contractors. See Federal contractors
Government Printing Office (GPO)
Appropriations, 2-27, 2-28
Government Reform Committee (House)
Homeland security bill, 7-7
Government securities. See Stocks, bonds, and securities
Government Securities Investment Fund
Debt limit, 6-11
Governmental Affairs Committee (Senate)
Homeland security bill, 1-6, 7-3, 7-6, 7-7, 7-20
GPO. See Government Printing Office
Graham, Bob, D-Fla.
Intelligence director proposal, 7-20–7-21
Intelligence failure investigation, 7-18
Prescription drug coverage, 1-7, 10-6–10-7
Trade negotiating authority, 18-5
Welfare overhaul, 15-5

Gramm, Phil, R-Texas
Bank insurance, 5-6
Corporate fraud bill, 11-5, 11-6
Energy bill, 8-5
Farm bill, 4-5
Homeland security bill, 7-7
PAYGO rules extension, 6-13
Supplemental appropriations, 2-42
Tax cuts, 16-6
Terrorism insurance, 11-11–11-13
Gramm-Leach-Bliley financial service overhaul law
Banks as real estate brokers, 2-36
Gramm-Rudman-Hollings law
Debt limit, 6-11
Grand Staircase-Escalante National Monument
Expansion, 2-22
Grants. See Block grants
Grassland Reserve Program
Creation and funding of, 4-4
Grassley, Charles E., R-Iowa
Farm bill, 4-5
Medicare provider payments, 10-5
Pension plan overhaul, 12-3
Prescription drug coverage, 10-6
Trade negotiating authority, 18-4, 18-5, 18-6
Grazing land
Environmental assessments, 2-22
Greece
NATO program funding, 2-31
Green, Gene, D-Texas (29)
Campaign finance, 14-9
High-speed Internet access, 17-4
Medical malpractice caps, 10-15
Greenspan, Alan
Accounting regulation, 11-4
Bank insurance, 5-6
Economic stimulus package, 1-5
Greenwood, James C., R-Pa. (8)
Human cloning, 17-5
Gregg, Judd, R-N.H.
Budget resolution, 6-10, 6-12
Supplemental appropriations, 2-42
Trade negotiating authority, 18-6
Welfare overhaul, 15-6
Gross domestic product
Deficit as percentage of, 6-14
Economic forecasting, 6-8
Guam
Military environmental violation, 7-13
TANF grants, 15-5
Gubernatorial elections
Election results, F-3–F-12
Guinn, Kenny
Yucca Mountain nuclear waste site, 8-8
Gulf of Tonkin resolution
Iraq war authorization resolution, 9-5
Gun control
Campaign finance amendment, 14-9
Guns
Armed pilots, 7-4, 7-8, 19-3
Gutknecht, Gil, R-Minn. (1)
Prescription drug coverage, 10-6

H

Hagel, Chuck, R-Neb.
Export-Import Bank reauthorization, 18-10
Prescription drug coverage, 10-6
Hall, Ralph M., D-Texas (4)
Medical malpractice caps, 10-14
Hamilton, former Rep. Lee H., D-Ind. (1965-99)
Intelligence commission, 7-21
Hannity, Sean
Lott controversy, 1-10
Hansen, James V., R-Utah (1)
Bear River agreement, 2-22
Hanssen, Robert
Spying revelations, 13-3, 13-4
Harkin, Tom, D-Iowa
Agriculture appropriations, 2-5–2-6
Farm bill, 4-4–4-7
Farm drought aid, 4-11
Labor-HHS-Education appropriations, 2-24
President's budget proposal, 1-5
Harman, Jane, D-Calif. (36)
Medical malpractice caps, 10-14

Hastert, J. Dennis, R-Ill. (14)
Appropriations
Labor-HHS-Education, 1-5, 2-3, 2-24
Status overview, 2-42
Supplemental, 2-43
Budget deficit, 6-13
Campaign finance, 1-6, 14-9
Corporate fraud bill, 11-6
Debt limit, 6-12
Homeland security, 1-7
House leadership and organization, 1-10
Intelligence failure investigation, 7-19
Investor tax breaks, 16-7
Iraq war authorization resolution, 9-4
Prescription drug coverage, 10-5–10-6, 10-9
Terrorism insurance, 11-11
Trade negotiating authority, 18-4
Unemployment benefits, 12-7
Hatch, Orrin G., R-Utah
Child pornography, 13-10
Human cloning, 17-5
Justice Department reauthorization, 13-3
Prescription drug patents, 10-8–10-9
Welfare overhaul, 15-5, 15-6
Hawaii
Special election, 1-11
Hayes, Robin, R-N.C. (8)
Textile imports, 2-42
Trade negotiating authority, 18-7
Hazardous waste. See also Nuclear waste
Brownfields cleanup, 8-10
Health, public. See Public health
Health and Human Services, Department of
Appropriations, 1-5, 2-3, 2-24
Bioterrorism preparedness, 10-10
Faith-based social action, 15-7
Homeland security budget, 6-4
Homeland security restructuring, 7-5
Overseas funding, 9-8
Prescription drug coverage, 10-5, 10-6
Prescription drug patents, 10-9
Rescissions and offsets, 2-43
Smallpox vaccine, 7-4
Health care. See also Hospitals; Medicare; Physicians
See also Prescription drugs
Abortion service refusals, 3-3–3-4
Bioterrorism preparedness, 2-44, 7-4, 10-10–10-11, 10-12
COBRA and economic stimulus package, 16-4
Community health center reauthorization, 10-15
Emergency preparedness centers, 7-21
Family caregiver tax breaks, 6-4
Medical device imports, 10-10
Medical device manufacturer fees, 10-11, 10-12–10-13
Medical device sterilization and reuse, 10-12
Medical malpractice caps, 10-9, 10-13–10-15
Military retiree benefits, 2-11, 2-13
Patients' rights, 1-4, 10-7–10-8
Veterans, 2-38–2-39, 2-44, 7-13, 7-21
Welfare overhaul, 15-3–15-6
Health, Education, Labor and Pension Committee (Senate)
Pension plan overhaul, 12-3, 12-5
Prescription drug patents, 10-8, 10-9
Welfare overhaul, 15-4, 15-6
Health insurance
District of Columbia, 2-14
Patients' rights, 1-4, 10-7–10-8
Prescription drug coverage, 1-7, 10-3–10-4, 10-6
Tax credits, 6-4, 16-4, 16-5, 18-3, 18-5, 18-7
Unmarried domestic partners, 2-14
Welfare overhaul, 15-5
Health Insurance Association of America (HIAA)
Prescription drug coverage, 10-4
Health research. See Medical research
Helicopters
Defense appropriations, 2-10, 2-12, 2-13
Defense authorization, 7-17
Helms, Jesse, R-N.C.
Supplemental appropriations, 2-43
Thurmond's profile, 1-14
Webcaster royalties, 13-11
Highway Trust Fund
Appropriations, 2-32